Managing Information Technology Resources in Organizations in the Next Millennium

1999 Information Resources Management Association International Conference
Hershey, PA, USA

May 16-19, 1999

Mehdi Khosrowpour
Pennsylvania State University
at Harrisburg

IDEA GROUP PUBLISHING
Hershey, USA • London, UK
URL: http://www.idea-group.com

Senior Editor: Mehdi Khosrowpour
Managing Editor: Jan Travers
Printed at: BookCrafters

Published in the United States of America by
        Idea Group Publishing
        1331 E. Chocolate Avenue
        Hershey PA 17033-1117
        Tel: 717-533-8845
        Fax: 717-533-8661
        E-mail: jtravers@idea-group.com
        Website: http://www.idea-group.com

and in the United Kingdom by
        Idea Group Publishing
        3 Henrietta Street
        Covent Garden
        London WC2E 8LU
        Tel: 171-240 0856
        Fax: 171-379 0609
        Website: http://www.eurospan.co.uk

Library of Congress Cataloging-in-Publication Data

Information Resources Management Association. International Conference (1999: Hershey Pa.)
        Managing information technology resources in organizations in the next millennium : 1999
Information Resources Management Association International Conference, Hershey, PA, USA, May 16-19,
1999 / [edited by] Mehdi Khosrowpour.
        p.   cm.
Includes bibliographical references (p.   ).
ISBN 1-878289-51-9
1. Information resources management Congresses. 2. Information technology--Management Congresses. I.
Khosrowpour, Mehdi, 1951-. II. Title.
758.64.I533 1999   99-20249
658.4'038--dc21   CIP

British Cataloguing in Publication Data
A Cataloguing in Publication record for this book is available from the British Library.

All papers that appear in this Proceedings have been subjected to a blind review by two anonymous reviewers.

Table of Contents

Web-based Teaching: Is It for Real

Anil K.Aggarwal,
University of Baltimore, MIS Area, 1420 N. Charles St., Baltimore, MD 21201
(410) 837-5275, fax: (410) 837-5722, aaggarwal@ubmail.ubalt.edu

Edward R. Kemery
University of Baltimore, Management Area
(410) 837-5064, ekemery@ubmail.ubalt.edu

ABSTRACT

As internet and intranet usage expands, so are their applications in different areas. Web-based systems are being used for shareholder reports, accounting systems, for collecting consumer data and for advertising. Education is not far behind. In fact, many virtual universities are providing internet based courses. This poses a big problem for non-profit universities. How can they provide web-based education without compromising quality? This paper addresses many issues related to web-based teaching environment. We also provide our experiences with a pilot course. We feel web-based education is for "real" and non-profit universities can provide quality education. However market for such education may be limited to motivated suburban students who are looking for "information" from home.

INTRODUCTION

Technology is creating tremendous opportunities in most areas and education is no exception. Web is becoming a virtual library where information about anything and anybody is available at almost no cost. Education is not far behind. Many virtual organizations with little or no staff are emerging and providing full-fledged curriculums.

For traditional universities, the basic question is: Can the internet be used effectively for educational purposes? Can web-based teaching provide same quality as the traditional face-to-face environment? Should traditional universities go into web-based teaching and compete with virtual universities? Many traditional universities are joining the web bandwagon and have been very successful. This paper looks at web-based teaching and discusses some issues that must be addressed before web-based teaching becomes a reality.

WEB-BASED TEACHING

What is web-based teaching? Is it similar to distance learning where students are dispersed geographically but are taught at the same time? Is it similar to correspondence courses where students can learn anywhere on their own and take exams as needed? Or is some combination of the two? Two dimensions can be used to describe web-based teaching; time and place. Web-based teaching can be implemented from same-time same-place to any-time any-place environments. However, any-place any-time pedagogy creates an asynchronous learning environment students can use anywhere they have computer access. Correspondence degrees are the earlier examples of this. This is where web-based teaching can provide maximum contribution. Web board, web-assignments, web-based exams can all be used in this model. Education is available any time from any place and students can learn from home, office or wherever they are.

Issues In Web-based Teaching

Many issues arise when we discuss web-based teaching. Control and quality are the biggest challenges. Hardware and software are constantly changing and will not be considered in our discussion.

Control

Control refers to control for quality, ethics and information overload. We can provide an abundance of information through the web, but how do we control it before it becomes "information overload". How can we motivate students to "seek" useful information on the web? Homework, exams, papers and group assignments need to be submitted and graded. How can we ensure the ethics of this process? Current technology does not allow video and audio control in real time at a reasonable cost.

Quality

Quality refers to effectiveness of web-based teaching. Can we provide the same or better quality learning? Web-based teaching requires motivated students whose aims are to learn and not just to pass and get a grade. Will students learn modules on their own? How can face-to-face peer interaction be duplicated on the web? Web-based teaching requires a completely different approach. The goal is to translate face-to-face teaching environment to a web-based any-time any-place environment. This is not economically possible with current technology.

Student Evaluation

How should students be evaluated? Traditional in-class exams and class presentations are not appropriate instruments to measure student performance in web-based courses. We suggest the following:

- On-line tests and quizzes
- Web participation
- Take-home exams/papers
- Peer evaluation
- On-line ad-hoc exams

The following section discusses an experiment in web-based course.

AN EXAMPLE

Currently there is big push for offering a web-based MBA at our university, driven by economic reality and intrusion of many web-based programs. Last year several faculty were given a course release to develop web-based courses. At that time a web-based course was defined as a course offering some instructions/tutorials on the web and some in-class. Under this approach, also called the artisan approach, the course description clearly states that students will need access to Internet and classes will physically meet every other class period. Being an urban university with commuting student population this was very attractive for our students. A typical course includes the following:

- Web board for on-line discussions
- Links to various course-related resources
- On-line tutorials
- On-line communications through e-mail

This section describes a pilot course that was used to teach Seminar in Human Resource Management, a case-based, senior level undergraduate course. This course was offered in Spring 1998 and Summer 1998. The course contained several components — a web-based syllabus (see, for example, http://ubmail.ubalt.edu/~ekemery/mgmt419), cases and exercises that were stored on a server (and linked to the syllabus), and a web-board that allowed for asynchronous communication among students. The Spring 1998 course used technology to enhance the course — that is, students met in class as much as any other course. The Summer 1998 course was taught using the "artisan model" of web teaching. The artisan model is one in which students meet in class for 50% of the time, and interact on the web the remaining 50%.

The first day of class in the Spring of 1998 was interesting. There were many quizzical looks from the students, particularly when they learned of the cases and exercises that they must retrieve using a computer. Several students complained a bit because they had never had to use computer technology before; Most were silent; and, several seemed to enjoy the anticipation of this new twist.

As the semester progressed, the web-board sparked some lively debate both on the board itself and in class about the cases and related issues. In general, we believe the use of web-based technology enhanced student learning. We also believe many students felt the same way as is evident by the student comments provided at the end of the semester. It also reinforced our belief that students were having a quality learning experience.

Reactions to the Summer 1998 course was less positive. From the instructor's standpoint, motivation was low, as evidenced by in-class discussion and web-board participation. From the students' standpoint, several never did participate to a meaningful degree; Class attendance and web-board participation was spotty. This was disappointing because the only obvious difference between the two classes was that Spring 1998 course was taught using predominately face-to-face interaction (with web-enhancement) while the Summer 1998 course was taught with the artisan approach.

Table 2 shows several statistics for the two semesters.

Based on data (see table 2), it appears as though there were no meaningful differences in student participation over the two semesters. The number of student postings ranged from 6 to 43 in the spring semester. In the summer semester they ranged from 5 to 40. What is curious about these data is that the reward system differed in these classes. During the spring, web board participation was 15% of the grade, while in the summer it was 25%. Clearly more summer participation should be expected. The spring semester was 14 weeks long and the summer semester was only 8 weeks long. Perhaps it takes a while for student participation to gain momentum.

There were only 7 students in the summer class, while there were 27 during the spring. Of the summer students, only 4 participated consistently. During spring, about 20 participated consistently. While the percentage of con-

Table 1: Selected Student Comments From Spring 1998.

- I used the Web and library resources more in this class then any other I have taken to fully research each topic.
- Electronic Resources - Well, when you can gain access (this being a fine example), I think they are a plus. My "net" skills have been enhanced by taking this course. I would suggest that in the future, assignments such as "would you make a good expat", "BDI interview questions", etc. be used on the web.
- Electronic Resources were definitely a plus in my book. I had purchased my first computer in November '97 and was considering getting internet service by the time this class had begun. After the first meeting however, I decided this would be a wise investment. And it definitely paid off. Without the internet at home I think I would have been discouraged in the beginning and little frustrated. It is a lot easier to say that this part of the class was no big deal when you are sitting in the comfort of your own home. Anyway to get to the point, I have become internet proficient and research proficient on the net, and for all of us going into HR it is becoming a requirement, at some workplaces, to be able to get around on the net. Therefore, I definitely know I am ahead of the game (maybe) or at least part of the game. Thank you for forcing us to become technology friendly. The goal you had of encouraging us to be tech. friendly was achieved as far as I am concerned. More so for me probably because I was out of touch before. I was just entering our tech. age.
- Before this class, I have used the internet maybe twice for another class. I really got to understand all its capabilities. I overall enjoyed using both the internet to find outside resources and responding on the web board.
- You can never know enough about technology!!! Although I have used the Internet many times for my other classes, I have realized that there were some people who weren't very familiar with the use of Internet. This class encouraged students to use the available technology, which added great deal to their skills.
- Before this class, I had never used the internet. This class forced me to do so and I'm so grateful for that. I plan to continue to use it for personal interest. The information on the internet is tremendous and can be used for many things.
- Since, the case material is so current, this class has forced me to use the internet. In the past, I would often use the library.
- I just wanted to say that even though I am not a fan of computers, I definitely learned my way around them for this class. I really was not given a choice in the matter, if I wanted to pass this class. The web board allowed me to see how other classmates felt about topics in the class. When your are in class, there are always people who dominate the discussions and those who will always keep quiet. Because it was part of our grade, the web board gave us a chance to "hear" everyone's thoughts and concerns on class discussions and topics.
- I liked the idea of using the internet as a main tool for communication. Using the internet gives everyone an equal chance to voice his or her opinions. Also, there is so much information on the internet that is helpful for studying.
- I thought it was great that we used the web board as a learning tool this semester. As I said before, I've never used the web board in any of my other classes and I've learned to enjoy using it. Also, the supplemental materials provided by Dr. Kemery were beneficial. I've learned to use the Internet for educational purposes for a change.
- I have enjoyed the Web Board this semester. I found myself checking it frequently during the semester. There is clearly a place for this medium in the college curriculum, but it must be supplemented by human interaction. I can't image a H.R. graduate that has taken most classes on the Internet; being well rounded enough to function successfully in that position.
- New technology is very important to learn, every computer skill is important to know, when entering the job market. I can say, that when I leave this class, I have learned a lot, unlike other classes. And I know I will retain this information.
- I really enjoyed being able to use the web board to update our class assignments as well as let you know what was on our mind. It was very convenient especially since most people have the internet at home now. I think the web board is a good device that can be used to teach and I think you should use it next semester.
- Prior to this class, I had very little experience on the Internet/E-Mail/Web Board, but I knew that had to change. I had just taken a non-credit Internet/E-Mail course in January to learn the basics. This class helped me to become comfortable using the Internet, doing research (other than the library), and using a Web Board. The Internet has a wealth of information and presented a whole new research/learning dimension for me. In February, I took a basic Excel course and can practice at home to become more proficient.
- The Web board is a nifty way to communicate with many of the other class members that aren't as vocal during class. This is definitely the wave of the future in education and business.
- Before this class, I was not an internet user. While I'm glad that the web board requirements in this class have given me a general understanding of the internet, I don't see a real benefit in the manner it was required.

Table 2. Student and Instructor Web Board Postings Spring 1998 vs. Summer 1998

	Spring 1998	Summer 1998
Number of students	27	7
Minimum number of postings per student	6	5
Maximum number of postings per student	43	40
Average number of postings per week	1.52	2.3
Number of instructor postings	54	41
Average number of instructor postings	3.86	5.12

stant participators in each class was roughly the same, the absolute number differed dramatically. With a larger number of constant participants, more information was shared through the web board and thus students perceived a more positive experience during the spring.

Based on this experience it appears that web-enhanced teaching is more suited for regular semester and for motivated students who are "looking" to learn. Class size appears to have some affect on student participation and learning. Also, summer semester because of short duration may not be suitable for web-based learning because of time involved in learning the technology itself.

CONCLUSION

As with any new technology, this paper has raised more questions than provided answers. Since web-based teaching is a debatable issue it is actively being discussed in journals, Conferences and on the web itself. There are no clear cut directions as to which way is the best.

Our belief is that web-based teaching is for real, however "full" web-based courses as offered by virtual universities are not desirable for all students. They may be suitable for non-traditional students, who live far away from campuses, are on the road most of the time and self-motivated.

We should use technology for delivering information but should not allow technology to dictate education. A complete web-based education may produce robots who have very little social and interpersonal skills and may shortchange on content quality. This is not to say that web-based teaching should not be used but the "good" part of technology should be used to enhance face-to-face teaching environment.

REFERENCES

1. Aggarwal, A.K. , Issues in Web-Based Teaching, panel, AIS Conference, 1998
2. Brandt Scott, Teaching for Under of the Internet, Communications of the ACM, vol 40, no 10, 1997.
3. Thom Gillespie, Web -Ed for Information professional, Database, April/May, 1997
4. Kemery, Ed, Issues in Web-Based Teaching, panel, AIS Conference, 1998.
5. Emerging Digital Economy, Commerce Department report on Digital Commerce, 1998.

The Role of Personality Characteristics in User Information Satisfaction Measurement

Adel M. Aladwani
Department of QM & IS, College of Administrative Sciences, Kuwait University
E-mail: adwani@kuc01.kuniv.edu.kw

INTRODUCTION

Many information systems (IS) researchers and practitioners have considered User Information Satisfaction (UIS) as a very important indicator of IS success (Bailey and Pearson, 1983; DeLone and McLean, 1992; Doll and Torkzadeh, 1988; Doll and Weidong 1997; Galletta and Lederer, 1989; Gelderman, 1998; Ives et al, 1983; McKeen and Guimaraes, 1997; Melone, 1990; Palvia, 1996; Treacy, 1985; Woodroof and Kasper, 1998; Zmud, 1979). Despite the importance of UIS, many IS scholars have identified several conceptual and measurement problems associated with the construct (Melone, 1990; Galletta and Lederer, 1989). As a result, some IS researchers have recommended the incorporation of attitudes in future UIS research to gain a better understanding of the construct (e.g., Melone, 1990; Treacy, 1985).

Psychologists view attitudes as a two step process: an antecedent stimulus followed by an evaluative reaction (McGuire, 1969). Further, psychologists have investigated the effect of attitudes on behavior, the effect of behavior on attitudes, and the interaction between the two (Byrne and Kelly, 1981). By drawing on the psychology literature in general and on the personality literature in particular, we will try to re-evaluate the relationship between deep satisfaction (as an attitude) and the overt response to a user satisfaction measure in the context of IS research.

To achieve this goal, the paper will first review key UIS measures. Then, the paper will examine some of the assumptions of UIS measurement. Next, the attitude-behavior consistency assumption and its relevance to UIS research will be discussed. The conclusions and research implications will be discussed last.

THE MEASUREMENT OF UIS

UIS is, undoubtedly, the most widely used surrogate of IS success (Galletta and Lederer, 1989). DeLone and McLean (1992) numerated three reasons for UIS popularity. First, UIS has high face validity. Second, the available instruments that are used to measure other success dimensions (e.g., quality) are so poor that no body prefers to employ them. Finally, in contrast with the second reason, many instruments exist to measure UIS.

The UIS measures of Bailey and Pearson (1983), Ives, Olson, and Baroudi (1983), and Doll and Torkzadeh (1988) are vastly recognized in the literature. Bailey and Pearson (1983) reviewed the literature and came up with 36 factors that were believed to affect users' satisfaction. In addition, 3 more factors were included later based on a recommendation from three IS practitioners. The 39 factors were tested for completeness by comparing the list to interview responses of 32 middle managers.

Ives, Olson, and Baroudi (1983) factor analyzed the items in Bailey-Pearson instrument and 4 additional items using data from 200 subjects. The result was a reduced scale consisting of 13 items loaded on three factors: quality of the information product, user knowledge and involvement, and information systems' staff and services.

Doll and Torkzadeh (1988), after reviewing the satisfaction literature, developed a 12-item end-user satisfaction instrument that covered five dimensions: content, accuracy, format, ease of use, and timeliness. Responses from 618 end-users were used to test the instrument. However, Etezadi-Amoli and Farhoomand (1991) criticized the EUC satisfaction instrument. Later, Doll and Weidong (1997) cross-validated the EUC satisfaction instrument using confirmatory factor analysis and found that the EUC satisfaction instrument is robust. Swanson (1974), and Larcker and Lessig (1980) also developed satisfaction scales. Nevertheless, these scales suffer from numerous problems such as the limited focus on the product dimension of UIS and the serious reliability and validity limitations.

Although considerable efforts have been made to measure UIS, many scholars still report major conceptual and measurement problems associated with it. Melone (1990), for example, noted two major drawbacks in UIS research. First is that UIS research exists largely apart from theoretical frameworks in the behavioral sciences. Second is the lack of agreement among IS researchers on a unified conceptual definition of the UIS construct. Moreover,

Galletta and Lederer (1989) empirically evaluated one of the most cited and used UIS instrument and concluded that researchers need to develop more reliable measures of UIS.

Moreover, a common thread among the three reviewed UIS measures is the emphasis, in one way or another, on four major dimensions: the product, technical support, organizational environment, and the knowledge and involvement of the user. None of the measures taken into account the effects of *one's personality* on the relationship between one's information satisfaction as an attitude and one's expressive behavior as represented by the answer to some sort of a UIS tool.

The IS community may need to reflect upon the lack of congruence between the existing measures of UIS and the specific personality characteristics of the users. Better understanding of the UIS construct can accrue with the consideration of all relevant factors including the personality attributes of the users. The lack of consideration to the possible conformance between attitudes and behavior may result, in the final analysis, in an under optimum measurement of UIS. This is particularly true because different users have different responses to a particular instrument due to the various rationalities that users employ in either a calculated or an uncalculated manner. This assertion will be discussed in a later section.

REVISITING UIS: ON THE CONSISTENCY ASSUMPTION

Melone (1990) noted that McGuire (1969) definition of an attitude (an evaluative response to an antecedent stimulus) "incorporates much of what has been included in the research on user satisfaction." Further, Melone (1990) followed Fazio (1986) and Breckler (1984) to separate between the UIS (attitude) and the verbal/non-verbal responses.

Traditionally, IS researchers have assumed that users' feelings predict users' behavior with high reliability. Hence, IS scholars have paid scant attention to the factors that affect the attitude-behavior relationship. With the exception of Cheney's (1984) article, in which he explored the effects of programmers' characteristics on productivity and satisfaction, most of the IS articles have studied the effects of individual differences (ID) on IS success surrogates other than satisfaction. For example, Benbasat and Dexter (1982) investigated the effects of ID on IS success as measured by *usage*. Harrison and Rainer (1992) studied the influence of ID on knowledge workers computer skills.

The above reviewed studies concerned themselves with the cognitive and situational elements of individual differences. No attempt, as far as the author can tell, has been made to study the effects of personality attributes per se. Moreover, in his very influential article, Zmud (1979) reviewed and synthesized the empirical literature, up to that time, regarding the influence of ID *(cognitive, personality, and situational factors)* on MIS success to come up with numerous suggestions for future research. Three observations came up when reviewing the piece:

1 In the association between ID and MIS success as measured by user satisfaction, Zmud considered IS studies that cover two out of the three dimensions of ID. He considered the effects of both cognitive style and situational dimensions and did not mention any IS study that has investigated personality (the third dimension).

2 In citing the research on the effects of the personality dimension on MIS success, Zmud referred only to psychologists. The studies, however, focused on decision maker personality and information receiver perception. The first and second observations, imply that the personality dimension was not investigated in the IS literature.

3 In one of the impact paths of his ID-MIS success associative model, Zmud conceptualized the effect of ID on MIS success as one that is mediated by attitudes. This is contrary to what the psychologists would argue. Personal variables (one of the dimensions of ID) are viewed by many psychologists as important determinants of attitude-behavior relationship (e.g., Norman, 1975).

The previous discussion points to the need for reconsidering UIS measurement.

PERSONALITY ATTRIBUTES, ATTITUDE-BEHAVIOR CONSISTENCY, AND THE MEASUREMENT OF THE UIS CONSTRUCT

The psychology literature has extensively investigated the personality determinants of the attitude-behavior relationship. Worchel et al (1988) asserted that this wide interest, in part, is inspired by the jittery evidence to support the conventional wisdom that one should act according to how one feels. Other factors have also been hypothesized to influence the relationship of attitude to behavior including situational factors (e.g., Snyder and Swanson, 1976). In this paper, we consider the research on the effects of personality characteristics on the relationship between attitude and behavior.

Over a relatively long period, the psychology stream of research have investigated the impact of numerous personality determinants on attitude-behavior relationship (Zanna, Higgins, and Herman, 1982). Some of the personality characteristics that are believed to be pertinent to our case include self-monitoring (Snyder, 1974); self-awareness (Wicklund, 1982); and Moods (Kimble, 1990).

Self-monitoring

Snyder (1974) introduced the concept of self-monitoring to reflect the possible personality differences among people regarding the congruence between attitude and behavior. The author suggested that in a social setting an individual actively attempts to behave in accordance to either the surrounding situational signals (high self-monitoring) or knowledge about the internal state (low self-monitoring). An individual who is considered a high self-monitor demonstrates low attitude-behavior consistency. A low self-monitor person demonstrates high attitude-behavior consistency.

The attitudes (satisfactory feelings) toward an information product of a high self-monitor user may be concealed. When a UIS instrument is administered to measure the satisfaction of such a user, his/her answers may reflect other calculations consistent with some of the influences that are enduring at that particular moment. For example, the user may observe that his/her colleagues are applauding the information product of the system or that his/her boss is in favor of the system in general. In such a situation, a high self-monitoring user is more likely to abide to the pressure from the surrounding environment for some perceived gains. Therefore, the overt response of such a user(s) may distort the accuracy of the scale.

The social pressures on an individual's decision making process have been considered in the IS implementation research. For example, Lawrence and Low (1993) found positive correlation between top management support and individual user satisfaction. Davis, Bagozzi, and Warshaw (1989), although did not include the social pressure factor in their research model, affirmatively acknowledged the importance of social influences for system usage. The behavior of the low self-monitoring user usually follows his/her deep satisfaction beliefs.

Self-awareness

This personality factor involves imputing oneself into a particular situation, thus, strengthening the attendance to the self (Wicklund, 1979; Scheier et al, 1978). Several classes of stimuli have been identified as having attracting (e.g., using first person pronouns in questionnaires) or distracting (e.g., showing a television programs during the questionnaire) effects on the self. A person in a self-aware state is expected to demonstrate high attitude-behavior consistency and vice-versa (Wicklund, 1982).

The findings of Wicklund (1979), Wicklund (1982), and Scheier et al (1978) give rise to many interesting implications to the user information satisfaction research. Provoking the self-aware state of a user during the administration of a UIS assessment tool can help direct the response of the user in accord with his satisfaction feelings. Therefore, stimulating one's self-awareness can lead to answers that are more reflective.

The dominant procedure to take record of users' attitudes (satisfaction) toward the system is through recording their nonverbal (written) responses. Consequently, using first person pronouns to personalize the written questions of a particular measure may have beneficial consequences such as achieving an increased interest in answering the questionnaire.

Although some UIS researchers used first person pronouns in some of the questions in their surveys, the constructed questions in these surveys did not reflect a systematic use of self-person pronouns. For example, Galletta and Lederer (1989) studied two UIS scales that of Ives et al. (1983) and a four-question summary scale. They reported the Ives et al. scale in a passive mode, while they reported theirs in an active mode.

Moods

The results of the research on moods, although not directly related to the consistency issue, suggest that hypersensitive moods may overwhelm the effect of attitude on behavior (Kimble, 1990). This remark has major implications for UIS research. One's satisfactory feelings toward an information product and his or her overt response to a UIS measure is not always straight forward as one may want to assume. The more intense the disposition of a user is when responding to a UIS instrument, the less the chance that the result will reflect user actual feelings.

The discussion in the previous sections points to the suggestion that UIS can not be judged in separation of the evident congruence between an individual's personality characteristics (e.g., moods) and the phenomenon under consideration.

CONCLUSION

The User Information Satisfaction construct is reassessed and a candidate answer to the apparent wide differences in its measurement is explored. The conventional attitude-behavior consistency assumption in the UIS literature is challenged. The effects that users' personality attributes may have on UIS measurement are discussed. Our analysis led us to believe that the overt response toward an attitude object is not necessarily directly related to one's previous attitudes.

Some implications for future research emerge from this study. First, there is a need to develop and empirically test a model that considers the interaction effects of personality characteristics on the relationship between satisfaction beliefs and overt response to a tool(s) that measure these beliefs. Conducting an experiment is the most likely research design here. Second, there is a need to examine how existing UIS instruments may be modified to consider users' personality traits. Finally, future user information satisfaction research may need to investigate which psychological measurement tools for personality would be best studied and under what circumstances.

REFERENCES

Bailey, J. and S. Pearson "Development of a tool for measuring and analyzing Computer User Satisfaction," *Management Science*, v. 29, 1983, pp. 530-545.

Baroudi, J. and W. Orlikowski "A Short Form Measure of User Satisfaction and Notes on Use," *JMIS*, v. 4, 1988, pp. 44-59.

Benbasat, I. and A. Dexter "Individual Differences in the Use of Decision Support Aids," *J. of Accounting Research*, v. 20, 1982, pp. 1-11.

Breckler, S. "Empirical Validation of Affect, Behavior and Cognition as Distinct Components of Attitude," *J. of Personality and Social Psychology*, v. 47, 1984, pp. 1191-1205.

Byrne, D. and K. Kelly *An Introduction to Personality*, 3rd. edition, Prentice-Hall, Englewood Cliffs, NJ, 1981.

Cheney, P. "Effects of Individual Characteristics, Organization Factors and Task Characteristics on Computer Programmer Productivity and Job Satisfaction," *Information & Management*, 1984, pp. 209-214.

DeLone, W. and McLean, E. "Information Systems Success: The Quest for Dependent Variable," *Information Systems Research*, v. 3, 1992, pp. 60-95.

Doll, W. and G. Torkzadeh "The Measurement of End-User Computing Satisfaction," *MIS Quarterly*, v. 12, 1988, pp.259-274.

Doll, W. and Weidong, X. "Confirmatory factor analysis of the End-User Computing Satisfaction instrument: A replication," *Journal of End User Computing* 9, 1997, 24-31.

Etezadi-Amoli, J. and Farhoomand, A. On End-User Computing Satisfaction. *MIS Quarterly, v.* 15, 1991, pp. 1-4.

Fazio, R. "How Attitude Guide Behavior?" in R. M. Sorrenino and E. T. Higgins (Editors) *Handbook of Motivation and Cognition: Foundations of Social behavior*, Guilford, NY, 1986.

Galletta, D. and A. Lederer "Some Cautions on the Measurement of User Information Satisfaction," *Decision Sciences*, v. 20, 1989, pp. 419-438.

Gelderman, M. The relation between user satisfaction, usage of information systems and performance. *Information & Management* 34, 1998, pp.11-18.

Harrison, A. and R. Rainer "The Influence of Individual Differences on Skill in End-User Computing," *JMIS*, v. 9, 1992, pp. 93-111.

Ives, B., M. Olson, and J. Baroudi "The Measurement of User Information satisfaction," *Communications of the ACM*, v. 26, 1983, pp. 785-793.

Kimble, C. *Social Psychology: Studying Human Interaction*, Brown Publishers, 1990, p.149.

Lawrence, M. and G. Low "Exploring Individual user Satisfaction Within User-Led Development," *MIS Quarterly*, v. 17, 1993, pp. 195-208.

Larcker, D. and V. Lessig "Perceived Usefulness of Information: A Psychmetric Examination," *Decision Sciences*, v. 11, 1980, pp.121-134.

McGuire, W. "The Nature of Attitudes and Attitude Change," in G. Lindzey and E. Aronson (Eds.). *The Handbook of Social Psychology: volume 3*, 2nd edition, Addison-Wesley, Reading, MA, 1969.

McKeen, J. and Guimaraes, T. Successful strategies for user participation in systems development. *Journal of Management Information Systems, v.* 14, 1997, pp.133-150.

Melone, N. "A Theoretical Assessment of the User-Satisfaction Construct in Information Systems Research," *Management Science*, v. 36, 1990, pp. 76-91.

Norman, R. "Affective-Cognitive Consistency: Attitudes, Conformity and Behavior," *J. of Personality and Social Psychology*, v. 32, 1975, pp. 83-91.

Palvia, P. A model and instrument for measuring small business user satisfaction with information technology. *Information & Management, v.* 31, 1996, pp. 151-163.

Powers, R. and G. Dickson "MIS Project Management: Myths, Opinions, and Reality," *California Management Review*, v. 15, 1973, pp. 147-156.

Scheier, M., A. Buss, and D. Buss "Self-consciousness, self-report of aggression, and aggression," *J. of Research in Personality*, v. 12, 1978, pp. 133-140.

Snyder, M. "The Self-Monitoring of Expressive behavior," *J. of Personality and Social Psychology*, v. 30, 1974, pp. 526-537.

Snyder, M. and W. Swann "When Actions Reflect Attitudes: The Politics of Impression Management," *J. of Personality and Social Psychology*, v. 34, 1976, pp. 1034-1042.

Treacy, M. "An Empirical Examination of a causal Model of User Information Satisfaction," *working paper, Center for ISR, Sloan School of Management, MIT*, 1985.

Wicklund, R. "The Influence of Self-awareness on Human Behavior," *American Scientist*, v. 67, 1979, pp. 187-193.

Wicklund, R. "Self-Focused Attention and the Validity of Self-Reports," in Zanna, Higgins, and Herman (Editors) *Consistency in Social Behavior: The Ontario Symposium (volume II)*, Lawrence Erlbuam, Hillside, NJ, 1982.

Woodroof, J. and Kasper, G. A conceptual development of process and outcome user satisfaction. *Information Resources Management Journal, v.* 11, 1998, pp.37-43.

Worchel, S., J. Cooper, and G. Goethals *Understanding Social Psychology*, Dorsey Press, Chicago, IL, 1988.

Zanna, M., E. Higgins, and C. Herman *Consistency in Social Behavior: The Ontario Symposium (volume II)*, Lawrence Erlbuam, Hillside, NJ, 1982.

Zmud, R. "Individual Differences and MIS Success: A Review of the Empirical Literature," *Management Science*, v. 25, 1979, pp. 966-979.

Object-Oriented Design Representation on Jasmine

Dr Fawzi Albalooshi

Department of Computer Science, University of Bahrain, P. O. Box 32038, Isa Town, Bahrain.
Tel: 0973-782340, Fax: 0973-682582, Email: fbalushi@batelco.com.bh

ABSTRACT

When thinking in building a software development environment the first problem we are faced with is information representation. In this paper we investigate the possibility of using Jasmine as a base for a software development environment that supports OO design and development. Using Booch's OO design notation we investigate the possibility of representing design information on Jasmine's OODB. We then look into the possibility of representing design information that uses UML. The similarity between the two notations suggests that they can share the same representation, thus multiple views of design information can be supported. We further investigate how code can be generated from the proposed representation. The capabilities provided by Rational Rose that support multiple design notations and code generation are compared with the capabilities that are possible by our representation.

Index Terms: Object-Orientation, design representation, code generation, multiple views, software engineering environment, repository, Jasmine, Booch, UML

INTRODUCTION

OO software development has gained a wide popularity for a number of reasons. The main is that they help in software reuse, which leads to a reduction in development time, costs, and effort. The structure of OO software is decoupled which supports code modification and correction, and leads to higher quality software.

In recent years researchers from academia and other organizations have shown interest in Multiple Views of Software Development (MVSD). They provide the user with different views of the system under development, such that each development stage is reflected by a view, and throughout the system's life cycle the views show its most recent state. Furthermore, they ease the development process, and ensure that the various presentations of the system are up to date, whether design, specification, or implementation. The availability of various notations assists in the task of developing the software. A developer is able choose the notation s/he is more familiar with, and there is a choice of notation available to introduce a new concept that cannot easily be captured by all notations. Automatic transformation between the notations can further speed the development process, and enables reverse engineering. In an empirical study carried out at Brown University [MR92] it was found that when increasing the number of views of a software system the performance of the programmers working on the system was increased. The study concluded that multiple views improved the performance of the software developers. As a long-term plan we aim at developing an environment supporting OO software development using multiple views. The bases of such an environment are three levels of integration, and they are, data, presentation, and control integration. Data integration is achieved by providing the tools with a common representation that they can share. Presentation integration is the degree of similarity between the tools to interact and provide their services to the user. Control integration is communication between the tools to provide the user with the most recent state of the system under development.

A good example of an OO software development environment that supports multiple views of a system is SPE (Snart Programming Environment [GH95]). The stages supported by the environment are analysis, design, specification, and implementation. Another example is PIROL (Project Integrating Reference Object Library [GHJK95]) that supports object thinking throughout. The environment supports OO development, the interface is OO, and the tools are developed O Orientedly. P. Rosch [Ros96] proposed a model that provided the basis for a representation and efficient processing of abstract objects in a multiple view design environment. Two implementations for his proposal were reported: EXPLOIT and the Multi-View-Engine. A widely used OO development environment is Rational Rose that supports UML, Booch, and OMT notations. This environment is discussed in more detail in section 6 where we present the capabilities of our proposed representation and the functionality that is provided by Rose.

In this paper we look into the problem of data integration as a first step in developing an environment. At first we surveyed the literature to obtain details of previous work in the area. A detailed discussion and investigation on the topic can be found in [LL94]. The work mainly investigated a number of tightly integrated environments that used abstract syntax trees and others that used attribute graphs to represent software development information. It was found that these two methods of representation were closely related to the syntax of programming languages and were not flexible enough to support a wider range of tools. The authors recommended the use of a canonical representation that represents software systems in general rather than a particular tool. The canonical representation was then instantiated into a subset of data representation to cater for the needs of specific tools. S. Chou, J. Chen, and C. Chung [CC96] also recommended fine-grained representation for its advantage in re-using classes and software. Based on these readings and other work on multiple view environments reported in [Alb97] we investigated the possibility of OO design representation on Jasmine.

JASMINE

To represent OO software design our first choice of database was an OO one. Jasmine is a product produced by Computer Associates International and FUJITSU LIMITED. It is a complete system that uses an OO database for application development. The database is used to hold class definitions and objects (class instances). A group of related classes are stored under a class family. A class can have two types of properties and they are instance-level and class-level. Instance level properties belong entirely to the instances, but class-level properties contain a value for all class instances. This value can be changed dynamically during processing. Similarly to properties there are two types of methods instance level and class level. Instance level methods perform calculations on individual class instances. Class level methods are used to perform calculations on the entire class instances. Additionally two more types of methods are supported by Jasmine and they are instance-collection-level methods, and class-collection-level methods. The first perform calculations on a collection of instances of a class, and the second perform calculations on instances of a collection of classes.

The database supports inheritance and multiple inheritance. One-to-many and many-to-many type of relationships can also be represented. The object database query language (ODQL) provides complete database access including data definition and access, and method writing. Jasmine provides integration with other databases, including, OpenIngres, Oracle, Sybase, Informix, SQLServer, and DB2. It has its own class library with support for multimedia and complex data types, such as, images, frame animation sequences, audio, and video.

An application-programming interface (API) is provided for access from C and C++, and bindings for direct access from Java applications. Other services provided by Jasmine include, client/server computing, locking and concurrency control, transaction management, recovery and restart, and database administration. More details on Jasmine can be found in [Com97].

Jasmine seems to confirm with many of the OODBMS concepts discussed in [GHS96] and [EN94], except for encapsulation, which is not explicitly supported. The main concepts are, object identity, structure, type constructors; encapsulation of operations, methods, and persistence; type and class hierarchies and inheritance; and complex objects.

BOOCH'S CLASS NOTATION AND ITS REPRESENTATION

The first OO design method we look into is Booch's [Boo94] for its clearness and wide use. In this method the main entity that represents a software component or a group of classes is the class category. It may contain one or more classes and may contain other categories. Classes can be any of six types and they are abstract, meta class, normal, utility, instantiated, or parameterized. Class relationships that are supported are meta, instantiation, association, inheritance, has, and using. The last four relationships can have a property, such as, friend, virtual, or static. Export control can be applied to relationships, class attributes and operations, such as, public, private, protected, and implementation. To represent Booch's class notation on Jasmine we need to store two types of information, and they are the definitions and the information about them. The definitions are the class categories, and the classes containing their attributes and operations that can easily be represented as Jasmine classes. The information related to the definitions include the relationship details, the class types, and export control. In the repository the information about the classes and their relationships can be stored as instances of two user defined classes. One defined to hold class details, let us call it class_det, and another to hold relationship details, let us call it relation. The details of these two classes are discussed in the next two sections.

Class Category and Classes

A class category may contain one or more classes, and zero or more categories. The notation can be represented on Jasmine as a class having a has relationship to every class and category it contains. An instance of class_det is needed having the category name and holding its type as a 'category'. For each relationship an instance of the class relation is required to represent the relationship between the category and any other category or class.

A notational class can be of the following types: abstract, meta class, normal, utility, instantiated, or parameterized. Any of the first four can be represented as a jasmine class with an instance of type class_det to hold its type. The notational attributes and operations can be represented as Jasmine instance-level attributes and methods respectively, making up the class members. The parameterized and instantiated classes have formal and actual parameters respectively that need to be represented. These two types can be stored as jasmine classes, and their parameters can be stored as class-level attributes, so that the formal and actual parameters are distinguished from the normal class parameters. To illustrate further consider figure 1, in it the class PlanSet is instantiated from Set. The Jasmine class definitions for the two are shown below, and further class details will be maintained by instances of type class_det as we explain in the following sections.

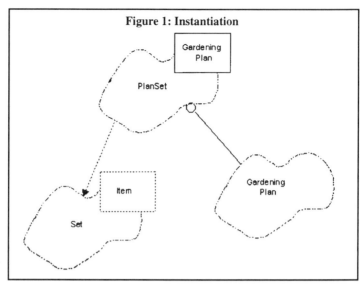

Figure 1: Instantiation

```
defineClass Set
{
    class:
        Item para1;
        .
        .
        .
}
```

```
defineClass PlanSet
{
    class:
        GardeningPlan para1;
        .
        .
}
```

The notational relationships between classes include, association, inheritance, has, using, instantiation, and meta. In Jasmine there is no way to represent relationships between classes explicitly by means of a link. Therefore we have chosen to use instances of a class that we defined to represent all relationships.

Relationships
The most basic relationships are meta and instantiation. The details that are needed to be stored for these two are relationship type, source class, destination class, and label. The Jasmine class declaration to hold these details is shown below.

```
defineClass relation
{
    instance:
        string type;
        string source;
        string destination;
        string label;
};
```

Properties of type string are needed to store the details. The association, inheritance, and has relationships further need two more attributes in addition to the existing ones. One to hold the relationship property, such as, friend, virtual, or static. The other to hold export control, such as, public, protected, private, or implementation. These two can be strings, holding the literals, or integers holding values to represent the literals. The new relationship class is as follows:

```
defineClass relation_2
    super: relation
{
    instance:
        string property;
        string export;
}
```

The using relationship needs two more Jasmine attributes in addition to the ones specified for relation_2, they are needed to hold cardinality. Therefore integer attributes are added, the first called from_card and the second to_card as follows:

```
defineClass relation_3
    super: relation_2
{
    instance:
            integer from_card;
            integer to_card;
}
```

To represent a relationship of any kind an instance of the appropriate class is used to store the details of the relationship. For example, to represent a using relationship an instance of relation_3 is used; to represent a has relationship an instance of relation_2 is used; and to represent an instantiation relationship and instance of relation is used. When creating instances of type relation, relation_2, or relation _3 we are faced with the problem of naming the instances. Practically the names must be generated by the system automatically and no user intervention is required. To make the names unique it is suggested to use serial numbers. Starting from 0 or 1, the number is appended to a predefined identifier such as 'Rel' to create a unique instance name. Each time a new instance is generated the serial number is incremented. A class-level attribute can be added to the class relation to hold the last serial number used. The class definition is modified to add the attribute as follows:

```
defineClass relation
{
    class:
        integer NextRelationNo default:0;
    instance:
        string type;
        string source;
        string destination;
        string label;
}
```

Properties of a class have access control associated with them such as private, public, protected, and implementation. The properties, their visibility, and the class type are maintained by an instance of a class called class_det. An instance of this class is created for each notational class represented by a Jasmine class. The class definition for class_det is as follows:

```
defineClass class_det
{
    instance:
        string type;
        Bag < string > properties;
        Bag < string > access;
}
```

EXAMPLE DESIGN

As an example representation consider the classes shown in figure 2 from [Boo94]. Figure 3 shows how the design would be represented on Jasmine. The Jasmine class definitions are shown in dotted boxes; solid boxes show instances of class_det containing the details for the notational classes, an instance for each class; solid boxes with thick borders are instances representing the relationships between the classes. Instance names representing relationships are prefixed with the keyword 'Rel', and the names of instances of type class_det holding details for each class are prefixed with the keyword 'Ins'. Designing and implementing a tool to maintain such design information is our next task following the investigation reported here. Jasmine has its own development environment, provides an interface to Java, and has C APIs, thus a tool that can access the database can be built using any of these languages. Details of maintaining the information at tool level can differ, depending on the language used and the tool functionality. The design representation proposed here is general and may need adjustments to suit the tool designed to maintain it.

UML

UML is short for Unified Modeling Language that unifies the notations of Booch, Rumbaugh, and Jacobson. It is expected to become the standard modeling language of the future, its standardization efforts are currently being carried out by the Object Management Group. Our discussion on OO design is not complete without considering UML and the possibility of representing it on Jasmine. When we discussed Booch's design method we mainly considered class diagrams and their relationships for possible representation on Jasmine. We will carry out a similar analysis for UML. Fowler [FS97] addressed and explained with examples the use of classes and various class types in UML. An interesting extension available in UML is the concept of stereotypes that is used to add

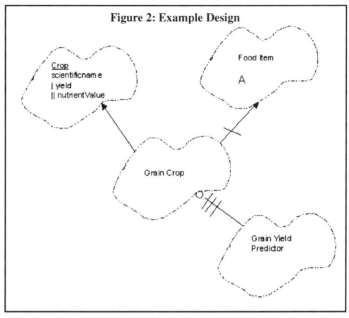

Figure 2: Example Design

any required semantic. All class types and relationships available in Booch's notation are supported by UML. A detailed discussion with illustrations can be found in [EP98]. Relationships in UML include: associations to represent conceptual relationships between classes; refinement to indicate greater level of detail, and is similar to generalization; dependency relationship to show that a class A is dependent on a class B, changes to any of the classes may result to changes to the other; generalization to represent inheritance; aggregation is the part of relationship; and composition which is stronger than aggregation, in that the part of object may belong to only one whole, and the parts are expected to live and die with the whole. Classes can have attributes and operations with different levels of visibility such as private, protected, and public. Figure 4 shows an example design using UML notation. Corporate customer inherits the customer properties; therefore they have a generalization relationship. A customer can have at least one or more orders; therefore the Customer class has an association relationship with the Order class. Figure 5 shows the same design using Booch's notation, and figure 6 shows our proposed representation on Jasmine. The same representation is suitable to store the design information for both notations with a minor difference, and that is, the object Rel_1 contains details of the relationship between Customer and Order, and has using as its type. This is due to the similarity between Booch's using relationship and association in UML. The similarity between the two notations can open the possibility of integrating both to share the same design information stored on Jasmine, thus supporting Multiple Views of design information.

CODE GENERATION

A major advantage for the representation proposed here is code generation. Depending on the details entered for the design, code can be generated from the stored information. Details such as, class names and their types; attribute names, types, an initialization details; and method names, return types, parameters, and code (preferably in the targeted programming language) can all be maintained through the design tool. From these details class specifications can be derived in a suitable OO programming language such as C++. Details of relationships between classes are available and can be extracted from the instances representing them. Sequencing of code units is a problem faced at this stage. During the design stage information is entered at random and order is not important, but to produce compile-able code that reflects the appropriate relationships between code units they must be presented in their correct order. As a simple example consider a declaration that is of a certain class type, the class must be defined sequentially ahead of the declaration. A solution to this problem would be to ensure that the information is stored in proper order at the design stage, thus ensuring the correct sequence of the generated code. Another solution would be to retrieve the information stored at the design stage in a special way that maintains sequencing, such as, checking for dependencies.

In our search for an OO development environment we found Rational Rose [Qua98] a product from Rational Software Corporation. Rose stands for Rational Object Oriented Software Engineering. It supports software modeling using UML, Booch, and OMT notations; supports automatic code generation to a number of OO languages including C++; and reverse engineering. We compared the capabilities that can be supported using our representation

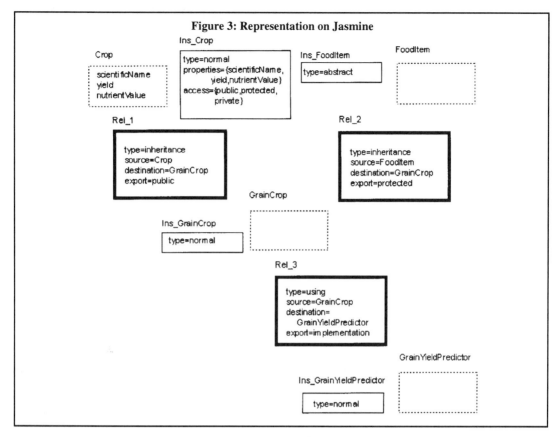

Figure 3: Representation on Jasmine

with that of Rose's. The design example shown in figure 4 was entered using UML notation. After that we changed the notation to Booch's, and the UML design was transformed to the one shown in figure 5. We carried on with our experiment to generate the code for the design. In Rose C++ code can be generated for selected design items through an option available in the tools menu. We choose to generate code for all three classes and their relationships, therefore a header and an implementation file for each class were generated. The generation of separate files for each class overcomes the problem of sequencing we mentioned in the previous paragraph. The generated header and implementation files for the Customer class are shown in figures 7 and 8. Many of the annotated code and comments have been removed to reduce the size of the code, and improve readability.

One of the important observations that we have deduced from this experiment is that similar code can be generated using our proposed representation. The Customer class has a relationship with the Order class; therefore the Order class's header file was included. Reading the instance Rel_1 we know that there is a relationship between Customer and Order, so we include the Order class's header file in the Customer's header file. Constructors and destructors can be automatically generated since they only need the class name, so does the assignment and equality operations. Signatures of operations, and attributes and their types can be included in their proper sections whether private, protected, or public. Get and Set operations can be automatically generated for the attributes. All these details are available and can be extracted from the Customer class stored in the database and the instance reserved for it. Get and Set operations for associations can be derived from the information available in the object representing the relationship, in this case Rel_1. The generated header file further contained the implementation of the Get and Set operations as inline functions that can easily be produced using the available information. The file Customer.cpp contained the implementation of the constructors, destructor, assignment, equality, and the specified functions. The details for these functions were not given and are left for the software engineer to specify. In our representation the default functions such as constructors, destructors, assignment, and equality can be generated automatically, and the user-defined functions can be included with their implementation details if they have been specified in the proper language.

CONCLUSION

At first we reviewed the literature for existing work on software design representation. Our aim was to find a

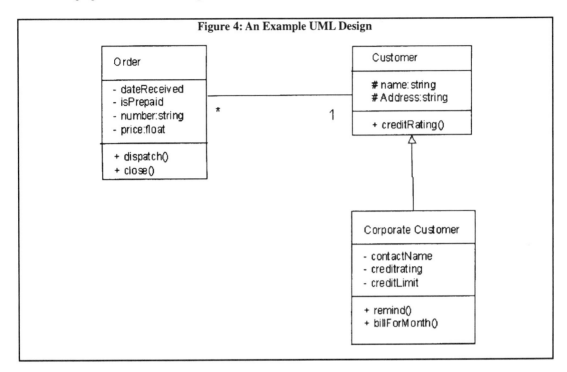

Figure 4: An Example UML Design

suitable representation for OO design information and learn from previous experiences. An important factor that effects the representation is the database model, and we chose to experiment on an OO one. Jasmine, a very recent product that uses an OO database was investigated for its suitability.

We then looked into two recent OO design notations, namely, Booch and UML. At first we proposed a representation for Booch's class notation on Jasmine, and illustrated the representation with an example design. After that we investigated the possibility of representing design information that uses the UML notation. The similarity between Booch and UML showed that they can share the same representation, thus both notations can be used to present the information. This is a very interesting feature as it would be possible to provide the user with two views one for each notation through which the design information can be manipulated. We further showed that it is possible to automatically generate code from the information stored.

To evaluate the capabilities that can be provided by the representation, we examined Rational Rose the dominant OO development environment in the market. The examination showed that our representation can be a suitable base for a development environment that provides software engineers with support similar to that provided by Rose. In Jasmine it is possible to code the class methods, and this code can be automatically incorporated in the classes generated from the design. We strongly believe that Jasmine's OODB can be a suitable database to represent OO design

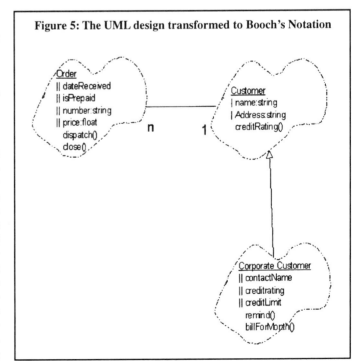

Figure 5: The UML design transformed to Booch's Notation

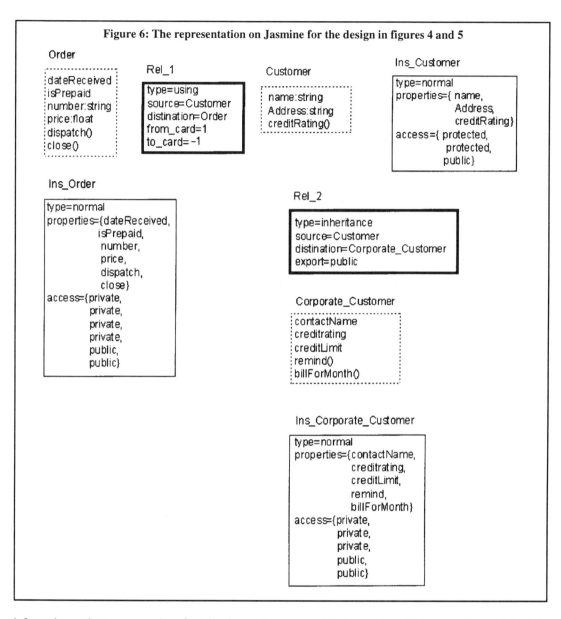

Figure 6: The representation on Jasmine for the design in figures 4 and 5

information, and can serve as a base for a development environment that supports multiple views. Our next step is to experiment further by building a development environment that uses the representation proposed here. The main components would be design tools that support notations such as Booch and UML, and functionality to automatically generate code.

REFERENCES

[Alb97] Fawzi Albalooshi. Multiple View Environments A Review. Department of Computer Science, University of Bahrain, PO Box 32038, Isa Town, Bahrain, September 1997.

[Boo94] G. Booch. Object-Oriented Analysis and Design with Applications. Addison-Wesley, 2nd edition, 1994.

[CC96] Shih-Chien Chou, Jen-Yen Chen, and Chyan-Goei Chung. A Repository for Object-Oriented Specification Reuse. Report on Object Analysis and Design, 2:17-24, 1996.

[Com97] Computer Associates International, Inc. and FUJITSU LIMITED. Jasmine Version 1.1 Evaluation Copy 1996, 1997, 1996-1997.

[EN94] Ramez Elmasri and Shamkant Navathe. Fundamentals of Database Systems. Benjamin/Cummings Publishing Company Inc., 1994.

Figure 7: The generated file Customer.h

```
#ifndef Customer_h
#define Customer_h 1

#include "Order.h"

class Customer
{
    public:

            Customer();
            Customer(const Customer &right);
            ~Customer();

            const Customer & operator=(const Customer &right);
            int operator==(const Customer &right) const;
            int operator!=(const Customer &right) const;
            Strings creditRating ();
            const UnboundedSetByReference<Order> get_the_Order () const;
            void set_the_Order (UnboundedSetByReference<Order> value);

    protected:

            Strings name;
            Strings Address;
            const Strings get_name () const;
            void set_name (Strings value);
            const Strings get_Address () const;
            void set_Address (Strings value);

    private:

            UnboundedSetByReference<Order> the_Order;

};

inline const Strings Customer::get_name () const {return name;}

inline void Customer::set_name (Strings value) {name = value;}

inline const Strings Customer::get_Address () const {return Address;}

inline void Customer::set_Address (Strings value) {Address = value;}

inline const UnboundedSetByReference<Order> Customer::get_the_Order () const {return the_Order;}

inline void Customer::set_the_Order (UnboundedSetByReference<Order> value) {the_Order = value;}

#endif
```

[EP98] Hans-Erik Eriksson and Magnus Penker. UML Toolkit. John Wiley and Sons, Inc., 1998.

[FS97] Martin Fowler and Kendall Scott. UML Distilled, Applying the Standard Object Modeling Language. Addison-Wesley, 1997.

[GH95] John C. Grundy and John G. Hosking. Software Environment Support for Integrated Formal Program Specification and Development. In Proceedings 1995 Asia Pacific Software Engineering Conference, 1995.

[GHJK95] B. Groth, S. Hermann, S. Jahnichen, and W. Koch. Project Integrating Reference Object Library (PIROL): An Object-Oriented Multiple-View SEE. In Software Engineering Environments, April 1995.

[GHS96] A. Goh, S.C. Hui, and B. Song. A Step/Express to Object-Oriented Databases Translator. In Proceedings of the SPIE - The International Society for Optical Engineering, volume 2644, pages 530-7, 1996.

Figure 8: The generated file Customer.cpp

```
#include "Customer.h"

Customer::Customer() { }

Customer::Customer(const Customer &right) { }

Customer::~Customer() { }

const Customer & Customer::operator=(const Customer &right) { }

int Customer::operator==(const Customer &right) const { }

int Customer::operator!=(const Customer &right) const { }

Strings Customer::creditRating () { }
```

[LL94] Chi-Chung Leung and Fred Long. Representing Ada Program Constructs in PCTE. In Proceedings of the PCTE '94 Conference, pages 262-83, December 1994.

[MR92] Scott Meyers and Steven P. Reiss. An Empirical Study of Multiple-View Software Development. In Proceedings of the Fifth ACM SIGSOFT Symposium on Software Development Environments, December 1992.

[Qua98] Terry Quatrani. Visual Modeling with Rational Rose and UML. Addison-Wesley, 1998.

[Ros96] Peter Rosch. User Interaction in a Multi-View Design Environment. In Proceedings IEEE Symposium on Visual Languages, September 1996.

Planning for Office Information Systems

Chandra S. Amaravadi

Department of Information Management and Decision Sciences, College of Business and Technology, Stipes Hall
435, Western Illinois University, Macomb, IL 61455
Ph:309-298-2034; Fx: 309-398-1696, Email: Chandra_amaravadi@ccmail.wiu.edu

ABSTRACT

Newer office information technologies such as groupware and workflow are enabling thousands of knowledge workers to share information and processing. Organizations can reap strategic and operational benefits by implementing such systems. The first step towards implementation is understanding the business needs in terms of the processes that need to be implemented, and the personnel responsible for carrying them out. Proper planning and analysis are important for the success of the implementation. An eight step methodology for planning and analyzing offices is presented. The methodology views the office as a collection of sub-structures such as the organizational, functional etc structures which are individually identified. It provides a technique for documenting these sub-structures, which serve as inputs into the design and implementation stages of the OIS development cycle. The method is technology independent and requires only a modest investment of resources.

INTRODUCTION

The information revolution has spawned numerous technologies geared towards automating the office. Whereas in the eighties many organizations invested in developing their PC and LAN infra-structures, there is a growing trend at the present time, towards implementing hi-end Office Information Systems (OIS) solutions such as groupware and enterprise applications. Included under this rubric are shared repositories, intranets, workflow, imaging systems and a growing number of customized applications[Radosevich '96]. Such applications are enabling thousands of knowledge workers to share information and processing and to offload many routine tasks to the system. Implementation of high end systems confers strategic and more frequently, operational advantages to the organization carrying out the implementation. For instance, the implementation of groupware can result in improved customer service or enable an engineer to identify the solution to a fatigue problem in a particular alloy. Organizations have to invest in an appropriate level of planning and analysis to reap the benefits of the technology.

In the Information systems area, a number of planning methodologies have been introduced under the aegis of enterprise planning, the most well known of which are the Business Systems Planning (BSP) methodologies [Carlson '79][Kerner '79]. In BSP, the analyst identifies the needs of the organization at the enterprise level by first identifying the processes and information classes relevant to the organization. Historically this was determined by a set of seven questions concerning the suppliers and orders in the company. Next, the analyst develops a set of matrices which depict relationships between the functions and processes in the organization and between processes and the information classes that they handle. The enterprise planning methods provide a broad overview of the organization's information classes and the specific processes responsible for creating, modifying or updating them. The planning information yielded by these methods can be utilized only for database planning rather than planning for applications. While there are no techniques geared specifically for carrying out IS planning (in a technical sense) there are a number of process oriented methodologies such as SADT, Warnier-Orr, Jackson and DFD. These have often been criticised for being too detailed and time consuming [Atkas '87].

However, neither the enterprise techniques nor the conventional analysis techniques are transferable to the office domain. Unlike conventional information systems, OIS involve smaller volumes, richer media types, richer user-behaviors, richer user-interactions and a lesser degree of automation [Braachi and Pernici '84]. Moreover these systems are frequently customized from off-the-shelf components rather than being developed from the ground up. Conventional techniques would therefore be too detailed, formal, unnecessary, time consuming and expensive. The enterprise techniques, with their data orientation, do not provide the degree of detail necessary for customization of an off-the-shelf package. Techniques in the OIS literature suffer from these and other limitations. For example, at the enterprise level, the OAM methodology and the OSSAD methodology provide a set of guidelines regarding the type of information to be collected and how it is to be collected [Sirbu et al. '82][De Antonellis and Zonta '90]. There are no graphical notations. At the process level, the TODOS conceptual model [Pernici et al. '91] perhaps takes the place of DFD and SADT in systems analysis and is similar to them in notation. Techniques such as the Critical Task Method (CTM) and OSSAD which are addressed at the activity/task level enable specifications in the form of verb and object as in "prepare proposal," "cancel trip request" etc [Harris '87] [De Antonellis and Zonta '90]. As with their MIS counterparts, the process and activity models in the OIS literature are richer, yet too detailed and too implementation oriented. The lack of graphical notations and vertical integration are other common problems of the office analysis techniques.

It is evident from the foregoing discussion that the enterprise techniques, the systems analysis and design techniques and the OIS techniques are not adequate when planning for Office Information Systems. There is a pressing need for a technique that that is informal and easy to use and yet can quickly uncover the business requirements. In this paper we will introduce such a technique and discuss its application to offices via the case study of the Drug and FDA affairs office.

PLANNING OBJECTIVES AND PHILOSOPHY

The OIS development cycle parallels the information systems development cycle except that in the former case, planning and analysis are not distinct phases. Since office systems are frequently developed by customization rather than by software development, they require more detailed planning and a lesser degree of analysis than conventional systems. The eight stage methodology discussed here results in outputs that are associated with both planning and analysis. The purpose of these front-end activities is to furnish a high level view of processes enabling them to analyzed, re-engineered and prioritized. The methodology will also provide inputs into the system selection process and implementation.

As with all methodologies, an OIS planning methodology must be abstract, hierarchical, technology independent (at least in the early stages) and easy to use. Abstraction in AEI-2 is achieved by limiting the anlaysis to the four essential sub-structures of the office [Amaravadi '89]: organizational, functional, process and application. These substructures focus respectively on work descriptions/reporting relationships, functions, processes and applications in the organization. They are individually modelled using a widely understood notation. A top-down approach needs to be followed in the analysis in order to provide the necessary planning perspective.

Technological issues should be deferred to the later stages of the methodology. Planning should be technology independent in the early stages, but once the process structure is understood, potential OIS technologies can be planned for and evaluated. A technological structure, which is one of the outputs of the planning process provides the framework for evaluating specific product offerings.

This structure expresses the business requirements using a structure chart or a tabular notation.

THE AEI-2 METHODOLOGY

The AEI-2 methodology is an extension of the OAM methodology referred to earlier and the AEI methodology [Amaravadi et al. '92]. OAM is based on the business systems planning methodology while AEI has its origins in Conceptual Dependency Theory in Artificial Intelligence. The former provides the overall sequence for the planning and analysis methodology while the latter provides the insights into the domain as pointed out earlier. The unit of analysis is the *office*, which can be a geographic unit, an organizational subunit or simply the locus of control. The methodology scales well to offices that are small as well as to those that have hundreds of employees. It is also applicable to a wide range of office types such as those with primarily clerical/administrative employees such as "purchasing" and "benefits" as well as to those having primarily knowledge workers such as "R & D" and "software development". The scope of the methodology is the planning and analysis parts of the system life cycle (see *Figure 1*).

Steps in AEI-2 Methodology

1. *Identify resources and scope of the study* — The resources required for the study would be a function of the size, type of office to be studied and number of offices to be studied. The methodology itself would not require more than an hour's training. The resource requirements for small offices such as the DFDA office (described subsequently in the case study) would be modest. A two person team could complete the study in a few days. The project team would preferably consist of a mix of senior and junior analysts, with the senior analysts developing the functional structure and the junior analysts concentrating on process structures. In the case of large offices or large numbers of offices, it is recommended that the study be carried out in a phased manner to allow for experience to cumulate as well as to minimize disruptions to staff. As with other information systems projects, the support of top management and co-operation of the staff are critical to the success of the effort.

2. *Identify organizational structure* – The staff structure or organizational structure is a fundamental component of any OIS and is analyzed first. It is developed in the form of *work descriptions* by referring to the personnel files or through interviews if there are no formal files. A *work description* for an employee could include the name, job

title, the person he/she reports to and a list of specific responsibilities. The work descriptions are cross-checked with the functional and process structures to ensure that their aggregation (or intersection in the case of overlapping assignments) adequately covers the process portfolio. In other words, are there any parts of the functional/process structure which have not been assigned to employees? Are there any processes that employees are carrying out, which are not included in the functional structure? The former case points to the need for revising job descriptions while in the latter case, the functional structure is revised appropriately.

3. *Identify functions and information used* — In keeping with the planning philosophy, we focus on the most important aspect of the office, namely its functions. *Functions* are the broad groups of processes, identifiable as the highest organizational level task descriptions. They are referred to by descriptive nouns such as product development, merchandising etc. In AEI-2, we start with the main function of the office and identify functions and sub-functions, down to the level of pro-

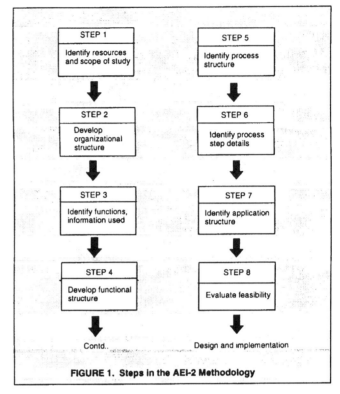

FIGURE 1. Steps in the AEI-2 Methodology

cesses, keeping in mind that functions are relative within an organization. For e.g. "Sales" would consist of sub-functions such as "Market research", "Sales forecasting", "Advertising etc." In large offices, these may be regarded as processes. *Processes* are the groupings of activities which are carried out together while activities are the smallest units of work. The main function of the office should be evident from the title of the office or from a mission statement if one exists. This can be identified by interviewing the person with overall responsibility for the office. Functions and sub-functions are identified by interviewing managers of each group in the office as well as the personnel next to them in rank. The information used or created by the functions/sub-functions are also identified at an aggregate level. These could include reports, forms, databases or raw data. For e.g. the "sales forecasting" function could use "historical sales" information and create "sales forecasts" as an output.

Table 1 — Types of Allowed Relationships Among Functions		
Abbreviation	Name of Relationship	Description of Relationship
SD	Structural Dependency	If two functions A & B are connected by an SD, it means that B is a part of A.
AD	Associative Dependency	If two functions A & B are connected by an AD, it means that B is done at the same time as A.
AOD	Alternative Dependency	If functions B and C are connected to a function A by an AOD, it means that B is an alternative to C.
TD	Time Dependency	If two functions, A & B are connected by a TD, it means that A is done after B.
ID	Information Dependency	If a function A has an ID to an item, it means, depending on the direction of the arrow that A either uses or creates the information item.

4. *Develop functional structure.* The functional structure is the overall structure of the functions, their relationships to other functions and their information needs/outputs. It represents the scope of the activity to be supported with an OIS. We will also refer to this as the *process portfolio.* AEI-2 has a graphical methodology to depict this structure which uses two major concepts to depict the functional structure: functions/sub-functions (depicted by ovals) and information (depicted by rectangles). As described earlier, "functions/sub-functions" are units of organizational activity while "information" includes any report, form or memo created/used by a function. (The functional structure is illustrated in *Figure 3* in the case study, to be discussed subsequently).

A function can have different types of relationships with other other functions/sub-functions. Functions can be part of other functions, they could be carried out at the same time or instead of or after other functions and so on. These different types of relationships are summarized in *Table 1* and illustrate the complexity of the office environment. It is primarily in this respect that an OIS methodology differs from traditional methodologies. There are more entity types and relationship types in the office domain, which can interact in complex ways. The ability to model these types of relationships is one of the strengths of this methodology. The functional structure is developed using the notation given in *Table 1*, reviewed with all managers and revised if necessary. It is an invaluable tool for communicating with users.

5. *Identify the process structure* -- The process structure consists of the relationships among steps or activities which comprise the process. Normally, there would be a sequential flow of activities in a process such as step1 followed by step2 followed by step3 etc. However, business processes sometimes have *branching, repetition or parallelism.* In branching, a process takes different paths depending on the value of a decision variable. Repetition is where a set of steps are repeatedly executed until some condition is satisfied. Parallelism simply means that activities are carrried out in parallel, i.e. at the same time. The process structure must be identified in terms of the steps and the order in which they are carried out. Decision variables and their values must be documented. The person with overall responsibility for process is interviewed to obtain this information. This information must be cross-checked with the persons who actually carry out the process. Either a flow charting or a tabular structure can be followed for documenting the process structure.

6. *Identify step details* -- The individual steps of a process or workflow involve a number of entities such as the documents used/created and the agents participating in them. These are identified by interviewing the person who carries out the steps and cross checked with the person having overall responsibility for the process. If there are constraints such as a step to be performed at a particular location, these should also be noted down. The step details are documented as textual annotations on the process structure.

7. *Identify application structure* -- In keeping with the planning philosophy, technological issues are deferred to the later stages of the cycle. At this stage, since the agent and functional structures are understood we can proceed with developing this structure. The *application structure* is a vendor/product-independent description of the features required to accomplish the process steps identified in the previous steps. It requires examining the functional and process structures to identify activities that have potential for automation. The application structure can be stated as tabular specifications or given in the form of a structure chart and accompanied by a narrative for maximum clarity. Focussing only on the features enables us to choose an OIS technology that best fits the business needs. In most cases, the technological structure would reflect commonly available features of applications software such as "fill" (from forms) "send" (from mail), "retrieve" (from database) etc. Clearly, this stage of the development cycle requires analysts with implementation experience.

8. *Evaluate Feasibility* — The feasibility of an OIS implementation is evaluated by comparing the features of available technologies with those in the application structure. There is a tradeoff between acquiring an integrated package that can satisfy most of the processing needs versus a mix-and-match approach where several components obtained from different vendors are integrated together. The former approach may result in a reduced implementation effort at the cost of the business requirements not being completely met. The latter approach provides increased flexibility and the ability to customize at the cost of a greater implementation and maintenance effort. The costs of the implementation must be weighed against financial and business considerations. Financial benefits can include staff reductions, increased productivity, greater throughput etc. Benefits to the business can range from improved sales and service to supporting organizational learning. As with good systems in general, a good OIS implementation can provide benefits that are disproportionately high in comparison to the initial investment.

A CASE STUDY

We will illustrate the methodology with the drug and FDA affairs (DFDA) office[1] of a large pharmaceutical company we will call PHC Inc. The DFDA organization chart is given in *Figure 2*. The office consists of fifteen full time employees and four part time employees. This study is mainly concerned with the field agents who report to the office managers as shown in Figure 2.

The primary mission of the DFDA office is to fulfill the Food and Drug Administration's (FDA) reporting requirements for drugs sold by PHC. Drugs sold by pharmaceutical companies can be prescription drugs or over the counter drugs (OTCs). Prescription drugs require a physician's prescription while OTCs can be purchased directly from drug stores. Consumers may sometimes have an *adverse reaction* (AR) such as headache or nausea to an OTC or a prescription drug. It is the job of the FAs to obtain the necessary documentation of these ARs. Information about an adverse reaction (AR) may be obtained in a number of ways: 1) directly from the consumer - consumers may call or write to PHC, 2) from the physician - doctors may sometimes report the adverse reactions of their patients, 3) from the pharmacy which dispenses the drug, 4) from other health care professionals such as nurses, or 5) from studies published in the medical

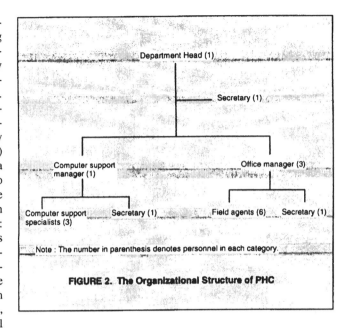

Note : The number in parenthesis denotes personnel in each category.

FIGURE 2. The Organizational Structure of PHC

literature. This information is obtained by periodically searching Medline, an online database of medical literature. The person reporting the adverse reaction is called a *reporter*.

The FDA requires information about ARs to be recorded on form FDA 1639. This form has details about the patient such as age, sex etc; details about the treatment, its duration, date and time of administration, concomittant drugs used; and the name of the person reporting the AR. Normally the FA mails FDA 1639 to the agent reporting the

AR such as the physician. For serious cases, the FDA requires reporting to be done within 15 days. When the drug is associated with a serious bodily dysfunction such as loss of sight or death, the head of DFDA becomes directly involved in collecting the AR information. On receipt of the form from the reporter, the field agent checks it for the terminology used to describe the AR as well as for any discrepancies. The terminology used must conform to the FDA-preferred terminology which is available from a thesaurus published by the World Health Organization.

A number of discrepancies could arise in the AR process such as one AR being reported and another being recorded or multiple cases being reported and only one case being recorded. If there are discrepancies, the FA tries to resolve it through direct contact with the reporter. The FDA requires documentation of each AR at the time it was first reported. Documentation could vary from the transcript of a phone conversation to detailed lab reports submitted by the reporter. Documentation is filed by the secretaries and archived every year by the Archives department of PHC.

Once a filled out 1639 form is

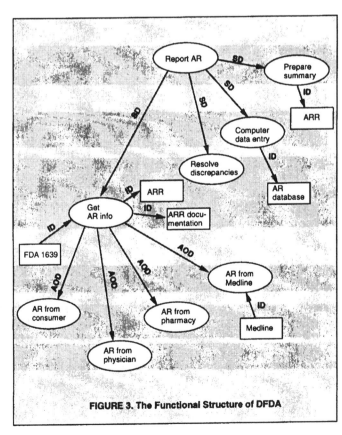

FIGURE 3. The Functional Structure of DFDA

checked for inconsistencies, it is sent to the computer support specialists to be entered into the DFDA database. Approximately 40-50 1639 forms are processed each day. For new drugs, FDA requires quarterly reporting of all ARs. For drugs which have been in the market for more than three years, FDA requires yearly reporting. The report is generally prepared by printing out all the AR reports for each drug, for the respective time period, from the DFDA database. In addition, the FA's prepare and attach summaries of the ARs to the report which is simply called the *adverse reaction report* or ARR.

DISCUSSION

The DFDA consists of only nineteen employees and is a small office, but it illustrates the workings of a typical office. The office has a significant amount of paperwork and there are different agents (both internal and external) who get involved in recording and reporting the adverse reactions. Within this office there are five distinct organizational positions, the head of the DFDA, Computer Support Manager, Office Manager, Computer Support Specialist, Field Agent and Secretary (as seen in *FIGURE 1*). In addition, the reporter (person reporting the AR) is an additional agent who is part of the process. The work descriptions of DFDA are detailed in *Table 2*. Being a small office, there are no mismatches between the work descriptions and the business structures.

The office has a clearly stated mission, that of reporting adverse reactions to the FDA which is shown as the highest level node of the functional structure in *Figure 3*. The functional structure illustrates the four major functions of the DFDA: obtaining the AR information, resolving discrepancies, entering the data and preparing summaries. These func-

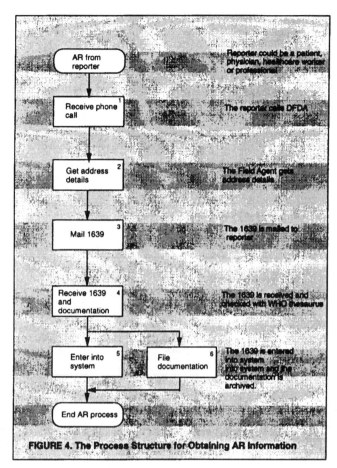

FIGURE 4. The Process Structure for Obtaining AR Information

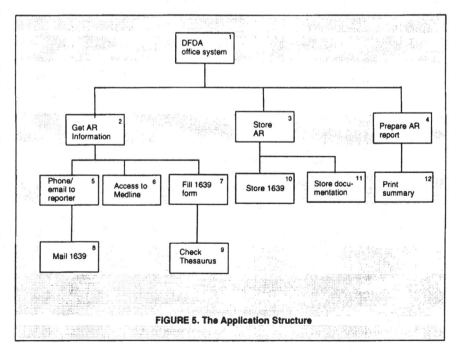

FIGURE 5. The Application Structure

tions are primarily handled by the field agents and the computer support personnel. As illustrated in *Figure 4,* the process structure highlights the details of obtaining the AR information. Similar structures must be developed for other processes, but as the DFDA is a small office, obtaining the AR information is the major process. There could be several important processes for larger offices, all of which need to be documented. A flowcharting-type notation is recommended as it enables the process structure to be absorbed at a glance. Descriptive comments provide details about the steps of the process. Notice in the process structure that there are activities such as "receive phone call" and "mail 1639" which are not shown in the functional structure. This highlights the major difference between the two structures, the functional structure shows the overall functions and their relationships, while the process structure shows details of a node in the functional structure. This type of abstraction, where a node is expanded to another structure can also be used for functional structure diagrams that are too large to fit on a single page

Table 2 — Work Descriptions at DFDA		
JOB TITLE	REPORTS TO	RESPONSIBILITY LIST
Head, DFDA	VP, PHC Inc.	Gets AR information in serious cases, Interacts with top management.
Computer Support Manager	Head, DFDA	Ensures computer support, Co-ordinates the specialists.
Office Manager Field Agent	Head, DFDA Office Manager	Manages field agents. Interacts with reporters, Gets AR information, Resolves discrepancies, Prepares summary reports.
Computer Support Specialist	Computer Support Manager	Enters AR data, Prints reports.
Secretary	Department staff	Receives phone calls, files AR documentation, types memos and reports.

The process structure in *Figure 4* also highlights another interesting aspect of the work, i.e. parallel activities. Note that after the 1639 and documentation are received (in step 4 of *FIGURE 4*), there are two parallel activities, "enter into system" and "file documentation." Parallel activities are significant in reducing the process throughput time and therefore an attempt must be made, to parallelize activities whenever possible. The application structure for the planned DFDA office system is illustrated in *Figure 5.* The application specifications have been given in the form of a structure chart. As stated earlier, this structure is developed by examining the functional and process structures for activities that can be automated.

Predictably, the major features of the system revolve around getting, storing and reporting the AR information. Obtaining the AR information involves contacting the reporter or searching the "Medline" database, both of which are identified as required features (Figure 5: modules #5 and #6). Note that "access to Medline" is listed as a feature even though it is currently automated. This implies that, access to the online database must be a feature of the implemented OIS also.

At this stage the feasibility of implementing an OIS is carried out. The case study highlights the challenges faced in automating offices. First, the volume of operations do not seem to justify automation. For the DFDA only 40-50 FDA 1639's are processed in a day. Does this volume justify an OIS implementation? It could for e.g. if making the AR information available to other departments of PHC would have a business advantage. Another challenge is that some of the activities are inherently manual and therefore cannot be automated. For e.g. resolving discrepancies or contacting the reporters are inherently manual and are carried out by the field agents. In the case of offices with a concentration of knowledge workers such as software engineering or design, the proportion of manual activities will be even higher. There are also other challenges faced in implementing office systems. A single software package usually does not satisfy the processing needs of the target office and some degree of customization will be required. Considerable MIS resources may be required to develop and maintain the customized system. But these could be offset by benefits such as a faster and more convenient access to information, reduced errors and reduced staffing requirements. For some offices, the planning process may identify a large process portfolio. In such cases, it would be necessary to prioritize processes based on weighing the expected benefits of automating each process against others.

The feasibility study is followed by design and implementation. If a process is to be re-engineered for efficiency, it is carried out in meetings involving the analyst, the MIS manager, the person supervising the process (the office manager in this case) and his/her superiors (the head of DFDA). Re-engineered processes must also be documented with appropriate notes on how processes were carried out before the re-engineering so that any potential problems during implementation may be resolved. The design and implementation stages can now proceed. If an integrated off-the-shelf package is chosen, there may not be much scope for customization. If the component approach with some in-house development is undertaken, the usual system development methods are followed. The choices of the IS manager for both approaches have been expanding [Radosevich '96], [The '94].

Fortunately, the technological structure enables managers to limit alternatives and to zero in on a feasible solution. In this case, an intra-net coupled with database capability (for the AR information) would serve the needs of the DFDA.

CONCLUSION

The AEI-2 methodology produces a set of outputs with only a modest investment in resources. These outputs are invaluable in understanding the workings of offices and proceeding with OIS implementations. Important among the outputs are the organizational structure, functional structure, the process structure and the technological structures. The functional structure is especially important because it captures the method of functioning of the office and should in fact be part of the OIS itself. Task descriptions can then be attached to the nodes of the functional structure and it can double as a repository of "how to" knowledge. This would be invaluable in organizational learning and in training new staff. Similarly, the process structure would be incorporated into workflow systems if they are selected as the solution. The technological structure provides a feature guide if selecting an off-the-shelf software or serves as a high level design if the customized approach is followed. The outputs of planning serve as useful inputs for the design, implementation and maintenance stages of the OIS development cycle. A successful OIS implementation can result in streamlined office operations, reduced costs and increased job satisfaction.

ENDNOTES

1. This case study was developed from interviews with employees at PHC Inc. who wish to remain anonymous.

REFERENCES

1. Aktas, Z. A., 1987. *Structured Analysis and Design of Information Systems*, Prentice-Hall, Englewood Cliffs.
2. Amaravadi, C. S. 1989. Towards a conceptual model for the office: An integrating approach. *Doctoral Dissertation,* University of Arizona, Tucson.
3. Amaravadi C.S., Sheng O.R., George, J.F., Nunamaker, J.F. "AEI: A knowledge-based approach to integrated office systems," *Journal of Management Information Systems* 9, no.1 Summer 1992, pp. 133-163.
4. Bracchi, G. and Pernici B., 1984. The design requirements of office systems. *ACM Transactions on Office Information Systems*, Vol. 2, No. 2 (April), pp. 151-170.
5. Carlson, Walter M., "Business Information Analysis and Integration Technique - The New Horizon," Database, Vol. 10, No. 4, Spring 1979, pp. 3-9.
6. De Antonellis V. and B. Zonta, "A Disciplined Approach to Office Analysis," *IEEE Transactions on Software Engineering* 16, no.8 , August 1990, pp. 822-828.
7. Harris, Sidney E. Critical task method: A language action formalism for support system design. *IEEE Technical Committee on Office Automation Newsletter,* Vol. 1., No. 2, May 1987, pp. 25-38.
8. Kerner, David V., "Business information characterization study," *Database* 10 (4), Spring 1979, pp. 10-17.
9. Pernici B., Barbic F., Fugini M.G., and Maiocchi R. " C_TODOS: An automatic tool for office system conceptual design." *ACM Transactions on Information Systems,* Vol. 7, No.4 October 1991, pp. 378-419.
10. Radosevich, L., "Keep your groupware options open," *Datamation*, November 1996, pp 110-120.
11. Sirbu M., Schoichet, S., Kunin, J. S., Hammer, M., and Sutherland, J., "OAM: An Office Analysis Methodology," *Proceedings of the Office Automation Conference,* San Francisco 1982, pp. 317-330.
12. Sasso, W. C., Olson, J. R., Merten, A. G. "The practice of office analysis: objectives, obstacles, and opportunities." *IEEE Technical Committee on Office Automation Newsletter*, Vol. 1, No. 2 May 1987, 11-24.
13. The, Le 1994 , Getting into the workflow, *Datamation*, Vol. 40, No. 19, October 1, pp. 65-72.

An Analysis Of Conflicting Ontological Assumptions In Information Modeling

John M. Artz, Ph.D.

Department of Management Science, The George Washington University, Washington, D.C. 20052

Phone: (202)994-4931, Fax(202)994-4930, Email: jartz@gwu.edu

ABSTRACT

Information modeling is a technique by which a database designer develops a conceptual model of a database depicting the entity classes that will be represented in the database. There are three competing ontological assumptions that guide the modeling process. The broadest characterization of these assumptions is realism verses conceptualism with social realism occupying a middle ground. The realist believes that the object classes exist in the real world waiting to be discovered. The conceptualist believes that object classes are constructed in the mind of the modeler based on observations about the application domain and the objectives of the information model. The social realist believes that classes exist as shared meanings among stakeholders in an application domain. This paper explores these assumptions and then reviews selected literature in information modeling to determine which assumptions are held by key authors. It concludes that most authors hold inconsistent views, and this inconsistency provides some important insights into information modeling while presenting serious problems for practitioners and students of information modeling.

ONTOLOGICAL ASSUMPTIONS IN INFORMATION MODELING

Perhaps one of the most perplexing problems in information modeling is the ontological status of entity classes. Simply put, this raises the question - Do entity classes exist in the world, or are they constructed in the mind of the modeler ? This seemingly esoteric question is important because the way in which one answers it has a significant impact on how one approaches the process of information modeling.

If entity classes exist in the world, independent of the mind of the observer, then the job of the information modeler is to discover those classes and record them in an information model. Hence, information modeling is a discovery process rather than a constructive process. If two modelers examine a domain and come up with different models, then one is wrong. One or the other (or possibly both) must bring their models into conformance with the real world. Further, an information model can be validated by ensuring its conformance with the real world. This is the realist position. To the realist, the challenges in information modeling are how to discover the existing entity classes and accurately represent those classes in an information model. Validation is not a problem for the realist because a model is valid if it correctly represents the real world. Realism can be detected when writers use the phrases 'real world' or 'as they exist in the real world' or more subtly when they refer to 'natural classes' or 'natural data relationships'.

If classes do not exist in the world, then it is the job of the information modeler to construct them. Thus, information modeling becomes a process of construction rather than discovery. The conceptualist position holds that classes exist only in the mind of the observer and are constructed according to objectives (probably not explicit) that guide the process of abstraction. The modeler selects certain facts from the application domain and constructs classes based on individual objects with similar attributes. Conceptualists believe that different models of an application domain cannot be determined to be correct or not correct. They can only be more or less useful for meeting the model objectives. This leads to a problems in both construction and validation of the information model. Construction is difficult because most of the literature on information modeling focuses on description of entities rather than construction of them. The literature is strangely silent on how to construct a set of entity classes to meet a set of modeling objectives. Validation is also a problem since the model cannot be compared with entities existing in the real world. It can only be evaluated with respect to the objectives of the model, again an area where the literature is strangely silent. The conceptualist position creates serious problems for information modelers because it requires that modeling objectives be defined before model construction and it requires some method of evaluating a model with respect to a set of objectives. Conceptualism can be detected in the literature when authors talk about 'abstraction", 'the problem to be solved', 'objectives', or the possibility of 'multiple representations' or 'multiple models.'

An intermediate position is social realism which assumes that entity classes exist as shared meanings within a social context. This is a realist position in that the classes exist independent of the mind of the modeler. Presumably if several modelers were to examine the same application domain they would eventually discover the same shared meanings and hence would produce the same information model. Validation is less problematic under the social realist position in that the model can be compared with the social reality, that is, the model agrees with what people in the application domain believe to be the entity classes or it doesn't. The social realist discovers the entity classes by talking with users and recording their usage of key words. Consensus is an important factor in the social realist approach because social reality is a shared understanding. If people do not agree on meanings then the realism assumption breaks down because different modelers may very well come away with different understandings depending on who they spoke to. Domain experts are important to the social realist position because the domain expert is the gatekeeper to the social reality. Social realism can be detected in the literature when authors talk about 'language', 'shared meanings', 'domain or subject matter experts', or modeling as a process of 'consensus'.

Realism is a shaky assumption from a philosophical perspective, but desirable from a pragmatic perspective. If entity classes exist in the world, where do they reside ? While there are ample instances of an entity class, nobody has ever seen the class itself, nor will they. The reason is that entity classes exist only in the mind of the observer and have no real existence in the application domain. The modeler examines the application domain and through a cognitive process of abstraction, derives a set of entity classes. Yet this process of abstraction is poorly understood and difficult to explain so modelers act as though the classes actually exist in the world and are being discovered. From a pragmatic perspective, realism is a desirable assumptions because it reduces the class construction process to one of simple discovery and provides an easy means of validation by requiring that the model simply conform to the real world.

Conceptualism is a much more justifiable position from a philosophical perspective, yet a nightmare in practice. Conceptualism recognizes the role of modeler and his or her cognition in the class construction process. Yet in practice it presents some severe problems. Since classes are constructed, how does the process of construction work ? What criteria are used in class construction ? Once classes are constructed, how do we know that the right classes have been constructed ? One answer is that classes are constructed by grouping objects with similar attributes. But that position raises the question of whether or not attributes exist in the world and opens up, once again, the three positions just described with regard to attributes. Another answer might be to say that the classes are right if they meet the objectives of the model, but that answers the question by raising two more: How do we define modeling objectives and how do we determine if a set of classes meets those modeling objectives ?

Most authors nod towards conceptualism, using terms like 'problem solving' or 'multiple models' but back off when it comes to the actual process of modeling where they will often fall back to a realist position by talking about modeling 'the real world'. Recognizing the faultiness of the realist position several authors have adopted an intermediate position of social realism. The more rigorous ones adopt social realism with respect to attributes. But the best that can be said is the literature is confusing and few authors have taken and articulated a consistent philosophical position.

AN ANALYSIS OF THE LITERATURE

The ontological assumptions made by practitioners are rarely articulated. They are more often manifest in their behavior. Practitioners may even claim to hold one belief while acting as though they held a conflicting view. Hence, in order to gain a sense of the variety of assumptions that are held in the field of information modeling, it is necessary to look at the recorded literature - widely read texts and papers -- to see what assumptions are being put forth.

Peter Chen's original article on the Entity-Relationship Model begins by establishing a clearly realist perspective. "The entity-relationship model adopts the more natural view that the real world consists of entities and relationships. It incorporates some of the important semantic information about the real world". [pp 9-10] This perspective is picked up by later authors. Andleigh and Gretzinger claim "The Entity Model describes the real-world relations for the information system." [pg. 383], while Teorey refers the model as including "the natural data relationships," again a strong indication of realism. Yet only a couple of paragraphs later in Chen's paper, he refers to a conceptual data model as "Information concerning entities and relationships which exist in our minds" [pg. 10] and "conceptual objects in our minds" [pg. 14] showing a clearly conceptualist perspective. In discussing whether a given object should be an entity or a relationship, Chen defers to the enterprise administrator who should decide so that "the distinction is suitable for his environment." [pg. 10] suggesting an objectives driven conceptualist view or a social realist view depending on the meaning of the word 'suitable'. He goes on a bit later to say "if we know an entity is in the entity EMPLOYEE, then we know that it has the properties common to other entities in the entity set." [pg. 11] suggesting extreme class realism. Since nothing is said , in the paper, regarding how to construct entities, the reader is forced to defer back to the realist position and use the 'real world' to guide the discovery and validation processes.

Only two years after Chen's original article, Kent [1978] thoroughly devastated the realism assumption in <u>Data and Reality</u> by raising question after question that could not be answered from the realist's perspective. "There is no natural set of categories.", he said, "The set of categories to be maintained in an information system must be specified for that system." [pg. 13] He goes on to say, "If we really did want to define what a data base modelled, we'd have to start thinking in terms of mental reality rather than physical reality. Most things are in the data base because they 'exist' in people's minds, without having any 'objective' existence." This is about as clear of a statement of conceptualism as one can find. Unfortunately, this work raised many, many more questions than it answered. This coupled with the fact that it is difficult to follow reduced its impact on the practice of modeling.

Later, Kent [1986] adopted a more conservative, fact-based, approach. The fact-based approach trades entity realism for attribute realism and allows class construction based on entities with similar attributes. "If we examine any field in a record, we find that it contains a character string. These character strings generally represent something in the real world". [pg. 181] Attribute realism is more believable than entity realism and provides an illusion of greater rigor. Unfortunately, it is equally difficult to justify ontologically. Just as we ask - where to the entities come from, we have to ask - where do the attributes come from ? Attribute realism acknowledges that entities are constructs but fails to recognize that attributes are similarly constructs.

Nijssen and Halpin also adopt a 'fact-based' approach but give the reader mixed signals with regard to their ontological assumptions. They recognize the fact that classes are constructed, but see this construction as guided by facts gathered from the Universe of Discourse. The ontological status of the Universe of Discourse is unclear. They say, "Recall that the UoD is the portion of the (typically) real world relevant to our application" [Pg. 35], which suggests realism. Yet they go on to say "Recall that entities are the basic objects or things that we want to talk about" [Pg. 37] which suggests that the Universe of Discourse is a social construct based on language usage. This view is reinforced by the statement that "The UoD expert or domain expert is familiar with the application area, and can clarify any doubtful aspects of the UoD." [Pg 14] These claims of social realism are further supported by the validation process - "Our conceptual schema design procedure facilitates early detection of errors by various checking arrangements including ongoing feedback to the user by way of examples." [Pg. 199] Here the model is being validated against user opinions, which suggests social realism.

It would appear that Nijssen and Halpin agree with Kent in being social realists with regard to attributes. Yet they refer to the modeling process as information design rather than analysis and refer to the modeler as a designer. Design suggests a constructive activity rather than analysis which is a recording activity. Further, they identify information systems development as a problem solving process and suggest that the problem be divided into sub-problems suggesting that objectives drive the process. Hence, underlying conceptualist assumptions are quite clear. The problem arises when it comes to actually constructing a model. They drop back to a social realism perspective citing the need for "a domain expert who can clarify doubtful aspects of the domain" and the need of the model to "describe the universe of discourse". Later on they state "If we design two different but equivalent conceptual schemas for the same application, then conceptually it doesn't matter which one we pick. They both model the same UoD." [pg. 216] Once again a clear statement of conceptualism and, hence, a full set of conflicting ontological assumptions.

Conflicting ontological assumptions are not uncommon. Shlaer and Mellor reflect the same confusion. At one point they assert "What is needed is a way to capture information so that it can be checked against the reality, rather that the different, and possibly inconsistent, 'user views' of reality" [pg. 3], which reflects a realist view of information modeling and a criticism of social realism. Then a few paragraphs later they say "What we need is a method by which we can lay out candidate definitions of the conceptual entities and examine the implications of those definitions" [pg. 4] which reflects a conceptualist view.

Flavin clearly stated that "the decomposition of the system of interest into its component objects is a function of the system, the observer, and their mutual interaction," [pg. 38] which again reflects a conceptualist perspective. While Flavin does provide implicit modeling objectives in terms of abstraction and classification, he does not discuss how to construct classes to meet a given set of information objectives. Instead he describes functional, transaction, and scenario analysis as a means of discovering entities. Hence, the ontology is unclear.

Veryard recognized this confusion and called the competing positions semantic absolutism and semantic relativism.

"There are two philosophical attitudes toward data modelling, known respectively as semantic relativism and semantic absolutism. According to the absolutist way of thinking, there is only one correct or ideal way of modelling anything: each object in the real world must be represented by a particular construct. Semantic relativists, on the other hand, believe that most things in the real world can be modelled in many different ways, using any of the basic constructs." [Veryard, 1984, pg. 7]

But it was not until Klein and Hirschheim [1987] that the problem was grounded philosophically. Klein and Hirschheim examined both ontological and epistemological assumptions in information modeling. They identified two ontological poles that they referred to a realism and nominalism. Nominalism and conceptualism are slightly different antirealist views. Nominalism asserts that things are what they are because we have named them that way. The collection of things that share a name need not have anything in common other than they fact that they share the same name. Conceptualism asserts that there are abstract mental entities called concepts which are abstracted from the particulars that we experience. The name that we apply to a thing is really the name of a concept that the thing is an instance of.

> "In its extreme form, that there is nothing common to a class of particulars called by the same name other than that they are called by the same name, nominalism is so clearly untenable that it may be doubted whether anybody has actually tried to hold it." [Woozley, pg. 203]

Extreme nominalism results in Wittgenstein's Family Resemblance problem, which, if it holds, makes information modeling impossible. [Artz, 1997]

Later Hirschheim and Klein changed their ontological assumptions to social realism with order versus conflict poles. [1989, 1995].

> "the 'order' or 'integrationist' view emphasizes a social world characterized by order, stability, integration, consensus and functional coordination. The 'conflict' or 'coercion' view stresses change, conflict disintegration, and coercion." [1995, pg. 47]

The social realist view is problematic because whether the social reality is stable or in a process of change, the entity classes that exist in usage may or may not be appropriately constructed to meet the objectives of the information model. Yet, as Hirschheim and Klein say, "The potential of objects to model imaginary, 'ideal' or socially constructed worlds has not, unfortunately, been widely recognized in the data modeling literature." [1995, pg. 62] Indeed, since conceptualism requires the construction of imaginary, possible worlds it is scrupulously avoided by researchers in information modeling. Yet the questions must be asked - Is it better to use faulty philosophical assumptions that are easier to work with or sound philosophical assumptions that may create problems in practice ?

Rumbaugh, et.al comes the closest of any of the non philosophers to correctly articulating a consistent set of assumptions. They claim that "In the real world an object simply exists" which is a safe assumption for modeling purposes since it refers to the independent existence of the instance rather than the class. They go on to say "Classification means that objects with the same data structure (attributes) and behavior (operations) are group together in a class." [pg. 2] This is clearly a conceptualist perspective since the grouping is a result of the process of classification. To emphasize the point further, they state, "A class is an abstraction that describes properties important to an application and ignores the rest. Any choice of classes is arbitrary and depends on the application." This is a clear statement of the conceptualist position. In defense of the other authors, conceptualism is more obvious in pure object-oriented systems because the objectives of hierarchy and reusability are much more clear. Validation of the model is easier since alternative models can be compared in terms of hierarchical coverage and component reusability. In a non object oriented database application, the objectives of the model are not as clear, nor are the criteria for validation. Hence, the conceptualist position is a little easier for object-oriented modelers to come around to than for information modelers.

On a closing note, it is interesting to note that practitioners are sometimes aware of deeper philosophical issues, but their concern is often brief. Coad and Yourdon, who published one of the first books on object-oriented analysis sum up the practitioner's scant concern:

> "As authors, it would be intellectually satisfying if we could report that we studied the philosophical ideas behind methods of organization, from Aristotle and Socrates to Descartes and Kant. Then, based on the underlying methods human beings use, we could propose the basic constructs essential to a requirements analysis method, and in particular to OOA [object-oriented analysis]. But in truth, we cannot say that, nor did we do it." [pg. 16]

CONCLUSIONS

The best that can be said regarding the ontological assumptions underlying information modeling is that there is a great deal of confusion. Few authors really hold the realist position as can be seen in their constant references to conceptualist ideas. Yet abandoning the realists position creates serious methodological problems in discovery and validation. Some have adopted social realism in a retreat from realism. This position handles the discovery and validation problems but is only slightly more tenable than realism. Social realism assumes that the classes which exist in the shared meanings of the stakeholders of the application domain are exactly the classes needed to meet the objectives of the information model. With luck this may be true, but it is unlikely. First, socially constructed classes are more likely to meet the objective of intellectual economy, than any processing or information objective. Second, social realism assumes that the application domain is static and that classes which have bee useful in discourse in the past will be useful for information derivation in the future. It seems that conceptualism is the only justifiable ontological position. Unfortunately, conceptualism requires that modeling objectives be explicitly articulated and that models be constructed to meet objectives and evaluated with respect to those objectives. There is much work to be done here, but since it appears that conceptualism is the only sound foundation for information modeling, it is probably time to get started.

BIBLIOGRAPHY

Andleigh, P. and Gertzinger, M., *Distributed Object-Oriented Data-Systems Design.* Prentice-Hall, 1992.

Artz, J. "A Crash Course in Metaphysics for the Database Designer", Journal of Database Management. 8(4). 1997.

Chen, P., "The Entity Relationship Model - Towards a Unified View of Data," Association of Computing Machinery Transactions on Database Systems. 1(1), 1976.

Coad, P. and Yourdon, E., *Object-Oriented Analysis.* Prentice-Hall, 1990.

Flavin, M., *Fundamental Concepts of Information Modeling.* Yourdon Press, 1981.

Hirschheim, R., Klein, H.K., and Lyytinen, K. Information Systems Development and Data Modeling: Conceptual and Philosophical Foundations. Cambridge University Press. 1995.

Hirschheim, R. and Klein, H.K., "Four Paradigms of Information Systems Development," Communications of the ACM., (32:10), 1989, pp. 1199-1216.

Kent, W., Data and Reality. North Holland Publishing Company. 1978.

Kent, W., "Limitations of Record-Based Information Models," ACM Transactions on Database Systems. (4:1), March 1979, pp. 107-131.

Kent, W., The Realities of Data: Basic Properties of Data Reconsidered. In Database Semantics(DS-1) T.B. Steele, Jr. And R. Meersman (eds.) Elsevier Science Publishers. B.V. North Holland. 1986.

Klein, H.K. and Hirschheim, R.A., "A Comparative Framework of Data Modelling Paradigms and Approaches," The Computer Journal. (30:1), 1987, pp. 8-15.

Nijssen, G.M. and Halpin, T.A., *Conceptual Schema and Relational Database Design: A fact oriented approach.* New York:Prentice Hall, 1989.

Parsons, J. and Wand, Y., "Guidelines for Evaluating Classes in Data Modeling," Proceedings of the 13th International Conference on Information Systems, 1992, pp. 1-8.

Rumbaugh, J., Blaha, M., Premerlani, W., Eddy, F., and Lorensen, W., *Object-Oriented Modeling and Design.* Prentice-Hall, 1991.

Shlaer, S. and Mellor, S.J., "Object-Oriented Systems Analysis: Modeling the World in Data," Englewood Cliffs, New Jersey: Yourdon Press, 1988.

Stamper, R. "Semantics," In Boland, R.J. and Hirschheim, R.A. (Eds.) *Critical Issues in Information Systems Research.* Chichester. John Wiley & Sons, 1987, pp. 43 - 78.

Teorey, T.J. *Database Modeling and Design: The Entity-Relationship Approach.* San Mateo, CA: Morgan Kaufman Publishers, Inc., 1990.

Veryard, R. *Pragmatic Data Analysis.* Oxford: Blackwell Scientific Publications, 1984.

Veryard, R. *Information Modeling.* New York: Prentice-Hall, Inc., 1992.

Woozley, A.D. "Universals," In Edwards, P. (ed.) *Encyclopedia of Philosophy.* Vol. 8, 1967, pp. 194-206.

C by Active Learning a Web-based Interactive C Programming Tutor

Dr Nicola Ayre

Faculty of Informatics, University of Ulster, Newtownabbey, County Antrim, BT37 0QB, Northern Ireland
Telephone: +44 (1232) 368830, Fax: +44 (1232) 366068, E-mail: n.ayre@ulst.ac.uk

Edward Wingfield

Institute of Technology, Tralee, County Kerry, Ireland
Telephone: +353 66 45600, Fax: +353 66 25711, E-mail: ewingfield@fexco.ie

ABSTRACT

The wide accessibility of the World Wide Web (WWW) makes it a perfect base for developing computer science courseware modules. Since learning involves more than just receiving transmitted information, courseware must be interactive and encourage student engagement, which is a challenge on WWW architecture.

This paper examines the issues involved in developing a fully interactive Computer based Training (CBT) package for the WWW. While standalone packages offer numerous benefits it was decided to exploit the many advantages of the WWW by taking an Internet approach to the implementation of the courseware. The courseware presented is called **C by Active Learning** and uses a combination of HyperText Markup Language (HTML), Java and Java Script. HTML was used to structure the individual lessons; the numerous animations and automatic multiple choice tests were developed using a combination of Java and Java Script.

KEYWORDS

Internet, World Wide Web, Courseware, C programming, Computer Based Training.

INTRODUCTION

The use of computers to provide an integrated environment for teaching a variety of disciplines has received much attention in recent years. The materials provided by such courseware varies greatly from the provision of lecture notes and lecture support material through to integrated and interactive tutorial packages. Marshall and Hurley (1996) notes that '*until recently courseware has existed as stand alone packages, however with the advent of the World Wide Web on the Internet and accompanying WWW browsers, such as Mosaic, Netscape and Hot Java, the provision of courseware has taken on a whole new dimension*'. However, it is becoming increasingly commonplace to utilise WWW technology as a vehicle for course delivery. Currently, the majority of courseware on the WWW is in the form of static pages. When used in this fashion, the web page becomes an alternative form of textbook or lab manual. This paper examines a different use of the WWW where the web page becomes an alternative form of the classroom itself.

Providing students with access to a book does not imply that students will learn. Learning occurs when the book is given in context within a wider educational framework. Biggs and Moore (1993) suggest that '*deep*' learning involves both: communication between learners and teachers, and learners being engaged in interactive learning processes. By similar analogy the provision of written and visual information in electronic format on the WWW is not in itself an effective teaching and learning tool.

Well designed CBT packages are powerful tools which allow students to learn by doing. To their disadvantage however, many lack tools which facilitate the communicative functions of learning. With the development of current Internet and WWW technologies it is now possible to design networked, interactive courseware which integrates some of the interactive functionalities of a CBT package as well as the electronic communication tools that are available for Internet users.

The economics of courseware development is forcing the production of educational software from a focus on courseware produced by the individual lecturer to the development of educational resources that can be shared and assessed from a wide variety of teaching sites. A new approach to CBT development was required - enter the WWW. Due to the development of the WWW and the subsequent introduction of graphical browsers such as Netscape, the Internet has moved from being a text only communications tool to serving as a powerful multimedia platform whose potential applications are immense. The WWW is ripe for teaching for a number of reasons (St Andrews, 1996):

- Cross-platform availability - as long as browsers are available for a particular platform the material can be viewed or executed.
- Distribution of material - once the material is published on the WWW it is published world-wide with no distribution problems or costs.
- Updating of material - standalone systems place a heavy emphasis on the end-user to be aware when upgrades are available and to initiate the updating process. With the WWW only the package located on the WWW server has to be updated.
- Data - the teaching package can be improved quite easily by taking advantage of new links to relevant material from anywhere in the world.
- Functionality - with the emergence of Java the multimedia capacities of the WWW are as sophisticated, if not more so, than those of traditional authoring packages.

These views are also supported by Cunningham (1996) who points out that the WWW provides a consistent interface over a range of platforms. While browsers obviously vary in detail a user familiar with one will easily be able to use any other.

PAPER OVERVIEW

This paper consists of eight sections, beginning and ending with an introduction and conclusion respectively. Section three explains the application domain for this work namely C programming for novices. The choice of an Internet approach is explained in section four followed by an overview of three pieces of courseware for teaching programming. The primary subject of this paper namely the courseware: C by Active Learning is extensively covered section six. The main evaluation findings are then presented.

THE APPLICATION DOMAIN

There is no doubt that programming is a difficult subject. Walsh (1989) found that postgraduate students learning programming for the first time had great difficulties solving relatively simple programming problems even after completing a programming course unit. C is more complex than traditional introductory programming languages however this added complexity can be minimised by the system presented - C by Active Learning. The authors felt that by teaching C the student would learn not only a sound introductory programming language, but also a powerful programming language which is in widespread use and in great demand.

A number of approaches to teaching programming have evolved in an attempt to make the experience more enjoyable and productive. One such approach is called CORE (Context, Objects, Refinement and Expression) which encourages the learner to actively form and test their own cognitive representations of the programming constructs (Boyle, 1990). The CORE approach focuses on the process of learning. In doing so new constructs are not introduced through formal definitions but rather through numerous examples. Having gained some understanding of the subject, the CORE approach seeks to refine this understanding through a series of questions with feedback provided. This enables the learner to test, refine and extend his/her knowledge of the subject area. The student therefore becomes actively involved in understanding the language rather than just passively assimilating information dictated by someone else. The last stage of the CORE approach encourages students to express their skills. The favored approach for programming is to get students to write working programs which express the skills they have just acquired.

The courseware presented in this paper was designed around the CORE approach to programming.

WHY USE AN INTERNET APPROACH?

There are many reasons to use Internet technology in courses ranging from purely administrative to truly learning related. Firstly, the Internet provides a very flexible way to distribute your materials world-wide and enables people to access that material from a variety of hardware and software platforms at any time. Material is therefore available instantaneously, avoiding the usual delays in distribution. Secondly, the interactive capabilities of the Internet can provide for increased student to student and student to teacher interaction through a variety of formats. This can allow for more immediate feedback to students regarding their progress, and to teachers so the materials can be adapted and enhanced. Finally, the multimedia capabilities of the Internet can provide a more exciting way of presenting material and a way to adapt material to the different learning styles of individual students. Some learners are more visually orientated than others, and some need a combination of visual and auditory stimulation to learn well.

As noted C by Active Learning takes an Internet approach and uses a combination of HTML, Java and Java Script. The following sub-sections highlight the most pertinent features of each 'language'.

HyperText Markup Language (HTML)

HyperText Markup Language or HTML is, in essence, an easily learned language for describing the structure of a document, not its presentation. Its presentation is determined by the WWW browser being used. The main advantage of this approach is that all packages developed in HTML are fully platform independent. HTML is therefore both a relatively simple language and one that offers considerable power in specifying the structure of a document.

Within C by Active Learning it was initially used to establish a template for each learning block. Each learning block has three generic page types: textual, question and answer material, and multiple choice tests. While HTML is very powerful at structuring page layouts it fails to offer any form of processing. As such, it was satisfactory for the first two pages types but not for the multiple choice tests. Here some mechanism was required to capture all student answers and effectively correct them. This was achieved through embedding Java Script code into the page.

Java

The WWW, due to its reliance on the HyperText Transfer Protocol (HTTP), by itself was not enough to create an attractive, real-time learning environment. HTTP is limited to asynchronous communication, without synchronous real-time communication any attempt to create true distance learning on the WWW is bound to be incomplete - enter Java. Java code is downloaded and executed on the local client, rather than on a remote server. This has allowed developers to avoid the WWW's latency problems. By overcoming the WWW's weakness in interactive operation, Java's superior responsiveness has turned distance learning on the Internet into an achievable goal (Gordon, 1996).

Java is a streamlined programming language for developing Internet applications. Java can basically be used in two different ways, as an application or as an applet. Java applications are standalone Java programs that can be run by using the Java interpreter. Java applets however, are run from inside a WWW browser. A reference to an applet is embedded in a web page using a special HTML tag. When a reader, using a Java-enabled browser loads a WWW page with an applet in it, the browser downloads the applet from a WWW server and executes it on the local system. The Java interpreter is built into the browser and runs the compiled Java class file from there. Java applets run inside a Java browser and as a result of this they have access to the structure the browser provides including an existing window, an event-handling and graphics context and the surrounding user interface. As such, we felt that the best way of developing the animation aspects of C by Active Learning would be by means of a Java applet.

Until recently browsers were static in nature in that they were limited to text, images and low quality audio. Interactivity was limited to selecting or fetching pages. With Javatised browsers, animations, audio and video, 3D capabilities and serious computing power can now be embedded into WWW pages. A CBT package developed using Java can thus exploit this exciting new language's many benefits and in doing so become a powerful interactive teaching tool.

Java Script

Java Script is a compact, object-based scripting language for developing client and server Internet applications. Java Script code can recognize and respond to user events such as mouse clicks, form input and page navigation. While based on a small number of data types representing numeric, Boolean and string values, Java Script was ideal for the calculations necessary to correct and provide feedback on the numerous Multiple Choice tests throughout C by Active Learning. This correction system was a vital factor in the overall effectiveness of the tutor in its ability to teach. Another important factor which contributed greatly to this effectiveness was the numerous animations throughout. For these use was made of pre-complied Java code in the form of Java applets.

AN OVERVIEW OF CURRENT SYSTEMS

To gain a deeper understanding of what constitutes a good programming language tutor, several CBT systems were assessed. An overview is presented of two standalone CBT packages before examining the additional benefits of an Internet approach by analyzing a WWW system.

Pascal by Active Learning

Pascal by Active Learning (Boyle & Margetts, 1991) is a standalone DOS based CBT package for learning the Pascal language. It was developed using the CORE approach (Boyle, 1990) in an attempt to involve the user as an active problem solver from the very start. Each of the twenty four learning blocks begins with a context screen which gives the student a view of the new constructs to be learned. Each new feature is then introduced through clear central examples. Later a series of questions and answers allow you to test, clarify and refine your understanding of the construct. Each block concludes by testing the students competence in Pascal by requesting that they write a program which incorporates the new construct.

The Pascal tutor does avail of some of the many benefits enjoyed by good CBT packages (Owens, 1992) for example it affords the user self-paced instruction and thus offers individualised training. However, it fails to avail of the many other advantages which could accrue from more advanced CBT packages. For example it only allows limited: practice opportunities, feedback and interactive practices. The tutor aids the student in understanding programming language features, but fails to give the user an appreciation for program behavior through its lack of program visualisation features.

As a package developed in 1991, the Pascal tutor is a novel way of learning the syntax of the Pascal language. However, more advanced packages take CBT to a higher level and in doing so avail of the many more advantages possible from good CBT packages. A prime example of one such package is CLEM.

CORE Learning Environment for Modula-2 (CLEM)

CLEM (Boyle et al, 1992) is a Windows based CBT package for learning Modula-2. Analogous to the Pascal tutor discussed in section 5.1, CLEM's design is based on the CORE approach. However, CLEM's use of a hypertext tool, GUIDE, running in a Windows environment permits a much richer environment to be constructed which supports enhanced interactivity and greater flexibility in use.

The overall structure of CLEM is presented to the student as an electronic book. This metaphor enables the student to quickly make sense of the basic functionality of the system while supporting him/her in making the transition into using its more powerful features. The new material is presented as examples rather than rules which means that the student must actively induce the underlying pattern or rule. Later the student can test out and refine the hypothesis with a series of carefully graded questions. Having completed a multiple choice test CLEM automatically calculates your results and offers advice accordingly.

The most impressive feature of CLEM is its direct linkage to a commercial compiler. Boyle et al (1992) describe the compiler aspect of CLEM as extending the CBT system. The student can select all programs and program fragments used in the system by simply clicking on the program text. The chosen fragments are contextualized in a full Modula-2 program presented in a window on the screen. These programs, at the click of an icon, can be transferred to the compiler environment where they can be compiled and executed in a window. Furthermore, learners can alter the programs before they are transferred. They can thus ask their own questions by altering selected features and use the compiler as a feedback resource. So essentially CLEM is exploiting its compiler link by allowing students to enter, compile and test their programs without leaving the CBT environment.

Although CLEM offers a multitude of features it ignores the program and algorithm animation aspect of CBT packages and as a result fails to exploit the power of graphics in teaching programming.

Cardiff C Course

Programming in C (Marshall, 1994) attempts to avail of many of the advantages of an Internet approach to CBT production. However it abandons the CORE approach to teaching programming and as such fails to involve the user to the same extent as some of the systems examined so far. Programming in C provides a very comprehensive coverage of the C programming language reinforced by the use of numerous examples. User interaction is however limited and it does not offer the student self paced instruction. It makes some use of the graphic display capabilities through its use of various font types. Unlike CLEM it fails to allow the student to actively practice and compile the example programs.

Programming in C, by its very nature, exploits many of the automatic advantages associated with the WWW. It is platform independent, avoids distribution costs, easy updating and its use of hypertext to structure the course and to provide numerous links to additional material enable the student to partake in exploratory learning (Kamouri, Kamouri & Smith (1986).

Drawing upon the material presented to date section 6 provides an overview of the most pertinent features of the courseware which resulted from the work identified in this paper.

C BY ACTIVE LEARNING - AN IMPLEMENTATION STORY

C by Active Learning can be divided into four different sections as shown in figure one.

Welcome

In the first section entitled 'Welcome' the student is introduced to the package and a brief description of the CORE approach is offered. A User Guide (on-line) is then offered to the student to help him/her gain maximum benefit from the package.

E-mail Link

The E-mail link embedded within C by Active Learning offers the student the opportunity to interact with the

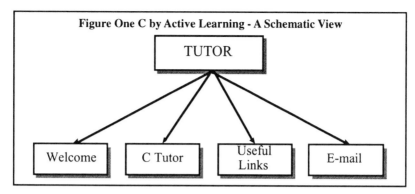

Figure One C by Active Learning - A Schematic View

teacher or with other students on the course. Regardless of how comprehensive the courseware is, a student will always have questions. The E-mail link enables the student to easily send queries to the teacher or to other students. The instructor can then respond either privately or publicly. A public response would be mailed to all students on the course.

Useful Links

The 'Useful Links' component of C by Active Learning is a prime example of the power an Internet approach offers to CBT development. Here links have been established to additional resources on the WWW. This has the effect of instantly improving the courseware by giving it additional scope and functionality. Most good books and papers offer further reading sections, providing the reader with the opportunity of exploring further literature on the subject. Through its 'useful links' section C by Active Learning not only provides a list of these further resources, but with the click of a button also retrieves them for the user. Boyle (1990) begins his paper on the CORE approach to programming by posing the question *'how can we develop more effective learning environments for programming?'* By providing numerous links to invaluable resources already on the Internet, C by Active Learning makes a large step in the right direction.

C Tutor

The 'C Tutor' component is made up of 10 learning blocks.

Block 1 - Writing a Simple C Program

The first learning block is designed to introduce the student to C programming. Unlike the remaining learning blocks, the first block cannot build from a previous framework. It must start from the very beginning. As such, Block 1 introduces the user by means of a very simple C program designed to print a sentence to the screen. A program to achieve this in C encompasses many important issues. Firstly, the user is made aware of the importance of including C libraries at the start of a program. Secondly, the user is introduced to the concept of a main program in C. The importance of the *printf* command for writing text to the screen is then highlighted. Finally, the block explains, at this early stage, the importance of including comments in a program in an attempt to improve the overall readability of the code.

The student's knowledge of these new concepts is then refined by means of numerous questions. The student is then offered a summary before being faced with a multiple choice test. This provides the student with an opportunity to test his/her knowledge before embarking on the project. The project, a simple program to test the student's ability to write text to the screen, has the effect of encouraging the user to practice the newly learned concepts. The first block therefore attempts to introduce the student to the basics of writing a simple C program in an interesting, interactive and effective manner.

Block 2 - Building on a Simple C Program

The second block has the task of taking the newly acquired concepts from block 1 and building on them. Emphasis is now put on refining the student's use of the *printf* statement. The \n escape sequence is introduced to enable the student to write programs which print sentences, on different lines, to the screen. While this is a small step forward from the material covered Block 1, it was felt that it merited a section of its own as the \n escape character can be the cause of many errors for the novice C programmer. Again refinement questions are used throughout this block and again the student is required to complete a carefully constructed multiple choice test and project. Both are designed to test the new concepts, including those introduced in block 1. At this stage the student has been given considerable exposure to C basics and is in a position to move on to more advanced concepts.

Block 3 - Introducing Numeric Variables

Learning Block 3 introduces the concept of numeric variables. It begins by highlighting a program which performs a simple calculation on two numeric variables, thus introducing format control specifiers to the student. As this can prove a difficult concept for the best of students, numerous questions and examples are provided.

Variables are one of the cornerstones of programming and as such it was felt that every effort had to be made to guarantee understanding. To this effect C by Active Learning offers the first of many animations. The animation, in the form of a slideshow, traces the execution of a simple program offering graphical displays of the variables throughout. The student can thus sit back and watch a step by step execution of a program containing numeric variables. Comments are provided throughout, graphical representations of the variables and changes to the variables all help to explain this crucial concept in programming.

All lecturers who have labored over blackboard box-and-arrow simulations of programs have actually been trying to help their students visualize program execution. The fact that so many educators employ such time consuming and error prone techniques is sufficient testimony to their faith in the advantages of a graphical simulation of such algorithms. Block 3 exploits these advantages by providing a clear, carefully designed animation.

Block 4 - Introducing Character Variables

Having been introduced to numeric variables Block 4 seeks to build on this newly acquired knowledge by introducing the concept of character variables. Character variables are another important concept in programming. However, due to the thorough coverage of numeric variables in Block 3 it was felt that this block did not warrant another animation. It does however challenge the student's knowledge with a multiple choice test and a project.

Block 5 - Introducing the Scanf Function

At this stage the student should be capable of writing simple yet complete C programs incorporating both character and numeric variables. Block 5 builds on this knowledge by introducing the *scanf* function. The *scanf* function enables the user to write programs which wait for and accept data from the keyboard. A simple program to calculate the area of a rectangle is used firstly to highlight the use of the *scanf* function and secondly to highlight the importance of prompting the user for data. The *scanf* function temporarily halts program execution, a concept new to the student, and as a result of this it was felt that an animation would be an ideal way to guarantee understanding of this new construct. The animation traces a programs execution simulating user input and highlighting graphically the effect of this interaction on the variables used throughout. Once again the block concludes with a multiple choice test and project.

Block 6 - Introducing Conditional Statements

All the basics of writing simple C programs should now be apparent to the student. Block 6 therefore has the task of introducing the subject of conditional statements. It was felt that of the many conditional constructs available in the C language the *if* statement was the easiest to understand and it therefore forms the basis of Block 6. The simple *if* statement is used to introduce the whole concept of the program making a decision based on user input. This forms a perfect framework to introduce the more complicated *if-else* statement. Conditional statements in any language can be difficult for a novice to understand. However, the whole concept that part of a program might never be executed, depending on user input, can be effectively demonstrated by means of an animation. The animation shows exactly what lines are executed and again by means of simulated user input, why they are executed. Once again a multiple choice test and project allow the student to test and express their newly found knowledge before continuing.

Block 7 - Introducing the Switch Statement

As programs become more complex the need for highly structured code becomes more apparent. The *if-else* construct, as explained in Block 6 can deal with just about any form of decision making. It can however result in code that lacks structure and that is difficult to read. Block 7 introduces the *switch* statement as a structured alternative to the *if-else* statement. Again numerous examples are offered highlighting when and when not to use a *switch* statement. An animation is not offered in Block 7 as it was felt that the animation in Block 6 gave sufficient coverage of the whole concept of decision making in a program. As with all learning blocks, Block 7 finishes with a carefully constructed multiple choice test and project.

Block 8 - Introducing Iteration

Block 8 has the task of introducing one of the most powerful concepts in programming, that of iteration. The C language has various constructs on offer to achieve iteration or repetition. However, in an attempt to give a more gradual introduction to looping Block 8 concentrates on the *for* loop. The usefulness and power of the *for* loop is clearly explained by means of numerous examples which clearly demonstrate how the *for* loop can be used to execute one or more statements a specified number of times. Block 8 offers an animation which demonstrates, in a graphical way, the workings of the for loop. Considerable emphasis is put on the *for* loops effect on the variables used throughout the sample program. A multiple choice test is then offered and finally the student is given the opportunity of expressing this newly discovered construct in the form of a challenging project.

Block 9 - Introducing While and Do While Loops

While the *for* loop is indeed a powerful construct, there are numerous occasions when the programmer does not want to specify how many times a set of actions will be carried out. Block 9 begins by highlighting this fact and then quickly introduces the *while* and *do while* loops in C by means of a sample program. As the two constructs are very similar it was felt that the one learning block would provide sufficient coverage. Various programs are used to highlight when to use one construct or the other. This knowledge is then refined by means of numerous questions each offering detailed answers. As three forms of iteration are now available to the student it was felt that an animation of the *while* loop would prove invaluable in avoiding any confusion. A multiple choice test gives the student the opportunity to test themselves on these two new types of iteration. The block then concludes with two projects. One to allow the student to practice the *while* loop and the second to practice the *do while* loop.

Block 10 - Introducing Arrays

Block 10 the last of the learning blocks making up C by Active Learning introduces the user to the most advanced topic so far, arrays. The user is immediately made aware of the need for and the power of the array by means of a sample program. The block continues by highlighting array declaration and then places considerable emphasis on the correct use of an array subscript. Block 10 also has the effect of summing up the content of the entire application as several constructs introduced in previous blocks, such as the *for* loop, are necessary for effective array implementation. As arrays are the first real data structure encountered by the student it was felt that a graphical demonstration of their correct use would prove invaluable. An animation is therefore offered which steps through a sample program highlighting the operation of an array. A graphical representation is offered of the variables, subscripts and arrays used throughout the program. The student can watch the array fill up with integer values and likewise watch as each value is printed to the screen. The block concludes with a multiple choice test and a challenging project. Every effort is made to give the student a compete understanding of arrays and equally important a taste for more.

EVALUATION & RESULTS

Over the last twelve months C by Active Learning has been used to complement more traditional teaching methods and as such was piloted by a number of students on introductory programming modules. The selected pilot groups were deliberately targeted as groups with limited, if any, programming experience and in particular no C programming experience. Using a questionnaire and a series of informal interviews and discussion sessions the students were asked to comment on the courseware in terms of its interface and more importantly on its content.

Interface Design

The overall findings were very encouraging. The students felt that the interface was consistent, clear, uncluttered and had a navigation system that was both simple to use and effective. It was interesting to note that a number of students indicated a preference for keyboard controls. As a result future versions will include both a mouse and keyboard navigational systems.

Tutor Content

Although a high quality interface is paramount we focused the majority of our evaluation effort on establishing how the tutor had 'performed' as an aid to teaching C programming. The evaluators were initially asked to comment on the quality of the descriptions used for the numerous programming constructs. As the most basic feature of the courseware it was vital to get these right. Over 90% of the evaluators were impressed with the explanations. As such we concluded that the Context and Object stages of the tutor had been pitched at the correct level for a high percentage of the students and that the explanations were comprehensive.

As numerous questions and projects were included throughout the courseware we were eager to elicit feedback on this refinement effort within the tutor. Although the questions were considered to be of a high standard a number of evaluators felt that some were too easy. As a result effort has been given to increasing the complexity of the questions in an incremental fashion that is, some the questions now build upon each other. This incremental approach has the effect of gradually increasing the difficulty of each question in a learning block. It was interesting to note that the suggested projects were considered to be just right by many students, but quite difficult by the rest. As a result the courseware now includes projects of different complexity within each learning block. This facilitates the complete beginner whilst providing more cryptic projects to challenge faster learners.

The evaluators were also asked to comment on the features provided by the tutor. The 'useful links' option was used extensively, but surprisingly the e-mail option had a relatively small uptake. The animations were used by every evaluator and were seen as one of the key features of the courseware. A number of students even asked if it would be possible to build more user control of the animations into the courseware. This seems to indicate that the animations at the very least piqued the imagination.

In the early stages of design considerable effort was made to integrate a commercial C compiler directly into the courseware. However, this proved to be technically impossible due to the security restrictions imposed by the applet security manager which prohibits an applet from accessing the local hard disk (McGraw & Felten, 1997). We felt it had to be guaranteed that every potential student could test his/her newly found skills and as such some form of workaround was required. The solution proved to be another example of the power of the Internet. A direct link was offered to a limited, but nonetheless effective shareware C compiler. This enabled all students to quickly download their own compiler which when combined with a standard text editor proved ideal for introductory C programming. Despite this workaround a number of students commented that the most frustrating feature of C by Active Learning was leaving the courseware environment to complete examples and projects. If and when the Java security restrictions are relaxed a direct linkup to a compiler would be an immediate advance.

CONCLUSIONS

The wide accessibility of the World Wide Web make it a perfect base for developing courseware modules. Since learning involves more than just receiving transmitted information, courseware must be interactive and encourage student engagement, which is a challenge on WWW architecture. The courseware presented in this paper, C by Active Learning, is the result of combining an effective approach to teaching (the CORE approach) with the individual strengths of HTML, Java and Java Script. Considerable emphasis has been placed on interactivity in the design of the courseware to promote learning and involvement. Thus, students are free to reflect on the material contained in the tutor, interact with it and create an understanding of it.

The world we live in is rapidly changing and as a result there is a growing need for flexible course delivery. C by Active Learning is testimony to the fact that the WWW is indeed an ideal platform on which to develop such flexible courseware. It is not intended to replace formal teaching methods, but instead provide considerable support to students when required. In the words of Du Boulay (1986) *'learning to program is not easy'*. C by Active Learning makes use of the latest Internet technology to make this learning process a little easier and a lot more enjoyable.

REFERENCES
Biggs, J. & Moore, P. (1993) *The Process of Learning*, Prentice Hall.

Boyle, T. (1990) "The CORE Approach to Developing Learning Environments for Programming", *Monitor*, vol. 1, no. 1.

Boyle, T., Gray, J., Wendl, B. & Davies, M. (1992) "Taking the Plunge with CLEM: the Design and Evaluation of a Large Scale CAL System", Department of Computing, Manchester Metropolitan University.

Boyle, T. & Margetts, S. (1991) "*Pascal by Active Learning Using the CORE Approach*", DP Publications.

Cunningham, S. (1996) "Teaching and Learning on the WWW", *Graphics and Visualisations*, Issue 45, pp. 3-5. Http://www.man.ac.uk/mvc//sima/articles/reading.html

Du Boulay, B. (1986) "Some Difficulties of Learning to Program", *Journal of Educational Computing Research*, vol. 2, no. 1, pp. 57-73.

Gordon, B. (1996) "JAVA A New Brew for Educators, Administrators and Students", *Educom Review*, vol. 31, no. 2.

Kamouri, A. L., Kamouri, J. & Smith, K. H. (1986) "Training by exploration: facilitating the transfer of procedural knowledge through annalogical reasoning", *International Journal of Man-Machine Studies*, vol. 24, no. 2, pp. 171-192.

Marshall, D. (1994) "Programming in C", http://www/cs.cf/ac.uk/Dave/C/CE.html

Marshal, A. D. & Hurley, S. (1996) "Interactive hypermedia courseware for the World Wide Web", *SIGCE Bulletin*, vol. 28, pp. 1-5.

McGraw, G. & Felten, E. (1997) "JAVA Security and Type Safety, *BYTE Magazine*, pp. 63-64.

Owens, M. (1992) "The Role of Computer Based Learning and the Teaching of Programming", *Conference Proceedings, Developments in the Teaching of Computer Science*, pp. 207-214.

St Andrews (1996) "Using the World Wide Web for Teaching", The Computing Laboratory, University of St Andrews. http://www.st-and.ac.uk/cl/cal/newsletter/5/teaching.html

Walsh, T. (1989) *Bringing Design to Software*, Addison Wesley.

A Conceptual Model and a Taxonomy of Queries for Audio-visual Databases

S. Balachandar

Department of Computer Science and Engineering, University of Texas at Arlington, 416 Yates Street, Suite 300, Arlington, Texas 76019 U.S.A.

sbalacha@cse.uta.edu

Ramez A. Elmasri

Department of Computer Science and Engineering, University of Texas at Arlington, 416 Yates Street, Suite 300, Arlington, Texas 76019 U.S.A.

elmasri@cse.uta.edu

ABSTRACT

Audio-visual databases will come into increasing vogue because multimedia data is inherently more expressive than alphanumeric data and technical barriers to the widespread use of audio-visual databases, like bandwidth constraints, and storage overhead, have been eroding. Traditional alphanumeric databases were given a boost by a conceptual framework in which to model real world entities and the relationships among them. Audio-visual databases too will benefit from a conceptual data model to represent the contents of audio-visual repositories. While some researchers have dealt with various aspects of data modeling in the context of video and audio, none has presented an integrated conceptual model, unifying the domains of audio and video. This paper is an attempt at such a synthesis. Since query based retrieval is a core function of a database, this paper presents a taxonomy of queries a typical audio-visual database would be expected to field.

Key Words: data model, frame, video segmentation, scene, shot, audio.

INTRODUCTION

Though multimedia data are richer in information content than alphanumeric data, conventional information systems have been based on a manipulation of alphanumeric data because of technical constraints that restrict the handling of images, video and audio. First, multimedia data is more voluminous than alphanumeric data. Second, because of the sheer size of multimedia objects, the performance characteristics of storage devices, processors and network bandwidth have proved to be bottlenecks to the widespread implementation of multimedia systems. However, technological evolution in these areas and breakthroughs in CPU & I/O scheduling algorithms and database indexing techniques are shattering the barriers to the adoption of multimedia content to augment the meaningfulness of traditional information systems. This has been demonstrated by prototypes such as QBIC [16] and Informedia [25].

Figure 1 provides a tabular comparison of the sizes of typical multimedia data objects. It can be seen that the richer the desired information content, the larger the size of the data object. It is both intuitive as well as borne out by Figure 1 that the richest information transfer is achieved with both video and audio media present.

Multimedia systems too can enjoy the benefits of more efficient storage, retrieval, and transaction management if shared database management systems were used in place of stand-alone file systems for individual applications [1, 2].

A well crafted data model is a prerequisite to developing an efficient database application. A data model is an abstraction of real world objects, their attributes and the relationships among these objects. A conceptual data model is a vehicle for the analysis of the data at hand and for decisions on the scope and boundary of the database. These decisions are based on the queries that will be posed to the database. There has been some work done in the area of modeling video data [3, 4, 5, 9, 10, 11, 12, 13, 14, 15, 16, 17, 18]. However, each of these papers lacks at least some of the issues raised and covered in this paper, as evident from the section entitled "Related Research." Further, there is little literature describing models that integrate the visual *and* audio components of video.

This paper proposes an integrated model for the conceptual modeling of audio-visual data. By modeling both audio and visual media in a single conceptual data model, it is possible to specify more queries for retrieval. Because query based retrieval is a core function of databases, a clear understanding of the types of queries a database would be expected to handle influences the database design. With this in mind, this paper presents a taxonomy of queries for

Figure 1: Sizes of representative multimedia objects	
Multimedia Object	Size
1 page of typed text	4000 bytes (assuming 50 line pages and 80 character lines)
A 400 page book	1.6 MB
A 4 inch X 5 inch black & white photograph	1.8 MB (assuming a resolution of 300 dots per inch and 8 bits per dot)
A 4 inch X 5 inch color photograph	5.4 MB (assuming a resolution of 300 dots per inch and 24 bits per dot)
1 second of full-motion uncompressed video with frame resolution of 640 X 480 pixels	27.65 MB (assuming 30 frames per second and 24 bits per pixel color representation)
A 2 hour movie with frame resolution of 640 X 480 pixels	199.07 GB (assuming 30 frames per second and 24 bits per pixel color representation)
1 second of stereophonic audio	176.4 KB (assuming a 44.1 Khz sampling rate & sample size of 16 bits)
A 5 minute of song recorded in stereo	52.92 MB (assuming a sampling rate of 44.1 Khz and sample size of 16 bits)

audio-visual databases. The rest of this paper is organized as follows. Section 2.0 starts with an exploration of relevant concepts about audio-visual data, goes on to examine the types of queries that an audio-visual database would be expected to field and then presents the conceptual model for audio-visual databases. Related research efforts are briefly described in section 3.0 and the points of contrast with this paper are highlighted. Section 4.0 concludes this paper with some suggested areas for future research.

CONCEPTUAL MODEL PRELIMINARIES

There are two fundamental approaches to data retrieval in a multimedia database system — *content based retrieval* and *annotation based retrieval.* In the latter approach, video must be processed in advance and items and other aspects of interest in the data must be identified, and these must be annotated and mapped to points in the video footage where they appear, to facilitate subsequent retrieval in response to user queries. Content based retrieval obviates the need for this pre-processing step because it relies on using image processing/computer vision algorithms to retrieve images and video segments based on *color, shape, texture,* and *object tracking.* While the fact that this method does not require a pre-processing step clearly makes it more attractive, it is not practically feasible to use this approach always. This is because the state of the art in the fields of image processing, computer vision and artificial intelligence does not yet lend itself to answering such questions, for example, as *"Find all video segments where the colt races ahead of the horse."* Such a query would be difficult to evaluate and answer even if a query-by-example approach was used where the database search engine is actually presented with the picture of a horse; still the system cannot easily distinguish between a colt and a horse. Therefore, annotation based retrieval will have a place till advances in image processing and artificial intelligence render content based retrieval a more reliable method. Reliability is measured in terms of precision of recall, i.e., ideally, all and only those video segments meeting the query conditions must be retrieved.

Video Concepts

A video segment consists of a sequence of still images that is presented at a rapid rate. This is the mechanism by which video simulates motion. Each of these still images is referred to as a *frame*. A *frame*, therefore, is simply the equivalent of one photograph. A *frame* is the atomic unit of a video segment, i.e., it is the smallest unit into which a video sequence may be broken down. In the case of full motion video, frames are presented at a rate of 30 per second. If frames were presented at a lower pace, one would view jerky motion, a la animation. For animation, the frame rate is 10 or 15 per second. Any raw video footage consists of a series of frames.

Since in video there are 30 frames to a second, it is easy to see that the number of frames in any length of video clip would be very high. A mere 5 minutes of full motion video would consist of 9000 frames. The primary goal of a video database is to provide an efficient means to search through video data for *items, features* and *actions* of interest; to this list can be added sound patterns should the video database also include an audio component. However, if one were to search through each and every frame, the task would be very inefficient.

Typically, an item of interest or an action of interest would, starting at a certain frame, span several frames. Given this fact, it is sufficient to search through only these starting frames, if only it is possible to process the video footage in advance and identify these starting frames. In fact the computer vision and image processing community has worked on this *segmentation* problem for a while. Several segmentation algorithms have been proposed. Hampapur

[6], Boreczky and Rowe [7], Hampapur, et al. [8], Dailianas et al. [22], and Ahanger and Little [23] provide a good survey of these. These algorithms analyze a length of full motion video and compare frames, looking for abrupt changes (typically a user can specify the permissible degree of abruptness as a parameter). Such abrupt changes would generally result with the appearance or disappearance of one or more items of interest. Any motion based *action* would also result in the identification of segments. Some algorithms also provide for identification of segments based on changes in the texture, color and shape of items that appear in the frames of the video footage. The algorithm or combination of algorithms to use for video segmentation depends on the nature of the subject matter of the video footage. [6, 7] provide a comparison of the various video segmentation algorithms. Video can also be segmented on the basis of sound patterns occurring in the video using speech processing algorithms [19, 20]. Additionally, segmentation can also be done on the basis of the occurrence of text in video footage [20, 21].

As we have seen earlier, a *frame* is the atomic unit of a video clip. A *shot* and *scene* are less granular units of a video clip. A *shot* is an uninterrupted sequence of video that is the result of one camera operation such as a wipe, dissolve, zoom, pan, fade, etc. A *scene* is a sequence of frames that capture a certain set of items of interest or actions of interest [7]. Examples of scenes may be "the child cutting the cake," "the player striking the ball," "the airplane taking off," "the teacher walking into the classroom," etc. Video segmentation algorithms actually attempt to identify, in a footage of video, scene change points and shot boundaries. Instead of analyzing every single frame to identify items and actions of interest, it is a lot more efficient to merely review the frames that mark a scene change or shot boundary with a view to identifying items and actions of interest.

After segmenting the video sequence into points that mark scene changes and shot boundaries, this subset of frames must be analyzed to identify items and actions of interest. This can be done automatically by algorithms developed by the pattern recognition and image processing community, or manually by a human expert conversant with the subject matter of the video. As far as the video database is concerned it matters little which approach is taken. Pattern recognition and image processing algorithms have a long way to go before they approach the accuracy of a human expert.

Taxonomy of Queries

This section presents a taxonomy of queries and for each query type presents some examples.

Item Occurrence Queries

This is a class of queries that calls for searching a video database for the occurrence of specified *items of interest*. Items of interest may be narrowed down through feature qualification. A *feature* is a characteristic about an item of interest, e.g., a *cargo* ship, a *green* shirt, etc. Examples of this class of queries include:

a) Find all video segments where a vehicle appears,
b) Find all video segments where a car appears,
c) Find all video segments where a yellow car appears, (here, the car, which is the *item of interest*, is qualified by a *feature* of the car, its color, which in this case happens to be yellow)
d) Find all video segments where a yellow Ford car appears, and
e) Find all video segments where a yellow Ford car and a child appear.

The level of detail about the car, i.e., the features about the item that must be captured in the data model depends on the application domain and on the type of queries that the database is expected to handle. For instance, if the application domain pertains to automobile racing, one would track as many features as possible about the car and not as many about the child, who is not central to the theme of the application, but is merely incidental to it. On the other hand, if the application pertains to kids' TV shows, one might track a lot more features about children than about cars. Such decisions and tradeoffs result from careful analysis by subject matter experts.

Action Queries

These queries represent search based on the occurrence of actions, e.g., *"Retrieve all video segments where a goal is scored"* in the domain of soccer. An *action* may be defined as a set of items of interest, referred to as the *subject*(s) of the action, doing something to a set of items of interest, referred to as the *object*(s) of the action. Examples of such queries include:

a) Find all video segments where the center-forward kicks the football into the goal; here the center-forward is the subject and football and goal are the object, and kicking the action,
b) Find all video segments where the hero drives a car; in this example, the hero is the subject, the car is the object and driving is the action,
c) Find all video segments where children run into the garden; here children represent the subject, the garden is the object and the action is running.

Spatial Queries

A spatial query is one whose search condition specifies the relative topological positions of one or more items of interest. A representative list of relative positions includes : *above, to the left of, to the right of, behind, below, in front of.* Depending on the subject matter of the video database, the granularity of the query conditions, and the desired level of the retrieval accuracy, the aforementioned list of relative positions can be made more sophisticated and comprehensive, and less granular. Some examples of spatial queries are:

a) Find all video segments where the sun is *above* the field,
b) Find all video segments where the brother is *to the left of* the sister,
c) Find all video segments where the father is *to the right of* the mother,
d) Retrieve all video segments where the car is *behind* the truck, and
e) Find all video segments where the book is *below* the pen.

Temporal Queries

A temporal query is one whose condition specifies the relative time order of the appearance of items of interest, specific to the performance of an action. These are some queries of this class:

a) Retrieve all video segments where the teacher arrives *before* the students,
b) Find all video segments where the students repeat *after* the teacher,
c) Show all video segments where the tiger and the clown enter the circus ring at the same time.

Sound Pattern Queries

The incorporation of the audio component of video is one of the main differences between this paper and other papers that have presented data models for multimedia in general and video in particular. Using the audio dimension can contribute significantly to retrieval performance. In this type of queries, the video database is searched for sound patterns specified in the query condition. Examples of these are:

a) Find all video segments where the bell rings.
b) Retrieve all video segments where thunder is heard.

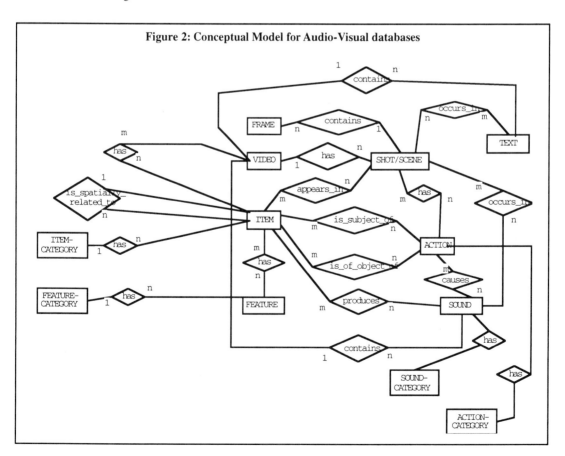

Figure 2: Conceptual Model for Audio-Visual databases

Text Occurrence Queries

Video databases that are interspersed with text can be searched by specifying text patterns in the query condition and by including an Optical Character Recognition (OCR) module to the database search engine. One of several access methods for text can be used [24].

Conceptual Model for Video

Based on the taxonomy presented in section 2.2, Figure 2 presents a conceptual model for audio-visual data, using the entity-relationship notation. Entity types are indicated within rectangles, relationships between entity types are indicated within diamonds, and the cardinality of a relationship is indicated as *1:n*, if it is a one-to-many relationship and *m:n* if it is a many-to-many relationship. In a relational implementation, entities would be converted to relations and a *m:n* relationship would be implemented as a pair of *1:n* relationships.

Relational Representation

Figure 2 provided an entity-relationship diagram of the conceptual model to analyze audio-video repositories and organize the information therein, into databases, thereby facilitating ready retrieval of segments of interest, without having to laboriously pore through endless reels of footage. The data pertaining to an audio-visual repository must be organized using the object or relational model. The primary advantage of the object model vis-a-vis the relational model is that it allows for the incorporation of methods (procedures) along with the data, thereby rendering the reuse of software components easier; however, the structure of the data elements and the relationship among them are not fundamentally altered. In this section, a relational schema corresponding to the conceptual model of Figure 2 is presented. A relational schema is presented instead of an object class diagram for only one reason: the relational model supports a high level query language -- SQL(Structured Query Language) — which can be readily used to craft queries for desired retrieval patterns. In contrast, the object model does not support such a high level language — retrieval is performed from object databases using languages such as C++ and Java. Means to convert a relational schema to an object-class diagram are presented in [1]. In the following schema, the following conventions are followed:

Entity names are in bold, upper case letters.

Attribute names are shown in the table, in lower case letters.

Primary Key attributes are shown in bold letters.

Foreign Key attributes are shown italicized.

Non key attributes are neither bold nor in italics.

The last column in each table is the ellipsis, to indicate the fact that there could be other non key attributes and that the list of non key attributes presented is not comprehensive.

Entity **VIDEO**

Video_ID	Video_description	Video-producer	Video-production-date	.....

Entity **ITEM**

Item_ID	Item_description	*Item_category_id*	.....

Entity **VIDEO-ITEM**

Item_id	Video_id	.....

Entity **ITEM-CATEGORY**

Item_category_id	Item_category_description	.....

Entity **FEATURE-CATEGORY**

Feature_category_id	Feature_category_description	.....

Entity **FEATURE**

Feature_id	Feature_description	*Feature_category_id*	.....

Entity **FEATURE-ITEM**

Feature_id	**Item_id**	.....

Entity **SHOT**

Shot_id	Shot_description	*Video_id*	.....

Entity **FRAME**

Frame_id	*Shot_id*	…..

Entity **SHOT-ACTION**

Shot_id	**Action_id**	…..

Entity **ACTION**

Action_id	Action_description	*Action_category_id*	…..

Entity **SOUND**

Sound_id	Sound_description	*Sound_category_id*	*Video_id*	…..

Entity **SOUND-CATEGORY**

Sound_category_id	Sound_category_description	…..

Entity **ACTION-CATEGORY**

Action_Category_id	Action_category_description	…..

Entity **SUBJECT**

Action_id	**Item_id**	…..

Entity **OBJECT**

Action_id	**Item_id**	…..

Entity **SHOT-SOUND**

Shot_id	**Sound_id**	…..

Entity **SHOT-ITEM**

Shot_id	**Item_id**	*Related_item*	Spatial_Relation	…..

Entity **TEXT**

Text_id	Text	*Video_id*	…..

Entity **SHOT-TEXT**

Shot_id	**Text_id**	…..

Entity **ACTION-SOUND**

Action_id	**Sound_id**	…..

Contributions of this paper

As indicated in section 3.0, a few researchers have done work in multimedia data modeling in general and video data modeling in particular. However the unique contributions of this paper lie in the fact that it presents an integrated conceptual model for video that unifies video, audio and text. In addition to integrating the media of video, audio and text in a single conceptual framework, the model presented in this paper also incorporates the notion of *action*, which is a powerful tool to pare down the results of searching through a video database. Additionally, this paper presents a systematic taxonomy of queries that could be posed to an audio-visual database.

RELATED RESEARCH

This section summarizes some of the other research efforts on the topic of multimedia data modeling. Each deals with one or more aspects of multimedia data modeling. However none presents a comprehensive conceptual framework to facilitate the modeling of audio-visual data. This is the main contribution of this paper, as emphasized in section 2.5. In addition to providing a brief description of the research effort, the shortcomings of the approach espoused in each of the papers are also explained.

Gibbs, Breiteneder and Tsichritzis [3, 10] present a model for the *interpretation, derivation* and *temporal composition* of audio-video data, starting from raw video which is typically stored in the form of binary large objects (BLOBs). An *interpretation* I, of a BLOB B, is a mapping from B to a set of *media objects*. A *media object* is defined as a timed audio/video/audio-video stream or sequence or a collection of a collection of temporally related timed audio/video/audio-video streams. A *derivation* is the process of producing another media object or sequence by applying transformation parameters to existing objects in the raw media BLOBs. The notion of *derivation* reduces storage requirements by allowing alternate views to be specified without the need for data replication. Additionally, updates are made easier because derivation renders it unnecessary to delete and reassemble video frames or audio sequences. *Composition* is the specification of the relative time order among the media objects that constitute a multimedia presentation.

While the Gibbs model provides adequately for the editing and presentation of audio-visual content, it does not provide for the easy retrieval of an audio-visual stream based on inherent items of interest or actions or sounds in a video stream.

Schloss and Wynblatt [11] have proposed a *Layered Multimedia Data Model*. The lowest layer, the *Data Definition Layer*, provides a logical interpretation of raw multimedia data to the higher layers. Above this layer, the *Data Manipulation Layer* provides services for grouping media sequences into temporally ordered presentations. On top of this, the *Data Presentation Layer* specifies the playback devices involved and the *quality of service* parameters such as play back rate, play back resolution, text font, etc. The top layer, the *Control Layer* provides a scripting language that allows for multiple multimedia presentations to be presented in some pre-determined sequence, following some desired logic. The Layered Data Model suffers from the same deficiencies as the Gibbs model.

In the Advanced Video Information System [12], Adali et al. segment raw video into a sequence of frames. In this model, *video objects, activity types* and *events* are identified and are related to *frame sequences* using the notion of *association maps*. Adali et al. propose a segment tree based data structure to represent these association maps. While this model is close to the one proposed in the current paper, in that it provides for the retrieval of video clips based on the presence of items of interest and actions, it does not allow for the retrieval of video segments based on the sounds inherent in them.

While Hjelsvold and Midstraum [4] do propose an entity-relationship based scheme for the capturing of video content, the main points of difference with our work is that they do not have mechanisms to allow retrieval by actions and sound patterns present in a video segment.

Day and his colleagues [13] have proposed a graph based model called Video Semantic Directed Graph (VSDG) to conceptually model video data. The authors suggest that the VSDG representation superimposed on an object oriented hierarchy leads to an architecture for handling video. The main deficiencies of this approach are that it does not allow for searching and direct access to video segments containing specified items of interest, actions, sounds etc.

Oomoto and Tanaka [14] have proposed an object oriented model called the Object-Oriented Video Information Database (OVID). OVID does incorporate the concept of a *video object,* which is similar to our *item of interest*; however, it suffers from an inability to allow retrieval of video content based on the sound component of video data.

Jain and Hampapur [15] propose a model called ViMOD (The Video Data Model), which provides for the searching of video content based on specified items of interest and their features. However ViMOD does not address the issue of retrieval by actions and sound patterns.

Query by Image Content (QBIC) [16] is a prototypical system developed to demonstrate *content based retrieval*, whereby repositories of images or video can be searched based on colors, shapes and textures. It also includes a *query by example* component that allows users to specify an example image and have the system retrieve other images/clips that look like that one, based on a combination of color, shape and texture. QBIC is not capable of retrieval based on actions and sounds. Also, image processing and computer vision algorithms are not accurate enough yet to perform retrievals with acceptable levels of recall and precision. The same problems afflict the work by Zhang et al. [17], which is also based on content-based retrieval.

LI and Ozsu [18] have proposed a data structure called the Common Video Object Tree (CVOT) wherein they map *salient objects*, which are identical in meaning to the *items of interest* in our paper, to video frames. The CVOT model does not provide for retrieval on the basis of actions and sound patterns.

CONCLUSIONS

This paper has proposed a conceptual model to represent the contents of audio-visual databases. This model integrates the media of audio, video and text. This conceptual model could be used as the basis to analyze video footage, with a view to creating a digital library or audio-visual database that could be used for fast and efficient retrieval of segments satisfying user specified criteria.

This paper assumes that raw video will be available in uncompressed format. An area of future research is to investigate the possibility of working with compressed video.

Another area of future research would be to conduct studies comparing the retrieval precision between automated and manual identification of items and actions of interest in frames that mark the beginning of shots and scenes.

Devising novel indexing schemes is yet another research area that can be pursued.

REFERENCES

1. Elmasri, R. and Navathe, S. B., [1994], *Fundamentals of Database Systems*, 2nd edition, The Benjamin/Cummings Publishing Company, Inc.
2. Batini, C., Ceri, S. and Navathe, S.B., [1992], *Conceptual Database Design*, The Benjamin/Cummings Publishing Company, Inc.
3. Breiteneder, C., Gibbs, S. and Tsichritzis, D., [1992], "Modelling of Audio/Video Data," *Proc. of 11th International Conference on the Entity-Relationship Approach,* Karlsruhe, Germany, October 7-9, 1992.
4. Hjelsvold, R. and Midtstraum, R., [1994], "Modelling and Querying Video Data," *Proc. of 20th VLDB Conference,* Santiago, Chile.
5. Li, J.Z., Ozsu, M.T. and Szafron, D., [1996], "Modeling of Video Spatial Relationships in an Object Database Management System," *Proc. of International Workshop on Multi-Media Database Management Systems,* Blue Mountain Lake, New York, August 14-16, 1996.
6. Hampapur, A., [1995], Designing Video Data Management Systems, Ph.D Thesis, University of Michigan, Ann Arbor, Michigan.
7. Boreczky, J.S. and Rowe, L. A., [1996], "Comparison of video shot boundary detection techniques," *Proc. of SPIE 2670,* pp. 170-179.
8. Hampapur, A., Jain, R. and Weymouth, T., [1994], "Digital Video Segmentation," *Proc. of 1994 ACM Multimedia Conference,* San Francisco, California, October 1994.
9. Baral, C., Gonzalez, G. and Son, T., [1998], "Conceptual Modeling and Querying in Multi-media databases," Journal of Multimedia Tools and Applications, Vol. 7, pp. 37-66, 1998.
10. Gibbs, S., Breiteneder, C. and Tsichritzis, D., [1994], "Data Modelling of Time Based Media," *Proceedings of SIGMOD Conference,* pp. 91-102, Minneapolis, MN, May 1994.
11. Schloss, G.A. and Wnyblatt, M.J., [1994], "Building Temporal Structures in a Layered Multimedia Data Model," *Proceedings of 2nd International Multimedia Conference,* pp. 271-278, San Francisco, CA, October 1994.
12. Adali, S., Candan, K.S., Chen, S.S., Erol, K., and Subrahmanian, V.S., [1996], "The Advanced Video Information System: Data Structures and Query Processing," *ACM Multimedia Systems Journal,* pp. 172-186, August 1996.
13. Day, Y.F., Dagtas, S., Iino, M., Khokhar, A., and Ghafoor, A., [1995], "Object-oriented Conceptual Modeling of Video Data," *Proceedings of 11th International Conference on Data Engineering,* pp. 401-408, Taipei, Taiwan, 1995.
14. Oomoto, E. and Tanaka, K., [1993], "OVID: Design and Implementation of a Video-Object Database System," *IEEE Transactions on Knowledge and Data Engineering,* Vol. 5, No. 4, pp. 629-643, August 1993.
15. Jain, R. and Hampapur, A., [1994], "Metadata in a Video Database," *ACM SIGMOD Record,* Vol. 23, No. 4, pp. 27-33, December 1994.
16. Flickner, M. et al., [1995], "Query by image and video content: The QBIC system," *IEEE Computer,* Vol. 28, No. 9, pp. 23-32, September 1995.
17. Zhang, H.J., Low, C.Y., Smoliar, S.W., and Wu, J.H., [1995], "Video parsing, retrieval and browsing: An integrated and content-based solution," *Proceedings of ACM International Multimedia Conference,* pp. 15-25, San Francisco, CA, 1995.
18. Li, J.Z., and Ozsu, M.T., [1997], "STARS: A Spatial Attributes Retrieval System for Images and Videos," *Proceedings of 4th International Conference on Multimedia Modeling,* pp. 69-84, Singapore, November 1997.
19. Pfeiffer, S., Fischer, S., Effelsberg, W., [1996], "Automatic Audio Content Analysis," *Proceedings of ACM Multimedia Conference,* pp.21-30, Boston, MA, November 1996.
20. Hauptmann, A., and Smith, M., [1995], "Text, Speech, and vision for video segmentation: The Informedia Project," *Proceedings of AAAI Fall Symposium, Computational Models for Integrating Language and Vision,"* Boston, MA, November 1995.
21. Lienhart, R., [1996], "Automatic Text Recognition for Video Indexing," *Proceedings of ACM Multimedia Conference,* pp. 11-20, Boston, MA, November 1996.
22. Dailianas, A., Allen R., and England, P., [1995], "Comparison of Automatic Video Segmentation Algorithms," *Proceedings of SPIE 2615, Photonics East 1995: Integrating Issues in Large Commercial Media Delivery Systems,"* Philadelphia, PA, October, 1995.
23. Ahanger, G., and Little, T.D.C., [1996], "A Survey of Technologies for Parsing and Indexing Digital Video," *Journal of Visual Communication and Image Representation,* Vol. 7, No. 1, pp. 28-43, March 1996.
24. Faloutsos, C., [1985], "Access Methods for Text," *ACM Computing Surveys,* Vol. 17, No. 1, pp. 49-74, March 1985.
25. Christel, M., Winkler, D., and Taylor, R. [1997], "Multimedia Abstractions for a Digital Video Library," *Proceedings of ACM Digital Libraries Conference,* Philadelphia, PA, July 1997.

The Impact of Problem Formulation on a Mixed-Motive Task

Reza Barkhi

Pamplin College of Business, Department of Accounting and Information Systems, Virginia Polytechnic Institute and State University, Blacksburg, VA 24061-0101

Phone: (540) 231-5869, Fax: (540) 231-2511, Email: reza@vt.edu

ABSTRACT

Despite the advances in Group Decision Support System (GDSS) research, the research on the impact of decision guidance and problem formulation tool on negotiation task has been limited. Problem formulation tools may provide managers with procedural guidance of how to structure collaborative problems. In a controlled laboratory experiment, I compare a GDSS that supports problem formulation with a GDSS that does not support problem formulation. The groups using a GDSS with the problem formulation tool outperformed the groups using a GDSS without the formulation tool but were less efficient. Important implications about the design of GDSS features and managerial concerns are discussed.

INTRODUCTION

Group Decision Support Systems (GDSS) may facilitate group communication and aid group members in solving problems by providing problem formulation capabilities. Nutt (1992) reports that the majority of managerial problem activities either completely ignore problem formulation or use ineffective tactics (Nutt, 1992). This research examines the impact of problem formulation on decision process and outcomes of GDSS users. Each group is given either a GDSS with problem formulation tool or one without problem formulation tool. All groups solve a mixed-motive negotiation task (McGrath 1984), where each member may have dual motives: compete, and cooperate. The research question is: will problem formulation tools for distributed groups lead to optimal decisions for the group or to misguided individual optimization under conditions of information asymmetry'

PROBLEM FORMULATION

Studies on individual use of Decision Support Systems (DSS) have shown that quantitative modeling and formulation tools improve performance (Benbasat and Schroeder 1977, Chervany and Dickson 1974). Modeling and problem formulation tools may improve process gains (Benbasat and Nault 1990) by reducing the problems arising from incomplete task analysis, incomplete use of information, and information overload. However, in group decision making situations (i.e. GDSS), models may require input from 'multiple users' and the problem formulation tool may not be effective if decision makers misrepresent or bias the model's parameters.

Problem formulation tools provide a systematic method to search the solution space (e.g. corner points of the solution polytope). On the other hand, 'What-if' methods scan the solution space by allowing the members to incrementally change the parameters and move towards a solution that may be an improvement compared to the previous solution. This "greedy" method may converge to a local optima. Hence, systematic search of the solution space is preferred to incremental approaches like 'what-if' or other greedy heuristics[1]. This implies that the use of the problem formulation tools may result in better solutions than the use of what-if methods. Given that decision makers adapt their strategies to the decision aids (Todd and Benbasat 1991), it is important to understand how decision aids influence decision strategies. Chu and Elam (1990) have shown that a decision aid may impose an 'induced restrictiveness' on solution strategy. Specifically, spreadsheet use imposes an incremental solution strategy which may result in a suboptimal solution for some problems.

Previous research on individual DSS generally favors optimization over 'what-if' solution methods for individuals. However, in a group setting with asymmetrical information and conflicting objectives, the dynamics of decision making may be different. For such groups, one member's optimal solution cannot be adopted by others. In addition, it may not be easy to synthesize an optimal solution for the group from the individual optimal solutions. Hence, it is not clear if the problem formulation tool is favored over a 'what-if' tool that is inherently an incremental approach. Faced with a negotiation task, group members may exploit their information asymmetry to misguide others. The problem formulation and optimization tool may induce each member to stay close to her optimal solution and thereby miss an alternative solution that may be best for all members.

In group negotiation, members may share information that may reveal their preferences. Based on the information members receive from others, they may make inferences about the preferences of others and adjust their solution to identify compromised solutions. This may reduce equivocality (Daft and Lengel 1986) and enhance convergence to a mutually acceptable solution. This process may help each group member to identify the commonalities in her view with that of others in an attempt to form a consolidated perspective and a group view of the problem (Sambamurthy 1989). Such a *convergent* approach may help the group to reach a mutually acceptable solution (Janis and Mann 1977).

Convergent approaches promote high consensus, while *divergent* approaches can lead to conflict resulting in weakened group's feelings of consensus and commitment to a final solution (Janis and Mann 1977). A divergent approach promotes improved quality of outcomes as it encourages a more comprehensive understanding of the issues. However, because it weakens the group's feelings of consensus it may not converge. The dilemma resulting from the tradeoff between decision quality and convergence may be overcome by taking a two-phase approach to problem solving. In the first phase, each individual generates solutions from her perspective and in the second phase each individual shares her solutions with others and evaluates other individuals' proposed solutions (Niederman and DeSanctis 1995).

Each member in groups supported by a GDSS with the problem formulation tool can find her optimal solution and propose solutions to others. Each member can evaluate the solutions proposed to her utilizing the 'what-if' capability and can make incremental changes to the solution in an attempt to find a mutually acceptable solution. Using the problem formulation tool and the 'what-if'capability, the decision makers are induced to take a two-phase approach. Each time they optimize with new parameters, they 'land' on a new region of the solution space. Then using the 'what-if' capability they perform a local search around that optimal solution to see if there exists any solutions that are in the vicinity of the optimal solutions and are also acceptable by others. This process continues until the group decides that the best solution identified thus far should be accepted so that the problem-solving process may converge.

Each decision maker using a GDSS without the problem formulation tool can use the 'what-if' capability. She does not have the problem formulation tool to find the optimal solution from her perspective. The problem formulation tool, in the face of information asymmetry and conflicting objectives, may not necessarily be a valuable tool. However, given that such a tool may change the dynamics of decision making to encourage users to adopt a two-phase approach, groups using a GDSS with the problem formulation tool should more effectively search the solution space resulting in improved solution quality. The groups that only have the 'what-if' capability are more likely to remain in one region of the solution space given that the 'what-if' capability is used for making incremental changes to a previous solution. Hence, groups without the problem formulation tool are more likely to converge faster but achieve lower quality solutions. Section 3 presents two propositions based on these concepts.

PROPOSITIONS

Effects on Performance

The groups with a GDSS that provides the problem formulation tool are more likely to search more diverse solutions than groups that incrementally move in the vicinity of a solution. More systematic search and a larger set of diverse solutions makes selecting a compromise solution less conflicting and may reduce equivocality (Niederman and DeSanctis 1995). A GDSS with the problem formulation tool facilitates a systematic search of the solution space and promotes a two-phased approach to problem solving. Hence, it should lead the users to a higher quality solution than a GDSS without the problem formulation tool. This suggests the following proposition:

Proposition 1: Distributed groups using a GDSS with the problem formulation tool will produce better[2] solutions than will distributed groups using a GDSS without the problem formulation tool.

Effects on Efficiency

Niederman and DeSanctis (1995) suggest that problem formulation capability directs the conduct of information search and helps reduce equivocality making the process more efficient. The problem formulation tool of the GDSS directs the conduct of information search and provides a systematic method of searching the solution space. Groups that have access to the problem formulation tool should be able to search the solution space more systematically. They generate optimal solutions and then use the 'what-if' capability to search the vicinity of the optimal solutions. This results in new information about the solution space. This information may be used to revise the model parameters, find new solutions, and continue searching the vicinity of the new solutions for new compromise solutions. On the other hand, the groups that use a GDSS without the formulation tool may start constructing the solution by incrementally revising the previous solution. This is likely to result in a local search. If the local search results in a local optima, the problem-solving process may prematurely converge.

In this paper, efficiency is measured by the time it takes to converge to a solution. Decision-makers that search a small region of the solution space using the incremental approach are likely to converge faster than those who search a large region using the problem formulation tool as well as the incremental approach. We, therefore, expect groups using a GDSS with the problem formulation tool to be less efficient than groups using a GDSS without the problem formulation tool. This suggests the following proposition:

Proposition 2: Distributed groups using a GDSS with the problem formulation tool will be less efficient than those without the problem formulation tool.

THE EXPERIMENT

Seventy two executive MBA students enrolled in a decision making course at a major American University were randomly assigned to eighteen four-member groups. The members represented managers of three departments (i.e marketing, production, and purchasing), and a group leader (i.e. executive vice president). Subjects were provided with a structured thirty minute in-class presentation about the task. Each student was assigned to a computer separate from others where he/she could not have face-to-face or verbal contact with others in the group.

Each department manager received a separate sheet that included the cost data for her department. This operationalized information asymmetry. The negotiators, to reach a final solution, had to resolve their differences by consolidating their perspectives through the exchange of their private information. The case study was required for the course and represented 10% of the course grade based on their performance on the task.

Task and GDSS

A group meets to select a subset of orders, with differential payoff impacts for each member, from a larger set of customer orders such that capacity limits are not violated. Each member has to maximize her payoff. In addition to deciding which orders to select, each member has to decide how much effort to expend on filling each order. The mathematical model of the problem is provided in Appendix. This model is used as the formulation component of the GDSS that has the problem formulation tool.

Two versions of a GDSS were designed. Common features include structured information exchange facilities, electronic chat capability, what-if capability, and the capability to capture group memory. The GDSS with the problem formulation tool may be close to the definition of a Level Two GDSS while the one without this tool may be close to the definition of a Level One GDSS (DeSanctis and Gallupe 1987). Based on Nunamaker et al.'s (1991) proposed framework, both GDSSs provide process support (i.e. group memory and information exchange via pre-defined templates), and task structure (i.e what-if capability). However, only the GDSS with formulation tool provides task support (i.e. problem modeling and formulation capability).

The problem formulation tool uses the information in a group member's database to formulate and solve a specific problem instance and displays the optimal set of orders with the corresponding reward to the user. Each participant may evaluate a proposed solution by using the GDSS's what-if capability. Both GDSS provide the 'what-if' capability. The 'Group Memory' capability keeps a history of all proposed solutions and textual messages.

TESTABLE HYPOTHESES
Proposition 1

Proposition 1 stated that GDSS groups with the problem formulation tool will make better decisions than will those without the problem formulation tool. Given that each member tries to maximize his/her reward since it is directly tied to his/her grade on this project, one measure of solution quality is task performance that is captured by the reward he/she achieves. The GDSS with the problem formulation tool facilitates a systematic search of the solution space and promotes a two-phased approach to problem solving. This should lead to a higher quality solution that will be reflected in higher reward on the task than a GDSS without the problem formulation tool, suggesting the following hypothesis:

H1: Member reward will be higher in distributed groups supported by a GDSS with the problem formulation tool than those supported by a GDSS without the problem formulation tool.

Proposition 2

Proposition 2 suggests that groups using the GDSS with the problem formulation tool will be less efficient than those without the problem formulation tool. Efficiency is measured by the time it takes for the group to converge to a solution. The groups with the problem formulation tool are likely to use a two-phase approach. Each member will search the entire solution space to find the optimal solution (i.e. diverge) and then will incrementally make changes to search the vicinity of her optimal solution for 'good' compromise solutions (i.e. converge). On the other hand, the groups without the problem formulation tool are likely to search one small region of the solution space, find the best solution in that region, and terminate their search. Searching a small region of the solution space will take less time than searching a large region. Hence, groups that have the problem formulation tool are more likely to search a large portion of the solution space and are likely to have a longer convergence time. This suggests the following hypothesis:

H2: The time to converge to a solution will be less in groups supported by a GDSS without the problem formulation tool than those supported by a GDSS with the problem formulation tool.

RESULTS

The t-test was used to compare the results between the two types of GDSS groups: with and without the problem formulation tool. The results are categorized by each proposition.

Proposition 1: Solution Quality

Table 1 displays the results of the experiment on the average rewards achieved by members of groups using the GDSS with the problem formulation tool and those without the problem formulation tool.

Table 1: Reward			
	Mean Value	Std. Dev.	N
Without Tool	83.34	30.40	27
With Tool	108.18	22.60	27

Member reward is higher for GDSS groups with the problem formulation tool than those without it. Hence, hypothesis H1, that reward will be higher in GDSS groups with the problem formulation tool than those without the problem formulation tool, is supported ($p<.005$, $t=3.407$). This means that the GDSS tool that supports problem formulation caused a change in the individuals' task performance (i.e. reward) and possibly her strategy that resulted in the observed statistical difference in performance. This implicitly questions the validity of the theories of behavior that emphasize the ability of groups to determine their own behavior, regardless of technological intervention[3] (Markus and Robey, 1988). Technological intervention seems to affect the problem solving strategy and performance of decision-makers. Hence, in designing specific GDSS features, one has to examine the impact such features may have on user behavior, decision strategy, and subsequently performance.

Proposition 2: Efficiency

Table 2 depicts information on the average time it takes to converge to a solution.

Table 2: Time taken to converge to a solution			
	Mean Value	Std. Dev.	N
Without Tool	96.33	9.13	9
With Tool	115.33	26.29	9

The results provide evidence to support hypothesis H2, i.e., the time to converge to a solution will be less in groups supported by a GDSS without the problem formulation tool than those with the problem formulation tool ($p < .05$). Given that the GDSS users with the problem formulation tool performed better (Proposition 1) and that they used a two-phase approach, they searched the solution space more comprehensively resulting in a longer convergence time.

SUMMARY

Table 3 summarizes the results of the hypotheses that compare GDSS groups with the problem formulation tool (PF) and those with no problem formulation tool (NPF). The problem formulation tool affects solution quality as measured by rewards that members receive in the simulated company. Groups with the incremental 'what-if' approach were more efficient with respect to the time it takes to converge to a solution. Higher efficiency, however, came at the expense of solution quality. These groups did not search the solution space as thoroughly as did their counterparts that had the problem formulation tool. The latter groups did not converge to a solution as quickly as the former groups that used a convergent approach. They, however, generated better solutions as they diverged in the solution space before they converged to a mutually acceptable solution (Janis and Mann 1977).

Table 3: Summary of hypotheses and their significance	
Proposition 1: Performance (Reward)	Statistical Support
H1: PF > NPF	s
Proposition 2: Efficiency (Time)	
H2: PF > NPF	s
s - supported at .05 level, ns - not supported	

This research, within a GDSS context, studied the impact of the problem formulation tool and discovered that the problem formulation tool improves solution quality. Furthermore, this study shows that technological intervention into the decision process can change the decision outcomes.

This is one of the few studies that investigates distributed GDSS supported decision making. Given that this type of group meeting and decision making is increasing in organizations with the growth of the Internet, it is hoped that this research stimulates more studies on distributed decision making in a computer supported setting.

ENDNOTES

1 It is noted that there are some problems like matroid problems (i.e. minimum spanning tree) where the greedy heuristic results in the optimal solution.
2 "better" will be defined once the task is explained and an objective measure of decision quality is specified later in the paper.
3 We acknowledge that in repeated experimentation, human subjects tend to learn to modify their behavior and may not be subject to limitations imposed on them by the technology. However, given the rapid changes in technology and the fact that suboptimal decisions are costly, organizations cannot afford to provide systems that lead so suboptimal decisions and assume that the users will eventually learn to overcome the limitations of the system. Hence, it becomes important to study how a particular technological intervention influences decision behavior.

REFERENCES

Benbasat, I., Nault, B.R. "An Evaluation of Empirical Research in Managerial Support Systems," Decision Support Systems, 6, (1990), 203-226.

Benbasat, I., Schroeder, R.G. 'An experimental investigation of some MIS design variables,' MIS Quarterly,1,1, (1977), 37-49.

Chervany, N.L., Dickson, G.W. 'An experimental evaluation of information overload in a production environment,' Management Science, 20, (1974), 1335-1374.

Chu, P.C., Elam, J. "Induced system restrictiveness: An experimental demonstration," IEEE Transactions on Systems, Man, and Cybernetics SMC-20 ,1, (1990), 195-201.

Daft, R. L., Lengel, R. H. 'Organizational Information Requirements, Media Richness and Structural Design,' Management Science,32,5, (1986), 554-571.

DeSanctis, G., Gallupe, R. B. "A foundation for the study of group decision support systems," Management Science,33,5), (1987), 589-609.

Janis, I.L., Mann, L. Decision Making: A psychological analysis of conflict, choice, and commitment, New York: The Free Press, 1977.

Markus, M.L., Robey, D. 'Information Technology and Organizational Change: Causal Structure in Theory and Research,' Management Science,34,5, (1988), 583-598.

McGrath, J. E. Groups: Interaction and Performance, Prentice -Hall, Inc., Englewood Cliffs, NJ; 1984.

McGrath, J.E., Groups: Interaction and Performance, Prentice-Hall, Inc., 1984.

Niederman, F., DeSanctis, G.. "The Impact of a Structured-Argument Approach on Group Problem Formulation," Decision Sciences,26,4, (1995), 451-474.

Nunamaker, J.F., Dennis, Alan R., Valacich, Joseph S., George, Joey F. Electronic Meeting Systems to Support Group Work. Communications of The ACM, 34, 7, (1991), 41-61.

Nutt, P.C. "Formulation Tactics and the success of organizational decision making," Decision Sciences, 23,3, (1992), 519-540.

Sambamurthy, V., Unpublished Ph.D. Dissertation, University of Minnesota, 1989.

Todd, P., Benbasat, I. "An experimental investigation of the impact of computer based decision aids on decision making strategies," Information Systems Research, 2, 2, (1991), 87-115.

Appendix

To operationalize a specific experimental task, the following terms are introduced:

PC_{id} = *Projected Cost of filling order i at department d. This is the best estimate the organization has regarding how much it should cost the department to fill an order.*

ADC_{ijd} = *Actual Departmental Cost of filling order i expending effort level j at department d. For varied levels of effort, the ADC differs and this information is internal to each department.*

$UDEC_{ijd}$ = *Uncompensated Departmental Effort Cost is the cost that the department d incurs for filling order i for effort level j. This information is internal to each department.*

Rev_i = *The Revenue generated by filling order i.*

The problem for each department i, with four discrete choices for effort levels and twenty orders to select from, is modeled as follows:

$$\text{Max} \sum_{i \in S} \sum_{j \in E} .15 \left[\left(\text{Re} \, v_i - \sum_{t \neq d, t \in D} ADC_{it} - ADC_{ijd} \right) - UDEC_{ijd} \right] X_{ij}$$

S.t.

$$\sum_{i \in S} Q_{ik} Y_i \leq \text{Capacity}_k \qquad \forall k \quad (k \text{ is a product})$$

$$\sum X_{ij} = Y_i \qquad \forall i \in S$$

where,

$$X_{ij} = \begin{cases} 1 & \text{if order i taken at effort level j} \\ 0 & \text{otherwise} \end{cases}$$

$$Y_i = \begin{cases} 1 & \text{if order i taken} \\ 0 & \text{otherwise} \end{cases}$$

Q_{ik} = Quantity of product $k \in K$ required in order $i \in S$

E = Set of effort level choices = 1,2,3,4

S = Set of orders = 1,2,3,....,20

D = Set of departments = 1 = Mrkt, 2 = Prod, 3 = Purch

K = Set of products = 1,2,3,4

Collaborative Electronic Group Interaction: A Test of Performance Impacts

Tonya Barrier
Associate Professor, CIS Department, 368 Glass Hall, COBA, Southwest Missouri State University, Springfield, MO 65804
Tel: (417) 836-4117, Fax: (417) 836-6907, Tonyabarrier@mail.smsu.edu

Ruth C. King
University of Illinois at Urbana, Department of Business Administration, 1206 South Sixth Street, 339 Commerce West, Champaign, IL 61820
(217) 244-8051, rcking@uius.edu

Vikram Sethi
Southwest Missouri State University, College of Business Administration, 368 Glass Hall, CIS Department, Springfield, MO 65804
Tel: (417) 836-5078, Fax: (417) 836-6907, vikramsethi@mail.smsu.edu

INTRODUCTION

Computer-based communication technologies (CBCT) such as electronic mail, computer-supported meeting systems or computer conferences have increased group collaboration. The proliferation of computer networks has removed the constraints inherent in the traditional face-to-face work groups. Computer-based communication technology has not only allowed us to work more efficiently than the traditional technologies, but has created new ways of doing business. Can group be thrown together to work electronically? Will there be any unexpected usage patterns or behaviors?

While traditional research on the effect of conventional media have examined the relationship between group communications and group performance, additional issues arise when studying advanced communication technology - computer-based communication technology environment. CBCT differs from traditional communication technology in several ways. CBCT is digital based. CBCT can be used in both synchronous and asynchronous modes, therefore it is more dynamic, flexible, and convenient than traditional synchronous media. In addition, CBCT usually has multiple features built in, such as text processing, calculating and networking, therefore, it allows more than just synchronous communications which is the primary function supported by most conventional communication media. Indeed, organizations are adopting advanced communication technology to facilitate electronic group work (Hiltz and Turoff, 1981; Olson and Primps, 1984; Eveland and Bikson, 1987). While many researchers have predicted that computer-based communication technology will revolutionize the way we do business, the way we see the place we live, and the vision we have of earth; the expected pervasiveness of CBCT in the organizations still remains in the exploratory stage in most organizations.

There are several limitations inherent in the studies described above. Most of the studies were conducted in an experimental laboratory setting, therefore the studies lack the "naturalness" of an organizational setting. In most laboratory studies, only one communication technology was used at a time to compare with face-to-face communication. These studies provide limited insights on the advantages and/or disadvantages of technology substitutions for face-to-face communications. The ability to generalize results of these studies is limited since communicators are usually provided with multiple communication alternatives in the organization. In addition, most studies were conducted at one point in time using a single task which involved no further group contact or collaboration beyond the initial encounter. However, group collaboration usually involves multiple interactions

It is, therefore, the intention of this study to:
1. build upon existing media effects research to examine the effects of CBCT on group collaboration.
2. design a study that mimics natural group collaboration conditions.
3. quantitatively and qualitatively document the processes and outcomes of group collaboration mediated by CBCT.

Specific research questions in this study are to investigate the role of CBCT in group collaboration and the possible effects this communication technology has on the group collaboration process. The term "communication technology" is used in this study to refer broadly to any medium, technique, or mode used in the exchange of information.

Thus, four commonly used communication technologies are included in this study: (1) face-to-face interaction, (2) telephone, (3) written document (letter, memo, note) and (4) CBCT.

In this study, the use of multiple communication technologies by group members is compared to the exclusive use of CBCT in conducting a group project. By comparing the behaviors of CBCT group with groups using multiple communication media, this study enhances the understanding of the behaviors of electronic work groups and the external validity of this study since the electronic work group is compared with groups in a natural communications environment.

RESEARCH BACKGROUND

The conceptual frameworks that this study are based on are the traditional social presence of media theory, media richness theory, information processing theory, and recent research on electronic meeting systems. Theoretical and empirical work on the social presence of media theory which can be traced to the early 70's (Chapanis, Ochsman, Parrish and Weeks, 1972; Short, William and Christie, 1976). This work theorizes that face-to-face communication is the standard or natural mode of communication and any other medium is sub-optimal since it reduces "naturalness" by reducing visual and vocal cues. Because nonverbal cues are filtered out in mediated communication, this theory proposes that group performance should be affected and group members will tend to perceive their collaborators as less personal. However, the findings of many empirical studies have shown that group performance (operationalized in most studies as ideas generation, accuracy of recall of information, or accuracy of judgement) was not significantly affected either positively or negatively by the presence of non-face-to-face communication medium (Williams, 1977; Rice & Associates, 1984).

Group members' perceptions toward each other are sensitive to the medium (Short et. al., 1976). This is especially true when the tasks shifted from simple, objective, and cooperative working conditions to more complex, subjective, and competitive working conditions (Wichman, 1970; LaPlante, 1971; Gardin, Kaplan, Firestone and Cowan, 1973; Short, 1974). These findings suggest that mediated communication can lead to more "depersonalized, argumentative, and narrowly focused responses, compared to face-to-face conversations" (Williams, 1977). Recent studies on computer-based communication technology point out that experienced electronic mail systems (E-mail system) users, demonstrated different behaviors from non-E-mail users (Hiltz and Turoff, 1981; Rice, 1984). These empirical studies found that E-mail systems were used to exchange both task-specific and social-emotional information (Siegel, Dubrovsky, Kiesler and McGuire, 1986; Steinfield, 1985; Sproull & Kiesler, 1986; Rice & Love; 1988; Finholt & Sproull, 1990). While some users viewed E-mail as a playful and fun tool (Steinfield, 1985), others viewed E-mail as a social equalizer in a group context (Siegel et al, 1986).

The social presence of media theory postulates that mediated communication will affect group performance because of lost cues. The media richness theory, however, posits that the match between the characteristics of the task and the kind of media lead to effective communications. (Steinfield, 1985; Daft and Lengel, 1984). Since each communication medium possesses different capacities or degrees of richness to facilitate meaning sharing, rich media such as face-to-face meeting is more suitable in dealing with task that requires interpretations or clarifications (Daft, Lengel and Trevino, 1987). Their empirical findings suggested that better performing managers preferred rich media to communicate tasks that are equivocal and hard to analyze and choose less-rich media, such as the telephone or a written note, to communicate factual or objective messages. Thus, a rich communication medium may not always be preferred. This view supports the theory of the social presence of media in which each communication medium conveys information differently. However, the media richness theory proposes that performance should not be passively constrained by the medium, instead, individuals should proactively choose suitable communication media based on the complexity of the task at hand. What is not clear in the media richness work is whether computer-based communication will be perceived as a suitable medium for tasks with varying degrees of complexity.

Information processing theory (Galbraith, 1973; Weick, 1979) posits that organizations are designed to facilitate the attainment of needed information. As work related uncertainty increases, so does the need for more pertinent information, and thus the need for information processing capacity increases. Organizations have two major information problems to solve: that of interpreting the environment (Weick, 1979) and that of coordinating various task activities (Galbraith, 1973). Interpreting the environment involves managers in the upper echelon of the organization. They read cues and define organizational strategy and technology. People in the core of the organization are mainly concerned with the coordination and execution of organizational activities which requires the processing of large amounts of information (Daft and Lengel, 1984). Thus, according to the information processing theory, it seems reasonable to suggest that CBCT may facilitate group's task coordination, and information processes.

RESEARCH HYPHOTHESES

This study hypothesizes that groups working electronically will demonstrate different attitudes (e.g., perception toward the collaborator) and performance outcomes than groups working under a multiple communication media setting. It further hypothesizes that CBCT will allow groups to accomplish an equal or greater number of tasks and also allow groups to apply the multiple capabilities inherent in CBCT to coordinate the collaboration process. In an attempt to better explain the dynamic nature of CBCT, this study measured group performance, perception of group collaboration, and coordination mechanisms.

RESEARCH METHODOLOGY

Sample Characteristics

Participants in this study were first-year MBA students at a major U.S. University. Sixty-five percent of the participants were male and thirty-five percent were female. The average age was 26 years. Students had an average of four years work experience. Participants were drawn from an introductory computer class offered to students who had little computer experience. The participants were randomly paired and assigned to one of two experimental conditions.

Collaboration Task

The two-member teams were given a seven-week time period to conduct a multiple-task research project. These tasks included but were not limited to: contacting and knowing the assigned collaborator, finding a mutually agreed upon research topic, searching for related literature, designing the project's outline, generating and evaluating ideas, exchanging information, coordinating the work load and schedules, editing the final report, and deciding on the authorship. The project deliverable was a five to seven page paper. To achieve this goal, team members had to engage in several interactions.

Design

Groups were randomly assigned to one of two communication conditions. The first set of groups was urged to conduct all communications via CBCT (referred to as the "CBCT-Urged Condition"). The second set of groups was told to use any available communication technologies that they wished to facilitate the research project and was referred to as the "Multi-Media Condition".

Computer training sessions were offered to all participants at the beginning of the study. Tutoring sessions, handouts, and quick-fix tips were also provided. Steps were taken to assure the anonymity of the participants who volunteered. In order to assure the maximum treatment effect, CBCT-urged groups were requested to turn in hard-copies of their E-mail communications. They were only given the collaborator's name and computer account number; while the multiple-media groups were provided with the collaborator's name, telephone number, computer account number as well as their in-school mailbox number. Forty-nine CBCT-urged and forty-seven multi-media groups were included in the final data analysis.

Data Collection and Measures

Data was collected during a seven-week period. Groups were asked to keep track of their interaction by filling out a standard contact sheet. Questionnaires were administered to collect perceptual measures. Final research reports were collected from each member. Hence, two identical papers were collected from each group. Term papers were then independently evaluated by two raters.

The group performance measure was obtained from the research report evaluations performed by two independent raters. The raters were two MIS PhD students who received detailed instructions regarding grading and were asked to divide the submitted papers into five groups according to the overall quality of each report. Raters were then asked to write down specific criteria used in separating the reports. Four operational dimensions of performance emerged from this exercise. These were used to determine the performance on a 7-point scale for each dimension ranging from very poor to excellent. The four dimensions were: (1)clear objective, (2) integration of different thoughts, (3)quality of reasoning and argument and (4)content interesting and relevant. Inter-rater reliability on overall performance was 0.83.

Perceptions of the collaborator were determined from individuals' responses to six items. Respondents rated their perception toward their collaborator on six 7-point Likert-type scales (e.g., trustworthy, friendly, cooperative, knowledgeable on the topic, skilled in writing, and skilled in computer mechanics) with 1 being lowest and 7 being highest.

To evaluate whether CBCT provided more than just communication functions, two other measures were used. The first measure was used to evaluate whether CBCT can be a group coordination mechanism. Four items were collected from the contact sheets: number of meetings by each group, communication mode used for each meeting, the duration (in minutes) of each meeting, and the number of issues addressed in each meeting. Each member was asked to keep his/her contact sheet. The data comparison of each group revealed a consistent record. Therefore, this helped assure the reliability of measures.

The second source was the post-study questionnaire where participants were asked to indicate the methods used to integrate individual efforts into a final report (e.g., whether a file was electronically transferred, manually merged, or retyped). Participants were also requested to document if any other interesting activities were carried out via CBCT. Additionally, opinions on this project were assessed from two open-ended questions. Each participant was asked to document the best (liked the most) and the worst (disliked the most) things that happened during this project. The richness of the data collected helped to assure a more quantitative and qualitative understanding of the effect of CBCT on the group collaboration.

RESULTS

Manipulation Check

The communication manipulation was checked by examining the E-mail messages and the contact sheets submitted by the groups. Since CBCT-urged groups were expected to conduct the majority of their communication via CBCT, their number of E-mail messages was expected to be significantly higher than groups that were not urged to use CBCT. The date on the E-mail message was checked against the contact sheet for confirmation. The CBCT-urged groups had an average of 8.84 E-mail messages per group compared with 3 E-mail messages per group in the multi-media groups ($X = 8.84$, 3, $F=143.02$, $p < 0.001$). The CBCT-urged groups were randomly checked to see if the communication condition assigned was clearly understood.

Group Performance

Although participants worked as teams on the research project, the basic unit of analysis was based on both individual and group data. One-way ANOVA was used to find the descriptive statistics for group performance, perception of collaborator and coordination activities. It is interesting to note that the ANOVA results on the group's overall performance was not affected by the communication technology ($X = 22.10$, 21.76, $F = 0.47$, N.S.). However, some of the performance's sub-dimension scores vary. CBCT-urged groups demonstrate statistically significant performance in their reasoning quality ($X = 6.05$, 5.00, $F = 42.49$, $p < 0.000$). On the other hand, multi-media communication groups performance was much better in integrating their thoughts ($X = 5.64$, 5.07, $F = 9.02$, $p < 0.05$).

Perception on Collaboration

Member's perception on collaboration was measured using six items: less trustworthy, friendly, cooperative, collaborator's knowledge, skill in writing, and skill in computing similarly. The results show that CBCT-urged groups perceived their collaborator as less trustworthy ($X = 5.70$, 6.48, $F = 35.09$, $p < 0.000$), friendly ($X = 5.89$, 6.60, $F = 38.59$, $p < 0.000$) and cooperative ($X = 5.81$, 6.60, $F = 28.33$, $p < 0.000$). The results also show that both groups perceive their collaborator's knowledge on the research topic, skill in writing, and skill in computing similarly.

Coordination of Activities

Four items were used to examine if CBCT can assist the coordination of group collaboration activities. The results suggest that CBCT-urged groups interacted significantly less frequently ($X = 7.32$, 9.17, $F = 48.12$, $p < 0.000$) but the duration of each interaction was much longer ($X = 35.21$, 28.35, $F = 83.47$, $p < 0.000$) than multi-media groups. In addition, CBCT-urged groups addressed less issues during each interaction and the issues they addressed were mostly project-oriented tasks ($X = 4.49$, 7.39, $F = 41.33$, $p < 0.000$). Lastly, more groups formed or merged their final project report electronically in the CBCT-urged condition than groups in the multi-media condition (17 groups vs. 6 groups).

Additional Comments on Collaboration

The groups listed the things they liked the most and the least in this project. Five hundred and twelve comments were collected with an average of 2.67 comments per member. Among these five hundreds comments five categories of attitude seemed to emerge. They are related to the project, the collaborator, the technology, the unexpected prize (the pleasant surprise), and the contextual factors. Examples of the comments can be found in Table 1.

DISCUSSION AND CONCLUSIONS

Can computer-based communication technology assist us to collaborate? In this study, we find the answer is yes. However, caution should be exercised in interpreting these results. CBCT can assist groups to perform equally well (overall), particularly the quality of the reasoning compared to groups working under normal communication conditions. This finding confirms previous previous media effect research However, groups using CBCT showed a

Table 1. Examples of Comments From the Groups		
Attitudes	CBCT-Urged	Multi-Media
Project	1.It was a fun exercise compared to a typical report. 2.The project had many different tasks and that kept it interesting.	1.I learned the value of looking at issues from different perspectives. 2.I gained an appreciation of how well a project can turn out by joint efforts.
Collaborator	1. I like having a "buddy" to work with. 2.I had a trustworthy timely! (More so than myself) partner.	1.The worst part was my collaborator's attitude toward my abilities. 2.The best part was getting to know a stranger.
Technology	1.Being in front of the computer to collect E-mails was nice. 2.Transferring files was at first difficult but we managed to overcome the problems.	1.The project allowed me an opportunity to overcome my anxiety with computers. 2.I dislike the options of using phone, paper and face-to-face interactions.
Unexpected Prize\Price	1.I sharpened my research skills. 2.My collaborator needs a writing lesson.	1.I learned to be more assertive. 2.I feel better prepared for the "real" world.
Contextual Factors	1.The computing resource of the school is not facilitating. 2 The communication restriction was very difficult to follow.	1 We seemed to be always pressured for time. 2 You learned how difficult it is to work with someone, who has a very busy schedule similar to your own.

lack of cohesive organization in their project reports. The joint effort developed via CBCT may be the simple addition of two individually produced halves. Such technology-induced joint-effort can be a concern and requires more attention.

However, groups using CBCT demonstrated much lower satisfaction toward their collaborator. This finding further confirms the results from previous research where e-mail users tended to "flame" and direct expressions when the nonverbal cues are not present. Comments from CBCT-urged groups also indicated that members were particularly concerned when their collaborators did not share the same view. The mediated communication made it more difficult for groups to communicate socially and to establish bonding.

Results from this study suggest that CBCT can be an activity coordinator. Groups in the CBCT condition spent less time interacting and a longer time typing and attending to project-specific tasks. Although some studies found users used e-mail to exchange task-specific and social-emotional information (Rice and Love, 1988; Steinfield, 1985), this study did not support those finding. This can be attributed to the time pressure each group experienced. CBCT-urged groups may take a longer time to establish effective communications via computers. CBCT-urged groups may also take longer time to express their ideas since communication access was through a keyboard, thus, reduce the opportunity to convey their social-emotional feelings. However in terms of coordinating task-specific activities, CBCT can be a sufficient mechanism.

The goal of group collaboration is to complete a project in a satisfactory manner in terms of both project quality and interpersonal relationships. The participant's comments revealed that challenges and meaningfulness inherent in the project are the trustworthiness, fairness, and dependability of the collaborator. These important factors can contribute to the success or failure of the completion of the task.

REFERENCES

Chapanis, A., Ochsman, R. B. Parrish, R. N., & Weeks, G. D. Studies in interactive communication: I, The effects of four communication modes on the behavior of teams during cooperative problem-solving, Human Factors, (1972), 14, 487-509.

Culnan, M. J. and Markus, M. L. Information Technologies, in Handbook of Organization Communication: An Interdisciplinary Perspective, F. M. Jablin, L. L. Putnam, K. H. Roberts and L. W. Porter (eds.), Sage Publications, Newbury Park, CA (1987).

Daft, Richard L., Lengel, Robert H., Trevino, Linda Klebe, Message Equivocality, Media Selection, and Manager

Performance: Implications for Information Systems, MIS Quarterly,(September 1987).

Daft, R. L., and Lengel, R. H., Information Richness: A new approach to managerial behavior and organizational design, Research in Organizational Behavior, 6 (1984) 191-233.

Drucker, Peter F., The Coming of the New Organization, Harvard Business Review,(January-February, 1988).

Eveland, J. D., and Bikson, T. K., Evolving electronic communication networks, An empirical assessment, Office: Technology and People, 3(2),(1987), 103-128.

Finholt, Tom and Sproull, Lee S., Electronic Groups at Work, Organization Science, Vol. 1, No.1 (1990).

Galbraith, J., Designing Complex Organizations, Addison-Wesley, Reading, Mass., (1973).

Galbraith, J., Organizational Design, Addison-Wesley, Reading, Mass., (1977).

Gardin, H., Kaplan, K. J., Firestone, J. J. & Cowan, G. A. Proxemic effects on cooperation, attitude, and approach-avoidance in a Prisoner's Dilemma game, Journal of Personality and Social Psychology, (1973), 27,13-18.

Hiltz, S. R. and Turoff, M., The Evolution ofuserbehaviorin a computerized conferencing system, Communications of ACM, 24(11), 1981, 739-751.

Huber, George P., A theory of the effects of advanced information technologies on organizational design,intelligence, and decision making, Academy of Management Review, Vol. 15, No. 1, (1990) 47-71.

Katz, Ralph, The influence of group longevity on project member responses to their work settings, Working Paper No. 1388-83, Massachusetts Institute of Technology, Sloan School of Management, (1983).

Kiesler, S., Siegel, J. and McGuire, T. W., Social psychological aspects of computer-mediated communication, American Psychologist, 39(10),(1984), 1123-1134.

LaPlante, D. Communication, friendliness, trust and the prisoner's dilemma, Unpublished master's thesis, University of Windsor, Windsor, Canada, (1971).

Markus, M. Lynne, Asynchronous Tools in Small Face-to-Face Grups, Information Systems Working Paper #3-90, Version 4.0, August, (1989).

McGrath, Joseph E. Groups: Interaction and Performance, Englewood Cliffs, NJ, Prentice Hall, (1984).

Olson, M. H., and Primps, S. B., Working at home with computers: Work and nonwork issues, Journal of Social Issues, 40(3) (1984), 97-112.

Peters, T. and Waterman, In Search of Excellence, 1982.

Rice, R. E., Mediated group communication, in The New Media, Communication, Research and Technology, R. E. Rice (ed.), Sage, Beverly Hills, CA, (1984).R

Rice, Ronald E. & Associates, The New Media, Communication, Research and Technology, by Sage Publications, Inc., Beverly Hills, CA. (1984).

Rice, R. E., and Love, G. Electronic emotion: Socio-emotional content in a computer-mediated communication network, Communication Research, (1988).

Rogers, E. M., The New Media in Society, Communication Technology, (1986).

Short, J. A. Effects of medium of communication on experimental negotiation, Human Relations, (1974), 27, 225-234.

Short, J. A., Williams, E., and Christie, B. The social psychology of telecommunications, London: Wiley International, (1976).

Siegel, J., Dubrovsky, V., Kiesler, S. and McGuire, T. W. Group processes in computer-mediated communication, Organizational Behavior and Human Processes, (37),(1986), 157-187.

Sproull, L. and Kiesler, S., Reducing social context cues: electronic mail in organizational communication, Management Science,(32:11), November (1986), 1492-1512.

Steinfield, C. Dimensions of electronic mail use in an organizational setting, Proceedings of the Academy of Management, (1985), 239-243.

Tjosvold, D. Team organization: an enduring competitive advantage. London: Wiley. 1991.

Weeks, G. D., and Chapanis, A. Cooperative versus conflictive problem solving in three telecommunication modes, Perceptual and Motor Skills, (1976), 42,487-917.

Weick, K. E., The social psychology of organizing, Addison-Wesley, Reading, Mass., 1979.

Wichman, H., Effects of isolation and communication on cooperation in a two-person game, Journal of Personality and Social Psychology,(1970), 16, 114-120.

Williams, Ederyn, Experimental comparisons of face-to-face and mediated communication: a review, Psychological Bulletin, Vol. 84, No. 5, 963-976, (1977).

A Structured Approach to Intranet Application Development

Shirley A. Becker

Computer Science, Florida Institute of Technology,150 West University Blvd., Melbourne, FL 32901
Tel: (407)674-8149, Fax: (407)674-8192, becker@cs.fit.edu

Ebru Gunaydin Bjarnason and Anita LaSalle

Computer Science & Information Systems, American University, 4400 Mass. Ave. NW, Washington DC
20016-811

ABSTRACT

This paper describes the technologies used to develop an Intranet application to support personal and team work processes in a software development environment. The application was built using a structured approach in order to support correctness and completeness in meeting user requirements. This approach required an integration of Computer Aided Software Engineering (CASE), database, and Web technologies in an effective manner. As part of the process, a common repository and formal specification guidelines are used as a foundation upon which the application is built. The process focuses on the quality goals as identified by the user, which are then used as the basis for completion conditions during development work.

INTRODUCTION

The popularity of Intranets is growing as organizations search for effective communication mechanisms (Bernard, 1996). An Intranet is a private network that uses internet protocols and technology including a centralized Web server for information management and a Web browser as a user interface (Lai & Mahapatra, 1997). One of the major benefits of using an Intranet application is that it permits the collection and dissemination of information quickly and efficiently between remote sites.

High quality Intranet application development calls for a structured approach to ensure data integrity, completeness, and consistency with user requirements. The structured approach described in this paper incorporates computer aided software engineering (CASE) technology for managing a conceptual and physical design, relational database technology for storing and retrieving information, and Web technology methodologies for remote user access.

The paper briefly describes the technologies that were used in the development of an Intranet application to support team and personal processes in a software development environment (Gunaydin Bjarnason, 1998) and a generalized structured approach to Intranet application development.

STRUCTURED METHODOLOGY

A structured approach, integrating CASE, database, and Web technologies is proposed based on a modified version of Barker's life cycle method (Barker, 1995) and the incremental development technique described by Mills (1988) and Karlsson (1996). Barker's life cycle may be considered an outgrowth of CASE technology as a formal approach for conceptual and physical designs of system applications. A modified version of the life cycle, shown in Figure 1, is a means for gathering user requirements and designing in small incremental building blocks. This approach is particularly important for development work that is driven by defined product or process goals because of its iterative expansion and feedback loops.

Each increment is part of a larger increment such that there is minimal integration complexity needed to link them. An increment has its own functionality that is expanded at the next level of incremental development. Within each development increment, there are several activities that are performed as many times as necessary to ensure correctness and completeness conditions are met. These activities, briefly described in terms of Intranet development work, include:

- *Strategy* - User requirements are gathered in terms of system functionality and the user interface (i.e., inputs and outputs). The user requirements include browser capabilities, screen layouts, information use in terms of read, update, and deletion capabilities, and security and access mechanisms among others. User requirements may be informally specified as inputs and outputs as they relate to system behavior.

Figure 1: Incremental Development Activities

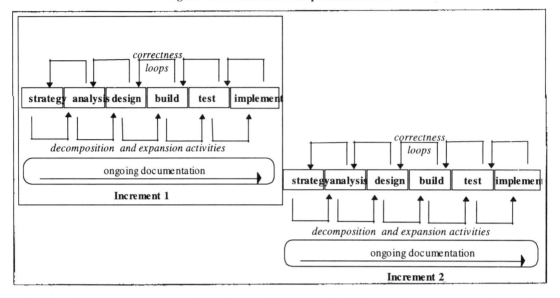

- *Analysis* - The user requirements are formalized and then reviewed with the user for correctness and completion conditions. The formalization of system behavior may be done using a specification language or a grammar that concisely defines system behavior. For interface logic, state diagrams of screen sequences may also be used to reduce functionality to a graphical level easily understood by users. During the analysis activities, an Entity-relationship diagram (ERD) is designed that represents the data requirements for the current increment of the Intranet application.
- *Design* - The ERD is translated into a physical set of objects including tables, constraints, and indexes. The analysis documents are expanded into design components that provide details on the uses of the system.
- *Build*- The design components that have been validated for correctness are expanded into script and database languages. In the case of Intranet development, the end-user support may require HTML, JAVA script, database manipulation language such as PL/SQL, or some other appropriate development tool.
- *Test* - The components are tested for quality and functionality in terms of the user requirements. The database is tested to ensuring that data integrity is maintained.
- *Implement* - The increment is deployed. Subsequently, it is expanded during the next increment under development.

For the application described in this paper, CASE technology (Oracle Designer/2000) was used to support the strategy, analysis, and design phases. A relational database and supporting objects were built as an expansion of the conceptual design produced by the CASE tool. A centralized database enhances the use of Intranet capabilities such that information can be retrieved and stored in a distributed fashion. A procedural query language and supporting script languages were also used to support a Web browser. All of these components are discussed in the following sections.

COMMON REPOSITORY

Throughout each development activity, a common repository evolves that contains terminology as an outgrowth of specification and design work. This shared repository contains terms that are produced throughout the life cycle phases but particularly during the strategy and analysis phases. During these phases of work, user requirements are transformed from "fuzzy" terms to precise and unambiguous definitions. Thus, when a term is used in future development work, it will not be misinterpreted, used incorrectly, or represented redundantly in the specification and design documents. It is proposed that for precision-sensitive terminology, a detailed definition be stored in the repository. For example, to avoid ambiguity in the definition of a team assignment, the repository would contain the following details. (See top of next page.)

The definition in the dictionary appears to be represented in a grammar-type structure. This ensures that the use of the phrase "team assignment" or its acronym will be understood to be comprised of lower level data definitions. Each new data definition that is introduced in the description of an existing one is also defined to a level where there is no need for further explanation.

Name: Team_assignment
Acrononym: tagn
Description: A component of work assigned to a team that will result in a set of deliverables.
Formal definition: <tagn> ::= <deliverable>*<deliverables>; /* zero or more deliverables */
            <deliverable> ::= <task>*<tasks>;
            <task> ::= <result><responsible_for><actual_completion>
                    <due_date><planned_resources><actual_resources>;
            <result> ::= artifact | document;   /* physical output */
            <responsible_for> ::= <identifier>;
             <actual_completion> ::= date;
            <due_date> ::= date;
            <planned_resources> ::= <digit>*<digit>;
            <actual_resources> ::= <digit>*<digit>;
            <identifier> ::= <digit>*<digit>;
            <digit> ::= 0|1|2|3|4|5|6|7|8|9;
tagn appears in: Specification of the team process page, team plan, and progress reports.

QUALITY GOALS

One of the problems with relying on technology for developing specification and design artifacts is that garbage put into these tools will produce garbage out to the user. To eliminate or minimize this potential, it is important to establish quality goals for the good use of CASE tools. Though tools will provide a documentation trail, repository of terms, and other pertinent data, they cannot guarantee that correctness goals will be met.

At the onset of development work, it is important to identify the appropriateness of a particular quality goal in using CASE technology to satisfy end-user requirements. The IEEE Software Specification Requirements (SRS) guidelines document (1994) is useful in providing guidance in establishing quality goals in terms of correctness, maintainability, completeness, and others. Table 1 presents an extraction of quality goals from the IEEE standards.

Quality goals play an important role in establishing completion conditions for each development activity such that it becomes apparent when one activity is completed and the next activity can begin. For example, completion conditions in meeting the precision goal ensure that an artifact is fully documented in the common repository, and has been team reviewed for clarity and precision in the functional descriptions of system behavior.

Table 1: Goals for Application Development	
Goal:	Description
Correct	All artifacts produced are correct in terms of capturing the "true" requirements of the user.
Precise & Unambiguous	Each artifact can be directly expanded into lower level details without interpretation.
Complete	Each artifact captures the necessary and sufficient system behaviors.
Consistent	Each lower level artifact captures the same behavior as its higher level counter parts. There is no conflicting terms or contradictory behavior.
Modifiable & Maintainable	Each artifact is supported by dictionary definitions, indexes, and other artifacts.
Holistic	Each artifact encompasses the whole system in terms of its relationships with other components (e.g., interfaces, operational modes).
Tolerant	Each artifact must be tolerant of mistakes made (e.g., incomplete, inconsistent) due to the size and complexity of the application under development.
Understandable	All parties using the artifact can understand it or have supporting artifacts to assist in understanding it (e.g., repository).

CASE TECHNOLOGY

Once a functional specification and high-level design have been validated in terms of its quality goals and completion conditions, the automated support offered by CASE technology becomes useful in maintaining intellectual control over lower level designs. The CASE technology used to build the Intranet prototype design has the capability of managing granular levels of design necessary for incremental development. Figure 2 illustrates the use of the integrated tools that manage information requirements in terms of data use, definitions and relationships. CASE technology provides a documentation trail necessary for version control, quality checks, and design modifications during iterative development work.

CASE support of Intranet development has been made easier by the automated generation of HTML code, query language, and other components. Perhaps more importantly is the shared capability of process and product information in the CASE repository. Historical and current information becomes available for assessing product and process goals. Several of the major benefits from using CASE to support Intranet development are summarized in Table 2 (this list is not meant to be all-inclusive but representative of CASE capabilities).

DATABASE TECHNOLOGY

CASE technology will produce both the conceptual and physical designs including index and constraints objects and query syntax. It is important that these design components are validated for correctness, completeness, and consistency to ensure a high level of data quality. Though the CASE tool may generate "correct" database objects (e.g., normalized), there may be user requirements that are not met as specified during the strategy and analysis activities. In the case of syntax checks, statistical tools may be used to determine the optimal query structure based on an assessment of data retrieval paths and the use of indexes. Indexes and constraints must be validated so that they are used to maximize system performance and maintain data quality. Analysis tools can assess the efficient use of indexes in terms of table sizes, number and type of joins, data selection criteria, as well as, the query syntax structure. The impact of a constraint object (e.g., foreign integrity constraint with cascading deletions) should also be analyzed in terms of meeting the long-term and short-term needs of the user.

The procedural query language, PL/SQL, was used in the prototype as a means of manipulating data in a relational database. During the build activities, PL/SQL is generated (using CASE technology) or written within required HTML (or Java script) language. For example, the following is a piece of PL/SQL code used to show team member names on a Web page.

Figure 2: Illustration of CASE Tool Set

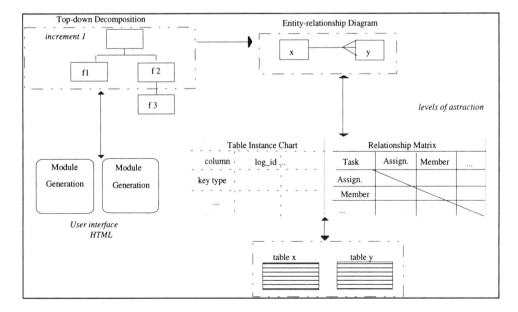

Table 2: Benefits of Using CASE Technology in the Development of Intranet	
Development Feature	Benefits of CASE
Quality Support	Built-in consistency checks and normalization of databases.
Configuration Management	Version control over design modifications automatically maintained.
Automated Expertise	Developers have automated expertise to assist in development work. Includes database design, creation and query and script language generation.
Traceability and Accountability	Information is readily accessible in a shared repository. Documentation is automatically generated from development work.
Reusability	Standard data formats and code generation support reusability.
Process Support	Customizable environment supports structured development work and process adherence.

```
procedure log_name
is
begin
htp.Centeropen;
DisplayTitle('Time Recording Log');
...
htp.FormSelectOpen('v_memid','Select name: ');
FOR member in (
        select f_namell' 'lll_name Name, mem_id
        from team_member
        order by l_name)
LOOP
htp.FormSelectOption(member, Name, cattributes=>'VALUE="'llmember.mem_idll'"');
END LOOP;
...
END;
```

It is important to note that this procedural language can be validated for correctness using traditional code verification techniques (e.g., stepwise refinement and verification as presented by Linger et al., (1979)). Also, team inspections may be held to validate the HTML and PL/SQL code to ensure consistency with specification and design artifacts and identify reusable components.

WEB TECHNOLOGY

There are three layers that comprise the physical design of the Intranet structure. Each of the three layers, Back-end, Middleware, and Front-end require an integrated toolset to support the implementation of the end-user requirements.

The back-end component developed for the prototype described in this paper is a relational database system with supporting SQL and PL/SQL code generation. It relies on the Web-server (Middleware) component for maintaining high performance, security, and reliability.

The Middleware component is the "Intranet" component that supports the user needs via the shared database. The Webserver is used to develop distributed applications on the Web using HTTP (HyperText Transport Protocol). It combines HTML code with data retrieval from a database enabling the development of complex Web applications necessary for data manipulation in a shared environment. When the web server receives a Uniform Resource Locator (URL) from a browser, it uses information from the database and the Operating System to handle a request.

The front-end component of the Intranet structure is the browser component that supports HTML and the application screens developed to meet the end-users needs. A screen snapshot is shown in Figure 3 whereby a task is inserted into the underlying database system. This screen illustrates how data is entered in the client environment that is then manipulated using the procedural query language on the server side.

Figure 3: The Insert A New Task Screen

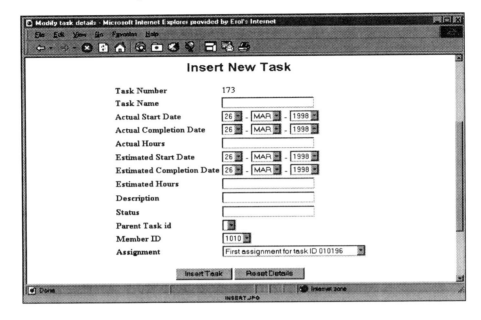

STRUCTURED METHODOLOGY TO INTRANET PROTOTYPE SYNTHESIS

Figure 4 shows how the three technologies previously described were applied implementing the distinct features of an Intranet application. The application, to support team-centered, multi-task, software projects, enables project team members to track project progress at the task-level. Team members use a Web-based tool to enter data about tasks and projects. The data is stored in project databases for use in project management.

As each enabling-technology is applied to product components, deliverables are generated that contribute to incremental builds. For the Web-based project support tool, this included: graphical models (i.e. ERDs) of data relationships, PL/SQL code that supported queries to the database, and embedded HTML to support web user interfaces.

LIMITATIONS OF ENABLING TECHNOLOGIES

One of the major lessons learned regarding the integrated use of CASE, database, and Web technologies is the misconception that the technology will necessarily enable implementations that satisfy user requirements. The final

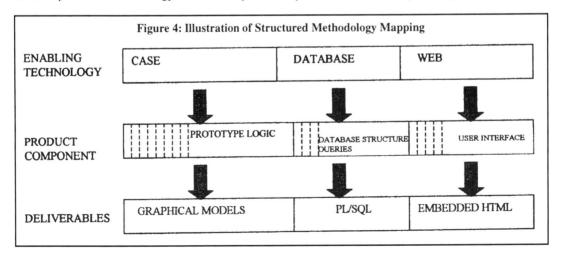

implementation components may be correct in terms of functionality but may not satisfy the user requirements because of a number of reasons including: performance, insufficient documentation, lack of user involvement, or design changes (known or inadvertent) that result in inconsistencies with higher level specification and design components, among other factors.

Correctness criteria needs to be established for each increment in the development life cycle in order to ensure high-quality early and continuously during development. Table 3 identifies correctness conditions for each life cycle activity based on the toolset used. Notice that these correctness conditions are applied across development activities as a means of promoting high quality within and across increments.

Another important consideration is process support for performing the life cycle activities. What is needed is a documented process whereby feedback is obtained early and often during development activities. To accomplish this, completion conditions need to be specified for each activity that is signed off by all parties involved. The condition sheet would not be signed-off until all completion conditions have been satisfied. This iterative approach to development may require one or more loops through each activity in order to ensure high-quality and process adherence.

Table 3: Correctness Criteria for Incremental Development	
Activity	Correctness Conditions
Strategy	Necessary and sufficient user requirements have been gathered. User requirements are validated with user in terms of input & output relationships.
Analysis	Formal specification documents are consistent with user requirements. Necessary and sufficient user requirements have been formally defined and validated.
Design	The conceptual and physical database designs sufficiently handle the data requirements specified during analysis and strategy activities. Specification documents are expanded into design language necessary to support the screen designs and data manipulation.
Build	The designs are expanded into code and database objects. These physical components are consistent with higher-level specification and designs. There are a sufficient and necessary set of objects and code generated to meet the user requirements.
Test	The build components are tested for reliability, performance, and correctness based on the user requirements documented in the strategy activity.
Implement	Sufficient documentation is provided to the user to support good use of the Intranet. Documentation includes valid and invalid behavior in order to provide ongoing support after the Intranet is put into operation.

CONCLUSION

The breadth of application and the complexity of Web technology continues to grow as more organizations realize the benefits associated with its use. The advent of script languages such as HTML and Java, web-based database support, and browser capabilities offer client/server environments the opportunity to develop complex applications.

What is needed, however, is a structured approach to developing web-based applications to ensure completeness, consistency, and correctness in meeting the end-user's needs. This paper described one such approach. Proven methodologies and technologies were applied in a structured, incremental way to product component builds, resulting in a reasonably seamless development life cycle. Future work will study team-based application of this technique to more complex Intranet application development projects.

REFERENCES

Barker, R. (1995). Case Method: Entity Relationship Modeling. Harlow, England: Addison-Wesley Publishing Company.

Bernard, R. (1996). The Corporate Intranet: Create and Manage An Internal Web For Your Organization. John Wiley & Sons, Inc.

Gunaydin Bjarnason, E. (1998). Personal Software Improvement Process, Masters Thesis, American University, Washington DC.

IEEE Standard 830-1993 (1994). Recommended Practice for Software Requirements Specification, Standards Collection on Software Engineering, IEEE Press, NY.

Karlsson, E.A. (1996). "A Construction Planning Process." Third Annual International Conference on Cleanroom Software Engineering Practices, College Park, Maryland.

Lai V.S., and Mahapatra, R. (1997). "The Implementation of Intranets to Support Corporate Distributed Computing Strategy: Some Hong Kong Experiences", Proceedings of the Americas Conference on Information Systems, Indianapolis, Indiana.

Linger, R., Mills, H.D., and Witt, B.I. (1979). Structured Programming: Theory & Practice, Addison-Wesley, Reading, MA.

Mills H.D. (1988). "Stepwise Refinement and Verification in Box-structured Systems." IEEE Computer 21(6).

Innovation And Information Technologies In Small And Medium Size Enterprises: The Case Of The Italian Shoemakers

Paola Bielli and Francesco Ciuccarelli

I.S. Department, L. Bocconi University, via F. Bocconi, 8, 20136 Milano, Italy

tel. +39.2.5836.6849, fax +39.2.5836.6893, e.mail: Paola.Bielli@uni-bocconi.it, Francesco.Ciuccarelli@sda.uni-bocconi.it

ABSTRACT

Nowadays Information Technologies represent one of the most important sources of innovation in business, but small and medium size enterprises still have difficulties in adopting them.

Innovation is a clear need for small and medium size enterprises facing competitors from emerging countries, but quite often in small and medium size enterprises innovation means to buy a new machine or to modify existing products.

Information and Communication Technologies (ICT) offer a broader range of innovation opportunities, including entering new markets, co-operating with producers in other countries, decentralising non core processes.

The reasons for resistance to changes are numerous and they derive from organisational, cultural, financial factors existing within the single enterprise and within the social environment it operates in.

Awareness and diffusion initiatives are a pre-requirement to enhance innovation in small and medium size enterprises. Besides, the active role of independent brokers selecting the best technical solutions for a certain environment and supporting small and medium size enterprises in the introduction step is a key success factor in many projects.

The research hypothesis bases on this approach and focuses on the *facilitator* as the enabling factor for diffusing ICT among small and medium size enterprises. Depending on the nature of the ICT and the specificity of the information needs, the *facilitator* plays different role to let small and medium size enterprises introduce ICT.

This state is quite evident in one of the Italian shoemaker districts in Italy - the Riviera del Brenta area (not far from Venice) - where a concentration of small producers is facing the competition both of other Italian districts and of Spain and Portugal.

These enterprises have founded a support centre, responsible for training the work-force on innovative technologies, for selecting the most suitable SW packages for business actors of the area and eventually for co-operating with local software houses in the development of new applications.

Results are evident: also small enterprises can afford innovation as they can find support in the surrounding environment.

The paper is organised into four sessions: the first session presents some theoretical concepts for innovation and ICT in small and medium size enterprises, and it defines the research hypothesis; the second session describes the shoemaker industry in Italy and in the analysed district, with the aim of defining the profile of the existing small and medium size enterprises and their attitude towards ICT; the third session illustrates some projects running in the area and concerning ICT while the last part draws some conclusions about the role of ICT in the innovation process within small and medium size enterprises.

Keywords: innovation, I.T. & small and medium size enterprises, introduction process of IT, IT diffusion, IT facilitator

INNOVATION, INFORMATION TECHNOLOGIES & SMALL AND MEDIUM SIZE ENTERPRISES

In highly competitive environments innovation[1] is often the key lever to gain or maintain dominant roles [Dematté, 1996]: it allows better effectiveness and/or greater efficiency thanks to new products, new services, new plants, new agreements, etc.

Innovation derives from two main sources: formal research and development investments and empirical experimentation within enterprises. While R&D efforts are explicitly mentioned in annual reports and national statistics - so that we can compare enterprises' and countries' propensity to R&D, empirical experimentation has no direct measures. On the opposite it is evident on the long range when enterprises show positive performances in the competitive arena.

The European Union is conscious of the relevance of innovation to sustain the competitiveness of European enterprises against aggressive players in other countries and greatly invests in innovation and research programmes.

Within this framework the Italian situation presents peculiarities: Italy is one of the countries with the lowest research and development expense rate (1.2% of GNP against 3% of North-European countries [Forlani, 1996]) and with the lowest number of researchers (in 1992 80,000 against about 200,000 in Germany), but at the same time Italian enterprises are able to keep their market shares and are world leaders in many industries.

In this case innovation derives from day-to-day experiments, creativity, technical know-how, knowledge of the market. Obviously these enterprises also invest in technology, but they do not develop technologies themselves; often innovation is a by-product of the introduction of a new machine or SW. Mainly small and medium size enterprises prefer this approach - often called incremental approach - which gives rapid feed-backs and tangible results through continuous improvements instead of dramatic changes - called radical innovation.

From the macro economical perspective the mentioned approaches will presumably bring to the international specialisation of countries: at one side those producing innovation; at the other side those consuming innovation [Demattè, 1996].

At the enterprise level they imply the ability of any firm - multinational or small business - to monitor the technology industry and the markets around the world to look for new business ideas or for new ways to solve old problems. In any case innovation is the key issue for competing at national and firm level.

As stated above, small and medium size enterprises are aware of the relevance of innovation, but they prefer incremental innovation. This derives both from unbiased reasons and from cultural factors.

First of all, the size of the enterprise - in terms of financial resources, personnel, available know-how, geographical coverage - represents an evident limitation to certain types of innovation: equipment for big volumes, too expensive machines, lack of competencies in the area are the frequent obstacles to radical innovation for small and medium size enterprises[2].

At the other side, as small and medium size enterprises have usually a strong entrepreneurial character, the preferences and the habits of the entrepreneur conditions the enterprise's choices. If the entrepreneur does not succeed in keeping the pace of technology development, he does not realise the opportunities related to technology and he hardly introduces new systems or new processes. Besides, as small and medium size enterprises are usually family business the risk assessment related to innovation is often affected by personal/family needs or perspectives[3].

Along with incremental innovation small and medium size enterprises tend to invest in cross-technologies [Gottardi, 1995], that is technologies enabling several types of processes and better co-ordination among different production steps (e.g. flexible cutting tools, production scheduling, warehouse management, CAD systems, etc.) as they are modular and they can be used almost for any batch size.

Information and communication technologies belong to the cross-technology class and they seem to offer the suited profile for small and medium size enterprises.

Literature identifies some factors influencing ICT adoption in small business [Bergeron and Raymond, 1992; Julien and Raymond, 1994 ; Iacovou, Benbasat and Dexter, 1995; Raymond and Bergeron, 1996]: environmental, organisational, decisional, psycho-sociological and informational contexts. The profile acquired by each one of the previous variable and the combination they reach strongly condition the choices of small and medium size enterprises in the IT field. In particular, the coherence between small and medium size enterprises' strategic orientation and strategic IT management can explain successfully or unsuccessfully enterprise's performances [Bergeron and Raymond, 1995].

The issue of IT diffusion in small and medium size enterprises assumes a special outline when small and medium size enterprises do not operate in independent environments, but they do belong to industrial districts or networks. The concept of *industrial district* is known in literature since Marshall's study [1961] and it refers to *a group of geographically concentrated firms specialising [..]* in *similar and complementary activities and developing [...] experiential knowledge*[4]. This implies that manufacturers can exploit external economies deriving from the know-how and abilities cultivated within the district by several actors of the business and social environment (e.g. unions, school systems, traditions, etc.).

In this context social factors, such as the imitation effect[5], play a relevant role to diffuse ICT among small and medium size enterprises and the presence of support centres and technology leading enterprises is a pre-condition to innovate.

Literature emphasises the role of the *facilitator* [Cash, Eccles, Nohria, Nolan, 1994 ; Franch and Zaninotto, 1995] in the inter-organisational information systems where co-ordination among different partners - often of small size - needs a supervision and support by superior actors, able to maintain the overview of the whole system.

The role of the facilitator can be analysed in details referring to ICT in general. Two useful dimensions for the analysis are the nature of the applications/systems which can be diffused among the small and medium size enterprises and the degree of personalisation/specificity small and medium size enterprises requires for solving the information needs. As shown in \h Figure 1 the facilitator's role has at least four different approaches: supporting the diffusion of existing applications, monitoring the offer of the ICT industry ; re-acting

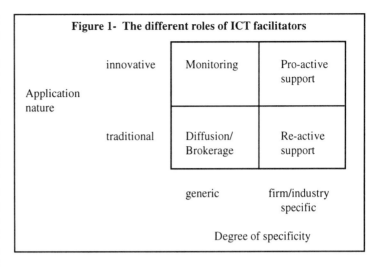

Figure 1- The different roles of ICT facilitators

to personalisation needs and pro-actively developing the most innovative/(firm/industry-) specific applications.

The four approaches can be shortly described as following.

- supporting the diffusion of existing applications - the facilitator does not intervene directly in the solution of the information/technology need, but it creates the awareness among the interested partners and, when necessary, suggests the most interesting suppliers/applications for the specific firm;
- monitoring the offer of the ICT industry - in this case the relevance of the facilitator role refers to the ability of understanding trends and perspectives. The facilitator is expected to monitor the offer of the supply side in order to suggest the most useful perspectives and the areas where it is convenient to invest;
- re-acting to personalisation needs - the specificity of the industry/enterprise requires ad-hoc solutions and the facilitator can support in the choice of the most suitable technology or in the selection of the supplier with the necessary competencies.
- pro-actively developing the most innovative/(firm/industry-)specific applications - the most challenging approach includes active participation of the facilitator in the solution of the innovation problem. *Facilitating* in this case implies requirement analysis, solution design, supervision of the realisation/implementation phases, final testing.

The implications of this classification scheme are relevant both for research and practice. At one side, research can analyse what the influence factors and the levers are in the four cited situations, in order to improve the effectiveness and the efficiency of this role. At the other side, the understanding of some positive or negative experiences in the introduction of ICT in small and medium size enterprises can improve considerably taking into account what the facilitator is expected to achieve and the means it has available.

In the next sessions the paper presents the situation observed in one industrial district in Italy, where the presence of one *facilitator* has obtained interesting results for the diffusion of ICT.

THE SHOEMAKERS IN ITALY

One of the driving forces of the Italian economy has been 'light manufacturing' (textile, clothing, hats and shoemaking industries, for example), in which the craft work has a prominent role.

The labour costs represent a high percentage of total costs, while investments in production facilities are not so relevant.

With 8.880 enterprises and 124.600 persons employed in 1996, shoemaking is one of the most relevant industries in Italy. The shoes produced in 1996 were 482,7 million (476,2 in 1995), and the revenues 15.669 billion lire (15.212 in 1995). Exported production is 84,3% (by volume) and 76% (by value) of total production; in 1995 the export value was 11.896 billion lire, and the pairs 426,7 million.

As described in the following paragraphs, shoemaking in Italy has a long lasting tradition, which goes back to the craft abilities at the end of the XIX century. Almost all the artisans and the persons employed in the first mechanised plants came from the agricultural industry.

During the first steps of the industry development, it was common to accept a part-time employment contract as a way to complete the reducing income from agriculture.

The high number of shoemaking enterprises and the low number of employees per firm (14 in 1995 e 1996) suggest that the small size of the enterprises and the low concentration rate are two main characteristics of that industry.

It is possible to differentiate production in terms of quality level (high, medium, low) or target groups (woman, man, kid or sportswear). Each segment is characterised by different distribution channels (retailing, specialised chains, department stores), manufacturing processes (manual steps, partially automated or fully automated activities) and available technologies (for product development and manufacturing processes).

In every district there are examples of each identified production type, even if there is evidence of a traditional district specialisation (e.g., sport shoes are produced only in Montebelluna, while Tuscany produces mainly high quality shoes). Nowadays, traditional shoe manufacturers are facing a growing competition both from other Italian districts and from abroad. A clear trend in the industry is 'niche focusing' (segmentation) is replacing district specialisation. Single manufacturers, independently from the district they belong to, select the most suitable target for their business structure, and the product system which better fit to target needs.

Shoemakers birth and development

Despite their economic and social relevance, not many studies have been conducted about the birth and development of the light industries, mostly because of the small size of the business, that means few information and studies coming from the enterprises themselves, especially on a historical basis.

This paragraph and the next one will individuate the driving forces underlying the birth of the Italian shoemaking industry and the development lines, founding on the following industry development scheme (\h Table 1).

Shoemaking industry development scheme (life cycle)
1. (1900-'20) mechanisation (the first mechanised plants)
2. ('30-'40) development (basically in the north regions)
3. ('50) consolidation and development of emergent districts (north-east, centre of Italy)
4. ('60-'70) industrialisation and high growth (export increase, especially in the emergent districts)
5. ('80) alternation of crisis and recoveries
6. ('90-2000) new opportunities

The first non mechanised plant for shoe manufacturing open at Vigevano in 1872. In 1898 is founded one of the first shoemaking plant of Veneto, in which all the production process are mechanised, like in the American, English and German plants of the same period.

The two World War can be defined as a 'watershed' in the shoemaking industry: the First World War period is characterised by the mechanisation; between the two Wars, as follows, there is a period of fast growth of the industry, despite the economic crisis following the First World War.

At the beginning of the First World War, there are 75 industrial shoemaker in Italy, equipped with sewing machines[6]. More than half of the factories are located in Lombardia and Piemonte, the rest placed in Veneto, Emilia, Campania, Toscana, Marche, Liguria, Calabria, Sicilia e Umbria.

Around 1910, in the Marche region, an entrepreneur set-up the first example of decentralised work organisation in the shoemaking industry. The network he managed is composed by around 200 workers at home.

In these early steps, the industry is starting to define it's characters: decentralisation of some or all the phases of the production process, a tight relationship with the social and geographical background, a wide attitude to approach new international markets.

In 1911, the first reliable 'Italian industrial census' shows 26.447 enterprises (almost all characterised by a small size) operating in the shoemaking industry, and 97.997 persons employed (10,8 and 4,2% of the totals).

The First World War has a significant impact on the industry widening the volumes of production (as it happened in others industries), that does not reduce after the War, and strengthening the industry structure.

The figures show the impact of the First World War on the Shoemaking Italian industry.

Table 1 - Production and export in the Italian shoemaking industry				
	Production (millions of pairs)			Export (pairs)
1921	22		1923	232.000
1925	25		1926	373.000
1930	29,6		1929	668.000 (source: *Anselmi, 1989*)

Table 2 - European shoes production (1930/1990/1995)					
Production (millions of pairs)					
	1930		1990		1995
England	118,9	CSI	820	Italy	476
Germany	80	Italy	425	Spain	187
URSS	48,9	Spain	202	France	152
France	45,3	France	177	England	103
Italy	29,6	Czechoslovakia	115	Portugal	97
Czechoslovakia	23,1	England	108	CSI	96
Belgium	15,1	Portugal	102	Czechoslovakia	72
Holland	13,2	Romania	92	Poland	55
Spain	8	Yugoslavia	80	Romania	52
Swiss	7,9	Germany	65	Germany	47
(source: *Anselmi, 1989; ANCI, 1990 e 1995*)					

In 1930 Italy is the fifth shoes producer in Europe, increasing the potential production by 50% in little more than ten years (1913-1925). As showed in \h Table 3, this is the beginning of a positive trend that has driven Italy to be the first European shoes manufacturer nowadays, producing twice as much the second manufacturer's pairs.

In the 30s, a new factor is starting to drive the product development and the competition: fashion, and the related attention the customer is starting to pay to the shoe as a part of his dressing style. There are social reasons and costume changes behind this pattern (like the influence of cinema, and press to the customers' behaviours, and the evolution of dressing styles). Anyway, it is clear that the international markets are demanding more and more high quality and superior styled shoes (that are the traditional Italian shoes' success factor). This fact is sustaining another problem: the human resources training and improvement. Only in 1956 the first training school addressed to the shoemaking industry (located in the Marche district) starts its courses.

Product specialisation, based on shoe models and labour division among manufacturers and districts, starts in this period. Some enterprises restrict their activity to women shoes or men shoes; the component manufacturers become independent units; districts begin to focus their production (economical or high quality products rather then women or men shoes).

The Second World War, differently from the First, has a negative impact on shoemaking industry, and the economic 'reconstruction' is getting very difficult.

The main constraints are lack of raw materials and poor demand, and the difficult relationship with the banking system.

In a European perspective, the shoemaking industry is lead by four countries: Germany, England, France and Italy. The first two are the most industrialised ones, whereas Italy and France are characterised by labour division and geographical specialisation (in terms of production phases).

In 1948 the economic recovery starts, and there is public acknowledgement of home workers. This is the moment when enterprises become aware of the necessity to approach foreign markets as a way to accelerate industrial growth. It is evident that internal demand is not sufficient to absorb the growing production capability, and that international demand of Italian shoes is growing more than the internal one. The United States are identified as one of the most relevant export markets.

Artisans are disappearing, basically in two ways: transforming their workshops into small factories, or being employed by bigger manufacturers.

Table 3 - Shoes export		
	Pairs exported	
1951	302.000	
1954	927.000	
1957	6.500.000	(*Anselmi, 1989*)

Shoes trade fairs are flourishing (the most important ones are located in Milano, Vigevano, Bologna and Riviera del Brenta), setting up a wide range of activities related to industry development. In this period the historical districts (Lombardia) are loosing edge compared with the emerging ones (Marche and Toscana above all).

The effort sustained by the Italian shoes manufacturer is testified by the increase in shoes export, as showed in the Table 3, and is being strengthened by the creation of the Common European Market.

In these years, the proliferation of shoes models is attracting the attention of industry operators: some of them consider the high number of models like a distinctive feature of Italian manufacturers; others are focusing the risks of this approach, in terms of production complexity and product identity.

The modern industrialisation of the Italian shoemaking industry, started around the '60, induces the rapid growth of the industry, based on two main factors:
• the flexibility of Italian small and medium size enterprises, especially in the regions with the presence of districts;
• the growing importance of international shoes markets.

The results of this process is summarised by production increase - from 73 millions pair (in 1960) to 270 millions pair (in 1970), by total employees increase in the industry and by the bigger average business size.

United States and Germany are the most relevant export markets for Italy, with the European Union countries absorbing from 30 to 40% of the total shoes export.

As showed in the chart below, the Eighties are characterised by crisis and recovery alternation, in which the production volumes range from 531 million pairs in 1981 to 407 million pairs in 1989. In this period, the end of the relentless growth of the industry and the increasing foreign competition are forcing shoemaking enterprises to reorganise, or to close down.

Starting from 1992 the industry lives a new positive trend, strongly driven by new challenges to the Italian shoemakers:
• the increasing importance of the distribution channels,
• the emergence of new potential markets,
• the foreign competition, focused on low and medium quality products.

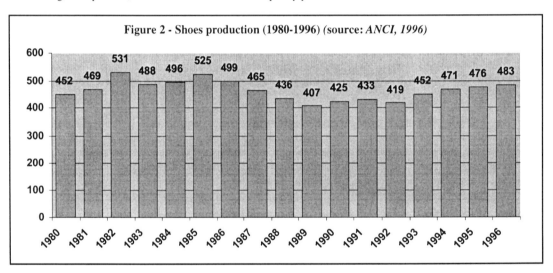

Figure 2 - Shoes production (1980-1996) (source: *ANCI, 1996*)

The shoemaking district of Riviera del Brenta

As seen in the paragraph 3.1, the Veneto region is one of the leading shoes district. In 1995 Veneto is the third district for number of enterprises and employees (1.456 and 24.958) after Marche and Toscana (ANCI, 1995). Veneto is the first region if analysed in terms of export (25,1% of the total export of Italian shoes.

In this region, it is possible to identify three areas, or districts, each one having its own peculiar characters: Riviera del Brenta (women's shoes of very high quality), Verona (lower quality shoes) and Montebelluna (sport and technical shoes).

The following features can describe the Riviera del Brenta area:
• High quality production (concentrated on women shoes - 97%),
• Labour intensive processes,
• Relatively high attitude to co-operate and to associate,
• High attitude to export (Europe).

STRATEGIC APPROACHES OF THE SHOEMAKING DISTRICT IN RIVIERA DEL BRENTA

In 1997 a research project aimed at analysing trends and perspectives of the shoemaking industry in Veneto[7] surveyed a group of shoemakers in Riviera del Brenta by direct interviews[8].

Purpose of the research project was the understanding of innovation paths, and in particular of ICT, common among the enterprises in the area.

One strong assumption of the research was the link between innovation and strategy: in the research model decisions related to innovation and ICT depend on the strategic options selected by enterprises.

The research identified four strategic approaches prevalent in the area:
1. product oriented approach,
2. creation of its own image/brand,
3. co-operation with one or more designers
4. subcontracting approaches.

1. Product orientation is the traditional approach of Italian shoemakers, based on product quality and wide range of products (measured by the number of different models included in the winter and the summer collections). The main variables affecting this approach are:
- wide range of models,
- low bargaining power towards distributors (wholesalers , purchase groups, chains of associated retailers in various European countries;
- product brand is rarely known by the final customer,
- high competition focused on price and price/quality ratio,
- growing competition from foreign producers (Spain and Far East),
- high number of direct competitors, similar in terms of competencies, product quality, catalogue,
- low market segmentation as the offer is generally targeted to female customers, without an in-depth analysis of their expectations (derivign from age, income, life styles, etc.).

While successful in the past, the product oriented approach shows potential limits in the future, mainly due to strong competition. Therefore, the enterprises in the area are looking for alternative behaviours. The ones depicted in \h Figure 5 are already present in Riviera del Brenta. Unfortunately few enterprises have already switch to new approaches, and the majority is still linked to the traditional one.

2. The second approach aims at conquering the direct contact with the final customer, through the creation of its own image and brand. The main features of this approach are:
- product brands are known to retailers and to final customers,
- low direct product competition,
- accurate market segmentation,
- limited range of models (collections include 20 to 30 models),
- partnership with distribution (franchising, joint-ventures, etc.) and with other supply chain actors.

While this approach overcomes the main limits of the traditional strategy (e.g. low bargaining power towards distribution and strong competition) it presents high risks and investments. Investments refer mainly to market analysis (in order to identify suitable market segments), to advertising and to distribution: usually it takes long before a brand is known by the market and it requires heavy investments in advertisements.

3. Integrating with one or more designers (via exclusive licences) is the third strategic option observed in the research. Adopting this approach involves the following issues:
- business strategy bases on coherence with licensed designer's styles,
- reduced independence in product design and development,
- widely known product brand or designer's name,
- no direct product competition,
- partnership with designers who usually take care of advertising and distribution,
- high flexibility in manufacturing and organisational structure.

The advantages of the third approach are clearly demonstrated by the quick growth rate (turnover) of the enterprises adopting it. The risk implicit in the second approach (creation of its own brand name) are taken over by the designer who has his/her own advertising policies and distribution channels. The main limit of this approach is the strong dependence from the designer: if the shoemaker deals only with one designer, its business completely depends on this counterpart. His/her mistakes in market analysis or his/her internal problems might have strong repercussions also on the shoemaker.

4. Subcontracting

The last approach evident in the area shows enterprises operating as pure subcontractor of bigger companies or stronger brand names. In synthesis, this approach is characterised by the following features:

- Pure production activities based on orders forwarded by bigger companies or strong brand names,
- Limited research and development,
- Several relations with different customers (often competitors) at the same time,
- Price and technical competencies are competitive variables.

Often the fourth approach is combined with the traditional one or with the creation of an independent brand name, as it produces a financial flows to cover the fixed costs of the main business.

As discussed in the following paragraph, the relevance of information and information systems in shoemaking enterprises differs, depending on the strategic approach adopted. Obviously if customers and designers play a relevant role for the enterprise I.S. supporting marketing (e.g. internet web sites) and external transactions (supply chain systems) are present in the enterprise; where product quality is more important, CAD and CAM systems might absorb heavy resources.

The pure core processes and the related technologies are different between high-volume/medium-quality producers (where technology is progressively replacing human activities) and high quality shoemaker branches (where manual activities - \h Figure 6 - can be hardly replaced or even supported by technologies).

5. Information and Communication Technology within the shoemakers' district in Riviera del Brenta[9]

The analysis of the shoe industry in Italy clearly shows that ICT might have different impacts in different branches, coherently with their specific competitive factors.

In the high-volume-low-cost-branch ICT can support the search for efficiency, while in the branches with the highest quality they should improve the image of the products.

As mentioned above, the Riviera del Brenta district produces high quality shoes whose image on the market is very strong and connected to the overall image of the *Made in Italy* fashion.

The production processes still have several human activities as automation and technology have not reached satisfying quality standard so far.

In terms of ICT, in general Italy is not among the fastest growing markets - +1.4% Information System expenses over GNP and 26 PCs for 100 employees[10] in 1996; but the regions with the widest presence of small and medium size enterprises (Northeast) have the highest growth rate in the ICT market (5.6% in 1996).

In the analysed area computer-based Information Systems - both in the administrative and technical departments - are highly specialised/personalised and respond to the branch needs (e.g. SW packages supporting inventory for shoemakers, production scheduling for shoemakers, etc.).

This state derives from the essence of the industrial district, where the concentration of manufacturers of the same industry/branch nurtures the growth of suppliers and related services.

In deed, for payroll systems and for general ledger applications small software houses in the area have produced their own packages specialised for the shoemakers (mainly in terms of glossary for warehouse management and for cost control) and then they have sold the packages to several local producers (pure market approach). Unfortunately for more sophisticated products (such as CAD systems or technical databases) this approach was weak.

While for traditional applications the market approach (demand represented by the manufacturers of the area and supply made of the SW houses nearby) is effective, innovative applications require some external support to be developed and diffused among the small and medium size enterprises of the area.

At one side innovative applications require relevant personalisation efforts - implying the study of the shoemakers activities, of their information needs, of their decision process - and small software houses have not the financial resources to afford the investment. At the other side a big Information Technology operator does not find the branch appealing as it bases on very small enterprises.

Moreover, the personal background of the majority of the entrepreneurs in the area is far from the ICT world and therefore they need support to become aware of the opportunities offered by these technologies.

A key role in the diffusion of ICT is played by Centro Veneto Calzaturiero, a support centre responsible for training and innovation within the area. Centro Veneto Calzaturiero is part of the shoemakers' association -ACRiB - and offers free and fee-based services.

In the last decade Centro Veneto Calzaturiero highly invested in ICT as they have the highest growth potential for this type of firms; in particular, CAD systems and technical databases have been developed and implemented in several enterprises.

For instance, one project - CALIGA - produced a database of images from the world of fashion and every-day-life useful for supporting the designers in the creation of new collections. The database is multidimensional so that the designer can search images through keywords, time period, images, articles, etc. Besides, Centro Veneto Calzaturiero itself has a workstation available for the smallest associates which cannot afford the system themselves[11]. The access and the use of the CALIGA database is one of the Centro Veneto Calzaturiero's services. Another even more interesting product is a technical database which support the design of the single shoe; it can be integrated with CAD and

CIM systems and with the I.S. of the small business (e.g. inventory system, orders from customer). This system has been developed within a common project of Centro Veneto Calzaturiero with an independent software house of the area, which has strong competencies in the shoemakers branch. The development costs are financed by Centro Veneto Calzaturiero and the software house can sell the product to Centro Veneto Calzaturiero's associates for a reduced price (less than 2,500 ECU including HW) and to any other manufacturer at a market price.

The brief presentation of the Centro Veneto Calzaturiero's experience is coherent with the facilitator model presented in paragraph 2.

For traditional applications Centro Veneto Calzaturiero organises awareness events (visits to technology producers/fairs, workshops, training), without being directly involved in technology development or adaptation; on the opposite, for innovative and industry-specific applications Centro Veneto Calzaturiero anticipates the associates' needs promoting the development of ad-hoc systems.

CONCLUSIONS

Apparently small and medium size enterprises do not invest in innovation, but the deeper analysis of their behaviour shows that they prefer incremental innovation instead of radical changes.

ICT are flexible technologies as they do not require big production batches and their cost is affordable also for small businesses.

The main obstacle to a large diffusion of ICT within small and medium size enterprises derives from the personal know-how of entrepreneurs and managers who privilege manufacturing or sales competencies instead of information management.

To overcome this problem a *facilitator* is needed: a support centre/organisation whose mission might be technology monitoring, adaptation of tools to small and medium size enterprises' needs, training of potential users, maintenance of the system. The tasks of the facilitator vary depending on the nature of the necessary innovation and the specificity of the requirements.

A successful example of the intermediary role is played by Centro Veneto Calzaturiero, a support centre in one of the shoemakers' districts in Italy, which developed or contracted several applications for the small and medium size enterprises in its area (e.g., specialised CAD packages, model databases).

The main results of the efforts are tangible: also the smallest enterprises in the district can afford sophisticated SW systems, enabling them to face the growing competition of foreign manufacturers.

The local environment also supports the effort, as Centro Veneto Calzaturiero co-operates with the education system in the area, training young workers on these technologies.

Both the theoretical framework and the practical case suggest new research fields aimed at analysing the role of support centres in diffusing ICT among SMEs and at understanding the variables explaining their performances.

ENDNOTES

1 Freeman [1974] defines innovation as technical management, engineering, manufacturing, marketing related to a new/improved product or to the introduction of a new equipment.

2 Gottardi [1995] presents similar factors for small and medium size enterprises in Veneto, the region analysed by this paper.

3 Demattè, Corbetta, 1993 ; Danco, 1982, Ward, 1990

4 Best, 1990, p. 233

5 see the Prato case in Kumar, Van Dissel and Bielli, 1996

6 The first mechanic sewing machines appeared in Italy around 1891, imported from United States.

7 The project was part of the Irene Relay Centre, lead by Enea, and financed by the programme Innovation of the European Union

8 The interview covered several topics, such as explicit strategy, expectations for the future, organisational structure and problems, financial data, production processes, attitude towards innovation, applications of ICT, etc. The research sample included 15 enterprises.

9 this session will be completed with quantitative measures in December 1997 when the data related to a field survey are fully available. The survey analyses the diffusion of ICT within a selected sample of small and medium size enterprises in the area (10).

10 for comparison, the U.S. have 3.1% of DP expenses and 67 PCs per 100 employees ; UK has 2.8% expenses and 45 PCs per 100 employees (source Assinform/nomos, 1997)

11 the cost of the database does not derive from the initial investment, but from the maintenance costs. If the enterprise is to small to update the images in the database its utility decreases sensibly. Centro Veneto Calzaturiero selects and introduces new images every season, keeping up-to-dated the system.

REFERENCES

ANCI, *L'industria calzaturiera italiana 1990/1995/1996 - Relazione economico statistica*, ANCI, 1990, 1995, 1996

Anselmi S., *L'industria calzaturiera marchigiana - Dalla manifattura alla fabbrica*, Unione Industriali del fermano, 1989

Assinform, *Rapporto Assinform sull'informatica e le telecomunicazioni*, Assinform, 1997

Becattini G., *The development of light industry in Tuscany : an interpretation*, Economic Notes, vol. 2-3, 1978

Bergeron F., Raymond L., *Planning of information systems to gain a competitive edge*, Journal of small Business Management, 1/92

Bergeron F., Raymond L., *The Contribution of IT to the Bottom Line : A Contingency Perspective of Strategic Dimensions*, Proceedings of the 16th ICIS, Amsterdam, 1995

Best M., *The New Competition*, Polity Press, 1990

Boccardi L., *Party Shoes,* Zanfi Editore, 1993

Cash J.I.Jr., Eccles R.G., Nohria N., Nolan R., *Building the information-age organisation : structure, control and information technologies*, Irwin, 1994

Clemens E.K., Row M.C., *Sustaining I.T. Advantage : The Role of Structural differences*, MIS Quarterly, 15-3 1991

Danco L.A., *Inside the family business*, Prentice Hall, 1982

Demattè C., *L'innovazione come arma competitiva*, Economia & Management, 4/1996

Demattè C., Corbetta G., *I processi di transizione delle imprese familiari*, studi e ricerche Mediocredito Lombardo, 1993

Forlani F., *Prodotti nazionali ad alta tecnologia. Un treno perso o ... meglio pensare ad altro ?*, Sistemi & Impresa, 9/1996

Franch M., Zaninotto D., *La diffusione degli IOS nei distretti industriali*, Proceedings of the Workshop Tecnologie dell'informazione e flessibilitaà nei mercati e nell'organizzazione, Trento, 1995

Freeman C., *The Economics of Industrial Innovation*, Penguin Modern Economics Texts, 1974

Gottardi G., *Stato e traiettorie evolutive delle tecnologie caratteristiche dei settori veneti maturi. Technology Assessment*, in Petroni, 1995

Iacovou C.L., Benbasat I., Dexter A.S., *Electronic Data Interchange and small Organisations : Adoption and Impact of Technology*, MIS Quarterly, Dec. 1995

Jarillo J.C., *On Strategic Networks*, Strategic Management Journal, Jan.-Feb., 1988

Johnston R.H., Lawrence P.R., *Beyond vertical Integration - the Rise of the Value-Added Partnership*, Harvard Business Review, July-August 1988

Julien P.A., Raymond L., *Factors of New Technology Adoption in the Retail Sector*, Entrepreneurship Theory and Practice, 4/1994

Kumar K., Van Dissel H.G., Bielli P., *The Merchant of Prato - revisited : towards a Third Rationality of Information Systems*, Research Papers, Erasmus University, 1996

Lorenzoni G*., L'architettura di sviluppo delle imprese minori*, Il Mulino, 1990

Malone T., Yates J., Benjamin R.I., Electronic Markets and Electronic Hierarchies, Communications of the ACM, 30-6, 1987

Marshall A., Principles of Economics, Macmillan, 1961

Merli G., Saccani C., *L'impresa olonico-virtuale*, Ed. Sole 24 Ore, 1994

Miles R. Snow C., *Organizations - New Concepts for New Forms*, California Management Review, 28-3, 1986

Nakane J. *Holonic Manufacturing Flexibility . The competitive Battle in the 1990s,* Production, Planning and Control, vol 2, 1990

Ordanini A., *I principali distretti calzaturieri italiani*, EGEA, 1995

Petroni G. (ed.), *Innovazione, sviluppo industriale e processi formativi nell'area veneta, CUOA, 1995*

Piore M., Sabel C., *The Second Industrial Divide*, Basic Books, 1984

Porter M., *Competitive Advantage : Techniques for Analysing Industries and Competitors*, The Free Press, 1980

Porter M., *Competitive Advantage : Creating and Sustaining Superior Performance*, The Free Press, 1985

Prahalad C.K., Hamel G., *The core competence of the corporation*, Harvard Business Review, May-June 1990

Raymond L., Bergeron F.,*EDI Success in small and Medium-sized Enterprises : A Field Study*, Journal of Organisationa Computing and Electronic Commerce, 2/1996

Rullani E., *Il valore della conoscenza*, Economia e Politica Industriale, n. 82, 1994

Sabel C., Herrigel G. Kazis R., Deeg R., *How to keep mature industries competitive*, Technology Review, April 1987

Tescaro M., Birolo A., *Calzature*, in Gottardi, 1995

Ward J.L., *Keeping the family business healthy*, Jossey-Bass Publishers, 1990

Williamson O., *Markets and Hierarchies*, Free Press, 1975

Integrating Earned Value into the Management of Software Development Projects

Daniel M. Brandon, Jr., Ph.D.

Christian Brothers University, School of Business, 650 East Parkway South, Memphis, TN 38104

Phone: (901) 321-3615, Fax: (901) 321-3566, E-Mail: dbrandon@cbu.edu

ABSTRACT

Software Development projects are notoriously difficult to manage due to several reasons including the fact that most of the project cost is typically labor and quantitatively determining progress is difficult. Upper management usually realizes the dynamic situation of software development but needs to have accurate projections of project deliverable dates. "Earned Value" has proven to be an extremely effective tool for project management and it provides very good estimates of actual project completion date and actual completion costs. However the effective use of earned value in software developments projects is rare, particularly outside of the US Government and its contractors. Application of earned value in software development is not obvious nor straightforward since earned value requires quantitative work packet specification and percent complete measurements which must be integrated into the organization's software development methodology. This article presents some ways to integrate earned value and software development methodology and also specific techniques to reduce associated earned value complexities.

Software development projects are difficult to manage due to several reasons including:
- Most of the project cost is typically labor
- Such labor typically has widely varying productivity, even within the same job category
- Quantitative methods for measuring task level progress are immature or not used
- Applications are being implemented in new environments (i.e. client/server and Internet) where prior task estimation data is sparse
- The underlying technology is changing rapidly, as are the associated tools, also making task estimations less reliable and increasing risk factors
- There are often unrealistic goals and pressures placed upon project managers and project teams to deliver software products "better/cheaper/faster"

Upper management needs to have accurate projections of project deliverable dates to plan associated release/migration efforts and other interdependent activities. Thus it is very important for project managers to be able to give upper management good estimates of when the project will eventually be completed and at what cost. "Earned Value" is a "progress versus plan" based approach to evaluate true performance of a project both in terms of cost deviation and schedule deviation. It also provides a quantitative basis for estimating actual completion time and actual cost at completion; earned value can provide an early warning of project time and/or cost problems as early as 15 percent into the project [Fleming & Koppelman, 1998].

EARNED VALUE

"Earned Value" is simply the value (usually expressed in dollars) of the work accomplished up to a point in time based upon the planned cost for that amount of work. While earned value methods are now internationally recognized for effective project management, these methods have not been widely applied on software development projects [Christensen & Ferens, 1995, *Acquisition Review Quarterly*]. Also earned value use is rare outside of the US Government and its contractors[Fleming & Koppleman, 1996].

There are several reasons for this lack of use, and these reasons involve the over complication of the surrounding methodology and procedures, and also the effort and human factors involved in gathering the necessary input data, reporting same, and integrating results with other management information systems. Methods for overcoming these obstacles for general projects was discussed in an earlier article by this author [Brandon, 1998]. This article will present some techniques which can be employed for software development projects in particular.

The Earned Value concept has been around in several forms for many years dating back to types of cost variances defined in the 1950's. In the early 1960's PERT (Program Evaluation Review Technique) was extended to include cost variances and the basic concept of earned value was adopted therein. PERT did not survive, but the basic earned value concept did. That concept was a key element in the 1967 DoD (Department of Defense) policy called Cost/Schedule Control Systems Criteria (C/SCSC). Early implementations of C/SCSC met with numerous problems most common of which was over implementation due to excessive checklists, data acquisition requirements and other paperwork, specialist acronyms, and overly complicated methods and tools. However, C/SCSC is now very effective and the government has accumulated many years of statistical evidence supporting it. Also in the last several years initiatives within DoD have been started to remove excessive and ineffective components of the C/SCSC [Abba, 1997]. The C/SCSC have now been successful, and have met the "test of time" for nearly three decades on major government projects [Abba, 1997]. Effective commercial use is still in its infancy, but Internet web sites have been set up to track progress of earned value research and practice:

> http://www.uwf.edu/~dchriste/ev-bib.html
> http://www.acq.osd.mil/pm
> http://www.pmi.org
> http://www.spmn.com

SOFTWARE DEVELOPMENT METHODOLOGY

Most software development groups or organizations have some type of formal or informal methodology (or lifecycle) indicating the processes and/or key practices that are to be performed in developing software. Earned value analysis is based upon measuring progress and effort against a planned baseline of work definition ("things to be done"). Thus it is natural when applying earned value analysis to software development projects, to base the work definition on the organization's software development methodology. Any type of methodology can be used (waterfall, overlapping waterfall, spiral, prototyping convergence etc.), but in this article the example will use a classical simple waterfall methodology:

- Requirements Definition
- Overall Design
- Detail Project Plan
- External Design
- Detain Design
- Implementation (Coding and Unit Testing)
- Integration
- Internal Documentation
- Training
- Installation

USING EARNED VALUE

"Earned Value" is basically the value (usually expressed in dollars) of the work accomplished up to a point in time based upon the planned (or budgeted) value for that work. The government's term for earned value is "Budgeted Cost of Work Performed" (BCWP).

Typically when a schedule is being formulated, the work to be done is broken down into tasks or "work packets" which are organized into a logical pattern usually called a "Work Breakdown Structure" (WBS). According to the PMBOK‰ [PMI Standards Committee, 1996], the WBS is a "deliverable-ori-

Figure 1: Work Breakdown Structure	
Level 1	**Level 2**
Requirements Defintion	External Requirements
	Standards Requirements
	Performance Requirements
	Interface Requirements
Overall Design	External Design
	Internal Design
Detail Project Plan	WBS & Packet Definition
	Baseline Plan
External Documentation	Overall Control & Menus
	Tables
	Sorts, Selects, Options
	Forms
	Reports
Detail Design	Standards for Inheritance
	Business Entities & Relationships
	Database Interface
	Validation
	Help Subsystem
	Communications
Implementation	Database Interface
	Validation
	Menus
	Tables, Sorts, Selects
	Forms & Reports
	Help Subsystem
	Communications
Integration	Basic System
	Help Subsystem
	Communications
Internal Documentation	Installation & Operation
	Inline Class Definition
Training	System Administrators
	Database Administrators
	Managers & Supervisors
	Support Personel
	Operators
	Users
Installation	Entity Maintenance
	Entry & Operations
	Production

ented grouping of project elements". The WBS is usually formulated in a hierarchically manner as shown for our example project in Figure 1, which has two of its levels shown and is following our example software development methodology. There are also other typical patterns of WBS for software development [Raz, 1998].

Each work packet is typically assigned to an organization for work management/responsibility. The organizational structure may also be represented in a hierarchically manner typically called an "Organizational Breakdown Structure" (OBS). The amount and type of cost to complete each work packet is then estimated. For software development projects, most packets involve only labor and the amount of work is estimated by using historical data and some specific technique such as "lines of code", "function point analysis", number and type of requirements involved, or by a percentage relative to some other work packet(s).

Resources to perform the work are identified (now or later) for each packet and may be coded by using a "Resource Breakdown Structure" (RBS). Each packet typically has one type of cost (labor, travel, materials, etc.), coded by an "Element of Cost Breakdown" (EOC) or simple general ledger account number. Thus each work packet is the intersection of these coding dimensions (WBS, OBS, RBS, EOC), and it has a detailed description plus an estimated cost, and dependent task(s) identification. "The work package usually has a short-time span schedule (40 to 100 hours), is limited to one performing department, and has defined completion criteria "[Kiewel, 1998]. There may also be other important criteria for defining work packet granularity [Raz, 1998].

Figure 2: Project Cost Plan

	Jan	Feb	Mar	Apr	May	Jun	Jul	Aug	Sep	Oct	Nov	Dec	Total
Requirements Defintion	10	5											15
Overall Design		5	5										10
Project Plan			5	5									10
External Documentation				5	5								10
Detail Design					10	15	5						30
Implementation						5	15	20	15	5	1		61
Integration									10	10			20
Internal Documentation										5	5		10
Training											5	5	10
Installation												5	5
Monthly Cost	10	10	10	10	15	20	20	20	25	20	11	10	181
Cumulative	10	20	30	40	55	75	95	115	140	160	171	181	

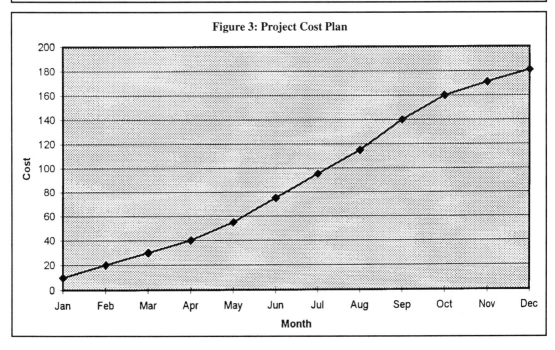

Figure 3: Project Cost Plan

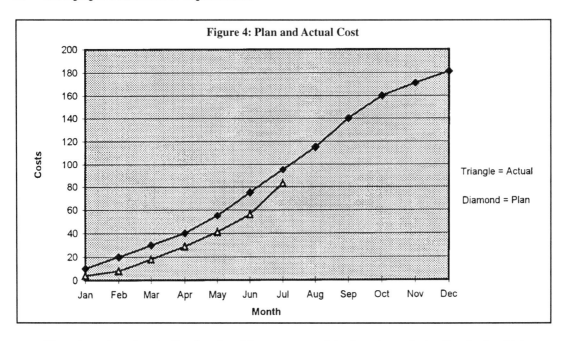

Figure 4: Plan and Actual Cost

The estimated cost is typically a function of the resources, and the dependent tasks is a list of tasks which must be completed before starting this task. These tasks are then typically input to a scheduling program which produces a time phasing of task start and end dates based upon: project start date, task resource needs, resource availability's, and task interdependencies. When these tasks are "rolled-up" the WBS hierarchically, the total cost plan is derived as shown in Figure 2 in spreadsheet form (for our example project) or as Figure 3 in graphical form. The government's term for this planned cost curve is "Budgeted Cost of Work Scheduled" (BCWS). With a full spreadsheet model, there would be a subsidiary spreadsheet for each level 1 task also (similar to Figure 5) or any task that was divided into subtasks.

As the project progresses, actual costs are incurred by the effort expended in each work packet. Hopefully these actual costs are measurable at least in total, as shown in Figure 4. The costs may or may not be practically measurable for each work packet which are at the lowest level of the WBS (this is discussed more later). However the relative amount of the things needed to be accomplished within the work packet that have actually been completed (% complete) can be estimated. The planned cost may change in time also, and thus work packets may need to be re-estimated or new ones added or deleted.

Since percent complete and earned value can be estimated for each work packet, the total project earned value at a point in time can be determined by a WBS rollup of the values. A WBS rollup example is shown in Figure 5. There are usually "level of effort" (or indirect or allocated) costs associated with a project. For earned value analysis, these can be left out, or their associated work packets can be assigned 100% complete.

The earned value can be projected onto the planned cost (BCWS) curve to graphically show deviations. This is illustrated in Figure 6, which shows the planned cost and actual cost curves for a project analysis on our sample project through July. Variances between the three values BCWS (planned cost), BCWP (earned value), and actual cost (ACWP) yield the earned value metrics. There are earned value metrics available for both cost and schedule

	Apr	May	Jun	Jul	Aug	Sep	Oct	Nov	Dec	Plan	% C	Value
Overall Control & Menus	2									2	100	2
Tables	3									3	100	3
Sorts, Selects, Options		1								1	0	0
Forms		2								2	60	1.2
Reports		2								2	65	1.3
Monthly Plan	5	5	0	0	0	0	0	0	0	10	75	7.5

Figure 5: External Documentation

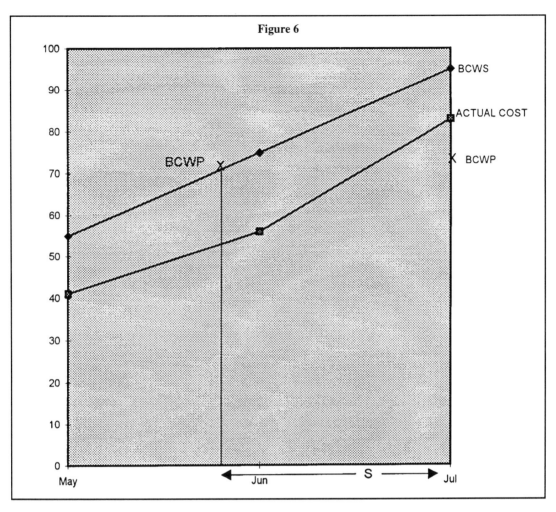

Figure 6

variances. The cost metrics are:

Cost Variance (Dollars) = ACWP - BCWP

Cost Variance (Percent) = (ACWP - BCWP) * 100/BCWP

Cost Efficiency Factor = BCWP/ACWP

Estimated Cost to Complete (EAC)= BCWS/(Cost Efficiency Factor)

There are other (EAC) formulas, and the most appropriate depends upon project type and when the EAC is calculated [Christensen, 1995, Journal of Cost Analysis]. Another popular EAC formula is:

EAC = ACWP + (Budget at Completion - BCWP)/(Cost Efficiency Factor)

Here ACWP is a "sunk cost" and (Budget at Completion - BCWP) is the estimated remaining work. Often a composite of the Cost Efficiency Factor and the Schedule Efficiency Factor (discussed below) is used, such as the product of the two factors. The schedule metrics are:

Schedule Variance (Dollars) = BCWS - BCWP

Schedule Variance (Months) = (BCWS - BCWP)/(Planned Cost for Month)

Schedule Efficiency Factor = BCWP/BCWS

Estimated Time to Complete =(Planned Completion in Months)/

(Schedule Efficiency Factor)

The schedule variance in time (S) is shown in Figure 6 along the time axis. In the variance formulas above, I have reversed the sign from the direction usually shown in the literature, so that a positive variance represents a cost or time overrun.

If earned value analysis is such a good measure of true project performance, then why is not used more in industry and in particular for software development. There appear to be several reasons for this. First commercial awareness of earned value is still low; corporate training courses rarely discuss earned value, and there is relatively

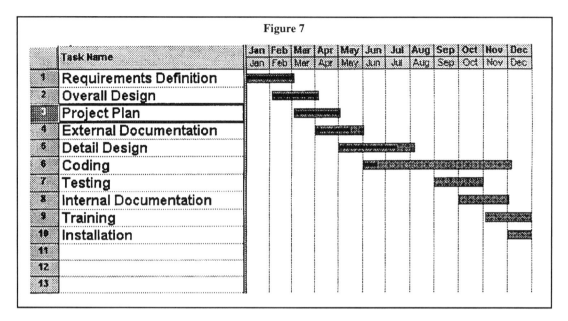

Figure 7

little in commercial print on the subject (Books and Journal Articles) [Brandon, 1998]. Even recent comprehensive books on software development project management do not include earned value [Hallows, 1998; Yeates, 1996]. Secondly the data acquisition required (for obtaining percent complete and actual cost numbers) if implemented in a "by the book" method is too costly and time consuming. Thirdly earned value reporting has not been handled in an easily implemented manner by project management software. And lastly there can be significant employee and contractor resistance problems when trying to put earned value into practice.

PROJECT MANAGEMENT REPORTING METHODS

Usually when project progress is reported, two types of information are presented: schedule data and cost data. Schedule data is typically shown in a Gantt or similar type chart as shown in Figure 7 for the example project here. Cost data is typically reported as actual cost (at some WBS level(s)) versus planned cost. The cost variance is often just reported at the total level as total actual cost incurred versus budget [Brandon, 1998].

The problem with these usual methods is that they do not provide a clear quantitative picture of the true project status, not do they provide a means for extrapolating project cost to complete or completion date. For our example project, observe at the Gantt chart (which also shows the task % complete as dark bars stripes inside the bars). We see that we are not over budget (actual cost of 83,000 versus planned cost of 91,000), but it is hard to say how much we are behind schedule and it appears we are not over spending.

However on this project we are well behind schedule and are over spending as the earned values analysis shows. The schedule variance is 0.67 months (behind schedule) and the cost variance is 10,000 dollars (over spent). The estimated time to complete is 15 months instead of the 12 months planned, and the estimated cost to complete is 289,000 instead of 254,000. The calculation of these numbers is via the previous formulas implemented in the spreadsheet of Figure 8.

EARNED VALUE ANALYSIS METHODOLOGY

Timely and reasonably accurate cost and progress data is necessary for earned value analysis, but the data acquisition process must be relatively inexpensive and "easy". Providing for easy and effective data acquisition requires that the methods used are "non-intrusive" yet provides for the necessary accuracy. Non intrusive means that very little extra effort is required by project team members or managers to provide the input data for the analysis. The goal is to implement the necessary data acquisition as a by product of existing corporate reporting or payroll procedures where possible. The key steps in the earned value process that need to be integrated with the organization's methodology are:

Setting appropriate work packet size
Appropriate definition of % complete
Obtaining % complete and effort information
Appropriate basis for costing

Figure 8: Project Earned Value Analysis - Thru July

	Jan	Feb	Mar	Apr	May	Jun	Jul	Aug	Sep	Oct	Nov	Dec	Plan	%C	Value
Requirements Defintion	10	5											15	100	15
Overall Design		5	5										10	100	10
Project Plan			5	5									10	100	10
External Documentation				5	5								10	75	7.5
Detail Design					10	15	5						30	75	22.5
Coding						5	15	20	15	5	1		61	10	6.1
Testing									10	10			20	0	0
Internal Documentation										5	5		10	0	0
Training											5	5	10	0	0
Installation												5	5	0	0
Monthly Plan	10	10	10	10	15	20	20	20	25	20	11	10	181		71.1
Cumulative	10	20	30	40	55	75	95	115	140	160	171	181			
Monthly Actual	4	4	10	11	12	15	27	0	0	0	0	0	83		
Cumulative Actual	4	8	18	29	41	56	83								

Schedule Variances

Budgeted Cost of Work Scheduled (BCWS)	95
Budgeted Cost of Work Performed (BCWP)	71
Schedule Variance (Dollars)	24
Schedule Variance (Months)	1.20
Schedule Efficiency Factor	0.7
Estimated Time to Complete (Months)	16

Cost Variances

Actual cost of Work Performed (ACWP)	83
Budgeted Cost of Work Performed (BCWP)	71
Cost Variance (Dollars)	12
Cost Variance (Percent)	13
Cost Efficiency Factor	0.9
Estimated Cost at Completion	211

WORK PACKET SIZING

If work packets are too small then there will be excessive reporting and paperwork required by project members and managers. If work packets are too big, then performance will not be measured frequently enough to allow corrective action. If project performance is to be measured monthly, then the work packets should be smaller than a month, such as a week or two. It is a best to tie the maximum size of work packets to the progress and effort data acquisition frequency (as further discussed below) where employee labor is a significant cost item (as is the typical case with software development).

DEFINITION OF % COMPLETE

Percent complete estimates must be provided for each work packet on a regular reporting basis. For most work packets, taking the time to calculate the percent complete based on the amount of completed versus the amount of work remaining (or the number of "things" completed versus the number of "things" in the work packet) is too time consuming and an unnecessary burden on project members. If the work packet size has been appropriately determined, then the packet estimates can be very rough without losing much accuracy on the overall project performance evaluation.

There are several methods that have been suggested for estimating software project percent complete that provide sufficient accuracy without much additional effort (Christiansen & Ferens, 1995). For example a very easy percent complete scheme is the "Weighted Milestone" method:

Have not begin work on packet	0 %
Working on packet	50 %

Finished packet	100 %

This works well for smaller work packets. Another method is the "Interim Milestone" method where a percent complete is allocated for each of several milestones.

In most software development methodologies, there is a review, verification, or testing step involved in each phase of the methodology (requirements, design, coding, etc.). Common completion and/or monitoring methods include self-checking, team leader reviews, peer reviews, walkthroughs, or even "Fagan Inspections" [Yeates, 1996]. Usually, by proper decomposition, that verification step can be subdivided and a portion placed in each work packet. For example in the implementation or coding phase, the verification step could involve unit testing and/or peer code review (even in pure "clean room" approaches, programmers are going to do some unit testing). With that being the case, the percent complete can be obtained by a standard interim milestone method where the milestones are:

Have not begin work on packet	0 %
Working on packet	50 %
Finished packet	75 %
Packet verified	100%

Figure 9 shows a possible set of interim milestones for the classical phases of the software development lifecycle.

Figure 9: Verification for Software Development Work Packets		
Phase	**Work Packet Definition**	**Possible Verification Method**
Requirements Defintion	Identification and itemization of Requirements	Customer Sign-Off
Overall Design	Adoption of standards, approaches, packages, libraries	Design Review Approval
Detail Plan	Detail project baseline plan	Upper Management Approval
External Documentation	Definition of user interfaces	Customer Sign-Off
Detail Design	Specification of each class (C++/Java) interface	Peer Review Approval
Implementation	Coding and unit test of each class/package	Unit Test Successful
Integration	Definition and execution of each test scenario	Succesful Scenario
Internal Documentation	Completion of all in-line and external specifications	Peer Review Approval
Training	Training users, operators, administrators, etc.	User Sign-Off
Installation	Place components in service	Customer Sign-Off

OBTAINING % COMPLETE AND EFFORT INFORMATION

To be fully successful any project management performance measurement system must be accepted by project team members and project managers. Thus it is very important that obtaining regular progress (% complete) and effort (man hours) information be easily obtainable. The effort required by team members to report their status must be insignificant relevant to the overall work being done. The easiest way to obtain percent complete and effort statistics is to include such information with existing regular reporting. Some organizations may have timecards and/or progress reports that are complete regularly. The proper time interval for most software projects would be weekly or bi-weekly, any more frequently would be bothersome, and any less frequently would now allow problems to grow before corrective action could be applied. The decomposition of overall work into work packets should be done so that most packets are completed in one or two reporting periods. Whether time cards or progress reports are used, the data obtained must include:

Work packed id
Percent complete
Hours expended

If time cards are used, all of an individual's time (paid time) should be accounted for including project discrete work, project "level of effort" work (where BCWP will equal BCWS, i.e. 100 percent complete), and non-project time (including time off). By doing so one system can be used for "time & attendance", payroll, and earned value project management.

COSTING BASIS

Earned value analysis uses a percent complete for each work packet as shown in Figure 5 to calculate an earned value for each packet. This value requires knowledge of the planned cost and the percent complete, it does not require knowledge of the actual cost. Schedule variations can be calculated without any knowledge of actual costs. The earned value cost variance for the total project only requires knowledge of the total project actual cost not individual work packet actual costs.

A major problem in many organizations is that actual costs, even at the total project level are not obtainable in a timely manner or properly segregated by project. In that case, it is necessary to set up a "feed forward" cost reporting system instead of the "feed back" cost system typically coming off the company's general ledger (Brandon, 1998).

For a feed forward system, resource utilization (usually in manhours) is tracked as well as percent complete, and the predicted cost is the resources utilized times the estimated resource rate. For labor, the hours worked is tracked each reporting period as well as the percent complete for each work packet. Using these two data items each reporting period, earned value can be calculated in one of three manners:

Expressing earned value in terms of manhours (or mandays)

Using the actual pay rate of project workers

Using categories of skills and skill levels

In the first option, the entire work plan is expressed in terms of manhours instead of dollars. This is the least accurate method, but the simplest.

In the second method, a table of "burdened" individual pay rates (pay rates multiplied by a factor which includes all overhead, benefits, etc.) is maintained. This is the most accurate of the three methods, but requires more data to be stored and maintained. There may also be confidentiality of information problems.

The third method is fairly accurate, yet simple; and it does not pose confidentiality problems. Categories are set up for skills (ie. analysts , programmers, etc.) and for skill levels (ie. programmer 1, programmer 2, etc.). For each category an average burdened rate is established ($ per manhour). Then each project worker is assigned one specific category. A spreadsheet or simple database program can be used for these tables also, and linked to the spreadsheet tables previously shown.

REPORTING RESULTS

Reporting earned value in many project scheduling tools is usually not easy. This is for several reasons. First getting actual costs onto a project so that it can be used in the system's earned value mechanism usually means getting actual costs onto each task, and in many systems getting actual costs onto the resources for each task. Second, setting up an automatic interface between your corporate systems (or departmental databases) and a project management systems is not trivial and usually not does use a standard format such as a spreadsheet. Thirdly, using the earned value mechanism in these systems is typically not straightforward and simple (Brandon, 1998).

As stated in the last section, actual costs or estimates thereof are only required for the entire project to find the cost variance and estimated cost at completion. A simple and straightforward way to do this is with a database product (i.e. Access, dBase, etc.) or spreadsheet as shown in Figure 8. This can be done manually, or interfaces to spreadsheet tools (i.e. Excel or Lotus) are relatively easy to set up.

When, and only when, there is a problem with a project do you need to "drill down" your earned value cost variance analysis to lower levels of the WBS; and only then for the WBS areas in which there appears to be a problem ("Management by Exception"). At that point you need to look at a spreadsheet like Figure 10, where the next level down WBS work plan has been augmented with actual costs (or estimates thereof).

Earned value methods have another advantage over current reporting techniques (Gantt Charts and Cost Versus

Figure 10: External Documentation

	Apr	May	Jun	Jul	Aug	Sep	Oct	Nov	Dec	Plan	% C	Value
Overall Control & Menus	2									2	100	2
Tables	3									3	100	3
Sorts, Selects, Options		1								1	0	0
Forms		2								2	60	1.2
Reports		2								2	65	1.3
Monthly Plan	5	5	0	0	0	0	0	0	0	10	75	7.5
Cummulative	5	10	10	10	10	10	10	10	10	10		
Monthly Actual	2	2	3	2								
Cummulative Actual	2	4	7	9								

Actual Cost of Work Completed	9
Budgeted Cost of Work Completed	7.5
Cost Variance (Dollars)	1.5

Budget). Since earned values are quantitative numbers expressed in dollars (for both cost and schedule deviations), these numbers can be rolled up, along an OBS for example, to give a picture of how all projects are performing in an organization.

INTEGRATION WITH SEI'S CMM

The Software Engineering Institute (SEI) has published the well known software development Capability Maturity Model (CMM) which identifies the process areas and key practices used by organizations at different levels of maturity (Paulk, 1993). Two of the key process areas for Level 2 (repeatable) are "software project planning" and "software project tracking and oversight". Each of the key process areas has a number of key practices, and the use of Earned Value Analysis provides for compliance with a number of these practices. For example under "software project planning" are the key practices "A software lifecycle with predefined stages of manageable sizes is identified or defined." and "Estimates for the size of the software work products (or changes to the size of software work products) are derived according to a documented procedure". Another example is under "software project tracking and oversight" where a key practice is "The project's software effort and cost are tracked, and corrective actions are taken as necessary".

Summary

Software development project management is typically dominated by labor costs and is difficult to manage especially in terms of obtaining good interim estimates of time to complete and cost at completion. This article has presented some techniques for effectively using earned value analysis to obtain completion time and cost estimates and thus better manage software development projects.

WORKS CITED

1. Abba, Wayne. "Earned Value Management Rediscovered", http://www.acq.osd.mil/pm/newpolicy/misc/abba_art.html
2. Brandon, Daniel. "Implementing Earned Value Easily and Effectively", Project Management Journal, Vol. 29, No. 2, June 1998
3. Christensen, David and Daniel Ferens. "Using Earned Value for Performance Measurement on Software Projects", Acquisition Review Quarterly, Spring 1995, 155 - 171
4. Christensen, David S., et al., "A Review of Estimate at Completion Research", Journal of Cost Analysis, Spring 1995
5. Fleming, Quentin and Joel Koppelman. Earned Value Project Management, Project Management Institute, 1996, [ISBN 1-880410-38-9]
6. Fleming, Quentin and Joel Koppelman. "Earned Value Project Management, A Powerful Tool for Software Projects", CROSSTALK, The Journal of Defense Software Engineering, July 1998, 19 – 23
7. Hallows, Jolyon. Information Systems Project Management, Amacom,1998 [ISBN 0-8144-0368-9]
8. Kiewel, Brad. "Measuring Progress in Software Development", PM Network, January 1998, 29 - 32
9. Lewis, James. Project Planning, Scheduling & Control, Irwin 1995, Chapter 10, 1995 [ISBN 1-55738-869-5]
10. Paulk, Mark, Bill Curtis, Mary Chrissis, Charles Weber. "Capability Maturity Model, Version 1.1", IEEE Software, Vol. 10, No. 4, July 1993, 18 – 27
11. Project Management Institute Standards Committee (1996). A Guide to the Project Management Body of Knowledge (PMBOK‰ guide), Project management Institute
12. Raz, Tzvi, Shlomo, Globerson. "Effective Sizing and Content Definition of Work Packages", Project Management Journal, December 1998
13. Yeates, Don and James Cadle. Project Management for Information Systems, Pitman Publishman 1996 [ISBN 0-273-62019-3]

Abstract Interaction Specification for Information Services

Wolfram Clauss & Jana Lewerenz
Computer Science Institute, Brandenburg Technical University
PF 101344, 03013 Cottbus, Germany
Tel.: +49-355-692711, Fax: +49-355-692766, {clauss,jl}@informatik.tu-cottbus.de

ABSTRACT

The design of human-computer interaction consumes a significant portion of the resources assigned to the development of state-of-the-art information services. The results, nevertheless, are frequently unsatisfactory: interfaces are platform-dependent and not very flexible. Information services call for a technology that raises interaction specification from system to application level and incorporates it into an integrated framework of structure, functionality, and user-interface design—creating the opportunity for paradigm-independent development and automatic translation for a multitude of target platforms. Particularly important are mechanisms that make such an abstract specification method accessible to designers at various levels of expertise.

INTRODUCTION

A trend in information systems is the shift from specifically trained users and a purpose-oriented computer infrastructure towards unexperienced, occasional users expecting to access information systems through whatever device they know and like. Interactive information systems, particularly if they offer public access, have to become *information services*.

Usability *is a decisive criterion for successful information services. Usability has two aspects, (a) adequacy to the task the system is to solve, and (b) an efficient and effective interaction with its human users. As appropriate interaction capabilities are essential for a system to serve its purpose, both aspects are highly inter-connected. Surprisingly, design techniques and tools do not systematically exploit this connection to achieve an improved design productivity. Is it necessary, for example, to spend a significant time and effort on issues like window and button placement, color, fonts, etc.,* besides *designing the complete structure and functionality of an application?*

The problem of productivity in interaction design is widely recognized. Design and implementation of interaction consumes an average of 45-50% of time and costs in current system development projects, up to 100% in extreme cases [MR92]. A more application-centered specification promises to decrease these efforts.

THE SCOPE OF INTERACTION ABSTRACTION

Flexibility of interaction. One major reason for unsatisfying productivity is that, in too many aspects, interaction design is directed towards proprietary environments. Interaction environments have a diversity of technical and social parameters, with respect to which an application is deployed.

- Technical environments may consist of different platform systems, communication protocols, devices, co-operating applications, etc. Specifically, a design technology should allow addressing a variety of *interaction paradigms* as distinct as window-based GUIs or natural-language interfaces, without the necessity of costly re-designing and re-implementing most parts of an application.
- Varying backgrounds and abilities of users form the social environment of an information service. Some aspects are different native languages, preferences and expectations, levels of expertise, cognitive abilities, etc., to which a high-quality interface must adapt.

Currently, these environments too often require a separate design/realization process, decreasing the efficiency of system development. Consequently, a higher degree of flexibility is necessary, which only automatic interaction generation offers. Therefore, the application specification *must* abstract from concrete environments.

Automatic interaction generation. Automatic realization of interaction has long received attention from researchers and practitioners. Schlungbaum/Elwert [SE96] provide a summary of existing projects. They point out that (a) automatically generated interfaces still lack ergonomic quality and that (b) specification languages used are difficult to learn and to use. We add that (c) automatic generation is still directed towards particular platform paradigms (typically graphical windowing interfaces and/or text-oriented forms interfaces), significantly decreasing the usability and maintainability of specifications. Further, (d) the focus on a specific paradigm makes the designer concentrate too early on transient details of the representation instead of *abstract behavior patterns* of the application.

Paradigm-independent and hierarchical interaction specification. In the following, we introduce *paradigm-independent* concepts for interaction specification (section 3). We keep specifications abstract with respect to possible physical realizations so that an automatic translation into different target paradigms is possible. This avoids thinking in terms of screen positions and graphical widgets and allows applying more universal concepts that can be used to address high-level graphical windowing systems, simple one-line displays, natural-language interfaces, etc. Instead of detering by details that concern the implementation on a particular interface system, interaction specification is raised towards a purely application-oriented level. Finally, mapping mechanisms are employed to automatically translate abstract specifications into different physical representations (section 4.2).

The process of interaction specification involves different classes of developers: from highly-specialized application template designers over customizing programmers to self-customizing users. To accommodate for diverse levels of experience, the use of a hierarchical specification methodology (section 4.1) is advisable. Thus, developers may trade a lower degree of ease-of-use for more details that can be manipulated and for greater influence on interaction structuring and composition.

We consider interaction specification as an *integral part* of the overall system specification [CT97]. Data structures, functionality, and interaction strongly relate to each other. They must be designed simultaneously, ensuring a high degree of specification consistency and completeness. Too often this integration does only happen informally *in the mind of the designer* who goes back and forth between different aspects during development.

ABSTRACT INTERACTION REQUIREMENTS
General Interaction Model

We base interaction specification on our integrated model for application design [CLS99]. Its main elements are data (structural elements) and processes (functional elements), which in turn are either computational processes or interaction processes. The designer structures and relates these elements using a variety of semantical concepts.

As a simple interpretation, consider ordinary computational processes as *internal* transformation units. The specified system incorporates concrete definitions on how to transform input data into output data. From a functionality-oriented point of view, interaction processes are nothing but *external* transformation units. They consume input data (e.g., to present it to the user) and produce output data (e.g., the user's typing). Here, it is the user who „magically" performs this transformation. (This process-oriented model uses the terms input and output in a reversed sense with respect to common interaction terminology.)

Information services generally have multiple, concurrently working users. To achieve a fully independent execution of individual interaction processes, they need to be completely localized. All information necessary for execution and control of a particular interaction process is incorporated into its run-time instance through (static) specification or (dynamic) parameterization. The complete specification of interaction processes includes the following components:

• The *input data type* captures the structure of data that is supplied to the interaction process by other processes. We employ a very expressive category-theoretic type system to put as much semantics as possible into this part.

Either the input data is directly provided to the user, or it controls the interaction process. The type information is necessary for selecting possible *corresponding* interaction patterns (for mapping the data to appropriate interface constructs). The type ·list(a)Ò, for instance, maps to scroll lists on a GUI, to verbal enumerations in a natural language interface, etc.

• The *output data type* specifies the structure of data that results from user input and/or from internal processing and is supplied to further processes.

The output type information serves two purposes:

1. Selecting appropriate interface constructs, e.g., selection boxes, slide bars, buttons, etc.
2. Controling the integrity checking of user actions. This is useful if the available constructs of a specific device do not support necessary correctness checks (i.e., the device is too „weak" for the requirements of the application).

• The *interaction process description* contains abstract properties of the data involved. It captures data *meaning* beyond structural information (types): the *concepts* to be communicated during interaction.

Interaction process descriptions contain the *contents* of non-explicit interaction rather than the *method* to communicate them. The methods, concrete materializations, are a matter of the automatic interaction generation, which is based on such abstract content descriptions and properties. Details concerning the content of interaction process descriptions are given below.

Variations in Functionally Equivalent Interaction Processes

Imagine you want to tell somebody who plans visiting you how he/she reaches your home. You do this either on the phone, by letter, or by e-mail.

- On the phone you would verbalize taking care to give information in small units so your visitor can make notes, and often reactivate context information to ensure he/she will not forget what you already told.
- A letter would allow to include a map so that hardly any textual information is necessary.
- In an e-mail (without attached images) you would again verbalize, but you can go straight ahead with your description since the reader has your e-mail as permanent reference.

Obviously, *how* you communicate is fundamentally different in each of those cases. But isn't the concept (*what* you communicate) always the same? Do you *think* differently about the way to your home because you talk or draw or write? No. This is a major intention and contribution of this paper: explaining the need and providing the means to abstractly capture the content of interaction, talking about concepts rather than concrete materializations. Only on the basis of abstract specifications is a flexible and automatic interaction realization possibleæexactly as humans do when they perform their everyday communications.

Content of Interaction Process Description

The interaction process description is the place to include abstract data characteristics and relations. These abstract properties are used to control the interaction realization, i.e.,

- to structure interaction steps (for breaking information down into smaller units) and
- to select appropriate interaction constructs and settings.

For a more sophisticated example, we now look at organizing a whole trip instead of simply visiting somebody. Imagine trying to find accomodation at a certain place and an appropriate transportation. The interaction processes involved are the input of the search information (get_flight_data, get_hotel_data), the display of flights and hotels found and the selection of one each (select_flight, select_hotel), and the display of the finally chosen flight and hotel (display_flight, display_hotel). Computational processes involved are the search for appropriate flights and hotels (find_flights, find_hotels).

Since you should have the choice of consulting your favorite travel agency either by phone (using a natural language interface), by a graphical windowing system or any other interface system, abstract interface specification as the basis for automatic interaction generation seems very appropriate.

We distinguish the following functionality-oriented attributes that an interface description can carry (besides input and output type information). Below, we give a more detailed overview of these typical abstract interaction process properties.

- Assisting data of the interaction process,
- Data characterizations, defining properties of the individual data elements that are related to the interaction, and
- Data relations, determining the relationships between these data elements.

These properties are *patterns* typical for interactive information systems. The language has to provide the necessary power to *express* these patterns. Application-dependent extensions are still possible, and a suitable specification language (whether textual or graphical) has to include generic constructs for these extensions.

Assisting data. This data is commonly (but not necessarily) constant, as opposed to data that other processes provide dynamically. Assisting data contains explanations, default information, etc.

In our travel agency, the name of the agency's place of business is used as constant assisting data in the get_flight_data process where it serves as default for the place of departure.

assisting_data (address_of_travel_agent, „Cottbus")
...
rel_default (place_of_departure, address_of_travel_agent)

Qualitative data characterization. Data can be associated with concept categories and/or usage patterns.

- Categoric characterization assigns particular semantics to a certain object. It is often captured by the type information itself. If we specify a type flight, the type-based mappings during interaction generation process this information, for instance to visually distinguish flight information from hotel information. Types (especially basic types) can additionally be enriched with categoric characterizations to supplement the mere type information.
- Usage characterization is motivated by speech act theory [Sea69] that distinguishes several illocutionary forces. These express the way of using language to achieve a reaction from the hearer. The classical illocutionary forces are:
- Assertives (the speaker identifies himself with the truth content of the fact uttered),
- Directives (the speaker tries to initiate a particular action by the hearer),
- Commissives (the speaker commits himself to some future activity),

- Declarations (the speaker tries to establish a fact as true by uttering it) and
- Expressives (the speaker states a particular mental attitude).

Commissives, expressives and declarations are not typical for information services (although in some cases they may be). Here,· we exemplarily focus on assertives and directives and on which possibilities exist to express their semantic properties.

Often the property of being assertion or directive can be inferred from the role the respective data is playing in an interaction process. Most information for the user (input data) will be assertions, and the system will simply display or utter these. Directives are employed to elicit information from the user (output data). Here, the system can use input fields, prompts, verbal requests, etc. Exceptions are input data not simply intended for informing the user but for invoking some reaction: Alerts, warnings, etc. are (functionally) input data and yet need to be explicitly characterized as directives since they aim at initiating some activity. Available means of expressing this property are, e.g., color, special fonts (textual or graphical interfaces), beeps (interfaces with audio facilities) or sharp voice and higher volume (natural language interfaces).

Quantitative data characterization. Quantitative characteristics measure the correspondence of data to certain criteria. We can think of application-independent criteria like relevance or priority. Relevance is useful to decide which data to drop or to make available only through hyper-links (in case of space restrictions). Priority controls the emphasis put on information, by particular color scheme, by font types, by data positioning, etc. Other criteria like expensiveness, age or duration are application-dependent.

Rules can modify characteristics, like most other properties. For instance, if a price limit on the flight is set, the price information of the flights found should be emphasized in the process select_flight (value „1" on a scale from 0 to 1).

> char_emphasis(select_flight,found_flights[flight.price]=
>   if flight_search.limit<>"none" then 1 else 0.5)

An expensiveness criterion to flights might visualize or verbalize a price ranking. In this case, the respective criterion is computed by the following rule:

> char_expensive(select_flight,found_flights[flight]=
>   flight.price/MAX(found_flights[flight.price]))

Data relations. *Data relations* capture different types of connections between information. We broadly distinguish quantifying, organizational and rhetorical relations.

- Quantifying relations are similar to quantifying characteristics. They measure the correspondence of data to different criteria. They do not, however, give an absolute measure but grade data in relation to each other. For instance, when hotel information is displayed in the process select_hotel, the name information has a higher priority than the date information: The name is displayed or uttered more prominently.

> rel_priority(date_of_departure=0.5*name)
> rel_priority(date_of_arrival=date_of_departure)

Quantifying relations can also be connected with rules.

- Organizational relations abstractly determine the arrangement of information in relation to each other. Adhesion specifies the connectivity between information items, i.e., how strongly data „belong" to each other. To realize adhesions, information is displayed close together (the one right below the other, within the same data window, etc.), put forward within one sentence/utterance and the like. If we ask for the start and end date of a journey, we want, for instance, to display the appropriate directives close to each other. Thus we specify a high adhesion (value „1" on a scale from 0 to 1).

> rel_adhesion(start_date,end_date,1)

Sequences determine a particular order in which data should be provided or elicited which is not functionally motivated but ergonomically. They are used to split large information „chunks" into smaller units and to utter them sequentially or to decide on a certain sequence to display information within a window.

- Rhetorical relations between data are motivated by text-related and conversation-oriented research [ABWF+97, MT87]. In refinement of a first rough classification [Lew98], we here distinguish between narrative and conversational relations.

Narrative relations concern dependencies between information to be conveyed to the user. Examples are elaboration, context, summary, etc. Presented with a set of possible hotels, there will, for instance, exist some additional information on each hotel, which is characterized as elaboration to the mere hotel name.

> rel_elaboration(found_hotels[hotel.name],
> found_hotels[hotel.info])

This information is either explicitly marked as elaboration and provided in conjunction with the name or it is made available via a hyper-link concept. Narrative relations can also adapt interaction to specific *requirements of the information service's environment*. They allow to cope with various user interest (level of detail) or space restrictions.

Conversational relations connect information to be provided to the user with information to be elicited. Typical examples are default, choice or suggestion. We already established the default relation between the address of a travel agent and the place of departure. Such relations are used to address specific constructs on the target interface system. Whereas in other cases input data is uttered and output data is elicited, it is here important to use a functionality which connects input and output data. It makes no sense telling there is some default for the place of departure and still requiring to type that information in. Rather users should have the choice between accepting the default or overwriting it.

The properties contained in the above classification are obviously completely application-oriented and independent from specific physical interaction systems. Yet they have a great power to control the flow and the appearance of interaction. Mapping mechanisms can exploit these properties

- To chose appropriate presentations (constructs and settings) for each information item and the relevant characteristics and relations,
- To select information items and properties according to the user requirements and interest and according to physical capabilities of the target interface system, and
- To structure interaction according to user abilities and system particularities.

Our intention is the presentation of a *methodology* for abstract specification and automatic realization of interaction. Therefore, the above classification is exemplary only. Application-dependent extensions are always possible and often required. The context model for this specification method offers the possibility to do so [CLS99].

The following section sets forth how this abstract machinery is made accessible both to designer and system, although the requirements from both perspectives appear rather contradictory.

SPECIFYING AND TRANSLATING INTERACTION REQUIREMENTS
A Hierarchy of Specification Languages

The emergence of new application fields and new interaction technologies is unpredictable. Thus, a design technique should be able to support a wide range of possible application domains and a variety of interface system capabilities. On the other hand, a complete language for interaction specification would have to contain a tremendous number of possible data characterizations and data relations. In section 3, we only gave a limited overview of fundamental concepts that it must typically support. Many reasonably complex specification languages for interaction are subject to the drawback stated by Schlungbaum and Elwert [SE96\l „SE96"]: they give rise to overwhelming difficulties in learning and using such a complex language.

The solution is, again, abstraction. A designer should have access to a language that he or she understands and that is appropriate to the current task. We group these different but inter-dependent languages into a *language hierarchy*. Several specification languages represent the trade-off between a lower level of expertise required and a smaller amount of influence on interaction composition and processing, and vice versa. At the same time, such a hierarchy does never need to be considered final; it is always open to the inclusion of further specification languages containing new specification elements if the application domain requires.

We illustrate this concept using an apparently simple specification task. Imagine languages that allow the definition of line spacing for a text-writing device (screen, printer, etc.). The following examples form a language hierarchy as explained.

- Such a language can be empty, meaning that the designer has no influence on this parameter and no learning effort at all.
- It can consist of a range of non-negative real numbers with the semantics that a number determines the line spacing as a multiple of a standard value. (This level typically occurs in word-processors.)
- The language can consist of pairs of two values indicating a lower bound and an upper bound in which the system chooses the optimum line spacing based on some pre-determined criteria. (Type-setting systems commonly offer this language.)
- ...
- In the extreme case, it might also be a Turing-complete programming language whose sole purpose is computing the optimum value for each line distance. This case offers highest flexibility but is most difficult to comprehend. For instance, the designer needs knowledge of type-setting rules and conventions, device properties, the semantics of all possible parameters for this computation, such as screen or paper size, used fonts, line and page content, visual distribution of objects, etc.

For general interactive system specification, we start with a specification language allowing us to define the input types and output types of all interaction processes and nothing else (i.e., the pure functionality of the interaction). The resulting, automatically generated interfaces will admittedly appear not very fancy. But with at least something achieved, the designer's motivation to continue using this method will keep up and allows stepwise learning and applying more complicated concepts. Fully functional prototypes are available earlier, and systems at that level are free of representational details. Step by step, more sophisticated specification languages can be introduced and applied. As long as we provide translations from existing languages (using parameterization), previous specifications continue to work.

It is important to notice that lower level (i.e., more detailed) languages completely cover the expressive power of their higher level counterparts. The semantics is richer at lower levels, such that the designer has a greater influence on details. However, it is not necessary (although possible) that syntactic constructs of higher levels are present at lower levels. It is sufficient if they are *definable*. This distinction of syntactic and semantic properties helps keeping the respective languages small.

Specification Translations

As previously proposed, we separate the translation of specifications for concrete target systems (i.e., the interface generation) into two steps. The reason behind this is to provide a *Lingua Franca* level between a set of application-oriented specification languages on the one hand and a set of concrete interaction languages (e.g., API libraries of a graphical user-interface) on the other hand. The two steps are the following:

1. A *paradigm-independent* translation of the high-level constructs of a given specification into a primitives-based intermediate language.
2. A *paradigm-dependent* translation from the intermediate language into a particular target system.

The latter step, the paradigm-dependent translation, is based on type mappings: input types and output types are mapped onto target constructs. A „style guide" defines those mappings. The preceding paradigm-independent translation serves the purpose of achieving such a primitives-based, but still paradigm-independent specification.

Translation into primitives-based specifications. A primitive in this sense is a language construct that each interface device can immediately handle, either directly or through execution of a device driver program. (The allegory to hardware devices is deliberate, although our „devices" might be as complicated as a complete graphical window system.)

The highest-level specification language (only based on input types and output types) is already primitives-based. Adding any new language element to capture more application semantics also includes to provide translations for it. In the following, such translations are sketched by examples:

• For *assisting information* further data elements (types) are introduced. The assisting data can now be handled exactly like common input and output data, i.e., further type mappings can be applied to them. The reason for „hiding" assisting information in the first place was to decrease complexity in large system developments, and this step promotes assisting data back into a first class citizen to enable its processing.

• *Data characteristics* result in the definition of new data types and in the definition of corresponding paradigm-dependent mappings.

We consider types as completely denoting the semantics of information. Characterizations can always be expressed by type refinements. The corresponding paradigm-dependent type mappings (see below) will then need to be extended to be able to cope with these refinements.

• *Relations* can also often be replaced by refined types. However, structural modifications are sometimes required, too.

Default relations, for instance, have to be replaced by a structure which introduces the 1-type (the one-element set) for capturing the users acceptance of the default value. Furthermore, an additional process responsible for the checking of the actual interaction process output needs to be included: If the output is of the type 1 then propagate the default value, else the newly entered value.

Another example are context or also elaboration relations. These mean that the respective context or elaboration information has to be added as additional input data to the interaction process in question, and that this data has to be used in a very specific sense.

For each additional interaction constructs to be included (besides the primitive constructs), our system architecture requires providing a translation mechanism, for instance as a macro library. The result of such translations are expressions in the intermediate language itself [CLS99]. They are still completely paradigm-independent.

For the realization of such translations, efficient and well-established formalisms are at our disposal. We use graph-rewriting techniques [Roz97] as transformation method, which are efficient because the underlying graphs are highly structured in average applications.

Type mappings. Type mappings are the base mechanism for the paradigm-dependent translation of primitives-based specifications for particular target systems. They are used to convert the types that occur in primitives-based specifications into concrete constructs of the system in question, e.g., a list of small cardinality into a list box (GUI), a verbal enumeration (natural language interface), etc.

Similar to the type structure of applications, each interface system offers a collection of basic and complex types that it can either present to or read from the user (a text-entry field is of type string, a button of type 1, multiple elements form a record or a union, depending on their structure, and so on). The paradigm-dependent translation "simply" has to integrate both sides by extending the respective type systems until they fit.

An old-fashioned command-line interface, for example, does not have a construct for reading a list of values from the user. A solution would be to supply the interface with a list-typed construct simply as a complex dialog that consists of a repeated data entry. As the system has internal knowledge of the structure of the type list, it can even derive this complex dialog behavior from that knowledge.

Frequently, many possible mappings are conceivable. One mapping can be selected accordingly to user preferences and to compositional guidelines. Preferences information ("style guides") determines this selection. As style guides can theirselves be manipulated at run-time, selection and, thus, user and system adaption, is dynamic. To express these type mappings, powerful parametric languages for semantically rich data structures are available (e.g., [BLS+94, Cla96, SF93]).

CONCLUSION

We have proposed a mechanism for interaction specification that allows the manipulation of a wide range of abstract representational aspects. We also have motivated the use of a hierarchical or multi-level language concept to give access to the specification for designers with different levels of expertise. At the same time, this approach ensures the extendibility of language hierarchies in case new aspects and features of interaction need to be addressed. We have not presented a specification language because we do not think there is *one* such language. Instead, we are interested in properties and patterns that languages for interactive systems should have.

We consider interaction specification as an integral part of the overall system development. In our approach, interaction specification remains completely abstract which frees the designer of considerations of implementational issues and which furthermore guarantees flexibility insofar as it remains usable for translation into a wide range of target systems. The trade-off is that developers would have to switch to the specification of What an interaction is to achieve instead of How it has to do this—which might be less intuitive, at least in the beginning.

In the long run, this approach seems to provide a solution for the problem that most applications outlive the paradigms of their interfaces. In the short run, it adds the flexibility of targeting multiple *very* distinct interaction platforms.

In order to increase system independence, we use two main translation steps to convert a specification: first, a paradigm-independent translation (using graph rewriting) to map into a primitives-based specification and, second, a paradigm-dependent translation (using type mappings) to translate the structural specification primitives into concrete target system constructs.

In a prototype we are currently developing, we have implemented the basic (still purely functionality-oriented) mechanisms of automatic translation. Step by step, we are also building a library of abstract interaction properties as described in the first parts of this paper to prove the advantage of abstract interaction specification.

ACKNOWLEDGMENT

We thank Bernhard Thalheim and Thomas Feyer from the database research group at Cottbus for fruitful discussions on this topic.
* Supported by the German Research Society, Berlin-Brandenburg Graduate School in Distributed Information Systems (DFG grant no. GRK 316).

REFERENCES

ABWF+97 Jan Alexandersson et al. Dialogue acts in VERBMOBIL-2. Verbmobil-Report 204, DFKI Saarbrücken, May 1997.

BLS+94 Peter Buneman et al. Comprehension syntax. *SIGMOD Record*, 23(1):87-96, March 1994.

Cla96 Wolfram Clauss. Using structural recursion as query mechanism for data models with references. *Proc. ER'96*, Cottbus, 1996.

CLS99 Wolfram Clauss, Jana Lewerenz, Srinath Srinivasa. Modeling concepts and translations for interactive information systems. Submitted for publication (see http://www.informatik.tu-cottbus.de/jl/publ/ps/pods99.ps), 1999.

CT97 Wolfram Clauss, Bernhard Thalheim. Abstraction layered structure-process codesign. *Proc. COMAD'97*, Madras, 1997.

Lew98 Jana Lewerenz. Dialogs as a mechanism for specifying adaptive interaction in database application design. *Proc. CAiSE'98, Doctoral Consortium*, Pisa, 1998.

MR92 Brad A. Myers, Mary Beth Rosson. Survey on user interface programming. *Proc. CHI'92*, Monterey, 1992.

MT87 William C. Mann, Sandra A. Thompson. Rhetorical structure theory: A theory of text organization. Livia

Polanyi, editor, *The structure of discourse*. Ablex, Norwood, N.J., 1987.

Roz97 G. Rozenberg, editor. *Handbook of Graph Grammars and Computing by Graph Transformations*. World Scientific, 1997.

SE96 Egbert Schlungbaum, Thomas Elwert. Automatic user interface generation from declarative models. *Proc. CADUI'96*. Presses Universitaires de Namur, 1996.

Sea69 John A. Searle. *Speech Acts: An Essay in the Philosophy of Language*. Cambridge University Press, 1969.

SF93 Tim Sheard, Leonidas Fegaras. A fold for all seasons. *Proc. 6th Conference on Functional Programming Languages and Computer Architecture*, Copenhagen, 1993.

Reformulating Information Technology Management Higher Education

Eli Cohen and Elizabeth Boyd
Informing Science Institute and the Leon Kozminski Academy of Entrepreneurship and Management
+1.616.785.0041, Eli_Cohen@acm.org

ABSTRACT

What job skills in information management do graduates of higher education require? This question has been asked and answered by academia, industry, and government. Unfortunately, each investigation constituency approaches the question from its own different perspective, and so each answers the question differently. This paper provides framework for understanding and integrating these and other competitive influences. It is the author's hope that this framework will serve as the theoretical foundation for global research leading to a curriculum model for information management instruction in higher education.

THE ISSUE

The wealth of nations depends on their ability to develop their workforces in the use of today's information technology (Reich, 1996; Greenspan, 1996). Yet the necessary changes to education require tremendous political will and leadership (Riley, 1998). To meet these pressing needs literally requires reformulating Higher Education.

The problem of keeping the information worker curriculum up-to-date is not new. Various groups have addressed the issue in the past.

APPROACHES TO THE PROBLEM

Professional organizations are one set of constituents who have addressed the issue of ensuring that the higher education curriculum on information systems remains relevant.

Professional Organizations and University Educators

The organization Association for Information Technology Professionals (formerly DPMA) has sponsored a model curriculum over the past two decades. This curriculum, in its last rendition, is co-sponsored by other IS professional organizations (Feinstein, et al., 1997). The current primary methodology in developing this curriculum model was to ask those teaching IS what topics they consider important. The curriculum development committee then organized the resultant learning objectives into categories and themes and, ultimately, into suggested courses.

The landscape of higher education has changed since the first DPMA model curriculum. The same topics that formerly were studied only by Information Systems departments are now taught in a variety of departments across campus (Cohen, 1995; Couger, 1996). Fields, such as Library Science, now consider knowledge of application design and development essential to their evolving field. Office Systems (formerly secretarial science) is evolving into End-User computing with its own curriculum (OSRA, 1996), and the traditional information systems department splits into subfields with their own curriculum models.

Lastly, on some campuses, computer science departments are expanding their curriculum beyond their own ACM curriculum model to incorporate more and more of the topics within information systems.

Departments of Labor and Commerce

The turf wars waged on campuses have little effect beyond academia. However, government policy issues on educating for a viable workforce affects all levels of society. Of all the governmental agencies, the departments of labor make the clearest cry for change.

US

In the US, reports of the Secretary (of Labor's) Commission on Achieving Necessary Skills (SCANS) (U.S. Department of Labor, 1992) provide the most cogent call for re-forming education. The commission's focus was to ensure that future generations of citizens are prepared to meet the demands of the modern workplace.

One of the outcomes of their research elucidates five necessary job skills for the 21st century: "effective workers can productively use:

- **Resources** — They know how to allocate time, money, materials, space, and staff.
- **Interpersonal skills** — They can work on teams, teach others, serve customers, lead, negotiate, and work well with people from culturally diverse backgrounds.
- **Information** — They can acquire and evaluate data, organize and maintain files, interpret and communicate, and use computers to process information.
- **Systems** — They understand social, organizational, and technological systems; they can monitor and correct performance; and they can design or improve systems.
- **Technology** — They can select equipment and tools, apply technology to specific tasks, and maintain and troubleshoot equipment." (U.S. Department of Labor, 1991)

The findings of SCANS reports are similar to those in other countries, such as Singapore, Malaysia, Australia, and New Zealand.

Likewise the U.S. Department of Commerce predicts a growing shortage in Information Systems workers in the coming decades (Ivens, 1998; Lerman, 1998).

Futurists

Futurists too espouse the need of future workforces to understand and use information tools. For example, Barry Jones (1995), a former Australian cabinet minister, warns of the need to re-form education. The same call is heard by British futurist Charles Handy (1990,1996) and Israeli-American Shoshana Zuboff (1988) , who point out how the nature of work itself is changing.

Lastly, management gurus, such as Walter Wriston (1988-89) and Peter Drucker (1998) write that the ability of a nation's workforce to use information is a competitive force and element of its sovereignty.

Corporation by-pass of university

Universities often encourage bridging the gap between employers' needs and the university curriculum. However, public universities, with their committee structures, are not well equipped for rapid change. Consequently, corporations are looking at other options for educating their workforce, including on-the-job training, apprenticeships, and mini-courses.

The point here is that if higher education is slow in meeting the needs of industry, industry will look elsewhere.

AN INTEGRATED APPROACH

Higher Education must consider the needs of a variety of constituencies. These include, but are not limited to, current and future employers.

Current needs of employers

All of the above approaches (to the problem of educating the future workforce to meet the information demands of the market) agree that the needs of current employers must be considered. The studies conducted by information systems organizations focus on specific information technology skills, such as knowledge of one computer language or communication protocol. Studies by governments focus on broader issues, such as the ability to communicate in one's native tongue.

Future needs of employers

Only the government and futurists have given much attention to the changing nature of the economy. The professional organizations have not dealt with the larger issues, such as the impact of the globalization of industry and the changing nature of work.

LIMITATIONS ON HIGHER EDUCATION

Higher Education, at least the traditional university model, is ill structured to meet the dynamic demands of the world in the information age. In particular, the departmental structure commonly followed by universities does not deal well with the reality that knowledge is not easily compartmentalized.

The problem with compartmentalizing knowledge

Within the university, typically one department exerts political pressure to prevent other departments from "invading their turf", i.e. teaching knowledge which they consider proprietary. In this author's experience, the rationale for such battles is often stated as the need to save the university money by reducing duplicated effort.

Unfortunately, as noted above, knowledge no longer is so easily compartmentalized. In industry, workers bring their specialized knowledge to their work team as most problem cross disciplinary lines. Even highly technical problems involve human and societal issues. (An information systems curriculum that ignores these realities is not complete.)

THE IS EDUCATION INFLUENCES FRAMEWORK

With the above in mind, let us now consider the IS Education Influences Framework. At its center is the university department, the student's primary source of knowledge about their future profession.

Four constituencies influence the content and level of material taught within the department: other departments at the university, other departments at other universities, the students, and the employers.

As noted above, other departments within the same university influence what and how information is presented to students. These are the "turf battles" mentioned above.

Departments at other universities likewise exert influences. One influence is through articulation agreements. Articulation agreements (of which courses at one university will substitute for courses at another) tend to limit the ability of the department to respond to change. Another influence is the tendency for instructors of a course to use and revise resources developed by other professors. Even the requirement some universities impose to retain a text book for a given number of years and the very content of that text book influences what is taught in a given course.

Employers typically exert sizable influence on the curriculum of a given university. A number of factors are involved in this influence; the hiring of graduates, donation of software, individuals serving on advisory boards and as guest lectures are some examples. In some cases, the software selection of a major employer actually determines the software used in the education of information systems students.

Lastly, the students themselves influence the curriculum. The student population of, say, Harvard, differs from the student population at most small schools in a number of ways, such as preparedness in academic skills, abilities to reason and plan, opportunities for summer internship and work after graduation. A student population with a high proportion of working parents requires a different set of expectation than one in which students live on-campus and have few outside responsibilities, demands and limitations.

Beyond the university, national forces influence the nature of the information systems curriculum. Such forces include the availability of resources. For example, Malaysia has set a goal of providing a college education to 80% of its students by the year 2020. Likewise, the U.S. Departments of Commerce, Labor, and Education reports indicates their interest in supporting higher education in information systems.

However, these national forces are not independent of one another. Globally, the forces of the market place to use technology to improve the quality of all products and for firms to compete globally influences all nations to promote the quality of information systems education.

CONCLUSION

There are a number of efforts by various constituencies that share a common goal: determining the current and future requirements for job skill training for information workers. However, these efforts have not yet been coordinated. This paper has outlined a framework for understanding and coordinating these various views and proposed

Figure 1 above depicts this IS Education Influences model.

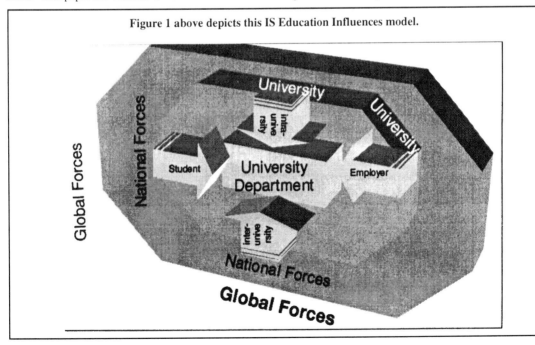

solutions. The next stage in this research will be the transformation of this framework into a unified set of goals and a set of model curricula to meet the needs of the global IS education community.

BIBLIOGRAPHY

Cohen, Eli and Elizabeth Boyd (1995) Active Learning and Reengineering the University: Andragogy Meets Technology, found at http://gise.org/seminar.htm on Jan. 14, 1999.

Cougar, Daniel. (1996) Invited Talk, Information Systems Education Conference, St. Louis, MO.

Drucker, Peter F. (August 24, 1998) "The Next Information Revolution". Forbes ASAP.

Feinstein, David L. et al. IS '97 (1997) Model Curriculum and Guidelines for Undergraduate Degree Programs in Information Systems. Association of Information Technology Professionals: Park Ridge, IL (USA).

Greenspan, Alan. (1996). "Alan Greenspan gives prepared remarks at Syracuse University" MSNBC Business Video, 12-03-1997.

Handy, Charles (1990). The Age of Unreason. Harvard Business School Press: Boston.

Handy, Charles (1996). Beyond Certainty. Harvard Business School Press: Boston.

Ivens, K. 1998. Shortage of IS professionals is growing fast. WinNT Magazine, December 7. Retrieved December 12, 1998 from http://WinNTmag.com/News/NewsStory.cmf?NewsID=1260.

Jones, Barry. (1995) Sleepers, Wake! Technology and the Future of Work.. Oxford University Press Australia: Melbourne.

Lerman, R. 1998. Is there a labor shortage in the information technology industry? Issues in Science and Technology, Spring 1998: 82-83.

Office Systems Research Association (1996), Office Systems Model Curriculum, found at http://pages.nyu.edu/~bno1/osra/model_curriculum/ on Jan. 14, 1999.

Reich, Robert B. (1996) "Labor Secretary Reich offers real-world advice to graduates" US Newswire -6-14-1996.

Riley, Richard W. (1998) Technology and Learning Beyond the Schoolhouse, http://www.ed.gov/News/980909.html

U.S. Department of Labor Employment and Training Administration (1991). What Work Requires of Schools: A SCANS Report for America 2000. The Secretary's Commission on Achieving Necessary Skills. , U.S. Department of Labor Employment and Training Administration: Washington, D.C.

U.S. Department of Labor Employment and Training Administration (1992). Learning a Living: A Blueprint for High Performance: A SCANS Report for America 2000. The Secretary's Commission on Achieving Necessary Skills. , U.S. Department of Labor Employment and Training Administration: Washington, D.C.

Wriston, Walter B. (1988-1989) Technology and Sovereignty. Foreign Affairs, pp. 64-75.

Zuboff, Shoshana (1988) In the Age of the Smart Machine: The Future of Work and Power. Basic Books: New York.

Knowledge Management and Coordination through Method Engineering and Metamodeling: Application of Computer Aided Method Engineering Technology in Industry

A.N.W. Dahanayake, Ph.D.

Faculty of Information Technology and Systems, Department of Information Systems

Delft University of Technology, P.O. Box 356, 2600 AJ Delft, The Netherlands

Telephone: 31 - (0) 15 785811, fax: 31 - (0) 15 2786632, E- mail: A.N.W.Dahanayake@is.twi.tudelft.nl

ABSTRACT

The application of Computer Aided Method Engineering technology to design and implement a knowledge management system that cooperate within number of users with varying information needs in the production industry is presented in this paper. The management and coordination of knowledge through method engineering and metamodeling in an industrial setting is evaluated and discussed.

Key words: knowledge management, coordination, method engineering, CASE, metamodeling

INTRODUCTION

Over the last few decades, computer systems have required increasingly complex software development support. Software engineering process was increasingly structured according to methods and techniques to simplify software development. A variety of CASE tools are available today, that support monolithic I-CASE methodologies, as well as method engineering tools that support any software development methodology. In theory Computer Aided Method Engineering has the strength to simplify and smoothen the software development process by crafting and generating required tools according to required methodology. In this paper the application of Computer Aided Method Engineering technology in an industry setting is evaluated to assess the flexibility in supporting knowledge management and coordination.

THE AVAILABLE KNOWLEDGE AND REQUIRED INFORMATION MODELS

Product development is a competitive industry that constantly have to improve their product development process in response to increasing competition from other industry members mainly due to the availability of new technologies and increased product complexity. These companies have similar product development processes and increasingly suffer from enormous time and quality pressures. The traditional isolated sequential method of product development and the traditional way of making small adjustments to the product development process is no longer appropriate in the modern industry. It was realized that multiple business functions have to be brought together at an early stage of product development process to process a customer demand with an optimum time to market interval, with the highest possible product quality and at a competitive price.

Even though it is common now a days, that the product development process is fully automated, the decision-making factors and knowledge about the product development process is not properly coordinated. A central issue of the early involvement in the product development process is optimization of the supply knowledge to the users such as schedule makers, rather than to the product producers. That means production knowledge must be available in time, at the right moment and in the right format for its users, who are not necessarily the production department. To achieve this it is necessary to determine and chart the knowledge that is created and/or used by the industrial engineering designs and then to determine where, when and how to structure the product development process information to realize company goals. That means the design and implementation of a knowledge management system that cooperate within a number of users with varying information needs and inter-operable tools is the problem that needs attention.

The research involved three industry partners (Texas instruments, Infala and IKU) with similar product development processes. The analysis carried out within a research project at Delft University of Technology [8] was as follows: The distinction between product knowledge and engineering knowledge is based on four types of information that describes the entire knowledge involved in the product development processes (see figure 1). The nature of this knowledge is explained below.

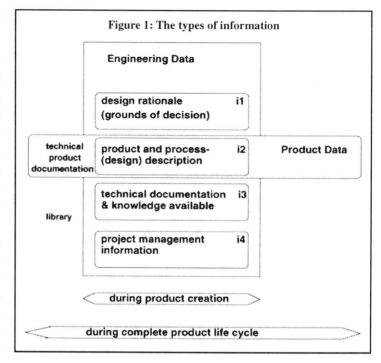

Figure 1: The types of information

Type i1 design rationale: consists of the arguments and reasons for taking design decisions, such as, simulation models, calculations, and test results that are usually concealed in the drawers and files of the engineer and are not accessible to anyone else, though information of this type could be of immense value for subsequent projects. Availability of a design rationale of earlier designs can encourage the re-use of parts of these earlier designs; this type of information is only valuable to the engineering department.

Type i2 product and process design description: defines the product and process design, using for example, drawings or computer models of the product design, prototypes, or lists of requirements, usually collected in a technical product documents. This type of information must be accessible to several departments.

Type i3 library information: expert knowledge is stored in the library, and where the knowledge can be found in catalogues or databases or requested from experts. This information is not specific to the running of a project and does not need to be managed within a project's database.

Type i4 project management information: this information is relevant to the project manager and should include information about costs, time consumed and milestones reached during the project's life.

To be able to make this information types available in the right from in the right place:
- The available knowledge has to be represented in a data model containing these types of information.
- The required models of management information have to be abstracted and represented in the required form.

In other words, these four types of information need to be represented in a generic model to be charted in the required form, using a set of automated tools, to improve the information access to the person who requires the information and where it is required. The development process, which is also described in the models, can be improved by tuning the development process to the information requirements and by tuning the activities of the process to each other.

Figure 2 represents the contents of a company specific data model and the way this data is represented and analyzed using diagram techniques for different tasks in the knowledge management system. This offers insight into and an overview of the products and the processes involved.

The data model includes the development process and the information structure, but also the users and producers of information, the time consumed in the development process, the systems used and the relationships between all these aspects. The data model is derived from the relationship between the product development method and the organization by splitting the organization into three objects:
-The acting system which is the subject
- The treated system, which is the object, called the information
- In between these two lies the action or process, the activity

These three elementary objects are considered to be appropriate to chart the relevant aspects of product and process development process, and they form the main building blocks of the data model.

The database building blocks are modeled in an object-oriented manner including attributes and relationships

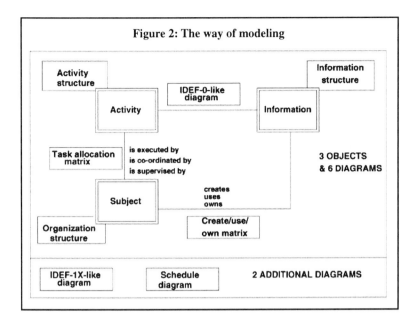

Figure 2: The way of modeling

between the objects.

The information users define a set of eight models. Out of these, three of them represent the relationships within the objects (one-dimensional) and another three represent the relationships between the objects (two-dimensional).

The three one-dimensional models are:
- Organizational Structure Chart (OSC) which gives the relationships within the subject object
- Activity Structure Chart (ASC) which gives the relationships within the activity object
- Information Structure Chart (ISC) which gives the relationship within the information object

The three two dimensional models are:
- IDEF-O {Integrated computer-aided manufacturing DEFinition-O-like} diagram which gives the relationship between activity and information objects
- Create/Use/Own Matrix (CUOM) which gives the relationships between information and subject objects
- Allocation of Tasks Matrix (TAM) which gives the relationships between activity and subject objects
    Further, two additional models are given.

WHY COMPUTER AIDED METHOD ENGINEERING

Product development process contains the engineering and product knowledge of one or several products. The data that contains this knowledge is distributed in terms of local models of the users and is used in an ad-hoc fashion. Normally these data can not cooperate and are not inter-operable because of the syntactical, semantic and conceptual differences. Therefore, it is required to transform these specific goal oriented islands of information concentrations into cooperative and inter-operable format.

The requirements of a Systems Engineering Environment that could be used to develop a knowledge management system for the product development process was identified using the service based framework given in [3].

The first requirement is a good modeling capability to develop a generic model of the product development process and as well as the models of the generic models of the required tools. In other words a metamodeling is a valid requirement.

Secondly, the required data models of the company specific models and the tools are required. The models have to be consistent and integrated properly to be able to provide cooperation and inter-operability. The requirement of a good modeling service with concepts, constraints and population derivation rules for integrity definitions is a paramount requirement.

As each tool is a part or a view of the generic schema, it needs to define type level as well as instance level views. It should have combinations, overlapping as well as hierarchies of views that can be manipulated. For example the metamodel of the task allocation matrix have to be a view of the concepts required from the product development process model. The task allocation matrix that user requires is a view of the data instances. A view definition service is required to represent different tools that could share a generic schema.

The system requires a number of different user interfaces according to the user requirements. For example an object can appear in two or more tools with different out looks, or representations. Therefore to be able to define user specific user interfaces a representationally independent user interface service is required. The above described requirements are necessary to generate different tools or methods.

A good storage and manipulation service is required that could handle all these layers of data. The storage and manipulation service has to be a layered database system, which contains the meta-meta, meta, data as well as the operational data.

The instance generation and performance have to be taken into consideration. A good query facility needs to be available to handle the dynamic nature of the stored data. Together with the storage and manipulation service, a transaction service is required with atomic and nested transactions that provide triggers, and could control pre and post conditions.

The logical and physical distribution models of the system have to be distributed among a client server system. This has to be coupled with concurrency and security services to maintain the systems credibility.

The above identified requirements are not available in a single automated Systems Engineering Environments. That means a Computer Aided Systems Engineering environment with a metamodeling and method engineering capability is the required level of automated support to develop the knowledge management system in product development industry. How the Computer Aided Method Engineering (CAME) environment is used to develop the knowledge management system is discussed in the following sections.

THE CAME APPROACH

Method engineering is the engineering discipline to design, construct and adapt methods, techniques and tools for the development of information systems [6]. Computer Aided Systems Engineering with a Method Engineering capability is a Computer Aided Method Engineering environment. There are many such environments normally called MetaCASE are available in the market. In this research an environment developed at the Delft University of Technology called Meta-CAME is used to develop the system required for this particular problem [2].

The Meta-CAME approach differs from other MetaCASE approaches, which focus more on the representation of the methods as first order logical theories, or graphical behavior of design objects. The Meta-CAME approach has some similarity to the MetaEdit+[5] approach from the viewpoint of conceptual modeling. Where the design of a method specification is akin to the development of a conceptual schema of a software repository and the design of a CASE tool resembles the design of an external view to a conceptual schema [1]. A specific difference of this approach with respect to the MetaEdit+ approach is the ability to define arbitrary process description and to support arbitrary process specification, which is important for selecting the suitable method or its parts for a specific problem area [4]. Also, specifically to this problem, the ability to define integrated schemas and data population according to data model's specifications, or the possibility to define executable models is an advantage of the Meta-CAME. The Meta-CAME is implemented on NeXTstep/Objective C Platform, integrating the research areas of MetaCASE and object-oriented service specifications.

The global philosophy behind a CAME environment is that such an environment has to provide the required design tools according to the chosen method particular to a problem situation (see figure 3). The CAME environment functions as a service based object oriented MetaCASE environment, which offers services required for modeling tools by a mechanism interpreting the required modeling knowledge and changing the visual representations to the required form with the use of a graphic object binding mechanism. Further, this environment offers mechanism for population of models specified according to such designed tools. The architecture of the service based CAME environment and a detailed description is available in [2].

SUPPORTING KNOWLEDGE MANAGEMENT AND COORDINATION

The product and process development information determines the underlying foundation of the Knowledge Management System (KMS). The underlying foundation or the metamodel provides the required building blocks for the knowledge management system. The KMS consists of tools for data modeling, population generation and facilitation of six types of tool generation. In addition to this a synonyms editor and a query facility was included. The design and generation of KMS using the CAME environment is as follows:

Data modeling and population generation

The general data model of the participating companies was composed of three building block objects: activity, information and subject, with each

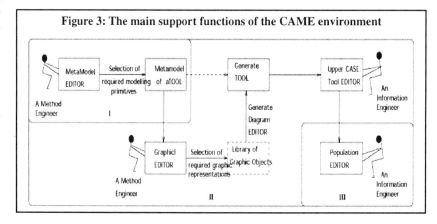

Figure 3: The main support functions of the CAME environment

object having several levels. The objects were used to determine the appropriate detail level of an example model and internal structure of the objects. A level is identified by a number that represents the position of the level within the structure of the object. The numbering used is similar to that used in the Structured Analysis and Design Technique (SADT) [7], a technique that is frequently used in the manufacturing industry and is sometimes called Integrated computer-aided manufacturing DEFinition (IDEF). For example, A0 is the main IDEF diagram in which the activities such as A1, A2,......Am, are presented. Subsequently, the activities are divided into A11, A12,....... and A21,A22,A23, etc., taking into account the hierarchical relationships between the activities. Each object is characterized by its type and is included at one level of an object and is represented by a type attribute.

Activity object

Figure 4 illustrates an activity object with its hierarchical structure of five levels; area of analysis, subdivision of analysis area, producer, task and activity or decision, and the attributes of each level. Each level describes processes with the lower level representing the same process in more detail. The attributes that appear in the levels of activities include the relationships between activity object and the other two main objects. The relationship between the activity object and the information object are included in the task level as required information and delivered information. All attributed levels of activities contain relationships between activity object and subject object, as the contents of these relationships are considered to be different, and these relationships are concerned with responsibility, coordination and execution activities.

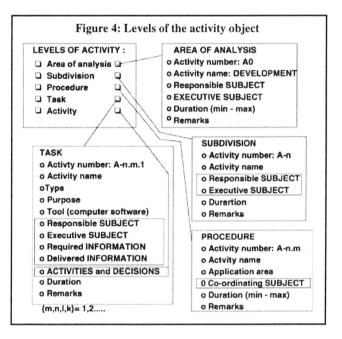

Figure 4: Levels of the activity object

Information object

The information object illustrated in figure 5 is composed of four levels; group of information carriers, information carriers, and group of information elements and information element.

Subject object

The subject object has five levels (see figure 6) and in addition to these levels, there are external subjects such as, client, supplier, competitor and external diverse.

The meta model

The concepts discussed under the three main building blocks were translated accordingly to define the meta model of the product development process using the meta model editor of the CAME environment, see figure 7. Before generating the KMS tools, the data model must be designed and populated. As the tools were intended to be used to present data, a KMS-Tool manager was introduced.

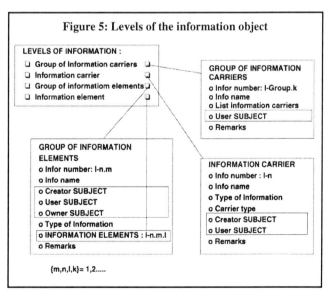

Figure 5: Levels of the information object

Therefore, a simple data model editor was designed within the KMS-Tool manager. This data model editor is a menu driven text editor, where multiple levels of required main objects are allowed to be defined. It enables the selection of relationships and attributes according to the company situations at each level of the three objects. The concepts that are required to appear in the data model editor are those of characters, and therefore, the concept to graphic-object counterpart definition was simple. The only difference was that a simple selection oriented data model editor was required. The data model editor allows the user to add the company specific data model, and this was designed specifically to the taste of the problem solver (see figure 8).

Population generation is associated with a population editor that allows the user to enter, modify or delete instances to the data model and is coupled to the KMS-Tool manger (see figure 9) which takes control of the main activities of the system. Multiple levels of main objects defined in the data model are described by a number of attributes. The population editor assigns values to each attribute and characterizes a main object instance at a certain level. Population editing is

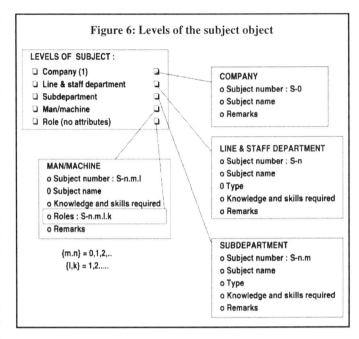

Figure 6: Levels of the subject object

menu driven, and the user selects a main object, the level of the object, and then the desired operation to be performed. For example, after an add operation, a form appears on the screen in which the attributes can be given a value to characterize the instance. This way straightforward add, delete, or modify operations are included according to the problem owners requirements. The population editor also consists a synonym editor, which enables the user to streamline the jargon usage. The synonyms can be defined and the preferred synonym option can be given. The `check synonyms option' can be selected for automatically translating the term used into preferred synonyms during the addition or modification of an instance.

In addition to population generation the KMS-Toolmanager gives the user access to extract and present the entered data in several ways, including simple listings, user defined listings, graphs, trees and matrices. The simplest way to extract data from the database uses the list option. The list button generates a list of all instances in the database. The query facility is associated with the query button, for selectively extracting instances of any kind to be

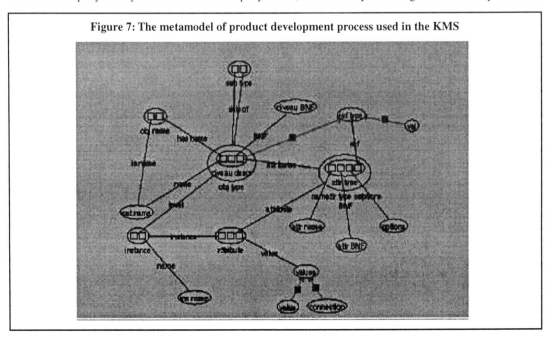

Figure 7: The metamodel of product development process used in the KMS

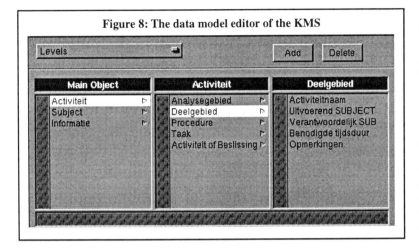

Figure 8: The data model editor of the KMS

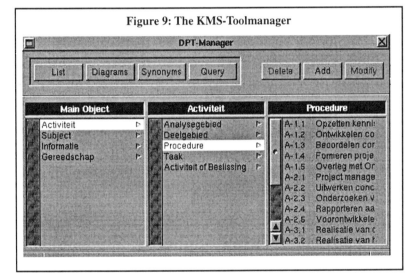

Figure 9: The KMS-Toolmanager

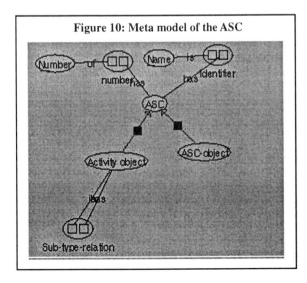

Figure 10: Meta model of the ASC

put on a list for further investigation. These additional options were built into the KMS-Toolmanager to fulfill user requirements.

Activity structure chart

The Activity Structure Chart (ASC) is a one dimensional tree structure of activity hierarchy relationships within the activity object. The attribute activity number of the activity object is the identification that determines the position in the ASC. The components that must appear in the ASC are the instances of activity object and its subtype relationships. The activity structure is maintained in the activity number attribute, and must be sorted out by extracting the required instances.

Figure 10 shows the metamodel that described the information architecture of the ASC. ASC-object is introduced to derive the activity structure chart together with a graphic object called tree-object. The tree-object is provided with the algorithm to calculate the positioning of the Activity-object instances in the hierarchy tree and for including the Sub-type-relationships and positioning rules. The tree-object places the tree chart from left to right on a page and is used for very large tree charts. The required concepts, graphic-object counterparts and their visual shapes including the calculations to generate activity structure charts are shown in table below. Figure 11 shows a part of an ASC generated using the CAME environment. The ASC is quite large owing to the number of object instances in the database and is not presented fully as it contains classified information.

The Information Structure Chart (ISC) and the Organization Structure Chart (OSC) are tools that represent tree structures similar to ASC. Therefore, they are not included as their definition and generation is similar to ASC.

Create/Use/Own matrix

The Create/Use/Own Matrix (CUOM) represents the relationships between the subject and in-

OS-object	Graphic-object	Shape
Activity-object	Activity-object	a square with activity name and number
Sub-type-relation	Sub-type-relation	a line; connecting path in the activity hierarchy
ASC-object	Tree-object	a tree chart spreading from left to right

formation object. This is a matrix that indicates whether a subject, is an information creator, user and/or owner using the letters C, U and O. Creator, user and owner are attributes of information object. The components that have to appear in the CUOM are the instances of subject and information object and the relationships between these are selected at each level of information object according to create, own and user attributes.

The matrix maintains the number and name of subject and information object, and they have to be sorted out by extracting the required instances.

The CUOM matrix is generated fist by designing the metamodel of this tool and using the following graphic object coupling. CUOM-object is introduced to derive a create/user/own matrix together with a graphic

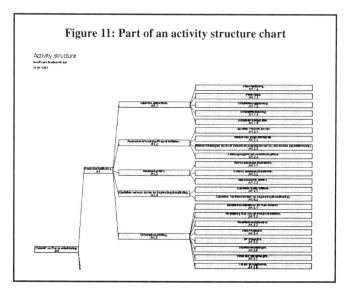

Figure 11: Part of an activity structure chart

object called the matrix-object. The matrix-object is provided with the algorithm to calculate the positioning of the subject and information object instances. The subject and information objects are given graphic text objects to include their name and number. The subject object instances with their name and number are placed horizontally one after another, top to bottom and the information object instances with their name and number are placed vertically from left to right. The matrix-object calculates the maximum number of subject and information object instances involved and the relationships between creator, user and owner attributes of the information object and places this information in the matrix. The matrix-object also takes care of drawing vertical and horizontal lines according to the maximum number of selected object instances. The CUOM is quite large owing to the number of object instances of the database and is not included due to the confidential nature of the data.

The Task Allocation Matrix (TAM) is similar to CUOM matrix except for the fact that it represents the relationships between the subject and activity object.

IDEF-0 like diagram

The Integrated computer-aided manufacturing DEFinition (IDEF)-0-like diagram represents the relationships between the information and activity object. This diagram is used to represent the relationships in a surveyable manner, and is slightly different from the original IDEF-0 diagram and therefore it is called an IDEF-0-like diagram. The boxes represent the instances of the activity object and arrows represent the instances of the information object. The incoming arrows to the left of the activity box represent the information required to carry out an activity, while the outgoing arrows to the right of the activity box represent the information delivered by the activity. The arrow reaching the activity box from the bottom indicate the tools used in the activity, each activity carries its decomposition up to the task level and maintains a hierarchy structure, is similar to Data Flow Diagram (DFD) technique.

The components that have to appear in an IDEF-0-like diagram are the instances of information and activity object and the relationships between these are selected at each level of activity object according to required and delivered attributes. The diagram maintains the number and name attributes of information and activity object, and these are being sorted out by extracting of the required instances. To generate the IDEF-0 like diagram first a metamodel is designed and further the following graphic objects were coupled: activity-object is provided with a graphic object an IDEF-activity graphic object as an adjustable box with activity name and number including an algorithm to calculate the activity decomposition up to task level. Information-object is provided with text graphic object to represent the name and number of the information object instance. The required relationship is given a graphic object with an arrow and a dot at the begin point. The delivered relationship provided with a graphic object, out going arrow. The tool relationship is provided with a graphic object, upward-arrow to indicate the value of the tool attribute. IDFE-object is introduced to derive an IDEF-0 like schema together with a graphic object IDEF-graphic-object. The IDEF-graphic-object is provided with an algorithm to calculate positioning of the activity object and information object instances in relation to the required and delivered attributes of the activity object. The IDEF-graphic-object places the required and delivered graphic objects by calculating their relative position, and also places the upward-arrow in the correct position indicate the tool attribute. The amount of information in one diagram is quite large owing to the number of object instances of the database population. Usually these diagrams are printed on large sheets of paper. Detailed models are not presented for reasons of confidentiality.

THE CONCLUSIONS AND DISCUSSION

The detailed evaluation of the KMS carried out by Vroom [8] on the strength of the CAME technology as a supporting platform for structuring the workflow information for optimizing the supply information can be summarized as follows. The modeling tools required to structure the production process of three production organizations were generated successfully. This was achieved by first modeling the schema description of the product development process and generating six tools to present data in the required form. The databases were populated with real information from the production processes of the participating organizations and each database contained around 3500 object instances. Performance was low but reliable, as the experiment was conducted using an index structure instead of an Object Oriented database. At the same time providing, IDEF-0-like graphic representations as well as matrix and tree structures demonstrated the degree of representational independence.

The CAME principle proved a step forward in conceptual modeling. It proved that the conceptual modeling is not limited to information systems development but also applicable to other engineering disciplines, when coupled with Computer Aided Method Engineering facility. The experiment proved the ability of the environment to support multiple methods, in this case, data modeling and six modeling techniques. The resulting models gave a method integration level as required and a reliable information retrieval and computational facility. It showed a stable tool set integration, multi-tool, and multi-method support by the performances in real-life situations of knowledge management system. The meta modeling technique described within the CAME environment supported the demands of integrity and consistency of repository that is required for KMS during concurrent access by different tools. The novel method specification and generation mechanism answered the needs of the highly diverse representational paradigms, i.e., graphic, tree and matrix structures and information processing requirements.

The environment and its underline theory based on metamodeling proved that the method engineering is a feasible approach for handling inter-operability and cooperation of knowledge management and coordination. The experiment was limited to a set of information presentation tools in a distributed environment. The requirement of not only the Database Presentation tools but also the ability to experiment with presented results was seen as one of the important issues. The ability to couple computational facilities within the architectural specifications by associating graphic objects with algorithms and procedures is a good indication that the platform is extendable to generate better knowledge management tools for decision support process. In reality the decision support tools need to be cooperative within the business information system. Therefore, in future the research will be conducted to assess this aspect. Further the main building block components of the datamodel will be coupled to simulation tools to further fine tune the decision making process. In this respect the research has shown the feasibility of method engineering in an industrial setting for developing knowledge management systems.

The Computer Aided Method Engineering technology is a feasible way to direct towards providing number of inter-operable tools for any software engineering methodology. The integration of legacy systems with new functionalities according to the organizational needs can be attained, with the use of Computer Aided Method Engineering, when available within a CASE environment. In this way Computer Aided Method Engineering can be directed towards designing and development of evolvable software systems for the benefits of future needs.

REFERENCES

[1] ANSI. Study Group on Data Base Management Systems: Interim Report 75-02-08. Technical Report 7(2), ACM SIGMOND Newsletter, 1975.

[2] A.N.W. Dahanayake. An Environment to Support Flexible Information Systems Modeling, PhD thesis, Delft University of Technology, The Netherlands, 1997.

[3] A. Dahanayake, J. Bosman, G. Florijn and R.J. Welke. A Framework for Modeling Repositories. In Proceedings of the 3rd workshop on NEXT Generation of CASE Tools, Manchester, UK, May 1992.

[4] A.N.W. Dahanayake, H.G. Sol and J.L.G. Dietz. A Fully Flexible CAME in a CASE Environment. In 16th International Conference on Conceptual Modeling - ER97, L.A., California, USA, November 1997. Springer-Verlag, Lecture Notes in Computer Science.

[5] S. Kelly, K. Lyytinen and M. Rossi. MetaEdit+ A fully Configurable Multi-User and Multi-Tool CASE and CAME Environment. In Proc. Of 8th International Conference CaiSE'96, Advanced Information Systems Engineering, Greece, June 1996. Springer-Verlag.

[6] K. Kumar and R.J. Welke. Method Engineering: A proposal for situational-specific methodology construction. Systems Analysis and Design: A Research Agenda, pages 257-269. 1992.

[7] D.A. Marca and C.L. McGrowan. SADT Structured Analysis and Design Technique, McGraw-Hill, 1987.

[8] R.W. Vroom. A general example model for automotive suppliers of the development process and its related information. Computers in Industry, 31:255-280, 1996.

Universities and Enterprises Cooperating Together

Khalid A. Fakeeh
King Abdulaziz University
e-mail: kfakeeh@kaau.edu.sa

ABSTRACT

Problem solving involves an analysis, design and implementation at a higher level thought-process and has always been more difficult to teach. The National Science Foundation recently funded a study which involved using information technology to identify new ways to learn and new ways to teach problem solving skills. These methods concerned cooperative programs involving both universities and industry. It was suggested that recent advancements in information, communication and computer technologies could enable a new and innovative approach to improving graduates' problem solving skills. This paper uses the NSF study and its teaching/learning paradigm to explore the possibility of universities and enterprises working together towards a common goal.

INTRODUCTION

Ever since business, industry and government started to complain that universities are unable to produce graduates that can function well in complex problem-solving environments there has been a general movement in higher education toward more "hands-on" learning in classrooms[7]. In Computer Science, teaching about analysis is not a problem. We start failing when it comes to the design and development of appropriate algorithms, especially in the design as it needs to be to solve the larger, complex problems. There is, however, a reason for this. Good design is an iterative process that requires the construction of trial implementation with a repetition of the analysis portion of the problem to make sure that the implementation is going to solve the problem. With the current academic environment , with fixed semesters and the need to assign grades, the design process is many times neglected. In general, the major limitation of university education is the lack of opportunity to expose students to real-life field problems.

A SOLUTION

Students tend to learn more by the "hands-on" approach, that is constructing and creating — working with materials and figuring out how to solve problems [1]. Good design of information systems requires a solid background in a set of concepts that are associated with the area we are working with [5], and the careful application of concepts to problems not previously solved by the student. Research has shown that the development of cognitive problem solving skills, with design a major part of the process, is enhanced by solving problems and having prompt, non-threatening feedback regarding the problem solutions [2].

How can we improve the ability of our students to work in complex problem solving environments and to provide designs for implementation that are robust and effective? The solution lies in having the students work on problems that are significant and challenging, that have complex structure and that require sustained effort to solve[6], those problems that are worked on in the enterprise environment every day. Thus, this will involve having the students actively figuring out problems.

METHODS

The National Science Foundation(NSF) recently funded a taskforce to identify new ways to learn and new ways to teach, in collaboration with the workplace. This taskforce included corporations such as Boeing, Citicorp, US West, and Elite Systems. They suggested that a new cooperation between the providers of educated information workers (academic institutions) and the consumers of the academic product (industry business and government) needs to be organized to work together for a common goal.

This taskforce identified three major weaknesses in the current approach to teaching about the production of reliable systems involving software [5]:

1. Teaching students problem solving and design skills, reinforced with laboratory experiences is not well done.
2. Teaching students to deal with complex information systems architecture, design and implementation is not well done.
3. Collaborative methods and experiences provided to students are very weak.

Because students should become more involved as dynamic rather than passive participants in the educational process and because students should be allowed to participate in the solution of very complex problems and be creative in their approach to solving the problems of real world systems, an environment should be created where there is a natural motivation for the student to be active in the problem solution activity and thus increase their ability to learn from the experience[4]. The taskforce proposed that a cooperative effort between the academic institutions and business, industry and government be developed .

THE COOPERATION

The basic ingredient in the proposed educational effort involved a university and a company that were willing to sit together and agree upon the need to cooperate and the methods of implementing an educational activity that would involve real students working with practicing developers with real problems in the development of systems.

The company and the university had to be willing to commit financial resources and manpower to insure the success of the educational effort. But the basic idea of the cooperative effort was to form systems development teams consisting of students in the university undergraduate program and professional members of the companies development staff. The projects being worked on would be regular complex information systems development projects that were part of the company's on-going activities. The students would remain on campus in their regular academic program but would be assigned to work with a company development team and the communications and coordination between the student developers and the full-time developers would use electronic communication means.

In the implementation of the educational effort, the company had to identify its working teams, its development processes, and the team leaders (who would be the educational facilitators within the working environment of the project). The company also had to identify projects that would be workable with the apprentice developers from the university. The company also had to establish the 2-way electronic communication links between the company and the university. It was the university's responsibility to identify lead faculty members to organize, supervise and provide ongoing education for the university participants in the development teams. The lead faculty members had to be familiar with both the academic and the industrial dimensions of the project.

The student apprentices for a project were required to be in the last 1/4 of their undergraduate program. They were also expected to have a strong foundation in information concepts and to have had some exposure to principles of software engineering. They should also be students who display a high interest in applying their knowledge to industry's problems and should be willing to abide by the confidentiality that is required by the cooperative project. Project organization was a joint responsibility of the industry and university team leaders with the industry team leader taking the lead role.

JUST IN TIME TEACHING/LEARNING PARADIGM

The taskforce designed a new teaching learning paradigm that illustrated how a collaborative working project, in close working relationship with industry developers, could provide a unique opportunity of new approaches to student learning and faculty teaching. This extended environment would be a break from the traditional semester based, lecture dominated environment, and would be made possible only with the integrated and effective use of information technology. Imaginative use of the available technologies through electronic means would expect to draw the industry and development environment close to the University class/laboratory facilities.

The major elements of the paradigm are:
- An on-going long term and relevant company information technology project.
- Faculty and students are full members of the collaborative project team.
- Information technology links the University classroom/laboratory facilities to the company design and development environment (2 way video, e-mail, shareware etc.) Students and faculty participate in all project meetings.
- Faculty and students contribute to the project solution.
- Based on the current focus of the project, faculty develop just-in-time learning modules for the students.
- The project is not bound by semesters even though students may have grades assigned each semester .
- Continuous measurement of the effectiveness of the paradigm toward project solution and learning goals.

According to this just-in-time teaching part of the paradigm the faculty members would be guided by what is going on with the project at the time. Interactive discussions and laboratory experiences would be developed as the project evolved. Potential solution designs could be prototyped in University laboratories by the students or in cooperation with the industry team members and the results shared electronically with the entire development team.

The Project
In developing the just-in-time teaching/learning paradigm with industry, the taskforce was able to identify the following benefits:
Students and faculty learn through experience by participating in industry problems and methods.

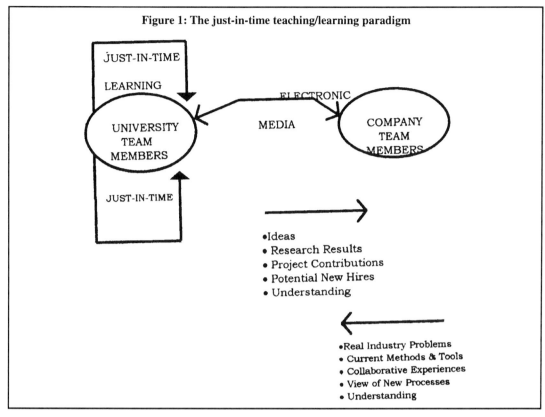

Figure 1: The just-in-time teaching/learning paradigm

- Company team members have professional development opportunities by participating with the student team in the just-in-time teaching learning sessions.
- Collaborative skills are developed in the cooperative experience.
- Faculty open interfaces focusing on the needs of industry.
- The company has early access to potential new hires, and students become familiar with the company.
- The company has access to bright minds and ideas, and potentially useful university research results.
- All participants gain working experience with information technology as an enabler.
- Working bridges between the company and the university are strengthened.

CAN IT WORK?

The NSF taskforce felt that it was imperative that the enterprise enhanced paradigm for education be evaluated and suggested both University and Company metrics to be considered. The following table (Table 1- Paradigm Success Factors) has been prepared to aid both the university and the enterprise in its evaluation.

As a result of this taskforce's efforts, two test sites have been identified and University and Industry working partners have committed to implementing the just-in-time teaching/learning paradigm. The two test sites are:

      Test site 1:   Seattle, Washington
                     University of Washington/Boeing Commercial Aircraft
                     completed Spring quarter 1996
      Test site 2:   Tempe , Arizona
                     Arizona State University/American Express (began Winter 1997)

Prototype documents that can be used as other participants begin to form working alliances will be produced and there will be a report generated by the task force on these projects detailing how the projects were selected and how the company and the university worked together.

CONCLUSION

Given the full implementation of the just-in-time teaching/learning paradigm in a collaborative effort between a university and an enterprise, not only should it be possible to create an ideal learning environment, but it provides an easier transition from school to employment for both the prospective employer and employee. Furthermore, the

Table 1 - Paradigm Success Factors					
University Measurement	Yes	No	Company Measurement	Yes	No
Was there a significant technical content to the problem solution?			Was there a significant technical content to the problem solution?		
Were there significant teaching/learning problem solving skills ?			Were the team's total problem solving and design skills enhanced ?		
Did the students learn from the experience?			Was there a reduction of cost of the total project?		
Did the faculty members learn from the experience?			Was there a reduction of time for the total project?		
Did the company members add value to the experience?			Was the solution for the identified problem correct?		
Was the communication between members good?			Did the university members add value to the project?		
Was it difficult to implement the paradigm?			Did the project provide access to new ideas and technology?		
Did the experience create potential placement for students?			Was the communication between members good?		
Did the experience create access to new ideas, technology and equipment?			Were you able to evaluate the students' potential in terms of future employees?		
Would the members repeat the procedure for future projects?			Would the members repeat the procedure for future projects?		
			Was there any skill improvement for team members?		

social process that results from the new teaching/learning paradigm is a bonus. Students learn by working with others; when they communicate what they know to others in writing and/or speaking, they are learning even more [3]. Working together allows each individual's talents to serve as resources for everyone else. An environment that focuses on the student as an active, collaborating and contributing member of the teaching/learning process provides a superior way to achieve meaningful and lasting learning. This just-in-time learning collaborative approach to the students advanced education will overcome most of the problems such as teaching problem solving skills, teaching complex information systems architecture, design and implementation and teaching students collaborative methods and experiences.

The truly interesting problems are in the large information systems that are worked on in enterprise environments everyday. The coupling of industry and education provides a unique opportunity to solve problems and have prompt, non-threatening feedback regarding the problem solutions.

REFERENCES

[1] Bloom, Benjamin S., *Human Characteristics and School Learning*. New York, New York: McGraw-Hill. 1976

[2] Forester, Tom. *Computers in the Human Context,* MIT Press, Cambridge, Massachusetts, 1991.

[3] Gagne, Robert M., Briggs, Leslie J.; *Principles of Instructional Design*, New York, NY: Holt, Rinehart and Winston. 1979

[4] Heller, Patricia Keith, Ronald, and Anderson, Scott (1992). "Teaching problem solving through cooperative grouping," *American Journal of Physics, 60 (7): 627-644.*

[5] Levine, Marvin, *A Cognitive Theory of Learning*. Hillsdale, New Jersey: Lawrence Earlbaum Associates. 1975

[6] Mulder, Michael C., *Educating the Next Generation of Information Specialists: A Framework for Academic Programs in Informatics*. Report of NSF Sponsored Task Force: DUE 9352944, University of Southwestern Louisiana Press. 1994. Presented at SCS/SIGCSE-95, Nashville, TN, March 1995

[7] Novack, Joseph D., *A theory of Education* . Ithaca, New York: Cornell University Press. 1977

[8] Travers, Robert M. W., Essentials of Learning: 4th edition. New York, New York: Macmillan Publishing co., Inc. 1977

A Decision Support System for Assessing the Benefits and Costs of High-speed Rail Grade Crossing Investments

Guisseppi A. Forgionne
Professor of Information Systems, University of Maryland Baltimore County, 1000 Hilltop Circle,
Catonsville, MD 21250
(410)455-3943, FAX: (410)455-1073, forgionn@umbc7.umbc.edu

ABSTRACT

The Federal Railroad Administration (FRA) has developed a series of rail and rail-related analysis tools that assist FRA officials, Metropolitan Planning Organizations (MPOs), state Department of Transportation (DOT), and other constituents in evaluating the cost and benefits of potential infrastructure projects. To meet agency objectives, the FRA wants to add a high-speed rail grade crossing analysis tool to its package of rail and rail-related intermodal software products. This paper presents a conceptual decision support system (DSS) that can assist officials in achieving this goal.

The paper first introduces the FRA's objectives. Next, there is a discussion of the models needed to assess the feasibility of proposed high-speed rail grade crossing investments and the presentation of a decision support system (DSS) that can deliver these models transparently to users. Then, the paper illustrates a system session and examines the potential benefits from system use.

INTRODUCTION

The Federal Railroad Administration has developed a series of rail and rail-related analysis tools that assist FRA officials, Metropolitan Planning Organizations (MPOs), state Department of Transportation (DOT), and other constituents in evaluating the cost and benefits of potential infrastructure projects. The FRA wants to add a high-speed rail grade crossing analysis tool to its package of rail and rail-related intermodal software products. This additional tool will improve upon the analysis provided by existing FRA software. It will be used by state and municipal agencies to identify, rank, and implement proposed high-speed rail grade crossing investments.

To meet FRA objectives, the developed tool must [14]:

a) be Windows-based user-friendly software that will function on a personal computer and be easily distributed to MPOs, state DOTs, and other constituents, free of charge,

b) provide a benefit-cost analysis that will assist the FRA and its constituents in promoting and developing high-speed rail projects,

c) include the Volpe Transportation Service Center's Accident Prediction Model as applied to high-speed rail in the Empire Corridor Case Study,

d) incorporate existing FRA costing models to evaluate the commercial feasibility of high speed rail,

e) include quantification of all the project associated costs, including crossing maintenance, and all the benefits of crossing improvements,

f) allow for the maximum amount of modification of variables to reflect regional conditions, and

g) provide output that will allow users to target investment and, wherever possible, reduce costs.

A decision support system (DSS) can be developed to support the desired analyses.

This paper presents a conceptual architecture for such a DSS. First, there is a brief overview of the FRA problem. Next, the paper presents the conceptual decision support system and illustrates how the DSS can assist users in evaluating the cost and benefits of potential high-speed rail grade crossing investments. The paper concludes with an examination of the potential benefits from system use and the implications for railway practice.

GRADE CROSSING EVALUATION

Car, truck, and other motor vehicle traffic will arrive at rail grade crossings according to patterns determined by demographic, economic, and roadway network factors. Train traffic will arrive at rail grade crossings according to patterns determined by schedules and railway network factors. The pattern of arrivals and the type of crossing will influence delays, the potential number and severity of accidents, pollution, and other measures of interest.

Crossings can have a variety of configurations to manage traffic. There can be a series of controls throughout the traffic corridor. Controls can be limited to the crossing itself. The controls can be technologically sophisticated or relatively simple. Each configuration will require a particular level of investment, and there will be a budget that limits the total grade crossing expenditure.

As a result, the FRA needs a methodology that will provide detailed and systematic analyses of a project's economic feasibility and potential impact on the FRA budget. Such analyses involve the process shown in Figure 1.

Investment Analysis

Any investment analysis begins with a forecast of the number of automobile, truck, and other motor vehicles arriving at rail grade crossings. Next, FRA officials forecast the number of high-speed trains arriving at the crossings in the corresponding time period. These two forecasts become the basis for predicting traffic delays, pollution, and other operating characteristics, by vehicle category, from specified crossing configuration alternatives.

The operating characteristics generate the benefits and costs that can be expected from a specified crossing configuration. Benefits less the corresponding costs provide the annual net benefit flows yielded by the configuration. Using these flows over the crossing's useful life, FRA officials can simulate the internal rate of return and net present value from the investment. Such financial outcomes then determine whether or not the project is financially feasible.

Once financial feasibility has been established, the FRA must allocate the available budget among the viable investments. Selections will be made on the basis of the investments' contribution to the budget-constrained overall net benefit to FRA constituents.

Process Support

The FRA needs a systematic methodology to project motor vehicle and train traffic and operating characteristics, simulate economic outcomes, determine financial feasibility, and objectively evaluate crossing alternatives. The methodology should create an audible procedure that: (a) formalizes and documents the investment performance and assumptions, and (b) defines the key relationships between this program performance and local indicators. An information system is also needed to deliver the methodology to railway officials and constituents.

There are a variety of variables that could impact the investment analysis. Among other things, there will be [1,2, 9]:

a) demographic, economic, and network factors that influence highway and train freight and passenger traffic,

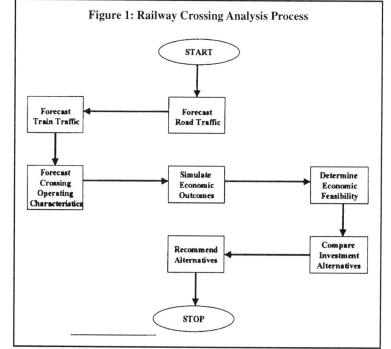

Figure 1: Railway Crossing Analysis Process

b) accident severity statistics, such as total predicted severity to highway vehicle and train occupants for different vehicle mixes,

c) costs, interest rate, benefits, and other financial statistics, and

d) waiting time, system reliability, and other grade crossing data.

These data are available from FRA, Federal Highway Administration (FHWA), Federal Transit Administration (FTA), and Federal Aviation Administration (FAA) documents and through reports generated by information systems of MPOs, state DOTs, and private organizations. However, the FRA does not have the staff to organize the collected data, develop a methodology for utilizing the data properly, or implement an information system that will deliver the data and methodology effectively to nontechnical persons.

The deficiencies and potential adverse consequences have lead FRA officials to seek improved support. Specifically, the FRA desires focused data, models, analyses, and reports that can be readily accessed and utilized by railway officials to objectively evaluate high-speed rail grade crossing investments. Such capabilities can be provided through a decision support system (DSS) [10, 12].

DECISION SUPPORT SYSTEM

To meet FRA objectives, the decision support system should be developed iteratively, using the Adaptive Design Strategy (ADS), by researchers working in conjunction with FRA officials, Metropolitan Planning Organizations (MPOs), state Departments of Transportation (DOTs), and other constituents [4]. It should be made available through an easy-to-use computer system with the conceptual architecture shown in Figure 2. As this figure shows, the decision support system interactively processes inputs into the outputs desired by railway officials. Figure 5 does not show that data for the DSS are captured and stored in a data warehouse.

Data Warehouse

Requisite data for the investment analysis will come from various internal FRA and external sources, and these data will be in a variety of different formats. However, the data must be extracted, reformatted, summarized, and focused for the DSS analyses and evaluations.

Pre-written computer programs automatically extract the data from their sources, place the data in a standard format, and capture the standard-formatted data in a data warehouse. To ensure that the computer programs are accurate, warehoused

data are tested against actual values. The testing ensures that these programs will reproduce the actual data exactly. Warehoused data are available to the railway officials through the DSS for browsing, editing, and display. Such analyses will enable sophisticated users with better data to manipulate all of the key input variables and assumptions [3, 5].

Descriptive statistical procedures (frequency and probability distributions, measures of central tendency, and measures of dispersion) and predefined rules are used to convert the warehoused data into the variables and formats needed for the DSS analyses and evaluations. These variables define and explicitly measure benefit and cost components common to high-speed rail grade crossing technologies. The DSS automatically creates Structured Query Language (SQL) calls to the data warehouse from user actions and then displays the called information in concise reports. Such analyses will minimize the data needs and technical expertise required of the system user [6].

Inputs

The decision support system has a database that captures and stores traffic conditions, local factors, and schedules. This database provides the parameters (metrics) needed for the investment models.

There is also a model base that contains forecasting, project evaluation, and resource allocation models. The forecasting model defines and explicitly measures the relationships between operating characteristics and grade crossing alternatives. This model is used to predict the operating characteristics (benefits, waiting times, accident incidences, and costs) that can be expected from each grade crossing alternative. The predictions are made as expected values and as confidence interval estimates. The project evaluation model converts each grade alternative's investment and net financial benefit flows over the alternative's projected life into financial outcomes, such as the internal rate of return, net present value, and other FRA-desired measures. This model enables FRA staff, state governments and DOTs, MPOs, and the private sector to evaluate the financial feasibility of proposed high-speed rail grade crossing investments. The resource allocation model defines and explicitly measures the relationship between the collection of feasible grade crossing alternatives and overall net benefit. This model determines the best combination of alternatives in the face of budget constraints.

Literature research, intensive consultation with FRA staff, state agencies, MPOs, transportation researchers, and private stakeholders, and empirical analysis are used to identify the specific determinants and equation forms. Values for the variables in the traffic arrival model will differ by region. Consequently, the DSS allows the user to manipulate the key model inputs and assumptions and thereby complete a more in-depth, regionally specific analysis. The predictions are generated as expected values and as upper and lower limits based on the confidence level specified by the user. In this way, the model provides a confidence interval that accounts for the uncertainty involved in the estimation.

Processing

The decision-maker (a railway official or staff assistant) uses computer technology to perform the investment

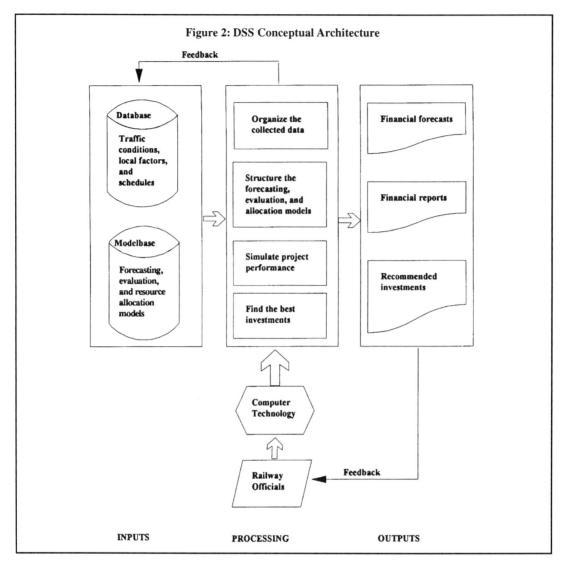

Figure 2: DSS Conceptual Architecture

analyses and evaluations. Currently, the system executes on an IBM-compatible Pentium-based microcomputer with 16MB of RAM, a color graphics display, and a printer compatible with the microcomputer. It runs the SAS information delivery system through the Microsoft Windows operating system. This configuration was selected because it offered a more consistent, less time-consuming, less costly, and more flexible development and implementation environment than the available alternatives.

Users initiate the processing by pointing and clicking with the computer's mouse on screen-displayed objects. The system responds by automatically organizing the collected data, structuring (estimating and operationalizing) the forecasting, project evaluation, and resource allocation models, simulating project performance, and finding the best grade-crossing investments. Results are displayed on the preprogrammed forms desired by railway officials. Execution is realized in a completely interactive manner that makes the processing relatively transparent to the user.

As indicated by the top feedback loop in Figure 2, organized data, structured models, and performance reports created during the analyses and evaluations can be captured and stored as inputs for future processing. These captured inputs are stored as additional or revised fields and records, thereby updating the data and model bases dynamically. The user executes the functions with mouse-controlled point-and-click operations on attractive visual displays that make the computer processing virtually invisible (transparent) to the user.

Outputs

Processing automatically generates visual displays of the outputs desired by railway officials. Outputs include

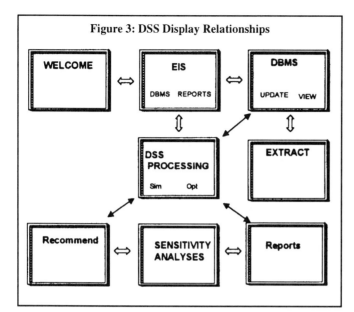

Figure 3: DSS Display Relationships

financial forecasts and reports and recommended grade-crossing investments. The reports are in the form of tables that display the forecasted net present value's and internal rate of return's lower limit (which has a 1% chance of occurrence), expected value, and upper limit (which has a 1% chance of occurrence) from the project. Recommendations display the mix of grade-crossing investments that generate the largest total net benefit from the available budget. The user has the option of printing or saving the reports and recommendations.

As indicated by the bottom feedback loop in Figure 2, the user can utilize the outputs to guide further processing before exiting the system. Typically, the feedback will involve sensitivity analyses in which the user modifies traffic conditions, local factors, schedules, or other pertinent factors and observes the effects on financial outcomes and recommended investments.

System Session

There is a FRA icon on the Windows desktop. By double clicking this icon, the user accesses the decision support system. Once in the DSS, the user performs the investment analyses and evaluations by navigating with point and click operations through the displays overviewed in Figure 3.

The Welcome display enables the user to access an embedded executive information system (EIS). Once in the EIS, the user can interactively access the data warehouse, by selecting the database management system (DBMS) button, or go directly to DSS reports, by selecting the REPORTS button. Selecting the DBMS button will enable the user to UPDATE the data warehouse and VIEW the contents of the existing or updated warehouse.

By selecting the UPDATE button from the DBMS screen, the user will be placed in the EXTRACT screen. Once there, the user will interactively select the data source for the updating operation from the predefined list. The selection reads data from the specified source, automatically reformats the data (if necessary), and automatically updates the data warehouse values.

Selecting the VIEW button from the DBMS screen will access a screen that prompts users for the desired information. These selections will automatically form the pertinent Structured Query Language (SQL) call to the data warehouse and generate the desired custom report.

Selecting the REPORTS button from the EIS display will run the investment analysis with the updated or existing data and bring the user to the DSS PROCESSING screen. Once there, the user can simulate economic (financial) performance from specified grade-crossing alternatives, by selecting the Sim button, or find the best grade-crossing investments, by selecting the Opt button. The decision support system will automatically form the DSS database from the data warehouse, operationalize the appropriate models, and perform the needed analyses and evaluations. A Sim button selection will display the results in the desired predefined format on the Reports screen, while an Opt button selection will display the results on the Recommend screen.

From either output screen, the user can perform sensitivity analyses on the results. By making the desired selection from the predefined "What If" list, the user can experiment with changes in: (a) traffic conditions, (b) key local factors, (c) investment statistics (such as the interest rate or the useful project life), (d) schedules, (e) grade-crossing alternatives, or (f) the available budget. Results from the what-if analyses are displayed on the SENSITIVITY ANALYSES screen. Such experimentation can continue in sequence, or the user can generate an entirely new experiment.

BENEFITS AND CHALLENGES

The existing FRA investment analysis relies on tedious manual procedures. These procedures often result in inaccurate, incomplete, and redundant data collection. The decision support system will identify all data relevant to the analysis and provide a mechanism that facilitates data entry while reducing errors and eliminating redundant inputs [13].

In addition, the decision support system will enable railway officials to improve the decision making required in the grade-crossing investment analysis. The decision support system will provide:

1) quicker analysis of the regional environment and its impact on grade-crossing operating characteristics, costs, and benefits,
2) operationally and computationally error-free financial feasibility and budget allocation evaluations,
3) more timely policy analyses and evaluations,
4) rapid sensitivity analyses of regional conditions, schedules, and policy changes, and
5) efficient flagging of data and information deficiencies.

These enhanced capabilities will enable FRA officials and their constituents to more efficiently and effectively manage the grade-crossing programs under their control [8].

The decision support system has some limitations that present profound challenges to the FRA and its constituents. This system relies on accurate and current data, and these data must be obtained from a variety of sources. At the present time, the FRA does not have a systematic way to systematically obtain the needed data on a continuous basis. In addition, the DSS models should be updated as new data become available. The updating will require technical expertise currently in relatively short supply at the FRA. Such expertise can be outsourced on a fee-for-service basis, or the expertise can be delivered virtually by extending the capabilities of the DSS [7, 11].

CONCLUSIONS

The DSS architecture is based on a combination of database, statistical, mathematical programming, simulation, and decision support techniques. Its deployment can enable the Federal Railway Administration to realize significant economic, management, and political benefits. Future enhancements, motivated by the challenges from the current system, promise to increase the power of the DSS and to further improve the FRA's ability to manage high-speed grade-crossing investments.

Partially because of budget cutting, there has been significant movement within the government to promote technology-based management innovations. Top-level policy makers realize that all government agencies can benefit from information technology initiatives, and the DSS's potential may convince them that the management of railway projects can be substantially enhanced with decision support. Consequently, the FRA's DSS-supported investment analysis can be offered as the standard for the process.

REFERENCES

1. Begur, S. V., Miller, D. M., and J. R. Weaver. "An Integrated Spatial DSS for Scheduling and Routing Home-Health-Care Nurses," *Interfaces*, 27(4), 1997, 35-48.
2. Couillard, J. "A Decision Support System for Vehicle Fleet Planning," *Decision Support Systems*, 9(2), 1998, 112-123.
3. Hoch, S. J. and D. A. Schkade. "A Psychological Approach to Decision Support Systems," *Management Science*, 42(1), 1996, 51-64.
4. Holsapple, C. W. and A. B. Whinston. *Decision Support Systems: A Knowledge-Based Approach*. Minneapolis: West, 1996.
5. Leidner, D., and Elam, J. "Executive Information Systems: Their Impact on Executive Decision Making," *Journal of Management Information Systems*, 10(3), 1993-1994, 139-155.
6. Mackay, J.M., and Elam, J. J. "A Comparative Study of How Experts and Novices Use a Decision Aid to Solve Problems in Complex Domains," *Information Systems Research*, 3(2), 1992, 150-172.
7. Maes, P. "Agents That Reduce Work and Information Overload," *Communications of the ACM*, 14(4), 1994, 31-40.
8. Moormann, J. and M. Lochte-Holtgreven. "An Approach for an Integrated DSS for Strategic Planning," *Decision Support Systems*, 10, 1993, 401-411.
9. Sander, R. L. and W. M. Westerman. "Computer Aided Train Dispatching: Decision Support Through Optimization," *Interfaces*, 13(6), 1983, 24-37.
10. Sauter, V. *Decision Support Systems*. New York: Wiley, 1998.
11. Silverman, B. G. "Unifying Expert Systems and the Decision Sciences," *Operations Research*, 42(3), 1994, 393-413.
12. Sprague, R. H. and H. J. Watson. *Decision Support for Management*. Upper Saddle River: Prentice-Hall, 1996.
13. Todd, P., and Benbasat, I. "An Experimental Investigation of the Impact of Computer Based Decision Aids on Decision Making Strategies," *Information Systems Research*, 2(2), 1991, 87-115.
14. United States Department of Transportation, Federal Railway Administration. "Development of Benefit-Cost Software for High-Speed Rail Grade Crossing Investments," DTFR53-98-R-00010. Washington: U. S. Government Printing Office, 1998.

Implementing Strategic IT Plans: Does Content Matter?

Petter Gottschalk

Department of Technology Management, Norwegian School of Management, Box 580, 1301 Sandvika, Norway
petter.gottschalk@bi.no, http://www.bi.no/people/fgl98023.htm

ABSTRACT

The need for improved implementation of information technology strategy has been emphasised in both empirical and prescriptive research studies. In this study, ten content characteristics of formal information technology plans were identified from the research literature as potential implementation predictors. A survey was conducted in Norway to investigate the link between plan and implementation. The analysis of 190 surveyed companies with strategic IT plans revealed a significant relationship between content characteristics of the plan and the extent of plan implementation. Two implementation predictors proved significant in the testing of hypotheses: description of responsibility for the implementation and description of user involvement during the implementation.

Keywords: Management of information technology, strategic information systems planning, formal information technology strategy, content characteristics, implementation predictors, survey research.

INTRODUCTION

The need for improved implementation of information technology (IT) strategy has been emphasised in both empirical (Earl, 1993; Lederer and Mendelow, 1993; Lederer and Sethi, 1988, 1992; Premkumar and King, 1994) and prescriptive studies (Galliers, 1994; Lederer and Salmela, 1996; Lederer and Sethi, 1996). These studies show that implementation is important for four reasons. Firstly, the failure to carry out the strategic IT plan can cause lost opportunities, duplicated efforts, incompatible systems, and wasted resources (Lederer and Salmela, 1996). Secondly, the extent to which strategic IT planning meets its objectives is determined by implementation (Earl, 1993; Lederer and Sethi, 1996). Further, the lack of implementation leaves firms dissatisfied with and reluctant to continue their strategic IT planning (Galliers, 1994; Lederer and Sethi, 1988, 1992; Premkumar and King, 1994). Finally, the lack of implementation creates problems establishing and maintaining priorities in future strategic IT planning (Lederer and Mendelow, 1993).

Lederer and Salmela (1996) have developed a theory of strategic information systems planning (SISP) which contributes to helping researchers study SISP and present their findings in an organised and meaningful manner. This paper adds to the body of empirical implementation research by evaluating the plan implementation link suggested by Lederer and Salmela (1996). The research question is presented in the next section, followed by the literature review, research model and research method. Finally, research results are provided and key study findings are discussed.

RESEARCH QUESTION

The theory developed by Lederer and Salmela (1996) consists of an input-process-output model, seven constructs, six causal relationships and six hypotheses. The input-process-output model provides the initial bases for the theory. The seven constructs are i) the external environment, ii) the internal environment, iii) planning resources, iv) the planning process, v) the strategic information systems plan, vi) the implementation of the strategic information systems plan, and vii) the alignment of the strategic information systems plan with the organisation's business plan. The seven constructs exhibit causal relationships among each other demonstrated by hypotheses. For this research on the implementation of strategic IT plans, the most important relationship in the theory is the effect of the plan on its implementation.

The plan implementation link inspired the following research question: "What content characteristics of formal IT strategy predict the extent of plan implementation?". IT strategy is defined as a plan comprised of projects for application of information technology to assist an organisation in realising its goals. The plan also comprises a gestalt view representing philosophy, attitudes, intentions, and ambitions associated with future IT use in the organisation. The term plan refers to a written document following Mintzberg's (1994) suggestion that when the word planning is used, the understanding should be that of formal planning. In this research, terms such as strategic information systems plan (Lederer and Sethi, 1996) and information technology strategy (Galliers, 1993) are treated as synonymous. Two observations formed the basis for the specific research question:

a) Organisations engage in strategic IT planning. Galliers (1994), Finnegan et al. (1997) and Kearney (1990) found that 75 percent, 76 percent and 80 percent respectively of those surveyed had a strategic IT plan. However, as discussed later in this paper, the survey in this research was conducted in Norway where the organisations are smaller than those in previous studies, leading to a potential expectation that there would be a lower percentage of organisations with a formal IT strategy. Similarly, an Australian survey found the proportion claiming to undertake strategic IT planning ranged from 58 percent in large organisations to 29 percent in medium-sized organisations and 19 percent in small organisations (Falconer and Hodgett, 1997).

b) Strategic IT plans are not implemented very extensively. Lederer and Sethi (1988) found that only twenty-four percent of the projects in the strategic IT plans surveyed had been initiated more than two years into the implementation horizon. In a study of four Norwegian organisations, approximately forty-two percent of the projects in the formal IT strategy had been implemented after five years (Gottschalk, 1995). Ward and Griffiths (1996, p.97) found that "despite a belief in its importance, in the past decade many organisations have developed perfectly sound IS strategies that have been left to gather dust, or have been implemented in a half-hearted manner". Taylor (1997, p.336), too, found that "all too often strategies remain 'on the page' and are not implemented".

Content characteristics of formal IT strategy as implementation predictors is an important research topic for two main reasons. Firstly, there is a lack of empirical research, and where it exists, implementation is included as only one of several issues (Lederer and Salmela, 1996; Lederer and Sethi, 1996). Secondly, the strategic IT plan is one of the main concerns of IS/IT managers today (Watson et al., 1997). In a survey conducted by Stephens et al. (1995), eighty percent of the chief information officers (CIOs) reported that they had responsibility for IT strategy. The documentation process is, however, challenging for CIOs both because it is a time consuming effort to write the IT strategy (Gottschalk, 1995), and because the plan contents chosen by the CIO may influence the extent of plan implementation (Lederer and Salmela, 1996). Despite the existence of literature suggesting that a formal IT strategy is neither a true template of an organisation's IT strategy process nor a reflection of its IT actions (e.g., Mintzberg, 1994), many organisations seem to concentrate on and struggle with their formal IT strategy implementation (Lederer and Sethi, 1996). Their struggle is the concern of this paper.

RESEARCH LITERATURE ON IMPLEMENTATION PREDICTORS

Though there exists an extensive range of literature on strategic information technology planning (e.g., Lederer and Mendelow, 1993; Raghunathan and Raghunathan, 1994) and on information technology implementation (e.g., Alavi and Joachimsthaier, 1992; Gill, 1996), specific literature on plan implementation has been relatively sparse. While the literature on strategic information technology planning treats implementation only as one of many phases,

Table 1: Organisational Practices Influencing IT Strategy Implementation

Earl (1993): Implementation Problems
E1 Resources were not made available
E2 Management was hesitant
E3 Technological constraints arose
E4 Organisational resistance emerged

Galliers (1994): Implementation Barriers
G1 Difficulty of recruiting
G2 Nature of business
G3 Measuring benefits
G4 User education resources
G5 Existing IT investments
G6 Political conflicts
G7 Middle management attitudes
G8 Senior management attitudes
G9 Telecommunications issues
G10 Technology lagging behind needs
G11 Doubts about benefits

Lederer and Salmela (1996): Effect of Plan on Implementation
S1 Contents of the plan
S2 Relevance of proposed projects in the plan to organisational goals
S3 Sections of the plan
S4 Clarity and analysis of presentation of the plan

Lederer and Sethi (1992): Implementation Problems
L1 Difficult to secure top management commitment
L2 Final planning output documentation not very useful
L3 Planning methodology fails to consider implementation
L4 Implementing the projects requires more analysis
L5 Planning methodology requires too much top management involvement
L6 Output of planning is not in accordance with management expectations

Lederer and Sethi (1996): Prescriptions for SISP
X1 Prepare migration plan
X2 Identify actions to adopt plan
X3 Identify resources for new tools
X4 Avoid/dampen resistance
X5 Specify actions for architecture
X6 Identify bases of resistance

Premkumar and King (1994): Implementation Mechanisms
P1 Monitoring system to review implementation and provide feedback
P2 Resource mobilisation for implementation
P3 User involvement in implementation
P4 Top management monitoring of implementation

the literature on information technology implementation lacks the gestalt perspective which is needed when plan implementation is to be studied. Furthermore, much of the reviewed research literature consists mainly of theory (e.g., Joshi, 1991), often lacking empirical evidence. For the testing of the plan implementation link in the theory of strategic information systems planning suggested by Lederer and Salmela (1996), it was nevertheless possible to identify existing literature as listed in table 1. The thirty-five organisational practices derived from the six research studies analysed constitute a comprehensive list of practices for the implementation of IT strategy.

In this reseach, the thirty-five organisational practices were reduced to a set of ten predictors (Gottschalk, 1998) as listed in table 2.

RESEARCH LITERATURE ON DEFINITION OF IMPLEMENTATION

The term implementation is given a variety of meanings in the literature (Montealegre, 1990). Nutt (1986) defines implementation as a procedure directed by a manager to install planned change in an organisation, whereas Klein and Sorra (1996) sees it as the process of gaining targeted organisational members' appropriate and committed use of an innovation. In table 3, the reviewed research literature on implementation is listed according to their particular definition of implementation. The first references in the table represent definitions where implementation

Table 2: Implementation Predictors derived from Organisational Practices		
Practices	Predictors	Measurement
E1 Resources were not made available G1 Difficulty of recruiting P2 Resource mobilisation for implementation X3 Identify resources for new tools	Resources	Multiple item scale by Lee (1995)
G4 User education resources P3 User involvement in implementation	Users	Multiple item scale by Chan (1992)
G5 Existing IT investments L3 Planning methodology fails to consider implementation L4 Implementing the projects requires more analysis X5 Specify actions for architecture	Analysis	Multiple item scale by Segars (1994)
Gilbert (1993), Salmela (1996), Teo (1994)	Environment	Multiple item scale by Segars (1994)
E4 Organisational resistance emerged G6 Political conflicts X4 Avoid/dampen resistance X6 Identify bases of resistance	Resistance	Multiple item scale by Lee (1995)
E3 Technological constraints arose G9 Telecommuncations issues G10 Technology lagging behind needs	Technology	Items from Teo, 1994; Lederer and Sethi, 1992; Byrd et al., 1995; Salmela, 1996
G2 Nature of business G3 Measuring benefits G11 Doubts about benefits S2 Relevance of proposed projects in the plan to organisational goals L6 Output of planning is not in accordance with management expectations	Relevance	Items from Teo, 1994; Lederer and Sethi, 1992; Segars, 1994; Chan and Huff, 1994; Hann and Weber, 1996
P1 Monitoring system to review implementation and provide feedback X1 Prepare migration plan X2 Identify actions to adopt plan	Responsibility	Ideas from Olsen, 1995; Ward et al., 1996; Gottschalk, 1995, and pilot tests
E2 Management was hesitant G7 Middle management attitudes G8 Senior management attitudes L1 Difficult to secure top management commitment L5 Planning methodology requires too much top management involvement P4 Top management monitoring of implementation	Management	Items from Lee, 1995; Jarvenpaa and Ives, 1991; Segars, 1994; Premkumar and King, 1994
S1 Contents of the plan S3 Sections of the plan S4 Clarity and analysis of presentation of the plan L2 Final planning output documentation not very useful	Presentation	Ideas from Lederer and Salmela, 1996; Hussey, 1996

Table 3: Stages of Implementation Completion		
Stage	Implementation completed when:	Reference
1	System is installed	Lucas (1981)
2	System is put to use	Brancheau, Schuster and March (1989)
3	Programs are adopted	Baier, March and Saetren (1986)
4	Organisation acts on new priorities	Floyd and Wooldridge (1992)
5	Changes are installed	Nutt (1986, 1995)
6	Not abandoned or expensively overhauled	Markus (1983)
7	Adoption has occurred	Lucas, Walton and Ginzberg (1988)
8	Innovation is adopted and used	Leonard-Barton and Deschamps (1988)
9	Systems are installed and used	Srinivasan and Davis (1987)
10	Change is accepted	Baronas and Louis (1988)
11	Systems are accepted	Ginzberg (1980)
12	Innovation is accepted and used	Alavi and Henderson (1981)
13	Systems are accepted and used	Bradley and Hauser (1995)
14	Control rests with users	Alter and Ginzberg (1978)
15	Change process completed	Joshi (1991)
16	Committed use occurs	Klein and Sorra (1996)
17	Post-application phase is consolidated	Rhodes and Wield (1985)
18	Satisfaction with system is achieved	Griffith and Northcraft (1996)
19	Intended benefits are realised	Alavi and Joachimsthaier (1992)

is completed at an early stage, while those that follow represent definitions where implementation is completed at a later stage. The numbers may, therefore, represent a scale of stages at which authors place their definition of implementation. Some authors find implementation to be completed when change is occurring, while others find it continues until intended benefits have been realised.

The purpose for using the stages in table 3 is not to defend a certain rank order of the authors along the axis of implementation completion, but rather to indicate that the authors have different opinions about when implementation is considered completed. The dimensions of IT strategy implementation may be summarised as illustrated in table 4. The purpose of the table is to develop alternative measures of IT strategy implementation.

In table 4, there are two dimensions of IT strategy implementation: the time dimension and the level detail dimension. The time dimension is the implementation stage derived from table 3, where the two extreme stages of implemented are "installed" and "benefits", while the middle stage is "completed". Benefits may be considered as the effect of the changes; that is, the difference between the current and proposed way work is done (Ward et al., 1996). The detail dimension refers to the implementation content which may be the whole plan, one or more projects in the plan, or one or more systems in one project. Implementation content thus refers to a plan consisting of one or several projects (Falconer and Hodgett, 1997), and a project consisting of one or several systems. The term project is defined as the means by which the organisation's technological, organisational, and external assets are mobilised and transformed (Williams, 1992, p.36): "Projects, or initiatives as termed in this study, then, are the vehicles through which an organization's competitive and technology strategies are operationalized into organizational outputs". For, according to Gupta and Raghunathan (1989, p.786), "the ultimate success of systems planning depends on the success of the individual projects covered by the plan". Both the time dimension and the detail dimension may certainly be challenged. The detail dimension, for example, may in an organisation be such that a large system is broken down into several projects, and a project may itself consist of several phases or stages. The main purpose of table 4, however, is to develop a definition and measures of implementation suitable for this research. As such, IT strategy implementation is here defined as the process of completing the projects for application of information technology to assist an organisation in realising its goals. As such, the column "completed" is essential for this research.

Table 4: Dimensions of IT Strategy Implementation			
Time / Level	Installed (Earl, 1993)	Completed (Lederer and Salmela, 1996)	Benefits (Premkumar and King, 1994)
Level			
Plan		3	4
Project	2	1	
System			

Implementation is measured in four different ways in this research based on the two dimensions of time and detail discussed above. The first plan implementation measurement (#1 in table 4) is concerned with completion of projects in the plan which were to be completed to date. The second plan implementation measurement (#2 in table 4) is concerned with completion of projects in the plan which are expected to be completed, or at least installed,

Table 5: Four Potential Implementation Constructs

Construct	Measurement of Construct
1 Implementation rate to date (Lederer and Sethi, 1988)	Divide projects actually implemented to date by projects scheduled to be implemented to date
2 Implementation rate to end (Lederer and Sethi, 1988)	Divide projects actually implemented to date by projects in the IT strategy and divide by percent of expired time horizon
3 Implementation extent (Coolbaugh, 1993; Ginzberg, 1981; Salmela, 1996; Ward et al., 1996; Williams, 1992)	*IT strategy has been implemented as planned* IT strategy implementation has been completed on time IT strategy implementation has been completed within budget IT strategy implementation has been completed as expected IT strategy implementation has achieved the desired results Deviations from the IT strategy have occurred during implementation You are satisfied with the IT strategy implementation
4 Contribution to organisational performance (Scale adopted from Teo, 1994, p.121, Alpha=0.87; one item added from Segars, 1994, p.154)	*Contribute to improved organisational performance* Contribute to increased Return on Investment (ROI) Contribute to increased market share of products/services Contribute to improved internal efficiency of operations Contribute to increased annual sales revenue Contribute to increased customer satisfaction Contribute to alignment of IT with business needs

by the end of the implementation horizon. The third implementation measurement (#3) measures completion of the whole plan in a gestalt perspective, while the fourth IT strategy implementation measurement (#4) is concerned with improved organisational performance from plan implementation. According to Ward and Griffiths (1996, p.102), the impact of an IT strategy implementation is not instantaneous; "it may, in fact take some time - two or more years - between embarking on strategic IS/IT planning for the first time and demonstrating any consequent impact on business practices and results". The operationalisation of these alternative implementation constructs is listed in table 5.

RESEARCH MODEL

Ten predictor constructs were listed in table 2, while four alternative implementation constructs were listed in table 5. To organise the research according to the theory of Lederer and Salmela (1996), a causal relationship between predictor constructs and implementation constructs is proposed in the research model as illustrated in figure 1. For each of the ten predictors, one hypothesis was formulated stating that the greater the extent of description of the content characteristic, the greater the extent of plan implementation.

RESEARCH METHOD

Data was collected through a survey. The CIO or person with CIO responsibilities was chosen as the informant for each organisation, following prior research such as Stephens et al. (1995), Earl (1993), Sabherwal and King (1995), and Teo and King (1997).

RESEARCH RESULTS

Of 1108 mailed questionnaires, 471 (43%) were returned. 190 subjects (40%) confirmed that they had a written IT strategy and provided information on its content characteristics. Ten content characteristics of formal information

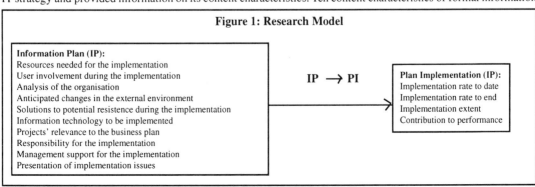

Figure 1: Research Model

Information Plan (IP):
Resources needed for the implementation
User involvement during the implementation
Analysis of the organisation
Anticipated changes in the external environment
Solutions to potential resistence during the implementation
Information technology to be implemented
Projects' relevance to the business plan
Responsibility for the implementation
Management support for the implementation
Presentation of implementation issues

IP → PI

Plan Implementation (IP):
Implementation rate to date
Implementation rate to end
Implementation extent
Contribution to performance

Table 6: Items for Measurement of Implementation Predictor Constructs		
Construct	Measurement of Construct	Alpha
Resources needed for the implementation Lee, 1995, alpha = 0.68	Financial resources needed for implementation Technical abilities needed for implementation Human resources needed for implementation Project team time needed for implementation External consultants needed for implementation (new) A "project champion" needed for the implementation (new)	.87
User involvement during implementation Chan, 1992, alpha = 0.82	Degree of systems-related training received by information systems users Users' understanding of systems' functional and technical features Users' participation in systems projects Users' involvement in the operation of information systems Participation in the ongoing development of information systems Users' support for the implementation (new)	.86
Analyses of the organisation Segars, 1994, alpha = 0.86	Information needs of organisational sub-units How the organisation actually operates A "blueprint" which structures organisational processes Changing organisational procedures New ideas to reengineer business processes through IT Dispersion of data and applications throughout the firm Organisation of the IT function (new)	.87
Anticipated changes in the external environment	Anticipated changes in competitors' behaviour Segars, 1994, alpha = 0.82 Anticipated changes in suppliers' behaviour Anticipated changes in customers' behaviour Anticipated changes in information technology Anticipated changes in government regulations (new) Anticipated changes in the economy (new)	.83
Solutions to potential resistance during the implementation Lee, 1995, alpha = 0.64	Solutions to resistance caused by job security Solutions to resistance caused by change in position Solutions to potential resistance caused by new skills requirements Solutions to potential resistance caused by scepticism of results Solutions to potential resistance caused by a unit's interests Solutions to potential resistance caused by our customers	.93
Information technology to be implemented New scale	Hardware to be implemented Communications technology to be implemented Databases to be implemented Applications software to be implemented Operating systems to be implemented A data architecture for the organisation	.89
Projects' relevance to the business plan New scale	Projects in accordance with the expectations of management Organisational goals for the projects Benefits of the projects to the organisation Projects that contribute to new business opportunities Competitive advantage from IT Strategic applications of IT	.88
Responsibility for the implementation New scale	Responsibility for the implementation on time Responsibility for the implementation within budget Responsibility for the implementation with intended benefits Responsibility for the stepwise implementation of large projects Responsibility for the implementation of high priority projects Responsibility for short-term benefits from initial projects Personnel rewards from successful implementation	.91
Management support for the implementation New scale	Management expectations of the implementation Management participation in the implementation Management monitoring of the implementation Management knowledge about the implementation Management time needed for the implementation Management enthusiasm for the implementation	.93
Clear presentation of implementation issues New scale	Evaluation of progress clearly Change management clearly A list of projects clearly A schedule for the implementation clearly Alignment of IT strategy with business strategy clearly	.83

technology strategy were measured in the questionnaire through sixty-two items as listed in table 6.

The Cronbach alpha for all multiple item scales were between 0.73 and 0.93 as listed in table 6. Alphas greater than 0.70 are considered evidence of reliability (Bagozzi, 1996).

Alternative implementation constructs were developed in table 5. The implementation extent scale was the most suitable measure for IT strategy implementation based on decision criteria such as statistical, methodological and theoretical considerations including the gestalt perspective. On a scale from 1 (very little extent) to 5 (very great extent), the CIOs reported an average implementation extent of 3.3.

The hypothesis testing was carried out using multiple regression analysis (Hair et al., 1998). All observations with missing values were excluded, reducing the sample from 190 to 151 valid cases. Table 7 lists the results of multiple regression analysis between the ten independent variables and the dependent variable implementation.

The full multiple regression equation with all ten independent variables explains 19% of the variation in implementation, that is, the adjusted R-square is 0.19. The F-value of 4.505 is significant at $p < 0.001$, indicating that the null hypothesis is rejected and that there is a significant relationship between content characteristics and IT strategy implementation. However, none of the content characteristics were individually significant implementation predictors. When stepwise regression (Hair et al., 1998) was applied, two of the ten predictors have significant coefficients in the multiple regression equation. Firstly, the description of responsibility for the implementation was associated with the highest explanatory power since it achieved the highest Beta coefficient. Next, the description of user involvement during the implementation proved to be the other significant predictor. The adjusted R-square of the stepwise model is 0.19. None of the remaining eight potential predictors are significant.

Responsibility was the first hypothesis to be supported in this research: the greater the extent of description of responsibility for the implementation, the greater the extent of plan implementation (H8). Implementation participants must accept responsibility (Markus and Benjamin, 1996), responsibility is a positive duty (Swanson, 1995), and tasks should be assigned to specific individuals (Bajjaly, 1998). Responsibility was measured by responsibility for implementation on time (Kaplan and Norton, 1996), responsibility for implementation within budget (Flynn and Goleniewska, 1993), responsibility for implementation with intended benefits (Ward et al., 1996), responsibility for stepwise implementation of large projects (Kaplan and Norton, 1996), responsibility for implementation of high priority projects (Gottschalk, 1995), responsibility for short-term benefits from initial projects (Nutt, 1995), and personnel rewards from successful implementation (Argyris and Kaplan, 1994).

User involvement was the second hypothesis to be supported in this research: the greater the extent of description of user involvement during the implementation, the greater the extent of plan implementation (H2). User involvement during the implementation is the engagement of people who will employ the technology and the systems after the implementation. User involvement was measured by a multiple item scale adopted from Chan (1992).

DISCUSSION

This empirical research confirms the plan implementation link suggested by Lederer and Salmela (1996) in their theory of strategic information systems planning. The total set of content characteristics of the plan has a significant impact on the extent of plan implementation - in other words, when it comes to implementing strategic IT plans, all factors are necessary and none is sufficient. With this in mind, however, description of responsibility for the implementation and description of user involvement during the implementation were the two specific content characteristics of formal IT strategy of particular significance as implementation predictors.

The most surprising result of this study, both from a theoretical and practical perspective, is the relative lack of importance of management support. All the leading research studies on which this research is based (Earl, 1993; Galliers, 1994; Lederer and Salmela, 1996; Lederer and Sethi, 1992, 1996; Premkumar and King, 1994) as well as all the general business literature (e.g., Applegate et al., 1996), seem to share a strong belief in the importance of management support for the implementation of IT strategy. It is interesting that management support, as reflected in management expectations, participation, monitoring, knowl-

Table 7: Multiple Regression Analysis between Implementation and Predictors				
Content characteristics as implementation predictors	Full regression Beta	Full regression t-test	Stepwise regression Beta	Stepwise regression t-test
Resources	.078	.766		
Users	.158	1.665	.233	2.892**
Analyses	.019	.170		
Changes	.138	1.407		
Resistance	-.065	-.628		
IT	.015	.173		
Relevance	.048	.449		
Responsibility	.189	1.672	.298	3.692**
Management	-.071	-.599		
Issues	.145	1.408		
Note: The statistical significance of the t-values is ** for p<.01 and * for p<.05.				

edge, time and enthusiasm, is of no significant importance in this study. Several explanations, however, may be offered. Firstly, there is the distinction between planning and implementing to be considered. Some argue that management is primarily involved in strategy-making, not in plan implementation (Mintzberg, 1994). Secondly, as long as responsibility for the implementation is defined, management support becomes less important (Gottschalk, 1995). Since responsibility is the relatively most important predictor in this research, the latter explanation may well carry weight. Next, the role of management is often to take on responsibility (Applegate et al., 1996), suggesting that management is important through responsibility. Furthermore, the rising top management mobility in recent years in Norway may also represent some explanatory power for the relative non-importance of management support for the IT strategy implementation (Gottschalk, 1995). Finally, the existence of a plan may serve to reduce the importance of management support (Lederer and Salmela, 1996).

The three main suggestions for future research are concerned with weaknesses of the presented research. Firstly, the research model suggested a connection between implementation of an IT strategy and the content of the strategy. Previous research has identified, as table 1 indicates, that much more complicated causal relationships might exist. Secondly, the importance of various implementation predictors may depend on contingency issues such as organisation size, implementation horizon and environmental turbulence (Salmela, 1996). Finally, future research may widen the scope by including both factors and processes in both the planning phase and the implementation phase (Mintzberg, 1994; Van de Ven and Poole, 1995).

An important practical contribution can be derived from the conducted research. In practice, the CIO is often responsible for the IT strategy process, as well as the IT strategy topics and the IT strategy plan (Gottschalk, 1995a; Stephens et al., 1995). When the CIO sits down to produce the formal IT strategy, this research provides clear priority on what to include in the plan document to increase the likelihood of its implementation. Description of responsibility for the implementation is important. Responsibility description should include responsibility for implementation on time, within budget, intended benefits, stepwise implementation of large projects, high priority projects and short-term benefits from initial projects. Description of user involvement during the implementation is the other important factor. User involvement description should include user training, understanding, participation, operation, development and support.

REFERENCES

Alavi, M. and Henderson, J.C., 1981. "An Evolutionary Strategy for Implementing a Decision Support System", Management Science, 27 (11), pp. 1309-1323.

Alavi, M. and Joachimsthaler, E. A., 1992. "Revisiting DSS Implementation Research: A Meta-Analysis of the Literature and Suggestions for Researchers", MIS Quarterly, Vol. 16 (1), pp. 95-116.

Alter, S. and Ginzberg, M., 1978. "Managing Uncertainty in MIS Implementation", Sloan Management Review, 20 (1), pp. 23-31.

Applegate, L. M.; McFarlan, F. W. and McKenney, J. L., 1996. Corporate Information Systems Management. Chicago, USA: Irwin.

Argyris, C. anad Kaplan, R.S., 1994. "Implementing New Knowledge: The Case of Activity Based Costing", Accounting Horizons, Vol. 8 (3), pp. 83-105.

Baier, V.E.; March, J.G. and Saetren, H., 1986. "Implementation and Amibiguity", Scandinavian journal of management studies, May, pp. 197-212.

Bajjaly, S.T., 1998. "Strategic information systems planning in the public sector", American Review of Public Administration, Vol. 28 (1), pp. 75-85.

Bagozzi, R.P., 1996. "Measurement in Marketing Research: Basic Principles of Questionnaire Design". In: Bagozzi, R.P. (ed.), Principles of Marketing Research. Cambridge, USA: Blackwell, pp. 1-49.

Baronas, A-M. K. and Louis, M. R., 1988. "Restoring a Sense of Control During Implementation: How User Involvement Leads to System Acceptance", MIS Quarterly, Vol. 12 (1), pp. 111-124.

Bradley, J.H. and Hauser, R.D., 1995. "A Framework for Expert System Implementation", Expert systems With Applications, 8 (1), pp. 157-167.

Brancheau, J.C.; Schuster, L. and March, S.T., 1989. "Building and implementing an information architecture", DATA BASE, Summer, pp. 9-17.

Byrd, T.A.; Sambamurthy, V. and Zmud, R.W., 1995. "An Examination of IT Planning in a Large, Diversified Public Organization", Decision Sciences, 26 (1), pp. 49-73.

Chan, Y. E., 1992. Business strategy, information systems strategy, and strategic fit: Measurement and performance impacts. Unpublished Doctoral Dissertation, Canada: University of Western Ontario.

Chan, Y.E. and Huff, S.L., 1994. "The development of instruments to assess information systems and business unit strategy performance", In: Venkatraman, N. and Henderson, J. (editors), Research in strategic management and information technology, UK: JAI Press, pp. 145-182.

Coolbaugh, J.D., 1993. An analysis of strategic planning in California cities, unpublished doctoral dissertation, USA: University of Laverne.

Earl, M. J., 1993. "Experiences in Strategic Information Planning", MIS Quarterly, Vol. 17 (1), pp. 1-24.

Falconer, D. J. and Hodgett, R. A. 1997. "Strategic Information Systems Planning, an Australian Experience", Proceedings of the Americas Conference on Information Systems, 15-17 August, USA: Indianapolis, pp. 837-839.

Finnegan, P.; Galliers, R. and Powell, P., 1997. "Investigating inter-organisational information systems planning practices in Ireland and the UK", Proceedings of the 5th European Conference on Information Systems, 19-21 June, Ireland: Cork, volume I pp. 281-294.

Floyd, S.W. and Wooldridge, B., 1992. "Managing strategic consensus: the foundation of effective implementation", Academy of Management Executive, 6 (4), pp. 27-39.

Flynn, D.J. and Goleniewska, E., 1993. "A survey of the use of SISP approaches in UK organisations", Journal of Strategic Information Systems, Vol. 2 (4), pp. 292-319.

Galliers, R. D., 1993. "IT strategies: beyond competitive advantage", Journal of Strategic Information Systems, Vol. 2 (4), pp. 283-291.

Galliers, R. D., 1994. "Strategic information systems planning: myths, reality and guidelines for successful implementation", in: Galliers, R. D. and Baker, B. S. H. (Eds.), Strategic Information Management. Oxford, UK: Butterworth-Heinemann, pp. 129-147.

Gill, T. G., 1996. "Expert Systems Usage: Task Change and Intrinsic Motivation", MIS Quarterly, Vol. 20 (3), pp. 301-329.

Ginzberg, M. J., 1981. "Key Recurrent Issues in the MIS Implementation Process", MIS Quarterly, Vol. 5 (2), pp. 47-59.

Gottschalk, P., 1995. Technology Management (in Norwegian: Teknologiledelse), Bergen, Norway: Fagbokforlaget publishing.

Gottschalk, P., 1998. Content Characteristics of Formal Information Technology Strategy as Implementation Predictors. Oslo, Norway: Tano Aschehoug publishing.

Griffiths, T.L. and Northcraft, G.B., 1996. "Cognitive Elements in the Implementation of New Technology: Can Less Information Provide More Benefits?", MIS Quarterly, 20 (1), pp. 99-110.

Gupta, Y. P. and Raghunathan, T. S., 1989. "Impact of Information Systems (IS) Steering Committees on IS Planning", Decision Sciences, Vol. 20 (4), pp. 777-793.

Hair, J. F.; Anderson, R. E.; Tatham, R. L. and Black, W. C., 1998. Multivariate data analysis. Fifth Edition, Englewood Cliffs, USA: Prentice Hall.

Hann, J. and Weber, R., 1996. "Information Systems Planning: A Model and Empirical Tests", Management Science, 42 (7), pp. 1043-1064.

Hussey, D.E., 1996. "A Framework for Implementation", In: Hussey, D.E. (editor), The Implementation Challenge, The Wiley Series in Contemporary Strategic Concerns, UK: John Wiley and Sons, Chichester, pp. 1-14.

Jarvenpaa, S.L. and Ives, B., 1991. "Executive Involvement and Participation in the Management of Information Technology", MIS Quarterly, 15 (2), pp. 205-227.

Joshi, K., 1991. "A Model of Users' Perspective on Change: The Case of Information Systems Technology Implementation", MIS Quarterly, Vol. 15 (2), pp. 229-242.

Kaplan, R.S. and Norton, D.P., 1996. "Using the Balanced Scorecard as a Strategic Management System", Harvard Business Review, January-February pp. 75-85.

Kearney, A. T. (1990), Breaking the barriers - IT effectiveness in Great Britain and Ireland. Report by A.T. Kearney for The Chartered Institute of Management Accountants, London, UK: A.T. Kearney Limited.

Klein, K.J. and Sorra, J.S., 1996. "The challenge of innovation implementation", Academy of Management Review, Vol. 21 (4) pp 1055-1088.

Kwon, T.H. and Zmud, R.W., 1987. "Unifying the Fragmented Models of Information Systems Implementation". In: Boland, R.J. and Hirschheim, R.A., Critical Issues in Information Systems Research, UK: John Wiley and Sons, pp. 227-248.

Lederer, A. L. and Mendelow, A. L., 1993. "Information systems planning and the challenge of shifting priorities", Information & Management, Vol. 24 (6), pp. 319-328.

Lederer, A. L. and Salmela, H., 1996. "Toward a Theory of Strategic Information Systems Planning", Journal of Strategic Information Systems, Vol. 5 (3), pp. 237-253.

Lederer, A. L. and Sethi, V., 1988. "The Implementation of Strategic Information Systems Planning Methodologies", MIS Quarterly, Vol. 12 (3), pp. 445-461.

Lederer, A. L. and Sethi, V., 1992. "Root Causes of Strategic Information Systems Planning Implementation Problems", Journal of Management Information Systems, Vol. 9 (1), pp. 25-45.

Lederer, A. L. and Sethi, V., 1996. "Key Prescriptions for Strategic Information Systems Planning", Journal of MIS,

Vol. 13 (1), pp. 35-62.

Lee, J., 1995. An exploratory study of organizational/managerial factors influencing business process reengineering implementation: An empirical study of critical success factors and resistance management. Unpublished Doctoral Dissertation, USA: The University of Nebraska.

Leonard-Barton, D. and Deschamps, I., 1988. "Managerial influence in the implementation of new technology", Management Science, 34 (10), pp. 1252-1265.

Lucas, H.C., 1981. Implementation - the key to successful information systems, USA: Columbia University Press, New York.

Lucas, H.C.; Walton, E.J. and Ginzberg, M.J., 1988. "Implementing Packaged Software", MIS Quarterly, 12 (4), pp. 537-549.

Markus, M.L., 1983. "Power, Politics and MIS Implementation", Communications of the ACM, 26 (6), pp. 430-444.

Mintzberg, H., 1994. The Rise and Fall of Strategic Planning. New York, USA: Prentice Hall.

Montealegre, R., 1994. Management's role in the implementation of information technology in an agroindustrial organization of a less-developed country, Unpublished Doctoral Dissertation, USA: Harvard University.

Nutt, P.C., 1986. "Tactics of Implementation", Academy of Management Journal, 29 (2), pp. 230-261.

Nutt, P.C., 1995. "Implementing Style and Use of Implementation Approaches", Omega, Vol. 23 (5), pp. 469-484.

Olsen, R., 1995. Rating Congruence between various Management Appraisal Sources, Unpublished Doctoral Dissertation, UK: Henley Management College.

Premkumar, G. and King, W. R., 1994. "Organizational Characteristics and Information Systems Planning: An Empirical Study", Information Systems Research, Vol. 5 (2), pp. 75-109.

Raghunathan, B. and Raghunathan, T. S., 1994. "Adaption of a Planning System Success Model to Information Systems Planning", Information Systems Research, Vol. 5 (3), pp. 326-341.

Rhodes, E. and Wield, D., 1985. Implementing new technologies, UK: Basil Blackwell, Oxford.

Sabherwal, R. and King, W. R., 1995. "An Empirical Taxonomy of the Decision-Making Processes Concerning Strategic Applications of Information Systems", Journal of Management Information Systems, Vol. 11 (4), pp. 177-214.

Salmela, H., 1996. The requirements for information systems planning in a turbulent environment. Doctoral Dissertation, Publication of the Turku School of Economics and Business Administration, Turku, Finland, Series A-1:1996.

Segars, A. H., 1994. Strategic Information Systems Planning: The coalignment of planning system design, its relationships with organizational context, and implications for planning system success. Unpublished Doctoral Dissertation, USA: University of South Carolina.

Srinivasan, A. and Davis, J.G., 1987. "A Reassessment of Implementation Process Models", Interfaces, 17 (3), pp. 64-71.

Stephens, C. S.; Mitra, A.; Ford, F. N. and Ledbetter, W. N., 1995. "The CIO's Dilemma: Participating in Strategic Planning", Information Strategy, Spring, pp. 13-17.

Swanson, D.L., 1995. "Addressing a theoretical problem by reorienting the corporate social performance model", Academy of Management Review, Vol. 20 (1), pp. 43-64.

Taylor, B., 1997. "The Return of Strategic Planning - Once More with Feeling", Long Range Planning, Vol. 30 (3), pp. 334-344.

Teo, T. S. H., 1994. Integration between business planning and information systems planning: Evolutionary-contingency perspectives. Unpublished Doctoral Dissertation, USA: University of Pittsburgh.

Teo, T. S. H. and King, W. R., 1997. "An assessment of perceptual differences between informants in information systems research", Omega, Vol. 25 (5), pp. 557-566.

Van de Ven, A. H. and Poole, M. S., 1995. "Explaining development and change in organizations", Academy of Management Review, Vol. 20 (3), pp. 510-540.

Ward, J. and Griffiths, P., 1996. Strategic planning for information systems, Wiley Series in Information Systems, UK: John Wiley and Sons, Chichester.

Ward, J.; Taylor, P. and Bond, P., 1996. "Evaluation and realisation of IS/IT benefits: an empirical study of current practice", European Journal of Information Systems, Vol. 4 (4), pp. 214-225.

Watson, R.T.; Kelly, G.G.; Galliers, R.D. and Brancheau, J.C., 1997. "Key Issues in Information Systems Management: An International Perspective", Journal of Management Information Systems, Vol. 13 (4), pp. 91-115.

Williams, K.L., 1992. An investigation of how organizations manage information technology initiatives, Unpublished Doctoral Dissertation, USA: The Florida State University.

Zmud, R.W. and Boynton, A.C., 1991. "Survey Measures and Instruments in MIS: Inventory and Appraisal", In: Kraemer, K.L.; Cash, J.I. and Nunamaker, J.F., The Information Systems Research Challenge: Survey Research Methods, Harvard Business School Research Colloquium, USA: Harvard Business School, Boston, pp. 149-180.

Key Issues in Information Systems Management in Norway: Extending Key Issues Selection Procedure and Empirical Study

Petter Gottschalk

Department of Technology Management, Norwegian School of Management, Box 580 , 1301 Sandvika, Norway

petter.gottschalk@bi.no, http://www.bi.no/people/fgl98023.htm, Tel + 47 67 55 73 38, Fax +47 67 55 76 78

ABSTRACT

Information systems (IS) departments face many challenges in today's rapidly changing environment. One approach to understanding the challenges faced by IS departments is to survey IS managers to elicit what they consider are key issues. Key issues in IS management surveys have been conducted for many years in many nations and regions. However, most of these surveys lack a theoretical basis for the selection of key issues. Furthermore, most studies have used a multi-round Delphi method. Recently, the analysis of key issues in IS management has been extended by a multimethod approach using Q methodology and interpretive structural modeling. This paper provides an overview of research approaches to key issues studies combined with results from previous research. The paper presents methodological issues and choices for a planned survey on key issues in IS management in Norway late 1998. A theory-based procedure for key issues selection is applied, and a multimethod approach for analysis is adopted.

INTRODUCTION

Information systems (IS) departments face many challenges in today's rapidly changing environment. One approach to understanding the challenges faced by IS departments is to survey IS managers to elicit what they consider are key issues (Watson et al., 1997). According to Niederman et al. (1991), the primary purpose of such studies is to determine which IS management issues are expected to be most important over the next three to five years and thus most deserving of time and resource investment, how much consensus exists about the relative importance of specific issues, and why some issues deserve more attention than others. IS vendors, professional societies, consultants, educators, and researchers need to be aware of IS executives' key concerns to serve their markets effectively.

Key issues in IS management surveys have been conducted for many years in many nations and regions. However, most key issues surveys lack a theoretical basis for the selection of key issues (Watson et al., 1997). Furthermore, most surveys have used only the Delphi technique in single or multiple rounds (e.g.; Brancheau et al., 1996; Galliers et al., 1994; Moores, 1996; Pervan, 1993; Wang, 1994). Recently, the analysis of key issues in IS management has been extended by a multimethod approach using Q methodology and interpretive structural modeling (e.g.; Morgado et al., 1995, 1998). This paper provides an overview of research approaches to key issues studies combined with results from previous work. The paper presents methodological issues and choices for a planned survey on key issues in IS management in Norway late 1998. There is a need not only to find out what the key issues are, but also to find out what causes these issues and to determine the diversity of view points so that there is no assumption of one single answer.

The specific purpose of this study is to use the research results to develop new educational programs. The Norwegian School of Management is in the process of developing both undergraduate and graduate programs in the area of IS management. An undergraduate program in information technology is to start in the fall of 1999, while a graduate program leading to the Master of Science degree in information management is to start later.

LITERATURE REVIEW

Over the past two decades, the US Society for Information Management (SIM) has periodically surveyed its members to determine the most critical issues in IS management (Brancheau et al., 1996). Surveys were conducted in

1980, 1983, 1986, 1990 and 1994-95, representing a valuable resource for key issues insights in a time perspective. These SIM studies have had a significant influence on key issues studies in other countries (e.g., Dekleva and Zupancic, 1996; Wang, 1994). IS key issues studies have been conducted in Australia 1993, Canada 1995, Costa Rica 1997, Estonia 1993, Europe 1993, Guatemala 1997, the Gulf Cooperation Council 1992, Hong Kong 1993, India 1992, Indonesia 1996, Poland 1994, the Republic of China (Taiwan) 1990, Slovenia 1993, South Korea 1995, and the United Kingdom 1993 (Watson et al., 1997). A Web-site (http://www.cba.uga.edu/iris/) has been established to report details of key issues studies. The results of two recent key issues in IS management studies are now considered. The first study listed in table 1 is the most recent US SIM study (Brancheau et al., 1996), while the second study listed in table 2 is the result of an international comparison of several key issues studies (Watson et al., 1997).

While table 1 is based on a survey in the United States in 1994-95, table 2 is based on surveys in eleven nations and regions in 1988-92. Six issues are present in both lists: strategic

Table 1: US SIM Issues in IS Management (Brancheau et al., 1996)

Rank	US SIM Issue
1	Building a responsive IT infrastructure
2	Facilitating and managing business process redesign
3	Developing and managing distributed systems
4	Developing and implementing an information architecture
5	Planning and managing communication networks
6	Improving the effectiveness of software development
7	Making effective use of the data resource
8	Recruiting and developing IS human resources
9	Aligning the IS Organization within the enterprise
10	Improving IS strategic planning

Table 2: International Issues in IS Management (Watson et al., 1997)

Rank	International Issue
1	Strategic planning
2	IS organizational alignment
3	Information architecture
3	Competitive advantage
3	Data as a resource
3	Human resources
3	Security and control
8	Integrating technology
9	Software development
9	IS's role and contribution

planning, alignment, information architecture, data resources, human resources and software development. The top three issues in the US SIM study are not present on the international list at all: infrastructure, business process redesign and distributed systems. In a time perspective, eight out of ten issues in the 1994-95 US SIM study were present in the top ten list from 1990 (Niederman et al., 1991). The two new issues emerging from 1990 to 1994-95 were business process redesign and distributed systems.

This research is concerned with key issues selection procedure and key issues survey approach: it is assumed that the ranking results of the studies presented above were influenced by selection procedure and survey approach (Watson et al., 1997). The most common selection procedure is to start with an old key issues list and let it be revised in multiple survey rounds (e.g., Brancheau et al., 1996). Few studies start from scratch by asking respondents to specify issues which they think will be key issues (e.g., Dekleva and Zupanic, 1996). This paper argues that key issues selections should be based on theory (Watson et al., 1997). The most common survey approach is the Delphi technique (e.g., Niederman et al., 1991). Few studies apply other methods (e.g., Morgado et al., 1995, 1998). This paper argues that key issues surveys should be extended by multiple techniques to gain insights into the relationships among key issues which can influence the final ranking. Table 3 compares methodological choices in key issues studies.

Key Issues Selection

Some key issues appear to emerge quickly. The sudden prominence of business process redesign in table 1, for example, indicates that IS managers may be too willing to respond to a current hot topic, and their attention may be too easily diverted from fundamental, long-term issues (Watson et al., 1997). If asked today, many Norwegian IS managers would probably rank "Year 2000" as a key issue. The Year 2000 issue is, however, both a short-term problem and an issue which is part of a bigger problem of maintaining software. Hence, the selection of key issues for survey research is associated with several problems as listed in table 4.

Study	Key Issues Selection			Key Issues Survey		
	List	New	Method	Respondents	Score	Nation
Badri (1992)	Old	No	1 round	CIOs	Rate	Gulf nations
Brancheau et al. (1996)	Old	Yes	Delphi 3 rounds	SIM members	Rate	USA
Burn et al. (1993)	Old	Yes	Delphi 3 rounds	Managers	Rate	Hong Kong
CSC (1997)	Old	No	Survey 1 round	IS executives	Rate	USA Europe Asia/Pacific
Deans et al. (1991)	Old	Yes	Survey and Interview	MIS managers	Rate	USA
Dekleva and Zupancic (1996)	New	Yes	Delphi 4 rounds	IS managers	Rate	Slovenia
Dexter et al. (1993)	New	Yes	Delphi 3 rounds	IT managers	Rate	Estonia
Galliers et al. (1994)	New	No	Delphi 1 round	Executives	Rate	UK
Harrison and Farn (1990)	Old	No	Survey 1 round	Professionals	Rate	USA Taiwan
Mata and Fuerst (1997)	Old	Yes	Survey 1 round	IS managers	Rate	Costa Rica Guatemala
Morgado et al. (1995, 1998)	Old	Yes	Q-sort ISM	IT managers	Rank	Brazil
Moores (1996)	Old	No	Delphi 1 round	MIS managers	Rate	Hong Kong
Olsen et al. (1998)	Old	No	Delphi 1 round	IT managers	Rate	Norway
Palvia and Palvia (1992)	Open	Yes	Seminar	Managers	Rate	India
Pervan (1993)	New	Yes	Delphi 3 rounds	IS managers	Rate	Australia
Pollard and Hayne (1996)	Old	Yes	Delphi 2 rounds	IS personell	Rate	Canada
Swain et al (1995)	Old	Yes	Delphi 1 round	Information manager	Rate	USA
Wang (1994)	Old	No	Delphi 1 round	IT manager	Rate	Taiwan
Wrycza and Plata-Przechlewski (1994)	Old	No	Survey 1 round	Seminar participants	Rate	Poland
This study	New	Yes	Q-sort ISM	CIOs	Rank	Norway

Table 3: Comparison of Methodological Choices in Key Issues Studies

The lack of theory is a major concern. Watson et al. (1997) suggest that a sufficiently relevant theoretical model, on which to base a new key issues framework, should be identified. They discuss role theory, managerial IS competencies and general management practices as "redesign" approaches to potential new key issues frameworks (Watson et al., 1997, p. 111):

Advantages of the "redesign" approach include the possibility that the framework be complete, consistent, parsimonious, and both regionally and temporally stable. Disadvantages include the lack of continuity with previous studies and the danger that the issues might become so abstract that they would cease to have meaning to IS managers and executives, thus breaking an important link to practice.

Niederman et al. (1991) made a theoretical contribution by classifying key issues along three dimensions and categorising them into four groups. The three dimensions were management versus technology issues (M/T), planning versus control issues (P/C), and internal versus external issues to IS management (I/E). The four groups consisted of:

Table 4: Key Issues Selection Problem	
Problem	Problem Description
Time	**Key issues change over time, critical issues in the early 1990s differ from critical issues in the late 1990s. Therefore, the use of previous key issues lists in new surveys has limitations.**
Fashion	**The IS profession is notable for its fashion swings. In the last few years the hot topics have included outsourcing, business process redesign and Internet.**
Events	**Certain events strongly influence ranking, for example the Year 2000 issue.**
Overlaps	**Some issues are not defined properly to avoid overlap with other issue(s).**
Granularity	**While some issues refer to broad general problems, other issues refer to more narrow and specific concerns.**
Theory	**Application of theory is lacking in key issues selection.**
Clearity	**Some issues are not formulated and communicated properly to understand the contents of the issues.**
Causality	**Some issues might, although ranked as unimportant, represent important drivers of other key issues. For example, recruiting and developing IS human resources might be an important driver of building an IT architecture.**
Reliability	**Interrater reliability measures the consistency by which issues are assigned to categories and dimensions. A test of five faculty members at the Norwegian School of Management resulted in a low interrater reliability for latest US SIM issues.**

- *Business relationship:* These issues deal with concerns external to the IS department. They focus on managing the relationship between IS and the business. The group included data resources, strategic planning, organisational learning, IS organisation alignment and competitive advantage.
- *Technology infrastructure:* These issues deal with technology concerns. They focus on the integration of technology components to support basic business needs. The group included information architecture, technology infrastructure, telecommunications systems, distributed systems, and electronic data interchange.
- *Internal effectiveness:* These issues focus internally on the IS function. They are concerned with those essential activities comprising the bulk of the IS function's work. The group included human resources, software develop-

Table 5: US SIM Issues Classified By Dimensions and Categories							
DIMENSIONS/	**Key Issues in IS Management**	**M/T**		**P/C**		**I/E**	
CATEGORIES	**1994-95 SIM Delphi Results**	**M**	**T**	**P**	**C**	**I**	**E**
Business relationship	Business Process Redesign	2			2		2
	Data Resources	7			7		7
	IS Organization Alignment	9			9		9
	IS Strategic Planning	10		10			10
	IS Role & Contribution	13		13			13
	Organizational Learning	14			14		14
	Competitive Advantage	17		17			17
Technology infrastructure	Responsive IT infrastructure		1		1	1	
	Distributed Systems		3		3		3
	Information Architecture		4	4		4	
	Communication Networks		5		5		5
	MultiVendor Open Systems		18		18	18	
	Electronic Data Interchange		19		19		19
Internal effectiveness	Software Development		6		6	6	
	IS Human Resources	8			8	8	
	IS Effectiveness Measurement	11			11	11	
	Legacy Applications		15		15	15	
	Outsourcing	20			20		20
Technology application	Collaborative Systems		11		11		11
	End-User Computing	16			16		16

Note: In table 1, the top ten key issues from the US SIM study were listed. In this table, the top twenty key issues from the same study are listed. Dimensions and categories are the same as in Brancheau et al. (1996, Appendix D). The numbers in the columns are the ranks of the key issues.

Table 6: Delphi Survey Problems	
Problem	**Description**
Consensus	Reported consensus in Delphi studies is somewhat illusory. Rather, what is reported traditionally is not consensus, but possibly an aggregation of concerns that are quite different for disparate groups of respondents.
Interaction	Independent consideration of key issues disregards interaction between issues. For example, an unimportant issue might be an important driver for a key issue.
Theory	Application of theory is lacking in key issues modifications.
Difference	Differences in rating scores are low, i.e. the full potential of scales is not utilised. For example, while a scale from 1 to 10 is provided, the highest rated issue achieves 9.10 and the lowest rated issue achieves 5.40 in the 20 key issues list in Brancheau et al. (1996).

ment, applications portfolio and IS effectiveness measurement.

• *Technology application:* These issues focus on the business application of specific information technologies. The group included CASE technology, executive/decision support, end-user computing and image technology.

However, classifying issues into dimensions and categories is a challenging task (Smith, 1995). In table 5, the latest US SIM classification is listed.

Table 5 can be used to identify both potentially missing issues and potentially overlapping issues. A total of 32 different issues are possible in this matrix by combining four categories with three double dimensions. Several potentially missing issues can be identified. For example, there are no business relationship issues involving technology. Several potentially overlapping issues can be identified. For example, there are four business relationship issues involving management-control-external.

Key Issues Survey

The dominating survey approach of key issues in IS management studies is the Delphi method. The Delphi method uses a series of linked questionnaires. Successive rounds of questionnaires summarize subjects' responses to the preceding questionnaire and ask respondents to re-evaluate their opinions based upon the summarized results. Questionnaire rounds are continued until a reasonable level of consensus is achieved (Brancheau et al., 1996). However, the Delphi survey approach is associated with problems (Morgado et al., 1998) as listed in table 6.

Morgado et al. (1998) suggest extending the analysis of key issues in information systems management by demonstrating two techniques that may provide greater insight into the concerns of IS managers than the traditional rating method used by most recent key issues studies. Their research used Q-sort (Brown, 1993, 1996) and interpretive structural modeling (ISM) (Warfield, 1991) based on a survey of banks in Brazil (Morgado et al., 1998, p. 3):

These approaches allowed us and the participating IT managers to gain a deeper understanding of the relationships among the key issues. A factor analysis on the Q-sort data identified three groups of banks with similar IT situations and strategies, and led to the conclusion that key issues can vary considerably among respondents. Application of ISM resulted in a revision of IT managers' perceived priorities and proved to be a significant contribution to their understanding of their key concerns.

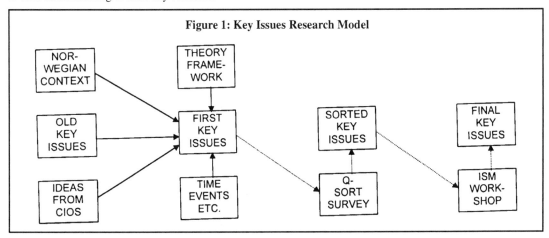

Figure 1: Key Issues Research Model

Table 7: Structured Sample of Key Issues for Q-sort

C	D	Key Issue	Sources	#
BR	MPI	*NA: BR only external*	*NA: BR only external*	
BR	MPE	Improving Links between Information Systems Strategy and Business Strategy	Expanded from Olsen et al. (1998) and Brancheau et al. (1996), and suggested by CIO; also found in general MIS literature (e.g., Ward and Griffiths, 1996; Robson, 1997)	1
BR	MCI	*NA: BR only external*	*NA: BR only external*	
BR	MCE	Making Effective Use of Data and Information Systems Resources	Expanded from Olsen et al. (1998) and Brancheau et al. (1996)	2
BR	TPI	*NA: BR only external*	*NA: BR only external*	
BR	TPE	Improving Interorganisational Information Systems Planning	Norwegian context: Most organisations are small and cooperative	3
BR	TCI	*NA: BR only external*	*NA: BR only external*	
BR	TCE	Improving Control, Security and Recovery Capabilities	Two low-ranked issues combined from Brancheau et al. (1996)	4
TI	MPI	Improving Information Technology Infrastructure Planning	Expanded from Olsen et al. (1998) and Brancheau et al. (1996)	5
TI	MPE	Planning Information Technology Projects for Competitive Advantage	Adapted from Olsen et al. (1998) and Brancheau et al. (1996)	6
TI	MCI	Managing the Technical Foundation of Information Systems	General MIS literature (e.g., Laudon and Laudon, 1998)	7
TI	MCE	Improving Availability of National and International Networks	Adapted from Dekleva and Zupancic (1996)	8
TI	TPI	Developing and Implementing an Information Architecture	Adopted from Olsen et al. (1998) and Brancheau et al. (1996)	9
TI	TPE	Planning Information Technology for Electronic Commerce	General MIS literature (e.g., Laudon and Laudon, 1998)	10
TI	TCI	Controlling a Responsive Information Technology Infrastructure	Adapted from Olsen et al. (1998) and Brancheau et al. (1996)	11
TI	TCE	Implementing Information Technology for Electronic Commerce	Expanded from Olsen et al. (1998) and Brancheau et al. (1996)	12
IE	MPI	Recruiting and Developing IS Human Resources	Suggested by CIO and adopted from Brancheau et al. (1996) and Olsen et al. (1998)	13
IE	MPE	*NA: IE only internal*	*NA: IE only internal*	
IE	MCI	Reducing IT Projects' Completion Time	Suggested by CIO	14
IE	MCE	*NA: IE only internal*	*NA: IE only internal*	
IE	TPI	Improving Computer Operations Planning	Adapted suggestion by CIO	15
IE	TPE	*NA: IE only internal*	*NA: IE only internal*	
IE	TCI	Improving Software Engineering Practices	Suggested by CIOs	16
IE	TCE	*NA: IE only internal*	*NA: IE only internal*	
TA	MPI	Managing Application Architecture Planning	General MIS literature (e.g., Laudon and Laudon, 1998; McNurlien and Sprague, 1998)	17
TA	MPE	Managing Internet Applications	General MIS literature (e.g., Laudon and Laudon, 1998)	18
TA	MCI	Measuring Benefits from Information Technology Applications	Adapted suggestion by CIO, Olsen et al. (1998) and Brancheau et al. (1996)	19
TA	MCE	Managing and Controlling End-User Computing	Adopted from Olsen et al. (1998) and Brancheau et al. (1996)	20
TA	TPI	Ensuring Quality with Information Systems	General MIS literature (e.g., Laudon and Laudon, 1998)	21
TA	TPE	Scanning Emerging Technologies	General MIS literature (e.g., Robson, 1997, p. 357; Laudon and Laudon, 1998; McNurlien & Sprague, 1998)	22
TA	TCI	Assuring Software Quality	General MIS literature (e.g., Laudon and Laudon, 1998)	23
TA	TCE	Implementing and Managing Knowledge Work Systems	Adopted from Olsen et al. (1998) and Brancheau et al. (1996)	24

Note: The first column lists categories (C) which are business relationships (BR), technology infrastructure (TR), internal effectiveness (IE) and technology application (TA). The second column lists dimensions (D) which are management (M) or technology (T), planning (P) or control (C), and internal (I) and external (E).

METHODOLOGICAL CHOICES

In this research, the survey approach is following the key issues selction procedure and empirical study illustrated in figure 1.

FIRST KEY ISSUES

A total of 32 different issues are possible in the matrix in table 5 by combining four categories with three double dimensions. However, business relationship is by definition concerned with external issues, thereby excluding internal issues; while internal effectiveness by definition is concerned with internal issues, thereby excluding external issues. Hence, to cover all categories and dimensions suggested by the theory framework (Niederman et al., 1991), a total of 24 issues have to be identified as listed in table 7. The key issues in table 7 are derived from old key issues lists (Olsen et al., 1998; Brancheau et al., 1996) and ideas from CIOs by consideration of the Norwegian context and formulation problems as illustrated in figure 1.

Q-SORT SURVEY

The Q-sort survey as illustrated in figure 1, is based on the first key issues list in table 6. The mailing took place in October 1998, and the results will be available in December 1998.

REFERENCES

Badri, M.A., 1992. "Critical Issues in Information Systems Management: An International Perspective", *International Journal of Information Management*, Vol. 12, pp. 179-191.

Brancheau, J.C.; Janz, B.D. and Wetherbe, J.C., 1996. "Key Issues in Information Systems Management: 1994-95 SIM Delphi Results", *MIS Quarterly*, Vol. 20 (2), pp. 225-242.

Brown, S.R., 1993. "A Primer on Q Methodology", *Operant Subjectivity*, Vol. 16 (3/4), pp. 91-138.

Brown, S.R., 1996. "Q Methodology and Qualitative Research", *Qualitative Health Research*, 6 (4), November, pp. 561-567.

Burn, J.; Saxena, K.B.C.; Ma, L. and Cheung, H.K., 1993. "Critical Issues in IS Management in Hong Kong: A Cultural Comparison", *Journal of Global Information Management*, Vol.1 (4). pp. 28-37.

CSC, 1997. *Critical Issues of Information Systems Management, 10th Annueal Survry of I/S Management Issues.* Computer Science Corporation (CSC), USA: California.

Deans, P.C.; Karwan, K.R.; Goslar, M.D.; Ricks, D.A. and Toyne, B. (1991). "Identification of Key International Information Systems Issues in U.S.-Based Multinational Corporations", *Journal of Management Information Systems*, Vol. 7 (4), pp. 27-50.

Dekleva, S. and Zupancic, J., 1996. "Key issues in information systems management: a Delphi study in Slovenia", *Information & Management*, Vol. 31, pp. 1-11.

Dexter, A.S.; Janson, M.A.; Kiudorf, E. and Laast-Laas, J., 1993. "Key information technology issues in Estonia", *Journal of Strategic Information Systems*, Vol. 24 (2), pp. 139-152.

Galliers, R.D.; Merali, Y. and Spearing, L., 1994. "Coping with information technology? How British executives perceive the key information systems management issues in the mid-1990s", *Journal of Information Technology*, Vol. 9, pp. 223-238.

Harrison, W.L. and Farn, C.-K., 1990. "A Comparison of Information Management Issues in the United States of America and the Republic of China", *Information & Management*, Vol. 18, pp. 177-188.

Laudon, K.C. and Laudon, J.P., 1998. *Management Information Systems - New Approaches to Organization & Technology.* Fifth Edition, USA: Prentice Hall International, Inc.

Mata, F.J. and Fuerst, W.L., 1997. "Information systems management issues in Central America: a multinational and comparative study", *Journal of Strategic Information Systems*, Vol. 6, pp 173-202.

McNurlien, B.C. and Sprague, R.H., 1998. *Information Systems Management in Practice.* Fourth Edition. USA: Prentice-Hall International, Inc.

Morgado, E.M.; Reinhard, N. and Watson, R.T., 1995. "Extending the analysis of key issues in information technology management", *Proceedings of the sixteenth International Conference on Information Systems*, Amsterdam, Netherlands, December, pp. 13-16.

Morgado, E.M.; Reinhard, N. and Watson, R.T., 1998. *Adding value to key issues research.* Athens, GA, USA: University of Georgia Working Paper.

Moores, T.T., 1996. "Key issues in the management of information systems: A Hong Kong perspective", *Information & Management*, Vol. 30, pp. 301-397.

Niederman, F.; Brancheau, J.C. and Wetherbe, J.C., 1991. "Information Systems Management Issues for the 1990s", *MIS Quarterly*, Vol. 17 (4), pp. 475-500.

Olsen, D.H.; Eikebrokk, T.R. and Sein, M.K., 1998. "Key Issues in Information Systems Management in Norway: An Empirical Study", *Proceedings of the NOKOBIT-98 conference*, 17-19 June, Norwegian School of Management, Norway: Oslo, pp. 1-17.

Palvia, P.C. and Palvia, S., 1992. "MIS Issues in India, and a Comparison with the United States", *International Information Systems*, April, pp.100-110.

Pervan, G. H., 1993. "Results from a study of key issues in Australian IS management", *Proceedings of the 4th Australian Conference on Information Systems*, University of Qeensland, Brisbane, Australia, 28-30 September, pp 113-128.

Pollard, C.E. and Hayne, S.C., 1996. "A Comparative Analysis of Information Systems Issues Facing Canadian Business", *Proceedings of the 29th Annual Hawaii International Conference on System Sciences*, pp. 68-77.

Robson, W., 1997. *Strategic Management & Information Systems*. Second Edition, UK: Financial Times, Pitman Publishing.

Smith, G.F., 1995. "Classifying managerial problems: an empirical study of definitional content", *Journal of Management Studies*, Vol. 32 (5), pp. 679-706.

Swain, J.W.; White, J.D. and Hubbert, E.D., 1995. "Issues in Public Management Information Systems", *American Review of Public Administration*, Vol. 25 (3), pp. 279-296.

Wang, P., 1994. "Information systems management issues in the Republic of China for the 1990s", *Information & Management*, Vol. 26, pp. 341-352.

Ward, J. and Griffiths, P., 1996. *Strategic Planning for Information Systems*, 2nd Edition, UK: John Wiley & Sons.

Warfield, J., 1991. "Complexity and Cognitive Equilibrium: Experimental Results and Their Implications". *Human Systems Management*, 10, pp 195-202.

Watson, R.T.; Kelly, G.G.; Galliers, R.D. and Brancheau, J.C., 1997. "Key Issues in Information Systems Management: An International Perspective", *Journal of Management Information Systems*, Vol. 13 (4), pp. 91-115.

Wrycza, S. and Plata-Przechlewski, T., 1994. "Key issues in information systems management. The case of Poland". *Proceedings of the 4th International Conference on Information Systems Development*, Bled, Slovenia, pp. 289-296.

Towards an E-commerce Business Strategy: A European perspective

Ray Hackney & Gareth Griffiths
Manchester Metropolitan University, Department of Business Information Technology
Aytoun Street, Manchester, M1 3GH
Tel: +44 (0)161 247 3735, Fax: +44 (0)161 247 6317, R.Hackney@MMU.AC.UK, G.Griffiths@MMU.AC.UK

Ashok Ranchhod
Southampton Business School, East Park Terrace, Southampton, SO14 OYN
Tel: +44 (0)1703 319541, Fax: +44 (0)1703 222259, Ashok.Ranchhod@SOLENT.AC.UK

ABSTRACT

There is a pervasive and continued interest in the fundamentals of formulating an organisational strategy through the opportunities afforded by information systems and technology (IS/IT). One specific classification of IS/IT is recognised in the form of electronic commerce (e-commerce). This paper defines and analyses such systems and considers their impact on competitive 'virtual' trading. It argues, in particular, the relationship between e-commerce and its potential influence on the value chain. The motivation for the paper is to consider the impacts such systems have on business performance. In this respect it is believed that their nature is recognised as offering different guidelines on approaches to organisational strategy. A European perspective is outlined with an emphasis upon various factors (environmental, economic, political, legal) and future organisational developments with reference to a number of industry examples.

INTRODUCTION

The emergence of EDI heralded the start of e-commerce. According to Graham et al (1996) the systems, utilising value added networks (VAN's) between major manufacturing organisations and their suppliers have impacted most notably on the improvement of operational efficiency, and to some degree the industrial forces, enhancing a firms competitive advantage (Barnett, 1995). Other e-commerce developments enabled large firms to connect proprietary links with their customers, examples include American Hospital Supply (Short and Venkatraman 1992) and airline computer reservation systems (Hopper 1990). These e-commerce developments are classified by Graham et al (1996) as Electronic Hierarchies and are most notably expressed within the value chain.

Although impacts were felt on operational activities and outbound logistics, the principle impact of e-commerce was felt within the purchasing department (Bartram, 1996). For example, Kwik-Fit were able to substantially reduce the cost of handling invoice paperwork (Graham et al 1996). This impact was felt within most large scale European manufactures, reducing internal procurement costs and shifting responsibility to suppliers, from the firms internal inbound logistics departments. As suppliers got effectively 'locked' in to a firms ordering system the sales function became less involved and the prime driver was service, quality and cost. These functions allowed retailers to concentrate on re-engineering other elements in the supply chain. Evidence from car manufactures within the UK such as Rover and Ford, support this argument, whereby their suppliers only supply them and therefore have very little bargaining power. As companies such as Tesco, Ford, Nissan and other large retailers reduced supply costs by introducing industry wide e-commerce systems, barriers to entry were raised, allowing them to attain a substantial competitive advantage (Graham et al 1996).

By the mid 1980's e-commerce was limited to operational efficiency. For example Ford's policy of using e-commerce for competitive advantage was challenged as such systems were widely adopted by other automotive manufactures. In addition as suppliers developed standard interfaces to their customers, their bargaining power was reduced as e-commerce was seen as a means of conducting business not a requirement. E-Commerce was essentially confined to impacting on the value chain, enhancing operational efficiency. Although the e-commerce market in Europe continues to grow steadily only 5% of trade in the western hemisphere is carried using the technology. Europe continues to fall behind America with detractors blaming the high cost of value added networks, integration with existing systems, maintenance overheads, and the necessity of re-engineering business processes as the main factors behind its slow take-up rate (Miller, 1997).

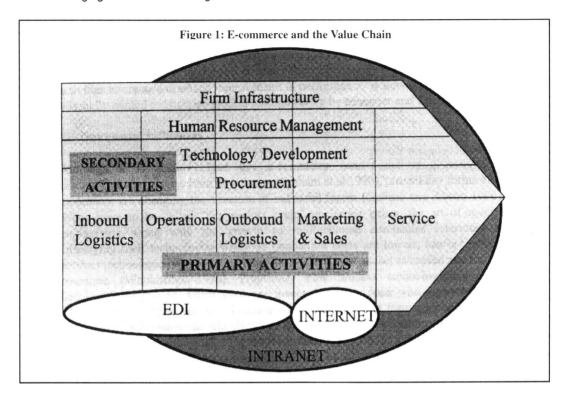

Figure 1: E-commerce and the Value Chain

These paradigm shifts translate loosely but accurately into four main modes of modern day e-commerce, namely: internet, intranet, extranet, electronic market place. These technological advances will impact more widely than with previous e-commerce developments, as how you communicate no longer depends on the technology but on what you want to do (Hoffman & Novak, 1996). However, despite this change, European business according to KPMG (Bennett 1996) is a long way off achieving industry and organisational wide adoption, reporting only 3% of transactions are made with e-commerce systems. E-commerce is continuing to contribute the majority of these transactions (Caston, 1997; Miller 1997).

Figure 1 illustrates an outline of these processes relating to the value chain and e-commerce.

Tesco, arguably one of the forerunners in utilising the benefits of e-commerce, have adopted sales based ordering. This system commences with information captured through electronic point of sale (EPOS) terminals, and electronically moves through the organisation to its EDI links with its suppliers. In this perspective the value chain has truly become an integrated system. Where in the past EDI was seen as an extra to enhance operational efficiency, e-commerce is now able to offer firms a friction-less value chain. Its impact in this instance has been in enhancing operational efficiency by reducing stock levels. These impacts are not limited to retailing, their effects are being felt within many other industries. The benefits that Tesco and other retailers are generating are being felt within many other industries, most notably;

• financial services : E-commerce has also changed the financial service industry. Amongst many other examples, banking transaction completed electronically have had the effect in reducing the cost of completing the transaction by a 10 - 15 fold factor (Miller 1997).
• media : 65% of television advertisements are placed electronically from editors personal computers with intranet and extranet technologies. This has led to reduced costs and increased control of information. Internet technologies have enabled large media firms to electronically advertise globally (Stevens 1997).

The exploitation of these technologies within a business must be managed so that there is a seamless web among invention, design, manufacturing, sales, logistics, and services those competitors cannot match (Thurlow 1996). E-commerce is enabling business to become enablers of process technologies, giving short term competitive advantages within the activities of the value chain, a process of reconfiguring activities to create a dramatic improvement in performance is now commonplace and originally named as business process re-engineering by Mammer and Champy (1994).

ENVIRONMENTAL INFLUENCES

Although it is acknowledged that e-commerce cannot deliver a sustainable competitive advantage within its industry (Graham et al 1996), present day forms of e-commerce are changing the structure of industrial forces (Guthrie and Austin 1996). What came to be called "the product cycle" no longer exists, the art of reverse engineering along with the growth of multinational companies interested in employing their technologies wherever production costs are lowest, has led to new product technologies which flow around the world almost as fast as capital and natural resources (Wooldridge 1996). Proprietary new product technologies are not necessarily employed where they are invented or by those who financed them (Thurow 1996). Firms are now therefore open to competition from a global business community, increasing the likelihood of new entrants and substitute products. By using e-commerce strategically, organisations have attempted to externally disturb the competitive forces at work in an industry and in so doing change the industry structure (Angehrn, 1997; Hackney & Ranchhod, 1998). For example, the impact that e-commerce has had in the financial services industry, from 'Big Bang' through to 24 hour electronic trading in equities. The once familiar open call system of the stock exchange has been replaced by buyers and sellers linking together electronically to buy and sell shares. A physical presence in the exchange is now no longer necessary (Peppard 1993).

Over the past few years, mainly as a result of open systems and advances in communications, organisations have begun to link to each other electronically. Instead of sending orders trough the post, which can take several days, they can now be sent electronically in real-time. The enabler of this is e-commerce which is the main factor in the creation of a global market place (Griffiths & Newman 1995). Earl (1989) argues that a business must produce a conceptual framework for managing technical change. He notes that *"it must be business driven and capable of giving tangible benefits, for example increased productivity, lower headcount."*. This has been addressed by Kosiur (1997) as shown in Figure 2.

In recent years many businesses grew by exercising economies of scale. This can be applied to e-commerce, but in a more limited sense because other principles can have just as great an impact. The Law of Digital Assets which was originally formulated by the Harvard Business School points out that, unlike physical assets, digital assets are used and not consumed and therefore can be used over and over again. Thus it will create more value for the business by continually recycling these assets through a large, infinite, number of transactions. However, they will not necessarily remain useful forever, so there will be a need to revise, enhance, improve and even repackage the products.

political environment

The impact of national government regulation on business has changed dramatically. Activities go to where they are unregulated and often that relocation can happen without anyone physically moving. Insurance and financial activities are electronically performed in Bermuda or the Bahamas, while almost all of those doing the activities are still sitting in their offices in New York or London (Thurlow 1996). This is able as a result of e-commerce, causing governance structures to potentially become obsolete (Cerny 1997). This has already happened in world finance where institutions base themselves wherever the political regulations are the most favourable. Within Europe this issue has now been fully recognised by the G10, whom acknowledge that fundamental steps need to be taken in order to safe guard regional regulations, such as tax and consumer protection (Miller 1997).

social-cultural environment

Why should anyone pay an German high school graduate 40,000 DM per year, when it is possible to get a better-educated Chinese for $35 per month who will work hard twenty-nine days each month and eleven hours per day in China? If one drives east from Germany, one quickly reaches countries with educational standards equal to

Figure 2		
Improve the organisation	Transform the organisation	Redefine the organisation
Product promotions	Customer relations	New products
New sales channels	Organisational learning	Business models
Direct savings	Information sharing	
Time-to-market		
Customer service		
Brand Image		

that Germany but where wages are only 5 to 10 percent as high. With e-commerce as the medium to link a global economy this scenario is a real concern for European business. E-commerce does not respect traditional economic barriers and therefore these socio-cultural influences will have an important effect on business operations. E-commerce is at present breaking the link between worker and employer and creating a global resource of potential labour (Miller 1997). Examples of Indian software developers solving European year 2000 problems, and electronically relaying the information from India to Europe via a satellite (Wooldridge 1996).

legal environment

As the environment becomes more global, there are a number of legal implications for business. For example, trademarks are becoming increasing hard to keep under control (Miller 1997). Recent examples of individuals registering themselves as internet business sites such as www.harrods.com have produced legal challenges. Producing companies will have to take on the responsibility of writing product descriptions in an international perspective as the role of intermediaries is eroded (Griffiths and Newman 1995). Copyrights will become hard to control, examples of music /TV /Film copyrights being distributed over the internet are abound. International agreement will have to be made. Huge losses could be suffered by the unwary who fail to take adequate measures to protect their intellectual property rights (IPR) in cyberspace. E-commerce has changed the environmental forces impacting on European business, which although has not translated into any major environmental changes, has created a period of flux. Consumers are able to make international comparisons of products, traditional industry forces are set to be changed (Miller 1996). This situation is referred to as punctuated equilibrium (Johnson and Scholes 1996), whereby a period of flux is followed by a major transformation. It is therefore considered useful to outline what are believed to be the future developments as a result of e-commerce.

FUTURE DEVELOPMENTS

The predictions for the use of IS/IT over the next five years is that it will become more part of the product, rather than enhancing incremental improvements through BPR. In this perspective e-commerce will become central

Figure 3: Kosiur, 1997	
Traditional E-commerce	**Internet E-commerce**
business-to-business only	business-to-consumers business-to-business business-to-public administration user-to-user
closed "clubs", often industry specific	open marketplace, global scale
limited number of corporate partners	unlimited number of partners
closed proprietary networks	open, unprotected networks
known and trusted partners	known and unknown partners
security part of network design	security and authentication needed
The market is a club	**The network is the market**
Business-to-business services	Business-to-consumer services
Traditional E-commerce • EDI and EFT • Messaging/E mail • Fax	Messaging services • E-mail • Fax
Online information services, e.g. Lexis-Nexis	Online information services, e.g. America Online, CompuServe
Electronic marketplaces/ transactions e.g. Industry.Net, electronic malls	Electronic marketplaces/ transactions, e.g. Internet home shopping

Threat	Security Solution	Function	Technology
Data intercepted, read or modified illicitly	Encryption	Encodes data to prevent tampering	Symmetric encryption; asymmetric encryption
Users misrepresent their identity to commit fraud	Authenticat'	Verifies the identities of both sender and receiver	Digital signatures
Unauthorised user on one network gains access to another	Firewall	Filters and prevents certain traffic from entering the network or server	Firewalls; virtual private networks

to a firms strategy rather than a magical universal panacea for incrementally improving business operations. In the next few years, as web sites become more interactive, the current business model which requires visitors to switch off their modems and pick up the telephone to place an order will disappear. The era of the internet, providing a standardised medium to enable all business's and consumers to digitally communicate any information, will have serious implications for European business. Most notably the internet will provide small firms a level playing field that big firms have enjoyed with the expensive standards based EDI, BACS and other such technologies. This new form of e-commerce will mean technology is a medium and not a competitive advantage.

Ultimately as information management becomes key to organisational success, e-commerce will enable new 'virtual' business's to emerge, these new businesses will have knowledge as a product and be able to operate anywhere. These new businesses will not be subject to traditional business thinking and will abide by new models. There are examples of electronic malls that have failed to attract customers are abound (Miller 1996), these illustrate the potential pitfalls of e-commerce and highlight the shortage of viable business models. In the end the most economical viable channel to market needs to be used, and not just because a new technology enables a firm to work differently. This is shown in Figure 3 where a comparison is drawn between traditional and internet e-commerce.

upstream changes
The growth of e-commerce has been inexorably linked to the growth of the Internet due to the potential size of the audience and hence customer base. The UK and Germany represents one of the largest markets of users in Europe. It is noted that many web users are well-educated, affluent consumers - an ideal target for consumer marketing. Booker (1995) found that an increasing number of consumers are buying goods electronically and initiating digital payments from these transactions.

Technological factors relate to innovation risk (Child 1997). Technology developments in e-commerce have also had an immense impact upon European business, transforming existing activities as well as creating entirely new ones, involving the collection, handling and transmission of information (Smith, 1997; Child, 1997). Technology also allows the tracking of individual customer behaviour which can be used to specify individual requirements. This allows the supplier to 'get it right first time'. Benetton utilise a system where a customised list can be created to enable any of it's customers to order its garments in any colour or size. Furthermore they can monitor relevant news groups to discern what is being said about their products or services. With existing physical sales channels, it is expensive to offer products as there is a need to determine which channel to use and how.

downstream changes
The fundamental socio-demographic impact e-commerce will have on businesses will be the mobilisation and globalisation of the workforce. Since it's advent there has been a reduction in the length of the working week, or type of hours worked which have contributed to the development of the flexible firm.(Mullins 1993). This has been essential in many of today's 24 hour businesses such as Dresdner Kleinwort Benson, where it is possible to work in a number of world time zones from the comfort of your home. As a result these workers may wish to shop outside of the 'normal' shopping hours. However, businesses are finding that the potential for this type of relationship is being threatened by concern over privacy. Due to the public awareness that organisations can tap into personal details, many customers are logging in under disguised identities or not responding to that organisation. Marketers have realised that there is a need to offer a *value exchange* (Abela 1997) whereby the customer is offered something in return for information. Through this a relationship can be built with customers, providing a non-stop focus group.

With these findings, many UK industries have taken the challenge with supermarkets, bookshops and music stores taking action. Tesco has for at least a year been at the fore front of home shopping with Tesco Direct, a 250 product gift service and a 20,000 product grocery service. Sainsburys are expected to follow suit with its own package resulting in what *Porter (1980)* describes as the threat of a substitute service or Cragg and Finlay's (1991) *'fast second'*. The cost of implementing such a system should be lower as Tesco would have paid for much of the initial research and development. In order to combat the demographic changes occurring, firms need to be flexible, adaptive and continually searching for new markets for their products and services.

ORGANISATIONAL IMPACTS
Although traditional companies are realising the potential, it is the new entrants that are using e-commerce to redefine current markets. Existing suppliers in these rapidly evolving markets often find it difficult to react with changing technologies. However, many of these companies have not allocated resources to include e-commerce as a method of gaining competitive advantage as funds are still injected into factory and support systems. In evaluating the financial services industry, it has been estimated by Ernst and Young (1997) that 75 per cent of financial companies will exploit the Internet in doing business with its customers. The insurance company, Eagle Star launched what is claimed to be the worlds first Internet based car insurance service, with personal and payment details being submit-

ted to the customer on-line. Other companies have adopted a 'a wait and see approach', in order to assess whether new technologies really do offer an ephemeral competitive advantage.

While this occurs, new entrants are redefining markets and are potentially infiltrating the market share of existing players. Amazon. Com. is the worlds biggest bookstore, yet it has no traditional premises. It encompasses what is known as the virtual organisation as the business exists entirely on line and has had the most profound effect on book retailing. Amazon demonstrates two particular virtues of Internet commerce. Amazon's virtual bookshelves claim to hold over 2.5 million books, ten times as many as the bookshop in the physical world. However Amazon only stock the top 400 best selling titles. Any remanding orders are fulfilled by Ingram Books, a neighbouring book distributor. For best sellers it charges 40% below list price and for nearly everything else 10% below the listed price. Without incurring the traditional overheads associated with running a book shop Amazon finds it easy to match or beat discounts of most conventional book sellers, even including shipping costs. The result of this virtual organisation is sales amounting to £14 million, almost three times the figure for its nearest on-line competitor. Amazon's second virtue as an organisation utilising e-commerce is that it offers a service, as well as being a point of purchase. It supplies information about books, offers reviews and interview while allowing on-line users to leave their own opinions. Amazon.com is already eroding the market share of high street retailers such as WH Smith and Dillons.

ECONOMIC AND POLITICAL FACTORS

European companies also assess their position in a globalised, information-rich economy as traditional supply chains are broken down and reformed. As markets become more open and businesses become more global, the assets of firms in trading economies become increasingly connected. New strategies will have to be developed to cater for the bargaining power of suppliers, buyers and new opportunities in different industries. New concepts of core competencies will emerge. Unfortunately the problem faced by numerous organisations is that as e-commerce is still relatively new, no formal planning models exist. Companies have attempted to adapt traditional formal models such as the McFarlan's (1980) Application Portfolio. However e-commerce is a fluid and fast changing tool for business that it cannot be used effectively within a rigid model.

downstream changes

Similarly, suppliers will need to re-assess their role in global product supply. Product differentiation, low cost producers flooding the market will be the fundamental issues facing producer companies and countries with market reach and supply being the critical issues. Specialist producers that do not compete globally will need to create "*channel masters*" to ensure access. Therefore changes in economy structure will require thought on the following strategies:

- Global vs. Local
- Virtual vs. Real
- Partnership vs. Independence
- Traditional vs. New
  (Adapted from Tapscott and Caston 1993)

Government, of course, is a key component of the market economy and will influence the ways in which businesses are run. The issue of tax has for some time been a matter for debate. Thoughts of a new 'internet tax' were after some time removed by the European Commissioner for the single market stating that the European Union should rely less on imposing fresh law and more on recognition of national regimes. This means that businesses will still have to pay taxes such as VAT in the traditional manner. There are also a number of political factors that will have an impact on the way in which businesses use e-commerce. The European Commission plans to promote business transactions and protect consumers buying and selling through e-commerce. There is currently a lack of a regulatory framework. New laws would need to consider rules to harmonise intellectual property, personal data protection as well as encryption technologies and digital signatures designed to protect legal documents.

A new framework would have to be based on existing single market principles to ensure the free movement of services, persons and goods. Failure to do so would result in a failure to be able to compete with the US who already have a framework in place. The five forces of competition would take effect on a global level and reduce the competitiveness of the European industry in various spheres. In considering law enforcement, companies must take into account the threats of misuses from launderers and take necessary action to prevent this. The Financial Action Task Force (FATF) are working pro-actively to ensure that as products such as Mondex evolve in European countries, they are made in ordinance with anti-money laundering policies thus protecting the cash and the economy in which it operates. It is hoped that this will help foster the constructive development of the regulatory and legislative frame-

Figure 4	
Stasis: Low quality use of e-commerce which is not easy to use, but one which is low cost. Closest to the current situation.	**Drift:** Low quality of use, easier to use, but the cost of using it will rise.
Consumers pays: High quality, access is easy but businesses will pass on the cost to customers. However 65 per cent[1] of customers say that they would not pay.	**Information at your fingertips:** Consumers choose most convenient method of e-commerce. May impact on ease of access as there will be no single route, but the quality of content will increase and the costs will be low.

work. Without these measures it is felt that many European businesses will not engage in e-commerce where large sums of money are exchanged.

upstream changes

The issue of Data Protection is also a concern to financial regulation. As standards and practises vary between countries, the consumer must be made aware of this to that they can make a well-informed decision as to a whether a product is acceptable in terms of it's handling of personal data. The security of the Internet is the main force restraining developments in e-commerce. Currently Abbey National, Lloyds TSB, NatWest and Barclays are participating in a Secure Encryption Transaction (SET) pilot to prevent perpetrators from intervening transactions. A third party element is also under development, its role simply to arbitrate transactions, to certify that the seller is who they say they are and to confirm that a transaction has taken place. In evaluating this 'PEST' analysis, four e-commerce paradigms are possible that will impact business over the next five years, as shown in Figure 4.

A fifth paradigm 'Nirvana' is possible but unlikely. It will consist of high quality content, ease of accessibility and low cost.

CONCLUSION

In light of these paradigms companies need to apply the fundamentals of business planning in their adoption of e-commerce. This is particularly important as the uncertainties of the Internet is high. Most European companies have an existing information infrastructure, linked into existing supply chains and target a particular set of customers, but find that existing toolkits such as the portfolio analysis do not seem to work. Therefore the universal network demands that these organisations will need to re-think the following:-

- Who are my customers? E-commerce offers companies new ways of interacting with both customers and suppliers.
- What position do I take up in my supply chain? E-commerce alters the speed and channels to markets.
- What type of infrastructure do I need to support this strategy?

Clearly, the key issues is to establish long term differentiation: This is not achieved through extending existing IS/IT systems to include intranets or Web sites but to become 'knowledge masters' in a particular area of specialisation which requires continuous improvement and development in business areas that generate high value. Increased operational efficiency: will occur as network technologies become prevalent in their existing operations.

For e-commerce to achieve credibility, both upstream and downstream, it must be supported by a quick and secure payments system. It is lucid that many European multinationals may find it challenging to promote e-commerce due to substantial investments in physical premises. There is a need to balance these investment decisions against the emergent e-commerce opportunities as resources are allocated for future expansion. The advantages that many European countries and in particular the UK carry are that they have powerful capabilities in hardware, software and services.

REFERENCES

Abela, A. (1997) Value Exchange and the Internet, McKinsey, Tokyo

Angehrn, AA (1997) The Strategic Implications of the Internet, Proceedings of ECIS'97, University of Cork, Ireland, June

Barnett, T (1995) Cyber Business : Mindsets for a Wired Age

Bartram, P (1996) Accountancy Age. Making Money with E-commerce. September

Bennett, P (1996) The European market to 2005', FT Management Reports

Booker, E (1995) AT&T usine internal Web to test digital payments, Web Week, Vol 1, December

Child, J (1997) Strategic Choice in the Origins of Action, Structure, Organisations and Environment: retrospect and prospect, Organisational Studies, Vol 18, No 1, pp 43-76

Cragg, P.B. and Finlay, P.N. (1991) 'IT: running fast and standing still?' Information and Management, 21, pp193-200

Cerny, P. (1997) Technology, Culture and Competitiveness, Routledge

Caston, A (1997) E-commerce, Caspian Publishing

Earl, M (1989) Management IT Strategies, Prentice Hall

Ernest & Young (1997) Internet Report, London

Graham, I, Spinardi, G, Williams, R (1996) The Impact of the Internet on the Value Chain, Journal of Information Technology 11, 161-172

Griffiths & Newman (1995)

Guthroie, R, Austin, L (1996) Competitive Implications of the Internet', Information Systems Management, Summer

Hackney R A & Ranchhod, A (1998) IS/IT Mediated Marketing: impacts on global biotechnology companies, IFIP8.7 (ICIS'98), Helsinki, December

Hoffman DL & Novak TP (1996) Marketing in Hypermedia Computer Mediated Environments: conceptual foundations Journal of Marketing, 60, 3, pp50-68

Hopper, M, D. (1990) Rattling SABRE - new ways to compete on information, 90, 118-25 Harvard Business Review

Johnson, G, Scholes, K (1996) Exploring Corporate Strategy, Prentice Hall

Kosiur (1997)

Mammer M & Champy J (1993) Reeengineering Recorporation: a manifesto for business revolution, Nicholas Brewby Pub, London

Miller, A. (1997) E-commerce, Caspian Publishing

Mullins, L. (1993) Management and Organisational Behaviour, Addison-Wesley

Peppard, J. (1993) 'IT Strategy for Business' 1993 Longman Group UK Limited

Porter, M,E (1980) Competing Strategy Techniques for Analysing Industries and Competitors, Free Press, New York

Stevens, T. (1997) 'Set Sale on the Net', Industry Week, 21st April 1997 pg 56-64.

Short, J.E, Venkatraman, N. (1992) Beyond Business Process Redesign, Sloan Management Review, 34, 7-21.

Smith (1997) The Intranet: Slashing the Cost of Business, Web Week, Jan

Tapscott, D. and Caston, A. (1993), Paradigm Shift, McGraw Hill

Thurow, L (1996) The Future of Capitalism, Nicholas Brealey Publishing's

Worthington, I & Britton, C (1994) The Business Environment, Pitman

Wooldridge, A (1996) The Witch Doctors, Heinnman

Risk in Partnerships Involving MIS Development: Lessons from a Re-engineering Case Study

G. Harindranath & J.A.A. Sillince

School of Management, Royal Holloway, University of London, Egham, Surrey, TW20 0EX, UK. Tel. +44 -1784 - 443787, Fax +44 - 1784 - 439854, g.harindranath@rhbnc.ac.uk; j.sillince@rhbnc.ac.uk

ABSTRACT

The paper develops five types of risk in partnerships involving software development and illustrates them with a case study of business process reengineering and information systems development. (1) Ownership risk is the risk that collaboration will lead to a loss of ownership or control of vital or valuable assets and depends on (i) the dependence of one partner on another; (ii) the market value of the final product to each partner; and (iii) the separateness of the partners' markets. (2) Uncertainty risk is the risk borne by a partner committing itself before another commits itself. (3) Control risk arises when responsibility is given to someone for decisions, which depend upon earlier decisions over which that person has no control. (4) Internal incompatibility risk is the risk of generating incompatibilities within business processes when reengineering takes place. (5) External incompatibility risk is the risk of generating incompatibilities between business processes when reengineering takes place.

INTRODUCTION

At the core of risk is the possibility of loss, which arises whenever uncertainty exists about the outcomes of possible actions (Yates & Stone, 1992a). It is the probability of loss which is actually described in practice, although a more thorough consideration of risk involves three important but imprecise elements: (1) the type of possible loss; (2) the significance of those losses; (3) how uncertain are those losses (Yates & Stone, 1992b).

Software risk management techniques are important devices for minimising unwanted problems in software projects (Baskerville, 1991; Boehm, 1989; Saarinen & Vepsalainen, 1993). Uncertainty arises from lack of understanding between business and IS staff (Reich & Benbasat, 1996). In projects where several partners collaborate, not only is uncertainty increased by each partner having different objectives, but by conflicting common objectives. On the one hand there is the need for widespread diffusion of information within a consortium, which contrasts strongly with the need for secrecy and appropriability within profit-seeking companies. This means that conflicting objectives exist when partners collaborate, making risk even more difficult to estimate (Catsbaril & Thompson, 1995). The case reported below is of the perceptions of risk by partners in a consortium involved in creating a new medical facility, involving reengineered working practices, software development, and building design. Hospitals can make several types of response to risks - they can vary prices, change service mix, or reduce variation in resource use (Friedman & Farley, 1995). The creation of an internal market within the UK's National Health Service (NHS) is forcing hospitals to pay increasing attention to financial planning and the management of business risks. Our analysis reveals a number of different types of risk associated with software development and consortium collaboration.

CASE STUDY

The context for this research is a major healthcare project at the Central Middlesex Trust (CMT), an acute hospital in the UK National Health Service (NHS) employing 1300 people and with an annual turnover of £50m. Funding, amounting to £16m, had become available through land sales and central government funding through the Private Finance Initiative (PFI) for the Trust to establish an Ambulatory Care and Diagnostic Centre (ACAD) adjacent to CMT. Five theatres for 20,000 cases per year were planned. This form of rapid service delivery and medical process redesign was adventurous and still at an early stage of diffusion into acute care, following successful though politically controversial experimental schemes of world-class quality in Australia, Switzerland and the USA (the Mayo Clinic).

ACAD required both radical changes to business and medical processes and social structures, because it focused on rapid throughput and computerised scheduling. Although 'greenfield' in being a new facility, it was sited within an existing medical complex and drew on the existing resources of that site. It was therefore an example of business process reengineering (BPR). Also ACAD required a careful relating of new systems to existing hospital functions and information systems (IS). The main top level business processes of ACAD were: to educate and prepare the patient; to regulate and direct referrals to improve predictability; to schedule on the basis of units of time, taking power from doctors and giving it to schedulers; to use predictable flows and processes to design jobs and workloads; to develop system, machine, manpower and building use to maximise effectiveness of jobs and clinical process flows; and to manage the patient quickly back into the community.

The information system needed had to network with General Practitioners (GPs), the main hospital at CMT and other NHS care centres, and had to solve complex scheduling problems, in order to shorten patient care from typically 4-10 days to one day.

The approach not only required radical restructuring of working practices but it also required new technology - for example MRI and CT scanning which enable rapid interactional diagnosis. The ACAD design also facilitated the performance of imaging-guided interventions, involving, for example, clinical procedures requiring imaging and endoscopy, or imaging and surgery.

Central Middlesex NHS Trust (CMT) was headed by a Chairman and also a Chief Executive, together with six Directors. A software developer, a hardware manufacturer, and a builder were involved as a Consortium in ACAD together with CMT. One of CMT's directors, the Director of Contracts & Clinical Activities, was also given the role of ACAD project manager. He acted as chairman of the ACAD Steering Committee, which included the Chief Executive, Chairman and other directors of CMT, together with representatives from the other Consortium partners, the ACAD architect, and the software requirements team. The user organisation was therefore ACAD; the client organisation was CMT; the project organisation was the Consortium; and the subcontractors were the Consortium members - the equipment provider, the software developer, and the construction company.

There were various Groups within ACAD. The Design Group commissioned architects who began design work on the new building between June 1996 and January 1997 based on a master plan, intending to commence construction by April 1997. The IS Group commissioned a software requirements team to produce a requirements document by April 1997, with the intention of software development by the Consortium partner responsible after that date. The Negotiation Group dealt with contracts and agreements between the Consortium partners.

All the meetings (20 in all) between July and November 1996 of the various Groups and Steering Committee were attended and recorded for later analysis. Problematic statements were later followed up by means of questioning participants. The negotiations between CMT and the Consortium suggest that there were five types of risk involved:

Ownership risk

Ownership risk is the risk that collaboration will lead to a loss of ownership or control of vital or valuable assets. CMT claimed that the principal intellectual property innovation arose from clinicians' reports on reengineering medical procedures, whereas other consortium partners claim that they add the main source of innovation. In particular, the Consortium software partner has claimed that its software design is appropriable. The implication of any one partner gaining the upper hand in such negotiations is that that partner then has a saleable product within the potentially vast ambulatory care market. Of course, each partner is adding unique value (BPR and IS cannot be disconnected in this way) to what is undeniably a productisation process.

Ownership risk is important within a collaboration, because it influences commitment (if we expect to lose assets due to the collaboration then we reduce commitment) and intimacy (ownership and control involve information, so that if we expect to lose ownership or control we will attempt to reduce information flows).

Three important partners were ACAD, with its knowledge of potentially new medical working practices, the software developer, with its knowledge of hardware and software technologies for delivering systems for imaging, diagnostics and scheduling, and the construction company, with its knowledge of hospital design. In terms of these three partners, the important dimensions of ownership risk were:

1) The dependence of one partner on another. For example, the ambulatory care concept was based on minimisation of the total time a patient spent in the facility and this was largely dependent on recovery time. So reengineering of working practices and caseload planning by ACAD depended on new scheduling software written by the software developer.

"Caseload planning should be based on recovery time. This will require a new form of scheduling" (Director of Contracts & Clinical Activity, CMT).

Moreover, even though the architect claimed that building design was unproblematic and certain, there were many design issues, which depended upon decisions about software systems and equipment:

"What are the implications of IS for building design? They must include (1) image storage and retrieval; (2) medical records (electronic or not); and (3) patient scheduling......... The building itself will depend to an extent on what kind of activities IS can do"(Software Engineer, Requirements Team).

Also software and equipment decisions were interconnected:

"Most equipment procurement is based on the assumption that paperless systems will be introduced to ACAD" (Clinical Director of Imaging, CMT).

Decisions about software systems also had implications for staffing levels:

"IS will bring staff numbers down" (Director of Contracts & Clinical Activity, CMT).

2)   The market value of the final product to each partner. All three parties could take away and reapply new knowledge, although such knowledge varied from partner to partner. ACAD could develop a new set of medical working practices which could be disseminated in manuals, training courses, and university education, and its copyright over such knowledge enabled it to derive income directly from this process or sell such rights to a specialised training company. The builder-architect could use the experience as track-record to gain further ambulatory care commissions. The software developer could reuse or modify improved versions of the code, which it was developing for ACAD and could sell it to other ambulatory care clients.

Awareness of the market value of ambulatory care involved considering in what way it was different from other medical services, which were already provided elsewhere, and of the market value and profitability of alternative mixes of medical services in the new facility:

"Someone wants cardiac stuff in ACAD. This is fantasy as the utilisation rate [of equipment] is 20% [and thus unprofitable] and there are teaching hospitals which are good at this. So this should be out [of ACAD]...... Consultation is out of ACAD except if it brings in money. If consultation is in ACAD then the facility will turn into another hospital. This is not what ACAD is about" (Director of Contracts & Clinical Activity, CMT).

One of the problems that arose during the negotiation process was that ACAD directors felt that, although each partner could potentially benefit from the large amount of new knowledge which the project would create, some partners wanted to regard the project in more conventional terms. These more conventional terms were to regard each partner as being told what to do and being fully paid for it, without the problems of negotiating and educating each other.

"There is tremendous intellectual value for the Consortium from this project. But they're being front-ended by salesmen who just want all the answers now. CMT needs to think through all the logistics. We are prepared to educate them" (Clinical Director of Anaesthetics, CMT).

"[The Consortium partner providing the building] seems more like a salesman and doesn't seem to be interested in a 'partnership' approach. They may not sign a contract until the IS uncertainties are sorted out. It may take at least 12 months" (Director of Contracts & Clinical Activity, CMT).

3)   The separateness of the partners' markets (the substitutability of final products). In the ACAD case, although working practices, software and building design were separate products, it was possible to represent them to the market in an integrated form as a 'total solution', giving the seller greater credibility and lower marketing costs, and giving the customer reduced complexity. Ideally, the partners should have worked together, creating this novel, total product. However, this ideal was difficult to achieve, because it was far easier for each partner to regard its product and its market as separate. For example, insufficient information was given to the software engineers about other partners' requirements:

"People here don't appreciate the need to articulate what they require from IT. They also don't like plans. They turn up late for meetings. The assumption is that they are always doing something more important" (Software Engineer, Requirements Team).

Uncertainty risk

This is the risk borne by a partner committing itself before another. It relates to the question of how long decisions should be postponed. In the ACAD case, the Consortium software partner had to complete, as one of its deliverables, an IS Building Design, documenting the IS related issues identified as having a material effect upon the internal design of ACAD. The building design was to be frozen, yet until IS issues had been resolved (particularly the issue of paperless IS, and the juxtaposing of specialities to minimise patient flow), there may have been calls for architectural changes, such as space for records storage.

This dimension of risk arises from the fact that some activities (theatre, imaging and exterior design) were relatively certain - for example:

"Considerable certainty exists about theatre, imaging and exterior design" (Architect).

On the other hand, other activities were not. These activities included (1) information systems' potential to simplify process flow; (2) multi skilling and nurse empowerment reducing process hold ups; (3) elimination of offices - all ACAD staff needed to be mobile so rooms were for multiple purposes; (4) elimination of departments and beds to maximise practitioner-patient contact time and to speed up throughflow.

However, one of the reasons why pressure was put on partners early on to settle the building design issues was as a way of reassuring the building Consortium:

"The Consortium only gets £3 million out of £18 million. So let's concentrate on the building and engineering of ACAD and give the Consortium a simple reassurance of their involvement" (Director of Contracts & Clinical Activity, CMT).

Uncertainty risk relates to a difficult problem for the Consortium - how could reengineering of processes occur at the same time as an IS specification:

"Reengineering of processes is taking place at the same time as the specification, and this is very, very difficult" (Director of Contracts & Clinical Activity, CMT).

BPR requires that business processes and IS be redesigned together, yet in practice there is more sequence than simultaneity. In the ACAD case, building design preceded IS requirements. Figure 1 shows how the building issues were seen to be driving the information system issues. One of the most important issues in Figure 1 was the question of the correct scope and boundaries of the new facility (Issue G) - how did it differ from conventional hospital treatment, how did it relate to the existing hospital, and how did it relate to GPs? An answer to these questions would provide some answers to questions such as the degree of computerisation required and staff numbers (Issue F). The new facility was envisaged as needing a new approach to scheduling of treatment (Issue E) based upon caseload planning and recovery time (Issue D). Resolving these issues could then fix the building design more precisely (Issue B) which could then make information requirements more certain (Issue A).

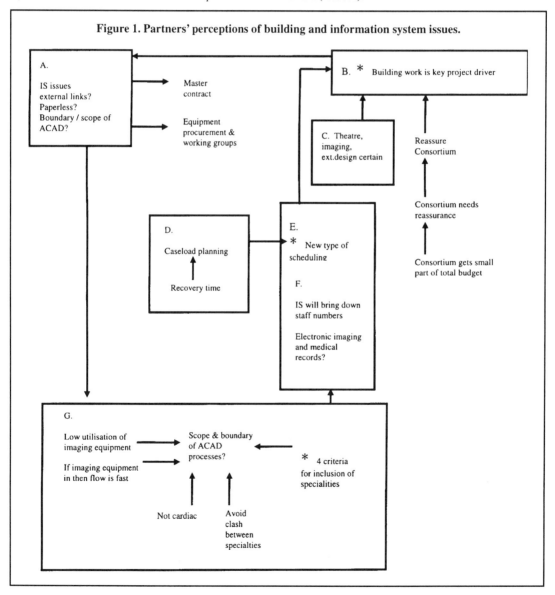

Figure 1. Partners' perceptions of building and information system issues.

This means that some activities (e.g. building design) must be done with no knowledge about other activities (e.g. IS design), increasing the risk for particular Consortium partners, who then seek to cover their risk in various ways. Despite evidence that avoidance of delays as a management concept is not widely used in the software industry (Carmel, 1995), the perception of this risk by two of the three private sector Consortium partners became clear during the case study.

The components of uncertainty risk are therefore (1) the proportion of diagram elements (the issues in Figure 1) which should be and are simultaneous; (2) the proportion of diagram elements which should be and are not simultaneous; (3) the length of time that the situation described by (2) persists. Members of a collaboration will tend to be more able to deal with uncertainty risk when there is high commitment from collaboration members, because the expectation of a long-term mutually beneficial relationship leads to higher trust and a longer payoff horizon.

Control risk

This type of risk arises when responsibility is given to someone for decisions, which depend upon earlier decisions over which that person has no control. It is the risk of unknown bad effects of a previous decision by another partner. Control risk can be reduced by co-ordination mechanisms such as vertical authorisation and horizontal deals (Nidumolu, 1995). In vertical authorisation, a superordinate person or group is given responsibility for earlier decisions, and must ensure that earlier decisions help later ones. In a sense the Steering Group was supposed to ensure this consistency, although it was only as effective as the trust and group-mindedness of each of its partner members. Horizontal deals also ensure consistency, this time by spelling out responsibilities and deadlines. The ACAD case was punctuated by a number of points when contracts were used in this way between partners. For example, the Consortium building partner was concerned that it would have to manage and operate a building which was not designed by itself, where IS-relevant design defects (e.g. defects relating to networking or communication facilities) might come to light later.

The components of control risk are therefore (1) the proportion of user requirements which should be and are met by the partner; (2) the proportion of user requirements which should be and are not met by the partner; (3) the length of time that the situation described by (2) persists; (4) the legal, financial and safety consequences of incorrect or incomplete user requirements determination.

Internal incompatibility risk

This is the risk of generating incompatibilities within business processes when reengineering takes place. This partly depends upon human relations factors which suggest separation of staff from each other for reasons of personal relationships or professional rivalry:

"To schedule certain kinds of activity may be a bad thing. Some specialities cannot stand each other" (Chairman, CMT).

or because of cultural contamination of the new facility by old 'bad' working practices and attitudes:

"We may need totally new staff for ACAD. If you move an entire department like "Eyes" into ACAD you will get the old "Eyes" social structure and this is not good for ACAD" (Director of Contracts & Clinical Activity, CMT).

Incompatibilities also arise from a poor relationship between existing and new information systems. Changing a business process causes changes to data flows and data types which then are not adequately dealt with by old information systems. In the ACAD case, images were intended to be ubiquitously available within ACAD but unavailable at the main hospital, severely curtailing any possibility of continuity between consultation (in CMT) and treatment (in ACAD).

There was also the problem of how to relate new and old information systems:

"Existing IS are outdated by at least 10 years. They don't provide all the information even at present" (Software Engineer, Requirements Team).

The components of internal incompatibility risk are therefore (1) the proportion of data flows within each business process which have compatible source and destination; (2) the cost of the making new information systems simpler and less functional merely to enable them to be compatible with the existing information system; (3) the cost of the existing information system being improved to enable it to be compatible with the new information system.

External incompatibility risk

This is the risk of generating incompatibilities between business processes, and between new and existing information systems when reengineering takes place. Integration between ambulatory and other treatment regimes is an acknowledged problem of the radical changes to business processes brought about by the ambulatory care concept (Suber, 1996). Barrows et al., (1994) found that although ambulatory care is aimed at cost reduction, one of the significant factors raising costs was the need for compatibility with IS serving old business processes. Sources of incompatibility are technical (different data models, normal forms, data formats and data sets), design-related (unique or domain-dependent designs - Kohane *et al.,* 1996), business-related (IS for a business process still based on old requirements), cultural (user resistance or politicisation of the IS development process within the user organisation), financial (new IS requires too-expensive adapting of legacy IS), security-related (new and old IS having different security procedures) or safety-related (when different safety standards or protocols are used).

In the ACAD case, communication between ACAD and GPs will either necessitate expensive modifications to upgrade GPs' IS or else expensive modifications to create a paper-based ACAD system able to be posted out to GPs.

"Are we having paper? Will it come over the next few years? What about the boundary of ACAD and external links to GPs?" (Software Engineer, Requirements Team).

Similarly, the new ACAD information system will need to connect to the existing information systems of the main hospital (CMH):

"What will be the relationship between ACAD and the main hospital systems?" (Software Engineer, Requirements Team).

A question raised by this relationship was who pays for the links and who pays for reducing the data incompatibilities?

" Who pays for external links from ACAD and what's ACAD's boundary? My own view is that what's most important is that CMT should fit into ACAD, not ACAD fitting into CMT. This means that CMT will incur extra costs" (Clinical Director of Anaesthetics, CMT).

Another type of incompatibility is the incompatibility arising from staff working both at ACAD and CMH, two facilities which will have different working practices and objectives:

"If someone is "inside" ACAD they should not be called out to the main hospital every time there is a need" (Director of Contracts & Clinical Activity, CMT).

Old information systems create many different problems, including the need to enforce consistency, the effect of raised maintenance costs, the difficulty of using information from multiple sources (Li *et al.,* 1994), and the creation of a shared vocabulary (Barrows *et al.*, 1994). New system owners probably wish to overlook old systems, and indeed current cost justification schemes encourage short term ignoring of inherited IS, information and expertise (Hinton & Kaye, 1996), yet many connections between old and the new IS are usually necessary. It is important to identify those connections, the owners of the connected processes, and the ways in which connections are protected or ignored. Much will also depend on the old system owner (CMT in the case study) and how much it is prepared to spend to make it compatible or to alter or replace parts of it. This extra work may include creating intermediate systems, which can make use of old systems, but which interface with the new IS (Meistrell & Schlehuber, 1996; Vanmulligan & Timmers, 1994). These three roles (new system owner, old system owner, and owner of connections between old and new systems) require some kind of agreement between relevant parties.

It may be that doctors' expectations of a paperless ACAD (electronic prescribing, case notes taking, doctors using notepads, image and medical records storage, transmission and retrieval, JIT scheduling and complete tracking of all intervention) were too high. At the start of the project no commercial electronic scheduling system existed which was easily useable in a health context. Complete digitisation may have been too expensive and intermediate solutions needed to be considered, partly because of the need to communicate with old CMT systems and GPs and others who were not at that time using electronic media for all information flows. Complete electronic tracking of patient intervention may have been too expensive and may have needed to be relaxed to attend just to entry and discharge data, leaving the period between the two untracked and hence flexible. The Consortium software partner had to complete, as one of its promised deliverables, an Information Systems and Technology Strategy, which defined a plan to ensure that the resourcing of IS in ACAD and the information, systems and technology architectures defined and agreed for ACAD "fitted with" and complemented the resourcing and corresponding architectures used by the main hospital. There would be problems of data transfer, and patient referrals from the main hospital, but options still existed. For example, interaction between the two systems could have been minimised or made compatible. This raises the question of what the factors are which lead to decision-makers deciding on compatibility rather than a new standalone system. Another question is about data ownership by GPs, Trusts, the Department of Health and others, and about the boundaries where data transfer is difficult.

BPR will be bounded by several constraints relating to old systems. Examples of constraints are: (A) A constraint to maximise utilisation rates of shared equipment increases the amount of necessary interaction (e.g. A CT scanner will be cited within CMT and ACAD patients will use and do bookings for it); (B) A constraint to outsource equipment increases the amount of necessary interaction (e.g. ACAD will outsource sterilisation equipment, and will also store film off site).

An agreement between relevant parties would therefore need to take account of (1) the type, access rights, security status and number of data flows between old and new IS; (2) how these are changed by BPR; (3) who own the business processes affected and whether or not they are prepared to spend money to increase compatibility; (4)

the implications of disputes over data ownership; (5) the consequences of different compatibility-creating options for new IS, old IS and new-old IS connection owners; (6) the implications of constraints internal to business processes on flows between new and old IS.

The components of external incompatibility risk are therefore (1) the proportion of data flows between business processes which have compatible source and destination; (2) the cost of the making new information systems simpler and less functional merely to enable them to be compatible with the existing information system; (3) the cost of the existing information system being improved to enable it to be compatible with the new information system; (4) the ease of insulating working practices from outside influences; (5) whether or not the relevant parties are prepared to pay for incompatibilities to be minimised.

CONCLUSIONS

We have suggested ways of assessing the different types of risk involved in any BPR-IS project. This could be extended by means of quantification of the risks, although it is accepted that many of the factors will remain as categoric rather than as scaleable data. More important is the typology of risks as an aid to communication. Communication of IS and business executives' perceptions is of central concern to organisations wishing to achieve change (Lederer & Mendelow, 1986). These perceptions include cross-references between IS and business plans, mutual understanding and congruent long term vision between IS and business executives, and executives' self-ratings of congruence (Reich & Benbasat, 1996). We suggest that an additional dimension of congruence will be perception of risks. Where linkage between IS and business executives is low, we would expect business executives to be most concerned with ownership risk (relevant to business-related assets), uncertainty risk (relevant to when they should make decisions) and control risk (relevant to their reading of what is their 'territory' or span of control) and to underestimate internal and external compatibility risk (with its relevance for incompatible data flows). Conversely, we would expect in low linkage contexts for IS executives to be most concerned with internal and external compatibility risk, and to underestimate ownership, uncertainty and control risk.

Any BPR-IS project will be bedevilled by existing IS. Even the case study described above, a new building attempting to achieve a new approach to working practices, still had to relate itself to the main site and outside purchasers. Old IS is therefore of crucial importance. We have suggested a number of tasks, which need to be tackled in order to create some understanding between the project participants with regard to this problem.

REFERENCES

BARROWS R.C., CIMINO J.J., and CLAYTON P.D., (1994), 'Mapping clinically useful terminology to a controlled medical vocabulary', *Journal of the American Medical Informatics Association,* 211-215.

BASKERVILLE R.L., (1991) 'Risk analysis as a source of professional knowledge', *Computers and Security,* 10, (8), 749-764.

BOEHM B.W., (1989) *Software risk management,* IEEE Computer Society Press, Washington DC.

CARMEL E. (1995), 'Cycle time in packaged software firms', *Journal of Product Innovation Management,* 12 (2), 110-123.

CATSBARIL W., and THOMPSON R., (1995), 'Managing information technology projects in the public sector', *Public Administration Review,* 55 (6), 559-566.

FRIEDMAN B., and FARLEY D., (1995), 'Strategic responses by hospitals to increased financial risk in the 1980s', *Health Service Research,* 30 (3), 467-488.

HINTON C.M., and KAYE G.R., (1996), 'The hidden investments in information technology - the role of organisational context and system dependency', *International Journal of Information Management,* 16 (6), 413-427.

KOHANE I.S., GREENSPUN P., FACKLER J., CIMINO C., and SZOLOVITS P., (1996), 'Building national electronic medical record systems via the World-Wide-Web', *Journal of the American Medical informatics Association,* 3 (3), 191-207.

LEDERER A., and MENDELOW A., (1986), 'Issues in information systems planning', *Information & Management,* 10 (5), 245-254.

LI P., KRAMER L., PINEO S., and KULP D., (1994), 'Evolving a legacy system: restructuring the Mendelian Inheritance In Man database', *Journal of the American Informatics Association',* 344-348.

MEISTRELL M., and SCHLEHUBER C., (1996) 'Adopting a corporate perspective on databases - improving support for research and decision-making', *Medical Care,* 34 (3), 91-102.

NIDOMOLU S., (1995), 'The effect of co-ordination and uncertainty on software project performance - residual performance risk as an intervening variable', *Information Systems Research,* 6 (3), 191-219.

REICH B.H. and BENBASAT I., (1996), 'Measuring the linkage between business and information technology objectives', *MIS Quarterly,* 20 (1), 55-81.

SAARINEN T., and VEPSALAINEN A., (1993) 'Managing the risks of information systems implementation', *European Journal of Information Systems*, 2 (4), 283-295.

SUBER R., (1996), 'Chronic care in ambulatory settings - components of an integrated care system', *American Behavioural Scientist*, 39 (6), 665-675.

VANMULLIGAN E., and TIMMERS T., (1994), 'Beyond clients and servers', *Journal of the American Medical Informatics Association,* 546-550.

YATES J.F., and STONE E.R., 1992a, 'The risk construct', 1-23 in Yates J.F., Risk-taking behaviour, Wiley, Chichester.

YATES J.F., and STONE E.R., 1992b, 'Risk appraisal', 50-81 in Yates J.F., Risk-taking behaviour, Wiley, Chichester.

Information Technology Diffusion in Hospitals in the United States

Albert L. Harris

Dept. of Information Technology & Operations Management, Appalachian State University, Boone, NC 28608
(828) 262-6180, Fax: (828) 262-6190, harrisal@appstate.edu

Pete Kiefert

Science Applications International Corporation. 1953 Gallows Road, Suite 170, Vienna, VA 22082
(703) 610-8888, kiefertp@yahoo.com

ABSTRACT

The healthcare industry in the United States spent over $11 billion in 1996 to purchase products and services to support automated information systems. Those expenditures are expected to grow to over $20 billion by 2000. What kind of automated systems are hospitals investing in? What is the level of information technology diffusion in U.S. hospitals? The purpose of this paper is to report the results of a hospital survey that sought the answer to these and other questions regarding information technology diffusion in U.S. hospitals.

Results showed that financial type applications were the most developed in hospitals. In this area, hospitals generally used vendor supplied, off-the-shelf products. Applications focusing on the quality and effectiveness of patient care were less automated in most hospitals than financial type applications. Surprisingly, point of care and computer-based patient records were among the lowest in automation in U. S. hospitals. The Internet is the most widely used technology, even though it is relatively new among hospital technologies. The source of information systems applications in U.S. hospitals is heavily concentrated with three vendors. Finally, U.S. hospital administrators seem moderately or highly satisfied with most of the automated system in use. The results of this project point out several areas for further research in information technology diffusion in U. S. hospitals.

INTRODUCTION

Healthcare reform has placed an even greater importance on the use of information technology (IT) and hospital information systems (HISs) within the hospital environment to assist in providing more efficient and effective care. As a result, the Healthcare industry has spent $11.6 billion in 1996 to purchase products and services to support automated information systems. [1] It has been estimated that by the year 2000 the healthcare information technology market will grow to $20 billion.[2] The major problem is that these expenditures may not translate into more effective and cost saving operations. [1] Information technology has had a great impact on hospitals in the recent years. It is difficult to say with any degree of certainty what types of applications are being used and what their effects are on the organization. The extensive list of information systems software available for hospitals alone raises many questions: What kind of HIS applications are hospitals currently pursuing? What are the sources of software?

The purpose of this paper is to examine the most commonly used HIS applications, the application providers and satisfaction levels of these applications. The benefactors would be two fold. First, hospital administrators will become aware of the array of available software applications and other administrator's reactions to those applications. Second, providers will become aware of the market's reaction to currently used HIS applications in an attempt to predict future trends in the HIS market or make needed adjustments in current systems.

METHODOLOGY

A mail survey, utilizing a four and five point Likert scale, was conducted of randomly selected general hospitals with more than 50 beds in the continental United States. The sample was selected from a alphabetical listing in the 95/6 American Hospital Association Guide of all the member hospitals. The survey was sent to 223 hospitals and 49 useable surveys were returned, for a response rate of 22%.

Hospital demographics, including number of beds, percent of hospital's budget spent on IT, and yearly spending for new or upgraded software, were identified. Current information systems (IS) used in the hospital were also identified. Software categories used in the survey to identify current IS use included:
- Admissions/Discharge/Transfer (A/D/T)
- Case Mix management

- Chart Tracking
- Clinical Laboratories
- Computer-Based Patient Records (CBPR)
- Diagnosis
- Financial Management
- Food Services & Nutrition
- Material Management
- Medical Records Abstracting
- Nursing Support
- Pharmacy
- Point of Care
- Quality Assurance
- Radiology, and
- Scheduling.

In each of these categories, respondents were asked to identify their extent of use of information systems as 'currently used,' 'project started,' 'evaluating options,' or 'do not plan to use.' Hospitals were asked to identify where they obtained their software for each category identified above. Choices for sources of software included custom developed by hospital IS personnel, custom developed by a vendor, or vendor supplied, off-the-shelf software.

The extent of use of certain information technologies was also explored. Hospitals were asked to identify their level of use for:

- Bar coding
- Bedside terminals
- Direct hook up with physicians
- Electronic data interchange
- Internet
- Light/touch pens
- Optical character recognition
- Portable terminals
- Touch screens
- Voice recognition.

Finally, the hospitals' satisfaction levels were assessed in several different ways. First, the ability of the information systems to increase services, reduce costs, and improve efficiency was explored. Second, an overall satisfaction level was identified. Third, satisfaction with specific implementation issues, including reliability, training, ease of use, flexibility, and technical support were measured. And finally, reasons for not implementing or upgrading software were explored.

RESULTS

Eighty-three percent of the hospitals that are members of the American Hospital Association are categorized as general hospitals. Forty-eight percent have between 50 and 199 beds. The 48% is evenly split between hospitals with 50-99 beds and 100-199 beds. Table 1 displays the distribution of respondents by the number of beds compared to the AHA distribution. Except for the 100-199 and the 0-49 bed category, which was not included in the survey population, the distribution of respondents by bed size is similar to the distribution with in the AHA.

Forty-five of the 49 respondents knew the percentage of the hospital budget that was spent on information technology (IT). Of the 45 respondents, 44.4% indicated the hospital spent between 0 and 2 percent of its budget on IT. An additional 40% indicated that the hospital spent 3-5% of its budget on IT. In other words, according to the survey, 84.4% of the responding hospitals spent 5% or less of their budget on IT. These results matched that of the 1997 HIMSS/HP Leadership Survey. The 1997 HIMSS/HP Leadership Survey found that approximately 84% of respondents, who knew how much of the hospital's budget was spent on IT, believed that IT spending accounted for 4.9% or less of the hospital budget. [3]

Table 1: Distribution of Survey Respondents by Number Beds							
# Beds	0-49	50-99	100-199	200-299	300-399	400-499	500 or more
Survey	0%	25%	44%	8%	10%	4%	8%
AHA	23%	24%	24%	13%	7%	4%	6%

Forty-five of the respondents were also aware of the hospital's average yearly spending on IS software. Sixty-two percent believed the hospital spent between $15,000 and $150,000 a year. Only 8.8% felt the hospital spends over $500,000 in an average year. This seemed to match very closely with the 500 or more bed category. Eleven percent believed the average yearly spending in IS software was between $150,000 and $249,999, while another 11% believed it was between $250,000 and $499,999. This 22% again seemed to match closely with the 200-499 bed categories, which also totaled 22% of the survey distribution.

The applications used for this survey could be categorized as either financial or service type systems. The financial applications are primarily concerned with the hospital's bottom line. Service type applications are focused on the quality and effectiveness of patient care. The financial applications, Admission/Discharge/Transfer (A/D/T), financial management, material management and medical record abstracting, were the four most commonly used applications. Table 2 shows the distribution of the extent of use for the different applications under consideration. Ninety-six percent of all respondents use medical record abstracting software. Ninety-four percent of the respondents either use an A/D/T application or are starting an A/D/T application project. Material management application was used by 92% of the respondents.

As a whole, the mean score suggest that most applications are either being used currently or a project has been started. Point of care systems were the least used with a mean response of only 2.5. Eighty-seven percent of the respondents that do not use or have not yet started a project to automate their point of care system are currently evaluating options.

Table 3 shows the distribution of responses to the type of technologies used within the hospital. Portable terminals seem to be receiving much more attention than bedside terminals. Fifty-three percent of the respondents either use portable terminals or have a project started utilizing portable terminals. Only 27% use or have started a project utilizing bedside terminals.

The most common technology used was the Internet. Eighty-five percent of the respondents reported using the Internet in some manner within the hospital. Electronic data interchange (EDI) was a close second, with 84% of the hospitals using it in some manner. Bar coding also ranked high with 66% of the respondents reporting using bar codes in some departments within the hospital. The Internet, EDI, and direct hook up with physicians were the technologies used most throughout hospitals.

Table 4 shows the distribution of respondents' answers to "How did you acquire the software applications?" According to the survey, vendor supplied, off-the-shelf products were the most common source of acquiring IS applications. In that category, Medi-Tech was the most commonly used vendor for 10 out of the 16 applications listed in the survey. HBO and Company was the second most popular source of HIS software. HBO & Company

Table 2: Extent of Use of Hospital Information System Software Applications.

Software Application (Answer Value)	Number of Respondents				
	Currently Used (1)	Projected Started (2)	Evaluating Options (3)	Do Not Plan to Use (4)	Mean Answer Value
Admission/Discharge/Transfer	45	2	1	0	1.1
Case Mix Management	34	3	10	1	1.5
Chart Tracking	31	4	8	5	1.7
Clinical Laboratories	39	2	6	0	1.3
Computer Based Patient Records	18	9	20	1	2.1
Diagnosis	34	1	7	4	1.6
Financial Management	45	0	3	0	1.1
Food Services & Nutrition	25	4	12	7	2.0
Material Management	44	2	1	1	1.1
Medical Records Abstracting	45	0	1	1	1.1
Nursing Support	28	4	13	3	1.8
Pharmacy	43	2	3	0	1.2
Point of Care	10	7	26	4	2.5
Quality Assurance	24	4	18	1	1.9
Radiology	34	3	9	2	1.6
Scheduling	24	9	15	0	1.8

Table 3: Extent of Use of Hospital Information System Technologies.						
	Number of Respondents					
Technologies (Answer Value)	Used Throughout Hospital (1)	Used in some Departments (2)	Project Started (3)	Evaluating Options (4)	No Plans to Use (5)	Mean
Bar Coding	0	32	4	11	1	2.6
Bedside terminals	4	6	3	21	14	3.7
Direct Hook Up with Physicians	9	15	4	15	3	2.7
EDI	9	29	3	3	1	2.1
Internet	11	30	4	3	0	2.0
Light/Touch Pens	5	3	1	11	27	4.1
Optical Character Recognition	1	10	3	11	21	3.9
Portable Terminals	5	15	5	16	6	3.1
Touch Screens	0	11	1	9	27	4.1
Voice Recognition	0	7	0	16	25	4.2

dominated in A/D/T, financial management, material management (the three most commonly used software applications, all of which are classified as financial-oriented applications), and point of care applications. Although SMS never clearly dominated a particular category, they were usually close behind Medi-Tech and HBO and Company in many of the application areas. No other vendor had a significant position (at least 5% of the total applications) in providing any software applications in U. S. hospitals. A very distant second method of acquiring HIS software was to have a vendor custom develop the software. Very few IS applications were developed by hospital IS staff.

The final issue covered by this survey is the levels of satisfaction with current IS applications. Respondents were asked if they strongly agreed, agreed, did not know, disagreed or strongly disagreed with whether their currently used IT applications have increased services, reduced cost and improved efficiency. Sixty-six percent agreed and 12.8% strongly agreed that services were increased. Similarly, sixty-four percent agreed and 19.1% strongly agreed that efficiency has been improved. There was not strong consensus on the HIS applications helping to reduce cost. Although 46.8% agreed and 2.1% strongly agreed that costs were reduced, 19.1% disagreed, putting some doubt in this area with many respondents.

Table 4: Distribution of Source of IS Applications						
	Custom Developed		Vendor Supplied			
Application	Hospital IS Staff	Vendor	HBO & CO.	MEDI-TECH	SMS	Other
Admission/Discharge/ Transfer	0	4	13	12	8	8
Case Mix Management	1	4	6	11	8	8
Chart Tracking	2	3	7	9	4	9
Clinical Laboratories	1	4	7	10	2	17
Computer Based Patient Records	1	4	6	6	5	6
Diagnosis	0	5	6	6	3	10
Financial Management	1	4	12	10	8	10
Food Services & Nutrition	2	6	3	8	3	8
Material Management	0	5	14	9	3	11
Medical Records Abstracting	2	5	8	12	6	12
Nursing Support	2	2	5	7	5	7
Pharmacy	0	3	11	12	5	14
Point of Care	0	2	5	4	1	4
Quality Assurance	2	4	3	5	5	9
Radiology	1	3	7	10	6	9
Scheduling	0	1	6	10	4	8

Technical Area (Answer Value)	Number of Respondents					
	Extremely Low (1)	Low (2)	Moderate (3)	High (4)	Extremely High (5)	Mean Answer Value
Technical Features	1	4	27	15	1	3.2
Reliability	0	3	9	25	11	3.9
Training	1	7	21	16	2	3.2
Ease of Use	0	6	26	15	1	3.2
Flexibility	1	15	19	8	5	3.0
Tech Support	0	12	15	19	2	3.2
Overall Satisfaction	0	2	24	21	1	3.4

Table 5: Degree of Satisfaction with Technical Areas

We asked for the most common reasons for not implementing a new or upgraded software application. The most common reasons were the lack of financial resources and a system was recently implemented or updated. On the other hand, the least common stated reason was that the current applications are working fine. Ninety-one percent reported that their current systems were working fine and this was the reason they were not implementing or upgrading their HIS applications.

Finally, Table 5 shows the evaluation of respondents' degree of satisfaction in seven different technical areas. Overall respondents were moderately or highly satisfied with the automated systems used within their hospitals. The highest degree of satisfaction was with reliability in which 52% of respondents ranked their satisfaction levels as high. Flexibility ranked the lowest relative to satisfaction levels. Thirty-one percent of the respondents felt that the degree of flexibility was low and 40% felt it was only moderate.

CONCLUSION

Financial-oriented applications (i.e. A/D/T, Financial Management, Materials Management, etc.) are more likely to be used by most U. S. hospitals than service-oriented applications, which could be a result of time. Financial-oriented systems are usually the first applications to be developed in most industries. The service-oriented applications, those focused on the quality and effectiveness of patient care, will become more likely to be automated as time goes by and more hospitals assess the benefits of these types of systems. The most popular source of HIS applications is vendor supplies, off-the-shelf products.

The HIS software market in the United States seems to be dominated by three providers (vendors): Medi-Tech, HBO and Company, and SMS. These three competitors control almost 50% of the market and the remainder of the market is scattered among numerous other vendors.

Although one of the newest technologies, the Internet is one of the most widely used technologies in U. S. hospitals. This is probably because it is relatively inexpensive to implement and use. The next two technologies used most by U. S. hospitals, EDI and bar coding, are generally associated with financial-oriented systems. As financial-oriented systems seemed to be more widely used by U. S. hospitals, technologies that these systems use would seem to be the most widely used also. This seems to be the case here.

Overall, information technology diffusion in hospitals in the United States seems to be progressing, but it does not seem dominating. If the application and technology deals with financial or business management, then it is generally being used. If the application and technology deals with the quality and effectiveness of patient care, then it is generally lagging. Is this because medical personnel hold back technological advances or is there another reason? Many businesses learn to use technology for a competitive advantage. Is this possible in hospitals and the hospital environment?

IMPLICATIONS FOR FURTHER RESEARCH

This research effort looked at information technology diffusion in hospitals in the United States. Two areas of further research emerge from this study. First, more research needs to be done on various areas reported here. For example, is there a connection between source of application and satisfaction level? What is the relationship between size of hospital and types of applications used? Why aren't hospitals more proactive in implementing information technology? To this end, an expanded base of responses is needed. Additional surveys and responses of U. S. hospitals are being planned.

The second area for further research deals with the difference between information technology diffusion in U. S. hospitals and hospitals in other parts of the world. Are hospitals in Europe or the more industrialized Far Eastern countries (for example, Japan) utilizing information technology better in their hospitals? To this end, research partners in other parts of the world are sought for collaborative research.

Additional research in information technology diffusion in hospitals is needed. This study is meant to be the forerunner in research in this area.

BIBLIOGRAPHY

1. Dorenfest, Sheldon I., A Look Behind the Rapid Growth in Healthcare IS, Healthcare Informatics, http://www.healthcare-informatics.com/issues/1997/0697/doren.htm
2. A Market to Die For, DigitalSouth, Fall 1997, pp. 55-59
3. 1997 HIMSS/HP Leadership Survey Results, http://www.hmiss.org/results97.htm

The Impact of IT Investment on Firm Performance

Qing Hu

Department of Information Systems and Operations Management, Florida Atlantic University, Boca Raton, FL
33431
qhu@fau.edu

Robert Plant

Department of Computer Information Systems, University of Miami, Coral Gables, FL 33124
rplant@exchange.sba.miami.edu

ABSTRACT

The promise of increased competitive advantage has been the driving force behind the large-scale investment in information technology (IT) over the last three decades. There is a continuing debate among executives and academics as to the measurable benefits of this investment. The return on investment (ROI) and other performance measures reported in the academic literature indicate conflicting empirical findings. Many previous studies have based their conclusions on the statistical correlation between IT capital investment and firm performance data of the same time period. In this study, using the Granger causality models and three samples of firm level financial data, we found no statistical evidence that IT investments have caused the improvement of financial performance of the firms in the samples. Implications of these findings as well as directions for future studies are discussed.

INTRODUCTION

In the highly competitive global economy, top managers of businesses and organizations are constantly faced with the dilemma: Does it pay to invest in information technology (IT) provided that there are other investment opportunities? The case literature of the 1980's and 90's attempted to show that IT provided competitive advantages to firms by adding value across all aspects of the value chain, improving operational performance, reducing costs, increasing decision quality, and enhancing service innovation and differentiation (Applegate, et al, 1996; Porter and Millar, 1986). The underlying theory is that these operational and strategic improvements should lead to corresponding improvements in productivity, revenue, and profits for those firms which consistently make higher investment in IT than their competitors.

There are several empirical studies that support this argument. Brynjolfsson and Hitt (1996) estimated that the net marginal product of IT staff is about $1.62, and that of IT capital is about 48% or better, which are at least as large as these of other types of capital investment. Mitra and Chaya (1996) showed that the firms that spent more on IT achieved lower cost of production and lower total operating cost when compared with their peers in the same industry, indicating that IT investment indeed improves operational efficiency.

However, not all studies of industry and firm level financial data have shown positive causal relationship between IT investment and improved firm performance. Morrison and Berndt (1990) found that in the manufacturing sector, every dollar spent on IT only delivered on average about $0.80 of value on margin, an indication of over-spending in IT. Loveman (1994)'s study of 60 business units found that IT investment has a negative output elasticity, indicating that the marginal dollar would have been better spent on other categories of capital investment. Even though such a negative impact of IT on a firm's output seems unlikely and counter-intuitive, it is consistent with the findings of Hitt and Brynjolfsson (1996). Their study of 370 firms showed that IT stock has negative impacts on firm performance measures, such as return on assets, return on equity, and total return, though the magnitude of such impact is quite small.

Closer examinations of these studies reveal that the impact of IT on firm performance was tested using the IT capital data and the performance data of the same time period. Under such circumstances, the positive and significant correlation between IT capital variables and the firm performance variables has no inherent implication of a causal relationship, no matter how this correlation is established: whether it is through Canonical correlation as in Mahmood and Mann (1993), economic production functions as in Brynjolfsson and Hitt (1996) and Rai et al (1997), or t-test as in Mitra and Chaya (1996). This is because one can equally reasonably argue, given the same test results, that it is the higher revenue or profit that caused the firm to spend more on IT capital, or that firms allocate more capital spending when they anticipate better financial performance in the coming years.

In this study, we investigate the impact of IT investment on firm productivity and performance using well accepted causal models based on firm level financial data. We argue that no matter what theoretical or empirical models are used, with the currently available testing techniques, it is unlikely that using concurrent IT and firm performance data would yield conclusive causal relationship between the two. We further submit that it would be more convincing to conclude that IT investment does impact firm performance if it can be shown that the IT investments in the preceding years are significantly correlated with the output level of a firm in the subsequent year, but not vice versa.

RESEARCH MODEL AND HYPOTHESES

We argue that the causal relationship, if it exists at all, between IT investment and firm performance, could not be established with any degree of certainty using concurrent IT data and performance data with conventional statistical techniques. The commonly used models in many of the previous studies, such as simple and multiple linear regression, the economic productions models or the structural equation models based on instantaneous causation assumption, are certainly inconsistent with the first condition, and questionable with the third condition at the best.

On the other hand, there are plenty of theoretical arguments and empirical testimonies in the literature that IT investments indeed have impact on firm performance. According to Porter and Millar (1985), the three most important benefits that IT can provide to a firm are reducing cost, enhancing differentiation, and changing competitive scope. From this point of view, the impact of IT investment on firm productivity and financial performance can be hypothesized as follows. IT investment increases IT capital in a firm, which leads to three main results. First, improved efficiency of operation and decision making, which reduces the number of employees, other factors being equal; or more products or services can be produced or offered, other factors being equal. Second, product innovation and differentiation, which increases the market share or demand, other factors being equal. Finally, broadened competitive scope, which leads to a larger market for the product and services, other factors being equal. In any of the cases or as a combined result, the net effect of IT investment should be the increased productivity and better financial performance.

Meanwhile, it has been noted in many studies (e.g., Brynjolfsson, 1993; Brynjolfsson et al, 1994; Loveman, 1994; and Osterman, 1986) that it would take a few years to realize the effect of IT capital investment on the bottom-line of firms. The logic behind this type of argument is convincing. The greatest benefits of any IT initiatives come not from replacing old computers with new ones or manual processes with automated ones, in which the effect of investment can be realized immediately, but from organizational and procedural changes enabled by the investment in IT, often know as business process reengineering (BPR). The effect of such changes may take years to realize (Hammer, 1990; Stoddard and Jrvenpaa, 1993). There are good reasons for such lagged effect. Significant IT projects usually take years to implement. Organization structures need time to adapt in order to take the advantage of the new or improved systems. Employees need time to be trained and re-skilled. Finally, customers and the market are the last of these time-delayed chain reactions to respond which ultimately determines the firm performance.

In light of the preceding argument, the following research hypotheses are developed for testing the causality between IT investment and firm performance:

Hypothesis 1: The increase in IT investment per employee by a firm in the preceding years (t-j, j =1, 2, …n) may contribute to the reduction of operating cost per employee of the firm in the subsequent year (t).

Hypothesis 2: The increase in IT investment per employee by a firm in the preceding years (t-j, j = 1, 2, …n) may contribute to the increase of productivity of the firm in the subsequent year (t).

Hypothesis 3: The increase in IT investment per employee by a firm in the preceding years (t-j, j = 1, 2, … n) may contribute to the sales growth of the firm in the subsequent year (t).

Hypothesis 4: The increase in IT investment per employee by a firm in the preceding years (t-j, j = 1, 2, …n) may contribute to improvement of profitability of the firm in the subsequent year (t).

The preceding hypotheses can be summarized into the following research model, as shown in Figure 1. The solid arrow lines represent the hypothesized causal relationships in this study, and the dashed arrow lines represent the causal relationships proposed in the previous studies.

We use the weaker causal relationship "contribute" rather the stronger relationship "cause" in the hypotheses simply to reflect the fact that IT investments alone would not cause the stated effects. Many operational, technological, and economic factors play significant roles in the performance of a firm. Since we have no control over those other factors, we shall not proclaim that IT investment "causes" these stated effects even if the statistical tests show the existence of the causal relationships between IT investment and these effects.

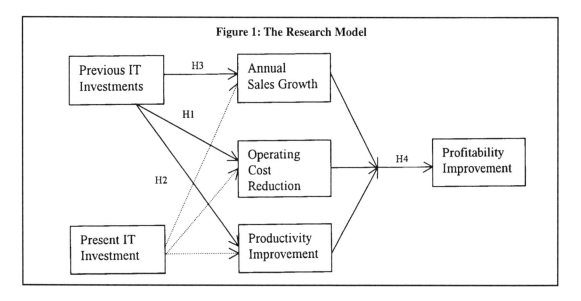

Figure 1: The Research Model

DATA AND METHOD

Data

One of the major difficulties pertaining to economic studies of IT impact on business is to obtain reliable company IT related data, such as IT budget, IT stock value, replacement value, and IT staff, etc.. This is because most companies, even the publicly traded ones, regard these data as private and competitive information. Without empirical validation, theories of IT impact on corporate performance or the value of IT to business competitiveness can only be regarded as hypotheses. Academic researchers have explored various

Table 1: Characteristics of Firm in the Data Sets

DESCRIPTION	DATA SET #1	DATA SET #2	DATA SET #3
Years Covered	1990-1993	1991-1994	1992-1995
Number of Companies	56	62	42
Revenue, μ (σ), billions	10.82 (13.54)	11.19 (13.73)	12.74 (14.93)
IT Budget, μ (σ), millions	348.88 (763.76)	357.77 (759.32)	412.85 (834.03)
Employee, μ (σ), thousand	56.28 (82.64)	58.09 (83.32)	58.64 (82.53)
Firms in Industry Groups			
Aero/Auto	4	5	4
Airline/Air Freight	3	2	0
Banking	10	9	7
Chemical	3	3	3
Computer/Electronics/Telecom	6	13	8
Consumer	1	2	1
Energy/Natural Resources	9	9	6
Financial Services	5	0	1
Food	1	3	2
Manufacturing	4	3	4
Healthcare	2	3	2
Pharmaceutical	1	2	1
Publishing	3	0	0
Railroad/Transportation	1	0	0
Retailing	1	3	2
Wholesale	2	0	0

* Firms in the three data sets are not mutually exclusive, rather they overlap with each other to a fair degree. About 50% of the companies overlap in any two adjacent data sets, and about 30% companies overlap in all three data sets.

avenues for firm level IT data sources. Most of them relied on data published in industry trade publications and databases.

It would be extremely beneficial if different studies used the same set of data sources, so that theories and inferences could be validated utilizing different research frameworks and methodologies. Unfortunately, among these sources that have firm level IT data, only the *ComputerWorld* (CW) and the *InformationWeek* (IW) databases are publicly available. To test our hypotheses, we need a set of companies that have IT data available for at least four consecutive years. These companies must also be publicly traded on one of the three major exchanges (NYSE, AMEX, and NASDAQ) so that their financial data can be obtained using the widely available Compustat database. For this study, we decided to use the IT data published in a high quality industry publication, *InformationWeek* (IW). IW publishes an annual list of 500 companies that it considers as the largest users of information technologies in the United States. These companies were selected based on their revenue as recorded in the Compustat database.

Like other databases, the companies in the IW 500 lists vary from year to year. In addition, the IT investment data of about half of the listed firms were either not available or estimated by the editors of IW. In order to create reliable and accurate data sets that can be used to test our causal models and hypotheses, we constructed three separate data sets, each of which contains a set of firms that have non-estimated IT data for four consecutive years. Then we matched these firms with the Compustat database and acquired other financial data for each of the firms. The characteristics of the three data sets are shown in Table 1.

It can be seen that the companies included in the three data sets have similar characteristics: they are mostly large corporations, on average, with an annual revenue about $10 billion, and annual IT spending about $340 million, and employing about 56 thousand people. The companies are well distributed in a variety of industries, with Banking, Computer/Electronics/Telecom, and Energy/Natural Resource having a slight lead over other groups.

Method

In order to test the causal relationships submitted in our research hypotheses, we must rely on the established causal modeling methods. Among those, the Granger causal model (Granger, 1969) is chosen for its compliance with the pre-conditions of causality and flexibility. Even the instantaneous causation can be accommodated in the model. Let X_t and Y_t be two time series data, the general causal model with consideration of possible instantaneous causality can be written as:

$$X_t + b_0 Y_t = \sum_{j=1}^{n} a_j X_{t-j} + \sum_{j=1}^{n} b_j Y_{t-j} + \varepsilon_t$$

$$Y_t + c_0 X_t = \sum_{j=1}^{n} c_j X_{t-j} + \sum_{j=1}^{n} d_j Y_{t-j} + \eta_t \tag{1}$$

where ε_t and η_t are two uncorrelated white noise error terms with zero means.

This definition of causality implies that Y causes X if some b_j is not zero, and X causes Y if some c_j is not zero. If both of these events occur, there is said to be a feedback relationship between X and Y. If b_0 is not zero, then the instantaneous causality is occurring and a knowledge of Y_t will improve the "prediction" or goodness of fit of the first equation for X_t, and vice versa if c_0 is not zero.

Substituting X and Y in the causal model with firm IT data and performance data, we can derive a set of models for testing our research hypotheses. However, before we present the causal models specific to these hypotheses, we need to define each of the variables used to represent IT investment, operating cost, sales growth, productivity, and profitability. To minimize the impact of firm size variations in our samples, it is decided that we should use per employee metrics wherever it is applicable.

IT Investments. The three data sets provide annual IT spending of each firm for four consecutive years. Instead of using the actual values, the change of the annual IT investment per employee is considered as the most appropriate measure for studying the impact of IT on firm performance, defined as follows:

$$\Delta I_t = \frac{I_t / E_t - I_{t-1} / E_{t-1}}{I_{t-1} / E_{t-1}} \tag{2}$$

where I_t and I_{t-1} are the IT investments by the firm in year t and t-1, E_t and E_{t-1} are the number of employees of that firm in year t and t-1, and ΔI_t is the percentage change of IT investment per employee over the preceding year.

Operating Cost. If IT investment has any impact on firm performance, the operating cost should be the most sensitive area. A firm's operating cost is measured in terms of its selling, general, and administrative expenses as reported in its annual report. In this study, we are more interested in the change of operating cost than the cost itself. Therefore, we define the change of operating cost as follows:

$$\Delta C_t = \frac{C_t / E_t - C_{t-1} / E_{t-1}}{C_{t-1} / E_{t-1}}$$

(3)

where C_t and C_{t-1} are the selling, general, and administrative expenses in year t and t-1, and E_t and E_{t-1} are the number of employees of that firm in year t and t-1, respectively. ΔC_t is the operational cost reduction per employee.

Sales Growth. Annual sales growth rate is an important indicator of the competitiveness of a firm. If IT investment has any impact on firm performance, it should be reflected in the changes of sales from year to year. In this study, the sales growth is calculated as follows:

$$\Delta S_t = \frac{S_t - S_{t-1}}{S_{t-1}}$$

(4)

where S_t and S_{t-1} are the annual sales of a firm in year t and t-1, and ΔS_t is the annual sales growth rate from year t-1 to year t .

Productivity. Labor productivity is defined in general as the output per unit time of labor. In this study, the output is measured in terms of sales, and the time unit is one year. Thus labor productivity of a firm is defined as the annual sales per employee, and the change of productivity is defined as follows:

$$\Delta P_t = \frac{S_t / E_t - S_{t-1} / E_{t-1}}{S_{t-1} / E_{t-1}}$$

(5)

where S_t and S_{t-1} are the annual sales of a firm in year t and t-1, E_t and E_{t-1} are the number of employees of a firm in year t and t-1, and ΔP_t is the change of productivity of the firm from year t-1 to year t.

Profitability. A firm's profitability is measured in terms of the classic ROA (Return on Assets). Since this measure is usually calculated in percentages, the annual change of profitability is simply defined as:

$$\Delta ROA_t = ROA_t - ROA_{t-1}$$

(6)

where ROA_t and ROA_{t-1} are the Return on Asset of a firm in year t and t-1.

We can see that, compared to the conventional regression analysis used in many previous studies, including the studies using economic production models, the tests based on Granger causality model are able to eliminate the chance of confirming false causal relationship resulted from mis-specified regression models.

RESULTS

We estimated the model parameters using least-square linear regression method provided in the SAS software package based on the causality models defined in equation (1) and the three data sets as described in Table 1. The results are presented in Tables 2 through 5. Notice that since we only have the data for four consecutive years, and we are using the year-to-year changes as variables, the upper limit (n) for subscript j in all the models is two (j = 1, 2).

Since multi-year financial data are involved in the regressions, inflation becomes an important factor. Before

Table 2: The Causal Relationship between IT and Operational Cost			
		Data Sets	
	1990-1993	1991-1994	1992-1995
Parameters		*Operational Cost as the Effect*	
R^2-adj	-0.0459	0.1627	0.1120
F statistic	0.6312	**3.0202	1.9335
Intercept	4.8519 (1.2325)	1.2415 (0.4125)	***9.1060 (3.3979)
a_1	-0.0853 (-0.2480)	-0.0083 (-0.0594)	*-0.4417 (-1.9457)
a_2	-0.0870 (-0.2129)	**0.3893 (2.2898)	-0.0942 (-.3434)
b_0	0.0836 (1.6596)	0.0768 (0.9193)	0.0808 (1.2834)
b_1	0.1489 (1.1798)	-0.0900 (-0.8141)	-0.0898 (-1.3426)
b_2	-0.0154 (-0.2345)	0.0729 (0.8941)	-0.0708 (-0.8610)

Table 3: The Causal Relationship between IT and Productivity

Parameters	1990-1993	1991-1994	1992-1995
		Data Sets	
		Productivity as the Effect	
R^2-adj	0.0374	0.2568	0.0731
F statistic	1.4273	***5.2165	1.6471
Intercept	2.8143 (1.0971)	4.5869 (2.0858)	10.7476 (4.1925)
a_1	0.3107 (0.3077)	-0.0727 (-0.7407)	-0.2226 (-1.5291)
a_2	0.1966 (0.7719)	***0.4988 (3.4739)	0.0951 (0.4678)
b_0	-0.0619 (-1.4358)	*0.1217 (1.9925)	*0.1143 (1.8257)
b_1	-0.1270 (-1.6106)	-0.0483 (-0.6531)	-0.0253 (-0.3766)
b_2	-0.0367 (-0.6435)	0.0696 (1.1894)	-0.0356 (-0.4753)

Table 4: The Causal Relationship between IT and Sales Growth

Parameters	1990-1993	1991-1994	1992-1995
		Data Sets	
		Sales Growth as the Effect	
R^2-adj	0.0563	0.3027	-0.1177
F statistic	1.6562	***6.2953	0.1362
Intercept	7.8706 (1.5032)	***6.9156 (4.6003)	***12.2512 (2.8656)
a_1	0.2652 (0.7117)	***0.2457 (2.9643)	0.0146 (0.0485)
a_2	0.5320 (1.6358)	***0.4640 (3.8513)	0.1064 (0.4357)
b_0	-0.1440 (-1.5658)	-0.0153 (-0.3686)	-0.0760 (-0.6748)
b_1	-0.0119 (-0.0607)	*-0.0909 (-1.9744)	-0.0454 (-0.3803)
b_2	-0.0595 (-0.4986)	-0.0115 (-0.3250)	0.0369 (0.3260)

Table 5: The Causal Relationship between IT and Profitability: ROA

Parameters	1990-1993	1991-1994	1992-1995
		Data Sets	
		ROA as the Effect	
R^2-adj	0.0822	0.0512	0.0824
F statistic	1.9851	1.6588	1.7362
Intercept	-0.1784 (-0.3515)	0.6810 (0.7691)	0.7811 (1.2644)
a_1	0.0443 (0.3210)	**-0.3516 (-2.1276)	-0.2356 (-1.1410)
a_2	***-0.3526 (-2.6759)	**-0.5123 (-2.4413)	-0.0180 (-0.1105)
b_0	0.0078 (0.9466)	0.0110 (0.4681)	0.0169 (1.0543)
b_1	***0.0470 (2.6962)	-0.0208 (-0.7515)	0.0054 (0.3160)
b_2	0.0007 (0.0649)	0.0105 (0.4964)	0.0207 (1.0912)

conducting the regressions, we inflated the financial figures of the preceding years to the real dollar values of the subsequent year (t) based on the annual percentage change of implicit price deflator of the Gross Domestic Product, as published in the Survey of Current Business (US Department of Commerce, 1997).

In all tables, the numbers in parentheses are the two-tailed t-statistics of the regression parameters, and the statistical significant levels are represented as: *** for $p < 0.01$, ** for $p < 0.05$, and * for $p < 0.1$.

DISCUSSION

The preceding tables presented a large amount of data about the estimated causality models and their associated testing statistics. To facilitate our discussion, these results are summarized in Table 6 and organized based on the research hypotheses.

The results in Table 6 speak out laud and clear: there is no convincing evidence that IT investments in the preceding years have made any significant contribution to the subsequent changes in any of the four categories of firm performance measures: operating cost, productivity, sales growth, and profitability. In the cases of operating cost (H1), $p<0.05$ level. The only noticeable significant b parameter is the one for the effect of IT investment on the ROA in the 1990-1993 data set ($b_1 = 0.0470$, significant at $p<0.01$ level). The implication is that the increase of IT investment in the time period of 1991-1992 had contributed to the increase of ROA in 1993 of the firms in the data sets. However, given the overall non-significant tone of the results, this one case of significance is not enough to be considered as convincing evidence to conclude that IT investment has a positive impact on firm profitability.

We also found no evidence to support the hypothesis that there is an instantaneous causality between IT invest-ment and firm performance, as implicitly assumed in many of the previous studies when concurrent IT data and performance data are used to test the causal relationship. According to the principle of Granger causality, if there exists an instantaneous causal relationship between IT investment and firm performance, then either coefficient b_0 or c_0 would be significantly different from zero. Examining Tables 2 through 5, none of the b_0's is significantly different from zero at the $p<0.05$ level. This result casts serious doubt on the research methodology that uses concurrent data for testing causal relationship between IT investment and firm performance.

Table 6. Hypotheses with IT Investment as Cause and Performance as Effect

Hypotheses	Data Sets		
	1990-1993	1991-1994	1992-1995
H1	$b_1 = b_2 = 0$	$b_1 = b_2 = 0$	$b_1 = b_2 = 0$
	No support	No support	No support
H2	$b_1 = b_2 = 0$	$b_1 = b_2 = 0$	$b_1 = b_2 = 0$
	No support	No support	No support
H3	$b_1 = b_2 = 0$	$b_1 < 0^*, b_2 = 0$	$b_1 = b_2 = 0$
	No support	Negative impact	No support
H4	$b_1 > 0^{***}, b_2 = 0$	$b_1 = b_2 = 0$	$b_1 = b_2 = 0$
	Partial support	No support	No support

Significant level: *** $p<0.01$, ** $p<0.05$, * $p<0.1$

CONCLUSIONS

We have shown, through tests using the Granger causality models and firm level data, that the hypothesized positive causal relationship between IT investment and firm performance cannot be established at acceptable statis-tical significant levels. The results of this study have a number of significant implications for future studies of the economic value of IT investment. The first is that most firms, if not all, may have failed to capitalize on their investments in IT through reengineering business processes (Hammer, 1990) and other organizational changes. Year after year firms adjust, usually upward, their IT budget based on previous year's level simply because their competi-tors and other members of the industry are doing the same. New versions of software and ever more powerful hardware replace the existing ones, even if they are still adequate for the applications they support. Detailed exami-nations of how firms actually allocate their IT budget and the subsequent changes are warranted and may shed some light on why IT investments have failed to show at the bottom line of organizations.

Second, overspending in IT by firms may be another complicating factor. Marginal analysis by Morrrison and Berndt (1990) shows that every additional $1 spent on IT only delivers $0.80 in output. This is essentially the same as the findings of two other studies (Brynjolfsson and Hitt, 1996; Hitt and Brynjolfsson, 1996) using different data sets. A recent report by Sentry Technology Group based on a survey of 16,000 large U. S. companies estimates that as much as $66 billon—nearly 10% of total IT purchases—could go into the "inefficient" IT spending category, including purchases of unused or underused hardware, software, and services (Violino, 1997a). "It has become so easy to spend a lot of money on hardware, software, and maintenance – and not necessarily see any return," said one executive (Violino, 1998, p61). Policies and practices for better IT asset management may be another important area that has been overlooked by both practitioners and academia.

The last is the issue of measurement. Although most studies of the economic value of IT, including the present one, have attempted to associate IT investment with aggregated firm performance measures, such as ROA, other alternatives have been proposed. Barua, Kriebel and Mukhopadhyay (1995) advocate the use of intermediate vari-ables (e.g., capacity utilization and inventory turnover) to study the impact of IT since they reflect the direct impact of IT investment. From a different perspective, Brynjolfsson (1996) suggests that if the impact of IT investment fails to show up the in the statistics of producers' performance data, it should be reflected in the surplus that consumers have benefited from lower prices of the products due to the use of IT by the producers.

While both studies provided empirical evidence that support the hypotheses, one central question is: no mater how much IT has contributed to the consumer surplus or the capacity utilization rate, what is the value of IT investment to shareholders if it fails to increase the profitability of a for-profit-organization? "Business leaders, IS executives, consultants, and academics for years have debated whether it's necessary or even desirable to measure IT's return on investment. But the discussion is being cut short by CEOs and chief financial officers with their eyes on the balance sheet. Before granting funds for a major project, these execs are demanding to see the expected payback – in financial terms they understand." (Violino, 1998, p61).

It seems that we have raised more questions than provided answers in this study. This is perhaps a reflection of the on going debate about the economic value of information technology and how it should be measured properly (Violino, 1997b; Vilino, 1998). It is our hope that this study will assist in moving the focus of future research on the economic value of IT from the discovery of statistical correlations to the development of new metrics and methodologies that are appropriate for evaluating the causal relationship between IT investment and firm performance.

REFERENCES

Applegate, L. M., F. W. McFarlan, and J. L. McKenney, *Corporate Information Systems Management: Text and Cases*, (4th Ed.), Irwin, Chicago, IL. 1996.

Barua, A., C. Kriebel, , and T. Mukhopadhyay, Information Technologies and Business Value: An Analytical and Empirical Investigation, *Information Systems research*, 6, 1, (1995), 3-23.

Brynjolfsson, E., The Productivity Paradox of Information Technology, *Communications of the ACM*, 36, 12, (1993), 67-77.

Brynjolfsson, E., The Contribution of Information Technology to Consumer Welfare, *Information Systems Research*, 7, 3, (1996), 281-300.

Brynjolfsson, E. and L. Hitt, Paradox Lost? Firm-level Evidence on the Returns to Information Systems Spending, *Management Science*, 42, 4, (1996), 541-558.

Brynjolfsson, E., T. W. Malone, V. Gurbaxani, and A. Kambil, Does Information Technology Lead to Smaller Firms? *Management Science*, 40, 12, (1994), 1629-1645.

Granger, C. W. J. Investigating Causal Relations by Econometric Models and Cross-Spectral Methods. *Econometrica*, 37, 3, (1969), 424-438.

Hammer, M. Reengineering Work: Don't Automate, Obliterate, *Harvard Business Review*, July-August, 4, (1990), 104-112.

Hitt, L. and Brynjolfsson, E. Productivity, Business Profitability, and Consumer Surplus: Three Different Measures of Information Technology Value, *MIS Quarterly*, 20, 2, (1996), 121-142.

Loveman, G. W. An Assessment of the Productivity Impact on Information Technologies, in *Information Technology and the Corporation of the 1990s: Research Studies*, T. J. Allen and M. S. S. Morton (eds.), Oxford University Press, New York, NY. 1994, 84-110.

Mahmood, M. A. and G. J. Mann, Measuring the Organizational Impact of Information Technology Investment: An Exploratory Study, *Journal of Management Information Systems*, 10, 1, (1993), 97-122.

Mitra, S. and A. K. Chaya, Analyzing Cost Effectiveness of Organizations: The Impact of Information Technology Spending, *Journal of Management Information Systems*, 13, 2, (1996), 29-57.

Morrison, C. J. and E. R. Berndt, Assessing the Productivity of Information Technology Equipment in the U. S. Manufacturing Industries, National Bureau of Economic Research Working Paper #3582, Jan, 1990.

Osterman, P. The Impact of Computers on the Employment of Clerks and Managers, *Industrial and Labor Relations Review*, 39, 2, (1986), 175-186.

Porter, M. E. and V. E. Millar, How information gives you competitive advantage, *Harvard Business Review*, July-August, (1985), 149-160.

Rai, A., R. Patnayakuni, and N. Patnayakuni, Technology Investment and Business Performance, *Communications of the ACM*, 40, 7, (1997), 89-97.

Stoddard, D. and S. Jarvenpaa, Business Process Reengineering: IT - Enabled Radical Change, Harvard Business School, 9-191-151, 1993.

U. S. Department of Commerce, *Survey of Current Business*, 77, 4, (1997), D34-36.

Violino, B. Out of Control, *InformationWeek*, June 9, (1997a), 36-46.

Violino, B. Return on Investment, *InformationWeek*, June 30, (1997b), 36-44.

Violino, B. ROI in the Real World, *InformationWeek*, April 27, (1998), 60-72.

A Lexicon of "Excellent" Systems Analysts Skills: Determining Operational Definitions of Attributes

M. Gordon Hunter
St. Francis Xavier University, Antigonish, Nova Scotia, B2G 2W5, CANADA
Tel: (902) 867-2439, Fax: (902) 867-2448, E-mail: ghunter@stfx.ca

ABSTRACT

This article proposes a lexicon for the attributes associated with "excellent" systems analysts. In general, good systems analysts must be able to deal with users. While sufficient technical knowledge is taken for granted, the good systems analyst must also possess skills in interpersonal relations, and communication. Further, in order to perform well the systems analyst should have some knowledge of the user's functional area. The SEI sponsored P-CMM is a personnel management framework for the information systems industry. While it indicates what should be done, it does not indicate how to carry out the recommended programs. Identifying and defining those important skills is a necessary task in improving the management and productivity of systems analysts. The lexicon proposed here may be employed in a number of ways by the personnel management function of an organization. The definitions proposed here will provide some further guidance in the effort to improve the productivity of systems analysts.

INTRODUCTION

In the past few years many research projects have investigated the skills necessary to perform the function of systems analyst. Without question, the results of these research projects have contributed to the general understanding of the function. However, as reported on in the following section, it has been difficult to operationalize this understanding. Further, some research has focused more upon a specific aspect of the function without a thorough consideration of the interaction affects amongst all the applicable aspects.

This article proposes a lexicon for the attributes associated with "excellent" systems analysts. Previous research is reviewed regarding a definition of systems analyst. Also, a number of projects are reported upon which investigated the skills associated with the function of systems analyst. The article then briefly discusses the research conducted to investigate interpretations of "excellent" systems analysts. The main emphasis, however, is upon the results obtained from a series of research projects. A lexicon is proposed which reflects an interpretation of the data gathered and which will support the operationalization of various aspects of personnel administration of systems analysts.

RELATED RESEARCH

While many definitions of "systems analyst" exist in the literature, the following seems to be an acceptable representation. Whitten and Bentley (1998) describe a systems analyst as one whom,

"... facilitates the study of the problems and needs of a business to determine how the business system and information technology can best solve the problems and accomplish improvements for the business". (Whitten and Bentley, 1998:8).

Previous research (Awad, 1985 and Nordbotten, 1985) has suggested that good systems analysts must have abilities in two major areas. First, systems analysts must be able to deal with users. That is, for example, systems analysts should have good interpersonal skills, should be able to communicate, and should have knowledge of the user's functional area. Second, systems analysts should have sufficient technical knowledge so they understand the capabilities of computers and are able to gather and interpret facts.

Also, some time ago, Vitalari (1985) suggested that a concept is emerging regarding High-rated Domain Knowledge. He does not, however, indicate any detail regarding this concept. Martin (1982) presented a list of factors, which may relate to improving the productivity of systems analysts. This list of factors is included here in Figure 1.

Vitalari and Dickson (1983) investigated the problem solving thought processes of high and low rated systems analysts. Supervisors were asked to rate systems analysts using behaviourally anchored rating scales that were originally developed by Arvey and Hoyle (discussed elsewhere in this document). Vitalari and Dickson contend that, "...

successful systems analysts behave differently in solving analysis problems than do those that are less successful." (Vitalari and Dickson, 1983:253). While the report concludes with many valuable suggestions (such as; highly rated systems analysts seemed to understand the importance of interpersonal relations), the authors noted that, "The results indicates that there are more similarities in the problem solving behaviour of analysts than differences." (Vitalari and Dickson, 1983:258). It should be noted that supervisors of systems analysts were asked to nominate high-rated and low-rated systems analysts. Perhaps, this method actually does not result in differentiated groups, as the authors had planned.

Litecky (1985) also suggested interviewing is an important task performed by systems analysts. Interviews are the systems analysts largest source of data for problem solving and systems design.

Barrett and Davis suggest, "A good systems analyst must be an expert in personnel management and possess excellent communication skills." (Barrett and Davis, 1986:18). The authors present a description of Carl Jung's theory of personality and suggest "The ability to identify your own personality leanings and the personality of some-one else is a valuable skill in the interpersonal situation of the interview." (Barrett and Davis, 1986:19).

Figure 1: Factors that Improve the Productivity [of] Systems Analysis

- Avoidance of the writing of requirements documents and specifications, where possible, this may be replaced partially or completed with prototyping using the software discussed in this book.
- Interactive screen, report, and dialogue design.
- Use of interactive computerized tools for accomplishing formal design and techniques.
- Avoidance of hand-drawn charts of excessive complexity and the replacement of these with computer-drawn charts.
- Skill with application generators, report generators, and dialogue generators so that these can be used efficiently and fast.
- End users doing as much of their own application creation as possible.
- End users obtaining their own information with database query languages and information retrieval systems.
- End users generating their own reports.
- Good training and skilled motivation of end users to do the above.
- An Information Center approach to support the end users in the above and to generate applications for them.
- Salesmanship by systems analysts to encourage the spread of end-user employment of the software and information systems. Concentration on early adapters in the end-user community.
- Automation of database design [2] and good management of the database environment.
- Database systems with formal descriptions of triggers that cause database actions and descriptions of those actions. Logic associated with the database rather than with individual applications.
- Recognition of the distinction between Class 3 and Class 4 databases. Simple, fast, implementation of Class 4 databases.
- Use of self-documenting techniques and the creation of interactive documentation and HELP functions in end-user software.
- Motivation of systems analysts by creating better job satisfaction. This can result from working with users to finish a job, seeing it in actual use, and adjusting it to be as effective as possible. The analysts see the direct effects of their creativity. This helps to build their own effectiveness.

Source: Martin, James. Application Development Without Programmers. Prentice-Hall, Inc., Englewood Cliffs, 1982, p. 339.

Maxwell (1986) investigated the personal characteristics of successful information systems analysts. Maxwell used the critical incident technique to gather data from 197 respondents. All respondents were members of the Association for Systems Management in a particular geographic region. Job titles included Executive Officer, MIS Director/Manager, Supervisor, Project Leader, and Other. Maxwell, it is noted, has defined a successful information systems analyst, as follows:

> "An employee whose primary role is to perform information systems analysis and design activities directed at creating, implementing, improving, and maintaining computer-based information systems that meet the prescribed needs of the organization and its functionaries." (Maxwell, 1986: 94)

It seems this is a definition for information systems analysts in general. There does not seem to be, within this definition, a component, which supports the differentiation of successful information systems analysts. Maxwell also prepared a ranked list of personal characteristics based on frequency of occurrence. Figure 2 shows the results of this analysis. Other than presenting this data Maxwell does not pursue its use in any manner.

More recently, McCubbrey and Scudder (1988) asked 10 MIS practitioners to comment on the importance of a supplied list of skills regarding systems analysts. The list was the result of previous work by Nunamaker, et al (1982). The results of the McCubbrey and Scudder research project are shown in Figure 3. The skills have been rated based upon participant responses according to a standard Likert scale (Less important 1 2 3 4 5 more important).

According to the authors, the results suggest that communication and organisational skills are important for systems analysts of the future. Guinan (1988) also found that the individuals involved in information system development could improve the quality of their interactions with more knowledge about effective communication.

Cheney, et al (1989) asked 79 senior information managers to comment on skill requirements of, amongst others, systems analyst/designers as a further follow-up to the previous two projects. Structured interviews were used to gather the data. The following conclusions were reached regarding systems analyst/designers.

"The trend for systems analysts/designers is toward increased knowledge of people and problem-solving skills, and away from developing application software. As the purchase of packaged software technology becomes the norm, Software Package Analysis is and is expected to become a valuable skill for systems analysts/designers. Consistent with the role of using technology to find solutions, Database Management Systems skills are also viewed as being increasingly more important now and in the future." (Cheney, et al, 1989:335).

The research projects described above all attempt to determine a better understanding of systems analysts and what they do. However, while these projects identify the importance of a skill, they do not indicate the relative importance. Trends in skills may be shown, but not relative to a skill set. Some projects highlight skill categories, but not in sufficient detail to support action. Other projects identify "highly rated" systems analysts, but do not discuss how these individuals were actually identified. Thus, no data are available with which to be able to differentiate systems analysts. The research projects reported on in this article attempted to address the concerns expressed about the projects reviewed in this section.

Figure 2: Ranking Analysis of Selected Personal Characteristics for all Responses

Characteristics	Number of Responses	Percent of Responses	Ranking
Works well with others	70	17.5	1
Compromises	49	12.5	2.5
Communicates well with others	49	12.2	2.5
Thinks, reasons and creates order	46	11.5	4
Functions with objectivity	36	9.0	5
Considered technically competent	28	7.0	6
Possesses high, personal, ethical standards	27	6.7	7
Views a situation as a system	26	6.5	8
Motivates and develops others	22	5.5	9
Manifests patience	21	5.2	10
Manifests a positive nature and personality	12	3.0	11
A self-starter, motivated	6	1.5	12
Prefers Less-structured environments	3	0.7	13
Pursues organized plan for personal and professional continuing education	2	0.5	14.5
Manifests sensitivity and loyalty to employing organization	2	0.5	14.5
Functions with tact and consideration	1	0.2	16.5
Possesses a career instead of just an information systems orientation	1	0.2	16.5
Total Responses	401	100.0	

In 1995, the Software Engineering Institute (SEI) has proposed a framework, People - Capability Maturity Model (P-CMM). The purpose of P-CMM is to enhance the ability of software organizations to manage personnel in order to improve their software capability. The P-CMM framework provides a description of a continuous improvement process for organizations to adopt in the management of their information systems personnel. While the framework outlines the concepts underlying capability maturity regarding personnel, it does not indicate how to implement these concepts. Hunter (1998) has proposed a method, based on his research, which may be used to implement the P-CMM framework. Not only does the proposed method support the concepts outlined in P-CMM, it also grounds the data obtained within the specific organization.

While the next section of this article briefly describes the various research projects, which used the method, the emphasis of the remainder of the article will be on the results obtained.

RESEARCH METHOD

George Kelly (1955 and 1963) first proposed personal Construct Theory. He suggested that individuals, based upon their past experience, would devise and internalize a system of personal constructs which they would employ to deal with current or anticipated situations. A technique developed by Kelly to study an individual's personal construct system is the Role Construct Repertory Test (RepGrid). The RepGrid technique has been employed to investigate a number of areas beyond the original application by Kelly. It has been used to study problem construction (Eden and Jones, 1984), for market research (Corsini and Marsella, 1983), and knowledge acquisition for expert system development (Latta and Swigger, 1992; and Phythian and King, 1992).

Hunter has employed the RepGrid technique in a number of projects, which consisted of interviewing a total of 87 research participants at four fieldwork locations. Three of the locations were in Western Canada. The fourth was in Singapore. At each location research participants were identified who were associated with a group related to Information Systems Professionals (either systems analysts or their supervisors) or Business Professionals (those who interacted with systems analysts from a functional perspective).

One-to-one interviews were conducted which maintained confidentiality and allowed the researcher to pursue research participants' comments to a fair degree of detail. Constructs were elicited from the research participants through the use of the RepGrid. The comments made by the research participants were based upon their experience with specific systems analysts in their organization. In order to understand what a research participant meant by a particular construct, it was necessary to attempt to understand the content of the construct. Thus, during the elicitation of each construct detailed interviews were taken. This process generated a vast amount of rich qualitative data. Various themes and sub-themes were identified as emerging from the data. These themes represent the start of the process to develop the lexicon proposed in this article.

Figure 3: Survey Results

SKILL	AVERAGE
1. People Skills:	
Hear and listen	4.3
Describe behavior by economics/psychology	3.6
Describe/predict task/time behavior	3.2
2. Model Skills	
Formulate and solve simple models	3.3
Recognize appropriate models	3.6
View situation as system	2.9
Apply system to organisation	2.7
Perform economic analysis	3.8
Present written summary of project	4.0
Present written detailed description of subparts	3.1
3. Computer Skills	
Knowledge of hardware/software	3.1
Program in a higher language	3.6
Program a defined problem	3.0
Develop multiple logical structures	3.0
Develop multiple implementations	3.3
Develop specifications	2.6
Knowledge of sources	3.4
Develop major alternatives for system components	3.5
Develop economic analysis for alternatives	3.6
Create "rough-cut" feasibility evaluations	3.8
Develop task management and database components	2.6
4. Organisational Skills	
Knowledge of purposeful organisation structure	3.9
Knowledge of functional areas	4.5
Identify functional area key issues and problems	4.3
Knowledge of typical functional roles and behavior	4.0
Identify short-term/long-term effects	3.9
Identify appropriate information needs	3.9
Knowledge of IS needs at organisational levels	4.1
Knowledge of information gathering techniques	4.1
Gathering information systematically	3.9
Specify alternative information transfers	3.5
Make "rough-cut" analysis of alternatives	3.7
Develop positive and negative impacts	3.9
Develop specifications for needs	2.6
5. Societal Skills	
Articulate position on issues	3.5
Perceive and describe impacts on society	3.6
Perform "rough-cut" specifications of impacts	3.5

Initially, Hunter (1992, 1993, and 1994) identified the skills and personal characteristics which members of various audiences identified as contributing to an interpretation to what constitutes an "excellent" systems analyst. In subsequent work, Hunter and Beck (1996a and 1996b) and Hunter and Palvia (1996) and Palvia and Hunter (1996) replicated and expanded the investigation of this area. The result of these investigations is a vast amount of rich and in depth data relating to audience members' interpretations of the domain of discourse. While the previous articles have contributed to an improved understanding of systems analysts, operational definitions have not been developed based upon the data gathered in the earlier research projects. While Hunter (1995, 1997 and 1998) has proposed a method for implementing a skill assessment process, it will be necessary to develop operational definitions of the appropriate attributes. This article addresses this lack of definition by analysing the data gathered from the previous research projects and proposing a lexicon of skills for "excellent" systems analysts.

Figure 4: Definitions of Themes

Theme	Definition
Attitude	personal belief about how to approach work, users and staff
	Examples: "analyst realizes it's his duty to check into reported errors"
	"will work overtime"
	"keen about analysing what user wants"
Knowledge	understanding of a particular subject
	Examples: "knows how system will interface with other systems"
	"knows which parts of system are correct"
	"knows existing application packages"
Communicate	exchange (send or receive) of messages with others
	Examples: "can express self well"
	"gives programmers feedback at the end of each project stage"
	"will explain things to team members"
Plan	anticipation of activities and organization of tasks
	Examples: "prepares a schedule of who and by when"
	"allows time for each activity"
	"can fit in with other projects"
Investigate	gathering of facts about a particular aspect
	Examples: "determines how request will affect current situation"
	"tries to understand what user wants"
	"finds out from users how they handle the situation now"
Flexible	readiness to change based upon external clues
	Examples: "doesn't have a solution in mind"
	"willing to try different things that are untried"
	"open to suggestions from project team"
Thorough	consideration of aspects at a detailed level
	Examples: "analyst checks out entire system"
	"goes into depth in new system"
	"analyst looks at solution from all sides"
Design	incorporation of necessary functions in a system for current and future use
	Examples: "system provides what user wants"
	"system is easy to use"
	"ensures present system can be changed to meet future needs
Experience	length of time spent working in an area or on a system
	Examples: "has worked on system for a long time"
	"has worked in this area"
	"doesn't need guidance about how to solve problems"
Involve User	include functional user in tasks
	Examples: "will work with user deciding how to make a change"
	"will offer user other alternatives"
	"forces user to think more about the request"
Delegate	assignment of duties to staff and monitoring progress
	Examples: "leaves members free to use their own style"
	"works well with subordinates"
	"distributes he work load"
Creative	internal generation of new ideas
	Examples: "tries to think in ways not thought before"
	"generates lots of ideas"

PROPOSED LEXICON

The themes and sub-themes emerged from the research data. In previous research it has been shown that the themes have a relative level of importance. This aspect will not be discussed here. Instead, this article will concentrate upon presenting, in the form of a lexicon, proposed definitions of these themes, based upon the detailed interview notes obtained from the research participants.

The more important aspects, which emerged from the research, suggest the research participants interpreted "excellence" in systems analysts based upon such general categories as "communicate", "attitude", " knowledge", "investigate", and "experience".

The proposed lexicon is presented in Figure 4. Along with the proposed definition for each aspect some examples are included to further explain the meaning of the word.

The results of this research project seem to present a more thorough description of what constitute the skills and personal characteristics of "excellent" systems analysts than does some of the earlier research. Figure 5 presents a mapping of the current results onto the results obtained previously by Maxwell (1986) and McCubbrey and Scudder (1988). Both of the previous research results do not present as thorough coverage of the domain of discourse. Maxwell's results concentrate mainly upon the theme of "attitude", while the McCubbrey and Scudder results seem quite sparse. These disparate results may be the result of the type of research method employed within each project. Maxwell used the critical incident technique, while McCubbrey and Scudder supplied a list of skills. First the supplied list approach would be very limiting regarding any new aspect not considered by the researchers. Second, while the critical incident technique would be an improvement in flexibility, Maxwell did not differentiate between "excellent" and non-"excellent" systems analysts in his grouping of research participants.

Figure 5: Map of Proposed Lexicon onto Previous Research

Themes (FIGURE 4)	Maxwell (1986) (FIGURE 2)*	McCubbrey and Scudder (1988) (FIGURE 3)*
Attitude	7,10,11,12,13,15,16,17	
Knowledge	6	3,5
Communicate	3	1
Plan	4,8,14	2
Investigate		
Flexible	2,5	
Thorough		
Design		
Experience		4
Involve User		
Delegate	1,9	
Creative		

*- The numbers in these columns represent the items presented sequentially in Figures 2 and 3.

CONCLUSION

There is a need for an organizational strategy regarding the evaluation of systems analysts in a number of areas. The current response to systems analyst productivity has resulted in the application of a plethora of tools and techniques. Thus, an investigation of the individuals involved in information systems development has provided information regarding another important component of systems analyst productivity. To improve productivity systems analysts should be more carefully selected and should be trained according to their skill deficiencies. The basis for systems analyst selection and training will vary from one organisation to another. Identifying and defining those important skills is a necessary task in improving the management and productivity of systems analysts. The lexicon proposed here may be employed in a number of ways by an organization. Personnel management will vary from one organization to another. The definitions proposed here will provide some further guidance in the effort to improve the productivity of systems analysts.

REFERENCES

Awad, Elia M. Systems Analysis and Design. 2nd Edition, Homewood, Illinios, Richard D. Irwin Inc., 1985.

Barrett, Robert A. and Bruce C. Davis. "Successful Systems Analysts Hone Their Communication Skills". Data Management, April, 1986, pp. 18-21.

Cheney, Paul H., David P. Hale, and George M. Kasper. " Information Systems Professionals: Skills for the 1990's".

Proceedings of the 22nd Annual Hawaii International Conference of Systems Sciences, IEEE Computer Society Press, 1989, pp. 331-336.

Corsini, Raymond and Anthony J. Marsella. Personality Theories, Research and Assessment. Itasca, Illinois, Peacock Publishers, Inc., 1983.

Eden, Colin and Sue Jones. "Using Repertory Grids for Problem Construction". Journal of Operations Research, Vol. 35, No. 9, 1984, pp. 779-798.

Guinan, Patricia J. Patterns of Excellence for IS Professionals - An Analysis of Communication Behavior. Washington, ICIT Press, 1988.

Hunter, M. Gordon. "Managing Information Systems Professionals: Implementing a Skill Assessment Process". Special Interest Group on Computer Personnel Research, March 26-28, 1998, Boston, Massachusetts, pp. 19-27.

Hunter, M. Gordon. "People-Capability Maturity Model: A Proposed Implementation Method". 8th International Conference of the Information Resources Management Association, May 18-21, 1997, Vancouver, Canada.

Hunter, M. Gordon. "Managing Systems Analysts: A Proposed Decision Making Process". International Conference on Global Business in Transition, Prospects for the Twenty First Century, December 14-16, 1995, Hong Kong, pp. 527-534.

Hunter, M. Gordon. ""Excellent" Systems Analysts: Key Audience Perceptions". Computer Personnel, April, 1994, pp. 15-31.

Hunter, M. Gordon. "A Strategy for Identifying "Excellent" Systems Analysts". The Journal of Strategic Information Systems, Vol. 2, No. 1, March, 1993, pp. 15-26.

Hunter, M. Gordon. "The Essence of "Excellent" Systems Analysts: Key Audience Perceptions". Doctoral dissertation, Department of Management Sciences, Strathclyde Business School, University of Strathclyde, Glasgow, Scotland, UK, 1992.

Hunter, M. Gordon and John Beck. "A Cross-Cultural Comparison of "Excellent" Systems Analysts". Information Systems Journal, Vol. 6, No. 4, 1996a, pp. 261-281.

Hunter, M. Gordon and John Beck. ""Excellent" Systems Analysts: The Singapore Context". Asia-Pacific Journal of Management, Vol. 13, No. 2, October, 1996b, pp. 25-46.

Hunter, M. Gordon and Shailendra Palvia. "Ideal, Advertised, and Actual Systems Analyst Skills: The Singapore Context". Information, Technology & People, Vol. 9, No. 1, 1996, pp. 63-77.

Kelly, G. A. A Theory of Personality. Norton, New York, 1963.

Kelly, G. A. The Psychology of Personal Constructs. Norton, New York, 1955.

Latta, Gail, F. and Keith Swigger. "Validation of the Repertory Grid for Use in Modelling Knowledge". Journal of the American Society for Information Science, Vol. 42, No. 2, March 1992, pp. 115-129.

Litecky, Charles R. "Better Interviewing Skills". Journal of Systems Management, June, 1985, pp.36-39.

Maxwell, Paul David. "A critical Analysis of the Personal Characteristics of Successful Information Systems Analysts". Doctoral dissertation, Boston University, 1988.

Martin, James. Application Development Without Programmers. Englewood Cliffs, New Jersey, Prentice-Hall Inc., 1982.

McCubbrey, Donald J. and Richard. A. Scudder. "The Systems Analysts of the 1990's". Management of Information Systems Personnel, Proceedings of the 1988 ACM SIGCPR Conference, New York, ACM, 1988, pp. 8-16.

Nordbotten, Joan C. The Analysis and Design of Computer-Based Information Systems. Boston, Houghton Mifflin Co., 1985.

Nunamaker, Jay F., Jr., J. Daniel Couger, and Gordon B. Davis. "Information Systems Curriculum Recommendations for the 80's: Undergraduate and Graduate Programs". Communications of the ACM, Vol. 25, No. 11, November, 1982, pp. 148-149.

Palvia, Shailendra and M. Gordon Hunter. "Information Systems Development: A Conceptual Model and a Comparison of Methods Used in Singapore, USA, and Europe". Journal of Global Information Management, Vol. 4, No. 3, Summer, 1996, pp. 5-16.

People - Capability Maturity Model (P-CMM), Draft Version 3.0. The software Engineering Institute, Pittsburgh, 1995.

Phythian, Gary John and Malcolm King. "Developing an Expert System for Tender Enquiry Evaluation: A Case Study". European Journal of Operations Research, Vol. 56, No. 1, January, 10, 1992, pp. 15-29.

Vitalari, Nicholas P. "Knowledge as a Basis for Expertise in Systems Analysis: An Empirical Study". MIS Quarterly, September, 1985, pp. 221-241.

Vitalari, Nicholas P. and Gary W. Dickson. "Problem Solving for Effective Systems Analysis: An Experimental Exploration". Communications of the ACM, Vol. 26, No. 11, November, 1983, pp. 252-260.

Whitten, Jeffrey L. and Lonnie D. Bentley. Systems Analysis and Design Methods. Irwin McGraw-Hill, Boston, 1998.

A Model and Research Project into Social Navigation of Information

Dr. Ric Jentzsch

University of Canberra, Faculty of Information Science and Engineering, Canberra, ACT , 2601, Australia

Phone 61 2 6201 2424, Fax: 61 2 6201 5227, E-mail: Ricj@ISE.Canberra.edu.au

ABSTRACT

This research paper describes the background and key concepts of social navigation of information. A model of social navigation of information is presented. This model seeks to explain how people within social networks act as sources and pointers to knowledge. This paper compares the various perspective's that authors have presented on the subject of social navigation of information. The components that make up social navigation are discussed within a framework. Finally a research project is described. Future research directions in tacit information and social navigation of information are described.

Keywords: Social navigation, knowledge management, information sharing.

INTRODUCTION

Changes to modern organisations, brought on by changes in organisational infrastructures, are causing disruption and discontinuity in the sharing of implicit information. Most accessible and shareable information in modern organisations is explicit. Explicit based information is structured information held in enterprise databases. Although the management of explicit information continues to increase in modern organisations, implicit information management is not well managed, nor is the value well assessed.

The question of how to manage implicit information or at least make a good portion shareable has not been well established. Answers to the question of shareable information becomes even more important as modern organisation's environment continues to change and their use of information technology, using such technologies as e-mail, Intranet, Internet, groupware, and client server computing, continues to increase implicit information.

The concept of social navigation of information is not new. For years humans have grouped together in ones, twos, threes, and more, in a social context, and shared knowledge. Many of the concepts have been going on for centuries. What is new, is that there are new ways in which it is and can be done. In other words there now exists new ways that implicit information can be made more visible and shareable. These new ways, in some fashion, incorporate and augment the existing traditional social structure of information and knowledge sharing. These new ways, technology based, present social navigation through new mediums, ie. the Internet and intranet.

INFORMATION VS KNOWLEDGE

Information has been defined by various authors [Hoffer 1996, Kendall 1996] and from various perspectives [Hawryszkiewycz 1998, McFadden 1996]. In social navigation, information is something that a requestor requires at a point in time in order to do, proceed, or accomplish some task. Knowledge is what is held by the respondent (disseminator), a piece of which (information) is needed by a requestor. Knowledge is the accumulation of information over time and categorised, in some way, by the knowledge holder. Information is specific, whereas knowledge is the sum total of related information. In the social navigation context, a requestor requires a piece of information and to obtain that information they seek out, via navigating a social network, possible knowledge holders within a social network.

SOCIAL NAVIGATION

Traditional information and knowledge management techniques work well with explicit information and knowledge. Explicit information and knowledge is readily documented, stored and accessed through information systems. Traditional information system fails to adequately deal with tacit (implicit) information and knowledge. Collective memories belonging to communities (social networks) are not just a way of accumulating and preserving knowledge, but also a way of sharing and developing additional, and often, new knowledge. These collective memories consist of tacit information and knowledge. Tacit information and knowledge is personal, context-specific, not easy to formulate, and not readily communicated using via traditional methods. Social navigation of information provides new insights into tacit information and knowledge by describing how it exists within a social network, how knowledge of its existence is learned, how we can find the information or knowledge that is needed, and the value of the information once gained (trust).

The concept of social navigation has been explored to various degrees from different perspective's by several authors [Dieberger 1997, Dieberger 1998, Dourish et al. 1994, Kafer et al. 1997, Spence 1998]. In this section we examine several differing views of social navigation of information, and attempt to present a model that codifies the common elements of these different views. This model forms the basis for the discussion of the research into social navigation. This model is only a starting point for research projects into social navigation of information.

An early attempt, at providing an understanding of social navigation of information, was made by Dourish and Chalmers [1994]. They focused mainly on spatial environments to describe the process of moving between one item and other as a result of the actions or presence (or absence) to other. Examples of this include moving toward a cluster of people or selecting an object because other people have selected the object.

Dourish and Chalmers [1994] then go on to explore social navigation within the non-spatially-organised information environment. Using the example of World Wide Web (Web) home pages and collaborative filtering systems they go on to show how social navigation is used to find information within an information space.

A simular description of social navigation was developed by Erickson [1996]. Basing his work mostly on personal experience, he explored social navigation in the context of Web personal home pages. Personal home pages generally contain an eclectic mix of personal and professional information. This information, that can appear on personal home pages, includes such things as professional publications, links to interesting sites, pets, hobbies, research interests, and links to colleagues.

For Erickson, personal home pages can be seen as a deliberately constructed representation of an individual, and within that representation, links to "socially salient pages" may emerge [Erickson 1996]. These links, in turn, provide us with some understanding of the home page owner, her / his interests, colleagues, and friends. Although this presents a limited social network it does present many interesting concepts and ideas.

Like Dourish and Chalmers [1994], Erickson [1996] goes on to describe how personal home pages can act as a type of social filtering mechanism where information can be found by relying on another person's interests. For example, rather then using a Web search engine to find information, a user might go to a friend's home page because he / she has a similar interest in the topic.

Picking up on the work of Erickson [1996], Dieberger [1997] examines how tools can be modified or developed to support the sharing of information pointers, in this case URLs for Web pages. As with Erickson's [1996] descriptions of Web personal home pages, the information pointer sharing facilities described by Dieberger [1997] allows us to use other people as information filters. In this context we might depend on how other people feel about a movie or television show before making a decision to see the movie or show.

Both Dourish and Chalmers [1994] and Erickson [1996] introduce an important insight into the understanding of social navigation of information. That is, that other people can be pointers, or providers of pointers to a source of the information that is sought. They also implicitly show that we must know something about the other person in order to use them as a pointer to information.

The models presented by both Dourish and Chalmers [Dourish et al. 1995] and Erickson [Erickson 1996] could be described as social or collaborative filtering, rather then social navigation of information. In both models, people are trying to limit or filter information to a subset of the knowledge available.

Kanfer, Sweet and Schlosser [1997] more recent definition of social navigation of information is based on the process of using knowledge of one's social network and the accompanying distribution of knowledge to find information. This introduces the idea that social navigation of information somehow involves the use of a social network and its knowledge base.

From these differing views and perspectives into social navigation of information, we can draw out several key ideas.

- first information can be derived from either a spatial or non-spatial environment,
- second, non-spatial environments, such as the Web, can be used in social navigation of information,
- third, URLs can be used as a tools to aid in information sharing,
- fourth, people, in virtual or tangible environments, can be used as a network for information acquisition, and
- fifth, social networks are a viable source of specific types of information that are likely to be pursued and found via the use of social navigation of information.

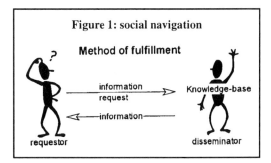

Figure 1: social navigation

Our resulting model codifies three primary key agents: process of navigation (with methods of fulfilment), the social network (knowledge base), and the information need (requestor need).

PROCESS OF SOCIAL NAVIGATION

An integral part of social navigation of information is the process of navigation. Needham [1998] in a similar context, referred to this process as the "herd instinct". It is like racing through the supermarket trying to find what you are looking for [Needham 1998]. Thus social navigation within any space must

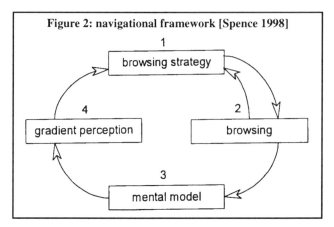

Figure 2: navigational framework [Spence 1998]

consider three basic questions: "Where am I now?" this is the starting point of the navigation process, "Where do I go from here?" this is the direction of the navigation, and "How do I get from here to there?" this is the method that is used to go from where I am to where I want to be.

Spence [1998] presents a generic navigation framework for both real and virtual environments. He discusses navigation as consisting of four activities.
• browsing strategy formulation
• browsing
• context or mental modelling
• gradient perception

The first two activities described by Spence [1998], browsing strategy formulation and browsing, work together to decide the method of fulfilment. Browsing is done using random navigation, a systematic strategy navigation, or some combination of both in trying to find out what is out there.

The third activity, termed by Spence [1998] as context modelling or mental modelling, describes how a mental map or plan in locating available information. The mental model is a conceptual version of the process of navigation. Information held in the mental model is used in the fourth activity, gradient perception, to decide possible courses of action. Thus the four activities all involve the method of fulfilment or process of navigation.

As Spence pointed out, the whole process of navigation is governed by an over all purpose, a goal or a destination [Spence 1998]. During the gradient perception activity this purpose is used to decide if the goal has been satisfied, or the destination reached. If not, the gradient perception activity will help to generate a new, or revised browsing strategy.

Navigation can be ordered and systematic or it can be dynamic, frustrating, and a random activity. Rather then moving through Spence's [1998] four activities in an ordered way, requestors may cycle between two activities, without moving to the next activity. Some activities may be performed in parallel or skipped such as forming a browsing strategy while browsing the space. The process as a whole may be heavily bias by our previous experiences in navigating thus determining a pre-established method of fulfilment.

SOCIAL NETWORK

The second component of social navigation of information is the social network that is to be navigated. Informally a social network can be seen as one or more people connected by a set of social relationships, such as friendship, co-working, clubs, or any common interest in which information is casually exchanged. An understanding of the formation, and on going growth of a social network is vital in understanding the process of social navigation of information.

The discussion of social networks presented here takes an egocentric view of relationships. Within the egocentric view of relationships, one person is considered as central, with all other relationships examined as they interact with the central individual [Erickson 1996].

Members of a social network can be described as egos and alters (requestors and disseminators). Ergos and alters represent the members. Relationships between different members of a social network can be described as ties. Ties can be direct, as linking ego A directly to alter B, or indirect, as in linking ego A to alter B, ego B to alter C, ego C to alter D where the indirect tie is between A and D. A tie connects a pair of individual members by one or more relationships. Relationships can be seen as the 'why' of the tie, and can described in terms of content, direction, and strength.

A tie may involve more then one relationship such as between A to C. Each relationship will pass content, which describes what is exchanged between the two individuals - personal information, social pleasantries, resources, support, etc.

A relationship direction describes the flow of content between the individuals. A relationship may be describes as directed, for example one individual may give some form of content, while the other receives the content, or it may be undirected, with both individuals maintain the relationship with no specific direction to it, as in a social friendship.

The final characteristic of a relationship is its strength. A relationship's strength can be seen as a function of the intimacy of the relationship, characterised by the type and value of the content passed through it and the frequency of communication (daily, weekly, monthly, etc). In many ways strength can also be seen as the degree of friendship. Implicit to a relation's strength is the degree of trust and empathy shared by the two individuals. In this case trust management becomes an issue.

A tie can consist of more then one relationship, the more relationships within a tie the more multiplexed the tie is. As pointed out by Garton et. al [1997], multiplex ties tend to be more intimate, voluntary, supportive, and durable.

As discussed by Stokman and Zeggelink [1996] social networks are dynamic, with members of a social network constantly evaluating and re-evaluating their relationship with other members and reacting to the introduction of new members. As such, social networks are self-organising. The order often seen in a social network is a result of the interactions and decisions of individuals (and their personal preferences, attitudes, and personal goals), rather then adherence to some overall plan.

Social networks are also inherently discriminatory. Membership to a social network is decided by individuals according to their personal goals and desires. Personal preference and likes/dislikes play an important part in selecting individuals for membership within a social network.

Simplistically, social networks consist of three key activities: the activity of introducing new members into the network, the activity of evaluating and re-evaluating the placement of new or existing members within the network, and the on going maintenance activity of the social network. Each of these activities are described below.

During our normal day to day lives we are presented with many new ties and relationships. For example, shopping, sports, or local interests. Many of these ties are highly situational and transient. The deepening of the initial relationship and the search for additional relationships between two individuals is dependent on several factors. The first factor is the desire to add members to their social network [Stokman et al. 1996], and the second factor is the cultural acceptability of attempting to deepen a new tie and its associated relationship.

The second activity of a social network is evaluating and re-evaluating the placement of new or existing members within the network. As described by Stokman et. al [1996] and Garton, et. al [1997], ties between individuals within a social network can be seen as consisting of one or more relations. Each relation has associated with it a measure of its strength, content and direction. These elements work together to form the level or type of tie, binding two individuals together. Thus the placement of the individual within a social network.

Evaluation and re-evaluation of the placement of individuals within our social network is an on-going, cyclic process. We learn about other people via self discloser; the process of sharing information about yourself with another person. We use this information, along with observations of the other persons actions, our underlying social network goals, and implicit and explicit sounding out actions [Stokman 1996] to help decide where we would like to place the individual within our social network [Kanfer et al. 1997].

The final activity performed is the on going maintenance of a social network. Maintenance may be an implicit result of using the social network, or it may be a deliberate action designed to maintain a social network. The stronger the tie binding two individuals, the less explicit maintenance is required, simply because using the tie and relationship may form normal occurrences within our daily activities.

Garton, et. al [1997] describes several important characteristics of social networks, these include the networks range, and egos centrality and the roles different egos play within the network. A social network's range can describe its size and scope. It is not easy to determine the size or scope of a social network especially heterogeneity networks because of their complex structure.

CHARACTERISTICS INFORMATION

The final component of the social navigation of information is the type of information likely to be gathered via the social network's social navigation. We use the term information in its broadest sense, ie all possible things. Within this very broad and classical definition of information there exists many different specialisations of information, ranging from simple facts, or data through to processed or applied facts, through to opinion, knowledge, experience and skills [Miller 1998].

Three key properties can be used to differentiate between types of information:
• the amount of interpretation performed on it,
• how well it can be externalised, and

• the value of the information.

The degree to which the 'raw' information is interpreted has been used as the classic description of information by many authors [Keating et al. 1994]. Simply put, factual information under goes little interpretation, while knowledge, experience and skills involves a lot of interpretation [Keating et al. 1994, Miller 1998].

A second key characteristic used to differentiate between types of information is its how well it can be externalised, that is how easy is it to record and communicate the information. Explicit information is information which can be readily recorded. It can be packaged, communicable, transferred and expressed in formal, shared language. Tacit information is the opposite. It is often personal, it is often context-specific, hard to formulate, hard to communicate and more difficult to express in a shared language [McAulay et al. 1997, Miller 1998].

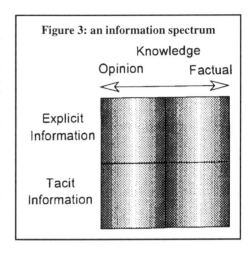

Figure 3 graphically illustrates an information / knowledge continuum. The continuum running along the top of figure 3, shows the degree to which the information can be interpreted, ranging from opinions based on knowledge to knowledge based on facts. The left side of figure 3 shows the degrees with which the information can be externalised: explicit or tacit.

Social network knowledge can be involved in the full spectrum of information, ranging from explicit opinions to factual knowledge, all of which is accessible via social navigation of information. How information can be discover and obtained via social navigation of information, and the knowledge held either exclusively or shareable, within a social network, is part of the question of this research.

The third property that differentiates information is its value to the requestor (navigator). The value of information is determined by the navigator's goals and objectives. The value of that information is both temporal and within a context. The value of information depends on what other information has been gathered before and the time at which the information is being requested.

VIRTUAL SOCIAL NAVIGATION

With the development of the Internet infrastructure and the growing use of Intranets, virtual social navigation of information becomes more of a reality. Remember social navigation consists of three elements in its model:
• process of navigation
• social network
• information / knowledge

There are several uses and ways in which the process of social navigation can help the navigator find the information they seek. From an Internet view, figure 4 shows one way in which personal home pages might point to things commonly referred to as "favourite sites" or "interesting sites", that provide information that the navigator wants.

Other ways associated with social navigation can include: guest books, hit counters, notes, and even graffiti. Each potentially builds a virtual social network of information.

INFORMATION NEED

When seen as a navigation process, social navigation of information can be seen as navigating a social network and the knowledge contained within the network to fulfil some information need. However, before any type of navigation occurs there needs to be an information need. This forms the goal of what Spence [1998] calls the purpose of navigating.

As with most forms of navigation, social navigation of information will often begin with the development of a browsing strategy [Spence 1998].

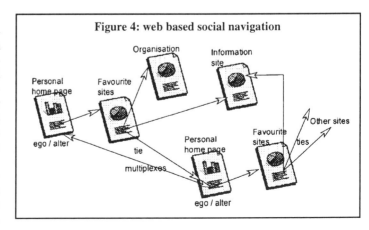

Figure 4: web based social navigation

In the context of social navigation of information, this activity is aimed at finding information via the best person, or persons, or a knowledge base (via browsing) to satisfy the information need. The mental model of social networks is used to help decide the best way of achieving, ie. finding the information needed.

Once this initial strategy has been decided, browsing of the members of a social network can take place. Browsing is the seeking, or the asking based on a communications protocol. It is meant to be an active process where individuals within a social network communicate. As with navigation of a physical space, building a mental model while navigation a social network involves building a model of what information or objects exists within the space. When building a mental model of a social network, the individuals, the ties between the ego and the alters and the types of knowledge that the alters may hold, are modelled.

An interesting difference between social navigation and other forms of navigation is the expansion of the space during the navigation process. When navigating a physical space, the space being navigated is likely to remain relatively constant over the information need. However, during the navigation of a social network we might find our social network expanding. As a result of our initial browsing, we might discover one or more potential in-direct links which may be likely sources of information, or we might deliberately seek out new ties and relations.

The final activity of the navigation process is gradient perspective. As with navigation of a physical space, during the gradient perspective activity of social navigation of information we compare what we currently know (the mental model) with the over all purpose of navigating, to help select the most 'rewarding' direction or path. In this case the most 'rewarding' direction may be a person mostly like to have the information we need or most able to point us in the best direction. The result can also acquaint the requestor with another social network where the knowledge on this topic and similar are held.

As with navigating any space, social navigation of information can stop for many reasons and at any point during the navigation process. Navigation may stop because the purpose of navigation may have been fulfilled (information need satisfied), the original question has altered, or the problem was solved during the navigation process. Another possibility is that there may be no more time to continue navigating for the information needed, or the cost of continued navigation out weighs any potential benefits to be obtained.

Remember that social navigation of information may appear to be an orderly and linear process, where in reality social navigation of information is more likely to be a dynamic chaotic process. Some activities may be performed in parallel, while other activities may be jumped over all together. The whole process may be effected by intangible factors such as personal preferences, personal goals, group goals, or even a tangible factor.

KNOWLEDGE TYPES WITHIN A SOCIAL NETWORK

Figure 3 illustrates two key characteristics of information, its externalisation, and the amount of interpretation performed on it. As previously discussed, information can be seen as explicit or tacit, and ranges on a continuum from knowledge based on simple opinions to complex knowledge based on facts through experiences. Within a social network the whole range of information, as illustrated in figure 4 exists, and is accessible via social navigation of information.

While all types of knowledge may exist within a social network, not all types of knowledge is actively searched for via social navigation of information. As previously discussed, the type of relations tying an ego to an alter, its strength, and the history of content passed through it affect how a social network is navigated, as well as affecting the type of information we seek via social navigation. This dictates what type of knowledge (in the form of information) is acceptable to seek through parts of our social network.

As shown by several authors [Kanfer et al. 1997, Keating et al. 1994, McAulay et al. 1997, Miller 1998, Rogers, 1993] social navigation of information is generally used as a method for seeking out tacit, and highly interpreted information (bottom right side of figure 4), rather then explicit, factual, un-processed information (top left quadrant of figure 4). In fact, much of this type of knowledge only exists within a social network, and is only accessible via social navigation of information.

Rogers [1993] showed that complex and/or novel ideas are more likely to be communicated through a social network then by any other means. He showed that we learn about innovations and their worth, almost exclusively via social navigation of information. Rogers [1993] also describes how the success or failure of a new or complex idea is closely related to how well it can be communicated through a social network.

McAulay, et. al [1997] pick up on Rogers [1993] theme. Using examples from financial management, they show how tacit, highly interpreted information is vital in making complex business decisions, and how successful executive officers actively rely on their social network, and social navigation of information to seek out this information when making complex business decisions. In figure 4 this decision process covers the tacit information - opinion to factual - based on experiences that are not explicitly stored.

Finally, Kanfer et. al [1997] describe how memory within a group can be seen as a social process. Each group member acts as a knowledge base for specific types of information that is important to the group. This knowledge, which may cover the full spectrum of information types, is available only via social navigation of information.

RESEARCH PROJECT

Thus far we have described a model of social navigation of information, the background concepts, and issues that support the model. While the discussion has implicitly assumed that most, if not all of the activities involved were performed with little or no computer support, this research explores how some or all of the process of social navigation of information can be supported using technology. In using technology, in supporting social navigation of information, we can be in a better position to capture and retain some of the tacit information that is being lost as dynamic changes in modern organisations continues. In particular is it possible, through a combination of information and knowledge management technologies and computer mediated communications technology, to support components of the social navigation of information?

Here we want to get more value out of the existing social navigation or use social navigation of information in a more productive way in today's organisation. We might encourage each employee to have a home page on the Internet or / and Intranet and derive tacit information from the pages. However, as Schrage [1998] pointed out, in encouraging this, it might mean that the real business competition would be coming from within where employees build customer and client loyalties using their personal page(s) rather than the organisation's.

A research project that has just begun, is to develop the social navigation of information model based on a specific context. In this approach we have set up a virtual resource centre (VRC) for users. This VRC provides users with the opportunity to ask questions and view previous responses. The navigator (requestor) attempts to find information based on the help function concept. In the virtual resource centre a help session is established between a requestor and the knowledge base. A requestor forms a question, via a text box, in the virtual resource centre. The question and the response are posted to a knowledge base (disseminator). The system first provides a list of similar questions and responses, with a percentage of confidence in the matching to the requestor's question. A side note identifies other questions that requestors have asked on related topics. This initiates a virtual social network based on the common topic of the question.

A second part, allows the navigator to browse the VRC to identify other questions that have been asked. External links are provided for additional information on the topic. This provides a means for the requestor to look up other questions and responses. The VRC provides a high level information sharing environment for the information users.

A third part, is when the knowledge base can not provide adequate information, then a knowledge expert (disseminator) is contacted or external links are provided. The knowledge expert's response becomes part of the knowledge base. The provides access to experts or those who might have the knowledge of the specific topic(s). In this context, we are attempting to address the questions of: "How can an understanding of social navigation augment existing information systems?" And second, "How can we more efficiently or better support users in a social navigation of information concept?"

An area that is being investigate the referencing to other users. The requestors might want to see information on who has requested similar information. This would allow the requestor(s) to seek out other users in discussing the information they needed. This is a more difficult area as there are concerns with confidentiality, personal rights, security, and related issues. This part is not yet envisioned for the VRC research project. The overall concept that the VRC is taking, is similar to what is done by Amazon.com with books.

The development and research into a VRC will enable researchers to collect data and analyse a control group involved in the social navigation of information. The data is used to develop a framework for identifying social navigation information content, direction, strength, and value.

CONTINUING AND FUTURE RESEARCH

The research in this area has brought out many questions on the use of social navigation of information and its resulting value of information. Within the model being developed, it is hoped that some of the following questions can be either answered (fully or partially) or additional avenues of research identified.

Some of the research questions that are being explored are:
- to what level can social navigation be applied to existing information and knowledge management?
- how can social navigation be applied to information and knowledge management in the dynamic changing environment of modern organisations?
- can a model of social navigation of information help support the growing numbers of remote workers?
- can an understanding of the elements of social navigation of information aid the development of 'virtual information environments' that are socially based, rather then information based.
- can social navigation of information be applied to educational environments: locally, nationally, and globally?
- what cultural connotations are inherent in social navigation?

• can business organisations use social navigation of information to support or advance their competitive strategies?

REFERENCES

Benyon, D. and Munro, A. (1998). "Using agents in Social Navigation." http://orgwis.gmd.de/projects/SAW/ benyon.html.

Dieberger, A (1997). "Supporting Social Navigation on the World-Wide Web." International Journal of Human-Computer Studies. Special issues on innovative applications of the Web, Vol 46, pp 805-825. http://www.lcc.gatech.edu/~dieberger/IJHCS_SocNav_abstract.html.

Dieberger, A (1998). "Social connotations of spatial metaphors and their influence on (direct) social navigation." Position paper at the Workshop on Personalized and Social Navigation in Information Spaces, Stockholm, March 1998. http://www.lcc.gatech.edu/~dieberger/ SocNav_Stockholm_3_98.html.

Dourish, P. and Chalmers, M. (1994). "Running out of Space: Models of Information Navigation." In Proceedings of the Conference on Human Computer Interaction (British Computer Society). Glasgow.

Erickson, T. (1996). "The World Wide Web as Social Hypertext." Communications of the ACM, 39(1): 15-17.

Garton, L., Haythornthwaite, C. & Wellman, B. (1997). "Studying Online Social Networks." Journal of Computer-Mediated Communication, 3(1).

Kanfer, A., Sweet, J. & Scholosser, A. (1997). "Humanising the Net: Social Navigation with a "Know-Who" Email Agent"." In Proceedings of the 3rd Conference on Human Factors and the Web. Denver, Colorado.

Hawryszkiewycz, I. T. (1998). Introduction to System Analysis and Design. 4th edition, Prentice Hall.

Keating, C., Robinson, T. & Clemson B. (1994). "A Process of Organisational Learning." In Proceedings of IEEE International Engineering Management Conference.

Kendall, P. A. (1996). Introduction to System Analysis & Design: A Structured Approach. Richard D. Irwining Publishing Company.

Hoffer, J. A., George, J. F., Valacich, J. S. (1996). Modern Systems Analysis and Design. The Benjamin / Cummings Publishing Company.

McAulay, L., Russell, G. & Sims, J. (1997). "Tacit Knowledge for Competitive Advantage: Management Accounting." December.

McFadden, F. R., and Hoffer J. A. (1996). Modern Database Management. 4th edition. The Benjamin / Cummings Publishing Company.

Miller, T. (1998). "Knowledge Management Levers of Change." In Proceedings of the 11th National Technology in Government Conference. Canberra.

Needham, K. (1998). "Herd instincts." Sydney Morning Harold. 25 April.

Rogers, E. (1993). "Diffusion of Innovations." The Free Press, New York.

Schrage, M. (1998). "When employees launch their own web sites." Computerworld, New Opinions. 18 May.

Spence, R. (1998). "Navigation in Real and Virtual Worlds." In Proceedings of the Workshop on Personalised and Social Navigation in Information Space. Stockholm.

Stokman, F. N. & Zeggelink, E. P. H. (1996). "Self-Organising' Friendship Networks." in proceedings of the Frontiers in Social Dilemmas Research, eds Liebrand, W. B. G. & Messick, D. M. Springer, Berlin.

Modelling the Rationale of Methods

Par Ågerfalk and Kenneth Åhlgren
Orebro University, Dept. of Informatics
SE-701 82 OREBRO, SWEDEN
E-mail: {pak | kan}@esa.oru.se, Phone: +46 19 303000

ABSTRACT

This paper presents a meta-modelling approach that allows the argumentative dimension of a method to be modelled by systematic treatment of modelling primitives concerning activities and goals, and their relationships. It is argued that the capture of a methods rationale is imperative if the purpose of modelling is to understand or learn a method, or to combine existing methods. Applications of the approach are presented and elaborated. Suggested applications are: the construction of context-sensitive help systems in CASE-tools; method reconstruction; verification of proposed method achievements; consistency checking of aggregated activities; and evaluation, adoption, implementation, and combination of existing methods.

Keywords: action, goal, intention, meta-modelling, method, methodology engineering, model, rationale, software engineering, systems development.

INTRODUCTION

Traditional approaches to meta-methods and methodology engineering are, in general, restricted to the conceptual aspects of the modelled methods [for example, Hey93, Kum92]. Methods can be viewed as normative conceptualizations in the sense that they direct the method user's attention by means of chosen modelling primitives, that is, by means of the concepts that are focused, or searched for, and that constitute elements in the methods of the various kinds of models. The primitives used in traditional, conceptually oriented meta-methods are thus restricted to concepts (entities), attributes, and relationships.

We believe that what to focus must be in parity with the purpose of the modelling (or model). An implication is that for some purposes, a conceptual meta-model is sufficient. Such meta-model usage includes, but is not limited to:
• Implementation of methods in computerized tools (for example, CASE) during which a formal description of the method is needed.
• Conceptual overviews in, for example, method handbooks.
• Creation of languages to enable inter-subjectivity (defined below) regarding concepts and notation, for example, the unified modelling language (UML) [Boo99].

What a conceptual meta-model can never capture is the method's prescribed activities and their rationale. We understand a method's rationale to be the argumentative dimension of the method. The capturing of that dimension is imperative if the modelling purpose is, for example, to understand or learn a method. The rationale is also important when communicating methods, when constructing, reconstructing. or combining methods. and when evaluating methods.

What, then, constitutes a method? Basically, a method is a way of doing things, a kind of process, that is, an internalized successful pattern of activities, with the purpose of achieving some effect or goal. A method can also, in its externalized form, be viewed as a normative prescription for actions. Such a process can often be characterized as social interaction [Ber89] between developers, users and other systems stakeholders. In addition, a method, and the communication of its results, always implies the use of some concepts which can be expressed in some notation (textual or graphical, and more or less formal), which corresponds to the conceptual dimension mentioned above. This notion of method is quite common in the literature. For example, Rumbaugh [Rum95], as well as Blaha and Premerlani [Bla98], describes the concept of method in terms of concepts, notation and process. How, then, do methods exist? Methods can exist as actions or as results of actions (situational existence). Other "method existences" are methods as prescriptive guidelines (generic existence), and methods more or less implicit in various kinds of tools such as CASE-tools (implicit existence), cf. [Gol94a].

This paper deals with methodology-based analysis and design of methods, or methodology engineering. The focus is on methods for such engineering, that is meta-methods, and their possibilities for directing attention towards primitives concerning a method's rationale. Since the rationale can be viewed as the reasons and argumentation for prescribed actions, this paper's primary focus is on analysis of method activities (which constitute the method's process) and method goals (in the sense of, for example, intention) and, in particular, the relations between these two concepts. Note that various results of method actions might also be associated with goals. We do not present this approach as an alternative to conceptual method modelling but rather as a complement-they are both needed and serve different purposes.

A method's activities, together with some sequence constraints among them, form what we call the method's process. Such a process can be partially understood in terms of the questions asked to find the elements that constitute modelling primitives (which questions and how they are asked). If a method has been externalized and stated explicitly, for example, in a handbook, that statement can consist of several different components. It might consist of prescriptions regarding modelling concepts and their notation. It might consist of prescribed activities, questions and rules. Finally, it might consist of effects and qualities regarding the expected results. Such results can be formulated as either direct results or more indirect ones. Statements about expected results can, to some extent, be seen as arguments and thereby rationales for the method. Unfortunately, these arguments are not always made explicit within handbooks and other forms of description. On the other hand, sometimes the expected results are the only way in which the method is represented.

Methods represent knowledge and experiences [Gol94a] and, therefore, methods also represent rationale. A method user thus inherits both the knowledge and the rationale of the method creator. A method user is forced to rely on the method creator's judgements and normative statements. To be successful the method user, therefore, has to both understand and ultimately internalize the creator's arguments and perspective on the problem domain. As mentioned above, methods exist in several different forms. Two forms of method existence that deserve special attention are situational existence (or methods in use) and generic existence (or methods at a type level). Situational existence is the result of an interpretation, and an accomplishment, of the generic method by a method user. Such interpretation is a function not only of the generically existing method but also of the user's pre-knowledge, experience, values, rationale, tacit knowledge, and so on, cf. the infological equation as proposed by Langefors [Lan66]. The generically existing method is, in the same manner, an externalization of the method creator's expressible conceptualization of the subject area of the method.

We argue that a wider perspective on methods can be applied with the use of primitives additional to the traditional ones: concepts, attributes, and relationships. The added primitives suggested in this paper are action, actor, role, action object, goal, and intention, which all aim at understanding the rationale of methods.

THEORETICAL FOUNDATIONS

This chapter describes the main theoretical work that has influenced our work on rationale analysis. It is not an attempt to be an exhaustive description but rather to point out some important foundations and influences in order to serve as arguments for, and definitions of, the concepts we use.

Conceptual modelling aims at describing the meaning of concepts, and their relationships in order to get an accurate "image" of the studied piece of reality. Such an approach seems to be what Austin [Aus62] refers to as a "descriptive fallacy", assuming that language is merely used for descriptive purposes. Our approach aims at understanding the intentions of, and arguments for, activities. This approach emanates from the so-called "speech act theory" [Sea69]. Speech act theory emphases what people do while communicating, that is, actors using language to perform actions. In order to communicate, actors must share enough pre-knowledge to be able to conceptualize some part of the world in the same manner. Such sharing, or commonality is known as inter-subjectivity. Thus, communication is the process of one actor communicating something (acting), with some purpose, to another actor. That other actor then interprets the communicated "something" and reacts in response, so that a social interaction is taking place. We use the terms "internalize" and "externalize" when reasoning about methods in the context of social interaction. Internalizing means "making something to your own" and externalizing is the process of making something internalized communicable to others. However, sometimes the knowledge of an actor is difficult, or even impossible, to verbalize. One can do things but cannot explain how they were done, or even why. These are expressions of "tacit knowledge" [Mol96] and "hidden rationale" [Sto91], which are parts of what Polanyi refers to as "the tacit dimension", or "we

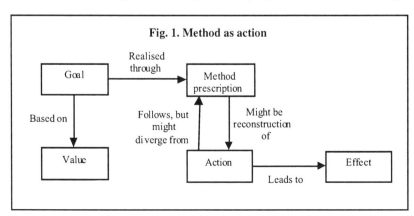

Fig. 1. Method as action

can know more than we can tell" [according to Mol96].

To know something and to be able to argumentatively discuss it in a dialogue with others constitute what we call rationality. Our notion of rationale is thus based on Goldkuhl's [Gol94a] "argumentative rationality" which in turn is influenced by Habermas's social-critical concept of rationality [Hab84]. In this view, well-founded knowledge is characterized as being [Gol94a] discursive, re-constructive, critical, and congruent. The discursive dimension is a part of all the others and discursive rationality means that knowledge is socially transferable by the use of arguments in inter-subjective dialogues.

To focus means to direct attention to certain kinds of phenomena (or kinds of terms, to be precise). Some of these are recognized as primitives, that is, kinds of modelling elements. This means that the focus is determined by the questions asked to analytically abstract the phenomena. Methods include prescriptions that direct attention towards such primitives. The prescriptions are, in some sense, realizations of the method's goals, which are always based on some values. The action prescriptions are then instantiated in actions during method use, which lead to an effect. On the other hand, if actions are performed, and observed to be "good" in some sense, they might eventually become institutionalized [Ber89] into a method (situational existence). Such institutions might then be reconstructed into methods at a generic existence level. Figure 1 illustrates how these concepts are related.

ACTIONS, GOALS AND RATIONALE

The proposed analysis focuses on three activities that can be logically separated, even though they are typically performed in parallel (see Fig. 2). The first activity, activity analysis, is concerned with the methods process: activities, actors, prerequisites, results, and possible sequence restrictions. The second activity, goal analysis, is concerned with the method's goals. Here, the concept of "goal" is used in a broad sense and includes notions such as intention, reason, value, and effect. The third activity, rationale analysis, is concerned with the relations between the primitives used in the other two activities. The real essence of the modelling is reached, motivated, and illustrated by the applications in which it may be used, that is, when combining the analysis results.

Method actions, and thereby intentions (which in turn are underpinned by rationale), exist on different levels of abstraction, just as do methods per se. Method user actions, based on prescribed activities, are intentional at the situational level of method existence. The method creator, on the other hand, had some intention in mind when stipulating the method actions in the first place. Therefore, the method actions are also intentional at the generic level of method existence. In this paper, we will pay attention mainly to the generic level of method existence. It is, however, important to distinguish between the two levels, and in some cases the relation between them is the main object of study. The latter is the case, for example, when reconstruction of a method is taking place. Reconstruction is the process of externalizing a method and generalizing it from situational to generic existence. This is often done with the purpose of making implicit methods communicable in the form of handbooks or tools etc., or as part of method integration efforts.

To summarize, an actor associated with a role performs some action that has some outcome. Both the action and the outcome are associated with some intention that in turn is related to one or more goals.

One can argue that the three analysis activities mentioned are not really analysis but rather data collection. The collected data is then analysed in what we call different applications or contexts. We do, however, retain the term analysis to be consistent with the names of the activities in MA/SIMM from which the first two are chosen.

Throughout this chapter we will use a brief example of our approach. The method we have chosen to analyse is the Object Modelling Technique (OMT) as described by Blaha and Premerlani [Bla98]. The specific part of OMT we will consider is the creation of the object model, that is, the first phase of the method. The activity analysis is performed on "Listing tentative classes", one activity within the object-modelling phase [Bla98, pp. 127-129]. Note that this example is not given with any special purpose, or application, other than to show how the analysis might be performed and documented.

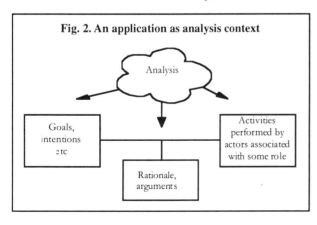

Fig. 2. An application as analysis context

Analysis

Goals, intentions etc

Rationale, arguments

Activities performed by actors associated with some role

Activity Analysis

Activity analysis is performed according to the corresponding method component in the SIMM-family of methods. Goldkuhl and ≈gerfalk [Gol98] present activity analysis in the context of requirements engineering and Goldkuhl and Fristedt [Gol94b] discuss its use within methodology engineering.

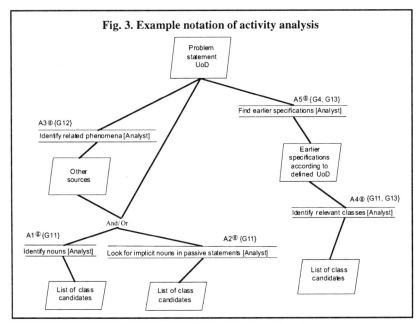

Fig. 3. Example notation of activity analysis

During activity analysis, different method actions and their relations to each other are described. The relations are constituted by sequence restrictions between activities and the possibility that one activity requires the result of another activity as input. In conjunction with activity analysis, the different actors, the performers of method actions, and other stakeholders are identified and allocated to the actions they perform or to the action objects that they may represent. Usually, the role name is used but sometimes the name of the actor is more appropriate, for example, when there is a need to distinguish between different actors sharing the same role.

To summarize, activity analysis means analysis of:
• Actions and action structure.
• Performers of actions, that is, actors associated with some role.
• Results and prerequisites of actions (or action objects), which may be either in the form of information or material (which includes, for example, documents and human resources).

Figure 3 shows an example notation of activity analysis extended with mappings from activities to sets of goals. In the model the Gs identify goals and the As identify activities.

One important aspect of activity analysis is that it is performed contextually rather than compositionally [Gol92]. One strength of the contextual approach, among others, is that it allows analysts to model phenomena in the contexts in which they are used, without having to worry about compositional restrictions. The activity analysis is preferably documented with Action diagrams as shown in Figure 3 (see also, for example, [Gol92, Gol98]).

Goal Analysis

Goal analysis, like activity analysis, is performed according to the corresponding method component in the SIMM-family of methods. Goldkuhl and Rôstlinger [Gol93] introduced goal analysis as part of Change analysis and Goldkuhl and Fristedt [Gol94b] discuss its use within the context of methodology engineering. It is important to notice that our use of the term "goal" includes other notions associated with intentional action such as intention, motivation, reason, effect, and purpose.

During goal analysis, the goals of the method are identified and elaborated. One important issue is the analysis of relations between goals in goal/sub-goal hierarchies (or networks). A sub-goal is, by definition, a goal but it is also a means of achieving the higher goal to which it is related. In a goal hierarchy there can also be goal conflicts, with one goal contradicting another.

To summarize, goal analysis means analysis of:
• Goals.
• Relationships between goals in goal-hierarchies (means and contradictions).

Figure 4 shows an example notation of goal analysis (a goal graph) and Figure 5 shows the corresponding goal statements in a goal definition table.

The goal analysis is preferably documented in a Goal graph in conjunction with a goal definition table, as shown above in Figures 4 and 5 [c.f. Gol93].

Rationale Analysis

During rationale analysis the actors, roles, prerequisites, results and activities identified during activity analysis are explicitly related to goals identified during goal analysis. For the purpose of the analysis it is not necessary to

Fig. 4. Example notation of goal analysis

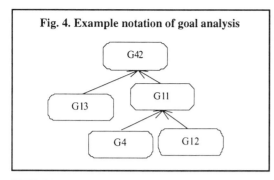

Fig. 5. A goal definition table

G4	Definitions reused from previous efforts.
G11	Class candidates found.
G12	All available sources of information considered.
G13	Integration with earlier applications enabled.
G42	All possible class candidates found.

distinguish between all modelling primitives from activity analysis. Therefore, we group all such instances together to form a set called the activity set. The rationale analysis thus aims at identifying a relation from the activity set to the set of goals. This analysis can be performed in two different ways. Either the elements of the activity set are iterated and related to goals, or the goals are iterated and related to activities. Normally these two approaches are both used alternately during the analysis. Sometimes the activities are well described and understood and it is straightforward to start with them, and perhaps identify new goals. In other cases, all that is known are perhaps vague goals with no intuitive relations to activities. Often, the purpose of the analysis implies the most convenient way to work (see the applications below).

The known rationale of the example can thus be modelled as a relation R (A (G where A={A1, A2, A3, A4, A5} is the set of activities and G={G4, G11, G12, G13, G42} is the set of goals, such that R={(A1, G11), (A2, G11), (A3, G12), (A4, G11), (A4, G13), (A5, G4), (A5, G13)}.

Applications

The information gathered during analysis of activities, goals, and rationale can be used in several different contexts; we describe some important ones below. Note that this is not meant as an exhaustive list but rather as examples of applications of our approach.

Context-sensitive help systems

One possible application is the creation of more usable context-sensitive help systems in, for example, CASE-tools. The system can keep track of the current activity and keep relations to goal descriptions as meta-data. This way the system can suggest different action patterns and motivate the different proposals argumentatively. Today, most context-sensitive help systems are focused on what to do in a particular activity but frequently fail to motivate the proposed actions.

Method reconstruction

Reconstruction of a method, as described above, is the process of generalizing a successful pattern of activities to an externalized representation. In order to communicate such a method, it is quite common to write a method handbook. The goals that are related to the activities can then be used to motivate those activities and thereby serve as a rationale for the method. It has become increasingly popular to augment method handbooks with a meta-model, for example, UML [Boo99] and OOA [Coa91]. Such models could be more argumentative with the use of our approach.

Verification of proposed achievements

Statements about the (positive) effects of using a particular method often accompany method descriptions. Such "political" statements can typically be regarded as goals. By verifying that every such goal is related to at least one activity it is possible to verify that they are made operational in the method.

Consistency checking of aggregated activities

Activities are often made up of other activities and thereby form activity aggregates. Examples of such aggregates are method phases like "object modelling" [Bla98]. Such phases can be compositionally divided into smaller activities, which in turn can be recursively divided into even smaller activities. Each activity aggregate can be related to one or more goals. The same holds for all activities that are part of the aggregate. It is possible to verify that all activities within the same activity aggregate are related to goals that are either related to the activity aggregate as a whole or to a sub-goal of such an activity. Such analysis can be used to verify that method activities are consistent with regard to goals. It can also be used during method construction to decide whether a proposed activity should be a part of a particular phase or step. If the proposed activity's goals do not appear in the phase's goal hierarchy it is doubtful that it should be a part of that phase at all.

Consistency checking can easily be formalized, in a mathematical sense, and automated by a computerized tool.

Evaluation, adoption, implementation and combination

Evaluation of methods is always done with some purpose. One common purpose should be a need to choose a method for adoption in a project. Such adoption always includes implementation of the method in a particular organizational context. By understanding the goals of the organization and comparing them to the proposed method, or methods, a better match can be reached. The goals could then be compared based on the arguments used.

At times. one single method does not satisfy the needs of a particular development situation, for example, when one method is used in one development phase and that method does not cover the following phases. At other times. more than one method is needed even in the same phase. In both cases, it is important to understand both what to do and why that should be done, in order to combine methods.

RELATED RESEARCH

Nilsson [Nil99] presents a meta-modelling approach used to verify that it is possible to integrate two or more methods. The modelling primitives used are intentions, concepts, and ways of working, which result in three different meta-models. The meta-models within the same categories are compared and integration possibilities judged by meta-model matching. If, for example, some goals are contradictory then integration is not recommended. If, on the other hand, all goals are supplementary or corresponding, it is possible to integrate the methods. The approach assumes that all method goals are made operational or that the ways of working (the action structure) really lead to stipulated goals. Our approach could be used to verify such assumptions, which would make Nilsson's approach more convincing.

Another approach to method assembly is proposed by Brinkkemper et al. [Bri98]. Their approach uses a three-dimensional classification scheme to categorize method fragments. Even though it is comprehensive, their categorization does not include the intentional dimension of methods.

Our theoretical influences are much the same as those that constitute what is known as the language action perspective (LAP) on communication modelling. Flores and Ludlow [Flo80] as well as Goldkuhl and Lyytinen [Gol82] made early contributions to LAP and Winograd and Flores [Win86] carried out seminal work. LAP emphasizes what people do while communicating and it has been used and elaborated in various research efforts, most notably in business modelling. One meta-method that builds explicitly on LAP is MA/SIMM [Gol94b]. Hence, we are strongly influenced by MA/SIMM and its contributions to understanding the action dimension of methods. We do, however, believe that the analysis, as proposed by Goldkuhl and Fristedt [Gol94b], should be carried one step further. Such an extension is not only implied as a consequence of the perspective of systems development as a social phenomenon, it is also needed in order to understand a method's rationale.

Tolvanen et al. [Tol93] discuss a methodological approach based on three levels of information architecture named GOPRR. The levels are named the ISD level, the ISD meta-level, and the ISD meta-meta-level. Their approach aims at capturing the dynamic aspects of methods as well as the conceptual. It does not, however, capture the argumentative dimension.

Design patterns [Gam95], and more recently analysis patterns [Fow97], are attempts to externalize tacit knowledge within a particular domain. Their approach aims at reuse and inheritance of actions developed by more experienced analysts and designers. We argue that we should go one step further and analyse the rationale behind such patterns in order to achieve better understanding of them. With such understanding we can be more successful, by reaching higher precision in interpretation when internalizing the patterns.

Nimal Jayaratna [Jay94] holds as a high ideal that the "whys" of a method are important when discussing and evaluating methods. We do, most certainly, identify ourselves with that ideal. What we propose is a systematic, and theoretically justified, approach to modelling and analysing those "whys", that is, what we believe are the main constituents of a method's rationale.

CONCLUSIONS

This paper has discussed an approach to meta-modelling that covers the argumentative dimension of methods. It is important to notice that the approach presented is meant as a complement, and not as an alternative, to conceptual approaches. The approach directs attention to activities and goals, and their relationships.

However, it is not only actions that are related to intentions and goals. Concepts used in a method are used for some reason. The same is also true for notation, documentation, and so on. The existence of such relationships is implied by the fact that all method aspects are actually results of action at the meta-level, actions performed by the method creator. It is, however, beyond the scope of this paper to discuss the use of rationale in conjunction with such non-activity-related aspects of methods.

The applications presented suggest that the proposed kind of modelling depends on the actual application context. We cannot really tell how to perform the analyses without some specific purpose. The suggested applications are: construction of context-sensitive help systems in CASE-tools; method reconstruction; verification of proposed method achievements; consistency checking of aggregated activities; and finally (and perhaps most importantly), evaluation, adoption, implementation, and combination of existing methods.

The proposed approach should make at least parts of the tacit dimension visible.

REFERENCES

[Aus62]   J. Austin. How to do things with words. Oxford University Press (1962).

[Ber89]   P. Berger and T. Luckmann. The social construction of reality. Anchor Books, New York (1989).

[Bla98]   M. Blaha and W. Premerlani. Object-oriented modeling and design for database applications. Prentice Hall (1998).

[Boo99]   G. Booch, J. Rumbaugh and I. Jacobsson. The Unified Modeling Language User Guide. Addison-Wesley Longman, Inc. (1999).

[Bri98]   S. Brinkkemper, M. Saeki and F. Harmsen. Assembly techniques for method engineering. In proceedings, 10th Intl Conference on Advanced Information Systems Engineering (CAISE'98). Pisa, Italy, June 8-12 (1998).

[Coa91]   P. Coad and E. Yourdon. Object-oriented analysis. Yourdon Press, Object International, Inc. (1991).

[Flo80]   F. Flores and J. Ludlow. Doing and speaking in the office. In Fick and Sprague (Eds, 1980) Decision support systems: Issues and challenges. Pergamon Press (1980).

[Fow97]   M. Fowler. Analysis patterns: Reusable object models. Addison-Wesley Longman, Inc. (1995).

[Gam95]   E. Gamma, R. Helm, R. Johnson and J. Vlissides. Design patterns: Elements of reusable object-oriented software. Addison-Wesley Longman, Inc. (1995).

[Gol92]   G. Goldkuhl. Contextual activity modelling of information systems. In proceedings, 3rd Intl Working Conference on Dynamic Modelling of Information Systems, Noordwijkerhout (1992).

[Gol94a]   G. Goldkuhl. V‰lgrundad metodutveckling. ("Well-founded method development", in Swedish). Research report, IDA, Linkˆping University (1994).

[Gol94b]   G. Goldkuhl and D. Fristedt. Metodanalys: En beskrivning av metametoden SIMM. ("Method analysis: a description of the meta-method SIMM", in Swedish). Research report, IDA, Linkˆping University (1994).

[Gol82]   G. Goldkuhl and K. Lyytinen. A language action view of information systems. In proceedings, 3rd Intl conference on information systems, Ann Arbor (1982).

[Gol98]   G. Goldkuhl and P. J. ≈gerfalk. Action within Information Systems: Outline of a requirements engineering method. In Dubois et al., proceedings of the 4th Intl workshop on requirements engineering: foundations for software quality (REFSQ'98). Pisa, Italy, June 8-9 (1998).

[Gol93]   G. Goldkuhl and A. Rˆstlinger. The legitimacy of information systems development: A need for change analysis. In Proceedings, IFIP Conference on Human-Computer Interaction, London (1993).

[Hab84]   Habermas J. The theory of communicative action 1. Reason and the rationalization of society. Beacon Press (1984).

[Hey93]   M. Heym and H. ÷sterle. Computer-aided methodology engineering. Information and software technology. Vol. 35, No. 6/7 (1993).

[Jay94]   N. Jayaratna. Understanding and evaluating methodologies: NIMSAD, a systemic framework. McGraw-Hill International (1994).

[Kum92]   K. Kumar and R. J. Welke. Methodology engineering: A proposal for situation-specific methodology construction. In Cotterman, Senn (Eds. 1992), Challenges and strategies for research in systems development. John Wiley & Sons Ltd. (1992).

[Lan66]   B. Langefors. Theoretical analysis of information systems. Studenlitteratur, Lund, Sweden (1966).

[Mol96]   B. Molander. Kunskap i handling. ("Knowledge in Action", in Swedish). Daidalos, Gothenburg (1996).

[Nil99]   A. G. Nilsson. The Method Developer's Toolbox: Chains and Alliances between Established Methods. In Nilsson, Tollis and Nellborn (Eds. 1999). Perspectives on Business Modelling. Springer Verlag, Heidelberg, Germany (1999).

[Rum95]   J. Rumbaugh. What is a method? Technical Paper, Rational Software, Inc. (1995).

[Sea69]   J. R. Searl. Speech acts. An essay in the philosophy of language. Cambridge University Press, London (1969).

[Sto91]   E. Stolterman. Designarbetets dolda rationalitet: En studie av metodik och praktik inom systemutveckling. ("The hidden rationale of design work: A study in the methodology and practice of systems development", in Swedish). Doctoral dissertation, UmeÂ University, Sweden (1991).

[Tol93]   J-P. Tolvanen, K, Lyytinen. Flexible method adaption in CASE environments - the meta-modelling approach. In Scandinavian Journal of Information Systems, vol. 1, no. 5, pp 51-77 (1993).

[Win86]   T. Winograd and F. Flores. Understanding computers and cognition: A new foundation for design. Ablex, Norwood (1986).

Deriving a Methodological Perspective for Business Process Management and Business Process Change

Antony Bryant

Professor of Informatics, Leeds Metropolitan University, The Grange, LS6 3QS Leeds, United Kingdom
a.bryant@lmu.ac.uk

Jurgen Vanhoenacker

PricewaterhouseCoopers Management Consultants, 16, Rue Eugène Ruppert, L-1014 Luxembourg, Luxembourg
jurgen.vanhoenacker@lu.pwcglobal.com

ABSTRACT

The initial response to BPR was for many to see it as a new fad, or fashion. On the other hand many organizations embraced it in its simplistic form, since it echoed many aspects of the spirit of the early 1990s - and coincided with many of the worst excesses of short-termism, commercial myopia and bad management from that period. This led to scepticism, disbelief, and disavowal; with disclaimers even from some of the originators of BPR. But the phenomenon cannot be ignored. Despite all the well-argued critiques of BPR, there is still a profound basis to the work that has burgeoned since Hammer and Champey's, and Davenport's, books appeared.

This paper seeks to preserving the key insights of BPR, while moving forwards. We seek to articulate the methodological basis for BPR projects and initiatives; offering a form of transparency and justification for activities that have often been lacking in such features.

The BPR literature is all too often reliant on a mixture of anecdotes and slogans. If there is any methodological basis on offer, it is often poorly explained, taking too much for granted, and highly unspecified. Some business analysts and professionals either reject the process perspective entirely, or fail to comprehend how the endless list of modelling techniques, the variety of decision making guidelines and numerous staffing prescriptions 'fit together' into a comprehensive whole to facilitate their decision making. Consequently many fail to mobilize, exploit and capitalize on the organizational knowledge base, which is needed for business process change.

In this paper, we explain some of these methodological shortcomings, and offer a framework for developing a more inclusive, integrative and adaptive approach to the field of what we term *I-BPM* - Integrated Business Process Management. The framework reflects our belief that successful business process change demands a degree of conceptualization and co-ordination across a variety of key dimensions. Furthermore the paper elaborates on how this concept of methodological fit can be applied at various conceptual levels. Illustrations from an I-BPM effort in the Financial Services Industry illustrate our ideas.

RE-EVALUATING THE BUSINESS PROCESS PHENOMENON

The early enthusiasm for BPR rapidly evoked an equally exaggerated scepticism and now, a decade later we are entering a period of re-evaluation and re-assessment. There is still no definitive outcome from this, but if nothing else BPR has focused attention on the process aspects of organizational existence, now a crucial aspect of business analysis and information management.

A consequence of the fervour and disdain that marked the emergence of BPR has been the way it has drawn people's attention to the question of effectiveness and success of reengineering and other change-oriented projects. Ironically it may have been Hammer himself who was largely responsible for this when he was quoted as saying that '80% of BPR projects fail'. This was immediately seized upon by critics of BPR, and led to the preponderance of research findings by advocates and critics keen respectively to refute or corroborate this statistic. Two key aspects were for the most part unnoticed or neglected -

- Was an 80% failure rate higher than that found with other projects concerned with fundamental change and redirection?
- What constituted 'failure' in such instances?

These are important issues but we wish to consider other key aspects, particularly the methodological bases of reengineering. In so doing, we hope to illuminate aspects of organizational practice that are often ignored by the methodological support upon which reengineering has relied. Many reengineering or change-management practitioners either take methodological concerns for granted or, more likely, are confronted by methodology overload; and can no longer appreciate when, why and how, one or other business process technique should, or can be used in their efforts.

This situation cannot be remedied by application of existing methodologies, since their focus is different or too narrow. They emanate from a highly normative, mechanical view of business reality, whereby IT has been elevated to the role of primary, or even sole change vector: Business processes are treated like Lego pieces that can be pulled apart and reassembled [29]; an influence partly inherited from software engineering approaches [14, 17, 18, 22, 31]. This despite caveats in the early writings of BPR advocates, that specifically warned against 'throwing computers at problems'. Furthermore, there is the paradox that many guiding concepts of the business process movement retain significant 'Taylorist' influences, including the mistaken assumption that business processes were *engineered in the first place*. All this leads to a contradiction between the practice and the research [4, 8, 13, 33, 40].

We wish to resolve this contradiction, starting from the proposition that business process change is highly context sensitive; always contingent upon the peculiarities of a specific decision making situation. The core of such change is the effective management of changing business processes - whether or not they are thought to need 'reengineering', and perhaps regardless of how they came to develop in the first place. Our approach to all business process change is to treat it as an organizational learning exercise, and we do not judge *a priori* whether a radical business transformation is by definition better than a local optimization of a functional work process. We use the term 'Integrated Business Process Management' (I-BPM); an amalgam of general managerial action concerned with business processes. This helps circumvent the endless discussion on the distinctions between different management approaches centred on analysis and change of business processes.

EXPANDING THE FOCUS - THE METHODOLOGY TRIANGLE

I-BPM aims to provide organizations with the means to manage their business processes, including questioning the validity of and necessity for existing working practices, and justifying and comparing potential changes. I-BPM facilitates and promotes business process change, resulting in an increase in organizational knowledge. This can be accomplished with the utilization of various methodologies, tools and techniques; although we would maintain that many of the existing and 'obvious' ones are inadequate or inappropriate.

We consider a methodology to be a prescriptive device that guides actions and decisions. It is akin to Lyytinen's definition of an information systems development methodology (ISDM) -

'an organised collection of concepts, beliefs, values and normative principles supported by material resources. The purpose of the ISDM is to help a development group successfully change object systems, that is to perceive, generate, assess, control, and perform change actions in them' [40].

Regardless of the exact form in which a methodology appears, three fundamental components need to be explicitly integrated. These can best be visualized as the Methodology Triangle.

The Methodology Triangle illustrates the necessary requirements for any methodological support for business process change. The 'Formalism' component represents the dimension of the information elements required in designing business process change. The 'Algorithm' dimension refers to the proper decision making discipline; and the dimension of 'Organism' underlines the often overlooked importance of competence, skills and roles with respect to business process change. All three aspects have to be considered if business process change is to be successful; and any methodology has to exhibit a high degree of *'methodological fit'* as a prerequisite for effective business process knowledge management.

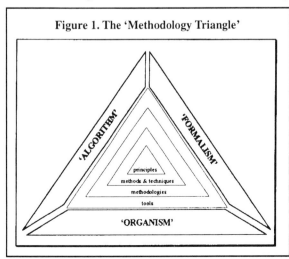

Figure 1. The 'Methodology Triangle'

'ALGORITHM'

'FORMALISM'

principles

methods & techniques

methodologies

tools

'ORGANISM'

THE SPARTA FRAMEWORK

Current methodologies, claiming to support business process change tend to reflect a high degree of technological determinism. (Again, this echoes within BPR criticisms similar to those offered by Lyytinen concerning information systems methodologies.) This deficiency derives from the assumptions that many early BPR advocates borrowed, often unwittingly, practices emanating from software engineering. Hence the observation that BPR methodologies do not distance themselves from software development methodologies, and furthermore that many 'BPR tools' are simply CASE-tools in new guises [4, 34].

Two fundamental principles of business process change distinguish it from software development. First, changing business processes emanates from a refusal to accept any facet of organizational existence as immutable, without first seeking clarification of core processes and key assumptions [6]: The *principle of discontinuity*. Conversely, software engineering practice can only commence once some firm set of requirements has been authorized.

Second, process professionals face decision situations that are highly unstructured. The problem has to be fitted into a 'frame' before any solution can be developed: The *principle of dynamic complexity* [32]. This is distinct from the principle of *detail* complexity that guides software engineering, sometimes referred to as 'step-wise refinement': Software engineering practice is quite correctly focused on the technicalities of the potential solutions to determined problems. Whereas I-BPM addresses elements of discontinuity and dynamic complexity, embedded in business processes, conventional software engineering methodologies focus on issues of stability and detail complexity. Rather than mimicking a software engineering methodology, an I-BPM methodology has to resemble an organizational double-loop learning device for acquiring the crucial understanding of 'why?' a business process exists in the first place - rather than a tool that merely describes the details of 'how?' a business process operates.

The Methodology Triangle suggests the need to validate and integrate knowledge from different disciplines into a comprehensive methodological support. Consequently developing effective I-BPM methodologies has to draw upon a wide inter-disciplinary basis, and cannot simply re-use SE approaches. One approach is to use Systems Theory as a foundation for integration [1, 5, 7], resulting in a language to describe different phenomena in terms of a set of interrelated components that together form a comprehensive whole manifesting emergent properties. We have developed such a model that contains six fundamental functional components that provide the bases for any form of methodological support for business process change [37, 38]:

I-BPM as a System of Systems	'ORGANISM'	'ALGORITHM'	'FORMALISM'	
Feedback System	Reporter	Observation	Flow-Activity-Flow (FAF) Construct	'SOLICITOR'
Abstraction System	Sensemaker	Introspection	Intention-State (IS) Construct	'PROCESSOR'
Openness System	Diplomat	Diversion	Intention-State-Intention (ISI) Construct	'ACCEPTOR'
Questioning System	Challenger	Discursion	Positive State-Intention-State (+SIS) Construct	'RESISTOR'
Leverage Identification. System	Animator	Deracination	Negative State-Intention-State (-SIS) Construct	'TRAFFICATOR'
Servomechanistic System	Negotiator	Conversion	Inverted Activity-Intention-Activity (AIA⁻¹) construct	'ASSESSOR'
	Organizational System	Decision Making System	Modelling System	

If business process change can be considered to be the result of learning, and if learning is achieved by design, *"then there must be an architecture to support it"* [21]. The SPARTA Framework provides this architecture, with six functional components as follows:

1. Solicitor: 'soliciting' of basic information with respect to an underlying business process and the appreciation of process breadth.
2. Processor: 'processing' of information in terms of the dynamics of business processes ('Why?') instead of aiming for the infinite details ('What?').
3. Acceptor: 'acceptance' of different and contradictory interpretations of the same problem situation, rather than rushing to an early judgement, which too often leads to preclusion of a number of change options.
4. Resistor: 'resistance' towards taking for granted seemingly familiar and obvious elements that underlie business processes, and seek to develop a more profound explanation of working practices.
5. Trafficator: identification of change directions ('a trafficator') and business process change levers, as a means to break commonly accepted frames of references.

6. Assessor: 'assessment' of the nature and validity of a proposed business process change, **leading to a consensus and a proper level of ambition, which is shared by a critical mass of organizational stakeholders.**

GOING A STEP FURTHER: DEVELOPING A META-MODEL

SPARTA provides an outline against which we can locate the principles of I-BPM. In order to provide the framework with the prescriptive power needed for methodology development, we can develop a *meta-model* that formalizes the content of each cell and enables integration with the other cells. A similar meta-model could be used as a conceptual data-schema for I-BPM tool builders for their repositories.

To develop this metamodel the dimensions of Formalism, Algorithm and Organism can be treated as objects of a meta-modelling exercise[1]. A detailed account of the meta-modelling strategy lies beyond the scope of this paper. Here we simply offer some meta-model concepts, particularly those concerning with the underlying systems concepts of components, interrelations and emergent properties.

The SPARTA Formalism meta-concepts

A basic component of Formalism is the '*business process dimension*'; concerned with different ways of looking at business processes; the logical sequence of its activities, the information structures they act upon, the people who execute the business process activities, and so on. This dimension has can be modelled with a distinct "*unique basic model*", consisting of a basic entity type and a basic connector type. ER-diagramming is based on the data-entity/relationship/data-entity model.

We have identified seven basic entity types for I-BPM:
1. business process activity (Activity),
2. activity flow (Flow),
3. intended organizational state (State),
4. underlying intention (Intention),
5. actual organizational state (State^{-1}),
6. new intention (Intention^{-1})
7. new business process activity (Activity^{-1}).

These can be combined into six modelling primitives, which can be implemented using existing modelling techniques. The Flow/Activity/Flow (FAF) modelling primitive might be implemented using Data-Flow diagrams or Process Flowcharts. The FAF construct represents a business process in terms of a logical flow of activities. The details of each formalism are beyond the scope of this paper, but two central concepts deserve further clarification.

The concept of *Intention* is a basic modelling variable. It evokes the implicit and explicit assumptions and rationales that people use as part of their working practices. Usually these are implicit and unquestioned: Once rendered explicit, they focus attention on the 'why?' questions underlying organizational action. For instance a state defined as 'validated cheque' (STATE) might emanate from an intentional statement of the form 'in order to confirm the signature' (INTENTION). Intentional structures can be modelled using systems diagrams, similar to those proposed by Senge [32]. The +SIS (State-Intention-State) construct refers to the identification of a reinforcing loop amongst a set of intentions. The existence of a similar positive feedback loop explains why people stick to a specific working pattern. On the other hand, it is quite possible that the intention is never realized in practice; hence the distinction between the intended state and the actual state.

The −**SIS** construct acts as a balancing loop amongst a set of intentions. Specifically it represents a negative feedback loop that challenges ingrained thinking patterns and motivates a reconsideration of an existing working pattern. The integration of these semantic and syntactical elements enables us to assess the *dynamic complexity* in I-BPM decision situations. This construct develops from the potential discrepancy between intended and actual states. The negative feedback loop is called into play to redress the gap between intention and performance.

The second important element of the SPARTA Formalism meta-model is the notion of the inverted version of a basic modelling variable. This encompasses any meaningful alternative, including the converse, to an original modelling statement. Thus an intentional statement "in order to divest myself of my responsibilities" (INTENTION^{-1}) might well be an inverted version of the original intention "in order to identify typing errors" (INTENTION) that underlies the existence of "a reviewed report" (STATE). Inversion could vary from simple negation to a 'less mathematical' alternative of an original statement. The role played by this set of inverted entity types, integrated into modelling techniques, is that it prompts us to consider the elements of *discontinuity* in I-BPM decision making situations.

Within the constraints of the M.E.R.O.DE. modelling prescriptions, the figure below presents a conceptual object-relationship diagram for the overall SPARTA Formalism meta-model:

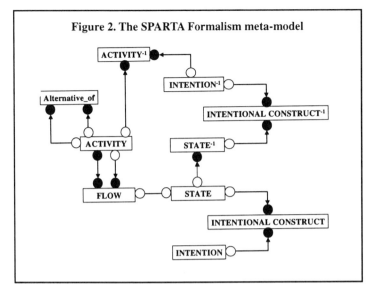

Figure 2. The SPARTA Formalism meta-model

Here is a brief illustration of how this Formalism meta-model was "instantiated" in a real-life banking case. This was concerned with an I-BPM project for an asset management process. A simplified account of this 'business process story' is as follows: « The moment a customer places (ACTIVITY) a securities purchase order (FLOW), the account manager sends (ACTIVITY) a hand-written order notification (FLOW) to the middle-office for customer cash position control (ACTIVITY) before sending an order validation (FLOW) to the back-office for final settlement of the transaction (ACTIVITY). The fact that the order notification forms arrive at the middle-office (STATE) was, amongst others, justified 'because account managers should not deal with administrative control work' (INTENTION). The fact that account managers did not effectuate this type of control (STATE) however was offset by the fact that, in reality, they actually had real-time access to this type of customer information (STATE^{-1}). This new observation gained in importance 'because it only takes a couple of seconds to verify customer cash positions' (INTENTION^{-1}). This insight resulted in the new working pattern that customer securities orders were directly entered into the system by the account manager (ACTIVITY^{-1}) for automatic cash position control. »

In the above banking case, the ACTIVITY and FLOW constructs (FAF) were presented as a flowchart model of the securities business process. The STATE and INTENTION constructs (IS, ISI, SIS) were described and analyzed within a simple MS Excel spreadsheet form and with 'a type of' conceptual mapping technique, used during workshops. Finally, the alternative working pattern (AIA^{-1}) was formalized and discussed by means of a more textual 'model'.

The SPARTA Algorithm meta-concepts

The SPARTA Algorithm focuses on decision making activities for I-BPM. Whereas the SPARTA Formalism meta-model constructs define the type of information about business processes that is considered important, the SPARTA Algorithm components define how this information is created, how it evolves over time and how it 'materializes' into knowledge. Metaphorically speaking, the Algorithm components of decision making activities 'give life' to the Formalism meta-objects. There are six different decision making activities for I-BPM: Observation, Introspection, Diversion, Discursion, Deracination and Conversion. These can each be implemented using different decision making techniques, such as structured interviews, brainstorm sessions or group workshops.

The priority of each will depend on the type of I-BPM exercise being performed. For example, Discursion activity, with the objective of 'leaving no stone unturned', will be more important in reengineering settings than might be the case for simple process automation. Moreover, depending on the culture of the organization, the Algorithm components can vary in terms of formal rigor and procedural prescriptions. For instance, the Diversion activity, aiming at uncovering the implicit intentions[2] that underlie a specific working pattern, might well be accomplished through a series of structured workshops (using techniques such as Nominal Groups), and be given the label of 'The Discovering Phase' in the overall project. In turn, the 'Conversion' activity, which aims at arriving at a consensus, might be achieved through a series of open discussions, using a technique such as Force Field Analysis, and be given the label of 'The Validation Phase' in the overall project. (Whether or not such gatherings are feasible or effective will depend on the culture of the organization itself.)

Following the logic underlying the SPARTA framework, this set of decision making activities, constitutes a comprehensive whole; manifesting the emergent property of a double-loop learning cycle. It results in the creation of new knowledge; transcending the traditional activity of merely describing a business process in infinite detail and justifying the status quo (i.e. single-loop learning). The SPARTA Algorithm meta-model concepts act as 'information functions' upon the Formalism meta-objects. In other words, from a meta-model perspective, the Observation activity is a function which represents information from its environment in terms of business process activities and flows:

The Observation activity as modelled above could be identified in the banking case as follows:

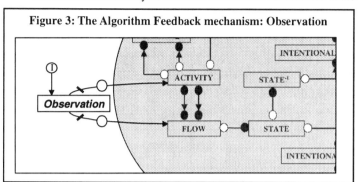

Figure 3: The Algorithm Feedback mechanism: Observation

« From the moment the securities management business process had been identified for analysis, the initial step consisted in acquiring a first overall picture of what the business process looked like (i.e. the OBSERVATION activity). This decision making activity was labelled as 'the process description phase' in the overall I-BPM project. Furthermore, the activity had been organized along structured group interviews with a particular stress on open-ended questions about the logical process flow (e.g. 'What are the most important activities you consider in this process?'). The objective of this phase was to get a quickmap picture of the business process while identifying the major business process steps and the ways in which they are connected (cf. instances of ACTIVITY and FLOW objects). As a result, multiple N:M relationships had been identified between instances of the ACTIVITY and the FLOW meta-objects. This quickmap served as the focal point for all members of the I-BPM project team and enabled them to arrive at a common definition of the business process before proceeding with further analysis (cf. INTROSPECTION, DIVERSION,…). Moreover, the interviews were organized in such a way as to avoid the danger of 'getting lost' in the infinite detail that might underlie each and every business process activity identified. Therefore, no stepwise refinement or 'functional decomposition', similar to what is often done in IS projects, was allowed on the securities management business process quickmap. »

The SPARTA Organism meta-concepts

The SPARTA Organism addresses the organizational roles to be fulfilled in I-BPM contexts. This dimension has traditionally not received the methodological attention it deserves. This largely a result of the mechanistic and technology-oriented approach of BPR. Human activity was treated as simply another company resource to be scrutinized in business process analysis [13, 40]. This deficiency partially explains why many early BPR modelling tools, although intrinsically interesting and potentially useful, never gained wide use in business practice, since their target audience did not possess the proper skills to handle the techniques themselves, nor could people interpret the business process models that resulted from their application.

Overall, the core motivation for integrating organizational issues into I-BPM methodologies is that human/social aspects have to be considered explicitly. This has always been highly problematic in business process management. Modelling abstract parts of systems is less complicated than attempting to capture the complexities of social interaction; and it is always tempting to ignore what is most difficult to accomplish. This evasion is cited in much of the critical literature [3, 12, 40]. The SPARTA Organism deals with the so called 'people factor' as a priority at the start of any change exercise. The objective is to address such aspects proactively, rather than dealing with them once a business process solution has been inflicted on the workforce.

The SPARTA Organism should be looked at as a system, with components constituting a comprehensive whole. This is evoked by the concept of *a role*; and implies the notion of an actor or agent. Roles are associated with the execution of activities. An actor executing an activity successfully should have the proper skills. So there are three prerequisites to a role: An actor, an activity and a skill set[3].

We should be able to assess the set of skills and actors that are present in an organization, and incorporate them in change programmes. This will provide a means to assess the (intrinsic) learning capability of an organization and take appropriate action. We should be able to assess whether a specific organization, with an existing set of actors and skills, is capable to assume the roles that are important in, for instance, a reengineering project. The Organism dimension also develops the realization that human resource management experience is a necessary feature of any I-BPM methodology or tool.

Some roles can be considered as generic; e.g. 'Challenger' or 'Negotiator'. The 'Challenger' role is designed to generate creative tension or even conflict in a business process study, and could be allocated to an external consultant, for obvious political reasons. In particular the 'Negotiator' role is critical as a servomechanism in the SPARTA Organism. The objective is to create sufficient momentum to introduce organizational change and simultaneously anticipate the degree of organizational resistance. In practice the 'Negotiator' role encompasses facilitating skills to mediate between different parties; to identify and build a 'winning coalition'.

We have deliberately integrated the constituents of role as core meta-model objects. A specific role can be seen as a function that inquires into the set of skills and actors, and generates the sufficient input that triggers a SPARTA Algorithm component. The latter in its turn 'freezes' the information into a business process model. A representative implementation for the 'Reporter' role is provided below:

Figure 4: The 'Reporter' ROLE object

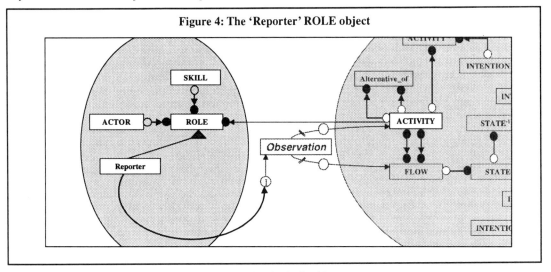

Again, these meta-model concepts were identified in the banking case:

« External consultants explained to top management the objective of the Observation activity (cf. AC-TIVITY) that was labelled as 'the process description phase'. Furthermore, a request was made to organize a set of structured group interviews with persons that were able to provide an overall and 'objective' picture of the securities management business process (cf. REPORTER role). Basically, various process participants, including internal process customers (cf. ACTOR instances) were identified to participate. A couple of years of experience, preferably in various departments of the bank, as well as an outspoken ability to communicate freely and an ability to provide a structured view on working practices (cf. SKILL instances), formed the focus for the selection of these interview participants. »

AN INTEGRATED APPROACH TOWARDS BUSINESS PROCESS CHANGE

The formalized framework (meta-model) serves as a vehicle to structure different types of discussions on the business process phenomenon. Once the principles behind SPARTA are fully understood, the individual components can be manipulated like a 'Rubik's Cube'. The framework can be 'read' in different ways: with 'vertical' and 'horizontal' perspectives each revealing different aspects of the business process phenomenon.

The vertical perspective essentially offers a project management view of I-BPM efforts. The Formalism dimension read from top to bottom offers a minimal set of project deliverables for any business change program. Similarly, the Organism dimension suggests a generic project team definition; indicating the minimum set of skills that must be available for business process change activities to be initiated. This underlines the necessity for a degree of *organizational preparedness* in the current business situation, and also to proceed with business process change. Other organizations might be said to have an inherent organizational 'attitude' or culture that is conducive to encouraging and completing business process management initiatives. Finally, the vertical view along the Algorithm dimension indicates the various activities that should be 'phased and scheduled' into an overall business process change program. Decisions need to be taken regarding which Algorithm components should be grouped together in which project phases, and their relative importance in terms of planned time and resources to be allocated.

Reading SPARTA along its vertical axis encourages an integrated approach towards I-BPM project management. It addresses project phases and deadlines, and staffing requirements and project 'outputs'. If this vertical view seems overly complex, seeking to account for three facets and six dimensions, the benefit is that it stresses the ways in which these components are related to each other. This remedies any tendency to a partial view of project management, which is all too often observed in practice [8]. The vertical view of the framework goes some way to answer the need of many process professionals who want to know where to start and how to prepare for a I-BPM project.

The horizontal perspective prompts a multidimensional view of I-BPM. For any single strand across the structure, there will be related or complementary strands above or below: This suggests that any action undertaken within

I-BPM contexts must be performed with an eye to the wider context. Activities have to be integrated in a *'contextual fit'*. This requires a balance between Formalism, Algorithm and Organism for successful decision-making about business process change.

This provides a more formal basis for several 'rules of thumb' in change or reengineering projects. For instance, with regard to any specific process modelling technique, the framework immediately indicates the necessity for skills analysis and clarification of activity sequencing and co-ordination. Also, while assessing the importance of uncovering the underlying rationales of working patterns, the framework suggests a set of decision-making techniques and roles to be observed to uncover this type of information. The horizontal view of SPARTA highlights the concern that no matter how sophisticated a modelling technique might be, it will be completely useless without the relevant competence and decision-making discipline.

Business process change is contingent upon very specific features of a particular decision making situation. The horizontal view suggests that generic concepts must be tailored to the idiosyncrasies of the organization. For example, the banking case reported on a trade-off made along the 'Solicitor' component of SPARTA. While observing the lack in graphical process mapping skills for handling a sophisticated FAF process modelling technique, the Bank resorted to a more comprehensive matrix representation of its business process, thereby adopting more discipline in its use. The outcome was a lower level of ambition at the Formalism level, due to a lack of 'Organism'-capability, offset by an increased level of ambition on the Algorithm side, while proceeding through the analysis in a much more disciplined way. Overall, the notion of trade-off and compromise is intrinsic to SPARTA, and makes this an explicit concern in every business change effort. This is not merely to say that SPARTA is flexible; it is actually stressing that SPARTA cannot be applied *without* some balancing and trade-offs. An appropriate equilibrium between contending forces has to be an aspiration - balancing information, analysis activities and organizational skills as a prerequisite for successful business process change.

The horizontal and vertical two views together force process professionals to assess the totality of their process management efforts, modelling techniques and roles. Any location within the framework affords a perspective from which to evaluate the importance of any issue in an I-BPM project. For us SPARTA is a holistic construct: A similar notion of 'Gestalt' underlines the idea of Peppard that "*a reason why many organizations have problems with BPR is that difficulty lies in bringing together all these elements under one initiative*" [29]. SPARTA is a means to appreciate why and how all these elements can and should fit together in an overall business process change effort.

The framework offers a structure against which the plethora of techniques, methodological guidelines and team-composition directives, presented in the popular business process literature, can be compared and integrated. For instance, while confronted with the overwhelming number of process mapping techniques of a methodology, the process professional often fails to appreciate the intrinsic utility of the activity itself; or assumes that a specific technique is useful in contexts where it is barely appropriate. SPARTA enables process professionals to identify situations where a technique is used simply for the sake of the technique itself. It enhances appreciation of the decision making activity, and stresses the need to assess what kind of information is needed before being able to start simulating a new business process. Even more, use of the SPARTA model might suggest, for instance, the importance of simulation activity as a basic consensus building instrument, while enabling process participants to change process variables that will affect simulation. In other words, all actions taken by the process professional can be motivated along the framework. Likewise, while inquiring into the usefulness of explaining existing working practices, instead of adopting a clean slate approach, SPARTA suggests the importance of providing process participants with an outlet to express their (personal) rationales and values that could motivate their daily professional activities. SPARTA provides perspective and focus to the process professional.

Furthermore, the framework could be used as an instrument to define the functional coverage of a business process change effort. As such it is possible to define degrees of generic functional coverage depending on the type of process change effort that will be undertaken. SPARTA will differ if the change effort concerns a radical reengineering, a design of a workflow system for an existing business process or an implementation of a Total Quality Management system. In other words, the nature and the degree of methodological fit will vary with the variety of business process management types. This functional component addresses the concept of validating and building consensus around an identified business process change that seems worthwhile. Once a winning coalition has been built, a new SPARTA cycle is triggered which will formalize the decision for one or another I-BPM archetype. The latter could range from a company-wide radical reengineering program to a more localised project aiming at rationalizing an existing business process without inducing major changes, such as defining a quality system. Our framework too provides a basis for determining the ideal mix of decision making dimensions with respect to a number of I-BPM archetypes. Whereas, the objective of this paper is not to provide an exhaustive SPARTA mapping for all possible I-BPM archetypes, below is suggested a generic mapping for the implementation of an ISO 9000 compliant quality system on a business process, that might have resulted from a second iteration in a SPARTA cycle:

	'ORGANISM'	'ALGORITHM'	'FORMALISM'	
Feedback System	Process Participants	Quality Planning	ISO compliant Process Model	'SOLICITOR'
Abstraction System	Quality Manager	Quality Training	Quality Procedures	'PROCESSOR'
Openness System	/////	/////	/////	'ACCEPTOR'
Questioning System	/////	/////	/////	'RESISTOR'
Leverage Identification System	Internal Quality Auditor	Internal Quality Audit	Request for Corrective Action (RCA)	'TRAFFICATOR'
Servomechanistic System	Quality Manager	Management Review / External Quality Audit	Quality Plan / ISO 9000 Certificate	'ASSESSOR'
	Organizational System	Decision Making System	Information System	

A further application of the SPARTA framework might be in conducting a gap analysis or project audits, respectively before and after the completion of an I-BPM project. In cases where a process change effort did not succeed, the framework could be used as a tool for -diagnosing the causes of failure, and indicating ways in which such 'failures' could be the basis for learning and understanding. This could be done while indicating the absence of components and the (lack of) time spent on one or other activity. In a similar way, the framework not only promotes recognition of the causes of failure, but also it enables the process professional to qualify or characterize the nature of the causes identified. Many of the much-cited - but poorly understood, or inadequately analyzed - pitfalls of reengineering could be better acknowledged as fundamental mismatches in terms of the SPARTA framework. For instance, a project might have failed due to a lack in skills or understaffing of the project, or an over-rigidity in formal planning, or misinformation; or a combination of all three. We like to refer to this as the concept of *'diagnostic fit'*, suggesting the idea that a failure of business process change should always be explained in as complex and varied a manner as is appropriate to the project itself. Simplistic explanations are rarely adequate for complex phenomena. It has been cited in the literature that many reengineering efforts eventually failed despite the definition of a sophisticated redesign blueprint. Some of the major pitfalls or 'mismatches' typically encountered in these situations are those where severe organizational resistance blocked implementation because process participants were not involved in the analysis, or where an extreme focus on details dominated the analysis and prevented the participants from appreciating the global picture [40]. A similar diagnosis in SPARTA 'vocabulary' could be indicated as follows:

	'ORGANISM'	'ALGORITHM'	'FORMALISM'	
Feedback System	Senior Staff Expert	Process Analysis	IDEF1, DFD, Flowcharts,...	'SOLICITOR'
Abstraction System	Senior Staff Expert	Process Analysis	/////	'PROCESSOR'
Openness System	/////	/////		'ACCEPTOR'
Questioning System	/////	/////		'RESISTOR'
Leverage Identification System	External Consultant	Benchmark With Best practices	Benchmark Report	'TRAFFICATOR'
Servomechanistic System	Senior Management	Senior Management Approval	/////	'ASSESSOR'
	Organizational System	Decision Making System	Information System	

APPLYING SPARTA AT DIFFERENT CONCEPTUAL LEVELS

It has been suggested above that the power of SPARTA resides in its integrative character, enabling us to express different notions of consistency and complementarity - i.e. of 'fitness'. Once this is understood, SPARTA can be used as a tool to structure a discussion on the business process phenomenon at other conceptual levels. Indeed the SPARTA logic proves to be applicable to any situation where the element of 'learning at the level of a process' is present or where knowledge-creation is a central theme.

In the first place, we could apply the framework as a learning instrument at the 'micro' level of a single business process, which embodies an element of knowledge-creation: This would include most business processes. As examples we could refer to a product development process, a customer complaints handling process, an IT planning process, a supplier selection process, a marketing process, and so on. All these processes thrive on an increase of 'knowledge' (e.g. a new product, new supplier information,...). Here SPARTA acts as *'process description tool'*. Other 'knowledge-based' business processes operate on a set of information elements, which could be embedded in various representation and communication tools (i.e. document forms, data files, procedures, memos, spreadsheets, etc.), on a set of activities (i.e. control, copy, verify, classify, phone, etc.) and on a set of roles (i.e. a process owner, an expert, a supervisor, a customer, a case manager, etc.). As an illustration of the above idea, a possible process description of a credit approval process might be represented as follows:

A similar discussion could be established at the aggregated level of all business processes of a particular industry. As such, it is reasonable to assume that the business process models and the knowledge that is reflected in, for instance, an insurance claim process of company X, a claim process model of the Swiss Insurance Industry and a customer request process model of the service industry, show major similarities. This development of generic business process models has already been done in information systems development where industry data models and process models have been developed for the healthcare industry, financial services, and other domains. SPARTA could also be used as an instrument to develop similar generic models of business processes, as has been done for industry-specific ISO 9000 process frameworks[1]. From this perspective SPARTA serves as an *'aggregation tool'*. A set of roles, at the level of the industry, could be used to identify participants in this discussion - e.g. labour unions as a servomechanism, industry associations as 'reporters', consumer groups as 'challengers', and so on: As well as a set of 'Formalisms' (cf. the 'white' and 'green' papers issued by the European Commission, environmental standards such as the EMS-ISO 14001).

There are still possibly further levels that could be considered in developing the business process phenomenon. Overall, our objective has been to demonstrate the integrative character of the SPARTA framework as a valuable contribution to this endeavour. Our message is that the viability of the 'business process discipline' thrives on *synthesis and integration* rather than on *analysis and segregation* of concepts and disciplines.

REFERENCES

1. Ackoff R.L., Redesigning the future: a systems approach to societal problems, New York, John Wiley & Sons, 1974.
2. Andrews D.C. & S.K. Stalick, 'Business Reengineering, the survival guide', Prentice-Hall, Englewood Cliffs, 1994.
3. Ascari A., Rock M. & S. Dutta, 'Reengineering and Organizational Change: Lessons from a Comparative Analysis of Company Experiences', European Management Journal, Vol. 13, No. 1, 1995, pp. 1-30.
4. Avgerou C., Cornford T. & A. Poulymenakou, 'The challenge of BPR to the Information Systems Profession', New Technology, Work and Employment', Vol. 10, No. 2, 1995, pp. 132-141.
5. Bertalanffy L. von, General systems Theory: Foundation, Development, Application, New York, George Braziller, 1973.
6. Bryant A. & D. Chan, 'Goal Directed Development; Confronting Organizational Legacy', Proceedings of the 6th annual Business Information Technology (BIT) Conference, Manchester Metropolitan University, Manchester, 7/11/1996, pp. 143-154.
7. Checkland P. & J. Scholes, Soft Systems Methodology in Action, New York, John Wiley & Sons, 1990.
8. Coombs, R. & R., Hull, 'BPR as 'IT-enabled organizational change': an assessment', New Technology Work and Employment, Vol. 10, No. 2, 1995, pp. 121-131.
9. Davenport, T.H., 'Why Reengineering failed; the fad that forgot people', Fast Company, Vol. 1, No. 1, 1995, pp. 70-74.
10. Davenport, T.H., Process Innovation; Reengineering Work through Information Technology, Harvard Business School Press, Boston, Massachusetts, 1993.
11. Dedene G. & M. Snoeck, 'M.E.R.O.DE: a Model-driven Entity-Relationship Object-oriented Development method', ACM SIGSOFT Software Engineering notes, Vol. 13, No. 3, 1994, pp. 51-61.
12. Drew S., 'BPR in Financial Services: Factors for Success', Long Range Planning, Vol. 27, No. 5, 1994, pp. 25-41.
13. Grey C. & N. Mitev, 'Reengineering organizations: a critical appraisal', Personnel Review, Vol. 24, No. 1, 1995, pp. 6-18.
14. Grover V., Teng JTC & KD Fiedler, 'Information Technology Enabled Business Process Reengineering: An Integrated Planning Framework', Omega, Vol. 21, No. 4, pp. 433-447, 1993.
15. Hall G., Rosenthal J. & J. Wade, 'How to make reengineering really work', Harvard Business Review, Novem-

ber-December 1993, pp. 119-131.

16. Hammer M. & J. Champy, Reengineering the Corporation: a manifesto for Business Revolution, New York, Harper Business, 1993.

17. Harmon P., 'Business Process Reengineering with Objects - Part II', Object-Oriented Strategies, Vol. 5, No. 1, 1995, pp. 1-13.

18. Henderson J.C. & N. Venkatraman, 'Strategic Alignment: Leveraging information technology for transforming organizations', IBM Systems Journal, Vol. 32, No. 1, 1993, pp. 4-16.

19. Holland D. & S. Kumar, 'Getting Past the Obstacles to Successful Reengineering', Business Horizons, May-June 1995, pp. 79-85.

20. Huizing A., Koster E. & W. Bouman, 'Balance in Business Reengineering: an empirical study on and performance', PrimaVera Working Paper Series, University of Amsterdam, May 1997.

21. Johnson L. & M. Stergiou, 'The Necessary Architecture of Self-Regulating Teams', Proceedings of the ME-SELA '97 Conference, 1997, pp. 93-98.

22. Khalil A.E.M., 'Implications for the Role of Information Systems in a Business Process Reengineering Environment', Information Resources Management Journal, Winter 1997, pp. 36-43.

23. Kuhn T.S., The Structure of Scientific Revolutions, University of Chicago Press, Chicago, 1970.

24. Lyytinen, K., 'A Taxonomic Perspective of IS Development', in Critical Issues in IS Research, Boland, R. J., and Hirschheim, R.A., (eds) Wiley, 1987

25. Lohse G.L., Min D. & J.R. Olsen, 'Cognitive evaluation of system representation diagrams', Information & Management, Vol. 29, 1995, pp. 79-94.

26. Martinez E.V., 'Successful Reengineering Demands IS/Business Partnerships', Sloan Management Review, Summer 1995, pp. 51-60.

27. McGrath G.R. & I.C. MacMillan, 'Discovery-driven Planning', Harvard Business Review, July-August 1995, pp. 44-54.

28. Pacanowsky M., 'Team Tools for Wicked Problems', Organizational Dynamics, 1994

29. Peppard J., 'Broadening Visions of Business Process Reengineering', Omega, Vol. 24, No. 3, 1996, pp. 255-270.

30. Petrozzo D.P. & J.C. Stepper, Successful Reengineering, New York, Van Nostrand Reinhold, 1994.

31. Schnitt D.L., 'Reengineering the Organization using Information Technology', Journal of Systems Management, January 1993, pp. 14-20,41,42.

32. Senge P., The Fifth Discipline; the art and practice of the learning organization, New York, Doubleday, 1990.

33. Stoddard, D., Jarvenpaa S. & M. Littlejohn, 'The reality of Business Reengineering: Pacific Bell's Centrex Provisioning Process', California Management Review, Vol. 38, No. 3, Spring 1996, pp. 57-76.

34. Taylor J.A. & H. Williams, 'The transformation game: IS and process innovation in organizations', New Technology, Work & Employment, Vol. 9, No. 1, 1994, pp. 54-65.

35. Turner I., 'How to reengineer Successfully I', Manager Update, Vol. 5, No. , Winter 1994, pp.

36. Turner I., 'How to reengineer Successfully II', Manager Update, Vol. 6, No. 3, Spring 1995, pp. 1-7.

37. Vanhoenacker J., Bryant A. & G. Dedene, "Rethinking BPR Methodologies; an alternative framework", Proceedings of the BPR'97 Europe Conference, London, June 1997.

38. Vanhoenacker J., Bryant A. & G. Dedene, "The BPR Holon; a framework for (re)orienting methodological developments for BPR", Proceedings of the Fifth World Conference on Systemics, Cybernetics and Informatics (SCI'97), Caracas, Venezuela, July 1997.

39. Verhelst M., Objectgerichte systeemontwikkeling; een praktische aanpak met JSD en M.E.R.O.DE, Deventer, Kluwer, 1992 (in Dutch).

40. Willmott H., 'The odd couple?: reengineering business processes; managing human relations', New Technology, Work and Employment, Vol. 10, No. 2, 1995, pp. 89-98.

41. Zachman J.A., 'A Framework for Information Systems Architecture', IBM Systems Journal, Vol. 26, No. 3, 1987, pp. 276-292.

ENDNOTES

1 We have adopted the M.E.R.O.DE. methodology to structure our meta-modelling effort [11, 39].

2 cf. « why do we do what we do at all ? »

3 As an illustration, we could conceive the role of a policeman as a person x (actor) that has a thorough knowledge of traffic rules (skill) in order to intervene successfully at the site of a car accident (activity).

4 As an example, we could refer to the SPICE model as an ISO 9000 compliant and generic process model for the software development industry.

User Satisfaction as a Measure of the Success of Information Technology Applications in Small Business

Stephen Burgess

Victoria University of Technology, Department of Information Systems, Footscray Campus, PO Box 14428, MCMC Melbourne, Victoria, Australia, 8001

Telephone: 61 3 9688 4353 Facsimile: 61 3 9688 5024, Email: Stephen.Burgess@vu.edu.au

ABSTRACT

This paper examines the concept of using measures of user satisfaction as a means to determine the success of information technology (IT) in small businesses. Current (cost saving) uses and potential (strategic) uses of information technology in small business are reviewed. This leads to a discussion of the methods used to evaluate the success of such uses of IT. User satisfaction is one of the more common measurement methods used. Interpretation of this type of success measure needs to be balanced with the understanding that expectations relating to what IT can do for the business may differ amongst different users and different businesses. A study of 134 Australian small businesses with computers examined user satisfaction of IT application performance. Respondents were generally satisfied with the performance of their IT applications. The least satisfied industry area was 'Professionals', which may reflect that their expectations of IT performance were higher than those of other industry areas, rather than a 'lesser' performance of IT applications in that area.

Software applications were divided into two categories, office 'suite' software and specialised applications. Both categories reported a better success rating in the business areas that the applications were most frequently used in. This may indicate that the success rating for the software applications improves when they are used in areas of the business that are more appropriate for that particular application. Conversely, it also indicates that there may be areas of the business that applications are being used in that are not as suited to the use of that application.

INTRODUCTION

There are a number of methods that have been used to measure the success of information technology (IT) in small businesses. This paper concentrates upon one of those methods, measures of user satisfaction. Results of a study of user satisfaction related to information technology applications in Australian small businesses are reported and analysed.

DEFINITIONS

Small Business - Small Business can be defined as a business which is independently owned and managed and which is closely controlled by the owner/managers who also contribute most of the operating capital. Typically small businesses in the non-manufacturing sector employ less than 20 people and in the manufacturing sector less than 100 people, though this is not a strict definition (Australian Bureau of Statistics, 1990).

Micro Business - Any small business with one to five employees can be classed as a micro business.

THE USE OF IT IN SMALL BUSINESS

There are a number of key differences in the use of information technology between small and larger businesses (Doukidis, Smithson and Lybereas, 1994; Naylor and Williams, 1994; Bergeron and Raymond, 1992; Palvia, 1996):

• Small businesses generally have fewer resources available to devote to IT projects.
• Small businesses generally offer a limited number of products or services, often to a very specific market.
• Small businesses have very little control over forces that are external to the organisation, which means that they face greater uncertainty.
• Small businesses generally do not have their own separate IT department.
• Small businesses are, however, more flexible and therefore able to more easily reorganise their business around IT.
• Small businesses generally have less formalised planning and control procedures. In many cases the owner/man-

ager does not have the time, the resources or the expertise necessary for such tasks. This means that formal IT project evaluation (such as the use of internal rate of return or discounted cash flow analysis) and review procedures are seldom used.

Current IT Applications

This section examines the types of applications that small businesses use on their computer systems.

IT can be used to assist the organisation in a number of ways. Traditionally, IT has been used in small businesses to save costs or improve efficiencies by improving the execution of core business tasks (Alter, 1993). Examples of these traditional uses of IT in small business are (Baker, 1987; Garsombke and Garsombke, 1989; Kirby and Turner, 1993; Soh and Leow, 1994):
• accounts payable
• payroll
• account receivable
• financial statements/ general ledger
• stock ordering/purchasing systems.
• general administration
• sales and marketing

As well as this, small businesses make use of 'office' applications such as word processing, spreadsheets and database packages (Burgess, 1998).

Potential 'Strategic' Use of IT

Another way of using IT to assist the organisation is by improving products or services (Alter). The use of IT for strategic advantage occurs where an organisation plans and implements IT projects that aim to achieve more than just the cutting of costs. These strategic IT projects are intended to:
• Add value to products or services to make them more attractive to the buyer by using strategies such as being the low cost producer, producing a differentiated product or filling a specialised market (Porter and Millar, 1985).
• Assist organisational growth/ establishment of alliances with other organisations (Frenzel, 1992).

This section examines the strategic use of IT use in small business. A number of studies of computerised small businesses (Garsombke and Garsombke; Holzinger and Hotch) identified some of the benefits of computerisation as:
• being able to respond to customers
• having control over operating costs
• being able to effectively manage resources
• increase in production output
• increase in profit margin
• increase in sales
• reduced lead times
• increase in return on investment
• improved material flow
• reduced throughput time
• increase in market share.

This list shows that the potential benefits of information technology to small businesses go far beyond the mere saving of costs.

In many cases the potential strategic use of IT in small business is limited or not understood. There is, however, a realisation amongst small businesses that there must be a more proactive focus towards the use of IT than in the past (Garsombke and Garsombke). Much more can be done to improve the use of IT by small businesses in this area:
• Small business leaders often " wait and see then react" and are usually are left behind. (Garsombke and Garsombke).
• Some businesses make relatively little use of IT and this is mainly tactical or operational in nature, whereas others truly lack a strategic approach to their utilisation of IT (Kench and Evans,1991).
• "Microcomputer technology can be adopted to great advantage by many small businesses, but visions as to how it can and should be used have been too limited" (Lincoln and Warberg, 1987, p.9).
• Strong potential exists at the operational level, but also at the administrative and strategic levels for small businesses. (Bergeron and Raymond).

An examination of the applications used by small businesses (refer previous section) shows that although some small businesses do use IT for strategic purposes, they mainly concentrate upon improving the execution of core business tasks. This notion is supported by a number of studies world-wide (Naylor and Williams). This could be because the adoption of IT in small businesses is often a reaction to pressure from suppliers and/or customers, rather than a proactive strategy designed to improve the firm's strategic position (Lebre La).

SUCCESS FACTORS

A number of factors have been identified as being important in the successful implementation of Information Technology (IT) in small business. Although not a direct focus of this paper, it seems appropriate to list some of these factors as drivers for the successful implementation of IT (and subsequent measurement of the level of success). These factors are (Swartz and Walsh, 1996; Naylor and Williams, 1994; Zinatelli et al, 1996; Yap and Thong, 1997):

- Factors relating to involvement of personnel
- Involvement of Owner/Managers in the implementation of IT
- Involvement of end-users in development and installation
- Training of users
- Factors relating to the applications chosen for computerisation
- The use of disciplined planning methodologies in setting up applications
- The number of analytical/strategic (versus transactional) applications being run
- Factors relating to levels of IT expertise
- The level of IT expertise within the organisation
- The role of the external environment (especially consultants and vendors)

MEASURING IT SUCCESS IN SMALL BUSINESSES

The success of IT implementations relate to the extent to which the system contributes to achieving organisational goals (Yap and Thong). There have typically been three methods used to evaluate the success of IT systems in small businesses. These are (Naylor and Williams; Zinatelli et al):

- Measures of system usage
- Impact upon organisational performance
- Measures of user satisfaction.

System usage is often measured using data automatically collected from the system. For instance, this may be the number of record updates, reports being requested and so forth. The impact of IT upon organisational performance is difficult to assess, as so many other factors can directly or indirectly effect organisational performance (Naylor and Williams).

Another way determine the level of IT success is to measure small business user satisfaction with information technology. Such measures of user satisfaction have one major problem - they are linked with user expectations (Naylor and Williams). For instance, an owner/manager understanding the strategic benefits that IT can provide may be less satisfied with a simple transactional system than an owner/manager who is unaware of these strategic benefits. This is despite the possibility that they be reviewing systems that perform in a similar manner.

The study results reported in this paper (which relate to different ways of measuring user satisfaction) should be interpreted in this light.

The Study

A study was conducted under the auspices of Small Business Victoria (a Victorian State Government department) in March/April 1997. The study consisted of a survey sent to a number of small businesses. The survey method was chosen because of the investigative nature of the project, the geographic flexibility that the method provides and the relatively low cost (in time and money) when compared with personal interviews (Zikmund, 1991).

Two versions of the survey were mailed out to each potential respondent. The first version was the traditional paper-based survey. The second version was a disk-based version of the survey that worked in the Windows/MS DOS environment, prepared using the programming language Delphi. The questions were identical in the paper and disk versions of the survey. The disk version was mailed out in the hope that the novelty value of receiving the disk might encourage an increased response rate.

A number of questions were asked in the following categories, so that some analysis may be carried out over a number of different areas:

- Industry
- Region
- Premises
- Number of Employees
- Success (see Study Categories)

There was only one question that investigated the 'non' use of computers. Potential respondents that fitted this category were requested to tick one box indicating that they did not use computers. This was to encourage non-users of computers to respond as well.

Survey: First Mailout

The intention was to survey approximately 500 Victorian small businesses.

Small Business Victoria (SBV) Sample

Between 2 August 1996 and 26 February 1997 there were 33,080 recorded enquiries made at SBV offices. Of these, 536 were made by existing businesses that had supplied their complete addresses. Each second entry was selected from this list. After the removal of duplicate entries, a total of 258 small businesses were sent surveys. SBV records showed that some 70% of these small businesses were micro businesses (one to five employees).

Dun and Bradstreet (D&B) Sample

Due to the large percentage of micro businesses in the SBV sample, another sample of small businesses was identified. This was taken from a list commissioned from Dun and Bradstreet by the Small Business Research Unit at Victoria University of Technology of Australian small businesses with one to nineteen employees. From this list of 2517 firms, the third entry was selected, followed by each fifth entry after that. To reduce the sample to the desired size, only Victorian, New South Wales and Australian Capital Territory firms were then extracted. This amounted to 233 firms in total.

Note:
1. After including the Dun and Bradstreet sample, the breakdown between micro (56%) and other small businesses (44%) was more even.
2. Small businesses were given the option to reply anonymously. In these cases it was impossible to determine which sample they were included in.
3. After receipt of some returns, it was obvious that they could no longer be classified as small businesses according to the definition used. It was decided to exclude these from the overall return percentages, even though they did respond to the initial mailout.

Response to first mailout

Table 1. Response to First Mailout.				
Sample Details	**SBV**	**D&B**	**Anon.**	**Total**
Initial sample	260	233		493
Incorrect address/ firm no longer in business	8	24		32
Not a small business	3	6		9
Actual sample	**249**	**203**		**452**
Did not wish to participate	2	1		3
Did not use computers	27	19	1	47
Filled out Disk Survey	22	18		40
Filled out Paper Survey	35	27	1	63
Total Filled out	**57**	**45**	**1**	**103**
Returned Total	**86**	**65**	**2**	**153**
Returned Percentage	**35%**	**32%**		**34%**

Survey: Second Mailout

The follow up was sent out in early April (3/4/97) to all non-respondent organisations (a total of 323). This was broken up into 178 surveys sent to potential respondents on the SBV list and 145 to organisations on the Dun and Bradstreet list. This turned out to be more organisations than were required because some returns were received from the initial mailout after the follow up was sent out.

Only the paper survey was sent out in the follow up mailout.

Table 2. Response after Second Mailout.				
Sample Details	**SBV**	**D&B**	**Anon.**	**Total**
Actual sample	**249**	**203**		**452**
Did not wish to participate	2	1		3
Did not use computers	44	25	1	70
Filled out Disk Survey	22	18		40
Filled out Paper Survey	52	41	1	94
Total Filled out	**74**	**59**	**1**	**134**
Returned Total	**120**	**85**	**2**	**207**
Returned Percentage	**48%**	**42%**		**46%**

This return rate is considered to be excellent, given the time constraints that are placed on small businesses.

Of the 204 respondents, 134 were computer users. This equates to a percentage of 66%.

A Comment on Data Analysis

The following analysis relies upon the direct comparison of means, which are calculated from a sample (as described above), and various subsets of that sample. It is difficult to apply a particular statistical test on such samples as they do not each have the same number of observations (therefore, there are no ordered pairs of observations to be analysed). As well, the sample and sub-samples are all decidedly non-normal in distribution (in fact, they are quite skewed), therefore the less specific non-parametric tests would have to be applied anyway. Because of these reasons, the decision was made to directly compare the means of the samples and sub-samples alone, and to observe the sub-samples that fall 'above' or 'below' the average (mean) for the particular sample being observed.

Success Ratings

Australian small businesses in the study were requested to rate the success of their software applications. The possible rating was from 1 (complete success) to 5 (complete failure). This occurred across two major categories of software, office software (word processing, spreadsheet, database and presentation/ graphics packages) and specific software (twenty separate specific software applications that were identified).

Respondents were requested to indicate the success rating for each area of the business that the software was used in. The areas identified were:
• Accounting
• Administration (described as 'Admin' in the following tables)
• Inventory/ Stock Control (Inventory)
• Marketing
• Operations/ Production (Production)
• Personnel/ Human Resource Management (Personnel)
• Planning
• Purchasing
• Research and Development (R&D)
• Other.

Respondents were also requested to indicate their industry. These industries were later placed into industry categories. These categories were:
• Building/ Construction (Building)
• Finance/ Property/ Business Services (Finance/ Property)
• Manufacturing
• Professional
• Recreation/ Personal/ Other Services (Recreation)
• Wholesale/ Retail
• Other.

The following table represents the average rating for each software category.

Table 3: Average Success Ratings for Small Business Applications.

Type of Software	Average Rating
Office Software	1.92
Specific Software	1.94
Overall	1.93

These results indicate that, at a general level, respondents were generally satisfied with the performance of their IT applications (a response of '2' was described in the scale as 'adequate performance'). This result is consistent with a number of other small business studies (Fink, 1997; Zinatelli et al).

The following table represents software success levels indicated across business area. The shaded areas indicate where the average for the particular business area is less then the overall average (that is, considered to perform better) for the particular software type.

The ratings were most successful for software used in the accounting, administration and operations/ production areas of the business.

There is some evidence to support the theory that there may be differences in levels of satisfaction related to the use of IT across industries (Harrison et al, 1997). The following table represents software success levels indicated across industry category. The shaded areas indicate where the average for the particular industry

Table 4: Average Success Ratings for Small Business Applications, by Business Area.

Industry Area	Office Software Rating	Specific Software Rating
Accounting	1.89	1.79
Admin	1.67	1.77
Inventory	2.25	2.01
Marketing	1.81	2.06
Production	1.81	1.90
Personnel	2.05	2.03
Planning	1.92	1.96
Purchasing	2.06	2.11
R&D	2.27	2.19
Other	2.26	2.04

area is less then the overall average (performs better) for the particular software type.

The ratings were most successful for software used in the Finance/ Property/ Business Services and Manufacturing industry categories.

Notice the average ratings in the Professional industry area for both Office and Specific software. This industry area registered the worst success rating in both categories. This may reflect one of the problems mentioned earlier with the use of measures of satisfaction as a means of determining the success of IT in small business. If the expectations of owner/managers and/or employees in the various industry categories are different, then perhaps the levels of success ratings cannot accurately be compared across industry categories.

Table 5: Average Success Ratings for Small Business Applications, by Industry Category.

Industry Category	Office Software Rating	Specific Software Rating
Building	1.64	1.99
Finance/ Property	1.60	1.52
Manufacturing	1.66	1.62
Professional	2.28	2.60
Recreation	2.03	1.96
Wholesale/ Retail	2.17	2.04
Other	1.79	2.17

The success ratings will now be examined for the two major software categories that have been identified, office software and specific software.

Office Software

The following table shows the reported overall usage (and average success rating) reported by respondents for each office software application.

Table 6: Average Success Ratings for Office Applications

Office Application	Usage (%)	Rating
Word Processing	87	1.86
Spreadsheet	71	1.83
Database	57	2.02
Graphics	38	2.20

These initial results suggest the possibility that the more frequently used packages are the most successful.

The following table shows some further detail relating to these office packages. The figures shown in the previous table are repeated. In addition, usage levels are shown for primary business area and industry area usage. In this instance, 'primary' means the areas that are the two most frequent users of the particular software application. The shaded areas indicate where the success rating for the business area and/or industry category that is the most frequent user of the software is less than the average rating for the software.

Table 7: Average Success Ratings for Office Applications, by Business Area and Industry Category Primary Users.

Specific Application	Usage (%)	Rating	Primary business areas of usage			Primary industry category usage		
				Usage (%)	Rating		Usage (%)	Rating
Word Processing	87	1.86	Admin	85	1.61	Professional	100	1.93
			Marketing	65	1.68	Recreation	100	2.05
Spreadsheet	71	1.83	Accounting	78	1.74	Professional	93	2.25
			Admin	68	1.61	Building	79	1.82
Database	57	2.02	Admin	64	1.73	Finance/ Property	80	2.29
			Marketing	47	1.97	Other	70	2.10
Graphics	38	2.20	Marketing	55	1.82	Other	55	1.87
			Admin	35	2.06	Finance/ Property	40	2.11
						Wholesale/ Retail	40	2.48

Notice that, for each application, there has been a better success rating reported for the primary area that the application is used in. This is not the case for industry area. This may indicate that the success rating for the software application improves when it is used in areas of the business that are more appropriate for that particular application. This premise will be further examined in the next section, which examines specific software applications.

Specific Software

The following table shows the reported overall usage (and average success rating) reported by respondents for each specific application.

Table 8: Average Success Ratings for Specific Applications

Specific Application	Usage (%)	Rating
Accounting	78	1.84
Documents/ Records Management	45	1.80
Internet Browser	34	2.35
Payroll/ HRM	34	1.61
Desktop Publishing	31	1.86
Electronic Mail	28	2.33
Statistics	26	1.88
Electronic Diaries	22	1.94
Financial Management	20	1.87
Tracking	19	2.15
Scheduling	15	1.67
Drafting/ Design	13	1.96
Point of Sale	12	1.95
Internet Home Page	12	3.12
Operate Machinery	10	2.00
Project Management	10	1.47
Automating Decisions	9	1.55
Bookings	8	1.91
Monitoring	6	1.94
Intranet	3	1.25

It is interesting to note that there is little evidence in the success ratings for specific software applications to indicate that the more frequently used packages are the most successful.

The following table shows further detail, relating to the most frequently used specific applications. These applications represent those were used in at least 30 organisations, this being the number of observations which can arbitrarily be considered as a sufficiently large sample (Sincich, 1996).

Usage levels are shown for primary business area and industry area usage. The shaded areas indicate where the success rating for the area that is the most frequent user of the software is less than the average rating for the software.

The results here support the claims made in the previous section. In six out of seven applications, there has been a better success rating reported for the primary area that the application is used in. This only occurred in three out of seven applications for industry area. This supports the notion that the success

Table 9: Average Success Ratings for Specific Applications, by Business Area and Industry Category Primary Users.

Specific Application	Usage (%)	Rating	Primary areas of usage			Primary industry usage		
				Usage (%)	Rating		Usage (%)	Rating
Accounting	78	1.84	Accounting	94	1.66	Manufacturing	88	1.66
			Admin	45	1.70	Professional	87	2.39
Documents/ Records Management	45	1.80	Admin	63	1.79	Other	60	1.96
			Accounting	40	1.71	Wholesale/Retail	55	1.96
Internet Browser	34	2.35	R&D	54	2.08	Professional	67	2.61
			Marketing	50	2.04	Recreation	41	2.30
Payroll/ HRM	34	1.61	Accounting	59	1.59	Manufacturing	67	1.50
			Admin	52	1.71	Wholesale/Retail	45	1.94
Desktop Publishing	31	1.86	Marketing	71	1.90	Other	50	1.50
			Operations	32	1.69	Wholesale/Retail	45	1.94
Electronic Mail	28	2.33	Admin	70	1.88	Professional	47	2.71
			Marketing	38	2.43	Finance/Property	40	1.25
Statistics	26	1.88	Admin	54	1.58	Professional	33	2.07
			Accounting	46	1.69	Recreation	29	1.82
			Planning	46	1.81			

rating for the software application improves when it is used in areas of the business that are more appropriate for that particular application.

CONCLUSION

User satisfaction is one of the common methods used to measure the success of IT in small businesses. Interpretation of this type of success measure needs to be balanced with the understanding that expectations relating to what IT can do for the business may differ amongst different users and different businesses. A study of 134 Australian small businesses with computers examined user satisfaction of IT application performance. Respondents were generally satisfied with the performance of their IT applications. The least satisfied industry area was Professionals. This may reflect that their expectations of IT performance were higher than those of other industry areas, rather than a 'lesser' performance of IT applications in that area.

There was strong indication that software applications reported a better success rating in the primary business areas, or business areas that the applications were most frequently used in. This may indicate that the success rating for the software applications improves when they are used in areas of the business that are more appropriate for that particular application. Conversely, it also indicates that there may be areas of the business that applications are being used in that are not as suited to the use of that application.

REFERENCES

Alter, Steven Information Systems: A Management Perspective, 2nd. Edition, Benjamin/Cummings, California, 1996.

Australian Bureau of Statistics, Small Business in Australia, Australian Government Publishing Service, Canberra, 1990.

Baker, Dr.William H, Journal of Systems Management: Status of information Management in Small Businesses, April 1987

Bergeron,F. and Raymond,L.,'Planning of Information Systems to Gain a Competitive Edge' Journal of Small Business Management, January 1992, pp.21-26

Burgess, Stephen, 'Information Technology in Small Business in Australia: A Summary of Recent Studies', United States Association for Small Business and Entrepreneurship 12th. Annual Conference Proceedings, Northern Illinois University, Clearwater, January 1998, pp.283-291.

Doukidis G.I., Smithson Steve, and Lybereas, Takis 'Trends in Information Technology in Small Businesses', Journal of End User Computing, Vol.6, No.4, Fall 1994, pp.15-25.

Fink, Dieter. 'Information Systems Success in Small and Medium Enterprises: An Evaluation by Australian Public Accountants, Australian Journal of Information Systems, Vol.4 No.1, September 1997.

Fuller, Ted. 'Fulfilling IT Needs in Small Business; A Recursive Learning Model', International Small Business Journal, Vol.14, No.4, July-Sept 1996, pp.25-45

Garsombke,W and Garsombke,D.J. 'Strategic Implications Facing Small Manufacturers: The Linkage Between Robotization, Computerization, Automation and Performance', Journal of Small Business Management, Oct 1989, pp.34-44.

Harrison, David A., Mykytyn, Peter P. Jnr., Riemenschneider, Cynthia K., 'Executive Decisions about Adoption of Information Technology in Small Business: Theory and Empirical Tests', Information Systems Research, Vol. 8 No.2, June 1997, pp.171-195.

Holzinger, Albert G, and Hotch, Ripley. 'Small-Business Computing - Small Firms' Usage Patterns', Nation's Business, August 1993, pp.39-42.

Kench,R and Evans,M., 'IT: The Information Technology Dichotomy', Marketing Intelligence and Planning, Vol. 9 No 5, 1991, pp.16-22.

Kirby, D.A. and Turner, Martin, J.S. 'IT and the Small Retail Business', International Journal of Retail and Distribution Management, Vol.21, No.7, 1993, pp.20-27.

Lebre La, R.R. 'IT Diffusion in Small and Medium-Sized Enterprises: Elements for Policy Definition', Information Technology for Development, Vol.7, No.4, 1996, pp. 169-181.

Lincoln,D.J. and Warberg,W.B., Journal of Small Business: The Role of Microcomputers in small business marketing, April 1985

Naylor, J.B. and Williams, J. 'The Successful Use of IT in SMEs on Merseyside', European Journal of Information Systems, Vol. 3, No. 1, 1994, pp. 48-56.

Palvia, P.C. 'A Model for Measuring Small Business User Satisfaction with Information Technology', Information & Management, No.31, 1996, pp. 151-163

Porter, Michael E. and Millar, Victor E. 'How Information Gives You Competitive Advantage', Harvard Business Review, Vol.63, No.4, July-August 1985, pp.149-160

Sincich, Terry. Business Statistics by Example, 5th. Ed., Prentice-Hall, New Jersey, 1996.

Soh, Christina and Leow, Dolly 'The Use of Information Technology in Small Business: A Survey of Singapore Firms', Proceedings of the 5th. Endec World Conference on Entrepreneurship, Nanyang Technological University, Singapore, 1994, pp.350-359.

Swartz, Dr. Ethne and Walsh, Dr. Vivien, 1996, 'Understanding the Process of Information Management in Small Firms: Implications for Government Policy', 19th. ISBA National Conference Proceedings, Birmingham, pp. 387-399.

Yap, Chee-Sing and Thong, James Y.L. 'Programme Evaluation of a Government Information Technology Programme for Small Businesses', Journal of Information Technology, No.12, 1997, pp.107-120.

Zikmund, William G, Business Research Methods, 3rd.Edition, The Dryden Press, USA, 1991

Zinatelli, N, Cragg, PB, and Cavaye, ALM. 'End User Computing Sophistication and Success in Small Firms', European Journal of Information Systems, No.5, 1996, pp. 172-181.

The Societal Impact of the World Wide Web - The real challenge for the 21st Century.

Janice M Burn

School of MIS, Edith Cowan University, Churchlands Campus, Perth, W.A., Australia 6018

Tel: 618 9273 8718, Fax: 618 9273 8332, E-Mail: j.burn@cowan.edu.au

ABSTRACT

This paper addresses the impact of Information Technology (IT) and the World Wide Web (WWW) on the 21st Century and the challenges which we will face as responsible members of a dynamically changing society. Reviewing the spread of potentially alienating technology, the paper highlights the implications for change with reference to the "haves" and the "have-nots"- developing societies, economically disadvantaged groups, women and children. The author argues that insufficient attention is given to the organisational, sociological and cultural factors which may inhibit an effective transformation to an Information Society and contends that failure to acknowledge these issues and incorporate these into future IT developments may lead not to virtual reality but rather to virtual rape.

DEVELOPMENT OF THE INTERNET

Until the early 1980s the IT environment was a "mainframe" environment. Then, in the 1980s, it shifted radically to a desk-top environment and in the 1990s shifted again to a "network" architecture which includes client-server computing and open networks like the Internet. While it is difficult to compare client-server implementation across countries the percentage of applications is rising rapidly and is expected to continue. This has to be examined at two levels: the rates of PC diffusion and connectivity. In terms of no. of corporate PCs per 100 white-collar workers, leading countries such as Norway, Switzerland and the US had more than 100, major Western European countries 60-80 and Japan only 24. As for PCs connected to LANs 64% of corporate PCs are on a network in the US but only 21% in Japan (Dataquest, 1995). Corporate cultures in Asia may be far less conducive to on-line management.

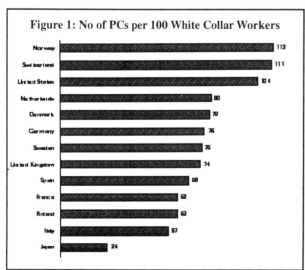

Figure 1: No of PCs per 100 White Collar Workers

The Internet now reaches into every part of the globe with the number of host computers connected to the Internet increasing from 3.2 million in July 1994 to 6.6 million in July 1995, 12.9 million in 1996, 16.1 million by January 1997 and 19.5 million by July 1997 (Network Wizards). This is more than a ten-fold increase since July 1993.

The 1995 estimates from the Internet society indicated that some 90 countries, just under 5 million machines and some 50 million users worldwide were connected to the Internet. (NBEET). The 1998 CommerceNet figures produced by Nielson suggest a world total population of Internet users as 120.54 million (although one must accept that these estimates are an inexact science). These figures tend to mesmerize but also to hide the real facts - that distribution worldwide is sadly skewed - the USA, Canada and Europe account for over 102 million of these users (CommerceNet, 10/16/98).

The West against the Rest?

In 1995, the world IT market as measured by the revenue of primary vendors was worth an estimated US$ 527.9 billion. Between 1987 and 1994, its growth rate averaged nearly twice that of GDP worldwide. It was particularly high in Asia climbing from 17.5% of world share to 20.9% of world share during that time. Nevertheless this

**Figure 2: No of Host Computers Connected to the Internet
1993 - 1997**

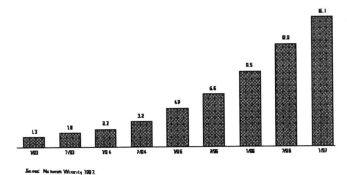

Source: Network Wizards 1997.

strong growth did little to redress the geo-graphical imbalance in the world IT market - markets outside Asia and the OECD area (ROW) accounted for only 4% of the world total. Table 1 shows examples of Worldwide IT markets and corresponding GDP figures. The IT Divide is still very large - China with a population of 1.2 billion people (more than 1/5th of the world population) accounts for only 0.6 of the IT market!

From a world population of 5.53 billion, ROW accounts for 82.6% of the total yet from a world GDP of US$25,223 billion, ROW accounts for only 19.2% (decreasing >2% over the last 7 years) and from a total IT market of US$ 455 billion, ROW accounts for only 8.4%.

The IT market has remained concentrated within the G7 countries at around 88% with the United States accounting for 46% of the market. Growth in hardware has been mainly driven by PCs and workstations with the price/performance ratio steadily decreasing. This has seen an increasing convergence of PCs and consumer electronics through joint development of hardware and specific software for use on the Internet. In terms of installed PC base the US was by far the world leader with 86.3 million units well ahead of Japan (19.1m), Germany (13.5M) and UK (10.9m). In the US this averages at 32.8 PCs per 100 inhabitants!

The technology gap is strikingly apparent in telephone usage where consumers in the United States make an average of **2170** calls per inhabitant annually, which converts into just under seven calls a day.

Table 1. Worldwide IT Market and GDP (selected figures)				
	1987	1994	IT Growth	GDP
North America	47.4	45.1	9.1	5.9
Japan	15.2	16.9	10.2	6.3
Europe	29.1	27.6	9.1	5.9
DAEs	1.7	2.8	7.6	16.7
China	0.3	0.6	22.6	10.0
India	0.2	0.3	20.0	2.3
Phillipines	0.0	0.1	25.5	9.0
Argentina	0.1	0.3	37.8	14.6
Venezuela	0.0	0.3	26.2	2.8
World	235 110	455 000	9.9	5.7

Figure 3 Share of OECD Member Countries in world population, GDP and IT market 1987 - 1994

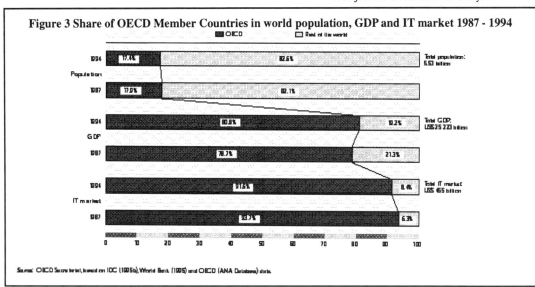

Source: OECD Secretariat, based on IDC (1995b), World Bank (1995) and OECD (ANA Database) data.

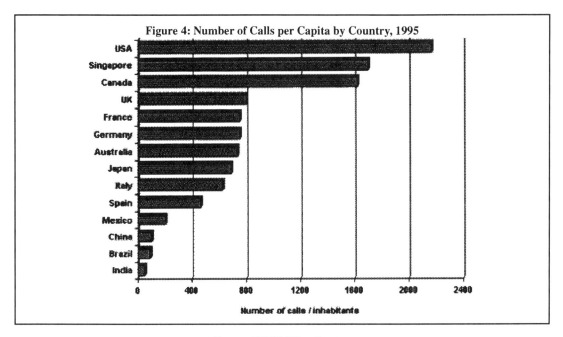

Figure 4: Number of Calls per Capita by Country, 1995

Source: ITU/MTI estimates

The difference between the United States and that of the Latin American and some of the Asian countries is even more striking. **The average American makes ten times as many calls as the average Mexican, 20 times as many calls as the average Chinese, and 40 times as many as the average Indian.** As the developing countries make greater inroads into extending their networks and their inhabitants succeed in integrating the telephone more into their daily lives, it is to be expected that their telephone usage will eventually start to catch up to that of the more developed countries.

The technology invasion has nevertheless offered developing countries amazing opportunities to leapfrog over stages of growth in their programs for industrialisation and advancement and yet the drive for informatisation can often occur only at the expense of other basic infrastructure needs which are regarded as norms for advanced societies.

China aims to enter the 21st Century as an information economy yet has an average GDP which is only 1/50th of the US; Argentina has a school life expectancy of less than 4 years compared to over 16 in Australia and India boasts a female adult illiteracy problem of 62.3%. The statistics are even more horrifying when comparisons are made with rural communities with only 7% of the rural population in China and 2% in Argentina, having access to sanitation.

	1995 US$ gdp pc	School life expectancy	Adult (F) illiteracy	Economic Rural Activity %	% access to sanitation
Table 2. Worldwide Indicators (selected figures from UN statistics 1995)					
USA	26037	15.8	3.1	59.9	*
Japan	41718	14.8	*	50.0	*
UK	18913	16.3	*	52.8	*
Australia	20046	16.2	*	48.1	*
China	582	*	27.3	72.9	7
India	365	*	62.3	*	14
Philippines	1093	11.0	5.7	49.0	67
Argentina	8055	3.8	3.8	41.3	2
Vietnam	270	*	8.8	74.1	15

These figures indicate ever widening gaps in the basic infrastructures required to become a fully developed civilization and will inevitably lead to significantly different degrees of cyberspace implementation.

LIFE IN CYBERSPACE

Cyberhomes?

Almost four out of ten homes in the US already have a personal computer and one in three of these has a modem enabling the computer and telephone to be connected. By the year 2000 at least half of all US homes will have two or more telecommunications lines. One reason is home-working, a factor in 37 million homes. Most home workers are self-employed but 8.4 million work at home for companies.

More than 500,000 people have already made telephone calls on the Internet, using microphones and loudspeakers installed as part of multimedia. An advantage over conventional phone is ability to share documents and pictures - worked on by both simultaneously. CU-SEE ME technology has revolutionised communications. The technology already exists for a PC user to be able to watch any channel from a choice of tens of thousands.

At present the median age of users is 32 years, 64% have college degrees and 25% have an income larger than $80,000. Half of Internet users have managerial or professional jobs and 31% are women. There are now more than a million web sites for them to visit.

IT household penetration rates worldwide is directly related to household income. In Australia (1996) the penetration varied from 9.5% (income below US$ 9,630) to 52% (income above US$ 42,222) with an average for all households of 29.5%. Other factors are:

• age - households where the head is between 35-44 and 45-54 years of age have the highest penetration linked to higher income levels and the presence of teenage children.
• education
• employment status and occupation - the existence of a home-based business is a significant motivation to acquire a home computer - 46% of such households in Australia had computers compared to 30% of all households and 20% of households without a business.
• location of households - in every state of Australia computers had penetrated a far greater proportion of households in capital cities than in rural areas. City households accounted for 72% of all home computers. In the Australian Capital territory (ACT) penetration is more than 12% above national average.

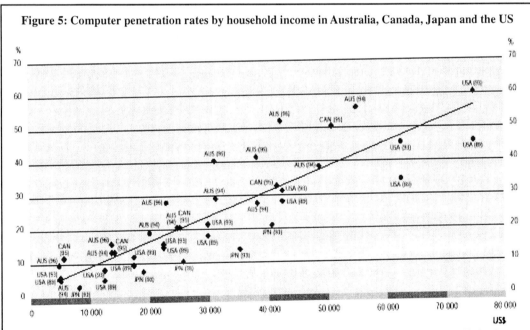

Figure 5: Computer penetration rates by household income in Australia, Canada, Japan and the US

Sources: Australia: Australian Bureau of Statistics (1994, 1996b) Household Use of Information Technology
Canada: Statistics Canada (1996b) Access to the Information Highway: Canadian Households
Japan: Economic Planning Agency in JEIDA (1995), PC White Paper
United States: US Bureau of the Census (1993b) Computer Use in the US

Cyberslums?

The sad truth is, however, that the groups that are the most disadvantaged in terms of computer and modem penetration are the most enthusiastic users of on-line services that facilitate economic betterment and empowerment.

Low-income, minority, young and less educated computer households in rural areas and central cities actively engage in searching ads for employment, taking educational classes and accessing government reports on-line. Somewhere societal priorities have gone wrong.

Falling Through The Net II - a 1997 survey of the Digital Divide in the US shows that whilst there is expanded information access there is a persisting "digital divide" which has actually increased since the last survey in 1994. The least connected are typically lower income groups, Blacks and Hispanics, but geographical locations (urban city centre and rural), age, education and household type are all factors leading to disadvantaged groups. The following are profiles of groups that are among the "least connected," according to the 1997 data:

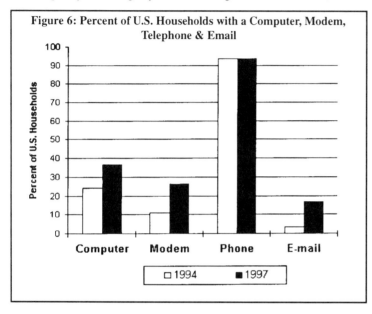

Figure 6: Percent of U.S. Households with a Computer, Modem, Telephone & Email

• **Rural Poor** - Those living in rural areas at the lowest income levels are among the least connected. Rural households earning less than $5,000 per year have the lowest telephone penetration rates (74.4%), followed by central cities (75.2%) and urban areas (76.8%). In 1994, by contrast central city poor were the least connected.

Rural households earning between $5,000-$10,000 have the lowest PC-ownership rates (7.9%) and on-line access rates (2.3%), followed by urban areas (10.5%, 4.4%) and central cities (11%, 4.6%).

• **Rural and Central City Minorities** - "Other non-Hispanic" households, including Native Americans, Asian Americans, and Eskimos, are least likely to have telephone service in rural areas (82.8%), particularly at low incomes (64.3%). Black and Hispanic households also have low telephone rates in rural areas (83.2% and 85%), especially at low incomes (73.6% and 72.2%). As in 1994, Blacks have the lowest PC-ownership rates in rural areas (14.9%), followed by Blacks and Hispanics in central cities (17.1% and 16.2%, respectively). On-line access is also the lowest for Black households in rural areas (5.5%) and central cities (5.8%), followed by Hispanic households in central cities (7.0%) and rural areas (7.3%).

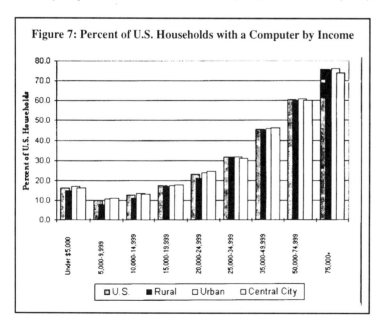

Figure 7: Percent of U.S. Households with a Computer by Income

• **Young Households** — Young households (below age 25) also appear to be particularly burdened. Young, rural, low-income households have telephone penetration rates of only 65.4%, and only 15.5% of these households are likely to own a PC. Similarly, young households with children are also less likely to have phones or PCs: those in central cities have the lowest rates (73.4% for phones, 13.3% for PCs), followed by urban (76% for phones, 14.5% for PCs) and rural locales (79.6% for phones, 21.2% for PCs).

• **Female-headed Households** - Single-parent, female households also lag significantly behind the national average. They trail the telephone rate for married couples with children by ten per-

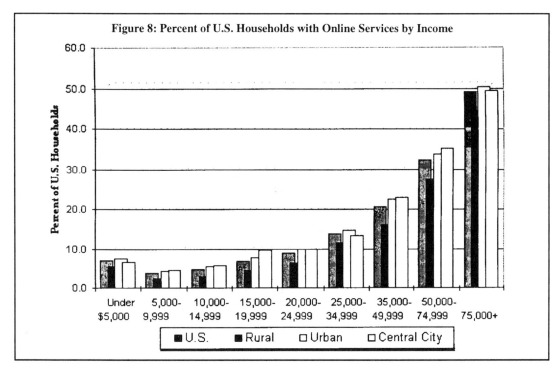

Figure 8: Percent of U.S. Households with Online Services by Income

centage points (86.3% versus 96%). They are also significantly less likely than dual-parent households to have a PC (25% versus 57.2%) or to have on-line access (9.2% versus 29.4%). Female-headed households in central cities are particularly unlikely to own PCs or have on-line access (20.2%, 6.4%), compared to dual-parent households (52%, 27.3%) or even male-headed households (28%, 11.2%) in the same areas.

In Australia, the picture is very similar. The report "Women's Access to Online Services" produced by the Office of the Status of Women in December 1996 states "The Governments' focus on commerce has meant that the social consequences of becoming an 'information society' have been largely ignored. This may have been exacerbated by the apparent lack of women in decision-making positions in industry and relevant departments." The most recent data from ABS estimated 262,000 users who indicated use of the Internet at home with about 178,000 men and 84,000 women (68%: 32%). Women's representation amongst email users was even lower with only 26%. Women over the age of 55 were extremely poorly represented. However, perhaps a more important issue is "What access opportunities are open to women who don't have a computer and modem at home?" AGB McNair estimate that in the region of 13% of Australian women over the age of 14 have ever accessed the Internet!

There are astonishing exceptions to the rule - one example is Women Farmers. The DSS CRP case studies found that women farmers "were the enthusiasts, the main drivers, while their husbands, if they had no prior computer experience, were reluctant to touch the CIN (Community Information Network). Weather information, farming practices, health and education were all foci but further email was used to develop support networks, thereby reducing social and cultural isolation. Strangely it is not only those women typically identified as culturally isolated (aboriginal, non-English speaking, remote communities such as mining) but also professionally educated women whose need for professional support, continuing education and contact with like-minded peers is not adequately met.

Increasingly, education, health, legal services and social communications are moving to computer based technology. The success of the Ipswich Global Infolinks project "SeniorNet" is another startling example. One resident said "I personally find the Internet to be a fascinating medium where any information seems available - - which opens up a whole new world for elderly people and keeps the mind active - - -there is no age limit to having a good time surfing the net - - -" (des Artes, 1996).

Cyberwork

The Internet is used widely to trade and persuade. More than two and a half million people have already bought goods and services using their computers. The value of the trade in 1996 was around $1 billion, with growth expected to reach anywhere between $7 billion and $170 billion a year by early in the next century. Music sales are popular. One site sells 25,000 CDs every day, allowing people to hear samples before they order. The world's busiest site is a CD site, able to send out a staggering 100 megabits every second - that is the equivalent of 6,000 volumes of Encyclopedia Brittannica every minute.

Magazines are also picking up large readerships. Just a few months after launch, the electronic EMAP magazine collection was receiving 350,000 "hits" or different access requests every week. In the first four months of 1996 alone the number of major sites (domains) on the web rose from 170,000 to 300,000. This is a vast investment, with each site costing up to $1 million.

In mid-1993, the ANN group, one of the pioneers of electronic marketing, announced the development of the Industry.Net Online Marketplace to serve the needs of buyers and specifiers of products and services purchased and specified by industry professionals. By late 1994, the Industry.Net Online Marketplace had grown to include hundreds of companies who began using it to announce new products, provide customer support information and, in general, promote their companies through electronic marketing programs. The Wall Street Journal reported, "Industry.Net has emerged as perhaps the most popular network for the manufacturing sector..." Today, the Industry.Net Online Marketplace is the largest industry-focused Web site on the Internet, including over 10,000 new products (1,000 more are added every month), company catalogs, seminar schedules and other marketing materials from over 450 of the industry's leading companies. Industry.Net usership has grown to over 350,000 and expects over 1 million users in 1995.

Users are now visiting the Industry.Net Online Marketplace by the thousands. Current visits by qualified buyers and specifiers are now running at over 40,000 per month and it's expected to have traffic exceeding 1 million buyers and specifiers this year. At the click of their mouse, users can instantly see all the new products of a given type announced within the past 6 months (computers, valves, controls, machine tools, software, etc.) and instantly interact with the manufacturers. In addition, they can visit trade shows on-line and get information from exhibitors who are Industry.Net participating companies - all from their personal computers anywhere in the world. Along with the global nature of today's business, Industry.Net reports that 18% of the buyers and specifiers visiting its online marketplace are from foreign users located in over 26 countries throughout the world. In addition to including information directly in the Industry.Net Online Marketplace, companies can also create their own Web site in the Marketplace with a unique Internet address.

CyberBanking

From September 1994 to July 1996 the number of banks on the Internet grew from 20 to 1,178. By May 1997 the number was over 2000, growing at around 350 - 400 every quarter. A large survey of European banks has found that 56% of those with web-sites are planning to provide full on-line net banking by the end of 1997. Wells Fargo, is a typical success story in retail banking with over 200,000 net accounts in early 1997. From October 1996 to March 1997 the number of financial institutions offering full Internet transactions leapt from around 15 to over 70. Traditional banks are struggling to keep up with non-banking competitors who are intent on grabbing market share. Unlike traditional banks, they have no culture to fight and are able to move fast. The stampede onto the net is gathering pace with an explosion of alliances between banks, food retailers, insurance companies, software houses, media companies and Internet service providers.

The most dramatic changes are being seen not in retail banking but in share trading with discount brokers now offering unlimited trades for $12 or less. 1.5 million people are already selling and buying stock on their PCs, increasing at 100,000 a month.

Cyberbanking Market Growth

- 8 million European homes will receive broadband interactive services by 2000. Only 280,000 homes have these services now. Source: Datamonitor Inc
- The greatest take-up of electronic shopping channels by retailers will come from 1997-9. Most retailers outside traditional mail order expect 13% of their sales to be via home shopping within two years, rising to 26% in ten years.
- 70% of respondents expect to be receiving customer orders via the World Wide Web within two years. Source: "Electronic Shopping & the Retail Offer", a Cap Gemini survey of retail opinion across Europe.
- Between now and the year 2001, annual growth in use of online computer banking in the EU is expected to be 75%. - Datamonitor Report. Source: The European
- A study of 45 banks in Europe, the US, Asia and South Africa found that the low cost of telephone banking makes it likely that this channel will account for a third of banking transactions within a few years. Home banking should account for 12% of banking transactions by 2000.
- KPMG says the use of fees (home banking) in Australia is still at an embryonic stage and user-pays fees are being foisted on consumers 'fairly crudely', instead of being used to persuade customers to use cheaper delivery channels. Source: Australian Financial Review
- 73% say banking at home will take off. Source: Barclays Bank Study

- There will be 7.8 million PC banking customers in Europe by 2001.Source: Network Week
- 4 million use phone banking in the UK - 1997 Source: Reuter News Service

The Demise of Television?

Commercial television is entirely financed by brief adverts which fund long periods of high quality television. Television companies are independent of any advertiser, and sell space into programs they have already commissioned (with rare exceptions). However, on the internet the operation is becoming reversed, with major companies setting up their own entertainment stations, looking to tempt internet surfers into their area, and hold them there long enough to keep hitting them with adverts for their products. This is an all out war against other Internet users and against conventional television. The success of a campaign in future will be measured not just by television ratings but also by millions of mouse clicks. So long as a company can be sure of attracting a big enough number of participants (because internet audiences like to be very interactive), then they might be willing in time to cut television advertising budget and shift it into net entertainment. Internet users are a prime target audience because of their relatively high incomes, and because they are cutting down on television.

Television companies are now uncertain what television will even look like beyond 2000, let alone what sort or programmes people will want to watch once they have 500 or more channels to chose from - not including a billion internet pages and tens of thousands of internet videos to connect to. Video-rental shops on street corners are likely to take a real hammering and many will go out of business unless they find a new product by 1999.

While many internet sites at the moment are run by companies looking to sell their own products (banks are a good example), others have been set up to sell advertising space just like any other media company. An example might be a virtual reality area which is free to join but which contains high profile adverts for a number of different products and services. IBM and Microsoft spent around $800,000 million on net advertising in 1996. Spending on Internet ads rose by 83% in the first six months of 1996 to $71.1 million. Advertising works on the knowledge that the average net user looks at two hundred pages a month, and many of them are in upper income groups. Internet advertisers can be invoiced on the number of times a user selects their product pages. Each cluster of ten or a hundred visits then triggers another tiny amount onto the advertiser's bill. In this way advertisers know exactly what they are getting for their money. At present Internet traffic is estimated to flow mainly from servers to clients (80:20) with US accounting for 63.8% of hosts indicating that much of the information obtained by Internet users comes from US corporations.

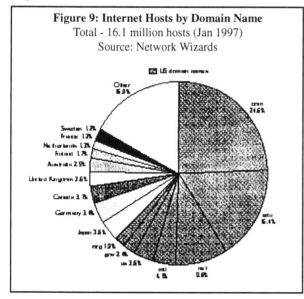

Figure 9: Internet Hosts by Domain Name
Total - 16.1 million hosts (Jan 1997)
Source: Network Wizards

The implications for the workplace overall are significant:
* Internet life is measured in dog years
* Organisational structures are changing and so are organisations
* Outsourcing has increased and so has homeworking
* Power has shifted even more to large organisations
* Employment shifts are noticeable by sector, operational and managerial levels

We are witnessing the wholesale disappearance of work accessible to the urban poor (Wilson, 1996). Without intervention, unemployment, poverty, and out-migration will likely increase, exacerbating the structural problems typical of rural areas ((OTA, 1996).

The implications for all responsible people are that they must become involved and be proactive as users, decision-makers and regulators of the Internet.

The Real Challenge?

Consider these words which come from the Cyberspace declaration of independence
- "Cyberspace is a world that is both everywhere and nowhere
- A world that all may enter without privilege or prejudice accorded by race, economic power, military force, or station of birth
- A world where anyone, anywhere may express his or her beliefs

- A world where legal concepts of property, expression, identity, movement and context do not apply
- A world of no matter"
     Hopefully it is in our hands to make our new world matter and for it to be a cybercivilisation to be proud of.
     "We will create a civilisation of the Mind in Cyberspace. May it be more humane and fair than the world your governments have made before"
     Cyberspace declaration of Independence (Barlow, 1996)

REFERENCES

Australian Broadcasting Authority (1996) Investigation into the Content of On-Line Services: Report to the Minister for Communications and the Arts, June 1996.

Australian Broadcasting Authority, News Release 65/1996, p4

Australian Bureau of Statistics (1995) Computing Services Industry, Australia 1992-93, ABS Catalogue No 8669.0, March 1995.

Australian Bureau of Statistics (1998) Household Use of Information Technology, Australia. Cat no. 8146.0.

Barlow, J. P. (1996) http://www.cse.unsw.edu.au/dblp/db/indices/a-tree/b/Barlow:John_Perry.html

CommerceNet http://www.commerce.net/research/stats/wwstats.html (10/16/98).

Dixon, P. (1999) http://www.globalchange.com/cyberr_index.htm

Novak, T.P. and Hoffman, D.L., Bridging the Digital Divide: The Impact of Race on Computer Access and Internet Use, Science, April, 17, 1998.

OECD (1997). Information Technology Outlook http://www.oecd.org/

OECD (1998). Electronic Commerce. http://www.oecd.org/subject/e_commerce/summary.htm

Office of the Status of Women, Department of Prime Minister and Cabinet, Australia, Regulating the Internet: Issues for Women, Dec, 1996.

Office of the Status of Women, Department of Prime Minister and Cabinet, Australia, Women's Access to Online Services, Dec, 1996.

The Emperor Has No Clothes – Time to Address the Virtual Organisation

Janice Burn, Peter Marshall, Martyn Wild
School of MIS, Edith Cowan University, Churchlands Campus, Perth, W.A., 6018
Tel: 618 9273 8718, Fax: 618 9273 8332, E-Mail: j.burn@cowan.edu.au

ABSTRACT

This paper looks at organisational value in relation to virtuality. It challenges the notion that the virtual organisation is the answer for the 21st Century and further suggests that with the basic concepts of virtual information management being so poorly understood there are likely to be far more actual failures than virtual realities. The paper attempts to redress some of these imbalances by providing some clear definitions of virtual organisations and different models of virtuality which can exist within the electronic market. Degrees of virtuality can be seriously constrained by the extent to which organisations have pre-existing linkages in the marketplace and the extent to which these can be substituted by virtual ones, but also by the intensity of virtual linkages which support the virtual model.

Six virtual models are proposed within a dynamic framework of change. In order to realise the flexibility promised by virtuality organisations must align themselves along the virtual strategic perspective and then match this with the virtual model for structural alignment. The virtual value which may result has then to be examined in relation to the structure /strategy alignment model and to both the virtual organisation and its component alliances. The Virtual value Model (VVM) identifies factors which may inhibit or promote effective business value realisation.

This paper further proposes a research agenda for the 21st Century which places far greater emphasis on qualitative rather than quantitative studies.

INTRODUCTION

The value of going virtual is often espoused in the management literature but there is very little empirical research to show that value and "virtuality" are directly related. Indeed, there are so many fuzzy concepts related to virtuality that any broad statement made with regard to virtual organisations must be regarded with suspicion. It could be argued that there is a degree of virtuality in all organisations but at what point does this present a conflict between control and adaptability? Is there a continuum along which organisations can position themselves in the electronic marketplace according to their needs for flexibility and fast responsiveness as opposed to stability and sustained momentum?

While there may be general agreement with regard to the advantages of flexibility the extent to which virtuality offers flexibility and the advantages which this will bring to a corporation have yet to be measured. There is an assumption that an organisation that invests in as little infrastructure as possible will be more responsive to a changing marketplace and more likely to attain global competitive advantage but this ignores the very real power which large integrated organisations can bring to the market in terms of sustained innovation over the longer term (Chesbrough and Teece, 1996). Proponents of the virtual organisation also tend to underestimate the force of virtual links. Bonds which bind a virtual organisation together may strongly inhibit flexibility and change rather than nurture the concept of the opportunistic virtual organisation (Goldman, Nagel and Preiss, 1995). Aldridge (1998), suggests that it is no accident that the pioneers of electronic commerce fall into three categories:
• Start-ups, organisations with no existing investment or legacy systems to protect;
• Technology companies with a vested interest in building the channel to market products and services;
• Media companies, attracted by low set-up costs and immediate distribution of news and information.

When is a virtual organisation really virtual? One definition would suggest that organisations are virtual when producing work deliverables across different locations, at differing work cycles, and across cultures (Gray and Igbaria, 1996; Palmer and Speier, 1998). Another suggests that the single common theme is temporality. Virtual organisations centre on continual restructuring to capture the value of a short term market opportunity and are then dissolved to make way for restructuring to a new virtual entity. (Byrne, 1993; Katzy, 1998). Yet others suggest that virtual organisations are characterised by the intensity, symmetricality, reciprocity and multiplexity of the linkages in their networks (Powell, 1990; Grabowski and Roberts, 1996). Whatever the definition (and this paper hopes to resolve some of the ambiguities) there is a concensus that different degrees of virtuality exist (Hoffman, D.L., Novak, T.P., & Chatterjee, P.1995; Gray and Igbaria, 1996; Goldman, Nagel and Preiss, 1995) and within this, different organisational structures can be formed (Palmer and Speier, 1998; Davidow and Malone, 1992, Miles and Snow, 1986). Such structures are normally inter-organisational and lie at the heart of any form of electronic commerce yet the organisational and management processes which should be applied to ensure successful implementation have been greatly under researched (Finnegan, Galliers and Powell, 1998; Swatman and Swatman, 1992). Further it is suggested that the relationship between tasks and structure and its effect on performance has not been studied at all in the context of virtual organisations. (Ahuja and Carley, 1998).

This paper tries to address these aspects and remove some of the ambiguities surrounding virtual values. Firstly, a definition of virtual organisations is developed and related to the concept of virtual culture which is the organisational embodiment of its virtuality. This may take a variety of different virtual models which will reflect the strength and structure of inter-organisational links. The paper identifies six virtual models - the Virtual Alliance Models (VAM) and suggests that each of these will operate along a continuum and within a framework of dynamic change. In order to maximise the value derived from the VAM the organisation needs to ensure that there is a consistency between the alignment of its Virtual Strategic Positioning (VSP) and the VAM and the organisation and management of internal and external virtual characteristics. The ability of the organisation to change from one VAM to another or to extend itself as a virtual entity will reflect the extent to which an understanding of these concepts has been embedded into the knowledge management of the virtual organisation as a Virtual Organisational Change Model (VOCM). These change factors are the essential components through which virtual value can be derived and from which it can be measured as presented in the Virtual Values Model (VVM). Finally, the paper outlines an agenda for future research which calls for far more in-depth, qualitative studies of virtual success and failure related to the real value derived from virtual operation.

VIRTUAL ORGANISATIONS AND VIRTUAL CULTURES

Virtual organisations are electronically networked organisations that transcend conventional organisational boundaries (Barner, 1996, Berger, 1996, Rogers, 1996), with linkages which may exist both within (Davidow and Malone, 1992) and between organisations (Goldman, Nagel and Priess, 1995). In its simplest form, however, virtuality exists where IT is used to enhance organisational activities while reducing the need for physical or formalised structures (Greiner and Mates, 1996). Degrees of virtuality then exist which will reflect
- The virtual organisational culture (strategic positioning)
- The intensity of linkages and the nature of the bonds which tie the stakeholders together (internal and external structures)
- The market (IT dependency and resource infrastructure, product, customer)

Culture is the degree to which members of a community have common shared values and beliefs (Schein, 1990). Tushman and O'Reilly (1996) suggest that organisational cultures that are accepting of technology, highly decentralised, and change oriented are more likely to embrace virtuality and proactively seek these opportunities both within and without the organisation. Virtual culture is hence a perception of the entire virtual organisation (including its infrastructure and product) held by its stakeholder community and operationalised in choices and actions which result in a feeling of *globalness* with respect to value sharing (e.g. each client's expectations are satisfied in the product accessed), and time-space arrangement (e.g. each stakeholder has the feeling of a continuous access to the organisation and its products). The embodiment of this culture comes through the Virtual Strategic Perspective (VSP) which the organisation adopts.

Networks can be groups of organisations but also groups within organisations where the development and maintenance of communicative relationships is paramount to the successful evolution of a virtual entity. However, the ability to establish multiple alliances and the need to retain a particular identity creates a constant tension between autonomy and interdependence, competition and cooperation (Nouwens, J., & Bouwman, H., 1995). These relationships are often described as value-added partnerships based on horizontal, vertical or symbiotic relationships. These in turn relate to competitors, value chain collaborators and complementary providers of goods and services all of whom combine to achieve competitive advantage over organisations outside these networks. The nature of the alliances which form the virtual organisation, their strength and substitutability define the inherent virtual structure.

Markets differ from networks since markets are traditionally coordinated by pricing mechanisms. In this sense, the electronic market is no different but further "central to the conceptualisations of the electronic marketplace is the ability of any buyer or seller to interconnect with a network to offer wares or shop for goods and services. Hence, ubiquity is by definition a prerequisite" (Steinfield, Plummer and Kraut, 1995). There are different risks associated with being a market-maker and a market-player and different products will also carry different risks. Criteria for successful electronic market development include products with low asset specificity and ease of description and a consumer market willing to buy without recourse to visiting retail stores. (Wigand and Benjamin, 1995). Necessarily, the most important asset to an electronic market is the availability of pervasive Information and Communication Technology (ITC) infrastructures providing a critical mass of customers. A virtual organisation is both constrained

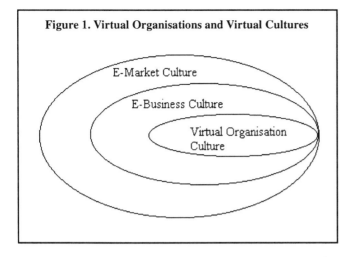

Figure 1. Virtual Organisations and Virtual Cultures

E-Market Culture

E-Business Culture

Virtual Organisation Culture

and supported by the electronic market in which it operates and the stage to which its business environment has developed as an e-business.

Figure 1 shows this set of relationships.

Despite the growth of online activity many firms are nervous of the risks involved and fear a general deterioration of profit margins coupled with a relinquishment of market control. Nevertheless, as existing organisations are challenged by new entrants using direct channels to undercut prices and increase market share, solutions have to be found that enable organisations to successfully migrate into the electronic market. The authors suggest that there are six different models of virtuality which may be appropriate.

MODELS OF VIRTUALITY

This paper identifies six different forms of virtual organisations as:

Virtual faces
Co-alliance models
Star-alliance models – core or satellite
Value-alliance models – stars or constellations
Market-alliance models
Virtual brokers

Put simply, virtual faces are the cyberspace incarnations of an existing non-virtual organisation (often described as a "place" as opposed to "space" organisation, Rayport and Sviokola, 1995) and create additional value such as enabling users to carry out the same transactions over the Internet as they could otherwise do by using telephone or fax e.g. Fleurop selling flowers or air tickets by Travelocity. The services may, however, reach far beyond this enabling the virtual face to mirror the whole activities of the parent organisation and even extend these e.g. the web-based versions of television channels and newspapers with constant news updates and archival searches. Alternatively they may just extend the scope of activities by use of facilities such as electronic procurement, contract tendering or even electronic auctions or extend market scope by participating in an electronic mall with or without added enrichment such as a common payment mechanism. There is obviously an extremely tight link between the virtual face and the parent organisation. This model can be actualised as an e-shop, e-auction or even e-mall

Co-alliance models are shared partnerships with each partner bringing approximately equal amounts of commitment to the virtual organisation thus forming a consortia. The composition of the consortia may change to reflect market opportunities or to reflect the core competencies of each member (Preiss, Goldman and Nagel, 1996). Focus can be on specific functions such as collaborative design or engineering or in providing virtual support with a virtual team of consultants. Links within the co-alliance are normally contractual for more permanent alliances or by mutual convenience on a project by project basis. There is not normally a high degree of substitutability within the life of that virtual creation.

Star-alliance models are co-ordinated networks of interconnected members reflecting a core surrounded by satellite organisations. The core comprises leaders who are the dominant players in the market and supply competency or expertise to members. These alliances commonly based around similar industries or company types. While this form is a true network, typically the star or leader is identified with the virtual face and so the core organisation is very difficult to replace whereas the satellites may have a far greater level of substitutability.

Value-alliance models bring together a range of products, services and facilities in one package and are based on the value or supply chain model. Participants may come together on a project by project basis but generally coordination is provided by the general contractor. Where longer term relationships have developed the value alliance often adopts the form of value constellations where firms supply each of the companies in the value chain and a complex and continuing set of strategic relationships are embedded into the alliance. Substitutability will relate to the positioning on the value chain and the reciprocity of the relationship.

Market-alliances are organisations that exist primarily in cyberspace, depend on their member organisations for the provision of actual products and services and operate in an electronic market. Normally they bring together a range of products, services and facilities in one package, each of which may be offered separately by individual organisations. In some cases the market is open and in others serves as an intermediary. These can also be described as virtual communities but a virtual community can be an add-on such as exists in an e-mall rather than a cyberspace organisation perceived as a virtual organisation. Amazon.com is a prime example of a market-alliance model where substitutability of links is very high.

Virtual Brokers are designers of dynamic networks (Miles and Snow,1986). These prescribe additional strategic opportunities either as third party value-added suppliers such as in the case of common web marketing events (e-Xmas) or as information brokers providing a virtual structure around specific business information services (Timmers, 1998). This has the highest level of flexibility with purpose built virtual organisations created to fill a window of opportunity and dissolved when that window is closed.

As discussed previously each of these alliances carries with it a set of tensions related to autonomy and interdependence. Virtual culture is the strategic hub around which virtual relationships are formed and virtual links implemented. In order to be flexible, links must be substitutable, to allow the creation of new competencies, but links must be established and maintained if the organisation is going to fully leverage community expertise. This presents a dichotomy. The degree to which virtuality can be implemented effectively relates to the strength of existing organisational links (virtual and non-virtual) and the relationship which these impose on the virtual structure. However, as essentially networked organisations they will be constrained by the extent to which they are able to redefine or extend their virtual linkages. Where existing linkages are strong e.g. co-located, shared culture, synchronicity of work and shared risk (reciprocity) these will both reduce the need for or perceived benefits from substitutable linkages and inhibit the development of further virtual linkages. Figure 2 provides a diagrammatic representation of these tensions and their interaction with the Virtual Alliance Models (VAM).

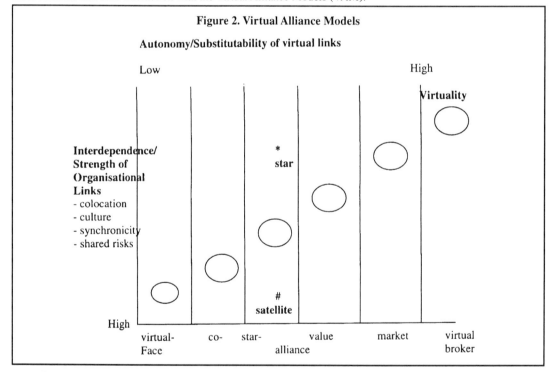

These six models are not exclusive but are intended to serve as a way of classifying the diversity of forms which an electronic business model may assume. Some of these are essentially an electronic re-implementation of traditional forms of doing business, others are add-ons for added value possibly through umbrella collaboration and others go far beyond this through value chain integration or cyber communities. What all of these have in common is that they now seek innovative ways to add value through information and change management and a rich functionality. Creating value through virtuality is only feasible if the processes which support such innovations are clearly understood.

VIRTUAL ORGANISATIONAL CHANGE MODEL

These six forms of virtual organisations all operate within a dynamic environment where their ability to change will determine the extent to which they can survive in a competitive market. Organisational theorists suggest that the ability of an organisation to change relates to internal and external factors (Miles and Snow, 1978), including the organisation's technology, structure and strategy, tasks and management processes individual skills and roles and culture (DeLisi, 1990; Venkatraman, 1994) and the business in which the organisation operates and the degree of uncertainty in the environment (Donaldson, 1995). These factors are also relevant to virtual organisations but need further refinement.

Moore (1997) suggests that businesses are not just members of certain industries but parts of a complex ecosystem that incorporates bundles of different industries. The driving force is not pure competition but co-evolution. The system is seen as "an economic community supported by a foundation of interacting organisations and individuals - -Over time they coevolve their capabilities and roles, and tend to align themselves with the direction set by one or more central companies" (p. 26). The ecosystems evolve through four distinct stages:

- Birth
- Expansion
- Authority
- Death

And at each of these stages the system faces different leadership, cooperative and competitive challenges.

Table 1. E-Market Ecosystem

EcoSystem Stage	Leadership Challenges	Cooperative Challenges	Competitive Challenges
Birth	Maximise customer delivered value	Find and Create new value in an efficient way	Protect your ideas
Expansion	Attract Critical Mass of Buyers	Work with Suppliers and Partners	Ensure market standard approach
Authority	Lead co-evolution	Provide compelling vision for the future	Maintain strong bargaining power
Renewal or Death	Innovate or Perish	Work with Innovators High Barriers	Develop and Maintain

This ecosystem can be viewed as the all-embracing electronic market culture within which the e-business maintains an equilibrium. The organisational "virtual culture" is the degree to which the organisation adopts virtual organising and this in turn will affect the individual skills, tasks and roles throughout all levels of the organisation . Henderson and Venkatraman (1996) identify three vectors of virtual organising as:

- Virtual Encounters
- Virtual Sourcing
- Virtual Work

Virtual encounters refers to the extent to which you virtually interact with the market defined at three levels of greater virtual progression:

- Remote product/service experience
- Product/service customisation
- Shaping customer solutions

Virtual sourcing refers to competency leveraging from:

- Efficient sourcing of standard components
- Efficient asset leverage in the business network
- Create new competencies through alliances

Virtual Work refers to:

- Maximising individual experience
- Harnessing organisational expertise
- Leveraging of community expertise

Figure 3. Virtual Organisational Management

Where the third levels all relate to an organisation with an "information rich" product and the highest degree of use of ICT. If we view this as the virtual culture of the organisation then this needs to be articulated through the strategic positioning of the organisation and its structural alliances. It also needs to be supported by the knowledge management processes and the ICT. These relationships are depicted in a dynamic virtual organisation change model as shown below.

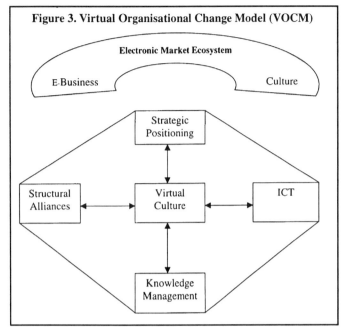

Figure 3. Virtual Organisational Change Model (VOCM)

The degree to which virtuality can be applied in the organisation will relate to the extent to which the VOCM factors are in alignment. When these are not aligned then the organisation will find itself dysfunctional in its exploitation of the virtual marketspace and so be unable to derive the maximum value benefits from its strategic position in the VAM framework.

VIRTUAL VALUES RESEARCH FRAMEWORK

The VAM framework depicted in Figure 2 shows the opposing structural tensions which will pull the VAM in different directions and which may therefore force the organisation into a less favourable strategic position. This same framework can be used to view the six models along a continuum which relates the extent of substitutability of virtual linkages (virtual structure) to the extent of virtuality as embedded in the organisation (virtual culture) and hence identify the strategic positioning which will be the most effective in value return.

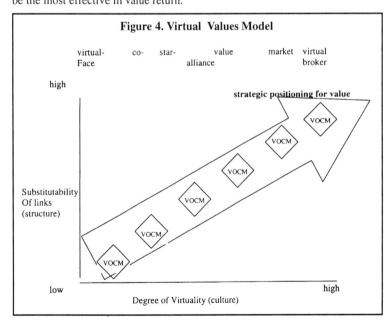

Figure 4. Virtual Values Model

This model shows the ideal positioning for each of the virtual models. The organisation then needs to examine the VOCM factors in order to evaluate effectiveness and identify variables for change either within that VAM or to move beyond that VAM according to the virtual culture. Change directions should be value led but there is as yet very little empirical research to identify how value is derived in a virtual organisation. For virtual organisations performance measurements must cross organisational boundaries and take collaboration into account but it is also necessary to measure value at the individual level since it is feasible that one could be effective without the other (Provan and Milward, 1995). There is also an interesting difference of perception. Ahuja and Carley (1995) have completed one of the few empirical studies of the relationship between structure and performance in a virtual setting and conclude that perceived outcomes were seen as highly productive when tasks and structures were "in fit" but when measured objectively showed no correlation. This would suggest that future research cannot be based solely on quantitative measurement but also cannot rely on anecdotal evidence or subjective "feel good" analysis. Research into virtual organisations must embrace reality at a number of different levels.

The concluding section of this paper outlines where and how the authors believe research efforts should be directed.

RESEARCH AGENDA.

This paper has looked at organisational value in relation to virtuality and identified a number of different areas where research must focus in order to ensure that the virtual organisation does not (as with most other recent hype issues in information systems research) become a dinosaur before it has a chance to really change the world. First there needs to be an acceptance of the multifarious forms which the virtual organisation can assume and the realisation that there is no "one good way" for the virtual organisation to grow. Much of the existing literature on organisational change may be as valid in relation to virtual organisations as to traditional organisational forms but in order to assess this there must be in-depth analysis of the change process over a number of different business and electronic markets. Failures need to be evaluated and not just successes but longer-term studies are needed to help understand the sustainability factors which relate to virtual organisations.

Second there needs to be a directed effort towards evaluating information systems practices in light of virtual organisations. Strategic planning processes need to take into account the collaborative strategies as well as the individual; information systems requirements need to capture the views of the stakeholders who are now frequently the customers or even more complex the desired customer; information management needs to embrace virtual organising, knowledge management, service customisation and alliance interactions.

Third we need to apply more realistic and comprehensive measures of value benefits which encompass both objective and subjective assessments. Values apply to all the stakeholders in the virtual community and so include the customers as well as the alliance members. Sociological approaches are required to evaluate the impact of virtual access on the community and particularly to identify the repercussions for societies where web access is not a reality or a priority.

Finally, there must be a move towards more qualitative research with multiple paradigms for research methodologies. This means that IS researchers have to become deeply involved with organisations as they manage their way through the change process. This needs a commitment from academia to release research staff for organisationally based research work and also a definite commitment from organisations to allow researchers access to their change processes and the business impacts of such changes.

The authors are committed to leading a research programme which will be highly collaborative with government , public and private organisations and also to establishing a virtual network of both practitioners and scholars where the change management practices will be both shared and practiced. A team of ten researchers are currently engaged in evaluating the virtual values model in a variety of different business areas (Small and Medium Enterprises (SMEs), the information industry, retail industry, government and travel industry), from a variety of perspectives such as competitive advantage, strategic planning, change management and value-added business benefits. This research would benefit from cross-cultural comparisons to reflect the global realities of the virtual world and researchers and practitioners elsewhere are encouraged to engage with us in this work.

REFERENCES

Ahuja, M. K., & Carley, K. M. (1998). Network structure in virtual organizations. Journal of Computer-Mediated Communication [On-line], 3 (4). Available: http://www.ascusc.org/jcmc/vol3/issue4/ahuja.html

Aldridge, D. (1998). Purchasing on the Net – The New Opportunities for Electronic Commerce. EM – Electronic Markets, Vol 8, 1, pp 34-37.

Barner, R. (1996). The New Millenium Workplace: Seven changes that will challenge managers and workers. Futurist, 30:2, pp 14-18.

Berger, M. (1996). Making the Virtual Office a Reality. Sales and marketing Management, SMT Supplement, June, pp 18-22.

Byrne, J. (1993). The Virtual Corporation. Business Week, pp 36-41.

Chesbrough, H. W. and Teece D. J. (1996). When is Virtual Virtuous? Harvard Business Review, Jan-Feb, pp 65-73.

Davidow, W. H. and Malone, M. S. (1992). The Virtual Corporation, New York: Harper Business.

DeLisi, P. S. (1990). Lessons from the Steel Axe: Culture, Technology and Organisation Change. Sloan Management Review,

Donaldson, L. (1995). American Anti-Management theories of Organisation. Cambridge UK., Cambridge University Press.

Finnegan, P., Galliers, B. and Powell, P. (1998);. Systems Planning in an Electronic Commerce Environment in Europe: Rethinking Current Approaches. EM – Electronic Markets, Vol 8, 2, pp 35-38.

Gray, P. and Igbaria, M. (1996). The Virtual Society, ORMS Today, December, pp 44-48.

Goldman, S. L., Nagel R. N. and Preiss, K. (1995). Agile Competitors and Virtual Organisations: Strategies for Enriching the Customer, New York: Van Nostrand Reinhold.

Grabowski, M. and Roberts, K. H. (1996). Human and Organisational Error in Large Scale Systems. IEEE Transactions on Systems, Man and Cybernetics, 26:1, pp 2-16.

Greiner, R. and Metes, G. (1996). Going Virtual: Moving your Organisation into the 21st Century. Englewood Cliffs, NJ: Prentice Hall.

Henderson, J. C., Venkatraman N., and Oldach S. (1996). Aligning Business and IT Strategies. In Competing in the Information Age: Strategic Alignment in Practice (Ed. Jerry N. Luftman), Oxford University Press, Chapter 2, pp. 21-42.

Hoffman, D.L., Novak, T.P., & Chatterjee, P. (1995). Commercial scenarios for the Web: Opportunities and challenges. Journal of Computer-Mediated Communication [On-line], 1 (3). Available: http://www.ascusc.org/jcmc/vol1/issue3/hoffman.html

Katzy, B. R. (1998). Design and Implementation of Virtual Organisations. HICSS, Vol , pp .

Miles, R. E. and Snow, C. C. (1986). Organisations: new concepts for new forms. California Management Review 28, 3, Spring, pp 62-73.

Moore, J. F. (1997). The Death of Competition: Leadership and Strategy in the Age of Business Ecosystems. New York, Harper Business.

Nouwens, J., & Bouwman, H. (1995). Living apart together in electronic commerce: The use of information and communication technology to create network organizations. Journal of Computer-Mediated Communication [On-line], 1 (3). Available: http://www.ascusc.org/jcmc/vol1/issue3/nouwens.html

Palmer J. W. and Speier, C. (1998). Teams: Virtualness and Media Choice, Proceedings of HICSS, Vol , pp .

Powell, W. W. (1990). Neither Market nor Hierarchy: Network Forms of Organisation. Research in Organisational Behaviour, 12, pp 295-336.

Preiss, K., Goldman, S. L. and Nagel, R. N. (1996). Cooperate to Compete. New York: Van Nostrand Reinhold.

Provan, K. and Milward, H. (1995). A Preliminary Theory of Inter-Organisational Network Effectiveness: A Comparative Study of Four Community Mental Health Systems. Administrative Science Quarterly, 14, pp 91-114.

Rayport, J. F. and Sviokola, J. (1995). Exploiting the Virtual Value Chain. Harvard Business Review, 73 (6), pp 75-86.

Rogers, 1D. M. (1996). The Challenge of Fifth generation R and D. Research Technology Management, 39:4, pp 33-41.

Schein, E. (1990). Organisational Culture. American Psychologist, 45, 2, 109-119.

Steinfield, C., Kraut, R., & Plummer, A. (1995). The impact of electronic commerce on buyer-seller relationships. Journal of Computer-Mediated Communication [On-line], 1 (3). Available: http://www.ascusc.org/jcmc/vol1/issue3/steinfld.html

Swatman, P. M. C. and Swatman, P. A. (1992). EDI System Integration: A Definition and Literature Survey. The Information Society (8), pp 165-205.

Timmers, P. (1998). Business Models for Electronic MarketsEM – Electronic Markets, Vol 8. 2, pp 3-8.

Tushman, M. L. and O'Reilly, III, C. A. (1996). Ambidextrous Organisations: Managing Evolutionary and Revolutionary Change. California Management Review, 38, 4, pp 8-29.

Venkatraman, N. (1994). IT-Enabled Business Transformation: From Automation to Business Scope Redefinition, Sloan Management review, Winter, pp .

Wigand, R.T., & Benjamin, R.I. (1995). Electronic Commerce: Effects on electronic markets. Journal of Computer-Mediated Communication [On-line], 1 (3). Available: http://www.ascusc.org/jcmc/vol1/issue3/wigand.html

Use of an Artificial Neural Network to Predict the Likelihood of Renal Deterioration in Meningomyelocele Patients

Chi-lien Lee, Sky Chaleff, Rajiv Thakkar, Ilhami Surer, Linda A. Baker, Steven G. Docimo, and James Clements
Park B2-202, 600 N. Wolfe Street, Johns Hopkins University, Baltimore, MD 21287
(410) 614-3444, chilien1@welchlink.welch.jhu.edu

ABSTRACT

An artificial neural network (ANN) is a computer-based model that emulates a biological neural network (40). Artificial neural networks can be trained to solve a variety of pattern recognition and classification problems and have been used successfully by numerous business organizations (41). Most recently, they have become an alternative technique which medical professionals may use to solve medical classification decision problems (9,15,20,39). In this project, an artificial neural network model was designed to predict the probability of renal deterioration in meningomyelocele (MMC) patients. The raw clinical data (109 variables) from years 1975-1997 on 260 MMC patients (124 males, 136 females) were gathered from clinical charts and entered into a relational database. Mean patient age was 14 (range 1-51). Once the data entries were verified by the clinicians, the patient data was transformed into a digitized format. Twenty digitized clinical parameters were entered as input data into the artificial neural network software. The data sets were first randomized and then grouped by a variety of sampling methods such as the cross validation approach, allowing generalization of both the training and testing data sets. By using commercially available neural network and statistical software, neural network models and logistic regression models can be created. Moreover, the significance of all of the variables available in the database will also be examined in order to provide more information for clinical diagnosis. The results will be analyzed by comparing the area under the Receiver Operating Characteristic (ROC) curves. The ROC curve is a well-known method in laboratory medicine for characterizing the accuracy of a test over the full operating range of the normal/abnormal decision threshold.

ARTIFICIAL NEURAL NETWORKS

An artificial neural network (ANN) is a computer model originally designed to simulate the function of the human brain itself (13). ANNs were originally created in the late 1940's and the need for additional techniques to solve non-linear processing problems has recently revived ANN technology. Since the 1990s, neural networks have been applied to a wide range of problems including pattern recognition, control, and optimization. Examples include noise control in air-conditioning systems, credit card fraud detection, character recognition, loan approval, and anti-lock brake control (41).

Besides the frequent improvement in predictive accuracy, ANNs are increasing in acceptance because of an increased availability of user-friendly neural network software packages and high-speed processors. By far, the most popular ANN architecture is the back-propagation neural network. It has been successful in a broad area of decision problems and was developed as an alternative technology for nonlinear regression estimation (2,3,4,5,6,11,18,21,23,24,26,27,37, 41).

An artificial neural network is a learning system that mimics certain characteristics of the human brain, thus coming under the broad category of artificial intelligence (13,31). They are composed of highly interconnected processing units that duplicate the neurons in the brain. The interconnections between the neurons are called weights, which duplicate the axons and dendrites of the neurons, which connect the neurons to each other. The intelligence of an ANN is contained in the weights of the connections between the neurons. Each neuron is a processing unit and does not hold state information about the knowledge the neural network is representing.

ANNs learn to discriminate knowledge the same way humans do. Humans learn by being presented with known facts and then correlating them with known outcomes. ANNs are presented with a pattern of data to be recognized and the expected outcome to that pattern of data. As the ANN learns the patterns of data and what the expected outcome is, the ANN can generalize about patterns in the correlation between the data and outcome.

An ANN consists of many neurons (processing units) connected together as shown in Figure 1. The neurons are grouped into layers. The ANN presented in Figure 1 is a 3-layer network. The first layer is the input layer, which is where the data is presented to the network. The last layer is the output layer that shows the response of the network given the input. The layers between the input and output layers are called the hidden layers, as they have no contact with the outside world. These add to the non-linearity learning. (14,26).

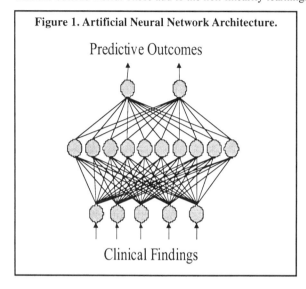

Figure 1. Artificial Neural Network Architecture.

Predictive Outcomes

Clinical Findings

Artificial neural networks are developed by collecting historical data on a problem, separating the data into training and testing sets, defining the network architecture, and then training the system. If the ANN can successfully learn to predict the results of the training set, then the system is evaluated on how well it can predict the results of the test data.

Artificial neural networks have numerous benefits over traditional computer-based systems. They can process data in parallel, they learn, they can handle noisy and incomplete data, and they don't need to be programmed using traditional techniques. However, they are limited in that they cannot explain their results, they require significant amounts of historical data, training can be excessive and tedious, and the software packages still need to be more user-friendly (40).

BACKGROUND OF MENINGOMYELOCELE

Meningomyelocele (MMC) is a common birth defect, affecting 1 in 1,000 births in the United States (Figure 2). This congenital anomaly, one of several forms of spina bifida, is the result of abnormal development of the spinal cord and its coverings and most commonly occurs in the low back region of the spine. At birth, a sac is seen on the surface of the low back that contains the abnormal spinal cord.

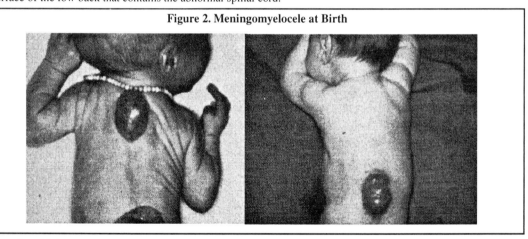

Figure 2. Meningomyelocele at Birth

In addition to this MMC, these children typically have abnormalities in their brain (Arnold-Chiari malformation) which leads to fluid accumulation within the brain (hydrocephalus). The common end result of these abnormalities is neurological damage, which can vary in its type, location and degree. Patients with lumbar MMC typically have loss of function of lower extremities and may also have bowel and bladder dysfunction. Due to the susceptibility of the MMC to infection, surgery is performed soon after birth to provide covering over the MMC and to shunt the hydrocephalus. However, this does not repair the neurological damage.

The urological management of children with spina bifida has two paramount goals. First and foremost is the preservation of kidney (renal) function. The kidneys can be damaged by bacterial infections or by high bladder pressures which impairs urine drainage from the kidneys. Renal deterioration, urinary tract infection and renal calculus disease have been the greatest sources of morbidity and mortality in the spinal bifida population surviving past infancy (18). The second goal is urinary continence—a prerequisite to social integration of these children in school and into adulthood. The strategies to achieve the first goal have followed two paths in recent years. Traditionally, frequent radiological studies have been performed to screen for evidence of renal deterioration; if deterioration is detected, action is taken to prevent progression (36). A more aggressive strategy is to use urodynamics, an invasive pressure/volume study of the urinary tract, to screen the urinary tract for risk factors for future renal deterioration (1). These risk factors include a high urinary leak point pressure, high pressure uninhibited bladder contractions and bladder-sphincter dyssynergy. In all of these situations, the kidneys may be chronically exposed to high pressures, resulting in hydronephrosis and loss of renal function. If these risk factors are present, an aggressive regimen of anticholinergic medication and intermittent clean urinary catheterization is undertaken in order to prevent renal deterioration from occurring in the first place. The assumption for this is that avoiding early deterioration will provide long-term benefit to the health of the patient (16).

Unfortunately, there is no strong scientific evidence that either management strategy is either more cost-effective or more beneficial to the renal well being of the child. In order to shed some light on this controversy, as well as to analyze other measures of urological outcome, a computerized relational database was designed which contains the important urological information relating to the patient with spina bifida. The clinical management scheme used and the radiological and urodynamic parameters observed during the first five years of life will hopefully predict the possibility of deterioration of renal function, as evidenced by changes in the imaging results of the kidneys by ultrasound or intravenous pyelogram (IVP). Therefore, this neural network examines the clinical data during the first five years of the patient's life and predicts the likelihood of renal deterioration after the first five years of life.

MATERIALS AND METHODS
Data Set

As described earlier, meningomyelocele is a severe, congenital disease of young patients. These patients are at high risk for genitourinary complications and therefore a preventative radiological imaging and medical management regimen would be practical. However, cost-containment issues necessitate that this regimen be practical in its frequency and price. Therefore, the preventative regimen and medical interventions need to be tailored to the needs of the individual patient.

The clinical parameters that are perceived by the pediatric urologists to bear significance upon the future state of renal function in MMC patients are depicted in Figure 3. This figure demonstrates the relationships of signs, symptoms, radiological testing results and treatments for the MMC patients. Abbreviations: PVR- Postvoid Residual, UIT-Urinary Tract Infection, IVP- Intravenous Pyelogram, Uninhib Contr- Uninhibited Detrusor Contractions, DLPP- Detrusor Leak Point Pressure, DSD- Detrusor Sphincter Dyssynergia, VP shunt- Ventriculoperitoneal Shunt, DOB- Date of Birth, hydro- hydronephrosis, US- renal and bladder ultrasound, pyelo- pyelonephritis, Avnl UDT- Abnormal Urodynamics Testing, CIC- Clean Intermittent Catheterization.

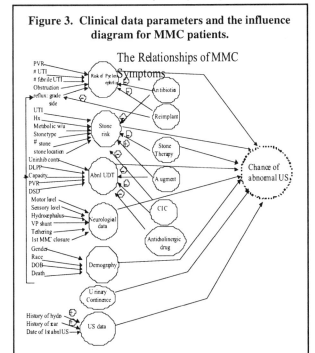

Figure 3. Clinical data parameters and the influence diagram for MMC patients.

The first column shows raw data parameters that factor into various risk categories, seen in the second column. The second column is a higher-level abstraction of information from the first column. The risk categories can then be ameliorated by medical or surgical treatments, seen in the third column. Therefore, they have arrows pointing back to the related higher level abstractions. The signs above the arrows reflect the impact the parameter has upon the risk. The final net risks then impact upon the ultimate chance of developing an abnormal renal ultrasound. All of the higher level abstractions affect the chance of an abnormal ultrasound.

Since these complex, non-linear relationships all factor into this disease, an ANN would be a suitable model to predict the likelihood of renal deterioration in MMC patients. The outcomes of this model will allow urologists to tailor the frequency of ultrasound imaging of the kidneys, thereby trimming the costly life-long surveillance in MMC patients.

We created a relational database in FileMaker Pro 3.0 for the specific purpose of recording parameters of urological interest of patients with spina bifida. With the approval of the Joint Commission on Clinical Investigation at the Johns Hopkins University School of Medicine, longitudinal information from the medical records of the 260 patients followed in the Spina Bifida Clinic at the Kennedy Krieger Institute are being entered into this database. This is an extensive review of 109 variables, and includes the original spinal lesion, neurosurgical procedures including cord untethering, all urological radiological studies from birth, method of bladder emptying, urological surgery, calculus disease history, all urinary tract infections and organisms and the results of all urodynamic studies. At this time, the data has been collected from the records kept in the Urology department, the records of the Spina Bifida Clinic at the Kennedy Krieger Institute and the inpatient records of the Johns Hopkins Hospital. After raw data was entered, the data was re-verified by pediatric urologists to ascertain accuracy.

Data Definition

The data preparation and selection in this study has shown to be very complicated. As was expressed before, the data is represented in a relational database. A demographic record is represented for each patient. There are 19 databases related to the patient databases that hold all the medical records of the patients, including prognosis and medical examination data. As the disease progress, several examinations are applied to the patients as needed. Certain tests used for monitoring patients' conditions were taken several times and recorded both results and dates in this database. Most of the records in the database represent the prognosis of this disease in the textual format as to digital coding system. Many descriptions are very specific that could affect the ability of the neural network to generalize the interrelationships. For example, the upper left side of the kidney could be too specific, as contrasted with just a problem with the kidney.

Variable Selection

The study will use the first three years of data after the patient was born and then to predict the likelihood of abnormal ultrasound examinations between age five to ten. Some of the data is from an early age patient who hasn't had a chance to receive any of the treatments so that the records will not be used. Many of the factors, for the same reason, will not be used. The physician chooses the best candidates for correlation from the remaining factors. These include the number of febrile urinary tract infections (UTIs), past ultrasound examines, first abnormal urine reflux, motor and sensory levels of the MMC, first abnormal IVP, bladder capacity, urinary capacity and demography data such as gender, race and ethnicity (17,19,21,25,28,33,36).

The other possible way to use this data to predict the possibility of abnormal ultrasounds has been analyzed. The predictive outcome for this model will be to predict if the next the ultrasound examination would be abnormal based on the last known reading of the patient chart combined with what problems and treatments the patient has had.

The time-series nature of this database, along with great variability of when patients had certain problems, if they had them at all, makes this data set difficult to fit into the neural network paradigm. Therefor, transforming the data in the original database into digital format will be necessary so that an ANN model can use it. These conditions include the number of occurrences of a particular problem, the places on the body a symptom appeared, the first place on the body the symptom appeared, number of years since a symptom last showed up or treatment was last given. In this project, a coding scheme described multiple occurrences of an illness into one number will be used. There are other possibilities that will also be explored for its predictive possibility

Training and Generalization

Training the neural network is usually an iterative process. Input-output pairs that are input data and the expected outputs are repeatedly presented to the ANN. At the end of iteration the actually output of the network is compared with the expected output that was presented to the ANN. When the error value goes above a certain user-defined value, the weights on the interconnections between the neurons adjusted to better represent this input-output relationship. It will usually take the ANN numerous iterations before the weights are adjusted properly for the network to recognize the pattern, if it can at all. When the error between the output and expected output fall below the user-defined error value, the network has learned the interrelationships between the data. During the iterative process, if it can, the network can generalize the interrelationships between the data so that it can recognize most if not all the training data.

Testing

The final step in training the neural network is to test it. A testing data set of input-output pairs was held back from being trained on. Therefore, when this data is tested against the neural network, it is known that the network did not just memorize all the patterns without creating generalizations about the interrelationships. The testing data set is presented to the network. The output of the network is compared with the expected output. The effectiveness of the network's prediction capability can then be presented as a percentage of input data it properly classified.

Neural Network Architecture

The ANN in this study, is a feed-forward network and will be trained using the back-propagation algorithm learning algorithm. It will consist of one input, one output and one or two hidden layers. Adding extra hidden layers can sometimes help in detecting more complex interrelationships in the data. The number of hidden nodes will be in the range of ten to fifteen. This will be increased if good prediction results are not attained at these levels. The nodes will be randomly initialized between –3 and 3. Input variables will be linearly scaled, independent of each of, to capture all the data the physician uses in determining the change that a patient might be a candidate of having an abnormal ultrasound in the future. For example, a person could have a temperature between 50 and 110, which could be scaled down to between –3 and 3. If the temperature were 55, the network would see approximately –3.3. The output will be scaled to between –1 and 1. When possible, more then one element will be used to represent the outcome is dichotomous since it may improve the patterns established in the network (12).

Network Training Criteria

The training-stop criterion is very important to define so that overfitting effect for the ANN does not occur in this study. The overfitting effect means that the network has memorized the data instead of extracting the generalization from the data. The desire training process will be to try to minimize the mean squared error (MSE) and stop when the MSE stops decreasing.

STATISTICAL METHODS

Data Sampling by Cross Validation

In the cross validation methods the database is randomly separated into two sets. The ANN is trained on the first set and tested against on the second set. This is done several times to reduce the selection bias. The average is the cross validation estimate (8,10,29,30,38). It has been determined that the optimal split is 25%-50% of the data should be for testing data set (10). This study will probably use several different splits: 50% for training and 50% for testing, 75% for training and 25% for testing, and finally 95% for testing and 5% for testing.

Discriminant Analysis and Hierarchical Cluster Analysis

Since the mechanism of neural network is a "black box", the predictive performance of the neural network models depends on the designer's choices such as rules of thumb or trial and errors. Moreover, due to the nature of the complex disease prognosis, we proposed to use some other statistical methods to help the creating data set process. The discriminant analysis is the procedure generates a discriminant function based on linear combinations of the predictor variables, which provides the best discrimination between the groups (7,35). Hierarchical cluster analysis is a multivariate statistical technique that separates samples into groups or classes by minimizing the within-group variance and maximizing the between-group variance (35). It attempts to identify relatively homogeneous groups of cases based on selected characteristics.

Logistic Regression Analysis

For logistic regression analysis, we will use the same training and testing data sets used for creating neural network models. After creating the models, the area under ROC curve will be calculated and compared to the created neural network models.

Experimental Design Summary

This experiment will go through the following steps. The variables will be selected. According to the information in the database, the representing predictive variables will be determined. The relational databases will be transformed into PC format that can produce records in the format, which allows one record per patient and has the data and the expected results. These records will be sampled according to the selected sampling method. The ANNs will be trained and tested against the training and testing data sets created by the sampling method. At the end, the prediction percentages will be analyzed.

Possible Results and Validation

We have no previous data on the correlation of the data variables used in the study and the results being predicted. Therefore, it is possible that a correlation between the data and expected results can not be determined or only weakly determined. This could have for a number of reasons. First, the data is in a time-series format. After transforming process the data could lose its predictive power. Second, there are many variables in this database. It is possible that selected variables do not have any correlation with the output. Third, the data is very noisy and incomplete. Transforming the incomplete data could also cause data to loose its predictive value.

The validation of the testing results will be done against a statistical method using receiver-operating characteristic (ROC) plots. The ROC can be used as an index of diagnostic accuracy. It is useful because they provide a unifying concept in the process of test evaluation (34,42). Diagnostic accuracy is critical for the physician's decision making because it measures a test's ability to distinguish between possible outcome states. The ROC plot provides a comprehensive view of the test's ability to make the distinction being looked at over all the thresholds of the decision (42). A plot for a test with no predictive ability will be a line with a 45% angle through the middle. The greater the area under the curve the greater the predictive ability of the test.

REFERENCES

1. Bauer, S.B., *et al.*, *Predictive value of urodynamic evaluation in newborns with myelodysplasia.* Jama, 1984. 252(5): p. 650-2.

2. Buchman, T.G., *et al.*, *A comparison of statistical and connectionist models for the prediction of chronicity in a surgical intensive care unit.* Crit Care Med, 1994. 22(5): p. 750-62.

3. Cenci, M., *et al.*, *The PAPNET system for quality control of cervical smears: validation and limits.* Anticancer Res, 1997. 17(6D): p. 4731-4.

4. Doig GC, *et al.*, *Modeling mortality in the intensive care unit: Comparing the performance of a back-propagation, associative-learning neural network with multivariate logistic regression.* In: Proceedings of the Seventeenth Annual Symposium on Computer Applications in Medical care. McGraw-Hill, Inc., Washington, DC, 1993, pp.361-365.

5. Duh, M.S., *et al.*, *Prediction and cross-validation of neural networks versus logistic regression: using hepatic disorders as an example.* Am J Epidemiol, 1998. 147(4): p. 407-13.

6. Dybowski, R., *et al.*, *Prediction of outcome in critically ill patients using artificial neural network synthesized by genetic algorithm.* Lancet, 1996. 347(9009): p. 1146-50.

7. Erkki Pesonnen. Is Neural Network better than statistical methods in diagnosis of acute appendicitis? Medical Informatics Europe'97. IOS Press, 1997: p377-381.

8. Efron B. Estimating the error rate of a prediction rule: Provement on cross-validation. J. Am Statistical Assoc. 1995; (78):p.316-31.

9. Forsstrom, J.J. and K.J. Dalton, *Artificial neural networks for decision support in clinical medicine.* Ann Med, 1995. 27(5): p. 509-17.

10. Gong G. Cross-validation, the jackknife, and the bootstrap excess error estimation in forward regression logistic regression. J. Am Statistical Assoc. 1986;81 (393):108-13.

11. Guh, J.Y., *et al.*, *Prediction of equilibrated postdialysis BUN by an artificial neural network in high-efficiency hemodialysis.* Am J Kidney Dis, 1998. 31(4): p. 638-46.

12. Hartzberg, J., *et al.* BrainMaker User's Guide and Reference manual , 4th edition, Sierra Madre, Calif., CA scientific software, Sierra Madre, Calif, 1990. Chapter 4: *Designing Neural Networks.* Pp. 79-108.

13. Hebb DO. The organization of behavior. New York : John Wiley & Sons, 1949.

14. Kattan, M. *A model for explaining and predicting the effectiveness of machine learning techniques. Ann Arbor, Mich.: University Microfilms international*; 1993

15. Kattan, M.W. and J.R. Beck, *Artificial neural networks for medical classification decisions [editorial].* Arch Pathol Lab Med, 1995. 119(8): p. 672-7.

16. Kattan, M.W., M.E. Cowen, and B.J. Miles, *Computer modeling in urology.* Urology, 1996. 47(1): p. 14-21.

17. Kaufman, A.M., *et al.*, *Decreased bladder compliance in patients with myelomeningocele treated with radiological observation.* J Urol, 1996. 156(6): p. 2031-3.

18. Kaufmann, S.J., *et al.*, *The application of neural networks in predicting the outcome of in-vitro fertilization.* Hum Reprod, 1997. 12(7): p. 1454-7.

19. Kinsman, S.L. and M.C. Doehring, *The cost of preventable conditions in adults with spina bifida.* Eur J Pediatr Surg, 1996. 6 Suppl 1: p. 17-20.

20. Leon, M.A. and J. Keller, *Toward implementation of artificial neural networks that "really work".* Proc AMIA Annu Fall Symp, 1997: p. 183-7.

21. Lette, J., *et al.*, *Artificial intelligence versus logistic regression statistical modeling to predict cardiac complications after non-cardiac surgery.* Clin Cardiol, 1994. 17(11): p. 609-14.

22. Likothanassis, S.D., Adamidis, P., Giogios, C. use of neural networks in medical expert systems. Medi. Inform., 1995. 20(4): p. 349-357.

23. Lucek, P.R. and J. Ott, *Neural network analysis of complex traits.* Genet Epidemiol, 1997. 14(6): p. 1101-6.

24. Maclin, P.S. and J. Dempsey, *How to improve a neural network for early detection of hepatic cancer.* Cancer Lett, 1994. 77(2-3): p. 95-101.

25. McLorie, G.A., *et al.*, *Determinants of hydronephrosis and renal injury in patients with myelomeningocele.* J Urol, 1988. 140(5 Pt 2): p. 1289-92.

26. Naguib, R.N. and G.V. Sherbet, *Artificial neural networks in cancer research.* Pathobiology, 1997. 65(3): p. 129-39.

27. Orr, R.K., *Use of a probabilistic neural network to estimate the risk of mortality after cardiac surgery.* Med Decis Making, 1997. 17(2): p. 178-85.

28. Partington, M.D. and D.G. McLone, *Hereditary factors in the etiology of neural tube defects. Results of a survey.* Pediatr Neurosurg, 1995. 23(6): p. 311-6.

29. .Picard RR, Berk KN. Data splitting. American statistics. 1990 (44): p.140-7.

30. Rocker EB. Prediction error and its estimation for sub-selected models. Technomertrics. 1991 (33): p.459-68.

31. Rosenblatt F. *Principles of neurodynamics.* New York: Spartan Books. 1959.

32. Rumelhart DE, Hinton GE, Williams Rj. Learning internal representations by error propagation. In : Rumelhart De. McClelland JL, (eds). *Parallel distributed processing: Explorations in the microstructures of cognition.* Cambridge, MA: MIT Press, 1986; (1): p,318-62.

33. Samuelsson, L. and M. Skoog, *Ambulation in patients with myelomeningocele: a multivariate statistical analysis.* J Pediatr Orthop, 1988. 8(5): p. 569-75.

34. Swets, J.A., *Measuring the accuracy of diagnostic systems.* Science, 1988. 240(4857): p. 1285-93.

35. M. Norusis. SPSS for windows professional statistics release 7.5., SPSS Inc., Chicago, 1995.

36. Teichman, J.M., *et al.*, *An alternative approach to myelodysplasia management: aggressive observation and prompt intervention.* J Urol, 1994. 152(2 Pt 2): p. 807-11.

37. Tewari, A., *Artificial intelligence and neural networks: concept, applications and future in urology.* Br J Urol, 1997. 80 Suppl 3: p. 53-8.

38. Tourassi, G.D. and C.E. Floyd, *The effect of data sampling on the performance evaluation of artificial neural networks in medical diagnosis.* Med Decis Making, 1997. 17(2): p. 186-92.

39. Tu, J.V., *Advantages and disadvantages of using artificial neural networks versus logistic regression for predicting medical outcomes [see comments].* J Clin Epidemiol, 1996. 49(11): p. 1225-31.

40. Turban, E, Decision Support and Intelligent Systems, 5th Edition, Prentice Hall, 1998.

41. Widrow, B., Rumelhart, D., and Lehr, M., *Neural Networks: Applications in Industry, Business, and Science, Communications of the ACM, March, 1994, 37(3): p.93-105.*

42. .Zweig, M.H. and G. Campbell, *Receiver-operating characteristic (ROC) plots: a fundamental evaluation tool in clinical medicine [published erratum appears in Clin Chem 1993 Aug;39(8):1589].* Clin Chem, 1993. 39(4): p. 561-77.

Using the Internet to Assist with Subject Delivery: A Case Study

Paul Darbyshire

Dept. Information Systems, Victoria University of Technology, P.O. Box 14428, Melbourne City MC, Victoria, Australia

Fax : (03) 9688-5024, (03) 9688-4393, Paul.Darbyshire@vut.edu.au

Stephen Burgess

Dept. Information Systems, Victoria University of Technology

Fax : (03) 9688-5024, (03) 9688-4353, Stephen.Burgess@vut.edu.au

ABSTRACT

The Internet offers versatility for the delivery of education, with a potential still largely untapped. While many institutions are exploiting the Internet for distance education, the overwhelming majority of educators use the Internet to supplement existing modes of delivery. The Internet can be used to supplement the delivery of material and/ or, to aid in the administrative functions necessary for efficient subject coordination. Efficient subject coordination is necessary to enhance the learning experience of the student, and this can be impaired by a variety of factors, including the extra burden of multi-campus subject administration. This paper presents a case study of using the Internet as both an educational material supplement and a subject administrative tool for coordinating many tutors and lectures in a multi-campus environment. This subject had not previously used the Internet in this way before and figures on student participation use of the Internet for both of the above functions are collated from usage surveys.

Keywords : internet, education, subject, coordination, administration

INTRODUCTION

The Internet is providing a low cost and flexible option for training in a number of subject areas. Students do not have to be on campus or in class to gain access to a number of subject functions, both administrative and academic in nature. More than 180 graduate schools and 150 undergraduate colleges and universities offer distance education via the Internet (Phillips). Many more would be using the Internet as a medium to support their teaching in a number of different ways. These range from the presentation of lecture notes to complete interactive teaching packages (Charp).

A number of interactive commercial teaching packages have recently come on to the market which support teaching on the Internet, and these include TopClass, Learning Space and Lotus Domino. With packages such as these, many aspects of subject delivery can be managed via the Internet, providing flexibility for both academic staff, and ultimately for the student. With learning material and administrative functions available via the Internet, a standard World Wide Web (Web) connection and browser may be used to provide and read supplementary material, submit and collect assignments as well as for the management of academic discussion and publication of results.

Anecdotal evidence suggests that the versatility this offers to students and staff is usually well received. Research, (Freeman, 1997) has shown that a TopClass based system had a positive reception from a large group of students. The Internet has been used in the Department of Information Technology of Victoria University for some time, and a small system has evolved over this period to aid in subject administrative functions via the Internet (Darbyshire, Wenn 1998). A small grant was received in 1998 to examine the integration of this administrative system with subject delivery. Although, many aspects of this are covered by the commercial systems now appearing, there was little available when the project first began.

In the first semester 1998, we used the administrative components of our evolving Web Based Learning Administration (WBLA) system, together with Web based course material, to try and administer a multi-campus subject via the Internet. This subject had not been administered via the Internet previously, and involved four lecturing staff and four tutors over two campuses. In the following sections we discuss the general aspects of Subject delivery, and then present the results of the usage case study conducted, using our Web based subject coordination system.

ASPECTS OF SUBJECT DELIVERARY

There are two overall aspects to subject delivery, these are the educational and administrative components. Delivery of the educational component of a subject to students is the primary responsibility of the subject coordinator. It is this task which is the most visible, from a students perspective. The administration tasks associated with a subject form a major component of subject coordination, but these responsibilities are not immediately obvious or visible to the students. However, if the administration tasks are performed poorly or inefficiently, the effects of this become immediately apparent to both subject tutors and students alike, and can be the source of much discontent.

There are a variety of factors that can effect performance of content delivery and administrative functions. These include change in subject content due to changes in the discipline area, enrolment numbers, coordination of other lecturing staff and subject tutors, and multiple campus subject coordination. However, it is essential that all aspects of subject administration be carried out as efficiently as possible, so as not to distract the students from their goal, which is to learn.

The next two sub-sections briefly highlight the administrative and educational tasks involved in subject coordination, and indicate where we have used the Internet to supplement or carry out these functions.

Administrative Tasks

There are a number of administrative tasks associated with subject coordination, and these include
• Student enrolment
• Assignment collection
• Grades distribution and reporting
• Informing all students of important notices
We have used the Internet, in the form of a system of Web pages to help perform all of these functions. A detailed discussion of the Web based implementation of these functions can be found in (Darbyshire, Wenn 1998).

Student Registration/ Enrolment

Actual student enrolment in their courses and subjects is currently a faculty responsibility. As the use of the Internet in administrative functions is still relatively new, the system we use is not integrated with the university database. However, in order to carry out subject administrative functions, a database must be maintained with student ID numbers and names for the current enrolment. This does necessitate the entering of this data into the locally maintained database.

To alleviate the subject coordinator of this responsibility, this aspect of the system is user driven. Thus the students enter this data themselves in their first tutorial via the Internet. This actually serves two purposes, the first has already been discussed, while the second is to introduce students to aspects of the system from their first class.

Assignment Submission

There are many elements involved in assignment collection and marking (Byrnes et al 1995), and the components identified by Byrnes that we facilitate by use of the Internet, are given in the list below
• Distribute assignment and guides
• Arrange for multiple point collection noting date and time
• Record marks and comments
• Distribute marked assignments
• Provide and distribute a sample solution
• Answer queries on assignment marks
• Collect re-submitted assignments
• Distribute remarked assignment and comments
• Collate all assignment results for final submission
To submit an assignment, a student fills out a form embedded in a Web page, including the name and local path of the assignment file they are submitting. The assignment is then transmitted to a Web server via the standard http protocol, and stored in a special directory. The date and time of submission are also recorded. The student receives instant notification of receipt by receiving a listing of assignment submissions with dates and times displayed in the browser.

As only standard Web forms are used, this operation can take place from anywhere at any time of the day or night, providing a great degree of flexibility for the student, and subject coordinator. The assignments do not have to be re-distributed to the tutors, as any authorized member of the subject team can then access these submitted assignments from any standard Web browser (Darbyshire 1998).

Assessment and Grades Distribution

There is a scope for the development of assessment techniques using the Internet. Current 'online' efforts of evaluation are often trivial and not properly tested (Charp). Many distance education programs require their students to travel to a local or regional centre for moderated final subject assessment (Hettinger).

Some desired features of an online system are (Charp):
- A help system
- A variety of levels for different users
- An assessment or evaluation system
- Feedback summaries for users.

At this stage, the integration of on-line assessment is being investigated, with the most likely outcome as a series of automatically generated multiple-choice Web pages. Some commercial systems already provide this (WBT Systems 1997), however in many instances more flexibility is needed for effective use. It is envisaged that these generated tests would be initially used as a series of self-assessment procedures embedded at various points in the on-line educational material. The use of Java applets, together with a Microsoft Access data base placed on a Web server containing the multiple-choice question stems, distractors and answers is currently the focus of the grant mentioned in the Introduction.

Currently, only assignment grades and comments are distributed back to the student via the Internet. To maintain privacy, the students can only view their own grades for a particular assignment after the provision of a password, which they supply upon registration into the system. Comments on their work are also entered by the tutor/lecturer, which they can view with their grade.

Notice Boards

Important notices are distributed to all students via the use of an electronic notice board. The use of this notice board takes on a greater importance when a subject is taught over many campuses on different days. This allows us to reach all students within an acceptable time frame with notices on assignment submission dates, cancellations, supplementary reading etc... Sophisticated managed discussion systems can be found in many system, (WBT Systems 1997), however we have found that a simple notice board for these 'Subject Announcements' is satisfactory, and is best kept separated from any discussion groups where important messages may become lost in the crowd.

The notice boards are actually maintained as a series of threaded discussion groups via an ODBC data source accessed via SQL statements through a series of special Web pages (Darbyshire 1998). There is one threaded discussion for each subject, and only authorized members of a subject team may place messages on these notice boards.

Educational Tasks

There are many 'educational' tasks that can be performed over the Internet. Some of these are (Kubala):
- Online class discussions (using, for instance, chat or listserv facilities)
- Course outline distribution
- Assignment distribution
- Class notes distribution
- Answers to student queries (email; listserv).

Just how many of these are actually performed relate to a number of factors, such as the amount of face-to-face contact between lecturers and students. Although we are using the Internet to supplement traditional face-to-face teaching, we have included all elements contained in the above list in the subject Internet trial, for the purposes of providing flexibility to both students and staff. Thus the traditional problems of students misplacing handouts, and staff not having any more copies can easily be addressed.

A number of products currently available to assist in 'educational' tasks are available. Some of these tasks include (Kursh):
- Authoring materials
- Newsgroup and/or chat features
- 'Shared whiteboard' feature
- Interactive discussions
- Shared applications.

We have implemented all the above educational tasks/ features using the current Web standards, thus any standard Web browser can access them. This provides the greatest possible flexibility to students.

Delivering Course Material

Course material was first delivered as a traditional lecture, and then supplemented with educational material for access over the Internet. The supplementary course material is generated as a series of standard Web pages using a number of tools. These included Microsoft's Publisher 98, Netscape Communicator's composer facility, a standard text editor, and some simple graphics packages including Paint Shop Pro.

Supplementary material placed on-line for Web access, included lecture handouts, lecture notes and slides where available, further reading material references, Web-links where appropriate, tutorial material, assignments and course guides.

All material could be accessed from any of the faculty or University laboratories, as all are connected to the Internet. However, many students opt to access the material from home, as they either have direct access to the university network, or their own connection through an Internet Service Provider (ISP).

Student/ Lecturer/ tutor Contact

Lecturer/ tutor/ student contact is encouraged at all times. However, given the changing nature of University employment, with more contract staff being employed on limited contracts, face-to-face contact is not always available. This also becomes exacerbated with multi-campus delivery, and has been the subject of many a student complaint when staff, (through no fault of their own), are permanently based on one campus, and students on other campuses have limited physical contact. In assisting subject administration by use of the Internet, this is one of the main areas we hoped to address.

In trying to maintain student contact, or at least provide possible avenues other than physical contact, use of email and a discussion group was encouraged. All students at Victoria University are given email accounts, so all have access to this facility from the University laboratories at least. A discussion group was also provided as part of the WBLA system so students could maintain an on-going 'academic' discussion, or post once-off messages.

The discussion group was implemented in the same way as the subject notice boards, as a threaded message facility maintained via and ODBC data source and a series of web pages with SQL access to the data source. The discussion group is open to general Web access, however only registered students in the WBLA system can post messages, by providing their registration ID and password which is attached to each threaded message. On-line chat facilities are currently banned in all faculty laboratories.

Other Concerns

There are a number of other concerns to take into account when using the Internet for subject delivery. These are security, Robustness of the technology and equity of access. These are briefly discussed.

Security

There are two aspects to security in the current system. Firstly, security of the administrative functions provided for authorized staff becomes particularly important when student grades are stored on-line. Secondly, security features for the students must be adequate to ensure their confidence in the system, and hence their continued use of it. The WBLA system is implemented on a Microsoft NT server, running NT Server 4.0 and IIS 4. This provides flexibility in security implementation.

Security for staff members is implemented as a two-tier system. All Web pages facilitating staff administrative functions are located in a directory with general Web access removed, requiring authorized staff to supply an NT user/password combination. The WBLA system then requires the entry of its own user/password combination, which is stored in an ODBC database. On successful initial entry, a transient security cookie is maintained in the user Web browser for the current session, granting them access to administrative functions.

Security for students is currently only required for very few functions. These include
• User details/password change
• Assignment Submission
• Grades lookup
• Discussion group participation

Consequently, when required, a standard user ID/ password Web page is displayed, requiring the students registration ID and password combination. On successful entry the appropriate function is permitted.

How Robust is the Technology?

The technology must be reliable. For successful trials, it is necessary for lecturers and students to be familiar with the interfaces that are to be used. Technical staff must also be competent and responsive to the needs of lecturers and students (Kubala). To this end, the use of the Web pages on the Internet to facilitate subject delivery is a good choice. The Web is controlled by standards which, while still evolving, have been in place for some time, and most first year students have had some experience with the Web and Internet through secondary school.

Equity of Access

Equity of access to the Web is often overlooked as educators become caught up in the rush to embrace the new media. We would view this as more of a problem if we were not merely supplementing subject delivery with the use of the Internet, but using it to replace some of the current services. All of the faculty's students currently have adequate access to University and faculty computer laboratories, which are connected to the Internet. While those without home access may lack the flexibility that Internet services can offer, we are not forcing students to move to this medium for the current trial.

To date, none of these concerns have been raised with us by students (the people who would be affected), only by concerned staff members. This may become an issue in future.

ADVANTAGES AND PROBLEMS

Most of the reported advantages of this type of subject delivery relate to cost savings, efficiency, flexibility and/or convenience for the students (Kubula; Phillips; Hettinger).

Lecturers can actually gain feedback in the form of web site analysis. This includes knowing what web pages have been accessed the most, how long has been spent on the pages, what files have been downloaded by students, the popular access times, and so forth.

The nature of the delivery mechanism means that materials must be kept up-to-date. Kubula suggests that it can be an advantage if the subject has been taught in the traditional mode before attempting to convert it (completely or partly) to online mode.

Some concerns have been about possible social problems, especially with distance education over the Internet. The possibility exists of people becoming addicted to use of the internet, or stressed at the bulk of information to be sorted through, using it to avoid personal interactions and other similar problems (Eddy and Spaulding).

VICTORIA UNIVERSITY OF TECHNOLOGY CASE STUDY

As previously discussed, the system we are using for the current case study has evolved over a period of time, and has been named 'Central Point', (Darbyshire, Wenn 1997). The intent is to provide a single point of access to students, and staff in the department, for subjects delivered on the Internet. This includes an initial point of access for educational material provided by subject coordinators, subject notice boards, student discussion groups, assignment collection, grades distribution, and staff administrative functions.

No style or limitations are imposed on Web pages designed by subject coordinators. Rather, Central Point provides links to the initial subject home pages only at this stage. The main functions of Central Point are to provide one common set of administrative functions for all subjects, controlled by standard Web page access. This facilitates use of the system by students, as these administrative features will be the same for all subjects they study whose coordinators make use of the system.

In 1998 a small Personalized Access and Study (PAS) grant was provided by the Center for Professional Development center of the University, to help us integrate the educational and administrative components of Central Point. This case study is the first step of that process.

One subject that used Central Point as its centre of operations was BCO3444, 'The Information Environment', in Semester One 1998. This subject examines the effect of external influences (predominantly the Internet) on businesses and seemed the ideal vehicle to pilot the Central Point scheme. The subject was offered at the two largest campuses of the university, Footscray and St.Albans. The various administrative and educational tasks discussed above, were employed during the pilot and are examined below.

At the end of the semester (in the last lecture), students were requested to fill out a questionnaire regarding their use of the Central Point system and the subject's Web site. All students present at that lecture completed the questionnaire. Some 71 students completed the questionnaire, 36 from Footscray and 35 from St.Albans. The vast majority of these (83%) were full time students.

All of the students that did not register with Central Point were situated at St.Albans. This is because registration was made compulsory at Footscray, but not at St.Albans. This meant that 77% of the students at St.Albans voluntarily chose to register with Central Point. It should be mentioned here that the developers of Central Point were based at the Footscray campus, thus were more readily available to staff members having initial difficulties. This may have been an influencing factor with success or lack of success with some tutors experiences using the Central Point site.

Table 1 Respondent profile		
Campus	**Status**	**Registered with Central Point**
Footscray (51%)	Full time (83%)	Yes (89%)
St.Albans (49%)	Part time (17%)	No (11%)

Administrative Tasks

The subject administrative tasks we were most interested in obtaining student usage figures for were those of assignment submission, and grades distribution. Successful implementation of these administrative functions on the Internet not only provides a more flexible service to students, but also unencumbers the subject coordinator from physically collecting and date stamping assignments. It also allows a common collection date for assignments from multiple campus locations to be easily enforced. This is also a feature easily extended to distance education models.

Assignment Submission

Students were requested to indicate whether or not they had submitted an assignment through Central Point during the semester. The following table shows the results to this question.

Footscray students were told that they had to submit the assignment through Central Point. St.Albans students were not told this. One quarter of them attempted to submit their assignment through Central Point.

Students that had submitted their assignments through Central Point were also requested to indicate why they had chosen to do this. The majority of Footscray students indicated it was 'because they were told to'. Other responses were:

- Ease of use (8 responses)
- It was convenient (6 responses)
- To see if it worked (1)
- My assignment was in electronic format anyway (1).
- Its a bit risky (1)

These responses reflect the advantages of Internet course delivery that were identified earlier.

Table 2 Assignment submission through Central Point			
Response	Overall (%)	Footscray (%)	St.Albans (%)
Yes, from home	8	14	0
Yes, from work	5	3	7
Yes, from school	46	75	7
No, but I tried	9	8	11
No, I did not try	32	-	75

Assignment Results

One of the key areas identified earlier was the provision of feedback to students in the online system.

Students were requested to indicate whether or not they had accessed assignment marks through Central Point during the semester. The following table shows the results to this question.

There was only one tutor at Footscray. The tutor used Central Point to enter all of the students marks. The vast majority of students accessed them throughout the semester. One tutor did not enter the assignment marks on Central Point at St.Albans. Even taking this into account, less students accessed their marks (proportionally) at St.Albans than at Footscray.

Table 3 Assignment mark access through Central Point			
Response	Overall (%)	Footscray (%)	St.Albans (%)
Yes	63	94	22
No, my tutor did not enter the marks on Central Point	8	3	15
No, I did not know how to	5	0	11
No, I did not try	24	3	52

Educational Tasks

The educational material provided for the subject's Web site was previously discussed. This included, lecture overheads, lecture notes and handouts where available, assignments, tutorial material, further references and Web links where appropriate.

Students were requested to indicate which academic features of the subject web site that they had used during the semester. The following table shows the results to this question.

Use of Discussion Groups

The students were not asked to indicate their use of the on-line discussion facility on the questionnaire as this was easily monitored externally. The use of the provided discussion group facility was poor at best. Students were given the opportunity in tutorials to trial this, which many did with a simple test message. However, during the rest of the semester, only a handful of notes were posted, and given the size and multi-campus delivery of the subject, this was obviously not a successful feature of the system.

A similar result on discussion groups was

Table 4 Use of Academic Features			
Academic Feature	Overall (%)	Footscray (%)	St.Albans (%)
Read or printed off assignment details	90	92	89
Downloaded lecture notes	76	75	77
Read or printed off the course outline	73	72	75
Followed tutorial links **during** a tutorial	70	78	63
Followed tutorial links **outside of** a tutorial	45	50	40

obtained on a prior trial of an earlier version of the system (Darbyshire, Wenn 1998). This seems to be a reoccurring trend that may require further study. However, it may be that standard email provides more functionality than we were able to build into the threaded discussion group.

COMMENTS ON RESULTS

The results of the trial are encouraging despite some of the varied figures. What is clear is that there is a greater participation rate from both campuses in obtaining educational material from the Internet, than there is in assignment submission and grades collection. Although participation was high in the administrative functions at the Footscray campus, students were told to use it. At the St.Albans campus where usage was not actively encouraged, participation was low. There are a number of factors that we believe influenced this. Location on the Footscray campus of the Central Point developers for ad hoc queries, more sessional staff at the St.Albans campus and lack of on-line documentation for students in using the system.

Hesitation in using the assignment submission facility at the St.Albans campus may also be due to perceived security problems. A survey on satisfaction with an earlier version of the Central Point system, Darbyshire and Wenn (1998), showed that the student main concern over security was with submitted work. Students were not convinced that their submitted assignments were 'safe', and mistrusted such systems. Students still seemed to prefer physically handing their assignment to their tutor.

From the figures in the Table 2, the vast majority of assignment submissions via the Internet occurred at the University, with only 17 percent at Footscray campus occurring from home or work. It is interesting to note that this is the exact same figure of part-time students from Table 1, though conclusions cannot be drawn from the collected data. We believe these figures show that flexibility for assignment submission can still be achieved although the majority of students may not be using the system outside of the University.

The figures from Table 4 show a wider acceptance for obtaining educational material from the Internet. These figures show encouraging use of the Internet for students following up supplementary material placed thereon. With the acceptance of the Internet for such material, subject coordinators and tutors now have at their disposal a versatile tool for providing material to students at any time, removing the restrictions of the once-a-week handouts. This added flexibility can only be to the benefit of students whose subject coordinators make use of such a system.

While the tutors and lecturing staff were not formally polled for their response to the system, anecdotal evidence suggests that they would make more use of such a system in future. It should be noted that all assignments submitted through the central point system were successfully received by the system server and no data corruption occurred. There was however, some problems reported with students emailing assignments as attachments to email. Assignments received through the Central Point system were able to be easily accesses by tutors, providing more flexibility for staff as to where and when the did their marking.

CONCLUSION

The data collected from this trial has been useful in so much as it has provided us with some areas for future concentration. There needs to be more functionality added for staff members. Particular attention needs to given to the manner in which assignment results are placed on the Web, and further integration of the educational component with the administrative tasks needs to be addressed. Students need to be encouraged to use the system, particularly the assignment submission facility if both staff and students are to benefit from increased flexibility.

BIBLIOGRAPHY

Charp, Sylvia, 1996, 'Courseware, Assessment and Evaluation', <u>Technical Horizons in Education</u>, Vol.24, No.2, September, p.4

Byrnes, R., Lo, B., and Dimbleby, J., (1995), "Flexible Assignment Submission in Distance learning", WCCE'95.

Darbyshire, P. and Wenn, A., 1997, 'Central Point – cyber classroom', <u>http://busfa.vut.edu.au/cpoint/cp.htm</u>

Darbyshire, Paul and Wenn, Andrew, 1998, 'Cross-Campus Subject Management Using the Internet', IRMA'98, Boston MA

Eddy, John Paul and Spaulding, Donald, 1996, 'Internet, Computers, Distance Education and People Failure: Research on Technology', <u>Education</u>, Vol.116, No.3, Spring, pp.391-393

Freeman, M., (1997), 'Flexibility in access, interaction an assessment: the case for web based teaching programs', Australian Journal of Educational Technology, Vol.13, No.1

Hettinger, James, 1997, 'Degree by E-mail', <u>Techniques,</u> Vol.72, No.7, October, pp.21-23

Kubala, Dr Tom, 1998, 'Addressing Student Needs: Teaching on the Internet', <u>Technical Horizons in Education</u>, Vol.25, No.8, March, pp.71-74

Kursh, Steven, 1998, 'Going the Distance with Web-based Training', <u>Training & Development</u>, Vol.52, No.3, March, pp.50-53

Phillips, Vicky, 1998, 'Virtual Classrooms, Real Education', <u>Nation's Business</u>, Vol.86, No.5, May, pp.41-44

WBT Systems, 'Guided Learning – Using the TopClass Server as an Effective Web-Based Training System', WBT Systems White Paper, 1997, <u>http://www.wbtsystems.com</u>

Forecasts and Trends for Electronic Commerce

Paul Foley
Leicester Business School and Visiting Professor, School of Information
Systems, University of South Australia

David Sutton
School of Information Systems, Faculty of Business and Administration, University of South Australia, City
West, North Terrace, Adelaide, South Australia 5000, Australia
(61) 8 8302 0436, Fax: (61) 8 8302 0992, david.sutton@unisa.edu.au

Chanaka Jayawardhena
Leicester Business School, De Montfort University, The Gateway, Leicester, LE1 9BH, England
(44) 116 257 7269, Fax: (44) 116 251 7548, pdf@dmu.ac.uk

ABSTRACT

This paper takes a sober look at recent studies about Internet growth and trade between 1996 and 2000. Analysis of more than 85 studies of Internet statistics reveals considerable diversity in estimates and forecasts. A review of how forecasts have changed over time is presented alongside an overview of current estimates and forecasts for key Internet statistics.

The potential for growth in electronic commerce is affected by two factors - supply of information provided by businesses and demand for goods and services from users. These two factors are reviewed separately and conclusions are put forward about the number of people using the Internet, the characteristics of potential purchasers, the industries most likely to be affected by electronic commerce, and the volume of trade which could be transacted using the internet in the future.

All studies agree that there will be significant long-term growth in the number of Internet users and growth in Internet trade. Early forecasts, made in 1996, made some of the highest predictions for Internet use. More recent forecasts have been considerably lower. The opposite trend has been observed in forecasts for electronic commerce. Forecasts for Internet trade have been continually revised upwards in recent years, particularly amongst forecasts made in 1998. However, few studies distinguish between the volume of business to business and business to consumer (or online shopping) trade. Many people have misinterpreted total Internet trade statistics as being online shopping. Most surveys suggest online shopping (business to consumer trade) is currently less than ten per cent of total Internet trade.

INTRODUCTION

Some amazing statistics have been put forward for the growth of the Internet and World Wide Web and the potential for trade. It is nonsense to believe forecasts that one billion people will be using the Internet by the year 2000 (Webster, 1996; Eccles and Palmer, 1997) or to give credence to wild predictions that US$1,000 billion of world trade will be transacted using the Internet in 2002 (Internetnews.com quoted in Nua, 1998).

There is no easy way to measure any statistic regarding the growth of the Internet, but many businesses are becoming concerned about its potential impact on their company. This paper takes a sober look at recent studies about Internet growth and trade. An understanding of the potential impact of electronic commerce (also known as Internet trade) should be central to the development of any strategy to develop applications on the Internet or better inform those considering its potential impact on existing businesses.

Many businesses developing Internet technology (such as Microsoft and Netscape Communications), those providing access to the Internet (such as CompuServe and America on Line) and others that sell the technology are doing very well. But many businesses using the Internet to promote trade are struggling. The number of losers exceeds the number of moneymakers by at least two or three to one (Rebello, 1996a, Waltner, 1996). A little like China, the Internet is a potentially huge market, everyone believes there is money to be made, but few have so far figured out how to do it (Strickland, 1997).

The paper is divided into four parts. The first part provides a definition of electronic commerce and analyses the different roles that the Internet can have in the trading process. The second part examines demand for the Internet by users and Internet user characteristics. It also examines purchasing behaviour and identifies industries that are most likely to be affected by electronic commerce. The paper concludes with a review of the key issues for anyone trying to use or interpret Internet statistics and it addresses the question of whether the predicted boom in electronic commerce is rhetoric or reality.

COMMERCE AND THE INTERNET

The Internet is said to represent a level playing field (Allen, 1996; Pitt et al, 1996) posing minimal barriers to entry for businesses seeking new markets and distribution channels. But it is unclear how electronic commerce is cannibalizing existing marketing outlets or how much trade is the result of expansion in new and existing markets, such as on-line games or gambling. Even in new markets there is likely to be some capture of resources from other activities (other things being equal) as disposable income is spent on new activities.

Electronic commerce can be defined as the exchange of information, goods, services and payments by electronic means (Harrington, 1995). The Internet provides a medium for communication. In some cases it can facilitate all the elements of Harrington's (1995) definition, but it is equally possible for transactions to be completed using a range of communication media, including the Internet. For instance it is possible a purchase could be initiated by stumbling across a page on the World Wide Web while browsing, further information could be sought by Email, a telephone call may be required to get detailed technical information which could be received by fax, and finally a visit to the distribution depot or retailer could be made to collect and pay for the goods. This diversity of uses for the Internet in a purchasing decision is a feature rarely commented upon by many papers that provide estimates and forecasts for electronic commerce.

The Internet may play a role in 'ordinary' purchases such as the example above or it could become central to business operations at all stages of the marketing process. The primary focus of this paper is a review of literature forecasting electronic commerce and investigating the processes involved in the final part of the trading process where a purchase is completed by making an on-line order using the Internet.

DEMAND FOR THE INTERNET AND ELECTRONIC COMMERCE

The potential for electronic commerce is affected by *demand* from users and *supply* by businesses or other organisations. Demand is affected by three key factors. Firstly, the number of people using the Internet now and in the future. Secondly, the characteristics of people (and businesses) using the Internet. Thirdly, and probably most importantly, purchasing behaviour on the Internet. Together with an examination of the goods and services purchased by Internet users these factors allow the analysis of current and future demand for goods and services on the Internet.

This paper provides an introduction to Internet demand by reviewing more than 85 reports and predictions of Internet use and trade were accumulated between June 1996 and December 1998. Sources include newspapers and magazines as well as academic journals and consultants reports (the relatively high purchase cost of several consultants reports led to only key results being obtained from press releases). In addition, numerous Web based newsletters, daily reports and email services were also examined. No survey of this nature could ever be regarded as complete. But many of the key players, such as Forrester, Jupiter, IDC, eMarketer and NUA have been quoted and cross-referenced on many occasions. All monetary figures quoted in this paper are United States dollars.

Demand: Internet Connectivity

One of the fundamental factors affecting the potential for electronic commerce is the number of people connected to the Internet. The number of people using the Internet is a popular topic for commercial organisations and analysts. Primarily, because it represents the potential market for electronic commerce. However, calculating the number of users is not easy. Many groups appear to extrapolate or produce estimates from data about Internet hosts, the number of users served by Internet Service Providers (ISP's) and other figures, many of which are themselves estimates. A complementary approach is the use of household or business surveys of Internet use. Problems arise in comparing survey results because response rates, survey sizes and definitions of what constitutes Internet use vary.

Despite these problems many organisations use a variety of methods to estimate the number of Internet users. Indeed, the Wall Street Journal suggested that information about information technology can be more valuable than the technology itself. With reports often costing more than US$ 2,000 for the most basic estimates or forecasts and businesses such as Hewlett Packard spending US$ 4million a year on market research it is obvious why so many forecasters have moved into the area of Internet predictions.

Regrettably, methodologies and calculations are rarely elaborated in forecasts or publications. Any comparison of estimates is made more difficult because studies provide data in different ways. Some present data as the number of users, others provide information about the number of computers, some record the number of households connected. Few distinguish between household users and commercial users accessing the Internet from businesses or other organisations. Therefore caution must be exercised when comparing estimates or forecasts.

Despite these caveats and reservations it is still interesting to examine predictions. In the context of this paper an 'estimate' is a current or historical calculation of the variable being investigated. A 'forecast' is a prediction about the future value of the variable (thus based on estimates).

Figure 1 shows results of estimates and forecasts for the number of Internet users for the period 1996 - 2002. This data was collected from 37 studies published between June 1996 and November 1998. There are several interesting and amusing features about these predictions.

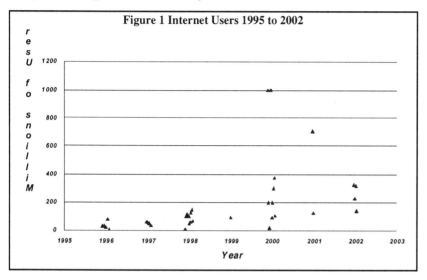

Figure 1 Internet Users 1995 to 2002

Firstly, the number of forecasts of future Internet use matches the number of reports providing estimates of past or current Internet users. Interestingly, many of the initial forecasts made in 1996 make some of the highest predictions for Internet use in 2000. Three 1996 reports predicted 1 billion users in 2000. Some organisations are reported as making significant changes to earlier forecasts only a few months after they have been made. For instance in March 1996 Rasmussen reported IDC as estimating 80 million users on the Net in 1996. In 1997 Steven Systems reported IDC as estimating the number of Internet users in 1996 at 40 million. A downward revision of 50 per cent.

Figure 2 removes five of the more extreme predictions for 2000 and 2001 presented in Figure 1 (four of these were 'early' forecasts made in 1996). Clearly, as earlier parts of this paper highlighted, confidence cannot be placed on any forecast and certainly not on any single report being more or less accurate than any other. Nonetheless, greater convergence in estimates and forecasts is apparent if these 'outliers' are omitted. If a linear trend line is also added to Figure 2 correlation improves and convergence is apparent. However, it must be emphasised that the selection of reports for inclusion is subjective and there is no reason why a linear trend should exist. We are continually collecting and analysing estimates and forecasts to examine trends and investigate whether a linear relationship is appropriate to model user growth on the Internet (see http://www.dmu.ac.uk/ln/ecommerce/welcome.htm).

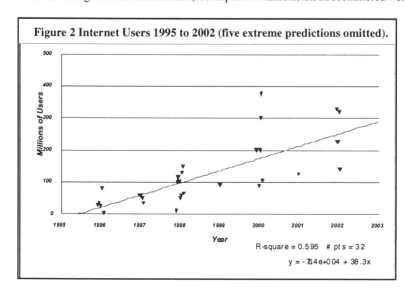

Figure 2 Internet Users 1995 to 2002 (five extreme predictions omitted).

R-square = 0.595   # pts = 32

y = - 7.64e+004 + 38.3x

Based on the linear regression line inserted in Figure 2 an overview of all reports would predict the number of users as 175 million in 2000, rising to approximately 252 million users by 2002.

Internet user characteristics

Internet users have been characterised as being dominated by young, well-educated, professional and affluent males (Tamer, 1996). However, recent surveys suggest that people using the Internet are becoming more representative of the population as a whole (Chandrasekaran, 1997; GVU,

1998). Once again comparison between studies is difficult because of their different survey techniques (such as on-line questionnaires for individuals and household telephone surveys), the non-random selection methods used by on-line surveys and differences in the questions asked (Tamer, 1996). Therefore care must be taken when comparing results. Comparison of general trends is more robust than analysis of key variables between surveys. However, even within general trends there is potential for spurious results since respondents to all on-line Internet surveys are 'self-selecting' and 'converted'. The novelty or attractiveness of participating in surveys of Internet use is likely to be highest for some users and not others, for example by gender, age or the simple fact that new Internet users may find on-line surveys a novelty, more experienced users may not.

The United States appears to be leading the trend in greater adoption of the Internet by the population at large. Early users in the United States did fall into the usual characterisation of male affluent dominance. However, on-line surveys reveal that the proportion of female users in the US has risen from 5 per cent in 1994 to approximately 39 per cent in 1998 (GVU, 1998). Two household surveys undertaken in 1997 also found an increase in Internet use by women. Jupiter Communications estimate 40 per cent (Hamilton, 1997) and Chandrasekaran (1997) reported that a telephone survey of 6,600 households found 42 per cent female users. In Britain, where the Internet market is starting to mature, the percentage of female users reached 35 per cent in 1997 (NOP Research, 1997). Elsewhere male dominance was still prevalent: 85 per cent in Europe and Australia (GVU, 1997; Australian on-line survey, 1996) and 90 per cent in Japan (IDC, 1997a).

Internet users are predominantly young but the average age of users is increasing. A GVU (1998) on-line survey in April/May 1998 found an average age of 35.1 compared with 33.0 two years earlier. European users are generally younger than US respondents (30.2 and 36.5 years old respectively; GVU, 1998). Users also appear to be more affluent than the general population. Average US household income in 1995 was $42,400, Internet using households had an income of $66,700 (DuBrow, 1995), Diamond (1997) suggests the average had fallen to $55,000 in 1997 and GVU estimate an average figure for US users of $54,000 in 1998. A higher proportion of those with managerial and professional jobs are Internet users in comparison with the US as a whole which had 34 per cent in this category in 1994 (DuBrow, 1995): 59 per cent of users in 1994 had managerial or professional jobs (DuBrow, 1995), 50 per cent in 1995 (Chandrasekaran, 1997) and 39 per cent in 1997 (Chandrasekaran, 1997).

Internet purchasing behaviour

Predictions of the level of Internet trade are even more difficult to calculate than those for Internet connectivity. It is hard enough to know how many people are using the Internet let alone what they are doing when they are using it. Several additional difficulties arise when trying to estimate Internet trade. Firstly, there is no commonly accepted definition of what constitutes electronic commerce. Secondly, it is difficult to distinguish whether a purchase is purely facilitated by, or a result of, the Internet. For example a purchase made on the Internet could be stimulated by a newspaper advert. Equally a terrestrial purchase can be made after gathering information on the Internet. The computer manufacturer, Dell, exemplifies this difficulty. They carry out the majority of their business through a combination of Internet and telephone sales and recent reports suggest some confusion between the amounts of trade attributed to each medium.

Finally, and most importantly, many reports appear to aggregate or confuse the volume of transactions carried out between businesses (commonly called business to business) and trade between vendors and customers (commonly called business to customer or online shopping). The significance of these two categories is highlighted later.

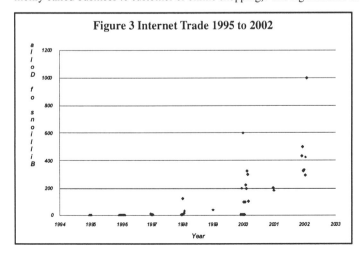

Figure 3 Internet Trade 1995 to 2002

Figure 3 shows Internet trade volume estimates and forecasts from 51 different reports for the period between 1996 and 2002. All forecasts are for total Internet trade (i.e. business to business and business to customer trade). A number of similarities and differences can be observed between Internet trade reports and Internet use forecasts examined in the previous section.

Firstly, unlike Internet use predictions, reports on Internet trade tend to have been revised upwards in later years. For instance, 60 per cent of 1996 predictions for 2000 estimated Internet trade volume at less than US$ 7 billion. The average forecast in 1997 for

Internet trade in 2000 was US$ 62 billion, by 1998 predictions had risen to an average forecast of US$ 260 billion of Internet trade in 2000. Individual organisations have also made significant readjustments to their forecasts. In May 1998, Nuá quoted IDC as forecasting US$ 333 billion of Internet trade in 2002, five months later the same source quoted IDC as revising its forecast for the same year to US$ 425 billion.

Internet trade reports are also characterised by some very extreme values. The same caveats as highlighted previously concerning the subjective nature of selecting results for presentation must once again be acknowledged. Nonetheless Figure 4 shows a linear trend line after excluding two outliers. If the trend is correct it indicates Internet trade of US$ 177 billion in 2000 and US$ 276 billion in 2002. Internet trade forecasts appear to be predicting significant increases in future years and a linear relationship may not be appropriate. We will continue to analyse estimates and forecasts to investigate whether a non-linear relationship may be more appropriate (see http://www.dmu.ac.uk/ln/ecommerce/welcome.htm).

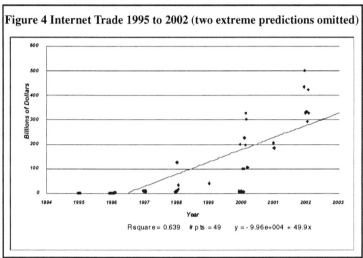

Figure 4 Internet Trade 1995 to 2002 (two extreme predictions omitted)

Rsquare= 0.639   # pts = 49   y = - 9.96e+004 + 49.9x

Internet use reports showed a steady convergence in predictions over time. However, convergence in views about Internet trade volume is not matched by agreement about the size of the two different Internet markets. An IDC forecast in September 1998 estimated that 21 per cent of Internet trade in 2002 would be in the business to customer market. Most other forecasters predict that this market will only comprise less than a tenth of total Internet trade volume. This failure by many forecasters and analysts to distinguish between business to business and business to consumer markets is significant. Business to business electronic commerce has been delivered via Electronic Data Interchange (EDI) systems over private networks for approximately 20 years. EDI therefore has a relatively long history. EDI trade is thought to be 14 times larger than the current level of Internet trade (Sun Microsystems, 1998). However, over the next five years it is predicted that EDI and Internet trade will both grow to approximately US$ 450 billion per annum, with 30 per cent of EDI traffic running over the Internet (Sun Microsystems, 1998).

It is possible that a high proportion of the business to business trade on the Internet is a migration from traditional EDI systems as business transfer these activities to the World Wide Web. Several companies, such as EDI Network, now offer a service converting EDI systems into Web based Internet systems. In effect this could be mere substitution of one computer network with another, and not "new" trade.

Much of the recent stock market speculation has concentrated on consumer oriented companies, such as Yahoo, Excite, Amazon.com and eBay operating in the business to consumer market. If estimates that this market comprises only ten percent of overall Internet trade were correct in 1998 the size of the business to consumer market would therefore be approximately US$ 3.5 billion. Trade at this level is obviously significant, but to provide a comparison the two largest 'big book' general merchandise marketers in the United States had total catalog sales of US$ 5.5 billion in 1995 (J C Penney US$ 3.7 billion and Spiegel US$ 1.8 billion; Kiley, 1996).

What do people buy?

The characterisation of early web users as young professional men, educated and technically knowledgeable is also the demographic profile of typical purchasers of CDs, adult entertainment, computer software and other 'boys toys' (Cyr, 1996). Users are purchasing some goods more frequently than others on the Web. Computer hardware and software, books, music, adult entertainment and travel (GVU, 1998; Hodges, 1996; Waltner, 1996; Weekend Australian, 1997) are consistently reported as the main items purchased. Smith Shi and Salesky (1994) suggest that the key characteristics for merchandise purchased on-line are items :-

• where product information is an important part of the purchase decision, but where pre-purchase trial is not critical (e.g. computers not cars)
• where audio or video demonstrations are useful (e.g. CDs and videos)
• which can be delivered electronically (e.g. computer software)

- that are unique (e.g. collectibles, speciality foods)
- items purchased regularly, where convenience is valued (e.g. packaged goods).

The passage of time has shown most of these predictions were accurate, but the last two have generally not proved as useful. Analysis of items purchased on the World Wide Web, see Table 1, has generally confirmed that early predictions about the products which would become most suitable for electronic commerce have been correct.

Smith Shi and Salesky (1994) concentrated on the characteristics of merchandise. This approach ignores two other important factors. Firstly, by concentrating on merchandise they did not consider services. Several more recent studies have highlighted the growth of services offered on the World Wide Web, particularly financial and insurance services (Birch and Young, 1997; Greenwood and Stutz, 1998).

Table 1. Items most frequently purchased on the World Wide Web			
Study (year) / Product	Activmedia (1997) Rank (%)	Intelliquest (1996) Rank (%)	GVU (1998) Rank only
Computer hardware and/or software	1st (21 %)	1st (24 %)	1st
Books/Magazines/ Information	2nd (13 %)	2nd (12 %)	2nd
Travel	3rd (6 %)		3rd
Finance/Investment Reports	4th (4 %)	3rd (10 %)	4th
Real Estate	5th (2 %)		
Flowers		4th (8 %)	

Secondly, by concentrating on products they failed to consider the process through which a purchase is undertaken. The unique characteristics of the electronic commerce process have been very attractive to some purchasers. Two additional factors, to those put forward by Smith Shi and Salesky (1994), also become important when the process of undertaking electronic commerce is considered. They were both highlighted in the October/November 1996 GVU on-line survey (1997) as the two primary advantages of electronic commerce. The two additional characteristics are concerned with the process of purchasing merchandise on-line are:-

- ease and privacy of transaction (e.g. adult entertainment, gambling and possibly flowers)
- availability of information about price where products are standard comparison items, particularly entertainment goods (e.g. CDs and videos)

Although none of the surveys in Table 1 record the importance of adult entertainment or gambling there is anecdotal evidence, concerning the most frequently read pages on the Web, to suggest they are significant (Cowley, 1997). The adult entertainment and/or pornographic industry, with around 60,000 Web sites, is said to account for over 23 per cent of all consumer sales (NUA, 1998). This suggests that 'privacy' of transactions is important

CONCLUSION

Many of those developing Internet technology or providing access to the Internet have a strong vested interest in the real or perceived expansion of the Internet and electronic commerce. Internet consultants, journalists and perhaps even academics have equally pressing reasons to ensure the popularity of this relatively new method of communication.

The relative youth, wealth and professional status of early Internet users was extremely attractive to many businesses contemplating electronic commerce. However, the characteristics of Internet users is stabilising in the US and this trend is likely to be mirrored in other countries. Late adopters have a profile much more like the population at large. The stability of user characteristics in the US (who are slightly younger and more affluent than the general population, 40 per cent are females) may be disappointing to those who targeted youthful, wealthy professional males. But it should provide greater confidence for the majority of Internet traders.

The key characteristics that facilitate electronic commerce concern the nature of the *product* and the *process* of undertaking trade on the Internet. The sale of products such as CDs, videos, computer software and books, which are amongst the most popular electronic commerce merchandise, is enhanced by the capability of the Internet to provide audio or video demonstrations and other product information where this is influential in the purchase decision. The ability to deliver goods or services, such as computer software (the most popular electronic commerce item) and investment reports, electronically is also important. Two advantages in the way trade is conducted (process) through the Internet are also highlighted by users. These are the ease and privacy of electronic commerce transactions (particularly for adult entertainment and gambling) and the speed and convenience with which the lowest prices can be found for standard comparison items such as CD and books.

Analysis of more than 85 studies and forecasts of Internet use and trade reveals considerable diversity in estimates and forecasts. All the studies agree that there will be significant long-term growth in the number of Internet users and growth in Internet trade. Most forecasts predict exponential growth in Internet use. The number of people using Internet host computers is obviously important information but it is impossible to count the number of users. Despite this difficulty 37 studies have estimated or forecast the number of Internet users. Early forecasts, made in 1996, made some of the highest predictions for Internet use in 2000. More recent forecasts have been considerably lower. The average estimate for the number of users in 2000 is 175 million, rising to approximately 252 million users in 2002. Recent forecasts for 2000 and 2002 are beginning to converge. However, it unknown whether these changes are the result of more sophisticated techniques or simply a better understanding of other organisations' predictions and therefore a desire to conform.

Predictions of the level of Internet trade are even more difficult to calculate than those for Internet connectivity. Nonetheless, there are almost twice as many reports about Internet trade as there are about the number of users. Unlike Internet user predictions, reports on Internet trade have continually been revised upwards in recent years. Convergence in Internet trade forecasts is also evident, particularly amongst forecasts made in 1998. Estimates suggest an average Internet trade volume of US$ 261 billion in 2000 rising to US$ 358 in 2002.

A conflict appears to have arisen. Many forecasters and analysts have been downgrading predictions for the number of future Internet users considerably during recent years. Despite these reductions in the number of Internet users many of the same analysts have been making significant increases in predictions about the volume of Internet trade in the future.

There are only two ways this potential conflict can be resolved. Firstly, if the proportion of Internet users (businesses and individuals) making purchases increases growth in Internet trade could grow. However, recent reports suggests a plateau of about 19 per cent of Internet users undertaking purchases may exist. GVU surveys had been showing a steady increase in consumer purchasing behaviour, but the last time this data was presented (for their survey undertaken in April/May 1997) a decline in purchasing behaviour to 18.7 per cent of respondents, from 18.8 per cent in a similar survey six months earlier was recorded. Other surveys (Srinivasan et al, 1998; Chandrasekaran, 1997) have also suggested relative stability in purchasing patterns. The second way this conflict could be resolved is if the level of purchases undertaken by those users who do buy goods and services increases significantly.

Few studies distinguish between the volume of business to business and business to consumer (or online shopping) trade. This is important because many people have interpreted Internet trade forecasts as being online shopping. Most surveys, which provide an interpretation, suggest online shopping (business to consumer trade) is currently less than ten per cent of total Internet trade. More than 90 per cent of Internet trade is estimated to be business to business commerce. To put the potential for online shopping into perspective it is worth highlighting that business to consumer Internet sales in 1998 are unlikely to have exceeded the combined catalog sales of $5,500 million achieved by J C Penney and Spiegel in 1995.

Finally, we believe that it is important to investigate geographical purchasing patterns from online providers, in addition to the existing preoccupation with trade volumes and the number of users. The migration of consumers from terrestrial suppliers to Internet suppliers in a different locality or country could have an impact on some companies, localities or certain types of shops. If purchases are made outside of the locality of existing suppliers less money will be circulating in that local economy and multiplier effects, creating jobs and trade, will be lost. More needs to be done to investigate this potential impact of Internet trade.

AUTHORS NOTE

The authors are continually monitoring Internet surveys. The latest surveys, trends, analysis and hot links to survey sites for reports mentioned in this paper can be found at the International Electronic Commerce Research Centre home page http://www.dmu.ac.uk/ln/ecommerce/welcome.htm. This Web site also contains details of all the references mentioned in this paper.

Prediction of Usability: Comparing Method Combinations

Erik Frøkjær

University of Copenhagen, Department of Computing, Universitetsparken 1, DK-2100 Copenhagen, Denmark
+45 35 32 14 56, fax: +45 35 32 14 01, erikf@diku.dk

Marta K. Larusdóttir

EJS hf., Grens·svegi 10, 108 Reykjavìk, Iceland
+354-563 30 00, fax: +354-563 84 13, marta@ejs.is

ABSTRACT

The effectiveness of three methods for uncovering and assessing usability problems has been derived from usage reports from 17 groups of evaluators with 3 evaluators per group. The evaluators were third year computer science students. The methods investigated were Cognitive Walkthrough, Heuristic Evaluation, and Thinking Aloud. The effect of combined use of two evaluation methods was investigated by first doing either Cognitive Walkthrough or Heuristic Evaluation followed by Thinking Aloud. When used alone, Heuristic Evaluation detects significantly more problems than Cognitive Walkthrough. Thinking Aloud after prior use of Heuristic Evaluation seems superior in detecting usability problems when compared to any other methods, and it also eliminates an important weakness of Heuristic Evaluation when used by non-experts, namely its proneness to indicating false problems.

Keywords: Usability evaluation, experimentation, method combination, predictive power, effectiveness, individual differences, Heuristic Evaluation, Cognitive Walkthrough, Thinking Aloud.

INTRODUCTION

The purpose of this study is to compare the effectiveness of predicting usability problems by three widely taught and applied usability evaluation methods (UEMs). Usability problems are considered to be those that will influence the users of the system during practical use. The three UEMs selected for the study are Thinking Aloud (TA) [15, 18] and the two inspection methods, Heuristic Evaluation (HE) [20, 18] and Cognitive Walkthrough (CW) [22, 25]. For the first time, the effect of combined use of two evaluation methods is investigated by having the same evaluators use one of the inspection methods, then TA, on the same user interface. Further, we have examined whether the UEMs tend to waste efforts by addressing so-called false problems a false problem being a usability problem registered that in practice influences no or very few users. For each method, the time spent by the evaluators in learning the techniques, and in preparing and doing the evaluation has been recorded. The evaluators were third year computer science students in the final semester of their bachelor program. The number of evaluators in this study was 51 -- higher than in any other previously published study of the effectiveness of UEMs.

Since the early nineties researchers have carried out studies comparing and contrasting some of the methods brought forward to uncover usability problems of interactive computer systems, e.g. [8, 3, 14, 2, 13]. As pointed out by John and Mashyna [11], Gray and Salzman [5], and Baecker et al. [1: p. 87], these studies still have to be considered preliminary. Baecker et al. ask for studies where combinations of inspection methods and empirical usability testing are evaluated. The present study takes up exactly this line of research.

The term a usability experiment is here used as a common designation of either an empirical usability evaluation, here TA, or an inspection based usability evaluation, here HE or CW.

THE DESIGN OF THE EXPERIMENT

Evaluation Methods Selected

Of the three UEMs, CW and HE were selected because these two inspection methods seem to be the most widely taught and used in Europe and in the United States. TA is a very common method for usability testing, and we knew from previous studies [12, 16] that computer science students and system designers are able to make quite effective use of this method without heavy training.

We decided to make use of more recently published descriptions of the methods than were available to earlier prominent method evaluation studies, e.g. [8, 14, 3, 2], although we emphasized to use introductory descriptions prepared by the original authors of the methods. Direct comparisons with results from earlier studies were hereby made problematic, but it would be so for a number of other reasons, see below in the section Comparative Discussion.

The evaluators were introduced to the methods in a uniform manner. They received descriptions of HE by [18: pp. 19-20 and pp. 115-165]. CW was introduced by [19: Chapter 5]. TA was introduced by [18: pp. 181-191 and pp. 195-198] and by [15: pp. 51-56].

The Method Evaluators

The evaluators were 51 students in their third year of a bachelor degree in computer science. The evaluators' mean age was 25.1 year; 75% were male. One third of the evaluators was or had been working in industry as software designers or programmers, typically on a part time basis. Participation in this method evaluation project was a mandatory, grade-giving part of a semester course in Human-Computer Interaction. The students could decide whether the researchers were allowed to include their results in this comparative study. All collected data were anonymously related to the individual evaluator and his or her group. Nearly half of the evaluators had heard about TA before, but less than five percent had ever used it. Only 10% had heard about CW and HE, none had used any of them.

The general computing and system development skills of the student evaluators are not too far from the typical level of programmers and software developers in industry in Scandinavia, and probably in many parts of Europe. This statement is based on the fact that these third year students already have, or easily obtain, responsible positions as software developers.

Software Tools Selected for Evaluation

The evaluators evaluated either one or both of the following two software tools for usability problems: (1) An experimental text retrieval system TeSS giving access to documentation of certain programming tools [6], or (2) the graphical text editor Asedit, a Unix-based shareware program developed by Andrzej Stochniol. The evaluators received a short user manual about TeSS. Asedit includes hypertext on-line help facilities and user documentation. TeSS and Asedit are quite simple systems to an audience like the evaluators, and could be used for practical tasks after a few half hours introductory training. Only 10% of the evaluators had heard about TeSS, none had used it. None had heard about Asedit.

The Experimental Procedure

During a two-week period 17 groups of 3 evaluators performed 28 usability experiments following one out of three evaluation programs, see Table 1. The evaluator groups were randomly assigned to one of the evaluation programs each starting by evaluating one of the two software tools using one of the two inspection methods. The

Table 1. The procedure of the experimental method evaluation.			
Preparation	Voluntary group formation, 51 students made 17 groups, 3 individuals in each group. Each group was randomly assigned to one of three evaluation programs.		
Evaluation Program no.	1	2	3
Usability experiment name 1. Week	**CW** 6 groups evaluated TeSS using CW	**HE** 5 groups evaluated TeSS using HE	Control 6 groups evaluated Asedit, 3 using CW and 3 using HE
Result	6 LUPs	5 LUPs	6 LUPs (not used)
Usability experiment name 2. Week	**CW-TA** 6 groups evaluated TeSS using TA 6 LUPs	**HE-TA** 5 groups evaluated TeSS using TA	**TA** 6 groups evaluated TeSS using TA
Result		5 LUPs	6 LUPs
Data Analysis	The authors combined the 28 LUPs on TeSS (6 from CW, 5 from HE and 17 from TA) for making the A-LUP list for TeSS		

second week all groups evaluated the same software tool TeSS using the TA method.

After one weeks work with one of the inspection methods each group submitted a List of Usability Problems (LUP) to the research group, (see description below). After still one week the groups submitted the LUPs based upon TA.

By leaving out Asedit from the TA evaluation we obtained to have 6 groups to meet TeSS for the first time (Evaluation Program 3 in Table 1). This could make it possible to identify, and maybe to compensate, for a learning effect or an effect where evaluators who had first used an inspection method might be biased in their empirical testing, wanting to confirm the usability problems they had already found.

As recommended by Nielsen [18], a strict procedure of the evaluations forced the students to carry out and report individual evaluations using HE or CW before they opened discussions with their group members for reaching a common result and preparing the group's LUP. For the TA tests another 51 computer science students acted as subjects. Groups of 3 subjects were randomly assigned to each group of TeSS evaluators. These students had followed similar evaluation programs as the TeSS evaluators, but instead of TeSS they evaluated a Unix-based email-system, Elm, which was familiar to them. The purpose of this arrangement was two-fold: (a) to be able to assign subjects without prior knowledge of TeSS to the 17 groups for their TA sessions; and (b) to let the students experience that systematic use of UEMs would reveal a rather large number of severe usability problems, even in tools they were accustomed to. The evaluator groups followed the same procedure for their TA tests. The procedure was: (a) the group developed a set of test tasks for each of the three subjects to solve; (b) one member of the evaluator group functioned as a moderator who asked the subjects to solve the test tasks one by one and during this encouraged the subjects to think aloud; (c) another member of the evaluator group functioned as a registrant who wrote down the usability problems that each of the subjects came upon; (d) the third member of the evaluator group observed and was a subject in a pilot test to prepare for the TA tests. As a result of the TA tests the groups handed in a LUP for each of the 3 subjects, and a combined LUP for the TA experiment, which are used in this study.

The reasons for a group-based evaluation program were that we wanted the students to benefit from mutual discussion during their process of training the usage of either CW or HE. Also we wanted them to be able to have different roles in the TA tests, as a moderator, an observer, and a registrant. We expect a group-based evaluation program to be quite realistic for system developers. In a corporate environment Karat et al. [14] found group-based walkthroughs superior compared to individual walkthroughs.

The Data Collected

The evaluators described the results of each usability experiment in a List of Usability Problems (LUP). Each entry in such a list consisted of a problem description, and the evaluators' severity rating of the problem according to the scale in Table 2.

Table 2. The three point scale used by the evaluators to grade the severity of the usability problems.

- Highly Critical Problems (HCP), i.e. problems that decisively in?uence whether or not the user is able to perform the ongoing operation and complete the task. It is strongly recommended that such problems should be corrected before the system is put into operation.
- Severe Problems (SP), i.e. problems that impede the user's work substantially and have some in?uence on whether the user can perform the ongoing task. Such problems should at least be corrected in the next version of the system.
- Cosmetic Problems (CP), i.e. problems that impose only slight inconvenience to the user. Such problems should be corrected when a convenient opportunity turns up.

In this scale, the descriptions about when the problems should be corrected was only meant as an indicator of the severity of the problem. The evaluators in their classifications were not supposed to take into consideration any other aspects than usability. Severity classifications similar to those presented in Table 2 are used in many other UEM studies.

Additionally we have collected background information about each evaluator's study activities, professional work experience, prior knowledge about the UEMs and software tools similar to the tools selected for this study.

DATA ANALYSIS

As a common reference for the assessment of the evaluator groups' LUPs, we formed an Authorized List of Usability Problems (A-LUP) of TeSS. This list contains all usability problems identified in the 51 evaluators' 28 usability experiments. The A-LUP identifies each problem, describes the problem shortly, and grades the severity of the problem. Table 3 gives an overview of the usability problems registered, arranged according to the categories of the A-LUP.

Identification of Problems

The identification of the problems of the A-LUP was done by collecting all the problem descriptions from the 28 LUPs. The problem descriptions were grouped according to the different parts of the interface of TeSS. Descriptions of identical problems were registered as one; and descriptions which covered more than one problem were split and registered accordingly. We preferred the problem descriptions in their concrete forms avoiding slipping into more general expressions of problem types. We expected concrete problem descriptions to be more useful during the appraisals of the groups' LUPs against the A-LUP.

Table 3. Categories of problems included by the Authorized List of Usability Problems (A-LUP) with total number of problems by each category.

```
107 Usability Problems
    3   Highly Critical Problems, HCP
   38   Severe Problems, SP
   66   Cosmetic Problems, CP
 14 False Problems
 34 Neutralized Problems
    8   Evaluators' error
    5   User's choice of an extreme manner of operation
    7   Not a usability problem related to the software tool evaluated
    2   Programming error
    2   Not reproducible
    5   Meaningless
    5   Underlying system
155 Total number of identifed problems
```

Neutralized Problems

Some of the problems registered were not directly attributable to TeSS. Such problems were identified independently of the severity of the problem and they have been neutralized, i.e. they have not been taken into this comparative analysis. The problems neutralized were categorized as either (1) evaluator's error, (2) user's extreme and intricate manner of using TeSS, e.g. what programmers sometimes call "crash-testing", (3) not a usability problem related to TeSS, (4) not reproducible, (5) meaningless problem description, (6) problem of an underlying system, in the case of TeSS the X Window System or Unix.

False Problems

Some problems from the LUPs we considered to be false problems in the sense that -- if such a problem would be taken to justify a change of the evaluated software tool -- we would expect this change to have no or even a negative effect on the usability of the system.

We registered 14 false problems. As an illustration we can mention "TeSS at DIKU ought to be in Danish". We do not consider this issue to be of relevance in this particular context. The body of texts made searchable in TeSS are programming manuals written in English, and the intended users of TeSS are computer science students who are quite familiar with the English language. Further, TeSS is only available through the Unix-based computer network of the department, where practically all the other software tools offer an English-oriented user interface only.

Identifying a problem as false can raise many complicated questions and discussions. We have been restrictive in using this category. For instance, there are only three false problems that have been identified by more the one LUP.

The Severity of the Usability Problems of the A-LUP

The important grading of the severity of the usability problems of the A-LUP was established as follows. First, in the high end, with the strict definition of a Highly Critical Problem, we could take over the HCPs of TeSS from an earlier study, based on feed-back from 83 subjects working 648 hours on-line with TeSS during their solution of 25 information retrieval tasks [6]. With regard to the severe and cosmetic problems, the accumulated results from the 17 TA experiments were taken carefully into account, but because of large variances, see section 4, the grading was not just a matter of computing the evaluators' mean grading. We decided that no problem identified by more than one TA experiment as being severe or highly critical was graded less than a SP, i.e. a noticeable usability problem. In this way we adjusted towards the evaluators' final assessments after their TA sessions avoiding disputable grading of potential SPs as CPs.

RESULTS AND DISCUSSION

This section first presents the results of the statistical analysis of the effectiveness of the methods in identifying the usability problems of TeSS. Then the effectiveness of the methods in revealing the proper severity of the identified problems are examined.

As background information concerning the time spent, an average evaluator, as a member of a group of evaluators, used respectively 22 hours, 29 hours and 24 hours doing a complete CW, HE or TA. The differences are statistically significant, but not large enough to be really important. These figures include from 6 to 9 hours for an evaluator to read the description of the method, to reach an understanding of its techniques, and to prepare the usability experiment in collaboration with the other members of the evaluator group.

Predicting Usability Problems

As to the effectiveness of the methods in predicting usability problems, our study shows a significant differ-

significant, see Table 4. With HE an average group of evaluators finds 19% of all the usability problems of TeSS, while an average group using CW finds 10%.

HE and TA performed by a group of three evaluators on an average uncovered approximately 80% more usability problems than a group using CW. Compared to the users' actual activity during system interaction the strict GOMS-like walkthrough built into CW seems to have an unrealistically narrow focus.

Nielsen [17] has reported that 3 developers using HE found approximately 40% of the usability problems of a software tool. He asked 31 computer science students, in their first year, to evaluate an interface in which 16 usability problems had already been identified. Our groups of 3 evaluators found only half as many problems as could be expected from Nielsen's experiment. A possible explanation could be that our system, although being rather simple, was definitely more complex than the walk-up-and-use interface investigated by Nielsen.

Table 4. The mean percentage of usability problems from the A-LUP found by a group in one usability experiment using the specific UEM.

Usability Evaluation Method (UEM)	CW	HE	TA
Mean percentage of the usability problems	10%	19%	18%
Standard deviation (σ)	4%	5%	9%

Our A-LUP includes 107 usability problems, compared to Nielsen's 16. Our result indicates that more HE evaluations than usually recommended have to be carried out in order to cover the problems of a specific user interface of even small systems properly. But readers of this kind of studies have to be cautious drawing quantitative, general conclusions from the results. The specific circumstances differ markedly between the studies, so what is significant is probably only the relative effectiveness of the methods within each study.

The effect of combining results of using the inspection methods and the TA method is presented in Table 5.

Table 5. The mean percentage of usability problems from the A-LUP found by a group in one TA experiment, containing three TA sessions, after prior use of CW (CW-TA) or HE (HE-TA).
TA indicates the six control groups, see Table 1.

	CW-TA	HE-TA	TA
Mean percentage of the usability problems	15%	25%	18%
Standard deviation (σ)	7%	11%	9%

Although the figures show a quite substantial mean improvement for HE-TA as compared to CW-TA and to TA, HE-TA is not significantly better (p=0.22 by an F-test). There are important variances among the groups within each of the three evaluation programs. This indicates that the individual differences among evaluators have important effects [7], even in our group-based evaluations.

Predicting the Problem Severity
Incorrect grading of problem severity may have unpleasant effects because the resources for correcting usability problems are always limited, i.e. not all problems can be corrected; and each correction has a risk of introducing new usability problems. If evaluators assign the problem severity too high, valuable resources are wasted on correcting problems of little or no significance. If evaluators assign a problem severity too low, there is a risk that a severe problem is overlooked. A cost-conscious project manager would normally not use time to correct problems that are classified as cosmetic. Table 6 presents how the usability problems graded as HCP by the present authors were graded by an average group of evaluators. The most remarkable result is how the HCP, when found by CWs, are graded as only CP in 39% of the instances. It seems that CW leaves the evaluators with a weak feeling of problem severity.

Table 7 presents how the usability problems graded as SP by the present authors were graded by the groups of evaluators. A SP graded as HCP isn't a big problem; but if SP are graded as CP then the users will probably continue

Table 6. The Highly Critical Problems of the A-LUP as graded by the groups of evaluators.

Graded as	CW	HE	TA	CW-TA	HE-TA
HCP	17%	33%	33%	6%	53%
SP	28%	47%	17%	17%	13%
CP	39%	7%	11%	33%	13%
Total of Found HCP	83%	87%	61%	56%	80%
Not Found HCP	17%	13%	39%	44%	20%

Table 7 presents how the usability problems graded as SP by the present authors were graded by the groups of evaluators. A SP graded as HCP isn't a big problem; but if SP are graded as CP then the users will probably continue to be substantially impeded in their work with the system, because the large number of usability problems typically detected by these evaluation methods makes it necessary to give CP a very low priority during repairing or re-designing of the system. When using TA the evaluators tend to misjudge the SP as CP.

Table 7. The Severe Problems of the A-LUP as graded by the groups of evaluators.					
	CW	HE	TA	CW-TA	HE-TA
Graded as					
HCP	3%	6%	8%	7%	9%
SP	6%	15%	10%	11%	15%
CP	4%	4%	7%	7%	12%
Total of Found SP	13%	25%	25%	25%	36%
Not Found SP	87%	75%	75%	75%	64%

Table 8 presents how the usability problems graded as CP by the present authors were graded of the groups of evaluators. Here we find a proneness to overestimate the severity of the CP by evaluators using HE. CW identifies only few CP.

Table 8. The Cosmetic Problems of the A-LUP as graded by the groups of evaluators.					
	CW	HE	TA	CW-TA	HE-TA
Graded as					
HCP	0%	2%	1%	1%	1%
SP	1%	4%	3%	3%	5%
CP	3%	5%	8%	4%	10%
Total of Found CP	5%	12%	12%	8%	16%
Not Found CP	95%	88%	88%	92%	84%

In summary, this examination of the groups' ability to indicate properly the severity of the identified usability problems shows a mixed pattern. CW seems to lack guidance for the evaluators to grade especially the HCP realistically. HE seems to lack guidance in grading the CP properly, an important weakness because of the typical large number of CP, see Table 3.

False Problems

Table 9 shows that the three methods differ significantly with regard to identifying false problems, i.e. problems that in practice influence no or very few users. A HE experiment on the average identifies 23% of the false problems on the A-LUP, TA identifies 1%, and CW none. Most of the false problems are graded as CP, but again HE stands out with a considerable part of false problems graded as SP. This is a serious weakness of HE, which however can be redressed by using TA afterwards.

Table 9. False problems					
	CW	HE	TA	CW-TA	HE-TA
Grades as					
HCP	0%	0%	1%	0%	0%
SP	0%	11%	0%	0%	0%
CP	0%	11%	0%	1%	1%
Total of Found False Problems	0%	23%	1%	1%	1%
Not Found False Problems	100%	77%	99%	99%	99%

Practical Advice

Table 10 shows the mean percentage of problems found by one group by using either one or two methods. Here CW&TA means that all the problems found by one group using first CW and then TA have been gathered, no matter whether the group finds a problem with one or both methods (see Table 1, evaluation program no. 1). HE-TA gives the best prediction of the usability problems of TeSS compared to each of the other methods or method combinations involved in this experiment. HE-TA could even be argued to be better than using the two methods HE&TA, because HE-TA nearly avoids all the false problems and limits the number of CP.

A practical advice based on this study to a manager of a software project could therefore be to concentrate on only the noticeable problems (HCP and SP) detected by TA evaluations; but he or she should encourage the evaluators to prepare for the TA evaluations by studying the system under evaluation by means of HE.

Table 10. The mean percentage of problems of the A-LUP found by one group by using one or two methods. Concerning the evaluation designations, see Table 1.

	Inspection methods		Think Aloud methods			Two methods used	
	CW	HE	TA	CW-TA	HE-TA	CW&TA	HE&TA
HCP	83%	87%	61%	56%	80%	94%	87%
SP	13%	25%	25%	25%	36%	30%	47%
CP	5%	12%	12%	8%	16%	10%	24%
All problems	10%	19%	18%	15%	25%	19%	34%
False problems	0%	23%	1%	1%	1%	1%	24%

Comparative Discussions

No previous study has investigated the effect of using two evaluation methods on the same user interface and comparing this with using only one method. Our result -- that the combination of first doing HE then doing TA seems superior in predictive power -- has relevance to practitioners interested in how to maximize the effectiveness of their usability evaluation program.

Many other studies have compared the predictive power of selected UEMs. The most influential of these, according to Gray and Salzman [5], are the studies [8, 14, 17, 3, 21]. Gray and Salzman [5] found methodological flaws in all these studies and call much of what we thought we knew regarding the efficiency of various UEMs into question.

Discussion Related to Jeffries et al. (1991)

Jeffries et al. [8] studied four methods: HE, guidelines, CW (in an earlier and more complex version than the one we have used) and usability testing. The specific form of the usability testing used in the study by Jeffries et al. is not identified by references or described in the paper, but presumably it had similarities to our TA tests. Four user interface specialists did the HE, a team of 3 software engineers did the guideline evaluation, a team of 3 software engineers did the CW, and 6 regular PC users participated in the user testing group.

Concerning the study by Jeffries et al, Gray and Salzman [5] summarizes that (a) the conclusions regarding one UEM versus another, and (b) the claims made about the types of problems found by each UEM, are problematic. There are uncontrolled differences among the evaluator groups, and the small number of evaluators and usability experiments result in statistical insignificance.

Jeffries et al. found that HE uncovered the most problems, including more of the serious ones, and that usability test also did a good job compared to guidelines and CW. The usability testing failed to find many of the serious problems, a result that corresponds to what we found for the TA tests, see Table 6. One explanation could be that usability testing is highly dependent on the tasks used as basis for the TA process. In the method descriptions very little is explained to the evaluators about how to construct these tasks. Unless the set of test tasks is comprehensive and adequate to cover all facets of the system, it is problematic to let a number of usability tests, or TA tests, have the final word in determining the severity of the problems of a specific user interface.

Another observation in the study by Jeffries et al. is that especially HE runs the risk of finding too many problems, "some of which may not be the most important ones to correct". This agrees with our study, see Tables 8 and 9. This is particularly a problem when the method, as in our study, is used by people who are not user interface specialists. Many ordinary system developers who will be trained and involved in usability evaluations in industry will tend to pursue many cosmetic or even false problems. Training material and probably even the procedures of HE should be modified to address this aspect more directly.

Note that CW in our study practically avoids false problems, so this method has some kind of filter towards this. Why not try to utilize this in a modified version of HE? The idea to include task scenarios during the HE is one possibility used by Karat et al. [14] -- another idea strongly suggested by the results of the present study is to combine TA testing into HE in some way.

We do not find an improvement when CW is followed by TA as compared to just using TA. This might not be too surprising. The approaches of CW and TA have clear similarities by virtue of the predefined tasks to be studied. You could look upon CW as a simulated TA evaluation focused by a GOMS-like walkthrough. But HE and CW represent different filters towards the user interaction, as witnessed empirically in our study and in other studies, e.g. [2]. This leads to the idea of intertwining some kind of heuristic walkthrough with CW. It would be interesting to see such methods developed and empirically tested.

Discussion Related to Desurvire et al. (1992)

In Desurvire et al. [3] groups of evaluators did usability evaluations using CW, HE and a laboratory usability test. Their study focused on how the selected methods functioned as tools for evaluators with different types of expertise, i.e. human factors experts, users of computer systems and the software engineers of the system under evaluation. The HE and the CW groups used "paper flow-charts organized by task" to complete six tasks. The user testing group used a prototype of the interface, according to information from H. Desurvire to Gray and Salzman [5]. The user testing group had 18 participants; the six inspection UEM groups had 3 participants each, but the 3 software engineers participated in both HE and CW.

Concerning the study by Desurvire et al., Gray and Salzman [5] summarizes: "The prerequisites for an experimental study -- statistical conclusion validity and internal validity -- were severely lacking. ... We believe that there is nothing that can be safely concluded regarding UEMs or expertise based on this study."

The design of the experimental method evaluation used by Desurvire et al. differs markedly from ours making it meaningless to go into detailed comparisons. The main conclusion in their study, that a laboratory based usability test is clearly the most effective to uncover the problems, cannot be compared to our results. Our TA tests are much more restricted in the approach and the invested efforts than the laboratory usability testing of the Desurvire et al. study. They use human factor experts to do the testing and collect the results from 18 users to establish their 'authorized' usability list. We use students with knowledge and experience comparable to well-informed, non-expert system developers in industry to make or supervise the usability evaluations. On the other hand, we draw results from 51 evaluators. The indication of the Desurvire et al. study [3] -- that HE is better than CW to predict usability problems, especially when used by human factor experts -- was confirmed in our study with computer science students as evaluators.

Discussion Related to Karat et al. (1992)

The Karat et al. [14] compared user testing with a walkthrough technique that combined scenarios with guidelines, i.e. a set of 12 usability heuristics. There were 48 participants in the study. They were predominantly end users and developers of GUI systems, along with a few user interface specialists and software support staff. The participants were randomly assigned to three method conditions: user testing (two groups of 6 individuals), individual walkthrough (two groups of 6 individuals) and team walkthrough (two groups with six teams of 2 individuals per team). One group in each condition evaluated one office system, whereas the second group evaluated a second office system.

Concerning the study by Karat et al., Gray and Salzman [5] summarizes:

"This study handled most of the threats to internal validity well ... The mixed nature of the groups limits the generalization of their findings. ... The main failing of this study was with statistical conclusion validity. Few statistical tests were reported, and those that were reported failed to control for the Wildcard effect (Remark by Frøkjær and Larusdottir: Here "Wildcards" are participants who are significantly better or worse than average and whose performance in the onditions of the study do not reflect the UEM, but their Wildcard status.) Hence, although the results regarding the superiority of user testing to walkthroughs may be interesting and suggestive, they may not be generalizable beyond this study's testing conditions."

A direct comparison of the Karat et al. study with the present one is impossible because: (a) the walkthrough method used by Karat et al., which is combining techniques known from both cognitive walkthrough and heuristic evaluation, is quite different from both CW and HE used in our study; (b) the participants' professional backgrounds are different from those of the evaluators in our study.

We mention just one of the important results found by Karat et al, namely that team walkthroughs were more effective than individual walkthroughs. This supports the idea used in our study of taking reports from groups of evaluators as the unit of measurement instead of reports from individual evaluators.

Discussion Related to Cuomo and Bowen (1994)

Cuomo and Bowen [2] compare the three inspection-based evaluation methods CW, HE, and the Smith and Mosier guidelines. Their objective was to learn more about what types of usability problems the selected methods were suited to uncover.

The study by Cuomo and Bowen was based on results from only one evaluation experiment with each method. We had experiments by five or six groups for each method or method combination. Another important difference is that Cuomo and Bowen's evaluators were highly educated and specialized human factors professionals with a solid knowledge also about the domain area of the system evaluated.

Using Norman's seven stage model of user activity, Cuomo and Bowen were able to show that the CW almost exclusively identified issues within the action specification stage, while guidelines and HE cover more of the stages.

We have not tried any detailed analysis of this kind, but our results seem to support their main conclusions. Thus, Table 10 shows that HE has induced the evaluators to take a wider view of the usability problems. When HE and TA tests are combined the coverage is the widest.

Cuomo and Bowen also conclude that CW was best at predicting problems that cause users noticeable difficulty as observed during a usability study. But they have no statistical support for this conclusion, and their data supporting this point actually show very small differences between CW and HE; and our results differ at this point. Tables 6 and 7 present how the highly critical and the severe problems, i.e. the problems we consider to impede users, have been uncovered and properly graded much better by the groups doing HE or TA than the groups doing CW.

Discussion Related to John and Marks (1997)

John and Marks [10] present a case study that tracks usability problems predicted with six UEMs, namely claims analysis, CW, GOMS, HE, user action notation, and simply reading the specification. The predictive power of each UEM is assessed by comparing the predictions given by it to the results of user tests. They also measure what they call (a) the persuasive power of a method, i.e. a measure of the number of identified problems that led to changes in the implemented code, and (b) the design-change effectiveness which gives information about how the implemented changes may reduce the number of problems users experience, leave performance the same, or introduce more problems than before.

John and Marks's results are based upon only one evaluator using each of the methods; the involved evaluators are quite different in their educational and professional backgrounds; and the evaluations are based upon written specifications, not a prototype or a running version of the evaluated system. Although their study proposes interesting new concepts of importance for more adequate comparisons of UEMs, the "lessons learned" reported seem to us very uncertain and not relevant in comparison with ours. (See also John Carroll's critique of the study by John and Marks which is commented upon in [9].)

CONCLUSIONS

The effectiveness of predicting usability problems using either HE or TA was found to be significantly higher than using CW. A usability experiment performed by a group of three evaluators using HE or TA on an average uncovered approximately 80% more usability problems than a group using CW. The strict GOMS-like walkthrough built into CW seems to impose an unrealistically narrow focus compared to the users' actual activity during system interaction.

HE and TA were found to be complementary in the sense that they revealed somewhat different problems. We have found that one usability experiment using TA after a HE experiment on an average reveals about 25% of all the usability problems, while TA used after CW reveals only 15%. But this difference is not statistically significant because of quite large variances among the six evaluator groups trying this method combination. The individual differences among evaluators seem to have important effects, even in our group-based evaluations.

The combination CW and TA has lesser predictive power than HE-TA. This might not be too surprising as both CW and TA are based upon the evaluator's task scenarios; and these task scenarios can not be expected to cover all aspects of the evaluated system when the system is more complex than walk-up-and-use systems.

All methods are well capable of uncovering the Highly Critical Problems (HCP). But reaching a good coverage of the Severe Problems (SP) by just one of the methods seems impossible to an average group of inexperienced evaluators. The combination, first HE and then TA, improves the coverage of Severe Problems from 25% to 36%. Moreover, this combination eliminates one of the most important weaknesses of the HE method when used by non-experts, namely the proneness to addressing many false problems.

In brief summary, this study shows that the idea of combining HE and TA, as brought forward in the literature [1: p. 87], effectively improves the methods suitability to uncover the important usability problems of smaller interactive software -- without disturbing the picture by false problems, or over-graded Cosmetic Problems (CP).

A practical advice to managers of software projects would be to concentrate on only the noticeable problems (HCP and SP) detected by a number of TA evaluations, done by evaluators prepared for their TA evaluations by a study of the system under evaluation by means of HE.

ACKNOWLEDGMENTS

We thank Heather Desurvire, Morten Hertzum, Jakob Nielsen and John Rieman for their highly constructive critique of a preliminary design of this evaluation project, giving us many judicious proposals for improvements. We are exceptionally grateful to Rolf Molich who not only offered his advice during the preparation of the project, but continued to support us with his experience and ideas during the accomplishment of the study. Niels Bulow Andersen, Jette Holm Broløs, Bjorn fior Jonsson, Morten Hertzum, Kasper Hornbæk, Peter Naur, Ketil Perstrup, Kristian Bang Pilgaard, and Gudmundur Valsson read an earlier version of the paper and gave us numerous indispensable proposals for clarifying the presentation. Finally, we owe thanks to all the students who decided to participate in this research project by offering their exertion and enthusiasm as evaluators.

REFERENCES

1. Baecker, R.M., Grudin, J., Buxton, W.A.S., and Greenberg, S. [Authors and eds.] (1995) *Readings in Human-Computer Interaction: Toward the Year 2000*, Second edition, Morgan Kaufmann Publishers, Inc., San Francisco, California.
2. Cuomo, D.L., and Bowen, C.D. (1994) Understanding usability issues addressed by three user-system interface evaluation techniques. *Interacting with Computers*, 6, 1, 86-108.
3. Desurvire, H. W., Kondziela, J. M., and Atwood, M. E (1992) What is gained and lost using evaluation methods other than empirical testing. In Monk, A., Diaper, D., and Harrison, M. D. (eds.) *People and Computers VII*, Cambridge University Press, Cambridge, U. K.
4. Dix, A., Finlay, J., Abowd, G., and Beale, R. (1993) *Human-Computer Interaction*, Prentice-Hall, Englewood Cliffs, N. J.
5. Gray, W. D., and Salzman, M C. (1998) Damaged Merchandise? A Review of Experiments That Compare Usability Methods, *Human-Computer Interaction*, Vol. 13, pp. 203-261.
6. Hertzum, M., and Frøkjær E. (1996) Browsing and Querying in Online Documentation: A Study of User Interfaces and the Interaction Process, *ACM Transactions on Computer-Human Interaction*, 3, 2, pp 136-161.
7. Jacobsen, N. E., Hertzum, M., and John, B.E. (1997) The Evaluator Effect in Usability Tests, *Proc. ACM CHI '98, Late-Breaking Results*, pp. 255-256.
8. Jeffries, R., Miller, J. R., Wharton, C., and Uyeda, K. M. (1991) User interface evaluation in the real world: A comparison of four techniques, *Proc. ACM CHI '91 Conference*. (New Orleans, LA, 28 April - 2 May) ACM, NY.
9. John, B. E. (1998) On our case study of claims analysis and other usability evaluation methods, *Behaviour & Information Technology*, Vol. 17, 4, 244-246.
10. John, B. E., and Marks, S. J. (1997) Tracking the effectiveness of usability evaluation methods, *Behaviour & Information Technology*, Vol. 16, 4/5, 188-202.
11. John, B. E., and Mashyna, M. M. (1997) Evaluating a Multimedia Authoring Tool, *Journal of the American Society for Information Science*, 48(11):1004-1022.
12. Jørgensen, A. H. (1990) Thinking-aloud in user interface design: a method promoting cognitive ergonomics, *Ergonomics*, Vol. 33, pp. 501-507.
13. Karat, C. (1994) A comparison of user interface evaluation methods. In J. Nielsen and R.L. Mack (eds.) *Usability Inspection Methods*. New York: John Wiley, 1994.
14. Karat, C., Campbell, R., and Fiegel, T. (1992) Comparison of empirical testing and walkthrough methods in user interface evaluation, *Proc. ACM CHI '92 Conference*, (Monterey, California, 3 - 7 May).
15. Molich, R. (ed.), Beyer, P., Carstensen, P., Jørgensen, A. H., and Pedersen, F. H. (1986) *Brugervenlige edb-systemer*, Teknisk Forlag, København. In Danish. New edition: Molich, R. (1994)) *Brugervenlige edb-systemer*, Teknisk Forlag, København.
16. Nielsen, J. (1992) Evaluating the thinking-aloud technique for use by computer scientists, In Hartison, H. R., and Hix, D. (Eds.), *Advances in Human-Computer Interaction*, Vol. 3, Ablex. Norwood, N. J.
17. Nielsen, J. (1992) Finding usability problems through heuristic evaluation, *Proc. ACM CHI '92 Conference*, (Monterey, California, 3 - 7 May).
18. Nielsen, J. (1993) *Usability Engineering*, Academic Press, San Diego.
19. Nielsen, J., and Mack, R.L. [Eds.] (1994) *Usability Inspection Methods*. New York: John Wiley.
20. Nielsen, J., and Molich, R. (1990): Heuristic evaluation of user interfaces, *Proc. ACM CHI '90 Conference*, (Seattle, WA, 1 - 5 April).
21. Nielsen, J., and Philips, V. L. (1993) Estimating the relative usability of two interfaces: Heuristic, formal, and empirical methods compared. *Proc. ACM InterCHI'93 Conf.* (Amsterdam, The Netherlands, 24-29 April).
22. Polson, P., Lewis, C., Rieman, J., and Wharton, C. (1992) Cognitive walkthroughs: A method for theory-based evaluation of user interfaces, *International Journal of Man-Machine Studies*, 36.
23. Shneiderman, B. (1992) *Designing the User Interface: Strategies for Effective Human-Computer Interaction*, 2. edition, Addison-Wesley, Reading, MA.
24. Weinstein, S. (1992) *The Elm Mail System: A Replacement Mailer for all Unix Systems*, Use Net Version (2.4 Release System), DIKU, København.
25. Wharton, C., Rieman, J., Lewis, C., and Polson, P. (1994) The cognitive walkthrough method: A practitioner's guide. Published in Nielsen, J. and Mack, R. L. (eds.) *Usability Inspection Methods*, Wiley, New York.

Transferring Lessons Learned from Traditional Structured Methods to the Object Oriented Environment

Kay M. Nelson
The University of Kansas, Division of Accounting and Information Systems, Summerfield 350B, Lawrence, Kansas 66045
(785) 864-7529, FAX (785) 864-5328, **knelson@ukans.edu**

H. James Nelson
The University of Kansas, Division of Accounting and Information Systems, Summerfield 350B, Lawrence, Kansas 66045
(785) 864-3765, FAX (785) 864-5328, **jnelson@ukans.edu**

Mehdi Ghods
The Boeing Company, P.O. Box 3707 MS 6C-FL, Seattle, WA 98124-2207
(425) 234-8947, FAX: (425) 234-5460, mehdi.ghods@boeing.com

Holly E. Lee
The University of Kansas

ABSTRACT

This research investigates specific traditional structured methods for their contributions to the performance of information systems development teams. The attitudes of the development teams towards structured methods and the satisfaction of the teams with training in structured methods are used as mediating factors in this investigation. The results are then mapped to the Object Oriented environment.

This research is supported by The Boeing Company

INTRODUCTION

The term structured methods refers to a philosophy of software development which emphasizes an adherence to a set of consistent rules or methods throughout a project (Yourdon 1989). These methods include broad programs such as Systems Development Lifecycles and Methods and Information Engineering as well as individual techniques such as structured programming, data flow diagramming, data modeling, and object oriented methodologies. Perhaps the newest, most visible, but least understood of these methodologies are the Object Oriented methods. The specific set of rules or methods that organizations use can come from a variety of sources. Organizations often implement their own methodologies for software development, using tools and techniques borrowed from a variety of formalized methodologies. Commercially produced methodologies are also widely used, usually obtained from software vendors and consultants.

The primary objectives of traditional structured methodologies can be summarized as follows: (Martin and McClure 1988)
• Achieve high-quality programs of predictable behavior
• Achieve programs that are easily modifiable (maintainable)
• Simplify the development process
• Control the development process
• Speed up system development
• Lower the cost of system development
    Graham (1994) summarizes the benefits of Object Oriented (OO) methodologies as:
• reuse
• higher quality due to reuse of tested objects and modules
• flexibility
• more naturalistic applications

- ease of maintenance
- ability to reverse engineer and trace requirements

The focus of traditional structured methods is function and procedure with data shared by functions or processes (Bordoloi and Lee 1994). In OO methodologies, data and procedure are encapsulated within the object. Therefore, the primary focus is on data modeling rather than process modeling. This difference in focus does not require that all of the knowledge gained through the use of traditional structured methods be put aside when adopting OO languages and methodologies. Rather, a need exists to map traditional methods that have shown performance results in the organization to the OO paradigm. This mapping should be a conceptual one in that the logic remains the same while the mechanics and focus of the methodology are adapted for OO. Training seems to have the largest single cost when converting to OO methodology (Conway 1993). Reusing knowledge gained from the traditional structured methods environment is one way of reducing these training costs by focusing on the *concepts* that produce the best results and adapting them to new development paradigms.

This research examines specific traditional structured methods for their contribution to traditional development team performance. The attitude of the team toward structured methods and the satisfaction of the team with training in structured methods are used as mediating variables in this examination. Correlation analysis and stepwise regression are used as analysis methodologies. The results of these analyses are then mapped to the OO environment.

WHY STRUCTURED METHODS MAKE A DIFFERENCE

Structured methods, as a general concept, can make a difference to application development projects in many ways (Atkas 1987, Graham 1994, Topper et.al. 1994). Using structured methods can effect development team efficiency and effectiveness. The overall quality and business value of the delivered system can be improved. User satisfaction with product attributes such as the format of information, the content of information, ease of use of the system, timeliness of information, and accuracy of information, as well as overall user satisfaction are also impacted by structured methods.

Structured methods can reduce the impact of differences in programmers' abilities (Yourdon 1986). Structured methods seek to formalize the instinctive good practices of experienced programmers in a way that can be taught to programmers of all experience and ability levels. This is especially critical in a new paradigm such as OO, where most of a development team may be relatively inexperienced. Examples of programming practices are the breaking down of a large system into modules, well organized coding or classes, and complete and accurate documentation (Topper, Ouellete, and Jorgensen 1994).

Yet another reason why structured methods impact developer efficiency and effectiveness is the percentage of time developers actually spend programming. Brooks (1995) states that normally only one sixth of development time is spent writing code. OO programming requires even less code than structured programming with procedural languages because of its feature of inheritance and polymorphism (Bordoloi and Lee 1994). Structured methods not only structure the programming process, but the management processes which are involved in application development, such as meetings, reporting, documenting, inspecting, testing, and communicating (Topper et.al. 1994). These processes exist in both the traditional and OO environments.

Structured methods can also impact the quality and business value of a system. The structured methods performed at the beginning of application development are especially critical for quality and business value. Estimation provides an early analysis of costs to benefits. Data/process models, enterprise models, and design inspections can insure that the system being developed is the one needed for the business (Topper, Ouellete, and Jorgensen 1994). The role of users in enterprise modeling and design inspections can result in increased quality and business value. Code or object inspections and other forms of testing can contribute to quality by insuring delivery of a minimum defect product (Chaar, Halliday, Bhandari, and Chillarege 1993).

The user satisfaction measures of timeliness, accuracy, format, and content of information in the system, as well as ease of use of the system are impacted by structured methods. High levels of initial user satisfaction will result in lower system maintenance costs (Yourdon 1986, Topper, Ouellete, and Jorgensen 1994). While maintenance to keep pace with changes in the business process will always be a reality, a system that meets user needs up front will require fewer changes to meet users' current needs.

The Role of Attitudes in Structured Methods

The attitudes of developers toward structured methods can make a difference in performance. The Theory of Reasoned Action (TRA) (Fishbein and Ajzen 1975, Ajzen and Fishbein 1980) provides a way of understanding the relationship of attitudes toward technology and technology performance. In this theory, a person's performance of a behavior is a result of behavioral intention (BI) to perform the behavior. This BI has two components, the person's attitude (A) and subjective norms (SN) about the behavior.

$$BI = A + SN$$

BI is defined as the strength of a person's intention to perform a behavior. A is defined as positive or negative feelings about performing the behavior, and SN refers to a person's perception of how people important to him or her feel about performing the task.

Davis (1986) adapted the TRA into a Technology Acceptance Model (TAM) specifically designed to model user acceptance of information systems. TAM differs from TRA in that it does not include SN as a determinant of BI. Davis, Bagozzi, and Warshaw (1989) tested this model and confirmed that for user acceptance of information systems, SN is not a significant indicator of BI. This same study demonstrated that BI is determined by A and perceived usefulness U.

$$BI = A + U$$

This implies that all else being equal, people form intentions to perform behaviors which they hold positive attitudes towards and perceive they can have positive results with.

Sherif, Sherif and Nebergall (1965) found in several studies that groups exhibit group behaviors and attitudes. As the knowledge base, expectations, and realities of a group become more cohesive, cooperation and group behaviors begin to appear (Sherif 1962). Groups begin to exhibit a single attitude which can exhibit itself in contrast to that of other groups, such as an "us against them" group attitude

Ancona (1990) also found that the external interactions of groups have patterns similar to the internal patterns of the members of the group. In this research, when individual members of a development team exhibits attitudes toward structured methods, the group itself will display these attitudes. These attitudes, according to the TAM model, will lead to behavioral intentions and usage of structured methods.

The Role Of Training

Formal training in structured methods also impacts both structured methods and team performance. It is not only the quantity and quality of training received that matters, it is the level of satisfaction with this training on the part of developers which impacts usage and performance. In other words, great training is only great training if the student perceives it as such. The ability to conceptualize the ideas behind structured methods and to see potential benefits from using them can be gained through good training programs.

STRUCTURED METHODS IN THIS STUDY

This study measures the structured methods of data/process modeling, design inspection, code inspection, enterprise modeling, estimation, standards, metrics collection, and user training. These methods were chosen using a traditional systems development lifecycle model and an information engineering type of model (Topper, Ouellete, and Jorgensen 1994). Figure 1 shows these models and the structured methods constructs they represent in the center of the figure.

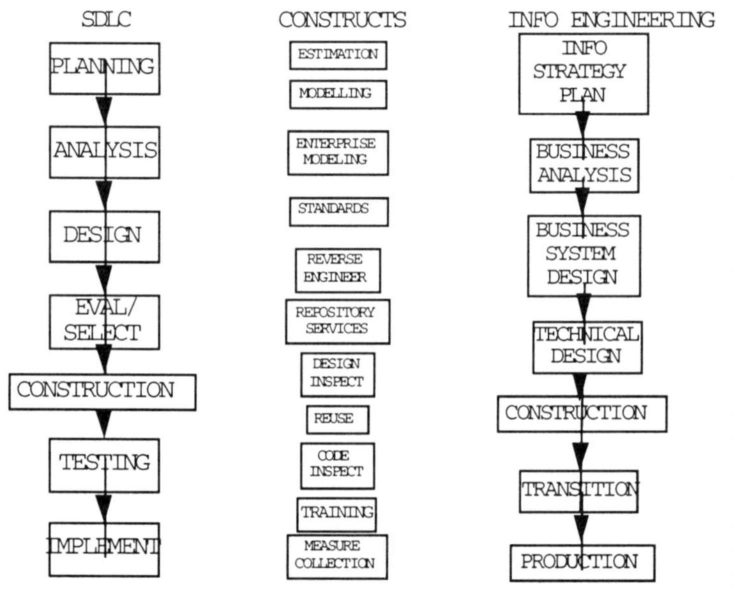

Data was not available for all of the constructs, therefore, the methods listed above were chosen for measurement and analysis.

Data/process modeling is defined as producing data models, process/function models, and as modeling the distribution of data and process. Data/process modeling allows system developers to capture the nature and flow of information in the system during early phases in development.

Design inspection is defined as performing walkthroughs and reviews of the system design with users. The purpose of design inspection is to look for flaws, weaknesses, errors, and omissions in the design before the code is written (Chaar, Halliday, Bhandari, and

Figure 1. Initial Models and Constructs

Chillarege 1993).

Code inspection is defined as performing walkthroughs and reviews of the code once it has been written. The purpose of code inspection is to look for flaws, weaknesses, errors, and omissions in the code before it is put into production (Chaar, Halliday, Bhandari, and Chillarege 1993). This is especially critical since defects are much less likely to be detected once a system is in production (Yourdon 1986).

Enterprise modeling is defined as using observation and interview data to model the business model. Enterprise modeling depicts the tasks and activities as well as the flows of the business process. It can be used to generate process diagrams for the information system. Another purpose of enterprise modeling is to communicate the flow of information in a way comprehensible to the user.

Estimation is defining application priorities and dependencies, product scope, and preliminary project feasibility. Estimation allows I/S organizations to forecast the time and cost required to produce a system. This information can be communicated to users and be used as a project management tool.

Standards is defined as the enforcement of compliance with standards. Standards are put in place for software development for a variety of reasons. Standards can force developers to produce a product that is compatible with other systems in the organization. Standards in documentation allow easier maintenance by people other than the original developer. Standards can enforce both the way which systems are developed and the composition of the final system.

Metrics collection is defined as metrics data collected for the purpose of productivity measurement. Examples of these metrics and measures are source lines of code, function points, labor hours, and cost and complexity data. The data is generally used by organizations to undrestand the productivity of software development activities.

User training is defined as the percent of users who have been trained on the software application. Training is not included as a part of all structured methodologies, but can be a useful tool in the hand-off of the system from the developers to the users.

Attitude toward structured methods is defined as the attitude held by developers on the power, reliability, value, usefulness, and speed of structured methods.

Structured methods use is defined as the extent to which structured methods are used in the development team.

Satisfaction with structured methods training is defined as satisfaction with the amount and quality of formal education given in structured methods.

The structured methods described above were tested for direct effects on development team performance. In addition, attitudes toward structured methods and satisfaction with training in structured methods were used as mediating variable to test for effect on performance. The next section details the analysis performed on these variables.

METHODOLOGY AND RESULTS

In order to compare results across organizations, this study focused on large companies who had extensive in-house Information Systems departments. To control for project size, development projects had to be 12-to-18 months in planned duration. The selected projects were business applications with some strategic relevance to the company. Data were collected on 105 projects at 22 sites of 15 organizations in the US and Canada. Contributing organizations represent financial services, manufacturing, and high-technology industries from the Fortune 500. For each project, we surveyed the development team at the end of the requirements phase of the project. All of the 105 teams provided information on structured methods usage, attitudes, and training. The projects consisted of a variety of computing infrastructures, including mainframe, local networks, uncoupled work stations, mixed vendor shops, and rudimentary client-server systems. Performance data was collected from information systems and user managers who are considered the stakeholders of the systems.

The specific structured methods defined in the previous section were tested for impact on performance using stepwise regression analysis (Pedhazur, 1982, Cohen and Cohen, 1983). In stepwise regression, all of the structured methods are added to a model of performance based on a specific dependent

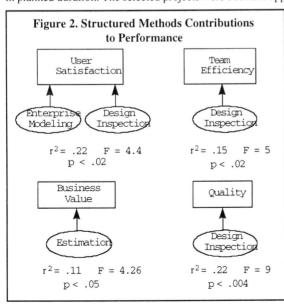

Figure 2. Structured Methods Contributions to Performance

User Satisfaction

Enterprise Modeling   Design Inspection

$r^2 = .22$ $F = 4.4$
$p < .02$

Team Efficiency

Design Inspection

$r^2 = .15$ $F = 5$
$p < .02$

Business Value

Estimation

$r^2 = .11$ $F = 4.26$
$p < .05$

Quality

Design Inspection

$r^2 = .22$ $F = 9$
$p < .004$

variable such as quality. The regression procedure adds variables one at a time, testing for contribution to performance, and keeping variables which contribute while dropping those that do not. Figures 2 and 3 show the results of the stepwise regression procedures. The number of teams in these regressions was 54.

Figure 2 shows the structured methods which contribute to team efficiency, overall user satisfaction, business value and quality. Design inspections are shown to be a significant contributor to team efficiency at the .02 significance level. Design inspections and enterprise modeling both contribute to overall user satisfaction with a system. Design inspections are significant at the .05 level, while enterprise modeling is significant at the .10 level. Design inspection also contributes to system quality as rated by the stakeholders of the system. Design inspection is significant at the .004 level. Estimation contributes to the business value as perceived by stakeholder of the system. Estimation is significant at the .04 level.

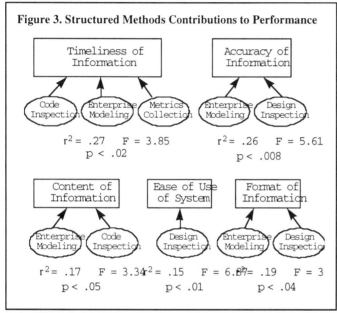

Figure 3. Structured Methods Contributions to Performance

Figure 3 shows that structured methods also contribute to the timeliness, accuracy, content, and format of information, as well as ease of use of the system. Code inspection, enterprise modeling, and metrics collection contribute to timeliness of information rated by the end users of the system. Code inspection is significant at the .10 level, enterprise modeling at the .06 level, and metrics collection at the .10 level. Enterprise modeling and design inspection contribute to accuracy of information and format of information. Enterprise modeling is significant at the .10 level for both accuracy and format, while design inspection is significant at the .02 level for accuracy and the .08 level for format. Content of information is impacted by enterprise modeling and code inspection. Enterprise modeling is significant at the .09 level, while code inspection is significant at the .07 level. Design inspections contribute to the ease of use of the system. Design inspection is significant at the .01 level.

Structured methods were also analyzed for direct effects on performance with attitude toward structured methods and satisfaction with training in structured methods used as mediating variables. Correlation analysis was used to detect relationships. Table 1 shows the relationship of structured methods to performance for teams with positive attitudes toward structured methods.

Table 1: Relationship of Specific Structured Methods on Performance (T3 part V) for Teams with Positive Attitudes Toward Structured Methods
n=30, * < .05, ** < .01

Method/Measure	User Satisfaction	Format	Accuracy	Ease of use	Content
Data/ process modeling	.35	.28	.22	.25	.31
Design Inspection	.42*	.34	.51**	.40*	.36*
Code inspection	.41*	.32	.49**	.35*	.37*
Enterprise Modeling	.39*	.34	.32	.36*	.37*
User Training	.35	.36	.22	.36	.33
Estimation	.00	-.02	.05	-.14	.01
Standards	.00	-.22	.04	-.32	.06
Metrics Collection	.03	-.14	.17	-.06	.15

Table 1 shows that design inspections, code inspections, and enterprise modeling have the strongest relationship to performance for teams with positive attitudes toward structured methods. Design and code inspections are related to user satisfaction, ease of use, accuracy and content of information. Enterprise modeling is related to the user satisfaction, ease of use, and content of the system. Table 2 shows the relationship of structured methods to

Table 2: Relationship of Specific Structured Methods on Performance for Teams Satisfied with Training in Structured Methods
$n=30, \ * < .05, \ ** < .01$

Method/Measure	User Satisfaction	Format	Accuracy	Ease of use	Content
Data/ process modeling	.52	.57	.45	.54	.55
Design Inspection	.42	.42	.41	.47	.34
Code inspection	.43	.38	.45	.38	.40
Enterprise Modeling	.69**	.70**	.59	.67**	.67**
User Training	.08	.16	.12	.13	.04
Estimation	.20	.26	.13	.25	.16
Standards	.20	.15	.18	.18	.18
Metrics Collection	-.00	-.13	.03	.09	-.09

performance for teams satisfied with training in structured methods.

Enterprise modeling is the only structured method which shows a positive correlation to performance for teams satisfied with training in structured methods. Enterprise modeling is related to user satisfaction, ease of use, format and content of information.

MAPPING THE RESULTS TO THE OBJECT ORIENTED ENVIRONMENTS

This research shows that structured methods do have direct impacts on development team performance. The use of design inspections contributes to user satisfaction, format and accuracy of data, the ease of use of the system, overall quality of work performed on the delivered system, as well as the efficiency of the development team. The use of code inspections contributes to content of data and timeliness of data. Enterprise modeling contributes to user satisfaction and timeliness, format, accuracy and content of the data. Estimation contributes to the business value of delivered systems. These results reinforce the need for interaction with the users of the system and an understanding of the business process which the system supports early on in the development cycle. The strength of the contributions of design inspection points to a verification process which is needed early on in development and performed in conjunction with users.

In a study of software validation, Chaar et. al (1993) found that design inspections detected defects in documentation of the system, function of the system, and system interfaces. These types of defects must be detected early in the lifecycle to insure that the system delivered is the system ordered. Design inspections can also lead to confidence on the part of the users that the development team is performing the work ordered (Yourdon 1986). In addition to being a method for error detection, design inspection is a management tool for good developer - user interface. Design inspections are also critical to OO development. Graham (1994) recommends reviewing both the prototype and the paper model with users and/or experts. By releasing current public versions of prototypes and paper models for discussion and criticism by users, OO developers can aid transition to the new system and enhance credibility and communication. Items examined in an OO design inspection include technical feasibility, reusability, use of library classes and duplication of function among classes.

The Chaar et. al (1993) study also found that code inspections revealed a high percentage of checking and documentation errors. The authors point out that in code inspection, a second inspection can be critical in eliminating operational semantic errors, which do not effect the content as much as the operation of the system. A first code inspection can detect content defects where a second may detect operational defects which can impact performance measures such as timeliness. The process of OO systems development is more incremental, concurrent, and iterative than structured development (Bordoloi and Lee 1994). Analysts, designers, and programmers all have the same focus on objects and can work with the object model concurrently. Thus, the boundaries between the phases in OO development become indistinct. This difference reinforces the need for code, or in this case, object inspections. Graham (1994) recommends testing every object as it its produced, and testing it again as it becomes part of a classification structure.

Enterprise modeling is a structured method present in many automated tools, and used extensively in the OO paradigm. This study shows that the use of enterprise modeling leads to a system that performs to the satisfaction of the user. These results emphasize the need for system development to be tied more closely to the business process. Problem areas in OO enterprise modeling include abstraction, problem decomposition, separating problem space and solution space, and distributing the behavior of the enterprise. One recommendation for solving these issues is to focus a large proportion of time on enterprise modeling issues, using examples, discussions, and analysis/design evaluations. This allows analysts to explore alternative representations of a problem from different perspectives

(Puhr, Nelson, Monarchi 1995). As in traditional structured methodologies, time spent up front in enterprise modeling pays off throughout the OO development process.

Structured methods also have a direct effect on development team performance when teams have a positive attitude toward methods or they are satisfied with the training received in methods. Once again, the specific methods of design inspection, code inspection and enterprise modeling are significantly related to development team performance. This suggests several things. The early verification, validation, and error detection provided by design and code inspections lead to a better overall product. However, these methods are time consuming and must be included as part of the original time schedule estimates. The same holds for the OO paradigm. The principal distinctive features of all the OO technologies from a managerial viewpoint, are the way objects model real-world features, the possibility of reuse, the easy extensibility of such systems and their richer semantic context. This also means spending more effort early on in projects, so that estimating practices must change to encompass this work (Graham 1994). Teams who have positive attitudes toward structured methods are more likely to be willing to take the time needed to perform these activities. Both design inspections and enterprise modeling bring the user into the development process. These methods allow early detection of disparities between user and developer expectations and understandings. Design inspections and enterprise modeling may be methods which lead to an accurate capture of user needs and requirements.

Teams who are satisfied with training in structured methods achieve results through the use of enterprise modeling. Perhaps it is this training which "sells" a development team on the value of this structured method. Mangers have long recognized the need to link development activities to the enterprise (Yourdon 1986), and training in structured methods appears to be a way of transferring this need to developers. Puhr, Nelson, and Monarchi (?) have found that the concepts of OO methodology by themselves are not difficult to grasp, but that difficulty occurs in seeing how the concepts are manifested in designs and programs. Therefore, training may be even more critical to the successful use of OO methods than it is to traditional methods use.

This study has shown the importance of the structured methods of design inspection, code inspection, and enterprise modeling in traditional software development projects. Organizations should consider the importance of these activities when implementing a structured methodology, be it in the traditional or OO paradigm. This study shows a clear link between the use of methods and the performance of internally developed software. The lessons learned from these traditional versions of design inspection, code inspection, and enterprise modeling can be used by both practitioners and future researchers of the Object Oriented paradigm.

REFERENCES

Ajzen, I., and Fishbein, M., Understanding Attitudes and Predicting Social Behavior, Prentice Hall, Englewood, NJ, 1980

Aktas, A. Ziya, Structured Analysis & Design of Information Systems, Prentice Hall, Englewood, N.J., 1987

Ashok, Sheolikar, "An Approach to Structured MIS Development", *MIS Quarterly*, Vol. 5, No.4, December 1981, pp.19-33

Baker, F.T., "Chief Programmer Team Management of Production Programming", *IBM Systems Journal*, Vol. 11, No. 1, January 1977, pp.56-73

Banker, R. and Kauffman, R. "Reuse and Productivity in Integrated Computer-Aided Software Engineering: An Empirical Study", *MIS Quarterly,* 15,3, (September 1991), pp. 375-402

Bordoloi, Bijoy and Min-Hwa Lee, "An Object-Oriented View", *Information Systems Management*, Winter 1994

Brooks, Jr., Frederick P, The Mythical Man-Month, Addison-Wesley Publishing Company, Reading, Massachusetts 1975/1995

Chaar, J.K., Halliday, M.J., Bhandari, 1055 I.S., and Chillarege , R., "In-Process Evaluation for Software Inspection and Test", *IEEE Transactions on Software Engineering*, Vol. 19, No. 11, November 1993, pp. -1070

Chen, Peter P. "Entity-Relationship Model: Toward a Unified View of Data", *ACM Transaction on Database*, Vol.1, No. 1

Cohen, J. And Cohen P., Applied Multiple Regression/Correlation Analysis for the Behavioral Sciences, Lawrence Erlbaum Associates, Hillsdale, NJ, 1983.

Conway, J. "OOP: An academic perspective", *Education and Training Supplement to SIGS Publications*, 4-7, 1993.

Crinnion, John, Evolutionary Systems Development: A Practical Guide to the Use of Prototyping Within a Structured Systems Methodology, Plenum Press, NY, 1991

Davis, Fred. D., "A Technology Acceptance Model for Empirically Testing New End-User Information Systems: Theory and Results", Doctoral Dissertation, *Sloan School of Management, Massachusetts Institute of Technology*, 1986

Davis, Fred D., Bagozzi, Richard P., and Warshaw, Paul R., "User Acceptance of Computer Technology: A Comparison of Two Theoretical Models", *Management Science*, Vol. 35, No. 8, August 1989

DeMarco, Tom, Structured Analysis and System Specification, Yourdan Press, New York, 1978

Dolk, Daniel R., "Model Management and Structured Modeling:, The Role of Information Resource Dictionary Systems", *Communications of the ACM,* Vol. 31, No. 6, June 1988, pp. 704-718

Downs, Ed, Structured Systems Analysis and Design Method Application and, Prentice-Hall, Hertfordshire, UK, 1992·

Fenton, Norman, "Software Measurement: A Necessary Scientific Basis", *IEEE Transactions on Software Engineering*, Vol. 20 No. 3, March 1994, pp. 199-206

Fishbein, M., and Ajzen, I., Belief, Attitude, Intention, and Behavior: An Introduction to Theory and Research, Addison Wesley, Reading, Context MA, 1975

Gane, Chris, and Sarson, C., Structured Systems Analysis: Tools and Techniques, Prentice-Hall, Englewood New Jersey, 1979

Gane, Chris, Rapid System Development: Using Structured Techniques and Relational Technology, Prentice-Hall, Englewood New Jersey, 1989

Graham, Ian, Object Oriented Methods, Addison-Wesley Publishing Company, Wokingham, England, 1994

Henderson-Sellers, Brian and Edwards, Julian M., "The Object Oriented Systems Lifecycle", *Communications of the ACM,* Vol. 33, No. 9, September 1990, pp. 142-159

Martin, James and McClure, Carma, Structured Techniques: The Basis For CASE, Prentice Hall, Englewood Cliffs, N.J., 1988

Orr, Ken, Gane, Chris, Yourdan, Edward, Chen, Peter P., Constantine, Larry L., "Methodology: The Experts Speak", *BYTE*, April 1989, pp. 221-233

Orr, Kenneth T., Structured Systems Development, Yourdan Press, New York, 1977

Pedhazur, E.J., Multiple Regression in Behavioral Research, (2nd ed.), Holtz, Reinhart & Winston, New York, 1982.

Puhr, Gretchen I., Nelson, H. James, and David E. Monarchi, "Teaching Object-Oriented Systems Development: Challenges and Recommendations", *Object Oriented Systems*, 2, 1995

Ross D.T. and Shoman, K.E. Jr., "Structured Analysis for Requirements Definition", *IEEE Transactions on Software Engineering*, Vol. SE-3, No. 1, January 1977

Sanden, Bo, "Entity Lifecycle Modelling and Structured Analysis in Real-Time Software Design—A Comparison", *Communications of the ACM,* Vol. 32, No. 12, December 1989, pp. 1458-1466

Sherif, Carolyn W., Sherif, Muzafer and Nebergall, Roger E., Attitude and Attitude Change, W.B.Saunders Company, Philadelphia and London, 1965

Sherif, Muzafer (ed), Intergroup Relations and Leadership, John Wiley and Sons, Inc., New York and London, 1962

Stevens, W.P., Myers, G.J., and Constantine, L.L., "Structured Design", *IBM Systems Journal*, Vol. 13, No. 2, 1974

Topper, Andrew, Ouellete, Daniel, and Jorgensen, Paul, Structured Methods: Merging Models, Techniques, and CASE, McGraw-Hill, Inc., NY, 1994

Tung, Sho-Huan, "A Structured Method for Literate Programming", *Structured Programming*, Vol.10, No. 2, 1989, pp. 113-120

Vessey, Iris and Weber, Ron, "Structured Tools and Conditional Logic: An Empirical Investigation", *Communications of the ACM,* Vol. 29, No.1, January 1986

Yourdan, Edward, Managing the Structured Techniques: Strategies for Software Development in the 1990's, Yourdan Press/Prentice Hall, New York, 1986 (2)

Yourdan, Edward, Modern Structured Analysis, Yourdan Press/Prentice Hall, New York, 1989 (1)

Yourdan, Edward, Techniques of Program Structure and Design, Prentice hall, Englewood, New Jersey, 1975

Types of Business Objects Used to Model an Information Architecture During Information System Planning

Rui Gomes
Escola Superior de Tecnologia e Gestão
Apartado 574, 4900 Viana do Castelo, Portugal
Phone: +351.58.828801/2 Fax: +351.58.827636
Email:rgomes@estg.ipvc.pt

António Dias de Figueiredo
Departamento de Engenharia Informática
Universidade de Coimbra, Polo 2
3030 Coimbra, Portugal
Phone: +351.39.790021 Fax: +351.39.701266
Email:adf@dei.uc.pt

ABSTRACT

There is no standard definition to business object, however we consider OMGs (Object Management Group) as the closest to the business language. Although it mentions that the business object can be represented in a programming language (implementation perspective), it understands the object as an active thing in the business domain, defining its characteristics in a natural or modeling language. This definition does not establish links between an active thing in the business domain and the software object, and doesn't suggest how to derive the business object from the business.

This paper presents, in a representation perspective (Wand 1997), the types of business objects we can use to build a conceptual model of an information architecture during the organization information system planning, pointing out in each specification the way they relate within the business. The use of these objects is illustrated with a specific example drawn from the shipbuilding industry.

Keywords: Information system planning, information architecture, business object, types of business objects.

INTRODUCTION

Information System Planning (ISP) is the activity of producing a plan where we consider "Management Objects" at two levels – Organisation, and Information System (IS) – to build a global view of the IS and include the necessary components for its implementation (Amaral 1995). Management objects of the information system are the specification of the information architecture, the identification of applications and services to support the organisational processes, and the definition of "Application and Services Development". One of the most important IS "Management Objects" is the Information Architecture, because it lets us identify opportunities for obtaining competitive advantages. It also lets us establish and maintain connections between the organisational objectives and the resources involved in the development project of its applications. Finally, it lets us define the business areas and development project boundaries, so that we can co-ordinate the development projects and derive the required technological and organisational infra-structures.

The difficulty of communicating and making understood the information architecture modelled using the Entity-Relationship Model (Earl, 1993; Goodhue et al. 1992; Kim and Everest 1994) and the growing impact of object orientation (OO), first in the field of programming, and more recently in the models for businesses and their supporting IS (Martin 1992, Jacobson 1994, Gale 1996), led us to develop an object-oriented method to analyse the information architecture, when planning the information system of the organization (Gomes and Figueiredo 1998).

To develop this method firstly, we identified how the various OO analysis and design methods identify the objects for system modelling, we developed an object oriented information architecture, for an enterprise of the ship industry (Shipyard of Viana do Castelo – Portugal), that is as independent as possible from the structure of the enterprise, what made possible the test and creation of a set of concepts, steps, and supporting techniques that allowed to delineate the method. Within the concepts of this method, we only present the different types of businees objects that we use to build the conceptual model of the information architecture of the information system.

DEFINITION OF BUSINESS OBJECT

There is no standard definition of business object, although several attempts have been made, first by the BOMSIG (Business Object Management Special Interest Group), and then by the BODTF (Business Object Domain Task Force), both OMGs. However it is possible to say that the interpretation given to this term has developed from what is considered as a software object to an object that represents an active business thing, simulated in a software component. Being difficult to separate both interpretations, we consider that the first three given definitions are closer to software object, and the other two to an active business thing, simulated in a software component;

- business object is the data structure gathered by an event or enquiry from several objects for display at the user interface – the response – a kind of database view. It is a presentation layer thing – often a block of data displayed on a screen that users see as one coherent thing (e.g., a composite of an Order with all its Order Lines and a description of the Stock ordered on each Order Line), (Jacobson 1996).
- business object is a generalisation from which application classes can inherit – say transaction rather than credit or debit, or farm animal rather than cow or pig (Partridge 1996);
- business object encapsulate traditional lower-level objects that implement a business process (i.e., they are a collection of lower-level objects that behave as single, reusable units), (Sutherland 1995);
- business object is simply an entity in an entity relationship model, but with business rules and processes attached to it – a life history with operations and constraints allocated to event-effects (Ramackers 1996);
- business object is a representation of a thing active in the business domain including at least its business attributes, behaviour, relationships and constraints. A business object may represent a person, place or concept. The representation may be in a natural language, a modelling language, or a programming (OMG BODFT 1996).

We consider OMGs definition to business object, as the one which is closest to the business language, for understanding the object as an active thing in the business domain, defining its characteristics in a natural or modelling language , although it mentions that the business object can be represented in a programming language (implementation perspective). This definition doesn't establish links between an active thing in the business domain and the software object, and doesn't suggest how to derive the business object from the business.

TYPES OF BUSINESS OBJECTS USED TO BUILD A CONCEPTUAL MODEL OF AN INFORMATION ARCHITECTURE DURING INFORMATION SYSTEM PLANNING

Before defining the types of business objects used, it will be necessary to consider the entreprise as an open system and its information system, as an information sub-system supported by computers with the aim of recording and supporting management services and organisational operations and explain our understanding about the followings concepts:

- Information Architecture of the Information System illustrates the relationship between the different types of business objects of the information architecture that can be supported by information systems. The Information Architecture is described by the resource and product objects and by its relationship with the activity objects corresponding to the activities of the functional business model, Figure 1.
- A functional area is a

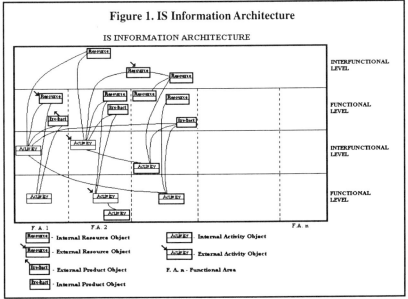

Figure 1. IS Information Architecture

grouping of business functions that materially contributes to the margin or value of products or services of the enterprise according to Porter's value chain.

• A function is any set of actions performed in the course of the business. This definition is only based on the actions performed, not in the way the enterprise is structured or conducted.

• An activity results from a functional decomposition, it is oriented to a single-action, executed repeatedly, and has an identifiable outcome.

Business Objects

Definition

We define a business object as "a representation of a thing active in the business domain, including type, ISP(Information System Planning) attribute, name, definition, business attributes, responsibilities, and relationships, being:

Type – clarifies the object role in business modelling, based on specific caracteristic and relationships.

ISP Attribute – caracterizes the object value concerning the business strategy.

Name – term used by business "experts" to classify a business object.

Definition – states the meaning and purpose assigned to a business object by business experts.

 (Business) Attributes – facts about the business object relevant to fulfiling its purpose.

Responsabilities – the actions acquired by a business object (they can be performed or not) to fulfill its purpose.

Relationship – an association or agregation between business objects that reflects the interaction of their business purposes.

A business object may represent, for example, a person, place or concept, being its representation in a natural or modeling language.

Types of Business Objects

Activity Object

The activity object corresponds to an activity, both for a primary functional area and for a support functional area, and it is responsible for controlling the information for its execution. It holds responsability for the sequence of operations performed to produce a product (accomplish its objective). This objective will be a future state for the activity object, which will be evaluated through the state of its attributes. The responsibilities corresponding to the state transitions of the activity object are not considered, as well as the responsabilities corresponding to the dependency of other activity objects.

To the ISP attribute characterization of the activity objects we use the chain value analysis (Porter, 85), improved with success critical factors inside the chain and, considering the predominant type of acquired responsibilities by each activity object, we will classify that attribute as principal critical or non-critical and of support critical or non-critical. So, if the object acquires responsibilities corresponding to the principal activities development of the value chain, related to success critical factors, it will be given the attribute of principal critical; if it acquires responsibilities corresponding to the principal activities development of the value chain, not related to success critical factors, it will be given the attribute of principal non-critical; if it acquires responsibilities corresponding to the support activities development of the value chain, related to success critical factors, it will be given the attribute of support critical; if it acquires responsibilities corresponding to the support activities development of the value chain, not related to success critical factors, it will be given the attribute of support non-critical.

Between activity objects, we can refer these types:

• The internal functional activity object, that only uses resource objects of the functional area to which it belongs. This object is illustrated in figure 2.

• The internal inter-functional activity object, that uses resources objects (functional and inter-functional) of various functional areas. This object is illustrated in figure 3.

• The external functional activity object, that represents an action resulting from the external environment of the enterprise, using resource objects of the functional area to which it belongs. This object specification differs from the internal functional activity object, represented in figure 2, only by the inclusion of "External Agent" item after "Attributes" item.

The external inter-functional activity object, that represents an action resulting from the external environment of the enterprise, using resource objects of various functional areas. This object specification differs from the internal inter-functional activity object, represented in figure 3, only by the inclusion of "External Agent" item after "Attributes" item.

Figure 2. Specification of the internal functional activity object

Object Name:		
Type	Internal functional activity	
Definition		
ISP attribute		
Functional Area		
Attributes		
Responsabilities gained in its functional area		

Responsabilities gained by the objects that it uses		
Functional resource object	Responsabilities	
Product object	Responsabilities	

Responsabilities of their dependent activity objects			
Functional Area			
Activity	Activity object	Responsabilities	
Behavioural pattern			
Support to IS			

Figure 3. Specification of the internal inter-functional activity object

Object Name:		
Type	Internal inter-functional activity	
Definition		
ISP Attribute		
Functional Area		
Attributes		
Responsabilities gained in its functional area		

Responsabilities gained by the objects that it uses		
Functional resource object	Responsabilities	
Inter-functional resource object	Responsabilities	
Product object	Responsabilities	

Responsabilities of their dependent activity objects			
Functional Área			
Activity	Activity Object	Responsabilities	
Behavioural pattern			
Support to IS			

Resource and Product Objects

We can talk about several resource object types; conceptual, human and financial, etc, some tangibles and others intangible. We consider as resource object the object that corresponds to the information needed to execute an activity. We consider as product object the object that corresponds to the information resulting from an activity execution. The product objects created by an activity object are used as resources in others activities. But in some cases, the activity objects themselves can be the resource object for other activity objects too.

To the resource and product object ISP attribute characterization, we use the portfolio proposed by Ward (Ward. Et al. 1996), figure 4, which categorizes the information in strategic, high potential, operational key and support. So, considering the predominant type of acquired responsibilities by each object, we classify the attribute as strategic, high-potential, key operational and support. If the object has acquired responsibilities corresponding to the information supply, both internal or external, that is crucial to strategic business processes and prominently associated with objectives or measures of success, it will be given the attribute the strategic value; if the objects has acquired responsibilities corresponding to the information supply to primary activities and value enhanced by horizontal integration, it will be given the attribute the key operational value; if the object has acquired responsibilities corresponding to the information supply needed for supporting business but little strategic value, it will be given the attribute the support value; if the object has acquired responsibilities corresponding to information supply with high potential value to the business, but not confirmed, it will be given the attribute the high potential value.

Between resource and product objects, we can refer these types:

- The internal functional resource object is created inside the enterprise by its activities and is only used by activity objects corresponding to activities of the same functional area, acquiring its responsibilities as a result of its use by those activities. This object is illustrated in the fig. 5.

- The internal inter-functional resource object is created inside the enterprise by its activities

Figure 4. Value of the information to the business

Strategic	High Potential
Critical to business and of greatest potential value	Potential value to business may be high, but not confirmed
Essential for primary processes and value enhanced by horizontal integration	Needed for supporting business but little strategic value
Key Operational	Support

and is used by activity objects (inter-functional) corresponding to activities within various functional areas, acquiring its responsibilities as a result of its use by those activities. This object is illustrated in figure 6.

- The external functional resource object, is related to external agents that supply resources to it and is only used by activity objects corresponding to activities of the same functional area, acquiring its responsibilities as a result of its use by those activities. This object specification differs from the internal functional resource object one, represented in figure 5, only by the inclusion of "External Agent" item after "Attributes" item.

- The external inter-functional resource object is related to external agents that supply resources to it and is used by activity objects (inter-functional) corresponding to activities within various functional areas, acquiring its respon-

Figure 5. Specification of the internal functional resource

Object Name:	
Type	Internal functional resource
Definition	
ISP Attribute	
Functional Area	
Attributes	

Responsabilities gained from being used by avtivity objects that creates it		
Activity	Activity object	Responsabilities

Resource objects with which is aggregated
Resource object

Structural pattern	
Support to IS	

Figure 6. Specification of the internal inter-functional resource object			
Object Name:			
Type	Internal inter-functional resource		
Definition			
ISP Attribute			
Attributes			
Responsabilities gained from being used by activity objects that creates it			
	Activity	Activity object	Responsabilities
Responsibilities gained from being used by activity objects of different functional areas			
Functional Area			
	Activity	Activity object	Responsabilities
Functional Area			
	Activity	Activity object	Responsabilities
Functional Area			
	Activity	Activity object	Responsabilities
Resource objects with which is aggregated			
Resource object			
Structural pattern			
Support to IS			

sibilities as a result of its use by those activities. This object specification differs from the internal inter-functional resource object, represented in figure 6 only by the inclusion of "External Agent" item after "Attributes" item.

The product object corresponds to the information resulting from the execution of an activity.

- **The internal product object corresponds to the information resulting from the execution of an activity within a functional area, holding responsibilities acquired within a functional area. Its only purpose is to be consulted by other business activities. This object is illustrated in figure 7.**

- The external product object corresponds to the information resulting from the execution of an activity within a functional area, holding responsibilities acquired within a functional area. Its purpose is both to be consulted by other business activities as well as by external business actors. This object specification differs from the internal product object one, represented in figure 7, only by the inclusion of "External Agent" item after "Attributes" item.

EXAMPLE

Objects of the IS Information Architecture

We present the objects "Estimate_Labour" and "Block" used in the conceptual modelling of the IS information architecture of Viana do Castelo shipyard.

Evaluation of the IS Information Architecture

An evaluation of the IS information architecture for a Viana do Castelo shipyard has been carried out with the business users and IS professionals of the firm, and has shown that the resource, product and activity objects has a set of characteristics and responsabilities that show how they are derived from the business. They also refer that these objects facilitate the capture of the high level information that is important for the business and that they increase the mutual understanding and communication among stakeholders.

CONCLUSIONS

In this paper we present some definitions about a business object and we go futher into proposing a new definition following a representation perpective so that the business objects can be used in conceptual information

Figure 7 – Specification of the internal product object		
Object Name		
Type	Internal Product	
Definition		
ISP Attribute		
Functional Area		
Attributes		
Responsabilities gained from being used by the activity object that creates it		
Activity	**Activity object**	**Responsabilities**
Use by activity objects		
Functional Area/Activity/Activity object		
Product objects with which is agregated		
Product object		
Structural pattern		
Support to IS		

architecture modeling.

We also described the types of business objects used to build a conceptual model of an IS information architecture when performing the organization information system planning and we illustrate it with some examples in the shipbuiding industry.

We also point out that these types of business objects show how they are derived from the business and that the information architecture modelled through them capture the high level information that is important during information system planning.

REFERENCES

Amaral, L. , PRAXIS – Um referencial para o Planeamento de Sistemas de Informação, Ph.D. Thesis, University of Minho, 1995.

BOMSIG, OMG Business Application Architecture - White Paper, 1995.

Earl, M.J., Experiences in strategic information systems planning. MIS Quarterly 17(1) 1-20, 1993.

Gale T. , Eldred J., Getting Results with Object-Oriented Enterprise Model, SIGS Books, 1996.

Gomes, R., Figueiredo A., "A method to define the object Information Architecture of na Information System", Proceedings of the Third CaiSE/IFIP8.1 International Workshop on Evaluation of Modeling Methods in Systems Analysis and Design, I,1-12, Pisa, Itália, 1998.

Goodhue, D.L., Quillard, J.A.,Wybo, M.D., Strategic data planning: lessons from the field, MIS Quartely 16 (1) 11-34, 1992.

Jacobson, I., The Object Advantage - Business Process reengineering with Object Technology, Addison-Wesley Publishing Company, 1994.

Jacobson, I., Use Case Engineering Tutorial in OOPSLA´96 Conference, San Jose Convention Centre, San Jose, California, 1996.

Kim, Y., Everest, G,C., Building and IS architecture: collective wisdom from the field, Information and Management 26,1-11, 1994.

Martin, J. , Odell, J., Object Oriented Analysis and Design, Prentice Hall, Englewood Cliffs, NJ, 1992.

OMG Business Object Domain Task Force, OMG Business Application Architecture White Paper, 1996.

Partridge, C., Business Objects Re-engineering for RE-use. Butterworth Heinemann, Oxford, 1996.

Porter, M.E., Competitive Advantages: Creating and Sustaining Superior Performance, The Free Press, New York, 1985.

Ramackers, G., BPR with Extended Use Cases and Business Objects in Object World'96 UK Conference, Queen

Figure 8 – Specification of the internal inter-functional activity object "Estimate _Labour"

Object – Estimate labour	
Type	Internal inter-functional activity
ISP Attribute	Principal critic
Definition	Activity that calculates the cost of a ship.
Functional Area	Marketing and Sales
Business Attributes	Ship Total_Labour/Area Total_Labour/Type_of_work
Responsibilities gained in its functional area	Identify areas(ship) Compare specifications(area, type_of_ship) Calculate labour/area(ship) Identify type_of_work Calculate labour/type_of_work Exchange labour Distribute labour/months

Responsibilities gained by the objects that it uses	
Resource object	**Responsibilities**
Preliminary_drawing	Inform area
Areas(ship)	Inform characteristics
Previous.labour.records/area	Inform labour/area
Previous.labour.records/ship	Inform area/type_ship

Inter-functional resource object	**Responsibilities**
Section	Price/hour (section)
Exchange_rate	Exchange

Product object	**Responsibilities**
Estimate_Labour	Inform document_topics

Responsibilities of their dependent activity objects		

Functional Area: Design Area

Activity	**Activity object**	**Responsibilities**
Produce Ante-Project	Ante_Project	Perform calculations
		Perform preliminary drawings

Behavioural pattern	No
Support to IS	Yes

Elizabeth Conference Centre, London, 1996.

Sutherland, J., The Object Technology Architecture: Business Objects For Corporate Informmation Systems, Symposium for VMARK Users, Albuquerque, USA, 1995 b.

Wand, Y., "Using objects for systems analysis, COMMUNICATIONS of the ACM, Vol 40, n°12, 1997,104-110.

Ward, J., P. Griffiyhs, Strategic Planning for Information Systems, 2d ed. John Wiley & Sons, 1996.

Figure 9 – Specification of the internal inter-functional resource object "Block"

Object - Block	
Type	Internal Inter-functional resource
ISP Attribute	Key operational
Definition	One of the parts of the ship hull that result of the building strategy
Attributes	Ship Block_number Structure Weight Installation_sequence Products Fabrication_Stage Inspection Subcontract

Responsibilities gained from being used by activity object that creates it

Functional Area: Design Area

Activity	Activity Object	Responsabilities
Define construction units	Model_parts	Inform characteristics

Responsibilities gained from being used by activity objects of different functional areas

Functional Area : Design Area

Activity	Activity Object	Responsibilities
Plan Blocks installation	Installation	Inform installation sequence
Split Blocks	Block_division	Create products

Functional Area : Planning Area

Activity	Activity Object	Responsibilities
Planning of cutting, pre-fabrication and installation of blocks	Planning	Identify fabrication_stage, activity

Functional Area : Production Area

Activity	Activity Object	Responsibilities
Organise subcontracts	Subcontract	Inform on subcontract

Resource objects with which is aggregated

Resource Object
Products

Structural pattern	Yes
Support to IS	Yes

Case Study on a Healthcare Reengineering Project: How It Can Fail

Minh Huynh
Binghamton University, School of Management, Binghamton, NY 13902-6015
Email: br00328@binghamton.edu; Tel: 607-777-2371

Sal Agnihothri
Binghamton University, School of Management, Binghamton, NY 13902-6015
Email: agni@binghamton.edu; Tel: 607-777-2125

ABSTRACT

In this paper, we present key principles and the limitations of business process reengineering (BPR). We then present a case study of a BPR project in a healthcare environment. The purpose of this case study is to explore the reality of how a BPR project is initiated, formulated, and implemented in a hospital setting and how it can fail. In the final discussion, we analyze the possible reasons for the failure of the BPR project and discuss their implication to the implementation of BPR in general.

INTRODUCTION

Just in the past few years, Business Process Reengineering (BPR) has been one of the hottest topics in management. The remarkable success of the best-seller book "Reengineering the Corporation - A Manifesto for Business Revolution" by Michael Hammer and James Champy (1993) is evidence. According to Hammer and Champy, "Reengineering" is termed for the fundamental rethinking and radical redesign of business processes to achieve dramatic improvements in critical, contemporary measures of performance, such as cost, quality, service, and speed. Many executives (according to some surveys show that as many as 88% of large corporations) have initiated BPR projects as a way to turn their companies around, to regain their competitive edge, and eventually to boost their profitability.

The critical reappraisal of BPR in itself is interesting proposition. Despite the claims of the tremendous success in BPR as presented by Hammer and Champy as well as other reengineering proponents, there exist problems within BPR approach. Many researchers have studied the actual practices of BPR in organizations and reported the lessons learned (for example, Caron et al., 1994; Stoddard and Jarvenpaa, 1995).

In 1993, a survey of over 500 CIOs by Deloitte & Touche's Consulting Services reveals that although a growing number of CIOs are involved in reengineering projects, BPR projects usually bring with it big-time problems and very often failure. Even Michael Hammer, the guru of reengineering, admitted that most reengineering projects are fraught with problems and estimates as many as 70% of these projects are failing (Moad, 1993). Davenport and Stoddard (1994) identify, discuss, and dispel the reengineering myths. The survey in literature on the topic of BPR reveals a wide-range of possible causes that may contribute to the failure of BPR projects. Among those possible causes are the followings:
• Reengineering function rather than process.
• Selecting wrong process to reengineer.
• Lacking the detailed methodology to do reengineering.
• Reengineering under a constraint financial budget and insufficient staff resources.
• Ignoring the cost/benefit factor.
• Ignoring the existence of surrounding context.
• Ignoring the effect of changes on workers.
• Lacking inputs from those at the front lines of the process.

Bashein et al. (1994) discuss the organizational preconditions that set the stage for BPR success or failure. Based on the literature survey related to BPR, the conditions that can influence the outcome of a BPR project are summarized below.
• BPR project may not succeed when it relies solely on the use of information technology for the redesign of the process. Although the use of information technology is essential, it is not a sufficient condition for the success of creating a new process. A deeper understanding of the logic and structure under the current practices is required. This means BPR must take into account not just the technological choice but also the critical factor of human

interaction embedded within the process.

- BPR project may not succeed when it relies solely on the top-down approach. The support and commitment from the management leadership is no doubt crucial in BPR, but these alone cannot successfully transform the process. It is important to make BPR acceptable and beneficial to users of the process. Hence, BPR requires a strong participation and partnership from those at the front lines of the process. This means BPR must be established on an effective two-way communication between those at the top management and those closest to the process.

- BPR may not succeed when it is used to set unrealistic expectation. When management initiates BPR with a hope of solving a complex problem and trying to create major impact in a short time, the results are often disappointment. The reason lies in one of BPR's basic assumptions that to redesign process, one needs to throw away the existing process and start from scratch. This assumption ignores the existence of a surrounding context. Since none of the process can exist in a vacuum or by itself, process has to exist in a larger environment with which it must interact and by which it must be constrained. Hence, starting from scratch is just a costly illusion.

- BPR may not succeed when it focuses on the different way of doing the same thing rather than trying new things to meet new demands. BPR's narrow focus on just the process can be fatal, because in some cases changing the process may be the wrong way to solve the organization's problem. The case of Britannica is an example of how reengineering would be an inappropriate solution to the company's problem. In the age of multimedia, when CD-ROM version of encyclopedia has been developed and is widely available, reengineering production of the old paper-based encyclopedia will not help. The important point is that BPR should stress not just redesign, rethinking, but also reinventing the process to meet the dynamic changes in the business environment.

THE CASE STUDY

We now present a case in which BPR is applied in a project for the design, development, and implementation of a critical information system at a hospital. We will also discuss and analyze why BPR project at this organization failed to achieve its goals. Our objective is to demonstrate how the complexity in the process, the human interactions involved, and the existing technological infrastructure can affect the outcome of BPR and eventually reveal important limitations in the BPR approach.

The management of a local hospital, located at a rural community at the Northeast of the United States, was interested in a hospital-wide Order Communication Management System (OCM) in order to undertakings to improve its quality and performance. The objective of such a system is to communicate and process orders primarily from doctors efficiently. These orders are patient related and are related to, for example, tests, x-rays, medications etc. At present, a paper-based order processing system is used like most other hospitals around the country. The problems caused by an inefficient ordering process will increase hospital and patient costs due to delays, errors, and waste of resources. To start the OCM plan, the management organized a working committee to guide the project. This committee consisted of a Vice-President, a Chief Information Officer, an Administrator Resident, a Manager of Nursing, a Laboratory System Coordinator, a Radiology System Coordinator, and a MIS Coordinator. In addition to the hospital staff, a university team consisting of a doctoral student and a professor was also invited to serve on the committee as outsiders to facilitate and work on the project.

Because the OCM plan involved many complex processes, determining where to begin, what to do, and how to apply BPR turned out to be an enlightening task for the committee. The new OCM process would affect not only human interaction but also technology integration across different departments. The wide-range of needs from various departments must be addressed; the diversity of orders within the hospital must be accommodated; and the different requirements in order-handling procedures must be satisfied. The effect of drastic changes would have a far-reaching repercussion in the way the hospital will operate in the future. Because of the complexity and the extensiveness in the proposed OCM plan, the BPR project conducted by the university team had to start with a process on a smaller and more manageable scale.

Define the scope of the study:

With the time and resource constraints, the scope of the study was limited to West wing[1] (WW) unit, one of the largest wings in the hospital. Because of the important role and the significant contribution of WW, the team found that WW is a good representative of the units in the hospital. Understanding the process in WW could provide valuable insights to the operation of other units in the hospital as well. Although work detail of WW could be different from other units, the overall procedures in ordering were very much similar among the units. Hence, the team predicted that any successful measures to improve the ordering process at WW would potentially be applicable and transferable to other units as well.

Understand the current process and identify problems:

After specifying the objective of the study, the university team started to examine the current order processing system. Being outsiders to the hospital gave us an advantage of seeing things from an objective perspective. We looked at the process without worrying about the constraints and organizational politics. We first examined the ordering process at the WW unit. This unit was specialized in heart patients. One general manager was responsible for all the activities with the WW unit. The unit had a staff of 40 nurses and 3 unit clerks and had 35 beds.

We interviewed the floor manager, nurses, unit clerks, and a doctor to learn about the order processing system, and observed the activities at the reception center where most of the activities occurred. We identified several problems related to the order processing at WW. Some of the major problems include poor scheduling, no standard procedure for getting things done, lack of coordination, and inefficiency of paper charting practice. We also gained a better understand of how an actual order was initiated, processed, and completed and identified several problems associated with the current process.

In addition to WW, we toured and interviewed personnel in two other departments, which interact with WW very closely. The System Coordinator of the first department shared with us her vision of an OCM. According to her, the system should provide users at her department an on-line electronic access to the patient's record. From the system, the users should be able to view, retrieve, and update information related to the patient. Furthermore, the users should be able to look up the patient's chart and schedule for certain tests. She also mentioned three other features desirable in the new system. One, the system should be able to alert the users when the test is done and the result is available. Two, the system should be paperless so that there would be no more reliance on paper and forms for processing an order. Three, the system should provide a central link to all departments in the hospital so that order could be entered directly from anywhere and be processed on-line in a timely manner.

From our interview with the users in the second department, we learned that the basic requirements for OCM system were similar to those at the first department. However, the System Coordinator of the second department pointed out several specific enhancements that she wanted to incorporate in the new process. To reduce error, she would like information for orders to be captured at the source. The process should allow a Unit Clerk at each floor to enter their orders to the Laboratory directly from the system. There should be no phone call or filling out of a paper form. She would like to enhance the current label using bar code system. She was also interested in simplifying the order preparation and processing with more automation to reduce the training time.

From the WW unit's perspective, the system with scheduler was most desirable. The users wanted to access scheduling information and make decision on patient's daily activities chart so they could better plan their works. Also, a feature which allows direct order entry onto the system to bypass the paper and handwriting forms was desirable.

Develop Flowchart:

The next task for the team was to translate the actual steps of the existing process into a flowchart. This required a deep understanding of the logic, structure, and information flow in the current process. The flowcharts are revised several times with the comments from people involved. The final flowchart helped us gain a broader perspective on the existing process, allowed us to locate a possible process flaws, identify bottlenecks and non value-added steps. It also helped us to come up with the measures of effectiveness for an order processing system. Finally, it gave us a foundation for the design of an ideal order processing system.

Collect data:

Considering the objective of the study and the constraints in time and resources, we came up with the following categories of data. In order to substantiate the important contribution of WW and to justify our selection of WW as the site of the study, we collected data related to patient census. This included number of admissions, discharge, occupancy rate, length of stay, and patient days of both WW and the whole hospital. We then collected data on the volume of orders processed by both WW and by the whole hospital. This data would give us some evidence on the magnitude of the problem in the order processing system. By surveying the staff, we collected data to identify the root causes of the problem in the current order processing system. Using the survey, we also collected data related to the measures of effectiveness in an order processing system, which in turn, would enable us to locate the flaws in the system, to recommend changes, and to assess the effect of implemented changes.

Analyze data:

The record of all inpatient procedures for the past data revealed that the hospital had processed an average of 95,000 orders per month. According to data collected on in-patients for a six months period, WW contributed approximately 25% of all procedures processed in the hospital. It had more patients than any other units. The occupancy rate was around 80-90%. The duration of patient stay varied between 3 to 5 days. For the survey, we tabulated all the questionnaires completed by nurses, clerks, doctor, and patient. From the result of our survey, we were able to identify the following causes of the problems in the existing ordering process. They include illegible writing on the order, poor communication between doctors and nurses, poor scheduling, and errors and inconsistencies on the order.

According to our original plan, the next phase would involve the second round of our data collection. This time, we would focus on data relating to the root causes of the problem and on the measures of the effectiveness in the ordering process. We would design a check sheet for use in the data collection. The purpose of this data was to allow us understand the impact of the current problems on the system. Using this, we also can measure the improvement when the processes are reengineered.

Mean while, we also started redesigning the process. The approach we took was to start with an ideal process, which were not subject to any organizational, budgetary, and technological constraints. We developed the ideal process into a flowchart that showed how an order was processed under a new system. We also explored the current and emerging information technology to be incorporated into our ideal system. We searched for creative applications that are currently used at other sites or have potential use in the hospital environment.

As a first step in moving towards this ideal system, we suggested a simpler redesign, which considers the existing constraints. The revised system should overcome the flaws in the current manual-driven process. The approach is the automation of the current ordering process with the available information technology. The objectives are to eliminate the paper work and to make use of a computerized scheduling system.

We presented our recommendations to the committee. Although the committee liked our recommendations, due to several occurring within the organization including management restructure, the results of the study were not been implemented.

LESSONS LEARNED

One of the limitations of this project was the absence of two-way communication and the lack of partnership effort between the top-management and the front line employees. First of all, the BPR project in this hospital was initiated without any strong sponsorship from the management. This is evident in the fact that no resources are committed or specifically allocated for the project. Although the leadership involved both the vice-president and CIO, their roles were quickly disappeared soon after the project started. Secondly, the senior management did nothing to convey the BPR message and its importance to the employee. Most of the people whom we came in contact had little idea what the OCM plan is. Each of them had different reaction of our BPR effort. In one occasion, Radiology System Coordinator explicitly indicated that whatever the change is, they did not want to lose control of their systems. Thirdly, there was little participation in the project from people who were the actual users of the system or closest to the process. Neither doctors nor nurses served on the OCM committee. This perhaps attributed to the poor response rate from the doctors in our survey. In fact, when we received only one completed survey from the doctor, we could sense their negative attitude towards the overall OCM project. If doctors, who would be the ultimate users of the new OCM system, did not care and failed to participate in the project, the chance for the acceptance of the new system would be slim.

The misleading information that we got from the MIS coordinator during our data collection process provides an interesting insight of an internal conflict among key parties involved in the project. This is another indicator of poor communication and cooperation, which has to be resolved for the BPR project to be successful.

From these observations, it is logical for us to predict that when the BPR project has neither the support from the top management nor the participation from the front line people, it will get little chance to succeed as demonstrated in this case study.

When the OCM plan was first proposed, the vision was to build a system with central links to support the ordering processes throughout the hospital. BPR was the chosen approach, because the plan was directed toward the innovative use of information technology to support the hospital mission. However, as the study proceeded, the team realized that the actual ordering process was far more complex than expected. It was not a simple replacement of one system with another. When the logic and the structure of the current process was unveiled, the task of reengineering became monumental. First, there were issues related to human factors that must be resolved. For instance, the management needs to galvanize the support and cooperation from users such as doctors, nurses, system coordinators, etc. Secondly, there were existing technological infrastructures that must be integrated to the redesign. For instance, the management needs a strategy to analyze the cost/benefit issue involved the disposition or reuse of the existing investments in computer systems, lab equipment, and other software applications at both the Laboratory and the Radiology. Simply abandoning all of previous investments may not be an attractive option. Hence, in a complex process, it is difficult to justify the decision of redesigning it from scratch. Here is another evidence to disclaim the virtue of "start with a clean sheet of paper" approach.

In the case study, we also see a real world situation in which a project is always facing constraints. For instance, there was a priority in budget allocation that restricted resources committed for the BPR project. When the priority was shifted, so did the resources. Hence, the change in resource support can have a drastic impact on the direction and momentum of the on-going project.

One the methodological problem associated with this case study is the confusion in applying BPR approach. When the process was too complex, we could not redesign the process directly. We had to first break the complex process into smaller and more manageable processes, then we focused on one of the smaller processes. Since we worked on the smaller process, we might not apply all the principles in BPR. In essence, we no longer did reengineering and hence we could achieve only an incremental change. This is contradictory to the fundamental objective of reengineering, which is to make radical changes.

In retrospect, we find that the organization was not ready for reengineering. It lacked management commitment. It did not have a strong leadership with clear vision. It had no strategy in establishing two-way communication needed in the BPR. It could not get users such as doctors, nurses, and those at front line to actively participate and provide input for the BPR initiative. The lack of management commitment was also evident in the fact that there was no funding to support the project. Basically, the management approached the project with an exploratory attitude. Their strategy was to incur neither cost nor risk in the proposal of new system. As a result, the penalty for not implementing the proposed system was negligible. It would not be the case if a paid consultant from conducted the study. Perhaps, the management would feel more committed toward the project.

REFERENCES

Bashein, Barbara J; Markus, M Lynne; Riley, Patricia; 1994. "Preconditions for BPR Success," *Information Systems Management, 11* (2), 7-13.

Caron, J. Raymond; Jarvenpaa, Sirkka L.; Stoddard, Donna B. (1994). " Business Reengineering at CIGNA Corporation: Experiences and Lessons learned from the First five years," *MIS Quarterly, 18* (3), pp. 233.

Davenport, Thomas H. (1993). *Process Innovation: Reengineering Work through Information Technology.* Harvard Business School Press, Boston

Davenport, Thomas H.; Stoddard, Donna B. (1994). "Reengineering: Business change of mythic proportions?," *MIS Quarterly, 18* (2), pp. 121.

Hammer, M. & Champy, J. (1993). *Reengineering the Corporation - A Manifesto for Business Revolution,* New York: Harper Business, a division of HarperCollins Publishers, Inc.

Moad, Jeff. (1993). "Does reengineering really work?" *Datamation, 39*(15), pp. 22-28.

Stoddard, Donna B.; Jarvenpaa, Sirkka L. (1995). "Business Process Redesign: Tactics for managing Radical Change", *Journal of Management Information Systems, 12* (1), pp. 81.

ENDNOTES

1 Disclaimer: The "West wing" unit is a fictious name used to protect the confidentiality of the actual site.

Data Communication Security Issues for Multi-Media Hospital Information Systems

L. J. Janczewski and P.P. Singh

The University of Auckland, Department of Mgt Science and Information Systems, Private Bag 92019,
Auckland, New Zealand

phone: +64 9 373 7599, fax +64 9 373 7430, email: lech@auckland.ac.nz

ABSTRACT

Interest in the Multi-Media based Hospital Information Networks (MMHIN) was the foundation of a research project aimed at analysing the various security aspects of this new technology with a special emphasis on utilising it in the New Zealand hospitals. Several subprojects have been carried out already and this paper describes the next project from this series.

The objective was to evaluate security issues related to the telecommunication part of the multi-media hospital information systems. Major parts of the MMHIN telecommunication security: the Certification Architecture and the Security Protocol are proposed and discussed. Also a description of the status of the medical information domain in New Zealand including the law related to security issues is reported.

INTRODUCTION

Information technology is being deployed rapidly in the administration of health information in hospitals. The storage of patients' records has changed from the traditional paper-based systems to the current partially computerised systems. In recent years, system development for hospitals have started utilising Internet/Intranet technologies to develop Multi-Media based Hospital Information Networks (MMHINs).

Interest in the MMHINs was the foundation of a research project aimed at analysing the various security aspects of this new technology with a special emphasis on utilising it in the New Zealand hospitals. Several sub-projects have been carried out already:
• Laying foundations for the multimedia hospital information systems (Janczewski, 1996)
• Considerations in the development of a reference monitor for MMHIN (Janczewski/Low,1998)
• Privacy protection models in MMHIN (Janczewski/Keng, 1998)

This paper describes the next project from this series. The objective was to evaluate security issues related to the telecommunication part of the multi-media hospital information systems.

The paper starts with the description of the status of the medical information domain in New Zealand including the law related to security issues. Then constraints related to the security of the multi-media hospital information systems are presented. Special emphasis will be made on the telecommunication part of the system. The major part of the paper is the description of the proposed Certification Architecture and principles of the Security Protocol.

NEW ZEALAND HEALTH SYSTEM

The New Zealand Health System is made up of public, private and voluntary sectors that interact to provide and fund health care. Over 75% of health care are publicly funded. The Ministry of Health provides policy advice to the Government on health and disability support services. The four Regional Health Authorities (RHA) are responsible for purchasing health and disability service for New Zealanders, including public health services. There are 23 Crown Health Enterprises (CHE) grouped into the four RHAs. They generally provide health care and disability support services for a particular geographical region. For instance, in Auckland (population around 1 million and the biggest city in the country), there are three CHs operating: Waitemata, Auckland Healthcare and South Auckland Health.

The regional health authorities subsidise the cost of general practitioners' fees and some prescription costs. Although the majority of the health care is publicly funded, many New Zealanders now have their own health insurance through private companies to cover the costs of staying in hospitals and operations. These operations are available through the public system but usually there are lengthy waiting lists (unless life threatening) and with private health insurance this enables access to medical attention immediately.

The protection of patients' privacy is covered under the *Health Information Privacy Code* introduced in 1994. The relevant guiding principles for national health information are:
• the need to protect patient confidentiality and privacy,
• the need to collect data once, as close to the source as possible, and use it as many times as required to meet different information requirements,
• the need for standard data definitions, classification and coding systems,
• the requirement for national health data to include only data which is used, valued and validated at the local level,
• the need for connectivity between health information systems to promote communication and integrity.

The Code of Practice is based on the *Privacy Act*, introduced by the New Zealand Parliament in 1993, which in turn used the *OECD Privacy Principles* as a blue print for development.

A unique feature of the Privacy Code is that it postulates *unique identifiers*. The Privacy Act in Principle 12 states: "An agency shall not assign to an individual a unique identifier that, to that agency's knowledge, has been assigned to that individual by another agency, unless those two agencies are associated persons within the meaning of section 8 of the Income Tax 1976". This means in practical terms that in New Zealand it is impossible to use such popular identifiers as Inland Revenue Number, Driver Licence Number, etc for identifying the patients. This regulation was introduced to make data matching more difficult and, as a result, provide better protection of individuals' privacy. Currently (fall of 1998) the Privacy Act 1993 is undergoing revision and there are strong suggestions that the clause about the unique identifiers will be abolished as not being a significant guardian of patients' privacy.

Nevertheless, the national health information system currently runs the following nation-wide databases:
• *National Health Index* (NHI)
  Basic personal information of anybody being attended by medical professionals
• *Medical Warning System* (MWS)
  Information about patients infected with socially dangerous diseases (like AIDS)
• *National Minimum Dataset* (NMD)
  Basic information about patients being treated in hospitals
• *Patient Throughput Statistics* (PTS)
  Summary of services provide by medical facilities

In 1987 Health Level 7 (HL7) was founded to set up standards for the electronic interchange of clinical, financial and administrative information among independent health-care oriented computer systems.

A survey was conducted [Singh, 1997] within this project framework to determine the level of computerisation of medical records and privacy protection in the New Zealand hospitals. The current system could be characterised as following:

Each CHE (Crown Health Enterprise) stores their patients NHIs and MDS plus relevant documents and correspondence. The main purpose of that database is to provide a summary of a person's contacts with the CHE and treatment. This data is distributed across many different departments such as laboratory, radiology, patient administration, etc. Electronically stored information is relatively minimal and used mainly in such areas as patient administration data. Little protection is therefore needed for these records because the information is not so sensitive. Each CHE must maintain links with the Ministry of Health, to exchange data required by regulations. Also it is worth mentioning that many hospitals outsource their IT services to such organisations like EDS. Fig 1 depicts major parts of the hospital network for Auckland Healthcare, being the biggest healthcare provider in the country.

DATA COMMUNICATIONS

As there is not much data communication between hospitals and external organisations, information security in this aspect is not well developed, if any at all. The only form of external data communications is through e-mail, plus links with the Ministry of Health, as indicated in Fig 1. Most of the hospitals have private wide area network so the security concerns are not very high. In most cases, the only form of security is restricted physical access to communications equipment plus use of an individual password. However, as the cost of utilising Internet falls, it is inevitable that hospitals will move away from private X.25 networks and towards the Internet. One of the hospitals is currently developing security software utilising encryption algorithms. Also the New Zealand Health Information Systems launched a project aimed at building extensive Intranet system (Health Information Systems, 1998). Part of it is a program for introducing a set of security measures.

With the current trends in the growth of Internet, it holds a promising future for its utilisation in the Health Industry. However, there are number of problems to be overcome before a National Health Information network becomes a reality. These problems are as follows:
• **Bandwidth** - Currently the highest bandwidth available for Internet usage in New Zealand is primarily ISDN, which offers speeds of up to 128 BPS. For effective communications within HIN, higher bandwidths need to be

utilised.

- **User resistance** - This presents a major challenge as medical staff, particularly doctors do not tend to view computers very favourably. The user interface design is crucial in addressing this issue and with adequate training, this problem can be easily solved.

- **Security** - this is perhaps the most important issue. Due to the explosive growth of the Internet, a number of security holes have been found in the existing architecture and protocols. This has been an advantage as it means that solutions to these problems have been also proposed and tested. This has resulted in the development of more robust security protocols and applications.

- **Integration of records** - This would have presented a major challenge if all the records were currently stored on computers. So it is more a problem of actually transferring data from hardcopy to computers. The HL-7 group has already established data standardisation to some extent. However, some problems are anticipated due to the legacy data.

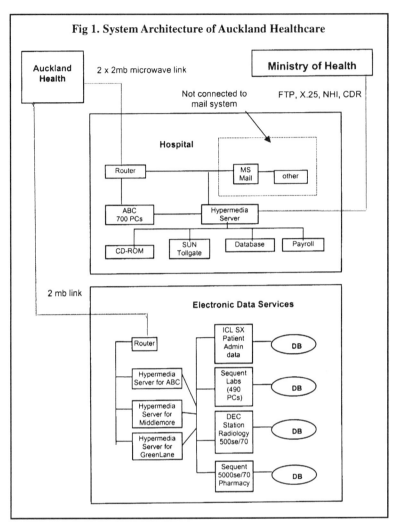

Fig 1. System Architecture of Auckland Healthcare

The major issues regarding MMHIS are the certification structure and the development of a protocol allowing secure transfer of information with authentication and non-repudiation capabilities. The following parts suggest possible solution to these problems.

CERTIFICATION STRUCTURE

There are two main structures for certificate management, Hierarchical and Networked (or peer-to-peer). In the hierarchical structure all the certificates are arranged in a tree-form relationship, similar to the relationships between data in the hierarchical database management system. Privacy Enhanced Mail (PEM) uses that type of certification structure.

In the network structure the users' keys are certified by someone the user knows and trusts. For example, if Alice want Bob's key and she has got Barry's keys which she trusts to be correct, and Barry has Ben's keys which he trusts to be correct, then Alice can get Bob to certify Ben's key and get this certificate either from Bob or Barry. In this way, the peers certify all the keys. This structure is used in the Pretty Good Privacy (PGP) system.

It is also possible to set up a structure which is a hybrid of the hierarchical and networked certificate structure. This involves the Certification Authority (CA), which is the root of the hierarchical system, replacing the peers in the cross-certified structure. Instead of a central authority certifying CA under it, other CAs certifies the CAs.

Looking at the advantages and disadvantages of the various structures, for MMHIS a purely hierarchical structure is recommended. The assurance existence of certification paths, absence of certification loops and difficulty of managing certification authorities leads to this recommendation.

Having a hierarchical structure does not necessarily mean that a central body will be responsible for the certification of all medical workers in the country. In fact, in the Zergo report in United Kingdom (Anderson, 1996), this is exactly what was proposed, having a single third party to manage keys for the whole National Health System. This idea was severely criticised and rejected by the clinical professionals who saw this as an attempt to transfer control of professional registration bodies to the NHS executive. In response, the Department of Health backed down and instead decided that the trust structures in the electronic world should mirror those in existing practice. However, according to Anderson, this set-up is unlikely to work. The natural place to administer any kind of access is where the rest of the employee registration is done. In the health service, this would mean in general practices, hospitals and community care facilities, and any attempt to centralise will be expensive, and keys should be managed locally.

Because of the size of the health infrastructure in New Zealand, these problems apply here as well. It is suggested that for all the hospital workers, the registration authority should be the hospital, which could also certify the GPs who are physically close to it. An intermediate body could service other individuals.

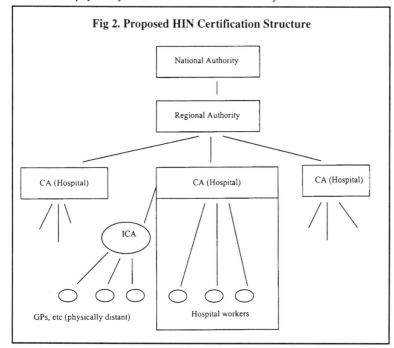

Fig 2. Proposed HIN Certification Structure

The Intermediate Certification authority's (ICA) task would be to help a user, who is physically distant from a CA, to register. The ICA would perform identification and authentication of the end-user and vouch for her/his authenticity in a signed message that it sends to the CA. So the overall HIN certification structure could look as in Fig 2.

The most widely recognised standard public-key certificate format is that defined in the Directory Authentication Framework X.509. The structure of the X.509 v3 is presented in Fig 3.

Some modifications of the X.509 certificate are required to accommodate an additional field that would contain the identifier for the ICA. However, that ICA identifier can be placed within the optional Issuer unique ID field. This may be the preferred approach since any modification to the X.25 format is not then required.

One addition to the X.509 certificate used for MMHIN is a "role" field. A user may have different roles like doctor, nurse or admin staff at different times, or even simultaneously. The information accessible would depend on the role of the person. For example, the nurse on duty will not be able to see all the information about a patient, but only what he/she needs to know, while a doctor will have access to almost all the records of his or her patients. A certificate should be issued for each role a person has, which for most people would be only one; however, there may be some exceptions. Another reason is that the access control mechanism can use the certificate of the person to determine the access rights for this purpose. The reason for this is for future integration with other infrastructures or even with X.500 for

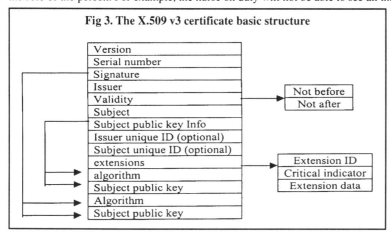

Fig 3. The X.509 v3 certificate basic structure

global inter-operability.

HIN COMMUNICATION PROTOCOL

The communication protocol defined below is used for assuring authentication and non-repudiation properties of both parties. It is based on the handshake principle.

Before the Handshake protocol is initiated, the client must obtain the public key (via certificates) from the server. Since there won't be a great number of servers, the certificate will not have to obtain frequently; thus the first component of the protocol is presented separately from the second (Handshake) phase.

$$\text{Message 1: A} \Rightarrow \text{S: A,B}$$

A sends a message to the server requesting the certificate of B. B here can be another server or a client. This message contains the identity of both A and B.

$$\text{Message 2: S} \Rightarrow \text{A: CB}$$

The server sends back the certificate of B to A. Both message 1 and 2 are sent open, there is no need to encrypt these messages.

Begin of the Handshake protocol

$$\text{Message 1: A} \Rightarrow \text{B: } \{N_A, CA\}_{KB}$$

A sends a nonce and its certificate to B, requesting a session key. The message is encrypted with B's public key, which would have been extracted from the certificate in the first phase of this protocol.

$$\text{Message 2: B} \Rightarrow \text{A: } \{N_{A+1}, K_{AB}\}_{KA}$$

B generates a session key and sends it to A with the nonce incremented. The session key and the nonce are encrypted with A's public key. Encryption and nonce increment are implemented for assuring authenticity of B.

At the beginning of each connection the server must be authenticated to the client and vice versa. Also the exchange of session keys should be performed. The messages used during that phase are listed in Fig 4.

Fig 4. Handshake messages	
Message	From
CLIENT_HELLO	Client
SERVER_HELLO	Server
HELLO_DONE	Client
ERROR_DONE	Either
DISCONNECTION_NOTIF	Either

In contrast to the Hello messages of Internet protocols such as PCT and SSL the HELLO message of HIN is much simpler as the certificate of the server is obtained from another source then requested from the server. The server certificate will actually be obtained from the local CA, for example, the hospital CA database will contain most of the certificates of the users on the network. The server certificate will be requested from the local database server which would already have been verified.

The overview of the Handshake Protocol in establishing communications between a client and a server is depicted in Fig 5.

The server sends the HELLO_REQUEST to the client if the server wishes to initiate a connection. The server should then wait for a CLIENT_HELLO message.

The client may send a hello request in reply to a HELLO_REQUEST from the server or on its won accord. The CLIENT_HELLO message contains the following data:
• Protocol version number
• Client certificate
• Client random number
• Compression option
• Encryption algorithm
• Encryption mode

This message is encrypted using the public key of the server, which would have been obtained by the client from their local Certificate Database.

The server sends the SERVER_HELLO message in the response to a CLIENT_HELLO. Alternatively, the HELLO_ERROR message may be sent if the server refuses a session request. The SERVER_HELLO message contains the following:
• Protocol version number
• Client random number +1
• Compression option
• Session ID
• Session Key

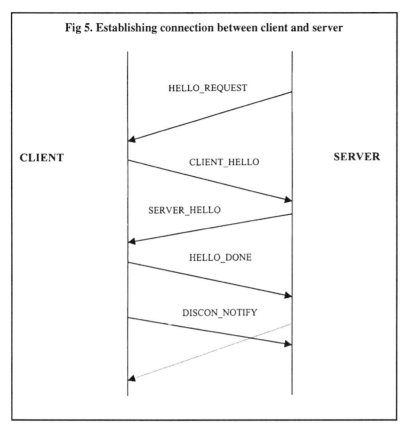

Fig 5. Establishing connection between client and server

This information is encrypted using the public key of the client derived from the certificate obtained from the CLIENT_HELLO message. Once the client has received the SEVER_HELLO, it sends a confirmation message indicating that the parameters are valid and it has accepted the use of the particular session key. This is again sent after encrypting it with the server's public key.

DISCONNECTION_NOTIFY is sent by either party and indicates that no more messages will be sent after this one. An ERROR_MESSAGE is issued when an error results from the messages being exchange. The alert message gives severity of the error message as well as the description of the error. The alert messages are also encrypted like other messages. Each error message is either fatal or non-fatal. If it is a fatal error, then the session must be discontinued immediately. If the error is non-fatal, either party could re-send the message or discontinue the session voluntarily until the problem has been fixed.

The limited space here prevent the authors to present details of the protocol such as
• Key management activities
• Key generation, certification and distribution
• Internal structure of certificates
• Obtaining certificates
• Verification of certificates
• Semantics of the messages, etc.
Details of the suggested secure MMHIN protocol could be find in (Singh, 1997).

CONCLUSIONS

This project attempted to present solution to the four most important security aspects of data communications in MMHIN:
• Data confidentiality
• Data integrity
• Data origin authentication
• Non-repudiation.

The suggested certification architecture attempted to find solutions for ensuring that only the intended party reads the data by providing means of obtaining a valid key for encryption. This certification architecture was unique as it utilises a combination of local and central databases to maintain keys, but at the same time using a global standard certificate structure - the X.509 v3. This is to ensure a smooth possible transition to a Global Certification Network if such network becomes a possibility in the future.

Due to the fact that this project presented only an overview of the architecture, further investigation need to be conducted regarding the hardware, software and the communication infrastructure of such a system. Possible project should aim on determining, for example:
• type of database used for storing the certificates,
• other database-specific issues such as maintaining updates, deletions and additions

• hardware and software specifications
• economic feasibility analysis

Though current costs of hardware and other technologies may not make this a feasible solution for the whole network, small-scale implementations should be possible as a test bed for future systems. The suggested certification architecture may even be applied to other organisations and industries and later integrated into an inter-organisational infrastructure if there will be needs for it.

REFERENCES

Anderson, R.J. "Security in Clinical Information Systems", British Medical Association, January 1996

Health Information Systems, 1998, Health Intranet Project, also in http://www.nzhis.govt.nz/projects/intranet.html

Janczewski, L. Data Security Framework for Hyper-media Based Health Information Systems, in: Notes on Information Security Management, ed. Von Solms, R., Port Elizabeth Technikon, South Africa, 1996

Janczewski, L., B. Keng, Privacy Protection in Hyper-media Health Information Systems from a Law Point of View, in Information Security; Small Systems Security & Information Security Management, ed. Eloff, J.H, Von Solms, R. IFIP, 1998.

Janczewski, L., Lo, B.K.W., Reference Monitor for Hypermedia-Based Hospital Information Systems, in Global IT Security, ed. Papp, G., Posh, R., Osterreichische Computer Gesellschaft, Austria, 1998.

Singh, P.P., (1997), "Data Communications Security for a Hypermedia Health Information Network", MCom Thesis, Department of Mgt Science and Information Systems, The University of Auckland, 1997.

Telecommunications Planning, Budgeting and Training in Small Organizations

Karen Ketler and John R. Willems
School of Business, Eastern Illinois University, Charleston, Illinois 61920
Phone: (217) 581-6906; (217) 581-6916, Fax: (217) 581-7244, E-Mail: cfjrw@eiu.edu

ABSTRACT

Telecommunications may be the strategic weapon of the 1990s. In order to gain insight into the impact of budgetary allocations on telecommunications planning and on telecommunications training, a nationwide survey was undertaken. The exploratory study, reported in this article, found a noticeable weakness in the development of an organizational telecommunications plan. In addition, there was a relationship between the development and implementation of a plan and adequate budgetary funding for the telecommunications function, including training. The researchers concluded that as organizations researched the development of a telecommunications plan, they would discover the strategic uses of telecommunications and allocate appropriate funding of the function. In addition, MIS managers expressed dissatisfaction with their training in telecommunications, especially on the managerial or strategic applications of telecommunications. However, as organizations increase their budgetary allocations to telecommunications, improved training on the managerial and technical issues were noted. No improvement was noted in the standard or clerical application area.

INTRODUCTION

As organizations look forward to the twenty-first century, they are re-emphasizing the importance of strategic planning in the hopes of locating a niche for a competitive advantage. Telecommunications technology appears to be the instrument for innovation in many organizations. Additional telecommunications services are available during airline flights, in hotel rooms and literally everywhere. Using cellular phones and laptop computers, data can be sent across a wireless network (King, 1997).

Airline flights now provide fax, e-mail and other technological innovations. These services are now provided due to the keen observation of airline personnel who noticed that several boardings were delayed because travelers in the airport were utilizing telecommunications technology until the last possible minute ("A moveable office", 1996).

Similarly, hotels are providing similar telecommunications technology in the guest rooms. AT & T offers a comprehensive reservation system for members of the Small Luxury Hotels of the World group. This system combines telephone and internet technology. Customers accessing the web site will be able to instantly establish a phone line and book a reservation through TeleService (Bittle, 1996). However, telecommunications technology is also providing innovative problems for the hotel systems. Consumer groups sometimes claim that hotels charge too much for phone calls. Thus, justifying the expense to guests for the additional technology is often difficult. Other problems include detecting and preventing fraud such as "dial-a-porn" services. The final problem noted, was preparing for the future, including the trend to cellular and other wireless devices, and videoconferencing technologies (Carson, 1995; The Telman Group, Inc., 1995).

Planning for the future is difficult for all organizations. In a 1995 survey, less than 25% of the 6500 respondents indicated that they currently use videoconferencing. But 57% indicated that they plan to implement it by the new century (Edwards, 1995). Yet, little information about how organizations plan for the future of telecommunications has been noted in the literature.

In order to explore how organizations plan for telecommunications, including the training of their managers, a nationwide survey was undertaken. In the next section of this paper is a literature review of some of the innovations in telecommunications in industry, including issues on planning and training. A discussion of the methodology of the survey is contained in the third sections. The results and conclusions of the survey are contained in the fourth and fifth section.

LITERATURE REVIEW

Originally, only major corporations could afford to use a videoconferencing system, but as prices drop, videoconferencing is becoming an alternative for nearly every organization. It allows people on different continents to hod meetings as if they were in the same room. The quality of videoconferencing has improved so much that Funrise Toy, located in Woodland Hills, California uses it for formal approval of advertising artwork. In addition, telecommunication technologies increase their efficiency and productivity (Edwards, 1995).

Telecommunications technology is also used to quickly coordinate activities between suppliers and customers. This tightens the bond between customers and suppliers and is used as a strategic weapon by many organizations. Southwestern Bell in Arkansas has invested $231 million to make Arkansas a leader in telecommunications technology. Digital technology, combined with fiber optics technology will make it possible for business and residential customers to transmit high-quality voice, data, and video locally or globally in a matter of seconds. Arkansas officials hope that the telecommunications technology will help to recruit new businesses to the area ("Southwestern Bell Telephone Company: innovations in telecommunications", 1995).

Southwestern Bell also offers videoconferencing through public telephone lines. Schools districts are currently using the service for distance learning. They only need to purchase basic monitors and computers. They no long incur the costs of a dedicated network. Similarly, hospital and doctors use videoconferencing services to assist in diagnostics at remote locations. Similar uses of videoconferencing is also occurring in developing nations ("Meeting the world face-to-face: videoconferencing helps Latin firms conduct business globally", 1995).

Organizations utilizing videoconferencing report a reduction in travel costs ranging from 20% to 50%, plus an increase in productivity. Some organizations report that videoconferencing is used to enhance professional development. Employees use videoconferencing to expand their areas of expertise with seminars and instant access to experts in their fields. Videoconferencing costs about $2500 to implement on a desktop computer, and about $44,000 for a higher performance group systems. ("Meeting the world face-to-face: videoconferencing helps Latin firms conduct business globally". 1995)

Organizations are realizing that it is not enough to have these new technology. Organizations must also restructure themselves in order to effectively utilize them (Johnson and Ciandella, 1995). Technology is merely a means to an end, where the end is the organizational goals and objectives. Yet, technology requires planning and training. But it is difficult to train managers on a new way of thinking, "thinking outside the box".

Stenton resource Center, a telecommunications giant, launched a new learning organization program originally targeted at the marketing department. Goals of this program included 1) stretching personal creativity, 2) intelligent risk taking, 3) challenging business processes, 4) empowering others, and 5) coaching. New projects and innovations from the learning forum resulted in a $72 million increase in revenues (Berry, 1998).

It is difficult to train managers to think innovatively. Add the problems associated with predicting the technology of the future and managers have an impossible task. Cooper and Lybrand's Information/Communications Consulting Group and Thinking Tools have developed a computer game for honing the management skills of professionals in the telecommunications industry. The game, called TeleSim, allows users to manage a Bell operating company for 10 years in approximately 30 minutes on a computer (McCarthy, 1996).

Telecommunications technology, through the use of distance learning, is increasing the effectiveness of corporate training when employees are located around the word. Distance learning can provides access to the best instructors and courses at lower costs and smaller time commitments. On-line training is the method in highest demand. It has produced innovations in areas such as course topics, performance assessment tools, on-line registration, curriculum planning and courseware development (Davy, 1998). Educational institutions must be at the forefront of this new trend so that they can assist organizations to effectively use this new telecommunications technology to achieve the corporate goals and objectives. Organizations must make sure that their managers and employees have access to training on this and other telecommunications innovations.

The exploratory study reported in this article was undertaken in order to gain insight into the planning and managerial training in telecommunications technology, with special emphasis on budgetary allocations to the telecommunications function. In particular, the primary objectives of the study were:

1. to determine if organizations are developing and implementing a plan for their evolving telecommunications function.
2. to determine if there is a relationship between the development and implementation of a telecommunications plan and MIS managers' satisfaction with budgetary allocations to the telecommunications function.
3. to determine if there is a relationship between the MIS managers' satisfaction with budgetary allocations to the telecommunications function and their satisfaction with managerial telecommunications training.

METHODOLOGY

In accordance with the above objectives, the following three hypotheses were formed:

1. The degree to which organizations are developing and implementing a telecommunications plan will be uniformly distributed from one end of the spectrum to the other. There will be organizations which have not started a plan while others will have developed and fully implemented their plan.
2. As organizations develop and implement their telecommunications plans, MIS managers' satisfaction with budgetary allocations to the telecommunications function will increase.
3. There is a direct relationship between the satisfaction of MIS managers with the budgetary allocation to the telecommunications function and their managerial training in telecommunications.

In particular, as MIS managers' satisfaction with the budgetary allocation to the telecommunications function increases, telecommunications training will emphasize unique managerial/strategic implications of telecommunications in their training as opposed to standard applications, such as e-mail and voice-mail.

Questionnaire

A questionnaire was developed and pilot tested. It consisted of two parts. The first part requested information about the respondents and their organizations. Information about the respondent included his/her position and management level. Organizational information included the type of business, the size of the organization in employees, and the number and types of computer systems.

The second part of the questionnaire solicited information in order to accomplish the above objectives. The questionnaire asked the respondents to indicate the degree of their satisfaction with the budgetary allocation to the telecommunications function. The statement was "Budget allocation for telecommunications has been favorably considered by management". The responses to the above question were recorded on a 5-point Likert scale where values ranged from 1 for strong disagreement to 5 for strong agreement. Similarly, the MIS managers were asked to indicate their agreement or disagreement with the statement: "Telecommunications is vital to the organization".

In addition, the questionnaire requested information about the development and implementation of the organizational telecommunication plan was solicited. Each respondent was requested to indicate whether or not his/her organization had a telecommunications plan. The respondents indicated their response on a 6-point scale ranging from 0 to 6. Zero indicated that the organization does not have a telecommunications plan. A response from 1 through 5 indicated the percentage, ranging from 0% to 100%, of the telecommunications plan which has been implemented.

Finally, information was sought about the quality of training for management on a list of thirty issues within the telecommunications area. The respondents were asked to rate the quality of managerial training on each telecommunications issue on a scale from 0 to 5 where

0 = no training
1 = poor
2 = below average
3 = average
4 = above average
5 = excellent

From a pilot study, it was expected that these issues would be grouped into four categories based on a factor analysis. The categories were: 1) standard telecommunications applications, 2) emerging telecommunications applications, 3) technical issues and 4) managerial or strategic issues.

While the factor analysis from the current study supported the four categories, there were a few surprises about the individual issues within the categories. For example, surfing the web was not considered a standard application, but an emerging application. Similarly, data security was not considered a technical issue but a managerial or strategic issue. Table 1 lists the thirty issues and their categories.

Subjects

The Disclosure Database was used to obtain the sample. The Disclosure Database contains financial and management information on over 12,000 public companies. Company data is extracted from annual and periodic reports filed with the U. S. Securities and Exchange Commission (SEC). The Disclosure Database includes records for companies that provide goods and services to the public. Approximately fifteen hundred small organizations were sought for the sample. The researchers randomly selected several of the smaller organizations from the database only to discover that they were no longer in business or had moved and left no forward information. In order to minimize this problem, the researchers selected 1411 organizations with sales between 10 million and 40 million. Six responded with a letter indicating a policy of not completing surveys or an apology for lack of time to complete it. Of the remaining 1405 surveys, 106 usable forms (7.5% rate of return) were received as can be seen in Table 2.

There were several reasons for the low rate of return. First, the survey was mailed to "Information Systems Manager" as opposed to an individual by name. Although the Disclosure Database listed the officers in the organizations, many of the organizations were so small, there were only two or three officers. It was difficult for the researchers to ascertain which officer was in charge of the information systems function.

Another reason for the low rate of return was the technical nature of the questionnaire. A few respondents indicated unfamiliarity about several of the telecommunications issues. Finally, some subjects expressed hesitation about rating their organization as below average. This was a significant concern in this survey since many of the results indicate an inadequate emphasis on the training and use of telecommunications.

ANALYSIS OF THE RESULTS

Demographic Data

Although the response rate was low, the questionnaire was completed by a relatively high level of management. Forty-eight percent were senior managers, forty percent were middle managers and twelve percent were supervisory or lower management. The organizations represented a variety of businesses. Table 3 indicates the types of businesses in which the respondents were employed.

It was interesting to note the average number of employees in the organization as 678 while the average number of employees in the telecommunications area was approximately five. The ratio of one telecommunications employee to 136 organizational employees appeared quite inadequate.

Finally, the average number of personal computers in the organizations responding to the survey was approxi-

Table 1. Groupings of Telecommunication Areas				
Telecommunication Issues	Category			
	Standard Applications	Advanced Applications	Technical Issues	Managerial Issues
Voice Mail	X			
Electronic Mail	X			
Facsimile Devices	X			
Video Teleconferencing		X		
Voice Teleconferencing		X		
Telecommuting		X		
Surfing the Internet		X		
Web Page Development		X		
Conducting Business on the Internet		X		
Voice/Data Integration			X	
Environmental Restrictions			X	
Equipment Capability			X	
Telecom Software Availability			X	
Telecom Terminology			X	
Electronic Data Interchange (EDI)			X	
Local Area Networks (LAN)			X	
File Transfer Protocol (FTP)			X	
Network Management and Control				X
Data Security				X
Telephony				X
Information Mgt of Telecom				X
Managing Innovation and Technology				X
Telemarketing				X
End User Telecom Needs				X
Data Transmission Management				X
Strategic Planning of Telecom				X
Telecom for a Competitive Advantage				X
Use of PC for Telecom				X
Vendor Selection				X
Data Integrity				X

Table 2. Response Rate	
Questionnaires Mailed	1411
Forms Returned	122
Usable	106
Unusable	6

Table 3. Type of Organization	
Type of Organization	Percent of Respondents
Manufacturing and Processing	29.7
Finance, Banking and Insurance	40.6
Educational Institutions	1.0
Wholesale and/or Retail	7.9
Transportation, Communications, Utilities	3.0
Health Services and Hospitals	3.0
Software Vendors	7.9
Others	7.0

mately 321 with a standard deviation of 883, while the number of mini-computers averaged 10 with a standard deviation of 25. And lastly, the average number of mainframe computers in the organizations was just over 1 with a standard deviation of 3.85.

Hypotheses Testing

While 20% of the respondents disagreed with: "Budget allocation for telecommunications has been favorably considered by management", 48.6% agreed with the statement. Surprisingly, 31.4% were neutral. This was significant considering only 3.9% disagreed with the statement that telecommunications is vital to the organization. Over 90% agreed with the latter statement.

Hypothesis One

The first hypothesis was:
The degree to which organizations are developing and implementing a telecommunications plan will be uniformly distributed from one end of the spectrum to the other. There will be organizations that have not started a plan while others will have developed and fully implemented their plan.

Responses from the question about the development and implementation of a telecommunications plan ranged from 0 to 5 where:

0 = Organization does not have a telecommunication plan
1 = The company does have a telecommunication plan, but none of the plan has been implemented
2 = The company does have a telecommunication plan, but only approximately 25% of the plan has been implemented
3 = The company does have a telecommunication plan, and approximately half of the plan has been implemented
4 = The company does have a telecommunication plan, and approximately 75% of the plan has been implemented
5 = The company does have a telecommunication plan, and all or nearly all of it has been implemented

What was surprising about the results was overwhelming negligence in the development and implementation of a telecommunications plan. While the use of telecommunications as a strategic weapon is evolving in the 1990s, few organizations have emphasized planning for this powerful weapon.

Approximately 50% of the organizations have not developed a telecommunications plan. Only 2.9% had a fully developed and implemented telecommunications plan. These organizations noted that although the plan was implemented, it is undergoing continual evaluation and modification. Table 4 summarizes the responses to this question. The distribution was not uniform (Chi square=94.25,p<.001). More organizations than expected had not planned for the telecommunications function.

Table 4. Organizational Development and Implementation of an Telecommunications Plan

Statement	Percent Responding
Organization does not have a telecommunication plan	49.5
The company does have a telecommunication plan, but none of the plan has been implemented	1.9
The company does have a telecommunication plan, and approximately 25% of the plan has been implemented	16.2
The company does have a telecommunication plan, and approximately half of the plan has been implemented	14.3
The company does have a telecommunication plan, and approximately 75% of the plan has been implemented	15.2
The company does have a telecommunication plan, and all or nearly all of it has been implemented	2.9

Hypothesis Two

The second hypothesis was
As organizations develop and implement their telecommunications plans, MIS managers' satisfaction with budgetary allocations to the telecommunications function will increase.

This hypothesis was tested by performing a correlation analysis between the degree of agreement/disagreement with the budgetary allocation statement and the degree of development and implementation of the telecommunications plan. The correlation coefficient was .31998 which was significant at .0009. Thus, it was concluded that as organizations research, develop and implement a telecommunications plan, they recognize the importance of the telecommunications function to the organizations. This recognition was realized in the form of favorable budgetary allocations.

Hypothesis Three

The third hypothesis was

There is a direct relationship between the satisfaction of MIS managers with the budgetary allocation to the telecommunications function and their managerial training in telecommunications.

In particular, as MIS managers' satisfaction with the budgetary allocation to the telecommunications function increases, telecommunications training will emphasize unique managerial/strategic implications of telecommunications in their training as opposed to standard applications, such as e-mail and voice-mail.

Respondents indicated that, on twenty-one of the thirty telecommunications issues, the satisfaction of MIS managers with the quality of managerial training improved as their satisfaction with the budgetary allocations to the telecommunications function. Table 5 identifies the issues, the category of the issue, the mean of the respondents rating of the quality of their training, the correlation statistic (between the quality of managerial training on the issue and the agreement with budgetary allocation statement) and the probability value.

What was most surprising was the low ratings which the information systems managers' gave to the quality of their training on telecommunications issues. Only one of the thirty issues received a satisfactory rating. This issue was Local Area Networks. All other issues were rated below average.

Statistical analysis of the quality of the telecommunications training by category yielded the conclusion, that although all areas were rated below average, the standard applications area was rated higher than the advanced applications, technical issues and managerial issues (F = 28.08, p = .0001).

The researchers anticipated that there might be a "halo effect" between the respondents satisfaction with the budgetary allocation to telecommunications and their satisfaction with their telecommunications training. Thus, their interest became focused on the nine issues which were not significant. These issues included all three issues in standard application area, and three of the six issues in the emerging application area. There was no statistical correlation between the respondents satisfaction with the telecommunications budgetary allocation and the quality of their managerial training on two of the seven technical issues. But only one issue of the fourteen managerial issues was statistically insignificant.

As organizations increase their telecommunications budget, improved training on the managerial issues, and to a lesser degree, the technical issues, was noted. No improvement was seen in the standard or clerical application area. Organizations generally provide training on the clerical applications of telecommunications, such as e-mail, voice mail and facsimile devices, regardless of the budgetary allocation. These issues apply to nearly all employees. However, training on specialized managerial issues, such innovative and strategic issues, was slighted when budgets were tight. These training issues are more specialized and unique. The researchers concluded that as organizations increase their telecommunications budgets, telecommunications training evolves from standard issues to strategic issues.

It was surprising to note that the strongest correlation (r = .38267, p = .0001) between the quality of managerial telecommunications training and budgetary allocation was on the issue "Surfing the Internet". This issue also has had unexpected results on the pilot study and in a study of marketing managers. In the pilot study, the results were the similar. The respondents rated "Surfing the Internet" as the area in which their managerial training was the weakest (Ketler, 1998). Similarly, in a survey of marketing managers, the respondents expressed great dissatisfaction with their training on "Surfing the Internet". It was the second lowest rated issue from a list of twenty-nine areas (Willems, forthcoming). Thus, it seems that managers do not feel that they have an understanding of the potential of the internet. Managers are consistently asking for additional training on the internet.

Similarly, the second strongest correlation (r = .38226, p = .0001) between the MIS satisfaction with the telecommunications budgetary allocations and their telecommunications training was on the issue: Use of telecommunications for a competitive advantage. This issue supports the concept that as organizations increase their telecommunications budgets, managerial training tends to focus on the strategic issues.

SUMMARY

As managers develop plans for the telecommunications area, which are consistent with the strategic goals and objectives of the organizations, budgetary allocations to the telecommunications functions increase. Furthermore, as budgets grow in the telecommunication area, improved managerial training on strategic issues was noted.

However, nearly half of the organizations responding to the survey reported in this article indicated that their organization has no plans for the telecommunications functions. A relationship was noted between the development and implementation of a telecommunications plan and satisfaction with the budgetary allocations to the telecommunications function (r = .31998, p = .0009).

Table 5. Quality of Training Available to Information Systems Managers in the Telecommunications Issues and Factors

Telecommunication Issues	Category			
	Category	Mean of Training Quality	Correlation Statistic	Probability Value
Voice Mail	Standard	2.56	.18301	.0713
Electronic Mail	Standard	2.62	.19815	.0505
Facsimile Devices	Standard	2.85	.15424	.1274
Video Teleconferencing	Advanced	0.86	.04453	.6734
Voice Teleconferencing	Advanced	1.75	.17536	.0882
Telecommuting	Advanced	1.61	.30095	.0027*
Surfing the Internet	Advanced	2.42	.38267	.0001*
Web Page Development	Advanced	1.75	.22004	.0286*
Conducting Business on the Internet	Advanced	1.59	.18114	.0728
Voice/Data Integration	Technical	1.86	.28930	.0037*
Environmental Restrictions	Technical	1.73	.18728	.0648
Equipment Capability	Technical	2.35	.26643	.0077*
Telecom Software Availability	Technical	1.99	.24579	.0147*
Telecom Terminology	Technical	2.07	.33076	.0008*
Electronic Data Interchange (EDI)	Technical	1.91	.10722	.2934
Local Area Networks (LAN)	Technical	3.15	.22475	.0258*
File Transfer Protocol (FTP)	Technical	2.36	.20855	.0384
Network Management and Control	Managerial	2.57	.16082	.1137
Data Security	Managerial	2.57	.27726	.0055*
Telephony	Managerial	1.98	.29285	.0036*
Information Mgt of Telecom	Managerial	2.31	.24684	.0153*
Managing Innovation and Technology	Managerial	2.34	.24803	.0138*
Telemarketing	Managerial	1.69	.25311	.0127*
End User Telecom Needs	Managerial	2.11	.20947	.0374*
Data Transmission Management	Managerial	2.33	.21693	.0310*
Strategic Planning of Telecom	Managerial	2.10	.31794	.0013*
Telecom for Competitive Advantage	Managerial	2.04	.38226	.0001*
Use of PC for Telecom	Managerial	2.33	.27921	.0051*
Vendor Selection	Managerial	2.27	.23927	.0183*
Data Integrity	Managerial	2.30	.27035	.0068*

Training Quality: 0 = none, 1 = poor, 2 = below average, 3 = average, 4 = above average, 5 = excellent *significant at p < 0.05;

MIS managers expressed great dissatisfaction with their training on telecommunications issues. There was minimal satisfaction on only one issue, local area networks. They rated their managerial training on the remaining twenty-nine issues as unsatisfactory.

Further analysis of this dissatisfaction showed that there was a relationship between the quality of managerial training and the budgetary allocations. As organizations increase their telecommunications budgets, telecommunications training evolves from standard issues to strategic issues. Thus, in order to assist organizations in achieving their strategic goals and objectives, the researchers suggest that organizations study the potential of telecommunications and devise a plan for the telecommunications function.

REFERENCES

1. "A moveable office" (1996). Air Transport World. October, 1996. p. 136.
2. "Southwestern Bell telephone Company: innovations in telecommunications". Arkansas Business. July 31, 1995. p S26.
3. Berry, M. (1998). "Leaning 'next practices' generates revenue". HR Magazine. July, 1998. pp. 146-151.
4. Bittle S. (1996). "Small Luxury Hotels testing new AT&T on-line booking plan". Travel Weekly. September 5, 1996. p. 5.

5. Carson, G. K. (1995). "Telecommunications: a wake-up call". Hotel & Motel Management. March 20, 1995. pp. 36-37.

6. Davy, J. A. (1998). "Education and training alternatives: today's online learning gets up close and personal. Managing Office Technology. April, 1998, pp. 14-15.

7. Edwards, J. (1995). "Transforming the telephone". Nation's Business. August, 1995. pp. 49-50.

8. Johnson, B. and Ciandella, D. (1995). "Technology, management-speak keys to success in the 90s". National real Estate Investor. December, 1995. pp. 48-51.

9. Ketler, K and Willems, J. (1998). The Positives and Negatives of Managerial Telecommunications Training". (Proceedings of the Association for Computing Machinery - Special Interest Group on Computer Personnel Research Conference, 1998), pp. 184-194.

10. King. S. (1997). "Using wireless technology to send data is on horizon". the Kansas City Business Journal. August 1, 1997, p. 6.

11. "Meeting the world face-to-face: videoconferencing helps Latin firms conduct business globally". Latin Finance. September, 1995. p. TT28-30.

12. The Telman Group Inc. (1995). "Top 10 Telecommunication Challenges Facing Hotels Today". March 20, 1995. pp. 36-37.

13. Torkzadeh, G. and Weidong X. (1992). "Managing Telecommunications by Steering Committees". MIS Quarterly. June, 1992. pp. 187-199.

14. Willems, J. and Ketler, K. (forthcoming). "Telecommunications Issues: The Marketing Managers' Viewpoint". Marketing Intelligence and Planning.

Managing Key IT issues for Australia and New Zealand using the Critical Success Factors Technique

Dr Vijay K. Khandelwal

School of Computing & IT, University of Western Sydney, P.O. Box 10, Kingswood NSW, Australia

Phone: +61-2-9685 9236, email: v.khandelwal@uws.edu.au

Mr Jeff R. Ferguson

School of Computing & IT, University of Western Sydney, P.O. Box 10, Kingswood NSW, Australia

Phone: +61-2-9685 9232, email: j.ferguson@uws.edu.au

ABSTRACT

This paper analyses the current key management issues of the Australian and New Zealand IT executives. It establishes the validity of Critical Success Factors (CSFs) as a tool to identify and prioritise these issues, and using the stages theory determines the current level of maturity of IT in Australian/New Zealand organisations. It has been found that the recent emergence of the year 2000 issue has pushed aside several key strategic IT issues, thereby impacting the growth of IT in organisations. To manage effectively in this complex environment the IT executives need to reprioritise their agendas and move onto more mature CSFs if they want to provide real business value to their enterprises.

INTRODUCTION

There is little doubt that the role of the IT executive is changing with alarming speed. The major issues that the IT manager is facing today are no longer educating end users in IS tools, or developing quality standards for IT, or even IT for competitive advantage; which just a few years ago were among the top IT management issues in Australia (Khandelwal and Hosey 1996). Our most recent findings show that current key IT management issues are alignment of IS with business, information architecture development, and technical skills of IT staff. This, on top of transitory yet crucial areas such as achieving year 2000 compliance, are making the job of IT manager even more challenging. Throughout the profession there is an acceptance that the role of an IT executive has changed dramatically in just a few years from being technically or managerially oriented, to being business oriented. In a complex environment such as this it is important that the IT manager clearly understands today's IT management issues, and takes timely and suitable action to manage them for success.

The purpose of this study is to determine the key management issues of IT managers in Australia and New Zealand. A number of investigations have been carried out in the past to determine the key issues of Australian and New Zealand IT managers (for example, Dampney *et al.* 1984, Hansell *et al.* 1985, and Broadbent *et al.* 1992). This study updates the earlier investigations, and establishes Critical Success Factors (CSFs) as a quality management tool for the measurement and control of critical IT issues. Further, by mapping the CSFs on to the stages of growth of IT (Mutsaers *et al.* 1997) the study determines the level of maturity of IT in organisations across Australia and New Zealand.

CRITICAL SUCCESS FACTORS (CSFs)

The concept of Critical Success Factors (CSFs) was first introduced by Rockart (1979) as a mechanism to identify the information needs of chief executive officers. Since then it has become widely used in a number of situations. Rockart had based the CSF concept on the idea of "success factors" first discussed in the management literature by Daniel (1961). CSFs are defined as those few key areas where things must go right for the business to flourish. If the management doesn't pay attention to these areas the organisational performance would suffer. The emphasis here is on "few" and "must go right". The number of CSFs for a given situation is typically limited to between five and nine. This is because it is the ideal number of issues to which management can provide constant attention until they are successfully achieved (Miller 1956).

Although introduced initially to determine the information needs of managers, the current use of Critical Success Factors has grown to cover all legitimate areas of management. Examples of these are the use of CSFs for management of the Year 2000 project (University of Texas 1998), and the CSFs for identification of global business drivers (Ives *et al.* 1993). The CSF technique has been assessed for reliability and consistency by comparing the results of management studies carried out for identifying the key concerns of IS managers. The results published (Munro 1983) confirm that it indeed is a reliable technique.

Individual and generic CSFs

Although the CSFs aim at organisational objectives, each individual manager of an organisation can have a different set of CSFs. In a company for example, the Marketing Manager may have a different set of CSFs to the Personnel Manager. The CSFs for the Marketing Manager may include Market success, Profit margin, and the Performance of the sales staff, while those of the Personnel Manager may be Human resource planning, Occupational health and safety, and Staff rewards.

Studies have shown that CSFs can be synthesised (Rockart 1982). While each manager in an organisation may have different, individual CSFs, the whole organisation may have its own, aggregated set of CSFs (organisational CSFs). This argument has been extended to include CSFs for a group of organisations belonging to an industry (industry CSFs), or CSFs for a group of managers in a particular role belonging to different organisations (occupational CSFs), giving rise to the concept of generic CSFs. Thus there could be generic CSFs for manufacturing managers, or generic CSFs for the retail industry. This concept can be further broadened to incorporate geographic regions of the world. We can thus, for example, have IT management CSFs for Australia and New Zealand which will define those few factors that are required by Australian and New Zealand IT management for their success.

Temporality, maturity and CSFs

CSFs can either be ongoing, or they can be temporal. The Year 2000 problem is an example of a temporal CSF the proper management of which is essential for the success of an organisation for a period after which it will cease to be critical. On the other hand, strategic IT planning is an example of an ongoing CSF because the IT plans need to be updated on a regular basis for the organisation's success.

Because of the changing circumstances a manager's priorities may change from time to time. What is critical for the manager today may in time be accomplished and thus cease to be critical. Conversely what is non-urgent today may become critical in the future. The same would apply to organisations, industries, geographic regions, etc. With time, as an organisation grows and matures, it may possess a differing set of Critical Success Factors. A less mature IT function of an organisation for example may have cost reduction, office productivity, and executive information systems as its CSFs, whereas the CSFs of a more mature organisation may include competitive advantage, linking with external organisations, and work management. In other words a less mature IT function may have deployment of IT for cost reduction as one of its topmost issues. But once it is successfully achieved the IT function may move on to more mature issues, such as, IT for competitive advantage. The CSFs can thus be used as a tool to measure the maturity of an organisation, industry, or a geographic region.

It is implicit in the above argument that CSFs are temporal. We assert, notwithstanding the earlier statement that the CSFs can either be ongoing, or temporal, that all CSFs can be defined in a way that they are temporal. For example, strategic IT planning can be defined as, implementing the process to develop long term IT plan incorporating platforms, standards, priorities and resources. This CSF will then be considered as having been achieved as soon as a process to develop the strategic IT plan is implemented. The assumption is that once this process is implemented the ongoing updating of the IT plan would be an integral part of this process. All CSFs would thus belong to a point in time, although they may differ in their degree of temporality. It is this feature of the CSFs which can be used for determining the level of maturity of an organisation (or an industry, etc.). Organisations that are more mature will have a different set of CSFs than those that are less mature, changing their CSFs as they grow. This, together with the CSF performance measurements, can be an effective tool for management to identify their level of maturity and the actions required to achieve success.

METHODOLOGY

Identifying the CSFs

To determine the CSFs a number of techniques exist. Prominent among them are structured interviewing Bullen and Rockart (1981), focus groups, the Delphi technique Brancheau *et al.* (1996) and the group interview (Khandelwal 1992). Each of these techniques have their respective strengths and weaknesses. In the structured interviewing technique interviews are carried out by an analyst to zero-in on the Critical Success Factors of individual managers. Two, or sometimes three, interviews are required to obtain the CSFs of a particular manager. The focus groups technique involves a group of managers who collectively discuss and decide upon their generic CSFs guided by an experienced facilitator. This approach obviously is much more effort effective as it employs group synergy and takes significantly less time. The Delphi technique involves a number of iterations through the same set of managers, and while this makes it a slow and somewhat inefficient process, it is an ideal technique when little initial information about the CSFs is available. Finally, the group interview approach is similar to the focus group approach except that it starts with a number of pre-prepared CSF constructs and proceeds quickly to identify the CSFs. This technique is very effort-effective, and in our view gives superior output. Needless to say the development of quality CSF constructs is an important prerequisite for this technique.

For determining generic CSFs of a large number of managers dispersed throughout a large region we have developed a modified survey approach which utilises the strengths of the above techniques, and has been used for several past years. In brief the approach involves the following steps:

1. Identifying a number of CSF constructs. This is a list of possible CSFs, as high as 40, covering the needs of the whole group of managers. An important consideration here is the correct identification and definition of the constructs (Khandelwal *et al.* 1998).

2. Designing a survey instrument. The survey instrument consists of the constructs, and their definitions, for rating by the respondents on a Likert scale such as the one given below.

    1 = Critical for this year
    2 = Important for this year
    3 = Nice to have this year
    4 = Not required for this year

Because CSFs are temporal, an additional option for the respondents to indicate that the construct is already achieved must be included because if the construct is already achieved none of the above options are meaningful.

3. Mailing the survey instrument along with a briefing to the target managers. The managers are asked to identify the importance to them of each construct on the pre-defined scale. Space is provided for additional items that the respondents may choose to add. In the end they are asked to name their top five CSFs distilled from the above list.

4. Analysing this data to arrive at the final CSFs for the entire group. The analysis process generally includes a number of follow-up interviews.

This technique has been found to be extremely efficient and has been used with very positive outcome (Khandelwal and Miller 1992, and Khandelwal and Hosey 1996).

Data Collection

For the purpose of this study 38 constructs (Khandelwal *et al.* 1998) were identified for inclusion on a survey instrument which was sent to the heads of IT functions of the top 900 private sector, and 900 largest public sector organisations in Australia, and 100 of each in New Zealand. The top private sector organisations were selected based on their annual revenue, whereas the largest public sector organisations were selected based on the number of their employees. The constructs were identified from extensive literature search of current IT issues, MIS Quarterly Keyword Classification Scheme for IS Management (Scanlan 1997), IT management surveys carried out in the US and Europe (for example CSC 1997, Brancheau *et al.* 1996, and Benjamin and Blunt 1992), and Australian surveys on related subjects (Watson 1989, Khandelwal and Miller 1992). Space was also provided on the survey instrument for additional CSFs that the respondents wished to include. For each of the CSF construct on the survey instrument the respondents were asked to rate the criticality of the construct to them on a four-point Likert scale of 1 (Critical for 1998), 2 (Important for 1998), 3 (Nice to have in 1998) and 4 (Not for 1998), or *N* (Not applicable. CSF already achieved). After rating each of the CSF constructs the respondents were asked to review the list, select their top five CSFs, and write them in order of importance in the space provided on the survey instrument. Finally the respondents were asked to estimate the percent certainty that they would assign to actually achieving each of their top five CSFs during 1998.

Analysis of the data

A total of 186 organisations returned the completed survey instrument representing New South Wales (36%), Victoria (16%), South Australia (9%), Western Australia (11%), Queensland (12%), Australian Capital Territory (4%), Tasmania (2%), Northern Territory (1%), and New Zealand (9%). All percentages shown are rounded off to the nearest whole number. The organisations belonged to a wide range of industries namely building & construction, commercial, mining, education, finance & insurance, government, local councils, health, legal, manufacturing, production, retail, service, utility and wholesale/distribution. The difference between the percentages of questionnaires sent and received in any category was within ±11% signifying a relatively unbiased sample. Of all the responses received 44% were from private sector and 56% from public sector.

As mentioned earlier the survey instrument had space provided for additional CSFs that the respondents may wish to add. In all 14.5% respondents chose to include an average of 1.5 additional CSFs each. Close examination the additional CSFs revealed that they fell into two broad categories. Firstly there were those which were a subset of the

CSF constructs already on the survey instruments, for example, "Trading partner year 2000 compliant"and "Retention of IS staff". These were incorporated in "Achieving year 2000 compliance", and "Management of IS human resource" respectively. Secondly there were CSFs which in fact were not issues but rather solutions of the issues, for example, "Increase IT budget". These responses were excluded from the analysis.

Responses for each of the CSFs were tallied and the percentage responses for each point on the Likert scale were then determined. In addition, responses for CSFs identified as being the "top five" were compiled and the percentage of respondents listing each of the CSFs in their top five was determined. Finally, the "percent certainty of achieving in 1998" for CSFs identified in the top five was determined by averaging the percentages given by the respondents for each CSF. Subsequently, to obtain more detailed information on specific CSFs, and to understand the issues therein, a number of respondents were personally interviewed.

KEY IT MANAGEMENT ISSUES

Based on the above analysis the most critical issues facing IT management in Australia and New Zealand, in order of significance are as follows.
1. Achieving year 2000 compliance
2. Alignment of IS and organisational objectives
3. Strategic IT plan development
4. Disaster recovery planning
5. Integrating systems
6. End user service management
7. Information architecture development
8. Technical skills of IS staff

These results are presented in Figure 1 from which it is evident that by far the most critical issue identified by the IT executives is the problem of year 2000 (Y2K) compliance, with 61% respondents listing it as one of their top five issues. These results support the extraordinary attention that this subject is getting in the

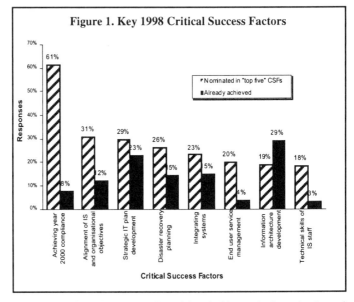

Figure 1. Key 1998 Critical Success Factors

press, management seminars, and the like. However it is disturbing to note that with only 21 months from the date of survey until "Y2K day", only 8% of the organisations have successfully achieved year 2000 compliance. Obviously a major effort combined with serious management commitment is mandatory for the remaining organisations to achieve success in this CSF.

The next two most critical, and somewhat related CSFs are Alignment of IS and organisational objectives, and Strategic IT planning. In fact Alignment of IS and organisational objectives has been rated as a top IT management issue in most surveys around the world for many years (Watson 1989, Brancheau et al. 1996, CSC 1997). Our own earlier studies (Khandelwal and Miller, 1992, Khandelwal and Hosey 1996) have ranked it in first place among both the public and private sector organisations in Australia during the past six years. Considering its continued importance it is disappointing to see that only 12% of the organisations have been successful in aligning their IS with business objectives. Further it is significant to note that the sudden prominence of the year 2000 issue has pushed aside the key strategic issues such as Alignment of IS and organisational objectives, and Strategic IT planning, thereby impacting the growth of IT in organisations.

Another noteworthy finding is that Information architecture development, despite having a large number of organisations having achieved it, still rates as one of the major issues for the remainder of the organisations. The same applies to Strategic IT plan development. These organisations obviously have some urgent catching up to do in these areas.

Finally two CSFs namely Technical skills of IS staff and End user service management, have the lowest achievement rates of all the CSFs. We believe these two CSFs represent significant opportunities for the IT managers to improve their performance.

LEAST IMPORTANT CSFs

Figure 2 shows the analysis of the four CSFs that were ranked as least important (in order, with the least important first).

CSF	Not for 1998	Already achieved
Running IS as independent business	55%	26%
Public domain software and shareware utilisation	48%	19%
Use of emerging technologies	44%	7%
Outsourcing IS	41%	32%

Figure 2. Least important CSFs showing responses rates

It is evident from Figure 2 that Running IS as independent business, and Outsourcing IS, have both a high rate of achievement among the respondents together with a high percentage of the remaining respondents listing them as "Not for 1998". It may therefore be concluded that in most cases the organisations who wished to outsource IS, or run IS as a profit centre, have already done so, with the remaining ones no longer showing any further interest in these two areas.

A low achievement rate for Use of emerging technologies indicates that there is a justified realisation among IT management that technology by itself is not going to address the information delivery issue. Technology is merely an enabler. Many IT managers are of the view that trying out a leading edge technology for the sake of technology can be fraught with risks. Some others believe that they are nowhere near exploiting the full potential of existing technologies, and therefore do not see any merit in using emerging technologies.

CERTAINTY OF SUCCESSFULLY MANAGING KEY CSFs

The underlying reason for identifying the key CSFs is so that an organisation can focus appropriate management attention on those factors and, therefore, optimise the organisation's chances of success in the time period under consideration. A mapping of the relative importance of the key CSFs against respondents' rating of certainty of their success is shown in Figure 3.

Given the purpose of identifying the CSFs, examination of Figure 3 indicates that managers of IT functions are very optimistic about achieving their key CSFs within 1998, rating the certainty of achieving the top eight CSFs between 67%-90%.

The two CSFs with highest level of certainty of achieving success in 1998 are Strategic IT plan development (90%) and Disaster recovery planning (84%). It is of interest to note that currently only 23% and 15% of these CSFs respectively, have been achieved by the respondents (Refer Figure 1). The top ranking CSF "Achieving year 2000 compliance" also rated a very high 82% confidence level of being achieved in 1998. These CSFs wherein the respondents have shown an extremely high level of confidence in successfully achieving in 1998 are opportunity areas to be exploited by the organisations.

On the other end of the scale of the key CSFs, "Technical skills of IS staff" and "End user service management", have the lowest achievement rates (3% and 4% respectively). These two CSFs have also rated the lowest level of confidence in being achieved in 1998 (67% and 70% respectively).

It should be noted that "Alignment of IS and business objectives" which has been one of the top ranking issues for several years rated only a 74% success rate in being achieved in 1998, which suggests that this will be a continuing highly ranked CSF at least in the near term.

Further analysis has demonstrated some significant differences in the certainty of achieving the key CSFs between the public sector organisations and private sector organisations.

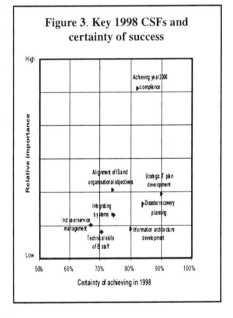

Figure 3. Key 1998 CSFs and certainty of success

CSF	Certainty of achieving in 1998		
	Public sector	Private sector	Difference
Achieving year 2000 compliance	78%	88%	10%
Disaster recovery planning	80%	90%	10%
End user service management	70%	59%	11%
Technical skills of IS staff	65%	76%	11%

Figure 4. Difference in certainty of achieving key CSFs- Public and private sector

Figure 4, for example, shows the key CSFs with at least 10% difference in certainty of achievement between the public and private sector organisations. It is evident that only in the achievement of End user service management is the public sector IT management significantly more confident than their private sector counterparts. In other CSFs, namely, Achieving year 2000 compliance, Disaster recovery planning, and Technical skills of IS staff, the private sector takes the lead over the public sector.

It may be concluded from the above that public sector organisations need to put urgent emphasis on the critical issues of resolving the year 2000 problem, implementing disaster recovery plans, and ensuring that their IT staff are properly trained. Further analysis that underscores the above finding is the relatively small difference (1%-6%) between the importance attached to these three CSFs by public and private sector organisations. On the other hand 26% respondents from the public sector listed End user service management as one of their top 5 CSFs, while only half as many from the private sector did so. It is clear that the private sector organisations need to put increased emphasis on managing end user service.

MATURITY OF IT IN ORGANISATIONS
The Stages Theory

One of the purposes of this study was to determine the level of maturity of IT in organisations. To do this use was made of the stages theory mentioned earlier which is probably one of the most well known and widespread frameworks of the development of IT in organisations (Mutsaers *et al.* 1997, Nolan and Koot 1992). The theory provides an insight in the way IT evolves, and offers the IT management the possibility of managing this complex phenomenon.

The stages theory identifies three eras, data processing (DP) era, information technology (IT) era, and network (NW) era, that an organisation will pass through in its information technology growth. These eras are themselves subdivided into three stages each (Initiation, Contagion, and Control stages for DP era; Integration, Architecture, and Demassing stages for IT era, and Functional infrastructure, Tailored growth and Rapid reaction for the NW era) as they undergo their S-, or growth curve (Figure 5). The curve represents both the growth of the information technology and the organisation's learning experience as it progresses through these eras. Each era is characterised by a period of evolution, followed by a period of stability, ending with a period of discontinuity, before the start of the next era. The discontinuity is more a revolution rather than an evolutionary transition. For example, the transition from DP era to IT era is characterised by technological discontinuities in the form of personal computers, data communication networks, and robotics, and the transition from IT era to NW era is characterised by business discontinuities in the form of strategic alliances with customers and suppliers, access to external data, and outsourcing.

The stages theory provides the IT management with a powerful tool to determine where on the curve they currently are, and to predict the actions they need to take to achieve their future goals. To do this the management needs to recognise and understand the indicators of each stage. These indicators, characterised by business, management and IT issues, described in Mutsaers *et al* (1997), are summarised in Figure 6.

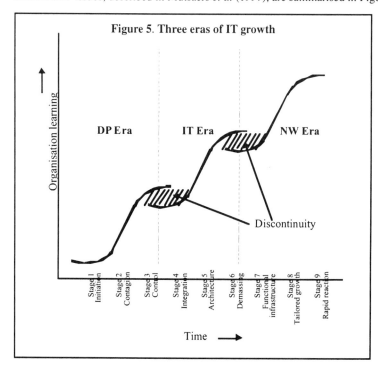

Figure 5. Three eras of IT growth

As discussed earlier the temporal nature of the CSFs makes them a very useful tool to identify the position on the growth curve the IT function of an organisation is at. To do this the CSF constructs were mapped against the characteristics of different stages of growth. This mapping was determined through a systematic matching of the definition of the stages (Mutsaers *et al.* 1997) and the definitions of the CSF constructs (Appendix). The outcome of this is shown in Figure 7. It should be noted that two of the constructs namely, Achieving year 2000 compliance, and Management of IS human resource have been excluded from this mapping because they are not related to the growth, or maturity of the IT function. In situations where the CSF construct was called by a name different than the ones used in Figure 7 the definition of the construct was

Figure 6. Key indicators of stages of growth

Era	Stage	Key indicators	
DP	1.	Initiation	Operational support, largely finance and accounting.
	2.	Contagion	Rapid expansion. Little control. IT expenditure growing 20% to 40%.
	3.	Control	Control of high automation cost. DP steering committee. Use of methods/standards. User participation to develop systems.
IT	4.	Integration	Integration of applications. Old systems replacement to facilitate integration. IT enables new business methods. Systems justified for business contribution. Users assume greater control over their own computing.
	5.	Architecture	Information dispersed. Data management is critical. New systems focus on strategic business objectives. Rapid increase in top management involvement.
	6.	Demassing	Disbanding of central IT. Business unit has responsibility for deployment of IT. Outsourcing of processing becomes a commodity. Clear trend towards maintenance of legacy systems.
NW	7.	Functional infrastructure	Translation of business architecture into a new additional layer of functional infrastructure. Continuous shift towards open and public platforms. IT staff get accustomed to powerful tools. Organisations develop strategic alliances with their customers and suppliers. Focus is to develop applications according to quality standards, at high speed and low cost. The focus will move from system integration to flexible module integration. There will be continuous shift towards a client-server environment. Attempts of truly integrated office automation.
	8.	Tailored growth	IT infrastructure centres operated as profit centres. Expansion of the functional support for users by adding top layer applications that use the functionality provided by the functional infrastructure. Vast amounts of external servers are available and accessible via public networks.
	9.	Rapid reaction	Adaptation of functionality with dynamic business team changes. Many required adaptations performed by the users by simply changing the parameters. All development of new applications will have the character of pragmatic engineering with high efficiency.

Figure 7. Mapping of CSFs and stages of growth

Stage 1 (Initiation) CSFs
No CSF constructs included

Stage 2 (Contagion) CSFs
No CSF constructs included

Stage 3 (Control) CSFs
Reducing IS costs
Strategic IT plan development
Project management methodologies
End user service management
IS-user partnership

Stage 4 (Integration) CSFs
Integrating systems
Assessment of business value of IT
IT for competitive or significant advantage
Retiring obsolete systems
Data availability to users
Executive information systems implementation

Stage 5 (Architecture) CSFs
Information architecture development
Distributed systems
Alignment of IS and organisational objectives
Disaster recovery planning
Security of IS facilities
Educating senior management in IT

Stage 6 (Demassing) CSFs
Reviewing IT in organisation
Outsourcing IS
Business skills of IS staff
Reengineering of business processes
Reduction of software maintenance

Stage 7 (Functional infrastructure) CSFs
Adoption of open systems platform
Technical skills of IS staff
Linking with external organisations
Quality standards for IT
Software development productivity
Developing modular applications
Educating end users in IS tools
Workflow and work management implementation
Client-server systems
Office systems facility

Stage 8 (Tailored growth) CSFs
Running IS as independent business
Achieving end user autonomy
Public domain software and shareware utilisation

Stage 9 (Rapid reaction) CSF
Use of emerging technologies

Figure 8. Most and least important CSFs and the stages of growth			
Most important CSFs	**Stage**	**Least important CSFs**	**Stage**
Alignment of IS and organisational objectives	5	Running IS as independent business	8
Strategic IT plan development	3	Public domain software and shareware utilisation	8
Disaster recovery planning	5	Use of emerging technologies	9
Integrating systems	4	Outsourcing IS	6
End user service management	3	Reducing IS costs	3
Information architecture development	5	Distributed systems	5
Technical skills of IS staff	7	Achieving end user autonomy	8
Median	5	Median	8
	(IT era)		(NW era)

used for matching purposes

Maturity of IT in Australian and New Zealand Organisations

The mapping for the most important CSFs against the stages of growth shown in Figure 8 clearly shows that the seven most important CSFs lie between stages 3 and 7, with the median at stage 5 (IT era), indicating that Australian and New Zealand IT managers at present are largely establishing control, integration and architecture in their IT in organisations. As would be expected most of the lowest ranked CSFs are in the higher stages of growth with the seven lowest ranked ones at the median stage of 8 (NW era). It may thus be concluded that once the current most important CSFs are achieved the IT managers have plans to focus on more mature CSFs. What is of concern however is the fact that the mapping of prioritised CSFs of six years ago (Khandelwal and Miller 1992) resulted in almost identical trend indicating that the IT in organisations are not maturing quickly. This combined with the transitory yet crucial issue of year 2000 compliance is expected to slow the pace of growth and the maturity of Australian and New Zealand IT in organisations.

CONCLUSION

The role of IT executives is becoming increasingly complex. In Australia and New Zealand there are a number of major issues confronting the IT executives. Our investigation of the IT Critical Success Factors has shown that of the three eras of growth, namely the DP, IT and NW eras, the Australian and New Zealand IT in organisations are currently in the process of stabilising themselves in the IT era, and are looking ahead at the NW era. While they have a high degree of confidence that the current issues will be resolved, similar studies from the previous years indicates that the progress may be slow. The crucial issue of year 2000 is delaying management action on the other critical items even further.

For an effective management of these issues it is important that IT executives prioritise them according to the criticality of the issues to them, establish measurements for managing the issues effectively, and monitor their performance. Without actions such as these they will continue to struggle with the day-to-day activities, and will be unable to deliver business value.

REFERENCES

Benjamin, R.I. and Blunt, J. (1992) Critical IT Issues: The Next Ten Years, *Sloan Management Review,* Summer, pp. 7-19.

Brancheau, J.C., Janz, B. and Wetherbe, J.C. (1996) Key Issues in IS Management: 1994-95 SIM Delphi Results), *URL http:www.colorado.edu/infs/jcb/home.html.*

Broadbent, M., Hansell, A., Lloyd, P. and Dampney, C.N.G. (1992) Managing Information Systems in Australia and New Zealand: Requirements for the 1990s. *The Australian Computer Journal,* 1, pp. 1-11.

Bullen, C.V. and Rockart, J.F. (1981) *A Primer on Critical Success Factors,* Center for Information Systems Research, Sloan School of Management, Working Paper No. 69, June 1981.

CSC (1997) *The Tenth Annual Survey of I/S Management Issues,* CSC, Cambridge, Massachusetts.

Dampney, C.N.G., Hansell, A.E., Brothwick, K. and Gilmour, P. (1984) Directing information systems in an organisation: what is important and why? *Proceedings of the Joint International Symposium on Information Systems,* Sydney, Australia, pp. 241-260.

Daniel, R.D. (1961) Management information crisis, *Harvard Business Review,* 5, 111.

Ives, B., Jarvenpaa, S.L. and Mason, R.O. (1993) Global business drivers: Aligning information technology to global business strategy, *IBM Systems Journal,* 1, pp. 4-16.

Hansell, A.E., Gilmour, P., Dampney, C.N.G. and Goodair, G. (1985) Macquarie University surveys of Australasian Share Guide computer installations, 1984-85. *Proceedings of ASG/13, Australasian Share Guide,* Melbourne.

Khandelwal, V.K. (1992) *Information System Study,* Opportunity Management Program, IBM Corporation, New York.

Khandelwal, V.K. and Hosey W.L. (1996) 1996 Critical Success Factors for Quality IT Management, *University of Western Sydney, Technical Report,* 10/95.

Khandelwal, V.K. and Miller, H.R. (1992) Critical Success Factors for Quality IT Management, *University of Western Sydney, Technical Report,* 92001.

Khandelwal, V.K., Hosey W.L. and Ferguson, J. (1998) Australia: Critical Success Factors for Quality IT Management, *University of Western Sydney, Technical Report, Technical Report No. CIT/1/98.*

Miller, A.M. (1956) The Magical Number Seven, Plus or Minus Two: Some Limits on Our Capacity for Processing Information, *The Psychological Review,* 63, pp. 81-97.

Munro, M.C. (1983) An Opinion...Comment on Critical Success Factors Work, *MIS Quarterly,* September 1983, pp. 67-68.

Mutsaers, E, J., van der Zee, H. and Giertz, H. (1997) *The Evolution of Information Technology,* Nolan Norton & Co., Utrecht.

Nolan, R.L. (1979) Managing the Crisis in Data Processing, *Harvard Business Review,* 2, pp. 115-126.

Nolan, R.L. and Koot, W.J.D. (1992) *Nolan Stages Theory Today.* Nolan Norton & Co., Melbourne, Australia.

Rockart, J.F. (1979) Chief executives define their own data needs, *Harvard Business Review,* 2, pp. 81-93.

Rockart, J.F. (1982) The Changing Role of the Information Systems Executive: A Critical Success Factors Perspective, *Sloan Management Review,* Fall 1982, pp. 3-13.

Scanlan, S. (1997) Keyword Classification Scheme, MIS Quarterly Roadmap, *URL http://www.tjt.or.id/rms46/isr-ssche.html#EL.*

University of Texas (1998) Y2K- Critical Success Factors, University of Texas System Administration, *URL http://www.utsystem.edu/oir-year2000/success.htm.*

Watson, R.T. (1989) Key Issues in information systems management: An Australian perspective- 1988, *The Australian Computer Journal,* 2, pp. 118-129.

MSEEC - A Multi Search Engine with Multiple Clustering

Peter Hannappel, Reinhold Klapsing, and Gustaf Neumann, Information Systems and Software Techniques,
University of Essen, Universitätsstraße 9, D-45141 Essen, Germany
Tel.: +49 (0201) 183 4074, Fax: +49 (0201) 183 4073, {Peter.Hannappel, Reinhold.Klapsing,
Gustaf.Neumann}@uni-essen.de

Adrian Krug
Support Delivery Engineering, Hewlett Packard, Berliner Straße 111, D-40880 Ratingen, Germany
Tel.: +49 (02102) 90 6650 , Fax: +49 (02102) 90 6300, Adrian_Krug@hp.com

ABSTRACT

This paper presents a scalable architecture for a multi search engine for web documents with multiple cluster algorithms (MSEEC [16]). Querying multiple primary search engines in the Internet (or in an intranet) can increase information coverage but may result in an overwhelming amount of matching documents. In this paper we use clustering techniques to find a set of similar documents which are presented to the user by a suitable cluster title. The scalable and modular architecture of our search engine MSEEC allows the addition, removal or replacement of cluster algorithms and interfaces for querying primary search engines. Processing information with different cluster algorithms results in alternative clusters which can give the user different views of the same information. This paper introduces a novel clustering technique that is based on the LZW (Lempel, Ziv, Welch) compression method.

INTRODUCTION

A prerequisite for the reuse of knowledge is accessibility. In order to profit from previous work it is necessary to access and contribute documents containing the knowledge. Open protocols can provide an infrastructure for information exchange over heterogenous systems. The web technology is suitable to build distributed information and authoring systems where people are able to search and retrieve digital documents. When the web technology is used within an enterprise we talk about an intranet. Due to the huge amount of available information in the web and the limited accessibility of intranets no single database can store all information. Lawrence and Giles argue in [11] that searching in multiple databases can increase the information coverage. However, finding the right information in the sometimes overwhelming amount of search results is a challenge.

This paper presents MSEEC, a novel multi search engine for web documents which is able to provide a synopsis of the matching documents to the user by applying cluster algorithms on the search results. In Section 2 we describe approaches for finding information in the web including multi search engines, catalogs and clustering techniques. We present a short overview of related work on clustering of web documents.

Section 3 describes the architecture of MSEEC and introduces the required terminology. Section 3.2 presents the cluster processing environment of MSEEC. Linguistic processing (Section 3.2.1) can be used optionally to filter and to transform the input data before the cluster algorithms are applied. Section 3.2.2 introduces a modified version of the theme detection method [6], Section 3.2.3 presents the novel LZW-based phrase detection method. The generation of the cluster trees is described in Section 3.2.4. Section 4 gives a summary and presents some ideas for future developments.

WEB BASED SEARCH AND RETRIEVAL OF DIGITAL DOCUMENTS

Generally the following approaches can be used to find information in the web:

a) *Brute force search (no guidance)*: Primary search engines can be used to search for web documents containing a certain query term. A web robot automatically collects (new or modified) web documents which are used to build an index. The search engine provides an interface to accept queries and uses the index to generate a list of references to the documents containing the search term. However, Lawrence and Giles [11] argue that currently no primary search engine indexes more than about one third of the indexable web.

b) *Use of additional information (meta data) to guide search*: Meta data such as key-words or topics can be used to structure the site of an information provider. Web catalogs are manually generated hierarchies of web information. A web catalog provides access to documents that are categorized by humans (see e.g. [21]) such as that similar documents can be found at a common place. Brin and Page [4] argue that human maintained web catalogs can cover popular topics effectively but are subjective, expensive to build and maintain, slow to improve and cannot cover all topics. Meta information assigned to web documents can be used to guide the search by properly classifying and structuring the information (e.g. RDF [10] or PICS [17]). Meta information can be used in resource discovery to provide better search engine capabilities, in content rating, in cataloging for describing the content and content relationships available at a particular web site, etc [10]. However, Marchiori [14] argues that it will take some time before a reasonable number of people start using meta information to provide a better web classification and that currently no one can guarantee that a majority of the web documents will be ever properly classified via meta information. Meta information can also be provided to intelligent software agents to facilitate knowledge sharing and exchange for automating specialized search tasks [15].

c) *On the fly structuring of results of (a) or (b) to improve accessibility*: The results from (a) or (b) can be huge amounts of matching documents that are hard to evaluate by a user. Structuring of the results by grouping of the documents based on similarity measures can help to condense information by presenting only a symbol for a set of similar documents. A user can select a set of similar documents by means of the symbols for further processing. Clustering (see Section 2.2) can be used to find a set of similar documents and a suitable symbol (cluster title) for a document set.

Multi Search Engines

A *secondary search engine* processes the results of a primary search engine. Resource consumption is much less because of using the already existing index of the primary search engine (e.g. bandwidth, disk storage and computational power to build an index are not needed).

A secondary search engine using multiple primary search engines (called multi search engine) warrants the utilization of the disjunct information covered by primary search engines. Furthermore it is possible to use multisearch engines in such a manner that one primary search engine's advantage can overcome a disadvantage of another primary search engine (e.g. the primary search engine with the most recent pages may not be the most comprehensive). Moreover a multi search engine can provide a unique interface to different databases [18]. Thus it is possible to query primary search engines and arbitrary databases (e.g. special purpose databases) with the same query term (Note: from a point of view of an enterprise the combination of internal and external information can be provided).

A multi search engine has the following properties. A user does not need to know specific properties (such as query syntax) of the primary search engines. The query term formulated by a user is modified automatically to be suitable for each primary search engine. The basic logical operators (e.g. AND, OR) should be supported by the query interface. The results returned by the primary search engines are merged and presented in a unique format and duplicate entities should be removed. The secondary search engine should be able to detect modifications of the query or result syntax of a primary search engine and should either adopt itself or provide an easy interface for the adoption to reduce the cost of maintenance. The architecture of a multi search engine should scale in order to provide an easy way of adding or removal of primary search engines.

Clustering of Search Results

Clustering is the process of grouping distinct entities based on similarities. Similar entities are joined to clusters which are joined with other entities or clusters. The result of the cluster processing are cluster trees. There are various criteria and measures that can be used to compute the similarities between entities. This section discusses cluster criteria which can be used to cluster web documents.

- *URI as cluster criterion*: An URI (Uniform Resource Identifier) [2] is used to reference web objects. Using an URI as a cluster criterion is based on the idea that URIs which partially match against each other refer to similar content. It is a spatial criterion specifying the locality of a web server and further a locality of a resource in a web server's information space. Resources with spatial closeness can be considered as containing similar information. The domain name (a part of the URI) can be considered as a natural cluster. The top-level domain name (e.g. .de) can sometimes be used as an indicator for the language of the document.

- *Link structure as cluster criterion*: Web documents contain references (links) to other (parts of) web documents. These links point to related information that the author considered as relevant for the document. Using the link structure as a cluster criterion is based on the idea that documents referring each other (even over a link chain) contain similar information (see for example [3,19]). The quality of this cluster criterion is potentially high if the links are assigned by a human.

  Another use for exploiting link information is described in [13] where the match of a document is determined by the content of the document itself but also by the content of the documents that can be reached via links (which obtain lower weight).

- *Recurring text patterns as cluster criterion*: Using text patterns as cluster criterion is based on the idea that a set of web documents containing similar information also contains recurring text patterns. The text patterns can be cat-

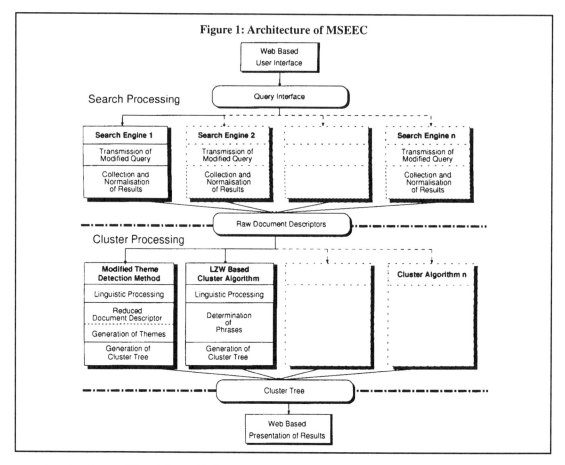

Figure 1: Architecture of MSEEC

egorized into themes [6] and phrases [1,7].

In this paper we use the output of the primary search engines for clustering. This output is processed in order to determine significant pieces of text such as phrases or themes.

We present a modified version of a theme detection method in Section 3.2.2 and a novel method for phrase detection in Section 3.2.3. The phrases or themes are collected in document descriptors which are the basis for clustering. Our architecture allows that other phrase or theme detection methods can be added to our system to provide different groupings of the search results.

A MULTI SEARCH ENGINE WITH MULTIPLE CLUSTER ALGORITHMS

MSEEC [16] is a novel multi search engine for web documents with post processing capabilities to merge and condense information in form of cluster trees. The current implementation contains two methods for cluster processing, but can be extended by other clustering methods in a flexible way. Most processing steps of MSEEC can be controlled through parameters. A user can switch on or off the use of a certain primary search engine or a cluster algorithm dynamically.

Architecture of MSEEC

The query interface of MSEEC (see Figure 1) accepts a query consisting of a query term (a search string with boolean operators), parameters for the multi search engine (selection of primary search engines, number of solutions) and various parameters controlling the cluster generation. These parameters are used for example in the linguistic processing of the results, for selecting and controlling of the cluster algorithms.

To simplify the query formulation we provide a simple user interface for the casual user or an advanced interface where all parameters are available to a experienced user. Figure 2 shows in the top section a user interface for the casual user.

Before the query is transmitted, it's syntax is modified to be suitable for the specific primary search engine. The primary search engines are queried in parallel. The results of the primary search engines are collected and

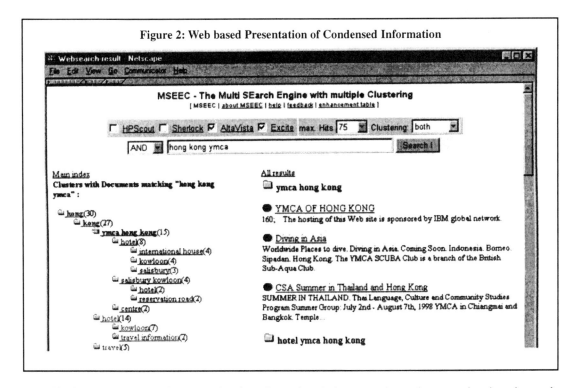

Figure 2: Web based Presentation of Condensed Information

normalised to generate a raw document descriptor for each web document. A raw document descriptor is a tuple containing the obtained information for each document. It contains the reference to the full document (URI [2]), the title and a text description of the document (leading text fragment) and some other contextual information such as the name of the primary search engine etc.

The raw document descriptors are passed to the cluster processing environment which is described below in more detail. In short it performs some linguistic processing on the raw document descriptors and invokes the selected cluster algorithms that generate the cluster trees as a result .

Figure 2 shows an example of a generated cluster tree. Each node of the tree represents the subsumed documents. The nodes are labelled with the cluster titles generated by the cluster algorithms and are implemented as a hypertext link to the associated documents. When such a link is activated the cluster contents are presented in the right half of the display (see Figure 2). Every document is presented based on information of the raw document descriptor.

The Cluster Processing Environment

The cluster processing environment of MSEEC consists of two major components, (a) the linguistic processing component and (b) the cluster algorithms. Both of these components can be controlled by parameters supplied through the query, such as - for example - the linguistic processing can be performed in a different way (e.g. for a different language) or turned off.

The input of the cluster processing components of MSEEC are the normalized raw document descriptors returned from the multi search engine. These document descriptors are passed to the linguistic processing component that returns the processed document descriptors. These are again the input of the cluster algorithms. The clustering environment of MSEEC allows several cluster algorithms to be used. In our current implementation we use a modified version of the theme detection method (see Section 3.2.2) and a newly developed method for phrase detection (see Section 3.2.3).

Linguistic Processing of Document Descriptors

For information retrieval linguistic processing of the query or of text descriptors is an important step to improve the query results. The most important forms of linguistic processing are stemming, the elimination of non-words and explicit treatment of word senses.

Stemming [8] is used in order to reduce variant word forms to common roots which represent a much smaller vocabulary. The reduction to the reduced vocabulary improves the ability of the system to match the query and the document vocabulary. A stemming algorithm processes a word and computes from the word the common root typically by removing word affixes (pre- or suffixes) using tables of common particles and some heuristics. Examples for stemming transformations are words ->word, policies -> policy, or presented -> present. Note that the stemming algorithms and heuristics are language dependent. The number of possible word forms in English is much less than that for German or even Hungarian for example.

Another simple approach to reduce the vocabulary and to detect meaningful words is the elimination of non-words and words with very low semantic content. These words (such as articles or pronouns) occur very likely in about every document. Therefore these words are bad candidates for query terms and as words characterizing the documents' content (which is important for clustering). A list of non-words for every supported languages can be easily kept in a table, which can be used to eliminate these words from the document descriptor. However, if the query term contains solely non-words (as for example in the search for the pop group "the who") this elimination must be omitted.

Another important area of linguistic processing in information retrieval is the multiple word senses and the treatment of synonyms. The disambiguation of word senses can be used to differentiate between various meanings of a word and can reduce the number of relevant matches [9] but requires a significant degree of text understanding. The treatment of synonyms and homonyms can be used to increase the number of matches.

The current implementation of MSEEC supports word stemming and non-word elimination. As noted above linguistic processing is language dependent. Therefore the linguistic processing component has to obtain a parameter to select the language. MSEEC uses linguistic processing only on document descriptors and not on query term.

Clustering based on the Modified Theme Detection Method

The *theme detection method* [6] is based on the idea to find recurring text patterns (called *themes*) in a collection of texts. A theme consists of one or more significant words describing the content of a text. We implemented a modified version of the theme detection method that differs from the original by (a) separating the linguistic processing from the theme detection method and by (b) generating multiple themes used for cluster titles rather than producing a single theme that characterizes a document (or a set of documents) best. In the following we informally describe the steps of the theme detection method we implemented in the current version of MSEEC. For the formal and detailed description of the theme detection method see [6].

For each processed document descriptor a *reduced document descriptor* is generated. In a first step, for each

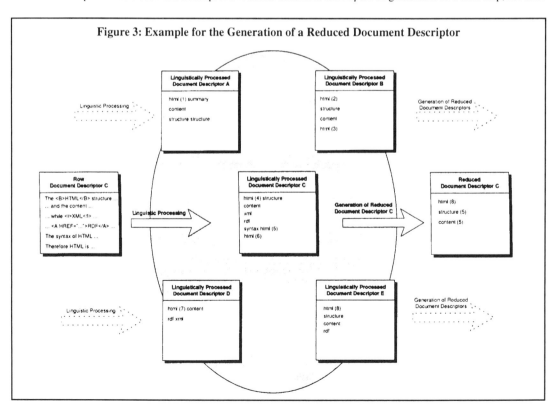

Figure 3: Example for the Generation of a Reduced Document Descriptor

word contained in a document descriptor the ranking is determined. The frequency of the occurrence of each word (out of the set of the document descriptors) in all document descriptors determines a measure for the ranking of a word. The context of a word in a document descriptor can optionally influence the weighting of the ranking. A word belonging to the title is assumed to be more important than a word belonging to the document body and is more likely to be kept in the reduced document descriptor. From this word list (contained in the reduced document descriptor) all words having less frequently than a threshold are removed, since they do not contribute to clustering.

In the next step, the text in the document descriptor is reduced by keeping only the words with the highest rankings from the word list (bounded to a maximum number per document descriptor). The result is called the reduced document descriptor. Figure 3 shows a simplified example of a generation of a reduced document descriptor with 5 as the ranking threshold.

The reduced document descriptors are the source of theme detection. From every reduced document descriptor the word with the highest ranking is selected and is taken into account as a theme candidate. Then it is checked over whether the theme candidate is part of more than one reduced document descriptor (*valid theme candidate*). If so, the word with the second highest ranking is added to the theme and builds a new theme candidate. If the test fails the theme candidate is dropped and the theme candidate without the last added word is kept.

This algorithm iterates through all words of the reduced document descriptor and builds a set of themes. For every theme the list of document descriptors that contains the theme is kept. The computed themes can be used as cluster titles for the final step of the clustering algorithm where the cluster tree is built (see Section 3.2.4).

The theme detection module can be controlled by various parameters by the user to control the threshold, weight factors and an upper bound for number of computed themes.

Clustering based on the LZW-Method for Phrase Detection

While the last section describes theme detection, this section introduces a novel approach for phrase detection we developed. Like a *theme a phrase* consists of terms that occur in a text. Phrases can be used as cluster titles as well as themes. Contrary to a theme the words in a phrase must occur in the same order in proximity in the document.

The purpose of the phrase detection algorithm is to identify similar or common used word phrases in different documents that can be used for its characterization. Croft, Turtle and Lewis [7] distinguish statistic and syntactic methods for phrase detection. A statistic method for phrase detection constraints phrases by the number of occurrences and co-occurrences of its component words and/or proximity between occurrences of components in a document. A syntactic method for phrase detection additionally to the above constrains forces constraints on syntactic relationships among its component words. We propose a new statistic method of phrase detection that is based on the widely used LZW compression algorithm [12,20]. This compression algorithm identifies patterns that do often occur in data to encode the patterns in another more compressed form in order to save storage. We do not use this method in MSEEC for compression but for the determination of often recurring text patterns in the document descriptors.

The LZW compression algorithm as suggested by Lempel, Ziv, Welch [12,20] is used for data compression. The LZW algorithm adapts dynamically to different data by building an encoding table during a single pass through the data (instead of using a fixed predefined encoding table). The LZW compression algorithm takes a stream of data as input (e.g. 8-bit characters). The output of the algorithm is a stream of encoded and compressed values (2x tokens, depending on size of encoding table). The algorithm needs an internal storage buffer (ISB) to keep track of a list on input tokens as well as a fixed size encoding table (ET) to encode the token lists.

The LZW compression algorithm has several properties that make it quite valuable for phrase detection: It detects often used token phrases automatically, the phrases are extended on the fly, the algorithm needs only a single pass which has the advantages of run time efficiency and incrementality (for incremental clustering see [5] also).

For *phrase detection* in documents we modify the LZW algorithm in various aspects:

- *Words as basic units*: While the original algorithm works on characters the modified version works on words as input tokens. Therefore the coding table and the coding sequence are words and recurring text phrases.
- *Phrase rating*; In order to identify the most characterizing phrases of a document we introduce a rating which is based on the frequency multiplied by an optional weight factor that is influenced by the location of the word phrase. Phrases in the title of a document for example receive higher weights than phrases from other parts of the document.
- *Enhanced encoding table*: The encoding table needs additional fields to keep track of the rating of each word phrase as well as the document descriptor of the detected word phrase.
- *Unbounded encoding table size*: For the LZW compression method the first data has higher impact on the structure of the coding table than later data since once ET becomes full no new phrases can be added and potential phrases from later processed documents are ignored. By unlimiting the size the phrase candidates from all documents are treated equally.

In the following the pseudocode of the *LZW-based Phrase Detection Algorithm* is presented:

```
PHRASES := {}
foreach ‹DOCUMENT,ID› ∈ DESCRIPTORS
    PHRASE := "
    foreach WORD in DOCUMENT
                EXT_PHRASE := PHRASE    WORD
                if (EXT_PHRASE ∉ PHRASES)
                        FREQUENCY(PHRASE)++
                        DOCIDS(PHRASE) := DOCIDS(PHRASE) ∪ ID
                        PHRASE := WORD
                        PHRASES := PHRASES ∪ PHRASE ∪ EXT_PHRASE
    else
                PHRASE := PHRASE    WORD
    endif
  endfor
endfor
(Note:       denotes concatenation of words, plural of a variable denotes a set)
```

In the first step the set PHRASES is initialized to null. The phrase detection algorithm is applied on all documents (document DESCRIPTORS). Foreach document the variable PHRASE is set to null. It is concatenated with words iteratively. The concatenation of the PHRASE and a WORD (EXT_PHRASE) is proven to be in the set of PHRASES. If this is false a new phrase is detected. The rating of each phrase is updated after each detected phrase (table FREQUENCY). For every phrase a table of document descriptor IDs is maintained which are pointing to the documents containing the phrase (table DOCIDS). Further the value of WORD is assigned to the variable PHRASE and the set PHRASES is extended by the value of PHRASE and EXT_PHRASE. If the EXT_PHRASE is in the set of PHRASES (an already known phrase is detected) the PHRASE is concatenated with the value of WORD and the next iteration step is entered. If all document descriptors are processed the algorithm terminates. The set of phrases and the tables of related rankings and document descriptor IDs are passed to the cluster tree generation module (see Section 3.2.4).

Generation of Cluster Trees

The output of the theme detection and the phrase detection methods is passed to the same cluster tree generation module. The themes and phrases are used as cluster titles and do solely determine the structuring of the cluster trees. Each node in a cluster tree represents the documents contained in the whole subtree. In order to keep the presentation of the cluster's tree small it is possible to limit the number of nodes in a tree (by merging clusters with a high similarity) and to limit the depth of the tree (by merging clusters deeper than a certain depth in the tree). These parameters can be controlled by the user through query parameters.

The tree generation tries to find for every group of document descriptors (denoted by the cluster title) a parent (ancestor) node that is less specific, which means that it contains a subset of the words of the cluster title. The algorithm starts with an arbitrary (e.g. the longest) cluster title T0 and eliminates in step 1 these cluster titles that contain words not in T0 (see Figure 4). In step 2 the longest titles are kept as candidates for the parent cluster, in step 3 the cluster title with the most frequent document descriptors is chosen as the parent cluster.

These three steps are performed for every cluster title. If no parent cluster can be determined the cluster title is regarded as a root of a tree. Therefore this algorithm does not result in a single but multiple cluster trees (cluster forest).

The maximum depth of a cluster tree can be determined by a query parameter. If the specified depth is ex-

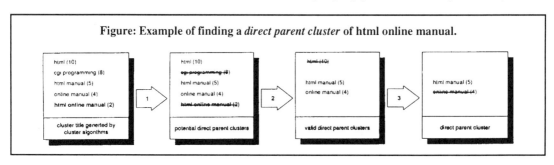

Figure: Example of finding a *direct parent cluster* of html online manual.

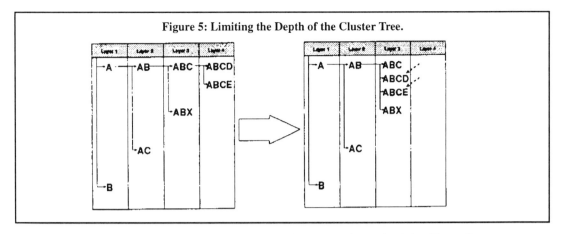

Figure 5: Limiting the Depth of the Cluster Tree.

ceeded nodes from deeper subtrees are merged with the node at the maximum depth (see Figure 5).

From our experience with users the phrase detection method returns more intuitive results for the cluster titles than the theme detection method. One reason is the more natural word order. Beyond that the phrase detection method is faster than the theme detection method. On the other hand the theme detection method returns better results for less related documents whereas the phrase detection method fails to detect interesting common phrases. For example for the texts "The Salisbury House Hong Kong" and "Hong Kong, The Salisbury House" the phrase detection method is able to detect the phrases "Hong Kong" and "Salisbury House" but is not able to connect these phrases which is no problem for the theme detection method.

CONCLUSION AND FUTURE WORK

This paper presents a scalable architecture using a secondary search engine to query multiple information servers. The additional layer introduced by a secondary search engine can be used to provide a unique query and result interface to multiple primary search engines. The design of the system as a secondary search engine reduces the consumption of resources by using the index of primary search engines. The use of multiple primary search engines has the advantage that it can result in a higher coverage of indexed web documents and allows to select different sources for certain queries. This enables us to query databases in an intranet and the Internet with a single query. The results can be merged for further processing. Thus internal and external knowledge can be combined.

Queries may return excessive amounts of matching documents that can overwhelm a user. We use cluster algorithms to give the user a better synopsis and some guidance to differentiate between the matches. We introduce a modified version of the theme detection method and a novel approach for phrase detection which are suitable to cluster the results returned by a secondary search engine. The cluster algorithms can also be combined in such a manner that one algorithm's advantages can overcome a disadvantage of other cluster algorithms.

Of course there are various areas where we think we can improve the system. One interesting area is to invest more on the users perception of the cluster algorithms, to allow the user to navigate through the information space based on cluster algorithms with different similarity measures. It should be possible to reach different types of clusters through links from the user interface.

Another area with high potential for improvements is the linguistic processing, which is currently based on simple heuristics. It appears to be useful to provide the user with mechanisms for specifying additional non-words that should be ignored in a query.

From our experiences we would expect even better results from the phrase detection algorithm by enhancing it to allow skipping of words. This could be implemented by changing the internal storage buffer to a stack of buffers. The depth of the stack would directly determine the maximum word skip distance.

To reduce the maintenance work of the multi search engine a more sophisticated pattern recognition would be of advantage to parse the results of the primary search engines.

From our experience we believe that the accuracy of recognition of phrases and the usefulness of the system for retrieval is satisfiable but asystematic evaluation and comparison with other approaches have still to be made.

BIBLIOGRAPHY

1 Peter G. Anick and Shivakumar Vaithyanathan. Exploiting clustering and phrases for context-based information retrieval. In 20th Annual International SIGIR Conference on Research and Development in Information Retrieval, pages 314-323. ACM, 1997.

2 Tim Berners-Lee, Roy Fielding, and Larry Masinter. Uniform resource identifiers (URI): Generic syntax. RFC, category: Standards track, IETF, August 1998. ftp://ftp.nic.de/pub/rfc/rfc2396.txt.

3 Rodrigo A. Botafogo. Cluster analysis for hypertext systems. In 16th Annual International SIGIR Conference on Research and Development in Information Retrieval, pages 116-125. ACM, 1993.

4 Sergey Brin and Lawrence Page. The anatomy of large-scale hypertextual web search engine. In Proceedings of the Seventh International World Wide Web Conference, volume 30 of Computer Networks and ISDN Systems, pages 107-117, April 1998.

5 Fazli Can. Incremental clustering for dynamic information processing. ACM Transactions on Information Systems, 11(2):143-164, April 1993.

6 David K.Y. Chiu and David R. Brooks. Detecting themes in web document descriptors. In Proceedings of WebNet97 - World Conference of the WWW, Internet & Intranet, pages 123-128. AACE, 1997.

7 W. Bruce Croft, Howard R. Turtle, and David D. Lewis. The use of phrases and structured queries in information retrieval. In 14th Annual International SIGIR Conference on Research and Development in Information Retrieval, pages 32-45. ACM, 1991.

8 Robert Krovetz. Viewing morphology as a inference process. In 16th Annual International SIGIR Conference on Research and Development in Information Retrieval, pages 191-202. ACM, 1993.

9 Robert Krovetz and Bruce Croft. Lexical ambiguity and information retrieval. ACM Transactions on Information Systems, 10(2):115-141, April 1992.

10 Ora Lassila and Ralph R. Swick. Resource description framework (RDF) model and syntax specification. Technical report, W3C, January 1999. Proposed Recommendation, http://www.w3.org/TR/PR-rdf-syntax/.

11 Steve Lawrence and C. Lee Giles. Searching the World Wide Web. Science, 280(5360):98, April 1998.

12 Abraham Lempel and Jacob Ziv. A universal algorithm for sequential data compression. IEEE Transactions on Information Theory, IT-23(3):337-343, May 1977.

13 Massimo Marchiori. The quest for correct information on the Web: Hyper search engines. In WWW6 - The sixth international World Wide Web conference, pages 265-276, 1997. http://www6.nttlabs.com/HyperNews/get/PAPER222.html.

14 Massimo Marchiori. The limits of web metadata, and beyond. In Proceedings of the Seventh International World Wide Web Conference, volume 30 of Computer Networks and ISDN Systems, pages 1-9, April 1998.

15 M. Montebello, W. A. Gray, and S. Hurley. An evolvable personal advisor to optimize internet search technologies. In Database and Expert Systems Applications, 9th International Conference, DEXA 98, pages 531-540, 1998.

16 MSEEC (current) home page. http://nestroy.wi-inf.uni-essen.de/MSEEC.html, January 1999.

17 Martin Presler-Marshall, Christopher Evans, Clive D.W. Feather, Alex Hopmann, Martin Presler-Marshall, and Paul Resnick. PICSrules 1.1. Technical report, W3C, December 1997. W3C Recommendation, http://www.w3.org/TR/REC-PICSRules-971229.

18 Erik Selberg and Oren Etzioni. Multi-service search and comparison using the MetaCrawler. In Proceedings ot the 1995 World Wide Web Conference, 1995.

19 Ellen Spertus. Parasite: Mining structural information on the web. In WWW6 - The sixth international world wide web conference, pages 201-214, 1997. http://www6.nttlabs.com/HyperNews/get/PAPER206.html.

20 Terry A. Welch. A technique for high performance data compression. IEEE Computer, 17(6):8-19, June 1984.

21 Yahoo home page. http://www.yahoo.com/, January 1999.

Information Overload in Organizational Processes: A Study of Managers and Professionals' Perceptions

Ned Kock

Dept. of Computer and Information Sciences, Temple University, 1805 N. Broad St., Wachman Hall, Rm. 313,
Philadelphia, PA, 19122, USA
kock@joda.cis.temple.edu

ABSTRACT

The information overload phenomenon has been receiving increasing attention in recent years, particularly in the popular business and information technology literatures. While prescriptions and computer tools have been developed to reduce information overload based on "commonsense" assumptions, few careful research investigations have been conducted. We contribute to filling this research gap with an analysis of quantitative and qualitative information overload perceptions evidence collected from a sample of managers and professionals. Our findings suggest that, contrary to prevalent beliefs, task productivity and outcome quality are not strongly linked with information overload. Additionally, we found that time pressure is a stronger determinant of information overload than amount of information processed. These and other findings are discussed from a process-centered perspective, and academic as well as organizational implications are explored.

INTRODUCTION

The topic of information overload has been the subject of much speculation, at least since the 1970s, when Alvin Toffler warned us about the problems and opportunities of a "symbolic" society (Toffler, 1970). More recently, the topic has been linked with the emergence of the Internet (Kiley, 1995), and, particularly, the explosion in the amount of data easily available through web sites since the development of the World Wide Web in the early 1990s.

Many "commonsense" assumptions, such as that information overload is a negative phenomenon that should suppressed or eliminated, have been widely used as a basis to discuss and propose preventive prescriptions and remedies to the "information overload problem". The development of computer tools to deal with performance problems purportedly caused by information overload has been a common theme in the popular computing literature (Foley, 1995). Yet, careful research investigations of issues related to information overload have been scarce.

We provide an overview of information overload and its determinants, from a process-centered perspective, by summarizing prior research findings through a causal model. We then investigate this model based on quantitative and qualitative research data obtained from twenty-two respondents holding management or professional appointments in organizations located within the metropolitan area of Philadelphia.

Our investigation was framed on two main research questions drawn from the model, and led to several findings. Some of these findings are counterintuitive, and contradict assumptions held by software developers and management consultants. This adds relevance to the findings, while providing a new way of looking at the information overload phenomenon.

A PROCESS-CENTERED VIEW OF INFORMATION OVERLOAD

The development of a process-centered view of information overload should combine assumptions derived from the process redesign and management literature with traditional assumptions about the information overload phenomenon. From a process-oriented standpoint, individuals carry out interrelated activities that make up the various processes whereby organizations produce and deliver goods and services to their customers. The execution of process activities incorporates the following characteristics (Davenport, 1993; Davenport and Short, 1990; Davenport and Stoddard, 1994; Earl, 1994; Hammer and Champy, 1993; Harrington, 1991; Kock et al., 1997).

- Process activities are carried out in a repetitive and standardized way, following a process design. Such design may change, from time to time, as a result of reengineering or incremental process improvement efforts.
- Individuals cooperate as members of a process team in order to accomplish a well-defined task, such as to provide a service or manufacture a part.
- Descriptive information needs to be exchanged among process team members so process activities can be effec-

tively accomplished.
- Specific knowledge and skills to carry out different activities are usually held by different individuals of a process team, in a somewhat fragmented way.
- The number of different types of expertise (i.e. knowledge and skill sets) needed to perform process activities correlates the amount of descriptive information that has to be exchanged among process team members.

Information overload has been studied from many different perspectives, which have their roots in different disciplines and modes of investigation. In the field of cognitive psychology, information overload has been traditionally seen as a function of the volume of information to which a person is subjected (Evaristo, 1993). Information overload occurs whenever the amount of information exceeds an individual's information processing resources (O'Reilly, 1980). This standpoint has been incorporated in the majority of business and organizational studies of information overload, which albeit scarce, have led to a number of generic propositions. The most relevant for an analysis of information overload from a process-centered view are summarized below.

- Information overload depends on the nature of the task accomplished through a process (Casey, 1982; Schneider, 1987). Such nature is defined by task attributes; one of the most important, from a cognitive standpoint, being task complexity (Daft and Lengel, 1986; Daft and Weick, 1984).
- The decision style of a process team member can affect how efficiently information is processed (Glazer et al., 1992; Holsapple and Whinston, 1996), and therefore can be a determinant of information overload.
- As the number of information exchange interactions involving a process team member increases, so does the number of information processing interruptions he or she is subjected to (assuming that information processing is not instantaneous, requiring a finite amount of time to be completed). Such interruptions can affect information processing efficiency (Speier et al., 1997), and therefore cause information overload.
- The amount and nature of knowledge and skills possessed by a process team member affects his or her information processing speed and quality (Camerer and Johnson, 1991; Chervany and Dickson, 1974), and therefore influences information overload.
- A task accomplished through a process is affected by the information overload experienced by process team members. More specifically, information overload affects task productivity and outcome quality (O'Reilly, 1980).

Figure 1 is a causal model that incorporates individual and task factors affecting information overload, and depicts its impact on task productivity and outcome quality. It integrates the process assumptions and information overload propositions listed above, and provides the basis for a process-centered investigation of information overload. Both individual and task factors are grouped on the left hand side of the figure as independent variables. The variable *information overload* acts as an intervening variable that mediates the influence of individual and task-related variables on task productivity and outcome quality.

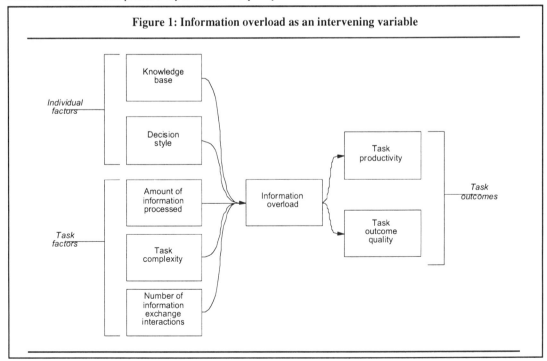

Figure 1: Information overload as an intervening variable

The process-centered view of information overload depicted in Figure 1 can be used as basis for the understanding of how individual and task factors comparatively influence information overload, and how this influence is reflected in task productivity and outcome quality. This research tries to contribute towards such understanding by providing answers to two research questions that have not been answered by the extant research literature on information overload:

• Does information overload significantly affect task productivity and outcome quality?
• Are individual factors comparatively more or less important than task factors as information overload determinants?

Although information overload is generally believed to be a negative phenomenon (Wurman, 1989), some view it as a force behind the building of specialized knowledge and skills (Lord and Foti, 1986). Such contrasting views highlight the importance of the first research question, as an answer should clarify whether information overload has an impact on task productivity and outcome quality, and thus whether it should be the focus of organizational redesign and other management efforts.

The importance of the second question is due also to the normative nature of its answer, which complements the answer to the first question. It clarifies the main type of factors that influence information overload and their nature - either human or structural. An answer to the second research question can help organizations decide whether task or individual attributes should be managed to control the influence of information overload.

DATA COLLECTION AND ANALYSIS

The study was based on qualitative and quantitative research data collected from a sample of twenty-two MBA students enrolled in a one-semester MIS course in the School of Business Management, Temple University. The distribution of students according to industry and job title is shown in Table 1. Nearly all respondents held management or professional appointments in organizations located within Philadelphia's metropolitan area. They were asked to answer a questionnaire in class over approximately two hours, and were given partial course credit for their participation. In order to reduce question misinterpretation bias, the researcher was available in class during the completion of the questionnaire to answer any queries.

Table 1: Respondents' industries and job titles		
Industry	**Respondents**	**Job titles**
Apparel manufacturing	1	Designer
Automobile manufacturing	1	TQM assistant
Clothing	1	Buyer
Computer service	1	Programmer
Construction and development	2	Project director, Civil engineer
Education	1	Program consultant
Electrical manufacturing	1	Sales representative
Financial services	4	Credit manager, Market analyst, Credit analyst, Asset recovery compliance manager
Health care	6	Research fellow, Marketing manager, Nurse, Nursing director, Physician, Medical education program coordinator
Insurance	1	Account underwriter
Legal services	2	Legal intern, Director of administration
Telecommunications	1	Telecommunications service coordinator
Total respondents = 22		

The data collection instrument was designed to incorporate measures for each of the constructs discussed in Figure 1, as well as open-ended questions in which the respondents have been asked to either explain their answers or provide additional qualitative information regarding their perceptions. Construct details, including operational definitions and measures, are presented in the Appendix. Two types of construct measurement scales were used in the instrument. These were continuous ordinal scales (e.g. for the measurement of the average number of work-related decisions per day) and five-point interval scales (e.g. for decision focus measurement). A set of twenty unstructured interviews informed the selection of semantic differential terms used in the development of the interval scales (Sommer and Sommer, 1991).

The analysis was geared at providing answers to the two research questions discussed in the previous section. That is, the research data were analyzed with the aim of establishing the existence and comparative strength of links between individual and task factors and perceived information overload, as well as between perceived information overload and its impact on task productivity and outcome quality. This was attained by the calculation of both descriptive statistics for each of the measurement items, and Spearman product-moment correlation coefficients for each par of construct measurements. The use of a non-parametric technique (i.e. Spearman's) required that the continuous ordinal scales be first converted into ranked ordinal scales, before the Spearman correlation coefficients were calculated (Pervan and Klass, 1992; Spatz, 1997).

SUMMARY OF RESULTS

The analysis is summarized into a set of descriptive statistics for each of the construct measurement items, and correlation coefficients for construct pairs, both shown in Table 2. The last five rows at the bottom of the table show descriptive statistics that have been calculated before continuous ordinal scale measurements were ranked. The Spearman coefficients of correlation were calculated after ranking.

The correlation coefficients between the measures of information overload intensity and information overload impact on productivity and outcome quality were respectively .06 and -.17, both statistically insignificant at the .01 level. Also, row 11 of the table shows that no statistically significant (for $P < .01$) correlation exists between information overload intensity and any of the other measures. However, if P were lowered to .05 on a one-tailed test, a significant correlation could be inferred between information overload intensity and decisional scope.

A further analysis of the coefficients in bold and within parenthesis suggests the correlation links below. Each of the construct measurement items, represented below in italic, is defined in the Appendix.

• *Pages written* is strongly correlated with *number of work related decisions* and *pages read*. That is, the number of pages of documents a respondent writes per day increases with the number of decisions made and the number of pages read.
• *Number of information receiving interactions* is strongly correlated with *pages written* and *number of information giving interactions*. That is, the number of daily interactions in which the respondent receives information increases with the number of pages written and the number of interactions in which the respondent provides information to others.
• *Skill acquisition in months* is very strongly correlated with *work knowledge acquisition in months*. That is, the number of hands-on work months needed by a respondent to learn to perform his or her job increases with the number of months of formal education needed.
• *Number of different work related activities* is strongly correlated with *number of information receiving interactions*. That is, the more different daily activities a respondent performs, the higher is the number of information receiving interactions.
• *Information overload impact on quality* is strongly correlated with *information overload impact on productivity*. That is, respondent perceptions regarding information overload impact on task outcome quality were similar to perceptions regarding its impact on task productivity.

An analysis of qualitative responses to a question concerning the three main reasons why individuals experience information overload revealed the predominance of *time pressure* as the main cause of information overload (see Table 3). This was followed by *poor prioritization*, *amount of information received*, and *multiple demands*, as the most frequently cited causes. These reasons are self-explanatory, with the exception perhaps of *poor prioritization* and *multiple demands*. Poor prioritization refers to the individual's inability to prioritize tasks optimally. Multiple demands refers to the individual's perception of task fragmentation intensity, which is linked to the number of differ-

Table 2: Descriptive statistics for construct measurement items

	1	2	3	4	5	6	7	8	9	10	11	12	13
1 No. of work related decisions	1												
2 Decisional scope	.35	1											
3 Decision rationality	-.52	-.44	1			Coefficients of correlation *							
4 Pages read	.45	.29	-.19	1									
5 Pages written	(.61)	.24	-.27	(.58)	1								
6 No. of info. giving interactions	(.54)	.14	-.15	.40	.46	1							
7 No. of info. receiving interactions	.41	-.03	-.03	.42	(.55)	(.59)	1						
8 Work knowledge acquisition in months	.25	-.02	-.08	.19	.27	.31	.31	1					
9 Skill acquisiton in months	.28	-.06	.06	.10	.20	.26	.29	(.91)	1				
10 No. of different work related activities	.30	.30	.08	.53	.35	.55	(.58)	.27	.16	1			
11 Info. overload intensity	.02	.40	.13	.03	.18	-.15	-.12	-.20	-.03	.10	1		
12 Info. overload impact on productivity	.32	.44	-.18	.07	.32	-.05	.17	-.24	-.07	.06	.35	1	
13 Info. overload impact on quality	.13	.31	-.11	-.07	.07	-.15	.01	-.44	-.24	-.17	.27	(.79)	1
Standard deviation	12.1	1.1	1.2	23.3	8.5	17.1	14.0	49.4	38.8	5.6	1.1	0.9	1.3
Median	3.0	3.0	3.0	22.0	6.0	15.0	10.0	56.8	29.1	5.0	3.0	3.0	3.0
Mean	7.9	2.7	2.9	27.0	8.2	21.3	15.4	71.3	37.9	7.2	2.8	2.6	2.5
Minimum	1.0	1.0	1.0	4.0	1.5	3.0	2.0	2.0	0.1	3.0	0.0	1.0	0.0
Maximum	50.0	4.0	4.0	100.0	40.0	56.0	56.0	180.0	180.0	25.0	4.0	4.0	4.0

* Spearman coefficients; N = 22; P < .01 (two-tailed test) for coefficients within brackets

Table 3: Frequency distribution of top four qualitative answers to the question:
What are in your opinion the three main reasons why people feel information overloaded?

Answer	Frequency	Percentage
Time pressure	14	64%
Poor prioritization	9	41%
Amount of information received	5	23%
Multiple demands	4	18%

Chi-square = 7.75, P = .0514, df = 3

ent activities and individual has to perform within a given time period (e.g. a day).

A Chi-square test of the frequency distribution on Table 3 suggests a near 95 percent probability that the particular distribution of answers observed is not due to chance, or that it is caused by an underlying perception trend. The nature of this statistical test implies the assumption that the answers are provided independently. Even though this assumption may not be accurate, as each respondent was asked for three main reasons, and there might have been a tendency of some respondents to consistently provide a pair of (or three) reasons together, the statistical significance of the test has not been affected. The reason is because, if there was a tendency to group reasons in the same answer, this would have negatively affected the significance of the Chi-square test (i.e., towards an increase in P, and a consequent decrease in chance probability). Moreover, other answers with frequency lower than four were disregarded in the analysis, which also increased P. Therefore, even though the resulting P is slightly higher than .05, we can reasonably assume that the probability that the frequency distribution is due to chance is actually lower than 5 percent.

DISCUSSION AND CONCLUSION

The results of the analysis suggest a negative answer to the first of the two research questions around which this study was conducted - Does information overload significantly affect task productivity and outcome quality? That is, our research data supports the conclusion that there is no clear relationship between information overload and the efficiency or quality of tasks. This contradicts most of the extant academic literature on information overload falling into the general banner of "organizational research", which has traditionally seen it as a condition that should be reduced or eliminated because of its deleterious influence on task performance (Casey, 1982; Chervany and Dickson, 1974; Glazer et al., 1992; O'Reilly, 1980). The same is true for the popular computing and business literature on the subject, which is crowded with descriptions of computer tools and "commonsense" prescriptions to reduced and information overload (Berghel, 1997; Frank, 1984; Jander, 1993; Maes, 1994; Meglio and Kleiner, 1990; Wheelwright, 1995).

Yet, the finding that task performance and information overload are unrelated can be explained based on cognitive psychology findings, notably those from "schema" theory. The concept of *schema* was developed as a reaction to the traditional memory studies pioneered by Ebbingaus, where arbitrary materials and sensorial stimuli were used to determine factors influencing memory formation and information recall (Gardner, 1985). The development of the concept of schema is credited to Bartlett (1932). He used an Indian folk tale called "The War of the Ghosts" to show that existing mental structures strongly affected the formation of memory and recall performance. Such mental structures were called *schemas*. They were used by Bartlett's study subjects to process the facts presented to them in the tale. Fundamentally, Bartlett's studies show that individuals holding different schemas would interpret the tale, which is filled with strange gaps and bizarre causal sequences, in significantly different ways.

In essence, schemas are information-processing structures used by individuals to interpret, make decisions, and perform actions in response to sensorial stimuli. A person can develop schemas through communication (vicarious learning), experience (experiential learning), or a mix of communication and experience. Lord and Foti (1986) view information overload as a transitory sensation that is experienced by individuals developing schemas that will allow them to upgrade their performance in job-related tasks. Such view is consistent with our finding that task performance is unrelated with information overload intensity because information overload may, for some process team members, transitorily precede increased performance. As such, information overload will not decrease performance, but increase it. Yet, this would occur in a fleeting way that, as we see it, could not be easily perceived by process team members.

Our data analysis allows us to provide a *positive* answer our second research question - Are individual factors comparatively more or less important than task factors as information overload determinants? The two most significant constructs influencing information overload intensity were, as indicated by Spearman coefficients, decisional scope (statistically significant at .05 level) and work knowledge acquisition in months (not statistically significant, but yielding the second highest Spearman coefficient). Both constructs belong to the *individual factors* construct type (see Appendix), as opposed to *task factors*. One implication of this finding is that individual characteristics of process team members are more influential in determining information overload than the structure of organizational processes.

Finally, this research points to the somewhat counterintuitive finding that information overload is more generally seen as related to the pressure to perform tasks within a certain timeframe, than to the amount of information that has to be processed. This finding is consistent with a few previous studies, which we see as exceptions, pointing in the same general direction (Evaristo, 1993; Schick et al., 1990). It is also consistent with the notion that individual factors influence information overload more than task factors. Individual factors, such as decision-making style and amount of expertise, are likely to affect task completion time much more strongly than task factors, because task factor are more contingent on process structure and thus are more or less constant for different individuals. That is, tasks factors are more contingent on job title and respective responsibilities than on individual traits.

The findings above provide the basis for a new framework to understand the information overload phenomenon. In light of them, we conclude that it is possible that information overload, at controlled levels, can have a positive impact on task performance. This research does not gives us any clue as to what is the optimum level of information overload (or information load), but our findings suggest that it is likely to vary from person to person. Our findings also suggest that individual characteristics can be used to categorize people according to their propensity to experience information overload, and adjust individual levels accordingly. This can be done by manipulating task-related time constraints.

FUTURE RESEARCH

This research presents and discusses findings based on quantitative and qualitative research data collected from a relatively small sample base. While the sample was large enough to perform Spearman correlation analysis, a larger sample could lend significance to a few links between information overload and variables that were found to be insignificant in our research. These could provide a clearer picture of the information overload determinants. Thus, a suggestion for future research is to simply increase the size of sample of individuals studied.

It is known from prior methodological studies that question-order bias may affect findings obtained with questionnaires and structured interviews. The strength of this effect depends on attributes of the question set, which in most cases are contingent on basic research questions. As these are used in the design of data collection instruments, question set attributes cannot be easily manipulated. Yet, question order bias can be reduced or eliminated by breaking a respondents' sample into several sub-samples, and using different listings of the same research questions in different sub-samples, where the order of the question listings is randomly determined. Therefore, as the sample of respondents increases in the future, this treatment should be employed. Additionally, a Cronbach alpha (or similar) reliability test should be conducted to assess the extent to which question set attributes contribute to question-order bias. Such test should correlate quantitative answers from different sub-samples.

Finally, future research should also contemplate changes in the list of questions asked from respondents. Such changes should be informed by the findings of this research, so as to provide a stronger basis for answering the two initial research questions. They should also allow for the development of new information overload models that highlight different facets of the phenomenon and provide answers different research questions. Our experience suggests a combination of questions leading to quantitative and qualitative answers as an adequate framework for this.

REFERENCES

Bartlett, F.C. (1932), *Remembering*, Cambridge University Press, Cambridge, MA.

Berghel, H. (1997), Cyberspace 2000: Dealing with Information Overload, *Communications of the ACM*, V.40, No.2, pp. 19-24.

Camerer, C.F. and Johnson, E.J. (1991), The Process-Performance Paradox in Expert Judgment, *Toward a General Theory of Expertise*, Ericsson, K.A. and Smith, J. (Eds), Cambridge University Press, Cambridge, MA, pp. 195-217.

Casey, C.J. (1982), Coping with Information Overload: The Need for Empirical Research, *Cost and Management*, V.56, No.4, pp. 31-38.

Chervany, N. and Dickson, G. (1974), An Experimental Evaluation of Information Overload in a Production Environment, *Management Science*, V.20, No.10. pp. 1335-1344.

Daft, R.L. and Lengel, R.H. (1986), Organizational Information Requirements, Media Richness and Structural Design, *Management Science*, V.32, No.5, pp. 554-571.

Daft, R.L. and Weick, K.E. (1984), Toward a Model of Organizations as Interpretation Systems, *Academy of Management Review*, V.9, No.2, pp. 284-295.

Davenport, T.H. (1993), *Process Innovation*, Harvard Business Press, Boston, MA.

Davenport, T.H. and Short, J.E. (1990), The New Industrial Engineering: Information Technology and Business

Appendix: Construct measurement items

Construct type	Construct	Measurement items	Description
Individual factors	Knowledge base	Work knowledge acquisition in months	Number of months of formal education and hands-on practice needed to perform work-related activities well
		Skill acquisition in months	Number of months of hands-on practice needed to acquire skills to perform work-related activities well
	Decision style	Decisional scope	Five-point scale: 0 (focus on details) -- 4 (focus on the big picture)
		Decision rationality	Five-point scale: 0 (very intuitive) -- 4 (very rational)
Task factors	Amount of information processed	Pages read	Average number of equivalent written pages read per working day
		Pages written	Average number of equivalent written pages written per working day
	Task complexity	No. of work related decisions	Average number of relevant work-related decisions made on a working day
		No. of different work related activities	Average number of different work activities performed per working day
	Number of information exchange interactions	No. of information giving interactions	Average number of information giving interactions per working day
		No. of information receiving interactions	Average number of information receiving interactions per working day
Information overload	Information overload intensity	Information overload intensity	Perceived information overload intensity experienced at work (five-point scale)
Task outcomes	Task productivity	Information overload impact on productivity	Perceived information overload impact intensity on work productivity (five-point scale)
	Task outcome quality	Information overload impact on quality	Perceived information overload impact intensity on work quality (five-point scale)

Process Redesign, *Sloan Management Review*, V.31, No.4, Summer, pp. 11-27.

Davenport, T.H. and Stoddard, D.B. (1994), Reengineering: Business Change of Mythic Proportions?, *MIS Quarterly*, V.18, No.2, pp. 121-127.

Earl, M.J. (1994), The New and the Old of Business Process Redesign, *Journal of Strategic Information Systems*, V.3, No.1, pp. 5-22.

Evaristo, R. (1993), *An Empirical Investigation of the Impact of Information Characteristics and Information Technology on Individual Information Load*, PhD thesis, Carlson School of Management, University of Minnesota, MN.

Foley, J. (1995), Managing Information - Infoglut - New Tools can Help Tame an Ocean of Data, *InformationWeek*, October 30, pp. 30-33.

Frank, R.A. (1984), Combating Information Overload, *Business Communications Review*, V.14, No.2, pp. 2-4.

Gardner, H. (1985), *The Mind's New Science*, Basic Books, New York, NY.

Glazer, R., Steckel, J.H. and Winer, R.S. (1992), Locally Rational Decision Making: The Distracting Effect of Information on Managerial Performance, *Management Science*, V.38, No.2, pp. 212-227.

Hammer, M. and Champy, J. (1993), *Reengineering the Corporation*, Harper Business, New York, NY.

Harrington, H.J. (1991), *Business Process Improvement*, McGraw-Hill, New York, NY.

Holsapple, C.W. and Whinston, A.B. (1996), *Decision Support Systems: A Knowledge-Based Approach*, West Publishing, St. Paul, MN.

Jander, M. (1993), Midlevel Managers Ease SNMP Information Overload, *Data Communications*, V.22, No.17, pp. 53-57.

Kiley, K. (1995), The Cyberspace Database Information Overload, *Catalog Age*, V.12, No.9, pp. 56-59.

Kock, N.F., Jr., McQueen, R.J. and Corner, J.L. (1997), The Nature of Data, Information and Knowledge Exchanges in Business Processes: Implications for Process Improvement and Organizational Learning, *The Learning Organization*, V.4, No.2, pp. 70-80.

Lord, R.G. and Foti, R.J. (1986), Schema Theories, Information Processing and Organizational Behaviour, *The Thinking*

Organization, Sims, H.P., Jr. and Gioia, D.A. (Eds), Jossey-Bass, San Francisco, CA, pp. 20-48.

Maes, P. (1994), Agents that Reduce Work and Information Overload, *Communications of the ACM*, V.37, No.7, July, pp. 31-40.

Meglio, C.E. and Kleiner, B.H. (1990), Managing Information Overload, *Industrial Management and Data Systems*, V.1, No.1, pp. 23-26.

O'Reilly, C.A. (1980), Individuals and Information Overload in Organizations: Is More Necessarily Better?, *Academy of Management Journal*, V.23, No.4, pp. 684-696.

Pervan, G.P. and Klass D.J. (1992), The Use and Misuse of Statistical Methods in Information Systems Research, *Information Systems Research*, Galliers R. (Ed), Blackwell Scientific Publications, Boston, MA, pp. 208-229.

Schick, A.G., Gordon, L.A. and Haka S. (1990), Information Overload: A Temporal Approach, *Accounting Organizations and Society*, V.15, No.3, pp. 199-220.

Schneider, S.C. (1987), Information Overload: Causes and Consequences, *Human Systems Management*, V.7, No.2, pp. 143-154.

Sommer, B. and Sommer R. (1991), *A Practical Guide to Behavioral Research*, Oxford University Press, New York, NY.

Spatz, C. (1997), *Basic Statistics: Tales of Distributions*, Brooks-Cole, Pacific Grove, CA.

Speier, C., Valacich, J.S. and Vessey, I. (1997), The Effects of Task Interruption and Information Presentation on Individual Decision Making, *Proceedings of the 18th International Conference on Information Systems*, Kumar, K. and DeGross, J.I. (Eds), The Association for Computing Machinery, New York, NY, pp. 21-35.

Toffler, A. (1970), *Future Shock*, Bantam Books, New York, NY.

Wheelwright, G. (1995), Information Overload, *Communications International*, V.22, No.1, pp. 55-58.

Wurman, R.S. (1989), *Information Anxiety*, Doubleday, New York, NY.

To Err Or Not To Err, That Is The Question: Novice User Perception of Errors While Surfing The Web

Jonathan K. Lazar
Department of Information Systems, University of Maryland Baltimore County, 1000 Hilltop Circle, Baltimore, MD 21250
Phone 410-455-2851, Fax 410-455-1073, jlazar1@umbc.edu

Anthony F. Norcio
Department of Information Systems, University of Maryland Baltimore County, 1000 Hilltop Circle, Baltimore, MD 21250
Phone 410-455-3938, Fax 410-455-1073, norcio@umbc.edu

ABSTRACT

Novice users frequently make errors as they attempt to perform new tasks. These errors tend to frustrate novice users. In the networked environment, there is an increased opportunity for users to perceive that they make errors. Much of the research on errors was done before the networked environment was widespread, and the research does not address this new task environment. This paper introduces the concept of a "situational error." A situational error is when a user has entered their commands correctly to reach a goal, but the user is not able to reach their goal due to outside factors such as network bottlenecks and remote site failures. Situational errors are described in detail, and are placed into the traditional taxonomies of errors. Methods for designing systems and training to assist novice users in responding to errors are also presented.

INTRODUCTION

As users learn to use a new application of computer technology, they frequently make errors (Greif and Keller, 1990; Lazonder and Meij, 1995; Norman, 1983). These errors tend to frustrate users (Arnold and Roe, 1987; Carroll and Mack, 1984). There is an extensive body of literature classifying the different types of errors that novice users make when interacting with computer systems. However, much of this literature was created before the networked environment and the Internet were prevalent. The current literature does not address many of the user-perceived errors that can occur in the networked environment. The purpose of this paper is to introduce the concept of a "situational error."

SITUATIONAL ERRORS

When users are connected to a network, whether it is a local area network, or the Internet, they have task goals in mind. They may want to print a document, retrieve a file from the Internet, or access the latest news from a web site. Novice users may have the "traditional system" mindset, which is that, if they enter their commands in a correct manner, then they will be able to reach their goal. However, in the networked environment, this is not always the case. A user's task goal may require the use of a network resource which is not available or is not functioning properly. Even if the user enters all of their commands in the appropriate manner, they may not be able to reach their task goal. We have named this a "situational error." A situational error is when a user's task goal requires the use of a network resource, which is not available or is not functioning properly.

Why would a situational error occur? There may be a problem with the connection from a user's computer to a local area network. There may be a problem with the connection between a local network and an Internet Service Provider. Domain name service may not be set up correctly, so users on a local network may not be able to access sites on the world wide web. A network resource may not be properly configured. A remote site may have failed, or there may be a bottleneck somewhere on the network (Johnson, 1998). Regardless of why users could not reach their goal, many novice users do not have a good understanding of the technologies and protocols that support their network, and therefore, cannot understand when they do not meet their goals (Johnson, 1998). Therefore, the user may view this occurrence as an error. Should this even be considered an error? This depends on the working definition of error. The next section discusses the various definitions of errors.

CLASSIFICATIONS OF ERROR DEFINITIONS

Within the literature, several different definitions of errors have been proposed. To understand errors, it is important to examine the many definitions of error. Arnold and Roe point out that within error definitions, there are two very different views of errors (Arnold and Roe, 1987). One set of error definitions is *user-centered*; the other set of definitions is *system-centered* (Arnold and Roe, 1987).

User-centered definition of error

Users want to complete their tasks successfully. User-centered definitions consider errors from the point of view of the user. User-centered definitions of error view an error as when a user's desired action is not carried out (Norman, 1983). Users are concerned with reaching their goals, and from the users' point of view, errors keep them from reaching those goals. Some of the user-centered definitions of error that have been presented in the literature are "when a user's intention or goal is not attained," (Arnold and Roe, 1987, p. 204) and "the non-attainment of a goal" (Frese and Altmann, 1989).

User-centered definitions do not blame users for errors. User-centered definitions of error only state that errors keep users from reaching their goals. Zapf et. al. point out that for an error to be defined as such, a specific program or system must be designed to perform the task that the users want (Zapf et al., 1992). If the user has a specific goal, but the program or system is not designed to perform the tasks to reach such a goal, then this is called a functionality problem (Goodwin, 1987). For instance, if a user attempts to use a statistics program to browse the web, this would be considered a functionality problem, not an error, because the application (the statistics program) was not designed to meet the user's task goal (browsing the web). According to these classifications, a situational error is still an error, since functionality is not a problem. The applications and systems are designed to perform the tasks to reach the users' goals.

System-centered definitions of error

System-centered definitions of error view errors from the system's point of view; user goals are not addressed. System-centered definitions of error are more technically-oriented. From the system's point of view, if something cannot process successfully, it is due to an error on the user's part. System-centered definitions of error blame the users (Lewis and Norman, 1986). Some of the system-centered definitions of error in the literature include:
- An action that violates a rule (Frese and Altmann, 1989).
- Something that the system cannot respond to (Lewis and Norman, 1986, p. 411).
- Actions that are inappropriate (Booth, 1991).

Although system-centered definitions of error blame the user for errors, it is pointless to blame a user (Zapf et al., 1992). In human-computer interaction research, the focus is on assisting and designing for users (Dix et al., 1998; Preece et al., 1994; Shneiderman, 1998). Assigning blame doesn't help the user. Instead, it is important to focus on assisting the user in reaching their goal.

USER PERCEPTION OF ERROR

How do users perceive these situational errors? Do users perceive these errors are their own fault? Or do users perceive them as someone else's fault? With traditional classifications of errors, novice users tend to blame themselves for making an error (Carroll and Mack, 1984; Lewis and Norman, 1986). Errors intimidate novice users more than expert users, who are confident in their abilities (Carroll, 1990). Expert users tend to blame anyone or anything else (the program, the manual, the system designer) before they blame themselves for an error (Carroll, 1990). Expert users may not even consider a situational error an error at all. Expert users are used to dealing with errors and other odd situations, and may just consider these errors as par for the course (Somekh and Davis, 1997). Will these same patterns of blame appear with situational errors? Experimental work needs to be done with users and situational errors.

When a situational error occurs, the user has taken an action, by performing a set of commands, in the appropriate manner. The user then expects to get the appropriate result. However, through no fault of their own, the user cannot achieve their goal. What may frustrate the user even more is the fact that they have performed the same actions previously, with a successful result. The user may wonder why, in this specific situation, is the same set of commands not producing the same result? This can be confusing to the user.

TRADITIONAL CLASSIFICATIONS OF ERRORS

How do situational errors fit into the traditional classifications of errors? The classification system for user errors that is prominent in the HCI world is provided by Donald Norman. At the highest level, Norman separates errors into two types: mistakes and slips (Norman, 1983). Norman defines a mistake as when users choose the wrong commands to reach their goals (Arnold and Roe, 1987; Norman, 1983). A mistake has also been called a conceptual error (Booth, 1991). A slip, on the other hand, is when a user's intended command is correct, but the user makes an error (such as a spelling error) in entering their commands (Norman, 1983). Within slips, there are many different classifications. For instance, Norman defines mode errors, description errors, capture errors, activation errors, and data description errors.

Mode errors

Frequently, applications and systems have different modes. A keypress while the system is in one mode will provide a different action then the same keypress when the system is in a different mode. A mode error is when users believe that a system is in one mode, when instead, it is in another mode (Norman, 1988). Users then perform their actions with the mistaken belief that the system is in a certain mode. Because the system is in a different mode, their actions may have results other than what the users intended, and user does not reach their goals.

Description errors

Many times, different actions or procedures are carried out using a similar set of commands. A description error is when users perform a procedure in a correct manner, but perform it on the wrong file, item or object (Norman, 1983; Norman, 1988). An example of a description error could be to send a business colleague the wrong file as an e-mail attachment. The user performed the procedure in the correct manner, saving a file in the correct directory, uploading it to their e-mail account, and correctly attaching it to their e-mail message. However, these procedures were performed on the wrong file. Description errors frequently occur when objects, files, or items, look similar or are physically close to each other.

Capture errors

A capture error is when there is overlap between one set of commands and another, and the user performed the wrong sequence of commands (Norman, 1983). When attempting to perform one set of commands, another set of commands, which is similar, "takes over" (Norman, 1988). There are many commands that are similar. In some of these cases, the commands partially overlap. For instance, a keystroke sequence of control-alt-delete reboots most personal computers. If the key sequence control-alt by itself performed a procedure, it is expected that many times, users would mean to type only control-alt, but instead would type control-alt-delete.

Activation errors

An activation error occurs when users fail to complete all of the required procedures to reach their intention (Norman, 1983). This may be due to other events that have occurred while users are performing the appropriate actions. These other events take away the users' attention, causing them to forget the exact procedures to execute and the order in which the procedures should be executed (Norman, 1983). Norman later renamed this specific type of error as a "loss-of-activation" error (Norman, 1988).

Data-driven errors

A data-driven error is based on the arrival of data to our senses (Norman, 1988). Users may be in the process of entering data, when someone tells them that the current ballgame score is 3 to 1, Orioles winning. The users then may enter the numbers 31 instead of the actual data that should be entered. This differs from an activation error, because it does not completely end the users' procedure. The user can continue with the procedure, however, they will have entered incorrect data at an earlier point.

Situational errors

A situational error does not fit into any of these traditional classifications of errors. A situational error cannot be considered a slip. Since the user does not carry out the commands incorrectly, a situational error is not a slip. Furthermore, since the user has chosen the correct commands to reach their goals, a situational error is not a mistake. In mistakes and slips, it is assumed that the user caused an error. However, there is no classification for when a user selected the correct commands, and entered the commands in the correct manner, but was still not able to attain their goal. Other error classification schema have been presented in the literature (Zapf et al., 1992), but they, too, do not address these situational errors.

DESIGNING FOR SITUATIONAL ERRORS

How can system designers and trainers assist novice users in responding to situational errors? There are two possible approaches to assisting users in responding to errors: system design and training design.

System design

Systems should be designed in a way that they assist the users in responding to errors. For instance, Lazonder and Meij state that users need to be aware of the error as quickly as possible, so that they can attempt to correct it (Lazonder and Meij, 1995). If users are not immediately aware of an error, the error can be compounded over time, into a larger error which is harder to recover from (Carroll and Carrithers, 1984; Carroll and Mack, 1984). Lazonder and Meij also emphasize the location of the error message. If an error message is displayed in a dialog box superimposed on the center of the active screen, users will be likely to notice it (Lazonder and Meij, 1995). However, if an error message is displayed in the lower right hand corner of the screen, and no other signals (graphics, sounds, etc.) draw the user's attention to the error message, the user might not even notice the error message (Lazonder and Meij, 1995).

The error messages themselves should be designed in a way that is clear and easy for the user to understand. Both Brown and Shneiderman emphasize the importance of easy-to-understand error messages (Brown, 1983; Shneiderman, 1998). A bad example of an error message, as described by DuBoulay and Matthew, is the error message "fatal error in pass zero" (DuBoulay and Matthew, 1984). In their anecdotal experience with students, novice users have had trouble understanding the meaning of that message (DuBoulay and Matthew, 1984).

In an experiment with 22 novice programmers, Shneiderman found that error messages that are easier for the user to understand and interpret can result in users being better able to respond appropriately to errors (Shneiderman, 1982). Shneiderman suggests that error messages should 1) be specific, 2) be positive, and 3) tell users what to do to respond to the error (Shneiderman, 1998). In their conceptual paper, Arnold and Roe go one step further, by encouraging system designers to not just tell the users what to do, but to give users information about the different alternatives that they have to respond to the error (Arnold and Roe, 1987). This can facilitate recovery from the error.

To assist novice users in responding to situational errors, more information needs to be provided to the user. What is Domain Name Service? What is a "404" error? The novice user may not know what these things are. Therefore, it may be necessary to provide the novice user with further information, such as a message saying "There is an error on the network, but it is not due to your actions." Another approach, such as "The network is experiencing problems; please try again later" might be appropriate. This is similar to the phone company message "All circuits are busy. Please try again later." These error messages let the novice user know that, although they may not be immediately able to reach their task goal, that 1) this is not their fault and 2) they should attempt their goal again later that day.

Training design

Since users may perceive that there are many more errors when learning to use the Internet, user training should focus on assisting users in responding to these errors. Alternative approaches for training have been suggested, to help novice users deal with errors (Dormann and Frese, 1994; Frese and Altmann, 1989; Frese et al., 1991; Nordstrom, Wendland and Williams, 1998). Error management training, introduced by Frese and Altmann in 1989, focuses on turning errors into positive opportunities for learning (Frese and Altmann, 1989). Users are given a set of "error heuristics," telling them that errors are not bad, but that errors are good opportunities for learning, and that they can figure out an appropriate response to the error. Another approach is exploration, in which users are given an overview of their task environment, and how to navigate through it (Carroll and Mack, 1984; Carroll and Mazur, 1986; Frese and Altmann, 1989). This replaces the traditional training method, where users are given a specific list of exactly what to type in order to reach their task goal. By familiarizing users with the structure of their environment, exploratory training might assist users in understanding why they weren't able to reach their task goals. Conceptual models may also assist users in gaining a better understanding of the structure of their task environment (Santhanam and Sein, 1994; Sein, Bostrom and Olfman, 1987). Conceptual models are graphical or mathematical representations of a system that correspond closely to the real-world system (Santhanam and Sein, 1994). With a better understanding of their task environment, users might not become as frustrated with situational errors, since they would understand the cause of their errors. Since errors are more prevalent in the networked environment, it is important to train novice users to better respond to errors.

SUMMARY

This paper serves as an introduction to the concept of situational errors. Errors can frustrate novice users, and in the networked environment, there is an increased opportunity for users to make the form of error known as a situational error. It is important to understand what a situational error is, and know how to design systems and training to assist users in responding to errors. Experimental work with users is needed to learn more about situational errors and how users are affected by them.

REFERENCES

Arnold, B., and Roe, R. (1987). User errors in human-computer interaction. In M. Frese, E. Ulich, and W. Dzida (Eds.), Human computer interaction in the workplace (203-220). Amsterdam: Elsevier Science Publishers.

Booth, P. (1991). Errors and theory in human-computer interaction. Acta Psychologica, 78(1/3), 69-96.

Brown, P. (1983). Error messages: The neglected area of the man/machine interface. Communications of the ACM, 26(4), 246-249.

Carroll, J. (1990). The nurnberg funnel: Designing minimalist instruction for practical computer skill. Cambridge, Massachusetts: MIT Press.

Carroll, J., and Carrithers, C. (1984). Training wheels in a user interface. Communications of the ACM, 27(8), 800-806.

Carroll, J., and Mack, R. (1984). Learning to use a word processor: By doing, by thinking, and by knowing. In J. Thomas, and M. Schneider (Eds.), Human Factors in Computer Systems (13-51). Norwood, N.J.: Ablex Publishing.

Carroll, J., and Mazur, S. (1986). LisaLearning. IEEE Computer, 19(11), 35-49.

Dix, A., Finlay, J., Abowd, G., and Beale, R. (1998). Human-Computer Interaction. (2nd ed.). London: Prentice Hall England.

Dormann, T., and Frese, M. (1994). Error training: Replication and the function of exploratory behavior. International Journal of Human-Computer Interaction, 6(4), 365-372.

DuBoulay, B., and Matthew, I. (1984). Fatal error in pass zero: How not to confuse novices. Behaviour and Information Technology, 3(2), 109-118.

Frese, M., and Altmann, A. (1989). The treatment of errors in learning and training. In L. Bainbridge, and S. Quintanilla (Eds.), Developing skills with information technology (65-86). Chichester, England: John Wiley & Sons.

Frese, M., Brodbeck, F., Heinbokel, T., Mooser, C., Schleiffenbaum, E., and Thiemann, P. (1991). Errors in training computer skills: On the positive function of errors. Human-Computer Interaction, 6(1), 77-93.

Goodwin, N. (1987). Functionality and usability. Communications of the ACM, 30(3), 229-233.

Greif, S., and Keller, H. (1990). Innovation and the design of work and learning environments: The concept of exploration in human-computer interaction. In M. West, and J. Farr (Eds.), Innovation and creativity at work: Psychological and organizational strategies (231-249). Chichester, England: John Wiley & Sons.

Johnson, C. (1998). Electronic gridlock, information saturation, and the unpredictability of information retrieval over the world wide web. In P. Palanque, and F. Paterno (Eds.), Formal Methods in Human-Computer Interaction (261-282). London: Springer.

Lazonder, A., and Meij, H. (1995). Error-information in tutorial documentation: Supporting users' errors to faciliate initial skill learning. International Journal of Human-Computer Studies, 42(2), 185-206.

Lewis, C., and Norman, D. (1986). Designing for error. In D. Norman, and S. Draper (Eds.), User-centered system design (411-432). Hillsdale, NJ: Lawrence Erlbaum Associates.

Nordstrom, C., Wendland, D., and Williams, K. (1998). To err is human: An examination of the effectiveness of error management training. Journal of Business and Psychology, 12(3), 269-282.

Norman, D. (1983). Design rules based on analyses of human error. Communications of the ACM, 26(4), 254-258.

Norman, D. (1988). The psychology of everyday things: Harper Collins Publishers.

Preece, J., Rogers, Y., Sharp, H., Benyon, D., Holland, S., and Carey, T. (1994). Human-Computer Interaction. Wokingham, England: Addison Wesley Publishing.

Santhanam, R., and Sein, M. (1994). Improving end-user proficiency: Effects of conceptual training and nature of interaction. Information Systems Research, 5(4), 378-399.

Sein, M., Bostrom, R., and Olfman, L. (1987). Conceptual models in training novice users. Proceedings of the Human-Computer Interaction- INTERACT '87, Stuttgart, Germany; 861-867.

Shneiderman, B. (1982). System message design: Guidelines and experimental results. In A. Badre, and B. Shneiderman (Eds.), Directions in Human/Computer Interaction (55-78). Norwood, N.J.: Ablex Publishing.

Shneiderman, B. (1998). Designing the User Interface: Strategies for Effective Human-Computer Interaction. (3rd ed.). Reading, Massachusetts: Addison-Wesley.

Somekh, B., and Davis, N. (1997). Getting teachers started with IT and transferable skills. In B. Somekh, and N. Davis (Eds.), Using information technology effectively in teaching and learning (138-149). London: Routledge.

Zapf, D., Brodbeck, F., Frese, M., Peters, H., and Prumper, J. (1992). Errors in working with office computers: A first validation of a taxonomy for observed errors in a field setting. International Journal of Human-Computer Interaction, 4(4), 311-339.

An Exploratory Study on the Role of Information Technology in Asian Economic Crisis

Ook Lee

Department of Business Administration, Hansung University, 389 Samsun-dong-2ga, Seoul, Korea

E-mail) leeo@hsel.hansung.ac.kr, Tel) +822-760-4412, Fax) +822-760-4217

INTRODUCTION

The economic turmoil that started in Thailand and was spread throughout Asian countries in 1997 was truly historic in terms of its scale and speed; never before these many countries which were seemingly sound in economic fundamentals were crushed in such a short period. The scholars now argue that the so-called Asian economic model was to blame and thus, a structural breakup of current economic systems is essential for recovery, which is also the view of the IMF. However we should not ignore the fact that the so-called Asian economic model which means concentrations of resources to a few big conglomerates guided by the interventionist government had been the major reason of elevating poor Asian countries to the level of economic development which includes higher standard of living. For the last thirty years or so, the Asian countries developed their economies in this way and received many praises from Western scholars. And suddenly everything collapsed; the scholars are blaming the Asian economic structure itself as the culprit. The author of this paper who is from South Korea was able to observe the devastating process of economic downturn personally and can not just accept the view of Western scholars and the IMF. Until summer of 1997, South Korea was doing well and its economic fundamentals such as GDP, inflation, and unemployment rate were sound. For just several months, the South Korean currency was depreciated more than 80% and, then came all the economic troubles such as business failures, soaring unemployment rate, and contracting economy. As an IS scholar, the author of this paper became suspicious of the origin of this economic disaster and started to conduct research on the alternative theory that can explain the phenomenon. The hypotheses of this paper on the origin of the Asian economic disaster are two fold. The first hypothesis is that the economic downturn came because of sudden and steep depreciation of their currencies. The second hypothesis is that the sudden and steep depreciation of currencies against US dollar is due to the advanced IT that could move an astronomical amount of money in the lightning speed, which led to investor's panic to sell the particular currency. In this paper, the defense of these two hypotheses will be presented; other reason such as the appreciation of US dollar that started from mid 1990s will be also cited.

ECONOMIC CRISIS CAUSED BY CURRENCY CRISIS

In general, the economic crisis happens in the following order(Hanke, 1997a):

1. Central bank creates a lot of credit that leads to inflation.
2. Balance-of-payments crisis happens due to the inflation.
3. Balance-of-payments crisis leads to currency devaluation.

This used to be the usual pattern of the nations that had economic crisis in the past. For example, most of Latin American countries during 70s suffered hyperinflation and contracted economy that led currency devaluation. This is why IMF which had the job of rescuing these countries always ordered the austerity measure on the governments of these countries such as reduced money supply from the central banks. And this policy is used again in Asian countries that are suffering now. The reduced money supply inevitably led to higher interest rate and many business bankruptcies, which actually increased the unemployment much higher than before. This policy is aimed at preventing hyperinflation and stabilizing the currency. But the author of this paper would like to suggest that the economic disaster can happen in the reverse direction of the above flow.

Namely the economic turmoil can happen as following way:

1. Currency devaluation that happened suddenly and deeply leads to the balance-of-payment crisis since many companies become not being able to afford to pay the debt or product price which is denominated in foreign currency in trade.
2. Balance-of-payments create inflation since product that are imported become very expensive.
3. Inflation leads to put pressure on the central bank to tighten money supply, which means higher interest rates.
4. Higher interest rates lead to many business failures that cause high unemployment rate.

Thus in the reverse way, we can show that the economic crisis which can be measured by the unemployment rate can be caused by the currency devaluation which happened suddenly and deeply. In other words, it is possible to destroy an economy by destroying the currency. The argument that currency stability is the key to the economic stability is well illustrated in nations such as Hong Kong and Argentina which adopted currency board system(Hanke, 1997b), The currency board system is a monetary authority that issues notes and coins convertible into a foreign "anchor" currency such as US dollar at a truly fixed rate and on demand(Currency Boards, 1998). In other words, countries with currency board system can avoid the speculation on their currency and achieve currency stability which also leads to the economic stability. Currency boards are worth considering in any country where the national currency has not performed as well in the long term as the major internationally traded currencies such as US dollar. Among central banks, only about 50 percent in developed countries and 5 percent in developing countries issue currencies that have performed as well in the long term as the major international currency such as US dollar(Currency Boards, 1998). In other words, otherwise sound economy of a nation can be ruined by the attack of currency speculators. For example, unlike other Asian countries, Hong Kong's currency is well standing even though the Asian financial turmoil caused mild recession. And the reason for Hong Kong's resilient financial system is their currency board system which prevents speculative attack by the currency trading funds(Finance and Development, 1997). The only Asian country that had real economic difficulty before the Asian economic crisis of 1997 was Thailand. Thailand had been in serious recession already in 1996 due to the collapse of real estate markets. Thus it is correct that the currency dealers and their currency dealing information systems decided that Thai currency, Baht, was overvalued. And in the summer of 1997, the Baht was indeed attacked and depreciated at an incredible speed(Meltzer, 1997). This can not be called as a case that brought the economy down by attacking the currency as mentioned before since the economic process was inevitably heading in due course toward the currency devaluation. But what was surprising was the speed and the rate of depreciation of the Thai currency, which became the ominous sign of what was coming to the Asian economies. The currency trading funds attacked all of Asian currencies after Thailand's fall and succeeded in making those currencies devaluated almost everywhere except for Hong Kong. Even the fall of Asian currencies forced countries like Brazil to take a preventive measure such as raising interest rates and tax raises, and spending cuts so that the Brazilian currency did not look overvalued(Economist, 1998a). In other words, the currency trading systems and the traders look for overvalued currencies all over the world and when they find it, they attack the currency mercilessly particularly against the US dollar which has begun its appreciation from mid-90s. The continuing position of strong US dollar makes many developing countries' currencies look overvalued regardless of the current economic situation. For example, Indonesia was doing well until the summer of 1997 and suddenly after the fall of Thai Baht currency, it became the target of the currency trading funds and lost 80% of its value in about a month(Hanke, 1998a) and the depreciation of Indonesian Rupia currency continued with no end in sight. IMF blamed the system of crony capitalism of President Suharto and demanded the dismantling of the current economic system. But they ignored the fact that the very "crony" capitalistic system achieved remarkable economic development and the country was not in bad shape before the attack on its currency began. This is why president Suharto was so interested in establishing the currency board system; he knew that the origin of the country's economic problem lied in the unstable currency. Other Asian countries which were never in bad economic conditions were Malaysia, Taiwan, and South Korea and they were all attacked by the currency trading funds and their currencies significantly and sometimes drastically depreciated.

The idea that the unstable currency brings about the economic instability was an old idea. Some goes back to the 19th century-the Latin Monetary Union, German currency union, and the gold standard(Economist, 1998b). The desire to bring the ever-lasting stability of currency to the European countries has become the basis for the introduction of European common currency, the Euro. They understand that the single currency was the only way to achieve currency stability which would lead to the economic stability. The reason that the various currencies of the world are not stable is because they are tradable and the bad guys of Wall street who are currency traders would make profit out of unstable currencies, which happened to grow to a trillion dollar business already in 1992(New York Times, 1992). By mid-90s, due to the strength of the US economy, the US dollar started to appreciate against almost all currencies in the world. And the currency traders using the very sophisticated information systems attacked and attacked many seemingly "overvalued" currencies. Even the US government recognizes that the currency depreciation is the cause of the economic turmoil in Asia of 1997. In Federal Reserve Bulletin(Federal Reserve Bulletin, 1998) reports that on November 17 1997, the Bank of Korea announced it would stop intervening to support the Won, a decision thought to be prompted by declining levels of foreign currency reserves, which led to massive business failures and IMF rescue packages. Unlike the normal economic flow of disaster, this one was, in fact, caused initially by the currency devaluation in all of Asian countries except for Thailand. Even in 1998, no countries are safe from attacks from currency traders and their trading information systems if their currency seemed to be overvalued. For example, Russian currency, Ruble, as Hanke(1998b) predicted, had been in free fall recently. The net foreign exchange reserves declined from $18.6billion to $14.8 billion in just 3 months. A ruble devaluation will send shock waves into central and eastern Europe. It will also induce a further deterioration of the international financial environment. Now we can suggest with confidence that the currency speculation alone can cause the economic turmoil based on many empirical evidence presented here. But how come it happened in the late 90s? The answer is the advancement of information technology, which will be discussed in the later chapter.

CURRENCY BOARD SYSTEMS

To strengthen the hypothesis that the economic turmoil can be caused by the currency turmoil, in this chapter, we present various examples of nations that adopted currency board systems which allowed them to fight off the currency speculation and achieved the economic stability.

Firstly, Hong Kong adopted the currency board system in 1973. Since then it has maintained currency stability and economic prosperity except for several periods of cyclic recessions. Passell(1997) analyzed the difference of the monetary policy of Hong Kong to its Asian neighbors such as Thailand which had currency troubles and pointed out that a country like Thailand where poorly regulated and undercapitalized banking system was not able to survive the attack on their currency whereas a country like Hong Kong with the currency board system was able to conserve the currency stability by guaranteeing to hold enough foreign currency to buy back every bit of local currency. Even though Hong Kong is suffering a recession now which was brought by Asian economic crisis, its economy did not collapse as in countries such as Thailand, South Korea, and Indonesia. Even an article from the Economist(Economist, 1997)argues that Hong Kong's currency board system might force a quick recovery from the current recession. The reason for this is that Hong Kong's currency board system is forcing the country to confront its past financial excesses swiftly. In Hong Kong's efficient markets, prices adjust with astonishing speed; the bubble in the stock market is gone; property prices took a just a few months to find sharply lower levels. In other words, Hong Kong's economy is not collapsing due to the currency board system which otherwise must have become the victim of currency speculation.

Among other countries which adopted a currency board system, Argentina stands out as the model for Latin American economic policy. On April 1, 1991, Argentina installed a currency board system to halt the hyperinflation. Argentina's currency board stopped hyperinflation. As a result, Argentina today has the lowest inflation rate in Latin America(Hanke, 1995; Starr, 1997). With a stable currency came an economic boom as it happened in other countries which adopted the currency board system. Then came Mexico Peso crisis which resulted in drastic depreciation of Mexican currency which led to the serious economic crisis. But during that time, argentine currency was rock-solid and the economy was stable.

These examples demonstrate that currency stability is the key to the economic stability. Thus currency speculation or attack on the particular currency can cause economic disaster as it happened in Asia of 1997.

ADVANCEMENT OF IT IN CURRENCY TRADING

Currency speculation has been around for long time, but why, at the late 90s, did the currency speculation become so destructively powerful as seen in the Asian crisis? The answer is the advancement of information technology that is used in currency trading systems. The destructive force can be said to come from the lighting speed of movement of a very large amount of money, say, several billion dollars per second. Namely, since so much money is used to attack the particular currency in such a short time period, there is no way to defend the currency without using much more amount of money; some Asian countries such as South Korea did try this method of using billions of foreign exchange reserve in vain and became bankrupt. Today's IT can move billions of dollars in a second and this ability is cunningly used in the currency trading system.

In early 90s, the dominant currency trading system was the Reuter Monitor Dealing service which processed the foreign currency exchange transactions. This kind of IT service was a newly growing market due to the technological development such as computer networks and computer technology itself. For example, Crockett(1990) describes a currency trading company called Quotron Systems Inc. which was a rival company to the Reuter Monitor Dealing service. Quotron claimed that its system called F/X Trader could provide subscribers with faster transaction processing and support more trades simultaneously than a rival company such as the Reuter service. However in 1992, Reuter fought back with the new system called Dealing 2000, an automated trading system that promised to revolutionize the way banks traded currencies(Maremont, 1992).

We can see clearly the direction of the advancement of currency trading systems from this example. Namely the technology aimed at developing faster transactions which meant faster movement of money and at developing bigger amount of trades which meant the movement of larger amount of money. These two aims were achieved during 90s due to the amazing development of computer technology. In other words, in 1990, the earlier mentioned F/X Trader was running on DEC MicroVAXs and IBM's PS/2s which were connected through DECnet local area network and RS-232 links. We can notice that how much the computer and communication technology advanced for the last 7 years when we examine their hardware/software/communication ware. In 1997, the computer and communication technology used in currency trading systems became potent enough to achieve the ultimate goal which was the faster movement of the larger amount of money that could break a targeted currency. Without the development of such advances in computer technology such as worldwide fiber-optic communication lines which can move incredible amount of data at the lightning speed and computers that can process transactions of astronomical volumes of financial data in seconds, the demise of Asian economies of 1997 could have not happened because their currencies were not able to depreciate in such a short period with such a fast speed. The point is that if the currency devaluation had happened over a longer time period at the smaller volume of transactions each time, the Asian economies would not have suffered the currency crisis and currency-crisis-induced economic crisis since their economic fundamentals such as growth rates and inflation rates of Asian countries were sound except for Thailand.

Most big foreign-exchange banks have invested a lot of time and money developing proprietary foreign-exchange trading systems for their clients. Most of the systems let corporations and investors do almost all their foreign-exchange transactions electronically, communicating directly with their banks' trading desk for execution, i.e., transaction(Ensor, 1997). Electronic dealing allows investors to deal quickly. For example, Fuji bank's wholly owned subsidiary, Fuji Capital Markets Corp. installed the Informix Online Dynamic Server(Bank Systems and Technology, 1996). This installation resulted in near real-time global trade data communication achieving 75% improvement in high-volume portfolio hedging. Another proprietary currency trading system that is popular among major banks is EBS(Electronic Brokerage System). It claims that average transaction volumes in excess of US $70 billion are made per day on the EBS electronic dealing system(EBS, 1998).

Nowadays, more powerful currency trading systems are developed and used. Besides, due to the growth of the Internet, now ordinary people can participate the currency trading using the currency trading system, which used to be exclusively within the realm of banks. And this phenomenon will accelerate the dangerous currency speculation business. For example, Redman(1998) reports that by the end of 1998, roughly 1/2 of all multibranch banks will provide home banking, which might include currency trading if the customer installs the propriety system software, access via a direct-dial PC modem connection, or the Internet. Let alone the banks, there are more and more individual investors who are interested in dealing currency which is possible through the Internet. Such services can be found in Forex Trader, E-FOREX, WEBFOREX, AND CTS(Forex, 1998; E-FOREX, 1998; WEBFOREX, 1998; CTS, 1998). All of these services claim that their systems guarantee real-time Internet currency dealing.

Banks who are major players of currency trading are themselves adopting new technology. For example, Washington Mutual Bank has automated its fund transfer operations with the FEDplu$ Funds Transfer client/server system from Fundtech Corporation(Orenstein, 1997a). The new system is expected to increase speed and efficiency in money transfer, which can be very useful in currency trading. Another similar example is NationsBank. It installed a new intranet-based multicurrency payment service, which made transferring funds overseas become faster and easier(Orenstein, 1997b). Other banks are also innovating in technology regarding currency trading. First National Bank of Chicago started to use PayBase payment software from Bottomline Technologies Inc.(Luhby, 1998). This system could print foreign currency checks that incorporated the local banking rules of individual countries, which made the movement of funds easier. CS First Boston bank introduced the Web-based Global Research Library using Illustra technology from Informix Software(Bosco, 1997). This system allowed faster access and analysis which must be useful in currency trading. In fact, this system supported 3,000 users including bankers, analysts, and traders. Chase Manhattan Bank even used Artificial Intelligence technique in creating a real global cash-management system which became more important in international currency trading(Gluck, 1997). The system called PaySource used a form of artificial intelligence to navigate through the variability of check clearing and payment systems among nations of the world. Bankers Trust was also engaged in innovating in trading technology. It purchased Object Design Inc.'s ObjectStore object database to minimize the development time of its new international trading system(Bank System and Technology, 1997). The new system could store and manage sophisticated financial data on an object database and incorporate live feeds from 20 different trading systems in various parts of the world. In other words, faster analysis and decision making was made possible due to this system. This software runs in Windows NT environment in various powerful hardware platforms, which were never available in early 90s; the IT development made it possible to run these very sophisticated and powerful systems that could influence world currency markets in a negative way, i.e., sudden steep depreciation of a currency.

PROGRAM TRADING IN STOCKS AND CURRENCIES

On October 19, 1987, the worst day in the history of the New York Stock Exchange, the Dow-Jones average dropped by 508 points. Among reasons for this fall, the most important finding was the role of program trading which can lead to trading development that are automatic and can not be stopped once they begun(Nadler, 1988). A survey which measured changes in investors' preferences and attitudes after 1987 crash showed that elimination or control of computerized program trading was cited most frequently as a measure that would bolster investors' confidence(Boyles and Carr, 1989). Thus circuit breakers were introduced by the New York Stock Exchange in 1988;

circuit breakers were an attempt to prevent excess price volatility by preventing program trading, i.e., shutting down trading and cooling off the market(Santoni and Liu, 1993). This rule required that if the Dow Jones Industrial Average moved 50 points in either direction during the day, all computer program trading orders could be only entered for stocks moving in the opposition direction to the prevailing trend. Willoughby(1996) reports that in 1995, the curbs had hit 29 times. This tells that market is more volatile due to the program trading as Hogan et al.(1997) identified that program trading did lead to a higher market volatility. The reasons that program trading can cause that kind of trading developments are considered to be the speed of the movement of money(stocks) and the size of money(stocks). In other words, program trading can move astronomical amount of money(stocks) in a lightning speed, which might cause "panic disorder" in investors who mistakenly believe the direction set by the program trading and sell everything(Powell, 1989).

Essentially, the program trading in stock markets operates in the same way as in currency markets. Namely, computers move stocks/currencies in dealings of stocks/currencies. Thus the danger is the same as following. As program trading in stock markets caused panic because of the speed of movement of money(stocks) and the size of money(stocks), program trading in currency caused panic in Asia because of the speed of movement of money(currency) and the size of money(currency). This fact is the evidence for our hypothesis that currency crisis in Asia of 1997 was due to the Information Technology such as computerized currency trading or program currency trading.

HOW CURRENCY TRADING SYSYEMS BREAK CURRENCIES

Currencies require active management to yield significant returns, which means that it needs computerized support(Lequeux, 1997). And it frequently requires speculation; one has to master the skill of looking through all relevant information from many nations and speculating on the future of the nations' currencies. The speculation part is the one that is heavily supported by computers which collect, analyze, and recommend regarding currency dealing. These currency trading systems can make stupid decisions which can be induced by "group think" of computers. In other words, the currency trading system might act as following steps:

1. The system A thinks that South Korean currency is overvalued at a rate of 5%.
2. The trader A follows the advice from the system A and starts to sell South Korean currency.
3. The system B after 1/1000 second later after the system A's action detects there is a movement toward selling of South Korean currency and recommends to sell.
4. The trader B follows the advice and starts to sell South Korean currency.
5. The same routine might repeat about 1,000 times at one second(probably more), which means several billion dollar attack on the South Korean currency at one second that leads to the depreciation of 80%, rather than 10% which was originally predicted, of the South Korean currency.

This fits Jeanne(1997)'s idea that there exists self-fulfilling speculation in currency crises. The computers do perform "group think" since they check the environment at every micro-second and try to adjust its view on the changed world. And trading actions accelerate since as time goes by, the more the environment changes, the more the system recommends to sell(the system rarely recommends buying due to the continuing appreciation of US dollar since mid-90s). Following graph summarizes this argument rather clearly.

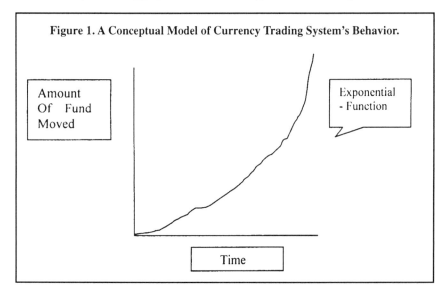

Figure 1. A Conceptual Model of Currency Trading System's Behavior.

Amount Of Fund Moved

Exponential - Function

Time

Due to the difficulty in collecting empirical data, the graph could not be drawn as a precise model. It is rather a conceptual model for computerized currency trading system's behavior during the Asian currency crisis of 1997. In this kind of environment, investors get " panic disorder" and follow the pattern of computer's "group think" pattern, which is selling like crazy.

CONCLUSION

The only country whose currency was considerably overvalued was Thailand during Asian economic crisis of 1997. All other nations had good economic fundamentals, but still they fell victims of currency speculation which seemed to be fueled by computerized currency trading systems as program trading did to the American stock market in 1987. The subsequent economic hardships were natural for countries whose currencies were seriously devaluated. And IMF brought money and so-called restructuring plans to these nations, which could backfire by creating even worse economic disasters such as very high unemployment rates which happened in Latin America during IMF's rein there. The Western scholars blamed all kinds of different business practices done in Asia. For example, the United States Comptroller of the Currency, Ludwig complained that inconsistent accounting rules allowed Asian banks to conceal inadequate capital levels and other problems(McConnell and Anason, 1998). But once again we should not forget that with that kind of accounting rules, Asian economies prospers for the last 30 years. James(1998) correctly worried about the challenges of managing globalization. He observed that the world lacks the mechanism to deal with more intense global trade and investment, i.e., currency speculation. As a conclusion, the author of the paper would like to propose a world-wide cooling-off mechanism for currency trading systems as done in the American stock market. If this is unrealistic, then all of developing nations should adopt the currency board system in order to prevent the recurrence of Asian currency and economic crisis of 1997 which has a real possibility of comeback any time in the future. Eventually probably the best and permanent solution could be to adopt a world single currency.

REFERENCES

Bank Systems and Technology. "Bankers trust propels international trading system using object database", (32:2), 1997, pp. 10.

Bank Systems and Technology. "Fuji Capital globally integrates systems", (33:12), 1996, pp. 15.

Bosco, P. "Data goes dynamic, and complex", Bank Systems and Technology (34:2), 1997, pp. 39.

Boyles, G. V. and Carr, D. R. "Black Monday 1987 Revisited", Business and Economic Review (35:2), 1989, pp. 8-21.

Crockett, B. "Quotron Unveils New Currency Trading Net", Network World (7:37), 1990, pp. 27-28.

CTS, World Wide Web, http://www.currencytraidngsystem.com, 1998.

Currency Boards, World Wide Web http://www.erols.com/kurrency, 1998.

EBS, World Wide Web, http://www.ebsp.com, 1998.

Economist. "Can Brazil hold the line?", (346: 8053), 1998a, pp. 35.

Economist. "The history of an idea", (346: 8063), 1998b, pp. 4.

Economist. "A rubbery sort of economy", (345: 8041), 1997, pp. 78-79.

E-FOREX, World Wide Web, http://www.eforex.com, 1998.

Ensor, B. "Obstacles on the path to electronic trading", Global Investor (107), 1997, pp. 30.

Federal Reserve Bulletin, "Treasury and Federal Reserve foreign exchange operations", (84:3), 1998, pp. 174-179.

Finance and Development, " Capital flow sustainability and speculative currency attacks", (34:4), 1997, pp. 8-11.

Forex, World Wide Web, http://inusa.com/tour/forex.htm, 1998.

Gluck, A. "Creating a global cash-management game plan", Bank Systems and Technology (34:2), 1997, pp. 28-31.

Hanke, S. "The reluctant fireman", Forbes (161:7), 1998a, pp. 110-111.

Hanke, S. "Is the ruble next?", Forbes (161:5), 1998b, pp. 64.

Hanke, S. "Good news from a bad news spot", Forbes (159:4), 1997a, pp. 106.

Hanke, S. "Rock-solid Hong Kong", Forbes (160:11), 1997b, pp. 46.

Hanke, S. " Why Argentina is solid", Forbes (155:10), 1995, pp. 92.

Hogan, K. C., Kroner, K. F., and Sultan, J. "Program trading, nonprogram trading and market volatility", Journal of Futures Markets (17:7), 1997, pp. 733-756.

James, D. "How the world may end up paying for the allure of globalization", Business Review Weekly: BRW (20:2), 1998, pp. 62-63.

Jeanne, O. "Are currency crises self-fulfilling? A test", Journal of International Economics, (43:3/4), 1997, pp. 263-386.

Lequeux, P. "A new benchmark for dynamic currency management", Global Investor (106), 1997, pp. 26-28.

Luhby, T. "1st Chicago unit automates foreign checks", American Banker (163:88), 1998, pp. 15.

Maremont, M. "Reuters unveils supertrading", Business Week (3253), 1992, pp. 44.

McConnell, B. and Anason, D. "OCC criticizes standards of regulators in Asia crisis", American Banker (163:41), 1998, pp. 2.

Meltzer, A. H. "Asia afloat", National Review, (49:22), 1997, pp. 44.

Nadler, P. S. "A Look at Black Monday, One Year Later", Secured Lender (44:6), 1988, pp. 20-25.

New York Times. "Cashing in big: The bad boys of currency", (142:49193), 1992, Section 3, pp. 1.

Orenstein, A. F. "Seattle-based institution automates wire transfers", Bank Systems and Technology (34:5), 1997a, pp. 26.

Orenstein, A. F. "NationalBank rolling out net-based service for making multicurrency payments", Bank Systems and Technology (34:3), 1997b, pp. 14.

Passel, P. "Economic Scene", New York times. (147:50961), 1997, pp. D2.

Powell, D. "Toward the Automated Stock Exchange", Computing Canada (15:21), 1989, pp. 1-4.

Redman, R. "On-line programs to multiply in'98", Bank Systems and Technology (35:4), 1998, pp. 11.

Santoni, G.J. and Liu, T. "Circuit breakers and stock market volatility", Journal of Futures Markets (13:3), 1993, pp. 261-277.

Starr, P. K. "Government coalitions and the viability of currency boards: Argentina under the Cavallo Plan", Journal of Interamerican Studies and World Affairs (39:2), 1997, pp. 83-133.

WEBFOREX, World Wide Web, http://www.ectx.com/webforex, 1998.

Willoughby, J. "Program trading played role in stock market's tumble", Investment Dealers Digest (62:13), 1996, pp. 4.

Processing Updates on Complex Value Databases*

Hartmut Liefke and Susan B. Davidson

Department of Computer and Information Science, University of Pennsylvania, 200 South 33rd Street,
Philadelphia, PA19104

liefke@seas.upenn.edu and susan@cis.upenn.edu

ABSTRACT

Query languages and optimization techniques for complex and object-oriented databases have been extensively studied by the database community. Languages for updating such databases, however, have not been studied to the same extent, although they are clearly important since databases change over time. We have therefore developed a language for updating complex value databases called CPL+. The syntax of CPL+ is concise and optimizable.

To argue that the rewrite rules produce updates with fewer accesses and updates to stored values, we present an execution model for CPL+ and an abstract storage model for a complex value database. We develop the notion of a *workspace* - i.e. the set of persistent objects that are accessed or updated within an update. Based on this measurement, we illustrate how rewriting of update expressions can reduce the cost of updates.

INTRODUCTION

Although query languages for complex value databases have been well studied ([1, 22,4]), the issue of updating such databases has not. Update languages - for any model - are, however, important since databases are not static but change to reflect the world that they model. Such changes can trigger updates at the instance as well as the schema level, and while both are important for now we only address changes at the instance level. Schema updates and schema evolution have been studied thoroughly, for example in [4,18].

While there exist standardized update primitives for SQL [11], object-oriented databases generally implement updates through methods, i.e. functions associated with classes. Methods are most often written in imperative languages, such as C++ or O_2C, and compiled into executable programs. This leads to three problems: 1) The capabilities of rewriting and optimizing updates is limited, 2) Updates are implemented in system-specific, proprietary languages and cannot be applied to other databases, 3) Methods (i.e. updates) must be compiled and added to the schema before they can be used. That means that updates cannot be changed or created easily.

In contrast to using methods for updates, we believe that users should be able to explicitly specify updates by describing the parts of the database instance that have to be changed. As an example, suppose our database contains a relation Employees(Name, Salary) and we wish to increase the salary of any employee named "Joe" by $5,000. In SQL-92 this could be written as

    UPDATE   Employees E
       SET   S.Salary= S.Salary+5000
     WHERE   S.Name= "Joe"

The syntax is terse, specifying only the pieces of the database that are to be altered. In complex value databases, the need for a terse specification of updates is even greater than in relational databases due to the deeply nested structures involved. Consider a company database in which this employee information is nested inside one component of a company record: Each company has a set of employees with a name and a salary. Each employee is affiliated with a set of projects. Each project in a company has a description. Using {...} for sets and $[a_1:..., ..., a_n:...]$ for records, we can describe such a database using the following complex type:

    Companies:{[Name: string,
                Employees: {[Name:string,Salary:real,Projects:{string}]}
    ]};

Updates such as changing the salary or inserting/deleting projects of employees cannot be specified in a conventional (relational) update language.

Starting in Section 2 with a query language called Collection Programming Language (CPL), we describe CPL+, a concise and optimizable update language for complex value databases. In Section 3, we discuss a general storage and execution model for updating complex value databases using CPL+. We describe two techniques called *evaluation-on-demand* and *deferred deletion* for efficient update processing and we introduce the notion of a *workspace* as a measurement of the update cost. In Section 4, we illustrate how existing CPL+ optimizations reduce the workspace. We conclude in Section 5 with a discussion of related issues on updates, additional work that has been done, and an indication of future research.

CPL: A QUERY LANGUAGE FOR COMPLEX TYPES

The Collection Programming Language (CPL) is based on a complex type system that allows arbitrary nesting of the collection types - set, bag and list - together with record and variant types [6,22]. For the purposes of this paper we will restrict our attention to bags (i.e. multi-sets) as the only collection type - thus, we leave the problem of duplicate removal during update processing for future work. We also do not consider issues of classes and object identities, although extensions to CPL can be made along these lines [8,6]. The set of CPL types is therefore given by the syntax:

$$t ::= \text{bool} \mid \text{int} \mid \text{real} \mid \text{string} \mid \dots \mid [a_1:t_1,\dots,a_n:t_n] \mid <b_1:t_1,\dots,b_n:t_n> \mid \{t\}$$

The types bool, int, real, string, etc. are built-in base types. $[a_1:t_1,\dots,a_n:t_n]$ constructs record types from the types $t_1,\dots,t_n$; $<b_1:t_1,\dots,b_n:t_n>$ constructs variant types from the types $t_1,\dots,t_n$; and $\{t\}$ constructs set types from the type t. For example, the schema of a database for the company could be the following:

```
[Persons:{[  Name :string, Salary:real,
             Occup:<Empl :{string},Manag:string>]},
 Projs:{[    Name:string,Budget:int]}]
```

Values in CPL are constructed as follows: $[a_1:e_1,\dots,a_n:e_n]$ for records, giving values of the appropriate type for each of the attributes; $<a:e>$ for variants, giving a value of the appropriate type for one of the labels; and $\{e_1,\dots,e_n\}$ for sets. The following is a valid value of the given type:

```
[Persons:{  [Name:"Tom",Salary:34000,Occup:<Empl:{"Proj1","Proj3"}>],
            [Name:"Ellen",Salary:36000,Occup:<Empl:{"Proj2","Proj3"}>],
            [Name:"Peter",Salary:78000,Occup:<Manag:"Proj3">]},
 Projs:{   [Name:"Proj1",Budget:100000],[Name:"Proj2",Budget:20000],
            [Name:"Proj3",Budget:50000]}]
```

We consider a database schema to consist of a type, and an instance of the database to be a value of that type. Note that we are ignoring issues of integrity constraints, and assume nothing about the correctness of instances beyond type correctness.

Queries in CPL

The syntax of CPL resembles, very roughly, that of relational calculus. However there are important differences in order to deal with the complex type system we have mentioned. The important syntactic unit of CPL is the *comprehension* [20,21], which can be used with collection types. As an example of a set comprehension, the following extracts the name and salary of all people who earn more than $40000:

```
{[Name:p.Name,Sal:p.Salary] | \p<-Persons, p.Salary>40000 }
```

The variable p is successively bound (indicated by the backslash, "\p") to each element of Persons; "<-" is a set-generator. For each p, if p.Salary>40000 the value [Name:p.Name,Sal:p.Salary] is constructed; all such values are then combined in a set to form the final result. Note we use the literal Persons as an entry point to the database. It represents the attribute Persons of the database with record type Company. Comprehension syntax is derived from a more powerful programming paradigm on collection types, that of *structural recursion* [5].

Another important concept of CPL is *pattern matching*. Instead of binding an element of a collection to a variable name using the expression \p, it is possible to specify variable bindings and conditions using patterns. The following example returns the name and the project budget for each manager named "Tom":

```
{[ManagerAge:a,ProjBudget:p.Budget] |
    [Name:"Tom",Age:\a,Occup:<Manager:\proj>,...]<-Persons,
    \p<-Projs, p.Name=proj}
```

Each expression in CPL has a type that can automatically be inferred. The type of the result of the previous query, for instance, would be {[ManagerAge:int,ProjBudget:int]}. The query also illustrates how to form the join of two sets by using two set-generators.

Extending CPL with Updates : CPL+

An update is a function from an instance of a given database schema to another instance of that schema. For example, the update "Increase Ellen's salary by $5000" applied to database of the correct type will return a new value of this type. Often, we tend to think of a database schema as giving a set of *named* values, as in the example from the previous sections. Here, the schema has two named values - Persons and Projs - and the database is a record type.

One could use CPL to express the new database value as function of the new value. Using the given schema, we could increase Ellen's salary as follows:

Persons == { [Name:n,Age:a,Occup:i,Salary: if (n="Ellen") then s+5000 else s)]
      | [Name:\n,Age:\a,Salary:\s,Occup:\i]<-Persons};

This form of complete update is cumbersome to specify and inefficient if executed as written - we are rewriting the entire set of Persons when only one record of one set is updated.

Since updates have side-effects, we cannot consider updates as CPL expressions that can be used in other CPL expressions. In the rest of the paper, we therefore distinguish updates *upd* from CPL queries *expr* by using prefix @ for update expressions: @*upd*. The syntax of expressions *upd* is given by the following grammar:

upd ::=   *ID* | a:=upd | <<b: upd>> | *if* cond *then* upd$_1$ *else* upd$_2$ | *if* cond *then* upd | (upd) |
        expr | {upd} | *insert* expr | upd$_1$;upd$_2$ | pat=>upd | *delete*

Here, *expr* denotes a conventional CPL expression, and *cond* is a CPL-expression of type bool. The construct *pat* denotes a *pattern matching* expression, which is described later. An update is always executed on a given persistent value in the database. This value is called *update value* and is an implicit parameter of CPL+ updates. The update constructs have the following meaning:

The *identity update* ID represents the identity function, and does not change the value in the database. The *record update* a:=*upd* updates the attribute a$_i$ for the given record value by performing update *upd* on it. The *variant update* <<b:upd>> tests if the branch for the given variant value is b; if it is, then the update *upd* is performed on the branch value. Expression if *cond* then *upd$_1$* else *upd$_2$* evaluates condition *cond* and, depending on the result, performs either *upd1* or *upd2*; if *cond* then *upd* is syntactic sugar for if *cond* then *upd* else ID. Expression (*upd*) is used to group updates syntactically together.

The update expression *expr* denotes a *complete update*: The update value is completely replaced by the value of the CPL expression *expr*. The *collection update* {*upd*} updates each element of the set by applying *upd*. The expression insert *expr* updates a set by inserting the elements of set *expr*. *upd$_1$;upd$_2$* denotes a *sequence* of updates. The primitive delete deletes the element from the containing set. Note that delete can only be applied to elements of sets. Thus, it must occur in collection updates {...}, such as in if *cond* then delete. Recall that sets in CPL+ have the semantics of bags or multi-sets, since we not consider duplicate removal during the update process.

As in CPL, we use patterns to select subvalues and introduce variables. The update expression *pat*=>*upd* tries to match the update value with the pattern *pat*. If the value matches, then the variables in *pat* are bound to the respective parts in the value and update *upd* is performed. Otherwise, the update is not performed. The syntax of patterns is:

pat ::= _ | expr | \x | <b:pat> | [a$_1$:pat$_1$,...,a$_n$:pat$_n$]

Pattern _ matches anything and pattern *expr* matches the object whose value is equal to the value of *expr*. The pattern \x binds variable name x to the value. The pattern <b:pat> matches those variant values that have branch b and whose branch values matches *pat*. Pattern [a$_1$:pat$_1$,...,a$_n$:pat$_n$] matches record values that have attributes a$_1$,...,a$_n$ whose values match *pat$_1$*,...,*pat$_n$*, respectively. Variables bound in an attribute pattern a$_i$:pat$_i$ can be used in subsequent attribute patterns a$_j$:pat$_j$ with j>i. For instance, the pattern [a:\v,b:v] matches a record value, whose attributes a and b have the same value.

The update *upd* in *pat*=>*upd* does not change the value of the variables bound in *pat*. For example, consider the update \a=>(a+2;a+5), which can be applied to any integer value. The first update a+2 increases the value by 2; the second update a+5 increases the value by 5. However, variable a in the second update represents the value *before* the first update occurred. Therefore, the entire update will only increase the value by 5. To increase the value by 7, one could use update (\a=>a+2;\a=>a+5).

Let us illustrate CPL+ by two examples for the Company database:

Example 1: Increase Ellen's salary by $5000.

@Persons:={ \e => if e.Name="Ellen" then (Salary:=e.Salary+5000)}

Variable e is successively bound to each element of the set Persons. If the condition e.Name="Ellen" evaluates to true for an element, then the salary is raised by $5000. It is also possible to use pattern matching:

@Persons:={ [Name:"Ellen",Salary:\s] => (Salary:=s+5000)}

Note the difference to the update expression given at the beginning of this section. Rather than specifying the complete new set of persons, only the part that has to be updated is mentioned.

Example 2: Consider an update that removes all affiliations to project "Proj3" from the database. This update entails two different tasks: 1) remove the project from the project list of all other employees and 2) set the project name of the associated managers to the empty string "". The resulting update expression is as follows:

@(Persons:={ Occup:=<<Empl:{"Proj3" => delete}>>};
    Persons:={ Occup:=<<Manag:"Proj3" => "">>})

Update expressions can only be applied to values of the correct type. An update of the form Persons:=..., for instance, can only be applied to record values that have a Persons attribute. The details of the underlying type system based on partial records and variants and subtype polymorphism can be found in [12,13].

AN ABSTRACT EXECUTION MODEL FOR CPL+

To understand how CPL+ expressions are evaluated and to analyze their cost, we must define a storage and execution model. Unlike the relational model where the storage model is straightforward (tuples of the same relation are clustered together on pages), there are many possible storage models for sets of non-fixed length values. The choice of which model to use is influenced by many factors, such as the expected size of a collection (i.e. whether it typically has many or just a few elements), and the expected type and frequency of queries and updates performed on the database. Furthermore, auxiliary structures such index trees or access support relations reduce the cost of queries, but increase the cost of updates. We therefore present in this section a general model that is an abstraction of different possible physical implementations.

An Abstract Storage Model for Complex Values

A complex value can be represented as a tree. A node of the tree represents a subvalue in the database. A record value has an outgoing edge for each of its attribute values. A set value has an outgoing edge for each of its elements, and a variant value has one outgoing edge for the branch of the variant value. The outgoing edges of records and variants have labels corresponding to the attribute and branch names used in the type.

The tree representation of the database example in Section 2 is shown in Figure 1. We distinguish three different types of nodes: record nodes, variant nodes, and set nodes.

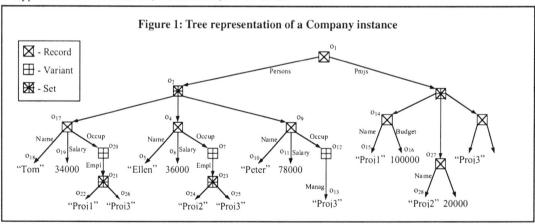

Figure 1: Tree representation of a Company instance

The physical representation of the value tree depends on the actual storage model. For instance, elements of sets could be clustered together on pages. The efficient physical representation of sets often requires additional persistent data structures, such as indexes or clustering information.

For our purposes, we make the following assumption: Each node in the tree has a unique location on the persistent storage and has an *object identity*, as shown in   Figure 1. The associated value of an object identity contains the object identities of its subvalues. The value of a record node is a tuple of the object identities of the subnodes. The value of a variant node is a pair of a branch identifier (such as Empl or Manag) and the object identity of the underlying node. The value of a set node is a set of object identities of the subnodes. The value of a base node is the base value itself (i.e. the string value, the integer value, etc.)

Although the physical representation of such object identities and values can vary, we can assume that the value of an object can be accessed (*object access*) or updated (*object update*). The cost of executing a CPL+ update depends on the number of single object accesses and object updates. The set of all objects accessed while processing a CPL+ update is called the *access workspace* of the update. The set of objects that are updated, inserted, or deleted is called the *update workspace*. Both sets they can contain the same object multiple times, since an object can be accessed and updates multiple times.

Optimizations, such as caching, clustering, and indexing, will reduce the (average) time of object lookups and updates. However, we can assume that the following property holds:
• An update upd_1 which accesses only a subset of the objects that are accessed by another update upd_2 will be faster when applied in a real database environment.

Although this assumption is quite intuitive, it is not always satisfied. Consider a simple database LRU cache with two initially empty entries and consider an access sequence $[o_1,o_2,o_3,o_1]$. Clearly, each read will cause a disk access. Consider now the sequence $[o_1,o_2,o_1,o_3,o_1]$: Here, we only need three disk accesses, since object o_1 is in the cache for the second and third access. Fortunately, scenarios as in the example above are quite rare and can be avoided by several techniques.

Executing CPL+ Updates

An update is performed on a given node in the tree, i.e. it is parameterized by a specific object identity o. The value of o must be of the correct type. Updates in CPL+ are performed in the following way:

Update ID leaves the database unchanged. Update $a_i:=upd$ loads the value of o and performs update upd on the object identity obtained by the projection a_i of the value. Update $<<b_i:upd>>$ loads object o. If the value is a variant with branch b_i, then update upd is performed on its branch object identity. Update if *cond* then upd_1 else upd_2 evaluates condition *cond*. Depending on whether the result is true or false, update upd_1 or upd_2 is executed for object o. Update *expr* evaluates CPL expression *expr*, stores the result persistently, and changes the old value of o to the new persistent value.

Update $\{upd\}$ loads the set value of o, iterates over this set of object identities and updates each element in the set by performing upd. Update insert *expr* first evaluates CPL expression *expr*, which yields a set value. The result is made persistent and added to the existing set. Update $upd_1;upd_2$ first executes upd_1 on o, and then executes update upd_2 on o, whose value has already been changed by upd_1. However, upd_2 is not executed, if o is an element of a set and has been deleted by upd_1 (using delete). Update *pat* => *upd* tests whether the object matches pattern *pat*. If the object matches the pattern, then variables in *pat* are bound to the appropriate persistent objects and update *upd* is performed on o. Update delete removes object o from the containing set. This update is only valid if o is an element of a set.

Consider the following update again:
@Persons:={\p => if p.Name="Ellen" then Salary:=p.Salary+5000}

Variable p is bound to a person in the set of persons. For each person, attribute Name is loaded. If the name is "Ellen", then we increase the salary by $5000. Figure 2(a) shows how the update is performed on the set of persons. Bold edges indicate that the value must be traversed in order to retrieve or update the object at the end of the arrow. In the given instance, we have to read the name of each person (assuming that Name is not necessarily a key). If the name is "Ellen", then we increase the salary by $1000. The access workspace for this update is $\{o_1,o_2,o_{17},o_{18},o_4,o_5,o_6,o_9,o_{10}\}$ and the update workspace is $\{o_6\}$.

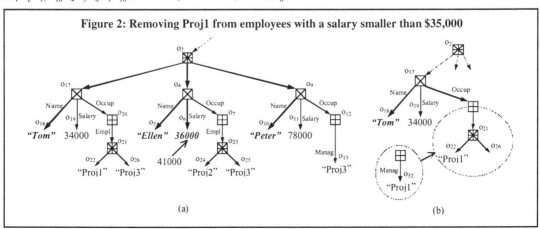

Figure 2: Removing Proj1 from employees with a salary smaller than $35,000

(a)

(b)

A second update example changes person "Tom" to be the new manager of project "Proj1": @Persons:={ \p => if p.Name="Tom" => Occup:=<Manag:"Proj1"> }. The update iterates over all persons and reads its name. If the name is "Tom", we replace the value of attribute Occup by the value tree representing <Manag:"Proj1">. Figure 2(b) illustrates the update. The object identity o_{20} **of attribute Occup does not change, only its value changes. The access** workspace is $\{o_1,o_2,o_{17},o_4,o_5,o_9,o_{10}\}$ and the update workspace is $\{o_{20},o_{21},o_{22},o_{26},o_{32}\}$. Note that we assume that object deletions and insertions are classified as updates. A finer distinction between different classes of workspaces is used in [12].

Finally, consider an update that removes all employees from project Proj1 who earn less than $35000. This entails removing project "Proj1" from the set of projects of each employee who has a salary bigger than $35000:

@Persons:={\p=> Occup:=<<Empl:{"Proj1"=> (if p.Salary<35000 then setdel)}>>}

This update iterates over all persons. If the person is an employee, then the system iterates over all projects. If a project has name "Proj1" and if p.Salary<35000 is true, then the project is deleted from the set of projects for this employee. \h Figure 3 shows how the update is performed on the given database instance and which objects are accessed. The access workspace is $\{o_1,o_2,o_{17},o_{20},o_{21},o_{22},o_{19},o_{26},o_4,o_7,o_{23},o_{24},o_{25},o_9,o_{12}\}$ and the update workspace is $\{o_{21},o_{22}\}$.

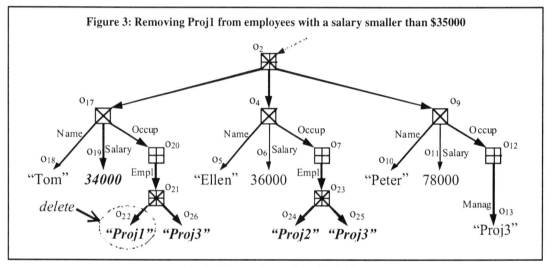

Figure 3: Removing Proj1 from employees with a salary smaller than $35000

Evaluation-on-demand for Variables

In the previous examples, variable p was bound to a person in the set of persons. It would be inefficient to load the entire subtree associated with variable p in order to evaluate subsequent CPL expressions, such as p.Salary+1000. In particular, there could be other attributes of persons, such as Children, that have large values that are not needed for answering the query.

Instead of binding variables to the complex *value* represented by the tree, we bind a variable to the *node* - i.e. the object identity representing the node. Whenever parts of the value are accessed (using projection, set iteration, or variant branching), we load the value of the object from disk and extract the object identities needed to answer queries. This evaluation strategy is called *evaluation-on-demand*.

Consider a projection such as p.Salary. We access the record value associated with object identity p and extract the object identity for the salary node. Then, the salary value can be accessed using this object identity (e.g. in p.Salary+1000). CPL also allows us to perform projections and other operations on constructed values such as [Name:"Test",Salary:p.Salary]. Since such values do not correspond to persistent values, we distinguish two types of CPL values:

• A *persistent object* refers to an object in the persistent database. The value of an object can be retrieved or modified. For example, p and p.Salary are persistent values.
• *Transient objects* are values that were created within CPL expressions and are represented in memory. For example, p.Salary+1000 is transient since the sum is computed in memory. Complex transient values can contain persistent object identities, such as in the expression [Name:"Test",Salary:p.Salary].

Each CPL expression returns either a persistent or transient object. It is possible to *dereference* such identities and to obtain the corresponding value. The formal framework for this mechanism and the complete evaluation model for CPL can be found in [12].

Deferred Deletion

A variable bound within a CPL+ update pattern refers to the value at the time of the binding. Consider the following update, which performs two updates on Ellen's salary:

Persons:={\p => if p.Name="Ellen" then (Salary:=p.Salary+1000;

Salary:=p.Salary+2000) }

The salary is first increased by $1000 and then by $2000. However, the second update is based on p.Salary, which refers to the salary *before* the first update occurred. Therefore, the overall increase will be $2000. If variable p is bound to the identity of a person, then the value of p.Salary would be affected by the first update. In the following, we discuss a technique call *deferred deletion* to solve this problem.

A primitive update replaces a given subtree of the database by a new subtree. Instead of deleting the old subtree immediately, we allow access to that tree *in the context of a variable*. Figure 4 shows how the deletion of the old salary is deferred.

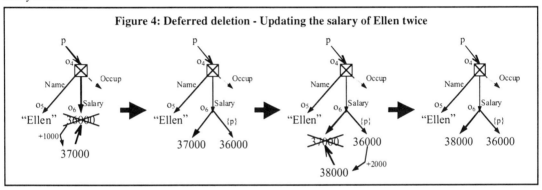

Figure 4: Deferred deletion - Updating the salary of Ellen twice

First, we want to replace the current salary ($36000) by the new salary ($37000). As a result, we replace the old value by the new one, as shown in the second picture. However, the system also keeps the previous value and annotates it with the set of variables that are currently bound ({p} in the example). Thus, there are two values stored for the salary of "Ellen": The current (default) value is marked with a bold arrow and the old value is marked with an arrow labeled with the current set of bound variables.

The second update is based on the old value. The current value is replaced, but the variable *p* still references the old salary. When the update is finished, the old value edges are removed from the tree.

In general, we can identify the following two rules:

1. When a complete update occurs in the database, the old value is stored under an edge annotated with the current set of bound variables. Variables that occur in the annotations of other edges for the same object are not considered. Afterwards, the new value is stored under the default edge and represents the current value.

2. If a variable becomes unbound, then the variable identifier is removed from the respective path annotations. If path annotations become empty, then the edge and the value are removed.

An update variable *x* within a CPL expression describes the context it is evaluated in. That means the access to the object is done with respect to context *x*. Traversing down in the value tree using projections and set iterations does not change the variable context. Keeping track of path annotations requires additional data structures, which can be kept in memory.

OPTIMIZATIONS

CPL+ allows various optimizations through rewriting. The purpose of optimization in general is to reduce the cost of performing some operation. In this section, we illustrate optimizations and show how the workspace is reduced. A more detailed description of the optimization process can be found in [12].

Consider the update that removes all affiliations of project "Proj3":

@(Persons:={ Occup:=<<Empl:{"Proj3" => setdel}>>};

Persons:={ Occup:=<<Manag:"Proj3" => ""'>>})

Performing this update as written means that the set Persons is traversed two times. Each time, the Occup attribute must be loaded and the branch must be checked. The first update part has the following access workspace: $\{o_1, o_2, o_{17}, o_{20}, o_{21}, o_{22}, o_{26}, o_4, o_7, o_{23}, o_{24}, o_{25}, o_9, o_{12}\}$. The second update part accesses the following objects: $\{o_1, o_2, o_{17}, o_{20}, o_4, o_7, o_9, o_{12}, o_{13}\}$. For small sets, a memory cache can be used to avoid the second loading. However, if the set of persons is large, there will be cache misses and the objects will have to be loaded from disk twice.

In CPL+, it is possible to merge the iterations in the following way:

@Persons:={Occup:= <<Empl :{"Proj3" => setdel}>>;
<<Manag:"Proj3" => ""`>>}

In this update, only one iteration over persons is needed. Consequently, the overall access workspace is smaller: $\{o_1, o_2, o_{17}, o_{20}, o_{21}, o_{22}, o_{26}, o_4, o_7, o_{23}, o_{24}, o_{25}, o_9, o_{12}, o_{13}\}$. Figure 5 shows the objects that are accessed during the update processing and which objects are deleted or modified.

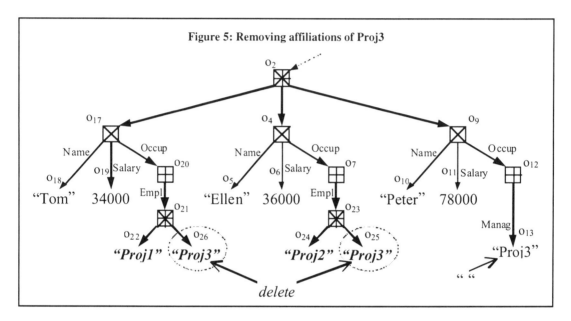

Figure 5: Removing affiliations of Proj3

In general, any sequence $\{upd_1\};\{upd_2\}$ can be rewritten as $\{upd_1;upd_2\}$. This optimization is called *vertical loop fusion* and is part of a class of rewriting rules called *update composition*. Other important update composition rules are $a:=upd_1;a:=upd_2 \ddagger a:=(upd_1;upd_2)$ and $<<a:upd_1>>;<<a:upd_2>> \ddagger <<a:upd_1;upd_2>>$.

Similar to rewriting in the relational algebra, it is desirable to perform selections as early as possible. In CPL+, we can move filters (i.e. expressions if *cond* then *expr1* else *expr2*) to the outside of complex updates. This class of optimizations is called *filter promotion*.

Reconsider the following update: Remove all employees from project Proj1 who earn less than $35000.

@Persons:={\p => Occup:= <<Empl: {"Proj1" =>
(if p.Salary<35000 then setdel)}>>}

Figure 3 shows that every project of every employee is loaded into the memory: Since condition p.Salary>40000 does not depend on the project or the employee, it is possible to delegate the condition to the outside of the updates:

@Persons:={\p => if p.Salary>35000 then Occup:= <<Empl:{"Proj1" => setdel}>>}

Thus, only projects of the persons with a salary >$40000 are considered (\h Figure 6). The access workspace of the update is $\{o_1, o_2, o_{17}, o_{19}, o_{20}, o_{21}, o_{22}, o_{26}, o_4, o_6, o_9, o_{11}\}$.

Filter promotion can increase the cost of the update under certain conditions. In the original expression, it is possible that condition c is not evaluated at all. The optimized expression, however, leads to an evaluation of c in *every* case. If c is a complex condition that requires accessing a large set of objects, then the rewriting can lead to higher execution costs. In the example, the salary of "Peter" (o_{11}) must be loaded to check whether it is smaller than $35000. In the original version, the update firstly analyses the attribute Occup before checking the salary.

On the other hand, the rule for filter promotion can lead to significant cost improvements if the set has a lot of elements, since c is only evaluated once instead of multiple times. While in general we assume that the average cost reduction achieved outweighs the average cost increase, it is clear that these rules are best used with instance-level statistics to guide their application. This is a topic for future research.

Other rewriting rules for CPL+ exist, such as the simplification and elimination of updates and pattern expressions, and can be found in [12].

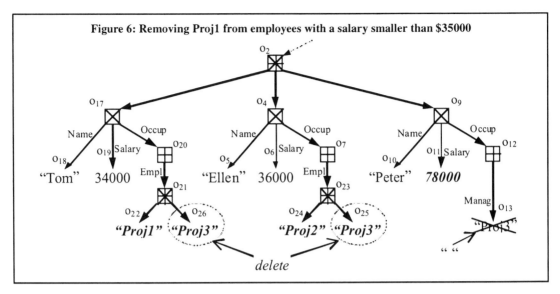

Figure 6: Removing Proj1 from employees with a salary smaller than $35000

CONCLUSIONS

This paper presents an update language and an execution model for complex value databases based on the functional query language CPL. We describe how updates in CPL+ are processed on a given database instance. We introduced two important techniques: *evaluation-on-demand* and *deferred deletion*. Evaluation-on-demand minimizes the number of object accesses for a given update. Deferred deletion is an efficient mechanism for providing old value semantics for variables bound within CPL+ updates. We introduce the notion of a *workspace* - the set of objects accessed or updated while processing an update, and we show how typical updates are processed and what workspace they have. Furthermore, we illustrate how CPL+ optimizations can reduce the workspace and lead to more efficient updates.

While the logical specification of updates in relational and deductive databases has been investigated (e.g. [7,16,2]), the design, implementation and optimization of update languages in object-oriented and complex value databases has received little attention (e.g [14]). Other techniques, such as monads [15], linear logic [3], and extensions of the lambda calculus [19], have been used for incorporating stateful functions in functional languages. In this paper, we introduce update as top-level language construct based on an imperative paradigm with notions of sequential execution, context, and side effects.

We implemented a prototype for CPL+ based on the execution model described in this paper. The set of optimization rules and the type inference algorithm described in [12] has been implemented. In [12], we also show that the cost of an update does not increase during optimization, except in certain cases.

Various interesting practical and theoretical problems remain to be investigated. Since CPL is currently being used for querying multiple, heterogeneous database systems [9], the issue of what updates across databases mean and how to optimize them has to be addressed. Lastly, CPL+ is a concise and optimizable algebra, which can be the basis for more user-friendly languages, such as OQL-like or visual update languages.

ACKNOWLEDGMENTS

*This research was supported in part by DOE DE-FG02-94-ER-61923 Sub 1, NSF BIR94-02292 PRIME, ARO AASERT DAAH04-93-G0129, and ARPA N00014-94-1-1086. We would also like to thank Peter Buneman for the original idea and Val Tannen for many helpful discussions.

BIBLIOGRAPHY

[1] S. Abiteboul and P. Kanellakis. Query languages for complex object databases. *SIGACT News*, 21(3):9-18, 1990.

[2] S. Abiteboul and V. Vianu. Datalog extensions for database queries and updates. *Journal of Computer and System Sciences*, 43(1):62-124, August 1991.

[3] S. Abramsky. Computational interpretation of linear logic. *Theoretical Computer Science*, 111:3-57, 1993.

[4] F. Bancilhon, S. Cluet, and C. Delobel. A query language for the O_2 object-oriented database system. In *Proceedings of 2nd International Workshop on Database Programming Languages*, pages 122-138. Morgan Kaufmann, 1989.

[5]   V. Breazu-Tannen, P. Buneman, and S. Naqvi. Structural recursion as a query language. In *Proceedings of 3rd International Workshop on Database Programming Languages*, Naphlion, Greece, pages 9-19. Morgan Kaufmann, August 1991. Also available as UPenn Technical Report MS-CIS-92-17.

[6]   Peter Buneman, Leonid Libkin, Dan Suciu, Val Tannen, and Limsoon Wong. Comprehension syntax, *SIGMOD Record*, 23(1):87-96, March 1994.

[7]   E. Bertino D. Montesi and M. Martelli. Transactions and updates in deductive databases. *IEEE Transactions on Knowledge and Data Engineering*, 9(5):784-797, 1997.

[8]   S.B. Davidson, C. Hara, and L. Popa. Querying an object-oriented database using {CPL}. In *Proceedings of the Brazilian Symposium on Databases*, October 1997.

[9]   Susan Davidson, Christian Overton, Val Tannen, and Limsoon Wong. Biokleisli: A digital library for biomedical researchers. *Journal of Digital Libraries*, 1(1), November 1996.

[10] C. Hara and S.B. Davidson. Inference rules for nested functional dependencies. Technical Report MS-CIS-98-19, University of Pennsylvania, June 1998.

[11] SQL, ISO. Standard 9075. *Information Processing Systems. Database Language SQL*, 1987.

[12] H. Liefke and S.B. Davidson. An execution model for {CPL+}. Technical Report MS-CIS-98-29, University of Pennsylvania, Philadelphia, August 1998.

[13] H. Liefke and S.B. Davidson. Updating complex value databases. Technical Report MS-CIS-98-06, University of Pennsylvania, Philadelphia, May 1998.

[14] R. Hull M. Doherty and M. Rupawalla. Structures for manipulating proposed updates in object-oriented databases. In *SIGMOD Conference*, pages 306-317, 1996.

[15] S. L. Peyton-Jones and P. Wadler. Imperative functional programming. In *Proceedings of 20'th ACM Symposium on Principles of Programming Languages*, Charlotte, North Carolina, January 1993.

[16] R. Reiter. On specifying database updates. *Journal of Logic Programming*, 25(1):53-91, 1995.

[17] John F. Roddick. Schema evolution in database systems - An annotated bibliography. *SIGMOD Record*, 21(4):35-40, December 1992.

[18] Andrea H. Skarra and Stanley B. Zdonik. Type evolution in an object oriented database. In Bruce Shriver and Peter Wegner, editors, *Research Directions in Object Oriented Programming*, pages 392-415. MIT Press, Cambridge, Massachusetts, 1987.

[19] J.C. Springer. *Implementation of Functional Languages with State*. PhD thesis, University of Illinois at Urbana-Champaign, 1996.

[20] P.W. Trinder. Comprehensions, a query notation for DBPLs. In *Proceedings of 3rd International Workshop on Database Programming Languages*, Nahplion, Greece, pages 49-62. Morgan Kaufmann, August 1991.

[21] P.W. Trinder and P.L. Wadler. Improving list comprehension database queries. In *Proceedings of TENCON'89* Bombay, India, pages 186-192, November 1989.

[22] Limsoon Wong. Querying Nested Collections. PhD thesis, University of Pennsylvania, August 1994. Available as University of Pennsylvania IRCS Report 94-09.

Supplementing Traditional Instructor-Led Instruction with Computer-Based Instruction in an Introductory Information Systems Course

Susan K. Lippert
Management Science Department, School of Business and Public Management, The George Washington University, Washington, DC 20052
(202) 994 - 6831 (o), (202) 994 - 4930 (f), lippert@gwu.edu

Mary J. Granger, Ph.D.
Management Science Department, School of Business and Public Management, The George Washington University, Washington, DC 20052
(202) 994 -7159 (o), (202) 994 - 4930 (f), granger@gwu.edu

Sharon R. Lydon
Management Science Department, School of Business and Public Management, The George Washington University, Washington, DC 20052
(202) 994 - 7375 (o), (202) 994 - 4930 (f), slydon@gwu.edu

ABSTRACT

Two popular techniques for teaching software productivity packages in a university environment are traditional hands-on instructor-led and self-paced computer-based instruction. Mastery of these packages is not seen as acquiring knowledge, but attaining a level of proficiency with a software package. Using computer-based instruction in conjunction with or in place of traditional instructor-led instruction, faculty teaching information systems are beginning to address the shift in the emphasis of the introductory information systems course from computer literacy to information literacy. This study uses an explanatory research design to examine the effectiveness of using computer-based as a supplement to traditional instructor-led. The outcomes from the instructor-led class of Spring 1998 and from the instructor-led/computer-based instruction class of Fall 1998 will be tested for significance.

INTRODUCTION

"Computer software training refers to the planned, structured, and formal means of delivering information about how to use a specific computer software application. Despite the overall improvement in computer skills in the workplace, computer software training continues to take a larger and larger portion of the human resource development budget as people struggle to keep their computer skills in pace with the rapid changes in computer technology" (Harp, Taylor and Satzinger 1998).

In a 1997 survey, employers identified computer skills required of recent university graduates (Davis 1997). Eighty-three percent of the respondents indicated that computer literacy were either important or very important in the hiring decision. Some of the desired skills include word processing, spreadsheet competency, graphics, presentation skills, database and a familiarity with Internet documents (Perry 1998). However, there is an ongoing debate on the appropriateness of teaching software productivity packages in a university. Mastery of these packages is not seen as acquiring knowledge, but attaining a level of proficiency with a software package. Additionally, the introductory information systems course in its present form is being replaced with a focus on information literacy rather than computer literacy (Khan 1997). Using self-paced computer-based instruction in conjunction with or in place of traditional instructor-led instruction, faculty teaching information systems are beginning to address this shift.

Two popular techniques for teaching software productivity packages in a university environment are traditional instructor-led and self-paced computer-based. Traditional instructor-led, often known as the lecture method, is perhaps the widest used of other instructional techniques. In a business environment, the lecture method is still the most popular, and it appears that this method will survive (Cohen 1988). Since 44% of Fortune 500 firms used self-paced computer-based instruction in 1990 (OTA 1990), it might be assumed that the percentage is higher today.

Computer-based training (CBT) is software enables the mastery of a skill; it need not be a computer skill, however, this paper focuses on the acquisition of software productivity skills. CBT is a modularized, self-contained, self-paced, interactive instruction (Fritz 1997). It is an effective method for developing conceptual and applied knowledge (Preston & Chappell 1990), and is usually a practical and lower-cost alternative for acquiring a level of proficiency with software productivity software. However, some training in computer usage may need to precede the use of CBT software.

Since CBT enables self-paced instruction, users are able to revisit parts of the training which they did not understand nor comprehend completely, repeat learning sequences requiring additional time or skip ahead through sections of known information. CBT is appropriate for use in group, classroom, or individual delivery settings, as stand-alone instruction or in conjunction with other training methods such as lectures. Since users can install CBT on their own machines either at work or at home, this method enables learners to complete their instruction on their own time and at their own pace. CBT software may also provide administration and off-line analysis of testing to aid in the evaluation of desired skill levels.

A 1995 study (Bowman et al 1995) found students using CBT to learn software skills performed as well as those with an instructor. However, in a 1998 study of licensed users (Harp, Taylor and Satzinger 1998), there was a preference for instructor-led training, but there is no evaluation of performance. In this study, both the traditional instructor-led and self-paced computer-based instruction were combined in an introductory information systems computer lab. As in previous semesters, this portion of the course concentrates on the mastery of web-based skills and software productivity skills, such as word processing, spreadsheet competency and presentation graphics. In order to compensate for different learning styles and the uneven skill levels of the students, computer-based software was included as part of the computer lab instruction. Students attend an instructor-led lab, and then CBT provides an opportunity for them to repeat unclear or difficult sections. Therefore, the responsibility for mastering the software is transferred from the instructor to the learner (Squires and McDougal 1981).

This study uses an explanatory research design to examine the effectiveness of using computer-based instruction as a supplement to traditional instructor-led instruction. For the student, the objective of the computer lab is mastery with the software applications. They complete homework assignments using each of the required skills and the grades on the individual tasks measure the student's proficiency level. The outcomes from the instructor-led class of Spring 1998 (control group) and from the instructor-led/CBT class of Fall 1998 (treatment group) will be tested for significance.

Research Question

The following question was asked in this study: Do students at a medium-sized university in the eastern United States who receive traditional hands-on instructor-led instruction supplemented with multimedia computer-based instruction tutorials and drill-and-practice achieve higher assignment grades (a performance measure) than students who receive only traditional hands-on instructor-led instruction.

Research Hypotheses

In view of the research question, six null hypotheses were advanced:

$H_{o,1}$: There is no difference in assignment grades between students receiving traditional hands-on instructor-led instruction and students receiving traditional hands-on instructor-led instruction plus multimedia computer-based instruction tutorials and drill-and-practice as a supplement.

$H_{o,2}$: There is no difference in Netscape assignment grades between students receiving traditional hands-on instructor-led instruction and students receiving traditional hands-on instructor-led instruction plus multimedia computer-based instruction tutorials and drill-and-practice as a supplement.

$H_{o,3}$: There is no difference in Windows assignment grades between students receiving traditional hands-on instructor-led instruction and students receiving traditional hands-on instructor-led instruction plus multimedia computer-based instruction tutorials and drill-and-practice as a supplement.

$H_{o,4}$: There is no difference in Word assignment grades between students receiving traditional hands-on instructor-led instruction and students receiving traditional hands-on instructor-led instruction plus multimedia computer-based instruction tutorials and drill-and-practice as a supplement.

$H_{o,5}$: There is no difference in Excel assignment grades between students receiving traditional hands-on instructor-led instruction and students receiving traditional hands-on instructor-led instruction plus multimedia computer-based instruction tutorials and drill-and-practice as a supplement.

$H_{0.6}$: There is no difference in PowerPoint assignment grades between students receiving traditional hands-on instructor-led instruction and students receiving traditional hands-on instructor-led instruction plus multimedia computer-based instruction tutorials and drill-and-practice as a supplement.

Subjects

Eighty-four undergraduate business students from a medium-sized university in the eastern United States participated in this study. Participants were obtained from four sections of a core business course in information systems. The average age of the subjects participating in the study and their prior computer experience will be determined. The number of females and males in the sample will be included. T-tests will be used to indicate differences between the subjects in terms of self-reported computer skills. The primary unit of analysis in this study is the group (Singleton, Straits, Straits, 1993).

Method

The computer laboratory meets for one two hour session each week across six weeks. Class sizes were limited to twenty-five students due to computer restrictions within the laboratory. Student assignment to laboratory sections occurred through a common university registration procedure. Each semester, students selected from one of five lab sessions that best fit their schedule. The same instructor taught the four lab sessions under study (two from spring 1998 and two from fall 1998). The instructor had previously taught the laboratory four times prior to the spring 1998 session.

Since students in different sections discuss course content, requirements, and expectations, to avoid compensatory rivalry among participants (Singleton, Straits, & Straits, 1993), control and treatment were not administered during the same semester. Data for control sections were collected in spring 1998 and for treatment sections in fall 1998.

To control for potential experimenter bias, an identical set of classroom protocols and procedures was followed by the instructor in each of the treatment sections. Lecture notes were followed very closely, and the same material in an identical sequence and form over the same time period was presented to the students in each class. Furthermore, the project assignments were identical for the four sections involved in the study. The primary difference between the sections was the use of the multimedia computer-based instruction as a supplement to the traditional hands-on instructor-led instruction.

Figure 1: Distribution of Participants			
	Date	Code	Number of Participants
Spring 1998	Tuesday	C1	21
	Friday	C2	21
Fall 1998	Tuesday	T1	24
	Friday	T2	18

This study consists of two groups:

a. Students receiving traditional hands-on instructor-led instruction, from this point forward known as the IL group (instructor-led group). This group, composed from spring 1998 students, is also the control.

b. Students receiving traditional hands-on instructor-led instruction supplemented with multimedia computer-based instruction, from this point forward known as the MS group (multimedia supplement group). This group, composed from fall 1998 students, is also the treatment.

Experimental Manipulation

The experimental manipulation involved the use of multimedia computer-based instruction tutorials, drill and practice checkpoints, and self-paced hands-on exercises. All students, in both the control and treatment groups, received traditional hands-on instructor-led instruction. Students in the treatment group complete self-paced multimedia computer-based instruction tutorials, drill and practice checkpoints, and self-paced hands-on exercises. All students complete project assignments. Figure 2 graphically depicts how both groups were handled. The experimental manipulation is repeated for each of the productivity tools taught in the following respective order: Netscape, Microsoft Windows, Microsoft Word, Microsoft Excel, Microsoft PowerPoint, and an integration exercise that integrates skills learned in each of the applications.

Students in the treatment sections (T1 and T2) completed an initial survey designed to collect demographic information, computer experience, and prior familiarity with the productivity tools employed in the experiment. Students in the control sections (C1 and C2) completed an e-mail version of the same survey ex post during the beginning of the fall 1998 semester. Five-point Likert-type scales were used to measure perception items. Three-point scales were used to measure computer experience.

At the onset of each class, students in all sections (both control and treatment) received traditional instructor-led instruction. A reference manual written expressly for this course was required reading for all students. Reading material from the reference manual on the topic was previously assigned and the students were asked to complete the

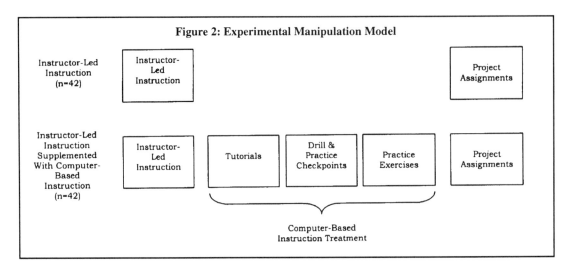

Figure 2: Experimental Manipulation Model

assigned readings prior to each class meeting. The objective of the lecture was to highlight the key concepts in the productivity package and provide students an opportunity to master relevant keystrokes through a step-by-step instructor-led example.

Participants in both the control and treatment sections completed a project assignment designed to challenge their ability to build upon skills learned during the instruction and explore additional concepts beyond the presented material. Since the study was conducted in a School of Business, all project assignments were developed to emulate business-type problems students may encounter. Students have one week to complete the project assignment. The following week, the instructor begins lecturing on the next productivity application. Figure 3 provides a schedule of the administration of the lecture and project assignments over the six-week period.

Participants in the treatment received the same traditional instruction from the instructor as those students in the control group. Students in the treatment group completed the computer-based instruction supplement either on a university computer or a personal computer. Projects were the same for both groups. The treatment consisted of three phases:

1. *Step-by-step tutorials* in which the CBI instructed students on the productivity tool's concepts and keystrokes;
2. *Checkpoints* where students were quizzed on concepts learned in the tutorials by the CBI through short answer questions or fill-in-the-blank responses; and
3. A short 5-10 minute *practice exercise* selected by the instructor.

The lecture instructor was available during weekly office hours to discuss content or process issues either relating to the lecture or to the computer-based instruction.

Figure 3: Instruction Sequence and Project Assignments		
	Spring 1998	Fall 1998
Netscape		
Instructor-led Instruction	X	X
Computer-Based Instruction		X
Project Assignment	X	X
CBI Evaluation		X
Microsoft Windows 95		
Instructor-led Instruction	X	X
Computer-Based Instruction		X
Project Assignment	X	X
CBI Evaluation		X
Microsoft Word		
Instructor-led Instruction	X	X
Computer-Based Instruction		X
Project Assignment	X	X
CBI Evaluation		X
Microsoft Excel		
Instructor-led Instruction	X	X
Computer-Based Instruction		X
Project Assignment	X	X
CBI Evaluation		X
Microsoft PowerPoint		
Instructor-led Instruction	X	X
Computer-Based Instruction		X
Project Assignment	X	X
CBI Evaluation		X
Integration of All Applications		
Instructor-led Instruction	X	X
Project Assignment	X	X

Data Collection

Data for this study were collected at several intervals. Students in the treatment sections (T1 and T2) completed an initial survey designed to collect demographic information, self-reported computer experience, and self-reported prior familiarity with the productivity tools employed in the experiment. Students in the control sections (C1 and C2) completed an e-mail version of the same survey ex post during the beginning of the fall 1998 semester. Five-point Likert-type scales were used to measure perception items. Three-point scales were used to measure computer experience.

The instructor determines project assignment grades. A standardized scoring instrument was developed for each project assignment and followed very closely across all sections to ensure grading consistency. The same scoring instrument and point distribution was used to evaluate project assignments for all sections (T1, T2, C1, and C2).

The CBI evaluation instrument[1] asked students to evaluate the CBI over seven measures (completion time, content, instruction quality, technical quality, motivation, ease of use, overall product). All items were measured on five-point Likert-type scales. The same questionnaire was used after each treatment in order to evaluate the participants' perceptions of that productivity tool.

Completion time assessed the students' perception of time required to complete each of the treatment components (tutorials, checkpoints, and practice exercises). The item was assessed using a five-point Likert-type scale (1=too little, 3=about right, 5=too much). The remaining six measures included: content (consisting of eight items such as appropriate for intended student population, responses to student errors helpful and non-judgmental); instructional quality (consisting of twelve items including learner control of rate and sequence of presentation and review; technical quality (consisting of 14 items including product stability, quality of various media); motivation (consisting of five items including motivation to learn more and effectiveness of feedback); ease of use (consisting of fifteen items including clarity of directions, ability for self-pacing, and error corrections); and an overall product score. The five items (content, instructional quality, technical quality, motivation, and ease of use) were assessed using five-point Likert-type scale (1=strongly agree, 2=agree, 3=disagree, 4=strongly disagree, 5=not applicable).

The questionnaire also contained open-ended questions eliciting the participants' comments on strengths and weaknesses of the CBI compared to the instructor-led instruction.

Figure 4: Data Collection Methods
CBI Checkpoints and Practice Exercise Grades are collected but not included as part of this study.

	Spring 1998	Fall 1998
Initial Questionnaire	E-mail Questionnaire (Sent Fall 1998)	Paper Questionnaire (Beginning of semester)
CBI CheckPoints	CBI Validated by Instructor	CBI Validated by Instructor
Practice Exercise Grades	Assigned by Instructor	Assigned by Instructor
Project Assignment Grades	Assigned by Instructor	Assigned by Instructor
CBI Evaluation	Questionnaire (after each treatment)	Questionnaire (after each treatment)

Data Analysis

The process of data analysis enables the researcher to evaluate the hypotheses in light of the data collected, accept or reject the hypotheses, and revise decisions in light of new information (Meier & Brudney, 1993). All hypotheses are evaluated at a .05 significance level.

Descriptive statistics including the mean and standard deviations for the project assignment grades will be evaluated. T-tests will be used to indicate differences between the subjects in terms of self-reported computer skills. Independent sample t-tests will be used accept or reject the hypotheses. There may be a correlation between prior computer experience and student performance (project assignment grades). However, it will not be controlled for if the correlation is non-significant. However, if the correlation is significant, an analysis of covariance will be performed where prior computer experience is the covariate. If outcomes are correlated, an artificially high effect will result. If there is overall significance, separate analysis of variances will be run to determine which individual impact was significant. If the hypotheses appear to have an interaction effect resulting from multiple hypotheses, a Bonferoni test will be used to separate the effects.

SUMMARY

Data collection will be completed by the end of the semester. Preliminary results and anecdotal evidence

Figure 5: Statistical Tests		
	Control Group	Treatment Group
Descriptive Statistics Mean Standard Deviation	 Arithmetic Average Distribution of Grades	 Arithmetic Average Distribution of Grades
T-test	Comparability of Groups	
Independent Sample T-test	Significance test to accept or reject hypotheses	
Analysis of Covariance	To control for prior computer experience, if variables are correlated	
Bonferoni Test	To control for interaction effect between multiple hypotheses, if effect occurs	

indicate student grades are higher for those receiving instructor-led instruction supplemented with computer-assisted instruction (exact applications and significance not yet available). Students with a high proficiency level with the software applications prefer a single instruction method. Students with less computer experience indicate a preference to practice difficult or unknown skills at their own pace, on their own time, outside the realm of the traditional classroom environment. Instructor feedback indicates that students in the treatment group asked questions throughout the instruction timeframe rather than wait until the last minute as typical of their control group counterparts. The small sample size (N=84) presents a limitation to this study. Since true randomization was not a possibility in this university environment, the study's generalizability is limited.

FUTURE

Implications for this research affect both university instruction and corporate training. A 1996 ASTD survey of major corporations' training practices indicates that over 70% of training were instructor-led while only 9% were delivered through CBT. Harp, Taylor, and Satzinger (1998) found that overall preference for instructor-led training over computer-based training was not statistically significant, which they concluded implies that CBT may be a lower-cost substitute for instructor-led training.

Although training students to use the software packages is the development of a *skill*, where the emphasis is on *skill* rather than acquisition of *knowledge*, universities continue to provide productivity software instruction. This focuses on *skill* development rather than *problem-solving* or *decision-making* issues. The undergraduate introductory information systems course is a prerequisite to others in the curriculum. Currently the university is considering the use of computer-based instruction in place of the instructor-led computer laboratory. The instructor-led laboratory will then be able to focus on the *use* of these productivity tools for business applications and *decision making* rather than the acquisition of the *skill*. As a first step in this transition, an aim of this study is to assess student performance in mastering productivity skills through the use of computer-based instruction as a supplement to traditional instructor led instruction[1].

REFERENCES

American Society for Training and Development Benchmarking Forum. (1996). *Current Industry Statistics 1996 Training Statistics*. [Electronic data file]. Alexandria, VA: American Society for Training and Development. Available: www.astd.org.

Bowman, B.J.; Grupe, F.H., & Simkin, M.G. 1995. Teaching End-User Applications With Computer-Based Training: Theory and An Empirical Investigation, *Journal of End User Computing*, 7(2), (April 1, 1995), 12-18.

Campbell, D.T. and Stanley, J.C. *Experimental and Quasi-Experimental Design for Research*, Chicago: Rand McNally, 1963.

Cohen, D.J. 1988. Training Methods During the Last 25 Years: A Review and Survey. Published in the *Proceedings* of the Eastern Academy of Management.

Davis, P. 1997. What Computer Skills Do Employers Expect From Recent College Graduates?, *T.H.E. Journal*, 25(2), (September 1, 1997), 74-78.

Fritz, M. 1997. Is Web-Based Training New Hype In Old Wineskins?, *E-media Professional*, 10(6), 69-71.

Harp, C.G, Taylor, S.C., & Satzinger, J.W. 1998. Computer Training and Individual Differences: When Method Matters, *Human Resource Development Quarterly*, 9(3), 271-283.

Heller, R.S. 1991. Evaluating Software: A Review of the Options, *Computers Education*, 17(4), 285-291.

Khan, M.B. 1997. Changing Computer Skills of Incoming Undergraduate Business Majors, *Journal of Educational Technology Systems*, 26(1), 55-66.

Meier, K.J. and Brudney, J.L. *Applied Statistics for Public Administration*, 3rd ed., Fort Worth: Harcourt Brace College Publishers, 1993.

NCET (1992) Choosing and Using Portable Computers, Coventry, National Council for Educational Technology.

Perry, W.R. 1998. What Software Skills Do Employers Want Their Employees To Possess?, *Business Education Forum*, 52, (February 1998), 35-38.

Preston, J.C. & Chappell, K.E. 1990. Teaching Managers Leadership, *Leadership & Organization Development Journal*, 11(5), 11-16.

Singleton, R.A, Jr.; Straits, B.C.; and Straits, M.M. *Approaches to Social Research*, 2nd Ed, Oxford, Oxford University Press, 1993.

Squires, D., and McDougall, A. (1994) *Choosing and Using Educational Software: A Teacher's Guide*. London: The Falmer Press.

U.S. Congress, Office of Technology Assessment. *Power On! New Tools for Teaching and Learning*. OTA SET-379. Washington D.C. (U.S, Government Printing Office 1988).

U.S. Congress, Office of Technology Assessment. *Worker Training: Competing in the New International Economy*. OTA-ITE-457. Washington, D.C. (U.S. Government Printing Office, September, 1990).

ENDNOTES

1 The CAI evaluation instrument was created using: U.S. Congress, Office of Technology Assessment. *Power On! New Tools for Teaching and Learning*. OTA SET-379. Washington D.C. (U.S, Government Printing Office 1988); Heller, R.S. 1991. Evaluating Software: A Review of the Options, *Computers Education*, 17(4), 285-291; TECC and California Library Media Consortium for Classroom Evaluation of Microcomputer Courseware; and NCTM Software Evaluation Checklist.

Method Support for Developing Evaluation Frameworks for CASE Tool Evaluation

Björn Lundell
Department of Computer Science, University of Skövde, SWEDEN
email: bjorn@ida.his.se
Fax: +46 500 464725 Phone: +46 500 464600

Brian Lings
Department of Computer Science, University of Exeter, UK
email: brian@dcs.exeter.ac.uk

Per-Ola Gustafsson
Skövde Systemutveckling AB, Skövde, SWEDEN
email: per-ola.gustafsson@swipnet.se

ABSTRACT

Whatever CASE tools are developed to support database applications development, the process of tool selection will continue to be a major factor influencing successful adoption. In this paper we consider the necessary organisational preparation for CASE tool selection, describing a method for the development of an evaluation framework which is based on application requirements. The proposed method offers organisations considering CASE tool adoption an important complement to current practice, as exemplified in the 1995 ISO standard for CASE tool evaluation. We report on a field study which exemplifies the use of this method in an organisational setting.

Keywords: CASE tool evaluation, Evaluation framework, Empirical methods, Standards, Field study

INTRODUCTION

Huff *et al.* (1992) claim that the vendor's price of a CASE tool represents only a small portion of the true adoption cost of CASE (p. 45) and there are documented cases in which difficulties in initial evaluation have led to bad experiences which cause organisations to be wary (e.g. McComb, 1994).

The ISO standard for CASE-tool evaluation and selection (ISO, 1995) (hereafter referred to as the standard) provides organisations that intend to adopt CASE tools (p. 1) with guidance on identifying organisational requirements for CASE tools (p. 1). The scope of the standard is broader than this, in that it also provides support for tasks that are to be undertaken at a later stage in an evaluation effort.

In this paper, we propose a method for identifying key factors which are to be used for organisational evaluation of CASE tools. The proposed method assists an organisation in the important task of establishing an evaluation framework, which is widely accepted as a necessary pre-requisite for any CASE tool evaluation effort. Essentially, the method addresses what to measure, as a necessary complement to current practice of CASE tool evaluation (typified by the standard) which, in our view, is more focused on how to measure. Subsequent aspects of evaluation covered in the standard are not of relevance here, since we are proposing a method which aims to support the establishment of an evaluation framework which is based on organisational requirements for CASE tools.

The underlying methodology we have adopted as a foundation for the method outlined here is presented and analysed in Lundell and Lings (1998). Below, we exemplify the method through a field study in which it is applied by evolving a partial framework which is then used in a pilot evaluation of two commercial CASE-tools.

The Problem of CASE evaluation

Many CASE-tool characteristics have been suggested in the CASE literature as potentially relevant to an organisation's evaluation framework. Some authors suggest CASE-tool characteristics which are rather broad, while others' characteristics are described at a more detailed level of abstraction (e.g. Dixon, 1992, suggests around 400 different CASE-tool characteristics). To identify a definitive set of characteristics whilst maintaining a common understanding among all different stakeholders involved is a difficult (we would say impossible) task. The standard acknowledges this difficulty (ISO, 1995, p. 25).

The context: Methodology

Much has been written on the issue of how organisations should undertake an evaluation effort in a CASE adoption process. While some of these contributions are *methodologically* oriented (e.g. Bubenko, 1988) other contributions are more *method* oriented (e.g. the standard). For the purpose of this paper, we classify contributions on two levels (see Figure 1).

Pre- CASE tool usage refers to activities that takes place before the tool being evaluated actually is adopted and in real use in the organisational setting. Such activities include any organisational effort with respect to selection of CASE tools. *Post-* CASE tool usage refers to reported experiences from actual adoption and use of CASE technology. Such evaluation is therefore reflective (e.g. Orlikowski, 1993).

A *context-free* evaluation is characterised by being technology centred. Tools are evaluated against a (largely fixed) pre-determined framework, and the evaluation can take place anywhere. We classify the standard as largely promoting context-free evaluation, although it does acknowledge (without methodological support) the need to vary the framework in response to organisational setting. By contrast, an evaluation *within an organisational setting* assumes support for framework development in response to specific application requirements in the context of actual or planned development methods.

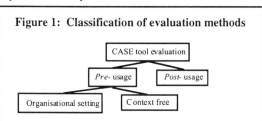

Figure 1: Classification of evaluation methods

Methodologically, it is possible to identify a preponderance of quantitative methods for context-free evaluation, and a dominance of qualitative methods within organisational settings. The latter almost exclusively concern post-usage evaluations. We classify our own method for CASE tool evaluation as *pre*-usage, *within an organisational setting*.

The Organisational Setting

In this section we provide some background information on the IS development company Skövde Systemutveckling AB (hereafter referred to as SSAB), in order to characterise the organisational setting of the field-study.

SSAB has developed a system (CLARA) to support the management of non-conforming product in manufacturing. The customer, Collins & Aikman Inc., is an international corporation which is a supplier to the car-industry. Using an iterative methodology, the system was developed in close cooperation with Collins & Aikman Automotive Systems Skara (hereafter referred to as CAS), which is one of this company's plants.

The first version of the system has been in use at CAS since May 1995, and successively evolved as new requirements have been identified. Some of these requirements originate within the car-industry in general (e.g. as expressed in QS9000), while others originate from the specific car-industries that are customers of CAS. Other requirements are identified within CAS, as a result of analysis by different stakeholders within the organisation, in order to achieve competitor advantage. Yet others are initiated by SSAB, and can be viewed in terms of product enhancement. The current version has about 20 different windows, 25 software modules, and approximately 20000 (Delphi) lines of underlying application code, and is offered for use with several commercial DBMSs.

The nature of the problem being addressed can be characterised as highly dynamic, since it is important for CAS to satisfy changing requirements imposed by the car industry. From SSAB's perspective, the system to be engineered is therefore exposed to an evolving set of requirements which originate in different organisations (SSAB, CAS, and the car-industry) and different standards (primarily ISO9001 and QS9000).

Overview of the paper

The rest of this paper is organised as follows. First, we introduce our method for CASE tool evaluation, which includes a brief presentation of its methodological underpinnings together with an indication of both process and deliverables. We also set the scene for the field-study (2). This is followed by an illustration of the use of our method, and its different phases, in a field-study (3). Thereafter, we analyse the outcome of the field-study, and discuss our findings (4). Finally, we present our conclusions (5).

METHOD

The first generative phase of the method to be reported is presented and analysed in Lundell and Lings (1998). We here identify and describe a second phase, which acknowledges the importance of prototyping within the overall development of an evaluation framework.

Underlying methodology

Our method for CASE-tool evaluation is theoretically underpinned by a qualitative research methodology, it being informed by Grounded Theory (Glaser and Strauss, 1967). An important characteristics of the approach is its strong emphasis on the generative phase, in which an emerging framework is closely linked with its underlying data. During the generative phase the process aims to reach a consensus among stakeholders so that concepts are shared. A pilot evaluation of commercial CASE-tools provides, from this perspective, further data for continued framework development. This process will be illustrated in the field-study (see section 3).

Method output

In applying the method, an organisation is attempting to generate a framework for an evaluation of CASE tools as they might satisfy organisational and application requirements. The framework will consist of a set of critical factors identified for the organisation. In order to capture the precise understanding within the organisation of these factors, they should be fully characterised: a second outcome of the method. Unlike the standard, we do not assume that these characterisations need to be in the form of agreed and itemised subcharacteristics. This may be the outcome of a particular application of the method, but (as in the field study reported) they may equally be in the form of rich descriptions.

Outline of method: Phases

The generation of an evaluation framework is an evolutionary process involving data collection, coding and analysis (see Figure 2). There is no sequential nature to these activities; each can affect (and trigger) the others so that, in essence, all activities are going on together. This is characteristic of qualitative methodologies.

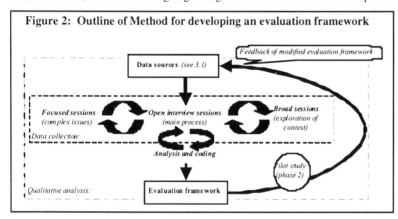

Figure 2: Outline of Method for developing an evaluation framework

In practice, we identify two phases to the method because we wish the resulting evaluation framework to be informed both by organisational requirements and by current CASE technology. The second phase is entered when an emerging framework is used in a pilot evaluation of CASE tools, the pilot itself being used to refine the framework and then as a data source when cycling back to phase 1. The overall process stops when the emerging framework is considered stable and effective.

Goal and scope of the field study

For the purposes of the field study, the method was abridged so that a pilot evaluation framework could be developed. This was done during phase 1. Instead of continuing data collection and coding until a full and stable evaluation framework had emerged, the goal was to proceed initially until at least two key factors had been agreed. Data collection and analysis then proceeded concentrating on issues relevant to these factors. The resulting "pilot" framework could then be used in phase 2 in the evaluation of two commercial CASE tools. This allowed us to study refinement in the context of available technology.

FIELD STUDY

In the field study one of the developers of the method took the role of 'analyst', responsible for developing the evaluation framework. A second author, now a senior systems developer at SSAB, represented the organisation in the role of 'interviewee'.

Background of interviewee

It is of significance in the field study that the interviewee was versed in qualitative methods. He was earlier responsible for IS development in a number of projects at the Swedish Social Insurance Organisation, Försäkringskassan, and was involved in the introduction of Grounded Theory in one of its regional projects during 1990-93 (Försäkringskassan, 1993).

Phase 1: Data collection and analysis

During phase 1 of the field study, the analyst searches for indications of patterns in the available underlying data, aiming to characterise factors for the evolving evaluation framework. A number of different sources were available for· the study, though not all were used in the pilot. Firstly, internal documents from the development organisation were provided, including: annotations, internal reports (including previous experiences of CASE-tool adoption), requirements specifications, various kinds of manuals, prototypes and implemented systems (both beta- and delivered systems). Secondly, public sources that address CASE-tool adoption were collected, such as the standard, books and reports.

Data collection and analysis was performed over six half day sessions in the organisational setting. Before the first session, the company provided the analyst with some organisational documents aiming to provide a general background.

At each session, an open interview format was used in the data collection process. However, these were interrupted with complementary special sessions. Some of these were more focused, with both the analyst and the interviewee concentrating on a single issue, perhaps in the form of a concrete example. Others were more relaxed, with the analyst deliberately allowing the session to be very broad, sometimes thereby facilitating a breakthrough in understanding and clarification of diffuse concepts. The use of more relaxed sessions was considered a useful complement to the rather exhaustive two-way dialogue. It is also our opinion that shifting both the level of abstraction and focus of the data collection process during ongoing sessions helped to avoid the pitfall of over-simplification in defining the framework for evaluation.

Before most (not all) interview sessions an agenda was prepared by the analyst in the form of a checklist of issues thought to be significant before the session. Such an agenda was always kept hidden from the interviewee and was not allowed to dominate discussion; in some cases it was even abandoned during a session.

The early sessions focused on the problem to be solved by SSAB and the requirements for that problem, as expressed by SSAB's analysis of the organisational situation at CAS. CASE-related issues were very much in the background at this stage, since it was believed that an in-depth understanding of the problem to be solved needed much more than a study of requirements as expressed by the interviewee:

'The organisational way of working within this area implies a set of routines, approaches, techniques, etc. to solve these problems. These constitute a basis for the successive development of the IS. Over time, as the systems are used, the organisational routines are improved. Furthermore, again, over time the IS and the routines will gradually be 'integrated' in the evolving process. Roughly, you could think of it as a chicken and egg situation.'

Ideally, CASE-tools will provide support for future development, for which organisational requirements are vague and gradually evolving. Such needs are closely related to expectations and attitudes towards the scope for tasks to be assisted by the tool. A good example of this concerns SSAB's requirement for 'traceability', which was revealed in successive interviews to contain many facets. For example, with respect to traceability of requirements, it became clear that the organisation requested support for traceability not only for design and modelling activities, but also for the very early phases of analysis - prior to requirements specification (something which the standard's set of characteristics does not address).

In fact, it can be argued that SSAB's requirements for traceability do not fit well with how that particular CASE-tool feature is considered in the standard. It emerged from in-depth sessions that the interviewee considered transparency to be a special form of traceability, and used the term when appropriate, as in the following clarification:

'By transparency I also mean that the tool should support various kinds of "intelligent" assistance with interlinking concepts from various documents, models and representations, to thereby hopefully get a deeper understanding of how various things are related to each other ... I think it is important to have support both in the very early phases, even if there is a very tentative idea of what the requirement will look like later on, as well as for the massive amount of design and implementation oriented representations'

When comparing SSAB's requirements for traceability with the standard's pre-structured set of characteristics, a number of mismatches can be identified. For example, the standard refers to traceability in the characteristic 'Specification Traceability Analysis' (ISO, 1995, p. 33), as part of the verification process: 'Analyses normally address information from the level of requirements specification through design data.' This omits consideration of traceability between concepts, which is required by SSAB even when using very tentative representations and models prior to fixing the requirements specification. The standard does not cover such aspects, but recommends augmentation for such situations (ISO, 1995, p. 25).

Analysis revealed a number of features relevant to SSAB. The evaluation criteria eventually chosen for the pilot represent critical features, aspects of which had led to an earlier decision not to use a commercial CASE-tool from inception:

• Design transformations (especially logical database design) with preserved semantics (i.e. support for a 'true two-

way mapping' between layers)
- Maintenance of (conceptual and implementation oriented) data models
- Transparency between models or parts of models, both at the schema and instance level.

Other factors included: version management; keeping track of artificial key generation; and generation of DDL-code for the latest version of Oracle (an absolute requirement, but one needing interpretation with respect to specifying acceptable conformance delays).

Partial framework for pilot study

Although the method assumes continuation until the emergent criteria are stable, for the pilot study the three critical factors identified above were selected for refinement. Below, we summarise the outcome of this refinement by describing the characteristics identified with each.

Design transformations:

With respect to database design, many CASE-tools provide support for some variation of the ER model, to be used in the conceptual database design phase, and its transformation into an implementation oriented model, typically SQL. Besides many approaches for the task of transforming a conceptual data model into an implementation oriented model for a target DBMS (forward engineering), there also exist many approaches for the reverse engineering process, in which a conceptual data model is extracted from an implementation oriented data model. Many modern CASE-tools provide support for both the forward and reverse engineering processes.

SSAB requires a two-way mapping between the conceptual data model and the SQL-level which is *information preserving* (Fahrner and Vossen, 1995). Furthermore, it must be possible to customise (or control) the forward generation, due to implicit needs from the use of other tools, such as reporting tools by which staff at CAS access (parts of) the underlying database, as well as other legacy MISs. This implies that SSAB requires 'assisted', and not 'automated' design transformation support from the CASE-tool.

It may be argued that changes in the model should not be allowed at the SQL-level, i.e. all changes should be done at the conceptual level followed by a 'regeneration', or a maintenance activity provided by the tool at the conceptual level. For the situation in the field-study, legacy requirements on the implemented system make this inappropriate.

Transparency:

The interviewee from SSAB considered *transparency* to be a special form of *traceability*, and used the term when appropriate. By transparency we refer to any kind of functionality that assists both the CASE-tool user and the stakeholder to *explore* and *perceive* various inter-related concepts kept in different models, possibly at different levels of abstraction. It is important to clarify that this aspect of CASE-tool functionality was considered important from SSAB's perspective, in that parts of the representation kept in the CASE-tool internal data would be to facilitate external validation. SSAB also had a specific requirement for using populated models.

Maintenance:

The efforts required for SSAB's maintenance of the system are significant. The nature of SSAB's chosen development process can, so far, be characterised as 'evolutionary' in that the system has been developed in close relationship with the customer. Given the situational conditions under which this system has been developed, SSAB considers such an approach necessary in order to be able to achieve a good resulting product. Although there are benefits regarding the resulting product the evolutionary development process has had negative implications in terms of maintenance. Also, new requirements are successively being placed on the system to be engineered, especially from within the car industry. SSAB attempt to 'maximise' flexibility in the solution through their choice of data (Moody and Shanks, 1994).

That the CASE-tool provides an adequate level of abstraction for expressing the conceptual schema, from which the underlying database structure should be generated, is an important aspect of maintenance. It was established that the tools should support (some variation of) the Information Engineering notation, as it was judged in SSAB to have an adequate level of abstraction from a designer's perspective and likely to be supported in many CASE tools.

SSAB's requirement for maintenance includes *information preservation* in the design transformation *over time*. Given a truly dynamic specification, this is related to what has been discussed by Wieringa (1996):

'Product evolution by updating the product specification requires at least modifyability of the specification itself, but in addition, it requires traceability of the specification in the forward and backwards directions' (p. 78)

Phase 2: pilot evaluation

Among the platforms on which the system is currently being offered, the Paradox platform has the 'weakest' expressive power and so was selected for this analysis. Two popular CASE-tools were chosen for the pilot evaluation: PowerDesigner 6.1 DataArchitect (Sybase Inc.) and ERwin3.5 (Logic Works Inc.), hereafter referred to as *P* and *E*.

Design transformations:

We applied the reverse engineering functionality provided in *P*, using ODBC to access the existing Paradox version of CLARA. In the underlying database, each entity is transformed to an individual relation except the three entities 'Anmärkning', 'Individuell anmärkning' and 'Huvudaktivitet'; these are all transformed to the single relation 'Anmarkning' for legacy reasons. The resulting schema from this transformation was *significantly* different from the operational one (shown in Figure 3).

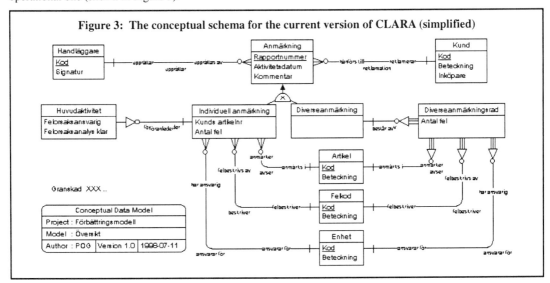

Figure 3: The conceptual schema for the current version of CLARA (simplified)

We found a number of unexpected (and incorrect) transformations:

- for several foreign keys that existed in the underlying database. During the reverse engineering process, they could not be identified and so resulted in 'dangling' entities. Strangely, *some* foreign keys were correctly identified by the tool. For example, the relationship from 'anmärkning' to 'felkod' was correctly identified, while the relationship from 'anmärkning' to 'artikel' could not be identified.

- which identified a relationship at the conceptual level that does not exist in the underlying database. The transformation draws a one-to-one relationship in the conceptual schema between two entities ('felkod' and 'handläggare') which does not have a relationship in the underlying database (other than via yet other entities).

Other results were more understandable due to the semantically 'poor' implementation schema. In particular, the conceptual schema produced from the transformation has no grouping of entities in relations, lacks super-/sub types (the underlying database contains no 'clue' which the tool can use), lacks a participation constraint in one-to-many relationships (interpreted as 'optional'), lacks role names, and has a layout of the schema which differs significantly from the one shown in Figure 3.

No additional meta-data or user input was provided to guide the reverse engineering process, such as availability of all keys and inclusion dependencies, a set of functional dependencies, or a database instance (Fahrner and Vossen, 1995, p. 235 (table 4)). In our understanding of *P* the method used for transformation can not take user input, and is only guided by what is available (in terms of keys) in the underlying DBMS.

Due to the unexpected result with the reverse engineering process, it was decided that a subset of the existing CLARA conceptual schema should be drawn in each tool manually to constitute a starting point for further analysis of forward engineering.

Using *P* and Paradox, the IE schema was forward engineered to generate a Paradox database using ODBC. Unfortunately, we did not manage to generate any foreign keys in the Paradox database. Instead, these keys appeared as secondary indexes. Since *P* managed to identify some such definitions during the reverse engineering process, we found this lack of support somewhat surprising. After reverse engineering, forward engineering resulted in the renaming of some attributes; which ones it was not possible to predict. Such renaming is problematic for existing application programs. An additional, more serious problem, is that renaming even affects the attributes that belong to foreign keys that *are* correctly identified during the reverse engineering process.

Both tools assist forward engineering of the IE schema to scripts for generating Paradox databases, and SQL-schemes for Oracle version 8. Neither of the tools supported designer led design decisions. For the forward engineering process, this lack meant that neither tool was able to produce the existing CLARA. With the *P* tool, we could not transform the three entities 'Anmärkning', 'Individuell anmärkning' and 'Huvudaktivitet' into one single relation ('Anmarkning') at the SQL-level. However, we managed to transform the two entities 'Anmärkning' and 'Individuell anmärkning' into one relation ('Anmarkning'). With the *E* tool the same three entities were transformed into three distinct entities.

The use of conceptual names in the Swedish language was found to be a problem with *E*. Since we used the Swedish national characters for entities and attributes at the conceptual level, the resulting SQL-code was incorrect since no alternative naming (at different levels of abstraction) were found in the tool. *P* supported this by using an associated 'code' (that is unique within the tool and only uses the characters A-Z) for each conceptual name, using (system generated) unique naming when necessary. However, it was found relatively easy to alter codes that were found inappropriate at the SQL-level, after a manual inspection of the resulting SQL-schema. The designer's 'control' over the resulting names was found to be sufficient.

Transparency:

Using the IE notation in both tools, neither provided support for natural language paraphrasing, or populated models (i.e. to explore the models using 'instance' data as a complement to the model). When considering Moody's (1996) claim that '[a] number of CASE tools' (p. 228) support such facilities, this finding was somewhat disappointing. However, when the conceptual models are designed and each role-name therein is used, the reporting facilities in both tools was found to be rather impressive.

The *P* tool's ability to generate html-documents was found to be a useful facility, especially if people are geographically distributed. The *E* tool's ability to generate many different types of reports also impressed. However, both tools seemed focused on providing detailed and extensive reporting on implementation oriented aspects.

Maintenance:

Maintenance of the development information includes both maintenance of the conceptual (part of) the specification, and the design oriented (part of) the specification. It also includes maintenance of design decisions made during design transformations. Other related factors include the maintenance and preservation of internal consistency in the complex development solution.

Since both tools suffered in terms of the generated SQL-schema, a manual change has to be performed (either in the SQL-script before it is being generated, or directly on the schema in the DBMS). However, since information of such changes cannot be 'known' to any of the tools, the development information (as kept in the tools) does not exactly reflect the structure of the underlying system. Consequently, annotations and notes must be attached to the models in both tools.

Refining the framework

In order to facilitate a two-way mapping, each design decision made by the designer during the design transformation process must consequently be maintained. Both tools support the 'attachment' of various notes and annotations to the development information. It is possible to annotate both for schemes and various individual concepts (such as entities, relationships, attributes and domains). For both design transformation and transparency therefore the framework was refined to include the characteristic that notes and annotations be 'attachable' to any concept, or set of concepts which are part of a model. Furthermore, it should also be possible to attach such annotations to a design transformation provided by the CASE-tool. For example, if the developer wants to add a database-trigger to the SQL-schema which has been generated by the CASE-tool (using a forward engineering functionality), it must be possible to somehow link this database trigger with the conceptual level.

In practice, it proved rather difficult to obtain a good overview of all such information. Our impression is that both tools treat this contextual information as a 'supplement' to the formal part of the development information which is manipulated with the tools. For example, each such annotation is 'attached' in each model (see for example 'Granskad' in Figure 3) and is not a first class object. If the designer deletes a relationship at the conceptual level, all annotation previously made for that particular relationship will be lost without warning. A characteristic concerning annotations as first class objects was therefore added.

ANALYSIS

When applying the method, the investigator needs to be experienced with qualitative techniques, but the interviewee need only be sympathetic to the special form of data collection being used during phase 1 of the method; something we would claim is true for any method. If there is no belief in a method, it is unlikely to help.

Phase 2 of the study is a more traditional, in-depth exploration of the support for a few organisational factors when assessing commercial CASE-tools. The benefit of the original phase of empirically grounded factors was brought home to the company when they reviewed the guidance in the ISO standard. It was clear that the level of abstraction in the standard's definitions of its criteria, and its structure was not sympathetic to their perceived needs. Consequently, it would have been very difficult to use without some clear refinement method.

For example, the subcharacteristic 'Construction' (p. 29), which is part of the characteristic 'Development process' (p. 26), has two atomic subcharacteristics which, in a database context, are defined at significantly different levels of abstraction. We consider, in the context of this study, the atomic subcharacteristic Database Schema Generation:

'attributes relating to its ability to generate database schema based upon user-supplied information' (p. 29)

to be part of another atomic sub-characteristic, Code generation, within the same subcharacteristic:

'attributes relating to its ability to generate code in one or more specific languages based upon designing data available to CASE tool.' (p. 29)

'NOTE 2 - Typical code generation capabilities include general purpose code generation, database generation, query generation, screen display/menu generation. Another form of code generation is the direct generation of executable code.' (p. 29)

We believe this is illustrative of the difficulty with providing an a-priori structure. This is especially difficult when we 'instantiate' the general structure with an empirically grounded interpretation (such as data from our field study).

The difficulty of deciding when to consider an evaluation framework fully developed and proceed to later stages of an evaluation effort, is difficult, as with termination of any analysis phase (see Bubenko, 1998).

In the field study reported, we have illustrated the two phases of the method. When developing a full evaluation framework for an organisation, it is possible that one would need to go through several cycles. From the method's perspective, phase 2 can essentially be characterised as a (very) special form of data source, to be used as input when refining the evolving evaluation framework. As can be seen in the overview of the method (Figure 2) it is not the method's intention that one should start with an 'empty' evaluation framework when initiating phase 2, because in such a situation one would lose the empirical grounding. In this respect, phase 2 in our method is different from a pure 'laboratory experiment'.

Finally, having concentrated on a few 'key factors' which are considered relevant to the organisational setting, we claim that this situation has a potential for a high level of external validity. This has emboldened us to highlight two key features in the conclusions as having implications for CASE tool vendors.

CONCLUSIONS

In this paper, we outline a method for the important task of building an evaluation framework for CASE tool evaluation. The method is consistent with the approach represented in the ISO standard, typifying current practice.

We report on experiences of a field study using the method in a complex database application domain. Key phases in the method are demonstrated, and findings from the field study presented in the form of a prototype evaluation framework. This framework is then used in a pilot evaluation of two commercial CASE tools. Such pilot evaluation is an essential component of the refinement phase of the outlined method, giving feed-in from current CASE technology.

Finally, although this was not a goal of the field study, we identified two issues which might inform future development of CASE tools: adopting CASE technology in the context of legacy systems which place a constraint on the forward engineering of database design, and the treatment of annotations as first class objects. Our impression from the pilot evaluation is that, in a sense, the 'A' in CASE seems to have been interpreted as 'automated' by the CASE-vendors instead of 'aided', and that flexibility in a designer's control of this automation is rather limited.

REFERENCES

Bubenko, J. (1988) Selecting a strategy for computer-aided software engineering, SYSLAB, University of Stockholm, SYSLAB Report No. 59, June 1988.

Bubenko, J. (1998) Challenges in Information Systems Engineering, Invited talk at the *3rd Baltic Workshop on Data Bases and Information Systems*, 13-17 April, Riga, Latvia.

Dixon, R. L. (1992) *Winning with CASE: Managing Modern Software Development*, McGraw-Hill, New York.

Fahrner, C. and Vossen, G. (1995) A survey of database design transformations based on the Entity-Relationship model, *Data & Knowledge Engineering*, **15** (3), 213-250.

Försäkringskassan (1993) *Slutrapport: Kvalitetsmätning - Ett Projekt för Bättre Uppföljning*, Final Report, 1993-08-13, Diarienummer: 33-1993:76, Försäkringskassan Skaraborg, Sweden *(In Swedish)*.

Glaser, B. G. and Strauss, A. L. (1967) *The Discovery of Grounded Theory: Strategies for Qualitative Research*, Weidenfeld and Nicolson, London.

Huff, C. C. (1992) Elements of a realistic CASE tool adoption, *Communications of the ACM*, **35** (4), 45-54.

ISO (1995) Information Technology - Guideline for the evaluation and selection of CASE tools, ISO/IEC JTC1/SC7/WG4, ISO/IEC 14102:1995(E).

Lundell, B. and Lings, B. (1998) An empirical approach to the evaluation of CASE-tools: Method experiences and reflection, In Siau, K. (Ed.) *Third CAiSE/IFIP8.1 Int. Workshop on Evaluation of Modeling Methods in System Analysis and Design (EMMSAD'98)*, 8-9 June 1998, Pisa, Italy, pp. N:1-12.

McComb, M. E. (1994) CASE Tools Implementation at Amtrak - Lessons Almost Learned, *Journal of Systems Management*, **45** (3), 16-20.

Moody, D. (1996) Graphical Entity Relationship Models: Towards a More User Understandable Representation of Data, In Tallheim, B. (Ed.) *Conceptual Modeling - ER '96: 15th Int. Conference on the Entity-Relationship Approach*, Springer-Verlag, 7-10 Oct. 1996, Cottbus, Germany, pp. 227-244.

Moody, D. L. and Shanks, G. G. (1994) What Makes a Good Data Model? Evaluating the Quality of Entity Relationship Models, In Loucopoulos, P. (Ed.) *Entity-Relationship Approach - ER '94: 13th Int. Conference on the Entity-Relationship Approach*, Springer-Verlag, 13-16 Dec. 1994, Manchester, UK, pp. 94-111.

Orlikowski, W. J. (1993) CASE Tools as Organizational Change: Investigation Incremental and Radical Changes in Systems Development, *Management Information Systems Quarterly*, **17** (3), 309-340.

Wieringa, R. J. (1996) *Requirement Engineering: Frameworks for Understanding*, John Wiley & Sons Ltd., Chichester, England.

Factors Affecting Information Technology Usage: A Meta-analysis of the Experimental Literature

Mo Adam Mahmood, Laura Hall
Information and Decision Sciences Department, University of Texas at El Paso,
El Paso, TX 79968
Tel: (915) 747-5496, Fax: (915) 747-5126, email: mmahmood@utep.edu

Daniel Leonard Swanberg
American Hospital Supply Corporation, El Paso, TX 79975

ABSTRACT

With an estimated investment of over 1 trillion dollars to date on information technology (IT) products and applications, one would hope that there exists a corresponding improvement in organizational performance and productivity. The level of IT usage has widely been accepted as an important indicator of IT effectiveness within organizations. The present research defines and validates the construct of IT usage using a meta analysis.

INTRODUCTION

The availability of information technology (IT) within organizations, over the last two decades, has increased tremendously. The rapid growth of the personal computer industry, substantial decreases in computer unit costs, and simultaneous increases in computer power and speed have made vast amounts of information readily available to individuals in organizations.

IT effectiveness can have a profound impact on organizational success. With an estimated investment of over 1 trillion dollars to date on IT products and applications, one would hope that there exists a corresponding improvement in organizational performance and productivity. The level of IT usage, according to DeLone and McLean (1992), has been widely accepted as an indicator of IT effectiveness within an organization.

It appears that the past research studies relating to IT usage fall into four general categories. The first group deals with the actual amount of individual use of an IT system based on the individual's perception of the convenience and usefulness that the system provides in performing his or her job (DeLone and McLean, 1992). The second category studies the characteristics of the individual end users themselves and the degree to which they employ IT systems (DeLone and McLean, 1992). The third type explores, based on the level of maturity of IT systems within an organization, the increased use of specific types of IT applications such as expert systems (Coakes and Merchant, 1996) while the fourth focuses on the characteristics of the organizations themselves such as size of the organization and to what level does the organization and its management support the implementation and use of IT systems (King and Teo, 1994).

The purpose of the present research is to define and validate the construct of IT usage. It accomplishes that by analyzing the empirical results of various studies over a period of time covering a broad scope of characteristics of both users and information systems and examines the relationship between these characteristics and the level of IT usage within organizations. The meta-analysis method is employed to gather and combine the results of a number of independent research studies measuring various factors affecting IT usage within organizations over the time period of the study. Combining a divergent set of results from a number of studies becomes challenging in view of the fact that not all the studies agree on the effects of identified factors and their impact on IT usage.

The most overriding and important reason for developing IT usage construct is that IT usage is an important driver of IT effectiveness within organizations. By developing a better understanding of the factors affecting IT usage, strategic managers should be able to shape policies within their organizations to maximize the effectiveness of their efforts to stimulate IT usage and in the process increase organizational performance and productivity.

RESEARCH HYPOTHESES

The present research focuses on the various dimensions of IT usage since it is an important driver of IT effectiveness within organizations. It is, therefore, important to understand how the various factors across many diverse research studies affect IT usage. The literature in the area reveals that the factors affecting IT usage fall into four major categories: perceived convenience and benefits, individual user characteristics, organizational IT maturity level, and organizational structural characteristics. These are discussed in details in what follows.

Perceived Benefit for the Individual User

The improved ease and convenience of use, both in applications software and systems software, have been found in the literature to correlate to the increasing use of systems. According to Davis, Bagozzi, and Warshaw (1989), perceived ease of use has a significant effect on intentions to use a specific system. Ferratt and Vahlos (1995), based on research conducted in Greece, indicated that the availability of cost effective microcomputers is a major factor in increased use. .

Evidence in the literature also suggests that there is a link between the usefulness of a software and its usage. Adams, Nelson, and Todd (1992), for example, found that usefulness is an important determinant of system use. Baroudi, Igbaria, and Parasuraman (1996) and Davis, Bargozzi, and Warshaw (1989) provided substantial support for the proposition that perceived usefulness is the main motivator of increased use of information technology. This leads to the first two hypotheses.

H1: *Individuals within organizations will increase their usage of IT systems in direct proportion to the perceived ease of use of these systems.*

H2: *Individuals within organizations will increase their usage of IT systems in direct proportion to the perceived usefulness of these systems.*

Characteristics of Individual IT Users

The question of what motivates particular types of end users to utilize computers has been studied with interesting results that appear to depend on psychological factors of various groups of individuals. Baroudi et al. (1996), for example, found that training, skill level, and organizational support were also found to be significant factors in this study. They also established that acceptance increases with educational level.

Two studies, performed several years apart, revealed that education and training in IT use is a positive motivating factor in actual increase of usage (Huff, Igbaria, and Pavri,1989; Igbaria, Meile, and Schiffman, 1992). Similar results were also uncovered in other countries including Taiwan (Igbaria, 1992) and Finland (Igbaria, Iivari and Maragahh, 1995)

On the other hand acceptance and usage tends to fall dramatically, the higher the professional level of an individual within the organization. The most interesting factor discovered in these and other studies by Lederer and Mahwhinney (1990) and Lee (1986) is that while IT usage declined in general with higher levels in the organization, those at highest levels of organizations reported virtually no IT usage.

H3: *Information Technology systems usage increases in direct proportion with higher educational level of the individual user.*

H4: *Information Technology systems usage increases inversely proportional to the professional level of the individual user.*

H5: *Information Technology systems usage increases with higher levels of computer related skills of the individual user.*

H6: *Information Technology systems usage increases with greater amounts of computer system related training of individuals within organizations.*

H7: *Information Technology systems usage increases with higher levels of positive attitude of the user toward IT systems.*

Organizational IT Maturity and Strategic Applications

As organizations themselves gain experience with the use of IT, a stronger propensity to use IT may be found. Increased usage of specific types of IT systems have also emerged in organizations as IT systems have matured. In researching systems usage, Coakes and Merchant (1996) found that, "A factor that did affect usage was the maturity of computer usage within the organization." Based on a research that studied the usage of data base management systems in 288 Fortune 500 companies, Grover and Teng (1992) states that a positive relationship between the age of information systems in organizations and usage exists.

Morgan and VanLengen (1993) found a positive relationship between the maturity level of information technology in organizations and the usage level of most types of IT applications except for the use of IT systems for strategic management which had a significant negative relationship. Paramount in this category are systems designed for the strategic and competitive use of IT. The major areas found to help an organization's decision making process included alignment with business planning, competitive pressure, and management vision and support. Liberatore and Stylianou (1994) identified Strategic Market Assessment System (SMAS) as a significant management decision making tool. Extejt and Lynn (1996) uncovered extensive use of various software systems utilized by union and management negotiators in collective bargaining decision making. This leads to the eighth and ninth hypotheses.

H8: *The proliferation of the use of IT systems employed by an organization increases with the level of maturity of these systems.*

H9: *Organizations that focus on IT systems for strategic applications rely increasingly on specific IT applications for decision making purposes.*

Organization Characteristics and IT System Usage

Existing characteristics of organizations prior to implementation of an IT application can have an impact on the level of IT systems use. These include organization size and the level of organizational support for IT systems. Baroudi et al. (1996) found that organizational support had a direct effect on the use of microcomputers. Schiffman, Meile, and Igbaria (1992) found organizational support, among other factors, affecting system usage.

Fisher, Lind, and Zmud (1989) found organizational size as a significant predictor of microcomputer usage. Grover and Teng (1992) indicated that a positive relationship exists between organizational size and the use of a system. Park and Jih (1993) unearthed the fact that the level of contribution of MIS to a firm's success seems to be related to the size of the firm. This leads to hypotheses tenth and eleventh.

H10: *Information Technology systems usage in organizations increases with an increase in the level of organizational support for these systems.*

H11: *Information Technology systems usage in organizations increases with greater levels of size of the organization.*

METHOD

Meta Analysis

Meta analysis is a statistical technique for combining the results of independent studies (Green and Hall, 1984, Hedges and Olkin, 1985; Rosenthal, 1984). The meta-analysis approach was chosen for the present research for several reasons: first, it is the analysis of analyses (in other words, it enables the synthesizing of literature by combining the findings of a number of studies). Second, each data point used for analysis is obtained from an individual study rather from an individual subject. Third, a meta-analysis also can include studies over a large time and scope, potentially validating the factors over time. Lastly, since technology changes over time, the impact of factors at various stages of technological development can be combined.

Sampling Procedure

The study covers the empirical research studies in the IT usage area over the period from 1979 to 1996. An electronic search using ABI/INFORM was conducted of a number of sources of research studies in the area including *Communications of the ACM, Information & Management, Journal of Accounting and EDP, Journal of Computer Information Systems, Journal of Management Information Systems, MIS Quarterly, Management Science, Decision Sciences, and Academy of Management Journal.* Studies reporting only quantitative data analysis and the significance level of the data were included.

Coding Procedure

A total of seventy-three studies were identified in the literature search. Of these twenty-eight were eliminated because their data could not be utilized for this research. The remaining forty-five studies with data pertaining to the hypotheses tested are included in the present research. For each study, the corresponding relationship that was analyzed, the one tailed p values, and the number of samples in each study were recorded. According to Rosenthal's guidelines, when results were reported as "not significant", a p level of 0.50 and a Z of 0.00 were recorded.

Analysis Procedure

For each p value, an associated standard normal deviate score (Z) was also tabulated. The individual Z values were obtained from the table entitled *Areas in One Tail of the Normal Curve at Selected Values* (Croxton, 1949). Using these values the effect size r was estimated for each effect of interest using a method described by Rosenthal (1984). Then a table of *The Transformation Z for the Correlation Coefficient (CRC Standard Probability and Statistics Tables and Formulae)* was used to determine the individual Z_r for each study testing a specific relationship. To determine the overall level of significance and size of the relationship, the combined Z_r and effect size, r, were then calculated using Stouffer's method described in Rosenthal (1984).

With these values, three aspects of each relationship were tested. First, the overall effect level was tested. The following guidelines were used to classify effect size, large for $r > 0.50$, medium for $0.10 < r < 0.50$, and small for r

< 0.10 (Cohen, 1977). Second, the overall significance level was determined using the individual Z data (Rosenthal, 1984). Lastly, the degree of heterogeneity was measured using chi squared values calculated from the individual Z data (Wolf, 1986). The significance of the chi squared values was determined using p values from *Table III, Statistical Methods for Research Workers* (Fisher, 1936).

RESULTS

This section presents the meta-analysis results on various effects investigated in this research. More specifically, it provides information on how large and how significant are these effects and also provides information on the degree of heterogeneity among the Z scores and effect sizes.

Results on Perceived Ease of Use

Thirteen studies measured the effect of perceived ease of use on the amount of usage of IT systems. These studies estimated the amount of IT usage by time and/or frequency of computer use. Where both were indicated, only the time data was recorded in this analysis. The combined normal standard deviate of these studies is $Z = 8.817$. The combined effect size is $r = 0.695$, a large effect size according to Cohen (1977). The level of significance for the individual study Z data is p< .0001. The Z scores were not found to be heterogeneous to a significant degree, X^2 (d.f. =12)44 = 6.052, $p < .92$.

Results on Perceived Usefulness

Thirty-one studies measured the effect of perceived usefulness on the amount of usage of IT systems. Some studies calculated the amount of IT usage by time and/or frequency of computer use. Other studies used the amount of charge-back or the number of different tasks completed as indicators of IT usage. The combined normal standard deviate of these studies is $Z = 13.778$. The combined effect size is $r = 0.968$, a large effect according to Cohen (1977). The level of significance for the individual study Z data is $p < .0001$. The Z scores were not found to be significantly heterogeneous, X^2 (d.f. = 30) = 35.484, $p = 0.24$.

Results on the Educational Level of the User

Eight studies measured the effect of the level of completed years of education of the individual on the amount of usage of IT systems. The studies assessed the education level by completed levels of traditional education, high school, bachelors degree, masters degree, and doctorate degree. The skill level was indicated by the amount of time of completed computer related courses and classroom based systems training. The combined normal standard deviate of these studies is $Z = 4.566$. The combined effect size is $r = 0.314$, a medium effect according to Cohen (1977). The level of significance for the individual study Z data is $p < .0001$. The Z scores were not found to be significantly heterogeneous, X^2 (d.f. = 7) = 5.518, p=.599.

Results on Professional Level of the User

Eight studies measured the effect of the professional level of the user on the amount of usage of IT systems. These studies used the level of management within the organization as the indicator of the professional level of the user. The amount of usage was measured by various indicators of time or frequency of use. The correlation's were tested in an inverse relationship, that is the higher the level within the organization of the user, the less the amount of IT usage was measured. The combined normal standard deviate of these studies is $Z = 5.297$. The combined effect size is $r = 0.398$, a medium effect according to Cohen (1977). The level of significance for the individual study Z data is $p < .0001$. The Z scores were found to be slightly heterogeneous, X^2 (d.f. = 7) = 12.15, p = .097.

Results on Skill and/or Experience Level of the User

Ten studies measured the effect of the computer related skill or experience level of the user on the amount of IT systems usage. These studies used number of years of systems experience or self reported skill level of the individual user as the indicator of the skill or experience level of the user. The amount of usage was measured by self-reported indicators of time or frequency of use. The combined normal standard deviate of these studies is $Z = 8.038$. The combined effect size is r = sage was measured by various indicators of time or frequency of use. The combined normal standard deviate of these studies is $Z = 6.031$. The combined effect size is $r = 0.497$, a medium effect according to Cohen (1977). The level of significance for the individual study Z data is $p < .0001$. The Z scores were not found to be significantly heterogeneous $X^2 = 7.079$, $p = 0.53$.

Results on Level of Positive Attitude of the User

Twelve studies measured the effect of the level of positive attitude of the user on the amount of usage of IT systems. The level of positive attitude was measured through indicators of perceived enjoyment and general satisfaction with system quality. The amount of usage was measured by indicators of time or frequency of use. The combined normal standard deviate of these studies is $Z = 7.34$. The combined effect size is $r = 0.588$, a large effect according to Cohen (1977). The level of significance for the individual study Z data is $p < .0001$. The Z scores were not found to be significantly heterogeneous, $X^2 = 14.774$, $p = 0.195$.

Results on the Level of IT Maturity Within the Organization

Seven studies measured the effect of the maturity level of the IT systems within the organization on the amount of usage of IT systems. The studies measured the maturity of IT systems by the amount of time the systems had been in place, the number of different types of IT applications employed by the organization, and also by the amount of IT tasks that were completed. The combined normal standard deviate of these studies is $Z = 7.399$. The combined effect size is $r = 0.500$, a large effect according to Cohen (1977). The level of significance for the individual study Z data is $p < .0001$. The Z scores were found to be heterogeneous, X^2 (d.f.= 6) = 2.294, $p = 0.89$.

Results on the Strategic Applications of IT within Organizations

Ten studies measured the effect of the use of strategic applications on the amount of usage of IT systems. The studies measured the amount of IT usage by time and/or frequency of computer use. Where both were indicated only the time data was recorded in this analysis. The combined normal standard deviate of these studies is $Z = 6.061$. The combined effect size is $r = 0.554$, a large effect according to Cohen (1977). The level of significance for the individual study Z data is $p < .0001$. The Z scores were found to be significantly heterogeneous, $X^2 = 11.481$, $p = 0.29$.

Results on the Effects of Organizational Support Level on IT Use

Ten studies measured the effect of organizational support level on the amount of usage of IT systems. The studies measured the amount of IT usage by time and/or frequency of computer use. Where both were indicated only the time data was recorded in this analysis. The combined normal standard deviate of these studies is $Z = 7.388$. The combined effect size is $r = 0.796$, a large effect according to Cohen (1977). The level of significance for the individual study Z data is $p < .0001$. The Z scores were not found to be significantly heterogeneous, $X^2 = 3.892$, $p = 0.92$.

Results on the Effects of Organization Size on IT Use

Seven studies measured the effect of organization size on the amount of usage of IT systems. The studies measured the amount of IT usage by time and/or frequency of computer use. Where both were indicated only the time data was recorded in this analysis. The combined normal standard deviate of these studies is $Z = 2.822$. The combined effect size is $r = 0353$, a medium effect according to Cohen (1977). The level of significance for the individual study Z data is $p = .0024$. The Z scores were not found to be significantly heterogeneous, $X^2 = 6.535$, $p = 0.374$.

DISCUSSION

To summarize the meta-analysis results, the usage of IT systems within an organization is strongly affected by the perceived usefulness of the system by the user, the perceived ease of use, skill level, and the level of positive attitude of the individual towards IT systems within the organization. These results were all statistically significant and all showed a large combined effect size. In all cases the results across studies were consistent. These results are congruent with the qualitative review of literature in the area. .

The effect of educational level, training level, and professional level were also significant on IT system usage. In all but one case, the results across studies were consistent. All the relationships had a medium effect although education effect had a direct relationship to usage while professional level, as expected, had an an inverse relationship. Therefore, while more educated individuals tend to use IT to a greater degree, the higher up the organizational ladder those individuals rise the less they use IT systems. Again, the qualitative review of the literature in the area supports these findings.

The usage of IT systems in organizations is also affected by the organizational characteristics such as IT maturity level, level of strategic applications, organizational support, and organization size. These results were all statistically significant and all but one showed a large combined effect size. In all cases, the results across studies were consistent. These results are also consistent with the qualitative review of literature in the area.

As obvious from the earlier discussion, the present research also investigated the heterogeneity of the effect of each of the eleven factors on IT usage across studies. It found all but one effect to be not significantly heterogeneous. This implies that these studies were consistent and significant for the direction of these effects. This makes a strong case for the validity of these results.

As obvious from the earlier discussion, the present research also investigated the heterogeneity of the effect of each of the eleven factors on IT usage across studies. It found all but one effect to be not significantly heterogeneous. This implies that these studies were consistent and significant for the direction of these effects. This makes a strong case for the validity of these results.

One exception is the professional level of the user. The results regarding the effect of the professional level of the user on IT system usage indicated a highly significant medium level of effect. These results, however, showed a low level of heterogeneity among the studies included for investigating this effect (p = .097). A closer scrutiny of these studies reveals that the study by Mawhinney and Lederer (1990) is an outlier because its z score and effect size are zero. This implies that, at least according to this study, the professional level of the user is not important in determining IT systems usage. This is not as surprising as young and technologically savvy managers move up the ladder to more senior positions, the professional level of these managers will perhaps have less and less impact on their IT usage. This, however, does not explain why the professional level effect sizes are still significantly heterogeneous even if the study by Mahwhinney and Lederer (1990) is removed. There is not a clear reason for this later heterogeneity. One possible explanation is that the subject population and IT systems for these studies are too dissimilar to be homogeneous.

CONCLUSIONS

In general, the results of this meta-analysis lead to the conclusion that there exists a strong and significant positive relationship between the perception of ease of use and the perceived usefulness of an IT system to the actual amount of usage that will occur. Individual perceptions, therefore can be considered the foremost driver of IT use in organizations. Another factor that indicates a high level of IT usage is the organizational support of IT within an organization. This suggests that organizations where management dedicates a high level of resources to support IT tend to foster greater use of IT systems within that organization. Although the factors of skill level, training level, and positive attitude were found to have a substantial effect on IT usage, the magnitude of these effects were lower than those of the perceptions of the user and organizational support. This suggests that while these factors are key elements in promoting IT usage, they are probably not as powerful in driving this usage.

A moderate level of heterogeneity was found in the studies that investigated the effect of the professional level on IT usage within organizations even though the effect itself was highly significant. This suggests conflicting findings as to the effect level in different studies in these areas. Managers should exercise caution in using the results based on this effect.

REFERENCES

To be furnished on request.

The WWW-based Presentations as a Complementary Part of Conventional Lectures in the Basics of Informatics: Is It Worth it?

Pekka Makkonen, Lecturer

University of Jyväskylä, Department of Computer Science and Information Systems, P.O. Box 35, Fin-40350
Jyväskylä, Finland

Tel: +358-14-603090, Fax: +358-14-603011, E-mail: pmakkone@jyu.fi

ABSTRACT

Hypertext and the WWW appear to affect learning positively enabling the constructivist learning environment to support a student's knowledge construction and a more active student role. However, the problems associated with them may endanger the benefit on learning. Thus, the role and the forms of hypertext and the WWW must be discussed.

Because of the common problems of "information overload" and "lost-in hyperspace" we suggest guided tours in the form of a slideshow presentation as a solution to organize a hypermedia presentation on the WWW for learning the basics of informatics. These slides include links to the appropriate supporting web sites. In addition to the idea of a guided tour, based on cognitive flexibility theory, we also suggest that the use of search engines and directories must be promoted.

This paper describes the use of guided tours as a complementary part of conventional lectures in the learning of the basics in informatics. We claim that learning can be promoted in the spirit of constructivism, situated action and cognitive flexibility organizing a course work based on guided tours as well as search engines and directories. We analyze the benefit of an optional course work including the use of guided tours and in addition the use of search engines and directories on the WWW. We assess the learning outcomes of the students comparing the students who have completed the optional course work to the students who have not participated in the optional course work.

Learning outcomes were significantly better in the group of students who completed the optional course work. The results confirm both the theoretical discussions presented in this paper and our previous results.

INTRODUCTION

During the 90s the reform work of teaching has reached universities. For example, Isaacs [10] and Rosenthal [20] have reported several problems in regard to traditional lecture based teaching. These problems include ineffectiveness, promoting passivity and isolation in students. In the context of technology and related sciences, some revisions have been suggested to improve lecturing as a teaching method by activating students using e. g. cooperative learning in small groups and essay-writing assignments about technical topics [10]. From this perspective lecturing has its possibilities by correcting previously mentioned problems, but also other learning methods must be considered. In informatics a course work utilizing information technology and its new possibilities may be a good and natural alternative for conventional lectures.

Hypertext reflects a human's way of thinking and provides an opportunity to process information and interrelatedness between information cues [13]. Since hypertext and hypermedia enable an alternative view for learning supporting knowledge construction and individual learning, it can be an alternative for conventional lectures or textbooks. Thus, hypertext and hypermedia provide an ideal environment for learning based on a constructivist approach. One alternative for the conventional lectures is a hypermedia presentation on the World Wide Web (WWW).

Hypertext and hypermedia do not typically offer an explicit mechanism to help learners better interpret and assimilate information, the context surrounding its creation and use, or the perspectives on the information of the author or other learners [25]. Simply improving information access without supporting learning leads directly to the problems of "information overload" and "lost-in hyperspace". Thus, students need some degree of guidance as well as the form and structure of hypermedia presentations must be discussed.

In this paper we introduce our approach to use the WWW to overcome previously mentioned problems and to take advantage of the features of the WWW as a complementary part of conventional lectures. The WWW provides both the possibility to organize information in a strict form (e. g. using trails and guided tours) and also opportunities for free "surfing" with its advantages and disadvantages. To realize the benefits of the WWW we suggest the solution of three layers. These layers are (a) the support of guided tours as a slide show on the WWW, (b) the support of appropriate links, and (c) the support of search engines and directories. We analyze the power of our approach based on comparing the learning outcomes of the students who participated in our optional course work to the outcomes of those who did not participate in the optional course work.

The paper is organized as follows: In section two we describe the character of learning of the basic concepts from the perspective of psychology. Section three describes constructivism as a view of learning. In section four we discuss the opportunities of the WWW in learning. The fifth section presents our experiment and results. In section six we draw conclusions based on our results.

NATURE OF LEARNING CONCEPTS

Our study recognizes hypertext as a knowledge construction tool and learning as knowledge construction. Thus, we understand learning especially from the perspective of the constructivist theory (constructivism). According to constructivism, an individual learns new concepts in relation to his/her prior knowledge [19] (for more details about constructivism, see section 3).

The psychological perspective of our research can be divided into the perspective based on cognitive psychology and the perspective based on developmental psychology. In this section we introduce these perspectives. They both emphasize that learning is knowledge construction, which makes them suitable for our research.

Perspective of Cognitive Psychology

From the perspective of cognitive psychology we distinguish declarative and procedural forms of knowledge. Declarative knowledge represents cognizance or awareness of some object, event, or idea [22]. Declarative knowledge of ideas is often characterized as schemas [21], which are ideational constructs that are defined by attributes that they inherit from other schemas. Procedural knowledge describes how learners use or apply their declarative knowledge. Ryle [22] describes this type of knowledge as knowing how. An intermediate type of knowledge is structural knowledge, which mediates the translation of declarative into procedural knowledge and facilitates the application of procedural knowledge. According to Diekhoff [9], structural knowledge is the knowledge of how concepts within a domain (e.g. in informatics) are interrelated. It describes how declarative knowledge is interconnected.

The basics of informatics include two kinds of learning. First, students learn to understand the field of informatics and its basic concepts. Second, students learn to use computers and utilize instructions to facilitate the use of computers. These two goals emphasize the learning of both declarative and procedural forms of knowledge. Since both forms of knowledge are important, we argue that the structural form of knowledge is important. Structural knowledge enables learners to form the connections that they need to use scripts or complex schemas [12].

It is typical for the basics in informatics that the basic concepts form structures. For example in our basic course on informatics the themes (for more details about the contents of the course, see subsection 5.1) form structural knowledge. Thus, we comprehend learning as a knowledge construction process of both declarative and structural knowledge. In this process a learner's goal is to approach an expert's knowledge structure which is the same as the requirements of a course.

Perspective of Developmental Psychology

From the perspective of developmental psychology conceptual knowledge can be approached using Collis's [7] modification of Piaget's stages of development. This approach creates a basis for evaluating learning outcomes emphasizing the quality of learning concerning a single concept and interrelatedness between the concepts.

Based on Piaget's stages of development a SOLO (Structure of the Observed Learning Outcome) taxonomy has been developed which divides learning outcomes into five classes. These classes reflect the quality and the awareness of a learning outcome. Learning outcomes (i.e., definitions of concepts) can be classified as follows using the SOLO taxonomy [3]:

1. Prestructural.
2. Unistructural.
3. Multistructural.
4. Relational.
5. Extended Abstract.

A student's response can be classified according to the capacity, relating operation, and consistency and closure of his/her response. Pre-structural responses are based on irrelevant or inappropriate data (level 1). Unistructural responses are based on conclusions on one aspect (level 2). Multistructural responses are based on isolated relevant data (level 3). Relational responses are based on relevant data and an understanding of the interrelations of different data in responses (level 4). Extended abstract responses are based on an understanding of data and interrelations both in the context of a question and in unexpected situations (level 5).

CONSTRUCTIVISM AS A VIEW OF LEARNING

In this section we introduce constructivism as a view of learning especially from the perspective of the use of the WWW. Widely known and discussed views associated with (computer supported) learning are behaviorism and its opposite constructivism. Behaviorism is interested in a student's behavior (reactions) in relation to teaching (stimulus), while constructivism is interested in the mental processes which affect the behavior of a student [19]. A traditional lecture is mainly based on the behaviorist approach while course works and projects are typical constructivist learning.

Constructivism asserts that learners construct knowledge by making sense of experiences in terms of what is already known [4]. In constructivist learning the concept of a mental model is essential. Learning is comprehended as the development of a learner's mental models (or declarative and structural knowledge). Constructivism is an essential basis when applying the WWW for teaching and learning [4]. While the goal of constructivism is to recognize and help to facilitate a learner's ability to construct knowledge when applied to teaching information retrieval on the Internet, it also provides the teacher with a structure for teaching. By focusing on concepts and connecting them to mental models, instructors and teachers can gain both confidence and control over the amount of material they cover in the small blocks of time usually allotted to teaching and training. Integrated with experiences that learners use to alter and strengthen mental models, the constructivist approach to teaching information retrieval also gives users a needed structure to get the most out of the Internet.

Despite the promise of constructivism several researchers emphasize the meaning of guidance. For example, Silverman [24] points out that providing the right amount of traditional instruction, students seem to favor constructivist environments. He suggests different tools to support constructivist lessons.

THE WWW IN LEARNING

Vast information resources are available to teachers and students via the WWW. However, the problems inherent in any information system such as disorientation, navigation inefficiency and cognitive overload are multiplied on the Internet [4]. However, these problems can be overcome using a suitable pedagogical approach and/or appropriate tools. Constructivism that mentioned in section three is the basic approach for the Internet solutions in learning. Additionally, it is useful to discuss the use of the WWW from other perspectives. In this section we introduce trails and guided tours as a way to improve the usefulness of the WWW. In addition, we introduce the concepts of situated action and cognitive flexibility, since these concepts are useful while applying the WWW for learning.

One way to organize a presentation on the WWW is trails and guided tours. Trails connect a chain of links through information spaces [2]. These can include multiple "recommended" trails through a network. Guided tours restrict users to the trail prohibiting detours. While trails lower cognitive overhead (or overload) by recommending the next logical link to take, guided tours reduce overhead further by removing all other choices. Thus, they can also prevent the phenomenon of lost-in hyperspace.

The term situated action emphasizes the interrelationship between an action and its context of performance [6]. The success of a computer supported learning environment depends not just on the software, but on the context in which that software is used [5, 14]. Situated action emphasizes a person's responsiveness to the environment and focuses on the improvisory nature of human activity [18]. Situated action theory emphasizes the local management of activity as mediated by relevant environmental cues [1, 24]. The implications for learning are that appropriate actions are generated from a recognition of appropriate opportunities given by the context. In addition to situated action theory, Jacobson et al. [11] emphasize also the meaning of cognitive flexibility theory affecting hypertext based learning. This theory proposes that complex knowledge may be better learned for flexible application in new contexts by employing case-based learning environments that include features such as: (a) use of multiple knowledge representations, (b) link abstract concepts in cases to depict knowledge-in-use, (c) demonstrate the conceptual interconnectedness or web-like nature of complex knowledge, (d) emphasize knowledge assembly rather than reproductive memory, (e) introduce both conceptual complexity and domain complexity early, and (f) promote active student learning.

Based on above it is important to comprehend the views of learning while outlining courses as well as comprehending ways to use the WWW in learning. We stress three issues. First, we must discuss what the right amount of traditional (behaviorist) teaching is. Second, we must analyze what the right way to use the WWW is. Active learning must be promoted and the pitfalls of the WWW must be avoided. Third, scaffolding support is needed to support constructivist learning.

METHODS

We pursued a study concerning a WWW-based course work based on the idea of trails and guided tours supported by the use of search engines and directories. In this section we describe our experiment, sample, measures and tests, followed by the results of our study.

Experiment

At the University of Jyväskylä the themes of a course introduction to automatic data processing are introduction (including the themes Meaning of Automatic Data Processing, Information Society and Problems Utilizing Computers), presentation of data in the PC environment, computer software, hardware technology, data communications, and the meaning of information technology in business. The course usually lasts 10 weeks including lectures (8 hours), compulsory practical exercises (18 hours) in basic skills with personal computers and the Internet as well as the final examination. The course of spring 1998 lasted the same amount of time including the previously mentioned activities and in addition material and activities on the WWW to support the lectures in the constructivist fashion.

Our approach to use the WWW for teaching and learning was combining
- idea of trails and guided tours on the WWW,
- both behaviorist teaching/learning and constructivist learning,
- situated action, and
- cognitive flexibility theory.

In the WWW-based learning the basic point is situated action. The constructivist approach is the commonly accepted principle for learning. As mentioned in section two the structural form of knowledge is typical for informatics, it is natural to approach the learning and teaching of it from the perspective of constructivism. However, in our context students need guidance at the beginning of learning. Thus, the traditional learning methods in the behaviorist manner must be accepted as a part of teaching and learning methods.

We introduced our approach for the students and administered the pre-questionnaire at the beginning of the course. The results of it [15] support our approach. Over 58% of the students considered both the lectures and printed lecture notes and the material on the WWW significant or strongly significant (based on a 5-point Likert scale ranging from strongly insignificant to strongly significant). Additionally, below 9% of the students considered both the lectures and printed lecture notes and the material on the WWW insignificant and none of them strongly insignificant.

We organized our lectures realizing the previously mentioned approach. Thus, the lectures consisted of
- printed lecture notes, which all students got at the beginning of the course,
- conventional lectures,
- lecture notes on the WWW including the links to the supporting sites, and
- optional course work in regard to lecture notes on the WWW.

Because of our context, we claim that conventional lecture and printed lecture notes are needed as a behaviorist part of a course, but lecture notes on the WWW provide an opportunity to the constructivist approach. The lecture notes on the WWW were organized in the form of a slide show using Microsoft Powerpoint 97 and its Internet assistant. These tools enable that the slides in each lecture can be organized in the strict form of a guided tour on the WWW supporting a student who is at the beginning of learning in informatics and not familiar with computers and the WWW. Each slide of a slide show can include a set of links to interesting WWW sites and in this manner a slide show can also be comprehended as a trail. Our slides included the links concerning the critical concepts to the appropriate link pages, which were evaluated to support the learning of these concepts best. The selection of the links on the slides was based on the list of critical concepts to learn produced by the group of the teachers (n=12) of informatics in our university. Since the slides are on the WWW, a student can also support her/his learning using search engines and directories. Thus, the form of a lecture is flexible and it can be seen as a trail or a guided tour depending on the situation and information needs. This enables different views and brings a real constructivist way of learning, since the role of instructional media shifts from one which seeks to maximize the communication of fixed content and/or skills to one in which students engage themselves in the knowledge construction process. In this sense our approach is also consistent with cognitive flexibility theory.

To realize the benefit of the lecture notes on the WWW we organized a course work in which students were expected to enter their findings in their personal diaries. These findings included their opinion about (a) the general form of presentation, (b) the links provided by the teacher, and (c) the links found by the students themselves using search engines and directories. Additionally, the students were expected to give various examples about what they have learned during the course work. To promote the students' participation in the optional course work, the students got credits by completing the course work for the final examination. Although course work is a constructivistic part of the course, the teacher's office hours were available as an additional resource to promote their work. The students had six and a half weeks for the course work before the final examination. The work was expected to be realized as a personal work or in groups of two or three students.

Sample

One hundred and three students, 78 females and 26 males, whose mean age was 23 years (range 19-42 years), entered the course and completed both pre- and post-treatments. All students were familiar with university lecturing. They familiarized themselves with the use of a WWW browser and basic search engines and directories (i. e., Altavista and Yahoo) before the introduction of the optional course work. All students studied informatics as a minor and were required to participate in the practices concerning the use of personal computers and the Internet (18 hours) and they all had the same exercises concerning these matters. Participating in the lectures (8 hours) and the course work was optional.

Forty-six of them, 38 females and 8 males, whose mean age was 22 years (range 19-40 years), participated in the optional course work. 17 of them completed the course work individually, 23 in the groups of two students and 6 in the groups of three students. The students used 13 hours (range 5-30 hours) for the course work on an average. They attended 6.5 hours in the lectures and used 43 hours for the whole course on an average.

Fifty-seven students, 39 females and 18 males, whose mean age was 23 years (range 19-42 years) did not complete the optional course work. These students attended 4.9 hours in the lectures and used 31 hours for the whole course on an average.

Measures and Tests

We utilized a SOLO taxonomy based measure to clarify learning outcomes and their quality (see subsection 2.2). Both the pre-treatment and the post-treatment contained 15 separately selected items. These items were chosen randomly from 88 critical concepts to learn of the whole learning area. 88 critical concepts were selected by the group of the teachers (n=12) of informatics in our university. In each test respondents produced 15 definitions of randomly selected basic concepts. The responses of the students were ranked from 1 to 5 based on the quality of learning. The basis for the rankings was the contemporary definitions of these concepts that were included in the material on the WWW.

In the responses the students were expected to define concepts using certain sentences clarifying the basic properties of each concept and connections between these properties. Additionally, based on the SOLO taxonomy the students were also expected to express alternative definitions for the concepts and the meaning of a concept in a larger sense, if they noticed it necessary.

The pre-treatment was administered at the beginning of the first lecture. Since our intention was to study the effect of the WWW as a complementary part of conventional lectures and lecture notes, the post-treatment was administered as the first part of the final examination. Both in the pre- and post-treatments the students had as much time as needed to produce their responses.

Results

We compared learning supported by the WWW (the experimental group) and learning without the support provided by the WWW (the control group). The dependent variable was the quality of learning (based on a SOLO taxonomy based measure). Since the data based on the responses of the students disagreed with the normal distribution, the Mann-Whitney test as a non-parametric test was appropriate for this experiment.

The pre-treatment Mann-Whitney test showed a significant difference between the experimental group and the control group (p=.018). The mean for the experimental group was 1.59 and the mean for the control group was 1.67. Cronbach's alpha to show the reliability in the pre-treatment was 0.72.

The post-treatment Mann-Whitney test showed that the difference between the experimental group and the control group was significant (p<.001). The mean of the experimental group was 2.62 and the mean of the control group was 2.46. Cronbach's alpha to show the reliability in the post-treatment was 0.77.

The learning outcomes of the students who had completed the optional course work were better compared to the students who had not completed the optional course work based on the WWW. The students who participated in the course work were in worse situation at the beginning of the course, but after the course and the course work the learning outcomes were significantly better in the experimental group. The results can partly be caused by the lower attendance of the control group in our lectures (difference is 1.6 hours between the experimental group and the control group). However, since the students in the experimental group used 13 hours for the course work on an average and these students used the WWW 10 hours more than the students in the control group, we argue that the WWW-based course work had the greatest influence on learning.

DISCUSSION

The results of this paper support the use of guided tours in the form of a slide show. The finding confirms both Bieber's and his colleagues' [2] discussion concerning the benefit of guided tours and trails and the results of pre-questionnaire where we found that the students have a positive attitude to the idea of the WWW as a medium to present lectures [15]. Our preliminary analysis of the students' course works [16] also supports the results of this paper. We found that especially the form of a slide show, links and appropriate link pages are beneficial in learning. Search engines and directories are less effective in learning than guided tours in the form of slide shows or links and link pages (destinations) [16]. However, we claim that search engines and directories may be more effective after the basic course in informatics when students are more familiar with these tools. In learning in the constructivist manner computers and their applications can be comprehended as cognitive tools, in other words, tools for knowledge construction. According to Mayes [17], these tools are more effective in the hands of an experienced user.

A qualitative analysis of the course work answers is needed. In the course work students were required to give reasons for their ratings and analyzing this information will clarify what the reasons for the success or the failure are.

The results of this paper provide more evidence to promote the use of the WWW for the learning of basic concepts especially in the context of informatics. Our results in this and the previous papers support both the constructivist learning and the use of guided tours supported by the links. Brandt [4] points out that teaching and learning based on constructivism must concentrate on concepts and connecting them to mental models. The WWW-based guided tours provide these concepts in a strict and controlled form and links provide connections to a student's mental models. Thus, the course work of three layers provides a real basis for constructivist learning as a complementary part of conventional lectures. However, more evaluation from the perspective of constructivism may be needed. Motivation is important to evaluate, since in constructivist learning it is important that students are actively engaged in learning and knowledge construction [8, 12]. Additionally, as mentioned in section four cognitive flexibility theory stresses the meaning of activity. Thus, the evaluation of motivation is also meaningful from this point of view.

Our results are consistent with situated action theory and cognitive flexibility theory. From the perspective of situated action theory our previous paper [16] showed that the basics of informatics is the right context for guided tours supported by appropriate links preventing the pitfalls in the use of the WWW ("information overload" and "lost-in-hyperspace"). This paper confirms these results. Since our use of the WWW as a whole has enabled better learning in the sense of knowledge construction, it also supports the meaning of cognitive flexibility theory as a basic point in applying hypertext and the WWW for learning.

REFERENCES

[1] Agre, P. E., Chapman, D. (1987). Pengi: An Implementation of a Theory of Activity. Proceedings of AAAI-87, Los Altos, CA, pp. 196-201.

[2] Bieber, M., Vitali, F., Ashman, H., Balasubramanian, V., Oinas-Kukkonen, H. (1997). Some Hypermedia Ideas for the WWW. Proceedings of the 30th HICSS, Vol. 4, Wailea, Hawaii, pp. 309-319.

[3] Biggs, J. B., Collis, K. F. (1982). Evaluating the Quality of Learning. The SOLO Taxonomy (Structure of the Observed Learning Outcome). New York: Academic Press.

[4] Brandt, D. A. (1997). Constructivism: Teaching for Understanding of the Internet. Communications of ACM, Vol. 40, No. 10, pp. 112-117.

[5] Bruckman, A., De Bonte, A. (1997). MOOSE Goes to School: A Comparison of Three Classrooms Using a CSCL Environment. Proceedings of CSCL 97. Toronto, Canada, http://www.oise.utoronto.ca/cscl/.

[6] Chen, C., Rada, R. (1996). Modelling Situated Actions in Collaborative Hypertext Databases. Journal of Computer Mediated-Communication, Vol. 2, No.3, http://www.ascusc.org/jcmc/vol2/issue3/chen.html.

[7] Collis, K. F. (1975). A Study of Concrete and Formal Operations in School Mathematics: A Piagetian Viewpoint. Melbourne: Australian Council for Educational Research.

[8] Cunningham, D. J., Duffy, T. M., Knuth, R. A. (1993). The textbook of the future. In McKnight, C., Dillon, A., Richardson, J. (Eds.), Hypertext. A psychological perspective (pp. 19-49), New York: Ellis Horwood.

[9] Diekhoff, G. M. (1983). Relationship Judgment in the Evaluation of Structural Understanding. Journal of Educational Psychology, 71, pp. 64-73.

[10] Isaacs, G. (1994). Lecturing Practices and Note-Taking Purposes. Studies in Higher Education, Vol. 19, No. 2, 1994, pp. 203-216.

[11] Jacobson, M. J., Maouri, C. , Mishra, P., & Kolar, C. (1996). Learning with Hypertext Learning Environments: Theory, Design, and Research. Journal of Educational Multimedia and Hypermedia, Vol. 5, No. 3/4, pp. 239-281.

[12] Jonassen, D. H. (1992). What are Cognitive Tools? In Kommers, P. A. M., Jonassen, D. H., Mayes, J. T. (Eds.), Cognitive Tools for Learning (pp. 1-6), Berlin: Springer-Verlag (NATO ASI Series).

[13] Jonassen, D. H. (1993). Effects of Semantically Structured Hypertext Knowledge Bases on Users' Knowledge Structures. In McKnight, C., Dillon, A., Richardson, J. (Eds.), Hypertext. A Psychological Perspective (pp. 153-

166), New York: Ellis Horwood.

[14] Koschmann, T. (1996). Paradigm Shifts and Instructional Technology: An Introduction. In Koschmann T. (Ed.) CSCL: Theory and Practice of an Emerging Paradigm (pp. 1-23), Mahwah, NJ: Lawrence Erlbaum.

[15] Makkonen, P. (1998a). The WWW-based Presentations as a Complementary Part of Conventional Lectures in the Basics of Informatics. Proceedings of the ACM Conference on Integrating Technology into Computer Science Education, Dublin, Ireland, pp. 162-165.

[16] Makkonen, P. (1998b). Benefit of the WWW-based Presentations as a Complementary Part of Conventional Lectures in the Basics of Informatics. Proceedings of the 21st IRIS, Vol. 2, Aalborg, Denmark, pp. 583-591.

[17] Mayes, J. T. (1992). Cognitive tools: A Suitable Case for Learning. In Kommers, P. A. M., Jonassen, D. H., Mayes, J. T. (Eds.), Cognitive Tools for Learning (pp. 7-18), Berlin: Springer-Verlag (NATO ASI Series).

[18] Nardi, B. (1996). Studying Context: A Comparison of Activity Theory, Situated Action Models, and Distributed Cognition. In Nardi, B. (Ed.), Context and Consciousness (pp. 69-102), Cambridge, MA: MIT Press.

[19] Risku, P. (1996). A Computer-Based Mathematics Learning Environment in Engineering Education. Jyväskylä: University of Jyväskylä, Department of Mathematics, Report 71.

[20] Rosenthal J. (1995). Active Learning Strategies in Advanced Mathematics Classes. Studies in Higher Education, Vol. 19, No. 2, 1994, pp. 223-228.

[21] Rumelhart, D. E., Ortony, A. (1977). The Representation of Knowledge in Memory. In Anderson, R. C., Spiro, R. J., Montague, W. E. (Eds.), Schooling and the Acquisition of Knowledge. Hillsdale, NJ: Lawrence Erlbaum.

[22] Ryle, G. (1949). Collected Papers, Vol II. Critical Essays. London: Hutchinson.

[23] Silverman, B. G. (1995) Computer Supported Collaborative Learning (CSCL). Computers in Education, Vol. 25, No. 3, pp. 81-91.

[24] Suchman, L. (1987). Plans and Situated Action: The Problem of Human-Machine Communication. Cambridge, UK: Cambridge University Press.

[25] Wan, D., Johnson, P. M. (1994). Computer Supported Collaborative Learning Using CLARE: The Approach and Experimental Findings. Proceedings of the ACM Conference of Computer-Supported Cooperative Work, pp. 187-198.

An Empirical Investigation of the Impact of Telecommuting on the Career Advancement Prospects of Professionals

Donna Weaver McCloskey, Ph.D.
School of Business Administration, Widener University, One University Place, Chester, PA 19013
Phone (610) 499-4318, FAX (610) 499-4614, Donna.W.McCloskey@Widener.edu

Magid Igbaria, Ph.D.
Programs in Information Systems, Claremont Graduate School, 130 East Ninth Street, Claremont, CA 9711
IgbariaM@cgs.edu

ABSTRACT

The fear that telecommuting will have a negative impact on career advancement prospects has been a barrier to employee acceptance of telecommuting. This study sought to examine whether professionals who telecommute did indeed experience less advancement prospects than their non-telecommuting peers. The results indicate that this fear is unfounded. Telecommuting did not have a direct or indirect effect through job performance evaluations on career advancement prospects. Additionally, the level of telecommuting participation did not have an impact on career advancement. Employees who telecommuted more frequently did not experience significantly different job performance evaluations or career advancement prospects than those who telecommuted less. The paper concludes with the limitations of this study and directions for future research.

INTRODUCTION

Telecommuting has been found to offer many advantages to organizations and employees. In addition to increasing productivity (Hartman, Stoner and Arora, 1992; Weiss, 1994) and increasing retention and recruiting (DiMartino and Wirth, 1990), telecommuting has also been found to contribute to cost savings from the reduction in office space and related overhead expenses (Jacobs and VanSell, 1996). Employees who telecommute have reported many benefits including eliminating long commutes (DiMartino and Wirth, 1990; Mahfood, 1992), decreasing personal costs such as transportation and parking (Fuss, 1995) and increasing flexibility to balance work and family commitments (DuBrin, 1991). But despite these many potential benefits, there are still fears about the impact of this work arrangement on career outcomes. Many employees have said they will not telecommute, despite the many benefits to themselves and the organization, because they fear that the work arrangement will have an adverse effect on their career advancement prospects (Connelly, 1995).

The impact of telecommuting on career advancement has been the subject of a great deal of speculation, yet it remains one of the least understood aspects of this work arrangement. Generally, managers and employees believe telecommuting will limit visibility and consequently, restrict career advancement opportunities (Hooks, 1990; Stanko and Matchette, 1994). Employees believe limited career advancement opportunities is one of the greatest disadvantages of telecommuting (DuBrin and Barnard, 1993). However, anecdotal evidence suggests that telecommuting may contribute to higher productivity and, consequently, greater advancement opportunities (Riley and McCloskey, 1997; Solomon and Templer, 1993; Wagel, 1988). In a pilot study Bell Atlantic found 27% of the managers who telecommuted had higher work ratings and several were promoted at a time when promotions were not common (Weiss, 1994). Other research has suggested telecommuting will have no impact on career advancement prospects (Olson, 1989). Pilot study results have provided mixed information on the promotability of telecommuters. For example, in a small study of nine remote employees conducted by Olson (1983) it was reported that four employees felt their promotability was not effected, two felt their promotability was increased because their work was recognized and rewarded and three believed their promotability was hindered due to less visibility.

It is very important for both researchers and practitioners to understand how telecommuting impacts work outcomes, specifically career advancement prospects. The advantages of telecommuting will only be realized if employees choose to participate in this work arrangement. Despite the promises of societal, organizational, and individual advantages, employees are fearful to accept a work arrangement that may have an impact on their career. Organizations should be concerned with the impact of telecommuting on career advancement prospects as well. It has been suggested that should employees choose to telecommute and then experience limited career advancement opportunities that they may sue because they have been discriminated against due to perceived inequities of treatment (Fitzgerald, 1994). In addition to avoiding litigious threats, it is important for organizations to understand the impact of telecommuting on career advancement so that programs and training can be designed to reduce the potential negative outcomes of telecommuting and therefore encourage employee participation.

Empirical research has not yet adequately addressed this issue for professional employees. This study addresses this need by examining whether there are differences in career advancement prospects between professional telecommuters and non-telecommuters. In addition to examining whether career advancement prospect differences exist, this research also examines why this occurs. This research seeks to establish (1) whether telecommuters and non-telecommuters receive different job performance evaluations from their supervisor's which lead to differences in advancement opportunities, (2) whether telecommuting has a direct effect on career advancement prospects and (3) whether increased telecommuting participation leads to more negative career advancement prospects.

RESEARCH MODEL

The model, contained in Figure 2, posits that the work arrangement may have a direct effect on career advancement prospects as well as an indirect effect through job performance evaluations.

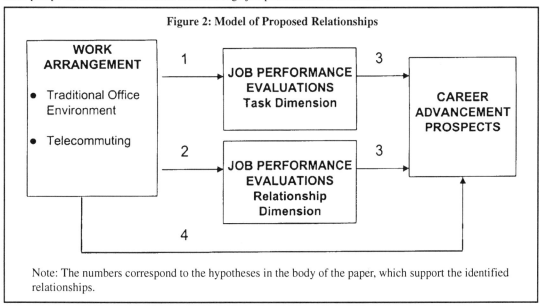

Figure 2: Model of Proposed Relationships

Note: The numbers correspond to the hypotheses in the body of the paper, which support the identified relationships.

Job performance evaluations play an important role in assessing an employee's promotability (DeCotiis and Petit, 1978; Stumpf and London, 1981). Job performance has been found to be comprised of two dimensions, task and relationship (Greenhaus, Parasuraman and Wormley, 1990; Igbaria and Baroudi, 1995). The task dimension addresses factors concerning the performance of work, including such characteristics as productivity, job knowledge and accuracy. The relationship dimension contains psychological and personality factors, such as attitude, cooperation, commitment and loyalty. The contradictory belief that telecommuting both helps and hinders career advancement may in fact be true. Telecommuting may result in a positive impact on the task dimension of job performance and a negative effect on the relationship dimension.

One of the heralded advantages of telecommuting is that employees are able to minimize distractions when working outside of the office and are therefore able to work more productively. Prior research and pilot studies have found telecommuters to be more productive than non-telecommuters (DuBrin, 1991; Hartman, Stoner and Arora, 1992; Solomon and Templer, 1993) and more productive on the days they are telecommuting (Ross, 1990). In addition to productivity gains, telecommuters have also been found to perform higher quality work (Fuss, 1995; Olson, 1989; Riley and McCloskey, 1997). An increase in the quantity and quality of work would result in more favorable job performance evaluations on the task dimension.

Telecommuting is not an appropriate work arrangement for everyone. It has been suggested that organizations screen participants to ensure that the work arrangement will be successful. Experts have suggested only those employees who are knowledgeable of their job, responsible and self-motivated should be allowed to participate in telework arrangement (Wright, 1993). Given that the task dimension taps qualities that telecommuters are perceived to have, such as responsibility, and other work outcomes that are frequently a result of telecommuting, such as productivity and high quality work, it would be expected that telecommuters would score very high on this dimension of job performance.

H1: Telecommuters will receive higher job performance evaluations on the task dimension than non-telecommuters.

Telecommuters may be viewed as being less committed and loyal to the organization (Mahfood, 1992) and are thus less likely to be considered for promotion. By participating in a telecommuting program supervisors may perceive the employee is putting his/her family life ahead of work responsibilities. Hooks (1990) found that 37% of those who participated in alternative work arrangements, such as telecommuting, believed their careers were damaged because the supervisors questioned their competitiveness and commitment. The relationship dimension of job performance reflects the supervisor's impression of an employee's loyalty and commitment. If supervisors believe telecommuters are not as committed as non-telecommuters, they may rate telecommuters lower on the relationship dimension of job performance.

H2: Telecommuters will receive lower job performance evaluations on the relationship dimension than non-telecommuters.

Research has found job performance evaluations to be the most powerful predictor of career advancement prospects (Igbaria and Wormley, 1995; Stumpf and London, 1981). Both the relationship and task dimensions of job performance evaluations have been found to have a significant, positive effect on promotability assessments (Igbaria, 1991; Igbaria and Greenhaus, 1992); however, the task dimension has been found to be a much stronger predictor (Greenhaus et al., 1990; Igbaria, 1991). This suggests that the most important factor contributing to future promotability is the ability to do the job well, not the supervisor's perception of loyalty, interpersonal relationships and other relationship oriented job performance factors.

H3: Both the task and relationship dimension of job performance will have a positive impact on career advancement prospects although the task dimension will have a stronger effect than the relationship dimension.

Other factors may also have an impact on advancement opportunities. Telecommuters may lose contact with peers and will no longer be tapped into informational networks. Relationships in informal social networks have been found to be an important factor on organizational advancement (Kanter, 1979; Tsui, 1984). If an employee is out of the office and does not maintain informal communication with colleagues on such things as training opportunities, new projects and job postings, s/he may hinder advancement opportunities. The "out of sight, out of mind" adage is certainly believed to be true (Haddon and Lewis, 1994; Shellenbarger, 1993). An employee may receive positive job evaluations but still not receive promotions because they are not seen and consequently not thought of at promotion time. Hartman, Stoner and Arora (1992) found that most telecommuters believed their career advancement had been hindered due to both decreased visibility and limited access to information and networking. This research proposes that telecommuting, in addition to impacting job performance evaluations, has a direct effect on career advancement prospects.

H4: Telecommuters have less career advancement prospects than non-telecommuters.

Experts have suggested that employees limit the amount of time they telecommute so they do not hinder their advancement opportunities (Wright, 1993). In a small study Ramsower (1985) found that satisfaction with advancement opportunities declined with increasing telecommuting participation. This research explores whether increased telecommuting participation does indeed result in even more limited career advancement prospects.

Researcher has found that with a high level of telecommuting participation productivity actually declines (Bacon, 1989). A high level of telecommuting participation may result in a lower job performance rating on the task dimension.

H5: Professionals who have a high level of telecommuting participation will receive lower job performance evaluations on the task dimension than professionals who have a lower level of telecommuting participation.

A supervisor may question the loyalty and commitment of a person who telecommuters most of the time but not an employee who only telecommutes occasionally. High levels of telecommuting participation may therefore result in lower evaluations on the relationship dimension of job performance, which could consequently limit career advancement prospects. Ramsower's (1985) findings offer limited support. Employees who had a high level of telecommuting participation were less satisfied with career advancement opportunities than employees who telecommuted less.

H6: Professionals who have a high level of telecommuting participation will receive lower job performance evaluations on the relationship dimension than professionals who have a lower level of telecommuting participation.

Hypothesis 4 proposed that telecommuting would have a direct, negative impact on career advancement prospects. The more an employee telecommutes, the more negative this relationship would become. Employees with a high level of telecommuting participation have even fewer opportunities for networking and are more likely to be forgotten at promotion time.

H7: Professionals who have a high level of telecommuting participation will have less career advancement prospects than professionals who have a lower level of telecommuting participation.

METHODOLOGY

Overview of the procedure

Telecommuting policies and experiences may vary widely from organization to organization. For this reason, it was deemed reasonable to conduct this research with a sample from one large organization. Representatives from the corporate headquarters of a large telecommunications firm were introduced to this research project and agreed to participate. A statewide survey found that there were 225 professional employees telecommuting. The organization provided the names, internal mailcodes and work phone numbers of these telecommuters. A "fan out" method was employed to identify non-telecommuters. The telecommuters, in addition to answering the questionnaire, were asked to identify both their immediate supervisor and a non-telecommuting employee who most closely matched their present position and level. The identified non-telecommuters then received a questionnaire. The non-telecommuters were asked to identify their supervisor. Each identified supervisor was asked to complete a brief questionnaire. In addition to demographic questions, supervisors are asked to respond to questions concerning the job performance and career advancement opportunities for the employee.

Sample

Completed questionnaires were received from 89 telecommuters (40% response rate), 71 non-telecommuters (49% response rate) and 97 supervisors (61% response rate). Since our analyses required responses from both employees and their supervisors, we were interested in the number of employee-supervisor pairs. We received useable responses from 53 telecommuter-supervisor pairs and 44 non-telecommuter-supervisor pairs.

As contained in Table 1, the telecommuters and non-telecommuters are very similar to one another. There is, however, a significant difference in the gender composition of these two groups. The gender distribution of the telecommuters was fairly equally split (51% men and 49% women) whereas the non-telecommuters were predominantly men (70% men and 30% women).

Table 1: Comparison of the Demographic Characteristics of Telecommuters and Non-telecommuters

	Telecommuters (N=53)	Non-telecommuters (N=44)	t
Age	45.45	45.59	.096
Number of children	1.72	1.84	-.506
Hours worked per week	47.89	46.70	-.822
Job tenure (years)	5.88	6.76	.714
Org. tenure (years)	19.91	22.27	1.548
			Chi Square
Gender			
male	27 (51%)	31 (70%)	3.087*
female	26 (49%)	13 (30%)	
Education			
high school	6 (11%)	5 (11%)	5.291
some college	21 (40%)	25 (57%)	
bachelors degree	14 (26%)	9 (20%)	
graduate degree	11 (21%)	3 (7%)	
Marital Status			
married	33 (62%)	35 (80%)	6.647*
unmarried, living w/ partner	5 (9%)	6 (14%)	
unmarried, not living w/ partner	14 (26%)	3 (7%)	
Salary			
$30,001-45,000	5 (9%)	5 (11%)	7.703
$45,001-60,000	15 (28%)	22 (50%)	
$60,001-75,000	27 (51%)	16 (36%)	
$75,000-90,000	3 (6%)	0 (0%)	
$90,001-115,000	2 (4%)	1 (2%)	
$115,001-130,000	1 (2%)	0 (0%)	
p £ .05*	p £ .01**	p £ .001***	

There is also a statistically significant difference in the distribution of marital status for telecommuters and non-telecommuters. Although the majority of both groups were married (62% of telecommuters and 80% of non-telecommuters), there is greater variation in the marital status of the telecommuters. Twenty six percent of the telecommuters reported they were unmarried and not living with a partner and 9% reported being unmarried and living with a partner compared to 7% and 14% of the non-telecommuters, respectively. The data collection process resulted in a sample of telecommuters and non-telecommuters from similar managerial and professional job types. A chi-square analysis revealed that there was not a significant difference in the distribution of job titles among the telecommuters and non-telecommuters.

Measures

All of the respondents were asked to respond to a series of demographic questions. Gender and marital status were coded as dichotomous variables (1 = male, 2 = female and 1 = married, 2 = unmarried, living with partner and 3 = unmarried, not living with partner). Respondents were also asked to indicate the highest level of education they have achieved on a four level scale from (1) some high school to (4) graduate degree. Respondents were asked to indicate the number of children they have. Age, job tenure and organizational tenure were obtained with open-ended questions and were measured in years. Number of hours worked per week was obtained with an open-ended question and measured in hours per week. Respondents were asked to indicate their current salary on a nine level scale from (1) less than $30,000 through (9) more than $140,000 and indicate the proportion of this salary in their total family income from (1) 0-19% to (5) 80-100%. All respondents were also asked to indicate their job title in an open-ended question. Telecommuters were asked to indicated what percentage of their work time they spend telecommuting on a five point scale from (1) all or almost all the time – 100-80% to (5) little to almost no time – 20-1%.

Job Performance Evaluation. Job performance was assessed using a measure developed by Touliatos, Bedeian, Mossholder and Barkman (1984). The supervisor was asked to respond to the extent that the employee exhibits 22 qualities on a 5-point scale from (1) unsatisfactory to (7) excellent. One quality from the original measure, promotability, was excluded due to the overlap with a separate construct, career advancement prospects. Items were average to form a composite score for the two dimension of job performance, task (alpha = .93) and relationship (alpha = .94).

Career Advancement Prospects. Each individual's career advancement prospects were assessed by their supervisor's response to the following inquiry: "How would you assess this employee's chance for promotion sometime during his or her career in this company?". Responses were made on a three point scale: (1) slight chance, (2) good chance and (3) very good chance. This measure has been used by a number of researchers (Greenhaus, et. al., 1990; Igbaria and Baroudi, 1995).

Data Analyses

This research proposes a model of relationships concerning the impact of a work arrangement on job performance evaluations and career advancement prospects. Hierarchical multiple regression was used to see if there is support for the proposed model. Prior to entering the study variables it was necessary to enter, and therefore control, demographic variables that may cause spurious effects. The sample of telecommuters and non-telecommuters were found to differ significantly on gender and marital status. It was therefore necessary to control for both gender and marital status so that conclusions regarding differences in the work arrangement were not confounded by demographic differences. This research explores whether the level of telecommuting participation impacts job performance and career advancement prospects. The sample of telecommuters was split into high and low participation categories. Employees who spent less than 20% of their work time telecommuting were considered "low" (N=36 and those who spent 20% or more of their work time telecommuting were considered "high" (N=17) .

RESULTS

Telecommuting was not found to have a direct or indirect effect on career advancement prospects. Hypothesis 1 proposed that telecommuters would receive higher job performance evaluations on the task dimension of job performance evaluations than non-telecommuters. As indicated in Table 2, this hypothesis was not supported. Hypothesis 2 proposed that telecommuters would receive lower job performance evaluations on the relationship dimension than non-telecommuters. As indicated in Table 3, this was also not supported. Hypothesis 4 stated that telecommuting would have a direct, negative impact on career advancement prospects. The results of the regression used to test this hypothesis are contained in Table 4. This hypothesis was also not supported. Hypothesis 3 was the only hypothesis that was supported. It posited that the two dimensions of job performance evaluations would have a positive impact on career advancement prospects. The results of the regressions used to test this hypothesis are contained in Table 4. Both the task and relationship dimension of job performance evaluations were found to have a significant impact on career advancement prospects.

Table 2: Direct, Indirect and Total Effects on the Task Dimension of Job Performance Evaluations

	Total	Direct	Indirect	R^2	ΔR^2
Gender	.111	.149	-.038	.012	
Marital Status	-.071	-.083	.012		
Work arrangement	-.047	-.047		.014	.002

p £ .05*   p £ .01**   p £ .001***
work arrangement (1=telecommute and 0=does not telecommute); gender (1=male and 2=female); marital status
(1=unmarried and not living with a partner and 2=married or living with a partner)

Table 3: Direct, Indirect and Total Effects on the Relationship Dimension of Job Performance Evaluations

	Total	Direct	Indirect	R^2	ΔR^2
Gender	.176	.207	-.031	.048	
Marital Status	-.203	-.215	.012		
Work arrangement	-.057	-.057		.051	.003

p £ .05*   p £ .01**   p £ .001***
work arrangement (1=telecommute and 0=does not telecommute); gender (1=male and 2=female); marital status
(1=unmarried and not living with a partner and 2=married or living with a partner)

Table 4: Direct, Indirect and Total Effects on Career Advancement Prospects

	Total	Direct	Indirect	R^2	ΔR^2
Gender	.053	-.021	.074		
Marital Status	-.001	.105	-.104	.003	
Work arrangement	-.148	-.116	.264	.023	.020
Job Performance Evaluations - Task	.309*				
Job Performance Evaluations - Relationship	.307 *			.355	.332

p £ .05*   p £ .01**   p £ .001***
work arrangement (1=telecommute and 0=does not telecommute); gender (1=male and 2=female);
marital status (1=unmarried and not living with a partner and 2=married or living with a partner)

This research proposed that the negative outcomes of telecommuting would increase with telecommuting participation. These hypotheses were not supported. Hypothesis 5, 6 and 7 proposed that employees with a high level of telecommuting participation would receive more negative job performance rating on the task and relationship dimension and would have less career advancement opportunities than those employees who telecommuted less. As indicated in Tables 5, 6 and 7, level of telecommuting participation did not have a significant impact on the two dimensions of job performance or on career advancement prospects.

DISCUSSION

The fear of compromising career advancement prospects has had a negative effect on telecommuting participation. Employees fear that by telecommuting they will be sacrificing career advancement opportunities. This research offers evidence that this feared outcome does not occur. Telecommuting did not have a negative impact on job performance evaluations and there was not a significant difference in the supervisor's assessment of career advancement opportunities for the telecommuters or non-telecommuters. This is a very positive outcome that begins to alleviate the greatest concern of this flexible work arrangement. Employees can participate in this mutually beneficial work arrangement without fearing the work arrangement will have a negative impact on advancement opportunities.

Table 5: Direct, Indirect and Total Effects on the Task Dimension of Job Performance Evaluations

	Total	Direct	Indirect	R^2	DR^2
Gender	.084	.085	-.001	.007	
Level of Telecommuting Participation	.005			.007	.000

p £ .05*   p £ .01**   p £ .001***
work arrangement (1=telecommute and 0=does not telecommute); gender (1=male and 2=female); marital status (1=unmarried and not living with a partner and 2=married or living with a partner); level of telecommuting participation (0=low and 1=high)

Table 6: Direct, Indirect and Total Effects on the Relationship Dimension of Job Performance Evaluations

	Total	Direct	Indirect	R^2	DR^2
Gender	.152	.153	-.001	.023	
Level of Telecommuting Participation	.018			.023	.000

p £ .05*   p £ .01**   p £ .001***
work arrangement (1=telecommute and 0=does not telecommute); gender (1=male and 2=female); marital status (1=unmarried and not living with a partner and 2=married or living with a partner); level of telecommuting participation (0=low and 1=high)

Table 7: Direct, Indirect and Total Effects on Career Advancement Prospects

	Total	Direct	Indirect	R^2	DR^2
Gender	.136	.071	.065	.019	
Level of Telecommuting Participation	-.130	-.136	.006	.035	.016
Job Performance Evaluations – Task	.403*			.343	.308
Job Performance Evaluations – Relationship	.179				

p £ .05*   p £ .01**   p £ .001***
work arrangement (1=telecommute and 0=does not telecommute); gender (1=male and 2=female); marital status (1=unmarried and not living with a partner and 2=married or living with a partner); level of telecommuting participation (0=low and 1=high)

LIMITATIONS AND DIRECTIONS FOR FUTURE RESEARCH

This research offers evidence that despite the myths and fears, telecommuting does not have a direct or indirect negative impact on career advancement prospects. Future research should test the generalizability of these findings by addressing the study limitations. First, this research was conducted at one organization that was committed to making telecommuting work. There was support for telecommuting from the highest levels of the organization and training was provided for the participants and their supervisors. It is possible that that this organization was able to minimize the impact of telecommuting on career advancement prospects through these efforts.

Second, it has been suggested that telecommuters can maintain their advancement opportunities by coming to the office regularly (Fitzgerald, 1994). This study found that increased telecommuting participation did not have an impact on advancement opportunities. Overall this sample did not have a high level of telecommuting participation. It is possible that this sample did not telecommute frequently enough to experience an impact on their job performance evaluations and career advancement prospects. Employees who spent more than 20% of their work time telecommuting were considered to have a "high" level of telecommuting participation. The majority spent 20-39% of their work time telecommuting. Differences may have been found if the employees in this sample telecommuted for a majority of their work time. Researchers should examine whether there are differences in job performance evaluations and career advancement prospects between professional employees who do not telecommute and those who telecommute more frequently than the current sample.

Although additional research is needed to confirm these findings, this study provides evidence that the greatest employee barrier to telecommuting, the fear of limited career advancement, is unfounded. Additional research should assess the generalizability of these findings. Both organizations and employees can benefit from a well-structured telecommuting program. If employees can telecommute without compromising their career advancement, they would be more willing to participate, thus reaping additional benefits for both themselves and their organizations.

REFERENCES

Bacon, Donald C. (1989). Look Who's Working at Home, Nations Business, 77, 20-31.

Connelly, Julie (1995). Let's Hear it for the Office, Fortune, 131(4), 22-23.

DeCotiis, T. and Petit, A. (1978). The Performance Appraisal Process: A Model and Some Testable Propositions, Academy of Management Review, 3(3), 635-646.

DeSanctis, Gerardine (1984). Attitudes Toward Telecommuting: Implications for Work-at-Home Programs, Information and Management, 7(3), 133-139.

DeSanctis, Gerardine (1983). A Telecommuting Primer, Datamation, 29(10), 214-220.

DiMartino, Vittorio and Worth, Linda (1990). Telework: A New Way of Working and Living, International Labour Review, 129(5), 529-554.

DuBrin, Andrew (1991). Comparison of Job Satisfaction and Productivity of Telecommuters vs. Inhouse Employees, Psychological Reports, 68, 1223-1234.

DuBrin, Andrew and Janet C. Barnard (1993). What Telecommuters Like and Dislike about Their Jobs, Business Forum, 18(3), 13-17.

Fitzgerald, Kevin M. (1994). Telecommuting and the Law, Small Business Reports, 19, 14-18.

Fuss, Dianne (1995). Telecommuting: The Ways of the Future, Telecommunications, 15-21.

Greenhaus, Jeffrey H., Parasuraman, Saroj and Wormley, Wayne (1990). Race, Organizational Experiences and Career Outcomes, Academy of Management Journal, 33, 64-86.

Haddon, Leslie and Alan Lewis (1994). The Experience of Teleworking: An Annotated Review, The International Journal of Human Resource Management, 5(1), 193-223.

Hartman, Richard I; Charles R. Stoner and Raj Arora (1992). Developing Successful Organizational Telecommuting Arrangements: Worker Perceptions and Managerial Prescription, SAM Advanced Management Journal, 57(3), 35-42.

Hooks, Karen L. (1990). Let's Give Alternative Work Schedules a Chance, Journal of Accountancy, 170(1), 81-86.

Igbaria, M. (1991). Job performance of MIS professionals: An examination of the antecedents and consequences. *Journal of Engineering and Technology Management*, 8, 141-171.

Igbaria, Magid and Baroudi, Jack (1995). The Impact of Job Performance Evaluations on Career Advancement, MIS Quarterly, 19(1), 107-122.

Igbaria, Magid and Wormley, Wayne (1995). Race Differences in Job Performance and Career Success, Communications of the ACM, 38(3), 82-92.

Igbaria, M. and Greenhaus, J.H. (1992). The Career Advancement Prospects of Managers and Professionals: Are MIS Employees Unique, Decision Sciences, 23(2), 478-499.

Jacobs, Sheila M. and Mary VanSell (1996). Telecommuting: Issues for the IS Manager, Information Systems Management, 13(1), 18-22.

Kanter, R.M. (1979). Differential access to opportunity and power in R. Alvares (Ed.), Discrimination in Organizations, San Francisco: Jossey-Bass.

Mahfood, Phillip E. (1992). Homework: How to Hire, Manage and Monitor Employees Who Work at Home. Chicago, IL: Probus Publishing.

McCloskey, Donna Weaver and Magid Igbaria (1998). A Review of the Empirical Research on Telecommuting and Directions for Future Research in The Virtual Workplace, Magid Igbaria and Margaret Tan (Eds.), IDEA Group Publishing, Hershey, Pennsylvania.

Olson, Matgrethe H. (1983). Remote Office Work: Changing Work Patterns in Space and Time, Communications of the ACM, 26(3), 182-187.

Olson, Margrethe H. (1989). Organizational Barriers to Professional Telework in Eileen Boris and Cynthia Daniels (Eds.) Historical and Contemporary Perspectives on Paid Labor at Home. Urbana: University of Illinois Press.

Ramsower, Reagan Mays (1985). Telecommuting: The Organizational and Behavioral Effects of Working at Home, UMI Research, Ann Arbor, Michigan.

Riley, Francine and Donna Weaver McCloskey (1997). Telecommuting as a Response to Helping People Balance Work and Family in Integrating Work and Family: Challenges and Choices for a Changing World, S. Parasuraman and J. Greenhaus (Eds.), Quorum Books, Westport, Connecticut.

Ross, (from N. Lamar Reinsch, 1997 – The Journal of Business Communication)

Schepp, Brad (1990). The Telecommuter's Handbook, New York: Pharos Books.

Shellenbarger, Sue (1993, December 16). I'm Still Here! Home Workers Worry They're Invisible, Wall Street Journal, B1, Col. 1.

Solomon, Norman A. and Andrew J. Templer (1993). Development of Non-Traditional Work Sites: The Challenge of Telecommuting, Journal of Management Development, 12(5), 21-32.

Stanko, Brian B. and Rebecca J. Matchette (1994). Telecommuting: The Future is Now, B&E Review, October-

December, 8-11.

Stumpf, S.A. and London, M. (1981). Capturing Rater Policies in Evaluating Candidates for Promotion, Academy of Management Journal, 24(4), 752-766.

Touliatos, J., Bedeian, A.G., Mossholder, K.W. and Barkman, A.I. (1984). Job-Related Perceptions of Male and Female Government, Industrial and Public Accountants, Social Behavior and Personality, 12, 61-68.

Tsui, A.S. (1984). A Role Set Analysis of Managerial Reputation, Organizational Behavior and Human Performance, 34, 64-96.

Wagel, William H. (1988). Telecommuting Arrives in the Public Sector, Personnel, 65, 14-16.

Weiss, Julian M. (1994). Telecommuting Boosts Employee Output, HRMagazine, 39(2), 51-53.

Wright, Phillip C. (1993). Telecommuting and Employee Effectiveness: Career and Managerial Issues, International Journal of Career Management, 5(1), 4-9.

Semantic Domains for Information Modeling

Antonio Badia

Computer Science and Computer Engineering, University of Arkansas, SCEN 232, Fayetteville, AR 72701

e-mail: abadia@godel.uark.edu, Phone: (501) 575-7662, Fax: (501) 575- 3817

INTRODUCTION

The relational model, as defined originally, made the concept of domain orthogonal to the data model. Conse-quently, the concept received little attention and was hardly developed. Recently, several factors have highlighted this weaknesses of the relational model. Interest in heterogeneous information integration proved the need to capture more meaning about the domains involved ([ESR],[LNE]). Also, the difficulty to model complex entities in the real world on the relational model has led to the idea of letting users supply abstract data types to the database ([CAR]). This idea has not surfaced without a long debate on the notion of domain in the relational model ([CAM],[DAT],[DAW]).

Semantic data models ([HK]) and knowledge representation formalisms ([REA]) have always been more care-ful about representing domain information in order to capture more data semantics; however they usually lack a strong notion of domain. In this paper we propose to define a concept of domain that captures more semantics and that can be used as the basis for work on schema integration, semantic query optimization, and any other task that requires real-world semantics. This notion of domain is different from others in the literature in that it uniformly applies to simple (attribute) domains and to complex (entities, relationships) domains; it covers both structural and semantic information, it takes context into account and it sharply separates specification from implementation. While each one of these characteristics is present to some degree on same data models, no work that we are aware of tries to combine them all.

The structure of the paper is as follows. In the next section we give some examples of applications of the extended concept of domain, to give the reader a feel for the importance of the concept, and discuss related research to illustrate the current state of the art. In section 3, we present the basic definitions of the extended concept of domain. We deal with each aspect on a separate subsection. Our approach is intuitive; the presentation is informal and is illustrated with examples to give a feeling for the intended use of the concept. Finally, in section 4 we summa-rize the ideas of the paper and point out some issues that deserve further research.

MOTIVATION AND RELATED WORK

Our basic idea is to consider every value in the database as belonging to a domain. With the domain, we associate metadata (data about the data) which gives information about how to manipulate the data in more intelli-gent ways. It may seem that making everything a domain puts a burden on the system designers, but this concept allows to capture more useful semantics, and this semantics is vital for advanced applications.

Applications

The work of [ESR] and [LNE] shows that integration of heterogeneous information will depend on how much semantics we have managed to capture, since it is the only way to overcome problems with synonyms, different (partial) representations of the same information, etc.

Example 1:

Assume we are interested in integrating the information of two databases which have related data in slightly different format. The following two term descriptions of individuals would match, provided that
• *age* has transformation functions to solve the scale difference,
• *first-name* has a function that OKs partial string matches, and
• *zipcode* in address has functions to go from one
implementation to another.

Note that certain conflicts could be solved automatically: the difference in order of fields in both tuples does not matter (since tuples have no order), and the fact that fields are slightly different can be handled by a unification procedure ([BAD]), in which information that does not directly conflict is combined.

```
(employee1 ((structure tuple last-name first-name age address department)
            (last-name Jones)
            (first-name James)
            (age 30) % age in years
            (address 100 Frier FYV 72701)
            (department shoes))

(employee2 ((structure tuple first-name last-name address age)
            (first-name J.)
            (last-name James)
            (address 100 Frier FYV "72701")
            (age 3600) % age in months
```

Semantic information is also vital for semantic query optimization, in which the knowledge about the domains that are mentioned in a query is used to arrive to an equivalent, but easier to process, query.

Example 2:

Assume a query that asks for employees that are 75 years or older. This query can be determined to return an empty answer without ever looking at the database extension, by checking the information in the domain *Employee*. Note that this query will return an empty answer in any database state in which the domain description holds. Thus, it probably would be very useful to explain to the user why the answer to the query is empty, since it probably reveals a misconception by the user. This is a technique used in cooperative query processing ([GM],[DI],[LAC]).

Finally, we note that the generation and management of metadata to capture more information about data is an important step in the development of a data warehouse. It is acknowledged that the quality of the Decision Support environment depends greatly on the quality of the data in the Data Warehouse. Since this data usually proceeds from a variety of heterogeneous sources, it must be cleansed, checked and put in a global format before it can be entered in the warehouse. The importance of this phase has been made evident in the literature ([BK]).

Literature Review

There has been a large amount of research on the area of schema integration (and in general, heterogeneous information integration) lately (see [HULL] for an excellent overview) which has motivated interest on expanded concept of domain. We will mention only research that has directly influenced the work presented here.

The work of [LNE] examines schema integration from the point of view of attribute integration. The authors present a list of characteristics of attributes (uniqueness, cardinality, domain, static semantic integrity constraints, dynamic semantic integrity constraints, security constraints, allowable operations and scale) which try to capture as much as possible of the semantics of attributes. Two attributes are considered basically equivalent if there is a mapping from the domain of one to the domain of the other which is an isomorphism (i.e. it maps each characteristic of one attribute into a corresponding characteristic of the other attribute, and it has an inverse with the same property). If the map does not have an inverse, the equivalence is weak. The main difference between the concepts is that strong equivalence permits updates on values on one domain, as these can be meaningfully mapped into the other domain. If the map extend over the domains of the attributes (i.e. every possible value), the equivalence is equal. If the map involves the subset of the domain of attribute A and the whole domain of attribute B, it is said that A is contained in B. When no mapping (weak or strong) occurs, the attributes are considered disjoint. Integration of attributes is based on the exact relationship between attributes. If two attributes are strongly equivalent, they can be integrated by unionizing their domains (since their characteristics are basically the same). If A is contained in B, A is considered a subclass of B. If they are disjoint, a new class is formed (certain conditions ensure that the two attributes in question can be meaningfully combined) and both attributes are considered (disjoint) subclasses of the new class. Based on this relation at the attribute level, equivalence of pairs of objects or relationships is defined based on whether an equivalence exists among the key attribute(s) of those objects or relationships. Integration of objects and relations is likewise based on the possible integration of attributes in the object or relation.

The work of [ESR] starts with the observation that values need, in order to be properly interpreted and integrated, a context which gives as much of their meaning as possible. In order for different systems to be able to interoperate, values are transformed into semantic values by adding to each attribute a context. The context gives information about the meaning, properties (like the source, quality and scale) and organization of an attribute. Also, conversion functions which express how certain values in a context can be transformed into values in another context are given. A context mediator examines the context of values and their conversion functions to make sure that values can be meaningfully compared, manipulated and transformed. This work is developed in the framework of the relational model. An extension of SQL, called Context-SQL, in introduced that extends SQL with the ability to provide contexts for values so that any operations requested in the SELECT of WHERE clause of a query can be analyzed by the query mediator.

The work of [CBH] utilizes the framework of Description Logics (DLs) to represent descriptions of sets of individuals. In DLs, a description is a composite term that is built from primitive classes and restrictions on the properties individuals may have, expressed by some constructors. Thus, DLs can be used to express information about attributes. An operation on descriptions, called the Least Common Subsumer (lcs) is introduced, and its relationship to other well-known operation on DLs (subsumption) is studied, in order to determine the properties and complexity of lcs. Intuitively, this operation computes the largest set of commonalties between two descriptions, and therefore it seems specially well suited for the task of information integration(3). Technically, a description C is the lcs of descriptions A and B if C subsumes both A and B and there is no other description D such that D also subsumes A and B and is subsumed by C. The operation lcs is based on the least upper bound (lub) of the partial order generated by the constructors. Those constructors are, in many cases, similar to the functors we have defined to capture characteristics of the domain. This coincidence is not surprising, since for the lcs operation to work as a integration of data, as much as possible of the domain semantics must be expressed in the terms.

BASIC DEFINITIONS

The basic intuition is that every value is part of a domain. A domain is the pool of values for attributes, objects and relations. Thus, all the things allowed in our ontology should come from a domain. However, the domain is more than a list of values; it gives meaning to the values on it. In order to capture the semantics associated with the data, we need to describe domains in as much detail as possible. Descriptions of domains will contain several types of related information, like structural information, semantic (contextual) information, operations allowed, and possible implementations (note that this information is usually characterized as metadata).

What kind of information defines a domain? In [ESR], a semantic value is defined as a value plus and environment (contextual information). This includes metadata for meaning, properties (source, quality, precision), organization and conversion functions. Also, a context mediator is used to go from values in a context to values in another. For [LNE], there are a series of properties that are deemed necessary for information integration: uniqueness, cardinality, domain extension, static integrity constraints, dynamic integrity constraints, security constraints, allowable operations and scale. It is clearly impossible to come up with a list of properties that will provide us with the data meaning as appropriate for each intended use. Instead, we give a list of aspects that are considered necessary and suggest ways in which each one can be captured.

Throughout the paper, examples are written in italicized font, and a functional notation is used, with *(age (min-value 0))* meaning the minimum value for elements of domain *age* is 0. Sometimes *age* will be called a functor in this context. In order not to get confused with terminology from other approaches, we call the attributes that define a domain <u>characteristics</u>. In the next subsections we introduce each characteristic separately.

Domain Structure

A domain is defined intensively, in that we do not list of all the elements (in infinite domains, this is clearly impossible; but even for finite domains, listing the elements is not sufficient to have a domain), but declare information about the domain to characterize it as completely as possible . It will not always be possible to describe domains completely; therefore, we distinguish between primitive and defined domains (1):

- primitive: there is no set of necessary and sufficient conditions to define the domain. As a consequence, individuals need be asserted as instances of them. What can be asserted for such domains are constraints (i.e. necessary conditions).
- defined: necessary and sufficient conditions can be given. As a consequence, a (total) predicate belongs? can be defined for the domain (i.e. one that always returns "yes" or "no" for any individual). Note that this does not mean that such domains are absolute or context-independent; only that at the present we can give a complete definition for the values on it.

Example 3:

Consider the domain *age*. The value of *age* (for humans) must be a number between 0 and 150. Note that this not absolute (some day medical sciences may allow people to live longer) and is context dependent: age limits are not the same for humans and other animals (the next subsection deals with context-dependent aspect of domains in more detail.). Thus age is considered a derived domain. On the other hand, the domain *last-name*, intended to cover English proper nouns for people, cannot be analytically defined -a list of names must be given, a list that probably is going to change over time.

This first distinction gives us a difference between the concept of domain and the concept of abstract data type:

an abstract data types do not put any limitation into what can be an element of the data type.

Because the domain is going to provide values not only for attributes, but also for entities and relations, we must admit domains that have complex structures. Thus, a second distinction (orthogonal to the first one) must be made based on the structural composition of a domain, which is represented explicitly. From this point of view, two types of domains are distinguished:

- simple: the values are considered atomic or not decomposable.
- complex: the values have internal structure. This structure is described by one of the following functors:
  - tuple, which takes an indeterminate number of domains as arguments. Order is not important on a tuple, and arguments may be heterogeneous.
  - set takes a single domain as argument.
  - sequence takes a domain and a natural number as arguments. The intended meaning is that the sequence has as many arguments as the natural number, all belonging to the domain. Order is important on a sequence, and obviously the sequence is homogeneous.
  - list takes an indeterminate number of domains as arguments. Order is important on a list, and arguments may be heterogeneous.

Note that since tuple arguments may be heterogeneous, we have covered all the combinations of ordered/non ordered structures with heterogeneous/homogeneous elements.

Example 4:
We define the domain *employee* has having a tuple structure and as arguments domains *last-name* and *age*.

Context
Contextual knowledge is necessary in order to understand the meaning of values. In this kind of knowledge we include several pieces of information:

- context, i.e. relativization of values to a given situation. Domains may have slightly different semantics when they are part of another domain. Complex domains get part of their semantics from the domains that are part of their structure. However, the complex domain may add to or change the semantics of those domains; that is, a domain A may have somewhat different semantics when it is part of another domain B than when it is part of another domain C (domains C and B be considered contexts for A). A complex domain may also constraint the way its component domains interact.

Example 5:
Obviously a lot of the semantics is context dependent. The maximum age could be set at 150 for people (a pretty safe limit) but it should be 25 for a cat or a dog. Thus, when used as the value of the attribute of a certain domain, the set of allowed values changes. Sometimes the change is very subtle; any domain should be considered as a possible context in which the same attribute may yield different values.

Assume a domain *People* and subdomains *Employee* and *Relative*. Because mandatory retirement at 70 is a policy of the business, in the context of *employee* the domain *age* has a maximum value of 70. However, relatives may have any age that a person can have, and therefore inherit the maximum value of *age* in *People* unchanged.

- constraints that hold of all values in the domain. For complex domains, constraints usually assert dependencies among the component domains. This includes functional dependencies from the data model, or business rules. Note that there is a distinction between properties of the domain as a whole and properties of the elements in the domain. For instance, that all employees have a maximum age of 70 is a property of the elements, but we attach it to the domain *employee* because it only happens in that context. Asking that each employee name be unique is a property of the domain as a whole. The difference is important to reasoning methods: to check that the first type of constraint holds, we have to examine each element of the domain separately; to check the second type, all elements of the domain must be compared to each other.
- operations that are allowed on elements of the domain. These are operations involving only the domain elements (or domains that are part of it, in the case of complex domains). Two operations are required for a derived domain:
     -a membership predicate;
     -an equality (and inequality) predicate;

Operations are characterized by signatures. Signatures only give the type of an operation, and they are expressed as input-type,…,input-type ->output-type. This is clearly not sufficient, but here we concentrate on the declarative aspects of domain.

Example 6:
The operation *initial:name ->Character* is attached to the domain *name*. The *operation get-name: employee -*

> *name* is attached to the domain *employee*.

Domain Representation

The semantic concept of domain must be implementation independent. To this end, the data type used to implement it in a computer is just another attribute of the domain. More than one data type is allowed, in which case the attribute is multi-valued, and low -level (internal) conversion functions must be declared to allow an equality predicate to be implemented over all the elements of the domain.

Example 7:

The type *age* can be implemented as a string ("42"), an integer (42) or a real (42.00). If more than one of these representations are allowed, then conversion functions are necessary, so that we can meaningfully compare and manipulate values in different representations. Note that for three different representation, six different functions are necessary: their signatures are *string -> integer, integer -> string, string -> real, real -> string, integer -> real, real -> integer*.

In general, for n different implementations, n * (n –1) operations will be necessary.

The representation of complex domains is more problematic, as programming languages may differ greatly on the built-in types offered. Besides types for record (structure) and array, it is unclear how to refer to data types in general. We note, however, that the important part of the characteristic is the presence of conversion functions that allow representation independence.

Example 8:

Most database systems have utilities to dump the contents of a table in a system file, usually by transforming data from its internal representation to ASCII. Another utility is usually provided for the inverse task (reading information from a file in ASCII and populating a table in the database with it). Such utilities have an implicit representation of the domain and of the conversion functions. A distributed heterogeneous database system that deals with both relational databases and system files would have to be aware of the difference in implementation and the conversion functions in order to integrate the information.

Hierarchies

Organization of attributes in hierarchies plays an important role in reasoning about the properties of the attributes, especially reasoning about attribute and schema integration ([BAN],[SGN]). Therefore we allow for expression of relationships among domains. Domains may be organized in a hierarchy; the concept of inheritance applies. However, the relations among attributes may be more complicated than mere class-subclass links. Since we are interested in capturing structural relations, we allow the subdomain, disjoint from, overlaps with, partition and part-of functors to be used.

It is assumed that simple domains are disjoint from each other. Note that this holds even if the extensions happen to overlap or even coincide. For instance, extensions for domains age and *width* are likely to overlap notably. However, we know that they denote completely different information, and consider them disjoint (and disallow comparisons and other operations between the two, unless an operation relating the two is explicitly declared -an even that can be done only under certain circumstances). For complex domains, the relationship part-of holds between the complex domain and the domains that make up its structure.

Example 9:

Our previous example assumes that *Employee* and *Relative* are subdomains of domain *Person*. We would usually state that they are disjoint. Domain *age* is a part of both subdomains, as well as part of the domain *Person*. On a university model, domains *Faculty*, *Student* and *Staff* are subclasses of *Person*, and may not be disjoint, but overlapping. All three subdomains together may, from the point of view of our modelling, exhaust the domain *Person*, in which case they constitute a (non disjoint) partition of the domain.

Operations on Domains

All our operations are defined in the context of a domain. This seems to create a problem, however, in the following sense. The operations that are internal to a domain were already described in subsection 3.2. Since in principle no two simple domains are compatible, there should not be operations that involve more than one domain. But in some cases some domains must be operated upon together. For these cases, high level (external) conversion functions have to be provided. Since each operation must be attached to a domain, the only way for an operation to involve two or more different domains is if they are related to each other in some way. For example, an operation that relates *name* and *age* must be attached to *Employee*. If *name* and *age* were not part-of the domain *Employee* (and *name* and *age* were not related by some other structural relation) then an operation relating the two would not be possible. We take the point of view that this restriction is meaningful and that operations not related to any particular domain are better left to an external part of the system, for instance a query language processor(2).

Example 10:

The domains Length and Width must be multiplied to obtain a
surface. However, they are both subdomains of domain Dimension, so
a proper operation can be defined (although said operation must be attached to
Dimension).

Relations and Views

We have treated some entities as tuples of elements from some previously defined domains. It is clear that relationships can also, in this sense, be defined as domains. Thus, we model relationships as special domains, their extension being but one of the characteristics that we want to capture. A relationship is a domain with a certain fixed structure and certain characteristics: <u>arity</u>, <u>tuple-structure</u> and <u>extension</u>. Other properties (like being transitive, having keys, or functional dependencies) can also be expressed as characteristics in the context.

Example 11:

The relation *works-for*, relating domains *Employee* and *department*, is a domain with arity two, and tuple structure *(tuple employee department)*. The value of the characteristic *extension* would be a set of tuples with the given structure. Note that while this seems to imply that relations must operate on the entities themselves (as opposed to keys or identifiers representing them) the view that we are developing here is purely conceptual, and does not constraint in any way possible implementations.

An important note must be made here: set-valued characteristics are allowed, and therefore the above relation could be expressed (as it is done in the object-oriented model) by having an attribute *department* in the domain *Employee* and an attribute *employees* in the domain *department*. We take the point of view that one technique is not better than the other, and that probably both of them should be included in a good model. This represents some extra work in making sure that both techniques work together smoothly -i.e. that for any employee *e* and department *d*, *(e, x)* is in the extension of *works-for* (where *x* is an element of *e.department*), *(y,d)* is in the extension of *works-for* (where *y* is an element of *d.employee*), and nothing else is in the extension of *works-for*. This attitude, called semantic relativism in [BS], has long been a tenet of some knowledge representation formalisms. It allows for a neutral perspective on the modeling of information, and is usually accompanied by a redundancy on the language that expressed queries (i.e. expression like *e.department*, *works-for(x,y)*, *d.employee* are all allowed and used in querying the knowledge-base). Current data models (relational, object-oriented) take a unique point of view and model information from a unique perspective.

Views are nothing but new domains created by giving necessary and sufficient conditions in the definition. Thus, in this framework views are not different from other (derived) domains, and we can represent and reason about views just like any other domain. Thus, a view is obtained by combining other domains and putting further constraints on some or all of these domains (or on the way the domains are related).

Example 12:

The view of employees that work on the Marketing department could be defined by setting the property *department* of *employee* to "Marketing", or by getting the employees attribute of the "Marketing" object from domain *department*.

CONCLUSION AND FURTHER RESEARCH

We have introduced a strong notion of domain that helps capture more data semantics. This idea of domain includes information about the domain's internal structure, necessary (and if possible, sufficient) conditions for values to belong to it; contexts in which the domain may be used; operations that are allowed on elements of the domain (internal operations); place of the domain on a hierarchy of domains, possible representations for its elements, and (external) operations that may relate a given domain with others. We have seen that such a strong notion of domain is able to support knowledge-dependent operations, like heterogeneous information integration and semantic query optimization.

The notion of domain introduced here tries to be very general; however, it can be expanded in several ways. One of the more appealing is incorporating the idea of prototype. By specifying which attributes are necessary and which ones are optional for a concept to belong to a class we bring further flexibility to the framework. Also, it should be possible to give default (typical) values for (some of) the necessary attributes, and combine that with inheritance to allow for some sort of non monotonic reasoning ([MCA]). With these extensions, the formalism could be used to model semistructured data ([MAGQW]), since it is very flexible as to the structure of the domain and can express constraints on that structure.

We have made very little use of the idea of hierarchy. Term-based formalisms (like the psi-terms of [HBA], [AIT] and description logics ([BOR], [BOR2])) rely heavily on subsumption, a partial order on terms, to reason about terms denotation. We allow complex interactions to be expressed, and therefore it would be interesting to see if a counterpart of subsumption (or some other order-based technique) could be used in this framework.

Possible uses not mentioned here include data analysis and cleaning for data warehousing, and definition of ontologies for heterogeneous database systems. Both are very active areas of research currently, and it seems clear that their reliance on manual methods can only be alleviated by knowledge-based methods.

ENDNOTES
(1) This distinction is already made in [CL].
(2) In some systems, a special domain called *top* is allowed which is considered to subsume any other domain. In that case, the restriction on operations just described does not really limit the system.
(3) Surprisingly, the authors of [CBH] do not point out the possibility of using their technique for information integration in that paper.

BIBLIOGRAPHY
[BK] Ballou, D. P. and Kumar Tayi, G., Enhancing Data Quality in Data Warehousing Environments, Communications of the ACM, January 1999, vol. 42, no. 1.

[CBH] Cohen, W., Borgida, A. and Hirsh, H., Computing Least Common Subsumers in Description Logics, in Proceedings of AAAI-92.

[HBA] Holsheimer, M., de By, R. and Ait-Kaci, H. A Database Interface for Complex Objects, Technical report, Digital Paris Research Laboratory, March 1993.

[MAGQW] MuHugh,J. Abiteboul, S, Goldman, R., Quass, D. and Widom, J. LORE: A Database Management System for Semistructured Data, SIGMOD Record, vol. 26, number 3, September 1997.

[ESR] Sciore, E., Siegel, M. and Rowenthal, A. Using Semantics Values to facilitate interoperability Among heterogeneous Information Systems, ACM Transaction on Database Systems, June 1994.

[LNE] Larson, J., Navathe, S. and Elmasri, N. A Theory of Attribute Equivalence in Databases with Application to Schema Integration, IEEE Transactions on Software Engineering, vol. 15, number 4, April 1989.

[CLN] Calvanese, D., Lenzerini, M. and Nardi, Danielle A Unified Framework for Class-Based Representation Formalisms Proceedings of the Conference on Principles of Knowledge Representation, Bonn, 1994.

[BOR] Borgida, A. On the Relative Expressiveness of Description Logics and Predicate Logics, Artificial Intelligence, vol. 82, 1996

[BOR2] Borgida, A. Description Logics in Data Management, IEEE Transactions in Knowledge and Data Engineering, vol. 7, number 5, October 1995

[BS] Brachman, R. and Schmolze, J. An Overview of the KL-ONE Knowledge Representation System, Cognitive Science, vol. 9, 1985.

[BAN] Beck, H., Anwar, T. and Navathe, S. A Conceptual Clustering Algorithm for Database Schema Design, IEEE Transactions on Knowledge and Data Engineering, vol. 6, number 3, June 1994.

[NS] Nebel, B. and Smolka, G. Representation and Reasoning with Attribute Descriptions, in Blasius, Hedstuck, Rollinger, eds. Sorts and Types in Artificial Intelligence, Lecture Notes in Artificial Intelligence, 418, Springer-Verlag, 1990.

[HULL] Hull, R. Managing Semantic Heterogeneity in Databases: A Theoretical Perspective, invited tutorial for PODS 97.

[AIT] Ait-Kaci, H. An Algebraic Semantics Approach to the Effective Resolution of Type Equations, Theoretical Computer Science, vol. 45, 1986.

[SGN] Seth, A., Gala, S. and Navathe, S. On Automatic Reasoning for Schema Integration, International Journal of Intelligent and Cooperative Information Systems, vol. 2, n. 1, 1993.

[BIG] Blanco, J., Illarramendi, A. and Goni, A., Building a federated Relational Database System: An Approach Using a Knowledge-Based System, International Journal of Intelligent and Cooperative Information Systems, vol. 3, n. 4, 1994.

[CL] Catarzi, T. and Lenzerini, M. Representing and Using Interschema Knowledge in Cooperative Information Systems, International Journal of Intelligent and Cooperative Information Systems, vol. 2, n. 4, 1993.

[CAR] Carey, M. J., Mendoza Mattos, M. and Nori, A. Object-Relational Database Systems: Principles, Products,nd Challenges (Tutorial). SIGMOD Conference 1997.

[CAM] Camps, R. Domains, Relations and Religious Wars, SIGMOD Record, vol. 25, n. 3, 1996.

[DAT] Date, C.J. A Response to R. Camp's Article, SIGMOD Record, vol. 25, n. 4, 1996.

[DAW] Darwin, H. In Reply to Domains, Relations and Religious Wars, SIGMOD Record, vol. 25, n. 4, 1996.

[HK] Hull, R. and King, R. Semantic Database Modeling: Survey, Applications and Research Issues, ACM Computing Surveys, vol. 19, n. 19, 1987.

[REA] Brachman, R.J. and Levesque, H. J., editors, Readings in Knowledge Representation, Morgan Kaufmann, 1985.

[GM] Gaasterland, T., Godfrey, P. and Minker, An overview of cooperative query answering, Journal of Intelligent Information Systems, vol. 1, 1992.

[DI] Demolombe, R. and Imielinsky, T. Non standard queries and non standard answers, Oxford University Press, 1994.

[LAC] Larsen, H.L., Andreasen, T. and Christiansen, H. Proceedings of the 1996 Workshop on Flexible Query Answering Systems, Roskilde University Center, 1996.

[MCA] McCarthy, J. Applications of Circumscription to Formalizing Common Sense Reasoning, Artificial Intelligence, vol. 28, 1986.

[BAD] Badia, A. Semantic Unification: A Tool for Information Integration, to appear in the proceedings of AIDA'99.

Information Technology in Banking: A Resource-based Analysis

Tanai Khiaonarong and Jonathan Liebenau
Department of Information Systems, London School of Economics, Houghton Street, London WC2A 2AE
Tel: +44 171 9556044, Fax: +44 171 9557385, E-mail: T.Khiaonarong@lse.ac.uk and J.L.liebenau@lse.ac.uk

ABSTRACT

This paper applies a resource-based view to examine the use of information technology in banking. After reviewing the basic concepts and recent developments under this perspective, two mini-case studies are presented, discussing the key role of IT and the main sources of innovation in each commercial bank. An analysis of the two cases suggests the following. Although there has been an increase of IT investment to gain competitive advantage, the sustaining of this advantage still depends on the stock of staff skills. Such resources are intangible, unique, and are much more difficult to replicate than physical resources. This suggests that IT investments may gain, but not sustain, a firm's competitive advantage, for which the latter requires a firm to acquire, accumulate, and advance its stock of skills.

INTRODUCTION

Does information technology (IT) contribute to competitiveness in commercial banks? Although competitiveness may be gained, can it be sustained? To address these questions, we examine the role of IT in banking using a resource-based approach. Our research objective is to examine the range of IT-related resources in firms, and identify and assess the sources of innovation. The research method involved the use of interviews with senior-level executives involved in IT-related areas in two of the largest international commercial banks based in Thailand. In addition, analysis of archival material, including company annual reports, company magazines, internal documents, and newspaper articles were used. The paper is organised into five sections. Section 2 provides a brief overview of the resource-based approach. Section 3 presents two mini-case studies of commercial banks situated in Thailand, examining their use of IT and identifying their sources of innovation. Section 4 discusses the competitiveness of the two banks based on a resource-based view, while the final section concludes the paper.

THE RESOURCE-BASED APPROACH

The resource-based perspective is a relatively recent view of studying how a firm's unique set of resources influences its growth (Foss, 1997). This view argues that firm competitive advantage is sustained through a set of unique resources. Penrose (1959, p.25) was one of the earliest proponents of this view, arguing that 'it is never *resources* themselves that are the inputs in the production process, but only the *services* that the resources can render'. This implied that firms are conceptualised as a 'bundle of resources' and differ in their innovative capabilities while they transform resources into potential services, making them distinct and influencing their growth. Itami (1987) illustrates these resources as 'invisible assets', including the knowledge, skills, and experience of committed people.

The importance of resources has also been emphasised in strategic management studies. For example, Chandler (1962) argues that the structure of firms follows its strategy, suggesting that *entrepreneurial* decisions and actions affect *operating* decisions, particularly in the allocation and reallocation of resources. Andrews (1987) points to the central role resources in corporate strategy in converting distinctive competence into competitive advantage. Kay (1993) introduces the term distinctive capabilities, which represents a firm's source of competitive advantage including architecture, reputation, innovation, and strategic assets.

Although the role of resources has been identified as important, there has been less emphasis on the analysis of their attributes. For example, Porter (1990) argues that a nation's competitive advantage is determined by four major attributes in his 'diamond' framework, including factor conditions, demand conditions, related and supporting industries, and firm strategy, structure, and rivalry. This structural view of resources, however, overlooks their underlying behavioural attributes (Nonaka and Takeuchi, 1995, pp. 46-47). Prahalad and Hamel's (1990) core competence argument acknowledges the importance of behavioural aspects in collective learning in firms, but does not analyse the acquisition of competence. Stalk et al (1992) further argue that core competence has a strong orientation towards the production and technological aspects of the firm along specific points in the value chain, and suggests that the concept of capabilities complement this with a more visible and broadly-based analysis in the whole value chain.

The shortcomings of the research-based view are a lack of a comprehensive theoretical framework and empirical research. For example, Nonaka and Takeuchi (1995, p. 49) argue that the resource-based approach does not address how different parts in a firm interact over time to influence innovation, and introduce an analytical framework based on examining explicit and implicit knowledge. Robins and Wiersema (1995) suggest that empirical research in the resource-based view has been relatively difficult due to the concepts of capabilities and tacit knowledge, which resists direct measurement.

However, proponents of resource-based theory suggest that the approach contribute to a new theory of the firm, incorporating a range of related theoretical perspectives (Conner, 1991; Mahoney and Pandian, 1992). There has also been the development of theoretical frameworks in support of these arguments. Wernerfelt (1984) developed an economic analysis approach, focusing on the relationship between resource-product matrices. Barney (1991) introduced a firm resource model, which analysed the potential of firm resources based on their value, rareness, imitability, and substitutability attributes. Grant (1991) developed a framework to analyse the relationship among firm resources, capabilities, competitive advantage, and strategy. Peteraf (1993) argues that there are four conditions influencing competitive advantage. This included superior and heterogeneous resources, imperfect mobility of resources, *ex post* limits to competition (competition which is limited *subsequently* after a firm has gained a superior position over competitors), and *ex ante* limits to competition (competition which is limited *prior* to a firm gaining a superior position over competitors). More recently, resource-based perspectives have shared a common characteristic with evolutionary views of the firm, leading to attempts to synthesise the two approaches (Foss et al., 1995; Montgomery, 1995). Such integration has also been compared by the '4 Rs' relationship, focusing on the link among the concepts of resource, routine, replication, and rent (Winter, 1995, p. 148). In sum, the resource-based view has been a widely applied approach, suggesting that its use may potentially become 'automatic' rather than 'noteworthy' (Wernerfelt, 1995, p.173).

In information systems research, IT has been seen as a type of strategic resource, which is a source of sustained competitive advantage to firms, sectors and countries (Clemons, 1991; Clemons and Row, 1991; Mata et al., 1995). For example, Ciborra and Andreu (1998, pp.90-96) applied the resource-based approach in developing an organisational learning model, which emphasises the relationship among strategic, capabilities, and routinisation loops in core capability development. Grant and Liebenau (forthcoming) combined evolutionary and resource-based views in developing an organisational information systems capabilities framework, which focuses on the relationship among routines, contexts, and resources. However, the resources related to IT are not exclusively embodied in computer hardware and software components. For example, Ross et al (1996) argue that there are three IT assets that have an interdependent relationship, including human assets, technology assets, and relationship assets. Powell and Dent-Micallef (1997) also suggest that IT was not a sole source of sustained competitive advantage, but rather its use in leveraging intangible and complementary human and business resources, including culture, strategic technology planning, and supplier relationships. These IT assets may also be viewed as a firm's physical resources, organisational resources, and human resources. We examine these issues in the following sections.

THE COMMERCIAL BANK CASES

This section presents two mini case studies of commercial banks. The organisations were selected as they are among the largest international commercial banks, in addition to being two of the largest banks, which have widely invested in IT in Thailand.1 The cases represent two firms seeking to use IT to develop new financial products and services, to provide innovative banking services, and to gain competitive advantage in local and foreign financial markets. In each case, we provide a brief background of the bank, discuss the role of IT, and identify the main sources of innovation.

Siam Commercial Bank

Siam Commercial Bank (SCB) was officially established in 1906, following its transformation from a 'Book Club' set-up in 1904. The Book Club, which is a private trust, formed the modern basis of the bank, providing basic banking functions such as deposits, loan extensions and foreign exchange. It was operated by local people and primarily served Thai and Chinese clients in the local business community. The bank became the first Thai commercial bank formed after the first foreign commercial bank began operations in the country in 1888. Most importantly, it has served as a model for many Thai commercial banks in the early and modern periods. In 1996, the bank was ranked the fourth largest Thai commercial bank in terms of total assets, and the 211th largest international commercial bank (KTB, 1997). Today, the bank's chief executive officer has adopted the learning organisation concept (Senge, 1990). This is further supported by the bank's strategy in developing knowledge workers who are 'enknowledged personnel performing quality work to best serve our customers.' Bank restructuring based on the principle of customer-based business process management has also contributed to a flatter organisation with small business teams capable of responding rapidly to customer needs.

Role of IT

SCB has been progressive in the use of IT. This has been partly due to senior-level management support, which has helped shape the company's visions and strategies. For example, the active involvement of the chief executive officer has led to investments in data warehousing technology to learn more about the bank and, more importantly, customer information (*The Asian Banker*, 15 August 1997). Furthermore, the chief executive officer has clearly defined two main objectives in the use of IT, which were (1) to facilitate daily banking activities between the bank and customers, and (2) to develop new methods in delivering financial services (*SCB Technologies*, November 1996, pp. 8-9).

More interestingly, the bank surprised the banking community in early-1998 by announcing an increased investment in its IT budget by 2-3% over its Baht 900 million investment in the previous year (*Bangkok Post*, 14 January 1998). This was despite the country's financial crisis, which caused a change in exchange rate regime, a devaluation of the local currency, and the cutting of costs across companies. Moreover, in response to the financial crisis, the bank established a non-profit organisation to serve as a job placement centre for potential employers and employees, and providing language and computer training for unemployed IT professionals (*Bangkok Post*, 27 August 1997).

Such an aggressive strategy was well supported by the bank. For example, the bank's technology group first executive vice president suggested that the organisation's continued investment in IT was based on the transformation of problems into opportunities, particularly during the period of financial crisis in the country. In support of this argument, the bank noted that the development of an Intranet and inventory control system helped reduce internal expenses to approximately Baht 13 million annually, and moreover, reduced non-performing loans to approximately 6% (Bangkok Post, 10 December 1997). Bank functions related to IT are mainly organised in the Technology Group. In addition, the Information System Audit Department located within the Human Resource and Control Group also has a technological role. The Technology Group, following the initiation of ideas in the early-1980s and a reorganisation in 1996, reports directly to the bank's chief executive officer, and is divided into five main units (*SCB Technologies*, May 1996, pp. 6-7).

Firstly, the technology policy division overlooks broad technological developments and provides a centre of co-ordination. It prepares and monitors policies, plans, and the bank's expenditures in IT. Secondly, the system engineering department develops, implements, tests, operates, and maintains the bank's computer systems. Thirdly, the technology and process engineering department overlooks the management of the bank's two man computer centres, controls the operating systems, and manages the bank's data warehouse located in mainframe computers. Moreover, it also overlooks the purchase of computer equipment. Fourthly, the business relations department manages the bank's call centre, promotes the use of IT in the bank and to the public, and finally, overlooks the bank's customer information facility system, credit monitoring, and collection system and black list system. And lastly, the applied technology department conducts research into the use of new information technologies, maintains computer software, and manages computer hardware, software and communication standards. This last function has played a particularly important role in building and strengthening bank capabilities, which will later be discussed.

IT Development Plans

In 1983 the bank prepared two major technological development plans. The first nine-year plan covered the period between 1983-1991, and the second six-year plan between 1992-97. The first plan was divided into 3 phases, each covering a three-year period. The first phase was aimed to improve customer services with IT. During this phase, the bank introduced the first ATM in Thailand in 1983. This major development became a very successful innovation as the bank's customer's bases expanded and market share increased. This later required central bank co-ordination of ATM-related activities introduced by other Thai commercial banks accordingly.

In the second phase, the bank used IT to automate routines and to increase productivity. In bank automation, paper documents, work processes and the required time to accomplish tasks were reduced. While work processes were shortened, this increased the speed in delivering customer services. This was further supported with an office automation project aimed to facilitate the flow of information within various working units in the bank. In the third and last phases of the first plan, the bank prepared plans for the IT society. IT projects were aimed to strengthen the bank's overall technological infrastructure further. For example, a management information system was developed to connect four main sub-systems related to customer, financial, marketing, and personnel management. Additionally, the bank has co-operated with large computer vendors like IBM to modernise its hardware and software technologies.

The second plan is also divided into 3 phases, each covering a two-year period. In the second plan, efforts have been directed to strengthen the existing technological infrastructure of the bank, including the upgrading of computer, telecommunications, and database technological capabilities to support ongoing and forecasted expansion of banking activities.

Bank Automation and Innovation

Computers were first introduced into the bank in 1975. This was primarily to support deposit functions located at the bank's head office. Early use of IT was extended to more sophisticated bank operations, and financial products and services. The pioneering ATM provided a new method of delivering payment services, and was widely adopted by other local commercial banks, which diffused nation-wide accordingly. In the 1990s, the bank once again became a pioneer in introducing on-line electronic banking communications in Thailand, particularly in tele-banking and info-banking systems.

In 1996, the bank relocated its head office to a new building, which reflected its adjustment to globalisation. The new 'intelligent building' incorporates the use of modern IT, and includes building automation features over-looking control, safety, security, telecommunications, and energy-saving systems. Moreover, an office automation system connected by the bank's local area network provides a communication channel to both bank customers and departments located within the building. In the early 1990s the bank introduced two major changes. They were the adoption of customer-based business process management and organisational restructuring at the bank's head office. Price Waterhouse was contracted to advise on improving the bank's commercial lending and counter services. The consultants studied customer requirements and modified the bank's work processes to help address their needs. This partly resulted in the increased use of IT.

The bank recently developed relationship banking 2020 (RB 2020). This project was jointly developed with IBM and helped shift the bank's focus from account-based system to a customer-based system. RB 2020 restructured the way retail banking was delivered to bank customers since the early 1970s, and moreover, has an analytical capability that assists in identifying the most suitable services for a particular target group of customers. This project, introduced by the bank in early 1996, was to be widely diffused and installed in over 400 bank branches nation-wide. The bank has adapted and applied object-oriented technology to facilitate the delivery of many financial services. For example, loan authorisation systems were built based on expert systems, which has decision-making capabilities based on a 100-points scale. If a loan application scored high points, the computer approved the loan. Otherwise, an average or low score further considered or rejected the application accordingly. Furthermore, the bank built a mobile loan authorisation system, which efficiently analysed and approved a customer loan application data, following on-line verification by portable computers with the bank's head office. Such services provided new channels for delivering financial services and moreover, improved customer convenience.

IT is also applied to improve personnel management and promotion (*SCB Technologies*, December 1996, pp. 8-9). In 1994, the bank's human resource and control group introduced a personnel information system that recorded all personnel particulars including education, work experience, and training. In 1995, an employee promotion system was subsequently introduced. This was aimed to support the bank's concept of a learning organisation. The second system was later enhanced to support decision-making in personnel promotion, and was aimed to make personnel information widely available to specific bank departments and nation-wide branches.

Sources of Innovation

The sources of innovation can be grouped into five main areas. The first source is from the bank's applied technology department (*SCB Technologies*, June 1996, pp. 6-7). This department, established in 1996, conducts research and development into the application of IT in financial services. Departmental tasks are grouped into five different teams - IT standards, technology selection, research and development, prototype, and support services. After the research and development team creates a new innovation, it is tested by the prototype team and considered for bank-wide diffusion by the systems engineering department. The department, for example, introduced a pilot electronic commerce project using the Internet and a newly established transaction centre in late 1997 (*The Nation*, 3 June 1998). As a result, SCB became one of the earliest commercial banks in the country to provide Internet-based banking services, in the form of 'SCB Cash Management' for retail customers, which provides account and statement inquiries, funds transfers, and bill payment services (*The Nation*, 26 November 1997). In addition, 'SCB Trade' provided corporate customers with international trading related services. The bank's first executive vice president responsible for the technology group describes the role of this office.

'In our applied technology office, staff would observe new products and examine what is appropriate for the bank. We try to recruit new staff who have recently completed their university studies and not rely on recruits with old working experiences. These recruits can be out-of-date easily. For example, the head of our applied technology office has a recent doctoral degree from a Japanese university with several months of working experiences acquired from that country. We try to attract new people.'

The second source is from co-operation with computer companies. Computer firms have introduced many innovative products and ideas to the bank, as suggested previously in IBM's involvement in RB 2020 development. In 1995, the bank's collaboration with Lines Technology led to the development of electronic systems that helped identify target customers, and provide personalised products and services. This included the introduction of the SCB video banking system that provided individual bank customers on-line financial, business and stock market information. In 1998, the bank, in collaboration with a local computer company, jointly developed a smart card system for a major university in the country, and further announced an aggressive strategy of entering into joint-venture partnerships with computer hardware companies (*Bangkok Post*, 14 January 1998). Furthermore, in response to the country's financial crisis, increased investments in IT were focused on the development of software with computer software companies. In co-operation with IBM, the bank planned to develop the first Workspace on Demand pilot project in Asia, which aims to reduce the ownership cost of IT by shifting from a personal computer to network computer working environment, resulting in a 'Zero Administration Environment' (*Bangkok Post*, 14 January 1998).

The third source is from bank-affiliated companies. Such companies created management and technological capabilities, and served as a consulting arm to strengthen the bank's competitiveness. In 1991, an affiliate company called Siam Information and Processing Company Limited (SIPCO) was established, mainly for the purpose of processing air tickets for the International Air Transportation Association. Thereafter, this company expanded its activities to outsourcing services, consulting services, and developed advanced software applications for the banking and financial services sectors, which also became beneficial for the bank. Most interestingly, the company provides a packaged banking solution software, which uses modern software development tools, such as object orientation and rapid prototyping. In 1994, the bank established Siam Commercial Link (SCL). The objective was to aid the development of new value-added industries through the transfer of technology. SCL includes two divisions. The first is a 'technology link', which serves to form international business collaborations, and the second is a 'management link', which aims to handle the recruitment of mid-level and top-level managers. In 1996, the bank entered a joint-venture agreement with the National Science and Technology Development Agency. As a result, SCL was renamed as Science Commercial Link. This served as a source of venture capital for domestic and overseas companies wanting to enter partnerships or invest in technology-related areas in Thailand. In other areas, the bank was also innovative. In 1995, SCB Business Services installed new software and security systems that permitted customers of Mastercard to obtain cash advances from Cirrus-affiliated ATMs around the world.

The fourth source is from the strengthening of staff capabilities. A major source of technology originates from employees. Senior-level management, particularly the bank's chief executive officer, has driven much of the bank's technological initiatives. Bank employees are sent to international seminars and computer trade exhibitions. Bank staffs learn, acquire and transfer new sources of skills and technology to the bank. The bank's first executive vice president responsible for the technology group describes the importance of skilled staff.

'We do not hire or have a high degree of dependency on consultants. A major source of innovation originates from bank staff. We have opportunities to attend seminars, read books or follow related developments. This includes staff in the technology group and other departments. Our managers have the opportunity to undertake training and make bank visits. This is similar for other employees. Every year, our employees have the opportunity to attend overseas seminars and computer shows such as COMDEX and CEBIT. Over 10 of our staff attend these exhibitions every year. So the sources of technology derives from these managers and staff.'

Moreover, staff are trained and retrained on a continual basis. Two training centres provide general programs that help educate and train staff on the bank's background and specific skills in banking. Video-conferencing systems also help staff in inter-office communication, meetings and information exchanges. The bank has planned agreements with local technological universities to offer computer courses at the bank's premises. Upon completing the courses, bank staff will obtain postgraduate degrees either in management information systems or computer science. The bank's first executive vice president responsible for the technology group further notes the importance of staff development programs.

'The training centre is only a tool for improving the quality of staff on a continuous basis. The centre is not aimed to increase the number of employees. I think that what is more helpful is the organisation of a postgraduate course for our staff. For example, the quality of entry-level staff varies from different disciplines and educational institutions. Technology is rapidly changing. The postgraduate course can help upgrade them. Our employees are very interested in this project and have a positive demand for it.'

Lastly, the bank's dependency on consultants is minimal. Computer software for minor programs, such as in client-server related projects, are developed in-house. To leverage such capabilities, the bank can readily consult its in-house research and development department or affiliated companies. However, for major programs that are unavailable in the market, software packages are purchased from outside sources and later modified to suit the bank's requirements. The bank maintains that this principle is necessary, as the organisation cannot continually depend on consultants. The bank builds its own capabilities by using purchased software packages as basic program structures which have to be adapted to rapidly changing user requirements. The bank also changed its work processes by outsourcing selected technology functions to overseas companies thereby focusing on more important and efficient areas. For example, this included the replacement of old methods of developing software from COBOL to object-oriented computer languages.

Summary

Strong senior-management support in IT suggests that the bank is a leading and forward-looking financial institution in the country and perhaps in Asia. Apart from investing heavily in IT, the bank has also gradually created capabilities through the set-up of an in-house research and development capability, the development of human resources, the co-operation with computer companies, and the establishment of bank-affiliated companies.

Thai Farmers Bank

Catalyst of Re-engineering

TFB was established by the Lamsam family in 1945. Although Bangkok Bank, the biggest bank in the country, may have claimed to pioneer re-engineering in the early-1980s, TFB was the catalyst of this change in the early-1990s. Apart from gaining wide publicity for its proactive bank re-engineering programs, the bank's successful use of IT to gain competitive advantage in the 1980s has also attracted international attention, resulting in a case study conducted by the Harvard Business School (Cash and Mookerjee, 1990). At the organisational level, the bank has set a mission of "the spirit of excellence", as well as the philosophy of "dedication to banking excellence", which aim to provide high-value added financial services and support to clients, while balancing societal and national concerns (TFB Annual Report, 1995). In 1996, the bank was ranked as the third largest Thai commercial bank in terms of total assets, and the 182nd largest international commercial bank (KTB, 1997; *The Banker*, various issues).

Innovation has become a major factor contributing to the bank's leadership. Bank re-engineering, in particular, helped strengthen the bank's capabilities and competitiveness, and further prompted preparations for more efficient working processes that are comparable to and competitive with international banking standards. Most importantly, the bank's senior-level management has played a key role in initiating the use of advanced information systems and supporting the reengineering of bank branches nation-wide. Back in 1984, the bank's chairman demonstrated his complete support to the senior vice president of the computer department in adopting ATMs, which followed recommendations made from a study of such machines at Banco International, Mexico's fourth largest commercial bank (cited from Cash and Mookerjee, 1990, p. 1).

'I still want to see the first Bangkok branch go on-line by the year-end, most of the others by the end of next year, and also 15-20 up-country branches. Siam Commercial Bank already has on-line branches and over 50 ATMs in Bangkok. Unless we catch up fast, they will capture a significant portion of our market share. You will have to manage a turnaround. I know you can do it. You have my total commitment of the bank's resources for this project.'

Role of IT

The bank's computer department was established in 1975. As the department head was technically-oriented, there was a weak link with business strategy, and moreover, there was an emphasis on batch retail processing systems, without considering the emergence of on-line systems being introduced by competitors (Cash and Mookerjee, 1990, p. 5). This changed in 1983, when the bank's chairman became involved in technology planning, established a high-level technology committee, and contracted a consulting company called Peat Marwick. As a result, the bank wrote-off its existing systems and considered the installation of IBM mainframe computers to support on-line computing.

As of 1997, the bank's use of IT is focused in four main areas. Firstly, the information system-processing department overlooks banking operations, including the gathering of input data, the processing of output information, and the backing-up of information on a 24-hour daily basis. Secondly, the information system-engineering department develops the bank's computer software. Thirdly, the telecommunication department supports inter-bank functions. And lastly, the newly established research and process development department, which studies and advises on the improvement of the bank's business processes, conducts research related activities.

The bank's president started and supported re-engineering in the early 1990s. In 1993, the president, who is a Harvard Business School graduate, attended a seminar on re-engineering organised in the United States by Michael Hammer (Hammer and Champy, 1993). As a result, such ideas formed the basis for organisational reforms, a change which was not only radical to the bank, since it was established in the mid-1940s, but also to the local banking community. Nevertheless, the bank's president was capable of communicating and convincing employees the main concepts and contributions behind re-engineering.

Firstly, foreign consulting firms helped the bank re-think. In 1992, early feasibility studies conducted by Booz Allen and Hamilton suggested a focus on retail banking businesses. Two more consulting companies were contracted, including Immacon focusing on bank restructuring, and Andersen Consulting concentrating on IT strategies. In 1993, a joint team of 11 employees, between the bank and IBM, helped develop a new computer system to pilot the bank's first branch re-engineering. Together, these gradually build the bank's managerial and technological capabilities, and have led to re-engineering without the use of foreign consulting companies (*The Economist*, 11-17 October 1997, pp. 128-9).

Secondly, the bank learned to re-design itself. The bank's president took a progressive position towards re-engineering by selecting 6 bank staff to jointly work with the consulting companies. This included research and analysis into the problems of the bank's current business processes and a comparative study of financial service delivery between Thai commercial banks and their foreign counterparts. The results suggested that Thai financial institutions were constrained by multiple working processes, which unnecessarily slowed the time to provide customer services. As a result, this early work materialised in the establishment of the bank's own research and process development department.

The bank re-designed its branches and business processes. For example, the front and back offices were rearranged to increase customer services areas to 80-90 percent (TFB interview, 1997). Financial services were grouped into five main service stations - cash services, personal services, general services, loan and marketing services, and electronic services. In electronic services, for example, this included the automation of routines such as in updating of bank balances or in depositing of cheques. Furthermore, the bank restructured its branch services, foreign service centres, liabilities, credit authorisation, funds transfer, and credit card services.

Lastly, IT helped the bank re-tool. This included the development of new computer systems and self-service machines for customers. For example, computer software was re-coded, and personal computers replaced dumb terminals, which connected the computer file servers located among branches and the bank's communication networks. In addition, bank tellers working with personal computers were empowered to authorise transactions within a predetermined amount of money, without seeking prior supervisory approval, which helped provide improve customer services and reduced overall cost.

The results of re-engineering suggested successful operating performances. This is based on the comparison between the time required to deliver a specific service before and after branch re-engineering. Generally, the average time in providing financial services required approximately 60-72 percent less time (TFB Annual Report, 1995). For example, the maximum and minimum time which was required to cash a cheque was approximately between 10-5 minutes before re-engineering, as compared with approximately 5.2-1.6 minutes after re-engineering (TFB Annual Report, 1995). As of 1997, the bank has claimed that re-engineering has reduced annual remuneration by 6.36 percent, when compared to figures in the previous four years, and moreover, has also reduced the number of employees to 15,740 from 16,400 in 1995 (*Bangkok Post*, 16 April 1997).

In sum, re-engineering was progressive and sequential. The performances of the first re-engineered pilot branch proved successful. Thereafter, the bank aimed to re-engineer all remaining branches located nation-wide by 1996 with an average of 30 branches per month. The bank benefited from both managerial and technological innovations. For example, the adoption of a unitary queuing system meant that a single file of customers waited for the first available position, in contrast to standing in several queues, and moreover, bank tellers were empowered with modern computer systems to authorise basic financial transactions.

Sources of Innovation

The sources of innovation can be grouped into four main areas. The first and most important source is bank personnel. Personnel development has become one of the bank's priority, as it has experienced a shortage of skilled staff was as early as the 1980s. During this period, the bank was required to strengthen the capabilities of the computer department, in order to support ATM development plans, by recruiting employees experienced in data communications and on-line system skills. Although the bank has experienced the problem of 'brain drain', whereby the turnover of employees in the computer department was less than 5 percent annually between 1975-1983, the chairman strongly emphasised the importance of developing personnel who are well qualified and educated (cited from Cash and Mookerjee, 1990, pp. 1-2).

> 'My top priority over the next two decades was to build a cadre of high-quality professional managers in the bank. I decided to develop people in the bank rather than shop around for people from outside. We gradually raised salary levels to match Bangkok Bank, to attract bright, young people. We also set up a scholarship to sponsor a few Thai Farmers Bank employees each year for advanced degrees at U.S. schools. These students had to sign a bond to work two years at Thai Farmer Bank, for each year of schooling. Many of them are still with us. Today we have the most qualified people in the industry: many

of our managers have MBAs from Harvard, Wharton, Chicago, etc.'

The policy towards retaining and training employees, rather than recruiting, has also been adopted during the period of bank re-engineering. In some bank branches, although re-engineering affected 70 of the 200 employees, or one third of the workforce, unemployment did not increase (*The Economist*, 11-17 October 1997, pp. 128-9). Alternatively, the bank reduced the recruitment of new employees and strengthened the skills of existing employees by retraining and reassigning them to newly established branches. Such was the case for employees who were affected by the automation of cheque processing routines, who were retrained.

The bank resolved redundancy caused by re-engineering in several ways. This included the set-up of marketing teams, the conducting of research into bank customers, the building of computer databases and the retraining of staff. Moreover, the bank expected employees to be regularly trained or retrained twice a year at its learning centre. This centre, a simulated bank branch environment, provides training courses ranging from the improvement of foreign language proficiency to IT skills. Employees are trained to understand the bank's working processes so that they be familiar with each departmental requirement, which the bank believes would facilitate employees to work efficiently.

In addition, the bank encourages employees to undergo training locally and abroad. For example, the bank acquired training from computer vendors in a project connecting electronic mail, included in the Lotus Notes software package, with the Internet. In other areas, the purchase of a specific computer software from an overseas company may involve the set-up of a team which travels overseas to examine the software and learn possibilities in modifying them to suit the bank's requirements. In return, the team reports and presents the materials acquired from the international software firm to other employees.

The second source is the management of information. Apart from supporting technological improvement programs, the bank's president has also initiated innovative ideas, which manages the use of information. For example, in responding to the country's financial crisis, the president has initiated an information-based internal risk management division in the bank, which is in addition to a 'command centre' previously set-up to monitor world news through electronic media for senior-level management (*The Nation*, 3 June 1998). The bank's first vice president for information systems processing illustrates how information, in addition to IT, has become the bank's source of innovation.

'In the past, Thai Farmers Bank relied on employee experiences to make adjustments to every specific situation. Today, we give increased importance to information. We examine and analyse information such as the bank's budget. That is why my department was renamed from computer processing department to information systems processing department. Being a computer centre is not well defined. Thai Farmers Bank has given great importance to information in evaluating everything.'

The third source is the research and process development department. Early re-engineering experiments led to the development of this department, which gradually acquired skills and know-how from working co-operatively with consulting companies. As a result, the department has served as the bank's consulting arm in re-engineering related areas. For example, the department initiated plans to introduce an Internet-based banking service, which is an investment of approximately Baht 10 million awarded to a local computer company (*Bangkok Post*, 1 April 1998). From 10 corporations co-operating during the pilot phase, the department expects to provide such services to all 1,500 corporate customers of the bank. Furthermore, the department works on the identification of innovative ideas from senior-level management (TFB interview, 1997). After idea generation, a research group, consisting of relatively young employees aged below forty, some holding doctoral degrees, studies the bank's current business processes, searches for new computer software, and suggests alternative approaches for improvement. For example, the loan approval process was studied and an approach was suggested to shorten the approval time from 1 month to 7 days. In other areas, research projects have also considered the improvement of bank branches, international trading activities, credit scoring, and the analysis of consumer behaviour.

The fourth, and perhaps an increasingly unimportant source, are consulting companies. Through such contacts, the acquisition of managerial and technological capabilities was made possible, and later served as a basis for building company capabilities. As re-engineering has continued without the presence of foreign consultants, the bank remains relatively independent for such sources of know-how. This may be seen as the specific reason behind the set-up of an internal research and process development department, which acts as the bank's own consulting arm. For example, the bank's policy in computer software development is relatively flexible (TFB interview, 1997). They are developed in-house, provided that there is an adequate source of skills from staff, as experienced by the joint-development of a new computer system with IBM employees for the bank's first pilot re-engineered branch. Otherwise, the bank purchased and modified an internationally well known software package, which has already been the case for supporting international trading and financial management.

Summary

Although the bank was not a pioneer of re-engineering, it was a major catalyst for such radical changes.

Through relatively strong senior-level management support, the bank demonstrated that IT played a key role in gaining competitive advantage back in the early 1980s, and more importantly, has shown that this potential relied on personnel development. In addition, other important sources of innovation included the set-up of an in-house research and process development department, and the innovative management of information. Although consulting firms were a main source of innovation in the early periods of re-engineering, there are signs that the bank has been decreasing its dependency on such sources.

DISCUSSION

This section analyses the competitiveness of the two banks based on a resource-based view. The two firms shared four common characteristics: reputation, skilled staff, re-engineering programmes, and IT investment. In retrospect, these characteristics may be seen as resources, which can be replicated. However, the replication rate of resources varies, and this is where the potential sources of sustained competitive advantage may be found.

Role of Reputation

The first common characteristic is the reputation behind banking leadership. As a result of having a large market share of the local banking industry, in terms of total assets and total deposits, the two commercial banks have gained and maintained a positive reputation with their customers and competitors. In 1996, SCB's market share was approximately 11 percent for total assets and 10 percent for total deposits, while TFB's was approximately 13 percent and 14 percent respectively (KTB, 1997). The two banks are also among the largest regional and international commercial banks. In comparison with 200 commercial banks in the Asian region in 1997, TFB ranked 22nd, while SCB 28th (*The Banker*, 1997). Similarly, in comparison with 1000 international commercial banks in 1996, the rankings were 182nd and 211th for each respective commercial bank (*The Banker*, various issues). Such rankings suggest that the size of commercial banks may have been an important factor influencing their international standings. Moreover, they may also indicate the preparedness of the commercial banks to compete regionally and internationally. Nevertheless, such figures do not fully explain the relatively strong fundamentals, which have originated from banking policies directed towards developing resources, particularly in personnel, IT, and bank re-engineering.

Role of Skilled Staff

The second common characteristic is the use of skilled staff. This ranged from skilled senior-level management who help form long-term banking visions and strongly supported the commitment of organisational resources towards investments in personnel development. Such characteristics have helped the two commercial banks acquire, apply, and advance modern management techniques, which strengthened their managerial capabilities. The main sources of skilled staff can be organised into two main groups.

The first group is senior and middle management executives. A majority of senior-level bank executives from the two commercial banks were educated in foreign universities and hold high-level positions such as president, chairman, and chief executive officer. This includes personnel who have earned academic degrees ranging from economics to business administration from some of the world's most outstanding universities. For example, the president of TFB, who was a catalyst behind branch reengineering and bank computerisation, studied at the Harvard Business School (TFB Annual Report, 1995). The president and chief executive officer of SCB, who is a former central bank official, is an economics graduate from the University of Pennsylvania and the Massachusetts Institute of Technology (SCB Annual Report, 1995). Such high educational qualifications were also common characteristics shared by a large number of mid-level managers who were ranked among senior vice-president positions. The board of directors also played an important role in the two commercial banks. This includes individuals who have become influential figures in the country's political and economic affairs. SCB has a former Prime Minister and a former assistant central bank governor represented on its board (SCB Annual Report, 1995), while a former Police Department director general is a board member at the TFB (TFB Annual Report, 1995). In these cases, although the commercial banks may not have benefited directly from bank-specific skills, the political skills and connections possessed of influential individuals provide a potential source of competitive advantage, which is necessary in conducting the bank's affairs with other key figures in both the public and private sectors.

A large number of senior-level bank executives also have prior professional banking experiences. One key institution that is a source of skilled staff is the central bank, which has adopted a longstanding policy in promoting human resource development. Since the early 1950s, the central bank scholarship program has provided financial assistance to educate eligible Thai students in leading overseas universities, for which this group of students work in return for the central bank upon completing their studies. In some cases, central bank officials are sought for by Thai commercial banks. In other circumstances, they are a source of skilled staff. The chief executive officer of SCB, for example, has worked as the central bank's director of the financial institution supervision and examination department, prior to joining the commercial bank.

The second group of staff is lower-level personnel. From early-1990s to mid-1990s, the two commercial banks invested in the building of staff training centres, which provided a simulated branch bank environment. Entry-level employees were trained on basic banking knowledge and on improved working processes, which are supported through modern computer-based information systems. In other cases, the training centres provided experienced employees to update their skills through training seminars. In addition, the training centres also provided re-training programs. Although many bank personnel may have been made redundant through re-engineering, bank policies were aimed at reducing the recruitment of new employees, and increasing the efficiency of the current workforce. Such policies was supported through an increased use of IT, which empowered bank clerks, for example, in authorising a predetermined amount of cash withdrawal or loan application. The two banks also experienced a decline in employee growth rates between 1995-1996. This may have been partly a result of reengineering, which was popularised in the mid-1990s, and the promotion of progressive bank policies favouring the training and retraining of current personnel, as compared with the recruitment of new employees.

In sum, skilled staff was a major factor influencing innovation in the two banks. Firstly, senior-level management demonstrated relatively strong support to strengthen managerial and technological capabilities. Bank managerial capabilities, for example, were strengthened with the acquisition of former central bank officials and the appointment of influential individuals in the bank's board of directors. Secondly, lower-level employees received training, and in some cases re-training, according to bank policies promoting personnel development. The two banks were committed to human resource development through the set-up of specialised training centres, which provides training on foreign languages and basic computer skills. Moreover, bank personnel also received re-training, particularly in cases which responded to reengineering programs, which was aimed to prepare them to work with improved business processes and computer systems.

Role of Re-engineering

The third common characteristic is the introduction of re-engineering programs. Such changes have been a response to increased competition in the Thai banking system, resulting from financial liberalisation initiated in the early 1990s. For example, local and foreign commercial banks were allowed to operate international banking facilities, increasing the availability and flow of foreign capital in and out of the country. Moreover, the two banks faced competition from non-bank financial institutions, for example, finance firms, securities companies, and insurance companies, which were allowed to provide a range of similar, and in some cases, more competitive and innovative financial services.

Re-engineering began with the contracting of consulting companies. This ranged from foreign firms providing management and IT consulting. The main management advice was aimed at organisational restructuring, for example, to create flatter organisational levels, and to promote teamwork among bank personnel. Additionally, consulting companies helped formulate IT strategies, and in some cases, assisted the development of computer-based information systems. Re-engineering was aimed to improve current business processes. Routine functions in current working processes were identified and modified accordingly, which was followed with use of IT to increase operational efficiency. Re-engineering started at bank head offices as pilot programs, and thereafter, the operational results, before and after the program, were evaluated and diffused to bank branches located nation-wide accordingly. In some cases, bank personnel were also retrained to learn changes in working practices.

There were, however, reservations to re-engineering. Although the two banks realised the importance of consultants in re-engineering, they have initiated projects to decrease the dependency on consultants. For example, this included the set-up of in-house teams to work closely with consultants, and as a result, this joint-team effort helped the banks learn more about re-engineering in general and about their current problems in particular. Furthermore, one of the commercial banks established a new research and process development department to support re-engineering, while another formed an independent company serving as the bank's own consulting unit. Such initiatives increased their indigenous capabilities in re-engineering and reduced their complete reliance on consultants.

Role of IT

The fourth and final common characteristic is the increased use of IT. The mini-cases illustrated how the banks pioneered the use of IT in banking in their own unique ways. For example, this may have been the introduction of ATMs or Internet-based banking applications. As a result, such early mover advantages have positioned them as technology pioneers, leading both mid-sized and small-sized commercial banks in major technological applications. Large and risky investments in IT projects were initiated by the two banks to test the market, and if the pilot project was successful, they were generally replicated by the two latter groups, whose aims are to catch up in technology to gain a competitive parity. Nevertheless, the large commercial banks have committed significant investments in IT, partly to maintain their market shares in the sector.

The two banks maintained their dominant market share in ATM units during 1988-1996. However, the growth rates in ATM units of the large commercial banks have become increasingly lower than the mid-sized and small-sized commercial banks categories. In 1989, the figures were 17.26 percent (large banks), 17.07 percent (mid-sized banks), and 17.31 percent (small-sized banks) for each group respectively. By 1996, the difference in growth rates widened, being 29.80 percent (large banks), 41.38 percent (mid-sized banks), and 31.42 percent (small-sized banks) for each group respectively (KTB, 1997). Such changes indicate the relatively high rate of replication in ATM technology, which further suggest that IT may not become a potential source of competitive advantage.

There were also clear IT strategies and plans. By forming strategies through the assistance of consulting companies, senior-level management has helped in preparing plans, which ranged from long-term to short-term periods. Such plans formed the basis for bank computerisation through IT investments, and served as early exercises, whereby the four commercial banks were required to invest in human resource development, particularly in the retraining of bank personnel to suit new and increasingly efficient working processes. In addition, the two banks pioneered the use of IT in banking. For example, SCB successfully introduced ATMs, while TFB popularised re-engineering in the country.

In sum, the two banks promoted the use of IT in two main areas. Firstly, this was to automate bank routines, and formed a part of wider programs in branch re-engineering, including the use of new computer systems connected to terminals located in the front office. In addition, this empowered bank clerks and increased the physical area for serving customers, shifting non-customer related work to the back offices, which, in turn, used computers to process routine transactions. Secondly, this was to improve customer services and satisfaction. While IT improved current working processes, it also increased efficiency in delivering banking services to customers. In addition, IT was applied to support a range of financial services, including, for example, the authorisation of loan applications. Other innovative services, for example, telephone-based banking, electronic banking, and Internet-based banking, were introduced accordingly.

Replication of Resources

In cases where commercial banks shared common characteristics, as discussed above, there may be competitive parity among firms. Alternatively, some commercial banks may distinguish themselves on the uniqueness of specific resources, which may become a source of sustained competitive advantage. Such uniqueness may vary in their rate of replication, which is further influenced by a set of attributes characterised in physical, organisational, and human resources.

Firstly, the replication of physical resources is slightly difficult. The mini-case studies suggested that IT, which is a physical resource in form, were being increasingly acquired, applied, and advanced by the large commercial banks. The ATM provides one illustration. Although SCB enjoyed early-mover advantages in the early-1980s, when it pioneered ATMs, other commercial banks replicated such technologies. TFB was one of these earliest competitors, which rapidly responded by developing telecommunications and on-line computer capabilities to catch-up with the technology leader. There were more interesting changes in the 1990s, as suggested by the growth rates in ATM units among mid-sized and small-sized commercial banks outgrowing their larger counterparts. Although this may be partly due to the initiation of co-operative computer networks among a group of commercial banks, it also suggests that the smaller firms have focused and expanded their banking activities into the retail market. This high rate of replication in ATM technology further suggest that such physical resources are a weak source of competitive advantage, as they are homogenous, mobile, and readily available to purchase in the markets.

Nevertheless, some interesting developments have been emerging. For example, commercial banks have developed and modified their own computer software to support ATMs, as compared to purchasing them. This suggests the building of software development capabilities, and more interestingly, commercial bank affiliated companies are increasingly becoming an important source of innovation. Such affiliated companies can develop, in the long-term, innovative financial products and services, which are unique. Furthermore, if successful, the company can create an appropriability regime to protect such innovations, which may potentially become a source of sustained competitive advantage.

Secondly, the replication of organisational resources is moderately difficult. Although commercial banks have the resources to invest in IT, the linkage with company strategy is equally important. The case of re-engineering provides one illustration. Through recommendations made by consulting companies, commercial banks have learned to a great extent about their working processes, and more importantly, how to improve them. However, the application of recent re-engineering concepts and modern management techniques may not suit each commercial bank similarly, as their organisations have unique characteristics. In order to address such issues, some commercial banks have initiated an in-house research unit to work closely with consultants, expecting to learn more about their organisations themselves, and most importantly, to be capable of initiating the re-engineering of other potential processes on their own. For this research unit to be a source of sustained competitive advantage, however, there is a need for skilled bank personnel to conduct studies, analyse alternative, and make recommendations.

And thirdly, which follows on from the previous point, the replication of human resources is always difficult. For example, since specific skills residing in bank personnel are intangible, they are not clearly coded and difficult to transfer. Such expertise, for example in designing an information system, is tacit knowledge to a specific person and may be difficult to articulate. Thus, the education and training of specific individuals become an organisational routine or the repository of knowledge for the organisation. This stock of skill is one of the most important sources of innovation an organisation could use to gain or sustain competitive advantage. Therefore, it is not surprising that the commercial banks committed resources in this area by investing in training centres and the supporting of further education for bank personnel. Such strategies seek to develop and support employees in specific technical skills, and who are familiar and trained to work with computers and re-engineered working processes. Most importantly, however, is the acquisition of personnel at the senior-management level. Although such policies are not explicit, it has become one of the common characteristics among the two banks. Such individuals have been recruited, or in some cases appointed, to acquire managerial skills. In addition, it is also interesting to note that in Thailand, where a large number of commercial banks are family-controlled, there has been the appointment of influential figures in the country to key organisational positions. This has largely been to gain and maintain political and social connections in government and business. Thus, such invisible human resources are unique and difficult to transfer, but would provide a potential source of competitive advantage.

CONCLUSION

This paper has shown that although commercial banks have invested in IT to gain competitive advantage, such initiatives may not be sustained. Although there may be early mover advantages, the replication of IT resources, in their physical form, may be similarly adopted among other firms, creating competitive parity. In order to sustain competitive advantage, commercial banks have to rely on a unique set of resources to strengthen their stock of skills. This may be through the extension of their reliable reputation in the delivery of innovative financial services, the tailoring of re-engineering programmes to distinguish themselves from competitors, and the acquisition and training of skilled staff.

ENDNOTE

1 See Top 1000 by country, *The Banker*, various issues. The world rankings of international commercial banks is based on Tier One capital and is defined by the Bank for International Settlements. Tier One includes common stock, disclosed reserves and retained earnings, but excludes cumulative preference shares, revaluation reserves, hidden reserves, sub-ordinate and other long-term debt, which are defined as Tier Two capital.

REFERENCES
Andrews, K. (1987). *The Concept of Corporate Strategy*. Homewood, Irwin.
The Asian Banker, various issues.
The Bangkok Post, various issues.
The Banker, various issues.
Barney, J. (1991). Firm Resources and Sustained Competitive Advantage. *Journal of Management* 17 (1): 99-120.
Cash, J.I., and Mookerjee, A.S. (1990). Thai Farmers Bank. Harvard Business School Case Study No. 9-190-079.
Chandler, A. D. (1962). *Strategy and Structure: Chapters in the History of Industrial Enterprise*. Cambridge, MIT Press.
Ciborra, C., and Andreu, R. (1998). Organizational Learning and Core Capabilities Development. In R. D. Galliers, and Baets, W.R.J. (eds.), *Information Technology and Organizational Transformation: Innovation for the 21st Century Organization*, Chichester, John Wiley and Sons: 87-106.
Clemons, E. K. (1991). Corporate Strategies for Information Technology: A Resource-Based Approach. *Computer* (November): 23-32.
Clemons, E. K., and Row, M.C. (1991). Sustaining IT Advantage: The Role of Structural Differences. *MIS Quarterly* (September): 275-292.
Conner, K. R. (1991). A Historical Comparison of Resource-Based Theory and Five Schools of Thought within Industrial Organization Economics: Do we have a New Theory of the Firm? *Journal of Management* 17 (1): 121-154.
The Economist (1997). Re-engineering in Thailand. Economist. 345: 128-129.
Foss, N. J., (ed.) (1997). *Resources, Firms, and Strategies: A Reader in the Resource-Based Perspective*. Oxford, Oxford University Press.
Foss, N. J., Knudsen, C., and Montgomery, C.A. (1995). An Exploration of Common Ground: Integrating Evolutionary and Strategic Theories of the Firm. In C. A. Montgomery (ed.), *Resource-Based and Evolutionary Theories of the Firm: Towards a Synthesis*. London, Kluwer Academic Publishers: 1-17.

Grant, G. G., and Liebenau, J. (forthcoming). The Strategic Dimensions of Information Systems Capability: An Evolutionary and Resource-Based View.

Grant, R. M. (1991). The Resource-Based Theory of Competitive Advantage: Implications for Strategy Formulation. *California Management Review* 33 (3): 114-135.

Hammer, M., and Champy, J. (1993). *Reengineering the Corporation: A Manifesto for Business Revolution*. New York, Harper Business.

Itami, H. (1987). *Mobilizing Invisible Assets*. Cambridge, Harvard University Press.

Kay, J. (1993). *Foundations of Corporate Success*. Oxford, Oxford University Press.

KTB (1997). Key Financial Data of Thai Commercial Banks, 1988-1996. Bangkok, Business Research Department, Krung Thai Bank Public Company Limited.

Mahoney, J. T., and Pandian, J.R. (1992). The Resource-Based View within the Conversation of Strategic Management. *Strategic Management Journal* 13 (5): 363-380.

Mata, F. J., Fuerst, W.L., and Barney, J.B. (1995). Information Technology and Sustained Competitive Advantage: A Resource-Based Analysis. *MIS Quarterly* 19 (4): 487-505.

Montgomery, C. A., (ed.) (1995). *Resource-Based and Evolutionary Theories of the Firm: Towards a Synthesis*. London, Kluwer Academic Publishers.

The Nation. various issues.

Nonaka, I., and Takeuchi, H. (1995). *The Knowledge-Creating Company: How Japanese Companies Create the Dynamics of Innovation*. Oxford, Oxford University Press.

Penrose, E. T. (1959). *The Theory of the Growth of the Firm*. Oxford, Basil Blackwell.

Peteraf, M. A. (1993). The Cornerstones of Competitive Advantage: A Resource-Based View. *Strategic Management Journal* 14 (3): 179-191.

Porter, M. (1990). The Competitive Advantage of Nations. London, Macmillan.

Powell, T. C., and Dent-Micallef, A. (1997). Information Technology as Competitive Advantage: The Role of Human, Business, and Technology Resources. *Strategic Management Journal* 18 (5): 375-405.

Prahalad, C. K., and Hamel, G. (1990). The Core Competence of the Corporation. *Harvard Business Review* (May-June): 79-91.

Robins, J., and Wiersema, M.F. (1995). A Resource-Based Approach to the Multibusiness Firm: Empirical Analysis of Portfolio Interrelationships and Corporate Financial Performance. *Strategic Management Journal* 16 (4): 277-299.

Ross, J. W., Beath, C.M., and Goodhue, D.L. (1996). Develop Long-Term Competitiveness Through IT Assets. *Sloan Management Review* 38 (1): 31-42.

SCB Technologies, various issues.

SCB. Siam Commercial Bank Annual Report, various issues.

Senge, P. M. (1990). *The Fifth Discipline - The Art and Practice of the Learning Organization*. New York, Doubleday.

Stalk, G., Evans, P., and Shulman, L.E. (1992). Competing on Capabilities: The New Rules of Corporate Strategy. *Harvard Business Review* (March-April): 57-69.

TFB. Thai Farmers Bank Annual Report, various issues.

Wernerfelt, B. (1984). A Resource-Based View of the Firm. *Strategic Management Journal* 5 (2): 171-180.

Wernerfelt, B. (1995). The Resource-Based View of the Firm: Ten Years After. *Strategic Management Journal* 16 (3): 171-174.

Winter, S. G. (1995). Four R's of Profitability: Rents, Resources, Routines, and Replication. In C. A. Montgomery. (ed.), *Resource-Based and Evolutionary Theories of the Firm: Towards a Synthesis*. London, Kluwer Academic Publishers: 147-178.

Structuring and Systemizing Knowledge on the Internet - Realizing the Encyclopedia Concept as a Knowledge Medium

Ulrike Lechner, Beat Schmid, Salome Schmid-Isler, Katarina Stanoevska-Slabeva
Institute for Media and Communications Management, University of St. Gallen, Müller-Friedberg Strasse 8, CH-9000 St. Gallen, Switzerland
Tel.: +41 71 224 2401 or +41 71 224 2297, Fax: +41 71 224 2771, EMail: {firstname.lastname}@unisg.ch

ABSTRACT

We reconsider the encyclopedic concept as a knowledge medium for the scientific community in the Internet. Referring to the ancient concept of encyclopedia, we reconstruct the encyclopedia for the new interactive carrier of information as a knowledge medium, representing and organizing knowledge for the scientific community anew on Internet. We envision those knowledge media as communication spheres for agents and exemplify them with the performance of the NetAcademy project.

INTRODUCTION

The quantity of knowledge that is generated nowadays and the speed at which it is distributed distinguish the modern information society. Despite the enhanced availability of information, its applicability remains far behind the potentials. Information overload is one aspect of this problem. The central challenge nowadays is to turn information into knowledge, i.e. into information that becomes active in humans. In order to achieve this we recall and apply the ancient concept of encyclopedia and revive it to take full advantage of the features and potentials of new carrier of information [Schmid 97b, Schmid-Isler, 98a].

In the paper we propose a holistic approach for structuring and organizing scientific knowledge in the Internet, which takes advantage of the potentials of interactive information and communication technology by applying the following core concepts:
• encyclopedia as an encompassing concept for management of given, i.e., defined knowledge,
• computational media as a holistic concept for the organization and management of the knowledge creation process.

In the introduction of the paper our concept of encyclopedia, of computational media and their potentials are given, referring to the example of the NetAcademy platform, a medium for the scientific community on the Internet. The content of the paper, after that, is organized as follows: Section 2: Analysis of knowledge management and encyclopedia, section 3: General model for computational media; section 4: Computational encyclopedia as an instantiation of the general model; Section 5: The NetAcademy as a computational encyclopedia. Section 6 concludes the paper.

THE CONCEPT OF ENCYCLOPEDIA

In this section about knowledge management we first refer to the achievements which have been made from the times since, in ancient Greece, the notion of encyclopedia was born, until the 18th ct. where, with the encyclopedia editors Diderot and d'Alembert, the concept of the encyclopedia reached maturity [Schmid-Isler 98]. We then investigate if and how these solutions remain valid and how they are to be developed according to the advantages of today's new media.

The Historical Context

Since reflection and philosophy began, they focused on the theme [Schmid-Isler et.al. 98a]: How to foster, how to manage knowledge?. Let us refine this quest by three issues:
• What are the criteria for categorization of knowledge?

- What are the criteria for validity of knowledge?
- What are the successful methods to accomplish order?

In the western world it was at the Greek philosopher Platon's academy (founded 386 b.c. in Athens, being closed down by the Christian emperor Justinian 529 a.d.), that the first principles of systemizing knowledge and the first methods to generate knowledge were elaborated. These principles were:

- Establishing a *repository* for shared knowledge, aiming at an encompassing accumulation of knowledge (encyclopedia translates as: an encompassing circle for education);
- Establishing an *academy* for the scientific community, i.e. regular congregations for wise men to reason about knowledge and abduct new knowledge by doing so;
- Establishing a *method* to ensure congruent reasoning.

Following the three principles will be explained in more detail.

Encyclopedia as Knowledge Repositories – (1) Managing Knowledge

Encyclopedia means a compendium of knowledge, either general or specialized, focusing on one field of interest [Columbia 94], [Schmid-Isler 98a]. Encyclopedia are often compared to dictionaries. While a dictionary is basically devoted to words, an encyclopedia refers to both data on and discussion of each subject covered. An almanac is a periodical publication containing much ephemeral data.

The first and most important aim of Encyclopedia is to document and maintain authentic knowledge, ensuring and testifying its preservation over time and space. Secondly, it is to provide adequate categorization and systematization of knowledge, providing easy access on knowledge for any interested person.

There are different approaches to classify knowledge, e.g., to structure knowledge in a *pre-established order* (as in the artes liberales and any religious schools), or in a *hierarchic classification* (as Carl Linné used in his category system for biology and zoology), or in a *alphanumerical list* (as is the case in common dictionaries), or in a *ranking order* according any given preferences and value judgement [Schmid-Isler 98].

- Classification criteria provide a compact meta-description of knowledge.

Organization of Communities: Academia and University – (2) Distributing Knowledge

Arguing about cognition and establishing orders for knowledge has been a noble tradition in philosophy since reflection was born. As Snell states, reasoning about knowledge started in ancient Greece since their language has the unique characteristic to build abstract terms, which philosophy surmises [Snell, 80]. Congregations of wise men got established at specific places, academias, as a means to discuss and teach knowledge. Platon's academia, Aristotle's lykaion, the monastery schools, the hence arising universities (since the 11th ct.) and, since the Italian Renaissance beginning in the 15th ct., the academies [Schmid-Isler 98a]: They all eventually established conventions about the *processes of academic acknowledgement* for the scientific community. Measures to guarantee scientific quality in accordance with established methods have been developed referring to the academic career, to exams and titles, to quality assessment processes, to reviewing, publishing and intellectual property rights etc.

- The main aim of Academies is to provide the methods and organizational framework (roles and protocols) according to which the processes of teaching, evaluating and generating knowledge are performed.

Methods to Accomplish Order – (3) Creating Knowledge

Along with the concepts of the encyclopedia and of the academy there was a continuing reflection and quest for a general method to assure congruent reasoning about knowledge. Platon was convinced that only *mathematics* could offer certainty in the ocean of the arbitrariness of reasoning about truth [Whithead 47]. It was Leibniz, a German philosopher and mathematician, who introduced the constructive or operational component which allows a systematic development of knowledge [Peckhaus 97]. He turned the discipline of logic into a discipline of mathematics by substituting „truth" with: „proven by calculation".

- Today, we dispose of an instrument which allows the application of mathematics and calculation onto processes of any kind, allowing to delegate reasoning about knowledge, which was a privilege to mankind, onto machines – onto the *computers*.

The Encyclopedia Knowledge Cycle

The above described three aspects of knowledge (1) management, (2) distribution and (3) creation are closely related to each other. The encyclopedia as a repository of given knowledge is the base for knowledge distribution and generation. The result of reasoning, using various methods, and therefore of generating new knowledge, will flow into a next generation of encyclopedia. Thus, the three aspects together form a spiral of knowledge generations, which will further be called the Encyclopedia Knowledge Cycle [G. Mazzola, 1997].

The Encyclopedia Knowledge Cycle distinguishes two approaches to foster knowledge (c.f. 1):

- *The encyclopedic method.* This is an encompassing management of given knowledge, founded on library and information science. This method deals with structuring, categorizing, filtering and organizing authentic knowledge, making it accessible for a given community by the means of an appropriate repository, say an information carrier.
- *The epistemologic method.* This is the process-orientated method that continuously puts knowledge on the test-bed. Founded on Platons method to strive for knowledge [Bormann 78], the epistemologic method (or reasoning) means to view knowledge either as something that has to be developed following a method, or to view knowledge and its development methods as something that has to be reviewed.

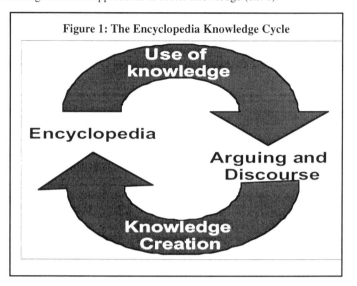

Figure 1: The Encyclopedia Knowledge Cycle

The two methods are closely interrelated: The encyclopedia, as a historically verified means to secure and identify the commitments of a scientific community, is dependent on methods to gain cognition – episteme - providing the means for further growth and liability of knowledge. Reasoning in quest of cognition eventually crystallizes new facets to the encyclopedia.

With reference to the technologies and media applied for the realization of encyclopedia, the interrelationship between the two aspects could be realized with a different degree of tightness. Knowledge repositories are, since ancient times,

- on the one side, living (or: understanding) information carriers, i.e. human beings which are able to open a dialogue about the information while conveying it to a person,
- on the other side, dead (or: mute, ignorant) information media as signs, pictures, text scrolls, books, movies and the like, which are not interactive.

Dead media, though capable of documenting a precise state of knowledge, are cut off the reasoning process. There are several explanations for this, let us mention three of them: (1) discrete dynamics of update versus continuos dynamic of knowledge generation; (2) methods are not applicable directly to the contents on the carriers, and (3) discourse happens out of the medium.

Due to those shortcomings, traditional i.e. mute encyclopedia are prone to loose their importance for the knowledge generation process. Moreover, in a paper based encyclopedia the reader has to inference over the given content by himself, which means tracing cross references and the like. Electronic interactive media make it possible to delegate this task to the machine. E.g., Electronic Encyclopedia available at CD-ROM or hypertext Systems allow an easy tracking of hyperlinks and cross-references. But, besides providing enhanced access to information, the first generation of electronic encyclopedia follows the traditional encyclopedia concepts and suffer from the same drawbacks as being observed by printmedia-based encyclopedia.

- With the emergence of artificial knowledge repositories, capable to interpret the information they carry and with their union with the telecommunication technology (i.e. Internet), we are facing unprecedented possibilities to revolutionize and revive the concept of an Encyclopedia Knowledge Cycle by accordingly uniting the concept of Encyclopedia with the concept of academic arguing to an encompassing knowledge source.

Chances and Challenges for the Encyclopedia Knowledge Cycle in the Information Age

The convergence of information and communication technology resulted in a new interactive medium [Schmid, 97a]. The characteristics of this new medium deeply affect the principles of systemizing knowledge already mentioned:

- Today, the World Wide Web develops into a huge repository of unstructured knowledge bits and bytes. As the contents eventually run there, a structuring of encyclopedic manner has to be built. (First successful attempts, although limited in their effectiveness, have been made with the Search Engines and Web Directories like yahoo or altavista.)

- Today, the Internet allows for remote knowledge exchange, file accumulation and almost synchronous cooperation activities of people around the world, anytime. No wonder, the organizations based on communication, as academic institutions, are challenged by deep changes. Virtual universities [Noam 96], tele-learning and various platforms for the accumulation, dissemination and discussion of knowledge are emerging, facilitating and altering academic.research methods.
- Today, the overpowering dominance of computational logic applies to almost everything. Provided there is a formal representation of knowledge, reasoning can be performed more and more by computers, thus enhancing and liberating human vocations.

Despite the described achievements, the already described challenge remains the same: How to manage knowledge? But, the paradigms for this challenge have changed: For centuries, the scientific community stored and generated knowledge mainly by means of writing and printing, while today knowledge increasingly gets accumulated, disseminated and reviewed on interactive networks.

- We are aware, that we need to develop a new scientific approach to meet this change of paradigms facing the encyclopedic and the epistemologic tradition of the academic world. We thus suggest the inclusion of the Media Metaphor.

COMPUTATIONAL MEDIA – A CONCEPT FOR STRUCTURING KNOWLEDGE AND KNOWLEDGE MANAGEMENT

We reconsider the notion of a medium as a carrier of information and explore a new notion of medium as a concept to structure and activate information. Media are envisioned as spheres for communities of agents and they are modeled as multi-agent systems. We call this notion of a medium the computational media metaphor and the media we model according to this model computational media [Lechner/Schmid, 99]. Computational media comprise the following components:

1. *Logic* to represent information in its relation to the real world. It comprises a logic as the means to represent information as well as possible worlds relating this logic to the semantics of the community using the medium.
2. *Channels*, to distinguish and distribute knowledge over space and time and to facilitate co-ordination among agents. The channel system encompasses communication mechanisms and corresponds to the notion of a medium as a carrier of information.
3. *Organization*, comprising both a set of roles defining the rights and obligations of agents and protocols defining processes and communication relations of the community.

Communities of human and artificial agents, striving towards a common aim, employ this organized channel structure to process and to communicate information.

The three components of a medium establish a structured way to compose a medium. E.g. two media may have the same logic– however differing channels, i.e., differing means to distinguish and address agents and different co-ordination mechanisms and facilities, yield a different media.

This model captures several characteristics of "new media" as they are established by information and communications technology. A medium is no longer an isolated carrier of information – it is a component in a net of interwoven media. Media can share e.g., logic, or channels and an agent may participate in several media. Media can be (provided they have an appropriate organization) considered to be channels in encompassing media.

COMPUTATIONAL ENCYCLOPEDIA

We define computational encyclopedia as computational media that apply the paradigm of the encyclopedia knowledge cycle for structuring and systemizing the knowledge repository and for facilitating knowledge creation and management processes.

Let us describe how we envision and model computational encyclopedia as a holistic approach to knowledge management on the Internet. We begin with a description of a *computational encyclopedia* according to the *computational media metaphor*. For structuring and defining the organization of the computational encyclopedia we employ two orthogonal concepts:

1. According to the domain of discourse into volumes: the computational encyclopedia can be organized as a collection of what we call "*volume*" (encyclopedia).
2. According to the encyclopedia knowledge cycle into „*views*" representing the encyclopedic and epistemologic method.

Computational Encyclopedia as a Computational Medium

Following the concept of computational media, the vision and model of a computational encyclopedia as a sphere for communities of agents is described. We start with the organization, as the requirements towards agents and channels and continue with a detailed description of both the components channels and logic and the community of agents.

The *organization* of a computational medium comprises a set of roles and processes (protocols). An encyclopedia mirrors the roles, science has developed for assuring the quality of knowledge, i.e. peer-review processes for publications and editorial boards with roles as editor, reviewer, author, member of editorial board. Those roles have certain rights to access the knowledge in the encyclopedia and certain obligations in the encyclopedia knowledge cycle. There is furthermore the role of a search agent with the knowledge about applied categorization and systematization including the capability for answering queries presented to it.

The *channels* are carrier of information and as such relate agents and facilitate the communication between agents. Channels can be described in the logic and can be computed at run-time. Thus, the adequate documents containing information as well as changes in the categorization and systematization can be reflected.

The *logic* represents the domain of discourse as well as the systematization and categorization in a computable manner. Thus, it represents the means to reason about the documents of the encyclopedia according to the systematization and categorization. Possible worlds relate the knowledge represented on a medium to their semantics. Since computational reasoning is at present hardly possible for documents as files themselves, the contents are represented in the logic by meta-information, including, e.g., keywords, author, data etc. Thus, here the document itself is the semantics of such a representation in the medium. Both the logical representation and the extra-logical semantics are part of the medium itself. The agents' knowledge consists of subsets of the information that can be represented with the logic.

Volumes of the Computational Encyclopedia

An entity of channels and logic organized to support a community of agents dedicated to creation and communication of knowledge in a well defined domain of discours, define a specific volume of an encyclopedia.

The mere representation of knowledge is not enough. Systematization and categorization of knowledge are essential aspects of the Encyclopedia. Thus, each volume may have its own systematization for the knowledge and its own means to implement reasoning about the knowledge.

The language chosen to describe the domain of discourse in the different volums might be heterogeneous. Thus, to form an encyclopedia, those volume encyclopedias have to communicate via a mediation or translation mechanism.

Views of the Computational Encyclopedia

The views distinguish the encyclopedic and the knowledge generation aspect of the holistic medium. We consider two views (c.f. 1): (1) the encyclopedic view and (2) the knowledge generation view on the computational encyclopedia.

The Encyclopedic View

Encyclopedia contain the agreed upon knowledge of the community in form of definitions. Thus this view is constituted by channels containing such knowledge. This specific role of the channels is denoted by their organizational description. Thus, the organization with the roles determines which agents and channels participate in which medium. Encyclopedia have an order on the knowledge they present, and this order is customizable and implemented by the channels. The encyclopedia can have several systemizations and categorizations implemented each as a sets of channels. The channels are the base for intelligent search agents, providing hereby point wise access to the database.

The encyclopedia grants access to the information it contains to any visitor, while it allows only selected participants, i.e., the ones capable and allowed of playing the role of an editor of the encyclopedia to edit the encyclopedia and its entries.

The Epistemological View

The epistemological view reflects the ongoing process of scientific discussion. Thus, this view comprises channels together with their meta-description reflecting the arguing aspect of knowledge creation as publications, discussions, proposals and the like. Again, the role of this channels is denoted by their organizational description. The meta-information, which includes a list of keywords expressed in logic manner, makes the documents contained in the medium accessible for processing. Some of the keywords stem from the Encyclopedia and the relations between the Encyclopedia terms allow semantic access to the documents.

This view represent the documents and the relations between them as it is common in the traditional media: publications are browsable by appearance data (as in a journal), according to a common topic (as in a conference proceeding) or by searching for any keyword in the meta-information (as in a library with a sophisticated catalogue including semantic relations).

This view uses the paradigm of reviewing processes for quality management and supports them accordingly. Thus agents representing humans play the roles of author, editor, member of the board, reviewer in this medium. An other important agent is the search engine capable of intelligent retrieval and combination of knowledge based on the applied logic.

Inter-View Processes – Implementing the Knowledge Cycle

The (two) views on the holistic medium are characterized by different channels and organization. However, the holistic concept of the Encyclopedia implements via inter-view channels and processes strong connectivity between the links based on the common logic and aim. Note that documents (or any other agent) can -in different roles – participate in both views. Both views have their own processes (e.g., of quality management). However, there are inter-view channels and processes, that provide a more tighter integrating of the two organizational views. Let us describe them.

In the Encyclopedia view, e.g., a committee of editors decides upon which documents (or part of documents) are considered to be authentic. The document itself with the meta-information becomes part of the encyclopedia view while remaining in its old role in the arguing view:

When part of a document becomes (by playing a role in the encyclopaedia) part of the encyclopedia, technology can be employed to represent this concept in an adequate structure. Namely by changing the document in a hypertext and by linking the encyclopedia role to the document(s) it originated form. An authentic contribution changes stepwise from a linear document to a hypertext and towards playing a role in the encyclopaedia.

Our approach, in particular, supports the notion of an encyclopedia to be the basis for knowledge generation. New publications can be designed with hyperlinks to entries in the encyclopedia view instead of including the full text. For the representation in the medium, links are adequate, while when playing, e.g., in another medium the role type "conventional, flat publication" the hyperlink to encyclopedia is represented by its full text.

With such a structured representation of documents those documents become accessible as subject of logic reasoning themselves. Relations via those hyperlinks can be employed to reason about the contents in documents and, more important, about the semantic relations between documents.

THE NETACADEMY: A COMPUTATIONAL ENCYCLOPEDIA

In this chapter, we present the NetAcademy project [Schmid, 97b], [www.netacademy.org] as a prototype for the new concept of a computational encyclopedia. The NetAcademy is designed to be a virtual platform for the scientific community, fostering creation of knowledge and supporting the whole lifecycle of knowledge. Following we will explain the application of both the encyclopedia knowledge cycle and the metaphor of computational media in the NetAcademy.

Implementation of The Encyclopedia Knowledge Cycle in the NetAcademy

In the figure given below the entrance page of the NetAcademy is depicted:

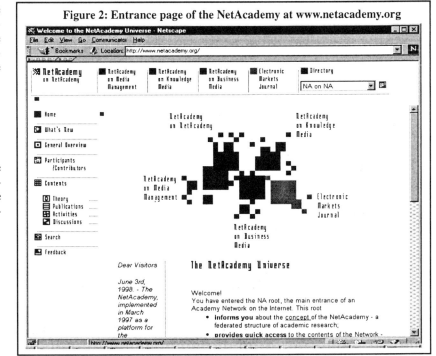

Figure 2: Entrance page of the NetAcademy at www.netacademy.org

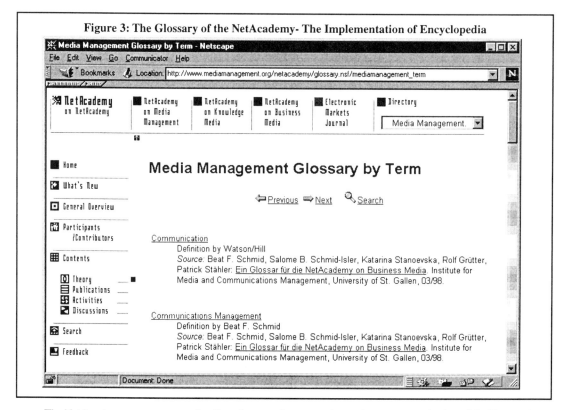

Figure 3: The Glossary of the NetAcademy- The Implementation of Encyclopedia

The NetAcademy entrance page visualizes the recursive structuring and content organization of the NetAcademy. *The horizontal bar* represents the width (choice) of research volumes settling on the platform. Each volume is related to a specific community conducting research in a well defined domain of discourse. Currently, three volumes are active:

• The Community on Business Media (www.businessmedia.org), which deals with research on electronic markets and E-Commerce, including the peer-reviewed online academic Journal „EM –Electronic Markets"
• The Community on Knowledge Media (www.knowledgemedia.org), which is concerned in innovative approaches, technologies and methodologies for knowledge management.
• The Community on Media Management (www.mediamanagement.org), which is a research space concerning the definition and management of the effects of new media on the economy, society, politics, law and culture.

The vertical bar represents the organizational views of the NetAcademy. The NetAcademy provides services for the scientific community following the epistemological view. Those services are online publication, mechanisms for search and retrieval of information and quality assurance processes. The glossary with the publication database, represent the epistemological view of the knowledge cycle (c.f. 3).

The Encyclopedia aspect of the NetAcademy, the *NetAcademy as Encyclopedia* is implemented by the glossary [Schmid et al. 98], as well as the search engine based on it [Stanoevska-Slabeva et al. 98]. The glossary provides a collection of keywords with their definitions and explanations. This glossary, presented in an alphabetical order of keywords is essentially the virtual counterpart of a traditional encyclopedia.

The realization of the glossary based on the Q-Technology for representation and processing of ontologies [Schmid et al. 96] provides further value-add. Based on this technology relationships between terms, such as *"is-a"* or *"part-of"* can be expressed in the glossary's semantic net and used for intelligent search [Stanoevska-Slabeva et al. 98]. Thus, the glossary allows to define and customize relations between the keywords for different domains of discourse. Based on the federated paradigm for integration of heterogeneous information sources [Sheth et al 90], it furthermore allows to relate different versions of encyclopedia or the domain specific vocabularies to a mediating vocabulary of the universal encyclopedia, i.e., the Encyclopedia having different domain-specific volumes [Stanoevska-Slabeva 97].

The NetAcademy as an Application of the Computational Media Metaphor

The NetAcademy instantiates the computational media metaphor as follows: The *community of agents* of the medium are the publication database, the registration database and the search engine as well as the participants and the guest account. The *channels* are the different types of publications with their meta-description. The *logics* of the NetAcademy is the glossary of a NetAcademy and the search and query mechanisms implemented on it. This comprises the terminology a NetAcademy employs and establishes a set of connections between channels and agents via the semantic relationships defined in the logic. The *roles* in the NetAcademy for participants are author, reviewer, editor. We distinguish furthermore (plain) publications and publications which are part of the glossary [Schmid et al. 98], i.e.; which play a role in the encyclopedia view on the NetAcademy. The *processes* in a NetAcademy is the publication process including steps as submission, selecting reviewers, reviewing, evaluating and sending the answer to the reviewer. The possible world of a NetAcademy is the aspect or view of the world, a NetAcademy refers to.

The NetAcademies together form a federation [Sheth et al. 90] of communicating NetAcademies. A NetAcademy is an agent-channel combination, processing knowledge and transporting knowledge over the time. There is only one distinguished role in the NetAcademyNet, the role of the "NetAcademy on NetAcademy", featuring the communication between NetAcademies. The protocols in the NetAcademy are the Inter-NetAcademy searching, mediating and retrieving of information. The logics of this medium is the mediation mechanism, i.e., the mediation between the different vocabularies. The configuration of the media establishes the federated structure. The NetAcademy on NetAcademy is the root of the NetAcademyNet.

Each NetAcademy features its own domain of discourse and a glossary for it. The glossary allows to relate different discourses of domain – according to homonyms and synonyms. Thus, we obtain a collection of related, domain specific encyclopedia. Moreover, this forms an open distributed and decentralized structure: any community can join with their encyclopedia an established Net of Encyclopedia, by providing the semantic link between the NetAcademies. Thus, the concept is open and provides hereby an additional competitive advantage to conventional encyclopedia which are closed systems managed in a centralized way

The contents of the NetAcademy are provided by the scientific community and the quality assurance mechanisms of the scientific community for publication apply not only to the normal publications but to the distinguished entries in the Encyclopedia. Definitions being part of publications can become part of the Encyclopedia. Thus, the Encyclopedia aspect of the NetAcademy is a real handbook for the scientific community. Naturally, by providing links between the Encyclopedia and the normal knowledge base of the NetAcademy, the Encyclopedia in the NetAcademy becomes much more attractive for researches. It is an excellent means to search for specific information in a collection of publications of a scientific community by using the semantic links between different terms and by providing the relevant and related publications online.

CONCLUDING REMARKS

We envision for the future a living computational encyclopedia for the scientific community, where bits of knowledge continuously cluster like a crystal to an intelligible and redundant system of universal knowledge. Compared to conventional encyclopedia, computational encyclopedia are no longer a static repository of organized knowledge (comparable to cut flowers), but a living organism of evolving knowledge in the different stages of a lifecycle (comparable to a flourishing garden). The main competitive advantages of such new forms of encyclopedia are:

- *Accessibility*: The access as is offered by Internet is democratic, i.e., for everybody, any time, anywhere, to the same conditions and the encyclopedia becomes ubiquitous, i.e., independent from physical locations.
- *Effectiveness and efficiency*: The costs of establishing a conventional encyclopedia and keeping it up to date are huge. An encyclopedia, which is interwoven with a strongly motivated community generating and relying on the knowledge collected in the Encyclopedia provides an efficient means to keep the knowledge base up to date. Moreover, changes in the encyclopedia take immediately world-wide effect ensuring hereby effectiveness of the encyclopedia.
- *Organization and Navigation*: The new carrier for encyclopedias provide convenient ways to access the knowledge or to search for knowledge as well as manifold ways to relate knowledge. Several different organizational views can be laid upon the contents presented in an encyclopedia expressing different systematization, organization and representation paradigms. Thus, there is no need to stick with one predominant organization paradigm, or with mainly linear orderings of contents as media on traditional carriers have to do.

We perceive our approach of a holistic medium distinguishing an Encyclopedia view to be a prototype for the new forms of organization of knowledge management and the new media that emerge. For example we could refine the organizational structure of computational encyclopedia and consider it as a dictionary, as a journal, as a conference proceedings, as a newsletter and possible much more different organizations of knowledge.

ACKNOWLEDGEMENTS

We are indebted to the Bertelsmann Foundation and the Heinz-Nixdorf Foundation, the partner organizations of the Institute for Media and Communications Management. The NetAcademy project received funding from those partner organizations. The Swiss National Funds sponsored projects related to the NetAcademy and Ulrike Lechner received funding from the Grundlagenforschungsfonds of the University of St. Gallen.

We are particularly indebted to the NetAcademy team for the implementation of the NetAcademy: David-Michael Lincke, Dorian Selz, Petra Schubert, Siegfried Handschuh, Bernd Schopp. However, the participants, editors and executive editors made the concept and its realization to a living community. We are indebted to them for manifold contributions. We would like to thank all the members of the Institute for Media and Communications Management for stimulating discussions.

BIBLIOGRAPHY

[Bormann 78] K. Bormann "Platon: Die Idee. In: Grundprobleme der grossen Philosophen, Series UTB Vandenhoeck, 1978.

[Columbia 94] The Concise Columbia Electronic Encyclopedia, 1994, Columbia University Press. Online http://www.encyclopedia.com/

[Lechner et al. 99] U. Lechner, B. Schmid. Logic for Media – Towards the Computational Media Metaphor. To appear in: Proc. of the 32th Hawaiian Int. Conf. on System Sciences (HICSS 99), 1999.

[Mazzola 97] G. Mazzola. „music@encyclospace". Klangart 1997. URL: http://www.ifi.unizh.ch/groups/mml/musicmedia/

[Medoc 97] Medoc." MEDOC-the online computer science library, 1997. URL: medoc.informatik.tu-muenchen.de.

[Noam 96] E. Noam. What is the v.i.i.: About the institute., 1996. URL: http://www.ctr.columbia.edu/vii/mwhat.html.

[Peckhaus 97] V. Peckhaus. "Logik, Mathesis universalis und allgemeine Wissenschaft. Leibniz und die Wiederentdeckung der formalen Logik im 19. Jahrhundert". Akademie Verlag Belrin, 1997

[Schmid 97a] B. Schmid. "IKT als Träger einer neuen Industriellen Revolution" in: Komplexität und Agilität, Festschrift W. Eversheim, hrg. G. Schuh, H.P. Wiendahl, Springer Verlag Heidelberg, 1997

[Schmid 97b] B. Schmid. "The concept of a NetAcademy." Institute for Information Management, University of St. Gallen, 1997.

[Schmid 98] B. Schmid, "Wissensmedien". Gabler-Verlag, 1998. In preparation.

[Schmid et al. 96] B. Schmid, G. Geyer, W. Wolff., R. Schmid., K. Stanoevska-Slabeva. „Representation and automatic evaluation of empirical, especially quantitative knowledge", Final Report of the SNF (Swiss National Fond) Project No. 5003-034372, March 1996.

[Schmid et al. 98] B. Schmid, S. Schmid-Isler, R. Grütter, K. Stanoevska, and P. Stähler. Ein Glossar für die NetAcademy on Media Management.www.netacademy.org, 1998.

[Schmid-Isler 98] S. Schmid-Isler "The Academic Concept Reconsidered: Platon, Leibniz, Xanadu and the NetAcademy", NA-Publikation No. 823, URL: www.netacademy.org., Submitted. 1998.

[Sheth et al. 90] M.P. Sheth, and J.A. Larson „Federated Database Systems for Managing Distributed, Heterogeneous, and Autonomous Databases", in: ACM Computing Surveys (22:3), 1990, p.p. 184-264.

[Snell 80] Snell, B."Die Entdeckung des Geistes: Studien zur Entstehung des europäischen Denkens bei den Griechen", Vandenhoeck/Ruprecht, 1980.

[Stanoevska-Slabeva 97] K. Stanoevska-Slabeva. „Neugestaltung der Unternehmensplanung mit Hilfe eines prozessorientierten Planungsinformationsystems", Dissertation Nr. 2007, University of St.Gallen 1997.

[Stanoevska-Slabeva et al. 98] K. Stanoevska-Slabeva, A. Hombrecher, S. Handschuh, B. Schmid. "Efficient Information Retrieval: Tools for Knowledge Management". In: Proceedings of the Second European Conference on Practical Aspects of Knowledge Management, 29.-30. October, 1998, Basel, Switzerland.

[Whitehead 47], A.N. Whitehead, Essays in science and philosophy, 1947]

A framework for Post-implementation Evaluation Aimed at Promoting Organizational Learning: A Case of Looking into the Past to Solve Problems of the Future

Keith Miller
Department of Computing, Manchester Metropolitan University, John Dalton Building, Chester Street, Manchester, M1 5GD, UK
Dennis Dunn
Department of Business Information Technology, Manchester Metropolitan University, Aytoun Building, Aytoun Street, Manchester, M1 3GH, UK.
E-mail: K.Miller@doc.mmu.ac.uk. Facsimile: +44 161 247 1483.

ABSTRACT

The notion that IS evaluation has an important role to play in achieving organizational learning is well documented in the literature. However the high number of reported failures are a testament to the inability of the IS discipline to learn how to develop and adopt information systems successfully. Our research focuses on post-implementation evaluation, a key stage in which the learning can take place, and we use results of interpretive case studies to gain insights into improving practice. In the paper, we integrate concepts from two distinct research paradigms, IS evaluation and organizational learning, with our empirical work to develop an evaluation framework which can promote learning.

INTRODUCTION

The pace of technological change continues unabated. The organizations which will thrive in such volatile conditions must have the ability to learn, and learn quickly, in order to exploit new technologies and to make innovative use of mature ones. We believe therefore that learning is crucial within the IS context. We focus on the post-implementation phase to consider learning because the outcomes of the investment are known, and it should be possible to reflect on project activities and results without affecting progress or morale. A number of authors have noted that IS evaluation, particularly post-implementation audits, can act as feedback mechanisms which can help organizations learn (e.g. Avegerou, 1996; Willcocks, 1992). However according to the literature this learning is rarely achieved in practice (Miller & Dunn, 1997; Ward et al., 1996). It has been well documented that IS evaluation is intrinsically problematical due, principally, to difficulty in assessing intangible benefits and attributing causality in relation to benefit achievement (see for example Farbey et al., 1993). Some authors (e.g. Serafeimidis & Smithson, 1995; Walsham, 1993) have suggested that a more broadly-based approach to evaluation which incorporates qualitative elements can address these problems. However, neither the use of IS evaluation for promoting learning, nor the use of qualitative approaches to address problems of evaluation have been well developed, which makes the research presented here timely.

The work makes use of the field organizational learning. Organizational learning concepts have been adopted by many disciplines in a search for improvement. Our work assimilates ideas from the management science view of organizational learning. We take a broad view of the concept, which suggests that it encompasses the ways in which organizations construct and organize their knowledge in order to improve efficiency and adapt to their environment (Dodgson, 1993).

The next section of the paper reviews literature relating to IS evaluation and organizational learning. Section three describes the research approach and section four reports the key findings. This is followed by a presentation of a framework for post-implementation evaluation which aims to facilitate organizational learning. Section six discusses the framework in relation to the empirical research and literature. Finally, we draw conclusions and make recommendations for future work.

IS EVALUATION AND ORGANIZATIONAL LEARNING THEORY
IS Evaluation

Much of the work in the mainstream literature documents a formal and rational approach to evaluation based on financial assessment, using techniques such as return on investment and cost benefit analysis. Symons (1991) notes that financial evaluation techniques lay a heavy emphasis on audit of costs and return on capital, the result of which is to discourage innovation and favour short term payback. In addition she and others (e.g. Willcocks, 1992; Farbey et al., 1993) identify that, increasingly, benefits are strategic and intangible, and that these types of benefits do not lend themselves to being analysed by traditional financial methods. While there have been some novel attempts to deal with the problems of intangible benefits (e.g. Brown, 1994), the typical response from the IS evaluation community has been to develop more sophisticated versions of existing methods e.g. information economics (Parker et al., 1988). However Ballantine et al., (1996) suggest there has been a low take up of these methods.

Some authors advocate looking at IS evaluation from more than one perspective, in particular developing a more qualitative approach (e.g. Symons, 1991; Walsham 1993). Symons' influential work proposes a more broadly-based evaluation based on the three layer framework shown in figure 1. She argues that an examination of the interaction between content, context and process enables the qualitative and social impacts of IS to be drawn out. These impacts are crucial to the assessment of strategic investments where the benefits are often intangible.

Post-implementation evaluation of IS projects, which is the primary focus of the research, may be viewed as a post-installation audit of the product of the IS investment, plus an analysis of lessons learned by management, (Keen, 1987). The evaluation, often known as a post-implementation review (PIR), usually consists of an assessment of the performance of a system against stated objectives a short

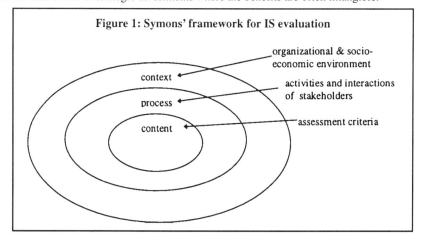

Figure 1: Symons' framework for IS evaluation

context ← organizational & socio-economic environment

process ← activities and interactions of stakeholders

content ← assessment criteria

period after it has become operational. Other methods include assessment of user satisfaction and assessment of system use. While many authors note the theoretical benefits to be gained, the empirical work on post-implementation evaluation practice suggests that PIRs are not performed routinely (Miller & Dunn, 1997) and that, if they are conducted, their use is primarily to effect project closure (Kumar, 1990). Overall, we find there is little detailed study of post-implementation reviews, with notable exceptions in the work of Kumar (1990) and Norris (1996).

Organizational Learning

Since Argyris and Schon introduced the concept of organizational learning (1978), it has been adapted by many disciplines in an effort to improve effectiveness. The work of Senge (1990) in the related area of Learning Organizations, for example has done much to stimulate research activity. The Learning Organization may be viewed as an ideal or a concept where the focus is on using environmental issues as a basis for promoting learning. The emphasis on learning in the approach is commendable, however the resources required to become a learning organization are significant and be beyond the scope of many. Our research builds more on insights from the organizational learning literature which can be applied in a more selective and pragmatic way. Dodgson (1993) in his review of the literature makes a number of observation which are relevant:

• organizational learning is predicated on individual learning, thus procedures for promoting individual learning should be developed;
• deliberate strategies are required to co-ordinate lessons learned in order to promote learning;
• a culture which is open and reflective counteracts the tendency of organizations to maintain the status quo.

The importance of organizational culture is also significant for the work and has been noted by a number of authors (e.g. Schein, 1993; Brown and Duguid, 1991).

RESEARCH APPROACH

The empirical research was carried out in 1996/97, and was divided into two phases. The first consisted of a survey of 150 medium and large UK companies. The key findings from the survey were:

- organizations continue to place a low emphasis on the post-implementation evaluation - a champion is needed to counteract this tendency;
- a clearer focus on the two key advantages (i.e. ensuring benefit achievement and achieving organizational learning) is required;
- overall, the most effective PIR tasks were review of implementation and assessment of users' views;
- some organizations are receptive to the idea of incorporating qualitative assessment into evaluation.

The detailed findings from the survey are reported elsewhere (Miller & Dunn, 1997). The principal vehicle for gaining an understanding of post-implementation evaluation was an analysis of interpretive case studies of practice in the UK financial services sector. Walsham (1995) identifies a general growth in the use of interpretive case studies for IS research, and reports that they are useful for developing concepts, generating theory, drawing implications in a domain of activity and contributing rich insights. A multiple case approach was used because the evidence from them is considered more compelling than a single case (Yin, 1989). Three institutions from the UK financial sector were chosen. Selecting organizations from the same sector reduced the number of confounding factors and improved the potential for generalizing results in that domain. In-depth interviews were carried out with senior IS and user personnel in the three organizations. In this way it was possible to obtain the perspectives of the two key stakeholding groups involved in the evaluation process. The interviews were semi-structured, and although they were taped, interviewees were frank and sometimes critical of organizational practice. The framework was derived by synthesising the key outcomes from the analysis of the case studies, and integrating these with the main issues from the literature review and survey analysis. Initially a basic framework model based on the main findings was generated. The empirical and literature findings were then examined in some detail to identify relevant issues. These were related to the basic model which resulted in refinements to the framework. At several points the framework was tested for consistency and coherence by ensuring the stages were in a logical sequence and that the content was in agreement with other findings. The overall research design was viewed to robust since there were two forms of triangulation incorporated. Firstly, there were two strands to the empirical work (i.e. a survey and case studies), and secondly, two perspectives were gained from each organization. This had the effect of improving the reliability and generalizability of the research results.

RESEARCH FINDINGS

It was noted in the previous section that the survey results are reported elsewhere, this section therefore presents only the case study findings. In the first part of this section a background to the cases and a summary of findings are presented. This is followed by the key issues to emerge from the analysis of the case studies. InsCoA had been bureaucratic organization, with traditional insurance values, but it was in the process of moving to more dynamic, open operation. In so doing it was adopting a 'no blame' culture. The company had in the past used conventional post-implementation audits. Currently PIRs were carried out infrequently because they were thought to be of little benefit, however some post-project business reviews had been conducted with success. InsCoB was a dynamic organization, which had enabled it to grow rapidly. The company had a quality management programme in place which emphasised its commitment to customer service. The IS manager had recently introduced a traditional PIR process in which IS staff carried out questionnaire-based interviews with users. The process focused on IS issues. BankA had been through a major organizational change recently and had also had moved to centralize some of its business functions. Like InsCoA, it was moving to a 'no blame' culture. The bank was a mature user of IT and had a mandatory, traditional PIR procedure. Group-based sessions were used for some reviews. Business and technology PIRs took place. A summary of the responses from IS and user personnel in the three organizations is given in the three tables below. The categories in the table were derived from the survey analysis and literature, and they formed the basis of the interviews.

The key issues arising from analyzing the findings will now be described. Learning within the IS function was weak. Only InsCoB claimed any success, however the users in this company did not perceive any improvements arising from the PIR process. In the other companies traditional modes of dissemination, such as making the results available in a report, were found to be too passive. It was particularly surprising to find in BankA, which had a thorough procedure, that no mechanisms to promote learning existed. It was in the user areas where learning from post-project reviews was observed. In InsCoA and BankA, business reviews had been carried out successfully by users. In the former, a team was created to review a re-organization. The review sessions were mostly group-based, and the results were taken back to those affected by a member of the review team. In this way it was believed that good practice was identified and spread quickly and effectively. The use and success of business reviews in comparison to technical reviews is in itself a significant finding.

Table 1: Perspectives on post-implementation evaluation from InsCoA

	InsCoA	
	IS Perspective	User Perspective
Rationale	ensure benefit achievement, learn lessons	learn lessons, ensure benefit achievement
Learning	suggested reviewing plans as a source of lessons, learning lessons down to good management	in a business review reports prepared from PIR sessions which were used by managers to 'sell' findings
Politics	politics could be a factor, there were mechanisms to reduce its affects, e.g. 'no blame' culture	politics would play a part, move to a 'no blame' culture would reduce the effects
Problems	PIRs do not receive priority, need to move on to next project, 'soft' benefits difficult	documents too large & not used, difficult to assess 'soft' benefits, focus on bad practice
Subjective assessment	acknowledged it takes place, prefers objective measures	was used in a review she authorised
Suggestions to improve PIRs	should be set up jointly with users, should use presentation to market findings	group & individual sessions needed, modular PIR needed, timing is important

Table 2: Perspectives on post-implementation evaluation from InsCoB

	InsCoB	
	IS Perspective	User Perspective
Rationale	feedback mechanism for customers, learn lessons	useful for IT department, may help with next project
Learning	achieved by developers analyzing PIR questionnaires, meetings between IS personnel	no evidence of learning apparent
Politics	politics could play a part, particularly on large projects, effect should not be over-played	probably could play a part, close user & IS staff relationship would help reduce effect
Problems	none identified, noted PIR process was new & had not been assessed	use of questionnaires seen as 'wooden', did not understand some questions
Subjective assessment	used in investment appraisal, prefers objective measures	no comments made
Suggestions to improve PIRs	group discussion appropriate	group-based session useful, business should play a greater role

Table 3: Perspectives on post-implementation evaluation from BankA

	BankA	
	IS Perspective	User Perspective
Rationale	learn lessons, close project, assess benefits	learn lessons
Learning	lessons were learned by those involved in the PIR process, dissemination of results poorly achieved	PIR report sent to participants, reports lodged in a central register which can be accessed by personnel
Politics	acknowledged politics could affect outcome, move to 'no blame' culture could help reduce effects	politics can have an effect, role of facilitator important in ensuring it does not have a serious effect
Problems	benefit assessment a problem due to change, varying stress placed on PIRs process	assessment of 'soft' benefits difficult, not enough priority given, people not around
Subjective assessment	not perceived to be a problem if spread of personnel involved	subjective views used, but prefers objective measures
Suggestions to improve PIRs	more active approach to marketing results, PIRs in smaller chunks	take care in choice of facilitator, use group sessions

Organizational culture was found to be a contributing factor to the success of business reviews in InsCoA and BankA. Both users cited the creation of a 'no blame' culture as assisting the generation of open discussion. The culture had been introduced in both companies as part of new quality management systems. Users and IS personnel acknowledged that engendering the 'right' culture was difficult to achieve since it involved attitudinal change, but progress had been made in both companies.

Assessment of intangible benefits was found to be problematical. Only in BankA was there a specific approach to assessment, which involved checking the consistency of project outcomes with strategic direction and organizational culture. In addition a list of the estimated value of the benefits, expressed in monetary and non-monetary terms, was produced by the review team. In the other two organizations managerial judgement was used to appraise intangible benefits. In essence this amounted to tacit use of qualitative assessment. As part of the general research aims, views were sought on using qualitative approaches to appraise benefits. There was agreement that explicit use of qualitative assessment would be useful. Two interviewees (i.e. IS manager in InsCoA and user manager in BankA) felt strongly that tangible benefits should be the primary basis for evaluation.

FRAMEWORK

An eight stage framework (see figure 2) which covers the life cycle of an IS project was derived from an analysis of the empirical results and the literature. This section describes the operation of the framework. It is discussed in the next section. The first stage, orientation of stakeholders, aims to ensure that the participants in the evaluation process have the necessary predisposition and knowledge to contribute effectively. Education in relation to organizational culture and organizational learning are particularly important. The cultural education relates to an attempt to create an open environment in which learning and innovative thinking are encouraged and blame is discouraged. The organizational learning relates to making stakeholders aware of ways in which the organization and individuals can facilitate or inhibit learning. The final element is to educate stakeholders on the way in which the framework operates. Workshops would be an effective way of inculcating concepts.

The second stage, define PIR role, is part of the project initiation procedure. It aims to state which of the framework stages are applicable to the project, and gain the project sponsor's authorisation for their inclusion. The evaluation should be sponsored jointly by the business and IS areas. If it is decided to conduct a full scale PIR (i.e. carry out stage 6), then details of benefits to be assessed and the ways in which they can be measured need to be established. The projected benefits and costs should be documented and analyzed in order to define relevant measures. Methods of benefit assessment should be reached by negotiation among key stakeholders.

The third stage aims to capture the data necessary to make an assessment of benefit achievement. It may be that the capture is a once off exercise e.g. a customer survey, or there may be a need for data to be captured on an ongoing basis. The third stage would only be carried out if a full scale PIR was being conducted.

Figure 2 Framework for post-implementation evaluation

Framework for post-implementation evaluation			
project phase	framework stage	framework activity	key: [..] = optional
pre-project	**1. orientate stakeholders**	cultural orientation organizational learning education PIR education	
project initiation	**2. define PIR role**	define PIR stages to be executed [state benefits to be assessed] [state relevant benefit measures]	
system building	**[3. capture benefit measures]**	capture measures relevant for benefit assessment, through to stage 5	
project completion	**4. close project**	close project mini-review; distribute findings flag need for PIR if necessary	
	[5. assess development]	assess development process assess planning process	
benefit accrual	**[6. conduct PIR]**	prepare for review review system performance review benefit achievement review user & IS roles	
post-PIR	**[7. disseminate PIR findings]**	collate findings market key findings set up findings for easy access	
	[8. manage benefits]	drive out benefits	

The fourth stage, should be conducted shortly after project completion and aims to effect project closure. It should include a formal sign off and transfer of responsibilities. It is proposed that a short mini-review is carried out, minimally, between the project sponsor, a senior user and the IS project manager. The personnel involved should consult briefly with colleagues prior to the review. The purpose of this review is to highlight issues which require immediate action or may provide useful knowledge for others in the organization. If there is a full scale PIR carried out, it may take place at a much later time, thus the mini-PIR serves to ensure that urgent issues are addressed without delay.

Stage five may follow on from project completion or it may be incorporated into the PIR process. It consists of an assessment of system development and planning and aims to help improve these functions. A similar approach to that suggested for the PIR proper should be adopted. It should be led by an IS project manager who is independent of the project concerned. In the first part of the review session, participants should be encouraged to reflect openly on their project experiences. In the second part, the development and planning processes and their outputs are examined to identify any lessons learned. The results of this stage should be fed into stage 7, disseminate findings. This stage is optional.

The sixth stage is the post-implementation review itself . The timing of this stage will be dependent on when sufficient benefits have accrued. The first part of this stage is preparation for the activity by the facilitator. The role of the facilitator is crucial throughout the stage. An independent, trained facilitator should be chosen to conduct the review. The facilitator should collate and summarise relevant documentation such as system objectives and benefit achievement statistics. This documentation should not be submitted ahead of the review to participants. Prior to the review, participants should reflect on their role in the project in order to gain their perspective on outcomes. A group session, involving users and IS personnel, will be the main review activity. The make up of the review team should be drawn up with a view to balance the need to get a spread of opinions and the need to have a manageable number of people present. It will be the facilitator's responsibility to guide discussion and record the outcomes of the process. The group session should be divided into three parts. In the first, participants should reflect critically on their experiences and identify what went well and what went badly. In the second part, a summary of ideas generated in the first should be used along with the documentation produced in the preparation for the PIR to examine objectively system performance, benefit achievement, and performance of IS and personnel. Specific areas which should be considered include how the outputs relate to business goals, the impact of the system on users and the organization, and an appraisal of the implementation process. The final part of the group session should be a debriefing where the facilitator reports on the outcomes from the session. This stage is optional.

The seventh stage, which should be carried out immediately following the PIR, aims to disseminate the results. Two categories of outcomes may emerge. The first category relates to substantial findings which can deliver immediate benefits to the organization. These findings should be marketed actively to the relevant parties. It may be through a presentation to those affected or by an e-mail message. The second category relates to useful findings which should become part of organizational procedures. These should be incorporated into a repository of good practice. It is proposed that an electronic repository be used for the purpose. Stage seven would only be conducted if a PIR had been carried out.

The final stage, manage benefits, aims to ensure that all potential system benefits are delivered. Areas of shortfall or opportunities for realising further benefits are identified from the PIR results, and these are used to generate the actions needed to remedy problems or exploit opportunities.

It will have been noted that several stages are optional. This allows the post-implementation evaluation carried out to be determined by the nature of the project and the type of outcome expected. The possibilities run from a basic project close out activity (i.e. stages 1, 2 and 4) to full scale evaluation with substantial efforts made to incorporate learning and drive out benefits (i.e. all eight stages).

DISCUSSION

This section explains how the empirical insights and the existing body of knowledge support the framework. The overall development was guided by the rationale for PIRs which emerged from the analysis of the case studies and is supported by the survey findings i.e. the main reasons for conducting a PIR are to learn lessons from project experiences and to ensure benefit achievement. A further factor which has influenced the framework is the notion that it is important to deliberately adopt strategies and structures for learning (Dodgson, 1993). Three stages are particularly significant in this: stage one, where participants gain an appropriate orientation, stage six where there is an emphasis on using the review for learning lessons and finally in stage seven where lessons learned are disseminated.

The case studies provide strong support for cultural education being a pre-requisite for a successful PIR, and this aspect is embodied in stage 1. The adoption of a 'no blame' culture as a mechanism to promote learning is consistent with observations from the field of organizational learning. For example it has been observed that individuals in Japan are not allocated blame (responsibility is taken by the group) and that this may contribute to the levels of learning achieved (Jones & Hendry, 1992). Heller (1996) too offers support for a 'blame-free' environment as away of encouraging innovation. The personnel in the case studies were clear that a 'no blame' culture was not easy to achieve and this may prevent effective deployment of the framework.

There are two elements of the second stage which are drawn directly from the analysis of the empirical data. The first is the modular nature of the framework, which means that it is inherently flexible. The business manager at InsCoA specifically stated that she thought a modular PIR, which allowed a 'fast track' version to be conducted, was needed. Two reasons for the flexibility emerged from the empirical data: one was it acted as a resource saving device, and two it was unlikely that performing PIRs on all projects would be cost effective since few 'new' lessons would emerge each time. The second is benefit assessment. Both phases of the empirical work identified the difficulty of appraising intangible benefits. However by reaching decisions on the measures for intangible (and other) benefits through negotiation, it is argued that they are more likely to be used and believed in the review process. Also an insight from the IS manager at InsCoA suggested that if decision makers knew that the benefits they projected were going to be analyzed, they would apply more effort to ensure they were realized. This stage and the next of capturing relevant data have some resonance with Ward et al.'s benefit management model (1996).

Parts of the fourth stage, close project, were prompted by the two factors. The perception of the PIR as a close out function was confirmed by the IS manager at InsCoA, and it was also identified as a significant factor from the survey and the work of Kumar (1990). The implication drawn from this is that a PIR's role as a project closure device is a fact of organizational life. The view taken here is that by making the closure action explicit, it clarifies and distinguishes the position of the PIR proper.

Stage 5, assess development, has traditionally been a major function of the PIR (Keen, 1987). This was found to be the case in InsCoB and with many survey respondents. The implication drawn from this was that appraisal of these functions was useful and should be incorporated into the framework.

The empirical evidence provides substantiation for a number of elements of stage 6, conduct PIR. The use of a facilitator-led group sessions was strongly supported by the user manager at BankA and some other interviewees. The notion of multiple stakeholder reviews has been around for some time in IS evaluation (Kumar, 1990) and also in the field of evaluation research (Rossi and Freeman, 1993), but the practice is not widely adopted. There was general agreement in the case studies that subjective judgement was employed tacitly in evaluation. The framework makes explicit use of qualitative assessment. The interpretation of the benefit measures and causality, in terms of benefit achievement, is achieved by discussion among stakeholders. The case studies suggested that qualitative assessment should be used in conjunction with objective measures.

One area element of the framework is in conflict with case studies findings. It has been suggested that no information about the project is sent to those participating in the PIR, which is in contrast to conventional practice. Rather individuals are asked to reflect on their experiences of the project. This saves time on the part of the participants, and more importantly allows a form of goal-free evaluation to take place as proposed by Scriven (1972). We believe this is justified because of the potential advantage of identifying benefits or costs which are unexpected. If the review was based on prepared material there would be a danger that it would focus on this and not uncover issues in other areas.

There was strong evidence from both the case studies and the survey that an active approach was needed to disseminate the results of the PIR, as proposed in stage 7. The case study of BankA highlighted the situation that even where resources were put into the PIR process there was a danger of lessons not being incorporated. Interviewees in InsCoA and BankA stated in view of the pressure employees were under, a more active form of dissemination should occur. Presentation was the most popular choice.

The final stage relates to benefits assessment. The IS manager in InsCoA was particularly strong in his desire to see benefits 'driven out'. As recognized by Ward et al. (1996) this is the natural culmination of the benefits assessment process.

CONCLUSIONS

The ability to learn from the results of IS investments is crucial in order to exploit the potential from emerging organizational forms and novel technologies. The evidence from this research is that IS evaluation is currently under-utilized in its capacity to improve organizational learning. The framework proposed in this paper has synthesized theory from different disciplines and empirical research. We believe the flexibility of the framework (some stages are optional) and its grounding in practitioner experience make it inherently usable and cost effective in operation.

The research has confirmed and extended the view that post-implementation evaluation, and indeed IS evaluation in general, is a process which is dependent on the perceptions of individuals and the cultural environment in an organization. Objective measures are an important input into the process of evaluation, but the construction of meaning from such data is also significant. In addition to promoting learning, the evaluation proposed has identified ways in which qualitative assessment can be used to address the weaknesses in appraising IS investments which have intangible benefits. There is evidence from the empirical work to suggest cultural changes taking place in some organizations is creating the right climate for the proposed form of evaluation to take place. More work is required to develop and refine these concepts in the field.

REFERENCES

Argyris, C. & Schon, D., (1978), *Organizational Learning: A Theory of Action Perspective*, Reading, Addison-Wesley.

Avegerou, C. (1996), 'Evaluating Information Systems by Consultation and Negotiation', *International Journal of Information Management*, (15) 6, 427-436.

Ballantine J A, Galliers R D & Stray S J (1996) Information systems/technology evaluation practices: evidence from UK organizations. *Journal of Information Technology*, 11, 129-141.

Brown A (1994) Appraising intangible benefits from information technology investment. In *Proceedings of the First European Conference on IT Investment Evaluation*, Henley, September, 187-199.

Brown, J.S. and Duguid, P. (1991) 'Organizational Learning and communities-of-practice: toward a unified view of working, learning, and innovation.' *Organizational Science*, 2(1), 40-57

Dodgson, M. (1993), 'Organizational Learning: A Review of Some Literatures', *Organization Studies*, 3, 375-394.

Farbey, B. Land, F. & Targett, D. (1993), *How to Assess Your IT Investment,* Butterworth-Heinemann, Oxford.

Heller, R., (1996) 'Slipping up on route to the top', *Management Today*, 1, 21.

Jones, A.M. & Hendry, C.M. (1992) *Learning Organizations: a review of literature and practice*, HRD Partnership, London.

Keen, J. S. (1987), *Managing Systems Development* (2nd ed), Wiley, Chichester.

Kumar, K. (1990), 'Post Implementation Evaluation of Computer Based Information Systems: Current Practices', *Communications of the ACM,* 33(2) 1990, 203-212.

Miller , K. and Dunn, D., (1997), 'Post-implementation of information systems/technology: a survey of UK practice' In proceedings of the Fourth European Conference on the Evaluation of Information Technology, Delft, October, 47 - 55.

Norris G D (1996) Post-investment Appraisal. In L Willcocks (Ed*.) Investing in Information Systems,* 193-223. Chapman Hall, London.

Parker M, Benson R & Traynor H (1988) *Information Economics: linking Business Performance to Information Technology*, Prentice Hall, London.

Rossi P.H. and Freeman H.E. (1993) *Evaluation: a systematic approach*, (5th ed), Sage Publications, London.

Schein, E.H. (1993) 'On dialogue, culture and organizational learning.' *Organizational Dynamics.* 22(2),40-51

Scriven, M. (1972) 'Pros and Cons about Goal-Free Evaluation', *Evaluation Comment*, 3(4),1-4.

Senge P.M. (1990) The Fifth Discipline: The Art and Practice of the Learning Organization, Century Business, UK

Serafeimidis, V., and Smithson, D., (1995), 'The management of change for a rigorous appraisal of IT investment: the case of a UK insurance organization' in Doukidis, G, Galliers, B, Jelassi, T, Kremar, H & Land, F (Eds) *Proceedings of the 3rd European Conference on Information Systems, Athens, Greece*, June 1 - 3, 1995, 221-233

Symons, V.J. (1991), 'A Review of Information Systems Evaluation', European *Journal of Information Systems*, 1(3), 205 - 212.

Walsham, G. (1993), *Interpreting Information Systems in Organizations*, John Wiley and Sons, Chichester.

Walsham, G. (1995) 'Interpretive Case Studies in IS Research: Nature and Method', *European Journal of Information Systems*, 4, 74-81.

Ward, J., Taylor, P. & Bond, P. (1996), 'Evaluation and realisation of IS/IT benefits: an empirical study of current practice', *European Journal of Information Systems*, 4, 214-225.

Willcocks, L. (1992), 'Evaluating Information Technology investments: research findings and reappraisal', *Journal of Information Systems*, 2, 243-268.

Yin, R., K., (1989) *Case Study Research: Design and Methods*, Sage, London.

Cross-national CAI Tool:
A Management Decision Making Learning Tool
Focusing on Competitive
and Economic Market Analysis

Dr. Robert J. Mockler
Joseph F. Adams Professor of Management, St. John's University, Jamaica New York
114 East 90th St (1B), New York, NY 10128
Tel: 212 876 5856, Fax: 212 996 6967, e-mail: mocklerr@stjohns.edu

Dr. Dorothy G. Dologite
Professor, Computer Information Systems, School of Business ,Department of Statistics and Computer
Information Systems, Baruch College, City University of New York, 17 Lexington Avenue, New York, New York
10010
Tel: 212 802-6232, Fax: 212 996-6967, e-mail: dgdbb@cunyvm.cuny.edu

Dr. Mikhail Y. Afansiev
Professor, Moscow State University, School of Economics, Head of Department, Central Economic and
Mathematical Institute (CEMI), 32, Krasikova St., 117418 Moscow, Russia
Tel: 011-7-095-32-4344, Fax: 011-7-095-32-7015

ABSTRACT

This paper develops a new and improved CAI tool for learning management decision-making using advanced and traditional CIS technologies. Three professors from Russia and the United States joined to develop an advanced expert system, which differentiates itself substantially from predecessors in the following aspects:
1. it expands to focus more on management decision making learning rather than technical skills learning alone;
2. it is cross-nationally useful since it has been used in Russia and the United States with the respective language modules integrated into the same tool, therefore accommodating language differences;
3. it is able to measure not only results more accurately, but also outputs - the impact of the system on the user's ability to correctly reply to questions;
4. it combines traditional computer technologies with artificial intelligence; and
5. it integrates competitive (free) market and economic (controlled market) analysis.

INTRODUCTION

The project and expert system developed through the project described in this paper was initiated by professors from the University of Moscow and Central Economic and Mathematical Institute, from St. John's University, New York, and Baruch College, City University of New York.

The American professors visited Moscow in 1991 and again in 1993 where they gave seminars, workshops, and classes in expert systems, artificial intelligence, and free market strategic planning. At that time, they studied the possibility of joint research projects with professors from Moscow State University, involving their two areas: computer aided instruction (in Russia) and expert systems/free market planning (in the United States). This initial discussion and work led to a grant from IREX (International Research Exchange Board) — USIA in the fall of 1996 for the Russian professor to spend three months in New York working at St. John's University with the American professors. This work led to the development of a working prototype system, which is now being used at the Russian and United States universities and institutes involved.

This paper describes this system and how it was developed. The system had the following distinguishing

characteristics:
- it expands to focus more on management decision making learning rather than technical skills learning alone;
- it is cross-nationally useful since it has been used in Russia and the United States with the respective language modules integrated into the same tool, therefore accommodating language differences;
- it is able to measure not only results more accurately, but also outputs - the impact of the system on the user's ability to correctly reply to questions;
- it combines traditional computer technologies with artificial intelligence; and
- it integrates competitive (free) market and economic (controlled market) analysis.

On one level, there were the obvious benefits arising from using computer aided education to facilitate learning, a documented way to improve learning in the United States, and a necessary tool in Russia and other developing nations where textbooks are not readily available to students. It is especially useful at the undergraduate level because it enables the students to learn the mechanical aspects of a subject on their own, and, therefore, enables the professor to focus on more interesting and advanced aspects of the subject when interacting with students.

On another level, the project proved useful in integrating two cultures — the ones of Russia and the United States — in a real and permanent way, since that integration was preserved in a system that is used in both countries at major educational institutions.

A third extraordinarily useful dimension to the system's benefits grew out of the great need in Russia to acquire knowledge of and skills in competitive (free) market thinking and management. This system development has an integrated built-in module, which introduces and provides guidance in free market planning so that this perspective is automatically built into the educational process in Russia at major educational institutions. This perspective can ultimately make major contributions to Russia's prospering in the rapidly changing multinational competitive market environment faced by business managers today and in the future.

At the core, the idea was a very simple one: marrying an advanced technology (expert system) with conventional data based computer information systems technology. Furthermore, it was relatively easy to combine the Russian and English versions because of the facility in English of most business students in business education programs in Russia. In addition, the receptivity to free market thinking has increased substantially over the past five years in Russia, as has the interest of the United in the growing markets in the former Soviet Republics. Once the basic technologies and groundwork were laid over the years between 1993 and 1996, the actual creation of the new prototype system was relatively straightforward, as the following sections will discuss.

The next section of the paper provides a brief review of related literature, including the following topics: 1. Disciplines using CAI, 2. Reasons for considering CAI, 3. Measures of effectiveness, and 4. Instructional approaches employed. After the literature review, this paper describes the background of the tool being discussed, namely the preliminary work of the three participating professors, geographically divided into two parts — Russia and the United States.

LITERATURE REVIEW

The growing importance of CAI and its related fields in today's learning/educational environment is evidenced by the vast amount of research material in the field of CAI. CAI (Computer-Aided/Assisted Instruction) is also known as CBI (Computer-Based Instruction); CBT (Computer-Based Training); CAL (Computer-Assisted Learning); and ITS (Intelligent Training System) [Computer-mediated communication …, 1994; and Maul & Spotts, 1993].

Content and Level of CAI Use

CAI and CAI applications are used to support learning in a wide range of educational areas. These include: acquiring computer software [Bellm, 1997; and Filipczak, 1997], language, writing, reading, and handwriting skills [Gordon, 1994; Harris, 1994; Jagtman & Bongaerts (1994); Maneekul, 1996; Schulz, 1993; Torres Ortiz, 1994, and Wolf, 1985]; learning mathematics, statistics and scientific subjects [Carrier, Post & Hack, 1985; Cavin, Cavin & Lagowski, 1981; Fletscher, Hawley & Piele, 1990; Hale, 1986; Kracjik, Simmons & Lunetta, 1986; Mausner, et al., 1983; Phalakonk, 1994; and Wahl, 1995]; military training [Orlansky & String, 1979]; and studying photography [Smart, 1994], economics [Hyperlecturing …, 1994]; and political economics [Zatschek, 1996].

Leidner and Jarvenpaa (1995), and other studies [e.g., Using computer simulation …, 1992], describe various opportunities for, and the need of, CAI training methods in the area of management development and education. Other studies support the close relation of IT technology to management education and training [Alavi, Wheeler & Valacich, 1995; Alavi, Yoo & Vogel, 1997; Schlechter, 1990; and Sweeney & Oram, 1992].

The levels at which CAI is used include special education [Koscinski, 1995; and Shiah, 1995], elementary, secondary and collegiate – undergraduate and graduate – education [Daiute, 1985; Henderson, Landesman & Kachuck, 1985; Skinner, 1990; and Stanton, 1994].

This paper focuses on cross-cultural (U.S. and Russian) applications of CAI in the business management and decision making teaching field at the graduate and undergraduate levels.

Reasons for CAI Use

Several reasons account for the fact that CAI applications have recently become more attractive to teachers, trainers, and employers.

- The fact that educational institutions in the United States are facing a crisis is well known [Bronner, 1998]. Studies have emphasized that American 12th graders scored close to last compared with other industrialized nations and that this has not been an isolated incident but a continuing pattern. President Clinton responded to the results of the study with the words, "This week, America got a wake-up call on education." [Clinton decries …, 1998].
- In order to stay economically competitive internationally, the US economy needs workers with more sophisticated skills [Measelle & Egol, 1992]. To fill this need, a new educational system has to be developed in which, among other things, the learning experience and student engagement in the learning process has to increase.
- The use of information technology in general and CAI applications in particular can help achieve this goal. Other research supports this view [Bardach, 1997; Gandz, 1997; Loupe, 1997; and Osin & Osgold, 1996]. Wulf (1995) concludes that information technology will transform the university of the next millenium to an unprecedented degree. Higher education will flourish, but the most successful universities will be the ones that take part of the technological revolution.

CAI Effectiveness

The results of CAI applications research and the uses to which CAI has been effectively put today are varied. In terms of acquired knowledge and increased learning ability, CAI applications are almost all at least as effective as traditional teaching methods [Clark, 1991; Harris, 1994; Jurenovich, 1994; and Kim, 1994]. Since this body of research demonstrated that CAI did not always improve teaching and learning performance, CAI has had only a fairly moderate impact, especially at the college level until recently. This has been in part due to the fact that traditional teaching technologies — chalk and blackboard, overhead projectors — are not only perceived as adequate methods of communicating textbook material to the student, but instructors are also more familiar with them.

Studies, however, have established CAI's superior effectiveness for various subjects on different levels over traditional teaching methods [Bellm, 1997; Gordon, 1994; Shiah, 1995; and Foley McInerney, 1995]. A 1995 benchmark review of more than 130 recent academic studies, for example, concluded that using technology/computer supported instruction improved student outcome in language, arts, math, social studies, and science [Bailo & Sivin-Kachla, 1995]. In addition, CAI can be more cost effective than traditional methods, which are labor intensive [Alavi, 1994; Burston, 1993; Fletscher, Hawley & Piele, 1990; Maul & Spotts, 1993; Orlansky & String, 1979; and Wuebker-Battershell, 1994].

The project described in this paper found CAI especially effective where instructors with Western expertise and textbooks are not readily and widely available, as it is the case in Russia [Applegate, 1997; Kulik, 1997; MacWilliams, 1997; and Medvedev, 1997]. The newly developed CAI system also proved useful in the United States for learning operations management tools and for learning how to integrate operations management decision making with strategic planning.

Instructional Methods Used in CAI

CAI utilizes the computer as a teacher [Taylor, 1980]. The computer and its software programs (applications) perform tasks that were traditionally handled by a human teacher/tutor, and, therefore, assume the role of an instructor. The most commonly used traditional instructional methods implemented in CAI are categorized by various authors as [Hackbarth, 1996; Heinrich, et al., 1996, Newby, et al., 1996; Steinberg, 1991; and Thompson, Simonson & Hargarve, 1992]: Drill and Practice; Tutorial; Simulations; Instructional Games; and Problem Solving.

BACKGROUND: PRIOR SYSTEMS DEVELOPMENT WORK BY THE AUTHORS

Russia

The Russian professor began his work on computer aided education tools during 1986 when he was put in charge of courseware development to support economics teaching at the Central Economics and Mathematics institute (CEMI) of the Russian Academy of Science. He continued this work while working on his doctoral degree at Moscow State University between 1989 and 1993. This early work led to a development of a working CAI system, which was introduced into undergraduate courses at Moscow State University and other Moscow educational institutions in 1990. Since then, a number of improvements and refinements have been introduced, based on the use of the system by over 500 students in Moscow State University alone.

The original "Courseware" developed in Russia was created to reduce the gap between theory, as covered by economists in standard business courses in Operations Research, and practical skills in operations research methods to make management decisions. In foreign universities, this goal was achieved by converting Operations Research courses to courses in Production and Operations Management.

During the courses where "Courseware" is used, students are supposed to do considerable *individual* work using the new "Courseware". The "Courseware" contains 21 subject areas, each one offering between 8 and 10 decision making situations. Some of the subjects deal with such business problem situations as production volume, blending, cutting, assignment, transportation, and allocation. Others deal with practical business situations involving queuing, inventory, and project management. In keeping with the original orientation of the courses, Operations Research, these situations were based on mathematical tools, such as network models and Pert/CPM. Supporting software packages based on operations research techniques, such as STORM and AB.POM, were originally used in the "Courseware" program. The system and their problem situations were largely quantitative-based.

The system works by providing a menu from which the type of situation could be selected by the student. The student would then be presented with a problem on the computer screen, would proceed to solve it, and would then enter his/her answer. The computer would then check the answer against the correct one generated by the supporting software without telling the student the answer. This general process is shown in Figures 1 and 2.

Those not having a correct answer were guided (through references to appropriate reading material related to

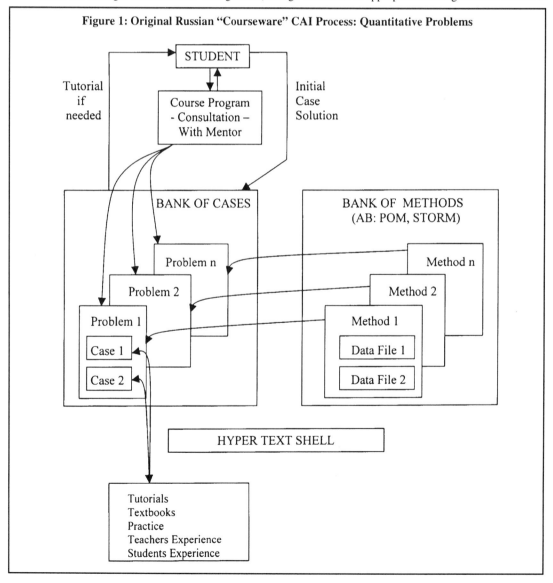

Figure 1: Original Russian "Courseware" CAI Process: Quantitative Problems

STUDENT

Tutorial if needed

Course Program
- Consultation –
With Mentor

Initial Case Solution

BANK OF CASES

BANK OF METHODS
(AB: POM, STORM)

Problem n

Method n

Problem 2

Method 2

Problem 1

Method 1

Case 1

Data File 1

Case 2

Data File 2

HYPER TEXT SHELL

Tutorials
Textbooks
Practice
Teachers Experience
Students Experience

the kind of error they made) in working the problem situation over again until they finally got the correct solution.

The system, over the years, was able to accumulate the test scores of students as they progressed in learning, and, therefore, the system has a very accurate statistical measure of the value of the software in relation to other kinds of traditional teaching, such as lectures and supervised labs. The results were very encouraging since they showed that use of "Courseware" was a more effective way to teach. In addition, they required considerably less time of the instructor who was then able to devote more time to individual student coaching in advanced problems. This result is confirmed by United States studies, which showed that learning individually through computer aided instruction tools is a more effective way to learn.

The Russian professor is widely published in the field. His books include: Foundations of Industry Planning Optimization (Moscow: Naudia Publishing Company, 1988); "Methods of Estimation of Production Efficiency," Atlantic Economic Journal, v.20, n.1, 1992; and Computer Assisted Instruction for Economists (Moscow University Publishing House, 1993). His doctoral dissertation (Moscow State University) was entitled Computer Technologies of Economic Education Electronic Aids for Teaching and Their Application (1993); his undergraduate degree was in Mathematics (Moscow State University, 1973).

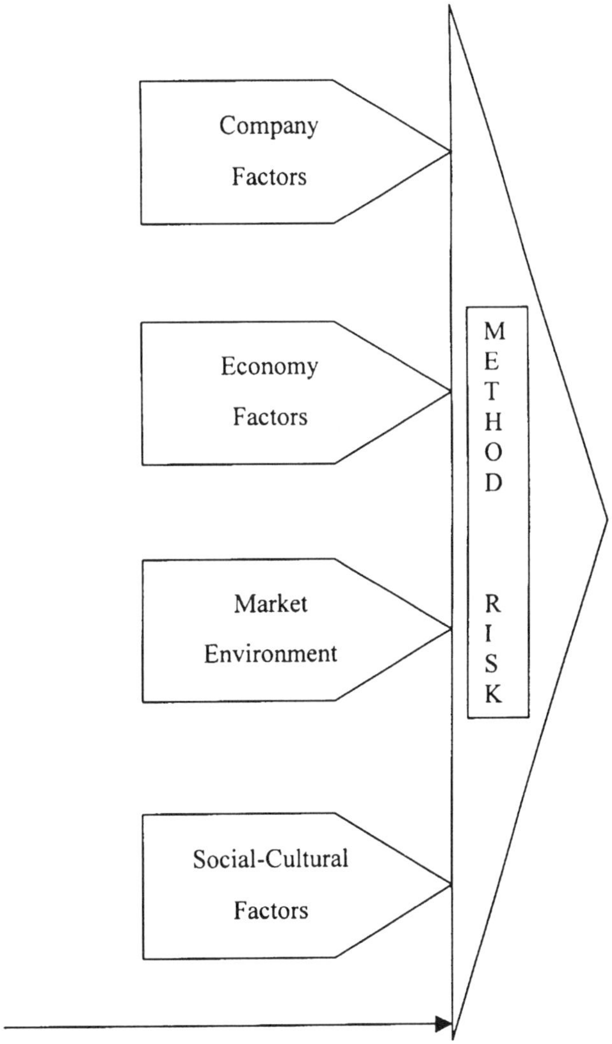

United States

In 1989, one of the American professors did two studies of expert knowledge-based systems (Knowledge-Based (Expert)

Figure 2: Dependency Diagram - Qualitative Problem: New Venture Method of Entry Situatation - Overview

Systems for Management Decisions and Knowledge-Based (Expert) Systems for Strategic Planning) and one on planning systems (Computer Software to Support Strategic Management Decision Making: A Comprehensive Review of Available Existing Conventional and Knowledge-Based Applications), all published by Prentice Hall. In 1992, the American professors had three books on expert systems all published by Macmillan: Expert Systems: An Introduction to Knowledge-Based Systems (co-authored); Developing Knowledge-Based Systems Using and Expert System Shell: A Guidebook for General Business Managers and Computer Information System Technicians (includes 19 Sample Prototype Systems and a Development Shell) by one of the professors (this book has been translated into Chinese); Developing Knowledge-Based Systems Using VP-Expert (by the other American professor). Together the two American professors co-authored the recent Multinational Cross-Cultural Management: A Context Specific Process published by Greenwood Publishing Group, a Division of Elsevier Science Publishers.

Many of the expert systems developed by them were used to support learning in their courses taught at St. John's University, New York, and Baruch College, School of Business, City University of New York.

DESCRIPTION OF THE SYSTEM

The new system incorporating expert system technology, which was developed during the fall of 1996, built on the original "Courseware" system — for example, the first four panels: (1) the title, (2) the main menu, (3) general

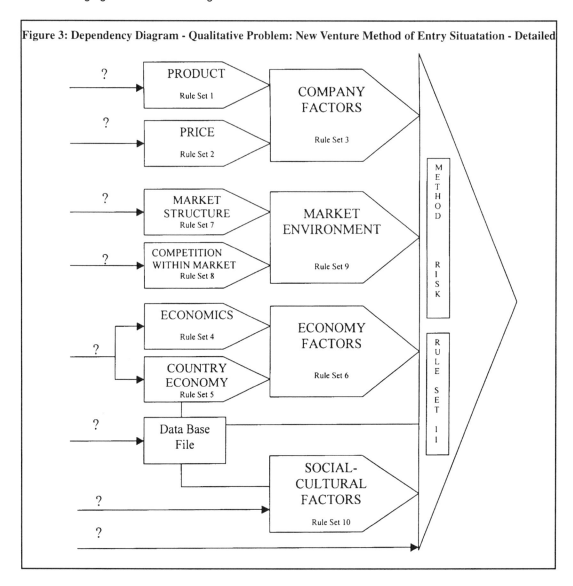

Figure 3: Dependency Diagram - Qualitative Problem: New Venture Method of Entry Situatation - Detailed

information on the subject and additional reading (a sort of tutorial the student could review before going on), and (4) the problem situation to be dealt with. This was done in both Russian and English.

The difference was that in the new system version developed, the menu contained an additional group of subjects about management decision making situations in a free market environment and the tutorial concerned planning in a free market environment; the problem was a qualitative not quantitative one (for example, determining method of entry into a new overseas area). To begin the exercise, the user would then enter the expert system by pressing "consult". The overall outline of the method of entry situation is shown in Figures 3 and 4.

At this point, the introductory panel given in Figures 5 is shown. There then follows a series of questions, which cover not only the traditional economic factors, but also briefly some competitive market factors. These are also shown in Figure 5.

At the end of the consultation, student answers are compared to benchmark answers, as in the original "Courseware" system, and the student is graded. Students who missed key points are then coached, as in the original system, and asked to redo the consultation. Two levels of student responses are tested. First, they are graded and tutored on their knowledge of the economy involved, since the system contains a database of the "correct" factor values (Figure 6). Second, they are graded and tutored on their skills in making management decisions in specific management situations. This is shown in Figure 7.

Figure 4: Introductory Panel and Questions to be asked by the System

Western Corporations' Strategic Partnership Service Assistant
Developed by Dr. M.Y. Afanasiev, Moscow State University
In collaboration with
Dr. R.J. Mockler and Dr. D.G. Dologite, St. John's University
And
Zicklin School of Business, Baruch College, City University of New York
For further information, contact
Dr. D.G. Dologite and Dr. R.J. Mockler
Fax: 212 996-6967, Tel: 212 876-5856

Questions:

COMPANY FACTORS
1.   PRODUCT
What kinds of product are you going to sell in {country_name}?
Does your product quality meet or exceed that of competing products?
Is your product design advanced?
Is your packaging attractive?
What product improvements do you feel should be made?

2.   PRICE
Are competitive products or substitute products of similar design or function available in the market of {country_name}?
Can you offer competitive prices?
Do you offer attractive sales terms?
Can you make a profit at the prices and terms you are considering?
If you cannot make a profit over the short term, do you anticipate making a profit over the long term or making some other
        kind of contribution to {country_name}?

MARKET ENVIRONMENT
1.   MARKET INFRASTRUCTURE
Is available advertising media adequate?
Are there adequate available distribution channels?
Will it be necessary to create new distribution and advertising channels?
Is good customer service important to your success?
If it is very important, does the present retailing system support these services?

2.   COMPETITION WITHIN THE MARKET
Is the market highly competitive?
Are there significant market barriers to entry by new competitors such as your company?
Are there many substitute products available?
Are there adequate supplies and suppliers for any components or parts you may need
        from producers within {country_name}?

ECONOMIC FACTORS
What country are you considering to have a partnership with?

1.   ECONOMICS
After examining political risks, financial stability and incentives, government regulation, interest rates and level of criminal
        activity, do you consider the investment environment favorable in {country_name}?
After considering competitive prices, do you estimate you can price your product at a level that is profitable in {country_name}?
Are there tariffs, duties, and taxes in {country_name}?
Is it possible to freely purchase foreign currency in {country_name}?

2.   COUNTRY ECONOMY
Labor costs in {country_name} are high, medium, low?
Is the economy in {country_name} expanding?
Are there opportunities for short term profits in {country_name}?
Is the market size in {country_name} adequate for the products now offered, considering the competition and level of income?
Is adequate skilled labor available in {country_name}?
Can you get inexpensive raw materials in {country_name}?
The fluctuation of {country_name} currency exchange rate is high, medium, low?
The inflation in {country_name} is high, medium, low?

SOCIAL-CULTURAL FACTORS
Will people from your business organization be willing to locate in {country_name} where you will be doing business?
Is language an issue when doing business with {country_name}?
Are there differences in religious beliefs? Are they an issue when doing business with {country_name}?
Are there differences in attitudes towards work? Are they an issue when doing business with {country_name}?
Do you anticipate major resistance to foreign businesses or to change and newness when doing business in {country_name}?
Do you expect to counter major differences in ways of doing business, such as different distribution and banking payments
        systems, to be an issue when doing business in {country_name}?
Do you expect differences in political systems to be an issue when doing business in {country_name}?
Do you expect different attitudes towards gift giving and bribery to be an issue when doing business in {country_name}?
Do you expect different attitudes towards other social-cultural issues to create difficulties when doing business
        in {country_name}?

CONCLUSION: THE IMPACT OF THE SYSTEM

A comparison of Figures 1 and 7 highlight the development process involved in this project. The basic framework of the system remained the same in both the older Russian version and the newer cross-national version, so that the new system was in fact cross-national. In addition, it was used in both countries' educational systems at major institutions in Russia and the United States.

A third major difference was that in the newer version the underlying expert system's qualitative management decision situation module replaced the quantitative operations research (production-operations management) software (AB.POM, STORM) used by the old system. The impact of this is twofold: first, it introduced and integrated newer artificial intelligence technology with traditional operations software; second, it introduced situationally oriented management thinking, an entrepreneurial orientation critical to success in rapidly changing world markets.

The fifth major difference was the addition of the free competitive "Market Environment" segment in the new system. This "Western" segment was balanced with an old "controlled" market thinking segment, which involved broader economic studies, such as those done in the past (country "Economic Factors" in Figure 4) This was done to help introduce a balanced analytical perspective.

This particular system is designed for undergraduate students, as such it provides only a brief introduction to

---

Figure 5: System Recommendation Panel of Newly Developed Integrated CAI System

Western Corporations' Strategic Partnership Service with {country_name}
Service Assistant recommendations:

FACTORS:
   Company Factors - {inter_knowl}.
   Economic Factors - {macro_econ}.
   {country_name} Economy Factors - {country_econ}.
   Market Infrastructure - {market_infrastructure}.
   Competition within Market - {competition_within_market}.

   Recommended Method - to use {method}

WARNINGS:
   Market Environment is {market_environment}.
   Level of Risk is {risk_level}.

Figure 6: Examples of Country Specific "Correct" Factor Values in the CAI System

Factor Code		Russia	China
COUNTRY	=	Russia	China
N1	=	3	3
N2	=	8	8
N3	=	7	7
LABOR_C	=	medium	low
ECONOMY_G	=	no	yes
SHORT_R	=	yes	yes
MARKET_S	=	yes	yes
SKILLD_L	=	yes	no
MATERIAL_C	=	no	yes
INVEST_E	=	no	yes
SELL_P	=	yes	no
TARIFFS_C	=	yes	no
CURRENCY_C	=	yes	yes
EXCHANGE_R	=	medium	medium
INFLATION_	=	high	medium
LANGUAGE_C	=	no	yes
LEGAL_S	=	yes	yes
RELIGIOUS_	=	no	no
ATTITUDE_W	=	no	no
ATTITUDE_C	=	no	yes
ATTITUDE_L	=	no	yes
POLITICAL_	=	no	no
GIFT_A	=	no	yes
METHOD_D	=	Russian_agency_or_trading_company	your_joint_venture_with_Chinese_firm
METHOD_N	=	Russian_purchasing_agents	Chinese_purchasing_agents_in_the_West
WAYS_B	=	yes	yes

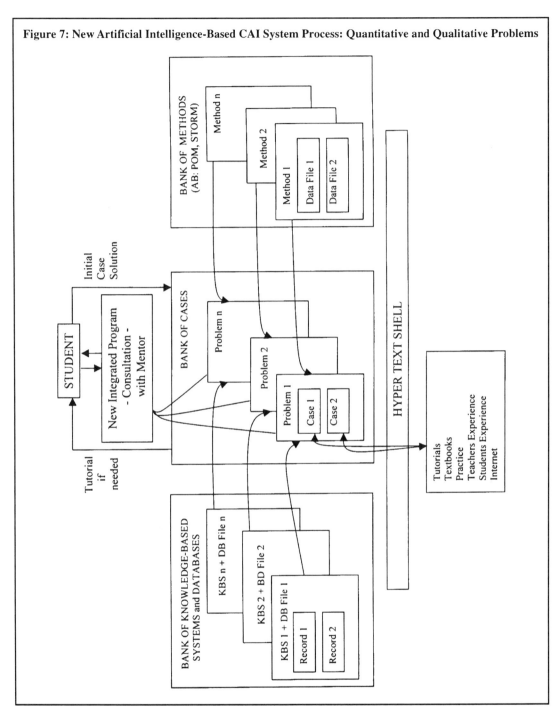

Figure 7: New Artificial Intelligence-Based CAI System Process: Quantitative and Qualitative Problems

the basic approach involved and a basis for introducing the subject of competitive market planning. The system is simple in concept and execution for these reasons.

This new system provides a learning perspective from a management decision making (rather than technical or technique learning) viewpoint; at the same time, it directs the discussion into competitive free market economy. Introducing the subject of free market versus controlled economy planning is in the minds of Russian business educators a major step in redirecting the educational system there to meet the growing emerging needs of Russian businesses.

A last distinction of this system is that results can be measured, so outputs can be measured as well as the results used to improve the learning experience along the way. Hopefully, this will continue as the system is used in both countries during the coming years, and results are exchanged between countries as the system is refined and further developed.

Publications of the Authors

Afanasiev, M.Y. (1988). Foundation of industry planning optimization. Moscow: Naudia Publishing Company.

Afanasiev, M.Y. (1992). Methods of estimation of production efficiency. *Atlantic Economic Journal, 20*(1).

Afanasiev, M.Y. (1993). Computer assisted instruction for economics. Moscow University Publishing House.

Afanasiev, M.Y. (1993). Computer technologies for economic education: Electronic aids for teaching and their application. Doctoral dissertation (Moscow State University 1993).

Dologite, D.G. (1992). Developing knowledge-based systems using VP-Expert. New York, NY: Prentice Hall/Macmillan Publishing Company.

Mockler, R.J. (1989a). Knowledge-based systems for management decisions. Englewood Cliffs, NJ: Prentice Hall.

Mockler, R.J. (1989b). Knowledge-based systems for strategic planning. Englewood Cliffs, NJ: Prentice Hall.

Mockler, R.J. (1992a). Computer software to support strategic management decision-making: A comprehensive review of available existing conventional and knowledge-based applications. New York, NY: Prentice Hall/Macmillan Publishing Company.

Mockler, R.J. (1992b). Developing knowledge-based systems using and expert system shell: A guidebook for general business managers and computer information system technicians (includes 19 sample prototype systems and a development shell). New York, NY: Prentice Hall/Macmillan Publishing Company.

Mockler, R.J. , & Dologite, D.G. (1992). Expert systems: An introduction to knowledge-based systems. New York, NY: Prentice Hall/Macmillan Publishing Company.

Mockler R.J., & Dologite, D.G. (1997). Multinational cross-cultural management: A context specific process. Westport, CT: Greenwood Publishing Croup, a division of Elsevier Science Publishing Company.

REFERENCES

Alavi, M. (1994). Computer-mediated collaborative learning: An empirical evaluation. *MIS Quarterly, 18*(2), 159.

Alavi, M., Wheeler, B.C., & Valacich, J.S. (1995). Using IT to reengineer business education: An exploratory investigation of collaborative telelearning. *MIS Quarterly, 19*, 293.

Alavi, M., Yoo, Y., & Vogel, D.R. (1997). Using information technology to add value to management education. *Academy of Management Journal, 40*, 1310.

Applegate, J., (1997, November 16). Moscow a blooming mecca for the entrepreneurial spirit. *Denver Post*, p. K 14.

Bailo, E.R., & Sivin-Kachla, J. (1995). Effectiveness of technology in schools. 1990-1994. Washington, DC: Software Publishers Association.

Bardach, K.C. (1997). Patterns and trends in executive education. *Selections, 14*(1), 18.

Bellm, M. (1997). New media provide new ways to teach. *Control Engineering, 44*(7), 32.

Bronner, E. (1998, March 2). Freedom in math class may outweigh tests. *New York Times*, p. 1.

Burston, J. (1993). Exploiting available technology. *CALICO Journal, 11*(1), 47.

Carrier, C., Post, T.R., & Heck, W. (1985). Using microcomputers with fourth-grade students to reinforce arithmetic skills. *Journal for Research in Mathematics Education, 16*, 45.

Cavin, C., Cavin, E.D., & Lagowski, J.J. (1981). The effect of computer-assisted instruction on the attitudes of college students toward computers and chemistry. *Journal of Research in Science Teaching, 18*, 329.

Clark, R.E. (1991, February). When researchers swim upstream: Reflections on an unpopular argument about learning from media. *Educational Technology*, p. 34.

Clinton decries test scores: He, GOP spar over dismal U.S. math, science result. (1998, March 1). *Detroit News,* p. A5.

Computer-mediated communication in instructional settings. (1994). *Communication Education, 43*, 171.

Daiute, C. (1985). Issues in using computers to socialize the writing process. *Educational Communication and Technology Journal, 3*, 41.

Filipczak, B. (1997). CBT on the rise. Training, 34(12), 71.

Fletscher, J.F., Hawley, D.E., & Piele, P.K. (1990). Costs, effects, and utility of microcomputer assisted instruction in the classroom. *American Educational Research Journal, 27*, 783.

Foley McInerney, M.E. (1995). A comparison of computer-assisted instruction with teacher-managed instructional practices. Dissertation Abstracts International, A 55/07, 1907.

Gandz, J. (1997). The death of teaching: The rebirth of education. *Ivey Business Quarterly, 62*(1),11.

Gordon, R.B. (1994). The effects of computerized instruction on the improvement and transfer of writing skills for low-skilled and below average-skilled sophomore students, considering student gender, ethnicity, and learning style preferences. <u>Dissertation Abstracts International, A 55/01</u>, 23.

Hackbarth, S. (1996). <u>The educational technology handbook: A comprehensive guide: Process and products for learning</u>. Englewood, NJ: Educational Technology Publications, Inc.

Hale, M.E. (1986). Improving research in computer science learning. *Journal of Research in Science Teaching, 23*, 471.

Harris, G. (1994). A study of computer-assisted instruction for reading achievement in college reading improvement courses. <u>Dissertation Abstracts International, A 54/07</u>, 2429.

Henderson, R.W., Landesman, E.M., & Kachuck, I. (1985). Computer-video instruction in mathematics: Field test of an interactive approach. *Journal for Research in Mathematics Education, 16*, 207.

HyperLecturing and linkages. (1994). *American Economist, 38*(2), 58.

Jagtman, M., & Bongaerts, T. (1994). Report_COMOLA: A computer system for the analysis of interlanguage data. *Second Language Report, 10*(1), 49.

Jurenovich, D.M. (1994). Measuring the impact of computer-assisted instruction on the academic performance of high risk students in the developmental classroom. <u>Dissertation Abstracts International, A 55/06</u>, 1475.

Kim, J.H. (1994). Case-based cognitive modeling: A student modeling methodology for an intelligent tutoring system. <u>Dissertation Abstracts International, A 55/01</u>, 75.

Koscinski, S.T. (1995). Comparison of teacher-assisted and computer-assisted instruction using constant time delay to teach multiplication facts to students with mild disabilities. <u>Dissertation Abstracts International, A 55/12</u>, 3810.

Kracjik, S., Simmons, P.E., & Lunetta, V.N. (1986). Improving research on computers in science learning. *Journal of Research in Science Teaching, 23*, 465.

Kulik, A.N. (1997). Trends in the development of political science in Russia. *Russian Social Science Review, 38*(6), 4.

Leidner, D.E., & Jarvenpaa, S.L. (1995). The use of information technology to enhance management school education: A theoretical view. *MIS Quarterly, 19*, 265.

Loupe, D. (1997, October 11). More computer training on tap state wants teachers technology-savvy. *The Atlanta Journal the Atlanta Constitution*, p. C7:1.

Macwilliams, B. (1997). Soros will spend up to $500-million on education and social services in Russia. *The Chronicle of Higher Education, 44*(10), A59.

Maneekul, J. (1996). The effects of computer-assisted instruction on the achievement and attitudes of private postsecondary vocational-technical students in a supplementary English course in Thailand. <u>Dissertation Abstracts International, A 57/04</u>, 1588.

Maul, G.P., & Spotts, D.S. (1993). Developing computer-based instructional courses. *Industrial Management, 35*(6), 9.

Mausner, B., Wolff, E.F., Evans, R.W., DeBoer, M.M., Gulkus, S.P., D'Amore, A., & Hirsch, S. (1983). A program of computer-assisted instruction for a personalized instructional course in statistics. *Teaching of Psychology, 10*, 195.

McLagan, P.A., & Sandborgh, R.E. (1977). Computer aided instruction - what it is - what it will cost you. *Training, 14*(9), 48.

Measelle, R.L., & Egol, M. (1992). New system of education: World-class and customer-focused. *Ohio CPA Journal, 51*(3), 39.

Medvedev, R. (1997). A prophet and his country ... . *Russian Life, 40*(11), 22.

Newby, T. J., Stepich,D.A., Lehman, J.D., & Russell, J.D. (1996). <u>Instructional technology for teaching and learning: Designing instruction, integrating computers, and using media</u>. Englewood Cliffs, NJ: Prentice Hall, Inc.

Orlansky, J., & String, J. (1979). <u>Cost-effectiveness of computer based instruction in military training</u>. Alexandria, VA: Institute for Defense Analysis.

Osin, L., & Lesgold, A. (1996). A proposal for the reengineering of the educational system. *Review of Educational Research, 66*, 621.

Phalavonk, U. (1994). Achievement and motivational effects of computer-assisted instruction for university mathematics in Thailand. <u>Dissertation Abstracts International, A 55/02</u>, 236.

Schlechter, T.M. (1990). The relative instructional efficiency of small group computer-based training. *Journal of Educational Computing Research, 6*, 329.

Schulz, R. (1993). What one has to know about methodology in computing. *CALICO Journal, 10*(4), 39.

Shiah, R.-L. (1995). The effects of computer-assisted instruction on the mathematical problem-solving of students with learning disabilities. <u>Dissertation Abstracts International, A 55/08</u>, 2347.

Skinner, M.E. (1990). The effects of computer-based instruction on the achievement of college students as a function of achievement status and mode of presentation. *Computers in Human Behavior, 6*, 351.

Smart, K.A. (1994). The effect of traditional versus multimedia augmented instruction on exposure time determination. <u>Dissertation Abstracts International, A 54/10</u>, 3722.

Stanton, D.G. (1994). Utilizing HyperCard for tutorial CAI in advanced professional training (Macintosh). Dissertation Abstracts International, A 54/10, 3722.

Steinberg, E.R. (1991). Computer-assisted instruction: A synthesis of theory, practice, and technology. Hillsdale, NJ: Lawrence Erlbaum Associates, Publishers.

Sweeney, M.T., & Oram, I. (1992). Information technology for management education: The benefits and barriers. International Journal of Information Management, 12, 294.

Taylor, R.P. (Ed.). (1980). The computer in the school: Tutor, tool, and tutee. New York: Teachers College Press.

Thompson, A.D., Simonson, M.R., & Hargrave, C.P. (1992). Educational technology: A review of the research. Washington DC: Association for Educational Communications and Technology.

Torres Ortiz, P. (1994). The use of computer-assisted instruction in the teaching of handwriting skills (Spanish-speaking). Dissertation Abstracts International, A 54/10, 3723.

Using computer simulations in management education. (1992). Management Education and Development, 23, 155.

Wahl, S.C. (1995). A computer-assisted instructional computer program in mathematical problem-solving skills for medication administration for beginning baccalaureate nursing students at San Jose State University (California). Dissertation Abstracts International, A 55/09, 2705.

Wolf, D.P. (1985). Flexible tests: Computer editing in the study of writing. New Directions for Child Development, 28, 37.

Wuebker-Battershell, R.B. (1994). A model for evaluation of the cost-effectiveness of integrated learning systems in a public school setting. Dissertation Abstracts International, A 54/07, 2426.

Wulf, W.A. (1995). Warning: Information technology will transform the university. Issues in Science and Technology, 11(4), 46.

Zatschek, O. (1996). WITUT: A knowledge-based computer-aided instruction system for political economy. Dissertation Abstracts International, C 57/03, 722.

Using Knowledge-engineering (Expert Systems) Cognitive Modeling Techniques to Nurture Professional Growth

Dr. Robert J. Mockler
Joseph F. Adams Professor of Management, St. John's University, Jamaica New York, 114 East 90th St (1B),
New York, NY 10128
Tel: 212 876 5856, Fax: 212 996 6967, e-mail: mocklerr@stjohns.edu

Dr. Dorothy G. Dologite
Professor, Computer Information Systems, School of Business, Department of Statistics and Computer
Information Systems, Baruch College, City University of New York, 17 Lexington Avenue,
New York, New York 10010
Tel: 212 802-6232, Fax: 212 996-6967, e-mail: dgdbb@cunyvm.cuny.edu

ABSTRACT

The paper concerns the professional development of entrepreneurs. It describes how cognitive modeling / mapping tools drawn from knowledge engineering (an Artificial Intelligence discipline in which they are used in developing expert systems) can be employed to help entrepreneurs both to make decisions <u>and</u> to grow professionally. The experiences described involve both the decision to become an entrepreneur and the decision involved in selecting a franchise offering. The paper begins with a description of underlying the cognitive modeling concepts and tools adapted and used.

This paper describes an approach to nurturing professional growth through cognitive modeling or mapping techniques. The techniques described here are self-learning tools which individuals can use on their own both to make decisions <u>and</u> to increase their expertise in their chosen business professional area. The focus in this paper is on entrepreneurs and entrepreneurial thinking.

The approach described in this paper starts with stories about experiences in decision making/action — experiences either of the students themselves or others. These are the specific instances referred to in Figure 1.

Each person is then systematically guided through analyzing the experience from two viewpoints (decisions/actions made and factors affecting decision/actions) and then creating a generalized model or situation diagram based on that analysis. This conceptual model is the start of the professional expertise development - the development of their professional knowledge base useful in guiding them in handling other increasingly challeng-

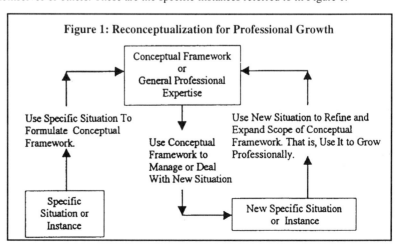

Figure 1: Reconceptualization for Professional Growth

Conceptual Framework or General Professional Expertise

Use Specific Situation To Formulate Conceptual Framework.

Use Conceptual Framework to Manage or Deal With New Situation

Use New Situation to Refine and Expand Scope of Conceptual Framework. That is, Use It to Grow Professionally.

Specific Situation or Instance

New Specific Situation or Instance

ing decision situations. Expert systems (artificial intelligence) cognitive modeling tools are used in doing this.

The project exercise then guides him/her through two more phases of the learning cycle, as shown in Figure 1. First, they make use of their "generalized" professional model to deal with subsequent situations involving related tasks or problems. Second, based on subsequent experiences they refine the initial conceptual model and in this way are initiated into the professional growth cycle. This step mimics prototype refinement and expansion processes.

LEARNING THROUGH MODELING EXPERIENCE

The basic approach described in this paper is a very familiar one. For example, when we interact with other people many of us gradually build mental models (patterns/concepts) of different types of people and how they might be expected to respond to what we say or do. When we meet new people, we use these continually developing mental models to try to anticipate reactions to our words and actions and adjust our words and actions to generate the responses from others we have learned to expect in the past from what we perceive to be similar types of people. We are not always right, and we are constantly refining, retesting and creating new patterns or models in our mind, as we pass through life and its learning experiences. For those of us who are mystery fans, it is a technique that Miss Marple uses in Agatha Christie's mystery novels to determine who might be a logical murderer suspect.

This same pattern building approach is used by business managers and leaders, as they gain experience in their professional fields and develop mental models of the heuristics ("if-then" rules of thumb) for handling more and more complex business situations. This mental modeling professional growth process, which can be learned and systematically pursued, is outlined in Figure 1.

The Origin, Definition and Description of Cognitive Modeling and Its Contributions to Learning

Human behavior, according to social learning theory, is in large measure learned through modeling — mainly behavior modeling [Decker 1986]. Behavior modeling is an effective way of teaching overt, observable behaviors/activities [Goldstein and Sorcher 1974]. However, behavior modeling falls short when applied to teach covert, cognitive/thinking skills [Harmon and Evans 1984]. Bandura [1969] was aware of these limitations and made use of cognitive modeling (or mapping) and its applications to training and learning. Rooted in behavior modeling, cognitive modeling is a type of observational learning which relies on making hidden mental processes visible to observers [Harmon and Evans 1984]. Cognitive modeling techniques can be used to create qualitative models [Card, Moran, and Newell 1983] useful in business decision making situations/tasks [Johnson and Payne 1985; Mockler 1992(B); Payne, Bettman, and Johnson 1988, Purcell 1990]. These studies show that with the help of cognitive modeling techniques, situation factors affecting a decision/task can be specified, the heuristics or reasoning steps involved be traced, and outcomes be determined.

There are two levels of professional training and development of interest to this study. One is the acquisition of knowledge and skills required performing a certain job or position, such as mechanical engineering or accounting. The second level deals with the acquisition of — that is learning and developing — cognitive (thinking) skills. These conceptual skills are needed to structure and apply related knowledge and previous job experiences to new business/management situations within an area of professional interest, and therefore help the learner (employee or manager) to grow professionally in their job.

This paper focuses on this second level of professional training and development for business management, a discipline involving often changing and new competitive marketing situations. It extends prior research work by integrating Artificial Intelligence (Expert Systems) techniques into the cognitive learning process of graduate (MBA) business students and participants of executive training programs. The cognitive modeling techniques discussed in this paper enable the learner to become aware of, articulate, and sharpen his/her own thinking (cognitive) processes. This is known as metacognition and is discussed in various studies [e.g. Chipman, Segal, and Glaser 1985 (A, B); McGilly 1994; Mulcahy, Shirt, and Andrews 1991; Phye and Andre 1986; Richardson, Eyseneck, and Piper 1987]. In general, these studies emphasize the importance of metacognition — that is learning how to learn — in personal and professional cognitive training and development. Acquiring the cognitive skills to learn how to learn, elevates the student/employee/ manager to a stage of the learning process at which s/he is able to control and monitor his/her own cognitive, and therefore, professional development. The cognitive modeling techniques described in this paper are invaluable tools to nurture a students/employees/ managers professional growth, by engaging him/her in a continuous cycle of constant learning on the job.

Cognitive modeling or mapping is used to teach cognitive skills [Schunk and Hanson 1989; Decker 1986]. I refer to these as "skills" because they are teachable and learnable. While some people have greater natural cognitive (thinking) skills than others, developed either through training and conditioning or through inherited traits [Begley 1996], individuals generally have some capacity to learn how to do this kind of learning/modeling better.

There are available many effective, easy to use techniques/tools for learning and teaching cognitive skills, techniques which could be built into any learning program or course. For example, twenty years ago, Edward de

Bono [1976] provided simple exercises and tools for learning and teaching cognitive skills, such as CoRT, a teaching thinking tool. CoRT is one of many specific tools de Bono discusses for helping people create generalized models of thinking processes (abstraction and inferential reasoning); the dependency diagrams and their underlying reasoning (that is, heuristics or rules of thumb) used in this paper are another cognitive mapping tool for helping people give useful form to concepts involving how to handle professional management decision situations.

Since then many books and studies have been written about how to teach and learn thinking skills. For example, Richardson, Eyseneck and Piper [1987], give a series of papers presented at a Society for Research in Higher Education / British Psychological Society (Cognitive Psychology Section) conference in 1985. The papers discuss the integration of cognitive psychology into higher education by merging the concepts and theories of human cognitive psychology with the evidence and practical implications of research on student learning. Gerard Nierenberg [1982] provided similar guidance.

The papers describe different ways to develop cognitive models and use them in teaching.

These include models or maps of reasoning steps involved in making decisions which are useful in helping learn how to reason more effectively. As in the following sections of this paper, ways are discussed first of how to model decision heuristics based on observing real life experiences, and second of how an individual can use these heuristic models both to make decisions and to gain greater expertise in decision making. In essence, the process moves from a descriptive cognitive mapping (an expert's experiences) to a prescriptive one (how a group of experts might do it more effectively).

Other relevant studies include Boud, Keogh and Walker [1985], Bourne, et al. [1986], Phye and Andre [1986], and Trehub [1991]. Additional studies in the related areas of cognition and artificial intelligence discuss the structure of human cognitive processes – how the human brain works — and their usage in and integration into knowledge engineering/expert systems technologies [e.g., Andriole and Ademan 1995; Lloyd 1989; Mockler 1992(A&B); Rothfeder 1985; Shepherd and Cooper 1982; Turner 1994].

Cognitive skills are needed, for example, in knowledge engineering, the artificial intelligence discipline guiding the mapping of the thinking/decision processes an expert goes through when making business decisions [Mockler 1992(B)]. The dependency diagrams (or maps) developed through this approach, which involves systematically restructuring an expert's thinking processes that were mapped, are then used to develop expert computer systems replicating the expert's thinking processes. For example, franchise selection situations are described below in which an expert consultant's decision processes were analyzed and mapped, and a decision model created. Such a model is given in Figures 2, 3(A-D), 5(A, B) below. These models were then used in making subsequent decisions and refined based on these subsequent decisions. Such a process enables an individual to increase his/her professional expertise by learning systematically from experience. Much of the work described in this paper draws upon knowledge engineering technologies.

Why Are Cognitive Skills Important

Regretfully, the thinking or reasoning skills that enable developing cognitive models and related thinking skills have diminished considerably over the years among graduates of United States schools. If not corrected, this will negatively affect the American society and the competitive advantage of the U.S. economy negatively. These shortcomings are documented in many studies [e.g. Denning and Metcalfe 1997; Drucker 1992; Fisher 1955; Flesch 1955, 1981; Maeroff 1981]. Drucker [1992], for example, highlights that "... for the first time in human history it really matters whether or not people learn." He emphasizes the need for the members of society — individuals as well as organizations — to learn how to learn, and that the responsibility of teaching the cognitive skills needed to achieve this will be shared by schools and colleges and by employers. Denning [1997] also stresses the importance of an individual's ability to adapt and learn. This means having the cognitive skills to apply acquired knowledge to new business situations, being able to learn from each new job experience, and being able to practice entrepreneurial skills — in the complex and uncertain changing business environment, as well as in society as a whole. Knowing how to learn through cognitive modeling or mapping, the subject of this paper, is one effective way not only to make that kind of adaptation easier but also to foster an individual's professional development.

In order to fill these many growing social needs of a changing society, educational institutions will have to change and business will have to pay more attention to employee professional development. One solution has been the development of corporate universities at individual companies [Authers 1998]. The techniques described in this paper are another step in helping fill this growing need for accelerated and more effective individual professional development.

The Importance of Growing Professionally in Business:

The growing number in business jobs such as chief learning officer, chief knowledge officer, manager of performance, or director of intellectual assets substantiates the growing importance to manage a firm's *intellectual capital,* that is " ... the knowledge, experience and ideas of people at every level of the firm" [Jay Stuller, 1998]. These executives of self-styled learning organizations, such as Motorola, encourage learning, professional growth, and self-actualization of its employees, because constant learning is advantageous for both the employees and the firms since it creates competitive advantage. Moreover, learning in business or on the job replaces loyalty as the main pillar of company cultures [Young 1995(A)]. Based on its research on employment strategies, the Institute of Management (IM) has consistently encouraged every worker/manager at every level to learn continuously throughout their lifetime. The IM emphasizes that the key to personal success is continuing professional development [Young 1995(B)]. Other studies and sources, such as Fisher 1997; Nelton 1995; Prestwood 1997; Sherman 1997; Ulrich 1998, confirm these facts and trends.

Professional growth depends on an individual's ability to systematically learn from experience. This paper focuses on the learning involved in acquiring cognitive (thinking) skills to create generalized concepts/models of decision making in areas related to an individual's profession. The construction of these cognitive models can be learned using cognitive modeling or mapping techniques drawn from Expert Systems (Artificial Intelligence) technologies, as shown in the following discussions. The approach has proven effective in a variety of learning situations. The following sections describe how cognitive mapping tools drawn from knowledge engineering (an Artificial Intelligence discipline in which they are used in developing expert systems) can be employed to help entrepreneurs both to make decisions <u>and</u> to grow professionally. The experiences described involve both the decision to become an entrepreneur and the decision involved in selecting a franchise offering.

EXPERIENCED-BASED LEARNING

Most everyone has read a story. Most of us are also able to write summaries of experiences we have had — that is, write or tell our own stories. If we think about the experience and it involved a decision or action on our part, we can be prompted to include in our story the reasons why we made the decision or took the action and why it did or did not work. We might also be able to sketch out the possible alternative decisions or solutions and the relationships among factors and our judgements about these factors that led to our decision or action. These are called the reasoning processes or heuristics — that is, rules of thumb at work.

The parts that need to be included in the story to make this a useful exercise are: the possible decisions or actions; the general situation factors affecting the decision and ways needed information was obtained; the specific situation factors considered in making the decision or taking the action; and the reasoning process (and judgements) which led from the factors to the decisions/actions.

Once such a story or stories are in hand — our own or someone else's - then we have a basis for teaching or learning key conceptual skills which an individual needs in order to learn from experience and grow professionally. The process involved is shown in Figure 1. The following discussions describe some learning experiences and techniques for using them to grow professionally. They present an orientation useful in any application learning program. For discussion purposes, however, the examples are limited to business management situations.

A SIMPLE INITIAL EXAMPLE OF THE LEARNING PROCESS

As a start describe some simple decision made recently. For example, the situation may involve a decision often facing business students and managers — whether to go into business for themselves or to work (or continue working) for someone else.

Initially, through reading, observation and/or experience one workshop participant, Betty Mercer, began to describe some of the requirements of going into business for herself: the financial investment, long hours and risk taking, skills appropriate to the business, ability to handle people (workers/customers), stamina requirements, and the like. After sketching out a profile of the perceived requirements, she began to explore her own capabilities to meet these requirements. These included temperament, interests, education and training, financial assets available, personal goals, any physical limitations, family obligations, and the like. The possible initial recommendation or decision, based on an analysis of these factors, would initially be "likely to succeed or not likely to succeed as an entrepreneur", depending how high or low she rated in each requirements factor area. Her initial outline of such a decision is given in Figure 2.

One is not expected to instantly arrive at a perfect outline or model. There may be a series of diagrams, which are hopefully "successively more accurate approximations of reality". One rarely fully replicates reality, especially in the management decision making/action area; one only works for a pretty good working replication or model. The emerging refinement process through which the model is refined might involve such tasks as reading some key books on the subject [for example, Cook 1987; Stevenson 1985; Timmons 1985], talking with local merchants and store owners, and reading cases and newspaper and magazine articles.

Clearly, more is involved in the decision than just a yes/no answer. One might want to identify one's own weak areas, such as work habits, so they can improve their chances of success by correcting bad habits, as is indicated under the recommendations box in Figure 2. One would also like to know what kinds of business they are best suited for. One would also have to determine how the comparisons are made between requirements and personal qualifications, and then expand the outline model as is done for the "interests" factor segment in Figure 2 and later in this paper. These decisions require more complex decision processes, which can be modeled at later stages. For the moment, only a basic model is being developed.

The same process could be gone through when examining the decision involved in determining which major subject to take at school or what kind of job to seek: First define the available options, the general job or profession requirements, and then the personal qualifications of the individual to meet those requirements. The pattern is then outlined as in Figure 2 or as in the other decision/action situations modeled in the figures, which follow. Once the pattern or model is outlined, then it is reused to evaluate each job opportunity or each of the available professional majors at school in relation to the individual's qualifications.

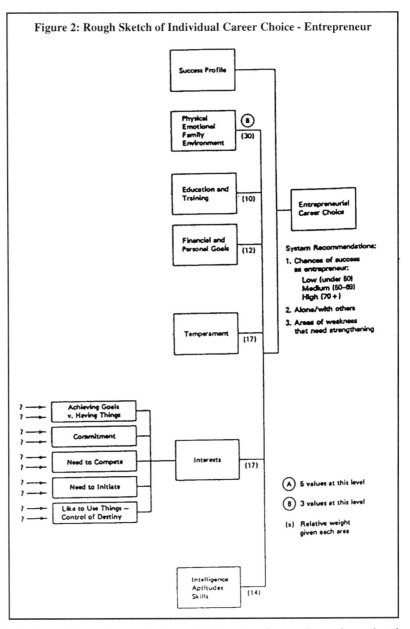

Figure 2: Rough Sketch of Individual Career Choice - Entrepreneur

At the same time one keeps refining the model or outline and in this way is able to do a faster and more thorough and systematic job each time, and at the same time revise the model.

In this sense, this initial example is an exercise in the professional growth process outlined in Figure 1.

AN EXTENSION OF THE FIRST EXAMPLE INTO A RELATED AREA

One seminar workshop participant discussed an experience he had recently when he was considering going into business for himself through buying a fast-food franchise. After he gathered preliminary information about franchising in general and about one offering in particular, he visited a consultant in the field for advice. He described his experiences this way.

Robert London, age 31, is a single male interested in a retail fast-food franchise. He has worked in investment banking for the last six years and prior to that worked in a branch of a suburban bank. He holds a bachelor and master's degree in business and lives in a rented apartment in a middle class suburban area near a major city. Rob engaged a consultant (expert) in the field to help him in deciding whether or not to purchase a Burger King franchise near his home.

The consultant first collected background information. In terms of general business prospects, the product was examined for growth potential and staying power. Since fast food products are common products consumed by many segments of the general population, ample demographic and market studies were available that showed that the overall growth prospects were modestly favorable.

However, an analysis of the local area revealed several weak points. The consultant found that the location Rob was looking at was already saturated with competition, including a McDonald's, a Wendy's and a Roy Rogers, all within a mile radius of each other. In addition, the franchise Rob was interested in would be located near an exit ramp to a major highway, but would be the last eating place that travelers would reach coming off of the highway exit.

Although the demographic profile of the local area matched the franchise's target market, the market area was not expected to grow significantly in the future. The consultant talked with small business owners in the area and found that general indicators called for only modest overall growth. Although the other franchises in the area seemed busy, the consultant's research indicated that competitors' sales had been fairly flat over the prior three years.

The consultant interviewed Rob to see if he was cut out to be an entrepreneur. Based on experiences Rob described from his past, he seemed capable of taking charge, organizing and handling multiple jobs, and dealing effectively with people. He had demonstrated determination and self-reliance to a high degree. Rob generally seemed competent enough to run his own business but lacked a willingness to take big risks. He had barely adequate financial resources to handle the franchise investment. These factors suggested that Rob examine franchise offerings.

Next the consultant examined the franchise offering under consideration. Burger King provides substantial initial assistance at no additional cost in the areas of operations, equipment maintenance, and training. However, they have a relatively high annual franchise payment, provide no assistance with financing, and subject franchisees to a wide variety of controls. Burger King, in business since 1954, has maintained excellent relations with its franchisees and business contacts. The company is predicted to increase its 4,000 units substantially over the next decade. Although a very reputable franchisor, Burger King's contract gives no guarantees of exclusivity of territory and contains some supplier tie-in purchasing agreements.

The consultant summarized her evaluation as follows:

- Business prospects. The general prospects were favorable. However, because of a stagnating local market and poor location, the local business prospects were considered unfavorable. The business prospects were, therefore, rated unfavorable overall.
- Individual resources and capabilities. Because Rob had favorable personal, financial, and business skills and resources, the overall rating was favorable in this key factor area.
- Franchisor offering. Franchisor support was favorable. However, due to the lack of financial assistance and only fair fee schedule, the reasonableness of the deal was rated average. Although Burger King's reputation is excellent, lack of exclusivity of territory and tie-in agreements yielded an average rating for the contract. The overall rating for the franchise offering was average.

Based on this analysis and evaluation, the consultant's overall rating of the venture was only fair. Knowing that the local area was not well suited to the particular franchise because of heavy competition, and that Rob would probably need some assistance with financing, the expert recommended looking for a more generously financed offering, with a similar product but in a better location.

Based on this experience and some reading he had done, Rob began to formulate his own version of the generalized approach to the franchising decision the consultant had used.

The typical recommendations made when evaluating franchise offerings seemed to include:

- Superior — actively pursue the offering.
- Very good — pursue the offering, but commit to it only after further analyses and evaluations are completed of factors such as local business prospects, and especially the competition.
- Fair — if the local business prospects are weak, examine a similar proposal in another location; if the franchise offering is a weak factor, look for another offering with a similar product and location, but through a different franchisor.
- Poor— Abandon the proposal.

The critical factors considered when evaluating franchise offerings appeared to include:

- The business prospects, both general and local
- Individual resources and capabilities, such as personality, financial position and work experience and skills.
- The franchisor contract, covering franchisor support, the reasonableness of the deal, and the franchisor character.

Based on this analysis, Rob prepared the outline shown in Figure 3A.

In general, the way the consultant reasoned from these factors (his "if-then" heuristics or rules of thumb) in reaching a conclusion seemed to be:

- A franchise offering would be considered superior if both the business prospects and franchise contract were favorable and the individual's resources were favorable or average.

- A franchise offering would be considered very good if both the business prospects and the individual's resources were favorable and the franchise contract was only average. It would also be considered good if the business prospects were average and both the franchise contract and the individual's resources were favorable.
- A franchise offering would be considered fair if both the business prospects and the individual's resources were average and the franchise contract was average or favorable.
- A franchise offering would be considered poor if any of the critical factors were considered unfavorable.

These conclusions of course could be modified in some instances through negotiation or through additional information.

In addition, Rob listed the questions the consultant asked answered in investigating the factor areas. The following is a sampling of them:

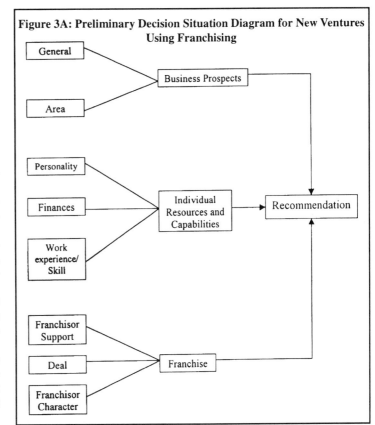

Figure 3A: Preliminary Decision Situation Diagram for New Ventures Using Franchising

- For Business Prospects: "After examining demographic characteristics such as age, income, and size of the target market, what is your estimate of the potential for growth in the market in general?"
- For Individual Resources and Capabilities: "What amount of money do you have and how much are you able to borrow?"
- For the Franchise Offering: "What is the failure rate of new franchisees in the past?" and "Has the general evaluation of the franchisor by former and current franchisees been favorable?"

After thinking more about the visit and reading more about franchising in general, Rob expanded the list of questions and drew the more detailed diagrams shown in Figures 3B, 3C, and 3D. One of them (Figure 3C) is a variation on the decision outlined in Figure 2, a variation appropriate to the particular requirements of the franchise situation and to Rob. Although still in fairly rough form, Rob felt that he now had the basis of a systematic approach to how to make these decisions in the future. He felt that he was beginning to develop a kind of professional expertise for making these decisions and concluded that he had wisely used his investment in the consultant's visit to grow professionally since he had increased his ability to make better decisions on his own.

Rob had done this through systematically organizing the scenario of his experience along the lines suggested in Figure 4.

What he did basically is systematically reconceive or reconceptualize his story to enable him to develop a generalized model of the approach that he could use in making these kinds of decisions in the future. His approach covered the specific information he had to gather from the situation (questions to be asked in relevant key factor areas), the possible decisions (recommendations), and the reasoning or heuristics (if-then rules of thumb) that went into making that decision. In other words he appeared to have learned how to learn from his experiences and so grow professionally. He also clearly had learned how to learn from experts he comes in contact with. He admitted later that he approached his job as loan officer at his bank in a similar way and had developed similar routine guidelines for making his decisions more quickly and effectively there.

Rob's experiences showed that it was possible to acquire or enhance a systematic approach to professional development through guidance and practice.

WAYS TO FURTHER PROFESSIONAL GROWTH

As seen from the experiences of Betty Mercer and Rob London, growing professionally as suggested in Figure 1 requires not only systematically creating general rules of thumb (heuristics) for handling different kinds of decision making/action situations. Professional growth also requires practicing using these guidelines, and refining and developing them. This process might involve your own or others' guidelines and experiences.

For example, the guidelines or conceptual framework developed by Betty Mercer and outlined in Figure 2 were subsequently modified and expanded by other entrepreneurs, experts and workshop participants who were considering becoming entrepreneurs. Several such expanded versions are given in Figures 5A and 5B.

The refinements may be made in any aspect of early working models or prototypes at any stage of their development. These refinements might involve more detail about factors and ways to explore them, additional

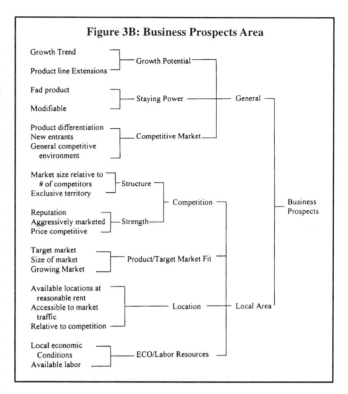

Figure 3B: Business Prospects Area

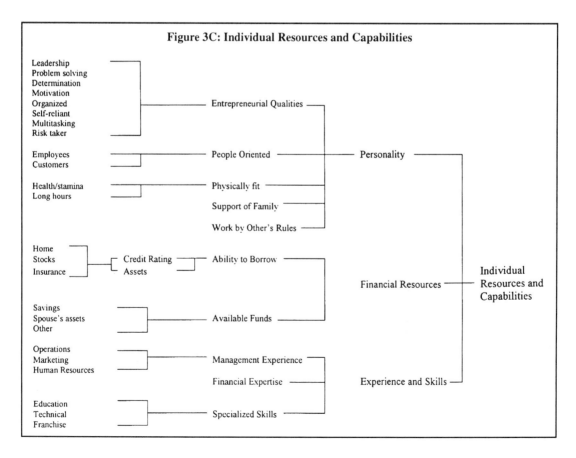

Figure 3C: Individual Resources and Capabilities

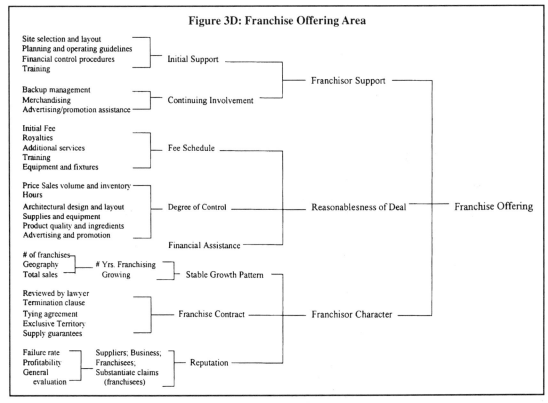

Figure 3D: Franchise Offering Area

options, or more sophisticated or different reasoning processes. For example, the extension in Figure 5B expands one segment, interests, of the model in Figure 5A, which itself is an amplification of the model in Figure 2. The point to remember is that the professional growth process described in Figure 1 is an adaptive, fluid, emerging process. The objective is simply to create a working visualization — or prototype — as a reference point to build on and experiment with in dealing with new situations.

One is not searching for an ideal "only" solution; there can be many good ways to model a decision making/ action situation. It is not a totally definite prescriptive or limiting process; it is a process that enables innovative, creative thinking. It is a process which simply involves searching for a useful and relatively accurate general guideline for decision making/action in the kinds of situations the manager/leader might face in the future in his/her professional work.

For those readers who wish to explore this process further, additional examples are given in other books by the author [1989, 1992(A, B), 1993, and 1997]. These references also include expert systems versions of the models which are on computer disks and which a reader can use and analyze. The basic approach in building all of these models and systems was the story telling approach used in this paper, during which stories are reconceived or

Figure 4: Helpful Steps in Developing Structured Decision Models

- Write a very detailed scenario (story) of how the task or decision under study is carried out in a specific situation, including such specifics as time, place, people involved, and other actual events which would occur on a given day in a real situation.
- Identify the recommendations which can be made in the kind of situation under study (limiting your answer to no more than four or five)
- Specify the three or four critical factors which are considered in making these recommendations and describe how these factors affect which recommendation is made
- List ten or twelve specific questions which need answering in order to obtain information about the critical factors used to make a recommendation
- If you are dealing with a diagnostic situation, reduce it to a technical manual outline and describe alternative ways this manual might be used to answer three or four specific questions or problems
- Reexamine samples of existing KBS and transfer the structured information to an expert systems shell.

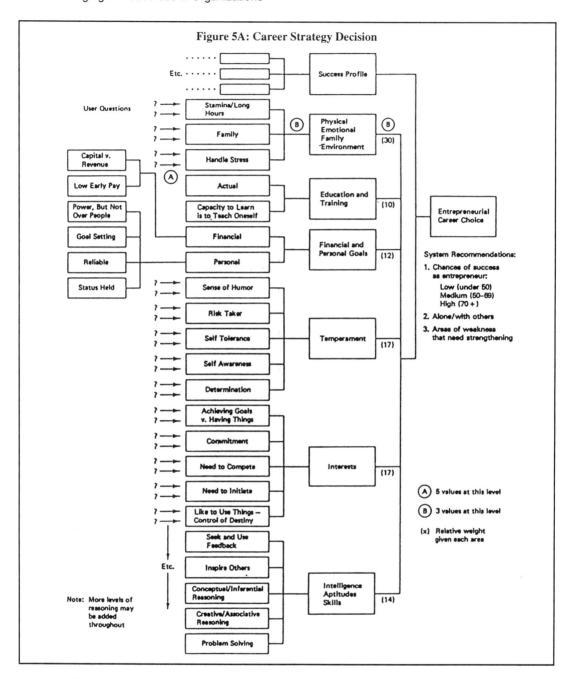

Figure 5A: Career Strategy Decision

reconceptualized along the lines shown in Figure 4.

THE UNDERLYING COGNITIVE SKILL

The underlying thinking (cognitive) skill involved in the professional growth described in this paper is a common entrepreneurial conceptual one, which is outlined in Figure 6. This is an "it all depends" process, that is, a context specific contingency process. It is a process, which has whimsically been referred to as an individual's basic survival process. The situations described in this paper are two kinds of application of this process. For example, the task in each situation was to identify the decision making/action process involved in a management situation of your choosing. The situation chosen was then studied in detail and in stages reconceptualized or reconceived along the lines shown in Figure 4 into a pattern which could be replicated in a decision/action situation diagram. Examples of such reconceptualizations were covered in this paper and illustrated in the accompanying figures.

Figure 5B: Career Strategy Decision: Interests Segment

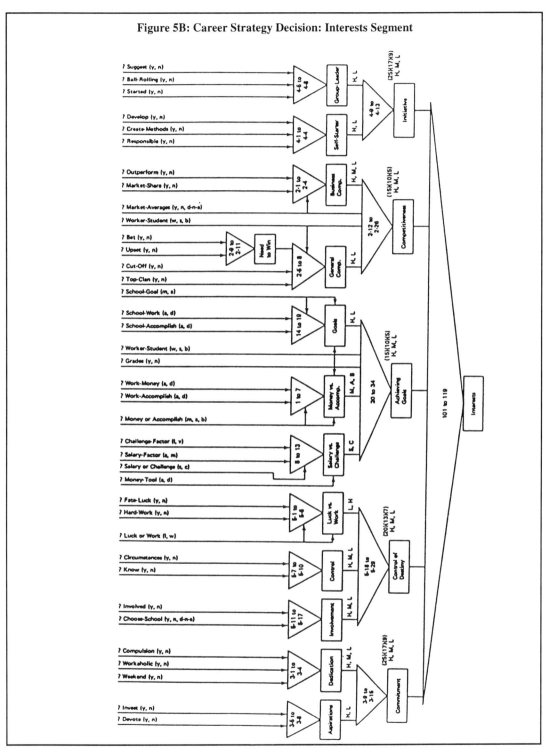

It is similar to the process one goes through when writing a paper or business report. One has a topic or task and a situation or research area. When one creates an outline for the paper or report, one is simply reconceiving or reconceptualizing the situation in a way appropriate for carrying out the task, as shown in the middle box in Figure 6.

The process outlined in the 3-box diagram in Figure 6 is only one of a wide range of cognitive processes and skills useful in management. It is useful in many areas of life —especially those involving new situations we encoun-

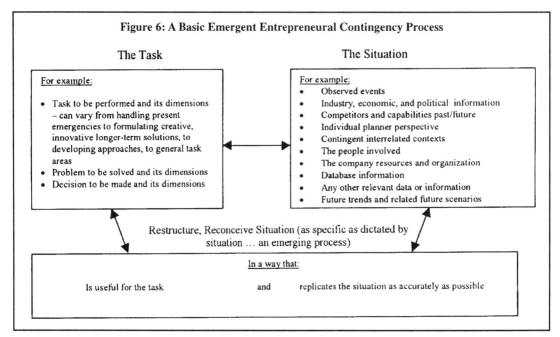

Figure 6: A Basic Emergent Entrepreneural Contingency Process

The Task

The Situation

For example:
- Task to be performed and its dimensions – can vary from handling present emergencies to formulating creative, innovative longer-term solutions, to developing approaches, to general task areas
- Problem to be solved and its dimensions
- Decision to be made and its dimensions

For example:
- Observed events
- Industry, economic, and political information
- Competitors and capabilities past/future
- Individual planner perspective
- Contingent interrelated contexts
- The people involved
- The company resources and organization
- Database information
- Any other relevant data or information
- Future trends and related future scenarios

Restructure, Reconceive Situation (as specific as dictated by situation … an emerging process)

In a way that:

Is useful for the task   and   replicates the situation as accurately as possible

ter, which is why it is considered a basic entrepreneurial process or skill. It has proved useful in both multinational and domestic business situations [Mockler 1993, 1997]. This process and the related professional growth process described in this paper are well grounded in both cognitive psychology and artificial intelligence disciplines, as noted at the beginning of this paper.

Fortunately, as seen from the discussions and exercises in this paper, it is a skill, which can be learned by most people with a little guidance, concentration and, of course, work. While it is not necessarily an easy-to-learn skill, it possible for the average person with persistence and determination to learn it.

Regretfully, it is also a cognitive skill which is especially lacking in graduates of United States schools. This paper and the techniques it describes are small steps designed to help overcome this deficiency.

SUMMARY CONCLUSION

The professional growth project described in this paper can be broken into four specific steps. First, one selects an appropriate topic and writes a short description of the management situation they have chosen for the project, using guidelines such as those given in this paper. Second, one prepares the story — a complete very detailed description of the situation, of the reasoning processes leading to decisions, and of the outcomes. This often requires some reconceptualization or restructuring of the description. One then highlights the decisions/actions involved and the reasons leading to them. Reasons for success or failure are also underlined. Third, one constructs a generalized model for handling the type of situation under study. This model includes questions asked to obtain needed information about the factors affecting decisions/actions. Fourth, this generalized model is then tested and refined through analyzing an additional situation and by studying the subject area in general. The major focus is on learning decision making/action in a specific area of interest — from a management decision/action, not technology, viewpoint.

In essence this teaching approach provides the student with guidance on how to grow professionally through using experiences to create their own professional heuristic guidelines. Such an exercise benefits them in many ways:

- they acquire increased professional knowledge in their area of interest, such as accounting, finance, marketing, and operations.
- they acquire this knowledge in a management application context, that is they learn to put their knowledge of a subject area to work in actual business situations.
- they go beyond case studies and learn how to learn from cases, as well as from their own experiences, and how to systematically increase their professional competency by learning how to generalize the knowledge learned in a systematic way.
- they learn to use that generalized knowledge to deal with new situations
- they acquire the capability to continue to grow professionally in a well focused and time efficient way.
  Education comes from a Latin word meaning to "draw out". The learning and teaching approach described in

this paper is based on that concept, since it works with ("draws out") one's experiences and one's ability to generalize (or conceptualize) those experiences. It is what is known as active learning, a way research tells us is the best (and perhaps major) way to learn, since it helps one learn how to learn.

REFERENCES

Andriole, Stephen, and Leonard Ademan 1995. Cognitive Systems Engineering for User-Computer Interface Design, Prototyping and Evaluation, Hillsdale, NJ: Lawrence Erlbaum Associates.

Authers, John 1998. "Motorola Leads the Way in the Corporate University Sector," *Financial Times*, June 18, p.7.

Bandura, A. 1969. Principles of behavior modification, New York: Hot, Rinehart and Winston, Inc.

Begley, Sharon 1996. "Your Child's Brain," *Newsweek*, February 19, pp. 55-62.

Boud, David, Rosemary Keogh, and David Walker (Eds.) 1985. Reflection: Turning Experience into Learning, New York: Nichols Publishing Co.

Bourne, Lyle E., Roger L. Dominowski, Elizabeth F. Loftus, and Alice R. Healy 1986. Cognitive Processes, 2nd edition, Englewood Cliffs, NJ: Prentice-Hall.

Card, S. K., T. P. Moran, and A. L. Newell 1983. The Psychology of Human-Computer Interaction, Hillsdale, NJ: Lawrence Erlbaum.

Chipman, Susan F., Judith W. Segal, and Robert Glaser 1985(A). Thinking and Learning Skills, Volume 1: Relating Instruction to Research, Hillsdale, NJ: Lawrence Erlbaum Associates, Publishers.

Chipman, Susan F., Judith W. Segal, and Robert Glaser 1985(A). Thinking and Learning Skills, Volume 2: Research and Open Questions, Hillsdale, NJ: Lawrence Erlbaum Associates, Publishers.

Cook, James R. 1987. The Start Up Entrepreneur: How You Can Succeed in Building Your Own Company Into a Major Enterprise Starting from Scratch, New York: Harper & Row.

de Bono, Edward 1976. Teaching Thinking, New York: Penguin Books.

Decker, Phillip J. 1986. "Social Learning Theory and Leadership," *The Journal of Management Development*," Vol. 5(3), pp. 46-58.

Denning, Peter J. and Robert M. Metcalfe 1997. Beyond Calculation: The Next Fifty Years of Computing, New York: Springer-Verlag.

Drucker, Peter 1992. Managing for the Future, New York: Truman Talley Books/Dutton.

Fisher, Edward 1955. "Reading Analysis is Called Lacking," *The New York Times*, April 29, pp. A1ff.

Fisher, Anne 1997. "Six Ways to Supercharge Your Career," *Fortune*, January 13, pp. 46-48.

Flesch, Rudolph 1955. Why Johnny Can't Read — and What You Can Do About It, New York: Harper & Row.

Flesch, Rudolph 1981. Why Johnny Still Can't Read, New York: Harper & Row.

Goldstein, A. P. and M. Sorcher 1974. Changing Supervisor Behavior, New York: Pergamon Press, Inc.

Harmon, Paul and Kay Evans 1984. "When to Use Cognitive Modeling," *Training and Development Journal*," March, pp. 67-68.

Johnson, A. and J. W. Payne 1985. "Effort and Accuracy in Choice," *Management Science*, Vol. 31, pp. 395-414.

Lloyd, Dan 1989. Simple Minds, Cambridge, MA: The MIT Press.

Maeroff, Gene I. 1955. "Reading Data Indicate Decline in Reasoning Ability," *The New York Times*, April 29, pp. A1ff.

McGilly, Kate (Ed.) 1994. Classroom Lessons: Integrating Cognitive Theory and Classroom Practice, Cambridge, MA: MIT Press.

Mockler, Robert J. 1989. Knowledge-Based (Expert) Systems for Management Decisions, Englewood Cliffs, NJ: Prentice-Hall.

Mockler, Robert J. 1992(A). Contingency Approaches to Strategic Management: Integrating Basic and Applied Research, Research Monograph, New York: Strategic Management Research Group.

Mockler, Robert J., and Dorothy G. Dologite 1992(B). Expert Systems: An Introduction to Knowledge-Based Systems, New York: Prentice-Hall/Macmillan Publishing.

Mockler, Robert J. 1993. Strategic Management: An Integrative Context-Specific Process, Harrisburg, PA: Idea Group Publishing.

Mockler, Robert J. 1997. Multinational Cross-Cultural Management: An Integrative Context Specific Process, Westport, CT: Greenwood Press.

Mulcahy, Robert F., Robert H. Short, and Jac Andrews (Eds.) 1991. Enhancing Learning and Thinking, New York: Praeger.

Nelton, Sharon 1995. "How to Broaden Your Skills," *Nation's Business*, December, pp. 49.

Nierenberg, Gerard I. 1982. The Art of Creativity Thinking, New York: Simon & Schuster.

Payne, J. W., J. R. Bettman, and E. J. Johnson 1988. "Adaptive Strategy Selection in Decision Making," *Learning of Experimental Psychology: Learning, Memory and Cognition*, Vol. 14, pp. 534-552.

Phye, Gary D., and Thomas Andre (Eds.) 1986. Cognitive Classroom Learning: Understanding, Thinking, and Problem Solving, Orlando, FL: Academic Press, Inc.

Prestwood, Donna C. L. 1997. "Seven New Principles of Leadership," *The Futurist*, Jan/Feb, p. 68.

Purcell, J. A. 1990. "A Cognitive Modeling Technique for Complex Decision Strategies," *Proceedings of the Human Factors Society 34th Annual Meeting*, pp. 254-258.

Richardson, John T., Michael W. Eyseneck, and David Warren Piper (Eds.) 1987. Student Learning: Research in Education and Cognitive Psychology, Milton Keynes, England: SRHE and Open University Press.

Rothfeder, Jeffrey 1985. Minds Over Matter: A New Look At Artificial Intelligence, New York: Simon & Schuster.

Schunk, Dale H. and Antoinette R. Hanson 1989. "Self-Modeling and Children's Cognitive Skill Learning," June, pp. 155-163.

Shepherd, Roger N., and Lynn A. Cooper 1982. Mental Images and Their Transformations, Cambridge, MA: MIT Press.

Sherman, Marilyn 1997. "Launch Your Career Through Learning," *Career World*, March, pp. 15-17.

Stevenson, Howard H., Michael J. Roberts, and H. Irving Grossbeck 1985. New Business Ventures and the Entrepreneur, 2nd edition, Homewood, IL: Irwin.

Stuller, Jay 1998. "Chief of Corporate Smarts," *Training*, April, pp. 28-37.

Timmons, Jeffrey A 1985. New Venture Creation, 2nd Edition, Homewood, IL: Irwin.

Trehub, Arnold 1991. The Cognitive Brain, Cambridge, MA: MIT Press.

Turner, Scott R. 1994. The Creative Process: A Computer Model of Story Telling and Creativity, Hillside, NJ: Erlbaum.

Ulrich, Dave 1998. "Intellectual Capital = Competence x Commitment," *Sloan Management Review*, winter, pp. 15-26.

Young, Doyle 1995(A). "Constant Learning," *Executive Excellence*, April, p. 19.

Young, Roger 1995(B). "It's Time to Learn to Help Yourself," *Management Today*, November, p. 5.

Policy Implications for Speedy Rural Telecommunications Development

Sufi M. Nazem & Bongsik Shin
University of Nebraska at Omaha, 6001 Dodge St., CBA 310E, Omaha,NE 68182
Phone: 402—554-2816, Fax: 402-554-3747 ,E-mail: Sufi N azem@unomaha.edu

ABSTRACT

The results of empirical analysis examining of rural telecommunications development and needed appropriate policy is reported in this paper. This cross-section study of forty-seven nations around the world finds that the development of rural telecommunications infrastructure lags behind that of urban areas, and the difference is greater among the poorer nations. Rural development appears to follow that of urban communities through a form of technology transfer. The process, however, is slow and pro-active public policy is needed to enable rural communities to participate in the emerging information society.[1]

INTRODUCTION

Communication, undoubtedly, is the key ingredient in developing a democratic society and only a democratic society can be transformed into the much talked about 'information society.' The democratic nature of the information society brings us a step closer to the so called 'global village' where everyone can communicate with everyone else freely anytime and anywhere. Although the notion of 'wired cities' [8] is no longer a new idea it is imperative that we recognize the fact that a large majority of the world's population lives and works in communities which hardly qualify as cities. Residents of these communities too need to fully participate in the information society of the next century. To facilitate such unrestricted communication the nations of the world need to move rapidly toward the creation of a 'universal global telecommunication network.' [16] This is a "must" and is an achievable goal. The questions remain to be asked, however, as to when and in what form could such a network become a reality?

Clearly, the above statement makes a fundamental assumption that the world of tomorrow will provide a communication infrastructure accessible to all the inhabitants of the globe and even beyond regardless of their geographic locations. Tomorrows infrastructure will be developed upon today's foundation and it is thus necessary to examine the existing communications infrastructure and development trends. In this process one issue that has long been debated in the United States and more recently in other countries is the notion of 'universal service.' Although universal service casts a broader net, historically it has focused on rural communities. Rural communities have enjoyed many privileges in the U.S. in comparison to their counterparts around the world, primarily because rural communities historically have played the central role in American life. Politically they provided democratic thoughts and economically they provided labor, food and natural resources that fueled and sustained the industrial revolution. [24] Consequently, rural telecommunication occupies an unique position in the United States today and provides a guiding light for all nations of the world. Any study of rural telecommunications benefits immensely from historical analysis of the development of rural infrastructure and services. The very concept of 'universal access' and 'universal service was originated in the U.S. and the rest of the world has much to learn from these developments.

The need for universal access in communication is now well recognized and rural infrastructure development has become a goal for many countries. The question is how well are we doing? The primary objective of the present research, therefore, is to evaluate the status of rural telecommunications around the world. Because of its long history, the logical starting point should focus on past developments in the U.S. and subsequently examine rural communications in other nations around the world. The focus of this research, however, remains the telecommunications infrastructure in rural communities around the world. In fact, this cross—section study includes countries from all nine telecommunications regions as defined by the International Telecommunications Union. The research examines the disparity in infrastructure development that exists among and within the nations. It further explores the process of rural telecommunications infrastructure development and the effect of public policy on this process.

STATE OF RURAL TELECOMMUNICATIONS

Rural communities have played a significant role in the development of the nation that is known today as the United States. [24] Naturally, in the U.S. the development of an infrastructure in the rural regions was simply expected as an extension of the natural technological progress. Telecommunications policy in the United States has always retained the notion of 'universal service' and rural telecommunications development has always enjoyed broad political support from the nation's lawmakers. The landmark Telecommunications Act of 1934 virtually guaranteed telecommunications access to rural residents. Over the decades, many subsequent policy reviews have reiterated such commitments to rural America. For example, the National Telecommunications and Information Administration (NTIA) reaffirmed this commitment in its policy study 'Telecom 2000'. [29] More recently, the Telecommunications Competition and Deregulation Act of 1996 also assured the preservation and advancement of universal service. [30] Section 254 of the Act is intended to protect universal service. To achieve this goal the Act retains many of the provisions of the 1934 Communications Act and mandates the creation of a Federal—State Joint Board for the purpose of recommending appropriate actions to the Federal Communications Commission (FCC) and the State Public Utilities Commissions (PUC). It further requires that the Joint Board evaluate universal services in the context of a local market changing from 'one characterized by monopoly to one of competition.' It is expected that the Joint Board and the FCC will oversee quality of service, access to advanced telecommunications, availability of information services and the price of telecommunications service, as well as access to information services for health care, education, economic development and other public purposes. In spite of the historical commitment to universal service, rural communities in the United States trail behind their urban counterparts. With rapidly emerging new services the future cost and quality of rural services and their availability remains uncertain. Judging by past experience, this is particularly true for rural areas in some southern states such as Mississippi and Alabama.

While policy in the United States has always recognized the need for telecommunications for rural residents and the Government as well as the industry has made conscious efforts to fulfill this need, much of the world is only just beginning to address the question of rural telecommunications. In. most countries, socio-political power has been concentrated in' the cities. Residents in rural areas hardly voice their needs and policy makers rarely attach priority to rural telecommunications. As a result the level of telecommunication service in the rural communities in most countries is meager at best. However, a recent shift in attitude towards the rural areas has been noticed, at least in some countries. This may partially be due to urban pollution and crime, though the effect so far has been relatively insignificant.

Over the past several years there has been unprecedented growth in telecommunications with innovative new technologies as well as the rapid technological convergence of voice, data, images and video transmission. Revolutionary transformation in the regulatory environment has also led to rapid growth in communication networks and services on a global scale. In spite of all these remarkable achievements and much rhetoric about the global information society, the lingering question remains as to how widely communications technology is accessible to the citizens of the world? Can everyone participate in the information—intensive future civilization? The much—publicized Maitland [18] report on the status of telecommunications access among nations dubbed those communities lacking telecommunications as the 'missing link.' It is still appropriate to ask 'is the missing link still missing?'

This general question is directed towards many countries with poor telecommunications infrastructure. While individual countries were the primary concern of the Maitland Commission the same set of questions are also valid for rural communities around the world. The status of rural communities is not only indicative of a nation's overall economic status it also reflects the prevailing national attitude towards rural residents. A common historical cultural phenomenon still persists in many countries which views rural folks as being backward. Historically, cities have been the seat of political power where rulers such as kings, queens and generals reigned and ordered the surfs in the villages to carry out their wishes. Technology has forced many changes in this historical attitude and communications technology may force permanent changes in an universal form.

RESEARCH METHODOLOGY
(a) General Hypotheses:

In this cross—section study telecommunications infrastructure is measured as the number of access lines per 100 inhabitants in a country. Thus, the key variables utilized in further analysis in this research are defined as:

TOTAL   =   Total number of access lines per 100 people
URBAN   =   Number of access lines per 100 people in urban areas of a country
RURAL   =   Number of access lines per 100 people in rural areas of a country
GNPPC   =   Per capita gross national products of a country

While national policy plays an important role in developing a telecommunications infrastructure it is largely a function of the economy of a nation. Past studies have found a strong relationship between telecommunications development and national income. [19] Development of rural telecommunications is no different from this economic reality. Thus, it can be postulated that development of rural telecommunications by and large depends upon national income. as measured by gross national product and services.

Thus, using the variable defined above, a functional relationship between rural telecommunications and income can be put forward as:

Rural   =   f(GNPPC)

Since national income or more precisely per capita national income has long been established as a major determinant of telecommunication infrastructure development disaggregation of countries by income appears appropriate. The sample countries, therefore, have been classified into two broad categories, one with per capita income of $2000 or less and the other with per capita income of over $2000. Thus, three sets of regression models have been estimated for further analysis, one set including all the countries in the sample and the other two sets comprising the lower and higher income countries.

Unlike the United States that has long pursued a policy of rural development and made an early commitment to rural telecommunication services, most countries have viewed rural telecommunications in the context of technology transfer from urban to rural areas. A general hypothesis can be put forward postulating rural telecommunications as a function of urban telecommunications, perhaps with some lag effect. Therefore, another functional relationship can also be put forward as:

Rural   =   f(Urban)

In fact, such a functional relationship can also be used to determine relative growth in the telecommunications infrastructure in urban versus rural areas among the nations of the world. For supplementary evidence several additional models have been developed using TOTAL and URBAN dependent variables.

(b) Data Sources and Classification:

This research is intended to include cross—section data from the nations of the world. However, the limited availability of comparable data has imposed some restrictions on the number of countries included. Thus, the study has been limited to those forty—seven countries from around the world for which complete information is available. The study, nonetheless, benefits from embracing a diverse group of countries, comprising both wealthy and poor nations, and the sample countries represent all nine telecommunications world zones, as defined by the International Telecommunications Union. Selected countries included in this research are listed in Appendix A. Data on telecommunications infrastructure used in this study have been obtained from AT&T compilation of world telephone statistics for the year 1991—92. [3] Data on income and population have been obtained from the United Nations Yearbook. [28]

The research has focused on penetration of telecommunications in sample countries and the proxy for infrastructure used is 'access lines per 100 people', as mentioned earlier. The ratio is computed for urban as well as for rural communities within each country. An urban area is generally defined as a community with a population of ^{100},OOOormore. However, some exceptions were made for those countries with large. populations in many mid—sized cities where appropriate data were unavailable. This usually has been the case in certain Asian countries with very high population density. A cut off point of one million inhabitants is used for Japan and South Korea, 200,000 for Brazil, and 350,000 for Taiwan. These exceptions were forced because of a lack of available data for smaller cities in those countries. Since this dividing line is used only for classification purposes and the analysis is carried out in ratio scale the results are unlikely to be influenced in any significant way. Raw data is grouped into two categories namely urban and rural. The aggregate data from all urban areas is then subtracted from national totals to obtain aggregate data for all rural areas within a country. Subsequently, the ratio 'access lines per 100 people' is computed for both urban and rural areas of each of the countries included in the study. Since the key ingredient for telecommunications service remains the access line, the rural—urban comparative study undertaken in this research is based upon the above ratios.

As mentioned earlier, in addition to the aggregate analysis, the regression models were also developed for two separate groups of countries, one for relatively low income countries with per capita income of less than $2000 per year and the other including higher income countries. Therefore, the data is further disaggregated and classified into these two groups of countries for subsequent analysis. It is expected that such a classification enables us to capture any differences that may exist between rich and poor countries. A statistical summary of aggregate data related to sample countries is included in Table 1. These summary measures expose the extent of disparity that exists among the sample countries. Regression models estimated from sample data are included in Tables 2, 3 and 4. Table 2 summarizes the models estimated from aggregate data including all sample countries whereas Tables 3 and 4 include models estimated from countries with higher and lower incomes respectively.

ANALYSIS OF RESULTS.

(a) Statistical Characteristics of Sample Countries:

A brief discussion of the statistical summary presented in Table 1 may be useful to appreciate the diversity in levels of infrastructure development among countries included in this research. The forty—seven countries included in this study represent a cross-section of the nations of the world. Per capita gross national products of these countries are centered around a mean income of US $6,104 and a standard deviation of US *$7,656,* clearly indicating that the

Table 1: Summary of the Indicator Variables				
Access Lines per 100 People	Per Capita Gross National Product	Urban	Rural	<u>Overall</u>
Mean	6104	21.45	12.91	15.42
Standard Deviation	7,656	20.04	16.83	17.68
Minimum	124	0.90	0.01	0.20
Maximum	27,497	64.90	48.92	54.10
Sample Size	47	47	47	43

sample countries represent a diverse group. In fact, the country with lowest per capita income is Ethiopia with income of $124 only whereas on the other extreme the country with highest per capita income of $27,497 is Switzerland. Similarly, telecommunication access to inhabitants of these countries is also extremely diverse. The lowest number of access lines per 100 inhabitants is again noted as a meager 0.02 for Ethiopia whereas the comparable number for Switzerland is 54.10, tracking the poorest and the richest countries in the sample. Diversity in access lines among the nations is further represented by the distribution of the variable 'access lines per 100 inhabitants' in the sample countries and is centered around a mean of 15.42 and a substantially larger standard deviation of 17.68. Composite measure of this diversity can also be seen as the statistical measure of coefficient of variation, which measures a relative variability of 92 percent for urban and 130 percent for rural areas. Clearly, greater diversity is more prevalent in rural areas compared to their urban counterparts.

Table 2: Aggregate Regression Models Including All Sample Countries (n=47)

Al	TOTAL	=	2•174 (1•89)	+	2•170 GNPPC (18•36)	R^2=0•880
Bl	URBAN	=	6•7l6 (4•58)	+	2•4l4 GNPPC (16•01)	R^2=0•848
Cl	RURAL	=	0•131 (1•10)	+	2•064 GNPPC (18•30)	R^2=0•879
Dl	RURAL	=	-4•559 (-5•11)	+	0•8l5 URBAN (26•64)	R^2=0•939
El	RURAL	=	-1•706 (1•89)	+	0•948 TOTAL (18•36)	R^2=•992
Fl	URBAN	=	4•338 (5•477)	+	1•ll0 TOTAL (32•667)	R^2=0•959

(b) Analysis of Aggregate Models:

As mentioned in the previous section, telecommunications infrastructure is generally a function of national income. The present study utilizes a similar notion in analyzing infrastructure development among nations where total number of access lines has been used as the key indicator in this process. The three primary regression models developed here have utilized three dependent variables as defined in section 111, namely TOTAL, URBAN, and RURAL, all representing the number of access lines per 100 people. The independent variable is the level of income, measured as per capita gross national income and abbreviated as GNPPC. In addition to these three primary models, three additional models representing rural to urban, rural to total, and urban to total relationships are also viewed as appropriate models to further this research. It can be postulated that rural development takes place through technology transfer from urban areas of a country and therefore can be viewed as a function of urban development. Urban areas benefit early from new technologies and a gradual deployment takes place in rural areas over a period time. To measure such a relationship a fourth model has been developed which defines RURAL as the dependent variable which is affected by the independent variable URBAN. The remaining two models are developed using TOTAL as the independent variable, only to confirm further the rural—urban relationship representing a form of technology transfer from urban to rural areas. These six aggregate models utilizing all 47 countries are included in Table 2, and are denoted as Al, B1, C1, Dl, El and Fl.

Each of the first three models shows a significant relationship between access lines per 100 inhabitants and per capita gross national income, as has been found in earlier studies on telecommunications development [19]. Model Al represents a highly significant relationship between total number of access lines and national income. Model B1 relating to urban areas and Model C1 relating to rural regions of the nations have also proved significant relationships with income. However, some important differences may be noted in these relationships. For example, the relative

Table 3: Estimated Regression Models for Higher Income* Countries (n=26)

A2	TOTAL	=	6•202 (2.605)	+	1•939 GNPPC (10.613)	R^2=0•817
B2	URBAN	=	14•391 (5.491)	+	1•976 GNPPC (9.827)	R^2=0•793
C2	RURAL	=	4.434 (1.466)	+	1•887 GNPPC (10.501)	R^2=0•814
D2	RURAL	=	-8•571 (-4.041)	+	0•905 URBAN (16.592)	R^2=0•917
E2	RURAL	=	-2•540 (-4•390)	+	0•971 TOTAL (52•383)	R^2=0•991
F2	URBAN	=	8•482 (5•323)	+	1•003 TOTAL (19•656)	R^2=•0939

*Countries with per capita gross national products of at least $2,000.

Table4: Estimated Regression Models for Lower Income* Countries (n=21)

A3	TOTAL	=	-0•307 (-0•75 1)	+ (6.552)	2•268 GNPPC R^2=0•688	
B3	URBAN	=	3•122 (1.153)	+	2•038 GNPPC (2•968)	R^2=0•396
C3	RURAL	=	-0•122 (-1•174)	+	0•954 GNPPC (2•632)	R^2=0•3 12
D3	RURAL	=	—0•882 (-1726)	+0•337 URBAN (3.947)		R^2=0•422
E3	RURAL	=	-0•493 (-1•833)	+	0•576 TOTAL (6•763)	R^2=0•690
F3	URBAN	=	2•678 (3•860)	+	1•078 TOTAL (3•914)	R^2=0•429

*Countries with per capita gross national products of below $2,000.

magnitude of change in telecommunications with respect to income between urban and rural communities within nations is interesting to examine. The rate of change for urban areas as estimated in Model BI is 2.414 and the comparable number for Model C1 representing rural communities is 2.026, which is substantially lower than that of its urban counterpart. The difference is statistically significant. These results suggest that rural communities receive less emphasis in the development of telecommunications infrastructure compared to their urban counterparts within a country. The fourth aggregate relationship between URBAN and RURAL is expressed in Model DI and essentially represents a lag effect in rural developments in relation to their urban counterparts. This significant regression model defines the urban-rural relationship by a slope of *0.815* indicating a slower transfer in telecommunications technology to rural areas. This value of the slope can be interpreted as rural areas only enjoying telecommunications facilities at approximately four—fifths the level of their urban counterparts. The statistically significant value of the intercept in Model Dl, which is —4.559, also suggests that there may be other unfavorable factors negatively influencing the rural communities. Rural areas appear to be adversely affected by some other arbitrary forces beyond relative income. This observation is further confirmed by the last two models, El and Fl, representing the RURAL-TOTAL and URBAN—TOTAL relationships. Slopes of these models are 0.948 for rural and 1. 110 for urban areas which indicate that urban communities enjoy a greater share of the infrastructure. It is noted in Model 131 as well as in Model Fl, both representing urban areas, that the intercepts are positive and statistically significant. At the same time, comparable coefficients in Models Dl and El representing rural areas are negative and statistically significant. Perhaps, these coefficients can be interpreted as some kind of preference coefficient of a socio—political nature which historically has worked in favor of urban areas. This may, however, also be contributed to by spatial factors in the ease of telecommunications which has traditionally favored areas with high population density. Regardless of the reasons, overall results seem to indicate that rural communities have suffered from a lower priority in the development of their telecommunications infrastructure compared to their urban counterparts.

(c) Analysis of Disaggregated Models:

Sample data is further subdivided into two groups of countries, the first including those countries with per capita gross national product of over $2,000 is referred to as higher income countries, and the second group with per capita incomes of $2,000 or less is referred to as lower income countries. The regression models for the higher income countries are presented in Table 3 and referred to as A2, B2, C2, D2, E2 and F2. These models are estimated utilizing data from 26 countries with GNPPC of over $2,000. The regression models for the lower income countries with GNPPC of $2,000 or less are estimated from the remaining 21 countries which fell in this category. These regression models are referred to as A3, B3, C3, D3, E3 and F3, and are included in Table 4.

An examination of models A2 and A3 representing total access lines as a function of income reveals some interesting differences between rural and urban areas. The slopes of these two models are 1.939 for A2 and 2.268 for A3 for the higher and lower income country categories respectively. These numbers suggest that the lower income countries are now spending a relatively higher portion of their national income in telecommunications development in comparison to the higher income countries. However, a greater proportion of investments is made in the urban areas in lower income countries than in those countries that arc classified as in the higher income category. This can be identified by careful comparisons of the slopes of the models B2 and C2 as well as B3 and C3. Marginal rates for urban areas are 1.976 compared to 1.887 for rural areas in higher income countries, indicating perhaps a more or less equal emphasis attached to infrastructure development in both urban and rural areas. The comparable marginal rates are 2.038 for urban and 0.954 for rural areas among the lower income countries as noted in models B3 and C3. Thus, in the case of lower income countries a significant difference exists between urban and rural areas with urban areas receiving a greater share of investment.

As noted above, urban areas certainly enjoy a greater priority among the lower income countries than in those countries classified as higher income. This difference may, in part, be attributed to the fact that urban areas in higher income countries have already developed their telecommunications infrastructures and more emphasis is now devoted to rural development. Some differences, however, may have been caused by public policy or lack thereof. Also, yet another dimension may be the rate of technology transfer from urban to rural communities. This is particularly true among those countries pursuing a free market policy.

The last three models, namely D, E and F represent physical relationships, providing some measures of the relative development of infrastructure between rural and urban areas. An examination of models D2 and D3 is particularly interesting. The slopes of these two rural —urban relationships are 0.905 for higher income and 0.337 for lower income countries. It appears that there is almost a one for one access line development between rural and urban areas in higher income countries while only one for three is the ratio among the lower income countries. A similar, though not identical, difference in the slopes of the two models E2 and E3, representing rural—total relationships may also be noted. The slope of the lower income countries

is significantly smaller than that of the higher income countries, almost a one to two ratio. On the other hand, little difference can be noticed in the slopes of models F2 and F3, representing urban—total relationships. From these results, it appears that the rural communities in rich countries are likely to get a fairer share of telecommunications access lines while rural communities in poorer countries can expect to find a lower priority for developing access lines in comparison to their urban counterparts. These findings provide further evidence of lagging technology transfer in rural areas of poorer nations around the world.

CONCLUSIONS AND LIMITATIONS

Needless to say, rural telecommunications infrastructure development lags its urban counterparts and this phenomenon appears to be a universal one. Such a difference can be noted among the wealthy as well as among the relatively poorer nations regardless of their geographic locations. Perhaps, much of this difference can be attributed to the prevailing concentration of economic and political power in the cities around the world. But, at least a part of this can be explained by lower population density in rural regions thus requiring a higher capital expenditure in developing traditional wireline telecommunications systems. Regardless of national income, rural communities are experiencing a substantial lag in telecommunications infrastructure development. The gap in terms of available access lines between urban and rural areas is found to be wider among the poorer nations.

Rural telecommunications systems appear to develop through a form of technology transfer from urban to rural areas within a country and this appears to be particularly true for the countries enjoy higher incomes. Early investment goes towards building urban infrastructures and then a gradual migration of technology takes place to rural regions. Naturally, in wealthy countries with urban infrastructures already in place rural development takes place at a faster rate than in poorer countries where urban development still remains the primary consideration. National policy favoring urban areas may also be another factor affecting rural telecommunication development in many countries. Spatial factor is yet another source of lagging rural infrastructure development. Sparsely populated rural communities generally require higher investment per access line than their urban counterparts. Wireless technology may, however, provide new opportunities for sparsely populated rural communities. Digital wireless technology being less capital intensive and more flexible certainly could contribute to the developing of rural infrastructures.

Appendix A: List of Countries Included in the Study

Dominion Republic	Greece	El Salvador
Jamaica	Hungary	Honduras
Puerto Rico	Italy	Paraguay
Trinidad and Tobago	Norway	Peru
U.S.A.	Portugal	Uruguay
Algeria	Spain	Venezuela
Cameroon	Switzerland	Australia
Ethiopia	Czechoslovakia	Malaysia
Morocco (200,000)	Germany FR	New Zealand
South Africa	Germany DR	Papua and New Guinea
Tanzania	Finland	Thailand
Tunisia	Bolivia (50,000)	Philippines
Zambia	Brazil (200,000)	Taiwan (350,000)
Zimbabwe	Chile	Japan (1 million)
Austria	Ecuador	Republic of Korea (1 million)
Belgium		

Note: Urban centers are with populations of 100,000 or more unless shown in parentheses.

However, technology transfer from urban to rural communities remains the key to rural telecommunications development. While political will and capital or lack of it may remain constraints for many emerging countries technology certainly provides choices and opportunities for telecommunications infrastructure development.

The results reported in this paper clearly demonstrate the differences in urban versus rural telecommunications infrastructures and the varying degree to which such differences exist among the wealthy compared to the poorer nations. It also raises questions about existing policy towards rural infrastructure development among the nations of the world. It is necessary for governments to recognize the critical need for communications infrastructure development in both urban as well as rural areas for their residents to participate fully in the rapidly emerging information society of the next century. If nations do not address this problem soon we may find rural communities will constitute a new 'missing link' even among relatively wealthy nations.

This study, while somewhat constrained by a lack of data certainly brings out some valuable information for making policy decisions. Further studies to examine telecommunications from a geo—political perspective using appropriately disaggregated data would be of great interest. Such studies could establish some interesting policy indicators for the development of national and global policy.

BIBLIOGRAPHY

1. Adler, Richard, Telecommunications, Information Technology, and Rural Development, Institute for the Future, Menlo Park, California, 1988.
2. Aspen Institute, Statement of Goals and Strategies for State Telecommunications Regulation, Third Annual Aspen Institute Conference on State Telecommunications Regulation, The Aspen Institute, Lanham, Maryland, 1988.
3. AT&T, "The World Telephones: A Statistical Compilation as of January 1991—92,"AT&T, Whippany, NJ 07981-9990.1993
4. Barkema, Alan D. and Mark Drabenstott, "Consolidation and Change in Heartland Agriculture," Economic Force Shaping the Rural Heartland, Federal Reserve Board of Kansas City, 1996.
5. Dillman, D. A. and Donald M. Beck, "Information Technologies and Rural Development in the 1990's," Journal of State Government, 61(1): 29—30, 1988.
6. Dillman, D. A., "The Social Impacts of Information Technologies in Rural North America," Rural Sociology, 50:1—25, 1985.
7. Dordick, Herbert S., "Toward a Universal Service," Universal Telephone Service, Institute for Information Studies, The Aspen Institute, Queenstown, MD 21658. 1991.
8. Dutton, William H., Jay G. Blumber, and Kenneth L. Kraemer, "Wired Cities: Shaping the Future of Communications," The Washington Annenberg Program, G K. Hall & Co., Boston, MA 1987.
9. Economic Research Service, Rural Economic Development in the 1980's: Prospects for the Future, U.S. Department of Agriculture, Washington, D. C., 1988.
10. General Accounting Office, Rural Development: Federal Programs that Focus on Rural America and Its Development, GAO, Washington, D. C., 1989.

11 General Accounting Office, <u>Telephone Communications: Issues Affecting Rural Telephone Service,</u> GAO, Washington, D. C., 1987.

12. Gillespie, T. M., "Telecommunications System for Rural Villages," <u>Telecommunications Journal,</u> Vol.49, No. 11, November 1982, pp.773—776.

13. Golschmidt, Douglas, "Financing Telecommunication for Rural Development," <u>Telecommunication Policy,</u> March 1984. pp.181—203.

14. Hardy, Andrew P., "The Role of the Telephone in Economic Development." <u>Telecommunications Policy,</u> December 1980.

15. Henry, Mark and Mark Drabenstott, "A New Micro View of the U.S. Rural Economy," <u>Economic Review,</u> Federal Reserve Bank of Kansas City, Vol.81, No.2, 1996.

16. Institute for Information Statistics, "Universal Telephone Service: Ready for the 21st Century?" The Aspen Institute, Queenstown, MD 21658.1991.

17. Intelsat, <u>Bridging the Gap III: A Guide to Telecommunications and Development</u>, Intelsat, Washington, D. C., 1989.

18. International Telecommunications Union, The Missing Link: Report of the Independent Commission for Worldwide Telecommunications Development, ITU, Geneva, Switzerland, 1984.

19. International Telecommunications Union, Telecommunications Indicators of the Former Soviet Union. ITU, Geneva, Switzerland, 1992.

20. Jussawalla, Meheroo, "Is the Communication Link Still Missing?!! <u>Telecommunications Policy,</u> Vol.16, No.6 (Aug.1992), *pp.485—503.*

21. Kerr, W. T. and B. C. Blevis, "Telecommunications Services for Rural and Remote Areas," <u>Telematics; and Informatics,</u> Vol.1, No.1, 1984, pp.37-46.

22. Kim, Jae-Cheol and Mm—Ho—Lee, "Universal Services Policy in Korea: Past and Future," <u>Telematics and Informatics,</u> Vol.8, No.1 and 2, pp.31—40.

23. Office of Technology Assessment, <u>Technology. Public Policy. and the Changing Structure of</u> <u>American Agriculture,</u> Washington, D. C., 1986.

24. Office of Technology Assessment "Rural America at the Crossroads: Networking for the Future,!! U. S. Government Printing Office, Washington, D.C., 1991.

25. OPASTCO, Keeping Rural America Connected, OPASTCO, Washington, DC 20036,1995.

26. Parker, Edwin B., Heather E. Hudson, Don A. Dillman, and Andrew D. Roscoe, <u>Rural America in the Information Age: Telecommunications Policy for Rural</u> <u>Development,</u> Aspen Institute, Lanham, Maryland, 1989.

27. Pelton, Joseph N., "The Globalization of Universal Telecommunications Services," <u>Universal Telephone Service,</u> Institute for Information Studies, The
Aspen Institute, Queenstown, MD 21658.1991.

28. United Nations, Yearbook of World Statistics, United Nation Organizations, NY. 1993

29. Department of Commerce, <u>NIIA Telecom 2000: Charting the Course for a New Culture U</u>.

30. U.S. Congress, Telecommunications Competition and Deregulation Act of 1995, U.S. Government Printing Office, Washington, D. C. 1995.

Shifting Paradigms of Teaching and Learning: Integrating the World Wide Web into Curriculum

Ali A. Nazemi
Computer Information Systems, Roanoke College, Salem, VA 24153
Phone: (540) 375-2217, Fax: (540) 375-2577, Nazemi@Roanoke.Edu

ABSTRACT

This paper investigates the impact of World Wide Web (WWW) technology on higher education and the resulted shift from traditional teaching methods to a more innovative teaching paradigm. This movement is fueled by a shift in the learning mode and styles of students which has evolved from traditional, text and lecture-based techniques to a hands-on, Web-based, interactive mode. A review of traditional teaching methods is used to show how multi-mode instructional techniques are used to impart information and knowledge to students. A brief study of individual learning styles shows how learning can vary from one individual to the next and how most of these styles can be accommodated through the utilization of technology in delivery of course material. Teaching techniques and learning styles are then overlapped to illustrate the areas where traditional methods fall short and where technology can bridge the gap between teaching and learning in such cases.

INTRODUCTION

The ever-increasing applications of web technology and modern, user-friendly web design tools provide a great opportunity for innovation and creativity in academic environment. The Internet and Web resources are being tapped as instructional tools in practically all disciplines be it with mixed results. In business education, the web technology not only provides an invaluable resource for case studies, research and data analysis but can be used as a tool for covering various business topics, concepts and processes through the use of on-line resources and Web-based course material. This study also addresses the trials, tribulations and triumphs of integrating WWW technology into business curriculum. A case study of a typical business course serves to illustrate a framework for effective utilization of the Internet and Web-based technologies in instructional delivery. This framework provides a fresh look at how technology can be incorporated in all aspects of business education both in and out of classroom. Finally, we will discuss some of drawbacks and barriers to the effective utilization of web resources. We will recommend some guidelines to overcome these barriers and discuss the essential elements for successful integration of technology into individual courses as well as the entire curriculum.

SHIFTING TEACHING PARADIGM

The primary goal of most educators is to provide an environment in which the students can learn and retain pertinent material effortlessly, and in some cases, while being entertained. A variety of tools and methods are used to help students with easier comprehension and retention of valuable knowledge. Courses are often revised and redesigned to make academic subjects more relevant to students' life experiences with the premise that this refinement would eventually result into an effective and well-organized series of presentations that are most beneficial to students. However, with every new generation of college students, it has become increasingly difficult to reach that magic formula, mainly because of the extreme diversity among today's college students. The framework proposed in this paper provide a guideline for designing academic courses so that the content and the delivery techniques can be changed without the need for a total overhaul of the course. Maintaining a high level of flexibility may be the only means to sufficiently accommodate the diverse student population. This solution, however, requires a complete change in philosophy of teaching and may require drastically different types of instructional delivery techniques.

To establish the appropriate background, a quick review of traditional instructional methods would be helpful. Faculty members have utilized a variety of instructional techniques over years and many continue to use such techniques with or without the use of technology. Some of these techniques include:

- Lectures/Discussions
- Case Studies
- Laboratory Work

- Field Work
- Simulation
- Problem-Solving Sessions
- Observation
- Brainstorming
- Use of Audiovisual Systems

Numerous studies have addressed the advantages of one method over others and have examined the level of effectiveness of each technique (Ronchetto, Russel). Most academicians, however, agree that often more than one technique must be implemented in order to communicate the material effectively to the students of diverse background (Alam & Rencis). In a typical course, class time is often divided into segments using various teaching techniques in an effort to enhance students' learning regardless of the individual learning style. This effort is often very time consuming and may be problematic in larger classes. To avoid this problem, many academicians have turned to computers and communications technology in search of new tools to enhance their teaching (Malasri, Quinnell, Schemmel).

There are basically two directions in which web technology can be incorporated into instruction. First, computer and communication technology can be used to enhance and support the existing traditional methods (Schemmel). In such a case, no changes are made to the content and delivery, rather technology is used to automate and computerize the existing methodology. This could be in form of computerized test banks, electronic transparencies and on-line tutorials. This approach, although an improvement over previous delivery techniques, does not take advantage of the capabilities of computers and provides little or no opportunity for student interaction. The second direction, which is the focus of this study, is to completely integrate technology into all aspects of a course (McIntyre). One of the advantages of this approach is that technology can fuse together a multitude of instruction techniques into a single, effective instructional aid. This can lead to the integration of technology into curriculum by introducing a common core component that can connect multiple disciplines. This technical core can be an important factor in improving students' ability to understand the material regardless of their learning styles, time limitations and geography. This is particularly important to the new generation of students who are accustomed to asynchronous modes of learning and are exposed to a variety of information sources and mediums long before entering college. Today's college students are exposed to computers at an early age either through playing computer or video games or through more sophisticated applications and programs that use images, sounds, animation, and videos. By the time these students enter college, many of them have used on-line services and have been sufficiently exposed to Internet resources. In other words, there has been a seismic shift in learning and in the way knowledge is transferred to the new generation of students. Many academic institutions have recognized this trend and have acquired or are in the process of acquiring the technological resources needed to satisfy the students' needs.

SHIFTING LEARNING PARADIGM

As we investigate the essential elements for successful integration of web technology in education, it is important to recognize the impact of technology on students with diverse learning capabilities. Learning styles vary in each individual according to individual's background, experience, attitude and personality. The challenge is to provide an environment that enhances students' comprehension regardless of their learning ability. Although, it may be impossible to create lecture presentations and course material that can support all types of learner, using multimedia and web-based instruction can help in achieving a large portion of this objective. There have been a plethora of research on the learning styles and its influences on teaching methods in academic community (Cordell, Malley, Russell). These studies have addressed a variety of learning styles from personal and societal perspectives. Russell, in his study of learning style inventory, recognizes seven types of learner described below:

Linguistic who learns by saying, hearing and seeing words. This learner type likes to read, write and tell stories and is good as memorizing places and dates. This learner learns best by repeating facts and benefits from lectures, case studies and written martial.

Logical/Mathematical who learns by categorizing, classifying material and working with abstract patterns and relationships. This type of learner likes to do experiments, work with numbers and solve problems by asking questions and explore relationships. Logical learner is good at math, reasoning and logic and is highly organized and methodical.

Spatial who learns by visualizing, dreaming and working with pictures and colors. This type of learner perhaps benefits the most from a multimedia environment that uses animation and pictures. This learner is best at using imagination, sensing changes and working with mazes and puzzles.

Musical who learns by rhythm, melody and music. This learner usually listens to music and enjoys jingles and sounds. This type learns best by picking up sounds, remembering melodies and noticing pitches and rhythms. This learner likes to play an instrument and responds well to music.

Bodily/Kinesthetic who learns by touching, moving and interacting with environment. This person likes three dimensional images, hands-on experiences and learns by doing. This type of learner is good at physical activities and crafts and likes to use body language in communicating with others.

Interpersonal who learns by sharing, comparing and cooperating with others. This learner benefits from group discussions and teamwork and likes to discuss and analyze material with friends and classmates. This person is good at understanding people, leading others, organizing and communicating.

Intrapersonal who learns by working alone, using self-paced instruction and individualized projects. This learner likes to work alone, pursues own interest and is good at focusing inward on felines and dreams. This type of learner can benefit from computerized tutorials and self-paced instructional material.

It may be difficult to identify a specific learner type without direct interaction with the individual, however, this may not be of significant importance. The important factor is how the course content and instruction delivery can be adjusted to reach as many individual learners as possible. This is precisely where technology can play an important role in broadening teaching scope to address various learning styles.

WEB TECHNOLOGY

One of the major focuses of this study is to examine how a web-based delivery system can be integrated into a course in a context most appealing to a variety of individual learners. To examine the relationship between teaching and learning, various instructional methods and learner types can be represented in a table format in which columns represent Learning Styles and rows represent Teaching Methods. The intersection of any column with a given row is the point where a specific teaching technique corresponds with a specific learner type. Exhibit 1 illustrates how such table can be constructed.

Exhibit 1

Teach./Learn.	Linguist	Logical	Spatial	Musical	Kinesthetic	Interpersonal	Intrapersonal
Lecture	High	Low	Low	Low	Low	High	High
Case Study	High	High	Medium	Low	Low	High	Low
Simulation	Medium	High	High	High	Medium	Medium	Medium
Labs	Low	Low	High	High	Medium	Medium	High
Field Work	Medium	Low	High	Medium	High	High	Low
Prob. Solve.	Low	High	Low	Low	Medium	Medium	Medium
Observation	High	Medium	High	High	High	High	Medium
Brainstorm	Low	High	Medium	Low	Low	Medium	Medium
Model Bldg.	Medium	High	High	Low	Medium	Medium	Medium
Use of A/V	High	High	High	High	High	High	High

Using this table, we can now identify how well a particular teaching method matches up with a given learning style. This is done by assigning weights to the level of effectiveness on a simple "Low", "Medium" and "High" scale. For example, a Visual learner will benefit the most from Audiovisual methods, Simulations, Field Works and Labs, so there is a good match between these techniques and the visual learner type. In such case, a "High" is placed in cells at the intersection of learner column and teaching style rows. Conversely, a Linguist does not benefit as much from Labs and Problem Solving sessions hence a 'Low" is placed at the intersection of Linguist with Labs and Problem Solving. A weight of "Medium" was assigned to cells where the impact of teaching was neither great nor small. These weights are assigned purely based on experience of the author and may vary among individuals and/or institutions.

By examining the "Low" and "Medium" cells in Exhibit 1, we can identify major areas where teaching styles and learning styles do not match and where technology can be instrumental in bridging the gap between teaching and learning. This is not to say that "High" areas do not benefit from technology enhancement rather "Low" and "Medium" areas are the ones requiring more attention.

To illustrate how web technology can be valuable, one can look at a situation where a Spatial or a Kinesthetic learner is involved in analyzing a written case study. In such cases, the author has observed that some individuals have a hard time visualizing the components of the case leading to weak analysis of the case problem. A case study represented in a multimedia format on a web page however allows a Spatial or a Kinesthetic learner to see and in some case to hear the primary characters and situations in the case resulting in better understanding of case problem and hence a more accurate analysis of the case. In a Model Building session, music, sound and animation can be used to accommodate the Musical and Linguist learner. A Groupware software or a chat session can be used in collaborative Problem Solving and Brainstorming situation allowing the Intrapersonal learner to be involved in team-oriented activities. Projects and assignments requiring the use of Internet resources can be used to enhance Lectures and Field Work. Numerous other examples can be provided on how technology and world wide web resources can be integrated in classroom instruction using on-line access to the Internet and to institutions' Intranets. In addition, CD-R, Laser Disc, Digital Versatile Disc (DVD), Computer Aided Instructional Tools and Multimedia technologies can accommodate individual learners in an asynchronous mode and time-frame.

INTEGRATING WEB-BASED TECHNOLOGY

To successfully implement web techniques into the curriculum, several important factors must be taken into consideration. First, we must ensure that educators are willing and able to incorporate new technology into their teaching. If the initial commitment in part of the instructor is lacking, it would be extremely difficult to undertake and sustain the curricular changes that are essential to the success of the project. This may require some formal training in part of the instructor as well as willingness to experiment with innovative approaches. This requires a change in the philosophy of traditional teaching to a new paradigm that may be hard to envision. It may require a complete rethinking of how knowledge (instructor's or otherwise) is transferred from one entity to another. Another factor to consider is the basic understanding of technology and its limitations. In some cases, we may have to identify the current level of technology used by each educator in order to estimate the scope of the required changes. For example, if an instructor is already using audiovisual aids in classes, the transition to web-based technique is much smoother than for those who use lectures as the only means for disseminating knowledge. A third factor is the academic discipline and the content of the specific course that is under consideration. Some academic disciplines (i.e. Religion and Philosophy) tend to be less conducive to the use of technology while others (i.e. Information Systems and Computer Science) are naturally suited for technology integration. The literature, however, suggests that more and more faculty members from less technology-oriented discipline are discovering new ways to incorporate web resources into their courses (Carver, Quinnell, Ward). Finally, institutions must be committed to providing necessary resources, facilities and services in order to successfully implement web-based projects. This requires cooperation from administrators, information systems department, webmaster, network administrators, and audiovisual and library staff.

TRIBULATIONS OF WEB-BASED TEACHING

Although, the web-based technology is becoming more prevalent in classrooms, it's benefits and drawbacks are yet to be fully understood or assessed. This has caused some to fear that the use of technology in classroom would mean abandoning those traditional classroom techniques that may have been successful in the past. They believe that incorporating technology in classroom would negatively impact the entire dynamics of the class by taking away the one-to-one interaction between faculty and student. They argue that technology in and out of the class will eliminate face-to-face interaction between the student and faculty resulting into fewer intellectual exchanges. This surely is a legitimate concern and poses yet another challenge to web site designers. It means that greater care must be taken to ensure that technology is used in an effective manner and with a clear understanding of its capabilities and limitations and not used merely for "technology sake". This author suggests that a dynamic and effective learning atmosphere can be accomplished by careful, structured planning and implementation and by maintaining flexibility in designing lectures and course contents. The framework suggested in this paper provides a blueprint for accomplishing these exact objectives.

Another drawback to successful implementation of technology in classroom is the high level of technical complexity of such systems that makes them less user-friendly compared to simple devices such as overhead projectors and video cassette players. This problem is magnified in cases where the system must be used interactively by both faculty and students. Very few educators have used interactive web pages in a classroom environment since this approach is difficult to set up and may require technical expertise beyond ones knowledge. In addition, a truly interactive, web-based course often means that the entire course must be redesigned requiring a great investment in time and effort.

Finally, the effectiveness of web-based teaching system is not immediately apparent even to those who do utilize them on regular basis. Very few studies have been conducted to assess the effectiveness of using the Internet and Web techniques in the classroom or to examine whether or not it can improve learning. Those few studies point out that there may be a problem with lack of motivation in part of students and lack of support and feedback that may lead to negative consequences (Bender, Quintana, Hiltz). Others indicate that Internet-based learning would be used by students to socialize rather than acquiring and retaining knowledge. (Tsikalas). There are also concerns regarding the amount of time and resources required to develop such systems and the logistics of integrating such systems into various academic disciplines. Currently, this author is in the process of conducting an experiment to study curricular ramifications of using web-based technologies as well as assessing the efficiency and effectiveness of using such techniques in a classroom environment. The results of the study will be reported at a later date.

THE FRAMEWORK

The second major focus of this paper is to illustrate how web-based technology has been implemented in the Business and Information Systems courses. Because of the nature of such courses, instructors must often utilize a variety of media such as overhead transparencies, audio tapes, videos, hands-on projects and case studies to convey the material·to the students. The following is a framework to illustrate how the use of technology has evolved from simple LCD panel to an Internet and web-based in a typical Information Systems course.

Trials

Initially, to make the lectures in these courses more organized and interesting, several graphics and hypertext software packages were utilized to develop a set of electronic transparencies for lectures and presentations. Animation and sound were later added to enhance the presentations and to provide a more realistic view of business environment. In addition, videos from real cases were used to show the use of IS in a real-world business case. This system, however, was controlled by the instructor and was only used during class period. The electronic transparencies were gradually integrated with a hypermedia software and was made available to the students outside the class. This, however, did not help in integrating other tools into the classroom and was seen by some as a set of fancy transparencies.

Multimedia ToolBook software was used to replace the graphics and hypermedia packages. This immediately allowed for a drastic improvement in presentations by providing the capability to cross-link the topics in a non-linear fashion. The system slowly evolved into the type of multimedia environment in which students would be able to not only interact with the system but change and enhance the presentation as well. Students' participation helped in refining the course content as well as the delivery method. Presentations were later enhanced by incorporating sound, animation and most importantly video clips relating to the topics under discussion. This allowed for a truly interactive classroom were students and the instructor could collaborate and exchange ideas while learning the material. Each screen in the presentations contains multiple objects that are linked to subsequent objects, pages, audio and video clips. This enabled students to navigate freely through the presentation and bring up more information as needed. The way ToolBook presentation were set up is basically the way Hyper Text Manipulation Language (HTML) operates making the transition from ToolBook-Based to Web-Based presentations quite easy. As the HTML tools evolved and became more user-friendly, more course material and information such as lecture notes, course syllabus and outline and assignments were transferred to web pages.

Integration

The next step in the process was to attempt to fully integrate web technology into other aspects of teaching such as the use of real-life cases, group discussions, team projects and on-line evaluations. This required a shift from the way the instruction took place in a traditional classroom environment to a wen-based approach. This shift is illustrated in table in Exhibit 2.

Exhibit 2	
Traditional Teaching Paradigm	**Web-Based Teaching Paradigm**
One-Way Lectures, Handouts	Interactive, Intellectual Exchanges, Electronic Posting or Handouts and Class Notes
Fixed Course Information and Syllabus	On-line, Flexible Course Content.
Paper-based Homework Assignments and Collections	Web-Based Assignments and Submissions
Group Discussion and Team Work	Bulletin Boards, Chat Rooms and Discussion Zones
Library-Based Research	Internet-Based Research
Project and Case Analysis	On-line Projects and On-line Case Discussion and Submission
Office Hours and Outside Help	E-Mail, Electronic Live Office Hours and Chat Sessions

As this table illustrates, we can use web technology to provide an environment were students are less dependent on the single source of information and are able to learn using multiple media from many sources. Web-Based material gives students a source that they can go to for information regardless of time and geographic limitations. On-line case analysis and submission gives students the capability to analyze cases individually or in groups and record or submit the results either during class or outside the class.

Special on-line bulletin board and conferences allow students in teams to share their ideas with team members without compromising privacy or interference from other teams. The results of electronic case analyses can be used to review material in the following class sessions or used as tutorials for students outside the class. Also, this allows for various points-of-view to be compared and contrasted by looking at the responses side-by side. This is made possible by using the HTML's dynamic links and buttons that allows the instructor to easily add material and objects to the existing pages. The use of Groupware software is also under consideration in order to make this process much more appealing.

A typical scenario would be in a case where the topic of the discussion is Expert System. In this case, the basic elements of a rule-based system is provided on-line in the course web page and the topic is discussed in the class prior to case analysis. In a separate page, the most important points of the case discussing a typical set of rules is provided with rules appearing one at a time. The students are then prompted to critique and analyze the rules and type in their responses in a text box. The response fields allow students to enter a long answer as they analyze questions or use radio buttons or check-boxes for multiple choice questions. These pages can then be saved for subsequent review or can be submitted to faculty over the Internet. The classroom environment becomes quite interactive when each student team provides responses and the instructor readily documents and compares various viewpoints.

This approach seems to appeal to most students and some use it after class to go over the class notes and other classroom discussions. There are, however, few drawbacks in using this system in every course. One major drawback is the amount of time that is needed to develop the effective web-based presentations. In order for the presentation to be fluid, more sophisticated hardware and software is required to capture and interconnect text, animations, sounds and videos. Also, a great deal of training is required to gain understanding of hypermedia links, VB and Java scripts and CGI and Perl programming. The learning curve, however, has somewhat flattened out with the introduction of new web tools. Another point of concern is the fact that setting up and using this system consumes a large portion of each class time leaving less time for discussions. This problem has been partially solved by using faster computers and better network and internet connections. Outside the classroom, students are encouraged to use campus network and web resources by designing assignments and homework in such way that requires students to use such resources to complete their assignments. These may include on-line research of industrial trends, business projections and company profiles. As part of Information Systems course requirements, students are expected to design individual and/or business web pages that are published on campuses web site. In addition, the use of on-line databases such as ABI-Inform, Wall Street Journal Index and other publications have been invaluable for student research and term projects.

CONCLUSIONS

As the Internet and web technologies become more popular, their use as an educational tool will drastically increase. In this study, we have discussed how technology can be instrumental in bridging the gap between teaching and learning. We are now at the threshold of a technological revolution in information delivery and must harness the power of computers to improve and enhance our teaching. This requires a shift from traditional educational paradigms to more flexible, innovative approaches to teaching. To improve the educational environment, a highly delicate balance between using technology-oriented techniques and other effective traditional methods must be maintained. Furthermore, a commitment to provide more time and resources must be made in order for these projects to be successful. There still remain some questions as to the effectiveness and the efficiency of the use of web technology in education. However, this author believes that through clear, careful planning for technology we can construct a new teaching paradigm that can be highly effective.

REFERENCES

Alam, J., Rencis, J., Use of Internet in Information Content Creation and Delivery for Promoting Active Cooperating Learning, *Computers in Education Journal*, 1998.

Arjomand, L. and Phillips, D., A Statistical Analysis of Student Performance in On-line vs Traditional Classes, *Working Paper*, 1998.

Bender, R.M., Creating Communities on the Internet: Electronic Discussion Line in the Classroom, *Computers in Libraries*, Vol. 15, No. 5, May 1995, pp. 38-43.

Carver, C. and Adams, W., Hyperdusciplinary Courseware: A Means of Integrating the Curriculum, *Computers in Education Journal*, 1998.

Cordell, B.J., A Study of Learning Styles and Computer-Assisted Instruction, *Computer Education*, Vol. 16, No. 2, 1991.

Hiltz, S.R., *Evaluating the Virtual Classroom, Online Education: Perspectives on a New Environment*, Praeger, 1990, pp. 133-183.

Hofstetter, F.T., *Multimedia Presentation Technology*, Wadsworth Publishing, 1994.

Hustedde, S.F., *Developing with Asymetrix ToolBook*, Integrated Media Group, Wadsworth Publishing, 1996.

Kearsley, G., Lynch, W., and Wizer, D., The Effectiveness and Impact of Online Learning in Graduate Education, *Educational Technology*, November-December 1995, pp. 37-42.

Keys, A.C., Asynchronous Distance Learning Issues for Business School Quantitative Courses, *SE INFORMS*, 1998.

Malarsi, S., Multimedia and Web-Based Instructions on Expert Systems, *Computers in Education Journal*, 1998.

Malley, John, Integrating Communication and Human Information Processing (HIP) Styles, Paper.

McIntyre, D. and Wolf, F., An Experiment with WWW Interactive Learning in University Education, *Computers & Education*, 31 (1998) pp. 255-264.

Martel, L.D., Profiles of the Integrative Learning Systems, Applications in Education, Corporation of Government Agencies.

Quinnell, K. and Beasley, J., Creating "On-Line" Examinations, *Computers in Education Journal*, 1998.

Quintana, Yuri, Evaluating the Value and Effectiveness of Internet-Based Learning, *Business Research Interest*, Winter 1997.

Ronchetto, J.R. and Buckles, T.A., Multimedia Delivery Systems: A Bridge between Teaching Methods and Learning Styles, *Journal of Marketing Education*, Spring 1992.

Russel, K., The Integrative Learning Systems, Workshop, SETIMS 1993.

Schemmel, J., Hall, K., and Dennis, Using Computer Technology to Enhance Instruction and Learning, *Computers in Education Journal*, 1998.

Smith, G. and Pallatto, J., *Building Applications with ToolBook*, Brady Publishing 1991.

Tsikalas, K., Internet-based Learning? Mostly students use the Net to socialized, *Electronic Learning*, Vol 14, No. 7, April 1995, Pg. 14.

Tway, L., Welcome to... Multimedia, MIS Press 1992.

Ward, M. and Newlands, D., Use of the Web in Undergraduate Teaching, *Computers & Education*, 31 (1998), pp. 171-184.

Wolfgram, D.E., *Creating Multimedia Presentations*, Prentice Hall Computer Publishing, 1994.

Diffusion of Translation Software: An Exploratory Study

Denise James
Merrick School of Business, University of Baltimore, 1420 North Charles St., Baltimore MD 21201

Fred Niederman
Merrick School of Business, University of Baltimore, 1420 North Charles St., Baltimore MD 21201
410-837-5276, 410-837-5722 (fax), fniederman@ubmail.ubalt.edu

ABSTRACT

Software programs that translate text from English to French, German to Spanish, etc. offer the potential for shattering barriers to cross-cultural understanding. It also offers the potential to facilitate international transactions and accelerate global careers. However, there are a number of attributes of spoken language that make such automated translation difficult. This exploratory study examines data collected from a sample of volunteer translators and interpreters in Maryland, USA. Study results regarding views of quality, software diffusion, precursors to translation software use, perceived ease of use, and costs/benefits of translation software are presented along with a proposed typology of potential translation software users.

INTRODUCTION

Global commerce and trade continues to increase in volume at an astonishing rate. Internet communication has been growing at exponential rates. Both of these trends indicate an increasing communication across national boundaries and, therefore, across cultural and linguistic groups. Translation software (TS) offers the potential for a wide array of individuals to access a broader spectrum of information without having to learn additional languages.

TS processes data and instructs machines to translate text from one language, such as French, into another language, such as German. It also instructs a machine to translate the language in a document by inputting text into a computer and receiving that same output, in a targeted foreign language (Hobby, 1997). TS is a tool that facilitates translation of languages; translation with this tool can occur with or without knowledge of the translated foreign language (Poliworld, 1998). Most, if not all, TS come with dictionaries that can be customized to particular environments to improve the quality of translations with the volume of words that can be created. Typical in most TS packages are spell checkers, verb conjugators, and grammar checkers. Further, TS may allow viewing source text through a split screen or a display window.

Interest in TS is evidenced by the entry of Berlitz International, Inc., world renowned for its leadership in language instructions, into this rapidly growing business area. The company has identified the translation of applications and multimedia to be a $1.7 billion industry. Spokespersons claim TS comprised 1/5th of its business in 1996, and further claim to be the largest supplier in this rapidly growing industry (Mullich, 1997).

Internet users are beginning to find translation functions built into products for use on microcomputers and minicomputers, thereby facilitating the translation of incoming and outgoing on-line correspondence for business and personal use (Kwon, 1997). The ability to review a machine translated, draft ready document, offers the possibility of an organization or individual to make international business decisions in the absence of a translator. It also offers the possibility of providing "rough translations" that allow professional translators to focus on smaller segments of text or to automate a portion of the translation function (Poliworld, 1997).

This paper presents and analyzes data derived from a sample of professional and volunteer translators. It examines ways in which TS users vary in their characteristics and, as a result, in the way that they use TS and the requirements they have for TS performance. It proposes a typology for categorizing TS users and distinguishing their characteristics.

THE TRANSLATION PROBLEM

The goal of using machinery to aid language translation has been pursued since the origination of computing machinery. Early efforts to convert statements to another language almost immediately revealed accurate translation to be exceedingly difficult. Because languages are based on the experiences and judgements of people living in different environments, basic concepts differ. The idea of many words for "snow" among people living in cold climates is well known. How then can a computer translate a single word for powdery snow into a language that has historically only been used by people living near the equator?

To deal with the complexity of human languages, TS programs use a variety of strategies. Most translate an entire sentence one word at a time then by phrases. The rules of grammar in the language are then incorporated to properly structure the target language sentence. The more similar the source language is to the target language, the higher the quality of the translation.

Localization of TS incorporates the cultural and language dependencies of indigenous users, to include: ambiguities, idioms, transliteration, spelling, notational conventions, and other culturally dependent elements. Neither ambiguities nor idioms translate well even when users share a native language. When some spelling errors occur, TS can not discern that it is spelling the correct word, only that a word is spelled correctly or incorrectly. Numbers, currency, time and date, all add up to "notational conventions" that must be addressed to aid cultural context. Each language brings these and a host of other culturally dependent peculiarities that are difficult for TS to translate. In contrast, human translators are likely to be familiar with the cultural context of both source and target languages. They are likely to resolve ambiguous segments and may vary from strict interpretations to convey larger meanings and intentions of the original document.

HOW GOOD IS TRANSLATION SOFTWARE (AS OF SEPTEMBER 1998)?

Neither TS nor human translators are able to provide users a translated document with 100% accuracy. The reported accuracy of TS programs is between 60% and 70%. Human translators possess the ability to reason, allowing them to discern cultural context, appropriate word variants and uses. TS will provide a user the general idea of most foreign translated documents to allow what is called "gisting." Such a translation is considered to be edit-ready when the requirement exists for a quality draft. Translators render numerous edits to their translations before delivering the finished translation. Where machines will always provide a document in its original format, layout, and without omissions; human translators cannot make that claim. Large and technical documents are suited for TS; technical documents use a limited and often redundant vocabulary. The speed of human translations is not necessarily increased as a result of redundant data.

Translation rates for popular commercial TS are reputed to be as high as 300,000 words per hour. However, the reported quality from trade journal anecdotal reports of these translations varies. There are few reports of TS generating immediately usable product (as acknowledged by typical warnings for TS translation). For example, graduate students are known to have fun creating gibberish by using Internet provided TS to translate poems such as "Casey at the Bat" into French, French into German, then German back into English.

On the other hand, software company SAP, used the TS product Logos to translate a 20,000 page document from English into French over a six month period. The project required human assistance to customize "product specific" dictionaries, and to edit the machine translated document. The product allowed SAP to translate twice the number of words in two thirds the time required by conventional methods. This was accomplished using only two thirds the number of persons working on the translation team. SAP plans to use TS to meet future translation needs (Hobby 1997). In this scenario, the TS is used as a component in a socio-technical system where the whole system (compared to traditional human only translation) generates organizational benefits.

TS programs are available (as of September 1998) in varying degrees of complexity and accuracy. They can be used on various hardware platforms, from the personal computer to the mainframe (Hobby 1997). Each software package has a unique set of operating requirements; although most are comparable. Minimum system requirements for one of the inexpensive programs ($49.Easy Translator by Transparent Language) are: Windows 3.1, or 95, or NT; have at least a 386 CPU; 8MB of RAM; 15MB of hard disk space; Navigator, Internet Explorer, or Mosaic browser (Finney, 1997).

DIFFUSION RESEARCH

Research in the diffusion of technologies began with examination of communication factors that facilitated the spreading use of agricultural, medical, and educational innovations (see Rogers and Shoemaker, 1971). This research stream was adopted in the area of information technology to examine patterns of diffusion of information technologies. This supporting research area was drawn upon to examine the degree to which information technologies behaved in the same manner as other technologies while being adopted by new users. It has also formed a basis for studying how various factors influenced the spread of particular technologies such as spreadsheets, end user computing, group support systems, imaging, budgeting software, and expert support systems. For a survey of diffusion research regarding information systems see Prescott and Conger (1995).

TS can be viewed as an emerging software technology. As such, the factors thought to influence its diffusion can be examined. For example, attributes such as ease of use are thought to influence the degree to which a technology will be adopted by new users. Although it is not expected that a great number of translators have necessarily adopted use of TS, this point in time presents an opportunity to examine the perceptions among translators that will influence their future adoption decisions.

STUDY ONE — METHOD

The Maryland International Committee (MIC) promotes international communication between the citizens of Maryland and members of the international community. The organization strives to stimulate interest and exchange between cultures through economics, education, training, seminars and conferences. The organization maintains the "Interpreters &Translators Guide," (ITG) which is a roster of language professionals that provide, for-hire services, volunteer services, oral interpretations and written translations. Many members speak several languages and include many for whom English is not their native language. This group is comprised of a broad range of individuals who all do at least some translation work. To the extent that translation software has become diffused through the community of those who would benefit from its use, this should be reflected in the behaviors, attitudes, and opinions of members of this group.

A survey questionnaire was designed regarding the diffusion of technology. Construction of questions was based on those validated by Moore and Benbasat (1991). TS was viewed as a new technology and questions were intended to ascertain the relative strength of various influences on their decisions regarding whether or not to use TS. In addition to modifying the questionnaire to refer specifically to TS, several questions were added pertaining to prerequisites to TS adoption (e.g. access to computer technology) and to perceived or expected costs and benefits of using TS.

A letter explaining the intent of the research along with a questionnaire was sent to each member of MCI, Interpreters and Translators. A total of 157 questionnaires were sent with 32 returned for a response rate of 20%.

Thirty-two participants responded to the survey. They range in age from 20 to 87. The mean age was 53. Fifty four percent of the participants were male; the remaining 46% were female. All participants held at a minimum an associates degree and 2 held doctoral degrees. Though one individual reported only one year of experience, the majority had 20 or more years. The average was 18. 8 years. Participants reported providing only a limited amount of translation services. The average participant translated 43 pages per week. Just over 40% of the respondents performed the services so infrequently that they claimed no pages of translation weekly, however, 25% reported translating 20 or more pages per week. Additionally, most respondents were familiar with computers to some degree. Almost all reported using word processing (27/32 — 84%) as well as several using spreadsheet, database, graphics and electronic mail. Finally, respondents generally reported that translation generates a small percentage of their income. More than half (56%) reported less than 10% of their income derived from translation. Participant professions included: educators 21%; language professionals 3%; consultants 18%; retirees 18%; computer professionals 6%; finance 6%; and specialized 6%. Complete tables of demographic information are available from second author on request.

Results of the survey showed two distressing occurrences (see Table 1). First, a very high percentage of data was missing. Given that the response rate was already fairly low, this finding raised additional questions. Second, the standard deviation for each question was quite high. This suggested that the sample consisted of a non-homogenous grouping of individuals in spite of the commonality of being interpreters or translators. This will be discussed in more detail in the next section.

Comments on open questions on the survey as well as telephone conversations with some of the respondents and non-respondents to the survey revealed a number of interesting points. Many of those listed provide only interpretation (oral rather than written translation) and, therefore did not feel the survey applied to them. Others who did not use and expressed having absolutely no intention of using TS also thought that the survey did not apply to them. Finally, a number of translators took the initiative to call the researchers to loudly and vigorously denounce TS.

Correlation analysis of the responses to the questions showed high correlations among four of the five constructs, all except for the two questions regarding costs and benefit analysis (see Table 1). The latter question regarding performing enough translating to make the investment significant, while logically related to costs and benefits, may have been viewed by respondents as a more general question regarding the amount of translating they perform. While there was high correlation among logically clustered correlations, there was also much significant correlation among what should be unrelated items. This suggests that the discriminant validity of the questionnaire is not high and that there may be fewer constructs than the literature would suggest. For example, questions regarding diffusion and those regarding ease of use would appear to form a single construct.

In spite of these reactions and questionnaire properties, the researchers found responses to a number of questions that provided interesting results and stimulated a new round of questioning (see Table 2). Average responses to questions involving the penetration of TS into the workplace of translators were quite low. Respondents did not envision many people in their field using TS, they tended not to know where to try out TS, and they have not had the opportunity to try it out. This is consistent with a technology that has not yet diffused through a target user commu-

		1	2	3	4	5	6	7	8	9	10	11
	Table 1: Questionnaire Correlations											
1	TS improves the quality of work I do.	1.00										
2	I would be too concerned about potential errors to use TS.	.59**										
3	In my profession, many people use TS.	.39	.01									
4	I know where I can try out TS.	.44*	.02	.65**								
5	I have used TS for long enough to try it out.	.39	.07	.54*	.99**							
6	Learning to use TS poses an obstacle to using it.	-.34	.27	-.17	-.25	-.28						
7	Learning to use computer HW would be a large obstacle to using TS.	-.04	.18	-.03	-.15	-.22	.58**					
8	I believe it is easy to get TS to do what I want it to do.	.61**	-.17	.42	.64**	.58**	-.18	.23				
9	I believe TS is easy to use.	.76**	-.30	.33	.59**	.61**	-.34	.10	.90**			
10	Learning to operate TS is easy for me.	.46*	-.27	.40	.45*	.46*	-.49	-.37	.45	.65**		
11	I don't see how TS would provide more benefit than cost.	-.41	.58**	-.27	-.10	-.08	.64**	.16	-.25	-.22	-.03	
12	Even if TS improved my effectiveness as a translator, I don't do enough of it to make it worthwhile.	-.52*	.41	.39	.10	.13	.01	.16	-.04	-.14	-.2	-.08

*   Correlation is significant at the 0.05 level (2-tailed).
** Correlation is significant at the 0.01 level (2-tailed).

nity.

What keeps TS from diffusing through a larger user community? Some of the possibilities include a perceived lack of quality, lack of access to hardware or software, difficulty in using the software, and a perception that the costs would not justify the investment. This was not apparent in the question asked regarding the impact of TS on quality of work. In this case responses were fairly evenly distributed across levels and the mean (3.67) was just below neutral. It is difficult, however, to project how someone who has never actually used TS would answer this question. Either it would reflect their expectation or it might be neutral simply because they did not know. Significantly, a full 25% of respondents (presumably weighted toward those who have not used TS) did not choose to answer this question.

Based on answers to questions regarding whether learning to use the hardware (mean of 2.17) and software (mean of 2.96) would be obstacles to using TS, apparently these weren't viewed as particularly significant. By the same token, responses to whether TS software is likely to be difficult to use were fairly evenly distributed and averaged very close to a neutral response. This makes sense considering the high penetration of word processing and moderate penetration of other software tools including spreadsheets, database, graphics, and electronic mail. Based on the data collected, respondents who did not adopt TS were not generally computer-phobic.

Regarding the perceived relationship between costs and benefits, respondents were largely bimodal and slightly negative. The average (3.81) shows a modest negative leaning, but the largest numbers of respondents were at the highest and lowest levels. Another question regarding whether the respondent does enough translation to make the investment worthwhile shows that all but five were generally below the threshold of viewing the investment as worthwhile.

In addition to the formal questions, several participants provided comments regarding their experiences with TS. One participant had tried earlier products, XL8, Trados Multiterm, IBM Translation Manager and Globalink Translate Direct. The participant felt translation software was not ready in its present form to be used as a good translation tool. He did however feel it could be useful with "repetitive tasks." Another translation software tool that he was familiar and impressed with, used an "asemantic database" with the purpose of ranking articles and rendering

Question	Mean	StD	1 Low	2	3	4	5	6	7 High	Missing
Table 2: Questionnaire Responses										
Quality										
Using translation software improves the quality of work I do.	3.67	2.14	6	3	2	3	5	2	3	8
I would be too concerned about potential errors to use translation software.	3.85	2.43	9	1	1	2	5	3	5	6
Diffusion										
In my profession, many people use translation software.	2.87	1.82	7	5	3	4	0	4	0	9
I know where I can go to satisfactorily try out various uses of translation software.	2.64	2.40	14	3	2	0	0	2	4	7
I have had the opportunity to use translation software for long enough periods to try it out.	2.86	2.35	10	3	2	0	0	4	2	11
Precursors										
Learning to use translation software would be a large obstacle to using it.	2.96	2.26	11	5	1	3	2	1	4	5
Learning to use computer hardware would be a large obstacle to using it.	2.17	1.89	17	5	1	2	1	1	2	3
Ease of Use										
I believe it is easy to get translation software to do what I want it to do.	3.36	2.19	8	3	3	3	1	5	2	7
Overall, I believe that translation software is easy to use.	3.96	2.01	5	2	1	6	2	7	1	8
Learning to operate translation software is easy for me.	3.95	2.17	5	2	1	5	2	4	3	10
Costs/Benefits										
It is difficult to see how translation software would provide more benefit than cost.	3.81	2.42	7	4	2	1	4	2	6	6
Even if translation software improved my effectiveness as a translator, I don't do enough of it to make the investment worthwhile.	5.08	2.22	4	1	0	3	2	6	9	7

answers to knowledge questions within a set of documents. Not yet cost effective, in the respondent's view, that database was maintained on a mainframe and was priced in the six figures. From his comments, it was discerned that a split screen was provided to allow one to see the source and translated text at the same time. The participant felt that both split screen areas were inadequate in size; preventing one from having good access to a larger portion of the text and from having adequate area for typing. He felt the time spent learning to adapt the software to the user's needs would be neither time nor cost efficient. Further, he noted that he uses a "syllabic keyboard" which keeps him from needing to perform single keyboard strokes. He added that he can translate 300 words in 20 minutes in comparison with the XL8 software, which required in excess of an hour.

Other participants had concerns with the idea that a computer could be capable of replacing human translations. One reason for the concern is that many words have multiple meanings with different combinations, imply different things, and have different variants. The ability of a human to reason allows one to render a credible translation, though not one without time consuming thought. Errors that are in the source text of a machine translated document that go undetected will render a greater error. Language nuances differ from one language to the next, i.e., in German, verbs are placed second in some sentences whereas in others it has a primary placement. Dialects and regional differences are further concerns for translators considering translation software.

The views of a few translators are that TS comprises only the use of dictionaries. They address the fact that a dictionary could not be all-inclusive and that the work of going in and out of the source document to access the dictionary would be too cumbersome. One participant felt that translation software would be useful in the completion of forms and stated this would eliminate the need for repetitive typing. The individual added however, that he did not view this as translating.

Especially interesting is that the reasoning of less knowledgeable translation software persons and the reasoning of the literate translation software persons were very similar to knowledgeable translators/interpreter persons. They believe language is contextual. Computers would need the ability to reason, to make decisions in order to make accurate translations.

STUDY TWO – METHOD

A number of individual translators, who translated for their livelihood, were identified through Internet and were e-mailed qualitative questions concerning their use and knowledge of translation software. Eleven professionals in the translation industry responded. No demographic information is available for these individuals.

Responses provided by these translators to the benefits found in translation software were similar to those of the surveyed translators. Two of the nine respondents felt translation software improved the possibility of communication where language could be a barrier. This group was partial to the effectiveness of translation aids; specifically regular language dictionaries, and online regular and technical dictionaries. They are touted as time savers that expedite finding vague, nebulous, and difficult to find words. Translation software's "gisting" ability is favored for certain language combinations when large but simple documents need to be translated right away. Further, the software is beneficial when translators are presented with lengthy documents with short turnaround times and where every detail of the document need not be known. Technical texts that use a great deal of recurring terminology, tend to translate well. In this situation customized dictionaries are believed effective.

Another value found in translation software is that on big projects, typing alone is a major task. With translation software time is saved in that your text is typed. With human translation there exists the possibility of oversight, omission, and combining unrelated sentences. Further, the document's text is always complete, it eliminates the need to format; with translation software the document's format is unchanged. Technical text with repetitive terminology that is combined with a customized dictionary may translate well.

Responses to the disadvantages of using translation centered on the software's inability to be subjective in its evaluation of information. The majority of the translators believed machines translate word for word and not contextually. It was said the one can not use the raw data that the computer gives you as is. Editing is always a requirement. Language requires flexibility to translate that the software could not have. Machines do not make intelligent decisions and people do not speak in the three word sentences that would be simple enough for software to translate. Language, being reflective of the speaker or writer, is often filled with metaphors, idioms, and slang. These language elements render text especially difficult to translate. For the above reasons, half of the members of this group believe the accuracy of translation software be only 50%.

The need to customize the dictionary was considered a disadvantage by two respondents because the process is tedious and time consuming. Two respondents indicated client had expectations of speedier translations because of the use of translation software. One felt clients familiar with the claims of translation software want to pay less for the services because they feel they can replace the translator with a good translation program. One respondent thought translation software was too expensive, and another felt the software required too much memory.

Translator's responses to the effectiveness of customizing a dictionary were similar. Most identified time needed to build customized dictionaries excessive. One translator indicated the ideal situation in which customization is indicated occurs when working with a client that has a long term project or projects and in that project the subject's and documents are similar. There was agreement from four of the participants that this is one of the few times that customizing a dictionary could be cost or time efficient. They stated, customization requires a huge human (time investment); with translation, time is always an issue. Another translator agreed in principle with customization for working on long-term projects or on projects that are similar. One translator, translates in several different language combinations, with ever-changing subject matter, does not believe customization to be useful. Another translator felt customization of the dictionary to be useful if used for word identification alone and not in conjunction with a machine translated document.

A TYPOLOGY OF TRANSLATION SOFTWARE USERS

Based on the literature reviewed and the respondents in two studies of the views of professional and volunteer translators, it is possible to propose a typology of potential TS users based on two dimensions. These dimensions are frequency/amount of use and need for accuracy. Figure 1 presents a graphic display of these dimensions. These dimensions summarize the issues that differentiate different concerns expressed by TS users. Several translators, including those who called the researchers following the first questionnaire, expressed serious reservations about the accuracy and quality of TS. It was also apparent from the demographics of those surveyed, that translators can vary

Figure 1: A Typology of TS Users.			
		Need for Accuracy	
		Low	High
Frequency/Amount of Use	**Low**	Casual User	Scientific/Research User
	High	"Gisting" User	Professional User

greatly in the amount of translation performed. Both of these dimensions can greatly affect the requirements a translation user would have for TS. For example, a need for extreme accuracy might require human translation, a rough draft using TS with extensive human polishing, or highly customized software and human polishing. In contrast, a lower need for accuracy may allow translation without human intervention, but users must accept that the probability of mistakes is not low.

Dividing each dimension into two segments, those with high and those with low needs, we can observe four distinct user types. At one extreme are the "casual users" who have a low need for accuracy and an infrequent use of TS. Examples of these users might be penpals from language classes in, for example, the US and Mexico. While learning the languages, the "good enough" translations may allow the correspondents to get to know each other and build camaraderie while continuing to study. Another example in the business world might be a manager following political developments in a particular part of the world that wants some sense of the thinking in a local newspaper. The translation must be good enough that basic ideas are conveyed, but not necessarily perfect in every nuance. Casual users are likely to be most concerned, in selecting TS products with low cost (since the cost isn't spread out among a high number of usages) and ease of use (since presumably there can be some deterioration in knowledge of how to perform the task between infrequent uses). Quality should be adequate and not grossly incorrect, but need not be perfect.

At the other extreme are the professional translators who have a need for highly accurate and high volume translation. People responsible for preparing user manuals in multiple languages is an example of this type of user. In this case, the translation must be of high enough quality that the user reading the text in his or her native language can follow instructions without making costly or time-consuming mistakes. Moreover the translation must be performed in a timely manner given the volume of material translated to be cost effective. Considering the present level of TS, a strategy for these users will probably include both a highly customized TS package and dictionary and human polishing. The key question in this environment is whether, for the particular organization, translators are effectively supported by the TS such that their work can be done more efficiently without loss of quality. In selecting TS for this type of user, quality and the ability to improve quality is the key consideration.

Two additional user types are the "scientific/research" users with a low volume of material that must be of the highest quality and the "gisting" user who scans a high volume of material but does not need high quality, except perhaps for a few selected extracts. In the former case, it is not clear that TS is of much value currently. Given the need for high quality, human intervention is still probably required. The low volume would in many cases render the costs of TS with high enough quality to be prohibitive. The later case may be where TS is most effective. A "gisting" user may be scanning a wide array of documents from another language looking for critical segments. Such a user might be scanning patents looking for those pertaining to a single technology or scanning an annotated bibliography looking for entries on a particular subject. Because the activity is high volume, the cost of the TS can be spread across a great deal of usage. Since the need for extreme accuracy is low, this is the case where human intervention is least necessary.

CONCLUSION

There is still much to learn about the relationship between language and the cultural experience of its speakers (and readers and writers). To the extent that people of different languages possess unique cultural experiences, there may always be a gap when concepts are translated from one language to another. Between "perfect translation" and "first draft quality' translation is a gap that promises to be increasingly narrowed as translation software is localized for particular purposes (following the Berlitz model) and as dictionaries of idioms and figures of speech are expanded.

The number of potential TS users is great. Overall use of Internet continues to increase internationally and with it the potential for TS to provide increasing access to larger numbers of people continues to grow. This study has shown that for some purposes translation software can provide "good enough" translation for informal transactions. This occurs when negative consequences resulting from misinterpretation are not highly likely. Additionally, there was value in having "first draft" quality translation for increasing the efficiency of some professional translators – particularly where the text to be translated is already in electronic format.

Four related research areas are important for continuing to narrow the gap. First, techniques such as the use of neural networks for assessing the probability that particular words and meaning are intended must continue to be expanded, tested, and adopted where helpful. Second, for the various kinds of potential users, sources of incremental benefit need to be identified and targeted for additional programming. This includes development of programs for translation between a greater array of languages (e.g. Arabic to Spanish; Mandarin to Norwegian). Third, for those seeking to obtain translation software, what are the appropriate criteria and procedures for selecting the technology that will give them the best match?

Finally, best practices for getting the most value from existing software as it evolves need to be promulgated. In many instances, users can already enhance the performance of translation software. Users can avoid nonstandard grammar and ambiguous constructions. Prior to initiating the translation process, documents can be pre-edited to facilitate good translation. Translation professionals currently believe that dictionary customization is time consuming, thereby, the value is increased when used on long term or extremely large projects. Additionally, user expectations need to be managed such that draft quality translation is valued for what it is rather than compared to the more expensive and time-consuming professional human translation. It should be noted that human translations is also not perfect – the best literature is often translated by multiple translators who bring different values, linguistic nuances, and fresh vision to the work.

This study is based on a small sample of translators and interpreters as well as a broad examination of current literature. Although the questionnaire is drawn from the validated instrument proposed by Moore and Benbasat (1991), most questions were reworded and several new areas of questioning were added. The sample size was insufficient for rigorous testing of the survey instrument, but the number of non-respondents and qualitative examination of comments by respondents indicated that the instrument as applied to this particular technology may not retain the characteristics observed by the instrument developers. Generalizations from this data should be made with caution. The intent is to bring an important and growing area of global enterprise software to the attention of the research community, rather than test an existing theory.

Human languages are living entities in the sense that they continue to grow and evolve. It is not clear that with any amount of refinement and increased computing power TS will ever provide flawless translation. For literary purposes, it is not even clear if there is such an entity as "perfect translation". However, continued refinement of TS offers the potential of providing increasingly valuable, if imperfect, tools for aiding varied user groups.

REFERENCES

Finnie, S. "Sites That Speak Your Language," Personal Computer/Computing 10(10) October 1997, p. 170.

Hobby, J. "Mind Your Language," Computer Weekly, February 13, 1997, 54-55.

Kwon, R. "It's a Small World After All," Personal Computer Magazine, 16(17), October 1997, 40.

Moore, G.C. and Benbasat, I. "Development of an Instrument to Measure Perceptions of Adopting an Information Technology Innovation," *Information Systems Research*, 2(3), 1991,192-222.

Mullich, J. "In Translation," *PC Week*, 4(14), April 7, 1997, p. A3 (2).

Poliworld, http://www.ghgcorp.com/poliworld/index, accessed 9/14/98.

Prescott, M.B. and Conger, S.A. "Information Technology Innovations: A Classification by IT Locus of Impact and Research Approach," *DATA BASE*, 26, 2 & 3, May/August, 1995, 20-41.

Rogers, E.M. and Shoemaker, F.F. *Communications of Innovations: A Cross-Cultural Approach*, Free Press, New York, 1971.

Transparent Language Inc., http://www.transparent.com, accessed 9/14/98. Note this address leads to homepage which leads to multiple software translation products and descriptions of each.

Populating a Data Warehouse with Mobile Agents

R.Dandu
Department of Computer Science, Iowa State University, Ames, IA 50011

L. Miller
Department of Computer Science, Iowa State University, Ames, IA 50011
lmiller@cs.iastate.edu

S. Nilakanta
Department of Logistics, Operations and MIS, College of Business, Iowa State University, Ames, IA 50011
nilakant@iastate.edu

V. Honavar
Department of Computer Science, Iowa State University, Ames, Iowa 50011
honavar@cs.iastate.edu

ABSTRACT

Data warehouses have become important decision-making tools for many organizations facing ever-growing amounts of data. The data warehouse approach typically builds a large archival data collection separate from the operational databases. Modeling and populating the data warehouse represent critical problems in the development of a successful warehouse environment.

Since the operational data sources are generally geographically distributed, populating the warehouse tables requires techniques that are capable of operating over network boundaries. In the present work we present a warehouse population strategy based on views that makes use of mobile software agents to retrieve data from the distributed data sources. A user interface is used to model the data warehouse table and launch the set of agents needed to retrieve the necessary data. We look at the model of our system and briefly look at our implementation.

Keywords: data warehouse, mobile agents

INTRODUCTION

Today's computing environment is characterized by increasing heterogeneity, distribution and cooperation. These characteristics increase the complexity of systems that require integration and inter-operation of heterogeneous and distributed hardware and software systems. The integration of these systems is of critical importance, since many organizations possess multiple databases, which have been designed for independent use.

The technology available today has allowed users to design complex applications that were not plausible just a few years ago. For example, the data warehouse has given corporations the ability to bring data from a variety of data sources together for analysis and report generation. The data warehouse environment has delivered many of the features promised by the research on decision support systems.

Formally, a data warehouse is a repository of integrated information for querying and analysis. As relevant information is made available, the information is extracted from its source, translated if necessary and integrated with the existing data in the data warehouse. At the warehouse, queries can be answered and analysis can be performed quickly and efficiently since the information is directly available with any semantic differences already resolved.

Creating a data warehouse design and populating the resulting data warehouse tables represent two of the interesting issues where currently available commercial tools are still inadequate. We looked at the first issue in [10], where we introduced a CASE tool for generating queries needed to define data warehouse tables. In the present work we look at the second issue. Our approach is based on using mobile agents to take data from a set of independent, geographically distributed relational database systems and add it to a data warehouse table.

In the next section we take a brief look at the mobile agent paradigm. Section 3 looks at the overall model and Section 4 is concerned with our prototype to test the feasibility of our approach. Conclusions and future considerations are given in Section 5.

MOBILE AGENT BASED COMPUTING PARADIGM

A mobile agent is a named program, which can migrate from one machine to another in a heterogeneous network for remote execution [5]. The main features of a mobile agent are autonomy and mobility. Mobile agents are autonomous as they decide when they want to migrate and where. Perhaps, scripts dispatched to a remote language interpreter provide the simplest form of mobile agents. A remote execution mechanism permits an application to dispatch and sequentially execute a script to a remote interpreter. Such scripted agents were popularized by Telescript [4], a language to script network agents. Development of mobile agent infrastructures has been an active area of research in recent years [3,5,6,9,11,13,15,16].

The mobile agent model has significant advantages over the traditional client/server model in some applications. For example, in the traditional Client/Server paradigm, functionality is associated with servers rigidly at their design time. A client can only invoke a fixed set of predefined services exported by each rigid server. These services remain constant until interfaces are redesigned, and the server is compiled, installed and instantiated anew.

The client and the server communicate with each other with a predefined communication protocol. The client sends a request to the server and a response will be sent back from the server to the client. In order to finish one task, the client and server may have to make many interactions. This may have poor performance and low efficiency in some situations, especially if the network has low bandwidth, long latency, or limited availability

We can view the mobile agent as an extension of traditional client/server model. Since the mobile agent model is bi-directional, this new peer to peer model can replace the traditional client/server model. Hence, on one hand, a client can send a mobile agent to the server and enhance the server functionality. On the other hand, the server can send a mobile agent to client to provide some services. It has much more flexibility than the two-tier client/server model. Another advantage of mobile agent based computing is that two mobile agents can communicate with each other and gain knowledge from their past computations.

In certain situations, the traditional client/server model may be better. If the interaction between the client and server for a particular service is very minimal and the code for the service is very large, it does not make sense to transfer the whole computation to the remote site every time the client wants this service. Ideally, we would want these two paradigms to co-exist.

Agent

ObjectSpace's Voyager [11] has been designed to help developers produce high impact distributed systems quickly. Voyager is 100% Java [8] and designed to use the Java language object model. Voyager allows us to use regular message syntax to construct remote objects, send them messages and move them between programs. The Voyager Object Request Broker (ORB) provides services for mobile objects and autonomous agents. It also provides services for persistence, scaleable group communication, and basic directory services.

Object Request Brokers like CORBA [1], DCOM [2] and RMI [12] support fundamental distributed computing. They allow developers to create remote objects and send them messages as if they were local. They often include features such as distributed garbage collection, different messaging modes, and a naming service. However, none of them support object mobility or mobile, autonomous agents.

Agent platforms like Odyssey [3] and Aglets [16] allow developers to create an agent, program it with a set of tasks, and launch it into a network to fulfill its mission. However, they have minimal support for basic distributed computing and treat agents differently than simple objects. Aglets use sockets and Odyssey uses RMI to move agents between machines. But, none of these platforms allow sending a regular Java message to a stationary or moving agent. As a result, it is very difficult for objects to communicate with an agent after the agent has been launched and for agents to communicate directly with other agents.

The unique feature of the Voyager environment is that it is the first platform to seamlessly integrate fundamental distributed computing with agent technology. Voyager supports both mobile objects and autonomous agents. In Voyager's point of view an agent is a special kind of object that can move independently, can continue to execute as it moves, and otherwise behaves like any other object. Voyager enables objects and other agents to send standard Java messages to an agent even as the agent is moving. In addition, Voyager allows us to remotely enable any Java class, even a third party library class, without modifying the class source in any way.

MOBILE AGENT MODEL

Our model consists of a set of computers $M = \{m_0, m_1, m_2, ..., m_n\}$, where m_0 is the machine that supports the data warehouse and $m_1, m_2, ..., m_n$ are the machines that support the data sources, $d_1, d_2, ..., d_n$, respectively. We model each computer, as supporting exactly one data source, but that is not critical to our approach. Each computer in M runs a compatible agent infrastructure (A). Today that means that each computer supports the same infrastructure (e.g., Voyager), but as vendors begin to support the evolving standards for agent infrastructures this will become more flexible. Figure 1 shows an instance where n is three.

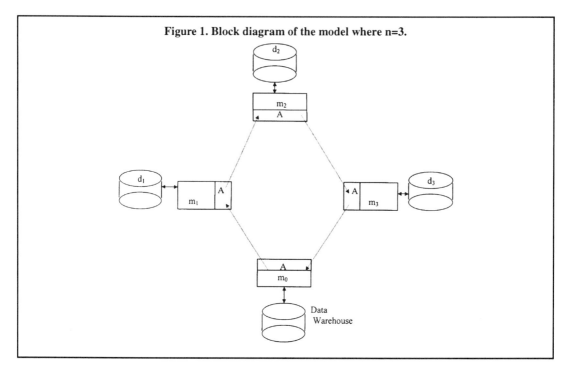

Figure 1. Block diagram of the model where n=3.

The model assumes the existence of a software module running on the machine m_0 designed to define the table (cube) in the data warehouse and launch the mobile agents used to contact the data sources and populate the warehouse tables. There are several possibilities for this software and we will look at a user interface in the next section that will perform both of the required actions. From the model point of view, all that is required is that the software provides sufficient information to define the table and the queries that can be posed to the individual data sources.

There is no restriction on the number of mobile agents launched, nor the number of data sources that an individual agent visits before returning to the launch site. The nature of what is allowed is really controlled by the type of data warehouse, the type of data sources allowed and the type of operations allowed. The latter issue is basically an issue of how complex the agents and the user interface is. For example, if a join is required before the data is placed in the warehouse, the model assumes that this will be accomplished by either the agent collecting the data or by the user interface when the agents return the data.

When unrestricted data sources are used, it is necessary to make the agent software equal to the task of brokering the semantic differences. This can be done either by tuning the agents to the individual data sources (e.g., views [18,19,20]) or by making the agents intelligent enough to understand the semantics of a variety of data sources (e.g., mediators [17]).

In the next section we look at our prototype to test the feasibility of the model. The prototype makes use of the Voyager agent infrastructure; relational databases as data sources and an object oriented data warehouse.

PROTOTYPE

This section looks at the feasibility of the model described in Section 3 by describing a prototype of the model implemented using relational databases as the data sources. We briefly look at the critical pieces of the prototype.

Agent Implementation

The agents in our prototype make use of JDBC (Java DataBase Connectivity) to make the connection with the individual databases [14]. While this is somewhat of an overkill (since JDBC would allow us to forego using agents at all), we made use of JDBC simply because it is an easy way to connect the software of a mobile agent to the local data source. Meanwhile, the mobile agent environment will be critical when we upgrade our prototype to use more than relational data sources. We will provide some additional information on our plans in the section on future considerations.

The JDBC API provides Java programmers with a uniform interface to a wide range of relational databases, and provides a common base on which higher level tools and interfaces can be built. JDBC is now a standard part of Java and is included in JDK 1.1. Leading database, connectivity, and tools vendors have already endorsed the JDBC

API and are developing products using JDBC. Three main goals of JDBC are
• JDBC should be an SQL-level API.
• JDBC should capitalize on the experience of existing database APIs.
• JDBC should be simple.

JDBC accomplishes its goals through a set of Java interfaces, each implemented differently by individual vendors. The set of classes that implement the JDBC interfaces for a particular database engine is called a JDBC driver.

The following steps show the basic aspects of using JDBC
1. Load the Driver implementation:
   The following function call can be used to load the JDBS driver.
   Class.forName("DriverImplementationClass");

2. Connect to the database:
   The connection can be done as follows.
   Connection con = DriverManager.getConnection(url, uid, passwd)
   where url is composed of hostname:port/subname
   eg: url = jdbc:msql://dazzler.cs.iastate.edu:1144/salaryDb
   uid = username, eg: "ravik"
   passwd= password needed to access the database, eg:""

3. Do the query on the database
   eg: ResultSet result = select.executeQuery("SELECT name FROM
   salary WHERE salary > 50000");

In a Java database applet/application, the only driver specific information JDBC requires is the database URL. Using the database URL, a user name, and password, the application will first request a java.sql.Connection implementation form the DriverManager. The DriverManager in turn will search through all of the known java.sql.Driver implementations for one that will connect with the URL you provided. If it exhausts all of the implementations without finding a match, it throws an exception back to the application.

A mobile agent class called *queryAgent* is the main class in our prototype. The *queryAgent* receives the query from the user interface. It goes to the machines listed in the registry that the user interface assigns, accesses the information from that particular database and finally returns to the machine where it started. The class *launch* which started the *queryAgent* receives the information from the *queryAgent* and displays the results on the screen. A sample itinerary is shown in Figure 2.

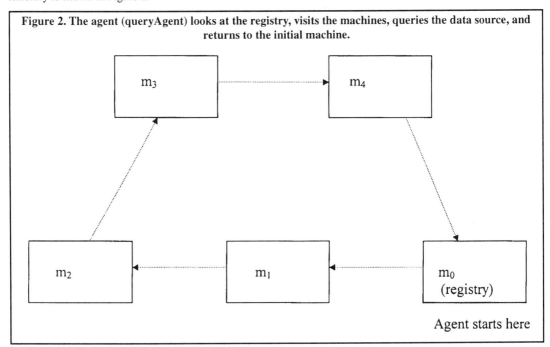

Figure 2. The agent (queryAgent) looks at the registry, visits the machines, queries the data source, and returns to the initial machine.

The launch class initializes the itinerary of the mobile agent. It loads all the database locations into the itinerary of the mobile agent from the registry. Once the initializing is done, the mobile agent is sent to the first location using the function: *moveTo(destination, function_name())};* This function moves the mobile agent to the destination and executes the function *function_name* when it reaches the *destination.* Then the user interface waits for the mobile agent to finish its work and return to the starting machine. This is done periodically by checking whether the mobile agent is parked in the initial machine. Once the *queryAgent* returns after finishing querying, the *launch* class retrieves all the information from the agent and places it in the data warehouse.

The query agent goes to a machine in its itinerary. At each machine:
• It loads the JDBC driver using
  Class.forName("com.imaginary.sql.msql.MsqlDriver");
• Connects to the database using the command
  Connection con=DriverManager.getConnection(url,uid,passwd);
  where, url = the location of the Driver,"jdbc:msql://dazzler.cs.iastate.edu:1144/dazzlerDb";
  uid = "ravik"
  passwd= ""
• After connecting it queries the database using the command
  Statement select = con.createStatement();
  ResultSet result = select.executeQuery("SELECT name FROM salary
  WHERE salary$>$50000");
the ResultSet result will have the people whose salary is above 50,000.
• Each of the results is added to a global Vector. Once all the sites have been visited this vector contains all the results. The agents goes back to the initial machine and parks. The user interface will get the results from the agent and places the results in the data warehouse.

User Interface

In the initial version of the prototype our focus has been on the agent environment. As a result, we have used a barebones approach to the user interface. However, we have a clear vision of what the user interface needs to look like and we briefly discuss that in the remainder of this subsection.

Our work on a CASE tool for modeling data warehouses [10] is the obvious starting point for the user interface/launch program. Our modeling CASE tool allows a user to model a warehouse table from the meta data on the data in the data sources. The CASE tool makes it possible for a user to click on the attributes required in the warehouse table and add any conditions that the user wishes to impose on the data.

Given the attribute list for the warehouse table, the modeling tool generates a correct (lossless) query over the relational databases that makeup the data sources. We have shown that a simple technique can be used to partition the generated query into the queries required for each individual data source. From the population agent's point of view, each resulting partition of the warehouse query would be the query that an agent would carry to the computer that supports the data source over which the query can be executed. The agents can then bring the data back to the user interface to allow the necessary joins to be formed.

Expansion of our current version of the CASE tool to incorporate the necessary features of the user interface is a rather straightforward process. The CASE tool has to be expanded to make use of the agent infrastructure and it will be necessary to incorporate a local database to allow the necessary operations, like join, to be executed against the incoming data from the partitions of the warehouse query. Neither feature is especially difficult to add to the current version of the software nor we expect to add it when we upgrade to the next version of the prototype.

Data Sources

The data sources used where individual relational databases stored on individual computers. We made use of Mini SQL [7] and ACCESS databases in our tests. The only issue in expanding the prototype to include other relational database systems would be the availability of the database software and the appropriate JDBC driver.

The issue of expanding to support non-relational database systems will be briefly discussed in the comments on future considerations.

Data Warehouse

The only critical feature of the warehouse is that it allows "batch" access for defining tables and adding data to any existing table definition.

In the prototype we made use of an object-oriented data warehouse designed and implemented at Iowa State University in the Department of Computer Science. The warehouse was built on the POET object-oriented database system. It has been designed to allow both interactive and "batch" access to the full range of warehouse capabilities (e.g., the data analysis tools, definition of materialized views (classes) as well as the basic data manipulation features. In the current prototype no real advantage was taken off of the fact that the data warehouse supports objects. Rather the issue was simply one of price – we already had our object-oriented warehouse in place so we did not need to obtain additional software.

In the next section we provide some conclusions and some future considerations.

CONCLUSIONS AND FUTURE CONSIDERATIONS

A mobile agent environment to define data warehouse tables and populate the resulting tables has been designed and a prototype has been implemented to test the feasibility. The prototype is based on using relational databases as the data sources.

The main future extension of our prototype will be to allow more than relational databases to serve as data sources. We are currently working on the use of object views [18,19,20] as the basis of the agent software. The result will be that the object-oriented views will allow an information manager to tune the agents to a wide variety of different data source semantics. We are currently implementing a system that will allow our CASE tool to make use of the object-oriented views to incorporate object-oriented databases and legacy information systems in addition to the relational database systems now being supported.

ACKNOWLEDGEMENT

The authors would like to thank Ji Hoon Yang for his help with the Voyager software and Darren Manning for installing **Voyager** on the department machines.

REFERENCES

[1] Common Object Request Broker Architecture Organization, CORBA homepage, March 23, 1997. http://www.corba.org/.
[2] Distributed Component Object Model home, Microsoft Inc. home page, September 21, 1997, http://www.microsoft.com/com/dcom.htm.
[3] General Magic Inc., Odyssey homepage, May 26 1997, http://www.genmagic.com/agents/index.html
[4] General Magic Inc., Telescript Technology Whitepapers, April 5, 1997, http://www.genmagic.com/Telescript/Whitepapers/index.html
[5] Gray R.S., Agent Tcl : A flexible and secure mobile-agent system, Fourth Annual TCL/TK workshop (TCL 96), January 8, 1996, http://www.cs.dartmouth.edu/agent/papers/index.html
[6] Harrison, C.G., D.M. Chess and A. Kershenbaum. 1995. Mobile Agents: Are They a Good Idea?, Research Report. T.J. Watson Research Center, IBM.
[7] Hughes Technologies. 1996. Mini SQL. Http://www.hughes.com.au
[8] Javasoft Inc., Javasoft homepage, October 12, 1997, http://www.javasoft.com/.
[9] Li W. and D.G. Messerschmitt. 1996. Java-to-Go Project, http://ptolemy.eecs.berkeley.edu /dgm/javatools/java-to-go/.
[10] Miller, L.L. and Sree Nilakanta. 1998. Data warehouse modeler:A case tool for warehouse design. Hawaiian International Conference on Systems Science. Pages 42-48.
[11] Object Space Inc., Voyager Project homepage, June 1, 1997, http://www.objectspace.com/Voyager/.
[12] Remote Method Invocation product specification, Javasoft homepage, October 12, 1997, http://www.javasoft.com/products/jdk/1.1/docs/guide/rmi/spec.
[13] Rothermel, et al. The MOLE Project. http://www.informatik.uni-stuttgart.de/ipvr/vs/projekte/mole.html.
[14] Taylor, Art. 1997. JDBC-Developer's Resource. Informix Press. Menlo Park, CA.
[15] White, J.E. 1997. Mobile Agents. In: Bradshaw, J.M. (ed). Software Agents, Cambridge, MA, MIT Press.
[16] Tokyo Research Lab, IBM, Aglet Workbench homepage, January 16, 1997, http://www.trl.ibm.co.jp/index.html.
[17] Wiederhold, G., and M. Genesereth. 1997. The conceptual basis for mediation services. IEEE Expert. Vol. 12. No. 5. Pages 38-47.
[18] Yen, C.H., L.L. Miller, A. Sirjani and J. Tenner. 1998. Extending the object-relational interface to support an extensible view system for multidatabase integration and interoperation. International Journal of Computer Systems Science and Engineering. To appear.
[19] Yen, C.H. and L.L. Miller. 1995. An extensible view system for multidatabase integration and interoperation. Integrated Computer-Aided Engineering. Vol. 2. No. 2. Pages 97-123.
[20] Yen, C.H., L.L. Miller and S.H. Pakzad. 1994. The design and implementation of the zeus view system. Hawaiian International Conference on Systems Science. Pages 206-215.

A Conflict-Free Protocol for Queries in Decision Support Systems

Chanjung Park
Multimedia Research Lab., Korea Telecom, 17 Woomyon-dong, Seocho-gu, Seoul, Korea
Phone:+82-2-526-6580, Fax:+82-2-526-5909, park@kt.co.kr

Seog Park
Dept. of Computer Science, Sogang University, 1 Sinsu-dong, Mapo-gu, Seoul, Korea
Phone:+82-2-705-8487, Fax:+82-2-704-8273, spark@dblab.sogang.ac.kr

ABSTRACT

Traditional concurrency control protocols for legacy operational systems resolve the data conflicts between transactions by using locks or timestamps. As a result, one of the transactions in a conflicting mode should be blocked to resolve the conflict between transactions. Queries are not the exceptions. In a query-intensive system such as a decision support system, if queries can execute their read operations without being interfered by update transactions, the system can achieve a higher performance than the existing transaction processing systems.

In this paper, we propose a new concurrency control protocol that eliminates the conflicts between queries and update transactions by maintaining multiple versions and using a new method, called mark. The mark scheme allows that each transaction has its own version selection point. In the proposed protocol, new version selection rules and an efficient version maintenance scheme are also presented. The proposed protocol is based on locking scheme and it provides a method to resolve deadlocks caused by locks.

Keywords: Concurrency Control, Transaction Management, Query Processing, Data Warehouse, Decision Support System

INTRODUCTION

In a traditional database system, multiple users share a database and the database system processes the transactions requested by the users concurrently. Thus, the database system must guarantee the correct executions of transactions. *Serializability* is the definition of correctness for concurrency control in a database system [2]. There are many research works on the concurrency control protocols that guarantee the serializable executions of transactions [5] [6] [7].

In order for a database system to ensure serializability, when a transaction manager schedules transactions, it uses some mechanisms such as locks or timestamps. These mechanisms cause either the blockings or the abortions of some transactions. Some of the commercial protocols maintain multiple versions for each data item in order to reduce the contentions when several transactions access the same data [3]. Hence, concurrency control protocols based on multiversions provide a higher level of concurrency than those, which are based on a single version.

Conventionally, transactions are categorized into two types: *(i) queries (or read-only transactions)* and *(ii) update transactions*. However, if there is no additional consideration, queries are blocked by update transactions, and vice versa even though a transaction processing system maintains multiversions. Especially, in a query-intensive environment such as a decision support system, if the conflicts between queries and update transactions can be eliminated, we can achieve a good performance of the system [10].

Many research works have provided the various efficient algorithms to reduce the conflicts between queries and update transactions [3] [4] [7] [9]. However, in [3], weaker levels of consistencies have been proposed. Thus, serializability cannot be guaranteed. [9] has satisfied serializability. However, in this algorithm, a parameter, namely a version period, is used. Therefore, if a wrong version period is used, transactions may read very old versions of data items. And the algorithm has not given a method to reduce the conflicts between update and update transactions.

In this paper, we propose a new concurrency control protocol based on locking which eliminates blockings between queries and update transactions completely. In addition, the proposed protocol reduces the conflicts between update and update transactions with a new method, called *mark*. In the mark scheme, both the read set and the write set of a transaction are used. In the existing protocols, all the transactions have the same version selection point such as the current time or the start time of the transactions. However, in the proposed protocol, each transaction has its own version selection point.

We also propose new version selection rules and an efficient version management scheme. Since our protocol is based on locking, deadlocks can occur. In this paper, we propose a new deadlock handling method. Our protocol ensures serializability and provides newer versions than [9].

The remainder of this paper is organized as follows. In Section 2, we present the correctness criteria for multiversion concurrency control protocols and the *Multiversion Two Phase Locking (MV2PL)* protocol. In Section 3, we define some terminologies that are used in the proposed protocol. We present a new concurrency control protocol based on locking for database systems. We then provide some examples to illustrate how transactions are scheduled by our protocol and the performance issues of our protocol are presented. After giving the correctness proof of the proposed serializability in Section 4, we conclude the paper in Section 5.

BACKGROUND

In this section, we first present the correctness criteria for multiversion concurrency control protocols. And then, we summarize the rules of MV2PL protocols and the method proposed in [9] as the related works of our protocol.

Correctness Criteria

The objectives of concurrency control in a database system are the avoidance of inconsistent retrievals and the preservation of the correct state of a database. In this section, we introduce some definitions presented in [2]. They are the correctness criteria for multiversion concurrency control.

Definition 1 A multiversion (MV) history H that indicates the order in which the operations of transactions are executed relative to others is *serial* if for any two transactions T_i and T_j that appear in H, either all of T_i's operations precede all of T_j's, or vice versa [2].

Definition 2 A serial MV history H is *1-serial* (or *one-copy serial*) if for all i, j, and some data item x, if T_i reads the value of x created by T_j, then $i = j$, or T_j is the last transaction preceding T_i that writes into any version of x [2].

According to Definition 2, in a 1-serial MV history, transactions always read the most recent versions. It is easy to see that the serial execution of transactions is correct. However, in order to maximize the performance of a database system, several transactions may be executed in an interleaved manner. Thus, correctness criteria for multiversion concurrency control should be defined.

Definition 3 An MV history H is *one-copy serializable* (or *1SR*) if its committed projection, $C(H)$, is equivalent to a 1-serial MV history, where $C(H)$ is the history obtained from H by deleting all operations that do not belong to committed transactions in H [2].

Related Works

In the *Two Phase Locking (2PL)* protocol [2], a write lock on a data item x prevents other transactions from obtaining read or write locks on x, to control the concurrent execution of transactions. The *Two Version Two Phase Locking (2V2PL)* protocol [2] relaxes these rules so that conflicts between read and write locks are eliminated. However, conflicts among write locks remain. Table 1 (a) shows the compatibility matrix for 2V2PL.

Table 1. Compatibility Matrices							
Holder Requester	Read	Write	Certify	Holder Requester	Read	Write	Certify
Read	Y	Y	N	Read	Y	Y	N
Write	Y	N	N	Write	Y	Y	Y
Certify	N	N	N	Certify	N	Y	N
(a) 2V2PL				(b) MV2PL			

On the other hand, the MV2PL protocol [1] removes all conflicts between read and write locks. Hence, each data item may have many versions that are written by active transactions, called uncertified versions. However, transactions can read only the most recently certified version in order to ensure serializability. Therefore, MV2PL has a certify lock which is used to delay the commitment of a transaction until there is no active reader of data items that are about to be overwritten. Certify locks conflict with read locks as well as with other certify locks. Table 1 (b) shows the compatibility matrix for MV2PL.

Let us consider the following history in Figure 1. In the history H_1, $r_i[x_j]$ indicates that T_i reads x certified by T_j, while $w_i[x_i]$ indicates that T_i writes x. Also, c_i is the certifying operation of T_i. According to the rules of MV2PL, when T_2 certifies its operation at time 3, it is blocked by T_1 because T_1 holds a read lock on x. However, T_2 can certify at time 3 without violating serializability.

Time Transaction	1	2	3	4	5	6
T_1	$r_1[x_0]$			$r_1[y_0]$	c_1	
T_2		$w_2[x_2]$	c_2 (blocked)	blocked	blocked	c_2

Figure 1. *Motivated Example History H_1*

On the other hand, [9] has proposed a transient versioning algorithm for queries. In this algorithm, queries can access old versions of data items without being locked and this algorithm offers a parameter, called a version period. When a transaction starts its execution, a specific version period is assigned to the transaction. While queries select versions at its version period, update transactions select versions on the basis of the current time. Therefore, if the length of a version period is long, transactions read very old versions. Otherwise, the number of versions maintained by a data manager increase. In the following section, we present a new protocol that eliminates the conflicts between queries and update transactions.

PROTOCOL

In this section, we define a new scheme, called *mark*, and a version selection point of each transaction T. And then, we present the rules and features of our protocol. After a data structure for keeping information of a version is defined and an efficient version maintenance scheme is presented, some examples to illustrate the behavior of the protocol are provided.

Terminology

We assume that each transaction T declares a read set, denoted by $R(T)$, which contains the data items read by T and a write set, denoted by $W(T)$, which contains the data items written by T. $R(T)$ and $W(T)$ are declared when T starts its execution.

Definition 4 While a transaction T holds a read lock on a data item x, if a certify lock on x requested by another transaction T' is permitted or while T' holds a certify lock on x, if a read lock on x requested by T is allowed, then we say T is *marked* by T'. And x is also marked.

According to the multiversion locking mechanisms, if a transaction holds a read lock on some data item x, other transactions cannot obtain certify locks on x, and vice versa. However, in our protocol, we eliminate the conflicts between read and certify operations.

Definition 5 For each transaction T, $VSP(T)$ is defined as the version selection point of T. Initially, $VSP(T)$ is set to $+\bullet$. When T is marked for the first time, $VSP(T)$ is changed to a positive integer.

For each transaction T, $VSP(T)$ has the following characteristics.

VSP_1 When T requests a read lock on x, if T is marked for the first time by other active transaction T' (i.e., T' holds a certify lock on x), then $VSP(T)$ is set to the time when T requests the read lock.

VSP_2 When T requests a certify lock on x, if T's which hold read locks on x are marked by T for the first time, then $VSP(T')$s are set the time when T requests the certify lock.

VSP_3 T can be marked several times. However, $VSP(T)$ is modified only when T is marked for the first time.

VSP_4 If T is not marked, then when T finishes its certify operations, $VSP(T)$ is set to its certification time.

In each of the following histories, we assume that the execution time of the first operation is set to 1, the execution time of the second operation is set to 2, and so on.

$$H_2 = \underline{r_1[x_0]}\ r_2[y_0]\ \underline{w_2[x_2]}\ c_2\ r_1[y_0]\ c_1$$

Let us consider the above MV history H_2. T_1 is marked by T_2 when T_2 certifies its operations. Thus, at time 4 (i.e., the execution time of c_2), $VSP(T_1) = 4$ and $VSP(T_2) = +\bullet$. After T_2 finishes its certification operation, $VSP(T_2)$ is set to the certification time, $4 + e$. In other words, $VSP(T)$ is treated as a virtual certification time of T.

Rules

We assume that a transaction T declares a read set $R(T)$ and a write set $W(T)$. In this section, before we present our protocol, we examine the cases that classified by the read sets and the write sets of any active two transactions.

(1) $R(T_i) \cap R(T_j) \neq \emptyset$

Since there exists no conflict between a read and a read operation, T_i and T_j do not mark with each other. Hence, they should read data items that are certified before their version selection points.

(2) $R(T_i) \cap W(T_j) \neq \emptyset$ (or $W(T_i) \cap R(T_j) \neq \emptyset$)

We consider the following history H_3. In this case, since T_i has a read operation on x, T_i can be marked by T_j.

However, if T_i certifies before T_j, then T_i is not marked. Therefore, there is no problem. However, if T_j certifies before T_i, then T_i is marked by T_j on a data item x. As a result, $VSP(T_i)$ is set to 5 (i.e., the certifying time of T_j). If T_i reads the data versions which are created before $VSP(T_i)$, then they can execute concurrently without violating serializability.

$$H_3 = r_i[x_0]\ w_j[x_j]\ w_i[z_i]\ w_j[y_j]\ c_j\ c_i$$

(3) $W(T_i) \cap W(T_j) \neq \varnothing$

In a protocol which maintains multiple versions, there exist conflicts neither between write and write operations nor between write and certify operations. Therefore, T_i and T_j do not mark with each other.

(4) $R(T_i) \cap R(T_j) \neq \varnothing$ and $R(T_i) \cap W(T_j) \neq \varnothing$

$$H_4 = r_i[x_0]\ w_k[x_k]\ c_k\ r_j[x_?]\ w_i[y_i]\ r_j[y_?]\ c_j\ c_i$$

$VSP(T)$ represents the virtual certification time of T. And the write operations after $VSP(T)$ cannot affect other transactions until its certification time. In an above history H_4, if T_j reads x_j and y_0 which is the earlier version of y_i, then serializability cannot be guaranteed. Thus, when a transaction T_j reads a data item x, a transaction manager checks if x is marked or not. If x is not marked, there is no problem. However, if x is marked, it checks whether there exist common data items which are both written by any transaction in MTL and read by T_j. If so, $VSP(T_j)$ is changed to $VSP(T')$, where T' is the transaction which is in MTL, is marked due to the data item, and has the smallest VSP. In H_4, T' is T_i.

(5) $R(T_i) \cap R(T_j) \neq \varnothing$ and $W(T_i) \cap W(T_j) \neq \varnothing$

This case is similar to the previous one. In the following history H_5, if T_i and T_j read the same version of x, then there is no problem. However, if not, there can exist a cycle caused by the third transaction T_k. In other words, if T_i is marked, then T_k's write operation on x should be hidden to T_j until T_i commits. Thus, the version read by T_j should be restricted by T_i. If T_i is not marked, $VSP(T_j)$ is not influenced by $VSP(T_i)$. Otherwise, $VSP(T_j)$ is set to $VSP(T_i)$. In general, $VSP(T_j)$ is set to $VSP(T')$, where T' is the transaction which is in MTL, is marked due to the data item, and has the smallest VSP.

$$H_5 = r_i[x_0]\ w_k[x_k]\ c_k\ r_j[x_?]\ w_j[y_j]\ w_i[y_i]\ c_i\ c_j$$

(6) $R(T_i) \cap W(T_j) \neq \varnothing$ and $W(T_i) \cap R(T_j) \neq \varnothing$

$$H_{6a} = w_i[y_i]\ r_j[y_0]\ w_i[x_i]\ c_j\ r_i[x_j]\ c_i \qquad \text{[no deadlock]}$$
$$H_{6b} = r_i[x_0]\ r_j[y_0]\ w_j[x_j]\ w_i[y_i]\ c_j\ (\text{abort } T_i) \qquad \text{[deadlock]}$$

In this case, T_i can mark T_j, and vice versa. If neither T_i is marked by T_j nor T_j is marked by T_i, then as shown in a history H_{6a}, there is no problem. In H_{6a}, T_i reads the version of x which is certified by T_j. However, if one of the transactions is marked, then due to their read sets and their write sets, one of them cannot continue executing its operations. In H_{6b}, since T_i holds a read lock on x and T_j holds a read lock on y, neither T_j can certify on x at time 5 nor T_i can certify on y at time 6. A deadlock occurs according to the rules of the MV2PL protocol. Even though they are scheduled by our protocol, serializability cannot be guaranteed because a cycle occurs. Therefore, at time 5, since T_j certifies its operations, T_i is aborted. The strategies for aborting one of the transactions are various.

(7) $R(T_i) \cap W(T_j) \neq \varnothing$ and $W(T_i) \cap W(T_j) \neq \varnothing$

In this case, if T_i is not marked by T_j, there is no problem. However, as shown in a history H_7, if T_i is marked by T_j at time 4, in order to guarantee serializability, we should devise an algorithm for resolving the conflict.

$$H_7 = r_i[x_0]\ w_j[x_j]\ w_j[y_j]\ c_j\ r_i[y_0]\ \underline{w_i[y_i]}\ (\text{ignored})\ c_i$$

We consider the following history H_8 in Figure 2. According to the MV2PL rules, at time 3, T_2 is blocked by T_1 until T_1 commits. On the other hand, with mark method, T_2 finishes its operations without blocking. Instead, because of the obsolete write operation of T_1, T_1 should be aborted to ensure serializability. However, the abortion of T_1 is unnecessary because there cannot exist a transaction that reads the version of x written by T_1 until T_1 certifies. Therefore, though the obsolete write operation of T_1 on x may be ignored, we do not lose serializability. It is very similar to the *Thomas Write Rules* [8].

Figure 2. Concept of Thomas Write Rules: An Example History H_8					
Time Transaction	1	2	3	4	5
T_1	$r_1[x_0]$			$w_1[x_1]$ *(ignored)*	c_1
T_2		$w_2[x_2]$	c_2		

In H_7, the write operations of the marked transaction, T_i, onto the data items that are written by both T_i and T_j may be ignored.

In the cases (8) ~ (11), two transactions T_i and T_j are update transactions because their write sets are not empty.

(8) $R(T_i) \cap R(T_j) \neq \varnothing$ and $R(T_i) \cap W(T_j) \neq \varnothing$ and $W(T_i) \cap W(T_j) \neq \varnothing$

T_i can be marked by T_j because $R(T_i) \cap W(T_j) \neq \varnothing$. And $VSP(T_i)$ is affected by $VSP(T_j)$ because $R(T_i) \cap R(T_j) \neq$

$\emptyset$ and $W(T_i) \cap W(T_j) \neq \emptyset$ (or $R(T_i) \cap R(T_j) \neq \emptyset$ and $R(T_i) \cap W(T_j) \neq \emptyset$). Like the previous case 7, T_i's write operations onto the data items written by both transactions are ignored to ensure serializability. As shown in a history H_9, T_i's write operation on x is ignored so that T_i precedes T_j in serialization order.

$$H_9 = r_i[x_0] \, r_i[y_k] \, r_j[y_k] \, w_j[x_j] \, w_i[y_j] \, c_j \, w_i[x_i] \text{ (ignored)} \, c_i$$

(9) $R(T_i) \cap R(T_j) \neq \emptyset$ and $R(T_i) \cap W(T_j) \neq \emptyset$ and $W(T_i) \cap R(T_j) \neq \emptyset$

Since $R(T_i) \cap R(T_j) \neq \emptyset$ and $R(T_i) \cap W(T_j) \neq \emptyset$ (or $W(T_i) \cap R(T_j) \neq \emptyset$), $VSP(T_j)$ is affected by $VSP(T_i)$ (or $VSP(T_i)$ is affected by $VSP(T_j)$). Like the above case 6, if T_i is marked by T_j, then one of the transactions should be aborted to resolve a deadlock. Otherwise, serializability cannot be guaranteed. Therefore, an earlier certified transaction continues its operation, while the other transaction should be aborted.

(10) $R(Ti) \cap W(Tj) \neq \emptyset$ and $W(Ti) \cap R(Tj) \neq \emptyset$ and $W(Ti) \cap W(Tj) \neq \emptyset$

In this case, since $R(T_i) \cap W(T_j) \neq \emptyset$ and $W(T_i) \cap R(T_j) \neq \emptyset$, a deadlock can occur. Therefore, the same operations which are described in case 6 and case 7 are performed.

(11) $R(T_i) \cap R(T_j) \neq \emptyset$ and $R(T_i) \cap (T_j) \neq \emptyset$ and $W(T_i) \cap R(T_j) \neq \emptyset$ and $W(T_i) \cap W(T_j) \neq \emptyset$

Since $R(T_i) \cap R(T_j) \neq \emptyset$ and $W(T_i) \cap W(T_j) \neq \emptyset$, $VSP(T_j)$ are influenced by $VSP(T_i)$ according to T_j's marking condition. Since $R(T_i) \cap W(T_j) \neq \emptyset$ and $W(T_i) \cap R(T_j) \neq \emptyset$, a deadlock can occur. The same operations described in case 9 are performed. In summary, the proposed protocol is described as follows:

M_1 When T starts, T declares its $R(T)$ and $W(T)$.

M_2 $VSP(T)$ is set to $+\bullet$ initially.

M_3 A marked transaction list, called MTL, is set to NULL.

M_4 There is no conflict between read and three operations, read, write, and certify. However, there exist conflicts between certify and certify operations.

M_5 When T starts, for a transaction T' in the MTL, a transaction manager checks if $R(T) \ll R(T') \, \pi \, \Delta$ and $W(T) \cap W(T') \neq \emptyset$ or $R(T) \cap R(T') \neq \emptyset$ and $R(T) \cap W(T') \neq \emptyset$. If so, $VSP(T)$ is set to the $VSP(T_s)$, where T_s has the smallest version selection point among the transactions in the MTL.

M_6 When T reads a data item x, a transaction manager checks if x is marked or not. If so, we define a transaction T' as the one that is in the MTL and has the smallest VSP. And it checks if there exists common data items between $R(T)$ (or $W(T)$) and the write set of the transaction T'. If so, $VSP(T)$ is set to $VSP(T')$. Otherwise, T selects the version of x which is the most recently certified before $VSP(T)$. If $VSP(T)$ is $+\bullet$, the $VSP(T)$ is interpreted as the current time.

M_7 The write operations of a transaction T are not deferred by other operations. A new version is written in the local space of T. After T certifies its write operations, the new versions written by T are opened to other transactions.

M_8 When T is marked by T', the followings are checked.

$M_{8.1}$ $R(T) \cap W(T') \neq \emptyset$ and $W(T) \cap R(T') \neq \emptyset$.

If the above condition is true, by Definition 4, T' requests a certify lock while T holds a read lock (or while T' holds a certify lock, T requests a read lock) on the same data item. Therefore, after T' certifies its operation, T is aborted to resolve a deadlock in addition to ensuring the serializable executions of transactions.

$M_{8.2}$ $R(T) \cap W(T') \neq \emptyset$ and $W(T) \cap W(T') \neq \emptyset$.

If the above condition is true, we ignore T's obsolete write operation on the data items which are also written by T' so that their execution result is the same as the one that T precedes T'.

M_9 When T executes its certify operations, if T is a marked transaction, then it is deleted from the MTL. If T is not marked, then $VSP(T)$ is set to its certification time.

Let us consider one example history in Figure 3. T_2 is marked by T_3 because of a data item x at time 6. $VSP(T_2)$ is set to 6. A MTL contains T_1. At time 14, T_2 is marked again because of T_6 on data items x and z. However, the $VSP(T_2)$ is not change by the property VSP_3. At time 14, T_5 is marked by T_6 because of x and z. Thus, the MTL is $\{ T_2, T_5 \}$. When T_1 reads a data item z, $R(T_1) \cap R(T_5) = \{ z \}$ and $R(T_1) \cap W(T_5) = \{ y, z \}$. Therefore, when T_1 reads z, T_1 does not read the version of z written by T_6. Instead, T_1 reads the previous version z_0, which certified before time 14. However, T_7 can read z_6.

Version Management

In this section, we propose an efficient mechanism to manage a version pool. Traditionally, concurrency control protocols based on multiversion locking use 2PL for write/write synchronization and version selection for read/write synchronization [2]. When a transaction chooses a version of a data item, the most recent certified version is commonly read. However, since there are marked transactions in our protocol, additional operations are required to maintain the versions of data items.

Figure 3. An Example History

Time Trans.	1	2	3	4	5	6	7	8	9	10
T_1									$r_1[y_4]$	...
T_2	$r_2[x_0]$				$r_2[y_4]$				$r_2[z_0]$	...
T_3		$w_3[x_1]$				c_3				...
T_4			$w_4[y_4]$	c_4						...
T_5							$r_5[z_0]$	$w_5[z_5]$		...
T_6										...
T_7										...

Time Trans.	11	12	13	14	15	16	17	18	19	20	21
...					$r_1[z_0]$					c_1	
...						c_2					
...											
...											
...	$r_5[x_3]$							$w_5[y_5]$	c_5		
...		$w_6[x_6]$	$w_6[z_6]$	c_6							
...							$r_7[z_6]$				c_7

Figure 4 shows the data structures for a version used in this protocol. *Value* is the field for storing a data value, *count* represents how many transactions read the version, and *timestamp* is the time when the version is certified. *Tlist* is the list for storing the transaction identifiers of the transactions that read the version. *Mark_flag* is the field for representing whether some transactions are marked due to the version or not. If *mark_flag* is 0, then there exists no transaction marked due to the version. Otherwise, *mark_flag* is 1. *Next_version_pointer* is the pointer that points to the next certified version of the data item.

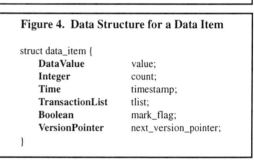

Figure 4. Data Structure for a Data Item

```
struct data_item {
    DataValue          value;
    Integer            count;
    Time               timestamp;
    TransactionList    tlist;
    Boolean            mark_flag;
    VersionPointer     next_version_pointer;
}
```

$$H_{10} = r_1[x_0]\ w_2[x_2]\ w_1[z_1]\ w_2[y_2]\ c_2\ c_1$$

For example, in an above history H_{10}, the versions of a data item x at time 5 are illustrated in Figure 5. At time 5, a transaction T_1 is inserted into MTL because T_1 holds a read lock on x. Thus, The mark_flag for x_0 is set to 1. The tlist field can be implemented by using either pointers or bit vectors. A data manager should keep the following rules:

1) When a transaction T requests a read lock on x, a data manager selects the version of x which has the biggest timestamp among data items whose timestamp values are less than $VSP(T)$. If T reads a version of x, namely x_i, the count of x_i is incremented by 1.

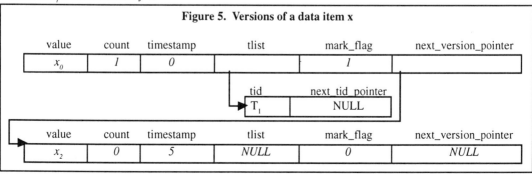

Figure 5. Versions of a data item x

2) T writes a version of each data item in its local space. Thus, after T certifies its write operations, other transactions can access the version T certifies.

3) When T requests a certify operation on x written by itself, the data manager checks if there exists the version whose count is zero. If there exists, that version is purged. Otherwise, a new version is appended to the version list of x. Initially, the count of a new version is set to zero.

4) When a transaction T commits, the count fields of data items read by T is decremented by 1.

Comparisons

We present several performance issues related to our protocol. And then, we compare our protocol with MV2PL and the algorithm proposed in [9].

First, our protocol eliminates the conflicts between queries and update transactions. That means compared with MV2PL, the opportunities of denials for lock requests are reduced. Hence, the blocking time of a transaction can be reduced. As a result, the proposed protocol provides a higher degree of concurrency than the existing protocols. In that aspect, our protocol is better than MV2PL.

Next, in MV2PL, deadlock problems are serious than in 2PL when there exist many transactions such that transactions in a conflict mode belong to the case (7) described in Section 3. For deadlock detection, undesirable repeats for acquiring locks may be performed. However, by using the read sets and the write sets of transactions, the proposed protocol can avoid wasting time. In addition, the method for resolving deadlocks is also provided in our protocol.

Figure 6. An Example History for a Comparison												
Time Trans.	1	2	3	4	5	6	7	8	9	10	11	12
T_1	$r_1[z_0]$		$r_1[x_0]$					$w_1[y_1]$			c_1	
T_2		$r_2[y_0]$					$r_2[z_0]$					c_2
T_3				$w_3[x_3]$	$w_3[z_3]$	c_3						
T_4										$r_4[x_3]$	c_4	

We compare our protocol with [9]. Let us examine the history shown in Figure 6. T_1 and T_3 are update transactions while T_2 and T_4 are queries. In MV2PL or [9], T_3 is blocked until T_1 commits. However, in our protocol, T_1 is marked by T_3 and T_3 can certify at time 7 without blocking. In other words, the conflict between update and update transactions is eliminated. The execution result of the above history is equivalent to the one that T_2, T_1, T_3, and T_4 are executed sequentially.

One more important advantage is that the proposed protocol provides newer active query T_1, T_4 has the same version period as T_1. Therefore, T_4 reads x_0 instead of x_4. On the other hand, our protocol provides a newer version to T_4 than [9].

Finally, in terms of the amount of storage for keeping multiple versions, we need to quantify through the simulation studies. In the near future, the performance results of our protocol can be given.

CORRECTNESS PROOFS

Theorem 1 *A multiversion schedule, H, is one-copy serializable (1SR) if and only if MVSG(H, <<) is acyclic [2].* ∎

Theorem 2 *Every history produced by our protocol is 1SR.*

Proof: Let $\{\ T_1, T_2, °, T_n\ \}$ be a set of transactions, and let H be a history produced by our protocol over $\{\ T_1, T_2, °, T_n\ \}$. Let cr_i represent the certification of T_i. Define a version order as follows: $x_i << x_j$ implies $cr_i < cr_j$. First, we examine the versions that a transaction T_i selects. If T_i is not marked, then the rules for selecting versions are the same as those of MV2PL, and only the most recent versions are selected. Otherwise, the versions read by T_i are those whose certify times are less than $VSP(T_i)$. We prove that $MVSG(H, <<)$ is acyclic by showing that for every edge T_i Æ T_j in $MVSG(H, <<)$, $VSP(T_i) < VSP(T_j)$ and if $VSP(T_i) = VSP(T_j)$, then $cr_i < cr_j$.

Suppose T_i Æ T_j is an edge of the serialization graph, $SG(H)$, of an MV history H which is a direct graph whose nodes are transactions and whose edges represent all conflicting relationships between two transactions. This edge corresponds to a reads-from relationship (i.e. for some x, T_j reads x from T_i). Then, since all transactions read certified versions of data items, $cr_i < cr_j$.

Next, we consider version-order edges. Let $w_i[x_i]$, $w_j[x_j]$, and $r_k[x_j]$ be operations in H, where i, j, k are distinct, and consider the version-order edge that they generate. There are two cases: *(i)* $x_i << x_j$ and *(ii)* $x_j << x_i$. The first case implies T_i Æ T_j is in $MVSG(H, <<)$. If T_i and T_j are not marked transactions, then by M_{10}, $VSP(T_i) < VSP(T_j)$. If

$VSP(T_i) > VSP(T_j)$, then T_i violates the rule M_9. In addition, by the definition of $<<$, $cr_i < cr_j$.

The second case implies $T_k \not\!\!\!\!\!\!\!\!\!\!\!\!\not E\, T_i$ is in $MVSG(H, <<)$. Then, by the property of MV2PL [2], either $cr_i < cr_j$ or $cr_k < cr_i$. However, by the definition of $<<$, if $x_j << x_i$, then $cr_j < cr_i$. And since certification operation follows either read or write operations, in case of $cr_i < r_k[x_j]$, $cr_j < cr_i < r_k[x_j]$. Therefore, we can notice that T_k is marked because it does not read the more recent version than x_j. As a result, $VSP(T_k) < VSP(Ti)$. If T_k is not marked transaction, T_k executes its certify operation before T_i does. Thus, $cr_k < cr_i$ and by M_{10}, $VSP(T_k) < VSP(T_j)$. Since all edges in $MVSG(H, <<)$ are in VSP order, $MVSG(H, <<)$ is acyclic. Therefore, by Theorem 1, H is 1SR. ∎

CONCLUSIONS

Traditionally, in order to ensure serializability, concurrency control protocols use locking scheme or timestamps. With these methods, queries are blocked due to the update transactions, and vice versa. However, if the blockings of queries are eliminated, we can achieve a better performance. This feature is especially adequate for query-intensive systems such as decision support systems.

The contributions of our paper are as follows. First, we proposed a concurrency control protocol which eliminates both the blockings of queries and the unnecessary delays of update transactions by using a new method, called mark. Compared with the existing protocols, the proposed protocol reduces the waiting time for finishing a transaction. In addition, it gives newer versions to transactions than the existing protocols.

Next, the proposed protocol with mark may consume more storage for maintaining multiple versions. However, recently, the power of computer hardware is sharply increasing. Along with the increase in the power, the cost has fallen as dramatically. Thus, for the systems such as decision support systems that execute many queries, the proposed protocol can provide faster response time than the existing protocols.

REFERENCES

[1] Bernstein, P. A. and N. Goodman, "Multiversion Concurrency Control - Theory and Algorithms," *ACM Transactions on Database Systems*, Vol. 8(No. 4), December 1983.
[2] Bernstein, P. A., V. Hadzilacos, and N. Goodman, *Concurrency Control and Recovery in Database Systems*, Addison-Wesley, 1987.
[3] Bober, P. M. and M. J. Carey, "Multiversion Query Locking," *Proceedings of the 18th VLDB Conference*, August 1992.
[4] Bober, P. M. and M. J. Carey, "On Mixing Queries and Transactions via Multiversion Locking," *Proceedings of the IEEE Conference on Data Engineering*, February 1992.
[5] Chan, A., S. Fox, W. Lin, A. Nori, and D. Ries, "The Implementation of an Integrated Concurrency Control and Recovery Scheme," *Proceedings of the ACM SIGMOD*, June 1982.
[6] Claybrook, B., *OLTP : On-Line Transaction Processing Systems*, John Wiley \& Sons, 1992.
[7] Hector Garcia-Molina and Gio Wiederhold, "Read-Only Transactions in a Distributed Database," *ACM Transactions on Database Systems*, Vol. 7(No. 2), June 1982.
[8] Korth, H. F. and A. Silberschatz, *Database System Concepts*, McGraw-Hill, 1991.
[9] Mohan, R. L. C. and H. Pirahesh, *Efficient and Flexible Methods for Transient Versioning of Records to Avoid Locking by Read-Only Transactions*, Technical Report, IBM Almaden Research Center, 1995.
[10] Mumick, I. S., "The Rejuvenation of Materialized Views," *Proceedings of the 6th International Conference on Information Systems and Data Management*, November 1995.

Delivering Desktop Services with Push Technology

Ravi Patnayakuni
Department of Computer and Information Systems, Temple University, Philadelphia, PA
Phone: 215-204-1911, Fax: 215-204-5082, E-mail: patnayak@joda.cis.temple.edu

Nainika Seth
Department of Management, College of Business and Administration, Southern Illinois University at Carbondale,
Carbondale, IL 62901, E-mail: naina_seth@hotmail.com

INTRODUCTION

The web provides an active mode of many to many communication in which users pull information relevant to their needs instead of a central agency pushing out information to them. This represents a shift in the way information is delivered within and across organizational boundaries. What is an interactive media from users point of view, is a much more passive mode of communication from the perspective of information providers. Information providers find that they have a limited idea of who and how often visits their website [Dickinson 1997].. For instance, to be affective, advertisers need to know the demographics of the audience they are sending their messages to.

The push mode of information delivery is heralded by some as a paradigm shift in information delivery on the web. Push when leveraged with other technologies such as filtering, search and retrieval, and intelligent agents can dramatically enhance an organization's ability to manage information. It is, in some ways akin to the broadcast media model of one to many communication but enables users to select the content and frequency with which they want the service to be delivered and providers to gather better customer information. But the real potential of the technology is not in having conventional information delivery transplanted on the web but in enabling personalized information systems.

The objective of this paper is to explore how organizations can effectively deploy push technology for information delivery based on the application domain in which it is used. The paper begins with a brief description of push technology. Soshanna Loeb's (1992) information filtering dimensions are used to examine the application domain and two usage scenarios are developed.

THE TECHNOLOGY

Different vendors use different terms to describe the technology and more and more vendors are offering new product and services everyday. For a comparison of push products see Levitt [1997].

For simplicity, Push technology can be considered to consist of three principal components: a server, a channel manager, and the channels themselves. Channels consist of programs and data/content files that are used to provide a service such as network applications, tickers or simply news content. Channel manager is the client software that keeps track of subscriptions and update schedules for each channel. The channels are stored and updated on servers and mirrored using the Internet and/or Intranet to be executed on client desktops.

A server may provide several channels or different channels may be provided by different servers. Because performance is critical in channel servers, they are streamlined and highly optimized. They can operate on a stand-alone basis or as extensions to popular HTTP servers. Channels on the server may be customized with plug-ins that can analyze channel feedback data and/or dynamically alter files sent to client desktops.

Users obtain channel services by subscribing to channels using web browser or channel manager software. Different vendors have different implementations of the subscription process. More often than not the channel manager will work with the browser to manage the process. Similarly there are several ways of launching channel content, it may be launched from the desktop by double-clicking an icon; or choosing it from the browser which launches the channel manager as a 'helper'; or it may be displayed in screen saver mode.

Each channel is updated on the basis of a default schedule set by the channel provider. The channel manager interacts with the channel's server to obtain the latest version of the channel. Automatic channel updating ensures, within the channel's update interval, that users have the latest version of a channel. A user can also customize channel updates on the channel manager or obtain an instant update. As the files associated with each channel are stored on the client's computer, the channels function like conventional applications, independent of network or server difficulties.

UNDERSTANDING THE APPLICATION DOMAIN

Work in the area of information filtering systems has examined the architecture and dynamics of end-to-end personalized delivery systems and identified certain dimensions to describe the application domain of these systems. Soshanna Loeb [1992] identifies these dimensions as user disposition, time scale, information delivery and information content. We draw upon these dimensions to develop a better understanding of the application domain for push technology.

The dimensions used to characterize the application domain of push technology are use and service categories, service lifetime, usage patterns, service attributes and media characteristics. Use and service categories are a very broad and general classification of user and service types. Service lifetime is the degree to which the value of the service is dependent on the speed of its delivery. Usage patterns refer to the style in which users use the service. Service attributes consist of the degree to which the services are customized. Media characteristics consist of the media richness and feed back ability. The objective of applying this categorization in the context of push is to raise issues and questions that need organizations need to deal with for effective service delivery.

Use and Service Categories

Two broad categories of users can easily be identified. Consumers are likely to be more casual users with uncertain information requirements. They are a moving target for service providers and are unlikely to provide substantive explicit feedback without elaborate persuasion. The other broad category is the employee who is on the corporate communications network. Their information and application needs are better defined and more detailed user profiles can be made available for service delivery. Needless to say there is going to be an overlap between consumers and employees. What distinguishes the two is the nature and intention of consumption, private versus corporate. It is much easier for the service provider to maintain control of the consumption process by establishing acceptable use policies and procedures for corporate as compared to private consumption.

Three broad categories of services can be distinguished, content, application and workflow. Service delivery is simplified by the use of open Internet based standards such as HTML and HTTP. However the availability of technology does not undermine the difficulty in managing requirements acquisition and service delivery. User expectations can escalate as the visibility of technology and its potential applications increase and the service provider may find that it is unable to meet these expectations.

The user categories of consumer and employee together with the three service categories provide a framework under which the different dimensions can be discussed. Figure 1 illustrates the matrix with examples of services that characterize each cell. Push technology can be used to deliver news and other broadcast content to consumers. Memos, notices or postings on formal and informal bulletin boards received by the employees are also classified as content. Applications are the extensions to games, software, educational material etc. delivered to consumers and the software patches, updates and new applications delivered to employees. If a user response triggers further events within the service it is termed workflow. Software that is centrally managed on the corporate networks is an application. A web site that informs customers when certain items of their choice go on sale is content. But if the customer responds to that information and the response triggers further events such as the use of existing customer profile and credit information to process the order or modification of future notification sent to that customer it becomes a part of workflow. Workflow applications automatically push different sections of a document to different departments for further action based on certain prespecified conditions or allow a team of employees to work together or a document or project. The objective of differentiating between content, application and workflow is to highlight significant issues in service development, delivery and maintenance.

Precise and structured user needs have to be identified for application and workflow services. For delivery of content, only topics and subject areas may be identified, information collected from various sources, organized in databases and presentation methods designed. Design, development and delivery of applications and workflow services require s, in addition, consideration of various technical and feasibility issues. Design and delivery of content would focus more on substantive, style and presentation issues. Maintenance and update of content services would be more frequent and simpler based on precise user needs. Update and maintenance of applications is likely would follow a longer

Figure 1: Use and service categories			
	Content	**Applications**	**Workflow**
Consumer	Direct Advertising, News	Game Extensions, Software Educational Material	Customer transactions
Employee	Company Bulletins, Memos, Notices	Software Updates, application delivery	Workflow Applications,

time cycle in view of the complexity in identifying user needs. Update of workflow services would require a modification of underlying organizational processes and may be less frequent because of the attendant costs. In specific organizational contexts other design, development and delivery issues can be identified for content, application and workflow services.

Service Lifetime

The value of a service to a consumer depends on the speed and timeliness with which it is delivered. Content services like company news have a very short service lifetime and are of little value to employees dealing with financial markets if not delivered instantaneously. In contrast some services, such as news digests, reference material or game extensions, have a longer lifetime and may be delivered with some time delay depending on factors like network traffic.

Service lifetime is usually the overriding criterion for service delivery independent of user category or nature of the service. Services that have a short lifetime need to be delivered quickly if not instantaneously. Service lifetime will also be an important consideration in the design of the user interface and notification, connectivity to network, and costing of services. Short lifetime services need to provide mechanisms to notify users with appropriate icons and sounds so that they can access the service immediately. Services with a longer lifetime can notify users in other less obtrusive ways such as e-mail. Services with shorter lifetimes are more suitable when users are connected to a network on a continuous basis and are likely to be designed under that assumption. Finally the lifetime of a service is an important factor in determining the cost of the service to consumers. Growing network traffic on the Internet is eventually expected to lead to different lanes on the information superhighway that operate at different speeds. The faster lanes will command a premium that consumers would be willing to pay for faster and reliable delivery of services.

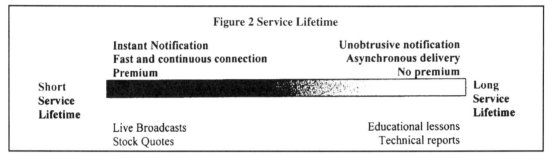

Figure 2 Service Lifetime

Usage Patterns

Not all users of a service intend to use it in exactly similar ways even if their use objectives are similar. While some like to use information in short frequent bursts, others may like to use the same information or service in long infrequent phases. From the point of view of the service provider, usage in small frequent bursts is likely to put a greater strain on network traffic at certain points in time. Many such users are also likely to be using the service at peak time, further straining the overloaded networks. For these users it also very important that the service or information be delivered synchronously as soon as it is available. Such users are much more likely to discern time lags in service delivery. This would reduce their satisfaction with service. Service providers can charge a premium for their service from these groups of users. Long infrequent users can be persuaded to use the service at off-peak times by providing them with monetary and non-monetary incentives to do the same. Services can be delivered to them asynchronously and do not require their immediate perusal.

Short frequent users, provide a rich demographic profile to service providers that can be used to improve service delivery on a continuous basis. Such users are connected for frequent short bursts, unobtrusive modes of data collection such as web usage logs, connect times, links followed, files downloaded, pages visited are more appropri-

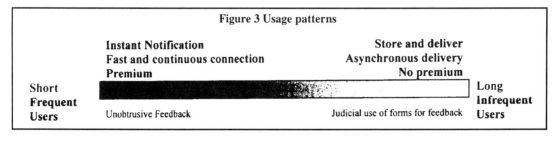

Figure 3 Usage patterns

ate. For infrequent users, profile forms can be used on a regular basis to collect information. Used judicially, obtrusive means of data collection may be less of less of a nuisance for long infrequent users than for short frequent users.

Service Attributes

Services such as workflow documents are customizable to the needs of individual users but many others such as software upgrades and news are delivered based on the broadcast model. Customization of services influences their mode and manner of delivery. Computer technology enables ever increasing customization of information services to the needs of users, the same cannot be said of the customizability of these services. Customization refers to the degree to which the service can meet individual user needs at the time of delivery, while customizability is the extent to which the users can modify the service in use. Hypertext documents and modular software is highly customizable by the users. They can choose their own organization of information rather than reading it in the linear order presented by the document author. Software users can select the modules they wish to use, ignoring other components of the software they are not interested in. Customizability is not always a desirable attribute. Sometimes authors and producers intend to limit the customizability of their services. Documents delivered in Adobe portable document format can force users to stick to a particular format and organization of documents. Workflow software can rigidly compel users to follow a series of steps and prevent them from choosing other sequence of steps of their choice. Non-customizable services seek to enforce the service consumption process of the user to a predefined sequence of steps, with the assumption that such a sequence is desirable for a variety of reasons. Low customizability may be enforced in workflow software to ensure that organizational processes are faithfully implemented. To see a discussion of customization and customizability in the context of decision support systems refer to Silver (1991).

When the service is customized to the needs to individual users, the premium for the service is likely to be high. It is important to collect user profiles and feedback in continuously improving the service to fit user needs. User profiles needs to be accurate and current and need to be regularly updated. User involvement in service design and delivery is critical in updating a customized rather that customizable service. Service providers need to be able to use intelligent agent based learning mechanisms to continuously learn from user experiences with the service.

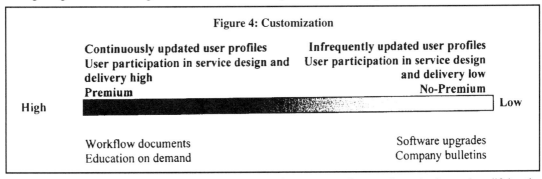

Figure 4: Customization

	Continuously updated user profiles User participation in service design and delivery high Premium	Infrequently updated user profiles User participation in service design and delivery low No-Premium
High		Low
	Workflow documents Education on demand	Software upgrades Company bulletins

If the service is customizable there would be a need for support to the users in navigating and modifying the service. This support can be incorporated in the software or content of the service. Additional support can be provided with offline and online support from the service provider. User groups and FAQ's on web ages can supplement and add value to support provided by the service provider. A judicial balance of different types of support based on relative costs and usage patterns is needed. The ability to customize the service reduces provider control on the consumption process. The service provider can use guidance and customer support to provide acceptable and preferred guidelines for the consumption of customizable services.

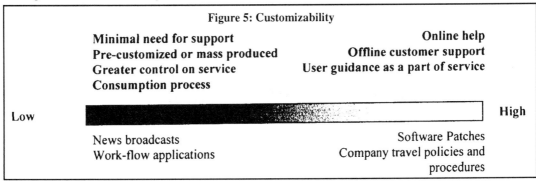

Figure 5: Customizability

	Minimal need for support Pre-customized or mass produced Greater control on service Consumption process	Online help Offline customer support User guidance as a part of service
Low		High
	News broadcasts Work-flow applications	Software Patches Company travel policies and procedures

Media Characteristics

Different media can be used in the provision of push services. Loeb (1992) classifies media as encapsulation media and transmission media. The media in which the information is encapsulated could be a text, audio, video or graphics. The media used for service transmission can be wireless, cable, Internet or radio. The media that users use to receive the service could be a network computer, PC, TV, personal digital assistant or a similar device.

The richness of the encapsulation media determines the required capacities of the transmission and reception media. In many cases the capacities of the transmission and reception media are limited, placing an upper limit on the appropriate richness of encapsulation media. Organizations can place a premium on media rich services to ensure that they are used only where necessary, preventing unnecessary traffic on the corporate network. The current practice of indiscriminate encapsulation media richness in the form of web pages jazzed up with complex graphics, pictures and backgrounds overloads public and private networks. Organizations can push only the links to media rich services rather than the services in their entirety. IS can provide local buffers for these services to reduce network loads. It would also be useful to analyze the use patterns of these services to better identify the location of buffers and the demand for these high cost services.

It is important for service providers to obtain relevant and immediate feedback on their services. Transmission and reception media capacity influences the richness of feedback that can be provided by users. Capacity can be asymmetric such that the bandwidth available to consumers is much lower than the bandwidth available to service providers. Consumers can watch TV broadcasts on their PC's but are limited by their modems in providing feedback or accessing additional information. Different reception media differ in the flexibility that they provide users in providing instantaneous feedback. Computer based reception media provide a higher level of control to users in providing feedback. TV provides less flexibility in manipulating text and images than a full function keyboard [Kalakota and Whinston 1996]. Asymmetries in feedback ability require that alternative modes of feedback are made available to some users and incentives are provided to them to encourage feedback. Service providers need to make an additional effort in organizing focus groups, panels and surveys to obtain user feedback. Conversely, the availability of rapid feedback places an additional burden on the service providers to establish a procedure for handing user feedback. Rapid feedback raises expectations of rapid response and even minor delays can cause user dissatisfaction. Service providers can provide single point of contact as well as multiple contact points and e-mail addresses of departmental executives. While some users may prefer to get in touch with a single person, others may have a clear preference about who they want to deal with. Very careful attention needs to be paid to back office operations in integrating the services pushed with information on the web sites and the day to day operations of business.

USAGE SCENARIOS

Two different scenarios that exploit push technology are presented. The first uses push technology to deliver instruction using multimedia and web based technologies. The second illustrates how project management can be supported on the web with push technology.

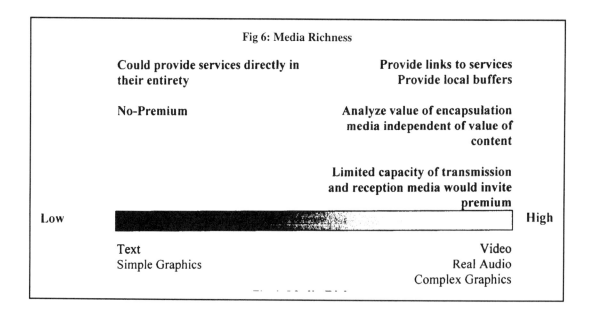

Fig 6: Media Richness

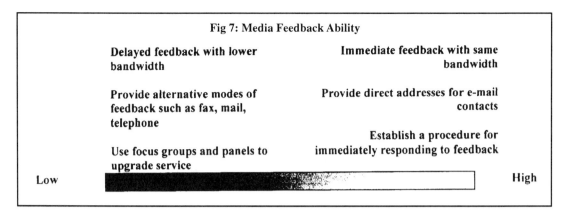

Fig 7: Media Feedback Ability

Delayed feedback with lower bandwidth

Immediate feedback with same bandwidth

Provide alternative modes of feedback such as fax, mail, telephone

Provide direct addresses for e-mail contacts

Establish a procedure for immediately responding to feedback

Use focus groups and panels to upgrade service

Low   High

Teachers MATE

Teacher's Multimedia Assisted Teaching Environment or MATE aims to assist teachers in planning and delivering interactive instruction over the web [Cybulski and Mackowiak 1997]. Under development at the Department of Information Systems, The University of Melbourne MATE supports the reuse of multimedia components for instructional delivery. In the environment, students can either work alone (off-line or on-line), in teams, or under the supervision of a teacher. The project illustrates a case where intelligent use of 'push' concept is used to create an interactive environment for learning.

Typically in the virtual classroom of Teacher's MATE, teacher's produce multimedia teaching material that can be presented on the web. Parsed into 'objects', the teaching material is classified and stored in a repository of multimedia components. The repository can then be used to compose and structure multimedia presentations, modules and courses. This makes reuse of multimedia objects a practical and attractive option. The repository can then be published in a form compatible with a web browser either as a network download or on a CD-ROM that can be distributed to students. A presentation server is used to deliver presentations and coordinate instruction sessions. Figure 8 gives a schematic of MATE architecture.

Students access a MATE presentation with the help of Java applets either from a local copy of the teaching repository or the presentation server. They can interact with teaching resources via embedded forms and Java applets to navigate between different pages of the material using existing hypertext links, obtain course updates, or do self-assessing exercises. Most of this can be done in an asynchronous mode, i.e. offline from home or at remote sites without a live network connection. For attending on-line presentation students may be required to log on to the presentation server. Once a lecture session begins, teaching material such as slides are automatically displayed on student computers. Instructors can display structured text and graphics, initiate animation sequences, or play sound and video. The sessions can be organized using a variety of templates that could have been predefined or specified on-the fly by the lecturer. The sessions are coordinated through the presentation server that sends requests to student machines to display the material from the local copy of the repository. During the course of a session, students can submit questions and requests to the instructor. The instructor can then use the feedback to alter the flow of the session or respond individually to the student. In responding to queries the instructor can either use material already available on the student machine by just sending appropriate requests or send it over the network. Those who are unable to attend live sessions can later retrace them using a

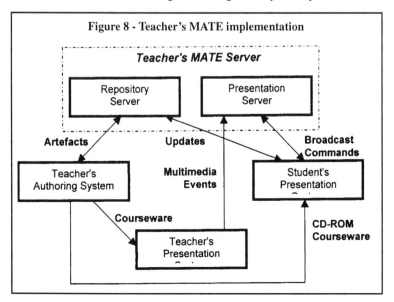

Figure 8 - Teacher's MATE implementation

Teacher's MATE Server

Repository Server

Presentation Server

Artefacts

Updates

Broadcast Commands

Teacher's Authoring System

Multimedia Events

Student's Presentation

Courseware

CD-ROM Courseware

Teacher's Presentation

navigation applet that can be downloaded from the presentation server. The delivery mechanism avoids sending huge multimedia files across the network minimizing bandwidth requirements. The repository can be 'differentially' updated periodically when network traffic is likely to be light.

MATE is an application that uses the push concept to deliver services to individual consumers. The architecture can quite easily be adopted for other usage contexts particularly in the corporate environment, such as training and on-line help. The environment provides for both on-line (short service lifetime) and off-line services. As most of the content and on-line sessions can be archived, the value of the service does not deteriorate substantially with time. Users do not have to be continuously on-line and most of the media traffic is likely to consist of applets and small text files. If video streaming is used then the media characteristics are likely to change. The potential for feedback and interactivity is quite high especially during on-line sessions but it can be expected that most of the communication is likely to be asynchronous. Using a combination of data replication (multimedia repository) and even broadcasting, MATE provides an efficient way of delivering multimedia instruction over the network.

Project Management

The use of teams to manage a variety of business projects is very much the norm in today's business environment. Most teams are geographically dispersed and have multiple centers of control, making communication, coordination and managing ongoing project activity a key factor between the success and failure of a project. Traditional project management applications are designed as single user tools for the project manager to track tasks, monitor milestone and follow up on deliverables and are not conducive to collaborative teamwork. Push technology can be effectively leveraged to manage project management applications over the network. This section discusses ActionPlan [Ly 1997] by Netmosphere to illustrate the application of push technology in a project management context.

A typical project involves the formulation of a project plan that identifies the goals of the project and the means to achieve them. Each member of the team is assigned responsibility for certain tasks required to complete the project. Over the life of the project, tasks may be added, deleted, shifted, reassigned, compressed. This requires a high amount of communication between team members. They need to receive updates about the status of tasks and the project as a whole. Use of e-mail for project coordination is unlikely to provide an integrated, consistent and current view of the project. With effective use of Internet technologies these hurdles can be overcome to support real-time collaboration for distributed teams.

The application uses the traditional client/server architecture consisting of clients that can connect to servers using Java applets. The application server, which may be housed in the same box as the web server and the push server, maintains a set of project-plans and to-do lists, and also manages the synchronization of all changes made to the documents by individual team members and the project manager. In addition the server also maintains user profiles for authentication and audit purposes. The server sends copies of project plans and to-do lists to thin clients for viewing and manipulation. Individual team members can check off completed tasks in their to-do lists and this information is then communicated to the server. The server then applies the modification to plan documents in real-time if necessary. The changes are then pushed to other clients in the system. One important consideration in the application architecture is the support for multiple users to edit the same objects simultaneously while maintaining their integrity. Using push technology, the application can provide efficient communication between clients and the server by only communicating changes made to documents. The application should be designed to resolve conflicts and maintain transactional correctness. The collaboration application for project management enables distributed teams to share information synchronized across different documents and to view up-to date information on these documents in real-time.

Discussion

The figure below compares the two scenarios on the application domain dimensions identified earlier. The placement of scenarios along the dimensions is illustrative and highlights the contrast between the two examples.

CONCLUDING REMARKS

Tremendous excitement surrounds push technology with a number of vendors vying for the market. On the other hand many Internet commentators have already written off the technology. Whatever the prognostications, push technology under its various names and guises is destined to leverage the many to many communication potential of the Internet. There are a variety of other issues that need to be considered in the application of push technology:

• User Profiles: The success of push technology hinges on the ability to construct a useful actionable user profile. Casual web users are unlikely to indulge in lengthy interactions to provide information about themselves or their needs. Developing a user profile needs to take this into account.

• Privacy: If information about users is collected explicitly, users need to be aware of what the information is used for and who has access to it. This may be particularly important in the corporate context where a more detailed user

Figure 9: Teachers MATE versus Project Management

Dimensions of the Application Domain	Teachers MATE	Project Management
Service Lifetime	Long	Short
Usage	Long	Short
Customization	High	Low
Customizability	Low	High
Media Richness	High	Medium
Feedback Ability	Medium	High

profile is needed to push relevant content and services to users. On the other hand if data is collected unobtrusively such as on usage behavior, a number of privacy and ethical issues are likely to come up.

- User Interface and Notification: Few would disagree that the web has contributed to the problem of 'information overload'. Add to that the notion of pushing information and many users are likely to protest. Most users are likely to be using their computers for other purposes and will need both obtrusive and unobtrusive mechanisms to notify them of any changes. The challenge is to develop a user interface that works with different filters to provide users a snapshot picture of what lies in their inbox.

REFERENCES

J. L. Cybulski and M. Mackowiak, "Teacher's MATE: Multimedia-Assisted Teaching Environment", Proc. of DITAM'97, University of Melbourne, October 1997, pp 56-61, http://mate.dis.unimelb.edu.au/jacob/publications/ditam-97/ditam.htm

J. Dickinson, "Pushing Users Around," Internet Computing, February 3, 1997, Http://www.zdimag.com/content/columns/techcom/970203/index.html

J. Hibbard, "Knowledge Management - Knowing what we know - Knowledge management, the process of capturing a comapany's collective expertise is big business," Information Week, October 20, 1997, Http://www.techweb.com/se/directlink.cgi?IWK19971020S0040.

D. L. Hoffman and T. Novak, "Marketing in hypermedia computer-mediated environments: Conceptual foundations," Journal of Marketing, v60, July 1996, pp 50-68.

R. Kakakota and A.Whinston, "Frontiers of Electronic Commerce," Reading, Ma: Addison Wesley 1996

R. Karpinski, "The changing face of Push," Internet Week, December 8, 1997, Http://www.techweb.com/se/directlink.cgi?INW19971208S0043

J. Levitt, "Rating the push products - The internet may become your company's primary source of personalized news. These nine push clients have the technology to make it so," Information Week, April 28, 1997, Http://www.techweb.com/se/directlink.cgi?IWK19970428S0047.

S. Loeb, "Architecting personalized delivery of multimedia information," Communications of the ACM, v35, December 1992, pp 39-48.

E. Ly, "Distributed Java Applets For Project Management on the Web," IEEE Internet Computing, May-June, pp 21-26, 1997.

Marimba, "Executive Summary," Marimba, Inc. Palo Alto, CA 94306, 1997a, Http://www.marimba.com.

Marimba, "Castanet white paper," Marimba, Inc. Palo Alto, CA 94306, 1997b, Http://www.marimba.com.

M.S. Silver, "Systems that Support Decision-Makers: Description and Analysis," John Wiley and Sons Ltd., Chichester 1991.

A Mutual Authentication Protocol
for Smart Cards

Deepak Rauniar and Syed.M.Rahman
School of Computing and Information Technlogy, Monash University, Churchill, VIC, Australia 3842
Tel: (03) 5122 6462, (03) 5122 6568, Fax: + 61 3 9902 6879, Email: {deepak.rauniar,
syed.rahman}@infotech.monash.edu.au

ABSTRACT

Smart cards will soon exist in virtually every area of our lives. These IC chip cards will soon control our access to a growing number of public facilities. The technology promises much and is very flexible - in the sense that it can be designed and manufactured to serve a multitude of purposes. The power of these cards lie in their ability to store and manipulate data, to handle multiple application on the card, and to perform secure transactions. Considering the sensitive nature of information that these cards will eventually carry, there is a strong need to protect these cards and hence the data inside the cards from misuse, be it from card theft or through a fake terminals. Authentication is one such technique, which provides the first line of defense in any security system. Authentication is the process whereby a process can verify the claimed identity of the other party in a communicating pair. In this paper, we propose a mutual authentication protocol for smart cards. The proposed protocol can be used to provide secure authentication between a smart card and a smart card terminal, where the smart card will eventually be inserted to access a service. The scheme provides a mechanism whereby a valid smart card can be distinguished from a fake one by the terminal. Our proposal also allows a smart card to distinguish an authorized terminal from an unauthorized one.

INTRODUCTION

As the world has evolved with the IT (Information Technology) revolution, so has emerged the need to process tremendous amount of information in our daily lives. Computers are no longer a tool that even some years ago, only few fortune companies could afford to shape their future. Over these years, computers have influenced our lives as never before – for better of course. No body has been spared with the benefits of the ongoing IT revolution - be it in an advanced country or what is known as a third world country [Caelli, 91]. Computers, and to be more precise the microprocessor behind them, have delivered us the ability to control, process and access information. It is this versatility of the microprocessor, that now a smart card provides, however in our own wallet [URL02, 98].

On the onset, a smart card may look like a regular sized credit card. However the similarity ends there. Simply speaking a regular credit card is a magnetic-strip card that is universally employed mainly by the banking sector. These cards act as a token, which the owner possesses to identify him-self in a financial transaction. However a smart card is smart-smart in the sense that instead of a magnetic-stripe, it has a microprocessor along with the necessary memories, a complete operating system and an application program embedded in the card. Thus these cards enjoy the versatility and the power that a microprocessor provides [Lindley, 97]. The power of these cards lie in their ability to store and manipulate data, to handle multiple application on the card, and to perform secure transactions [Tomkowiak, 96]. A typical card consists of a complete Central Processing Unit (CPU) with a memory (ROM) for the operating system. It also contains a main memory (RAM) and a memory sector for the application data. Further some cards contain an extra cryptographic processor to achieve high level of security [URL02, 98], [Rankl, 97], [Hendry, 97].

These cards provide a strong level of security with their ability to control who can access the information they possess. This is not possible in magnetic stripe cards. With the embedded microprocessor in the card, these cards possess the power to apply both symmetric as well as asymmetric cryptography, a powerful tool for any security system, to enhance security. Some of these cards also contain arithmetic coprocessors to enhance the overall computing power to support advanced public cryptographic algorithms, providing better security with minimum delay. For example, cards developed by Siemens and SGC Thomson can perform 512 bit RSA exponentiation in about 60 ms [Fuchsberger, 95].

The major disadvantage of the magnetic stripe card lies in the very simplicity of the concept, which has lead to financial fraud in massive scale. These cards simply cannot authenticate its owner. In 1991 alone, magnetic-stripe card fraud losses were estimated as high as £ 400 Million in UK alone [URL01, 98]. With the increased fraud and security concerns, smart cards offer a top security alternative. As per the latest study, it has been found that there has been a massive decrease in card fraud with the increase in the use of smart card (Figure 1) [Lindley, 97].

In a typical card system, there are generally three different entities associated with the system. Beside the cardholder i.e. the consumer of whatever goods or services that is offered by the system, there is the supplier of those services (e.g. supermarkets) as well as the operator of the card system (e.g. bank). Security functions of any system, including smart cards, revolve around three basic security requirements: integrity, confidentiality and availability. One of the major security concerns of present security system in general is the integrity problem. Like any other environment, in a smart card environment, three integrity issues arises [Konigs, 91] [Garfinkel, 97], [Bovelander, 95]:

* is the user genuine (user authentication).
* is the smart card genuine (card authentication)
* is the system genuine (system authentication)

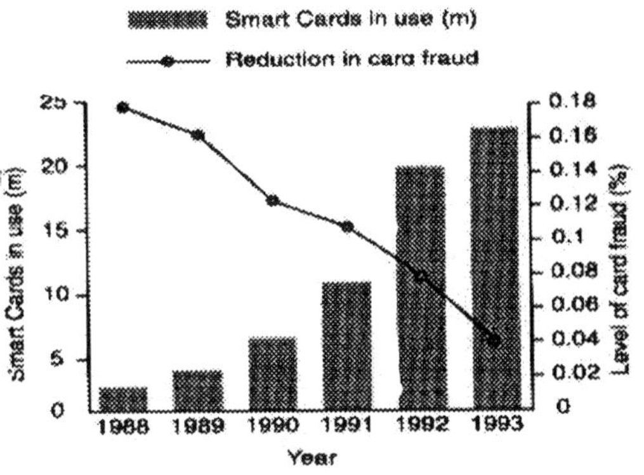

Given the fact that a single smart card can be configured to access a variety of applications (from

Figure 1: Graph showing the relationship between the increase in smart card and the level of bank card fraud in France for the period 1988 to 1993 [Lindley, 97].

financial to medical applications), eventually a smart card carries a wealth of data of personal nature. From a perpetrator's point of view, the returns in terms of unauthorized reading and hence obtaining data from a smart card is more rewarding than a magnetic stripe card, which carries data for only a single application. Hence smart cards are required to show high resistance as far as the overall security requirement is concerned, while showing high flexible as far as the support for multi-application is concerned.

Almost inevitably, in accessing security threats in a card system, it is implicitly assumed that some individuals will try to get the card system to produce goods or services for which he has not paid, often with the aid of stolen or doctored cards. In other words, it is assumed that it is the supplier of the services that is being defrauded and thus in most of the traditional systems the overall security revolves around identifying the genuine nature of the card (e.g. in bank automated teller machines). However, a full analysis ought to consider security threats from the points-of-view of all participants involved. In particular, the legitimate cardholder can be equally vulnerable to fraud as is evident from the following examples.

A cardholder can be at threat from bogus terminals (e.g POS terminals). Criminals can set up a bogus automatic teller (AT) or add a false front to a real AT. The terminals can be further designed to simulate a real terminal to fool a cardholder and thus induce him to insert his card and enter the security data (e.g. PIN) to access a service. After the card is inserted, the system can then make an unauthorized copy of the card data into its memory. Once the security related data is acquired the terminal can come up with a false message (e.g. the card has expired) prompting the cardholder to remove his card and leave. Armed with this information, a fraud can easily duplicate a new card and use it to make a genuine request together with the security information, emptying the cardholder's account as a genuine withdrawal [GLAS, 91]. Similar frauds are also possible at point-of-sale terminals. A dishonest merchant can always manipulate his terminal to obtain the necessary data from the card. It is also possible that the merchant manipulates his terminal in such a way that the cardholder authorizes payments of larger amounts than displayed at the terminal. These illustrations are but few examples where the cardholder can be equally at risk [Glass, 91], [Tempus, 96]. Given the fact that smart card can store a wealth of data of personal nature, the risk is more for smart card holders than magnetic stripe cardholders. Thus it becomes equally important from the card holder's point-of-view to check for the authenticity of the terminal before revealing any secret and eventually engaging in a transaction.

Since smart cards can execute complex cryptographic computations, in this paper we propose a mutual authentication protocol employing cryptographic techniques. The proposed protocol is influenced by the work of Nigel Jefferies, Chris Mitchell and Michael Walker [Jefferies, 95] and our protocol can be used to for mutual authentication purposes between a smart card and a terminal. Thus, once the protocol is executed in a smart card environment, besides the terminal authenticating the card, the smart card will also be satisfied about the authenticity of the terminal.

AUTHENTICATION

Authentication is a technique whereby a process (e.g., a smart card, terminal etc.) verifies the claimed identity of another distributed process over an insecure channel. A successful authentication results in authenticity, whereby a verifying process becomes sure of the identity of the claimant process as the one, which it claims to be [Oppliger, 96]. Proper authentication between distributed processes is important considering the insecure nature of the underlying physical channel where messages can be tapped, modified, deleted and initiated by an intruder. Authentication provides a mean through which distributed resources can properly verify the identity of the remote process before entering into a transaction.

Given the distributed model of computing that has evolved recently with an insecure channel bridging the distributed processes, providing proper identification of distributed processes is not an easy task and it is precisely this problem that authentication protocols solve. When processes are authenticated, typically by exchanging a series of messages depending on the protocols used, both the processes in a communicating pair become confident about each other's identity. They know for sure that they are not talking to someone else, who is impersonating as the other. In any computer system, generally there are three different levels of authentication that are involved -
• Authentication of the user with the system – User Authentication.
• Authentication of the distributed or remote process (smart card, remote computer etc.) with the system – Process/ Device Authentication.
• Authentication of the system itself.

Authentication of users with the system is done through passwords, PIN, Tokens or biometric techniques [Garfinkel 97], [Rankl., 97], [Hendry, 97], [URL03, 98] User authentication through password or PIN is done by having the user to type his password or Personal Identification Number (PIN) through a keyboard. This is matched against the stored password of the user inside the system. If the password matches, the user is authenticated and allowed to proceed further, else he is blocked from proceeding. With Token identification, the user is authenticated if he is able to present the physical token as required by the system. Typical example of such authentication is the use of access cards to open electronic gates. In Biometric identification, the user is uniquely identified by the system based on his unique, individual and biological properties. Fingerprint is one of the common examples of such authentication technique. Device as well as system authentication is generally done employing cryptographic, one way hash functions or zero knowledge based protocols [Kaufman, 95], [Schneier, 96], [Garfinkel 97], [Tanenbaum, 96]. These protocols employ complex mathematical computations to finally prove the identity to each other.

CRYPTOGRAPHIC AUTHENTICATION

The basic idea of a cryptographic authentication is that a claimant A proves his identity to a verifier B by performing a cryptographic operation of a quantity that either both know or B supplies. A uses a secret cryptographic key to make the operation on the quantity and hence to convince B [Oppliger, 96]. Figure 2. illustrates the general cryptographic model.

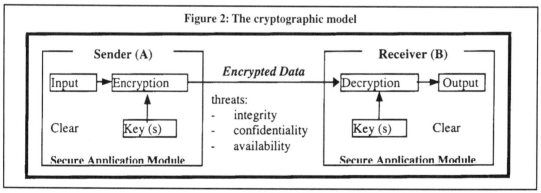

Figure 2: The cryptographic model

Cryptographic authentication is desired considering the inherent insecure nature of the underlying physical channel, which can be quite vulnerable to attacks from an intruder who can read, alter, destroy, and create messages at his will. In applications of remote/distributed computation, which crucially requires secure communication, authentication establishes a secure channel between distributed communicating processes [Wenbo, 94]. In any authentication scenario, there are ultimately two distributed processes to which the protocol serves. There is a prover, also known as a claimant - who desires to prove his identity to a remote process, in order to communicate securely or to access the service provided by the process. And there is a verifier, who verifies the claimed identity of the prover/ claimant before actually starting the communication or delivering the service. The claimant and the verifier are often also known as principals.

Two different strategies are possible for any claimant process to authenticate itself to a verifier process. In the first case, a claimant process can directly approach the verifier and prove itself to the verifier process. While in the second approach, a claimant process can prove itself to the verifier process by proving itself to a third party, whom the verifier process trusts. Based on the above strategies, authentication protocols can also be divided into two classes [Tanenbaum, 96], **[Kaufman, 95], [Schneier, 96], [Oppliger, 96], [Ford, 94]. The first class of authentication protocols provides direct mutual authentication between two distributed processes. While the second class of the protocols employ the services of an intermediary third party, which is trusted by everybody (also known as Key Distribution Center in networks), to provide authentication of distributed processes. These two approaches are discussed below:**

Direct Authentication.

In the direct authentication approach, the authentication is done directly between the two communicating processes as given in Figure 3. The process A proves its identity directly to the process B, with which it wishes to talk. Similarly, the process B also proves its identity directly to the process A in order to convince A that it is indeed talking to B. The authentication is done based on some shared secret or public key - private key cryptography technologies.

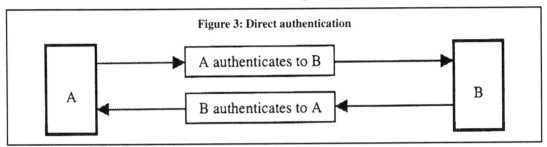

Figure 3: Direct authentication

The basic problem with this type of authentication is that key management is difficult. For a process to communicate with n other processes, it requires to maintain a minimum of n keys. The larger the number of processes it wishes to communicate with, the larger would be the number of keys to be managed. This can lead to a very frustrating scenario if the processes are human users and each key are stored in plastic cards (for better security), then each user would be required to maintain n cards at all times.

Authentication via a Trusted Third Party (KDC)

In this approach, authentication between any two processes is done employing the services of a trusted third party, which is known as KDC (Key Distribution Center) and trusted by everybody. The KDC essentially acts as a common secretary for all the processes in the system. It maintains a common database of everybody's key while each process shares only one unique key with the KDC. This model of authentication is depicted in Figure 4. For the purpose of authentication, the process wishing to talk e.g. A, to some other process e.g. B, approaches the KDC with a request for the key of process B, step (1) in the Figure 4. The KDC encrypts the desired key of the process B, which is also known as a ticket, with the key shared between the process A and the KDC and sends it to A (step (2)). This ensures that nobody else obtains a key from the KDC impersonating as somebody else. When A receives the encrypted key from the KDC, it decrypts it using its key and obtains the necessary key to authenticate to B. Then A and B mutually authenticate to each other (step (3) and (4)) with the help of the ticket.

Key management is relatively very easy with the protocols employing KDC because any process has to maintain only one secret key that is shared with the KDC and through the same, it can talk to virtually any other process in the list of KDC.

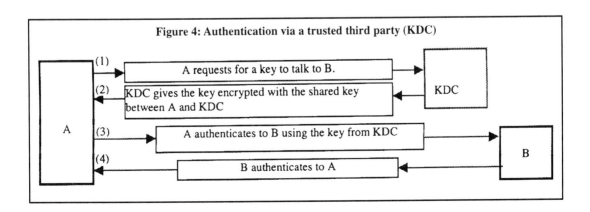

Figure 4: Authentication via a trusted third party (KDC)

AUTHENTICATION PROTOCOLS

The problem of authentication in the wake of an insecure channel is fundamental to the success of secured distributed computing. It is therefor highly desirable to provide secure solutions, so that protocols for these goals can be raised [Blake, 97]. A secure mutual authentication protocol is a two-party protocol, where both processes accept (at least with overwhelmingly probability) if their adversary is benign, but reject with overwhelmingly probability in the presence of an active attacker [Lucks, 97].

The core of any authentication protocol, which provides unidirectional/mutual identification of a distributed entity, revolves around challenge-response technique [Tanenbaum, 96], [Schneier, 96], [Stinson, 95], [Ford, 94], [Pfleeger, 89]. In a typical run of protocol employing challenge-response techniques, one of the processes involved issues what is known as a challenge to the other party, who in turn is required to come out with a proper response to the challenge. The party issuing the challenge is known as the challenger while the later responding to the challenge as the responder. The challenge itself typically involves a random number, and the responder is required to transform it in some special way (often involving its private key) known only to the bona fide party, and return the result. After receiving the result of its challenge, the challenger confirms it with the desired result, which also generally involves some computation locally by the challenger. If the result hence obtained matches with the desired result, then and only then the responder is authenticated. The grounds for such authentication is the fact that the responder has demonstrated the possession of a secret, which is supposedly known only to the bona fide party, and thus it is the bona fide party. By changing the roles of the challenger and the responder, mutual authentication is provided.

Apart from establishing the claim of a remote process in the wake of an insecure physical channel, most of the mutual authentication protocols also address with the issue of secure session key exchange between the authenticated processes [Tanenbaum, 96], [Schneier, 96], [Ford, 94]. A secure session key exchange between the authenticated processes involves the delivery of a new session key, which is randomly generated for each session. Once the session key is exchanged, all communication is encrypted with the session key, allowing only the bona fide processes to encrypt/decrypt the message. Hence the message remains hidden from an intruder in the absence of the session key. Further, the use of a new random session key for each session also serves to enhance the overall security and the efficiency of the system. Security is enhanced considering the fact that the secret key of the processes is used only for a short duration - just for authentication and session key exchange. Once the session key is securely exchanged, the session key is used to encrypt all communication between the authenticated processes. Thus at any time the compromise of a session key only makes those communications vulnerable involving the particular session key. If a session key is randomly generated and strictly used for only one session, the damage involved is restricted to a particular session. In contrast, if the secret key is used at all times for all purposes, a compromise of the key makes all the messages exchanged in all the sessions involving the key vulnerable. The damages hence caused can be severe [Wenbo, 94].

The efficiency is increased considering the fact that for authentication purposes, more advanced cryptographic technologies (e.g. private-key/public-key) can be used, however once the processes are authenticated, a small session key (e.g a symmetric key) can be used. Thus the actual messages can be encrypted/decrypted with relatively small processing power and minimum delay [Wenbo, 94]. Thus, briefly speaking a mutual authentication protocol addresses the following two different issues:

• Authentication of the distributed processes.
• Establishment of a random session key between the authenticated processes.

DIFFIE-HELLMAN KEY EXCHANGE

A key exchange protocol provides a mechanism such that when the protocol is finally executed, the two processes executing the protocol end up possessing a secret key. The secret key hence possessed remains secret to the processes running the protocol and any intruder who might have monitored the entire communication between the two processes over an insecure channel is unable to obtain the key. Dieffie-Hellman was the first public-key algorithm that was ever invented. It is also the first and best known key exchange algorithm which allows total strangers to establish a shared secret, in total broad daylight, even with an intruder carefully recording each message. Diffie-Hellman gets its security from the difficulty of calculating, discrete logarithms in a finite field as compared with the ease of calculating exponentiation in the same field [Schneier, 96], [Tanenbaum, 96], [Stinson, 95], [Ford, 94].

In the following paragraphs, we describe the protocol, by which two remote as well as unknown processes A and B can establish a secret key between them. To start with, A and B agree on a large prime, n and g, where $(n-1)/2$ is also a prime and g is primitive mod n. These integers are made public and A and B can agree to it over an insecure channel. Further, these numbers can even be common among a group of processes. In the next step, the process A picks up a large (e.g. 512 bit) number, x, and keeps it secret. Similarly, the process B picks up a large secret number, y. After that the protocol works as follows:

1)   Process A sends B a message containing (n,g, g^x mod n).
2)   Process B replies by sending g^y mod n.
      These steps are shown below in the Figure 5.

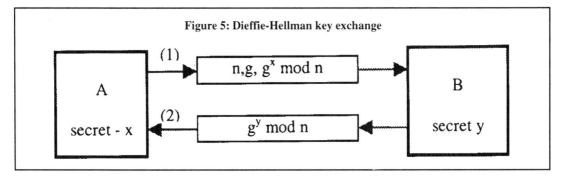

Figure 5: Dieffie-Hellman key exchange

After receiving message (1) from process A, process B raises it to the y th power and computes $(g^x \textbf{ mod n})^y$ **resulting in g^{xy} mod n. Similarly, process A also raises the message it receives from process B to the power of x resulting in $(g^y$ mod n$)^x$ and hence g^{xy} mod n. Now they both share a secret key, g^{xy} mod n. Even though an intruder, T, has seen both the messages, the security of the system lies in the fact that given n, g and g^x mod n, the intruder, T, can not find x. There is no practical algorithm for computing discrete logarithms modulo a very large prime number.**

The choice of n and g can have a substantial impact on the security of this system. As n increases, so does the difficulty of factoring number as large as n and thus the security of the system is increased. However as for value of g is concerned, it need not be a large number. Any g such that g is primitive mod n, can be chosen – for that matter g can be one digit number.

Man-in-the–middle attack

As Dieffe-Hellman only provides for key exchange and not authentication, there is no way that the process B can verify the authenticity of the first message from process A. An intruder process, T, can exploit this situation to deceive both the processes A and B as follows [Tanenbaum, 96]:

      Let x, y and z be the secret numbers of the process A, B and the intruder T.

1) Process A sends B a message containing (n,g, g^x mod n).
2) The intruder T, intercepts the message and modifies the message with her secret key to contain (n, g, g^z mod n).
3) Process, T, also sends g^z mod n to the process A.
4) The process B, assuming that the second message has come from process A, sends g^y mod n, as required by the protocol to the intruder process T.

      These steps are shown below in the Figure 6.

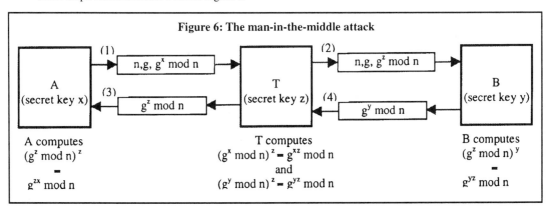

Figure 6: The man-in-the-middle attack

At the end of the message (4), every process does their local computation. Process A, computes the secret key (g^{zx} mod n) and so does the intruder, T. Similarly, process B computes the secret key as (g^{yz} mod n) along with the intruder. Process A, thinks it is talking to process B and so does process B. Both the processes are under the illusion that a secure channel has been established between them. On the contrary, the intruder process, T in the middle can capture every message between them and can even modify it without causing any suspicion.

TECHNOLOGY FRAMEWORK

In this paper, we show how the work of Nigel Jefferies, Chris Mitchell and Michael Walker can be designed to provide mutual authentication between a smart card and a terminal. In their work, the authors have shown how the services of a trusted third party can be employed such that two processes (over a computer network) can communicate securely over an insecure physical channel (e.g. public networks) involving one way communication such as emails. Their model is based on Dieffe-Hellman key exchange. However, unlike most of the popular protocols employing Dieffe-Hellman key exchange, in their protocol, the Dieffe-Hellman key is not computed and exchanged directly between the two processes involved. Instead a trusted third party i.e. the KDC computes the respective Dieffe-Hellman keys for each distributed processes. Whenever a process wants to send a mail to some other distributed process, the process obtains the Dieffe-Hellman key of the other distributed process from the KDC, encrypts the mail and sends it the other process. Since, the secret Dieffe-Hellman key is known only to the other process, only it will able to decrypt the mail [Jefferies, 95].

In this section, we show how the above model can be extended to provide authentication between a smart card and a terminal in a smart card environment. In the above model, we realize that there are three different entities, each having its own role. There are two distributed processes, which wish to communicate securely over an insecure network, and there is a third party, which is trusted by all the processes. We realize that a similar model exists in a smart card environment also. In a smart card environment too, there are two different distributed entities (the card and the terminal) which have their own security concerns, and there is a card operator, which is of course is a trusted party, since it is he who establishes the entire infrastructure of smart card/terminal. Further, given the fact that smart cards also possess remarkable computing power and can execute cryptographic computation to overcome threats arising from the physical channel and fake terminals, we feel that our protocol can easily be implemented in a smart card environment.

To begin with, in our protocol, every terminal set up by the card operator/service provider possess a secret Dieffe-Hellman key, y. This key needs not to be the same for all the terminals and can be different. Whenever the card operator issues a new smart card, he chooses a large prime, n and g (can be different for each card), where (n-1)/2 is also a prime and g is primitive mod n (as per Dieffe-Hellman requirement). He then selects a secret key x for the card (can be different for each card) and burns it into a inaccessible memory location (i.e. once the card is finally distributed to a customer, this memory location will not be any longer accessible). After that he computes (g^x mod n), signs (g^x mod n), g and n using his secret key (which can be verified by the terminal) and burns it into the smart card. In this way, the card operator as the KDC.

Now whenever a smart card is inserted into a terminal to access a service by a customer, mutual authentication (employing challenge-response technique) between the card and the terminal and hence secure transaction can be ensured as follows:

1) The smart card releases (gx mod n, g, n) to the terminal, where represents the signature of the card operator using a secret master key MK. A genuine terminal can easily verify this signature. The card also generates a random number, R1, and sends it to the terminal.

2) The terminal verifies the signature of the service provider. If the signature is verified then and only then further transaction takes place, else the card is rejected as an unauthorized card. It may be argued that this itself is the verification of the card. However at this point, we are interested in mutual authentication, such that the card can also verify the terminal before releasing its data. The terminal then extracts gx mod n and computes the session key, KS = gxy mod n, by raising its secret key, i.e. y over gx mod n. It also computes gy mod n using its secret key, y, over g and n received from step 1. The terminal generates its own random number R2, encrypts R1 and R2 with KS and sends it along with gy mod n to the smart card.

3) Once the smart card receives gy mod n, it locally computes the session key, KS = gxy mod n, by raising its secret key, i.e. x, over gy mod n. After, that it decrypts the encrypted message containing the random numbers R1 and R2 with KS. When it sees, its random number R1 back, it authenticates the terminal, on the ground that only a genuine terminal can compute the session key correctly from the signed message of step 1. The card then encrypts R2 with KS and sends it back to the terminal.

These three steps are shown in Figure 7.

When the terminal receives the encrypted message, it also tries to decrypt it using its key KS and when it sees its R2 back it authenticates the card as a genuine card. Thus in this way mutual authentication, and hence secured transaction (using the session key) can be provided between the card and the terminal.

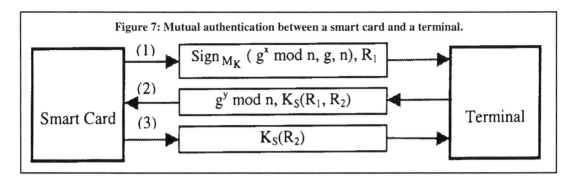

Figure 7: Mutual authentication between a smart card and a terminal.

ADVANTAGES OF THE PROPOSED SYSTEM

The proposed system provides a mechanism whereby mutual authentication can be provided between a smart card and a terminal. Given the limited resources that a smart card possesses, the above scheme is quite attractive. The above scheme is not computation as well as resource hungry as generally most of the public key cryptography algorithms often are. In our proposal, the bulk of the processing is done by the terminal and basically card processing is restricted to simply raising the quantity obtained in step (2) with the secret key to obtain the session key.

Our proposal allows the flexibility of having each terminal its own secret key. Thus the session key that is developed with a terminal is valid only for that particular terminal and is not a global proposition. This is in contrast with method where the key is developed based on information of the card by the terminal. In such system, if the master key of any one terminal is compromised, then the whole system crashes. In our system, if the master key (i.e. the secret key, y) is ever compromised, then only that particular terminal will be affected and the impact on the overall system is limited. Security is improved considering the fact that keys are not exposed until the terminal is able to verify the sign of the service provider. Further, our proposal is not vulnerable to man-in-the-middle attack.

CONCLUSION

Smart cards will soon exist in virtually every area of our lives. Even though, its current use is mainly focussed on electronic money, however in the future, it will also control our access to a growing number of public facilities. Considering the sensitive nature of information that these cards will eventually carry, there is a strong need to protect these cards and hence the data inside the cards from misuse, be it from card theft or through a fake terminals. In this paper, we have proposed a mutual authentication protocol for smart cards. The proposed scheme can be used to provide secure authentication between a smart card and a smart card terminal, where the smart card will eventually be inserted to access a service. The scheme allows a mechanism to distinguish between a valid smart card from a fake one as well as a valid terminal from a fake one.

REFERENCES

Blake.S.W, Menezes.A: "Entity Authentication and Authenticated Key Transport Protocols Employing Asymmetric Techniques", Security Protocols - 5th International workshop, pg 137-158, Paris, 1997.

Bovelander.E, Renesse.R.L.V: "Smartcards and Biometric: an Overview", 12th Compsec Conference, UK, 1995.

Caelli.W, Longley.D, Shain.M: "Information Security Handbook", Macmillan Publishers, New York, 1991.

Ford.W: "Computer Communications Security", PTR Prentice Hall, New Jersey, 1994.

Fuchsberger.A, Gollmann.D, Lothian.P, Paterson.K.G, Sidropoulos.A: "Public-Key Cryptography on Smart Cards", Cryptography: Policy and Algorithms, pg 250-269, Brisbane, 1995.

Garfinkel.S, Spafford.G: "Web Security and Commerce", O'reilly, Cambridge, 1997

Glass.A.S: "Why Should Secure Cards be Smart", Smart Card 2000, Elsevier Science Publishers, pg 39-49, North Holland, 1991.

Hendry.M: "Smart Card Security and Applications", Artech House, Boston, 1997.

Jefferies.N, Mitchell.C, Walker.M: "A Proposed Architecture for Trusted Third Party Services", Cryptography: Policy and Algorithms, pg 98-104, Brisbane, 1995.

Kaufman.C, Perlman.R, Speciner.M: "Network Security: private communication in a public world", PTR Prentice Hall, New Jersey, 1995.

Konigs.H.P: "Cryptographic Identification Methods for Smart Cards in the Process of Standardization", IEEE Communications Magazine

Lindley.R: "Smart card Innovation", Saim Pty Ltd, Wollongong, 1997.

Lucks.S: "Open Key Exchange: How to Defeat Dictionary Attacks Without Encrypting Public Keys", Security Protocols - 5th International workshop, pg 79-90, Paris, 1997.

Oppliger.R: "Authentication Systems for Secure Networks", Artech House, Boston, 1996.

Pfleeger.C.P: "Security in Computing", Prentice Hall, New Jersy. 1989.

Rankl.W, Effing. W: "Smart Card Handbook", Wiley, New York, 1997.

Schneier.B: "Applied Cryptography: Protocol, Algorithms and Source Code in C", Wiley, New York , 1996.

Stinson D.R: "Cryptography: Theory and Practice", CRC Press, Florida, 1995.

Tanenbaum.A.S: "Computer Networks", Prentice Hall, New Jersey, 1996.

Tempus House Of Publishers: "Smart Card Security: How Secure is the Smart Card", Journal Business Continuity, 4(3), pg 58-60, 1996.

Tomkowiak.S, Hofland.P: "A computer in your wallet", BYTE magazine, 1996.

URL01: "Fraud, Smartcards, Biometrics", Internet WWW page at URL < http://www.gare.co.uk/smart.html > accessed on 13-07-98.

URL02: "Smart Cards : The Latest in Finance Technology", Internet WWW page at URL < http://www.oberthurkirk.com/smartc.html > accessed on 10-07-98.

URL03: "Biometric Identification", Internet WWW page at URL < http://www.afmc.wpafb.af.mil/HQAFMC/LGL/LSO/LOA/bio.1>, accessed on 13-07-98.

Wenbo.M, Boyd.C: "On Strengthening Authentication Protocols to Foil Cryptanalysis", Computer Security-ESORICS'94, pg 193-204, Brighton, 1994.

Redesign of the Neuman-Stubblebine Protocol Using Confidentiality-Authentication Channels to Foil Replay Attacks

Syed M Rahman, Deepak Rauniar and Robert J. Bignall
School of Computing and Information Technology, Monash University, Churchill, VIC, Australia 3842
Email: {syed.rahman, deepak.rauniar, bob.bignall}@infotech.monash.edu.au

ABSTRACT

Recent advances in Information Technology have removed many of the physical barriers that inhibited information flow in the past. Never has information been so readily available as it is now. However, as information around the globe becomes more accessible, it has also become more vulnerable to misuse. Authenticating the identity of a distributed process in the face of a malicious active intruder is an exacting area of computer security. The design and implementation of authentication protocols is critical and of paramount importance in view of the fact that these protocols provide the first line of defense in setting up a secure communication session. In this paper we discuss one such authentication method, namely the Neuman-Stubblebine protocol, which provides mutual authentication between two distributed processes. We discuss the limitations of the protocol in terms of replay attacks as well as existing solutions to counter such an attack. Finally, we propose a redesign of the protocol employing the concept of confidentiality and authentication channels, such that the protocol is no longer vulnerable to a replay attack.

Keywords: distributed processes, authentication, protocols, cryptography, session key, Neuman-Stubblebine

INTRODUCTION

Information technology has exploited the power of microelectronics to provide unparalleled opportunities for users to access information, both in terms of effective use of local information and by the use of communication facilities to create world wide information systems. The recent advances in information technology have removed many of the physical barriers that inhibited information flow in the past. Never has information been so readily available as it is now. With the networking technologies that are available today, it is possible to connect to a distant computer over international communication lines and access information that would have been locked in a filing cabinet just a few years ago [Caelli, 1991].

However, as information around the globe has become more accessible, it has also become more vulnerable to misuse. With advances in technology, a whole new dimension has been added to the notion of information security. Infrastructure is required that minimizes the opportunities for misuse of sensitive information within the powerful technology based systems established for legitimate users. Over the years the need for strong mechanisms has emerged. These should ensure that the integrity and confidentiality of the information is maintained while maintaining transparent access to information and associated processing facilities by legitimate users. Furthermore, anyone who gains illicit access to information should be inhibited from exploiting the situation [Caelli, 1991].

The verification of the identity of a process in a distributed environment is the first logical step in providing security. In a secured system, only when the processes are properly verified should they be allowed to enter the system and access its information, otherwise their access should be blocked.

In this paper, we show how the Neuman-Stubblebine protocol can be redesigned to foil a replay attack. Neuman-Stubblebine, which is an excellent mutual authentication protocol that employs the services of a trusted Key Distribution Center to provide mutual authentication between two distributed processes, nevertheless suffers from a replay attack as described in section 5.

The term "process" in this paper is used to refer to any distributed entity that wishes to communicate securely over an insecure physical channel with another entity, and hence needs to be authenticated. Such entities are assumed to have some computing power at their disposal and may take the form of users with a terminal, servers, smart cards, etc.

AUTHENTICATION

Authentication is a technique whereby a process verifies the claimed identity of another process over an insecure channel. Authenticity refers to the result of a successful authentication procedure, whereby a verifying process becomes sure of the claimed identity of the claimant process [Oppliger, 1996]. Proper authentication between distributed processes is important in view of the insecure nature of the underlying physical channel where messages can be intercepted, modified, deleted or initiated by an intruder. Authentication provides the means whereby distributed resources can properly verify the identity of a remote process before entering into a transaction.

Given the distributed model of computing that has evolved in recent years with an insecure channel bridging the distributed processes, providing proper identification is not an easy task and it is precisely this problem that authentication protocols solve. When processes are authenticated, typically by exchanging a series of messages depending on the protocols used, both of the processes in a communicating pair become confident about each other's identity. They know for certain that they are not communicating with an imposter. In any computer system there generally are three different levels of authentication involved -
• Authentication of the user by the system – User Authentication.
• Authentication of the distributed or remote process (smart card, remote computer etc.) by the system – Process/Device Authentication.
• Authentication of the system itself.

Authentication of users by the system is done through passwords, PINs, tokens or biometric techniques [Garfinkel 1997], [Rankl., 1997], [Hendry, 1997], [http://www.afmc.wpafb.af.mil/HQ-AFMC/LGL/LSO/LOA/bio.1]. User authentication through a password or Personal Identification Number (PIN) is achieved by having the user type his password or PIN at a keyboard. This is matched against the password of the user stored in the system. If the password matches, the user is authenticated and allowed to proceed further, else he or she is blocked from proceeding. With token identification, the user is authenticated if he is able to present the physical token as required by the system. A typical example of such authentication is the use of an access card to open an electronically controlled gate. In biometric identification, the user is uniquely identified by the system based on his individual and unique biological attributes. Fingerprints are one common example of such attributes.

Device as well as system authentication is generally achieved employing encryption, one way hash functions or zero knowledge based protocols [Kaufman, 1995], [Schneier, 1996], [Garfinkel 1997], [Tanenbaum, 1996]. These protocols employ complex mathematical computations to conclusively prove the identities of the communicating entities.

CRYPTOGRAPHIC AUTHENTICATION

The basic idea of a cryptographic authentication is that a claimant A proves his identity to a verifier B by performing a cryptographic operation on a quantity that either both know or B supplies. A uses a secret cryptographic key to perform the operation on the quantity and hence to convince B [Oppliger, 1996].

Cryptographic authentication is desirable in view of the inherently insecure nature of the underlying physical channel, which can be vulnerable to attacks from an intruder who can read, alter, destroy, and create messages at will. In remote/distributed computing applications which crucially require secure communication, authentication establishes a secure channel between distributed communicating processes [Wenbo, 1994].

In any authentication scenario, there are ultimately two distributed processes, which the protocol serves. There is a prover, also known as a claimant, that desires to prove its identity to a remote process in order to communicate securely or to access the service provided by the process. There is also a verifier, who verifies the claimed identity of the prover/claimant before actually starting the communication or delivering the service. The claimant and the verifier are often also known as the principals.

Two different types of strategies are possible for any claimant process to authenticate itself to a verifier process. In the first case, a claimant process can directly approach the verifier and prove itself to the verifier process. In the second approach, a claimant process can prove itself to the verifier process by proving itself to a third party whom the verifier process trusts. Based on the above strategies, authentication protocols can be divided into two classes [Tanenbaum, 1996], [Kaufman, 1995], [Schneier, 1996], [Oppliger, 1996], [Ford, 1994].

The first class of authentication protocols provides direct mutual authentication between two distributed processes. For example, if a distributed process A wishes to authenticate itself to another distributed process B over an insecure channel, it directly contacts B and proves its identity to B. If mutual authentication is required, process B also authenticates itself directly to process A.

The general model of the protocol is as below:
1. A → authenticates → B
2. B → authenticates → A

The second class of the protocol employ the services of an intermediary or third party, also known as Key Distribution Center (KDC), that is trusted by everybody to provide authentication of distributed processes. For the purposes of authentication, a process, e.g. A, wishing to communicate with some other process, e.g. B, approaches the KDC with a request for the key of process B. The KDC encrypts the desired key of the process B, which is also known as a ticket, with the key shared between process A and the KDC and sends it to A. This ensures that nobody obtains a key from the KDC while impersonating somebody else. When A receives the encrypted key from the KDC, it decrypts it using its key and obtains the necessary key to authenticate to B. Then A and B mutually authenticate each other with the help of the ticket.

The general model of the protocol is as below:

1. A → request for a key to talk to B → KDC
2. KDC → KDC gives the key encrypted with A's secret key → A
3. A → authenticates itself to B using the key from KDC → B
4. B → authenticates itself to A → A

Key management is relatively easy with protocols employing a KDC because any process has to maintain only one secret key that is shared with the KDC and through this it can talk to virtually any other process known to the KDC. A KDC can be implemented as a single point for key management or it could be distributed geographically with multiple KDCs around the world.

In this paper, the proposed protocol employs the services of a trusted Key Distribution Center to authenticate distributed processes and also to establish a session key to encrypt the messages that are exchanged and thus hide them from prying eyes.

AUTHENTICATION PROTOCOLS

The problem of authentication in the presence of an insecure channel is fundamental to the success of secured distributed computing. It is therefore highly desirable to provide sound protocols for authentication [Blake, 1997]. A secure mutual authentication protocol is a two-party protocol, whereby both processes accept (at least with overwhelmingly probability) if the opposite party is benign, but reject with overwhelmingly probability in the presence of an active attacker [Lucks, 1997].

The core of any authentication protocol that provides unidirectional or mutual identification of a distributed entity revolves around challenge-response techniques [Tanenbaum, 1996], [Schneier, 1996], [Stinson, 1995], [Ford, 1994], [Pfleeger, 1989]. In a typical run of protocol employing challenge-response techniques, one of the processes involved issues what is known as a challenge to the other party, who in turn is required to come up with a proper response to the challenge. The party issuing the challenge is known as the challenger while the one responding to the challenge is called the responder.

The challenge itself typically involves a random number that the responder is required to transform in some special way known only to the bona fide party (often involving its private key) and return the result. After receiving the response to its challenge, the challenger compares it to the desired result, which also generally involves some computation locally by the challenger. If the responder's result matches the desired result, then and only then is responder authenticated. The grounds for such authentication rest on the fact that the responder has demonstrated the possession of a secret, which is supposedly known only to the bona fide party, and thus must be the bona fide party. By swapping the roles of the challenger and the responder, mutual authentication is achieved.

Apart from establishing the claim of a remote process in the context of an insecure physical channel, most mutual authentication protocols also address the issue of secure session key exchange between the authenticated processes [Tanenbaum, 1996], [Schneier, 1996], [Ford, 1994]. A secure session key exchange between the authenticated processes involves the delivery of a new session key, which is randomly generated for each session. Once the session key is exchanged, all communication is encrypted using it, allowing only the bona fide processes to encrypt/decrypt messages. Hence these messages remain hidden from an intruder who does not hold the session key. Further, the use of a new random session key for each session also serves to enhance the overall security and the efficiency of the system.

Security is enhanced in view of the fact that the secret keys of the processes are only used for a short duration - just for authentication and session key exchange. Once the session key has been securely exchanged, it is used to encrypt all communication between the authenticated processes. Thus at any time the compromise of a session key only makes vulnerable those communications involving that particular session key. If a session key is randomly generated and used strictly for one session only, the damage involved is restricted to that particular session. In contrast, if the secret key is used at all times for all purposes, a compromise of the key makes all the messages exchanged in all the sessions involving the key vulnerable. The damage thus caused can be severe [Wenbo, 1994].

Efficiency is increased in view the fact that for authentication purposes more advanced cryptographic technologies (e.g. private-key/public-key) can be used. However, once the processes are authenticated a small session key (e.g a symmetric key) can be used. Thus the actual messages can be encrypted/decrypted with relatively small processing power and minimum delay [Wenbo, 1994]. In summary, a mutual authentication protocol addresses the following two distinct issues:

- Authentication of the distributed processes.
- Establishment of a random session key between the authenticated processes.

NEUMAN-STUBBLEBINE PROTOCOL

The Neuman-Stubblebine protocol [Gurgens, 1997], [Schneier, 1996], [Syverson, 1993] is a mutual authentication protocol that employs the service of a trusted KDC to provide mutual authentication between two distributed processes. This protocol is capable of foiling a suppress-replay attack by an intruder. A suppress-replay attack is an attack that can be mounted by an intruder if the clocks of the distributed processes are not synchronized. For example, if a process A sends a message to B to which it also adds its time stamp and if A's clock is ahead of process B, then an intruder T can intercept the message and replay it later when the timestamp becomes current at B.

For our protocol definition, we assume process A wishes to communicate with process B. K_A and K_B are the keys that process A and process B respectively share with the KDC. K_S is a random session key that will be ultimately possessed by the two processes after executing the protocol. Random numbers R_A and R_B are the respective challenges of processes A and B.

The Neuman-Stubblebine protocol provides mutual authentication between two distributed processes A and B as follows:

1) Process A generates a large random number, R_A, and sends it to process B along with its identity.
2) Process B generates its own random number R_B. It adds a timestamp, T_B, to the message received from step (1) and encrypts the message using K_B. It sends the encrypted message along with its identity and R_B to the KDC.
3) The KDC generates a random session key K_S and sends the following two messages to Process A along with R_B.
   - The first contains Process B's identity, K_S, R_A and T_B, all encrypted with K_A.
   - The second contains Process A's identity plus K_S and T_B encrypted with K_B. The latter is also known as the ticket.
4) Process A, decrypts the message intended for it using its key and extracts the session key K_S. It authenticates the KDC as the source of the incoming message when it sees its R_A returned. It then sends the following two messages to Process B.
   - The ticket it received from the KDC for Process B.
   - R_B encrypted with K_S.

When process B receives message (4), it decrypts the ticket using K_B and extracts the session key. It then decrypts the second message with K_S and when it sees that its R_B has been returned correctly, it authenticates process A.

The protocol can be summarized as below:

1. A Æ B: A, R_A
2. B Æ KDC: B, R_B, $K_B(A, R_A, T_B)$
3. KDC Æ A: $K_A(B, K_S, R_A, T_B)$, $K_B(A, K_S, T_B)$, R_B
4. A Æ B: $K_S(R_B)$, $K_B(A, K_S, T_B)$

Features of the Protocol

- The protocol works efficiently even if clocks are not synchronized. As a matter of fact synchronized clocks are not required at all because the time stamp is relative to process B's clock. For authentication purposes process B just checks the time stamp that it generated itself.
- Once it has been executed, the protocol allows processes A and B to directly authenticate themselves within some predetermined time limit in just three steps, without relying on the KDC, as follows:
   1) Process A re-sends the message it received for B in step (3) along with a new random number.
   2) Process B encrypts process A's random number with the session key and sends it back along with its own random number.
   3) Process A encrypts process B's random number with the session key and sends the same to B.

   The protocol can be summarized as below:
   1. A → B: $K_B(A, K_S, T_B)$, R_{A1}
   2. B → A: $K_S(R_{A1})$, R_{B1}
   3. A → B: $K_S(R_{B1})$

Limitations of the Protocol

The protocol is vulnerable to attack by an intruder because there is no way for process B to authenticate the source of the message it receives in step (1). An active intruder process, T, can exploit this situation and mount an

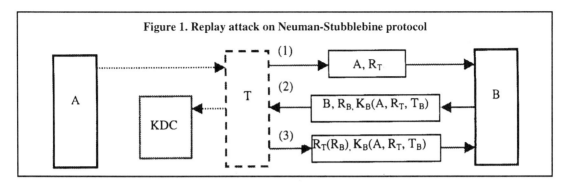
Figure 1. Replay attack on Neuman-Stubblebine protocol

attack impersonating process A as follows [Gurgens, 1997], [Syverson, 1993].

1) An intruder process T generates a large random number R_T and sends it to process B, impersonating process A and sending A's identity.

2) As process B can not authenticate process A at this stage, it adds as usual a time stamp to the message received from process T, and encrypts it with K_B. It generates its own random number R_B and sends the encrypted message, its identity and R_B to the KDC.

3) Process T intercepts process B's message to the KDC and blocks it from going to the KDC. As a result, the third message of the protocol is omitted. Process T encrypts R_B with R_T and sends it along with $K_B(A, R_T, T_B)$, as received from step (2), to process B, again impersonating process A.

These three steps are shown in figure 1.

The dotted line shows the original source and the recipients. When process B receives the message from step (4), it decrypts it using K_B and extracts the session key as R_T plus time stamp T_B. It then decrypts the second message with R_T and when it sees both its T_B and R_B correctly returned it authenticates process T as process A. Then process B uses R_T as the session key to communicate with process T.

Analysis

An intruder is able to mount a replay attack on the protocol by exploiting the fact process B is not able to distinguish between a random number used as a challenge and a session key [Gurgens, 1997], [Syverson, 1993]. This is not entirely unreasonable, since both are freshly generated random numbers.

One way the above attack can be avoided is by requiring process B to check that $K_S \neq R_T$. However, this also means an added level of cost (both in terms of memory as well as computation) while implementing the protocol.

This particular attack can also be avoided by including direction bits in the messages. However, this again implies an extra cost, and furthermore direction bits are not considered to be a general solution to repair a protocol [Syverson, 1993].

Another way of avoiding the attack is by reversing the order of T_B and R_T in step (2) [Gurgens, 1997], [Syverson, 1993]. However, in doing so, even though the replay attack is prevented, the protocol becomes vulnerable to a different attack as discussed in [Syverson, 1993].

PROPOSED MODIFICATION

In the preceding section, we analyzed how the replay attack can be avoided in the Neuman-Stubblebine protocol. However, as analyzed, the suggested approaches are basically implementation dependent and mean extra costs in terms of computing and memory. Furthermore, while the third approach was able to foil the replay attack, it made the protocol vulnerable to a different type of attack.

In the following sections, we show how the protocol can be redesigned so that an intruder can not mount the replay attack in the first place. Our design is influenced by the work of Colin Boyd and Wenbo Mao who in [Boyd, 94] promulgate the view that in any cryptographic security protocol two different logical channels exist. The first, namely the confidentiality channel, allows the sender of the message to decide those users who will be able to receive it. The confidentiality channel should ensure that the message does not become known to anybody other than the intended recipient. The second, namely the authentication channel, allows the recipient of the message to decide those users who must have sent it.

Redesigned Neuman-Stubblebine Protocol

For our protocol definition we again assume that process A wishes to communicate with process B. K_A and K_B are the keys that process A and process B respectively share with the KDC. K_S is a random session key that will ultimately be possessed by the two processes after executing the protocol. Random numbers R_A and R_B are the respective challenges of processes A and B.

Our proposed protocol provides mutual authentication between the two distributed processes as follows:

1) Process A generates a large random number, R_A, and sends it to process B along with its identity.
2) Process B generates its own random number R_B. It encrypts a timestamp, T_B with K_B and sends the encrypted time stamp along with its identity, process A's identity, R_A and R_B to the KDC.
3) The KDC generates a random session key K_S and sends the following sets of messages to Process A.
   • The first set of messages are for process A and contain
      (a) The session key, K_S, encrypted with K_A. This message represents the confidentiality channel for process A and ensures that the session key is available only to process A.
      (b) A hash of A's identity, B's identity, K_S and R_A all encrypted with K_A. This message represents the authentication channel for process A and allows process A to make a decision about the source of the message.
   • The second set of messages are for process B. They serve as the ticket and contain
      (a) The session key, K_S encrypted with K_B. This message represents the confidentiality channel for process B and ensures that the session key is available only to process B.
      (b) A hash of A's identity, B's identity, K_S, R_B and T_B all encrypted with K_B. This message similarly represents the authentication channel for process B and allows process B to make a decision about the source of the message.
4) Process A decrypts the message intended for it using its key and extracts the session key K_S. It then locally computes the hash and compares it with the hash received from the KDC (after decrypting it with K_A). It authenticates the KDC as the source of the incoming message when it finds the two hash results to be equal. Furthermore, the above hash also confirms to process A the freshness of the message (since the resultant hash is also a function of the value R_A freshly generated by process A). Process A then sends the ticket (received in step 3) to process B.

When process B receives message (4), it decrypts the first message using K_B and extracts the session key. It then locally computes the hash and compares it with the hash received from the KDC (after decrypting it with K_B). It authenticates the KDC as the source of the incoming message when it finds the two hash values to be equal (the grounds for this being that the hash involves T_B, which can only be known to the KDC besides process B). Furthermore, the above hash also confirms to process B the freshness of the message (i.e. it is not a replay of a previous message) since the resultant hash is also a function of the number R_A freshly generated by process A).

The protocol can be summarized as below:

1. A → B: A, R_A
2. B → KDC: A, B, R_A, R_B, $K_B(T_B)$
3. KDC → A: $K_A(K_S)$, $K_A(\text{hash}(A, B, K_S, R_A))$, $K_B(K_S)$, $K_B(\text{hash}(A, B, K_S, R_B, T_B))$
4. A → B: $K_B(K_S)$, $K_B(\text{hash}(A, B, K_S, R_B, T_B))$

In this way indirect authentication between process A and process B is provided with the help of the KDC. Then, using the session key that has been distributed, processes A and B can communicate securely over an insecure channel.

Improvements Due To Redesign

The proposed redesign is not vulnerable to the replay attack by an intruder as described in section 5.2. Thus our re-design improves the overall security of the Neuman-Stubblebine protocol.

In the original protocol, an intruder process was able to mount a replay attack because the encrypted messages in steps (2) and (4) were almost identical in their content. As analyzed in section 5.2, an intruder can exploit this fact to attack the protocol, by reusing the message generated from a previous step in a later step i.e. a message from step (2) is replayed in step (4). The intruder never needs to know the secret key of process B to mount the attack and hence successfully impersonate process A.

In our design, this point has been carefully dealt with. We recognize that there are two channels involved in any authentication and key exchange protocol. In our protocol there is a confidentiality channel and an authentication channel. The confidentiality channel is required to distribute the session key securely to the intended distributed process. Since the other components of the messages e.g. the random numbers, time stamps (except in step (2) where it needs to be kept confidential) etc. are required to ensure the authenticity of the source of the message, they are separated into the authentication channel.

The proposed protocol is quite effective in terms of the overall cost of implementation. The overall complexity of the protocol in terms of processing is actually reduced in view of the fact that only the session key needs to be encrypted in steps (3) and (4). As far as the hash is concerned it can be any simple one way function, not necessarily having the same complexity as required in a cryptographic computation.

CONCLUSIONS

In any security system, entity authentication offers the first line of defense. Authenticating the identity of a distributed process in the face of a malicious active intruder is an exacting area of computer security. A variety of authentication and key exchange protocols already exist in literature. However, protocols for authentication and key exchange have proved difficult to develop correctly despite their apparent simplicity in terms of the length and number of messages involved [*Boyd, 1994]. The design and implementation of these protocols are critical and of paramount importance in view of the fact that they provide the first line of defense in setting up a secure communication session. [Boyd, 1994].

In this paper, we have shown how the Neuman-Stubblebine protocol can be redesigned to foil a replay attack by an intruder. Even though solutions do exist to foil such attacks, these solutions require extra overhead in the form of direction information, memory requirements to hold the previous messages etc. In addition even though one of the existing solutions is able to foil the replay attack on the protocol, it open up the possibility of a different form of an attack. In this paper, we have taken a different approach to addressing the limitations of the Neuman-Stubblebine protocol. We have shown how the protocol can be redesigned using the concept of security channels (confidentiality and authentication) such that the replay attack can not happen. In addition, our proposal is cost effective in terms of implementation.

REFERENCES

Blake S.W, Menezes A: "Entity authentication and authenticated key transport protocols employing asymmetric techniques", Security Protocols - 5th International Workshop, pg. 137-158, Paris, 1997.

Boyd C, Wenbo M: "Design and analysis of key exchange protocols via secure channel identification", Advances in Cryptology - ASIACRYPT'94, pg. 171-181, Wollongong, 1994.

*Boyd C, Wenbo M: "Designing secure key exchange protocols", Computer Security-ESORICS'94, pg. 93-105, Brighton, 1994.

Caelli W, Longley D, Shain M: "Information Security Handbook", Macmillan Publishers, New York, 1991.

Ford W: "Computer Communications Security", PTR Prentice Hall, New Jersey, 1994.

Garfinkel S, Spafford G: "Web Security and Commerce", O'Reilly, Cambridge, 1997.

Gurgens S.: "SG Logic - a formal analysis technique for authentication protocols", Security Protocols - 5th International Workshop, pg. 158-176, Paris, 1997.

Hendry M: "Smart Card Security and Applications", Artech House, Boston, 1997.

Jefferies N, Mitchell C, Walker M: "A proposed architecture for trusted third party services", Cryptography: Policy and Algorithms, pg. 98-104, Brisbane, 1995.

Kaufman C, Perlman R, Speciner M: "Network Security: Private Communication in a Public World", PTR Prentice Hall, New Jersey, 1995.

Lucks S. (1997): "Open key exchange: How to defeat dictionary attacks without encrypting public keys", Security Protocols - 5th International workshop, pg. 79-90, Paris, 1997.

Oppliger R.: "Authentication Systems for Secure Networks", Artech House, Boston, 1996.

Pfleeger C.P: "Security in Computing", Prentice Hall, New Jersey, 1989.

Rankl W, Effing W: "Smart Card Handbook", Wiley, New York, 1997.

Schneier B: "Applied Cryptography: Protocol, Algorithms and Source Code in C", Wiley, New York, 1996.

Stinson D.R: "Cryptography: Theory and Practice", CRC Press, Florida, 1995.

Syverson P: "On key distribution protocols for repeated authentication", in ACM Operating Systems Review, Vol 27, No 4, pg. 24-30, 1993.

Tanenbaum A.S: "Computer Networks", Prentice Hall, New Jersey, 1996.

Wenbo M, Boyd C: "On strengthening authentication protocols to foil cryptanalysis", Computer Security-ESORICS'94, pg. 193-204, Brighton, 1994.

PLanning for System Security

Patricia Sendall

Associate Professor of Management Information Systems, Merrimack College, Department of Management, 315 Turnpike Street, N. Andover, MA 01845

978.837.5000 x4419 , 978.837.5013 (fax), psendall@merrimack.edu

ABSTRACT

The growing number and complexity of systems makes providing for a secure computing environment difficult. The problem of computing security is a complex one. There is a noticeable tendency within systems development projects to downplay or ignore the need for the modeling of security requirements, which include security policy (Freeman, 1994). It is more productuve and cost effective to address security requirements during the planning and design phase of the traditional systems development life cycle. Security that is added after the fact is not as effective and is more costly to implement and maintain (Bruce and Dempsey, 1997). This paper presents an overview of planning for enterprise-wide system security and policy-making.

PLANNING FOR SYSTEM SECURITY

With the proliferation of distributed systems, including local area networks, the Internet and World Wide Web, much has been written about safeguarding corporate data. How do we keep our intellectual property and corporate resources safe both from the and the inside? The literature is exploding with the latest standards and secure technology ready for implementation. However, what is sorely missing in contemporary research is guidance and recommendations regarding *the plan*. What do we first need to do before leaping into a secure system implementation?

According to leading cryptographer, Schneier (1997), when planning for system security, it is always better to assume the worst. Assume your adversaries are better than they are.

In a survey of 205 Fortune 1000 companies by Warroom Research LLC, Baltimore, 82.5 percent report that they have experienced break-in and about 90 percent admitted to having insider threat problems. Although most acknowledge that the biggest threat comes from inside the organization, more and more damaging attacks are coming from the outside (Higgins, 1997). Being proactive is the only way to minimize risk.

The traditional systems development life cycle (SDLC) includes five phases: planning, analysis, design, implementation and support (Whitten, Bentley & Barlow, 1994). Security considerations must be included throughout the SDLC, particularly in the planning and analysis stages. Failure to address security requirements early in the project merely delays potential problems. According to Chapman and Zwicky (1997), putting together a security policy is a great deal more amusing than dealing with the side effects of not having one.

Most organizations haven't codified policies for managing electronic records or invested time or money in this. Making the business case for infrastructure is the toughest challenge facing CIO's. It requires technical competence, communications skills and political savvy to convince senior management (May, 1997).

A secure computing environment is a business problem, not a technical one. Some researchers (Bruce & Dempsey, 1997) say that too much technology and too many standards with too little planning, and too little management, is a recipe for security risks, or worse, disaster. An overall security strategy must start with a current assessment of the level of security for the organization. It should include a review of the technologies used by the organization, its policies and procedures, and management directives.

To be able to provide security in a distributed environment, there needs to be demonstrated leadership and vision for security that can be applied across all areas of the enterprise. In order for any computer security program to succeed, it must have support from senior management (Alexander, 1997). A major challenge is to balance the cost of security solutions and controls against the risks these solutions are addressing.

Kahn & Abrams (1994) argue that it is prudent to enhance system security by anticipating failures and preparing for contingencies. By doing so, actions can be taken to avoid consequences. Information technology (IT) security needs to allocate resources to contingency resolution mechanisms that can be used to complement prevention mechanisms. Corporations cannot afford risk avoidance, therefore they must plan for contingencies. Information technology security must incorporate plans for these contingencies that will occur during system operation.

Unfortunately, available resources can be expected to continue to shrink, and therefore management can only afford pragmatic risk reduction. Security is, in general, a trade-off with convenience, and most people are not willing to forgo the convenience of remote access via networks to their computers. Inevitably, they suffer from some loss of security (Network Security White Paper (NSWP), 1995).

PRINCIPLES AND POLICIES

Before embarking on a secure system project, one must first understand the difference between principles and policies. Principles are statements of values, operation or belief that drive all of the elements of the security framework. The collection of principles provides the security philosophy under which the security architecture and security policies are developed. These principles can be thought of as rules by which the security policies and processes must follow. Security policies and procedures should be founded on business principles or statements of corporate philosophy.

To date, there are no specific standards associated with the development of security policy or procedures. The choices of policy topics and content are generally unique to each organization. The Information Systems Security Association's 1994 report, the Generally Accepted System Security Principles (GSSP), outlines 17 principles that can provide guidance to the development of the security principles defined by an organization.

In their paper on Internet security policies, Chapman and Zwicky (1997) provide the following definitions:
Policy-is what determines what "wars" you are going to fight and why; its primary purpose is to lay out a direction; it is a theory of what you're trying to achieve;
Strategy-is the plan for carrying out the war;
Tactic-is a method for carrying out a strategy.

Cobb (1997) offers the following definition:
Privacy-Denying other people access to certain information about ourselves.

A security *framework* defines the policies that provide direction for the implementation and maintenance of security measures to protect the information assets and services that support business activities of the organization. The objectives of a security policy framework are to effectively manage risk, maintain employee accountability for the protection of information assets, establish a basis for a stable process environment, assure compliance with applicable laws and regulations, and preserve management options in the event of asset misuse, loss or unauthorized disclosure. The security framework must be subject to an open process for continual development and improvement. The success of the security framework of policies can be measured by critical success factors (Bruce & Dempsey, 1997).

Security policy is one of the most important components with which to build the foundation of a security architecture. It is a way of communicating with users and managers what they need to know to make the decisions about security. It sets explicit expectations and responsibilities among the users and management (Chapman & Zwicky, 1996). The policy protects not only confidentiality, but also the availability of information, the utilization of the information, the authenticity of the information presented, and the integrity of the information. A security policy is actually a collection of individual policies that address specific topics or areas of concern. The absence of a policy may prevent an organization from taking an action even if an incident clearly violates the intent of the organization. Security policy is an area that usually gets some attention, especially when auditors are involved.

If a company has too little security, it can lose the organization to lawyers or attackers. What really matters is what an organization actually does, not what they have written down as policy. In their research on security policy making, Chapman & Zwicky (1996) warn that a policy that specifies what's supposed to be done, but not why, is doomed. In the absence of a formal security policy, it may be difficult to hold users accountable for their actions. According to Bruce & Dempsey,

"Policies may be required to legally protect the corporation from the action of an employee. Legal recourse to a security-related incident may not be possible if a governing policy does not define what is acceptable or unacceptable."

Getting Started

Security policies should be kept short and concise and should include:
• *Policy statement*-A formal statement of the corporate policy, should be specific and to the point.
• *Purpose*-Requirements, problem description, components and definition of the policy.
• *Scope*-Boundaries of the policy.
• *Compliance with policy*-Specific components, any deviation from, and applications of, the policy.
• *Penalties/Consequences*-for noncompliance with the policy.

According to Bruce & Dempsey (1997), before you begin writing your policy, some questions that should be asked and answered are:
• What does the organization need to protect?
• What is the security philosophy of the organization?

- What standards should be followed?
- Do the employees have access to all information?
- Who is responsible for security?

Based on the above questions, Bruce & Dempsey suggest a security strategy methodology which could include the following five phases:

Phase 1:   Assessment of current security practices, policies and procedures.

Phase 2:   Definition of overall objectives, including requirements analysis. Interview employees, including technologists and management.

Phase 3:   Assessment of alternative solutions and examination of the technology currently employed.

Phase 4:   Recommend solutions and course of action including risk assessment.

Phase 5:   Review future applications and directions; execute/implement the plan.

The evaluation team must conduct life cycle, configuration, and trusted distribution audits of all of the hardware, firmware, and software required according to the life cycle definition, configuration management, and trusted distribution plans (Mutispaugh, Ferguson, Bruce, & Alexander, 1994).

The strategy is to provide a direction for the future, not to find an immediate solution to every security concern. Strategic planning should begin with the assumption that you will not be able to meet every individual security objective put forward, and that not all objectives can be realized immediately. Also be aware that the strategy will change and evolve.

Policy Contents

It is necessary for IT managers and others to understand security policy development and content. But what is also important is what the security policy should *not* contain: technical details. The policy describes *what* is to be protected and *why*, and it leaves the *how* open so the technical staff can select the best implementation. A policy can guide you in selecting and implementing technology, but it shouldn't be used to specify it.

A clearly stated written policy must cover precisely how information, computers, and related resources are to be used by employees. The policy should spell out what the organization considers to be appropriate and inappropriate use of corporate computing resources, including the Internet.

The policy must succinctly detail the penalties for violating policy guidelines, or no one will take it seriously. One way to bolster a security policy is to distribute a set of guidelines for computer-related activities the company considers proper and improper, such as a section or two devoted to computer ethics and Internet behavior. Then, get the employees to buy in to the policy.

Some researchers (Alexander, 1997; Chapman & Zwicky, 1996; NIST, 1993) recommend that the following be used as the foundation for the content of a corporate computing policy:

1. Permission-The policy should state that the owner of the information or a senior manager must authorize the use of computer facilities by an employee. Employees should assume that all electronic files belong to someone, and therefore must be kept confidential.

2. Responsibilities-Employees are the owners of their own data and therefore have the responsibility of ensuring the information is adequately protected against unauthorized access.

3. Keep Passwords and Accounts Confidential-Advise employees to change their password frequently and avoid using passwords that can be easily guessed.

4. Unauthorized Access to Files and Directories-Employees should not circumvent computer security controls.

5. Unauthorized Use of Software-Employees are prohibited from loading unauthorized software onto any computer system without approval and from making illegal copies of software. If anti-virus software is installed, employees are required to use it.

6. Use for For-profit Activities-The company's computer systems are for the sole use of company business. Employees are prohibited from using corporate systems for personal or private financial gain.

7. Electronic Mail-E-mail systems should be used for company-related business only. Forging another's identity will be prohibited.

8. Harassment-Employees should not use corporate computers to insult anyone. This includes sexist, racist, obscene or suggestive e-mail.

9. Attacking the System-Employees must not attempt to deliberately degrade the performance of the corporate computer system.

10. Theft-All hardware, software and computer-related supplies and documentation are the sole property of the company.

11. Waste and Abuse-Eating, drinking, smoking around computing equipment is prohibited.

12. Networks-All networks must be used for company-related business only.

13. Enforcement Authority-Employees should be aware that the company will investigate any alleged abuse of its

computer resources.
14. Your Responsibility-Employees are responsible for their own actions.
15. Workplace Monitoring-The company reserves the right to monitor the system for signs of illegal or unauthorized activity.

A report by the National Institute of Standards and Technology (1993) also recommends that the policy include clear explanations of the policy where applicable, contain regular (non-legal) language, provide provision for reviews, and discussion of specific security issues.

A computer security policy is not a substitute for proper security controls. The policy's purpose is to demonstrate that you're serious about protecting the company's computer resources and to induce the employees to become a part of the solution rather than part of the problem. It defines ground rules. Once you have developed your policy, communicate it to every employee.

While the current literature is far from bursting with guidelines for system security planning, there is still some help available to the manager who is interested in doing so. The National Institute of Standards and Technology (NIST), through its National Computer Systems Laboratory (NCSL), publishes several publications about information systems security, including an executive's guide to information policies.

Once the governing principles and policies have been agreed upon, there is a challenge to provide the required security without requiring the user to jump through multiple hoops to access the distributed applications. Therefore, you want the best security that meets your requirements. When considering your plan, experts (Cobb, 1997; Chapman & Zwicky, 1996) suggest identifying each of the following:
• Affordability: How much money does the security cost? Because security budgets are never unlimited, it is important to focus protection on those attacks most likely to occur.
• Functionality: Can you still use your computers?
• Cultural compatibility: Does it conflict with the way people at your site normally interact with each other and the outside world?
• Legality: Does it meet your site's legal requirements? External factors include legal requirements, contractual obligations, and existing organizational policies. What is required is "due diligence," an attempt in good faith to take normal precautions.

There are a number of basic design issues that should be addressed by the person who has been tasked with the responsibility of designing, specifying and implementing or overseeing corporate security. The first and most important reflects the policy of how your company or organization wants to operate the system. The second design issue is what level of monitoring, redundancy and control do you want? You can form a checklist of what should be monitored, permitted, and denied. Start by figuring out your overall objectives, and then combine a needs analysis with a risk assessment, and sort the conflicting requirements out into a list that specifies what you plan to implement. The third issue is financial. It is important to try to quantify any proposed solutions in terms of how much it will cost to either buy or implement it (Network Security White Paper, 1995).

Freeman, Neely, & Heckard (1994) suggest a security policy modeling approach that can be applied to many types of systems, including networks and distributed systems. The approach is driven by security requirements and system architecture.

Security policy modeling, as a part of establishing a chain of reasoning between the security policy and the system implementation, is an accepted, required means of providing some of the necessary additional assurance.

Although many of the underlying security principles remain constant, security policy modeling methods have not kept up with the ever-increasing systems complexity. This has resulted in an increasing separation between security analysis and systems development.

There has been a perception that only one way exists to produce a policy model acceptable to security evaluation teams. The views regarding the need for security policy modeling and how such modeling is to be accomplished are changing. The approach is driven by security requirements and architecture rather than by forcing an existing generic model on a possible incompatible problem area.

A multi-level secure (MLS) development, integration or maintenance project has to address the incorporation of security technology within standard or traditional development disciplines. The significant contribution to system developers comes from assessing the security policy and placing its meaning within the framework of the system architecture. Matching policy statements to architectural components is very useful for (i) identifying and correcting inconsistencies in system security policy; (ii) providing an interpretation of policy suitable for the individual components; (iii) formulating system security requirements that correspond to security policy; and (iv) achieving a stable basis for a requirements interpretation and allocation to architectural components.

BASIC SECURITY ELEMENTS
When planning for system security, the following basic elements of security must be considered and included

in the plan:
* Information Integrity-Protects data from corruption; integrity is concerned with the reliability, accuracy, and management of data.
* Access Control/Authorization-Provides a means of enforcing authorization to use system resources.
* Confidentiality-Ensures that a user or process other than those that are authorized cannot access information.
* Authentication-A method of uniquely identifying a user, machine or application and verifying its identity; includes a clearly stated policy on passwords. Regardless of the motivation, user authentication systems like smart cards or non-reusable passwords are important parts of an overall security policy, but by themselves, do not provide adequate protection or security to an overall network (NSWP, 1995).
* Nonrepudiation-The ability to prevent denial that a message has been sent or received or an action taken; the message or action could only have been produced by the sender.
* Availability-Continuity, durability, recovery and consistency of data.

Internet and WWW

When planning for a secure computing environment, all of the interests within the enterprise must be represented. The implementation strategy must address such issues as IS security, change control, standards for the development, management and the deployment of this information. This strategy must also include the organization's formal policies for accessing Internet and web sites (Felmly, 1997).

Whether access is through the Internet or via a modem to a desktop, protecting corporate data is a critical issue. As the Internet becomes the most important communications medium of the new global economy, with growth estimated at 20% per month, more and more possibilities exist for an unwanted electronic intrusion from inside or outside your company (Network Security Crisis, 1995).

Companies, particularly those with new or existing Internet sites, need to take strong and specific measures to improve computer security. These measures include creating a TCP/IP service access policy, using strong authentication, and using a secure Internet gateway that can implement network access policy (NIST, 1993).

How detailed and complex should a network security policy be? A policy for Internet integration should be quite simple if it is designed to address only transactions between us (internal) and them (Internet). Garvin (1995) suggests that a more detailed policy is required if you intend to allow connections from the Internet through your firewall.

A web-access policy statement minimizes the organization's risk of being involved in web-related litigation. This policy statement should specify that access to the Web should only be for job-related purposes.

Committees made up of representatives from various constituencies from across the enterprise, have inherent limitations on their ability to formulate policies and act upon them. However, when strategy or policies spanning diverse organizational segments have to be created, creating a committee may be the best way in which to proceed. The IS auditor can encourage the formation of a working consensus, help foster senior executive support of the committee's work and ensure that all of the proper controls are in place.

Administrative controls should include policies stating that inappropriate materials cannot be accessed through the organization's Web connection. A good rule of thumb is to keep the control requirements general.

In a recent study (May, 1997), executives were asked, "Has Internet technology caused you to change your infrastructure requirements or plans?" Thirteen percent said "some." Sixteen percent said they were "still evaluating the question." Thirty-nine percent said "yes;" and 32% said "no."

As organizations and businesses begin to use the Internet to advertise their capabilities and distribute their products, sensitive data will increasingly become vulnerable to compromise and corruption (Securing Internet Information Servers, 1994).

According to Zalud (1997), some businesses see security concerns as a major impediment to growth into the WWW and Internet.

RISK MANAGEMENT: HOW MUCH SECURITY IS ENOUGH?

Pending laws will mandate that data security is a company's responsibility. The current standards for legal liability state that if you choose not to implement "reasonable" safeguards to prevent a dangerous event, you may be found guilty of negligence (Network Security White Paper, 1995).

Cobb (1996) states that in the face of massive enthusiasm for Internet technology in particular, the security professional must stress that "all security is relative" and advise that a practical answer to these problems has to be a compromise between vulnerability and risk. This takes system managers into the area of due diligence and liability.

To quote leading cryptographer Schneier, "The technology is not weak in and of itself, it is just badly implemented." Software engineers work for companies that have marketing departments with bottom lines. Schneier believes that we always need to be concerned about quality standards when encryption systems are developed under these circumstances.

Companies need to balance benefits with cost concerns. They should verify that their security concerns are well founded before they invest in an expensive security system they might not need. If a company provides too much security, it could slow the processing of online activity, perhaps raising costs unnecessarily (Row, 1997).

It is not possible to have a risk free (telecommunications) environment. Therefore, along with a sound security policy, organizations should establish a risk management process. Tompkins (1997) suggests that management establish an information security program using a risk-based approach. Historically, the governments and many regulated industries have used a threat-based approach to develop security policies, standards procedures and practices. Over the past few years, various security communities have recognized that a threat-based approach is not the most desirable approach. Corporations must and can provide a rational, cost-effective framework using risk management as the underlying basis for security decision making.

An information security program based on a risk management approach, assures implementation of security safeguards which are appropriate to the specific environment Risks should be ranked by priority.   The risk management process includes risk analysis, risk reduction analysis, management decision, development of risk reduction plans, implementation and maintenance of safeguards, review and audit.

Risk management is not a separate process from the life cycle management of information systems. It is an integral part of the life cycle comprehensive process for defining, analyzing, and managing the risks of operating automated information resources. It is an on-going process.

The implementation of a risk management approach will assure that there is a determination of viable threats in developing security policies, procedures and practices.

FUTURE DIRECTIONS AND CONCLUSIONS

While the traditional systems development life cycle is strongly grounded in the literature, emphasis on planning for enterprise-wide system security is not. With the proliferation of distributed systems, including local area networks, the Internet and World Wide Web, standardization and recommendations for secure computing policy will become prevalent. Traditionally, planning and policy making for system security has either been separate from the overall corporate strategy, it has been an afterthought, or not considered at all. While it will still be recognized that each organization is unique, and therefore so are their computing needs, greater emphasis needs to be placed on providing guidelines to assist IT executives in enterprise-wide policy making of secure systems.

The bottom line is that no longer can IT staffers put security planning on the back burners of the SDLC. When considering the value and importance of corporate data, it is essential that management is proactive, rather than reactive, to security planning.

REFERENCES

Alexander, Michael (1997). Net Security: Your Digital Doberman. Research Triangle Park, NC: Ventana Communications Group, Inc.

Bruce, Glen, & Dempsey, Rob (1997). Security in Distributed Computing: Did You Lock the Door?. Upper Saddle River, NJ: Prentice Hall PTR, Prentice-Hall, Inc.

Chapman, B., & Zwicky, E. (1996). Internet Security Policies. ConneXions, 10, 2-14.

Cobb, Stephen (1997). Building Trust and Security for Commerce on the Web. EDI Forum, 82-86.

Cobb, Stephen (1997). A Question of Privacy [On-line]. Available: http://www.ncsa.com/library/h.html

Cobb, Stephen (1996). Security Issues in Internet Commerce [On-line]. Available: http://www.ncsa.com/library/inetsec2.html

Dobry, Rob, & Schanken, Mary D. (1994) Security Concerns for Distributed Computing. Proceedings of the 10th Annual Computer Security Applications Conference, Orlando, FL, 12-18.

Felmly, Bradford (1997, July). Development, Implementation, and Audit or an Organization's Web Strategy. EDPACS: The EDP Audit, Control, and Security Newsletter, XXV, 1-15.

Freeman, J.W., Neely, R.B., & Heckard, M.A. (1994). A Validated Security Policy Modeling Approach. Proceedings of the 10th Annual Computer Security Applications Conference, Orlando, FL, 189-200.

Garvin, R. (1995). Debunking the Internet Security Hysteria. [On-line]. Available: http://www.btg.com/~rgarvin/security/debunk.html

Higgins, K.J. (1997). Under Attack.. Communications Week, 47-51.

Kahn, J.J. & Abrams, M.D. (1994). Editorial: Why Bad Things Happen To Good Systems and What To Do About It. Proceedings of the 10th Annual Computer Security Applications Conference, Orlando, FL, 306-307.

May, T. (1997). Electronic Commerce: 3 Truths for IS. [On-line]. Available: http://www.niitian.com/Briefs/2/NA1062.htm

Mutispaugh, D., Ferguson, J. , Bruce, G., & Alexander, J. (1994) Security for Electronic Commerce/Electronic Data Interchange (ED/EDI). Proceedings of the 10th Annual Computer Security Applications Conference, Orlando, FL, 32.

National Institute of Standards and Technology. (1993, July). Connecting to the Internet: Security Considerations. [On-line]. CSL Bulletin. Available: http://bilbo.isu.edu/security/csl/csl7_93.html

Network Security Crisis-A White Paper (1995). [On-line]. Available: http://www.zeuros.co.uk/cgi-bin/whtpap2

Row, H. (1997). The Electronic Handshake. CIO Magazine-Electronic Commerce Center [On-line], Available: http://www.cio.com/archive/ec_handshake/html

Schneier, B. (1997). Cryptography, Security, and the Future. Communications of the ACM, 40, (1), 138.

Securing Internet Information Servers. (1994, December) [On-line]. Available: http://ciac.llnl.gov/ciac/documents/ciac2308.html

Tompkins, T.G. (1997), A Systems Approach to Information Security Risk Management [On-line]. Available: http://www.ncsa.com/library/97072402.html

Whitten, Jeffrey L., Bentley, Lonnie D., & Barlow, Victor M. (1994). Systems Analysis & Design Methods (3rd ed.). Boston, MA: Richard D. Irwin, Inc.

Zalud, B. (1997). E-Commerce: New Security, New Threats. Security, 93.

Bridging the Gap between Practitioner-Educator Perceptions of Key IS Issues for Effective Implementation of IS Curriculum

Yongbeom Kim

Silberman School of Business, Fairleigh Dickinson University, Madison, NJ 07940

Telephone: (973) 443-8856, Fax: (973) 443-8804, E-mail: kim@alpha.fdu.edu

Sung J. Shim

Silberman School of Business, Fairleigh Dickinson University, Madison, NJ 07940

Telephone: (973) 443-8843, Fax: (973) 443-8804, E-mail: sshim@alpha.fdu.edu

K. Paul Yoon

Silberman School of Business, Fairleigh Dickinson University, Teaneck, NJ 07666

Telephone: (201) 692-7214, Fax: (201) 692-7219, E-mail: yoon@alpha.fdu.edu

ABSTRACT

This study is aimed to develop guidelines for effective implementation of information systems (IS) curriculum in rapidly changing technological and business environments. We conducted a survey of IS practitioners and educators regarding the perceived importance of thirty key IS issues. The survey results show that the two groups perceive differently the relative importance of twelve IS issues, while they agree on the relative importance of the remaining eighteen IS issues. Based upon the results, we suggest specific guidelines for effective implementation of IS curriculum by attempting to bridge the gap between practitioner-educator perceptions of IS issues.

INTRODUCTION

Information systems (IS) are essential in today's business environment, helping create competitive firms, manage global corporations, and provide quality products and services to customers. Further, rapid and continuous changes in technological and business environments pose new challenges as well as opportunities for organizations, calling for new knowledge, skills and training for IS personnel. In order to keep abreast of all these changes, IS educators should address the needs of industry and provide future IS personnel with proper education by constantly updating IS curricula.

Professional associations, such as the Association for Computing Machinery (ACM), Association for Information Systems (AIS) and Association of Information Technology Professionals (AITP), have proposed IS curriculum models to guide schools to develop appropriate IS programs. While such curriculum models prove to be useful (Couger et al., 1995), educators face some difficulties in implementing the models effectively. For example, schools may lack required resources (e.g., faculty, computing hardware and software, and laboratory facility) to support the proposed courses, and so they may have to limit course offerings. It is also difficult to maintain currency of the issues covered in the courses, as new issues continuously emerge and the importance of present issues changes. Although the proposed models suggest the specific issues to be covered in each course, educators still have to determine the extent to which each issue is covered in the respective courses.

The purpose of this study is to identify IS issues that are important to IS practitioners and IS educators and develop guidelines for effective implementation of IS curriculum by bridging the perceptual gap between the two groups regarding the relative importance of the issues. We first developed a list of thirty key IS issues from several secondary sources. Then, we conducted a survey of IS practitioners and educators regarding the perceived importance of the issues. Based upon the survey results, we attempted to provide specific guidelines for effective implementation of the IS'97 model curriculum. We hope that the guidelines will be useful in implementing the IS curriculum, particularly in assessing the relative importance of various IS issues and determining the extent to which the issues are covered in the respective courses.

RELATED STUDIES

Many studies have attempted to identify key IS issues and/or develop proper IS curricula by considering the concerns of IS practitioners and educators. They include, but are not limited to: (1) studies of critical IS issues as perceived by IS practitioners (e.g., Brancheau *et al.*, 1987; Brancheau *et al.*, 1996; Claudle *et al.*, 1991; Dean *et al.*, 1991; Dickson *et al.*, 1984; Niederman *et al.*, 1991), (2) studies of relationships between IS practice and research (e.g., Alavi and Carlson, 1992; Grover and Sabherwal, 1989; Palvia *et al.*, 1996; Szajna, 1994), and (3) studies of critical skills and knowledge requirements of IS professionals and academic preparation (Lee *et al.*, 1995; Ng Tye *et al.*, 1996; Trauth *et al.*, 1993).

From these studies, we note that it is important but difficult to maintain currency of key issues in IS curricula largely due to rapidly changing technological and business environments. Many of key issues identified in previous studies are getting outdated, while new issues are constantly gaining currency. Lee *et al.* (1995) and Trauth *et al.* (1993) also report that there is an expectation gap between industry needs and academic preparation despite a shared vision of future IS personnel. Ng Tye *et al.* (1996) note that two main reasons for the mismatch are failure of IS curricula to respond changes and lack of understanding between practitioners and educators.

METHODS

We first attempted to identify IS issues that are important to IS practitioners and educators by referring to three groups of secondary sources: (1) previous surveys, (2) articles published in major IS journals, and (3) introductory IS textbooks. First, we used the IS issues examined in previous surveys, including Brancheau and Wetherbe (1996), Brancheau *et al.* (1987), Dickson *et al.* (1984) and Niederman *et al.* (1991), as the basis for this study because of their wide acceptance (Deans *et al.*, 1991) and validity (Hartog and Herbert, 1986). Second, we reviewed the articles published in *MIS Quarterly, Communications of the ACM, Journal of Management Information Systems*, and *Information Systems Research* for the past five years for search of keywords. Finally, we reviewed the keywords in introductory-level IS textbooks, including Laudon and Laudon (1994), Martin *et al.* (1994) and Schultheis and Sumner (1995). We consolidated the IS issues and keywords from these sources. In doing so, we screened out those that are too technical (e.g., geometric algorithms, lambda analysis), from other disciplines (e.g., macroeconomics, marketing), and simply irrelevant (e.g., business history, travel industry).

Using the list of IS issues compiled, we prepared and pre-tested the survey instrument with several local IS practitioners and educators in order to test its validity. Their responses and comments were subsequently used to modify the questionnaire. Table 1 shows the resulting random list of thirty IS issues included in the questionnaire. The list includes seven new issues that was not covered in previous surveys of IS practitioners. They include four technical issues (client/server computing, groupware, the Internet, and software reengineering and maintenance) and three managerial issues (IS education and training, outsourcing, and IS ethics and legal issues). These new issues are marked with * in Table 1.

We mailed out the questionnaire to 900 IS practitioners and 350 IS educators in the United States. We asked prospective respondents to rate the extent to which each issue is perceived as important in the field over the next three years, using a seven-point Likert-type scale (i.e., 1 for the least important issue and 7 for the most important issue). We also collected some demographic data on the respondents and their organizations and industries. We received 201 responses (146 from IS practitioners and 55 from IS educators), repre-

Table 1. Key IS Issues Included in the Study

Issue Number	IS Issue
1	Competitive advantage and strategic IS
2	Enabling EDI
3	Telecommunications and networking
4	Having a responsive IT infrastructure
5	Management support systems (DSS/ESS)
6	IS development and tools
7	Developing and maintaining distributed systems
8	Integrating IT with existing systems
9	Multimedia and hypertext
10	Developing information architecture
11	IS human resources management
12	Understanding the role and contribution of IS
13	Aligning the IS organization with the enterprise
14	IS education and training*
15	Managing data resources
16	Measuring IS effectiveness and productivity
17	Outsourcing IT*
18	Improving IS strategic planning
19	Project management and IT investment
20	Improving information security and control
21	Facilitating and managing end-user computing
22	Organizational impact of IS
23	Client/server computing*
24	Disaster recovery
25	Managing global information systems
26	Groupware*
27	IS ethics and legal issues*
28	The Internet and electronic commerce*
29	Software reengineering and maintenance*
30	Organizational learning

Table 2. Characteristics of the Sample			
Practitioners (n = 140)		**Educators (n = 51)**	
Industry		Affiliation with	
Manufacturing (n = 45)	32%	Business school (n = 44)	86%
Service (n = 95)	68%	Other school (n = 7)	14%
		Affiliation with	
		Independent IS department (n = 19)	37%
		Interdisciplinary department (n = 32)	63%
Position		Position	
Executive (n = 21)	15%	Full professor (n = 17)	33%
Middle manager (n = 55)	39%	Associate professor (n = 21)	41%
IS developer (n = 64)	46%	Assistant professor (n = 8)	16%
		Other (n = 5)	10%

senting a response rate of 16 percent. But ten responses (six from IS practitioners and four from IS educators) were not usable due to lack of information. The remaining 191 responses (140 from IS practitioners and 51 from IS educators) were used as the sample for this study, representing an effective response rate of 15 percent.

Table 2 shows the characteristics of the sample we used. The sample distribution of IS practitioners seems skewed toward service industries (68 percent). However, the IS practitioner sample is relatively evenly distributed between executives/managers (54 percent) and IS developers (46 percent). Also, the sample distribution of IS educators seems skewed toward business schools (86 percent), interdisciplinary departments (63 percent), and senior faculty (74 percent). These characteristics of the sample should be kept in mind when interpreting results.

RESULTS

We asked IS practitioners and educators to rate the perceived importance of various variables related to the thirty IS issues. The means and standard deviations of all variables were first calculated. Then, we performed t test to see whether there are differences in means of variables between practitioners and educators. Table 3 shows the results of t test. The mean ratings of the variables range from 4.05 to 5.50 in the practitioner group and from 3.60 to 5.46 in the educator group. This result suggests that the issues included in this study are generally perceived as important by both practitioners and educators.

No significant difference is observed in eighteen variables between practitioners and educators, suggesting that both the groups agree on the relative importance of the related eighteen IS issues. But significance difference is observed in twelve variables between practitioners and educators (four variables at 0.01 significance level and eight variables at 0.05 significance level), suggesting that the two groups perceive differently the relative importance of the related twelve issues. Specifically, practitioners perceive eight issues as more important than educators do, whereas practitioners perceive the remaining four issues as less important than educators do.

In order to visualize the results in Table 3, we rearranged the thirty IS issues in a two dimensional grid by their relative importance, as shown in Figure 1. Quadrant I and III contain eighteen issues in which no significant difference of means is observed between practitioners and educators. Of the eighteen issues, Quadrant I contains eleven issues that are perceived as relatively more important by both the groups, and Quadrant III contains the remaining seven issues that are perceived as relatively less important by both the groups. On the other hand, Quadrant II and IV contain twelve issues in which significant difference of means is observed between practitioners and educators. Of the twelve issues, Quadrant II contains eight issues that are perceived as relatively more important by practitioners than by educators, and Quadrant IV contains the remaining four issues that are perceived as relatively more important by educators than by practitioners.

It is notable that most the issues in Quadrant II are those at managerial and organizational levels beyond anything associated with individual skills and knowledge. It seems that practitioners perceive managerial and organizational IS issues as more important than educators do. Also, the issues in Quadrant IV suggest that educators consider emerging issues, such as multimedia/hypertext and the Internet/electronic commerce, as more important than practitioners do, contrary to the old saying that educators tend to teach obsolete and irrelevant issues. There may be various reasons for the gap between practitioner-educator perceptions of IS issues, from individual propensities all the way to organizational contexts. Apart from these moderating factors, which are beyond the scope of this study, our results suggest that the two groups perceive differently the relative importance of some key IS issues.

GUIDELINES FOR EFFECTIVE IMPLEMENTATION OF IS CURRICULUM

We applied the results in Figure 1 to the IS'97 undergraduate IS curriculum model proposed by the ACM, AIS

Table 3. Comparison of Practitioner-Educator Perceptions of IS Issues

Issue Number	Practitioners Mean	Std. Dev.	Educators Mean	Std. Dev.	Mean Diff.	t	
1	5.50	1.520	4.96	1.737	0.41	2.06	*
2	4.57	1.641	4.52	1.515	0.05	0.19	
3	5.47	1.437	5.46	1.403	0.01	0.05	
4	5.21	1.496	5.04	1.399	0.17	0.69	
5	4.16	1.619	4.18	1.453	-0.02	-0.09	
6	4.96	1.398	5.02	1.507	-0.06	-0.27	
7	5.07	1.397	4.96	1.338	0.11	0.49	
8	4.95	1.602	4.69	1.432	0.26	0.99	
9	4.12	1.494	4.70	1.418	-0.58	-2.41	*
10	5.18	1.451	4.68	1.477	0.50	2.08	*
11	4.72	1.556	4.14	1.841	0.58	2.15	*
12	4.94	1.596	5.06	1.504	-0.12	-0.45	
13	5.11	1.577	5.14	1.325	-0.32	-0.13	
14	4.97	1.560	5.04	1.511	-0.07	-0.27	
15	5.08	1.465	5.08	1.140	0.00	0.00	
16	4.73	1.427	5.04	1.340	-0.31	-1.33	*
17	4.05	1.695	3.60	1.355	0.45	1.69	
18	5.17	1.628	4.40	1.539	0.77	2.89	**
19	4.64	1.499	3.94	1.449	0.70	2.85	**
20	5.21	1.393	4.86	1.242	0.36	1.59	
21	4.95	1.466	4.47	1.542	0.48	1.95	
22	4.51	1.505	4.65	1.601	-0.14	-0.56	
23	5.11	1.522	5.02	1.229	0.09	0.38	
24	5.29	1.538	4.29	1.500	1.01	3.97	**
25	4.27	1.856	4.29	1.458	-0.02	-0.07	
26	4.53	1.437	4.43	1.458	0.10	0.42	
27	4.11	1.709	4.73	1.668	-0.62	-2.20	*
28	4.23	1.756	4.92	1.552	-0.69	-2.44	*
29	5.19	1.477	4.69	1.278	0.49	2.07	*
30	5.04	1.595	4.06	1.533	0.98	3.74	**

Note: $* p < 0.05$; $** p < 0.01$.

and ATIP. Table 4 shows the proposed curriculum and this study's corresponding IS issue numbers arranged by quadrants in Figure 1. The IS'97 curriculum model recommends ten courses (97.1 through 97.10) required courses for IS majors and twelve courses (O-11 through O-22) as electives. As shown in Table 4, the curriculum model covers all thirty issues considered in this study.

Most the courses proposed in the curriculum model cover the issues in Quadrant I, indicating that the proposed curriculum model in general makes proper emphasis on the issues. But two issues in Quadrant I (IS organization alignment and client/server computing) are not covered in required courses but only in elective courses (O-11 and O-13). Since they are perceived as relatively more important by both practitioners and educators, we suggest to cover these two issues in required courses when to modify the curriculum model. Two required courses (97.3 and 97.6) and two elective courses (O-11 and O-20) cover some issues in both Quadrant I and III. Thus, the issues in Quadrant I (3, 6, 7, 8, 12, 13, and 20) with more emphasis than the issues in Quadrant III (2, 5, 17, 22, and 25) in the corresponding courses. The remaining three issues in Quadrant III (5, 21, and 26) may be covered with less emphasis in the corresponding courses, as they are perceived as relatively less importance by both practitioners and educators.

Of greater interest are the issues in Quadrant II and IV that practitioners and educators perceive differently their relative importance. We suggest to cover the issues in Quadrant II with more emphasis in the corresponding courses: competitive advantage/strategic IS and IS human resources management in 97.2; IS strategic planning in 97.3; information architecture in 97.4 and O-19; disaster recovery in 97.6 and O-14; software engineering and maintenance in 97.9; and project management and IT investment in 97.10. Also, we may need to invite more attention of practitioners to the issues in Quadrant IV, as the issues are perceived as relatively less important by them. In this regard, it may be necessary to develop a new course covering such emerging issues as the Internet/electronic commerce and multimedia/hypertext.

Table 4. IS Issues in Three Groups		
Issue Number	**IS Issue**	
2	Enabling EDI	
3	Telecommunications and networking	
4	Having a responsive IT infrastructure	
5	Management support systems (DSS/ESS)	
6	IS development and tools	
7	Developing and maintaining distributed systems	
8	Integrating IT with existing systems	
12	Understanding the role and contribution of IS	
13	Aligning the IS organization with the enterprise	Group I
14	IS education and training*	
15	Managing data resources	
17	Outsourcing IT*	
20	Improving information security and control	
21	Facilitating and managing end-user computing	
22	Organizational impact of IS	
23	Client/server computing*	
25	Managing global information systems	
26	Groupware*	
1	Competitive advantage and strategic IS	
10	Developing information architecture	
11	IS human resources management	
18	Improving IS strategic planning	Group II
19	Project management and IT investment	
24	Disaster recovery	
29	Software reengineering and maintenance*	
30	Organizational learning	
9	Multimedia and hypertext	
16	Measuring IS effectiveness and productivity	Group III
27	IS ethics and legal issues*	
28	The Internet and electronic commerce*	

Note: Group I – IS issues that both practitioners and educators agree on the relative importance; Group II – IS issues that practitioners perceive as more important than educators do; and Group III – IS issues that educators perceive as more important than practitioners do.

CONCLUSION

Using data from a survey of IS practitioners and educators, this study examined the relative importance of thirty key IS issues. The results show that the two groups perceive differently on the relative importance of twelve issues, whereas they agree on the relative importance of eighteen issues. We also attempted to bridge the gap between practitioner-educator perceptions of IS issues, and apply the results to the IS'97 curriculum model in order to provide specific guidelines for effective implementation of the curriculum model. It is important that both practitioners and educators have a shared vision of key IS issues and collaborate with each other in order to provide future IS personnel with proper education. In this regard, the guidelines suggested in this study will be useful in assessing the relative importance of IS issues and determining the extent to which they are covered in the respective courses.

Several limitations are recognized in this study. First, we considered thirty key IS issues. These issues may not be comprehensive, although they are found as important in other studies. In this regard, it is necessary to continuously update the issues by incorporating new emerging ones and discarding outdated ones. Further, it would be beneficial to examine changes of importance of IS issues in a longitudinal way. Second, the results of this study relied on the respondents' perceptions in measuring the relative importance of IS issues, and so they are liable to problems related to perceptual studies. Third, we used data from a survey of IS practitioners and educators at the national level but with relatively low response rate. The sample may not be large enough to represent the total population. In this regard, regional schools that provide graduates mostly to local organizations may conduct similar surveys of local IS practitioners to design and offer IS programs and courses that meet the needs of local organizations. These limitations are not exhaustive but rather important ones. Obviously, these limitations suggest several possibilities for future studies.

REFERENCES

Alavi, M. and Carlson, P. (1992). A Review of MIS Research and Disciplinary Development. *Journal of Management Information Systems,* 8(4), 45-62.

Brancheau, J. C., Janz, B. D., and J. C. Wetherbe, J. C. (1996). Key Issues in Information Systems Management: 1994-95 SIM Delphi Results. *MIS Quarterly,* 20(2), 225-242.

Brancheau, J. C. and Wetherbe, J. C. (1987). Key Issues in Information Systems Management. *MIS Quarterly,* 11(1), 23-45.

Caudle, S., Gorr, W., and Newcomer, K. (1991). Key Information Systems Management Issues for the Public Sector. *MIS Quarterly,* 15(2), 171-188.

Couger, J. D., Davis, G. B., Dologite, D. G., Feinstein, D. L., Gorgone, J.T., Jenkins, A. M., Kasper, G. M., Longenecker, Jr., H. E., and Valacich, J. S. (1995) IS '95: Guideline for Undergraduate IS Curriculum. *MIS Quarterly,* 19(3), 341-359.

Table 5. IS'97 Undergraduate Curriculum Model and IS Issues			
IS'97 Undergraduate Curriculum Model	Corresponding IS Issue Number and Group Number		
	I	II	III
97.1 Fundamentals of information systems	3, 6	1, 11	
97.2 Personal productivity with IS technology	21		
97.3 Information systems theory and practice	5, 8, 12, 25	18	
97.4 Information technology hardware and software	4	10	
97.5 Programming, data, file, and object structures	6, 15		9
97.6 Telecommunications	2, 3, 7, 20	24	28
97.7 Analysis and logical design	6, 7		
97.8 Physical design and implementation with DBMS	15		
97.9 Physical design and implementation with programming environments	6, 14	29	
97.10 Project management and practice		19	16
O-11 Information technology and organization strategy	13, 22	1, 30	
O-12 Organization, management, and evaluation of information resources	15		
O-13 Technology and development of client-server systems	7, 23		
O-14 Control, audit, and security of information systems	20	24	
O-15 Knowledge-based systems and methods	5		
O-16 Collaborative work, decision support, and executive support systems	5, 26		
O-17 Human-computer interaction and interface design	6		
O-18 Simulation methods and systems	6		
O-19 Advanced software and hardware architecture		10	
O-20 Alternative development methods and methodologies	6, 17		
O-21 IS professionalism and ethics			27
O-22 Communications networks	3		

Deans, P., Karwan, K., Goslar, M., Ricks, D., and Toyne B. (1991). Identification of Key International Information Systems Issues in U.S.-Based Multinational Corporations. *Journal of Management Information Systems,* 7(4), 27-50.

Dickson, G. W., Leitheiser, R. L., Wetherbe, J. C., and Nechis M. (1984). Key Information Systems Issues for the 1980's. *MIS Quarterly,* 8(3), 135-159.

DPMA (1991). *Information Systems: The DPMA Curriculum for a Four Year Undergraduate Degree,* Data Processing Management Association.

Gorgone, J. T., Couger, J. D., Davis, G., Feinstein, D., Kasper, G., and Longenecker, H. E., Jr. (1994). Information Systems '95 Curriculum Model - a Collaborative Effort. *DATA BASE,* 25(4), 5-8.

Grover, V., and R. Sabherwal, R. (1989). An Analysis of Research in Information Systems from the IS Executive's Perspective. *Information and Management,* 16, 233-246.

Hartog, C., and Herbert, M. (1986). 1985 Opinion Survey of MIS Managers: Key Issues. *MIS Quarterly,* 10(4), 351-361.

Holsapple, C. W., Johnson, L. E., Manakyan, H., and Tanner, J. (1994). Business Computing Research Journals: A Normalized Citation Analysis. *Journal of Management Information Systems,* 11(1), 131-140.

Laudon, K., and Laudon, J. (1994). *Management Information Systems: Organization and Technology,* 3rd. ed. Macmillan Publishing Company, New York.

Lee, D. M. S., Trauth, E. M., and Farwell, D. (1995). Critical Skills and Knowledge Requirements of IS Professionals: A Joint Academic/Industry Investigation. *MIS Quarterly,* 19(3), 313-340.

Martin, E., DeHayes, D., Hoffer, J., and Perkins, W. (1994). *Managing Information Technology: What Managers Need to Know,* 2nd ed. Macmillan Publishing Company, New York.

Ng Tye, E. M. W., Poon, R. S. K., and Burn, J. M. (1996). Information Systems Skills: Achieving Alignment Between the Curriculum and the Needs of the IS Professionals in the Future. *DATA BASE,* 27(4), 47-58.

Niederman, F., Brancheau, J., and Wetherbe, J. (1991). Information Systems Management Issues for the 1990's. *MIS Quarterly,* 15(4), 475-500.

Palvia, P. C., Rajagopalan, B., Kumar, A., and Kumar, N. (1996). Key Information Systems Issues: An Analysis of MIS Publications. *Information Processing and Management,* 32(3), 345-355.

Schultheis, R., and Sumner, M. (1995). *Management Information Systems: The Manager's View,* 3rd ed. Richard D. Irwin, Inc., Chicago.

Szajna, B. (1994). How Much is Information Systems Research Addressing Key Practitioner Concerns?. *DATA BASE,* 25(2), 49-59.

Trauth, E., Farwell, D., and Lee, D. (1993). The IS Expectation Gap: Industry Expectation versus Academic Preparation. *MIS Quarterly,* 17(3), 293-307.

A Model of Evolving Online Business

Joanne Silverstein, Ph.D.

School of Information Studies, Syracuse University, 809 Oakwood Street, Fayetteville, NY 13066

(315) 637-3285, jlsilver@syr.edu

INTRODUCTION

As the Web becomes home to thousands of businesses, it challenges their owners' and managers' concepts about goals, processes and practices. Given the number of businesses moving to online commerce[1], and the resources required, we may expect business organizations to spend large sums of money in attempts to harness the Web. For those businesses, however, we have little or no knowledge of how going online affects strategic planning, marketing and business processes, or business outcomes.

Considerable research exists about related topics, including electronic networking and communications, interface design, information retrieval, security and privacy, and strategic planning. While each of these may illuminate a small piece of the picture, none answers the overarching question: "What are the attributes of online business?" The goal of this research was to create a framework with which to identify and describe those attributes.

The framework resulting from this research comprises thirty-seven attributes, arranged in a two-part model of online brokers and online retailers. The framework will be of use to several groups of researchers and practitioners.

First, economists may use the model to investigate how online brokers will affect prices and competition in markets.

Second, marketing researchers may find the model useful for examining whether branding (or other kinds of differentiation) can combat the price-lowering effects of online brokers.

Third, practitioners can use the model to (a) identify their positions, both current and planned, in the framework, and (b) understand more clearly the market in which they will compete.

The remainder of this paper is organized as follows: A review of the literature is followed by presentation of the research question, the methodology, the results, and the implications of the results.

LITERATURE REVIEW: SOME TAXONOMIES OF ONLINE BUSINESS

A comprehensive discussion of the literature is precluded here by space constraints, but a representative perspective is set forth by Benjamin and Wigand (1995). They, among many others, argued that decreasing costs of IT would lead to (a) increased use of electronic markets to compare products, prices and services among more suppliers, (b) a restructuring of the value chain and (c) a proportional shift from electronic hierarchies to electronic marketplaces. They predicted that - as a result - market access, channels, and profit structures will be radically affected.

These predictions seem to be born out on the Web, but because of the Web's rapid growth and multiple business scenarios, are difficult to study. In an attempt to create useful models for studying online business, researchers have created various taxonomies. The three that follow are most helpful in understanding this research. The first describes a classification of effects that information technology has on business. The second and third taxonomies are categories of online businesses. While they do not form an overarching model of online business, these three taxonomies are helpful, particularly in providing an initial overview of the problem.

Malone, Yates and Benjamin

Most important to this research is the work of Malone, Yates and Benjamin (1987) who theorized about the effects of information technology on business. The authors predicted that IT would transform markets, changing them first from biased to unbiased, and then to personalized[2]. Ultimately, due to IT-based changes to markets, "...we... should expect fundamental changes in how firms and market organize the flow of goods and services in our economy".

The authors classified these predictions in a taxonomy of three electronic effects that influence online business:

1. The electronic coordination effect refers to the fact that information technology allows communication of more information in less time, and at lower cost.
2. The electronic brokerage effect describes the role of electronic markets in connecting many different buyers and suppliers, and enabling comparison of many products and vendors, quickly and inexpensively. The electronic brokerage effect is fundamental to this research.
3. The electronic integration effect occurs when information technology is used to closely integrate processes that create and use information.

These electronic effects are useful in studying electronic markets, and their concepts provide a perspective for observing online business.

Quelch and Klein

Quelch and Klein (1996) divided commercial Web sites into two categories. Already-established companies that use the Web as an ancillary marketing channel are known as Multi-National Companies (MNCs). MNCs begin by offering information to potential customers, then customer support services, and last, they enable online transactions.

Web start-up companies comprise the second category, and they operate according to a different model. By necessity, Web start-ups begin by conducting online transactions, then provide customer support for repeated visits. Web start-ups served as the focus for this research for this reason: When MNCs use the Web, the resources for those efforts may be drawn from existing budgets and rely upon existing organizational infrastructure. Start-ups, however, must rely on their online efforts alone, and it is in those organizations that Web-related phenomenon are most clearly observable.

Hoffman, Novak and Chatterjee

The taxonomy of Hoffman, Novak and Chatterjee (1995) includes two super-sets of categories for online business.

The first super-set is Web Traffic Control Sites, including three categories: malls, incentive sites, and search agents. These sites do not offer direct transactions.

The second super-set is Destination Sites. Destination Sites, including Internet presence sites, content sites, and online storefronts all of which are designed to generate and support transactions. The last category - online storefronts - is similar to Quelch's and Klein's Web startups.

In summary, taxonomies of Malone, Yates and Benjamin (1987), Quelch and Klein (1996), and Hoffman, Novak and Chatterjee (1995) help define online storefronts, which were the exclusive focus for this research.

RESEARCH QUESTION

The purpose of this study was to develop a description of attributes of online business, as defined in the previous section. It was a naturalistic study that began with the relatively vague question, "What is going on in online business?" and ended with the question "What are the attributes of online retailers and online brokers, and how do they act in online markets?"

The study adopted the perspectives of businesses' owners and managers. Other perspectives exist (e.g., customers', manufacturers', and Internet service providers). If, however, we fail to incorporate the perspective of online business owners and managers, we risk overlooking great stores of knowledge. Owners, managers, and designers are knowledgeable about new services and were able to report on strategic planning, resource allocation and consumer trends. Thus, the research was based on the following assumptions:
• important knowledge about online business resides in the expertise of online owners, managers and designers, and
• such knowledge is best investigated using naturalistic inquiry in respondents' context rather than presuming/testing for pre-determined variables.

RESEARCH METHODOLOGY AND SETTING

The broad scope of the question, the dearth of empirical research and the dynamic nature of the topic, suggested the use of naturalistic methods - specifically, analytic induction - to analyze the data. That is, data were scanned for similarities and organized into code categories. Relationships among the categories were explored and confirmed by comparison to subsequent data.

A. Data Gathering

This section provides a brief description of the scope of the research, sampling phases, unit of analysis, sample population, and sample size and instrument.

1. Scope of the Research

The literature offered little guidance for defining a population of online business owners and managers. The following boundaries, then, were established to define the scope of the research.

Only online storefronts in existence for more than six months, operating for profit, and offering direct sales via the Web were studied. Respondents had to illustrate at least four of sixteen characteristics of online business as suggested by the literature[3]. Sampling was stratified, then, not by product or industry, but by degree of exploitation of the Web's characteristics.

Although these boundaries helped to exclude millions of online entities from the sample, many potential respondents remained. Little was known about online business and its participants, and there seemed no clear way to further delimit the population. Miles and Huberman (1994, page 27), however, state that if little is known about the parameters or dynamics of a problem, research may progress through exploratory and confirmatory times; exploration called for at the outset, and confirmation nearer to the end. They label this "iterative sampling" and explain that:

...at each step along the evidential trail, we are making sampling decisions to clarify the main patterns...identify exceptions...and uncover negative instances where the pattern does not hold (page 29).

Iterative sampling provided the ability to investigate this broad research question, while - over time - narrowing the focus to the most interesting phenomena.

2. Sampling Phases

The sampling design of this research comprised four phases, and insured flexibility for the increasingly refined research questions that are characteristic of naturalistic inquiry (Marshall and Rossman, 1989). Each of the four phases (a) sampled somewhat different respondents, (b) resulted in exclusionary criteria that narrowed the sample for subsequent data gathering, and (c) generated codes, findings and hypotheses.

The four methods and phases of sampling were Opportunistic, Intensity,

Maximum Variety, and Stratified. This combination of sampling methods was advantageous because it allowed study of a population that was initially unknown, but that became better understood as research progressed. Analysis of data gathered in the last phase showed that the data had reached redundancy[4], and the study terminated.

3. Unit of Analysis

In a discussion of research study design, Babbie (1989, page 84) points out that the unit of analysis may be an organization, even in research that samples individual respondents. As described by Babbie, then, the unit of analysis for this research was the organization even though individuals were sampled. For the purposes of this research, sampled organizations are referred to both as "respondents" and "respondent sites". The word "interviewee" represents people - individuals who have contributed to the description of the respondent site, but they are not the unit of analysis.

4. Sample Population

Respondent sites were represented by "elite" interviewees. They are referred to as elites because they posses special knowledge about the organization they represent, not necessarily because of high status or position within the organization (Marshall and Rossman, 1989). Elites are desirable respondents because they can provide an overall view of the organization within its industry and market, are knowledgeable about organizational policies, histories, and plans, provide large amounts of contextual data quickly and respond well to one-on-one interviews.

For the purposes of this research, elites were owners or managers of online businesses. During the two-year study, owners and directors of marketing and strategic planning were interviewed. They represented the following retail sectors:

fine furniture
travel
boats
cars
eye care supplies
books
sports gear
smoking gear
collectible ephemera
medial care supplies for home use
wine and/or food (two respondents)
health food and natural beauty supplies (two respondents)
music (three respondents) and
computer hardware, software and peripherals (two respondents).

5. Sample Size and Instrument

The number of active online businesses is unknown and changes everyday[5], a fact that would hinder statistical analysis of online business. Naturalistic studies, however, are usually designed to generate rich descriptions, and are not dependent upon statistical representation. They often employ open-ended sampling instruments, and require fewer respondents than other methods (Miles and Huberman, page 30).

Bruner (1990) lists some advantages of using interviews, including that they allow interviewees to initiate topics and use their own perspectives in describing issues. Bruner suggests interviews also allow researchers to:
- learn the "language" and perspective of the respondent
- develop detailed and holistic descriptions
- identify variables and framing hypotheses for research.

Accordingly, this study employed the semi-structured interview, an open-ended instrument designed to generate a large amount of rich data. Nineteen respondent sites provided twenty-five interviews, three hundred and seventeen pages of transcription, and ninety pages of research notes. Interviews were conducted by phone and email, and transcribed and stored in electronic files.

In summary, data were gathered during semi-structured interviews, using open-ended questions to encourage narrative.

B. Data Analysis

This section presents a brief description of the methods used in analytic induction. The method requires a researcher to interactively perform the following four steps:
1. Assign codes to text units from transcribed interviews.
2. Integrate code categories and their properties, looking for mismatches or subsets. During category integration, relationships among the categories may emerge.
3. Consolidate until property lists are no longer in flux, and theoretical criteria emerge from the categories (Miles and Huberman, 1994 page 27).
4. Report the findings (results).

The first three steps occur throughout data collection, coding and analysis. There is, however shifting emphasis from exploratory to confirmatory activities as the work progresses.

In summary, this research used naturalistic inquiry to study the attributes of online business from the perspective of online owners and managers. Sampling strategies set boundaries and created a framework for the research. Analytic induction was used to identify hypotheses among the data. Data gathering and analysis continued throughout the research until redundancy was reached.

RESULTS

Data analysis revealed the existence of thirty-seven attributes of online business that occurred in distinct patterns. The attributes served as building blocks and enabled construction of a framework to view online business.

The framework consists of two categories of online business (online brokers and online retailers). Each category possesses three sets of attributes; identifying, supporting and shared. A brief description of the framework and its attributes is as follows:

A Online stores employ up to thirty-seven attributes to differentiate themselves.
B. Two kinds of online stores exist are distinguished by identifying attributes.
C. Brokers and retailers use different attribute sets[6].
D. Brokers and retailers share some attributes.

A. Online stores employ specific attributes to differentiate themselves[7].

It has been pointed out that the Web provides new opportunities for interaction between sellers and buyers (Rockart and Scott Morton, 1993; Ricciuti, 1995; Hoffman and Novak, 1996). This research shows that those opportunities are observable as thirty-seven attributes, each of which is grounded in the data. Specifically, online stores may:

1. allow buyers to search for information across vendors
2. allow buyers to search for information across products
3. compete based primarily on non-price features
4. compete based on reputation
5. compete based on price
6. set prices
7. take prices from buyers
8. bundle products according to customer preferences
9. offer special promotions
10. compete for vendors (in addition to customers)
11. generally act to lower prices
12. target certain demographic sectors for content and products
13. emerge as "new players" from unexpected circumstances

14. change or rearrange components of the traditional value chain
15. manage new components of strategic planning
16. allow customers to control the shopping experience
17. aim to provide positive shopping experiences
18. emphasize the visual aspects of a site
19. employ multi-language features
20. provide many levels of information
21. make a conscious decision whether to provide consistent information
22. use information to influence purchasing decisions
23. emphasize customer service
24. rely on "consumerization" (marketing directly to customers)
25. perform market research
26. employ economies of scope rather than economies of scale
27. use traditional media to cultivate customer relations
28. provide scarce products to achieve imperfect competition
29. "un-standardize" commodity products by infusing them with information
30. avoid selling products they manufacture because of channel conflict
31. capitalize on the global nature of the Internet
32. record personal data to more accurately market to existing customers
33. offer personalized accounts
34. create and use customized software and applications to "lock-in" vendors
35. design the interface to serve as a buying intermediary
36. balance effects of online communities vs. prospects of weak brokering
37. outsource many logistics.

B. Two kinds of online stores exist and are distinguished by <u>identifying attributes.</u>

Two of the above attributes were found to be mutually exclusive for two groups of respondent sites, and allowed a framework to emerge: The ability for buyers to compare across vendors for information (Attribute 1) was found only in online brokers. Thus, the presence or absence of Attribute 1 separated respondent into mutually exclusive groups, online brokers and online retailers. Attribute 1 is the identifying attribute for online brokers. Four respondents were in this category.

Attribute 2 is the identifying attribute for online retailers. Online retailers allow buyers to compare for information across many products, but not across vendors. Fifteen of the respondent sites fell into this group. At one such respondent site, for example, buyers can shop for different kinds of music and different artists. But the vendor (producer) of each is pre-selected, and prices are not challenged by other vendors offering duplicate items. The ability to compare across products is the identifying attribute of the group, known in this research, as online retailers.

C. Brokers and retailers use different attribute sets known as <u>supporting attributes.</u>

Online brokers and retailers each employ a set of supporting attributes - that is, attributes that are usually found in one category, but only rarely in the other.

Supporting attributes for online brokers deal mostly with product pricing, and are used only rarely by online retailers:

Attribute 5: Online brokers compete based on price

Online brokers specialize in offering price information. Their revenue models (flat fee per broker, or per item sold) depend not on the price of the product being sold, but on the number of transactions, or the number of participating (paying) vendors. This strategy inures online brokers to the concern for profit margin and encourages vendors to compete (via low prices) for buyers' interest.

Attribute 7: Online brokers take prices from buyers

Online brokers offer broad vendor selection and allow customers to compare and select from across vendors for price information, thereby influencing prices.

Attribute 10: Online brokers may compete for vendors

Online brokers use various strategies to attract and retain vendors, as well as customers. Providing vendor services may be as important to brokers as providing customer services. Tactics may include free data processing and storage, searchable databases, lookup tables, free scans, price listing, and live links and microsites to increase traffic.

Attribute 11: Online brokers generally act to lower prices

Online brokers attract vendors who compete with each other predominantly through price. Although retailers and brokers expressed expectations that online business would cost less to conduct and thereby lower prices, the phenomenon is more clearly observable in online brokers.

In summary, there are four supporting attributes for online brokers.

Supporting attributes for online retailers deal mostly with non-price features:

Attribute 3: Online retailers compete based primarily on non-price features

Because online retailers restrict the number of vendors for each product, there is little price competition. Customers may choose which product to buy, or whether to buy at all, but can not directly influence price. Online retailers interviewed for this research have used the following non-price-based features; personal (non-automated) e-mail responses, electronic magazines, memberships, access to one's personal buying records, chat lines, ancillary information (recipes and menus), mediated communication with performers, and sound and video samples.

Attribute 4: Online retailers compete based on reputation

Some interviewees spoke of the importance of reputation, using the word interchangeably with "branding". Within the context of information science, Dickson (page 310) explains that:

Customers...handle an enormous amount of information...(and) use selective attention, memory shortcuts and rules of thumb-in order to make decisions. With that reality in mind, potential buyers will often use symbols, such as brands, to stand for larger chunks of information and simplify information handling.

A brand is a conditioned cue that...comes to stand for something, be it quality, reliability, craftsmanship, exclusive styling, status or value... Consequently, buyers are willing to pay a premium for such quality and assurance.

The "premium" mentioned by Dickson has enabled traditional retailers to charge higher prices than brokers, and is similarly useful in online business.

Attribute 6: Online retailers set prices

Data show that online stores with limited vendor selection and non-price-based features usually dictate, or "set" the prices that buyers must pay.

Attribute 8: Online retailers bundle products according to customer preferences

Bundled products are offered as gift selections and as opportunities for buyers to sample desirable products in small quantities.

Attribute 9: Online retailers offer special promotions

Stores that set prices, restrict the selection of vendors and compete primarily on non-price-based features, employ special promotions as incentives to generate sales.

In summary, there are five supporting attributes for online retailers.

Figure 1. Identifying, Supporting, and Shared Attributes of Online Brokers and Retailers

Identifying Attributes of Brokers	Supporting Attributes of Brokers	Shared Attributes	Supporting Attributes of Retailers	Identifying Attributes of Retailers
1. Buyers search across vendors	5. Compete on price 7. Take prices from buyers 10. Compete for vendors 11. Lower prices	12. Target demographic sectors 13. New players 14. Change value chain 15. Manage new strategic planning 16. Customers control experience 17. Positive shopping experience 18. Visual aspects 19. Multi-language 20. Many levels of information 21. Consistent information 22. Influence decisions 23. Customer service 24. Consumerization 25. Market research 26. Economies of scope 27. Traditional media 28. Scarce product 29. Un-standardize products 30. Rarely manufacture 31. Global nature 32. Personal data 33. Personalized accounts 34. Software lock-in 35. Interface as intermediary 36. Weak brokering 37. Outsource fulfillment	3. Compete on non-price benefits 4. Reputation 6. Set prices 8. Bundle products 9. Special promotions	2. Buyers search across products

Table 1 Comparison of Offline and Online Brokers and Retailers

	Offline Businesses	Online Businesses[8]
Brokers	Allow comparison across vendors Take price from buyer Price-based competition Bring buyers and sellers together Rarely warehouse products Rarely own goods Rarely carry inventory Rarely provide financing May not assume risk	Allow comparison across vendors Take price from buyer Price-based competition Bring buyers and sellers together Rarely warehouse products Rarely own goods Rarely carry inventory Rarely provide financing May not assume risk
Retailers	Allow comparison across products Set price Non-priced-based competition Offer prepurchase, postpurchase and ancillary services. Usually warehouse products Usually take ownership of goods Usually carry inventory Usually provide financing Usually assume risk	Allow comparison across products Set price Non-price-based competition Offer prepurchase, postpurchase and ancillary services Rarely warehouse products Rarely own goods Rarely carry inventory Rarely provide financing *Rarely assume risk[9]*

D. Brokers and Retailers Have <u>Shared Attributes</u>

<u>Shared attributes</u> are a group of attributes often used by both brokers and retailer, including Attributes 12-37.

The results are illustrated in Figure 1 (Identifying, Supporting and Shared Attributes of Online Brokers and Retailers) and can be expressed as a group of statements:

Thirty-seven specific attributes are observable in use in online stores. Attributes are used by two kinds of online stores, brokers and retailers. While brokers and retailers share the use of some of attributes, several attributes are mutually exclusive.

Online brokers and retailers are currently clearly distinguishable from each other, but according to the data they are beginning to borrow each other's attributes. In terms of identifying, supporting and shared attributes, the models of brokers and retailers are starting to overlap, and may come to more closely resemble one another.

DISCUSSION OF IMPLICATIONS

Implications for Terminology are presented first. They provide a shared vocabulary for the subsequent discussion of Implications for Theory.

A. Implications for Terminology

Observations made during this research indicate that redefinition of the terms "broker" and "retailer" may be appropriate for discussion of online business (see Table 1 Comparison of Offline and Online Brokers and Retailers).

<u>Conventional (or offline) brokers are "merchants who...do not take title to goods and perform few functions"</u> (Kotler, 1994, p. 581). Brokers do not carry inventory, provide financing or take responsibility for customer satisfaction. They bring buyers and sellers together for a short time and are associated with wholesale activities.

<u>Conventional (or offline) retailers sell goods and services directly to consumers for their non-business use</u> (Kotler, 1994, page 558). Conventional retailers procure and own goods, carry inventory, provide financing, and are responsible for customer satisfaction.

By capitalizing on electronic coordination and communication, online retailers can employ characteristics of conventional brokers. For example, many online retailers - like conventional brokers - rely on warehousers and suppliers to assume customer risk, product cost and storage. Like conventional brokers, online retailers may also dropship products and outsource fulfillment. Thus, online retailers become less like conventional retailers as they share strategies of online brokers. The unique properties of the Web act to accelerate this sharing of strategies, and compel redefinition of some basic terms.

As seen in the upper half of Table 1, conventional and online brokers compete on price, allow customers to compare across vendors, and match multiple buyers and sellers.

Online brokers are similar to their conventional counterparts, and are defined in the following way: they **perform activities, enact policies and create design features that enable customers to compare information and/or prices across vendors**. This definition incorporates the electronic brokerage effect (Malone, Yates and Benjamin, 1987), specifically that, "the connection among many buyers and suppliers...decreases product costs, and increases the number and quality of alternatives considered".

The lower half of Table 1 shows that both conventional and online retailers compete primarily on non-price benefits and allow customers to compare information across products rather than across vendors.

Online retailers differ from conventional retailers in that they capitalize on the electronic coordination effect and adopt five characteristics of brokers (italicized entries in Table 1). As a result, online retailers are able to electronically "coordinate away" inventory, fulfillment and warehousing, and therefore, share some characteristics of both conventional retailers and brokers. Online retailers, then, are defined, in the following way: they **allow buyers to compare across products rather than vendors, and they compete primarily on non-price-based benefits.**

These new definitions for online retailers and online brokers are set out in Table 2 Definitions of Online Brokers and Retailers.

In summary, the electronic brokerage effect has allowed increased price comparison across vendors, and compels redefinition of the term "online broker[10]".

Similarly, the electronic coordination effect has allowed retailers to outsource some functions, and compels redefinition of the term "online retailer".

<table>
<tr><td colspan="3" align="center">**Table 2 Definitions of Online Brokers and Retailers**</td></tr>
<tr><td></td><td>Offline Businesses</td><td>Online Businesses</td></tr>
<tr><td>Brokers</td><td>Conventional Brokers "facilitate buying and selling, do not take title to goods and perform only a few functions" (Kotler, 1994, page 581)</td><td>Online Brokers are similar to conventional brokers **and in addition, perform activities, enact policies and create design features that enable customers to compare information and/or prices across vendors.**</td></tr>
<tr><td>Retailers</td><td>Conventional Retailers "sell...goods or services directly to final consumers for personal, non-business use" (Kotler, 1994, page 558)</td><td>**Online Retailers sell goods or services to final consumers and allow them to compare across products rather than vendors.**</td></tr>
</table>

B. Implications for Theory

The literatures of many disciplines are linked to online business. Thus, the implications for theory are organized here not by discipline, but by topic for consideration across disciplines. Implications include:

Models of online retailing and brokering are merging

Competition will increase between online brokers and retailers

Online brokers will be forced to put increasing emphasis on branding

Online retailers will be increasingly affected by the electronic brokerage effect.

Alliances among online retailers, brokers and other online entities will create an online oligopoly.

1. Models of online retailing and brokering are merging.

The implication for models of brokers and retailers is that they will adopt each other's identifying and supporting attributes, such that the models will begin to overlap. If brokers and retailers borrow sufficiently from each other's models, the models will begin to resemble each other, and perhaps approach a single model that allows buyers to search for information across both products and vendors.

Specifically, online brokers are approaching the model of online retailers by using the following attributes:

managing new components of strategic planning (Attribute 15)

aiming to provide positive shopping experiences (Attribute 17)

providing many levels of information (Attribute 20)

increased emphasis on customer services (Attribute 23)

capitalizing on the global nature of the Internet (Attribute 31)

design the interface to serve as a buying intermediary (Attribute 35).

As buyers capitalize on the electronic brokerage effect to compare information, online retailers will renew their consideration of pricing. Online brokers will take measures to differentiate themselves from each other, and from the growing competition of price-sensitive, online retailers.

2.   Competition will increase between online brokers and online retailers.

Findings show that online brokers and retailers are borrowing each other's strategies to win markets. One way to think about the likely evolution of online brokers and retailers is to consider the framework of Guttman, Moukas and Maes (1998). In a discussion of software agents and consumer behavior, Guttman, Moukas and Maes show that consumer buying behavior can be organized in six fundamental stages:
- need identification
- product brokering
- merchant brokering
- negotiation
- purchase and delivery
- product service and evaluation.

Although their framework was not intended for mapping out the future of online business, it provides a convenient framework for that discussion.

If we think of online retailers' identifying attribute (allowing buyers to search across products) as "product brokering", then online retailers may be seen to occupy the second category, "Product Brokering".

Similarly, the identifying attribute of online brokers is that they allow buyers to search across vendors, thus they occupy the third category, "Merchant Brokering".

Online brokers and retailers will be engaged in a long and difficult competition to occupy the remaining four categories of this framework. That is, to establish themselves, online brokers and retailers will find new ways to assist buyers in need identification, negotiation, purchase and delivery, and product service and evaluation.

3.   Online brokers will be forced to put increasing emphasis on branding.

Branding was mentioned by retailers, but not by brokers. Still, brokers use tactics that may be considered as branding devices (Mintzberg, 1988). For example, some brokers use dynamic, two-way communications to "talk" with customers. They emphasize the importance of fast, current information provision. Other brokers allow customers to post notes describing goods they want, and to create free personal home pages

Branding comprises both price- and non-price-related components (Mintzberg, 1988) and some brokers are attending to the non-price components in an effort to differentiate themselves from other online brokers.

4.   Online retailers will be increasingly affected by the electronic brokerage effect.

Online brokers offer buyers the ability to compare across vendors. As explained by the electronic brokerage effect, that activity acts to lower prices. All the brokers interviewed for this research articulated a desire to lower prices for buyers. And they leverage the competitive strategies of thousands of vendors to accomplish this goal. While online retailers can block the brokers' intelligent agents (designed to compare prices), it remains to be seen whether they can resist the forces of online brokers who:
1. may allow buyers to search for information across vendors
5. may compete based on price
7. may take prices from buyers
10. compete for vendors (in addition to customers)
11. generally act to lower prices
31. capitalize on the global nature of the Internet.

Off-line retailers rely on geographic friction to provide at least a local advantage. Online customers, however, can compare prices of online retailers anywhere in the world. This forces online retailers to compete on pricing, perhaps the most onerous component of branding.

5. Alliances among online retailers, brokers and other online entities will create an online oligopoly.

Online brokers use various strategies to attract and retain vendors, and increase traffic (Attribute 10). One way to increase traffic is to enter into a strategic alliance with a Web-based search engine. Retailers already use this strategy, but once a broker enters the scenario, retailers may not be willing to participate. Because brokers lower prices, the presence of a broker would tend to erode margins for retailers advertising in the same site or search engine. If, for example, a music broker is featured on a particular search site, a music retailer, selling more expensive CDS, may not want to share advertising or selling space. When search engines enter into alliances with brokers and retailers, the currently low barriers to entry will rise, along with the costs of competing in an oligopolistic market.

Rather than end the inquiry, these five implications initiate many new ones.

They suggest topics for future research, such as: Will retailers exert pressure on vendors not to work with online brokers? Can vendors afford not to participate in online brokerages? Will retailers pay to be included in online brokerages?

SUMMARY

This research provides researchers and practitioners with insights into the workings of online business, from the perspective of online business owners and managers. It contributes to the field in four specific ways:

First, the research findings **identify and describe thirty-seven attributes** of online business.

Second, the thirty-seven attributes occur in a configuration that **identifies and describes online brokers and retailers**, a distinction that will allow researchers and practitioners to understand more about the online business environment.

Third, the research provides justification for redefining some basic terms, (brokers and retailers) and **provides a shared vocabulary** with which to view the results.

Fourth, the findings **suggest five implications**, specifically, that:

1. Models of online retailing and brokering are merging
2. Competition will increase between online brokers and retailers
3. Online brokers will be forced to put increasing emphasis on branding
4. Online retailers will be increasingly affected by the electronic brokerage effect
5. Alliances among online retailers, brokers and other entities will create an online oligopoly.

The major contribution of this research is the model of online brokers and retailers within a framework of thirty-seven, gradually overlapping attributes. The broker/retailer model emerged from the data and was unanticipated by any a priori assumptions. The model was not described in the literature, in either empirical or theoretical works. It confirms the predictions of Wigand and Benjamin (1995), as well as Malone, Yates and Benjamin (1987) and may serve as a new and useful framework on which future research can build.

BIBLIOGRAPHY

Babbie, Earl. The Practice of Social Research. Belmont, California: Wadsworth Publishing Company, 1989.

Benjamin, Robert, and Rolf Wigand. "Electronic Markets and Virtual Value Chains on the Information Superhighway." Sloan Management Review 36.2 (Dec. 1995): 62-72.

Bruner, Jerome S. Acts of Meaning. Cambridge, Mass.: Harvard University Press, 1990.

Dickson, Peter R. Marketing Management. Fort Worth: The Dryden Press, 1994.

Guttman, Robert H., Alexandros G. Moukas, and Pattie Maes. "Agents as Mediators in Electronic Commerce." Transaction in Electronic Markets (Jan. 1998): www.electronicmarkets.org/electronicmarkets/electronicmarkets.nsf/index.html.

Hoffman, Donna L., and Thomas P. Novak. "A New Marketing Paradigm for Electronic Commerce." The Information Society 13.1 (Jan. 1997): 43-54.

Hoffman, Donna, Thomas P. Novak, and Patrali Chatterjee. "Commercial Scenarios for the Web: Opportunities and Challenges." Journal of Computer-mediated Communication 1.3 and http://shum.huji.ac.il/jcmc/vol1/issues/hoffman.html.

Kotler, P. Marketing Management Analysis, Planning and Control. Englewood Cliffs, New Jersey: Prentice-Hall, 1991.

Lincoln, Yvonna S., Egon G. Guba. Naturalistic Inquiry. Newbury Park: Sage Publications, 1985.

Malone, Thomas W., Joanne Yates, and Robert I. Benjamin. "Electronic Markets and Electronic Hierarchies." Communications of the ACM 30.6 (June 1987): 484-496.

Marshall, Catherine, and Gretchen B. Rossman. Designing Qualitative Research. London: Sage Publications, 1989.

Miles, Matthew B., and A. Michael Huberman. Qualitative Data Analysis. Thousand Oaks: Sage Publications, 1994.

Mintzberg, Henry. "Generic Strategies: Toward a Comprehensive Framework." Advances in Strategic Management 5.3 (1988): 1-67.

Porter, Michael E. Competitive Strategy: Techniques for Analyzing Industries and Competitors. New York: The Free Press, 1980.

Quelch, John A., and Lisa R. Klein. "The Internet and International Marketing." Sloan Management Review (Mar. 1996): 60-75.

Rockart, J., & Scott Morton, P. "Networked Forms of Organization". In Scott Morton, P. (Ed.), <u>The Corporation of the 1990s</u>, New York: Oxford University Press, 1993.

ENDNOTES

1. The number of online businesses is growing faster than all other kinds of online domains. As of October 10, 1998, commercial domains numbered approximately 3,000,000, up approximately 600% from the beginning of 1997 (Breakdown of Registered InterNIC Domains, Your Guide to Domain Name Statistics, NetNames, Ltd., http://wwwldomainstats.com/internic.cfm.)

2. Biased markets attempt to capture customers in a system biased toward a particular supplier.
Unbiased markets include products from many different suppliers. Personalized markets provide personal decision aides to help individual buyers select from many alternatives.

3. These characteristics are described in greater detail in "Information Technology and Electronic Commerce: Attributes of Emerging Online Business", Joanne Silverstein, doctoral dissertation.

4. In a discussion of redundancy in data gathering, Lincoln and Guba (1985) advise that: "(I)f the purpose is to maximize information, then sampling is terminated when no new information is forthcoming from newly sampled units." (page 202).

5. At the time of this writing, Web-auditing software cannot accurately audit demographic characteristics. Further complicating matters, a few individuals inflate the number of .com sites by reserving large numbers of domains that they hope to sell later, but that are not now operating online businesses.

6. For the remainder of this discussion, "brokers" and "retailers", unless otherwise specified, refer to online brokers and retailers. This research does not dismiss the conventional definitions of those words, but seeks to refine them for research about online business.

7. Differentiation is extensively discussed in several literatures. Most relevant to this research is the work of Porter (1980), Kotler (1994) and Mintzberg (1988) Porter clearly distinguishes price competition from differentiation through changes to the value chain. Kotler also excludes pricing from differentiation. Mintzberg's model, however, incorporates pricing as one component of differentiation, and it is that perspective that this research refers to when using the term "differentiation".

8. The definitions for the "Online Businesses" column were generated by analysis of the data from this research.

9. The lower, right cell of Table 1 contains five italicized entries that show the effects of electronic coordination, and differentiate online retailers from conventional retailers and online brokers.

10. The electronic brokerage effect will alter business for individuals as well as firms: Online customers use search engines to locate product information, thus becoming online brokers. This "customers as brokers" phenomenon will compel all online stores to reconsider how they set prices, accelerate the competition between brokers and retailer, and pose an interesting topic for future research.

Faculty Influence on Students' Knowledge in Information Technology Area

Judith C. Simon
Fogelman College of Business and Economics, The University of Memphis, Memphis, TN 38152
Tel: (901) 678-4613, E-mail: jsimon@memphis.edu

Khalid S. Soliman
Fogelman College of Business and Economics, The University of Memphis, Memphis, TN 38152
Tel: (901) 678-3699, E-mail: ksoliman@memphis.edu

ABSTRACT

For decades, research universities have placed more emphasis on research than on teaching, although studies have shown that more research productivity does not result in better teaching performance. In measuring teaching effectiveness, student evaluations have been the main instrument utilized. However, research has indicated that student evaluations are not good measures of performance. Through the development of information technology measurement instrument, this study compares students' acquisition of knowledge of computer concepts with instructor interaction, in an effort to provide more accurate measure of teaching performance.

INTRODUCTION

The issues of teaching effectiveness and the students' rights to have high quality education have come back to the top of the priority list of educators nationwide. The Academic Bill of Rights, presented by the Carnegie Foundation for the Advancement of Teaching in 1998, concluded that every undergraduate student at the nation's 125 research universities should have guaranteed high quality of education (Wilson, 1998). In that bill, the foundation stresses that undergraduate students should have comprehensive preparation for the future, opportunity to work with senior researchers, and access to first-class facilities. One of the issues for research institutions is the level of emphasis on research verses teaching. Additional concerns for information technology (IT) faculty are related to methods of measuring teaching effectiveness and lack of research regarding this issue within the Management Information Systems (MIS) area.

LITERATURE REVIEW

Research universities for a long time have emphasized on research and publications. One can not argue against the role faculty research plays as an important economic value in providing much-needed relief to universities' budgets (Murray et al., 1994) through grants. Another positive outcome of the research approach is that it has produced many useful concepts (Hollman et al., 1994). However, the practicality of much of the research was not effective. Many academics believe that few research findings were helpful to the business community (Dulek and Fielden, 1992). Furthermore, many business researchers demonstrate their "scholarly mastery" and methodologies on irrelevant data that provide results of no practical use to managers or business organizations (Behrman and Levin, 1984). Bell et. al. (1993) have found that greater research productivity is associated with less effective teaching performance. The time faculty might spend outside the classroom in developing and enhancing his/her teaching tools and methods is consumed by research activities. Accordingly, the attention that senior faculty have to give to their undergraduate students is limited. In some cases, students feel that they are "bothersome interruptions" to the faculty member's main activity of publishing (Clement, 1988). Consequently, on one hand, many students graduate from research universities without getting the appropriate preparation and the necessary tools to face the real world of business. On the other hand, many businesses complain that new graduates lack a coherent body of knowledge and the right mix of skills (Maglitta, 1996).

In the following sections, previous research related to effective teaching at research universities is discussed, followed by the research methodology for this study involving MIS faculty and students, and finally a discussion of the results, as well as conclusions and recommendations.

PREVIOUS EVALUATION OF TEACHING EFFECTIVENESS

The evaluation of teaching effectiveness at research universities has been under scrutiny. Research universities have realized that it is a pressing issue now a day. Different methods have been used in order to measure teaching effectiveness. Using student surveys, Centra (1981) has come up with several desirable instructor characteristics: 1) Instructor's ability to communicate well, 2) instructor's positive attitudes toward students, 3) instructor's extensive knowledge of the subject matter, 4) instructor's organizational skills, 5) instructor's enthusiasm about the subject, 6) instructor's fairness in exams and grading, 7) instructor's flexibility, and 8) instructor's encouragement of students to think for themselves. Tang (1997) has utilized students' evaluation methods to come up with factors that indicate teaching effectiveness including: 1) Instructor provides clear presentation of the material, 2) Instructor clearly answers students' questions, 3) Instructor treats students in a courteous manner, 4) Instructor prepares for each class. Singell et al. (1996) have studied inputs and the time allocation decision among different activities. They have found that distinguished professors spend less time on teaching than on other activities.

From the above analysis, we find that most of the studies were done utilizing one method. Bell et al. (1993) have indicated that the bulk of higher-education research has investigated the relationships between teaching effectiveness and research productivity by measuring teaching effectiveness using students' evaluation. However, students' evaluations do not actually reflect the true performance of the instructor (Gomez-Mejia and Balkin, 1992).

WHY THIS STUDY IS IMPORTANT?

As discussed in the above analysis, research has indicated that the true performance of the instructor is not accurately measured using students' evaluations, it is important to measure the effectiveness of an instructor using different methods. Measuring the knowledge the student acquired after taking a particular course can be an effective method to measure the instructor's performance and how effective he/she was in teaching the students.

By reviewing teaching effectiveness studies in the business field, we find that much research has been done in different areas such as: Accounting (Bell et al., 1993), Economics (Juster and Stafford, 1991), Insurance (Murray et al., 1994), Management (Tang, 1997), and Marketing (Enderwick and Akoorie, 1994). No research in the MIS area could be identified. To reflect the rapid growth of the MIS area and its popularity among business students in the 1990s, it is important to measure teaching effectiveness in that department.

Finally, many practitioners and academic researchers have come to agree that job requirements as well as the knowledge and skills of the MIS professionals are changing rapidly (Burn and Ma, 1997; Lee et al., 1995). Accordingly, it is important to examine teaching effectiveness in the MIS area, as professors' input in the classroom is essential in a young and dynamic area such as MIS.

RESEARCH METHODOLOGY

A survey instrument was utilized in order to conduct the study. The details of the research methodology are as follows:

Questionnaire

The survey instrument consisted of two sections. The first section of questions was designed to measure the students' perception of their self-competence in using computers and the importance of computers and their contributions to the business world and to society as a whole. A pool of questions was created both by writing new questions and by adapting questions from available scales: i.e. Davis (1993) and Kay (1993). In this way, 12 questions were selected for the first section of the questionnaire. These 12 questions were then presented to the students, accompanied by a five-point Likert scale, where 1=Strongly disagree, 2= Disagree, 3= Neutral, 4= Agree 5= Strongly agree (Appendix I). The second section of the questionnaire was a set of 40 multiple-choice questions to measure the students' general knowledge of IT. These questions had been tested in classes over several previous semesters.

Subjects

The subjects of this study were students enrolled in a course in IT concepts at a large university, which was taught by eight different instructors over a period of three semesters with multiple sections in each semester. The course is designed to introduce students to IT and to the use of computers in business applications. The answers from 659 students are considered to be valid for the test yielding a response rate of 79%.

Procedure

The subjects were presented with the two sets of questions twice, at the first (pretest) and at the last (posttest) class meetings of the semester. The rationale here was to measure the differences in the students' responses before and after the course.

DEVELOPING A MEASUREMENT INSTRUMENT

One of the main purposes of this study is to develop a measurement instrument in the IT area. In doing so, first we have to test whether the questions on the first section of the questionnaire were valid in measuring their perception of computers and IT. An exploratory factor analysis was utilized to develop the instrument. The analysis was done on half of the observations (330 observations), both to assess the construct's validity of measure and to determine underlying factors of computer perception among students. The factor analysis was conducted on 12 items using principal components analysis followed by a varimax (orthogonal) rotation to determine the underlying factors. The minimum eigenvalue for which a factor was to be retained was specified as 1.0. To validate the results, another factor analysis was conducted on the second half of the data (329 observations). The results of the validation process confirm the first analysis with regard to factor loading. All of the primary factor loadings are greater than 0.483, which demonstrates a strong correlation between the construct and the items. The results of the 3 factors and items within the factors are shown in figure 1.

The three factors observed from the analysis are: 1) Contribution of IT to society, 2) self-competence in using computers, and 3) the effect of computers on business employees. In general, the analysis suggests that the instrument is valid in measuring perceptions of IT. Specifically, it suggests that the instrument is valid in measuring the perception of the usefulness of computers and the perception of self-competence in dealing with them.

Figure 1: Results of Factor Analysis

Items	Factor 1	Factor 2	Factor 3
Q1	0.656		
Q2			0.536
Q3		0.773	
Q4		0.823	
Q5	0.754		
Q6			0.509
Q7	0.745		
Q9			0.620
Q10			0.483
Q11			0.649
Q12	0.706		

*Q8 was deleted because the factor loading was insignificant.

HYPOTHESES

After developing the instrument and measuring the students' perception of IT, the next step in the analysis was to test the effect of the instructors on the knowledge gained by the students with regard to IT by the end of the course. This was accomplished through Analysis of Covariance (ANCOVA) procedure to test the hypotheses. The independent variables are the eight instructors and the dependent variable is the score of both the pretest and the posttest. The students' general knowledge of IT is considered as a covariate. There are eleven sets of hypotheses. Each set corresponds to a question and tests 3 hypotheses, as follows:

H_a: The efforts presented by all the instructors in teaching are equal.
H_b: The students' answers in the pretest equal those of the posttest for all instructors.
H_c: There is no interaction between the instructors and the acquired knowledge by the students during the course period.

The results of the test are in figure 2.

DISCUSSION OF FINDINGS

The above analysis has generated significant findings that can be of interest to both researchers and practitioners. One major finding is that the test failed to reject the first hypothesis (H_a) for most of the items.

The only differences between instructors were detected in items related to students' interest in learning new ways of using computers, the dependency of businesses on computers, and students' concern about the accuracy of information. These findings can be related to the instructors' different backgrounds and knowledge of particular areas with regard to IT.

Another major finding from the analysis is that the test rejects the second hypothesis (H_b) for both items related to self-competence in using computers construct. This indicates that there was a significant change in the students' self-competence. However, that significant difference was not attributed to the efforts of the instructors, as the interaction results were found not significant. That significant difference could be attributed to the textbook used in teaching this course.

The most important finding of the analysis is that the test fails to reject the third hypothesis (H_c) for all items. It indicates that there is no interaction between the instructors and the IT knowledge of the students. In other words, the knowledge gained by the students while taking that course was not significantly attributed to the teaching methods presented by their instructors. This result is significant, as it points out that teaching effectiveness was the missing link here.

The interaction between the professors and their students represents a significant part of the higher education environment and the learning process. The transfer of knowledge environment, the share of experience and the participation in research projects are the core of the soft skills students need to acquire to be prepared for advance-

Figure 2: Results of ANCOVA

Hypothesis		H$_a$			H$_b$			H$_c$		
		F	p		F	p		F	p	
	Q1	1.259	0.268	FR	0.878	0.349	FR	0.219	0.981	FR
Contribution	Q5	0.460	0.863	FR	8.882	0.049*	R	0.678	0.691	FR
of IT to	Q7	2.518	0.015*	R	0.010	0.920	FR	0.335	0.938	FR
society	Q12	0.653	0.712	FR	0.381	0.537	FR	0.269	0.966	FR
Self-competence	Q4	1.466	0.176	FR	14.560	0.000**	R	0.766	0.616	FR
in using computers	Q3	1.935	0.062	FR	27.106	0.000**	R	1.356	0.221	FR
The effect of	Q2	1.575	0.140	FR	1.531	0.216	FR	0.647	0.717	FR
computers on	Q6	1.680	0.111	FR	11.366	0.001**	R	0.379	0.914	FR
business employees	Q9	3.434	0.001**	R	0.811	0.368	FR	0.675	0.693	FR
	Q10	1.132	0.341	FR	0.039	0.843	FR	0.424	0.888	FR
	Q11	3.004	0.004**	R	4.469	0.035*	R	0.481	0.849	FR

R: reject the null hypothesis, FR: fail to reject the null hypothesis.
Significant at $p < 0.05$, ** Significant at $p < 0.01$

ment.

Finally, in item Q11, the analysis shows a significant difference among instructors with regard to their effectiveness in discussing the accuracy of information issues with their students. Furthermore, there was a significant difference between pretest and posttest results. However, the analysis did not detect any significance to the interaction between students and instructors. This point needs to be tested further.

CONCLUSION AND RECOMMENDATIONS

Many academics around the country have realized the significance of the issue. As a result of an accumulation of unsatisfied customers (students and businesses), many research universities have started experiencing a decline in student enrollments. The public concern about the quality of undergraduate education is worth every bit of research universities' attention (Brunner, 1997). Research universities need to focus more on the satisfaction of their students in order to continue attracting more new students. This might be achieved by redefining the relationship between research universities and their faculty, specifically the faculty reward system.

Reward systems in most universities have greatly affected what we are experiencing now with regard to instructor's influence on the knowledge acquired by students. At these universities, reward systems focus on research as opposed to teaching. Faculty are encouraged by the reward system at their universities to be recognized (DeYoung, 1985). Excellence in teaching is "less highly regarded" and most of the time does not translate into promotions, pay raises or tenure decisions (Byrne, 1992; Kensicki, 1992). In most cases, an acceptable publication record or the potential for doing research has become a job prerequisite in hiring new faculty (Muller et al., 1998; Horwitz, 1994). Furthermore, studies have shown that the amount academics teach and their salary are negatively related (Gibbs, 1995).

Reward systems have to be revisited by many universities in order to set policies that reflect their commitment to providing the highest quality of teaching. Furthermore, effective measures should be in place to ensure that their policies are in effect, their students have been well served, and their faculty members are well rewarded for their high teaching skills.

REFERENCES

Behrman, J. W. & Levin, R. I. (1982). Are business schools doing their jobs? *Harvard Business Review*, January-February, 140-147.

Bell, T., Frecka, T. J., & Solomon, I. (1993). The relation between research productivity and teaching effectiveness. *Accounting Horizons*, 4, 33-49.

Brunner, R. D. (1997). Raising standards: A prototyping strategy for undergraduate education. *Policy Science*, 3, 167-189.

Burn, J. M. & Ma, L. C. K. (1997). Innovation in IT education - practicing what we preach. *Information Resources Mmanagement Journal*, 4, 16-25.

Byrne, J. (1990). Is research in the ivory tower 'fuzzy, irrelevant, and pretentious'? *BusinessWeek*, October 29, 62-64.

Centra, J. A., 1981. Research Report: Research Productivity and Teaching Effectiveness. Princeton, NJ: Educational

---

APPENDIX 1

Factor 1: Contribution of IT to Society
Q1: Computers have made a positive contribution to society as a whole.
Q5: I would enjoy using the Internet to search for information for a report.
Q7: I like to learn new ways of using a computer.
Q12: I believe that the Internet is valuable source of information.
Factor 2: Self-Competence in Using Computers
Q3: I could select by myself an appropriate new computer system for my home or office.
Q4: I could install by myself a new sound card.
Factor 3: The Effect of Computers on Business Employees
Q2: Computers have caused a decrease in available job opportunities worldwide.
Q6: I worry that I might press the wrong key and damage my computer hardware.
Q9: Businesses have become too dependent on computers for their operations.
Q10: I would get faster service at grocery and other retail stores if computer systems were not used for sales transactions.
Q11: I am concerned about the accuracy of information maintained on and distributed through computer systems.

Testing Service.

Clement, R. W. (1988). Management teaching can still be fun. *Business Horizons*, 1, 7-10.

Davis, F., (1993). User acceptance of information technology: system characteristics, user perceptions and behavioral impacts. *International Journal of Man-Machine Studies*, 38, 475-487.

DeYoung, A. J., (1985). Assessing faculty production: Penetration of the technical thesis into the status system of academe. *Educational Theory*, Fall, 411-421.

Dulek, R. E. & Fielden, J. S., (1992). Why fight the system? The non-choice facing beleaguered business faculties. *Business Horizons*, September-October, 13-19.

Enderwick, P. & Akoorie, M. E. M., (1994). The employment of foreign language specialists and export success -The case of New Zealand. *International Marketing Review*, 4, 4-18

Gibbs, G., (1995). Training lecturers to value teaching. *People Management*, 7, pp. 34-36

Gomez-Mejia, L. R. & Balkin, D. B., (1992). Determinants of faculty pay: An agency theory perspective," *Academy of Management Journal*, 5, 921-955.

Hollman, K. W., Hayes, R. D., Murrey, J. H. Jr, & Taylor, R. L., (1994). Insurance commissioners' attitudes toward research and publishing. *Journal of Insurance Regulation*, 2, 224-236.

Horwitz, T., (1994). Young Professors Find Life in Academia Isn't What It Used to Be. *The Wall Street Journal*, February 15, 1+.

Juster, F. T. & Stafford, F., (1991). The allocation of time: Empirical findings, behavioral models, and problems of measurement. *Journal of Economic Literature*, 4, 471-522.

Kensicki, P. R., (1992). Insurance academic world in crisis. *National Underwriter* (Property & Casualty/Employee Benefits edition), October 12, 9+.

Kay, R., (1993) An exploration of theoretical and practical foundation for assessing attitude toward computers: the Computer Attitude Measure (CAM)." *Computers in Human Behavior*, 371-386.

Lee, D. M. S., Trauth, E. M., Farwell, D., (1995). Critical skills and knowledge requirements of IS professionals: A joint academic/industry investigation. *MIS Quarterly*, 3, 313-340.

Maglitta, J.,(1996). IS schools: Need improvement. *Computerworld*,6, 78-83.

Muller, H. J., James L. Porter, J. L., & Rehder, R., (1988). Have business schools let down U.S. corporations? *Management Review*, October, 24-31.

Murrey, J. H., Taylor, R. L., Hollman, K. W., & Hayes, R. D., (1994). Risk and insurance faculty attitudes toward research and publishing. *CPCU Journal*, 3, 162-172.

Singell, L. D. Jr, Lillydahl, J. H., Singell, L. D. Sr, (1996). Will changing times change the allocation of faculty time? *Journal of Human Resources*, 2, 429-449.

Tang, T. L-P, (1997). Teaching evaluation at a public institution of higher education: Factors related to the overall teaching effectiveness. *Public Personnel Management*, 3, 379-389.

Wilson, R., (1998). Report blasts research universities for poor teaching of under graduates. *The Chronicle of Higher Education*, April 24, A12-A13

End-Users of the Next Millennium — Knowledge Workers Using Desktop Information Technologies

Valerie Spitler
Dept. of Information Systems, Stern School of Business, New York University, 44 West Fourth Street, Suite 9-181, New York, NY 10012
tel: 212-998-0827, fax: 212-995-4228, vspitler@stern.nyu.edu

INTRODUCTION

Firms continue to make enormous investments in information technologies (IT), but whether these investments pay off depends on how the technology is deployed, managed and used (Brynjolfsson 1993, Markus and Benjamin 1997, Strassman 1990, Panko 1991). One example of these investments is the desktop information technology (George, Iacono et al. 1995) that firms make available to their knowledge workers.[1] For many workers desktop information technologies are tools (Panko 1988) as important as the telephone for conducting business. However, desktop technologies can be applied to a multitude of tasks (communication, analysis, record-keeping, etc.), and they require both data and sophisticated manipulations and skills by workers to be useful in performing the worker's task. To capture the requirement for the worker to manipulate the information technology and data before applying it to a work task, I refer to the technology artifacts constructed by knowledge workers from desktop information technologies as 'constructed tools.'[2] This terminology also reflects the technology's close connection to specific and immediate work tasks. Understanding the process by which constructed tools come about and are applied to work tasks is a first step toward understanding how to manage this information technology and thereby realize economic benefits sought from investments in it.

Past research in information systems (IS) has focused on successful development and implementation of *systems* in firms (usually by IS professionals), but has virtually ignored the building and use of constructed tools by knowledge workers. The research presented here addresses two questions:

1. How can we characterize the constructed tools knowledge workers build and use?; and
2. Can we formulate a model for studying how constructed tools are built and used?

In order to answer these questions, I conducted a series of interviews at a management consulting firm and supplemented these interviews with observations of some of the workers as well as company documentation. I then used qualitative analytic techniques as proposed by Miles and Huberman (1994) and Strauss and Corbin (1990) to analyze these data and to build a conceptual model of tool construction and use.

PRIOR LITERATURE

Definition of 'Constructed Tool' Vis-à-vis 'Information System'

One of the main premises of the research is that constructed tools are different from information systems, and that therefore different research questions are likely to emerge when studying them. The discussion below elucidates the definition of constructed tools and compares them with information systems, including decision support systems (DSS) and user-developed applications (UDA).

The following is a definition of constructed tool and is explained vis-à-vis information systems in the paragraphs below.

constructed tool: the model, application or other artifact constructed by a knowledge worker (end-user) from general desktop information technology to support a specific and immediate work task for a relatively short period of time.

This definition indicates four important dimensions that, when taken together, differentiate constructed tools from information systems, including DSS and UDA. The first dimension concerns who has responsibility for development. In traditional systems and many DSSs, IS professionals have responsibility for developing the system. Like user-developed applications, however, constructed tools are developed by knowledge workers who are not IS professionals. The second dimension is the underlying technology used. Systems can be developed on many technology

Table 1: Comparing Systems and Constructed Tools			
	information technology artifacts		
	system		**constructed tool**
Dimensions	**system and DSS**	**user developed application**	
responsibility for development	IS staff	knowledge worker	knowledge worker
technology platform	diverse	common desktop technologies or other technologies	common desktop technologies
scope of intended use	replace or support organizational process	replace or support organizational process	support specific knowledge work tasks
intended duration of use	repetitive, on-going use	repetitive, on-going use	one-time or short-term use
cost	cost is usually a consideration: feasibility analysis or cost/benefit analysis conducted	cost may or may not be a consideration, usually the worker's time is the main consideration	cost is unlikely to be a concern since the hardware and software are already in place, worker's time or mistakes are likely the major costs
source in the IS literature	system: any IS textbook, e.g. Lucas 1990 DSS: Silver 1991, Sprague 1980,Gerrity 1971	Edberg and Bowman 1996 Sumner and Klepper 1987 Rockart and Flannery 1983	

platforms; constructed tools, by definition, are developed with common desktop information technologies. The third dimension is the scope of the intended use. Systems are, by definition, intended to replace or support organizational processes, generally involving many users (Lucas 1990, Silver 1991). Even user-developed applications, which seem to be nearest to constructed tools on the dimensions already discussed, have been defined as supporting organizational processes (Edberg and Bowman 1996) or departments (Sumner and Klepper 1987). Constructed tools, in contrast, are intended to support specific and immediate work tasks involving a limited number of workers. The final dimension in the definition is the intended duration of use. Systems are developed with the intention that they will be used repeatedly over a period of time, but constructed tools are intended to be used once or for a short period of time. Not in the definition, yet implied by the foregoing discussion, is one other important dimension, cost. For many systems, cost is an important consideration in the planning and development, as evidenced by feasibility analyses and cost/benefit studies. For constructed tools, cost is unlikely to be a consideration since the information technology is already in place with the expectation that workers will use it. Comparison across these five dimensions differentiates constructed tools from information systems; this comparison is summarized in Table 1.[3]

Models for Studying Constructed Tools

What models exist in the literature for studying the successful building and use of constructed tools in organizations? Models in the literature can be conveniently grouped under three headings: (1) prescriptive models of development of systems; (2) factor models of "IS success"; and (3) process models of development, use or implementation[4] of IT artifacts. Prescriptive models of systems development prescribe, usually to professionally trained IS developers or managers, how to build systems successfully. The second type of research models, factor models (or variance models) of IS success, assert that variances in individuals' characteristics, in perceived system features and in organizational factors are responsible for variance in "IS success," where IS success is measured in a multitude of ways (Seddon 1997, DeLone and McLean 1992). Recently IS researchers have begun to make use of process models to study the development, use and implementation of information systems. These models consider the process (rather than the antecedents or consequences of the process) of development, use or implementation as the phenomenon of interest (Shaw and Jarvenpaa 1997).

Existing studies in the IS literature have not addressed the questions of how to characterize the constructed tools knowledge workers build and use, nor have they provided an appropriate model for studying constructed tools. A model which is able to capture the dynamic nature of building and using constructed tools is required. Process models are suitable for these purposes. Therefore, I developed a process model of tool construction and use by conducting an empirical study using a grounded theory approach.

FIELD STUDY

Objective, Design and Methodology

The purpose of the study was twofold: 1) to gain an appreciation for the variety of constructed tools knowledge workers build and use, and 2) to begin to understand the process by which the tools get constructed and used in an organizational setting.

I approached a management consulting firm (Alpha) which expressed interest in the research topic and in participating in the research. This site was chosen based on a principle known as theoretical sampling (Strauss and Corbin 1990) to ensure that the phenomenon of interest would be highlighted. After discussing the topic and the organization at length with the Director of Human Resources at Alpha, he supplied me with the names of people who would be available for interviews about the research topic. The individuals identified included consultants at all levels in the organization, from Partner to Business Analyst. I was also provided with documentation about Alpha. The main documentation which I relied on were training manuals which describe how to approach, analyze and solve clients' problems as a consultant at Alpha.

I conducted eleven formal, semi-structured interviews (four partners, three managers, one associate, three analysts) and several informal, follow-up interviews at Alpha over a four-week period in October, 1997. Interviews lasted between 20 minutes and one hour; nine of the formal interviews were tape-recorded and subsequently transcribed. I took notes during unrecorded interviews and subsequently transcribed my notes. I followed the interviewing technique called conversational partners (Rubin and Rubin 1995) to gain trust of the participants and encourage them to share important details of their work. I also encouraged participants to speak about any constructed tools they had been involved with in their tenure at Alpha.

The qualitative data I collected at Alpha allowed me to answer my two initial questions. To analyze the data, I relied on several approaches. First, I discussed the data with colleagues who assisted in extracting categories and their properties. I also provided a written transcript of an early version of what is now section 3.3 to one of the partners who had participated in the formal and follow-up interviews; he ensured that what I had written reflected a reasonable account of the process of tool construction at Alpha, and he added further refinements. Finally, I used visual displays to represent and organize my data (Miles and Huberman 1994). Results are presented in the following two subsections.

Results: Characterization of Constructed Tools at Alpha

Alpha is a management consulting firm of approximately 150 consultants, providing services to a variety of clients. Services are provided by teams of consultants working on projects. Teams are composed of partners, managers, associates and business analysts. Typically partners sell the service to the client and subsequently manage the client relationship. Managers typically have responsibility for day-to-day operations for a project, and associates and analysts do the analytical work, including hands-on computer work.

Projects can be described as having overall objectives of solving a major client concern. The team then works using a consulting approach, breaking the problem into smaller sub-problems, which can then be solved. Consultants[5] use various constructed tools to tackle the sub-problems; many of these constructed tools are developed from general purpose office software (e.g., spreadsheet software, such as Excel or Lotus 1-2-3 and database software, such as Access or Paradox), and some are developed from specialized software (e.g., statistical software such as SAS).

In interviews it became apparent that consultants construct tools regularly as part of their solutions to clients' problems, even though training documents do not cover the use of technology in solving clients' problems.

Results: Tool Construction at Alpha

The process of tool construction at Alpha was gleaned from interview materials and from observing some participants using desktop information technology in their work. This process is described below.

Typically, a senior member of the team asks a junior member of the team to do a task.[6] For example, a manager or partner will ask a business analyst or associate to construct a spreadsheet to aid in an analysis. Senior people typically specify the task according to their own knowledge of software tools. Some senior people always specify that work be done using a spreadsheet since they know the spreadsheet tool and feel comfortable with neither database software nor database concepts. One business analyst expressed this issue as it manifest in the relationship with her client:

> "I ... spent a lot of time trying to smooth feathers with the client, explaining why I was doing this in Access and why it was difficult to work with Excel since they (the client) had already created a model (in a spreadsheet) before I got there."

Other managers, recognizing their own discomfort with database software specifically request a junior person who knows the software well to work on a project or task which requires the use of database software. One manager, who was supervising a business analyst in developing a database for a client remarked:

"...I must confess that I have never ever used a database, and I mean I'm an engineer and ... when it comes down to Access I promptly delegate. [followed by laughter]"

The conditions under which the request is made may vary and the amount of information passed from senior member to junior member may also vary. For example, a new business analyst explained the conditions under which he constructed a spreadsheet to predict labor costs for a new process:

"I had a brief five minute conversation with the associate who just ran down the numbers that he wanted that were estimates, like a percentage of the bucket. ... So, basically he just said okay I think 2% of bucket two ... is going to be put onto our new program and then 5% of three and 5% of four, and then I had to dig the volume numbers for the bucket off something that was faxed to me. I mean this is an estimate."

"But this was something that was presented to me at 12 and (the associate) said, 'Just get me something.'"

Sometimes a junior person will be supplied with a constructed tool and asked to perform an information task with the existing constructed tool. This may require the person to make adjustments to the constructed tool, or to abandon the constructed tool altogether as inappropriate for the task at hand. A business analyst, describing the modifications she made to a constructed tool which she inherited, had this to say about the quality of the inherited tool:

"(the person who created the constructed tool) used all the hard copies and hardcoded it into an Excel spreadsheet. So I was worried about the integrity of the data. ... he didn't have one data source, he had about five different ways of showing the (same piece of) data but each time he had a different way of showing the data he (hard-coded it, so that a change to a piece of data would have to be made multiple times in the spreadsheet, opening up the possibility for errors.)..."

The junior person (the one building the constructed tool) then works to complete the task. Sometimes several people work on different parts of the same constructed tool. A manager described how, as an associate, he had worked with two others to extract data from a spreadsheet:

"... all the data was in one place. Each one of us was trying to extract different information from it. So one of us was focusing on, say, wire transfer fees. Unfortunately the information was a huge mass of jumble and so one person was looking at that and one was looking at accounts payable, checks, things of that sort. So we were extracting different things..."

The approach followed by the person building the constructed tool also varies. The manager above described his approach to building spreadsheets:

"I don't plan the spreadsheet out in advance because I think it varies from (person to person). I just think in a certain way and as the thought keeps going I keep building columns and most often I don't find it necessary to tweak. I think it works out for me. It's almost like thinking on the spreadsheet ...In most cases, maybe the work I've done has not been that elaborate, but it's pretty obvious what needs to be done."

The amount of supervision varies. Sometimes junior people are expected to be self-motivated and to seek sources of assistance if they do not understand how to do something, do not have the requisite skills, or do not have sufficient information about the task structure. Other times, a senior person will give relatively more guidance. In the first case, junior people approach other business analysts or associates who have more experience with either the technology task, or the information task. They might also approach partners, managers or recognized specialists[7] for how to approach certain analyses. They may also ask their managers for guidance or may work with the client to gather data, assumptions and requirements of the task.

Because formal training covers only very basic concepts of tools, sometimes a junior person will be sent to training[8] to learn about a new tool a few days into a project. In other cases, the junior person is sent to the training at the beginning of the project in anticipation of the need to know a certain software tool.

Some people use many features of the software to develop a tool; others concentrate on the task, and develop a tool which might be considered less sophisticated but which completes the task, often in a shorter time. One manager explained the trade-off as follows:

"...one other person ... spent a huge amount of time trying to organize stuff and do all kinds of fancy things and at the end of which it took him a lot longer to get anywhere as opposed to just going and extracting what you needed. Maybe I have a strong bias. I just feel that most people, for whatever reason, end up getting too caught up on the fancy stuff that they can do with this as opposed to just use the tool and get out of it."

At some point, the junior person shows the fruits of his work. In the case of predicting labor costs cited above, the business analyst described what his supervisor does when seeing the completed spreadsheet:

"I know exactly what he does. The first thing that he does is audit that first cell and makes sure that I do the math right. He'll take this number and multiply it by the percentage that's supposed to be here and make sure that it's correct, that's the very first thing."

Once the constructed tool has been unveiled, further work may or may not be required to develop it. If it is not, the constructed tool is used for the task. Sometimes, at this stage if the work is inadequate, another person will take over the construction of the tool.[9]

Frequently, as the constructed tool is being developed, the task changes, or an ill-specified task begins to take shape. This may occur during the first instance of the task, or as the task is repeated for different projects. A partner explained how a task changed over time and how this change impacted tool selection for future projects:

"... initially, the emphasis was put on the quality and accuracy of data as well as on the speed at which we could train consultants to use the database tool which supported the analysis. For these purposes, Paradox was the perfect tool. Later on we discovered that the ability to produce easy-to-use and easy-to-read reports was more important. At that point, we switched from Paradox to Access."

This description of how tools get constructed at Alpha illuminates many aspects of the process and leads to the formulation of a model. In the next section I develop a model of this process and incorporate an evaluative component.

DISCUSSION: MODEL OF TOOL CONSTRUCTION

Before unveiling a model, different aspects of the process will be discussed. First, since the tool is constructed only as a result of the assignment of a task, task assignment is an important precursor to constructing the tool. There are many important issues surrounding the assignment of the task, including which people are involved and what they know, how the task is understood, how information about the task is communicated and under what conditions the task assignment is made. These issues surrounding the assignment of the task are likely to influence how the tool is actually constructed.

Second, the actual hands-on work of constructing the tool is a process with many facets. Issues such as which software is used, where data and assumptions come from, who actually constructs the tool and what they know, which sources of assistance are available during construction, and how much supervision there is during construction are all important parts of constructing the tool. The activities associated with the hands-on work of constructing the tool may be viewed as the heart of the process; it is preceded by the assignment of the task and is closely linked with use and assessment of the constructed tool.

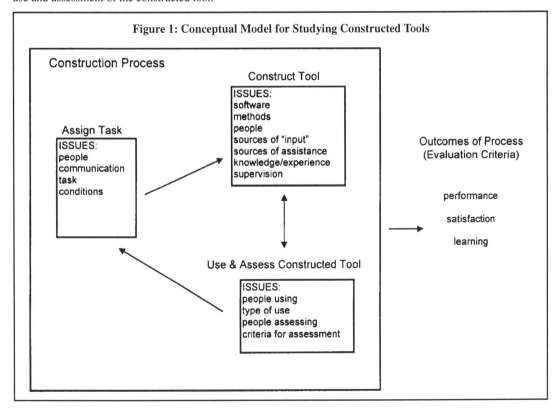

Figure 1: Conceptual Model for Studying Constructed Tools

Third, an assessment component is embedded in the construction process. As the constructed tool gets built, it is simultaneously used and assessed. Use and assessment are grouped together since it is difficult, if not impossible, to assess the constructed tool without using it, and in using a tool to do a task, one is likely to assess it, at least implicitly. Such issues as who uses the constructed tool and who assesses it, as well as the criteria used to make the assessment, are important. When the use and assessment are unsatisfactory or further enhancements are desired, either the constructed tool may get modified by those constructing it, the task may get modified, or the task may get re-assigned. These three aspects, task assignment, tool construction, and use and assessment of the constructed tool, are represented by the following model of the construction process.

This model shows the three main elements of the construction process for constructed tools, the relationships between these elements and the issues associated with each element. This representation shows the temporal sequence of events: first a task is assigned, then a tool is constructed, and finally the constructed tool is used and assessed. The two-way arrow between Construct Tool and Use & Assess Constructed Tool indicates a reciprocal relationship between these two elements. As indicated above, as the tool is being constructed, it is also being used and assessed; modifications and enhancements to the constructed tool occur as a result of this use and assessment. The arrow from Use & Assess Constructed Tool to Assign Task indicates that a task may be re-assigned if the constructed tool is deemed unsatisfactory for the task or if the tool does not work as envisioned. The absence of a two-way arrow between Assign Task and Construct Tool indicates that some type of use and assessment must occur for a re-assignment to be made. Re-assignments made independently of constructing the tool would be considered a new task and thus a new cycle of the construction process would begin. The entire three-step process, is referred to as the construction process.

Although the model describes the construction process beginning with task assignment and finishing with use of the constructed tool, it is incomplete since it does not capture evaluative outcomes associated with the process of construction. Since the goal of the research is to understand what contributes to *successful* tool construction, some type of evaluation must be included in the model. Whether tool construction is successful depends to a large extent on what is meant by success. Different criteria may apply depending on the circumstances. One criteria that could be used is that the constructed tool allows for the accurate and timely completion of the work task.

Other criteria are that those involved with the construction process were satisfied with the constructed tool itself and the process of construction, and that those involved learned new skills which will be valuable for future projects. (Finally, in some situations at Alpha, an important criteria is how easily the constructed tool can be passed to the client for the client to use.) The complete model, shown in Figure 3, includes these evaluation criteria under the heading 'Outcomes of Process.' Adding the Outcomes to the model is consistent with notions in evaluation research (Guba 1989).

CONCLUSION

The premise of this paper is that in order to make information technology pay off, we must understand better how it is deployed, managed and used. One area where new understanding is possible is knowledge workers' use of desktop information technologies. In this paper I have claimed and demonstrated in field work that knowledge workers create models, applications and other IT artifacts, which I have called 'constructed tools' and which differ from 'systems' as described in the literature. One of the main differences is that constructed tools are highly task-specific and therefore have a more limited scope and duration of use than do systems. They are also often constructed without the assistance of IS professionals. Whether knowledge workers are able to apply information technology in the form of constructed tools in productive ways will depend on the process by which these constructed tools are created and applied to information tasks.

In order to build a suitable research model, I conducted a qualitative research study in a management consulting firm. I used grounded theory techniques to collect and analyze data which led me to a preliminary conceptual model. The model indicates three important, interrelated concepts, each with a set of related issues. I added an extension to the model in the form of an evaluative component of the process of building and using the constructed tool.

This research contributes to the IS literature in two fundamental ways. First, it raises a new conceptualization of the IT artifacts created by knowledge workers in the course of doing their work. Secondly, it presents a preliminary research model which can guide future research in this area.

While contributing to the IS literature, this research is not without its limitations. The research does not pretend to present a complete model, but rather it provides an entry point for future research. In the quest for theoretical generalization, further refinement of the model may be obtained by collecting additional data at the study's research site or by collecting data at other sites. Refinement of the model may lead to the formalization of propositions which could eventually be tested. Testing would require further data collection and analysis, perhaps using a pattern-matching technique (Yin 1988), or using interpretive approaches (Orlikowski and Baroudi 1991, Walsham 1995).

Gaining understanding into how knowledge workers use desktop information technologies in the form of constructed tools may shed light on the productivity paradox, a problem which will, no doubt, continue to engage our attention into the next millennium.

REFERENCES

Brynjolfsson, E. (1993). "The Productivity Paradox of Information Technology: Review and Assessment." Communications of the ACM 36(12): 1287 - 1294.

Davenport, T. H., S. L. Jarvenpaa, et al. (1996). "Improving Knowledge Work Processes." Sloan Management Review (Summer): 53 - 65.

DeLone, W. H. and E. R. McLean (1992). "Information Systems Success: The Quest for the Dependent Variable." Information Systems Research 3(1): 60 - 95.

Edberg, D. T. and B. J. Bowman (1996). "User-Developed Applications: An Empirical Study of Application Quality and Developer Productivity." Journal of Management Information Systems 13(1): 167 - 185.

George, J. F., S. Iacono, et al. (1995). "Learning in Context: Extensively Computerized Work Groups as Communities-of-Practice." Accting., Mgmt. & Info. Tech. 5(3/4): 185 - 202.

Gerrity, T. P. (1971). "Design of Man-Machine Decision Systems: An Application to Portfolio Management." Sloan Management Review(Winter): 59 - 75.

Guba, E. G. (1989). Fourth Generation Evaluation. Newbury Park, CA, Sage Publications, Inc.

Lucas, H. C. J. (1990). Information Systems Concepts for Management. New York, Mitchell McGraw-Hill.

Markus, M. L. and R. I. Benjamin (1997). "The Magic Bullet Theory in IT-Enabled Transformation." Sloan Management Review(Winter): 55 - 68.

Miles, M. B. and A. M. Huberman (1994). Qualitative Data Analysis. Thousand Oaks, CA, Sage Publications.

Orlikowski, W. J. and J. J. Baroudi (1991). "Studying Information Technology in Organizations: Research Approaches and Assumptions." Information Systems Research 2(1): 1 - 28.

Panko, R. R. (1991). "Is Office Productivity Stagnant?" MIS Quarterly(June): 191 - 203.

Panko, R. R. (1988). End User Computing. New York, John Wiley & Sons.

Rockart, J. F. and L. S. Flannery (1983). "The Management of End User Computing." Communications of the ACM 26(10): 776 - 784.

Rubin, H. J. and I. S. Rubin (1995) Qualitative Interviewing: the Art of Hearing Data. Thousand Oaks, California, Sage Publications, Inc.

Seddon, P. B. (1997). "A Respecification and Extension of the DeLone and McLean Model of IS Success." Information Systems Research 8(3): 240 - 253.

Shaw, T. and S. Jarvenpaa (1997). Process Models in Information Systems. Information Systems and Qualitative Research. A. S. Lee, J. Liebenau and J. DeGross. London, New York, etc., Chapman & Hall: 70 - 100.

Silver, M. S. (1991). Systems That Support Decision Makers. New York, John Wiley & Sons.

Sprague, R. H. J. (1980). "A Framework for the Development of Decision Support Systems." Management Information Systems Quarterly December: 1 26.

Strassmann, P. A. (1990). The Business Value of Computers. New Canaan, CT, The Information Economics Press.

Strauss, A. and J. Corbin (1990). Basics of Qualitative Research. Newbury Park, CA, Sage Publications, Inc.

Sumner, M. and R. Klepper (1987). "Information Systems Strategy and End-User Application Development." Data Base(Summer): 19 - 30.

Walsham, G. (1995). "The Emergence of Interpretivism in IS Research." Information Systems Research 6(4): 376 - 394.

Yin, R. K. (1988). Case Study Research Design and Methods. Thousand Oaks, California, Sage Publications.

ENDNOTES

1 Davenport et al define knowledge work as "(work whose) primary activity is the acquisition, creation, packaging, or application of knowledge. Characterized by variety and exception rather than routine, it is performed by professional or technical workers with a high level of skill and expertise. Knowledge work processes include such activities as research and product development, advertising, education, and professional services like law, accounting, and consulting. We also include management processes such as strategy and planning." (Davenport, Jarvenpaa et al. 1996, p. 54) For purposes of this research, I consider knowledge workers who are not IS professionals.

2 A complete definition appears in Section 2.

3 A final point concerns the choice of the term 'constructed tool.' This term was chosen to reflect (1) the analogy of the craftsperson who uses a select tool to assist him/her in accomplishing a specific task and (2) the requirement for knowledge workers to skillfully manipulate data and information technology to *construct* such a tool before apply-

ing it to a work task. In the IS literature, the term 'tool' has often been used to describe IT hardware and software used to develop application systems — for example, end-user computing tools (Panko 1988) and DSS tools (Sprague 1980).

4 Implementation is used here in the broad sense of the word, including conception, development and use of the system.

5 Consultants at all levels, from partner to business analyst, are hired for their intelligence and are well educated, usually coming from elite educational institutions. They are good examples of knowledge workers. Their backgrounds in technology, however, vary widely.

6 This might happen in a team meeting, where all team members are present and brainstorming about the solution of the larger problem. Sometimes the manager outsources tasks. The task might be specified as an information task or as a technology task, or as a combination. An information task, by definition, does not specify how technology should be applied to the task; the worker uses his discretion. A technology task, by definition, is at the other extreme, specifying only to develop a tool, without specifying the corresponding information task. (This is really a pure definition and happens rarely, if ever, in reality). Finally, an intermediate approach is for the requester to specify both the information task and the technology task, e.g., build a spreadsheet to analyze these data, which is the most common approach at Alpha.

7 Specialists can be at any level of the organization. Their specialization results from having had experience in the problem area and is made known by word-of-mouth, internal presentations and/or publications.

8 Junior people generally receive one week of training when they join Alpha, then on-going training of about 1/2 day per month thereafter. The initial training covers general consulting skills such as problem-solving, conducting interviews and gathering data; it covers the basics of software tools. More advanced training on software tools such as Access, Excel and Solo (a presentation software) is given to junior people on an 'as needed' basis and is provided by outside firms, usually over 2-3 days for each tool.

9 In one case, a partner assigns a primary and a secondary person for each task. The primary person conducts the task, and the secondary person verifies that it is correct.

The Electronic Patient Record: Planning for a Successful Introduction

Dr. Robert A. Stegwee

Assistant Professor, Faculty of Management and Organization, University of Groningen, The Netherlands
Manager, Healthcare Consultancy Group, Moret Ernst & Young Management Consultants, P.O. Box 3101, 3502 GC UTRECHT, The Netherlands
Phone: +31 30 258 8752, Fax: +31 30 258 4242, E-mail: nlstegw2@mey.nl or r.a.stegwee@bdk.rug.nl

ABSTRACT

The introduction of a computerised patient information system (electronic patient record) in a healthcare organisation is a complex process, requiring a phased implementation over a number of years. It is important for the organisation to understand the full implications of the system and its introduction to be carefully planned. This contribution begins by briefly examining the motivation underlying the introduction of the electronic patient records system. The reasons for wanting to introduce the electronic patient record will determine how the system is tailored to meet specific requirements in order to respond, as much as possible, to the needs and wishes of the organisation. A systematic view of the elements contained in the electronic patient record shows that various scenarios are possible for introducing the system, as is illustrated by the example of how the system could work for an institution providing healthcare to mentally handicapped patients.

WHY AN ELECTRONIC PATIENT RECORD?

In recent years the need for computerised patient information has been a topic of discussion in almost every sector of healthcare. What was originally conceived as an electronic medical status has gradually developed, apace with other changes in the healthcare sector, into a more integrated electronic records system covering the full spectrum of healthcare services provided to individual patients. In some cases, patients are preferably referred to as clients, hence terms such as 'client monitoring system' and 'healthcare monitoring system' are used also. Since there are no strict definitions for such terms, there is little point in starting a discussion on terminology. [1] Thus, the term electronic patient record ('EPR') has been used throughout this article.

Various factors play a role in the decision to introduce the EPR. First, there is a need to simplify the registration system and to ensure, insofar as possible, that information only needs to be recorded once, thus avoiding the cumbersome process of having to type in the same details several times. This is called 'recording information at source'. Electronic linking of the administrative processes enables a more efficient processing of the information flows. Workload reduction and increased efficiency are also frequently cited as arguments for introducing an EPR system.

Second, there is a need for developing a more systematic approach to healthcare, whereby all disciplines work together towards a documented, integral approach to the individual patient. The advantage of such documentation is that it enables parties to learn from the methods applied and to evaluate and account for the chosen policy. This is particularly relevant in the face of today's increasing quality awareness and ever-more stringent (legal) requirements. The growing consensus that healthcare requires a multi-disciplinary approach, based on synchronised co-operation between the various disciplines, also implies that the communication between all parties concerned must be improved. It is no longer possible - as in the past - rely on verbal communication, hence a structured and documented approach is a precondition. Paper records, by definition, restrict the availability of information. In a multi-disciplinary approach, it is essential that the various teams involved should have access to a patient's record in different locations, at any time. [2] These are only some of the arguments in favour of developing and introducing the EPR.

There are some who dismiss the entire discussion surrounding the introduction of the EPR as just another episode in the digital onslaught, induced by a bunch of over-zealous IT experts fortunate enough to receive funding under government-funded stimulation schemes. The seeds of distrust are all too readily sown when the directors of the organisation or the government itself are seen to embrace these developments with enthusiasm, re-kindling old fears of big brother watching over the organisation's internal and external goings-on. [3] The possibility of this knowledge being used as a pretext for further cost cutting and efficiency measures is perceived by some as a real threat. However, there are proven benefits to be gained by the introduction of the EPR system. [4]

AVAILABLE SOFTWARE FOR THE EPR

The state of the software industry for EPR systems can broadly be divided into three categories. [5] The first approach is to integrate all relevant clinical data available in the hospital into one Clinical Data Repository (CDR). The functionality of these systems is usually limited to database viewing. Introduction of new data into the repository is governed by the traditional hospital or ancillary information systems, such as order processing and observation reporting procedures. A second approach is found in the storage of all relevant medical data into a combined Electronic Medical Record (EMR). The difference between a CDR and an EMR is that most of the data found in today's paper-based records are included in the EMR, often by scanning the paper versions of parts of the medical record. Often the EMR has extended functionality, beyond database viewing, to include orders, patient management and care plans. The third form of EPR systems is designed to actively support the healthcare professional in their day-to-day activities. Such a Computerised Patient Record (CPR) supports the active interpretation and structured charting of clinical data, includes protocols, and provides alerts, reminders and clinical decision support. Often CPR systems are linked to medical research.

Most hospital- or enterprise-wide implementations today are in the CDR - EMR range, with an emphasis on the CDR: a large database with a graphical viewer. CPR systems are often found in isolated departments, such as an intensive care / critical care unit. One of the disadvantages of current CPR systems is the fact that they were designed for individual hospitals or departments and with a focus on acute care. As such they are unable to support the continuum of care throughout an integrated delivery system. Other emerging applications are prerequisite to such an integrated implementation of an EPR: the implementation of a Master Patient Index, enterprise-wide scheduling and registration are hurdles facing a majority of healthcare facilities today.

Due to the limited functionality of current systems and the sometimes prohibiting cost of these systems, some healthcare providers are developing their own solutions to the EPR. These developments can often take advantage of the rapid changes in industry standards for hardware, software and communications. Based upon modern platforms, using technology like Windows NT, Netscape and XML, it has been shown that quick results can be delivered with a limited effort.

A STRUCTURED APPROACH TO THE INTRODUCTION OF THE EPR

The introduction of the EPR requires a carefully planned and structured approach. Working with the EPR implies some important changes in the daily activities of all parties concerned. Changes which will raise expectations on the one hand, and give rise to insecurity and opposition on the other. In the absence of a well-structured introduction plan, a project carrying such far-reaching implications as the EPR is almost certain to fail.

Those who have high expectations of the EPR will be disappointed if the system is not seen to immediately deliver all the advantages that incited their enthusiasm in the first place. Especially because the EPR offers few advantages in the early stages, its opponents and sceptics will only see their objections confirmed in the system's failure to deliver on its promises. A structured approach is therefore needed to achieve two things: first, it must ensure instant and tangible results for those required to make an extra effort. Second, efforts must be made to ensure that people's expectations are kept at a realistic level throughout the various stages of implementation and that they understand the ultimate objectives of the system and the time needed to achieve those objectives.

Having identified these basic issues, the next question is how to structure the implementation process. As the principal point of departure, the implementation will have a modular structure. Depending on the organisation's specific objectives and expectations, the various modules can be merged into a complete implementation scenario. A brief description of each of these modules and an implementation example are discussed below.

The EPR Modules

The introduction of the EPR serves different objectives and functionalities. The latter means that it must be possible to use the EPR for various tasks and functions. The implementation plan has to be based on clear segregation of the various elements. The key modules on which the EPR is built are described below. It is not necessary for an EPR to include all these modules. Details concerning the indicated care or the actual care assigned, for example, are mainly relevant to services provided under the Exceptional Medical Expenses Act (Algemene Wet Bijzondere Ziektekosten - AWBZ).

The following key modules of the EPR are recognised:
• basic information concerning the patient;
• healthcare requested, including a general case history and specification of the complaint or treatment request;
• indicated care or assigned care;
• analysis of specific problem, including a relevant case history and preliminary diagnosis;
• methodical description of healthcare programme;

- detailed description of proposed healthcare services and healthcare planning;
- description of care provided;
- results of care provided;
- quality of care provided;
- cost of care provided;
- costs to be declared for care provided;
- statistics and analysis of the process from the request to the care provided and results achieved.

The above modules can of course be further developed, as required. In relation to healthcare planning, for example, a more elaborate system has been developed for the entire patient logistics process. [6] However, these elements are not considered to be part of the EPR for the purpose of this introduction.

For the modules 'indicated care' and 'analysis', use can be made of knowledge systems supporting the care provider. In the modules 'healthcare programme' and 'healthcare planning', various protocols are followed for the treatment of specific conditions or the use of certain treatments.

Each module can be expanded to achieve a comprehensive support system tailored to the discipline in question.

The various modules, which are schematically represented in figure 1, are distinguished on the basis of their predominant character, i.e. administrative, support of direct care, or logistic. The time in the treatment process when the module is used, i.e. before or after the care is provided, is also indicated.

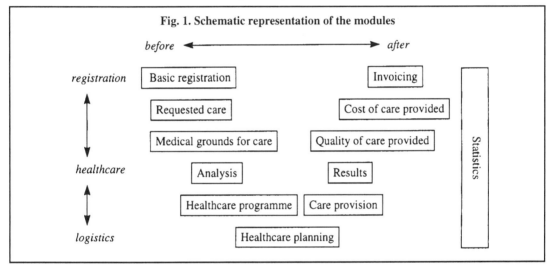

Fig. 1. Schematic representation of the modules

In the above diagram, the relationships between modules have been omitted as these will vary from one situation to the next. The treatment provided by a medical specialist, for instance, may involve the following cycle being repeated several times:
- referral by general practitioner in response to a complaint (requested care and indicated care);
- case history and preliminary diagnosis (analysis of problem and description of the healthcare programme);
- diagnostic research (healthcare planning, care provision and analysis of results);
- diagnosis (analysis of the patient's specific problem);
- identifying treatment (healthcare programme and planning);
- treatment (healthcare planning, care provision and analysis of results).

Combined with specific target groups, the above modules can serve as a basis for developing a range of scenarios for the introduction of the EPR. Naturally, there will be noticeable differences between the various scenarios depending on the nature of the organisation for which the system is developed.

An example scenario for an institution for mentally handicapped patients is described in the next paragraph. Achieving a proper balance between need and service provision is vital. In a general hospital, the emphasis understandably will be more on the medical side of the EPR, particularly so in the interaction with general practitioners and specialized medical departments, e.g. radiology, clinical chemistry, operating theatres and intensive care. [7]

Example of an Implementation Scenario

An institution for mentally handicapped patients has decided to introduce a modular EPR in stages, based on the specific characteristics and strategy of the institute. Despite an unsuccessful earlier attempt to introduce a comprehensive and integrated patient information system (largely on initiative of the IT department) the implementation plan as described below has broad support from staff as well as management. The following phasing is proposed:

1. Set up an integrated basic patient registration system.
2. Introduce a system for registering the care provided to individual patients, following a division between 'housing' and 'activities/recreation', and enabling immediate connections to be made between the care provided and the workload intensity in the various units.
3. Introduce a uniform care planning system, principally with a view to formulating and communicating the envisaged care programme. In addition, the information system should support the monitoring of the process of preparing and updating the care programme.
4. Electronically link the care registration system and the financial management system (FMS).
5. Introduce a care intensity methodology in the care planning to enable better planning for both patients and personnel, to be linked to a management information system (MIS).
6. Introduce a work pressure and cost price system within the care registration system, to provide detailed feedback on work pressure and to assist in achieving a better workload and cost control in the unit, with a link to the MIS.
7. Link the care registration system to the care planning in order to identify differences between planned and actual care and to draw connections between intensity of care and work pressure.
8. Link the external system regarding indicated care to the care planning system so as to analyse the demand and supply situation.
9. Introduce an intermediate planning phase in the route from the care planning through to care registration to achieve a more efficient and responsible use of human and technical resources in the care process. To achieve this, the personnel management system (PMS) must be extended to include information concerning the abilities and qualifications of personnel, and a description of the abilities and qualifications required for performing the activities outlined in the care plan. Basic information on allocated capacity is to be obtained from the MIS.

The architecture of the final situation is shown in figure 2. Because several of the connections between modules have changed over time, not all the intermediate steps described above are included. For example, there is no longer a direct link between the care plan and the realisation thereof as this connection is eventually made via the capacity planning module. On the right hand side, the client assets management system is shown. This module must be linked to the FMS to enable processing of collective expenditure for clients as well as accounting for cash expenses incurred on behalf of individual clients.

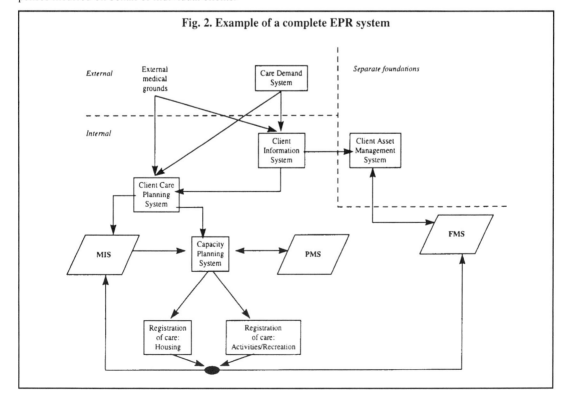

Fig. 2. Example of a complete EPR system

The above phasing covers a period of several years, and takes careful account of the required effort on the part of system users and IS staff, and the related costs to be incurred. In addition, the organisational developments required to successfully complete the elaborate IS infrastructure receive a great deal of attention. If not enough time and energy is invested to thoroughly and critically review the existing processes, past inefficiencies could be reintroduced in the new electronic structure. This could result in a computerised inheritance of organisational problems. Of course, the relationship of the new structure with the existing systems must also be considered.

An issue which warrants attention in its own right concerns the requirements dictated by the above developments with respect to the organisation's technical infrastructure. The resources to be invested in the introduction of the EPR are of a very different order than the present budget allocated to system management could provide. The standard of professionalism of the service department must keep pace with the introduction of the EPR. [8] As the day-to-day care provided as a whole becomes increasingly dependent on technology, systems must be available round-the-clock, including repair services after office hours. The provision of user support will attain a new dimension as the EPR system attracts new user groups who have no basic affinity with the registration processes.

Computer training will be a permanent aspect in the introduction programme for healthcare personnel, and will thus impose greater demands on the training capacity of the support departments. It will not be possible to simply purchase ready-made training courses from the established institutes, owing to the interaction of technology with the specific choices on the terminology used and nature of the care planning system. The importance of the training increases if the EPR is also used for management purposes. While mere financial data can be checked and corrected, the EPR will contain many times that amount of information, thus it is essential that all information is entered correctly from the outset. Furthermore, incorrectly recorded information could immediately lead to mistakes being made in the care provided to the patient. The latter aspect implies an intensive interaction between patient care and administrative processing; the administration must comply not only with the government directives but must also conform to agreements made within the organisation. In practice, these principles often collide. As a result, one is dealing with a vast flow of information which must be co-ordinated effectively, and which therefore requires a concerted effort on the part of the support staff.

The above scenario outlines the phased introduction of the various modules of an EPR in an organisation for mentally handicapped patients. The consequences in terms of the efforts required of personnel, costs, organisational developments and further professionalising the technical support services have been carefully considered. In essence, the proposal entails a practical and concrete plan for the provision of information with a long-term view.

CONSEQUENCES FOR YOUR OWN ORGANISATION

The introduction of an electronic patient record is not a matter to be decided without due consideration for all its consequences. The choices to be made with regard to the implementation process are often complex and require rank-and-file support within the organisation. The implementation must be kept in line with organisational developments, especially in areas where work processes need to be restructured or redesigned in connection with the introduction of the EPR. For example, a work methodology could be introduced in a nursing department prior to introducing the supporting information systems. [9,10] A tight, central co-ordination regime is needed to ensure effective interaction with the other information systems and technical infrastructure, without actually prescribing, in substantial terms, which aspects are to be included in the EPR. The overall responsibility for such a complex process must lie with the organisation's senior management or executive committee. The effort required at all levels in the organisation, both in terms of human and financial resources, warrants a commitment at the highest level.

By the same token, it is not necessary to approach the EPR project as a grand scheme from its early inception. An effective phasing of the project will offer sufficient scope for smaller developments, while ensuring that these can be adequately integrated in the system as a whole. It is thus particularly in the development and monitoring of the project phasing, including information systems planning and architecture, that the organisation will require the assistance of an external expert.

ENDNOTES
1 Tange, H.J., 'Het EMD heeft onze hoogste prioriteit. Maar ... wat is een EMD?', Informatie & Zorg, volume 27, no. 1, April 1998, pages 27-30.
2 Bemmel, J.H. van, 'Het kantelen van informatiesystemen', ZM Magazine, volume 13, no. 11, November 1997, pages 4-8.
3 'Big brother in zorgland : Zorgsector niet gebaat bij strakke sturing', NZi Notities, no. 63, April 1998, page 4.
4 Moret Ernst & Young, Zorgondersteunende Informatiesystemen: een praktische verkenning, report issued on behalf of the Ministery of Health, Welfare and Sport, May 1998.
5 Ernst & Young LLP, The Computerized Patient Record: Current Vendor Solutions, internal report, december 1997.

6 Vissers, J.M.H., Patient Flow based Allocation of Hospital Resources, thesis, Technical University of Eindhoven, 1994.

7 Informatisering en geÔntegreerde kwaliteitssturing in het ziekenhuis, results of a study carried out as part of the health stimulation programme (Volksgezondheid Transparant), Association for Hospital Information Processing in the North of the Netherlands (Vereniging ZINN [Ziekenhuis Informatieverwerking Noord-Nederland]), Groningen, 1995.

8 Stegwee, R.A., 'Information and Communication Technology Developments in the Dutch Health Care System'; In: Health Information Initiatives in the Netherlands, W. Dekker, et. al. (Eds), Amsterdam, The Dutch Association for Medical Records Administration (NVMA), april 1998, pp. 19-21.

9 Wieggers, J.G., 'Het electronisch verpleegkundig dossier: Werk in uitvoering!', Informatie en Zorg, volume 27, no. 1, April 1998, pages 14-21.

10 Abrahamsen, N.C. en R.K.J. van Valkenburg, 'Invoering van een elektronisch verpleegkundige dossier', Nederlands Tijdschrift voor Medische Administratie, volume 24, no. 92, June 1998, pages 35-37.

Web Site Management Strategies: An Information Management Issue

Craig Standing and Girija Krishnaswamy
School of Management Information Systems, Edith Cowan University, Joondalup
c.standing@cowan.edu.au, g.krishnaswamy@cowan.edu.au

ABSTRACT

Web sites have taken on strategic importance within large organisations. Despite this, many organisations are still grappling with their on-going management. Web sites have a number of features which make them quite different from traditional IS applications.

In this paper we explore the issues surrounding the on-going management of Web sites in large organisations and explore the notion of bureaucracy as a management strategy. A short case study of a large university is used to illustrate some of the key issues. Due to the complex relationship of organisational structure, Web strategy and Web site management policies, organisations need to think carefully about the amount of freedom or bureaucratic processes they put in place if they are to effectively manage this strategic resource.

INTRODUCTION

Many organisational Web sites now consist of hundreds, and in some cases, thousands of pages. The sites are often multi-functional and contain information on a vast range of topics. There is no disputing that Internets, Intranets and Extranets have taken on strategic significance within many organisations (Lawrence, Corbit, Tidwell, Fisher & Lawrence, 1998).

Web sites also evolve through time. Extra functionality is added and information is continually being added and updated. As a result the on-going management of Web sites has become an important issue (Fournier, 1998). This paper explores the issues surrounding the on-going management of Web sites as an organisational, customer/client and supplier resource.

Firstly, Web site development is compared with traditional IS development to determine the issues that need addressing in the management of Web sites. A number of problematic issues are raised in relation to the suitability of commonly used management structures and strategies for Web site management. A case study of a large Web site at a university is used to illustrate the nature of the problems and anomalies that can sometimes arise in large organisations. Finally, appropriate management structures and strategies for Web site management are discussed.

TRADITIONAL IS DEVELOPMENT

The traditional function of organisational information systems (IS) has been software development, maintenance and management, database development and administration, application package installation, and user support (Gordon & Gordon, 1996). In most cases the IS domain has been internal to the organisation and catering for the employees of the organisation (Whitten, Bentley & Barlow, 1994).

There has been a trend for the IS function to move from a centralised function to one that is distributed across the organisation (Hawryszkiewycz, 1998). Whilst this is true for some applications, the IS staff are still responsible for developing and managing the data/information resource, although they may be dispersed across the organisation in user departments. This IS responsibility often entails managing the appropriate database content and system design features across the organisation usually in collaboration with user groups. In many cases, the IS staff are the only ones with the expertise and authority to make the changes to systems. Despite the trend to distributed IS some applications are still centrally designed and managed; the payroll system being a typical example. There is still the fear for some managers that a move to distributed systems will mean a loss of control over the data and result in a lack of effective management of the information resource (Gordon & Gordon, 1996).

Projects are often suggested by user departments and groups and the future users are relatively clearly defined. Likewise, a specific aim in IS development is to clearly define and manage the scope of applications, in the hope that systems that have a well defined scope will be easier to maintain and manage and also behave more reliably (Whitten, Bentley & Barlow, 1994).

The IS function in organisations can be viewed from a bureaucratic perspective. According to Weber (1947), a perfect bureaucracy possesses:

1) *Rules and procedures* - information systems are designed with policies and procedures to help clarify the effective use of the system.

2) *Hierarchies of control and authority* - additions and developments in an organisational information systems require users to raise the issues with user management and if deemed acceptable are then raised with the IS department. Depending on the scale of the project it may need senior user management and senior IT management approval.

3) *Division of labour and expertise* - the IT/IS developments are carried out by experts in the field and as such there is a dependence on expertise and an adherence to a strict division of labour.

4) *Impersonality* - the IS department can use language and technical expertise to remain detached from user departments (Standing, 1998).

5) *Competence* - technical ability and expertise - changes to the information systems are made on the basis of technical competence and expertise.

6) *Record keeping* - is a large part of developing, maintaining and managing information systems.

Weber suggested that bureaucracy was the best administrative form for the rational pursuit of organisational goals.

HOW ARE WEB SITE APPLICATIONS DIFFERENT?

In this section we highlight a number of features of Intranet and Extranet applications that are quite different to many traditional IS development projects.

Web sites in many cases have evolved into multi-functional systems. They can be used for example for providing information to users or customers, for developing relationships with customers, for enabling customers to perform transactions, as well as a document management system for users internal to the organisation. Due to the multi-functionality there are frequently diverse stakeholders across the organisation (McKeown and Watson, 1997). Ownership of the Web site can be ambiguous as a result with the potential for the overall management of the Web strategy to be given little consideration.

The target audience for Internet web pages is a heterogeneous group, which is frequently not involved in the conceptualisation of web sites. The users can be internal to the organisation, and/or external customers, potential customers, and suppliers. These groups can live locally, or reside inter-state or overseas. Overseas users may have a different cultural and linguistic background and this may have to be considered in Web site development (Rockwell, 1998).

The content and functionality of Web sites changes through time. They are a type of evolutionary system and as such the notion of project completion is inappropriate. Even the standard six monthly update reviews used with traditional IS applications may be unsuitable for the rapid amount of change required. Web sites are living organisms which undergo constant changes. Thus a good web site 'is always evolving'. Web sites have a life-cycle which comprise of several sequential phases - from conceptualisation to implementation to updating to revision. Changes made to the Web site can be done by a variety of users as opposed to IS experts. These can be done through HTML code or more likely web authoring tools like Macromedia Dreamweaver, Microsoft Frontpage etc., that attempt to simplify the process of developing Web pages and applications.

Web site development lacks the type of specialised methodologies that exist for more traditional IS applications. Likewise evaluation of Web site efficiency and effectiveness cannot be done in the same manner as IS professionals have used with the typical core business applications.

MANAGEMENT STRATEGIES FOR WEB SITE EVOLUTION

As large organisational Web sites are continually evolving it is clear that some management strategy is required to keep the Web site strategy aligned to organisational goals and to keep a check on potential problems arising in content, functionality and design. Although Web sites typically have steering teams to plan and develop the initial Web site strategy and implementation, management structures are required to oversee the continual development of the system. Specialised enhancements and additions to the Web site are overseen by specially assigned committees or teams but a *meta-management structure* is required so that the function, content and design remain aligned to organisational goals.

A meta-management structure would need to plan its group composition, frequency of meeting, methods of communicating and the management of the on-going strategy of the Web site as part of the overall information systems infrastructure of the organisation. They would need to develop policies and procedures and effectively communicate these across the organisation. These are important to avoid the uncontrolled evolution of the Web site, the dangers of which are:

• Duplication of content and functionality

- Out of date and erroneous information content
- Inappropriate designs which adversely affect organisational image
- Inappropriate content which adversely affect organisational image; perhaps even resulting in loss of business or legal action
- Time spent in locating and updating content
- Inefficient use of an organisational resource (information - document management system)
- Lack of confidence in the Web site as an organisational resource
- The Web site being hi-jacked by sectional interests

The particular focus of this paper is to discuss appropriate strategies for Web site management. The management strategies can be analysed from a bureaucratic perspective and compared with management approaches used within the traditional IS function and in the organisation generally. Appropriate management approaches can be identified that are suitable for certain types of organisations and Web site strategies. Another aspect is how seriously the issue is taken within the organisation and the level of awareness of senior people.

It has been recognised that there are advantages and disadvantages associated with bureaucracies (Vecchio, Hearn, Southey, 1996). Table 1 lists the pluses and minuses of a bureaucracy for a Web site management strategy.

The issues just raised can be seen as being part of an information management strategy within the organisation and go beyond the usually narrowly defined Web site administration position found within large organisations (Fournier, 1998). Web site administrators can be responsible for analysing design issues, documentation and security issues and in some cases may advise on appropriate content. Their scope and authority may be limited though in some organisations. However, they still need to be advised on the suitability of adding certain functionality and content to the site.

Table 1: The Pluses and Minuses of a Bureaucratic Approach to Web Site Management			
Pluses of bureaucracy	**Pluses in relation to Web site management strategy**	**Minuses of bureaucracy**	**Minuses in relation to Web site management strategy**
Control	The management of the Web site is clearly visible and the Web site can be aligned to organisational goals.	Barriers to change	The decision making process (committees) becomes so protracted the Web site is not kept up to date and does not evolve.
Order	The Web site is easier to manage and use because it is clearly structured.	Reduced employee satisfaction	Staff do not feel 'owners' of the site and content - become alienated from participating.
Efficiency	It leads to an effective use of organisational resources and personnel.	Reduced discretion	Risks (experiments) are not taken and the potential rewards not realised.
Stability	The Web site can be used to support organisational goals and support the status quo.	Red tape	The rules, procedures and approval mechanisms are so involved it acts as a disincentive to staff to update and develop the Web site.
Rule by reason	That rational argument within the organisation determines the strategy, functionality, content and design of the Web site.	Power seeking	The staff responsible for the Web management strategy see themselves as owners of the site and do not encourage participation in its development and evolution.

CASE STUDY OF A LARGE UNIVERSITY

This short case study of a large university is used to illustrate the relevance of the issues and concepts raised so far in the paper. University web sites, unlike commercial organisations' web sites, fall into a category of their own. This is clear from the following statement taken from the University strategic plan:

... the University will plan for faculty, staff, students, alumni and the public to be able to transact all necessary business, exchange and obtain information, and work collaboratively from their offices, classrooms, and residences, through a dependable, responsive integrated voice-video-data network which transcends the limits of time and distance and supports worldwide ...

The University has a decentralised system of web site management and administration. Various faculties, schools and the administrative divisions of the University create, revise and update their web pages and upload them into the different servers. The organic unity of the site is overseen by the webmaster (not part of the IT division) in consultation with senior officials of the University, although this is done via a loosely coordinated approach. In reality they have little involvement with the distributed Web site activities. Thus at present, the classical elements of bureaucracy do not seem to prevail in the design and management of the web site. There is significant flexibility and freedom for individuals within the organisation to develop and add web pages to the site. This along with the training opportunities in web design tools made available to academic and non-academic staff members contribute to the process of site building. There is little central regulation and evaluation of individual, School and Faculty web pages at present.

Internet, Intranet and Extranet technologies are undergoing tremendous changes and acquiring increasing capabilities. This partly explains, along with the rapid evolution of the site, the less regulated approach being used. The University is in the process of organising three different functional groups: a web management group, a web content group, and a web systems group. This is intended to create an effective web site management strategy.

The current Web site management approach is far from being bureaucratic. The main evidence to substantiate this statement are as follows:
- There are few rules and procedures in place.
- There is no deep hierarchy of control and authority.
- There is little division of labour. Any one can develop and a web page to the site.
- The informal approach is in contrast to the bureaucratic mechanisms that are in place for many of the other processes within the organisation.

Although the University is intending to increasingly regulate the Web site content and design the management and development is currently organic in nature. To some extent it is "organic by accident". However, the less regulated approach has many benefits for staff and the University. It allows staff to take responsibility for changes and hence these can be carried out with minimum time delay. It also encourages staff to take on the ownership of the Web site and make it an effective part of the information infrastructure of the organisation.

DISCUSSION AND CONCLUSIONS

A quick look at web development processes in organisations would reveal that there is need for effective management. Web sites continually evolve and require a high level of integration, coordination and synergy between different groups. Some organisations may be in the process of developing proper organisational norms, rules and structure to manage web sites, as in the case study. Unlike the traditional IS management, the diversity of the users and the complexity of catering to different types of users, demand new management strategies. It is challenging to design web sites which are functional, user-friendly and creative at the same time.

Although we have used Weber's ideas on bureaucracy to guide the examination of Web site management and administration, it is clearly a simplified framework for such a task. Alternative organisational forms to the bureaucratic have been suggested as being more important for the business environment of the nineties (Robbins, Millet, Cacioppe, Water-Marsh, 1998). These include the organic structure, which has a flatter decision making structure and a less formal and deep hierarchy of control and authority. This type of organisational form has been put forward as one that can cope with rapid change and one that works well with motivated employees.

A number of organisational forms have been identified and these are listed in table 2 (based on Robbins et al, 1998). The simple structure is one where one person, such as a small business owner, has most or all of the authority for decision making. This style of management could be adopted for Web site management where one person (Webmaster) acts as the gatekeeper and has all the authority to make decisions.

The matrix form is based upon dual lines of authority where there are functional (departmental) hierarchies and hierarchies for the product which typically involve cross functional collaboration. This form of structure could be used in Web site management. Departments could have responsibility for there own site but also contribute to courses which might be a centralised responsibility.

The team based approach to management works within a bureaucratic framework. Responsibility is given to the teams which

Table 2: Web site management strategies	
Structural Form	**Structural Characteristics**
Simple	low degree of departmentalisation wide spans of control authority centralised in a single person little formalisation
Matrix	dual lines of authority combines functional and product departmentalisation
Team - network	the use of teams as a central device to coordinate work activities decentralised decision making to the team level cross-functional works within a bureaucratic framework
Organic	low horizontal differentiation adaptable duties low formalisation informal communication decentralised decision authority
Bureaucracy	Rigid hierarchical relationships Fixed duties High formalisation Formalised communication channels Centralised decision authority

operate in a cross functional manner. This style of management would appear to have merit for Web site management as the Web site can be viewed as an organisational resource rather than a number of discrete departmental entities.

Proposing a Web site management framework to help organisations decide on a suitable approach is clearly a complex task. However, a number of key factors are suggested for consideration in the development of such a framework. These are listed below.

Level of Risk

The Web site management approach needs to consider the levels of risk associated with possible breaches of data and information security. For example, information available to customers on the Internet would have higher levels of risk associated with it compared to data on an Intranet. However, levels of privacy and accuracy still have to be considered in relation to data on an Intranet. The more severe the consequences of a breach of security the more effort that is required in the development and monitoring of policies and procedures.

Organisational Form

The organisational structure needs to be considered when developing a Web site management strategy. One would expect that the two approaches would be the same or at least similar. If an organisational had an organic structure then the adopting a bureaucratic style of Web site management would be going against the culture of the organisation and possibly create a conflict in styles.

Levels of Change

In an environment where the data and information are changing rapidly then an overly bureaucratic approach would possibly create a barrier to change.

Levels of Creativity

If the Internet or Intranet is to be used in creative ways then again an overly bureaucratic management approach may act as a barrier to innovation.

Further research into the area will explore the relationships between the organisational structure, the goals of the Web strategy, the risk/freedom dichotomy, and Web site management strategies. It is hoped that this will lead to models of Web site management that will be useful to organisations coming to terms with this relatively recent addition to their information infrastructure.

REFERENCES

Fournier, R. (1998). *A Methodology for Client/Server and Web Application Development.* Yourdon Press.

Gordon, S. R. & Gordon, J. R. (1996). *Information Systems: A Management Approach.* Dryden.

Hawryszkiewycz, I. (1998). *An Introduction to Systems Analysis and Design.* Prentice Hall.

Lawrence, E., Corbit, B., Tidwell, A., Fisher, J., & Lawrence, J. R. (1998). *Internet Commerce: Digital Models for Business.* Wiley.

Robbins, S. P., Millet, B., Cacioppe, R. & Water-Marsh, T. (1998). *Organisational Behaviour.* Prentice Hall.

Rockwell, B. (1998). *Using the Web to compete in a global marketplace.* Wiley.

Standing, C. (1998). Myths and the art of deception in information systems. *Proceedings of the European Conference on Information Systems*, Aix-en-provence, France.

McKeown, P, G. & Watson, R. (1997*). Metamorphosis: A guide to the World Wide Web and electronic commerce.* Wiley.

Vecchio, P., Hearn, G., Southey, G. (1996). *Organisational Behaviour.* Harcourt Brace.

Weber, M. (1947). *The Theory of Social and Economic Organisations.* Translated by Henderson & Parson. New York, NY: Free Press.

Whitten, J. L., Bentley, L. D., & Barlow, V, M. (1994). *Systems Analysis and Design Methods.* Irwin.

Key Issues in Management of Information Systems in the Australian Environment.

Syed Arshad Usman / Andrew Robert Stein
Department of Information Systems, Faculty of Business, Victoria University Of Technology, PO Box 14428,
MCMC, Melbourne, Australia, 8001
Tel: 61-396884332 Fax: 61-396885024, Andrew.Stein@vut.edu.au

ABSTRACT

This research is an exploratory study of key Information Systems (IS) issues in the management of information systems in the Australian business environment. IS managers must be able to interpret trends in information technology, assess their impact on the organisation and decide which technologies to adopt. This process is becoming even more crucial as communications and information technologies are merging. Deciding on the proportion of resources allocated to business, technical, human resources, systems development or managerial problems is an important facet of the IS manager's job. This study sampled 79 organisations from the states of Victoria, New South Wales and Queensland in Australia. The key IS issues that made up the research instrument were compiled by analysing and conglomerating previous key issues surveys.

Three research questions formed the basis of this study. The first research question was to identify key IS issues in the management of information systems in the Australian business environment. Main findings for this question showed that two business issues, IS Strategic Planning and IS for Competition ranked top. The second research question compared the key IS issues identified in this study with previous Australian and international studies. The main finding in the Australian comparison showed that most issues stayed the same or increased in importance with previous surveys. The third research question identified four new trends highlighted by the IS respondents: managing Information Technology (IT) cost, the year 2000 problem, aligning IT to business now and in the future, and IS customer service considerations.

INTRODUCTION

Information is one of the assets that an organisation possesses. Information must be well managed like other assets and resources if the organisation is to be effective. Information, if badly managed, can lead to operational and managerial ineffectiveness and even to complete failure (Avision et al 1996). Few professions have seen as rapid a change over the past several decades as the field of information systems and services. Information systems today not only provide the backbone of information processing for organisations, they are also fundamentally changing the way organisations operate (Hammer et al 1990).

Changes in information technologies and changing patterns of use create different demands on the jobs of IS professionals and new expectations in the roles of IS professionals within organisations (Liebenau et al 1990). It is important for IS professionals to be aware of the key issues of information systems management so that they can serve the business community effectively.

This research is primarily a replication study to ascertain the current issues and trends in the information systems environment in Australia. A number of studies exploring the key issues in the management of information systems have been performed by other researchers: United Kingdom-Galliers, Merali & Spearing (1993); European-CSC (1993); United States-Niederman, Brancheau & Wetherbe (1991); United States-Lee, Trauth & Farwell (1995); Canada-Pollard & Hayne (1996); South Korea-Kim & Kim (1995); Hong Kong-Burn, Saxena & Cheung (1993); United States- Brancheau, Wetherbe, Janz (1994-1995) and in Australia-Pervan (1993, 1996). The major research objective is to ascertain the key issues in the management of information systems in the Australian business environment, and how these issues compare with previous international and Australian studies. A further objective is to ascertain emerging trends in information systems. To achieve the above objectives the following key research questions are proposed:-

RQ1: What are the key issues in information systems management in the Australian business environment?

RQ2: How do these key issues compare with international and previous Australian studies?
RQ3: Are there any emerging information systems issues?

CRITICAL IS ISSUES & KEY IS ISSUES MATRIX

Key IS issues and trends have been studied by previous researchers and can be shown to be divided into categories. Studies from Pervan (1993), Pervan (1997), Galliers et al (1993), CSC (1993), Niederman et al (1991), Lee et al (1995), Pollard et al (1996), Kim et al (1995), Burn et al (1993) and Brancheau et al (1994-95) have been analysed and have yielded a synthesised *"super set"* of key IS issues.

It would be possible to construct an entire research project compiling lists of key issues. It was felt that providing a *"super set"* through conglomeration would be sufficient to form the basis of a survey instrument for this research project. This approach of conglomerating was developed from Pervan (1997).

The Brancheau et al (1994-95) study was used as an initial template for the key IS issues. This study was considered as being recent enough to be relevant, and, expansive enough to be encompassing. Additional studies were analysed and the categories business, technical, human resources and systems development were created. All IS items from the studies were then recorded. The large grouping of IS issues was then formed into a *"super set"* of key IS issues. Several of the *"super set"* issues were synthesised by collapsing and conglomerating the issues from previous surveys(See Table 1). The synthesised group of issues includes; Business Process Redesign, also described as *"Implement new or changed computer-supported business processes"*. Improving Data Integrity and Quality Assurances described by many researchers as *"Effective use of the data resources"*. Integrating Data Processing, Office Automation, Factory Automation, and Telecommunications, also described as *"Integrate data types"*, *"Enabling electronic data Interchange and multi-vendor integration"*, *"Developing and managing EDI Interchange"* and also as *"Planning and integrating Multi-Vendor Open systems technology"*. Integrate Networks was described as *"Telecommunication technology"* and also as *"Planning and communication networks"*. The issue Improving Security and Control was also described as *"Information access and security"*. Train and Educate IS Professionals/ End users included *"Education of senior management"*, *"Train and educate end users"* and *"Facilitating organisational learning"*. Manage/Plan Systems Development/Implementation was variously described as *"Planning and using CASE technology"*, *"Implementing software process capability improvement"*, *"Systems reliability and availability"* and *"Improving systems development process"*. Improving Quality of Software Development was also described as *"Implementation systems evaluation process"*. It is important to note that several key issues cross over into multiple categories, for example, *"Education of senior management"* and *"Facilitating Organisational Learning"* could be both a human resources and a business category.

Table 1: Proposed Key Issues and Indicative References		
Proposed Key Issues	**Type**	**References**
Improving IS strategic planning.	B	Available on request
Using information system for competitive advantage.	B	
Facilitating/ managing executive and decision support system.	B	
Manage/plan systems development/ Implementation.	S	
Business process redesign.	B	
Planning for disaster recovery.	T	
Support end-user computing.	B	
Building a responsive IT infrastructure.	T	
Improving security and control.	T	
Integrating data processing, office automation, factory automation, and telecommunication.	T	
Specifying, recruiting, and developing human resources for IS.	H	
Improving quality of software development.	S	
Train and educate IS professionals/end users.	H	
Integrate networks.	T	
Improving data integrity and quality assurance.	T	

B:- *IS Business issues.* T:- *IS Technical issues.* S:- *IS System Development issues.* H:- *IS HR issues.*

THE SURVEY

The Organisation: The first section of the survey established industry sector and size. This was completed by the IS professionals and consisted of five short questions with multiple choice options (Zikmund, 1991).

Key IS management issues: The second section of the survey consisted of the 15 key information systems management issues in the Australian environment. Each issue was briefly described to help respondents gain a greater insight into the key issues. The question yielded a potential score from a minimum of one to a maximum of nine using Likert scales.

Sample

The sample for the main survey was selected from an Australian wide database of organisations. The database consisted of over 600 organisations with industry sector, size and state the being main groupings. Respondents were sampled from the states of Victoria, New South Wales, Queensland and selected organisations with number of employees greater than 500. The final sample consisted of 450 potential respondents. A total of 76 organisation returned a completed questionnaire for a response rate of 16.8%.

Demographics

Table 2 represents each respondent's industry grouping. Table 3 represents the size of the work force of the respondent's organisation

Table 4 shows the size of information systems department in the respondent's organisation.

Table 5 represents each respondent's position within the organisation and Table 6 represents each respondent's position within the IS department.

Data Assumption Testing

Before applying statistical procedures, data abnormalities and statistical assumptions were tested. Missing data and outliers were analysed. The sample size of 76 was not great enough to assume normality therefore frequency histogram and normal probability plots were both performed. Both graphical tests were inconclusive as to whether normality could be assumed. Skewness and kurtosis were analysed to determine normality as well as K-S Lillefors statistic (Coakes et al 1996). Normality was not assumed and therefore non-parametric statistics were employed.

The full 9 point Likert scale of the key IS issues was aggregated into 5 point likert scales. The Likert items 1 & 2 were combined to yield Strongly Disagree. Similarly items 3 & 4, 6 & 7 and 8 & 9 yielded Disagree, Agree and Strongly Agree respectively. Likert item 5 yielded Neither Agree nor Disagree.

RESULTS

Issues and Ratings

The results in Table 7 show the percentage (%) response for the key IS issues. Analysing the results from Table 7 yielded three possible broad groups of responses. These groups have been termed: unanimous agreement (ua), probable agreement (pa) and ambivalent (am). This type of grouping was also performed by Pervan (1996) his groupings included critical issues, important issues and problematic issues. Table 8 shows the issues rated by mean and standard deviation.

Table 2: Industry Groups after re-categorising others (N= 76)

Industry Group	No. of Respondents (N = 76)	Respondents (%)
Mining or Petroleum	15	20
Insurance or Financial Services	8	11
Banking or Lending	1	1
Services including Transport	14	18
Retail or Distribution	6	8
Manufacturing Industry	31	41
Public Sector	1	1
Education and Training	0	0
Total	76	100

Table 3: Size of Work Force (N= 76)

Work Force	No. of Respondents (N = 76)	Respondents (%)
Less than 100	1	1
Between 100 and 500	8	11
Greater than 500	67	88
Total	76	100

Table 4: Size of Information Systems Department (N = 76)

IS Staff Size	No. of Respondents (N = 76)	Respondents (%)
Less than 10	27	36
Between 10 and 50	27	36
Greater than 50	22	28
Total	76	100

Table 9 represents the key IS issues according to their rating with issue category and grouping also portrayed. Rating is presented according to the mean (m) in descending order. Ranking the IS issues and categorising the issues into unanimous agreement, probable agreement and ambivalent will allow us to compare our results with previous surveys as well as exploring why some issues are considered important by everyone yet other issues are not so important.

IS Issues by Industry Grouping

Table 10 shows crosstabulations between key IS issues and the industry group. The industry groups are made up of mining or petroleum (response rate - 20%), services including transport (14%), manufacturing industry (41%). These three industry groups were used because they made up the majority of the respondents within the survey. The issues in Table 10 are represented according to the rating in Table 9. Upon analysing the mean values two issues, BPR and Software Development may yield significant differences. The issue of BPR is of more importance to manufacturing industry (m =6.714, s =1.822) as compared to mining or petroleum industry (m =5.733, s =1.830). Software Development is of more importance to the manufacturing industry (m =6.129, s =2.183) and services including transport industry (m =6.214, s =1.311) than to mining or petroleum industry (m =4.266, s =1.940). Further analysis by kruskal-wallis one-way ANOVA shows that there is a clear difference between mining or petroleum and the other two groups in Software Development (p=.0358) and no difference for BPR.

Table 5: Level of Positions in Organisation (N= 76)

Positions	No. of Respondents (N = 76)	Respondents (%)
One Level below CEO	15	19
Two Levels below CEO	45	59
Three Levels below CEO	8	11
Four or more Levels below CEO	8	11
Total	76	100

Table 6: Information Systems Level (N=76)

Information systems level	No. of Respondents (N = 76)	Respondents (%)
Head of IS Section	60	79
One level below IS head	12	16
Two or more levels below IS head	3	4
Others	1	1
Total	76	100

Table 7: IS Issues by five point rating

Key IS management Issues.	Strongly Disagree (%) Likert 1&2	Disagree (%) Likert 3&4	Neither Agree nor Disagree (%) Likert 5	Agree (%) Likert 6&7	Strongly Agree (%) Likert 8&9	Gps
IS strategic planning	0	0	3	28	69	ua
IS for competition	0	1	6	44	49	ua
Systems development	0	9	11	38	42	pa
ESS and DSS	0	13	22	45	20	pa
BPR	1	10	19	42	28	pa
Disaster recovery	1	9	18	43	29	pa
End-user computing	1	12	8	51	28	pa
IT infrastructure	1	7	4	37	51	ua
Security and control	1	11	9	51	28	pa
Integrated systems	1	23	19	33	24	am
Human resources IS	7	19	10	43	21	am
Software Development	10	12	13	44	21	am
Education of IS staff	5	11	12	49	23	pa
Networking	3	9	8	37	43	pa
Quality assurance	1	7	12	45	35	pa

Table 11 presents the rating of the key IS issues according to industry grouping. The column rating gives the overall rating of the issues and each industry grouping can be compared by looking at their rating.

DISCUSSION
Key Australian IS issues
The purpose of the first research question was to ascertain the key IS issues in the Australian business environment and rank them from most important too least important.

RQ1: What are the key issues in information systems management in the Australian Business environment.

The key IS issues (Table 12) in the study are a mixture of business, technological, systems development and human resources issues. This clearly indicates the need for a balance between business, technical, systems development and human resources knowledge among IS professionals.

Among the respondents it is clear that the business issues (IS Strategic Planning, IS for Competition) are of more importance than other issues. This can be explained by the competitive nature of the business world and with IS professionals seeing information systems giving their organisation a business edge over their competitors. On the other hand human resources issues (Human Resources for IS, Education of IS Staff) are in the bottom group of issues. The reason for this may relate to the growing trends of outsourcing and contracting of IS personal. These practices obviate the need for organisations to develop human resource processes and policies for IS staff. An example would be the low priority given to training in new packages for IS staff. When a new package is adopted an organisation may outsource or contract new personnel to utilise the package. This need to outsource for IS skills is outlined by Baker (1997). This area is worthy of further study as there is an inherent contradiction in the rating of these issues. Information systems are developed and implemented by IS staff yet the respondents seem to place a low level of importance in enhancing the skills of these IS personnel. The impact of outsourcing upon busi-

Table 8: IS Issues by Mean and Standard deviation

Key IS management Issues.	Mean (μ)	SD (σ)
IS strategic planning	7.895	1.102
IS for competition	7.316	1.122
Systems development	6.750	1.576
ESS and DSS	6.184	1.529
BPR	6.421	1.619
Disaster recovery	6.513	1.763
End-user computing	6.316	1.683
IT infrastructure	7.171	1.509
Security and control	6.539	1.587
Integrated systems	5.882	1.932
Human resources for IS	5.803	1.973
Software Development	5.868	2.022
Education of IS staff	6.171	1.792
Networking	6.816	1.764
Quality assurance	6.737	1.535

Table 9: Rating of IS Issues (N = 76)

Key IS management Issues.	Issue Category	Mean (μ)	SD (σ)	Rating	Groupings
IS strategic planning	B	7.895	1.102	1	ua
IS for competition	B	7.316	1.122	2	ua
IT infrastructure	T	7.171	1.509	3	ua
Networking	T	6.816	1.764	4	pa
Systems development	S	6.750	1.576	5	pa
Quality assurance	T	6.737	1.535	6	pa
Security and control	T	6.539	1.587	7	pa
Disaster recovery	T	6.513	1.763	8	pa
BPR	B	6.421	1.619	9	pa
End-user computing	B	6.316	1.683	10	pa
ESS and DSS	B	6.184	1.529	11	pa
Education of IS staff	H	6.171	1.792	12	pa
Integrated systems	T	5.882	1.932	13	am
Software Development	S	5.868	2.022	14	am
Human resources for IS	H	5.803	1.973	15	am
ua: Unanimous agreement		pa: Probable agreement		am: Ambivalent	

Table 10: IS Issues by Industry Group (N=76)

Key IS Manage't issues. (Rated in order)	Mining or Petroleum		Services including Transport		Manufacturing Industry	
	Mean (μ)	SD (σ)	Mean (μ)	SD (σ)	Mean (μ)	SD (σ)
IS strategic planning	7.800	1.140	7.714	1.200	8.064	1.03
IS for competition	7.066	1.120	7.642	.8411	7.419	.992
IT infrastructure	6.600	1.760	7.500	1.163	7.322	1.62
Networking	6.400	1.720	6.928	1.974	6.741	1.91
Systems development	5.933	2.010	6.785	1.211	6.967	1.44
Quality assurance	6.866	1.680	6.785	1.711	6.645	1.40
Security and control	6.733	1.660	7.000	1.466	6.580	1.54
Disaster recovery	6.733	1.750	6.571	1.745	6.677	1.64
BPR	**5.733**	**1.830**	**6.571**	**1.085**	**6.714**	**1.822**
End-user computing	6.333	1.490	5.857	2.214	6.419	1.68
ESS and DSS	5.600	1.500	6.357	1.498	6.322	1.59
Education of IS staff	5.866	2.030	5.785	1.577	6.322	1.95
Integrated systems	5.600	2.060	5.642	2.177	6.193	1.99
Software Development	**4.266**	**1.940**	**6.214**	**1.311**	**6.129**	**2.183**
Human resources for IS	5.333	2.050	5.428	2.024	5.903	1.98

Table 11: Industry Grouping Rating by Key IS Issues Rating (N=76)

Key IS Issues Rating.	Mining or Petroleum	Services including Transport	Manufacturing Industry
	Rating	Rating	Rating
IS strategic planning	1	1	1
IS for competition	2	2	2
IT infrastructure	6	3	3
Networking	7	5	5
Systems development	9	6	4
Quality assurance	3	7	8
Security and control	4	4	9
Disaster recovery	5	8	7
BPR	11	9	6
End-user computing	8	12	10
ESS and DSS	12	10	11
Education of IS staff	10	13	12
Integrated systems	13	14	13
Software Development	15	11	14
Human resources for IS	14	15	15

ness performance as well as IS staff morale would be subjects worthy of study.

IS issues - Australian Comparison

Research Question Two compared previous Australian and international studies with the results from this survey.

RQ2: How do these key issues compare with international and previous Australian studies.

In Table 13 the issues have been divided into four categories, issues generally staying the same, issues increasing in importance, issues decreasing in importance and those issues where no trends was discernible.

Issues where ratings trended up were classified as increasing in importance. Similarly issues where rating trended down were classified as decreasing in importance. Issues that generally stayed the same in importance included, IS Strategic Planning, IT Infrastructure, Disaster Recovery, End-User Computing, ESS and DSS and Human Resources for IS. Issues that increased in importance to IS professionals included, IS for Competition, Networking, Systems Development, Security and Control, BPR and Integrated Systems. The increase in importance of Networking, Systems Development, Security and Control and Integrated Systems may be understood in terms of the development and improvement in technologies that guide these issues. The basis for this study was the rapid technological development that IS professionals must cope with and these issues are all heavily impacted by the advancement in internet and potential electronic commerce technologies. The issue that decreased in importance to IS professionals was Software Development. One reason for this may be that more and more organisations are using off the shelf software rather than software built from the ground up. Contracting out or outsourcing the software development process may also be a reason why this issue has decreased in importance. Issues that fail to show any trend include Quality Assurance and Education for IS Staff.

IS Issues - International Comparison

It was very difficult to compare Australian issues with previous international studies. The reason for this was the lack of uniformity among the issues selected for the survey in different countries. If a true comparison is to be made between the key IS issues among different countries then perhaps there has to be a uniform set of key IS issues. This might not be possible because of the different state of the IS environment in different countries. Another problem in comparing the international studies relates to the time frame of the surveys. In the IS field technology has a very short life span and IS issues can be born and lapse within the period of several years. The IS study by Niederman et al is from 1991, a period when the Year 2000 problem, the extensive use of the internet, and the potential of electronic commerce were unheralded concepts. Ideally an international study could gather views and would thereby provide a snap shot of IS issues across the globe. Table 14 attempts to summarise the differences in ranking between the key IS issues from eight international surveys and the current Australian one.

Issues that generally stayed the same importance to IS professionals included, IS Strategic Planning, IS for Competition, IT Infrastructure, Systems Development, Security and Control, Education for IS Staff, Integrated Systems. ESS and DSS was the only issue that increased in importance to IS professionals. Issues that decreased in importance to IS professionals included; Quality Assurance, BPR, Software Development, Human Resources for IS. Issues that failed to show any trend in importance included; End-user Computing, Networking, and Disaster Recovery.

Table 12: Grouping of IS Issues (N = 76)

Key IS management Issues.	Issue Category	Rating	Groupings
IS strategic planning	B	1	ua
IS for competition	B	2	ua
IT infrastructure	T	3	ua
Networking	T	4	pa
Systems development	S	5	pa
Quality assurance	T	6	pa
Security and control	T	7	pa
Disaster recovery	T	8	pa
BPR	B	9	pa
End-user computing	B	10	pa
ESS and DSS	B	11	pa
Education of IS staff	H	12	pa
Integrated systems	T	13	am
Software Development	S	14	am
Human resources for IS	H	15	am

Table 13: Key IS issues (1997) by Previous Australian Issues

Key IS management Issues.	Issue Category	Rating 1997	Rating** Pervan (1997)	Rating* Pervan (1993)	Trend
IS strategic planning	B	1	6	1	same
IS for competition	B	2	4	5	increase
IT infrastructure	T	3	1	2	same
Networking	T	4	5	15	increase
Systems development	S	5	31	25	increase
Quality assurance	T	6	19	7	no trend
Security and control	T	7	11	19	increase
Disaster recovery	T	8	8	10	same
BPR	B	9	18	NI	increase
End-user computing	B	10	9	11	same
ESS and DSS	B	11	14	13	same
Education of IS staff	H	12	3	12	no trend
Integrated systems	T	13	20	20	increase
Software Development	S	14	22	8	decrease
Human resources for IS	H	15	17	17	same

* Pervan (1993) Mean Importance.** Pervan (1997) Mean Importance. NI: Indicates not included.

Table 14: Key IS Issues (1997) by International Issues

Key IS management Issues.	Rating AUS (1997)	Rating Canada (1996) Pollard	Rating Korea (1995) Kim	Rating US (1995) Lee	Rating US (1994-95) Brancheau	Rating Hong Kong (1993) Burn	Rating UK (1993) Galliers	Rating Europe (1993) CSC	Rating US (1991) Niederman	Trends
IS strategic planning	1	11	6	14	10	2	1	12	3	same
IS for competition	2	8	4	NI	17	8	7	NI	8	same
IT infrastructure	3	1	1	NI	1	NI	NI	NI	6	same
Networking	4	3	3	15	5	9	NI	NI	10	no trend
Systems development	5	21	NI	3	NI	4	NI	11	16	same
Quality assurance	6	15	NI	NI	7	10	2	17	2	decrease
Security and control	7	NI	NI	13	NI	NI	6	NI	19	same
Disaster recovery	8	NI	NI	NI	NI	NI	NI	NI	20	no trend
BPR	9	9	2	NI	2	NI	3	1	NI	decrease
End-user computing	10	16	8	16	16	6	8	NI	18	no trend
ESS and DSS	11	NI	NI	NI	NI	NI	18	NI	17	increase
Education of IS staff	12	14	13	12	14	NI	8	14	5	same
Integrated systems	13	17	10	21	NI	10	NI	7	12	same
Software Development	14	4	12	19	6	7	4	NI	9	decrease
Human resources for IS	15	12	11	NI	8	1	NI	6	4	decrease

NI: Indicates not included in the survey.

IS Issues - New Trends

Research Question Three explored any emerging trends in IS management issues. This was conducted by asking participants to include any new issues, which they considered important and were not included in the survey. Table 15 contains only those issues that are repeated more than twice by the respondents.

RQ3: Are there any emerging information systems issues?

Table 15: Repeated Respondent Initiated New Key IS Issues

Proposed Key IS Issues	New Issues	No of Mentions
Managing IT cost	New Issue	5
Year 2000 problem	New Issue	3
Aligning IT to business now/future	New Issue	3
Customer service	New Issue	3

Managing IT costs was considered important by five respondents and could be due to the growing number of PCs (Personnel computers) or Network PCs in organisations. Advances in networking in modern organisations and the advent of rapidly changing IT technology have escalated the costs of running IS departments as described in Emma (1996).

The prospect of disabled computer systems and paralysed enterprises make the year 2000 problem one of the most significant and universal challenges ever faced by the IT industry. Solving the problem by rewriting date sensitive software to recognise the new millennium or replacing it will cost an astonishing amount, in excess of billions of dollars (Hayward 1997). This issue should be elevated to key status in the immediate short term future.

The alignment issue was considered important by three respondents and could be due to the rapid advances in IT industry with the business sector needing to align IT so that they can take full commercial advantage and be competitive (McLean et al 1996).

Customer service was mentioned by three respondents. Gone are the days when computers were expensive toys to be used only by selected personnel and the internal IT department was not affected by (Pitt et al 1995) competition and customer service issues. Due to the ease of computer use and drastically reduced computer prices, computer usage has increased enormously. There is now a need for IT departments to understand the need to be "a business within a business" and meet the demand for better customer service (Cearly 1997). Again internal IT departments are facing competition from outsourced IT companies.

When comparing the results from this survey with other Australian and international surveys two limitations arise. Firstly, the time frame of the previous surveys limits their usefulness when comparing results between countries. Secondly, every survey has a floating group of IS issues. Previous research by Brancheu (1994-95) consisted of Delphi studies to ascertain lists of IS issues. There will be a constant evolution of IS issues and future surveys will require a process for ascertaining developing issues.

CONCLUSION

Table 7 showed IS Strategic Planning, IS for Competition and IT Infrastructure are the most critical issues faced by Australian IS professionals. On the other hand Integrated Systems, Software Development and Human Resources for IS are the least important issues. It is possible to develop three groupings of issues, those that all respondents thought important, those that most respondents thought important and those that were somewhat ambivalent. The business issues, IS Strategy and IS for Competition, headed the list of crucial issues. The two human resource issues, Human Resources and Education for IS Staff, were amongst the least important. When comparing issues with previous Australian surveys most issues were either more important or about the same rating. Software Development was the only issue that decreased in importance from previous Australian surveys.

The increasing globalisation of IS and the business market place creates the need for international comparisons of IS issues. Global communications networks could be used to augment such studies. New issues that emerged from this study were: managing IT cost, year 2000 problem, aligning IT to business now and in the future and customer service considerations. There was a discernible difference in the rating of issues by different industry groupings. Further research probing the differences between industry groupings could provide the basis for future surveys.

REFERENCES

Avision, D. E. & Taylor, A. V., 1996, 'Information systems development methodologies: a classification according to problem situations', *Journal of Information Technology,* vol.11(2).
Baker, G., 1997, 'The soldiers have come to stay', *The Age,* November, pp. 11-16
Brancheau, J. C., Wetherbe, J. C. & Janz, D.B., 1996, 'Key Issues in Information Systems Management: 1994-95', *MIS Quarterly*, vol. 20, June, pp. 225-242.
Burn, J., Saxena, K.B.C., Ma, L. & Cheung, H. K., 1993, 'Critical Issues of IS Management in Hong Kong: A Cultural Comparison', *Journal of Global Information Management*, September, pp. 28-37.
Cearly, D., 1997, 'Get Real on Cost of Ownership', CIO Magazine, September, 1997
Coakes, J., & Steed, G., 1996, *SPSS for Windows*, John Wiley & Sons, Brisbane.
CSC Index., 1993, 'Critical Issues of Information Systems Management for 1993', *The Sixth Annual Survey of I/S management Issues,* CSC Index.
Emma, C., 1996, 'Discovering the cost of IT', *MIS*, April, pp.76-81.
Farwell, D., Kuramoto, L., Lee, D.M.S., Trauth, E. & Winslow, C., 1992, 'A new Paradigm for MIS: Implications for IS Professionals', *Information Systems Management.*
Galliers, R. D., Merali, Y. & Spearing, L., 1993, 'Coping with Information Technology? How British Executives Perceive the Key Information Systems Management Issues in the mid-1990s', *Journal of Information Technology*, vol. 9, pp. 223-238.
Galliers, R.D. & Baker, B.S.H., 1994, *Strategic Information Management*, Butterworth-Heinemann Ltd, London.
Hammer, M. & Champy, J., 1993, *Reengineering the Corporation*, Brealey Publishing, London.
Hammer, M., 1990, 'Reengineering work: Don't Automate, Obliterate', *Harvard Business Review*, July-August , pp. 104-112.
Hayward, B., 1997, 'Technology's top 10 trends', *MIS supplement*, October, pp. 7-15.
Keen, P. G. W., 1988, 'Roles and Skills for the IS Organisation', in *Transforming the IS Organisation*, ICIT Press, Washington, DC.
Kim, H. & Kim, J., 1995, 'Information Systems Management Issues for Korea', *Proceedings of the 1995 Korean MIS Conference.*
Lee, D., Trauth, E.M., & Farwell, D., 1995, 'Critical Skills and Knowledge Requirements of IS Professionals: A Joint Academic Industry Investigation', MIS Quarterly, vol.19 (3), September, pp.313-340.
Liebenau, J. & Backpush, J., 1990, *Understanding Information: An Introduction*, Macmillan, Basingstoke.
McLean, E., Turban, E. & Wetherbe, J., 1996, *Information Technology for Management: Improving Quality and Productivity*, John Wiley & Sons Inc, New York.
Niederman, F., Brancheau, J. C. & Wetherbe, J. C., 1991, 'Information Systems Management Issues for the 1990s',

MIS Quarterly, vol. 15, pp. 474-500.

Pervan, G. P., 1993, 'Results from a Study of Key Issues in Australian IS Management', *Proceedings of the 4th Australian Conference on Information Systems*, September, pp. 113-128.

Pervan, G. P., 1996, 'Results from a Study of Key Issues in Australian IS Management', *Proceedings of the 7th Australian Conference on Information Systems*, pp. 509-520.

Pervan, G. P., 1997, 'Information Systems Management- An Australian view of Key Issues', *Australian Journal of Information Systems*, (under review).

Pitt, L. F., Watson, R. T., & Kavan, C. B., 1995, ' Service Quality: A measure of Information Systems Effectiveness', *MIS Quarterly*, vol. 19(2), pp. 173-187.

Pollard, C. & Hayne, S., 1996, 'A Comparative analysis of Information systems Issues Facing Canadian Business', *Hawaii International Conference on System Sciences.*

Port, O., Gross, N., Hof, R. & McWilliam, G., 1994, 'Wonder chips', *Business week.*

Zikmund, G. W., 1991, *Exploring Market Research*, 2nd Ed, The Dryden Press.

Electronic Payment Systems – A Game-theoretic Analysis

Juergen Seitz, Eberhard Stickel, Krzysztof Woda

Dept. of Information Systems, Viadrina University, PO Box 776, 15207 Frankfurt (Oder), Germany

Phone: +49 335 5534 358, Fax: +49 335 5534 357, Email: { jse | stickel | kwoda} @euv-frankfurt-o.de

INTRODUCTION

Extraordinary growth of the Internet and its development as a new field of business transactions require new payment systems. Credit card-, check- or coin-based payment systems generally allow issuance and creation of money in a more or less unrestricted way by banks or non-banks. Money supply may be regulated by central banks (e.g. by means of reserve requirements for deposit accounts).

It should be expected that suitably adapted electronic money will lead to more efficient payment transactions since costs of transferring funds via the internet should be lower than costs of using the conventional banking system. Furthermore, electronic money is "borderless" and may be used by everyone having internet access and an internet-based bank (Tanaka, 1997). Consequences are an enlargement of new business opportunities and an expansion of internet-based electronic commerce.

There are some key elements to successful private electronic payment systems such as security, authenticity, anonymity, divisibility and two-way payment possibility (Seitz; Stickel, 1998). Currently there are over a dozen of proposals for electronic payment systems, which fully or partially fulfill these requirements. The goal of each new payment system is gaining the widest acceptability by consumers, merchants and producers. It is important to clearly note, that users have a choice among multiple electronic money providers.

In this paper we will analyze digital money systems by means of a microeconomic model and the use of game theory. We present all the actors involved, their roles and interactions, as e.g. competition or collaboration among the participants in the model. It is important to note that the payment systems do not only compete but are also able to collaborate. After discussing collaboration incentives we will consider from an economics point of view, what kind of collaboration is beneficial for competing digital money providers. Finally, we will analyze the added value aspect for the actors involved in our model of competing and collaborating firms and present a conclusion.

MICROECONOMIC MODEL OF COMPETING AND COLLABORATING PAYMENT SYSTEMS

Nalebuff & Brandenburger (1996) present a general model of competition with cooperating competitors. Using this model we will analyze electronic payment systems from a game-theoretic point of view.

Actors involved and their roles

We assume, that the providers of the payment systems operate within a simple market or environment with its own unique specifications. These specifications are formed by all the participants via their determined roles. Generally, there are four categories of participants in such models illustrating a given market or business environment: customers, suppliers, competitors and the suppliers of complementary products and/or services. Every participant has various relationships to other participants. Now, we attempt to outline such a model for electronic payment systems. At the beginning we assume, that in the core of our model there is a single firm or product – in our analysis it could be one of the digital money systems such as Ecash developed by DigiCash. The digital money system Ecash is the subject of interaction among the four categories of our model's participants. The role of the participants in the market of Ecash will be explained in Fig.1.

Along the vertical dimension in Fig.1 there are customers and suppliers:

- Customers are recruited from internet- or smart card-users and pay for products and services with digital money, e.g. with Ecash. The demand for Ecash by consumers will depend on how this digital payment system scheme will compare to other payment systems (e.g. in terms of security, anonymity or efficiency, ease and comfort of its usage, willingness of merchants to accept Ecash, BIS 1996).
- Suppliers are system architects, who develop new payment methods, service providers such as the network operators or the vendors of specialized hardware, software, and the system providers being responsible for transaction clearance (typically banks or bank-owned companies). The system architect and at the same time the supplier of

necessary software required to use Ecash is DigiCash founded by D. Chaum. Examples of institutions clearing Ecash transactions are Mark Twain Bank, St. Louis or Deutsche Bank AG, Frankfurt/Main (pilot project; cf. Seitz; Stickel 1998).

The horizontal dimension of the diagram consists of competitors and suppliers of complimentary products and services.

- Competitors of Ecash offering similar products/services to consumers are payment systems representing paper-based money and other electronic payment methods like CyberCoin, CyberCash, SET, Netcash or Mondex.
- Suppliers of complimentary products and/or services to our primary

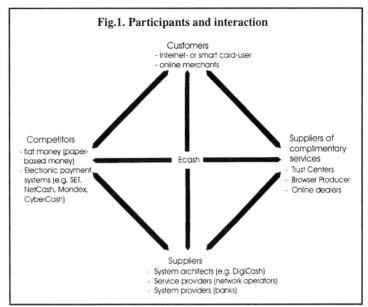

Fig.1. Participants and interaction

product (Ecash) complete the list of participants. Products are complimentary, if a customer having both products benefits more than if he would hold only one of them. Complimentary products or services increase the value of the primary good for the customer. In case of Ecash providers of such products and services are e.g. Trust centers controlling digital signature keys (increased security and authenticity), browser producers such as Netscape or Microsoft embedding in their products special security transfer protocols, online dealers selling information or products like the online bookstore "Laissez Faire Books" (Ecash as a non-national, global currency).

The model's participants may play multiple roles. The internet merchants or information providers are – by accepting Ecash – customers of that payment system, though they may also function as suppliers of complimentary services (e.g. offering round the clock information). For night shopping consumers or global stock investors this might be a complimentary service to the usage of Ecash. Electronic payment systems like CyberCash, NetCash or Ecash might cooperate against e.g. Trust Centers or central banks. The establishment of a single global Trust Center for all electronic payment systems would be certainly more efficient in terms of the technical implementation than the establishment of separate Trust Centers for each payment system. The central banks benefit from outlining regulations and laws jointly for all the electronic payment methods and not separately for each system (we do not consider what kind of regulations there are).

The position taken by the actors involved in the model may also change during time. Financial institutions like e.g. internet brokers trading stocks, bonds or more generally financial information usually cooperate with digital money providers. If a financial institution starts to issue its own electronic money, it becomes a competitor instead of a cooperating supplier. The other way round the payment provider supplying an online broker with digital money, could extend its services by offering online brokerage himself. He would then be a competitor of the financial institution. In both cases described above the participants stem from different branches.

In the following we will consider possible interactions such as competition and cooperation between Ecash and payment systems.

Competition between payment systems

Electronic payment systems compete with traditional paper-based payment methods and with each other. The competition between electronic money and existing fiat money (paper money, coins) is cost-driven, while the competition between electronic payment systems is based on wide acceptance. The latter leads to fights for market dominance (the winner takes all).

Electronic payment systems versus paper-based payment methods

For paper-based money, generally this is the official currency of a certain country, there is a legal obligation of acceptance. The private-issued digital money systems need to compete for the wide acceptability by consumers and businesses Therefore, they should be more efficient as traditional money in order to attract potential users.

One component of efficiency and consequently one way of comparing such systems is via costs. The aggregate costs of every payment consist of transformation costs (e.g. the fees for conversion from assets to cash and vice versa), transport and storage costs, costs for safety measures, as well as search and time costs needed for the completion of a transaction (Hakenberg, 1996). The charges for withdrawal of paper-based money may be related to the costs of transformation and clearance between electronic money and cash. The search costs for localization of places allowing withdrawal of money are low for fiat money because of a large number of bank offices and money withdrawal machines. For software-based electronic payment systems in the form of "values" stored on the PC, we may assume that search costs are equal to zero, while for smart card users charges for loading funds exist. Nowadays, the main problem of the search costs of electronic money lie in missing acceptance by a large number of merchants and institutions. The willingness of merchants to accept electronic money will depend on fees imposed by the issuer or operators, hardware costs and the reduction in the cost of handling money in comparison to traditional paper-based money. There are three types of costs that may be reduced by using electronic payment systems. The transport and storage costs are very high for fiat money because of its physical characters. Cash, being at high risk of robbery, must be kept in secure vaults and be guarded. The more cash is held or transported, the greater the risk and therefore the greater the investment in security measures of paper-based payment systems (Panurach, 1996). Transport costs for intangible electronic payment systems are generated from charges imposed by local internet access providers. Nowadays, many electronic payment methods are in the phase of construction or implementation. Therefore, safety costs consisting of costs for technical infrastructure and software (cryptography) are relatively high. If it is possible to exploit economies of scale these costs might decrease and eventually be lower than in case of paper money. Then, transport, storage and safety costs for paper-based payment methods might be an important reason to introduce and to accept electronic payment methods.

Competition between Electronic payment systems

Cost differences between commercially usable digital payment systems are much smaller than similar differences between certain digital payment systems and paper-based money. Therefore, the main channel for competition between electronic payment systems is in gaining exclusive rights to the point of sale of a large number of merchants and/or producers (Panurach, 1996). Thus, each system would compete for gaining market dominance which results in the creation of some sort of standard. Which system will be adopted finally depends largely on the details of the transactions and the needs of a payment system's potential users (e.g. micro-payments vs. pico-payments). To sum-

Table 1. Comparison of electronic payment systems						
	Ecash	CyberCash	CyberCoin	NetCash	Millicent	SET
System based on	Coin (token-based)	Credit card	Coin log-file)	Coin	Account	Credit card
Technical implementation	Software	Software	Software	Software	Software	Software (or chip card)
Transaction costs	Low	High	Low; suitable for transaction 0,25-10$	Low	Very low	High
Usability area	Pico-, Micro- Macro- payments	Macro- payments	Pico-, Micro-, payments	Pico-, Micro- payments	Pico-, Micro-, payments	Macro- payments
Security	Public key	Public key, Online verification for merchants	Public key, Online verification for merchants	Hybrid cryptography (public key)	Limited	Public key
Anonymity	Yes (blinding signature)	No	Partial	Partial	No	Partial (dual signature)
Person-to- Person- portability	Yes (currently with partici- pation of bank server)	No	No	Yes (with participation of bank server)	No	No
Extension possibility of the system	Difficult because of recording of every Ecash-	At the moment limited to one gateway server	At the moment limited to one gateway server	High through decentralised currency servers	High	High, worldwide

marize, key elements of a successful digital cash system can be seen in the degree of quality of new payment methods as security and anonymity. In Table 1 below we present a comparison of some electronic payment systems in terms of such quality factors.

The role of central banks in the model

Central banks play an important role in our. Depending on the position taken by these institutions they may be classified as to belonging to the class of suppliers of complimentary products and services (for example electronic money might be protected by a central bank's deposit insurance) or to competitors which are interested in limiting the issuance of electronic cash for financial institutions.

From the viewpoint of monetary policy electronic payment systems present a great challenge for central banks. In the central bank's balance sheet there are non-interest-bearing liabilities (issuance of banknotes and coins) and interest-bearing assets such as foreign reserve assets or claims. The resulting interest rate margin is a major source of income for the central bank. Now, we assume, that electronic payment systems (assuming that they will not be incorporated in the legal tender of a central bank) would partially replace conventional notes and coins. Results would be the decline in seigniorage revenues and shrinkage in central banks' balance sheets. However, losses would depend on the size of replacement of the real paper-based money by electronic money (BIS 1996). Another negative effect for central banks might be loss of control of the value of money and as a consequence there is danger with respect to stability of domestic financial markets. Therefore, central banks monitoring closely the development of electronic money have outlined several policy options. One would be issuing digital money themselves. The problem is lack of technological infrastructure and know-how. The Group of Ten (G-10) countries recommended to its member central banks that only credit institutions should be allowed to issue digital money (BIS 1996). Another policy option is expansion of reserve requirements to cover electronic money. To summarize, regulatory policy options of central banks may limit competition and innovation of electronic payment systems. Therefore, the primary goal of a central banks policy should be finding a trade-off between the innovative character of new payment systems and its traditional task of safeguarding the value of money.

Collaboration among Competitors

The limiting role of central banks to issuers of electronic money may trigger collaboration of digital money providers. In general, there are some important factors affecting benefits of collaboration among competing firms such as market structure, kind and degree of uncertainty faced by competing firms, their risk preferences, product relationship (substitutes or complements) and distribution of knowledge and ability. In our case it is plausible to assume oligopolistic competition and risk averse decision makers, as well as heterogenity of payment systems.

Collaboration incentives

An economic analysis of collaboration between competing firms was presented by Stickel (1997). Generally, there are two possible states related to the degree of collaboration. These states are influenced by the distribution of problem specific knowledge:
- Equal distribution of problem specific knowledge and ability – A firm does not risk to lose specific know-how to a competitor. Moreover, its development costs can be decreased via cooperation.
- Unequal distribution of problem specific knowledge – One firm has problem specific knowledge while others have not. There is danger of losing competitive advantages for such a firm.

It was shown by Stickel (1997), that in case of equal distribution of knowledge (and ability) there are incentives to collaborate for both firms. First, uncertainty may be decreased, second costs may be reduced significantly. In case of asymmetric distribution collaboration incentives are smaller for the firm having unique or strategic knowledge. However, even if one of the firms has unique and specific knowledge its competitors do not have, it may be advantageous to share this knowledge with competing firms. Stickel shows, that expected profits of risk averse firm (risk aversion is a rather plausible assumption) transferring its specific knowledge to competitors may decline, but its expected utility increases due to reduction of risk. To summarize, the resulting decrease in uncertainty may be sufficient incentive for digital money providers to collaborate. Using this explanation we now analyze possible forms of collaboration.

Collaboration between electronic payment systems

There are two possible forms of collaboration for competing firms related to equal distribution of problem specific knowledge (ability):
- Information sharing – Competing firms exchange problem specific information. In case of electronic money examples of information sharing could be cooperation among digital money providers in developing compatible secure transfer protocols, homogeneous software or foundation of a single Trust Center for global verification of

electronic money users. In the future, the providers of electronic payment systems may have the possibility to exchange electronic currencies. At the moment, customers buying products and services at various online merchants need to have "money" from different payment providers (nowadays, a merchant usually accepts only money from a single electronic payment system).

• Joint development of information systems - This should not be confused with collusion (or merging). In this case it would be possible to outsource the problem specific knowledge by the competitors to an independent third party. The result might be the wide adoption of an open standard developed by that third party (in fact, by the cooperating digital money providers), in which the client of a system could conduct transactions with any other seller whose intermediary uses the same system. An example for a joint development of information systems (as well as for information sharing) is the establishment of an open standard for electronic payments, based on credit cards, namely Secure Electronic Transaction (SET). In 1995 MasterCard in cooperation with IBM presented this transfer protocol named Secure Electronic Payment Protocol, while at the same time its competitor VISA together with Microsoft worked on another protocol: Secure Transaction Protocol. In early 1996, both sides agreed to develop only one standard to secure network transfer of credit card information. SET was chosen. Both competitors could save on development costs due to collaboration. Another advantage is cost reduction for merchants (in case of two systems, they should have e.g. different terminals to conduct transactions with customers of two credit card organizations)

CONCLUSION

This work discussed electronic payment systems from the perspectives of customers, suppliers and competitors. Using a game-theoretic model of competing firms we concluded that the actors involved in the model may play multiple roles, and that these roles may change over time. In view of added value for all participants we argued, that consumers will benefit if transformation time and search costs of using electronic money are lower than associated costs generated by traditional paper-based money. Merchants, producers and service providers may benefit through possibly higher sales and reduction of branch offices. The system intermediaries, financial institutions and other suppliers of complimentary services such as Trust Centers will achieve revenues consisting of royalties and other fees.

We analyzed the possible interactions such as competition and cooperation between payment systems. In case of competition between electronic payment systems and paper-based payment methods cost differences are an important factor. Especially, high transport, storage and safety costs for paper-based payment methods may contribute to further development of electronic payment methods. The main competition between electronic payment systems is in gaining wide acceptance by merchants and producers. The key success factor is system quality. Quality is influenced by factors such as security and anonymity. The introduction of electronic payment systems will also depend on the position taken by central banks. Their strict regulatory policy might limit the competition and innovation of new payment systems. Therefore, central banks should find a trade-off between the innovative character of new payment systems and their traditional tasks as e.g. safeguarding the value of money or ensuring the stability of the domestic financial markets.

Digital money providers compete for wide acceptability to gain market dominance. On the other hand, there are strong incentives for collaboration. Digital money providers could share problem specific knowledge in order to reduce risk. Outsourcing their development efforts to a third party may lead to the development of an open standard. Also, search and development costs for new payment methods and standards could be lowered. Furthermore, the actions of central banks may provide another incentive for collaboration. Collaboration in the context of this paper should not be confused with collusion. It is not argued that collaboration may lead to a decrease in the number of potential digital payment suppliers.

REFERENCES

BIS (Bank for International Settlements) (1996): "Implications for Central banks of the Development of Electronic Money", Basel, October 1996
Hakenberg, T. (1996): "Elektronische Zahlungssysteme im Wettstreit mit dem Bargeld". Sparkasse, No. 6, pp. 271-274 (in German).
Nalebuff, B.; Brandenburger, A. (1996): "Co-opetition". New York.
Panurach, P. (1996): "Money in Electronic Commerce: Digital Cash, Electronic Fund Transfer and Ecash", CACM 39, No. 6, pp. 45-50.
Seitz, J.; Stickel, E. (1998): "Internet Banking – An Overview". Journal of Internet Banking and Commerce 3, No. 1, http://www.arraydev.com/commerce/JIBC/9801-8.htm.
Stickel, E. (1997): "Collaboration Among Competitors – A First Economic Analysis". In: Wildemuth, B. (Ed.): Collaboration Across Boundaries. ASIS (Association of Information Science) Midyear Meeting. Orlando, pp. 106-113.
Tanaka, T. (1997): "Possible Economic Consequences of Digital Cash". First Monday No. 2, http://www.firstmonday.dk/issues/issue2/digital_cash.

A Web Based Intelligent Interface to Geographic Information Systems Using Agent Technology

Dr. Vijayan Sugumaran
Department of Business Administration, Le Moyne College, Syracuse, NY 13214-1399
Tel: (315) 445-4136, Fax: (315) 445-4787, Email: sugumara@maple.lemoyne.edu

INTRODUCTION

Geographic Information System (GIS) technology is increasingly being adopted by businesses for their analytical and visualization capabilities. While GIS has traditionally been used for managing facilities, natural resources etc., there is a growing interest in the use of GIS for decision support in the business environment. The Information Systems (IS) community has conducted extensive research in Decision Support technologies, however, very little has been done in the use of GIS for decision support and process/workflow management. Much of the GIS research has been performed by researchers in geography, urban systems planning, and engineering disciplines. One plausible explanation for the lack of involvement in the GIS technology by the IS community may be that GIS technology is very specialized and does not have a broad range of applicability. Moreover, these systems are difficult to use and have a very steep learning curve. With open system architecture and other enabling technologies such as Intelligent Agents, and new communication paradigms, GIS systems could be made user friendly and used effectively for decision support and process management.

There are many instances where GIS users do not perform complex operations using a GIS application, and also don't have to write to GIS databases constantly. They simply want to access certain data elements from the GIS database in order to carry out their day to day tasks. For example, in facility management, operators often print relevant maps in response to "trouble calls" and dispense them to the appropriate crew. In this case, it is sufficient for the operator to have read only access to GIS data; they do not have to run complex GIS application to access the necessary data. More over, there is a greater need for accessing the GIS data from any location using a low-end computer as opposed to executing a complex, resource demanding GIS application on a high-end workstation from a specific location. There is a major push towards providing web access to GIS data; using a simple browser interface users can quickly gain access to GIS data without having to run complex GIS applications. Part of this research focuses on the architecture of an environment that provides a web interface to traditional GIS database servers.

Intelligent agents has been receiving lot of attention lately, and early results indicate that the agent technology has the potential to change the way we think about computing, and systems in general. Researchers are focusing on designing autonomous intelligent agents that can support and augment human agents in their day to day work and decision making. One could envision a computing environment where the human agent can delegate routine/mundane tasks to these intelligent agents so that he/she can focus on more creative tasks.

We are currently witnessing the beginning of the application of intelligent agent technology towards GIS based decision making. Rodrigues et. al. [17, 18] have investigated the use of intelligent agent technology to create "spatial" agents to help in spatial decision making using GIS. This paper also focuses on the use of intelligent agent technology in providing an intelligent interface to GIS systems, and assist users in utilizing the GIS system in their day to day work. It is our view that with the help of intelligent agents, one could use the GIS effectively in their routine tasks. Also, by providing web interface to the GIS, these agents can be distributed and reside on different machines, and users can utilize these agents to access the necessary GIS data in carrying out their tasks.

The remainder of this paper is organized as follows. Following the introduction section, a brief description of the GIS technology and their potential uses is provided and the next section discusses the Web and GIS integration model. Then, a quick review the intelligent agent technology and the current developments in that area is provided, following which the use of intelligent agents in a GIS environment and the proposed agent based GIS environment is described. Next, a prototype that is under development for a large utility company which uses a GIS for their core business processes is described. This prototype implements a suite of intelligent agents to assist the users in planning related activities. Finally, the last section provides the summary.

GEOGRAPHIC INFORMATION SYSTEM

Compared to a typical DBMS which stores mostly textual data with limited processing capability, a GIS is capable of assembling, storing, manipulating, and displaying geographically referenced information, i.e., data identified according to their locations. Geographical information consists of both textual data ("attribute" or "aspatial" data) as well as spatial data (data which includes cartographic coordinates). Thus, a GIS not only provides users with tools for managing and linking attribute and spatial data, but also advanced modeling functions, tools for designing and planning, and imaging capabilities, that eventually support data analysis and decision making.

A GIS typically consists of the following key components: a) data entry, b) data management, c) data manipulation and analysis, and d) data output. The data entry component provides facilities for entering/capturing attribute and spatial data into the GIS database. Normally, data exists on paper maps, electronic maps, aerial photographs, or even satellite images. Data conversion and merging data from different sources is the primary function of this component. Data entry and conversion generally is a time consuming and expensive process, particularly if there are high accuracy requirements. Once the data is captured, the next step is to manage this data, which is the function of the Data Management component. Updates and changes must be made on a regular basis in order to ensure data integrity.

The Data Manipulation and Analysis component provides facilities that are utilized in specific GIS applications for manipulating and analyzing the data stored in the GIS. This component concentrates on what the end user wants from the data. Applications can include standard queries, map generation and production, marketing analysis, reports, data entry forms, work order tracking, trouble call routing, and dispatching etc. The Data Output component is responsible for generating outputs in the form of maps, tables, or text in both hard copy and soft copy. A GIS can produce great visuals if the data is accurate and well maintained.

Usually, GIS systems tend to be monolithic with proprietary display drivers, development tools, object models, database access and user interface tools. All the layers in such a system are tightly coupled and not open to other systems. As the GIS industry moves towards a componentware model, new developments in customization tools for GIS packages are opening the doors for new implementation approaches. The constant increase in the functionality provided by GIS packages is making them become large applications which are difficult to manipulate. The diversity of GIS applications has showed that some kind of interface must exist to provide collaboration between existing GIS tools and other kinds of software.

With the increase in both the number and quality of functionalities provided by existing GIS systems, there is a greater need for finding new and faster ways of executing GIS tasks. GIS users are under constant pressure to perform their tasks in shorter and shorter time frame while the systems are getting more complex and cumbersome to use. The gap between end user capability and the GIS tasks that must be completed keeps widening. Any support that would decrease this burden on the user will be a welcome change. To this end, the use of intelligent agent technology may offer partial solutions to the current state of affairs.

We argue that these intelligent agents would improve the way GISs are used. The use of GIS becomes more difficult as new software releases become available and functionality expands. The large amount of information manipulated is again to be considered. Agent functionality in this area could include the generation of templates for executed tasks, monitoring of these tasks and the constant dynamic re-formulation of the GIS user environment.

WEB INTERFACE TO GIS

The Web has drastically altered the computing landscape, in particular, information dissemination. More and more corporations are providing their valuable information, i.e., catalogs of their products and services, to customers on-demand through the internet. Many companies also share their operating procedures, manuals, human resource information, etc. via their intranets. There is a major push towards providing Web interface to commercial database and GIS software to enhance easy access to data. Several GIS vendors are introducing web based products for gaining read only access to GIS data without running GIS applications for performing simple tasks. In this research, we propose a model for integrating the Web technology and the GIS database, as shown in Figure 1, where the GIS users can use their favorite web browser to interact with the GIS database.

As shown in Figure 1, the GIS-Web integration model is based on client-server architecture, where the client can be a browser running an HTML based application or an intelligent agent assisting users with some task. The server side is a GIS Web Server which provides access to spatial data stored in the GIS Database Server. The GIS Web Server contains scripts and/or methods necessary for data retrieval and other spatial computations. Users can interact with the GIS through simple HTML forms, or delegate tasks to the intelligent agents on their behalf.

Web based applications may reside on an HTTP server connected to the corporate intranet from where any one can execute the application by downloading the appropriate HTML document. The HTTP server is the local intranet server which serves HTML pages, Active X controls, and client applications to the browser. These client applications are "browser-based thin clients" where GIS data can be queried and displayed. Users can interact with the system by

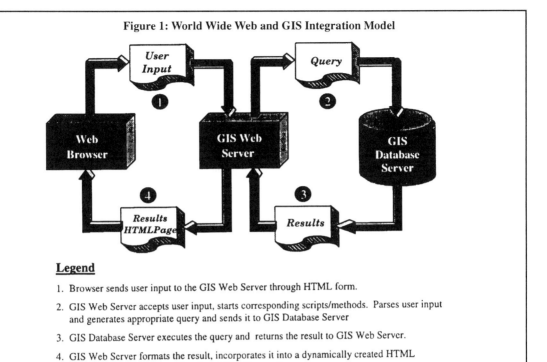

Figure 1: World Wide Web and GIS Integration Model

Legend

1. Browser sends user input to the GIS Web Server through HTML form.

2. GIS Web Server accepts user input, starts corresponding scripts/methods. Parses user input and generates appropriate query and sends it to GIS Database Server

3. GIS Database Server executes the query and returns the result to GIS Web Server.

4. GIS Web Server formats the result, incorporates it into a dynamically created HTML document, and serves it to the client (Web Browser)

specifying input using HTML forms and action buttons. The browser gathers user input and sends it to the GIS Web Server, which parses it. Based on this user interaction, the GIS Web Server executes the corresponding scripts and methods. For example, if the user is interested in obtaining certain GIS data, the Web Server generates the appropriate query and sends it to the GIS database server. The database server executes this query and retrieves the necessary data and sends it back to the Web Server. The GIS Web Server then, formats this query result and incorporates it into an HTML document, which is created on-the-fly. The Web Server then serves this document to the client, and the user can view this information using their browser. The Web Server can also send the information to an agent, if the agent initiated the session on behalf of the user. The Web Server can implement the scripts and methods using cgi-scripting, or Active X controls and Visual Basic.

INTELLIGENT AGENTS

There is considerable amount of research taking place not only in the academia, but also in the commercial sector on intelligent agents. Research on agents emerged initially from Distributed Artificial Intelligence, a branch of Artificial Intelligence that deals with the solution of complex problems by networks of autonomous, cooperating computational processes called agents. Development of intelligent systems is on the rise in recent years [5, 8, 12, 15, 19]. These systems contain agents (intelligent computerized assistants) that are capable of acting autonomously, cooperatively, and collaboratively to achieve a collective goal. Communication covers the exchange of information between cooperating agents. An agent by itself may not have sufficient information or expertise to solve an entire problem; hence mutual sharing of information and expertise is necessary to allow a group of agents to produce a solution to a problem. Collaboration involves joint work by a group of agents on a common task or sub-task. Finally, coordination means the integration and adjustment of the individual group member's work towards the common goal.

Several types of intelligent agents have been proposed and implemented, as evidenced in the agent literature [2, 7, 9, 16]. While there is no consensus on what the architecture of an agent should be, there is agreement on what are some of the properties of agents. Sycara et al. [20] list the following as desirable characteristics of intelligent agents: (a) taskable - take directions from human or other agents, (b) net-centric - distributed and self-organizing, (c) semiautonomous - perform tasks on its own, (d) persistent - doesn't require frequent attention, (e) active - able to initiate problem solving activities, (f) collaborative - delegate tasks to other agents and work cooperatively with other agents, (g) flexible – handle heterogeneity of agents and information sources, and (h) adaptive - accommodate changing user needs and task environments.

Application of agents in the GIS environment is actively being explored and a few projects have been reported in the literature where different types of intelligent agents are being employed to improve the use of GIS systems, as well as help in spatial decision making. In [1], Campos et al. describe an intelligent agent that provides interface to ARC/INFO GIS to help the naive users better interact with the system. This agent receives and processes user's request in plain English. The agent takes the user query and generates sequences of commands that ARC/INFO can understand. If the concepts known to the user are not confirmed by the ARC/INFO database, it interacts with the user to clarify the misconception. Once the GIS commands are executed, the agent presents the results to the user.

Rodrigues and Raper [18] report on developing an intelligent agent based interface for Smallworld GIS that helps users with their drawing and plotting tasks. Smallworld GIS is an object-oriented GIS which has been developed using an OO language called Magik. They have developed two types of agents using Magik. The controller agent monitors the GIS, and the task agent helps the user learn how to use a specific tool within the GIS.

Use of agent technology in addressing spatial decision making problems are on the rise. Ferrand [3] reports on a system that is used to solve complex spatial optimization problem encountered in the search for least environmental impact area. Papadias and Egenhofer [14] report on using agents in Qualitative Collaborative Planning. Agents represent topological, direction and distance constraints that are applied to a spatial planning problem. The focus of this work is on using spatial access methods that can effectively process qualitative constraints represented by agents. In [17], Rodrigues et al. describe a multi-agent based system called MA-MEGGOT, used for modeling geographic elements for environmental analysis in land use management. The system is aimed at establishing methodologies for evaluation and standard simulation in environmental quality description scenarios.

From the above mentioned research projects it is evident that there is a great deal of interest in applying agent technology to GIS environment. We are seeing only the beginning of this cross fertilization between Intelligent Agent technology and GIS technology, and lot more research is yet to be conducted. The agent technology seems to be a natural fit for making GISs user friendly and applicable in a variety of problem solving/decision making scenarios, other than their limited use in facilities management.

The following section describes the proposed agent based environment to make GIS user friendly, and assist the user in executing their day to day functions and business processes.

AGENT BASED GIS ENVIRONMENT

Several GIS prototype implementations have used one or more of the following types of agents: a) cognitive agents - agents that use explicit symbolic representations of their environment and of other agents in problem solving [13, 22, 4], b) reactive agents - agents that don't include a central symbolic model and do not use complex symbolic reasoning [21], c) interface agents - agents that assist users in dealing with one or more computer applications [11], and d) spatial agents - agents that can reason over representations of space and make spatial concepts computable [17, 18].

While each of the above mentioned type of agents were successfully used in projects related to natural resource management [17], modeling people-environment interactions in forest recreation [6], or modeling prehistoric settlement in northern America [10], these agents were designed specifically for that project and hence have a very narrow focus. Moreover, these agents were not distributed and hence did not have well defined inter agent communication, collaboration and coordination. In our work, we propose a more comprehensive agent based GIS environment where several types of intelligent agents coexist in a distributed environment, and these agents collaborate with one another in solving a particular problem. A schematic representation of the overall architecture of the environment is shown in Figure 2.

We define the following generic agents for a GIS environment: a) User Interface Agent, b) Monitoring Agent, c) Business Process Agent, and d) Application Program Interface (API) Agent. While we currently envision an agent based GIS environment to contain the above mentioned agent types, it should be noted that the architecture of the environment is "open" so that additional agent types can easily be integrated into the system. These agents are designed in such a way that they all use the same communication paradigm to interact with one another. The following paragraphs briefly describe each of the agent types.

User Interface Agent

User interface agents keep track of user actions and acquire knowledge on tasks, habits and preferences of users. These agents can start and execute tasks on behalf of the user or suggest actions for them to take. They provide the interface to the GIS and help with his/her daily work. They constantly learn the user preferences and profile and build a knowledge base of the way in which he/she works. These agents can also modify the user environment according to his/her preferred tools, or the commands that are executed the most. The user environment will constantly and dynamically evolve over time.

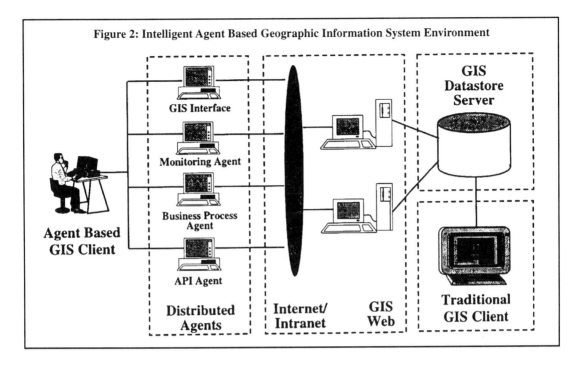

Figure 2: Intelligent Agent Based Geographic Information System Environment

Monitoring Agent

Monitoring agents are similar to control agents that monitor every event that occurs in the GIS and channels the relevant information to other appropriate agents. They keep track of the tasks/processes that are being executed within the GIS system. It keeps track of the "state" of objects within the GIS environment. When a specific event or user action causes the state of an object to change, the affected parties are notified. For example, all GIS objects are version managed and users "checkout" a particular object (i.e., make a copy of it) and work with it. After the changes have been made, the user has to "ckeckin" the object back. If another user is also working with a different version of the same object, conflicts may arise and the monitoring agent informs the user about possible conflicts and how to resolve them. The user can request the monitoring agent to enable or disable certain functions depending upon the task at hand.

Business Process Agent

Business process agents help the end users with the execution of typical business processes that the user is responsible for. They automate a specific function of the GIS and help the user learn how to execute a certain business process. These agents posses control and procedural knowledge needed to execute various processes, and carry the execution of a function through to the end. The business process agents are tightly coupled with the monitoring agents. They receive event information from the monitoring agents and use that information to suggest and perform further actions. Typical GIS business functions may include planning activities, adding new data to the GIS, trouble shooting and managing specific facilities, etc.

Application Program Interface (API) Agents

API agents provide interface to other software systems that may be needed in problem solving. They serve as interfaces between the GIS and external software packages like statistical packages, generalization algorithms, spatial models, etc. They also provide for an input interface for external commands, and are responsible for communicating with the external package, and finally integrating the results into the GIS data model. The interface agent can be as simple as a process object that sends some input to an application, or as complex as an application transparently integrated into the GIS.

PROTOTYPE IMPLEMENTATION

As a proof of concept, we are in the early stages of implementing a prototype agent-based GIS environment; the intelligent agents are being developed using Java and are integrated into the GIS. We are working with a large utility company that uses the Smallworld GIS system for managing their electrical and natural gas lines and related facilities. One of their core business process is to provide electric and gas connections to new customers. This involves a lot of planning work, and planners are typically not well versed with information technology, and in particular the GIS environment. Hence, we are developing an agent based interface to the GIS system to assist them in their daily planning activities.

When a customer puts in a request for new service, a work order is created and it goes through various phases such as planning, design, construction, completion etc. within the system. Each work order has a work order number, and several people access this work order before it is completed. A work order is assigned to a planner who is responsible for generating a design sketch, which shows how the service connection will be provided. For example, if the customer requests for a new electrical connection, the planner uses the GIS to sketch out how electrical wires are to be laid and its impact on existing infrastructure. Then a construction sketch is generated using which the construction crew installs the necessary cables and poles to establish the connection. Then the work order is completed and the GIS records are updated.

The agent based interface that we are developing would facilitate the planners and the designers to work with the GIS more effectively and the agents would guide them in their activities. For example, once a particular work order is assigned to a planner, with the help of the user interface agent, the planner can start the process of creating the work order sketch. The agent would bring up the appropriate location on the map and display the existing electrical objects. Then, the business process agent, which contains information about how to generate the work order sketch will guide the planner in putting together a plan that would adhere to all the business rules and constraints. The monitoring agent will be active in the background and alert the planner if any event that occurs within the GIS may have an impact on the current design.

Though several agent development languages are currently available such as Knowledge Query and Manipulation Language (KQML), Knowledge Interchange Format (KIF), Tool Control Language (TCL), Telescript, Java, Lisp, Smalltalk, C Language Integrated Production System (CLIPS) etc., we have chosen to use Java for implementing the agents because of its platform independence and interoperability. The GIS is in a networked environment (corporate intranet), and the agents are distributed on this network; hence they can reside on any machine connected to this network. Though we are in the preliminary stages of our implementation, early results are very promising.

SUMMARY

Geographic information systems have traditionally been difficult to use because of the complex nature of spatial and temporal data representation, presentation, and computation. However, with the advances in the intelligent agent technology, monolithic GIS systems can be made user friendly by providing intelligent interfaces. Intelligent agents can be deployed to help the user in accomplishing their day to day tasks. This paper has presented an agent based GIS environment which incorporates a variety of intelligent agents to guide the user in executing core business processes. The GIS can also be augmented with Web interface to improve access to spatial data. Though we are in the early stages of implementation, the prototype demonstrates the feasibility of implementing an effective agent-based GIS environment.

REFERENCES

[1] Campos, D., Naumov, A., Shapiro, S., "Building an Interface Agent for ARC/INFO," ESRI User Conference, Palm Springs, California, USA 20-24 May, 1996.

[2] Chavez, A., Moukas, A., and Maes, P. "Challenger: A Multi-agent System for Distributed Resource Allocation," *Proc. of Autonomous Agents '97*, Marina del Rey, CA, Feb. 5-8, 1997.

[3] Ferrand, N., "Modelling and Supporting Multi-Actor Spatial Planning Using Multi-Agents Systems," Proc. of the Third NCGIA Conference on GIS and Environmental Modelling, Santa Fe, Jan. 1996.

[4] Franklin, S., Graesser, A., "Is it an Agent, or just a Program?: A Taxonomy for Autonomous Agents," Proc. of Third Intl. Workshop on Agent Theories, Architectures, and Languages, Springer-Verlag, 1996.

[5] Genesereth, M., and Ketchpel, S. "Software Agents," *Comm. ACM*, Vol. 37, No. 7, pp. 48-53, 1994.

[6] Gimblett, H. R., Durnota, B., Itami, R. M., "Spatially-Explicit Autonomous Agents for Modelling Recreation Use in Complex Wilderness Landscapes," Complex International Journal. Vol. 3 1996.

[7] Hedberg, S. "Agents for Sale: First Wave of Intelligent Agents Go Commercial," *IEEE Expert*, Vol. 11, No. 6, pp. 16-19, 1996.

[8] Hendler, J. "Intelligent Agents: Where AI Meets Information Technology," *IEEE Expert*, Vol. 11, No. 6, pp. 20-23, 1996.

[9] King, D., and O'Leary, D. "Intelligent Executive Information Systems," *IEEE Expert*, Vol. 11, No. 6, pp. 30-35, 1996.

[10] Kohler, T., Van West, C., Carr, E., Langton, C., "Agent-Based Modeling of Prehistoric Settlement Systems in the

Northern America Southwest," Proc. of Third NCGIA Conference on GIS and Environmental Modeling, Santa Fe, January 1996.

[11] Kozierok, R., Maes, P., "A Learning Interface Agent for Scheduling Meetings," Proc. of ACM-SIGCHI Intl. Workshop on Intelligent User Interfaces, Florida, January 1993.

[12] Maes, P. "Intelligent Software: Easing the Burdens that Computers Put on People," *IEEE Expert*, Vol. 11, No. 6, pp. 62-63, 1996.

[13] Maes, P., "Modeling Adaptive Autonomous Agents, Artificial Life," 1: 135-162, 1994.

[14] Papadias, D., Egenhofer, M., "Qualitative Collaborative Planning in Geographical Space: Some Computational Issues," NCGIA Initiative, Sept. 16-19, 1995.

[15] Petrie, C. "Agent-Based Engineering, the Web, and Intelligence," *IEEE Expert*, Vol. 11, No. 6, pp. 24-29, 1996.

[16] Rich, C., and Sidner, C. "COLLAGEN: When Agents Collaborate with People," *Proc. of Autonomous Agents '97*, Marina del Rey, CA, Feb. 5-8, 1997.

[17] Rodrigues, A., Grueau, C., Raper, J., Neves, N., "Environmental Planning using Spatial Agents," Proceedings GIS Research in the UK 1997 (GISRUK '97), School of Geography, University of Leeds, UK, 9-11 April, 1997.

[18] Rodrigues, A., Grueau, C., Raper, J., Neves, N., "Research on Spatial Agents," Proceedings of the Third Joint European Conference and Exhibition on Geographical Information (JEC-GI'97), Austria Center, Vienna, Austria, 16-18 April 1997.

[19] Spector, L. "Automatic Generation of Intelligent Agent Programs," *IEEE Expert*, Vol. 12, No. 1, pp. 3-4, 1997.

[20] Sycara, K., Pannu, A., et al. "Distributed Intelligent Agents," *IEEE Expert*, Vol. 11, No. 6, pp. 36-45, 1996.

[21] Wooldridge, M., "Conceptualizing and Developing Agents," Proc. of The Agent Software Seminar, UNICOM Seminars, London, 25-26 April, 1995.

[22] Wooldridge, M., Jennings, N. R., "Intelligent Agents: Theory and Practice," Knowledge Engineering Review, 10:2, 1995

Federated Information Systems Architecture for Local Public Administration

Maurizio Panti, Claudia Diamantini, Luca Spalazzi and Salvatore Valenti
Computer Science Department - University of Ancona
60131 Ancona - Italy
{panti, diamanti, spalazzi, valenti}@inform.unian.it

ABSTRACT

The information flow through different actors is as desirable as difficult in a Public Administration scenario. It is desirable, since it allows coordination and cooperation among different activities, producing more timely and effective results. It is actually difficult, due to the rigid structure of a bureaucratic environment, which often produces very different structural views of the same objects or resources, depending on the aim an activity is carried on, its context, and the constrains involved. Thus it seems of particular relevance the study of methodologies of information integration and the development of technologies to support interoperability of autonomous information systems.

In this paper we concern with this topic in the context of a particular case study: the information system supporting the Territorial Framing Plan of an Italian district, analyzing a possible reference architecture for the interoperability and cooperation of information systems of the local public administration components involved in the plan.

DEFINITION OF THE INFORMATION SYSTEM FOR THE TERRITORIAL FRAMING PLAN

The aim of this section is to characterize the information system for the monitoring of the Territorial Framing Plan (TFP) as an open and cooperative system, outlining a reference model which allows to describe social, economical and cultural phenomena coming into the plan and their actual manifestations. On the other hand, the TFP allows representing the evolutions of both such phenomena and the model itself.

After a brief analysis of the kind of information that is relevant for the monitoring and of the involved actors, we consider some characteristics of the present information repositories in terms of data accessibility and usability.

The problem of an information system for monitoring "political instances" as TFP are, must be stated in terms of pre-existing, evolving information systems which are managed by the actors of the plan, rather than in terms of available technologies (e.g. communication networks, servers, computers, etc.). The term actor addressing any individual or collective private or public subject having a relevant role in the plan definition, and characterizing both information needs and products. Such information systems are often cited in acts, regulations and directives in an imprecise, informal way, without detailed specifications of their characteristics nor of the procedures to set for their effective running. Therefore, even if an attention to information and its circulation can be guessed from official documents, on the other side, they lack to grasp the fundamental fact that usefulness of such systems strongly depends on the presence of cultural, normative, organizational and technological tools to "put at work" information not only for operational tasks, but also for decision-making. The realization of a TFP as a result of interaction among various private and public subjects can be seen as the concrete ground to define a general project involving the development of such tools.

As a matter of fact, TFP is seen by districts, as the knowledge needed to produce a reference scenario within which to measure and coordinate political strategies devoted to the development of:
• cohesion and coexistence of economic, social, administrative, and cultural demands;
• infrastructures (means of communication, assistance, services or other);
• the location of district plants or centers;
• the utilization of historical and cultural areas to a greater advantage.

Furthermore, the TFP has a purposive aspect in terms of suggestions/directions of actions on the territory which can be taken as a sort of benchmark of the action model the TFP itself represents. In this framework the need of an information system which allows monitoring the realization of the TFP and provides the information needed to log its temporal evolution becomes relevant.

Since the goal is to produce and circulate information, the first fundamental step is the characterization of relevant information, and the management of its circulation by means of suitable tools which allows to realize a true communication, where sender and receiver understand each other.

Furthermore, since a TFP is a dynamic entity, whose contents can change and evolve in many respects, it turns to be necessary the continuous actor intervention thus raising the need of a representation supporting the external communication towards the actor community, besides a coherent internal representation of information.

Therefore, an important preliminary work is the deep analysis of the state of the information owned by the actors, their needs (related to the plan) and their ways of communication. Moreover, the monitoring of possible interactions and overlaps of parts of the TFP pertaining to different actors is of great importance, as well as actor's awareness of interactions and overlaps, which can be achieved only by communication. Thus the communication methods cannot be conceived just as networks of interconnected computers: they must include some mechanism of proactive information exchange and revision.

TFP is both a planning activity, producing real projects of intervention on road, health, industrial infrastructures etc., and a set of norms and methodologies by which to plan and control the consequences of the planning. Therefore the TFP has to adjust itself by adjusting its plans on the basis of the original norms and methodologies it born with, and also by adjusting such norms and methodologies. This result may be obtained imposing a steady although flexible set of relations among actors and their information systems, that is a flexible model of communication allowing mutual understanding between involved actors while saving autonomy. As a main consequence, the system supporting the TFP is mainly characterized by the capability of integration of heterogeneous solutions adopted by single actors.

The dynamical properties of a TFP adds another level of complexity on the support system, which has to handle modifications due to:

• internal actions causing revision/adaptation processes;
• external events, independent of its area of influence, like decisions assumed by neighbor districts or unforeseeable natural phenomena.

Therefore an open information system, easily reconfigurable to allow both the entrance of new actors and the exit of old ones, is required.

Features such as plurality, heterogeneity, dynamicity, reconfigurability make traditional information system paradigms quite inadequate, as the organization models they are based on (typically hierarchic or functional) are too rigid in terms of reconfigurability and too centralized both in terms of the definition of languages, protocols and information organization/conceptualization and in terms of control mechanisms.

Since the autonomy of each actor cannot be decreased to reduce the heterogeneity of the whole system in the adopted test-bed, it is necessary to study solutions that do not affect autonomy while maintaining a "reasonable" level of information interchange (communication of everything to everybody is utopian in the context of TFPs, which involve a wide variety of very different actors).

In the light of current research insights and available technology, an adequate model appears to be that of "federated information systems": that is a set of autonomous information systems which decide to share (part of) their data and processes in a cooperative perspective.

Actor's information systems

The variety of actors concurring to the definition and realization of the TFP (public and private companies, associations, etc.) have to be considered as provider/receiver of some kind of predefined information, as well as subjects which contributes to the modification of information flows, by generating new production/consumption centers of an information which may evolve in its structure, contents, communicability.

Actors may perform from time to time as:
• plans, scenarios and goals proposers;
• action/intervention planners, accomplishers and addressees;
• controllers/evaluators.

They act with various interests and goals in different, but not necessarily disjoint, domains such as:
• political / legislative;
• economical / industrial;
• administrative;
• technological;
• cultural / formative.

This simple taxonomy entails a number of different information needs, leaving the system with the burden of supporting communication and distribution of the relevant information to each actor, with the commitment to respect the constraints related to information quality features like timeliness, accessibility, communicability and relevance.

Information repositories

Denoting by information repositories the whole set of data stored ad managed by an actor's information system, we can distinguish the following categories of data/information:

1) structured and available in electronic format (e.g. files, records, and tables);
2) unstructured and available in electronic format (e.g. letters, resolutions, reports);
3) unstructured and not available in electronic format (e.g. hard-copy letters, resolutions, reports, etc.).

From a brief analysis of data in terms of availability and usability in a cooperative perspective, we can see that in category 1 archives are typically organized in files, with the access structures supported by the operating system (sequential, indexed, random, etc.), and only few recently automated organizations can be founded on DBMS; a formal documentation of the conceptual design rarely exists; a documentation of internal and external information flows together with a handbook of administrative activities rarely exists. In category 2 data are usually spread in more than one computer and organized for individual purposes end goals, except for resolutions whose repositories can be centrally organized; their classification is usually semantically poor and "protocol-oriented". Finally, in category 3 data are not available at all, and the possibility of recovery is very limited and expensive.

Almost all actors have automated information systems and possess large repositories of data belonging to the former category. Part of these data could be shared in a cooperative perspective. However, from a deeper analysis it turns out three main problems limiting cooperation:

- data heterogeneity;
- information contents heterogeneity;
- organization heterogeneity.

We note again that heterogeneity stem out from the autonomy of each actor in structuring its data, processes and information flows, and it is a major problem that must be dealt with. The main sources of data heterogeneity are due to different data structure, data representations and levels of abstraction.

With respect to contents, each system is dedicated to capture/provide data for internal processes, which results for the major part operational or control processes. They are unlike from actor to actor, their difference relying in the way they are identified, modified, managed; in the domains of interest (economic, financial, administrative, technical, political, etc.) and in the organizational structures and the way they act.

With respect to organization, each actor can adopt different architectural criteria: a single centralized system, many interconnected distributed autonomous systems and independent systems. A typical example is represented by geographical information systems, which in many Italian municipalities (but not only there!) are usually isolated from the other subsystems and simply used for technical-operative purposes, while it is known that they represent a decision support system of invaluable utility, if properly used.

In the public administration systems these repositories for data falling in the two latter categories are very huge. However, the automatic management of this information is usually limited to record operations, in a pure storing perspective, making difficult to exploit one of the main information sources in the public administration decisional processes.

REFERENCE MODELS

In this section we will give an overview of the most common models both of Federated Information Systems and of Agent-based Systems. Such models will be then compared with the requirements of the application domains in order to present our approach to Federated Information Systems for Local Public Administration.

Models for Federated Information Systems (FIS)

Information integration is defined as the task of providing a uniform access to autonomous and heterogeneous information sources. Furthermore, information sources may be classified as structured, as for instance relational databases, semi-structured, i.e. spatial data represented through quad-trees, or de-structured (text or images).

The basic components of a FIS are {She90}:

- a common data model - that should be flexible enough a) to represent different kinds of information from different sources and b) to cope with missing or wrong information;
- a common language - that could be used to submit queries to the integrated system. Also in this case, flexibility along with high expressiveness levels is required to cope with different functional levels of distinct information

sources;
• some tools for translation (to cope with syntactic relations), integration and mapping (to handle semantic relations)

In the last few years, mediators-based systems have become the reference architecture to integrate both structured semi-structured data {Wie92, Sub98, Ham97 and Are93}. Such systems are characterized by the presence of wrappers that are responsible of the translation of the data representation from the local model of the information source to the common one and of the queries from the common language to the information source language (fig. 1).

Mediators have been introduced to improve the management of the integrated system through the amalgamation of data coming from different sources and the handling of inconsistency. Furthermore mediators are used to handle user-formulated queries through reformulation plans and query optimization towards different information sources.

Two main approaches have been reported in the literature to the design of mediator-based systems that can be discriminated as query vs. data centered. The former put the emphasis on the ability of the mediator to answer queries: in this case it does not exist an explicit integrated schema of the common data model, and the semantic relations are defined as views. Different mediators are needed to answer different queries or to build distinct relations among data. Existing systems in this class provide the programmer who has designed the mediator, tools to integrate domains, information and to handle conflicts. {Gar97, Lev96, Sub98}

In the latter approach to the of design mediator-based systems, query formulation is an activity that stems out from the definition of an integrated schema requiring a partial or total unification of the local data models {Are93, Har97, She88}. In spite of the greatest number of prototypes based on a query-centered mediators that have been reported in literature, we believe that the applicability of such approach is reduced by the number of involved information sources, since

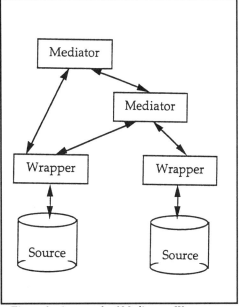

Figure 1 - A network of Mediators, Wrappers and Information Sources {Gai97}

semantic heterogeneity must be explicitly reduced by the programmer. Furthermore query centered mediators may rise the classical problems of information processing: reduced usability due to the fact that a limited amount of semantic relations and queries is implemented only, and dependence of data from applications rising problems of alignment and inconsistency.

Therefore we consider the development of models for automatic integration of common data schemata a strategic issue.

The FIPA Model

An open system is defined as a system in which it is possible to add at any time new modules that are able to interact with existing others without rewriting the existing software. Open systems are identified by two main characteristics: portability and interoperability.

Agent-based programming is becoming a valid approach to the design of distributed open systems {Gen94, Nwa96 and Woo94}. Since its origin a number of studies have been reported in literature dealing with the effective applicability of this approach both in the field of information systems and web design {Geo96, Lie95, Mae94, Pet96 and She93}. Up today both some reference models and standards have been defined.

The reference model selected for its applicability to our domain has been proposed by the Foundation for Intelligent Physical Agents (FIPA) {FIP97a through FIP97g} and will be discussed in following part of this section.

The definition of the agent may be found both in part-1 (Agent Management) and in part3 (Agent/Software integration) of the FIPA Specifications. The aim of such specifications is to highlight the technologies needed to design multi-agent systems, without any concern to the internal structure of agents. Therefore an agent can be seen as a module providing a number of services inside an integrated model of execution. Such a module may be used to grant access to external software, to human actors and to communication facilities. An agent is handled as a single entity, although different access levels for security reasons may be defined. An agent may belong to several owners, can be either static or mobile and may be associated to one or more addresses. The characteristics that an agent must necessarily possess in order to communicate with other agent are:
• unique identifier - a unique name that identifies the agent.

- birth platform - any agent can be registered to different platforms (i.e. sets of agents) but it can belong to a single birth platform: the one over which the agent has been created and that can solve any query about its identity.

The FIFA specifications give a wide emphasis to the integration of existing software to multi-agent architectures with the goal of providing a single tool to link external systems in a technology-independent approach. FIPA specifications provide both transducer-based and case-based solutions to the integration problem. Both approaches may de dedicated or general. Therefore, with reference to the situation depicted in fig. 2, agents 2 and j provide a transducer-based solution, while agent 1 provides a case-based solution; furthermore, the solution provided by agent 1 and 2 are dedicated, while the one provided by agent j is general.

Agents developed for dedicated solutions are able to interface only "a priori" chosen software: therefore dedicated solutions are less flexible than general ones, since any new software introduced requires the development of a specific agent.

The general solution suggested by FIPA is to rely on wrapper agents that can interface different software with distinct characteristics, dynamically. This solution is based on the capability of wrapper agents to use standard communication protocols and to invoke the activation of a connection with existing software through them {FIP97c}. Therefore wrapper agents must be parameterized with both the physical address of the software and the communication protocol adopted.

The second section of the FIPA specifications (FIPA-ACL) is devoted to the definition of a communication language among agents {FIP97b}. The FIPA-ACL specifications are introduced to single out a set of communication acts through the definition of their syntax, semantics and communication protocol. The communication among agents is defined keeping in account their mental attitudes: beliefs (i.e. the set of propositions that are believed true by the agent), concerns (i.e. the set of propositions that the agents is not sure to believe true) and intentions (i.e. the set of propositions that the agent desires to become true).

The message transport layer represents another important point: dealing with open systems imposes that different interfacing mechanisms could be used.

The FIPA specifications require that messages can be composed either by sequences of characters or by MIME-coded documents in order to simplify this task. Therefore the specifications are focused on the structure that messages must have. Every message contains the class of communication act involved along with a set of related parameters in a LISP-like syntax. As an example, a request for information is shown in fig. 3.

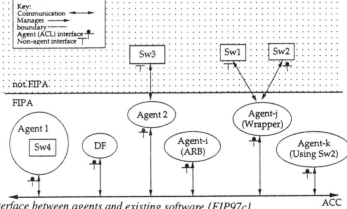

Figure 2 - Reference Model for interface between agents and existing software {FIP97c}

```
(request
:sender i
:receiver j
:content
(select name from employees where payroll > 20)
:ontology registry
:language SQL
:protocol FIPA-request)
```

Figure 3 - A message for asking information

"Content" is the mostly important parameter, since it defines message content (an SQL query in the example of fig. 3). The parameter "language" allows specifying the language used for the "content", to permit the existence of different languages in the same environment. "Ontology" defines the vocabulary used to allow the existence of different databases. Finally, "protocol" identifies the communication protocol used: (FIPA-Request in the instance shown in fig. 3).

The multi agent system selected by FIPA is based on federated system. Therefore an agent needing a service interacts with a facilitator instead of communicating directly with other agents. The remaining part of this sections will be devoted to the discussion of the following concepts: agent platform (AP), agent management system (AMS), directory facilitator (DF) and agent communication channel (ACC) that are introduced by FIPA model.

Agent Platform

The physical infrastructure inside which agents are employed is the agent platform. An agent platform is built up by a set of agents (fig. 4). Agents must register to a platform in order to communicate among them or with other platforms. Agents that have been created over a platform, mobile agents migrated onto a platform or asking registration as local agents must apply for the registration procedure to the platform.

Each platform must have an AMS, a DF and an ACC at least and may support different domains.

Agent domain

A logical grouping of agents and services is said agent domain. The arrangement into groups may occur for a number of motivations including (but not limited to) organisational, ontological, geo-political and contractual reasons. Directory Facilitators maintain the list of agent and services belonging to a domain: therefore only one DF is defined inside each domain. An agent may belong to different domains and agents from different platforms can support each domain (fig. 5).

The Agent Communication Channel provides the default communication method used by agents belonging to each platform: the Internet Inter-ORB protocol (IIOB). Needless to say, this does not prevent the use of other protocols.

An agent called AMS administers each platform. The AMS controls the use and the access to the ACC, is responsible both of agent-creation and deletion, handles the dynamical registration of agents to a platform and supervises agent migration (immigration / emigration). Finally the AMS provides a "white page"-like service, maintaining the list of agents registered to the platform they administer, along with their address.

The DF is the agent that manages a domain, maintaining a "yellow page"-like service being able to answer to queries devoted to identify both agents providing each service in a given domain and services provided by each agent. The DF agent for a given domain can be agent of another domain.

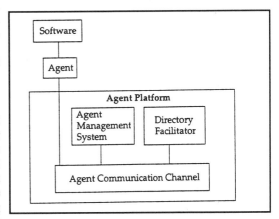

Figure 4 - Agent Platform {FIP97c}

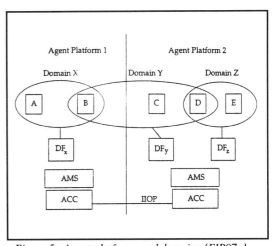

Figure 5 - Agent platforms and domains {FIP97c}

THE PROPOSED ARCHITECTURE

In this section we are going to present an overview of the architecture of the Federated Information System to be implemented. Our main focus will be the highlight of the domain characteristics that mostly affected the design of our solution.

From the description of the application domain it descends the necessity of keeping in account the following points:

- variety of information systems: there are a great number of different information systems in the domain, belonging to different agents (regions, provinces, and communes)
- actor autonomy: each actor is completely autonomous in the definition of its information needs, in the identification of the information to be regarded as public domain and in the design and implementation choices.
  Therefore each agent has to be considered as completely autonomous.
- dynamicity of the federation: the actors that belong to the federation may change in time: both for new entries and for the departure of old actors. The policy that must be adopted is to federate information systems in a gradual way: this policy being due to the autonomy of agents that may decide to join or to leave the federation at any time.
- dinamicity of the information systems: each information system may change over time either at the conceptual or at the logical/physical level.

Those characteristics strongly affect the system design since:

- it is impracticable to build a unique integrated schema: the autonomy of each actor being against the use of a unique integrated schema residing on another actor's node. Furthermore each actor has different information needs and thus a personal view of information, such different views may be partially incompatible each others. Finally the whole system may undergo a crisis if the actor hosting the unique integrated schema opts for leaving the federation.
- it is impossible to build global views and schemas "a priori" due to dynamicity both of the federation and of the information systems;

These specifications led to focus our attention on mediator-based systems in the realm of agent-programming more in detail we believe that it is necessary to adopt a solution where each agent is related to a mediator. A mediator is a static, autonomous, intelligent agent: autonomous means that it is able to solve by himself the problems that may rise due to heterogeneity, while intelligent means that has both knowledge (even if its view of the whole system may be incomplete and dynamic) and intentions. We selected agent-programming instead of distributed object-oriented programming since each module must be autonomous and intelligent. We selected static instead of mobile agents since having agents only short interactions with any site, the time requested to transfer them is greater that the time required by the communication process.

A possible architecture for the domain under examination is shown in fig. 6. With reference to the FIPA model the following observations can be done.

Wrapper Agents (WA)

We have chosen wrapper agent to interface information system sources. Wrapper agents translate queries in the format required by local data model, in the same way as mediator agents do. The WA may be able to answer queries related to both data and schemas of the involved databases.

Alike the wrappers defined by the FIPA model WA are used to interface agent-based software with legacy systems.

Mediator Agents (MA)

Each agent is completely autonomous and possesses different information needs. Furthermore inside the same organization completely different needs can co-exist: the information required by a Borough Council clerk are for instance completely different from those needed by the Technical Office manager. Therefore, each information need may be implemented as a personal view on the totality of involved information systems. This point alone may justify the need of mediator for each agent of the system. In fig. 6 the MAs responsible of reporting information in the domain both of thematic maps

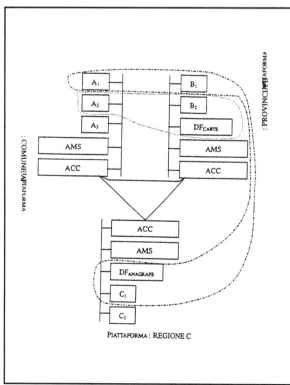

Figure 6 - Platforms and domains for the case study

and of registry-office of an Italian district are depicted.

An MA must possess:
- a personal view on the information systems of the federation. This view takes in account the information needs that must be satisfied by the agent and is dynamically modified as the requirements change.
- knowledge about allowed transactions. The transactions are designed taking in account the involved actors, the performed activities and the objects modified by the transactions itselves.
- knowledge about the justifications of any choice. The agent must be able to log its inferences for using them to justify its choices and to make the degree of confidence on its knowledge adjustable.

A mediator agent builds its own knowledge trough the interaction with other agents and with the human actor. More in detail it interacts with wrapper agents to access the original data schemas and with mediator agents to access their views.

When a query is submitted to an MA, it is redirected to the right wrapper agents if is referred to knowledge already owned by the MA. Otherwise, the MA must enlarge its view in order to contain the knowledge require to forward the query. This result may be obtained through the interaction with both WA (to access their original data schemas) and MA (to access their global views).

Thus the view of an MA is dynamically updated with the submission of queries by the user. It is straightforward to infer from the previous discussion that the view will be strongly influenced by the queries submitted by the user. The interaction with other MAs can be useful both to create new views {Dia98} and to improve the confidence on pre-existing views.

Agent platforms

We decided to have an agent platform for each actor. This permits the autonomy to each actor by allowing the management of his own agent and the selection of the services provided to other actors. In the example shown in fig. 6, three platforms devoted to Italian local public administrations are depicted.

Agent domain

In the considered application a number of different domains can be identified. The domain of thematic maps and the registry-office domain have been single out, but it is possible to identify a number of other interesting ones. All actors co-operating both to provide and to identify information in the domain of interest concur to belong to the domain itself. The same situation arises for the repositories hosting domain-specific information. This is the design rationale for adopting an agent domain for each sphere of interest. All WAs that interface information systems involved in a domain and all MAs that must create a view of the domain belong to the domain itself.

FINAL REMARKS

In this paper we tried to present an overview of a project funded by the Italian Ministry for University and for Scientific and Technological Research (MURST) that is currently under development.

We tried to discuss the analysis of the specifications imposed by the case study selected for the verification of the obtained results: the interoperability of information systems of different components of local public administration. As a reference for this work the mediator-based model for the integration of information systems and the FIPA defined agent model for open systems have been selected. The approach discussed has led to the rejection of the unique-mediator hypothesis for a solution adopting mediators and wrappers modeled as static, autonomous, intelligent agents.

References

{Are93} Y. Arens, C. Y. Chee, C. N. Hsu, C. A. Knoblock, "Retrieving and Integrating Data from Multiple Information Sources", in International Journal of Intelligent and Cooperative Information Systems, vol. 2, pp. 127—158, 1993.

{Dia98} C. Diamantini, M. Panti, L. Spalazzi, "Information integration in Local Public Administration Information Systems" (in Italian), Tech. Rept. T3-R05, InterData Project, University of Ancona, 1998.

{Fip97a} Foundation for Intelligent Physical Agents, Specification Part 1 — Agent Management, Geneva, Switzerland, October 1997.

{Fip97b} Foundation for Intelligent Physical Agents, Specification Part 2 — Agent Communication Language, Geneva, Switzerland, October 1997.

{Fip97c} Foundation for Intelligent Physical Agents, Specification Part 3 — Agent/Software Integration, Geneva, Switzerland, October 1997.

{Fip97d} Foundation for Intelligent Physical Agents, Specification Part 4 — Personal Travel Assistance, Geneva,

Switzerland, October 1997.

{Fip97e} Foundation for Intelligent Physical Agents, Specification Part 5 — Personal Assistant, Geneva, Switzerland, October 1997.

{Fip97f} Foundation for Intelligent Physical Agents, Specification Part 6 — Audio/Video Entertainment & Broadcasting, Geneva, Switzerland, October 1997.

{Fip97g} Foundation for Intelligent Physical Agents, Specification Part 7 — Network Management & Provisioning, Geneva, Switzerland, October 1997.

{Gai97} Gaizauskas R., Wilks Y, "Information Extraction: Beyond Document Retrieval", in Memoranda in Computer and Cognitive Science, University of Sheffield, CS-97-10 , 1997.

{Gar97} H. Garcia-Molina, Y. Papakonstantinou, D. Quass, A. Rajaraman, Y. Sagiv, J. Ullman, V. Vassalos, J. Widom, "The TSIMMIS Approach to Mediation: Data Models and Languages", in Journal of Intelligent Information Systems, 1997. Available @ http://www-db.stanford.edu/pub/papers/tsimmis.ps.

{Gen94} M. Genesereth, S. Ketchpel, "Software agents", in Communications of the ACM, vol. 37, N. 7, pp. 48-53, 1994.

{Geo96} M. Georgeff, "Agents with Motivation: Essential Technology for Real World Applications", in Proc. of the First International Conference on the Practical Applications of Intelligent Agents and Multi-Agent Technology, London, UK, 24th April 1996.

{Ham97} J. Hammer, J. McHugh, H. Garcia-Molina, "Semistructured Data: The TSIMMIS Experience", in Proc. I East-European Workshop on Advances in Database and Information Systems - ADBIS'97, St. Petersburg, Russia, Sept. 1997. Available @ http://www-db.stanford.edu/pub/papers/adbis97.ps.

{Har97} T. Harder, G. Sauter, J. Thomas, "Design and Architecture of the FDBS Prototype INFINITY", in Proc. EFDBS97 - Engineering Federated Database Systems, Barcelona, June 1997.

{Lev96} A. Levy, A. Rajaraman, J. Ordille, "Querying Heterogeneous Information Sources Using Source Description", in Proc. of the 22th Int. Conf. on Very Large Databases - VLDB'96, Bombay, India, 1996.

{Lie95} H. Lieberman, "Letitzia: An Agent that Assists Web Browsing", In Proc. of IJCAI-95, AAAI Press, 1995.

{Mae94} P. Maes, "Agents that Reduce Work and Information Overload", in Communications of ACM, vol. 37, N. 7, pp. 31-40, 1994.

{Nwa96} H. Nwana, "Software agents: an overview", in Knowledge Engineering Review, vol. 2 N. 3, pp. 205-244, October/November 1996.

{Pet96} C. Petrie, "Agent-based engineering, the Web, and intelligence", in IEEE Expert, December 1996.

{She88} A. Sheth, J. Larson, A. Cornelio, S. B. Navathe, "A tool for integrating conceptual schemas and user views", in Proc. 4th International Conference on Data Engineering, Los Angeles, CA, February 1988, IEEE.

{She90} A. Shet, J. Larson, "Federated Database Systems for Managing Distributed, Heterogeneous, and Autonomous Databases", in ACM Computing Surveys, vol. 22, N. 3, pp.183-236, 1990.

{She93} B. Sheth, P. Maes, "Evolving Agents for Personalized Information Filtering", in Proc. of the IEEE Conference on Artificial Intelligence for Applications, 1993.

{Sub98} V. S. Subrahmanian, S. Adali, A. Brink, R. Emery, J. J. Lu, A. Rajput, T. J. Rogers, R. Ross, C. Ward, "HERMES: A Heterogeneous Reasoning and Mediator System", submitted for publication, 1998.
Available @ http://www.cs.umd.edu/projects/hermes/overview/paper

{Wie92} G. Wiederhold, "Mediators in the architectures of future information systems", in IEEE Computer, vol. 25, N. 3, pp. 38—49, 1992.

{Woo94} M. Wooldridge, N. Jennings, "Intelligent agents: theory and practice", Knowledge Engineering Review, vol. 10, N. 2, pp. 115-152, October 1994.

Human-Centred Methods in Information Systems Development: Is There a Better Way Forward?

Steve Clarke and Brian Lehaney

The University of Luton, Department of Finance, Systems and Operations, Park Square, Luton, LU1 3JU, United Kingdom

Tel: 01582 734111, Fax: 01582 743143, Email: Steve.Clarke@Luton.ac.uk

ABSTRACT

Developers of information systems (IS) have long recognised the value of incorporating factors relating to human activity into the development process. The methods used vary from the simple insertion of some form of user needs analysis into a systems development life cycle method, to the softer approaches, which see the whole problem situation as one of interpreting participant views rather than designing systems.

This paper looks briefly at the history of IS development, and from this background determines the current status as dominated by functionalist, problem-solving, design issues, within which the needs of participants in the proposed system are given inadequate attention. These problems point to a failure of both hard and soft methods to offer a way forward in systems where human behaviour is a key element, and signify the need for an alternative approach. Drawing on similar difficulties faced in the domain of management science, a proposal is put forward for a method which is theoretically and practically defensible, and which allows hard and soft methodologies to contribute within a controlling framework.

This new approach offers significant benefits in IS development, better enabling debate and consensus-seeking as the central issues in place of problem-solving and design.

TECHNOLOGY-BASED APPROACHES TO INFORMATION SYSTEMS DEVELOPMENT

Pick up any standard text on information systems development (ISD) and certain factors consistently appear. The first is a strong adherence to pragmatism, with little or no explicit recognition of underlying theory. Following on from this adherence to pragmatism is the treatment generally of information systems development (ISD) as a technical, problem solving domain. This adherence to pragmatic problem solving leads to tensions when the system to be developed requires significant user input. Just as most of the systems development literature stresses the project management, methodological, pragmatic approach to ISD, so it also emphasises the need for discovering the requirements of users, basing this view on the observation that systems frequently fail to meet user needs (Reynolds, 1995 p.454). Most commonly, the incorporation of user requirements into information systems development (ISD) is achieved by including a user analysis stage within the existing problem solving approach (Wetherbe and Vitalari, 1994 p.211), with advice on how to undertake this user analysis often addressed only weakly. The argument for an alternative to these technology-based approaches is supported by the findings from a number of studies of systems failure. Boehm (1989 p.2) cites examples of such failures, and considers that, directly or indirectly, they contribute to as much as 50% of total systems cost.

In all of these instances, the systems development life cycle emerges, implicitly or explicitly, as the prime control element, resulting in a methodology which adheres to the functional engineering model, taking a structured, problem-solving approach: human complexity in the system is seen as something which can be analysed, and toward which a specification can be written. Beath and Orlykowski (1994), focusing on a three-volume text by Martin, mount a convincing critique of the interaction between users and systems professionals in information systems development (ISD), concluding that the commitment to user participation is revealed as ideological rather than actual, with users frequently shown to be passive rather than active participants in the process.

Through a thorough review of the information systems development literature, Lyytinen and Hirschheim (1987) make a compelling case for the argument that few information systems can be considered a success. The reason for claiming success is, they argue, largely based on an erroneous classification of how such success should be measured, which usually focuses on the extent to which the completed system meets the requirement specification laid out in advance. Lyytinen and Hirschheim promote the notion of expectation failure, or the failure of the system to meet the expectations of the key stakeholder groups, as conveying a more pluralistically informed view, and forcing a dynamic perspective of information systems development.

If technology-based approaches to information systems development provide an impoverished view of the domain, perhaps the solution is to be found in human-centred methods.

PEOPLE: THE HUMAN-CENTRED METHODS

The human-centred approach to information systems development (ISD) has given rise to the so-called 'soft' methods. It is argued that traditional 'engineering' approaches are 'hard' or functionalist, being based on a view of the world which sees it as composed of deterministic, rule-based systems, in contrast to which the soft methods take an interpretivist, ideographic stance.

An early attempt at incorporating human issues into what was seen as a technical domain was the ETHICS methodology. ETHICS (Mumford, 1985) was developed in the 1970s as a socio-technical methodology (Effective Technical and Human Implementation of Computer-based Systems), which follows an essentially problem-solving approach. More recently, Stowell and West (1994) have promoted the client led design (CLD) methodology, which takes the position that, since the information system results from social interaction, participants in that interaction ought to be central to systems analysis and design. In their view, information systems development needs to be *driven* by interpretivism, and not, at the technical development stage, "engulfed by functionalism." (Stowell, 1991). Consequently Stowell & West are critical of methods whereby soft, interpretative approaches such as soft systems methodology (SSM) are used to front-end a technological development, arguing that once the soft analysis is passed to the technical specialists the benefits of that soft analysis are largely lost.

In the next section, a critique of the perspectives taken on information systems development is put forward, suggesting that neither technology-based nor human-centred methods offer an adequate solution to the development of computer based human activity systems.

CRITIQUE OF THE CURRENT POSITION

Much debate has taken place in the last fifteen years or so regarding the relative merits of hard and soft approaches to information systems development (ISD) (Jackson, 1982; Checkland, 1994). This debate may be criticised, however, for giving rise to essentially *methodological* arguments: hard protagonists favouring the 'systems development life cycle' approaches under their various guises; soft thinkers promoting their own range of methods. By focusing on methodology, both the hard and soft schools exhibit shortcomings resulting from the lack of investigation of underpinning theory.

To address these issues it is necessary, therefore, to look beyond the practice of systems development, and return to the roots from which this practice evolved, thereby deriving an approach which successfully combines the human activity and technological elements of a problem situation. Within this paper, these roots are sought in social theory, a review of which is therefore undertaken to form the basis of this study.

SOCIAL THEORY: THE PARADIGM PROBLEM

Burrell and Morgan positioned all social theories into one of four paradigms: functionalist, inter-

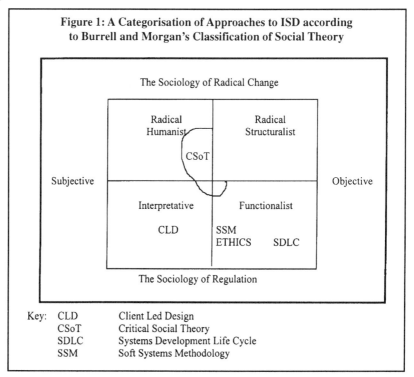

Figure 1: A Categorisation of Approaches to ISD according to Burrell and Morgan's Classification of Social Theory

The Sociology of Radical Change

Radical Humanist

Radical Structuralist

CSoT

Subjective

Objective

Interpretative

Functionalist

CLD

SSM
ETHICS   SDLC

The Sociology of Regulation

Key: CLD   Client Led Design
      CSoT   Critical Social Theory
      SDLC   Systems Development Life Cycle
      SSM   Soft Systems Methodology

pretivist, radical humanist and radical structuralist (Figure 1), according to the extent to which they were subjective versus objective or regulative versus radical. The subjective-objective dimension can be seen can be seen in terms of four elements: ontology, epistemology, a view of the nature of human beings, and methodology.

The ontological debate concerns the nature of reality, the two opposing extremes of thought being realism: that reality is external to the individual and is of an objective nature; and nominalism: that reality is a product of individual consciousness. Epistemology is concerned with the grounds of knowledge, or how the world might be understood, and this understanding communicated as knowledge. The two opposing extremes are positivism: knowledge is hard, real and capable of being transmitted in a tangible form; and anti-positivism: knowledge is soft, more subjective, based on experience and insight, and essentially of a personal nature. Human beings may be viewed on a scale from deterministic: determined by situations in the external world and conditioned by external circumstances; to voluntaristic: they have free will, and create their environment.

The view taken of ontology, epistemology and the nature of human beings directly influences the methodological approach which is adopted. A realist ontology, positivist epistemology and view of human beings as largely deterministic, leaves nomothetic methodologies as the appropriate choice. Such methodologies are characterised by a search for universal laws that govern the reality that is being observed. A nominalist ontology, anti-positivist epistemology and view of human beings as largely voluntaristic, indicates ideographic methodologies as appropriate: the principle concern would be to understand the way an individual interprets the world, with a questioning of external 'reality'.

Accordingly, the functionalist paradigm is, in Burrell and Morgan's terms, regulative in nature, highly pragmatic, often problem orientated, applying natural scientific methods to the study of human affairs (Burrell and Morgan, 1979 p.26). The early application of functionalism to business organisations is to be found in functionalist organisation theory, which can be traced from the work of F.W.Taylor (1856-1915). This laid the foundation for the 'classical school', contributors to which have been, for example, Fayol and Gulick. In Fayol's work, organisations are characterised in terms of a reality which can be investigated systematically, taking a highly mechanistic view of human beings, informed by an objectivist ontology and epistemology.

The interpretative paradigm is also regulative, seeing social reality as "…little more than a network of assumptions and intersubjectively shared meanings." (Burrell and Morgan, 1979 p.29-31). Burrell and Morgan argue that the ontological assumptions of interpretative sociologists lead them to seek an understanding of the existing social world from an ordered viewpoint, and do not allow them to deal with issues of conflict or coercion. Consequently, interpretivism suffers criticism from all sides. Functionalists see it as finding out about problem situations without any means of solving problems or, in effect, producing any 'hard' output. Radical thinkers criticise interpretivism for its support of the status quo - the existing power base: interpretivism is fine for achieving consensus, provided the conditions required for consensus-seeking pre-exist; it has no means of overthrowing existing power structures or of resisting coercion.

The radical humanist paradigm has much in common with the interpretative paradigm, being nominalist, anti-positivist, voluntaristic and ideographic, but unlike interpretivism "emphasises the importance of overthrowing or transcending the limitations of existing social arrangements." (Burrell and Morgan, 1979 p.32). The emphasis is on radical change and the attainment of potentiality through human emancipation, or release from 'false consciousness':
    " .. the consciousness of man is dominated by the ideological superstructures with which he interacts,
    and these drive a cognitive wedge between himself and his true consciousness. This .. 'false conscious-
    ness' inhibits or prevents true human fulfilment." (Burrell and Morgan, 1979 p.32).

An early recognition of the theoretical validity of a radical humanist approach to information systems development was by Hirschheim and Klein (1989), who saw neither the functionalist nor the interpretivist approach as adequate. Hirschheim and Klein view functionalism as the "orthodox approach to systems development", and argue that interpretivism offers an alternative to functionalism in so far as it does not accept there to be an objective reality but only socially constructed reality. However, its relativist stance makes it " … *completely uncritical* of the potential dysfunctional side effects of using particular tools and techniques for information systems development." Different systems development outcomes are simply viewed as the result of different socially constructed realities. Through the critical social theory of the radical humanist paradigm there is therefore the possibility of moving beyond a debate located firmly in the sociology of regulation to a critically reflective, radical position.

These paradigmatic considerations carry implications for ISD, which will now be investigated in more depth in the following section.

SOCIAL SYSTEMS THEORY: ITS APPLICATION TO INFORMATION SYSTEMS DEVELOPMENT

The functionalist-interpretivist debate, with the support of social theory, can now be taken further, and a foundation developed for ISD. This is the direction which has been pursued by part of the systems movement, from its origins in the so called Singer/Churchman/Ackoff school (Jackson, 1982; Britton and McCallion, 1994), through to present day systems thinkers. Jackson (1982) has argued that the soft methods of Ackoff, Checkland and Churchman all adhere to some degree to the assumptions of the interpretative paradigm, and identifies a third position which distinguishes hard, soft and emancipatory systems thinking. The argument is for a complementarist approach, which sees the strengths and weaknesses in each of the three areas and argues that each one must be respected for those strengths and weaknesses.

The effect of this is illustrated, in Figure 1, by positioning ISD approaches on the Burrell and Morgan grid. From the perspective of social theory, ISD methodologies are mostly functionalist, with some movement evident towards the interpretative paradigm. The pre-eminent soft methods such as ETHICS and soft systems methodology (SSM) seem to locate best at the interpretative end of the functionalist paradigm. SSM, for example, though usually seen as an interpretative method, is difficult to support in these terms from a social theoretical standpoint; its 'purposiveness' locates it as a functionalist method with high interpretative content. Certainly SSM fails to meet the test laid out by Burrell and Morgan (1979 p.32), that interpretivism "question(s) whether organisations exist in anything but a conceptual sense." Client led design surfaces as an attempt at a development approach to information systems entirely from the interpretative paradigm.

Critical social theory offers the possibility of encompassing functionalist and interpretivist issues, whilst offering progression to a more radical approach. Much work in this area has already been undertaken in the management science domain, and it is from here that further support will be sought in formulating an alternative framework for ISD.

CRITICAL SOCIAL THEORY: THE THEORETICAL UNDERPINNING

Critical social theory (CSoT) can be traced from the work of Kant (1724-1803), through Marx and the Frankfurt School. The two most widely accepted modern theorists are Foucault and Habermas, and it is to the latter that management science turned in the 1980s in order to develop a more radical view of its domain. Habermas (1971) sees all human endeavour as undertaken in fulfilment of three knowledge constitutive or cognitive interests (Table 1): technical, practical (in satisfaction of human interaction or communication) and emancipatory. It is these interests which can also be seen in Hirschheim and Klein's (1989) work. Jackson (1993) follows the cognitive categories of Habermas, and argues that in Western industrialised society the technical interest has been accorded too much primacy. Jackson goes further in asserting, again after Habermas, that, in fact, practical questions are re-defined as technical ones, effectively blocking the separation of what we ought to do from questions of how we ought to be doing it.

Table 1: The Theory of Knowledge Constitutive Interests (Oliga, 1991)				
Knowledge Constitutive Interest	Basis of Human Interest	Type of Interaction	Underlying Paradigm	Methodological Approach
Technical (control)	Labour (Instrumental action)	Man-Nature	Functionalist	Empiricism
Practical (Understanding)	Communicative (Interaction)	Man-Man	Interpretative	Hermeneutics
Emancipatory (Freedom)	Authority (Power)	Man-Self	Radical/Critical	Critique

Critical social theory (CSoT) applied to the field of information systems development (ISD) is appealing for its denial of the natural scientific principles on which study has largely hitherto been based. Seen through an instrumental framework, ISD appears as the design of a system to satisfy a known set of requirements - objective, verifiable requirements which are the same for all involved since they are independent of human opinion. CSoT refutes this, seeing our understanding of the world as determined by *a priori* conditions which are uncritically accepted. Critical theory seeks to expose these, and thereby release human beings from their 'false consciousness' to a position from which true potentiality can be attained.

From these roots came the development, in the domain of management science, of critical systems thinking, which is detailed below before moving on to the development of a critical framework for ISD.

CRITICAL SYSTEMS THINKING

It is essentially a quest for a theoretical underpinning - for a means of combining approaches adhering to different paradigms - that is the concern of critical systems thinking. A critical approach to information systems development, by recognising the merits of both hard (functionalist) and soft (interpretivist) methods, offers a way forward from the current emphasis on, at worst, solely technological issues, and at best a technological approach which has added to it some recognition of the need to deal with human activity. CST, it is argued, accepts the contribution of both hard and soft approaches, and, through critique, enhances awareness of the circumstances in which such approaches can be properly employed. The pragmatism of the hard approaches and the lack of theoretical reflection in the soft allow CST to expose both as special cases with limited domains of application. The value of CST in information systems interventions can be demonstrated through the Burrell and Morgan grid (after Burrell and Morgan, 1979 p.22). Burrell and Morgan's work, together with contributions from Oliga (1991), may be interpreted as shown in Figure 2 below.

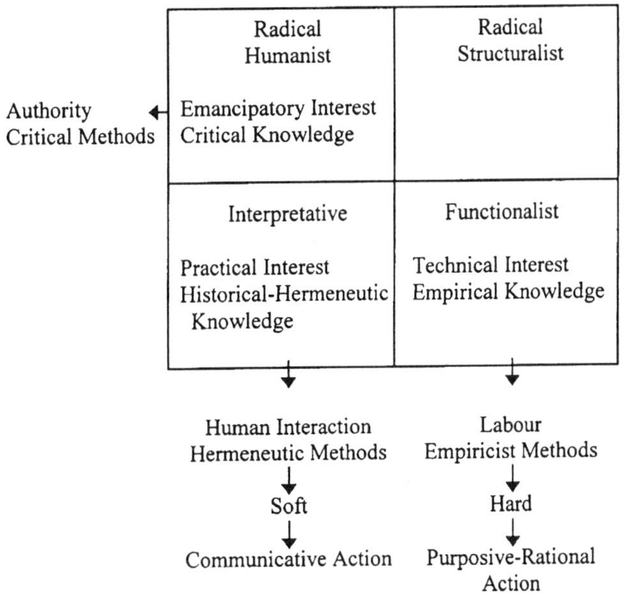

This perspective further supports the view that traditional, structured ISD largely emerges as serving the technical interest, with labour applied as purposive-rational action to achieve transformation by application of the means of production - in this case information technology. The alternative, evident in this domain since the 1970s but still limited in acceptance, is the service of the practical interest from the interpretative paradigm, relying on the communication of perceptions and consensus forming.

That critical systems thinking is true to the principles of critical social theory can be seen from its five key commitments (Jackson, 1991), the relationship of which to information systems have been investigated by Jackson (1992). These commitments are critical awareness, social awareness, complementarism at the level of methodology, complementarism at the level of theory, and human emancipation.

Critical awareness " ... {consists

Figure 2: The Social Validity of Hard, Soft and Critical Approaches

of} examining and re-examining taken-for-granted assumptions, together with the conditions which gave rise to them." (Midgley, 1995). Complementarism at the level of methodology rests on the encouragement of diversity and the concept that methodologies can do no more than "legitimately contribute in areas of specific context" (Flood, 1990 p.28). The objective of human emancipation, from an organisational standpoint, is to enable the achievement of human potentiality, which, it is argued, is enhanced where information systems are implemented in a way that promotes human well-being. The work particularly of Hirschheim, Klein and Lyytinen (Hirschheim and Klein, 1989; Lyytinen and Hirschheim, 1989; Klein and Hirschheim, 1993) gives further support to this view.

A Critical Framework for Information Systems Development

As has been argued, the foundations of a critical approach to organisational studies owes much to the work of Churchman (1968), which was built on foundations laid by Singer, and has been continued by Ackoff and other adherents to the systems school (see Britton and McCallion, 1994).

The work of Jackson and Keys (1984) proved a major turning point in the development of a critical framework which is true to the commitments of critical systems thinking. By looking at the range of problem contexts and at the systems methodologies available for addressing these contexts, Jackson and Keys have provided a unified approach which draws on the strengths of the relevant methodologies, rather than debating which method is best, and argued for a reconciliation focusing on which method to use in which context, controlled by a "system of systems methodologies". A number of developments have followed this initial work, a summary of which can be found in Midgley (1995). In developing a framework for information systems development (ISD), total systems intervention (TSI) emerges as the most promising basis, offering as it does a solid framework of inquiry, design and critique which most

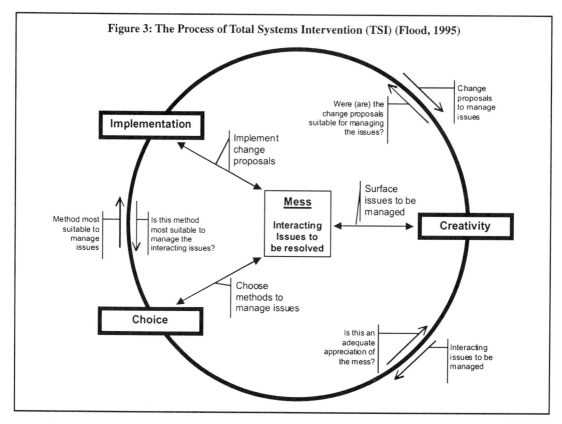

Figure 3: The Process of Total Systems Intervention (TSI) (Flood, 1995)

comprehensively actions the commitments of critical systems thinking (CST). In the following section, a review of the principles and practice of TSI is therefore undertaken as a foundation for an ISD framework.

TOTAL SYSTEMS INTERVENTION: THE PRACTICAL FACE OF CRITICAL SYSTEMS THINKING

Unlike the waterfall method implicit within SDLC, TSI uses an iterative and recursive framework. Participation, based on emancipatory principles, is key to this framework, and critique is embedded within it. TSI accedes to the view that ISD 'problems' are not amenable to engineered solutions, so that developing information systems is not best served by approaches based on step-by-step, project management techniques. The TSI ideology explicitly recognises the part played by both technical and human activities in organisations, and the extent to which human interpretation may in some instances so distort the so called 'real world' that study of the latter may become meaningless.

Implementation of the principles of TSI is through the three modes of critical review, critical reflection and problem solving, and the three phases of creativity, choice and implementation (Figure 3). In the problem-solving and critical reflection modes, the circle connecting the three phases of TSI is to be read in both a clockwise and anti-clockwise direction. Clockwise it directs the intervention; anti-clockwise it indicates critical reflection at each phase.

Problem Solving and Critical Reflection using TSI
Creativity

In the problem-solving mode, creativity progresses in the clockwise direction, surfacing the issues to be dealt with. In the critical reflection mode, creativity in an anti-clockwise direction receives the output of implementation, in the form of change proposals, to re-evaluate. Creativity in TSI was originally

Table 2: Metaphor in Organisational Analysis

Morgan	Flood
Machine	Machine
Organism	Organic
Brain	Neuro-cybernetic
Culture	Socio-cultural
Political	Socio-political
Psychic prison	
Flux and transformation	
Instrument of domination	

based exclusively on the use of metaphor. A key application of the use of metaphor to organisational studies has been undertaken by Morgan (1986), whose original eight metaphors, together with Flood's adaptation of them, are reproduced in Table 2 below.

Creativity has since been expanded (Flood, 1995) to include all techniques which may be categorised as 'brainstorming', including, in addition to the use of metaphors, lateral thinking (de Bono, 1977), idealised design (Ackoff, 1981), and phases 1 to 5 of soft systems methodology (Checkland, 1989). The creativity phase of TSI enables the situation to be seen from a number of different angles, allowing a clearer appreciation of the system and hence a more carefully guided intervention. The output is then synthesised by the use of techniques such as metaphors and lateral thinking, and re-contextualised to make choices about the issues to be managed (see Flood and Jackson, 1991).

Choice

Choice in the problem-solving (clockwise) mode receives the interacting issues to be applied to the problem situation, and in the critical reflection (anti-clockwise) mode reflects on whether creativity surfaced an adequate appreciation of the 'mess'. The choice phase of TSI aims to select appropriate intervention methodologies by employing a complementarist framework of designing, debating and disimprisoning (Table 3).

Table 3: The Complementarist Framework (Flood, 1995, p.183)		
Designing	Debating	Disimprisoning
Machine	Socio-Cultural	Socio-Political
Organic		
Neuro-Cybernetic		

In this framework, type of method can be chosen by asking which of the following questions is most pertinent (after Flood, 1995, p.185): How should we do it: this is addressing issues of design, and must therefore assume that consensus already exists; What should we do: addressing issues of debate, and therefore assuming non coercive consensus is achievable; Who will benefit / Why should we do it: addressing issues of disimprisoning, where disagreement, power or coercion are prime.

In the creativity phase, interpretivist methods are used to surface the main issues and prioritise them. Here in the choice phase, these issues must be taken forward toward implementation.

Implementation

Implementation in the problem-solving (clockwise) mode implements the methodologies most suitable to managing the issues surfaced within the problem situation, and in the critical reflection (anti-clockwise) mode reflects on whether these were the most suitable methods.

TOTAL SYSTEMS INTERVENTION AND INFORMATION SYSTEMS DEVELOPMENT

Space limitations for this paper prohibit the inclusion of case work undertaken using this approach. However, it has been tested in a major longitudinal information systems development (see Lehaney and Clarke, 1997; Clarke and Lehaney, 1998), and whilst issues requiring resolution have surfaced, the findings in general point to the value of future development of information systems development informed from a critical social perspective.

CONCLUSIONS

Information systems development (ISD) is dominated by pragmatic, problem-solving ('functionalist') approaches, against which soft ('interpretative') methods have been promoted as more relevant to the human-centred context of typical IS developments.

This paper argues that neither hard nor soft approaches offer an adequate basis for ISD, and points to a need for replacement with a framework which adequately serves both perspectives. Such a framework, it is argued, is to be found in developments based on critical social theory, from which total systems intervention emerges as currently the most theoretically and practically sound means of combining methodologies from different sociological paradigms within a critically reflective approach.

REFERENCES

Ackoff, R. L. (1981). *Creating the Corporate Future*. New York, Wiley

Beath, C. M. and W. J. Orlikowski (1994). "The Contradictory Structure of Systems Development Methodologies: Deconstructing the IS-User Relationship in Information Engineering." *Information Systems Research* 5(4): 350-377.

Boehm, B. W. (1989). A Spiral Model of Software Development and Enhancement. *Software Risk Management*. B. W. Boehm. Washington D.C., IEEE Computer Society Press: 26-37.

Britton, G. A. and H. McCallion (1994). "An Overview of the Singer/Churchman/Ackoff school of thought." *Systems Practice* 7(5): 487-522.

Burrell, G. and G. Morgan (1979). *Sociological Paradigms and Organisational Analysis*. London, Heinemann

Checkland, P. B. (1989). "Soft Systems Methodology." *Human Systems Management* 8(4): 273-289.

Checkland, P. B. (1994). *Systems Thinking, Systems Practice*. Chichester, Wiley

Churchman, C. W. (1968). *The Systems Approach*. New York, Dell

Clarke, S. A. and B. Lehaney (1998). Information Systems Intervention: A Total Systems View. *Modelling for Added Value*. R. Paul and S. Warwick. London, Springer-Verlag: 103-115.

de Bono, E. (1977). *Lateral Thinking*. Aylesbury, U.K., Pelican Books, Hazell Watson & Viney Ltd: 260.

Flood, R. L. (1990). *Liberating Systems Theory*. New York, Plenum

Flood, R. L. (1995). "Total Systems Intervention (TSI): A Reconstitution." *Journal of the Operational Research Society* 46: 174-191.

Flood, R. L. and M. C. Jackson (1991). *Creative Problem Solving: Total Systems Intervention*. Chichester, Wiley

Habermas, J. (1971). *Knowledge and Human Interests*. Boston, Beacon Press

Hirschheim, R. and H. K. Klein (1989). "Four Paradigms of Information Systems Development." *Communications of the ACM* 32(10): 1199-1216.

Jackson, M. C. (1982). "The Nature of Soft Systems Thinking: The Work of Churchman, Ackoff and Checkland." *Applied Systems Analysis* 9: 17-28.

Jackson, M. C. (1991). *Five Commitments of Critical Systems Thinking*. Systems Thinking in Europe (Conference Proceedings), Huddersfield, Plenum: 61-71.

Jackson, M. C. (1992). "An Integrated Programme for Critical Thinking in Information Systems Research." *Journal of Information Systems* 2: 83-95.

Jackson, M. C. (1993). "Social Theory and Operational Research Practice." *Journal of the Operational Research Society* 44(6): 563-577.

Jackson, M. C. and P. Keys (1984). "Towards a System of Systems Methodologies." *Journal of the Operational Research Society* 35(6): 473-486.

Klein, H., K. and R. Hirschheim (1993). "An Application of Neohumanist Principles in Information Systems Development." *Human, Organizational and Social Dimensions of Information Systems Development* A-24: 263-280.

Lehaney, B. and S. A. Clarke (1997). *Critical Approaches to Information Systems Development: Some Practical Implications*. Systems for Sustainability: People, Organizations, and Environments, Milton Keynes, U.K., Plenum: 333-338.

Lyytinen, K. and R. Hirschheim (1987). Information Systems Failures: A Survey and Classification of the Empirical Literature. *Oxford Surveys in Information Technology*. Oxford, Oxford University Press. 4: 257-309.

Lyytinen, K. and R. Hirschheim (1989). Information Systems and Emancipation: Promise or Threat? *Systems Development for Human Progress*. H. K. Klein and K. Kumar. Amsterdam, North Holland: 115-139.

Midgley, G. (1995). "Mixing Methods: Developing Systemic Intervention." *Hull University Research Memorandum* No. 9.

Midgley, G. (1995). *What is This Thing Called Critical Systems Thinking*. Critical Issues in Systems Theory and Practice, Hull, U.K., Plenum: 61-71.

Morgan, G. (1986). *Images of Organisation*. Beverly Hills, Sage

Mumford, E. (1985). "Defining System Requirements to meet Business Needs: a Case Study Example." *The Computer Journal* 28(2): 97-104.

Oliga, J. C. (1991). Methodological Foundations of Systems Methodologies. *Critical Systems Thinking: Directed Readings*. R. L. Flood and M. C. Jackson. Chichester, Wiley: 159-184.

Reynolds, G. W. (1995). *Information Systems for Managers*. St. Paul MN, West

Stowell, F. A. (1991). *Client Participation in Information Systems Design*. Systems Thinking in Europe (Conference Proceedings), Huddersfield, Plenum

Stowell, F. A. and D. West (1994). "'Soft' systems thinking and information systems: a framework for client-led design." *Information Systems Journal* 4(2): 117-127.

Wetherbe, J. C. and N. P. Vitalari (1994). *Systems Analysis and Design: Best Practices*. St. Paul, MN, West

Property Maps: A New Secondary Access Mechanism

Karen C. Davis
Database Systems Laboratory, ECECS Department, University of Cincinnati, Cincinnati, OH 45221-0030
karen.davis@uc.edu, phone: 513-556-2214, fax: 513-556-7326

Baskaran Dharmarajan
Microsoft Corporation, 3590 N. First St., Ste. 300, San Jose, CA 95134
baskd@microsoft.com

ABSTRACT

A new secondary access structure called a property map is introduced and illustrated with an example relational database. A property map concisely stores information about properties of data, where properties refers to enumerated, range, or boolean categorizations of data values. Property maps are a multi-attribute indexing structure that capture more semantics of an application than traditional multi-attribute techniques, although not as much fine-grained detail.

Property maps provide a superset of the functionality of bitmap indexes and support richer semantics. An overview of how property maps can be utilized for query optimization, for both query rewriting and query evaluation, is provided. It is anticipated that property maps will be useful in data mining and data warehousing scenarios where stored data, frequently executed queries, or discovered patterns can be characterized by our notion of properties.

INTRODUCTION

This paper introduces a new secondary access structure called a property map that concisely stores selected properties of data. A property map is similar to a bitmap index except that every value in a domain is not indexed; instead, query expressions that result in an enumerated, range, or Boolean value are stored and utilized for query optimization. A theoretical framework for using property maps to optimize queries is defined and we give an overview of the process. Query transformation consists of first identifying relevant parts of a property map for a particular query, then using them to rewrite the query to facilitate retrieval. The research reported here has been funded by the U.S. Department of Energy to explore the feasibility of using property maps for indexing the data generated by high energy nuclear physics experiments [6].

In order to illustrate the terminology and algorithms developed here, an example business application is given. The business has three departments, Sales, Production and Collection. Each of the departments maintains its own records of its business transactions. The Sales department has records of sales transactions. Each of the sales invoices goes into its respective ledger. Each ledger might contain multiple records representing multiple sales invoices. Similarly, the Production department has its own records of the quantity and cost of the various batches of products produced. The Collection department is responsible for collection of the sales amounts, possibly in multiple installments, from customers. The data is collected into three relations to provide a summary overview of the state of business at any time. The following is a description of the relations that appear in Figure 1. Keys are underlined, and the number of bytes occupied by each attribute is given in parentheses.

The attribute *productCode* represents a single product where the first byte represents a department (A to Z), the second byte represents a product category (0 to 9), and the rest of the bytes represent the series number and model number. The attribute *month* ranges from 1 to 12, and the year includes both the twentieth and twenty-first centuries. The ledger fields indicate where the original records are located that are the source for the summary information recorded in the relation. The relation *Sales* has the attributes *area1sales* and *area2sales* that give the sales amounts for area

---

Figure 1. A Sample Schema

Sales(<u>productCode</u> (10), <u>month</u> (1), <u>year</u> (1), <u>salesLedger</u> (4),
    area1sales (4), area2sales (4), sales(4))
Production(<u>productCode</u> (10), <u>month</u> (1), <u>year</u> (1), <u>productionLedger</u> (4),
    unitsProduced (4), costPerUnit (4))
Collection(<u>productCode</u> (10), <u>month</u> (1), <u>year</u> (1), collectionLedger (4), collection (4))

1 and area 2, respectively. The relation *Sales* also has the attribute *sales* that provides the total sales amount for all the areas. The relation *Production* has attributes *unitsProduced* and *costPerUnit* that represent the number of units produced and the cost incurred per unit, respectively. The relation *Collection* gives the collection amounts for each product per month and year.

The database administrator provides us with additional information that the following properties are of interest and queried often.

1 The attribute *category* is a calculated value and has values 0 to 9. It is based on the attribute *productCode*.

2 Most queries are for the last six months. The data before six months are considered historical. Out of these, the last quarter sales are most important.

3 Queries are requested over the area sales fields, *area1sales* and *area2sales*, as follows:
   a) Into what range did the area sales figure fall? The available ranges of interest for sales figure are 0 to 1 million, 1 to 2 million 2, to 3 million, and greater than 3 million.
   b) Is the area sales field greater than the area sales of the previous month for each area?

4 The properties of sales amount that are of interest are as follows:
   a) Are sales greater than the production amount for the same month (where production amount is calculated as the product of *unitsProduced* and *costPerUnit*)?
   b) Is the collection rate greater than, equal to, or less than .8? The collection ratio is a ratio of the collection amount to the sales amount for the past three months. The collection rate for the current month is not meaningful as the values are still volatile.

We now investigate how to use the above application semantics to improve data retrieval. One way is to design a secondary access structure that concisely stores the properties and provides efficient access to data. We propose that these properties be stored as a bit map structure. The bit map contains several bit strings, each of which represents the value of the properties for one tuple. Within a bit string, a single bit or a group of bits may represent a particular property. Bit maps are compact and can be efficiently manipulated by computers. For the additional application semantics provided above, Figure 2 represents a table of properties that we call a property map. We give an overview of the information that can be represented in a property map here. The details of the structure are explained in the following section.

The column "meaning" gives the values that the property can have and what the values mean. For example, the property *period* can have values from 0 to 7. A value of 0 for *period* means that the value of the attribute month in a tuple represents the current month. The column "bits" gives the number of bits required to represent the property. For example, *period* requires three bits to represent the eight values from 0 to 7.

One important characteristic that we observe in this table is the conciseness of the structure. The data in the example presented earlier in Figure 1 spans over 70 bytes per tuple. The properties of these tuples occupy only 15 bits

Figure 2. A Property Map Example

property name	description	values	meaning	bits
productCategory	product category	0-9	category code	4
period	range of months	0-7	0: current month	3
			1: previous month	
			2: 2 months prior to current	
			3: 3 months prior to current	
			4: previous quarter	
			5: previous 6 months	
			6: previous year	
			7: all years prior to previous	
area1salesRange	range of area 1 sales	0-3	0: 0-1M	2
			1: 1-2M	
			2: 2-3M	
			3: ≥ 3M	
area2salesRange	range of area 2 sales	0-3	(same as for area 1)	2
greaterSales	this month's sales compared to last month's sales	0-1	0: less or equal	1
			1: greater	
inventoryControl	this month's sales compared to production	0-1	0: less or equal	1
			1: greater	
collectionControl	collection rate compared to .8	0-3	0: less	2
			1: equal	
			2: greater	
			3: not meaningful	

when represented as a property map. Some of the properties are really pre-computed information rather than just characteristics of raw data; this avoids frequent re-computation if queries often use the information.

The example introduced in this section serves as a running example throughout this paper. Section 2 presents the structure of a property map and the associated terminology. Section 3 develops the theory that allows us to use property maps to optimize a query. Section 4 provides a brief overview of the query transformation and execution processes; first, properties useful in optimizing a given query are identified, then the query is rewritten, and then a retrieval strategy is generated. Conclusions and comparison to related work are offered in Section 5.

DEFINITION OF PROPERTY MAPS

Informally, a property can be thought of as a characteristic or categorization of data stored in a relation. Properties that are frequently queried upon are used to form property maps. More precisely, a property is a mapping of a function over attributes to bit strings. An example of a property is given in Figure 3.

Definition 2.1. A *property* is defined as $P(F(X))$ where X is a set of attributes, possibly singleton; $F:t(X) \to r$ is a many to one mapping from $t(X)$ to r; $t(X)$ is the extent of the relation formed by concatenating attributes in X; r is a value from a given range of values; $P:r \to b$ maps a value in a range to a bit string of fixed length.

Figure 3. An Example Property		
term	example	explanation
X	collection, sales	$t(X)$, the extent of X, contains tuples representing collection and sales for the past three months
$F(t(X))$	CollectionRate(collection, sales) $\to$ resultOfCollectionRate	CollectionRate() returns the value obtained by dividing the amount collected in the past three months by the sales amount for the past three months; for the current month, CollectionRate() returns a negative value.
r	resultOfCollectionRate	A real number between -1 and 1 representing the range of the function CollectionRate().
$P:r \to b$	resultOfCollectionRate $\to$ {00, 01, 10, 11}	P maps the value of resultOfCollectionRate to a string of two bits, where 00 means resultOfCollectionRate is less than 0.8, 01 means resultOfCollectionRate is equal to 0.8, 10 means resultOfCollectionRate is greater than 0.8, and 11 means resultOfCollectionRate is negative.

A property string (pstring) is a string of bits that represents the value of a collection of properties for a tuple. Values and pstrings for two example *Sales* tuples are given below.

Sales	productCode	month	year	area1Sales	area2Sales	sales
	A1EPRY2345	1	96	3.3 million	2.4 million	6 million
	A1EPRY2345	2	96	4.6 million	2.2 million	6.8 million

Definition 2.2. A *property string* is an ordered list of groups of one or more bits, where each B_i, $1 £ i £ n$, represents the value of a property. The concatenation of the bit strings B_1, B_2, ..., B_n in order is called a property string or pstring.

Assume that the current month is 2/96, collection for 1/96 for the product A1EPRY2345 is 4 million. In January 1996 1.2 million units of A1EPRY2345 were produced at $5 a piece; in February 1996 1 million units of A1EPRY2345 were produced at a cost of $7 per unit. The property values and composition of corresponding pstrings are given in Figure 4. Concatenating the values in the last column results in the bit string 000100111101000, which represents the pstring for the first *Sales* tuple above. A similar calculation for the second tuple results in the pstring 000100011101011.

A *property map (pmap)* is a concise representation of properties that serves as a secondary access structure. It consists of physical component (physical property map) and a description component (meta property map).

Figure 4. An Example Property String		
property name	value of relevant fields	B_i
productCategory	productCode = A1EPRY2345	0001
period	month/year = 1/96	001
area1salesRange	area1sales = 3.3 million	11
area2salesRange	area2sales = 2.4 million	10
greaterSales	(There is no previous month)	1
inventoryControl	production 6 million, sales = 6 million	0
collectionControl	resultOfCollectionRate = .66	00

A *physical property map (ppmap)* is a list of pstrings, stored as a continuous stream of bits. The continuous stream of bits is demarcated into individual pstrings and property values using the information in the meta property map described below. In other words, the physical pmap is meaningful for query optimization purposes only in the context of a meta pmap. An index into the physical pmap, pmap[tuple ID, property ID], gives the bit value of the property indicated by the property ID for the pstring indicated by the tuple ID.

A *meta property map (mpmap)* is loosely defined as the schema of a pmap. It describes the meaning of each property and its layout in the physical property map. We envision the mpmap as a set of property structures each representing one property. A property structure contains the following information:

1. *propID*: an identifier that uniquely identifies the property.
2. *propName*: a descriptive name for convenience of usage.
3. *propType*: the tag field that describes the type of the values that the property can have. The field propType and the field valueSet (described below) together indicate the range of the property (r). The tag is one of:
   - enumerated: the value of the property comes from a set of discrete values. The actual set is supplied with each property.
   - range: the value of the property comes from a range. The actual range is supplied for each property.
   - Boolean: the value of the property is true or false.
4. *disjunct$_p$*: a disjunct that describes the property. We use disjunctive normal form for queries (described in the next section.) Each disjunct in a DNF expression is actually a conjuctive expression. Each predicate in a property disjunct is called a property predicate and is denoted by the symbol "predicate$_p$" . The structure of a property disjunct is restricted on the basis of the value of the field propType. If the property is of enumerated or range type, the field disjunct$_p$ is a single predicate that is of the form <attribute-expression> and evaluates to a numeric value. Some examples for valid values for the field disjunct$_p$ are "area1sales," "area1sales + area2sales," and "CategoryOf(productCode)." Some examples of invalid values for the field disjunct$_p$ are "area1sales > area2sales" (more than one attribute expression), "area1sales > 3000000" (Boolean predicate), "productCode == A1EPRY2345" (Boolean predicate) and productCode (even though productCode is a valid attribute-expression, it evaluates to a string and not a number). For properties of Boolean type, the field disjunct$_p$ can have any valid conjunctive expression.
5. *valueSet*: the range of the property or the set from which the property takes values for each tuple in the view. We use a triple (lowerLimit, intervalSize, upperLimit) to describe the set.

   If the property is *enumerated*, then the values fall into the set {lower limit, lower limit + interval size, lower limit + 2 * interval size, ..., upper limit}. For example, if the triple is (0, 1, 3) then the set described is {0, 1, 2, 3}. In the physical pmap, these values are represented in their binary form as the bit strings {00, 01, 10, 11}.

   If the property is of type *range*, then the values fall into a range from a lower limit to an upper limit. This range is divided into intervals whose size is given by interval size. For example, (0, 100, 500) denotes the range of values from zero to infinity (the term "infinity" is used for a very high value limited by the word length of the computer on which the algorithms are implemented.) that is divided into the intervals 0 to 100, 100 to 200, 200 to 300, 300 to 400, 400 to 500 and 500 to infinity so that the corresponding bit representation in the ppmap is {000, 001, 010, 011, 100, 101}.

   For a *Boolean* property, the range is pre-defined as the set {false, true} with a corresponding representation of {0, 1}.

   The variables above describe the meaning of the property or what it represents. The following variables are used to describe how a property is represented in a ppmap.
6. *numberOfBitsUsed*: the number of bits that are used to represent the value of the property for each tuple.
7. *startingPosition*: the position or column from which the bits representing a property start in the pstring.
8. *statistics*: an array of statistics associated with the property. The meaning of the array depends upon the type of the property; in general, each position represents the percentage of tuples with the binary value for a property corresponding to the position.

The meta pmap for our running example is represented in Figure 5. (The statistics field is omitted for simplicity.)

The meta property structure described above has several limitations that we discuss below. All of the limitations can be removed if the algorithms that are discussed later in this work are updated to work with more complex value sets for enumerated and range properties or if new property types are defined to permit more expressive conditions to be represented by properties. We envision this work as a future enhancement.

1. Enumerated and range properties can have only numerical values.
2. Enumerated properties can have only discrete numerical values separated by intervals of equal size. For example, an enumerated property can have values such as {0, 2, 4, 8, ..., 20} and not values such as {0, 3, 4, 5, 7, 9, 10, ..., 20}, where the discrete values are spaced unequally in the interval 0 to 20.
3. Range properties can have values from a continuous range split into intervals that are equally sized except for the final interval. For example, a range property can have values in intervals such as {0 to 100, 100 to 200, 200 to 300, 300 to infinity} and not values in intervals such as {0 to 100, 100 to 150, 200 to 320, 320 to infinity}.
4. Comparison of attributes with string values such as "productCode == A1EPRY2345" and attribute to attribute

Figure 5. Meta Property Map

propName	disjunct$_p$	propType	valueSet	position	bits
product category	Category(productCode)	enum	(0, 1, 9)	0	4
period	Period(month, year)	enum	(0, 1, 7)	4	3
area1salesRange	area1sales	range	(0, 1, 3) M	7	2
area2salesRange	area2sales	range	(0, 1, 3) M	9	2
greaterSales	(month1 == month0 + 1) AND (sales0 > sales1)	boolean		11	1
inventoryControl	(unitsProduced * costPerUnit > sales) AND (production.month == sales.month)} AND (production.year == sales.year)} AND (production.productCode == sales.productCode)	boolean		12	1
collectionControl	CollectionRate(collection, sales)	enum	3	13	2

comparisons such as "area1sales > area2sales" can be represented by properties of Boolean type only.

THEORETICAL FRAMEWORK FOR PROPERTY MAPS

In order to identify which properties in a pmap are relevant to a query (where relevant means that they can be used to optimize the query), we first define the form of queries, then how they are compared to properties. If the set of tuples described by a property subsumes the set of tuples that answer a query, then it is relevant. We use a syntactic comparison for the predicates of queries and properties, called a coverlet. We then define cover for disjuncts in terms of coverlets. Based on these relationships, we develop a query reduction strategy that is used to efficiently retrieve the tuples that satisfy a query.

We view a query as a set of projections satisfying a disjunctive normal form condition. A disjunct in a query expression is denoted by the symbol "disjunct$_q$" and a predicate in a query disjunct is denoted by the symbol "predicate$_q$."

The Coverlet Relation

Assume that x is an attribute over a simple domain, q is a predicate$_q$ and p is a predicate$_p$. Let the set of pstrings that satisfy the predicate$_p$ p be pstringSet$_p$; the set of pstrings that correspond to the tuples that satisfy the predicate$_q$ q is pstringSet$_q$. Let -pstringSet$_p$ be the complement of the set pstringSet$_p$.

A coverlet is a relation between a predicate$_q$ and a predicate$_p$. It has a grade and a type. The grade may be one of exactcover, supercover, or subcover, and if the type is positive, indicates that pstringSet$_p$ is equal to, is a superset of, or is a subset of pstringSet$_q$, respectively. If the type is negative, then -pstringSet$_p$ has an exactcover, supercover, or subcover relationship with pstringSet$_q$, respectively.

Definition 3.1. The relation *coverlet(p, q)* between predicate$_p$ p and predicate$_q$ q is defined as follows:

1. If pstringSet$_p$ = pstringSet$_q$, the grade of the coverlet relation is exactcover and the type is positive.
   For example, let p be (x > 3) and q be (x > 3). The tuples described by p and q are identical.
2. If pstringSet$_p$ ... pstringSet$_q$ the grade of the coverlet relation is supercover and the type is positive.
   For example, let p be (x ≥ 3) and q be (x > 3); pstringSet$_p$ contains all the pstrings in pstringSet$_q$ and possibly others.
3. If pstringSet$_p$ Ã pstringSet$_q$, the grade of the coverlet relation is subcover and the type is positive.
   For example, let p be (x > 3) and q be (x ≥ 3); pstringSet$_p$ contains some of the pstrings that are contained in pstringSet$_q$.
4. If -pstringSet$_p$ = pstringSet$_q$, the grade of the relation coverlet(p, q) is exactcover and type is negative.
   For example, let p be (x < 3) and q be (x ≥ 3); pstringSet$_p$ and pstringSet$_q$ are disjoint, however, -pstringSet$_p$ and the set pstringSet$_q$ are the same (i.e., -pstringSet$_p$ = pstringSet$_q$).
5. If -pstringSet$_p$ ... pstringSet$_q$, the grade of the relation coverlet(p, q) is supercover and type is negative.
   For example, let p be (x < 3) and q be (x = 3); the set -pstringSet$_p$ contains all the pstrings in pstringSet$_q$ and possibly others (i.e., pstringSet$_p$ ... pstringSet$_q$).
6. If -pstringSet$_p$ Ã pstringSet$_q$, the grade of the relation coverlet(p, q) is subcover and type is negative.
   For example, let p be (x £ 3) and q be (x ≥ 3). The set -pstringSet$_p$ contains some of the pstrings that are contained in pstringSet$_q$, but not all.

Considering the simple case where q and p are identical on their left and right hand sides (for example, if q is (x < 3) and p is (x = 3), then their left and right sides agree), Figure 6 gives the grade and type of coverlet(p, q). This table is called the CoverletComputationTable and is used by our algorithms for computing the grade and type of a coverlet relation; proofs of the cases in the table are straightforward [1]. Expanding the coverlet computation is

---

Figure 6. Coverlet Computation Table

Comparison Operator in the predicate$_q$

predicate$_p$	<	≤	=	≥	>	≠
<	+/exactcover	+/supercover	-/supercover	-/exactcover	-/supercover	+/subcover
≤	+/supercover	+/exactcover	+/supercover	-/subcover	-/exactcover	-/subcover
=	-/supercover	+/subcover	+/exactcover	+/subcover	-/supercover	-/exactcover
≥	-/exactcover	-/subcover	+/supercover	+/exactcover	+/supercover	-/subcover
>	-/supercover	-/exactcover	-/supercover	+/subcover	+/exactcover	+/subcover
≠	+/supercover	-/subcover	-/exactcover	-/subcover	+/supercover	+/exactcover

---

considered a future extension of this work.

The Cover Relation

The cover relation represents the result of a comparison between a disjunct representing a property (disjunct$_p$) and a disjunct in the query condition (disjunct$_q$); it has a grade and a type.

Definition 3.2. The relation *cover(P, Q)* between disjunct$_p$ P and disjunct$_q$ Q is defined as:

1. If every predicate$_p$ in P has a coverlet relation with a predicate$_q$ in Q, every predicate$_q$ in Q has a coverlet with a predicate$_p$ in P, and all the coverlet relations are of the same type (either positive or negative), the grade of the cover relation is exactcover and the type is the type of the coverlet relations.

   For example, let P be "((x ≥ 3) AND (x ≥ y))" and Q be "((x > 3) AND (x = y))." The predicate$_p$ "(x ≥ 3)" in P has a coverlet relation with the predicate$_q$ "(x > 3)" in Q that is of type positive. The predicate$_p$ "(x ≥ y)" in P has a coverlet relation with the predicate$_q$ (x = y) in Q that is also of type positive. Thus every predicate$_p$ in P and predicate$_q$ in Q are involved in coverlets that are of the same type, namely, positive. In this case, cover(P, Q) is of grade exactcover and type positive.

2. If at least one predicate$_q$ in Q does not have a coverlet relation of the common type with any of the predicate$_p$ in P, but all the other predicate$_q$ in Q have coverlets of a common type (either positive or negative), the grade of the cover relation is supercover and the type is the common type of the coverlet relations of the predicate$_p$.

   For example, let P be "(x ≥ 3)" and Q be "((x > 3) AND (x != y))." The only predicate$_p$ in P, "(x ≥ 3)," has a coverlet relation with the predicate$_q$ in Q, "(x > 3)." But the predicate$_q$ "(x != y)" in Q does not have a coverlet relation with any of the predicate$_p$ in P. In this case, cover(P, Q) is of grade supercover and type positive.

3. If every predicate$_q$ in Q has a coverlet relation of a common type with some predicate$_p$ in P, but there is a predicate$_p$ that has no coverlet relationship with a predicate$_q$, the grade of the cover relation is subcover and the type is the common type of the coverlet relations of the predicate$_q$.

   For example, let P be "((x ≥ 3) AND (x > y)) "and Q be "(x > 3)." The predicate$_p$ "(x > y)" in P does not share a coverlet relation with any of the predicate$_q$ in Q. The only predicate$_q$ in Q, "(x > 3)," has a coverlet relationship with the predicate$_p$ "(x ≥ 3)" in P. In this case, the cover(P, Q) is of grade subcover and type positive.

A cover relation between P and Q depends on the coverlet relations between the predicates in P and Q to the degree that they exist and are of the same type. However, the grade of the cover relation between P and Q and the grade of the coverlet relations shared by the predicates in P and Q may vary. For example, if P is "(x > 3) AND (x ≥ y)," and Q is "(x ≥ 3) AND (x > y)," then cover(P, Q) is of type positive with grade exactcover. However, the coverlet relation between the property predicate "(x > 3)" and the query predicate "(x ≥ 3)" has a grade subcover and the coverlet relation between "(x ≥ y)" and "(x > y)" has a grade supercover. Even though the predicates in P and Q have coverlets with grade subcover and supercover, cover(P, Q) has grade exactcover. Note that cover alone is insufficient for query optimization; we define the reduction operation for query transformation using coverlet and cover in the next section.

QUERY PROCESSING

If a property in a property map is related to a query, it can have one of three grades: cover, supercover, and subcover. Subcover is not useful for query optimization. For cover and supercover, there are several cases of interest where a property can be used to optimize a query. These cases are discussed below. No additional disk access is necessary (the tuples retrieved using the property map are exactly the same as or a superset of the tuples satisfying the query.)

Reduction is used to define query transformation and transformed queries are evaluated in the subsequent sections. Algorithms for these activities, along with analysis of their computational complexity, are given elsewhere [6].

Definition 4.1. A query predicate q in a query disjunct Q can be *reduced* by a property P containing a property predicate p if and only if:

1. coverlet(p, q) holds with grade exactcover or supercover, and
2. cover(P, Q) holds with grade exactcover or supercover.

If a query predicate is not reduced by any property in the pmap, then the query predicate is said to be *unreduced*.

If a coverlet relation of a query predicate reduced by a property has grade supercover, then the query predicate is said to be *partially reduced*; otherwise, if the grade of the coverlet relation is exactcover, the query predicate is *fully reduced*. Similarly, if all the query predicates in a query predicate are unreduced, then the query disjunct is unreduced. If some of the query predicates in a query disjunct are partially reduced, then the query disjunct is said to be partially reduced; otherwise, the query disjunct is fully reduced (in this case, all the query predicates in the query disjunct are fully reduced).

If a query disjunct is unreduced, then the pmap is not useful in efficiently executing the query disjunct at all. The tuples that satisfy the query disjunct can be obtained through conventional query execution methods and may require additional disk access and selection. If a query disjunct is partially reduced, at least one of the coverlet or cover relations that lead to the reduction has a grade of supercover and so additional selection is required. In other words, the set of tuples that correspond to the pstrings that have specific values for the properties that reduce a given query disjunct may be a superset of the set of tuples that satisfy the query disjunct. If a query disjunct is fully reduced, no additional disk access or selection is required. In other words, the set of tuples that correspond to the pstrings that have specific values for the properties that reduce a given query disjunct is equal to the set of the tuples that satisfy the query disjunct.

Query Transformation

Our theoretical framework is utilized by a process called query transformation to identify properties that are useful in executing a query using a property map. Query transformation refers to the rewriting of a query such that a query predicate is replaced by a property expression (possibly with appropriate constant values substituted.) Note that our theoretical framework considers any property expressed as a conjunctive expression and any query in disjunctive normal form. In particular, we do not make any references to the structure proposed for meta and physical property maps. It is a topic for future investigation to use the theory developed here with other secondary access structures.

Definition 4.2. A query is *transformed* using a property map if all the query predicates in the query that are reducible using properties in the property map are reduced.

We now provide an example to illustrate the query transformation process.

The query: *select category from sales where (area1sales ≥ 3000000)* reduces to: *select category from sales where (area1salesRange == 11).*

The query needs tuples for which *area1sales* is greater than 3 million. Any pstring that has the value 11 for the *area1salesRange* property satisfies the criterion set by the query.

Query Execution

The query execution process performs the following steps to retrieve the set of tuples that satisfy a transformed query Q:

1. search for the pstrings where the property p is true in the property map,
2. retrieve the tuples corresponding to the pstrings that satisfy the property, and
3. remove tuples that do not satisfy Q.

The task in the first step is to search for a property expression of the form "<property > == <bit-value>" in the property map. To perform the search, we test if the part of the pstring that represents the property <property> has the value <bit-value> for each pstring in the property map. Note that the parts of a pstring that represent properties other than the property <property> are of no concern in the search. To mask out the properties that are not of interest in a search, we use a bit-mask structure called a *pmask*. To specify the value <bit-value> for which the search is conducted, we use a bit string structure called a *pfilter*. The values of the pmask and pfilter are such that if a string passes the test "pstring AND pmask == pfilter," the pstring satisfies the search condition "<property> == <bit-value>" and if a string passes the test "pstring AND pmask != pfilter," the pstring satisfies the search condition "<property> != <bit-value>." The test conditions "pstring AND pmask == pfilter" and "pstring AND pmask != pfilter" are called *filter formulae*. The process of applying a pfilter-pmask pair using a filter formula to each pstring in a set of pstrings is called *filtering*. For example, consider the query "give all categories of products for which area1sales greater than 3 million and area2sales greater than 2 million," that can be represented in SQL as:

select category from sales
where (area1sales ≥ 3000000) AND (area2sales ≥ 2000000)

The query reduces to:
select category from sales
where (area1salesRange == 11) AND (area2salesRange == 10)

The property expression *(area1salesRange == 11)* is the result of the reduction of the condition *(area1sales ≥ 3000000)* in the query and the property expression *(area2salesRange == 10)* is the reduction of the condition *(area2sales > 2000000)* in the query. The pfilter is derived by setting the bits corresponding to the property *area1salesRange* to the value 11 and setting the bit string corresponding to the property to the value 10. The pmask is derived by setting all the bits corresponding to the properties *area1salesRange* and *area2salesrange* to the value 1 and resetting all other bits to 0. The computation results in the pfilter 000000011100000 and pmask 000000011110000.

The general idea is that the pmask masks out all bits that are not of interest to a particular query and the pfilter contains the bit values of the properties such that the pstrings with the bit values satisfy a given property expression. The filtering process described here can be implemented very efficiently. Note that the pfilter and pmask contain the same number of bits as the pstrings in the ppmap. If the number of bits in the pstrings are not greater than the number of bits in the registers of the Central Processing Unit (CPU), pfilter and pmask can be held in the registers. If the pstrings are not wider than the data bus, each pstring can be fetched in one fetch operation.

CONCLUSIONS

We define the structure of a property map and describe its components. We develop a theoretical framework that enables the property map to be used in efficiently executing a query.

We compare property maps with a few other secondary access mechanisms that are similar to property maps, namely multi-attribute hashing [2] and bitmap indexes [9, 10]. Note that these are all general-purpose secondary access mechanisms, and property maps are more special-purpose since they essentially represent views rather than entire relations.

The record signatures used by multi-attribute hashing are analogous to pstrings in property maps. Each signature is comparable to the part of the pstring that represents the value of a property. The query signature is analogous to the bit pattern represented by a pfilter-pmask pair. The advantages of property maps over multi-attribute hashing are that property maps are based on properties whereas multi-attribute hashing is based on attribute values. This enables property maps to represent not only the characteristics of an attribute value, but also characteristics of relationships between two or more attribute values. In addition, property maps can represent characteristics of relationships between the data in two or more relations. These observations also apply to secondary access mechanisms based on attribute values, including Grid Files [4], variations of binary trees such as B+ trees, R-trees [5], k-d-B trees [11], and hB-trees [6].

The disadvantages of a property map when compared to multi-attribute hashing include the following. For queries where most of the attribute values are specified, unless hashing is used for retrieval, property maps perform the filtering process for all the pstrings in the property map, which is computationally more intensive than hashing. However, if hashing is used for retrieval of query answers, the filtering process can be avoided [1]. For queries where all the predicates are of the form, "attribute comparison-operator constant-value," using property maps might be costlier than using multi-attribute hashing because our query transformation process for property maps may be more computationally intensive (as it compares each query predicate to each predicate of a Boolean property.) The number of property predicates compared for a query predicate can be reduced by hashing for candidate properties [1].

It might be possible to extend multi-attribute hashing using property maps. In the extended version, record signatures are computed using the bit string values of properties rather signatures of attribute values. In other words, pstrings are used as record signatures. Query signatures are computed by placing a don't-care value "X" in pfilters at the bit positions where a pmask in the same pfilter-pmask pair has the value "0." Once the query signatures are computed (at the end of filter planning), we can use hashing instead of filtering for retrieving a query answer.

The similarities between property maps and bitmap indexes are:
• Both of them use bitmaps and bit-wise operations. While bitmap indexes represent each value of an attribute by a separate bitmap, property maps use a single physical pmap to represent the values. Property maps can model high cardinality data using range properties or Boolean conditions.
• Unless hashing is used, both property maps and bitmap indexes always process each of their members before answering a query. Both have high locality of reference and can be loaded in multiple retrievals without causing working set problems [5]. Two bitmap indexes representing different attribute values, unless stored adjacent to one

another, require retrieval from different parts of the secondary storage device. However, as the entire physical property map can be stored in subsequent blocks, property maps might be more efficiently retrieved than bitmap indexes.

A disadvantage of property maps when compared to bitmap indexes is that if a property map has properties other than those related to the ones in a query predicate, or an enumerated property for each query predicate ranging over all possible values, then the number of bytes retrieved for evaluating the query predicates is greater than the size of the corresponding individual bitmap indexes for the selected values.

As with multi-attribute hashing, property maps can be considered as an extended bitmap index, with each element representing more complex characteristics of data. Also, it is possible to apply our query processing algorithms to bitmap indexes by regarding each element in a bitmap index as representing a boolean property rather than an attribute value.

In a related effort, we develop a cost model and conduct analysis of the performance of property maps, as well as comparison to secondary access mechanisms. We implement a Signature Tree [3, 12] index over a property map, and compare its storage and retrieval performance to that of the hB-tree [6]. Our preliminary analysis shows significant improvements for storage for a very large example data set and comparable performance for disk retrieval times for point queries. We utilize an example from the ATLAS high energy nuclear physics project with 512 million instances [7]; our savings in storage is 5 times that of hB-trees (4 million disk blocks to 0.9 million disk blocks) and our disk access cost for a single point query is 6 accesses compared to 5 for an hB-tree. Further study is in progress.

ACKNOWLEDGEMENTS

Partial support provided by Department of Energy grant no. DE-FG02-97ER82428.

REFERENCES

[1] Dharmarajan, B., "The Property Map: A Theoretical Foundation and Query Optimization Algorithms," MS Thesis, ECECS Dept., University of Cincinnati, Cincinnati, OH 45221-0030, 1997.

[2] Faloutsos, C., "Multiattribute Hashing Using Gray Codes," *Proceedings of the 1986 ACM-SIGMOD International Conference on Management of Data*, Washington, D.C., May 28 - 30, 1986.

[3] French, J.C., *IDAM File Organizations*, UMI Research Press, 1985.

[4] Hinrichs, K., and J. Nievergelt, "The Grid File: A Data Structure Designed to Support Proximity Queries on Spatial Objects," Nr. 54, Institut fur Informatik, Eidgenossische Technische Hochschule, Zurich, Germany, July 1983.

[5] Guttman, A., "R-Trees: A Dynamic Index Structure for Spatial Searching," *Proceedings of the 1995 ACM-SIGMOD International Conference on Management of Data*, Boston, Massachusetts, June 18-21, 1984.

[6] Lomet, D.B., and B. Salzberg, "The hB-Tree: A Multi-attribute Indexing Method with Good Guaranteed Performance," *ACM Transactions on Database Systems*, Vol. 15, No. 4, Dec. 1990, pp. 625-658.

[7] MegaSoft Technologies/University of Cincinnati, "A New Secondary Access Mechanism for Indexing Very Large Data Sets," Department of Energy SBIR Proposal. Grant No. DE-FG02-97ER82428, September 1997.

[8] Nebel, B., "Computational Complexity of Terminological Reasoning in BACK," *Artificial Intelligence*, Vol. 34, No. 3, April, 1988.

[9] O'Neil, P., and G. Graefe, "Multi-Table Joins through Bitmapped Join Indices," *SIGMOD Record*, Vol. 24, No. 3, September 1995, pp. 8-11.

[10] Perrizo, W., K. Jian, S. Krebsbach, J. Zhang, and K. Nygard, "Method for Processing Views on Demand in Data Warehouse Environment," *Proceedings of the Ninth ISCA International Conference on Computer Applications in Industry and Engineering*, Orlando, Florida, December, 1996.

[11] Robinson, J.T., "The k-d-B tree: a Search Structure for Large Multidimensional Dynamic Indexes," *Proceedings of the 1981 ACM-SIGMOD International Conference on Management of Data*, Ann Arbor, Michigan, April 29-May 1, 1981.

[12] Tharp, A., *File Organization and Processing*, John Wiley and Sons, 1988.

Computer crime: interpreting violation of safeguards by trusted personnel

Gurpreet Dhillon

Department of Management; College of Business, University of Nevada, Las Vegas, USA

Tel: (702) 895 3676; Fax: (702) 895 4370, dhillon@ccmail.nevada.edu

ABSTRACT

A majority of computer crimes occur because internal employees of an organization subvert existing controls. This paper uses the theory of reasoned action to provide an explanation of the phenomenon of computer crime resulting because of a violation of safeguards by trusted personnel. A case study is used to generate an understanding of the nature of computer crime. In a final synthesis the paper draws out some generic principles that organizations should adopt to prevent computer crimes.

INTRODUCTION

This paper provides an explanation of the nature of computer crime resulting because of violation of safeguards by trusted personnel. Such an explanation is necessary since a majority of computer crimes within organizations take place because of illicit activities by internal employees. It has been reported that most violations of information system safeguards have been carried out by internal employees of an organization (an astonishing 61%). The actual figure is certainly higher since only 9% of the cases have been positively linked with outsiders (Strain 1991). In the US, a study by Brown (1991) reports that nearly 81% of computer crimes are committed by current employees. These insiders may be dishonest or disgruntled employees who would copy, steal, or sabotage information, yet their actions may remain undetected. In 1993 a fraud came to light against the UK National Heritage Department which had resulted in payments in excess of US$ 100,000 to fictitious organizations. This was a typical case where the organization had weak internal management controls that gave an individual the opportunity to subvert the financial system (Audit Commission 1994). In another case a small US based Internet service provider, Digital Technologies Group, had its computers completely erased, allegedly by a disgruntled employee. The dismissed employee was later arrested and faced a prison sentence of up to 20 years.

This paper is organized into five sections. Following a brief introduction, the second section explores the issue of computer crime by internal employees. A conceptual framework based on Ajzen and Fishbein's (1980) theory of reasoned action is presented. Section three presents the case study of violations of safeguards by trusted personnel. Theory of reasoned action is used to provide a qualitative explanation of the crime situations. Section four presents a discussion of emergent issues. Section five draws some general conclusions.

UNDERSTANDING THE ISSUE

Violation of safeguards by trusted personnel constitutes a kind of computer crime that is intentional in nature. Intentional acts could result in frauds, virus infections, and invasion of privacy and sabotage. Parker (1976) uses the term 'computer abuse' to describes such acts as vandalism and malicious mischief and places them in the same category as white-collar crime. White-collar crime is defined by Parker as "…any endeavor or practice involving the stifling of free enterprise or promoting of unfair competition; a breach of trust against an individual or an institution; a violation of occupational conduct or jeopardizing of consumers and clientele". Computer crime resulting because of violation of safeguards by internal employees can therefore be defined as a deliberate misappropriation by which individuals intend to gain dishonest advantages through the use of the computer systems. Misappropriation itself may be opportunist, pressured, or a single-minded calculated contrivance.

Computer crime committed by internal employees is essentially a rational act and could result because of a combination of personal factors, work situations and available opportunities (Backhouse and Dhillon 1995). Hearnden (1990) believes that most of the perpetrators are motivated by greed, financial and other personnel problems. Forester and Morrison (1994) suggests that sometimes even love and sex could provide a powerful stimulus for carrying out computer crimes. A survey conducted by the UK Audit Commission in 1994 found, in addition to personal factors, disregard for basic internal controls (password not changed, computer activities not traceable etc.) and ineffective monitoring procedures to contribute significantly to incidents of computer crime. An earlier study by Parker and Nycum (1984) found that in most organizations sufficient methods of deterrence, detection, prevention and recovery did not exist.

In another study Parker (1982) found that there was a wide range of opinions regarding the extent of computer crime. There were reports suggesting that only 374 cases were directly related to computer misuse, hence portraying computer crimes as being of minor significance. However at the same time nearly 150,000 computers had been installed within US organizations. Clearly the reported computer crime cases were an underestimation and what we actually see is just the tip of the iceberg. The UK Audit Commission study suggests that many individuals and organizations fail to recognize computer crime as a problem. Their survey found employees at the managerial and supervisory levels as falling short of understanding the risks that computer misuse presents. In fact two-third of the perpetrators were supervisors who had been in the organization for a minimum four years (Audit Commission 1994). Another study based in the US found an astonishing 31 per cent of computer crimes as being carried out by low paid clerks, 25 per cent by managers and 24 per cent by computer personnel (Oz 1994). Indeed Balsmeier and Kelly (1996) suggest that most organizations had no method to minimize or deter computer crime and that the rewards to behave unethically seem to outweigh the risks.

Conceptual framework

Given that computer crimes resulting from violation of safeguards by trusted employees are essentially rational acts, in this paper we adopt the theory of reasoned action (Ajzen and Fishbein 1980) to provide an explanation of a crime situation. Although theory of reasoned action has been acknowledged as a plausible means to analyze information technology acceptance within organizations, its use in evaluating crime situations has been rather limited. However the theory goes a long way in providing explanation of crime situations. Kesar and Rogerson (1998) use the theory to analyze technology misuse scenarios. They go further to draw out ethical principles that could be developed to prevent the occurrence of potential crime situations. In this paper we use the theory in a qualitative and an interpretive manner to analyze the case of computer crime at Kidder Peabody and Co. Prior use of the theory of reasoned action has largely taken the form of a quantitative hypothesis testing. This paper takes a more subjective qualitative approach. The theory of reasoned action is based on the assumption that human beings are usually quite rational and make systematic use of information available to them, that is, people think about the implications of their actions before they decide to engage or not engage in a given behavior (Ajzen and Fishbein 1980). Barring unforeseen events, Fishbein and Ajzen (1975) believe that a person will usually act in accordance with their intentions. Thus, the theory of reasoned action views a person's intention to perform or not perform certain behavior as the immediate determinant of the action. Hence, the key to predict behaviors lies with intentions and beliefs; where intentions are shaped by attitude towards the behavior and social norms, and beliefs are the ultimate source of those attitudes and norms.

In the theory of reasoned action, Fishbein and Ajzen advocate an approach where a small number of concepts are embedded within a single theoretical framework. Their approach explains social behavior that is not restricted to a specific behavioral domain (Ajzen and Fishbein 1980). In contrast to traditional measures of attitude used by ethics researchers, Fishbein and Ajzen stress on a model where attitude towards the performing or not performing a certain acts in a given, well defined situation is the attitude construct and not an attitude toward an object, person, or situation (Randall 1989). In other words, a person's performance or non-performance of a specific behavior with respect to some object usually can not be predicted from knowledge of the person's attitude towards that object. Instead, a person's attitude towards an object influences the overall pattern of his responses to the object, but it need not predict any action (Ajzen and Fishbein 1977).

The conceptual framework adopted by Fishbein and Ajzen assumes a casual chain linking beliefs and attitudes towards the behavior and the intentions to behavior. This is because the performance of the behavior may provide the person with new information that influences a person's beliefs, which in turn will start the causal chain again (Fishbein and Ajzen 1975). Although, the foundation of their conceptual framework is provided by their distinction between beliefs, attitudes, intentions, and behavior, the main concern of the conceptual framework is to examine the relation between these variables.

According to the theory of reasoned action, there are two major factors that determine a person's behavioral intentions: attitudinal (personal) component and a social (normative) component. That is, a person's intention to perform or not perform a particular behavior is determined by his attitude towards the behavior and his subjective norms. Further, a person's attitude towards the behavior is determined by the set of salient beliefs he holds about performing the particular behavior. Although subjective norms are also a function of beliefs, but these beliefs are of a different nature and deal with perceived prescriptions. That is subjective norm deals with the person's perception of the social pressures put on him to perform or not perform the behavior in question. Moreover Fishbein and Ajzen maintained that a researcher's attention on variables such as personality traits alone is misplaced and instead, researchers should focus on behavioral intentions and the beliefs that shape those intentions (Randall 1989). However they do recognize that such factors will have a possible effect on the behavior in question, therefore they are termed as external factors. Consequently, the key to predict behavior lies with intentions and beliefs.

Prior to examining the determinants of the behavioral intentions in both the cases, it is important to identify the behavior in question and the four elements of the behavioral criterion: action, target, context and time. This is because these are the essential prerequisites for predicting and explaining the behavior. Moreover, the lack of correspondence on any four elements can reduce the accuracy of prediction of the behavior. Although it is important to note that in this paper, we are not trying to predict the behavior under investigation. However when eliciting the salient beliefs that determine attitude towards the behavior, it is essential to ensure correspondence between these elements.

CASE STUDY

This section examines the computer crime situation at Kidder Peabody & Co. Theory of reasoned action is used in a qualitative manner to interpret the reasons behind the occurrence of computer crimes.

The case of insider fraud at Kidder Peabody & Co.

This case study looks into the illicit activities of Joseph Jett who defrauded Kidder Peabody & Co out of millions of dollars. Using the theory of reasoned action framework, this section reviews and analyses as to how, over a course of more than two and half years, Joseph Jett was able to exploit the Kidder trading and accounting systems to fabricate profits of approximately US$339 million. Joseph Jett was eventually removed from the services of Kidder in April 1994. The US Securities and Exchange Commission claimed that Jett engaged in more than 1000 violations in creating millions of dollars in phony profits so as to earn millions in bonuses. During the course of Jett's involvement with Kidder, he amassed a personal fortune of around $5.5 million and earned himself upwards of $9m in salary and bonuses. In 1993 alone, he made nearly 80% of the firm's entire annual profit of $439m.

Analysis of Jett's actions

This section deals with attitudinal and normative factors that contribute to Jett's engaging in illicit acts. This is followed by a review of the impact of these factors on the behavioral intentions. The behavior under investigation in the case of Kidder Peabody & Co is the intentional misuse of the accounting system. The four behavioral criterion with respect to Kidder can be described as: misusing (Action); accounting system (Target class); the need to show profitability of Kidder (Time period); Kidder Peabody and General Electric (Context). The next section examines the various factors that contribute to the behavioral intentions of Jett at Kidder.

Attitude

Prior to joining Kidder, Jett was aware of the manner in which the brokerage business was conducted and the specific conditions at Kidder. Jett realized the shortcomings of the accounting system and began tinkering with it. The management overlooked Jett's actions, especially because he seemed to be performing very well and was adding to the firms' profitability. Jett had been hired to perform arbitrage between Treasury bonds and Strips (Separate Trading of Registered Interest and Principal of Securities). Kidder relied heavily of Expert Systems to perform and value transactions in the bond markets. Based on the valuation of the transactions, Kidder systems automatically updated the firm's inventory and Profit and Loss statements. Jett found out that by entering forward transactions on the reconstituted Strips, he could indefinitely postpone the time when actual losses could be recognized in a Profit and Loss statement. Jett was able to do this by racking up larger positions and reconstituting the Strips. This resulted in Jett's 1992 trading profits touching a US$32 million record, previously unheard of in dealing with Strips. Jett's personal bonus was US$2 million. The following year Jett reported a US$151 million profit and earned US$12 million in bonus. It was only in March 1994 that senior management started looking into the dealing. This was because Jett's position included US$47 billion worth of Strips and US$42 billion worth of reconstituted Strips.

The factors presented in the scenario above clearly suggest that basic safeguards had not been instituted at Kidder. Although the junior traders at Kidder were aware of Jett's activities, the senior management did not make any effort to access this information. These factors certainly influenced Jett's beliefs and his intentions regarding the advantages and disadvantages of engaging in the illicit activities. As a consequence Jett manipulated the accounting information system and deceived the senior management at Kidder.

Social norms

As is typical of many merchant banks, bonuses earned are intricately linked with the profitability of the concern. Kidder offered substantial bonuses for individual contribution to company profits. Even within the parent company, General Electric, CEO Jack Welch told his employees that he wanted to create a 'cadre of professions' who could perform and be more marketable. This resulted in the employees being subjected to intense pressure to perform and having a focus on serving their self-interest. As a consequence, General Electric did not necessarily afford a culture of loyalty and truthfulness. The employees were inadvertently getting the silent message that they should 'look after themselves and win at any cost'. Critics claim that there was a certain hollowness of purpose beneath

Welch's relentlessly demanding management style (e.g. see Greenwald 1994).

Reports of ethical violations have also marred some of General Electric's traditional lines of business (Greenwald 1994). There have been allegations of conspiracy with De Beers mining company of South Africa to fix prices of industrial diamonds. The FBI is also investigating charges that General Electric had repeatedly ignored warnings about electrical problems that could compromise the safety of aircraft engines. Jack Welch dismisses these charges and contends that had General Electric not acquired Kidder Peabody, such discussions would not have surfaced. Irrespective of the nature of defenses put up by the General Electric senior management, the fact of the situation is that a dominant culture to win and an aspiration to be number 1 or 2 in every market, created an internal context within the organization such that unethical practices could be overlooked.

Effect of external variables

Prior to Joe Jett joining Kidder Peabody, no significant ethical problems had been reported at Kidder. Over the past few years the bank had been striving to perform satisfactorily, because at some stage the CEO wanted to dispose off the loss making brokerage unit. It had stayed clear of all sorts of rogue dealings, a phenomenon so common to any merchant bank. In fact lessons had been learnt from dealings in 'junk bonds' elsewhere. For example, the horror stories surrounding the demise of Drexel Burnham Lambert Inc haunted every major bank involved in the derivatives market.

Kidder Peabody and the parent company General Electric were determined to court political and business acclaim by recruiting a large number of people from ethnic minorities. The bank considered this to be a means of paying back to the society and perhaps gaining esteem from others by lending a helping hand to certain under-privileged sections of the society. Various investigative reports following the Kidder Peabody swindling case have reported that the only reason why Joe Jett got selected was because he happened to be a Black American. There are claims that Jett had falsified information on his CV, thus making it extremely impressive. The personnel department at Kidder took this information on face value and did not make any attempt to verify it. It follows therefore that Jett's risk taking character and involvement in unethical deeds may have influenced his beliefs.

Given the description of Joe Jett's behavior at Kidder Peabody, we can conclude that Jett's attitudinal factors played far more important a role than the normative ones. This lead to Jett engaging in illicit activities that ultimately led to the demise of Kidder.

DISCUSSION

In the previous sections we have used the theory of reasoned action to analyze the unauthorized activities of Joseph Jett at Kidder Peabody. The theory argues that an individual gets involved in particular acts as a consequence of a combination of a persons behavioral and normative beliefs. If a person's attitude to perform an illicit act needs to be influenced, one has to focus of changing the primary belief system. In this section, based on the theory of reasoned action and the case study, we have identified some key principles that an organization should adopt to manage the occurrence of computer crimes.

Formalized rules

In the literature it has been argued that if an organization has a high level of dependence on IT, there is a greater likelihood of it being vulnerable to computer related misuse (e.g. see Moor 1985). It is therefore important that organizations need to implement effective and systematic policies. The demand for establishing security policies within organizations has long been made by academics and practitioners alike, however such calls have largely gone unheeded. Formalized rules in the form of security policies will help in facilitating bureaucratic functions such that ambiguities and misunderstandings within organizations can be resolved.

With respect to formalized rules, Kidder Peabody presented an interesting situation. In fact the Securities and Exchange Commission demands that certain procedures should be followed. There are even explicit rules regarding supervision. However because of an increased pressure to perform and be profitable, many of the formal rules were overlooked. The case of Kidder Peabody and Co suggests that although organizations cherish to instill a culture of efficiency and good practice, poor communication often has a negative impact. The case also suggests that formal-ized rules are essential for the functioning of an organization and often something more is needs to be done. Perhaps there should be an adequate emphasis on informal or normative controls.

Normative controls

Clearly mere technical or formal control measures are inadequate to prevent computer-related crime. In other related work Dhillon (1997) sites cases where it was relatively easy for insiders to gain access to information systems and camouflage fictitious and fraudulent transactions. One of the most publicized examples of this kind of behavior is evidenced by the demise of the Barings Bank and the dealings of the rouge trader, Nick Lesson. In Kidder Peabody,

Jett was able to exploit a loophole in the accounting system to inflate the profits. It was possible to engage in criminal activities because the person involved was an insider. It therefore becomes obvious that no matter what the extent of formal and technical controls, prevention of insider fraud demands certain normative controls. Such controls essentially deal with the culture, value and belief system of the individuals concerned (for details see Dhillon 1997).

Employee behavior

Previous research has shown that besides personal circumstances, work situations and opportunities available allow individuals to perform criminal acts (e.g. see Backhouse and Dhillon 1995). Both in the case of Kidder Peabody the prevalent work situation and the opportunity to commit criminal acts affected the primary belief system of Jett, thus creating an environment conducive for a crime to be committed. This suggests monitoring of employee behavior as an essential step in maintaining the integrity of an organization. Such monitoring does not necessarily have to be formal and rule based. In fact informal monitoring, such as interpreting behavioral changes and identifying personal and group conflicts, can help in establishing adequate checks and balances.

CONCLUSION

This paper has used the theory of reasoned action to analyze the computer crime resulting because of violations of safeguards by internal employees. The analysis of the case suggests that organizations need to focus on the underlying beliefs that lead individuals to engage in intentional illicit acts, such as computer crime. The theory of reasoned action suggests that behavioral change is ultimately the result of changes in beliefs. Thus it is important that people within the organizations are exposed to information which will produce changes in their beliefs. In proactively managing the occurrence of adverse events, it is essential that we trace those changes in primary beliefs that result in particular attitudes and subjective norms.

REFERENCES

Ajzen, I, and M Fishbein. "Attitude-behaviour relations: a theoretical analysis and review of empirical research." *Psychological Bulletin* 84.5 (1977): 888-918.

Ajzen, I, and M Fishbein. *Understanding attitudes and predicting social behaviour.* Englewood Cliffs: Prentice Hall, 1980.

Audit Commission. "Opportunity makes a thief. Analysis of computer abuse.": The Audit Commission for Local Authorities and the National Health Service in England and Wales, 1994.

Backhouse, J, and G Dhillon. "Managing computer crime: a research outlook." *Computers & Security* 14.7 (1995): 645-651.

Balsmeier, P, and J Kelly. "The ethics of sentencing white-collar criminals." *Journal of Business Ethics* 15.2 (1996): 143-152.

Brown, R K. "Security overview and threat.": National Computer Security Educators, Information Resource Management College, National Defence University, Washington DC, 1991, Tutorial track NCSC.

Clinard, M B, and P C Yeager. *Corporate crime.* New York: The Free Press, 1980.

Croall, H. *White collar crime.* Milton Keynes, UK: Open University Press, 1992.

Dhillon, G. *Managing information system security.* London: Macmillan, 1997.

Dhillon, G, et al. *Computer crime at CEFORMA: a case study.* ETHICOMP 96. Madrid, Spain, November, 1996.

Fishbein, M, and I Ajzen. *Belief, attitude, intention and behavior: an introduction to theory and research.* Reading, MA: Addison-Wesley, 1975.

Forester, T, and P Morrison. *Computer ethics: cautionary tales and ethical dilemmas in computing.* Second ed. Cambridge: The MIT Press, 1994.

Greenwald, J. "Jack in the box." *Time* 144.14 1994.

Hearnden, K. "Computer crime and people." *A handbook of computer crime.* Ed. K Hearnden. Revised ed. London: Kogan Page, 1990.

Kesar S and S Rogerson "Attitudinal and normative components in information misuse: the case of Barings bank" *Effective utilization and management of emerging information technologies.* Ed M Khosrowpour. Hershey: Idea Group.

Mintzberg, H. *Power in and around organisations.* Englewood Cliffs: Prentice-Hall, 1983.

Moor, J H. "What is computer ethics." *Metaphilosophy* 16.4 (1985): 266-275.

Oz, E. *Ethics for the information age.* 1st ed: Business and Educational Technologies, 1994.

Parker, D B. *Crime by computer.* New York: Charles Scribner's Sons, 1976.

Parker, D B. "Ethical dilemmas in computer technology." *Ethics and the management of computer technology.* Ed. W M Hoffman and J M Moore. Cambridge, MA: Oelgeschlager, Gunn, and Hain, 1982.

Parker, D B, and S H Nycum. "Computer Crime." *Communication of the ACM* 27.4 (1984).

Randall, D M. "Taking stock: can the theory of reasoned action explain unethical conduct?" *Journal Of Business Ethics* 8 (1989): 873-882.

Strain, I. "Top bosses pose the main security threat." *Computer Weekly* October 3 1991: 22.

Information Technology and Sustainable Competitive Advantage: A Competence-Based Perspective

T. Ravichandran
Lally School of Management and Technology, Rensselaer Polytechnic Institute, Troy, NY 12180
Tel: (518) 276 2035, Fax: (518) 276 8661, Email: ravit@rpi.edu

Chalermsak Lertwongsatien
Lally School of Management & Technology, Rensselaer Polytechnic Institute, Troy, NY 12180
Tel: (518) 272-2990 Email: lertwc@rpi.edu

ABSTRACT

There is a growing debate whether Information Technology (IT) can be a source of sustained competitive advantage. The basic premise of this paper is that IT assets per se may not be a source of sustained competitive advantage. Instead, it is the IT-enabled competencies that organizations possess that lead to competitive advantage. We argue that IT-enabled competencies emerge due to complementarities between IT and other firm resources. We examine the role of one complementary firm resource- organizational learning capabilities in transforming IT assets into competencies. Based on a synthesis of the strategy and information systems literature we propose a process model of how IT leads to competitive advantage. The model stresses that organizations with a learning environment are more likely to gain embedded advantage from information technology than those that do not have a learning environment.

INTRODUCTION

Information Technology (IT) has long been recognized for its possible role in creating competitive advantage. However, theories that explain how and why IT can lead to competitive advantage are still relatively underdeveloped. Reich and Benbasat (1990) pointed out that research on IT and competitive advantage has emphasized "describing how, rather than systematically why" IT can lead to competitive advantage.

Accordingly, many researches previously have emphasized on the linkages between IT and the tangible business value, such as financial performance, and market share. However, the results from several findings have shown that IT may not have a direct connect to such a tangible value (Baker and Kauffman, 1988; Kettinger, et al., 1994). Rather, IT may have a link with strategic "intangible" assets such as corporate knowledge, organizational competence, core competence, distinctive competence (Prahalad and Hamel, 1990; Itami, 1987, Selznick, 1957). These intangible assets have been a central exploration of researchers in the resource-based perspective (Barney, 1991) area as a potential source of sustainable competitive advantage (Hall, 1991, 1992) due to its strategic attributes, valuable, rare, imperfectly imitable, and nonsubstitable (Barney, 1991).

The purpose of this paper is to examine why and how IT leads to competitive advantage. We propose that the real benefits of IT may reside in how IT assets are leveraged to develop organizational competencies (Hamel, 1994). We further argue that organizational learning plays an important role in this transformational process. The rest of the paper is structured as follows. We first present theoretical arguments as to why IT per se will not yield rents. We then review the theoretical underpinnings of the competence-based perspective and develop our theoretical model. Finally, we offer some concluding remarks.

IT AND SUSTAINABLE COMPETITIVE ADVANTAGE

Over the past two decades, several strategic frameworks have been proposed to identify IT applications that are likely to provide competitive advantage (e.g., Value Chain Analysis (Porter, 1980, 1985), Strategic Opportunity Matrix (Benjamin, et al., 1984), Consumer Resource Life Cycle Model (Ives and Learmonth, 1984), Pricing Model (Beath and Ives, 1986), Competitive Force Framework (McFarlan, 1984), Information Intensity Grid (Porter and Millar, 1985), Strategic Option Generator (Rackoff, et al., 1985), Causal Model of Competitive Advantage (Bakos and Treacy, 1986). Many case studies have explored how firms have employed IT to gain competitive advantage.

For example, WalMart has used the purchase/inventory/distribution system to reduce its inventory costs (Stalk, et al., 1992). GE (General Electric) has utilized the answer center technology to differentiate its service support from competitors (Porter and Millar, 1985). Similarly, Otis Elevator has differentiated its service operations by its Otisline system (Neumann, 1994). There is little doubt among academics and practitioners that IT could be a source of competitive advantage for firms.

However, there is a growing concern whether IT can provide long-term sustainable competitive advantage (Clemons, 1986; Vitale, 1986; Adcock, et al., 1993; Feeny and Ives, 1990). For example, Vitale (1986) warns that strategic IT applications may provide limited advantages to the innovator before being readily copied by competitors. A number of researchers have examined the conditions under which IT can produce sustainable competitive advantage. Porter (1985) focuses on first-mover advantages arguing that technological advantage arises when first-mover advantages (i.e., preempting customers through switching costs) outweigh first-mover disadvantage (i.e., development costs and learning curves). Clemons (1986) suggests two mechanisms for sustainable competitive advantage: switching cost and defensive barriers. Switching costs arise because many interorganizational systems have the ability to add electronic handcuffs to customers. On the other hand, defensive barriers (i.e., scale or scope advantage, superior managerial adaptability, existing infrastructure, and patents) provide a means to guard against imitation from competitors.

Despite attempts to identify conditions in which IT can be a source of competitive advantage the relationship between IT and firm performance remains unclear. Empirical studies suggest that IT may not have a direct impact on the long-term firm performance. For example, Banker and Kauffman (1988) found that there is no significant connection between investments in ATM and firm performance. Similarly, Floyd and Wooldrige (1990) also found no connection between ATM adoption and firm performance. Based on an analysis of 30 well-known cases, Kettinger, et al. (1994) found that in most cases market share and profits declined within five years of IT implementation. In fact, many consider IT as a strategic necessity rather than a differentiating factor in the market place (Clemons and Kimbrough, 1986; Clemons and Row, 1991; Kettinger, et al., 1994). Information technology is readily available to all firms in a competitive market and thus is not a rare resource capable of yielding rents. The strategic necessity hypothesis fits well with the resource-based view which posits that firm resources can be a source of sustained competitive advantage only if they are (1) valuable, (2) rare, (3) imperfectly imitable, and (4) nonsubstituable (Barney, 1991; Dierickx and Cool, 1989; Peteraf, 1993). In fact, some scholars even treat IT as a commodity and that any impact it might have on firm performance must come from how it is used to leverage firm specific intangible resources such as organizational culture, learning capabilities and business processes (Clemons and Row, 1991; Henderson and Venkatraman, 1993).

According to Clemons (199x) complementarity between IT and other firm assets is central to understand the relationship between IT and firm performance. Complementarity represents an enhancement of resource value and arises when a resource produces greater returns in the presence of another resource than it does alone (Teece, 1988). A resource complementarity can be a source of sustainable competitive advantage since it is protected from imitation or mobility due to its embeddedness i.e., the value of the resource is inextricably linked to the presence of another resource (Rumelt, 1984). For example, EDI systems may enable a firm to enhance its supplier relationships while the pre-existing supplier relationships maximize EDI's inherent information-sharing capabilities (Powell and Dent-Micallef, 1997).

COMPETENCE-BASED PERSPECTIVE

As a subset of the resource-based perspective which views a firm as a bundle of physical, organizational and human resources (Barney, 1991; Grant, 1991; Hall, 1992), the competence-based perspective views a firm as a bundle of skills, tasks and knowledge (Krough, et al., 1996; Hamel and Heene, 1994). Various definitions of competence such as invisible assets, core capability, internal capability, and embedded knowledge have been put forth. Essentially all these definitions emphasize an organization's ability achieve some tangible outcomes. In this study, we draw from McGrath et al. (1994) to define competencies as 'the organizational ability to reliably and consistently meet or exceed its objective.'

Organizational competencies are a source of sustainable competitive advantage since they are characterized by tacitness, complexity, and specificity (Reed and DeFillippi, 1990). Tacit knowledge represents knowledge that is difficult to codify and explicitly replicable (Nonaka, 1991). Complexity describes the range of interrelationships among skills and other knowledge-based competencies (Winter, 1987). Specificity represents the extent to which resources and skills are idiosyncratic to the firm and can be advantageously channeled toward particular customers (Reed and DeFillippi, 1990).

The link between competence and knowledge is fundamental to the competence based perspective (Leonard-Barton, 1992). In order to develop competencies a firm must develop and maintain the knowledge and skills embodied in human resources. It must also accumulate, structure and codify knowledge embedded in technical systems (e.g., databases, decision rules). It is the embodied knowledge in combination with technical systems that form the basis of competence (Itami and Numagami, 1992). In addition, managerial systems are required for creating and controlling knowledge. Finally, values and norms are infused through the first three dimensions.

It is obvious that organizational learning is essentially involved in the various aspects of competence development discussed above. Prahalad and Hamel (1990) argue that the underlying element of core competence is the specialized expertise (or knowledge) of an organization resulting from its collective learning, particularly about the ways in which diverse production skills can be coordinated and multiple streams of technologies can be integrated. Learning makes a two-way relationship between people and organization possible (Klien, et al., 1991). Along this lines, organizational competence then embodies: (1) the formation of a common conception of key activities and key competencies, and (2) the creation of procedures and systems which promote the fulfillment of key tasks (Akerberg, 1989). Knowledge embodied in human resources and embedded in the technical systems are acquired and codified into an explicit form and stored in organizational memory (Nonaka, 1991). The organizational memory then enables the firm to retain knowledge and build on the accumulated experience of pre-existing competence (Walsh and Ungson, 1991).

New ideas, markets, and products have much longer time horizons, more uncertain outcomes, and more indirect results than the exploitation of existing ideas, markets, and products (March, 1991). Competitive sustainability requires that organizations both explore the unknown and exploit the known. Several cases illustrate how double-loop learning has the capability to enhance organizational performance. Elkington and Burke (1989) found that managers who were forced to respond to environmental issues inadvertently increased profits because more efficient production methods were found when the status quo was challenged. The success of Dell Computer, American Express Travel-Related Services, 3M, Wal-Mart, American Hospital Supply, and many other companies offer examples of firms that have reconceptualized competitive recipes (Spender, 1989), competitive environments, and products and services (Hamel and Prahalad, 1989) because their executives engaged in double-loop learning.

In summary, organizational competencies are the source of sustainable competitive advantage. Competency development is essentially a knowledge drive process and an organization's learning capability can hamper or facilitate competence development. Extending this argument we propose that organizational learning capabilities play an important role in transforming IT assets into organizational competencies.

RESEARCH MODEL

IT serves an increasingly important role in many organizations in facilitating and enabling the development of organizational competencies. As Keen (1993) pointed out "the success of IT in such endeavors is inextricably linked with the effectiveness of fitting the pieces together. The wide difference in competitive and economic benefits that companies gain from information technology rests on a management difference and not a technical difference. Some business leaders are somewhat better able to fit the pieces together than others." In this study, we focus on one critical management difference - organizational learning capability.

Figure 1 depicts our conceptual model. The model reflects the basic arguments of the competence based perspective that firm assets by themselves may not be a source of sustained competitive advantage. Thus, IT assets are not expected to have a direct effect on an organization's ability to maintain its competitive position over a long period of time. This is consistent with the findings in the IS literature that investments in IT infrastructure have no relationship with firm performance. The model also depicts that interactions between IT assets and an organization's learning capabilities have a strong positive effect on IT-enabled competencies. IT-enabled competencies are a subset of organizational competencies that are inextricably dependent on information technology. We propose that the interaction of IT with the organizational learning create embedded competencies that could be a potential source of sustained competitive advantage.

DISCUSSION

A major concern of executives is whether their organization's increasingly large IT investments provide worthy returns. The so-called "productivity paradox" has focussed the spotlight on one aspect of this problem i.e, whether high investment in IT boosts worker output (Brynjolfsson, 1994). Despite significant efforts from academics, consultants and practitioners assessment of the business value of IT remains a challenge. Most studies attempt to measure the business value of IT using "tangible" financial performance as the output variables. However, real benefits of IT also involve "intangible" outcomes such as customer service, timeliness, and flexibility.

Unlike the many IT investment studies that link IT investment directly to firm performance, we propose that the interaction between IT assets and organizational learning creates an intermediate variable, called IT-enabled competence which in turn will be directly related to firm performance. Furthermore, we conceptualize firm performance in terms of measures such as market share and profitability that reflect both the tangible and intangible effects

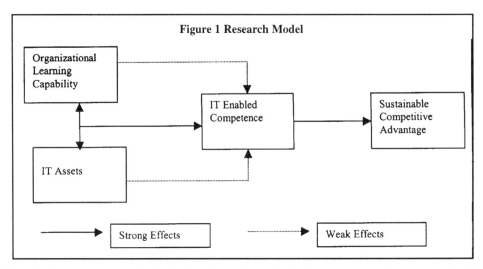

Figure 1 Research Model

of IT. IT enabled competencies are defined as the subset of organizational competencies that are caused by IT. These competencies entail large amounts of firm-specific investments of financial, technology, human, and organization resources that are developed over a considerable period of time and are not freely tradable. They can generate future streams of economic returns and, therefore, potentially be sources of sustained competitive advantage (Barney, 1991; Dierickx and Cool, 1989; Lado, et al., 1992).

Converting IT assets into business value may compass several layers of process complexity (Davenport, 1993). The systems development process of strategic IT application itself is complex. Moreover, the processes that establish value, monitor progress, and enable midcourse correction are also complex, involving significant uncertainty and a wide range of stakeholders (Davenport and Short, 1990). Each of these processes directly impacts value attainment. However, organizational learning is particularly critical in transforming IT assets into organizational competencies. Having deployed the IT initiatives, the firm may acquire some knowledge and insights that are useful for deploying other IT initiatives. A critical challenge is to gather the knowledge and make it available to those people who have the power to act on it (Henderson, et al., 1995). The process of acquiring and utilizing this knowledge is as important as the IT initiatives themselves. The organization's learning capability allows firms to create and enhance their competencies through the knowledge that is accumulated over time.

Research on strategic IT also points to knowledge as the key success factor for many strategic IT related projects. For instance, Kenny and Florida (1988) observed that Japanese firms are generally more successful in taking advantage of information technology that provides flexibility and responsiveness than are traditional Western "mass production" organizations. The authors posit that the primary reason for this success in Japanese firms is redundant knowledge and the robust exchange of information that exist among technical specialists and general managers within the organization. Learning is fostered by the ability of managers to discuss problems or opportunities effectively, exchange information openly, and posses a sufficient common degree of understanding about the information to be able to jointly work together toward common ends.

Organizational learning may also be important in explaining performance differences among firms that have similar IT assets. Goldhar and Lei (1995) in a study of CIM usage by organizations found that firms may be limited in how far they can improve their efficiency and flexibility by technology constraints. But, they can continue to seek faster responsiveness and integration by redesigning their organizations to promote new forms of learning. Faster responsiveness and capability to manage higher product variety depend not only on the technology but also on a firm's ability to learn and create new forms of knowledge. The richness of organizational learning is becoming a key asset that enables firms to separate themselves from their competitors.

Knowledge transferability (e.g., flow of knowledge and information) among IT workers and other line managers is also important in creating opportunities to leverage IT as is the role of overlapping information/knowledge exchanges for product and process innovations (Nonaka, 1991). Many Japanese firms encourage integration between IT and business by appointing managers to spend two or three years in an IT department as a job rotation scheme (Bensaou and Earl, 1998). The postings help them develop not only technical knowledge but also knowledge about how to get things done with IT and about who can help with what.

Flow of knowledge and information is also important for the success of strategic IT project implementation at the operational level. In a study of thirty-four software development projects, Leonard-Barton and Sinha (1993) found that, in addition to the quality and cost of the technology, and its initial compatibility with the user environment, two managerial processes were important in explaining successful implementation. These include the degree and type of user involvement, and the degree to which project participants deliberately altered the technology and adjusted the user environment in a process of a mutual adaptation. These two managerial processes essentially involve creation and channeling of knowledge.

CONCLUSION

Information Technology is a vital strategic business tool. However, IT alone may not be a source of sustainable competitive advantage since IT (i.e., hardware, software, services and personnel) is available to all firms. Even smaller players can often acquire the necessary technology through cooperative arrangements or by outsourcing (Clemons and Knez, 1988; Sager, 1988). However, the benefits resulting from IT applications can be more readily defended if the system exploits unique resources of the innovating firms so that competitors do not fully benefit from imitation.

Organizational learning enable the development of organizational competencies. Organizational learning enables firms to acquire and assimilate the new and unique knowledge through past experiences and experimentation. The advantages emerging from the interaction of IT assets and organizational learning capabilities are protected from imitation and mobilization by their embeddedness.

REFERENCES

References are available upon request. Please contact the authors.

The Intranet as a Knowledge Management Tool? Creating New Electronic Fences.

Sue Newell

Nottingham Business School, Nottingham Trent University, Burton Street, Nottingham, NG1 4BU. UK.

Jacky Swan & Robert Galliers

Warwick Business School, University of Warwick, Coventry, CV4 7AL. UK.

Harry Scarbrough

Leicester University, Management Centre, University Road, Leicester, LE1 7RH.

ABSTRACT

Intranets are often implemented with knowledge management as the primary focus. That is, intranet systems are seen as a tool for the more efficient sharing and creation of knowledge within organisations. In terms of knowledge sharing, intranets are viewed as tools to prevent reinvention through allowing individuals to store knowledge at one point in time, which can be mined and used by others at some latter point in time. In this way they can promote the more efficient exploitation of knowledge within companies. In terms of knowledge creation, intranets may be viewed as providing the virtual space for the exploration of new knowledge. In this paper we argue that, much of the prescription about the use of intranets adopts an impoverished view of both the knowledge exploitation and knowledge exploration processes. Moreover, the former is focused on efficiency (preventing reinvention), while the later is focused on innovation (doing new things differently). The tension between efficiency and innovation needs to be more clearly evaluated if intranets for KM are not simply going to become automating tools, reinforcing the traditional departmental barriers with even stronger electronic fences.

Key words: Knowledge Management, Intranets, Management Fashions, Organisational Learning.

INTRODUCTION

Knowledge Management (KM) as a topic has gained prominence, especially in the IS/IT literature over the last 2-3 years. KM could be described as the latest management fashion (Abrahamson, 1996). However, the growing emphasis on 'knowledge assets' (rather than labour or capital), 'knowledge work' and 'knowledge workers' as the primary source of productivity in contemporary society suggest that the interest in KM will be more enduring, even though the label may change (Drucker, 1993). For example, a KPMG research report on KM opens with the words "There is little doubt that we have entered the knowledge economy where what organisations know is becoming more important than the traditional sources of economic power – capital, land, plant and labour – which they command". Moreover, from a survey of 100 leading companies in the UK, only 2% considered that KM was a fad that would soon be forgotten, and 43% of respondents considered their organisation to have a KM initiative in place (KPMG, 1998). Similarly, Ruggles (1998) writes: "To a growing number of companies, knowledge management is more than just a buzzword or a sales pitch, it is an approach to adding or creating value by more actively leveraging the know-how, experience, and judgement resident within and, in many cases, outside of an organisation".

There is no single definition of KM, but in general the idea relates to unlocking and leveraging the knowledge of individuals so that this knowledge becomes available as an organisational resource which is not dependent on the particular individuals. KM then is about harnessing the intellectual capital of an organisation, recognising that knowledge, not simply information, is the primary asset to an organisation (Marshall, 1997). Much of the literature on KM is driven from an information systems perspective and is based on the belief that Knowledge Management Systems (KMS), for example intranets, can be used to capture and stockpile workers' knowledge and make it accessible to others via a searchable application (Cole-Gomolski, 1997). As such, Intranet systems are promoted as tools for KM. Intranets can facilitate both the exploration of knowledge -i.e. the pursuit and identification of new options, through sharing and creation - and the exploitation of knowledge -i.e. the use and development of things that are already known within the organisation but currently under-exploited, through capture and distribution. (Levinthal and March, 1993; Fletcher, 1997).Good practice examples include storing information on intranet-based repositories at Maritime

Telephone and Telegraph, harnessing existing documents by using intranet document managers at Hughes Space and Communications (Hibbard and Carrillo, 1998) 'knowledge-on-line' via the company-wide intranet at Booz, Allen and Hamilton, Inc. (Jahnke, 1998), and a cafe-style information service at ICL ('Cafe-Vik') via the global intranet (Lank, 1998).

In this paper we will argue that much of the positive prescription regarding intranet as a KM tool adopts a limited view of knowledge sharing (exploitation) and knowledge creation (exploration) processes. This means that the success of such tools is likely to be limited to specific contexts. This is supported by evidence, which demonstrates that there is no direct correlation between IT investment and business performance or KM (Malhorta, 1998; Strassmann, 1998). The paper has been based on our research in one particular global bank (referred to as 'Global'), which has been developing an intranet system with the intention of improving KM as well as on existing literature which takes a more critical view of the impact of communication technologies on knowledge creation and knowledge sharing (e.g. Earl, 1996; Clark and Staunton, 1989; Grant, 1996)..

THE EXPLOITATION OF KNOWLEDGE

In terms of the 'exploitation' of knowledge, the idea is that using intranets as KM systems can help to prevent reinvention within organisations. Reinvention is a common occurrence in organisations because people are unaware that what they are trying to do at a particular point in time has already been done (or at least something similar has been done) by another individual or group. So instead of learning from the past experiences of others, individuals or teams 'reinvent the wheel'. KM is based on the premise that the learning from a particular task should be codified and stored so that it is available to others at different times and places. A KM system then can be described as a linear process of:

Codification of Knowledge – Storing of knowledge – Mining of Knowledge – Application of Knowledge

However, this linear view greatly oversimplifies the knowledge sharing process.

Codification and Storing of Knowledge:

When individuals or groups undertake an activity, apply their existing knowledge to that activity and learn from that experience, they will have gained knowledge, which can potentially be useful to others in the organisation. Polanyi (1966) suggests that we should distinguish between the tacit and explicit knowledge gained. Explicit knowledge is that knowledge that can be easily expressed in formal, systematic language. So if the task involved negotiating a new order from a customer, there is some readily expressible knowledge that can be communicated, which might be useful for future negotiations, such as details about the customer organisation in terms of size, product mix, locations etc. The problem is that this does not automatically occur. Either the knowledge is not codified or else it is codified but not in a way that is useful or easily accessible – for example, it may be paper based and stored in a filing cabinet within a particular department which is difficult to access. The objective of an intranet-based KM system is to encourage individuals to store this explicit knowledge in a form that can be accessed by others for whom it might be useful.

The storing of explicit knowledge, however, is not seen to be the key to effective KM because, it is argued, it is the tacit knowledge which will typically be of more value (Grant, 1996; Hall, 1993). Thus, there will also be some tacit knowledge gained from a sales encounter. Tacit knowledge is rooted in action and involvement in the particular context and has both cognitive and technical elements (Nonaka, 1994). The cognitive element (know-what) relates to the mental models which humans develop to make sense of their experiences. It refers to the individual's view of what is or what ought to be. The technical dimension to tacit knowledge (know-how) refers to the skills needed in the particular context. So in terms of the example of learning from negotiating with a particular customer, the cognitive knowledge will relate to how those involved viewed the customer (as naïve, as competent, as full of future sales potential, as of limited future value etc.). The technical knowledge will relate to how best to approach this particular customer (using flattery, hard sell, wining and dining etc.).

As this tacit knowledge is potentially even more valuable to others, the emphasis for a KM system then, is to explicate this knowledge into more codified forms and store it on the organisational Intranet. Yet this type of knowledge cannot be easily articulated or transferred because it is personal and context specific. The attempt to codify tacit knowledge thus ignores the fact that some tacit knowledge is probably impossible to codify. For example, intuitions and hunches, which are a form of tacit knowledge (Nonaka, 1998), are not readily codified, since by definition they cannot be expressed. (The dictionary definition of an intuition being 'immediate apprehension by the mind without reasoning; immediate apprehension by a sense; immediate insight'). Thus, if an intuition could be fully expressed, this would demand reasoning and it would cease to be an intuition. Of course, some tacit knowledge could be codified, as Tsoukas (1996) points out – "tacit knowledge can indeed be linguistically expressed if we focus our attention on it". However, tacit knowledge is knowledge which cannot be communicated, understood or used without the 'knowing subject' (Popper, 1972). As Lam (1998) puts it: "The realisation of its (tacit knowledge) potential requires the close involvement and co-operation of the knowing subject". That is, it can be transferred only by example or observation and demands practical experience in the relevant context.

Moreover, in considering tacit knowledge in particular, the more fundamental question is WHY this tacit knowledge has not been codified in the past. There appear to be a number of explanations for this, but each 'reason' provides a fundamental challenge to the likely success of a KM strategy, which attempts to codify this tacit knowledge. Some of the most valuable tacit knowledge in a firm may not lend itself to capture (Gardner, 1998). This is because it is: too difficult to explain; too uncertain; too unimportant; too changeable; too contextually specific; too politically sensitive; or too valuable to the individual or group concerned. Therefore, that facet of tacit knowledge which is codified may, in addition to a general information over-load, result in knowledge which is:

• useless - if it is too difficult to explain
• difficult to verify- if it is uncertain
• redundant – if it is subject to continuous change
• irrelevant – if it is too context dependent
• trivial – if it is too unimportant
• difficult – if it is very time-consuming to codify
• politically naïve – if it is too politically sensitive
• inaccurate– if it is in short supply so that it confers personal advantages and is secreted by the 'knower'

The development of Intranets for KM then, typically fails to consider the multifaceted characteristics of knowledge, especially tacit knowledge. Tacit knowledge is not easily codified and is difficult to transfer. Moreover, even where knowledge could be codified, there are a variety of reasons why some knowledge remains tacit. The risk is therefore that the knowledge on intranets will only be that which is easily codified, rather than that which is really helpful and important. This was certainly evident in the case company, which had spent a considerable amount of resources developing their intranet system. When asked to give an example of the 'most useful knowledge' stored, interviewees responded with the example of the intra-site bus timetable! This was the timetable for the bus which travelled round the different company sites in the particular city, going at regular intervals every 20 minutes or so. Another example given was of the ability to track stationary orders so that an individual could have visibility about where their pencil order was in the system. It is doubtful whether these examples will revolutionise the knowledge base of the particular company.

The codification and storing of knowledge refers to the supply side of the KM process. Most emphasis in the literature is on this side of the process – "the idea behind knowledge management is to stockpile workers' knowledge and make it accessible to others via a searchable application" (Cole-Gomolski, 1997). Part of the reason for focusing on the supply of knowledge is the recognition that, because much of an organisation's knowledge is personal (in the abilities or skills of its employees), the organisation is vulnerable to losing that knowledge if the individual chooses to leave. An example is Xerox's missed opportunity when Steve Job left with the knowledge needed to develop the microprocessor for the first Apple computer. The solution is to capture and store knowledge so that it becomes the 'intellectual property' of the organisation, rather than of the individual. For example, in the survey referred to earlier (KPMG, 1998), 43% of respondents said that a relationship with a key client or supplier had been damaged by the departure of a key individual. However, as already seen, there are problems with this simplistic view of knowledge capture.

Rather, that attempting to grapple ownership of knowledge from the individual, a more effective solution may be to encourage key individuals to stay with the company through the more prosaic practices of human resource management. Enacting the idea that 'employees are our greatest asset', rather than simply espousing this rhetoric may be the more fundamental solution to the knowledge supply problems of a company. This is why Handy's idea of 'the empty raincoat' (Handy, 1995), which sees the future of work in terms of a migrant labour force, where individuals carry their accumulated knowledge from company to company on a contract base, may be an unhelpful vision of the future. Similarly, there is now recognition that the massive de-layering that took place in many companies during the late 1980s and early 1990s, resulted in a 'dumbing-down' of the organisation as much of its 'knowledge assets' was actually encouraged to 'walk out the door'. Again, it is unlikely whether exit interviews aimed at codifying and storing these individuals' knowledge would have substantially reduced the problem.

These problems were clearly evident in Global. They had de-layered in the 1980s and were using contract employees (consultants) to help develop their intranet. In one department they had 150 consultants working on the intranet project, alongside a handful of their own employees. The problem was that the technical expertise remained with the consultants while the business knowledge remained with the internal employees. Combining these two sets of knowledges to create the intranet as an effective KM system, was proving to be very difficult and problems were exacerbated by the different company loyalties of the consultants and the employees.

Mining and Application of Knowledge:

The mining and application of knowledge refer to the demand side (i.e. the demand among potential users for particular kinds of knowledge). While there are problems, as seen in the supply side, even less thought appears to have gone into the demand side. It is simply assumed by many developers of intranets for KM, that as long as they can encourage people to use the intranet to store knowledge, it will then automatically be used by others, especially if data mining applications are developed. But, even where knowledge has been codified and stored, it does not follow that this will be used or applied by others. This is because there is a failure to understand the difference between knowledge and competency or expertise. Competency or expertise is more than a 'bucket of knowledge'; it is the insight to be able to apply that knowledge (Dove, 1998). So as Sanchez and Heene (1997) observe, tacit knowledge is difficult to exploit organisationally even when it is clearly articulated. This is because to appropriate knowledge from someone else means having a shared code or mental model that enables the other to understand, value and accept that knowledge (Schwenk, 1986). That is, communication of knowledge is only possible between people who, to some extent at least, share a system of meaning (Trompenaars, 1995). In a sense this implies that the distinction drawn between tacit and explicit knowledge, as if they are two independent phenomenon, is too simplistic. Tacit and explicit knowledge are mutually constituted (Tsoukas, 1996).

This suggests that it is relatively easy to share knowledge across a group that is homogenous, but that it is extremely difficult where the group is heterogeneous. Yet, it is precisely the sharing of knowledge across functional or organisational boundaries, through using cross-functional and inter-organisational project teams that is seen as the key to the effective exploitation of knowledge (Gibbons, 1994). KM intranet systems developed to promote knowledge sharing typically fail to take into account the pre-existing organisational structures, norms and cultural values which leads individuals and groups to have divergent, possibly even irreconcilable, interpretations of what needs to be done and how best to do it. Knowledge is qualitatively different from information - it does not simply 'flow' from a sender to a receiver. As Nonaka (1994) writes: "In short, information is a flow of messages, while knowledge is created and organized by the very flow of information, anchored on the commitment and beliefs of its holder". Knowledge has to be continuously 're-created' and 're-constituted' through an interactive social networking process. This emphasises dialogue occurring through networks rather than linear information flows. However, while dialogue can promote mutual understanding between individuals (Senge, 1990), it is also the case that dialogue can expose deep-seated differences between individuals, especially when individuals come from very different epistemological positions (Newell, Swan & Preston, 1998). Where such fundamental differences are exposed, dialogue is likely to lead to conflict, rather than agreement, and the creation of new knowledge. This was confirmed by Dwyer (1990) who found that most of the respondents in the 12 UK organisations he was looking at, believed their organisation was incapable of promoting cross-functional co-operation in its teams.

Accepting the view of knowledge as socially constructed through a process of interaction, means that issues of power and social relationships come to the forefront. Adopting this perspective allows us to understand how Intranet technologies can be used to harden the boundaries around groups which restricts knowledge sharing and protects the expert power base of particular social groups: "An intranet is a powerful tool that, when used correctly can enhance communication and collaboration, streamline procedures, and provide just-in-time information to a globally dispersed workforce. Misused, however, an intranet can intensify mistrust, increase misinformation, and exacerbate turf wars". (Cohen, 1998).

This was very clearly evident in Global.. In this bank, 150 separate intranet projects were identified. The learning and sharing across these projects was minimal. For example, a number of the intranet projects had used a particular firm of consultants and in each case there had been problems with the relationship and the service provided by this consultancy. However, given that there was limited (no) communication across the intranet projects, the same mistakes with this consultancy continued to be made. Moreover, each of these intranet projects was sponsored by a different department. This meant that what was actually created in this bank were department-specific intranets that reinforced existing departmental boundaries with 'electronic fences', despite the fact the initial vision for developing the intranet was to create 'a global, networked bank'. Evidence suggests that this may not be uncommon in organisations, especially where functional and departmental boundaries remain strong (Cohen, 1998). Moreover, in many organisations, intranet developments are being financially supported at the local level by individual departments (KPMG, 1998). This again implies that intranet technologies may, in reality be as important in reinforcing pre-existing organisational boundaries as in stimulating knowledge sharing across the organisation.

In summary then, intranets developed as KM systems fail to understand both the supply of knowledge and the demand for knowledge in an organisational context. In terms of supply, much knowledge in organisations is not easily codified and transferred. In terms of demand, even where the knowledge is codified, it is still not necessarily easily acquired, used or applied.

THE EXPLORATION OF KNOWLEDGE

Discussions of the exploitation of knowledge are underpinned by a rather static view of organisations as information processing units whereby the fundamental task of an organisation is to solve problems more quickly by processing information more efficiently. Nonaka (1994) argues that this underplays dynamic processes of knowledge creation and innovation that give firms in contemporary society their competitive advantage: "Innovation, which is a key form of organisational knowledge creation, cannot be explained sufficiently in terms of information processing or problem solving. Innovation can be better understood as a process in which the organisation creates and defines problems and then actively develops new knowledge to solve them" (p. 14). In turbulent business environments the source of productivity is not the more efficient processing of information but the application of knowledge to knowledge itself in order to sustain innovation (Drucker, 1993). This dilemma between efficiency and innovation has been noted in the organisational literature for some time (e.g. Clark & Staunton, 1989). Yet most of the emphasis in the IS/IT literature has been on the efficient exploitation of existing knowledge rather than on more explorative processes which are central to the creation of new knowledges.

As seen, there are problems among writers on KM systems in the conceptualisation of the knowledge sharing process. These are even more evident when the focus shifts to knowledge exploration. In terms of exploration, a key element is 'redundancy' of information (Nonaka, 1994). The existence of extra information beyond that which is required immediately to solve problems can, paradoxically, enhance knowledge creation. The sharing of extra information not only helps to stimulate ideas about alternative possibilities for action but also promotes the sharing of tacit knowledge: 'since members share overlapping information, they can sense what others are trying to articulate' (Nonaka, 1994; p. 28). Yet the focus on the efficient exploitation of knowledge is likely to reduce the scope for such redundancy. For example, on the demand side a major problem many managers face is information overload (KPMG, 1998). The solution is seen to be to develop automatic knowledge mining tools, which give individuals only that information, which they specifically need for a particular problem based on recorded information of how that problem was solved in the past. While this may help to prevent 'reinventing the wheel', it is unlikely to stimulate the development of the future space car. In other words, if you only deal with situations based on the same information that has been used for that situation in the past then creativity, in terms of exploring novel approaches to situations, is unlikely to occur.

The problem appears to be that there is a lack of consideration of what avoiding re-invention may actually mean. Using the metaphor of the wheel to illustrate, the development of the car would not have gone far if engineers had followed the principle of avoiding reinvention and stuck to the traditional wooden wheel used on Victorian carriages. If intranets are used simply to transport a workable solution in one situation and apply it to a similar situation, then efficiency may be improved, but at the expense of innovation. Processes of exploration needed for knowledge creation would actually be undermined. In this sense, intranets would be actually be reinforcing old 'accepted' ways of doing things and so intensifying the 'iron cage' (DiMaggio and Powell, 1990).

Nonaka (1998) develops the concept of 'ba' as the necessary meeting place, which may be physical or virtual, for knowledge creation. That is, building on the theory that knowledge creation occurs when tacit and explicit knowledges are combined (Nonaka and Takeuchi, 1995), Nonaka argues that this needs to occur within some particular time and space location (i.e. within 'ba'). He goes on to argue that organisations need to create such spaces, if they are to promote knowledge creation, and hence be successful in what is being termed the knowledge age. The intranet may be a particularly useful tool for the purpose of creating the mechanism/location for such knowledge sharing – i.e. the intranet ba. Yet one must seriously question how far this essentially linear information tool can promote the 'community of interaction' which is seen to be so critical for the amplification and development of (especially tacit) knowledge (Nonaka, 1994). For example, Hansen (1998) looked at the way different organisational units within several large companies, acquired and used knowledge. He found that when units tried to use an intranet, which he described as a 'weak link', to exchange complex, tacit knowledge, they failed, because "electronic connections are fast, but they don't allow the interaction and interpretation required to share knowhow and expertise".

Nonaka (1998) develops the concept of ba, by differentiating 4 types of ba which stimulate the 4 types of knowledge combination needed to generate the full knowledge creation cycle: the 'originating ba' (facilitates the combination of tacit and tacit knowledge), the 'interacting ba' (facilitates the combination of tacit to explicit knowledge), the 'exercising ba' (facilitating the combination of explicit to tacit knowledge) and the 'cyber ba' (facilitates combination of explicit and explicit knowledge). The first four are all predicated on the need for face-to-face interaction. The intranet, on the other hand represents a cyber ba and cannot provide the location for these first three aspects the knowledge creation process. Rather, these aspects of the knowledge creation process require the physical space to engage in dialogue and share mental models with others, which in turn may encourage reflection about one's own mental models – a real bar, as opposed to a virtual intranet ba, is needed.. Developing the cyber ba may be possible through an intranet - indeed Nonaka (1998) argues that this combination process is best supported by utilising information technology - but this is only a very small part of the total knowledge creation process.

The core problem appears to be that knowledge is defined as a cognitive, analytical entity, which is possessed by individuals. The assumption is then made that Intranets can be used to capture and store this knowledge. One way of considering the difference between the intranet 'ba' and the dialogue-promoting 'bar' is to compare 2 models of the KM process (see Table 1). The cognitive model appears to underpin much of the IS/IT literature and certainly fits with most of what is written about intranets as KM tools. The community model, on the other hand, summarises the more realistic view, certainly when considering the issue of knowledge exploration rather than knowledge exploitation.

Table 1. Two contrasting views of the knowledge management process.

Cognitive Model	Community Model
Knowledge is objectively defined concepts and facts.	Knowledge is socially constructed and based on experience.
Knowledge is transferred through text – information systems have a crucial role.	Knowledge is transferred through participation in social networks including occupational groups and teams.
Gains from knowledge management include the recycling of knowledge and the standardization of systems.	Gains from knowledge management include greater awareness of internal and external sources of knowledge.
The primary function of knowledge management is to codify and capture knowledge.	The primary function of knowledge management is to encourage knowledge-sharing amongst and between groups and individuals.
The dominant metaphor is human memory.	The dominant metaphor is the human community.
The critical success factor is technology.	The critical success factor is trust.

THE UNDERLYING PROBLEM

The development of KM through using intranet technologies, therefore, fails to consider the difficulties and paradoxes involved in the social construction and creation of knowledge. Boland and Tenkasi (1995) reaffirm these problems when they write: *"The problem of integration of knowledge in knowledge-intensive firms is not a problem of simply combining, sharing or making data commonly available. It is a problem of perspective taking in which the unique thought worlds of different communities of knowing are made visible and accessible to others"* [p.39].

The lack of attention to these issues appears to arise because of the tendency of those writing about information systems to adopt a systems perspective. From a systems perspective the various components (subsystems) link logically together to constitute the organisational whole (Checkland, 1981). Thus, information systems are viewed as systems-oriented 'tools' to provide 'input' into various types of decisions (Tansley and Watson, 1998). The problem is that this perspective essentially views knowledge as a static stock (Nonaka, 1998). Moreover, it presents a reified view of the organisation; one which focuses on the inputs and the outputs but ignores the 'blackbox' of human interactions which lead to particular outcomes (Silverman, 1970). That is, it ignores the fact that organisation is the outcome of human activities. Information systems are presented as an unproblematic tool with the social exchange and political aspects of the ways they are devised and used largely ignored (Liff, 1997). In contrast, a processual analysis, focuses within the 'blackbox' and looks at the ways in which the organisational order is negotiated, sustained and changed over time. The focus is then on the ongoing social, political, cultural and economic dynamics, which constitute organisational life (Hosking and Morley, 1991). Considering intranets from this perspective requires a focus on sense-making processes (Weick, 1990) in order to understand why individuals use and engage with the systems in the ways they do.

When the 'blackbox' starts to be opened, not only does it draw our attention to the social, political, cultural and economic dynamics of the knowledge exploration and exploitation processes, but it also allows us to focus on the learning process that underpins the emphasis on KM. And while we tend to think of learning as always being positive, Henderson (1997) reminds us that learning can also be dysfunctional. This is because establishing what is 'right' and what is 'wrong' is difficult for an individual, but even more difficult for a group. For example, two independent observers may watch a sequence of events, but because of their very different mental models, what they 'see' is actually quite different. These heterogeneous perceptions are inevitable in organisations (Pfeffer, 1981) and means that, especially in the face of complex decisions, there is no single 'right' or 'rational' solution. Henderson (1997) concludes that "there is no real reason to suppose that organisations will improve understanding by improving learning, since it is likely that superstitious learning and other dysfunctional forms will frequently occur...If learning obstacles were overcome, organisations would merely assimilate superstitious and other unhelpful forms of learning at a faster rate. Managers would become even more vulnerable to the latest management fad or charlatan consultant". In other words, if knowledge was made 'less sticky' in organisations by detaching it from its source, then learning may well be improved but there is no reason to suppose that this will inevitably lead to improved decisions. We should be cautious about adopting a pro-learning bias, just as it is now recognised that much of the innovation literature adopted a pro-innovation bias.

By identifying these problems the paper hopes to stimulate alternative theorising about the use of intranets, and other IS-based KM tools, within organisations. Intranets clearly have a role in the new 'knowledge era'. In particular, they may facilitate the efficient exploitation of knowledge to reduce the amount of reinvention that occurs. However, even here it must be recognised that not all knowledge which is 'known' within an organisation is easily codified and transferred; nor that all knowledge which is supplied is readily found and applied. That is, that even in terms of improving the efficiency of knowledge utilisation within organisations, there is a need to recognise the problems associated with knowledge supply and demand. Relying on an intranet may actually reduce the sharing of important knowledge and lead to the reinforcement of departmental or functional boundaries by creating 'electronic fences'. This certainly appeared to happen in Global. There were 2 main reasons why this appeared to be happening:

1. Because intranets were being developed which were departmentally specific and which reinforced social and political divisions and so reduced integration across departments

2. Because there was some knowledge that could not and would not be codified and placed on the intranet. As people came to rely on the intranet they missed this important, typically tacit knowledge, that was available in other parts of the organisation.

In terms of knowledge exploration or knowledge creation, intranets may have an even smaller role to play. As Sveiby (1997) comments "unlike information, knowledge is embedded in people, and knowledge creation occurs in the process of social interaction". Knowledge exploration requires participation in a community of interaction, where tacit knowledge is shared over time and where there is necessary redundancy. The intranet 'ba' may facilitate this interaction, but there is also a need for face-to-face interaction, both formal and informal, so that the individuals can start to understand alternative views of 'reality' out of which may emerge creativity.

The need for such creativity should not be under-estimated. There are relatively few examples where a solution that worked well in one situation can be applied elsewhere without at least some modification because the context will be slightly different, especially in fast changing business environments. This was clearly evident in Global. For example, one of the intranet sites being developed was actually abandoned despite the fact that a lot of resources (both in terms of money and people's time) had been expended. The problem was that the designers had tried to copy a solution from elsewhere, and only found out when they started to 'roll-out' the intranet that in fact the system would not work on their particular infrastructure as the band-width was too small. A key issue here was that these designers had very little face-to-face interaction with the group from whom they had 'copied' the solution so the tacit knowledge of the solution provider, which included knowledge about bandwidth requirements, had not been shared.

Adopting intranets for KM may thus impede the knowledge creation process, by over-emphasising knowledge exploitation. This can lead to organisational stagnation as efficiency is promoted at the expense of innovation (Clark & Staunton, 1989). To prevent this there is a requirement to recognise the need for reinvention, which does not assume that solutions can simply be stored on the intranet and copied from one situation to another. There is also a need to understand that interaction in the social 'bar' is as important as is communication over the cyber intranet 'ba'. If organisations fail to recognise the limits of intranet technology, then the adoption of intranets may actually result in the building of electronic fences around intra-organisational boundaries.

REFERENCES

Abrahamson (1996). Management fashion. Academy of Management Review, 21, 254-285.

Boland, R.J. & Tenkasi, R.V. (1995). Perspective making and perspective taking in communities of knowing. Organization Science, 6, 4, 350-363.

Clark, P. & Staunton, N. (1989). Innovation in technology and organisation. London: Routledge.

Checkland, P. (1981). Systems thinking, systems practice. Chichester: Wiley.

Cohen, S. (1998). Knowledge management's killer application. Training and Development, 52(1), 50-53.

Cole-Gomolski, B. (1997). Users loathe to share their know-how. Computerworld, 31(46), p.6

DiMaggio, P. & Powell, W. (1990). The iron cage revisited: institutional isomorphism and collective rationality in organizational fields. American Sociological Review, 48, 147-160.

Dove, R. (1998). A knowledge management framework. Automotive manufacturing and Production, 110(1), 18-21.

Drucker, P. (1993). Post-Capitalist Society, Oxford: Butterworth-Heinemann.

Dwyer, L. (1990). Factors affecting the proficient management of product innovation. International Journal of Technology Management, 5, 6, 721-730.

Earl, M.J. (Ed.) (1996). Information Management: The Organizational Dimension, Oxford: Oxford University Press.

Fletcher, L. (1997). Information retrieval for intranets: the case for knowledge management. Document World, 2(5), 32-34.

Gardner, D. (1998). Knowledge that won't fit in a database - people. InfoWorld, 20(14), p.98.

Gibbons, M. (1994). The new production of knowledge: The dynamics of science and research in contemporary societies. London: Sage.

Grant, R. (1996). Toward a knowledge based theory of the firm. Strategic Management Journal, 17, 109-122.

Hall, R. (1993). A framework for linking intangible resources and capabilities to sustainable competitive advantage. Strategic Management Journal, 14, 607-618.

Handy (1995). The Empty Raincoat.

Hansen, M. (1998). Knowledge management: The well-connected company.

Henderson, S. (1997). Black swan don't fly double loops: The limits of the learning organization. The Learning Organization, 4, 3, 99-105.

Hibbard, J. and Carillo, K.M. (1998). Knowledge revolution. Informationweek, 5(663), 49-54.

Hosking, D. & Morley, I. (1991). A Social Psychology of Organising: People, processes and contexts. London: Harvester Wheatsheaf.

Jahnke, A. (1998). Shareware. CIO, 11(18), 10.

KPMG (1998). Knowledge Management research report.

Lam, A. (1998). Tacit knowledge, organisational learning and innovation: A societal perspective.

Lank, E. (1998). Cafe society. People Management, 4(4), 40-43.

Levinthal, D. & March, J. (1993). The myopia of learning. Strategic Management Journal, 14, 95-112.

Liff, S. (1997). Constructing HR information systems. Human Resource Management Journal, 7, 2, 18-30

Malhorta, Y. (1998). Tools at work: Deciphering the knowledge management hype. The Journal of Quality and Participation, 21, 4, 58-60.

Marshall, L. (1997). Facilitating knowledge management and knowledge sharing: New opportunities for information professionals. Online, 21(5), 92-98.

Newell, S., Swan, J. & Preston, J. (1998). Trust and inter-organisational networking. Paper presented at the 13th EGOS colloquim, Mastricht, July.

Nonaka, I. (1994). A dynamic theory of organisational knowledge creation. Organization Sciences, 5, 14-37.

Nonaka, I. & Takeuchi, H. (1995). The knowledge creating company. New York: Oxford University Press.

Nonaka, I. (1998). The concept of 'ba': Building a foundation for knowledge creation. California Management Review, 40, 3, 40-54.

Pfeffer, J. (1981). Power in organisations. Boston: Pitman.

Polanyi, M. (1966). Personal knowledge: Towards a post-critical philosophy. New York: Harper Torchbooks.

Popper, K. (1972). Objective knowledge: An evolutionary approach. Oxford: Clarendon Press.

Ruggles, R. (1998).The state of the notion: knowledge management in practice. California Management Review, 40(3), 80-89.

Senge, P. (1990). The fifth discipline: The art and practice of the learning organisation. London: Doubleday.

Silverman, D. (1970). The theory of organisations. London: Heinemann.

Strassmann, P.A. (1998). Taking a measure of knowledge assets. Computerworld, 32(4), p.74.

Sveiby (1997).

Tansley, C. & Watson, T. (1998). Managers, strategies and information technologies in international human resource management. Paper presented at the 6th conference on International Human Resource Management, Paderborn, Germany.

Trompenaars, F. (1995). Riding the waves of culture: Understanding cultural diversity in business. London: Nicholas Brealey.

Tsoukas, H. (1996). The firm as a distributed knowledge system: A constructionist approach. Strategic Management Journal, 17, 11-25.

Weick, K. (1990). Technology and equivoque: Sensemaking in new technologies. In: P.S. Goodman, L.S. Sproull and Associates. Technology and Organizations. Oxford: Jossey Bass.

Centralised Health Information Management In New Zealand: Advancing Health Or Invading Privacy?

Felix B Tan & Gehan Gunasekara
The University of Auckland, Private Bag 920]9, Auckland, New Zealand
Tel: +64 93737999. Fax: + 64 93737566
f tan @ auckland. ac. nz & g. gunasekara @ auckland. ac. nz

ABSTRACT

This paper reports on recent developments in the management of health information in New Zealand and the implications these initiatives have raised regarding individual privacy. Set up in]993 to implement the country's health information strategy, the New Zealand Health Information Service (NZHIS) has recently established a national health register. At the heart of this development are three national databases: the National Health Index, the Medical Warnings System and the National Minimum Data Set. These applications and their functions are presented. Also discussed is a number of other health information management initiatives currently being explored.

The paper contends that these initiatives under the guise of advancing the nation's health may instead be infringing the privacy and confidentiality of the nation's citizens. The paper further considers the application of New Zealand's privacy regime (the Privacy Act]993 and the Health Information Privacy Code) to the development of centralised health information management systems. It concludes by considering the possibility of hidden agendas despite the provisions of the nation's privacy rules.

INTRODUCTION

Purchasing and providing health services is an information—intensive activity. Millions of pages of information are recorded every year. Much of the information is relevant to the on going care of individuals. However, health information is plagued with problems of access, duplication and interpretation. Health information management in New Zealand is no exception. For example, the nation's health professionals requiring information for the care and treatment of patients have had to rely on fragmented information flows — as information needed for care or treatment of patients is collected at various sources. As a result, these professionals find it difficult to obtain relevant information in a timely and cost effective manner. There is a consensus in the country's health sector that the existing systems and organisational arrangements do not meet current needs and will not easily accommodate the requirements of the health sector reforms and the information needs of the future. In response to this, the 1991 Health Information Strategy outlines a framework for the development of health information services to meet the national requirements for health information.

This paper essentially describes recent developments in health information management in New Zealand initiated by the proposals in the 1991 Health Information Strategy. It discusses the role of the New Zealand Health Information Service (NZHIS) in the development of a national health register. It also considers the issue of privacy and confidentiality of the collection and use of health information. The paper argues that there is more than meet the eye. The government purports that a centralised health information management system should result in better health delivery by freeing up health resources (Ministry of Health, 1996), but at who's expense?

To set the scene, the paper begins with a background and an overview of the country's health information management. A review of the health information strategy initiative and a description of what has been implemented follows. A discussion of the issues around privacy and confidentiality ensues with special focus on the nation's privacy rules. It concludes by questioning the real motives of the New Zealand Health Sector and its Government for developing a centralised health register. The paper suggests that to date the initiatives have failed to take into account and comply with New Zealand's stringent privacy rules.

HEALTH INFORMATION MANAGEMENT IN NEW ZEALAND

Up to and until the early 1990s, health information at a national level was provided and used by the then area health boards, private hospitals and the Department of Health (Ministry of Health, 1991). A review of the health information systems and related services then identified significant problems with the existing national collections and services. Some of these problems related to (i) lack of quality standards and standard data definitions; (ii) problems of data accessibility and timeliness (iii) uncoordinated and overlapping points of collection; and (iv) a poorly maintained National Master Patient Index. The review concluded that the current systems do not meet existing needs, neither are they able to accommodate the new requirements of the future, or the new requirements of the health sector reforms. A further conclusion was that new data systems, processing and organisational structures are necessary to support the development of world class health care provision and management. There was a considerable consensus between, and within, working groups involved in the review on the need for change and the direction of that change.

In 1991, a national health information strategy was developed as a collaborative effort by the country's health sector (Ministry of Health, 1991). The strategy was designed to address the lack of relevant, timely, and accurate information. It provided a national framework for the development of health information services to meet the national requirements for health information. The strategy suggested the need to establish a new entity - the 'National Health Information Service' - to manage the national health information services in New Zealand. This new entity, described in the next section, would streamline many of the current activities and manage the services as a business.

NZ HEALTH INFORMATION SERVICE

The New Zealand Health Information Service (NZHIS) is a group within the Ministry of Health responsible for the collection and dissemination of health-related information. It was set up in 1993 to implement the country's health information strategy. Its primary goal is to make accurate information readily available and accessible in a timely manner throughout the health sector. The NZHIS therefore has responsibility for all aspects of health information management — from the collection, processing, maintenance and distribution of health data and statistics to the continuing development and maintenance of a national health information system, including the provision of appropriate databases, systems and information products (NZHIS, 1997a). The vision of NZHIS is to support the health sector's ongoing effort to improve health information management in New Zealand. The NZHIS has recently established a national health register which may be the envy of many larger, wealthier countries (Sybase, 1998). This centralised repository of health information is summarised in the next section.

THE NATIONAL HEALTH REGISTER

The national health register consists of several core applications implemented on the Sun Microsystems platform with multi-CPU servers. Running over public electronic highways, these applications contain information for secondary and tertiary health events from Crown Health Enterprises (CHEs). At the heart of this development are three national databases: the National Health Index (NHI), the Medical Warnings System (MWS) and the National Minimum Data Set (NMDS). These have been designed to incorporate stringent safeguards to protect the information they hold from unauthorised access or misuse, but also to make crucial information about patients and their health available to authorised users for legitimate purposes.

National Health Index

The National Health Index (NHI) is a population-based register of all healthcare users (patients) in New Zealand. Assigned to each patient is a unique identifier allocated on a random basis. The NHI holds details such as names, alternate names, addresses, date of birth, gender and ethnicity. This enables an individual to be positively and uniquely identified for the purposes of healthcare services and records. The NHI number is in fact not a number but a string of seven characters, the first three of which are letters and the last four are numbers. Details of the core fields, which are recorded in the NHI database for an individual, can be perused at NZHIS's online publication (http ://www .nzhis govt. nz/publications/NHI-MWS .html).

The NHI is developed essentially to help protect personally identifiable health data, particularly data held on computer systems, and to enable linkage between different information systems whilst still protecting privacy. Access to the NHI is therefore restricted to authorised users and is permitted by the Health Information Privacy Code 1994, under the Privacy Act 1993 (NZHIS, 1997b).

Medical Warnings System

The Medical Warnings System (MWS) is designed to 'warn" healthcare providers of the presence of any known risk factors that may be important in making clinical decisions about individual patient care (e.g. allergies, sensitivities, past significant history, etc). The MWS provides information on medical warnings and alerts, healthcare event summaries and donor information. These data are held nationally because of the clinical importance of quick access to the clinical information, and the relative geographic mobility of the New Zealand population. This enables a provider anywhere in the country to obtain potentially life-saving information about a specific patient in their care, once the patient has been uniquely identified. The responsibility for making sure that the content of the MWS is up to date will rest primarily with its users, the healthcare providers (NZHIS, 1997b).

National Minimum Dataset

The National Minimum Dataset (NMDS) is a single integrated collection of health data required at a national level for policy formulation and performance monitoring and evaluation. The NMDS provides a reliable, validated and comprehensive but selected set of information on (i) the health status of the New Zealand population; (ii) the factors which influence health status; (iii) health resources and their utilisation; (iv) the outputs, outcomes and impact of health services for national policy making; and (iv) the performance of the health sector (NZHIS, 1 997a).

The NHI, MWS and NMDS are central to effective national health information management. In addition to these, the NZHIS also maintains a national cancer registry and records mental health events (NZHIS, 1997a). The NZ Cancer Register has operated since 1948 and is a population-based tumour register of all primary malignant disease. It is regarded as one of the oldest cancer register in the world (Sybase, 1998). The mental health system is a register for all psychiatric patients currently in hospitals together with all admissions and discharges since 1974.

OTHER HEALTH INFORMATION MANAGEMENT INITIATIVES

Plans are now in place to expand the existing information base to include primary care information (NZHIS, 1997a). Considerable progress in this direction has been achieved, and various sites in primary care are operating with information systems that break new ground and offer significant advantages to patients, providers and purchasers. The use of electronic data interchange - for example, sending and receiving laboratory test orders and results or exchanging patient details for admission and discharge - is growing fast. Many provider groups are now making regular use of such facilities, or have pilot programs under way to explore their benefits. It will not be long before many of these programmes coalesce into larger groups offering more services and therefore greater benefits to both doctors and their patients (NZHIS, 1997b).

Although the core function of the NZHIS is the management of health information for the Ministry of Health, it has also established a business centre, offering its services on the open commercial market. The NZHIS has the flexibility to leverage its expertise to tender and bid for outside projects to generate additional revenue. An example of such external projects is the recent implementation of a pharmaceutical data warehouse. Funded by two commercial enterprises and in coordination with another agency responsible for managing pharmaceutical expenditure policy, the NZHIS was contracted to establish and store a data warehouse for all pharmaceutical information from across New Zealand (Sybase, 1998).

Every healthcare provider in New Zealand records and exchanges health information, and this is increasingly done in electronic format. The National Health Index (NHI) plays an important role in this process by providing a unique identifier for the whole health sector, including primary care. A wider use of the NHI would greatly improve the exchange of information between healthcare providers and make possible the integration of patient information from various sources. This can be facilitated by a Health Intranet (NZHIS, 1998). Pilot projects are currently underway to develop a proof of concept. This will test the practical benefits of the Health Intranet. When fully implemented, this initiative will provide a secure means of communications nationwide, with access to all health information systems for all healthcare providers registered to use the intranet.

ISSUES OF PRIVACY AND CONFIDENTIALITY

Most health information is collected in a situation of confidence and trust for the purposes of care and treatment. Assurances as to confidentiality and protection of privacy are vital components of the relationship between patient and health professional and are necessary if the latter is to obtain accurate information from the former in order to make an accurate diagnosis. It is therefore not surprising that the modern privacy rules overlap substantially with a much older law of confidentiality and the medical ethics of the profession. The notions of dignity and autonomy which underlie New Zealand's privacy law have also much in common with the idea of informed consent which is central to current medical practice (S lane, 1 998a). Against this backdrop it is strange that there has been to date very little public outcry over the development of a centralised health register in this country. This can be explained by two possible reasons. Firstly, there appears to be a lack of public awareness of the implications of these developments. According to a recent report prepared for the New Zealand Privacy Commissioner (Stevens, 1998), the issue of health information has bypassed public scrutiny. There are still many details to be addressed and debated. The lack of discussion involving all parties concerned has resulted in many doctors and even more patients being unaware of the type of patient details which are going to be collated and kept by health authorities. The same report goes as far as to suggest that there is something disquieting about the way health information is being managed in this country, with the health sector exhibiting a lack of openness about the various developments and plans in the collection of individual health information. As this program moves forward, it seems appropriate that more attention should be given to consultation with the public and debate within parliament. However this is more than a matter of good public relations: it is a legal requirement of New Zealand's privacy regime that individuals about whom information is collected are informed as to the purposes of the collection as well as the intended recipients of it.

Secondly, it might be thought that there is a high level of acceptance and trust amongst New Zealanders that the information collected will be used appropriately. For instance, information can be used to catch people defrauding the system by matching data from various agencies like inland revenue, accident compensation and social welfare. Data matching is now a practice since the middle of 1998. Television commercials advising the public about inter-agency data matching serve as a warning about defrauding the government. According to a senior health official interviewed by the author, the general population appears to be comfortable with the concept of a health number for tracking hospital admission and discharge; the use of a universal number by general practitioners; and the recording of allergies and health history on a national database. For example, Community Service Cards were first issued in early 1990s and today around 50% of the population carry them. These cards entitle cardholders to discounted consultations with general practitioners, but they do not contain the NHI number or any medical information. It appears that people are often surprised that these cards are not linked to their medical details and do not give their NHI number when swiped. An 'improvement' to this card is currently underway in the form of a medical smart card pilot. The smart cards combine Community Service Card details, NHI number and medical warnings of the cardholder. New Zealanders have a strong history in accepting the use of electronic systems, with the highest penetration of EFTPOS terminals in the world (New Zealand Bankers Association, 1995). This may explain the high level of acceptance of the development of a centralised health information system and the use of electronic health cards in this country.

On the other hand such acquiescence on the part of the general population cannot be assumed to exist. In the first place, while it is true that various data matching schemes between government departments exist (the Privacy Commissioner is empowered to sanction such schemes provided there are certain safeguards), the data matching schemes are targeted at what is perceived to be a minority anti-social element in the population. It is a very different thing to build up comprehensive health profiles of every single person, including law abiding citizens. Furthermore reported complaints to the Privacy Commissioner provide evidence that ordinary citizens are particularly sensitive about their health information or about the potential misuse by health agencies of information about them.

In one case, for example, a customer complained when a pharmacy (where she was due to collect medicines which had earlier been out of stock) delivered medicines to her home without prior warning — it was a case of the extra customer service not being appreciated. While a simple phone call would have avoided the problem an interesting question arises as to whether delivering medicines are directly connected with the pharmacist's purpose for holding the customer's name and address. Another complaint arose over the wording of a form asking parents to consent to immunisation. The form did not state how the information would be used. It also contained a number without explanation. The complainant assumed that children had been allocated identification numbers and that the information would be entered into a database. In fact the number was simply a batch coding for the vaccines, so that if something went wrong with one of the batches, the affected children could be contacted. Apart from statistical data, the main use of the information was in fact to inform the children's doctors so they would know whether to offer immunisation. These cases show a keen awareness by members of the public of their right to privacy.

NEW ZEALAND'S PRIVACY REGIME

At first sight New Zealand has a privacy regime which is well geared to the challenges posed by the development of a national health register. The Privacy Act 1993 (the Act) is radical in its application as it applies to both the public and private sectors — it applies to all "agencies" which are defined so widely that even individuals are subject to the Act. The Act governs the collection, use and disclosure of "personal information" (information about identifiable individuals). The Act also entitles individuals to access information held about them. Most importantly, the Act is information based, not document based. It does not therefore matter whether the information is stored or transferred through electronic means or through paper files —the same rules apply.

Central to the Act are the 12 Information Privacy Principles. For instance Information Privacy Principle 1 (IPP 1) requires that only information necessary for a lawful purpose of the agency is collected and that the collection must be necessary for that purpose. However this is also good information management practice. While the design of any data system proceeds backwards from the required outputs, one of the major health agencies recently put under scrutiny has been criticised because its outputs were evolving rather than having been stated at the outset (Stevens, 1998). IPP 3 is particularly important. It requires that an individual from whom information is collected is not only made aware of the fact of collection but also informed of the purposes for the collection and the intended recipients of the information. This most basic of requirements is evidently not always complied with especially when frontline health care providers are required to forward information about patients to central funding authorities (Slane, 1998a).

IPP 3 is relevant to Information Privacy Principles 10 and 11. IPP 10 requires that information held about an individual only be used for the purpose for which it was collected or for a directly related purpose. IPP 11 requires that personal information held by an agency not be disclosed outside that agency unless such disclosure is one of the purposes in connection with which the information was obtained, or is a directly related purpose. A crucial point here is that the purpose of the collection must be at the time of collection of the information. In other words, the purpose must have been communicated to the data subject (IPP 3). Otherwise, an agency could arbitrarily make up purposes for the information as it went along, or think of new uses for information it already has. This is contrary to the requirements of the Act. If the information is to be used or disclosed for purposes different to those articulated at the outset, consent must be sought from the individuals concerned.

One of New Zealand's major funding authorities (North Health) has been at the forefront of moves towards integrating primary health information (doctors and pharmacies) into its data depository. Through use of the NHI number the authority plans to collate and track individuals' attendance with different doctors, specialists, pharmacies, hospitals and other clinics over their entire lifetime (Stevens, 1998). However, in brochures encouraging the use of the NHI number, no explanation was offered as to the information which would be collected through its use or as to the ultimate uses and recipients of it. More seriously, in terms of IPP 3, no purposes for the compilation of the information were clearly stated. It has been rightly pointed out that while the agency may have been merely seeking to gather as much information as it could while not yet having formulated uses for it, such an approach is anathema to the Privacy Act (Stevens, 1998). The end of this discussion will focus on the real motives for establishing centralised health information management and as to whether any of these goals are sanctioned by the privacy regime.

Other Information Privacy Principles are of significance for centralised health information management. IPP 5 is the only principle specifically addressing the security of storage of information. The Privacy Commissioner has observed that the focus of the Act is not only in stopping leaks but also in determining where the pipes lead (Slane, 1998b). IPP 8 requires that agencies take steps to ensure information is accurate prior to using it — a step that would seem especially relevant in the health context. IPP 9 requires that information be retained for no longer than necessary. Last but not least is IPP 12, which relates to unique identifiers. Amongst other things, IPP 12 prohibits an agency from assigning, to an individual, the same unique identifier that has been assigned by another agency. It will shortly be seen that this last requirement has been specifically modified in relation to use of the NHI number.

It should also be noted briefly that the information privacy principles are, for the most part, not enforceable through the courts but rather through an alternative dispute resolution procedure beginning with the Privacy Commissioner (who acts in the first place as a conciliator) although a complaint can be taken to a tribunal which has considerable powers including the award of damages.

There are a number of qualifications and exceptions to the Information Privacy Principles. Some of these are stated within the principles themselves, for instance noncompliance for law enforcement and public health and safety purposes. Another common exception is where information is collected for research or statistical purposes provided it is to be published in a non-identifiable form. There are also grounds for denying access to personal information under 'PP 6.

The principles generally provide that non-compliance may be authorised by the individual concerned. This has the potential to cause serious mischief, particularly when agencies regard consent as a panacea. There is always the tendency to regard a one-off consent as sufficient. Consent must be not only informed but genuine. In the health arena patients are at the receiving end of an unequal power relationship and the Privacy Commissioner has referred to the "façade of patient control" (Slane, 1998b).

Finally the Privacy Commissioner is empowered to modify the information privacy principles (by prescribing greater or lesser standards than contained in the principles) in relation to specified matters by issuing codes of practice, which have the same force as the principles. This allows flexibility in adjusting the Act to the requirements of particular industries or types of information. Not surprisingly, one of the first codes of practice to be promulgated (there have so far been very few) was the Health Information Privacy Code 1994 (the Code) which is discussed next.

HEALTH INFORMATION PRIVACY CODE

In the introduction to the code three special characteristics of the health sector and health information are cited as the rationale for a separate code. These are: firstly, confidentiality of collection (in the context of a confidential relationship); secondly, the nature of the information (highly sensitive); and thirdly, ongoing use (health information may be required long after it has ceased to be needed for the original episode of care and treatment). It will be observed that of these the first two at least provide justification for more stringent standards than in the Act.

Despite this, the Code itself is an unremarkable document. The 12 Health Information Privacy Rules broadly follow the Information Privacy Principles. Perhaps the most useful feature is a detailed commentary, which is no doubt useful to health professionals. There are some modifications of the privacy principles. From the point of view of the present discussion the most significant alteration is in Rule 12(3) which allows specified agencies to assign the NHI number as an unique identifier. There are some safeguards. For instance Rule 12(6) provides that an agency must not require an individual to disclose any unique identifier assigned to that individual unless the disclosure is for one of the purposes in connection with which that unique identifier was assigned or for a directly related purpose. However as was observed earlier, it is extremely doubtful if these purposes have been communicated to the individuals concerned or indeed even articulated in the first place.

Rule 12(6) and its parent 'PP 12(4) are seriously flawed for another reason. They do not preclude the unique identifier being obtained from someone other than the individual concerned. In the moves described earlier by the funding authorities towards building up a data depository one of the steps has been to require every claim for subsidy payments (most prescriptions and laboratory tests as well as some doctors visits are subsidised by the Government in New Zealand) to be accompanied by the NHI number of the patient concerned. It is easy to see how an otherwise reluctant profession can be coerced into supplying the number. Yet as currently worded, they can be made to disclose the number for any purpose whatever.

The lack of adequate safeguards here is disappointing. When New Zealand's first privacy legislation was enacted in 1991, it served as a convenient smokescreen to allow the Government to proceed with plans for data matching. There is a danger that the Code will encourage similar complacency. Indeed it appear that the Health Ministry's statement in its web site that the Privacy Commissioner was involved in ensuring the highest standards of privacy were without foundation — the office had not even been consulted (Stevens, 1998).

HIDDEN AGENDAS?

What are the possible motives or the rationale for centralised health information management? A number of possible explanations have been given (Stevens, 1998). No doubt the fundamental concern (in New Zealand as in other developed nations) has been to control the cost of health care to the Government. One suggestion has been for "capitation" systems where individual customers are enrolled with a health management organisation and identified each time they seek a health care service so that costs can be referred back to the responsible organisation. If information is power then an interesting application of a complete patient database is as a means of wresting power away from the doctors who are seen as currently accountable to nobody for their economic efficiency.

Another explanation has been that the new systems will eliminate or reduce the incidence of fraud (especially over state health care subsidy payments). However these claims (for instance that as much as 11% of all claims are fraudulent) have been ridiculed — if hundreds of millions of dollars were indeed being lost it is hard to explain why to date little or no efforts have been spent on audit and fraud detection. In any case it is extremely doubtful that the elimination of waste is covered by the ambit of the law enforcement exceptions to the privacy principles.

A more radical plan has been hinted at. This is to set up, for planning purposes, a database which records, for every individual in New Zealand, a substantial degree of detail about symptoms as well as diagnoses and treatments (using a set of standard codes), and captures every health care transaction and the cost of that transaction whether or not it is state funded. Such a database would be a world first, and may well set New Zealand up as the world's foremost health research field and testbed. However such lofty goals (even if they exist) have not been articulated at the level of the individuals concerned which, as explained earlier, is a clear violation of New Zealand's privacy regime.

Cogent reasons exist, on the other hand, for not relying on centralised medical records. In making diagnosis and treatment decisions, good medical practice suggests not trusting information recorded by others, especially where the accuracy of the information is vital. There is little or no empirical research linking better patient health outcomes with centralised medical records. Hence a full and accessible patient health record may not necessarily be beneficial to the patient.

Finally, the authors argue that a less benevolent possibility exists for the use for centralised health records. if the tentative steps taken so far in New Zealand eventually mature into a comprehensive centralised record for every individual then it will be possible to give every individual a classification as either a good, average or bad health "risk". The utility of such information to insurance companies is obvious. It has been fashionable for some time, in New Zealand, to take an "insurer" view of health spending. There have been proposals for privatisation and accompanying cuts in Government health spending. One possibility, which may be attractive to the Government, will be the "farming out" of certain patients to the private sector. The existence of a precise "risk assessment" mechanism will undoubtedly assist this process.

CONCLUSION

In summary, this article briefly outlines recent developments in health information management in New Zealand. A centralised national health register is now in place with a few thousand PCs linked to a central IT client/server platform. This system now services around 30 hospitals and other medical services providing health care to New Zealand's 3.6 million population. The resolution of a number of issues pertaining to individual privacy and medical ethics are the current challenges facing the nation.

While New Zealand possesses a highly developed body of privacy rules which clearly apply to the initiatives highlighted these are evidently not always complied with. The privacy rules mandate the fostering of greater public awareness of the uses of information. To date this has been lacking. It remains to be seen how effective the Privacy Commissioner will be in his potentially powerful role in monitoring and regulating the initiatives for centralised health information management.

REFERENCES

Ministry of Health (1991) *Health Information Strategy for New Zealand,* 1991.

Ministry of Health (1996) *Improving Our Health Information System.* Http://www.health.govt.nzIHIS2OOO/ generallhis2ooo_news .html.

New Zealand Bankers Association (1995) *Annual Review]995,* Wellington. NZHIS (1 997 a) *Data & Services.* Http ://www.nzhis . ~ovt.nz/Service _guide. html.

NZHIS (1997b) *National Health Index and Medical Warning System.* Http://www.nzhis .govt.nz/publications/NHI-MWS .html.

NZHIS (1998) *Health Intranet Project.* Http://www . nzhis. govt.nz/projects/intranet.html.

Slane, B. (1998a) *Centralised Databases: People, Privacy and Planning.* A paper presented by the Privacy Commissioner to the New Zealand - Australia Health *IT* Directors Meeting, 18 February

Slane, B. (1998b) *Information Protection in Healthcare: Knowledge at What Price?* Address by the Privacy Commissioner to the Health Summit '98, 15 July.

Stevens, R. (1998) *Medical Record Databases: Just What You Need?* A Report for the Privacy Commissioner, April.

Sybase (1998) *NZHIS Health Register,* Sybase, 1,, Quarter, 16-17.

Balancing the Privacy Scales: A Framework for Managing Competing Values

Francena S. Warden, Ph.D.
Information Privacy Consulting Services, Hingham, MA 02043
(781) 749-3761, fwarden@lynx.neu.edu

Eileen M. Trauth, Ph.D.
College of Business Administration, Northeastern University, Boston, MA 02115
617-373-2759, 617-373-3166 (fax), trauth@neu.edu

ABSTRACT

In order to make privacy a reality it is necessary to develop viable ways of implementing, at the organizational policy level, the ideals embodied in privacy at the national policy level. But developing organizational policies involves acknowledging that privacy is not an absolute. Rather, it is a matter of striking the proper balance among competing interests. In order to help IS and general managers in this effort, a framework is presented which incorporates societal, legal, policy and technological perspectives on privacy. These perspectives are employed in considering the tradeoffs and issues associated with achieving a proper balance in establishing organizational privacy policy. This framework provides a conceptual mechanism for organizing and evaluating the volumes of information about the ever-changing topic of privacy.

Keywords: Information Privacy, Balance, Organizational Privacy Policy, Privacy Perspectives and Dimensions, Interdisciplinary Research

INTRODUCTION

In the movement toward making privacy a reality two important challenges arise. One is to develop viable ways of implementing, at the organizational policy level, the ideals embodied in privacy at the national policy level. The other is to develop organizational policies while acknowledging that privacy is not an absolute. Rather, it is a matter of striking the proper balance among competing interests. This paper reports on some of the findings from a research project directed at responding to both of these issues (Warden, forthcoming). This research is directed at developing a framework that identifies and represents the dimensions of privacy policy. The dimension examined in this paper is *balance*. This work contributes to the goal of better management of the information resource by providing tools to help the manager construct viable privacy policies. This paper, first, describes the framework and then discusses some of the issues associated with achieving balance. Finally, it provides guidelines and examples regarding the implementation of this framework.

METHODOLOGY

This research was based upon a critical analysis of the privacy literature from the 1960's through the 1990's. This literature included books, articles in scholarly journals, newspapers and magazines. This literature is interdisciplinary, in that it looks at privacy from multiple perspectives. This body of literature constituted the "data" that was analyzed by means of the interpretive methods of open coding and hermeneutic analysis. The goal of this research was to develop a framework to aid in the creation of organizational privacy policies by analyzing and synthesizing the body of knowledge that already exists.[1]

COMPONENTS OF THE FRAMEWORK

The framework consists of relating the *perspectives* on privacy to the *dimension* of balance. Four perspectives on privacy were employed in analyzing the literature: society, law, policy, and technology. Society is a relevant perspective, since privacy is primarily a social issue. As a member of society, an individual must balance his/her need for privacy with the need to interact in various contexts of society. The law is an important aspect of privacy, given that it is through the legal definitions that society addresses the right to privacy and redress for invasions of privacy. Policy is the manifestation of society's needs and desires combined with the law. Privacy policy appears under several different constructs, such as social policy, public

Table 1. Balance Dimension		
Perspectives/Dimension	BALANCE Groups	BALANCE Values
SOCIETY	Among Units in Society Gender and Strangers	Competing Values Processes and Mechanisms
LAW	Judicial Balancing	Immoral vs. Illegal Reasonable vs. Legitimate
POLICY	Public Sector Policy Private Sector Policy	Codes of Ethics Roles People Play
TECHNOLOGY	Communication Negotiation	New Ethical Issues Responsibilities of Computer Professionals

policy, and organizational policy. It may be explicit, such as executive decisions and corporate policy statements, or implicit, such as judicial decisions and market-driven actions.[2] Finally, technology has an important effect on privacy. Given various levels of technological understanding, individual expectations of privacy are inconsistent. This in turn creates a disconnect within society, requiring an emphasis on balancing competing values in a consistent yet realistic manner. It is incumbent on the technologically literate to explore methods of providing the appropriate levels of privacy, as defined by society. This is often accomplished through policy and law.

The balance dimension is a broad category that was constructed from several themes found in the literature. *Balance* refers to the process of weighing two equally important values and/or outcomes, especially among groups, and includes justification for both means and ends. As shown in Table 1, the balance dimension is composed of two sub-categories: balance among units of groups and balance of values. The balance among groups sub-category addresses the needs of individuals vis a vis groups – the interaction among units versus intimacy – as well as the needs of individuals and the social order. The balancing of values involves the identification of the relative importance of competing values. Different processes and mechanisms are used in the social, legal, and technical environments. There is not a simple process or mechanism for accomplishing an appropriate balance, and the point of "equilibrium" is constantly changing, in terms of time and place (context). Therefore, it is more appropriate to consider privacy as a continuum, along which there are various points of balance. Schoeman (1992, p. 156) also presents privacy as a continuum, contrasting privacy and autonomy: "[W]hereas privacy suggests involvement and intimacy, autonomy suggest isolation."

In terms of society, the extremes are absolute privacy (isolation and autonomy) and no privacy. Each individual must identify a comfort zone along this continuum, particularly with respect to the group(s) with which one is interacting, be it a small group or society at large, as well as the relative importance of the value. The laws must reflect society's values and provide for regulation, enforcement, and redress for loss of privacy. Voluntary policies in the private sector allow organizations to define the appropriate balance in particular contexts, given the culture of the organization. By incorporating the balanced expectations into communicated policy, both employees and employers have a sense of understanding and commitment to that policy. This allows for flexibility within bounds of that policy in specific situations due to business and technical-related change. The introduction of new technology requires a feedback process to assess the effect of the use of that technology on the adequacy of the existing policy, and laws. While the underlying values remain constant, the mechanisms for ensuring an adequate balance may change.

ACHIEVING BALANCE
Balance among Groups in Society
The balance among groups sub-category as it relates to the societal perspective includes a discussion of the needs of individuals vis a vis groups as well as the needs of individuals and the social order. A discussion of gender demonstrates that particular groups may have different needs and different mechanisms for meeting those needs. The discussion of strangers concerns people who, by definition, are not members of a group and present particular issues with respect to reputation and trust. This balancing act is played out with respect to each of the perspectives. For example, legal balancing involves which group is doing the balancing, from what authority and the biases of the law. Balancing with respect to policy involves the definition of public versus private sectors, as well as organizations (groups), and methods to address the democratic and equality aspects of each "group."

Westin (1967) discusses individuals' desire to balance the need for privacy with the need to be an active part of society. Moore (1984, p. 78) discusses balance in terms of "civilized society" and the need for private rights against the social order. The need for privacy, or protection from intrusion derives from the perceived difference between benefits and costs. He discusses alternatives to or substitutions for privacy, such as discretion — in the "sense of social rules against noticing or even discussing specific human actions," or direct participation in decisions affecting daily life. Culnan's (1993) research on consumer privacy made references to others such as Laufer and Wolfe's (1977) "Calculus of Behavior", Westin's (1991) "Willingness to Tradeoff Index", and the Code of Fair Information Practices. Culnan's position is that people will surrender a measure of privacy in exchange for some economic or social benefit.

Gender highlights one aspect of balancing among units: the influence of the composition of the units. Four authors who directly address gender as an issue are Pedersen (1987), Stone and Stone (1990), Loch and Conger (1996), and Moore (1984). Pedersen's (1987) research on patterns of privacy preferences found that women are more likely than men to prefer intimacy with family and intimacy with friends whereas men prefer isolation. His analysis includes the observation that women's preference for intimacy is due to a social orientation, whereas men seek isolation for security, and in order to be better prepared to protect themselves from others and from the elements.

Stone and Stone (1990) built upon Derlaga and Chaiken's[3] hypothesis that American cultural norms influence women to disclose more than men. As a result of socialization, women are prone to disclose information that exposes weaknesses, while men disclose information about their strengths. They note that females are more concerned about personal history, interests, values, and social adjustment than males who prefer larger interpersonal distances. Loch and Conger (1996) found that computer use is gender-biased. More males use computers and computer use is generally viewed as a masculine activity. They also found evidence of gender differences in ethical intention formation. Moore (1984) discusses gender in several cultures. It is primarily the men who constitute the public, women who constitute the private domain.

Another aspect of privacy among groups is the non-member or stranger. Nock (1993) wrote extensively on the "anonymous society of strangers," as it relates to the cost of privacy. He suggested that while having more strangers implied having more privacy, this privacy makes it difficult to form reliable opinions of one another. He discusses ordeals as rituals to determine whether an individual is telling the truth whereas credentials are something that enables a person to have credit or confidence. Credentials are the visible portion of public reputation. He develops these themes of credentials and ordeals, which are two elementary forms of overt surveillance required by the presence of strangers. One must augment credentials with ordeals, such as the lie detector, integrity testing, and drug testing, which are always used as the last resort when an individual's word can not be trusted.

Balancing Competing Values

The second sub-category in this framework is balancing values. From a societal perspective, the concern is with the processes and mechanisms that are involved in balancing competing values. The relative importance of values is key to the balancing process; it is when these values are equally important that the process becomes difficult. Examples of competing values are morality vs. privacy and the right of the individual to be left alone vs. the public's right to know.

Morality intersects with privacy when individuals' private behavior is in conflict with what society considers to be acceptable or moral. Examples are abortion, contraception, and homosexuality. The balance issue is whether private behavior should be of public concern. The social construction of reality involves society's objective reality (morality) and an individual's subjective experience of that reality (Berger and Luckmann, 1990). There are three possible outcomes. The individual may acquiesce to society's definition/conception of immorality and modify her or his behavior. Alternately, the individual may persist with the behavior, but only in private. Finally, society may change its perception and find the behavior to be acceptable, or at least, tolerable. In the first case, the individual no longer requires privacy; s/he is socialized into changed behavior. In the second case, society's willingness to leave the individual alone affords her or him the privacy needed.[4] In the third case, individuals change the reality of society through legitimation of the behavior. This is often evidenced by new legislation or policy outlining the acceptable parameters of the behavior (or more likely, the unacceptable parameters).[5]

Another set of competing values involves the public's right to know. At issue here is the individual's right to protection from invasion of privacy by the disclosure of private facts. From society's perspective, public interest or newsworthiness justifies disclosure. Chemerinsky (1991, p. 753) argues that it is "inconsistent with the First Amendment to allow liability for publishing true information." Nevertheless, the privacy invasion concern remains with public disclosure, regardless of whether the information is true or not. From this perspective the focus of attention is on the particular privacy interests that might justify interfering with First Amendment freedoms, regardless of the truthfulness of the information. Simitis (1987) observes that there is a constant adjustment of the boundary between the individual's right to be let alone and the public's need to be informed.

Kling and Allen (1996) consider five orientations with respect to competing values. The *privacy enterprise model* enhances the profitability of financial systems, often at the cost of consumers' privacy whereas the *statist model* values the efficiency of government institutions in order to emphasize citizens' obligations to the state. The *libertarian model* emphasizes civil liberties over other social purposes, such as profitability or welfare of the state. In the *neopopulist model* the emphasis is on the responsiveness of enterprises to the needs of ordinary citizens. Finally, the *systems model* considers the motivation of certain systems (such as financial ones) to be technically well organized, efficient, reliable, and aesthetically pleasing.

MANAGERIAL IMPLICATIONS FOR CREATING ORGANIZATIONAL PRIVACY POLICY

Gavison (1984) discusses the coherent values of privacy, noting that neither perfect privacy nor total loss of privacy is desirable. Instead, there must be a balance between privacy and interaction. It is not necessarily true that the more privacy people have, the better off they are. She identifies two clusters of concerns. One set, relating to the individual, includes freedom from physical access[6], promoting liberty of action[7], freedom from censure and ridicule, promoting mental health[8], promoting autonomy[9], promoting human relations[10], and limiting exposure. The second cluster, relating to society, includes protection of individual freedom in a society that is not tolerant of differences and endeavors to cope with a lack of consensus regarding the limitations of liberty.

Alderman and Kennedy (1995, p. 332) observe that sometimes the best safeguard is simply knowing that privacy cannot be expected. However, people are also learning to bargain for privacy by becoming more vigilant and altering their expectations. They propose the following solution:

This combination of education and altered expectations may hold the key to privacy protection in the future. There is a growing consensus that if the jumble of state and federal statutes, consumer pressure, and self-help is to be unified into meaningful privacy protection in the digital age, then we will have to do more than pass a law. The law in general, and each of us in particular, will have to make some fundamental adjustments in the way we think of personal information and electronic communication. In doing so, we will ultimately have to change our idea of what we can reasonably expect to keep private.

The managerial implications for balancing competing values center around a cost-benefit analysis. On the cost side of the ledger is commitment; on the benefit side is organizational privacy. There are clear costs associated with organizational privacy. Management must be willing to commit resources to this effort – staff members, time, and money – as well as their own visible support to the project. Commitment, then, involves four aspects: management support, responsibility, education, and technical expertise.

Management support is critical to the success of this process. By signifying their commitment to privacy in the workplace, management sets the tone for all employees. This support implies a willingness to allow staff members to participate in the formulation of privacy policy. Staff members from various areas of the organization will be involved, especially in the initial stages. Assignment of responsibility involves the identification of key team members, tasks, time-frames for completion, and deliverables that are mutually acceptable. In order to participate fully, some staff members will require education in the policy and technology aspects of the project. This education can be formal through participation in seminars or classes, or informally achieved through sessions with experts within the organization. Some technical staff members may require education in the business aspects of the organization. Technical expertise must be made available in the policy implementation phase in order to embed the policy into the electronic information systems effectively.

Indeed, a crucial part of organizational privacy policy is the role of information technology professionals with respect to policy formulation and implementation. New capabilities of information technology and new uses of information, present continuous challenges to privacy that society, and the law, have not adequately addressed. Rifkin (1991) cites several sources to argue that computer professionals are too sanguine about the topic. Others have shown that computer professionals do not incorporate privacy policy into their roles. Smith (1993, pp. 112-113) found that information systems executives at one bank in his study saw their role as one of implementing the requirements they are given, adding that "use of the data is not our job." At another bank, the view is similarly hands-off: "we make decisions not policies." At a credit card company, one IS professional responded, that "we're enforcers. . . vehicles for controlling release of information from a technical standpoint." These nonempowered viewpoints stand in direct contrast to calls for IS professionals to be concerned with privacy by assessing and advising people in the firm about policy activities (Weible, 1993).

Betts (1986) argues for greater participation by IS professionals on the basis of their fiduciary responsibility. It is the Chief Information Officer who has the legal responsibility to protect salary data, medical records and other employee information. It is this person's responsibility to ensure that the promises of confidentiality are implemented in the systems and operational context.

Straub and Collins (1990) introduce the notion of "information liability." They recommend creation of a high level committee to be responsible for setting policy and establishing procedures that would reduce the risk of such information liability. From this standpoint, IS managers are held accountable and firms expect these managers to monitor policy and legal issues related to information and computer systems. Further, IS managers work with the legal staff to develop organizational policy for information technology use and are responsible for disseminating approved information policy to the organization. At the opposite extreme of the "hands off" role, this role views the IS manager as the steward of personal data throughout the organization. They should have this role because they have knowledge of the potential liability, which can result from information processing behavior.

The investment in the costs of achieving organizational privacy yield clear benefits. First, implementation of public policy at the organizational level ensures that societal recognition of the need for policy is enacted in all spheres of life, not just in public spheres. The private sector can set an example by implementing the spirit – the essence – of public privacy policy even in those cases where technically the scope of the laws and regulations do not pertain. In addition, organizational privacy policy can complement public policy by voluntarily addressing the operational gaps. That is, organizational privacy policy operationalizes of the goals of laws and regulations in actual practice.

The second benefit involves expectations of both the employees and the employers. Having clear, explicit privacy policy in place sets expectations of privacy, and thus can minimize experiences of loss of privacy. Several lawsuits have been documented in the literature with respect to invasions of privacy in organizations. The existence of clear, explicit, communicated policy has been found to be critical in demonstrating the organization's expectations and intentions. Conversely, the absence of such policy has often been found to support the employee's expectations of privacy. In addition, by encouraging participation in the formulation of the policy, management provides an environment of shared understanding and expectations of privacy. This environment fosters loyalty on the part of the employees and can lead to a more effective and efficient workplace.

AN IMPLEMENTATION APPROACH: BALANCING COMPETING GROUPS AND VALUES WITH RESPECT TO LAW, POLICY, SOCIETY AND TECHNOLOGY

The preceding discussion of the privacy framework is made tangible in this section through examples and a discussion of its implementation. At the outset, a review of privacy issues and opportunities should be conducted. This review would be from the perspectives of laws, policies, society, and technology, and would consider issues of balance as they relate to competing groups and competing values. This review should then be built into an on-going process to be utilized when there are new/changed laws, creation or revision of internal policies, new relationships/services/products, and new/enhanced technologies.

Review of Laws

The purpose of this step is to review existing laws and regulations that pertain to the organization. Is the company in compliance in spirit? Do any of these laws directly or indirectly pertain to privacy? Would better compliance enhance privacy? The competing groups to be taken into consideration when reviewing the laws are the external groups — the law making and enforcing agencies – versus internal company management. The issues related to competing values involve balancing the need to know versus the need to ensure privacy. For example, in the financial services industry, banks need to balance their need comply with applicable privacy laws against their need to know enough about their customers. They need to know enough to ensure that they are not be dealing with criminals who would be performing illegal acts such as money laundering. They also need to know their customers' financial habits so that the banks can recognize unusual transactions.

Review of Policies

The next step is to review existing organizational policies that have incorporated privacy. This step also involves evaluating the effectiveness of these policies. The competing groups are those who are making the policies (management) and those affected by the policies (employees). An example is policy regarding e-mail as a company resource. Management expects the e-mail system, as a company resource, to be used only for legitimate business purposes. As a company resource, data (e-mail messages) can justifiably be monitored. This value needs to balanced against expectations of the employee that e-mail messages, including personal e-mails, are private.

Review of Society

While the previous step considered the expectations at the organizational level, this step considers societal expectations. In this example the competing groups are, once again, management and the employees. An example of competing values, is balancing the individual's right to privacy against the employer's desire to know about an employee's off-job behavior. Such off-the-job behavior might include drug use, alcohol consumption or smoking habits. The employer's argument would be that such off-job behavior can affect on-job performance and insurance costs.

Review of Technology

The purpose of this step is to consider the extent to which technology is the cause of the problem as well as to identify opportunities for using technology as the solution. The question that should be asked about existing technologies is whether they enhance privacy or create privacy issues. The competing groups might be the technically knowledgeable versus the technically illiterate. An example of competing values would be efficiency versus privacy. For example, efficiency goals might be served by giving widespread access to centralized data. On the other hand, privacy goals might be better served by having restricted access to databases on a need-to-know basis. This example illustrates how technology can be the source of a privacy problems but also the solution.

CONCLUSION

The framework discussed in this paper provides a consistent, explicit method of assessing the on-going adequacy of privacy policy in light of changes in the perspectives of society, law, policy and technology. It responds to the volumes of information about privacy issues and concerns generated by society. The framework addresses the legal aspects of privacy by showing how the spirit – the essence – of the laws and regulations can be incorporated into the creation and implementation of privacy policy. Policy, as both plan and practice, provides a method for considering of the privacy issues as well as a means of implementing solutions that address concerns. The importance of technology is acknowledged in the framework, but is put in perspective with the needs of law, policy and society.

ENDNOTES

1 See Warden (Forthcoming, pp. 123-179) for more detail on methodology.
2 See Trauth (1986) for a further discussion of implicit information policy.
3 See Derlega and Chaikin (1977).
4 An example of this case is the American military's policy of "don't ask, don't tell" with respect to gays in the military.
5 An example of this case is legalizing abortion and marijuana use for medicinal purposes.
6 Such arguments suggest that "by restricting physical access to an individual, privacy insulates that individual from distraction and from the inhibitive effects that arise from close physical proximity with another individual" (Gavison, 1984, p. 363).
7 This argument segregates the individual's conduct from knowledge of that conduct by others.
8 She suggests that Jourard (1966) links privacy and mental health due to pressures to conform to society's expectations.
9 Autonomy "requires the capacity to make an independent moral judgment, the willingness to exercise it, and the courage to act on the results of this exercise even when the judgment is not a popular one" (Gavison, 1984, p. 365).
10 Human relations of different intensities, the plurality of roles and presentations, and tolerance of others are of interest here.

REFERENCES

Alderman, Ellen and Caroline Kennedy. 1995. *The Right to Privacy*. New York: Alfred A. Knopf.

Berger, Peter L. and Thomas Luckmann. 1990. *The Social Construction of Reality: A Treatise in the Sociology of Knowledge*. New York: Anchor Books (Doubleday).

Betts, Mitch. 1986. "Safeguarding Privacy: MIS Confronts a Sensitive Challenge," *Computerworld* (7 July): 53-62.

Chemerinsky, Erwin. 1991. "In Defense of Truth," *Case Western Reserve Law Review*, 41: 745-756.

Culnan, Mary. 1993. "How Did They Get My Name? An Exploratory Investigation of Consumer Attitudes Toward Secondary Information Use," *MIS Quarterly*, 17,3: 341-363.

Derlega, V.J. and A. L. Chaikin. 1997. "Privacy and self-disclosure in social relationships," *Journal of Social Issues*, 33: 102-115.

Gavison, Ruth. 1984. "Privacy and the Limits of Law," *Yale Law Journal* 89: 421-71. Rpt. In *Philosophical Dimensions of Privacy: An Anthology*. 1984. Ferdinand Schoeman (ed.) Cambridge: Cambridge University Press: 346-402.

Jourard, Sidney M. 1966. "Some Psychological Aspects of Privacy," *Law and Contemporary Problems*, 31,2 (Spring): 307-318.

Kling, Rob and Jonathan P. Allen. 1996. "How the Marriage of Management and Computing Intensifies the Struggle for Personal Privacy," *Computers, Surveillance, and Privacy*. David Lyon and Elia Zureik (eds.) Minneapolis: University of Minnesota Press: 104-131.

Laufer, Robert S. and Maxine Wolfe. 1977. "Privacy as a Concept and a Social Issue: A Multidimensional Developmental Theory," *The Journal of Social Issues*, Privacy as a Behavioral Phenomenon, Stephen T. Margulis Issue

Editor 33,3: 22-42.

Loch, Karen D. and Sue Conger. 1996. "Evaluating Ethical Decision Making and Computer Use," *Communications of the ACM* , 39,7 (July): 74+.

Moore, Barrington Jr. 1984. *Privacy: Studies in Social and Cultural History.* New York: M.E. Sharge.

Nock, Steven L. 1993. *The Costs of Privacy: Surveillance and Reputation in America.* New York: Aldine de Gruyter, Inc.

Pedersen, Darhl M. 1987. "Sex Differences in Privacy Preferences.*" Perceptual and Motor Skills.* 64: 1239-1242.

Rifkin, Glenn. 1991. "Do Employees Have a Right to Electronic Privacy?" *New York Times (*8 December): F8.

Schoeman, Ferdinand David. 1992. *Privacy and Social Freedom.* Cambridge: Cambridge University Press.

Simitis, Spiros. 1987. "Reviewing Privacy in an Information Society," *University of Pennsylvania Law Review,* 135: 707-746.

Smith, H. Jefferson. 1993. "Privacy Policies and Practices: Inside the Organizational Maze," *Communications of the ACM,* 36,12: 105-122.

Stone, Eugene F. and D.L. Stone. 1990. "Privacy in Organizations: Theoretical Issues, Research Findings, and Protection Mechanisms," *Research in Personnel and Human Resources Management,* 8: 349-411.

Straub, Detmar W. and Rosann Webb Collins. 1990. "Key Information Liability Issues Facing Managers: Software Piracy, Proprietary Databases, and Individual Rights to Privacy,*" MIS Quarterly,*14,2 (June): 143-156.

Trauth, Eileen M. 1986. "An Integrative Approach to Information Policy Research," *Telecommunications Policy,* 10,1: 41-50.

Warden, Francena S. Forthcoming. *A Framework for the Development of Organizational Electronic Privacy Policy.* Ann Arbor, MI: University Microfilms, Inc.

Weible, Ricky Jay. 1993. *Privacy and Data: An Empirical Study of the Influence of Types of Data and Situational Context Upon Privacy Perceptions.* Diss. Mississippi State University.

Westin, Alan F. 1991. "Consumer Privacy Issues in the Nineties," Submitted for the First Conference on Computers, Freedom, Privacy, March 25-28.

—. 1967. *Privacy and Freedom.* New York: Atheneum.

Solving the millennium problem at a major Belgian Bank

Wim Van Grembergen •
UFSIA (University of Antwerp)
wim.vangrembergen@ufsia.ac.be

ABSTRACT

Organisations are facing the Year 2000 (Y2K) problem. This problem arises because most information systems developed over the past 30 years only use two digits to specify the year, which becomes a problem when the millennium rollover will happen. Past publications and the many websites devoted to the millennium bug have largely concentrated on the average North American firm. This case study is an analysis of the millennium project undertaken by a major Belgian Bank. The analysis focuses on the organisation and the different phases of the project, the cost estimation, offshore outsourcing as an alternative solution, and the relationship with the other costly maintenance project, the Euro-problem. A comparison with the international millennium status concludes this paper.

Keywords: Year 2000 problem, millennium bug, data change problem, millennium conversion, century compliance problem, Belgian banks

COMPANY AND SECTOR BACKGROUND

The case company is one of the leading banks in Belgium (hereafter, the case bank will be referred to as Belgian Bank). In 1997 the Belgian Bank was ranked number 104 on the world ranking of financial institutions. Its position as a leading Belgian bank is very relative because nowadays the competition within the European financial sector is tough and continuously new threats and opportunities emerge. At the beginning of 1998, a real merger mania was created ahead of the introduction of the European single currency: a major Belgian bank merged with two other Belgian financial institutions and there was a battle for control of another Belgian bank. Further, the millennium and Euro conversion are to be solved. Both conversions are expected to be very costly. For the insurance sector the EURO conversion is estimated to cost 9 billion Belgian Francs (approximately 250 million US dollars) (cf. Cap Gemini in *De Standaard*, August, 25, 1997). The high costs of both conversions and the loss of the currency exchange benefits due to the sole European currency are major problems within the banking sector.

BELGIAN MILLENNIUM STATUS

End 1997, PA Consulting Group conducted an international millennium survey including results for Belgium (PA Consulting Group, 1997). For Belgium this survey revealed that whilst awareness amongst IT professionals is as high as 81%, the message still is not getting through to senior management. On average only 55% of Belgian senior management are perceived to be fully aware of the implications and therefore of the likely costs involved. The same level of management involvement was detected for other European countries, whereas for the US 71 % was found. Another finding was that around 50 percent of the Belgian organisations surveyed did not have a formal millennium program and therefore were unable to give estimations on their century project:

- 42 % were unable to estimate the number of person-years required
- 29 % were unable to estimate the cost of their millennium program
- 44 % have not included the embedded systems such as elevators and security systems
- 26 % were unable to say how they plan to resource their millennium program.

The survey also indicates that Belgian organisations estimated that on the average they will have to spend up to 3.3 % of their turnover, and that 44 percent of planned human resource is going to have to be obtained externally which may be a major problem since within the IT industry a shortage of skills is beginning to occur. It is also observed that smaller organisations are lagging behind both in terms of awareness and action.

This paper describes the millennium situation of a major Belgian Bank. The conclusion will be that at this bank the awareness is high and that the conversion that really started at the end of 1997, is right on time (not too early, not too late). However, it is expected that the crucial time of the project will be 1998 and certainly 1999 when the modified systems will be tested and put into operation. The case presented can be seen as a good practices case. We share PA's opinion that "many of these (Belgian) organisations will fail to fix the problem in time, and it is likely that severe disruption to normal business operations will occur as a result".

Y2K AWARENESS

Already in the beginning of the 80's the Belgian Bank encountered concrete Y2K problems since some of their applications had data calculations that extended into the next century. The millennium bug first emerged when a 25 year loan was processed in the mortgage application. Even in 1997 problems occurred with an application that manages the safe-deposit boxes: the program refused a 3 year contract and crashed.

In 1985 the IBM relational database management system, DB2 was implemented and it was then that a first technical instruction about the Y2K-problem was issued. A first impact analysis was made in 1994 which resulted in 5,000 files and 15,000 programs that were found to be possibly affected by the Y2K-bug. This was also the start of more fundamental thinking about the millennium problem. One IT-professional (a data manager) was freed up for this activity and it resulted in concrete Y2K-instructions for new applications. From that moment on all newly developed applications had to be millennium compliant. At the beginning of 1996 a project team called EURO/2000 was established. Y2K surveys such as the PA Consulting Group survey reveal that the millennium awareness of senior managers is rather low with an international average of 55 %. There was no problem with senior management awareness and involvement at the Belgian Bank because some Board Members had been previously active in IT and consequently were familiar with the millennium problem.

It is commonly known that other equipment (embedded systems) such as elevators may be also Y2K impacted. An intelligent elevator computer has sophisticated programs that refer to internal calendars and take into account the day of the week. These day of week calculations may be completely wrong when the millennium rollover will happen and will be even more disturbed if they do not know that the year 2000 is also a leap year. It is very typical that also at the Belgian Bank there is currently (end 1997) no concrete project for solving these problems. Only recently some actions have been taken to start such a project in the sense that two Board members were made responsible for the other equipment conversion. Not only elevator computers suffer from the millennium bug. The Dutch airline company KLM is seriously considering the cancellation of some flights on January 1, 2000 keeping on the ground some types of planes until the rollover has happened (cf. *De Standaard,* 8-9 November, 1997).

Like the Belgian Bank most other Belgian financial institutions have already started addressing the millennium problem. However, it has been observed by the author and surveys of consultancy firms (cf. supra) that in industry, within small and medium businesses, and within Belgian government agencies, many are not fully aware of the big Y2K-problem and expect that ready-made solutions will be provided by the IT industry. De Jager (1996) thinks that it may be too late if one has to start yet with the Y2K project. What he calls a "systematic triage" is now in place: selecting the systems that are mission critical and making them at least year 2000 compliant. It is now (end 1997) quite clear that at the Belgian Bank all applications will be 2000 compliant on Saturday January 1, 2000. However, a kind of "triage" has been done: only the applications that are really business critical and client-oriented will be fully tested at that time. If after 2000 problems occur with the less tested programs, they will be taken out of production and will be converted as soon as is needed. This may be a very realistic option since it is believed that the right time to start fixing the century conversion was 1995 and as the repairs only started in 1997 it may be that only 80 % will be corrected by 1999 (Jones in Ragland (1997)).

RELATIONSHIP WITH THE EURO-CONVERSION

Besides the Y2K-problem, another problem is emerging in Europe: the introduction of the EURO that will become the standard currency from January 1999 and the sole legal tender from 2002. The problem arises because local currencies must be converted to EUROs; at least temporarily a two currency system has to be supported; some countries will be confronted again with decimal values and computations; and a solution must be found for the rounding off issue.

Although these technical issues are very similar to the Y2K-problem, the European currency normalisation is a more functional and strategic issue for commercial banks such as the Belgian Bank. EURO-compliant systems are to be developed that by the same token must provide additional functionalities to their clients. A typical example is the new representation of the daily bank statements: only in Euro currency or also in Belgian Francs? Because of the different nature and scope of the Y2K- and EURO-conversion, the Belgian Bank, like most other Belgian financial institutions, decided to solve them separately. However, the management of both projects is brought together.

THE Y2K-PROJECT ORGANISATION

"Most of the challenges in implementing a Year 2000 project involve project management" (Ulrich and Hayes, 1997). The Y2K-project seems to be an exercise in large-scale project management. Therefore, the Belgian Bank installed a separate Y2K-project team backed by substantial executive management support. This team will also be responsible for the millennium conversion of the recently acquired local banks.

The organisational chart of the EURO/2000-project brings out the bank's commitment to the Y2K-project: 9 internal people and 15 offshore people are full time involved in the Y2K-project supported by 5 to 6 external consultants. Most of the internal people have leading and co-ordinating responsibilities since the Y2K-conversion is maximally outsourced. An EURO/2000-steering committee with representation of the Board of Directors is supervising the project.

The Y2K-project consists of 4 teams. The "2000 team" co-ordinates the Y2K-modifications and testing, and is responsible for the strategy, the inventory, the impact analysis, and the prioritising of the sequence of providing the Y2K-readiness. The "DBA 2000 team" is responsible for the modification of the databases and also for the creation of testdata. The "Offshore team" is responsible for the construction and the unit tests below 2000. The "support team" assembles the program clusters for submitting to the outsourcer and accepts the clus-

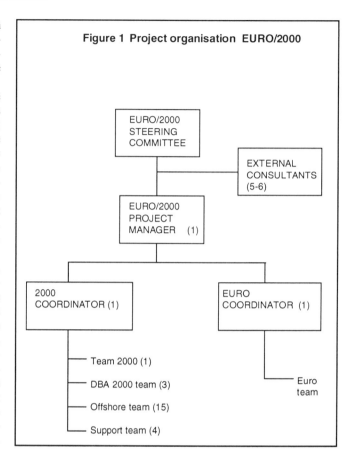

Figure 1 Project organisation EURO/2000

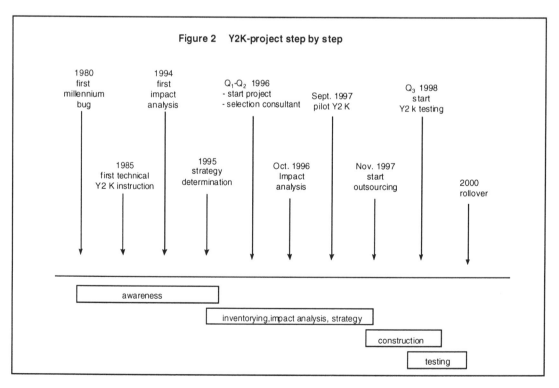

Figure 2 Y2K-project step by step

ters when made 2000-compliant. Together with the end users and the newly established test department they are also responsible for the acceptance testing below and above 2000.

Y2K METHODOLOGY

The success of a Y2K-project is dependent on a good methodology and good project management. Van Grembergen (1997 and 1998) proposes a five step model for the Y2K-conversion:
1. Strategy definition and inventory
2. Budgeting
3. Impact analysis
4. Construction
5. Conversion and testing.

Similar models can be found in Keogh (1997) and Ragland (1997).

The Belgian Bank's approach is very similar to the above model and consists of the following phases (Figure 2):
1. Inventory
2. Impact analysis
3. Prioritisation
4. Strategy
5. Construction
6. Testing
7. Implementation.

Inventory

The challenge of this step is to investigate in detail all hardware, software components and data bases in order to detect the hardware components, the program instructions and the data fields that have to be made Y2K-compliant. It has been observed by the author that in some cases taking stock of used hardware and software platforms may be a very painful experience. A major Belgian grocery chain needed several months to create an inventory of the hardware and software resources. Keogh (1997) gives an example of a particular company that spent 12 weeks conducting an inventory. At the Belgian Bank the inventory was made within 2 to 3 months.

The inventory contains the following components (Van Grembergen, 1997 and 1998):
• application inventory:
   . which applications will still exist after the year 2000?
   . which applications must be made millennium compliant?
• technical inventory:
   . which languages are used (COBOL, spreadsheets, ...)?
   . are the source codes available and where can they be found?
   . what are the different hardware and system software platforms and
      are they 2000 compliant?
   . what is the quality of the configuration management?
   . are good test procedures in place?
   . what are the skills of the technical staff and do they still possess knowledge about older systems and
      older programming languages such as assembler?

The inventory resulted in approximately 30 million lines of code (Table 1) to be examined for Y2K-compliance. A rough estimation of the total cost for the millennium conversion was made: 33 million US dollars. This estimation was based on the Gartner estimations (Hall and Schick, 1996): 1.10 US dollars per executable LOC (Line Of Code). This includes both impacted LOCs and LOCs that have not be changed, but not the non-executable lines such as COBOL comments and date definitions. It is the total cost for the different Y2K stages exclusive the tools costs, computer resources, and end user acceptance. In the Belgian business journals and newspapers it was called the billion bug (33 million dollars is approximately 1 billion Belgian Francs). The applied amount of 1.10 US dollars per line of code is believed to be realistic and is corroborated by other publications. In de Jager and Bergeon (1997) we find amounts ranging from $ .60 to $ 1.50; in Ulrich and Hayes (1997) $1 to $2 per line of code. However, Ragland (1997) reports somewhat higher estimates in the neighbourhood of $2 to $2.50 with higher figures between $5 and $8 for complex systems (weapons systems) developed in assembler language.

Based on the estimation of the number of lines of code, a first estimation of the needed person-years was calculated: an effort of 200 person-years was the result. In October 1996 this estimation was replicated using more accurate data of the detailed impact analysis with as outcome a reduced effort estimation of 70 person-years for the whole Y2K-project. We may use de Jager's and Bergeon's (1997) calculations to see whether this estimation is somewhat realistic. They assume that nearly 5 percent of all data processing operations are impacted by dates; that of these 5 percent of instances of data usage, 10 percent need millennium changes; and that each of these changes requires 1.3 hours of work. Translated into the situation of the Belgian Bank:

30,000,000 lines of code

1,500,000 instances of data usage (5 percent impacted)

150,000 changes (10 percent changes)

195,000 hours or approximately 135 person-years.

When we confronted the Y2K-project leaders of the Belgian Bank with these calculations, they agreed that their latest estimation of 70 person-years is probably too low. The reason is that at this point of time (December 1997) they have not yet a clear view on the testing activities and that they may have underestimated this phase. Currently, a separate testing organisation is set up and it is estimated that this will be a group of somewhat 50 people (this testing team will not solely be involved in testing the Y2K-conversions but will also be responsible for testing the ongoing new developments and the regular maintenance of the existing systems).

In the broad Y2K literature, we can find cost estimations for other organisations. Keogh (1997) e.g. states that it is very difficult to quantify the Y2K cost because there we do not have experience with such a huge change. He refers to estimates that appeared in the press and concludes that the cost could be higher than 100 million US dollars for a typical, large corporation. He also describes the case of an US commercial insurance company. Their inventory showed 8,500 COBOL programs and 45 IMS and 6 DB2 databases of which only 2,600 programs needed to be converted. It was detected that the source codes of 1,500 programs could not be found and surprisingly enough that another 1,500 programs were not being used (anymore) by the firm.

A problem at the Belgian Bank was that almost 50 % of the programs were written in PL/1 (see Table 1) which is more difficult to make Y2K compliant. COBOL-programs (only 2.3 %) seem to be more easy in detecting and modifying Y2K bugs. Moreover, the majority of Y2K conversion software is developed for COBOL which is only logical considering that most legacy systems are written in this language (the Belgian Bank seems to be an exception). A particular problem were the 500 to 600 assembler programs because only few internal programmers still did master this old programming language.

Software packages and custom-made software by third parties may present severe potential problems. At the Belgian Bank this is not a real issue since in-house development has always been a strategy and only 15 relatively small professional banking application packages were bought. A more critical question is whether the computer hardware and systems software will be millennium compliant on January 1, 2000?

Table 1. staff-build applications (languages)		
Platform	**Language**	**Million LOCs**
MVS	PL/1	14.5
	Natural	4.0
	CSP	2.5
	Assembler	0.4
	SAS	0.3
	COBOL	0.1
TANDEM	COBOL	2.2
	Tandem Assembly Language	0.6
HP/UNIX	C	3.0
SIEMENS/NIXDORF	PMS (Parameter Sprache) 2.2	
	Assembler	0.3
	total	**30.1**

The only way to find out is to contact the vendors directly. The result of this experiment was surprising: most service providers told the Belgian Bank that they are aware of the problem and are working on it, and some suppliers didn't even answer to the request. The status seems to be that few hardware and systems software is already 2000-compliant and that some of these conversions are not scheduled to be implemented until 1999. This may cause problems when the Belgian Bank wants to test the above 2000 situation. Further, it has been communicated by some providers that some products will not be supported after the year 2000.

The Belgian Bank is also tackling the millennium problem for personal computers. The PC inventory resulted in approximately 4,000 IBM and IBM compatible personal computers of which most are attached to a network. According to IBM (1996) all new models of IBM PCs shipped in 1996 and later will automatically update the century and many older models will be affected by date problems. However, the Belgian Bank experienced that the same models could have different and even older BIOS-versions and consequently could have a different year-2000 compliance. The only way to find out is to test each PC separately and run the simple test which consists of changing the system date to three minutes to 12 on December 31, 1999 and then turning off the computer and wait for 5 minutes. When the system is turned on back, it must read January 1 in order to be 2000 compliant (cf. de Jager and Bergeon, 1997). Further, one has also to check whether the different application programs such as Excel are also 2000 compliant. Currently, these tests are only conducted for some machines as a try-out and a software tool is evaluated that seems to be capable of doing these simple tests automatically for all the networked PCs. The strategy will be to upgrade the BIOS-versions that are not 2000 compliant and very old machines will simply be replaced. Standalone PCs will be hooked in a network or when this is impossible they will be replaced. The upgrading work will be outsourced because it is estimated to be a very labour-intensive assignment for which internal people can not be freed up.

Impact analysis

The first impact analysis in 1994 was executed by the staff of the external consultant. Data identification was done on the basis of a list of common datanaming conventions and specific-company standards. The analysis was conducted with the assistance of general scanning programs and queries of the data dictionary. In both cases it was a search for typical data names such as DEXPIRATION and DVALUE. The job was simplified because it was a standard policy at the Belgian Bank to start date data with the letter D. In 1996 a more detailed impact analysis was performed with a specific Y2K-tool, with as result that the hit-rate increased from 80 % to more than 95 %.

Prioritisation

Measuring the criticality of the different business applications and prioritising the sequence of providing their Y2K readiness is essential (IBM,1996). The desirability of the Y2K transition has to be based on the impact the Y2K problem has on the particular computerised application: a payroll system that is critical to uninterrupted operation and that will abend because of the millennium bug, will certainly be one of the first candidates to convert. As was explained above, all applications will be made 2000 compliant and a kind of "triage" is done in the sense that only the critical applications will be fully tested before the year 2000.

Strategy

The Y2K co-ordinator and the members of the Steering Committee have to define a strategy for coping with the millennium bug. Decisions were made whether
- to solve the Y2K problem solely or at the same time to reengineer some business systems;
- to make use of the opportunity to solve technical IT problems such as establishing good test procedures and good configuration management;
- to insource or outsource;
- vendor selection regarding the automated tools;
- choice between interpretation and expansion.

At the Belgian Bank it was decided to redevelop 12 % of the existing programs and to modify the remainder. The reasons for rebuilding some of the applications were that either they were very old legacy systems (e.g. the accounting system) and/or that they needed a new technology (e.g. the electronic banking system with internet).

The existing configuration management procedures proved to be effective. In less than three months the inventory of possibly impacted hardware and software was made. Moreover, no source codes were misplaced and could be easily identified, so the Belgian Bank had not to rely on the translation of executables to source code. However, the Belgian Bank did not have a specific organisation for testing and implementing applications. This shortcoming had been a discussion point for some time. The actual installation of a professional independent testing department has been accelerated by the Y2K project and it is considered by IT management as one of the opportunities of the millennium conversion (not only costs but also some benefits). Other opportunities were the retirement or replace- ment of old applications, the clean up of dead code, the introduction of tools such as debuggers and test tools, and the update of documentation.

It is essential that extra budgets are freed up for fixing the Y2K bug because the current systems development projects are not supposed to be placed on hold until the year 2000. At the Belgian Bank it was one of the first decisions that the Y2K-project should not disturb the regular maintenance and the development of new applications. Therefore, the millennium project was maximally outsourced and only some internal key people are involved in the management of this huge project.

The decision to outsource or insource the Y2K problem is one, which eventually has to be made. The Belgian Bank decided to outsource maximally. The reasons behind this decision were the freeing up of IT professionals for the ongoing work, bringing in specific, not in-house available Y2K expertise, and possible cost reductions. An external consultant (5 - 6 senior consultants) was made responsible for the general support of the 2000 project and for conducting the impact analysis. The construction and the unit tests are done by an India-based software company. In fact, offshore outsourcing is very suitable in the case of the millennium problem because in essence it is very technical. The particular India-based software house was chosen on the basis of lower wages and of the fact that the general manager had an American background and could bridge the cultural differences. Moreover, this offshore project will be evaluated in order to see whether this solution can be used for other IT projects. The offshore outsourcing project will be discussed more in depth in the next section of this article.

Construction

The two most popular solution strategies are the interpretation and the expansion approach. A variety of different terms are in use to describe these two options: procedural versus data change options (Eldridghe and Louton, 1996), and windowing techniques versus full conversion (IBM, 1996). Interpretation is the adjusting of the program logic to interpret the two-year digit as a century and year field. Simple interpretation algorithms define cut-off dates: e.g. before 50 is translated into the 21st century and after 50 becomes the 20th century (Table 2). This interpretation is a simple solution and only needs an adaptation of the program and has no need to expand the two-digit year data to a four-digit format in the programs and data bases. The restriction is that it cannot be implemented for dates of birth because a person born in 1901 will then be born in 2001. Expansion (Table 3) is a more fundamental solution: it involves modifying the source code and also the files and databases to be converted into four digit yeardates. At the Belgian Bank, it was decided to go for a mixed solution if possible the logical interpretation option because of cost and time considerations, and physical expansion only when it was really necessary. The physical approach was only used in the cases of dates of birth and files with company dates.

In case of data expansion, interface technology is needed that enables compliant programs to access unconverted data or, conversely, a noncompliant program to access converted data (Ulrich and Hayes, 1997). This solution is necessary because simultaneous conversion of all applications that use data is not possible. Figure 3 illustrates the interfacing strategy used at the Belgian Bank, which is commonly known as API or Application Program Interface (at the Belgian Bank the more popular name "I/O encapsulation" is used). The APIs are associated with I/O activities and can be used by Y2K compliant and Y2K noncompliant programs. An API used by a compliant program converts a 4-digit data representation into a 2-digit format during a write operation and vice versa during a read operation. A noncompliant program uses an API to reformat noncompliant 2-digit data to Y2K compliant data and vice versa.

Table 2. Logical solution at the Belgian Bank: a COBOL example

existing program

    if YYMMDD1 is greater than YYMMDD2

millennium compliant program

    if YY is less than 50
        then move 20 to XX
        else move 19 to XX

    if XXYYMMDD1 is greater than XXYYMMDD2

Table 3. Physical solution at the Belgian Bank

existing data base	*millennium compliant data base*
971206	19971206

existing program	*millennium compliant program*
02 YYMMDD picture 9(6)	02 YYYYMMDD picture 9(8)

Testing

The test situation in an Y2K project is very unique since you not only want to test whether the system is millennium compliant, but also whether the Y2K adapted systems can still work today. In order to test the after-2000 situation, a complete Y2K situation inclusive of Y2K modified hardware and system software, has to be set up. Of course, this test situation has to be clearly separated from the operational system to avoid contamination. It is now commonly accepted that the testing phase will take the bulk of the resources and time. Keogh (1977) mentions that about 40 % of the Y2K-process is testing. This can be more in case the installation has no good testing procedures and practices which is the case in most organisations (Ulrich and Hayes, 1977).

At the Belgian Bank the plan accounts for tests below 2000 and tests above 2000 (Figure 4). After the Y2K modifications, the system is run with dates of today and the results are compared with the results produced by the old system. In the case of compliance, the millennium version is put into production. The unit tests are conducted in India and include the debugging of individual programs. The Support Team in Brussels is responsible for the system testing, which determines whether the entire system operates as intended. Acceptance testing is the final testing by users and operational managers to decide whether they accept the system. The test program consists of "business as usual" situations and the different functions within the systems are individually tested. The reason

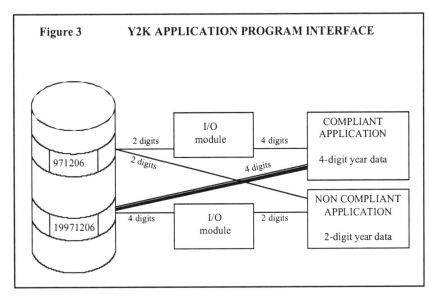

Figure 3   **Y2K APPLICATION PROGRAM INTERFACE**

for this thorough (regression) testing is that Y2K-changes may affect something else in the system that was not expected.

A first test above 2000 will be conducted by the newly installed test department with dates plus 28 years. The reason for doing this is that every 28 years you have the same calendar and again the results can be compared with these of a system run with dates before 2000. Additional specific tests are done for the rollover 1999-2000 and for specific dates such as February, 29, 2000. These tests are executed with an increased IPL date. Currently, the complete above 2000 tests can not be done because the computer manufacturers and other providers of hardware and system software did not yet deliver the Y2K-version of their hardware platforms, programming languages, database management systems, TP monitors, ... Moreover, the announcement of these Y2K-compliant resources has been recently postponed by IBM.

Testing takes 40 to 50 % of the total process of making your systems millennium compliant. Keogh (1997) reports of a US company with a purchasing system of 35 million lines of code. Their 2000 team spends two months developing the test plan and 6 months were necessary to complete the total test phase involving 100 managers and technicians often working 15-hour days. At the Belgian Bank it is estimated that testing will take more than 1 year (third quarter 1998 till end 1999) and that as many as 50 people of the new test department will be involved, not to count the end users and operational people involved in the acceptance testing.

OFFSHORE OUTSOURCING

Outsourcing of information services (see e.g. Van Grembergen and Vander Borght, 1997), and offshore outsourcing (see e.g. Kumar and Willcocks) as a special form of it, have become very popular issues in the 1990s. Offshore outsourcing seems to be an attractive alternative to fixing the Y2K problem. As being explained earlier, the Belgian Bank went for this solution. As in the US and other developed countries, Belgian organisations are also shifting to offshore sites for IT services. This was started in Belgium some five years ago with a large steel corporation that outsourced a technical mainframe conversion to an IT company in the Philippines. The Y2K problem, being also a technical conversion, is very suitable for outsourcing to an offshore site. It is the author's observation that this alternative for fixing the millennium bug is used by several Belgian companies.

The Belgian Bank has outsourced the work related to the construction and unit testing of their Y2K-project to a leading software export house in India that also caters a number of FORTUNE 500 customers in the US. The company was started in the year 1987 and now employs about 800 IT professionals. This provider was selected because he had millennium expertise and had management that had been living for many years in the US and therefore could bridge the cultural differences. Another issue was that their organisation is very flexible in the sense that new highly qualified IT professionals can be easily attracted if they are needed. As a local manager puts it: "it is a dream of any IT professional in India to find an opening in our company".

As been explained above, the Support Team assembles the clusters that must be converted. These clusters are put on a disc drive and are directly accessed and modified by the Indian programmers through a dedicated 64 KBPS link that has been established between the offshore site and the Belgian Bank. It is often stated that telecommunication facilities with offshore outsourcing may be a technical barrier. This was clearly not the case: the connections

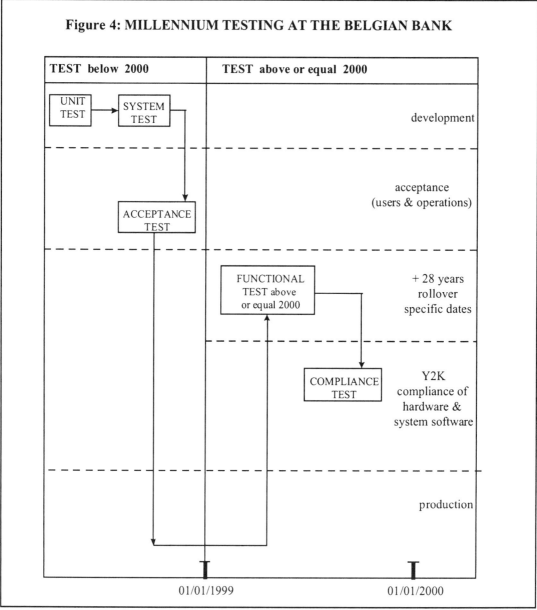

Figure 4: MILLENNIUM TESTING AT THE BELGIAN BANK

with India proved to be of good quality. The Indian provider has placed an on-site co-ordinator in Brussels as an interface between its client, the Belgian Bank, and the offshore team. This co-ordinator is responsible for resolving and clarifying issues raised by the offshore development team. Other communications between the remote partners are the daily use of telephone and e-mail, teleconferences and of course the regular visits of the Belgian project leaders to the Indian software house: frequent face-to-face contacts proved to be very necessary.

One major encountered barrier is the cultural difference between the Belgian and Indian IT professionals who became apparent when discussing work and assignments. Indian programmers and analysts seem to accept any assignment without discussion even if they know that it is not going to work out. This attitude caused major delays and some tension. Another barrier seemed to be that the Indian professionals had great technical experience in UNIX, C-language, personal computers, and PC software; things they learnt during their formal IT education. However, they had no knowledge of the mainframe environment and PL/1, two crucial technologies needed in fixing the millennium bug at the Belgian Bank. To overcome this problem, all of the Indian IT professionals involved received a thorough training, especially in PL/1.

The greater advantage of offshore outsourcing is the lower cost. However, the project leaders of the millennium project at the Belgian Bank are convinced that, taking into account the large telecommunication costs, the travel expenses and the additional costs of training the Indian IT professionals, this is not true. The major benefit is that in offshore countries there is a great supply of highly qualified IT professionals that can be contracted when needed. This is in contrast to the Belgian situation characterised by a scarcity of IT professionals partly due to the millennium and EURO problem. It is estimated that in Belgian more than 7,000 IT jobs are still vacant (EDS in *De Standaard* , March 27, 1997).

INTERNATIONAL BENCHMARKING

A major concern at the Belgian Bank is whether they are behind in understanding and action regarding the millennium conversion. An international benchmark is here in place. Table 4 and Table 5 compare the Belgian Bank millennium status with results drawn from the international millennium survey of PA Consulting Group (1997). In September 1997, PA surveyed IT Directors and Business Directors in fifteen countries. They received responses from approximately 1,000 organisations. Participating countries were UK, Ireland, France, Germany, Belgium, Czech Republic, Denmark, Sweden, Norway, USA, Australia, New Zealand, Hong Kong, Malaysia and Singapore.

PA's key overall findings from the survey are:
- awareness of the millennium problem is high amongst IT Directors: overall 87 % are fully aware of the millennium problem;
- only half of senior managers are aware of the millennium problem;
- to date only 56 % of the surveyed organisations have a formal program in place;
- too few organisations (on average 38 %) have now completed their millennium audit;
- embedded software issues are still not being addressed (only 44 % of the organisations have done so);
- on the average each organisation spends over 6.91 US $ million, ranging from 2.39 US $ million for the smallest organisations to 31.25 US $ million for organisations with an annual turnover over 1,000 US $ million;
- the millennium conversion will take an average of 58 person-years, ranging   from 3 person-years for the smallest organisations to 181 person-years for organisations with an annual turnover over 1,000 US $ million;
- it is estimated that 44 % of all resources will have to be supplied by external suppliers;
- smaller organisations are way behind in tackling the millennium problem.

Table 4. Millennium status Belgian Bank versus international status

	Belgian Bank	Banking Finance Insurance	Continental Europe	USA
Awareness IT management	100 %	93 %	78 %	100 %
Awareness senior management	100 %	72 %	49 %	71%
Millennium program in place	yes	79 %	57 %	71 %
Completed millennium audit	yes	52 %	39 %	50 %
Embedded systems included	not yet	60 %	36%	57 %
External human resources	66 %	NA	42 %	43 %

Table 5. International costs and human resources comparison

	Belgian Bank	International average
Estimated cost in US $ million	33	10.08
Estimated person-years	70	72

Table 4 reveals that the Belgian Bank is in line with the average international status and therefore can be called a good practice case. It is again indicated that there is still a problem with the embedded systems. The Belgian Bank has also a special position regarding the level of outsourcing of their millennium conversion. In fact, it is now estimated that more than 66 % will be supplied by external organisations primarily by a consultancy firm and the Indian software house. The estimated required 70 person-years seem to be in line with the international level (Table 5), whereas the estimated cost of 33 US $ million is considerable higher.

LESSONS LEARNED

This paper reviewed the millennium project of a leading Belgian bank.

A millennium project is just another example of a maintenance project. However, it differs from most maintenance projects because of its size. Some of the findings can be generalised to other (large) maintenance projects and to other IT projects such as the development of new applications.

Lesson 1: Establish the right strategies

Before starting a maintenance project, it is necessary to consider whether it is eventually more appropriate to rebuild or re-engineer the application rather than to make modifications. A careful review of the application portfolio at the Belgian bank revealed that 12 % of the applications had to be renewed because they were very old legacy systems and/or the implemented technology was outdated.

Lesson 2: Choose between insourcing and outsourcing

Another strategic choice is whether to insource or outsource. Most maintenance projects can be easily outsourced because of their technical nature. In the light of the contemporary shortage of IT professionals, offshore outsourcing may be the right solution. As is shown in this Y2K case, offshore outsourcing is a good option because it is very flexible in the sense that new highly qualified IT professionals can be easily attracted if they are needed. The case also showed that the key for success is constant and close management of the outsourcing process.

Lesson 3: Provide a good project organisation

Good project management is a critical success factor for maintenance and development projects. Especially when it is a project with a high business risk such as the Y2K project, a clear project organisation with well-defined responsibilities has to be established. As shown in this case, a senior manager has to be appointed who is responsible for the project and providing the resources needed and several experienced project co-ordinators are essential in managing the project and the programmers, in casu the offshore people.

Lesson 4: Establish good testing procedures

Each IT project and certainly major maintenance projects needs good testing procedures. This means that a good test organisation has to be set up with careful planning and excellent test data. Unfortunately, most IT organisations do not have a proper test organisation with as result poor testing and many errors and problems when the modified or new version is implemented and processed. The Belgian bank also suffered from this shortcoming and is now trying to establish a separate testing department for the Y2K project, which later on will be used for testing modified and new applications.

Lesson 5: Consider configuration management

The recent Y2K experience showed that for some companies it took several months before they had even established the inventory of hardware, software and data bases. Configuration management is an essential IT procedure which is necessary for major maintenance projects and other IT projects. Questions such as which data bases will be affected when modifying applications, which version of the application is now in production, and where to find the source codes can be easily addressed when an efficient configuration management is already in place.

CONCLUSIONS

It seems that solving the millennium problem is a huge and complex project. For our case company, this will cost approximately 33 million US dollars and a head count of more than 70 person-years will be required. At the Belgian Bank the awareness phase was started in 1994 and construction began at the end of 1997. It is expected that the different tests can be conducted end 1998 - end 1999 and that all business critical and client-oriented applications will be Y2K-compliant and fully tested on Saturday, January, 1, 2000.

The level of the IT department appears to be very critical to the success of a millennium project. The job will be easier when the IT department has good practices and procedures regarding testing and configuration management. At the Belgian Bank all source codes could be easily found and taking stock of hardware and system software was not a big issue because of the good configuration management. However, testing procedures were less developed and therefore a new testing department was established.

The millennium project of the Belgian Bank seems to be a best practices case. However, as in other European countries, the millennium status in Belgium is not favourable since a recent survey revealed that approximately 50 % of the organisations do not have a formal YAK-program yet. Moreover, it is the author's observation that small and medium Belgian companies do not even think about the problem and expect that later on, the IT industry will supply easy solutions. There is only one advice: if an organisation did not start yet, it needs to do so now and certainly a "systematic triage" approach will be required in order to survive the rollover.

ACKNOWLEDGEMENT

The author is thankful to the project manager EUROPE/2000 and the co-ordinator Year 2000 of the Belgian case company for providing all necessary information regarding this case study.

REFERENCES

de Jaguar, P. "Systematic triage",*http://www.year2000.com/,* 1996.

de Jager, P. en Bergeon, R. *Managing OO. Solving the year 2000 computing crisis.* John Wiley & Sons, New York, 1997.

Eldridghe, A. and Louton, B. "A comparison of procedural and data change options for century compliance", *http://www.year2000.com/,* 1996.

Hall, B. and Schick, K. *Year 2000 crisis: estimating the cost,* Gartner Group, Research note, 1996, KA.210-1262.

IBM, *The year 2000 and 2-digit dates. A guide for planning and implementation,* IBM, Poughkeepsie (NY), 1996.

Keogh, J. *Solving the year 2000 problem,* AP Professional Academic Press, Boston, 1997.

Kumar, K. and Willcocks, L. "Offshore outsourcing: a country too far?", *Proceedings of the 4th European Conference on Information Systems,* Lisbon, 1996, pp. 1309-1325.

PA Consulting Group, *Defusing the millennium bomb. An international survey of awareness and readiness,* London, 1997.

Ragland, B. *The year 2000 problem solver. A five-step disaster prevention plan.* McGraw-Hill, New York, 1997.

Van Grembergen, W. "The COBIT framework applied to the millennium conversion", *Computer Audit Update,* July 1997, pp. 17-21.

Van Grembergen, W. "Control and audit guidelines for the millennium conversion: an application of the COBIT model", *IS Audit & Control Journal;* August 1998, pp. 28-33.

Van Grembergen, W. and Vander Borght, D. "Audit guidelines for IT outsourcing", *EDP Auditing,* Auerbach 72-30-35, June 1997a, pp. 1-8.

Van Grembergen, W. and Vander Borght. D. "An audit of IT outsourcing: a case study", *EDP Auditing,* Auerbach 72-30-36, June 1997b, pp. 1-11.

Ulrich, W. en Hayes, I. *The year 2000 software crisis. Challenge of the century.* Yourdon Press, Upper Saddle River (NJ), 1997.

OTHER READINGS OF INTEREST

Brown, D. "So you think the year 2000 is just a mainframe problem", *Gartner Group Research Note, Strategic Planning, RDS-0596,* May 1996.

Castelluccio, M. "One year closer to doomsday", *Management Accounting,* January 1996.

de Jager, P. "Lock up your year 2000 staff", *Datamation,* May 1996.

de Jager, P. "Systematic Triage", *American Programmer,* February 1996.

Feiler, J. *Finding and fixing your year 2000 problem. A hands-on guide for small organisations and workgroups,* AP Professional, 1998.

Kappelman, L. and Cappel, J. "Confronting the year 2000 issue", *Journal of Systems Management,* July/August 1996.

Kearney, D. "Beating the clock", *InformationWeek,* April 1996.

Kelly, J. *Y2K. It's already too late.* JK Press, 1998.

Keuffel, W. "Coping with the year 2000 rollover", *Software Development Magazine,* August 1996.

Kilmar, T. and Wasserman, R. "The pros/cons procedure vs. data", *American Programmer,* February 1996.

Perry, W. *Year 2000 software testing.* Wiley, 1998.

Miller, S. *Year 2001. Reaching Y2K compliance after the deadline.* Digital Press, 1998.

Yourdon, E. and Yourdon, J. *Time bomb 2000. What the year 2000 computer crisis means to you.* Prentice Hall Computer Books, 1998.

A Task-based Measure of Perceived Effectiveness in Computer-mediated Communication

E. Vance Wilson and Joline P. Morrison
College of Business, University of Wisconsin-Eau Claire, Eau Claire, WI 54702-4004
Phone: (715) 836-3800, Fax: (715) 836-4959, Email: wilsonv@uwec.edu

ABSTRACT

Fit between task and technology is frequently cited as a critical element in system success. In the domain of computer-mediated communication, however, few mechanisms exist for quantifying this fit. This paper details the development and initial testing of a measure based on the well-known McGrath group task circumplex model.

INTRODUCTION

A key determinant in the success of computer mediated communication systems (CMCS) and group support systems (GSS) is the task they are used for (Huber, 1984; DeSanctis & Gallupe, 1987). Task models and theories exist in the domain of non-mediated groups (e.g., McGrath, 1984; Wood, 1986) but application of these to GSS and CMCS has been spotty and the results equivocal (Zigurs & Buckland, 1998). Although research findings repeatedly suggest that the fit between task and computer-mediated communication technology is important, researchers have not yet been able to comprehensively describe or measure the dimensions of appropriate fit.

This paper describes the development and initial testing of an instrument to measure the perceived effectiveness of CMCS based on task type (hereafter *PE measure*). The PE measure extends prior research in several ways. First, it operationalizes the four major dimensions of McGrath's task circumplex (McGrath, 1984; McGrath & Hollingshead, 1994), a model which frequently is used as a conceptual framework for studying GSS and CMCS (Dennis & Gallupe, 1993). Thus, it will be straightforward to integrate findings from studies that use the PE measure into the existing literature. Second, all four task types are incorporated into the PE measure, where prior research has focused primarily on generation tasks and, to a lesser extent, choice tasks. This comprehensive view of the overall task construct should benefit the process of theory-building as well as prediction in practical applications. Third, the PE measure has been tested successfully within heterogeneous task domains, suggesting that the instrument has validity and is relatively robust.

In the following sections we discuss the background and assumptions of our research and develop a set of hypotheses. Then we describe our research method, which involves developing and testing the PE instrument. Finally we discuss our findings and present our conclusions.

BACKGROUND

The task circumplex model is based on the assumption that all group tasks can be categorized within four main types (McGrath, 1984). These types are distinguished by two components: conceptual vs. behavioral orientation and cooperation vs. conflict emphasis (see Figure 1). The task types are:
- *Generation tasks*, including creativity tasks, e.g., idea generation and brainstorming, and planning tasks, e.g., planning and scheduling;
- *Choice tasks*, including intellectual tasks or solving structured problems, i.e., solution of problems that have a correct answer and similar logic problems, and decision-making tasks or solving problems that require consensus among group members;
- *Negotiation tasks,* including cognitive conflict tasks or resolving conflicts of viewpoint, and mixed-motive tasks or resolving motivational conflicts; and
- *Execution tasks*, including performance tasks where there is some objective standard, i.e., *excelling,* and contest/battle tasks where there is competition for victory, i.e., *winning.*

The first assumption of our research is that the different task types require distinct task-technology fit conditions, i.e., one task type might benefit from one particular technology feature, such as text-only messaging, while another task type might benefit more from a different technology feature, such as graphical message attachments.

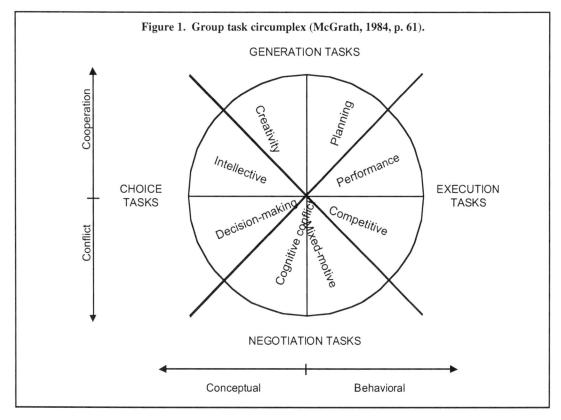

Figure 1. Group task circumplex (McGrath, 1984, p. 61).

Support for this assumption arises from theoretical and empirical bases. McGrath and Hollingshead (1994) theorize that three task types—generation, choice, and negotiation—are distinguished respectively by increasing information requirements. This idea parallels certain equivocal results that GSS research reports between generation and choice task types. In their review of the GSS literature, Dennis and Gallupe state:

> We are convinced that GSS technology can dramatically improve group performance and member satisfaction for generation tasks, where the group's objective is to draft a project plan, or produce a set of ideas, alternatives, opinions, information, and so forth.... We are less convinced that GSS technology can help groups facing a choice task, where the objective is to choose an alternative(s) from a pre-specified set. (1993, p. 74)

Our second assumption is that we can define a task-technology fit construct that is appropriate to CMCS. For this we turn to the related GSS domain, where Zigurs and Buckland define task-technology fit as "ideal profiles composed of an internally consistent set of task contingencies and GSS elements that affect group performance" (1998, p. 323). Part of this definition is directly applicable to our research-as we propose, first, to develop a profile of task variables based upon McGrath's task circumplex and, second, to develop a technology profile comprising a controlled CMCS feature set. The use of group performance as a measure is less relevant to CMCS than to GSS research. GSS and CMCS are distinct system types that, we argue, should be measured using different standards. The purpose of GSS is to increase overall group effectiveness (Huber, 1984), which is accomplished by supporting computer brainstorming, option-ranking, voting, etc. In contrast, CMCS emphasize support for effective communication (Turoff, Hiltz, Bahgat, & Rana, 1993), which is, only one of the overall factors that contribute to group performance. Thus, we propose to adapt Zigurs and Buckland's definition to the CMCS context by using *communication effectiveness* as the primary criterion of task-technology fit in the present study.

HYPOTHESES

Subsequent to a recommendation by DeSanctis and Gallupe (1987), McGrath's task circumplex frequently has been employed as a conceptual framework for task classification in GSS research. However, only two task types—generation and choice have been used extensively in empirical studies, and even these have not been tested systematically. Zigurs and Buckland note:

> There is one problem with how researchers have applied the circumplex, based on the fact that tasks

typically have elements of both the creativity (Generate type) and problem-solving (Choose type). In empirical work, even if authors classified a task in multiple categories of McGrath's circumplex according to the task's different phases, the subsequent analysis and discussion of results were typically combined across the entire group session. This practice makes it difficult to unravel task-technology fit issues. (1998, p. 323)

To answer these and related concerns, it would be valuable to develop an objective methodology for categorizing task types as they relate to task-technology fit.

A recent study of software development teams took initial steps toward creating such a methodology (Wilson, Morrison, & Napier, 1997). Subjects in this study used a combination of computer mediated communication and face-to-face (FTF) communication to complete a team project. Subjects were then asked to describe in their own words the activities for which they perceived the two communication channels to be most effective and least effective. Researchers organized this list to consolidate redundant items and categorized the list into six logical factors: the generate, choose, and execute task types of the McGrath task circumplex (subjects produced no comments that fit the negotiation task type category); socialization; communication speed; and communication completeness. They then returned the reduced list of activities to the entire subject pool and asked them to rate how effective they perceived each communication channel to be for supporting each activity relating to their team project. Analysis of the ratings showed relatively high reliability among items within each the three tested task types and indicated that,

for the three investigated task types the communication methods produced different hierarchies of perceived effectiveness. FTF communication supported execution tasks better than generation tasks ($p < .001$), but CMCS supported generation tasks better than both execution tasks ($p < .01$) and choice tasks ($p < .05$). Comparison between the hierarchies suggests that distributed software development teams may be able to create, plan, and coordinate fairly well. (Wilson *et al.*, 1997, p. 4)

These results support the idea that a comprehensive measure of perceived effectiveness can be successfully operationalized based upon McGrath's task circumplex. However, there are several issues that may thwart development. First, it is not known whether survey items created within the domain of software development will generalize well to other task domains. Second, in the Wilson *et al.* study relatively high intercorrelations of items *between* task types were found along with correlations reported *within* the tested task types, and it is not clear whether the survey items employed actually formed independent factors. Finally, it is only speculative that the negotiation task type can be represented successfully in such an instrument, since this was not previously tested. These issues could be addressed by developing a generalized PE measure that incorporates the negotiation task type and can be subjected to more rigorous analysis, leading to the following hypothesis:

H1: Perceived effectiveness of computer mediated communication can be distinctly measured for the four major task types of the McGrath task circumplex.

In order to be useful either as a basis for theory-building or for prediction in practical settings, a PE measure should provide similar outcomes for task domains that share similar characteristics and different outcomes between task domains that have different characteristics. This ability is a key test in establishing construct validity of the instrument, also called instrument validity (Davis, 1989). Cook and Campbell state, "assessing construct validity depends on two processes: first, testing for a convergence across different measures or manipulations of the same 'thing' and, second, testing for a divergence between measures and manipulations of related but conceptually distinct 'things'" (1979, p. 61). These criteria form the bases for Hypotheses 2 and 3.

H2: Groups with similar task domains will perceive the effectiveness of computer mediated communication similarly across the four task types.

H3: Groups with different task domains will perceive the effectiveness of computer mediated communication differently across the four task types.

In the remaining sections of the paper, we describe our research methodology and results, followed by a discussion of the findings.

RESEARCH METHOD

Our research design tested how communication effectiveness is affected by task-technology fit between two task domains (software development team project vs. general communication) and a controlled CMCS feature set. The research proceeded in two phases: instrument development and instrument testing. Procedures used for each phase are described in the following sections.

Instrument Development

To test Hypothesis 1 an instrument was developed to measure perceived effectiveness of computer-mediated communication. *Perception* of effectiveness was chosen in place of alternative primary attributes, e.g., objective evaluation of communication effectiveness. In this decision, we followed the suggestion of Moore and Benbasat, who justified their choice of perception measures of adoption of information technology innovation in this way:

> Primary attributes are intrinsic to an innovation independent of their perception by potential adopters. The behaviour of individuals, however, is predicated by how they perceive these primary attributes. Because different adopters might perceive primary characteristics in different ways, their eventual behaviours might differ. This is the root of the problem of using primary characteristics as research variables. Furthermore, studying the interaction among the perceived attributes of innovations helps the establishment of a general theory. (1991, p. 194)

In our study, subjects' perceptions were judged to be particularly relevant antecedents to a variety of important outcomes relating to effectiveness, e.g., satisfaction with the CMCS for a given task and subsequent decisions to use the CMCS for the task.

Items in the instrument were drawn initially from the instrument developed by Wilson *et al.* (1997). This instrument used nine generation task items, four choice task items, and six execution task items. Several items were specific to software development, e.g., the execution task item *debugging program code,* and these were rewritten prior to inclusion to be appropriate to general communication or were eliminated. With the objective of ensuring content validity through adequately representing each task type, the items were augmented by the two authors. The overall list was reviewed to verify that the emergent inventories fit within and were representative of the McGrath task type definitions through several review and reduction cycles. From the review a test instrument containing eight generate task items, eight choice task items, eight negotiate task items, and eleven execute task items was developed.

The test instrument asked subjects to rate each task item through a single question in one of the following forms, depending on the subject's task domain:

> Software development team project task domain question; *based on your experiences with computer mediated communication in your project team, how effective do you feel this communication method is for the following activities?*

> General communication task domain question; *based on your general experiences with computer mediated communication, how effective do you feel this communication method is for the following activities?*

Test items were operationalized as a list of activities, e.g., "Resolving conflicts" and "Making difficult decisions." Subjects rated their perceptions of effectiveness for each item using a five-position Likert scale ranging from (1) Very Ineffective to (5) Very Effective.

Instrument Testing

In the second phase of the research, the test instrument was administered to subjects, final inventories of items representing the task types were developed, and mean responses on the task type dimensions were analyzed between groups.

Subjects

Subjects were 167 undergraduate students enrolled in three different Information Systems courses at a university located in the U.S. Midwest. Participation in the study was a part of course requirements as reviewed and approved by the University Human Subjects Committee.

CMCS

Computer mediated communication was implemented using the controlled set of CMCS features provided by Eudora Pro software running under Windows 95/NT on Pentium PC computers. Eudora Pro is a popular text-based communication application that supports file attachments and features a graphical user interface that conforms to Microsoft Windows standards.

Procedure

The test instrument was administered during the final week of a 15-week course schedule. In one of the courses, students had used computer mediated communication both for general communication with the instructor and other students and for receiving course materials. Of the other two courses, one focused on 3GL programming and the other addressed database concepts and application development. In both of these latter courses, students participated in project teams of approximately four members. Projects were conducted over a three month period during which team members used both FTF communication and computer mediated communication to support their team projects. As previously discussed, the test instrument for students in the first course asked about perceived effectiveness of CMCS for "general" communication and for the latter two courses asked the same question about communication "in your project team."

RESULTS

Data Screening

Data from the 167 subjects were analyzed for completeness in responses to test items. Of these subjects, 12 did not mark responses to all the items, and these were removed from subsequent analysis. The remaining data were screened for outliers, particularly for those indicating reverse marking on the Likert scale, i.e., consistently marking 1 instead of 5 to indicate "Very Effective". No extreme outliers or reverse-marked scales were found in the data.

Item Evaluation and Reduction

A practical objective of instrument development is to achieve a parsimonious representation of the convergent underlying constructs. Thus, we conducted a *post hoc* analyses of correlation in the pooled data to eliminate items that showed low intercorrelations within the task type. This analysis resulted in the reduced instrument shown in Table 1. In its final form, the PE measure uses four items to measure each of four task types. Results from reliability analysis and exploratory factor analysis of the pooled data for these items are shown in Table 2. Although some intercorrelation was found between choice and negotiation task factors, generally the results suggest the PE measure satisfies the criterion of Hypothesis 1 by distinctly measuring perceived effectiveness in factors corresponding to the four major task types of the McGrath task circumplex.

Table 1. The PE Measure*.

Circle a number from 1 to 5 to answer your response to ALL of the following questions for each of the listed activities. *Please take your time and read the instructions completely.* The numbers are used in this way:

1	2	3	4	5
Very Ineffective	Somewhat Ineffective	Neither Effective Nor Ineffective	Somewhat Effective	Very Effective

Based on your experiences with computer mediated communication in your project team, how **effective** do you feel this communication method is for the following activities?

Activity					
Planning what tasks need to be done	1	2	3	4	5
Planning a meeting agenda	1	2	3	4	5
Planning when tasks need to be completed	1	2	3	4	5
Planning meetings	1	2	3	4	5
Making difficult decisions	1	2	3	4	5
Choosing when all of the alternatives seem about the same	1	2	3	4	5
Choosing when none of the alternatives seem very good	1	2	3	4	5
Making complex decisions	1	2	3	4	5
Negotiating who will be responsible for something	1	2	3	4	5
Resolving differences of opinion	1	2	3	4	5
Negotiating who will pay for something	1	2	3	4	5
Negotiating how to pay for something	1	2	3	4	5
Developing a presentation with other people	1	2	3	4	5
Improving a group presentation	1	2	3	4	5
Writing a report with other people	1	2	3	4	5
Editing a report developed with other people	1	2	3	4	5

***Item presentation order is randomized in actual administration**

Table 2. Reliability Analysis and Factor Analysis Results for the PE Measure.

Task Type	Item	Factor Loadings			
		1	2	3	4
Generation	Planning what tasks need to be done				.418
α = .77	Planning a meeting agenda				.736
	Planning when tasks need to be completed				.782
	Planning meetings				.524
Choice	Making difficult decisions		.733		
α = .81	Choosing when all of the alternatives seem about the same		.430		
	Choosing when none of the alternatives seem very good		.807		
	Making complex decisions		.588	.357	
Negotiation	Negotiating who will be responsible for something			.644	
α = .76	Resolving differences of opinion			.639	
	Negotiating who will pay for something			.584	
	Negotiating how to pay for something			.542	
Execution	Developing a presentation with other people	.708			
α = .83	Improving a group presentation	.561			
	Writing a report with other people	.746			
	Editing a report developed with other people	.670			

Kaiser-Meyer-Olkin (KMO) measure of sampling adequacy for this analysis = .878.
Factor extraction via Generalized Least Squares method and rotation via Varimax with Kaiser Normalization (Norusis, 1993). For clarity, factor loadings less than .35 are not shown.

Means Testing

Three subgroups were represented in the subject pool. Two of these groups had a similar task domain, i.e., project teams conducting software or database development. The third group's task domain was generalized communication that did not include a team project with specific deliverables. Means testing was conducted across the groups using one-way ANOVA and *post hoc* multiple comparisons were conducted using the Dunnett T3 method. Results of these analyses are shown in Table 3 and Figure 2.

Perceived effectiveness was very similar across all task types between the two project team subgroups, 3GL programming and database development. This finding suggests that where task domains are similar the PE measure converges appropriately, supporting Hypothesis 2. Significant differences do appear between the general communication group and both divergent groups on the Choice and Execution task types. This finding supports Hypothesis 3 and suggests that the PE measure is capable of discriminating between dissimilar task domains.

Table 3. Means Testing Among Subject Subgroups					
Task Type	**Group***	**N**	**Mean**	**S. D.**	**Analysis Results**
Generation	GC	62	4.08	.74	ANOVA F = .405, p = .667
	3GL	57	4.07	.85	*No significant differences among*
	DB	36	3.94	.82	*groups at a = .05*
Choice	GC	62	3.31	.82	ANOVA F = 19.33, p < .001
	3GL	57	2.46	.90	PostHoc
	DB	36	2.38	.87	GC <> 3GL, p < .001
					GC <> DB, p < .001
					3GL = DB, p = .960
Negotiation	GC	62	3.27	.74	ANOVA F = 2.90, p = .058
	3GL	57	2.95	.94	*No significant differences among*
	DB	36	2.91	.92	*groups at a = .05*
Execution	GC	62	3.23	.91	ANOVA F = 4.65, p = .011
	3GL	57	2.77	1.13	Post Hoc
	DB	36	2.67	.98	GC <> 3GL, p = .048
					GC <> DB, p = .019
					3GL = DB, p = .960

* GC = general communication; 3GL = 3GL programming project team; DB = database development project team

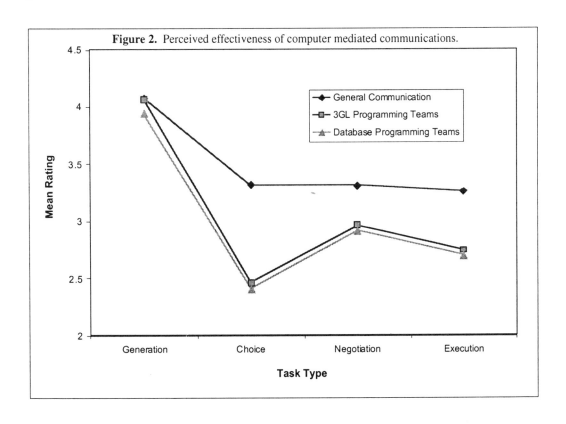

Figure 2. Perceived effectiveness of computer mediated communications.

DISCUSSION, LIMITATIONS AND CONCLUSIONS

Overall, the findings are encouraging. The PE measure proved capable of distinguishing between distinct constructs as evidenced in the factor analysis results. Although some intercorrelation occurs between the choice and negotiation task factors; this seems reasonable since choice is often intertwined with negotiation. Initial empirical testing indicates the PE measure has instrument validity as determined through convergent validity, which addresses whether items comprising a measure behave as if they are measuring a common underlying construct, and discriminant validity, which addresses whether the measurement item differentiates between objects being measured (Davis, 1989). These findings suggest the PE measure, as presently constituted, will be useful to CMCS researchers in providing descriptive analysis of communication effectiveness. In particular, the PE measure could facilitate task-based comparisons between alternative CMCS feature sets to help choose those features that are most effective in supporting specific group tasks.

Figure 2 provokes some interesting discussion points regarding the task domains that were studied. Subjects in all three tasks gave equivalent effectiveness ratings of CMCS for generation tasks. However, subjects in project teams reported significantly lower ratings for the choice and execution tasks and marginally lower for negotiation tasks (p = .058). One explanation is that, in general communication, subjects are more free to choose which tasks they will use CMCS to support and which they will save for FTF situations. Our subjects that were involved in team projects were required to produce specific deliverables within strict deadlines, which may have reduced their options and forced them to use CMCS. This initial finding suggests caution in the way we interpret results from different task domains. Clear overall differences are seen in our subjects' attitudes toward CMCS based on the task they performed.

Another interesting aspect is the range among the task ratings for the subjects in the various task domains. As predicted in previous research (Dennis & Valacich, 1993; Wilson *et al.*, 1997), the generation task was best task type supported by CMCS technology and the choice task was not supported as well overall (paired t test of pooled subjects, two-tailed, 154 df, t = 16.51, p < .001). However, within the team project task domains, negotiation and execution also were rated higher than choice (paired t test of pooled project team subjects, two-tailed, 92 df: negotiation vs. choice, t = 5.63, p < .001; execution vs. choice, t = 3.09, p = .003). Future work needs to investigate why CMCS falls down in supporting the choice task in this task domain, why it is perceived to support the negotiation and evaluation tasks better, and how the technology could be changed to support all three tasks at a higher level.

Although our hypotheses were supported by the results, several questions emerged from the research. First, although we can measure differences in communication effectiveness between task domains, it is not clear how to relate these measurements to specific task characteristics. If a choice task involves voting, for example, is this equivalent to an alternate choice task that involves development of consensus? Development of theory—along with theory's predictive and explanatory capabilities—likely will be hampered until research reveals more specific relationships than was possible in our research design. Potentially, this issue could best be addressed studying peoples' *perceptions* of task characteristics in the same manner that we studied perceived effectiveness. However, this idea is speculative at present.

Second, some areas within McGrath's task circumplex are not represented in the PE measure. For example, all the generation task items involve planning rather than creativity-oriented activities. This might have occurred because the CMCS being evaluated did not support simultaneous input or input feedback, but it also is possible that other causes exist, e.g., that creativity and planning are fundamentally distinct constructs. Future research needs to explore this issue by testing additional instrument items and using CMCS with different feature sets than the system we studied.

Finally, our study does not address individual or group differences among subjects. Although all subjects were enrolled in Information Systems classes on the same campus and during the same time period, it is possible that those who participated in an extended team project in which email was used extensively were sufficiently changed by the task that their views toward CMCS and their use of CMCS in general were altered. Because of concerns about experimental handling bias and learning effects, our research did not take measurements that could answer this question. However, it is well documented that such effects can occur. Future research should attempt to address this issue through employing different research designs, e.g., repeated measures.

This paper has described the development and validation of an instrument to measure perceived effectiveness in computer-mediated communication based on the tasks identified in McGrath's task circumplex. It provides a methodology that researchers can use to determine the impact of different task domains on perceived effectiveness of a CMCS as well as the perceived effectiveness of different CMCS when addressing similar tasks. Our research also raises questions for future research, in particular the question of how CMCS can support choice, negotiation and execution tasks more effectively.

REFERENCES

Cook, T. D., & Campbell, D. T. (1979). *Quasi-experimentation*. Boston: Houghton Mifflin Co.

Davis, F. D. (1989). Perceived usefulness, perceived ease of use, and user acceptance of information technology. *MIS Quarterly, 13*(3), 319-340.

Dennis, A., & Gallupe, R. B. (1993). A history of group support systems empirical research: Lessons learned and future directions. In L. M. Jessup & J. S. Valacich (Eds.), *Group support systems: New perspectives* (pp. 59-77). New York: MacMillan.

DeSanctis, G., & Gallupe, R. B. (1987). A foundation for the study of group decision support systems. *Management Science, 33*(5), 589-609.Galegher, J., & Kraut, R. E. (1994). Computer-mediated communication for intellectual teamwork: An experiment in group writing. *Information Systems Research, 5* (2), 110 – 138.

Galegher, J., & Kraut, R. E. (1994). Computer-mediated communication for intellectual teamwork: An experiment in group writing. *Information Systems Research, 5* (2), 110 – 138.

Huber, G. P. (1984) Issues in the design of group decision support systems. *MIS Quarterly, 8*(3), 195-204.

McGrath, J. E. (1984). *Groups: Interaction and performance*. Englewood Cliffs, NJ: Prentice-Hall, Inc.

McGrath, J. E., & Hollingshead, A. B. (1993). Putting the "group" back in group support systems: Some theoretical issues about dynamic processes in groups with technological enhancements. In L. M. Jessup & J. S. Valacich (Eds.), *Group support systems: New perspectives* (pp. 78-96). New York: Macmillan.

Moore, G. C., & Benbasat, I. (1991). Development of an instrument to measure the perceptions of adopting an information technology innovation. *Information Systems Research, 2*(3), 192-222.

Norusis, M. J. (1993). *SPSS for Windows professional statistics release 6.0*. Chicago: SPSS Inc.

Turoff, M., Hiltz, S. R., Bahgat, A. N. F., & Rana, A. R. (1993). Distributed group support systems. *MIS Quarterly, 17*(4), 399-417.

Wilson, E. V., Morrison, J. P., & Napier, A. M. (1997). Perceived effectiveness of computer-mediated communications and face-to-face communications in student software development teams. *Journal of Computer Information Systems, 38*(2), 2-7.

Wood, R. E. (1986). Task complexity: Definition of the construct. *Organizational Behavior and Human Decision Processes, 37*, 60-82.

Zigurs, I, & Buckland, B. K. (1998). A theory of task-technology fit and group support systems effectiveness. *MIS Quarterly, 22*(3), 313-334.

Organisational Learning and Information Systems: Reflections on the Experience of is Implementations for Nursing

Dr DA White
Sheffield Business School, Sheffield Hallam University, Shefield, S1 1WB
0044 114 2255130, D.A.White@SHU.AC.UK

Mr ZPF Swann
Shared Medical Systems (UK) Ltd, Sarum Gate, Sarum Hill, Basingstoke, Hants.
0044 1256 691344

ABSTRACT

This paper discusses the implementation of a computerised Nurse Management Information System into a National Health Service (NHS) hospital in the United Kingdom. Implementations may be seen as technically valid but fail to achieve genuine organisational gains. The concept of organisational learning has been suggested as a useful model for understanding the success or failure of IS development. Features of this implementation are discussed with reference to organisational learning. It was found that failures in organisational learning contributed to problems with the systems and restricted its innovative potential. It is proposed that organisational learning is a useful and important concept for understanding systems development in both a practical and conceptual way.

The views expressed in this paper are the authors and do not necessarily reflect those of the named institutions or companies.

INTRODUCTION

The successful implementation of information systems is dependant on an understanding of organisational processes. These processes are complex, powerful and difficult to map. Systems professionals and developers are increasingly urged to develop a wider understanding of organisational processes in relation to their effect on implementations. In this paper organisational learning (Argyris and Schon, 1978) is used to discuss a systems implementation and the efficacy of this concept for an 'enlarged view' of the systems problem is itself addressed.

INFORMATION IN THE NHS

The National Health Service (NHS) in the United Kingdom has invested heavily in computerised information systems in recent years in an attempt to manage the complexity of its operation and service delivery. The reported lack of information to manage the organisation of healthcare was a key feature of reform in the 1980's, (Steering Group on Health Service Information, 1982). This resulted in a drive to collect and create improved data sets on a national basis and, in a variety of initiatives, to change the nature of service provision and management.

Under the Korner initiatives (1982-84) (Steering Group on Health Service Information, 1982) data was systematically collected on service provision, theatre usage, patient survival and diagnosis. This was still considered inadequate, however, for a full understanding of resource utilisation, a fact noted in a statutory note referred to as the 1986 Health Notice.

The Resource Management Initiative (RMI) was put forward as a solution to this problem. It had, as its core premise, the need for the development of improved information management to support both clinical and operational decision making. Moreover, it recommended that clinicians be more closely involved in management decision making. Thus the framework was laid for the direct involvement of clinical staff in the development and use of information systems. The importance and impact of the RMI was further emphasised when it emerged as a cornerstone of the reforms enshrined in the far-reaching NHS Review, Working For Patients (Dept. of Health, 1989). Included among many key changes to be implemented by 1991 was:

"..improved information for managers and professional staff. This included extending the Resource Management Initiative to link up information on diagnosis and cost of treatment in order to provide a complete picture of the resources used in the treatment of hospital patients. The government was committed to introducing modern information systems to support both clinical and operational functions." (MacDougall and Brittain, 1992)

This aspect of the reform was embodied in Working Paper 11 (Department of Health, 1990) which laid out a series of short-term and long-term goals for the implementation of information systems in hospitals.

NURSE MANAGEMENT INFORMATION SYSTEMS

Nursing activity and information systems for nursing were a key area of these reforms and developments. Through the RMI £120,000 was contributed towards the cost of purchasing a Nursing Management Information System (NMIS) in each acute unit in hospitals with over 250 beds. By the end of 1993 150 sites had completed, or were in process of implementing, a computerised nursing system. This represents a base expenditure of £18,000,000, although actual total expenditure is likely to be considerably higher. It is difficult to assess the true level of investment as there are no complete figures that include local and regional top-up expenditure to the amounts derived from RMI source funding. Moreover it has been demonstrated in other areas (Keen, 1991) that the real operational cost would lead to an increase by a factor of 2.4. However this development is assessed it represents a considerable IT investment both within the confines of the NHS and as a general item of public expenditure.

It is difficult to discuss a general model of nursing information systems in relation to individual implementations because practice and development differs across regions and individual units. National guidelines for the development of systems are the responsibility of the Information Management Group (IMG) of the NHS Executive. In general terms these have been elaborated through the publication of the NHS Information Management and Technology strategy document published in December 1992. Prescriptions for the design and implementation of nursing information systems can be found in a range of NHS Executive published guidelines (NHS Training Executive,1990; NHSME Resource management Unit, 1990). For our purposes here the general definitions found in strategic guidelines will serve for a working description of a conceptual model for a NMIS and its constituent modules.

Typically a nursing system comprises three main areas. These are:
• Care Planning & Evaluation
• Workload Assessment
• Rostering (planning and evaluation) including nursing personnel and time-out analyses

These are functions that may have been performed manually in some way and in some cases still are. There are significant advantages to computerised storage and retrieval in these areas and this is where main benefits have been identified in the planning of implementations. These functions have been recognised as not meeting all the information needs of the nursing function but "..help to answer a wide range of questions." (Audit Commission, 1992:4). A Nursing System may have connections to a range of other hospital systems, depending on the type of applications adopted and the pace and scale of local developments. A conceptual model that approximates to a working standard is shown in fig. 1.

There have been a range of significant and well documented criticisms of implementa-

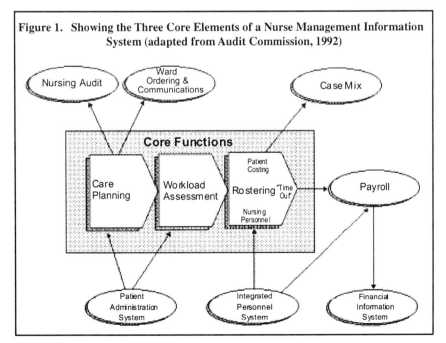

Figure 1. Showing the Three Core Elements of a Nurse Management Information System (adapted from Audit Commission, 1992)

tions of nursing systems. Most notable are those contained in the report by the Audit Commission (1992). In a full scale review of nursing system implementations criticisms were made on the nature of purchasing, the planning and design of systems, and the analysis of systems needs in relation to the changing operational and managerial nature of the service.

"The first generation of nursing management systems often appears to have been introduced piecemeal rather than as part of a holistic plan for meeting the information needs of the service and helping it to develop. Information is often geared to the perceived needs of old-style line management, even where new, slimmer management structures have been introduced, rather than to the needs of ward nurses acting as professionals" (Audit Commission, 1992).

A number of criticisms have been aimed at the failure of managers and systems developers to integrate the process effectively with the need and demand for organisational change.

"At the (resource management) pilot sites, systems were imposed rather than being agreed through discussion and reports thus held by senior nurse managers rather than being fed up from wards. The opportunity for nurses to establish proper professional management and clinical reporting arrangements was thus lost." (Keen and Malby, 1992).

Given the value of the investment described above it is not surprising that a deal of self-critical analysis has occurred both within the NHS management and amongst nursing professionals about the value and impact of computerised nursing systems. In one unit this has gone as far as abandoning an implemented system and commencing a fresh process of review (Mitchell and Lee, 1994). The scope of review has tended to focus on issues of project management, training and the nature of requirements formulation and purchasing.

We have discussed, elsewhere the need to shift the focus away from the use of the system itself to an understanding and use of the information product (Entwistle, Hutchins and White, 1992; White and Swann, 1995). This problem has been summarised by Buchanan (1991):

"The success or failure of any information system depends on the data produced being understood and utilised to improve and enhance the efficiency and efficacy of the organisation."

"The nursing workforce needs more knowledge about how to utilise the clinical and managerial information contained in the databases of systems, to manage resources better and to improve standards of patient care." (Buchanan, 1991).

ORGANISATIONAL LEARNING

The concept of organisational learning (Argyris and Schon, 1978) is well established and has been discussed and developed by many authors (Dodgson, 1993; Garvin, 1993). Its applicability to problems in information systems and new technology implementation has been highlighted in various ways by Boddy and Gunson (1994), Salaway (1987), Walsham and Han (1991) and Ciborra (1992).

Organisational learning can be discussed in relation to two main areas of application for Information Systems. Firstly, as a process of adaptation to changing circumstances and response to feedback from ongoing decision making. Learning and knowledge enhancement occurs as a process of questioning and changing the assumptions that underlie the rules which inform task behaviour in organisations. This can be seen as the implication that systems have for the ability of organisational members to process and use information to change assumptions about decision making actions in the context of their work.

"Organisational Learning means the process of improving actions through better knowledge and understanding" (Fiol and Lyles, 1985).

"An entity learns if, through its processing of information, the range of its potential behaviours is changed." (Huber, 1991).

It can be argued here that systems success depends on the ability and willingness of users to creatively employ the information product in a developmental way in relation to their own practice. This implies a continual, iterative process of using information to question and reformulate individual and collective 'theories-in-use' (Argyris and Schon, 1978) in relation to organisational objectives.

Secondly, organisational learning is assessed as a feature of the relationship between systems professionals and users in the process of information systems development and implementation. This reflects the problem of how consultation and participation is best understood and achieved in the context of the development process. Failure in systems design as a result of poor organisational processes and communication between designers and users is well known and extensively documented (Ives and Olsen, 1984). There is significant potential for conflict in this relationship which is counterproductive to good design and successful implementation (Edstrom, 1977; Markus, 1981). Reference to organisational learning has been made as a means of both understanding and harnessing the dynamic nature of this relationship (Salaway, 1987; Ciborra, 1992). In general it is proposed that the concept of organisational learning would facilitate improved project management practices and ensure greater systems development success.

This has been termed 'project learning' (Boddy and Gunson, 1994). They propose that the concept of organisational learning offers potential:

"..practices and creating mechanisms for groups of users to share experience of using systems in different circumstances, to exchange problems, and to generate new ideas" (Boddy and Gunson, 1994).

This reflects the findings that successful strategy formulation could be found as a result of a dynamic, and often informal, learning relationship between managers and IT specialists rather than any particular plan or methodology (Earl, 1990). A learning approach is seen as positively related to the successful design and adoption of Information System developments.

IMPLEMENTATION OF A NMIS

The implementation of a NMIS is discussed here. The authors were closely involved with the project, one as the project manager. Thus the discussion and any evidential data is produced from a perspective of action research with an emphasis on a qualitative mode of enquiry (Wood-Harper, 1985).

The hospital is an independent trust in the south of England with approximately 3,800 employees and an annual budget of £90 million. It has 834 inpatient beds split across two sites in a mix of old and modern buildings. Patient services are organised into 7 business units with annual inpatient activity in the order of 50,000 episodes.

The Trust was part of the second wave for resource management, and obtained three years of revenue funding for the project ending in July 1994. Implementation of a computerised nurse management information systems commenced in November 1992 following a lengthy regional procurement process. Selection and implementation of the systems was conducted through a consultative process with nursing staff participating in both the development of the Memorandum of Agreement (Specification) and choice of the product through a series of demonstrations and site visits. The systems includes modules for care planning, workload assessment, rostering and personnel.

The project was managed according to NHS guidelines which include the setting up of a project board and the use of the PRINCE project management methodology.

Training for the 1200 nursing staff was conducted off the wards in a purpose built facility by the project team. When the project was initiated the plan was to roll the system out to 35 wards over a 15 month period. The closure of a number of wards reduced this to 30 and the late delivery of the local area network and problems with funding for Health & Safety work resulted in 5 month delay. As part of the Trust's strategy to produce a Hospital Integrated Support System (HISS) by incremental steps the ageing Patient Admission System was replaced in April 1994 with a Patient Management System (PMS). Problems with this resulted in a delay to plans for an interface with the NMIS. The direct result being that nursing staff are still rekeying demographic information into the NMIS. This is an unsatisfactory and undesirable situation and has directly affected the acceptance of the system by nurse users.

Despite a number of technical, funding and project management difficulties, the project was viewed as an operational success. The mechanics of care planning, roster creation and nursing dependency measurement have been automated and the system was implemented within an agreed and expected framework. Care planning is now carried out using the computerised libraries that are available and the system forms the core database for hospital information. However, evaluation and investigation have revealed a gap between viewing the implementation as a technical success and as an organisational success. This may be described as the difference between a system that works and one that is used, consequently achieving true organisational validity (Markus and Robey, 1983).

A detailed study was conducted over a six week period of a busy acute surgical ward three months after the introduction of the NMIS. This revealed a number of problems with the nature of the care planning activities and consequent use of the system. Firstly, it transpired that the average time after admission for initial care plan creation was 16.5 hours and it was common practice for staff to stay behind at the end of their official shift to write and update care plans. Unfamiliarity with the system and problems with having to come to terms with it were cited and, clearly, these factors made a contribution to such a finding. But a more fundamental issue emerged in that the system was simply not perceived as integral to the work that the nurses were engaged in. They viewed it as an administrative chore to be completed - eventually - rather than a central element in the planning and management of the delivery of care on the ward. Consequently the potential of the system for information to be used in a dynamic way to inform and drive the decision processes of care was being lost. Clearly the time lag incurred in practice means that the system does not reflect the current health status of patients which is critical if it is to be part of the decision making process as envisaged. The system was being used to record but not to inform.

Further evidence of the systems usage in this way was revealed by analysis of the activities of rostering and workload planning. Central to staffing plans on wards is the construction of 'off-duties' which allow for planned absences and rest days of nurses. The majority of wards were found to be still drawing up their off-duty rosters on paper without reference to, or keying them into, the system. The aim of using the computerised system is that staffing is planned in relation to a measurement of workload demand derived from the process of care planning. The ward sisters responsible for this function were operating an informal manual procedure based on their local knowledge, experience and opinion. It became clear that a culture among ward managers which values information about resource utilisation was far from developed.

A third problem area of usage that emerged was with the process of care planning in the goal setting of care interventions and their evaluation. A key goal of the system was that it would enable better evaluation of interventions through the use and monitoring of the available trend information and make a contribution to the process of clinical audit. This is a crucial information-based activity which is central to the mission of nursing care and part of an overall drive for quality improvement.

It was found that goal setting tended to be poor. They were often far too global in nature and not defined with evaluation in mind. For example, a patient following a hip replacement would, by definition, be assessed as having a problem of reduced mobility. This would lead to a goal statement on the care plan of, for example:

"Patient will be able to walk out of the hospital in 10 days from surgery with the aid of crutches"

This is not inaccurate but it is not a goal against which progress can be assessed on day one or day two. This presented no real problems under the original manual system where interventions were subsequently and separately recorded. So if on day two the patient stood with the aid of a physiotherapist the nurse would record the event and add any appropriate commentary about such actions. However the NMIS follows a text book model of care planning in which the goals are evaluated rather than just a recording of interventions. This means that goals must be constantly re-evaluated and care plans updated in a constant and dynamic way. The process used by the nurses in practice is actually quite non-dynamic. The activities of assessment (including the formulation of nursing diagnosis), planning care, implementation and evaluation were performed in a linear fashion and there was little feedback on the basis of the evaluation. This reflects a classic view of the nursing process.

The introduction of the computerised NMIS resulted in the concept of care planning becoming a major issue. The processes in use with the manual paper-based system were inadequate for using the new system. For the computerised system to become useful in the way it is envisaged requires a change in professional practice to a more dynamic and questioning model of action in which outcomes are evaluated more responsively, resulting in the constant assessment of goal setting and even diagnosis. Such a model for care plans exists in the nursing literature with the spiral care

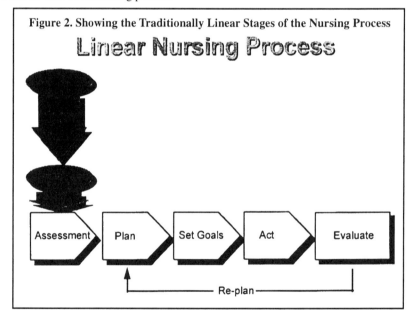

Figure 2. Showing the Traditionally Linear Stages of the Nursing Process

Linear Nursing Process

Assessment → Plan → Set Goals → Act → Evaluate

Re-plan

plans advocated by Barnett (1985). This method makes the care plan more dynamic by taking the patient's condition through a series of sub-goals towards the achievement of a global goal.

The sub-goals will be set according to each day's assessment, and then evaluated before the next cycle. If managed correctly the potential is to facilitate a more definitive articulation of goals for each patient, making the care plan more responsive for each patient's condition and thus a more complete record of the prescribed care and its outcomes (Barnett, 1985; Walters, 1986). Moreover there are greater benefits in that better goal evaluation leads to a wealth of quality related information that can be used by hospital managers in the negotiation of contracts with the purchasers of healthcare from the hospital. Such a regime of planning and evaluation was not feasible under manual recording systems because of the clerical burden of updating required. A computerised system has the potential to realise such a move but it requires a shift in the philosophy of practice at ward level and a recognition of the interrelationship between systems use and nursing process. It was clear from the evaluation that this shift was not occurring and indeed there was resistance to it.

The conclusion that can be drawn from our investigation of the actual use made of the system in relation to local ward-based decision making is that the computerised NMIS is not being employed to change and inform the nursing process. It has achieved technical but not organisational validity and the anticipated wider developmental and strategic benefits are not being realised. A relationship between the system and the process of delivering and managing care has yet to be established which would promote an information culture in which the NMIS is a central focus in clinical and managerial innovation. This can be discussed with reference to a model of organisational learning which may illuminate why this is not occurring.

DISCUSSION

Argyris and Schon (1978) identify and discuss three types of organisational learning: single-loop, double-loop and deutero-learning. Single-loop learning is based on a drive for effectiveness and involves the detection and correction of error. Responses to error, detection and consequent modifications of behaviour or actions occur within existing

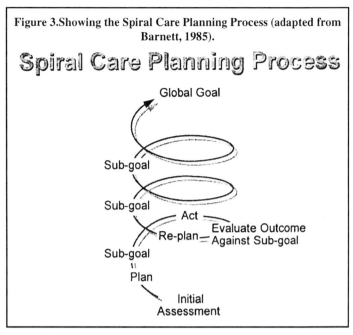

Figure 3.Showing the Spiral Care Planning Process (adapted from Barnett, 1985).

organisational norms. Double-loop learning requires the organisational norms themselves to be questioned, challenged and possibly changed. Response to reported error takes the form of joint enquiry between an individual and a collective level in the organisation. The key to double-loop learning is that organisational as opposed to just individual processes are assessed and amended. The ability to learn itself and to understand the processes that have affected or encouraged that ability reflects the third level known as deutero-learning. This requires a collective reflective response that identifies both behaviours and structures through which learning has occurred on both an individual and organisational dimension.

Boddy and Gunson (1994) have described how the management of information system projects can be seen to migrate through learning styles from single-loop to deutero learning. This migration is summarised below:

Type 1 Overcome administrative burden by automation of well-designed but overloaded manual system
Type 2 Change nature of structure and business through availability of timely, accurate management information previously unavailable
Type 3 Encourage a culture of action and experimentation serving to reinforce and enhance the prevailing learning style

The problems encountered with the use of the NMIS and the apparent failure to integrate it into the nursing process can be seen as a problem of the organisation's inability to move from type 1 to type 3 learning. The operation of the NMIS in relation to care planning is locked into a type 1 model of learning. Existing routines and processes have been automated and the nature of information use is limited to relatively low-level error detection and control. Consequently nurses are content to set quite limited goals and continue to record them in the same way that they did on the manual system. Their theories-in-use are predicated on a linear process model encouraged and reinforced by the previous structure of recording under the manual system. To achieve level 2 learning requires a move to a more dynamic planning model as discussed earlier (Barnet, 1986). It is interesting that such a model is available and clearly reflects a more innovative and reflective learning style which may, in fact, be closer to the real view that nurses hold about the nursing process. But the system is not perceived in this way and is seen as a barrier to the process rather than the enabling tool which it could be.

This apparent contradiction may be a product of a distinction between practical and discursive consciousness (Giddens, 1984) producing a dichotomy between espoused and actual theories-in-use. The consequence of this would be a resistance to the computerised system based on a view that it does not reflect the "..dynamic and qualitative ways in which nurses practice their science." (Rundell, 1993). In fact it is the theories-in-use held by nurses which are restricting such practice. The system is criticised but the processes that surround it, which are legitimated and routinised, are ignored. This presents itself as a significant issue of organisational learning which is influencing the take up of the system and the use of the available information.

Moreover they have very little incentive to adopt more innovative styles which would reflect a move to level 2 or 3 learning. The nursing function is currently organised in a strict hierarchical structure which reflects a traditional command and control ethos. There is very little scope for empowerment in the decision making process and this clearly affects the way that information is used and perceived. It is clear that double-loop learning demands and involves wider changes of organisational structure and process.

In this case this would mean redefining the hierarchy and the social structure of power relations in major and radical ways. Process innovation (Davenport, 1993) on this scale is currently beyond the scope of the implementation but will be required if the higher stages of learning are to be achieved. While the IT can be seen as a key enabler (Hammer and Champy, 1993) the danger is that "..we are currently implementing systems which are based on the existing systematic nursing process." (Swann, 1993). This process is reactive rather than innovative and the systems may block redesign by reinforcing and legitimating old ways of thinking and old behaviour patterns.

BARRIERS TO LEARNING

The above discussion has suggested a number of behavioural and structural barriers to achieving organisational learning which have affected the implementation of the NMIS. Two main organisational factors in this project can be highlighted for consideration as inhibiting the development of a learning environment for systems development. These are:

1. The particular structural features of the hospital as a human service organisation (Harshbarger, 1974). A hospital, as a professional bureaucracy, has very complex social and structural arrangements. These can best be understood by reference to a model of conflicting domains suggested by Kouzes and Mico (1979) and elaborated in the diagram below.

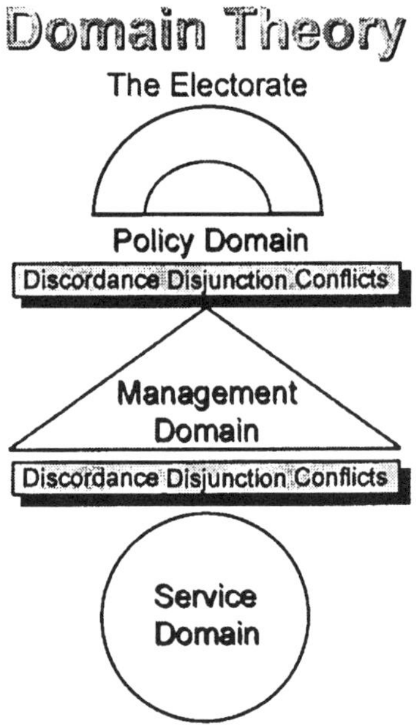

In this model the organisation is described not as a unitary hierarchy but as three identifiable domains with different and conflicting world views, modes of work, processes and success measures. The characteristics of the three domains can be summarised as follows.

Figure 4. Showing the 3 domains of a Health Care Organisation (adapted from Kouzes and Mico, 1979)

The Policy Domain refers to the level of the organisation at which governing policies are formulated. It is concerned with the translation of public policy and in bargaining and negotiating for resources.

The Management Domain controls and manages the resource base of the organisation and tends to reflect a "technocratic-bureaucracy" paradigm. This now includes the assumption that hospitals should be more "business-like" and it has generally assumed responsibility for the information systems developments in the NHS in recent years. It has developed into a career management group who employ a range of business and management tools in their mode of work.

The Service Domain is the point at which services are provided to clients and is populated by those who see themselves as having the right to control what they define as professional practice. Principles of autonomy and self-regulation dominate this area.

There is considerable potential for conflict between these domains, in particular between the management and service domains, due to the contradictory principles, structures and processes. This significantly affects the way that information as a concept and a resource is viewed and treated. The NMIS implementation was viewed as a product of the management domain and therefore, by definition, not part of the clinical process. This has contributed to the uptake described above, as developments are viewed with suspicion. It is very difficult for the systems implementors to suggest changes in process as this would be seen as an interference with professional practice. Thus the cultural divide promoted by this structure has been a major inhibitor to learning and development.

2. The systems development and project management process. The acquisition and implementation of computerised information systems in the NHS is typified by the use of structured design methodologies and linear project management tools such as the PRINCE method (PRojects IN a Controlled Environment). This project was no exception as NHS guidelines dictate that having these structures in place is a prerequisite of acquiring funding. The main elements are the Project Board, Project Manager, Stage Manager and Project Assurance Team. Meetings, documentation and progress evaluation are essential features of this process. On the surface PRINCE seems a satisfac-

tory quality assurance tool but it has a number of weaknesses which make its use with complex systems implementations problematic. Firstly, in common with all structured methods it places an emphasis on tasks at the expense of "softer" organisational and cultural issues which are central to success. Secondly, it promotes a bureaucratic environment with an emphasis on documentation and reports which is diverting for implementors. Thirdly, this emphasis on management control effectively stifles the sort of end-user experimentation which has been identified as vital for innovative development.

In summary a creative and learning environment for systems development was difficult to achieve due to the nature of the authority and control structure of the organisation.

CONCLUSION

We have discussed the experience of this implementation through the analysis of organisational learning. Such an analysis has illuminated a number of problem areas in relation to the impact of the system, its use and the development process. Identified barriers to learning present significant obstacles to achieving the wider, strategic benefits available from computerised information systems. It is proposed that the concept of organisational learning aligned to flexible development methodologies based on prototyping could promote an effective and valid environment for more successful systems interventions.

REFERENCES

Argyris and Schon (1978), Organisational Learning: A theory of action perspective, Addison-Wesley.

Audit Commission (1992), Caring Systems: A handbook for managers of nursing and project managers, London, HMSO.

Barnett (1985), "Making Your Care Plans Work", Nursing Times, January, 9: 24-27.

Boddy and Gunson (1994), Contrasting Results from the Computer Networks: Is organisational learning a useful perspective?. Paper presented at the British Academy of Management Conference, Lancaster, September.

Buchanan (1993), How to get the best value from your nursing system. In: Thompson, J. (ed) Conference Proceedings - Managing information for the benefit of patients. London: British Computer Society Nursing Specialist Group: 119-121.

Ciborra (1992), From Thinking to Tinkering: The grassroots strategic information systems. Proceedings of The International Conference on Information Systems, New York.

Davenport (1993), Process Innovation: Reengineering work through information technology, Harvard Business School Press.

Department of Health (1989), Working for Patients, CM 555, London, HMSO.

Department of Health (1990), Working for Patients: Framework for information systems overview, Working paper 11, London, HMSO.

Dodgson (1993), "Organisational Learning: A review of some literatures", Organisation Studies, 14 (3): 375-394.

Earl (1990), Approaches to Strategic Information Systems Planning: Experience in twenty one UK companies. Proceedings of the International Conference on Information Systems, Copenhagen.

Edstrom (1977), "User Influence and the Success of MIS Projects: A contingency approach", Human Relations, 30 (7): 589-607.

Entwistle, Hutchins and White (1992) 'One hospitals experience'. In: Scholes, M Barver, B (eds), Conference proceedings, Informatics for the nursing profession. London: British Computer Society Nursing Specialist Group.

Fiol and Lyles (1985), "Organisational Learning", Academy of Management Review, October.

Garvin (1993), "Building a Learning Organisation", Harvard Business Review, 71, July-August.

Giddens (1984), The Constitution of Society, Polity Press.

Hammer and Champy (1993), Reengineering the Corporation: A manifesto for business revolution, Nicholas Brearly Publishing.

Harshbarger (1974), The Human Service Organisation. In: Dermot and Harshbarger (eds), A Handbook of Human Service Organisations, Behavioural Publications.

Huber (1991), "Organisational Learning: The contributing processes and the literatures", Organisational Science, February.

Ives and Olsen (1984), "User Involvement and MIS Success: A review of research", Management Science, 30 (5): 586-603.

Keen (1991), Shaping the Future: Business design through information technology, Harvard Business School Press.

Keen and Malby (1992), "Nursing Power and Practice in the United Kingdom National Health Service", Journal of Advanced Nursing, 17: 863-870.

Kouzes and Mico (1979), "Domain Theory: An introduction to organisational behaviour in human service organisations", The Journal of Applied Behavioral Science, 15 (1): 449-469.

MacDougall and Brittain (1992), Use of Information in the NHS, Library and Information Research Report 92, British Library.

Markus (1981), "Power, Politics and MIS Implementations", Communications of the ACM, 26 (6): 430-444.

Markus and Robey (1983), "The Organisational Validity of MIS", Human Relations.

Mitchell and Lee (1994), Ward Information Needs Review. In: Richards (ed), Conference Proceedings, Current Perspectives in Healthcare Computing, BJHC: 552-557.

NHS Training Executive (1990), Guide to the Implementation of Nursing Information Systems

NHSME Resource Management Unit (1990), Nursing Information Requirements: Identification and computerisation.

Rundell (1993), A New Information Paradigm for Nursing. In: Richards (ed), Proceedings for Health Care Computing Conference: 403-411.

Salaway (1987), "An Organisational Learning Approach to Information Systems Development", MIS Quarterly, June: 245-264.

Steering Group on Health Services Information (1982), First Report to the Secretary of State, London, HMSO.

Swann (1993), Soft Systems and the Organisational Impact of a Nurse Management Information System, MSc Dissertation, Sheffield Business School.

Walsham and Han (1991), Structuration Theory and Information Systems Research. Proceedings of The International Conference on Information Systems, Copenhagen.

Walters (1986), "Computerised Care Plans Help Nurses Achieve Quality Patient Care", Journal of Nursing Administration, 16 (11): 33-39.

White and Swann (1995), The Use of Information in the Care Process: The need for a learning model of systems development in nursing. In: Richards, B. (ed), Conference proceedings in Health Care Computing, BJHC.

Wood-Harper (1985), Research Methods in Information Systems: Using action research. In: Mumford et al. (eds), Research Methods in Information Systems, North Holland.

Quality in a Respecification of DeLone and McLean's IS Success Model

Carla Wilkin and Bill Hewett
School of Management Information Systems, Faculty of Business and Law, Deakin University,
Warrnambool, Victoria, Australia
Tel: +61 3 55633511, Fax: +61 3 55633320, Email: carlaw@deakin.edu.au

ABSTRACT

The exploration of IS (Information System) Effectiveness has been significantly shaped by DeLone and McLean's (1992) IS Success Model. Their taxonomy comprised six major categories with 'temporal and causal' interdependencies. With quality as the focus of the quest for effectiveness of product and service in related disciplines and as part of their IS Success Model, this concept is now investigated in relation to evaluating IS Effectiveness. The result has been respecification of the IS Success Model and the proposal of a quantitative instrument to measure IS Effectiveness.

Keywords: Quality, IS Effectiveness

INTRODUCTION

A major challenge for the delivery of effective information systems is implementation which properly addresses the needs of the system users. However, to focus on system implementation, whether this involves software sourced from third parties or customized software, is to undervalue the important role service plays in delivering an effective IS function. This paper argues that an effective IS function is built on three pillars: the systems implemented, the information held and delivered by these systems, and the service provided in support of such. The common foundation for these pillars is the concept of "user needs".

Meeting or exceeding user needs forms the basis of current quests for quality. But for effective performance of the IS Function, we must achieve consensus about the definition of quality applicable to this environment, and then determine how quality can be assessed.

The paper is structured as follows. A review is made of the varying definitions of quality, with the two meanings of service explored in an IT context. With respecification of the IS Success Model to incorporate quality as the central component, we then explore a new approach for determining IS Effectiveness.

THE VARYING DEFINITIONS QUALITY HAS ACQUIRED OVERTIME

In reviewing the literature, it seems that while quality is an important force in attaining economic growth, a global definition doesn't exist. Depending upon context and era, the term has been varyingly defined as: value (Cronin and Taylor 1992; Garvin 1988); conformance to product and production to specifications (Levitt 1972; Crosby 1979); fitness for use (Juran et al 1974); meeting and/or exceeding customers' expectations (Gronroos 1983, 1990; Parasuraman et al 1984; Zeithaml et al 1990; Buzzell and Gale 1987); and undoubtedly more. Consequently the "notion of information system *quality* is ambiguous" (Kriebel 1979 p29).

But, with the "mix of industries in advanced economies changing rapidly in favour of service industries, especially quaternary [information technology]", this ambiguity needs attention (Stamford 1996 p2). Indeed there has been widespread movement away from the technical definitions of quality, to a service-oriented definition of meeting and/or exceeding customers' expectations.

Marketing has taken this focus, but the premise seems equally valid for IT where the difficulty of achieving quantifiable quality-control techniques applies too. For both, it is customers who demand higher levels of quality, and customers who provide critical judgements, so it would seem sensible to measure quality in their terms for IT too.

As Table 1 demonstrates, the focus for quality has changed, from imposition of standards to definition through the views of a wide range of stakeholders. With such an approach the pursuit of quality is closely linked to service.

SERVICE IN AN IT CONTEXT

Strong parallels exist between the characteristics of a service and those of IT. Zeithaml et al (1985) defines service characteristics as intangibility, inseparability, heterogeneity and perishability, and since IT arguably pos-

Table 1. Changing Views of Quality (Source: Kerzner 1998 p1042)

Past Understanding of Quality
- The responsibility of blue-collar workers and direct labor employees working on the floor.
- Defects hidden from the customers (and possibly management)
- Problems lead to blame, faulty justification, and excuses
- Corrections accomplished with minimum documentation
- Increased quality, increased project costs
- Product/business focus (internal)
- Close supervision of people required for achievement
- Achieved during project execution

Present Understanding of Quality
- Everyone's responsibility, including white-collar workers, indirect labor force, and overhead staff
- Defects highlighted and brought to attention for corrective action
- Problems lead to cooperative solutions
- Documentation essential for "lessons learned" so mistakes not repeated
- Improved quality saves money, increases business
- Customer focus (outward)
- Stakeholders independently produce quality products
- Achieved at project initiation by planning within the project

sesses each of these (see Table 2), it is a service.

When considering the role of delivered IT, its function relates to both classical customers whose demands are serviced through IT, and to stakeholders who use IT to perform their jobs. Therefore, service is provided by the information system itself and by the IS unit which facilitates this system.

In relation to the IS unit, service is delivered through its function in ensuring acceptable system performance; sufficiently trained users; and technical facilities with the capability of generating the information desired. Pitt et al (1995 p183) included Service Quality in the IS Success Model, to acknowledge that the IS department "delivers information through both highly structured information systems and customized personal interactions" such that "effectiveness of an IS unit can be partially assessed by its capability to provide quality service to its users". An entirely independent study (Wilkin 1996) provided supportive evidence that the effectiveness of the IT service department could be measured in terms of Service Quality.

Seddon (1997) contested Pitt et al's extension and excluded Service Quality from his IS Success Model, arguing that an Information System was best defined as either an individual application of IT or a group of applications. Such a narrow description would exclude the role of an IS unit in contributing to the effectiveness of delivered IT, and in reality exclude a significant variable.

Table 2. Characteristics of Service in Relation to IT

Characteristics of service	Meaning (Zeithaml et al 1985)	Evidence in service industries	Evidence in IT	Associated problems characteristic to service industries & IT
Intangibility	inability to taste, touch or see	hotel room or meal visible, delivery process not.	printed IT output visible, delivery process not	incapacity to protect service through patents lack of easy means to display or communicate service difficulty re price setting
Inseparability	goods are produced then sold and consumed but services sold first, then produced and consumed	service must be sold before it is produced and consumed (i.e. telephone service)	delivered IT packages must be bought, before information produced	involvement of customer (user) in production difficulty of production
Heterogeneity	high variation in performance	operators handle situations different-ly therefore consis-tent delivery difficult	IT users interact differently with same system there-for service to end users varies	difficulties with standardization and quality control
Perishability	inability to save	hotel rooms unused cannot be "banked" for next day	IT capacity not in use one day, non transferable	

Hence we have adopted the broader definition of IS by von Hellens (1997 p802), so it is "defined in terms of its function and structure: it contains people, processes, data models, technology, formalised language in a cohesive structure which serves some organisational purposes or function".

The information system is another level at which service exists with respect to delivered IT. Here the whole system provides service to user stakeholders, for people want not merely a machine but one which serves their needs; and not merely data and information but material appropriate to their requirements. In this sense, the service provided by the system relates both to internal customers (stakeholders) when IS is used to meet job requirements and to classical customers when IS facilitates purchase requests.

TOWARDS RESPECIFICATION

Therefore, with delivered IT classified as a service, what marketing lessons offer potential for IT research? Is it even appropriate to look at the connections between the two? It is significant that the effectiveness of service for marketing has really been explored in terms of service quality. This focus on quality as the key to effectiveness is a rather different approach from that taken by IT, where DeLone and McLean's IS Success Model has delineated most avenues of approach.

Figure 1. Interdependent Success Components in Information Systems (Source: DeLone and McLean 1992 p87)

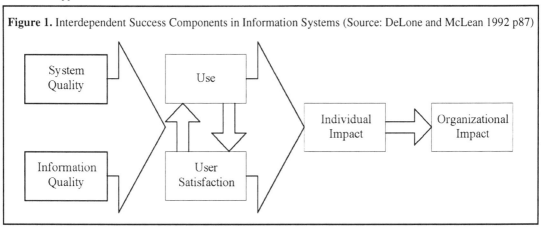

Their taxonomy (see Figure 1) includes quality in terms of System and Information Quality, but the principal means to measure IS Effectiveness has been through Use and User Satisfaction. There are four reasons for reconsidering this focus.

1. Research (particularly Seddon 1997) has revealed problems with measurement of Use as an accurate indicator of IS Effectiveness. One problem was the confusion between concepts 'benefits from use' and 'IS Use', when time spent with a system was equated to more benefits, ignoring influential factors such as work rates and expertise. Another arose when IS Use was interpreted as future use, hence measuring a behavior not IS Success. Further, IS Use could only be measured after the system had actually been used and impacted upon the individual and organization, contrary to the Success Model.
2. User Satisfaction and Use are shown in the model to be interdependent, when some of the literature suggests that each independently reflects IS Effectiveness. For example, where use is voluntary, then a measure of success is the extent of use, but when it isn't voluntary, then success concerns the user's overall degree of satisfaction (Moynihan 1982). Further, an empirical study (Baroudi et al 1986) concluded that user involvement in system development led to both user information satisfaction and system usage, with user information satisfaction leading to system usage, but not the reverse. The proposition of interdependency was also questioned in the finding of a pathway (assuming voluntary use) of ease of use $\Rightarrow$ usefulness $\Rightarrow$ usage (Davis 1989).
3. Focussing on User Satisfaction implies a particular view of the IT facility, namely support for users rather than output. Melone (1990) also argued that where system usage was tightly linked to work, an IT facility could be effective without satisfied users. Further, User Satisfaction could be inaccurately reported because self esteem encouraged certain users to support their established positions.
4. Careful investigation of a number of User Satisfaction instruments reveals some confusion about what is actually measured. User Satisfaction could indeed be used to predict outcomes like usage or variables like training needs, but Galletta and Lederer (1989) cautioned about choosing instruments and interpreting results. Seddon and Kiew (1996) agreed, suggesting that the variables so measured were likely to cause satisfaction, rather being themselves measures of User Satisfaction.

In seeking another approach for evaluating IS Effectiveness, DeLone and McLean's own words are pertinent. As quality was their term for framing the system and information components, that term was the next point of consideration. Was it preferable/achievable to measure quality directly rather than through surrogates like Use and User Satisfaction? Is there a difference between satisfaction and quality?

SATISFACTION AND QUALITY

While DeLone and McLean (1992) don't actually define quality, their tables of empirical measures use production terms like response times, resource utilization and investment utilization for System Quality, and others like accuracy, precision and completeness for Information Quality. Hence, their focus is technical.

When distinguishing between satisfaction and quality some have defined **customer satisfaction** in terms of the user's attitude/feeling as a result of a specific transaction. Oliver (1981) described it as a consumer's emotion about a specific transaction. Seddon (1997 p246) called it a "subjective evaluation … on a pleasant-unpleasant continuum", while Spreng and Mackoy (1996 p17) defined it as an "affective state that [was] the emotional reaction to a product or service experience". **Quality** was generally regarded as a global judgement about a product's (or service's) overall excellence (Parasuraman et al 1986).

Teas (1993 p30) suggested that service quality and customer satisfaction could be meaningful with reference to specific transactions and to global evaluations. Even with single transactions, he found that evaluations of quality led to satisfaction, with both value-judgements occurring simultaneously. Complexity grew when there was aggregation of experiences (Figure 2). Then, users' global views of a service were multi-faceted to include satisfaction, perceptions of service quality and perceptions of product quality. Here, Service Quality and Customer Satisfaction were related to both specific transactions and global judgements with satisfaction part of the process by which stakeholders derive judgements of quality (Bolton and Drew 1991; Carman 1990).

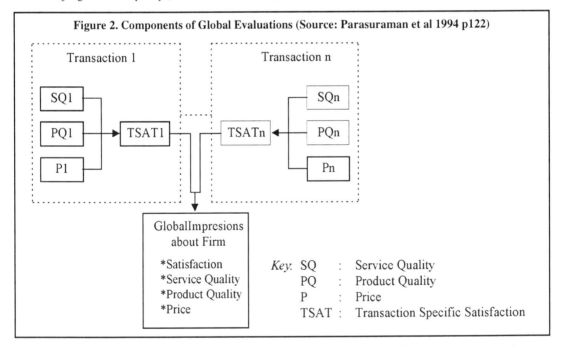

Figure 2. Components of Global Evaluations (Source: Parasuraman et al 1994 p122)

A supportive empirical study (Spreng and Mackoy 1996) proposed that satisfaction was the result of a comparison of perceptions of service received with expectations of what *will* happen (predictive expectations); and service quality was the result of a comparison of perceptions of service received with expectations of the service which the service provider *should* provide (ideal expectations or desires). They found that (see Figure 3) satisfaction and service quality were distinct constructs; that desires affected satisfaction; that the disconfirmation of expectations (what will happen) did not significantly affect service quality; but that expectations did indirectly have a positive effect on service quality (through perceived performance).

They concluded that **satisfaction** resulted when expectations of what "will happen" were disconfirmed by the perceived performance and that service **quality** was derived by comparison between desires and perceived performance.

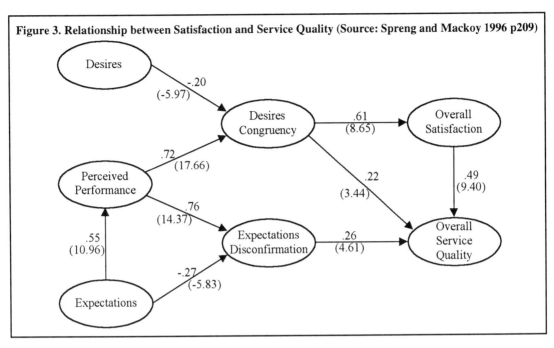

Figure 3. Relationship between Satisfaction and Service Quality (Source: Spreng and Mackoy 1996 p209)

The relevance to current research was twofold. Firstly, "managers should not believe that merely meeting (or exceeding) predictive expectations will *satisfy* consumers" for desires did have an impact (Spreng and Mackoy 1996 p210). Secondly, expectations did influence perceptions of performance and needed to be evaluated.

A reasonable conclusion would be that since the quest for IS success should be focussed beyond merely what a customer may think *will* happen, on a further horizon (what *should* happen), then measurement of *quality*, not of *satisfaction*, should be the focus of IS Effectiveness.

QUALITY IN THE IS SUCCESS MODEL

It is hard to escape the challenge of Iacocca (1988 p257) that quality "doesn't have a beginning or a middle. And it better not have an end. The quality of a product, and of the process in arriving at that product, has to go on and on to become part of every employee's mind-set...Quality is not something you can buy; it's something you must attain - through people".

Certainly, for delivered IT, much work has been done regarding technical quality, but there is also a need to effectively manage or evaluate IT quality in humanistic terms. Surely, stakeholders are the most knowledgeable source of information about effective system functions, the information generated and/or IT support services. By collating their myriad views in a quantitative and structured manner to match the principal facets of System, Information and Service Quality, then an opportunity exists to evaluate IS Effectiveness.

In the IS Success Model of the 1990s, Service, System and Information Quality are thought to impact in three ways: on end-users in their capacity to meet the needs of clients and management; on external customers with whom the company does business; and on the organization's management who would consider the strategic effects of such processes.

In Figure 4, Quality is positioned to provide the key information regarding the quality of the system, information and service unit as they impact on stakeholders. This proposition sustains the underlying belief in DeLone and McLean's model, that user involvement in delivered IT should produce increased positive outcomes for the user, the organization and the customer, and aligns with Drucker's (1988) plea that IS Success is achieved in terms of meeting the needs of professional users for quality, timely information.

The new model features quality as a key determinant of IS Success with sufficient work done on Service Quality to show the usefulness of this approach. Comparative instruments to measure Information and System Quality are being developed (see Measuring Effectiveness). The assumption is that most respondents are trained so that they know what they want, which aligns with identified IT trends regarding the merging of computing and communication technologies to deliver an integrated, cross-functional facility, with the IS department as a service provider rather than facility provider. The benefits of this new model, include:

• acknowledgment of greater expertise among users and consideration of a broader audience, including customer

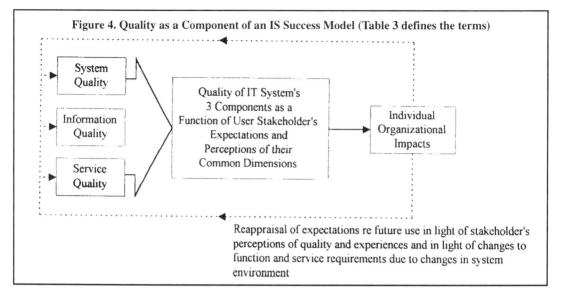

Figure 4. Quality as a Component of an IS Success Model (Table 3 defines the terms)

views and organizational interests;
* the use of two key variables, expectations and perceptions, to identify underlying reasons surrounding the importance of a particular component;
* direct measurement of the key issues rather than through surrogates;
* provision of detailed information directly relevant to System, Information and Service Quality;
* elimination of problems regarding interdependency; and
* a clear focus upon the functional effectiveness of IT, relevant to comparative and competitive advantage.

MEASURING EFFECTIVENESS THROUGH INFORMATION, SYSTEM AND SERVICE QUALITY

Research must now focus on an instrument which accommodates multi perspectives, including organization, management and the more classical end-user stakeholders; which is relatively easy to administer; and which evaluates the clients' own knowledge. Marketers have achieved this through measurement of customers' expectations regarding provision of a service and their perceptions of the service actually delivered.

The relevance of customers' expectations to the IS Success Model is justified on several grounds. Pitt et al (1995, 1997), Wilkin (1996), Kettinger and Lee (1997), Wilkin and Hewett (1997) and Watson et al (1998) have found that this approach generated pertinent insights regarding IS Effectiveness. All used the SERVQUAL instrument, by which Parasuraman et al (1984, 1986, 1991, 1994) explored these two notions through a disconformity measure whereby, a measure of quality, denoted G, was equated to the disconformity that arose from deducting Expectations from Perceptions (i.e. $G = P - E$). Expectations required respondents to consider their *"ideal"*: Perceptions focussed on the actual organization for which a measurement was sought. Later research extended Expectations to evaluate both the desired service level (can be/should be) and the adequate service level (acceptable), forming a "Zone of Tolerance" (Parasuraman et al 1994).

The applicability of $G = P - E$ to IT was tested in a comparative study (Wilkin 1996), with measurement made of two unrelated IT facilities who were providing support to similar groups of IT users. The resultant instrument (Wilkin and Hewett 1997) demonstrated that Expectations and Perceptions effectively measured Service Quality provided by support teams in an IT context, and further promised to be a useful measurement of humanistic aspects of quality in an IT context.

FRAMEWORK FOR DETERMINING THE QUALITY OF DELIVERED IT APPLICATIONS

When applying a new instrument, compatible with SERVQUAL, to measure stakeholders' expectations and perceptions of the tangibles, reliability, responsiveness, assurance and empathy aspects of Information and System Quality, the focus will initially be upon strategic stakeholders (CEOs and management) and practical stakeholders (end-users).

Using the grid approach, often adopted by Harvard researchers, we can obtain more global perspectives of delivered IT quality within an organization by plotting the views of these two groups, using the *vertical* axis to depict

Table 3. Components of the New IS Success Model (Reference Figure 4)

Component	Meaning	Relevant Aspects	Contributing Authors
Information System (implicit)	"defined in terms of its function and structure: it contains people, processes, data models, technology, formalised language in a cohesive structure which serves some organisational purposes or function."	Characteristics and type of information system impact upon three components (System Quality, Information Quality and Service Quality) and consequently on user stakeholder evaluations of quality.	von Hellens (1997 p.802)
IS Success	Global judgement of the degree to which these stakeholders believe they are better off.	Term used interchangeably with effectiveness by DeLone and McLean (1992) who adopted Mason's (1978 p227) relabelling of "effectiveness" as "influence" which was defined as "hierarchy of events which take place at the receiving end of an information system which may be used to identify the various approaches that might be used to measure output at the influence level".	Seddon (1997); DeLone and McLean (1992).
System Quality	Global judgment of the degree to which the technical components of delivered IT provide the quality of information and service required by stakeholders including hardware, software, help screens and user manuals.	Handbooks; user interfaces; terminals; output; response; errors; demands; break downs; back up facilities; disaster recovery systems;responsiveness; simple/quick processes; database integration; time reduction; confidence; usefulness; ease of operation; helpfulness; behavior; safe feeling; help screens; flexibility; forgiveness;usefulness; response patterns; user isolation, inadequacy, uncomfortability, job security, accessibility.	Larcker & Lessig (1980); Moynihan (1982); Ives et al (1983);Doll & Ahmed (1985); Srinivasan (1985); Doll & Torkzadeh (1988); Davis (1989); Galletta & Lederer (1989); Adams et al (1992); Segars & Grover (1993).
Information Quality	Global judgment of the degree to which these stakeholders are provided with information of excellent quality, with regard to defined needs excluding user manuals and help screens (features of System Quality).	Visual appeal; appropriate display; precision; clarity; consistency; accuracy; lack of ambiguity; timeliness; security; completeness; ease of correction; sufficiency; helpfulness; capacity to improve productivity and job effectiveness/performance; relevance; sequence; controllability; readability; value; applicability; understandability; non-replacement for jobs, judgement; job specificity; ease of use; support for key aspects.	Larcker & Lessig (1980); Moynihan (1982); Ives et al (1983); Doll & Ahmed (1985); Srinivasan (1985); Baroudi et al (1986); Doll & Torkzadeh (1988); Galletta & Lederer (1989); Adams et al (1992); Segars & Grover (1993).
Service Quality	Global judgment or attitude regarding assessment of excellence of service, provided by the IS support personnel.	Modern-looking equipment; visually appealing facilities; neat appearance (staff); materials visually appealing; service performed as promised; dependability; rightness at time promised; error-free records; notice re services; prompt service; helpfulness; availability; behavior instilling confidence; safe feeling; courtesy; knowledge; individual attention; convenient operating hours; care; best interests at heart; understanding of specific needs.	Parasuraman et al (1984, 1986, 1991, 1994); Pitt et al (1995); Wilkin (1996); Kettinger & Lee (1997); Pitt et al (1997); Van Dyke et al (1997); Wilkin & Hewett (1997); Watson et al (1998).
Quality of IT System's 3 Components as a Function of User Stakeholder's Expectations & Perceptions of their their Common Dimensions	Assessment of delivered quality of IS as a function of expectations and perceptions measured through audience consideration of System, Information and Service Quality.	Disconformity between stakeholders' expectations and perceptions of the level of performance of relevant aspects of System Quality, Information Quality, and Service Quality.	Parasuraman et al (1986, 1991, 1994); Baroudi et al (1986); Buzzell & Gale (1987); DeLone & McLean (1992); McNealy (1993).
Individual Organizational Impacts	Acknowledgement and consideration of the implications of the audience's views of the whole IS.	Performance; cost reduction; cost benefit analysis; changed perceptions; extent of computer application; understanding of decision context; change in user activity; job satisfaction; competitive advantage; comparative advantage; job efficiency; job flexibility; time saving.	DeLone & McLean (1992); Seddon (1997).
Stakeholder	"An individual or group of individuals with a common interest in the performance of the supplier organization and the environment in which it operates".		AS/NZS ISO 9000.1:1994 p2

opinions of practical end-users and the *horizontal* to depict those of the same organization's strategic stakeholders. Four levels of quality (Excellent Quality, Strategically Aligned, Practically Aligned and Poor Quality) are identified to rate an organization's application (see Figure 5).

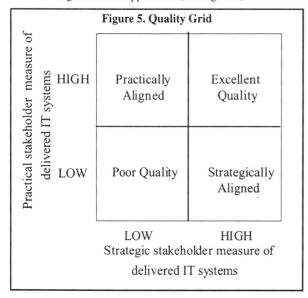

Figure 5. Quality Grid

Excellent Quality applications are those which all stakeholders perceive to be delivering IT applications of an excellent quality.

Strategically Aligned applications are those where an organization might be a candidate for Business Process Re-engineering or Business Re-structuring. Clearly the IT function is well aligned with the corporate strategies but work is needed before practical users see IT as relevant to gaining competitive position (Broadbent and Weill 1993).

Practically Aligned applications indicate that the IT function planning has not been synchronized with the corporate strategic thrust.

Poor Quality applications are those that are currently perceived by stakeholders as delivering inappropriate, inefficient or unreliable results. Training and rework are normal solutions.

IMPLICATIONS FOR FURTHER RESEARCH

Historically IT developers and managers have measured the quality or effectiveness of IT through surrogates such as use and user satisfaction. What this research proposes is consideration of IT as a service and measurement of IS Effectiveness as a function of quality of an information system through evaluation of stakeholders' Perceptions and Expectations of the System, Information and Service Quality.

REFERENCES

Adams, D.A., Nelson, R.R., and Todd, P.A. (1992) Perceived Usefulness, Ease of Use, and Usage of Information Technology: A Replication, *MIS Quarterly*, 16 (2).

AS/NZS ISO 9000.1 (1994) *Quality Management and Quality Assurance Standards – Part 1: Guidelines for Selection and Use*, Standards Australia and New Zealand.

Bailey, J.E., and Pearson, S.W. (1983) Development of a Tool for Measuring and Analyzing Computer User Satisfaction, *Management Science*, 29 (5).

Baroudi, J.J., Olson, M.H., and Ives, B. (1986) An Empirical Study of the Impact of User Involvement on System Usage and Information Satisfaction, *Communications of the ACM*, 29 (3).

Bolton, R.N., and Drew, J.H. (1991) A Longitudinal Analysis of the Impact of Service Changes on Customer Attitudes," *Journal of Marketing*, 55 (1).

Broadbent, M., and Weill, P. (1993) Improving Business and Information Strategy Alignment: Learning from the Banking Industry, *IBM Systems Journal*, 32 (1).

Buzzell, R.D., and Gale, B.T. (1987) *The PIMS Principles Linking Strategy to Performance*, The Free Press, New York.

Carman, J.M. (1990) Consumer Perceptions of Service Quality: An Assessment of the SERVQUAL Dimensions, *Journal of Retailing*, 66 (1).

Cronin, J.J. Jr., and Taylor, S.A. (1992) Measuring Service Quality: A Reexamination and Extension, *Journal of Marketing*, 56.

Crosby, P.B. (1979) *Quality is Free: The Art of Making Quality Certain*, New American Library, New York.

Davis, F.D. (1989) Perceived Usefulness, Perceived Ease of Use, and User Acceptance of Information Technology, *MIS Quarterly*, 13 (3).

DeLone, W.H., and McLean, E.R. (1992) Information Systems Success: The Quest for the Dependent Variable, *Information Systems Research*, 3 (1).

Doll, W.J., and Ahmed, M.U. (1985) Documenting Information Systems for Management: A Key to Maintaining User Satisfaction, *Information and Management*, 8 (4).

Doll, W.J., and Torkzadeh, G. (1988) The Measurement of End-User Computing Satisfaction, *MIS Quarterly*, 12 (2).

Drucker, P.F. (1988) The Coming of the New Organization, *Harvard Business Review*, January-February.

Galletta, D.F., and Lederer, A.L. (1989) Some Cautions on the Measurement of User Information Satisfaction, *Decision Sciences*, (20).

Garvin, D.A. (1988) *Managing Quality: The Strategic and Competitive Edge*, The Free Press, New York.

Gronroos, C. (1983) *Strategic Management and Marketing in the Service Sector*, Marketing Science Institute, Cambridge, MA.

Gronroos, C. (1990) *Service Management and Marketing: Managing the Moments of Truth in Service Competition*, Lexington Books, Massachusetts.

Iacocca, L. (1988) *Talking Straight*, Bantam Books, New York.

Ives, B., Olson, M.H., and Baroudi, J.J. (1983) The Measurement of User Information Satisfaction, *Communications of the ACM*, 26 (10).

Juran, J.M., Gryna, F.M. Jr., and Bingham, R.S. (eds.) (1974) *Quality Control Handbook*, 3rd edn., McGraw-Hill, New York.

Kerzner, H. (1998) *Project Management: A Systems Approach to Planning, Scheduling, and Controlling*, 6th edn., John Wiley & Sons Inc., New York.

Kettinger, W.J., and Lee, C.C. (1997) Pragmatic Perspectives on the Measurement of Information Systems Service Quality, *MIS Quarterly*, 21 (2).

Kriebel, C.H. (1979) Evaluating the Quality of Information Systems, in *Design and Implementation of Computer-Based Information Systems*, N. Szyperski and E. Grochla (eds.), Sijthoff and Noordhoff, The Netherlands.

Larcker, D.F., and Lessig, V.P. (1980) Perceived Usefulness of Information: A Psychometric Examination, *Decision Sciences*, 11 (1).

Levitt, T. (1972) Production-line Approach to Service, *Harvard Business Review*, 50 (5),.

McNealy, R.M. (1993) *Making Quality Happen - A Step by Step Guide to Winning the Quality Revolution*, Chapman and Hall, London.

Melone, N.P. (1990) A Theoretical Assessment of the User Satisfaction Construct in Information Systems Research, *Management Science*, 36 (1).

Moynihan, J.A. (1982) What Users Want, *Datamation*, 28 (4).

Oliver, R.L. (1981) Measurement and Evaluation of Satisfaction Processes in Retail Settings, *Journal of Retailing*, 57 (3).

Parasuraman, A., Berry, L.L., and Zeithaml, V.A. (1991) Refinement and Reassessment of the SERVQUAL Scale, *Journal of Retailing*, 67 (4).

Parasuraman, A., Zeithaml, V.A., and Berry, L.L. (1984) A Conceptual Model of Service Quality and Its Implications for Future Research, *Marketing Science Institute,* (84-106).

Parasuraman, A., Zeithaml, V.A., and Berry, L.L. (1986) SERVQUAL: A Multiple-Item Scale for Measuring Customer Perceptions of Service Quality, *Marketing Science Institute*, (94-114).

Parasuraman, A., Zeithaml, V.A., and Berry, L.L. (1994) Reassessment of Expectations as a Comparison Standard in Measuring Service Quality: Implications for Further Research, *Journal of Marketing*, 58.

Pitt, L.F., Watson, R.T., and Kavan, C.B. (1995) Service Quality: A Measure of Information Systems Effectiveness, *MIS Quarterly*, 19 (2).

Pitt, L.F., Watson, R.T., and Kavan, C.B. (1997) Measuring Information Systems Service Quality: Concerns for a Complete Canvas, *MIS Quarterly*, 21 (2).

Seddon, P.B. (1997) A Respecification and Extension of the DeLone and McLean Model of IS Success, *Information Systems Research*, 8 (3).

Seddon, P.B., and Kiew, M-Y. (1996) A Partial Test and Development of DeLone and McLean's Model of IS Success, *Australian Journal of Information Systems*, (4:1).

Segars, A.H., and Grover, V. (1993) Re-Examining Perceived Ease of Use and Usefulness: A Confirmatory Factor Analysis, *MIS Quarterly*, 17 (4).

Spreng, R.A., and Mackoy, R.D. (1996) An Empirical Examination of a Model of Perceived Service Quality and Satisfaction, *Journal of Retailing*, 72 (2).

Srinivasan, A. (1985) Alternative Measures of System Effectiveness: Associations and Implications, *MIS Quarterly*, 9 (1).

Stamford, D (1996) Workplace 2010 Forces That Will Shape the Future of Work in Australia, Unpublished Manuscript, DETAFE, South Australia

Teas, R.K., (1993) Expectations, Performance Evaluation, and Consumers' Perceptions of Quality, *Journal of Marketing*, (57).

Van Dyke, T.P., Kappelman, L.A., and Prybutok, V.R. (1997) Measuring Information Systems Service Quality: Concerns on the Use of the SERVQUAL Questionnaire, *MIS Quarterly*, 21 (2).

von Hellens, L.A. (1997) Information Systems Quality Versus Software Quality A Discussion from a Managerial, an Organisational and an Engineering Viewpoint, *Information and Software Technology*, 39 (12).

Watson, R.T., Pitt, L.F., and Kavan, C.B. (1998) Measuring Information Systems Service Quality: Lessons From Two Longitudinal Case Studies, *MIS Quarterly*, 22 (1).

Wilkin, C (1996) Service Quality as a Measure of the Correlation Between Employees' Expectations for Performance and Their Perceptions of Current Performance, Unpublished Honors Thesis, Deakin University.

Wilkin, C., and Hewett, W.G. (1997) Measuring the Quality of Information Technology Applications as a Function of Use, In D J Sutton (ed.), ACIS 97, University of South Australia, Adelaide, *Proceedings of the 8th Australasian Conference on Information Systems*, Adelaide, September 29 - October 2.

Zeithaml, V.A., Parasuraman, A., and Berry, L.L. (1985) Problems and Strategies in Services Marketing, *Journal of Marketing*, 49 (2).

Zeithaml, V.A., Parasuraman, A., and Berry, L.L., (1990) *Delivering Quality Service: Balancing Customer Perceptions and Expectations*, The Free Press, New York.

Automatic Generation of Database Schema for Structured Hypermedia Documents

Ken C. K. Law, Horace H. S. Ip and Fang Wei

Image Computing Group, Department of Computer Science, City University of Hong Kong, 83 Tat Chee Avenue, Kowloon, Hong Kong

Tel : 852-27844229; Fax: 852-27888614; Email : csweif@cityu.edu.hk

ABSTRACT

In this paper, we propose a layered model for hypermedia document systems and use this model in the design and implementation of a prototype hypermedia document system. The design of the hypermedia document system requires the storage structure to be closely coupled with the logical structure of a specific class, in order to maintain data integrity and dependency, and to optimize for access control. We focus on some important components in our system: parser, tree-generator and database-schema-manager. The parser and tree-generator are used to check the syntax and semantics of the document structure description and generate a tree structure as the document internal representation which can be visualized for the purpose of data capturing and navigating. In determination of the tables and fields of database in database-schema-manager, we introduce the algorithm and procedure to generate the final database schema from the document structure tree. The advantages and benefits of this approach are to allow the design and implementation of hypermedia systems to be automated and simplified.

INTRODUCTION

At present, electronic publishing have stepped from text-based documents into multimedia-based documents. People can make full use of multimedia technique to gain more information easily and conveniently. But this lays harder burden on both computers and computer's technicians.

In our group, we are exploring a hypermedia document system research which resulted in the creation of HMDOCS (Hypermedia Document System). The purpose of HMDOCS is to develop a generic and advanced high performance hypermedia information and communication system with a particular focus on layered model for system, document structure, database model, and document interchange among diverse systems.

The conventional hypermedia document systems based on static file structures are not appropriate for handling a large amount of multimedia data under dynamic environment. Except for few recently developed systems such as SEPIA [Haa92] and application in [BAK97]. And most of the hypermedia systems are implemented on a database which is application-specific. It is a tedious job for people to manually design and create database for every situation, and could better be done by machine automatically.

The first step towards the design of such multimedia document system is to provide an integrated and homogenous way to describe, organize, and structure multimedia information objects and to represent the relationship between them in a single entity called a multimedia document. A mapping mechanism is also employed between multimedia document description and database schema.

In our research, Open Document Architecture(ODA) [ISO94] is employed for representing multimedia documents, its generic logical structure is described using ASN.1 [Ste90]; at the same time, ODBC [Mic94] technique is applied to create a multimedia database based on a RDBMS.

Using the mapping mechanism, system can automatically create a multimedia database schema for a documents class [ISO94], based on the generic logical structure and contents of these documents, and can dynamically store and retrieve data objects while the documents are being authored or presented. The database's schema corresponds to the generic logical structure of the document class. This mechanism manages data for the document system, which is transparent to the user. It should be noted that a class of document is a set that is composed of some documents with same generic logical structure [ISO94].

The remainder parts is organized as following: Section 2 gives a brief introduction of ODA. used in HMDOCS and the architecture of HMDOCS. Section 3 describes the extension of ODA and ASN.1. Section 4 briefly describes the relationship between DBMS and multimedia document system. Section 5 addresses the implementation of automatically mapping from document architecture description to database schema. In section 6, a medical hypermedia document system to handle Cardiac Catheterization Record (CCR) is designed to verify our proposed approach. Section 7 concludes our work and suggests our future working direction.

OVERVIEW OF HMDOC

HMDOCS consists of three levels (see Figure 1). The upper layer is the Runtime Layer (RTL) that provides the functionality for users to create , access, view, and manipulate the multimedia document. The middle layer is the Document Description Layer (DOCDL) that defines the logical structure of the document. The

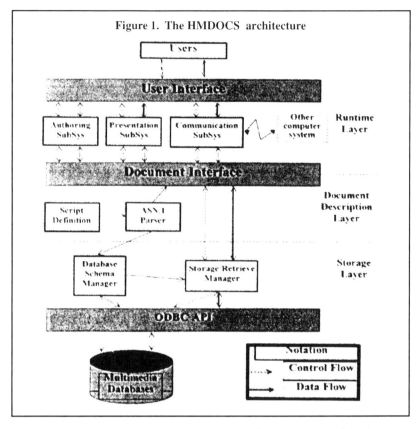

Figure 1. The HMDOCS architecture

lower layer is the Storage Layer (SRL) that contains one or more databases for storing the contents of the document classes. Each database corresponds to a multimedia document class [ISO94] and will be created automatically based on the document structure. DOCDL is the key component of our system model. It not only provides a mechanism for relating a document storage structure with its logical structure, but also provides a document interface for RTL manipulating multimedia data. In addition, an addressing mapping procedure is defined to locate the physical address for the RTL. The SRL contains media items, as well as structural information. Therefore the system architecture proposes a straightforward and natural method to relate the document logical structure with the corresponding storage structure, which plays an important role in the system. In this paper, we focus on the DOCDL and SRL.

MULTIMEDIA DOCUMENT STANDARDS

To encode and represent multimedia information in the multimedia/hypermedia systems, many document standards are deployed, such as office document architecture (ODA) [ISO94], SGML [Mc98], HyTime [Der94] and HTML [HTML98], etc.

ODA, a standard for a document architecture, emphasizes the efficient exchange of documents between different systems, and provides the logic structure, which is very important in our proposed model. As a result, ODA is adopted to describe and represent multimedia documents within our model.

ODA and ASN.1 in HMDOC

The Open Document Architecture (ODA) is a object-oriented document architecture that differentiates between a logical and a layout view of a document. Therefore a document in ODA is described by two independent but related structures, both of which are defined as hierarchies of objects, where objects can be either composite objects or simple objects. The *logical structure* represents the outlining of a document. Attributes of various types describe the property of objects or groups of objects, while logical expressions define the relation within the document. In this paper, focus is only on logical structure.

The role of ODA in this system

The hierarchical document logical structure to relational database mapping is based on *key-propagation*, which is similar to the process of database normalization, which eliminates the redundant data in relational schema. Firstly, we present some concept definitions used in our model:

- node: There are two types of nodes: simple nodes and composite nodes. A simple node is a set of some monomedia objects which may be retrieved and displayed as a single unit. A composite node is a collection of some simple nodes.
- attribute node: An attribute node is a subnode and the relationship with its parent node is an *object-attribute*. The *object-attribute* is a loose concept and the information contained in it is the attributes of its parent node, that includes contents information and relational information.
- entity node: Most documents are composed of a number of data objects. These components are not just attributes, but entities in themselves, which can be identified in the whole hierarchy. In this case, if the node has a parent node, they will have *component-aggregate* relationship.
- identifier node: It is an attribute node that contains an attribute as the identifier of its parent node.
- attribute: Every item contained in the leaf node will be called an attribute.
- key : An attribute that can identify the leaf node.
- item type: Nodes are composed of several information items that can be divided into two types: attribute item and key item. Key item can identify its corresponding node directly or indirectly. Others are attribute items.

In order to facilitate the mapping from the document structure model to the storage model, we also introduce two concepts: *global* node and *local* node into our model. If the key value of an identifier node or key item is unique in the whole document class, the node or item is a *global* one, otherwise it is a *local* one. An entity can be identified within the domain of document class by its unique key value of an identifier, so it must be a *global* node .

Our extension to node

The following symbols are prefixed at the front of a node item name or an attribute item name, to express the type of the node or item.

- The symbol "*" represents local identifier node or local key feature;
- The symbol "**" is similar to "*". The main difference is that it has a global feature. A global item must be a unique one.
- The symbol "+" means a unique feature.

If a node is an entity node, the relationship between the node and its parent node is that of an *aggregate-component* relationship, that is to say, the subtree itself is a generic logical structure of a subdocument; otherwise the node acts as a set of attributes of its parent node. Their relationship is an *object-attribute* relationship. It should be noted that an entity node, an identifier node or a node with a REP or REPOPT feature must have an identifier node or key as its item.

An example to describe the generic logical structure of a document class

In order to explain the above concept, let us use the following example. For simplicity and clarity, we only depict part of the generic logic structure of a medical document class "Patient" as shown in Figure 2.

The node **Patient** is the root node, **PersonalData** is an identifier node, **Physical-Situation** is an attribute node, Section is an entity node. In the node **PersonalData, PatientID** is the key for identifying this node and it is also used as an identifier of the node **Patient** because **PersonalData** is the identifier node of the node Patient as there are no two patients whose PatientIDs are the same. **IDNo** is an unique attribute, and other items are normal attributes.

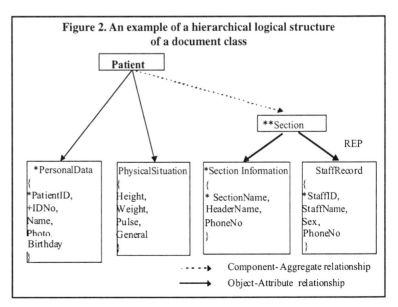

Figure 2. An example of a hierarchical logical structure of a document class

REP

- - - - ▶ Component- Aggregate relationship

⟶ Object-Attribute relationship

RELATIONSHIP BETWEEN DBMS AND MULTIMEDIA DOCUMENT SYSTEM

In contrast with other applications, as DBMS just serves as a basic tool for a multimedia document system to manage its data in our system, it is not necessary to develop a stand-alone system. It is just a part of a multimedia document system, Figure 4 shows the role that the DBMS acts in a multimedia document system.

In our system, documents are organized by document class. A document class is a set of specific document with the same generic logical structure. So, with respect to our system, a document information system consists of some document classes and each document class contains some specific documents (depicted in Figure 3).

IMPLEMENTATION OF THE MAPPING

Script definition and the parser

Script definition contributes to defining the generic logical structure for a document class using ASN.1. As we use the ODA model, a logical structure will be a tree structure. It will be a document template for creating specific document. Since ASN.1 only provides syntax rules, it does not contribute to the semantic parts. To construct a valid logical structure, there should be some semantic constraints. Therefore, we define *valid node* and *valid tree* for this purpose.

- *Definition of a valid Node (Rule 1):*

Given a node N, its subitem set is S_N, then N is a valid node if the following rules are kept.

1. $N \notin S_N$, et. One node can not be its own subnode.

2. Let $I \in S_N$ and $A(I)$ is an attribute function, $A(I) = \begin{cases} 1 & I = SubnodeItem \\ 0 & I = AttributeItem \end{cases}$; then

   $\forall I_1, I_2 \in S_N \Rightarrow A(I_1) = A(I_2)$, et. one node can only have subnode items or attribute items, but can not have both of them.

3. Let N is an entity node, an identifier node, or a node with **REP** or **REPOPT** feature, then $\exists I \in S_N$, where I is an identifier node or key attribute item.

- *Definition of a Valid Tree (Rule 2)*

Let $SetN$ is the set of the node in the tree(T). $f(N)$ represents the parent node of the node N. T is valid tree if the following rules are kept:

1. $\exists R \in SetN \& f(R) = \varnothing$ and $\forall R' \in SetN \& f(R') = \varnothing \Rightarrow R = R'$, et. a tree must have one and only one root node.

2. $\forall N \in SetN \& N \ne R \Rightarrow f(N) \ne \varnothing \& | f(N)| = 1$; et. every node except the root node has a parent node no more and no less.

3. If node N is a leaf node and I is its item, I must be an attribute item.

The script definition actually specifies a special tree. The *Parser*'s task (see Figure 5) is to analyze the syntax and semantics of the description and generate a tree structure as the document internal representation. It is divided into three levels. The first level tests whether or not the syntax is correct; the second level is to test the validation of one node. The last is to validate the whole tree's structure.

If the parser passes through the three levels, a tree corresponding to the document logical structure would be created. At the same time, a document interface is generated for the runtime layer to manipulate the specific document contents. Using the user interface based on the formal description of the document structure, a user can retrieve, insert or update the document content through a very simple point and click paradigm.

DB schema manager

A database schema describes the data structure used by a database application, which includes all of the database objects, attributes of the objects, relations between the objects and the methods attached to the objects [Gil91].

Determine the data objects

To build a database schema, the first step is to determine the data objects involved in the database. In a relational model, a data object responds to a table and its attributes are the fields of the table. However, relational tables design is domain-dependent, which should be the result of the study of its data usage, business needs, and performance requirements. In this system, we assume that a leafnode corresponds to a table, named **contents table**. Moreover, there are additional tables corresponding to some interior nodes, called **connection tables**, for representing the relationship between the tables. In addition to the above types of tables, there are other domain-dependent tables, called **system table, media tables, link table**, and **anchor table**. The system table is for storing document name and status. Media tables are responsible for holding the large objects such as image, sound and graphics. Link and anchor tables are used for hyperlink information. The structure of the content and connection tables dynamically depend on the generic logical structure of document classes.

Determine tables' fields

Actually, a database schema structure is hidden in the tables, it is the relationships of these tables that determine the schema structure. Moreover, a record in a table must have some fields that can uniquely identify the record. Therefore designing a table's fields is a crucial step for creating a database schema. Before describing the approach, we need to introduce two concepts first.

• *Subtree identifier* : In a document logical structure, one node must have a corresponding subtree, the leafnode's subtree is itself and the rootnode's subtree is the whole tree. Some of the subtrees

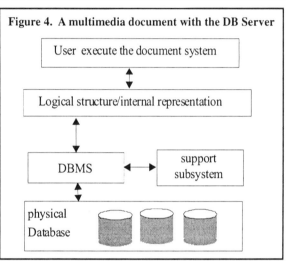

Figure 3. The data model of the multimedia document information.

Figure 4. A multimedia document with the DB Server

have an attribute to identify it within the whole tree or the upper level subtree, corresponding to its parent node. The attribute is called the identifier of the subtree. If a node has the REP or OPTREP option of occurrence, or is an entity node, the subtree identifier is needed here. But it is not necessary for other nodes.

• *Parent identifier* : Parent identifier is a set of attributes that can uniquely identify its parent node within the whole information system. These attributes will be called *parent identifier* of the node here.

Considering the normalization of the data in the tables, we also introduce some tables, called the connection tables. Each connection table corresponds to one parent node in a logical structure tree. These tables only have attributes for describing the relationship between other tables.

To generate *Subtree identifier* and *Parent identifier* we give the following rules:

Back-propagation rule: Determine subtree identifier (**SI**).

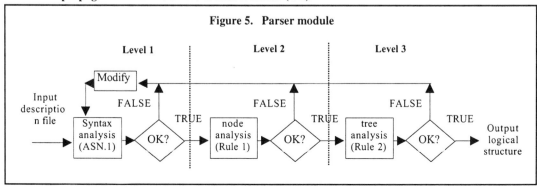

Figure 5. Parser module

1. If a node $\underline{N0}$ is a leaf node and an attribute can identify it, the attribute will be SI of $\underline{N0}$, goto 3;
2. Otherwise, $\underline{N0}$ is not leaf node. Calculating the SIes of its son nodes, if a son node ($\underline{NI}$) is an identifier node and has a SI, the SI of $\underline{Ni}$ will be transferred to $\underline{N0}$. Goto 3;
3. If $\underline{N0}$ does not have a SI, and the option of $\underline{No}$'s occurrence is REP or OPTREP or $\underline{N0}$ is an entity node; a default identifier will be created as SI of $\underline{N0}$.

Forward-propagation algorithm: **Deducing parent identifiers (PI).**

1. The root node does not have PI, PI is NULL;
2. For a node $\underline{N0}$ which is not the root node, assuming its parent node is $\underline{Nf.}$ If $\underline{Nf}$ is a entity node goto 3, otherwise goto 4.
3. If the SI of $\underline{N0}$ and its parent node ($\underline{Nf}$) are the same, PI of $\underline{N0}$ is NULL; otherwise, PI of $\underline{N0}$ is the PI of the $\underline{Nf}$. goto 5;
4. If the SI of $\underline{N0}$ and its parent node ($\underline{Nf}$) are the same, PI of $\underline{N0}$ is just PI of $\underline{Nf}$; otherwise, PI of $\underline{N0}$ consists of SI and PI of the $\underline{Nf}$. goto 5;
5. end.

Structure mapping procedure

The structure mapping procedure for generating the database schema is presented in 8 steps.

1. Using the back-propagation algorithm to generate the subtree identifiers.
2. Using the forward-propagation algorithm to generate the parent identifiers.
3. Creating new connection tables. If the node, which is neither the root node nor leafnode, is an entity node, a connection table will be created. The fields of the table consist of its parent identifier and subtree identifier.
4. Adding necessary attributes to the leaf node. If a leafnode is not an entity node and its subtree identifier is not global, the parent identifier and its items consist of the fields of the table that is corresponding to the node.
5. Creating media tables for unformatted data objects such as image table, graphic table, and audio table etc.. All of the tables have two fields: one is the data object itself whose type is LONGBINARY; another is the identifier of the data objects and its type is INTEGER. Moreover, there are some other fields for recording additional information.
6. Creating system tables. System tables include two tables: one is to store the specific document name and its' identifier within the multimedia document class, another is to record the status of a specific document.
7. Dividing tables. If a table has some LONGBINARY field, this field's type will be changed as INTEGER. It is a pointer to a specific media table. The data object will be saved in its corresponding media table. We call the new type field as referential field.
8. Annotating field. In order to add annotation on the nodes, each table will be added an additional field for storing the annotation information.

Through this procedure, a database schema is automatically generated based on a document class structure.

As an example, in Figure 6 we apply the above rules to the *Patient* document class example as shown in Figure 3. In the process of the back-propagation, the *subtree identifiers* of each node are determined, the *subtree identifier* of

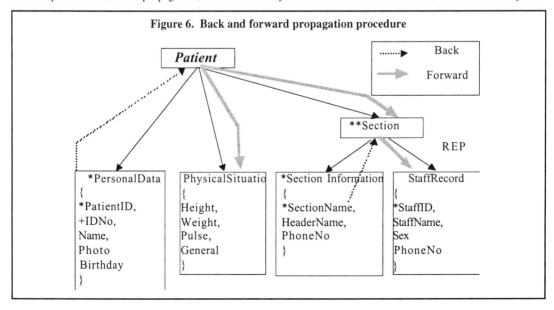

Figure 6. Back and forward propagation procedure

the node *Patient* is *PatientID* that is back-propagated from the node *PersonalData*. For the node *Section*, the *subtree identifier* is *SectionName* that comes from the node *SectionInformation*. In the process of the forward-propagation, the *parent identifiers* are determined. Both *PhysicalSituation* and *Section* have the *parent identifier* (*PatientID*) that is propagated from the node *Patient*, the *parent identifier* of the node StaffRecord is *SectionName*, propagated from the node *Section*. Other nodes' *parent identifiers* are NULL.

Therefore, there are four contents tables corresponding to the four leafnodes:

PersonalData   { PatientID, IDNo, Name , Photo, Birthday, SysAnnotation };
PhysicalSituation   { *PatientID*, **Height, Weight, Pulse, General, SysAnnotation** };
SectionInformation   { SectionName, HeaderName, PhoneNo, SysAnnotation };
StaffRecord   { *SectionName*, **StaffID, StaffName, Sex, PhoneNo, SysAnnotation** };

and a connection table corresponding to the node *Section*:
Section   { PatientID, SectionName, SysAnnotation }.

Data relationship

In a relational model, there are four basic table relationships: one to one, one to many, many to one, and many to many. These relations are just the reflection of the real world, and they may exist in a multimedia document. But in the ODA standard, there are nothing serving for this, so we introduced the concept of the GLOBAL and UNIQUE into the ODA standard (see the Section 3). Therefore these four relationships will be represented in the document generic structure.

- *one to one* : If the occurrence of the subnode is OPT or REQ and at the same time the subnode is UNIQUE and GLOBAL, the relationship of the node and its parent node is *one to one*.
- *one to many*: If the occurrence of a node is REP or OPTREP and it also is UNIQUE and GLOBAL, the relationship is *one to many*.
- *many to one* : If the occurrence of a node is OPT or REQ and it just is a GLOBAL node, the relationship between the node and its parent node is *many to one*.
- *many to many* : If the occurrence of a node is REP or OPTREP and it also is a GLOBAL node (a entity), the relationship between the node and its parent node is *many to many*.

Integrity control

Referential integrity allows the user to define relationships between column values in different tables [9]. The referential integrity can prevent the user from introducing inconsistencies into the data. SQL enforces referential integrity by utilizing the concepts of primary and foreign keys and creates a unique index on the primary key to prevent duplication. It also introduces referential constraints to control deletion of the primary keys. Herein we present the method to determine the primary key and foreign key. An example is given in Figure 7.

- Choose the primary key

Let *SI* and *PI* represent subtree identifier and parent identifier of a node respectively. The primary key is determined by there factors: the node feature GLOBAL and UNIQUE, and the occurrence option REP or OPTREP. The rule determining the table's primary key is shown in Table 1:

- Choose the foreign key

1. Foreign key in the leafnode tables. If there are some referential fields in the table, these fields are the foreign keys of the table, their parent tables are media tables.
2. Foreign key in the connection tables. If there are some tables (Tset) whose primary key is the SI of one connection table, SI is the foreign key of the connection table and Tset is the parent tables.

After creating these referential structures, the integrity of the data can be warranted. But this increases the overhead of the system. So a referential structure is not recommended when requirement on performance is necessary.

Update the logical structure

For a multimedia document information system, its generic logical structure is relatively stable and seldom changed. It is sometimes unavoidable to change the environment or requirements.

Table 1. The rule for determining the table's primary key			
Entity Node or not	REP/OPTREP	UNIQUE or NOT	Primary Key
Yes	Yes	Yes	SI
Yes	No	Yes	SI&PI
Yes	No	No	PI
otherwise			PI&SI

So, the schema that has been auto-matically generated from this hier-archical structure also needs to be updated.

In our system, two functions are supported to update the logical structure:

1. *Add node-items* in parent nodes. We can add subtrees in the original logical structure. It will result in altering the schema of the corresponding database. Additional tables will be added into the database. It is clear that these nodes can not be the identifier node, otherwise, the original logical structure is incomplete.

2. *Add attribute-items* in the leafnode. The system supports adding new attribute items in a leafnode. As a leafnode corre-

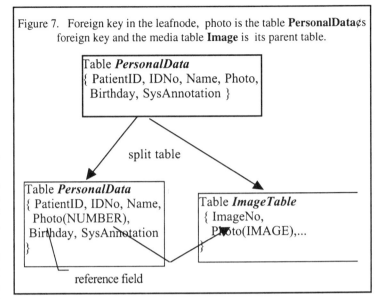

Figure 7. Foreign key in the leafnode, photo is the table **PersonalData¢s** foreign key and the media table **Image** is its parent table.

sponds to a table in the related database, adding attribute items will lead to altering the table structure, e.g. a new column will be added in the table. Obviously, the new attribute items can not be the *key*.

Arbitrarily altering the logical structure is not permitted here due to the integrity of the data. Altering items that would result in lose of the information is also forbidden.

Hyperlink

A hyperlink is a relationship between two anchors, called the head and the tail of the hyperlink. Anchors are identified by an anchor address. A hyperlink could contain information about itself and the nodes to which it links. Information contained by a hyperlink includes what the link does, what the link is pointing to and how the link relates the two (or more) nodes.

In our system, The links may be either implicit or explicit, Implicit links are derived from the structure and the order of the nodes, sometimes it is implemented by database search operations. For instance, the leafnode with REP or REPOPT feature will have a implicit link to directly point the objects of the first, previous, next, and last one, if it exists. Explicit links employed in the system connect any two nodes or monomedia items and are used to represent non-hierarchical relationships. Explicit links can also be divided into to two categories: *Static Hyperlinks* and *Spa-tial-temporal Hyperlinks*. The static links can also be further divided into three kinds: *Link-to-annotation*, *Replace* and *Go-To*. *Spatial-temporal Hyperlink* handles the relationship between active medias or active media and static media. A set of link tables are designed in our system (see Figure 8).

Anchor table is used for recording the anchors in the document class, the field ObjectType denotes the type of the media, such as IMAGE, SOUND, and GRAPHICS etc. ObjectID is the media identifier or primary key value of the component tables. Specific description describes the *hot region* in the media for a monomedia object .

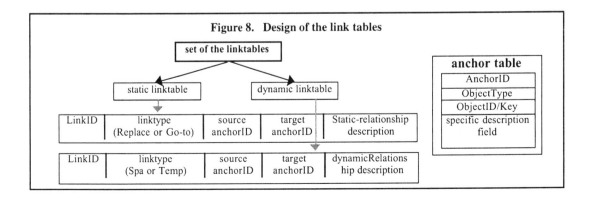

Figure 8. Design of the link tables

Figure 9. Application Interface for CCR

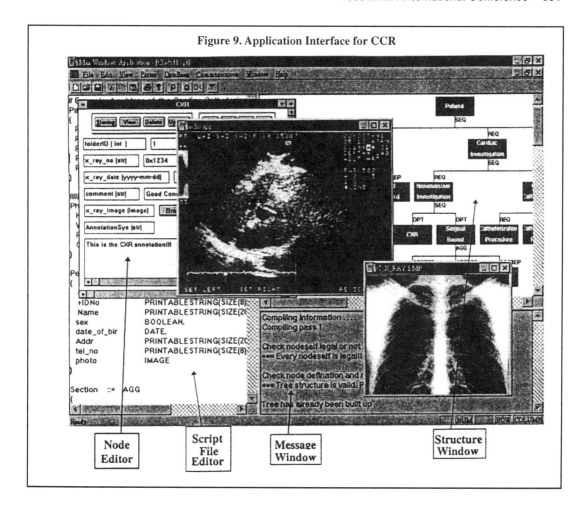

APPLICATION IN CARDIOLOGY

We demonstrate the possibility of this approach by applying our methodology to automatic defining the database schema and the associated database tables for the medical documents used in Cardiac Catheterization Record (CCR).

A CCR may contain such information as free hand text, form filled text and data, images, graphics, sound and video, which as a whole is treaded as document class. A tree dialog user-document interface is shown in Figure 9. In the Structure Window, the output of the internal tree structure representation is visualized to help user to retrieve information as a navigation tool, as well as can be used as a means for multimedia data capturing with Node Editor. The validation information and other system messages are given in the Message Window. The description of the corresponding visualized tree structure is shown in Script File Editor. This application shows that this model is well-suited to be applied on the field of complex structured hypermedia documents.

CONCLUSION AND FUTURE WORK

In this research, we mainly concentrate on creating a tool to help a hypermedia document system manage its large quantities of multimedia/hypermedia information. From the user¢s viewpoint, these data are just like to be stored in the nodes of the structure tree. It should be noted that since the database is created automatically, it is impossible to be more efficient than a database designed manually. Therefor the performance of the system will be effected.

Further developments with respect to our system include an improvement of retrieving and distributed application. In addition, since it is necessary to search a whole document database for supporting information retrieval, an efficient indexing schema for structured document should be added.

REFERENCES

[BAK97] K. Bohm, K. Aberer and W. Klas. Building a Hybid Database Application for Structure Documents. Multimedia Tools and Applications. 5, 275-300 (1997).

[Der94]   S. J. DeRose. Making hypermedia work : a user's guide to HyTime. Press: Boston : Kluwer Academic, 1994.

[Gil91] D. Gilor. SQL/DS Performance techniques for improvement. Press: John Wiley & Sons, Inc., 1991.

[Haa92] J. Haake, et al. SEPIA: A Cooperative Hypermedia Authoring Environment. Proc. of the 4th ACM Conf. on Hypertext (Hypertext'92), ACM Press, 1992.

[HTML98] http://www.ncsa.edu/General/Internet/WWW/HTMLPrimer.html. A Beginner's Guide to HTML, Internet Information, 1998.

[Int86] M.. N. Intermedia: The Architecture and Construction of an Object-Oriented Hypermedia System and Application Framework. In Proc. ACM Conf. on Objected-Oriented Programming, Systems, Language, and Applications, Sep. 1986.

[ISO94] ISO/IEC 8613:1994, Information technology — Open Document Architecture (ODA) and interchange format.

[Mc98] S. McGrath PARSEME.1ST SGML For Software Developers. Press: Prentice-Hall, Inc. 1998.

[Mic94] Microsoft ODBC 2.0 Programmer Reference and SDK Guide. Microsoft Press, 1994.

[Ste90] D. Steedman. Abstract Syntax Notation One (ASN.1) The tutorial and Reference. The Camelot Press, 1990.

Fluid Interactions: Describing the development of an Open System.

Andrew Wenn

HPS University of Melbourne & Department of Information Systems, Victoria University of Technology
email:Andrew.Wenn@vu.edu.au, phone: 61 3 9688 4342, fax: 61 3 9688 5024

The kind of systems we envisage will be open-ended and incremental – undergoing continual evolution.
In an open system it becomes very difficult to determine what objects exist at any point in time.

Hewitt, C. and de Jong, P. (1984)
Open Systems

INTRODUCTION

This paper is about an open system, an heterogeneous assemblage of computers, cables, modems, people, texts, libraries, buildings, dreams and images. I have attempted to capture some of its nature through the use of several vignettes that may give the reader a small insight into parts of it's being. Consider the system, VICNET as it is called, as a node of a much larger network, what I have attempted to do is to unfold this node to reveal the social and technical worlds contained therein, but I also fold the VICNET node in on itself so that it becomes part of a much larger sociotechnical system – the Internet. This process of folding I refer to as a topological transformation and it is by studying transformations of this type that may help us understand how open systems come into being and evolve.

BACKGROUND

In 1995, the Premier of Victoria, officially launched VICNET, Victoria's Network. VICNET is a collaborative project between Royal Melbourne Institute of Technology (RMIT) and the State Library of Victoria (SLV) by the State Government of Victoria as part of its commitment to "restore Victoria's library system and develop its capability to take full advantage of modern technology" (OMA, 1994). After many months of negotiations during which time a pilot scheme was established to test the feasibility of the project, VICNET had finally gone public. VICNET is an information provider connected to the Internet, which aims to provide access for all Victorians to the world of electronic information.

The public launch was simply the "coming-out" of the results of many months of work during which time: equipment was purchased, installed, configured and tested; staff were hired; documents formatted using HTML and published; and negotiations between a variety of organisations took place. The launch however did not mean that VICNET was complete – far from it – all that it indicated was that it was ready to enter the public arena and start to discharge its responsibilities.

Within VICNET there are a number of subgroups who attempt to operate cooperatively and run the system. There are the central staff whose salaries are paid out of the government grant, volunteer workers who donate their time to mark up documents, sponsors who have provided either money, discounted equipment or both, people from outside who provide information to be stored on the primary computer or links from the VICNET site to their own pages, the libraries that will provide public access terminals, and the people who will search for information.

In a wonderful study of the early electrical distribution networks, Hughes (1983) has shown that by considering them as heterogeneous sociotechnical networks of power we can understand why things happened they way that did. One method of analysing heterogeneous assemblages is to use Actor Network Theory (ANT) (Callon, 1986; Latour, 1987; Law, 1987; Law, 1994; Singleton & Michael, 1993) but before describing the mode of analysis it would be appropriate to comment on the means of data collection and presentation.

A NOTE ON METHOD

The material used in this paper is a small part of that which I collected whilst undertaking an ethnographic study of the early days of VICNET. Ethnography is a valuable method to use if one wishes to study the underlying culture and emergence of a system although this doesn't preclude the use of quantitative data where it helps build a picture of the system's development.

Much of the material came from unpublished documents kindly lent to me by the VICNET staff, other sources included interviews and email discussions with people whom I have never met but who chose to answer all my questions via the medium of the internet. Although some might criticise the use of material obtained via email interviews, especially from people whom I have never met, by comparing information obtained by email with events that actually happened or materials from other sources, one can validate the data and hence establish the reliability of the material. In fact as Van Maanen (1982, page 15) reminds us "qualitative research is marked more by a reliance upon multiple sources of data than by its commitment to **any one source alone**" (my emphasis). I feel that using electronic media, provided suitable care is taken to verify the material obtained, makes it possible to obtain a richer set of data than would otherwise be possible, from a larger range of geographically disparate sources.

By its very nature qualitative research tends towards the holistic, trying as it does to reveal as many influences as possible on the "thing" being studied (Myers, 1995). In a paper of this length and type, it is very hard to present, and for you the reader to make sense of, that whole. I have chosen to discuss just four aspects of VICNET to give you a glimpse of the complexity of and to underline some of the difficulties that arise when trying to describe a system that is both open and heterogeneous. The first vignette shows how quickly the equipment inventory of the VICNET site at the SLV grew in the 18 months since it was first established as a trial scheme, and offers some reasons for this growth. Vignette two offers a glimpse of how VICNET and a remote organisation coalesced to change the nature of both participants – a fluid topology in the sense used by Mol and Law (1994). The third vignette attempts to illustrate how VICNET can be seen as a vehicle for bringing remote information back to Victoria. In fact the system seems to fold the space occupied by the internet bringing the remote points closer together – in this way VICNET transforms the space occupied by the internet. Systems may also encounter resistance to their development or reconfiguration and this is illustrated in the last vignette where difficulties are encountered with the equipment being used, lack of confidence on the part of the user and a clash of cultures. In choosing these vignettes I am acutely aware of the fact that we have to understand large scale infrastructure projects from a multiplicity of views which will include "work practices of designers and users, the emergence of large-scale technical systems, and the encoding and decoding of information" (Neumann and Star, 1995). VICNET is revealed as infrastructure, as an organisation within the SLV community, and as the people or external organisations using it to gather or publish information as they attempt to become part of an ever widening system – in short networks of the social and technical.

As mentioned previously, Actor Network Theory (ANT) has been applied to the analysis of sociotechnical systems. In brief, ANT is a theory that seeks to use a neutral vocabulary to treat with impartiality all entities (human and non-human actors) involved in a system so as to reveal the powers and associations that bring that system to some sort of closure - referred to as "Black-boxing" (Latour, 1987). Although it might seem that because one of the fundamental components of VICNET is a computer network and as such is "hard-wired" it is perhaps salutary to realise that it is an assemblage of artefacts and as such constitutes an actor network.[1] That is a network of the social, technical, human and non-human. Bruno Latour in a recent paper reminds us that "[n]othing is more intensely connected, more distant, more compulsory and more strategically organized than a computer network." (Latour, 1997, p. 1) A technical or even a computer network is not a metaphor for an actor network. Actor networks may be local, may lack compulsory paths and nodes that are strategic centres, they are also not purely social networks which analyse, without touching, the way humans interact with the social and natural worlds. ANT aims at accounting for the very essence of societies and natures. (Latour, 1997, p. 1)

One problem that I have with ANT is that it tends to be too centralising, focussing on one actor which attempts to stabilise the identity and roles of the other actors. (See also Singleton & Michael, 1993) It also does not lend itself well to the analysis of groups of sociotechnical systems that develop in a diversity of spaces. Sociotechnical systems that may for whatever reasons gravitate towards or move apart from each other as things evolve.

For these reasons I move away from ANT and employ the concept of topology as Mol and Law have done. They argue that " 'the social' doesn't exist as a single spatial type" (Mol and Law, 1994, p. 643) but can be seen as a range of spaces in which various actions may take place. Objects may cluster together in regions around which boundaries can be drawn, there are networks where the distance between nodes is determined by the relationship between them and particular form of the node. To some extent the connections between, and thus, the shape of the network between objects or nodes on the network will depend on the obligatory passage points and interessements or groups of actions that are imposed in attempts to stabilise the network. (Callon, 1986, p. 207) Mol and Law (1994, p. 643) also identify social regions that can act as fluids. In a fluid space one cannot easily determine entities "[a] fluid world is a world of mixtures". (Mol and Law, 1994, p. 661) Fluids can flow and intermingle like water droplets on a sheet of plastic, fluid regions will also have different viscosities which will determine how fast they change. I also wish to introduce is the idea of a sheet or surface which can be deformed, something like a rubber sheet that can be stretched or folded in on itself thus making it easier to picture the transformations. All of these can be seen in action in the evolution of the open system that is VICNET.

OPEN SYSTEMS

Hewitt and de Jong's (1984) characterization of open systems is useful when we consider the development and use of the internet. They saw open systems as continually evolving in an incremental manner, containing no global objects holding it all together and consisting of a growing number of independent communicating sites. (Hewitt and de Jong, 1984, pp. 149, 157) These are just the properties that the internet exhibits. We have standards that are incrementally evolving just consider HTML. Web sites, email servers and the like can be developed and managed independently of each other provided they use the appropriate protocols e.g. TCP/IP, HTTP, MIME etc. There are no global objects on the internet it is a set of communicating subsystems each of which can be considered as being open as well as will be demonstrated in the next section.

AN EVOLVING SYSTEM

One way the system can be represented is in terms of the hardware and software in use at the VICNET site located in the State Library of Victoria PABX/computer room. Looking at the changes that have occurred over time will help to give a feeling for the systems evolution, albeit from a local viewpoint.

At the time of the launch VICNET essentially consisted of the equipment as shown in Table 1; this having been bought from the first grant allocation. Although the original equipment purchases were adequate for the pilot scheme and the first few months of operation, they were fairly rudimentary in terms of what the development group planned.

Since that time, a number of factors have led to an increase in equipment as shown in Table 2 and the list is still growing (as is the number of staff employed at the SLV VICNET site) although the latest changes are not shown here. Increases in the number of users brought with it concerns for reliability hence some of the new purchases were made to provide some redundancy. Other purchases (modems and 64Kbps ISDN lines) were made just to cope with the demand for access from actual and potential subscribers and to enable more of public libraries access to VICNET. To improve the management and presentation of information and to aid in the construction of databases a Microsoft NT based server with Microsoft Access and the Emwac server software was installed. Concerns about security and management led to a swap from the free CERN WWW (world wide web) server software to the Netscape Commerce server.

Because of the factors mentioned above, it makes no sense to draw a boundary

Table 1 Computer and communications equipment used by VICNET in November 1994. (Kurzeme, 1994)[2]

Item	Quantity	Description
CPU	1	Sun Microsystems SPARCserver 20 Model 51
		64 Mb memory, 6.3 Gb hard disk, 10 Gb tape drive
Operating system	n/a	Operating system Solaris 2.4
Other software	n/a	Other software, C compiler and SunNet manager
Httpd software	n/a	CERN httpd
Router	1	Telebit Netblazer 40 with 3 LAN ports, 32 async ports and 2 sync
Modems	2	Dataplex racks with 32 28.8 Kbps modem cards
Terminal adapter	1	JTEC J1200 ISDN
Ethernet Hub	1	Synoptics 2813
AARNet Link	1	64 Kbps ISDN B-channel
Telecom lines	20	

Table 2 Computer and communications equipment used by VICNET in May 1996. The items highlighted with the light grey are ones that existed previously but their quantity or nature changed whilst those highlighted with the dark grey are new additions. [3]

Item	Quantity	Description
CPU	many	Sun Microsystems SPARCserver 20 Model 51
		64 Mb memory, 6.3 Gb hard disk, 10 Gb tape drive
Operating system	n/a	Operating system Solaris 2.4
Other software	n/a	Other software, C compiler and SunNet manager
Httpd software	n/a	Netscape Commerce server
CPU	1	NT Server
Operating system		Windows NT
Other software		Emwac httpd, MS Access
Router	many	Telebit Netblazer 40 with 3 LAN ports, 32 async ports and 2 sync
Modems	60	Dataplex racks with 32 28.8 Kbps modem cards
Terminal adapter	1	JTEC J1200 ISDN
Ethernet Hub	1	Synoptics 2813
AARNet Link	11	64 Kbps ISDN B-channel
Telecom lines	many	

around the human and non-human artefacts involved at some particular point in time and say "this is VICNET" – it (VICNET) is not invariant, the quantity and type of equipment changes frequently as does the number of people and organisations involved in its structure. Regions can coexist and the way they hold together and co-constitute this thing called VICNET varies both spatially and temporally. There is a fluidity to the evolution – as Mol and Law say "[w]e're looking at *variation without boundaries and transformation without discontinuity.* We are looking at flows. The space with which we're dealing is fluid." (Mol and Law, 1994, p. 658)

INFLUENCES TO-ING AND FLOWING

Unless public libraries continually redefine themselves, and see their broad business as information and recreation not books, we will end up exactly the same way as the Mechanics Institutes and the subscription lending libraries.

...

It seemed important to me that we should redefine ourselves as information providers and navigators. (Mackenzie and Trembath, 1996, p. 147)

One of the first public libraries to participate in the extension of VICNET was the Mornington Peninsula Library Service (MPLS). They were seeking a way of modernizing the library's image and of redefining their place in the 'modern world' and VICNET offered just this opportunity. Following discussions with VICNET, Nepean Net was established which has ties back to both the local Mornington Peninsula community and to VICNET (Figure 1) This co-constitution brings with it local (to the peninsula community) advantages:

The big advantage is the very positive image of the service that is generated, of being seen as innovative. Publicity is easy to get, especially in local papers. It has captured the imagination of our [City] Commissioners, our [the MPLS] management group and others in the organisation as well as the local community. (Mackenzie and Trembath, 1996, p. 147)

The MPLS is in another region, distinct from the original SLV one, with a different set of stakeholders to charm. It is simultaneously local and global. Local in that it has local concerns for its image and provision of access to information, but global also as information can be obtained from and sent to the larger world. It simultaneously allows other Victorians (and indeed the world) to see and access the local peninsula community.

Libraries as we all know are heterogeneous assemblages of staff, books, buildings, computers, rules and regulations, borrowers, book browsers, financial reports and funding grants. VICNET also consists of a variety of human and non-human artefacts. Imagine that both VICNET and the

Figure 1. The Nepean Net home page at http://www.nepeanet.org.au/ with links to local services and VICNET. It acts both to make the Mornington Peninsula Library visible to the world as well as providing a navigation aid to the world's knowledge, for the local community.

Welcome to

Nepean Net

The Mornington Peninsula, Victoria, Australia

CLICK HERE -> What's New: PENINSULA WINERIES

Connect to Vicnet - Victoria's Network

For more information about Nepean Net contact Webmaster
The html code and page design for this site is by:

Arkins & Stewart

Internet Technologies

MPLS are droplets of fluid each made up of heterogeneous entities – each has their own boundary. Now imagine that these droplets are on a surface and something causes this sheet to fold in on itself. The droplets deform, roll and combine with each other to co-constitute a larger entity, the boundary becomes larger but there are still heterogeneous entities within. Just as raindrops can be shaken apart so may droplets break up – not necessarily returning to their original state. If the raindrops can be seen as heterogeneous regions then consider that social networks, such as the MPLS, appear in regions and regions can flow together to create a larger one and the networks within may also come together. VICNET now has a link to Nepean net, its state has altered, while the MPLS has a link to VICNET – it has undergone a change of state, it has been transformed and made visible to other regions.

INFORMATION FLOWS – GENEALOGY AND VICNET

From its inception VICNET has always been seen as a community, where people with similar interests could contact one another and exchange ideas and knowledge. "VICNET aims to create a rich information environment for Victorians." (Hardy, 1994, p. 2) One of the first public interest user groups on VICNET was the Genealogy Special Interest Group. In an article for the VICNET Newsletter, John, the co-ordinator of the Group says of the VICNET service:

> I envisage VICNET, through the Genealogy Special Interest Group, acting as a catalyst to this large group. It would act as a bulletin board enabling people to share information and assist one another. It would pace [sic] regional Victorians on a more equal footing with their city-based cousins. It would allow access to a range of databases of interest to historians. (Holt, 1994, p. 4)

It is about including Victorians who are remote from the city and hence the genealogical resources of the State Library. VICNET extends boundaries and incorporates others into its sociotechnical milieu, and as it does so, the others may bring with them new information or assistance. VICNET is being co-constituted.

Via email, I interviewed John some eighteen months after the publication of that article. Here is a transcript of part of that interview.[4]

Andrew: Was this initial enthusiasm warranted?

John: Yes, very much so. The amount of material on the net about family history is overwhelming!

> ...

> ... I am constantly staggered at the amount of trouble people will go to to answer a query from another person across [sic] the globe. It restores ones faith in human nature.

Andrew: Do you think that VICNET has helped place regional Victorians on an equal footing with their metro counterparts in respect to the access to genealogical resources?

John: Most assuredly. Except that in my own case, living mainly at Camperdown, I still don't have a local provider which makes things difficult!

With VICNET comes the possibility of joining country and metropolitan regions together. Information has the potential to flow from region to region. However, at the time of writing, the information couldn't flow from VICNET to the rural city of Camperdown (some 160 Km from Melbourne) because a local internet service provider was not available there. There was in fact some resistance to the growth of our technical network. More evolution in the open system was needed; other parts – computers, cables, modems and interested parties had to be persuaded that this system was one that was worthwhile being part of. In the actor network terminology they had to become interested in the development of the system and enrolled.[5]

John has also used the internet to find relatives both in Australia and overseas. Taking one instance of how he did this reveals the fluid nature of the information gatherers and sources.

John: ... I have personally discovered several Australian relatives locally by using the web, and have spend a happy time meeting them and their family. More excitingly for me, I have finally located information on a small school attended by my late father-in-law in UK. All I knew was that he went to Prices [sic] School, and that its blazer had a lion embroidered in gold. He was born in Manchester and I had assumed the school was in that area. ... In desperation about six weeks back, I put a message on the web asking for help with this problem ... I chose one of the numerous genealogically exclusive newsgroups

> ...

> In only two days I got back an encouraging response, and after several messages back and forth, I now have a complete history of this public school, founded in 1721, closed in 1908 located right at the bottom of England near Southampton. And my correspondent is even going to the County Record Office to check the enrolments for the period 1905-1915 ... He has already been to his local library, located a history of the school and scanned it into his computer. He then sent the whole multipage article to me via the net. Without the web this sort of discovery would have been impossible!

One of John's objectives was to gain access to difficult to find information about his relatives. Traditional means of correspondence between the UK and Australia didn't work. How do you write to someone you don't know on the other side of the globe and get them to find information?

Once access to the internet is gained it becomes a way of finding relatives and information about them – it works to make the previously invisible visible. VICNET allows John to bring the world closer, he can send out a message to a bulletin board, asking for help to find a school that he knows his father-in-law attended. Someone from this region replies and the remaining actors in this bulletin board are no longer necessary – the regions of the bulletin board and John no longer interact. The unknown becomes the known. The space and the network are reconfigured to create a more direct link between the two correspondents. By sending out a message asking for help in finding an invisible school in the UK not only has the school been rendered visible, but a flow of information between regions was established. The heterogeneous nature of these regions is also revealed to us as interlocutors. John's correspondent enrolled the services of a number of different artefacts; the library, documents of the school's history and a scanner which transformed the printed text into a electronic one. The resulting stream of binary 1s and 0s was then sent via another heterogeneous hard-wired network to John. England and Australia were brought closer together.

One way of picturing this is to think of John's Southampton correspondent as being situated in one region on a large rubber sheet, John situated in Camperdown in Victoria, Australia. The sociotechnical system that is VICNET acts on this sheet to fold it (continuously deform it, to use the topological parlance) so that the regions come closer together allowing the information to flow.

SLOWING DOWN THE FLOW

Another group to express an interest in VICNET was the Koori (the indigenous Australians) community. Peter, a Koori studying at Ballarat University, encountered the VICNET home page whilst surfing the web and telephoned VICNET and was asked to become involved in setting up a home page for Kooris in Victoria. Ballarat is approximately 110Km from Melbourne and once again we see the topological transformation at work folding the space occupied by VICNET and the Koori community to bring them closer together. Peter created a first page which was subsequently installed on VICNET and was given some software to enable the development of a more comprehensive site because as he says, "I want to redo it as I feel it is of inferior quality but there are very few people around our area that have much experience with Internet let alone Homepages."[6]

Lack of experience is one thing preventing the creation of a site pleasing to Peter but there are also other things acting to increase the viscosity of our fluid region and hence slowing the coalescence. Some are technical, others are financial:

... tomorrow we have some advisers arriving which I'm looking forward to, hopefully we can get some good programs to use. But there are frequent computer problems which waste enormous amounts of time, if technology was more reliable I would be more inclined to put more effort into it. We also need more funds to buy extra storage gear, zip drives etc.

He also adds, when speaking of equipment, that access is also a problem. Peter runs classes for other Kooris which include lessons on how to use the internet and cultural content, in general these internet classes work well with

elders getting involved ... because five day courses are done over fifteen days but I have to wait for holidays before [getting] access to desktop computers that have to be dismantled and assembled and a bus used for transportation. But submissions for laptops are turned down.

Many of the participants "are unemployed, depressed, just out of gaol, hate schools" and lack many of the written and oral skills that are needed for many things. Peter sees the multimedia capabilities of the internet as making "sessions more exciting and lessening the dependency on these skills".

Peter is ambivalent when asked whether having Koori information available on VICNET has been worthwhile but,

I get a few interesting letters but more exchange is occurring through chat groups and a homepage avoids repeating yourself; they can get location objectives and details from it. One chap from Sweden visited our campus years ago and when he saw the homepage he just wrote to say hi which is good for maintaining feedback.

... again it is fantastic for long distances. Indigenous students here swap general messages with native Americans. I constantly ask advice from overseas groups.[7]

Throughout our exchange there is an element of pride sneaking in. Pride in the fact that indigenous peoples can, despite the myriad of cultural differences, create a presence on the internet and get email from Sweden and the native Americans. One can detect a rising sense of equity and justice tempered by the fact that financial aid is very hard to obtain. Moral and social issues of pride, equity and justice flow through Peter's email. Despite the lack of support from "the ones in power" it is possible for the Koori community to have access to technologies. Using the technology, they can gain a sense of community with other indigenous peoples, seek advice and feedback and later on, maybe even give advice. The regions of the Koori and Western Technical cultures meet and intermingle allowing the Koori community in Victoria to become more visible.

VICNET AS AN OPEN SYSTEM/TOPOLOGICAL TRANSFORMATION

If we think of topology as the study of the way things act under continuous deformations then perhaps we can see VICNET as acting to deform the information space. This artefact (VICNET), acts, in the mathematical sense, like a transformation that folds the map of the territory in such a way that the distance between the two diminishes. This is a topological transformation, a study of things that remain invariant under continuous deformations. (Kac and Ulam, 1979) The introduction of an artefact acts to deform our territory, our regions. (Mol and Law, 1994) It performs in a similar way to one of Latour's immutable mobiles (Latour, 1986) acting to bring territories closer together. I would now like to extend this topological investigation even further into the realms of the fluid. (Mol and Law, 1994)

Picture a flat surface with a large number of pools of fluid (raindrops for instance) randomly spread across it. These pools are slowly spreading out over the surface. Because of imperfections on the surface, the rate of spread is uneven and the pools do not always maintain a uniform shape or boundary. As they spread, they may meet and combine with others thus increasing the size of the pool hence expanding the boundary. If we were to look in these pools we would see a variety of entities, it can be a region of mixtures (Mol and Law, 1994, p. 660) – our raindrops may contain dust, or chemicals from the atmosphere or even micro-organisms – but things within the pool exist in relative harmony. Conditions may change but all things in the pool are informed of the change, the raindrop may dry up or the chemicals may crystallize out either way the composition of the pool alters affecting the environment for the other entities.

The way VICNET evolves can be likened to these pools. There are regions, for instance libraries, where many entities co-exist. The boundaries of these regions may change in shape or character and interact with other libraries, coalescing as did the boundaries of the Mornington Peninsula Library and the State Library to form one larger pool. We can also deform our flat surface, let's say we fold it in on itself, the raindrops will run together more quickly.

In the case of the Nepean Net VICNET co-constitution several deformations were performed. It brought the Mornington Peninsula Library Service and the local papers, community and city commissioners closer together. The world of the Peninsula was brought closer to users elsewhere in the world.

Imagine that the SLV VICNET node and the MPLS are fluid droplets each made up of heterogeneous entities, each having their own boundary. These droplets are on a surface and something deforms it causing it to fold in on itself, the droplets combine to co-constitute themselves into a larger entity, the boundary becoming larger. In a similar way, we see information flow as the regions of John and a school in the United Kingdom coalesce; as those of the Ballarat Koori community intersect with VICNET we can add pride, access and understanding tempered with technical and financial problems that increase the viscosity of the fluid regions thus slowing down the coalescence.

One way of thinking about this open system is as a fluid topology where pools of liquid (centres of interest) can come together (form an alliance) or split up due to other pressures. Another might be to consider it as a topological transformation of a surface where the web acts to bring things closer together. There are multiple ways of seeing this – just as VICNET has multiple meanings – no one particular point of view should have privilege over any others. It is helpful to remember, at this point, that this is only one ordering out of many, because as Mol and Mesman say: "... semiotics also allows one to assume that everything which is noise in relation to one order, is information in another. It's not chaos, but another kind of tune." (Mol & Mesman, 1996:433) It would be incorrect to see the surface as doing all the work, it is our sociotechnical networks that help to deform the sheet also.

FLOWING TO A CONCLUSION?

So, to paraphrase Mol and Law, (Mol & Law, 1994:664) how does VICNET flow? Both slowly and quickly one is tempted to answer, there are regions of differing viscosity, some move fast to join up with others, some more slowly, our study helps reveal why. There are repulsions, attractions and frictions between regions each serving to determine the shape of the territory. As regions join the shape and nature of the pool boundary changes but some things inside remain the same. The system is undergoing continual evolution but it is difficult to determine what exists at any given point in time. Open systems such as VICNET may never be completely described, treating them as fluid topologies at least allows us to get a feel for the way they roll towards wherever it is that they are headed.

Now to the watershed. Why is this way of thinking about open systems is useful?

Throughout this paper, I have attempted to show that there are a variety of social and technical, human and non-human actors that can come together to form networks – social networks. Networks such as John and his genealogical interests and U.K. contacts, the MPLS and the local Mornington community, The VICNET group and the associated equipment at the SLV, Peter and the Koori community at Ballarat. All have their local issues which we can focus on and we can see them as regions each different from the other, but these regions can and do interact – flow together or apart to help shape the global entity we may call VICNET. We are no longer forced to see things as having to happen through some central agency. The true heterogeneity of the assemblage is revealed on both a macro and micro scale.

REFERENCES
References available on request.

ENDNOTES
[1] Star and Ruhleder (1996) in their examination of large scale information spaces also provide us with a timely reminder that such infrastructures are not just carriers of information alone but that "computers, people and tasks together make or break a functioning infrastructure" (page 118). There is no divide between the social and the technical.

[2] Even this table is out of date, as I compiled it more equipment and software was being purchased and installed. But of course, there must be some cutoff point or this story would never have been told.

[3] This table was compiled from information supplied via Email from Adrian Bates of VICNET on 20 May 1996 and 3 June 1996.

[4] Email, John, 8 June 1996.

[5] In the more formal terminology of ANT there had to be an interessement, a persuading of other parties who could supply the missing pieces and become caught up in the network.

[6] Email, Peter 26 May 1996. Peter was even doubtful that I would receive this message because the equipment was playing up.

[7] Peter made the remark that "snail mail" (the ordinary postal service) just does not have the same response rate.

The Security of Information Communications

Dr. H.B. Wolfe

Information Science Department, University of Otago, P.O. Box 56, Dunedin, NEW ZEALAND

Phone: +64 3 479-8141, Fax: +64 3 479-8311, Hwolfe@commerce.otago.ac.nz

ABSTRACT

Encryption provides the only real security for storing sensitive information, communicating securely and doing business via the Internet. This paper addresses some of the pertinent issues surrounding this important security technique describing and discussing cryptographic algorithms, secure protocols, and constraints that govern them. It attempts to dissolve the myth that America is the only source of "strong" encryption and further demonstrates the futility of restrictive laws that govern the export of such products.

INTRODUCTION

Computers are an important part of society today and many people use them as routinely as phones were used in the past. The computer is, after all, just another tool. The Industrial Age brought us the opportunity to significantly expand our abilities to produce. Those things formerly produced by hand are now produced faster, with greater accuracy, in quantity, by machine. This net effect can be equated to an extension and enhancement of our body's physical capabilities to be able to manipulate and produce more, faster and with greater precision.

The Computer Age has brought with it the ability to extend and expand the storage of information and improve our ability to retrieve and manipulate that information. This can be equated to an extension of our individual intellect, memory and evaluation processes – our mind. We can store our innermost thoughts, plans and ideas on our computer - each of which may be extremely personal and/or private.

What you think, can be kept private by not exposing it to anyone – controlled by the individual. And so too can one's plans and ideas be kept private. What you type into your computer, however, cannot be kept private in the same way. Moreover, a Court of Law does not view information stored on a computer to be private nor do various law enforcement units Both have the authority and can and will seize, explore, assess and evaluate information found there [1, 2]. Very few people consider that their information, which may be stored on the computer, is public and can be demanded by a Court of Law or confiscated and obtained by Law Enforcement – without their cooperation or permission. In a court of law you can be asked to provide information and be held in contempt if you refuse but the important issue here is that YOU get to choose. If that information resides on a computer in plain text form YOU do **NOT** get to choose.

Electronic security in this day and age covers a wide variety of techniques. One of the most important areas that must be addressed is that of communication and commerce on the Internet. The Internet is an insecure medium to say the least. Private conversations between two individuals over the Internet are not and should not be considered to be private either. It has been reported that these conversations are routinely monitored by NSA (the American National Security Agency) at the fifteen, or so, key switches through which the vast majority of Internet traffic passes [3]. These folks, if the reports are true, are monitoring conversations (by computer) for key words that fit their particular agenda and they act upon information gathered via this method. The issue here is not about guilt or innocence but about privacy. One cannot and should not expect that private conversations carried out over the Internet will remain private under any normal conditions.

Another insidious but less obvious fact about Internet use is that messages once sent, are not discarded nor do they disappear forever. Although you may purge a message from your computer it is still being held elsewhere [4,5]. Your Internet Service Provider (ISP) will have a copy and usually, at one or more of the relays through which messages must pass, copies of messages are archived and kept for differing time periods. The message is also kept at the ISP at the destination as well. Most ordinary users are not aware that messages sent six months ago may be able to be retrieved from one or more of these sites. That fact could have serious legal ramifications for the sender and possible consequences for the receiver as well.

CRYPTOGRAPHY

At this time cryptography, in one form or another, is really the only effective method that can be used to protect Internet transactions and communications. While this tool cannot prevent interception, it can inhibit or stop unauthorized persons or organizations from making use of your private or personal information - without your agreement and cooperation. Unauthorized means anyone who you have not expressly given permission to read your private communications. The author does not distinguish between law enforcement, intelligence or any other unwelcome intruder. They are all the same. There are arguments for and against allowing law enforcement and intelligence to have unlimited access to all communications. This paper, however, does not distinguish between "good" intruders and "bad" intruders.

Cryptography is the art or science of hidden writing. Plain text (your message in readable form) is modified using an algorithm (like a mathematical equation) that requires at least one special variable (your unique/secret key that no one else knows) to create ciphered text (your message in unreadable form). At the destination the person who the message is intended for must know that "unique/secret key" and specific cryptographic algorithm in order to be able to unlock the ciphered message. Exchanging that secret key emerges as a significant weakness in the whole scheme.

All encryption is not created equal nor does it necessarily provide equivalent security. It would be wrong to intimate that merely using some form of encryption to protect your communication is enough. There are other factors at work here as well and they have to do with the politics of privacy. I have often heard it said in New Zealand "if you have nothing to hide then it shouldn't matter who reads your communications". Of course, that opinion is naïve and foolish and does not represent reality in any meaningful way. Real privacy does not make any distinction about the qualities of private information. It is either private or it is not. Legal, illegal, good or bad, none of these descriptors are relevant.

A SHORT PRIMER IN CRYPTOGRAPHY

For the average user, cryptographic products come in two flavors. *Symmetric* cryptography means that you use the same key to encrypt as you use to decrypt. *Asymmetric* cryptography, also known as "public key cryptography", means that you have two different but related keys (one public and one private) one is used for encrypting and the other related key for decrypting.

Symmetric systems are the older of the two and vendors often use the key size (in bits - an example: the Data Encryption Standard - DES uses 56 bit keys) to describe the relative security provided by the algorithm. This is but one dimension that describes that security and should not be misinterpreted to be the only attribute that measures the actual safety provided. Strong algorithms implemented badly provide weak protection. The Data Encryption Standard (commonly used in the banking industry) when it was adopted as the US standard in the mid-1970's was claimed, by those who adopted it, to be extremely secure. One of the principal weaknesses of symmetric cryptography is the secure exchange of the secret key.

In the past it has been argued that a brute force attack on the Data Encryption Standard would take as much as 2,300 years to decrypt and that a sixty-four bit algorithm would take as much as 584,542 years [6]. In the example, one would be encouraged to conclude that algorithms of that length or greater are not breakable - in our lifetime.

The DES was publicly defeated in 1997 for the first time using an estimated 70,000 computers working in concert for 96 days. It was defeated in 1998 for the second time using 52,000 computers working in concert for 39 days. On the 17th of July 1998 a single, purpose built, machine (known as *DES Crack*) working for fifty-six (56) HOURS defeated the DES for the third time. The *DES Crack* machine was not especially designed for speed and only runs at 40 MHz. That could probably be increased ten fold without serious modification. *DES Crack* is the first publicized non-government attempt at building such a machine and has a good deal of room for improved efficiencies - and these will undoubtedly be made [7]. Today, strong symmetric encryption is thought to be 112 bits or greater.

Asymmetric systems provide the very important advantage of not requiring the secure exchange of keys in order to communicate securely. Each user's "public key" can be kept by a trusted third party that certifies its authenticity or exchanged much more easily than the symmetric system. The RSA public key crypto-system was introduced in 1978 (created by Ronald **R**ivest, Adi **S**hamir & Leonard **A**dleman). At the time it was thought that it would take "40 quadrillion years to factor" - this system's security is based on the difficulty associated with factoring large prime numbers. The creators issued a challenge in 1977 to defeat a key pair consisting of a 129-digit number (equates to 426 bits). On the 27th of April 1994, after 100 quadrillion calculations coordinated using the CPU's of some 600 participants, the RSA-129 was defeated [8]. Today, strong asymmetric encryption is thought to be 768 bits or greater.

The important lesson to be learned from the material described above is that there is really no 100% solution. With larger keys, either system can approach a level of computational security that would be acceptable in today's business community. However, these examples have addressed brute force attacks only (brute force attacks try every possible key or attempt to factor every combination of prime numbers within the key range). The field of cryptanalysis is prolific and there are other attack strategies that can be successful with various encryption algorithms (some examples: linear cryptanalysis, differential cryptanalysis, plain text attacks, and differential fault analysis to name just a few). To use this tool effectively, the user needs to consult an expert or spend the time necessary to achieve a reasonable depth of understanding of the discipline. *Note: "strong" cryptography refers to the way encrypted messages are attacked. An algorithm is said to be "strong" if using all of the computing power in the world to attack it would not produce a decrypted result within a time frame to make that result useful.*

CRYPTOGRAPHIC PRODUCTS:

There are a number of cryptographic products available around the world [9, 10], however, cryptographic products created in the US cannot legally be exported unless they have in some way been significantly weakened in their level of security. Coincidentally, we have a community of interest in New Zealand and there are several products that have been created there and elsewhere around the world that stand up to scrutiny - in other words - these products provide strong encryption. There is a firm in Christchurch that produces cryptographic hardware devices (SignalGuard by CES) [11]. This system is useful for secure communications between branches of organizations and does not require any computing resources (for the encryption/decryption process) for its use. The unique aspect of SignalGuard is that it does not encrypt "data". Instead it encrypts the analog signal without respect to any specific data that might pass over the analog communications channel.

Two crypto systems have been developed independently in Auckland. The first by Peter Smith and is called LUC and is a public key system [12, 13]. The second is produced by William Raike and is called RPK and is also a public key system [14, 15]. Internationally, it could be argued that the most commonly used crypto system used in the world is called **P**retty **G**ood **P**rivacy (**PGP** – a hybrid public key system). PGP was initially produced by Phil Zimmermann, however, there have been several others who have assisted with its development. PGP can easily be obtained from the Internet from various sites [16]. It is illegal to download it from a US site to a site outside the US [17, 18, 19]. Of course, that is a silly and wholly unenforceable law and PGP is freely available at many sites outside the US .

There are a couple of products from Finland that hold a great deal of promise due to their very user friendly interface and the choice offered to users of a range of strong encryption algorithms. The first is TeamWare Crypto (a symmetric key system) and that's available from Fujitzu (NZ) [20]. The second is F-Secure Desktop produced by DataFellows [21]. There is an algorithm (**IDEA** - **I**nternational **D**ata **E**ncryption **A**lgorithm) that can be licensed from a company in Switzerland called Ascom Systec AG [22]. IDEA is thought to be one of the most secure of symmetric algorithms available today and is one of the algorithms used in PGP. These products are a sample of what can be acquired outside the US easily and at a reasonable cost; however, the list should not be misconstrued to be complete nor as an endorsement of any product. Each, however, can provide strong encryption to users and offers the choice of different strong cryptographic algorithms.

Encryption products of the types mentioned here can be used not only for securely communicating over the Internet but also for storing private information. A recent example of where such measures might have been prudent occurred in New Zealand. The police executed a search warrant on three parties, one of whom was an attorney representing the other two. While searching the attorney's office the entire hard disk on her computer was copied and taken away. Subsequently, it was determined that the warrant was illegal. By that time, however, the client attorney privilege and client privacy had been breached for all of the attorney's other clients (whose case information was also stored on the hard disk). This, of course, could have been avoided if the entire hard disk had been encrypted using strong encryption.

INTERNET PROTOCOLS THAT USE CRYPTOGRAPHIC TECHNIQUES:

The discussion of cryptography thus far presupposes that the user will control their use of such products. For most users this is yet another activity that can go wrong and/or impede their activities and further complicates their use of the tool. Resistance is bound to occur. **V**irtual **P**rivate **N**etworks (**VPN**) have been designed and created to give control of the cryptographic function to the VPN owner and provide a secure environment within an organization for communications - some using public networks. The network administrator gets to choose the specific crypto algorithm to be implemented. In so far as the user is concerned, they operate as usual without any need to be concerned with cryptography. These systems are private as indicated and as such do not solve the problem of communication outside of the VPN.

There are, however, a number of protocols for communicating over the Internet that offer various levels of cryptographic security. For the most part these are designed to provide for secure transactions so that business can be transacted safely. Some of the more common examples are **S**ecure **M**ultipurpose **I**nternet **M**ail **E**xtensions (**S/MIME**), **S**ecure **H**yper**T**ext **M**arkup **L**anguage (**S-HTTP**), **S**ecure **S**ockets **L**ayer (**SSL**), **S**ecure **E**lectronic **T**ransactions (**SET**),

Point to Point Tunneling Protocol (**PPTP**), and there several others.

It is important to note that of the five protocols listed, three have been successfully attacked either because their cryptographic algorithm was weak or because the implementation of an otherwise strong algorithm was flawed (S/MIME, SSL, PPTP). One successful attack has been implemented in the form of a screen saver program [23] that quite happily performs a brute force attack on the 40-bit RC2 keys (RC2 for Ron's Code or Rivest's Cipher is the name of the variable key-size crypto algorithm). Of course, that screensaver/crypto attack program is readily available from the Internet. It is also worth mentioning that even though a protocol may have been successfully attacked, that does not mean that it cannot be improved such that the flaw or weakness no longer exists.

In April, Netscape released its source code onto the Internet minus the cryptographic portion. Within seventeen hours a new secure version of Netscape (called Cryptozilla) with strong encryption (128 bit) was readily available over the Internet throughout the world [24, 25]. The export version of Netscape, according to US law, was hobbled and contained only 40 bit encryption. The FBI argues that it needs "an immediate decryption capability which is available to law enforcement upon presentation of proper legal authority (to include the state and local levels) of encrypted communications or electronically stored information" [26]. The question needs to be asked: Are we prepared to give up freedom and privacy for the illusion of safety? The next question is: Who's going to protect us from law enforcement agencies with less than sterling track records?

All cryptographic products purchased from the US are intentionally hobbled as a result of US legislation that limits the strength of products that can legally be exported. Currently, it's okay for Americans to have strong encryption but it's definitely not okay for non-Americans to have strong encryption. The rationale for taking this position is the topic of heated debate around the world. However, the fact remains that folk outside America cannot buy strong encryption products from the US and therefore look elsewhere to spend their money on products that do offer that kind of protection.

The notion that one system or another is unassailable is a fiction and judging by the facts of history unsupportable. Successful attack is not about whether it can be done but rather of when it will be done. It is neither prudent nor reasonable to conclude that <u>ONLY</u> law enforcement nor only the US has access to good cryptographic knowledge, tools, and digital intercept equipment. Producers in the US are being penalized and missing out on a sizable market for their products as a result of backward unenforceable legislation that, in today's world, serves no purpose other than to give the illusion that only America can have secure communications.

REFERENCES:

1. *UK Customs Now Do Random Computer Checks For Porn*, an example of private information intrusion, http://www.infowar.com/class_1/class1_081898f_j.shtml
2. *Sci/Tech UK Customs check for laptop porn*, by Chris Nuttall, 13 August1998, BBC News, an example of private information intrusion, http://news.bbc.co.uk/hi/english/sci/tech/newsid_150000/150465.stm
3. *Is NSA Sniffing the Internet?*, June 1995, http://www.kimsoft.com/korea/nsa-net.htm
4. *Critics have no right to anonymity online, Canadian Court rules*, by Andy Harmon, 15 July 1998, an example of accessing previous Internet traffic, http://www.infowar.com/class_1/class1_071598b_j.html-ssi
5. Internet providers on defensive after Philip ruling, by Keith Damsell, Financial Post, 11 July 1998, an example of accessing previous Internet traffic, http://www.canoe.ca/FTPechnology/jul11_internetpr.html
6. *GSM Security and Encryption* by David Margrave, George Mason University - 1994, http://radiophone.dhp.com/gsm/gsm-secur/gsm-secur.html
7. Electronic Frontier Foundation, *Cracking DES: Secrets of Encryption Research, Wiretap Politics & Chip Design*, Sebastopol, California, O'Reilly & Associates, 1998, ISBN 1-56592-520-3.
8. Fun_People Archive 27 Apr: *R.S.A. 129 falls, taking the squeamish ossifrage with it...*, http://emoire.net/~psl/Fun_People/1994/1994AKV.html
9. The Commerce Department Report noted that in many of the countries surveyed, "exportable U.S. encryption products are perceived to be of an unsatisfactory quality." Elizabeth Corcoran, "Encryption rules Hurt Exporters, Study says," Washington Post, (January 17, 1996), p. A11.
10. But a 1996 survey by Trusted Information Systems, Inc. notes that "the quality of foreign products seems to be comparable to U.S. products." An updated survey finds 656 foreign products of which 281 use DES. See http://www.tis.com; NRC, pp. 127-128 (quoting 1996 report by Trusted Information Systems). Contesting the idea that foreign-made encryption is of inferior quality, James Bidzos of RSA notes that foreign developers can simply study U.S. patents. Stenographic Transcript of Hearings, subcommittee on Science, Technology, and Space, United States Senate, hearing on S. 1726, The Promotion of commerce online in the digital era act of 1996, or "PRO-CODE," Wednesday, June 12, 1996 (Statement of James Bidzos) p. 61.
11. CES Communications, Ltd., specializing in securing communications and improving the quality of transmitted signals, Christchurch, New Zealand. 28 September 1998. http://www.cescomm.co.nz/

12.   "The LUC family of public-key cryptographic algorithms"; 28 September 1998; New Zealand; http:// www.luc.co.nz/

13.   Lucas functions as used in the context of cryptography are used in a way similar to exponentiation. However to quote Bob Silverman of Mitre Corporation, this "amounts to the discrete log problem for a PARTICULAR sub-field of a finite field". *Newsgroups: sci.crypt*, 29 December 1992, http://www.funet.fi/pub/crypt/mirrors/ ftp.dsi.unimi.it/LUC/luc_vs_rsa.

14.   "RPK Public Key Cryptography"; 28 September 1998; New Zealand; http://www.rpkusa.com.

15.   The Discrete Logarithm Problem (in the context of cryptography is also known as an elliptic curve system) requires calculating two unique integers (a public key and a private key) that will generate a specific shared point on an elliptic curve. To quote Roderick Simpson; that "final point, when converted to an integer, acts as the secret key and can be used to pass information securely". "It's precisely the inability of the attack algorithms to solve the elliptic logarithm problem that allows the user to get essentially the same security from a 163-bit ECC (elliptic curve crypto) system as they would from a 1024-bit RSA or DSA system". *Wired*, Issue 5, 12 December 1997, http://www.wired.com/wired/5.12/geek.html.

16.   Pointers to Cryptographic Software; 28 September 1998; Finland; http://www.cs.hut.fi/ssh/crypto/ software.html#crypto++.

17.   ITAR - International Trade in Arms Regulations, http://www.eff.org/pub/Crypto/ITAR_export/ itar_registry_govt.document.

18.   Executive Order 13026, "Administration of Export Controls on Encryption Products", 15 November 1996, http://www.bxa.doc.gov/Encryption/eo13026.htm.

19.   Bureau of Export Administration of the United States Commerce Department, Annual Report, March 5[estimated date], 1998.

20.   TeamWare Group; *TeamWARE Crypto*; Helsinki, Finland; 28 September 1998; http://www.teamw.com/ teamware/products/twcrypto.htm.

21.   F-Secure FileCrypto: Data Fellows Ltd, PL24 FIN-02231, Espoo, Finland. 28 September 1998. http:// www.Europe.DataFellows.com/f-secure/filecrypto

22.   Ascom Systec AG; *IDEA* (International Data Encryption Algorithm); 14 April 1998; Switzerland; http:// www.ascom.ch/systec/security/ideafuture.html.

23.   Counterpane Systems Inc., Windows 95-compatible S/MIME 40-bit RC2 Cracking ScreenSaver, http:// www.countepane.com/smime.html

24.   Mozilla Crypto Group; "Putting Strong Cryptography back into Mozilla"; 11 April 1998; http://mozilla-crypto.ssleay.org/index.php.

25.   Michael Stutz; "Cryptozilla Thwarts Feds Crypto Ban"; Wired; 3 April 1998; http://www.wired.com/news/ news/technology/story/11465.html; (6)Mozilla Crypto Group; "Mozilla Crypto Group Achieves SSL Enabled 'Cryptozilla' in under 1 Day"; 2 April 1998; http://mozilla-crypto.ssleay.org/press/19980401-02/index.php.

26.   Encryption: Impact on Law Enforcement, Federal Bureau of Investigaton, Information Resources Division, Quantico, Virginia, http://ww.jya.com/fbi-en7898.htm

ADDITIONAL SOURCES OF USEFUL INFORMATION:
27.   Schneier, Bruce, *Applied Cryptography*, 2nd Edition, New York, John Wiley & Sons, Inc., 1996, ISBN 0-471-11709-9.

28.   Schneier, Bruce, *E-MAIL SECURITY: How to Keep Your Electronic Messages Private*, New York, John Wiley & Sons, Inc., 1995, ISBN 0-471-05318-X.

Using Public Web Sites to Communicate with Suppliers

Dale Young, Ph.D.
Decision Sciences and MIS, Miami University, Oxford, Ohio 45056
Telephone (513)529-4472 Fax (513)529-9689 E-mail YoungLD@muohio.edu

ABSTRACT

The World Wide Web (Web) is dramatically affecting how organizations conduct business. The most significant dollar volume of business transactions on the Web, for the next several years, will be business-to-business sales. This study examined how Fortune 100 firms use their public Web sites to communicate with their suppliers. The study looked at the predominant categories of Web-based communication between Fortune 100 firms and their suppliers and identified the following categories: product quality and product price, electronic communications between trading partners, supplier diversity programs, supplier business relationships, and supplier resources.

INTRODUCTION

The World Wide Web (Web) is dramatically affecting how organizations conduct business. The most significant dollar volume of business transactions on the Web, for the next several years, will be business-to-business sales (IDC, 1998a). Organizations have found the Web to be a cost efficient and relatively secure means of interacting with trading partners. These trading partners include suppliers, customers, and third parties such as financial institutions. Because the use of the Web for business transactions is an important, emerging application of information technology, and because of the significant impact electronic commerce is expected to have on the U.S. and world economy in the near future, this research examines a single component of the on-line economy. This is a study of how Fortune 100 firms use their public Web sites to communicate with their suppliers.

BUSINESS-TO-BUSINESS ELECTRONIC COMMERCE

Electronic business is business-to-business, or business-to-consumer, commerce that takes place over the Internet. Deloitte and Touche defines electronic commerce using the term e-business. Their definition focuses on "Web-enabling core business processes" to more efficiently provide customer service and sell goods or services (Stewart, 1998). This study focuses on the communication that takes place between a supplier and the firm that uses the supplier's goods.

The dollar volume estimates for business-to-business activity across the Web are significant, between $400 billion by 2002 (IDC, 1998a) and $800 billion by 2003 (Essick, 1998). Before these transactions occur, there must be formal contacts and the establishment of a business relationship between the two trading partners. In the past a seller (e.g., a parts supplier) would make a personal contact, or respond in writing, to a buyer (e.g., an auto manufacturer). We are witnessing the electronic transformation of these interactions. Now a supplier can go to a manufacturer's Web site, get the detailed information required, and apply to become a trading partner on line. This research project focuses on how the large buyer organizations are "talking to" their suppliers through the Web.

Certainly there are other avenues firms have used for years to make these supplier contacts, such as buying offices, published guidelines for both existing and potential suppliers to follow, and formal requests (often called a "request for proposal"). But the Web itself is a new communication medium for firms to use in making these contacts. In the last three years businesses have actively sought to use the Internet, more specifically the Web, as a medium for commercial interaction.

The Focus of This Study

This project is purposely focused on supplier relationships. This subset of trading partner interactions enables a focus on how Fortune 100 firms interact with the companies that supply them raw materials for processing, or finished goods for resell. Because supplier firms tend to be smaller than the manufacturers or retailers they sell to, the Web sites in the study are those of firms that tend to dominate the trading relationship.

Businesses buy from suppliers, add value through a variety of processes, and offer goods or services to their customers. The business-to-customer relationship, which is at the opposite end of the supply chain from the business-to-supplier link, is much broader and is an entirely separate study. ("Customer" here means another business, not an individual consumer.) Excluded in this supplier study are Web sites such the oil companies that encourage site visitors to become a dealer for their gasoline products. Also excluded are commercial bank Web sites that offer businesses a variety of on-line banking products and services, and insurance companies that use the Web as a way of attracting potential agents. This study's focus on *public* sites excludes *internal* sites that are accessible to exiting suppliers by use of a password.

This paper reviews current surveys and projections about the status of business-to-business electronic commerce. It then describes the methodology used to collect data from the public Web sites of Fortune 100 firms. Following the data collection is the presentation of the findings and a discussion to give some additional meaning to the data.

CURRENT ELECTRONIC COMMERCE SURVEYS

The trading partner aspect of electronic commerce has been overlooked in the rush to put up Web sites and manage the technical details such as Web servers and bandwidth for incoming communication lines. Practitioner journals evaluate hardware and software used to build Web sites, run short case descriptions of how firms are managing issues such as security and transaction volume, and touch on business issues such as the effectiveness of Web advertising.

Electronic commerce is a small percentage of the total global economy today (Essick, 1998). Both IDC and the Organization for Economic Cooperation and Development predict that business-to-business commerce will constitute 80% of the on-line economy by 2002 (Essick, 1998; IDC, 1998a). IDC predicts strong growth in electronic commerce in both the United States and Western Europe (IDC, 1998b), but the largest percentage of on-line commerce will be conducted in the United States (Essick, 1998).

Business-to-consumer sales across the Web are a small portion of the total commercial activity on the Web today (eMarketer, 1998). The Web-only bookseller Amazon (on the Web at *Amazon.com*) is in direct competition with brick-and-mortar retailers such as Barnes and Noble. Although the firm has yet to turn a profit, Amazon has a higher stock market valuation than Barnes and Noble (Mayer, 1998). Other business-to-consumer sites on the Web that are gaining significant amounts of publicity include travel sites (e.g., *travelocity.com* and *1Travel.com*), music "stores" (e.g., *CDNow.com*), and the "portal" sites that started a few years ago as Web search engines (e.g., *Yahoo.com* and *Netcenter.com*).

Corporations are using their external Web sites for a variety of reasons, including: publicity, trading partner support, revenue generation, advertising, and subscriptions (Gardner, 1998). In the *Internet World* survey (Gardner, 1998) 60% of the sites are being used for customer or business partner support. In contrast, less than 34% of the Web sites are used for direct revenue generation through transactions such as selling merchandise.

Electronic commerce enables efficient internal processes, dramatic changes in the types of services offered, and a global reach for a firm's products and services (Stewart, 1998). Electronic commerce is more than simply a technology change, "it's about the changes in institutions that must take place to take advantage of this global network. It's forcing CEOs to think about their businesses in very different ways" (Wilder, 1998). Businesses are now able to build electronic relationships with anyone in their supply chain. The first step in building these electronic relationships is to set up direct channels to trading partners such as suppliers (Stewart, 1998). Companies can better manage their supply chain by soliciting bids from a global set of suppliers, using these established electronic channels, and reduce cycle times (Stewart, 1998).

In summary, business-to-business commerce is expected to be a significant portion of the rapidly growing electronic commerce market for the next several years. A number of businesses are already using public Web sites to interact with trading partners. These trading partner interactions enable new business processes, especially concerning the procurement of goods and services. The role of trading partner relationships is therefore an important component of the emerging digital economy. Examining public Web sites is one way of determining how organizations interact with the trading partners who supply them goods and services.

RESEARCH METHODOLOGY

This is exploratory research. The unit of analysis is the public Web site at each Fortune 100 firm. The goal of this study is to examine and categorize the content of Web-based communications of large corporations to their suppliers.

An obvious question is "Why select Fortune 100 firms?" There are two reasons - convenience and resources. The "convenience" argument is simple; the Fortune list is widely accepted in the business and academic communities, it is easy to find, and there is a wealth of company data included with each year's Fortune rankings. The "resources" argument acknowledges that these firms are large, they have the funds to cover the development and maintenance of a public Web site, and they are dominant in the trading relationship (because of their size) and so can "tell" suppliers how business transactions are to take place.

The findings from this study will be of interest to both practitioners and academics, especially those working with Internet-based electronic commerce. This study seeks to answer the following research questions:

RQ1: What are the predominant categories of Web-based communication by Fortune 100 organizations to their suppliers?

RQ2: What business objectives of Fortune 100 firms are suggested by the categories of Web-based communication to their suppliers?

In simplest terms these questions ask: What are you saying to your suppliers?, and Why are you saying this? The first research question is answered by categorizing the content of Web site supplier communication. For example, one category is communication to prospective trading partners that are minority/female owned businesses. The second question explores business objectives. Why would a retailer tell a potential supplier that specific merchandise must be price competitive with goods already in the store?

This project requires several distinct steps to identify specific Web sites and then to perform a content analysis on the Web pages of the sites where firms interact with current or potential suppliers. The Web site addresses (i.e., the Uniform Resource Locator) for most of the firms on the 1998 Fortune 500 list are found at the Pathfinder site (Pathfinder.com). This study looks at the first 100 firms on the list. When the Web site address was missing from the Pathfinder data, the Web search engine AltaVista was used to find the address. Pathfinder also lists data such as annual sales and earnings, and number of employees.

The following steps were taken to collect the data for this study:
• Created/tested a survey form used to perform the review of the Fortune 100 public Web sites.
• Visited each Fortune 100 Web site and conducted the initial site review using the tested survey form.
• Completed a content analysis of the sections of the Fortune 100 sites where supplier communications were identified in the initial site review.

Several graduate students participated in the development and testing of the survey form on a random sample of the Fortune 100 sites.

The content analysis requires reading each of the pages with trading partner content on each Web site where supplier relationships are discussed. While reading I noted recurring topics across sites, topics that are unique to a company, the methods firms use to encourage additional contacts (e.g., electronic mail), the presence or absence of secured areas (requiring a sign-on by the trading partner), and comments to encourage business with minority/female-owned businesses. Strauss (1987) discusses this type of coding of published materials where a body of material is categorized, internal and external comparisons are made, and similarities and differences are explored before the researcher draws conclusions about the topic being studied.

FINDINGS

At the time this survey was taken fifteen firms in the Fortune 100 make comments to suppliers using their public Web sites. These are multi-billion dollar firms operating in ten different industries. The list contains four retailers, two companies in the electronics business, two aerospace firms, and one firm each in seven other industries.

Table 1: Fortune 100 Companies with Supplier Comments on their Public Web Site			
Rank	Company	Industry	Supplier Section on Web Site
1	General Motors	Motor Vehicles & Parts	Global Supplier Network
4	Wal-Mart	General Merchandisers	Vendor Proposal Guide
5	General Electric	Electronics	Trading Partner Network
8	Mobil	Petroleum Refining	U.S. Supplier Diversity Policy
11	Boeing	Aerospace	Working Together w/ Suppliers
13	State Farm	Insurance	EDI Homepage – Purchasing
23	Kmart	General Merchandisers	Kmart Vendor Communications
25	JC Penny	General Merchandisers	The Partnership Program
32	Lockheed Martin	Aerospace	Small Business Opportunity
55	USX/US Steel	Steel	Supplier Information
69	Columbia/HCA	Healthcare	Info. for Prospective Vendors
76	Nabisco	Food	Building Supplier Diversity
83	Federated	General Merchandisers	Accelerated Sales & Stock Turn
90	Sprint	Telecommunications	Supplier Diversity
100	Raytheon	Electronics	Small Business Programs

Category	Description	Companies Mentioning	% of Sites
Product Pricing	Vendor must be price competitive	GM, Wal-Mart, GE, Kmart, Columbia, Sprint	40%
Product Quality	Firms mention high or consistent quality	GM, Wal-Mart, Kmart, US Steel, Columbia, Nabisco, Sprint	47%
Small, Minority, Women-owned Business	Programs to certify & develop business with small firms	GM, Wal-Mart, Mobil, Boeing, Kmart, JC Penny, Lockheed, Columbia, Nabisco, Sprint, Raytheon	73%
Electronic Order Linkages	EDI support is often required	GM, Wal-Mart, GE, Boeing, State Farm, Kmart, JC Penny, Columbia, Federated	60%
Sales, Inventory, & Payment Data	Data available in password-protected areas of site	GM, Wal-Mart, Kmart, JC Penny, Columbia, Federated	40%

Table 2: Most Frequent Categories of Supplier Communication

The firms range in revenue from General Motors ($178 billion) to Raytheon ($13.7 billion). Boeing and Columbia both reported a loss for the year; the other thirteen firms reported profits for 1997.

Table 1 lists in order by 1998 Fortune ranking firms that use their public Web sites to communicate with existing or prospective suppliers. Note that there is little consistency in how these large firms title the Web pages where they "talk to" their suppliers. These fifteen firms mention several different issues in their communications with suppliers. The most frequently mentioned categories of these communications are product price and product quality, minority programs, and electronic linkages with trading partners.

Table 2 lists the categories of communication to suppliers that appear on five or more (i.e., at least one-third) of the Web sites in the study. Note that under the heading "Percentage of Sites" many firms make statements in multiple categories.

The issues of *price competitiveness and product quality* are critical, and are often mentioned on the same Web page. Columbia/HCA uses the terms "quality and cost effectiveness" together. Columbia/HCA states that "the supplier is encouraged to use creative and innovative approaches in order to improve service and quality, and to contain costs." Sprint seeks the "best value overall" covering quality, service, delivery, and pricing. GM uses the terms "pharmaceutical mentality" when discussing quality and "achieve continuous price reductions" when discussing pricing. Wal-Mart's stated goal is "to drive costs out of the total system."

A number of the Fortune 100 firms use their public Web sites to develop business with *small, minority, and women-owned businesses*. This is the category that received the most frequent number of mentions in these Web sites. This section of a Web site often contains a letter from the company president/CEO as a way of expressing company commitment to the program. Vendors are asked to provide proof or certification from a government agency that they qualify to do business in this category. JC Penney mentions certification by the National Minority Supplier Development Council and the Women's Business Enterprise National Council. Sprint adds "disabled veteran-owned business" to their listing. In response to government regulations, Raytheon wants small/women-owned firms, handicapped workshops, and minority institutions to participate and says "We want to make it easy for you to join our team." Suppliers in the United States must source five percent of their GM business with minority companies.

Several firms require *electronic linkages for ordering*. Federated charges a fee to vendors for sending paper invoices. State Farm uses and encourages EDI but does not require it. Columbia tells suppliers they must interface into Columbia/HCA's Electronic Order Entry System. Wal-Mart "expects its merchandise suppliers to be able to participate in EDI transactions once they become Wal-Mart vendors and are assigned a specific Vendor Number." GE's Trading Process Network has evolved from an internal system to an external service "that enables buyers and sellers to do business-to-business electronic commerce."

Firms are concerned about their ability to *share sales and payment data electronically* with suppliers. All four retailers in the study (Wal-Mart, Kmart, Federated, and JC Penny) provide vendors with sales, inventory, and payment or accounts payable data. These data are in password-protected areas of the site. Wal-Mart has a Web-based application called "Retail Link" that enables vendors to "...plan, execute, and analyze their business and thus provide better service to our common customers."

Several other issues are less frequently mentioned but equally as important as those listed in Table 2. The four retailers (Wal-Mart, Kmart, Federated, and JC Penny) note the importance of *labor law compliance* by vendors. GM, Boeing, Federated, and Kmart discourage *gifts to company employees* from vendors. Columbia/HCA tells vendors they must be able to handle the *volume of orders* they will send; Columbia/HCA and Nabisco include Web-based questionnaires that help determine the *financial stability* of prospective vendors. GM, Wal-Mart, and JC Penny require suppliers to be *listed with Dun and Bradstreet*. Columbia and Nabisco also look for vendors who can provide *national distribution* of products and services, as opposed to local or regional coverage. (Wal-Mart asks suppliers about "geographic service region" in the on-line questionnaire.) Columbia/HCA specifies a national account manager and a *single point of contact* between themselves and the vendor.

The first research question asks about the predominant categories of Web-based communication between Fortune 100 firms and their suppliers. This exploratory study has identified the following categories:

- product quality and product price,
- electronic communications between trading partners,
- supplier diversity programs,
- supplier business relationships (such as labor law compliance and gift policies), and
- supplier resources (to fill orders on time, provide nation-wide coverage, financial stability).

The first three items appear on multiple sites (i.e., over one third); the individual components of the last two items on the list appear less frequently. These large firms are telling suppliers what they want in supplies/components and raw materials, how interactions are to take place, and what their expectations are for conducting the business relationship. These categories also reveal the desire of these firms to trade with a diverse set of suppliers.

The second research question deals with business objectives that are suggested by the predominant categories of communication.

- The quality and price category acknowledges competitive pressures and both consumer and business demand for value in products. Because the end consumer is value conscious, manufacturers and retailers must demand value from their supplier firms.
- Stressing electronic interactions reveals a desire to improve internal efficiency and to lower cycle times. Placing sales and inventory data on-line assist vendors in keeping inventory low without running out of needed stock.
- Diversity programs are driven by government mandate and by a desire to be an exemplary corporate citizen. The president's letters and other pages reveal these joint objectives for supplier diversity.
- The business relationship category suggests that firms are concerned about negative publicity and legal action arising from supplier business practices that are either illegal or unethical. This issue is especially important to retailers that are buying goods produced in other countries.
- Finally, the resource category expresses a concern about the ability of the supplier to deliver contracted products and services over an extended period of time.

In summary, the business objectives revealed by these Web-based communications cover:

- the demand for value generated by the competitive environment,
- internal efficiency and the need to maintain critical stock levels to satisfy customers,
- corporate citizenship and avoidance of negative publicity, and
- the desire for long-term, stable relationships with financially sound trading partners.

DISCUSSION

Some of these findings are not surprising. Competition is driving total quality initiatives and certification programs such as ISO 9000. Large manufacturers and retailers have been demanding EDI compliance from suppliers for several years. The public Web site of large corporations is an extension of existing corporate communications and policies for both product quality/price and electronic interactions.

The resource requirement and diversity programs seem to be in conflict. Small or disadvantaged businesses may have a problem meeting the financial and production requirements listed on the application forms appearing at these Web sites. Public Web sites do seem to be a popular way to publicize a firm's desired to do business with minority and women-owned suppliers.

Why is the sample so small? Only 15% of the Fortune 100 Web sites featured public access to supplier information. Other large manufacturers and retailers on the Fortune 100 list certainly have established programs in place to make these types of communications to their suppliers. They have chosen, for reasons not explored in this study, to use their public Web site for other types of communications than the ones listed here. Given the nature of these communications, many firms that buy raw materials or products for resell should be including these categories somewhere on their public Web pages.

Public Web sites certainly seem to be an appropriate forum for presenting this form of communication. These Web sites are an efficient means of communication to trading partners who are Web-enabled. If a supplier has the resources to be EDI enabled, they most likely have some type of link to the Internet. The policies are available for public viewing; diversity programs, for instance, may help to improve the public image of the firm. Listing corporate charitable contributions is a related way some firms use their Web sites for "corporate citizenship" publicity.

Sharing sales and inventory data in password-protected areas of a Web site is efficient, but it also requires a rethinking of business relationships. The retailers and others who share this data are opening up their internal, operational databases to trading partners. This action certainly involves a higher level of trust than previous arms-length interactions.

Firms place materials on a Web site by direct choice. Because this supplier content is a matter of choice, the categories of information identified in this study are important issues to these firms. Researchers should be careful about drawing conclusions based on the frequency of appearance of specific items on a limited number of company Web sites. However, when 60-70% of extremely large firms in a sample mention the same items, in this case minority programs and electronic ordering, we should infer that that these issues represent critical operational matters that are recognized at the highest executive levels in these firms.

LIMITATIONS AND CONCLUSIONS

There are some obvious limitations to this study in its current stage. The sample is very small (i.e., fifteen firms), which reduces the generalizability of the findings. Public Web sites change daily so a survey of Fortune 100 firms taken at a different date will probably find other companies that have added these types of communications to their sites, and some that may have removed these types of supplier communications. The researcher did not seek access to "private" sites that require a user id/log-in to these Web sites. The study is limited to a particular group of trading partners - suppliers. Other forms of trading partner communications, not reviewed in this study, are present on public Web sites. Despite these limitations, the study did uncover some interesting forms of public communications between very large buying firms and their current or prospective suppliers.

The findings from this study will be of interest to academics who study electronic commerce and trading partner interactions. The findings will be valuable to practitioners who manage Web sites and who seek to develop closer relationships with existing and potential trading partners using outlets such as public Web sites. The findings should encourage practitioners to include these types of communications on their public Web sites, because of the example of the Fortune 100 firms in this study.

REFERENCES

EMarketer.com (1998). http://www.emarketer.com/estats/welcome.html

Essick, K. (1998). "E-commerce Will Play Small Part in Global Economy." The Industry Standard, September 28, 1998, http://www.thestandard.net

Gardner, E. (1998). "More Work - But More Money." *Internet World*, October 5, 1998.

IDC, International Data Corporation (1998a). "IDC's Internet Commerce Market Model® Predicts Buyers on the Web Will Increase Nearly Tenfold by 2002." http://www.idc.com/

IDC, (1998b). "Internet Commerce Revenues in Western Europe to Reach $30 Billion by 2001." http://www.idc.com/

Mayer, C. (1998). "Does Amazon.com = 2 Barnes & Nobles?" New York Times on the Web, July 19, 1998. http://www.nytimes.com/library/tech/98/07/biztech/articles/19amazon.html

Pathfinder.com (1998). http://pathfinder.com/fortune/fortune500/500list.html

Stewart, T. (1998). "The E-Business Tidal Wave." http://www.deloitte.com/tidalwave/

Strauss, A. (1987). *Qualitative Analysis for Social Scientists*. Cambridge University Press, New York.

Wilder, C. (1998). "IBM's Gerstner: Overcome Fear of Internet." *Information Week*, May 28, 1998.

Marketing for E-Commerce

Sana'a AlMoumen

Computing Department, Lancaster University, Lancaster LA1 4YR, UK

E-mail: sanaa@comp.lancs.ac.uk, Tel: +44-1524 65201 Ext. 94537, Fax: +44-1524 593608

Ian Sommerville

Computing Department, Lancaster University, Lancaster LA1 4YR, UK

E-mail: is@comp.lancs.ac.uk, Tel: +44-1524 593795, Fax: +44 1524 593608

EXTENDED ABSTRACT

In our research, we are concerned with the principles and the techniques of marketing as currently practiced through commercial web sites. The objective of the work is to understand the requirements of marketing and to provide guidelines on how these can be reflected on the design of web sites to support e-commerce. This work has been conducted as part of a long term research goal, to find an effective approach by which the requirements for e-commerce systems can be efficiently specified, which viewpoints should be considered, and how these may affect the required design of e-commerce systems. The main goal of this research is to provide guidance to developers of e-commerce sites on marketing issues and how these issues may influence the design of e-commerce systems. We believe that such guidance is necessary because the competition to be first on the Web has affected the quality level of the services and products promoted by many organizations. Most reports suggest that promoters are disappointed with the current level of online sales . In many cases, it seems that web site designers are unaware of the dif ferent marketing techniques that organizations can apply to meet their customers' needs, and to get the full benefit of Web features that support effective interaction with their customers. Good e-commerce marketing practice offers unique Web services that maintain customer loyalty and motivates them to re-visit the web site. Customers should enjoy the flow of the information browsed and the ease of accessibility. Organizations may get them involved interactively in the marketing process, collect customer feedback and give them the power to participate in keeping the web site active. Good web site design can mean that organizations can use their customers to promote their products and services by supporting communication facilities that allow them to share their experience in using the firm's products.

BACKGROUND INFORMATION

Organizations increasingly turn to the Internet with great expectations for their business development, and business performance. The Internet offers the opportunity to increase revenues by targeting new global markets and web managers will spend $3.5 billion for Web development products and services in 1999, up from the $1.2 billion expected in 1998. Most of that spending has to do with online transaction systems and other needs of consumer-directed web sites (ActivMedia 1998).

"Doing business on the Web is really doing business as usual with a twist. The twist is using the powerful capabilities of the Web to build virtual personal relationships with customers, that begins with effective marketing". The purpose of the presented work is to introduce an approach by which the requirements of a traditional marketing viewpoint can be elicited with a view to reflecting these requirements in the design of an e-commerce system.

DISCUSSION OF THE WORK

In this paper we discuss an initial analysis of how businesses are using their Web sites to market their products (goods/ services), how they invest on the Web to achieve their strategy's goals and how to facilitate their interaction with customers. For the purpose of our work, we have adapted some of the marketing models and applied them systematically in the analysis of e-commerce web sites. An analysis of web sites for e-commerce from a marketing perspective can be useful in two ways: firstly, as guidance to assess an existing e-commerce system for the purpose of improvement, secondly, as an analysis approach to provide input to a new design for e-commerce systems.

In our approach, we have concerned the importance of studying how of the organization strategy influences the design of a commercial Web site that aims towards globalization of the business. We have investigated the marketing principles that should influence the design of web sites for e-commerce. The work is based on a common marketing strategic model, and we have analyzed two commercial web sites that appear to be based on different marketing strategies. Depending on the implications of the web business activity classification, we have applied one of the common marketing mix models, that is appropriate for marketing services; the (six Ps). The 'six Ps' (product, price, promotion, place, people, and process) marketing mix has been inherited from the basic marketing mix framework the (four Ps namely: product, price, promotion, place), which has been subject to some refinement for service marketing. The two cases that have been assessed have been drawn from the same business segment, which is the computer industry (manufacturing/retailing): The "Dell Computer Corporation" http://www.dell.com, and the "Tiny Computers" Web site "http://www.tiny.com/index.html". Our assessment has been conducted by analyzing some important service characteristics. In addition, the analysis has examined the applicable target market variables and tactics through the adopted models. Our analysis has indicated how far the web functions, services or features have been based on marketing components and how these components have been represented on the web to target a potential customer segment or segments. We also discuss the extent to which these organizations have been successful in applying an appropriate positioning strategy for their marketing mix.

The analysis also assesses the management of the relationship (interactivity, accessibility, support, time, availability and so on), between the organization and its web customers. "The potential rewards of the marketing process on the web are great, but the challenge lies in experimenting with interactivity on the Web to learn how to establish a variety relationship with each customer". In addition, we have studied in detail how the applied techniques facilitates the communication with the Web site users, and what is the level of interaction has been achieved through the web site services that we have studied.

It appears to us from our analysis of the two cases of Web sites-according to our approach in discovering the requirements of marketing, that the Dell Computers site has been clearly influenced by marketing considerations planned for an effective positioning strategy through their Web site, and focused on providing many Web services for customer support and communication for selling, tracking orders, facilitating the payment procedure, providing sufficient information for both customers, investors and other business relationships, that is by applying a cost effective strategy. However, there were some flaws in representing some of the marketing mix components in the site design. By contrast, the other site that we analyzed seemed to have been designed from a solely technical perspective and showed very little evidence of input from marketing.

CONCLUSION

Our work on the requirement engineering process for E-commerce from the marketing viewpoint revealed a significant relationship between the business strategy concerns, policies, procedures, the differential advantage of the marketing mix and the Web-based business success that raise the profitability of the electronic commerce system. This success can be achieved by a well specified Web site design that can be derived from the business strategy and the application of a well-planned poisoning strategy for the marketing mix components. We have found that by following our approach in requirement discovery, a lot of marketing components can be defined and specified according to the business goals, concerns, and capabilities. Our work provides guidelines in developing an effective electronic commerce Web site. We have introduced some solutions to overcome Web-based marketing problems. We have defined the scope of focus where Web site developers should take essential part in specifying the requirements that should be applied in building such kind of commercial Web site. As we have seen, that there is a strong relation between the success of a Web-based business-as Dell Web site case-and the application of the requirement specification for the positioning strategy of the business marketing mix "differential advantage" components. In addition, we have found that managing the relationships with customers or businesses through an effective services design, is the main issue that should be carefully designed in order to overcome all the Web-based services implications.

Further information about the work is available from; http://www.comp.lancs.ac.uk/computing/research/cseg/98_rep.html - (CSEG/18/98), or ftp://ftp.comp.lancs.ac.uk/pub/reports/1998/CSEG.18.98.pdf.

The Influence of National Culture on Attitudes Towards Information Ethics: A Comparative Study

Abdulridha Alshawaf
College of Adminstrative Sciences, Kuwait University
Alshawaf@kuc01.kuniv.edu

Ajay Adhikari
Kogod Gollege of Business Administration, American University
aadhika@american.edu

Advances in technology and the globalization of business have propelled us in the information age. While information technology has served as a catalyst in facilitating and speeding up local and global communication it has also given rise to problems and issues surrounding its use. A number of factors (political, technical, and cultural) have been suggested as capable of hindering the use and international dissemination of information technology (Hill et al. 1998; Eining & Lee 1997). Of these factors, the cultural factor may be the most intractable given that culture imbues the social, religious, and political mores of a society and is learned rather than logically transmitted and is, therefore, difficult to change (Belkaoui 1990; Hofstede 1980).

The purpose of this project is two fold: to examine the role of culture on information technology and, to investigate whether the culture of the work place (organizational culture) influences attitudes towards information technology. The research instrument for the study will be adapted from Eining and Lee (1997) and will consist of four case scenarios dealing with information ethics issues (privacy, accuracy, property, and access). The research instrument will be administered to upper-level business students at Kuwait University and an American University. Additionally, employees of Kuwaiti banks will also be targeted. The responses of Kuwaiti students will be compared with those of the U.S. students on social issues surrounding information technology. The responses of Kuwaiti students and banks' employees will be contrasted to isolate effects due to experience.

The information provided by the study will be useful in increasing our understanding of how culture impacts IT related ethical issues. This is important in the context of the development and marketing of software packages; international information technology transfer; and the debate on intellectual property rights.

A New Framework for Strategic Information Management

Dr. Okan Geray

Bogazici University MIS Dept. , Suadiye Kaptan Arif sok. No: 9/22, 81070 Istanbul TURKEY

Tel: (90) (216) 3616042, Fax: (90) (212) 2659813, E-mail: gerayoka@boun.edu.tr

Mehmet N. Aydin

Bogazici University MIS Dept., Bogazici University, Hisar Campus, B.229, Bebek, Istanbul TURKEY

Tel: (90) (212) 2631540-1935, Fax: (90) (212) 2659813, E-Mail: aydmehme@boun.edu.tr

ABSTRACT

In this paper, we establish a new formal Strategic Information Management (SIM) Process to achieve sustainable competitive advantage. A new information management framework is established to aid in strategic decision making. Strategic Information Management is explained in this new context and parallels are drawn from classical Strategic Management (SM) theory. The suggested Strategic Information Management process entails identification, analysis, choice and implementation of strategic information options. A set of criteria has been defined to evaluate the competitive advantage of strategic information options. Trade offs in SIM process have been illustrated with simple examples. This paper treats information management from a strategic perspective. However, the proposed SIM process handles strategic, tactical and operational level bi-directional information flows in a structured and well-organised manner. We believe that strategic management coupled with the suggested formal SIM process will be much more effective. Essentially, the SIM process will form the solid underlying infrastructure and framework for strategic management.

INTRODUCTION

Strategic management has played a key role in organizations. In the past few decades, it has been applied to business context with varying results. Several definitions of strategy [1], [2], [3], [4] involve decision making and planning in a certain time frame with respect to changing external and internal conditions. Strategic management (SM) is an approach for businesses to cope with changing external environments, markets, stakeholders, resources, etc.

Organizations establish a vision based on their core values, core purpose and goals [5]. In the face of challenging complex and dynamic environments, they formulate strategies to achieve their long-term vision. Strategic management (SM) can be regarded as a process to define a vision and to steer an organization in the direction of its defined vision from its current state. SM process involves three main steps: strategic analysis, strategic choice and strategic implementation [4]. In order to carry out these three steps in the SM process organizations have to acquire, analyze and make use of relevant, consistent, accurate, timely and affordable information. Hence information plays a crucial role in formulating and implementing a strategy.

In this paper we aim to develop an approach to integrate information management with SM. A new formal process, namely strategic information management (SIM) process, is recommended for more effective information management. The SIM process identifies and aims to provide and manage required information in the SM process. The suggested SIM process also enables proper implementation of formulated strategy by aligning information systems with strategic goals and objectives.

THE STRATEGIC MANAGEMENT PROCESS

In this section we will focus on different aspects and information requirements of the SM process. Table 1 shows the main steps and some sample sub-steps and approaches in a formal SM process. One can easily notice that the formal application of the SM process will entail information from many sources. The analysis performed in the SM process will require information from possibly both internal and external sources. Fundamentally, information will guide the strategic decision-making.

Consequently the SM process needs to identify its own information requirements. In this paper we suggest a new process, namely strategic information management (SIM) process, which will provide the required information to the SM process after a systematic and thorough analysis.

THE STRATEGIC INFORMATION MANAGEMENT PROCESS

Organizations need information to carry out the approaches used in the SM process shown in Table 1. The strategic analysis, choice and implementation steps will all require information and information-related changes. The first two of these steps, namely strategic analysis and strategic choice, will need to acquire information. On the other hand the last step in the SM process, strategic implementation, may need to lay out a new information infrastructure and reshuffle the information flow in an organization. The SIM process is responsible for determining strategic information options to satisfy all the information requirements of the SM process. In other words, for each SM process information requirement the SIM process will generate, evaluate and determine the best strategic information option. Therefore the SIM process will act as a supplementary process to the SM process, and will interact and interrelate with it as shown in Figure 1.

	Table 1. Strategic Management in a Nutshell	
Strategic Management Step	Substeps	Approach
1. Strategic Analysis	Industry Structure Analysis	Porter's five forces [3], structure-conduct-performance analysis, strategic triangle [2], supply chain analysis, PEST analysis, competitor analysis, etc.
	Product\Market Analysis	Size and growth of the market, product and market segmentation, demand and supply structure, etc.
	Resource and strategic capability analysis	Value Chain analysis [6], SWOT analysis, core competencies, operational and organizational assessment, etc.
	Culture and stakeholder expectations analysis	Core values, core purpose, mission, stakeholder analysis, etc.
2. Strategic Choice	Strategic option generation	Porter's generic strategies [3], mergers, acquisitions, market based approaches, etc.
	Evaluation and decision making	Feasibility, suitability, decision trees, scenarios, cost benefit analysis, etc.
3. Strategic Implementation	Planning and Allocating Resources	Operational and process design, financial, manpower, asset planning, etc.
	Organization Structure determination	Structure design, definition of roles and responsibilities, management systems and control, etc.
	Change Management	Planning the transition, commitment and buy-in, training, recruitment, etc.

Strategic Information Analysis

The information requirements of the first two steps of the SM process (strategic analysis and strategic choice) will be input to the SIM process. The SM process may require obtaining information about the industry structure, stakeholders, competitors, internal capabilities, etc. The SIM process will analyze these requirements. This analysis step devotes time to determine the underlying issues for information sourcing and capability. Any insight and methodological approach will be extremely valuable at this stage. Careful and comprehensive analysis will be a prerequisite for forming sensible strategic information options at the next stage. Internal and external sources of information may need to be investigated meticulously. Finally at the end of this analysis step the SIM process will be ready to form alternatives for each required information of the SM process.

Strategic Information Choice

After the analysis step, the SIM process will generate the strategic information options to obtain the required information of the SM process. These options among many other things may include the source, the retrieval, the analysis and the presentation aspects of the information.

For example the SM process of a manufacturing firm may require information about the market shares of competitors in a given industry. This is an example of information requirement of the SM process. The SIM process will take this requirement as input and will generate strategic information options to provide this required information to the SM process. After a careful analysis, the strategic information options of the firm might be:

• to carry out its own market research through its own marketing organization;
• to use a third-party market research firm;
• to cooperate with its competitors to disclose market share information;
• to form alliances with its own distribution and sales channels to provide market share information, etc.

In this illustrative example the source aspect of the information is emphasized, however these options will be detailed even further within the SIM process. The above strategic information options are only for the "market shares of competitors in the industry" information requirement. The SM process may in general require internal (cost, productivity, sales, process, performance, etc.) or external (benchmarking, stakeholder, industry, etc.) information. The SIM process will generate strategic information options for all the required information from the SM process.

Now that the required information from the SM process and the corresponding strategic information options from the SIM process are available, the SIM process will evaluate its own strategic information options. The purpose of this step is to find out the best corresponding strategic information option for each and every information requirement of the SM process. Naturally the SIM process will need a set of criteria to evaluate the strategic information options. In this paper we propose four main criteria for the evaluation phase:

1. **Content of the information:** This criterion refers to the suitability and the reliability of the strategic information option to satisfy the information requirement of the SM process.

2. **Timeliness of the information:** This criterion measures whether the strategic information option provides the required information at the required time, and if necessary, at distinct required time intervals.

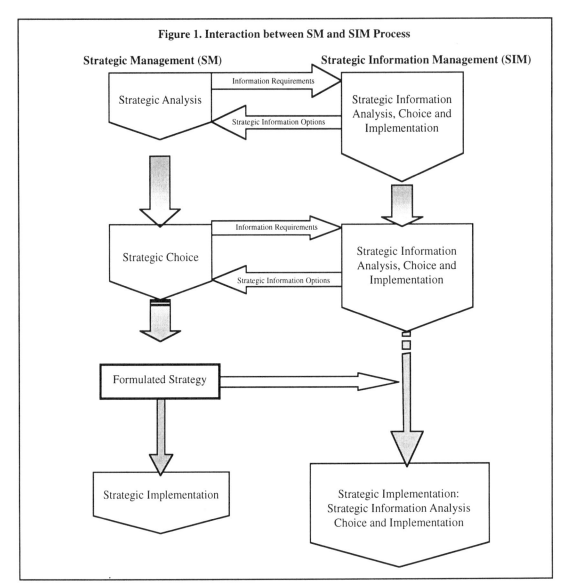

Figure 1. Interaction between SM and SIM Process

3. Location of the information: This criterion indicates whether the strategic information option will provide the required information at the right place, i.e. whether whoever needs the information will acquire it or not.

4. Cost of the information: This criterion shows at what cost the strategic information option provides the required information. This cost figure includes all the extra resources, infrastructure, prerequisites, etc. to provide the required information.

These criteria enable a cost/benefit analysis of the strategic information options. Each option must be evaluated based on these criteria. The strategic information options will differ in terms of these criteria. During this evaluation phase, organizations may use different schemes to determine the best strategic information options (more than one due to multiple information requirements, i.e. one best for each requirement). Finally after the evaluation step, the SIM process will determine the best strategic information option for each required information of the SM process.

Strategic Information Implementation

The strategic information choice step in the SIM process determines the best strategic information options (one for each information requirement of the SM process). The next step is to implement all the best options. At this step the SIM process will take all the actions necessary to implement the best strategic information options. Key tasks and resources are identified and planned. Any information flow and infrastructure related issues are determined and necessary changes are made. Sometimes the information requirements from the SM process may easily be obtained through a simple internal report, for example last year's sales and operating profit. But sometimes it may require obtaining external market insight and data, which may only be provided by another organization.

Note that the implementation of best strategic information options will, in turn, provide the required information to the SM process. Having been equipped with the required information, the SM process can now perform its own strategic analysis and strategic choice steps. These steps will employ the information obtained from the best strategic information options. A strategy will eventually be formulated as a result of these two steps in the SM process [4].

The last step in the SM process is concerned with the implementation of the formulated strategy. Depending on the formulated strategy, the SM process may entail tactical, operational and organizational changes. The SM process should come up with detailed implementation plans regarding all those changes. Key performance measures for the processes and the organization should be determined based on the vision and the new formulated strategy. The value-based measures [7] and balanced scorecard [8] are just two examples of determining such key performance measures. Performance measures should normally be determined for all entities affected by the formulated strategy within the organization. Basically this is a hierarchical strategic mapping between the performance measures and the organizational entities. The ultimate aim is to align the organizational activities with the strategic objectives of an organization.

Strategy Implementation: Strategic Information Analysis, Choice and Implementation

Strategic implementation in the SM process also involves information management. Once again the SM process will input its results, this time the formulated strategy, to the SIM process. The SIM process will identify information (and/or data) requirements within the organization resulting from the formulated strategy in the SM process. This identification phase must be thought out and planned very carefully. The information implications of the formulated strategy must be assessed and mapped to all affected entities within the organization. Any gap between the current and the desired information requirements must be analyzed scrupulously. This conceptual phase will then yield the final information requirements. This strategic information analysis phase will aid the information managers to see the rationale behind formulated strategies.

Having identified the information requirements, the SIM process will proceed to find alternate ways of creating information systems to implement the formulated strategy. In other words the SIM process will then generate strategic information options to implement the information requirements. Since various information requirements will arise for different entities within the organization, the SIM process might end up with several different strategic information options. Even coexisting complementary solutions may result as a viable strategic information option (for ex. a computer information system may coexist with a manual system).

For example a firm with multiple global distribution centers might decide to reduce its inventory cost as a generic cost reduction strategy. This strategy is the result of the SM process. SM process also determines key performance indicators (such as the inventory levels of distribution centers, transportation costs, etc.). To implement this strategy, the SIM process first determines all the information requirements within the organization, that is who needs what information and when. This identification is certainly a tedious and cumbersome step. Then the SIM process generates the following strategic information options:

- A decentralized and local information system for every distribution center;
- A decentralized information system for every distribution center interconnected through batch interfaces;
- A centralized on-line enterprise requirements planning (ERP) system among all distribution centers.

Note that without further analysis it is impossible to state which strategic information option is the best one to implement the generic cost reduction strategy. Therefore the SIM process needs to evaluate all the strategic information options. This step is analogous to previous strategic information choice step explained in Section 3.2. The SIM process once again uses the same set of four criteria as explained in Section 3.2 to determine the best strategic information option. At this evaluation step, strategic information options will be weighed against each other. The feasibility and the suitability of each option will be assessed. Different organizations may utilize different techniques for selecting the best option. Analytical techniques, simple models, sensible judgment, etc. may all be employed in arriving at the best option. As a result of this evaluation step, the organization determines the best strategic information option to implement the formulated strategy. Finally the SIM process is responsible for ensuring a proper and smooth information infrastructure implementation for the SM process. The size of this strategic information implementation step differs depending on the formulated strategy in the SM process. Some strategies will involve simple information processing changes; some will involve major information infrastructure changes accompanied by process reengineering and organizational changes. The SIM process is responsible for identifying, planning and accomplishing all the information related changes to implement the formulated strategy in the SM process.

ADVANTAGES OF THE SIM PROCESS

The suggested SIM process is a formal approach to information management. The SIM process enables an organization to view information management from a strategic perspective. The close interaction with the SM process will bridge the gap between information systems and top management. It will provide a particular context in which information management will be crucial to understand from the policy and decision-makers' perspective.

With a well-thought and well-implemented information system, the formulated strategy will be much easier to implement, track and if necessary modify. The SIM process, when carried out intact in conjunction with the SM process, will form a solid framework for achieving tangible results during the implementation of the formulated strategy. The harmony and alignment among organization, strategy and information blocks in Figure 2 play a critical role in the SM process. The SIM process intends to create a new and better information structure integrated with the strategic management of an organization. A properly designed information system will play a key role in enabling the critical information flow within an organization.

The SM coupled with the SIM process will focus on strategic performance implementation. The SIM process with the evaluation of strategic information options will deliver cost effective and beneficial strategic execution results.

CONCLUSION

In this paper we have established a new formal strategic information management process. We have identified linkages of this process with the strategic management process. The proper application of this process will ensure alignment of information systems with the strategic goals and objectives of the organization. The suggested SIM process is a step-by-step approach requiring close interaction with the SM process.

The SIM process may prove to be a powerful capability in strategy execution. In today's business world, information management is becoming a significant competency. Having the right information at the right place and time with the right cost may turn out to be a sustainable competitive advantage. Those organizations that know how to manage information in line with their visions and strategies will most likely be the survivors of tomorrow. The SIM is a simple tool to achieve this.

REFERENCES

[1] Giles, L.; translated from Chinese *Sun Tzu On the Art of War: The oldest military treatise in the world*, 1910.

[2] Ohmae, K.; *The Mind of the Strategist*, Penguin Books, 1982.

[3] Porter, M. E.; *Competitive Strategy*, Free Press, 1985.

[4] Johnson, G. and Scholes, K.; *Exploring Corporate Strategy*, Prentice Hall, 1997.

[5] Collins, J. C.and Porras, J.I.; *Building your company's vision*, Harvard Business Review, Sep-Oct, 1996.

[6] Porter, M. E. and Millar, V. E.; *How information gives you competitive advantage*, Harvard Business Review, July-Aug., 1985.

[7] Copeland, T. and Koller, T. and Murrin, J.; *Valuation: Measuring and the Value of Companies*, 2nd. Ed., John Wiley & Sons, New York.

[8] Kaplan, R. S. and Norton, D.P.; *Using the balanced scorecard as a strategic management system*, Harvard Business Review, Jan-Feb, 1996.

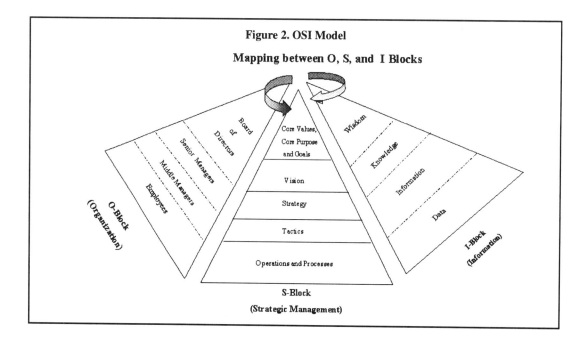

Figure 2. OSI Model

Mapping between O, S, and I Blocks

Consensus Management in a Generic Management Support Tool

Dr Nicola Ayre

School of Information & Software Engineering, University of Ulster, Newtownabbey, County Antrim, BT37 0QB, Northern Ireland

Telephone: +44 (1232) 368830, Fax: +44 (1232) 366068, E-mail: n.ayre@ulst.ac.uk

ABSTRACT

This paper reports on preliminary attempts to integrate consensus management with a generic management support tool called MATUM.

INTRODUCTION

Decision making has conventionally been considered an art or talent, gradually acquired through years of experience (learning by trial and error). Within any decision if more than one criterion is applicable or involved then the realm of multiple criteria decision making (MCDM) is entered. As individuals we are well versed in making decisions involving multiple and often conflicting criteria. On a personal level we cope with this type of decision without the use of any formal approach. Within a business context the number of criteria involved (many of which can be conflicting) may be substantial, reflect different viewpoints and change with time (Harhen, 1990).

Buchanan (1994) notes that '*the multiple and conflicting criteria that decision makers encounter in decision making situations need to be explicitly considered*'. In order to handle the complexity inherent in current business contexts, computer-based tools, such as decision support systems (DSS) are increasingly available. Decision support tools which can facilitate multiple criteria modeling help decision makers organise and synthesise this information (Ayre & Anderson, 1995). MATUM (Multi-Attribute Tool for Uncertainty Management) is one such support tool.

MATUM was originally conceived and developed over a two year period (Ayre, 1994). MATUM is a generic intelligent decision support system (IDSS) which has been applied to a number of domains for example site and property selection, and more recently to student (candidate) selection within the Faculty. The initial research was done in conjunction with an industrial sponsor - Digital Equipment Corporation and the focus was simply to look at different ways to facilitate management decision making under conditions of uncertainty.

MATUM fully supports decision making as an iterative process allowing the decision maker to express the flair, intuition, judgment and creativity at the heart of every good decision maker (Lucey, 1991). In keeping with the traditional role of DSS and IDSS within business environments (Bidgoli, 1989), the system is not intended to take away or replace the decision maker's judgment, ability or experience, but rather to enhance it.

WHY CONSENSUS MANAGEMENT?

MATUM has been used in a variety of decision making domains, but on each occasion only by individual decision makers. Individual decision makers use the tool in isolation, when two or more are involved in the decision making process the tool's recommendations from their respective interactions are manually compared. Differences in opinion are resolved by a process of negotiation.

Although most decision makers do some work in isolation many decisions are derived using group-based decision making activities. As Keen (1981) notes '*the lonely decision maker striding down the hall at high noon to make a decision - is true only in rare cases*' rather '*most decisions are taken only after extensive consultation*' (Gray & Nunamaker, 1996). In light of these comments recent efforts have focused on providing MATUM with the functionality to directly compare and appraise the underlying trends behind the responses of individual decision makers. Essentially the tool is trying to detect any underlying bias that may exist on the part of the individual decision maker and through the application of consensus theory attempt to arrive at the decision recommendation that has the highest level of agreement or consensus.

CONSENSUS MANAGEMENT - AN APPROACH

A number of methods exist to help establish whether a workable consensus has been achieved within group-based assessments. One such method is the '*concept of a neighbourhood consensus function*' (Dodd & Donegan, 1990). The concept of neighbourhood consensus works on the principle that each decision attribute score is regarded as being <u>around</u> a point rather than <u>at</u> the point. By taking this approach a set of scores (that is, the scores from each decision maker) for each decision attribute can be summarised by a function. The opinion profile for the group of decision makers, on a particular attribute, can then be derived from the graph of the function. The maximum value of the function and the point in the range at which it occurs offer a measure of the consensus and the focus of the opinion respectively (Dodd & Donegan, 1990). This approach has the advantage of being able to cope with the varying precision of individual decision makers.

Figure One A Schematic View of MATUM

A SCHEMATIC VIEW OF MATUM

MATUM has four main components: a knowledge-base or model repository, a knowledge input tool, a model evaluation tool and a sensitivity analysis tool, see figure one.

The Model Repository

The Model Repository (knowledge-base) supports the development of new multi-attribute decision models and stores existing ones. Within MATUM a decision model consists of:
- A tree-like hierarchy of evaluation criteria or attributes - the value tree.
- The weights associated with each attribute and a final normalised weight for each branch at twig-level.
- A definition for every attribute included in the model.
- One or more decision options, where a decision option represents one unique outcome of the decision making process. Each decision option holds the scores awarded to that option for each of the model attributes and a final overall score assigned to that option.

The Knowledge Input Tool

The knowledge-base is maintained through a Knowledge Input Tool (KIT). KIT allows the user to create and modify decision models, whilst still maintaining the integrity of the knowledge-base. Integrity is maintained through a series of validation and verification rules which check all user input.

The Model Evaluation Tool

The Model Evaluation Tool (MET) is based on Multiattribute Utility Technology (MAUT) (Edwards & Newman, 1982; Edwards, von Winterfeldt & Moody, 1989). MET 'runs' a model for any given set of decision options. In the early stages of a run MET is closely coupled with KIT. KIT prompts the user for actual values or scores for each twig-attribute for each decision option. MET contains a number of rules which use these actual values and the attribute's definition description to perform a numerical transformation on the values. When the transformations are complete MET obtains the aggregate of the two sets of numbers held in the model: the importance weights, one for each attribute, and the transformed scores awarded to each decision alternative on each attribute. This aggregate is achieved using a simple linear equation.

The Sensitivity Analysis Tool

The Sensitivity Analysis Tool (SAT) does not support a full MAUT sensitivity analysis as discussed in Edwards & Newman (1982). However, in keeping with its role as a DSS MATUM does support a form of sensitivity analysis. The decision maker can run a decision model with a variety of different 'scores' being input, for example, she could assess the effect of increasing the size of office available from 140sq. feet to say 200 sq. feet. Alternatively she could alter the ranks, definitions or both, previously input or add additional attributes to the value tree.

RESEARCH APPROACH

The approach currently being pursued is that of enhancing the modeling component of MATUM - the Model Evaluation Tool (MET) by the integration of a neighbourhood consensus algorithm, based on the work of Dodd (1993). When the system is used by an individual decision maker there is no consensus to be reached. When two or more decision makers are involved in the decision making process a consensus of opinion or **group-based perspective** is required.

When instructed to compute a group-based perspective the tool will focus on the scores awarded to each decision alternative on each attribute by each individual decision maker. The role of the consensus algorithm is to establish the degree of agreement between the decision makers for each attribute. As consensus is reached on each individual attribute it is added to the <u>consensus set</u> for the decision option. Upon completion of this set, that is all twig-attributes have been considered, it is again aggregated with the importance weights to establish an overall group-based perspective on the range of decision options available.

The initial approach being taken appears conceptually sound however, two significant practical problems have emerged. Firstly, integrating the mathematics behind the consensus algorithm and those behind MAUT is proving extremely complex. Secondly, after reviewing a number of paper based scenarios it has become obvious that depending on the range of attribute scores under consideration, a satisfactory mathematical consensus is not always definable. As yet, no satisfactory solution to this problem has emerged.

CONCLUSION

The research outlined in this paper is still very much in its infancy and needs to overcome some significant problems. Despite this the basic concept, from a theoretical perspective, appears sound and worthy of further attention. Recent discussions with local business men and women regarding the expected functionality of the tool have also proved highly encouraging.

REFERENCES

Ayre, N. (1994) *Uncertainty Management in Business Decision Making: A Pragmatic Perspective*, Doctoral Thesis, University of Ulster.

Ayre, N. & Anderson, T. J. (1995) "Knowledge-Based Uncertainty Management - An IDSS Approach", in *Intelligent Systems, Series D: System Theory, Knowledge Engineering and Problem Solving*, vol. 1, pp. 69-76, Kluwer Academic.

Bidgoli, H. (1989) *Decision Support Systems, Principles & Practice*, St. Paul:West Publishing Company.

Buchanan, J. T. (1994) "An Experimental Evaluation of Interactive MCDM Methods and the Decision Making Process", *Journal of the Operational Research Society*, vol. 45, no. 9, pp. 1050-1059.

Dodd, F. J. & Donegan, H. A. (1990) "The Representation and Combination of Opinions", *Proceedings of ILIAM 6*, pp. 17-29.

Dodd, F. J. (1993) *Consensus and Prioritisation in Analytic Hierarchies*, Doctoral Thesis, University of Ulster.

Edwards, W. & Newman, J. R. (1982) *Multiattribute Evaluation*, Sage University Paper series on Quantitative Applications in the Social Sciences, 07-026, Beverly Hills: Sage Publications.

Edwards, W., von Winterfeldt, D. & Moody, D. L. (1989) "Simplicity in Decision Analysis: An Example and a Discussion", in *Decision Making, Descriptive, Normative, and Prescriptive Interactions*, (eds. D. E. Bell, H. Raiffa & A. Tversky), pp. 443-464, Cambridge: University Press.

Harhen, J. G. (1990) "*Knowledge Based Modelling to Support the Determination of Manufacturing Strategy*", Doctoral Thesis, Graduate School of the University of Massachusetts.

Keen, P. G. W. (1981) Remarks at the closing plenary session, First International Conference on Decision Support Systems, Atlanta.

Lucey, T. (1991) *Management Information Systems*, 6th ed., London: DP Publications Ltd.

Gray, P. & Nunamaker, J. F. (1996) "Group Decision Support Systems", in *Decision Support for Management*, (eds. R. H. Sprague & H. J. Watson), pp. 330-349, N.J.: Prentice-Hall.

An Exploratory Study: Supporting Web-Based Collaboration for Multimedia Systems Design

Seung Baek
Department of Management & Information Systems, Saint Joseph's University, Philadelphia, PA 19131
Tel: 610-660-3437, Fax: 610-660-1229, E-mail: sbaek@sju.edu

Jay Liebowitz
Department of Information Systems, University of Maryland - Baltimore County, Baltimore, MD 21250
E-mail: liebowit@umbc.edu

Srinivas Prasad & Mary Granger
Department of Management Science, The George Washington University, Washington, DC 20052
E-mail: prasad@gwis2.circ.gwu.edu, E-mail: granger@gwis2.circ.gwu.edu

Authors thank Electronic Learning Facilitator, Inc. (Bethesda, MD) for helping in the system design and evaluation.

1. INTRODUCTION

Multimedia is an umbrella term generally referring to the seamless integration of text, sound (such as spoken words, music, or sound effects), visual images (such as still photographs, motion pictures, or animation), or other electronically represented information under computer software control (England & Finney, 1996; Tway, 1992). Therefore, a multimedia project generally requires a collaborative effort among many developers with a variety of backgrounds, such as personnel, context experts, instructional designers, users or clients, and so forth (Alber, 1996; England & Finney, 1996). Because each of them possesses totally different backgrounds, training, and experiences, communication among them is always problematic. Unifying a design team that is comprised of members from different disciplines, with different skills and different ways of describing multimedia, might be a major problem that project managers must solve in order to complete projects successfully. Also, when team members are located at different functional groups within a firm or in separate firms, their collaboration becomes more difficult. The major issue in the collaborative design environment is making designers, with their own unique interests and individual perspectives, come to a common understanding of what they are building, sharing information, and coordinating their individual design efforts. While a great deal of research and theories exists for designing more effective multimedia applications with respect to content, structure, and presentation (Isakowitz et al., 1995; Maybury, 1993; Park & Hannafin, 1993), very little attention has been paid to the actual coordination process that individual designers incur or groups undergo in a collaborative design process for multimedia systems (Streitz, 1996).

Designing a multimedia system can be characterized as a learning, communication, and negotiation process among design team members (Alber, 1996; England & Finney, 1996). Throughout the interactive process, the team members integrate knowledge and skills from various domains. Teamwork, cooperation, coordination, and communication among team members are very important in a collaborative design process for multimedia systems. One obvious recommendation is to promote actively the acquisition, sharing, and integration of knowledge within a design team (Walz et al., 1993). In order to enhance knowledge exchange and resolution of conflicts among team members, many real-world design teams construct a shared memory (Walz et al., 1987, 1993). However, because many design teams manage the shared memory in an ad hoc manner, and just store formal knowledge, such as users' manuals and user analysis reports, they cannot manage the dynamic evolution of knowledge that occurs throughout a design process (Walz et al., 1993). In order to manage and speed the evolution of knowledge, it is necessary to develop new tools that encourage design partici- pants to bring their knowl- edge and skills to bear on the design. Also this should be accomplished without forc- ing on them mediation through explicit description. This research aims to design and evaluate a tool that can facilitate expression, trans- mission, and evaluation of ideas on the Web.

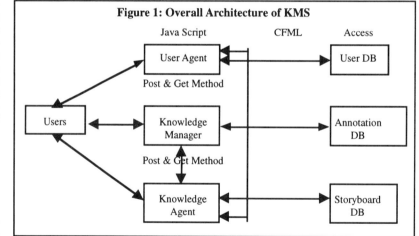

Figure 1: Overall Architecture of KMS

2. KNOWLEDGE MANAGEMENT IN MULTIMEDIA SYSTEMS DESIGN

Multimedia systems design consists of three ba- sic cognitive activities, which are usually performed by a group of designers: selecting information, structuring contents, and selecting media (England & Finny, 1996). By analyzing application domains and target audiences, designers decide what informa- tion should be contained in a multimedia system. Then, they identify a hierarchical relationship (content structure) among the selected information sources. Finally, they decide how the selected information should be presented in a multimedia system. These activities are very closely related, rather than separated.

The storyboard allows designers to streamline these activities (Kiddo, 1992). The storyboard shows how one frame relates to adjacent ones, as well as to the whole concept, and what media are needed to achieve a particular effect (Kiddo, 1992). By using storyboards, design team members can explicitly communicate and negotiate how narration, images, texts, special effects, and background music/images are brought together and linked together to form a final presentation. By helping designers create, exchange and share storyboards, we can enhance their knowledge communication and sharing activities.

3. KMS-BASED DESIGN ENVIRONMENT

A web-based collaboration environment for multimedia systems design consists of three intelligent agents: user agent, knowl- edge manager, and knowledge agent. The intelligent agents are designed to support the KM activities on the Web. Each agent consists of a knowledge base and a set of production rules that manage its knowledge base and generate adequate interfaces for designers. In order to perform their tasks, the agents communicate with other agents through HTTP communication protocols. An agent might request information from other agents. The knowledge bases are implemented using Microsoft Access. The rules are implemented using Java Script. For the interface between Java Script and Access, we use the CFML (Cold Fusion Markup Lan- guage). The overall system architecture is shown in Figure 1. By communicating with each other, agents dynamically generate the interfaces.

4. EVALUATION STRATEGY

For evaluating the KMS-based design environment, we formed two experimental teams. The first team (called the distributed team) used the KMS as a brainstorming tool within a totally virtual working space. Its members were geographically distributed, and they could communicate with each other only by using the KMS. The second team (called the local team) used the KMS as a design tool for representing its design knowledge. Unlike the distributed team, the local team used face-to-face meetings as well as the KMS in order to share design knowledge.

The distributed team was recruited through the USENET News Group (comp. multimedia). We conducted a three-day workshop with them. During the workshop, they did not have any chance to meet each other in order to discuss their tasks. In three days, by using the KMS, they generated 30 storyboards and 50 annotations. On the last day of the workshop, we asked them to fill out the questionnaire. The questionnaire asked the four designers about their subjective judgments and personal preferences toward the KMS-based design environment. We conducted the follow-up interview by using either e-mail or phone. Throughout the interview, we received more descriptive feedback about the KMS-based design environment.

The local team was formed from a local multimedia company. The designers actively participated in designing the KMS. They selected a proper project for the KMS-based design environment among their on-going projects. Before they designed storyboards by using the KMS, they had a series of brainstorming sessions to analyze an application domain. Also, they decided their tasks and roles under the KMS-based design environment. Two junior designers mainly created and revised storyboards, and a senior designer primarily reviewed the storyboards and provided annotations. Unlike the distributed team, the local team used the KMS for supporting the final stage of storyboarding, the detailed storyboard design. Since the designers already created storyboards roughly in the previous face-to-face meetings, they focused on refining their storyboards in the detailed storyboard design stage. Also, they used the face-to-face meeting as well as the KMS. We conducted a one-month workshop. In this workshop, the team created 20 storyboards and 10 annotations by using the KMS. We received feedback using the same questionnaire that we used for the first team. We also conducted a semi-structured interview afterward.

The questionnaire was designed using a multi-attribute decision making approach, called the Analytic Hierarchy Process (AHP) model. The approach enabled us to identify the relative usefulness of the KMS-based design environment under more than one criterion or attribute. There are many conflicting and competing user needs for constructing an ideal collaborative design environment. Individual users (designers) have totally different preferences for these needs. Therefore, in order to explore the usability of the new design environment, we need to consider all attributes that are valuable to designers. We chose the multi-attribute approach as an appropriate method for evaluating the KMS-based design environment. Keim et al. (1997), Liebowitz (1985), Maiden et al. (1997), and Sinha and May (1996) show the usefulness of the multi-attribute approach as a strategy for evaluating software or proposed features of new software products. In this research, we used the AHP model for evaluating the usability of the KMS-based design environment.

To evaluate the KMS-based design environment based on the AHP, we went through the following steps: constructing a hierarchy by decomposing the problem; designing the questionnaire for pair-wise comparison of attributes within the hierarchy.

Step 1 – Decomposing the problem

The first step in using AHP is the development of a hierarchy of attributes by decomposing the problem into its basic

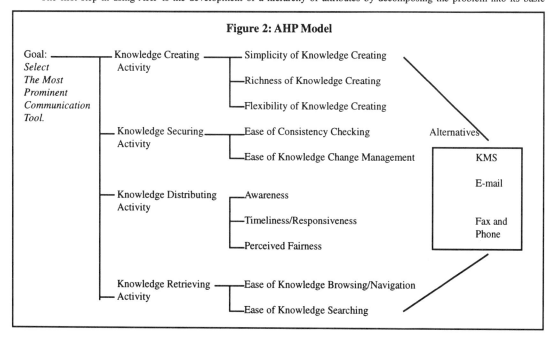

Figure 2: AHP Model

Goal: Select The Most Prominent Communication Tool.

- Knowledge Creating Activity
  - Simplicity of Knowledge Creating
  - Richness of Knowledge Creating
  - Flexibility of Knowledge Creating
- Knowledge Securing Activity
  - Ease of Consistency Checking
  - Ease of Knowledge Change Management
- Knowledge Distributing Activity
  - Awareness
  - Timeliness/Responsiveness
  - Perceived Fairness
- Knowledge Retrieving Activity
  - Ease of Knowledge Browsing/Navigation
  - Ease of Knowledge Searching

Alternatives

KMS

E-mail

Fax and Phone

components. There are many attributes that are important to designers who share their storyboards in a virtual working space. However, they might have a totally different set of attributes that they considered important. In order to explore how the KMS-based design environment affects the KM activities of multimedia designers, at first, we needed to identify a set of attributes for evaluating the KMS. We conducted a series of semi-structured interviews with four multimedia designers from a local multimedia company. First, we collected characteristics of an ideal design environment through e-mail. Then, through the team interviews, we categorized the collected characteristics into sub-categories.

The structure of the hierarchy is depicted in Figure 2. The first level of the hierarchy consists of the overall goal – selecting a promising communication tool for multimedia systems design. The second level contains the main factors that we need to consider when evaluating media. Since the focus of this research is to evaluate the new design environment by exploring how different communication media affect the KM activities, the four basic KM activities are in the second level. The third level describes the sub-factors influencing the second level of the hierarchy. The third level is composed of the driving factors that can enhance the effectiveness of each KM activity. As we mentioned, these factors were identified throughout a series of interviews with four professional multimedia designers. Finally, the fourth level consists of alternatives that will be evaluated based on the attributes in the second and third levels of the hierarchy. Based on the interviews with multimedia designers, we identified three most common

---

Figure 3: A Sample Question in Questionnaire

2.4 What is the most important factor when you share design knowledge (ideas) with your team members within a virtual environment? **Please compare the importance of the following three factors.**

- Awareness: You can be fully aware of a sense of identity, purpose, and consciousness to yourself in a design team.
- Timeliness/Responsiveness: You can easily get meaningful feedback from other designers in a timely manner.
- Perceived Fairness: Everyone can participate in design equally.

Intensity
1=Equal 2=Moderate 3=Strong 4=Very Strong 5=Extreme

Awareness	5 4 3 2 1 2 3 4 5	Timeliness
Awareness	5 4 3 2 1 2 3 4 5	Fairness
Timeliness	5 4 3 2 1 2 3 4 5	Fairness

---

communication media (e-mail, fax and phone). We also found that designers frequently used phone with fax. The evaluation task was to compare the importance of each communication media in the bottom-level of the hierarchy under 10 different effective measures.

Step 2 – Designing the Questionnaire for Pair-Wise Comparisons

The second stage of the AHP utilizes pair-wise comparison to establish the relative importance of the attributes within each level of the hierarchy. In order to determine the importance that an attribute will contribute to the overall utility, a series of comparisons are made. In the AHP, the pair-wise comparison provides a means of converting the subjective judgement about the attributes into the numeric values, the priorities (Dyer & Forman, 1992). The questionnaire was designed by way of pair-wise comparisons. Figure 3 shows an example question in the questionnaire.

The designers were asked to compare two factors at a time. Their ratings showed between the two factors, which was more important, as well as how many times more important it was. If they thought that the two factors were equally important, they would circle "1". Otherwise, they circled the number on the side of the more important factor in order to indicate how many times more important the factor was than another factor in the same row.

5. RESEARCH FINDINGS

The purpose of the section is to explore the impacts of KMS-based design environment on KM activities within the two different design teams. By using the questionnaires and the interviews, the opinions and needs of the two design teams about KMS-based design environment were captured.

First, the AHP model was used to investigate how well KMS-based design environment satisfied the users' performance expectations on the effectiveness measures that were identified in the previous chapter. Second, to support and elaborate the findings from the questionnaires, the data collected via the interviews was analyzed. Throughout the two phases of the data analysis, the impacts of KMS-based environment was investigated.

What is the most important KM activity in designing a multimedia system in a virtual working space?

Two experimental design teams had different opinions about the relative importance of the knowledge distributing and the knowledge securing activities in designing a multimedia system within a virtual working space. The distributed team selected the knowledge distributing activity (0.39) as the most important KM activity, and the local team selected the knowledge securing activity (0.4) as the most important KM activity (See Figure 4). However, both teams had similar opinions about the relative importance of the knowledge creating (Distributed Team: 0.2; Local Team: 0.17) and the knowledge retrieving (Distributed Team:

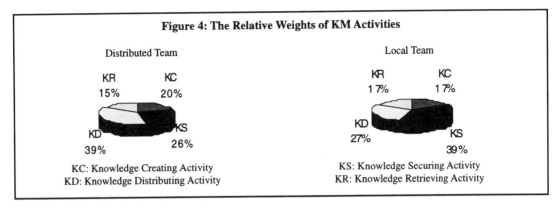

Figure 4: The Relative Weights of KM Activities

Distributed Team

KR 15% KC 20%

KD 39% KS 26%

Local Team

KR 17% KC 17%

KD 27% KS 39%

KC: Knowledge Creating Activity
KD: Knowledge Distributing Activity

KS: Knowledge Securing Activity
KR: Knowledge Retrieving Activity

0.15; Local Team: 0.17) activities.

Their different design environments might affect their judgments toward the relative importance of the KM activities. The distributed team worked together in an ill-structured design environment. Because its designers were recruited via the USENET (comp.multimedia), they did not meet each other during the design process. All designers were identified by their e-mail addresses. In addition, they did not know their experimental tasks until the workshop started. Under this kind of ill-structured environment, designers might try to interact with each other to identify their roles and tasks as much as they can. In the process of their interactions, the knowledge distributing activity might be a critical activity. Therefore, the designers in the distributed team considered the knowledge distributing activity (0.39) as the most important KM activity in designing a multimedia system.

Unlike the distributed team, the local team worked together in a well-structured design environment. Its designers were recruited from a local multimedia company. They experienced working together in a virtual working space. They knew each other pretty well. Also, since the experimental task was selected from their on-going projects, they already knew about the task before the actual workshop started. Prior to the workshop, in order to identify user and system requirements and to specify their individual tasks at the workshop, the local team had a series of face-to-face meetings. While they used KMS for designing a multimedia system, they also scheduled regular bi-weekly meetings to review what each of them accomplished or discovered during the previous weeks. They worked in a virtual working space mainly for reviewing and refining the results of their previous face-to-face meetings, and for outlining the incoming meetings. Throughout the process, they designed the storyboards in detail. Since they performed their pre-specified tasks in a virtual space and interacted with each other within a well-structured way, any duplicated design efforts were not observed. Their major concern was integrating their individual task accomplishments with the team project achievement, rather than interacting continuously with each other in order to organize the environment. Therefore, even if the designers in the local team still said that the knowledge distributing activity (0.28) was more important than other KM activities (knowledge creating activity - 0.17 and the knowledge retrieving activity - 0.17), they chose the knowledge securing activity (0.4) as the most important KM activity. They were mainly interested in storing and indexing properly their new knowledge in order to integrate their knowledge with other designers' knowledge.

How well does the KMS-based design environment support KM activities in a virtual working space?

Based on the relative importance of the KM activities of each team, the research investigated the teams' judgment of the impacts of KMS-based design environment on their KM activities. The two teams agreed that KMS was more preferable to other communication media, such as e-mail and fax/phone, with respect to creating, securing, and retrieving knowledge in a virtual working space. However, they had different preferences about KMS with respect to distributing knowledge in a virtual working space. The local team said that KMS was the least preferable choice in terms of supporting distributing knowledge activity. The distributed team still preferred KMS to other media in terms of supporting the knowledge distributing activity. However, the priority difference between KMS and other media with respect to supporting the knowledge distributing activity was much smaller than the priority differences that observed from other KM activities. Both teams agreed that KMS did not support the knowledge distributing activity as much as it supported other KM activities.

Why did not the KMS-based design environment support knowledge distributing activity?

Throughout the semi-structured interview, we identified why KMS did not support the knowledge distributing activity as much as it supported three other KM activities. In the case of the distributed team, since its designers did not know each other, even if KMS helped them to distribute their knowledge widely, they had a hard time in coordinating individual design efforts. Without supporting the socialization of team members, KMS could not enhance the knowledge distributing activity.

On the other hand, since designers in the local team knew each other and their tasks and goals in advance, they did not criticize the inability of KMS to support their socialization. However, they complained about its inability to deliver timely and responsive feedback. Since the local team, unlike the distributed team, worked together for a longer time and was involved with multiple projects simultaneously, its designers gave much more weight on the timeliness/responsiveness of feedback. In order to enhance the timeliness and responsiveness of KMS-based design environment, proper incentives that can make designers use KMS regularly should be implemented.

6. CONCLUSIONS

Two evaluation studies showed that KMS-based environment was a promising environment for multimedia systems design. More specifically, they indicated that KMS-based environment supported knowledge creating, knowledge securing, and knowledge retrieving activities for multimedia systems design, but it did not support knowledge distributing activity as much as it did for other KM activities. Additionally, the research found that the social interactions between the group members played an important role in the success of the collaborative multimedia systems design and that KMS-based environment did not support the socialization of design teams. Its inability in supporting the socialization directly linked to its low performance level in supporting the knowledge distributing activity.

Since designers in the distributed team did not know each other, they had a hard time to coordinate their design efforts. Although KMS-based environment reduced the gap between the continually changing knowledge and the awareness of the existence of such knowledge by distributing knowledge actively, it did not help them to integrate effectively their knowledge with others'. Without knowing each other personally, the designers resisted sharing critiques among themselves within a virtual working space. In the case of the local team, the inability of KMS in providing timely information did not enable the designers to maintain their socialization processes that they could experience at the face-to-face meetings. Therefore, they limited the usage of KMS during a design process. To make KMS more effective in distributing knowledge within a virtual working space, designers need to be motivated for the regular use of KMS. Within both experimental groups, proper management strategies can enhance the usability of KMS in supporting the knowledge distributing activity.

7. REFERENCES

References available upon request to Seung Baek at Saint Joseph's University

Comparing a Web-based and Traditional Course

Harry Benham and Barbara Ellestad
College of Business, Montana State University, Bozeman, MT 59717-3040
hbenham@montana.edu, ellestad@montana.campuscw.net

Using Internet technologies to delivery distance education has generated a great deal of interest. Numerous schools have either initiated distance education programs using Internet technologies or converted existing distance education programs to use Internet technologies. Visible examples of these initiatives are the Western Governor's University (http://www.wgu.edu) and California's Virtual University (http://www.california.edu). There is a great deal of anecdotal evidence describing development of Web-based courses and experiences with the initial offering of a Web-based course. But little direct evidence comparing Internet delivered distance education with traditional classroom instruction exists. Below we provide some preliminary results comparing the same course delivered in a distance, Web-based format and a traditional format.

COURSE DESCRIPTION

The course studied is an introductory computer literacy course delivered to in excess of 500 students each semester. A Web-based version of this course was developed and pilot tested during the Spring 1998 Semester. Fall Semester 1998 the Web-based version went into full production.

Course Resources

Materials available to students are identical. Students have a textbook, lab manual, and access to on-line lectures and tutorials. On-line discussions and the ability to e-mail instructors is available to both the Web-based and traditional versions. Students in the traditional version have lectures to attend and scheduled labs staffed by teaching assistants. Unlike a true distance education situation, students in the Web-based version have the opportunity to attend an 'open lab' staffed by teaching assistant for hands-on help with lab assignments. No attempt was made to limit access to the traditional lectures. It is possible that students in the on-line section could have attended the physical lectures.

Assignment Procedure

Assignment to the traditional and Web-based version was based on when the student enrolled. The first 350 students to enroll were assigned to the traditional version. All subsequent enrollments were assigned to the Web-based version. Sophomore, Junior, and Senior students had an opportunity to enroll toward the end of the Spring 1998 semester. Freshmen who attended summer orientation sessions were able to enroll during the summer. Those students who arrived on campus for the first time at the beginning Fall 1998 Semester could only enroll in the Web-based version of the course. This assignment procedure was not random. Consequently, it is necessary to look at the demographics of the on-line and traditional versions of the course for possible systematic bias.

Course Conduct

Comparison of the on-line and traditional versions of this course was complicated by the manner in which the course instructors' chose to conduct the class. Attendance at the traditional versions physical lecture or lab sessions was not required. Consequently some students assigned to the traditional version opted to behave as if they were in the on-line version. This self selective behavior presents a confounding influence in our analysis

DATA DESCRIPTION

Three sources of data are available: course performance measures, a pre-course survey, and a post-course survey.

Course Performance Measures

As a computer literacy course, course content covers both computing concepts and hands-on proficiency. Performance on computing concepts was measured by student scores on midterm and final examinations. Hands-on proficiency was measured as the cumulative total on all computer assignments. In addition, an overall course score is available as a summary measure of course performance.

Pre-Course Survey

Technically administered during the second week of the course, this survey was conducted to gather demographic information and gage the student's initial knowledge and attitudes. Demographic questions included the student's age, gender, class, number of credit hours being attempted, number of hours normally worked each week, and the students self reported level of computer expertise. In addition a "Microcomputer Playfulness" instrument [Webster & Martocchio, 1992] and the "Computer Self-Efficacy" instrument [Compeau & Higgins, 1995] were included. The Microcomputer Playfulness instrument yields a scale measuring an individual's tendency to interact spontaneously, inventively, and imaginatively with microcomputers. It was thought that promoting levels of comfort and familiarity with microcomputers that would enable an individual to interact with them spontaneously and inventively was an approximation of the goal of an introductory computer literacy course. The Computer Self-Efficacy instrument is a dynamic measure of an individual's confidence in his or her ability to accomplish a specific task using a computer.

Post-Course Survey

Similar to the pre-course survey, this survey will be administered during the last week of the course. The "Microcomputer Playfulness" and "Computer Self-Efficacy" instruments will be repeated in order to observe any changes in these two measures. In addition, a number of questions were asked enabling us to classify each student as 'behaving as if' they were enrolled in the on-line version or the traditional version.

RESULTS

Valid responses were received from 425 students. Of these respondents, 101 were assigned to the on-line version of the course. But because of the manner in which the course was administered, students who were assigned to the traditional physical lecture version of the course had the option of using the on-line resources and not participating in the physical lectures and labs. Additionally, students formally enrolled in the on-line version were able to attend physical lectures and labs. Consequently, a behavioral measure based on reported attendance at physical lectures and labs were used in addition to identify those taking the course on-line. By this second definition, 218 students behaved "as if" they were enrolled in the on-line version of the course. Table I contains a breakdown of enrollment in the traditional and on-line versions of this computer literacy course for both definitions. Based solely on these numbers, it would appear that some student respondents clearly preferred the on-line version to the traditional version. Before turning to course performance measures, we need to consider how the on-line and traditional samples differ.

Table I: Enrollment Figures		
Course Version	**On-Line Definition**	
	Assigned Section	**Behavioral**
Traditional Course	323	206
On-Line Course	101	218

Comparison on Traditional and On-Line Samples

There was a significant difference between the traditional and on-line samples in class. Using section assignment to indicate the on-line course, the on-line course had a disproportionate number of Freshmen students while Sophomores, Juniors, and Seniors were under represented in the on-line section. Since students had little or no choice about the section they were able to enroll in, the most likely explanation of this difference between the two samples is that the Freshmen registered later and consequently were more likely to be assigned to the on-line section. When one uses observed behavior to differentiate between those who took the course in a traditional manner and those who used the on-line method, Freshman continued to be over represented in the on-line course although the effect is not quite as pronounced.

The two samples also differ significantly on age. Students eighteen years of age and younger are over represented in the on-line version of the course. One's first instinct is to assume that class in college and age are highly correlated so that the age variable is simply reproducing the class effect discussed above. However, there seems to be more to it than that. The over representation by the youngest students increases when one changes from the assigned section definition of on-line to the observed behavior definition of on-line. The youngest group of students was the most likely to behave as-if they were enrolled in the on-line section.

Gender appears to have no impact on the traditional and on-line samples. In total, enrollment was 39% female and 61% male. Regardless of on-line definition, the sample gender proportions are very close.

The two samples differed significantly according to the student's credit hour load. Using the assigned section definition, the on-line version of the course was over represented by students attempting less than twelve credit hours. This phenomenon could be due to the section assignment procedure where part-time students may tend to register at the last moment and thus be assigned to the on-line section. Changing to the behavioral definition for who was taking the course on-line, one sees students attempting less than twelve credit hours dropping from 40% of the on-line students to 35%. Interestingly, students with a "normal" course credit load of 12 to 15 credit hours remain stable at 45% of the on-line students while students with credit hour loads of 16 or more increased from 14% to 19% of the on-line students. Our preliminary figures don't explain why we see these differences but it is certainly possible that part-time students and students with extra heavy loads appreciate the additional flexibility offered by an on-line course!

In addition to academic responsibilities, many students work and attend school simultaneously. One might posit that students with heavy work schedules would be more likely to prefer on-line versions of a course. Our figures show no evidence of such a phenomenon. If anything the proportion of heavy workload students in the on-line course as defined by behavior is less than the proportion of heavy workload students in the on-line assigned section.

One might argue that students are entering college with a greater degree of computer sophistication. Even in a basic computer literacy course, those students with more skills might tend to prefer an on-line version. Our data show no systematic difference between the on-line and traditional samples on the basis of self-reported computer experience.

The two samples are not directly comparable. Regardless of which on-line definition was employed, the on-line course sample was statistically different from the traditional course sample in terms of college class, age, and credit hour load. A student in the on-line section was more likely to be a Freshman, was more likely to be in the youngest age category, and to be either a part-time student or a student with a unusually heavy academic load. Gender, computer experience, and hours worked did not appear to differ between samples.

Comparison of Student Performance

Although there are systematic differences between the on-line sample and the traditional sample, it may still be worthwhile to look differences in student performance across samples. Student scores are the traditional measures of student learning. A key question is whether student learning is enhanced or hindered in an on-line environment. We have student scores on four course performance measures: lab assignments, the midterm exam, the final exam, and total score.

Lab assignments covered a range of elementary computer skills. The skills demonstrated in these lab assignments included e-mail usage, searching the Internet, creating and formatting word processing documents, moving and copying files over a network, and spreadsheet fundamentals. There were twelve individual lab assignments at 10 points each. We looked at the sum of all twelve lab assignments. In the traditional version of the course, the mean lab score was about 101.7 while the mean lab score for students in the on-line version of the course was around 104.4. Table II contains the precise values which are dependent on the on-line definition being used. The figures suggest that the on-line students did better, and in fact the difference is just statistically significant at a 5% level.

The midterm and final exams tested knowledge of computer concepts, terms, and definitions. Using the assigned section definition to distinguish between students in the traditional version and the on-line version, the mean midterm and final exam scores for the traditional version were 75.7 and 70.3 respectively. The corresponding on-line version mean scores were 75.4 and 68.6 respectively. These figures suggest that the on-line students' performance suffered relative to the students in the traditional version of the course. However these observed differences were not statistically significant. Using the behavioral definition to distinguish between the two versions, yields traditional version midterm and final mean scores of 76.6 and 71.2 respectively. The corresponding on-line mean scores were 74.8 and 68.8. The difference between the midterm scores is statistically significant at a 5% level. The difference between the final scores is significant only at a 10% level.

The course score is a weighted average of lab scores, midterm, final, and other minor factors such as participating in a visit to the local computer museum. Using this performance measure, the figures suggest that the on-line students do marginally better by one definition and marginally worse by the other. In neither case are the results statistically significant. Table II contains the mean scores for each on-line definition.

Comparison of Playfulness and Self-Efficacy Scales

In addition to the traditional assignment and exam score performance measures, we also have pre and post observations on two scales: Microcomputer Playfulness and Computer Self-Efficacy. The microcomputer playfulness scale measures measuring an individual's tendency to interact spontaneously, inventively, and imaginatively with microcomputers. In order to be able to interact with microcomputers in such a manner, an individual must be comfortable and familiar with microcomputers; the microcomputer would have achieved the status of a trusted tool. Table III shows the mean pre and post course values for this scale. The values are stable at approximately 36. There is virtually no difference between the pre and post course values for this scale nor is there a noticeable difference between the traditional course sample and the on-line course sample. Perhaps the level of familiarity necessary for imaginative, inventive interaction with a microcomputer is beyond the level that can be reasonably expected of students in an introductory computer literacy course.

The Computer Self-Efficacy

Table II: Performance Differences					
Performance Measure		**Traditional**	**On-Line**	**Difference**	**z**
Assigned Section Definition	Lab Scores	101.8	105.4	3.6	1.96*
	Midterm	75.7	75.4	-0.3	-0.26
	Final	70.3	68.6	-1.7	-1.09
	Score	83.9	84.2	0.3	0.24
Behavioral Definition	Lab Scores	101.7	103.6	1.9	1.04
	Midterm	76.6	74.8	-1.9	-2.11*
	Final	71.2	68.8	-2.5	-1.69+
	Score	84.4	83.6	-0.8	-0.62
* Significant at 5% level + Significant at 10% level					

scale measures of an individual's confidence in his or her ability to accomplish a specific task using a computer. A computer literacy course which emphasizes specific task oriented skills such as sending e-mail, formatting a word processed memo, and creating a simple spreadsheet should enhance an individuals perception that they can be successful using a computer to accomplish specific tasks. The figures in Table III support this view. Overall, there is an approximate 10 point improvement from the pre course Self-Efficacy scale mean and the post course mean. For each course type, the measured improvement is highly significant. However, there is no statistically significant difference between on-line and traditional versions of this course regardless of how on-line is defined. Thus this computer literacy course does increase individuals' perceptions that that they can successfully accomplish tasks using a computer. It doesn't seem to matter whether the course is on-line or taught in a traditional format.

CONCLUSIONS

In this paper, we have presented some preliminary results of a study comparing one course offered in a traditional format with students attending lectures and lab sections and also offered in a Web-based on-line version where students have access to on-line lecture notes and tutorials. The results presented here indicated that the traditional format students' demographics differed from those of the on-line students. Those in the on-line version of the course were more likely to be Freshmen, more likely to be in the youngest age category, and more likely to have academic loads above or below the "normal" range.

The traditional academic performance measures suggest that students in the on-line version of this course did slightly better on their computer assignments and slightly worse on concept exams. While some statistically significant results were found, those results do not appear to be of a practical significance. A difference of less than two points on a 100 point exam does not represent a substantive difference.

The same finding of no difference extends to the Microcomputer Playfulness and Computer Self-Efficacy scales. The computer literacy had no discernable effect on the playfulness measure. On the other hand, the course had a strong positive impact of the self-efficacy scale. But whether the course was taken on-line or in the traditional format had no discernable effect on Computer Self-Efficacy.

The tentative conclusions of this preliminary analysis would be twofold. First, some students appear to have a definite preference for on-line instruction. Recall that the formal assignment of students had only about 100 in the on-line version of the course. Yet when offered the opportunity to behave as if they were in the on-line version, over 100 additional students took the on-line option. Second, there don't appear to be any substantive differences in student learning as a result of taking a course on-line rather than in the traditional format.

There are caveats to mention regarding the above conclusions and the ability to generalize based on these results.

Table III: Scale Differences					
Scale Measure		Traditional	On-Line	Difference	z
Assigned	Pre-Play	35.4	36.5	1.1	1.32
Section	Post-Play	36.4	37.4	1.0	1.42
Definition	Play Diff.	0.1	0.5	-0.4	-0.48
	Pre-Self	60.3	62.3	2.0	0.92
	Post-Self	71.1	73.0	1.9	1.21
	Self-Diff	10.7	9.0	-1.7	-0.87
Behavioral	Pre-Play	35.7	35.6	0.0	-0.04
Definition	Post-Play	36.6	36.7	0.1	0.20
	Play Diff.	0.9	0.7	-0.2	-0.25
	Pre-Self	60.4	62.0	1.6	0.89
	Post-Self	71.6	71.6	0.1	0.06
	Self-Diff	10.7	9.9	-0.8	-0.48

First, the conclusion concerning student learning is based on the assumption that various scores are sufficient measures of learning achievement. Many argue that a significant portion of the learning experience stems from interpersonal interactions and may not show up immediately in exam scores.

Second, all the data analyzed pertain to an introductory computer literacy course. There is little controversy about the proper definition of ROM and there aren't many subtleties to the correct total of a column of numbers in a spreadsheet. In would be improper to generalize from these results and say that on-line versions of a foreign language, history, or botany course would not degrade student learning.

Additional caveats specifically about this study are also in order. Our sample only covered about two thirds of the enrolled students. Why didn't the remaining students participate in the study? If it was because they were so uncomfortable or unskilled at using the information technology used in their on-line course that they either didn't know of the opportunity or couldn't figure out how to participate, then the samples are seriously biased and the results suspect. Did having both the on-line and the traditional version available simultaneously adversely impact the traditional course delivery? And finally, one must trust our manufactured indicator of on-line or traditional course.

Yet the finding of "on-line or traditional format doesn't seem to make a difference" is consistent with a recent report comparing student performance in an introductory macroeconomics course available on CD-ROM or traditional class setting. No significant differences were found in academic outcomes. [Raine, 1999].

REFERENCES

Compeau, D.R. & Higgins, C.A. (1995). Computer Self-Efficacy: Development of a measure and initial test. *MIS Quarterly* 19: 189-221.

Raine, George. (1999). "'Cyberlearning' Causes Rift Within the Ivory Tower," *San Francisco Examiner*. January.

Webster, J. & Martocchio, J.J. (1992). Microcomputer Playfulness: Development of a measure with workplace implications. *MIS Quarterly*, 16:201-226.

Discovering A New Pedagogy For A New Medium

Barry Brownstein

Merrick School of Business, University of Baltimore, 1420 N. Charles Street, Baltimore, Md. 21201

410.837.4960 (voice), 410.837.5722 (fax), bbrownstein@ubmail.ubalt.edu

"If we can change the price and performance of bandwidth and long distance, if we can collapse distance and time, something big is going to happen"[1] - Joseph Nacchio, CEO Qwest Communications

This paper begins with the premise that something big is going to happen to higher education as a tidal wave of fast inexpensive bandwidth engulfs us over the next few years. The movement toward web- based teaching is just one manifestation of technological change. This paper is directed to those who feel we can *plan* for the advent of the new technology and design new programs now. Unfortunately we can no more plan for the new technology than the mid-nineteenth century coal field owner could plan for the revolution that the discovery of oil was going to bring. We cannot *plan* but there are steps that we can take.

PARADIGM BLINDNESS

To plan within the teaching model that we know now for something that is as revolutionary as inexpensive, fast bandwidth, is to guarantee paradigm blindness. Fast, inexpensive bandwidth will make possible teaching and collaborative models that we can hardly conceive of now. Our paradigms, our mental models of the world, "our basic ways of perceiving, thinking and valuing" are seldom stated explicitly, instead they exist as unquestioned understandings.[2] To not question our mental models leaves us certain to catch the deadly illness of paradigm blindness. "Who the hell wants to hear actors talk" said H.M. Warner in 1927. "The concept (FedEx) is interesting, but in order to earn better than a 'C' the idea must be feasible" said Fred Smith's professor in business school.[3] To be blinded to new ways of doing things by our current beliefs is to be human, but there are steps that we can take to mitigate the damage. The steps are be humble! Be humble! Be humble! Understanding, that as philosopher Karl Popper put it, "the more we learn about the world, and the deeper our learning, the more conscious, specific, and articulate will be our knowledge of what we do not know, our knowledge of our ignorance" is the penicillin for paradigm blindness.[4]

Cheap fast bandwidth will revolutionize learning and pedagogy. However, when we attempt to meet this challenge through planning we can only draw up plans within paradigms that we already know. Therefore, we believe that web teaching is putting our lecture slides or the publisher's textbook slides on the web. This is not likely to be what web-teaching will become. We can learn a lesson from the early days of television. In the first television ads an announcer stood in front of the mike reading radio copy. No one in 1950 could have conceived of a television advertisement of 1960 or 1998. Planning by design locks erroneous misconceptions into place. Thus to announce now that 'web-teaching will be as follows' is the equivalent of forever entrenching the 1950 television ad.

I can hear the concerns voice by my colleagues in academia- 'but we have to do something.' Doing something can be worse that doing nothing, but I am not going to propose doing nothing. Before we can do anything innovative we need to be reminded of Dee Hock's (founder and former CEO of Visa) maxim: "the problem is never how to get the new innovative thoughts into your mind, but how to get the old ones out".[5]

Working within their current paradigms many educational institutions behave in the following ways:

- Most courses can be taught using "tell them and test them" pedagogies by professors providing little more than information.
- The challenge of Internet teaching is thought of in the context of how to get the professors notes (or worse the publishers slides for the book being used) on the web.
- Little or no attention is paid to the questions of appropriate pedagogies for this new medium.
- The essential facts about what is needed to respond to new challenges are assumed to be knowable rather than something to be discovered.

MAKING OUR BOAT GO FASTER IS NOT GOOD ENOUGH

Not only do our paradigms make it difficult to change, but innovation within a paradigm is likely to fail. In the 1800's hauling icebergs and chopping them up provided ice. With the advent of the icemakers, not one icehauler made the transition to selling ice through icemakers. Why? They saw their business as hauling ice not as providers of ice. Similarly with the rise of the steam engine the only reaction of sailing ships was to try and make their boats go faster.[6] Had they seen themselves as providing transportation instead of sailboat services, they may have met the challenge of adopting the new technology. The cautionary tale for the University is clear: are Universities centers that facilitate learning or centers that provide courses that we fill with students? The answer will determine the survival of the University.

We are at the point that we recognize that new competition is coming and that change is necessary. Unfortunately at this point we may be like the 19th century sailing ships, reacting by trying to go faster. Many colleges have barely started the process of experimenting with new web pedagogies. Putting our lecture notes on the web is a not a new pedagogy. Instead putting our lecture notes on the web is simply translating what we do now into a new medium - the equivalent of the television announcer reading radio ads. An obvious question is what segment of the student market would pay to read our lecture notes on the web and consider this an education. I think there may be such a segment, more interested in buying a degree then in genuine learning. Do colleges want to position ourselves for this segment? To be sure, that model will enjoy some demand from a group of students who are buying a degree.

At this point, the cynic may wonder why students will not flock to "buying degrees". There are good reasons why this is impossible. One is the reputation of a school that does this would quickly suffer. The competitive nature of an increasingly world-wide job market puts pressure on students to migrate to institutions that genuinely facilitate learning. As economist and futurist James Davidson explains, due to technology: "the economic value of memorization as a skill will fall while the importance of synthesis and creative application of material will rise."[7] The successful schools will be those who are thinking genuinely about new course designs, trying collaborative learning experiments and rethinking the role of professor and student.

KNOWLEDGE VS. INFORMATION
The logic of inexpensive fast bandwidth is clear; the price of information will fall at an ever-exponential rate. Universities in the business of selling information will find the price that they can get for this information everfalling.

Although the price of information has fallen, the cost of creating new knowledge has not fallen as rapidly. Knowledge is not the same as information. Information is simply facts, knowledge involves conceptual understanding and is frequently tacit.[8] Educator Parker Palmer explains that knowledge is knowing something with familiarity gained through experience.[9] In other words, what we make of information. Due to technology there is little value added in providing information relative to facilitating the growth of knowledge.

Knowledge as distinguished from information, is the capacity to use creatively information. In the age of information, the value of someone who can creatively use information has gone up. How does this effect higher-ed? The "tell them and test them" model of education, where students are seen to be empty vessels waiting to be filled up with information from the all wise professor is a relic. A relic that was always antithetical to the human spirit but made some economic sense when the value of creative thinking was less important. In today's global fast changing world, innovation is crucial and to simply imitate is a recipe for disaster. Thus a course that does not teach students how to creatively apply and synthesize material, but simply teaches them a textbook's distillation of important information and formulas will find that too is a relic. The university will find that the market value of such a course will fall dramatically. Putting your lecture notes online and then giving multiple choice tests on line will not be the new model of higher education.

It is my belief that technology will not create a cold sterile climate where students learn solely by setting in front of a computer screen. Instead the climate will be rich in personal interaction and collaborative learning. This new learning climate will create new opportunities for the university to improve upon its traditional role of facilitating the discovery of new knowledge. Technology expedites the process by which new knowledge is created because it facilitates the discovery of what is meaningful and facilitates a interpersonal collaborative discovery process.

SOME THOUGHTS ON COLLABORATIVE LEARNING
Nobody knows specifically what new pedagogies look like. We can consider what general principles will drive the new pedagogies while being unable to predict the form the new pedagogies will take. Technology reduces the cost of information and of collaboration. Our age of innovation and entrepreneurship will value students who can creatively apply material just as the factory age valued students who passively followed orders. This will lead to the following changes:
- Learning will become increasingly a process for which the student is equally responsible for and not something that is done to them by the instructor.
- Students will become active acquirers of knowledge instead of passive acquirers of information.
- Students will increasingly value that which resonates from their own life-long learning experience rather than passively valuing that which they have been told.
- Learning will be a continuous process rather than taking place at a fixed time and place.
- Curriculum will be driven by the marketplace and thus the needs of students rather than by the needs of the faculty and the institutions. Much as the Internet is underspecified to meet the needs of its users, the curriculum of the future will be reduced in specification.

The question remains how do we discover the new pedagogies necessary to facilitate greater collaborative learning that facilitates the growth of new knowledge. Once we realize that useful knowledge is dispersed, we realize that the essential ingredients are open-mindedness, imagination and a willingness to be corrected. In other words humbleness.

USEFUL KNOWLEDGE IS DISPERSED
Since we are not in the habit of questioning our paradigms, many of the important questions in life do not surface or are assumed to have given answers. So as we consider the important questions of how to respond to changing technology, pedagogy is assumed to be given. In his seminal essay *The Use of Knowledge in Society,* Nobel Laureate Friedrich Hayek pointed out that assuming important knowledge to be given begs the whole question since we are assuming that which we do not know and can only discover.[10]

Thus the challenge *is not* how to utilize a given body of knowledge about which we can all agree. Instead Hayek points out that our actual problem "is a problem of the utilization of knowledge that is not given to anyone in its totality."[11] In other words the knowledge that we need to develop new pedagogies does not exist in concentrated form but can only be discovered. Our challenge becomes how to utilize, discover and grow useful knowledge about how to meet the challenges of technology.

PLANNING FOR CHANGE BY DESIGN VS. THE DISCOVERY PROCESS

What we can all agree on is the need to meet the challenges of technology. What we do not agree on is how to get there. I believe we can discover the components of a new program but not design them. The difference is more than semantical. Design implies a Newtonian world where all works like an orderly machine. Just put the pieces together and start the engine. This world of management through design is ending as quickly as technology's growth rate becomes more exponential. It is ending because human design can not adopt to change as quickly as a decentralized trial and error.

To discover new pedagogies, the first step is to see the 'old furniture' in our mental models that clutter our mind and inhibit discovery. The first piece of 'old furniture' to overcome is the belief that we can 'design' and plan new web programs. We all want progress to be orderly so we tend to rely on leaders, experts or authorities to design and plan our responses to change. Friedrich Hayek reminds us we typically conceive "of order only as as the product of deliberate arrangements."[12] We all desire more order. When things are orderly more of our expectations are met and we experience less uncertainty. However, Hayek points out that as conditions become more complex and the future more uncertain, adaptation to the unknown future can be achieved more effectively by decentralizing decision making. This is because such an order "will utilize the separate knowledge of all..., without this knowledge being concentrated in a single mind , or being subject to those processes of deliberate coordination which a mind performs."[13]

What Hayek is referring to is that in addition to a familiar hierarchical forms of order there are self-generating spontaneous orders. For example, no one invented language, it evolved through the interaction of millions. The Internet is the ultimate example of a spontaneous order. A chief characteristic of spontaneous orders is that "its degree of complexity is not limited to what the human mind can master."[14]

In the physical sciences developments in chaos and complexity theory parallels Hayek's ideas.[15] The differences between a linear Newtonian systems and complex systems have major implications as we think about responding to new technologies:

- Complex systems are self-organizing, they are far from equilibrium and they allow for discovery and entrpreneurship. Newtonian systems are closed systems tending toward equilibrium.
- Complex systems are inherently unpredictable but not random. Newtonian systems are predictable.
- Complex systems are synergistic and very sensitive to initial conditions. Newtonian systems are additive and not very sensitive to initial conditions.

In a world of complexity, planning for the future is of dubious value. While, the world of complex systems is not a random one, however it is *very* sensitive to the initial conditions. The initial conditions are set by our organization's culture, incentives, and infrastructure.

Dee Hock, founder and former CEO of Visa, uses the word Chaord to denote an organization that embraces the principles of creating order out of seeming chaos. He points out that when Visa was founded it was "beyond the power of reason to design an organization to deal with such complexity and beyond the reach of imagination to perceive all the conditions it could encounter." [16]

Thus 'design' by decentralized discovery allows experimentation to discover what really works. A discovery process can only take place one step at a time. So what can we do to begin this discovery process of new Internet pedagogies. Setting the initial conditions that make experimentation possible is necessary. The preconditions that are necessary to ignite the discovery process are for both simple incentives and infrastructure to be in place.

SO WHAT CAN WE DO?

"People ask: Where's the plan? How do we implement it? But that's the wrong question because an organization isn't a machine that can be built according to a blueprint" [17] - Dee Hock

"...the knowledge of the circumstances of which we must make use never exists in concentrated or integrated forms but solely as dispersed bits of incomplete and frequently contradictory knowledge which all the separate individuals possess."[18] - F.A. Hayek

The discovery process is like going up a flight of stairs in the pitch black. As you step on the first step, the second step lights up, but not until you step on the second step does the third step light up. The seduction of rational planning is clear, it gives us the delusion of control. However, our delusions stifle discovery and innovation. The spontaneous order has no power until it is relied on. So like a non-swimmer taking a swimming class and learning of the principle of flotation, we cannot get the benefits of the discovery process until we go in the ocean and try to float.

If we understand that useful knowledge is dispersed and that 'there are no ultimate sources of knowledge' then we realize that our challenge is to create the conditions so that knowledge that is not given to anyone in totality can be utilized. Here are some ideas.

Dee Hock warns us that "an organization's success has more to do with clarity of shared purpose, common principles and strength of belief in them than to assets, expertise, operating ability or management competence, important as they may be." [19] Just as a market place depends upon the 'rule of law' and property rights to function properly, the workplace is dependent upon proper values and conduct to function efficiently. Wayne Gable and Jerry Ellig, of George Mason University, have itemized some of the values that allow decentralized knowledge to be efficiently utilized. They are "humility, intellectual honesty, openness, receptiveness to new ideas, treating others with dignity and respect and recognizing and using everyone's unique knowledge and abilities."[20] It goes without saying then that hoarding information, and staking out a position without developing an understanding to support it are damaging to the mission of the organization.

Another precondition to growing and utilizing knowledge, is to improve the flow of information and the capacity to collaborate in the University. An Intranet would seem to be an essential item in an University. Software such as Lotus Domino/Notes is a billion-dollar business because it allows companies to save money through reducing the cost of collaboration. Any software or hardware that facilitates new ways of students collaborating with students or faculty collaborating with students will be useful to discovering new pedagogies. Trying to experiment with new pedagogies without powerful collaborative software is like trying to teach without a blackboard thirty years ago.

Related to this point, reform and decentralization of management information systems (MIS) has to be discussed and implemented. A centralized bureaucracy making decisions on the purchase of software and other issues flies in the face of what the new technology and Internet is bringing. The Internet in the words of David Isenberg is a 'dumb' network in that its intelligence lies in the users and providers and not in a centralized core.[21] Nicholas Negroponte of MIT warns that the concept of a MIS director with centralized power is an anachronism.[22]

Compensation and incentives, in meaningful monetary rewards, are necessary to encourage experimentation and grow new knowledge. Taking this step would also involve a genuine dialogue in the University community on the nature of being a professor. Resources are fixed and real choices have to be made between rewarding genuine innovations in teaching, significant research and trivial 'research ' papers that will never be read by more than the editor, referees and author. At the same time, those who are rewarded for experimental teaching have to be held accountable. Besides providing monetary rewards, providing real incentives means that any professor not in the business of pushing forward their teaching horizons in a demonstrable way will be evaluated as unsatisfactory in their job performance.

Many will find the above strong medicine. In any case, stronger medicine in the form of market discipline is coming our way. In some instances tenure gives perverse incentives not to innovate, to do unimportant research, to neglect responsibilities to students. Increasingly though professors that can not field courses which are marketable nationally will be themselves unmarketable. Unfortunately, in some quarters of academia the market is anathema. We cannot continue to defend courses and curriculum that are no longer meeting tests of market viability and usefulness. The role of the academy in helping to facilitate the growth of knowledge and our obligations to that are paramount.

In recognition that increasingly the arena of competition for all institutions will be virtual and national, Universities should explore alliances and consortiums with other schools. Such alliances and consortiums would allow students to take and transfer courses from any school in the network. The goal is to get the network as big as possible. The message of the Internet is that closed proprietary systems fail. Apple computer had a superior product, but by failing to license their hardware they kept their price artificially high and dramatically lost market share.

The future of cheap bandwidth is approaching rapidly. If our response to the new competition is similar to the sailing ship's response to the steam engine - try to go faster- we will suffer the same fate as sailing ships. That fate will be well deserved and justly earned.

ENDNOTES

1 Quoted by David Isenberg at http://www.isen.com
2 Joel Barker, *Paradigms*, (New York, New York: Harper Business, 1994) p.31
3 See http://www.foresight.org/News/negativeComments.html for many interesting erroneous predictions
4 Karl Popper, *'Knowledge Without Authority'* in Miller ed. *Popper Selections* (Princeton: Princeton University Press, 1985) p.55
5 Dee Hock, *Institutions in the Age of Mindcrafting* at http://www.cascadepolicy.org/dee_hock.htm
6 I am indebted to David Isenberg for this example, see his essay *Rise of the Stupid Network* at http://www.manymedia.com/david/stupid.html
7 James Davidson and William Rees-Mogg, *The Sovereign Individual*, (New York: Simon and Schuster, 1997) p. 45; see for a more complete discussion of the changing job market: William Bridges, *Job Shift,* (Reading, Mass.: Addison-Wesley, 1995)
8 Michael Polanyi, *The Tacit Dimension,* (Gloucester, Mass.: Peter Smith, 1983)
9 Parker Palmer, *The Courage To Teach,* (San Francisco: Jossey-Bass, 1998) pp. 50-52
10 Friedrich Hayek, *'The Use of Knowledge in Society'* in *Individualism and Economic Order* (Chicago: Regnery, 1972) pp. 77-91
11 ibid. p. 78
12 Friedrich Hayek, *'Cosmos and Taxis'* in *Law Legislation and Liberty v1* (Chicago: University of Chicago, 1973) pp. 35-54
13 ibid. pp41-42
14 ibid. p. 38
15 see for instance David Parker and Ralph Stacey, *Chaos, Management and Economics* (London: institute for Economic Affairs, 1994).
16 Dee Hock, *The Chaordic Organization* at http://www.newhorizons.org/ofc_21clidhock.html, p.6
17 Hock *Institutions in The Age of Mindcrafting*
18 Hayek, The Use of Knowledge in Society, p. 77
19 Hock p.11
20 Wayne Gable and Jerry Ellig, *Introduction to Market- Based Management* (Fairfax,Virginia: Center for Market Processes) p. 37
21 Isenberg
22 Nicholas Negroponte, *Being Digital,* (New York: Alfred Knopf, 1995) p. 229

Are CMC Inherently Supporting Democratic or Authoritarian Decision-Making? – A Field Study in an Australian University

Dubravka Cecez-Kecmanovic, Debra Moodie, and Lesley Treleaven
University of Western Sydney Hawkesbury, IS-KOMO Research Group, Faculty of Management, Locked Bag #1
Richmond NSW 2753 Australia
Ph 612-9852-4157; Fax 612-9852-4185; E-mail: Dubravka@uws.edu.au

ABSTRACT

This paper explores the use and impact of Computer Mediated Communications (CMC) employed in restructuring an organisation. An on-going field study of the organisation-wide consultation, enabled by CMC during a strategic change process in an Australian university, examines the impact of e-mail and intranet in (re)shaping management practices in the university. In particular, the paper focuses on the features of a authoritarian/bureaucratic versus participative/democratic dimension of management. The study indicates that CMC technologies have significant potential to produce changes along this dimension. Furthermore, early results suggest that the control and ownership of CMC as a channel for the creation, sharing and legitimation of organisational knowledge are important in generating such changes.

1 INTRODUCTION

As Computer Mediated Communications (CMC) are increasingly permeating all aspects of organisational life, we perceive them less as *tools* and more as a productive *social space*. The potential of CMS to enable new forms of social interactions that overcome not only physical and temporal but status-related barriers as well and to provide equal access to information sources and participation in public discussions, raises hopes that this new social space may democratise organisations and, more specifically, organisational decision-making. On the other hand, the potential of CMC to enable effective control and surveillance of organisational members and to thereby support and strengthen existing power structures and social inequalities raises fears that the new social space will inevitably make hierarchical structures and autocratic decision-making more efficient and thereby more powerful. Both hopes and fears have been substantiated, perhaps some may argue even fuelled, by research findings (Mantovani, 1994).

Sproull and Kiesler (1991a,b) found consistency between CMC and the ideals of freedom of speech, equality of participants, and participatory, democratic decision-making. They demonstrated that CMC affect social inequalities: soften the status-related barriers; decrease the informational and emotional distance between the centre and peripheral employees; and create opportunities for new connections among people. Similarly Dubrovski et al. (1991) found that in CMC, compared with face-to-face communications, status inequalities are attenuated and the difference in participation between high and low status members decreased. The equalising effect of CMC and contribution to more equitable participation was also reported earlier by McGuire et al. (1987) and Siegel et al. (1986).

While the above research results provide evidence confirming the democratising potential of CMC, many other studies confirm just the opposite. Adrianson and Hjelmquist (1991) could not confirm that CMC contributed to equal participation and reduction of status differences. Rice (1990) found that CMC tend to enforce rather than reduce status-related differences. Several other researchers (Bikson and Eveland, 1990; Bikson et al., 1989; Child and Loveridge, 1990) have identified that CMC are effective in overcoming physical barriers but they do not necessarily address social barriers as they are designed to support existing power structures and hierarchies. Studies thereby conclude that CMC are more likely to facilitate existing relationships and interaction patterns.

Some inconsistencies in the research findings have been attributed to the different populations involved in research (students vs managers) and their varying experience with CMC (Prashant, 1997). After a critical review of the contradictory evidence, Mantovani concluded that "CMC does not necessarily foster democracy in organisations. It depends on the social context, on the history of each organisation, and on the regulations ruling the specific network application" (1994, p. 57). This conclusion, however, does not answer but rather reiterates the question: what are the impacts of CMC's interaction with the social context, given a particular history and the attributes of a technological application? Furthermore, the democratising potential of CMC remains very much an open question.

In this paper, we present a different approach to the exploration of CMC in a social context. We attempt to observe the use of CMC in everyday organisational life, collect data from the field and interpret and make sense of the use and impacts of CMC within a particular context (Cecez-Kecmanovic et al., 1998, 1999; Moodie et al., 1998). Here we present the results from an on-going field study of the use of CMC (e-mail and intranet) in a strategic change process in an Australian university (which we shall call Sygma University). We analyse and interpret research findings with reference to a bureaucratic and authoritarian management model versus a participative and democratic management model (Clarkson, 1989). The question we address in this paper is: What impacts, if any, have the use of CMC (e-mail and intranet) in the strategic change processes had on (re)shaping models of management practice in the institution?

We will first introduce a *authoritarian/bureaucratic* versus a *participative/democratic* management model in the following section. Then, in section three we will briefly describe the field study - the research site, methodology and research results. In section four, we will discuss research findings and interpret the observed changes in the use of CMC as they relate to the shifts along the bureaucratic/democratic dimension. The concluding remarks and some further implications of this study are presented in section five.

2 AUTHORITARIAN VS DEMOCRATIC MANAGEMENT MODEL

Organisational contexts differ in many ways. A basic dimension for differentiation is the underpinning value system. An organisational context that places the highest priority on equality, freedom and the dignity of the people is fundamentally different from one in which equality is disregarded, freedom is suspended and obedience to superiors required. In academic institutions particularly, where the relationship between the espoused system of values and actual behaviour is often explicitly questioned, to put it nicely, this dimension of organisational context is vital in understanding the use and impacts of CMC.

Two antithetical value systems determine the polarities between which an organisational context may be classified:

• **Authoritarian/bureaucratic** value system at one end, and
• **Democratic/participative**, value system at the other.

These value systems underlie two contrasting paradigms of management: the old, industrial model of management and the new, post- industrial model of management (Clarkson, 1989). Table 1 summarises Clarkson's characterisation of these models.

The management model characterised by bureaucratic and authoritarian values (left column of Table 1) assumes work activity is broken down into single, narrow tasks and hierarchical structures in which supervisors are responsible for the direction and control of their subordinates. As Clarkson emphasises, this old model of management relies for its effective functioning on "the authority of position or rank and on the coercive use of power when necessary" (Clarkson, 1989, p13). External controls are imposed on people at every level of the hierarchical structure, causing low levels of trust between people at different levels. Dependence on authority and the coercive and manipulative use of power leads to feelings of powerlessness and anger.

The participative, democratic management model (right column of Table 1) is based on adaptable and flexible structures of working teams in which a manager is a "manager of learning". Open inquiry, risk taking, innovation and creativity are encouraged resulting in organisational learning. The essential features of this new model are the sharing of power, information, knowledge and authority (Clarkson, 1989). Members of the organisation participate in appropriate and relevant decision-making processes, that are collaborative and consensus-based.

As this short elaboration of authoritarian/bureaucratic versus participative/democratic dimension suggests, we are dealing here with a complex phenomenon with many overlapping aspects, and not a simple 'variable' that can be observed and 'measured'.

3 FIELD STUDY

3.1 Research Setting

The Sygma University is situated in a semi-rural area on the outskirts of a large metropolitan centre. It was originally established in 1891 as a single-purpose college and became a university in 1989, as part of a federated structure. It has an enrolment of approximately 6000 students, and can thus be regarded as a small university. The staff body comprises of approximately 250 academic staff distributed over five faculties and 420 general staff members including administrative staff, technical and scientific officers.

The field study focuses on a complex strategic change process in Sygma University, initiated at the end of 1996, conducted as a consultative process throughout 1997 and implemented in 1998. The strategic changes were motivated by shifts in government policies and a concomitant decrease in government funding, increased competition in the higher education sector and economic and social changes in its environment. The aim of the consultative process was to increase awareness of these changes across the University community and to consult the various staff about the organisational changes necessitated by such shifts.

The consultative process involved face-to-face forums, a planning conference, small discussion groups and a CMC system based on e-mail and the intranet. All documents, announcements, proposals, discussion papers, and other relevant material were distributed via e-mail to all Sygma members, academic and general (administrative and technical support) staff. Public discussions about major documents and proposals were also conducted via e-mail. In the second half of 1997, documents and e-mail messages generated in the consultative process were posted on the Sygma intranet.

2.2 Research Methodology

We started the field study in the second quarter of 1997 after the approval of the research proposal by the Sygma Ethics Committee. As participants in the consultative process, three of us had free access to all of the documents, messages, discussions, and other materials. We also participated in forums, group meetings and the planning conference. In addition, we conducted semi-structured interviews with academic and general staff (46 so far) in order to identify individual experiences, attitudes, feelings and insights regarding the consultative process and the use of CMC (Atkinson 1992; Rosen, 1991). The interviews were transcribed. Data collection included all sections of the Sygma University. The data has been subject to analysis within the framework described in Table 1.

2.3 Research Results

The field data from the consultative process indicate that the use of CMC evolved through three phases:

Table 1 Characteristics of Authoritarian/Bureaucratic versus Participative/Democratic Model of Management (adapted from Clarkson, 1989)

MANAGEMENT MODELS

AUTHORITARIAN and BUREAUCRATIC	PARTICIPATIVE and DEMOCRATIC
Hierarchical, rigid structures; Individual responsibility Work activity broken down into single, narrow tasks; Supervisors direct and control the work of their subordinates;Top executive is *brain* and *mind* of an organisation, responsible for its performance.	**Flexible, adaptive structures; Individual and group responsibility** Work performed by groups in adaptable, flexible structures; A manager is a "manager of learning" who creates environment for open inquiry, risk taking, innovation and creativity.
Authority of power The legitimation of power based on positions (ranks) within a hierarchical organisational structure; Controlled access to information and communication channels.	**The authority of knowledge** Authority of power is subordinated to the authority of knowledge; Information and knowledge are widely shared; communication channels are open and accessible to all members.
The coercive use of power Autocratic management style using directives, instructions, monitoring , control, and reporting; Vertical flows of information along the hierarchical structure: directives and instructions downward, reporting upward.	**The sharing of power** Democratic management style based on consensual decision making, collaboration and cooperation among empowered individuals; Open expression of views and critical discussions leading to learning.
Dependence on authority An individual perceived as an island whose faith depends on the boss; Subordination and obedience to superiors demanded; Lack of trust between superiors and subordinates.	**Mutual interdependence** An individual as part of a community (a group, a department, an organisation) contributes and shares in its success and failures; Interdependence and high level of trust among people lead to collaboration.

(a) An initial sporadic phase

After the members of the executive distributed five strategic papers via e-mail to all Sygma members and invited them to reply and express their views, the response was slow, cautious and lacking focus. As one interviewee put it: "..*it started very slowly and very cautiously with people waiting to see if they had permission to speak.*" Everybody was invited to participate, e-mail was available to all staff but still some felt that the consultative process was not meant for them. Sporadic responses by staff did not trigger other staff's responses. E-mail at this phase was still perceived as just another medium for top-down distribution of information from the executive to the members.

(b) A reactive phase

After Sygma President announced (by e-mail and intranet) a first draft of the proposal for University restructuring and invited staff to respond, a two-way communication was established. According to the interview data, the members learned that e-mail gave many of them an opportunity to express their opinions, to oppose or support some changes in the proposed document and to protect their own and their section's interests. Although staff responses to the proposed restructuring document were distributed by e-mail to everybody (via a special e-mail feature of Sygma-all), the interaction between staff and President was seen only as a two-way communication. While eager to respond to the President's proposal and express their (individual or group) views, staff did not engage in the dialogue with other staff members ("*We've had very little conversation, dialogue*"). However this phase is characterised by the opening up of the consultative process and increased dynamics of interactions. Based on staff feedback, the President made some changes and proposed a final version of the restructuring document.

(c) A disciplined phase

A more disciplined phase evolved as staff engaged in planning the implementation of the restructuring. Staff was selected to participate in implementation teams required to design the detailed restructure within different sectors of Sygma. Several teams worked in parallel, created numerous working documents most of which required quick response from other teams and the executive (in order to coordinate solutions and resolve conflicting issues). The use of e-mail enabled effective interaction within teams (and their working parties) and coordination between different teams. In addition, the intranet became a major, unique repository of up-to-date documents available any time to all members of Sygma. Both e-mail and the intranet were deeply embedded into implementation planning process. The activities in physical space and in electronic space were mutually dependent. While the general allocation of work to teams and the final approval of implementation documents were determined by the President, and thereby disciplined and constrained, many teams working in the physical/electronic space exhibited genuine freedom of expression, creativity, individual and group initiative and responsibility, mutual understanding and cooperation, and most importantly, a sense of community building.

4 DISCUSSION

The rich data collected in the field, but presented here only very briefly, provide opportunity to examine CMC in a particular social context, ie in a period of a major organisational change. From this evidence and from our observations, we could not conclude that the use of CMC at Sygma produced a major shift of the management model in Sygma either toward left or right along the bureaucratic/authoritarian and participative/democratic dimension (Table 1). Having said that, we would, however, claim that there is some evidence that several micro, but still significant, changes from the incorporation of CMC in the consultative practice of the University have emerged. These changes are often subtle, not necessarily consistent, affecting some aspects of the model in Table1.

Data from the initial sporadic phase indicate that the deployment of e-mail, with a one-to-many interaction facility, did not change interaction patterns in the institution. Staff perceptions of hierarchy, authority and responsibility for the University's future did not change at this phase. The use of e-mail by the executive to consult with staff was understood as *"more of the same"*, even as *"a token gesture"*. These attitudes toward the use of e-mail in this phase can be explained by staff assumptions about e-mail as another communication medium owned and controlled by the executive (drawing probably from the analogy with printed medium such as the official University newsletter).

However, with the persistence of the President and some members of the executive in seeking responses from staff via e-mail they gradually changed their attitudes. In particular, the announcement of the President's restructuring proposal triggered a deluge of responses by staff members. This phase of the consultation took the form of a two-way communication between President and staff. This process was experienced as open and transparent and the President (and the executive) as more cooperative and willing to listen. However, the understanding of the President's responsibility and the presence of the authority of power have not been affected. The underlying change in this phase was related to the decrease of status-related barriers and staff feeling less distant from the executive. This is consistent with the research findings by Sproull and Kiesler (1991a,b) and Dubrovski at al. (1991)we mentioned in the Introduction.

The use of e-mail and the intranet in the disciplined phase was much more uneven across the implementation teams. Those teams that fully embraced CMC and engaged in an intensive process of creating and publishing documents (on the intranet) at an accelerating pace, experienced significant changes, despite the fact that the institutional framework of decision-making had not been changed. Participants of these teams reported feeling empowered and energised at the time. The cooperative nature of the activity and the spirit of free exploration within such teams encouraged their creativity and innovation. They felt ownership of the way they used e-mail and intranet as channels of knowledge creation and sharing. These changes were, however, limited to these teams and were not reported by other parts of the institution. They are nevertheless important for our understanding of the use of CMC.

5 CONCLUSION

Are CMC inherently supporting democratic or authoritarian decision-making? Our field study enabled a deeper understanding of the use of CMC and the ways they affect various aspects of management. The study suggests that CMC have significant potential to produce changes, however subtle, fragmented, unevenly distributed and inconsistent, ultimately leading to a shift along the authoritarian/bureaucratic versus participative/democratic dimension. Furthermore, our study emphasises how important the control and ownership of the channels for the creation, sharing and legitimation of organisational knowledge might be to this shift.

Moreover, we become aware that CMC introduce a new social space in which participants perform linguistic acts of self-positioning, somewhat less constrained by power relations and other social pressures usually experienced in face-to face interactions in physical space. In this social space, participants experience new modes of presence in organisational life instituted by new communicative practices of 'self-constitution' and 'we-constitution' (as a group or community). Consequently, models of management in organisations, as we have known them, will be seriously challenged by the newly developing technologies of CMC.

REFERENCES

Adrianson, L. and Hjelmquist, E. (1991) Group Processes in Face-To-Face and Computer-Mediated Communication, *Behaviour and Information Technology,* 10, 4, 281-296.

Atkinson, P. (1992) The Ethnographic Imagination: Textual Constructions of reality, Routledge, London.

Bikson, T.K., and Eveland, J.D. (1990) The Interplay of Work Group Structures and Computer Support. In J. Galegher, R.E. Kraut, and C Egido (Eds.), *Intellectual Teamwork – Social and Technological Foundations of Cooperative Work,* Hillsdale, Erlbaum, pp. 245-290.

Bikson, T.K., Eveland, J.D. and Gutek, B.A. (1989) Flexible Interactive Technologies for Multi Person Tasks: Current Problems and Future Prospects, In M.H. Olson (Ed), *Technological Support for Work Group Collaboration* (ed.), Hillsdale, Erlbaum, pp. 89-103.

Cecez-Kecmanovic, D., Busuttil, A., Moodie, D., and Plesman, F. (1998) Contextual Determinants of the Use of an Organisational Support System in Academia, *IFIP Conference on Context-Sensitive Decision Support Systems,* Bled, Slovenia, pp. 31-43.

Cecez-Kecmanovic, D., Moodie, D., Busuttil, A. and Plesman, F. (1999) Organisational Change Mediated by E-mail and Intranet – an Ethnographic Study, *Information Technology and People,* 12, 1.

Child, J. and Loveridge, R. (1990) Information Technology in European Services – Towards a Microelectronic Future, Oxford, Blackwell.

Clarkson, M.B.E. (1989) Values: Moving from the Old Paradigm to the New. in *Learning Works: Searching for the Organisational Futures* (eds. S. Wright, and D. Morley), The ABL Group, York University, Toronto, pp. 9-19.

Dubrovsky, V.J., Kiesler, S. and Sethna, B.N (1991) The Equalising Phenomenon: Status Effects in Computer-Mediated and Face-to-Face Decision-Making Groups. *Human-Computer Interaction,* 6 pp. 119-146.

Mantovani, G. (1994) Is Computer-Mediated Communication Intrinsically Apt to Enhance Democracy in Organisations?, *Human Relations*, 47, 1, pp. 45-62.

McGuire, T.W., Kiesler, S. and Siegel, J. (1987) Group and Computer-Mediated Discussion Effects in Risk Decision-Making. *Journal of Personality and Social Psychology*, 52, pp. 917-930.

Moodie, D., Cecez-Kecmanovic, D., Busuttil, A. and Treleaven, L. (1998) The Social Impacts of Organisational Support Systems: An Interplay Between Actors, Technology And Contexts, The Conference *Re-Working the University*, Brisbane, December.

Prashant, B. (1997) Face-To-Face versus Computer-Mediated Communication: A Synthesis of the Experimental Literature, *Journal of Business Communication*, 34, 1, pp. 99-120.

Rice, R.E. (1990) Computer-Mediated Communication Systems Network Data: Theoretical Concerns and Empirical Examples, *International Journal of Man-Machine Studies*, 32, pp. 627-647

Rosen, J. (1991) Coming to Terms with the Field: Understanding and Doing Organisational Ethnography. *Journal of Management Studies*, 28, 1, 1-24.

Sproull, L. and Kiesler, S. (1991a) Computers, Networks and Work, *Scientific American*, 265, 3, pp.84-91.

Sproull, L. and Kiesler, S. (1991b) Connections: New Ways of Working in the Networked Organisation. Cambridge, MIT Press.

Being flexible by being *WISE* – Two case studies of Web-based teaching and learning

D. Cecez-Kecmanovic

IS-KOMO Research Group, Faculty of Management, University of Western Sydney Hawkesbury, Locked Bag #1 Richmond NSW 2753 Australia
Ph: 612-9852-4157, Fax: 612-9852-4185, E-mail:Dubravka@uws.edu.au

C. Webb

Centre for Higher Education Development, University of Western Sydney Hawkesbury, Locked Bag #1 Richmond NSW 2753 Australia
Ph: 612-4570-1337, Fax: 612-4570-1606, Email: Ca.Webb@uws.edu.au

P. Tayler

ITC Education Unit, University of Western Sydney Hawkesbury, Locked Bag #1 Richmond NSW 2753 Australia
Ph 612-4570-1864, Fax: 612-4588-5867, E-mail: P.Tayler@uws.edu.au

ABSTRACT

The paper reports preliminary results from a qualitative study of the adoption of a particular Web based teaching and learning environment as an extension of face-to-face teaching and learning in two subjects ('Electronic Commerce' and 'Computer-Mediated Communications'). More specifically the paper explores a new aspect of flexibility enabled by social interactions within a technologically mediated learning environment. Bulletin board type discussion, as our preliminary results indicate, provides new opportunities for students' meaning making and co-construction of understanding, for students' deep immersion in learning tasks, and high motivation and personal involvement in a learning process.

1 INTRODUCTION

The paper reports preliminary results from an on-going research and development project aimed to create and evaluate a Web-based Interactive Study Environment (*WISE*) in the University of Western Sydney Hawkesbury (UWSH). The objective of *WISE* is to provide an innovative pedagogical environment to facilitate flexible collaborative learning and teaching using Web-mediated technologies. It has resulted from the necessity to increase the flexibility of educational opportunities the University affords both to its local students in the large catchment area of Greater Western Sydney and to the increasing numbers of students from other regions of Australia and the world who choose our programs of study. In rejecting the notion of polarity between a *real* university and a *virtual* one, UWSH has chosen to integrate on-line learning environments to complement and enhance more traditional same-time, same-place facilitation of learning. The development of *WISE* has been supported at the institutional level to provide the infrastructure needed to facilitate on-line education at UWSH.

WISE is an attempt not only to advance on-line delivery using the Web but more importantly to enable a significant shift from the traditionally individualistic culture of knowledge custodianship to the necessarily collaborative culture on which high quality flexible learning approaches depend (Laurillard and Margetson,1997). Our approach has been squarely focussed on "establishing and nurturing learning communities within which [new] knowledge can be developed", and on providing "opportunities to collaborate, to engage in conversation about teaching and learning" (Taylor, Lopez and Quadrelli, 1996: xiii). The development of *WISE* has been, in itself, an example of very effective collaboration amongst staff in separate areas of the organisational structure, including IS academics, staff and educational developers, instructional designers, and IT support staff.

Perhaps the most important characteristic of our approach to the development of the technologically-mediated infrastructure to support flexible teaching and learning has been its firm grounding in our philosophical commitment to a learner-centred pedagogy. The key elements include a concern for high quality student learning outcomes, a view of knowledge as a socially created and shared phenomenon, a view of teaching as the process of immersing learners and teachers in the social community of knowledge sharing, a view of pedagogy as the process of mediating between learners, teachers and knowledge, and finally a view of *learning technologies* as the channels to support this mediation of learning. The theme of collaborative learning has been a logical choice for UWS Hawkesbury whose reputation for innovations in experiential and enquiry-based learning is widely recognised (Candy *et al*, 1994, p. 271).

WISE consists of a core educational software package, WebCT, extended with a range of templates for collaborative learning and teaching activities and assessment tasks, and an interface with the Student Registration System, Financial Information System and Human Resources Information System (under development). The user interface of WebCT has been slightly transformed to suit the specific requirements of *WISE*. *WISE* has been experimentally implemented in a number of subjects offered in 1998, and will be further tested during 1999 before being fully mainstreamed in 2000.

The paper reports results from a qualitative study of the adoption of *WISE* as an extension of face-to-face teaching and learning environment in two subjects ('Electronic Commerce' and 'Computer-Mediated Communications'). More specifically the paper explores the meaning of flexibility introduced by this new learning environment in real life situations. While flexibility in terms of time, place and pace of off-campus Web based learning and teaching has been the subject of significant investigation, what flexibility actually means in on-campus situations has been relatively overlooked.

The next section of the paper briefly summarises the research framework. The field study is described in section 3 including the description of the data collected from two case studies. Analysis and interpretation of results are presented in section 4 and concluding remarks in section 5.

2 RESEARCH FRAMEWORK

A review of literature reveals that significant improvements in learning processes have been achieved by adopting pedagogies that foster active learning based on a constructivist conception of learning, cooperative learning and problem-based learning (Slavin, 1987; Alavi, 1994; Wilson, 1995; Cecez-Kecmanovic, 1996; Marjanovic et al., 1995). These conceptual shifts have often been accompanied by the deployment of new educational technologies in learning and teaching processes. Recent developments in Web based technologies and their diffusion in educational processes have created new opportunities for active learning. The purpose of our study is to explore these new opportunities.

Many studies address the comparative advantages and disadvantages of computer supported or technologically mediated learning versus traditional, face-to-face learning environments (see eg. Alavi, 1994). The proliferation of technology use in the learning process has been accompanied by an emphasis in research studies on determining whether technologies do indeed provide more flexible and economic replacements for face to face forms of teaching and learning. However, it is not this aspect of technology-mediated learning environments which has inspired our research. We are intrigued by the mutual interrelations between physical space and electronic or virtual space and their blending into a flexible learning environment. We wanted to explore how students make sense and create meaning in this new environment. More specifically, we have identified that the interaction students have with each other is crucial to their development of understanding. We were therefore interested in investigating the nature of students' interactions in their own process of constructing understanding. Therefore our study was qualitative by nature and did not attempt to define and measure variables but rather to explore the phenomena in the actual teaching and learning situation and improve our understanding.

3 FIELD STUDY

The study involved the adoption of *WISE* in two subjects in the Information Systems (IS) major of the Bachelor of Commerce program in the Faculty of Management. The students enrolled in the subjects were full-time students, from highly diverse ethnic, cultural and socio-economic backgrounds. In addition to face-to-face lectures and tutorials, *WISE* was implemented as a complementary teaching and learning environment to facilitate the undertaking of tutorial tasks and participation in group discussions.

We collected the electronic transcripts of bulletin board discussions, after securing permission from the students to use this material without identifying them by name in our study. Based on the transcripts of discussions we were able to analyse their interactions, their process of constructing shared understanding, and their reflections on their own experience in the use of the technology in this process by applying qualitative data analysis techniques (Miles and Huberman, 1984). We coded these transcripts first by identifying the issues and themes raised by students and then by aggregating them in broader categories.

3.1 Case study 1 – Electronic Commerce subject

The Electronic Commerce (EC) subject was taught in the first semester of 1998 as a core second year subject in the Information Systems (IS) major. 21 students enrolled, all from the IS major. Week 10 teaching was conducted differently from others: there were no face-to-face tutorials and lectures. Instead this week's topic Intelligent Agents (IA) was studied via *WISE*. First, students were required to read two papers on IA: one was provided as a hard copy and the other was available on the Internet. Students had a week to discuss the two papers, compare and contrast their content, and examine the major issues by logging on to a forum (a bulletin board) in *WISE* from the place of their choice (one option being students' computer labs on campus). Students registered in the forum using their real names. After the discussion they were required to submit a short essay interpreting the major issues highlighted by the two papers. Note that while students were computer literate and had some knowledge about Web technology this was the first time they had used *WISE* (or WebCT) in a subject.

The discussion was prompted by the instructor who described the task, pointed to the Code of Conduct of the University and focused their attention to the discussion questions and expected outcome. The number of contributions was 56 containing altogether 7200 words.

From the very beginning students started to interact among themselves with just a few references to the instructor. Only one students started her comment by telling the instructor that she had read the articles. In all other cases students either implicitly assumed talking to each other or explicitly started by saying *"Hi everyone!"*.

Students interacted with each other referring to somebody's discussion, idea or comment, often expressing an agreement, *"I agree with John.."*, *"I support this [statement].."* or rarely disagreement, adding often new arguments. This was typical of 32 out of 56 contributions. The topic did not provoke much dispute.

Students' discussion started with comments about the two papers which triggered raising and commenting on relevant issues, exploration of some further ideas and identification of new problems and questions. The frequency of these contributions was as follows:

The discussion was open, uninhibited, spontaneous, sometimes including personal views such as: individual experiences and their evaluation, excitement with the technology, prediction of the future of the technology, etc. Students appeared to feel free to experiment (a student participated once by posting a picture), to share what they learned and experienced (eg. a student suggested a reading on a URL address), or to share their frustrations with reading the papers (some had difficulties understanding them).

The instructors did not intervene in the discussion much. On only three occasions did the instructors raise some new questions to stimulate the discussion.

It was interesting to observe how students reacted to those who joined the discussion late or demonstrated lack of knowledge from the papers. While the instructors did not comment on this issue at all, students did:

"How are we suppose to have an intelligent and informative ..discussion if someone .. does not perform [his tasks]"

"Another rorter .. we need valuable contribution from students, this assists us all in the electronic commerce subject".

The major problem in this learning task was uneven participation: 8 students participated only once; 8 participated 2-4 times; 3 were very active and participated 7-8 times; 2 students did not participate at all. Instructors participated 12 times including initial introduction and instructions.

3.2 Case study 2: Computer Mediated Communications subject

The subject Computer Mediated Communications (CMC) was taught in the second semester of 1998 by the same instructors. The subject is a core second year IS subject but is a recommended elective in other majors. 41 students enrolled, three quarters from IS major, one quarter from accounting, marketing, humanities and other majors. The subject was designed assuming constructivist conceptions of learning: students engage in an activity using the technologies they are studying. This included videoconference, groupware for face-to-face meetings, e-mail and bulletin board (*WISE* forum). The discussion in the forum took 6 weeks and incorporated experiences from the use of other technologies. Students participated with their real names.

Reference to or comment on the 2 papers		25 entries
Including:		
- summary of ideas	6	
- critical comments	4	
- expression of need for more reading	2	
Raising relevant issues		**20 entries**
Explore other issues		**32 entries**
Including:		
- usefulness of technology	5	
- comparisons/analogies	5	
- impact of technology	3	
Identification of new problems and raising questions not mentioned in the papers		**12 entries**

The discussion started with the a general topic of the characteristics of good communication in a workgroup situation with reference to students' experience from face-to-face and technology-mediated work situations. After that the focus was changed (by instructor's prompting) to the factors, such as cultural background, gender, familiarity with participants, that potentially influence students' engagements in discussion on the *WISE* forum. Students logged in 113 times, producing discussion totalling 14,311 words.

The forum discussion in this subject was designed as a more flexible learning activity, did not have a strict time schedule, and was more open in terms of topic and content compared to the previous EC subject. It was going on in parallel to face-to-face lectures and tutorials.

The discussion did not have the feel of a learning task in a subject; rather it looked more like a spontaneous interaction among people with a personal interest in the topic. What characterises the discussion from the outset was:

- thoughtful and engaging discussions,
- strong arguing of particular views and opinions,
- serious, longer and more elaborated contributions,
- exploration of particular statements and claims in a sequence of students' contributions raising pro and contra arguments
- reference to and reflection upon students' personal experience from this or other subjects and from outside university,
- refinement in exploration of issues, increase in precision in describing them as the discussion progressed.

The evidence from the discussion shows an important feature which was not present in EC case. Students expressed strong opposing views on the major issues and built consensus in subgroups on each view. Very often they started their comment by agreeing or disagreeing with a particular view before providing further arguments. For instance one group argued that Web based discussion is less inhibiting, as participants *"don't see each other"*, *"don't see others' reactions"* and that gender, race, cultural background do not influence the way participants engage in the discussion:

"The idea and opinion is important, the rest is irrelevant to me".

"everyone [in the discussion] is equal even the lecturers seem to be almost at the same level".

The other group claimed the opposite that:

"factors as cultural background, gender, familiarity with other participants, do influence the way we engage in discussion via WebCT".

The new discussants entered the debate by siding with one view or the other. A student used the example of their going-on discussion to argue that:

"The point of differing views and opinions, from individuals with different backgrounds allow a collaborative and informative discussion on issues in relation to CMC. It is evident [that] our diversity of cultural and religious backgrounds in this subject affected [the way] we put forward the decisive issues".

This particular part of the discussion is an illustrative example of how students' own experience with the technology made them reflect on the way they approached their interactions via WebCT and derive an understanding of the use of technology in mediating debate. They reflected on their own shared construction of meaning and the emerging two opposing views.

The discussion brought students' personal experience and their attitudes toward other fellow students into focus, which invigorated the debate but increased tension as well. Apart from the two cases of open conflict (in 4 entries) among two participants, the discussion was generally tolerant.

Similar to the first case study the level of students' participation was uneven: 16 students participated only once; 16 participated 2-4 times; 7 were very active and participated 5-13 times; 2 students did not participate at all. The level of participation of IS students was much higher then non-IS students: 31 IS students participated 101 times and 10 non-IS students 12 times.

4 DISCUSSION

The evidence from the two case studies suggests that the use of *WISE* to mediate students' discussion on any-time-any-place basis was very well accepted by students and contributed to their increased interest in the subjects, deeper immersion in the learning tasks and increased motivation to learn. In both studies it was evident that students:

- focused on the topic expressing clearly their positions; they reported much fewer distractions compared to face-to-face discussions
- engaged personally in the debate, expressing views and opinions freely and without inhibition
- engaged in an unconstrained debate driven mostly by their own interests in the subject matter (more present in the second study)
- established interpersonal relationships, including some rare expressions of negative attitudes
- were satisfied with their ability to express themselves, and to relate to others, and
- were reflective about the effect of the medium for discussion on the nature of their interactions.

In the second case study in particular, students approached new concepts by relating to and sharing their own past experiences and knowledge as well as reflecting on the present experience with the subject. The evidence from the use of *WISE* as an open space for discussion, in parallel with traditional face-to-face lectures and tutorials, indicates that the students engaged in meaning making and the co-construction of understanding that was important beyond the completion of tasks in the subject. Their engagement was often personal, distinctive, self-reflective, and sometimes even passionate. They engaged deeply with the topics discussed and with each other. As the evidence shows, they demonstrated conceptual thinking and ability to confront different arguments and views. The evidence from this study is consistent with other studies on constructivist learning environment and its contribution to learning outcomes (Wilson, 1995).

A significant problem in both case studies was the big difference in students' participation and contribution to the discussion. 10% of students in the first and 5% in the second subject did not participate at all. 38% in the first and 39% in the second subject participated only once. Students from non-IS major contributed much less to the discussion compared to IS students (average participation rate of non-IS students was 1.2 times and for IS students 3.3 times). Unequal participation in the second case study indicates the relevance of the students' background and computer literacy. However prior familiarity with *WISE* itself did not appear to make a difference. Further studies are needed to understand high differences in participation rates and explore strategies to equalise participation.

We have to indicate that the field setting of our study implied some limitations. The fact that both subjects are in the IS field could have had some impact on the issues studied. Second, the instructors were involved as researchers in the study which could have possibly affected the interpretation of the results.

5 CONCLUSION

In this paper we presented preliminary results from an on-going research of a particular Web based teaching and learning environment. In the two case studies we explored how students engage with the subject matter and with each other in the new social space of the technologically mediated learning environment. Our studies indicate that bulletin board type discussion provides new opportunities for students' social interactions, involving sharing of experiences and co-creation of understanding and deep immersion in learning tasks, high motivation and personal commitment.

Understanding of this aspect of flexibility – social interaction and collaboration within the extended social space - is becoming increasingly critical in designing learning environments and developing curricula. As the technological push and market forces are driving us towards ever increasing investments in technological infrastructure, it is becoming even more important to examine opportunities for pedagogical innovations. Our preliminary research study indicates a need for deep investigation of this new social space and the opportunities it provides for enhancement of learning outcomes. A better understanding of the new ways learners and teachers engage in collaborative learning and knowledge co-construction in the technologically mediated social space, we believe, will increase our ability to develop innovative pedagogies and to design genuinely flexible learning environments.

REFERENCES

Alavi, M. (1994) Computer-Mediated Collaborative Learning: An Empirical Evaluation, MIS Quarterly, Vol. 18, No. 2, pp. 159-174.

Candy, P.C., Crebert, G., and O'Leary, J. (1994) *Developing Lifelong Learners through Undergraduate Education*, National Board of Employment, Education and Training, Commonwealth of Australia, Canberra.

Cecez-Kecmanovic, D (1996) A Collaborative Electronic Classroom — An Emerging Teaching and Learning Environment, *University in the 21 Century - Education in a Borderless World,* Electronic publication, British Council and IDP Education Australia, Singapore.

Laurillard, D. and Margetson, D.(1997) *Introducing a Flexible Learning Methodology: Discussion Paper*, Occasional Paper No. 7, Griffith Institute for Higher Education, Griffith University.

Marjanovic, O., Cecez-Kecmanovic, D. and Bonner, R. (1995) Electronic Collaborative Classroom, ASCILITE'95 - Learning with Technology, p306-312.

Miles, M.B. and Huberman, A.M. (1984) *Qualitative Data Analysis: A Source Book of New Methods,* Sage, Beverly Hills, CA.

Slavin, R.E. (1987) *Cooperative Learning: Student Teams*, National Educational Association, Washington.

Taylor, P.G., Lopez, L., and Quadrelli, C. (1996) *Flexibility, Technology and Academics' Practices: Tantalising Tales and Muddy Maps*, Evaluations and Investigations Program, Higher Education Division, DEETYA, Canberra.

Wilson, B.G. (1995) *Constructivist Learning Environments: Case Studies in Instructional Design*, Educational Technology Publications, Englewood Cliffs, NJ.

Impact of Internet on Information Systems Skills Requirement

Abhijit Chaudhury
Department of Management Science and Information Systems, University of Massachusetts, Boston, MA02125
Tel: 617-287-7738, Chaudhury@umbsky.cc.umb.edu

H. Raghav Rao
SUNY- Buffalo

ABSTRACT

The World Wide Web (WWW) is today the breeding ground for innovative application types and technologies. How are these different from mainframe and client/server technologies? What is the impact, if any, of these technologies on the skill set that an IS professional needs to have?

This paper provides an answer to the above questions. It provides a framework for studying the impact of newer application types and basic technologies on the skill sets that IS professionals are expected to have. This understanding can best proceed from an appreciation of the fundamental differences that separate mainframe, client/server and web based technologies.

I. INTRODUCTION

While the late 1980s saw a major platform shift from mainframe-centric systems to client/server systems (Orfali, Harkey and Edwards 1993), the late 90s are seeing a similar shift into World Wide Web (WWW) systems. Late 90s are witnessing a similar transition into WWW based platforms. This is evident from increased demand for web-related skills and proliferation of web related tools. Trade journals carry news about Universities introducing Webmaster certification (Computer World, page 33, Sept 7, 1998), and high signing bonuses for web-related skills (Computer World, page 56, Sept 7, 1998). A more systematic study was done by Horizon Consulting Limited in Newfoundland, Canada, about shortages among IS skills. According to their study, web related skills such as Java, HTML and Web technology were among the top eight skills most in demand (Table 6.0, 1997).

Is WWW development an evolutionary extension of mainframe and or Client/Server (C/S) technologies? Or is there a fundamental and an abrupt change in platform characteristics that makes applications possible in the web world that were not even conceivable in the C/S world? This paper will argue on behalf of the second option. The paper will describe the web as a special kind of C/S platform, but with deep differences in the building blocks that go in making up the web. If the Web represent a major discontinuous transition, how does that impact on the skills and knowledge of tools that information systems professional need to have in this new emerging world? The paper will trace how the skill set is changing as we migrate from the C/S world to the web.

II. EVOLUTION OF APPLICATIONS

There are many ways to think about and classify IS applications. Zuboff (1988) classified systems according to their purpose. She divided them into systems that automate and systems that *informate* (a word she coined). The former encompasses transaction-processing systems. These systems automate an existing process by substituting computers for manual labor. Systems that informate, have their primary goal as informing business users about the business. This class includes all reporting and traditional management information systems. Morton (1991) extended this classification by adding a third class of applications. His third class included systems whose goal is to bring about organizational transformation. Such applications include inter-organizational systems such as Electronic-Data- Interchange (EDI) and collaborative systems such as Lotus Notes.

To understand the major difference between the above applications and the web-based applications, let us visit some popular sites such as home.microsoft.com or www.amazon.com. The first aspect to note is that these popular sites are built for visitors who may be students, researchers, business people or housewives. The sites are designed to focus attention on products and services that the company offers. The Microsoft site provides several web channels that a user can subscribe in the manner of TV channel. These web channels relate to different subjects such as sports, weather or general news. One can log into one of the web channels and have video clips or sound clips downloaded relating to a news item.

Unlike traditional IS application, web applications are organized in terms of documents. In general, the documents on web sites can be categorized as:

- Content-oriented documents. Such a document has a variety of contents such as text, sound and images. The author of the document determines the content and the document as such resides on the server. Such a document is said to have a static *structure*, because the document that exists on the server is the document that is sent over to the browser and displayed.
- Structure-oriented documents. Such a document does not exist in a pre-defined form. Instead, depending on the input from the user a query is executed on a database and the result of the query is then formatted as an HTML document that is sent to the browser. Such a document displays output from a database.
- Interactive documents. These documents allow the user to send information back to the web server. This information could be in the form of hypertext link, an e-mail, or parameters to a query to be executed over the database. The basic purpose of these documents is to provide interactivity.
- Generally, in advanced web sites, we find documents that are simultaneously content-oriented, structure-oriented, and interactive. A good example of such a document is found on the web site www.amazon.com.

Table 1: Evolution of Applications

Type	Application Purpose	Target Population	Platform
Transaction Processing Systems	Automate business processes relating to order processing, accounting, inventory control	A company	• Mainframe • Client/Server • WWW
Management Reporting Systems	Automate periodic and standard report preparation function	A company	• Mainframe • Client/Server • WWW
Office Productivity Applications and Decision Support Systems	• To assist individual in their office tasks • To make decision better and quicker	• Home users of computers • Individual managers in a company	• Mainframe (Use of statistical tools such as SAS on the mainframe) • Client/Server (Use of spreadsheets, word processors)
Collaborative and communication	To assist in exchange of electronic mail and in collaborative activities	Small groups within a company	• Mainframe (Use of e-mail) • Client/Server (Use of Lotus Notes) • WWW (Use of Web sites for community activities)
Web broadcasting	Parallel to the functions served by daily newspapers and television	The entire population at large	• WWW
Shop-front	Functions as a substitute for catalog and brochures	The entire population at large	• WWW
Entertainment and education	Receive audio and video clips relating to online training and entertainment	The entire population at large	• WWW
Business to business electronic commerce	Automating ordering and invoicing systems	Multiple companies	• Mainframe (Electronic Data Interchange) •WWW

We are now in a position to identify the differences between applications that run over the mainframe or client/server system and those that run over the web. These can be categorized into three dimensions.

- First, the target population. In case of mainframe or c/s application the population is limited to business whereas it is usually the general population in the case of web. Web sites such as home.Microsoft.com or www.Amazon.com are designed for a very varied clientele.
- Second, the purpose of the application. In the case of mainframe or c/s, the applications have their objective to further specific and well-defined business process or decision-making. In case of web based application that is not necessarily the case. The home page of home.Microsoft.com is not designed to further any business process.
- Third, the application contents and style. In the case of mainframe or c/s, the applications are primarily text-based with a rich interface for users to interact with the system. The content is primarily text-oriented. In case of web, the content is far richer. They are not only graphic in nature but also carry multi-media elements such as animation, and streaming video or sound. The opening page of www.amazon.com provides several such elements.
. Table 1, provides a synopsis of the points made in this section

III. EVOLUTION OF PLATFORMS

An IS platform consists of components. These components are workstations that interface to the users, communication networks, servers, and the applications and the databases that run on these servers. An IS architecture defines the logical framework that is used to interconnect these various components. Different architectures can all be described as different variations to basic theme, the theme of a client/server system.

World Wide Web Platform

The World Wide Web (WWW) is a part of the Internet system. The Internet is a vast *distributed* system made up of millions of servers and so is WWW. A distributed system stores information across many computers. Hypermedia is the basis of the WWW. Media refers to kind of data or information that is sent over by the web server to the browsers. It can be a plain text file, an audio file, an image, or a video clip. Hypermedia is a way of linking these documents, where you have links and you can jump form one topic to another by using these links. As you choose different links and move around from one document to another, you may be jumping from one server on the web to another without knowing it, while the WWW handles all the connections.

The WWW is also a client/server system. In such a system, the server is a repository of information and the clients are computers that request for this information. In the case of WWW, the browsers on our personal computers act as clients and the web servers act as servers. Often, the web server has to process a client's request before it can send over the information. For instance, on www.Amazon.com if you query about a book, the web server has to perform the following functions:

- The web server has to send the query to a database
- Obtain the result from the database
- Format the result in a proper form for the browser to display, and
- Send the results back to the client browser

The WWW is a distributed client server system. Because the information is distributed over many Web servers, it is sometimes described as n-tier distributed client/server platform. These servers manage a collection of web pages. Web servers are often dedicated machines that act as repository for web pages. It consists of:

- Hardware, the machine which could be a personal computer, a workstation or a mainframe computer.
- On the hardware runs an operating system such as Windows NT, Unix or some mainframe operating system such as VMS.
- The web server software runs on top of the operating system. Some of the popular web sever software are Microsoft's Internet Information Server, NCSA, CERN and MacHTTP.

In order to display the web pages a user needs to have a WWW client program called browser. Common browser programs are Netscape Navigator, MOSAIC, Microsoft's Internet Explorer, and many others. The browsers run over a variety of platforms such as Windows, Unix, MacOS, etc. In the WWW, any server running on any platform can interact with any browser running over any client machine. This makes the content of the WWW system universally available all over the Internet.

While the web is a form of client/server, there are many fundamental differences between a C/S platform and the web. First, unlike the C/S architecture the power of web architecture comes not from a single server but from a multitude of servers acting in concert. The WWW is a system of distributed servers. Second, as we move from one move from web server to another the process is totally transparent. This is made possible through the use of Hypertext Transfer Protocol (HTTP) that is memory-less. One does not need to set up and close a session in order to jump from one web server to another (refer to Appendix A for a detailed note on protocols used on web). Third, the communication takes place over the wide area networks built up from leased telephone lines. Fourth, since the content of the communication may consist of audio or video, the interface devices have to more than graphic. They should have the necessary hardware and software to allow audio clips, video clips and streaming audio and video transmissions to run. Table 2, provides in a summary form the differences between the mainframe, the traditional client/server and the web platforms.

IV. EVOLUTION OF SKILL-SETS

In this section, we concentrate on the evolution of IS skill-sets. We focus only on technical skills. We discuss this issue with

Table 2. Evolution of Platforms

Type of Platform	Interface devices	Databases	Communication platform	Architecture
Mainframe	Primarily character-oriented	Relational and hierarchical record-oriented databases	Slow speed wide area networks	1-tier
Client/server	Graphical user interfaces	Relational record-oriented databases	High-speed local area network and private wide area networks	1 and 2-tier
World Wide Web	Multi-media (sound, video and graphics) interfaces	Relational record oriented databases plus document based, and multi-media objects databases	Wide area networks running over telephone lines	n-tier distributed server platform

respect to three factors. First, is the domain knowledge. If an IS person is developing an accounting application, he must have a good understanding of accounting processes and standards. Similarly, somebody developing an order entry system should have a deep familiarity with that business process. Second, an IS person needs to possess basic technical skills related to programming, systems analysis and database design. Finally, the IS person must be familiar with the tools that he is expected to work with. We call the first domain knowledge, the second core IS skills and the last tool literacy.

How has the requirement for domain knowledge, core IS skills and tool literacy changed with the advent of the web? One way to gauge this change is to look at the emergence at new job classifications and the change in requirements for old ones. Let us take a look at the new job classifications that are coming up for WWW world. Some of these are web designer, web architect, producer (artists, illustrator, animation expert), web master, etc.

Morris and Paul (1998) have categorized these new titles into several roles (page 87). These are web master, analyst, quality assurance, producer (content developer such as graphic artists), web designers, programmers and database designers. Some of the roles are prevalent in the world of client/server or the mainframe and these are programmer, database designers, analyst and quality assurance. Newer roles include producers, web designers and web masters.

Web Designers, Producers and Masters: Domain Knowledge, Core Skills and Tool Literacy:

Unlike the client/server and the mainframe world, the data that appears on the interface is not limited to texts. It may include images, sound, animation, etc. Producers are content developers who work in these media. They usually specialize in one specific media such as sound, video, graphic art, etc. They bring along their skills in those media to develop contents on the web. The domain knowledge of web producers includes knowledge of subjects such as advertisement and mass communication. Their core skills include proficiency in the different art media. They need to be familiar with tools such as Macromedia Director, Adobe Photoshop and Microsoft's Image Composer.

The web designer is the one who designs and enforces aesthetic standards on the web. What the designers design, the producers develop. Like the producers, the domain knowledge of web producers includes subjects such as advertisement and communication. Similarly, their core skills include proficiency in the different art media. They need to be familiar with tools such as Macromedia Director, Adobe Photoshop and Microsoft's Image Composer

The roles of web designer and the producer are critical in web applications such as web broadcasting, shop-front applications, entertainment, etc. Their roles are limited in applications that focus on transactions or business to business electronic commerce. Much of technology progress on the web is related to the rich media types. Audio or video clips or streaming audio and video, and virtual reality are impacting the core skills and tool literacy that designer and the producer is supposed to bring on to the job.

The position of a webmaster is similar to that of a project manager of a development team. A webmaster needs to be familiar with different web technologies such as CGI, Java, Javascript, etc (refer to Appendix A). She should have the ability to manage cross-functional teams and coordinates technical development staff with content providers in other areas of business (Computer World, October 5, 1998, page75)

Programmers, Database designers, Analysts and Quality Assurance: Domain Knowledge, Core Skills and Tool Literacy

The traditional roles of programmers, database designers and analysts are changing too. This follows from the change in the type of applications that run on the web and the altered nature of the platform. The purpose of the web applications is rarely purely business and the platform is very different from that of the mainframe or the client/server. All data interchange between the client and the back-end database is mediated by the web server. This makes the platform a kind of n-tier distributed client/server system.

There are three classes of programs that run on the web: on the client side browser, on the web server and on the database server. The data that arrives at the client end, that is the browser is usually in the form of an HTML document. Knowledge of HTML or the meta-language XML (Extensible markup Language) is necessary to develop documents or channels for the web. The programmer is expected to familiar with the means of integrating multiple media elements in his documents. Currently, the programs that run on the web server employ scripting languages such as VBscript or Perl. The requirement of a database designer is least affected by the advent of the web.

The domain knowledge that programmers, analysts and quality assurance people need to bring to their job depends very much on the nature of the application. If the applications are transaction oriented then the domain knowledge they need is similar to the world of mainframe and client/server. If the applications are oriented towards collaborative activities or community building exercises, their domain knowledge need to include understanding of group processes, nature of communities, and a broad knowledge of sociology and anthropology.

With the rapid proliferation of tools for web development, the requirement for tool literacy for programmers, analysts and quality assurance people are now very different. Totally new tool environments are being created. For instance, Microsoft's Visual InterDev and a product called SilverStream. Table 3 below summarizes the points made in this section.

VI. CONCLUSION

The focus of this paper has been on the question: Is WWW development an evolutionary extension of mainframe and or Client/Server (C/S) technologies? Or does it imply a fundamental and an abrupt change in platform characteristics that makes applications possible in the web world that were not even conceivable in the C/S world? This paper agued on behalf of the second

Table 3: Evolution of Skill-sets		
Mainframe	**Client/Server**	**World Wide Web**
Role: Application Development (programmers and quality assurance) Core-Skills: Understand business processes and decision-making and build applications to support them Tool literacy: Development is limited to a single vendor's proprietary environment. Familiarity with COBOL language and CICS environment	Role: Application Development (programmers and quality assurance) Core-skills: In addition to mainframe, learn about GUI interfaces and event-driven programming Tool literacy: Development is limited to a few vendor's proprietary environment Alternative development environment include Microsoft' environment such as Visual Basic, Microsoft's Transaction Server and SQL server Visual Basic or PowerBuilder with Oracle	Role: Application Development (programmers, quality assurance, web producers and web designers) Core-skills: In addition to client/server, learn about development of web-based interactive systems, development of television-style channels. Familiarity with HTML and XML and scripting languages such as Java Script and VB Script Tool literacy: It is mostly an open environment where many vendors compete to provide tools to similar specification Development within Microsoft's Visual InterDev environment or using Java based environment such as SilverStream
Role: Systems Analysis and Design Core-skills: Traditional waterfall method	Role: Systems Analysis and Design Core-skills In addition to mainframe, learn about rapid application development, joint application development, etc	Role: Systems Analysis and Design Core-skills In addition of client/server, learn to use new metaphors such as that of theatre (Laurel 1993) and building architecture (Mitchell 1996) to design web sites and web application
Role: Data Designers Core-skills: Hierarchical and relational databases for records relating to business objects and events Tool literacy: Databases such as DB2	Role: Data Designers Core-skills Design and implement relational databases for records relating to business objects and events Tool literacy: Databases such as Oracle and Microsoft SQL server	Role: Data Designers Core-skills In addition to client/server, learn about document databases, and databases containing multi-media objects Tool literacy: Databases such as Oracle and Microsoft SQL server

option If the Web represent a major discontinuous transition, how does that impact on the skills and knowledge of tools that information systems professional need to have in this new emerging world? The paper traced how the skill set is changing as we migrate from the C/S world to the web.

(References can be provided on request)

Opportunities and Obstacles of Outsourcing Software: Compare China with India

Qiyang Chen, John Wang, Qiang Tu

School of Business Montclair State University , Upper Montclair, NJ 07043

ABSTRACT

This paper is an attempt to highlight the current issues of outsourcing software in countries in Asia, especially in China and India. It addresses the crucial factors to be a successful software outsourcer in the region. The paper compares China with India in terms of the software exports to identify the common issues and differences in software export. It also presents some strategic concerns for further development.

INTRODUCTION

Information technology is diffusing rapidly into all industrial and service sectors and is now seen as one of the most crucial technologies affecting global economic growth. Software is vital of all components of information technology. It is estimated that the software industry is responsible for 5% of GDP in U.S. [1]. Jobs in this area are growing rapidly as well. According to the survey from the ITAA, there nearly 200,000 IT jobs standing vacant in U. S. companies, and annually production of qualified IT graduates from domestic colleges is less than 40,000 [2].

Software industry is rapidly changing and hence it is not easily defined. It has grown and diversified to enter every aspect of business industry. Software industry is extremely labor-intensive and skill-intensive. Costs of computer programmers and other skilled labor have become major expense in development of information systems [3].

Software industry now is losing its strategic distinction because of its global availability, Internet accessibility and easy copy. As businesses develop their strategies in the information age, there is more emphasis on technology-enabled capabilities - not only for operational efficiency but also for strategic effectiveness [4]. One of the analysis performed by a national temporary personnel service indicates that up to half of large U.S. companies are investigating the feasibility of outsourcing some or all of their software functions [4].

GLOBAL FEATURES OF SOFTWARE DEVELOPMENT

In addition to the significant features of labor/skill intensity, the difficulties and advantages in technology know-how also attract various vendor and clients in software outsourcing business. For example, U.S. companies' advantages in developing emerging software technology will make various foreign outsourcers to lower their bids just for get in touch with the new technology. On the other side, any advantage on a particular technology can vanish fair quickly. U.S. companies have to transfer their technology know-how into profit or cost efficiency in timely manor. This is because of the following unique features of software industry:

- The technologies in software can be dispersed around the world widely and quickly, including the technologies to create, distribute, and operate software.
- The software technology is intangible; and can be modified after initial production to create a new product.
- The software technology has no clear distinction between production tools and final product.
- The technology can be transportable across various computer platforms and networks.
- Exported software has to meet the application requirements in foreign sites.

With increasing production and use of software, emerging economies in south east Asia such as India, China, Singapore, Hong-Kong, Taiwan, etc. all have software industries with annual growth rates of 30-40% [5]. One of the reasons for such fast growth is that the software industry is a highly desirable industry and got strong governmental support in all these nations. Software industry does not require a lot raw material but skilled manpower, and is not in any way damaging to the environment. With relatively small investment, right governmental policies and legislation, a developing country's IT/IS society can catch up the progress of the emerging software technology very quickly. Compare to the conventional industry, the unique features and applications of software industry shorten the technological distance between the developing countries and developed countries.

GLOBAL SOFTWARE OUTSOURCING

Outsourcing software development has become a prominent business practice in which a company contracts all or part of its software projects to one or more outside suppliers (outsourcers). As companies strive for an ever more delusive competitive advantage in today's global economy, more companies in developed countries opted to dismantle internal IT/IS departments by transferring IT employees, facilities, hardware leases and software licenses to third party vendors. Outsourcing software development, or the strategic use of outside software resources, has become one the most critical topics and most widely implemented management tool for organizational change.

As the world's largest software industry, U.S. continues to outsource its software development globally. It has become the largest software outsourcing client in the world. This is due to it being the first-entrant in the field of computer and software. Most world class software vendors are sited in U.S. It has the largest base of software installation [5]. There is general compatibility with a large number of installed software. Intellectual property right has been regulated and executed by US standards. There are many quality educational institutes for programming and computer science.

The growing software market offers firms to recruit critical resources to develop quality software, including skilled engineers to develop software, efficient markets channel to distribute software, strong support from academic research centers, and an active capital market to support risky investment.

US software outsourcing business is not only the largest domestically but also internationally. Table 1 shows the average revenue for the past five years.

Global outsourcing of software growth in world market has been almost exponential since late 1970's. Growth of software market in past twenty years has been exponential. The past five years' average revenue worth roughly $350 billion [6]. Internationalization was fueled by the desire to reduce labor costs and shortage of software skills in developed countries, which lead to large backlog of software projects.

Globalization of software outsourcing is also favorable due to the nature of the industry. There is standardization of job activities based on structured system analysis. Given current programming languages and hardware environments, as well as the Internet facilities, the technology and activities of software production can be regulated and monitored, no matter where the development taking place, hence it allows the internationalization of software services [7].

Studies show that for the innovative and strategic applications, they are unlikely to be ideal for outsourcing from countries having weaker law enforcement of security and piracy issues [8]. Never the less, the cost benefits of outsourcing are significant enough for companies to outsource. It is not only advantageous to outsource but also imperative for a company, in order to remain competitive and bring new technological advancement and most importantly stay ahead of competition.

SOFTWARE OUTSOURCERS: CHINA VS INDIA

Currently, the software industry in India is estimated to be worth $1.2 billion U.S dollars. If we add in in-house development that takes place at many large commercial/corporate end-users, the total software industry is near $2 billion, where as ten years back the software industry in India was less than $10 million. The growth rate for the Indian software industry in the last five years has been 46%. Despite these high growth rates, India's share in the world software market is very low [10]. Currently, the software industry employs more than 125,000 people and continues to be the fastest growing sectors in Indian economy.

Compare to Indian software industry, China started late. According to research conducted by International Data Corp., the compounded annual growth rate for software service in China between 1995 and 2000 will be 43 percent, with

Table 1. Market share of software outsourcing in past five years [7].

Country	Market Share %
US	57
Japan	13
UK	8
Germany	7
Canada	6
France	3
Others	6
Total	100

the total market size forecasted to reach $784 million by the year 2000. For this reason, many IT companies are placing high hopes on the future potential of the professional services market in China and are currently laying the groundwork they believe necessary for future success which include finding outsourcing partners for IT/IS development. The total IT market in China is forecasted to average 37 percent annual growth from 1995 to the year 2000, while over the same period the software services market is forecasted to grow at 43 percent.

On the other side, software export in India worth US$ 24 million in 1985 and with in a few years, the turnover has grown multifold; in 1996-97, a total export of $785 million was achieved and it is expected to reach an export level of $1 billion by 1998. Chinese software export industry got in touch with global software market since mid 80's while the major efforts were in the transplanting Chinese version of various software and data processing business. Table 2 shows the comparison of export proportion in several software service categories.

International companies landed in India and China, including IBM, Microsoft, Novell, Oracle, AT&T, Fujitsu, Motorola, Digital, Hewlett Packard. GE, AT&T, Reebok, Levies, Caterpillar, Citibank, American Airlines, British Aerospace, are partnering with local software industries. Three types of software development arrangements currently exist [9,10,11]:

• Subsidiaries of foreign vendors or foreign software users.
• Joint ventures between foreign and local IT/IS firms.
• Outsourcing of foreign based projects to local contractors. Foreign firms established a wholly owned subsidiary to develop and maintain its proprietary.

Internet has become a communication channel for software development. China's Internet infrastructure has been made up of four, largely separate national networks: (a) ChinaNet, the primary commercial network, run by the Ministry of Information Industry. (b) The golden Bridge Network (GBNet), a much smaller competing commercial network, owned by Jitong Corporation. (c) China science and Technology Network (CSNet), the nation's high technology researches network. (d) The China Educational and Research network (CERNet), linking China's academic and learning institutions from grade school to post-graduate level [12,13].

Both China and India enjoy the following advantages over some of other nations, which promote software exports:

Cheap labor: Manpower cost is relatively low. A typical programmer with 3 years experience in both countries might earn less than $200/month – approximately 15 times less than his or her American counterpart. Plus the Chinese/Indian labor has reputation for being flexible and amenable.

Highly trained and skilled personnel: Both China and India have the world's second largest pool of scientific manpower. It has a growing number of more than 3.5 million technical personnel with more than 41,000 IT/IS graduates annually.

Quality: Various training programs and certification processes ensure the quality of software personnel and services. For example, 37 Indian software companies have acquired ISO 9000 certification and about 70 more are in the pipeline. In China, there is a cooperate policy in many large IT firms to have employee to pass the certification tests.

State-of-the-art Technology: A survey shows that more than 65% of Indian software companies use the state-of-the-art technologies in their software development process. The state-of-the-art technologies include the use of Computer Aided Software Engineering (CASE) and Fourth Generation Languages (4GLs) in software development; adoption of Graphical User Interfaces; Object-oriented programming techniques; etc. Acquiring high computing equipment is no longer a major obstacle for software project as the price of such equipment is going down dramatically. The declining cost of telecommunications facilities that can lower cost of delivering the programmers' output to their clients around the world.

Table 2. A comparison on proportion of exports in each category [4]

| Country | Proportion of exports in each category % | | |
	Software service	Software packages	Data entry
India	70	15	15
Philippines	39	20	41
Singapore	25	58	17
China	17	56	27

Establishing Partnership: The huge market opportunities in China and India are very attractive to foreign enterprises. One of the ways of stepping into the local market is to provide outsourcing projects to the local societies so that to establish a positive relationship for the further market development. For example, a software vendor may outsource a project that transforms its product to be able to process the local dialects or languages. Such project will bring the hard currency to the local society and facilitate sales in the local market.

On the other side, both China and India also share some common problems.

Brian Drain: Software outsourcing projects are dwarfed by a problem that undermines growth polices in all developing countries - the problem of the brain drain. A local programmer who participated in an outsourcing project may have good opportunity to immigrate to a developed country where he/she can improve his/her standard of living as a result of dramatic wage differential cited above. Furthermore, the developed IT/IS societies offer the real prospect that a skillful foreign programmer can capture vast financial rewards for his/her skills and initiative. This phenomenon has caused a lot political debates in both China and India for years.

Software Piracy: Although both governments have implemented various policies to disfavor piracy but it still plagues the software industry, especially in China.

Low-end projects: The contracted projects are mostly fell into the categories of low-end products, such as utility programs, drivers, peripheral systems software, and simple data processing, such data entry and report generation. Majority of such projects does not need sophisticated software technology.

Competition: There is a rising competition from other developing nations in the region, such as Pakistan, Singapore, Philippine, Thailand, and etc. [5].

THE STRATEGIC CONCERNS FOR CHINESE OUTSOURCER

Compared to Chinese software industry, Indian software society is mature and therefore is positioned better as software outsourcer in global market. This challenges the Chinese IT/IS society to address the issues that hamper its efforts to be a successful bidder for the foreign software contracts. The following concerns are strategic for successful outsourcing environment. These issues also underline certain differences between Chinese outsourcers and Indian outsourcers.

Governmental restrictions: Chinese IT/IS society should try to alleviate as much business restrictions conflicting foreign client's interests as possible, meanwhile try to clearly state which domains are not allowed for foreigners to step in at first place.

Cultural and language barriers: Cultural differences can present managerial problems in outsourcing business in developing countries. Cultural differences are daunting to many foreigners, especially when governmental regulations involved. Communication is key to reconcile problems caused by culture issues. In addition, unlike Indian IT/IS society where the English is common media, Chinese IT professionals have to pay attention to its language skills to improve the communication with its foreign clients.

Protecting intellectual property rights: Fundamental intellectual property rights in China are relatively weak. How to enforce the laws and policies in this field is crucial to the success of executing contracts.

Reduce the uncertainties and hidden Cost reduction: The hidden cost should be recognized and minimized well. The high quality products delivered on time are the first. Credibility can be established by avoiding the negative surprises.

Political uncertainty: Providing a stable political environment for foreign investment is very important to keep foreign investments and contracts continually flowed into a developing country. The political uncertainty is not under the control of local IT/IS society. However, it is local society's responsibility to advice foreign client to accommodate the political environment.

Flexibility to change: Due to the nature of uncertainties and difficulties in global outsourcing business, it would be more practical for an outsourcer to be flexible to the changed proposed by its clients. Therefore, as the new entrant, an outsourcer should try to avoid those projects that require extensive system analysis.

CONCLUSION

The good news is that the appreciation for intangibles has been gradually increasing in China and we can expect this trend to continue. Factors spurring this increase in appreciation for intangibles include government incentive programs to increase awareness of software export, growing IT sophistication among professionals and end users, and increased first-hand experience with large project implementation.

Another factor that will lead to greater need for China's software export is the growing international competition that the country faces in international export markets. As China's mainly export-driven economy continues to develop, there is growing recognition among IT decision-makers that the country will need to invest heavily in IT in order to remain competitive in the future. This investment will need to put towards activities that can increase competitiveness through efficiency such as professional IT/IS services.

The most important factor behind a successful outsourcer is the understanding to outsourcing business, a closer relationships with clients and suppliers in specific vertical markets. Connections to reputable international outsourcing consulting firms will bring significant benefits to Chinese IT/IS society.

REFERENCES

[1] R.Anderson, Internal audit taps new sources," Journal of Business Strategy, 17(2) (1996), 22-24.

[2] S.Baker, Calling all nerds, Business Week, March 10, 1997.

[3] H.Czepiec and J.Landers, Skill requirement for a global workforce: The international business employers' perspective, Proceeding of Western DSI Annual Conference, 1996, pp. 298-300.

[4] "International Trade in Computer Software," Stephan E. Siwak and Harold W. Fuchtgoth-roht, Quorum Books, 1993.

[5] V.Gurbaxani, The new world of information technology outsourcing, Communications of ACM, July, 1996, 23-25.

[6] G.Hamel and C.K.Prahalad, Competing for the Future, Harvard Business School Press, Boston, MA, 1994.

[7] Outsourcing Institute, Talking the pulse of outsourcing, http://www.outsourcing.com, 1997.

[8] M. Lacity, L.Willcocks and D.Feeny, The value of selective IT outsourcing, Sloan Management Review, 37(3) (1996),.13-25.

[9] ChinaNet, http://www.asiainfo.com, June, 1998

[10] "India's Software Industry: State policy, Liberalization and industrial development," Richard Heeks, Sage Publication, New Delhi, 1997.

[11] "India's Software Industry: State policy, Liberalization and industrial development," Richard Heeks, Sage Publication, New Delhi, 1997.

[12] International data group (IDC) report, http://www.idgchina.com/NEWS/August97/IDC-Report.htm

[13] Zixiang, T., China's new internet regulations: Two steps forward, one step back, Communications of the ACM, Vol. 40, No. 12, 1997.

Exploring the Browsing Semantics of Information on the WeB[1]

Cheung, Shing-chi and Lam, Chi-yung
Dept of Computer Science, Hong Kong Univ.of Science and Technology, Clear Water Bay, Hong Kong
Tel: +852 2358-7016 Fax: +852 2358-1477, Email: {scc,chiyung}@cs.ust.hk

ABSTRACT

The complexity of the Web makes it difficult for users to understand the browsing semantics; the problem is aggravated with the incorporation of dynamic behaviour into information structure using facilities supported by JavaBeans and CORBA. This motivates the need to model HTML documents for rigorous analysis. In this paper, we propose a framework in the Calculus of Communicating Systems (CCS) to unify the modelling of HTML documents based on structure, content and dynamic behaviour. Interesting queries regarding the document, like accessibility, ordering, reachability and mirror site verification, can be answered. The process is automatable via the use of a tool called the Concurrency Workbench (CWB). Equivalence of two models in terms of behaviour can also be verified. An extended example is used throughout this paper as an illustration.

1 INTRODUCTION

With the staggering increase in the popularity for the WWW (World Wide Web), computer users interact with *HTML (HyperText Markup Language* [4]) *documents* – a form of hypertext [1] – much more frequently than before. Over the years, HTML is gaining more complexity, and both the content and the structure of HTML documents become more sophisticated. As a result, users and authors alike face challenges:

- Accessibility: parents would like to ensure that their children will not be able to get access to pages with pornographic materials starting from their homepage.

- Ordering constraint: a courseware author needs to make sure that revision materials should pre-

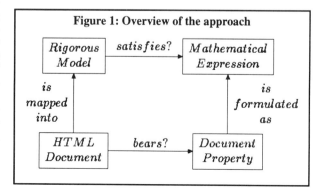

Figure 1: Overview of the approach

cede the quiz in any browsing path.

- Reachability: a medical professor wants to know whether the conclusion on recent advancement of cancer cure can be reached from any page in his HTML document. Also, it is helpful for a user to know if a page on cancer cure can be visited during web surfing from the page that the user is reading.
- Mirroring property: an author wishes to ensure that the *browsing semantics*, i.e. the manner in which information is to be visited and presented to the user through navigation [8], would be preserved when a new document substitutes the old one. This reduces the chance of getting lost (or disorientation) in cyberspace navigation *[1]*.

In addition, the incorporation of such new components as CGI (Common Gateway Interface) scripts adds dynamic behaviour to such documents. This further complicates the challenges because the structure, semantics and dynamic behaviour of an HTML document are now interrelated. For instance, some interactive HTML documents will lead users to different pages depending on the answer submitted. This will affect the reachability of some pages.

The use of a *rigorous model* on which analysis is carried out is helpful in resolving these challenges. HTML documents — in future discussion, HTML documents include dynamic components as well, if any — are first mapped to a model. Then, either properties that we would like the documents to satisfy are expressed in a mathematical form, which can further be analysed rigorously with the model, or the model itself can be utilised to guide users in the browsing process (say, solving the disorientation problem). From Figure 1, we argue that the mapping captures the essential properties of the HTML documents. With the support of mathematical tools, whose correctness are well established, we claim that the satisfaction or violation of a property in the model infers respectively the possession or lack of the corresponding property in the corresponding HTML document.

Previous hypertext modelling approaches are either restricted to hypertext without dynamic components, or to modelling without support for analysis or property verification. Our approach differs in the following aspects:

- mapping the Web-based information system to a concurrent system and modelling it using *CCS (Calculus of Communicating Systems)* which supports concurrency and synchronisation [5];
- providing a unified notion for different facets of the Web-based information system, namely, structure, semantics and dynamic behaviour, under CCS;
- expressing browsing properties of the Web-based information system as temporal logic (modal m-calculus) formulae for model checking.

The remainder of this paper is organised as follows. A brief discussion on some related work is explored in the next section. Then, a case study is presented alongside with the theory of the model in Section 0. Discussion on the analysis of the model will be given in Section 4, and a brief conclusion will be made before we end the paper.

2 RELATED WORK

Relatively little work has been done on the verification of hypertext documents. Attempts to reason about the features of hypertext systems were made [8]. Trellis, the model proposed by Stotts et al., makes use of Petri Nets [7] on which browsing semantics are defined. Nevertheless, the analysis is limited, and the approach may not be ideal in the domain of WWW. The authors do not make a serious effort to model dynamic components as well.

More recently, Stott et al. [9] suggest the use of automaton (termed *links-automaton*) for further analysis. While this model can help verify browsing properties by model checking, several points should be noticed. Firstly, dynamic behaviour embedded in the hypertext itself is ignored as those transition links in the automaton represent hyperlinks only. Secondly, modelling and analysis are separated. It may not be always easy to find a perfect mapping from a hypertext system to the corresponding links-automaton. Thirdly, the authors do not provide a way of abstracting the model by means of composition and information hiding, which is very important for web-based information system, as the scale is extremely large.

According to the work by Turine et al. [10], hypertext documents are modelled based on *Statecharts*, where both the structure and browsing semantics of hypertexts are specified. With this model, synchronisation of simultaneous display can be formulated, and problems like access control, tailored versions and node reachability are solved. The emphasis of this paper, nevertheless, is on navigation and browsing. No general modelling of dynamic behaviour is mentioned, and the examination of hypertext properties is not very comprehensive. Moreover, the model does not provide a discussion for the labelling of links, which can be interpreted semantically in our approach.

Figure 2: Greeting page in our example	Figure 3: Overview page in our example	Figure 4: Lifestyle page in our example
Welcome to ABC Travel Agency We hope that you can find relevant information on Hong Kong, the Pearl of the Orient [Enjoy!]		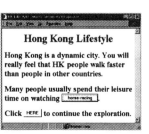

Figure 3: Overview page in our example

Figure 4: Lifestyle page in our example

In the field of information retrieval, researchers advocating the confluence of hypertext and information retrieval often see the need for making use of both the structure and content of hypertext. For instance, Chiaramella et al. [3] propose using *Conceptual Graphs* to represent both structure and content to take advantage from the combination of hypertext and information retrieval approaches. Wilkinson et al. [11] justify the combined approach that involves content, context, structure and attributes of hypertext for queries and retrieval. Many of these approaches, however, make use of graph models to represent their ideas. With only nodes and links but no tools or semantics supported, it is not easy for browsing semantics like concurrency and synchronisation to be expressed [8].

3 MODEL CONSTRUCTION

To have a successful modelling, rules must be defined to map HTML documents of a web-based information system into CCS notation. In this section, we will illustrate the process through an extended example.

Consider an HTML document written for a Hong Kong Travel Agency. After receiving a greeting message (Figure 2), users can choose to learn more about Hong Kong, or to have an on-line quiz (Figure 3). If the former link is chosen, a variety of topics can be further pursued (Figure 5). Of these topics, there is a page on Hong Kong lifestyle that contains a link to information on horseracing (Figure 4). There is also another page on places of fun in Hong Kong providing links to entertainment activities in Hong Kong. Some link may contain materials not suitable for youngsters, like "Night Life" (Figure 6). More details on the document will be unveiled as the discussion goes on.

A brief introduction to CCS, or *process calculus*, is in place. For an in-depth explanation, please refer to [5] and [2]. CCS is a formalism to specify the basic concepts of a reactive and distributed system which consists of *agents* communicating with one another to achieve system unity. Each agent has a number of *states* connected by *transitions*. These transitions, constituting the behaviour of the agent, are defined by *actions* and *operators*.

It is, then, straightforward to map fragments of an HTML document as states, and hyperlinks as actions. For each *link anchor* (i.e. a physical element in the source whose activation will lead the user to the destination of a link), we assign one or more actions to reflect the content information of link destination. This distinguishes our approach from [10] in that the authors do not place emphasis on the link annotation, while we believe that only by annotating links with semantics will queries on document content itself be carried out. Note that, as exemplified later, actions in our model are not confined to describing content information.

With reference to Figure 2, the user will reach a page as shown in Figure 3 if the anchor Enjoy! is triggered. The HTML document can be modelled as follows, where the system will have a change of state from A (the opening page) to B (the destination page) on action *overview* (triggering of Enjoy!):

$$A \overset{def}{=} overview \cdot B$$

This expression introduces the first operator: *prefix operator* (•). The same expression can be represented in an alternative form called *Labelled Transition System (LTS)*:

$$A \xrightarrow{\;overview\;} B$$

If the author wants to further annotate the destination as *hongkong*, the corresponding modification is:

$$A \xrightarrow{\;hongkong\;} \bullet \xrightarrow{\;overview\;} B$$

In the formulation, a special state V is introduced to the model. It can be thought as having a "virtual" start page which contains an anchor to the real homepage of the system. In this way, the content of the real homepage can be described. Returning to our example, the following expression can be added based on the discussion so far:

$$V \overset{def}{=} travelAgent \cdot A$$

Figure 5: List-of-topics page in our example

Figure 6: Fun-places in our example

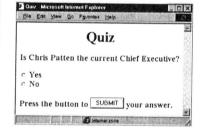

Figure 7: Online quiz in our example

Figure 8: Page shown when the answer is correct

Figure 9: Page shown when the answer is wrong

If there are multiple links to choose from a particular page, *summation operator* (+) can be used for modelling. Referring to Figure 3, a user can either choose anchor Learn more about HK! or Take a Quiz!. We can express it as follows:

$$B \overset{def}{=} background \cdot C + quiz \cdot D$$

Intuitively, once *quiz* is triggered due to the choice of anchor Take a Quiz! (say), the system will behave in accordance with the definition of D (the quiz page: see Figure 7).

The real power of the calculus is revealed when dynamic behaviour is modelled. Suppose we have to submit the answer of a true-or-false question to the web server in the quiz page (Figure 7). Based on the correctness of the answer checked by the server, different pages will be presented (see Figure 8 and Figure 9).

The behaviour on the client side can be modelled as in Figure 10, while one high-level model (with answer-checking mechanism abstracted away) of the server is shown in Figure 11. Note that an action can have parameters, as in *submit(ans)*, where *ans* is the answer for the true-or-false question. Also, actions like *correct* or *wrong* do not refer to any anchor in the document. Rather, they are used to represent the dynamic behaviour involved in the interaction between the client and server during the answer-checking process. Actions like *correct* and are called *complementary actions*, which serve for the purpose of synchronisation.

The incorporation of synchronisation is accomplished by the use of *composition operator* (|) in several ways. If the server does not store any information for later use by the client, we can simply regard the interaction as a *session*: the session ends when the interaction is over. With respect to our example, the server is modelled as shown in Figure 12. The formulation will then be $D=D1|S2$. Note that a new instance of S_2 is created every time when the quiz page is visited.

If the server stores information for future use (say, keeping the number of questions answered correctly by the user), we would instead formulate[2] as $V=travelAgent \cdot A|S1$. The server is instantiated at the beginning and will keep running. Only one server exists throughout the whole scenario.

Whatever the case, it can be thought of having both the client and server (or server session) running in parallel. After the client receives the action *userInput(ans)*, it emits the action *submit(ans)*. The server (or server session), on receiving this action (as indicated by the complementary action, *submit(ans)*), checks for the correctness and then emits either *correct* or *wrong*. When the server (or server session) is doing its job, the client cannot proceed but only stop at the dummy state, until it receives either *correct* or *wrong*.

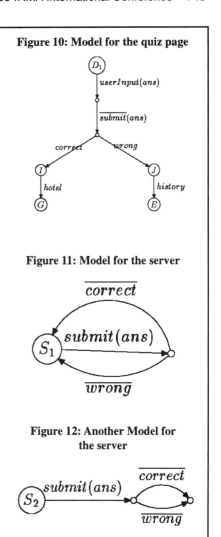

Figure 10: Model for the quiz page

Figure 11: Model for the server

Figure 12: Another Model for the server

One important concept is that such synchronised actions will then be hidden after applying the composition operator to become *internal action (t)*, which is not observable. This helps abstract away unimportant details of the system: when viewed externally, a user will not notice the presence of such actions as *submit(ans)* or *wrong*.

If actions are to be only involved in synchronisation, it is a good idea to restrict their occurrences so that they cannot act independently. This is the function of *restriction operator* (\).

4 ANALYSIS ON THE MODEL

Once the model is formed, we can formulate the desired properties and carry out model checking for verification. In the following subsections, we will use an automated tool called the *Concurrency Workbench (CWB)* [6] to answer the challenges discussed at the beginning of the article. CWB is a tool that allows users to specify agent behaviour in CCS and formulate property propositions in *modal m-calculus*, a particular temporal logic.

4.1 Modelling in Action

With reference to the discussion in Section 0, we obtain a list of agent expressions to be inputted in CWB environment. Figure 13 shows a typical session in CWB. Note that command agent specifies an agent expression, and the complementary actions are represented as correct and 'correct.

With the use of *daVinci*, a graph viewer, a transition diagram of the agent V can be generated automatically and is shown in the Appendix.

4.2 Safety and Liveness Properties Checking

Many properties fall into the following two classes: *safety* and *liveness*. A safety property asserts that the system never enters an undesirable state, whereas a liveness property asserts that the system eventually enters a desirable state.

The task is therefore to transform the queries to modal m-calculus logic formulae. The discussion that follows serves mainly for illustrating how temporal logic can be applied to different kinds of property verification in the domain of Web-based information systems. Please refer to Figure 13 for the sample interaction session.

- The challenge of whether some page is inaccessible can be modelled as a safety property. Provided that no corresponding action appears in the navigation path, the property is preserved. As an illustration, suppose a user wants to know if any indecent materials will be encountered when our extended example is navigated through. Assuming that the action is named *nightlife*, the formula expressing this property is:

$$vX.[nightlife] \text{ ff} \wedge [-]X$$

The query should return "false", which indicates that information on nightlife is provided via one particular link. We can actually make use of CWB to work out that path (see Figure 14).

- Page-ordering constraint problems can similarly be modelled as a safety property. If a user wants to make a query on whether the page on Hong Kong lifestyle always precedes the page on horseracing (note that we require such an ordering whatever the navigation path), a corresponding formula is shown below, where *a* and *b* represent actions for links to Hong Kong lifestyle page and horseracing page respectively:

$$vX.[a] \text{ tt} \wedge [b] \text{ ff} \wedge [-a,b]X$$

The query returns "true" based on the model checking. On the other hand, if we modify the document such that access to the page on horseracing is provided when a user answers the quiz question correctly, the answer to the query should be "false". This shows how the inclusion of a dynamic component affects the result.

- Let us investigate the reachability problem. Based on different needs, we have different reachability properties. In the following discussion, reachability of the quiz page is explored.

Case 1: If we just need to make sure that the quiz page is reachable via **some** navigation path from the starting page, we can make use of the safety property for inaccessibility by making a negation: a violation of the inaccessibility property implies that the target is reachable, and vice versa. The property is formulated as I, where

$$\Phi = \neg \left(vX.[quiz] \text{ ff} \wedge [-]X \right)$$

Evidently, the result of the query should return true.

Case 2: Suppose we need to ensure that the quiz page is reachable (via **some** navigation path) regardless of where the current location is. The property can be expressed as:

$$vY.\Phi \wedge [-]Y$$

where F is the expression defined in the last case. Note that the query returns "true". The quiz page can still be reachable via the action *history* even when other anchors like Hong Kong Lifestyle was selected earlier, because there is always an anchor that leads back to the page entitled "Explore Hong Kong".

Case 3: If we have to make sure that the quiz page is reachable (via **any** navigation path) from the starting page, liveness

Figure 13: A sample session of CWB for our example

```
X xterm                                                   _ □ ×
Edinburgh Concurrency Workbench, version 7.0,
Fri Oct  6 11:36:58 BST 1995

Command: * Agent definitions *
Command: agent A = hongkong.overview.B;
Command: agent B = background.C + quiz.D;
Command: agent C = history.E + lifestyle.F + hotel.G + funplace.H;
Command: agent D = userInput%0%.'submit%0%.(correct.I + wrong.J) +
                   userInput%1%.'submit%1%.(correct.I + wrong.J);
Command: agent E = hongkong.overview.backAnchor.B;
Command: agent F = horseracing.K + background.backAnchor.C;
Command: agent G = background.backAnchor.C;
Command: agent H = nightlife.L + background.backAnchor.C;
Command: agent I = hotel.G;
Command: agent J = history.E;
Command: agent K = background.backAnchor.C;
Command: agent L = background.backAnchor.C;
Command: agent S = submit%0%.('correct.S + 'wrong.S) +
                   submit%1%.('correct.S + 'wrong.S);
Command: agent V = (travelAgent.A | S)\{correct,wrong,submit%0%,submit%1%};

Command: * Inaccessibility property *
Command: prop NotAccessible = max(X.[nightlife]F & [-]X);

Command: * Automatic checking by CWB *
Command: cp(V, NotAccessible);
false

Command: * Ordering constraint property *
Command: prop Ordering = max(X.[lifestyle]T & [horseracing]F &
                          [-lifestyle,horseracing]X);

Command: * Automatic checking by CWB *
Command: cp(V, Ordering);
true

Command: * Situation if the correct answer for quiz leads to horse-racing *
Command: agent I = horseracing.K;

Command: * Automatic checking by CWB *
Command: cp(V, Ordering);
false

Command: * Converting back to the original definition *
Command: agent I = hotel.G;

Command: * Reachability -- Case 1 *
Command: prop Reachable1 = ~max(X.[quiz]F & [-]X);

Command: * Automatic checking by CWB *
Command: cp(V, Reachable1);
true

Command: * Reachability -- Case 2 *
Command: prop Reachable2 = max(Y.~max(X.[quiz]F & [-]X) & [-]Y);

Command: * Automatic checking by CWB *
Command: cp(V, Reachable2);
true

Command: * Reachability -- Case 3 *
Command: prop Reachable3 = min(X.<->T & [-quiz]X);

Command: * Automatic checking by CWB *
Command: cp(V, Reachable3);
false

Command: * Reachability -- Case 4 *
Command: prop Reachable4 = max(Y.min(X.<->T & [-quiz]X) & [-]Y);

Command: * Automatic checking by CWB *
Command: cp(V, Reachable4);
false
```

property comes to play. The corresponding formula is F2, where

$$\Phi' = \mu X.\langle - \rangle \text{tt} \wedge [-quiz] X$$

The query returns false since a user can repeat navigating on pages related to background of Hong Kong without the need to choose the anchor to quiz page.

Case 4: This is the strictest of all cases. Suppose the quiz page has to be reachable (via **any** navigation path) no matter where the current location is, the formula should be:

$$\nu Y.\Phi' \wedge [-] Y$$

where F2 is the expression defined in the last case. Obviously, if the query for the previous case fails, this query should return false also.

As observed from the examples, these formulae share a similar structure. In other words, they can be categorised from which a common pattern can be derived. One possible way of easing the burden of users in manipulating these expressions is to parameterise the formulae such that users only need to select from a list of formulae and then supply the necessary information.

5 CONCLUSIONS

We have presented a framework in process algebra to unify the modelling of HTML documents based on structure, content and dynamic behaviour. The framework can be deployed to answer interesting queries regarding the document, like accessibility, ordering, reachability and mirror site verification. Automated support can be provided through the use of some analysis tool, such as the Concurrency Workbench (CWB). We plan to realise the model through *Extensible Markup Language (XML)*. By extending the document type of HTML, documents on the WWW can be readily analysed. This necessitates further study on how to derive CCS expressions from HTML.

Figure 14: A simulation run to illustrate accessibility of pages on nightlife

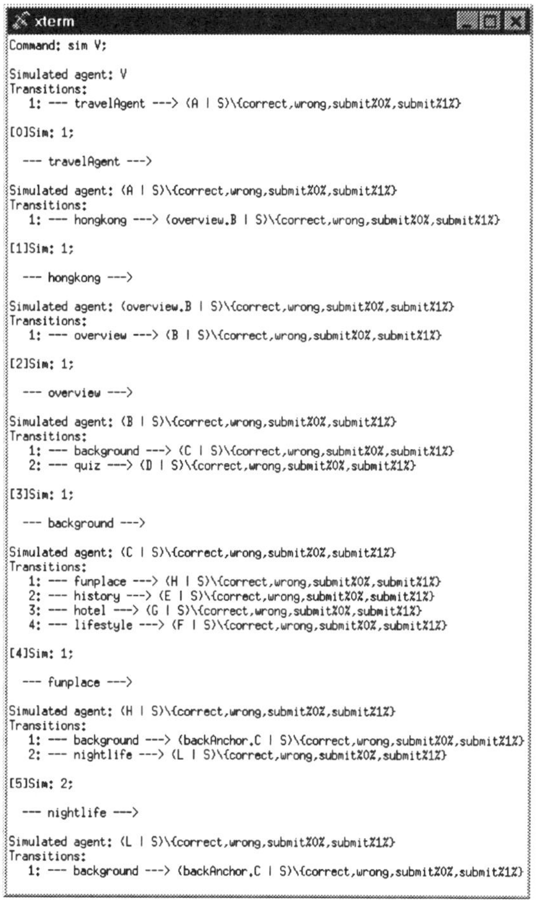

ENDNOTES

[1.] This work is supported in part by the Hong Kong University Grant Council under grant HKUST6088/97E.

[2.] Actually, this formulation can be applied to servers storing no information, as what our final model will be.

REFERENCES

[1] M. Agosti, "An Overview of Hypertext," *Information Retrieval and Hypertext*, pp. 28,31, 1996.

[2] G. Bruns, *Distributed Systems Analysis with CCS*. London: Prentice Hall, 1997.

[3] Y. Chiaramella and A. Kheirbek, "An Overview of Hypertext," *Information Retrieval and Hypertext*, pp. 139-178, 1996.

[4] W. Consortium, *HTML 4.0 Specification*, 1998.

[5] R. Milner, *Communication and Concurrency*. London: Prentice Hall, 1989.

[6] F. Moller and P. Stevens, *The Edinburgh Concurrency Workbench (Version 7)*, 1994.

[7] J. Peterson, *Petri Net Theory and the Modeling of Systems*. Englewood Cliffs, N.J.: Prentice Hall, 1983.

[8] P. D. Stotts and R. Furuta, "Petri-net-based Hypertext: Document Structure with Browsing Semantics," *ACM Transactions on Information Systems*, vol. 7, no. 1, pp. 3-29, 1989.

[9] P. D. Stotts, R. Furuta, and C. R. Cabarrus, "Hyperdocuments as Automata: Verification of Trace-Based Browsing Properties by Model Checking," *ACM Transactions on Information Systems*, vol. 16, no. 1, pp. 1-30, 1998.

[10] M. A. S. Turine, M. C. F. de Oliveira, and P. C. Masiero, "A Navigation-Oriented Hypertext Model Based on Statecharts," in *Proceedings of the Eighth ACM Conference on Hypertext*, pp. 102-111, 1997.

[11] R. Wilkinson and M. Fuller, "An Overview of Hypertext," *Information Retrieval and Hypertext*, pp. 257-271, 1996.

Factors Used In Software Packages Selection In Venezuela's Manufacturing Industry

Prof. Leopoldo E. Colmenares
University Simon Bolivar, Department of Technology of Services
Fax: 58-2-3372315, e-mail: lcolmen@usb.ve

1) INTRODUCTION

Software packages selection is an important issue for the bussiness strategy in the 90'. The biggest advantage of purchasing off-the-shelf software is that it provide economies of scale, while reducing the risk of implementation (Chau, 1996). The rules and key issues for software selection and as exposed in numerous books and articles may be good guidelines to select software packages in any country (Schwab and Kallman, 1991), but due differences in social and organizational characteristics may make that theses rules don´t be applied in a developing country like Venezuela. Furthermore, it is necessary to identify factors being used for managers in Venezuela to select software packages, and compare them with key issues mencionated in literature, so managers wiil be able avoid to forget use of basic aspect of software selection. This research investigate factors used by managers to select software packages in Venezuela's manufacturing industry and compare them with factors exposed in literature.

2) PROBLEM STATEMENT

One of most notable trend in developing information systems in the 1980s was the increased pressure on firms toward greater reliance on external sources for software (Sato,1997). Due to the enormous decline in price of computer equipment as a result of technological advancements during recente years, the computers becomes more and more feasible for many kind of new users, especially for smaller and medium firms (Martin, 1992). This issue, together with the large assorment of application software packages for many corporate functions such as inventory control, production programming, production control and son on, have increased the use of software packages in Venezuela's manufacturing industry. Table 1 shows the software packages application sales for last four years.

Therefore, due growth use of application software packages by Venezuela's manufacturing industry is very important to know which factors are being used for managers in order to evaluate and to select software packages, so we can to compare them with factors and key issues listed in literature to make the right selection and call atention about diferences founds.

3) RESEARCH OBJECTIVE

The main objective of this reseach is to investigate factors used in the application software packages selection process by managers in Venezuela's manufacturing industry and to compare them with factors mencionated in literature in order to make the right selection, and to call attention in missing or do not used factors, so individual managers in Venezuela will be able to understand the main factors and take care of them in order to selecting the right software package for their organizations.

4) THEORETICAL BACKGROUND

To accomplish the objective of the research, it will be listed advantages and disadvantages of to buy software packages and will be reviewed the software selection process, so we can identify key issues in order to build the questionnaire.

Table 1. Application software packages annual sales in Venezuela		
Year	Bs. '000000	% Annual Growth
1994	11050	105,4
1995	16320	48,2
1996	41976	157,1
1997	53625	27,9

Source: IDC World Wide Black Book. 1995-1997. Data not available for 1998

4.1) Advantages and Disadvantages of Software Packages

The advantages versus the disadvantages of buying software packages have been discussed by several authors. Next we will do a summary of advantages and disadvantages. (Sato, 1997)

In general, key factors that favor the buy decision include the following:

1) Specialized Skills: Firms can easily gain good perfomance and a variety of functions using with the lastest skill and technology which they can not retain internally.

2) Staff Utilization: Scarce in-house resources can be reserved for applications that are company-specify or confidential and they can not be safely subcontracted. An organization can also avoid the difficulties of hiring and managing huge numbers of its own technical staff. Savings in staffing take place not only in application pragramming, but also in system construction, system operation and system maintenance.

3) Cost savings: Since the vendor expects to sell a number of packages, developmental costs are amortixed over a number of users.

4) Time saving: Software packages can save installation time as well as money, and thus provide earlier returns on the investment.

5) High quality: Given the potencial for multiples sales, an established vendor can afford a higher investment in a product's development and support. Users can enjoy greater reliability achieved through exhaustive debugging and the corıtinual correction of bugs reported by users, better documentation and trainning materials and better customer support.

For all their advantages, software packages also have some important limitations:

1) Selecting a satisfactory package is not a easy task. This is not a minor issue, in some cases the effort merely to find a suitable product adds significantly to its total installation cost.

2) Vulnerability to the fluctuating business fortunes of outside software suppliers must be considered. Financial failure of the vendor may cause major problems, in some cases triggering a large emergency investment in a operation in which the firm had no desire to invest.

3) Difficulty in maintaining confidentiality regarding data and the type of business practice being implemented may be a problem.

4) Lack of competition: A software package is often "one-of-a-kind" and may be the only available software for the problem.

5) Loss of flexibility: Users are often faced with a gap between the package characteristics and the user´s operating enviroment. Serious problems may result if the user modifies the package or its standards, habit and procedures to resolve this discrepancy.

4.2) Software Packages Selection

The selection process of software packages requires choosing among a variety of them. Then, is necessary to conform a committee that will develop carefully the tasks necessaries to accomplish succesfully the software packages selection process. For do this process, a structured approach to making the selection must be used rather than informal or subjectives ways of acquiring software packages. Generally, the selection process have five steps. (Figure 1)

1) **Defining users requirements:** A key issue in software package selection is fit. A logical approach to determining fit is to find out what systems and procedures are currently in place, it must be considered what should be done rather than is being done. Requirements should be classified by importance, such as "Mandatory", "Opcional", etc. It is important too identify the technicals requirements, i.e. hardware required, database manager, operating system and so on. It should be emphasized at this stage that is helpful hiring consultants services in order to get the "best practices" in the area being selecting the software package.

2) **Search packages vendors:** Once the firm has listed its requirements, it should then identify software packages that may meet them. There are a number of useful ways for seeking software packages:
- Computers magazines.
- Consultants.
- Attend trade shows.
- Other users.

3) **Request for proposal (RFP):** After requirements analisys is developed and vendors are contacted, the firm is ready to obtain proposals from vendors to provide software. To obtain these proposals, the selection committee should prepare a formal document called Request for Proposal (RFP). This document outlines the organization's requirements and asks that interested vendor submit a formal proposal showing in detail how they will satisfy these needs. The RFP should be written clearly, consistently and completely. RFP should to include questions that will allow to firm to evaluate factors such as: software documentation, vendor support, vendor's personnel qualification, software customization experience, etc. A rule of thumb for the RFP; it is important, then ducument it. Is a request is not writen down, then it probably wiil not performed or will not be binding on the vendor.

4) **Evaluation:** In order to evaluate packages and vendors, firm must develop two different process: collecting data on software package and its vendor and to apply a software selection approach.

4.1) **Collecting data:** In order to collect data from software pack-

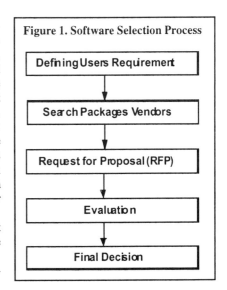

Figure 1. Software Selection Process

Defining Users Requiremert

Search Packages Vendors

Request for Proposal (RFP)

Evaluation

Final Decision

ages and vendors firm should developing the next tasks:
- Evaluate vendor's proposal: vendor's proposals should be reviewed to ensure that they contain all the information requested and meet RFP requirements. Proposals that fail this review should be rejected or returned to the vendor for corrections. Time and cost estimates as well as profiles of the vendor personnel who will work in the implementation and support the software package must be a part of the reply. At this level of evaluation, all the selection committee is trying to do is to identify a few vendors who have complied with all or most of the elements set forth in the RFP. The committee is not trying to select the "best" vendor at this point, but is reviewing the proposals to weed out those vendors who have submitted inferior proposals, and identify those which are worthy of more stringent evaluation.
- Vendor's presentation: once the initial review has been performed, the remaining vendors should be invited to make a detailed presentation. To make this as effective and helpful as possible, each vendor should be informed of the specified format for the presentation, its objectives and the time allowed. The vendor should be told that these presentation are to be working sessions, with ample opportunity for the participants to ask detailed questions. The vendor's representative should be knowledgeable enough to answer specific question from the user's standpoint.
- Visiting users: interviews and visits with the others users who are currently using the vendor's package are an important means of gathering information. It is normally better to visit two or even three users sites. Users will be ask about questions regarding the perfomance, special functional requirements and how they were handled and the level and quality of support from the vendor. In turn, the visiting members committee have the responsibility to prepare a specific list of questions for the firms being visited. This will streamline the visit, assuring a consistent approach for each the selected vendors.
- Visiting vendors: visist the vendor's headquarters should be planned like the users visits. The purpose of these vists is to reach agreement on the ability of the package to handle the firm requirements and to review the vendor support capabilities. It is importnat to get initial commitments on support including programming, training and education on the begining of the process.
- External information: here is intend be evalaute the ability of the vendor to remaing a going concern over the life of the system. May be used an independent auditor's report on the financial statement of each vendor. Credit rating agencies and banker can provide information on the general business practices of the vendor and its perfomance in meeting its obligations, too vendors must be investigate for liens and and pending ligitation.
- Benchmarks: frecuently is necessary to execute an evaluation of the perfomance of the software. Performance is generally defined as the response time of a system or the volume of input it can process in a given period of time. Benchmarks can be used to evaluate the perfomance of the new system, the firm can ask the vendor to run the programs at its location, or on some other user's computer system (assuming it is the same as one proposed).

4.2) Software selection approachs: in order to select the right software package for the organization, should be used a structured approach or method. More widely used methods for software packages selection are: (Martin, 1992)
- **Certificacion method:** in this approach committee consider whether in their opinion the software package do have a certain minimum set of functions which they regards to be essential. In case a software package supports that minimum set of required functions it passed the evaluation. Thus, an accepted software package is a candidate recommended by the committee.
- **The checklist:** the checklist consists of a table with the functions which have been didtinguished, on one axis, and the software packages which suppot the intended application, on the other axis. An marker is placed in the appropiate box if a software package contains the function mencionated limiting the answer to "yes" or "no". Software package that have most "yes" should be the package selected.
- **The ranking method:** a widely used method for evaluating packages is the ranking approach. This systems is very similar to the cheklist approach. In this approach software packages (or vendors) are scored quantitatively with respect to how well they perform with regard the functions or requirements being listed. Each function deemed important in the selection process is given a relative weight. The committee rates each vendor with respect how its package rates for each function. Finally, each set of vendors rating is cross-multiplies by the function weights, thereby producing a total score for each vendor. The vendor (or package) receiving the highest total may be the selected.
- **Benefit-Cost evaluation:** benefit-cost analyses in which estimates of cost are compared to estimates of the value of benefits are a familiar way to evaluate alternatives. Usually, the timing of costs and benefits is considered in developing an estimate of the rate of return on the capital invesment. Software package with highest benefit-cost ratio should be marked how the suitable software package.

5) The Final Decision: at this point, sufficient information should be available to allow the firm to reach a final decision. However, the final decision is not a simple as merely selecting the vendor with the highest score on the rating (ranking) systems. Whereas technical perfomance criteria are more quantitative and objective, general perfomance criteria are qualitative and subjective. Furthermore, if two o more vendors are close in the final ratings, the selection committee might declare a tie, and look for additional reasons to justify choosing one vendor over the other. If management then decidies the winning package is too costly, highly rated but lower-cost packages may be considered. Sometimes, the final decision is made by a firm's president or director based on the selection process completed by the selection committee. Some firms may select a vendor in the expectation of additional benefits later in the negotiating process.

5) METHODOLOGY

To collect data a questionnaire was sent to 60 managers of diferent manufacturing organizations in Venezuela with a recient (later two years ago) experience in selecting a software package. The questionnaire was sent to the president or general manager of firm, with a cover letter explaining the research objectives and asking to direct the questionnaire to the person who was responsible for the organization's software package selection decision in the most recent packaged software purchased. Questionnaire (see Appendix 1) had a list with a set of questions in order to identify factors and task that they used to select a software package.

A space was provided for respondents to add further factors or task. The language used was Spanish. It were received 22 usable responses (a 36,7 response rate); of these 15 firms had purchased a software package in the past 12 months (68,2 %). The 22 usable questionnaires sample was used for analisys. Table 2 shows the characteristics of the sample organizations.

6) RESULTS

Results of research exhibit the lack of formal methods to accomplish the software packages selection process in Venezuela's manufacturing industry. Only two firms (9,1 %) ask "yes " to question about use of formal procedures for selecting software packages. One firm (4,5 %) did use consultants services for selecting last year an application software package. Firms ask the question about methods to select software packages as showed in table 3.

It not a surprise that most of firms do not using a formal method (68,1 %) and that 5 firms ask question 3 with the use of certification method, because in this method "the criteria which were used remain unclear in most cases" (Martin, 1992). It important highlight that organizations using formal procedures to select software packages are the same using the ranking approach.

None of firms used a formal RFP to support the process of software evaluation, rather than 4 firm used a "questionnaire" to collect data from vendor's. In referent to specific factors evaluated in software selection process responses are showed in table 4.

Table 4, show clearly that important factors or key factors are not being widely considered by Venezuela's manufacturing industry managers in the software packages selection process. Anothers key issues like investigate financial and legal aspect from vendors are being missing in software selection process in Venezuela's manufacturing industry. None firm report ask for external information about vendors.

7) CONCLUSIONS

Use of software packages to satisfy informacion needs has become commonplace in many business firms. Indeed, from a time or cost perspective packaged software is frecuently preferred over in house developed systems. In order to accomplish successfully task of software packages selection, have been developed formal approach and guidelines. Firms in developing countries, like Venezuela, should take care of investment in information technology such as software packages invesment. Using recognized and widely tested approachs to software selection is a way of guarantee success in using the software and the consequent return of invesment. This research conclude that managers in manufacturing industry of Venezuela are not using formal methods to evaluate software packages. Results of selecting a software package in such way, may result in undesirables consequences for organization in a short period of time.

8) REFERENCES

Chau, P. Factors used in the selection of packaged software in small business: Views of owners and managers.Information and Management. Vol. 29. pp. 71-78. 1996.

Martin, H.H. Evaluation methods of standard software with respect to their effectiveness. International Journal of Production Economics. Vol. 24. pp. 249-261. 1992.

Shawab, S. and Kallman, E. The software selection process can't always go by the book. Journal of System Management. pp. 9-37. May. 1991.

Table 2. Descriptive data of the sample organizations

Average age of firms	32.8
Av. years of using computer	23.5
# firms with mainframes	2
# organizations with minis	16
# firms with LAN	4

Table 3. Method used to selecting software packages

Method	# Firms	% Firms
Certification	5	22,7
Checklist	-	-
Ranking	2	9,1
None	15	68,1

Table 4. Factors Evaluated

Factor	# Firms	% Firms
Vendor Support	3	13,6
Documentation	-	-
Vendor Personnel	-	-
Visit Vendor	2	9,1
Software Demo	22	100
Visit Vendor's customers	1	4,5
Cost	22	100
Benchmarks	-	-

Sato, Yoshikazu. Software package and vendor selection for corporate systems development. Master Thesis. Massachusetts Institute of Technology. 1997

APPENDIX 1

Software Packages Selection Questionnaire

1) Your firm have formal procedures for selection of software packages?

2) Your firm to hire consultants service for selection of software packages?

3) What method use your organization to select software packages ?

4) Your firm evaluate vendor support to select software packages ?

5) Your firm evaluate software's documentation in the software packages selection process ?

6) Your firm evaluate vendor's personnel qualification in the software packages selection process ?

7) Your firm to develop a RFP to obtain vendor's information in the software packages selection process ?

8) Your firm visit another vendor's customers with the same software packages being evaluated in the software packages selection process ?

9) Your firm to develop benchmarks with software packages being evaluated in the software packages selection process ?

10) Your firm evaluate software packages costs in the software packages selection process ?

11) Your firm ask the vendors for a demo of software packages being evaluated in the software packages selection process ?

12) Your firm visit the vendor's office in the software packages selection process ?

13) Your firm to investigate vendor's financial status with an independent auditor's report in the software packages selection process ?

14) Your firm to investigate if vendor have liens or pending ligitation in the software packages selection process ?

Developing Prototyping Skills:
The Onion Method

Jakov Crnkovic,
Associate Professor, Computer Information Systems Department, The College of St. Rose, Albany, NY 12203
Tel: (518) 454-5163, Fax: (518) 454-2100, e-mail: crnkovic@rosnet.strose.edu

William K. Holstein, Distinguished Professor
School of Business, University at Albany, State University of NY, Albany, NY 12222
Tel: (518) 442-4929, Fax: (518) 442-2568, e-mail: holstein@albany.edu

We (and our students) have entered the information systems support era. The focus of information systems now includes decision support for higher-level managers and is beginning to include vast amounts of external data on customers, competitors, markets and the environment. Users of these newer systems are much more sophisticated and demanding, and the role of "professional" developers has changed dramatically.

Earlier systems were developed as large mainframe systems over long periods of time with little user involvement. Contemporary decision support systems are often PC- or client/server-based. Development cycles are shorter and more iterative, and users are usually heavily involved in building the models used by the system and in the design and testing process.

As we have shifted our students' attention toward the development issues in decision support systems, we have given less emphasis to traditional systems development methods and more to prototyping. Over the past several years, we have developed an effective methodology for teaching prototyping skills. We call it the "Onion Method" because it involves a several-step process that begins with a simple prototype using manual methods, followed by a spreadsheet application, and then proceeds to "peel down" to successively more sophisticated prototypes using more (and more "live") data and more powerful development tools. A wide range of software tools can be used. We use packaged textbook software tools, applications such as Microsoft Office, and productivity software such as Oracle and Express.

The result is a process that develops confidence and prototyping skills in undergraduate and beginning graduate students. The process also focuses attention on key elements of the eventual system that are important for success. These elements include the user interface, the structure of the database, the tools and models that are built into the system, and procedures for modifying or

Layer	Description
1	Create a manual model
2	Convert the manual model into spreadsheet form
3	Add a user interface with buttons for options and "if-then" decision making
4	Add a module to produce graphical output. Discuss the model itself and model based decisions. Is there room for improvement?
5	Add a new criterion function based on total "performance" (additive model). Run and discuss possible problems when using the revised criterion.
6	Refine the new model by introducing a multiplicative option. Use the model several times to explore the sensitivity of product acceptance to the choice of criterion.
7	Shift the system from a spreadsheet to a database program. Add product data. Produce sample queries and reports.
8	Build a simple financial model based on the database. Add financial data to discuss profitability.
9	Add a simple inventory model. Analyze deterministic and stochastic demands over time. Compare to EOQ or other models.
10	Create a simple expert system with rules for decision making and forecasting based on overall performance of the prototype decision support system.

supplementing the database or system models.

The Onion Method can be applied to several categories of problems: model building, where the focus is on soft data and using mathematical models, model sensitivity, where the focus is mainly on hard data and simulation analysis, and model understanding, using both soft and hard data and emphasizing problem-finding as well as problem-solving.

As an example of the method, consider a "Gatekeeper Model" to assist supermarket buyers in accepting or rejecting new products offered by suppliers. In the supermarket industry, buyers may reject new products "at the gate," or later if sales do not develop according to expectations. The proposed model is designed as an aid to decision making.

The basic model, derived from an article in the literature, summarizes a condensed set of five factors or characteristics of a new product offering which are associated with acceptance or rejection by supermarket buyers. If the rating on any factor is below a minimum threshold, the product will be rejected. The process begins with the students preparing a manual flow model of the process. They try several simulated products with the model to reach "accept" or "reject" decisions.

Subsequent "layers" of the prototyping process require the programming of the model using a spreadsheet, the testing and further development of criteria for acceptance or rejection, and addition of a product database. The "peeling" of the various layers are summarized in the table below.

We have used this methodology in our own institutions, as well as in programs in Argentina, Yugoslavia and Hungary. Our students have developed a substantial inventory of multi-level models that we have used to teach prototyping skills. Samples are available from the authors on request.

We use the Onion Method in many different ways. For introductory classes, we use prototypes that do not go beyond two or three layers. For more advanced classes, we iterate through several prototype versions for a single case to expose students to many different aspects of the system. The method has value for modeling even the simplest systems such as break-even analysis, Pert/Cost, or forecasting.

Our experience is that the Onion Method improves teaching effectiveness and helps to develop analytical and prototyping skills.

EIS Design Issues: The Special Case of E-commerce

William K. Holstein
Distinguished Service Professor, School of Business, University at Albany, Albany, NY 12222
Tel: (518) 442-4929, Fax: (518) 442-2568, e-mail: holstein@albany.edu

Jakov Crnkovic
Associate Professor, Computer Information Systems Department, The College of Saint Rose, Albany, NY 12203
Tel: (518) 454-5163, Fax: (518) 454-2100, e-mail: crnkovic@rosnet.strose.edu

INTRODUCTION

Executive Information Systems have become a widely accepted innovation. More and more senior executives are using them. Yet there has not been much discussion of EIS applications in another highly innovative area – in virtual companies or in companies that deal largely with electronic commerce. We think that at least one reason for this is that future EIS applications in E-commerce will have to deal with some fundamental issues that are, as yet, relatively poorly understood. This paper explores requirements for systems to support senior management decision-making in the E-commerce environment.

The Web has sparked an explosion of entrepreneurial activity and experimentation with new business models and systems. The following quote from Everett Rogers' classic book on innovation captures the need for the "further information" that managers must have about the Web and E-commerce – information that executive information systems might provide:

An innovation presents an individual or organization with a new alternative or alternatives with a new means of solving problems. But the probabilities of the new alternatives being superior to previous practice are not exactly known by the individual problem solvers. Thus, they are motivated to seek further information about the innovation to cope with the uncertainty that it creates.[1]

Our objectives for this paper are two: 1) to frame the issues that developers of executive information systems for E-commerce applications must face, and 2) to signal our interest in these issues in order to attract comments and contributions of others who are interested in pushing forward in this area. We invite comments, criticism and ideas from others who are attempting to build systems to support high-level decision making in the virtual business world. We face momentous challenges as we try to serve a new and exciting class of users, and would welcome others to join us in this endeavor.

Most of this paper is taken up with six hypotheses that deal with the differences between Executive Information Systems to support electronic commerce (virtual business) and traditional EIS systems that support executives in conventional businesses, henceforth referred to as "real" businesses. Before we start on the issues of EIS applications, we provide some brief background on the E-commerce industry and executive information systems.

THE E-COMMERCE ENVIRONMENT

Most E-commerce companies are new and, almost by definition, small. Like the vast majority of new ventures, most E-commerce companies are undercapitalized, have cash flow problems, and difficulties in planning and utilizing capacity. (There are notable exceptions with eye-popping market valuations, yet most of the value accrues to the stockholders, not to the firm itself.) Most E-commerce firms are traversing new, unexplored terrain and creating markets and niches that did not exist only a few years ago. They operate with someone else's money on very slim or alarmingly negative margins with a dearth of reliable information. Their environment is characterized by relatively low barriers to entry and rapid copying of new ideas and business processes.

Diversification of business activities based on innovations is welcome in e-commerce. Because of that, many established real (traditional) companies acting like the fast followers devoted substantial parts of their business to E-commerce. The lines in E-commerce are blurring. Some E-commerce companies have been virtual companies from the start and will remain so, e.g. Amazon.com. Others that were founded as virtual companies are migrating to conventional operations (stores) as well, e.g. Gateway Computer. Still others started as conventional operations but are moving into virtual operations, e.g. Barnes and Noble or Victoria's Secret. Egghead Software is a particularly interesting case. They have moved all the way from a chain of software stores to an entirely virtual company with no conventional stores left. We will thus see electronic commerce popping up in many situations beyond pure Internet companies.

The (young and technically savvy) managers of E-commerce firms (or e-commerce departments of mixed firms) are changing all the rules. They are nothing like the managers found in "your father's industry" as noted in the following quotes:

(The CEO of Seattle-based Internet startup Honkworm International) is just 34, but he sits on the board of directors or advisers of seven other Internet-commerce companies – some of whose CEOs, in turn, sit on his. They know one another's forecasts, marketing plans, and new-product launches. They even share their financials, which ensures that scarcely a competitive secret escapes the group's notice.[2]

Another CEO of an Internet startup quoted in the same article says:

What we now see among individuals is first and foremost a loyalty to their networks ... the rock in the storm is not the individual, or even his organization. It's his peer group.[3]

This is not surprising in an industry that is burning, rather than making, money. A good connection to the next dose of capital is an imperative.

When rules and norms are carried in the heads of a handful of young entrepreneurs and venture capitalists, what kind of "decision support" do high-level executives need and want? We don't know the answer, but assert that the answer is dramatically different from the needs of more traditional managers operating in a more conventional milieu.

Before departing our consideration of the E-eommerce environment, we would note that we are considering an industry that is truly phenomenal. Worldwide Web commerce revenue was $12 billion in 1997; more than $7 billion of that came from transactions completed directly on the World Wide Web. Web transactions were expected to and grow to $220 billion by 2002.[4] In early January, America Online, Inc. announced that its members spent fully $1.2 billion shopping online during the 1998 holiday season – an average of $80 from each of its online accounts.[5]

Lest we get too carried away about the nature of change brought on by the E-commerce revolution, consider the following quote:

Web commerce is changing the way a lot of companies do business, but it's not everything it's pumped up to be. ... It's a major trend that's reshaping businesses and the IT that runs them. But ... it doesn't change some fundamental rules of business.

Doing business on the Web successfully takes capital, innovative leadership and execution, marketing savvy, perseverance, and the intelligent application of IT. As the Internet continues to speed the pace of change in the coming years, many aspects of business will be altered and transformed – but those guiding principles will always remain.[6]

Thus, as we consider decision support for virtual business, we can assume that many of the lessons that we have leaned about EIS in traditional companies will hold in the virtual world as well.

Executive Information Systems and Decision Support

The term "Decision Support System" generally refers to hardware and software harnessed together to support a decision-making process. In a Decision Support System, the role of the computer is to handle and transform the data. The role of the manager is to make the decisions.

Executive Information Systems "extend" the DSS concept:

• to a higher level of management,

• to a more varied and less structured suite of decisions, and

- to less repetitive problems.

Here is a definition of EIS from an early study of 20 companies by Rockart and Treacy (bold face emphasis added):

All of these systems have as a major purpose, **the provision of information to top management** for the **monitoring** of the organization's activities, **analysis** as to the reasons underlying favorable or adverse trends, and the **development of the future path** which the organization plans to pursue. In sum, the **systems support the planning and control processes** in an organization.[7]

A key word in this definition of EIS systems above is "monitoring." A common perception of top management is that they monitor operations with highly aggregated, summarized information – the kind of stuff contained in the White House "briefing book" that is provided to the President each morning. In fact, for many senior executives in traditional companies, quite the opposite is true. They want, and many of them now get, detailed or "microdata" and "microinformation" from the trenches in a very timely manner. With handheld computers, scanners and satellite transmission of data from stores to headquarters, senior executives in companies such as Frito-Lay and Wal-Mart are provided, as soon as they come to work in the morning, information on what happened as late as yesterday afternoon, together with the ability to "drill down" to very detailed data by product, region, etc. We assert that this ability to monitor at the detail level will also be important in Executive Information Systems for E-commerce.

Executive Information Systems are unique among information systems in two important respects:

1)   they are very personal and must be tailored to the specific needs and interests of the executive(s) that they support, and

2)   they support large, important, high-level decision making such as whether to enter a virtual business, or how to manage and control a mixture of business operations that operate in both E-commerce and regular business.

An obvious difference is the different mindset of executives in the real and virtual worlds and the completely different nature of the decisions that they must make.

SIX HYPOTHESES

Data: Our first hypothesis deals with data. Much of the data in a real company's EIS is typically rich, judgmental and soft (future- and externally-oriented). In a virtual company, the data will be quite different. Consider this ten year old quote:

Duracell's CEO asked the computer to "drill down" for more data to explain the difference in the performance of hourly and salaried work forces in the U.S. and overseas. At the end of the data-browsing session the real problem was found: too many salespeople in Germany wasting time calling on small stores.[8]

What was the source of the data that led to the problem? Obviously the EIS had data on the time that sales personnel spent with customers and, further, could relate the time spent to the size of each customer visited by each salesperson. This could come only from sales call reports which, in most companies, are submitted in paper (handwritten) form and are not captured in an information system.

In a virtual company there are no salespeople, no call reports and, often, relatively little data on customers. Without the organized input of salespeople and customers from the marketplace, virtual managers will ask different questions and will value different data.

The previous quote from Inc. magazine about networking by E-Commerce executives and the following quote suggest to us that EIS for E-Commerce will be much more involved with people and relationships than EIS in real companies.

As you move to the Internet, it's not just the transactional data sets anymore; it's information about what is going on in the company, information about people, the ability to have relationships much deeper in the organization.[9]

Including data and information on "people" and "relationships" within and outside the company in an EIS is not a trivial issue. To one manager the information in e-mail from customers is important:

I came to discover I could understand more about our products by reading consumer's e-mail than I could be reading our own engineering reports.[10]

But, reading voluminous e-mail from tens of thousands of customers without filtering, indexing and classification rules would be a huge waste of time for a busy executive. E-commerce EIS applications will probably require many more procedures to extract meaningful information from masses of poorly organized data than conventional systems.

Introduction of the "open" e-commerce (which assumes the whole process of commercial business, not just sales to final customers) and migration of EDI systems towards Internet will enlarge importance of building and managing databases and building Web Information Systems (WIS). Initially, WIS manages huge amounts of simple sales data.

Finally, consider the data implications of the following quote:

Web information systems are revolutionizing commerce. For starters, the Web reduces to nearly nothing many marginal costs of doing business, such as communications and customer service. Startup companies such as Amazon.com and CDNow have outperformed the leading national chains by successfully adapting traditional telephone and catalog sales models to exploit these radical economics.[11]

What data will be required to determine that traditional models are being effectively "exploited?" Effectiveness, in this sense, involves comparisons and benchmarks to evaluate performance against external standards, which means the competition. Which competition? other sellers of the same product? other virtual vendors selling different products with the same technology?

Data Gathering: Our second hypothesis follows naturally. Data gathering in virtual companies is quite different than in real companies. Virtual firms can gather customer data, but only that which the customer chooses to provide – sometime no more than a cookie – and its quality may often be suspect. No intermediary (salesperson, clerk, service person) is there to verify and interpret developments and assumptions in the customer's world. On the other hand, a large volume of transactions in a virtual environment can lead to a vast store of data about customers and preferences, as Amazon.com has accumulated on reader interests, reactions, and cross-selling opportunities.

Three quarters of all sales on the Internet are made to one quarter of Internet users. This surprising fact was revealed in a recent survey on Internet commerce. Reaching this core group of purchasers can mean the success or failure of an on-line business.[12]

It means that virtual retailers will need to seek out and identify the most valuable Internet shoppers. Stated otherwise, customer segmentation will be an important issue for E-commerce competitors.

This suggests, in turn, that data on transactions (e.g. purchases, payment methods, shipping preferences), interaction (e.g. browsing behavior and related transactions), and demographic characteristics will be needed to identify productive segments. An EIS to guide executives toward profitable segments and strategies for customizing Web content and reducing attrition will be quite unlike any applications now seen in the real world.

In E-commerce, marketing and merchandizing will not be the only issues. The role of trading and other partners across the whole supply chain is more important than in real companies, which typically manage more of the value chain themselves or carry inventories to lessen dependence on suppliers. We foresee a situation in which gathering data from and sharing data with a wider variety of partner organizations will be necessary in the virtual world.

Online commerce is clearly redefining the opportunities open to most merchants. Lower costs, greater market reach, and the prospect of improving customer service are drawing a substantial number of players to the Web. In large numbers, consumers too, are beginning to realize the convenience and economic power of shopping and buying online. ... In order to reap the apparent benefits of electronic commerce, however, merchants must embrace several new technologies. They must also learn to communicate electronically with consumers and an increasing number of business partners.[13]

Models: Extracting meaningful information from available data leads to our third hypothesis: models, tools and routines for processing data and leading users to actionable information will vary considerably in the two environments.

Here, we take a broad view of "models," not just models to elicit actioanble information from available data, but managing more general models. E-commerce executives will need help in finding effective business models, as noted in the first quote below. E-commerce EIS applications will have to deal with things such as the "environment" and the "platform" referenced in the second quote.

These early successes, though impressive, barely tap the Web's potential for transforming commerce. The next generation of Web-based businesses will not merely adapt existing business models and organizations; they will invent fundamentally new ones that ate inconceivable without the Net. Their focus will not be on selling things from a Web site but rather on using the Web to link buyers, sellers, and organizations in innovative ways. Moreover, they will exploit emerging technology that is making the Web accessible to computers as well as people.[14]

The Internet is driving an entirely new kind of commerce revolution – providing an environment for more intelligent, productive and responsive relationships to customers. ... To compete for this huge opportunity, e-businesses need a solid electronic commerce platform built for a spectrum of Internet business strategies for both short- and long-term growth.[15]

As noted earlier, many traditional business functions and tasks like competition will still be important in the E-commerce environment. E-commerce companies will have to enhance competitiveness by lowering overall costs, focusing on profitable groups of customers, and by differentiating their products and services from those of their competitors.

We are outlining tall orders here, if E-commerce EIS applications are to have an impact on decisions that determine the character and future of the business.

E-commerce EIS models will also need to deal with (and make sense of) large amounts of data, probably much larger amounts than are found in traditional EIS applications. Egghead Software expected more than 2 million visitors in its first year of operation in a virtual environment. The shear volume of data that can be extracted from virtual transactions demands efficient processing and knowledge-based procedures. In real companies, there is more time, richer information, and often more people available to hunt for meaning in the data.

Time: Consideration of time leads to our fourth hypothesis. Time moves faster in the virtual world. Change, growth, new competitors, new classes of customers come more quickly than in the real world. An EIS must be built and maintained to survive in this rapidly changing environment. Our hypothesis is that an E-commerce EIS must be developed and produced faster and it must perform faster than the EIS for a real firm.

Flexibility: Often, in the virtual world, fewer services are provided to buyers than in the real world and alternative sources are more easily found and checked. Our fifth hypothesis is therefore that the market is likely to be more price sensitive and customers more fickle and less loyal. Push technology and other fancy high-tech techniques will be less important than features that Web buyers will value – easy identification and location of relevant information the ability to personalize information to a high degree. Managers who understand this will win. Managers who are supported by a dynamic, flexible EIS, and can quickly adapt to the shifting attitudes and needs of customers, will win sooner.

Users: Finally, as we noted earlier, it is important to emphasize the differences in managers and culture in the two environments. Our final hypothesis is that EIS systems to support virtual company managers will have to deal with more computer-literate users and faster-paced decision making. The systems will also have to provide models that reflect user interests and abilities that are quite different than those of managers in real companies. Although the following quote refers more to Web users than managers of E-commerce firms, we think it is valid:

Most users aren't like us. They don't like change and don't care that a system uses the Web, any more than they cared that its predecessor used C... (users) expected the standard interface concepts such as double-clicking to open topics and dragging-and-dropping to move items...Interface design is important.[16]

Interface design for an E-commerce EIS certainly is important, largely because of the interests and preferences of its user(s).

Traditional approaches, utilizing simple menu structures and easy navigation, color, graphics, etc., will no doubt continue to be important, but knowing type of users we have will force us to think about possible different approaches. What will be good enough for them? May be future EIS will be driven by voice recognition software, using higher levels of built-in expertise and artificial intelligence.

In summary, those of us who are attempting to build systems to support high-level decision making will indeed have continuing challenges as we try to enter the virtual business world and serve a new and exciting class of users.

ENDNOTES

1 Everett Rogers, The Diffusion of Innovations, 4th Edition, Free Press, 1995.
2 Welles, Edward, "Not Your Father's Industry," *Inc.,* January 1999
3 ibid, pg. 26
4 International Data Corporation, *1997 Web Sellers Survey.*
5 Rebecca Quick, "AOL's Members Spend $80 Each Shopping on the Web," *Wall Street Journal,* January 5, 1999.
6 Clinton Wilder, "E-commerce: Myths and Realities," *Information Week,* December 7, 1998.
7 Rockart, John F. and Michael E. Treacy, "Executive Information Support Systems," Working Paper No. 65, Center for Information Systems Research, Sloan School of Management, MIT, Cambridge, MA, November 1980.
8 Main, Jeremy, "At Last, Software CEO's Can Use," *Fortune,* March 13, 1989, p. 77.
9 Wayne Brothers, CEO of Teledyne Waterpik, quoted in "Transforming the Enterprise," *Information Week,* September, 1998.
10 Wayne Brothers, CEO of Teledyne Waterpik, ibid
11 Jay M. Tenenbaum, "WIS and Electronic Commerce," *Communications of the ACM,* July 1998.
12 Scott Cunningham, Steve Rabin, "Retail Trends: Customer Segmentation and EC," *Electronic Commerce World,* December 1998
13 Tom Litle, "Effective Order Processing – Part 2," *Electronic Commerce World,* December 1998.
14 Jay M. Tenebaum, "WIS and Electronic Commerce," *Communications of the ACM,* July 1998.
15 Karl Salnoske, Stig G. Durlow, "The Customer-Driven Supply Chain," *Electronic Commerce World,* December 1998.
16 Alan Dennis, "Lessons from Three Years of Web Development," *Communications of the ACM,* July 1998.

Repositioning The Academic Library For The Next Millennium

Robert Danford
Widener University, Chester, PA 19013
610.4087/610.499.4465 (f) robert.e.danford@widener.edu

Dr. Deborah Leather
Towson University, Towson, MD 21252
410.830.2498/410.830.3760 (f) dleather@towson.edu

Institutions are composed of people, facilities and traditions. We will discuss how librarians react to change and how services and facilities can be molded in times of fiscal and technological turmoil.

The "Electronic Revolution" or the "Digital Age" may impose the greatest restructuring of libraries since the introduction of the card catalog over 100 years ago. At that time, libraries of all types were collections of books arranged by size, color, language, building, maybe roughly by subject. There was little available to the user to mine the collection other than crude lists and the personal help of librarians or scholars. The idea of a card catalog brought profound and unexpected changes in the library profession and industry.

The card catalog offered the possibility of greatly enhanced indexing, allowing for the more sophisticated use of the collection and allowing the user to be somewhat in charge of his or her trek through the world of knowledge represented in the catalog and the collections—a change in the user interface, so to speak.

Because the card catalog has been such a part of our academic lives, it may be hard to imagine the upheaval which its introduction caused. Consider the basics, the construction of the cabinetry itself. Few people outside the profession realize that an entire industry was formed to design, produce and sell catalog cabinets to libraries. And one can imagine the torture librarians and library funders went through in trying to come up with the money to buy this new resource—something which was going to offer tremendous benefits but which wasn't going to generate any funds.

These advances came with costs, of course. In addition to the cost of the cabinetry, the profession had to shift its personnel allocations to adapt to:

- New departments such as Cataloging, Catalog Maintenance and Classification so that the monster could be fed.
- New approaches to dealing with the public as catalogs became placed in the public area, necessitating that users be trained in the use of the resource.
- New approaches to training the professionals who would wrestle with cataloging and indexing, standard setting and information exchange.
- Increased workloads as circulation increased because of greater awareness of the collections.
- Adjusting to long term costs, especially in technical services, that were not easily seen and appreciated by the using public.

Libraries for the most part adopted subsequent technologies with relative ease and with the same aplomb that the rest of society accepted them. Typewriters, telephones, copiers, video, audio and even microforms, somewhat less joyfully, became routine in libraries as they did in society at large. Should we even mention electricity?

The introduction of digital technologies, however, may be causing the same type of trauma that the introduction of card catalogs to libraries did a century ago. Digital technologies offer the same quantum increases in indexing, sophistication in collection use, a more individual user interface and the ability to mine the investment in resources that the card catalog did. But such "opportunities" offer similar shocks to the status quo.

Modern library administrators, just like their predecessors, have to contend with:

- The need to form, fund and manage new departments such as hardware and software maintenance, network maintenance and telecommunications.
- New approaches to dealing with the public as they need training in search strategies, use of the WWW, basic computer skills and as they approach the library via telephone lines, networks and the Internet.
- The need for new breeds of professionals with enhanced skills in the use of technology and, increasingly, in the production of electronic resources.
- Increased workloads and varied workflows which cannot be easily managed by the staff as they may be dependent upon user wishes.
- Adjusting to new long term costs. The need to maintain and to upgrade machinery is of a magnitude not formerly known in libraries.

All of these are similar to the dislocations which occurred and were handled 100 years ago. Except for the need for more shelves, another card catalog cabinet every so often, and slowly rising energy costs, the infrastructure costs of libraries were rather meager, especially when contrasted with the invisible costs associated with maintaining an academic library technology infrastructure (power, furniture, networks, etc.)

Added to the continuing maintenance of an infrastructure is the problem of not owning that which the infrastructure delivers. A book, and even a serial volume, represented a one-time cost with the library owning the physical unit. Aside from copyright restrictions and outright theft, the volume was an owned item and available until the library sought to discard it or relocate it. Nowadays we manage licenses which allow us to use information in various ways, but we do not own much of anything—we even sign contracts which limit our use of an electronic resource and with variable assurance that the information will even exist beyond our contract date or beyond our ability or willingness to pay the fee.

There are added and hidden costs to using online or electronic journals—we find unintended effects on and relationships with formerly non-related departments:

- We may set de facto standards, or raise the bar, on departments who may not have the machines to access our systems (Netscape, Windows95/98, etc.)
- We may affect configurations in student labs.
- We incur the need for network maintenance, authentication, loading, etc.
- We must deal with relatively uncontrolled cost increases to maintain or to replace obsolete equipment, operating systems, new standards, and new or changed vendors of equipment, systems, etc.
- We often face uncontrollable duplication within or between "packages," forcing customers to pay for more than absolutely necessary to get vital information.
- We face a potential problem involved with having one interface and one access point. Too often there is little or no redundancy if/when a service, a network or a server goes offline. As we funnel more users through fewer access points, the possibility that greater numbers are affected by single problems grows.
- And we may promote time lost in "navigation" — offering larger and larger numbers of journals, for example, requires that users spend more time winnowing through results and requires that librarians and database designers spend more time in constructing credible tools to manage use of larger and larger databases.

Another major issue which librarians must deal with and which deserves its own discussion is the World Wide Web. Most newer library systems and most current database vendors offer their services via a web interface, forcing libraries to teach users how to use the web. It also forces librarians to be able not only to manipulate the web but to become adept at constructing web sites to offer standard library services (Reserves, Directories, ILL requests, Reference questions, "Bibliographic" Instruction) via web pages and via interactive web instructional modules. Such dependence upon web services requires that librarians become writers and publishers to an extent not present before.

The other side of the coin is that the user population is increasingly "remote" as it accesses services via the electronic infrastructure. Whether the student is in the dorm, at the Greek house, back at home on vacation, or in the library around the corner from the reference desk, he or she is removed from the librarian(s) and must be served via distance learning techniques. In this technological age, one of the major values of librarians is, of course, to be able to help people navigate and mine the electronic resources which are the advertised backbone of our modern services. Another major value is the ability to make connections between disparate services and to make connections between the modern electronic versions of information and the older non-electronic versions of information which libraries, schools and colleges have invested in for centuries.

These issues pose organizational questions for the institution, but what of the library's physical structure? Libraries have often been cited as the "Heart of the University" and "The Center of the Campus." For many years, library buildings have been ornate and impressive palaces devoted to housing some of the most expensive investments a college or university has made. Indeed, it made sense to house as many resources and as many experts as possible in a central location to foster synergy between disciplines and to help make connections between users and information.

Introducing technology into libraries has had profound effects upon these buildings. Leaving aside the well-known and not unique issues of A/C, conduit, power supply, lighting, drilling through massive walls, displacement and dislocation of services to accommodate digital systems, the buildings have been affected in other ways. Technology has prompted a wave of decentralization which affects the purpose and use of the former "Hearts of the Campus." With the user population being on-campus but out of the building, being off-campus or even being out of state or out of the country, we have to reevaluate the use of the massive buildings which symbolized the heart and power of the university.

But will the building disappear? No, but we may need to recast its appearance and purpose. It is commonplace to see students of all ages at Borders and Barnes and Noble working away on term papers, using computers and being comfortable. There are obvious lessons to be learned, but just offering coffee in the library isn't one of them. It would be quite instructive for college presidents to walk through one of these stores to see their students among hundreds of thousands of books, tapes, Cds, newspapers, journals and software packages. Librarians need to see the same thing and take lessons. What do these alternative structures offer that we don't:
• Multiple copies.
• Immediate access.
• Comfortable surroundings.
• Convenient hours.
• Food and drink.
• Generally easy access to a Kinko's.
• Parking.
    What do we offer that they don't:
• Systematic arrangement designed for research.
• Indexing.
• Thoughtful collections developed with curricular coordination.
• Free borrowing.
• Assistance in the use of materials.
• Knowledge of subject matter.
• Knowledge of the uses to which information will be or should be put to in the institution.
• Depth as well as breadth in collections.
    Will we become "virtual" campus centers? Librarians will spend time in their offices constructing web pages and devising services for the use of the remote user. Remember, those remote users will be in dorms, in offices, on the next floor as well as be off-campus. We will be available for the walk-in trade as before, but we will know that users may also be remote at times. But if people don't need to come to the library, how will we market our services? How will we try to insure that our population actually learns of our services? Not by just offering another web page.

We will be going to offices, to classes, to dorms, to special-interest housing (Honors, French, Gay) to teach how to use our services and to advertise our services. How else can we compete with the variety of services found on any campus network? In the real world, we as professionals just can't assume that students will opt to search for library services when those services must compete with ESPN, pornography, rock and roll and other commercial pages. We will have to leave the central building to keep the service central to the educational experience.

One of the greatest technological impacts libraries face now is how technology effects service delivery. No longer is instruction a simple show and tell of the card catalog, the layout of the library, and the general formats of printed indexes and abstracts. Librarians must keep up with interminable changes in electronic search engines, electronic information, and general hardware and software tools to ensure proper assistance to its user population. This means that all library staff have to deal with a rate of change that is incessant and ubiquitous. The more we learn, the more we need to keep up.

How many of us have heard over the years, "now that I have a 16 MB (or 24 or 36) RAM, 300 MHz, and assorted other computer doodads, I can effectively do my job and stay on top of the information gorge"? It has taken us time to comprehend that technology will be continually changing and that technology will be in the information design driver's seat for a very long time. It has also taken us time to understand how technology is rendering changes to libraries, facilities and services

And while we want to believe that technology is not the driving force, in reality, it is. Students and faculty are doing research and gathering information in different ways. When we talk about information literacy these days, there is more emphasis on computer literacy, like it or not. Our users are demanding different space configurations, more customized attention, and more places to hook up or work at computers. There is no question that this is a period of major transformation for the academic library.

The academic library community has been wrestling with the idea of library transformation for over a decade. There have been organizational changes that included combining the library with computing services, moving to teams in lieu of the traditional library line organizations, adding new service centers in and outside the library walls, and even changing of the library degree to a Master's in Information Science or the like. Most of these changes have come and gone; and with it the feeling that it had little impact on the academic library. To many, the changes appeared to be mostly smoke and mirrors. Yet, unlike what some professionals expected, we have not been able to go back to business as usual. Something is breathing down our necks. What is it?

The pressures are user independence and the rapid speed of the evolution of technology. In a profession that has been characterized by durability of the services provided and a sense of physical place, a number of our core values are being challenged. How to serve our users effectively and how to provide access to information are being questioned by faculty, students, and administrators alike. On the one hand, there is a feeling that our time has come — we ARE the information gurus. On the other hand, there is a belief that what we were trained to do is no longer important to many of our constituency — they don't understand us.

As we approach the new millennium, we need to decide just what is our role and assert ourselves accordingly. In times of true transformational change, there is a great deal of risk and speculation taking place. The first tenet to embrace during this period is no one has THE right answer, or stated alternatively, there is no one answer. This is good since the academic library environment has never been directed by just one answer. The second principle is that the changes at this time are obtrusive and we need to break down the change into manageable parts. Finally, miscalculations or misjudgments will be made, but it will be better to take chances and encourage staff and service alterations, than to remain stagnant and fall further behind. How do we approach these imposing changes? First we start with certain assumptions and work from there.

Assumption #1. *Library work has changed.* Very few, if any, academic libraries have as large a technical services department now as they did five years ago. Automation of technical services tasks, publishers' support services, a move to electronic information, limited operational budgets, and tightening materials budgets have reduced the need for "backroom" staff. Many professional positions have been redeployed from technical services to reference and reader services. Much of the cataloging and acquisitions work has been reassigned to paraprofessional staff. Reference service has expanded to include more complicated individual user assistance. For instance, more information customization in addition to general hardware and software support is expected.

Assumption #2. *Overall staff sizes have not increased.* While many academic libraries have had the ability to redeploy staff, there has been little support on most campuses to significantly increase the overall size of academic library staffs in the last five years. Shifting staff from one department to another gave most academic libraries relief through the first phase of the web explosion. But user expectations and needs have grown exponentially, and the short-term relief has already vaporized. Because technical service staff have shrunk to a bare minimum and demands on reference and reader services staff continues to be pushed to the limit, burn out and lethargy are becoming more common-place administrative problems.

Assumption #3. *There is demand for more library staff with higher level technical skills.* A big question facing academic libraries is at what skill level should library staff be technologically. Is there a need to have library staff who can support most of the technical computer and networking demands in the library? If yes, should that expertise be contained in one or two computer techies or should a larger number of library staff be trained to handle such support activities? How and what type of training should be provided to keep staff technologically current? Will staff with other degrees or skills sets, at the very least, complement or even more dramatically supplant staff holding the MLS? Each academic library will have to decide how to approach these question based on factors specific to the individual institution.

Assumption #4. *There is greater need for staff development and cross training.* Library staff are requesting more skill upgrades than in the past. There is also more concern by staff and library administration to cross train library employees, especially in those areas where departments have been downsized. This need for continual retooling has led to other complications, money being the least of the inconveniences. First, there is the matter of maintaining appropriate staffing levels at service stations. Second, there is a need to determine who actually needs what retooling. Finally, the library administration needs to insist that staff development be a recurrent requirement and develop a 3-5 year plan accordingly.

Assumption #5. *No one organizational structure for libraries has proven to be the best answer.* Since the late 1980s, there have been experiments with different organizational patterns. The models have included the merger of the library with all or some of computing, telecommunications, faculty development, teaching/learning centers, and multimedia departments. The head of such campus departments has usually come from the computing or library environment. In more rare cases, a faculty or academic administrator outside the computing or library field was named chief officer of the reorganized division. Many of these organizational structures have already been reconstituted or discontinued, returning the library to a more traditional reporting structure.

Assumption #6. *There are library staff who believe it is only a matter of time until libraries will be back to business as usual.* Since certain organizational changes due to technology have come and gone, there are seasoned library staff who believe that the current response to technology is just a fad, albeit an influential one. Like other trends in librarianship, technology will find its rightful place in public service. Once university administration gets over the technological mania, academic libraries will be able to put technology in its proper place – as just one of many resources available to the users of the library.

This is a time for academic libraries to deal with the monumental changes through formal planning. Yet, there is little to guide library administrators since
• Many organizational approaches in the academic setting have faltered,
• There is not an archetype to copy from the public, special, or medical library environment, and

• Current principles on organizational change in the private sector are also in question. As stated by Jeffrey Bennett:

Our hypothesis at Booz-Allen & Hamilton is that there is a more fundamental reason for many failed transformation efforts. In particular, some of us believe that the basic vision that guides many change experts is flawed. Their "unconstrained vision," or view that mankind is infinitely perfectible, drives their change initiatives to solutions that break down in implementation, either because these solutions cannot cope with the complexities of the real world or because they encounter overwhelming organizational resistance. (*Strategy and Business*, Issue 12, 1998, p. 22)

Using this hypothesis as the baseline, academic libraries should consider the use of constrained or bounded change to deal with the major transitions effecting its operations. Using the precepts of constrained change, the organizational culture is seen as a given and purposely creating a departmental culture is abandoned. Constrained change, rather, focuses on those aspects of the organization that can be more easily transformed, namely staff and operational designs.

Using the constrained change approach in a library, one will focus on:

• Reviewing current staffing structures,
• Assessing current staff knowledge, skills, abilities,
• Setting staff benchmarks,
• Building an action plan for real time changes,
• Designing actual change events,
• Determining who will manage what aspects of the change,
• Assessing the commitment, innovation and results of the change.
• Modifying the action plan as needed.

Distributed Web Based Assignment Submission and Access

Paul Darbyshire

Dept. Info. Systems, Victoria Univ. of Technology, P.O. Box 14428, Melbourne City MC, Victoria, Australia
Tel : (03) 9688-4393, Fax : (03) 9688-5024, Email : Paul.Darbyshire@vut.edu.au

ABSTRACT

With the increasing use of Web based instruction techniques by educators for delivering course material, it must be remembered that subject management is also an important task carried out by the subject coordinator. A Web based instruction system must be backed up by an efficient Web based subject administration system. Although the subject administrative tasks are usually transparent to some degree to the students, if they are performed inefficiently, they become immediately obvious and in the worst case can distract the students and staff from the learning process. One of the administrative tasks that can consume much of the coordinator's time is that of assignment collection, redistribution to tutors, collection of results, and return to students. This paper discusses Web based assignment management, and describes in detail the functioning of such a system designed for use at Victoria University of Technology which runs many multi-campus subjects. This system provides the functionality for a Web based assignment 'box', and provides access to this assignment box to authorized staff from any Web browser.

INTRODUCTION

There has been much written in the area of Computer Aided Learning (CAL) and Computer Managed Learning (CML) in recent years. Indeed, with the Internet now the dominant force in educational communication, Web Based Learning (WBL) (Darbyshire, Wenn 1998) is the more appropriate term. There have been some very good commercial and non-commercial courseware products produced in the last two years that allow delivery of educational material via the World Wide Web (Web). These include such products as TopClass, LearningSpace, Virtual-U and WebCT.

The focus of such courseware products has been understandably towards the delivery and management of educational material, with some attention also to the management of discussion groups via the Web. However, the delivery of a University subject to a student population involves more than a one way dissemination of information, but includes the input and feedback from a number of assessable tasks throughout the semester. Regardless of what material is taught, or the mechanism used to deliver such material, the written assignment still remains the basic unit of assessment for the vast majority of educators.

Effectively managing the tasks associated with collection, distribution, marking, recording and returning assignments take a great deal of the instructors' time, and a Web based system can be used to provide flexibility in these tasks. Byrnes et al (1995), identifies assignment management as one of the components which should be included in a reasonable CML system, however, an effective Assignment Management System (AMS) has been largely overlooked by the developers of most courseware systems until very recently. Many criticisms have been directed to various products over the years, and courseware developers were challenged (McCandless 1977), to work more closely with educational instructors.

In a comparative analysis of on-line delivery applications (Landon 1998), six major courseware products were compared. These were WebCT, Virtual-U, TopClass, Learning Space, Web course in a Box, and CourseInfo. Four of these now include an implementation of an assignment submission box, providing various degrees of functionality. At Victoria University we have been working on this problem for some time, before the reasonable availability of such commercial systems. Costs still become a prohibitive factor, and often the structure of such systems sometimes do not provide the flexibility required, or the purchase of component modules of these systems (McCandless 1977).

In the following sections we discuss some of the aspects of Web based assignment submission, and then provide a detailed description of the system we have implemented. The results of using this system over the last 12 months and future developments and directions are presented.

WEB BASED ASSIGNMENT MANAGEMENT

A number of systems have been developed which help manage the assignment life-cycle. Most systems just facilitate the assignment delivery process, but systems have been described which attempt to automatically mark the assignment (Hassan 1991). Such systems require stringent restrictions on the format of the assignment, and thus by necessity reduce the flexibility able to be offered by computerized systems. Byrnes et al (1995) describes the flexibility that should be required of such a system, and describes their implementation of a GUI driven interface for assignment submission over a network using an Internet connection. A flexible assignment submission system should address each of the following points without neither time nor geographical constraints.

- flexibility in time of assignment submission
- flexibility in location for submission and return
- flexibility in format of assignments
- flexibility in management of assignments
- flexibility in distribution to tutors.

An assignment management system based on use of the Web is able to provide flexibility in all the above points because of the nature of the Web. The system described by Byrnes (1995) is based on client-server architecture, and uses specific client software to handle submission. The Web is governed by international standards (W3C 1998), thus a system based on the application of these Web standards should require only an Internet connection and any Web browser that supports the current standards. Thus anyone with Web access can participate in the assignment submission and management system from any location at any time.

At Victoria University of Technology, there are 14 campuses in and around the Melbourne metropolitan area. Currently, due to the nature of many of the campuses, a subject is not taught at more than 3 campuses. One subject coordinator may be responsible for teaching and grading all work at a number of campuses, or there may be many lecturers and tutors responsible for grading written work at these campuses. In either case, manual methods for collecting assignments, distributing them to tutors, collecting results and returning the assignments are usually inadequate. A computerized system addressing the points above is required for efficiency and flexibility.

Rather than delegate tutors local to each campus the responsibility of collecting assignments, a Web based system can provide for distributed submission to a centralized Web assignment box. This also addresses any problems in regards to leniency of different tutors to deadlines. The deadline for an assignment can be set at any time, as students do not have to see a tutor/ lecturer, or physically place it in a drop-off box at a specific location. This is particularly useful to part-time students who have access to the Internet from home or work.

Flexibility in assignment format is essential as different subjects have different requirements. Some may require submission of multi-media documents containing graphics and sound, while others may require the submission of program executables and source. Standard HTML allows the inclusion of 'file' fields on HTML forms. This automatically places a 'browse' button beside the field which, when clicked, invokes the local platforms file selection dialog box. Unfortunately, recommendations contained in RFC 1867 (Nebel, Masinter 1994), a recommendation for HTML forms based file uploading, have not been fully implemented in most Web browsers. Thus, only standard text files can be uploaded through this facility.

This facility can be extended however with the use of third party software, and is only required at the Web-server end, making this transparent to the clients, (students and users of the system). Cold Fusion, (Allaire Corp.), has been installed on one of the Universities Web-servers to implement this and provide other functionality, thus any file type may be submitted to the Web assignment box. The only restriction we placed on students is that they cannot submit a file of a type for which the Department of Information Systems has no compatible software for viewing. This restriction is only a department restriction and not a restriction of the systems capability, thus different departments can implement different degrees of flexibility.

It should be noted that emailing assignments as attachments to academic staff members is an alternative to Web based submission, and is generally available to students at most institutions. This has been subjected to trials previously (Darbyshire, Wenn 1998). Submission by email is difficult at best, and with the plethora of email systems available, there is usually no standard procedure. Also, with the varied document types being submitted, different mail servers with different registered MIME types may handle the attachments in different ways, possibly leading to unreadable or corrupted attachments at the receiving end. Automatic notification of receipt is also difficult.

To maintain flexibility, the contents of the assignment box must also be made available to subject tutors and lectures via the Web. This functionality can be provided by a series of Web scripts and pages allowing distributed assignment access via the Web. This allows flexibility for staff members involved in the subject, in both the time and location they choose to access the submitted assignments. Security must be maintained during these functions to ensure that only authorized staff members have access to the Web assignment box.

A Web based system providing similar functionality to the one described in this paper is briefly documented in (Tregobov 1998). This has been developed in parallel with our system, and, while providing similar functionality in regards to assignment submission, differs in respect to the way results and comments are passed back to students.

DESCRIPTION OF SYSTEM

The Web based assignment collection and distribution system is developed using a series of standard HTML pages and Cold Fusion scripts. Cold Fusion is a product that runs as a service on a Unix, Windows NT or Windows 95/98 server. This service interfaces with the Web-server service and allows extra Cold Fusion tags to be embedded in HTML pages. These tags are ignored by the Web-server and passed to Cold Fusion for processing. They allow special functions to be performed not easily accomplished with standard HTML. These include functions such as file processing, directory manipulation and processing of SQL commands.

The first step in a student submitting an assignment requires filling out an assignment submission form as shown in Figure 1. The file for submission is chosen by selecting the 'Browse' button, and then the file to submit. Choosing the 'submit' button after the form is completed performs two actions. Firstly a database record containing fields corresponding to the form is created in a submissions database, and secondly, the file selected for submission is transferred to the appropriate 'Web assignment box'. A Web assignment box is just a special directory to which assignments are uploaded. Rather than place all assignments in the one assignment box for all subjects, an assignment box is created for each individual assignment by the subject coordinator (Darbyshire, Wenn 1988). Which assignment box the file is submitted to, is determined by the selection of the subject and assignment number in Figure 1. Entries are checked for a valid assignment box only at this stage. This separation of assignments by subject and number keeps assignment boxes manageable in size and aids in security.

Students can make more than one submission, and their different submissions are sorted by date and time in descending order. This easily enables the tutor to select the latest assignment for marking. In subjects where students may be required to submit many files for one assignment, students are instructed to use a standard ZIP compression utility to compress the files to be submitted into a single ZIP file for submission.

A feature incorporated into the assignment management system is the instant notification to students of the receipt of their

Figure 1 Assignment submission form

Subject	Object Oriented Systems	Assignment No.	
Id No.		First Name	
Password		Last Name	Campus Footscray
Partners			
File to Submit		Browse...	
	Submit		

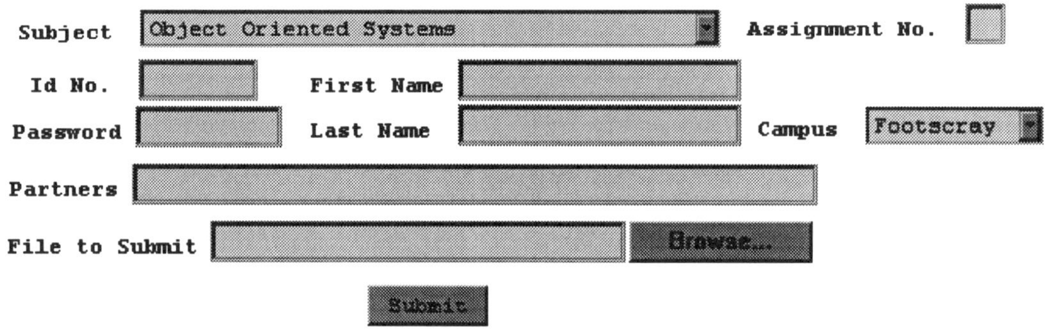

assignment. This feature is difficult to implement in email-based submission. Notification is implemented as a Web page dynamically populated by entries in the assignment box, and displayed as soon as submission is complete. A partial form showing such data is shown in Figure 2.

Experience has shown that immediate confirmation to students of their submission gives them confidence in use of the system. The result is that they are more likely to use this facility again. A trial (Darbyshire, Wenn 1988) highlighted the fact that most student concerns over system security were for the safety and confidentiality of their submitted work. A bad experience in using the system once was likely to result in them not using the system any further in future. This facility is also made available as a menu option, so partners involved in group work can check for successful submission at any time.

Once submission is complete, the assignment box needs to be accessible by all staff involved in teaching and grading

Figure 2 Successful submission listing

You have Successfully submitted your assignment -

Confirmation List for Object Oriented Systems, Assignment 2, is as follows

Id	First Name	Surname	Date Submitted	Partners
9607948	Michael	Ellis	06-Oct-1998	
9713081	Robert	Zejnula	06-Oct-1998	9708838 Brad Tasker
9607256	Peter	Stein	05-Oct-1998	
9609342	sione	teumohenga	05-Oct-1998	

assignments for the subject. This is achieved by two mechanisms. Firstly, a database is available which enables the subject coordinator to create subject teams. This is basically a list of authorized staff members who are granted certain privileges in dealing with aspects of the subject. One such privilege is access to any of the subjects' assignment boxes. Security is implemented as a two-tier security system. As a first tier security measure, the scripts enabling access to the assignment boxes are placed in a special directory with general Web access removed. Thus to access them the user must supply an NT username/ password combination, granted only to authorized staff members. As a second tier security measure, the assignment management system requires its own username/ password combination, Figure 3, which, when successfully entered, results in a transient security cookie being passed to the users browser.

The authorized staff member can then select the assignment box they wish to access. This is done by choosing the subject and assignment number from the HTML form presented in Figure 4. Once the 'Select' button is clicked, the assignment management system then verifies the users security cookie against a list of authorized subject team members. If the user is not an authorized subject team member, access to the selected Web assignment box is denied.

When a Web assignment box is successfully 'opened', the authorized staff member has access to all assignments submitted to the assignment box. This is achieved with a Cold Fusion script that dynamically builds a HTML form to be presented to the staff member. This form is populated by entries from the submission database, selected via an SQL search, with the Surname field of the entry being presented as a 'selectable' HTML link to the appropriate file in the assignment box. The resultant HTML form presented to the staff member looks like the partial list shown in Figure 5.

The Web page shown in Figure 5 is a standard Web page, where the Surname has been made into a HTML link, linking to the assignment that was submitted by the corresponding student. Clicking on the surname results in the browser asking if you wish to open or download the file in question. Downloading via the http protocol results in an exact copy of the file that was submitted by the student. As this functionality is provided by a standard Web page, all that is needed to access the assignment box is an Internet connection and standard Web browser. This offers a great degree of flexibility to staff members, who can access these at any time from any Web connection.

The submission of feedback to students

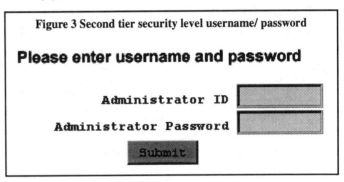

Figure 3 Second tier security level username/ password

Please enter username and password

Administrator ID

Administrator Password

Submit

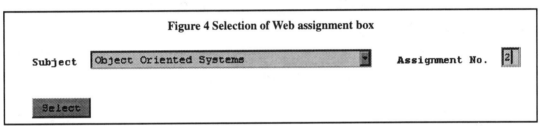

Figure 4 Selection of Web assignment box

Subject   Object Oriented Systems   Assignment No. 2

Select

is currently facilitated by completion of the Web form shown in Figure 6, and posting to a database. This Web form contains a field for a list of student ID numbers, as the assignment may have been a group assignment, the mark obtained, and a list of appropriate comments. These comments and the grade obtained, can be viewed by students from any Web browser by supplying their ID number and password combination upon request. Statistics on the average, lowest and highest grades are also supplied. The statistics functionality was added at the student behest.

The overall structure of the assignment management system can be seen in Figure 7. This structure has evolved over a period

Figure 5 Staff access to Web assignment box

Assignment Access for Object Oriented Systems, Assignment 2, is as follows

Id	First Name	Surname	Date Submitted	Partners
9508320	Steven	Bonnici	03-Oct-1998	n/a
9507706	Chris	Coghlan	25-Sep-1998	
9607948	Michael	Ellis	06-Oct-1998	
9608991	Dimitrios	Georgakakis	25-Sep-1998	nil

of time, and continues to evolve as enhancements are made and further functionality is added.

RESULTS

The Web based assignment management system has been used by a select group of subjects for a period of 18 months. Trials have proved extremely successful, with much of the mundane work involved in assignment collection and redistribution now performed automatically. Having one Web based central assignment box has provided much needed flexibility for staff and students in the participating subjects. Anecdotal evidence from part time students suggests that this group of students in particular, find it a great relief from the pressure of their busy schedules, in that they do not often have time for the odd trip to University to submit a single assignment, thus avoiding late penalties.

This system has allowed us to set common assignment collection dates for multi-campus subjects, where previously different dates were set depending on the subject coordinator's schedule. For staff members involved, they can actually begin accessing submitted assignments from another campus on the day of submission, thus improving turn-around time for student feedback. This is an important gain, as it has often been the source of much anguish.

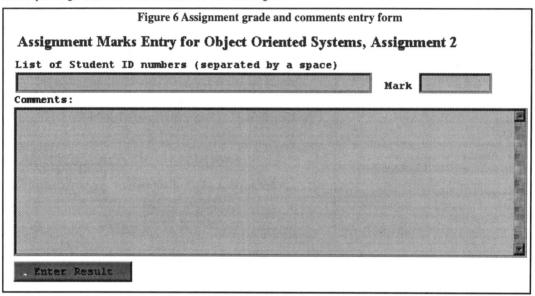

Figure 6 Assignment grade and comments entry form

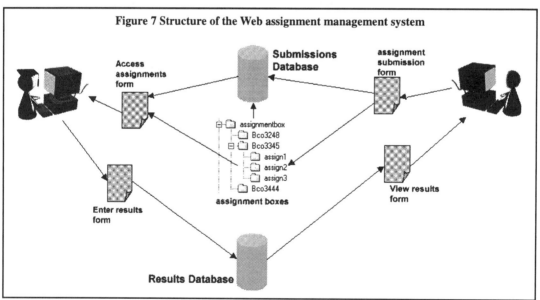

Figure 7 Structure of the Web assignment management system

The success of the trials to date has provided valuable feedback enabling us to tune some of the functions, and prompted us to instigate a staff information session, in order to offer this functionality to other interested staff members. This will be ready for full use in Semester 1, 1999.

CONCLUSIONS

Although, the trials have been largely successful, there is much in the way of staff and student comments, which have provided us with valuable feedback for possible future directions, and functionality to implement. The system is continuing to evolve, as it is also part of a larger Web based subject management system. Development is slow, as the designers continue to improve their knowledge and expertise in use of the software products, and work can only be performed in rare, free time.

The area in most need of attention in the system described above is that of feedback to students. More flexibility is needed in the return of comments, which at the moment is done through filling out a single form. This does not allow the commenting of assignments in a manner academics are familiar with and has attracted criticism from staff involved in the trials. Feedback to students in the form of annotations to their submitted assignments is essential (Byrnes et al 1995). This is also the predominant view of other staff members in the department. Development in this area has already begun and will hopefully be completed before the beginning of Semester 1 1999.

REFERENCES

Brunelli, P., Gunn, L., (1998), 'Putting the Web to Work: Streamlining Work Flow via an Institutional Intranet', Cause/Effect, Volume 21, Number 1, pp. 42-44, http://www.educause.edu/ir/library/html/cem9818.html

Byrnes, R., Lo, B., Dimbleby, J., (1995), 'Flexible assignment submission in distance learning', IFIP World Conference on Computers in Education VI, WCCE'95,

Darbyshire, P., Wenn, A., (1996), 'Experiences with Using the WWW as a Multi-campus Instructional Aid', Proceedings – 'Teaching Matters Symposium 1996', Victoria University of Technology, Melbourne, Australia

Darbyshire, P., Wenn, A., (1998), 'Cross Campus Subject Management Using the Internet", Proceedings IRMA'98, Boston MA

Darbyshire, P., Wenn, A. 'Central Point : cyber classroom', http://busfa.vut.edu.au/cpoint/cp.htm

Hassan, H., (1991), 'The Paperless Classroom', Proceedings of ASCILITE '91, pp.267-276

Landon, B., (1998), 'Comparative Analysis of On-line Educational Delivery Applications', http://www.ctt.bc.ca/landonline/, 10/10/98

McCandless, G., (1997), 'Are Software Publishers in Touch with Higher Ed Needs?', Cause/Effect, Volume 20, Number 2, pp.53-54, http://www.educause.edu/ir/library/html/cem9720.html, 12/10/98

Nebel, E., Masinter, L., (1995), 'RFC 1867 Form-based File Upload in HTML', http://sunsite.auc.dk.RFC/rfc/rfc1867.html, 15/10/97

Tregobov, A., (1998), 'The Web-Based Assignment Submission System', Proceedings N.A. Web'98, http://www.unb.ca/web/wwwdev/naweb98/montue98.html, 1/10/98

W3C (1998), 'HTML 4.0 Specification', W3C recommendation REC-html40-19980424, http://www.w3.org/TR/REC-html40 , 2/12/98

Introducing New Technology and Equipment Who Participates in the Decision Process

Dale Davis
Eastern New Mexico University, Portales, NM 88130
505-562-4331, fax: 505-562-4331, davisd@email.enmu.edu

Bill Brunsen
Eastern New Mexico University, Portales, NM 88130
505-562-2744, fax: 505-562-2252, brunsenb@email.enmu.edu

ABSTRACT

In the long arc of history, technological change has been incremental until two centuries ago. It was not until the late 1920's and early 1930's that scientific inquiry was begun into how and why workers react when change is introduced into the workplace. It has only been in the last fifty years that we have begun to come to grips with the phenomenon of "...the rate of change increasing at an increasing rate."

As a result of the recent and continuing research, we now know with some certainty how to reduce the resistance of workers to the introduction of new technology. What we need now is for the decision-makers to create the conditions that will lessen that resistance.

In this paper the authors summarize the research findings of the efforts to explain worker resistance to change. They use a contemporary example to demonstrate worker resistance and discuss alternative courses of action that might have reduced or avoided the resistance.

INTRODUCTION

The authors have been researching the phenomenon of resistance to change for a number of years. This research has, in the main, concentrated on how employees resist the introduction of new processes and procedures. Little attention was given to the manner in which new technology and procedures were introduced into the workplace. It would seem that the next (logical) step would be to study specific cases of successful and unsuccessful efforts to implement change. From this step, one could attempt to develop generalizations or "rules of thumb" about what seems to work and/or not work in attempting to reduce or eliminate resistance to change.

Recently, an incident occurred which caused the writers to recast the direction of their research and pursue this line of thought. This paper is the first effort in this new direction. In short, the authors are now beginning to address the issue of how the decisions are made, by whom, and when new technology is to be introduced into the workplace.

The authors are aware of a situation where new software was introduced for all the personal computers at a university. This software controlled the e-mail and impacted all faculty and administrators on the campus as well as all other personal computer users who had e-mail accounts. The new software program is an excellent program and it allows the user to accomplish all manners of tasks that could not be done with the old software. Regardless, there was, and continues to be no small amount of resentment towards the two individuals who made the decision to adopt the new software.

From what the President of the Faculty Senate could determine, it seems that the University Computer User Committee had asked its members to solicit input regarding the (proposed) new software. When no feedback was received, the two individuals made the decision on their own, creating all manner of "hate and discontent" in the faculty and among other users who now feel that they were not provided an opportunity for input - there was no consultation with the users. This may be a situation where the Computer User Committee members did not solicit user input from their colleagues, but it is certainly another example of decision-makers speeding up the decision process at the expense of building some kind of (before the fact) consensus regarding the decision — in this case, the software adoption.

BACKGROUND

From the beginning of human history, technological change was slow and incremental until the late eighteenth century. The European peasant farming his small plot in the Middle Ages would probably have been comfortable with the farming methods still in use in Europe and North America in the late 1700's. Until recently, evolutionary change has been the rule throughout history. With the advent of the Industrial Revolution in Europe the pace of change began to increase, ever so slowly at first, but gradually accelerating until we now live in an era where change is increasing at an increasing rate.

Very little of the change that has occurred during the past two centuries was welcomed by either the leaders or the led. The protectors of the established order, regardless of the order, had a vested interest in the status quo and devised all manner of stratagems to delay if not completely thwart change.

Whether it was the keeper of the keys to the hereafter, i.e., the priest and/or the shaman, or those who ruled by "divine right," any change endangered their authority. The religious sector took extreme measures to stifle what they pronounced as heresy. One need only consider the forced recantation of Galileo in this regard. They realized that any and all change threatened their established order. And both groups relied upon the officer corps of the military to force, when and where necessary, compliance. (It is not surprising that when the armed forces ceased to obey, the resulting conflicts tended to, at least temporarily, eliminate the religious hierarchy and the monarchy, as well as the officer corps.) And what of those who were to be led, what was their reaction?

Historically it has been to resist, often violently, any change that would affect how they earned their living and lived their lives. The term "Luddite" has become a part of our vocabulary to identify those who respond to the introduction of new technology in the workplace by "smashing the machinery." To be fair to the original Luddites, one does not have to go back to the nineteenth century for an example of this condition. A more recent manifestation of this resistance took place no more than twenty years ago with the widespread adoption of the "Bar Code" and the "scanner" at the checkout counter in our modern retail establishments. Various consumer groups attempted, and were often times successful in creating boycotts of the stores who were beginning to use the new technology. Why? Because it was new and could not be trusted. The authors believe that the operative term in all of this is "NEW." New is, or can be different. Something different frequently requires one to learn, and by definition, to change.

It was not, however, until after "The Great War," i.e., what today is referred to as World War I, that any meaningful research was begun to ascertain how one could improve the likelihood of effecting change without resistance and/or violence. In part, this was due to the fact that those who mandated changes never gave much thought to how change affected those most concerned with the results of change in the workplace. In the late nineteenth century there seemed to be nothing but positive results flowing from the Industrial Revolution. The old triumvirate of the Church, the Monarchy, and the Officer Corps/Aristocracy had been expanded to include a "new elite." A group known as the Industrial Elite now demanded their place in the order and justified their demand with a bankrupt philosophy called "Social Darwinism." In effect, there was no need to consult those who were to use the machinery when new machinery was to be introduced. The users of the machinery were, after all, somewhere down the "food chain" and the leaders were the "kings of the jungle." The results wrought by the Great War began to change all of that kind of thinking.

At the end of World War I, the Austro-Hungarian Empire was history. Czarist Russia was in the throes of a continuing revolution and the last of the Czars and his family was dead. The English Empire was a hollow shell, although it would take another twenty years to be recognized as such. Great change was in the air - - - political, social, and increasingly, technological. As an aside, I would remind you that people alive today have seen flights ranging from the first short flight on the sand dunes of North Carolina to the flight when man set foot upon the moon. All in a single life-span. It was not, however, until the late 1920's that the effects of change in the workplace upon the workers began to be studied with any scientific methodology.

Beginning with the research conducted at the Hawthorne Plant of Western Electric by Elton Mayo and his colleagues, reputable scientific inquiry into the question of why workers reacted to change as they did began to develop. Although the researchers were only willing to speculate about various possibilities and would not make explicit assertions, they did conclude that the level of interest shown by the supervisors (in the workers) seemed to have a positive effect on the productivity of the workers. The de facto hiatus imposed on this type of research by World War II was not, in retrospect, all that bad of a thing. As had World War I, the demands of World War ratcheted up the pace of implementing technological change.

The work of Coch and French profited by what had been learned prior to World War II and the great technological changes effected during that war. One of the leading characteristics of industry in the United States is, and has been, to adopt technology and then adapt it to the methods of accomplishing work. One troublesome result of this, insofar as managers and workers are concerned, is the frequent and necessary changes in how the individual accomplishes her/his work. This need for frequent change often results in increasing resistance to change by those directly affected - - the workers. Coch and French addressed this phenomenon in their landmark study shortly after World War II. One of their conclusions was that:

It is possible for management to modify greatly or to remove completely group resistance to change in methods of work. This change can be accomplished by the use of group meetings in which management effectively communicates the need for change and **stimulates group participation in planning the changes**. (Emphasis added) (Coch and French, p. 532)

The authors contend that effecting change(s) requires a different approach than that currently in use. The writers are aware that "time is money" and that leaders do have deadlines by which decisions must be made. On the other hand, using lack of time as an excuse for lack of proper planning and implementation simply does not wash.

Michael Fullan, in an excellent small book titled Change Forces: Probing the Depths of Educational Reform (1993), enumerates what he refers to as the Eight Basic Lessons of the Paradigm of Change.

Lesson One: You Can't Mandate What Matters (The more complex the change the less you can force it)

Lesson Two: Change is a Journey, not a Blueprint (Change is non-linear, loaded with uncertainty and excitement and sometimes perverse)

Lesson Three: Problems are Our Friends (Problems are inevitable and you can't learn without them)

Lesson Four: Vision and Strategic Planning Come Later (Premature vision and planning blind)

Lesson Five: Individualism and Collectivism Must Have Equal Power (There are no one-sided solutions to isolation and groupthink)

Lesson Six: Neither Centralization Nor Decentralization Works (Both top-down and bottom-up strategies are necessary)

Lesson Seven: Connection with the Wider Environment is Critical for success (The best organizations learn externally as well as internally)

Lesson Eight: Every Person is a Change Agent (Change is too important to leave to the experts, personal mind set and mastery is the ultimate protection)

(Fullan, 21-22)

SUMMARY

As Toffler pointed out in his thoughtful book, Future Shock, we live in an age where the rate of change continues to increase at an increasing rate. The marvels of technology have impacted the workplace and, for good or ill, will continually impact it. Managers cannot escape it.

Given that change will continue to occur, it behooves all of us to pay attention to how we handle change, particularly the introduction of new technology into the workplace. We as managers "know" what is best, but unless those who work with and for us are convinced of what is best, it seems obvious to the authors of this paper that resistance and/or resentment will invariably accompany the introduction of new technology. This need not be the case.

With some forethought and the willingness to allocate the time necessary to involve those who will use the new technology, the writers believe that the resistance and resentment can be reduced if not eliminated.

According to John Dewey, if people's behavior is to be altered, this will not effectively be accomplished through the direct attempt to change minds. Instead, the more indirect route of altering the environment in which people live must be prescribed. (p. 6) We can do no less as we attempt to effect change.

In the incident previously discussed, it would seem that "there's enough blame for all." The issue is whether the dissatisfaction could have been reduced or avoided. The answer is probably yes. The Computer User Committee members should probably have consulted with their constituencies and reported back to the decision-makers with any feedback. When this feedback did not develop, the decision-makers should probably have contacted the committee chair and/or members to confirm that the committee had understood the need for feedback and/or that they had understood and there was no concern. Whoever "dropped the ball," the users were not pleased with the adoption "without consultation" and a great deal of animosity was created that could have been avoided. It would seem that adherence to the Coch and French quotation on page 6 of this paper would have been good advice and good practice.

REFERENCES

Coch, L. and French, J. R. P., Jr. "Overcoming Resistance to Change," Human Relations, 1948, Vol. I, 512-532.

Dewey, J.A. The Influence of Darwin Upon Philosophy and Other Essays in Contemporary Thought. (1910) New York: Henry Holt and Company.

Fullan, M. Change Forces: Probing the Depths of Educational Reform. (1993) Bristol, PA: The Falmer Press, Taylor & Francis, Inc.

Hofstadter, R. Social Darwinism in American Thought. (1945) Boston: Beacon Press.

Mayo, E. The Human Problems of an Industrial Civilization. (1933) New York: MacMillan and Co.

Adaptive Learning Systems: A Prototype Model For Small Business Entrepreneurs To Successfully Implement Information Technology

Dessa David

Zicklin School of Business - Baruch College; Graduate Center, City University of NY, New York, NY 10010

(212) 802-6262, (212) 802-6253 (fax), Dessa_David@baruch.cuny.edu

INTRODUCTION

Businesses are the veins of worldwide economics. In the United States this holds true. Small businesses are a vital part of the United States economy. They account for the majority of businesses in the United States. As of 1996, they accounted for 99% of the 23.3 million nonfarm businesses within the United States. They also accounted for 51% of the private gross domestic product [Small Business Administration, Office of Advocacy, The Facts About Small Business, 1997; Small Business Answer card 1998]. In today's world: the Information age, the small businessperson is under tremendous pressure to implement Information Technology. The promises of IT to the small businessperson is alluring: *competitive and strategic advantages, status, increase productivity, automation of tedious tasks, reduction of errors, the internet and its global marketplace, business leveraging, a new technological savvy consumer, decreasing cost of hardware* are just a few of the motivating factors for IT implementation. Despite its allure, IT implementation poses some challenges. IT implementation can be costly and risky. The small business entrepreneur brings special properties to the table. Their limited budgets, lack of technological expertise, limited managerial staff, limited resources, time constraints, uncertainty of IT effectiveness, fear of relinquishing control to an outside consultant, are factors that enhance the risks for making the incorrect technological decisions. This can prove detrimental to a small business. At worst case, an *incorrect decision or lack of decision* can cost the small businessperson his entire company.

Studies exist that measure the success of IT implementation and benefits of various factors such as user participation in IT implementation [Montazemi, 1988; Doll et al 1988]. Successful implementation of IT within a small business can positively affect the business. IT promises businesses benefits that were never dreamt possible a few years ago. It can radically assist the small business entrepreneur in achieving his business goals. **However, the entrepreneur remains virtually unassisted in his/her decision-making and control for implementing Information Technology.** To minimize these risks, the entrepreneur must either have the expertise or tools must be developed to assist/support his/her decision making. Research exists on IT implementation but few are tailored to the small businessperson. [Ein-Dor and Segev, 1978; Pollard 1998] research findings show that studies geared towards large businesses cannot be generalized to small business. A review of the literature demonstrates a lack of framework and/ or tools to assist small business entrepreneurs to successfully implement IT.

The primary objective of this research is to provide an approach for successful implementation of IT for the small businessperson. This can be used by researchers and practitioners to develop tools to assist the small businessperson incorporate technology in his business. The birth of this research is based upon observations from practice, as well as reviews from research literature.

WHY DOES THE ENTREPRENEUR NEED SUPPORT IN HIS DECISION TO IMPLEMENT IT?

There is a competing climate among businesses to adopt information technology. IT is being viewed more and more as an extension of businesses today. For the small businessperson, the pressures and pull for adoption of IT are not different from other businesses. Many factors contribute to this allure. The declining cost and user friendliness of technology make it even more appealing. To the entrepreneur deciding to implement technology can be a complex decision. Though, IT promises benefits, it is not without great risks [Atkinson, 1991]. Generally, a small businessperson has much more at stake than the larger companies. Statistics illustrate that small business entrepreneur seek outside funding for their business less than their larger counterparts for their businesses [SBA]. This can be interpreted as a small businessperson stands to lose more from making an incorrect decision.

Several studies have been conducted to determine the factors that influence successful adoption of IT [Delone, 1988; Seddon, 1997]. According to [Delone, 1988], the knowledge of the chief executive is the most important determinant to successful IT implementation. Other factors are important but knowledge of the CEO is the most weighted determinant. He stated that outside expertise could not substitute the chief executive's knowledge. [Raymond, 1988] found that managers with computer education and training … used computers more often and in more ways. [Atkinson, 1991] also supported the theory of the involvement of managers in IS strategic planning by stating that " senior managers need to have some idea of the potential a technology might hold for the organization. " [Cragg, 1993] lends additional support to role of the CEO's knowledge of IT as a motivator for information technology implementation when he concluded from his research that one of the major inhibitors of information technology implementation is the lack of IS knowledge. These findings are particularly important since we are seeking ways to assist the entrepreneur in minimizing his risks when deciding to implement IT. What can be perceived from this is that entrepreneurs need to have means of realizing the net potential benefits that IT has to their organization.

In a small business there is usually a lack of large managerial staff- the entrepreneur is usually the decision-maker. He/She understands the factors that are critical to the survival of his/her business. Normally, the entrepreneur wears many hats. He/She is his/her own managerial team. When making complex decisions, which require support, the small businessperson may often find himself alone or dependent on outside help. Outside advice are suspect to the bias of the advisor. With such great risks, the small businessperson needs whatever support that can help him/her improve the quality of decisions made in the successful implementation of IT.

What is success?

There are a variety of literatures that specify ways for measuring the success of IT in business. Many cite success as IT use, end user satisfaction [Doll, 1988], [Delone, 1988], the evaluation of the CEO on actual use and impact of computer applications on business. [Agarwal, 1994] presents measurements that are based on a holistic view. It is clear to me that success must be measured in terms *of the extent information technology has assisted the business in realizing or surpassing its business goals.* Information Technology must possess a business value to the businessperson in order to be considered a success. To evaluate the success of IT, a holistic view of the business and the environment within which it exist must be envisioned.

Major emphasis have been focused on the measurement of the success of IT; and topics like why projects fail but little attention has been focused on specifying framework to implement the results of the research. This **void needs to be filled.** To truly realize the full potential of information technology for the small business entrepreneur research must be done to support the development of tools to assist him where he lacks expertise. The small business entrepreneur needs tools that can assist him/her acquire the knowledge that he/she lacks when making IT implementation decisions. In order to decide on implementation IT, one must perceive the potential net benefits of IT. I strongly believe that one's positive perception of the successful IT implementation is premised in a knowledge of the potential benefits of IT and the objectives of the business. Thus, there must be a way for transferring that knowledge to the small business entrepreneur in the first place. This view that the small business entrepreneur craves the knowledge of net benefits of information technology before making a decision to adopt is supported by [Pollard, 1998; Cragg et al, 1993].

What tools are currently available?

In computer science, particularly the field of artificial intelligence, whenever there is the need for transfer of knowledge, knowledge based systems are used. Knowledge based systems, that are designed to give expert advise are generally called expert systems (ES). Although one can find varying definitions for expert systems, an expert system is a computer program that imitates the knowledge of a human expert in a limited domain and can assist in solving problems experts generally solve. Another special type of system, which assists users in making decisions, is called decision support systems (DSS). DSS defined by [El-Najdawi et al 1993] is a set of computer-based tools used by managers to assist them in their decision making. A special type of DSS tailored for executives are called executive Information Systems (EIS). These systems play definite roles in successful IT implementation [Agarwal, 1994; J. Elam et al, 1995; J. Sullivan et al 1989]. Decision support systems lend support to the decision-maker for his/her decisions, which otherwise can be very time consuming to acquire. It usually saves the decision-maker time in reaching a decision. Expert systems are used to supplement expert advice where it is limited. [Sharma, 1998] showed that repeated use of an expert system by non-experts can really improve the decision-making capability of the non-expert. Executive information systems have been heralded by executives as a central source of important information to assist in decision making, planning and control. These systems, although they can help in the decision process of IT implementation in small businesses, are with limitations.

Limitations: DSS are only applicable to problems that are quantifiable. They are not adaptable to various user levels or environmental changes. They lack the ability to respond to certain knowledge and styles of the user and adjust advice to that user. The ultimate decision relies heavily on the control of the decision-maker. Traditional expert systems are also not accommodative to adjust dynamically to changes of the use and the environment. They are normally static in their approach and generally restricted to a specific task. Executive information systems are design with great benefits for a decision-maker but it lacks the flexibility of qualitative decision-making, too costly and requires too much special architecture to lay roots within small businesses. The traditional decision support paradigms lack the dynamic adaptation necessary for effective high-level decision support.

Overcoming the limitations of these decision support tools can be advantageous for the decision-maker. A system that can learn and adapt its advice autonomously based on user's competency levels, continuous feedback, cognitive styles, and environmental changes while retaining the strengths of the existing support systems will be an invaluable support tool for the small businessperson in his decision making. A system that can incorporating the businessperson ideas in the model places the entrepreneur in a unique position of making IT implementation decisions, and retaining control of outside consultants. He/She now can feel a level of support and increased confidence about his/her decisions. A system that can learn from the user and render an appropriate level of support can be a lifelong asset to a small businessperson.

WHAT IS AN ADAPTIVE LEARNING SYSTEM (ALS)?

A look at the literature reveals different types of systems that can be classified as adaptive learning systems. Names generally fitting the profile are: Intelligent System, Expert Support Systems, Adaptive decision support system, Intelligent decision support systems, Active intelligent decision support systems, Self-improving expert systems. There is no universal standard at this time. The common thread that runs through these systems are, that they must

- be interactive,
- posses a knowledge base
- have Problem solving component
- learn
- adapt support autonomous

The proposed model for the adaptive learning system must have the following characteristics:

- assist in decision making
- must be dynamic: adapt support/advise autonomously
  - based on competency level of user
  - decision styles
  - environment
- learn from the user
- knowledge base
- give explanation for decisions
- always give decisions based on holistic view
- warn and engage the user when the user makes unreasonable requests
- tutor user
- cost effective
- easy to use
- customizable interface
- nurturing
- degrade gracefully

Basically, the system will become his trusted assistant: his 'consultant in a can.' It will provide the needed support and control that small business entrepreneurs lack in IT implementation today. It will borrow strengths from the various decision support technologies that exist. Support for such systems that require a fusion of the strengths have been asked for in a variety of the literature dealing with support technology. [Agarwal,, El-Najdawi et al, 1993]

How does it work?

An entrepreneur may need to find out the benefits of a certain technology such as networking his office. If this is his/her initial contact with the system, he/she will be asked several questions which will be used as a basis for a user's profile. It will be a "getting to know you session". An interaction continues where the decision- maker will complete a business profile of his/her business: this will include goals and all constraints. The decision-maker then inputs the specifics of the tasks he/she needs support for. From this point the system begins to keep history profiles on the user, business, tasks. Before giving an answer, the system will ask several questions and give interim messages/reports. The decision-maker can also input feedback. During this time, the adaptive learning system will utilize knowledge from its databases, learn any specifics of this current task and tailor support for the particular user. The adaptive learning system will then present an optimal solution based on the decision-maker's cognitive style, as well as any environmental impacts followed by alternatives. The user at this point can continue to engage the system concerning the solutions it provided.

By keeping a history profile and invoking its learning mechanisms, the adaptive learning system will vary the level of support it provides for the decision-maker over time. The adaptive learning system can be described as self-learning. The system promises a support that is more efficient and effective than its existing predecessors.

By virtue of the small business entrepreneur's involvement in implementing technology, a sense of control is felt for the direction of his business. Based on the perceived net benefits of the adaptive learning systems the following hypotheses were developed.

Hypotheses: H1: The quality of decisions made by small business entrepreneurs who use the Adaptive Learning System will improve compared to those who did not.

H2: Small business entrepreneurs after repeated use the Adaptive Learning System will have higher competence levels on the impact of successfully implementing information technology as opposed to those who did not

H3: Even after extensive uses of the Adaptive Learning System and the confidence about making decisions are realized by the small business entrepreneur, he will still realize value from the Adaptive Learning System.

H4: The risks affiliated with the decisions to implement IT will be greatly reduced after using the Adaptive Learning System

H5: The small business entrepreneur who uses the Adaptive Learning System will feel a reduced level of dissatisfaction if information technology fails to meet his needs.

H6: The use of the Adaptive Learning System in making adoption decisions about IT provides him with a stronger sense of control about the implementation process.

H7: The Adaptive Learning System will act as an intelligent assistant.

When the entrepreneur acquires sufficient confidence in decision making, the adaptive learning system will adapt autonomously and act as a support/sound board for his decisions. The adaptive learning system will adapt dynamically to render the appropriate level of effective decision support.

CONCLUSION AND DIRECTIONS FOR FURTHER RESEARCH

My observation from practice and review of the literature reveal that practitioners and researchers should concern themselves with issues for effective IT implementation. It is evident that small businesses play an important role in our economy. Information technology promises small businesses revolutionary ways of realizing their business functions. By ensuring that small businesses take advantages of the net benefits of IT, we are boosting our economy. Information technology for the small businessperson is not just a tool to automate tasks, it possess strategic and competitive advantages. It promises him business leveraging.

Research to enhance IT within businesses needs to continue. There is a need for research customized towards exploring the strategic benefits of information technology for the small business entrepreneur. The results of this research can be used to develop tools and practices that the entrepreneur can use to take advantage of information technology.

My research interest continues to lie in ways to help the small businessperson successfully implement technology. Avenues for further research will be: refinement and validation of my proposed model; examination of applicable user interfaces for the entrepreneur; review of machine learning technologies applicable for the adaptive learning system prototype.

REFERENCES

1] R. Agarwal, S. Brown, M. Tanniru, Assessing the Impact of Expert Systems: The experiences of a small Firm, Expert Systems with Applications, 1994,vol.7, no. 2, 249-257
2] R. Agarwal, M. Tanniru, Assessing the organizational impact of information technology, Int. J. Technology Management, Special Issue on Strategic Management of Information and Telecommunication Technology 1992, vol. 7. Nos. 6/7/8. 626-643
3] R. A. Atkinson, Capturing the full impact of IT, Journal of Information Systems Management, Summer 1991, 53-56
4] A. Ben-David, Y. Pao, Self-improving expert systems, an architecture and implementation, Information and Management 1992, vol. 22, 323-331
5] H. Barki, J. Hartwick, Rethinking the concept of User Involvement, MISQ, March 1989
6] A. K. Baronas, M. R. Louis, Restoring a Sense of Control during Implementation: How User Involvement leads to acceptance, MISQ, March 1988
7] E. T. Bonk, The information revolution and its impact on SME strategy: The Asia Pacific Economic Cooperative Forum as a model, Journal of small business management, January 1996
8] P. B. Cragg, M. King, Small-Firm Computing: Motivators and Inhibitors, MISQ, March 1993
9] W. H. Delone, Determinants of Success for Computer Usage in Small Business, MISQ, March 1988
10] W. J. Doll, G. Torkzadeh, The measurement of end-user computing satisfaction, MISQ, June 1988
11] J. J. Elam, D. G. Leidner, EIS adoption, use, and impact: the executive perspective, Decision Support Systems 1995, vol. 14, 89-103
12] M.K. El-Najdawi, A. O. Stylianou Expert Systems: Integrating AI Technologies, Communications of ACM 1993, vol. 36 n12, 55-65
13] B. Fazlollahi, M. A. Parikh, S. Verma, Adaptive decision support systems, Decisions Support Systems, 1997, vol. 20, 297-315
14] V. Grover, J. Teng, A. H. Segars, K. Fiedler, The influence of information technology diffusion and business process change on perceived productivity: The IS executive perspective, Information and Management , 1998, vol. 34, 141-159
15] D. A. Harrison, P. P. Mykytyn, Jr., C. K. Riemenschneider, Executive Decisions About Adoption of Information Technology in Small Business: Theory and Empirical Tests, Information Systems Research, June 1997, vol. 8, no. 2
16] C. W. Holsapple, R. Pakath, V. S. Jacob, J. S. Zaveri, Learning by problem processors Adaptive decision support systems, Decisions Support Systems, 1993, vol. 10,85-108
17] V. S. Lai, A survey of rural small business computer use: Success factors and decisions support, Information and Management, 1994, vol. 26, 297-304
18] A. L. Lederer, A. L. Mendelow, Convincing Top Management of the Strategic Potential of Information Systems, MISQ, December 1988
19] G. M. Marakas, Decision Support Systems in the 21st Century, Prentice Hall, 1999
20] D. Mirchandam, R. Pakah, Four models for a decision support system, Information and Management, 1999, vol. 35, 31-42
21] A. R. Montazemi, Factors affecting Information Satisfaction in the context of the small business environment, MISQ, June 1988
22] S. Piramuthu, N. Raman, M. J. Shaw, S. C. Park, Integration of simulation modeling and inductive learning in an adaptive decision support system, Decision Support Systems, 1993 vol. 9, 127-142
23] C.E. Pollard, S. C. Hayne, The changing faces of information issues in small firms, Int. Small Business Journal, Apr – June 1998, vol. 16, no. 3, 70-87
24] H. R. Rao, R. Sridhar and S. Narain, An active intelligent decision support system – architecture and simulation, Decision Support Systems, 1994, vol. 12, 79-91
25] L. Raymond, The impact of Computer training on the attitudes and usage behavior of small business managers, Journal of Small business management, July 1988\
26] T. D. Rishel, O. M. Burns , The Impact of Technology on Small Manufacturing Firms, Journal of Small Business Management, January 1997
27] P. Seddon, . A respecification and extension of the Delone and Mclean model of IS success, Information Systems Research, 1997
28] S. Sharma, Effect repeated use of Expert Systems on Decision Making Capability of Non-Experts, presented Decision Science Institue, Las Vegas, Nevada November 1998
29] J. J. Sullivan, G. O. Shively, Expert System Software in Small Business Decision Making, Journal of Small Business management, January 1989, 17-26
30] P. Taitt, I. Vessey The effect of User Involvement in System Success: A contingency Approach, MISQ, March 1988
31] J. Y. L. Thong, C. Yap, K. S. Raman, Top Management Support, External Expertise and Information Systems Implementation in Small Business, Information Systems Research June 1996, vol. 7, no. 2

Information Infrastructure: Human And Technology Aspects

Apiwan Dejnaronk

Department of MIS, College of Business and Management, University of Illinois at Springfield,
Springfield, IL 62794-9243

Phone: 217-206-7833, Fax: 217-206-7543, email: Dejnaronk.Apiwan@uis.edu

BACKGROUND

According to the survey of information systems management issues for the 1990s, information infrastructure has been ranked as number six among twenty key issues found important among senior information systems executives (Niederman, et al. 1991). The structure and dimensionality of information infrastructure is an important theoretical issue that has not received much attention during the past years. Since knowledge of information infrastructure is still limited and based largely on anecdotal evidence, this area needs to be systematically studied.

Information infrastructure provides a foundation for information generation and dissemination in organizations. This infrastructure is considered critical to the firm's competitiveness (Darnton & Giacoletto, 1992). Many previous studies regarding information infrastructure emphasize the capability of technology (i.e., hardware, software, and telecommunication networks) and the capability of organization (i.e., control and coordination mechanisms) in generating information that can be shared firm wide (Broadbent, et al., 1996; Galbraith, 1973; Huber, 1982; and Porter & Roberts, 1976). In fact, technology or organization would be meaningless without people who operate it. Therefore, the aspect of human resource in an information infrastructure area needs to be closely examined.

DEFINITION AND COMPONENT OF INFORMATION INFRASTRUCTURE

At the preliminary stage of study, the only research question addressed here is what constitutes information infrastructure. Drawing upon the IS/IT literature, the working definition of information infrastructure can be stated as:

the capability of technological, human resource, and organizational foundation shared throughout the entire organization in a form of information and support services.

Three aspects of information infrastructure addressed here are: technology, human resource, and organization. It is useful to think of information infrastructure as a combination of these aspects because of two reasons. First, the three aspects are mutually exclusive. Second, it is believed that they are equally important. For example, Feeny & Willcocks (1998) suggest that both business (i.e., human and organization) and technology perspectives should be addressed in a study of information infrastructure.

RESEARCH MODEL

Thoroughly searching the IS/IT literature, we develop a model to measure the capability of information infrastructure. In this model, shortcomings in the literature (e.g., failure to recognize the emerging perspective and limited view to only the role of technology in information infrastructure) are addressed. The proposed model consists of three dimensions.

1. *Technological Infrastructure* refers to the capability of information technology (i.e., software, hardware, and telecommunication, and networks) that is in place to collect, transport, store, transform, and distribute information. The availability of information technology (IT) reflects the firm's ability to provide information to its employees. For example, firms that provide many IT services and links among business units, customers, and suppliers are considered to have high capability of technological infrastructure (Broadbent, et al., 1996).

2. *Human Resource Infrastructure* refers to the ability of personnel to operate and manage technology, to understand business functionality, and to communicate with each other in a comprehensible way. This capability can be captured through skills, experience, and education. Information systems (IS) skills include knowledge and expertise in both technology-related and business-related areas. For example, four types of essential IS skills are technical specialties, technology management, business functional, and interpersonal skills (Lee, et al. 1995).

3. *Organizational infrastructure* refers to the capability of the organization to guide and influence behaviors of organizational members. The concept of organizational infrastructure is drawn upon the structural aspect of a social system including rules and norms designed to regulate individuals' behavior and eventually to achieve corporate goals (Holesapple & Luo, 1996). Structural factors that constitute organizational infrastructure create capability for the organization to value information and use it effectively. Such those factors are reward, training, IS policy, leadership, and work team.

RESEARCH METHODOLOGY

In operationalizing the information infrastructure construct, an organization will be used a business unit as a unit of analysis.

We believe that a decision regarding information requirements is made at the business unit level. Since IS executives are knowledgeable of their firm's information infrastructure, they are selected as samples of this study.

To answer the research question posed earlier, we plan to conduct both interview and survey. The preliminary test of the proposed model to verify underlying dimensions of the information infrastructure construct (face validity) will be done through an interview with IS professional and practitioners. The results will be used to refine the original instrument and to make the final findings more generalizable (Doll & Torkzadeh, 1988).

For a survey, a questionnaire will be mailed to IS executives in the randomly selected firms. Cross-sectional data from the survey will be used to verify unidimensionality and validity the information infrastructure construct in the proposed model. Statistical techniques such as factor analysis and structural modeling will be used to analyze the data.

EXPECTED CONTRIBUTIONS

The contribution of this study is to make explicit the meaning of information infrastructure and the criteria for measuring information infrastructure capability. The proposed model will be empirically tested and the final result will contribute to both practice and research. For practice, an expected contribution is to provide a guideline for information infrastructure investment — both technology and people. For research, two contributions are to define the information infrastructure construct and to verify unidimensionality and validity of the construct.

CONCLUSION

Information infrastructure is one of the information systems issues that are unexplored. Perhaps this issue is so rudimental that it is often overlooked and assumed to be already embedding properly in organizations. This study attempts to define the domain of information infrastructure by performing a comprehensive literature review. This provides insights which is necessary in the theory development phase where the intent is to develop a theory to explain factors underlying information infrastructure in an organization.

REFERENCES

Reference is available upon request.

Group Meeting Support Systems — Impacts On Classroom Discussions

Charlene A. Dykman, Ph.D.
University of Houston-Downtown, One Main Street, Houston, TX 77002
(713) 221-8578, DykmanC@zeus.dt.uh.edu

Group Support Systems began with the age of electronic mail as American businesses, global organ-izations, and the public sector, have used this form of Groupware to shrink the world, to negate time zone impacts, to disseminate information more rapidly, and to improve decision-making activities. When the sterile, two-dimensional aspects of e-mail hindered full and accurate communication, teleconferencing evolved. Although a more expensive approach to organizational communication, teleconferencing allows richer communication with audio and video, as well as the textual communication of e-mail. The added expense comes from the dedicated resources needed to provide the capability. Teleconferencing also requires that communicating participants be available at the same time, something that e-mail does not demand. However, the ability to share graphics, to see and analyze subtle facial expressions, and to reach immediate agreement on issues may offset the negatives of synchronizing participation as well as the expenses involved.

Electronic mail and teleconferencing, as older types of Groupware, have evolved into specialized software that supports group meetings and group decision-making activities. Systems such as GroupSystems, by Ventana, the subject of this study, allow dispersed or non-dispersed groups to interact, share thoughts and views on issues, to rank order possible solutions, to seek consensus through various statistical capabilities and to vote on solutions that have been identified. All of this is accomplished anonymously for the participants. As these systems become more common, organizations and people are beginning to understand that such systems are both a technological and social invention. There is always an emphasis on the technical aspects, from the hardware and software infrastructure required to the actual button-pushing instructions for using various parts of the system. However, without an understanding of the social and behavioral impacts, the promised benefits of these systems may never be realized and negative impacts may result for participants who wish to influence others to accepts their ideas and opinions.

GROUP SUPPORT SYSTEMS AND THE SETTING

Group Support Systems are defined as "...interactive computer-based environments that support concerted and coordinated team effort toward completion of joint tasks" (Nunamaker, et. al, 1996-97), and "...information technology that will provide the higher levels of coordination and cooperation needed to support individuals working together in organizations (Vandenbosch and Ginzberg, 1996-97). The electronic meetings that are facilitated by these systems are going to be different than traditional meetings in an office setting. Electronic meetings support decision-making based on the premise that communication through an electronic medium will ameliorate the negative influences found in a traditional meeting environment. For example, electronic meeting participants need not be as "... sensitive or wary when making suggestions that seem to oppose those made by others." (Lim and Benbasat, 1996-97).

GroupSystems, by Ventana Corporation, is a very popular electronic meeting support system that offers a group of tools used to support brainstorming, list building, information gathering, voting, organizing, prioritizing, and consensus building. This paper describes a seminar class built around the use of GroupSystems. This class was about the social impacts of information technology. While this was not a tightly controlled research effort, insights into the use of this particular system to facilitate class discussion were gained. Topics in this class ranged from privacy and pornography on the Internet to a discussion about access to technology creating a new caste system in society.

The first four weeks of the class, with two class meetings each week, were spent discussing one topic per week in a traditional seminar format. The first session was used to identify and prioritize the issues related to the topic and the second session was spent brainstorming solutions to address each issue, categorizing the ideas and prioritizing the solutions. This was done for four weeks and four topics. The second set of four topics was discussed using GroupSystems as an aid to the brainstorming, the prioritizing and the general consensus-seeking activities. The first four weeks of discussions were held in a traditional classroom and the second four weeks of GroupSystems based sessions, were held in the new Technology, Teaching, and Learning Center at the University of Houston-Downtown. The TTLC awarded a competitive grant to support this study. Student opinions and reactions were solicited throughout the process of using GroupSystems. The students are all mature, mostly full-time employed professionals finishing up degree requirements. They are able to relate this type of technology to appropriate uses in their own firms and their opinions about using such a system reflect a working-world orientation.

We made use of several of the components of GroupSystems in this study. Brainstorming allows users of GroupSystems to freely communicate ideas regarding the assigned topic. These idea-generating tools allow meeting participants to anonymously key in ideas and submit them for the rest of the group to see. In GroupSystem's anonymous environment, the meeting participants can freely state their assumptions without facing retribution or scorn for giving critical answers. Following an electronic brainstorming session, meeting participants might choose to categorize the ideas developed into a smaller, finite group of ideas that encompass the free-thinking ideas generated. These various categories of ideas then could be electronically disseminated to the meeting participants for comments using a feature such as the Topic Commentor.

GroupSystems has a feature that assures anonymity and encourages open and honest comments to be submitted. Anonymity has been important in laboratory studies where groups using GSS produce more unique ideas and ideas of higher quality than groups using standard techniques by allowing meeting participants to explore issues that they may be reluctant to address in a face-to-face situation. Full disclosure of feelings and opinions may be given without fear of retribution.

The GroupSystems voting tool enhances the potential impacts of the brainstorming module and the anonymity feature by allowing for voting in a rank-order, Likert scaled, and yes/no format. The voting tool is designed to give the users computerized statistical data immediately following the vote. The amount of data communicated as well as the format of display of this information is decided by the leader of the meeting and is not automatically displayed without facilitator intervention. The participants can look at the display of voting results, and decide to narrow the range of possible results to the top three choices and vote again if desired. Instantaneous feedback, coupled with the aspect of anonymity, allows for far greater sense of ownership of the voting results by the meeting participants. This sense of ownership has been shown to be critical in the successful implementation of decisions in an organization. In a face-to-face discussion, fears of not being "politically correct" or of revealing one's own prurient interests in a topic such as regulating pornography on the Internet, could change the course of the meeting outcome.

THE TEAMWORK ASPECT

In the United States, teaming people together to focus on a specific problem has become a popular organizational trend. It is assumed that decisions reached by a group of people will be superior, because a diversity of ideas will be encouraged, to decisions reached by an individual and implemented downward through a hierarchy. A group decision will encourage ownership and acceptance of the decision. However, because teams and groups are made of humans, they are susceptible to "Groupthink". This is a process when "trust and mutual support among group members create a surreal euphoria that befuddles even the most astute decision-makers, luring them into conclusions that fly in the face of reality" (Thierauf, 1989).

There are many examples of Groupthink, such as the Bay of Pigs invasions and the Space Center Challenger explosion, in our history. Groupthink has even been recognized in Hollywood via the movie, The Twelve Angry Men. The "euphoria that befuddles" is a risk in face-to-face meetings and discussions especially when one is dealing with socially unattractive topics. GSS has offered a simple solution to the problem by having the participants interface with a computer screen instead of with each other. This does not completely eliminate Groupthink; however, it does greatly encourage and motivate independence of thought. It allows Member X to communicate concerns in spite of the aggressive nature of other group members in giving their opinions and directing the meeting based on those opinions.

Group size and group proximity are other important variables. As the size of a group increases, the number of potential information exchanges rises geometrically and the frequency, duration, and intimacy of the information exchange all decline. As group size increases, there is more confusion regarding information being disseminated and discussed and how to utilize that information in a problem-solving opportunity. Group Support Systems the information processing tasks for a large group as efficiently as for a small group. They also provide efficient handling of information for groups spaced over distributed areas.

Studies have shown that strategic decision-making is enhanced by input from all possible interested parties. GSS makes this possible to do. A distributed group such as a team over Mining and Refining for an oil company can be geographically dispersed and still use the utilities of a GSS to solve an optimization problem about shipping raw materials to the refineries. In today's flattened workplace environment, not all groups are small, stable, permanent teams and not all groups are under the same roof. Electronic meeting systems are able to handle these particular realities very nicely and can greatly contribute to effective decision-making processes.

Group Support Systems bring groups and teams closer together through their enhancement of honest and open communication. In this study, the group, when using GSS, tended to be lighter and more jovial in communications with each other, especially when discussing divisive topics using this media. It was more difficult to keep the students on topic in the GSS facilitated discussions than in the traditional classroom discussions. Joking and kidding around were much more apparent in the electronic communications.

PLANNING THE MEETING

The planning of meetings using a GSS requires far greater effort than planning traditional meetings. The person convening the meeting must prepare the agenda carefully in order for the technographer to develop the supporting electronic materials. The technographer is the expert in the actual use of the system, setting up instructions for the meeting participants, receiving and formatting results of votes at the server station and dissemination of information back to the participants as requested. A student assistant, trained in the basic use of GroupSystems, functioned as the technographer for this class. Research has shown that meetings that are carefully planned are going to be much more successful at task accomplishment than those that are held with only a loosely defined agenda. In fact, it appears that the greatest benefit resulting from the use of GSS is that it forces the thorough definition of meeting goals and preparations. GSS can be a very powerful tool in the hands of someone who is interested in moving a group in a certain direction.

An interesting dilemma exists with the use of GSS. In some ways, using a Group Support System for meetings, discussions, and decision-making empowers the soft-spoken, less aggressive meeting participants. They will no longer be run over in deliberations by the outspoken, fast thinking type of person, who can thoroughly dominate a discussion and push ideas and opinions to the forefront of the debate. If you are one of these more reticent people, this can be a positive situation for you. GSS can be a real blessing in such a situation because no one knows the source of the ideas that are offered over the system. Each idea or suggestion would receive equal consideration.

On the other hand, there is a real downside to GSS that the vendors and the academics have failed to acknowledge. This is the reality that control of the meeting now resides very firmly in the facilitator. Opinions can be solicited, and these may be "out of the box" ideas, and these systems are flexible enough to handle them and incorporate them into the evolution of the meeting. However, participants are still, to a significant degree, restrained by the initial formatting of the meeting as envisioned in the planning stage. When someone is going to call a meeting to discuss something, often the topic is sent out in the memo and participants convene for a free-flowing discussion. The use of a Group Support System requires the person convening the meeting to think, ahead of time, about just how the discussion might flow, what directions he/she wants it to take, what the issues are that might arise, etc. The technographer then prepares the instructions for participants, structures the brainstorming with stimulating questions, structures voting layouts as needed, etc. This can give enormous, unrecognized power to the person calling and structuring the meeting. If this type of preparation is not done, the meeting probably will not be a positive experience for the participants, as developing the auxiliary GSS templates, instructions, voting schema, etc., while participants twiddle their thumbs, will not make for satisfied decision-makers.

GROUP SUPPORT SYSTEM SETTINGS

Group Support Systems require special settings that are designed to allow the team or group to utilize all features of the GSS. Groups and teams are more productive when they become absorbed into the electronic discussion without competing influences. GroupSystems by Ventana can be implemented to two ways. The first is in a dedicated setting with workstations, overhead projection facilities, and technographer workstation, clustered in a room where the meetings take place. This entails a major commitment on the part of the implementing organizations. The University of Arizona, a site of significant GSS research, has two GSS facilities, one for large groups and one for smaller groups. The Claremont Graduate School has a one-size-fits-all style of facility. In all such cases, the facilities are built with the Group Support System as the hub and the meeting environment is built around this hub.

The typical meeting room has large monitors and many workstations. The large monitors display the information, such as votes and statistics, generated by the GSS and the group and meeting proceedings can by recorded, analyzed, and summarized for constituencies who are affected by group decisions (Thierauf, 1986). Moreover, in a large meeting room where the leader might by invisible due to the amount of workstations, there is often a monitor dedicated to the use of the technographer. This role is equivalent to being the interface between the GSS and the group. The GSS is controlled by the actions of the technographer, as instructed by the leader of the meeting.

A second approach to using GroupSystems is in a distributed environment, similar to a typical client-server implementation. Meeting participants engage in the discussion as they wish, at different times in the sanctity of their offices. Being present at the same time is not needed for effective collaboration. GSS technology is equipped with group memory that allows all members to join in an electronic meeting when they have the time. This is especially effective with international decision-making activities. Meeting agendas, brainstorming instructions, and voting criteria are disseminated to the client computers in private work areas. Participants may respond when and as they wish. Obviously, this decision-making process will take longer than in a room dedicated to facilitating Group Support System based meetings.

There are been little research to date on the actual differences in decision outcomes using both types of implementation. There has also been little research into participant satisfaction with the process when GSS is implemented in a distributed mode. The Federal government, as perhaps the largest user of GroupSystems by Ventana, has several agencies that are using this system, both in a dedicated facility and in a distributed fashion. Interesting insights are likely to result from these efforts.

CURRENT RESEARCH KNOWLEDGE

A major work has recently been published that presents an analysis of the results of twelve years of research regarding Group Support Systems in organizations. This paper "Lessons from a Dozen Years of Group Support Systems Research: A Discussion of Lab and Field Findings" (Nunamaker, et. al., 1996-97), details the current state of knowledge that has been derived from many efforts to understand this technology and its use in organizations. These findings are:

- GSS and Organizational Buy-In to Decisions - As people interact using GSS, sharing ideas, opinions, biases, and judgments, a unified shared vision emerges and key constraints from both sides get incorporated into the decision.
- Leadership - GSS does not replace leadership, nor does it imply a particular leadership style. GSS can help a group reach a clearly defined goal much more quickly, but in the absence of clarity and definition, the group process can fall apart very quickly. Numerous instances have been cited of the democratization of the group interaction when using GSS. Autocratic leaders, while they can shape the overall agenda of a meeting, find their personal power to force ideas and decisions to be greatly reduced when using GSS. For this reason, GSS can be a two-edged sword in organizations and some managers will not use it because it does level the playing field for their employees.
- Role Clarification - The process of communicating one's visions and beliefs is greatly facilitated by the synchronicity and anonymity of GSS. Software modules designed for stakeholder analysis help to clarify the various roles that different organizational groups are playing in the decision process. Assumptions of these groups are brought to the surface and more widely satisfying decisions are made.
- GSS and Participation in Organizational Activities - In traditional meetings, 20 percent of the participants do 80 percent of the talking. In GSS supported meetings, the input of participants is nearly equal. Anonymity and parallel input surely play a part in this finding. However, this is not always a good thing in the eyes of all participants. In organizations that base a reward system on individual performance, information access, or specialized knowledge, persons possessing these have been shown to resist GSS sessions where information is shared and ideas are contributed anonymously.
- Lessons about Anonymity - The anonymity aspect of GSS results in a much higher volume of ideas and far more creative out-of-the-box thinking. It is easier to separate ideas from the politics behind them and often the big picture is more likely to emerge. However, often the leaders/bosses find the anonymity factor to be a difficult issue to deal with. Participants are far less hesitant to tell it like it is, to get things off their chests, and to be critical of coworkers, management, etc.
- GSS and Productivity - Nearly all research in the field has shown increases in productivity as a result of using GSS. An early field research, conducted at an IBM plant, lasted a year and involved thirty groups using GroupSystems to solve problems in production line quality. Decisions made by the GSS group saved an average of 50 percent in labor cost over teams making decisions conventionally. Comparable results have been shown over and over again at Boeing, BellCore, the U.S. Army, and similar organizations.

CONCLUSIONS

Collaborative technologies change how we work in organizations. As professionals we need to be prepared to integrate these technologies into our work, to embrace their beneficial qualities. Corporations, as well as meeting participants, will benefit from recognizing the potentially powerful social and organizational impacts of this technology. The systems are not simple to use or to assimilate into the life of an organization. As a result, the focus tends to be on the issues of "how to use" and "what button do I push to make something happen". While these issues are important, failure to understand how to use Group Support Systems to gain the advantage in encouraging acceptance of your ideas may have an enormous impact on your career success. Adopters of this technology must understand the power of the facilitator in planning meetings and make certain their goals are incorporated into the planning. Similarly, participants must learn how to communicate persuasively using a keyboard and the written word to sell ideas and influence others. The force of personality will not be available when the playing field becomes level for all decision-makers through the use of Group Support Systems.

REFERENCES

Coleman and Khanna. Groupware: Technologies and Applications. Princeton Hall. New Jersey. 1995.

Dykman, C. Electronic mail systems: An Analysis of the Use/Satisfaction Relationship. Doctoral Dissertation. University of Houston. 1986.

Johansen, R. Groupware: Computer Support for Business Teams. The Free Press. New York. 1988.

Lim and Benbasat. "A Framework for Addressing Group Judgment Biases with Group Technology." Journal of Management Information Systems. Pages 7-24. Winter, 1996.97.

Nunamaker, Briggs, Mittleman, Vogel, and Balthazard, "Lessons from a Dozen Years of Group Support Systems Research." Journal of Management Information Systems. Pages 163-203. Winter, 1996-97.

Stohr and Konsynsky. Information Systems and Decision Processes. IEEE Computer Society Press. California. 1992.

Thierauf, R. Group Decision Support Systems for Effective Decision-Making. Quorum Books. New York. 1989.

Vandenbosch and Ginzberg. "Lotus Notes and Collaboration: Plus ca change..." Journal of Management Information Systems. Pages 65-82. Winter, 1996-97.

Logic Modeling of Cooperative Database Systems

M. Enciso, C. Rossi,

E.T.S.I. Informática, Campus de Teatinos, Universidad de Málaga, 29071 Málaga, Spain

Enciso@lcc.uma.es, Phone number +34 952 133309

J.M. Frias, A. Mora

{jmfrias,amora,rossi}@ctima.uma.es

E.T.S.I. Informática, Campus de Teatinos, Universidad de Málaga, 29071 Málaga, Spain

ABSTRACT

This work presents a new approach for database modeling, based in a general framework presented in [1]. The main objective is to combine the advantages and to avoid the disadvantages of both graphical and formal methods. The modeling process starts from an Entity/Relationship model that is automatically translated to a logical model. Then we apply some transformations to remove redundant information. Finally we re-engineer an improved graphical model. We consider this approach appropriate for cooperative Systems Development due to its capability to integrate several models.

1. INTRODUCTION.

Most of the methodologies for Information Systems Development split the model construction task into two related subtasks: Data Modeling and Process Modeling [2]. There are two main approaches to build these two models:

• *Graphical methods,* such as the Entity /Relationship data model [1] or the Data Flow Diagram process model [7]. Their main advantages are: their notations are simple and they are easy to learn and use. On the other hand, they present serious disadvantages: it is difficult to combine several models (even when they describe the same system); they have limited expressive power, therefore we cannot express some constraints; the model validation is difficult, since we cannot express all the rules needed to check the model soundness.

• *Formal methods*, such as logic or algebraic specifications [5]. They are a solid tool, but its construction, maintenance and comprehension are complex. These features make these methods inappropriate for inexperienced developers, and inadequate to encourage the final user participation in the evaluation and refinement of the models. These problems reduce in practice the use of formal methods in Information Systems Development.

Our approach combines the advantages and tries to avoid the disadvantages of both graphical and formal methods. The basic idea is to use graphical methods to construct the models and formal methods to combine them and to prove the soundness. This idea is presented in [5]. The steps in the proposed system modeling are:

1. Starting from a graphical model, we apply a translation process that automatically generates a logic model.

2. Then we apply some formal transformations to improve the model. Currently, we have developed transformations to remove redundancies.

3. Finally, we re-build an improved graphical model. In other words, we apply a re-engineering technique.

This is an iterative process. The model quality can be optimized repeating the application of these three steps.

This paper is focused exclusively on data model design. We consider that the initial graphical model is expressed in the widely accepted Entity/Relationship notation [1].

We will use logic as formal method. First order logic is sufficient to satisfy the objectives of this work. We will use Prolog to automate the process.

The technique proposed above can be applied in a *Computer Supported Cooperative Work* (CSCW) [6] System Development process. Particularly, we can use this approach to face up the problem of integrating several system models defined by different analysts. There are some well-known problems in the model integration task:

• The conflict produced when several analysts define some data as an attribute, while others represent this information as an entity set.

• The use of synonymous and homonymous terms.

• The existence of redundant information.

This third issue is the main goal of this paper. In the cooperative data modeling, different analysts build a set of Entity/ Relationship models. The automation of our method leads to a CSCW tool (in fact it is also a CASE tool) that detects redundant relationships. The search of these relationships is made by means of algorithms based on the construction of the transitive closure of the relationship of the entire model. A very important goal in our work is to have an efficient method to calculate the transitive closure of the relationships. We use the BTC' algorithm introduced in [3]. The details of this process will be explained in section 3.

Note that the redundancy usually arises when different data models are joined. For example, a binary relationship R_1 of the data model M_1 may be redundant with the information of another model M_2, and this redundancy is induced by a chain of binary relationships defined over a collection of entities sets that does not occur in M_1.

The above technique only treats with binary relationships. To increase the scope of this technique we apply a method to remove n-ary relationships (with n>2). In this method, n-ary relationships are substituted by induced or equivalent binary relationships (see section 2). In some sense, this approach is related with those works concerned with *Normal Form Entity/Relationship Diagrams* [4].

2. PRELIMINARY RESULTS.

In this section, we present some results that will be needed in the rest of the paper. Due to space limitations, we do not present them formally neither we prove them.

From now on, we will read a *"many to many"* relationship as a relation, a *"many to one"* (or *"one to many"*) relationship as a function and a *"one to one"* relationships as an injective function. This leads directly to the following definition:

Definition 1

Let *Order* be a process that compute the order of the relationship induced by a chain of binary relationships. This process will apply recursively the following two rules (rules of the relation composition operator):
• *Only the composition of two injective functions produces an injective function.*
• *Only the composition of two functions produces a new function.*

Note: our Prolog predicate defined for this process looks at the right (resp. left) element of the order label of the relationships and generates a right (resp. left) *"one"* order label if and only if all the order labels are *"one"*. In other case, a *"many"* order label is assigned.

Our main goal is the elimination of redundant information. So we give the following definition:

Definition 2

A binary relationship R, between the set of entities A and B is redundant if there exists an ordered list of set of entities, $[E_0, E_1, ..., E_n]$, and a chain of binary relationships, $R_1:R_2:...:R_n$ where R_i is defined over E_{i-1} and E_i for all $i \in \{1..n\}$, such that
• $E_0 = A$
• $E_n = B$
• The order of R is the same of the relationship induced by the chain $R_1:R_2:...:R_n$
• The meaning of R is equivalent to the meaning of the chain of relationships.

Note that the last property is unavoidable and it implies an on-line participation of the analyst in the redundancy removal process.

The following result allows ensures that we can treat only with binary relationship

Proposition 1

Let R be an n-ary relationship, it can be substituted by an equivalent set of binary relationships if and only if in R participates, at most, only one set of entities with order "many". To illustrate this result, we present the following figure, that represents the case of a generic relationship R defined over three sets of entities A_1, A_2, A_3.

Proposition 1 may be proved directly from the properties of the relation composition operator.

3. THE REDUNDANCY REMOVAL PROCESS

To reduce redundancy in the Entity-Relationship model, we remove those binary relationships whose meaning corresponds with the meaning of a chain of relationships that appear in the model. To carry out this task, we must execute the following steps:
• *Split*: Split the n-ary relationships into an equivalent set of binary relationships, if it is the case.
• *Induce*: Generate the binary relationships induced by the n-ary relationships that can not be split.
• *RRR_BTC'*: Compute the transitive closure of the model and remove the redundant relationships.

Now, we describe these three processes:

3.1 Split Process

This separation only can be achieved when in this relationship participates, at most, only one set of entities with order "many" (see *Proposition 1*). If the target relationship satisfies this property, we split the relationship as it is described in *figure 1*.

3.2 Induce Process

If the above process can not be achieved, then we compute all the binary relationships induced by the n-ary relationships, as it is presented in *figure 1*. These binary relationships are not physically added to the model (they are provisional relationships).

3.3 RRR_BTC' Process

To detect redundant relationships, we compute the transitive closure of the relationships of the target model. Then we eliminate all the redundant relationships detected obtaining a more refined model.

Now we present the redundant relationships removal algorithm, which is based in the Basic Transitive Closure algorithm (BTC) presented in [3]. We will call RRR_BTC' to our algorithm. This algorithm traverses the graph depth first, marking the nodes to avoid visit them twice. The algorithm processes the nodes following an inverted topological order: it builds up the set of the

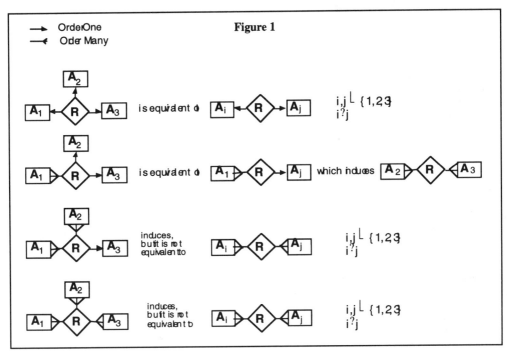

Figure 1

descendants of a node after computing the sets of the descendants of its children. The algorithm structure induces an intensive use of the backtracking in Prolog.

From now on, we will use the following notation:

G: A Graph.

E: The set of nodes (the sets of entities of the model)

$R_{ij}^{(k)}$: The k-edge between E_i and E_j (a relationship of the model).

S_i: The set of children of E_i, ($S_i = \{E_j \mid$ there exists a edge R_{ij} in $G\}$.

G^*: The Transitive Closure of G.

M_i/U_i: The Marked/Unmarked nodes of the graph.

D_i: The set of descendants of the node E_i ($D_i = \{E_j \mid$ there exists a edge R_{ij} in $G^*\}$).

The underlying strategy of RRR_BTC' are the following:

• It orders the nodes topologically.

• It computes the descendants of a given node following an inverse order, i.e., to compute the set of descendants D_i, it first computes the sets of descendants D_j, for all E_j child of E_i.

When the algorithm visit each node E_i, it computes the induced relationships with origin in E_i and checks if some of them causes redundancies. This is a schema of the above process:

Induced(E_i, E_j, D_j)
for all $E_a \in D_j$
    if R_{ia} is a relationship of the model then
            Propose_to_Remove R_{ia}
end if

In the following presentation of the RRR_BTC' algorithm, we will use this notation:

• The *number(G)* procedure numbers the nodes of the graph G. It is a simple procedure which is described in [3].

• The array *popped(k)* k ∈ {1..n} stores the nodes in their topological order.

• The function *node_popped(i)* outputs the node E_k such that *popped(k)*=i.

• The procedure *Induced(Ei, Ej, Dj)* builds up the set of all the induced relationships that start at E_j, end in a node of Dj and pass through Ej.

• The procedure *Propose_to_Remove Relationships(E_i, E_j, D_j)* proposes to the analyst remove the relationships that start at E_j end in a node of Dj and pass through Ej.

The algorithm may be implemented as follows:

proc RRR_BTC'

Input: $G=(E, S_i)$

Output: $D_i = M_i$, ($U_i = \emptyset$)

Number(G)
for i=1 to n do
    $U_i = S_i$
    $M_i = \varnothing$
end for

for i=n downto 1 do
    I=node_popped(i)
while $\exists j \in U_I - \{I\}$ do
        Induced(E_I, E_j, M_j)
        Propose_to_Remove Relationships(E_I, E_j, M_j)
$M_I = M_I \cup M_j \cup \{j\}$
        $U_I = U_I \cup U_j - M_I$
    end while
end for

4. EXAMPLE

To improve the comprehension of this technique, we present an illustrative example. We do not show the attributes of the set of entities and we will number the relationships instead of naming them. We have an Entity/Relationship model that represents several rules of an organization. In the following explanation we will label each rule with the relationship that represents the rule in the model. Each employee belongs only to one department [R2], but the employee can develop different tasks

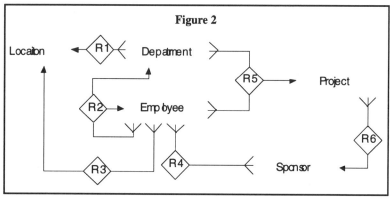

Figure 2

for several departments [R5]. These tasks are focused on the development of only one project (each employee can collaborate with any department only in one project) [R5]. Each project has only one financial sponsor [R6].

We store the information that relates the employees with the sponsors [R4]. On the other side, each department is located in only one place [R1] and each employee has an address [R3] that must correspond with the location of his department. We associate each employee with a supervisor [R2].

This information is described with the following data model in Figure 2.

The Prolog specification of this model is the following:
% o: one, m: many
entity(location).
entity(department).
entity(employee).
entity(project).
entity(sponsor).
relationship(r1,[(location,o),(department,m)]).
relationship(r2,[(departament,o),employee,o),(employee,m)]).
relationship(r3,[(employee,m),(location,o)]).
relationship(r4,[(employee,m),(sponsor,m)]).
relationship(r5,[(department,m),(employee,m),(project,o)]).
relationship(r6,[(project,m),(sponsor,o)]).

In the first step, we *Split* the n-ary relationship R2 into two equivalent many to one relationships:
- R2.1 (an employee belongs to only one department).
- R2.2 (an employee has only one supervisor).

In the *Induce* process we obtain two inferred many to many relationships from R5:
- R5.1 (the projects related with the departments).
- R5.2 (the projects related with the employees).

From the above situation, we deduce that R3 and R4 are redundant with the relationships chains R2.1:R1 and R5.2:R6 respectively. Finally, the process RRR_BTC' removes these two relationships, rendering a more refined model.

In the Prolog specification, we transform these two relationships in two new predicates that derive new information (extensional database) from the original one (intensional database). With this solution, the relationships are not fully eliminated and the users may reference them.

The resulting formal logic specification is the following:

entity(location).
entity(department).
entity(employee).
entity(project).
entity(sponsor).
relationship(r1,[(location,u),(department,m)]).
relationship(r2_1,[(departament,u),(employee,m)]).
relationship(r2_2,[(employee,m),(employee,u)]).
relationship(r5,[(department,m),(employee,m),(project,u)]).
relationship(r6,[(project,m),(sponsor,u)]).
induced_relationship(r3,[r2_1, r1]).
induced_relationship(r4,[r5_2, r6]).

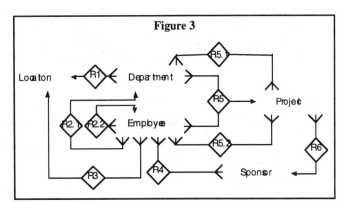

Figure 3

REFERENCES

[1] P. P. Chen. *The Entity-relationship Model: Toward a Unified View of Data.* ACM Transactions on Database Systems, Vol. 1, No 1, 1976

[2] I. Hawryszkiewycz. *Introduction to Systems Analiysis and Design.* 4 Ed. Prentice Hall. 1998.

[3] Y. Ioannidis, R. Ramakrishnan, L. Winger. *Algorithms Based on Graph Traversal.* ACM Transactions on Database System, Vol 18, N° 3, September 1993.

[4] T. W. Ling, P. K. Teo. *A Normal Form Object-Oriented Entity Relationship Diagram.* Proceedings of Entity-Relantionship Approach-ER'94. Springer-Verlag. 1994.

[5] D. Robertson, J. Agustí. *Automated Reasoning in Conceptual Modeling.* Addison Wesley, to appear in 1999.

[6] K.Spurr et al. *Computer Support for Cooperative Work.* Wiley 1994.

[7] E. Yourdon. *Modern Structured Analysis.* Prentice Hall 1989.

A Rule-Based, Adaptive Approach to the Design and Implementation of Data Warehouses

Henrik Engström
Department of Computer Science, University of Skövde, P.O. Box 408, S-541 28 Skövde, Sweden
henrik@ida.his.se, +46 500 464706

Sharma Chakravarthy
Computer and Information Science and Engineering Department, University of Florida, P.O. Box 116120,
Gainesville, FL 32611-6120
sharma@cise.ufl.edu, 352/392 2697

Brian Lings
Department of Computer Science, University of Exeter, Prince of Wales Road, Exeter EX4 4PT, United Kingdom
brian@dcs.exeter.ac.uk, +44 1392 264055

ABSTRACT

A data warehouse contains data integrated from a number of heterogeneous and distributed sources. Changes in the sources should be reflected in the warehouse, which can be performed in a number of different ways depending on warehouse requirements and source functionality. Materialisation of a data warehouse can be considered as a generalisation of the *view materialisation problem.*

The choice of a policy for maintaining a view has been shown to depend on a number of factors. In this paper we argue that

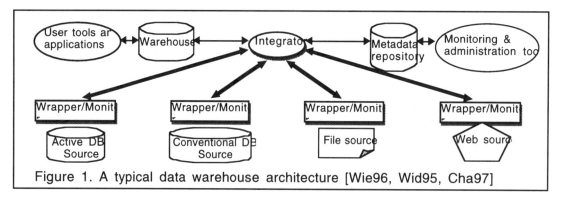

Figure 1. A typical data warehouse architecture [Wie96, Wid95, Cha97]

there is a need for a flexible infrastructure for incrementally maintaining (or updating) materialised views in order to fully utilise the advantages of a data warehouse. We discuss the potential of using a rule-based approach for view maintenance to enable dynamic adaptation of view maintenance policy and change detection in response to evolving prerequisites and observed behaviour.

INTRODUCTION

Data Warehousing

Data warehousing was introduced in the commercial world in the beginning of the 90s in response to market needs for decision support [Kim96, Rou95, Cha97]. From a usage perspective, a data warehouse can be seen as a database which collects and stores data from different data sources [Gup95, Wid95]. A manager may then, for example, perform extensive and complex queries based on company sales data, without affecting the performance of source databases [Ham95]. Other potential advantages are reduction of response time [Wid95], providing temporal views [Yan98], and to make data continuously available from sources which periodically go off-line [Rou95, Ham95].

The users access the contents of the warehouse (see Figure 1) through different tools, such as query languages, spreadsheet programs, web browsers and data mining applications. The data stored in the warehouse is retrieved from sources such as plain files, html-pages, active and conventional databases [Wid95]. The integrator is responsible for coordinating data retrieval from the sources and integrating the results into the warehouse. A source may need to be extended, through the use of a wrapper/monitor, to provide the necessary services to the integrator.

From an architectural point of view, the data stored in a warehouse can be seen as materialised views over the source databases [Gup95, Wie96]. Views are commonly used mechanisms in relational databases; in many cases the concept of a view is equated with relational view. There are, however, examples of views over data using object-oriented and other data models (Abiteboul et al. [Abi97], for instance, give suggestions on how to define views over semistructured data). In its most general form a view can be seen as an arbitrary function (or query) over some data sets. If the result is computed and stored then the view is said to be materialised. View maintenance is the task of changing a stored view according to changes made to base data.

A warehouse view differs from a centralised view in that it is typically read only [Cha97, Wid95]. That is, the sources are not updated even if the materialised data were to be updated. The sources are typically not sensitive to changes to the warehouse data and are decoupled from the warehouse. This means that source updates are committed independently and changes may have to be detected through polling [Ham95]. Central control, as offered by global transactions, can not be assumed in a warehousing environment [Wid95].

The Problem

One driving reason for introducing data warehouses and materialised views is to get performance advantages. The data is stored locally to get short response times and reduce the load on the sources. There have been many studies showing that maintenance mechanisms have an important impact on the performance of a system [Sri88, Seg90, Col97]. Some of the factors affecting the choice of maintenance policy are typically not known in advance, but must be estimated. Other factors change dynamically, impacting negatively on earlier optimisation decisions. This makes it reasonable to believe that maintenance policy is not a static property, but may need to change as a system evolves.

Ceri and Widom [Cer91] have shown that materialised views in an active DBMS can be maintained through automatically generated rules. There have been some reported efforts on developing these ideas for a data warehouse environment [Zho95, Ham95]. In this paper we present some initial ideas on how active rules could be further utilised in a data warehouse environment. Our primary concern relates to the highlighted parts of figure 1 and in particular how to provide flexible rule-based middleware for warehouse maintenance. It should be noticed that materialised views have been deployed for other purposes in the data warehouse context. It is common that some multidimensional conceptual model is used for warehouse data and views can be used to pre-compute some aggregations along different dimensions [Wu97]. This is done within the warehouse environment (using the base views derived from the sources) in order to improve query performance. In this paper we primarily focus on first level views.

What we envisage is an infrastructure, which supports different maintenance policies and offers ways to change policy dynamically. Ideally, the system should adapt to the outcome of 'uncertain' factors, such as update frequency.

BACKGROUND

Materialised view maintenance has been a research topic for more than a decade [Han87] and many of the results can be applied directly to a data warehouse environment. There have been efforts on realising adaptive techniques [Rou95] and on using rule systems [Cer91] but no project, that we are aware of provides a dynamic, and adaptive mechanism for supporting multiple maintenance policies. In this section we present work related to our problem.

Choice of a Maintenance Policy

A *view maintenance policy*, as used in this paper, determines when and how [Cha97] a materialisation should be updated as a response to base data changes. To start with, there is a choice on how to perform the actual update of a stored view. One solution, for example, is to reapply the defining query (i.e., recompute the view). Depending on the nature of the query definition it may be possible to use incremental maintenance. Additional information structures can be introduced and maintained in order to increase performance [Zho95].

Maintenance timing determines when to refresh a view. The most commonly mentioned maintenance timings are immediate, periodic and on-demand. With immediate (also called eager) maintenance the view is refreshed immediately after a source update is detected. Periodic timing maintains a view at periodic intervals such as once a day or once a week. A view inspection or some other external event triggers maintenance when timing is on-demand. Periodic and on-demand are sometimes collectively referred to as deferred maintenance. Maintenance timing should however not be confused with currency [Seg90] of a view. In a traditional database, views normally reflect all committed changes to the base tables immediately. In a warehousing environment it is, however, not always possible or even desirable that a view should reflect the current state of its sources.

Several projects have considered the issue of selecting the most appropriate policy for a given situation. Hanson [Han87] compares the performance of, amongst other things, deferred and immediate maintenance in a centralised environment. Hanson shows that the efficiency of a policy depends on the structure of the underlying database and on update and query distribution. For future work, he suggests that an adaptive method to choose maintenance policies should be devised.

Srivastava and Rotem [Sri88] use a queuing model to determine an optimal maintenance strategy. They identify the need to consider both the system's viewpoint (to minimise processing) and the user's viewpoint (to minimise waiting). They show that the relative importance given to the user's and system's viewpoint has an impact on the choice of policy. A restriction in their work is that the only system cost considered is the number of disk accesses. They suggest that the model should be extended to include communication cost. Apart from this we believe that storage cost is worth considering as auxiliary storage structures can be used to, for example, reduce response time. The results of Srivastava and Rotem depend on the assumption that views should always be current. If this assumption is removed then currency has to be considered in the user's viewpoint. This is typically the case in a warehousing environment.

Segev and Fang [Seg90] suggest that the currency requirements for a view should be explicitly specified and used when a maintenance policy is determined. They show that utilising the currency specification can reduce the cost of maintaining a distributed materialised view.

Colby et al. [Col97] argue that there is a need to support several maintenance policies. They consider three policies; immediate, deferred (on-demand), and snapshot (periodic), and present results from a simulation study showing that all three policies may give performance advantages depending on the circumstances.

Active Rules for View Maintenance

Active database technology was introduced as a means to enable a DBMS to handle active tasks, specified as event-condition-action (ECA) rules [Wid96]. An early application for active databases was view maintenance. Ceri and Widom [Cer91] have shown that maintenance rules may be automatically generated for certain views. Their target environment is an active relational database system and the views are defined using SQL select expressions. By analysing the table references in a view expression, maintenance rules are generated that either re-compute or incrementally refresh the view. As an example, if a view meets the requirements of being incrementally maintainable, each base table referenced in the definition will yield one rule for insertions, one for deletions, and two rules for updates. Ceri and Widom [Cer91] use active capabilities in a centralised environment and determine the policy statically, under the assumption that incremental maintenance should be used whenever possible. They indicate that different rule assertion points may be used to determine maintenance timing, but no details are presented.

The ideas from active database research have been widely accepted. Most commercial database systems offer some form of active capability. Recently there have been several projects aimed at applying the ideas outside the environment of a centralised DBMS [Gat98, Cha98, Ber97]. The active capabilities are said to be unbundled from the DBMS into a heterogeneous, distributed environment. The driving idea is to enable a dynamic, flexible infrastructure for tasks such as workflow management, cooperative information systems, and health care monitoring. Some effort has also been directed to utilising active functionality for warehouse maintenance.

Adaptation

Adaptation, as we define it, is the iterative process of setting system parameters using available metadata and observing changes to metadata. The metadata can contain estimations of system behaviour, design goals and other system properties. The selection of policy can be seen as applying a function which takes the metadata as parameters and returns the system parameters. In a similar way as for view maintenance, there is a question of when and how to adapt system parameters. They can, for example, be recomputed immediately after each new observation, periodically or on some other event (e.g. user demand). The adaptation can be performed either on-line or off-line. The 'function' used to compute values for the system parameters can be more or less automatic. At one extreme it is a decision taken by the system designers (based on their experience) and at the other extreme it is a formal mathematical function.

OUR APPROACH TO ADAPTIVE WAREHOUSE MAINTENANCE

The primary focus in our work is on how to provide the necessary infrastructure to enable a dynamic (on-line) adaptation of maintenance policy. For this purpose a rule-based approach is likely to be appropriate. The advantages of using rule-based middleware is that it hides the source details, offers a declarative well stablished interface and most importantly offers a highly dynamic modelling of behaviour. It would be relatively easy to achieve this in a centralised, homogeneous environment by enabling and disabling different rule sets (such as those described by Ceri and Widom [Cer91]) but the prerequisites in a warehouse environment gives a different, more complex situation. The Whips [Ham95, Wie96] and H2O [Zho95] projects present some efforts in this direction but no work, as far as we know, addresses the issue of dynamic adaptation of maintenance policies.

In Whips, passive sources are extended with monitors which detect changes and report them to the integrator. The integrator uses a rule-based engine to update the warehouse according to source changes. Immediate maintenance with different consistency levels is used and it is assumed that differences in source capabilities may be hidden through wrapping. Hammer et al. [Ham95] give clear indications that active rules may enable adaptation to metadata changes but they have, to the best of our knowledge, not reported any results on maintenance policy adaptation. In H2O, Zhou et al. [Zho95] present a taxonomy over the solution space for data integration. The taxonomy covers most of the maintenance aspects discussed above but a focus is chosen on sufficiently active sources and incremental, immediate maintenance.

We believe that a specialised rule middleware is needed which utilises inherent source capabilities and provides an infrastructure that may realise any maintenance policy. The active functionality we consider is the definition, management, and execution of rules including the definition and detection of events. These services may be tailored for this purpose in line with the suggestions of Gatziu et al. [Gat98]. To do this we need to analyse the requirements on the rule architecture, derived from the nature of view maintenance in a warehouse environment. In the rest of this section we elaborate on architectural implications, using a simple, figurative example.

An Illustrative Example

ACME Toys Ltd is a small international company with offices in London, Paris and New York. London and Paris are responsible for stock-in-trades and distribution while the production and head office is located in New York. Each branch has its own computer system (a node) connected to the others through a network (see Figure 2). In London there is a passive object-oriented inventory database storing the currently available items and in Paris they have an active relational database for the same purpose. The managers in New York have a data warehouse containing the total number of items in stock each day during the last 13 months. The databases run on different platforms and are updated by applications outside the scope of the warehouse system. The London node is extensible which means that it is possible to implement new services. The Paris node is not extensible.

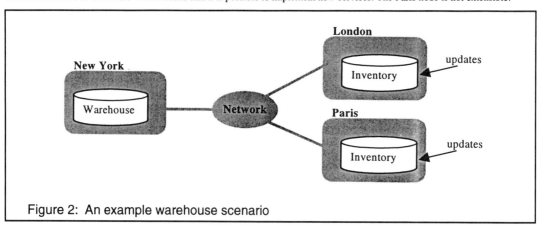

Figure 2: An example warehouse scenario

The initial design goal is to provide a warehouse with data that is at most one day old and with a minimal impact on the operational systems in London and Paris. At first the warehouse is incrementally maintained, but later the system designers realise that it is more efficient to recompute the view. After a while, the managers wish to do a different kind of analysis, which requires that current data should be available for querying.

All these changes should be performed without having to take the warehouse or the systems in London and Paris off-line.

Implications for Rule Architecture

Rule-based middleware may be used to maintain the warehouse in the example above. Ideally it should adapt the maintenance policy to meet the design goals (represented as metadata). To do this it has to be possible to set and alter system parameters dynamically. One such parameter is maintenance timing. Initially, the system designers in the example may choose to use periodic maintenance under the assumption that the sources are updated frequently. If it is later observed that the update intensity is low it will be better to maintain the warehouse immediately (if the changes occur once a week for example). As a further example of how the system may need to adapt as a consequence to observed behaviour: on-demand maintenance may be an optimal policy when the inspection intensity is low. It could, however, be replaced with immediate during periods of high user activity.

The London database is unable to perform automatic change detection and will have to be extended with a polling process to simulate immediate detection. The localisation of this activity is an issue, which affects system performance. By extending the London node, communication is significantly reduced (compared with remote queries from New York). On the other hand there is an additional load on the node in London. The polling frequency is another system parameter, which affects the impact on the system and may be explicitly controlled. There is no reason to detect changes once a second in London if New York allows one-day delay. In a similar way the maintenance strategies will have implications for change detection. If incremental materialisation is used it is probably a good idea to detect changes in London, but when recompute is introduced it may be more efficient to cease polling.

The heterogeneity of the sources affects the choice of policy as well as the work of the rule-system. When the most current data is required the Paris node may be using immediate maintenance while the London node may be forced to use on-demand maintenance. The polling process will always have an average delay proportional to the polling frequency. The integrator has to know which services the nodes provide to be able to make an optimal decision.

We believe that the source capabilities need to be characterised and recorded as metadata accessible for the integrator as well as the rule middleware. In the example above this metadata may include the currency requirements, the update intensity in the sources, the capabilities of the sources as well as the relative importance of storage, processing, communication, currency, and response-time. To be able to perform automatic policy adaptation the system should detect changes to metadata. This may include observed system behaviour (update intensity in the sources) as well as changes to declared metadata.

SUMMARY

Active technology has been used successfully in a number of areas. It has been shown that rules may be used to maintain materialised views in a centralised database environment and there have been some efforts to bring these ideas into the data warehouse environment. One problem in such an environment is to determine when and how to maintain the warehouse; the sources may have different capabilities and some system resources may be more critical than others. This paper discusses the potential use of active technology for multiple maintenance policy support. We believe that active technology could be deployed in the design and implementation of data warehouses providing a flexible and dynamic infrastructure. Optimally this flexibility should be used to make the view maintenance policy adaptable to observed system behaviour. Our goal is to explore the architectural implications for a rule system aimed at supporting dynamic, adaptive view maintenance in a warehouse environment, and to provide such a system.

Acknowledgements

We would like to thank Mikael Berndtsson, Björn Lundell, Jonas Mellin and Lars Niklasson for their valuable comments.

REFERENCES

[Abi97] S. Abiteboul, R. Goldman, J. McHugh, V. Vassalos, Y. Zhuge. Views for Semistructured Data. Workshop on Management of Semistructured Data, 1997

[Ber97] M. Berndtsson, S. Chakravarthy, B. Lings. Extending Database Support for Coordination Among Agents. International Journal on Cooperative Information Systems, 6(3-4), 1997

[Cer91] S. Ceri, J. Widom. Deriving Production Rules for Incremental View Maintenance. VLDB, 1991

[Cha98] S. Chakravarthy, R. Le. ECA Rule Support for Distributed Heterogeneous Environments. ICDE, 1998

[Cha97] S. Chaudhuri, U. Dayal. An Overview of Data Warehousing and OLAP Technology. SIGMOD Record, 26(1), 1997

[Col97] L. S. Colby, A. Kawaguchi, D. F. Lieuwen, I.S. Mumick, K.A. Ross. Supporting Multiple View Maintenance Policies. SIGMOD Conference, 1997

[Gat98] S. Gatziu, A. Koschel, G. von B Itzingsloewen, H. Fritschi. Unbundling Active Functionality. SIGMOD Record, 27(1), 1998

[Gup95] A. Gupta, I.S. Mumick. Maintenance of Materialized Views: Problems, Techniques, and Applications. IEEE Data Engineering Bulletin, 18(2), 1995

[Ham95] J. Hammer, H. Garcia-Molina, J. Widom, W. Labio, Y. Zhuge. The Stanford Data Warehousing Project. IEEE Data Engineering Bulletin, 18(2), 1995

[Han87] E. N. Hanson, A Performance Analysis of View Materialization Strategies, SIGMOD Conference, 1987

[Kim96] R. Kimball. The Data Warehouse Toolkit. John Wiley & Sons, 1996

[Rou95] N. Roussopoulos, C. Chen, S. Kelley, A. Delis, Y. Papakonstantinou. The ADMS Project: Views "R" Us. IEEE Data Engineering Bulletin, 18(2), 1995

[Seg90] A. Segev, W. Fang. Currency-Based Updates to Distributed Materialized Views. ICDE, 1990

[Sri88] J. Srivastava, D. Rotem. Analytical Modeling of Materialized View Maintenance. ACM PODS, 1988

[Wid95] J. Widom. Research Problems in Data Warehousing. CIKM, 1995

[Wid96] J. Widom, S. Ceri. Active Database Systems: Triggers and Rules For Advanced Database Processing. Morgan Kaufmann Publishers, 1996

[Wie96] J. L. Wiener, H. Gupta, W. J. Labio, Y. Zhuge, H. Garcia-Molina, J. Widom. A System Prototype for Warehouse View Maintenance. ACM Workshop on Materialized Views: Techniques and Applications, 1996

[Wu97] M. C. Wu, A. P. Buchmann. Research Issues in Data Warehousing. BTW'97, 1997

[Yan98] J. Yang, J. Widom. Maintaining Temporal Views Over Non-Temporal Information Sources For Data Warehousing. International Conference on Extending Database Technology, 1998

[Zho95] G. Zhou, R. Hull, R. King, J.C. Franchitti. Data Integration and Warehousing Using H2O. IEEE Data Engineering Bulletin, 18(2), 1995

Learning, Teaching and Browsing with Nestor®1

Liliane Esnault

Professor of Information Systems and Organization - E.M.LYON, 23 Av. Guy de Collongue - BP 174 -69132
ECULLY Cedex - France
Tel (33) 4 78 33 78 00 - Fax (33) 4 78 33 61 69, esnault@em-lyon.com

Romain Zeiliger
GATE - CNRS, 38 Chemin des Mouilles - 69131 ECULLY Cedex - France
Tel (33) 4 72 29 30 09, zeiliger@gate.cnrs.fr

ABSTRACT

This paper presents a pedagogical initiative in learning and teaching a course titled : "Impacts of IT on Organizations : The Net Comp@ny".

In order to meet the more and more compelling requirements of their environment, companies have to design and implement new frameworks of organization. Information Technology play a significant part in the increasing complexity of the companies' environment as well as in providing efficient responses for companies to compete at a higher level in the economic game. "The Net Comp@ny", the generic company studied in the course, is such a typical company of the 3rd millenium.

There are two kinds of information systems in the Net Comp@ny : traditional Information Systems as Structured Information Systems (SIS), and new Information Systems referred as Document Information Systems (DIS).Networked documents are as necessary as structured data bases to optimize the functioning of the Net Comp@ny. It is thus of first importance for tomorrow managers to understand and practice networked information management

From October 1998, the course takes place in a new way. Students gather information through a browser, called Nestor, which will have them act as **active producers** in the pedagogical process.

The papers presents the first results of the observation of groups of students in this new pedagogical process and environment.

INTRODUCTION

This paper presents a pedagogical initiative beginning on October 1998 at E.M. LYON, France. It deals with learning and teaching a course titled :
"Impacts of IT on Organizations : The Net Comp@ny"
using both "traditional" course sessions (in class room, with the professor and/or a speaker), interactive information research through the Internet, and collaborative group work. The last two items are dealt with through a browser, called Nestor, developed in the Gate laboratory (CNRS) with educational specifications added to the usual browser functions.

OBJECTIVES AND CONTENT OF THE COURSE

In order to meet the more and more compelling requirements of their environment, companies have to design and implement new frameworks of organization. Information Technology play a significant part in the increasing complexity of the companies' environment as well as in providing efficient responses for companies to compete at a higher level in the economic game.

"The Net Comp@ny", the generic company studied in the course, is such a typical company of the 3rd millenium. It is wired around its worldwide business network, its Intranet, providing its employees and managers the right information at the right place on the right time. Sharing its Extranet with partners, clients, and suppliers, it is able to offer the best prices, the best quality of products and services, the highest reactivity and flexibility. Connected to the Internet, it has the greatest awareness of its customer needs, the greatest knowledge about new technology and innovation, the greatest ability to hire competencies....

Such a new organization has not emerged at once. It is the result of the evolution of a number of factors, both related to internal companies organization, and environmental variables.

The purpose of the course is to study three of these factors : the way companies are structured, the way people are working together, and IT evolutions [Esnault, 94]. The course uses a historical approach, divided into three "Ages" (the '60-'70s, the '80-mid '90s, and the late '90s-2000s).The three organization frameworks are the Machine Bureaucracy and Adhocracy (From Mintzberg), and the Networking Organization. The three technological era are the centralized informatics, the micro-informatics and the open networks. Transferring some concepts used in the IT networks area to the organizational area seems to provide new management issues in these complex dynamic organizations [Esnault, 96].

INFORMATION MANAGEMENT IN THE NET COMP@NY

There are two kinds of information systems in the Net Comp@ny :

✔Traditional Information Systems are referred in the course as Structured Information Systems (SIS). They are mainly based upon the Operational Data Bases of the Company, and consist of the Operational and Decisional

Applications. The up-to-date implementations will deal with DatawareHouses, Datamining tools, EISs, and modular ERPs. Information is stored in structured tables, and user access it through structured applications (accounting, finance, human resources, sales, etc. applications) or structured interfaces (forms, reports, query languages, etc.). These Information Systems are implemented and maintained by IT professionals, driven by users' teams and users' needs.

✔New Information Systems are referred in the course as Document Information Systems (DIS). They consist of the flexible organization of all the communication information that is acquired, produced, exchanged, within the Company and between the Company and its environment, as textual or multimedia documents : mails, Web pages, scanned documents, news, photos, video sequences, ads, etc. Now, this information is generally accessed in the Company via Intranet interfaces, and stored in files of html format. Information pieces are networked together by hypertext linksµ. Each user is able to produce his or her own information network by finding, selecting, storing, producing the right information for his or her own needs.

In structured applications, the user is guided by
- the nature of the application
- the field of data
- the procedures programmed
- the standardized interfaces
- an access by query which favors a systematic search.

Furthermore, an application is generally used in a functional context : accounting by accountants, sales by sales people, CAD by drawing engineers, etc. Information in data bases is supposed to be true, valid and usable. Categories of information are conventional and well known (clients, products, employees, orders, invoices, financial boards, etc.).

Document information is a much less structured and organized area. It concerns a huge amount of information that differ by
- their source / origin
- their nature / subject
- their object / purpose
- their sender / author
- their form
- their life-cycle
- and are accessed by navigation, which favors explorative search and serendipitous discovery.

One is not even sure of the truthfulness or validity of this information. Validity may even be a relative notion [Harper, 98]. Information is not classified, arranged in universal categories. Each producer has his or her own categories, quite his or her own "language. The amount of information is growing exponentially, producing cognitive overhead and disorientation for users [Zeiliger 97].

Education is one necessary component to build something like an "information management ethical behavior". In companies that have implemented Intranet Communicative Applications, people insist on the necessary users' responsiveness in managing the information shared. In the Net Comp@ny, there is a subtle balancing between centralization and decentralization, between control and delegation, between hierarchy and autonomy [look for examples in Hastings, 93]. The same occurs regarding information management There is a complementarity between applications pushing information to users and users pulling the information they need from the network. So that everybody has to become more responsible for the information he or she gets, uses or produces.

Networked documents are as necessary as structured data bases to optimize the functioning of the Net Comp@ny. It is thus of first importance for tomorrow managers to understand and practice networked information management, to better understand information world. For example :
- What kind of information do I possess, need or master ?
- Can I draw links between all these information pieces ?
- Can I give a structure ?
- What could I transmit to whom ?
- How could I record the paths from an information to another ?
- Etc.

The usual browsers are not providing tools efficient enough to help users build their own landmarks, store organized representations, or share collaborative working spaces [Elliot, 95 ; Zeiliger, .98].

PRESENTATION OF NESTOR

From October 1998, the course takes place in a new way. Students gather information through a browser, called Nestor, which will have them act as active producers in the pedagogical process.

Implementing the approach: the NESTOR browser.

NESTOR is a Web client which runs on Microsoft Windows 95/98/NT platforms. Support to constructive navigation in NESTOR is implemented through a set of features that provide means for a range of navigational and information-structuring activities. Graphical user interface (GUI) - the human-computer interaction mode which prevails on the desktop - seems more adequate for constructive tasks which require re-arranging collections of objects. The basic idea in NESTOR design is to combine the hypertext access window of a standard Web browser with a GUI window favoring constructive activity. The GUI window can be thought of -at first- as a map of the visited Web subspace. Most navigation operations are available in both windows and provide a crossed feedback. The GUI (map) window is interactive and allows for re-arranging as well as creating new objects (documents, links, annotations, search keywords and conceptual areas). Most objects can serve for navigational operations.

We now list the main features of NESTOR and outline how they implement the constructive navigation approach.

a) representing self navigational experience : while the user performs navigational operations with the Web browser, NESTOR automatically draws a graphical representation of the Web subspace which has been visited. Every visited document is represented as a graphical object called a "document-object" (default shape of document-objects is a circle whose size depends on the number of departing links, or a square when the document does not contain any hotword). Visited links are represented as arrows. The object layout is automatic and favors the point of view of the user's. As long as the user traverses to a new document by clicking on a hotword, document-objects and arrows follow a straight line (figuring a "user's route"); the object corresponding to the currently displayed document is highlighted (providing situational cues for the user's position in the visited. This graphical representation is dynamic : users can modify the graphical layout by moving the objects (direct manipulation, the arrows follow accordingly). The graphical representation is interactive : any visited document can be accessed directly by double-clicking on the corresponding graphical object (facilitating the "Hub and spoke" process). This graphical representation can be thought of as a personal "map". The appearance of the map is customizable. Use of maps is expected to increase the visual feedback in practical navigation operations and facilitate orientation.

b) constructing a personal web : at the beginning the map reflects the visited subspace, i.e. public documents and their public links. Then, users can create personal documents and personal links, and inter-weave them with the public network (our Web browser incorporates an HTML editing component). Personal links are represented as dotted arrows while public links appear as solid arrows. Public documents need not be aware they are linked. Building thematic maps and creating personal hypertext are activities that are expected to promote plan-based navigation.

c) note-taking : After a while, the map reflects the visited subspace of the public network as well as the network built by the individual user. The process of inter-weaving the public and the personal network can be thought of as a sort of note-taking mode. Web network is annotated with a network of notes. Annotations can be attached to every visited document (be it public or personal). Annotations can be used to navigate. A separate HTML window - named the "bag"- is available to allow gathering of information selected in the visited documents along the navigation process. When pasting information into the bag, NESTOR includes a return link to the source document. The "bag" constitutes just a handy HTML clipboard. It can also be used for navigation. The information gathering and note-taking activities are expected to help user structure their thoughts.

d) creating keywords objects and conceptual areas: a few other objects can be created and incorporated to the maps : keywords, conceptual areas and sub-guides. Keywords -created by users- are automatically searched for in the visited document's text and highlighted if found. Keywords object are also extracted from the search motors queries. The keywords objects have a "checking" script through which users can define how the system should detect that they appear in a document. Conceptual areas are objects which can help structuring the maps : visited documents can be pinned into a given area so that they are moved when the area is moved. Users can collapse or expand conceptual areas;

e) creating and saving navigational objects : all objects created by users (maps, keywords, conceptual areas, annotations and routes) can be saved to a file and retrieved. Those objects are considered as "navigational objects" because they allow new navigational operations. «Conceptual orientation» is facilitated through creating and arranging such objects and using their navigational properties and methods. The generic term "map" is used in the software to refer to such collections of navigational objects. Merging maps is allowed.

f) sharing maps : NESTOR allows navigational information to be published and shared by a group of people. Simple URLs as well as whole maps can be published. A list of the published URLs is maintained on the local server. NESTOR users are warned whenever they navigates to a URL which has been previously published by one of their colleagues. In that case, annotations attached to the document (by the publisher) are available, as well as the map. This map cannot be modified, but it can be used to navigate. Bags can be published too. Synchronous communications (chat and map exchange) are provided through a customized mIRC component. Computer mediated communications and collaborative navigation are expected to help users identify meaningful information (a process Harper describes as «collaboratively defining institutional matters of relevance» or in short a «world-known-in-common» [Harper,98]).

OBJECTIVES OF THE PEDAGOGICAL INNOVATIVE PROCESS

There are several levels of objectives to be reached through this experience

✔Use the browser as a more attractive way to access information, both local (in-house course documents, case studies, etc.) and non-local (web sites, distant libraries, etc.); in the case, of this course, the objective (information management) is also part of the content of the course;

✔Use the browser tools to create individual knowledge maps within the course area;

✔Use the group work functions in the browser to produce and publish collective knowledge maps and documents on topics related to the course; this work may then be integrated to the corpus of the course, as it is directly produced in the good format;

✔Use the group of students as an experimental population to :
• evaluate the impact of the tools on the pedagogical process from viewpoint of both teacher and students,
• define possibly new pedagogical relationships and situations,
• investigate the way students gather information through navigating on the Web;

✔use the universality of the tools to develop international cooperation between groups of students working on related subjects or case studies.

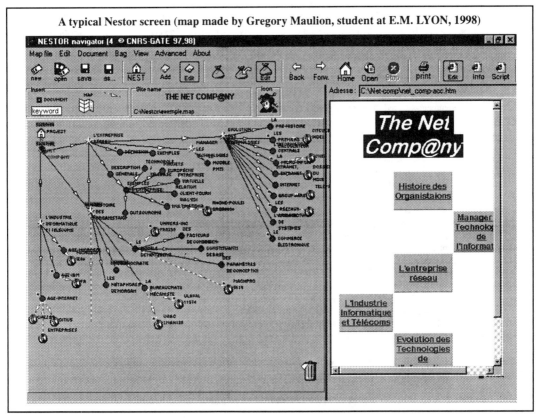

A typical Nestor screen (map made by Gregory Maulion, student at E.M. LYON, 1998)

FIRST RESULTS AND APPRECIATIONS

Students' work with Nestor

The first group was build of 32 students. They had two tasks to do :

✔An individual work that consisted in browsing the course and enriching it with external web sites. Examples of subjects chosen were :
- history of IT with sites related to IT museums,
- sites related to Mintzberg, one of the major authors in the course,
- courses, in Germany or in Canada, closely related to the local course;

✔A group work ; in the previous years they had to do a "research" text file on subject related to the course. This year, they had exactly the same specifications, but the result had to be presented as a map, containing not only annotated websites, but also documents presenting the subject, a synthesis and their opinion. The relationship with the course was supposed to be featured directly by the map.

They had also to fulfilla questionnaire evaluating :
- their ability to use Nestor : they found it rather easy, and suggested interesting improvements;
- the relevance of the exercise they had to do : they found them rather well suited, despite some technical problems;
- their opinion on possible uses of such a tool in companies : for what kind of documents or applications. They cited several kinds of survey, case studies, training at the workplace, economic intelligence, synthesis on a theme.

Students' opinion on Nestor

What they liked in working with Nestor was :
- Use the same tools to search, find, store and produce information
- Access to both local and distant information in the same way
- Store links and contents
- Mark texts with annotations
- Deal with concepts (keywords) and areas
- Have a spatial representation of the area
- Browse either by content or links, directly on the map
- Store all sites and documents related to a given theme, with personal opinion and remarks

Their main critics were directed to technical imperfections (some have been fixed since) and ...the too small size of the screens.

A few statistical data

Nestor provides with a lot of information about its use, through an historical record of every operation made with Nestor. This record can be searched by date, or by type of operation, or by many other means. One can also calculate statistical data. Here are some of this data for the group of students.

There was a total amount of 24008 browsing operations between October 14th and December 18th, which split into :

hotwords : 32%	back : 8%	open : 2%
access by map : 47%	next : 0%	home: 4%
		misc: 7%

Among all documents visited, 87% are visited more than once, thus there are 13% x 24008 = 3121 different documents visited. When documents are visited again, it is through the map by 53%. The amount of browsing incidents is 16% (which is weak).

Concerning the location of visited documents :

40,4% are in the course corpus

7,5% are personal documents in Nestor

40,6% are distant documents (http)

Here are the counts of operations numbers for some criteria:

THE PROFESSOR POINT OF VIEW

Building the local course corpus :

One of the objective was to experiment tools where professors themselves could produce their own documents, without spending more time than producing traditional ones, and, if possible, being more efficient. One of the problem was then to find a software editing tool that could allow one to produce html pages as easily as text with a word processor or diagrams with a graphic editor, and also to reuse existing documents.

Reaching some courses objectives

One important thing is to convince the students that the Internet is not only a place to surf on. It is not sufficient to collect potentially interesting sites. But they have also to perform in-depth study of the contents, develop a critical approach of information (by cross-controlling through several sites, identifying precisely the owner of the site, etc.) and select the relevant pages and only these ones.

Another objective was to have them think more in-depth about information management in the Net Comp@ny, and to understand this question about responsiveness of people regarding the information that they publish on professional networks. They are beginning to understand that, using the World Wide Web, the question is not to *find* information, but to sort, validate, synthesize, compare, organize information before publishing or sharing it with their colleagues, boss...or professor.

Delivering the course content

Nestor may also be used in the classroom to show slides and websites. It is more interactive than a tool like MS-Powerpoint, for example, because it allows to go by hypertext links instead of following a linear progression. But this may also be somewhat disorientating for the student ... and the professor.

FURTHER DEVELOPMENTS

Naturally, this is just the beginning of the experiment. A lot of questions remain to be answered, providing a lot of further research to be conducted, among which :

✔there is an open area regarding collaborative aspects in Nestor. Due to technical problems in the local area network, there was little collaborative work in this session ; this will be improved in the next sessions by using a dedicated server;

✔it will be very interesting to study more in-depth the topology of students' map, to better understand how they gather information, how they make their own way toward knowledge, and how they like to represent this knowledge; so that professors could try to deliver their course contents in a more adaptive form, leaving each student build his or her own path toward a higher level of skills;

✔an experiment will take place in 1999 concerning several groups of students in several European universities ; it will be of greatest interest to follow this experiment from pedagogical and cultural points of view;

✔the traditional pedagogical methods and organization are drastically changed when using such tools. It is not clear whether the changes may happen on a step by step basis, or if there must be something like a "big bang" for a complete corpus or teaching area.

BIBLIOGRAPHY

[Elliot, 95] Elliot, G.J., Jones, E., Cooke, A., Barker, P., (1995), Making sense : a review of hypermedia in higher education, *proceedings of ED-MEDIA'95*, AACE.

[Esnault, 94] Esnault, L. (1994), Facing the Local-Global Challenge : an IT Platform Model for the Networking Firm, in *Proceedings of the International Resources Management Association*, , Idea Group publishing, Harrisburg, Penn.

[Esnault, 96] Esnault, L., L'entreprise-réseau, une nouvelle frontière pour les managers, in *Actes du colloque CIMRE'96*, Lausanne 1996

[Harper, 98] Harper, R., (1998), Information that Counts: Sociology, Ethnography and Work at the International Monetary Fund, *Workshop on Personalized and Social Navigation in Information Space*, Hook, Munro, Benyon eds., http://www.sics.se/humle/projects/persona/web/wprkshop/.

research engines		countries		suffixes	
Yahoo	1601	.fr	4236	.com	4058
Alta Vista	585	.de	119	.net	669
Nomad	486	.uk	102	.edu	100
Infoseek	33	.it	22		

[Hastings, 93] Hastings, C. (1993), *The New Organization : Growing the Culture of Organizational Networking*, McGraw-Hill Book Company Europe, London.

[Zeiliger, 97] Zeiliger, R., Reggers, T., Baldewyns, L., Jans, V., (1997), Facilitating Web Navigation : Integrated tools for Active and Cooperative Learners, in *proceedings of the 5th International Conference on Computers in Education, ICCE'97*, December 97, Kuching, Sarawak, Malaysia

[Zeiliger, 98] Zeiliger, R., (1998), Supporting Constructive Navigation of Web Space, *Workshop on Personalized and Social Navigation in Information Space*, Hook, K., Benyon, D., Munro, A., eds., 16th-17th March 98, Stockholm, Sweden.

ENDNOTES

1 ® Registered by Gate-CNRS - France
2 ® Registered by Gate-CNRS - France

A Formal Approach to Describe Design Patterns

Laura Felice and Marcela Ridao

ISISTAN. Facultad de Ciencias Exactas. , Dpto Computacion y Sistemas Universidad Nacional del Centro, Tandil, Argentina.

Paraje Arroyo Seco. (7000)Tandil. TE:(54)2293-440363. FAX(54)2293-440362, e-mail:{lfelice,mridao}@exa.unicen.edu.ar

1. INTRODUCTION

Most authors [1,2] describe design patterns as a structured but informal expression. For example, [1] contains descriptions of patterns using text and diagrams, and they have grouped patterns into three major categories: Creational, Structural and Behavioral. These descriptions can be viewed as an informal recipe or process for producing instantiations of specific patterns in languages such as Smalltalk or C++. An untrained software designer interested in using patterns in his developments is compelled to understand both the pattern motivation and intent. Besides, he has to analyze the example code given as a part of the pattern description to use it appropriately. Thus, the designer is greatly oriented to the specific language and to the particular problem losing the abstract understanding of the pattern.

In this paper, we present a formal approach to describe design patterns based on an algebraic formalism. This work is part of a project whose purpose is to formalize the software development process, from the Analysis and Design phases to the efficient code generation, using the Object-Oriented (OO) paradigm.

There are several methodologies for OO system analysis and design based on informal models. These informal techniques can lead to ambiguous or inconsistent system constructions, where correctness verification, derivation of properties, and automatic optimization are difficult to achieve. On the other hand, formal languages for OO specification and information systems such as TROLL [3], Object-Z [4], Maude [5], ObjLog [6] and GSBL [7] have also been developed. These languages have the following advantages:

• High-level language features along with a formal semantic
• Powerful analysis and verification techniques can be applied

Using formal methods in early phases of the software development process allows to discover bugs in a stage where the majority of errors tend to reside in practice. This is a great benefit, since errors at this phase have a high and costly impact on the subsequent phases of the software development.

As the use of design patterns has become very common in the OO community, and considering the above-mentioned formalism advantages, we think it is appropriate to give a formal framework to these patterns that capture a wealth of experience about the design of OO software.

2. THE FORMAL LANGUAGE

In this work, we are using GSBL+[8] to specify design patterns. This is an algebraic formalism which is concerned with OO software reuse, integrating UML diagrams with OO code based on a rigorous approach. In this way, the formal specification of class diagrams allows the simulation and formal testing independently of different implementations and the mapping to efficient OO code. This method translates UML diagrams formal specifications into efficient code, using a library of reusable components. The translation is based on the transformation of these components by means of algebraic operators like renaming, restriction, extension and composition. Following, we describe the above mentioned language.

GSBL+ extends and integrates GSBL [7] language with mechanisms for error treatment, explicit parameterisation and restriction of specifications.

The mechanism of the language that creates the new specification is the class definition [Fig1]. GSBL+ specifications are considered structured objects. This structure is based on two relations associated to two specifications building mechanisms. The OVER relation defines which specifications are considered components of a given specifications. The specification is extended by the components declared in <overlist>. Similarly, the SUBCLASS-OF relation defines which specifications must be considered subclass or superclasses of a given specification. Note that the SUBCLASS-OF relation is conceptually linked to the inheritance relation in the object oriented level and the OVER relation to the client one.

The DEFERRED clause declares new sorts, operations or equations that are incompletely defined, i.e. there are not enough equations to specify the new operations or there are not enough opera-

Fig. 1 - GSBL+ Class Syntax	
Incomplete Specification Syntax	**Complete Specification Syntax**
CLASS class-name[<parameterlist>]	**CLASS** class-name[<parameterlist>]
EXPORT <exportlist>	**EXPORT** <exportlist>
OVER <overlist>	**BASIC CONSTRUCTORS** <constructorlist>
SUBCLASS-OF <subclasslist>	**OVER** <overlist>
DEFERRED	**SUBCLASS-OF** <subclasslist>
SORTS < sortlist>	**EFFECTIVE**
OPS <opslist>	**SORTS** <sortlist>
EQS <varlist><equationlist>	**OPS** <opslist>
EFFECTIVE	**EQS** <varlist><equationlist>
SORTS <sortlist>	**END-CLASS**
OPS <opslist>	
EQS <varlist><equationlist>	
END-CLASS	

Fig. 2 - GSBL+ Package syntax	
PACKAGE nombre-package [parameterlist] **IMPORTING** <importing-list> **CLASS** $class_1$_name ...... **CLASS** $class_2$_name	**CLASS** $class_n$_name .... **ASSOCIATION** association_name$_1$ .... **ASSOCIATION** association_name$_n$ ..... **END-PACKAGE**

tions to 'generate' all values of a given sort. A GSBL+ specification is implicitly parameterised in its incomplete parts.

The EFFECTIVE clause either declares new sorts, operations or equations, that are completely defined, or completes the definition of some sort or operation, belonging to some superclass, that was not completely defined.

A class may introduce any number of new sorts; if one of them has the same name as the class, this sort is considered the sort of inteeerest of the class.

The syntax of a class specified with the second technique includes the BASIC CONSTRUCTOR clause that refers to generator operations and dos not contain DEFERRED clause.

2.1 Class diagrams

The UML class diagrams can be specified by means of the Package, another modular construction provided by the language that allows the combination of classes and relationships and to have a control of the their visibility.

The Packages can comprise any number of classes and associations, they are organized in a import hierarchy and can be parameterized. A system of packages can include incomplete classes, and can also be used to express granularity in a design. Each class belongs to only one Package and can be exported to other Packages. The package syntax is shown in the figure 2.

3. DESIGN PATTERNS FORMALIZATION

Each design pattern is a description of a solution to a problem that frequently occurs in software design. The application of that description results in a collection of a few objects that form a specific instantiation of such a design problem [9].

The acceptance of reusable descriptions, such as design patterns, is highly dependent on easily comprehensible definitions and unambiguous specifications. In the present examples, we address both issues in the formal description of a design pattern.

In sections 3.1 and 3.2, we present a brief description of the patterns Interpreter and Iterator, according to the taxonomy presented in [1], as well as the formal specification of each one.

3.1 Interpreter

Intent

Given a language, this pattern defines a representation for its grammar along with an interpreter that uses the representation to interpret sentences in the language.

Motivation

If a particular kind of problem occurs often enough, then it might be worthwhile to express instances of the problem as sentences in a simple language. Then an interpreter may be built to solve the problem by interpreting these sentences.

The Interpreter pattern describes how to define a grammar for simple languages, represent sentences in the language, and interpret these sentences.

Applicability
This pattern can be used when there is a language to interpret, and it is possible to represent statements in the language as abstract syntax trees. The use of the Interpreter pattern is appropriate when:
• The grammar is simple. For complex grammars, the class hierarchy for the grammar becomes large and unmanageable. Tools such as parser generators are a better alternative in such cases. They can interpret expressions without building abstract syntax trees, which can save space and possibly time.
• Efficiency is not a critical concern. The most efficient interpreters are usually not implemented by interpreting parse trees directly but by first translating them into another form. For example, regular expressions are often transformed into state machines. But even then, the translator can be implemented by the Interpreter pattern, so the pattern is still applicable.

Structure

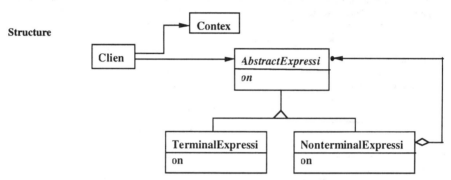

Participants
• AbstractExpression
  - Declares an abstract Interpret operation that is common to all nodes in the abstract syntax tree
• TerminalExpression
  - Implements an Interpret operation associated with terminal symbols in the grammar
  - An instance is required for every terminal symbol in a sentence
• NonterminalExpression
  - One such class is required for every rule $R::= R_1 R_2...R_n$ in the grammar
  - Maintains instance variables of type AbstractExpression for each of the symbols R_1 through R_n
  - Implements an Interpret operation for nonterminal symbols in the grammar. Interpret typically calls itself recursively on the variables representing R_1 through R_n
• Context
  - Contains information that's global to the interpreter
• Client
  - Builds an abstract syntax tree representing a particular sentence in the language that the grammar defines. The abstract syntax tree is assembled from instances of the NonterminalExpression and TerminalExpression
  - Invokes the Interpret operation

Formal specification
The specified classes in the package summarize all the pattern behavior as described in the most relevant bibliography. In our approach, the complementary behavior that can be deduced from the thorough analysis of the pattern informal description is specified by means of classes being **imported** and **used** in the package and the relationships between them. The behavior of these classes is **deferred** until a particular instantiation of the pattern occurs. Following, we briefly describe the domain and the responsibilities corresponding to these classes:
Sequence, Boolean and Nat can be considered as primitive types in any algebraic specification
Symbol: the domain is the set of symbols that can be present in an expression
Context: contains global information about the grammatical rules
Operator: the domain is the set of operators that can be present in an expression, and the responsibilities are related to the operators behavior
Result: it may be composed by additional outcomes produced by the interpreter, such as intermediate code, final code.

3.2 Iterator
Intention
Provide a way to access the elements of an aggregate object sequentially without exposing its underlying representation.

Motivation
An aggregate object such as a list should give a way to access its elements without exposing its internal structure. Moreover,

you might want to traverse the list in different ways, depending on what you want to accomplish. But it is not desirable to bloat the List interface with operations for different traversal, even if it could be possible to anticipate the ones we'll need. It might be also needed to have more than one traversal pending on the same list.

The key idea of this pattern is to take the responsibility for access and traversal out of the list object and put it into an iterator object. The Iterator class defines an interface for accessing the list's elements. An iterator object is responsible for keeping track of the current element; that is, it knows which elements have been traversed already.

For example, a List class would call for a ListIterator with the following relationship between them:

Before you can instantiate ListIterator, you must supply the List to traverse. One you have the ListIterator instance, it's possible to access the list's elements sequentially. The CurrentItem operation returns the current element in the list, First initializes the current element to the first element, Next advances the current element to the next element, and IsDone tests whether we've advanced beyond the last element, that is, the traversal is finished.

Separating the traversal mechanism from the List object lets us define iterators for different traversal policies without enumerating them in the List interface. It can be seen that the iterator and the list are coupled, and the client must know that it is a list that's traversed as opposed to some other aggregate structure. Hence the client commits to a particular aggregate structure. It would

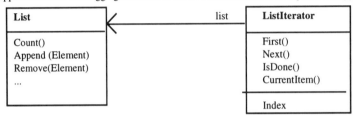

be better if we could change the aggregate class without changing client code. This can be done by generalizing the iterator concept to support polymorphic iteration. To do that, we define an AbstractList class that provides a common interface for manipulating lists. Similarly, we need an abstract Iterator class that defines a common iteration interface. Then we can define concrete Iterator subclasses for the different list implementations. As a result, the iteration mechanism becomes independent of concrete aggregate classes.

Applicability
• To access an aggregate object's contents without exposing its internal representation
• To support multiple traversals of aggregate objects
• To provide a uniform interface for traversing different aggregate structures

Structure
Participants
• Iterator
  - Defines an interface for accessing and traversing elements
• ConcreteIterator
  - Implements the Iterator interface
  - Keeps track of the current position in the traversal of the aggregate
• Aggregate
  - Defines an interface for creating an Iterator object
• ConcreteAggregate

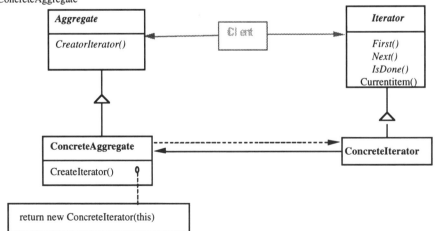

- Implements the Iterator creation interface to return an instance of the proper ConcreteIterator

New classes hierarchy

Such schemes as the Iterator are frequently used in the OO environment as well as abstract data type. For this reason, class libraries for those structures are very useful. One of the major tasks in OO software development is to identify recurrent patterns and build reusable classes to encapsulate them [10]. Thus, the future developers will resource to 'ready-made' solutions. Classes in the Iteration library should be focused to obtain these benefits.

In libraries for OO language such as C++ or Eiffel, a number of classes hierarquically depending on Iterator class can be found. This hierarchy is clearly richer than the one proposed by [1], because of the additional abstract behavior that allows a more clear understanding of the classes being defined. On the other hand, the description given in [1] compel to analyze code for specific problems to obtain the same clarity.

Hence, we propose to formalize this pattern by adding behavior and abstract classes to the previous structure, in order to obtain the above mentioned advantages. So, we have contrasted Containers class hierarchy from the taxonomy given in [10] against the pattern description in [1]. Consequently, we propose to modify the above structure by adding new classes to Aggregate and Iterator hierarchies. The new classes are AbstractCollection_Aggregate and AbstractTraversable_Aggregate for the former and AbstractCollection_Iterator and AbstractTraversable_Iterator for the latter. This new hierarchy is shown in figure 4.

New classes have been conceived adding behavior by means of more abstract functions that will be completely defined when the class get instantiated in a later phase.

Notice that we haven't included ConcreteAggregate and ConcreteIterator classes in figure 5. It is due to the fact they are concrete instances of the abstract classes in the specification.

It can be seen that the instantiation of this pattern classes gives rise to a big number of significant functions. However, these functions have not sense at this abstraction level. For example, we could identify Hierarchical and Linear classes as subclasses of AbstractTraversable_Iterator and we could define Down and Up functions for

---

Fig.1 - GSBL+ Specification of interpreter pattern

```
PACKAGE INTERPRETER
IMPORTING Sequence[Symbol], Boolean, Context, Operator, Result
OBJECT CLASS Abstract_ Expr
USES Operator, Sequence[Symbol]
PART OF
Shared Non_Terminal_Expr
DEFERRED
OPS
    Create_AE: Sequence[Symbol] —> Abstract_Expr
    Recognize: Abstract_Expr —> CP[Boolean, Result]
END_CLASS
OBJECT CLASS Terminal_Expr
USES Sequence[Symbol], Boolean, Nat, Context
SUBCLASS OF Abstract_Expr
EFFECTIVE
OPS:
    Create_TE: Sequence[Symbol] —> Terminal_Expr
DEFERRED
    Recognize_TE: Terminal_Expr x Context —> Boolean
EQS: seq: Sequence[Symbol]; cont: Context
    Recognize_TE (Create_TE(seq),cont) ( Validate (seq)
END_CLASS
OBJECT CLASS Non_Terminal_Expr
USES Operator, Sequence[Symbol], Boolean, Result
SUBCLASS OF Abstract_Expr
EFFECTIVE
OPS
    Aggregate_AE: Abstract_Expr x Abstract_Expr x Operator —> Non_Terminal_Expr
    Get_Op: Abstract_Expr(ae) —> Op
      pre:{ae ( Terminal_Expr}
    Get_Expr1: Abstract_Expr(ae)—> Abstract_Expr
      pre:{ae ( Terminal_Expr}
    Get_Expr2: Abstract_Expr(ae)—> Abstract_Expr
      pre:{ae ( Terminal_Expr}
    Is_TE_expr1: Abstract_Expr —> Boolean
    Is_TE_expr2: Abstract_Expr —> Boolean
    Recognize: Non_Terminal_Expr —> CP[Boolean, Result]
EQS: seq: Sequence[Symbol]; expr1,expr2: Abstract_Expr; op:Operator
    Get_Op (Aggregate_AE(expr1,expr2,op)) ( op
    Get_Expr1 (Aggregate_AE(expr1,expr2,op)) ( expr1
    Get_Expr2 (Aggregate_AE(expr1,expr2,op)) ( expr2
    Is_TE_expr1(Create_AE(seq)) ( True
    Is_TE_expr1(Aggregate_AE(expr1,expr2,op)) ( Is_TE_expr1(expr1)
    Is_TE_expr2(Create_AE(seq)) ( True
    Is_TE_expr2(Aggregate_AE(expr1,expr2,op)) ( Is_TE_expr2(expr2)
    Recognize (Create_AE(seq)) ( Recognize_TE(seq)
    Recognize (Aggregate_AE(expr1,expr2,op)) (
    If(Is_TE_expr1(expr1))
        If(Is_TE_expr2(expr2))
          Operate(op,expr1,expr2)
        else
      Operate(op,expr1,Recognize(expr2))
        else
        If(Is_TE_expr2(expr2))
          Operate(op,Recognize(expr1),expr2)
        else
      Operate(op,Recognize(expr1),Recognize(expr2))
END_CLASS
OBJECT CLASS Client
USES Abstract_ Expr, Sequence[Symbol], Boolean, Result
DEFERRED
OPS
    Invoke_Recognize: Sequence[Symbol] —> CP[Boolean, Result]
END_CLASS
END_PACKAGE
```

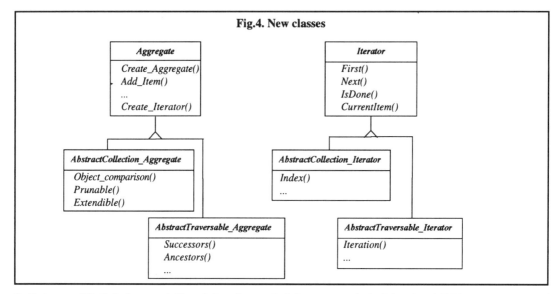

Fig.4. New classes

the first one, and Forth for the second. Nevertheless, these methods have no sense in the father class definition.

Client class has not been considered in the specification, because clients have not responsibilities in this pattern. However, this class has been included in the structure to show the interaction between pattern participants and clients.

3.3 Chain of Responsibility

Intention

Allow coupling the sender of a request to its receiver by giving more than one object a chance to handle the request. Chain the receiving objects and pass the request along the chain until an object handles it.

Motivation

To understand the motivation, consider a context-sensitive help facility for a graphical user interface. The user can obtain help information on any part of the interface just by clicking on it. If no specific help information exists for that part of the interface, then the help system should display a more general help message about the inmediate context. The problem here is that the object that ultimately prives the help isn't know explicitly to the object that initiates the help request.

The idea of this pattern is to decouple senders and receivers by giving multiple objects a chance to handle a request. The request gets passed along a chain of objects until one of them handles it. The first object in the chain receives the request and either handles it or forwards it to the next candidate on the chain, which does likewise. The object that made the request has no explicit knowledge of who will handle it. We say the request has an **implicit receiver.**

To forward the request along the chain, and to ensure receivers remain implicit, each object on the chain shares a common interface for handling requests and for accesing its **successor** on the chain.

Applicability

This pattern should be used when:

• More than one object may handle a request, and the handler isn't know a priori. The handler should be ascertained automatically.

• You want to issue a request to one of several objects without specifying the receiver explicitlly.

• The set of objects that can handle a request should be specified dynamically.

Structure
Participants

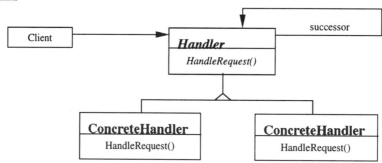

- Handler
  - defines an interface for handling requests.
  - implements the succesor link.
- ConcreteHandler
  - handle request it is responsible for.
  - can acces its successor.
  - if the ConcreteHandler can handle the request, it does so ; otherwise it forwards the request to its successor.
- Client
  - inititates the request to a ConcreteHandler object on the chain.

Formal specification

In this pattern we can observe dynamic properties, since it is uncertain when request attention takes place. The most appropriate formalism to specify situations of this nature must include Temporal Logic in their specifications.

The formalism used in this work is actually being extended to allow these aspects.

4. CURRENT WORK AND CONCLUSION

Currently, we are studying the complete catalog [1] of design patterns in order to provide a complete formalization. Since some patterns, like chain of responsibility, have a dynamic behavior, it has become necessary to consider the extension of the used formalism. The study of this extension is also a part of the project in which this work is included.

We think that the effort to give a formal description for so a popular methodology in OO community is valuable, since this work will provide a more detailed and precise understanding about the patterns application.

5. REFERENCES

[1] Gamma E. et al -"Design Patterns: Elements of Reusable OO Software" - Addison-Wesley-1995
[2] Buchmann F. et al - "A System of Patterns" - John Wiley & Sons Ltd-1996
[3] Jungclaus R. et al - "TROLL - a language for OO specifications of information systems" - ACM Transactions on IS, vol.14 N/2-1996
[4] Smith G - "A logic for Object-Z" - Technical Report 944, Department of Computer Science, University of Queensland, Australia-1994
[5] Meseguer J. and Winlker T. - "Parallel Programming in Maude" - Proceedings of Research Directions in High Level Parallel Programming Languages, Francia-1991
[6] Briggs T. and Werth J. - "A Specification Language for OO Analysis and Design" - ECOOP¥94 Proceedings, LNCS 821-1994
[7] Clerici S. and Orejas F. - "The Specification Language GSBL" - In Recent Trends in Data Type Specifications, LNCS 534-1990
[8] Favre L. - "Un mÈtodo para la reusabilidad de software OO: GSBL+" - Reporte TÈcnico ISISTAN, UNCPBA-1998
[9] Alencar P. et al - "A Formal Architectural Design Patterns-Based Approach to Software Understanding" - 4th Workshop on Program Comprehension Proceedings, Germany-1996
[10] Meyer B. "Reusable Software" The Base Object-Oriented Component Libraries. Prentice Hall Object- Oriented Series-1994.

Fig.5 - Iterator pattern specification using GSBL+

Formal specification
PACKAGE ITERATOR

OBJECT CLASS Aggregate
USES Item, Nat, Boolean, Iterator
EFFECTIVE
OPS
   Create_Aggregate: —> Aggregate
   Add_Item: Aggregate x Item —> Aggregate
   .?._Item: Aggregate x Item —> Boolean
   Empty_Aggregate: Aggregate —> Boolean
   Occurrences: Aggregate —> Nat
DEFERRED
OPS
Create_Iterator: Aggregate —> Iterator
EQS: it, it1: Item; a: Aggregate
   .?._Item (Create_Aggregate(),it) (False
   .?._Item (Add_Item(a,it1),it) (
     If(Equal(it1,it))
      True
     else
      .?._Item (a,it)
   Empty_Aggregate(Create_Aggregate()) (True
   Empty_Aggregate(Add_Item(a,it)) (False
   Occurrences(Create_Aggregate()) (0
   Occurrences(Add_Item(a,it1)) (1 + Occurrences(a)
END_CLASS
OBJECT CLASS AbstractCollection_Aggregate
SUBCLASS OF Aggregate
EFFECTIVE
OPS:
   Object_comparison: AbstractCollection_Aggregate(ac_a) x Item(it2) x Item(it3) —> Boolean
     pre:{Occurrences(ac_a) >= 2 .and. .?._Item (ac_a,it2) .and. .?._Item (ac_a,it3)}
   Prunable: AbstractCollection_Aggregate —> Boolean
   Extendible: AbstractCollection_Aggregate —> Boolean
DEFERRED
OPS:
   Prune: AbstractCollection_Aggregate(ac_a) x Item —> AbstractCollection_Aggregate
     pre:{Prunable(ac_a)}
EQS: it2,it3: Item
   Object_comparison(ac_a,it2,it3) (
     If (equal(it2,it3))
      True
     else
      False
   ...
END_CLASS

OBJECT CLASS AbstractTraversable_Aggregate
SUBCLASS OF Aggregate
DEFERRED
OPS:
   Successors: AbstractTraversable_Aggregate —> AbstractTraversable_Aggregate
   Ancestors: AbstractTraversable_Aggregate —> AbstractTraversable_Aggregate
   ...
END_CLASS
OBJECT CLASS Iterator
DEFERRED
OPS
   First: Aggregate —> Item
   Next: Aggregate —> Item
   IsDone: Aggregate —> Boolean
   CurrentItem: Aggregate —> Item
END_CLASS
OBJECT CLASS AbstractCollection_Iterator
DEFERRED
OPS
   Index: AbstractCollection_Aggregate —> Nat
   ...
END_CLASS
OBJECT CLASS AbstractTraversable_Iterator
DEFERRED
OPS
   Iteration: AbstractTraversable_Aggregate —> Item
   ...
END_CLASS
END_PACKAGE

Putting Your Finger on it – Patient Identification in a Multi-name Society

Stewart T. Fleming

Dept. of Computer Science, University of Otago, PO Box 56, DUNEDIN, New Zealand.
stf@cs.otago.ac.nz, Tel: +64 3 479 5728, Fax: +64 3 479 8529

David Vorst

ANGAU Memorial Hospital, PO Box 3798, LAE, Papua New Guinea.
lae.hmoip@global.net.pg, Tel: +675 472 1164, Fax: +675 472 1603

ABSTRACT

Papua New Guinea (PNG) is located on the eastern half of the island of New Guinea in the South Pacific. As a developing country, there are many concerns over access to healthcare, particularly for the rural population. The rich diversity of the many cultural groups raises problems of identification that is vital during patient admission to healthcare centres. In this paper, we describe research work in progress to improve the reliability of patient identification and matching to medical records. We are working on developing a system using biometric data, in this case a fingerprint, to confirm the identity of an individual. This research was initiated by ANGAU Memorial General Hospital and the Papua New Guinea University of Technology in Lae after a national meeting of Chief Executive Officers and Australian Technical Advisors in April 1998. The research is funded by the Papua New Guinea University of Technology

1. INTRODUCTION

A developing country is one that has the potential for economic strength, but lacks skills, capital or technical equipment to immediately exploit its own resources. People of these nations may have poor healthcare, limited education and inadequate nutrition. The developing nations are those at the low- and low/medium end of the United Nations Development Index.

Papua New Guinea falls into a very strange category. It has massive potential wealth in the form of mineral resources, timber, coffee and other cash crops. As a former protectorate, it enjoys a large contribution of Australian monetary aid delivered through the Australian Agency for International Development (AusAID). However, PNG does not live up to its potential, being ranked towards the low end of medium human development - 129th in the United Nations Development Index for 1998 (UNDP, 1998.) Its problems are due to the difficult terrain, extreme climate, economic and political instability. It is a country rich in diversity of culture, with over 800 languages and many distinct tribal groups. For a country where many regions were not discovered until as late as 1930, it represents a unique challenge to our ideas of cross-culturalism and the universality of information.

The immediate concern of healthcare managers in Papua New Guinea is with the reliable identification of patients and matching to the correct medical record. Conventional methods of identification are difficult because of the following factors:
* large, shifting population,
* multiple names used by individuals,
* lack of basic infrastructure to support information transfer between health centres,
* unreliable personal identification,
* environmental factors limiting access to health centres, basic record keeping and uptake of Information Technology.

PNG is a challenging environment for economic development due to its difficult topography, limited infrastructure and low level of human resource development. Many rural areas are extremely remote and cannot be accessed by road. Difficult topography and the remoteness of many rural areas make high-bandwidth communication difficult and unreliable. Regulated telecommunications infrastructure makes low-cost communication unlikely in the near future.

2. CONTEXT OF THE RESEARCH

2.1. Socio-Cultural context

Healthcare in PNG is provided through urban and rural centres by the National Department of Health, provincial governments and private aid organizations, mostly religious missions.

PNG is at a stage in its development where there is significant migration of people, from rural to urban centres and back again. There is a struggle between the tribal identity and the sense of nation. For 90% of the population, the village identity and the support of the *wantok[1]* system is strongest.

In PNG, there are over 800 separate languages and more than 700 distinct cultural groups. Police Motu, Melanesian Pidgin and English act as common languages between these groups. The many influences that act on the people of PNG provide much diversity and complexity. In building information systems to support this complex diversity, we must take these cultures into account.

2.2. Technical context

The devices that we take for granted in the developed world when interacting with personal computers – system units, storage devices, mouse, screen and keyboard – are actually fragile and prone to failure in an adverse environment, such as found in PNG. The breakdown of equipment causes intense frustration, particularly amongst those learning computer skills for the first time.

In PNG we often experience failure or degraded performance of simple pieces of equipment such as computer mice (internals gummed up with dust and dirt), floppy disks (mould grows rampantly on disk surface and disk drive heads), keyboards (dust, dirt and moisture), Pentium CPUs (dust, dirt and insects prevent cooling fan operation, causing overheating.) In fact, the environmental conditions in coastal regions are such that simply installing equipment voids manufacturer's warranty (temperature, humidity, and power out of tolerance.)

Unless expensive, ruggedised computers are introduced, the only solution is to provide environmental protection. While air-conditioning and power conditioning can be provided in urban centres, this is impossible in the rural bush areas. The uptake of high technology will be limited unless personal computer manufacturers achieve significantly higher reliability in an uncontrolled environment. The Husky portable computer (www.husky.co.uk/uk/products/fcfeat.html) is one step in this direction.

Difficult environmental conditions put up barriers to high-capacity, low-cost, reliable telecommunications. Many faults are found in the local loop due to poor-quality connections or where wired connections degrade due to corrosion. Repeater stations in remote locations suffer failures, or valuable solar panels and batteries are stolen. The infrastructure of a developing country may not have redundant capacity to take account of network failures.

Supply of electrical power is a problem, particularly to rural areas. In PNG, the domestic supply voltage is 240V AC on *average*, not nominal. Over-voltages, brownouts and blackouts are common. The infrastructure does not extend to rural areas, forcing them to fall back on generators, solar power or batteries. The inadequate power infrastructure is a major barrier to foreign investment in PNG.

2.3. Similar work

Our research involves the capture of biometric data for patient identification and the establishment of a central database of partial medical records keyed on patient index linked to the biometric.

Biometric data has been used in pilot studies in developed countries to combat benefit fraud, for example in Connecticut (digital imaging), Illinois (retinal scanning) and Los Angeles County (fingerprinting) in the United states and in the Spanish social security ID system. The situation there is that the biometric verification is to prevent is one person giving multiple false names at separate benefit offices to make false claims. In our case, the multiple names are all valid, point to the same person and the biometric confirms identity. Biometric data is also used to verify healthcare eligibility (BTT, 1997).

A thorough treatment of the issues surrounding human identification is given by Clarke (Clarke, 1995.) Clarke's paper gives a discussion of western-style naming conventions that is an interesting contrast with the ones that we have found for Papua New Guinea.

A feature-by-feature comparison of fingerprint devices is given by Network Computing magazine (NCC, 1998.)

3. RESEARCH IN PROGRESS

3.1. Fingerprint scanner

The original proposal was to provide a reliable means of patient identification using some form of biometric. Fingerprint scanning was selected as the least intrusive form of scanning. Prototype databases and scanning systems have been developed and the system is ready for field trials.

The prototype system is based around a laptop computer for portability and a Sony FIU fingerprint scanner (Sony, 1997.) Custom software has been developed using Microsoft Visual Basic and Microsoft Access. Initial tests have been conducted using this system for data capture and identification. A data model has been drawn up to represent the problem area. The key concept is that of identity, rather than patient name. Identification in the system is centred on patient identity and is achieved by the verification of multiple authoritative pieces of identification. That is, forms of identification such as patient names, birthplace, driving licence, passport, health books etc. (where available) are used to identify candidates for a patient master index. The biometric identification is then used to confirm identification and locate the patient master record.

A prototype system has been constructed using the software development kit made available with the Sony unit. This system can enter patient information into a database and acquire photographic and biometric (fingerprint) identification. The system can then verify identity and indicate the patient master index.

The proposed system is mobile. This is essential to allow data to be captured at the rural health centres. It is not essential to gather data prior to patient admission. However, it is advantageous to gather name and biometric data, tied to the village of birth to 'seed' the central database. As the rural health centres become more and more the focus of primary health care intervention, it would be possible to capture biometric data locally and feed that information first to the regional hospital and eventually into the central database.

3.2. Patient Master Index

In the long run, a central Patient Master Index would be established for the entire country. This would give all patients a unique index number and leave existing unit record (UR) or medical record numbers to remain under local hospital control. However, as new patients are admitted, the master index number and the unit record number can become one and the same. Our use of a biometric identifier allows the medical record to become independent of 'name' as such, since the index number will be tied to the biometric.

3.3. Naming Conventions

As part of this research, we investigated some of the ways that PNG citizens use to identify themselves. As one might expect from such a diverse culture, there are no general rules and conventions vary from one cultural group to another.

PNG culture has both patrilineal and matrilineal societies. The lineage of a particular society is of critical importance for many cultural considerations, particularly land ownership (Iatu, 1998.) A typical example from a patrilineal society common throughout the mainland is described.

When a male child is born he is given the name of a significant relative who is usually deceased. 'Significant' can include a whole range of things. For example if a person in the village died at an early age then the child is given that name so that the deceased can live out the rest of his life cut short by misadventure or illness. Children are also named after features of the landscape including trees.

The oldest child will also be given a clan name. This is the name of the clan e.g. the clan could be named after a bird plus the ancestor who is the first member of the clan.

As it is possible for two or more children to have the same name, it is not uncommon for a child to be given a village name to distinguish him from the others.

It is also common for children to be given a baptismal name(s) as a result of the Christian influence in the country. Indeed many children have been baptised twice and have therefore two 'Christian' names, which usually includes a name and surname.

The concept of surname was not known in New Guinea before western influence and most people adopt a surname as the 'system' requires it. A PNG citizen can change his or her name at any time officially by deed poll, or unofficially just because they want to.

In some cultures names tend to be very long and have been shortened to make it easier for others outside the village or group to pronounce it. These shortened names are also fairly common and the longer the name is used 'outside' the village or clan the more it moves away from the original 'long' name.

The western influence now makes it more common for urban dwelling people to follow western conventions using first names and surnames.

In matrilineal societies, for example among the Tolai people of New Ireland, all of the above generalizations hold but the naming of the eldest daughter is paramount.

There is a clash of conventions when a person travels from a village and arrives at an urban health centre. While the patient has an innate sense of their own identity, admissions staff must record sufficient information to distinguish and identify this patient. A biometric is the obvious way to bridge the gap, to preserve the sense of self and fulfil the requirement for unique identification.

3.4. Search Strategies

For those citizens born in urban centres, birth certificates and a reliable birth date may be known. For those born in rural centres, that information may not be known – birth dates are often estimates. However, the sense of village identity is strong and the name of village of birth is an important parameter for cutting down the number of search candidates to verify identity.

Search strategies on the central database would only be necessary where the patient index was not known. The search would locate possible candidates and the biometric comparison would confirm the identity.

3.5. The patient medical record

The telecommunications infrastructure that would be required to support a national database of medical records might be too difficult or expensive to extend to all medical centres. How would such a system cope with the movement of people from rural to urban centres, or from one region to another?

The key here is that in PNG, physical transport between points is still difficult and expensive and journeys by grassroots people are not undertaken lightly. The patient medical record does not need to be instantaneously transmitted or accessed across the country. It just needs to arrive at the point of care before, or at the same time as the patient.

We envisage a situation where a central database would not contain the medical record as such, but would contain pathology and radiology results and list the hospitals visited and when. Existing UR or medical record numbers would remain within each hospital system.

A patient medical record could be encoded and stored on a portable form, such as a plastic swipe card with magnetic-coded information or an optical card (Shiina et. al., 1991, Benson, 1990.) Our portable record would also include the biometric template to confirm identity.

4. FURTHER WORK

The next phase of the research is to undertake successively larger scale field trials. The aims of these trials will be to:
• develop appropriate procedures for the acquisition of personal details and biometrics,
• test the system configuration in the target environment, including rural health centres,
• increase the number of records held so that search strategies can be optimized.

Initial work indicates that high-quality identification data can be obtained. The fingerprint template data and matching method are such that an exhaustive search to match fingerprints is not practical.

Additional information is required to allow searching and matching to take place in an acceptable time interval. A variety of search strategies are required to enable identification to be verified.

However, the early field trials also indicate some problems with the reliability of the unit in being able to acquire fingerprints. There are basic research issues to be resolved, including age-related stability of the fingerprint, cleanliness requirements prior to scanning and possible inter-patient infection. The field trials aim to resolve these issues and to establish procedures for the use of biometric identification in healthcare facilities in PNG and to estimate the reliability and efficiency of data capture in this environment.

We believe that the integration of healthcare systems is possible within PNG, despite the difficulties that we have highlighted.

1. The telecommunication industry in PNG is scheduled for deregulation in 2000. The national carrier Telikom is upgrading infrastructure and increasing rural coverage prior to deregulation. The necessary telecommunications infrastructure already exists in some parts of the country and ISDN-type connections will be available from July 1999. From December 1998, the Iridium satellite-based communication system became operational in PNG, providing a viable alternative to the terrestrial communications network for the first time.
2. Urban healthcare centres and national health policy remain under the control of the national Department of Health, providing a body with authority to integrate at the correct level.
3. As a former Australian protectorate, PNG attracts significant funding from Australia. A 5-year Aus$50m rural health project funded by AusAID is at the design stage and provides an opportunity to advance the concepts presented here.

The work that we have done to uncover some of the cultural naming conventions used in PNG could be formalized and extended by ethnographic or anthropological researchers.

5. CONCLUSIONS

The use of biometrics in patient identification has the potential to revolutionize healthcare in Papua New Guinea. The presence of a portable, rugged system for reliable identification makes it possible to extend data collection to remote areas. Localized data collection with reference to a fixed point is of significant importance where there is a large shifting population. The harsh environment and the diverse cultural factors in the country make this a challenging research project.

The value of this research is that it takes an approach of preserving diversity. We recognize that people on both sides – healthcare providers and patients – have different identification needs and seek to bridge the gap by using a common characteristic – the biometric – rather than eliminating the difference by imposition of a homogenous system.

The value of the biometric data in our proposed system is to confirm the identity of a person who may use more than one name. We have uncovered some of the conventions amongst some cultural groups in PNG. Other developing nations that have a similar level of complexity in cultural naming conventions may benefit from this work.

REFERENCES

Bolyanatz, A., 1996. *Musings on Matriliny: Understandings and Social Relations Among the Sursurunga of New Ireland*. In: *Gender, Kinship, Power*. M.J. Maynes, A. Waltner, B. Soland, and U. Strasser, Eds. pp. 81-97. London: Routledge.

Benson, T., 1990. *Health cards—the move toward standards*. Journal of Medical Systems 14:147-50.

Clarke, R., 1994. *Human Identification in Information Systems: Management Challenges and Public Policy Issues*. Information Technology and People Vol. 7 No. 4, p. 6-37.

Iatau, M.D. and Williamson, I.P., 1998. Using the Case Study Methodology to Review Cadastral Reform in Papua New Guinea. The Australian Surveyor, Vol. 42, No. 4, 157-165.

Shiina, S., Nishibori, H. M., Fujita, I., and Y. Tsumori., 1991. *Practical use of optical cards in medical care*. Proceedings Fifteenth Annual Symposium in Computer Applications in Medical Care 1991, pp. 861-3.

United Nations Development Programme, 1998. *Human Development Index 1998*. United Nations, New York.

Healthcare Eligible on the Web? Biometric Technology Today, 1997, Vol. 4, No. 9, February 1997.

Six Biometric Devices point the finger at security. Network Computing, June 1, 1998.

Sony Fingerprint Identification Unit. Biometric Digest, May 1997, pp. 1, 8.

ENDNOTE

1 Wantok- lit. "one talk", a person from the same village, region or culture as yourself; friend or acquaintance; one to whom there is a binding obligation to provide mutual support.

Detecting Health Care Fraud Using Intelligent Data Mining

Guisseppi A. Forgionne, Aryya Gangopadhyay, and Monica Adya
Information Systems Department, University of Maryland Baltimore County, 1000 Hilltop Circle,
Baltimore, MD 21250
(410)455-3206, FAX: 410-455-1073, E-Mail: forgionn@umbc7.umbc.edu

ABSTRACT

There are various forms of fraud in the health care industry. This fraud has a substantial financial impact on the cost of providing health care. Money wasted on fraud will be unavailable for the diagnosis and treatment of legitimate illnesses. The rising costs of and the potential adverse affects on quality health care have encouraged organizations to institute measures for detecting fraud and intercepting erroneous payments. This paper presents an artificial intelligence methodology for facilitating the process, illustrates the use of the methodology, and discusses the implications for health care practice.

INTRODUCTION

Fraud in health care transactions refers to knowingly and willfully offering, paying, soliciting, or receiving remuneration to induce business that health care programs will reimburse. There are various forms of fraud in the health care industry. Among other things, fraud can result from internal corruption, bogus claims, and unnecessary health care treatments. For instance, waiving a patient's co-payment when billing third party payers and not disclosing the practice to the insurance carrier has been deemed as fraud and resulted in prosecution (Tomes 1993).

Fraud has a substantial financial impact on the cost of providing health care.   Medicaid fraud, alone, costs over 30 billion dollars each year in the United States (Korcok 1997). According to CIGNA HealthCare and Insurance groups, the healthcare industry is loosing an estimated $80 to $100 billion towards fraudulent claims and false billing practices (http://www.insurance.ibm.com/insur/cigna.htm). Investigators have shown that fraud is found in all segments of health care system including medical practitioners, drugs, X-rays, pathology tests etc.

The timely detection and prevention of fraud will not only provide significant cost savings to insurance companies but will also reduce the rising cost of healthcare. Money wasted on fraud will be unavailable for the diagnosis and treatment of legitimate illnesses. In the process, research monies may be reduced and critical research may be delayed. Ineffective and cost inefficient treatments may continue. Administrative effort may be diverted to fraud detection instead of being concentrated on the effective management of health care practice. As a consequence, patient care may suffer and health care costs may continue to soar.

In the past, claim fraud has been identified through complaints made, among others, by disgruntled health care competitors, beneficiaries and recipients, present or former employers of providers. A significant volume of false claims, however, still go undetected. Consequently, fraud is still rampant in the health care system. The rising costs of, and the potential adverse affects on quality health care, have encouraged organizations to institute measures for detecting fraud and intercepting erroneous payments, especially through electronic means.

Early cases of health care fraud have applied to gross issues such as kickbacks, bribes, and other fairly transparent schemes. Increasingly, however, the Office of the Inspector General has demonstrated a willingness to pursue cases that are in the gray area and courts have tended to interpret antifraud statues more broadly so as to make criminal prosecution more likely (Steiner, 1993). With the increasing number of health care transactions and persecution of situations with such uncertainty, it is possible to increase the chances of detecting fraud through the use of information technology. This paper presents an artificial intelligence methodology for facilitating the process. In particular, we propose the use of data mining and classification rules to determine the existence or non-existence of fraud patterns in the data.

The paper begins with an overview of the types of health care fraud. Next, there is a brief discussion of issues with the current fraud detection approaches. The paper then develops information technology based approaches and illustrates how these technologies can improve current practice. Finally, there is a summary of the major findings and the implications for health care practice.

HEALTH CARE FRAUD

Health care fraud can result from internal corruption, bogus claims, unnecessary health care treatments, and unwarranted solicitation. As in any commercial enterprise, unscrupulous provider or payer employees can misappropriate health care payments for personal purposes. Providers can also issue claims for treatments that were never, or only partially, rendered. Corrupt health care providers also can induce patients to undergo unnecessary, or even unwanted, treatments so as to inflate charges to the payers. In addition, unethical providers can willfully solicit business from unprincipled, or unsuspecting, patients for the sole purpose of generating billable procedures and treatments. According to a 1993 survey by the Health Insurance Association of America of private insurers' health care fraud investigations, majority of health care fraud activity is associated with diagnosis (43%) followed by billing services (34%). In Medicare, the most common forms of fraud includes billing for services not furnished, misrepresenting the diagnosis to justify payment, falsifying certificates of medical necessity, plans of treatment and medical records to justify payment and soliciting, offering, or receiving a kickback (http://www.hcfa.gov/medicare/fraud).

Due to the documentation typically required by payers, all forms of health care fraud will leave a paper, or electronic, trail that can serve as the basis for detection. However, the transactions useful for fraud detection will generally be buried in the documentation. Furthermore, these transactions may be from disparate sources and in diversified formats. Often, the needed transactions are also discarded as a normal part of transmitting claims from providers to payers.

Another major barrier to fraud detection is the reactive nature of the current approaches. For the most part, detection relies on: (a) complaints made by disgruntled interested parties, (b) random examinations by payers of provider submitted records, and (c) occasional detailed studies by public and private oversight agencies (Tomes 1993). Since such methods tend to be relatively narrow in scope, few fraud cases will be detected in this manner. Even in the identified cases, detection will be time-consuming, costly, and difficult to correct.

INFORMATION TECHNOLOGY-BASED STRATEGY

Information technology can be utilized to develop a proactive and effective health care fraud detection strategy. In this section, we propose a system that relies on current advancements in information technology, particularly in the area of Artificial Intelligence (AI). In particular, this strategy is based on concepts related to data warehousing and data .

Data needed to support the identification of fraud routinely flow, often electronically, between health care providers and payers as medical transactions. By filtering and focusing the transactions, warehousing the focused data, and creating tailor-made data marts for the appropriate recipients, requisite information can be made available for significant data mining analyses. Artificial intelligence then can be used to help providers and payers detect the underlying fraudulent patterns in the data and form effective proactive correction strategies.

Data Warehousing

Data warehousing involves the physical separation of day-to-day operational data from decision support systems. Benefits of data warehousing include clean and consistent organization-wide data, protection of transactional and operational systems from user's query and report requirements, and effective updating and maintenance of applications. The more significant purpose of the data warehouse is to support multi-dimensional analyses of both historical and current data. A multi-dimensional model is developed using the MOLAP (multi-dimensional on-line analytical processing) design. Several data cubes are populated with historical and current data. An example of a three-dimensional data cube consists of patient demographics, time, and procedure code as the dimensions, and the payment as the measure. The actual analysis could require dimensionality reduction such as a time-series analysis of payment records for patients that underwent a given treatment. In this case only two dimension of the data cube are investigated. Such an analysis could be required to establish a historical pattern of the amount of payments made for a given medical procedure, sudden changes of which may cause an alarm for further investigations. Average values of payment amounts for medical procedures over a given data set can be used as a normative value to trigger any significant variations in current payment amounts. Other examples of multi-dimensional analyses includes pivoting or cross tabulating measures against dimensions, dicing the cube to study a sub-population of the data collected over a period of time, and rollup or drill down along dimensions to study any changes that might have taken place along individual dimensions.

Data Mining and Classification Rules

Data mining is an emerging technique that combines AI algorithms and relational databases to discover patterns without the use of traditional statistical methods (Borok 1997). It employs complex software algorithms to identify patterns in large databases and data warehouses. Data mining can facilitate information analysis using either a top-down or a bottom-up approach (Limb and Meggs 1995). While bottom-up approach analyses the raw data in an attempt to discover the hidden trends and groups, the top-down data mining tests a specific hypothesis.

Effective data mining relies on an effective and representative data warehouse. By definition, data mining is a pattern discovery process that requires large volumes of data to infer meaningful patterns. Once the data is "mined" from the warehouse and patterns are cataloged, the patterns themselves can be converted into a set of rules (Borok 1997). These rules that explain health care behavior will be coded into a rule-base and be used for analyzing individual instances.

Classification rules deal with identifying a class of regularities in data. A classification rule is an expression $(l_1 \leq X_1 \leq U_1) \wedge (l_2 \leq X_2 \leq U_2) \wedge \ldots (l_k \leq X_k \leq U_k) \rightarrow (l_y \leq X \leq U_y)$, where $X_1 \ldots X_k$ are attributes used to predict the value of Y, and $l_1 \ldots l_k$, $U_1 \ldots U_k$ are the lower and upper bounds of the corresponding attribute values, respectively. As an example, in detecting health care fraud, a classification rule would be $X \rightarrow (Y \leq l_y)$ or $(U_y \leq Y)$, where X is a surgical procedure and (l_y, U_y) is the prescriptive range of values for the payments made (Y).

A classification rule is said to have a support s if the percentage of all cases satisfying the conditions specified in the rule equals or exceeds the support. In other words, s is the ratio to the total number of cases where both X and Y values are within the specified ranges. The confidence c of a classification rule is defined as the probability that, for all cases where the value of X falls within its specified range, the value of Y will also be within the range specified for Y. In other words, c is the ratio of cases where the values of X and Y are within their respective specified ranges, to the total number of cases where only the X values are within the specified range. Both support and confidence can be user or system specified as percentages or ratios.

If the support for a certain rule is low, it indicates that the number of cases is not large enough to make any conclusive inference. In that case, no further analysis is done with the current data set. If the support is large but the confidence is low, the rule is rejected. If both the support and confidence exceed the values specified by the user (or system) then the rule is accepted. Such a case would trigger a flag for a potential fraud and recommend further investigation, which is done by isolating the cases that triggered the flag.

Application

Take the instance of determining physician charges for a surgical procedure. Since charges for this procedure may vary somewhat by physician, location of the practicing facility, regulations of the insurance provider etc., it is challenging for the fraud detection scheme to identify an acceptable range of charges. This requires understanding the physicians' practice procedures, determining the practice patterns implicit in the data, and possibly identifying practice patterns over the past few weeks. Data mining can discover such patterns in the historical data. More importantly, it can uncover atypical patterns of practice within a group. For instance, mining on a large sample of nationwide data may identify that for a simple dental procedure, physicians charge a fee of $45.00 to $60.00 in the state of Maryland. If there are sufficient number of cases in the data warehouse that support the correlation between the procedure and the range of charges, then the support and confidence in this rule will be high. Otherwise the rule will be rejected and will not be included in the rule-base. If the rule is accepted, a new case regarding this procedure can now be compared against the rule and can trigger a fraud alert if the charges deviate significantly from those specified in the rule.

In another instance, data mining may support the analysis and understanding of temporary conditions which may be triggered as a fraud alert but are really not so. Suppose the classification rules above indicate an increase in the incidence of emergency hospitalizations that in other regions around the area. This can set up a trigger whereby further analysis may reveal the presence of a high risk construction facility for the next two years. This will allow the health care providers to prepare for the situation both during and after the construction activity and possibly aid in the prevention of emergency situations at this facility. Similar analysis can be used for chronic conditions such as breast or lung cancer in specific regions.

FRAUD DETECTION SYSTEM

The fraud detection methodology can be made available through an easy-to-use computer system with the conceptual architecture shown in Figure 1. As this figure shows, the system interactively processes inputs into the outputs desired by health care users.

Inputs

The fraud detection system has a data base that captures and stores historical, and industry standard, data on health care providers, claims, and payments. These data are extracted from the data warehouse that captures the relevant transactions from the providers to the payers, and vice versa.

Provider information includes the name, address, ID, and other demographics. Claims information includes the patient ID, procedure code, charge, billing dates, and other financial statistics. Payment information includes the patient and provider IDs, deductibles, co-payments, covered remuneration, and relevant payment dates.

Figure 1 Fraud Detection Conceptual System Architecture

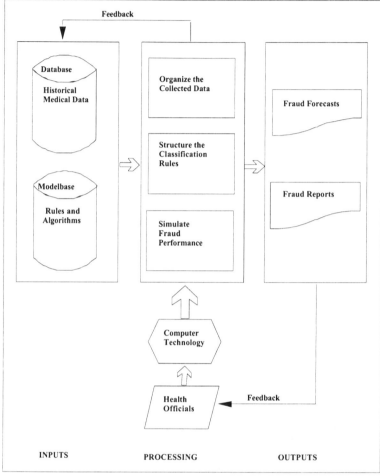

There is also a model base that contains classification rules and artificial intelligence algorithms. The classification rules would establish lower and upper limits, supports, and confidence levels for each covered procedure from historical data and industry standards. These rules would be derived through the data mining tool, and the classification algorithm would determine the support and confidence of the classification rules.

Processing

The health official (health plan administrator, auditor, or other staff assistant) uses computer technology to perform the fraud detection analyses and evaluations. Computer hardware includes an IBM-compatible Pentium-based microcomputer with 16MB of RAM, a color graphics display, and a printer compatible with the microcomputer. Software includes the SAS information delivery system running through the Microsoft Windows operating system. This configuration was selected because it offered a more consistent, less time-consuming, less costly, and more flexible development and implementation environment than the available alternatives.

Users initiate the processing by pointing and clicking with the computer's mouse on screen-displayed objects. The system responds by automatically organizing the collected data, structuring (estimating and operationalizing) the classification rules, and simulating fraud performance. Results are displayed on the preprogrammed forms desired by health officials. Execution is realized in a completely interactive manner that makes the processing relatively transparent to the user.

As indicated by the top feedback loop in Figure 1, organized data, structured classification rules, and fraud performance reports created during the system's analyses and evaluations can be captured and stored as inputs for future processing. These captured inputs are stored as additional or revised fields and records, thereby updating the data and model bases dynamically. The user executes the functions with mouse-controlled point-and-click operations on attractive visual displays that make the computer processing virtually invisible (transparent) to the user.

Outputs

Processing automatically generates visual displays of the outputs desired by health officials. Outputs include fraud forecasts and reports. These reports are in the form of tables and graphs. Each table displays the forecasted payment value relative to its lower and upper limits for a specified medical procedure. The corresponding graph highlights deviations outside the limits and allows the user to drill down to the supporting detail (which includes the provider, any extenuating circumstances, and other relevant information). The user has the option of printing or saving the reports.

As indicated by the bottom feedback loop in Figure 1, the user can utilize the outputs to guide further processing before exiting the system. Typically, the feedback will involve sensitivity analyses in which the user modifies support and confidence levels, upper and lower limits, or other pertinent factors and observes the effects on fraud performance.

CONCLUSIONS

The fraud detection system presented in this paper is a combination of data warehousing, data mining, and artificial intelligence technology. This system offers the health care official a tool that will support a proactive strategy of health care fraud detection. The system's use can reduce the time and cost needed to detect health care fraud, and the system can substantially lower the public and private expenses associated with such fraud.

To achieve the potential benefits, health care officials will have to meet significant challenges. First, a data warehouse must be established to capture the relevant transactions. In particular, there must be continuous user-involvement including careful upfront examination of business requirements and identification of quality and standards. The warehouse must be iteratively developed to deliver increasing value to the organization. Second, to support effective data mining, data marts must be formed to filter and focus the data for fraud detection. A strategy must be formulated for developing the tool. Once again, because of their domain knowledge, users must play a central role in such development. Finally, users must be convinced about the efficacy of the fraud detection system and trained in the use of the proactive technology.

REFERENCES

Borok, L. S., 1997, "Data mining: Sophisticated forms of managed care modeling through artificial intelligence: Review", Journal of Health Care Finance. 23(3): 20-36.

Korcok, M., 1997, "Medicare, Medicaid Fraud: A Billion-Dollar Art Form in the US. Canadian Medical Association Journal, 156 (8), 1195-1197.

Limb, P.R., and G.J. Meggs, 1995, "Data Mining -Tools and Techniques", British Telecom Technology Journal, 12(4), 32-41.

Steiner, J. E., 1993, "Update: Fraud and Abuse Stark Laws", Journal of Helath and Hosp., 26, 274-275.

Tomes, J.P., 1993, Healthcare Fraud, Waste, Abuse, and Safe Harbors: The Complete Legal Guide, Probus Publishing Company, Chicago, IL.

The Case For Teaching
Object-oriented Cobol

Tanya Goette

Georgia College & State University, ISC Dept. CBX 12, Milledgeville,GA 31061

912-445-5721 tgoette@mail.gcsu.edu

ABSTRACT

This paper explores reasons why object-oriented COBOL should be the object-oriented (OO) language taught by Information Systems Departments within Colleges of Business. Because COBOL is the most widely used business programming language, many institutions teach COBOL in their structured programming language course. It seems more efficient to teach students OO extensions to a language that they have already learned than to teach an OO language that is completely new to the students. This paper proposes that institutions teach OO COBOL and explains the basics of OO COBOL.

The IS '97 Model Curriculum and Guidelines for Undergraduate Degree Programs in Information Systems (1997) suggest an information technology course in programming, data file, and object structure (p.19) as well as an Information Systems Development course in physical design and implementation with a programming language (p.20). The guidelines suggest teaching OO development in the second course if it has not been taught previously. This paper presents arguments for making OO COBOL the language that should be taught in the second course.

REQUIRED COURSES

AACSB limits the number of required major courses that can be taken by students. Furthermore, many institutions also require that the major courses must be able to be completed in a two year time frame. According to a study by Adekoya and Quaye (1998), programming courses account for approximately 25% of the courses required for an IS degree in an AACSB institution. If eight courses (two per semester for four semesters) are required for the major, then only two of these are programming courses.

Programming Languages Taught

While many institutions offer a variety of programming languages as electives, the two required courses generally consist of a third-generation structured language and an OO language. COBOL followed by C++ or Java are popular choices. Courses in a structured language are being taught because in spite of the benefits of OO, most development is not currently being done with OO methodologies (Douglas & Massey, 1996; Fayad, Tsai, & Fulgham, 1996). Undergraduates that are being employed as business programmers typically use COBOL as their development language (Douglas & Massey, 1996). The demand for COBOL programmers is not expected to decrease. A study by Arnett and Jones (1993) indicated that 90% of mainframe users expect to remain with COBOL for business applications. Most institutions must meet the demands of the employers in their region by producing graduates literate in COBOL.

Typically, C++ is the OO language of choice because when companies are doing OO development, it is the most used language (Douglas & Massey, 1996). Java is also gaining popularity because of its use in WWW programming. One of the major problems with OO development is the long learning curve (Fayad, Tsai, & Fulgham, 1996). Many developers believe that learning OO development concepts requires a major paradigm shift. If there is a long learning curve, then why are institutions using C++ to teach OO development? Students tend to get bogged down in learning the new language rather than concentrating on the advantages of OO development. Therefore, it would make more sense to add extensions to a language that the students have already learned rather than requiring that a new language be learned in order to accomplish OO development.

OBJECT-ORIENTED COBOL

The 9X standards for COBOL compilers are including OO extensions for the COBOL language. The popular PC based COBOL compiler by Micro Focus already has OO extensions available. In addition to Micro Focus, IBM, Computer Associates, Allegiant Legacy, Software Technology Corporation, NiGSun International, Inegri Point Software, and AcuCorp (Krishnamurthi, 1998; Stern & Stern, 1999) all have software available to make COBOL web ready. There are also textbooks available that teach OO COBOL (most assume the student already knows COBOL). By using a programming language that the students have already learned to teach OO development, the course can place the emphasis on OO techniques rather than spending the majority of class time learning the basics of the programming language.

OO COBOL Basics

For anyone not familiar with object-oriented techniques, there are a myriad of books available on the subject, so this paper will not give a detailed explanation (see www.yourdon.com/index.htm for recommendations). However, the basic idea is to reuse previously developed code, or objects. These objects contain both data and procedures. COBOL already uses the Copy and Call verbs to share code, so referencing previously developed objects within another program is a natural extension of the language.

In Object COBOL, classes are source entities that package data and procedures together. Scope is the range of accessibility for each data item in a class. Invoking an object method can change an object's data values by sending a message consisting of an object reference, a method selector, and optional input and/or output parameters to an object (Stern & Stern, 1999).

Some basic OO additions to COBOL are: (1) a class header in the Identification Division that gives the Class-ID name and from what classes it inherits; (2) a Class-Control statement in the Environment Division for associating the logical class name with the physical disk file; (3) a new object reference data type in the Working-Storage Section for defining object classes and object instances; and (4) a new verb, Invoke, in the Procedure Division for creating and sending messages to objects (Stern & Stern, 1999; *Getting Started*, 1995).

For instructors that would like to learn more about Object-Oriented COBOL, Wilson Price teaches three day seminars on OO COBOL at various locations (click on Cobol University at www.objectz.com). The seminar allows hands-on labs to practice the programming extensions.

CONCLUSION

The vast majority of legacy systems are in COBOL. With the latest General Accepted Accounting Principles for capitalizing the costs of internally developed software, it makes sense to enhance existing COBOL applications (Yancey, 1998). There are also commercially developed OO COBOL applications. Sterling Commerce, Banking Systems Division, announced the general availability of a product written entirely in OO COBOL in September of 1998 (Webb, 1998). (See www.extra.newsguy.com/ ~oocobol for more information.) However, many companies are scared off OO development because their programmers believe they would have to not only learn new development techniques but also a new development language (Douglas & Massey, 1996). It would be much easier to convince developers to use OO techniques if a new language did not have to be used. OO COBOL can be used to solve this problem. If institutions produce graduates that not only understand OO techniques but also understand the existing COBOL systems, then these individuals should be able to lead programming teams into the use of OO methodologies.

REFERENCES

Adekoya, A. A. & Quaye, A. K. M. "An Evaluation of the Level of Contribution of Programming Language Courses to Undergraduate Information Systems Preparation: An Exploratory Study", Presented at the Twenty-eighth Annual Meeting of the Southeast Decision Sciences Institute, Roanoke, Va., February 1998.
Arnett & Jones. "Programming Languages Today and Tomorrow", Journal of Computer Information Systems, Summer 1993, pp. 77-81.
Douglas, D. E. & Massey, P. D. "Is Industry Embracing Object-Oriented Technologies?", Journal of Computer Information Systems, Spring 1996, pp. 65-72.
Fayad, M. E., Tsai, W. & Fulgham, M. L. "Transition to Object-Oriented Software Development", Communications of the ACM, (39:2), 1996, pp. 108-121.
Getting Started, Micro Focus Personal COBOL for Windows 3.1 with Object Orientation, 1995.
"IS '97 Model Curriculum and Guidelines for Undergraduate Degree Programs in Information Systems", 1997.
Krishnamurthi, M. "The COBOL Dinosaur: Does It Face Extinction?", Proceedings of the Ninth Annual Conference of the International Information Management Association, 1998, pp. 60-65.
Stern, N. & Stern, R., Structured COBOL Programming, 8th Edition, John Wiley & Sons, New York, 1999.
Webb, G. "Introduction to Collection Classes", The COBOL Report, (2:6), 1998, p.4.
Yancey, T. "Software Capitalization Changes", The COBOL Report, (2:6), 1998, pp. 5-6.

Globalizing Information Systems: An Evolutionary and Resource-based Perspective

Gerald Grant

School of Business, Carleton University, 1125 Colonel By Drive, Ottawa, Ontario K1S 5B6, Canada
Telephone: (613) 520 2600 Ext. 8006 Fax: (613) 520 4427, Email: gerald_grant@carleton.ca

INTRODUCTION

Firms operating in global environments face significant challenges harnessing and leveraging global capabilities, resources and competencies. To achieve their strategic objectives they must be able to effectively coordinate company-wide business processes while simultaneously maintaining the autonomy and flexibility of business operations in local markets. It is generally presumed that effective coordination and control of global operations can lead to the achievement of significant economies of scale and provide the basis for competitive advantage in both global and local markets. At the heart of the globalization agenda for most companies is the belief that the use of information and communications technologies will make it possible for them to achieve the efficiencies and competitiveness envisaged (Cross, Earl, and Sampler, 1997). In fact, it has been suggested that investments in information technology (IT) can give firms a basis for increased coordination and control or can provide direct competitive advantage in world markets (Ives and Jarvenpaa, 1991). A recent survey of 500 innovative users of IT in the United States, by Information Week magazine, confirms that many companies have begun to make significant investments in deploying global IT architectures. The survey found that over 85% of the companies regard the deployment of global IT architectures and standards as a key business priority in the next twelve months (Information Week, Sept. 14, 1998, p. 64).

IMPLEMENTING GLOBAL IT ARCHITECTURES

Decisions to implement global information systems architectures involve significant change to organizational structures and relationships. They may require substantial re-engineering of business processes and significant restructuring of traditional roles and responsibilities (Cross, Earl, and Sampler, 1997). Attempts to implement global information systems may even challenge the validity of proven and profitable approaches to organizing the business. Historically, most companies operating in multinational markets adopted a decentralized architecture for delivering information systems. That is, IT systems were developed and deployed to serve the needs of the local business unit or country organization. Companies faced with the challenge of competing both locally and globally are seeking ways to deliver the flexibility that this requires. The achievement of strategic flexibility is necessary if firms are to become and remain competitive in the new competitive environment (Hitt, Keats, and DeMarie, 1998)

While the pressures of globalization are forcing companies to consider the implementation of global IT architectures, there is insufficient understanding of how this is best done. Firms attempting to deploy global IS infrastructures have come to realize that "harnessing IT on a global scale presents management with problems that are far more challenging than those encountered in sharing systems across domestic divisions" (Ives and Jarvenpaa, 1991). Although a significant amount of the difficulties are technological in nature, many of them are related to the firm's history, management, culture, structure and business processes. Implementing global IT architectures is an onerous task, particularly for companies with long traditions of decentralization and significant local autonomy.

RESEARCH OBJECTIVES

This research seeks to develop a deeper understanding of the key issues faced by organizations and managers involved with implementing global information systems. Specifically, we plan to explore the factors that promote or inhibit the deployment of enterprise-wide IS architectures in global companies. We wish to provide explanations for these factors as well as suggest management approaches for successfully managing the process of implementing global IS architectures. We are also interested in how global firms develop organizational information systems capability. IS capability is "the organizational capacity to orchestrate investment in designing, acquiring, deploying, exploiting and sustaining computer-based information systems to support the strategic and functional objectives of the business" (Grant, 1996). We will use the IS capability framework suggested by Grant (1996) to provide us with an integrative structure for effectively investigating, analyzing, and interpreting information systems capability within and across organizations. The framework identifies three strategic dimensions of information systems capability, namely routines, resources, and contexts. Routines refer to key activities undertaken by management and non-management personnel in conceptualizing, designing, coordinating and executing organizational functions related to the implementation of computer-based information systems. Resources refer to organizational endowments that form the basis of IS capability development. Contexts focus on the general, business and firm environments that influence organizational IT-related investments and the path-dependent nature of such investments.

RESEARCH METHOD

We use the case study as our primary investigative method. Case studies are particularly valuable because they allow a more in-depth exploration of factors affecting the deployment and exploitation of information systems. This will help build the already strong tradition for case study research that exists in the IS field (Lee, 1989; Markus, 1983; Cross, Earl, and Sampler, 1997; Brown and Magill, 1994). We intend to present our initial findings from a case study carried out in a multinational company that is currently involved in deploying a global ERP financial system. The company has operations in over 30 countries employing some 33,000 employees. The project is expected to cost between US$80 - 100 million dollars.

The case study is based on a series of interviews with key business and IT managers who have global or regional responsibilities. The interviews general last for one to one hour and fifteen minutes and are tape-recorded. The interviews follow a semi-structured format. A list of issues has been identified and for the most part is submitted to the interviewee prior to the interview session. Although we attempt to follow the outline, interviewees are allowed substantial latitude in addressing the issues raised.

CURRENT STATE OF THE RESEARCH
At the time of this writing, in-depth interviews had been held with twelve (12) senior managers who have direct or indirect responsibility for global or regional businesses or for the deployment and management of IT systems and services. The interviewees included: an executive vice president with overall responsibility for IT worldwide, two vice presidents, the controller, chief internal auditor, regional director for Europe, along with other senior managers and IT project directors.

The interviews are in the process of being transcribed and edited. They will then be codified and analyzed with the aid of QSR NUD*IST, a software package for qualitative data analysis. This is a time consuming process but is expected to yield rich empirical data.

PRELIMINARY INDICATIONS
At a very preliminary level, the interviews indicate support for the notion that implementing global IT architectures is a complex and onerous task. Deploying global IT systems will require organizations to undertake significant organizational and process changes. We have indications that the existing organizational culture plays a significant role in defining the approach to and outcomes of enterprise-wide IT systems deployment. The successful deployment of global IT systems requires more than consent from top-level management. It demands the articulation of a clear and well-understood strategic vision and the exercise of prescient and proactive strategic leadership. Only then can organizations enact the significant, even radical, restructuring that deploying ERP systems require.

On another level, the construct "globalization" with regards to information systems has been challenged. What does globalization mean? Is it to be equated with centralization? Does it mean having the same hardware, software, and telecommunication systems in every location throughout the company? Or does it simply mean creating global standards for information storage, access and exchange? The exploration of these issues are critical to understanding how organizations can best configure and deploy IT-based systems to support their global operations.

CONCLUSIONS
As companies seek to gain and sustain competitive advantage from pursuing a globalization strategy, they need to acquire and deploy information and communication technologies that will make enterprise-wide communication, collaboration and control possible. The indications are that implementing global IT systems is more complex than most managers envision. Success will depend on the strategic leadership and vision provided by those at the very top of the organization and well as the willingness of managers at all levels to enact the organizational and process changes required to make the systems viable.

REFERENCES
Brown, C. V. and Magill, S. L. (1994) "Alignment of the IS functions with the enterprise: toward a model of antecedents," MIS Quarterly, December, pp. 371-403.
Cross, J., Earl, M. J., and Sampler, J. L. (1997) "Transformation of the IT function at British Petroleum," MIS Quarterly, December, pp. 401-423.
Hitt, M. A., Keats, B. W. and DeMarie, S. (1998) "Navigating the new competitive landscape: Building strategic flexibility and competitive advantage in the 21st century." The Academy of Management Executive, vol. 12, no. 4 (November), pp. 22-42.
Grant, G. G. (1996) "The strategic dimensions of information systems capability: case studies in a developing country context," Unpublished Ph.D. Thesis University of London.
Ives, B. and Jarvenpaa, S. L. (1991) "Applications of global information technology: key issues for management," MIS Quarterly, March, pp. 33-49.
Lee, A. S. (1989) "A scientific methodology for MIS case studies," MIS Quarterly, March, pp. 33-50.
Markus, M. L. (1983) "Power, politics, and MIS implementation," Communications of the ACM, (26:6) June, pp. 430-444.

IT Diffusion: National Best Practices

Tanya Gupta

LCSPR, World Bank; Tgupta@worldbank.org

Abir Qasem

Department of Computing and Mathematics, Embry Riddle Aeronautical University; qasema@db.erau.edu

INTRODUCTION

The effective use of computer and information technology (IT) contributes to an increase in an organization's capability in delivering its products and/or services. Companies that wish to survive and compete in this information era are finding that effective use and management of IT is fast becoming the single biggest contributor to their competitive advantage and thus, also to their bottom line. As a result, in recent years, we have seen an exponential growth in the literature that deals with effective IT management. Although a country is a large and a complex organization and its economy can benefit as much from the effective use of information technology as any corporation, IT management at a national level has been widely ignored in IT literature.

This paper presents a set of best practice for management of IT at a national level. To arrive at these best practices we have defined an abstract term "diffusion" to encapsulate the details of various IT management approaches. This abstraction helped us in identifying and classifying the national IT initiatives from a large amount of literature. After the general classification we have taken four successful Asian countries and gathered their specific practices under those general categories. Once we have the specific practices grouped, a simple frequency count revealed interesting insight into national level IT best practices.

RESEARCH METHODOLOGY

Source of information

We have reviewed articles, popular literature, country reports, government documents and the Internet for information regarding the IT diffusion initiatives of more than 30 countries. We believe that web presence is one of the indicators of technology diffused organizations. Therefore, our prime source of information for this paper was government reports on successful IT deployment and management that have been posted on the web.

Complete Diffusion: The information utopia

Since government documents were our primary source we needed a mechanism to filter out reports that dealt with successful IT deployment and management initiatives from a myriad of bureaucratic jargon.

To do so, we defined an abstract term, diffusion, which encapsulates the state of an organization, when all of its resources are using information technology to its fullest potential. In order for IT to be an active contributor to national economic growth a country has to diffuse IT in its economic activities. Complete diffusion of IT is an ideal condition that is reached when all entities/activities that contribute to the economic growth of a country are exploiting IT to its maximum potential.

Diffusion initiative Taxonomy

We examined our sources looking for "IT diffusion initiatives." Once we had filtered all the relevant information, we performed semantic grouping, where we clustered similar initiatives and identified eight general categories under which all the diffusion initiatives could be classified. The eight general categories are as follows: strategic IT management, marketing the IT image, accelerating IT diffusion through financing of IT production, IT human capital, managing coordination and interaction of IT elements, IT-related infrastructure and standards, IT research and development and legal IT related issues.

We used this taxonomy to collect the data from government initiatives taken in Japan, Singapore, Korea and India within the above categories. The focus was on Asian countries as most of western countries have already diffused IT to a large extent. Therefore, the best practices that we are trying to develop will have much higher utility to a developing country.

We collected and presented our data in table 1. We used a discrete binary numbering scheme to identify the popular initiatives. Therefore one should use discretion in applying the findings as a continuous scale may have been more appropriate. Thus, the numbers should not be used to rank the countries because it only denotes the presence of an initiative but does not really express the extent of such an initiative. A more specialized scale will have to be developed to capture this information

We classify all the initiatives and use them in their respective categories. The number 1 and 0 represent the presence and absence of initiatives for a country in a given category. The matrix can be used to rank the initiatives, that is to find out the most popular initiatives among successful countries. One should note that some good initiatives may score low since it was not popular among countries.

For example "Handling interministerial and interdepartmental conflict" was not a common initiative, however much of the analytical literature (as opposed to country studies) surveyed highlight the importance of this measure.

NATIONAL BEST PRACTICES

The countries focused mostly on infrastructure and standards, human capital and the financing of IT production. 85% of all possible initiatives were taken in the area of infrastucture and standards 80% was true of human capital and 70% for financing IT production. Japan and Singapore focussed more on the overall strategy which is why they may have been more successful overall in IT diffusion. These were also the most active countries in terms of initiatives taken. Singapore undertook 93% of all possible initiatives captured in the study and Japan undertook 86% of all possible initiatives. Studies show that Japan and Singapore have more developed IT-intensive economies among the countries studied. They also have the strongest economies. This study shows a correlation between the robustness of economy and the number of initiatives taken in the area of IT diffusion. Although this study is empirical and does not establish causation, this preliminary evidence shows that this is an area worth exploring in future research.

Least effort was given to managing coordination and interaction of IT elements. This was interesting as much of the literature and cases studies show that this is a crucial area for IT diffusion. Japan, particularly faced some problems as they did not lay enough

Table 1: IT Diffusion Initiatives					
Legend: J is Japan, I is India, K is Korea, S is Singapore and C is Cumulative					
Country	J	I	K	S	C
IT Initiatives	25	15	22	27	
A. Strategic	4	0	3	4	11
1. Civil Services Computerization	1	0	1	1	
2. National Committee	1	0	0	1	
3. Total quality emphasis and encouragement in software development by government	1	0	0	1	
4. Phased and comprehensive plans	1	0	1	1	
5. Promoting domestic market	0	0	1	0	
B. Marketing	2	2	3	3	10
1. Marketing national plan	0	0	0	1	
2. International office	0	0	1	0	
3. Active trade organizations and networking entities	1	1	1	1	
4. Participation in trade fairs	1	1	1	1	
C. Financing IT production	3	4	4	4	15
1. Subsidies or sponsorships	1	1	1	1	
2. Tax breaks/holidays	0	1	1	1	
3. Low interest loans	1	1	1	1	
4. Venture capital financing	1	1	1	1	
D. Human Capital	5	3	3	5	16
1. Vocational institutions	1	1	1	1	
2. Accrediting/Certifying Institutions	1	1	0	1	
3. Graduate and Postgraduate technical education	1	1	1	1	
4. Manpower surveys	1	0	0	1	
5. Continual revision of standard of technical curriculum	1	0	1	1	
E. Managing Coordination and Interaction of IT elements	1	0	1	2	4
1. Handling interministerial and interdepartmental conflict	0	0	0	1	
2. Partnerships between business/government/academia	1	0	1	1	
F. Infrastructure and standards	5	3	4	5	17
1. Organizational (Optic fiber, ISDN, Satellite use, digitization)	1	1	1	1	
2. Large number of projects	1	1	1	1	
3. Large amount of money invested	1	1	1	1	
4. Standards	1	0	0	1	
5. High number of telephones	1	0	1	1	
G. Research and Development	3	2	2	2	9
1. R&D Expenditure	1	0	1	1	
2. Technology spawning institutions	1	1	1	1	
3. EPZ's, Technopolis, Science cities, export zones etc.	1	1	0	0	
H. Legal	1	0	1	1	3
1. Intellectual Property Rights and other laws	1	0	1	1	

emphasis on managing the various IT elements.

The table revealed a set of IT diffusion best practices. Some of these are as follows:
- Civil Services Computerization
- Total quality emphasis and encouragement of software development by government
- Promoting domestic market
- Marketing national plan
- Maintaining an international office
- Having active trade organizations and networking entities
- Providing low interest loans
- Introducing accrediting/certifying institutions
- Improving the quality of graduate and postgraduate technical education
- Continual revision of standard of technical curriculum
- Handling interministerial and interdepartmental conflict
- Promoting partnerships between business/government/academia
- Focussing on organizational aspects (Optic fiber, ISDN, Satellite use, digitization)
- Increasing R&D Expenditure
- Promoting technology spawning institutions
- Promoting EPZ's, Technopolis, Science cities, export zones etc.
- Tackling Intellectual Property Rights and other legal issues

CONCLUSION AND FUTURE WORK

Although we may not find a country that is 100% IT diffused, a number of countries ranging from economically developed United States and Japan, to the more recent Asian success stories like Singapore, Korea, and India provide evidence of significant levels of IT diffusion. In fact, in some cases, the countries have succeeded in creating wealth through the effective use of information technology despite their financial misfortunes. We have also seen that a lot of countries failed to take advantage of the opportunities that information technology provided. These best practices may be used as a guideline for development of a national IT diffusion plan. It may also be used as an assessment tool by international development organizations such as World Bank and the United Nations in determining the feasibility of a loan request from a country that wants to borrow money for national IT diffusion projects.

Asian countries on the verge of development that wished to use information technology as a tool to attain economic development have had comprehensive strategies towards use of IT diffusion. Demonstration projects such as Civil Service computerization have commonly been incorporated into this strategy. The national plans for IT diffusion have been characterized by phased strategic plans, national-level committees, total quality emphasis on the software industry and to some extent promotion of the domestic market.

Marketing has also been used as a tool to promote IT. Some countries like Singapore have promoted their national IT plans worldwide and tried to sell themselves as "an intelligent island". Participation in trade fairs have also been common. Countries like Korea have concentrated on having offices internationally and promoted trade organizations actively. Financing IT production ultimately leads to IT diffusion. Subsidies, sponsorships, tax breaks, holidays, low interest loans and venture capital financing have been used extensively by almost all the countries surveyed to finance IT production. Promoting human capital is a step that has been taken before the other initiatives. Development of educational institutions including vocational institutions, accrediting and certifying institutions, manpower surveys and upgrading technical curriculum are initiatives that have been taken.

Most of the literature surveyed recommended that governments take strong measures towards promoting coordination and interaction of IT elements. Particular emphasis on handling interministerial and interdepartmental conflict as well as promoting partnerships between business/government/academia has been given in literature surveyed as well as in some of the government plans. However in reality most of the governments failed to implement this. Even though this is not a common measure it may be a useful component of IT diffusion initiatives. Most of the countries surveyed have planned for the development of infrastructure and standards. Organizational aspects such as optic fiber, ISDN, satellite use and digitization have been emphasized. The number of projects implemented and the number of telephones connected, the amount of money invested and the development of standards have been noted.

Research and development information was captured through the filters of R&D expenditure, technology spawning institutions and presence of EPZ's, Technopolis, Science cities, export zones etc. The primary area of interest in the literature reviewed in the area of legal issues has been Intellectual Property guarantees. Korea is the rare case where the legal system has been actively used to promote IT. The macroeconomic measures are too detailed to discuss in this paper so a very general judgment has been made with regard to economic development. We have looked for low interest rates, stable domestic government stable exchange rate and balanced budget etc. to determine the existence of a stable macroeconomic environment.

Governments in the Asian countries reviewed here, for the most part, have been active in promoting the diffusion of information technology. There is no doubt that the active efforts of the government has contributed, at least to some extent to the effective diffusion of information technology . It is also an accepted fact that effective diffusion of information technology contributes to economic development. Other developing countries, specially in Asia would do well to study the successful government initiatives and try to duplicate them with appropriate modifications in their own countries.

REFERENCES (paper)

Evenson, Robert E. and Gustav Ranis (1990). "Science and Technology: Lessons for Development Policy". Westview Press.
Heeks, R.B. (1996). "India's Software Industry: state policy, liberalization and industrial development". Sage Publications.

Hanna, Nagy, Sandor Boyson and Shakuntala Gunaratne. (1996). "The East Asian Miracle and information technology: strategic management of technological learning. World Bank Discussion Paper Number 326.
Hanna, Nagy. (1994). "Exploiting Information Technology for Development: a case study of India. World Bank Discussion Paper Number 246.
The World Bank Annual Report (1996). Washington D.C.

REFERENCES (Internet)

Japan
http://infoma.nttls.co.jp/infomofa/
http://itri.loyola.edu
http://jin.jcic.or.jp
http://kogcov.cc.keio.ac.jp
http://pears.lib.ohio-state.edu/science/
http://www-ntt.jp/square/
http://www.bekkoame.or.jp
http://www.crl.go.jp
http://www.cs.arizona.edu/japan/
http://www.denken.or.jp
http://www.fuji.stanford.edu
http://www.glocom.ac.gp/news/
http://www.ifnet.or.jp/~daruma/
http://www.iijnet.or.jp
http://www.itd.rr.navy.mil
http://www.jicst.go.jp/www/Institute/
http://www.jw.stanford.edu
http://www.kiis.or.jp/kiis/
http://www.mpt.go.jp
http://www.nacsis.ac.jp
http://www.orl.go.jp
http://www.ota.gov
http://www.pobox.com/~konrad/
http://www.rcot.or.jp
http://www.ta.doc.gov/aptp/

Singapore
http://198.68.10.246/khir/sdp/
http://dxm.org/techonomist/
http://iagent.iti.gov.sg/siro
http://www.asianconnect.com:8080/nlline
http://www.commerceasia.com
http://www.gov.sg
http://www.gov.sg/molaw/mbwcisd/
http://www.informatics.com.sg
http://www.ncb.gov.sg
http://www.opentech.com.sg
http://www.psb.gov.sg
http://www.rand.org
http://www.sedb.com
http://www.sp.ac.sg/jsist/
http://www.stee.com.sg
http://www.tbv.com.sg/tbv/

http://www.tdb.gov.sg
http://www.techlib.isi.edu
http://www.webdire.com-sg
http://www.worldbank.org

Korea
http://cair-archive.kaist.ac.kr
http://flower.comeng.chungman.ac.kr
http://home.sprynet.com/sprynet/jochov
http://iicat.snu.ac.kr
http://iit.disc.co.kr
http://jazz.seri.re.kr
http://kor-seek.chungman.ac.kr
http://korea.www.com
http://nyangdan.hit.co.kr
http://sunsite.sut.ac.jp/asia/korea/
http://www.kist.re.kr
http://www.kois.go.kr
http://www.korea.web.com
http://www.korealink.com
http://www.lgeds.lg.co.kr
http://www.miwon.co.kr
http://www.sjinfo.co.kr
http://www.tit.ac.kr

India
http://budget.allindia.com
http://cdacb.ernet.in
http://gurukul.ucc.american.edu
http://spiderman.bu.edu/misc/india/
http://sunsite.sut.ac/jp/asia/india/
http://www.eepc.gov.in
http://www.incharweb.com
http://www.india-net.com
http://www.india2001.com
http://www.indiagate.com
http://www.indiagov.org
http://www.indiaplus.com
http://www.indiaworld.com/
http://www.inetindia.com
http://www.internetindia.com
http://www.meadev.gov.in
http://www.soft.net/
http://www.tourindia.com

Culture's Web: How Not to Alienate the Aliens

Brian M. Harmer

School of Communications and Information Management, Victoria University of Wellington, New Zealand

Telephone: +64-4-472 1000, Fax: +64-4-495 5235, E-mail: brian.harmer@vuw.ac.nz

INTRODUCTION

We have had a reasonably long time in which to take advantage of the commercial opportunities provided by the Internet in general and the world wide web in particular. Yet there is a perception that many businesses have failed to come to terms with the consequences of the Web. Some businesses saw that new technology would extend the boundaries of their market, yet apparently failed to grasp the meaning of a global reach. Some have chosen consciously to confine themselves to a domestic market despite their use of a channel of communications with global capability. Business is carried out entirely within the cultural environment of the vendor's local market.

A second group operates as if in a purely domestic market, but gratefully accepts trade with foreign customers as a windfall extension to their business. Unless the volume of business which occurs in this manner becomes important to the vendor, it is likely that business will be conducted in the cultural milieu of the vendor.

The third group of businesses are those which perceive that a global network gives access to a global and culturally diverse market, and consciously set out to win the business of customers throughout the world by doing business in a culturally sensitive manner.

This study examines the validity of the third view and some practical aspects of making the transition if it is considered appropriate.

A PRAGMATIC VIEW

According to linguistic studies, a mere 6.4% of the world's population speak English as their first language (Grimes, 1996). Fortunately for most monolingual anglophones, a very large proportion of countries with developed education systems, encourage the learning of English as a second language. However, even if speakers of English as a second language were as numerous as those for whom it is a native language, there is still an enormous percentage of the global population who speak or understand no English at all. Thus at first glance, language appears to be a major issue. However, the most recent IP survey by Network Wizards (1998), shows that 26 million Internet hosts, or 70% of all the hosts in the world are based in the United States of America. This, together with other factors, alters the weight which might otherwise need to be given to the apparently overwhelming language imbalance.

The countries in which the first or dominant language is English, contain 450 million people who enjoy 35% of the world's aggregated GDPs and a quarter of the world's 787 million installed phone lines (Grimes, 1996; ITU, 1998).

Network Wizards' (1998) most recent annual survey finds that there are just over 36 million Internet hosts in the world. Combining these figures with the ITU's (1998) teledensity statistics enables us to look at the market made accessible via the web. Ninety nine percent of all Internet hosts are to be found in the top sixty countries ranked on the basis of the number of Internet hosts per capita. They have 75% of all the world's telephone lines, and a stunning 86% of the world's aggregated GDPs. In very broad overview, the English-speaking countries from the top sixty have 80% of all Internet hosts. Hosts in French language countries account for a further 2%, while German language countries have 4% and Spanish and Portuguese speaking countries just 1% each. Japan has 4% of all Internet Hosts. It must be speculated that the Internet-connected people whose native language is not yet accounted for, are multilingual to a sufficient extent to be able to make functional use of the Internet in one of the dominant languages.

However much social scientists might deplore the skewed distribution of global communication resources, these are the realities of the world in which would be Internet vendors must operate. The table below, which is derived from the ITU and Network Wizards' data, demonstrates that English is, by a very large margin, the dominant language of the Internet.

These figures provide a degree of vindication for the English speaking, US based web developers. They appear to show that a purely domestic approach will suffice to reach the lion's share of the Internet enabled market. However, the 3.4 million hosts in English speaking countries outside the United States of America represent an aggregate GDP of almost US$2.8 trillion and an average per capita income of $16,300. While lower than average US incomes, by world standards, these are affluent nations, and are thus of interest as potential markets.

THE CULTURE PROBLEM

Businesses shape their strategy to respond to the environment in which they operate (Porter, 1980). Where they have

Countries from the top 60 hosts/capita by Language Group	Total Population (millions)	Aggregated GDPs (US$ Billions)	Number of Internet Hosts	% of world total Hosts
English	438.4	10,412.5	29,209,940	79.7%
Japanese	126.2	4,595.2	1,352,200	3.7%
German	90.3	2,581.2	1,286,542	3.5%
French	66.4	1,851.5	643,056	1.8%
Spanish	92.9	966.7	340,200	0.9%
Portuguese	199.8	883.8	209.000	0.6%

a product which is so differentiated from its competition as to be in great demand, they can afford to pick and choose which customers to service. Where there is vigorous competition, businesses generally make more effort to become the preferred supplier. This shift in comparative power between the vendor and customer usually means that the vendor does more to meet the expectations of the customer. The customer, being free to choose among options where all else is more or less equal, is likely to choose the vendor with whom the process of buying provides the most gratification, or perhaps the least offence.

Shopping in "real life" illustrates the point. Few of us will return to an establishment where we have been treated discourteously, or where the service was otherwise poor. If the assistants are inattentive, if pricing information is not clear, if the premises are not clean and tidy, or if we feel in any way that the business is not treating us with respect, it is likely that we will walk out without making a purchase. We need not justify our opinion or subsequent actions to the vendor. Our own perception is everything, and we vote with our feet. There is rarely a second chance for a vendor to make a good first impression. Conversely, good service inspires loyalty, and customers will sometimes pay a premium in order to retain it.

In the context of our own home town, most of us will operate with confidence when it comes to knowing how to interact with courtesy. We know how to be polite because we have grown up immersed in the rules appropriate to our own culture. We have no difficulty saying "Sir" or "Ma'am", "please" or "thank you", or might even invite the customer to "have a nice day". These simple courtesies cost us nothing, and signify to the customer our willingness to afford them respect. If we were to be transported to a foreign environment, we might be less sure of our ground. There are people who don't know when Thanksgiving or Halloween is, who do not appreciate a firm handshake, and who regard direct eye-contact as impolite, or even impertinent. Unless we take the trouble to learn how respect is given in their environment, even in a textual way, we run some risk of offending, or at best failing to impress the customer.

Arguably, the web has placed us in precisely this dilemma. Every wired vendor has been transported by means of technology into the environment of every potential customer. The choice the vendor now has, is whether or not to compete for that customer's business. The brief examination of Internet demographics above, hints that the vendor may be wise to consider which markets are worth competing for. There is little commercial advantage to be had in preparing persuasive arguments for people who can't afford to buy the product or service in the first place. Equally, it is futile to adapt the organization's sales pitch to cultural groups which, because they are not actually Internet-enabled, will never read them.

The use of technology as a form of intermediation introduces new problems of its own. For a variety of reasons, people seem to make less effort to be courteous when communicating through electronic channels. From a vendor perspective this is sometimes manifested in a metaphorical shrug of the shoulders and a "take it or leave it" attitude.

ADAPTATION TO THE MARKET PLACE

In the same way that customers appreciate the ritual courtesies that they encounter in a real life store, on the web they appreciate efforts made by the vendor to acknowledge their existence as an individual. We observe a recognition of this in the provision of fields on web forms for honorifics such as "Mr.", "Dr.", "Ms." or "Mrs.". The principle is extended by the creation of web pages in the native language of the target market. Most organizations which trade globally have such targeted web pages. The Mazda organization's web site (http://www.mazda.com) is a good example of this practice, with links to points of presence in nineteen different countries, using the appropriate language for each, and in the cases of Canada and Switzerland, they are appropriately bilingual.

A common irritant to non-US web surfers is the bland assumption that many aspects of the American culture or infrastructure apply elsewhere. Consumer protection law varies from country to country. Trade regulations also vary. In Germany, for example, vendors may not process credit card transactions until two weeks after delivery of the goods or service. This is a considerable disincentive to web based trade. Product restrictions vary between jurisdictions, and items which are legal in the US are not necessarily acceptable elsewhere. An automotive security device which consists of an electrified steering lock is easily available in the United States, but is outlawed as a "prohibited weapon" in New Zealand. On the other hand, citizens of countries other than the United States have little or no ethical dilemma when it comes to doing business with Cuba.

Unless the newly launched "Euro" currency makes inroads, the United States dollar reigns supreme as a safe and acceptable currency for international trade, though this presents some difficulty for organizations based outside the United States. It is generally a condition of doing business with credit card companies, that merchants must raise transactions in their local currency. This can be a disincentive to potential buyers to whom prices in unfamiliar units seem high. Furthermore, it presents a risk to the buyer if the local currency is more volatile than the comparatively stable US dollar.

Sometimes simple assumptions cause intense frustration to local buyers. Not all countries have a federal system of government, so that customers in such countries have no use for a field which specifies "state". Many web sites have forms on which the state code is a mandatory entry (Mosley-Matchett, 1997). Even worse, such forms often require the customer to select one from a pull down list of the 50 states. The customer is thus required, not to deal with an irrelevant field, but also to enter a spurious value. Pull down lists in themselves present a danger, if all the appropriate options for international trade are not covered. More than one web designer decided that Australia was a sufficient approximation for the residents of New Zealand. This is akin to suggesting that Canada and the United States are synonymous. Likewise, zip codes are far from universal, though they too are mandatory fields in a number of web forms.

A television viewer in Hershey PA would be surprised, and after the first novelty had passed, annoyed if persistent advertising appeared for a hairdresser in Petaluma CA. The same danger arises on banner ads and supplementary windows associated with commercial web sites. A New Zealand researcher might be understandably frustrated by such a supplementary window which advertises a bargain hotel room in Boston, near the Tea Party ship. Regardless of the bargain this might represent to people in the North Eastern states of America, it is outrageously irrelevant to the inhabitants of the South Pacific. Another source of potential irritation is the difference in seasons and time zones. An American organization promoting their mid-winter bargains in December might easily overlook the fact that customers in Australia, Brazil, Argentina, South Africa and New Zealand are enjoying the warmth of mid summer. Time zones are generally less of a problem unless customer service is an issue. A desperate customer on a Monday morning in Australia or New Zealand may well be exasperated to discover that it is still Sunday in California, and nobody is answering e-mails, or even the telephone.

Differences such as these remind the buyer that the vendor is thinking domestically, and gives some grounds for the buyer to experience the same kind of frustration which occurs when a face to face shopper is ignored by sales staff.

CONCLUSIONS

It is up to the vendor to decide how hard to try to avoid alienating potential customers. Conceivably, if the product is so exotic, or represents such value for money by comparison with local options, then the potential international customer might overlook all but the most direct provocations. Is the cost of the added complexity of web sites, and the additional level of required interaction with distant customers worth the added revenue? Some vendors, most notably Amazon.com and Dell Computers have aimed at an international market from the outset. Others such as Egghead, have expanded their reach slowly and cautiously.

This exploration draws attention to some interesting areas for future research, including a scrutiny of the processes for a more rigorous analysis of the potential benefits and problems of entry to each national market.

REFERENCES

Grimes, B.F.(Ed.) (1996). *Ethnologue: Languages of the world.* International Academic Bookstore.

ITU (1997). *Telecommunications industry at a glance: Basic indicators: population, GDP, main telephone line and main lines per 100 people, 1997* [Online] Available: http://www.itu.int/ti/industryoverview/at_glance/basic.pdf Accessed 10 January, 1999

Mosley-Matchett, J.D. (1997). Remember it's the world wide web. In *Marketing News.* 31 (2): 16. January 20

Network Wizards (1998). *Internet Domain Survey, July 1998.* [Online] Available: http://nw.com/zone/WWW/report.html

Porter, M.E. (1980). *Competitive strategy: Techniques for analysing industries and competitors.* New York: The Free Press, 1980

NETNEWS Classification via Batch Routing and Updates

Wen-Lin Hsu and Sheau-Dong Lang
School of Computer Science, University of Central Florida, Orlando, FL 32816-2362
{hsu, lang}@cs.ucf.edu, TEL: (407) 823-2524, FAX: (407) 823-5419

ABSTRACT

We propose a batch scheme for categorizing NETNEWS articles and updating the news database. We use two inverted lists, one to store the training dictionary, and the other to buffer the new articles, for updating and routing purposes. Our experimental results using real NETNEWS articles and newsgroups demonstrate (1) the batch technique improves the efficiency of both routing and updating operations; and (2) updating improves the routing accuracy and the database storage.

1. INTRODUCTION

As large amounts of information and data are represented in textual form, text categorization and retrieval become increasingly important issues in today's information society. Text classification (categorization) is the process of deciding the appropriate categories for a given document. Classification tasks include determining the topic area of an essay [1]; deciding what folder an email message should be directed to [6]; and deciding what newsgroup an article belongs to [10]. This last task is the focus of the present paper.

The performance of a news dissemination and storage system is measured by its efficiency in time and space requirements, and by its effectiveness in routing the news articles to the proper categories. Routing news articles one at a time is neither efficient nor realistic. This is because groups of related articles often are submitted at the same time, and because routing in batch mode is more efficient, when the batch size is controlled appropriately. An issue related to routing concerns the subjects being discussed in the newsgroups. Since new terms and new topic groups may occur and outdated terms should expire, it is beneficial to update the term structures periodically in order to maintain a high level of routing accuracy. However, updating the internal representation after receiving each new article is inefficient and does not necessarily improve the accuracy. Therefore, batching techniques could also be applied to updating the internal representation.

In this paper, we propose a batch scheme for categorizing NETNEWS articles and updating the news database. Our implementation is based on the vector space model commonly used in information retrieval systems [1]. In this model, we first extract the distinct words out of each article, discard the insignificant words based on a standard stoplist [1], and apply a standard stemming algorithm to transform the words to their stems [1]. Then, each news article is represented by a vector of the terms (stems) the article contains and, similarly, each newsgroup is represented by a vector of the terms that belong to the articles of the newsgroup. Standard similarity measures between the term vectors can be used to select the newsgroup that is most similar to each news article. Since there is a large number of terms involved in a news database, we are interested in the issues of reducing the storage requirements and improving the news routing efficiency, by applying the batching techniques.

The remainder of the paper is organized as follows. Section 2 briefly describes the most relevant work. Section 3 explains our implementation details. Section 4 reports the experimental results of routing the news articles and updating the news database, by using real NETNEWS articles and newsgroups. Finally, Section 5 concludes the paper and points out directions for further research.

2. RELATED WORK

Several applications of text classification to NETNEWS articles have been reported in the literature. The Newsweeder project [4] uses user relevance feedback to classify future documents. The work reported in [10] classifies news articles based on the existing newsgroup categories. It uses the IR system SMART [7] as the underlying system, and a learning technique that forms "metadocuments" to represent the topics. In [2], the authors investigate automatic web page categorization for IR systems using the knowledge base (KB) technique. In order to reduce the size of the KB and to speed up the processing time, three methods using weights to filter out less-important words are used in their experiments.

The work in [3] explores the use of Support Vector Machines (SVM) for learning text classifiers from examples; a related work applies the Bayesian approach to filtering junk mails [6]. A recent work [9] describes a technique of incremental updates of the inverted lists for text document retrieval. Two kinds of the inverted lists are maintained: shorter inverted lists are maintained in memory while longer lists are kept on the disk. Periodically, the longest memory-bound lists are written to the disk. Another work [11] concentrates on the removal of redundant words using corpus statistics in text categorization. Each word in the training text is associated with a "word strength" indicating its importance. Work has also been done on batch updates in B-trees [5] for efficiency purposes. It is shown how searches in B-trees can be performed concurrently with batch updates to improve the system performance.

3. OUR METHOD

Our implementation uses the inverted list structure to represent the newsgroup articles and the terms they contain. We use the standard tf-idf weighting formula to compute the similarity between the articles and the newsgroups, in order to route the articles to the proper newsgroups [1]. Basically, for each term i and each newsgroup q, the term frequency tf_{iq} is the total number of times term i occurs in newsgroup q. Similarly, the inverse document frequency idf_i of term i gives a value that is inversely proportional to the number of newsgroups that contain term i. Each newsgroup q is represented by a vector of weights w_{iq} with i ranging over all the terms i contained in the newsgroup q, defined as follows:

$$ w_{iq} = \left(0.5 + \frac{0.5t\, f_q}{maxt\, f_q} \right) \times idf_i $$

Similarly, each news article d is represented by a vector of weights w_{id} with i ranging over all the terms i contained in the article d. The similarity between a newsgroup (vector Q) and a news article (vector D) is computed using the following Cosine coefficient formula:

$$ similarity(Q, D) = \frac{\sum_{i=1}^{n} (w_{iq} \times w_{id})}{\sqrt{\sum_{i=1}^{n} w_{iq}^2 \times \sum_{i=1}^{n} w_{id}^2}} $$

The inverted list is implemented as an array of term structures, in which each term structure contains the term and its associated statistics. In addition, each term is associated with a newsgroup (NG) list containing the newsgroups in which the term occurs. Both routing and updating utilize an inverted list to store the dictionary terms. In addition, a second inverted list is used to buffer the newly arrived articles during routing and updating. Hashing is used to insert terms into both structures to ensure near-constant search time. Figure 1 shows the structure of the inverted list used in our experiments.

Through extensive experiments, we determine the optimal number of articles to be buffered before updating and routing. In the process of updating the structure, we first include the new terms and new topic groups into the term structure. We then eliminate unwanted terms, which could be the least important, misspelled, or "outdated" terms, i.e., terms that only occur for a short period of time. We keep the "core" terms that persistently occur over a long period of time. These words represent the newsgroups and need to be represented in the term structure.

4. EXPERIMENTAL RESULTS

We performed experiments using the NETNEWS articles from the following six newsgroups: "rec", "arts", "autos", "music", "travel", and "food". These groups have 519, 96, 16, 20, 8, and 12 sub-newsgroups, and 243359, 82183, 70167, 27828, 17986, and 14588 terms, respectively. These articles were the news articles submitted to NETNEWS from June through August of 1997 in the newsgroups specified above.. We use the articles in June to train the term structure, and use the articles in July and August to test the performance in our experiments. Figure 2 shows parts of the hierarchy of the newsgroup categories.

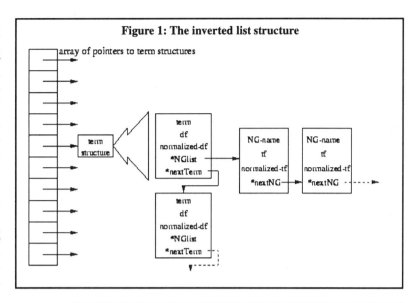

Figure 1: The inverted list structure

4.1. Routing Articles

Our first experiment investigates the performance in execution time of routing the news articles, using buffers of different sizes to batch the articles. Figure 2 plots the routing time in batch mode with buffer sizes of 10, 20, 50, 100, 200, and 500. The vertical axis of the figure shows the relative time required for batch routing with 1 being the routing time with zero buffering, and the horizontal axis represents the batch (buffer) size. As can be seen in the figure, the routing time improves when the batch size increases to a threshold value, around 50 to 100, beyond which some routing times deteriorate to that of using no buffers. The decreased efficiency can be attributed to the computational overhead of setting up and maintaining the buffer.

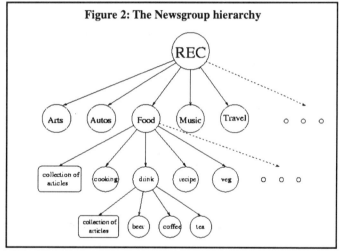

Figure 2: The Newsgroup hierarchy

4.2. Updating The Term Structures

Since new terms and new topic groups may occur and outdated terms should expire, it is beneficial to update the term structures periodically in order to maintain a high level of routing accuracy. There are two issues involved in updating the term structures. One is about adding new terms and groups into the term structure to keep the training structure up to date; the other is about removing the outdated terms to improve the storage requirement and efficiency. Our next experiment investigates the effects on routing accuracy of adding new terms and new topic groups. Table 1 shows the results (routing accuracy) of applying this update strategy using different batch sizes. The batch size *n1* varies from 0 (no buffering) to 500 for 5 of the newsgroups, but varies from 0 to 5000 for the newsgroup *rec* because it is a much larger newsgroup (more sub-newsgroups and news articles). We notice that the routing accuracy increases as the batch size increases, but the improvement levels off when the batch size becomes large.

Updating the term structure by adding the new terms and groups always improves the routing accuracy. However, there is a trade-off between the time and space requirements vs. the routing accuracy, because updating without removing the terms would make the term structure continue to grow in size. Figure 4 shows the percentage of increases in time and storage when the term structure is updated in every 100 articles (1000 articles for newsgroup *rec*). The vertical axis represents the percentage of the increases, using the time and space of no updating as the baseline.

Our third experiment studies the effects on routing accuracy of deleting the outdated terms. Table 2 shows the results of routing accuracy with varying update frequencies. The buffer size *n1* indicates the number of articles that are buffered before the term structure is updated; every *n2* such updates we scan the term structure for outdated terms and delete them.

We should comment that removing words too frequently (*n2* is small) may eliminate the core words in the dictionary; hurting the routing accuracy. On the other hand, removing words too infrequently makes routing inefficient in time and space requirements. Thus, reducing the size of the term structure by removing outdated terms at appropriate times makes updating more efficient without sacrificing accuracy.

Figure 5 shows the improvement in time and storage requirements by removing words after every 10 updates where each update buffers 100 articles. The vertical axis shows the percentage of reduction in time and memory space.

5. CONCLUSION AND FUTURE WORK

In this paper, we proposed a batch scheme for categorizing NETNEWS articles and updating the news database. Our experimental results showed that routing the news articles in batch mode is more efficient compared to routing individually, when the batch size is chosen properly. We also studied the overhead in time and space when the term structures are updated periodically. Adding new terms and deleting outdated terms both improve the routing accuracy. Since the latter also reduces the storage requirements, it could offset some of the updating overhead.

Incremental updating is not a novel technique in information retrieval applications. In text categorization, AI/Learning techniques involving complex computations have been reported in the literature [8, 10]. Our approach of updating the news articles is very simple because it uses the time as the single factor to determine the updating frequency. As future work, we plan to perform a systematic study on how to choose an optimal batch size for routing the news articles and

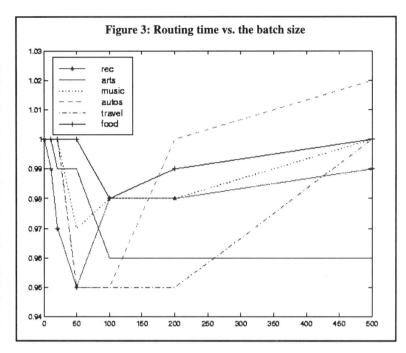

Figure 3: Routing time vs. the batch size

Table 1: Routing accuracy vs. the update batch size

n 1	0	500	1000	2000	5000
rec	23%	*27%*	27%	27%	26%

n 1	0	50	100	200	500
arts	27%	31%	*31%*	31%	31%
music	28%	33%	*33%*	33%	33%
autos	29%	*29%*	28%	27%	27%
travel	34%	42%	42%	*42%*	40%
food	26%	*61%*	60%	58%	53%

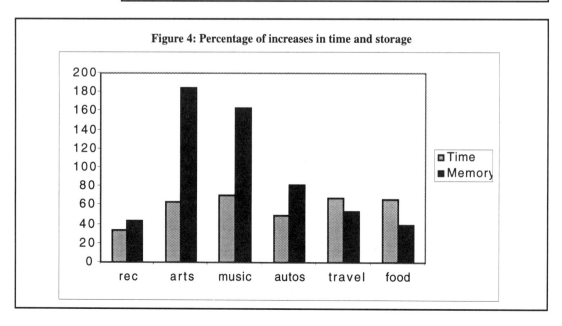

Figure 4: Percentage of increases in time and storage

Table 2: Routing accuracy vs. updates and term removal				
n1/n2	500/10	500/100	1000/10	2000/1
rec	26%	**28%**	27%	27%

n1/n2	50/10	50/100	100/10	200/1
arts	27%	**32%**	29%	31%
music	27%	**33%**	30%	33%
autos	29%	29%	**30%**	29%
travel	41%	**42%**	42%	42%
food	60%	**60%**	59%	58%

Figure 5: Percentage of improvements in time and storage

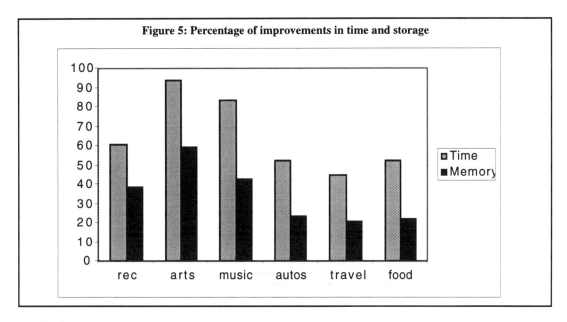

updating the term structures.

REFERENCES:

1. W.B. Frakes, and R. Baeza-Yates, *Information Retrieval: Data Structures & Algorithms*, Prentice Hall, 1992.
2. H. Mase. "Experiments on Automatic Web Page Categorization for IR system", technical report, Stanford University, 1998.
3. T. Joachims. "Text Categorization with Support Vector Machine: Learning with Many Relevant features", *Proceedings of ECML*, 1998.
4. K. Lang. "Newsweeder: Learning to Filter NETNEWS", *Proceedings 12th International Conference on Machine Learning*, pp. 331-339, July 1995.
5. K. Pollari-Malmi, E. Soisalon-Soininen, and T. Ylönen. "Concurrency Control in B-Trees with Batch Updates", *IEEE Trans. Knowledge and Data Eng.*, 8:6, Dec. 1996.
6. M. Sahami, S. Dumais, D. Heckerman, and E. Horvitz. "A Bayesian approach to filtering junk e-mail", *Proceedings of AAAI'98 Workshop on Learning for Text Categorization*, 1998, Madison, Wisconsin.
7. **G. Salton. *The SMART Retrieval System - Experiments in Automatic Document Processing*, Prentice Hall, 1971.**
8. S. Scott, and S. Matwin. "Text Classification Using WordNet Hypernyms", *Proceedings of the Workshop on WordNet in Nat. Lang. Proc. Sys.*, 1998.
9. A. Tomasic, H. Garcia-Molina, and K. Shoens, "Incremental Updates of Inverted Lists for Text Document Retrieval", *Proceedings of SIGMOD*, 1994.
10. S.A. Weiss, S. Kasif, and E. Brill, "Text Classification in USENET Newsgroups: A Progress Report", *Proceedings of the AAAI Spring Symposium on Machine Learning in Information Access*, 1996
11. Y. Yang, "Using Corpus Statistics to Remove Redundant Words in Text Categorization" *JASIS*, 1996.

One Method for Highpass Minimum-phase Filter Design

Gordana Jovanovic-Dolecek and Guillermo Espinosa Flores-Verdad
INAOE, Department for Electronics, P.O.Box 51&216, Puebla, Pue. Mexico
Phone and fax: + (22) 47-05-17, Email:gordana@inaoep.mx , gespino@inaoep.mx

ABSTRACT

A new practical design approach for highpass minimum phase FIR filter design is presented. The method uses the interpolated FIR (IFIR) technique, and the mipizing process. The cascade of combs and integrators (CIC) is used as an image suppressor in IFIR structure. The novelty of this technique is that mipizing is applied only on the shaping filter.

1. INTRODUCTION

The design of FIR linear phase filters is often an attractive alternative to its IIR equivalent. For some applications, such as in telecommunications, the high-degree FIR filters introduce the unacceptable high delay. Much lower delay time can be achieved with minimum phase (MP) filters that satisfy the same amplitude specifications. This is why the design of minimum-phase FIR filters has become an important issue, [1]. The design of MP FIR filters, which starts with a high order linear phase (LP), has many advantages, [2]. Having designed the high-order LP filter, it is necessary to find its Z-plane roots, and to fold all zeros which lie outside the unit circle to their reciprocal radius position, *(mipizing process)*. The problem arises in applying the mipizing process to a high order filter. In order to overcome this problem (in [3]), we proposed the use of Interpolated FIR (IFIR) filters.

The basic idea of IFIR filters is to implement a high order FIR filter as a cascade of two FIR sections of a much less order. In Fig. 1 is given a two-stage IFIR structure for the design of a lowpass filter.

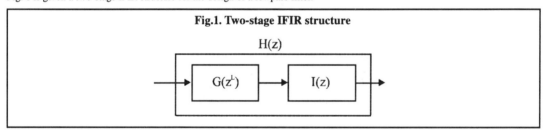

Fig.1. Two-stage IFIR structure

H(z)

$G(z^L)$ I(z)

The filter $G(z)$ is the *shaping filter*, and $I(z)$ is the *interpolator or image suppressor*, which is designed to attenuate extra-unwanted passbands of $G(z^L)$. The filter $G(z^L)$ is obtained by introducing L-1 zeros between each sample of the unit sample response of the filter $G(z)$. The design of the filters $G(z)$ and $I(z)$ is given in [4]. The filters $G(z)$ and $I(z)$ have much less order than the prototype filter, and so the process of mipizing can be easily applied. If the filter $G_i(z)$ is mipized then the corresponding filter is mipized too, [3].

The compression of the spectrum reduces the computational complexity by a factor of L, but we must also add in the complexity given by the design of the filter $I(z)$. In this paper we propose to use cascaded integrators and combs (CIC), as the interpolation filter.

2. IFIR-CIC STRUCTURE

The system function of the CIC filter is given as

$$H(z) = \left(\frac{1}{L} \frac{1-z^{-L}}{1-z^{-1}} \right)^K = \frac{1}{L} \sum_{n=0}^{L-1} z^{-n} \tag{1}$$

where K is called the *stage*. As it is seen in equation (1), all coefficients are equal to 1, and therefore it is not needed to perform any multiplication. All zeros are on the unit circle. Thus, the CIC filter is naturally a MP filter, and it is not necessary to apply the process of mipizing. The frequency response of the CIC filter can be expressed as

$$H(e^{j\omega}) = \left\{ \frac{\sin \frac{\omega L}{2}}{L \sin \frac{\omega}{2}} e^{-j\omega[(L-1)/2]} \right\}^K \tag{2}$$

Therefore, this is a linear phase low pass filter. The frequency response has nulls at integer multiples of $2\pi / L$. This makes it a natural candidate for eliminating images introduced by $G(z^L)$, provided that the baseband of the filter $G(z^L)$ is a narrowband. The proposed IFIR–CIC structure is given in Fig.2.

This algorithm is composed of three main stages. First, the IFIR-CIC structure of the corresponding LP filter is designed. In the second step the mipizing is applied on the shaping filter. Finally, lowpass filters are transformed into highpass filters, changing the sign of every second coefficient of the corresponding impulse response. Therefore, the CIC filter is transformed into a highpass filter. The mipized shaping filter is transformed into a high pass filter only if L is odd, [4]. The Remez algorithm is used for the design of the $G(z)$ filter. The entire structure of both $G(z)$ and $I(z)$, is implemented in MATLAB.

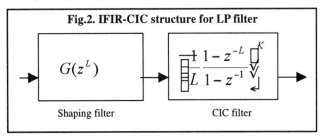

Fig.2. IFIR-CIC structure for LP filter

$$G(z^L)$$

$$\left[\frac{1}{L}\frac{1-z^{-L}}{1-z^{-1}}\right]^K$$

Shaping filter   CIC filter

Example 1.

We designed a highpass MP filter with $\omega_p = .99, \omega_s = .97$, passband ripple .25, and the stopband attenuation 60 dB. The prototype LP filter has an order of N=248. The MP filter has been designed using the IFIR-CIC structure. For L=8 and K=3 the order of the shaping filter was 30. The results of the design are given in Fig.3.

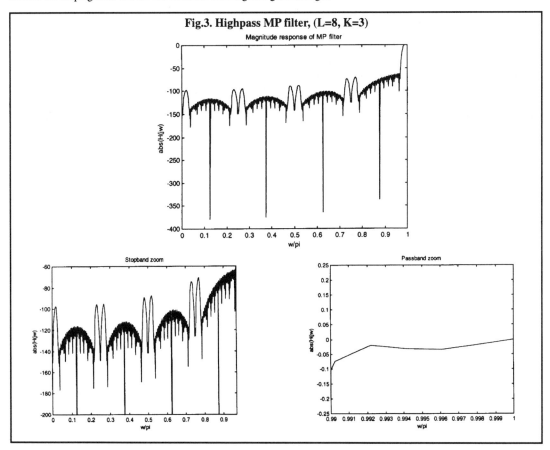

Fig.3. Highpass MP filter, (L=8, K=3)

The group delays of both prototype linear-phase filter and the designed minimum phase filter are given in the Fig.4.

3. CONCLUSION

In conclusion we can say that the proposed approach presents an efficient alternative to existing procedures for the design of highpass FIR minimum phase filters of a very high order. We propose to use the mipizing technique on the IFIR structure. Cascaded integrators and combs (CIC) are used as an interpolation filter in the IFIR structure. Thereby, the mipizing is only necessary to apply on the shaping filter, which has much less order than the prototype linear phase filter. The computational complexity is significantly

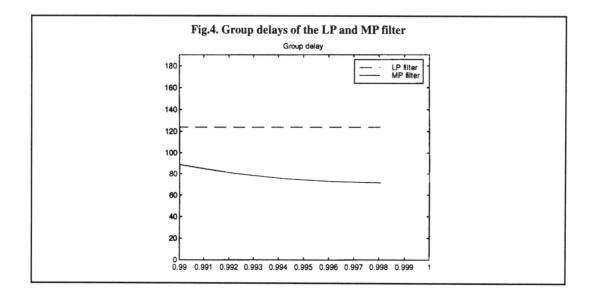

Fig.4. Group delays of the LP and MP filter

decreased because CIC structure does not require any multiplication. The main disadvantage is that the CIC filter has a very wide transition band, but a very narrow passband, so its intended usage is only for narrowband highpass MP filters. In addition, it is possible to adjust the number of stages K of the CIC filter in order to satisfy the magnitude specification.

Acknowledgement: This work was supported by a CONACYT grant, number 211290-5-3009PA

REFERENCES
[1] R. Boite, H. Leich, "A new procedure for the design of high order minimum phase FIR digital or CCD filter", Signal Processing, North Holland Publishing Company, pp.103-108, No.3, 1981.

[2] I.Kale, G.D. Cain and R.C.S. Morling, "Minimum-phase filter design from linear-phase start point via balanced model truncation", Electronics Letters, pp 1728-1729, Vol.31, No20, Sept.1995.

[3] G.Jovanovic-Dolecek, J.Diaz Carmona, "Low-pass minimum phase filters design using IFIR filters", Electronic Letters, pp.1933-1935, vol.33, No.23, 6th November 1997.

[4] Nuevo, Y., Dong, C.Y, and Mitra S.K, "Interpolated finite impulse response filters", IEEE Trans. on Acoustic Speech and Signal Processing, vol. ASSP-32, pp.563-570, June 1984.

Work Stress Factors Among Information Systems Professionals in Manitoba

Eugene Kaluzniacky

Business Computing, University of Winnipeg, 4M60 - 515 Portage Ave., Winnipeg, Manitoba, Canada, R3B 2E9

Ph: 1-204-786-9417, Fax: 1-204-786-1824, e-mail: eugene.kaluzniacky@uwinnipeg.ca

ABSTRACT

The purpose of this research in progress is to assess the degree of reported job stress among IS professionals in Winnipeg, Manitoba, Canada and other Manitoba centres, and to determine which hypothesized factors are reported by a majority of employees as being major contributors to their stress. Analysis will then be carried out to investigate a significant relationship between reported degrees of experienced stress, perceived stress factors, and personal characteristics of the employee, the computing environment (technical and managerial) and the employing organization.

INTRODUCTION

The first phase of this project has consisted of a literature survey and a series of interviews with selected local IS workers. This effort has provided a clearer understanding of factors and issues to include in a "Stress Assessment Questionnaire". The second phase has involved development, testing and administration of the survey instrument. This is still being carried out. The finalhase will encompass data entry, data tabulation and analysis along with identification and presentation of noteworthy results.

Insights from this exploratory research should be of significant value to middle and higher-level Information Systems managers as well as to Human Resource staff. Organizations which are expecting a significant contribution to effectiveness and competitive advantage from investments in innovative information technologies should indeed be interested in maintaining a work atmosphere conducive to creative effort. Also, this initial work is expected to give rise to other, related research studies and to initiate practical efforts in education and support for affected Information Systems personnel.

MOTIVATION FOR RESEARCH

"Organizational effectiveness" is a common phrase in today's business management environments. Economic conditions and technological capacity are initiating comprehensive re-organization of many businesses, large and small. The "Total Quality Management" concept is being increasingly promoted. In this setting, organizational Information Systems departments are often themselves being downsized and re-engineered in order to support cost-effectively new organizational structures and strategic directions.

With basic, computerized reporting systems mostly in place, IS professionals are being relied upon to produce, with often demanding deadlines, innovative computer applications which enhance the competitive position. In addition, the IS workers are faced with rapidly and continuously changing technologies and methodologies, a phenomenon likely not evidenced before in history. While technological change has had an impact on individuals in many professions, this change is even more immediate, more direct for the IS worker. He / she is often forced to change working languages, equipment, and even entire development paradigms amidst comprehensive re-structuring with its initial ambiguities and amidst ever increasing demands.

Few professionals are faced with as much direct obsolescence of key skills as are computer programmers. Moreover, the change required in skills and in entire mind set (as, for example, in the object-oriented paradigm) is not a one-time occurrence. As pointed out by noted IS consultant Ed Yourdon in his "career survival" newsletter, today's software engineers face a real dilemma: "What's the point in learning to be really good at something if it's going to become obsolete at the rate of 20% per year?" [22].

Also, North American computer professionals collectively are facing increasing competition from counterparts in India, South America, Russia, etc., since programs can be written and tested for a fraction of the cost in such locations and transmitted electronically to the required site[21]. Change and uncertainty have undoubtedly characterized the working climate for today's IS professional. Furthermore, the effectiveness of potentially impactful computer applications often depends on successful, synergistic communication between systems analysts (developers) and organizational managers (end-users). As evident in considerable literature, such communication is often severely hampered by profoundly differing perspectives on the organization held by managers and systems analysts. For the IS analyst, there is the pressure to use a (communication) skill in which he often has had little training. On the other hand, the user, often, may have little appreciation for the environment and work detail of the analyst and may impose what the analyst feels are unrealistic deadlines and expectations.

Thus, there is considerable reason to believe that the IS professional (applications programmer, data or systems analyst etc.) today is significantly more at risk of serious "burnout" than his counterpart of 20-25 years ago. In his 1984 effort, Technostress [2], Craig Brod points out that "high performance (requirements) with high technology can exercise a dangerous influence on the human personality... anyone who is constantly working or playing with computers is at risk". Psychologist Mary Riley points out dysfunctional behaviours arising when "high touch has not kept up with high tech". Khosrowpour and Culpan[11] have published a stress-related study applied to individuals working in computer-related fields. In it, they remark: "Information processing professionals see change in technology as a pre-requisite for their existence, yet the speed of this change can have profound psychological and physiological effects". In their survey with 231 responses, "a large majority agreed with the statements that change in computer technology creates pressure". The authors conclude that " the men and women who plan, design, and monitor these systems have experienced greater technostress in their jobs and environments". Such technostress is not at all likely to disappear in the foreseeable future.

Recently, an April, 1997 article by Robert Glass in Communications of the ACM [5], reports programmer stress as being "extremely common and extremely problematic" and points out that ".. deep thinking is easily affected by stress". Locally, a number of IS professionals have echoed concerns about rising stress levels in their jobs and have indicated their willingness to be part of a concerted effort to provide stress relief. However, it is felt that before such a problem can be addressed with adequate, practical assistance, the existing problem must be better understood. Although considerable stress research literature exists in the context of organizational management in general, specific stress studies applied to the computer field are not abundant. In addition to the above quoted study, Ivancevich, Napier, and Wetherbe reported on "An Empirical Study of Occupational Stress, Attitudes, and Health Among Information System Employees"[8]. Stress management articles, such as the one by Kleiner and Geil[12], Engler[3], and Fujigaki[4] have appeared in computer professionals' journals.

RESEARCH METHODOLOGY

This research attempts to expand on the work of Khosrowpour and Culpan in analyzing not only the stress effects of rapid technological change, but also of factors such as re-structuring and / or downsizing of the IS department, apparent obsolescence of skills, stringent user deadlines, and lack of management support. Relationship between geographical location (Winnipeg vs. other Manitoba centres) and degree of reported stress can be examined. Results of this initial effort can provide valuable insight for IS workers, their managers, and also for other Information Systems researchers.

Literature review

The first phase of this project has involved a survey of stress-related research literature, particularly as applied to work in business organizations. Relevant articles have been collected, classified, and summarized (e.g., Igbaria et al.[6], Li and Shani[13], Singh[16], Sonnentag et al.[17], and Weiss[19]). Attempts were made to extract information as to: i) perceived causes of work stress (e.g. Jick and Burke[10]), ii) personal factors related to experienced work stress, iii) categorization of identified stressors (e.g. Ivancevich and Matteson[9]) and iv) effectiveness of efforts initiated to reduce occupational stress (e.g. Newman and Beehr [14]). Such a preliminary orientation provides an initial frame of reference for current work and could also initiate a "clearinghouse", possibly Web-based, of occupational stress related literature for specific stress management programs for IS professionals in the future.

Stress models applied to IS

In literature attempting to analyze stress within the IS profession, it is accepted that occupational stress is related chiefly to the interaction of the person factors with work environment factors. Ivancevich et al. [7] propose a model which first identifies Work Environment Stressors as related to i) Job (time pressures, job scope, obsolescence), ii) Role (ambiguity, conflict) iii) Career (development) and iv) Organization (rewards, change, communication). They then identify Person (Individual) Factors such as self-confidence,ecisiveness, tolerance of ambiguity and locus of control. Stress ("the physical or psychological condition of a person that puts him or her under strain, and that threatens the person by stimulating him or her beyond their limits"[1]) arises from the interaction of Work Environment and Person Factors and results in Outcomes which can be classified as i) Psychological (satisfaction, commitment, tension), ii) Physical / Behavioural (blood pressure, cholesterol, smoking, drinking) and iii) Organizational (absenteeism, turnover). Young [20], in histudy, has also applied an adapted version of this model. Wastell and Newman [18] present an eclectic model of work-related stress and organizational behaviour similar to the one above, cast in cause-effect terms. It identifies Sources of Stress at Work (physical working conditions, role factors, interpersonal conflict, over/under promotion, job insecurity and organizational change). These sources interact with Individual Characteristics, Organizational Context, and Work Group Factors, yielding Individual Symptoms (e.g., poor health, absenteeism, resistance to change, ego defense mechanisms) as well as Group Symptoms (e.g., groupthink, internecine strife).

Stress questionnaire

The second phase of the research involves the development of a "Stress Assessment Questionnaire" to be distributed to different types of IS workers in Winnipeg, Manitoba, Canadand other Manitoba centres (e.g., Portage, Brandon, The Pas, Thompson, Churchill). The questionnaire, to be answered anonymously, is motivated by an adaptation of the model of Ivancevich et al. Work Environment factors considered include location (Winnipeg, or smaller centres), full or part-time work, and type of organization / industry, as well as rapid change in technology and methodology. Person factors include highest level of formal education, motivation factors related to the Enneagram personality types [15], and degree of emotional dependency on the job. Outcomes consider common physical symptoms as well as commonly experienced feelings. There is an opportunity for the person to assess (on a 7-point Likert scale) the degree of his / her experienced job stress, the degree of severity of common symptoms, and the degree of perceived contribution to this stress of commonly identified factors. Some of these factors are general enough to apply to a variety of occupations, while others are related specifically to facets of IS work.

In addition, respondents are asked for an assessment of their decreased productivity due to excessive work stress and for an identification of four most prominent stress factors. Respondents are also asked to identify and assess stress-relieving techniques which they have tried seriously. As well, they are asked to rank working condition improvements which would likely reduce their stress significantly and to identify most desirable IS stress relief efforts which could be undertaken by employing organizations and professional associations.

PRELIMINARY RESULTS

Questionnaire distribution has been ongoing since January, 1998. To date, over 60 responses have been received and preliminary tabulations have been done. Over 200 responses are expected at the completion of the survey. Following are initial highlights:

How stressful is your current position?
Stressful	- 34%
?	- 17%
Not that stressful	- 49%

How close to burnout are you?
Not close	- 70%
?	- 11%
Close	- 18%

How reasonable are your deadlines?
Reasonable	- 45%
?	- 11%
Not reasonable	- 43%

Is rapid change a characteristic of your job?
Yes	- 67%
?	- 11%
No	- 22%

Has IS stress level increased in the last 8 years?
No	- 10%
Moderately	- 23%
Significantly	- 47%
Dramatically	- 20%

Why has it increased?
Rapid changes, need to perform more with less, increase in computer use, unrealistic expectations of users...

Commonly experienced feelings:
frustration
pride in accomplishments
being overwhelmed
anxiety

Common stress symptoms:
decrease in energy
anxiety
muscle tension
headaches
upset stomach
negative thinking
insomnia

Effective techniques for de-stressing:
aerobic exercise
relaxing music
massage
prayer

Are IS managers not aware enough of employee stress?
Yes	- 39%
?	- 28%
No	- 33%

Is there significant absenteeism due to stress?
Yes	- 54%

?	- 30%
No	- 16%

Should there be a specific effort to combat stress in the IS profession?

Yes	- 50%
?	- 31%
No	- 19%

While the above are preliminary results with over 80% of responses coming from one company, some points are noteworthy. It does not appear that stress is affecting nearly everyone of the respondents. There seems to be a group of fairly satisfied workers who are energized by their work. However, a significant fraction is reporting stress symptoms which will likely continue to impede their work performance. Absenteeism may be an increasing problem. Also, it is worth noting that 50% of the respondents favour a concerted effort to combat stress within the IS profession.

Further analysis should provide insight into questions such as: i) what is the motivation level of different types of IS workers, as well as the main motivating factor, ii) how close are the individuals to "burnout", and do they feel likely to develop a serious illness within x years, iii) what are the common perceived stress factors among IS professionals (rapid change, unreasonable deadlines, work overload, lack of feedback etc.), iv) what are the common experienced stress symptoms, v) what are the most common feelings experienced by IS personnel at work, and do these differ with position type, vi) what stress relief techniques have been seriously tried, and with what degree of success, viii) should IS personnel be managed differently than other business personnel, and ix)what are the main working condition improvements that employing organizations could initiate.

Subsequent analysis would provide crosstabulation with various demographic characteristics of the respondents to highlight areas of statistical significance.

REFERENCES

[1] Bonoma, T.V., and Zaltsman, G, Psychology for Management, Kent Publishing Company, Boston, 1981.

[2] Brod, Craig, Technostress, Addison-Wesley, 1984.

[3] Engler, Natalie, "IS Managers Under Stress", Open Computing, January, 1995.

[4] Fujigaki, Yuko, "Stress Analysis: A New Perspective on Peopleware", American Programmer, July, 1993.

[5] Glass, Robert L., "The Ups and Downs of Programmer Stress", Communications of the ACM, April, 1997.

[6] Igbaria, M. et al., "Work Experience, Job Involvement, and Quality of Work Life Among Information Systems Personnel", MIS Quarterly, June, 1994.

[7] Ivancevich, John, Napier, H., and Wetherbe, J. "Occupational Stress, Attitudes and Health Problems in the Information Systems Professional", Communications of the ACM, October, 1983.

[8] Ivancevich, John, Napier, H., and Wetherbe, J. "An Empirical Study of Occupational Stress, Attitudes and Health Among Information Systems Personnel",Information & Management 9(1985).

[9] Ivancevich, John, and Matteson, M. "Organizational Level Stress Management Interventions: A Review and Recommendations", Stress Management Interventions, 1987.

[10] Jick, Todd, and Burke, R. "Occupational Stress: Recent Findings and New Directions", Journal of Occupational Behaviour, Vol. 3. 1-3, 1982.

[1 1] Khosrowpour, Mehdi, and Culpan, O. "The Impact of Management Support and Education: Easing the Causality Between Change and Stress in Computing Environments", Journal of Educational Technology Systems, Vol. 18(1), 1989-90.

[12] Kleiner, Brian, and Geil, Stephen, "Managing Stress Effectively", Journal of Systems Management, September, 1985.

[13] Li, Eldon and Shani, A. "Stress Dynamics of Information Systems Managers, A Contingency Model", Journal of Management Information Systems, Spring, 1991.

[14] Newman, John, and Beehr, Terry, "Personal and Organizational Strategies for Handling Job Stress: A Review of Research and Opinion", Personnel Psychology, Spring, 1979.

[15] Palmer, Helen, The Enneagram in Love and Work, Harper, 1995.

[16] Singh, G., "Computer Professionals: Trends in Their Experienced Role Stress and Job Satisfaction", Abhigyan (India), Spr., 1990.

[17] Sonnentag, S. et al., "Stressor-burnout Relationship in Software Development Teams", Journal of Occupational and Organizational Psychology, Dec., 1994.

[18] Wastell, D., and Newman, M. "The Behavioural Dynamics of Information System Development: A Stress Perspective", Accounting, Management, and Information Technology, Vol. 3, No. 2, 1993.

[19] Weiss, Madeline, "Effects of Work Stress and Social Support on Information Systems Managers, MIS Quarterly, March, 1983.

[20] Young, Rudolph, "Occupational Stress and the Information Systems Professional", Technical Report, Department of Accounting, University of Cape Town, 1992.

[21] Yourdon, Edward, Decline & Fall of the American Programmer, Yourdon Press, 1992.

[22] Yourdon, Edward, "The Ongoing Saga", Guerilla Programmer, February, 1994.

E-Commerce: "The Business Engine of the Future"

Sherif Kamel
American University in Cairo 1101 Corniche El-Nil Street, Garden City, Cairo, Egypt
Tel: + 202 340-4592, Fax: + 202 339-1343, E-mail: skamel@aucegypt.edu

INTRODUCTION

The information and communication technologies are the driving forces affecting the way people think, work, invest, and communicate among other impacts. As we approach the 21st century, newly innovated information and communication technologies promise businesses and societies major growth and developmental opportunities across different sectors helping pave the way towards a more efficient and dynamic digital global market place. One of the emerging information and communication technology trends is electronic commerce that is growing to be the vehicle to do business in the 21st century. Electronic commerce with its on-line transactions and the purchase and selling of information, products, and services digitally will prevail in the next millennium with its consumer to business and business to business modalities.

Electronic commerce represents a dynamic model for the information society. However, people and organizations are not yet prepared for it. There is a need for more and better training and education as well as awareness creation and readiness by governments and public authorities. Consumers will need to become familiar with information technology for communicating and ordering goods and services electronically. Moreover, from a socioeconomic perspective there is a need for public and widespread participation in the evolving information society, to avoid the risk of creating classes of information 'haves' and 'have-nots'.

For Egypt, as a developing country, electronic commerce brings about the same type of decision representing both a challenge and an opportunity for development and growth such as increasing trade, promoting investment, and facilitating business transactions. Projections for the volume of transactions of e-commerce show that the world's electronic-based trade can reach a 1 trillion US dollars by the beginning of the 21st century. Such an opportunity holds a lot of promise for the economic development of Egypt, providing it with new opportunities for penetrating international markets which is especially true for small and medium sized enterprises that lack the resources that can enable them to promote themselves globally.

With the dawn of the 21st century, one needs to address the opportunities that electronic commerce holds for Egypt. Such an issue compares with that that occurred more than a hundred years ago, when the world's economy evolved from an agricultural society to an industrial society. Had it not made this shift, Egypt would have been left behind, unable to survive in the New World order. Electronic commerce as a medium for foreign trade is a catalyst for export, implying an increase in Egypt's exports and a better formula for its balance of trade that will eventually have a positive impact on the economy. Electronic commerce could also enable Egypt to experience a more open economy and increase its comparative advantage worldwide.

ELECTRONIC COMMERCE IN EGYPT

The role of information and communication technologies is increasingly affecting socioeconomic and business development globally. From that perspective, Egypt in its strive to lift-up its developmental process has formulated a national plan to prepare itself for a more competitive and global market environment enabled by the information age.

Strategic Objective

To realize electronic commerce there is a need to formulate national policies that are compatible with the global electronic commerce environment, develop the national information infrastructure, implement collaborative projects between the government, the industry, and the private sector and develop the know-how required.

Window of Opportunities

The Global Information Infrastructure Commission announced in 1997 that the overall movement to on-line commerce will bring network generated revenues to over 1 trillion US dollars during the first decade of the next millennium illustrating the trend towards a growing importance of electronic commerce. This represents a window of opportunities for Egypt. It is believed that failure to adapt to the growing electronic trends will result in negative implications with respect to business development in the years to come. Electronic commerce represents a vehicle for global competition for Egyptian firms by helping in sustaining and leveraging their position in the global market place. Electronic commerce offers tax, fiscal, labor, social, and economic administrations, many possibilities to simplify, accelerate, and reduce the cost of business transactions. It also provides an opportunity to slim down the structures of the government itself by reducing the distance between government administration and the individual leading to government transparency. Therefore, the government of Egypt has been investing time and effort to provide the optimal environment and support from its organizations for electronic commerce.

The use of electronic processes in commerce gives firms the ability to offset drawbacks and create advantages in competition, strengthen their innovative capacities, and develop new markets. It is anticipated that a rapidly growing share of world trade will be through global information networks. Electronic commerce offers firms the chance to market their products and services globally by pushing a button without any trading intermediaries being involved making markets more open and more efficient. Competitive small and medium sized firms will benefit from electronic commerce by adapting more flexibly and more rapidly to changes in consumer wishes, and by shortening the product life cycles.

Through electronic commerce new goods and services will become tradable across borders in a digital form implying an increased consumer choice. Firms in many sectors will soon realize that cost savings from the use of electronic commerce and the opportunities that it provides will be vital to maintain competitiveness. Consumers benefit from increased choice by being able to compare and choose instantly from a wide range of offers where a one-to-one relationship is replacing traditional mass marketing and mass-distribution, bringing more responsive service.

A Challenge Ahead

There are a number of challenges that face the full-fledged implementation of electronic commerce in Egypt. These challenges relate to financing, regulations, legislation and technology. The Internet is truly a global medium lacking the clear and fixed geographic lines of transit that historically has characterized the physical trade of goods. Thus, while it remains possible to administer tariffs for products ordered over the Internet, but ultimately delivered via surface or air transport, the structure of the Internet makes it difficult to do so when the product or service is delivered electronically. Therefore, Egypt advocates that the Internet be declared a tariff-free environment with regard to electronic commerce.

With respect to electronic payments, there has been an accelerated trend in the form of prepaid cards and electronic money that are less costly and easier to handle than conventional payment systems. In Egypt, it is important to realize that moving from a highly regulated and traditional financial system into a system that advocates electronic commerce, will not be an easy step to take. The highly paper dependent work cycles are deeply engraved in the corporate culture. Thus, the newly digital format will be highly resisted by the management levels. There is an urgent need for awareness, training and cultural adaptation and that is the challenge that the Egyptian government in cooperation with the private sector is currently undertaking.

With respect to privacy, electronic commerce will only thrive if privacy rights of individuals are preserved and balanced with the benefits associated with the free flow of information. Therefore, the national information infrastructure must be secured and reliable. If the Internet users do not have confidence that their communications and data are safe from unauthorized access or modification, they will unlikely use the Internet on a constant and consistent medium for commerce. Therefore, Egypt is encouraging the development of a voluntary market-driven key management infrastructure that will support authentication, integrity and confidentiality.

With respect to intellectual property, sellers need to know that their intellectual property is preserved and buyers need to be confident that they are obtaining authentic products. Therefore, international agreements establishing copyright, patent, and trademark protection are necessary to prevent piracy and fraud. Hence, the protection of intellectual property rights constitutes one of the challenges faced by Egypt as it enters an age where information and knowledge make up and empower the economy. In recent years, Egypt has devoted substantial attention to the protection of intellectual property rights to be able to compete in an evolving information and knowledge based era. Egypt has embarked on a full-fledged program to combat intellectual property infringement by improving the legislative framework through issuing and amending copyright laws, strengthening the institutional capacities dealing with intellectual property rights, and promoting awareness on the institutional and individual levels as to the importance of protecting intellectual property rights.

With respect to technology, the telecommunications services in Egypt are relatively expensive and the bandwidth is limited. Respectively, the role of the government becomes vital in setting the policies and encouraging the private sector investment by privatizing government controlled telecommunication firms and by promoting and preserving competition within the industry. The objective is to avoid the inflation of prices, providing a better service, eliminating monopolies and the insuring that on-line service providers can reach end-users on reasonable and nondiscriminatory terms and conditions. Today, Egypt is upgrading its data communications infrastructure facilities. The government is mainly focusing on the deployment of basic telephony service countrywide to reach high penetration in the society and supporting free flow of information across international borders through the Internet such as web pages, news, information services, virtual shopping malls, and entertainment features products.

With respect to human resources, the Egyptian government is implementing a massive awareness plan for electronic commerce demonstrating its potential commercial use covering small and medium enterprises, government entities and individuals. Efforts are also put to build the awareness of the new generation to the benefits of electronic commerce to be able to develop the business sense from a very young age and realize the practical benefits of using the Internet. For example "Little Shopper" is an electronic commerce web site for children. It is a government initiative initiated by the ministry of education to provide Internet connectivity to two thousand Egyptian schools.

A Successful Partnership

The government plays a crucial role in all phases of electronic commerce penetration in Egypt. It tries to balance its regulatory and controlled roles with the ability to let the market determine the business environment. It encourages industry self-regulation with minimal government intervention with respect to imposing bureaucratic procedures. A non-traditional policy of bottom-up governance is being instituted and the existing regulatory framework is currently amended to reflect the needs of the new electronic age. The government's task is to create a flexible legal framework for electronic commerce that matches its development pace and permits optimal flow of information.

The success achieved through government-private sector partnership in commercialization of the Internet services will push the deregulation of other value-added services. Coherence, transparency and coordination should be the government's guiding principles in the information age. Currently, a government entity is being formed to protect the Internet consumer from possible electronic commerce crimes. The goals of the association "Internet Consumer Protection Organization" are to protect and guide Egyptian consumers, promote electronic commerce among Egyptian merchants on national and international levels, and diffuse awareness and trust in electronic commerce in Egypt.

The Egyptian government is continuously interacting with representatives of the industry and the business community in an attempt to gradually give the private sector the liberty to be the driving force of electronic commerce in the country. It should be the private sector's role to lead Egypt towards being electronic commerce ready.

AGENDA FOR THE FUTURE

The millennium is bringing the restructuring of national and global economies introducing non-traditional forms of trade coupled with non-traditional approaches in dealing with emerging technologies and global information infrastructures. Governments worldwide should retain a critical role as facilitators of the infiltration of electronic commerce in the society, as a new technology and as an innovative business culture with many requirements to support it at the legal, financial, and technology levels. Electronic commerce defined simply as electronic delivery of a product or service implies that customs and taxation regulations must be altered. Electronic payment systems must ensure interoperability in a global environment. Standards must be developed and implemented on the national level, and must be compatible with global standards. Privacy, liability, intellectual property protection and security are all major questions to be undertaken. A uniform legal framework that recognizes, facilitates, and enforces electronic transactions worldwide is needed.

The liberalized telecommunications and information infrastructure must exist to ensure suitable market access. Private sector investment, promoting and preserving competition must be encouraged. Technical standards need to be determined to guarantee interoperability. The government has a critical role in paving the way for the practical implementation and utilization of the technology. Moreover, the government must have a non-regulatory supervisory role when needed to protect consumers, provide transparency and create a predictable legal environment. Governance should be bottom-up where the government should act as a coordinator between the private and public sector. Finally, business awareness and a sense of confidence in electronic commerce must be established among the community in Egypt.

Over the past two decades, Egypt has witnessed socio-economic prosperity and development, positively impacting society, raising standards of living and reducing unemployment. Shifting to a market based and liberalized economy, Egypt has adopted notable adjustment programs which have led to accelerated economic growth rates, decreased budget deficit, controlled public spending, decreased inflation rate, an improved balance of payments, and stable exchange rates. The World Economic Forum's "Global Competitiveness Report 1996" has ranked Egypt as 29th in competitiveness among 49 countries.

CONCLUSION

Born global, electronic commerce encompasses a wide spectrum of activities, some well established, although most of them very new. Driven by the Internet revolution, electronic commerce is dramatically expanding and undergoing radical changes engendering a wide array of innovative businesses, markets and trading communities creating new functions and new revenue streams. Electronic commerce presents enormous potential opportunities for consumers and businesses worldwide. Its rapid implementation is an urgent challenge for commerce, industry and governments. To reap its full benefits, the development of efficient distribution channels and cross-border network is necessary for the physical delivery of goods ordered electronically. The World Trade Organization Agreement on basic telecommunication will contribute directly to the emergence of a global marketplace in electronic commerce. Similarly, recent international agreements to eliminate tariff and non tariff barriers should rapidly bring down the cost of key information technology products, encourage the take up of electronic commerce and reinforce competitiveness.

Considering the essentially cross-border nature of electronic commerce, global consensus needs to be achieved. Therefore, it is important to pursue international dialogues, involving government and industry, in the appropriate multilateral form, as well as bilaterally among different trading partners. This includes international cooperation to fight against organized cross-border crime on new communication networks. Promoting a favorable business environment will involve reinforcing awareness and confidence in electronic commerce for customers, as well as encouraging best practice among businesses. In parallel, public administrations will have a key role to play through their procurement power and their early implementation of key electronic commerce technologies.

To conclude, this research presented the concept of electronic commerce worldwide with reflections on the Egyptian experience with a set of proposals for action to promote and diffuse the electronic commerce culture in Egypt.

REFERENCES

Choi, Soon-Yong, Stahl, D.O and Whinston, A.B. (1997) The Economics of Electronic Commerce. Macmillan Technical Publishing, Indianapolis.
Clinton, W and Gore, A. A Framework for Global Electronic Commerce. http://www.iitf.nist.gov/eleccomm/electroniccommerce.htm
Ehrens, R. (May-June 1996) Doing Business on the Internet. On the Internet.
European Commission. A European Initiative in Electronic Commerce. http://www.cordis.lu/esprit/src/ecomcomx.htm.
Kalakota, R and Whinston, A. (1996) Frontiers of Electronic Commerce. Addison Wesley, London.
Kamel, S. (1995) Information Superhighways, a potential for socio-economic and cultural development. Proceedings of the 6th International Information Resource Management Association Conference, Idea Group Publishing, Hershey.
Kang, S. (1998) Adoption of the Internet and the Information Superhighway for Electronic Commerce. Proceedings of the 31st Hawaii International Conference on Decision Sciences, IEEE Computer Society, Los Alamitos.
Kini, A and Choobineh J. (1998) Trust in Electronic Commerce: Definition and Theoretical Considerations. Proceedings of the 31st Hawaii International Conference on Decision Sciences, IEEE Computer Society, Los Alamitos.
Lowy, A and Ticoll, D. and Tapscott (Eds.) (1998) Blue Print to the Digital Economy. McGraw-Hill. New York.
Lynch, D.C and Lundquist, L. (1996) Digital Money - The New Era of Internet Commerce. John Wiley & Sons, Inc. New York.

Information Management in Public Healthcare: A Case of a Small Municipality Federation

Jarmo Tähkäpää

Turku School of Economics and Business Administration, Institute of Information Systems Science,
P.O. Box 110, FIN 20521 Turku, Finland
Tel. +358-2-338 311, Fax +358-2-3383 451, Internet: jarmo.tahkapaa@tukkk.fi

Pekka Turunen

Turku Centre for Computer Science (TUCS), P.O. Box 110, FIN 20521 Turku, Finland
Tel. +358-2-338 311, Fax +358-2-3383 451, Internet: pturunen@ra.abo.fi

Kalle Kangas

Turku School of Economics and Business Administration, Institute of Information Systems Science,
P.O. Box 110, FIN 20521 Turku, Finland
Tel. +358-2-338 311, Fax +358-2-3383 451, Internet: kalle.kangas@tukkk.fi

ABSTRACT

Traditionally, information technology (IT) has mainly been exploited for the design of technical instruments, and for treatment and analysis systems development in the field of public health care. However, due to changes in the health care environment, the amount as well as the supply of information needed has increased. This has caused a need also for other kinds of information systems than just for care. Especially, systems for enhanced economical issues are required. The control and coordination of ever-swelling flows of information need right kinds of information management strategies. Such strategies still have to be aligned with the organization's overall management.

Creation of a working information management strategy (IMS) is, however, a difficult task, especially in a small organization. Mostly, such organization do not have any staff specialized into the problem area. Furthermore, they do not have any knowledge of advancements in information systems (IS) and technology. Usually, there are enough resources neither to control, nor to develop IS. Most often, someone manages IS issues as an avocate. In such organizations, IS mainly leads to entities with overlapping and unmatching parts which do not work together. Therefore, in the long run, ISs in such organizations are difficult, or at least expensive to maintain.

In this paper we address two issues: First, we introduce an IS strategy design model. The model is basically developed for the profit business field. Therefore, it is worthwhile to see whether it fits into the non-profit public sector, especially into health care environment. Second, we aim to address the key factors, which force the public sector to develop information management strategies. Through a case study, we aim to discuss how information management strategy to public sector health care can be developed, and present some preliminary findings of our research.

INTRODUCTION

Traditionally, in most European countries, governments finance and support public health care. Although the ratio of public expenditure to total health expenditure varies from country to country, more than a half of services are provided by the public funding in several European countries. (Cf. World Health Organization Regional Office for Europe Copenhagen). Therefore, economic efficiency has not been the key issue in health care activities. Consequently, there has not been so much need to develop the activities the way private enterprises do. But while the public sector is trying to decrease its expenditures, it is also forced to pay attention to the effectiveness of its service production. Furthermore, the private sector has intensified competition. This in turn can lead to a situation where a certain, large part of health care, which has traditionally been produced by the public sector, will be produced by private firms. In doing so the private sector can make the necessity of the public health care questionable - at least in the present form. This challenge forces the public health care to reconsider its business strategies. In competition with private organizations, the public sector tries paradoxically to follow the strategic trends. The public sector seems to be in lack of knowledge and resources to create strategies for their own environment.

We claim that information systems are one of the key issues in strategy design. The amount and acceleration speed of changes in information technology is increasing. This is also true in health care and medicine. IT becomes faster and more complicated to coordinate. To control this development, a comprehensive and goal-directed information management strategy is needed.

AIM OF THE RESEARCH

Aim of our research is twofold. First, we introduce an IS strategy design model. The model EMIS (Evolutionary Model for

Information Systems Strategy Design) is designed mainly as a general framework for designing strategies for business enterprises. We aim to discuss whether it fits to the public health care environment. Public health care in Finland is financed mostly by government funding. Therefore, the model probably needs some changes.

Second, we discuss how to create an information management strategy to municipal health care. In the first phase our aim is to develop, based on empirical findings and existing theory, clear guidelines for small municipalities to create information management strategies (IMS). These instructions should be defined so that a municipality health care organization could design its IMS on its own. This is an important issue for small public sector health care organizations, because they lack knowledge and resources to do that. The idea of a formal "Ansoff-type" (Ansoff, 1965) information system strategic planning model was rejected in the private sector already in the late 1970's. In all, the formal planning paradigm has suffered severe drawbacks ever since then. However, public sector health care still represents some kind of normative and bureaucratic way of management. The main idea of our guidelines is to design a modular and flexible model to prevent the problems mentioned above.

This is an ongoing research. In this paper we try to indicate the factors having influenced in the changing environment of public health care and the consequences for IS. We also present some preliminary findings from the field. Conclusions include some issues, which need further discussion as the research proceeds.

THEORETICAL BACKGROUND

There are a few important issues that organization should notice in strategy creation (cf. Reponen, 1993). First, management must know what and where the company wants to be in the future. This has been a fact in private sector for a long time, but not in public health care. In the future, creation of IM strategy, however, needs this consideration to act as a part of the strategy.

Secondly, to be able to use information systems strategically, an organization must have a clear business strategy. However, there are differences in creating business strategies in the public sector and in the private sector. The life cycle phase of a product is not so relevant in public sector health care as it is for example in the car industry. But the generic strategies, competitive position (especially in this new situation) and main strategic plans have to be considered.

Thirdly, there should be enough information about new technological possibilities. One has to consider which of them could benefit one's own strategy and functions. Fourthly, to be able to procure new systems, which are adaptable to the existing system, the state of the own information systems must be identified. In small public health care organizations this function has been too often ignored.

Fifthly, the previous experience in the field of information management might be useful to explore. Plans should be based on general knowledge of the area. Finally, learning from practical examples of other organizations is useful in preventing mistakes.

The framework used in this study is developed at the Turku School of Economics and Business Administration. It is called the EMIS-model (Evolutionary Model for Information Systems Strategy Design). There is an ever-growing pile of papers and thesis written on the use of the EMIS-model (e.g. Reponen, 1993; Reponen, 1994; Reponen, 1994; Reponen et al., 1996; Leino, 1995; Kangas 1996). It has been successfully used in numerous companies. (e.g. Viitanen, 1998; Reponen, 1993). In this study, we aim to extend the model into health care in the public sector.

Basic assumption of the EMIS-model is that information technology has an increasingly competitive importance and a company should self find its edge. However, IT should not be overemphasized, but should be seamlessly aligned with the overall business strategy. An enterprise's management should be forced to consider and self understand the IT possibilities in the company. Only that way, the effective use of IT is possible. (Reponen et al., 1990)

During the strategy generation process all participants in the organization should have internalized it. Through this, the strategy is much easier to implement. Strong involvement in the project gives the participants also a feeling of the strategy to be their own. Understanding the integration of business and IM strategies is a matter of learning by doing and therefore business management should create an environment where this learning is possible (Reponen, 1993).

The fundamental premises of the EMIS-model are (Leino, 1995 p. 44):

- the project must have management support
- all three essential interest groups (top management, operational management and information systems management) must take part into the project and support it
- information systems de-

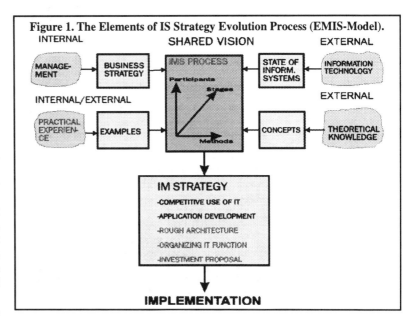

Figure 1. The Elements of IS Strategy Evolution Process (EMIS-Model).

sign must be based on the current situation, i.e., the design itself is an evolutionary process - information systems and business goals must converge

"*The model* (see Figure 1, below) *can not be perceived as an exact how-to algorithm for IS Strategy formulation, but more as a mental construct of agendas to be taken into account in planning and maintaining IS strategies.*" (Kangas 1996 p. 92-93)

The empirical part f the study is conducted as an action research. There is always a strong interaction between the scientist and practitioners in action research. In information strategy formulation this interaction emerges either in the research oriented work or in practical formulation of the information strategy itself (Reponen, 1992). In our case the interaction between the organization and the researchers has been good. We have conducted several interviews and interactive training sessions where the basic needs and goals of the organization have crystallized.

AN ILLUSTRATIVE CASE

Background

There are about 450 municipalities in Finland. The municipalities have autonomy and self-government by the clauses of Finnish constitution. Municipalities produce basic services, such as health care and education, for their inhabitants. Very often small municipalities form a federation (57 % of the municipalities) to produce services in order to create economies of scale. Public health care in Finland is mainly free for Finnish citizens, although there are some municipalities, which charge about 30 dollar per year. Health care in Finland offers a high quality basic treatment, and is therefore very much exploited.

About 30 % of the municipalities' income originate from government subsidies, but this share has decreased every year. The rest is collected in the form of s.c. community taxes and various payments on the services. During the 1990's, several factors have changed environment in the public health care.

The state subsidy system has changed in 1993. The change has been directed to the effectiveness and economic improvement of service production. The communities have more freedom to organize their services based on the local needs. Together with changes in national health laws, this means freedom for communities. They can buy some of the basic services from the private firms or from other municipalities. According to new national health laws communities are not obliged to produce their health services by themselves, although they have to organize them. The consequence has been that local health care providers have to pay more attention to the economic effectiveness of their service production.

Municipalities had to start using a new accounting system in 1997. They also start using quality measures based on the ISO 8402 and ISO 9004-2 standards. Together with the reasons described above, these two changes have caused the need for renewal projects in the aged information systems

One of the local governments has started a nation wide pilot program, which aims to develop a smart card for health care use. The aim of the program is to introduce a health card for every citizen in Finland. The card will carry electronically important information about the citizen, and medical authorities in every part of Finland will have access to any individual citizen's health information. When the program is finished, it will have a strong effect in health care in Finland. These effects cover a wide variety of sociological and technological issues. In the technological side are issues such as systems integration, as well as use of Internet and smart card. The social effects involve the functional change in moving the focus into the customer as well as moving to seamless service chain and ambulatory care of senior citizens.

The Case Organization

The case organization in this research is the Paimio-Sauvo health care federation of municipalities. The federation is located in South-Western Finland, and is formed by the city of Paimio and the municipality of Sauvo. It serves about 13, 000 people, and offers basic health care services for them. The main health center (community hospital) is located in the city of Paimio, and a smaller is in the municipality of Sauvo. The total number of employees is about 100.

The federation is a typical basic health care organization in size and in functions in the Finnish scale. It is therefore suitable as a case organization. We believe that the Paimio-Sauvo project represents a fairly new way of thinking among health care providers in Finland and in Europe (see Checkland & Hollwell 1998). The federation has started a large program aiming for better service quality and cost-effectiveness. Information systems are essential part of the program.

The federation has a fairly short experience in patient care computer systems. Only two years ago it moved from a manual system to a Windows'-based computer environment in the reception of patients. Earlier only administration used computers. The federation has not, however, formulated a real information management strategy.

The old system has been simple, producing only numerical information and statistics mainly for government authorities. There has been no system to support decision-making in the federation. Now as competition with other organizations (private and public sector) is expected to increase in the future, (cf. Salminen & Niskanen 1996; cf. Heinonen 1997; cf. Valtionvarainministeriö 1997, p. 50-51; see Moskowitz & Nassef 1997; cf. Kim & Michelman 1990; cf. Checkland & Hollwell 1998; cf. Friedman and Cornford 1989), such a system is required. The situation is totally new for the organization because it is not used to compete with anyone. Therefore the federation needs a carefully designed strategy to meet the challenge.

FINDINGS SO FAR

Integration

Health care information systems have traditionally been oriented for supporting patient care. To produce and maintain effective health care services, organizations have to consider their strategies in a new way. An essential part of these strategies are information systems. It seems that different stakeholders of information management strategy projects (Ruohonen 1991) represent a somewhat dualistic thinking in the area of health care. First, the information systems should support cost-effective decision-making for administrative people. Secondly, they should support clinical decision-making of the physicians. Thirdly, there has to be integration between these two separate ways of thinking. This way the clinical systems can support cost-effective decision-making through giving information about cost-benefit factors of different treatment possibilities (cf. Checkland & Hollwell. 1998, cf. Hallman).

General Strategies

General strategies should be generated through careful consideration of the organization's operational environment. Unless the general strategy is not well prepared and analyzed, also the information systems - based on that strategy - could not serve all the functions of the organization in the long run. Strategic planning in the public sector organizations is usually not a well-known area (cf. Turunen 1998). The relationship between business strategy and information management strategy is often a two-way relation (Earl, 1989 p. 62, Reponen, 1993 p. 6). Even a business strategy can be based on information technology. However usually, the purpose of IMS projects is not to formulate the organization's vision, or to define its whole business orientation. Public health care organizations also usually lack general strategy. Therefore, we aim to create in our model some alternative scenarios to improve the planning of 'business' strategies.

Learning

In our case the changes in the organization and the way of managing and producing information have taken place in fairly short period. The public health care sector has traditionally been a stable. Radical changes do not happen so often, and the organizational culture is rigid and difficult to change. But, the case organization faces strong demands to adopt the changes.

However, the organization has to see these changes as resources, and turn them to competencies as a part of its strategy development. Units already have their standard work practices and resources. They only have to learn to master them effectively. This way they can exploit changes in information technology and organization to create a learning environment for competence leveraging. (cf. Andreu & Ciborra, 1996,).

The possibilities of competition are not realized by all employees. There is a belief that the position of public health care is going to remain stable, and there will be no competition. This makes the required functional changes difficult to carry out.

Technological Issues

The role of the systems vendors is essential in developing and maintaining the systems in the future, especially in package implementation such as this (cf. Manwani & Kangas, 1998). Very often the interest of the supplier diminishes after the sale and implementation of the systems. The vendors should be obliged to present and maintain all the possibilities of the system.

When an organization that has no experience and knowledge to acquire technical equipment's the result is usually doomed to fail. Due to this, use of external consultant or other professionals is even more than recommendable. In our case for example there is a unit in which there are eight employees, eight PC's, nine printers and five operation systems. No need to say that they are not compatible, and are difficult to maintain. The lack of knowledge and time has been the major reason for this configuration.

Training

In the implementation of new systems, employees have to be trained carefully (Auer, 1995). This secures effective use of systems, all the way from the beginning. It is also important to create a future training system, for all employees (also temporary ones).

The effectiveness of the information systems is correlates to employees' using skills. In the worst case, use of the information system can be harmful for the work routines. In our case some of the employees said that after the patient care system was taken in use the routines became slower. These employees didn't use the system regularly and had thus forgotten some of the initial training. This opinion, however, was not a common one, but indicates the importance of training.

Also the use and maintenance of support systems has to be clear for all employees. Only that way, interruptions in the systems' effective use of can be avoided. Getting instant answer for the problems from the support system enhances the learning of the employees as well.

The responsibility of developing and maintaining the systems has to be clearly accredited to someone. The responsible person must have enough information and resources to perform the tasks.

CONCLUSIONS AND DISCUSSION

Information management strategies have been a must in many fields of private sector for a long time. In the public sector strategies have more or less had a secondary position. Therefore, there is a considerable gap between the public and the private sector. Gradually, the importance of also managing information systems - not just acquiring them - has become clearer to the managers in public sector. They are starting realize that the integration of business strategies and information management strategies - so that they support each other in an effective way - is a vital issue also in the public sector.

The use of basic resources is effective in public health care. Integrating them with IT resources gives organization its competence to face the challenge in changing environment. As Andreu and Ciborra (1996) point the process of integrating them is a path-depending learning process, which starts with a set of existing resources. These resources can be tangible or intangible assets but they are tied semipermanetly to the firm (Andreu & Ciborra, 1996). In our case organization the learning process has begun. It is aiming to integrate organizational objectives and the potential of information technology in the long run.

The production of health care services in most European countries is based on public health care. In Finland, for example, the utilization rate of services is high. This due to the fact that the services are free (or there only a nominal fee), and the quality of treatments in the local health centers is high. However, the activity has based itself highly on governmental subsidization. Now the stake of the government is decreasing. Thus public health care is in a situation where it has to increase its efficiency. There is also an increasing threat of competition from the private sector.

To be able to take the challenge, public health care organizations have to reconsider their strategies. They have to create and evaluate new information on how to support their strategies. We aim to develop a solution, an information management strategy for public health care. It should show a way for public health care organizations how to effectively use their information systems to support the ever-increasing information demands (both quantitative and qualitative). From the EMIS-model we aim to develop an applied model for the public sector.

The research outlined here should be able to respond to two problems. First, how a business-based model fits into the public sector environment. Secondly, how to create information management strategy for public sector health care. The empirical part of the research is carried out in a typical Finnish health care organization, which is in the process of developing its activities and total strategies. This research is a part of that development.

The main findings at the moment implicate that there has not been enough need and interest to evaluate and develop information systems. Therefore, their effective use has been incomplete. There are several examples of incomplete use of information systems from various fields. Those examples, as well as the fundamental questions of differences between public and private sector in creation of information management strategies are examined further.

Our findings seem to indicate that the framework, originally designed for private sector, can also be used in the public health care environment. However the infrastructure in the public sector for this kind of project differs from the private sector. That difference needs further research.

Further discussion is also needed about creating a general strategy, which could be aligned with respective information management strategy. In our case the general strategy has been formulated, in contrast to the common trend in other health care organizations. As the manager of our case organization says "the public sector has probably not yet wasted enough money to faulty IT acquisitions".

In Finland the whole public health care sector is only beginning to formulate a general strategy characteristics for its environment. Therefore the formulation of information management strategy in this area requires extensive research. We believe that our study gives a good starting point for future research.

REFERENCES

Auer, Timo (1995) *Information Systems Related Organizational Maturity: A Conceptual Framework and an Assessment Method.* Publications of the Turku School of Economics and Business Administration. Series A-7:1995.

Andreu, Rafael – Ciborra, Claudio (1996) Core Capabilities and Information Technology: An Organizational Learning Approach in Moingeon, Bertrand & Edmondson, Amy (Eds.) *Organizational Learning and Competitive Advantage.* SAGE Publications, London.

Checkland, P. and Holwell S. (1998) *Information, Systems and Information Systems -making sense of the field.* John Wiley & Sons. Chichester.

Friedman, A.L. and Cornford, D.S. (1989) *Computer systems development - History, Organization and Implementation.*

Heinonen, Jarna (1997) *Asiakaslähtöisyys ja kunnallisen yksikön kilpailukyky - käsitteellisen ajatetelun ja empiirisen havainnoinnin dialogi.* Lisenciate theses. Publications of the Turku school of economics and business administration. Series D-2. Turku. Kirjapaino Grafia Oy.

Kangas, Kalle (1996a) *"Information Resources Management in the Russian Trade of a Finnish Conglomerate",* Licentiate Thesis, Turku School of Economics and Business Administration, Turku (Unpublished)

Kim, K.K. and Michelman, J.E. (1990). *An Examination of Facors for the Strategic Use of Information Systems in the Healthcare Industrty.* MIS Quarterly 14(2) 201-215.

Leino, Timo (1995) *Yrityksen tietohallintostrategian suunnitteluprosessia tukevan päätöksen tukijärjestelmän rakentaminen.* Turun kauppakorkeakoulun julkaisuja D-2:1995.Turku.

Moskowitz, Ellen H. and Nassef, David T. (1997) *Integrating Medical and Business Values in Health Benefits Management.* Californian Management Review. 40(1) 117-139.

Reponen, Tapio, Ruohonen, Mikko, Suomi, Reima (1990) *Strategisen Tietojärjestelmä-suunnittelun tausta, kehitys ja sisältö* in Tietotekniikkastrategian kehittämismalli (ed. Hannu Salmela), Turun kauppakorkeakoulu, Sarja A-4:1990

Reponen, Tapio - Wood-Harper Trevor – Pihlanto, Pekka – Carlsson, Christer (1992) Action Research in Information Strategy Formulation and Implementation. In: *Action Research in Management Information Systems Studies,* edited Liisa Von Hellens. Publications of Turku School of Economics and Business Administration. A-3:1992. 52-64. Turku.

Reponen, Tapio (1993) *Six Tests of EMIS Approach in Information Systems Planning.* Publications of the Turku School of Economics and Business Administration. A- 2:1993. Turku

Reponen, Tapio, (1993) Information Management Strategy - an Evolutionary Process. *Scandinavian Journal of Management* 1993:9(3), 189-209.

Reponen, Tapio (1994a) Organizational information management strategies. *Journal of Information Systems* 1994: 4, 27-44.

Reponen, Tapio (1994b) Strategic Information Systems Planning Workshops: Lessons from Three Cases, R.D. Galliers, E.M. Pattison and T. Reponen, *International Journal of Information Management* 1994:14, 51-66.

Reponen, Tapio - Pärnistö, Juha - Viitanen, Jukka (1996) Personality's Impact on Information Management Strategy Formulation. *European Journal of Information Systems,* Vol. 5, No. 4, 161 - 171.

Ruohonen, Mikko (1991) *Strategic Information Systems Planning – Analyzing Organizational Stakeholders and Planning Support Activities.* Publications of the Turku School of Economics and Business Administration. Series A-2:1991.

Salminen, A. and Niskanen, J. (1996). *Markkinoiden ehdoilla? Arvioita markkinaohjautuvuudesta julkisessa sektorissa.* Helsinki: Oy Edita Ab.

Turunen, Pekka (1998) *Sustaining competitive advantage in the public sector - An example of geographic information system in Vaasa city.* Proceedings of the 21st Information Systems Research seminar in Scandinavia. 8-11 August, 1998, Saeby, Denmark.

Valtionvarainministeriö Hallinnon kehittämisosasto (1997) *Näkökulmia tilaaja-tuottaja -ajatteluun.* Oy Edita Ab. Helsinki.

Viitanen, Jukka (1998) *The Information Management Strategies in the Global Network Organization.* Publications of the Turku School of Economics and Business Administration. Series A-6:1998.

World Health Organization Regional Office for Europe Copenhagen (1996) *European Health Care Reforms. Citizens' Choice and Patients' Rigths.*

Creating Efficient Implementations from Express Information Models

Hilary J Kahn and Nick P Filer

Department of Computer Science, University of Manchester, Oxford Road, Manchester M13 9PL UK

e-mail: hkahn@cs.man.ac.uk, tel: +44 161 275 6156, URL: http://mint.cs.man.ac.uk/

INTRODUCTION

The use of specification as an integral part of design and implementation is accepted as part of most design methodologies. However, specification techniques differ in the degree of formalism they offer. For example, VDM [7] and Z [8] are both mathematically based formal specification languages, but IDEF1X [3, 10] is a semi-formal graphical method. The goal of using specification may also differ. In some cases, the expectation is that the specification will be used by people to enhance their understanding of a given domain without necessarily leading to implementation. In other cases, the specification is seen as a definition of the domain for use explicitly as the basis for implementations. Such implementations are commonly created manually, following the specification. The implementations may also be checked by validation tools based on the same specification.

In the world of ISO 10303, the Standard for the Exchange of Product Model Data (STEP), the specification is really intended as the basis for automated implementation of data sharing and exchange, through file representations and programming interfaces. This interoperability is, in theory, achieved using automatically generated files and programming interface (PI) calls based on the specification. The format of the automatically generated files is fixed according to Part 21[5] of the STEP standard; a series of separate parts specify language bindings for the PI. To some degree, this approach assists interoperability but the insistence on a fixed file format and a predefined programming interface style means that the implementor of tools built on the specification has no control over issues such as processing efficiency or levels of abstraction in software development.

The STEP specification method is based on a descriptive method that is part of the STEP Standard. This descriptive method, EXPRESS (ISO 10303-11) [2], is entirely language based, although there is a diagrammatic variant (EXPRESS-G) which can support much of what EXPRESS can represent. EXPRESS constructs are reminiscent of those in other languages such as Ada, C and SQL, but its fundamental style is object oriented.

This paper addresses the issue of using EXPRESS as a specification language for the automated generation of implementations, but doing so in a way that enables the implementor to have control over the implementation effectiveness and processing efficiency.

The work described here is taking place in the context of a European collaborative project called STEPWISE, involving companies in the aerospace, computer systems and oil industries. Each company intends to use the improved EXPRESS-to-implementation route slightly differently but all are looking for efficiency and flexibility as key factors in their implementation strategies.

STEP OVERVIEW

It is a characteristic of domains such as the automotive, process, construction and aerospace industries that they involve complex design and manufacturing challenges, in an environment with intricate supplier chains and cross-company, globally distributed collaborations. These domains therefore require significant support to allow information and data of all kinds to be shared in an effective manner.

The STEP standard has been created in an attempt to address these issues. It provides a way in which data created in one company can be distributed to others, either through file transfers or via PI calls operating on compliant databases. Hence one goal is that Computer-Aided Design (CAD) and Computer Aided Manufacturing (CAM) systems should be able to work against common data repositories. As a result, users will be less tied to specific design or manufacturing systems, and data, once captured, will be re-usable throughout the life of the product. The potential improvements in interoperability this approach offers promise significant cost reductions in transfers between suppliers and customers.

To ensure that systems can interoperate in this way, it is necessary that they share a common understanding of the information that they are handling within a given domain. The definition of the scope of a given domain is captured in an **application activity model**, often represented in IDEF0 [9]. The common understanding of the information needed in scope is captured as an '**information model**' in EXPRESS or IDEF1X.

The information models in STEP are at one of two levels. The first level defines **integrated resources** that are the building blocks common to the different application domains. For example, a model of basic geometric concepts such as point and conic is provided to underpin other models that include geometric objects. These higher level models, called **application protocols**, focus on specific application domains. Two examples of relevance to this project are AP214 (Core Data for Automotive Mechanical Design Processes) [1] and AP221 (Process Plant Functional Data and its Schematic Representation)[12].

An application protocol is developed first as an **application reference model** (ARM), an information model that is concerned only with the domain of interest. This is then mapped into the integrated resources to produce an **application integrated model** (AIM) which becomes the implementation model (data model) for the application protocol..

The implementation strategy in STEP automatically defines a file format (STEP Physical File) for exchanging data based on the AIM. To support dynamic exchange in a database-like way, a **Standard Data Access Interface** (SDAI) [6] is defined also based on the AIM. It includes abstract operations to create and delete instances of the EXPRESS entities in the AIM, as well as operations to modify instance data by reading and setting attribute values. So, according to the STEP methodology, interoperability is achieved because application protocols all map into the integrated resources via the AIM. Concrete implementations of SDAI are provided as bindings for various languages including C and IDL.

It is not clear that the STEP methodology provides a good way of supporting interoperability as is claimed. However, industries find specification in EXPRESS very valuable and they are looking for more flexible ways to go from an EXPRESS information model (specification) to a file format or PI implementation The work described here is being carried out in this context.

EXPRESS LANGUAGE

EXPRESS is used to model or represent a domain or 'universe of discourse'. Within an EXPRESS model, the domain is represented by one or more schemas, which group together objects with related meaning and purpose. The language supports data types of various kinds, including simple types (e.g. INTEGER or STRING), aggregations (e.g. SET, LIST), user defined types and enumerations.

An entity is a key construct in EXPRESS; it is used to describe concepts or objects of interest in the domain being modelled. An object is characterised by its attributes, its relationships to other entities, rules and constraints.

EXPRESS has a mechanism for specialisation and generalisation of entities. It is possible to create a hierarchy of entities in which each node in a given path is a specialisation of the nodes above and a generalisation of the nodes below.

The following figure presents a hierarchy of entities in which the most general concept is that of 'dwelling'; 'house' and 'apartment' are particular cases of 'dwelling', and 'detached_house' and 'terraced_house' are particular cases of 'house'. In such a hierarchy, the more general objects are called the supertypes of their specialisations. The less general objects are called subtypes of their generalisations. EXPRESS supports single and multiple inheritance as well as complex relationships (ONE OF, AND and ANDOR) between the subtypes of a supertype.

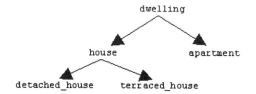

If a supertype is declared to be ABSTRACT, the supertype object is not directly instanced. The implementation can only create instances of its subtypes.

Constraints in EXPRESS may be applied to specific entities or types (using WHERE, UNIQUE and INVERSE rules), or may be applied across the whole model (using e.g. the EXPRESS RULE construct).

In the example below, the entity apartment_block is defined as being at some address (inexactly shown here as just a string), containing an unspecified number of apartments. An apartment, which is a kind of dwelling, is constrained to be on one floor only (in this artificial example). It is contained in a given apartment_block (as shown by the INVERSE constraint).

```
ENTITY dwelling
    SUPERTYPE OF (ONEOF(house, apartment));
    number_of_floors         : INTEGER;  (* number of storeys in the dwelling*)
. . .
END_ENTITY;

ENTITY apartment_block:
    address                  : STRING;  — not good style!
    contained_apartments     : SET [1: ?] OF apartment;
END_ENTITY;

ENTITY apartment
SUBTYPE OF dwelling;
    Floor_number             : INTEGER
INVERSE
    containing_block:    apartment_block FOR contains;
WHERE
    number_of_floors = 1;
END_ENTITY;
```

STEP PHYSICAL FILE

Implementation of an EXPRESS model as, for example, a STEP Physical File, allows instances of data that conform to the model to be created. The file format defines a series of items (identified by #number used for reference). The format does not impose processing constraints such as define before use .

The following example shows an instance of apartment_block (at an address on El Camino Real) and instances of two of the apartments within that block. One apartment is on the 4th floor; the other is on the 1st floor. Note that the inverse relationship does not get recorded in the data file explicitly. The ordering of the items in the file is immaterial and constraint information is not enforced.

```
#3   = APARTMENT_BLOCK ('16251 EL CAMINO REAL, BURLINGAME, CA', (#31, #2, ....))
#2   = APARTMENT (1, 4)
```

#31 = APARTMENT (1, 1)

It is clear that the STEP Physical file is not optimised in any way for efficiency of processing or clarity of representation. It is this type of problem that the STEPWISE project is addressing.

OVERVIEW OF STEPWISE

STEPWISE retains the concept of automated generation of implementations directly from EXPRESS information models, but in contrast to the STEP methodology it allows the user to determine the implementation strategy.

The STEPWISE architecture is based on a process of transformations that is guided by configuration information defining what information in the models is to be changed, added or deleted in order to produce the desired implementation. The process is broken down into a sequence of model manipulations. An EXPRESS model is input into each manipulation stage. The model is then modified to achieve some specific effects and an updated model in EXPRESS is output. The process is illustrated below.

By breaking down the modification process into a sequence of stages, the process is easier to define. In addition, it becomes possible to experiment with 'what if' model modification to assess the effectiveness of specific implementation strategies.

Model modifications may include:
- removal of entities or entity attributes. This may be used to allow an implementation to focus on specific subsets of a domain (i.e. support domain views) or omit attributes not required in a given implementation
- addition of entities or entity attributes. This capability may be used to provide additional attributes such as object keys for efficient implementation or enhance the coverage of the model
- modification of model hierarchy through the addition or removal of inheritance structures. This capability is essential to provide support for targeting specific implementations such as mapping to relational database tables or navigating OO databases.

When modifications are made to a model, the process maintains the original model semantics as far as is possible mainly through the inclusion of additional constraints.

For example, consider the following EXPRESS model extract derived from Page 159 of [2].

```
ENTITY person
  ABSTRACT SUPERTYPE OF (ONEOF (male, female)AND ONEOF (citizen, alien));
END_ENTITY;

ENTITY male
  SUBTYPE OF (person);
END_ENTITY;

ENTITY female
  SUBTYPE OF (person);
END_ENTITY;

ENTITY citizen
  SUBTYPE OF (person);
END_ENTITY;

ENTITY alien
  ABSTRACT SUPERTYPE OF(ONEOF (legal, illegal))
  SUBTYPE OF person;
END_ENTITY;

ENTITY legal
  SUBTYPE OF (alien);
END_ENTITY;

ENTITY illegal
  SUBTYPE OF (alien);
END_ENTITY;
```

This models states that a person may be either a male or a female and (at the same time) may be either an alien or a citizen. A person who is an alien may either be legal or illegal.

A simple implementation of this model in a relational environment might perhaps create a number of different tables to handle all the different entity types. One way to ensure that the mapping to a relational implementation would create a single table is to remove (flatten) the hierarchy and create a single, more complex person entity definition. However, to retain the precise semantics of the original model additional constraints are needed. For example,

```
ENTITY person;
  a:      OPTIONAL li;     (* flag for legal or illegal*)
  b:      mf;              (* flag for male or female*)
```

```
    c:          ca;                 (* flag for citizen or alien*)
WHERE
(* the legal/illegal flag only exists if the person is an alien *)
li_c:           ((c=alien) XOR NOT (EXISTS (a))); END_ENTITY;


TYPE li =  ENUMERATION OF (legal, illegal); END_TYPE;
TYPE mf =  ENUMERATION OF (male, female); END_TYPE;
TYPE ca =  ENUMERATION OF (citizen, alien); END_TYPE;
```

A single operation called from the STEPWISE configuration information, flattens the hierarchy, identifies the additional types and attributes required, and outputs a modified person object as shown. The result can then be mapped efficiently to an implementation that retains the information in the original model and the constraints on attribute values and relationships.

STEPWISE INFRASTRUCTURE

The STEPWISE methodology provides a range of transformations that can be applied to any EXPRESS model. The implementation provides a set of methods callable from the configuration handler to carry out the operations. The manipulations that can be carried out include the simple addition or removal of attributes and objects, flattening levels of hierarchy (as illustrated above) and re-writing hierarchies in terms of their constituent leaf nodes. There are also functions for adding levels of hierarchy, for example when adding an object_id to a selection of entities.

The support that is needed for these semantically-rich operations on EXPRESS models is quite different from that normally provided for modifying specifications. In the common case, modifications are made at the textual level either by standard or special editing systems. Such editors may help the user to make the textual changes in a syntactically correct way, but they are not capable of automating the re-writing nor nof ensuring that model semantics are retained.

The STEPWISE infrastructure that has been designed and developed at the University of Manchester provides the required functionality. The infrastructure system core consists of a Java-based EXPRESS processor that manipulates a read/write EXPRESS Abstract Syntax Tree. It provides both an in-memory and a persistent representation of an EXPRESS model definition, and an object-oriented API that operates on the in-memory representation. It maintains consistent reference resolution as the model is manipulated and is therefore able to underpin the higher-level model transformations with complete knowledge of side-effects caused by the manipulations.

The following figure shows the components of this infrastructure. The User Layer allows the user to configure the EXPRESS information model by issuing a series of model manipulation instructions. These are mapped to the Jex API and then applied to the Jex in-memory tree. A parser loads the tree initially and an EXPRESS writer outputs the modified EXPRESS model.

In the current implementation, the configuration information is described in Python or can be called directly from a Java Program.

STEPWISE EXAMPLES

Object Replacement: Basic Manipulation

The following example shows the output of the runtime system operating in 'noisy' mode. The task is the replacing of an EXPRESS enumeration type definition for flower_colour by an entity of the same name specifying the information in terms of R, G B values.

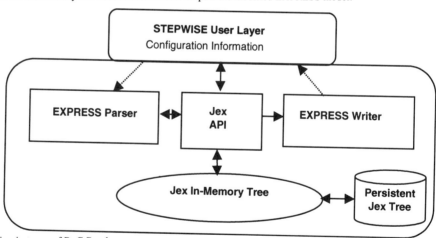

The relevant part of the original model contains the following:

```
TYPE
   flower_colour = ENUMERATION OF (red, yellow, white);
END_TYPE;


ENTITY plant
  ABSTRACT SUPERTYPE OF (ONEOF (greenhouse_plant,  outdoors_plant));
      colour             : flower_colour;
      latin_name          : plant_name;
      english_names        : OPTIONAL SET [1 : ?] OF plant_name;
  UNIQUE
      the_latin_name_of_a_plant_species_is_unique : latin_name;
```

END_ENTITY;

After the operation has been executed the entity plant is unaltered but the TYPE has been replaced by:

```
ENTITY flower_colour;
    red         : INTEGER;
    green       : INTEGER;
    blue        : INTEGER;
END_ENTITY;
```

The output generated in 'noisy' mode is:

Construct the flower_colour entity...
Try adding the flower_colour entity...
    Scope clash within Model.Schema(mr_jones_garden) between existing
    Model.Schema(mr_jones_garden).Type(flower_colour) and potential insertee
    Entity(flower_colour)
Remove the flower_colour type...
    Model.Schema(mr_jones_garden).Entity(plant).ExplicitAttribute(colour).
    NamedType.Ref is newly unresolved
Try adding the flower_colour entity...
    Model.Schema(mr_jones_garden).Entity(plant).ExplicitAttribute(colour).
    NamedType.Ref is newly resolved to Entity(flower_colour)

As can be seen, an attempt to add the new entity without removing the enumeration type definition for flower_colour, identifies a scope clash. This is corrected by removing the enumeration type definition. As a result a reference to flower_colour is left dangling (unresolved). When the new entity flower_colour is added, the reference is satisfied and the operation is complete. In a practical system this 'noisy' output would normally be suppressed unless significant errors are identified.

Adding an Object ID: Higher level operation

In this example, the user is converting the conceptual model to one in which all objects have an object identification (OID) for use in navigating an implementation based on the model..

The operation in this case does significant automatic model analysis before carrying out the task.

In particular, it

- identifies all top-level objects in the model. That is those objects that are the topmost element of a supertype hierarchy or are independent of any hierarchy
- creates a new supertype hierarchy with each of the identified top-level objects as a subtype in an appropriate relationship
- gives it an OID attribute (to be inherited by its subtypes)
- ensures that the OID is unique in the model
- generated any constraints needed

The relevant section of Python [11] code to achieve this is:

```
aoid = Add_OID('model.ex');
aoid.investigate_model()
aoid.generate_oid_entity()
```

These will of course be wrapped into a single call at the end-user level once the software system is released for use.

CURRENT STATUS

The work described in this paper represents work in progress by the University of Manchester on the STEPWISE project. The basic infrastructure described is in place (January 1999) and the system can apply a range of simple and complex manipulations to EXPRESS models. The software has not yet however achieved 'production' status. Apart from completing and fully testing the system, work is also now in hand to investigate the types of manipulations users need for specific implementation strategies. In addition, we are looking at the final stage of converting an implementation model in EXPRESS into an actual implementation such as an efficient file format. The STEPWISE web page (http://www.stepwise.org) will be updated with information on current progress in these areas.

ACKNOWLEDGEMENTS

The work described here is being done as part of ESPRIT Project 25110 supported by the Commission of the European Communities. This support is most gratefully acknowledged. Technical input from our partners in this project, Alcatel (France), ICL (UK), Prism Technologies (UK), Monsell EDM (UK) and the University of Hagen (Germany) has, of course, contributed to framing the current solution. More information about the project and the partners may be found at http://www.stepwise.org. The authors would most particularly like to thank the following members of the Mint Group in the Department of Computer Science at the University of

Manchester. Their involvement past and present in the design and development of the STEPWISE system has been of paramount importance: Alan Williams, Nigel Whitaker, Tim Francis, Denis Reilly and Rosa Macias Verde.

REFERENCES

1. Part 214: Application protocol: Core data for automotive mechanical design processes, Reference Number ISO 10303-214, ISO, Switzerland 1994.
2. Industrial automation systems and integration: Product data representation and exchange: Part 11: Description methods: The Express language reference manual, Reference Number ISO 10303-11:1994, ISO, Switzerland 1994.
3. Integrated Definition for Information Modeling (IDEF1X), Reference number FIPSPUB 184, Federal Information Processing Standards Publications 1993. Available from http://www.idef.com/
4. Industrial automation systems and integration : Product data representation and exchange:
5. Part 21: Implementation methods: Clear text encoding of the exchange structure, Reference Number ISO 10303-21:1994, ISO, Switzerland 1994.
6. Industrial automation systems and integration: Product data representation and exchange: Part 22: Implementation methods: Standard data access interface specification, Reference Number ISO/DIS 10303-22, ISO, Switzerland 1993.
7. Cliff B Jones "Systematic Software development Using VDM", Prentice Hall, 1990
8. J. M. Spivey "The Z Notation: A Reference Manual" Prentice Hall 1989
9. SofTech Inc, Integrated Computer Aided Manufacturing (ICAM) Architecture Part II Volume IV – Function Modeling Manual (IDEF0)
10. GEC Production Resources Consulting : Integrated Information Support System (IISS) Volume V – Common Data Model Subsystem, Part 4 – Information Modeling Manual – IDEF1 Extended
11. Mark Lutz "Programming Python" (Nutshell Handbook), O'Reilly and Associates, 1996
12. Part 221: Application protocol: Functional data and their schematic representation for process plant Reference Number ISO 10303-221, ISO, Switzerland

Data Quality in the Practice of Actuarial Science: Further Evidence from the Field

Barbara D. Klein
University of Michigan-Dearborn, 4901 Evergreen Road – 1070 SOM, Dearborn, MI 48128-1491
(313) 593-5268, Fax: (313) 593-5636, bdklein@som.umd.umich.edu

1.0 INTRODUCTION

Between one and ten percent of data items in critical organizational databases are estimated to be inaccurate (Laudon, 1986; Madnick and Wang, 1992; Morey, 1982; Redman, 1992). As computerized databases continue to proliferate and as organizations become increasingly dependent upon these databases to support business processes and decision making, the number of errors in stored data and the organizational impact of these errors are likely to increase. Two main approaches to this problem are validating data as they are input to or stored in databases (e.g., Morey, 1982) and (2) depending on users to detect and correct errors. A research program examining the efficacy of the second approach is underway. To data, several studies have been completed in this research stream. The first study was a field study in one business domain (actuarial science) showing that at least some users of information systems detect errors in data in organizational settings (Klein, 1997). Three laboratory experiments were then conducted to examine the impact of base rate expectations, incentive structures, and error detection goals on performance in the detection of errors. The conclusions drawn from the laboratory experiments are that incentives and error detection goals affect error detection performance and that base rate expectations developed through direct experience affect error detection (Klein, 1996; Klein et al., 1997). A field study was conducted to link the findings of the laboratory experiments to practice in organizations. Interviews were conducted with consumer product managers, inventory managers, and municipal bond analysts. Findings suggest that high levels of incentives to detect data errors, perceptions about the materiality of data errors, and perceptions about the base rate of errors are associated with incidents of error detection (Klein et al., 1996).

The research proposed here is a second field study conducted in the domain of actuarial science. Since the initial interviews with actuaries were conducted (Klein, 1997) additional insights into data quality have been developed through the laboratory experiments and through field interviews with other professionals (consumer product managers, inventory managers, and municipal bond analysts). A theoretical model of error detection has also been developed (Klein et al., 1997). This second field study of data quality in the practice of actuarial science applies these insights and the new theoretical framework to the development of a new interview protocol.

2.0 THEORETICAL FRAMEWORK

A theory of individual task performance and theories of effort and accuracy in decision making underlie this research.

2.1 Theories of Individual Task Performance

Theories of individual task performance provide some general guidance for identifying conditions under which users detect errors in data. For example, experience seems to affect performance in general and may affect performance in error detection. One theory we could use is Campbell's (1990; Campbell and Pritchard, 1976) theory of individual task performance. This suggests that experience (e.g., Weber et al., 1993), knowledge, and effort (e.g., Payne, 1982; Payne et al., 1988) all affect error detection.

Campbell's (1990) theory argues that performance on a particular component of a job is a function of an individual's declarative knowledge, procedural knowledge and skill, and motivation. Declarative knowledge is defined as knowledge of the facts required to complete a task. Procedural knowledge refers to skill-based knowledge about how to perform a task. Declarative knowledge and procedural knowledge are said to be partially a function of education, training, and experience; and motivation is said to be a function of three choices: the choice to expend effort, the choice of the degree of effort to expend, and the choice to persist in task performance. The theory suggests that experience and motivational influences can only affect job performance through changes in declarative knowledge, procedural knowledge and skill, or the three choices related to effort.

Error detection is viewed here as a very specific component of some jobs that is influenced by these determinants, and performance is viewed in this research as the successful or unsuccessful detection of an error in data. We argue here that variation in declarative knowledge and procedural knowledge affect error detection performance and that differences in expectations about the base rate of errors in data and assessments of the payoffs of error detection affect the rate at which errors are detected through the choices related to effort.

2.1.1 Experience and Knowledge

Studies of expert performance suggest that significant amounts of experience are necessary for the development of expertise (e.g., Ericsson and Chase, 1982; Johnson et al., 1992a; Johnson et al., 1992b). This suggests that the actual number of errors that users of data encounter will influence performance if they recognize the problem and try to detect the errors. A high base rate of errors has the potential, when adequate feedback occurs, to facilitate the development of declarative knowledge about the number and types of errors in data. Users working with data containing many errors also have more opportunities to develop the procedural knowledge and skills needed to detect errors than users working with data with a low base rate of errors. Thus, users in domains with a high base rate of errors may develop effective strategies for error detection, and performance in the task of error detection may be enhanced.

2.1.2 Effort

Effort expended to detect errors may be a function, at least in part, of expectations about the base rate of errors in data and of user assessments of the payoffs of error detection. Campbell's (1990) theory of performance suggests that choices about the degree of effort to expend in the detection of errors will influence performance. Analysis of the data collected in the study of the actuaries suggests that there are several factors that influence these choices when users work with imperfect data. Factors influencing choices related to effort in error detection are discussed below.

Expectations about the Base Rate of Errors in Data. As users expect more errors in data, greater effort may be devoted to this task. Compared to users who expect a low base rate of errors in data, users who expect a high base rate of errors may expend more effort to detect errors simply because they expect to detect more errors at any level of expended effort. There is evidence from the first study of actuaries that expectations about the base rate of errors in a source of data influence effort. For example, one user reported that she considers the base rate of errors in published mortality tables to be low and that she does not attempt to find errors in these tables. There is also evidence from the work of Weber et al. (1993) that at least some decision makers are sensitive to base rates in the generation of hypotheses in diagnostic tasks.

Payoffs of Error Detection. A specific task described by a subject in the first study of actuaries will be used to illustrate the impact of assessments of payoffs on error detection performance. In this incident an actuary was using data provided by a client. The objective was to determine whether an organization's financial reserves for its pension fund were sufficient. This judgment typically depends in part on the pay rate and the number of years of organizational service of each employee in the organization. The data provided by the client contained this information along with other personnel information for each employee as of the end of the year. Imagine a specific case in which this data (as of the end of 1996) contains a record holding information about an accountant in a position requiring a CPA certificate in which the value of the Date of Birth field is "December 31, 1971" and the value of the Number of Years of Service field is "10".

A user working with this dataset might or might not suspect that the data in one of these fields is inaccurate (i.e., it is unlikely that a firm would hire an accountant at the age of 15). An actuary analyzing a pension fund might be likely to detect this error because it is quite material to the judgment about the sufficiency of the firm's pension reserves. On the other hand, a payroll manager reviewing the same dataset might be unlikely to find the error because errors in the Date of Birth and Number of Years of Service fields are not material to a firm's payroll.

Materiality. Thus, beliefs about the materiality of an error may influence the degree of effort expended to detect the error. Users may expend more effort to detect errors that they believe will have a significant impact on their calculations or decisions. There is evidence from the first study of actuaries that the impact of data errors on the work being performed using the data is explicitly considered in the determination of the level of effort to expend in error detection. For example, one actuary stated that there are some types of errors that he does not try to detect when pricing insurance because the errors would not have a significant impact on his calculations.

Incentives. Organizational incentives may also play an important role in users' assessments of the payoffs of error detection. For example, an error in data that is successfully detected may generate additional work for the detector; and an incentive system that discourages the use of time to investigate and correct errors may create an environment in which many errors in data go unnoticed.

Ease of Verification and Correction. The ease with which an error can be corrected may also influence the degree of effort expended to detect the error. For example, it is possible that individuals won't try very hard to detect an error if (a) it is difficult to confirm that a suspected error is actually an error, or (b) if a confirmed error cannot be corrected. Perceived payoffs of error detection may be quite low if detected errors cannot be corrected.

2.2 Theories of Effort and Accuracy in Decision Making

An underlying assumption of theories of effort and accuracy in decision making is that humans will devote no more mental resources or effort to a task than what is demanded by task requirements. This suggests that performance in the task of error detection may be sensitive to the specific performance requirements implicit in payoffs for error detection. Payne (1982; Payne et al., 1988; Johnson and Payne, 1985) has demonstrated that task demands influence the selection of information processing strategies. Cryer et al. (1990) built on Payne's research to examine the impact of incentive schemes on information use and on task performance. Cryer et al. (1990) found that an incentive scheme rewarding accuracy would lead to more normative information processing and higher levels of task performance while an incentive scheme rewarding the minimization of effort would lead to the use of heuristic processing and lower levels of task performance. This finding supports the contention that error detection performance may be sensitive to variation in payoffs.

3.0 RESEARCH METHODOLOGY

Five actuaries have been interviewed. None of these actuaries had participated in the initial field study of data quality in actuarial science (Klein, 1997). To control for selection bias, potential interviewees were asked to participate in a study of the use of data in their work. The terms "error detection" and "data quality" were not used when recruiting subjects. Data were collected using a semi-structured interview. Several of the questions in the interview protocol are a variation on the critical incidents methodology developed by Flanagan (1954). These questions were designed to elicit descriptions of incidents in which the interviewees successfully detected errors in data and incidents in which errors were missed.

The semi-structured interviews were recorded and transcribed. An analysis of the interview transcripts will be performed using methodologies outlined by Miles and Huberman (1994) and King (1994). A coding scheme based on the theoretical framework was developed, and the transcripts will be coded using this scheme.

Results of the analysis of the interview transcripts will be presented at the conference. Descriptions of the reported error detection incidents, strategies used to find data errors, and a description of data errors that were missed will be presented. Perceptions of payoffs for error detection (materiality, incentives, and ease of verification and correction) and the base rate of errors in the domain will also be presented. A discussion of the extent to which the interview evidence supports the theoretical framework developed in this research stream as well as new theoretical insights will be presented.

REFERENCES

Campbell, J. P. (1990). Modeling the performance prediction problem in industrial and organizational psychology. In M. D. Dunnette and L. M. Hough (Eds.), Handbook of Industrial and Organizational Psychology (2nd ed., Vol. 1, pp. 687-732). Palo Alto, CA: Consulting Psychologists Press, Inc.

Campbell, J. P., & Pritchard, R. D. (1976). Motivation theory in industrial and organizational psychology. In M. D. Dunnette (Ed.), Handbook of Industrial and Organizational Psychology (pp. 63-130). Chicago: Rand McNally College Publishing Company.

Cryer, E. H., Bettman, J. R., & Payne, J. W. (1990). The impact of accuracy and effort feedback and goals on adaptive decision behavior. Journal of Behavioral Decision Making, 3, 1-16.

Ericsson, K. A., & Chase, W. G. (1982). Exceptional memory. American Scientist, 70, 607-614.

Flanagan, J. C. (1954). The critical incident technique. Psychological Bulletin, 51, 327-358.

Johnson, E. J., & Payne, J. W. (1985). Effort and accuracy in choice. Management Science, 31, 395-414.

Johnson, P. E., Grazioli, S., & Jamal, K. (1992a). Fraud detection: Sources of error in a low base-rate world. Paper presented at the 10th European Conference on Artificial Intelligence Research Workshop on Expert Judgment, Human Error, and Intelligent Systems, Vienna, Austria, August 1992.

Johnson, P. E., Grazioli, S., Jamal, K., & Zualkernan, I. A. (1992b). Success and failure in expert reasoning. Organizational Behavior and Human Decision Processes, 53, 173-203.

King, N. (1994). The qualitative research interview. In C. Cassell and G. Symon (Eds.), Qualitative Methods in Organizational Research (p. 14-36). Thousand Oaks, CA: Sage Publications.

Klein, B.D. (1996). Base rate expectations and the detection of errors in data: Direct experience versus information. Proceedings of the Second Americas Conference on Information Systems, 197-199.

Klein, B.D. (1997). How do actuaries use data containing errors?: Models of error detection and error correction. Information Resources Management Journal, 10(4), 27-36.

Klein, B.D., Goodhue, D.L., & Davis, G.B. (1996). Conditions for the detection of data errors in organizational settings: Preliminary results from a field study. Proceedings of the 1996 Conference on Information Quality, 24-52.

Klein, B.D., Goodhue, D.L., & Davis, G.B. (1997). Can humans detect errors in data?: Impact of base rates, incentives, and goals. MIS Quarterly, 21(2), 169-194.

Laudon, K. C. (1986). Data quality and due process in large interorganizational record systems. Communications of the ACM, 29, 4-11.

Madnick, S. E., & Wang, R. Y. (1992). Introduction to the TDQM research program. Total Data Quality Management Research Program Working Paper #92-01.

Miles, M. B., & Huberman, A. M. (1994). Qualitative data analysis. Thousand Oaks, CA: Sage Publications.

Morey, R. C. (1982). Estimating and improving the quality of information in a MIS. Communications of the ACM, 25, 337-342.

Payne, J. W. (1982). Contingent decision behavior. Psychological Bulletin, 92, 382-402.

Payne, J. W., Bettman, J. R., & Johnson, E. J. (1988). Adaptive strategy selection in decision making. Journal of Experimental Psychology: Learning, Memory, and Cognition, 14, 534-552.

Redman, T. C. (1992). Data quality: Management and technology. New York: Bantam Books.

Weber, E. U., Bockenholt, U., Hilton, D. J., & Wallace, B. (1993). Determinants of diagnostic hypothesis generation: Effects of information, base rates, and experience. Journal of Experimental Psychology: Learning, Memory, and Cognition, 19, 1151-1164.

Development of an Instrument Assessing the Quality of Data from Internet Sources

Barbara D. Klein
University of Michigan-Dearborn, 4901 Evergreen Road – 1070 SOM, Dearborn, MI 48128-1491
(313) 593-5268, Fax: (313) 593-5636, bdklein@som.umd.umich.edu

1.0 INTRODUCTION

Despite anecdotal evidence that problems with the quality of data available through Internet sources such as the World Wide Web can occur (e.g., Calishain, 1997), little research measuring the objective quality of this data or users' perceptions of the quality of this data has been done. It is unknown, for example, whether users of the World Wide Web consider information that they retrieve from the Web to be every bit as believable, accurate, complete, and relevant as information they retrieve from a university library.

A study of user perceptions of the quality of data retrieved from Internet sources is being conducted. The study applies the considerable research that has been done on the dimensions of data quality. The remainder of the paper discusses this body of research on the dimensions of data quality and the methodology of the present study.

2.0 DIMENSIONS OF DATA QUALITY

A significant volume of the literature on data quality is concerned with defining the term. Both purely conceptual definitions and definitions derived from empirical observation have been offered.

Data quality is generally thought of as a multi-dimensional concept. In a discussion of the quality of information systems, Davis and Olson (1985) identify three aspects of quality that refer to characteristics of data: accuracy, precision, and completeness. Accuracy refers to a judgment of whether the system contains the correct values. Two aspects of completeness are noted. The first refers to whether all needed data items are stored in the system, and the second refers to whether the relevant time periods are attached to data items.

Huh et al. (1990) define four dimensions of data quality: accuracy, completeness, consistency, and currency. They define accuracy as agreement with either an attribute about a real world entity, a value stored in another database, or the result of an arithmetic computation. They say that completeness must be defined with respect to some specific application and that the term refers to whether all of the data relevant to that application are present. Consistency refers to an absence of conflict between two datasets. Currency refers to whether the data are up-to-date.

Fox et al. (1993) discuss the same four dimensions of data quality. In the Fox et al. (1993) framework accuracy refers to whether a data value matches some value considered to be correct. They note that assessments of data accuracy can be difficult because it can be difficult to determine the correct data value. Currency refers to whether a data value is up-to-date. A value is said to be out-of-date if it is not currently accurate, but it was accurate at some time in the past. In this framework, completeness means that a collection of data contains values for all fields that should have values (i.e., those values for which "null" is not a valid attribute) and that no records are missing. A collection of data can be incomplete if existing records are missing values for one or more field or if entire records are missing. In this conceptualization, consistency refers to whether data values conform to constraints that have been specified for that data. It does not refer to consistency of data values across databases or across records. Fox et al. (1993) note that, although a necessary condition of high quality data, consistency does not guarantee accuracy. They note that it is important to consider consistency in a discussion of data quality because it is generally easier to check for constraint violations than to ensure that data values are accurate with respect to the attributes of the entities that the data describe.

Zmud (1978) and Madnick and Wang (1992) offer empirically-derived definitions of data quality. Zmud (1978) used factor analysis to examine the dimensionality of the construct of information. Four dimensions were derived: quality of information, relevancy of information, quality of format, and quality of meaning. Zmud includes the concepts of accuracy, truth, quantity, reliability, and timeliness in the relevancy dimension. The quality dimension refers to the concepts of applicability, helpfulness, significance, and usefulness.

Madnick and Wang (1992) describe four components of data quality: completeness, accuracy, appropriateness, and consistency. This taxonomy is based on observations of defective data in organizational databases.

Wand and Wang (1994) acknowledge that evaluations of whether data are of sufficient quality are dependent on the task for which the data are used. However, they argue that system designers need a definition of data quality that is task-independent because designers can not necessarily control the way in which data are used. They identify four dimensions of intrinsic data quality: completeness, lack of ambiguity, meaningfulness, and correctness. These dimensions are said to be applicable across a set of applications that are put to different uses.

Despite considerable overlap among these conceptualizations of data quality, some definitional problems remain. For example, it has been noted that the concept of data accuracy is not entirely straight-forward. The work of Agmon and Ahituv (1987) illustrates that a single definition of data quality is not well accepted. They apply concepts of manufacturing quality control to information systems in order to define data reliability. They argue that there are three dimensions to the reliability of data. The first, internal reliability, refers to whether a data item conforms to specified validation checks. The second, relative reliability, refers to whether the data item conforms to user requirements. The third dimension, absolute reliability, refers to whether the data item reflects reality.

Maxwell (1989) notes that one's perception of the accuracy of a collection of data is not necessarily stable over time. He notes that changes in business requirements or government regulations can drastically change perceptions of whether data are accurate enough for users' requirements. He illustrates this idea by noting that prior to the implementation of the Consolidated Omnibus Reconciliation Act (COBRA) many users of personnel data were not terribly interested in the accuracy of employees' home addresses. However, organizations now need accurate home address information because they must communicate with employees after they leave an organization.

3.0 THE DATA CONSUMER PERSPECTIVE

Wang et al. (1994) departed from earlier taxonomies of data quality by creating a framework of dimensions of data quality from the perspective of data consumers. Two surveys of data consumers were conducted to generate a comprehensive list of data attributes. In the first survey, data consumers were asked to list attributes of data quality. 118 attributes were generated. In the second survey, data consumers rated the importance of these 118 data attributes and an exploratory factor analysis of their responses was performed. Twenty dimensions of data quality were extracted. A second study was then performed in which subjects were asked to sort these twenty dimensions into four conceptually-derived categories (accuracy, relevancy, representation, and accessibility). Fifteen dimensions (encompassing 50 data attributes) emerged from the sorting study. The dimensions are believability, accuracy, objectivity, reputation, value-added, relevancy, timeliness, completeness, appropriate amount of data, interpretability, ease of understanding, representational consistency, concise representation, accessibility, and access security. Wang et al. (1994) argue that their framework is a tool for measuring data quality. Strong et al. (1997) discuss data quality problems in three organizations using this framework.

4.0 RESEARCH METHODOLOGY

A survey based on the Wang et al. (1994) framework has been developed. This framework is an appropriate foundation for this study because we are interested in perceptions of the quality of data provided through the Internet from the perspective of the consumers (users) of this data.

The survey will be administered to sixty graduate students following the completion of a course project requiring the use of the Internet as a tool for conducting research. The survey asks two kinds of questions. First, questions about the importance of the 50 data attributes found by Wang et al. (1994) are asked. Second, questions about the extent to which the 50 data attributes describe data from Internet sources used for the course project are asked. All questions are asked in the context of the course project that respondents have conducted prior to completing the survey. Two sample questions (one of each type) are shown below.

How important was it to you that the data you used for the course project was accurate?
Extremely important   1 2 3 4 5 6 7 8 9   Not Important At All
Data used for the course project from Internet sources were accurate.
Strongly Disagree   1 2 3 4 5 6 7   Strongly Agree

Factor analysis will be performed to test for consistency with the dimensions found by Wang et al. (1994). Reliability and validity of the instrument will be evaluated following the methodology of Straub (1989). Results of the tests of reliability and validity of the instrument as well as user perceptions of the data quality of Internet sources along the fifteen dimensions developed by Wang et al. (1994) will be presented at the conference.

REFERENCES

Agmon, N., & Ahituv, N. (1987). Assessing data reliability in an information system. Journal of Management Information Systems, 4(2), 34-44.

Calishain, T. (1997). Official Netscape guide to Internet research. Research Triangle Park, NC: Ventana Communications Group, Inc.

Davis, G.B., & Olson, M.H. (1985). Management information systems: Conceptual foundations, structure, and development. New York: McGraw-Hill Book Company.

Fox, C., Levitin, A., & Redman, T. (1993). The notion of data and its quality dimensions. Information Processing & Management, 30, 9-19.

Huh, Y.U., Keller, F.R., Redman, T.C., & Watkins, A.R. (1990). Data quality. Information and Software Technology, 32, 559-565.

Madnick, S.E., & Wang, R.Y. (1992). Introduction to the TDQM research program. Total Data Quality Management Research Program Working Paper #92-01.

Maxwell, B.S. (1989). Beyond data validity: Improving the quality of HRIS data. Personnel, 66(4), 48-58.

Straub, D. (1989). Validating instruments in MIS research. MIS Quarterly, 13(2), 147-166.

Strong, D.M., Lee, Y.W., & Wang, R.Y. (1997). Data quality in context. Communications of the ACM, 40(5), 103-110.

Wand, Y., & Wang, R.Y. (1994). Anchoring data quality dimensions in ontological foundations. Total Data Quality Management Research Program Working Paper #94-03.

Wang, R.Y., Strong, D., & Guarascio, L.M. (1994). Beyond accuracy: What data quality means to data consumers. Total Data Quality Management Research Program Working Paper #94-10.

Zmud, R.W. (1978). An empirical investigation of the dimensionality of the concept of information. Decision Sciences, 9, 187-195.

Managing the Human Challenges of Information Systems Education and Research

Virginia Franke Kleist

Assistant Professor, MIS, Division of Management, Industrial Relations, and Marketing, College of Business and Economics, West Virginia University, PO Box 6025, Morgantown, WV 26506-6025

Voice: (304)-293-7939, FAX: (304)-293-5652, E-mail: kleist@be.wvu.edu

ABSTRACT

There are human challenges associated with the profession of information systems (IS) education and research, which are caused by the effects of rapid technological advance. As the next century begins, it is an appropriate exercise to pause, reflect and examine the relationship between the changing times in which we live and the associated difficulties of the information systems education profession. This conceptual essay identifies five technologically driven challenges faced by IS professors, and offers five practical suggestions which may contribute to the better management of the influences of technological change on work effectiveness.

Business did not routinely use electricity at the beginning of this century. In the early 1900's, competitive, strategic advantage did not rely on videoteleconferencing, email, airplane travel, cellular phones or coast-to-coast overnight express delivery. At that simpler time, horses with wagons or trains moved freight around our cities. Markets were local or perhaps regional, but rarely national or global in composition. Information about business activity in far away places came slowly via the mail, with the limited bandwidth telegraph, or later the telephone, reserved for important and sporadic communication. At the end of the same century, business information is manipulated using computers, and is transmitted using electronic on/off digital pulses of microwave, electricity or light. Today, high bandwidth pipes of business data are sent continuously via satellites, microwave radio and fiber optic cables. The mainframes of the 'sixties yielded to personal computers in the 'eighties, and then the two technologies converged with telecommunications to form Internets and Intranets after a mere three decades. As a result, the current business environment bears little resemblance to that found earlier. It is possible that the technological change expected to come in the next century may prove to be even more interesting. As information systems educators and researchers, we conduct research and teach about the management of information systems in an exciting, but personally challenging Information Age.

This conceptual paper will examine five challenges for information management educators which are related to living in this special time in human history, as well as present five suggestions for overcoming these potential threats as we advance from here into the next century. The theme of this essay is that the human challenges of continued rapid technological change on the practice of information systems management education might be effectively managed by making positive, sensible and thoughtful choices.

RESPONSE TO CHANGES IN INFORMATION TECHNOLOGY

The speed of change of information management technology has been remarkable. The graphics based interface to the Internet, commonly called the World Wide Web, which most of us use daily, is only three years old. In the intervening three years, Internet modem technologies now run at 56K speeds instead of 19.9 kbps, the Netscape browser has replaced Mosaic, and WYSIWYG webauthoring tools are available instead of HTML. It was only ten years ago that we used the A: of DOS, 2400 baud telephone acoustic coupler modems, and 8088 processors which used a large floppy just to boot and run programs. As IS professionals, we are always challenged to stay current on new software releases, and are frequently seeking a new computer upgrade of one kind or another. Continued change due to technological advance is stressful, particularly when it occurs at the same time that we as educators face other tensions from tenure battles, budget cuts, larger classes and higher teaching loads.

The converse of the problems of the speed of technological change is the outrageous marvel and wonder of it all. Year after year, the one constant behind the threatening aspects of the relentless technological turmoil is the ever-increasing sophistication of the technology. Alvin Toffler calls this time period in history "Powershift," where the traditional manufacturing activities of industrialized nations have declined, and knowledge production has increased in influence (Toffler 1990). We are information systems educators in the midst of a global transformation to a knowledge-based economy.

It was Francis Bacon who said, "Knowledge is power." Today, it is the access to information that yields power. Researching and teaching about information access are among the core responsibilities of an information systems professor. Marshall McLuhan refers to the development of a knowledge-based "Global Village" (McLuhan 1992). Many of our information management students have laptop computers that dial up annual reports, visit e-commerce web sites or email their classmates for a team project. As researchers, we find bibliographies in our specialty areas of interest, and communicate extensively with colleagues at institutions all over the world. The on-line world creates a "virtual community" for information and social exchange (Rheingold 1993). The first point of this essay is that the new technology can be both fearful and wonderful, and we as professors can choose to positively respond to it with excitement and interest.

KEEPING UP WITH THE NEW TECHNOLOGY

As information systems educators, we are paid to be to the experts in this new Information Society. As professors, we should be expected to be competent with the ever-changing technology. The mind numbing, constant need to upgrade our skills can take away from our inherent enthusiasm for new technological advances. An IS professor in the '80s might have needed to know about technologies like Wordstar, Lotus 1-2-3, IRMA boards, Novell Netware, 3270 port emulators, 10K hard disk drives and ethernet connections in order to function well in the job. An information systems professor today will need to know about zip drives, SAP, NT servers, Java, C++, Oracle Developer 2000 and domain name assignments. An IS professor of tomorrow will need to throw out at least half of his or her technical skill set in the next five years, and re-learn yet another repertoire of information management technologies. An information systems professor is threatened with obsolescence every day. In short, an IS educator's work is never done. An information systems professor without a working currency in the medium is ineffective. It may be that we are better able to rise to this unending challenge if we choose to reacquaint ourselves with our own intrinsic love of learning in order to be successful educators.

EXCLUSION VERSUS INCLUSION IN THE INFORMATION SOCIETY

A third reflection appropriate for an essay about the human challenges for professors of information management, is the consideration of those persons excluded from an education of how to use information technology. Information systems academicians encounter a rich array of new technology on a daily basis. Some information systems educators have acquired skills that could be put to work for those who have not been exposed to information technology expertise. It is possible that IS academic professionals may be able to apply knowledge gained for the benefit of others who have not had the opportunity to be included with the technology explosion in society. Examples of approaches that share a working knowledge of information systems include taking on a project to coordinate donated corporate computers, helping to install a new computer system at a child's nursery school, or arranging a LAN network for a community center. The third point for consideration by an educator in information management, when reflecting at the end of the century, is to maintain an awareness of the greater effects of information technology on society, and to ensure that these benefits are more universally shared.

EDUCATION VERSUS TRAINING IN INFORMATION SYSTEMS

Students in information systems study a widespread assortment of current technologies and software tools in their classes in systems analysis and design, human computer interaction, database management and client server. They also may learn about electronic commerce, Internet economics and information systems strategic planning. The MIS student faces a busy and difficult curriculum. Education is wisdom, a quest for intelligence, and a learned ability to establish a coherence and understanding of some complex phenomenon. Education builds a large framework for a student to build upon as more experience adds to her knowledge base. Training is a smaller idea. Training gives a glimpse of only a piece of a field. The curriculum for training students in information systems changes with each semester. The curriculum for educating students in information systems never changes. Our information systems students are hired based upon what they have been trained in, but they are successful based upon how well they are educated. As information systems educators, we need to be certain that we are indeed educating our students.

THE INFORMATION SYSTEMS PROFESSOR IN THE SHORT VERSUS THE LONG RUN

In the long run, it would be best if information systems as a field disappeared from the business school curriculum. It has been said that there are no Vice Presidents of Electricity anymore, when referring to the practice at the turn of the century to manage the use of electricity within firms. It may also be true that there will be no more educators of information systems in the future. As the user interface substantially improves, the solutions in information systems should become simple enough that we are not necessary anymore. As technology gains in sophistication, the management problem should become the more fundamental one of managing information, not managing information technology. Indeed, we have seen the beginnings of this new trend happening. Knowledge management, intellectual capital, and working knowledge are the currently vogue terms which are used to focus on the idea that *what* is more important than *how* in terms of business information. As information systems professors, it is meaningful to look at the management of information problem as well as the mechanics of applying the technology. After all, the unchanging business problem at the end of the next millennium will be one of information too, just as it was before electricity came along.

On another note regarding the long run, current students appear to be extraordinarily focused on a very narrow definition of success. Of perhaps more importance for information systems educators to convey to our students than the details of what we teach (whether management, information or systems) is the important distinction that success in their lives is more important than success in their careers. Sometimes these are the same, sometimes not. If we succeed in achieving this transformation of our student's perspective of their own dependent variable over the long run, we might also come closer to addressing one of the reasons why we were motivated to be professors in the first place.

In conclusion, as we proceed into the next century, it is an appropriate time to take stock of the human effects of the change of technology on our profession. The exponential curve of technological change might continue to rise, or perhaps it has lost some of its energy and may begin to level off, or even dip. A sense of wonder, a bit of enthusiasm, cultivating the willingness to learn and share what we know, and a long run point of view are some of the practical approaches which we might wish to adopt in order to better manage the challenge of continued information technology change. Our two primary jobs are to research the relationship of information technology to the information management problem, and to educate, not train, the business minds for the new millennium. How we choose to respond to the relentless and inexorable force of technological change in our personal and professional lives will determine if we are able to successfully accomplish our responsibilities.

BIBLIOGRAPHY

McLuhan, M. and B. R. Powers. (1992 (Paperback ed.)). The Global Village: Transformation in World Life and Media in the 21sr Century. New York, Oxford University Press.

Rheingold, H. (1993). The Virtual Community: Homesteading on the Electronic Frontier. Reading, MA, Addison-Wesley Publishing Company.

Toffler, A. (1990). Powershift. New York, Bantam Books.

Towards an Understanding of Online Degree Programs

Harry L. Reif

James Madison University, CIS/OM Program, Harrisonburg, VA 22807, 540.568.8122 (Voice), 540.568.8122 (Fax),
ReifHL@jmu.edu

S. E. Kruck

James Madison University, CIS/OM Program, Harrisonburg, VA 22807, 540.568.3016 (Voice), 540.568-3273 (Fax),
KruckSE@jmu.edu

BACKGROUND

During the past decade, we have witnessed an increase in both the number and types of online course offerings by four-year colleges and universities in the United States and in other regions of the world. This increase can be linked to the advent of on-campus multimedia capabilities, which has resulted in the reengineering of numerous courses. Likely candidates for online courses are those courses offered regularly, have moderate to high enrollment levels, and where a shortage of professors precludes offering as many sections as might be demanded. As campuses added sophisticated communications links to meet their on-campus demand for Internet access, the added bandwidth provided a logical delivery mechanism to extend the traditional campus classroom to off campus locations.

Two basic types of off-campus courses dominate. The first type utilizes television type broadcast technologies to extend the traditional classroom. Using television cameras, desktop microphones, and dedicated telecommunications links, students in remote classrooms participate and interact in real-time with peers in other similarly equipped classrooms. This learning modality requires that all students and the professor are physically located in their respective classrooms at the same time. The professor can control interactions using a special console to entertain questions and video links from any of the subscribed locations.

A second type of off campus course more closely resembles the self-paced instructional model where students complete coursework at times and locations convenient to them according to a prescribed sequence and timetable. Students acquire course materials and interact with the professor using the Internet. Email is the primary communications vehicle. Some courses offer student to student interaction using electronic "bulletin boards", or web boards, listservs, and chat rooms where students can easily interact with each other concerning course-related topics. Group projects are even possible using this model.

LINKING COURSES TO DEGREE PROGRAMS

Most online courses are part of some type of degree program. Often, they supplement traditional course delivery methods where students require scheduling flexibility or where enrollment demands do not warrant offering particular courses on-site. We are beginning to see instances where institutions are offering certain degree programs entirely online.

A common thread is that credits offered for online courses are only available for courses that are listed in the university's catalog. Much like the traditional degree programs, there are limited opportunities to transfer in credits that are external to the institution. One rationale offered by many institutions for the limited ability for students to transfer external credits into their programs rests with accreditation agency standards requiring that credits be issued by the degree granting institution.

PROBLEM STATEMENT

At this time, there is no type of central clearinghouse that publishes, reviews, or evaluates available online course offerings. Given the current existence and expected growth of online course offerings, and given the potential of these courses to be offered in virtually any location, should accreditation and degree granting institutions reexamine their attitudes and policies regarding the recognition and cross-articulation of online course offerings? This research seeks to gather information regarding the existence of degree programs supported entirely by online course offerings. It also seeks to identify existing articulation agreements between higher educational institutions regarding the acceptance of online course credits delivered by other institutions. Finally, this research seeks to identify existing barriers in the accreditation process that would preclude the offering of degrees using coursework produced by other universities.

The authors recognize that these questions only begin to highlight the multitude of issues that such inter-university degrees would raise. These issues include those related to ownership of course content, fee structures, and course content quality control issues. Nonetheless, the authors feel that the movement away from the traditional educational paradigms requires that alternative degree earning options be examined for their feasibility, economic viability, efficiency, and consumer demand. In the absence of higher education's consideration of these issues and willingness to reengineer1 its current practices, we will continue to see the development of corporation specific solutions such as those already in existence at Motorola, GTE, Anderson Consulting and others that have been developed to allow employees to enhance their education while remaining productive in the workplace.

METHODOLOGY

The authors are surveying universities based in the United States offering online Information Systems courses. The purpose is to gather data regarding:

- Program content
- Program cost
- Required equipment
- Transferability of other online coursework
- Degree conferment

The survey is limited to United States-based universities. This search found the preponderance of online course offerings are developed and delivered by US-based institutions. The focus upon information technology related programs recognizes that information technology curricula meet the criteria outlined above (suggesting that these programs are best suited to courses where there are a shortage of instructors), where the students and faculty are already predisposed to working with technology to solve problems.

CONTRIBUTIONS

This study will add to the literature in two distinct ways. First, it will produce a comprehensive listing of courses and degrees available online. Second, it will investigate the transferability of coursework. This information will form a basis for the accrediting bodies, such as the AACSB, to develop accreditation standards for online degree programs.

ENDNOTE

1 Reengineering: The fundamental rethinking and radical redesign of business processes to bring about dramatic improvements in performance (Hammer, Michael & Champy, James, Reengineering the Corporation, Harper Collins, New York, 1993, pp. 32)

Decentralized Business Training: Case Interactive Networked Business Game

Timo Lainema
Turku School of Economics and Business Administration, and Turku Centre for Computer Science, P.O. Box 110, 20521 Turku, Finland
+358 2 3383 11, Fax: +358 2 3383 451, E-mail: timo.lainema@tukkk.fi

1. INTRODUCTION

The competitive environment around most businesses and companies is changing with accelerating speed. For example, competition is becoming world-wide, new products are developed faster, new producing technologies are emerging, and new delivery channels are available. Organizations are in the midst of whole new challenges and are seeking for better competitive position and productivity.

There is a demand for the training methods to be able to describe the characteristic of the recent and future environment and to train the employees to be able to operate effectively and productively in this turbulent environment. Regardless of the level of productivity improvement desired, people as decision-makers and as responsible for task execution need to understand thoroughly what they are part of in order to be able to cope with every day tasks. While the world around businesses is changing with growing speed the business game processing methods are still quite the same as 25 years ago.

In the future the use of management games in learning will probably be at least as common as today (Elgood, 1996): *Technological development will certainly not slow down, and one will be able to simulate more situations with greater realism and greater ease. ...work will be seen as an activity that should be rewarding in itself, and enjoyable, and therefore something to which game-playing can reasonable be linked.*

Considering the recent developments there is a distinct demand for new training tools which enable distributed, interactive, real-time learning. What is suggested here is that – compared to more traditional business training – decentralized business game training and the use of Internet tools could be in many ways a better practise in business training. While writing this paper the author is on the final phase of constructing such an interactive learning tool which will be used in decentralized business training.

2. THE NEED FOR DISTANCE BUSINESS EDUCATION

As organisations have converted to an information age economy, they have also decentralized their organisational power and authority (Hesse, 1995). This has lead to a situation where decision-making power is as near the front line of operations as possible. And this - together with the advances is communication technologies - has allowed organisations to decentralise themselves geographically. By decentralizing activities organisations aim to reduce complexity, increase flexibility, improve efficiency, and create new strategic opportunities (Jackson and van der Wielen, 1998). These dispersed organisations are called virtual organisations and are designed to overcome time-and-place constraints associated with rigid bureaucratic structures. What has emerged is a new type of organisation that often relies on telework.

For people as employees in this new environment, the change has been a rapid one. It is obvious that technologies develop so fast that people have serious problems in trying to adapt to all changes. Teleworking involves several changes in the working practise compared to a non-teleworking environment. These changes may concern, for example (Jackson and van der Wielen, 1998):
- Self-management by the workers themselves
- Reduced input control
- Output-oriented management and supervision
- Skills involved in managing the psychological and social boundaries between work and non-work
- A need for better knowledge management and organisational learning

- Issues of commitment, loyalty and organisational identity
- Better team-building skills and trust between the parties

If the change is so obvious and the areas of change are so many, it is distinct that also the business training should be adjusted to correspond to this development. Compared to more traditional business training, tele-training could be in many ways a better practise in training virtual business.

Distant learning is a category of training, which is technology-based, and where the instructor and students are separated geographically (Whalen and Wright, 1998). The decentralized tailored business game could be one answer on how to:
- train the employees to understand the company modes of action
- visualize the holistic structure and goal of the company
- make the employees become acquainted with each other through the organisation
- make the employees learn distant co-operation with each other
- make the employees learn to cope with new communication technology
- orientate new tele-working employees to organisational issues

While it is often difficult to gather the employees of a company simultaneously in same room for training, a decentralized tailored business game could be a medium to train these abilities needed. Whalen and Wright (1998) mention five reasons for organising distance learning instead of traditional classroom style training:
1. ability to take courses at a convenient location
2. access to expert instructors regardless of geographical location
3. interactivity of technology-assisted instruction that adds value to the learning experience
4. reduction of costs for the employer
5. increased employee access to training because of reduced costs

In case of decentralized business game training, an addition to this list could be the benefit of learning to use realistic tele-working tools in a virtual tele-working environment. If it really is so that the real-world environment similitude of the business game enhances the learning process, then the decentralized business game should enable more effective learning of virtual working.

3. ADVANCED BUSINESS GAME TECHNIQUES

This paper will describe a solution for implementing a business game where several groups of participants each make up companies which compete against each other. It is essential that the business game environment is constructed in a similar way to the real world environment. This means that the connection between the players, the supply market, the customers and the capital market needs to be interactively (real time) processed. What is essential is the role of time in decision making and the communication between the companies and different stakeholders. If the participants of the game are decentrally located, the business game training situation can be made to resemble the actual virtual business environment and teleworking.

So far the computer based business games have worked in batch-process mode which means that the model can not illustrate the actual functioning of real world decision making. The batch-processing model works in a linear order in which (figure 1):
1 the participants first enter their decisions for the first business term or season,
2 the decisions are given to a game model which includes the game rules and operates with the decisions,
3 the game model gives the results for the participants from the first term
4 this iteration is continued from 1 as many iterations as needed in order to meet the goals given for the learning program

A batch-processed business game works in a way where all the decisions from all the competing companies are first made for the whole season to be simulated. Then the simulation phase takes place and all the decisions are processed as a batch, all decisions being equal in the process.

The problem with the

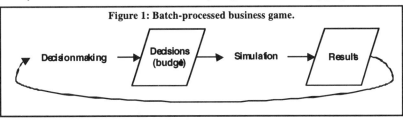

Figure 1: Batch-processed business game.

Decisionmaking → Decisions (budget) → Simulation → Results

batch-processing method is that world very rarely works in such a sequential order. There are hardly no business areas where the decision makers first enter all their decisions for the next budgeting term, then rest during all the actual term, and enter again the business in the end of the term to analyze the term results executed and to prepare the next budget.

What is suggested here is that decisions making and having results from the decisions made should be in interactive real-time mode as they are in the real-world environment. Interactive mode means that decisions are made continuously when in the game model and game market situations occur which need to be reacted to by the participants. In the interactive model decisions are made as soon as they are needed or at least as soon as the decision-maker notices that the market situation needs actions from him.

To sufficiently realistically represent the turbulent business decision environment the significance of time must be included. This is accomplished by building a business game, which includes internal time - a game which works as a normal business environment so that different business events and decisions are processed, executed, and decided on in virtual real-time. The only exception is that the internal simulation time is accelerated compared to the real world.

In a real-time processed business game all the events and processes take place continuously. If not necessary, the simulation processing does not stop at all. The participants who steer the company see all the market events and internal processes on-line. What ever happens can be seen instantly and reactions also can be carried out instantly. The game works exactly as in real world business environment with the exception that the internal simulation time is exhilarated compared to the real world (figure 2).

Real-time processing demands a platform, which offers on-line connections between the different parties in the business game.

This means a network environment. With the use of a computer network the technical solution of the game becomes decentralized. With present network technology the participating computers (i.e. competing companies) can be geographically decentralized. The distances between the parties can be considerable without any disadvantages

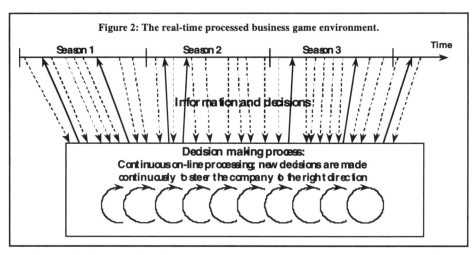

Figure 2: The real-time processed business game environment.

for any of them, because the data transfer times are insignificant compared to duration in human decision making.

With this structure based on a network the different entities (companies, suppliers, customers and funding organisations) are distributed. But with the network environment the entire functional decision making inside the company can also be decentralized. In this form the company transaction data bases are maintained in the network server and can thus be shared with several workstations, all working on the account of one company (figure 3). Because the company databases are shared, the different company workstations can also be geographically distributed. In this structure the collaboration between the company branch offices and remote members is vital and it is possible only with teamwork between the offices.

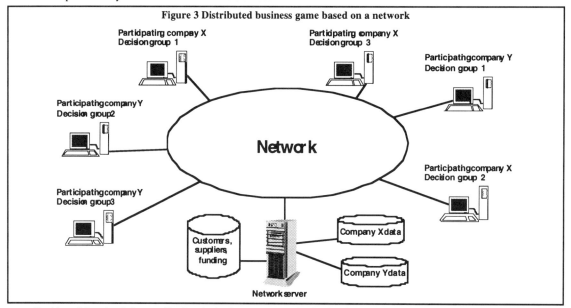

Figure 3 Distributed business game based on a network

Besides of functional decentralization the business game can be further developed to describe the present state of telework technology. In the case of figure 3 the branch offices need to have methods of communicating with each other. This can of course be realized with conventional financial indexes and accounts. These lay the ground for business decision-making, but are insufficient for effective cross-functional collaboration. But there must also be diversified communication about the goals of the business entity and common agreements on these. Fortunately present telecommunication technology serves several instruments to accomplish communication between remote offices. Thus, the new business game could include cross-functional e-mail, voice mail, Internet phone, videophone, and so on, to support the internal company communication.

The impact of time in real-time and batch-processed business games in some company operations and processes is described in table 1. The examples in the table illustrate just some of the deficiencies in batch-processed games compared to real-time processed games.

4. STATE OF THE RESEARCH

While writing this paper the author is on the final phase of constructing an interactive real-time processed decentralized business game. This game will be used in co-operation with two industrial partners for which the game will be configured. In January 1999

Table 1: The impact of time in real-time and batch-processed business games in different company operations and processes.

Operation / Process	Batch-processing mode	Real-time processing mode
Reacting to sudden opportunities in the customer market	The speed in which the opportunities are reacted by does not have any significance, because all the companies deliver their decisions (or at least their decisions are processed) at the same moment. The fastest decision-maker does not benefit from fast decision making. E.g. no company has any advantage of adapting early to customer needs.	The true nature of decision speed is described, because faster decision maker always responds first to any external events. For example, the company that fastest adapts to changing customer needs can gain new market share.
Speed of delivery process	The speed of delivery process has no (or minimal) significance as a competitive advantage.	The time of delivery might have a crucial impact on which company the customer will order from.
Response to misleading production plans	A misleading production plan can not be straighten until the decisions for the next season are being made.	A misleading production plan can be straighten as soon as it is discovered. This means that good observers have advantage of being good observers.
The advantage of faster product development	In some cases the speed of the product development process does not have any significance. E.g., consider two companies (A and B) developing similar novel products. Company A develops the new product during the season in half of the duration of the season. Company B develops the new product during the season but it takes all the length of the season. In this case the company A has minimal - or none - advantage of being faster in the development process.	The company being faster in development processes earns all the benefit it deserves from being faster. E.g., it can benefit from being the only provider of the novel product by demanding higher price from the product.

the game has been played twice with small test groups of participants. The following screen copies demonstrate the functioning of the game model. These very screen copies illustrate a configured game interface for the other of the industrial partners. The process of a delivery is simulated.

The first pilot game event is planned to be held in December, 1998, and the game model will be in productive use beginning about April 1999. After the completion of the game construction, the aim is to study the use of this business game on training and to survey the possibilities, benefits, and disadvantages of the game compared to conventional business game training. Because of the decentralized nature of the game the distance learning aspects are the very focus of this future research.

By May 1999 the researcher will have some preliminary experience on the suitability of the game training in the field of distance business training.

Figure 4: The user interface of the real-time processed business game.

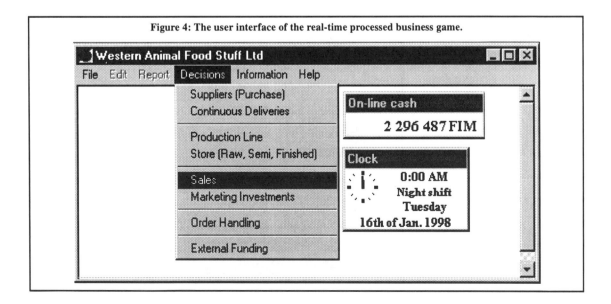

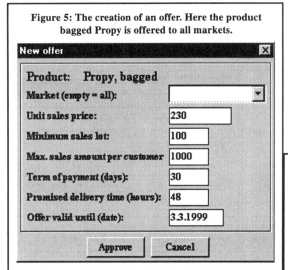

Figure 5: The creation of an offer. Here the product bagged Propy is offered to all markets.

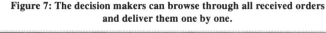

Figure 6: The company has received a bulletin informing about an order from a customer / several customers.

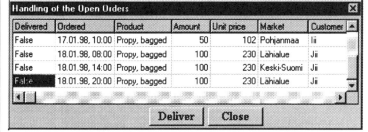

REFERENCES

Elgood, Chris (1996). Using Management Games. Gower Press.

Hesse, Bradford, W. (1995). "Curb Cuts in the Virtual Community: Telework and Persons with Disabilities". In Proceedings of the Twenty-Eighth Annual Hawaii International Conference on System Sciences, IEEE Computer Society Press.

Jackson, Paul, J. and van der Wielen, Jos, M. (1998) "Introduction: actors, approaches and agendas: from telecommuting to the virtual organisation". In Teleworking: International Perspectives (edited by Jackson, Paul, J. and van der Wielen, Jos, M.), Routledge, 1998.

Whalen, Tammy and Wright, David (1998). Distance Training in the Virtual Workplace. In The Virtual Workplace (edited by Magid Igbaria and Margaret Tan). Idea Group Publishing, 1998.

Figure 7: The decision makers can browse through all received orders and deliver them one by one.

Delivered	Ordered	Product	Amount	Unit price	Market	Customer
False	17.01.98, 10:00	Propy, bagged	50	102	Pohjanmaa	Iii
False	18.01.98, 08:00	Propy, bagged	100	230	Lähialue	Jii
False	18.01.98, 14:00	Propy, bagged	100	230	Keski-Suomi	Jii
False	18.01.98, 20:00	Propy, bagged	100	230	Lähialue	Jii

Figure 8: The company creates a delivery on the basis of the received order. The transport mode for the delivery is selected. During all these decisions and events, more than two days of the internal game time has been elapsed.

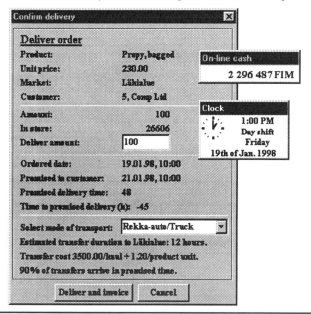

Line Managers' Supervision of the Development and Use of Information Systems (IS): Administration Through Planning and Control of IS Effects

Tor J. Larsen, Ph.D.
Associate Professor, Department of Technology Management, The Norwegian School of Management, P.O. Box 580, 1301 Sandvika, Norway
Telephone: (+47) 67 55 71 78, Telefax: (+47) 67 55 76 78, Email: TOR.J.LARSEN@BI.NO

ABSTRACT

The principle of requisite variety requires that an IS evaluation system must reflect the complexity of the information system (IS) innovation process and the interaction between the social and technical aspects of an IS. This may be achieved through paying attention to how people in their own minds define an IS (the IS axis), the questions that should be asked about a particular IS component (the IS issue axis), and people's role in the evaluation as participants in the IS evaluation process and as users of evaluation results (the actor axis.) In the IS innovation idea phase people have thoughts about IS effects, during the creation phase IS effects are analytically defined and partially documented through prototyping, and in the usage phase the real IS effects will emerge - regardless of the IS effects one has thought about or analytically documented. The objective of an appropriate IS evaluation system is to minimize the distance between real IS effects and IS effects thought of and analyzed in the IS development process. The tool to achieving this end is the IS effects worksheet.

INTRODUCTION

For an increasing number of organizations the importance of information has matured to the level where information is regarded as a fundamental business element in addition to men, money, machines, and management (Keen, 1991; Morton, 1991; Larsen, 1993). Yet, harvesting the benefits from IS investments may resemble the dangerous task of walking through a dense mine-field in a pitch dark night without map and torch. Some claim that the users view as much as 80 per cent of IS efforts as partial or complete failures (Mowshowitz, 1976; Harvey and Lesson, 1987; Vowler, 1991).

These reports may exaggerate of the true state-of-affairs. However, as Keen (1991) pointed out, business organizations do not know the true cost of IS since the ratio of known versus hidden costs for in-house developed IS may be as high as 1:4 and for installation of off-the-shelf standard packages as much as 1:7. The introduction of IS also often results in unforeseen social effects, rearrangement of jobs, and knowledge requirements (Zuboff, 1988). Also, IS is often blamed for not delivering the information people need to do their jobs, a problem that is specifically taxing at the managerial level (Wetherbe, 1991).

The problems of not knowing the effects of IS investments may be a challenge to academicians (since there are so many black holes to fill) and troublesome to IS managers (since it is so difficult to argue for and defend the value of IS projects.) However, it is a paramount worry for line managers since they, at the end of the day, are left with the responsibility for the bottom line business results.

Line managers need a coherent framework and a practical approach within which their planning and control of IS can take place. The view presented in this article is that the planning and control of IS effects is an approach that will increase line managers' ability to direct the development as well as use of IS. In the following section the framework for IS effects is developed. Next, the process of developing IS effects are discussed, followed by concluding remarks.

A FRAMEWORK FOR IS EFFECTS

Three questions are discussed; First, which IS or part of an IS should be evaluated? This is labeled the IS evaluation axis. Second, what are the issues and questions? This is called the IS issue axis. Third, who takes an active part in the evaluation and who uses evaluation results? Here the term actor axis is employed, as portrayed in Figure 1.

The three axes need elaboration.

THE IS AXIS - Which IS or Part of an IS Should be Evaluated?

For the developers of IS the question of what to evaluate may seem redundant. Obviously, the IS to be scrutinized is the computer system they make.

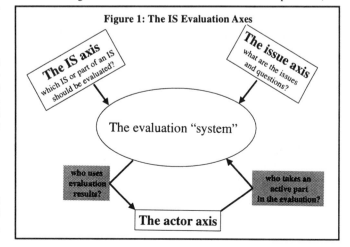

Figure 1: The IS Evaluation Axes

The IS axis
which IS or part of an IS should be evaluated?

The issue axis
what are the issues and questions?

The evaluation "system"

who uses evaluation results?

who takes an active part in the evaluation?

The actor axis

From the line managers' point of view that simple answer is ambiguous. First, managers have a dual relationship to IS. Some systems support the managers' own job. Line managers are also the custodians of organizational interest since they carry responsibility for IS quality on behalf of subordinates and other interest groups with direct or indirect relationship to the managers' area of responsibility.

Second, within most line managers' area of responsibility a host of different IS applications usually are in place. Some are basic organizational systems (for example, order processing, production planning and control, payroll, personnel, accounting, or office automation), others may be labeled decision support (for example, budgeting, customer credit evaluation, or product and customer evaluation), and the line managers may have an executive information system (EIS) available to them.

The recent trend of integrated IS applications illustrates the problem. For example, the quality of an Executive Information System (EIS) cannot be evaluated in isolation since a good EIS is highly dependent upon the quality of the organizational IS applications that deliver information to the EIS. An IS for collaborative work or office automation contains elements from many of the traditional basic IS applications. Last but not least, users may not easily understand the difference between an organization's intranet, extranet, or internet. Users are concerned with how well IS support their jobs. They may not be overtly interested in or know the names IS experts use for IS modules hidden behind menus, screens, and reports. In conclusion, for the user an IS cannot be precisely described technically but is a social construct.

Another integration effect is that users no longer limit their IS concerns to applications strictly within their own organizational unit or area of responsibility. That is, users in marketing may have opinions about the quality of IS in production, and users in production have an increasing need for evaluating the quality of IS in sales and marketing. And everybody has a legitimate interest in the quality of budgeting and accounting systems. The obvious effect of integrated IS is that a particular user is not interested in the total IS, only the *job relevant elements* of it.

However, the question of what is an IS user element remains unclear. In the literature on IS effects the application to be considered is taken for granted. Based on a survey of the most recognized published research within this domain, DeLone and McLean (1992) concluded that an IS success model should contain the elements of system quality, information quality, use, user satisfaction, individual impact, and organizational impact. Seemingly, researchers have not discovered the need for a clear definition of what to evaluate. The focus has been on how to evaluate.

The dangers of unclear definition of the elements of an IS that users take advantage of are two-fold. First, a lack of clear IS definition may result in lumping incompatible IS elements together. An evaluation including several IS different elements may result in averaged data. Second, users may be asked to evaluate IS elements they have no direct need for and/or practical experience with. The negative implications here are lack of user interest, unreliable results, and averaged data. The total end result is data that may not accurately define IS strengths and problems; prerequisites for initiating improvements.

This author suggests that both a top down and a bottom up approach must be used to determine the IS to be evaluated. This is an example of what Van de Ven (1986) has coined the part-whole relationship, that is, the difference between individual employee needs and organizational requirements.

The bottom up approach builds the bridge between the users and the users line manager who carries responsibility for a portfolio of ISs. The basis for defining the elements of an IS that users perceive as an atomic unit is the job tasks employees perform. Job tasks require IS support. Consequently, the definition of an IS user element is: "The user perceived atomic unit of an IS that supports a job task." Examples of job tasks and IS user elements for three employee positions are shown in Table 1.

The elements employees define may be combined to represent larger ISs within a line manager's area of responsibility. A larger IS may represent a traditional functional area (for example, production planning, sales, human resources planning, or managerial accounting.) A larger IS within a manager's area of responsibility is denoted "IS manager element." An IS man-

Table 1. Examples of Employee Positions, Job Tasks, and Required IS User Elements

Employee category	Job tasks	Required IS user elements
Marketing director	Stay informed about competitor activities	IS for competitor intelligence
	Identification of good customers	IS for customer analysis
	Capture market share	IS for competitor intelligence IS for customer analysis IS for order processing IS for inventory control IS for distribution IS for production plans
Sales person	Know if product can be delivered	IS for inventory control IS for production plans IS for sales forecast IS for next week's special campaigns
	Determine order delivery	IS for distribution
Production planner	Determine next week's production requirements	IS for inventory control IS for sales forecast IS for next week's special campaigns IS for production plans
	Allocate work-force	IS for production IS for personnel

ager element is defined as: "(A part of) an IS that supports a particular manager's area of responsibility." Obviously, managers may carry responsibility for several IS manager elements. The concept of the IS manager element allows evaluation within traditional business units (for example, production and marketing) although the IS application is an integrated system. The total evaluation of an IS application would be the sum of evaluation within each IS manager element.

This would allow for differentiation of evaluation among sub-user groups. For example, users in production may want to evaluate the quality of ISs targeted for marketing because production would benefit from having access to these ISs. Likewise, users in marketing may evaluate the quality of relevant production ISs. The main objective is, of course, to avoid a limited and narrow evaluation. That is, although those who are the traditional target users of an IS application may be satisfied with their IS support, users outside the target domain may not be of the same opinion.

An executive officer may ask how his firm can measure its business benefits from detailed IS elements. His argument would be that the most important business value does not stem from one particular but from the synergetic effect of many IS elements. Of course, the executive officer is right.

The answer to the executive officer's critique is the top down approach. In addition to the IS elements that individual employees use, IS should be evaluated for its contribution to business. However, an overall general business evaluation of IS would be too broad in scope and, therefore, imprecise and of little value. An organization must specify business value in regard to identifiable business processes or interest parties. Candidate business processes are product and business administrative processes, product and business technological processes, product and business product innovation, and product and business integration processes (Swanson, 1994). Interest parties may be vendors, customers, competitors, or new entrants (Porter, 1985). Once defined, each of these domains (hereafter called a "IS business domain") can be evaluated separately and the underlying IS applications, IS manager elements and IS user elements can be mapped to them. An example of this is shown in Table 1 where the marketing director's responsibility to capture market share may require support from many IS elements.

Good management practice tells us that a decision body - a group of managers or a particular manager - must be responsible for an IS business domain, otherwise purposeful action cannot be taken (Checkland, 1981). The members of the decision body may not be direct users of the IS elements within a particular IS business domain. They may have vague ideas about the underlying IS applications and IS elements. The inherent danger here is that if the decision body has an unclear perception of what the IS business domain is and what its corresponding IS applications and IS elements are, the evaluation of the IS business domain has no concrete frame of reference. That is why it is important that the IS business domain is given a concrete and good descriptive label and that the contributing IS applications and IS elements are mapped to it.

The enlightened executive officer and, even more probable, the corporate information officer would forward the view that the quality and functionality of IS strategy, common IS rules and regulations, and information technology (IT) infrastructure may not be adequately measured if the evaluation is only based on users' and decision makers' definitions of IS business domains, IS applications, IS manager elements, and IS user elements.

The point raised here is that organizations need guidance structures (hereafter labeled "IS platforms") that may determine IS application quality (Keen. 1991). Therefore, the IS platform is a candidate for evaluation in its own right. The starting point here may be that each part of the IS platform (for example, IS strategy, IS rules and regulations, IT infrastructure) is given a clear name and description. Each part of the IS platform may be broken down into meaningful sub-sets (for example, separate rules and regulations for end-user computing, outsourcing, or IS usage cost allocation). Where appropriate, IS business domains, IS applications, IS manager elements, and IS user elements may be mapped to these sub-sets.

As we have seen, the determination of what IS aspects to evaluate is a complex issue. The principal components may be arranged in a hierarchy, as shown in Figure 2.

THE ISSUE AXIS - What Are the Issues and Questions?

Managers have always controlled the development of IS features through the development and control of conceptual and concrete goals, objectives, and benefits (Cortada, 1980; Farbey, Land, and Targett, 1993; Remenyi, Sherwood-Smith, and White, 1997). The usual practice is to develop goals and objectives for the positive aspects of an IS, a perception of IS innovation outcome that the term "benefits" bluntly expresses. Seemingly, when an implemented IS functions in unpredicted or undesirable ways the term negative effects is employed. In hindsight, many claim, the problematic areas should have been controlled for in the development process. Impacts that strong interest groups may view as negative - reduction in staff or radical changes in work practice – are often not explicitly addressed or for political reasons treated as a hidden agenda, frequently in an intuitive manner (Weinberg, 1992, 1993, 1994). As shown in Figure 3, these concepts can be arranged within the two dimensions of "positive versus negative IS outcome" and "planned versus emerging IS outcome."

The proposition made here is simple. The more issues that are included in the planning of an IS development the higher the probability of implementation and usage success. It seems dysfunctional to differentiate between goals, objectives, benefits, and effects, since each of these terms denote areas that need attention to ensure the best outcome. Because it is time to avoid the limitation of focus that often is inherent in "goals" and "objectives" and evade the naïve IS view inherent in the term "benefits", the term "IS-effects" is preferred. A simple for this choice, but of critical importance, is that managers must consider all aspects of the IS innovation. Since undesired results are so common, and since the term "effects" more often is used in this respect, effects denotes more effectively the positive as well as negative aspects of an

Figure 2: Hierarchy of Components

IS platform
    IS strategy
    IS rules and regulations
    IT infrastructure
IS business domain
IS application
IS manager element
IS user element

IS innovation.

The most taxing challenge is that any dependent construct/variable may be viewed as an effect and any independent construct/variable may be seen as an effect trigger. In research, the focus is frequently on detailed aspects, and justly so since the aim is to understand the meaning of constructs/variables and their interdependencies in depth. The relatively recently established IS World Catalogue on research aid and tools clearly reflects this research scope (see http://www.umich.edu/~isworld/reshome.html.) However, a manager must understand IS-effects in its totality. Since research more often than not explains IS-effects fragmentally mangers must use judgement.

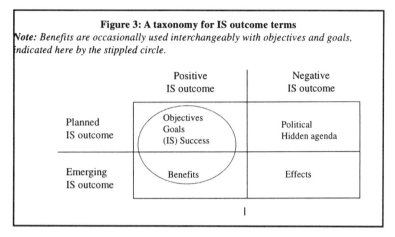

Figure 3: A taxonomy for IS outcome terms
Note: Benefits are occasionally used interchangeably with objectives and goals, indicated here by the stippled circle.

Obviously IS frameworks are forwarded (for example, Morton, 1991; DeLone and McLean, 1992; Olaisen, 1993; Allen and Morton, 1994). Most frameworks do not describe IS-effects and cannot be directly or easily used as the basis for practical IS effects planning and control.

However, IS-effects is a popular theme in its own right. The shortcoming of early contributions is the limited focus on economical issues (Cortada, 1980). Researchers and practitioners have recognized the need for a broader definition of areas where IS-effects occur and that some of these effects, although critical to the organization, cannot be expressed in dollars and cents. Although making progress, some recent contributions do not succeed in bridging theory with practice (see, for example, Remenyi, Sherwood-Smith, and White, 1997).

According to Wilson (1993), IS-effects can thematically be divided into the seven areas of functional productivity, user utility, impact on the value system and chain, comparative performance, business alignment, targeting assessment, and management vision. The division into effect areas is a valuable contribution. The problem is that the author does not present arguments that proves that these are clearly separated and not overlapping IS-effect areas. Nor does the approach guarantee that the areas included cover the business domains where experience tells us IS-effects will certainly occur.

Using DeLone and McLean (1992) as their conceptual basis, the contributors in Garrity and Sanders (1998) present comprehensive approaches to IS success. Yet, the book contains variations of the original DeLone and McLean IS success model - telling us that in the minds of the contributors this model is not stable or complete. Also, the book focuses on research instruments rather than on line management IS-effects issues. Perhaps this is why key line management concerns such as business value (Hitt and Brynjolfsson, 1996) is not explicitly included in the DeLone and McLean model.

The suggestion forwarded here is that the basis for defining IS effects is the concept of the IS artifact (Larsen, 1998). An artifact is a phenomenon or object created through a human activity system (Checkland, 1981; Checkland and Scholes, 1990). The artifact spans the core business activity level, the information needs and requirements level, the IS/IT expert level, the IS level, and the database level. The levels correspond with established views on the development of IS s; business issues as the basis for information definition, which determines the design of the IS framework and applications, that decide the database design and functionality. The addition is the IS/IT expert level which reflects the experience that IS/IT experts more often than not are integrators between the business environment and the IT.

Within each of the five levels effects might occur; business activity effects, information needs and requirements effects, IS/IT expert effects, IS level effects, and database effects. Adopting the principle in DeLone and McLean that technology effects explains organizational effects, the causal chain would be from database effects to business activity effects.

The five effect areas do not explicitly include the "human factor." At a minimum human activity is the combination of organizational structure and networks, formal groups, informal groups, and individual actors (Larsen, 1998). Effects occur among IS/IT experts and among line employees. Thus, IS/IT effects include IS/IT organizational structure and networks, IS/IT formal groups, IS/IT informal groups, and IS/IT individual actors. Conversely, within the "line" effects occur in the line organizational structure and networks, line formal groups, line informal groups, and among line individual actors.

The placement of line effects is made on the two observations that by and large IS/IT determines line effects (in musical terms, it is the theme that the line uses to make their own variations) and the line effects mostly determine information needs and requirements effects. The effect areas are shown in Figure 4.

THE ACTOR AXIS - Participation and the Use of Evaluation

The two most contrasting principles of organizational action that may determine IS innovation participation are mechanistic versus organic (Burns and Stalker, 1994). The characteristics of the mechanistic approach are top-down hierarchical, managerial, and expert oriented. In an IS project the evaluation would more likely than not be carried out by the project manager and the IS/IT experts. In the minds of the decision makers economical benefit and return on investment may dominate.

As Weinberg (1992, 1993, 1994) pointed out, the organic approach builds on the assumptions that the volume and rate of change creates the need for delegation. A small team of top mangers (line as well as IS/IT) cannot fully grasp the social and technical problem content. The knowledge that is required to ensure IS innovation success is dispersed throughout the organization and among customers and vendors. Organic oriented IS projects would put emphasis on the definition of stakeholders, stakeholder participation,

Figure 4: Effect Areas and their Suggested Causal Relationships, with Examples.

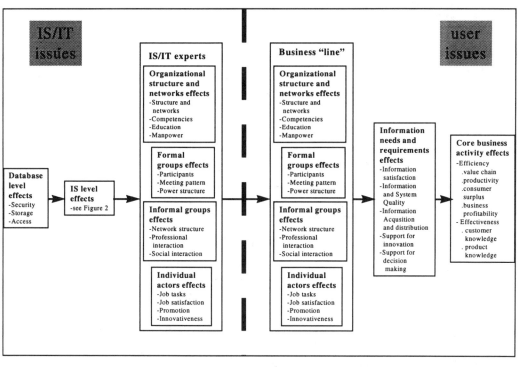

knowledge requirements for participation, and the definition of the broad specter of effects that might occur. Some of these effects may be translated into dollars and cents. Non economical effects are documented to yield a "rich picture" of positive, neutral, and negative change aspects. In essence, decision makers must consider seemingly incomparable IS project effects simultaneously.

It is of critical importance to recognize that we cannot by default say that the organic approach is the best. The organic prin-

ciples carry the impressions of being democratic and human oriented - virtues highly appraised today and, therefore, perceived as most relevant. However, there is no trustworthy research documentation. Obviously, applying mechanistic principles on highly complex social and technical will increase the failure probability drastically. But the opposite might be equally true, that is, adapting organic principles in situations where top managerial control and top-down principles are correct may also drastically increase the failure probability. In conclusion, the IS innovation characteristics determines the mix of mechanistic and organic principles employed in any IS project. The main prerequisite to ensure organizational learning is that the participation pattern is documented.

Decision makers may not want to use raw evaluation data from detailed effect items.

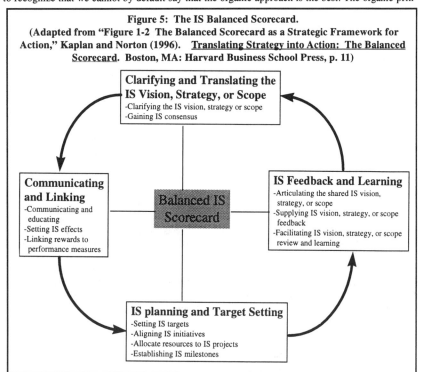

Figure 5: The IS Balanced Scorecard.
(Adapted from "Figure 1-2 The Balanced Scorecard as a Strategic Framework for Action," Kaplan and Norton (1996). __Translating Strategy into Action: The Balanced Scorecard.__ **Boston, MA: Harvard Business School Press, p. 11)**

They may want to see key aspects that would help them understand the IS value added. The relatively recent "Balanced Scorecard" approach (Kaplan and Norton, 1996) may be translated into IS issues, as shown in Figure 5.

Obviously, the issues presented here might not be those of critical concern to IS decision makers. They are introduced to illustrate the difference between documentation of detailed IS effects and managerial issues. The fact that IS innovation still might be a risky investment underlines the need for developing conceptual frameworks for IS evaluation.

THE PROCESS OF DEVELOPING IS EFFECTS

The development of IS effects can be viewed on a macro and micro level. The macro level is defined as the conceptual development of IS effects as a function of the IS innovation (Larsen, 1998). The IS innovation process spans from the birth of the idea that a new IS is needed until the day the IS is disconnected, see Figure 6.

One of the most severe traditional IS evaluation shortcomings is that effects have not been systematically treated throughout the IS innovation process. The most blatant error made is the traditional and obligatory post IS project review that many organizations conduct. Since detailed effects have not been documented as in integrated part of the development process the post review can not be based on good data. This is perhaps why so many post reviews are limited to financial analyses showing wishful bottom line positive return on investment.

Valuable macro analyses depend on the quality of the detailed effect documentation. The development of detailed effect documentation needs a worksheet. The worksheet should contain the effect items. For each item stakeholders should be identified. The degree of importance should be documented. The expected effect level should be included. Building on Gilb's (1976) software metric principle the highest acceptable effect level and the lowest acceptable effect level should be

IS Innovation Phases						
Idea phase		Creation phase		Usage phase		
Idea percolation	Idea molding	Change process definition	Change creation	Change anchoring	Change refinement	Change termination
perceptions about probable effects	socially recognized probable effects	macro effects analytically documented	micro effects analytically documented and prototype verified	recognized effects for freezing IS functionality	recognized effects that may lead to smaller projects that may run trough innovation phases from idea percolation to change anchoring	macro effects that document IS failure
Effect View as a Function of Innovation Phase						

noted for critical effect items. The industry standard performance rate for some of the effect items would allow for benchmarking. The method for measuring the effect should be included together with the cost figure for what it would cost to execute the measurement procedure, the reason being that it may cost more to measure an effect than its worth. Last but not least, each effect should be expressed in financial terms whenever possible. Each IS component would need a separate worksheet. The worksheet is illustrated in Figure 7.

The worksheet indicates that the evaluation process may be voluminous and elaborate. Obviously, one cannot include every detailed IS effect. The selection of focus and inclusion must be guided through the definition of critical aspects and experience.

CONCLUDING REMARKS

Because most IS innovations are complex interactions among social and technical issues, more attention should be paid to the development of theoretically sound IS evaluation practices and frameworks. The principle of requisite variety says that the complexity within a given system must mirror the complexity in its environment (Van de Ven, 1986). Therefore, the objective to establish valuable IS evaluation requires that the IS evaluation reflects the complexity in our ISs. The means to achieving this end, this article suggests, are paying attention to how actors define IS (the IS axis), the careful development of questions that should be asked (the issue axis), and the two employee roles of participants in the evaluation process and users of IS evaluation results (the actor axis.)

The breadth and depth of an IS evaluation changes as the IS innovation process runs its course. In the idea phase people have thoughts about what the IS effects might be. In the creation phase IS effects are analytically developed and in some cases documented through prototyping. In the usage phase the real IS effects emerge. An IS evaluation system must have the capability to handle these IS evaluation stages. The effects worksheet is an example of a practical tool which also allows for prioritizing among effect issues. Obviously, the number of IS components and corresponding effects that logically may be scrutinized is so vast that choosing IS components and IS effect issues is a critical task in its own right.

The implementation and use of an IS is the moment of truth. When in use IS effects will materialize regardless of effects thought of or analytically developed. Thus, an appropriate IS evaluation approach will minimize the difference between real IS effects and "before implementation" considered IS effects. Achieving this goal would mean the end of ritual post audit IS exercises.

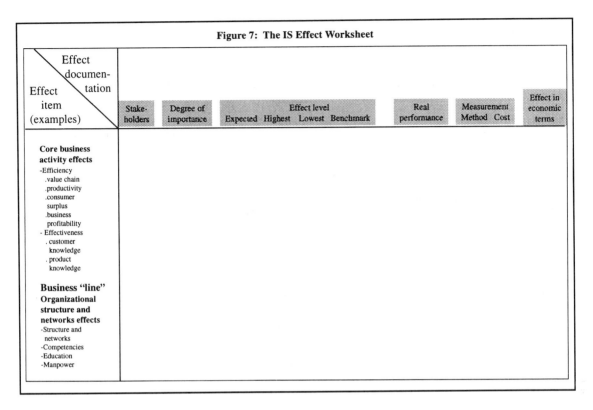

Figure 7: The IS Effect Worksheet

REFERENCES

Allen, Thomas J. and Morton, Michael S. Scott (1994). Information Technology and the Corporations of the 1990s: Research Studies. New York, NY: Oxford University Press.

Burns, Tom and Stalker, G.M. (1994). The Management of Innovation. Oxford, England: Oxford University Press, Third Edition.

Checkland, Peter B. (1981). Systems Thinking, Systems Practice. Chichester, England: John Wiley & Sons.

Checkland, Peter B. and Scholes, J. (1990). Soft Systems Methodology in Action. Chichester, England: John Wiley & Sons.

Cortada, James W. (1980). EDP Costs and Charges: Finance, Budgets, and Cost Control in Data Processing. Englewood Cliffs, NJ: Prentice-Hall, Inc.

DeLone, William H. and McLean, Ephraim R. (1992). "Information Systems Success: The Quest for the Dependent Variable," Information Systems Research, Vol. 3(1), March, pp. 60-95.

Farbey, Barbara, Land, Frank, ands Targett, David (1993). IT Investment: A Study of Methods and Practice. Oxford, England: Butterworth-Heinemann Ltd.

Garrity, Edward J. and Sanders, G. Lawrence (Eds.) (1998). Information Systems Success Measurement. Hersey, PA: Idea Group Publishing.

Gilb, Tom (1976). Software Metrics. Lund, Sweden: Studentlitteratur.

Harvey, D. and Lesson, C. (1987). "The Management Barrier," in Griffiths, P. M. (Ed), Information Management in Competitive Success: State-of-the-Art Report. Pergamon Infotech Limited.

Hitt, Lorin M. and Brynjolfsson, Erik (1996). "Productivity, Business Profitability, and Consumer Surplus: Three Different Measures of Information Technology Value, " MIS Quarterly, Vol. 20(2), June, pp. 121-142.

Kaplan, Robert S. and Norton, David P. (1996). Translating Strategy Action into Action: The Balanced Scorecard. Boston, MA: Harvard Business School Press.

Keen, Peter G. W. (1991). Shaping the Future. Cambridge, MA: Harvard Business School Press.

Larsen, Tor J. (1998). "Information Systems Innovation: A Framework for Research and Practice," in Larsen, Tor J. and McGuire, Eugene (Eds.), Information Systems Innovation and Diffusion: Issues and Directions. Hersey, PA: Idea Group Publishing.

Larsen, Tor J. (1993). "Globalization of Information Technology: Here to Stay or a Passing Fad?" in Khosrowpour, Mehdi and Loch, Karen (Eds), Global Information Technology Education: Issues and Trends. Harrisburg, PA: Idea Group Publishing, pp. 122-155.

Morton, Michael S. Scott (1991). The Corporation of the 1990s: Information Technology and Organizational Transformation. New York, NY: Oxford University Press.

Mowshowitz, A. (1976). The Conquest of Will: Information Processing. Reading, MA: Addison-Wesley.

Olaisen, Johan (1993). Information Management: A Scandinavian Approach. Oslo, Norway: Scandinavian University Press.

Porter, Michael E. (1985). Competitive Advantage: Creating and Sustaining Superior Performance. New York, NY: The Free Press.

Remenyi, Dan, Sherwood-Smith, Michael, with White, Terry (1997). Achieving Maximum Value from Information Systems: A Process Approach. Chichester, England: John Wiley & Sons Ltd.

Swanson, E. Burton (1994). "Information Systems Innovation Among Organizations," Management Science, Vol. 40(9), September, pp. 1069-1092.

Van de Ven, Andrew H. (1986). "Central Problems in the Management of Innovation," Management Science, Vol. 32(5), May, pp. 590-607.

Vowler, J (1991). "A Risky Investment that Business has to Make," Computer Weekly, Vol. 6(November.)

Weinberg, Gerald M. (1992). Quality Software Management, Volume 1: Systems Thinking. New York, NY: Dorset House Publishing.

Weinberg, Gerald M. (1993). Quality Software Management, Volume 2: First-Order Measurement. New York, NY: Dorset House Publishing.

Weinberg, Gerald M. (1994). Quality Software Management, Volume 3: Congruent Action. New York, NY: Dorset House Publishing.

Wetherbe, James C. (1991). "Executive Information Requirements: Getting It Right," MIS Quarterly, Vol. 15(1), March, pp. 51-65.

Wilson, Diane D. (1994). "Assessing the Impact of Information Technology on Organizational Performance," in Banker, Rajiv D., Kauffman, Robert J., and Mahmood, Mo Adam (Eds.), Strategic Information Technology Management: Perspectives on Organizational Growth and Competitive Advantage. Harrisburg, PA: Idea Group Publishing.

Zuboff, Shoshana (1988). In the Age of the Smart Machine: The Future of Work and Power. Oxford, England: Heinemann Professional Publishing.

Multimedia Design and Development: A Team-Centered, Collaborative Curriculum

Anita J. La Salle and Gene McGuire,
Computer Science and Information Systems, American University, 4400 Massachusetts Avenue NW, Washington, DC 20016
(202) 885-3305 Phone, (202) 885-1479 Fax, lasall3@ibm.net

Michael Graham and Charlotte Story,
Design, American University, 4400 Massachusetts Avenue NW, Washington, DC 20016

Jean-Cristophe Hyacinthe and Ann Zelle,
Communications, American University, 4400 Massachusetts Avenue NW, Washington, DC 20016

ABSTRACT

This paper describes a radical new undergraduate curriculum, the BS in Multimedia Design and Development (BS/MMDD). This multidisciplinary, team-centered, collaborative program, developed at American University by the departments of Design, Computer Science and Information Systems, and the School of Communication, focuses on educating practitioners to work in and manage multimedia production teams. The curriculum described here recognizes that those teams are populated by designers, technologists, and communicators who share some core expertise but who differ in some specialization areas. The BS in MMDD meets a growing need in the USA and globally for professionals in the burgeoning field of multimedia design and development. Graduates of this program will help organizations develop and manage their information resources in multimedia environments.

A. BACKGROUND AND MOTIVATION

In recognition of the emerging field of multimedia design, the Departments of Art and Computer Science and Information Systems, together with the School of Communication at American University, created an undergraduate major designed to provide the necessary education and training for this new discipline.

The BS/MMDD blends courses, practices, technologies, and skills from graphic design, computing and communications - it is truly an integration of several disciplines, not a supplement to any existing program.

The goal of the BS/MMDD is to produce graduates who enter the work force as professionals who manage and direct the design and development of multimedia presentations integrating text, graphics, animation, audio, and video. Reflecting the different skills that are required to accomplish this integration, the degree involves a collaboration between three units and offers a blend of design, technology and communication hitherto unknown on most campuses.

The motivations for the creation of this program come from several arenas. Computer scientists are increasingly more involved in the human interface of technology; graphic designers have migrated from the drawing board to an electronic platform; and communications experts in photography, video, audio, and journalism play a critical role in the production of human interfaces to electronic media. Examples of how computer knowledge, design, and communications know how are blending can be seen in a number of emerging technologies:

• The inclusion in the publishing industry of multimedia "texts."
• The proposed delivery of interactive multimedia television to every household in the U.S.

- The transformation of the practice of graphic design because of the impacts of multimedia techniques.
- The emergence of multimedia as the basis for educational technology.
- The production of web-based material for commerce, government, education, and citizenship.
  What do these activities have to do with this curriculum?

1. Publishing and Multimedia

The dissemination of knowledge through the printed textbook is rapidly being supplanted by learners interacting with "electronic texts." A dilemma faced by both publishers and authors is how they will build the authoring infrastructures that will permit the production of interactive, multimedia texts to meet the burgeoning demand for both formal and informal education. At the same time, authors are faced with a radical shift in thinking about how to disseminate their knowledge — static words on static pages do not lend themselves to electronic-based, interactive, multimedia learning.

A new kind of publishing work force is evolving, one where experts in journalistic, graphical, video, and audio presentation of information work in teams with technology and content experts to develop interactive texts. Publishers recognize that few college curricula prepared graduates to work in this evolving field and that publishing organizations do not have the personnel to serve the new publishing paradigms.

The curriculum described in this document is designed to produce graduates who not only meet the needs of the textbook publishing industry but also the needs of any publishing enterprise from advertising to entertainment. Computer-based publishing is transforming presentation of information so that newspapers, advertising brochures, magazines, encyclopedias and other reference repositories, training materials, games, and other printed materials are delivered in electronic (and largely interactive) formats. The preparers of these electronic-based media need to be specially trained (in graphics, computing, communication and new design metaphors) to produce such materials on electronic platforms.

2. Interactive Multimedia Television

Communications carriers are developing Interactive Multimedia Television (IMT) to deliver retail, educational, governmental, and other services directly to the household through interactive user selections of services. The delivery format is interactive-multimedia based with high reliance on graphics, video, text, and sound. The metaphor used is the "Shopping Mall." Through their television sets, users find providers of services and products through a multimedia front-end. They then use customized multimedia interfaces to select services and/or products remotely from the actual location of the provider. For example, using the mall-metaphor, if a subscriber wishes to locate a recorded performance of Beethoven's Ninth Symphony by the Berlin Philharmonic, the subscriber may locate (by navigating through a graphical multimedia front-end) a music provider (i.e., record shop) in the information "mall" and search the provider's holdings (using a customized search front-end) for the particular recording desired. Likewise, customized multimedia front-ends are being developed that permit the subscriber to browse providers' holdings (again using multimedia) with no particular product or service in mind. The browsing functionality is more graphical, interactive, and robust than currently delivered through web browsers.

IMT providers do not anticipate that they will amass the work force capable of building the customized multimedia front-ends that retailers and other service and retail providers require. They envision that new industries will rapidly proliferate that provide the multimedia productions for the "residents (i.e., the stores) of the malls." The program described in this paper will prepare graduates to function as practitioners in these new cottage industries, and, in fact to be entrepreneurs themselves in their own start-up companies.

3. The Graphic Designer and Multimedia

The world of the graphic designer has been revolutionized by the introduction of computing technologies. Paper-based design executions have been largely replaced by computer-based conventions. In an electronic environment, it is not enough for practitioners to understand traditional graphic design principles, they must also be able to integrate these principles with electronic platforms, some of which automate many of the non-creative aspects of producing a design. Graphic designers have to be cognizant of computing systems and software in order to produce and compete effectively.

Most university design programs have already made dramatic progress in combining technology with a traditional design education. The advent of multimedia design has added a new more complex dimension to this blend. For the field of multimedia this relationship must be pushed further to a point where the line between designer and computer specialist is less defined.

The requirements for a sound multimedia education involve the efforts of the graphic design and computing programs as well as communication programs — it is truly a combination of several fields, not a supplement to either program.

The curriculum described in this paper is intended to produce graduates who can function as graphic designers in a computing-based work environment, and to expand their graphic design capability to include the production of multimedia.

4. Multimedia in Educational Technology

The "talking-head" aspect of the classroom knowledge-transfer experience is an aging paradigm, one that is being replaced by experiential classroom learning with learners taking a more active role in their education. Multimedia-based lecture materials are rapidly augmenting and replacing the blackboard/chalk model. In the USA, both at preK-12 and college levels, we are seeing classrooms renovated to accommodate multimedia projection systems. School and business learning environments are building educational technology delivery infrastructures that include not only equipment and space for multimedia-based education but also the teams of professionals who support the instructor who is developing multimedia for a "lecture" environment.

In addition to lecture augmentation, multimedia makes enormous contributions to the field of computer-based training. Both on-line and off-line, self-paced, consistent, training in skills and concepts is a growth area of multimedia application.

The curriculum described in this document will prepare graduates to work in Educational Technology centers that produce materials in this rapidly growing field.

5. Production of Web-Based Materials

Nationally and globally, commerce, education, government, and citizenship are migrating to the World Wide Web. The demand for a workforce in this area is so profound that neophytes, who may produce creatively-mediocre media, flourish in a market where "time-to-web" can make or break a product or service. Also, a new trend is to contract off-shore for such production to compensate for workforce shortages in the USA. The BS in MMDD will produce professionals who understand the inter-related complexities of journalistic knowledge, visualization capabilities, and the technology need to support web-based product production.

The design of a degree that crosses university departmental boundaries poses a challenge. However, the kind of degree described here transcends traditional departments' foci and calls for some creative approaches to collaboration. In a number of existing "traditional" curricula where multimedia education might reside, localized curricular constraints may pose barriers to integrating such a degree into existing offerings including:

- Computing curricula that are concentrated in Computer Sciences are not flexible enough to incorporate sufficient graphic design education or communications knowledge for multimedia development.
- Information Systems curricula may not be technical enough to provide solid foundations in multimedia technology and are constrained by the number of electives in graphic design or communications that could be fit into a program of study.
- Video production curricula tend to concentrate on the production of dynamic visualization and are thus insufficient for development of textual and graphical aspects of multimedia production.
- Graphic Design, as well as communication programs, also have their primary focus in a single area and do not accommodate the breadth of courses needed to develop MMDD practitioners.

Educational Technology may be the area where multimedia design and development could potentially find a "home." However, traditional educational technology programs concentrate on pedagogy more than on design and development and the necessary supporting technologies.

The blend of technology and visual, written, and oral communication that this program offers is the essence of multimedia design. It provides the strongest background available for pursuit of a multimedia career.

B. SOURCE OF STUDENTS AND EMPLOYMENT OPPORTUNITIES

Because of the eclectic nature of a multimedia degree, students are likely to come from a variety of backgrounds including:

- students with an aptitude for art and design who are attracted to the technology-based aspects of multimedia design and development.
- students who have a proclivity for the technology of computing and also have an artistic sense that they wish to develop and apply.
- students who want to pursue careers in publishing as it migrates away from solely print-based media.
- students in communication who anticipate the broadening of career paths enabled by the growth of multimedia.
- students graduating from 2-yr schools with preparation in such areas as art, computer-aided-design, graphics, communication, and video who want to continue their education and broaden their career potentials.

The demand for multimedia design and development experts is driving both educational opportunities and advances in multimedia technical capabilities. In the New York Times and Washington Post, for example, "Multimedia Expert" listings for job openings already appear. During the past several years, a number of print and electronic journals, magazines and catalogs have appeared covering topics including: esoteric theoretical issues about media network performance, integration of multimedia in preK-12 education, media hardware and authoring software, and essentially every aspect of the development, use and evaluation of multimedia.

C. CURRICULUM CONTENT: BACHELORS OF SCIENCE IN MULTIMEDIA DESIGN AND DEVELOPMENT

The focus of the B.S. degree in Multimedia Design and Development (BS/MMDD) is to prepare graduates to enter the work force as professionals who design and develop multimedia presentations integrating text, graphics, animation, audio, and video delivered electronically through a range of mechanisms ranging from stand-alone systems to the World Wide Web. Reflecting the different skills that are required to accomplish this integration, the program blends courses, practices, technologies, and skills primarily from graphic design, computing, and communication.

1. Role of Teams

Central to the program is the role that teams play in the development of multimedia, a focus on portfolio development, and the integration of systemic skills and knowledge into content knowledge including: project management from "Requests for Proposals" through product deployment, legal and ethical issues relating to multimedia, oral and written communication skills, critical analysis, cultural diversity and its role in multimedia, the global economy and its impact on systems development, and rapid technology transfer and its impact on the practice of the profession.

In what may be a unique approach toward curriculum design, from the beginning, students are trained to be a part of a production team. However, academic preparation is different depending on the practitioner's role on the team.

As shown in Figure 1, all students in this program begin with a common core of courses (Groundwork) to prepare them to study the principles applied to multimedia. These courses contribute to student understanding of the components of multimedia including images, language and vocabulary, and technology foundations. Next, all students take a series of courses (Immersion) where they learn to use the tools and products of multimedia and study the influence of these tools on visualization and the creative process.

The concepts of successful teaming begin to be stressed in both the Groundwork and Immersion courses as is the development of a portfolio of individual and team deliverables. After the immersion courses, students branch off into their area of concentration (Specialization) chosen from Computing, Design, or Communication. After completing Specialization courses, all students in the program merge again into upper division teams (Union) where they collaborate (applying their particular specialization expertise) in Multimedia Practicum projects and research. Coops and Internships also play an important role in the program where students are

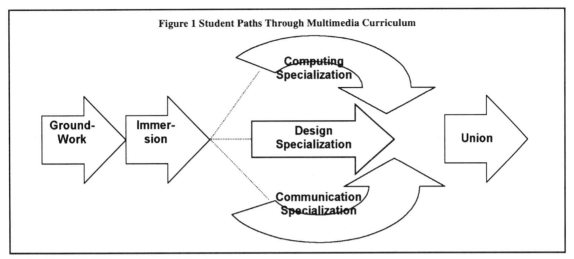

Figure 1 Student Paths Through Multimedia Curriculum

involved in real projects at various employer-sites.

2. Multidisciplinary Pedagogy: Course Distribution and Content

This program requires students to complete 120 credit hours in four years including the following multimedia-related course sequence (Note: the numeric notations in [ ] indicate American University's course designations).

Groundwork Courses:

A total of 24 credit hours including:
- Visual Literacy (3): Ways of understanding visual images in a variety of contexts: art, media, (including film, photography, television, and graphic design), and drawing. Students learn about aesthetics as well as the production aspects of visual images; they discover intuitive dimensions of seeing as well as the major influence of culture on visual images. [17.105]
- European Art: From Cave to Cathedral (3): Students are provided analytic tools for understanding art history. [07.100]
- Understanding Music (3): Introduction to musical language through listening and comprehension, the fundamentals of acoustics, melody, harmony, form, texture, and color in a wide range of music. [67.110]
- Design: Form, Space and Vision (3): Integrates visual principles, materials, and the design process to solve graphical communication problems. Develops a fluency in visual language to form a basis of aesthetic judgement and develop methods of analysis and inquiry that underlies creative thinking. [05.225]
- Design: Color, Theory and Practice (3): Theory, visual properties, and psychological and physiological effects of color including using color to communicate ideas. [05.220]
- Creativity and Computers (3): Explores how computers enhance the creative process including computer graphics, multimedia in literature and art, synthetic music, and virtual reality systems for simulating stage productions. [64.200]
- European Art: Renaissance to the Present (3): An introduction to architecture, sculpture, and painting in the western world. [07.101]
- Programming Concepts I (3): Basic concepts of computer programming and graphical user interface development, programming algorithms, design, testing, and implementation for maintainability. [64.234]
- Portfolio Review: Throughout the program and at major milestones, student portfolios are reviewed by faculty teams and students give presentations to students and faculty about the content and evolution of their portfolios.

Immersion Courses

A total of 16 credits including:
- Basic Photography (3): Technical and aesthetic principles of photography and basic principles of the camera. [17.430]
- Design Techniques I (3): Development of technical skills, creative thinking, and basic organizational presentation processes. [05.348]
- Fundamentals of Audio Technology and Lab (4): Anatomy of audio components; generation, transmission, and detection of sound; properties of sound; electricity and magnetism. [50.101,102]
- Basic Visual Media Production (3): Fundamental technical and aesthetic considerations involved in visual media production including principles and procedures of sound recording and editing, cinematography, editing visual images, and production planning. [17.431]
- Multimedia I (3): Introduction to the concepts of multimedia including the integration of visual, textual, and audio media. [86.200]
- Portfolio Review: (see above)
    Specialization (Students chose one Specialization area from Computing, Design, or Communication) - 15 credits

Computing Specialization Requirements

- Computer Hardware and Systems Software (3): Covers the major hardware and software components of computer systems as well as issues related to their use by organizations including feasibility analysis and hardware and software selection. [64.325]
- Introduction to Systems Analysis (3): Analysis and design through the systems development life cycle including structured analysis

and the tools used in the systems development life cycle. [64.455]
- Database Management in Computer Info. Systems (3): Design, development, and control of databases and applications software based upon databases including database models, logical and physical database design, applications development and database administration. [64.440]
- Designing and Writing Computer Documentation (3): Appropriate documentation for each stage of the systems development life cycle including guidelines for writing and evaluating system and user documents. [64.465]
- Client-Server Computing (3): Issues relating to the distribution of computing functions and data across networks including distributed data, local and wide area networking, transaction processing, and design of user interfaces to client-server systems. [64.442]
- Portfolio Review (see above)

Graphic Design Specialization Requirements
- Structural Drawing (3): Freehand perspective and structural analysis of form including traditional and alternative perspective systems, proportion, and tonal rendering. [05.349]
- Typography: Theory and Practice (3): Theory and analysis of letter forms as design and symbol including typefaces, arrangement and setting. [05.350]
- Design Techniques II (3): Exploration of advanced typographic problems, information organization, and project development and presentation. [05.351]
- Typography: Color and Design (3): Exploration of structure, space, and color in visual communication through the study of type faces and the arrangement of words. [05.353]
- Structural Drawing (3): Structural analysis of form and freehand drawing from simple geometric forms to complex forms of architecture and nature. [05.230]
- Portfolio Review (see above)

Communication Specialization Requirements
- Writing for Mass Communication (3): Stresses basic writing techniques for informing a mass audience with intensive practice in writing for mass media. [17.200]
- The Image From Camera to Computer (3): A survey of the development of photographic imagery from its advent in the early nineteenth century through contemporary twentieth century work. [17.527]
- Location Film and Video Production (3): Small-format video production emphasizing planning, treatment, sound, location issues, and visual design. [17.434]
- Writing for Visual Media (3): Techniques of writing scripts for media including screenplays, public service announcements, commercials, and scripts for non-theatrical productions. [17.482]
- Basic Digital Imaging (3): Digital effects for media production including tools and options. [17.519]
- Portfolio Review (see above)

Union
A total of 15 credits including:
- Multimedia II (3) and Multimedia III (3): Integrative, advanced courses where current multimedia technologies, techniques, practices, and project management approaches are applied in a team setting. Courses are project-centered. [86.400, 450]
- Multimedia Research and Development (3): Students explore, individually and in teams, application areas for multimedia in preparation for the major project produced in Multimedia Practicum. [86.420]
- Multimedia Practicum (3): Teams propose, analyze, design, document, build, and test a major integrative project of their own specification. [86.460]
- Coop (3): Students are required to participate in cooperative education in local industrial or government offices. [86.392]
- Capstone Project and Portfolio Presentation: The program culminates in individual and team presentations of work that evolved during portfolio production and during Multimedia Practicum.

The remainder of the 120 credit hours are elective credits. Students are encouraged to explore cohesive elective selections. For example, a student who wishes to pursue a career in medical multimedia might be encouraged to concentrate electives in biology.

Table 1 depicts this curriculum as offered over four years.

CONCLUSIONS
The bachelor's degree program described in this paper is rigorous. The Groundwork, Immersion, Specialization, and Union courses, individual and team projects, and team experiences are all designed to prepare graduates for a professional career. Graduates are expected to enter the workforce with the knowledge and skills to be immediately productive and to possess the capability to engage in life-long learning in a volatile field that is likely to change very rapidly. While skills are integrated into this curriculum, the focus is on principles, concepts, and bodies of knowledge that are likely to endure. We are confident that students who complete the program will be recruited worldwide, will prove to be valuable assets to their employers, and will be responsible for producing high-quality, high-integrity multimedia. We are also confident that this is a program that can be adopted by most universities.

REFERENCES
Multimedia: a hands-on introduction, Dave D. Peck. Published: Albany, NY: Delmar, 1997.
PC multimedia: an introduction to authoring applications, Francis Botto. Published: Oxford: Boston: Butterworth-Heinemann, 1995.
The universal machine: a multimedia introduction to computing, Glenn Blank, Robert Barnes. Published: Boston, Mass: McGraw Hill, 1998.

Table I Four Year Schedule for MMDD Bachelor Degree								
Semester	1	2	3	4	5	6	7	8
1. General Education Courses (30)	17.105 07.100	05.220	—.—	—.—	—.— —.— —.—	—.— —.—		
2. Groundwork Courses (15)	67.110 05.225	64.200 07.101	64.234					
3. Immersion Courses (16)			17.430 05.348 50.101 50.102	17.431 86.200				
4. Specialization Courses (15) (from CSIS, Design or Communication)					64.325 64.455 05.349 05.350 17.200 17.475	64.440 05.351 17.434	64.465 64.442 05.353 05.230 17.482 17.519	
5. MMDD Union Courses (15)							86.392 86.400 86.420	86.450 86.460
6. College Writing (6)	—.—	—.—						
7. College Mathematics (3)		—.—						
8. Electives (20)				—.— —.—		—.—		—.— —.— —.—
Total (120)	15	15	16	15	15	15	15	14

Exploring the digital domain: an introduction to computing with multimedia and networking, Ken Abernethy, Tom Allen. Published: Boston: PWS Pub. Co., c1998.

Caught in the act: a look at contemporary multimedia performance, photographs by Dona Ann McAdams ; introduction by C. Carr ; afterword by Eileen Myles. Published: New York, NY: Aperture Foundation, 1996.

Authorware: an introduction to multimedia: for use with Authorware 3 and higher, Simon Hooper. Published: Upper Saddle River, NJ: Prentice Hall, c1997.

An introduction to the issues and applications of interactive multimedia for information specialists, by Nicholas Givotovsky. Published: Washington, DC: Special Libraries Association, 1994.

Multimedia technologies for training: an introduction, Ann E. Barron, Gary W. Orwig; illustrated by Ted Newman. Published: Englewood, Colo.: Libraries Unlimited, 1995.

Multimedia presentations on the go: an introduction and buyer's guide, Martha C. Sammons. Published: Englewood, Colo.: Libraries Unlimited, 1996.

Digital video: an introduction to MPEG-2, Barry G. Haskell, Atul Puri, and Arun N. Netravali. Published: New York: Chapman & Hall: International Thomson Pub., 1997.

Caught in the act: a look at contemporary multimedia performance, photographs by Dona Ann McAdams; introduction by C. Carr; afterword by Eileen Myles. Published: New York, NY: Aperture Foundation, 1996.

Exploring the digital domain: an introduction to computing with multimedia and networking, Ken Abernethy, Tom Allen. Published: Boston: PWS Pub. Co., c1998.

Multimedia Telecommunications, Whyte, Bill, Published: August 1997, International Thomson Publications.

Art Of Interactive Entertainment Design, Dombrowerm Eddie, Published: August 1997, McGraw-Hill Publishing.

Publishing Digital Video, Ozer, Jan, Published: October 1996, Academic Press Professional.

Multimedia: Computing, Communications and Applications, Steinmetz/Nahrstedt, Published: May 1995, Prentice Hall.

An introduction to the issues and applications of interactive multimedia for information specialists, by Nicholas Givotovsky. Published: Washington, DC: Special Libraries Association, 1994.

Multimedia technologies for training: an introduction, Ann E. Barron, Gary W. Orwig; illustrated by Ted Newman. Published: Englewood, Colo.: Libraries Unlimited, 1995.

Comprehensive Guide To Lingo, Rosenzweig, Gary, Published: August 1996, International Thomson Publications.

Contextual Media, Barrett, Edward, Published: September 1997, MIT Press.

Digital Television, Benoit, Herve, Published: July, 1997 John Wiley & Sons.

Director Extras Book, Shupe, Rich, Published August 1997, International Thomson Publications.

Multimedia Technology For Applications, Sheu, Bing J., Published: February 1998, IEEE Press.

Midi Files, Young, Rob, Published: October 1996, Prentice Hall.

Multimedia Systems, Buford, John F., Published: February 1994, Addison Wesley.

Open Distributed Processing And Multimedia, Blair, Gordon, Published: November 1997, Addison Wesley.

Software Publishers Association Legal Guide To Multimedia, Smedinghoff, Thomas J., Published: September 1994, Addison Wesley.

Multimedia presentations on the go: an introduction and buyer's guide, Martha C. Sammons. Published: Englewood, Colo.: Libraries Unlimited, 1996.

Digital video: an introduction to MPEG-2, Barry G. Haskell, Atul Puri, and Arun N. Netravali. Published: New York: Chapman & Hall: International Thomson Pub., 1997.

Caught in the act: a look at contemporary multimedia performance, photographs by Dona Ann McAdams; introduction by C. Carr; afterward by Eileen Myles. Published: New York, NY: Aperture Foundation, 1996.

Exploring the digital domain: an introduction to computing with multimedia and networking, Ken Abernethy, Tom Allen. Published: Boston: PWS Pub. Co., c1998.

Beyond Midi, Selfridge-Field, Eleanor, Published: September 1997, MIT Press.

Design For Multimedia Learning, Boyle, Tom, Review Published: December 1996, Prentice Hall.

Electronic Publishing On Cd-Rom, Cunningham/Rosebush, Published: August 1996, O'Reilly and Associates.

Emerging Multimedia Computer Communication Technologies, Irwin, J. David, Published: January 1998, Prentice Hall.

Flash 2 Web Animation Book, Milburn, Ken, Published: August 1997, International Thomson Publications.

Looking Good Online, Bain, Steve, Published: September 1996, International Thomson Publications.

Mastering CD-ROM Technology, Boden, Larry, Published: October 1995, John Wiley & Sons.

McGraw-Hill Multimedia Handbook, The, Keyes, Jessica, Published: May 1994, McGraw-Hill Publishing.

Media Engineering, West, Steve, Published: June 1997, John Wiley & Sons.

MPEG Digital Video Compression Standard, Mitchell/Pennebaker, Published: December 1996, International Thomson Publications.

Second Generation Client-Server Computing by D. Travis Dewire, McGraw Hill, 1997.

Distributed Information Systems: From Client/Server to Distributed Multimedia, by Errol Simon, McGraw Hill, 1997.

The Essential Client/Server Survival Guide, by Orfali, Harkey and Edwards, Wiley, 1996.

Survey Customers through the Web: A New Research Method

Chang Liu
Dept. of Information Systems, College of Business, Shippensburg University, Shippensburg, PA 17257
Tel: 717-532-1674, Email: chliu@ark.ship.edu

Gary Armstrong
Dept. of Information Systems, College of Business, Shippensburg University, Shippensburg, PA 17257
Tel: 717-532-1674. Email: grarms@wharf.ship.edu

ABSTRACT

Web sites are being widely deployed throughout industry, education, government, and other institutions. In the world of practice, the importance of the use of Web technology for electronic commerce activities has been presented by many researchers. In this study, we present a new way of conducting marketing research through the Web. The result should benefit business organizations for conducting marketing research for their customers.

I. INTRODUCTION

Interest in the Internet and, more specifically the World Wide Web (or Web) has soared recently. The usage of the Internet has been profoundly changed. Today, business applications of the Internet greatly exceeded traditional non-commercial uses as a result of Web access [Dieckmann 1995]. Electronic commerce, electronic marketing, and electronic shopping mall are no longer the buzz words, rather they are the reality in our daily life. An important characteristic of Web-based marketing is its electronic communication to support the interaction between customers and the business enterprise [Benjamin 1995]. This two-way, on-line communication between customers and firms will facilitate building real-time, customized one-to-one relational markets. Therefore, it generates a strong appeal for the study of a research method to survey customers through the Web.

II. RESEARCH OVERVIEW

A survey development through the Web has the advantage of reduced cost and reduced response time compared to mail-out surveys or interviews. It also allows marketing researchers to reach some subjects who could not respond to surveys otherwise [Komenar 1997].

The initial survey efforts through the Web should be a form design. Forms are one of the most popular features on the Web. They allow research subjects to interact with the text and graphics being displayed on their computers. Researchers design a question-naire in a form format by giving a number of research questions in which the research subjects can enter information and/or choose options. When finished, they can click a submit button to send the survey to a Web server for data collection and processing.

Server scripts are needed here in order to process research data. Server scripts are extensions to Web servers. With the server scripts, the Web has been transformed into a place of interaction allowing research subjects to interact with the HTML pages instead of just reading or browsing static documentation. The CGI (Common Gateway Interface) scripts traditionally being applied as a standard for the communication between a Web server and its clients' computers. The scripts can be written in C, C++, Visual Basic, or Perl languages. Usually, the scripts reside within a special directory such as cgi-bin at the server side. When a research subject submit a form (survey questionnaire) to a Web server, the server will call the script to process data embedded in the form and provide a feedback in a HTML format back to the client computer. With the advancement of Active Server Pages (ASP), many Web develop-ment tools enable designers to add power processing for their applications through the use of ASP. ASP is a way to combine HTML, client-side, server-side script in one file to produce dynamic Web pages for applications [Van Hoozer 1998]. Therefore, rather than writing sever scripts using programming languages, research designers can use these tools such as Microsoft Visual InterDev to build dynamic Web based applications through the use of Active Server Pages. The script programs or ASP can also interact with a database server to store and retrieve research data. Figure 1 describes the interaction between research subjects and research designers during a survey process.

III. DEVELOPMENT PROCESS

Designing a good survey instru-ment involves selecting the questions needed to meet the research objectives, testing them to make sure they can be asked and answered as planned, then putting them into a form to maximize the ease with which respondents can do their jobs. The Web-based survey design is not an exception. Based on the au-thors experiences, the following stages were set up for a Web survey develop-ment:

Web Server

1) deciding research objectives and re-search scope;
2) designing research questions and their measurement scales;
3) pre-testing the questionnaire to confirm that the questions and their measurements are appropriate, correct, and understandable;
4) designing a Web form to contain research questions;
5) programming CGI script or designing Active Server Pages to link with the Web form;
6) testing and modifying the research design on the Web;
7) distributing the survey to research subjects electronically through the Web;
8) collecting and analyzing data.

IV. SURVEY ON DESIGN QUALITY OF WEB SITES: AN EXAMPLE

Figure 2 displays a sample screen of a research design in the Web form. When research designers distributed the survey through the Web, the research subjects can fill in the information or check appropriate option boxes and then submit the questionnaire to a Web server which is used to administrate the survey.

A server side script (here we use Perl language for demonstration) will be called to process the Web input. Figure 3 displays this server script. All respondents inputs will be recorded to the assigned variables for the data collection and data process. Research designers or those who administrate the survey will also receive an electronic copy of the survey result for each respondent.

V. CONCLUSIONS

This paper discusses how to conduct marketing and/or information systems research through the Web site. An example was also included to demonstrate the research development process. Indeed, business firms can reduce cost and save a lot of time to adminis-trate surveys if applied properly. The Web technology marks a new era of marketing research.

REFERENCES

Benjamin, R. I. (1995), "Electronic Markets and Virtual Chains on the Information Super highway," Sloan Management Review, 36(2), pp. 62-72.

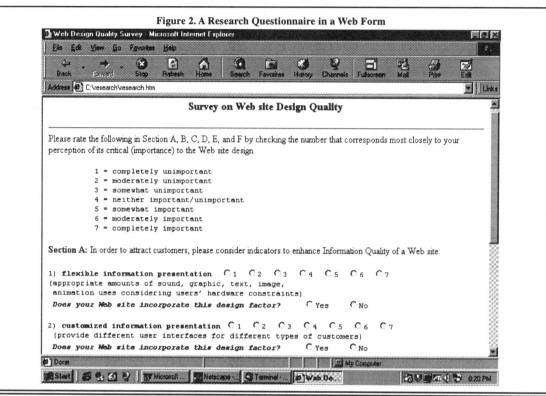

Figure 2. A Research Questionnaire in a Web Form

Figure 3. Perl Server Script Handling Web Form Input from Research Subjects

Dieckmann, M. (1995), "Doing Business on the World Wide Web," Managing Office Technology, 40(6), pp. 41-43.
Komenar, M. (1997), "Electronic Marketing," Wiley Computer Publishing.

The Application Research of CSCW in the Enterprises of China

Lu Liu, Gang Li, Qing Yu, & Xianglong Zou
School of Management., Beijing University of Aeronautics & Astronautics, Beijing, P.R.China, 100083.
Tel&Fax: 8610 8231 4476(H), Email: gxia@buaa.edu.cn or lulu@dept8.buaa.edu.cn

ABSTRACT

A conceptual framework of CSCW is developed which consists of group, tasks and technique. Based upon a real CSCW system, called as CECSCW (Chinese Enterprise-oriented Computer Supported Cooperative Work), a classification of the tasks in CSCW is presented. The CECSCW system supports group's members to accomplish different kinds of tasks: general, subject-based, decision-oriented, and project-oriented tasks through data sharing, communication facilities, control mechanism, and decision-support tools. The application research with CECSCW is conducted and analyzed.

Keywords: CSCW, CECSCW, Group, Task, Facility

1. INTRODUCTION

The information systems in China have been rapidly developed in the last decade. In most large-scale enterprises in China there are some separate information systems served individually to different business purpose: inventory management, accounting, quality management, office automation and etc. Unfortunately, a unified information system has not emerged yet in most organizations of China. That is the reality of today's information system in China enterprises.

Let us look at the other aspects of the issue. The circumstances what today's enterprises in China are faced with are full of severe competition. In order to win the competition position on the global market, an enterprise should overcome the competitors in such aspects as the variety, cost, quality, service and delivery time of the products. The today's enterprises are different greatly from the conventional enterprises in many aspects. The geographic distribution of an enterprise may be across districts, cities, provinces or countries. As the competition becomes more intense, the cooperation, both in an enterprise and inter-enterprises, plays more and more important role. It is realized by more and more people in China that Computer Supported Cooperative Work (CSCW) is an enabling technique to realize the communication, information sharing, coordination and cooperation in an organization or inter-organizations. More important, CSCW can serve as a platform to integrate separate information systems in an organization in order to realize organization's short and long term strategy goals.

CECSCW (Chinese Enterprise-oriented CSCW) is a general CSCW system which has been designed and implemented for enterprise application in China by Management School of Beijing University of Aeronautics & Astronautics. The research is supported by National Natural Science Foundation of China and National 863 High Tech Project. People of an organization can communicate and share information through CECSCW based upon a 1computer network at any time and any place. CECSCW supports group members to accomplish different kinds of task coordinately. It also provides a unified platform to integrate individual information systems, such as operational information systems, EDI, OA, DSS and so on. CECSCW requires only basic and simple hardware and software environment to install and use, Windows NT or NetWare environment. Some case studies are conducted with CECSCW.

2. A CONCEPTUAL FRAMEWORK OF THE CSCW

A conceptual framework of CSCW consists of three components: group, tasks and technique. They are interacted and interrelated. Among them, group or group members are the executors of the tasks. The task is the object of the group activities and the link of group members. The technique or environment is the media through which group members can accomplish different tasks. The performance of a CSCW system is determined by three kinds of factors. They are inherent factors, process factors and out-

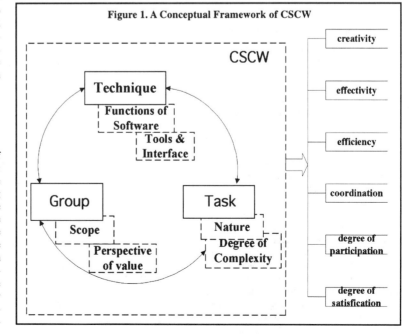

Figure 1. A Conceptual Framework of CSCW

CSCW

Technique
Functions of Software
Tools & Interface

Group
Scope
Perspective of value

Task
Nature
Degree of Complexity

creativity

effectivity

efficiency

coordination

degree of participation

degree of satisfaction

put factors. The inherent factors imply those related to the group, task and technique separately. For example, one of the inherent factors of the group is scope which implies the size of a group; small, middle or large size. Another is the perspective of the value of the group members. Their perspectives of the value may be common or totally different. The inherent factors of the task are nature and the degree of complexity of the task. We are going to discuss them later. The inherent factors of the technique are such factors related to software itself, such as the functions, tools, interfaces, performance of the software. The process factors, which result from the interaction of the three aspects, affect a work process, when group works with CSCW system, to move forward or backward to the goal. The output factors affect a CSCW system's performance. They are such parameters like creativity, efficiency, effectiveness, coordination, degree of participation and satisfaction.

A conceptual framework of CSCW is illustrated in Fig.1.

3. THE CLASSIFICATION OF THE TASKS IN THE CECSCW SYSTEM

Watts et al [1] described four types of group tasks. They are pooled; sub-tasks are independent and can be performed in parallel, sequential; the output of one sub-task is the input to the next task, reciprocal; the output of a participants is input to the other participant and matrix; a hybrid of pooled and sequential.

The classification of group tasks may be different if the focus of consideration or background of application are varied. Here we present a different classification of group tasks, which are formed as the foundation of design of the system, based on the investigation and analysis of group's activities and tasks in some large enterprises in China. First, two kinds of tasks, private task and public task can be divided according to the range of participants. Everyone can join a public task, but for the private task, only the people whom are allowed by the creator of the task can participate in it. Another view to classify the tasks is according to the features of the tasks. Four types of tasks are presented. They are general task, subject-based task, decision-oriented task and project-oriented task.

• General task

There is no definite objective for this kind of task. The members present suggestions, ideas, issue comments and etc. about some interesting issues. This kind of task is used for brainstorming or the collection of the problems or opinions.

• Subject-based task

Every member presents his (her) ideas or opinion around a definite subject. The coordinator will collect and synthesis these comments and opinions, control and guide the process toward the final consensus.

• Decision-oriented task

Member may play three different roles in the implementation of this kind of task. They are coordinator, participant and analyzer. The analyzers create the alternatives and present them to the group members. The participants evaluate these alternatives by using decision-support tools. The coordinator synthesizes all members' comments and then derives a group decision making to notify everybody.

• Project-oriented task

This kind of task supports the management of workflow. The task is broken down to several sub-tasks, which can be performed in parallel, sequential or hybrid of both. And each of sub-tasks can be comprised of some phases. The analyzer defines the implementation phases to form a task template according to typical workflow. The process of implementation of the task can be controlled and coordinated. The suitable tools are available to support every phase of the task according to the member's demand.

The CECSCW system supports all these kinds of task through its functions, control mechanism and various tools. It also provides members with some decision-support models, like AHP model.

Besides pre-defining four kinds of task, people can define new kind of task and then create the task process template through CECSCW. Fig.2 illustrated a task classification in CECSCW.

4. THE APPLICATION CASE STUDIES OF CECSCW IN CHINA ENTERPRISES

We conducted some application case studies with CECSCW in the Southern Power Machinery Corp. of China, SPNC, which is located in Zhuzhou City of Hunan Province, Shanghai Automobile Parts Manufacturing Co., and Yulin Machinery Manufacturing Co. All of these companies are state-owned.

The scale and the production style of those enterprises are different. For the size of the companies, above enterprises are large, medium and small respectively. For the production characteristic, above enterprises are technique intensive or labor intensive. They represent the current enterprise production styles in China.

The application areas include total quality management, company strategy forming, and business process reengineering etc.

Recently, the Chinese enterprises are transferring from the central planning system to marketing system. The executives of these enterprises are focusing on reforming the previous unreasonable production and management process, improving the quality and reducing the cost of products continuously. Most of managers of an enterprise are involved in these tasks. In other words, nearly every task in an enterprise needs people work together coordinately.

Figure 2. The Classification of Tasks in CECSCW

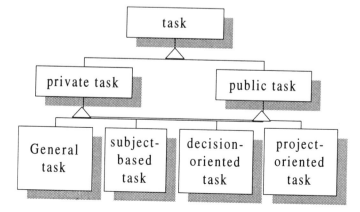

CECSCW provides people with electronic work environment and facilities in supporting accomplishment of these tasks.

5. A CASE STUDY-PROCESS REDESIGN OF OUTSOURCING PARTS MANAGEMENT BY CECSCW

One case study is the process redesign of outsourcing parts management in the Southern Power Machinery Co. of China (SPMC) with the CECSCW system.

5.1 Background

SPMC is one of the largest machinery manufacturing company in China. SPMC produces different kind of motorcycles. One motorcycle is composed of over one hundred parts. Most of these parts are produced by other factories. The outsourcing parts management is one of the most important processes in the SPMC, which affects the cost, quality and cycle time of the product. In order to occupy more dominant market

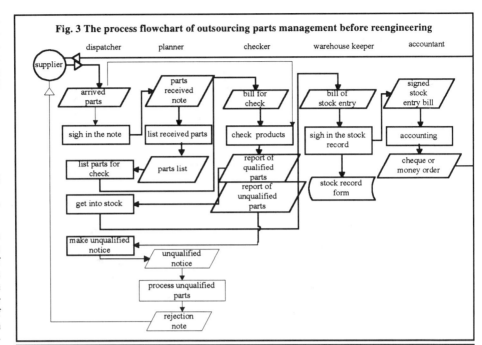

Fig. 3 The process flowchart of outsourcing parts management before reengineering

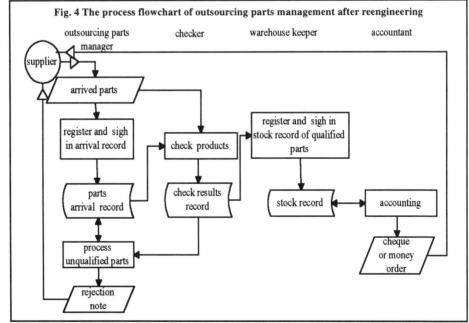

Fig. 4 The process flowchart of outsourcing parts management after reengineering

share, improve the quality and reduce the cost, the company wants to redesign its original process so as to raise productivity. The CSCW supports the managers to find the problem in previous unreasonable process and then guides the design of new process.

5.2 The Implementation of Process Reengineering with CECSCW

Business reengineering is the radical redesign of business processes, combining steps to cut waste and eliminating repetitive, paper intensive tasks to improve cost, quality, and service and to maximize the benefits of information technology. [7]

CECSCW is taken as a common platform to realize Business Process Reengineering (BPR) in these factories. The process of BPR is a group decision making process in fact. It is composed of four phases: to find problem, to diagnose the cause, to modify the old process or present a new process and to implement the new process.

Phase 1: To find problem

A general task called as "about BPR of outsourcing parts management' is set up. The electronic board is used to notice all members that they have to join this public task. It is said that every member may review the previous process and make the comment

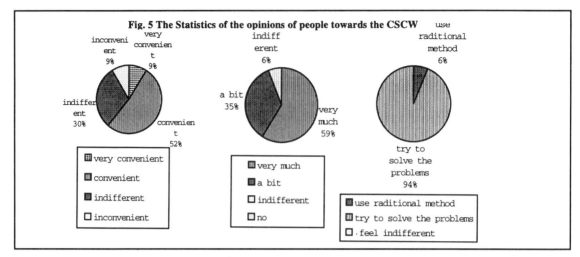

Fig. 5 The Statistics of the opinions of people towards the CSCW

and send it through mail and conference tools before the deadline. The members can read others comments in the conference mailbox. After several days, over one hundred comments have been received which sent by the members in the company and then analyzed by the organizer. By this way, some very important results have been obtained what as follows.
• The activities of the process were conducted in sequence, so the time of the period was quite long.
• The process of review and approval of the outsourcing parts was so complicated, that coordinating activity became more difficult.
• The supply parts could not be provided in time.

Phase 2: To diagnose the cause and give the suggestion

In order to find the causes of the delay of supply parts, a subject-based task is set up for some people in CECSCW to collect their opinions. It was the "diagnosis of outsourcing parts management". Managers from the departments of quality assurance, process design and supply were asked to join it. The original process flow chart, some descriptions and relevant data are given and accessible by all of the members. The members discuss around the subject in this virtual conference. The results show, which are obtained with a cooperative editing tool, the delay of the supply parts results from the function redundancy, the engineering message transferring repeatedly and the low efficiency. Some suggestions are made such as eliminating some repetitive, paper-intensive work; arrange some jobs in parallel not in sequence.

The members were asked to rethink and improve the old process or present a new process.

Phase 3: To obtain a new process

The organizer established a decision-oriented task with CECSCW, which is named as "alternatives selection". He invited other management experts besides the original members. Through the diagnosis phase a number of alternatives was obtained. To rank the alternatives is a decision task, which should be supported by decision models.

The alternatives were evaluated and compared with each other by the Analysis of Hierarchy Process model provided by CECSCW. Members' comments were gathered, evaluated, summarized and synthesized by the organizer continuously. At last, the rank of the alternatives is made. The best satisfied alternative process is selected and presented to every member at last.

Phase 4: To implement the new process

A project-oriented task named as 'outsourcing parts management' was set up aimed to manage and implement the new process. The manager who is in charge of outsourcing parts management created the task and then to create the task template with the tools provided by CECSCW. The coordinating and dispatching of the task is conducted automatically by the system under the control of template. E.g., after signing the receipt of parts, which have just arrived, the manager inputs the data of the parts. Then the inspectors are asked to test the parts. The test result of a part may be qualified or unqualified. After the testing, the state of the part is recorded in the system. The system will notice the responsible persons to treat them in different cases according to the test result or state of the part.

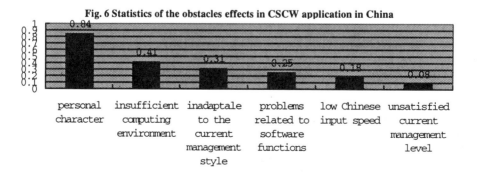

Fig. 6 Statistics of the obstacles effects in CSCW application in China

5.3 Results

Fig. 3 shows the previous process of outsourcing parts management and Fig.4 shows the new process. There are some important differences between two processes.

First, some redundant activities are canceled, and some activities are merged. Second, the number of people involved in new process in reduced. CECSCW supports the new process and workflow through its functions such as data sharing, information communication, and collective composition facilities.

After the implementation of process reengineering of the outsourcing parts management with CECSCW, both labor and time are saved. The period from parts' arriving to parts' entering into the warehouse will be one day from the previous several days. So the cost is reduced.

6. SURVEY
We conducted a survey among these participants who were involved in these case studies with CECSCW. The purpose of this survey is as follows:
• To collect the participants' attitude towards the CSCW
• To find the main obstacle of CSCW application
• To improve the CECSCW software
We sent some questionnaire to the participants and analyzed them. Some questions were as follows:
• What is your comment on the convenience of CECSCW? It is convenient or not?
• How do you like CECSCW compare with the traditional group communication or work media?
• What are you going to do when you meet with some problems in using CECSCW, give it up to turn into using traditional method, or try to solve the problem?
The results of the statistics show that over 60% managers are willing to use CECSCW system in their work for its convenience. About 60% people like it very much. Most of them will to try to solve the problem other than give it up when meet with obstacle in using CECSCW. Fig. 5 shows the result of this survey.

What are the obstacles for managers using CECSCW system in their work? Investigation shows the main obstacles are personal character, unsuitable management style, having no suitable computer network, the shortcoming of the software function, the low Chinese character input speed and so on, in the sequence of importance. See Fig. 6.

The results of the survey show that CECSCW is an applicable CSCW system for enterprise application in China. The case studies and survey show that CSCW has a bright future in China and on the other hand, there are still a lot of work have to be done to put forward the application both in scope and degree.

REFERENCES
[1] Watson Richard T., Bostrom Robert P. and Dennis Alan R., Fragmentation to Integration, in Groupware in the 21st Century: Computer Supported Co-operative Working Toward the Millennium, Adamantine Press, London, England, 1994, pp29-39.
[2] Ellls C A,Glbbs S J,Reln G L, Groupware: some issues and experiences. Communications of the ACM, January 1991.
[3] Brand Quinn Post, Building the Business Case for Group Support Technology, Proc. of the Hawaii International Conference on System Sciences, 1992.
[4] Roxanne S, Turoff M, The Network Nation: Human Communication via Computer, MIT Press,1993
[5] Michael Hammer & James Champy, Reengineering the Corporation-A Manifesto for business revolution, 1993.
[6] Whitescave James, Czech R M, Reddy S, et al. EIES2-A Distributed Architecture for Supporting Group Work. New Jersey Institute of Technology, U.S.A., 1990.
[7] Kenneth C. Laudon, Jane P. Laudon, Management Information Systems, Prentice Hall, Inc. 1998.
[8] Liu Lu, Lifan, CSCW and BPR, Office Automation. Vol. 17, No.4-2, Nov.1996, Japan.

ENDNOTE
1 This paper is partially founded by Nature Science Foundation of China (79970004) and National High Tech. 863-CIMS Foundation (9509-002).

Asynchronous Collaborative Learning: The Mitigating Influence of LearningSpace™

Dr. Hao Lou and Dr. Craig Van Slyke
Ohio University, 226 Copeland, Athens, OH 45701
Tel. 614-593-1799/E-mail: lou@oak.cats.ohiou.edu

Dr. Wenhong Luo
Worcester Polytechnic Institute, 100 Institute Road, Worcester, MA 01609
Tel. 508-831-5181/E-mail: luo@wpi.edu

ABSTRACT

This paper reports an on-going research related to the impacts of a popular online distributed learning technology, LearningSpace™, by IBM/Lotus Development Corporation. In particular, the ongoing research project investigates the relationship between students' opportunities for face-to-face collaboration and their perceived learning and satisfaction with participation.

INTRODUCTION

According to a recent report in *Forbes* (June, 1997), over one million higher education students are currently taking courses online. In addition, the explosion of the Web has led to a corresponding explosion in the number of courses that include at least some online components.

This paper reports research related to the impacts of a popular online distributed learning technology, LearningSpace™, by IBM/Lotus Corporation. In particular, the ongoing research project investigates the relationship between students' opportunities for face-to-face collaboration and their perceived learning and satisfaction with participation, as expressed in the following research question.

Does the presence of LearningSpace mitigate the negative influence of separation on students' perceptions of their learning and on students' satisfaction with their level of class participation?

LearningSpace™

Lotus LearningSpace™, which runs on the Lotus Domino Server, provides an integrative learning environment for creating and delivering training and education through the Web. LearningSpace™ courses are instructor-facilitated, collaborative learning experiences that combine the anyplace, anytime benefits of distributed learning with the "being there" advantages of a traditional classroom – interactions among students, communication among the members of project teams, and direct feedback from the instructor (Lotus, 1998).

Five specialized interactive course database modules were created using the course tool in LearningSpace‰. These five modules allow users (instructors and students) to engage in problem-solving activities, debates, discussions, and learning exercises, as well as access and use stored information. Moreover, students can receive personalized feedback from instructors. The five course modules are:

Schedule – This module publishes and stores the course materials such as the syllabus, assignments, and learning objectives. These course materials are also integrated with a group calendaring system online. In addition, it also provides students with access to the assignment materials and evaluation resources LearningSpace™ such as quizzes, surveys, and self-assessments.

MediaCenter – The MediaCenter is the central repository of all course-related content – readings and supplemental materials as well as media in multiple forms – audio, video, and graphics. In addition, it can integrate live information from Web sites and content from existing computer-based training (CBT) applications.

CourseRoom – This is an integrated module that supports collaborative team work on assignments and projects. By allowing participants to choose privacy levels, the CourseRoom supports multiple levels of communication within teams and between students and instructors.

Profiles – This module provides a repository of student-created "personal home pages" – publicly accessible descriptions of themselves that support the team's sense of online community. Each student's profile also contains a secure, private repository of the student's graded assessments and assignments.

Assessment Manager – This is an "instructor-only" tool that is used for creating and reviewing tests and surveys. The grading process is managed here.

LITERATURE BACKGROUND

Students value interaction with other students and instructors. This interaction is particularly important in classes that employ collaborative learning. As the name implies, collaborative learning requires students to interact with one another in order to accomplish learning objectives.

In a distance learning environment, face-to-face interaction and collaboration is often difficult due to physical separation. However, advanced computer technologies, such as groupware, are often used to mediate the physical separation and alleviate distance limitations to a degree (Alavi, et al., 1997).

A number of studies have investigated the role of technology mediated learning. Alavi (1994) found that students who utilized a group decision support system (GDSS) in a collaborative learning setting exhibited higher learning, both on the basis of an objective measure and on self-reported learning. However, the students in the present study actually met in the same location at the same time, allowing students to collaborate face-to-face, as well through the GDSS. One group of students in this study are restricted, as a practical matter, from collaborating face-to-face. Thus for these, the technology mediation represents a replacement of face-to-face collaboration, rather than the addition to face-to-face as in Alavi (1994).

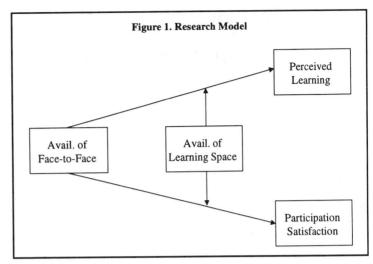

Figure 1. Research Model

Alavi, et al. (1995) found no differences in learning satisfaction and outcomes of students in three collaborative learning environments, two of which involved desktop video conferencing (DVC). The present study differs in that it considers a technology with different characteristics. LearningSpace™ primarily supports asynchronous interaction, while DVC represents synchronous interaction.

Examination of previous research leads to the development of the following propositions.

Proposition 1a: The availability of face-to-face interaction is not related to students' perceived learning when students collaborate through LearningSpace‰.

Proposition 1b: The availability of face-to-face interaction is not related to students' satisfaction with participation when students collaborate through LearningSpace‰.

It is believed that even when face-to-face collaboration is not practical, students are able to collaborate through LearningSpace™. If this technology mediated collaboration acts as an acceptable substitute for face-to-face collaboration, then there should be no differences in perceived learning or satisfaction with participation. Figure 1 illustrates this.

RESEARCH APPROACH

A study is underway to investigate the validity of these propositions. Students of three courses in two universities are involved in the study. The courses offer varying degrees of opportunity for students to interact face-to-face. However, all courses provide LearningSpace™ as a tool for collaboration with fellow students, interaction with instructors, and access to various learning materials. In addition, all courses utilize a collaborative learning model, which requires significant interaction among students.

The courses represent three different levels of face-to-face interaction. One course is an integrated undergraduate course that involves multiple instructors from different departments in the College of Business of a large Midwest university. The students in this course are all traditional on-campus students, and have considerable opportunity for face-to-face interaction outside of class. LearningSpace™ is employed to supplement face-to-face interaction. The second course is part of an Executive MBA program. Students are all employed full time, and generally only meet face-to-face during their weekly class session. In addition, these students are geographically dispersed, which presents a barrier for meeting outside of class. Thus, LearningSpace™ is a primary means for collaboration outside of classroom. Nevertheless, students still have the opportunity to work face-to-face during class sessions. The final course is a completely Web-based class offered by a university in the Northeast. There are no face-to-face class meetings. LearningSpace™ is the main course delivery vehicle.

At the end of the term for each course, students will complete a survey designed to measure perceived learning and satisfaction with participation. Items are derived from Alavi, et al. (1997). The responses from each class will be compared and hypotheses derived from the propositions stated earlier will be tested using multivariate analysis of co-variance. Data collection and analysis are scheduled to be complete prior to the date of IRMA 99. Complete results will be presented at the conference.

REFERENCES

Forbes (June, 1997), "I got my degree through e-mail." *Forbes*, June 19, 1997.

Alavi, M.; Yoo, Youngjin; Vogel, Douglas R. (1997). "Using information technology to add value to management education." *Academy of Management Journal*, Vol. 40, No. 6, December 1997.

Alavi, M.; Wheeler, Bradley C; Valacich, Joseph S. (1995). "Using IT to reengineer business education: An exploratory investigation of collaborative telelearning." *MIS Quarterly*, Vol. 19, No. 3 September 1995.

Alavi, M. (1994). "Computer-mediated collaborative learning: An empirical evaluation." *MIS Quarterly*, Vol. 18, No.2, June 1994.

Lotus Development Corporation (1998). "LearningSpace – Solutions for anytime learning." *A Lotus Development Corporation Strategic White Paper*, November 1998.

An Empirical Investigation of Employee Perceptions of Outsourcing Success of Information Technology Operations

Lynda Roberson Louis

Nova Southeastern University, School of Computer and Information Sciences, Information Systems Doctoral Program

(504) 246-96120, (504) 245-5067 (fax), louisl@scis.nova.edu

INTRODUCTION

Outsourcing has been defined as the contracting out of all or parts of a company's functional work. In recent years, the outsourcing of Information Systems (IS) or Information Technology (IT) functions has become a common business practice for small and large companies alike. Gupta & Gupta (1992) say that outsourcing in the IT industry means using an external agency to process, manage, or maintain internal data and provide information related services. These services include data processing, accessing external databases for business information, systems integration, facilities management, contract programming, global networking, configuration management, gathering business intelligence, and implementing turnkey projects. Numerous researchers, including Antonucci & Tucker III (1998), Earl (1996), Gurbaxani (1996), and McFarlan & Nolan (1995), have identified various reasons why companies are choosing to outsource its IT operations. These include, but are not limited to:
- Reduce or control operating costs
- Make capital funds available
- Cash infusion
- Resources not available internally
- Function difficult to manage or out of control
- Improve business focus
- Access to world-class capabilities
- Accelerated reengineering benefits
- Shared risks
- Focus on core competencies
- Free resources for other purposes.

Selective outsourcing, whereby a company will chose to outsource only part of its IT functions and retain control of the rest, is also an emerging trend (Lacity, Willcocks, & Feeny, 1996; Slaughter & Ang, 1996). Selective outsourcing leads to a relationship that is viewed more as a partnership of responsibilities and accountabilities between the firms involved. When more than one firm is chosen for the outsourcing venture, the arrangement is viewed as a strategic business alliance between the firms.

PROBLEM

While most outsourcing initiatives attempt to open a line of communication between upper management and affected employees, little effort is made to assess and incorporate employee perceptions into the outsourcing deal. Not enough attention is given to integrating employee concerns about outsourcing into the outsourcing process. Management is presented with a preconceived list of personnel issues from the outsourcing firms that it readily adopts. Management does not seek input from employees to assess the impact that the impending deal may have on these employees. Perceptions of employees may produce negative impact on the success of an outsourcing deal. Will knowing how the employees perceive the outsourcing venture and integrating these perceptions into the process lead to a more successful outsourcing relationship and deal?

GOAL

The objective of this research is to investigate the effects of Information Technology employees' perceptions about outsourcing IT functions in relationship to their career objectives and whether this perception affects outsourcing success. This investigation will seek to answer hypotheses that propose a relationship between factors both associated with outsourcing and identified in the literature search, and employee attitudes about outsourcing effects on their careers. The hypothesis will be formulated based on the following set of research questions drawn from an extensive review of outsourcing literature:

1. What effect has the outsourcing had on the employees who were outsourced?
2. What effect has the outsourcing had on employees retained in the company that outsourced its IT functions?
3. What are the employees perceived views of the outsourcing process: either positive or negative?
4. What is the perception of the employees involved in outsourcing of whether the move will/did enhance or hinder their IT career objectives?
5. What is the employees' level of perceived change in commitment from either company (outsourcee and outsourcer) toward furthering the employees' career objectives?
6. What effects do the employees perceive that their attitudes about the outsourcing initiative will/will not impact the success of the overall outsourcing relationship between the companies?
7. What is the perception that the quality of service provided by the outsourcer will be affected by the employees' attitudes toward the

outsourcing?
8. What are the employees perceived effects of the outsourcing initiative as a result of communication by either company? Was enough communication done up front to contribute to the employee perception of the impact of the outsourcing? Has enough communication continued following the transition of employees to contribute to the employees' perceptions of the impact of the outsourcing?

RELEVANCE, SIGNIFICANCE OF RESEARCH AND LITERATURE REVIEW

An investigation into IT/IS outsourcing literature revealed that a wealth of information exists on this topic in general. Frameworks and strategies for achieving an outsourcing deal are presented by researchers such as Grover, Cheon, & Teng (1994b), Lacity & Hirschheim (1993a) and Loh & Venkatraman (1992). Successes and failures of outsourcing based on factors such as management of the contracts are discussed by Benko (1993), Guterl (1996) and Mullin (1996). Antonucci & Tucker III (1998) discussed perceived benefits from management's perspective. Economic perspectives are given by Alpar & Saharia (1995) and Aubert, Rivard, & Patry (1996). Barrett (1996), Duncan (1995), Gerston (1997), and Quinn & Hilmer (1994) state that often companies will outsource so that they can strategically concentrate on their core competencies, which is unusually not IT. Lacity, Hirschheim, & Willcocks (1994) state that senior executives view IT as a utility and not a competitive weapon, thus making IT a prime candidate for outsourcing.

McLellan (1993) identified three core personnel issues that are both economic and strategic benefits to outsourcing: cost economies, enhanced career opportunities and reduced staff turnover, and removal of the salary sub-units. Lacity, Hirschheim, & Willcocks (1994) studied why outsourcing deals often fail to produce the results anticipated. They note that while many outsourcing deals list access to technical talent as a reason for outsourcing IT functions, this tactic can often backfire when a company's current perceived incompetent staff is transitioned to the vendor. They contend that the only way to ensure access to the technical skills desired is to build this requirement into the contract.

Barrett (1996) contended that ultimately outsourcing is concerned about people and jobs. He noted that in the deal between Hughes Aircraft and vendor Computer Science Corporation (CSC), 950 jobs were eliminated from Hughes but transitioned to CSC. Although Hughes made great efforts to ensure that the transitioned employees received similar benefits and pay packages with CSC, the results from this process were not without problems. Twenty-five (25%) percent of the Hughes IT staff quit prior to the transition, one-third (1/3) of the staff embraced the move and one-third (1/3) hated the change.

Eckerson (1992) discussed the importance of developing an effective line of communication during the transition process. He discussed Electronic Data Systems' (EDS) well-defined strategy for managing the transfer of employees to the company. EDS has developed a three-phase approach to communication. During the pre-transition phase, which spans three weeks to six months, EDS deals with details of benefits, compensation and personnel policies. The second phase goes into effect once a contract is secured. Then EDS will send in a staff to facilitate discussion groups, man hot lines, and meet individually with employees expected to transition into EDS. The post-transition phase involves the continued efforts to focus on problems and questions associated with benefits, and the beginning of training and education programs that focus on EDS company values, its mission and approaches.

Khosrowpour, Subramanian, Gunderman, & Saber (1996) studied the perceptions of IS professionals, how outsourcing affected them, and career and communications issues related to outsourcing. They state that successful outsourcing deals effectively with the human factors and that this requires management to understand what perceptions exist within the employee ranks. Their research identified the following human factors as critical to this issue: attracting and retaining talented IS professionals, employee resistance to outsourcing, job security, morale, productivity, training, and opportunities and career paths. These same set of issues are supported, all or in part, by Gupta & Gupta (1992), Laribee & Michaels-Barr (1994), Lee, Trauth, & Farwell (1995), Longnecker & Stephenson (1997), Richey (1992) and Wray (1996). None of these other researchers, however, offers a study addressing these factors from the employees' perspectives.

Gupta & Gupta (1992) state that IS employees often feel threatened and demoralized by outsourcing. They stress the need to involve key IS/IT personnel in the decision process so that these employees have a full appreciation of why outsourcing is necessary and what the implications of these decisions are. They contend that doing so leads to a more successful outsourcing venture.

Laribee & Michaels-Barr (1994) cite examples of early outsourcing ventures that resulted in the loss of IS jobs after the transition to the vendor. They contend that this issue emphasizes the need for careful planning for employees' needs during an outsourcing transition. Transition of employees affects morale and productivity. They note that communication is crucial to a successful transition process. They assert that the message to relay is that the decision to outsource is based on sound business objectives and that the job is valuable and appreciated. They contend that the three types of employees involved in outsourcing - those retained in the company, those transitioned to the vendor, and those laid-off - each must be handled differently. They offer management advice on how to effectively handle each type of employee to ensure a smooth process.

Lee, Trauth, & Farwell (1995) studied the changing face of IT and the effect this will have on future job skills and knowledge requirements. They say that outsourcing is causing a shift in the needs for IS knowledge and skills and companies and academia must adopt to this change in order to ensure a competent work force.

Longnecker & Stephenson (1997) contend that companies should develop a viable plan to deal with human resource problems associated with outsourcing. They state that challenges to the outsourcer are change management, employees' perceived loss of control and development opportunities, training and retaining employees, career transitions, and vendor staffing. They also assert that communication is key to addressing and resolving these human resource issues. They say success is gained when these issues are planned for and understood early in the process.

Richey (1992) addressed the effects of downsizing, including outsourcing, on employee job performance, morale and loyalty. He points to the importance of communication as a key enabler of effectively dealing with employees. He contends that the employee perception of this communication has a definite impact on the above factors.

Wray (1996) discussed the role of a company's human resource (HR) department in the outsourcing process. The key, he says, is communication. He stated that HR should prepare early to address issues from employees and should interact with the vendor HR to secure as much information and identify key issues. Both HR groups should know the employee concerns, which he asserts include benefits, options, job content/requirements, and security, and jointly develop a plan to address these issues.

The above research and articles demonstrate that the issues associated with outsourcing cover a wide spectrum. An important undercurrent to most outsourcing research and articles that address human resource issues is the need to communicate. Nearly all the researchers report that this communication is based on issues predetermined by upper management and the vendor companies, and not those perceived by the employees. To achieve effective communication and not adversely affect the outsourcing venture, these human resource issues cannot be ignored.

Khosrowpour, Subramanian, Gunderman, & Saber (1996) have the only published study addressing employee perceptions of outsourcing as of 1998. They suggest that their research can be extended by studying and comparing successful and unsuccessful outsourcing deals in relationship to the impact on people and organizations. Their research addressed the perspectives of IS professionals who may or may not have been directly involved in an outsourcing deal. This research will focus on how outsourcing affected retained and transitioned employees directly involved in the outsourcing in an attempt to identify a relationship between the employee perceptions and factors associated with outsourcing successes and failures. This research will be an initial attempt to validate results from the Khosrowpour, Subramanian, Gunderman, & Saber (1996) study against a more specific IT population. The results should contribute to helping management understand the effect of human resource issues from the employees' perspective and better use this information to formulate strategies for handling an outsourcing initiative. Since this is an area lacking in the outsourcing field of knowledge, these results should help lead to more successful IT outsourcing ventures.

RESEARCH PLAN

This study seeks to investigate the effects of outsourcing IT functions on information technology employees in terms of their career objective and its impact on outsourcing success. This research focuses on how outsourcing has affected retained and transitioned employees directly involved in outsourcing in an attempt to identify a causal relationship between the employee perspective and human factors identified in previous research and outsourcing successes. The research will evaluate the following human factors associated with outsourcing as viewed or expressed by employees directly involved in U. S. outsourcing deals over the past five (5) years. These factors are: attracting and retaining talented IS professionals, employee resistance to outsourcing, job security, morale, productivity, training, and opportunities and career paths and advancements. Results of this study are intended to contribute to helping management understand the effect of issues from the employee perspective, and thus assist management in its outsourcing efforts that will benefit both the company and the employee.

This is an empirical investigation taking the form of a survey submitted to members of prominent IT/IS national organizations. For inclusion in the results, the participant must have been affected directly by an outsourcing deal. The survey instrument will be validated through the Institutional Review Board at Nova Southeastern University prior to its use. It will then be pre-tested on a select population prior to beginning the study. The anticipated benefit of this research is to provide insight to management on how better to incorporate employee concerns into the outsourcing process, while maintaining the goal of the overall outsourcing initiative.

ABREVIATED LIST OF REFERENCES

Alpar, P., & Saharia, A. N. (1995). Outsourcing information systems functions: An organization economics perspective. Journal of Organizational Computing, 5, 197-217.

Antonucci, Y. L., & Tucker III, J. J. (1998). IT outsourcing: Current trends, benefits, and risks. Information Strategy: The Executive's Journal, 14(2), 16-26.

Aubert, B. A., Rivard, S., & Patry, M. (1996). Development of measures to assess dimensions of IS operation transactions. Omega-International Journal of Management Science, 24, 661-680.

Barrett, R. (1996). Outsourcing success means making the right moves. Available: http://www.reengineering.com/articles/jul96/InfoManagement.html [1998, January 21].

Benko, C. (1993). Outsourcing evaluation: A profitable process. Information Systems Management, 10(2), 45-50.

Duncan, N. (1995). Buying core competencies? A study of the impact of outsourcing on IT infrastructure flexibility. Available: http://hsb.baylor.edu/ramsower/acis/papers/duncan.htm [1998, January 21].

Earl, M. J. (1996). The risks of outsourcing IT. Sloan Management Review, 37(3), 26-32.

Eckerson, W. (1992). Outsourcing: Tending to the people issues. Network World, 9(12), 23,26.

Gerston, J. (1997). Outsourcing in client/server environments. Information Systems Management, 14(2), 74-77.

Grover, V., Cheon, M. J., & Teng, J. T. C. (1994). A descriptive study on the outsourcing of information systems functions. Information & Management, 27(1), 33-44.

Gupta, U. G., & Gupta, A. (1992). Outsourcing the IS function: Is it necessary for your organization? Information Systems Management, 9(3), 44-50.

Gurbaxani, V. (1996). A new world of information technology outsourcing. Communications of the ACM, 39(7), 45-46.

Guterl, F. (1996, March 1). How to manage your outsourcer. Datamation, 42, 79-83.

Lacity, M., & Hirschheim, R. (1993). Implementing information systems outsourcing: Key issues and experiences of an early adopter. Journal of General Management, 19(1), 17-31.

Lacity, M., Hirschheim, R., & Willcocks, L. (1994). Realizing outsourcing expectations: Incredible expectations, credible outcomes. Information Systems Management, 11(4), 7-18.

Lacity, M. C., Willcocks, L. P., & Feeny, D. F. (1996). The value of selective IT sourcing. Sloan Management Review, 37(3), 13-25.

Laribee, J. F., & Michaels-Barr, L. (1994). Dealing with personnel concerns in outsourcing. Journal of Systems Management, 45(1), 6-12.

Lee, D. M. S., Trauth, E. M., & Farwell, D. (1995). Critical skills and knowledge requirements of IS professionals: A joint academic/industry investigation. MIS Quarterly, 19, 313-340.

Loh, L., & Venkatraman, N. (1992). Determinants of information technology outsourcing: A cross-sectional analysis. Journal of Management Information Systems, 9(1), 7-24.

Longnecker, B., & Stephenson, J.-M. (1997). HR's role in outsourcing. Journal of Business Strategy, 18(4), 53.

McFarlan, F. W., & Nolan, R. L. (1995). How to manage an IT outsourcing alliance. Sloan Management Review, 36(2), 9-23.

Mullin, R. (1996). Outsourcing: Managing the outsourced enterprise. Journal of Business Strategy, 17(4), 28-36.

Quinn, J. B., & Hilmer, F. G. (1994). Strategic outsourcing. Sloan Management Review, 35(4), 43-55.

Richey, M. W. (1992). The impact of corporate downsizing on employees. Business Forum, 17(3), 9-13.

Slaughter, S., & Ang, S. (1996). Employment outsourcing in information systems. Communications of the ACM, 39(7), 47-54.

Wray, G. N. (1996). The role of human resources in successful outsourcing. Employment Relations Today, 23(1), 17-23.

The Field of Dreams: If you build a class Web site will they come? - A Case Study

Ross A. Malaga
Assistant Professor, Information Systems, University of Maryland, Baltimore County, Baltimore, MD 21250
malaga@umbc.edu

ABSTRACT

The use of Web sites to support lecture based classes and distance education has been gaining in popularity. The author surveyed students in an introductory information systems class concerning their use of and attitudes toward the class Web site. The author then conducted an experiment to determine if students in a class with Web based supporting material perform better than students in a class without Web based support. The results indicate that students need to be shown how to use the Web site.

INTRODUCTION

Due to their knowledge of the technology involved, information systems instructors have taken a lead role in using World Wide Web sites to augment their traditional lecture based teaching. In some institutions entire IS programs are offered online.

Since building a class Web site can be very time consuming it is important to know what content and features will work best to help students in learning the course material. In addition, it is important to understand why students use or don't use the Web site. If you build it, will they come?

THE NEED FOR WEB SITES IN IS EDUCATION

Perhaps more than any other subject information systems is a perfect match for online course content. After all online content allows students to view the technology they are studying in action. In addition, the rapid pace of change in the information systems field necessitates a content delivery medium that can be rapidly updated.

Out of Date Information

The development of new information technologies proceeds at an incredible pace. However, the traditional information systems textbook can be as many as eighteen months to two years out of date. Even a recently published textbook can be made obsolete by advances in technology. For instance, "Essentials of Management Information Systems: Organization and Technology", an introductory information systems text published in 1997, stated that, "Most voice [input] systems still have limited vocabularies of several hundred to several thousand words and can accept only very simple commands [1 pg. 150]." Advances in the field of voice recognition and the release of several continuous voice recognition software packages have made that passage in the textbook inaccurate only months after it was published. Similar examples can be found in almost any general information systems textbook.

Information systems students, should, and often do make use of the World Wide Web to find more up to date information. However, students often encounter three major problems when dealing with the Web:
- Inability to judge the reliability of information sources
- Inability to find relevant information
- Inability to relate online information to material covered in class.

Thus the use of a course Web site, developed by the instructor, with links to the most current information can prove to be a valuable tool in information systems education. The IS course Web site can act as a key ingredient to a distance education approach to the course, or it can provide support for a traditional in-class lecture style course. By creating the web site the instructor can ensure that the material is reliable and relevant. A well developed site will also integrate the Web based material with the textbook and lectures.

Improved Communication (with Instructor and with Other Students)

Over the past few years there has been a huge influx of students into information systems (and related) programs. Some programs do not have the instructors to keep up with demand. Thus some institutions have increased class sizes to the point where communication between the instructor and students has become difficult. In addition, many students in these programs have outside obligations (jobs and/or families) that do not allow time for interaction with fellow students.

A well designed course Web site can help alleviate these problems. The site can make use of discussion forum software for asynchronous communication and chat rooms for synchronous communication among small groups.

Financial Considerations and the Move Toward Distance Education

Some schools are beginning to view distance education offerings as a major revenue generator. For example, the on-campus cost for a Duke University MBA is about $50,000. Compare that with the $82,500 Duke students pay to earn their MBA through Duke's online Global Executive MBA program [2].

The higher cost of distance education offerings is offset at many schools by a reduction or elimination of campus activity fees. However, the fact that some schools do charge more for their online programs demonstrates that students are willing to pay for convenience.

Clearly colleges and universities have gotten the message that distance education is in demand and can be profitable. From 1995 to 1996 the number of online course s offered at four year colleges increased by 40% to 1,218 [2].

IF YOU BUILD IT, WILL THEY COME?

In 1997 the author built a web site to support a traditionally taught (lecture based) introductory undergraduate information systems course in a business school. The rationale for building this site was a lack of up to date information in the course textbook and student complaints about the course in general. Specifically, students were not happy with the low level of interaction with the professor and fellow students necessitated by a large lecture style class. In addition, students wanted a means of assessing their own knowledge of the course material before exams. Thus, the initial goals of the course Web site were:

- To augment the textbook and lectures with current information
- To provide feedback to students concerning their progress in the course
- To improve communication between students and the instructor
- To facilitate greater communication between students
- To experiment with the technology in order to move the course toward a distance education paradigm

The Web Site

The Web site (http://icasit.gmu.edu/rmalaga/mis201/mis201.htm) was developed around an online syllabus (see figure 1). This syllabus was the same as the paper based one handed out to students at the beginning of the semester. However, the online version provided a links to the online material for each topic. Each topic page (see figure 2) included a list of learning objectives, a hyperlinked table of contents for sub-topics, a button to launch a Java based quiz applet, and the actual material. The purpose of the online material was to update the textbook. The online material included a paragraph or two, written by the instructor, introducing the material and pointing out where the textbook was out of date. The material also provided links with other academic and commercial sites that had relevant information. For example, in a section of voice recognition links were provided to various software vendors, such as Dragon Systems, and Kurzweil.

Figure 1. Web Based Syllabus

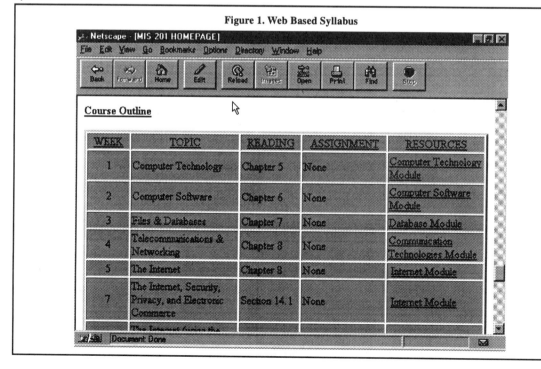

Figure 2. Topic Page

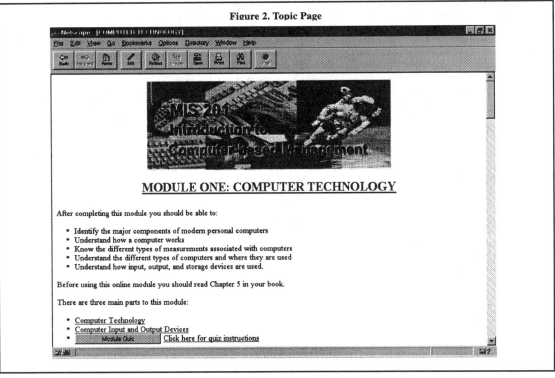

In order to facilitate greater communication, the course Web site also included a discussion forum area. This discussion forum was built using Lotus Domino and supported asynchronous communication only. In order to encourage students to use the discussion area, postings were counted toward the student's class participation grade.

Figure 3. Web Based Content with Hyperlinks

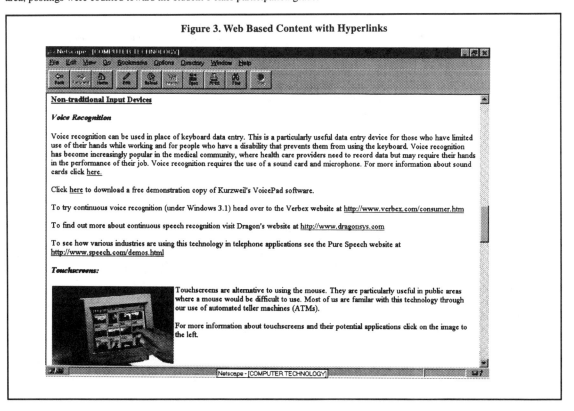

The Java based quiz program could be used by students to assess their knowledge of the topic material before the actual exam. The quizzes were not used in determining the student's grade. As a matter of fact, only the student was able to view his or her quiz grade. The quizzes used a multiple choice format. Ten questions were randomly selected from a database of approximately twenty questions for each topic. The applet totaled the student's score and reported a quiz grade to the student. Due to the random selection of questions students could take the quiz a number of times before all questions were viewed.

The Initial Survey

In order to determine if students would use the Web site and if the site would help in the learning process a survey was developed. Since the online material covered only the first part of the semester, students were surveyed at the time of the mid-term exam. At that time 97.7% of students indicated they had visited the class Web site. When student's were asked if they felt the Web site had helped them learn the course material, 96.5% indicated it had.

Most of the students, 88.5% had taken at least one of the online Java based quizzes. Many of the students who did not take an online quiz indicated that their browser was not capable of handling Java. Of those students who took the online quizzes 97.7% felt the quizzes had helped in learning the course material.

The online discussion area led to different results. Of those students who visited the class Web site 88% participated in the online discussion. Of the students who participated only 32% felt it had helped them learn the course material.

Hypotheses

Based on the results of the initial survey a follow-up study was designed to compare students who used the Web site with students who did not. The follow-up study was based on the following hypotheses:

H1: Students who visited the class Web site and read the online content would receive a higher mid-term grade than students who did not visit the Web site.

H2: Students who used the online quizzes would receive a higher mid-term grade than students who did not use the online quizzes.

EXPERIMENTAL DESIGN

In order to test the hypotheses an experiment was designed. The experiment had one dependent variable, mid-term exam grades, and two independent variables, course Web site use and online quiz use.

The Experiment

In the Spring 1998 semester, six sections of the course were offered. It was determined that three sections would be told about the course Web site while the other three would not. It was felt that at least some of the students who were not told about the Web site in class would learn about it from friends in other sections. It was determined that this problem could be handled by surveying the students in both groups about their Web site and online quiz usage.

The six sections were taught by four instructors. All of the instructors agreed to give the same multiple choice mid-term exam. Two instructors taught two sections each, while the other two instructors each taught one section each. The instructors with two sections told one section about the Web site. The students in that section were provided the URL on the syllabus and in class. In addition, the instructor told the class many times that the material on the site would help them on their midterm exam.

Results

The results of the experiment were completely unexpected. The surveys indicated, that despite the instructor's encouragement, less than one percent of the students told about the Web site actually visited the site. This poor response rate eliminated the possibility of further analysis, but it did raise important questions and concerns. Why was the Web site visitation rate so low?

Analysis

The cause of the low site visitation rate was examined in light of the extremely high rate reported in the first survey. The only major difference was that the instructor in the first survey used an electronic classroom for lectures. This classroom was equipped with a PC connected to the Internet. Thus, the instructor was able to demonstrate the course Web site in class at the beginning of the semester. The instructor also demonstrated the online quizzes in the weeks before the mid-term.

CONCLUSIONS

Based on the first survey it appears that students believe that an online component aids in learning when used to accompany a traditional lecture based course. However, getting students to use the online material seems problematic. Merely providing an URL and mentioning the site in class is not enough. The instructor should demonstrate the site and how to use it in class. So if you build a class Web site will students come? Yes, if you show them how to get there.

REFERENCES

1. Laudon, K.C.a.L., Jane P., *Essentials of Management Information Systems: Organization and Technology*. Second ed. 1997, Upper Saddle River, NJ: Prentice Hall.
2. Gubernick, L.a.E., Ashlea, *I go my degree through E-mail*, in *Forbes*. 1997. p. 84-90.

An Empirical Study of Online versus Retail Pricing and Attitudes

Ross A. Malaga

Assistant Professor, Information Systems, University of Maryland, Baltimore County, Baltimore, MD 21250

malaga@umbc.edu

BACKGROUND

Economic and business theory suggests that online pricing of goods should be less than traditional retail pricing. This is primarily due to increased competition and reduced supply chains. These lower prices come with no human interaction, which may lead to reduced customer satisfaction.

In addition, studies have shown that potential online customers are concerned about the security of their credit card information and their personal privacy.

HYPOTHESES

This study attempts to determine if online pricing is actually less than local retail pricing. It also attempts to determine customer attitudes toward each type of shopping experience. The following hypotheses were developed from the existing literature.

H1: Prices for goods purchased via the World Wide Web will be less than prices for the same goods purchased at a local retail store.

H2: Customers will have a higher level of concern for the security of their credit card information when shopping online than when shopping at a local retail store.

H3: Customers will have a higher level of concern for the privacy of their personal information when shopping online than when shopping at a local retail store.

H4: Customers will have a higher level of overall satisfaction when shopping at a local retail store than when shopping online.

THE EXPERIMENT

Thirty-six items in nine product categories were chosen for comparison between shopping modes. The nine product categories were: 1) music, 2) computer software, 3) consumer electronics, 4) travel, 5) food, 6) clothing, 7) insurance, 8) home improvement, and 9) books.

Students in an electronic commerce seminar were assigned to shop for four items from the list. The students were instructed to go through the entire shopping process, stopping just short of actually paying for the item. Data was gathered about the price of each item, including tax and/or shipping were applicable. Students also completed a survey about their shopping experience.

PRELIMINARY RESULTS

The results of the experiment were surprising. A preliminary analysis of variance for online versus retail pricing shows that hypothesis one was not supported ($F_{1,418} = .376$, $p = .540$). An analysis was done for each product category which showed that the music category had significantly lower online prices ($F_{1,44} = 12.78$, $p = .001$).

The results of a preliminary analysis of customer attitudes supports hypothesis two ($F_{1,418} = 47.535$, $p<.001$), that customers are more concerned with the security of their credit card information online. Hypothesis three, that customers will have a higher level of concern for their personal information online was also supported ($F_{1,418} = 16.607$, $p<.001$). Hypothesis four, that customers will have a greater level of overall satisfaction with local retail stores, was also supported ($F_{1,418} = 11.620$, $p=.001$).

CONCLUSIONS

While this analysis is still preliminary it does raise an important question: if prices a not lower online and satisfaction is lower, what is the customer incentive for business to customer electronic commerce? Could we be going through a stage where customers are shopping online merely due to novelty?

Agreement Does Not Always Mean Acquiescence International IT Trade Agreements and National IT Policy

Hema Swamy, ABD
International Studies, Old Dominion University, Norfolk, VA 23508
hswamy@usa.net

Joan Mann, Ph.D
Information Systems, Old Dominion University, Norfolk, VA 23508
jmann@odu.edu

ORIGNAL ABSTRACT

The concepts of national information infrastructure (NII), global information infrastructure (GII) and the global information society (GIS) are all movements that promise revolutionary change if only nations would allow unfettered IT diffusion. Nations that champion IT diffusion have worked with intergovernmental organizations to create global agreements that are based on these concepts (NII, GII and GIS) and which ensure that IT diffusion is unhampered by trade barriers. It is appropriate, therefore, to view the global diffusion of information technologies as a movement with ideological overtones.

If indeed, these treaties have ideological overtones, then it is possible that some nations will sign the agreements for political reasons but yet, do not fully embrace the ideology behind them. The propositions of this paper are as follows: 1) recent intergovernmental agreements in IT trade incorporate an ideology of unfettered IT diffusion 2) the ideology of unhampered diffusion of IT is more beneficial to developed nations than developing nations 3) the internal policy of developing nations that sign the agreement will be strongly influenced by this ideology But at the same time, 4) participating nations may have internal economic policies that partially or totally contradict the spirit of the treaty that was signed.

If the above propositions are true, global IT managers must be aware that 'agreement may not be acquiescence' on the part of some nations. Inability to recognize this type of dual mindset may have serious consequences for the firm, whereas, sensitivity could lead to better public relations. Moreover, awareness or lack of awareness on the part of many firms could have positive or negative impacts on the degree to which the ideology is accepted or rejected.

The propositions are tested by examining recent IT agreements created by the World Trade Organization and then comparing their tenets to those set forth by IT policies in India. By analyzing the policies (both global and national) along with their relationship to the specific needs of nations (both developed and developing) we should be able to create a theoretical model which connects global IT policy with national IT policy. This model can then be tested with other countries or even other global agreements.

RESEARCH COMPLETED TO DATE

There have been four global agreements introduced by the World Trade Organization that impact global trade in information technology.

Information Technology Agreement

Focuses on unhampered global trade in information technology goods by eliminating tariffs, preventing anti-competitive subsidies and enforcing free market access.

General Agreement on Trade in Services

Permits freer movement of technical personnel and services between nations by opening up domestic services to competition from multinational enterprises and allows skilled labor free movement to nations with the highest demand.

Trade Related Investment Measures

Deregulates movement of capital by liberalizing restrictions on foreign direct investment and strategic alliances across countries.

Trade Related Intellectual Property Rights

Ensures profitability of R&D investments by allowing recognition of intellectual property rights and ensuring the collection of royalties

Proposition 1: Recent intergovernmental agreements in IT trade incorporate an ideology of unfettered IT diffusion

Given that three out of four of the agreements focus on unhampered trade, we can conclude that proposition one is true. WTO agreements encapsulate a perspective that favors unfettered IT diffusion from one country to another, not only in goods and services but also in labor and capital. Only the agreement on intellectual property rights allows a nation to protect its sovereign interests by protecting the intellectual capital of its domestic firms. It is also important to note that only the first agreement is specific to IT. The others influence IT by establishing the rules of competition. By ensuring that national markets in IT goods, services, labor and capital are kept open to global trade, the WTO is encouraging IT diffusion from IT producing nations to IT consuming nations (some of which also produce IT). Thus, the WTO agreements can be said to be export-oriented in that they focus on protection of export.

Proposition 2: The ideology of unhampered diffusion of IT is more beneficial to developed nations than developing nations

Two Roles of IT with Nation:
The global IT diffusion ideology makes the assumption that information technology is a strategic resource that a nation can leverage to gain increased economic growth. According to economic theory, technology stimulates economic growth both directly and indirectly. Technology stimulates economic growth indirectly when IT is used in various sectors of the economy (IT use) and directly when IT goods/services are created in a nation (IT creation).

Indirect growth occurs when IT is used by individuals, businesses and government to become more productive and/or adaptive (IT as Enabling Tool) or when IT is used as a substitute for labor (IT as Labor Substitute). Technology can also stimulate economic growth directly if the nation has a productive IT industrial sector (IT Industry). If the IT industrial sector is especially competitive then economic growth can occur from exporting IT. Whether IT impacts economic growth indirectly or directly, the assumption is that IT diffusion has enhances economic growth and through externalities improves the overall development of a nation.

The paragraphs below, however, argue that the global IT diffusion ideology as codified by the WTO favors nations that export IT over nations that import IT and/or have only domestic-oriented IT industry. Nations advanced in IT will benefit both from using/ selling technology internally and by exporting IT to other nations. Developed nations and developing nations that have not been able to export IT must either import technology as an enabling tool or as a substitute for labor cultivate their own IT industries. As will be shown below, WTO policies will be beneficial or detrimental to these nations depending on two parameters: the nation's level of industrialization and the maturity of its IT industries.

IT Exporting Nations and the WTO
The market for IT has become increasingly competitive on a global scale. Multinational enterprises from many nations extensively compete to garner global market share. The home countries of these multinationals reap economic benefits whenever their firms have a competitive advantage. It is only natural then that multinationals and their home countries would support global organizations that support free trade initiatives. Moreover, the home countries may become actively involved in negotiating agreements on behalf of their global firms. In fact, they may use the NII, GII and GIS perspectives to mask what is essentially a political agenda.

Nations that Do Not Export IT and the WTO
IT as Enabling Tool: There are many nations that do not have highly sophisticated IT industries. These nations will still want to use IT as an enabling tool to increase economic growth and will import IT when needed.

Developed nations whose IT industry is either non-existent or immature are able to import IT. They can successfully use IT for enabling purposes because they are industrialized (many industrial sectors can benefit from IT) and they have the capital and skilled labor to buy and adapt technology. The cost/benefit ratio of importing IT, therefore, is favorable.

Developing nations will, however, face many obstacles when trying to use IT as enabling tools. Developing nations have less industrialization and so there are fewer industrial sectors which can successfully use IT and the technology will require more adaptation because of inadequate power supply, lack of modern equipment, lack of standards. It will, therefore, be more difficult for developing nations to benefit from using IT. Developing nations are also at a disadvantage when negotiating joint ventures.

The costs of importing technology are also higher for developing nations. The emerging urban industrial sectors of developing nations are often much smaller than their rural agricultural sectors. By allocating funds to the industrial sector, the government must forgo other social goals as a tradeoff. Development and economic growth must always be balanced with competing basic social needs. Moreover, when negotiating joint venture and strategic alliances, developing nations and their firms may be at a disadvantage compared to developed nations.

IT as Labor Substitute: Using IT as a substitute for labor is beneficial to developed nations (whether they export IT or not) because there aren't enough skilled workers available. Those who become unemployed because of technology can be retrained/ reeducated for other skilled work. Economic growth will not be harmed in the long term. In developing countries, however, the unemployment is much higher and so every skilled position lost is critical.

IT Industry: Domestic IT industry will, if successful, save money on royalties for imports and provide economic growth through domestic sales. Later, if the domestic industry becomes globally competitive, economic growth will occur due to exports. Some nations may even choose to build an IT industry for export purposes only, if the nation itself cannot support enough demand for IT.

The WTO initiatives constrain the ability of the state to support and protect these fledgling industries. In this sense, the WTO initiatives can be labeled anti-statist. By removing the influence of the state, IT diffusion is controlled by market rules. In fact, the WTO initiatives encourage nations to see export as the primary objective when building IT industries, which may obfuscate other important considerations. Given that these nations may or may not have the infrastructure (transportation, capital, labor) nor the domestic demand to make IT industrial development possible, signing the agreement may give them false hope. Even if a developing nation is successful at building an export-oriented industry, it may have forgone development of other areas of the economy (including the provision of basic social needs) as a tradeoff. If externalities from these industries do not appear, it can lead to social upheaval.

Fledgling domestic firms may attempt overcome these difficulties by participating in joint ventures with multinational enterprises based in advanced IT countries. If, however, the domestic firms add only low value (ex: unskilled labor) or have their identities subsumed by the multinational (ex: franchise agreements) then the benefits to the nation overall, will be minimal.

The WTO initiatives which enforce free trade and support only export of IT will have different impacts on each depending on the whether the nation is developing or developed and the degree of maturity in the nation's IT industry. Table 1: demonstrates this point by describing the impacts in each case.

Table 1: Impact of Unrestricted IT Import on Domestic IT Industry		
Maturity of Domestic IT Industry	Developing	Developed
A few IT sectors have immature firms	Multinationals will overwhelm domestic No export Strategic Alliances will have low added value	Multinationals will overwhelm domestic No export except to underdeveloped or developing nations Strategic alliances will have higher added value
Some immature, some mature	Strategic alliances will vary in added value depending on industry More sophisticated negotiations May try to export too soon or may make export the primary goal	Mature industry can support immature + more sophisticated negotiations Export to lesser developed nations
Mature in all sectors	Will benefit greatly from strategic alliances with peers and non-peers Export to all types	Will benefit greatly from strategic alliances with peers and non-peers Export to all types

To summarize, if using IT was the only objective, then nations that export technology will benefit most from the WTO initiatives, less advanced IT nations will be limited to importing expensive IT or building their own IT industries. Of those less advanced IT nations, developed countries will fare much better than developing countries.

Proposition 3: The internal policy of developing nations that sign the agreement will be strongly influenced by this ideology

This proposition will be proven by researching the policies of the WTO member states that have signed the various IT agreements. Preliminary research on Malaysia and India, support the proposition. In Malaysia, IT is seen as a 'tidal wave' that leads to prosperity derived from competitiveness and better governance. In India, the National Information Technology Policy includes the following quote in the preamble,

"IT is a key source of industrial competitiveness and economic growth. IT has the potential to enhance competitiveness of key industries, modernise business infrastructure and services, alleviate information poverty and reduce delivery costs throughout the economy [National Information Technology Policy of India]"

Not only are nation's lured by the opportunities possible once these agreements are signed. They are also under pressure to sign because as net consumers, they cannot risk losing Most Favored Nation status [National Information Technology Policy]. The results of signing are not always completely beneficial (see Table 2 below)

Table 2: WTO Agreements and Their Impact on the Indian Economy		
Agreement Signed	Rationale for Signing	Impacts
Information Technology Act	Wanted to open foreign markets to its IT services	Foreign firms overran its inefficient firms
Trade Related Investment Measures	Wanted to attract foreign investment flows	Investment flows into Indian telecommunications increased until embargoes related to nuclear proliferations went into effect
General Agreement on Trade in Services	Wanted improve its position of supplier of services	Pressure to allow multinationals to enter banking, insurance and tourism increased Lost skilled labor to advanced nations through emigration
Trade Related Intellectual Property Rights	Without protection of intellectual property it would lose foreign direct investment and technology transfers Wanted to protect its own innovations from piracy	Didn't realize the cost of royalties to developed countries for technology it was using

The picture is not completely bleak for India. It used revenue from its IT industry to improve its infrastructure in education and communications both in rural and urban areas. It was also able to create national depositories for academic research. In the future, however, they will need to strengthen their domestic IT service industry by focusing on custom-made software and improving their ability to add value by managing IT projects not just handling development. Lastly, it must find a way to increase domestic sales by educating its existing industries to use IT and by encouraging other industrialization. All this must be done, however, at the same time as it tries to modernize its extensive agricultural sector in rural areas and build up its basic infrastructure.

Proposition 4: Participating nations may have internal economic policies that partially or totally contradict the spirit of the

treaty that was signed

No evidence to support this proposition was found in the national IT policy of India. Indian policy makers seemed blinded by the opportunities that the WTO agreements would give their domestic firms and failed to see the opportunities that signing would give to foreign firms. It seems that India was caught in a 'Catch-22' situation. If a nation can export IT, and then it can achieve economic growth but only if its IT industry is fully competitive and competitiveness is only determined by price/quality. Developing countries have structural and institutional constraints that prevent them from being competitive.

DISCUSSION

This paper successfully demonstrated that unfettered IT diffusion through WTO trade agreements is disadvantageous to developing countries and possibly even developed nations that do not export IT. In the short term, WTO agreements will result in the commercial transfer of technology from producing countries to consuming countries. Over the long term, this channel of distribution will become the dominant one because consuming nations will be unable to cultivate competitive industries of their own. The potential opportunities from IT diffusion are real but there may be unwanted side effects if WTO mechanisms are the vehicle for achieving IT diffusion.

The fourth proposition, that developing nations would have policies that contradict the global agreements was not supported. This result may be explained in several ways. First, national governments may be completely co-opted by the ideology of the agreements. Second, pressures to sign may force nations to agree and abide by the agreements. Third, nations may not be able to fully evaluate the potential risks in signing. Fourth, there may be opposition to the policy from others in the government, interest groups that are not in power and even the general populace but these voices are not represented by the policy. All of these possible explanations should be tested empirically. Still, the first three propositions are enough to question the external validity of the theory that equates technology use with economic growth and supports the idea that exporters should be aware of these issues. Just as anti-trust legislation protects national markets from unwanted affects of imperfect competition, the global marketplace must be protected as well.

SELECTIVE BIBLIOGRAPHY

Fagerberg, Jan, Technology and International Differences in Growth Rates, *Journal of Economic Literature,* September, 1994, V. 32.

India, National Information Technology Policy, *http://www.doe.gov.in.*

Maskus, Keith, Implications of Regional and Multilateral Agreements for Intellectual Property Rights, *The World Economy,* 1997, 20(5).

Palvia, P. and S. Palvia, Understanding the Global Information Technology Environment: Representative World Issues, in *Global Information Technology and Systems Management,* Westford: Ivy League Publishing.

Sharma, Salendra, The World Trade Organization and Implications for Developing Countries, *SAIS Review,* 1997, 17(2).

Shrivastava, Paul, Technological Innovation in Developing Countries, *Columbia Journal of World Business,* Winter, 1984.

Solow, Robert, A Contribution to the Theory of Economic Growth, *Quarterly Journal of Economics,* February 1956, 70(1).

Vasquez, Sergio and Jean-Benoit, Zimmerman, Computers and Developing Countries, in *The Information Society,* eds. J. Berleur, et al., New York, Springer Verlag, 1990.

IT Organisation in Multinational Companies: A Reflective Practitioner Perspective

Sharm Manwani

CIO, White Goods Europe, 55-77 High Street, Cornwall House, Slough, Berkshire, SL1 1DZ England

Henley Management College, Greenlands, Henley-on-Thames, Oxon, RG9 3AU England

44-1753-872441 (tel), Mobile 44-410-301715, 44-181-893-4953 (fax), smanwani@compuserve.com

1. INTRODUCTION AND METHODOLOGY

This research examines the evolving information technology (IT) organisation structure within a multi-billion pound multinational that is undergoing radical changes.

Multinational companies (MNCs) are a major user of IT. '*Multinational corporations use the most advanced applications and technologies and have by far the largest geographical scale and scope in their data processing operations*' (Roche, 1996: 130). Co-ordinating international IT is extraordinarily complex, with maximum responsibility but only limited authority over remote staff and locations (Cash et al, 1992). It is vital that both IT planning and investment are linked to business goals (Earl 1994, Willcocks 1992). The alignment of business and IT goals is not straightforward in a multinational, particularly one that is undergoing a transformation. Radical change often results in discontinuous business visions yet technology realities require an evolutionary approach to business processes; contemporaneously new organisational forms are being created moving from vertical hierarchies to horizontal networks and strategic alliances (Parker 1996).

One way of classifying IT structures is to separate the Corporate and the Business Unit roles; the following table is adapted from Earl, Edwards, & Feeny (1996); a specific addition is that a separate policy unit has been optionally included with the categories of *internal bureau* and *business venture*.

Table 1: IT structure configurations (adapted: Earl, Edwards, & Feeny 1996).			
Structure	**Characteristics**	**Business unit role**	**Corporate IT role**
Corporate service	Unified	Contact points	Total IT function
Internal bureau	Unified - Run as business - Protected?	IT Buyers	Service bureau Separate policy unit?
Business venture	Unified + External	IT Buyers	Service bureau Separate policy unit?
Decentralised	Distributed	IT Resource Control	Financial control Corporate support
Federal	Distributed	IT Resource Control	Policy + Shared Service? + Corporate support?

The federal structure has become the most dominant form with a decline in centralised configurations according to a survey of 14 large European organisations and subsequent research conducted by Earl, Edwards, & Feeny (1996). Each of the federal structures studied had evolved from a central form. The initial research concluded that the bureau would not remain as a dominant structure although it could become one of the sources of supply in a federal IS structure.

The later studies identified new trends and forms in federal organisations. These include one or more of the following:
- more central control to reduce costs through standards
- rationalisation of data centres
- control of architecture to ensure cross-business-unit synergies
- introduction of processes to share best practice on IT
- central guidance on improving IS performance
- shared information system across units to present common face to customer
- support for shared accounting centres
- support for global efficiencies or transfer of knowledge
- business-unit-independent operational/development centre to enable structure change
- outsourcing of operations and development
- IS management linked to business processes across units
- shift of responsibility to end users but with infrastructure centralised

Many of the above were classified as variations of federal structure by Earl et al (1996). This is rather a broad taxonomy but was seen as indicative of the adaptive nature of the federal model.

Brown & Magill (1994) classified IT structures in six large companies as *centralised, decentralised*, and *shared*. They found that the structure was not consistent across the IT groups. These findings supported a contingency approach in defining the IT organisation. A contingency research question addressed by Jarvenpaa & Ives (1992) was whether IT provides a global perspective that fits with the strategies proposed by Bartlett & Ghoshal. Four IT configurations were classified matching to the different multinational strategies.

The fit of the IT configurations to the IT managers' perceptions of business structure was above average (56 percent) but less than expected. One of the reasons postulated was that the companies were in a transition stage not captured by the research. Another factor was the impact of additional contingency variables, for example, senior management support or subsidiary resistance, which could influence the direction and pace of change of the IT configuration.

Table 2: IT configurations and cross-border strategies (adapted: Jarvenpaa & Ives 1992)		
Strategic Orientation	**Business structure**	**IT configuration**
Responsiveness	Multidomestic	Independent operations
Efficiency	Global	Headquarters-driven
Learning	International	Intellectual synergy
Combination of above	Transnational	Integrated IT

Ives & Jarvenpaa encouraged future researchers to examine in depth the instances in which IT structure does not match the business structure within a global context. They recognised the limitations of using only the senior IT manager from headquarters and suggested obtaining the perspective of general and functional management and also subsidiary management.

In response to this prior research, the IT organisational structure was studied within a large multinational code-named Household. The challenge within Household was to create an effective business-driven IT organisation within a background of major changes to the business organisation. This research-in-progress describes the development of the new structure from the reflective practitioner perspective (Heiskanen et al, 1997) of the CIO of White Goods Europe and highlights some of the lessons learned from the initial study.

2 CASE STUDY FINDINGS

The multinational group Household is European-based, producing and selling household durables worldwide through retailers. There is a network of about 300 companies worldwide generating a turnover of some 15 Billion US dollars. The case here concerns the largest business sector White Goods Europe (WGE) and its IT relationships with Corporate and Internal Services. Historically, the

Group and the Sector had grown through acquisition resulting in decentralised operating companies and IT departments. Nevertheless there was a strong Corporate influence in the setting of IT standards, a relatively low limit for budget approvals, and the provision of 'free' central network services.

During 1995 (prior to the author joining the case organisation in mid 1996) a regional IT structure was proposed and agreed by the Group IT Board. The aim was to regionally consolidate IT equipment and staff to benefit from economies of scale and maximise scarce IT resources. Three IT Regions were created - North, Middle, South Europe. Progress in setting up the regions was slow and one year after the author joined no major structural changes had taken place even though transitions had been agreed in the UK and Denmark to enable the reorganisation of IT Region North. One reason for this was that there was no alignment between the configuration of these IT regions and the business or legal entity structure of Household.

During the period of 1995 to 1997, a gradual transition occurred resulting in the creation of a White Goods Europe business sector. A key goal was to link the factories and sales companies through integrated pan-European processes. National responsiveness was still important hence the move was from a *multidomestic* to a *transnational* configuration (Bartlett & Ghoshal, 1989). According to Jarvenpaa & Ives (1992) this was predicted to result in a transition from *independent operations* to *integrated IT*. Support for this prediction was evident in the increasing demand for cross-border systems and data.

At a Group Management meeting in September 1997, it was agreed to create a new IT Services company as an extension to the regional IT concept. This fitted with the philosophy of the new Group CEO who had drawn a clear distinction between corporate responsibility (legal, risk etc) and the service role. About 1% of the 1000+ IT staff were required in the Corporate IT role, leaving 99% of the IT staff available to the IT Services organisation which was given a period of grace with the business sectors customers.

In parallel with this restructuring, the author proposed creating a team of functional IT & Process managers to ensure a consistent and integrated approach across WGE. This proposal was accepted by the WGE management team and the author was asked to take IT responsibility for all business functions in WGE and to create a network of 'IT buyers' to purchase IT solutions from the new IT Services group.

These changes in structure were significant in moving away from the mixed organisation of IT staff in business units, holding companies, and IT companies that was the heritage of the acquisition history of Household. Using the Earl, Edwards, & Feeny (1996) classification table, the intention was for Household to move from a mixed somewhat *decentralised* structure to primarily an *internal bureau* also viewed as an insourcing arrangement since the business sector had the choice of going outside after an initial period. In some areas, notably the production shop floor, WGE retained IT resource operating closer to a *federal* structure. The existence of a Corporate IT group was also more indicative of a federal approach.

In effect, the Group IT role was divided into two structures – one a small corporate group responsible for co-ordinating IT policies and procedures approved by the Group Management. The second group (of 1000+ staff) was IT Services, an internal organisation which was created as a separate product line.

In response, the author negotiated for WGE IT to work with Corporate IT to create the recommended standards and define IT architectures. Additional negotiations took place with IT Services. During the first year (1998), WGE would continue to use IT Services as its supplier for current services with no projected change in budget. For future services, WGE would benchmark IT Services who as a product line within Household were expected to make a profit that was used to invest in the future. In 1998, with the appointment of a new head of IT Services, the question was raised of it making external business and profits, potentially fitting to the *business venture* category.

It is revealing to compare the response and reactions in Household with the findings from Earl et al (1996). Generally the prior research found that the first devolution was to create a business unit IS manager and/or user support resources, and this happened in WGE. Subsequently, the development resource was often moved to the business units although where central operations were running well, there was less incentive for a change. In this case study, WGE controlled the financial resource, and in particular WGE processes controlled the development priorities even though IT Services managed its own development resource. Generally from the research sample, the business venture was considered unacceptable to business units. This is consistent with the discussions at Household where managers were nervous about being locked into a profit-making unit. While there were also reservations about the bureau approach these were less severe. Concerns were expressed by Business Sector representatives at the Group IT Board in April 1998 about losing staff in the transition and also about losing touch with the business units; again this finding was consistent with the study sample.

3 CONCLUDING REMARKS

The initial findings confirm the importance of creating appropriate organisational structures for the development of information technology solutions in multinational companies. They demonstrate that the taxonomies for IT configurations suggested by Earl et al (1996) and Jarvenpaa & Ives (1992) are useful ones, if somewhat limited to describe a complex multinational. There is a longitudinal perspective to this research and it is too early to predict what will be the final IT configuration.

The research will ideally be considered complete once the implications of the changes to the IT structure in Household are known and stable. Given the ongoing changes and the potential instability of the structure it may be necessary to select a time checkpoint. Further research in Household is being conducted to assess the IT infrastructure consequences of moving from a multidomestic position towards a more global strategy.

REFERENCES

Bartlett C A & Ghoshal S (1989), Managing Across Borders, Harvard

Brown C V & Magill S L (1994), 'Alignment of the IS functions with the Enterprise: toward a model of antecedents', MIS Quarterly, December 1994, p 371-403

Cash Jr J I, McFarlan F W, McKenney J L & Applegate L M (1992), Corporate Information Systems Management: Text and Cases, 3rd edition, Irwin

Earl M J, Edwards B & Feeny D F (1996), 'Configuring the IS Function', Information Management: The Organisational Dimension (editor M J Earl), Oxford University Press

Heiskanen A, Newman M, Similä J (1997), 'Bridging the Gap between Information Systems Research and Practice: The Reflective Practitioner Approach', Proceedings ICIS

Jarvenpaa S L & Ives B (1992), 'Organising for Global Competition: The Fit of Information Technology', Decision Sciences, volume 24 no. 3, p 547-575

Roche E M (1996), 'Multinational Corporations - the emerging research agenda', Journal of Strategic Information Systems, vol 5, p 129-147

Willcocks L (1992), 'Strategy development and delivery', Creating a Business-based IT strategy (edited by Brown A), Chapman & Hall

Information Technology Development and Critical Success Factors in China -- A Country-Level Study

En Mao

Ph.D. Program, Management Information Systems, Fogelman College of Business and Economics, The University of Memphis, Memphis, TN 38152

enmao@memphis.edu, (901) 452-3322, (901) 678-4189

ABSTRACT

China possesses one the strongest economies in the world. Since its implementation of the open door policy, China has made tremendous progresses in the economy and standard of living by reaching out to the global market. Facing fierce competition from the global market, Chinese companies must meet global standards. Consequentially, information systems (IS) and information technology (IT), heavily used by the western business world, are finding their way into the organizations in China. First, this descriptive study explores IT development in China. Then, recognizing the fact that the development of IT in China is not purely business-driven, we identify four factors, economy status, national culture, political system and government policies, and technological status that have significant impact on IT development in China. In addition, the study proposes a list of country-level critical success factors pertaining to successful diffusion of IT. Finally, the study discusses the implications of the study to policy makers in China, foreign companies, domestic companies, and researchers.

INTRODUCTION

Predicted to be the world's largest economy in the 21st century, China has captured attentions from around the globe because of its size, growth potential, and impact on the global market. China's population, consisting of a quarter of the world's population, makes up unarguably the most important target market of many of the U.S., European, and Asian multinational corporations. Not only is it a huge market, it is also a fast growing market. China's economy has been growing at more than 10% annually Since 1992, whereas, the U.S., 2.3% (CIA, 1997). A chart found in Appendix A compares the real GDP growth of China and those of other countries'. It indicates that the distinctive rapid growth rate of China surpasses not only developed countries but also some fast growing Asian counties. In addition, China's impact on other countries is unprecedented. For example, the trading deficit between the US and China has been consistently increasing for the past ten years; it has grown from $ 0.3 billion in 1985 to 42 billion in 1996 (CIA, 1997).

Obviously, a study of China is important. However, a study of the information systems development of China is even more critical because it is believed that information systems development will significantly affect the economic development of China (China Daily (8), 1998). Moreover, the development phenomena are unique. The development of information systems in China is a recent event that started around 1993. Most major development took place in the last two to three years. While most western countries are maturing in strategic and management-oriented information systems, many Chinese firms find themselves mere beginners of computerized transactional-based information systems.

The literature review indicates that research concerning China in the area of MIS is limited. The majority is practitioner-oriented and neglects the management aspect of IS. Many focus on narrow domains, for example, hardware or software. Some aim on specific types of organizations, such as state-owned enterprises (i.e. Dologite, Fang, Chen, Mockler and Chao, 1997). No research has attempted to portray multiple aspects of information systems development of China.

There are three goals of the study. First is to explore many aspects of the current development of IT/IS in China: hardware, software, IT services, IT professionals, and the Internet/network. Second is to depict the factors that affect the development of IT in China. Third is to propose a list of critical success factors pertaining to the current and future success of IT development in China. Those factors are mainly at country and industry level. Finally, some suggestions and implications are presented to researchers, Chinese policy makers, domestic companies, and foreign companies.

RESEARCH MODEL

MIS development in China has been, is, and will continue to be unique. A framework for MIS, proposed by Ives, Hamilton, and Davis (1980), recognized a set of environmental variables that affect information systems development. Environmental variables include social, political, cultural, economic, etc. (Ives, Hamilton, and Davis, 1980). These factors are extremely important and influential to the IS development in China. More importantly, the uniqueness of those factors contributed to the unique IS development environment in China. Unlike, the U.S., developments in the IS are more business-driven, whereas in China it has been more environmentally-driven. The recent boom was the result of a combination of governmental encouragement, intensive foreign investment, technological advances, and economic development.

A major foundation of the research model is the model proposed by Palvia and Palvia (1991). The model, proposed for global IT research, indicates that the level of economic growth, national culture, and political system and government policies have significant impact on IS development. In addition, Watson et al (1991) identified technological status as a predominant factor that influences IS development.

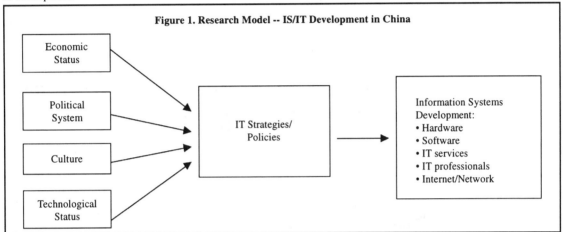

Figure 1. Research Model -- IS/IT Development in China

As shown in Figure 1, The model depicts that political, economic, cultural, and technological status factors are the driving forces that affect IT strategies and polices. IT strategies and policies then have direct impact on the development of IS/IT. We are interested in identifying those factors and describing IT development in China. The emphasis of the study is, however, not strategy/policy formulation. Furthermore, it is not the focus of this study to statistically prove the causal relationships suggested by the arrows. A separate study should be conducted to validate the model. This study is descriptive in nature.

INFORMATION SYSTEMS DEVELOPMENT

In 1997, China became the largest PC market in the Asia-Pacific region (Dietrich, 1997). The computer industry, including hardware, software, and information services, is growing at approximately 40 percent annually (China Daily (4), 1998). Yet, in China, business use of computer was virtually non-existence prior to 1980 (Lu, Qiu, and Guimares, 1988). In comparison, business use of computers in the U.S. started in the 1960s.

The development of information systems is unbalanced. The imbalances are apparent in two ways. First, domestic companies are lagging behind the foreign firms, which have dominated the developments since the 1980's (New Century Group Staff, 1997). Such big international players are Microsoft, IBM, Intel, Motorola, AT&T, etc. Most IT developments in China are contributed by the growth of joint ventures and solely foreign-owned firms (China Daily (4), 1998). Approximately 80 percent of Chinese businesses are small or medium businesses (China Daily (6), 1998). Lack of strong domestic presence in IT can be risky. The recent Asian financial crisis has dramatically reduced investment from the Asian countries (China Daily (2)). China must develop its strong domestic computer industry while maximizing the benefit from, not depending on, foreign investors.

Another imbalance is that most developments occur in big cities. In 1995, Beijing, Shanghai, and Guangzhou were the only three cities that had computer industries. Today, the developments have gone beyond those cities; however, they are still limited to large cities (Skillings (2), 1997). For example, Shenzhen, a major city in the south, dominates 30 percent of China's PC market (China Daily (2), 1998). This may create problems in setting business standards.

Software

The software industry in China is at its early developing stage. Even though the software industry first came into existence in the early 1980s (Yang, 1998), most companies in the computer industry only dealt with hardware before 1997 (China Daily (1), 1998). Currently, there are several thousands of software developing companies in China. Most are small and have around 50 employees (Yang, 1998). In 1997, application software held over 60 percent of the total software market, while system software was growing (registration) at the fastest rate, over 60 percent annually (China Daily (4), 1998).

Ministry of Information Industry oversees and funds software development in China. Intellectual property rights is a major concern of software companies. Higher educational institutions, where qualified developers can be found, play a major role in software development (China Daily (1), 1998; Yang, 1998). However, China is still far less competitive in this area compared to western counties. More disturbingly, Chinese and multi-lingual software are greatly lacking. Native Chinese software are overshadowed by sophisticated software vendors such as Microsoft. Much effort is devoted to modifying and customizing existing English-based software. It is believed that lack of Chinese-base software has prohibited the wide-spread of information systems.

Hardware

China's PC market grew by almost 60 percent in 1996 (China Daily (4), 1998). The number of PCs sold in China has been growing over 50 percent annually since 1992 (New Century Group, 1997). Currently (Spring, 1998), there are three million PCs in China; of which, 1.7 were sold in 1997. However, the domestic companies hold only 66 percent of the PC market in 1997. The Chinese have not mastered some of the advanced technology such as CPU technologies (Zhang, 1998). Computer hardware industry is mainly supported by Intel.

China is concentrating more on hardware than on software. Currently, there are about 100 firms that are licensed to produce PCs. However, foreign companies dominate the telecommunications industry. Over 90 percent of the telecommunications hardware installed in China was supplied by foreign investors (China Daily (7), 1998).

Hardware is updated rapidly. In their study of Chinese state-owned enterprises, Dologite, et al., (1995) found that the technologies employed in companies improved dramatically in just a few years. In an early 1991 study, there were only one occurrence of LAN and one of minicomputer. In 1995, however, IBM mainframes, Honeywell and Yolowata mainframes, HP minicomputers, VAX minicomputers, as well as networked 386 and 486 PCs were in operation.

IT services

The IT service sector is growing slowly, but it is expected to reach a faster growth rate in the next couple of years. The idea of IT services, such as IT planning and risk assessment, was excluded from business planning a few years ago. The level of IT spending in most companies is still inadequate (Peterson, 1997). There are several factors contributing to this problem.

One of the obstacles to IT investment is that businesses are not familiar with systems prices in China (Peterson, 1997). Second, the IT services, unlike hardware, is intangible, which is hardly appreciated by Chinese businesses. This is a universal problem to all other intangible assets and services. Intellectual property issues in China reflect this problem. Third, organizations are hesitant to outsource IT expertise. This is particularly true for large organizations. Currently, IT services firms are categorized into four groups: hardware vendors, software vendors, system and network integrators, and IT consulting firms (Peterson, 1997).

IT Professionals

IT professionals are greatly lacking in China. This is a major problem even in Hong Kong. Most of the IT professionals are young and concentrated in big cities (Yang, 1998). To make matters worse, retaining IT professionals within China has been a tough task. Many IT professionals received training overseas and never returned home (Zhang, 1998).

Internet/Network

By the end of 1997, there were 620,000 Internet users; of which 45 percent were commercial users (China Daily (5), 1998). E-commerce is developing rapidly in China. To sustain healthy growth of e-commerce, China is planning to improve its legislation and taxation concerning e-commerce (China Daily (5), 1998).

The major problem facing China's network development is network security. Security issues have been neglected since the beginning of the explosive growing of the Internet and network. CHINANET was attacked in July, 1997. One node was forced to reinstall the systems software. The incident brought the network to a halt for more than eight hours (Lemon (1), 1997). According to experts, China's network infrastructure is "extremely vulnerable" (Lemon (2), 1997). The government is responsible for investigating security violations, but it is not responsible for the security.

DRIVING FACTORS

The study identified a set of environmental factors at the macro-level. Those factors are China's unique economic, political, cultural environment, and technological status.

Culture

Today's China is the remains of a 2000-year-old empire. Once the world's most powerful country economically and militarily, China closed its door for a long period of time until the late 1970s when the open door policy was implemented (Franklin, 1994). To better understand national cultures, we examine the Chinese culture based on Hofstede's five dimensions of national culture: power distance, uncertainty avoidance, individualism versus collectivism, masculinity versus femininity, and long term versus short-term (1994).

Power distance refers to the degree of power inequality among people, more specifically, supervisors and subordinates (Shore, 1995). Chinese culture is high for this dimension (Paik, Vance, and Stage, 1996). This implies that the authority is more powerful. Moreover, recent studies conclude that Chinese organizations tend to be more hierarchical in nature because of the high degree of power distance. There has significant implication for the IS. IS structure is generally believed to be parallel with the organizational structure. If a Chinese firm was to implement a decentralized system, the firm would have to make major adjustments to its organizational structure to benefit from such system.

Uncertainty avoidance refers to the extent to which people feel threatened by a uncertain circumstance and avoid such situation by providing job security and establishing rigid rules (Shore, 1995). Traditionally, in a state-owned enterprise, employees are guaranteed life-time employment. Chinese culture is strong on this dimension. Some firms are relectant to automate their processes because first, manual labor is less expensive, and second, they do not want to create job insecurity.

Individualism refers to the degree that people focus on themselves as individuals rather than act as members of groups. The opposite is collectivism. In China, the society highly favors group activities. Usually, groups are formed in work settings. A high level of collectivism can work both for and against the implementation of IS.

Masculinity and femininity refer to values like assertiveness, performance, success and competition; the opposite of masculinity is femininity. Traditionally, males have been the dominating gender. However, this dimension is moving toward a more neutral status. The effect of this dimension on IS is yet to be determined (Shore, 1995).

On *long-term versus short-term* orientation, Chinese culture is long-term oriented. The implication for foreign investor would be that to be successful, they would expect to develop long lasting relationship with their Chinese partners.

Economic factor

The Chinese economy is growing steadily. Business growths, especially in the foreign invested sector, have directly affected the demand of information technology. The buying power of the 1.2 billion people of China is constantly rising. As more and more companies in western countries find themselves in saturating domestic markets, they find tremendous business opportunities in this vast market. More interestingly, the population is young compared to western countries. The medium age is 27.6, estimated in 1995 (Facts, 1998). These phenomena implicate the world power and center shifts in the near future.

Political Climate

The Economic Information Joint Committee was established in 1993 to formulate policies for the development of a national information infrastructure. This marked the beginning of the development of information systems and technologies in China. Later the committee focused on Internet development. Since 1993, more favorable policies towards foreign investors resulted in the recent rapid growth in computer industry. By early 1998, foreign investment accounts for almost 50 percent of the new IT projects (China Daily (3), 1998).

China has attracted significant foreign investment, $133 billion in the mid-1990s (The Economist, 1997). Favorable business policies contributed to the proliferation of joint-venture and sole-foreign-ownership firms, which exposed China to advanced information technology.

Technological Status

IT development depends on the level of technological status. For example, Internet development depends on telecommunications advancement. IT infrastructure is a major sector that has undergone tremendous construction. The telecommunications market is tightly controlled by The Ministry of Posts and Telecommunications (MPT) (Skillings (1), 1997)

China plans to install 123 million phone line by year 2000. Currently, foreign investors in the telecommunications market still face many hurdles. There are many parties involved in the process: government ministries, the provincial government, local posts, telecom authorities, equipment suppliers, and government agencies (Skillings (1), 1997).

COUNTRY LEVEL CSFS

Based on the understanding of the factors that affect IT development, we propose a list of CSFs that is meaningful useful to guide future IT development. There are two stages to determining the CSFs. First an extensive literature review in the area of IS/IT development key issues and CSFs is conducted. Common thread found in the studies that are relevant to the context of IT development in China is the foundation of the CSFs. The second stage is to firm and refine the CSFs. Two interviews with executives from a predominant Chinese IT firm are conducted.

There are country-specific MIS key issues studies of Hong Kong (Burn, Saxena, Ma, and Cheung, 1993; Burn and Szeto, 1998), Canada (Carey, 1992), Slovenia (Deans, 1991), Estonia (Dexter, Janson, Kiudorf, and Laast, 1993), India (Palvia and Palvia, 1992), Singapore (Rao, Huff, and Davis, 1987), and the Republic of China (Harrison and Farn, 1990). Some of the issues of China can be adopted from those studies.

In the Pacific arena, many country-specific MIS-related researches have been conducted – the Republic of China, Hong Kong, and Singapore. There are several studies done on the Republic of China (Harrison and Farn, 1990). Hong Kong was the focus of many studies (Burn, Saxena, Ma, and Cheung, 1993; Burn and Szeto, 1998). Singapore was also a popular target of IS research (Lally, 1994), (11). Those studies are extremely relevant. Even some key IS issues of China may be similar or common to those of other countries, significant differences can be found among different countries (Deans, 1991; Tractinsky and Jarvenpaa, 1995; Watson, Kelly, Galliers, and Branchear, 1991).

STONE is a leading computer company in China. One of the first private organizations, it was founded in 1981 The interviews took place in December 1997. One of the interviews was with the IS director at STONE. Another one is with the regional director in Beijing. Those interviews are preliminary. At the time, Stone's IS department had just acquired a new computing facility. The facility drew attention from Beijing's TV station. The interviews were informative. Many of the issues reported by the literature review were confirmed. Some new perspectives surfaced. Again, we are presenting county-level factors.

1. Understanding/awareness of MIS contribution

  The interview revealed that MIS department was not perceived positively nationwide. The effort and contribution of IT to businesses are rarely understood and known. Many times, IS personnel are blame for overspending and poor services. A widespread education campaign is needed to improve the perception of IS.

2. IT infrastructure

  China's infrastructure demands great attention and investment from the government and the foreign investors. This need will continue through to the next century. Internet development and network expansion depend on IT infrastructure. The Chinese government and businesses together must improve the infrastructure in terms of size and quality in order to continue to attract business as well as residential users.

3. MIS human resource. (Retaining, recruiting and training MIS/IT/DP personnel)

Lack of qualified personnel is one of the biggest obstacles to IT development in china. IT education and training must be improved. China needs to invest in IT training and education in schools and other institutions besides universities and higher educational institutions. To retain quality people, some large companies, such as STONE, find that offering flexible work schedule and autonomy help.
4. Information systems/technology planning
Planning activities of IS/T need to become a part of the business planning activities. Companies should be more proactive and open-minded to IT activities.
5. Government support
Utilization of IS/IT in government will help to improve the perception of IT. Also, government needs to show the support by providing incentives to organizations that are willing to adopt IT/IS.
6. Technology transfer
Chinese companies should take advantages of foreign investors' help. Foreign expertise brings in advanced management techniques and advanced technology.
7. Application software development
Software industry needs more support. Lack of Chinese and Multi-lingual software prevented many small local companies from becoming more IT sophisticated. More Chinese-language software can encourage more small and medium companies to use IT as well as more leisure users.
8. Software development and quality assurance standards
Software industry has been plagued by software piracy. More stringent regulations and policies are needed to discourage IRP violations and encourage software development and raise software standards.
9. Telecommunications
China is predicted to become the biggest telecommunications market. Large investment is needed for the growth of telecommunications infrastructure. This must be a joint effort from government, foreign investors, and local investors.

IMPLICATIONS

We identify the factors that have significant impact on IT development in China. Also, we propose a list of CSFs. Those factors have significant implications for policy makers, domestic companies, multinational companies from foreign counties, and researcher. The following discussions help those stakeholders to envision current problems and provide suggestions and solutions that will enable them to play better and more proactive roles in future IT development in China.

The research model implies that the success of IT development is dependent on the IT strategies and policies. Policy makers need to focus on policies that can stimulate a more balanced growth nationwide. To spur the growth in the domestic sector, which will truly boost the overall IT level, policy makers need to consider imposing more incentives for domestic companies, especially the small and medium companies. Furthermore, mainland companies should stay close to companies in Hong Kong, where most advanced information technologies (ie, Data warehousing; Mailloux, 1997) are being transferred from industrialized countries and implemented.

Foreign companies should take the advantage of current favorable investment policies in China. However, they need to be aware of the unique culture environment. To be successful in China, a foreign company needs to establish a long-term goal. There are many potential research areas. In the research model, there are other relationships worth examination. For example, the IT is believed to have impact on economic factors (Boisot & Child, 1996). Researchers are also encouraged to validate the research model.

CONCLUSION

IT/IS development in China is Unique. It is in an early stage. It is also a complex issue. The study descriptively presented the IT/IS development environment and circumstances in China. There are many driving factors of IT/IS development: culture, economic growth, political system, and technological status. These factors are dealt with as the environment of IT development. Insensitivity to any factor may hinder the future development of IT in China. Recognizing those factors will help us formulate better IT policies and strategies. CSFs proposed will serve as a checklist for IT planning at the country level.

There are many implications of this study. Policy makers, foreign investors, Chinese companies, and researchers all can benefit from understanding the IT driving factors and CSFs. Policy makers should take precautions when formulating new regulations and revising current regulations. More emphasis should be given to small and medium domestic companies that compose the main business force of China while maintaining open and favorable policies for foreign investors. Domestic companies need to be more proactive and lobby for more favorable IT investment projects toward them. They should continue benefiting from foreign expertise and transfer advanced management techniques and information technologies. Foreign investors need to be more long-term oriented in order to be successful. Furthermore, there are future research agendas. The research model needs to be validated. Studies concerning the relationships among the entities may bear meaningful and practical findings.

REFERENCE
Boisot, M.; Child, J. "From fiefs to clans and network capitalism: Explaining China's emerging economic order," Administrative science Quarterly, Vol (4), Dec. 1996, p600-628.
Brancheau, J. C, . and Wetherbe, J. C., "Key Issues in Information Systems Management," MIS Quarterly, March, pp. 23-46.
Burn, J. , Saxena, K.B.C., Ma, L., Cheung, H. K. "Critical Issues of IS Management in Hong Kong: A Cultural Comparison," Journal of Global Information Management. Vol 1, No 4, Fall, 1993, pp 28-37.
Burn, J. and Szeto, C. "Information Systems Management Issues in Hong Kong: A contingency analysis and comparison with the United Kingdom."

Carey, D. "Rating the Top MIS Issues in Canada," Canadian Datasystems, June 1992, pp 23-26.

(1)China Daily, News, "China Zone seeks software," May 11, 1998.

(2)China Daily, News, "China Shenzhen put high-tech top of agenda," May 11, 1998

(3)China Daily, News, "China Investment by overseas firms rises in Shenzhen," March 23,1998

(4)China Daily, News, "China computer sales to hit US\$ 20 billion," March 18, 1998

(5)China Daily, News, "China E-business IBM targets the market in China," February 25, 1998

(6)China Daily, News, "China HP promotes sales in smaller local firms," February 5, 1998

(7)China Daily, News, "China: Industry gives extra push IT expected to spur on economy," January 14, 1998.

(8) China Daily, "China: Industry gives extra push IT expected to spur on economy," January 14, 1998. P 6.

CIA. The world Fact Book. 1997. http://www.odci.gov/cia/publications/factbook/index.html

Computer Business Guide Book, in Chinese, 1998. p167.

Deans, P. C., Karwan, K.R., Goslar, M.D., Ricks, D. A., and Toyne, B. "Identification of Key International Information Systems Issues in U.S.-Based Multinational Corporations," Journal of Management Information Systems Vol 7 No.4, Spring 1991, pp. 27-50.

Dexter, A. S., Janson, M.A., Kiudorf, E., and Laast-Laas, J. Key Information Technology Issues in Estonia. The Journal of Strategic Information Systems. June, 1993, Vol 2, No 2, pp. 139-152.

Dietrich, Joy. "China Captures Top Spot in Asia-Pacific PC Market, Dataquest Says," IDG News Service, Paris Bureau. http://www.IDGCHINA.COM/NEWS/August97/DataQuest.htm

"Documents," Country: China. Kaleidoscope. 1998.

Dologite, D. G., Fang, M. Q., Chen, Y., Mockler, R. J., and Chao, C. "Information Systems in Chinese State-Owned Enterprises: An evolving strategic perspective," Journal of Global Information Management. Vol 5, No. 4, Fall, 1997, pp 10-21.

"Facts & Figures," Country: China. Kaleidoscope. 1998.

Franklin, B. "China: The emerging Economic Colossus," Vital Speeches, Vol. 60, No. 6, January 1, 1994, pp. 171-74.

Harrison, W. L., and Farn, C. A comparison of information management issues in the United Sates of America and the Republic of China. Information & Management, Vol 18, No 4 ,April 1990, 177-188.

Hofstede, G. H. "Management Scientists are Human," Management Science, Vol. 40, No. 1, Jan 1994, pp 1-13.

Huff, S. L. "Managing global information technology: You and the Computer," Business Quarterly, Vol (56); No. 2; p 71.

Ives, B., Hamilton, S., and Davis, G. B. "A framework for research in computer-based management information systems." Management Science, vol 26, No 9, September 1980, pp. 910-934.

Jarvenpaa, S. L.; Ives,B. "The global network organization of the future: Information management opportunities and challenges," Journal of Management Information Systems: JMIS. Vol. 10; No. 4; pp. 25-57.

Lally, L. "The Impact of Environment on Information Infrastructure Enhancement: A comparative study of Singapore, France, and the United states," Journal of Global Information Management. Vol 2, No 3, Summer 1994, pp 5-12.

(1)Lemon, Sumner. "Hackers Take Down Mainland ISPs," Computerworld Hong Kong. http://www.IDGCHINA.COM/NEWS/August97/Hackers.htm

(2) Lemon, Sumner. " Security Firm Flags China as High-Risk," Computerworld Hong Kong. http://www.IDGCHINA.COM/NEWS/August97/Security.htm

Mailloux, Jacqueline. "Hong Kong Eases into Data Warehouses," Computerworld Hong Kong http://www.IDGCHINA.COM/NEWS/August97/Hongkong.htm

New Century Group, "Chinese PC Companies Gaining Market Share," Computerworld Hong Kong. http://www.IDGCHINA.COM/NEWS/August97/ChinesePC.htm

Nolan, R. L. and Wetherbe, J. C. Toward a comprehensive Frameowork for MIS Research. MIS Quarterlyh, Juen 1980, pp. 1-19.

"Organization," Country: China. Kaleidoscope. 1998.

Peterson, Jared. "IDC Report: Mainland Warms to Professional Services," Computerworld Hong Kong, http://www.IDGCHINA.COM/NEWS/August97/IDC-Report.htm.

Paik, Y., Vance, C.M., and Stage, H. D. "The extend of divergence in human resource practice across three Chinese national cultures: Hong Kong, Taiwan and Singapore," Human Resource Management Journal. Vol 6, No. 2, 1996, pp 20-31.

Palvia, P; Palvia, S. "Understanding the Global Information Technology Environment: Representative World Issues" in Global information technology and systems management key issues and trends." P Palvia and S Palvia, and Roche (eds), Ivy League Publishing, (1996) pp. 3-30.

Palvia, P., and Palvia, S. "MIS Issues in India, and a comparison with the United States," International Information Systems, April 1992, pp. 100-110.

Purdue University Looks Within to Reduce the Number of Open I/T Jobs

Julie R. Mariga

Assistant Professor – Telecommunications and Networking Technology, Department of Computer Information Systems and Technology, Purdue University, West Lafayette, IN 47907-1421

Phone: (765) 494-0879, Fax: (765) 496-1212, Email: jrmariga@tech.purdue.edu

ABSTRACT

The number of open information technology (I/T) positions in the United States is currently at 346,000 and the number of qualified people graduating from undergraduate I/T programs to fill those open positions is around 42,000. Due to the shortage of skilled I/T professionals, companies and universities are having to be creative and develop in-house programs that will allow them to produce their own I/T professionals from among a pool of employees working in non-technical areas or possessing non-technical degrees. Purdue University has developed such a program that will help fill open computing positions by providing people with a solid educational foundation as well as current technical skills. This paper discusses the program Purdue has put into place to help overcome its shortage of qualified I/T professionals.

PROBLEM DEFINITION

According to the Information Technology Association of America there are 346,000 information technology positions currently vacant. The US Department of Commerce also states there will be more than a million new computer scientists and engineers, systems analysts, and programmers positions vacant between 1994 and 2005. Four-year educational institutions only produce a total of 42,000 graduates annually from computer and information sciences departments. Also, the number of incoming students enrolling in these programs is decreasing.

The problem is one that is felt around the world but it is especially critical at educational institutions due to their inability to compete with industry salaries in order to attract qualified I/T professionals. At Purdue University, in July 1997 there were 261 job openings on the West Lafayette campus. Of the 261, 47 were computer related jobs. Computer jobs account for 25% of the weekly job vacancies and that number is expected to continue to increase over time. Purdue I/T management recognized the problem and decided that they needed to be creative and develop some type of program that would allow them to utilize their existing employees and/or new hires that were qualified and wanted a career opportunity in the computer field. A feasibility report was completed in August 1997 at the request of the Executive Director of Management Information and the Department Head of Computer Technology. The feasibility report outlined the goal, problem, operational feasibility, schedule feasibility, economic feasibility, technical feasibility, and political feasibility of such an endeavor. Also, included in the report were the qualifications a potential candidate would need to possess and the process that would be followed to select candidates.

LITERATURE OVERVIEW

In a recent article, McGee (1998) states the number of college graduates with computer science degrees has dropped dramatically over the last decade, but that hasn't stopped companies from recruiting new graduates to fill I/T jobs. It's just forced some of them to reach out to grads with non-technical degrees. Math and science majors, even art, music, and history majors, are all being recruited for technology slots. It's not the degree that matters so much as a strong willingness to learn, companies say. Two companies that are hiring employees with non-technical degrees include EDS and CTG. EDS provides these employees with five weeks of training on programming languages and then the employees spend four weeks programming mock projects. EDS hopes to put 3,000 people through the program in 1998. CTG sends new employees through five weeks of programming training and hopes to put 600 new employees through the training in 1998.

According to Moad (1998), the I/T skills shortage is only going to get worse, driving up salaries and costing many companies revenues and profits. Driving the demand for people with I/T skills are massive year 2000 compliance projects, increasing systems complexity and new Internet commerce projects. Demand for people with I/T skills will continue to grow faster than the supply for at least the next two to five years. Last year, the number of I/T jobs in the United States grew by 13.8 percent, compared to a 9.6 percent annual growth rate between 1987 and 1994. I/T salaries are rising by an average of 20 percent per year compared with a 4 percent average increase rate for workers in other fields. The shortage also will force I/T managers to get better at recruiting and retaining people. Strategies should include helping universities produce more well-trained I/T workers and looking to offshore sources for I/T skills.

According to Callaway (1998), computer hardware and software vendors, the U.S. Department of Labor, universities, and nonprofit groups are reaching out to retirees, college students, teen-agers, laid-off professionals, the underemployed and folks who just want a career change—anyone who might be induced to join the I/T brigade. Last month, the Clinton administration got into the act at the Information Technology Association of America's National I/T Workforce Convocation in Berkeley, Calif., where officials announced plans to invest $28 million in projects to train more I/T workers, including laid-off laborers from other employment sectors.

PROGRAM OVERVIEW

After the completion of the feasibility report, a steering committee was formed by the Executive Director of Management

Information to further investigate the possibility of creating an educational program to increase the number of qualified computing professionals at the university. The steering committee consisted of a cross-section of professionals from the following areas: computer technology (an academic department), management information (the administrative computing division of the university), personnel services, student services, and sponsored programs. The steering committee reviewed the feasibility report and used it as the starting point to create the program. The objective of the program was to attract and develop professionals in computer information systems and technology by providing them with education and a supportive environment once their education was completed. To accommodate different competency levels and both internal and external candidates, the program included two components: Education and Practicum. The education component consisted of a series of six computer technology courses and the practicum component reinforced the knowledge and skills the candidates gained from the education. The program included four categories of participants:

1) Direct hires into the Practicum component
2) Direct hires into the Education component
3) Purdue employees who resign from their regular positions to accept an offer to participate in the program
4) Purdue employees who are sponsored in the Education component by their employing department.

Figure 1 provides an overview of the entire process that participants will go through from application through completion.

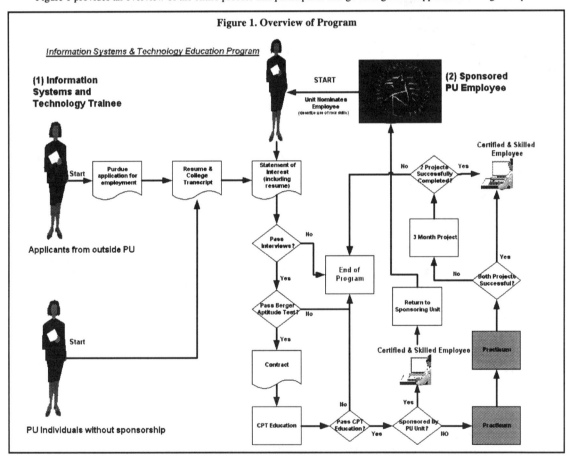

Figure 1. Overview of Program

The Education component includes four distinct curriculum tracks: basic computer literacy, advanced systems development, advanced programming, and advanced data and database management. The selected participants would go through the education component as a university employee and be paid during the process. The education would be provided to them free of charge and would count as university credit. Following the successful completion of the education component, department sponsored employees would return to their sponsoring departments for practical experience.

After completing the education component participants not sponsored by their department would complete at least two three month practicums that reinforce the education they just completed. If the participant successfully completes both practicums they would interview for one of the open computing positions on campus.

PROGRAM COMPONENTS

Selection Process

After receiving final funding approval for the program, the steering committee advertised the program through newspaper ads, internal publications, and via a web site. Applicants interested in being considered for the program had to write a statement of interest, send in a resume, fill out a Purdue employment application (if they were not already a Purdue employee), and submit a college transcript, if applicable. After the steering committee received all of the applications, selection was based on the following criteria:

1. Candidates went through a screening interview made up of interviewers from various departments. Interviewers were especially looking for candidates with:
- excellent communication and interpersonal skills
- strong ties to Purdue and/or the local community (in order to avoid investing in candidates likely to leave)
- basic computer knowledge
- a strong motivation and a keen interest in pursuing a career in the computing field.

2. Candidates passing stage one were then required to take the Berger Aptitude Test. The candidates had one hour and forty minutes to complete the test and had to score 27 or higher to move on to stage three of the selection process. The Berger Aptitude Test is used by many Fortune 500 companies, government agencies, and foreign companies. Organizations use the Berger Aptitude Test primarily to identify high aptitude candidates for programmer training. The candidate taking the exam does not need to have any prior programming experience. The exam uses a hypothetical language and is used to solve problems. The candidate taking the exam must apply rules of coding, looping, incrementing and branching as they write short programs. The candidates must also demonstrate the ability to be flexible by applying the language rules to solve more complex problems. The score is a strong indicator of a candidate's overall chances of success in programmer training and on-the-job performance. A score of 27 represents a probability that a candidate earning a 27 will have an 82% success rate during the training program and future job placement. Since Purdue is investing a tremendous amount of money and time in the training program it was imperative to increase the chances of the candidates being successful.

3. Candidates then went through a more in-depth interview called targeted selection. Interviewers were looking for candidates with:
- prior success in jobs
- ability to do college level work
- a firm belief that they could make a commitment to such a rigorous program.

The results of the three steps above were passed onto the steering committee who made the final decision about which 15 candidates would be selected for the program.

Following Acceptance

After offers were extended and accepted, candidates are required to sign a contract. A contract was established to assure that the candidates would not receive a free education and go to work somewhere else. The contract states that employees agree to refund 100% of the tuition and expense if s/he:
- Quits the education component at any time
- Fails to enter the practicum despite receiving a certification of completion in the education component.
- Fails to put forth a reasonable, good faith effort to successfully complete coursework and projects under the agreement, as determined by the project administrator, or
- Voluntarily terminates employment at the University within one year of entering the practicum

The contract also states that employees agree to refund 50% of the tuition and expenses if s/he voluntarily terminates his/her employment between the first and second years after his/her entry into the practicum. The contract also discusses grade expectations. The performance requirements of the contract states that the employee understands that the University will dismiss him/her from the program if s/he receives a letter grade of C or lower in any course. Also, if the employee completes the education component with an average letter grade of B or better, the University will present him/her with a Certificate of Completion signed by the appropriate University officials.

Commitment of Participating Departments

Participating departments are required to provide on-the-job-training. Each department must identify potential positions or projects for Practicum participants. The department must also identify the prerequisites for the position or project along with the knowledge and skills the employee will acquire through the assignment. The participating department must also outline the new job responsibilities of the employee after successful completion of the education component.

Orientation to Program

After the 15 candidates accepted the offered positions they went through an orientation program. The program included introducing them to the members of the steering committee, explaining to them why the program was being started, sharing with them an orientation to Purdue, and offering them a study skills course. The steering committee thought it was important to provide the candidates with some help on how to study since many of the candidates had been out of school for a long time. The study skills course covered the following areas:
- listening skills
- note-taking skills
- basic study skills
- memorization skills
- test-taking skills

Education Component

After completing orientation, the candidates entered the education component of the program. The education component consists of six courses in eleven weeks. As mentioned earlier, the candidates have certain grade expectations that they have to meet in order to stay in the program. The schedule for the education component is outlined in Table 1.

The education schedule was very rigorous and time consuming. The courses offered during the education component are the same courses that are offered to undergraduate students during a 17 week semester. The extremely demanding schedule is why it was very important for the steering committee to place a huge emphasis on the selection process. The program needed individuals that would be dedicated and make the type of commitment necessary in order to be successful in the education component. A typical day for a candidate during the education component was from 7:30 a.m. to 11:00 p.m. This is one reason why it is very important to find candidates that have good interpersonal skills who can work well with others since they will be spending a great deal of time together. The first group of candidates really worked well together.

Table 1. Overview of Education Schedule Schedule for Information Systems and Technology (IST) Education Program Pilot Implementation Summer 1998			
Dates	**Times**	**Element**	**Course Title**
May 18 – May 22	8:00 AM – NOON	Lecture	CPT 135
	1:00 PM – 5:00 PM	Lab	(Personal Computing Technology
May 26	8:00 AM – NOON	Exam	and Applications)
May 26	1:00 PM – 5:00 PM	Lab Practical	
June 1 – June 5	8:00 AM – NOON	Lecture	CPT 176
June 1 – June 5	1:00 PM – 5:00 PM	Lecture	(Information Technology
June 6 (Sat.)	8:00 AM – NOON	Exam	and Architecture)
June 8 – June 12	8:00 AM – NOON	Lecture	CPT 250
	1:00 PM – 5:00 PM	Lab	(Programming with
June 15	8:00 AM – NOON	Exam	Object Structures)
June 15	8:00 AM – 5:00 PM	Start Project	
June 16 – 17	8:00 AM – 5:00 PM	Complete Project	
June 22 – June 26	8:00 AM – NOON	Lecture	CPT 230
	1:00 PM – 5:00 PM	Lecture	(Data Communications)
June 29	8:00 AM – NOON	Exam	
July 6 - July 10	8:00 AM – NOON	Lecture	CPT 172
	1:00 PM – 5:00 PM	Lab	(Database Application
July 13	8:00 AM – NOON	Exam	Development)
July 13	8:00 AM – 5:00 PM	Start Project	
July 14 – 15	8:00 AM – 5:00 PM	Complete Project	
July 20 – July 24	8:00 AM – NOON	Lecture	CPT 280
	1:00 PM – 5:00 PM	Lab	(Systems Analysis and
July 27	8:00 AM – NOON	Exam	Design Methods)
July 27	8:00 AM – 5:00 PM	Start Project	
July 28 – 29	8:00 AM – 5:00 PM	Complete Project	

Practicum Component

After successfully completing the education component of the program candidates move into the practicum component. Candidates that are sponsored by their department go back to the department and start working on projects for the department. Candidates that are not sponsored have to complete two three month projects. The projects come from various areas on campus and a department interested in having a candidate complete a project has to provide the steering committee with information about the project. Items they have to provide include:
• brief project description
• estimated time frame for completion
• where the candidates office would be
• what computer hardware and software would be provided
• who the mentors will be

Each candidate is given both a technical mentor and a non-technical mentor.

The practicums vary in nature and the steering committee assigns students based on recommendations from the professors. Some example practicums include the candidates creating Microsoft Access databases for a variety of departments. The first round of practicums consisted of all MS Access projects and many of the candidates finished their practicum in four weeks although they were given twelve weeks to complete them. The second round of practicums will consist of some COBOL projects, a Brio query project, an Oracle project, and a web project.

Assessment of Program

Since a lot of time, money, and effort has gone into getting this program established it is very important to make sure every aspect of the program is properly assessed. There a number of assessment instruments that have been developed so that feedback can be collected and changes can be made if necessary. The table below outlines the various instruments that have been developed, identifies whether sponsored or non-sponsored candidates participate, identifies the timeframe for administration, and identifies who needs to complete the assessment.

Assessment Instruments

The End of Course instrument is to be filled out by each candidate and it is used to evaluate the overall effectiveness of the course and the instructor. The Education Component Assessment is filled out by each candidate at the end of the education component. This instrument is used to gather feedback about the selection and interviewing process and rates the overall curriculum as well as the instructors. The Practicum instrument is used to gather feedback from the candidates and supervisors about the practicum experience. The Intermediate instrument is completed by sponsored employees and their supervisors to gather feedback to make sure that the sponsored employee is using the education they gained. The Annual instrument is used to gather feedback from everyone,

Instrument	Sponsored	Non-Sponsored	Table 2. Overview of Assessment Schedule Timeframe	Trainee to complete	Supervisor of trainee to complete
End of Course	X	X	After each class	X	
Education Component Assessment	X	X	At end of the education component	X	
Practicum		X	At end of 1st practicum	X	X
Practicum		X	At end of 2nd practicum	X	X
Intermediate	X		6 months after education	X	X
Annual	X	X	12 months after education	X	X
Annual	X	X	Every year there after	X	X

non-sponsored candidates, sponsored employees, and supervisors. This instrument is used to gather feedback once everyone has had time to utilize their education with practical work experience and time to reflect on the past year.

CONCLUSION

The education program was offered for the first time during the Summer of 1998 and, by all accounts, was very successful. The candidates really came together as a group in the education component and continued to stay in contact after the education component. They all go to lunch every other week to keep each other updated on what they are doing. This is a very beneficial aspect of the program since they can learn from each other and share their experiences as they begin to build a network of professional peers. Also, many of the candidates keep in contact with the professors that taught them during the education component. This is also a very valuable benefit to the program since the students have another resource in the professors they had in class. We have received excellent feedback from the candidates so far about what we did right and what we can change in the future.

Some of the lessons we learned include:
• extending the education component to 13 weeks in order to provide more time in the more lab intensive courses
• keeping the study skills course in the program since many of them had not had a formal class in a long time
• keeping the orientation to Purdue and possibly expanding it to show how the University works and what the various departments do
• commending the targeted selection team for an excellent job at selecting a group of individuals that could work well together
• offering an additional programming course in place of the data communications course

Needless to say, if any other universities or companies consider putting together a similar program it is extremely important to spend significant time on the selection process.

Since the first offering of the program has been so successful, the program will continue in the future. The first iteration of the program offered a basic computer literacy set of courses to the candidates, while in the future the Computer Technology Department can offer a total of 10 courses per summer. In this manner, a new group of candidates can be selected to go through the basic computer literacy track while others can go through one of the advanced tracks. The courses that comprise the advanced track will be selected based on the university needs at that particular time. Some potential candidates for the advanced track courses include the first 15 candidates that completed the basic computer literacy track or other university employees that are already in computing positions but need to update their skills.

Purdue had a problem that many other universities and companies are facing. The University decided to be proactive in developing a program using existing educational resources that will help reduce the number of open computing positions around campus while offering new job opportunities to deserving individuals. By all accounts, this effort has been successful and worthwhile.

REFERENCES

Callaway, E. (1998). I/T openings: All may apply. Will training programs produce the people that I/T managers want to hire? PC Week [Online]. Available: http://www.zdnet.com/pcweek/news/0223/23jobs.html

Information Technology Association of America (ITAA) and Virginia Polytechnic Institute and State University. (March 1998). Help wanted 1998: A call for collaborative action for the new millennium, 6-7.

McGee, M. K. (1998). Nontech grads being hired for technology positions. Information Week [Online]. Available: http://techweb.cmp.com/iw/669/69canon.htm.

Moad, J. (1998). Study: Labor shortage to plague I/T for years. PC Week [Online]. Available: http://www.zdnet.com/pcweek/news/0630/02estaff.html

Application Portfolio Management – A Real Options Analysis

Anders Mårtensson
Department of Information Management, Stockholm School of Economics
Box 6501, SE–113 83 Stockholm, Sweden
Tel: +46 - 8 736 94 28, fax: +46 - 8 30 47 62, E-mail: anders.martensson@hhs.se

1 PROBLEM AREA

Management of information technology (IT) in general, and application portfolio management specifically, call for continuous attention. Short-term needs must constantly be met in a situation formed by long term effects of prior choices. Balancing short vs. long-term has become even more important due to the increasing complexity of application portfolios. From consisting of a few stand-alone applications, they have grown to large sets of interrelated applications, often with interactions with outside systems.

This research addresses management of application portfolios. A number of critical choices are of special interest. One is the acquisition strategy, i.e. the choice between make and buy. Development can be in-house, partially outsourced, or completely outsourced by acquiring a standard package. Another choice is between new and proven technology. Where in the technology life cycle should one invest? Due to the rapid development of information technology, timing is crucial. Each choice also forces the company to, actively or passively, take a stance on standards. What standards should be followed and what should be broken in favor of some "best of breed" solution?

2 RESEARCH OBJECTIVES

The overall research question guiding this research is *How are application portfolios managed in companies?* The more precise purposes of the research are:

A) to describe and characterize application portfolios

B) to describe and analyze application portfolio management in terms of considered factors, intended outcomes, and realized outcomes

3 THEORETICAL FOUNDATIONS

The research draws on two theoretical areas: application portfolios and IT infrastructures, which are the subject matter of interest, and real options, which are used as a tool for analysis.

3.1 IT Infrastructure and Application Portfolios

The importance of the IT infrastructure to the competitive strength of companies is well established (e.g. Keen 1991, Clemons and Row 1991) as is the role of flexibility (Duncan, 1995). Even though there is no universal definition of the concept IT infrastructure, most authors agree that the IT resources making up the infrastructure should be shared between different parts of the organization (e.g. Earl 1989, Keen 1991).

A slightly different way of approaching the problem is presented by Weill and Broadbent (1998) who, in addition to defining the concept, also focus on how management *views* firmwide infrastructure and thus how investments are analyzed. As an extension of Venkatraman (1991) they identify four different views of the role of the infrastructure:

None No firmwide infrastructure exists.

Utility Investments in infrastructure are based on cost savings alone.

Dependent Investments are driven by fulfilling business strategy.

Enabling Investments are made to provide strategic options.

On a different level, with less focus on the technology per se and more focus on the applications, the concept of application portfolios is pertinent. It was introduced by McFarlan (1981, 1984) who used a matrix to position companies according to the overall expected contribution of information systems to business success. The two variables used by McFarlan were *Strategic impact of existing operating systems* and *Strategic impact of application development portfolio*.

Later, Ward and Griffiths (1996) pointed out that companies are likely to have different systems with different strategic importance. They propose four different categories of applications for structuring application portfolios:

Support are important in order to run the business but not critical for the success of the business. The business can go on for quite a while even if the system were to break down. Examples of this kind of system are general ledger systems. Cost is basically the only way to gain a competitive advantage.

Key operational are vital for running the business. If they fail, parts of the business come to a complete standstill. The quality of the system is extremely important since any malfunctions are devastating. Examples of key operational systems are the reservation system of an airline and the electronic trading system of a stock exchange.

Strategic might help the company to gain competitive advantages in the future. Often time is very important since windows of opportunity tend not to last very long in a competitive market. These systems usually use fairly new technologies since they are pushing forward and trying to enable new business initiatives.

High potential are not usually used in the business but can rather be seen as insurance policies. Ward and Griffiths compare these systems with traditional research and development activities.

Another useful framework is a business factor matrix put forward by Lacity et al (1996). The matrix is used for suggesting suitable sourcing strategies for different applications. The two dimensions used are *Contribution to competitive or business positioning* and *Contribution to business operations*. The former deals with whether the IT activity distinguishes the company from its competitors, whether it is a *Commodity* or a *Differentiator*. The latter does not deal with the type of contribution but rather the extent of the contribution. This spectrum goes from *Useful* to *Critical*.

The business factors matrix (Lacity et al, 1996).		
Contribution to business operations	competitive or business positioning	
	Commodity	Differentiator
Critical	Critical to business operation but not distinguishing from competitors	Critical to business operation and distinguishing from competitors.
Useful	Provides incremental benefits but not distinguishing from competitors	Not critical to business operations but differentiates from competitors.

3.2 Evaluation And Real Options

Regarding evaluating IT investments, there is agreement on the difficulty of the task (see e.g. Farbey et al 1993, Keen 1991). There are a number of reasons for this. It is hard to estimate the cost of a new system as well as its lifetime, and the costs are hard to allocate since they usually are fixed and do not depend on utilization (Farbey et al, 1993). It is also important to take hidden costs, such as e.g. future maintenance, into account when an investment is made (Keen, 1991). Regarding the benefit side, it might in some cases be possible to estimate at the application level. For example, the effects of a new mail system might be convincingly measured. Estimating the benefits from more strategic systems is almost impossible (Keen, 1991). As the role of IT has changed from support to strategic initiatives, the benefits get more and more intangible, which make them harder to evaluate (Farbey et al, 1993).

This research applies a real options approach for analyzing the choices made in application portfolio management. Real options have been shown to be useful when evaluating IT investments in general and infrastructure investments specifically (Kogut and Kulatilaka, 1994). As strategic information systems and infrastructure typically provide companies with managerial flexibility or business growth opportunities they are well suited for an option modeling approach (Kambil et al, 1993). The idea of thinking of opportunities to make further investments as options is not new (see e.g. Kester, 1984).

More recently, the theoretical foundations of real options and their valuation have been developed (Dixit and Pindyck 1994, Trigeorgis 1996) as well as methods for practical applications (e.g. Luehrman, 1998). There are however one important difference between real and financial options to keep in mind apart from the obvious difference in evaluation complexity. Since real options are not tradable in the way financial options are, a real option must reflect a real capability of the company to actually exercise the option (Kambil et al, 1993). For financial options there are markets where they can be traded and thus an owner does not need to exercise the option. McGrath (1997) partly disagrees with this as she, at least in the case of technology commercialization, recognizes the opportunity to have the technology licensed out or spun off.

Basically, in an investment situation there are two types of real options. One deals with whether a decision must be made now or if it is possible to *wait-and-see*. The other deals with the *future flexibility* achieved after the decision (Trigeorgis, 1996). The latter can e.g. be options to invest further (call options) or abandon the project (put options). As an example, choosing a general standard software over an industry specific package can be justified by software growth options inherent in the general package, i.e. the options to invest further may outweigh the increased cost for adjusting the software for the specific industry (Taudes, 1998).

4 RESEARCH METHODOLOGY

A multiple case study consisting of six cases is planned and has been partly performed. Case studies are recommended for studying complex phenomenon that are little understood and exist in specific settings (Benbasat et al 1987, Eisenhardt 1989, Yin 1994). Given the purpose of this research a single case study is not deemed suitable. An overview is preferred to deep understanding of a single case since comparison between different application portfolios is one important part of the analysis. The usefulness of a framework for analysis of application portfolio is, at least at this time, deemed higher if it is based on a number of instances rather than a deep understanding of one case.

To enhance the possibilities of relevant inter-case analysis all cases are from the same industry, namely the financial industry. This industry is further narrowed by the selection criterion that the case companies all are stockbrokers active on the Stockholm Stock Exchange. Since they act on the same electronic market, their application portfolios have to conform to common external requirements and from time to time they are all forced to adapt their systems to changes in these external requirements. There are also interesting differences between the companies creating different conditions for the application portfolios. Examples of such differences are; company size, content of services offered (analysis or trade execution), targeted customers (private or institutional investors), and type of trading (own trading or customer orders).

The main data collection tool is semi-structured interviews (Rubin and Rubin, 1995), which are performed with line managers, users, executives, IT managers, and IT staff in order to cover different perspectives. The number of interviewees per company so far varies from six to about 15 since interviewing continues until the information added by additional interviews is deemed to be insignificant, i.e. the saturation point is reached (Glaser and Strauss, 1967). Whenever possible, interviews are supplemented with written information, such as written IT strategies, business strategies, documents describing application portfolios, minutes from meetings etc which enables data triangulation (Yin, 1994).

5 PRELIMINARY FINDINGS

Even though the data collection phase is not yet completed, some empirically based examples and preliminary findings are provided. First three miniature examples of critical choices in application portfolio management encountered in the case companies are presented. These choices are make-or-buy, new or proven technology, and stance on standards. Finally, some preliminary findings of general nature are presented.

5.1 Examples of Critical Choices

A few years ago, one company faced a make-or-buy decision when developing a strategic application. It was an innovative application so there were no existing packages but some small components used in other industries existed. The company chose to develop the application from scratch using outside consulting expertise. The existing components were rejected since the adaptation work required would have been large compared to the size of the components. Furthermore, developing from scratch was viewed as a way of increasing the window of opportunity for the application.

The make-or-buy decision is a central question in most IT projects. However, in many cases there is too much focus on the individual project and not enough focus on strategic thinking (Rands and Kambhato, 1996). Even though the make-or-buy decision is usually presented, or characterized, as a clear-cut yes-or-no type of question it is often more beneficial to apply a continuum approach (Rands, 1993). In this example, the company followed a rather pure make strategy, even though of course some standard components were bought, e.g. the database engine.

When one company faced a fundamental platform choice between a new and a proven technology, the company chose the new one partly based on predictions on future trends, but also partly based on a switching option (which was never not used). If the new technology would have turned out to be an inferior choice during the development phase, a readiness was kept to switch to the old technology.

Due to the rapid development of information technology, the timing of adopting a technology is crucial. There are a number of reasons for this such as the intrinsic uncertainty regarding new technologies, the intangibility of expected benefits, and the long-term perspective of committing to a technology (Scarso, 1996). The latter is especially true for infrastructure investments (Weill and Broadbent, 1998). In this example, a major advantage of the older more complex technology was speed. The IT department of the company predicted that the rapid technological development would make any performance problems with the new simpler technology vanish, and thus reducing the major advantage of the more complex technology. The switching option was an important factor since it reduced the risk of choosing the new technology.

One company has in some cases explicitly chosen to disregard existing corporate standards when acquiring major standard application packages. If e.g. an application is offered on several operating system platforms, the existing corporate standard is less relevant than the native platform of the application, i.e. ported versions are actively avoided. The major reason for this is that the company trusts its own ability to manage a different platform more than it trusts the provider to not lose quality and time when porting the package to other platforms.

The question of standards is omnipresent in management of application portfolios. The basic question is not if standards should be followed, but rather what standards should be followed and what should be broken. There are also different kinds of standards to follow (or break). Easily discernible are three different levels; product standards, industry standards, and corporate standards. Product standards are standards among all organizations, which e.g. relates to the possibilities of recruiting expertise. Industry standards relate to standards within industries or clusters of company, e.g. the Swedish financial industry. This may affect communication with other companies and the possibility of finding experts familiar with both the technology and the business. A corporate standard, which may or may not follow existing industry standards, means that the entire company follows the same standard, e.g. uses the same kind of system. Not using corporate standards means following a "best-of-breed" approach (Dewan et al, 1995). In the example quoted above, the cost of breaking the corporate standard and thus to maintain several platforms, is outweighed by the increased quality and decreased lead-times offered when using the native version.

5.2 Preliminary Findings

In this section three preliminary findings of general character are presented.

Relating to purpose A), a possible theoretical finding deals with the development from McFarlan by Ward and Griffiths that different applications belong to different categories. It seems that some applications belong to different categories depending on your organizational perspective and your use of them. This means that the model for structuring application portfolios might be an oversimplification, which is useful under some circumstances, but does not take into account that the character of an application might be in the eye of the beholder.

Relating to purpose B), two empirical observations might be noted. First, long term employee investments seem to be beneficial. Allowing slack and job switching might be costly in the short run, and is usually seen more as employee motivating than as directly beneficial for the company. However, job switching provides people with solid knowledge of both business aspects and IT, which in many cases is the key factor in application portfolio development. The combined IT and business perspective is fruitful, and often necessary, for IT based business development. There are many examples of the proactive role in innovative IT projects being played not by a specialist, nor a generalist, but rather by a general specialist, e.g. a former trader who switched into systems development.

Second, some companies finance in-house development of applications by selling it to others, even though this might not have been their intention from the beginning. The logic behind developing a system is that tailor-made business support is worth the cost. The option to sell the application to others is not always recognized when this decision is made. Once the application is completed this option is exercised with little concern of the initial logic. The long-term effects of this decision do not seem to be considered to any great extent. These effects may include restricted flexibility in the future since changes can not be tailored to the own company, but rather have to reflect the needs and wishes of the installed base and prospective customers. Thus, cashing in on the option to sell the system seems to be done without considering the flexibility options destroyed in the process. At any rate, the initial decision is not always a question of "buy or make", but sometimes rather "buy or sell".

6 REFERENCES

Benbasat, I., Goldstein, D., and Mead, M. (1987). "The Case Research Strategy in Studies of Information Systems", *MIS Quarterly* (11:3), pp. 369-386.

Clemons, E., and Row, M. (1991). "Sustaining IT Advantage: The Role of Structural Differences", *MIS Quarterly* (15:3), pp. 275-292.

Dewan, R., Seidmann, A., and Sundaresan, S. (1995). "Strategic Choices in IS Infrastructure: Corporate Standards versus 'Best of Breed' Systems". In DeGross, J., Ariav, G., Beath, C., Höyer, R., and Kemerer, C. (eds.), *Proceedings of the Sixteenth International Conference on Information Systems*, Amsterdam, The Netherlands.

Dixit, A., and Pindyck, R. (1994). *Investment Under Uncertainty*, Princeton University Press, Princeton, NJ.

Duncan, N. (1995). "Capturing Flexibility of Information Technology Infrastructure: A Study of Resources Characteristics and their Measure", *Journal of MIS* (12:2), pp. 37-57.

Earl, M. (1989). *Management Strategies for Information Technology*, Prentice-Hall, Hemel Hempstead, UK.

Eisenhardt. K. (1989). "Building Theories from Case Study Research", *The Academy of Management Review* (14:4), pp. 532-550.

Farbey, B., Land, F., and Targett, D. (1993). *How to Assess your IT Investment – A study of methods and practice*, Butterworth-Heinemann, Oxford, UK.

Glaser, B., and Strauss, A. (1967). *The Discovery of Grounded Theory: Strategies for Qualitative Research*, Aldine de Gruyter, New York, NY.

Kambil, A., Henderson, J., and Mohsenzadeh, H. (1993). "Strategic Management of Information Technology Investments: An Options Perspective". In Banker, R., Kauffman, R., and Mahmood, M. (eds.), *Strategic Information Technology Management: Perspectives on Organizational Growth and Competitive Advantage*, IDEA Group Publishing, London, UK.

Keen, P. (1991). *Shaping the Future: Business Design Through Information Technology*, Harvard Business School Press, Boston, MA.

Kester, C. (1984). "Today's options for tomorrow's growth", *Harvard Business Review* (62:2), pp. 153-160.

Kogut, B., and Kulatilaka, N. (1994). "Options Thinking and Platform Investments: Investing in Opportunity", *California Management Review* (36:2), pp. 52-71.

Lacity, M., Willcocks, L., and Feeny, D. (1996). "Sourcing Information Technology Capability: A Framework for Decision-Making". In. Earl, M. (ed.), *Information Management: The Organizational Dimension*, Oxford University Press, Oxford, UK.

Luehrman, T. (1998). "Investment Opportunities as Real Options: Getting Started on the Numbers", *Harvard Business Review* (76:4), pp. 51-67.

McFarlan, F. W. (1981). "Portfolio approach to information systems", *Harvard Business Review* (59:5), pp. 142-150.

McFarlan, F. W. (1984). "Information Technology changes the way you compete", *Harvard Business Review* (62:3), pp. 98-103.

McGrath, R. G. (1997). "A Real Options Logic For Initiating Technology Positioning Investments", *Academy of Management Review* (22:4), pp. 974-996.

Rands, T. (1993). "A framework for managing software make or buy", *European Journal of Information Systems* (2:4), pp. 273-282.

Rands, T., and Kambhato, P. (1996). "Software make or buy practices: towards a decision-making framework". In Willcocks, Leslie (ed.), *Investing in Information Systems: Evaluation and Management*, Chapman & Hall, London, UK.

Rubin, H., and Rubin, I. (1995). *Qualitative Interviewing: The Art Of Hearing Data*, SAGE Publications, Thousand Oaks, CA.

Scarso, E. (1996). "Timing the adoption of a new technology: an option-based approach", *Management Decision* (34:3), pp. 41-48.

Taudes, A. (1998). "Software Growth Options", *Journal of MIS* (15:1), pp. 165-185.

Trigeorgis, L. (1996). *Real Options: Managerial Flexibility and Strategy in Resource Allocation*, MIT Press, Cambridge, MA.

Venkatraman, N. (1991). "IT-induced business reconfiguration". In Scott Morton, M. (ed.), *Corporation of the 1990s: Information Technology and Organizational Transformation*, Oxford University Press, New York, NY.

Ward, J., and Griffiths, P. (1996). *Strategic Planning for Information Systems*, 2nd ed., John Wiley & Sons, Chichester, UK.

Weill, P., and Broadbent, M. (1998). *Leveraging the New Infrastructure: How Market Leaders Capitalize on Information Technology*, Harvard Business School Press, Boston, MA.

Yin, R. (1994). *Case Study Research – Design and Methods*, 2nd ed., Applied Social Research Methods Series, Volume 5, SAGE Publications, Thousand Oaks, CA.

A Primer for Information Technology as Used in Accounting Information Systems

Donald D. Martin

Central Missouri State University, 405 A Dockery, Warrensburg, Missouri 64093

telephone: 660.543.8560, fax: 660.543.8885, e-mail: dmartin@cmsu1.cmsu.edu

Since the invention of the computer in the 1940's, the rapid development of computer and telecommunications technologies has dominated thought about the role of information technology in colleges and universities. But future thought about planning for information technology is less likely to be concerned with technology than with the human factors at the interface between the machine and its user. Technology will continue to advance: Machines will become more powerful, so small, so reliable, and so inexpensive that none of these factors can be a major barrier to the proliferation of information technology throughout the activities of institutions of higher learning. Yet despite the rapid growth in numbers of machines in use and the quickening interest of students and faculty throughout the world, the information technology revolution has yet to be felt fully in educational institutions, nor is the technology used freely in instruction and administration as well as in research.

Information technology (IT), in its narrow definition, refers to the technological side of an information system. It includes hardware, databases, software networks, and other devices. As such, it can be viewed as a subsystem of an information system. Sometimes, the term IT is also used interchangeably with information system, or it may even be used as a broader concept that describes a collection of several information systems, users, and management for an entire organization.

DEVELOPMENTS AND TRENDS IN INFORMATION TECHNOLOGY

The primary reasons for this relatively minor impact are simply that the technology is still too complicated to use for many simple tasks, and it still is beyond any body ability to apply the technology to most of the more complex tasks. In business and in education computers have been successful in the great middle ground, where problems are routinized and sufficiently numerous to justify the considerable investment of human time normally required to master the devices and systems. Neither the simplest tasks nor complex ones performed just once normally justify the often complicated and idiosyncratic interface presented to the user; and the most complex and interesting tasks require cognitive algorithms that remain outside our grasp. The former category is typified by electronic mail and word-processing system, both of which have an important role to play in the educational institution. The latter includes problems of pattern classification and recognition inherent, for example, in translating natural languages, retrieving information from archival stores, assisting in programming algorithms, and performing other essentially cognitive and evaluative tasks (Luce and others, 1980).

This dichotomy will govern the strategy that may be selected to increase the use of information technology in the institution of higher learning, and it will certainly govern the development and design activities of the major manufacturers of information technology in the coming decades, for telecommunications capacity and computing power have become so great and their cost to small that equipment manufacturers must face the central problem of their future success: to provide convenient and effective means for nonspecialists to apply information machines to problems that intrinsically require the enormous capacity this technology makes available. These problems will involve vast amounts of computation and intricate organization of data and analysis. Where in the normal course of activities will be the ordinary person, the student, the faculty member, the administrator, find such problems?

In their early days, it was common to apply computers to problems that combined simplicity and precision of statement with large computational load. Such problems typically arise in mathematics (and, in another way, in administration) and involve the calculation of certain numbers, which may be the solution to an equation that represents some physical situation of interest, and for which the calculation proceeds in an interactive manner. There are certainly enough such problems that are profoundly interesting and worthwhile, but those people nevertheless constitute only a small fraction of the problems students and teachers face. The other problems are characterized by the opposite combination of attributes: small amount of interactive calculation. Whereas almost all of the former problems arise by abstraction from reality, the latter are, in many instances, more directly derived from perception and sensation. As the power of information technology increases and the scientific understanding of the properties of information grows correspondingly, the focus application of the technology will shift to those areas that now strikes other as more typically human, more subjective, and less structured.

As advanced as information processing machines now are, it still cannot match the human in the latter's characteristic sphere, although it is certainly coming close and can be expected to soon attain and surpass that goal. But it is advanced enough to allow the designer and the user the luxury of machine compatibility with human operational modes, whereas previously it was the human user who was forced, by the limitations of the machine, to adapt to its needs. This reversal of adaptive roles is another way to describe what is certain to be one of the main trends of development in the coming decades.

This trend, and the need for it, has been noted by writers in the past. In the context of higher education, the comprehensive Carnegie Commission study (Levien, 1972) correctly identified and predicted most of the technological developments of the past decade, but also noted that "the computer's role in research is not based solely on its primitive ability as a processor of numbers, but rests on a far broader base — its developed abilities as a processor of symbols, data, pictures, sounds, and events as well. Indeed, this listing is not exhaustive. Most of the people remain at the threshold of understanding the computer's ability to perform work for man." It still remains to give substance to this vision and to extend it beyond the boundary of research activities, although today most of them can say with some assurance that it will be done (O'Neil, 1981; Strassman and others, 1981).

The ability of machines to deal with pictures and events in an intelligent way will be measured largely by the understanding of the structure of information and the mental representation of knowledge. To the extent that progress is made on these fronts, the new technology will find increasing and deeper applications in the substantive work of colleges and universities.

In addition to adapting to the peculiarly human ability to organize and classify information and to find and define patterns in data, information machines must also adapt to the abilities of the human sensory system and the limitations of human memory. This is the essence of the problem of creating a "transparent" or "friendly" interface between the machine and its user. The possibilities and the inadequacies are both clearly exhibited in contemporary text processors and other systems intended to be used by large numbers of untrained or semi-trained people on a casual basis: just the use of information technology that should be the goal in institutions of higher learning where, after all, the principal objective of education (as of research) is to come to grips with thoughts, not with keyboards. But with rare exceptions these machines, as well as computers in general, still require that the user be very familiar with the machine and memorize many details. It still utilize non-intuitive sequences of keystrokes and commands to accomplish important tasks; they still take little account of the way people actually "process text" or possibly could process it, given human memory and other constraints under which people function. Computers still are designed, in many instances, from a point of view at odds with the realities of the human sensory system, which of necessity mediates all flow of information between the machine and its user. Twenty years ago there was a good excuse for the mismatched interface: the machines were too weak to accommodate to the complex needs and limitations of their users, and the designers were perforce preoccupied by the problem of getting the most out of them. Today, technology has advanced enough so that this explanation no longer carries force. Recent tentative forays by equipment manufacturers into information science and cognitive science, and the welcomed but still only occasional embodiment of human factors knowledge in machine features, suggests that this problem is gaining greater recognition and that more effort will be devoted to it in coming years.

Considered as a communication device, the human has a number of sensory channels for communicating with the external world. Of the sense of smell and sensation of heat we will have nothing to say. Touch plays a role — mostly one way — in current information entry systems, which generally depend on the tactile depression of keys requiring feedback from the touch sense for coordinated and efficient typing; similar feedback is necessary for motor control when writing is the input medium.

Sound provides one of the main channels for transmitting as well as receiving information. The receiving mode is capable of far greater discrimination, and hence capacity, than the transmitting mode, primarily because the latter consists only of coded atoms of speech (phonemes). There are fewer than 64 phonemes, and they are transmitted at about 10 per second, corresponding to some 60 bits per second of transmitted information if the speech sounds are not redundant. We can hear, and recognize, a far greater variety of sounds than phonemes of speech: the song of a bird, the rustle of leaves, the roar of the lion, the squeal of tires on pavement. However, speech input to an information machine simplifies the interface; and sound output, thought less significant, provides a valuable communication channel from the machine to the user. Recent developments in speech synthesis have resulted in toys — such as "Speak and Spell," which are acceptable to children, among the most unforgiving of users — and off-the-shelf modules that can be incorporated in the design of terminals, work stations, and other equipment. Thus many people may reasonably expect to find increased use of speech and other sound output as part of the dialogue machine maintain while it is being used.

IMAGE PROCESSING

Vision is by far the most important channel for human communication. It has the greatest channel capacity of all the sensory systems and the most refined pattern classification and analysis system. Vision is essentially a receiving channel; to transmit a visual signal, the human must employ the motor system to create motion and apply that motion either directly or by writing or otherwise creating a changed environment. Thus the receiving and transmitting aspects of the visual sensory channel are highly asymmetric in their capacity. This asymmetry may explain why the visual system has not enjoyed that degree of preeminence in ordinary affairs to which its superior channel capacity would seem to entitle it; it communication between people, no one can transmit information so quickly or in such quantity as to use the full capacity of the receiving apparatus. Indeed, the eye is not made for communication between people, although we have learned how to use it for that purpose by means of the printed word, the visual arts, and the artful smile; it is, nevertheless, really made to receive signals from a continually changing natural environment. When it is used to transmit thoughts through the modality of the printed word, the rate of communication is about 300 words per minute, or about 170 bits per second, some three times faster than speech. But the eye has the capacity to receive and analyze more than one million bits per second; indeed, this number is approximately the number of bits per second displayed by a color television tube, whose image occupies only a fraction of the field of vision. At the same time most the people know from experience that the resolution of the television image could not be significantly degraded without the degradation becoming evident, which shows that the eye assimilates at least that amount of information. It may assimilate much more, for the retina contains 125 million rods and the fovea, which is the region of acute vision, is packed with more than six million color sensitive cones. Each cone responds to changes of intensity that occur less frequently than about 60 times per second, and which may require as many as 8 bits for its representation. Even though these independent levels of discrimination are mutually constrained and the total channel capacity of the eye is not simply the product of these factors, the eye still tests the limit of a computer to keep pace with it. The display on a cathode ray tide of an image with an image with a degree of visual detail approximating the degree of resolution of which the eye is capable and stimulating smooth motion requires the computational capabilities of a relatively large computer.

The human vision channel has an unsurpassed ability to receive information, and it can do so at rates that approximate more nearly the operational speed of a computer than can any other human sensory channel; therefore, the vision channel is most compatible with the machine. Thus computer-generated imagery holds the greatest potential for simplifying the interface between the machine and its user. Contemporary methods that display text on a screen use this ability in a very limited way. Newer experimental techniques exploit ionic representations to convey information more efficiently than text, at least when the content is relatively well structured. Most of the people are familiar with the use of icons in place of text for efficient communication: Public rest rooms display icons of men and women in place of the word gasoline, a bed in place of motel, and a fork and knife in place of food. The use of icons is more common in Europe, where its relative independence of natural language is an advantage; precisely the same independence is an even greater advantage when machines will be used by people having greatly varying degrees of familiarity with the machines and the subtle functions they can perform. Thus we can expect to find an increasing use of the visual channel, and of representation by ionic metaphors, for communication between the machine and the user, and a corresponding requirement for still more powerful logic processors to generate the graphics and to store them.

The growth of computer-generated graphics as a tool for facilitating the use of information technology has important implications for the design of distributed information systems, for it suggests that the routine transfer of data from a terminal to a central processor, or from one terminal to another, or from a data bank to a terminal, will be measured against the norm of the visual channel of communication rather than of the acoustic channel. In terms of technology, the contrast is similar to that between the telephone line and the television cable — between 9,600 bits per second (data transmission rate) and 5 million bits per second. It is the contrast between baseband and broadband local area networks, and between the supporting computing power of an intelligent microcomputer terminal versus a powerful minicomputer work station. If there is one single important decision in the selection of technology for the needs of colleges and universities s decade or two from now, the choice of channel is probably that decision. The life of all other machines and systems typically is measured in years, but the electronic highway that ties machines together is passive and much less subject to obsolescence than the devices it connects, just as concrete highways become obsolete more slowly than the automobiles that traverse them. The electronic highway, like its concrete counterpart, requires a considerable capital commitment, at least by the budgetary standards of educational institutions, but it must be built broad enough to bear the traffic.

ALL-ELECTRONIC INFORMATION TECHNOLOGY

The third main theme of this paper is the trend toward full electronic information technology. It would be small exaggeration to assert that whatever is wrong with contemporary information technology is due to the non-electronic components. First, electronic working speeds far exceed mechanical working speeds, which means that mechanical input and output devices are mismatched to the electronic devices they serve. Second, reliability is a problem with non-electronic information technology. For reasons that cannot be probed here, electronic devices are inherently much more reliable than mechanical devices. It may not seem that way when one's digital watch breaks down, but in general it is the moving parts and the hot parts, if there are any, and the non-electronic interconnections that are the principal causes of failure in information technology. Usually the mechanical printer or the disk drive rather than the integrated circuit in the text processor is the culprit in equipment failure. Therefore, the trend toward higher integration of electronic elements (thereby reducing the number of inter-chip connections) and the replacement of mechanical and thermal devices by electronic or electro-optical ones will result in improved reliability. This trend also suggests that colleges and universities should adopt the goal of eliminating mechanical elements from their information processing systems.

These three main themes — (1) human factors of the machine interface, (2) image processing in distributed information systems and (3) all electronic information technology — from the background for the discussion in the following sections.

TRENDS IN COMPONENT TECHNOLOGY

Although it was suggested in the previous section that technological advance is not likely to be the dominant issue in planning for information technology in institutions of higher learning, it nevertheless will continue to be an important consideration because advances in technology affect the degree to which the interface between the machine and the user can be simplified and the complexity of the problems that can be accommodated on a personal work station. And, of course, changes in the cost structure are dependent primarily on technological innovation.

Microelectronic Storage and Processing Technology. Developments in microelectronics have virtually merged the concept of storage with the concept of processing capability in the sense that both have been reduced to common and physically similar fabrications realized as sandwiches layers of electrical conductors and insulators deposited on semiconducting wafers (typically made from silicon) less than a centimeter in diameter. Typical physical dimensions of the active elements (two-state switched called gates or transistors) of such an integrated circuit are measured in microns (millionths of a meter), a microscopic realm that verges on the world of quantum phenomena, wherein ordinary materials assume extraordinary properties, and the duality between the wavelike and particle like aspects of physical phenomena has practical and directly observable consequences.

Progress in the development of microelectronic storage and processing technology can be measured along many dimensions, among which the following six are particularly important in the context of their application to information systems:
1. Packing densities of active elements (logic gates per chip processors and bits for memory)
2. Processing performance (operations per second)
3. Reliability (mean time before failure)
4. Cost (dollars per logic gate or memory bit)
5. Power and power dissipation requirements (watts per logic gate)
6. Mass distribution (units marketed per unit time)

It is a remarkable fact, perhaps unique in the history of technology, that improvements in any of these six critical areas tends to stimulate advances in the other five. For instance, increased packing densities virtually automatically lead to greater operating speeds because the electron field propagating speed is close to the limiting speed of light, thus increases in operating speeds can result only from decreases in the distance between active circuit elements. For instance, if a logic gate or memory element can change its state in a picosecond , during this time light will travel about 30 microns; if electrical signals have to travel more than this distance from one gate to the next, the processor's rather than by the switching time of the circuits. For nanosecond changes of state, which are commonplace in contemporary integrated circuits, the corresponding distance is about 3 centimeters, which is greater than the diameter of an integrated circuit chip and consequently no limitation at all. Reliability is increased too because there are fewer macroscopic junctions and interfaces, where thermal fractures and other defects can concentrate; costs per active element fall because fabrication costs are spread over large numbers of elements per manufacturing operation for each silicon wafer; power requirements are reduced (and therefore total power dissipation requirements) because the smaller physical units require less power to drive electrons through them; and the opportunities for mass distribution increase because the portability, reliability, high performance, and low cost combine to create numerous possibilities for widespread application.

It is true that improvements in some of the areas have rather less pervasively beneficial consequences, but improvements in one category seem never to entail deficiencies in some other category; it is just not necessary to trade one desirable feature for another in this remarkable technology. But note that operating speed can be increased by increasing the power used to drive the circuit; the product of operating speed and power consumption is a characteristic parameter that has been decreased consistently by the successive introduction of different semiconductor sub-technologies (Hsiao, 1981).

BUSINESS ENVIRONMENT PRESSURES

To understand the role of information technology in the organization of the '90's, it is useful to review the major business environment factors that create pressure on organizations. The business environment refers to the social, legal, economic, physical, and political activities that impact business activities. Significant changes in the environment are likely to create major components of any organizations. There are five major components within an organization, they are organization structure and the corporate culture, technology, individuals and roles, management processes (planning, budgeting rewards), and the organization's strategy. These components are in equilibrium as long as no significant changes occur in the system. However, as soon as there is a change in the environment, or in any of the internal components, one or more of the components is also likely to be changed significantly. Now let's consider several major environmental factors.

Complex and Turbulent Environments. The environments that surround organizations are increasingly becoming more complex and turbulent. Advancements in communication, transportation, and technology create many changes. Other changes are the result of political or economic activities. Consequently, organization must take actions aimed to improve (or protect) their operations in such volatile environments. These actions may include better scanning of the environment, improvement, improved forecasting, flexible and adaptable planning, re-engineering of business processes, building business alliances, and quantitative and creative decision making. Organizations also restructure themselves. Information technology can be viewed as an enabler or supporter of such actions (Galbraith, 1993).

Strong Competition and a Global Economy. Pressures from international agencies, deregulation, improved technologies, and increased global communication have increased the level of competition worldwide. An example is the political changes in Eastern Europe, which created a large supply of skilled labor at a cost of $1 to $4 per hour. Inexpensive labor is also available in many countries of South African and Asia (Rhinesmith, 1993).

Global competition is especially intensified when governments become involved through the use of subsidies, tax policies, and import/export regulations and incentives. The competition is centered not only on prices, but also on quality, service level, and speed of delivery. Therefore, competition, which was previously confined within an industry or a region, is now becoming international. Rapid and inexpensive communication and transportation increases the magnitude of international trade even further. The nature of the competition is also changing. Competition used to be based on price, quality, and service (after the sale). Now companies compete also on rapid delivery times, and customizing products and services to the customers. Information technology can help companies compete globally and take advantage of globalization.

Social Responsibility. The interfaces between organizations and society are increasing and changing rapidly. Issues range from the state of the physical environment to the spread of AIDS. Corporations are becoming more aware of these interfaces and are willing to contribute toward improvements. Such contribution is known as social responsibility. Information technology can support many socially responsible activities. Example include Xerox Corporation of Los Angeles, which uses a decision support system to monitor equal opportunity programs (Turban and others, 1996).

Ethical Issues. The use of information technology raised many ethical issues ranging from surveillance of electronic mail to potential invasion of privacy of millions of customers whose are stored in private and public databases. Organizations must deal with ethical issues of their employees, customers, and suppliers. Ethical issues differ from legal issues. Since IT is new and rapidly changing, there is little experience or agreement on how to deal with its ethical issues. Also, what is ethical in one country may be unethical in another. Ethical issues are very important since they can damage the image of an organization as well as destroy the morale of the employees.

Changing Nature of the Workforce. The workforce is becoming diversified and is changing rapidly. There is an increasing number of female, single parents, minorities, and handicapped persons in all type of positions. Also, many employees continue to work more years than ever before. Information technology is helping the integration of some of these employees into the workforce.

Consumer Sophistication and Expectation. The consumer is continuously becoming more knowledgeable about the availability and quality of products and services. This results in a demand for better and customized products and services. For example, buyers of PCS want a computer that includes the options they like (Stalk and Weber, 1993). Customers also are demanding more detailed information about products and services. They want to know what warranties they receive, what financing is available, and so on, and they want the information quickly. Many companies are starting to treat the customer as a king. Companies need to be able to access information quickly to satisfy the customers.

Technological Innovations. Technology is playing an increased role in manufacturing and services. New and improved technologies create substitutions for products, alternative service options, and increased quality. Thus technology accelerates the competitive forces. What is the state of the art today may be obsolete tomorrow. There are many technologies that impact business in areas ranging from genetic engineering to food processing. However, the area that could have the largest overall impact is that of information technologies.

ORGANIZATIONS AND MANAGEMENT CHANGES

Changes in the business environment and in technology induce organizations to change the manner in which they operate. It has long been recognized that there are strong relationships among the environment, technology, organizational structure, people in the organization, organizational strategy, and management processes. As discussed earlier, significant changes in the environment are likely to change the equilibrium in internal parts of organizations. There is already evidence of some of these changes in many organizations. Changes in one country may impact others companies, creating more business pressures. The major factors that contribute to the pressure are as follows.

Business Alliances. Many companies realize that alliances with other companies, even competitors, can be very beneficial. There are several types of alliances: sharing resources, establishing permanent supplier-company relationship, and creating joint research efforts. One of the most interesting types is the temporary joint venture or strategies alliance, where companies form a special company for a teal corporation and, according to Byrne et al. (1993), this could be a typical business organization in the future.

A more permanent type of business alliance that links manufacturers, suppliers, and finance corporations is known as *keiretsu*. This kind of alliance can be heavily supported by information technologies ranging from electronic data interchange to electronic transmission of maps and drawings.

Decreased Budgets of Public Organizations. The U.S. budget deficit sky rocketed in the late '80's and early '90's. At the same time, the U.S. economy entered an economic recession. As a result, there was less funding available from federal, state, and municipal sources. The budget crunch forced organizations to streamline their operations and/or downsize them. For example, public universities were forced to reduce course offering. Information technology has become extremely important since it helps to cope with such changes. For example, intelligent computer-aided instruction allows increase in class sized by over 50 percent without reduction in quality.

Business Processes Re-engeering. Business processes re-engineering (BPR) refers to a major innovation — a quantum leap of change — in the manner for increased profitability or mere survival. Business process re-engineering involves changes in structure and in processes. The entire technological, human, and organizational dimensions may be changed in BPR. Over 70 percent of large U.S. companies claim to be re-engineering. As part of BPR, there are management realignments, mergers, consolidations, operational integrations, and reoriented distribution practices (Drucker, 1988).

Improvement Programs: TQM, JIT, and Others. BPR is a major undertaking. It is frequently compared to surgery, and like surgery, BPR may be risky. In medicine, there are alternatives and supplements to surgery, such as treating patients with drugs. These alternatives are less costly, take longer time, or have to be taken constantly. Similarly, there are several continuous improvement programs that can substitute for or supplement BPR. Two such programs are just-in-time (JIT) and total quality management (TQM).

Just-In-Time. The just-in-time (JIT) approach is a comprehensive production scheduling and inventory control system that attempts to reduce costs and improve work flow by scheduling materials and parts to arrive at a work station exactly at the time when they are needed. Such a system minimizes inventories and save space. It is comprehensive because it includes several other activities such as minimizing waste. While just-in-time systems can be managed manually, IT helps the implementation of large and complex JIT systems.

Total Quality Management. Total quality management (TQM) is an organization-wide commitment to continuous work improvement and meeting customers' needs. It is an organization effort to improve quality wherever and whenever possible. Information technology can enhance TQM by improving data monitoring, collection, summarization, analysis, and reporting. Information technology can also increase the speed of inspection and the quality of testing, and reduce the cost of performing various quality control activities.

Time-To-Market. Reducing the time from the inception of an idea until its implementation — time-to-market — is an important objective for many organizations because they can be first on the market with a product or they can provide customers with a service or product faster than their competitors do. Information technology can be used to expedite the various steps in the process of computer-aided design (CAD) computerized technology, Kodak Corporation was able to win race to develop the disposable camera against the Japanese (Turban and others, 1996).

Empowerment of Employees and Collaborative Work. Giving employees the authority to act and make decisions on their own is a strategy used by many organizations as part of their BPR or TQM. Empowerment is related to the concept of self-directed terms (Orsburn et. al., 1990; and Shonk, 1992). Management delegates authority to teams who can execute the work faster and with fewer delays. IT enables the decentralization of decision making and authority with a centralized control. It also enables employees to example, can give experts' advice to team members whenever human experts are not available. In with each other as well as to communicate with other terms. Collaborative work is a very important ingredient in a team-based organization, and it is heavily supported by IT.

Customer-Focused Approach. The 7-Eleven, Mercy Hospital, and many other companies are very customer oriented. They are beginning to pay more attention to customers and their preferences. Companies must re-engineer themselves to meet consumer demand. For example, at-from mass production to mass customization (Pine, 1993). In mass customization, a company produces large volume. But, in contrast with mass customization, items are made to fit the desires of each customer. Information technology is a major enabler of mass customization and other customer-focused approaches (Scott, 1991).

REFERENCES

1. Byrne, J.A., et al., "The Virtual Corporation," Business Week, February 8, 1993.
2. Drucker, P.E., "The Coming of the New Organization" Harvard Business Review, January/February 1988.
3. Galbraith J.R., and E.E. Lawler III, Organizing for the Future, San Francisco: Jossey-Bass, 1993.
4. Hsiao, M.Y., Carter, W.C., Thomas, J. W., and Stringfellow, W.R. "Reliability, Availability, and Serviceability of IBM Computer Systems: A Quarterly Century of Progress." IBM Journal of Research Development, 1981, 25, 435-465.
5. Levien, R. E. The Emerging Technology: Institutional Uses of the Computer in Higher Education. Carnegie Commission on Higher

Education and the Rand Corporation. New York: McGraw-Hill, 1972.

6. Luce, R. D., and Bresnan, J. "Behavioral and Linguistic Research Bearing on Information Science." Project Management Journal, June 1981.

7. O'Neil, H.F., Jr. Computer Based Instruction: A State of the Art Assessment. New York: Academic Press, 1981.

8. Orsburn, J. D., et al., Self-Directed Work Teams, Homewood, IL: Business One IRWIN, 1990.

9. Pine, J. B. II, Mass Customization, Boston: Harvard Business School Press, 1993.

10. Rhinesmith, S. H., A Managers Guide to Globalization, Homewood, IL: Business One IRWIN, 1993.

11. Scott Morton, M. S. (ed.), The Corporation of the 1990's: Information Technology and Organization Transformation, New York: Oxford University Press, 1991.

12. Shonk, J. H., Team-Based Organizations, Homewood, IL: Business One IRWIN, 1992.

13. Stalk, B. Jr., and A. M. Webber, "Japan's Dark Side of Time", Harvard Business Review, July/August 1993.

14. Strassmann, P., and Tanaka, R. I. Microcomputers: A Technology Forecast and Assessment to the Year 2000. New York: Wiley 1981.

15. Turban, E., McLean E., and Wetherbe J. Information Technology for Management: Improving Quality and Productivity. New York: Wiley 1996.

The Japanese Language Is Changing

Akira Matuura, Hosei University, Tokyo, Japan, 102-0071
Phone: 03-3264-9342

INTRODUCTION

Computer technology is now widespread in almost every aspect of Japan. It has facilitated what had been considered to be impossible before it came into being. It is changing not only our lives but also our ways of thinking and our language. What changes has it brought about?

Without computers, Japan as a whole would cease to function, including its banks, corporations, universities, hospitals and so forth. Computer technology gives such people as the elderly, disabled and handicapped easy access to various kinds of useful information and supplies them with a source of support and encouragement. Academics also enjoy a great deal of advantage, including easy access to a vast amount of information and exchanges of information among educational and other institutions. The Internet has also facilitated communication between people and groups beyond previous boundaries as if there existed no such limitations. It is quite evident that computer technology has given us various kinds of benefits although some drawbacks arising from its use remain to be removed.

Last year, my presentation focused on the written aspect of a changing Japanese Language in connection with computer technology. This time my main concern is directed to the spoken language, with some reference to its cultural aspects as well. As a background I will outline the language situation of Japan and the attitude toward language on the part of the people. Discussion will follow with special reference to changing aspects of Japanese brought about by computer technology. My presentation will conclude by summarizing a welcome sign of Japanese in favor of the internationalization of Japan and its language.

BACKGROUND

Viewed from outside, the Japanese Language is easy to learn as far as grammar and pronunciation are concerned. We have no noun inflexions and verb conjugations are rather simple. Vowels are as few as five and pronunciation is easy though a few difficulties exist for foreign learners. They may assume that written Japanese is also simple. As they proceed from the beginner's level to more advanced study, many of them are discouraged by Chinese characters. Our most complicated writing system in the world stands as a high wall facing foreign learners. We use three kinds of characters and letters, and Chinese characters play by far the most important role in our daily life. The number of Chinese characters used in writing is up to the individual. Some show off their knowledge of them by using as many of them as possible, while others prefer to write Japanese with very few of them. No one can deny the tremendously important part Chinese characters have played in forming Japan's culture as well as its language. But it must be pointed out that Chinese characters have been closely connected with the elite of society, so it is still associated with the concepts of prestige, authority and elitism. In this context it is no wonder that Japanese tend to pay more attention to a written language in which Chinese characters are used. It is quite common to see sentences whose meanings we can instantly understand with the help of Chinese characters but which are, when pronounced, incomprehensible due to the large number of homophones. Our language attitude is, thus, heavily dependent on written language but there are, surprisingly and regrettably, very few, if any, movements to alter this.

The younger generation is, however, beginning to say no to this Chinese-character dominated situation. Chinese characters are very difficult to master even for natives, to say nothing of foreign learners. I often see Japanese university students write incorrect Chinese characters. They are not to blame. The Chinese characters should be blamed in my view. Young people, who want to free themselves from such a heavy burden, prefer to use loanwords from English and English words themselves. They prefer both written and spoken language which are easy to master and are also comprehensible and communicative. They are so flexible that they are free from the old-fashioned and, in a sense, unreasonable elitism associated with Chinese characters. It is quite natural that they should turn their attention to taking advantage of computer technology which can offer them a wide range of opportunities to facilitate their new communication patterns. It would not be an exaggeration to say that computer technology, coupled with such a new way of thinking, will eventually produce a more globalization-oriented language, though ironically it was originally not intended for such a purpose.

DISCUSSION

I will now take up some cases in which the spoken language is becoming more dominant than the written one due to computer technology.

One of the most conspicuous phenomena is the language situation brought about by the introduction of cellular phone. In the big city where I live, it is a common scene in the train for not only commuters but also high school students and elderly people to speak loudly even though they appear to be alone. Without the existence of the portable telephone, such a situation would be unimaginable. In a sense, it is really astounding. In the train, particularly in big cities, people usually keep silent, except when they chat quietly among close friends. In this context conversation over the cellular phone looks and sounds unfamiliar, but sooner or later it will become part of our urban life. What is conspicuous is that a person talks loudly in public to someone else absent from the scene. This is clearly changing the situation of our spoken language. It makes people more positive and in a way defiant of restriction. The phone also helps expand the network of people never experienced before.

Personal computers are widespread and more and more documents are printed by them instead of through handwriting. This convenient device is now changing Japanese aesthetic value attached to handwritten Chinese characters. People are beginning to prefer the printed written language rather than the handwritten one. These few years I receive an increasing number of traditional New Year's Cards printed by computers. Another change is more fundamental. Some Japanese input Japanese with the keys of roman alphabet, without thinking of complicated Chinese characters due to the smaller number of its keys as compared with that of the two phonetic Japanese alphabets. This is really an amazing change. All they have to think of is just the sound. They are completely free from the yoke of Chinese characters. This habit will contribute to establishing a more comprehensible Japanese independent of confusing homophones of Chinese characters, with the result that the distance between spoken and written language will be greatly reduced.

E-mail is also playing a certain role in this area. Exchanges by E-mail are so popular as to be changing communication patterns among Japanese. Face-to-face communication is partly being replaced by E-mail. This means communication, for example, between bosses and people below them is becoming less formal. E-mail has the possibility of changing formal and honorific expressions used in formal correspondence and leveling it into one closer to spoken language. Also E-mail makes negotiations over glasses of beer or cups of sake less frequent. English expressions used in E-mail will cause language-mixing under the influence of English. Young Japanese are less resistant to this situation. So it will be more prevalent.

Voice-mail makes Japanese more aware of the spoken language than the written language. We will try to speak the language in a more easily understandable manner.

The Internet has a tremendous impact on the Japanese Language in that it takes Japanese people out of the confines of the Japanese archipelago. The language used there is mainly English but the importance of its impact lies in the fact that we instantly communicate with people all over the world. We can think and speak beyond the usual boundaries and expand our horizon, which means we are beginning to think and act globally. This will eventually lead us to think of drawbacks of our own language and try to make it more suitable for better communication in a global perspective. On the whole the changes mentioned so far will also result in reducing the Japanese trait of clearly distinguishing in-group people and out-group people and the Japanese traditions expressed in proverbs praising 'communication without verbal language,' or 'it's better left unsaid.'

CONCLUSION

In conclusion, computer technology is now changing the Japanese Language particularly among the younger generation. This change is not yet so noticeable but is in favor of the internationalization of Japan and its language. Of course, conservatives, laymen as well as the elite, would frown upon this and in fact computers can deal with more complicated Chinese characters, leading such people to advocate movement in the opposite direction. However, nobody will be able to hamper the progress of this change. Thus, I must conclude that computer technology is doing a great deal to contribute to language changes which have never been so widespread and fundamental in the direction of opening up Japan into an international community.

Continuous Improvement in the Development of a Computer Assisted Training System for Siemens Automotive

Kathryn McCubbin, Associate Professor and Students: Steve Allen, Doug Leidy, and Lanny Philips
Christopher Newport University, 1 University Place, Newport News, Virginia 23606
Phone: 757-594-7836, Fax: 757-594-7808, Mccubbin@cnu.edu

BACKGROUND

Problem Statement

The manufacturing industry is experiencing a serious shortage of skilled workers that threatens its future. A generation ago manufacturing was labor intensive using mainly manual operations. Automation of the manufacturing process during the last two decades has imposed greater computer skill requirements on that labor force. How can a global manufacturing organization economically retrain its employees in its transition from manual to robotic operations?

Student Research Project

The program in MIS included a course in business computer application design. Emphasis was placed on the design of real world, practical applications with which the students in their work place had experience. One of the students was employed as a robotics machine operator at Siemens Automotive. Maintenance and operational procedures called for him to use a physical manual that could be located át a distance from his station. In addition, the manual was not always timely regarding updates and international accreditation standards placed strict regulations on the contents of the manual. He designed a computer system that was simple in concept: providing electronic copies of the manual at each robotics station. However, it was the byproduct of this design that proved to be so effective. If the electronic manual provided optional tutorial features it could be used as an ad hoc training device. This meant that management could be more flexible in the assignment of operators to machines since a teaching device would be available should an operator need "brushing up" on a machine or if an unexpected fault developed. It would also provide for training of employees off the factory floor thus freeing critical resources. The conceptual design of a computer application system is only the beginning. To realize its advantages it must be implemented. This paper describes the evolution of that implementation. Such implementation would not have been possible without the aggressive and cutting edge management philosophy of Siemens Automotive.

The Company: Siemens Automotive, USA

In the mid 1980's Siemens Automotive, manufacturer of fuel injectors for automobiles, purchased Bendix Automotive in Newport News, Virginia. Its main customers are foreign and domestic automobile manufacturers. By 1988 Siemens was experiencing serious financial difficulty and the president, George Perry, knew there had to be a change in management philosophy if Siemens were to survive. The philosophy he chose was one of employee empowerment. It worked because George Perry "decided to turn the world upside down." He committed himself and the organization to three fundamental tenets:

People are not expendable;

We will pay for knowledge;

We will develop and retain a culture of trust in the organization.

John Olson instituted the practice of Company Wide Quality (CWQ). This is a six-step program involving the following:

Training and education;

Communication;

Improvement planning;

Employee involvement;

Productivity;

Reward and recognition.

It is implemented in three distinct ways. Through its REFLEXTIONS program Siemens deposits $50 for every implemented employee's suggestion into a central fund that is distributed equally to all employees at year-end. Through its Small Group Improvement Activity (SGIA) a cross-section of hourly and salaried employees, customers and suppliers brainstorm solutions to problems and develop implementation plans.i Through its Process Optimization with Early Results (POWER) program it dedicates teams full-time for 3 to 5 days to analyze and resolve specific problems.

Incidental practices that amaze more conventional outsiders include the fact that: all salaried employees have company credit cards; no administrative authorization is required for domestic business travel; domestic travel advances require little or no authorization and are obtained at ATM machines using the credit cards; decisions involving employees are made by the affected employees. Since the implementation of this management philosophy and practice in 1989:

Productivity as a measure of sales per employee is up 89%;

Customer reject rate on finished products has decreased by 43%;

Output is expected to increase by 33% in each of the next 2 years without increasing employment;

30% of total plant budget is invested annually in information systems and technology;

Manufacturing cost per unit was trimmed by 41%

Warranty costs were down 64%

Order-to-shipment lead times were slashed 75%;

There was 99.5% on-time delivery of all products.

As John Olson delights in pointing out "this turn around was accomplished with the same employees, the same work force." He credits employee training done in cooperation with the local community college for this fact.

The impact of international standards for businesses involved in global commerce was an important motivator for the change in management style. These standards, typically called the ISO 900x series of standards, impose severe quality requirements on businesses. Auto manufacturers have adopted an even more stringent set of standards.ii iii iv The auto manufacturers require that all of their suppliers are QS 900x certified. To become certified under these standards a company must have written procedures for all processes, these procedures must be followed by all relevant employees, an independent auditing team must certify that the employees' performances are consistent with the documentation, and the audit process must be continual. John Olson believed that the way to reach that level of quality was to empower each employee, to have her/him understand the importance of individual performance and continually try to improve upon it.

IMPLEMENTATION OF THE COMPUTER SYSTEM: PROCIS

Undergraduate and graduate students implemented the system. The faculty member served as the facilitator for implementation and liaison between Siemens Automotive development team and the students. The robotics machine chosen was the Swager, a machine used to combine the armature and casing of a fuel injector rod.

ProCIS: Phase 1

The computer system used VISUAL BASIC 5.0 and the Windows Explorer user interface format (using a mouse to explode and condense menus). It stored the Swager operations manual in an ACCESS database that contained both text and photographs. Video was excluded because of storage limitations. Audio was excluded because of the ambient noise of the factory floor. The text could be edited by invoking rather complicated VISUAL BASIC features. Either the text or the photograph was displayed. They could not be displayed simultaneously. A digital camera was used to photograph various parts of the machine. The major limitations of the pilot system were that the text and photographs were not shown simultaneously, the menu selection interface was cumbersome and the quality of the photographs was insufficient to illustrate the detail to which the text referred.

ProCIS: Phase 2

The user interface was redesigned so that a minimum menu was displayed at all times. Also, text and photographs were displayed together with the option of scrolling the photographs with the text or keeping the text fixed while scrolling the photographs. Forward and backward buttons were provided as well as "on the fly editing". A zoom effect for enhancing the text description of a process was accomplished by relating several, increasingly magnified photographs, with a single portion of text. The digital camera was discarded in favor of a 35 mm camera that provided significantly higher resolution. The ACCESS database was discarded in favor of a flat file system that dramatically decreased response time.

This version was field tested by a team of operational personnel on the production floor. Feedback from the field test was overwhelmingly positive and many suggestions were used in the design and implementation of the next phase. While Siemens management was satisfied with the basic design features of ProCIS it did not want to support a computer system that required the attention of software professionals each time a new machine was introduced on the production floor. Management also desired that the system operate on an NT network and provide that text be available in several languages. The latter would allow Siemens Automotive factories in several countries potentially to have access over the Internet to the same textual content in their native languages.

ProCIS: Phase 3

A feature termed "auto-population" was developed that allows a senior operations person to define a new machine, import the text of the corresponding manual, and electronically flag positions in the text where photographs and glossary items are to be inserted. Photographs would be scanned into bitmap files and automatically entered into the appropriate text. Software "hooks" are provided for five distinct languages of the user interface. The software implementation for this phase has been completed and initially reviewed by Siemens management. The efficiency and effectiveness of the "auto-population" feature awaits the assemblage of a Siemens Automotive team.

CONCLUSION

The pedagogy of higher education has changed dramatically from traditional class lectures to interactive formats that include student applied-research projects. Ideally, the project concept should originate from a real world experience of the student and be of interest to the larger university community. The advantages of this approach are many since the student, the university, the faculty member, and the community can all gain from the experience.

ENDNOTES

i Elmuti, Dean, "Sustaining high performance through self-managed work teams," Industrial Management, March-April 1996 v38 n2 p4 (5).
ii Foreign auto manufacturers also emphasize the importance of knowledge and training in manufacturing excellence.
iii Vasilash, Gary S., "Agility and other anguishing exercises in the auto industry," Production, Oct 1994 v 106 n10 p50 (10).
iv Pickard, Jane 'Tour de force, (Philip Ashmore, Nissan UK's personnel director)," People Management," March-April 1996 v 38 n2 p495).

A Unified Approach to the Determinants of IS/IT Outsourcing Success

Rajesh Mirani
Associate Professor of Information Systems, Merrick School of Business, University of Baltimore, 11 W. Mt. Royal Ave., Baltimore, MD 21201
Phone: (410) 837-5261, Fax: (410) 837-5722, E-mail: RMIRANI@UBMAIL.UBALT.EDU

INTRODUCTION

The outsourcing of information systems (IS) and/or information technology (IT) components such as applications development, systems operations, telecommunications, end-user support, and systems planning/management to external vendors has reached an all-time high. IS/IT outsourcing has also been the subject of much published research. Many of the published articles on this topic seek to provide guidance to chief information officers (CIOs) and other IS/IT executives by focusing on the question: What causes some outsourcing projects to succeed and others to fail?

Various answers to this question have been proposed. For example, one viewpoint that solely addresses applications development outsourcing is that commodity IS functions such as payroll are good candidates for outsourcing whereas applications that directly provide an organization with strategic advantage should always remain in-house, and that any violation of this maxim is bound to result in failure. Another school of thought seeks to extend this philosophy to all IS/IT realms with the argument that the more generic and less "asset-specific" an IS/IT function, the more likely it is to be successfully outsourced.

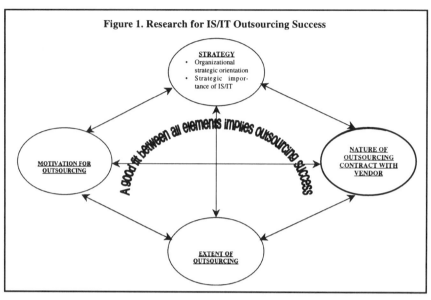

Figure 1. Research for IS/IT Outsourcing Success

Another perspective on this issue comes from a group of practitioners and researchers who contend that the foundations of a successful outsourcing endeavor lie in the nature of relationship forged between the outsourcer (vendor) and the outsourcee. There are two distinct schools of thought here. One likens this relationship to a partnership or even a marriage, where mutual trust, give-and-take, and assimilation of individual identities pave the path to success. The other (and more skeptical) theory offers the caution that vendors are motivated by their own profits and will provide only those services that are explicitly agreed upon in a written contract. Accordingly, followers of this school advocate extensive contract provisions to cover all possible contingencies on diverse issues such as services provided, charges incurred, price protection, response time, staffing, equipment ownership, sites covered, processing priority, security procedures, security inspection rights, contract termination, quality standards, continuity during dispute, and arbitration.

Yet another perspective on this topic sheds light on the reasons for organizations to consider outsourcing. A number of potential benefits of outsourcing have been identified. These include cost savings, infusion of cash and improvement of balance sheet figures, productivity gains, access to leading technology, and redirect internal focus on strategic uses of IS/IT. The catch, according to this line of thinking, is that organizations often expect specific benefits that are not realized for various reasons, and that this discrepancy between expected and realized benefits causes the outsourcing project to be viewed as a failure.

A UNIFIED PERSPECTIVE

The objective of this empirical research study is to include all of these divergent approaches in the synthesis of a unified perspective on outsourcing success. It will be shown that organizational strategy, the strategic importance of IS/IT to the organization, the motivation or reasons for outsourcing, the nature and extent of IS/IT functions outsourced, and the nature of relationship and contract with the outsourcer (vendor) are all key elements that determine outsourcing success. Furthermore, the success of any given outsourcing endeavor is determined not exclusively by one or more of these key elements but by how well they fit or match each other, to create a harmonious whole context. For example, an organization that relies highly on IS/IT for competitive advantage would be do well to steer clear of a cost containment focus and/or a heavily transactional relationship with the vendor and instead work towards a mutually nurturing relationship with a vendor that is capable of sustaining such a partnership. On the other hand, an organization where the strategic importance of IS/IT is low may well pursue outsourcing as a mechanism to contain costs, and would need to keep a tight rein on the vendor through specific cost-containment clauses in the contract. Figure 1 depicts this perspective in the form of a research framework for the study.

RESEARCH METHODOLOGY

The proposed methodology for this study is a cross-sectional survey of the highest-ranking IS/IT executives from hundreds of similar organizations in the manufacturing industry. Although the study will be exploratory in nature, the sample of organizations targeted will be as homogenous as possible (in terms of number of employees, annual sales, etc.) to prevent sample selection biases from creeping in and diluting the credibility of any findings. The results are expected to bolster the author's overall contention that there are various determinants of outsourcing success, and that they interact with each other to create an overall outcome (success or failure).

PARTIAL LIST OF REFERENCES

1. Chapman, Robert B. and Kathleen Andrade. *Insourcing after the Outsourcing: MIS Survival Guide.* New York: American Management Association, 1998.
2. Grabowski, Martha, and Sunro Lee. *Linking Information Systems Application Portfolios and Organizational Strategy*, in Khosrowpour,

Mehdi. Managing Information technology Investments with Outsourcing. Harrisburg, PA: Idea Group Publishing, 1995, pp. 55 – 82.

3. Johnson, Mike. *Outsourcing in Brief.* Oxford, Great Britain: Butterworth-Heinemann, 1997.

4. Klepper, Robert. *Outsourcing Relationships,* in Khosrowpour, Mehdi. Managing Information technology Investments with Outsourcing. Harrisburg, PA: Idea Group Publishing, 1995, pp. 218 – 243.

5. Klepper, Robert and Wendell O. Jones. *Outsourcing Information Technology, Systems & Services.* Upper Saddle River, New Jersey: Prentice Hall, 1998.

6. Lacity, Mary C. and Rudy Hirschheim. *Information Systems Outsourcing: Myths, Metaphors, and Realities.* Chichester, England: John Wiley & Sons, 1993.

7. Mylott, Thomas R. III. *Computer Outsourcing: Managing the Transfer of Information Systems.* Englewood Cliffs, New Jersey: Prentice Hall, 1995.

8. Nam, Kichan, Rajagopalan, Srinivasan, and Rao, H. Raghav. *Dimensions of Outsourcing: A Transactions Cost Framework,* in Khosrowpour, Mehdi. Managing Information technology Investments with Outsourcing. Harrisburg, PA: Idea Group Publishing, 1995, pp. 104 – 128.

9. Palvia, Prashant, and Parzinger, Monica. *Information Systems Outsourcing in Financial Institutions,* in Khosrowpour, Mehdi. Managing Information technology Investments with Outsourcing. Harrisburg, PA: Idea Group Publishing, 1995, pp. 129 – 154.

10. Williams, Oakie. *Outsourcing: a CIO's perspective.* Boca Raton, Florida: CRC Press LLC, 1998.

Defining New Models for Outsourcing

William H. Money, Ph.D.
The George Washington University, Associate Professor, Executive Masters In Information Systems Program,
University Center, 20101 Academic Way, Ashburn, VA 22011
(703) 729-8335; wmoney@gwu.edu

INTRODUCTION

Many organizations in today's complex environment have taken on properties attributed to virtual organizations by exercising options to extend their production of goods and services by arranging for the performance of key organizational activities by other firms. The performing firms utilize and expand their own key competencies by delivering the services required to many other organizations. This business activity has been described as the outsourcing of goods and services when it is delivered under a long-term contract.

Key services outsourced in the past have included the production of information systems, development of software, and delivery of software support. Contractual outsourcing activities of many organization have now expanded extensively into the broad areas of data center management, telecommunication, and help desk support.

The outsourcing services, agreements, advantages, disadvantages, and methods used to implement outsourcing have been addressed in a number of case studies. However, the more complex questions regarding the outsourcing activities performed, effective management and communication processes, and evolving nature of complex corporate relationships used to implement these managerial and service arrangements have received more limited attention in the literature. This paper will present an initial study of a relatively complex outsourcing relationship developed by three utilities and an information systems integration and development organization. The analysis indicates that the more traditional model of outsourcing is being modified (and greatly formalized) in a number of key areas. Understanding the changing nature of what has previously been called outsourcing poses a challenge for future MIS managers and developers. Effectively integrating this technique into an overall management strategy for the efficient provision of information services may require an increasingly complex formal business strategy supported by contractual rules and pre-planned management practices.

TRADITIONAL OUTSOURCING MODEL

The traditional outsourcing model is not fully described in any single literature. It is described in broad terms as an arms length relationship managed by a formal contract between the providing and using organizations. The arrangement are found in a wide variety of government, non-profit, business, and educational organizations. The general assumptions about the theory of benefits, contracting methods, typical outsourced systems and services, risks, research regarding attitudes, and management guidelines (wisdom) have been summarized below from the literature.

Theory of Benefits

The justification and theory and theory of outsourcing are based on the principles of economies of scale, and high price organizations must pay for scarce resources. Arguments favoring outsourcing and descriptions of successful relationships frequently suggest that the outsourcing organization acquires increased access (at potentially better rates) to the vendor's skilled workforce; economies of scale for services possibly shared with other organizations; and an increased ability to free up and apply its own scarce resources (capital) in other key business areas.

The rapid change occurring in the information technology and systems industries have also caused author's to suggest that there may be another factor that makes outsourcing particularly attractive. The broad argument is that the rate of change in the information systems industry is so rapid that companies are unable to rapidly depreciate their systems; unable to manage and quickly retrain information systems personnel; and unable to convince many personnel to fully learn and accept new development techniques and procedures. This rapid rate of change is also used to suggest that the non-outsourcing organization may have a greater risk of erroneously introducing software products and that are not fully developed when compared to the success of a vending organization. The implication is the outsourcing may reduce or mitigate the possible negative consequences for the outsourcing organization. The vendor organization is assumed to be capable of providing more highly trained personnel and services that spread the cost of training over many other organizations served , reusing development tools and techniques, and providing key services or a fixed cost basis that may be less that the costs of acquiring the services by an individual company.

Contacting Method and Payments

The traditional methods used to provide the services have varied, with many outsourcing arrangements involving the partial or compete transfer of computer resources (Caldwell, 1992) and personnel to the outsourcing vendor under a contractual arrangement. Contracting payments have typically been made on fixed schedules; treated as a capital buyout of the resources of the outsourcing firms by the providing firms; and treated as payments (fixed and variable) for service used or projected to be used. Many contractual relationships, services, clauses, and payment options appear to not be fully described in the literature for proprietary and competitive reasons.

Candidate Services and Systems

There are a number of theories and arguments which attempt to define and/or recommend the information systems, services, and technologies most suitable for outsourcing. The management wisdom suggests that some companies may turn over their more stable personnel, accounting, and purchasing systems to outsourcing firms. (Zwass, 1998) Other theories suggest that candidate outsourcing systems exist: where non-critical systems and those systems that don't require uninterrupted service; where systems present information management capability is limited or ineffective; and where outsourcing doesn't strip the organization of technical know how for future innovation in the IT area. (Laudon and Laudon, 1996)

A related theory suggests that information systems are increasingly becoming a significant component of the organization's capital budget. Organizations, which search for a method of controlling this expenditure, may improve control through outsourcing. (Caldwell, 1992) Hence, highly expensive systems requiring significant capital outlays may become viable outsourcing candidates.

These arguments for outsourcing candidates appear to be more ad hoc than scientific and in some cases possibly even contradictory. In addition, these examples appear to indicate that methods of defining outsourcing suitability criteria are not clear or uniform. Clermont (1991) has suggested that these candidate systems may be analyzed via a reward/penalty matrix that shows application which have a low reward for excellence and a low penalty for problems as good candidates for outsourcing. However, published applications of the use of this analytical selection approach were not identified.

Risks

It has been pointed out that there are various potential problems and risks associated with outsourcing. These include:
- Loss of control over the information systems technical decisions and costs of information systems (because the organization is now locked in a must pay whatever is demanded by the vendor providing the services)
- Loss of trade or secret information and competitive advantages
- Dependency upon weak vendor with poor results or services

Research

Studies of outsourcing satisfaction (Lacity and Hirscheim, 1993) have shown that not all firms are satisfied with the arrangements. Dissatisfaction arises from loss of control, dependency, failure of the vendor to have or provide talent, and unachieved savings.

Management and Guidelines

Most of the outsourcing literature expresses general guidelines for the activity. The contradictory and confusing guidelines include:
- not outsourcing proprietary or strategic systems that make an organization competitive; (McFarlan and Nolan)
- maintain capability to innovate with information systems, and maintaining qualified personnel; (Roche, 1992)
- negotiate carefully to avoid excessive outsourcing fees
- consider the need to reverse the outsourcing decision if the arrangement doesn't work (Appleton, 1996)
- manage the outsourcing arrangement

Zwass (1998: 489) has described outsourcing as a possible trend to toward corporate specialization around key competencies. He suggests that long term corporate partnerships may emerge from such arrangements if outsourcing organizations and vendors can refrain from opportunistic behavior and develop trust and mutual satisfaction.

Management of outsourcing is necessary, but the required practices and processes are not fully identified. Willcocks, and Feeny (1995) recommended that organizations constantly reevaluate outsourcing decisions, vendors in light of changing business conditions and services.

CASE STUDY

The Parties and the Relationship

The ten-year outsourcing relationship has been established among three utilities firms and an integrator of information services. It is unique because of the relationship between the utilities (to share service), and the outsourcing which actually occurs between the utilities (as customers) and the integrator. Two of the three outsourcing organizations have included all IT activities in the contractual arrangement, while the third has included its information technology and telecommunication capabilities. The vendor has a previous history of outsourcing and ongoing contractual activity in the information systems area in the utility industry. This overall outsourcing strategy is philosophically different from traditional contractual relationships because it represents an intentional partnership among the three utilities and with the integrator. The outsourcing contract covers a ten-year period (1998 - 2007).

A joint agreement among the three participating utilities, signed by the executives, formalizes the intention of these three organizations to work together to cooperatively develop a joint system and resolve differences during the development process. It also addresses the utilities need to jointly solve their Year 2000 problem and provide for sophisticated and functionally complete information systems in the future deregulated utility environment.

The outsourcing utilities have recognized that corporate cost saving possibilities exist which may be realized though economies of scale, and that a functionally improved information system may be cooperatively developed by the vendor and the outsourcing organizations which can meet the needs of other utilities.

Contract

The contact utilizes a model that provides for billing annual service charges for base resources such as existing employee salaries, benefits, office supplies, etc. The ten year agreement also includes a major development and implementation project planned as a three year effort, and names the vendor as a limited agent for administering, managing, supporting, operating, and paying under previously existing third party agreements. The systems development projects, known as joint projects, are provided by the vendor at an additional cost over the annual service charge. The vendor performs the work after preparing a project proposal with guaranteed maximum price. The required comprehensive proposals must detail any changes to the annual charges that would result from accepting the proposal.

The contract permits the nature of the relationship, services provided, and functions of the vendor to evolve and change over time. Specific tasks can be modified by the mutual agreement of the parties. Provisions in the also contract allow the annual service charge to be adjusted upward or downward; specify that staffing be approved by the utilities and stipulate that the vendor's employees may be replaced upon request. They also specify that the vendor take actions to retain experienced staff in order to maintain a high level of performance and minimum level of service. Staff not working on the current operating systems or supporting the present systems environment may be shifted to the development environment, but 'double-billing' for these resources is prohibited. Termination of the contract can occur for material or persistent breaches, convenience upon 180 days notice, and upon change of control of the vendor.

Services and Systems

Several services and systems are included in the outsourcing agreement. The first systems component calls for the continuing provision of as-is information systems and services including continued support, and maintenance of the systems environment with little or no development effort.

The second major service component calls for the vendor to develop an information systems to be used by all three utilities which includes the following core functions: (1) finance, (2) customer inquiry/billing, (3) work management, and (4) geographical information.

The outsourcing vendor is responsible for the following development related tasks on this project:
project management
design
testing
documentation
training
procuring hardware & software
interfacing with as-is systems

It is stipulated that each of these core functions will be treated as separate projects and that all three utilities will participate in the selection of the customer inquiry/billing, work management, and GIS systems, with the finance system vendor being pre-selected. Installation is varied across the three organizations (the GIS in one, work management in a second, and customer inquiry/billing in the third).

The contract identifies disaster recovery services that must be maintained at the level provided at the time of transition to the outsourcing agreement, and improved though project proposals for improving disaster response and recovery. Viruses must be addressed through the vendor's provision of reasonable measures to prevent viruses from being introduced into Customer's systems; removed by use commercially reasonable methods; identified as to the cause; and paid for by whomever introduced the virus if the cause/individual can be identified.

Finally, there is provision for change and growth in the contract. The outsourcing organizations may request that new and/or additional services be provided resulting in a corresponding reduction or elimination to one or more existing elements of the services.

Recognized Risks

Risks associated with development, management control, inclusion of staff, acquisition of staff, security, are addressed in the outsourcing contract.

Management Practices

The arrangement is managed via an management and executive committees consisting of two or more representatives from each organization that meets as often as necessary, but at least monthly, to discuss the status of the services Including:
Project Status

Comparison of the Outsourcing Models		
Model Components	TraditionalOutsourcing	Evolving Relationship
Theory of benefits	economies of scale, high costs incurred to obtain scarce resources	economies of scale, development of an effective system for the industry)with potential commercial viability)
Contacting methods	fixed schedules; capital "buyouts" of resources, payments (fixed and variable) for service used or projected to be used.	Negotiated for key services Proposal/acceptance for projects
Typical outsourced systems	stable personnel, accounting, and purchasing systems	(1) finance, (2) customer inquiry/billing, (3) work management, and (4) geographical information. (Systems are core, critical, and strategic)
Typical services outsourced	Not specifically identified	Maintenance and support services, development, telecommunication
Risks	Loss of control, locked in payments loss of trade or secret information Dependency upon weak vendor with poor results or services	Staffing, participation in decisions, lock in - identified in the contract. Mitigated via contractual requirements for performance, and negotiation for services and payments. Cancellation for breach.
Sources of satisfaction, dissatisfaction (attitudes)	Loss of control; dependency; failure to have or provide talent; and unachieved savings	Not yet assessed
Management guidelines (wisdom)	Recommend not outsourcing proprietary or strategic systems, maintain capability to innovate with information systems, maintaining qualified personnel; negotiate carefully; manage outsourcing arrangements	Outsourcing most systems and services. Personnel have been shifted to the vendor.

Baseline utilization
Performance standards & service levels
Prioritization of projects
Process improvements
Management Committee (Cont.)
Review business & information systems plans
Process, procedure, system, and technology improvements and changes

Disputes are resolved via a planning team formed with representatives from all the organizations. This team provides leadership and direction for the developed systems, approved the development plan, defines and forecast resources required for the project, prioritizes and approves the budgets for the developed system, and ensures participation and inclusion of utility personnel from all the participating organizations. This team also may define and evaluate objectives, substance, pricing, and performance of the development project; provide second level issue resolution for Joint Solution matters that line managers are unable to resolve; and report tot he participating organization regarding these issues.

DISCUSSION

The comparative analysis indicates that the more traditional model of outsourcing is being modified in a number of key areas. It is beginning to change in its intent for it appears to represent something more that just an arms length transaction for providing services. Zwass' (1998) description of outsourcing as a possible trend to toward corporate specialization around key competencies appears to articulate the intent behind this agreement. This is closer to a 10-year corporate partnership than a simple contract for support or a system. However, the trust and mutual satisfaction developed in the arrangement has not been assessed. It is also clear that the level of specific in the agreement is very high, and that a number of strategic application and functions are being addressed in this agreement. The more complex questions regarding the effective management and communication processes required for outsourcing, and evolving nature of complex corporate relationships used to implement these managerial and service arrangements are not addressed in this comparison.

CONCLUSION

There is clearly a significant need for both survey and case research dealing with outsourcing. Although the practice is growing, and changing key questions remain unanswered:

Is management truly improving its management of the information systems develop and support requirements for an organization when it employs this technique?

Does outsourcing develop economies of scale, and is it cost effective given the need to monitor and manage the relationship?

Are the cautions about not outsourcing critical systems and loss of key personnel founded upon facts and research? Should these recommendations been modified because of today' dynamic systems development environments?

How can outsourcing be managed well? What communication, monitoring, and decision tools are required?

How do organization develop and maintain the necessary mutual trust to continue the outsourcing relationship over time?

It appears that understanding the changing nature of what has previously been called outsourcing will pose a challenge for future MIS managers and developers. Effectively integrating this technique into an overall management strategy for the efficient provision of information services may require an increasingly complex formal strategy defined by contractual rules and pre-planned management practices.

BIBLIOGRAPHY

Appleton, Elaine L. Divorce Your Outsourcer? Datamation. August 1996, pp. 60-62.

Caldwell, Bruce. Blue Cross in Intensive Care, Beeps EDS. Information Week. January 27, 1992.

Clermont, Paul. Outsourcing Without Guilt. Computerworld. September 9, 1991.

Lacity, Mary C., Leslie P. Willcox, and David F. Feeny. IT Outsourcing: Maximize Flexibility and Control. Harvard Business Review. May-June, 1995.

Lacity, Mary C., and Rudy Hirscheim. Information Systems Outsourcing: Myths, Metaphors and Realities. Chichester, United Kingdom: Wiley, 1993.

Laudon, Kenneth C., and Jane Price Laudon. Management Information Systems. Upper Saddle River New Jersey, Prentice Hall, 1996.

Loh, Lawrence, and N. Venkatraman. Determinants of Information Technology Outsourcing. Journal of Management Information Systems. Vol. 9, no. 1 Summer, 1992.

McFarlan, F. Warren, and Richard L. Nolan. How to Manage an It Outsourcing Alliance. Sloan Management Review, Winter 1995.

Roche, Edward M. Managing Information Technology in Multinational Corporations. New York: Macmillan. 1992.

Zwass, Vladimar. Foundations of Information Systems. Boston, Mass.: Irwin/McGraw-Hill, 1998.

The Role of IS/IT in the Organizations for the Next Decade (Toward a Conceptual Grounded Theory)

Manuel Mora-Tavarez, MSc.
Department of Information Systems, Universidad Autonoma de Aguascalientes, Ave. Universidad 940, Aguascalientes, Ags.
México 20100
Phone: (5249) 14-72-06, Fax: (5249) 14-72-06, Email: mmora@correo.uaa.mx
Francisco Cervantes-Pérez, PhD.
Coordinator of Graduated Program in IS/IT, Instituto Tecnológico Autónomo de México, Ave. Camino a Sta. Teresa 930, México,
D.F. 11700
Phone: (525) 628-4066, Fax: (525) 616-2211, email: cervante@lamport.rhon.itam.mx

ABSTRACT

Practitioners and academics from Management field coincide on the industrial-based society from the 40's up to the 60's has shifted toward a new Information and Knowledge Society [LAW92, SIM97, DRU88, NOL91, QUI92, NON91]. Information & Knowledge are also considered key resources as much as: time, personal and money. It has also identified a new business world which is more turbolent, complex, hostil and competitive [HUB86, ROW96]. To deal with that, several organizational designs paradigms [SIM97, HUB86, HAM90, QUI92, NON91,VAN90, DAV98] have emerged in the last 15 years and all of them have a common propierty: are based on the use of IS/IT. With this premise, the role of IS/IT should be considered a critical issue. This paper addresses the problem of formulate the Role of IS/IT. We review motivations and relevance; then a first-trial Grounded Theory based research method [GLA69, STR90, ORL93, MYE97] is used with secondary sources of data –academic and commercial literature- to propose a conceptual theory about the the Role of IS/IT. In spite the theory proposed has an exploratory purpose, some insigths of explanatory and predictive use are given to show the potential utility of this theory. The theory proposed also guide to formalize the knowledge about how should be the the Role of IS/IT in the research stream of Strategic Management of IS/IT. Conclusions are discussed and finally a set of directions are recommended for further research.

I. INTRODUCTION

Twenty Century is already to finish. The humanity has generated more Information and Knowledge in the last one hundred years than the generated in all its full history [LAW92]. An awarded Nobel's Prize, Herbert A. Simon [SIM97] points out that scarcity of Information is not longer the problem but the time to the decision-makers select and deploy it to make better decisions. Practitioners and academics from Management field coincide on the industrial-based society from the 40's up to the 60's has shifted toward a new Information and Knowledge Society [LAW92, DRU88, NOL91, QUI92, NON91]. Peter Druker [DRU88], was one of the pioneers to alert to top executives about the incoming to age of an Information Society : "...the typical business will be knowledge-based ... and IT demands this shift". Moreover, several researchers and strategists – Quinn [QUI92], Nonaka [NON91], Leonard [LEO95], Sveiby [SEI95], and Davenport [DAV98] among others, have made an assestment about the creation of a Knowledge-Based Society. Some of the findings that reveales this shift of an industrial-based to a I&K based business society are the following: (a) about a 70% of the GNP in US is supplied by the service industries based on the I&K resources and nowdays some classic organizations considered like manufacturers define themselves like I&K intensive industries – for instance XEROX comp, anay does not sell photocopiers machines but offers services to the document management problem [QUI92]-; (b) international surveys [CWD97, GOV97, CWD98, INS98] show that the IS/IT markets in the US, Europe and Asia are growing in a very fast way as much as the investments in this field –since 1992 more than 90,000 new companies and 380,000 jobs related with IS/IT have been created in US, Canada, U.K., France, The Netherlands, Japan, Australia and Italy -; and (c) the " Productivy Paradox" established by the Nobel laureated economist Robert Solow and the Strassman's arguments [STR97] against the IS/IT contributions has been misunderstood at least in what is concerning with IS/IT according to new evidences [BRY93, LUL97, BRY98, IWK97, IWK98]. These findings lead to inquiry about the problem to set forht a theory about the Role of IS/IT in the current business organizations in the new I&K based economy.

II. MOTIVATIONS AND RELEVANCE.

This research has been motivated by the following reasons: (a) the necessity to help practitioners and academics to assest the role of a key player – i.e. the IS/IT function- in business organizations in the new business environment; (b) the complexity for practitioners and academics to understand from a general perspective the fast technological evolution and availability of new IS/IT; and (c) the fact that there is not even proposed a similar conceptual theory about the role of IS/IT in the organizations except by general frameworks or specific tools to classify particular issues of the IS/IT function. The relevance of this study relies on the great interest manifested by top executives in "squezze" the IS/IT to gain organizational benefits and obtain the best ROI over the greats investments made in IS/IT [CWD93, CWD98].

III. PRIOR MEANINGFUL RESEARCH.

Several frameworks or proposals have been formulated to understand the role of IS/IT in the organizations [GIB84, MCF83, MCF84, GIB85, WIS85, HUB90, NOL91, LUL96, MCN98]. Gibson and Nolan [GIB84] identified the evolution of a EDP Center in four stages – initiation, expansion, formalization and maturity-; the majority of the organizations were located in the expansion phase. McFarlan et al [MCF83] proposed a "Strategic Grid" where they classify the role of IS/IT in four categories - support, factory, turnaround and strategic- according to the strategic impact of the current and in-progress applications; the majority of the organizations are considered in factory or turnaround categories. McFarlan [MCF84] mapped the Porter's Five Forces Model [POR80] to inquiry five key questions about the use of IS/IT. This approach suggested a strategic role of IS/IT. Gibson & Hammer [GIB85], proposed a "Benefit/Beneficiary Matrix" to classify the impact of the IS/IT by type of beneficiary –individuals, functional unit or whole organization- and by type of benefit received –efficiency, effectiveness or transformation-. Adapted from this Wiseman's framework [WIS88] can be identified three roles of IS/IT: automation of operational activities; cross-functional integration of applications in a flexible architecture; and finally get the alignment of the IS strategy with the business strategy. George P. Huber [HUB90] proposed a theory of effects of advanced IT on organizational design, intelligence and decision making . His theory suggests that the availaility of advanced IT leads to the use of them, and this use leads to increase the accesibility of information which can change the organizational design, and the two lasts factors lead to improvements in the effectiveness of intelligence and decision making. Nolan [NOL91] proposed the shift of the role of IS/IT from a tactical support to a key enabler of strategic competitiveness. His model considers the dimensions of personal, organization and management. IBM Consulting Group, leaded by J. Lullman [LUL96] developed a "Strategic Alignment Model" which underlies the purpose of IS/IT to support the business strategy and the organizational infrastructure activities. Finally, McNurlin & Sprague [MCN98] establish that the real purpose of the IS/IT must be: " ... to improve the performance of people in organizations through the use of IT". Hence, the frameworks or models proposed are served to make-sense of the great problem of the Role formulation of IS/IT and the key finding of previous studies is the fact of some relevants questions are missing of answering, so the motivation of this exploratory study.

IV. RESEARCH METHOD

The research method used in this study comes from the field of Qualitative Research [MYE97, GLA67, ORL93, STR90] – the Grounded Theory Method -. Qualititive Research involves the use of qualitative data sources such interviews, documents and participant observations [MYE97]. The aim of Qualitative Research is the fact of the subject of study – behavior of human beings- has a differente attribute of subject of study from the natural world: the ability to talk and generate texts related to the phenomen of study. Case Study Research; Action Research; Ethnographic Research and Grounded Theory are four classic research methods used in Qualitative Research. Grounded Theory seeks develop theories from a interactive and systematic data gathering and analysing process. Grounded Theory generates concepts, categories and propositions [STR90].

This study uses this novel approach in IS research [ORL93] in order to derive a theory. Categories, concepts and propositions are identified in the collection and analysis of documents - in this case academics and commercial papers -. According to Glazer & Corbin: " ... the literature can be used as secondary sources of data." The study unit of data was a paper – i.e. any paper related with the problem of formulate the Role of IS/IT in business organizations-. It was used a theorical sample – not a statistical sample- as stated by Grounded Theory method. The cases were taken from prestigious journals and outlets like: HBR, MISQ, Management Science, Communications of the ACM, CIO Magazine, ComputerWorld, Information-Week, Financial Executive and several international reports generated by goverment and consulting agencies.

CATEGORY	CONCEPT	DATA
Table 1. Categories, Concepts and Data.		
1.- Impacts of the use of IS/IT.	C.1 Improvement of organizational performance.	D.1 "the use of IS/IT has improved the performance of the people in organizations; impacted on the effectiveness and efficiency of whole organizations; generated competitive advantages; demanded in order to compete; and changed the business rules of a whole industry".
	C.2 Improvement of decision making process.	D.2 "the use of IS/IT has improved the intelligence and decision making process; better decisions are taken from top executives who rely on information rather than on authority ; and decision makers needs special categories of information to make good decisions"
	C.3 Availability of Quality I&K Resources.	D.3 "I&K resources are nowdays as relevant as money, time and personal; well deployed are drivers to get competive advantages; and can be considered the foundations of high quality decisions."
2.- IS/IT performance.	C.4 Rigth User's Perception of the IS/IT performance.	D.4 "the users more motivated to use IS/IT are who have received tangibles benefits; are interested in introduce advanced IS/IT and have discovered that competitors are using IS/IT with a good level of peformance".
	C.5 CIO's Leadership of the IS/IT function.	D.5 "the excellente CIO is who has the vision of be lead the IS/IT to new business opportunities; understands the business problems as much as the technolological advances lead to a better performance of the IS/IT function and knows that could be the CEO of the same organization".
3.- Key foundations to the IS/IT performance.	C.6 Organizational Structure of the IS/IT function.	D.6 "a flexible organizational structure and quality-based with high specializated people offers better services of IS/IT to the organization".
	C.7 Relationship between CIO and CEO.	D.7 "a CIO has a strong relationship with other top executives when is invited to the tepee to discuss important problem of the organizations; has access to the strategic planning meetings and is respected by their business contributions rather than by his/hers technical knowledges".
	C.8 Organizational Structure Design.	D.8 "organizations based in decision-making paradigm are more suitable to deploy IS/IT and some organizations are started to track and monitor the impact of the decisions of top executives to evaluate the impact of the use of I&K resources – i.e. GM –"
	C.9 Fast development of IT.	D.9 "the integration of IS/IT with telecommunications has open a sea of business opportunities like e-commerce and the fast progress on IS/IT has disminished the costs of equipments and hardware so every competitor can reach advanced technology"

The research question of this study was formulated as: "What should be the Role of the IS/IT Function in modern business organizations in the new Information & Knowledge based economy ?

V. GROUNDED THEORY FORMULATED

A theory is a set of related propositions that specifies relationships among variables (constructs) to describe, explain, predict and or evaluate the behavior of some of them variables [BLA69, DUB69]. The data gathering and analysis tasks produced the categories and concepts –constructs- depicted in table 1.

The propositions derived of this conceptual theory – not hypothesis since the formers only involve conceptual relationships meanwhile the others considered measured relationships [WHE89]- are depicted in the figure 1.

VI. DISCUSSION

The following relationships can be derived of this grounded theory:

R1. The "Relationship of the CIO with the CEO" (C7), the "Organizational Paradigm" (C8), the "Fast Development IS/IT" (C9) and the "Organizational Structure of the IS/IT Function" (C6) lead to the "CIO's Leadership of the IS/IT Function" (C5). R2. The "CIO's Leadership of the IS/IT Function" (C5) leads to the "Rigth User's Perception of the IS/IT Performance " (C4). R3. The "Rigth User's Perception of the IS/IT Performance " (C4) lead to the "Availibility of High Quality I&K Resources" (C3).

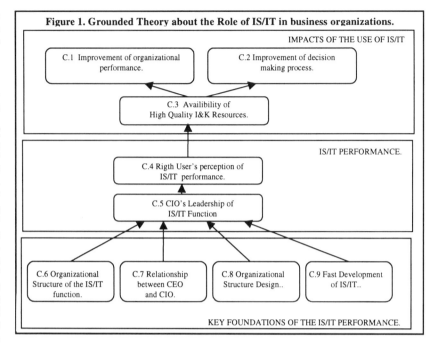

Figure 1. Grounded Theory about the Role of IS/IT in business organizations.

IMPACTS OF THE USE OF IS/IT

C.1 Improvement of organizational performance.

C.2 Improvement of decision making process.

C.3 Availibility of High Quality I&K Resources.

IS/IT PERFORMANCE.

C.4 Rigth User's perception of IS/IT performance.

C.5 CIO's Leadership of IS/IT Function

C.6 Organizational Structure of the IS/IT function.

C.7 Relationship between CEO and CIO.

C.8 Organizational Structure Design..

C.9 Fast Development of IS/IT..

KEY FOUNDATIONS OF THE IS/IT PERFORMANCE.

R4. The "Availability of High Quality I&K Resources" (C3) lead to "Improvements in Organizational Performance" (C1) and the "Improvements in the Decision Making Process" (C2). The descriptive utility of this theory can be considered through the following empirical evidences:

- R1 accounts for a "CIO's Leadership" exists in the organization where the constructs C6, C7, C8 and C6 are controlled. The evidence of the constructs C9,C8,C7 y C6 is given with the facts about the claim of the CIO have new non-technical skills and establish strong relationships with the others members of the business top team [AND97, HBR95]; the finding of the organizational structure design has been affected by the availability of IS/IT [HUB90]; the evidence of the fast evolution of IS/IT resources and the growing investment reported in this issues [CWD97, GOV97, CWD98, INS98] and the evidences about the impact of the internal organizational structure of the IS/IT area in its performance [CWD95, RUB95, IWK98b].
- R2 accounts for the "Right User's Perception of the IS/IT Performance" is satisfactory only when a CIO's Leadership really exists in the organizations [CWD93, CWD95, HBR95].
- R3 accounts for the "User's Perception of the IS/IT Performance" encourage to the access and availibity of high quality I&K Resources [FEI89, MUR98, TUR95].
- R4 accounts for the fact of in the new I&K based economy the decision making process will play a central role and the organizational performance will be affected seriously by the availibility of these kind of resources as much as money, time and personal resources [SIM97, HUB86, HUB90, QUI92, NON91, DRU88, DAV98].

Hence, a conceptual grounded theory of the Role of IS/IT in business organizations has been derived according to the research procedures established in Grounded Theory method. Moreover, we consider that this theory has some predictive and explanatory power. For instance, what could be the effect of overlook the introduction of advanced IT like Neural Networks or KBS ? Well, the theory predicts that this fact will affect to the availibility of high quality I&K resources for the decision makers due to the users will not perceive a good performance of the IS/IT function, which in turn is caused by a lack of CIO's leadership by not be aware of theses new IT's. This finding is very common in financial institutions in Mexico country in spite of the availability of these IT's from the 80's. In the explanatory dimension, for instance we could be interested in know why do not improve the decision making process if we have the best IT, our CIO has excellent relationships with the top executive team and the IS/IT function is well structured ? The explanation derived of this theory is that meanwhile the organizational structure design be not modified it will affect the quality of the decision making process.

VII. CONCLUSIONS AND RECOMMENDATIONS.

In this study we have addressed the problem to formulate a theory of the Role of IS/IT in business organizations. It was motivated basically by the great necessity to understand how the great investments on IS/IT can be deployed successfully in organizations in the new economic world which is turbolent, hostil and ill-structured. We review previous efforts which had missing links to answer important questions. Through a novel research method –Grounded Theory- from the Qualitative Research approach, we formulated a conceptual descriptive theory about the Role of IS/IT. Three categories, nine concepts and four propositions were derived to establish the theory. A set of evidences about the descriptive utility for practitioners and academics was discussed and two examples of predictive and explanatory utility were given. The authors acknowledge that this theory is only the first step to try to understand a current and relevant complex problem and suggest to further research: apply triangulation method to confirm or still correct the theory – i.e. path analysis – and gather data from other sources like interviews, observation and internal documents.

IX. BIBLIOGRAPHY

[AND97] Andrews, Phil and Tood Carlson, "The CIO is the CEO of the Future", CIO Conference, Naples, Florida, October 14, 1997.

[BAR95] Barabba, Vince, "Meeting the Minds", Harvard Business School Press, 1995.

[BLA69] Blalock, H. M. Jr., "Theory Construction: from verbal to mathematical formu-lations", Prentice-Hall, 1969.

[BYR93] Brynjolffson, E., "The Productivity Paradox of Information Tecnology", Communications of the ACM, Dec 1993.

[BRY98] Brynjolffson, E. and L. M. Hitt, "Beyond the Productivity Paradox", Communi-cations of the ACM, Aug 1998.

[CAS89] Cash, James I. Jr. And McFarlan, "Competing Through Information Technology", Harvard Business Press, Video , 1989.

[CWD93] Computerworld Magazine, "Squeeze Play", Management Secction, April 19th., 1993.

[CWD95] ComputerWorld Magazine, "Knowledge, Information, Learning and the IS Manager", May 1995.

[CWD97] ComputerWorld Magazine, Computer Industry News Story, 11/06/97.

[CWD98] ComputerWorld Magazine, "Global IT economy nears $2 trillion ", 10/09/98.

[DAV98] Davenport, David and L. Prusak, "Working Knowledege: How Organizations Manage What They Know", Harvard Business School Press, 1998.

[DRU88] Druker, Peter "The Comming of the New Organization", HBR Jan-Feb 1988.

[DRU95] Drucker, Peter, "The Information executives truly need", Journal of Information Week, May 1, 1995.

[DUB69] Dubin, R., "Theory Building", The Free Press, N.Y., 1969.

[FEI89] Feigenbaum, E., P. McCorduck and H.P. Nii, " The Rise of the Expert Company", Time Books 1989.

[GIB74] Gibson, C. & R. Nolan, "Managing the Four Stages of EDP Growth", Harvard Business Review, Jan-Feb 1974.

[GLA67] Glazer, B. & A. Strauss, "The Discovery of Grounded Theory: strategies for Qualitative Research", Aldine, Chicago, 1967.

[GOV97] US Goverment Report, "Evaluating Information Technology Investments", http:// www.whitehouse.gov/WH/EOP/OMB/infotech/infotech.html#A1.

[GRO98] Grover, Varun, James Teng and Kirk Fiedler, "IS Invesments Priorities in Contemporary Organizations", Commu-nication of the ACM, February 1998.

[HBR95] Harvard Business Review, Special Report on "The End of Delegation ? Information Technology and the CEO", Sep-Oct 1995.

[HAM90] Hammer, M., "Reengineering Work: Don´t Automate, Oliterate", Harvard Business Review, Jul-Aug 1990.

[HUB86] Huber, George P., "The Decision-Making Paradigm of Organizational Design", Management Science, May 1986.

[HUB90] Huber, George P., "A Theory of the Effects of Advanced Information Technology on Organizational Design, Intelligence and Decision-Making", Academy of Management Review, 1990, Vol 15, No. 1.

[INS98] InfoStrategy Company, "The Global Internet 100 Survey 1998", www.info-strategy.com/GI1000.

[IWK97] InformationWeek., "Where's Return On Investment?", November 17, 1997.

[IWK98a] Information-Week, "The Hidden Assump-tion", SecretCIO secction, February 16th., 1998.

[IWK98b] Information-Week, "Where to Find Innovators", September 30th. 1998.

[LAW96] Law, K "The Computists' Communique", electronic news, June 27, 1996.

[LEO98] Leonard, D. & Sussan Strauss, "Putting your Company's Whole Brain to Work", Harvard Business Review on KM, 1998.

[LUL96] Lullman, J., "Competing in the Information Age: Strategic Alignment in Practice", Oxford Press 1996.

[LUL97] Lullman, J. ,"Return On IT: Consider All Project Factors ", InformationWeek, August 11th., 1997.

[MCF83] McFarlan, W., J. Cash & L. Applegate, "Corporative Information Systems Management", Richard D. Irwin, 1983.

[MCF84] McFarlan, W., "Information Technology Changes the Way you Compete ", Harvard Business Review, May-Jun 1984.

[MCN98] McNurlin, B. & R. Sprague Jr., "Information Systems Management in Practice", 4th. Ed. Prentice-Hall, 1998.

[MUR98] Murray, Peter and Andrew Meyers, "The Facts about Knowledge", Special Report of InfoStrategy Co., http://www.info-strategy. com/knowsur1.

[MYE97] Myers, M., "Qualitative Research in Information Systems", on-line report, http: // www.auckland.ac.nz/msis/isworld / index.html.

[NOL91] Nolan, Richard L., "The Strategic Potential of Information Technology", Financial Executive, Jul-Aug 1991.

[NON91] Nonaka, I., "The Knowledge-Creating Company", Harvard Business Review, Nov-Dec 1991.

[ORL93] Orlikowski, W., "CASE Tools as Organizational Change: Investigating Incremental and Radical Changes in Systems De-velopment", MIS Quaterly, Vol. 17, No. 3, September 1993.

[QUI92] Quinn, James B., "Intelligent Enterprise", Free Press 1992.

[ROW96] Rowe, J., S. Davis and S. Vij, "Intelligent Information Systems: meeting the challenge of the Knowledge Era",Qoururm Books, 1996.

[RUB95] Rubin, Howard A., "Building an IT management flight deck", Computerworld Magazine, October 16th., 1995.

[STR90] Strauss, A. & J. Corbin, "Basics of Qualitative Research: Grounded Theory Procedures and Technoiques", Sage, London, 1990.

[SVE95] Sveiby, K. E., "The New Organizational Wealth: a Managing & Measuring Knowledge-Based Assests", Harvard Business Review, 1995.

[SIM97] Simon, Herbert A., "Administrative Behavior", 4th. Edition, Free Press 1997.

[SIF97] Sifonis, Jhon and B. Goldberg, "Strategic Management – Changing Role of the CIO –", InformationWeek, June 24, 1997.

[STR97] Strassmann, Paul A., "Will big spending on computers guarantee profitability", Datamation, Feb 1997.

[TUR95] Turban, E., "Management Support Systems", Prentice-Hall, 1995.

[VAN90] Van der Spek & A. Spijkervert, "Knowledge Management: dealing intelligently with knowledege", Kenniscentrum CIBIT, The Netherlands, 1990.

[WHE89] Whetten, D.A., "What constitutes a theoretical contribution", Academy of Management Review, no. 14, 1989.

[WIS88] Wiseman, Charles, "Strategic Information Systems", Homewood Irwin 1988.

An Expert System Of Peter Drucker's Knowledge

Robert Mullen and Madan Nangia

Southern Connecticut State University, 501 Crescent Street; New Haven, CT 06515

203-392-5856 phone; 203-392-5863 fax; MULLEN@SCSUD.CTSTATEU.EDU e-mail

BACKGROUND

Expert Systems have exploded in last decade of the 20th century to provide advice and assistance in various areas of managerial support. One area where these systems are applied is to capture the knowledge of a recognized expert so that managers can access that knowledge easily. This paper describes the development of such an expert system applied to the knowledge of Peter Drucker as an example of how such systems could be built. It has allowed two faculty members to integrate their respective expertise into a common product.

Since the early 1980s expert systems have been developed for the purpose of passing expertise from those with the knowledge to those who need the knowledge in a convenient and easily accessed manner. The idea is to tap the mind of the expert without the expert having to be present. In the 1990s with the focus on downsizing and need to cut costs in all area, managers of large corporations have turned to expert systems to provide advise when the cost of hiring an expert (consultant) or access to a previous expert employee who has been downsized is gone.

This paper addresses the area of advising corporation executives with knowledge from an expert in management – Peter Drucker. Drucker, at 89 , has not yet retired but may soon decide to do so. He is used as an example of the application of expert system technology to preserve knowledge from an expert after he retires or leaves a firm. It might be appropriate information for the Web. He is credited with 29 books with over five million copies sold. A recent biography, "The World According to Peter Drucker", by Jack Beatty covers the variety of topics which interest him.

NATURE OF THE STUDY/ISSUES ADDRESSED

This study involves the collaboration of two faculty members within the same department but representing different backgrounds. One from the Management Information Systems area with knowledge of the development of expert systems and the other from the field of Management who has personal association with Peter Drucker as his thesis advisor and mentor. This study provides a case example of how expert systems are developed.

RESULTS OF THE STUDY

The first step in the study is to bring together the specific knowledge for the project for the two participants. Figure 1 describes the components of an expert systems such that the Law professor could understand what was going to be involved. Figure 2 outlines the specifics areas of knowledge that Peter Drucker has published or addressed in some form so that an MIS professor could have some idea of the nature of the task at hand.

The second step is to organize the knowledge summarized in Figure 2 into statements of the form "if ... then ...." in order to build the knowledge base. The third step will be to design the appropriate dialog with an executive user of the system to question the executives action in such a way as to determine the advice that Peter Drucker would give as a recommended change most appropriate for the situation.

Figure 1. Components of an Expert Systems

Dialog Screen
Knowledge Base
Inference Engine
Presentation

Figure 2. Sample Outline of Knowledge Categories of Peter Drucker's Work

LEADERSHIP

Premises from Dr. Drucker's various works on leadership include the following examples from The Effective Executive; Harper & Row Publishing; New York, NY, 1966:
- To recognize a leader, ask what he or she has done well to set an example for the firm.
- To test your respect for a leader, ask if you had a son or daughter, would you be willing to have him or her work under that person.

MANAGEMENT

Premises from Dr. Drucker's various works on management include the following example from The Practice of Management; Harper ; New York, NY, 1954:
- Managers set objectives (establish vision for their firm), organize, motivate, communicate, measure, and develop people.

BUSINESS STARTEGY

Premises from Dr. Drucker's various works on business strategy include the following example from The Frontiers of Management; Harper & Row Publishing; New York, NY, 1986:
- People beyond their early sixties should ease out of managerial responsibilities.

FUTURE CHANGES

Premises from Dr. Drucker's various works on predicting the future include the following examples from Managing for the Future; Dutton Publishing; New York, NY, 1992:
- Buying customers by under-pricing boomerangs.
- One can use Market Research only on what is already on the market.
- The customer, not the maker, defines a market.

The last step is to describe the process of transforming the knowledge collected from the expert system into a meaningful presentation to the executive seeking advise. Figure 5 represents the initial design of that presentation.

CONCLUSIONS

This paper describes the development of an expert system applied to capture the knowledge of a well-known expert in the field of management. It has allowed two faculty members to integrate their respective fields into a common product.

REFERENCES WILL BE PROVIDED UPON REQUEST TO THE AUTHORS.

Figure 3. Developing the Expert System Knowledge Base

If ....Then ....
- If an organization lacks direction and vision, then you as a leader must provide it.
- If you have no vision for the organization, then you must develop one.
- If you have not communicated your vision to the organization, you must do so.

Figure 4. Dialog of the Expert System

- Do you regularly read management periodicals and books? Y__ N__
- Have you read any books or articles by Peter Drucker? Y__ N__
- If answered yes to above, how many books by Peter Drucker have you read? _____
- Do you think about the future of your firm? Y__ N__
- Have you communicated your vision of the future of the firm to the organization? Y__ N__
- Do you believe the organization understands your vision? Y__ N__

Figure 5. The Presentation from the Expert System

Based upon the description you provided of problems in your firm, Peter Drucker would have provided the following advice:
You must assume your expected role as leader.
You must communicate your vision to the organization.
You must determine that the organization understands your vision.

Adapting Information Systems to Global Operation

Robert Mullen and Shyam Lodha
Southern Connecticut State University, 501 Crescent Street; New Haven, CT 06515
203-392-5856 phone; 203-392-5863 fax; MULLEN@SCSUD.CTSTATEU.EDU e-mail

BACKGROUND

The decade of the 1990s has brought many significant changes to Information Technology (IT). More and more businesses are becoming involved in global operation and must adapt their information systems for this new global environment. This paper focuses on identifying the nature of the adaptation needed for information systems to become global in nature. Examples of firms who have successfully achieved the necessary change to become global will be cited. The results of this identification are reported in this paper.

INTRODUCTION

The decade of the is characterized as the decade of "networking". Business had to adapt their legacy systems of the 70s and 80s to accessibility via networks. The explosive business use of the Internet over the past few years has brought further change to IT. In addition to these technological adaptations, more and more businesses are becoming involved in global operation and must adapt their information systems for this new global environment involving countries outside the United States. This paper focuses on identifying the nature of the adaptation needed for information systems to be global in nature. Examples of firms who have successfully achieved the necessary changes will be cited.

NATURE OF THE STUDY/ISSUES ADDRESSED

This study involves searching the literature to identify information systems used by domestic business firms, analyzing their informational content, and determining what, if any, changes must be done to adapt these systems to global operation. A second search of large corporations which do operate globally will be done to compare the adaptations they have made to the required list developed from part one of the study. The result of this identification is reported in this paper.

RESULTS OF THE STUDY

The first step involved searching the literature to identify information systems which need to be reviewed for the impact of adapting these systems to operate in a global environment. A list for this step is shown in Figure 1.

Next, these information systems were analyzed for their informational content. A partial list of the informational content of these systems is shown as Figure 2.

Next, a list of adaptations or changes to the information content which the authors believe may be required to operate globally is shown as Figure 3.

The second step of the study is to search the appropriate literature to identify some firms who have successfully adapted their information systems for global operation as case examples to substantiate the first step of the study. Firms found from this search are identified in Figure 4.

CONCLUSION

This paper identified the information elements in information systems which may need adaptations to provide global use of these systems for firms. Although physical material can be easily moved from country to country, information systems for human use require adaptations. This paper may offer an explanation as to the rise of enterprise resource planning software and integrated software packages which have been adapted to global use such as SAP. Examples of firms who have successfully achieved the necessary change to become global were cited.

FIGURE 1. Information Systems Impacted by Globalization

Inventory Control Systems	Scheduling Systems	Accounting Systems
Just-In-Time Systems	Purchasing Systems	Marketing Systems
Capacity Planning Systems	MRP Systems	Human Resource
CAD Systems	Logistics Systems	Finance Systems

FIGURE 2. List of Information Content of the Information Systems in Figure 1

Part Identification	Costs
Vendor Identification	Quantities
Customer Identification	Dates
Location	Time
Units of Measure	Skills
Size	Dependents

FIGURE 3. Adaptations to Information Needed for Global Operation

- Part, vendor, customer identification must be standardized across the entire organization
- Units of Measure and size measurements must reflect local system in use (metric vs. U.S.)
- Costs must be converted to local currency values
- Dates must be in local format (American mm/dd/yy to Europeon dd/mm/yy)
- Time may have to reflect time-zone differences
- Location allows for appropriate postal zone code (US uses 9 digit ZIP, others 6-7 characters)
- Skills must be appropriate for country (English as language for countries outside US)

FIGURE 4. Example Firms with Global Operations

IBM Corporation
Xerox Corporation
Ford Motor Company with plants throughout the world

REFERENCES PROVIDED UPON REQUEST AND ARE INCLUDED IN HAND OUT

A Generalized Test Bed for Image Databases

Surya Nepal and M.V.Ramakrishna
Department of Computer Science, RMIT University, GPO Box 2476V, Melbourne VIC 3001
{nepal,rama}@cs.rmit.edu.au

ABSTRACT

With the advent of cheaper storage devices and the Internet, large databases of images have become possible. A user wants to retrieve images based on their contents from such databases. Many content based image retrieval (CBIR) systems have been developed. Most of these systems have the same/similar functionalities. They mainly differ in the features used for retrieval. A number of feature and object extraction algorithms, and similarity functions have been proposed and evaluated against different databases. Each such experiment has resulted in a new CBIR system. Withouthe standard test bed, it is difficult to say which one of these systems is better or worse than other. We are developing a generalized research test bed for CBIR systems, called CHITRA. Its aims are two fold. It is a CBIR system, which incorporates many new ideas developed including high level concept definition. The second aim is that it enables researchers to easily and readily test and evaluate new features, similarity measures, query processing techniques with out having to develop individual systems.

INTRODUCTION

The content-based image retrieval (CBIR) systems have attracted both academic and industrial interest in recent times. Commercial systems such as QBIC and Virage have been released [1]. Many prototype systems have been developed in the academic community such as VisualSEEk and NETRA. In all these CBIR systems,

- The user poses query by providing an example image, by selecting from pallets or patterns or by drawing sketches. He may also specify the features and their weights to be used in retrieval.
- The system correspondingly retrieves images based on similarity, and displays in sorted fashion. The system uses the similarity functions defined at the system level.

Many of the prototype CBIR systems have been developed to test the retrieval performance of a particular feature or similarity function on a specific collection. We observe that these CBIR systems differ in the features and image collections used for retrieval. It is well agreed that there is a great need of an image corpus that has images, queries, and measures of the relevance of images to queries generated painstakingly by human evaluators [3]. Such corpus must be flexible enough to add new features, similarity functions, and queries. This corpus must help image database community to compare their work to others and measure quantitative improvements in their image segmentation, feature extraction and similarity measurement algorithms. In the absence of such, it is impossible to compare the relative performance of different algorithms and techniques. We are developing CHITRA, a generalized content-based image retrieval system (GCBIR), in an attempt to meet this need.

The GCBIR system is based on the four layer data model shown in Figure 1[2]. The four layers are image representation layer, image feature layer, system semantic layer, and user semantic layer. The image representation layer stores the raw image data. Image and object feature information extracted from the images is stored in the image feature layer. The mapping from image representation layer to image feature layer is called feature extraction mapping. The mapping contains functions for feature and object extraction. The system semantic layer contains the similarity functions and the domain knowledge defined at the system level. In CBIR systems the user interacts with the system to pose queries and retrieve images. The

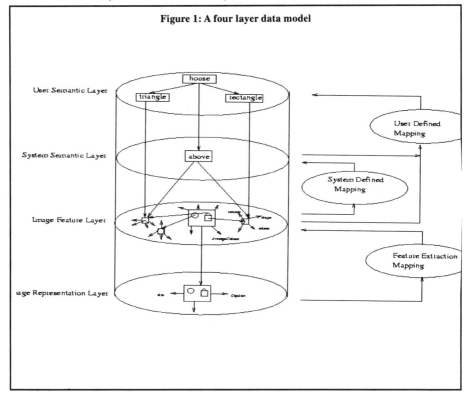

Figure 1: A four layer data model

top layer in our model is thus the user semantic layer. The user can interact with the system and define the high level concepts such as sunset and mountain based on the features and similarity functions available at the lower layers. The mapping from lower layers to user semantic layer is called user defined mapping. It contains the components related with user interaction such as relevance feedback technique.

The CHITRA is a CBIR system, and is a test bed for CBIR research. We can readily simulate many of the existing CBIR systems on top of it. The main characteristics/benefits of our system are,

- It allows users to create different databases and test the performance of algorithms on them individually or combined. This is against the current practice of having to use different collections of images used to test the performance of various algorithms (e.g., feature extraction, similarity measure, etc.) such as VisTex collection, Bordtaz collection and Corel Photo collections.
- One of the major areas of research in CBIR systems is developing new algorithms for feature extraction. Researchers now have to develop their own CBIR system to test their feature extraction algorithm on their databases. This makes hard to compare whether the proposed features are performing better or worse than other existing algorithms. Moreover, many comparisons have been made on different databases which does not really reflect the real quantitative retrieval performance of the features. CHITRA allows us to plug on new feature extraction algorithms, and compare their performances with other algorithms on different databases using different similarity functions.
- Finding algorithms/functions for similarity measurement is an another area of research. To the best of our knowledge, there has not been extensive experiments on the performance of features on different similarity functions. A pair of particular feature and similarity measure could give a better retrieval performance for a particular image collection. Our system allows us to test retrieval

performance of all pairs of features and similarity functions.
- Our system enables users to interact with the system using relevance feedback technique. If a user is satisfied with the result, then he/she can store the current session as a semantic definition. For example, the user can define a concept sunset if he is satisfied with the result obtained in the current session. Such user defined concepts can be used later to pose complex semantic queries such as sunset and mountain.
- A user can define his own query and relevant images within the database using human evaluators. This enables users to compare their algorithms using new queries (in addition to the default queries available with the system).

The specifications for features and similarity functions are being developed. Once CHITRA is ready, researchers can use it to measure the retrieval performance of their algorithms. Since CHITRA is also a CBIR system, one can use it directly for practical applications with the features and similarity functions provided with it.

We are developing CHITRA using SUN Solaris platform. The front end user interface is implemented in Java applets. It consists of popup menus for features, their weights and similarity functions. The user can compose a query using popup menus. Each user query is a set of triple: weight, feature, and similarity function. Queries can be composed by selecting features alone. In such cases, the system considers the default similarity functions and weights. The similarity functions associated with features can be changed during the interaction. Features are indexed using R-trees. We have developed a query processing strategy to process such queries using underlying R-trees. To the best of our knowledge, this is the first CBIR system that enables users to associate different similarity functions to features and change them dynamically during the course of user interaction.

In conclusion, it is well accepted and agreed in several conferences and workshops, that there is a lack of generalized test bed for CBIR systems. Our CHITRA system under development is an attempt to address this problem. The data model has been designed. Other works such as indexing structure, specifications for interfaces, graphical user interface and query language are under development.

REFERENCES

1 Myron Flickner, Harpreet Sawhney, Wayne Niblack, Jonathan Ashley, Qian Huang, Byron Dom, Monika Gorkani, Jim Hafner, Denis Lee, Dragutin Petkovic, David Steele and Peter Yanker. Query by image and video content: The QBIC system. Computer, Volume 28, Number 9, pages 23-32, September 1995.
2 Surya Nepal, M.V.Ramakrishna and J.A.Thom. Four layer schema for image data modelling. In Chris McDonald (editor), Australian Computer Science Communications, Vol 20, No 2, Proceedings of the 9th Australasian Database Conference, ADC'98, pages 189-200, 2-3 February, Perth, Australia, 1998.
3 Rohini K. Srihari, Zhongfei Zhang, R. Manmatha and S. Ravela. Multimedia indexing and retrieval. In 21st Annual International ACM SIGIR Conference on Research and Development in Information Retrieval (SIGIR98), Melbourne, Australia, August 24 - 28, 1998. Workshop.

Using Domain Knowledge to Validate the Discovered Knowledge

M. Mehdi Owrang O.
American University, Dept. of Computer Science and Information Systems, Washington, D.C 20016
owrang@american.edu; office # (202) 885-3159; fax # (202) 885-1479

ABSTRACT

Current database technology involves processing a large volume of data in order to discover new knowledge. Databases are full of patterns, but few of them are of much interest. In addition, databases are incomplete and redundant. Relational databases create new types of problems for knowledge discovery since they are normalized to avoid update anomalies, which make them unsuitable for knowledge discovery. In knowledge discovery, it is all too easy to generate a large number of patterns (or rules) in a database, and most of these patterns are actually redundant, inconsistent, useless and uninteresting to the user. But due to the large number of patterns, it is difficult for the user to manually process them to identify those patterns that are redundant, inconsistent and those that are interesting. A key issue in any discovery system is to ensure the consistency and accuracy of the discovered knowledge. We discuss the validation aspect of the knowledge discovery in databases. In particular, we propose to use domain knowledge (any data about the application database that is not explicitly stored in the database) to validate the set of discovered rules for redundancy, inconsistency, and triviality, accuracy, and completeness.

Keywords: Knowledge, Databases, Relational databases, Operational Databases, Knowledge discovery, domain knowledge, knowledge validation.

1. INTRODUCTION

Current database technology involves processing a large volume of data in databases in order to discover new knowledge. Knowledge discovery is defined as the nontrivial extraction of implicit, previously unknown, and potentially useful information from data [1,3,5-7,13,17,22,27]. Many organizations have started to develop or employ tools to discover knowledge from databases. For example, banks are analyzing data to find better rules for credit assessment. Similarly, several systems, e.g., RX [2], were designed to discover knowledge from medical databases. Recently, several tools have been developed for knowledge discovery in databases [10,28].

Databases contain a variety of patterns, but few of them are of much interest. A pattern is interesting to the degree that it is not only accurate but that it is also useful with respect to the end-user's knowledge and objectives [22,23,26]. Interestingness is driven by factors such as novelty, utility, relevance, and statistical significance [14,22,23,26].

Most knowledge discovery is being performed on operational relational database environment [1,5-7,25] that is not well suited for knowledge discovery. First, operational databases lack the summary data. Without discovery process on summary data, we may discover incorrect knowledge from detailed operational data [21]. Second, the operational relational databases are designed based on the normalization techniques in order to avoid update anomalies [4]. However, normalized tables are not good for knowledge discovery since they lose some of the hidden patterns as a result of the normalization process [1]. Also, knowledge discovery based on statistical significance could lead to inaccurate and incomplete discovery.

Much research in knowledge discovery has focused on ways of extracting interesting patterns from databases. However, it is critical to see what happens after a set of rules has been discovered from the database. Liu and Hsu [14] propose a fuzzy matching technique to perform the post-analysis of the discovered rules. In their approach, existing rules (from previous knowledge discovery) are regarded as fuzzy rules and are represented as fuzzy set theory. The newly generated rules are matched against the existing fuzzy rules to see if the rules generated represent what we know, and if not, which part of the previous knowledge is correct and which part is not; in what ways are the new rules different from our previous knowledge.

Databases include redundancy that could lead to discovering redundant knowledge. Also, databases are normally incomplete, thus discovered knowledge may be inconsistent and inaccurate. In knowledge discovery, it is all too easy to discover a large number of patterns (or rules) from a database, and most of these patterns are actually redundant, inconsistent, useless and uninteresting to the user. However, due to the large number of patterns, it is difficult for the user to manually process them to identify those patterns that are redundant, inconsistent and those that are interesting. Typically, we have some pre-conceived notion or knowledge about the domain (i.e., height and diagnosis are not casually related in a liver disease data set [1,6,20]). Therefore, we would like to know whether the generated rules are correct and complete, non-redundant and consistent, and non-trivial and interesting.

In this paper, we discuss the validation aspect of the knowledge discovery process. We propose to use domain knowledge (any data about the application database that is not explicitly stored in the database) to validate the set of discovered rules from the relational databases for redundancy, consistency, triviality, accuracy, and completeness. We also discuss how to avoid discovering redundant, contradictory and trivial knowledge.

2. PROBLEM WITH THE DISCOVERED KNOWLEDGE

Knowledge discovery systems rely on databases to supply the raw data for input and this raises problems in that databases tend to be dynamic, inconsistent (i.e., limited information, irrelevant attributes) , incomplete(i.e., missing values, attributes), noisy, and large[1,3,5,6]. Database inconsistency could lead to discovering redundant, contradictory, uninteresting, inaccurate, and incomplete knowledge. In the following, we show that the discovered knowledge could include these problems.

Redundant Knowledge:

Information often recurs in multiple places within a database. A common form of redundancy is a functional dependency in which a field is defined as a function of other fields, for example, profit = sales - expenses. The problem with redundant information is that it can be mistakenly discovered as knowledge even though it is usually uninteresting to the end-user. The discovered knowledge may contain redundancy when two pieces of knowledge are exactly the same (rules having the same premises and conclusions) or semantically equivalent [11,12,15,16,19]. In addition, the discovered knowledge may indeed be a previously known fact (i.e., a domain knowledge) rather than a new discovery. We have done several experiments on the CAR relation in Figure 1, using the IDIS discovery tool. We were interested to discover the relationship between the high way mileage and the rest of the attributes. In the CAR relation, we have the attribute Engine-Size which is the same as Bore*Stroke*Cylinders. The discovery tool discovered rules relating the high way mileage to Engine-Size and high way mileage to Bore,Stroke, and Cylinders. Thus, the rules relating high way mileage to Bore, Stroke, and Cylinders appear to be redundant.

Contradictory Knowledge:

There is a possibility of discovering knowledge that contradicts the domain expert's knowledge [1,3,5,19]. Consider the following rules discovered from the CAR relation in Figure 1:

Figure 1. Data Relation CAR.

CAR (Symboling, Losses, Make, Fuel-Type, Aspiration, Doors, Body, Drive, Engine-Loc, Wheel-Base, Length, Width, Height, Weight, Engine-Type, Cylinders, Engine-Size, Fuel-Sys, Bore, Stroke, Compress, Horse-Power, Peak-RPM, City-MPG, High-MPG, Price)

Rull 29:	CF=100.00%	"16" <= "High_MPG" <= "54"	IF "61" <= "Engine_Size" <= "326"
Rule 30:	CF=99.00%	"16" <= "High_MPG" <= "50"	IF "61" <= "Engine_Size" <= "234"
Rule 31:	CF=96.34%	"16" <= "High_MPG" <= "43"	IF "61" <= "Engine_Size" <= "183"

The above rules indicate that the smaller the Engine_Size, the lower the High_MPG, contrary to the domain expert's knowledge. One possible reason is that the relation does not have accurate data or the High-MPG may be dependent on other factors such as the existence of a turbo charger in addition to the Engine-Size of the car. In other situations, the discovered rules may contradict each other. The implication is that either the actual data values entered in the database is wrong or some relationships are missing from the database.

Inaccurate Knowledge

In general, summary data (aggregation) is never found in the operational environment. Without discovery process on summary data, we may discover incorrect knowledge from detailed operational data. The problem is that statistical significance is usually used in determining the interestingness of the pattern [9,23,26]. Statistical significance alone is often insufficient to determine a pattern's degree of interest. A "5 percent increase in sales of product X in the Western region", for example, could be more interesting than a "50 percent increase of product X in the Eastern region". In the former case, it could be that the Western region has a larger sales volume than the Eastern region, and thus its increase translate into greater income growth.

The following example [21] shows that we could discover incorrect knowledge if we only look at the detailed data. Consider the Table A1, where the goal of discovery is to see if product color or store size has any effect on the profits. Although the data is not large, but it shows the points. Assume we are looking for patterns that tell us when profits are positive or negative. We should be careful when we process this table using discovery methods such as simple rules or decision trees. A discovery scheme based on statistical significance may discover the following rules from Table A1 (in fact, we used discovery tool IDIS on Table A1 and it generated the following rules in this section):

Rule 1: IF Product Color=Blue Then Profitable=No   CF=75%

Rule 2: IF Product Color=Blue and Store Size> 5000 Then Profitable=Yes CF=100

The results indicate that blue products in larger stores are profitable; however, they do not tell us the amounts of the profits which can go one way or another. Now, consider the Table B1, where the third row in Table A1 is changed. Rules 1 and 2 are also true in Table B1. That is, from a probability point of view, Tables A1 and B1 produce the same results. However, this is not true when we look at the summary Tables A2 and B2, which are the summary tables based on Tables A1 and B1, respectively. Table A2 tells us that Blue color product is profitable and table B2 tells us it is not. That is, in the summary tables, the probability behavior of these detailed tables begin to diverge and thus produce different results. Similarly, if we look at Tables A1 and B1, we may discover that:

If Product Color = Green Then Profitable = No CF 60 % (3 records out of 5)

But, both summary Tables A2 and B2 tell us that Green color product is profitable. One possible explanation for such differences in the result is that the summary tables do not have all the information. In fact, it is the Green color products in small stores that are profitable.

Incomplete Knowledge

Most of the knowledge discovery has been done on the operational relational databases. The traditional database design method is based on the notions of functional dependencies and lossless decomposition of relations into third normal forms. However, this decomposition of relation is not useful because it hides dependencies among attributes that might be of some interest. To provide maximum guarantee that potentially interesting statistical dependencies are preserved, knowledge discovery process could use the universal relation [1,4] (although it may not be efficient) as opposed to normalized relations. In the following example, we show that knowledge discovery on a normalized relations may not reveals all the interesting patterns. Consider the relations Sales and Region [1] in Figure 2 which are in third normal form. Figure 3 shows the universal relation which is the join of the two tables in Figure 2. From Figure 3, we can discover that there is a relationship between the Average Price of the House and the type of Products Purchased by people. Such relationship is not that obvious on the normalized relations in Figure 2. This example shows that knowledge discovery on "well designed (i.e., 3NF)" databases according to the normalization techniques could lead to incomplete knowledge discovery.

Knowledge discovery based on statistical significance could also lead to incomplete knowledge discovery. Discovery schemes based on statistical significance discover hidden patterns based on occurrences of records. However, statistical significance alone may not be sufficient as patterns with low number of record occurrences may seem uninteresting and subsequently they are not discovered. For example, a discovery system that processes Table A1 may not discover the pattern:

Table A1. Sample Sales data.

Product	Product Color	Product Price	Store	Store Size	Profit
Jacket	Blue	200	S1	1000	-200
Jacket	Blue	200	S2	5000	-100
Jacket	Blue	200	S3	9000	7000
Hat	Green	70	S1	1000	300
Hat	Green	70	S2	5000	-1000
Hat	Green	70	S3	9000	-100
Glove	Green	50	S1	1000	2000
Glove	Blue	50	S2	5000	-300
Glove	Green	50	S3	9000	-200

Table B1. Sample Sales data.

Product	Product Color	Product Price	Store	Store Size	Profit
Jacket	Blue	200	S1	1000	-200
Jacket	Blue	200	S2	5000	-100
Jacket	Blue	200	S3	9000	100
Hat	Green	70	S1	1000	300
Hat	Green	70	S2	5000	-1000
Hat	Green	70	S3	9000	-100
Glove	Green	50	S1	1000	2000
Glove	Blue	50	S2	5000	-300
Glove	Green	50	S3	9000	-200

Table A2: Summary Sales table based on Table A1.

Product Color	Profit
Blue	6400
Green	1000

Table B2: Summary Sales table based on Table B1.

Product Color	Profit
Blue	-500
Green	1000

Figure 2. Relational database in third normal form.

Sales		
Client Number	Zip Code	Product Purchased
1111	11111	Wine
2222	22222	Bread
3333	11111	Wine
4444	33333	Wine
5555	44444	Wine

Region		
Zip Code	City	Average House Price
11111	Paris	High
22222	Peking	Low
33333	New York	High
44444	Moscow	High

If Product Color=Blue and Store Size > 5000 Then Profit=Yes,

since the statistical significance (or confidence factor) of the rule is too low (i.e., 25% , 1 record out of 4). In fact, it is the Blue product in large store (Store Size = 9000) that is profitable, and therefore it could be interesting to the user.

Uninteresting Knowledge:

As we noted, databases contain a variety of patterns with few of them are of much interest. A pattern is interesting to the degree that it is useful with

Figure 3. Universal relation based on the join of the tables in Figure 2.

Sales/Region				
Client Number	Zip Code	City	Average House Price	Product Purchased
1111	11111	Paris	High	Wine
2222	22222	Peking	Low	Bread
3333	11111	Paris	High	Wine
4444	33333	New York	High	Wine
5555	44444	Moscow	High	Wine

respect to the user's knowledge and objectives [9,23,26]. In our knowledge discovery of the CAR relation (Figure 1), some of the generated rules were uninteresting and/or known facts. For example, the tool discovered that "the smaller the Weight, the better High-MPG" which is a trivial discovery since it is a known fact (or a domain knowledge). Similarly, the discovered rule "the more expensive the car, the better High-MPG" which seems to be uninteresting since there is no relationship between the price of the car and the high way mileage.

Trivial Knowledge:

To provide maximum guarantee that potentially interesting statistical dependencies are preserved, knowledge discovery process could use the universal relation [4] as opposed to normalized relations. However, we should be careful when processing a universal relation since it could mistakenly lead to discovering a known fact (i.e., a functional dependency (FD)). Note that, when we denormalize the relations (joining them) to create the universal relation, we will have redundancies due to the functional dependencies among attributes. For example, consider the universal relation Sales/Regions in Figure 3. A discovery system may discover that:

If Zip Code = 11111 Then City = Paris

If City = Paris Then AverageHousePrice = High

The above rules indicate that there are relationships between Zip Code and City; and between City and AverageHousePrice. These relationships, however, do not represent new discovery since they are in fact the given functional dependencies that are true.

3. VALIDATION OF DISCOVERED KNOWLEDGE

Discovered knowledge has to be validated to assure its accuracy, consistency, and completeness. There are some similarity between the knowledge bases discovered from the databases and the ones defined for expert systems in that both could have redundant, contradictory, subsuming, and missing rules. Subsequently, the established validation schemes from expert systems could be used to detect rule anomalies in the set of discovered rules [11,12,15,16,18,19,24]. However, discovered rules from databases have special characteristics that introduce a new set of problems that require new techniques for testing. For example, for the knowledge base for an expert system, we have the domain expert(s) (who defined the rules) to verify the correctness, completeness, and consistency of the rules. However, the set of rules discovered from a database represent new knowledge (or decision making process) that are unknown even to domain experts. Also, rules defined for the knowledge base of an expert system are generally interesting and useful since they are there to represent the decision making process for the specified domain. However, rules in the knowledge base discovered from a database may or may not be useful and interesting. These rules are generated based on their statistical significance, which may not be enough of a reason. Therefore, we need new validation scheme for rule interestingness issue in the discovered knowledge base.

There are several approaches to validating the set of discovered rules. One possible scheme for knowledge validation is to include the discovered knowledge into the database to see whether it is correct by observing its interaction with the existing data [22]. A discovered rule is inconsistent with the database if an example exists in the database that satisfies the condition part of the rule, but not the conclusion part [9,12,16,18]. A straightforward approach to identify an inconsistent rule is to transform a rule of the form A ÆC into a query (C (A. If the query returns an answer that is not empty, then the rule is inconsistent. A knowledge base is inconsistent with the database if there is an inconsistent rule in the knowledge base. A knowledge base is incomplete with respect to the database if an example exists in the database that does not satisfy the condition part of any consistent rule.

Another scheme is to set aside some of your data in a vault to isolate it from the discovery process. Once the discovery process is complete, the results can be tested against the data hold in the vault to confirm the discovery's validity. If the discovery works, its observations should hold for the vaulted data. Similarly, we may verify the set of discovered rules with similar set of data, if possible.

Statistical techniques can be used to prove or disprove the newly discovered knowledge [22]. When databases are very large, with records in the millions, complete analysis of all the data for knowledge discovery may be infeasible. Discovery algorithms must then rely on some form of sampling, whereby only a portion of the data is considered. The resulting discoveries in these cases are necessarily uncertain. The discovered rules from a sample database can be invalid on the full database. Statistical techniques, however, can measure the degree of uncertainty. They can also be used to determine how much additional sampling would be required to achieve a desired level of confidence in the results. Piatetsky [22] presents a formal statistical analysis for estimating the accuracy of sample-derived rules when applied to a full database.

Finally, we can use domain knowledge (part of the meta data)[5,6,20] to validate the discovered knowledge. The discovered knowledge is checked to see whether it contradicts the available domain knowledge. If the discovered knowledge does not contradict the domain knowledge, then we may have some confidence in its accuracy.

3.1 Validation of Discovered Knowledge Based on Domain Knowledge

Domain or background knowledge can be defined as any information that is not explicitly presented in the database [1,3,5-7,9,20,25,27]. In a medical database, for example, we could say that the knowledge "male patients cannot be pregnant" or "male patients do not get breast cancer" is considered to be a domain knowledge, with some confidence depending on how close this domain knowledge is to be a fact. In general, domain knowledge is provided by the domain expert (although it may be generated automatically from the database) and represents some knowledge about some attributes in the database. It is also possible to derive domain knowledge from a set of given domain knowledge. The derivation process can be accomplished by using augmentation and transitive dependency rules the same way used to operate on functional dependencies in a database [4].

Formally, domain knowledge can be represented as X " Y (meaning X implies Y), where X and Y are simple or conjunctive predicates over some attributes in the database. Domain knowledge can take different forms. A data dictionary is the most basic form of domain knowledge [4]. Typical information in data dictionary includes: relationships among attributes (called functional dependency, FD), types of attributes, size of attributes, name of attributes, meaning of each attributes, format, constraints, Domain, usage statistics, access control, mapping definitions, etc. [4].

Domain knowledge can be used to test the validity of the discovered knowledge. In general, domain knowledge can be used to verify whether a contradictory discovered knowledge is indeed contradictory or if a possible consistent discovered knowledge is, in fact, accurate or inaccurate. Also, domain knowledge can be used to verify whether we discovered redundant and incomplete rules.

Validating Possible Contradictory Rules

Domain knowledge can be used to verify whether contradictory discovered rules are indeed contradictory or accurate. Consider our CAR relation in Figure 1 (with the added attributes Car Model and Car Year). Suppose one is interested to find what affects the High-Way mileage. A discovery system may discover the following knowledge:

Rule 1:   If Car Model=Honda AND Cylinders=4   Then Mileage = High
Rule 2:   If Car Model=Honda AND Cylinders=4   Then Mileage = Low

At first glance, it seems like the two discovered rules are contradictory. However, we have the available domain knowledge that cars produced after 1980 have special features that cause a better performance and better mileage. Thus, domain knowledge verifies that discovered knowledge is accurate rather than contradictory.

Domain knowledge can be used to avoid generating contradictory rules. We could use the domain knowledge to define more accurate hypothesis in order to avoid generating rules that seem to be contradictory otherwise. The basic idea is to expand the hypothesis to add more conditions based on the available domain knowledge. The process is to examine the set of available domain knowledge and find any of them that involve the goal defined for the discovery. In the above example, let's assume we have the domain knowledge (Car Year > 1980) ==> (Mileage = High).

Subsequently, we (or the discovery system) should include the Car Year attribute into the hypothesis. Then, we may get the following rules that do not seem to be contradictory.

Rule 1: If Car Model=Honda AND Cylinders=4 AND Car Year > 1980 Then Mileage = High
Rule 2: If Car Model=Honda AND Cylinders=4 AND Car Year <= 1980 Then Mileage = Low

Validating Possible Consistent Rules

Domain knowledge can be used to test whether possibly consistent discovered knowledge is accurate. For example, consider the data relation Patient (Name , Age, Drug X Administered, Side Effect , Has condition Improved). Assume that domain knowledge is, " Taking drug X does not deteriorate heart disease" and the knowledge discovered from the Patient data relation is," Drug X improves heart condition, although it has some side effects". To test the validity of this discovered knowledge, we could see if it contradicts domain knowledge. If it does, then either domain knowledge is wrong or the discovered knowledge is wrong (or both). In the above example, the discovered knowledge does not contradict domain knowledge, but goes one step beyond it by saying that the effect of drug X (e.g., anacin) on heart condition is not bad, but good. The fact that domain knowledge does not contradict discovered knowledge assures the validity of discovered knowledge with a confidence factor of x%.

Validating Possible Redundant Rules

Databases normally contain redundant data and definitions that could lead to discovering redundant rules. The redundant data / definitions are generally different syntactically. For instance, consider the CAR relation in Figure 1. The relation contains the attribute Engine_Size, Bore, Stroke, and Cylinder among other attributes. The redundant attribute Engine_Size is defined as: Engine_Size = Bore * Stroke * Cylinder. In our discovery experiment, we defined the High_MPG as the goal and the rest of the attributes as premise. The discovery tool IDIS discovered rules relating the Engine_Size to High_MPG as well as rules relating (Bore,Stroke,Cylinder) to High_MPG. Obviously, the discovered rules based on Engine_Size and (Bore, Stroke, Cylinder) are syntactically different, but they are semantically identical. We can define the redundant information in the database as domain knowledge and apply them in validating the discovered rules for possible redundancy. The basic process is to find all rules , call it R, that have the same conclusion from the set of discovered rules . For every two rules ri and rj in R, if there is a domain knowledge (i.e., X===> Y) such that ri (attributes in condition)=X and rj (attributes in condition)=Y or ri (attributes in condition)=Y and rj (attributes in condition)=X, then ri and rj are semantically equivalent rules, and therefore redundant. The choice of removing a redundant rule depends on whether we are interested in discovering more general rules or more detailed rules.

We can define the redundant information in the database as domain knowledge and apply them in the discovery process in order to avoid generating rules that are syntactically different but semantically equivalent. Before knowledge discovery, the user (or the discovery system) should check the available domain knowledge to find a domain knowledge that has attributes involved in the discovery hypothesis. If there is such domain knowledge, then the attributes in one side of the domain knowledge should be included in the discovery process (in the hypothesis). For the above CAR relation, we could use the Engine_Size attribute or the (Bore, Stroke, Cylinder) attributes in the discovery process. The choice depends on whether we are looking to generate more general rules or more detailed rules. The advantage of using this process is not only a gain in avoiding redundant rules, but also generating rules that are more meaningful.

Validating Possible Uninteresting Rules

Statistical significance is usually a key factor in determining interestingness [9,22,23,26]. If a pattern cannot be shown to be valid with some degree of certainty over a range of entities, then it is not of much use, and thus is not interesting. However, statistical significance alone is often insufficient to determine a pattern's degree of interest.

The specific factors that influence the interestingness of a pattern will vary for different databases and tasks, thus requiring outside domain knowledge [23,26]. For example, height and diagnosis may not be causally related if the database deals with liver disease; however, they may be causally related for physiotherapy. This domain knowledge can be used to verify the interestingness of the discovered rules. That is, if any of the discovered rules is the same as any of the available domain knowledge, then the discovered rule is not a new discovery and therefore it is not interesting. If the discovered rule does not contradict the available domain knowledge, then we have some confidence on the interestingness of the discovered rule. Otherwise, either the domain knowledge is inaccurate or the discovered knowledge, which requires us to use additional information, from domain experts or other data sources (summary data, historical data,..), to verify that.

Validating Possible Trivial Rules

A discovered knowledge is trivial when it is a known fact. In a relational database, functional dependencies are known facts that represent the relationships among attributes. To validate the set of discovered rules for triviality, we check the discovered rules against the set of available domain knowledge. If any of the discovered rules is the same as any of the functional dependencies, then we have a trivial discovered rule.

To prevent the discovering trivial knowledge, the functional dependencies are defined as domain knowledge and used in processing the data in order to avoid generating rules that are known facts. That is, in the discovery process, if a hypothesis is the same as an available domain knowledge (when the premise of the hypothesis is the same as the left hand side of an FD and the conclusion of the hypothesis is the same as the right hand side of the FD), then the hypothesis will generate a rule that would be a known fact and thus it should be removed from consideration for discovery.

Validating Possible Incomplete Rules

In an operational relational databases, there is a possibility that some knowledge are not discovered as a result of the normalization. Every decomposition involves a potential information loss that has to be analyzed and quantified, and traditional techniques from statistics and machine learning (minimum description length) can be used [1]. The chance of having complete/incomplete knowledge discovery depends on the discovery process. If knowledge discovery process uses the universal relation, then we could provide maximum guarantee that potentially interesting statistical dependencies are preserved. In case of the normalized relations, it depends on how the discovery process is performed on multiple relations. For instance, if the discovery process work on relations independently, then we may never discover that there is a relationship between Average House Price and the Product Purchased in the relations of Figure 3.

One possible scheme for validating the completeness/incompleteness of the discovered knowledge is to analyze the discovered rules (known as statistical dependencies) with the available functional dependencies (known as domain knowledge). If new dependencies are generated that are not in the set of discovered rules, then we have an incomplete knowledge discovery. For example, processing the Sales relation in Figure 2, we may discover that if Zip Code=11111 then Product Purchased=Wine with some confidence. We call this a statistical dependency which indicates that there is a correlation (with some confidence) between the Zip Code and the Product Purchased by people. Now, consider the Region relation in Figure 2, where the given dependencies are Zip Code —> City and City —> Average House Price which gives the derived new functional dependency Zip Code —> Average House Price due to the transitive dependency. By looking at the discovered statistical dependency and the new derived (or a given dependency in general), one may deduce that there is a relationship between the Average House Price and the Product Purchased (with some confidence). If our discovery process does not generate such a relationship, then we have an incomplete knowledge discovery which is the consequence of working on normalized relations as opposed to universal relation.

3.2 Avoid Blocking Unexpected Discovery

The main purpose of using domain knowledge is to verify the consistency, accuracy, and completeness of the discovered knowledge. Too much reliance on domain knowledge, however, may unduly constrain the knowledge discovery and may block unexpected discovery by leaving portions of the database unexplored. For example, if we use domain knowledge "male patients do not get breast cancer" in our validation process for the discovered knowledge "effects of drug X on patients with breast cancer", we may never discover that male patients can have breast cancer (an unexpected discovery, as found in [8]).

There are several things that we can do to improve the effective use of domain knowledge in knowledge discovery and to avoid blocking the unexpected discovery. First, the domain expert can assign a confidence factor to each domain knowledge and uses it only if the confidence factor is greater than a specified threshold. The assignment of a confidence factor to a domain knowledge depends on how close the domain knowledge is to the established facts. For instance, given known facts, a domain knowledge such as "male cannot be pregnant" should get higher confidence factor than domain knowledge that "Female over 65 and under 12 may not be pregnant" as the former can medically be proved to be true where as in the latter there may be a slight chance that female patients under 12 or above 65 can get pregnant. Second, if the size of the discovered rules is reduced too drastically after using some domain knowledge (due to rule redundancies and subsumption), then we may consider using fewer domain knowledge, or none of them, in order to avoid blocking unexpected discovery results.

4. CONCLUSION

We showed that rule discovery in operational relational databases could lead to inconsistent, incomplete, and inaccurate discovery. Subsequently, a discovery system should validate the discovered knowledge for its consistency and accuracy. We discussed the use of domain knowledge to validate the discovered knowledge for triviality, consistency, accuracy, and completeness.

Currently, we are studying mechanisms for gathering domain knowledge (i.e., from domain experts, and from automatic generation of domain knowledge from databases). Also, we are developing formal algorithms for validating the discovered knowledge for redundancy and contradiction, accuracy, and completeness. The problem with the use of domain knowledge in knowledge discovery is the likelihood of blocking unexpected discovery. This may happen as a result of using too much domain knowledge which may result in a large reduction in the set of discovered rules. We suggested assigning confidence factor to domain knowledge and using them when these confidence factors are high enough based on user specification.

The validation scheme based on domain knowledge can be used to validate the concepts discovered from object-oriented databases by representing the domain knowledge as concepts rather than rules. Similarly, we could use fuzzy terms in defining domain knowledge (with appropriate fuzzy sets describing the fuzzy terms) to validate the set of rules discovered from the fuzzy relational databases.

REFERENCES

1. Adriaans, Pieter and Dolf Zantinge, Data Mining, Addison-Wesley , 1996.
2. Blum, R.L., "Induction of Causal Relationships from a Time-Oriented Clinical Database: An Overview of the RX Project", Proceedings of the second National Conf. on Artificial Intelligence, Pittsburgh, PA. AAAI Press. PP. 355-357.
3. Brachman, Ronald J. And Tej Anand,"The Process of Knowledge Discovery in Databases", PP. 37-57,Advances in KnowledgeDiscovery and Data Mining, U.M. Fayyad, G. Piatetsky-Shapiro, P. Symth, Editors, AAAI Press/The MIT Press, 1996.
4. Date, C.J., An Introduction to Database Systems, Vol. 1, 5th Edition, Addison-Wesley, Reading, Mass., 1990.
5. Fayyad, Usama, Data Mining and Knowledge Discovery: Making Sense out of Data , IEEE Expert, Vol. 11 ,20-25, 1996.
6. Fayyad, Usama; Gregory Piatetsky-Shapiro; and Padhraid Symth, The KDD Process for Extracting Useful Knowledge from Volumes of Data, CACM, Vol. 39,27-33, 1996.
7. Han, Jiawei; Yandong Cai, and Nick Cercone, "Data-Driven Discovery of Quantitative Rules in Relational Databases", IEEE Transactions on Knowledge and Data Engineering, 5(1), PP. 29-40, 1993.
8. Hayward, John, Hormones and Human Breast Cancer, Springer-Verlag, 1970.
9. Hong, Jiarong and Chengjing Mao, "Incremental Discovery of Rules and Structure by Hierarchical and Parallel Clustering", Knowledge Discovery in Databases, AAAI/MIT Press, 177-194, 1991.
10. IDIS:the Information Discovery System,User's Manual,IntelligenceWare,Los Angeles,1994
11. Jafar, Musa and A. Terry Bahill,"Interactive Verification of Knowledge-Based Systems", IEEE Expert-Intelligent Systems
& Their Applications, Vol. 8, No. 1, PP. 25-32, 1993.
12. Keller, Robert, Expert System Technology - Development and Application, Yourdon Press, New York, 1994.
13. Kuok, Chan Man; Ada Fu; and Man Hon Wong,"Mining Fuzzy Association Rules in Databases ", SIGMOD RECORD, Vol. 27, No. 1, PP. 41-46, March 1998.
14. Liu, Bing and Wynne Hsu,"Post-Analysis of Learned Rules", Proc. of the AAAI-96 Conf. On Innovative Applications
of Artificial Intelligence, Portland, Oregon, PP. 828-834,1996.
15. Mengshoel, Ole Jakob and Delab Sintef,"Knowledge Validation: Principles and Practice", IEEE Expert-Intelligent
Systems & Their Applications, Vol. 8, No. 3, PP. 62-68, 1993.
16. Nikolopoulos, Chris, Expert Systems-Introduction to First and Second Generation and Hybrid Knowledge Based Systems, Marcel Dekker, Inc, 1997.
17. Nishio, Shojiro; Hiroyuki Kawano; and Jiawei Han,"Kowledge Discovery in Object-Oriented Databases: The First Step", Knowledge Discovery in Databases Workshop, PP. 299-313, AAAI Press, 1993.
18. O'Leary, D.,"Validation of Expert Systems",Decision Sciences,Vol. 18, No. 3, PP 468-486, 1987.
19. Owrang, M. Mehdi; Michael C. Frame; and Larry R. Medsker,"Testing for Inconsistencies in Rule-Based Knowledge Bases", Expert Systems Applications, EXPERSYS-90, PP. 281-286, 1990.
20. Owrang O., M. Mehdi,"The Role of Domain Knowledge in Knowledge Discovery in Databases", Microcomputers Applications, Vol.16 (1) 11-18, 1997.
21. Parsaye, Kamran,"OLAP & Data Mining- Bridging the Gap", Database Programming & Design, PP. 31-37, Feb. 1997.
22. Piatetsky-Shapiro, Gregory,"Discovery, Analysis, and Presentation of Strong Rules ", Knowledge Discovery in Databases, AAAI Press/MIT Press, PP. 229-247, 1991.

23. Piatetsky-Shapiro, G. and C.J. Matheus,"The interestingness of deviations", Proc. of the AAAI-94 Workshop on KDD, PP. 25-36, 1994.
24. Polat, Faruk and H. Altay Guvenir, "UVT: A Unification-Based Tool for Knowledge Base Verification", IEEE Expert-Intelligent Systems & Their Applications, Vol. 8, No. 3, PP. 69-75, 1993.
25. Sarawagi, Sunita; Shiby Thomas; and Rakesh Agrawal,"Integrating Association Rule Mining with Relational Database Systems: Alternatives and Implications", ACM SIGMOD RECORD, Proc. of the 1998 ACM SIGMOD, International Conf. on Management of Data, PP. 343-354, 1998.
26. Silberschatz, A. and A. Tuzhilin, "On subjective measures of interestingness in knowledge discovery", Proc. of the First International Conf. On Knowledge Discovery and Data Mining, 1995.
27. Simoudis, Evangelos, Reality Check for Data Mining, IEEE Expert, Vol. 11 (1996) 26-33
28. Szladow, A, Datalogic/R - Mining the Knowledge in Databases, PC AI, Vol. 7,40-41, 1993.

Software Family Life Cycle Development

Malgorzata Pankowska, Information Systems Department, University of Economics,
street Bogucicka 3, 40 226 Katowice, Poland, email: pank@figaro.ae.katowice.pl

ABSTRACT

Companies that understand the dynamics of product family evolution are better positioned to manage their design and manufacturing resources to competitive advantage. Software factories are noticed to know about that and they seem to develop families of software packages, even they lack of proper methodology. So the purpose of this paper is to present the methodological problems of software product family development. In the first part of this paper software systems are characterized from the product family point of view, next information systems development methodologies are criticized. Eventually software family life cycle model is presented.

Increasing market share in fiercely competitive markets can be achieved by tuning products for niche market demands and family product development. This results in a greater range of product variations, which must be produced at a lower cost and with the shortest possible design and production time, because in the emerging world of dynamic competition, companies face a two-fold challenge: they must decide on their short-run mix of variety and change, and over the long run they must find a way to expand both characteristics [Sanderson & Uzumeri, 1997, p. 31].

1 SOFTWARE SYSTEMS AS PRODUCT FAMILY

For physical products, a family is a set of products that share common technology and address related market applications. A product family evolves over time by incorporating new technologies into its designs and by targeting new customer requirements. According to Kotler product family is constituted by all the product classes that can satisfy a core need with more or less effectiveness [1991].

The software industry is becoming a parts manufacturing industry: building key parts which any user, work group, enterprise, or interenterprise partnership may acquire to build its customized computing environment. Correspondingly, the software market is becoming a standard-parts marketplace where customers with high-level problems to solve look for low-level, pluggable software components to assemble into higher-level solutions.

There are several ways in which products can vary: by actual content; by packing, formatting, and presentation; by distribution; and by degree of interactivity. The combination of different variations can lead to a range of distinct products within the product family, all derived from the same information repository. Providing users direct control over the packaging and content of the product itself can be a highly desirable product feature. Product family should map all new product initiatives across the business to balance risk and potential initiatives across the business to balance risk and potential return, short and long time horizons, or mature and emerging markets. Product family includes a combination of different products with both established and new technologies. Company should constantly monitor the parameters of its product family such as time horizon, risk, expected returns, required investments, and needed capabilities. It is very comfortable to have the product with versions for very major platform and market, frequently debugged and tested. Microsoft 's competitive strategy revolves around identifying mass markets quickly, introducing products that are Ñgood enough" rather than waiting until something is perfect, improving these products by incrementally evolving their features, and then selling multiple product versions and upgrades to customers around the world [Cusumano & Selby, 1997].

Software products family can include:

1. *Independently developed products.* Company develops family of products, however each of them is created, manufactured independently. When product A is completely sold out then product B life cycle begins. Product B has completely new characteristics in comparison with product A. This situation is common in case of complete transformation of company and transition to new technology implementation and usage.

2. *Interdependently developed products.* Selected functions and characteristics of software products are the same. All the products of the family or certain subgroups of products can have the same features. At the requirements main characteristics of products are established and collected in metadata repositories. Product Data Management module in CASE system makes easy design and modeling new product family as well as new release development [Griffiths & Clarke, 1997, Port, 1997].

3. *Independent products and dependent versions of products.* In software family products have different features, function and mar-

kets, however versions of a product are interdependent that essential characteristics of the products are maintained in long period of time.

4. *Dependent products and independent versions of a product.* That case means also transition to new technology implementation and usage. Each new release has new external features like new GUI or additional functions are included, however essential features stay the same in long period of time.

2 INFORMATION SYSTEMS DEVELOPMENT METHODOLOGIES

Information system (IS) development methodologies have in common a general preference for a top-down approach; that is, they begin with functional analysis (a very general view of the firm) and proceed through process and task analysis (a very detailed view of specific area). Most specify the content of the deliverables, and most include other project definition, management, and control information as well. These project-related items include checkpoints, walk-through, quality reviews, management reviews, funding reviews, and large numbers of approvals. The specific methodology followed by the firm my be home-grown or purchased from any one of a large number of firms who specialize in the development of methodologies. However that forms do not publish papers about family product development methodologies.

According to Modell the development of a software system, essentially a multistage cognitive process, typically involves five phases: requirements analysis, design, implementation, testing and maintenance [1996]. So information system is considered as stand alone, autonomic system with no relations to other similar systems, where any reusable components could be implemented.

The classic waterfall model of the software development process portrays the software development process as a series of development phases, with an iterative relationship between successive phases [Agresti, 1986]. The ordering of the phases assumes that there is iteration; each step may take place within preceding and succeeding phases, but rarely with other phases of the sequence. Since its presentation, all variations of the waterfall model have preserved its essence: software is developed as a sequence of general activities, focusing on the importance of design. The waterfall model has several shortcomings: It implies a uniform and orderly sequence of development activities. It does not accommodate the new development of software development, like rapid prototyping. It does not provide enough detail for process optimization. So it only partially addresses the issue of software products family development.

DeMarco defines an overall system development life-cycle, closely related to the waterfall model [1979]. This model assumes one software system development, however the options creation lets on new releases development, although DeMarco does not mention about that.

The spiral model addresses many of the problems identified in the waterfall model by including multiple paradigms in the system model development [Boehm, 1990]. This model allows combinations of the conventional, prototyping, and incremental models to be used for development as part of the spiral. Existing models of system life cycle do not adequately represent the iterative, concurrent and evolutionary nature of family products development.

3 INFORMATION SYSTEMS LIFE CYCLE VERSUS PRODUCT LIFE CYCLE.

There is a clear distinction between information system development life cycle and a product life cycle. The concept of a systems life cycle originated in marketing. It is an important concept in marketing that provides into a product's competitive dynamics.

However marketing thinking should not begin with a product, or even a product class, but rather with a need. The product exists as one solution among many to meet a need. The changing need level is described by a demand life-cycle curve shown in Figure 2. There is a stage of emergence (E) followed by stages of accelerating growth (G_1), decelerating growth (G_2), maturity

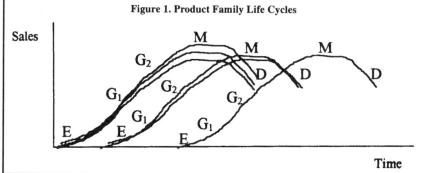

Figure 1. Product Family Life Cycles

Sales

M
M
M
G_2
G_2
D
D
D
G_1
G_2
G_1
G_1
E
E
E

Time

(M) and decline (D) (figure 1). Each demand-technology life cycle shows an emergence, rapid growth, slower growth, maturity and then decline.

A product life cycle can be considered as having five stages. Whereas a IS development life cycle outlines the steps that are taken to Ñgive birth" (creation) to a system and terminates when that system begins to perform. Clearly, the two concepts of life cycle are distinctively different, with an overlap at the beginning and (or according to some researchers) at the end- at the moment of IS elimination and rolling over by new generation IS. Particularly important tasks in each life cycle are presented on figure 2.

4 SOFTWARE FAMILY LIFE CYCLE MODEL

Successive products within a product family can be assessed by virtue of newness embodied in the core technologies and market applications of new products relative to prior products. An evolving product family will introduce new technology into product designs and target new customer requirements. However, the scope of change will be bounded. New technologies and market applications of a product family will be related to older ones: new technologies will be combined with and enhance existing core technologies and the resulting products will target existing and related market applications. The commonality of technologies and market leads to efficiency and effectiveness in manufacturing, distribution and service, where the firm tailors each general resource or capability to the needs of specific market niches.

Each product in family of related products has its own model life cycle. The aggregation of the model cycles constitutes the firm's product-family life cycle. Model change has two components -rate and type, the former reflecting the frequency, the latter the degree of change. The model is defined to be a product design

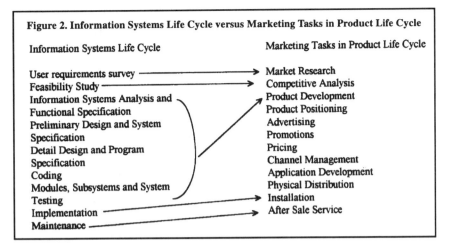

Figure 2. Information Systems Life Cycle versus Marketing Tasks in Product Life Cycle

Information Systems Life Cycle	Marketing Tasks in Product Life Cycle
User requirements survey	Market Research
Feasibility Study	Competitive Analysis
Information Systems Analysis and	Product Development
Functional Specification	Product Positioning
Preliminary Design and System	Advertising
Specification	Promotions
Detail Design and Program	Pricing
Specification	Channel Management
Coding	Application Development
Modules, Subsystems and System	Physical Distribution
Testing	Installation
Implementation	After Sale Service
Maintenance	

that differs sufficiently from other designs that the manufacturer assigns it a distinctive commercial designation and a product family to be a set of models that a given manufacturer makes and considers to be related.

Now product family development requires concurrent engineering. That is a systems engineering approach to the integrated coincident design and development of products, systems, and processes. Concurrent engineering is intended to cause systems acquisition, broadly considered to include all phases of the life cycle to be explicitly planned in order to better integrate user requirements to result in high quality cost-effective systems and thereby to reduce system development time through this better integration of life cycle activities. The basic tasks in concurrent engineering are much the same as the basic tasks in systems engineering.

Companies can gather preliminary requirements from either current or future customers. The current customer base can be elicited through the user groups, which often draw up formal prioritized lists of requirements for new releases. Requirements from future users often come through the marketing channel. Initial requirements and technical functional specifications are written that serve as a starting point to begin system building. Contingent on product characteristics these specifications may be highly detailed or only in skeletal form in anticipation of numerous changes. Specifications may have varying degrees of completeness, formality and granularity depending on the degree of newness of product.

Next phase satisfaction decision point can be arrived at when the developers are satisfied that the product has arrived at a stage all of its requirements have been discovered, scoped and are understood, usability issues are defined, market positioning considerations are satisfactory, initial external responses are positive, and managerial tradeoffs are resolved. Next the overall architecture is explicitly defined. The entire system designed is formalized. The design stage may be repeated because of quality failures, the design is modified to accommodate changes needed to support next Ñfamily member" development. The code stage may be relatively short for a new release of a mature product, or extended for a new product. The time spent on this stage, within the software industry, continues to be low. Alpha test is generally conducted inside the firm. Comprehensive rigorous testing takes place as a cooperative effort between developers and quality assurance personnel. Testing is conducted against requirements specifications. Beta test is generally conducted outside the firm with a favored group of customers that have some relationship with the firm. Final round of tests is conducted at the appropriate level of detail as assessed by development history and risk considerations. Software product family life cycle model is presented on figure 3. Particular phases are

Figure 3. Software product family lifecycle model

Figure 3 Software product family lifecycle model

REQuirement Phase
Document preliminary requirements and technical specifications
Modify requirements according to discovered requirements
MODel Phase
Feasibility study. Search for reusable components, interchange reusable components
New systems models and analysis.
DESign Phase
System design based on reusable components. Design review.
TESt Phase
System coding. Alpha and Beta testing. Defects removal. Final testing.
PRODuct Phase
Software product manufacturing

developed sequentially and parallel. Market and technology influence developments of products. Results of earlier phases are collected in repositories to be reused in later phases.

Family products are developed in software engineering environments (SEE) that support the configuration management of all of the software family products. The environment facilities are integrated. Sommerville identified three types of integration, namely data integration, interface integration and activity integration [1992]. The most expensive activity in managing long-lifetime systems is ensuring that, for all versions of the system, all of the documents associated with a version (specifications, design, code, user documentation) are complete and consistent.

5 COMPONENTS REUSABILITY

Concurrent engineering concerns compression of the phases of the life cycle, however family product development requires less intention to compress the time but rather development not only one product basing on use of reusable (sub)systems. Several reasons have been suggested to explain why the software reusability philosophy has gained little acceptance, most importantly: difficulty in estimating the impact of software reuse, scarcity of support tools to facilitate reusing software artifacts, and absence of information about the cognitive aspects of the software reusability process [Sen, 1997]. With the advent of CASE tools, design artifacts are continually being created in different projects. These artifacts, which are typically stored, can potentially be reused.

A design reuse process involves several necessary reuse tasks to help the software designer design an information system. First of it is necessary to identify reusable objects, classify and create them. In principle any software objects during the software development process can be reused; however, not everything that is reusable should be reused [Sen, 1997].

A fundamentally different approach -called object-oriented software- is now a reality. Object-oriented systems combine data and programs into chunks that are like objects in the real world. That is, object-oriented systems represent information in units called objects which consist of data and a set of operations to manipulate them. An object can be an invoice, a filing cabinet, a type of employee, or a computerized representation of a part in a jet engine. The outcome of an object orientation to software is reusable software elements that can be used for a large numbers of applications. The appeal of an object-oriented approach is that information in each object can be reused repeatedly in a variety of applications.

One of the primary benefits of this approach is to significantly reduce the number of design and programming errors by reducing the complexity and programming operations required to develop an application. Using objects to develop software programs also has the potential of increasing the productivity of the developers of software by reducing development life-cycle and increasing software portability [Tapscott & Caston, 1996].

A characteristic of an engineering discipline is that it is based upon an approach to system design which makes the maximum use of existing components. Design engineers do not specify a design where every component has to be manufactured specially but base their design on components which have been tried and tested in other systems. There are several kinds of reusable component: application systems, sub-systems, modules or objects, functions, or paper documents, operation service. Currently, application system reuse is widely practiced as software companies implement their systems across a range of machines. Function reuse is also widely practiced as use is made of standard libraries of reusable functions such as the UNIX C libraries and mathematical libraries. Component reuse for product family development, of course, does not mean the reuse of code. It is possible to reuse specifications and design. The potential gains from reusing abstract products, such as specifications, of the development process may be greater than those from reusing code components. Less adaptation may be required for abstract components compared to components which include program-level details. That why family products varies on design level. A product design that serves its originator beyond expectations is itself a resource. Product-family competition is transformed to product-design competition.

Ideally, once a reusable component has been constructed, it can be used without change. More commonly, however, it will be necessary to adapt the component in some way to take account of the particular requirements for the system being developed.

In family products development, the system requirements are modified according to the reusable components available. There are three requirements for software development with reuse:

1. It must be possible to find appropriate reusable components.
2. The reuser of the components must be able to understand them and must have confidence in their suitability.

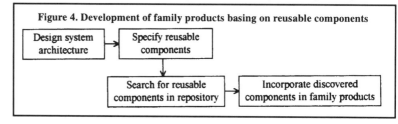

Figure 4. Development of family products basing on reusable components

Design system architecture → Specify reusable components

Search for reusable components in repository → Incorporate discovered components in family products

3. The components must have associated information discussing how they can be reused (figure 4).

An organization must have a base of properly catalogued and documented reusable components and this is a factor which inhibits systematic software reuse. The repository becomes the foundation from which a firm creates its families of information products [Meyer & Zack, 1996]. The greater the scope, depth, and complexity of the metadata structure data concerning prototypes, the greater the flexibility for deriving products and thus the greater the potential variety within the product family derived from that essential prototype forming product platform [Meyer, Selinger,1998]. The greater the complexity of the platform structure, however, the greater the cost and effort to maintain the repository, although repository of user requirements is constantly renewed. A well designed repository will enable a firm to mine the most value from the content for a given maintenance cost.

The levels of complexity and granularity and the associated scheme for structuring the repository can constrain basic product design. The more ways a firm can slice and dice its repository, the greater the potential for rapidly and efficiently creating products for new market niches.

In a multicycle product family development, the re-use of standard parts provides for efficient redesign and minimizes retooling of the manufacturing process. One benefit of design has been cost and time savings due to re-use of parts. When standard parts

cannot be used and changes in design and implementation are required, a shared design abstraction with a different physical realization can further reduce costs. Cost reduction is not only advantage development of product family. Product family development offers further advantages:
1. Increase of systems reliability
2. Reduction of overall risk and risk transferability from one product to another
3. Reduction of maintenance time and constant verification of repository of software data and models.

Much like warranties, product family can signal product quality. The greater the number of opportunities for using a product from a family, the more likely the buyer can evaluate the product prior to purchase, because of the learning that occurs during prior purchases and use.

SUMMARY

Assuming that methodologies to develop information systems are accepted by those who develop software, software life cycle is nearly the same as information systems life cycle. Scientists mainly focus on single system development methodologies, but companies need software family development methodologies for ordering and timing. Basing on traditional life cycle methodology and components reusability approach software family life cycle model was built.

REFERENCES

Agresti W., (ed.) (1986) New Paradigms for Software Development, *IEEE Computer Society Press*, IEEE Computer Society Tutorial.

Boehm B. (1990) A spiral model of Software development and enhancement, in R. Thayer and M. Dorfman (eds.), *System and Software Requirements Engineering*, IEEE Computer Society Press, 513-527.

Cusumano M.A., Selby R.W. (1997) How Microsoft Builds Software, June, Vol.40 No 6 *Communications of the ACM*, 54-61.

DeMarco T. (1979) *Structured Analysis and System Specification*, Prentice-Hall.

Griffiths A., Clarke CH. (1997) The Shift in Focus from ÑCost and Quality" to Ñagility" and the Implications for Data Management Strategy, *Proceedings of the Time-Compression Technologies'97* Conference, Gaydon, UK.

Kotler P. (1991) *Marketing Management, Analysis, Planning, Implementation & Control*, Prentice Hall.

Meyer M.H., Zack M.H. (1996) The Design and Development of Information Products, *Sloan Management Review*, Spring, 43-59

Meyer M.H., Selinger R (1998) Product Platforms in Software Development, *Sloan Management Review*, Fall, 61-74.

Modell M.E. (1996) *A Professional's Guide to System Analysis*, McGrawHill, NY.

Port S. (1997) PDM: A Time-Compression Technology for the Whole Life-Cycle, *Proceedings of the Time-Compression Technologies'97* Conference, Gaydon, UK.

Sanderson S.W., Uzumeri M. (1997) *Managing Product Families*, Irwin/McGraw-Hill, NY.

Sen A.(1997) The role of opportunism in the Software Design Reuse Process, *IEEE Transactions on Software Engineering*, Vol.23, No 7, July 1997, 418-435.

Sommerville, I. (1992) *Software Engineering*, Addison Wesley.

Tapscott D., Caston A.(1996) *Paradigm shift, The New Promise of Information Technology*, McGrawHill, Inc. NY.

The Road to the Electronic Classroom: Overcoming Roadblocks & Avoiding Speed Bumps

Raymond Papp
Department of MIS, Central Connecticut State University, New Britain, CT 06053
(860) 832-3293, PappR@ccsu.edu

The road to the electronic classroom is a journey filled with trial and error and learning. There are many reasons and rewards for undertaking the journey. Students use and interact with the technology they will employ in the work environment and faculty can devote more time to preparation and assisting students rather than to mundane, but necessary logistical tasks. Syllabi, exams, grades, and group interaction can be moved to the electronic realm. The Internet and networked servers, along with personal productivity software, make the journey less stressful and more pleasurable. Some tips for making a successful journey are also offered.

INTRODUCTION

I had just put the finishing touches on my course web page when a student planning to take my upcoming programming class walked into my office. "How many programs and tests will you require this term?" were the first words out of his mouth. (Why students are so concerned with "numbers" I will never understand). "Six programs and three tests, along with some group learning exercises," I told him, "but you can find all that information on my class web page. Here, let me show you..."

In an on-going attempt at continuous improvement, I have begun a journey down the road to a totally paperless classroom. The trip, thus far, has been smooth, however not without an occasional "roadblock" that must be overcome or a "speed bump" to make things interesting. This paper will discuss my progress toward a totally paperless classroom. I will point out what has worked for me, what has caused problems, and how faculty might incorporate some of what I have done in their own classes. I will conclude with some pedagogical implications and directions for the future.

The Traditional Approach

In the past, students received a syllabus from the instructor along with any necessary information regarding course policies, deadlines, supplementary readings, and other such material. Lecture notes were created by the instructor, possibly by hand or using a tool like Microsoft PowerPoint™, and then distributed to the students in the form of an outline. Exams, usually given several times each term, were updated and then duplicated on paper prior to class. Student projects or programs were turned in either on paper or on floppy disks, which then had to be scanned for viruses. A grade book, done using a spreadsheet, was then used to create a printout of current grades that was periodically posted on the instructor's door. Does this sound familiar? Are you still running your classes this way? There is a better way! It uses the Internet and your campus network to create an electronic, paperless classroom. Let's begin our journey.

THE NEW ELECTRONIC PARADIGM

Internet Syllabus/Web Page

The road to the electronic classroom begins with the primary classroom document, the syllabus. The Internet has revolutionized the way we teach (Bender, 1995; Chimi and Gordon, 1997; Granger & Lippert, 1995; Adams, 1998). It has made it possible to move much, if not all, of what we used to do on paper into the realm of electronic media. The traditional syllabus, often created using a word processor, can now easily be made into a home page using that same word processor. There is no need for the instructor to learn Hypertext Markup Language (HTML), the archaic and cumbersome language of the World Wide Web. It is quite easy to create a document with multiple pieces and parts, all linked together using hyperlinks (Purao, 1997; Falcigno, 1995). The instructor can also link his or her syllabus to other external sites on the web and even include sound and full motion video! My course syllabi have all been placed on the web and the only paper I give out to students is a hard copy of the syllabus on the first day, not because I want to give them paper, but because it is a school policy. Changes to the syllabus regarding dates of assignments and exams (usually the result of inclement weather cancellations here in snowy Connecticut), are immediately posted and broadcast to the students using a small applet that allows me to display a scrolling message of my choosing at the bottom of each web page.

Electronic Testing

As we journey farther down the road, we come to the use of electronic testing. Exams, once taken on paper and manually corrected by the instructor, can now be placed on-line and corrected automatically by the computer, should the instructor desire this. I have used a combination approach whereby students take an exam that consists of part multiple choice and part essay.

The multiple-choice portion is computer scored automatically, and the essay portion can be quickly graded on-line. I am using a product called Course Test Manager ™ developed by Course Technologies (see figure). The product was free with the course textbook and allows me to add questions and customize tests according to my needs. The program, stored on our school server, is accessible to students using any PC on campus, if necessary. I have used the exam scheduler option to create timed exams that require a password to take them. Students come to class, log in to the test manager, and enter the exam password which I provide to them. They then complete the exam in the allotted time. Once they are finished with the exam, the program grades the objective questions automatically and saves the grades in a log file, accessible only from the instructor's menu. Optionally, students may be allowed to see their score immediately upon completion of the exam and/or also view their exam answers on-line. (I choose to enable this feature a few days after the exam, thus allowing for make-ups and grading). By providing them with the ability to check their answers to the questions on their own time, valuable class time is saved for other instructional purposes. Office hours can be used to clarify any answers that students may not understand. The entire process is accommodating and expeditious and, based on their positive comments, students seem to love taking exams on-line. Many publishers are beginning to include such electronic testing programs with their textbooks. These programs make the instructor more productive and he or she can now spend additional time preparing.

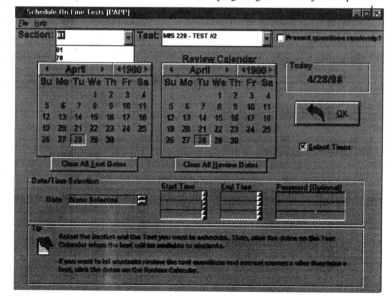

On-line Grades

Students always want to know what their current grade is for the class. Prior to the electronic classroom, the instructor had to field phone calls, answer e-mail, or use office hours to answer these questions. By using a spreadsheet like Microsoft Excel™, the instructor can keep an electronic grade book of course grades and then publish the file to their web site in HTML format. This allows students to access their grades whenever they wish and they no longer have to call or e-mail the instructor, except in cases of disagreement. I even go so far as to have an e-mail hyperlink on the grades page so students with questions or problems can send me an e-mail.

Electronic Assignment Submission

The best part of electronic submission, from an instructor standpoint, is the lack of floppy disks. My students previously submitted assignments (programs or papers) on disk, which then needed to be scanned for viruses. The students also frequently lost or damaged their disks. By having students submit their assignments to me electronically, these problems are avoided. Students either drag-and-drop their assignments into a secure directory on our school server or, if they are off-campus and unable to attend, use e-mail or FTP (File Transfer Protocol). The secure directory functions in much the same way as a postal mailbox. Items put into the box cannot be retrieved or viewed by the student. This prevents other students from copying someone else's work, yet facilitates the electronic transfer of files to the school's server. The drag-and-drop approach using either NT Explorer or FTP is preferable, since extraction of the programs or papers from e-mail messages becomes unneces-

Netscape - [http://www.sb.ccsu.edu/t pp/courses/220 sp'98.html]

File Edit View Go Bookmarks Options Directory Window Help

MIS 220: Contemporary Applications – Visual Basic
Spring 1998
Current Grades

Section 01: Mon/Wed 2:00-3:15																
	Program						Exam			Peer Learning Exercise					Current	
ID#	#1	#2	#3	#4	#5	#6	#1	#2	#3	#1	#2	#3	#4	#5	Average	Grade
0315	90	100	92	95			70	78		10	10	18			85%	B
4767	100	95	75	75			80	79		10	10	18			82%	B-
3811	100	100	20	105			77	69		10	10	20			77%	C+
4394	90	95	90	80			67	77		0	10	18			80%	B-
5289	90	90	90	95			84	77		10	10	18			85%	B
2204	100	90	92	110			100	97		10	10	20			95%	A
0762	100	95	90	95			79	81		10	10	19			88%	B+
1345	90	100	70	90			89	85		10	10	20			85%	B

Document: Done

sary. I have loaded a virus checker on my PC, so all programs, e-mail attachments, and files are automatically scanned and cleaned prior to viewing. If nothing else, I have eliminated the daily routine of scouring my hard drive for viruses using the anti-virus program. Students also like the secure directory (or "drop box" as they call it) since they can work on programs from the lab or from their rooms and then simply submit them electronically when they have finished. There are no disks to lose or get left behind. The only excuse seems to be the "Cyber excuse" (i.e. the server went down), which happens once in a great while.

Real-time Discussions

Using a program called WebBoard™ by O'Reilly Software, I have created discussion groups for each of my classes to enable students to post messages and ask questions at any time. They log into the program at their convenience using the Internet and a hypertext link from the course home page to read postings from me or other students. One unexpected, but nevertheless favorable result was the interaction between the students that occurred using this program. A student would post a question to the board and before I could answer it (and I checked it on a daily basis), other students would post an answer. This not only allowed students to learn from one another, but saved me from having to answer the same questions several times. Several other faculty members from my school were impressed with the program and have begun using it in their classes as well. The program also comes with a real-time chat feature that I am considering for use when I am not on campus. I am looking into the idea of holding at least some "virtual office hours" during which I could answer student questions from off-campus.

OVERCOMING ROAD BOCKS AND SPEED BUMPS

There have been few problems this year. The biggest roadblock has been a "learning curve" for some students. Many were not used to the idea of using a PC to do everything (view syllabi, take tests, etc.), however once they got used to the idea they frequently asked me, "How come everyone doesn't do it this way?" My answer to them is to talk to their instructors and suggest that they begin to move toward such a paradigm. I also tell my colleagues that they can call on me for help or suggestions at anytime.

Some of the "speed bumps" on the road to the electronic classroom included server problems, instructor access problems, and communication problems. The server has gone down briefly a few times this year, however never for more than a short time. The problem is usually due to human error of some sort (i.e. someone disconnecting an Ethernet cable).

My biggest problem has been one of access. I can run my entire class from my PC in my office. There are times, however, when I need to access my PC from off-campus. I have temporarily solved the problem by purchasing a ZIP™ drive, which I then take back and forth to work with me. The longer term (and more desirable) solution will occur later this year when the University installs a dial-up lines for faculty to reach the server. Since we have migrated to Windows NT and Office 97, the security issue is a lesser concern. The lack of dedicated dial-up lines is the current "roadblock".

I have also encountered a few communication problems with other users, particularly students using older systems from off-campus sites. They frequently cannot send file attachments using their e-mail and must resort to coming to campus to send their files. This might be a temporary problem as many local businesses begin the move to Windows NT or Windows 98 and the Microsoft Office suite.

Future Enhancements

Communication among students is an important part of the learning process. Since we are moving away from a mini-computer based e-mail server to a fully integrated client/server solution, it becomes increasingly necessary for students and the instructor to be able to communicate with one another at any given time (Zack, 1995). To facilitate such communication I have implemented a class discussion group whereby students can communicate with each other and with the instructor. Another approach that I am considering is the use of software packages that allow users to have real-time video and audio conversations using their PC and the Internet. Such video-conferencing and audio-conferencing might be useful when students are in physically different locations, such as with distance learning. This allows group interaction and communication, despite geographical isolation (Hall, 1997; McCormack, 1998; Motiwalla & Duggal, 1998). It might also be invaluable for conducting virtual office hours from an off-campus site (e.g. home). This option will be explored in the future for its practicality and applicability.

CONCLUSION

While the road to the electronic classroom is a journey fraught with trial and error, it can be a fulfilling and educational trip. The rewards of a fully implemented system are many. Students are happier, they are employing the technologies they will be using in the working world on a daily basis, and the instructor can devote more time to preparing and planning the course and spend less time with the logistics. In fact, it enables the instructor to devote more time to the classroom and to help students on an individual basis. The need to begin moving toward such a paradigm becomes clearer every day as the Internet moves further into the mainstream. The electronic classroom also paves the way for distance learning scenarios, something colleges and universities across the country are working toward (Bialaszewski, et. al., 1998; Fischer & O'Leary, 1998; Papp, 1998). In short, the electronic classroom is a good way to make classes more fun and applicable and teaching more rewarding and productive.

AFTERWARD

Shortly after this paper was written, I began to offer the same programming course outlined above in a distance learning environment as part of Connecticut State University's *OnlineCSU* initiative. I was one of twelve faculty members who participated in this pilot program to offer courses completely over the Internet. I "borrowed" a great deal of material from my traditional "on-campus" class, which was facilitated by the use of the electronic material developed for my on-campus course web site (Papp, 1998).

While discussion of the formation of the *OnlineCSU* program is beyond the scope of this paper, there were a number of issues that had to be worked out for this initiative to succeed. Concerns about faculty workload and time, ownership of the material, enrollment numbers, copyright issues, and whether or not distance learning would be accepted by the students were some of the major concerns that surfaced during the Fall of 1998. There was also concern by some of the faculty that such a program might jeopardize their on-campus classes and that all classes would be held electronically. Such fears, due largely to inexperience and lack of understanding of the technology involved, were quickly assuaged. Nevertheless, the process has been both exciting and challenging. Research is underway to compare the traditional class with the online class in an effort to determine whether any pedagogical differences exist with respect to student attitude and learning. Preliminary findings will be reported at the conference this spring.

REFERENCES

Adams, C. (1998). "The Skills Audit Approach to Facilitate Undergraduate Learning." *Proceedings of the 13th Annual Conference of the International Academy for Information Management*, Helsinki, Finland, 211-16.

Bender, R. (1995). "Creating communities on the Internet: Electronic discussion lists in the classroom." *Computers in Libraries*, 15:5, 38-43.

Bialaszewski, D., Burns, J., Dick, G., Papp, R., & Pencek, T. (1998). "Web-Based Teaching: Past, Present, and Future." *Proceedings of the 13th Annual Conference of the International Academy for Information Management*, Helsinki, Finland, 192.

Chimi, C. & Gordon, G. (1997). "Using innovative information systems techniques to teach information systems." *Proceedings of the 12th Annual Conference of the International Academy for Information Management*, Atlanta, Georgia, 161-166.

Falcigno, K. (1995). "HOME page, SWEET HOME page: Creating a web presence." *Database*, v18, (Apr/May 95), 20-28.

Fischer, D., & O'Leary, A. (1998). "Web-Based Distance Learning." *Proceedings of the 13th Annual Conference of the International Academy for Information Management*, Helsinki, Finland, 85-89.

Granger, M. & Lippert, S. (1995). "Enhancing the introductory information systems course: Using E-mail." *Proceedings of the 10th Annual Conference of the International Academy for Information Management*, New Orleans, Louisiana, 1-11.

Hall, B. (1997) *Web-based Training Cookbook*. John Wiley & Sons.

McCormack, J. (1998) *Building a Web-based Education System*. John Wiley & Sons.

Motiwalla, L., & Duggal, J. (1998). "Distance Learning on the Internet: a Virtual Classroom Approach". *Effective Utilization and Management of Emerging Information Technologies*, Idea Group Publishing.

Papp, R. (1998). "OnlineCSU: Course Delivery for the Next Millennium?" *4th Annual conference of the Connecticut Consortium for Enhancing Learning and Teaching (CCELT)*, University of New Haven, October 1998.

Purao, S. (1997). "Hyper-link teaching to foster active learning" *Proceedings of the 12th Annual Conference of the International Academy for Information Management*, Atlanta, Georgia, 197-205.

Zack, M. (1995). "Using electronic messaging to improve the quality of instruction." *Journal of Education for Business*, v70n4, 202-206.

Management Ethics in Virtual Organisations

Jerzy A. Kisielnicki, Warsaw University, Faculty of Management, Department of Management Information Systems, Poland -02-678 Warsaw, Szturmowa Str.3 phone (4822) 8471981, fax.(4822) 8471432.
e-mail jkis@wspiz.edu.pl

ABSTRACT

Virtual organisations being a new type of organisations are attractive for the users. However, their weakness is represented by the fact that they are not so popular as the traditional ones. In addition, the development of virtual organisations is hampered by a great deal of concern of various nature. The major concern is over the unethical behaviour of the whole organisation or any part of it. Thus the consequences are suffered by all virtually associated organisations. This report discusses the results of pilot research relating to the reliability assessment of both traditional and virtual organisations. Different groups of electorate of the two types of organisations have been involved in the research. The conclusions drawn may be of substantial help from the point of view of both theory and practice of virtual organisations formation.

VIRTUAL ORGANISATION AS A RESEARCH OBJECT.

The issues of virtual organisation functioning were presented in some earlier publications [J. Kisielnicki - 1997 and 1998]. The term 'virtual' derives from Latin words virtualis meaning 'effective' and virtus meaning 'power'. Thus, 'virtual' also means 'theoretically able to occur'. A virtual organisation is a completely new type of organisation which could be formed due to the development of the Information Technology and, especially, the functioning of the global information network and large data bases. This is also a response to the free market requirements and the necessity to adjust to its competitiveness. The term 'virtual organisation' has no generally accepted definition attached to it. It may be assumed to be a derivative of the term 'virtual reality'. Virtuality is determined rather by the description of characteristics than the existing physical features. Therefore, we speak of a virtual organisation, virtual services, a virtual journey, virtual activities. We assume that a virtual organisation is voluntarily established by the organisations which enter into various relations among themselves with the view of achieving an objective which is to produce benefit greater than if they operated in a traditional way. There is no need for their joint operation to conclude civil and legal agreements. The lifetime of such a relationship is determined by an organisation which first comes to the conclusion that its existance is no longer beneficial to it. The remaining organisations may, if they think fit to, continue their relationship without the organisation which has withdrawn from it, or enter into new relations with other organisations. A virtual organisation may not be perceived only from the point of view of a classic theory of organisation. Formally we can assume that we create virtual organisations in the situations to be presented as follows.

Let denote that:

Ω - is a set of all considered organisations;

O_i - is the i-th specific organisation, whereupon $\forall_i O_i \in \Omega$.

Every specific organisation can create relations (alliances). The choice is:

1. A group of virtual organisations W, where $W_k \in W$ - is the k-th specific virtual organisation, whereupon $\forall_k W_k \in \Omega$, $W_k \neq \Phi$, $L(W\kappa)>1$ where $L(W_k)$ - size of a virtual organisation.

2. A group of traditionally related organisations T, where $T_l \in T$ - is the l-th specific traditional organisation, whereupon $\forall_l T_l \in \Omega$, $T_l \neq \Phi$, $L(T_l) >1$, where $L(T_l)$ - size of a traditional organisation.

The organisation O_i cannot participate at the same time in the group W and in the group T, that is

$O_i \in T \rightarrow O_i \notin W$ and $O_i \in W \rightarrow O_i \notin T$

Every organisation realizes independently a unit profit accounting for $Z(O_i)$.

An organisation aiming at an increase in its profit has the following possibilities:

1. to increase a profit due to a virtual relationship - to realize a profit accounting for $Z_{wk}(O_i)$ - which is a profit of the i-th organisation when $\exists k O_i \in W_k$,

2. to increase a profit due to a traditional relationship - to realize a profit accounting for $Z_{Tl}(O_i)$ - which is a profit of the i-th organisation when $\exists l O_i \in T_l$,

Obviously respectively occurs:

$Z_{wk}(O_i)> Z(O_i)$.

$Z_{Tl}(O_i)> Z(O_i)$.

otherwise an organisation would not desire a relationship.

The organisation aims at earning the biggest profit possible and enters the virtual solution only if its profit $Z_{wk}(O_i)$ is higher than that in traditional relations or when functioning independently.

The organiasation traditionally related do not maximize a unit profit (for each organisation) but they maximize a total profit - for the organisation as a whole.

Calculating the total profit we obtain:

1. for the traditional organisations

$$Z(T_l) = \sum_{j=1}^{L(T_l)} Z_{T_l}(O_j) \geq \sum_{j=1}^{L(T_l)} Z(O_j) \quad where \forall j O_j \in T_l$$

2. for the virtual organisations
$$Z(W_k) = \sum_{j=1}^{L(W_{kl})} Z_{W_{kl}}(O_j) \geq \sum_{j=1}^{L(W_k)} Z(O_j) \quad where \forall j O_j \in W_k$$

Since in the traditional organisation we maximize the profit for the organiasation as a whole and in the virtual organisation we maximize the profit for every single organisation which belongs to it, the dependence occuring for hypothetical groups is as follows:
- profit of the group ($Z_T \geq Z_W \vee Z_T < Z_W$
- whereas the profit of a single organisation ($Z_{T1}O_i \leq Z_{wk}O_i$

The virtual organisation also aims at maximizing the profit in the short term. It results from the fact that decisions are made here in rapidly changing circumstances. The traditional organisation also maximize the profit in the longer term.

Probability of gaining the profit depends on the following basic elements:
1. speed and elasticity of adjusting to changes where the virtual organisations dominate,
2. organisation's positions on the market where the traditional organisations dominate then.

Let P_n denotes the probability of gaining the profit by the organisation, where n denotes a factor, for instance - ethics, which has an impact on the probability. We consider then the relation between $P_n(Z_{T1})$ and $P_n(Z_{Tk})$.

If the probability of gaining the profit is higher for the traditional organisation then such a type of organisation should be established. However, in the situation when at least one organisation of those which can enter the traditional organisation is able to reap a higher profit in the virtual organisation, that is $P_n(Z_{T1}(O_i)) < P_n(Z_{wk}(O_i))$, then such an organisation does not want to join the traditional organisation and tends to set up a virtual one.

Though, accordingly to the attitude of the remaining organisations it can be forced to join the traditional organisation. Then we are dealing with a situation of negotiations.

The possible decisive situations:
1. organisation O_i within the virtual organisation would gain the profit Z_w,
2. organisation O_i within the traditional organisation would gain the profit Z_t whereupon occurs: $Z_w > Z_t$,
3. the remaining organiasations which can establish the traditional organisation together with O_i:
- within the virtual organisation would gain the profit $\overline{Z}_w$
- within the traditional organisation would gain the profit $\overline{Z}_t$ whereupon occurs: $\overline{Z}_t > \overline{Z}_w$

That is why those organisations are likely to offer a bonus accounting for $\Delta < \overline{Z}_w > \overline{Z}_t$ to the organisation O_i for its access to the traditional organisation.

The organisation O_i unless it gets a bonus it will seek to enter a virtual coalition of other organisations from the set Ω which however do not belong to the competitive subset T_t. However, without the organisation O_i it can happen that the traditional organisation will not achieve expected results and the alliance of such a type will not be formed.

Objective and range of the presentation.

The research I have already completed qualifies me to put forward the following hypothesis: The development of virtual organisations primarily depends on the ability to cope with the concern over the unethical behaviour of the whole organisation of this type or its components. So we may say that the concern over the unethical behaviour represents an essential barrier to virtual organisations formation. The concern is voiced by the electorate of virtual organisations, that is the people and organisations directly interested in the outcome of their operations.

Justification of the above hypothesis and its applications are the basic subject of this report. The problem is of vital importance, the more so as virtual organisations are becoming the most dynamically developing type of organisations in these days.

The difficulties in presenting the report result from the fact that the two terms used in the headline, management ethics /often referred to as business ethics/ and virtual organisation, are hard to be clearly define.

Management ethics in virtual organisations.

Management ethics according to R. Griffin [1996 page 138] deals with rules of conduct followed by individual managers in their work. However, we think that the problem is of a broader nature since we take interest in the behaviour of the whole organisation. Individual managers obviously have impact on this behaviour, but in different ways. Such attitude stays in accordance to the opinions of T.M. Gariet and R.J. Klonowski [1986]. They list three areas, which are of particular interest to management ethics. These are:
- an organisation's attitude to its employee,
- an employee's attitude towards his or her organisation,
- an organisation's attitude towards other economic entities,
especially towards its clients and cooperating organisations.

Our interests particularly centre around virtual organisations' attitude towards other economic entities. E. Sternberg writes [1998 page 36 and the following ones] that management ethics is not an external option directed against business, but rigorous, analytical instrument of economic operations. There are different ways of measuring the management ethics value in economic operations. One of them is the harm done by lack of such ethics.

A virtual organisation is a type of organisation in which all the operations take place in a so-called information space, and their specific feature is the high speed of making decisions. In a traditional organisation any forms of cooperation and fulfilling orders go a long way of negotiations in which various specialists, including practicians, are involved. In the event that some doubts arise with regard to a partner's reliability, additional information is gathered about him or her, taking advantage, for example, of a business information agency or a court register. In case we establish virtual organisations in order to carry out a given task, formation procedures are highly simplified. The organisations frequently operate without legal agreements or they are very simplified. It is this high speed of making decisions that is conducive to admitting organisations conduct of which does not stay in accordance to the adopted ethic standard.

Apart from this high speed of making decisions, a virtual organisation is characterized by the following features:
• it does not have any legal authority,
• it may simultaneously enter into many deals done by similar virtual or traditional organisations,
• its links are not long-standing and they are maintained for as long as the effects produced by the joint operations exceed those given by one's own organisation,
• it is highly flexible, which means that it quickly adjusts to a changing environment,
• the participants of a joint undertaking have no prejudice against the others who are different in race, culture, etc.

The above listed features are conducive to establishing a virtual organisation by organisations which have adopted different systems of moral principles. While analysing the functioning of a virtual organisation engaged in real estate trading, the researchers encountered a barrier connected with cultural differences and, as a consequence, different interpretation of the term business ethics. When, for example, a virtual organisation is formed with a country from a cultural circle other than the European one, for the purpose of fulfilling a Polish client's order, a question is raised whether the managers of the two organisations observe the same rules of conduct. It may be stated that there are some universal values but, on the other hand, there are also manners which are specific only to a given cultural circle.

Ethical or unethical conduct of organisations occurs in a particular favourable context. The weak point of virtual organisations here is the fact that organisational contexts of the associated companies are unknown, which, of course, breeds unethical conduct.

Reliabilty assessment of traditional and virtual organisations.

Two forces affect each organisation, which is considering a sense of purpose of joining a virtual organisation. The first one is a desire to generate some additional profit resulting from an opportunity to carry out some additional tasks which such an organisation cannot perform on its own.

The second one is a fear that due to unethical conduct of one of the links chaining virtual organisations, such an organisation will suffer a decrease in the anticipated profit or even, at the worst, incur losses.

Table 1 sets out a comparative view of both traditional and virtual organisations presented by the groups of people who may be referred to as the electorate of these organisations.

For the purpose of the research completed among managers and students, the electorate was divided into the following groups: clients, suppliers, employees, bankers, government administrative staff, investors, university staff. These groups were formed on the basis of self-determination of their members who were asked to which group he or she wants to belong. The following two questions were put:

1. Which type of organisation (traditional or virtual) do you consider to be highly reliable?
2. On which organisation (traditional or virtual) have you set your hopes for the future?

The participants could attach their justification to their answers, but this was not compulsory. The second question was particularly important to the groups of employees and students. This question was a supplementary one, while the first question was a basic one.

Table 1: Reliability assessment of both traditional and virtual organisations - a comparative analysis.

Organisation electorate	Traditional organisation	Virtual organisation
1. Clients	+	-
2. Suppliers	+	-
3. Employees	+	-
4. Bankers	+	-
5. Government institutions	+	-
6. Investors	+	-
7. Universities /students/	?	?

Notes: + clearly positive opinion - negative opinion ? lack of clear answer

The research was conducted as part of training sessions organised for key managerial staff of large and medium sized organisations. Its weakness was the fact that generally it was only during the training sessions that the participants became familiar with the objectives and functions of virtual organisations. Only few of them had heard of such a type of organisations before. Therefore, one may suppose that the above clearly negative opinions on the reliability of virtual organisations are also caused by a fear of the unknown.

Slightly different was the situation in the students' group. The research was conducted among the final year students of the Polish and Japanese College of Computer Technology. The students knew in theory basic functioning aspects of virtual organisations.

Independently of the obtained answers, the researchers tried to make their work complete by discussing the causes of the reported concern over the operations and taking advantage of virtual organisations. The following comments were put forward in individual groups:

Clients - Two issues were raised in this group. The first one related to the quality problem. It is thought that not only the companies famous for their observance of morals will participate in the completion of deals. And if an end performer is known, its sub-performers are unknown. Therefore, all organisations should in great detail test the quality of virtual organisations' performance. The second issue raised was of a different nature. The concern results from imperfect legal regulations, namely a procedure in case of claims, since it may turn out that the organisation against which a claim has been made, is not operational any longer or has no legal successors.

Suppliers - the concern results from the goods being rejected or unduly used. It is thought that special attention should be paid to the settlement of accounts. It is a common belief that the following principle should be observed: 'Money first, goods second'.

Employees - In case of a virtual organisation, they are its potential employees, since they are now working in traditional organisations. Having been asked an additional question why they do not want to work for a virtual organisation, they answered that they fear, first, of the lack of stability and, second, unethical conduct, that is the employer's default on its obligation to pay. In addition, virtual organisations are of lower renown that traditional ones. A concern over very intensive work is still another problem.

Bankers - Banking sector employees openly say that a virtual organisation as a whole may not obtain a bank loan which, however, may be granted to a traditional organisation in spite of its operating within the structure of the virtual organisation. The concern is over the fact who is going to repay the loan. Moreover, if the virtual organisation has no joint assets, security for the loan represents here still another problem.

Investors - This group's members share their opinion on virtual organisations with banking sector employees.

Government institutions - Cooperation with virtual organisations is a major concern to this group's members, which results from the fact that there is no leadership in such organisations, they are unstable and often operate in the global space, and not only within the territory of a given country.

Summing up the research results, we may state that the majority of fears and concerns relates to possible unethical operations of this type of organisations.

Students - who act here as both a virtual organisation's employees and future clients, do not strongly raise the problem of their unethical functioning. They think there exist constantly improving security methods which are, for example, applied for the operations of virtual banks or Internet shops. What do they stress? The possibility of starting business operations even with a very small initial capital. Despite some concern, the students do not, however, present clearly polarized positions as the other groups' members. No ethical reservations are put forward here, but a lot of students think that having a professional career in mind, it is better to work for a stable and renowned organisation.

Ethical dilemmas related to the functioning of virtual organisations.

Quite different ethical problems are connected with the functioning of virtual organisations. One of them is a dilemma whether to conceal the fact of a given organisation being operational within a structure of virtual organisations. In other words, should the clients be informed that a virtual organisation has been established for the purpose of providing a given service or manufacturing a given product? Sometimes we have to cope with the reversed situation. An organisation uses the term 'virtual' to keep the client convinced that he deals with a modern organisation. But in fact, the organisation operates in a traditional system.

The class of management ethics problems connected with the functioning of virtual organisations involves, inter alia, fears of:
1. non-fulfilment by a virtually associated organisation of obligations towards another organisation associated in this way;
2. admitting an organisation which aims at discrediting its partner and, in fact, represents the interests of a competitor;
3. possibility of acting against the interests of a home country; for example, an organisation based in another country intends in this way to escape embargoes or other legal restrictions.

At this point a question may be asked: Do the above fears of unethical actions refer only to virtual organisations, and are not typical for many traditional organisations? The answer is affirmative.

However, especially virtual organisations create conditions conducive to unethical actions, which this report tries to prove. Such actions result, inter alia, from the facts mentioned above, which are: high speed of performing operations, a partner being earlier unknown, 'ad hoc' formation of organisations for the completion of only one undertaking, lack of appropriate legal regulations.

The general concern which appears while analysing the functioning of virtual organisations, is over the fact that the party guilty of unethical conduct will not take any consequences of it. These consequences may, however, be taken by those who acted in good faith and carried out tasks together with 'an unethical organisation'. One of the consequences is, for instance, a so-called 'damage to reputation'.

FINAL CONCLUSIONS

The above presented considerations show that management ethics problems are extremely important for the development of virtual organisations. What are the possibilities of solving such a complicated situation? It seems that solutions applied in the organisations such as negotiations, agreements, verification of partners' reliability, are acceptable only on a very limited scale. Following the path of these solutions may cause the decrease in competitive advantage of virtual organisations over traditional ones. Therefore, along with the progress in inventing new solutions relating to the data safety, much work should be parallelly done over ethical issues and methods of their solving in virtual organisations.

REFERENCES

T.M. Garret, R.J. Klonoski, Business Ethics, Prentice-Hall, Engelewood Cliffs, New-York , 1986

R.W.Griffin, Podstawy zarzadzania organizacjami, PWN ,Warszawa 1996

J. Kisielnicki; Wirtualna organizacja- marzenie czy rzeczywistosc, Computerworld, 16,1997 s. 58.

J. Kisielnicki: Virtual organization as a product of information sociaty; Informatica, vol.22,1,1998 p.3

D.J. Skryme; The Realities of Virtuality, in P.Sieber i J.Griese (eds.) Organizational Virtualness, Simowa Verlag Bern,1998.

E. Strenberg; Just Business, Business Ethic in Action, Warner Books,1995

The Information Security Toolbox

Prof. Rossouw von Solms
Department of Information Technology
Port Elizabeth Technikon, Private Bag X6011, Port Elizabeth 6000, SOUTH AFRICA
Tel: +27 (0)41 504 3604, Fax: +27 (0)41 504 3313, E-mail: rossouw@ml.petech.ac.za

Information has become a very important asset in most organizations today. For this reason, it is imperative that information and the associated resources are properly protected. Traditionally, information assets were protected through a set of physical and technical controls, introduced and maintained by the technical personnel in the Information Services Department. This scenario is no longer adequate and information security needs to be introduced, maintained and managed in a much more comprehensive way to ensure a proper and acceptable level of protection in modern business. The bulk of employees in an everyday organization work with information in an electronic format, and a large percentage of these people are barely computer literate, not to mention information security literate. A second aspect that was not addressed traditionally was the involvement of top management in the process of introducing information security. Information security is a business issue and not a technical issue any longer. For this reason, information security objectives, strategies and policies are required to introduce security in an orderly way into the organization. Therefore, a total new approach to introducing information security into an organization is required in the modern organization, specifically because information security and electronic commerce go hand in hand.

The objective of this paper is to introduce a new comprehensive approach to introduce information security in an organization. This approach will ensure that all information security objectives and policies are in line with business objectives and policies. This approach will also ensure that the most effective set of security controls is identified, introduced and maintained. Further, that a set of associated procedures accompanies each security control to ensure effectiveness. Through this approach, top management will get involved in the process and every user of information or associated resources will be forced to follow specific procedures to ensure a proper level of information security.

This new comprehensive approach to information security is the result of an extended research project and the results are currently being implemented in a software tool, called the Information Security Toolbox. Information Security Toolbox will be a forms-driven system that will cater specifically for small to medium sized organizations, but should also be useable in larger environments.

The Tool will firstly identify the requirement for and dependency on IT services in the organization. This will be done through some business analysis process. Based on this, security objectives will be deduced by the logic from the Toolbox. These security objectives will define a specific security requirement to be implemented in the organization. The security requirement will dictate an information security policy, spelling out clearly what the organization envisages to accomplish through their information security program. The individual policy statements will map onto some information security controls that need to be introduced to obtain the level of security spelt out in the policy. Each of these security controls will trigger some security procedures that need to be introduced in the organization to ensure that each control functions maximally. This whole process is summarized in figure 1.

It can clearly be seen from the architecture of the Toolbox, that the level of security required and dictated by the information security policy, is carefully analyzed through a thorough business analysis process, taking all relevant business objectives and policies into account. The security objectives are stated in terms of the five security services, namely, authentication, authorization, confidentiality, integrity and non-repudiation, as defined in ISO 7498-2. The controls can be drawn from any relevant security baseline manual. In the case of the Toolbox, it is based on the British Standard; BS7799.

The outputs from the complete process are:
• A complete Information Security Policy document,
• A set of security controls and
• A set of procedures that supports each security control.

The Information Security Policy document will include a definition of information security, a statement of support from top management, the security objectives, the individual security policy statements and lastly, penalties and disciplinary actions.

The set of controls will be drawn from BS7799, and depending on the policy, can vary from entry level security (the ten key controls) through to an advanced level of security, meaning full BS7799 security. The control procedures would be in the form of user procedures, help the users to effectively utilize the security controls. The Information Security Toolbox, should enable every small to medium sized organization to effectively define a security policy and automatically determines which BS7799 controls are required to implement this level of security. This should ensure that every organization can introduce a proper level of information security in an affordable way.

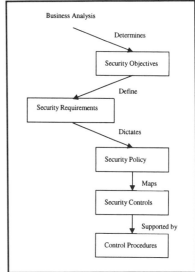

Fig. 1: Information Security Toolbox Architecture

Information Technology Sophistication in Health Care Institutions: Development and Validation of a Measurement Instrument

Guy Paré, Ph.D.
Associate Professor, Information Technology Department, Ecole des Hautes Etudes Commerciales, 3000, Cote-Ste-Catherine, Montreal, (Quebec), Canada H3T 2A7
Phone: (514)340-6812, Fax: (514)340-6132, E-mail: guy.pare@hec.ca

Claude Sicotte, Ph.D.
Associate Professor, Health Management Department, University of Montreal, C.P. 6128 Succ. Centre-Ville, Montreal (Quebec), Canada H3C 3J7
Phone: (514)343-5611, Fax: (514)343-2448, E-mail: claude.sicotte@umontreal.ca

It is widely recognized that major changes are underway in the delivery of health care in Canada. As a result of these changes, health care facilities are being forced to adopt and implement information technologies in order to deliver higher quality care to patients while at the same time holding down costs. A fundamental problem facing medical informatics and information systems researchers wishing to identify the effects of information technology (IT) on health care institutions is the necessity of characterizing IT for operationalization purposes as an independent, dependent or moderating variable within a conceptual framework. There exists no recognized characterization of IT in terms of its level of sophistication in health care organizations, and thus no validated instrument for use in empirical research and practice. Such an instrument should identify information technology's fundamental dimensions and position health care institutions on each of these dimensions, thus establishing an IT sophistication profile and allowing comparison between institutions. The objective of this research project is to take a first step toward an understanding of IT sophistication and the measurement and validation of this construct in health care institutions.

Following Raymond & Paré (1992) who developed a similar measurement instrument in the context of small manufacturing businesses, we initiated our study by performing an in-depth review of the different models and variables proposed in the information systems, health management and medical informatics literatures as characterizing explicitly or implicitly the concept of IT sophistication. From this review, we defined IT sophistication as a construct which refers to the nature, diversity and complexity of technological devices and software applications used to support clinical and administrative processes in health care institutions. The general framework for our classification of IT sophistication is presented in Figure 1.

Technological sophistication basically reflects the diversity and complexity of the hardware devices used by health care institutions, referring to various domains such as medical imaging, bar coding devices, data warehousing, wireless networks and PACS equipment. Functional sophistication consists of the processes or activities (e.g., vital sign recording, medication administration, staff scheduling, post-operative report dictation) supported by computer technologies. Finally, informational integration sophistication refers to the degree to which computer applications are integrated via a common database or any electronic communication link such as EDI. These three dimensions shall be assessed for each of the health care institutions' core activities, namely, patient care activities, clinical support activities (e.g., laboratory, pharmacy, radiology), materials management activities and financial management activities (Bourke 1994; Austin 1992).

After defining the building blocks of the concept of IT sophistication in the specific context of heath care institutions, we moved on to the operationalization of the various dimensions. The work of Singh (1997), Austin (1992) and Sicotte, Tilquin & Valois (1991) were instrumental during this phase as they helped us in elaborating a thorough classification of technologies, processes and integration applications in this context. The next step consisted of the actual elaboration of the measurement instrument.

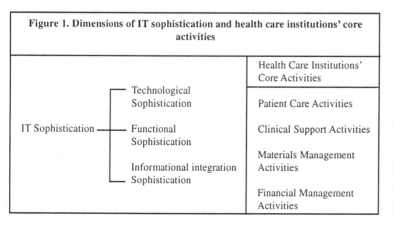

Figure 1. Dimensions of IT sophistication and health care institutions' core activities

IT Sophistication
- Technological Sophistication
- Functional Sophistication
- Informational integration Sophistication

Health Care Institutions' Core Activities
- Patient Care Activities
- Clinical Support Activities
- Materials Management Activities
- Financial Management Activities

Measurement of research constructs is neither simple nor straightforward. In order to ensure content validity, we decided to conduct interviews with the director of information systems, systems specialists and the heads of clinical departments at one of the largest and busiest hospitals in the province of Quebec. A total of 20 in-depth interviews were conducted. An interview guide was developed and used during each interview. Respondents were first required to identify the technologies and computer applications that were in use in their department or hospital-wide and discuss their particularities while focusing on the processes or functions being supported by these systems. Secondly, participants were asked to assess the degree of integration of the various applications in used in their department with other applications both within and outside their department. Finally, they were invited to share their knowledge about any other technologies and/or computer applications, possibly more recent ones, used in other institutions. The conclusions extracted from all the interviews were later used to bring modifications to the initial version of the instrument. As expected, the initial content of the questionnaire appeared to be measuring well the reality of IT sophistication in the hospital context. However, the interviews have brought an undeniably important pool of information that once incorporated into the questionnaire made it even more valid and representative of the reality.

In order to refine further our questionnaire instrument it was decided to perform a pre-test with a relatively small sample of individuals who give the researchers feedback on its pertinence before it is sent to the potential respondents. The questionnaire was sent to three representatives of the targeted population, namely, hospital information systems (HIS) directors. Following the mailing, we conducted one in-depth interview with each of the directors. The reviewers were very thorough in their comments which helped change the total feel of the questionnaire to make it more appealing. The major criticism that was made concerns the size of the questionnaire which was though to be too long. The order of the sections was also criticized and suggestions were made to reshuffle their sequence. Moreover, some comments were made about the use of the scales (wording) and suggestions were offered to improve them. In fact, most of the changes made specifically affected the format of the instrument without affecting its substance. The resulting measurement instrument will be presented at the Conference.

The next step of the current research project will be to complete the validation process of the IT sophistication measurement instrument (construct validity, predictive validity, and reliability) through an empirical study (survey) that will encompass the health care institutions in Canada. A fully validated instrument will then be used as a diagnostic tool by hospital managers interested in better situating their institution in terms of its adoption and use of information technologies. Ultimately, a validated tool will be useful in investigating the link between IT and health care organizations' performance.

REFERENCES

Austin, C.J. (1992). Information Systems for Health Services Administration. Fourth edition. Health Administration Press, Ann Arbor: Michigan.

Bourke, M.K. (1994). Strategy and Architecture of Health Care Information Systems. Springer-Verlag.

Raymond, L. & Paré, G. (1992). Measurement of IT Sophistication in Small Manufacturing Businesses. Information Resources Management Journal, 5(2), 4-16.

Sicotte, C., Tilquin, C. & M. Valois. (1991). La gestion de l'information dans les établissements de la santé: l'expérience québécoise. Presses de l'Association des hôpitaux du Canada.

Singh, K. (1997). The Impact of Technological Complexity and Interfirm Cooperation on Business Survival. Academy of Management Journal, 40(2), 339-367.

Creating a Business Transition Model in the Web Commerce

Minnie Yi-Miin Yen
University of Alaska Anchorage, afmyy@uaa.alaska.edu

Hao Lou
Ohio University, Athens, lou@oak.cats.ohiou.edu

I. INTRODUCTION

Today, it is important for an organization, no matter large or small, to develop and post its Web site to the public and conduct Internet-related business activities. This important strategic movement is usually driven by the requirements of extending company exposures, providing better user service, gaining competitive advantage, reflecting market demand and reducing operational cost. However, successful companies rarely support business strategy without rigorous planning, reviews, and concrete return-on-investment goals, except when it comes to this Web application development. This is because a lot of companies approach the Web at a tactical and experimental level without having business plans to support its development and expansion.

When more advanced Internet technologies were developed and being adopted in Web business development, creating Web sites that replace rather than simply supplement traditional methods of conducting business becomes possible. However, many organizations will face the challenge of figuring out what they can do, should do, and must do on the Web to gain its competitive advantage and market share in this dynamic electronic market place. Although it is realized that competitive advantage can be gained and sustained through a delicate balancing business act that is less about being first than it is combining the right vision with the right offering at the right time. How to develop an appropriate and flexible strategic plan is vital for developing and conducting an Web commerce (WC) business.

In this paper, we are trying to establish a transition business model to experiment the Web strategy evolution based on changing organization goals, technology availability, competitors' movement, customer demand, and cost. We hope this business model will be able to help management understand the situations and make decision in this highly strategic business-transforming endeavor.

II. WEB BUSINESS TRANSITION PHASES

There are a variety of driving forces which will influence an organization in its Web business development. These forces include organization's goals, its technological capabilities, competitors' movement, market demands, and costs. According to GartnerGroup's categorization, the Web business activities can be separated into the following phases:

1. Basic presence: This is the bare-minimum corporate site. The organization simply creates a digital form of corporate information and marketing collateral, and posts it on the Web. Basically, the information is largely static and just need to be updated periodically.
2. Prospecting: Organizations at this stage focus on marketing, but the tactics employed are far more advanced than traditional marketing. Beyond adding substantially more corporate, product, and service information than the first phase, the organizations in this realm are adding interactive features that allow them to collect visitor-specific information so that they can tailor content for every visitor who returns. The primary functions is to make visitors comfortable with the site by making it easy to use, providing personalized content, and linking the site to customer support functional area through different approaches such as E-mail.
3. Business integration: This marks the real corner stone movement of conducting Electronic Commerce business. Due to increased process efficiencies, the organization can expect profitability out from this phase and should make a strategic planning by creating the Web site as an established business channel and part of their bottom line. The businesses in this realm should feature lively online communities where current and potential customers meet. In this case, electronic transactions, e-mail based customer service, and advanced search techniques all create a high degree of customer comfort and interaction. However, this level of activities only supplements similar business processes performed offline. It doesn't replace them.
4. Business transformation: This level of activities can help to either create new Internet-based business or migrate traditional business to the Internet. Integrated back-office functions streamline supplier and customer communications and replace paper-based functions. This is the phase which organizations can expect to cut operating costs and increase both the breadth and depth of the sales channels and marketing base [Gartner Group].
5. Organization extension and integration: This level of Web business activities start to explore the most potentials and benefits of the Internet and at the same time, can get to be extremely complicated, from both technologies and organizational aspects. These business activities can be achieved in many forms, either as a way to outsource business processes or to better link themselves with their trading partners and customers. As companies move to this virtual- or extended-organizational structure, they will find a quite different business model with more functionally robust application. The available information technologies such as shared services, Internet delivery, intelligent agents and message brokers that can support this level of activities will be highly desirable and widely adopted.

III. THE WEB BUSINESS TRANSITION MODEL

In this project, a Web business transition model will be discussed and developed based on the above foreseeable Web business evolution patterns. There are three dimensions of factors will be put into consideration. The first dimension includes the driving forces of Web business development, such as organizational goals, market demands, and competitor's movement, etc. The second dimension includes the features of Web applications, such as content, functionality, organization structures and security, etc. The third dimension includes information technology capabilities such as information infrastructure, Internet delivery, agent technologies and their coordination and integration etc.

A. The Driving Forces Of Web Business Development

Web business development is a strategic movement for an organization. There are several driving forces, internal as well as external, to encourage the organization toward achieving its goals. First of all, the goals of the corporation, such as profit seeking, cost saving, customer service quality improving, etc. can all serve as a valid force to push the organization to adopt this new area of business. Other forces include stakeholders expectation, competitive advantage, new market penetration, and new business model innovation can all explore new business opportunities for the corporation. Web business process analysis can help to identify the reengineering operations streamlining opportunities. To understand the business driving forces associated with the analysis of an organization's strengths, weaknesses, opportunities, and threats can build up a foundation for the more detailed Web application systems design and planning effort.

B. The Features of Web Applications

Based on the requirements of the Web business, the functions of the web applications can be categorized into front-end merchandising, back-end fulfillment and other supporting features. The front-end merchandising features can include but not limit to the following areas: 1. Search capabilities, 2. Product content, 3. Product pricing, 4. Customer profiling, 5. Shopping basket, and 6. Product configuration. The back-end fulfillment features include 1. Order processing, 2. Payment, 3. Shipping, 4. Order tracking while the other supporting features include 1. Customer service, 2. Business image promoting and advertising, and 3. General security and privacy protection.

C. Information Technology Capabilities

As Web sites increasingly add dynamic behaviors and database-driven content, the skill for Web site developers and functions of the Web application development software become increasingly technical and complicated. Usually, the Web business applications have a heterogeneous staff, tools, and platforms. Due to the evolving and immaturity features of technology, many Web applications must implement complex features and characteristics through an aggregation of HTML, JavaScript, Java, SQL, third-party components and plug-ins, image maps, and software agents. All of these technologies must be maintained and applied in sync with each other.

IV. THE EXPERIMENT

We are trying to create an E-Commerce experiment market with a variety of Web business applications that will follow the business transition model with consideration of all three dimensions. Students who participate in this experiment will be separated into two groups, the developers and the customers. MIS major students who are taking Web design and development course will play as the roles of developers whose responsibility is to develop Web business applications based on the forces and requirements from both internal and external. The Business major students who are taking E-Commerce course or Management Information System course will play the role of customers, potential customers, and business partners. They are the ones actually use the Web to conduct shopping and also provide feedback and make request to change the way the organizations doing their businesses. All the Web applications will be developed with Lotus Domino.Merchant and they are created basically according to the different evolving phases described in section II. In this experiment, hopefully, by controlling the factors in three dimensions, the desirable business functions, and the available technologies, it can help us understand more about the business transition happen in the E-Commerce.

Eventually, this business transition model should be able to provide management general guidelines in the development of their Web business strategy and at the same time, it will help them in evaluating their Web development tools, budget and business plan.

Predicting the Success of Business Process Redesign Projects: The Australian Experience (Research-in-progress[i])

Ravi Patnayakuni
Department of Computer and Information Sciences, Temple University, Philadelphia PA 19122

INTRODUCTION

Michael Hammer (1990), in what may be considered as one of the most influential business management article in recent times, argues that Adam Smith's industrial paradigm is outdated in today's business environment. It is reasoned that the paradigm has for over two centuries ensured that work in organizations has been broken down into its most basic tasks and these tasks organized into functional units. As a result, the traditional hierarchical model of organization optimizes functional unit or sub-process effectiveness at the expense of an organization's core processes. Hammer proposed the practice of Reengineering[ii] which refers to the re-organization of work around an organization's core processes so that an organization most effectively meets the needs of its customer.

BPR is a planned program of change with the intention of achieving significant improvements in performance. Top managers are looking to BPR to maintain or advance the competitive position and profitability of their organizations with the objective of: decreasing costs, increasing customer service and output quality, decreasing product development time, and increase in the quality of work life of employees (Davenport and Short, 1990). Today business process reengineering (BPR) is an important phenomenon, growing rapidly in acceptance since the early 1990's. In a 1993 survey of 500 CIOs, conducted by Deloitte and Touche, it was found that the average CIO was involved in 4.4 reengineering projects in 1993 up from 1.6 projects in 1992 (Moad 1993). "Facilitating and managing business process redesign" was regarded by top IS executives as the second most important issue faced by them in 1994/95 (Brancheau, Janz and Wetherbe, 1996). Quite naturally, BPR has attracted a lot of interest from both practitioners and academics.

Although BPR has gained widespread acceptance, BPR initiatives have not always delivered the desired outcomes. Hammer and Champy (1994) stated that between 50 and 70 percent of reengineering projects do not achieve the goals set out for them. Recognizing the importance of understanding the factors that promote success of BPR efforts, a number of researchers have undertaken studies of BPR practices in the North American or European context (e.g., Grover, Jeong, Kettinger & Teng 1995, Clemons, Thatcher & Row 1995, Hall, Rosenthal & Wade 1993, Miles, Coleman & Creed 1995). Apart from the work done by researchers at the Melbourne Business School (Broadbent & Weill 1995, Broadbent et al. 1996, Butler 1993 & 1997) few studies have been done in the Australian context. Furthermore, while a variety of success factors have been enumerated and studied, we decided in particular to examine the diagnostic measure proposed by Hammer and Stanton in their book *The Reengineering Revolution*, published in 1994. The measure consisted of three factors labeled as reengineering leadership, organizational readiness, and style of implementation, as critical to the success of any BPR effort. We adopted this focus because, in addition to having been proposed by one of the originators of the concept it is, (1) most likely to be read and considered relevant by practitioners and (2) induced from practical consulting experience in contrast to being theoretically derived. The two objectives we have in this paper are to

1. Investigate the measurement and predictive properties of Hammer and Stanton's three critical success factors as enumerated in their diagnostic measure
2. Collect and analyze the data in the context of Australian business environment.

The rest of the paper is organized as follows. In the next section we briefly discuss the three factors outlined by Hammer and Stanton. The third section describes the methodology used in our study. The fourth section presents our analysis and some initial conclusions.

SUCCESS FACTORS

Hammer and Stanton's diagnostic measure highlighted the importance of three factors, reengineering leadership, organizational readiness and style of implementation. The diagnostic as proposed by them consisted of twenty questions[iii] that relate to the organizational context prior to reengineering. According to the measure, high scores on the diagnostic measure indicate an organization that is well positioned for success in its BPR efforts.

Management support and leadership in reengineering efforts has been identified in much of the literature as perhaps the most significant contributing factor to the success of an initiative. Top management support is necessary to develop faith throughout the organisation in the project and a respect for the project team (Hall et al. 1993, Hammer & Stanton 1994, Hoopes 1995). Hammer and Stanton (1994) place a strong emphasis on reengineering leadership in their diagnostic measure. The six points on leadership are rated highly be them in terms of the minimum numbers that an organisation should score before it attempts to embark on a reengineering project. They argue that management support is highly influential on the outcome of BPR initiatives and that senior managers can engender support for a project through the sheer force of their passion or belief.

A natural tendency in most people is to prefer the status quo to change. Employees will resist change, especially when it threatens to alter the way they do their work or their work related skills. Reengineering often demands an immense change in both organization structure and the way business is done and as such, resistance to change is inevitable. What makes reengineering a particularly complex exercise is, '...its cross-functional nature increases the number of stakeholders, thereby increasing the complexity of the effort (Davenport and Short, 1990:23)." This is reinforced by the questions on organizational readiness in the diagnostic measure. These questions refer to the organization's understanding, acceptance, and commitment to the proposed changes.

Managing a BPR initiative requires assigning team members time and responsibility to the projects and managing the communication both within the project team and between the team and the rest of the organization. "Many large scale projects fail because managers have underestimated the planning, logistical, and organizational complexity. Without a respect for the projects enormousness, well-meaning managers can easily be overwhelmed by its demands." In addition to project management and planning issues, Hammer and Stanton (1994) also cover process delineation issues under the umbrella of style of implementation.

The three factors of reengineering leadership, organizational readiness, and style of implementation overlap with many of the critical success factors identified by other studies, they also exclude factors like IT competence and infrastructure that are considered important by some. For the purpose of this study we restrict ourselves to the factors highlighted by Hammer and Stanton (1994).

METHODOLOGY

We adopted a quantitative approach towards collecting data to examine the influence of the three factors in predicting success of BPR efforts. Accordingly a questionnaire was developed and administered to business organizations in Australia to facilitate data collection from a large and geographically disperse sample.

Measurement

Hammer and Stanton published a set of 20 items that could be collectively used to assess the three organizational factors of reengineering leadership, organizational readiness and style of implementation. In order to improve the clarity of the questions and decrease ambiguity the original 20 items were expanded to 31 items. For each item the respondent was requested to indicate their agreement/disagreement with the appropriateness of a given statement to their organization on a five point Likert scale. The dependent variable adopted for this study was perceived project success, measured by one five-point scale question, which according to DeLone and McLean (1992) the most widely used measure of MIS success. The set of 31 items represents a subset of the questions in the survey instrument, which included questions on a number of other issues related to BPR. In this paper we maintain our focus on the three factors identified by Hammer and Stanton.

Sample

Data for the study was collected by a nation-wide mail survey of Australian organizations. The questionnaire was sent to senior managers in 1000 top Australian companies based on their revenue. The list contained both the private or public sector organizations. The questionnaire package sent to these organizations contained a cover letter addressed to the senior manager asking him/her to pass the enclosed questionnaire on to a project leader of a recent reengineering project. Each project leader was asked to respond to the questionnaire in the context of one specific project. The unit of analysis in this survey was therefore, a single process redesign project. The survey was completed in the early part of 1998.

We received a total of 207 responses of which 135 respondents indicated that they had not undertaken reengineering and 72 returned a completed questionnaire. The survey therefore produced a response rate of 20.7 percent. The potential for non-response bias was addressed by profiling both early and late responders and comparing the two groups according to techniques described by Fowler (1993). This analysis yielded no significant differences between the groups, suggesting that there was no non-response bias in the data collected.

Sample Profile

The average reengineering project leader had been employed with the current organization for 2.08 years and reported having an average of 10.5 months of experience with reengineering. A majority of the projects, in excess of 70%, were completed in less than two years. Project teams on an average consisted of 4 members. The scope of reengineering was single business division in 33 percent of cases, two or more divisions in 29 percent of cases, and organization-wide in 38 percent of cases. Responses indicated that consultants were used in 64 percent of the projects in the sample.

ANALYSIS & DISCUSSION

We began by analyzing the psychometric properties of the three factors. Only one factor, style of implementation, was found to be unidimensional in factor analysis with adequate reliability. The other two factors after subsequent analysis were broken down to leadership ability, leadership empowerment, organizational attitude towards reengineering, customer awareness and belief in leadership. All the factors were unidimensional and adequately reliable. Results of this analysis are summarized in table 1.

Next we examined the predictive ability of the diagnostic measure as proposed. When Hammer and Stanton explain how the diagnostic measure is to be used, they calculate a score for each organization that is a sum of each of the items in the scale. Accordingly we added up all the items and examined the correlation of this score to overall success of the BPR effort. The score had a correlation of 0.29 with the overall success measure which was significant at p = 0.005. This seems to suggest that Hammer and Stanton's diagnostic measure has good predictive ability. At the same time we have to take into account that the linear sum of all items

Table 1				
Factor	No. of Items	Eigenvalue	Variance Explained (%)	Reliability (alpha)
Style of implementation	6	2.641	44.02	0.73
Organizational belief in leadership	3	2.179	72.62	0.81
Organizational awareness of customers	2	1.574	78.9	
Organizational attitude towards reengineering	3	1.726	57.53	0.63
Leadership ability	6	3.892	64.86	0.89
Leadership empowerment	3	1.941	64.7	0.72

has as a scale has very poor reliability (alpha = 0.20) and that the measure has a number of dimensions which may or may not influence reengineering success. As such the diagnostic measure may not be a very reliable indicator of success. Also it is desirable to have greater insight into which factors are likely to contribute to successful BPR efforts.

A regression model with all the above factors as predictors showed that they were not significant predictors of BPR success (adjusted r squared of 0.02). A backward regression was used to find out which factors were likely to help in explaining the overall success in BPR. The analysis showed that organizational belief in leadership and the style of implementation, when used as independent variables produced a model that was significant at the p = 0.026. However, the coefficients for neither of the two variables were significant. This suggests that a more complex model needs to be used to explain the data. Accordingly we then tried to find out if the rest of the variables together explained any of the two independent variables. We found that they were indeed significantly associated with each of the independent variables. The three regression models are shown in Table 2. The results suggest a multi-level model of BPR success where organizational factors are likely to the style of implementation, and belief in leadership, which in turn is likely to influence the success of a BPR effort.

Initial results of the study reveal some interesting results. Hammer and Stanton's diagnostic measure consists of a number of underlying factors and have a more complex underlying structure then three factor structure indicated by them. Furthermore our analysis indicates a multi-level model of BPR success. If we examine the relationship between different factors, the relationships do seem to have face validity. Ability of the leadership, the extent to which leadership in the organization is empowered and the organization's atti-

Table 2			
Dependent Variable (N=88) Overall success of BPR project			
Adjusted R squared	F		Significance
0.060	3.807		0.026
Independent variables	Standardized coefficients	t	Significance
Organizational belief in leadership	0.171	1.269	0.208
Style of Implementation	0.143	1.065	0.290
Dependent Variable (N=88) Organizational belief in leadership			
Adjusted R squared	F		Significance
0.654	60.35		0.000
Independent variables	Standardized coefficients	t	Significance
Leadership ability	0.362	4.755	0.000
Leadership empowerment	0.388	4.858	0.000
Organizational attitude towards reengineering	0.247	3.576	0.001
Dependent variable (N=88) Style of implementation			
Adjusted R squared	F		Significance
0.592	46.506		0.000
Independent variables	Standardized coefficients	t	Significance
Leadership ability	0.465	5.615	0.000
Leadership empowerment	0.246	2.838	0.006
Organizational attitude towards reengineering	0.237	3.161	0.002

tude towards reengineering are likely to influence its belief in its leadership. Likewise the style of implementation is also likely to depend on these factors. Finally the style of implementation and organizational belief in leadership are more likely to directly influence the success of any BPR effort.

There are number of opportunities for further study. We need to employ more sophisticated tools of analysis such as path models to fully explicate the multi-level model that seems to be suggested by the data. We also need to corroborate our results with data collected from the rest of the survey in order to validate our conclusions.

Our conclusions are based on initial analysis and need to be interpreted with caution. There are also a number of limitations to our study. This is the first time that Hammer and Stanton's diagnostic has been investigated. Our results need to be replicated with more data. In the questionnaire, respondents were required to recall the organizational context at a point of time in the past order to answer many of the questions. The ability of the respondents to recall past events can potentially lead to errors. A survey based study that uses perceptual measures poses certain problems because of the potential for bias; however, for this research a mail survey was the most effective way to reach a large number of geographically dispersed respondents.

REFERENCES

Brancheau, J. C., Janz, B. D. and Wetherbe, J. C. (1996) Key issues in information systems management 1994-95 SIM Delphi results. MIS Quarterly, 20:2, 225-242.

Broadbent, M. and Weill, P. (1995). Busting up the Business: Different approaches to Business Process Redesign and IT Infrastructure Investments. MIS (Australia), 42-48.

Broadbent, M., Weill, P. and St. Clair, D. (1996). The implications of IT infrastructure for business process redesign. Melbourne Business School, The University of Melbourne: Melbourne.

Butler, C. (1993). The role of information technology in business process redesign: observations from the literature. Melbourne Business School, University of Melbourne: Melbourne.

Butler, C. (1997). Business Process Redesign: The Australian experience. Melbourne Business School, University of Melbourne: Melbourne.

Clemons, E. K., Thatcher, M. E. and Row, M. C. (1995) Identifying sources of reengineering failures A study of the behavioral factors contributing to reengineering risks. Journal of Management Information Systems, 12:2, 9-36.

De Lone, W. and McLean, E. R. (1992) Information systems success: the quest for the dependent variable. Information Systems Research, 3:1, 60-95.

Fowler, F. J. J. (1993) Survey research methods. Sage Publications: Newbury Park.

Grover, V., Jeong, S. R., Kettinger, W. J. and Teng, J. T. C. (1995) The implementation of business process reengineering. Journal of Management Information Systems, 12:1, 109-144.

Hall, G., Rosenthal, J. and Wade, J. (1993) How to make reengineering really work. Harvard Business Review, 71:6, 119-131.

Hammer, M. (1990) Reengineering Work: Don't Automate Obliterate. Harvard Business Review, 68:4, 104-112.

Hammer, M. and Stanton, S. A. (1994) The reengineering revolution: a handbook. Harper Business: New York.

Hammer, M. and Champy, J. (1993) Reengineering the corporation : a manifesto for business revolution. Nicholas Brealey Publishing, Allen & Unwin: London: St. Leonards, N.S.W.

Hoopes, J. (1995) Western civilisation versus the flat organisation. In Burke, G. and Peppard, J., (Eds.); Examining business process re-engineering: current perspectives and research directions, Kogan Page, London.

Miles, R. E., Coleman, H. J., Jr. and Creed, W. E. D. (1995) Keys to success in corporate redesign. California Management Review, 37:3, 128-145.

Moad, J. (1993). Does reengineering really work? Datamation.

ENDNOTES

i The study was partly funded by grant from the University of Melbourne, Australia. We also acknowledge the contribution of Felicity Murphy, Dr. Peter Seddon (University of Melbourne), and Dr. Sandy Staples (Kingston University) in conducting the study.

ii We use the term Business Process Redesign in the study to refer to business practices that have been variously referred to as Reengineering, Process redesign, Business Process Reengineering etc. The definition of BPR adopted in this study was:

A deliberate (planned) change, typically enabled by information technologies in an attempt to redesign a business process to achieve performance breakthroughs in measures such as quality, speed, customer service, and cost.

iii The original items and the items used in the study are not presented here due to space constraints. They are available upon request from the author.

Integrating the Internet and Teamwork Across Finance and Management Information Systems

Dennis Bialaszewski, Indiana State University, Terre Haute, IN 812-237-2113, 812-237-7675 (fax) sdjessie@mama.indstate.edu

Thomas Pencek, Meredith College, Raleigh, NC 919-760-8620, 919-760-8470 (fax) pencekt@meredith.edu

INTRODUCTION

The Internet is increasingly being integrated into the curriculum in schools of business. It is possible to use search engines such as Yahoo, Excite, etc., to search for information on a myriad of topics. Furthermore, many companies have structured home pages in which they provide certain information, such as annual reports. Moreover, teamwork is becoming a large part of the pedagogy and the Internet makes experiential learning via cyber teams a possibility. It is imperative that we offer our students the best possible education utilizing the new technologies. Corporate Advisory Boards continually provide feedback reinforcing the need for teamwork and now many companies are having teams communicating electronically through the Internet.

This paper discusses the planning of a group project between two schools, one in Indiana and the other in North Carolina. The class in Indiana is Introduction to Management Information Systems (MIS) and the class in North Carolina is Corporation Finance. Students from each school form a team to collect financial data. The data source is the EDGAR database as maintained by the Securities and Exchange Commission. The students will also explore the companies on their website. It is a follow up to a previous project two years ago. The project will take place during the Spring 1999 semester.

PROJECT

The project has three phases. Phase one consists of a getting to know one another and they communicate certain personal information about themselves. This information will include items such as hometown, major, etc. The students have to send an attachment of this information to each professor as a group report. This report is due in mid-February.

Phase two is where the students communicate their computer backgrounds to one another. Furthermore, they report the computer facilities of their respective schools to their teammates. This information is compiled and then reported to each professor. This report is due in late-March.

Phase three is the primary purpose of the endeavor. From the EDGAR database and the company's website, students will be required to compute certain financial ratios. These ratios are the profit margin and total asset turnover. These ratios determine the return on assets ratios. They will be required to compute these two ratios for two companies who are competitors in the computer industry. An example of this might be Dell Computer with Gateway. The students in the Corporate Finance class have assignment to explain what these ratios measure to the students in the MIS class. The students in the MIS class make a presentation to their professor on what they learned. This report is due in mid-April.

Planning this project presented some challenges. First of all, most of the students in the MIS class are freshman. The students in the Finance class are mostly seniors. The computer skills of the MIS students are assumed to be minimal. The professor at the North Carolina school has no idea of his student's computer abilities. Another problem was getting around the Spring breaks of the school since they didn't coincide.

Another issue dealt with the grading of the project. For the students to take such a project seriously, the professors agreed to have the project as a whole count as 20 percent of the student's grade. It was felt a lower figure would not provide a proper incentive for the students to do a good job. This was a problem previously where one school had a low weight assigned to the grade; it was found that these students did not put much effort into the project.

GOALS AND OBJECTIVES

One of the goals of the projects is to show how teamwork can be enhanced through the Internet. It will be an interesting test of teamwork since the students do not meet face to face. It is expected that the students in the Finance class see how the Internet can enhance their learning of financial statements and investing. Furthermore, they use real life companies who have financial statements that may be complex.

The integration of the two functional areas is an important consideration. From the MIS standpoint, the students learn about the uses of the databases and the Internet.

In the previous project, the following observations were made. Successful teams noticed they had a strong facilitator. However, they became aware of the consequences when the team depended on one individual. In a couple of cases, something happened to that individual and they could not complete the duties. Another issue is the timing issue where students waited until the last day to actually try to do the project. In the self-analysis by students at the end of the semester, they found the exercise to be quite useful. It is hoped that similar results are obtained.

REFERENCES

1. Bialaszewski, D., Pencek, T., Zaher, T., "Integrating the Internet into Finance Courses," Proceedings of Academy of Financial Services, 1995.
2. Bialaszewski, D., Case, T., Pencek, T., Oberholzer, M., and Wood, R., "Pitfalls to Avoid When Incorporating Electronic Teams Into Coursework," Proceedings of International Academy of Information Management, 1997.

Inter-Organizational Structures for Strategic Advantage

Anne Banks Pidduck (Computer Science Department) and David M. Dilts (Management Sciences Department)
University of Waterloo, Waterloo, Ontario, Canada 519-888-4567, Fax 519-885-1208, apidduck@uwaterloo.ca

INTRODUCTION

Recent research has shown that immediate dissemination of knowledge does not lead to better performance and at times actually hinders performance. [2] Our research is a study of the organizational structures of extended enterprises. Whenever an enterprise wishes to partner, they must share knowledge. Is there an optimum network of partners for knowledge sharing? For strategic advantage? To move the right information to the right people at the right time, we need excellent personnel and technology networks. If we are successful within the firm, we will want to extend this success to achieve competitive advantage against other firms in our market.

We are comparing different types of knowledge sharing networks within and between companies to determine whether one network is better than another network. Different reporting structures may hinder or improve knowledge sharing internally and externally, thus directly affecting the firm's success. Examples of knowledge sharing networks might be traditional hierarchical networks and peer-to-peer sharing networks. In the former, one person controls all knowledge management and sharing. In the latter, individuals within the organization are free to share ideas and suggest new ways of working to better the firm. If one network appears to work better than the others do, we want to find the optimum variables that contribute to the success.

Extending internal network structures, we are studying which firm will win when two or more firms are competing in a complex, chaotic environment. Given the same internal employee skills, finances, and physical assets, but better ways of working together, can one firm achieve greater success? Companies form strategic alliances and cooperative arrangements regularly to compete globally. They have organizational groupings within their command-of-control. How will the local structures compete with other organizations with other structures? Who will win, under what circumstances?

An interesting example of competing global networks is the battle among large computer, telephone and cable companies for their part of the Internet communications system. Multibillion dollar rewards and a worldwide customer base are available to the organization which can provide the first, fastest, cheapest, or best system for Internet use. The company with the best combination of people, information technology, networks and knowledge will achieve a tremendous strategic advantage.

Many new start-up firms are selling knowledge in one form or another. Established organizations are beginning to appreciate the value of their human and intellectual assets. Research and development and knowledge sharing are becoming a continuous, integral part of production system evolution. Continuing feedback and evolution with inter-firm collaboration can produce significant gains for many firms. Better, faster information does not necessarily equal better performance, however. Too much knowledge can produce information overload. This can overwhelm people, slow decision-making, require additional communication and hinder strategic advantage. Because of this, we must measure the information and the performance separately.

Part of our research is to examine the damage caused to organizational structures and knowledge sharing by one person leaving the company. Depending on the individual's knowledge and control and the network structure within and outside of the organization, strategic resources and advantage can be lost. Companies which can structure their information technologies and knowledge sharing networks better than their competition will be at less risk from the loss of key personnel.

A background literature search on extended enterprises, organizational networks, computer networks and knowledge-based systems has been completed. Information from each category is being combined with data from other categories to form the basis for our hypotheses. Hypotheses are being tested using intelligent agents controlling aspects of knowledge in an existing computer simulation system. Variables can be changed or manipulated as needed to produce additional experiments and results. The simulation system may also be extended if necessary to handle knowledge sharing within organizational networks and struggles between competing networks. Our final output would hopefully be a better theory, model, structure or network for extended enterprises. Potential applications of this work can be found in strategic IT management, organizational learning, distribution networks and supply chain management. Future work may include on-site research in competing or co-operative organizations. This could involve trials of our rival networks in representative business settings.

KNOWLEDGE SHARING NETWORKS

A number of inter-organizational networks for knowledge sharing have been classified and documented. The Hourglass structure (two triangles: one inverted over the other) identifies a traditional supply chain management structure. The large top and bottom identify large numbers of firms who provide supplies and purchase goods from the firm that is the small part in the middle. The Swarm structure shows a number of intersecting circles, identifying groups of people, departments, or firms working with other groups.

Quinn [7] identifies a number of 'intelligent enterprise' structures within individual organizations. These networks offer different methods of sharing knowledge. The Infinitely Flat organization has an extremely wide reporting span, requiring a well-designed central information system. Spider's Web organizations allow all personnel and groups in the organization to communicate with all others. There is no formal authority or hierarchy, and sophisticated, robust, wide area information systems are needed. International cooperative ventures among firms or international firms such as Arthur Andersen and Co. use this model. The independent nodes contain all the knowledge of their organization and interact directly with other independent nodes. Quinn describes other company and industry groupings, including Shamrock, Inverted, Starburst and the Japanese Keiretsu structures. Each may be appropriate in different situations to improve competitive positions.

Knowledge sharing networks are necessary and important in international business activities. Casson [1] discusses ownership and control of activities within an organization and factors that govern the diversification of the enterprise. For example, several firms may need to acquire or buy products from the same manufacturing facility. One firm can shut out another or several firms can get together in joint ownership of key facilities. The firms may then be competing in buying or selling in the same markets. This competitive behavior can undermine former co-operative behavior or vice versa. Organizational structures, working competitively or co-operatively as needed, will assist firms in international business.

INTER-ORGANIZATIONAL STRUCTURES

Hierarchical structures describe similar objects working together in a tree-like network. The network root is the 'control' object for the hierarchy. Each branch focuses on a specialized functional area of expertise. Entrepreneurs including Andrew Carnegie, Cornelius Vanderbilt, and Henry Ford believed that vertical integration, such as that in a hierarchical structure, could 'guarantee sources of supply and secure leverage on vendors.' [4] Firms in outlying branches of the hierarchical structure must be willing to be controlled by the organization at the root. Prahalad and Hamel [6] compare a diversified corporation to a hierarchical tree. Major limbs are the core competencies, smaller branches are business units, and the leaves and flowers represent the firm's products.

Star structures may be seen as a variation of hierarchical networks. The center of the star is the controlling organization and other subordinate firms must network according to strictly limited paths. Star networks are generally used only for closely-coupled organizations, either physically or functionally proximate. University recruiting may be used as an example of star structures. Both excellent high school students and professors are sought through a web of contacts radiating from individual universities. High schools are contacted for student recommendations in particular areas of interest to the university. Scholarships may be made available through local referrals. Students may be encouraged to participate in local university visits, camps or contests. Similarly, university professors are recruited from a number of external universities, often through personal contacts. Connections may be made at conferences, through previous academic visits, or from common research interests.

Bus structures are named for the long straight transit vehicle routes. [8] A number of organizations are connected in a row, like bus stops on a city street. One firm is in charge of information sharing for the group. The controller transmits information to others on the network through a continuous directed path. Bus structures are used extensively in computer systems as local area networks, connecting a number of personal computers. Built-in arbitration mechanisms are used on computer bus networks to handle simultaneous transmission and potential collisions, such as two computers trying to send information at the same time. [9] Similarly, the controlling organization in a bus chain needs to mediate information flow along the network. The bus structure allows organizations to work as individual entities while being loosely connected to a number of other businesses. The key to their effectiveness is the 'plug-in' capability and compatibility.

Ring structures consist of a peer group of firms working together in a circular network. [7] Alliances, such as that recently formed between Microsoft and Sun, are examples of ring structures. These networks involve equal partners sharing knowledge and working together for the good of all associate businesses. Information is traded around the group using a controlling organization or a shared data exchange. Rules can be established to negotiate direction of information flow and simultaneous access of individual firms. Organizations can institute their own alliance rules as needed.

The peer-to-peer structure involves a number of organizations working together on an equal basis with every other organization in the network. There can be similar organizations working together on related problems. Conversely, there may be very different organizations complementing each other's skills. Firms can focus on their own core competency with no concern for the work of other firms in the network. The Internet may be seen as a very-large-scale example of a peer-to-peer network. Organizations communicate directly with each other worldwide through their computer networks. This structure is also known as a Spider's Web [7], Complete network [9], and Swarm structure [5].

COMPUTER NETWORKS

Comparing our domain of organizational networks (structures) to computer networks, there are many similarities, warranting further research. A number of local and wide area computer network structures exist. Tanenbaum [9] describes ring and bus networks, complete networks, hierarchies and combinations of individual structures. Organizations make computer network decisions as appropriate, and then change, enhance or add to the networks at a later time. Organizational structures often follow the same pattern. Departments, groups and hierarchies are established to meet current organizational needs, and then are adjusted over time in response to new circumstances. As well, existing hardware or physical layout will often drive the choice of computer network. Similarly, organizational groups are often formed based on established principles or geographical proximity.

Computer networks are being developed to minimize the risk of humans damaging the network. Older networks will allow uninformed users to destroy the entire network if they try to move a computer connection incorrectly. Newer networks limit the individual's potential scope of harm by introducing hub technologies so that people can only destroy their own section of the network. These newer technologies are more expensive, but provide huge savings in trouble-shooting and in long-term maintenance.

Potential performance measurements are being developed for computer networks. Reliability is assured through network partitioning, so that all parts of the network won't go down if one part is faulty. Speed and efficiency performance is handled through clustering so that intranetwork traffic exceeds internetwork traffic. This particularly aids large-scale networks with lots of devices or long wires over a wide geographical area. Security issues are handled through different types of traffic (accounting, personnel, strategic planning) with different security needs having different local networks. Also, specific security needs (passwords, administrators, read/write restrictions) are controlled and monitored on an ongoing basis.

STRATEGIC ADVANTAGE

McGill and Slocum [4] proposed that structure in a 'smarter' organization is characterized by permeability (maximizing the flow of information), flexibility (the structure can change fast at any time), and network intimacy (people and decision-making authority are close to business processes). Maximizing the flow of information can "put the necessary resources in the hands of the people who need them. As needs and people change, the structure changes." This will blur lines between management and employees, between departments, between employees and customers, between the company and its vendors, and even between the company and its competitors. To achieve these goals and visions, organizations must be flexible, responsive and learn rapidly. Close contact with customers (part of the network) is necessary with the 'horizontal' (peer-to-peer) organization achieving the best new results, according to McGill and Slocum. Other issues or variables to be considered included maximizing profits, minimizing costs, type of task, and time constraints. Core competence was best kept in-house, but outsourcing meant stronger market linkages and external environmental changes with little or no internal control.

The measurement of performance in organizations, their environments and their sub-systems (individuals and groups) is multidimensional. [3] One generic measurement is "overall status of an organization in relation to its competitors, or against its own or external standards." Performance should be gauged across a profile of measures, such as 'the three Es' ñ economy, efficiency, and effectiveness. Unfortunately, because of balance of power issues, "powerful stakeholders tend to set the performance evaluation agenda." In spite of this assessment bias, Holloway et al [3] suggest that "measuring strategic performance is a difficult but necessary undertaking." To compare excellent organizations to others that are not so good, we must do regression analysis or use other statistical techniques across or within sectors. This is difficult because of the lack of standards for excellence measurement. Also, how can differences in measurement be controlled? Further, what is the impact of the measure used on behavior?

In the 1970's, Chrysler changed the structure of its organization from independent designers, engineers and manufacturing personnel to a structure where these people work with finance, purchasing, and other experts to jointly make decisions. [4] Senior management also changed from making final decisions (hierarchy) to ensuring that team decisions fit the company vision (overseer of a complete network). Many firms diversified in the 1960's, dividing their organizations into decentralized profit centers and treating them as independent small business units. Individual business units were then reviewed for market growth rate, relative market share and so on. This model provided the advantages of a peer-to-peer network among organizational units, but ignored possible synergies among small business units when they used the same sales force or research department.

In the late 1980's, Harley-Davidson moved away from a hierarchical functional form with vertical integration, manufacturing all its parts itself. [4] The firm now takes advantage of a just-in-time inventory, outsourced parts and a close relationship with suppliers who can manufacture goods cheaper than Harley-Davidson does. This has lead to reduced cycle time and cheaper costs.

McGill and Slocum [4] recommend a 'collaborative web of suppliers and customers'. To make this peer-to-peer outsourcing model work effectively, however, all firms must have a solid core competency. This should prevent a supplier moving directly to a customer, bypassing the center firm as happened to IBM. In 1981, IBM chose Intel for its microchips and Microsoft for its software. Intel and Microsoft quickly discovered that they could work together and no longer needed any expertise from IBM.

A modular network structure can entail sets of companies that come together quickly to do a job, sharing their expertise and resources. Networking organizations need excellent informational systems, core competencies, and opportunity. These firms come together for only a short time, so are less permanent and less formal than traditional structures. Within large organizations, divisions, functions and teams can get together concurrently, satisfy a customer need, and then disband. The advantage of this approach is speed and focus to satisfy the customer.

INTELLIGENT AGENTS

We will be using intelligent multi-agent simulation software to model the dominant organizational network structures and the people, products or locations (agents) in the organizations. Agents in the system are given different initial conditions: goals, background knowledge, experience, observations, and so on. Agents will also have an imperfect knowledge of other agents or other structures in the system. Variables will be measured, such as speed of knowledge transfer, length of the organizational contact, and volume of information required to solve the problem at hand. We can compare cooperative and competing agents, modeling organizations working together or against each other. Individual people or organizations, which are only out for themselves, can be modeled with selfish agents.

The particular problem of interest for our research is the interaction between group structures. Agents in the groups may be people, products or locations. The term 'agent' can identify any of the individual items. 'Multi-agents' are groupings of agents. Agents may be structured into work groups, supply chains or other clusters. These structures may work well as independent forces within a department or company. Once the structures begin working with other agents or groups of agents, however, independence may be lost and a new structure may be needed. Agents may be grouped into a hierarchical structure, a peer-to-peer relationship, a star network or a number of other structures. These groups may be competing for resources or they may be co-operating in joint ventures.

Representative research questions might include the following concerns. What is the best way to organize agents to maximize profits and minimize time? How do differing multi-agent network structures work together? Which structure is best for which task? Do time constraints change the interaction? If so, how? What is the effect of one or more agents or multi-agents leaving the work in the middle of an interaction?

Our approach to the above problem is the development of a computer model using existing chaos and complexity theory, intelligent software agents, and co-operative information systems. A variety of multi-agent structures may be simulated in software. The systems can then be set in motion to work co-operatively (or competing) with other multi-agent structures. Results can be observed and monitored over specific time periods. Variations in group structures, pairings, specific work and time should provide 'best' group structures for particular tasks under particular constraints, 'best' structures for co-operative work, and so on.

This work combines information systems and management with applications of software engineering and artificial intelligence. Existing systems, such as the Swarm Simulation System from the Santa Fe Institute and systems in use at the FedEx Center for Cycle Time Research at the University of Memphis, will be used to expedite computer modeling work.

CONCLUSION

We identified a number of inter-organizational structures for strategic advantage in this article. Although traditionally considered to be straight-line hierarchical structures, organizational networks may be viewed as star, bus, ring or peer-to-peer networks. Each of these structures provides a different opportunity for inter-organizational clustering. Different structures will also make a difference to the customer in terms of speed, cost, and quality of goods.

Corresponding organizational characteristics are being documented and compared across structures. Organizational characteristics such as the need for control, flexibility and speed will indicate a particular structure for a specific firm. Conversely, selection of an alternate network structure by a group of firms will affect various organizational characteristics for an individual firm. If we use that structure, what does it mean to our strategic advantage? Decision-making, time to market and other performance measures may therefore change, potentially impacting profit. The use of alternate inter-organizational structures may improve the work and potential gain of individual firms and may direct the success of all network members.

REFERENCES

[1] Casson, M. Enterprise and Competitiveness. Clarendon Press, Oxford University Press, Oxford, UK, 1990.

[2] Dilts, D.M. and Young B. Control in the Extended Enterprise; accepted by Management Sciences, September 1997.

[3] Holloway, J., Lewis & Mallory, Editors. Performance Measurement and Evaluation. The Open University (SAGE Publications), London, UK, 1995.

[4] McGill, M.E. and Slocum, J.W., Jr. The Smarter Organization. J. Wiley & Sons, New York, NY, 1994.

[5] Mills, D.Q. Rebirth of the Corporation. J. Wiley & Sons, New York, NY, 1991.

[6] Prahalad, C.K. and Hamel, G. The Core Competency of the Corporation. Harvard Business Review, May-June, 1990.

[7] Quinn, J.B. Intelligent Enterprise. Macmillan, Inc., New York, NY, 1992.

[8] Stallings, W. and Van Slyke, R. Business Data Communications, Third Edition. Prentice-Hall, Inc., Upper Saddle River, NJ, 1998.

[9] Tanenbaum, A.S. Computer Networks, Third Edition. Prentice-Hall, Inc., Upper Saddle River, NJ, 1996.

The effect of industry sector and value system on Internet Commerce benefit

Simpson Poon
Department of Information Technology, Murdoch University, Murdoch, Western Australia, Australia 6150
Email: spoon@it.murdoch.edu.au, Tel: +61 8 93606072, Fax: +61 8 93602941

ABSTRACT

Earlier studies of Internet Commerce suggest that there can be many determinants of Internet Commerce benefit. One such determinant is the influence of businesses from within the industry or along the value chain. In this study, we explored the effects of groups such as partner firms, competitors, suppliers and customers have on Internet Commerce benefit in a small business context. The results suggest that for small firms in the non-manufacturing industries, competitive advantage and information support relate positively to the experience of Internet Commerce benefit. Within a value system, the percentage of customers which participate in Internet Commerce strongly influences the experience of Internet Commerce benefit. However, suppliers online do not seem to contribute much to Internet Commerce benefit.

INTRODUCTION

Internet Commerce (a subset of Electronic Commerce) is now arguably one of the most addressed topics in Information Systems research. Internet Commerce has created trading paradigms that were not even imagined a decade ago. We adopted Zwass's (1996) definition of Electronic Commerce and modified it to define Internet Commerce as:

Internet Commerce is the sharing of business information, maintaining business relationships, and conducting business transactions by means of Internet-based technology.

Recently there has been a surge of Small Business Internet Commerce (SBIC) studies. These included longitudinal studies (e.g., Barker, 1994; Fuller and Jenkins, 1995; Barker, Fuller and Jenkins, 1997), surveys on business drivers (e.g., Lederer, Mirchandani and Simsand, 1996), studies of usage evolution (Abell and Lim, 1996; Abell and Black, 1997; Sieber, 1996; Fink et al., 1997), multi-method studies (Poon and Swatman, 1996; 1997; 1998), studies of international marketing and export (Hamill and Gregory, 1997; Bennett, 1997), studies of advertising (e.g., Auger and Gallaugher, 1997) and studies of business re-engineering (e.g., ITI, 1998). They conclude that small business is a key participant group of Internet Commerce and this has recurred over time. The results also present realities of Internet Commerce which are different from expected (e.g. slow uptake of Internet transaction).

Internet Commerce success among small firms depends on mapping adoption approach with expectation (Barker, Fuller and Jenkins, 1997). Some firms experience Internet success despite using commonly available technology because they fulfil onset expectations. However, the Internet as an effective advertising medium and the global electronic market has not been fully realised except in anecdotal examples (Poon and Swatman, 1998). However, the Internet has been an effective tool for customer support and information exchange. (e.g. email).

So far these studies had not focused on the effect of industry sector and value system on Internet Commerce benefit, therefore, we set out to examine this issue. We focused on what contribute to the experience of Internet Commerce benefit within an industry and along the value system of a small firm. Figure 1 illustrates the relationship between the industry sector and the value system. The value system illustrated includes both the physical and virtual value-chains (Benjamin and Wigand, 1995; Rayport and Sviokla, 1995). The virtual value-chain can be built using the Internet to support the information needs of the physical one.

BUSINESS ENVIRONMENT AND INTERNET COMMERCE BENEFIT

In this paper, business environment means the four parties (see Figure 1) a small firm interacts with during business activities. Earlier works (e.g., Cronin, 1995; 1996) suggest Internet Commerce can lead to operational and strategic benefit. How much of such benefit has been realised is debatable. For small businesses involving in Internet Commerce, early expectations of such benefit are now discounted.

The four indicators of Internet Commerce benefit were measured using a five-point Likert scale (5 – most positive experience; 1 – least positive experience), and they are:
- Obtain competitive advantage over non-online competitors
- Improved business performance since participating in Internet Commerce activities
- Improved supplier/customer relationship since participating in Internet Commerce activities
- Current benefits will continue if businesses keep on participating in Internet Commerce activities

Industry sector and Internet Commerce benefit

Studies of SBIC indicate that Internet Commerce adoption within an industry can affect the adoption strategy of other firms within the same sector (Barker, Fuller and Jenkins, 1997, Poon, 1998). In addition, if there is a preference to use the Internet to communicate and interact with firms in the same

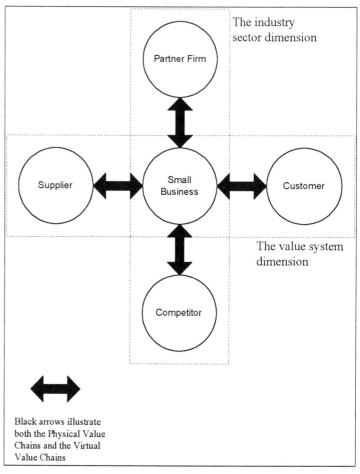

Figure 1 Relationship between Industry Sector and Value System

The industry sector dimension

Partner Firm

Supplier

Small Business

Customer

The value system dimension

Competitor

Black arrows illustrate both the Physical Value Chains and the Virtual Value Chains

sector, this may generate a need to adopt the Internet. For firms that find the Internet useful for information support, they might experience more Internet Commerce benefit.

To explore these, four hypotheses were formulated and divided into four categories. The issues examined were percentage of competitors participating in Internet Commerce (IC1), Internet as a preferred communication medium (IC2), being disadvantaged if not participating in Internet Commerce activities (IC3), and, the Internet provides information support (IC4).

Hypothesis IC1: The percentage of competitors online has a direct effect on the experience of Internet Commerce benefit.

Hypothesis IC2: There is no difference in Internet Commerce benefit experience between those who are in industry sectors that prefer Internet-based communication and those in other sectors.

Hypothesis IC3: There is no difference in Internet Commerce benefit experience between those who experience competitive advantage through Internet Commerce and those who do not.

Hypothesis IC4: There is no difference in Internet Commerce benefit experience between those who find the Internet is good for information support and those who do not.

Value system and Internet Commerce benefit

A value system contains a firm, its supplier and customer linked by a value-chain (Porter and Millar, 1985). Studies of inter-organisational systems and electronic markets reveal that parties on a value-chain can use their power to influence business relationships (Cash, Jr., 1987; Malone, Yates and Benjamin, 1989; Konsynski and McFarlan, 1990; Konsyski, 1992; Webster, 1994). For example, a large car manufacturer can coerce its small suppliers to adopt prescribed inter-organisational technology through power dominance (Webster, 1994).

The inter-organisational technologies discussed in these studies were either proprietary, custom-built or with narrow applicability (e.g. Malone, et al., 1989). Internet Commerce is quite different because the technology is non-proprietary and with wide applicability. Such technology renders traditional entry and exit barriers mentioned in earlier studies meaningless.

In our study, the effect of critical mass within the value system was explored by examining whether the percentage of customers and suppliers on the Internet has an effect on Internet Commerce benefit. Also examined was whether those who actually carry out Internet Commerce activities with the small firm would have a further effect.

Four hypotheses were set up to investigate the effect of value system on Internet Commerce benefit. Two hypotheses (VC1 and VC2) targeted the effect of the upstream value-chain (i.e. with a supplier).

Hypothesis VC1: The percentage of suppliers on the Internet will significantly influence the experience of Internet Commerce benefit.

Hypothesis VC2: The percentage of suppliers who actually engage in Internet Commerce activities with the small firm will significantly influence the experience of Internet Commerce benefit.

The following hypotheses examined the influence from the downstream value-chain.

Hypothesis VC3: The percentage of customers on the Internet will significantly influence the experience of Internet Commerce benefit.

Hypothesis VC4: The percentage of suppliers who actually engage in Internet Commerce activities with the small firm will significantly influence the experience of Internet Commerce benefit.

RESULTS AND ANALYSIS

The study sample

Survey research was adopted as the study method. The sample was collected from a number of Internet Directory services targeting Australian small firms (e.g. under the country category Australia or have an Australian contact telephone number). The sample consists of 224 small businesses each having a webpage and an email address. In this study, a small firm is one with less than 100 employees (DIST, 1995). 224 questionnaires were sent and 67 collected were useable. This constitutes a 30% response rate which compares favourably with other studies in similar topic areas (Abell and Lim, 1996; Auger and Gallaugher, 1997). We divided the sample into six industry sectors (see Table 1). Firms belonging to the Internet and related sector (e.g. Internet Service Providers, Website developers, etc.) were deliberately excluded from the sample because their specific nature could have biased the results.

The average number of years online was two. This indicated that their responses were experience-based. A high percentage of the respondents were from the knowledge-based and service sectors that do not physically manufacture goods. Although every effort had

Table 1. Characteristics of the study sample

Industry sector	% from this sector	Size of firm (persons)	% of this size
IT (non-Net) H'w & S'w	20.3	1 - 5	50.7
Music, Media & Publishing	13.0	6 -10	17.4
Business and Prof. Services	30.4	11 - 20	14.5
Retail and Wholesale	23.2	21 - 60	8.7
Tourism	4.3	61 - 100	2.9
Manufacturing	8.7	Not responded	5.8

been made to ensure a non-biased sample, there seems to be a low response rate from the Tourism and Manufacturing sector. There is a high percentage (80%) of micro-sized businesses with less than 20 persons.

The effect of industry sector on Internet Commerce benefit

Correlation analysis was carried out to examine whether the percentage of competitors online has a direct effect on Internet Commerce benefit (IC1).

Table 2. Correlation analysis for hypotheses IC1

	Comp. advantage over non-online competitions	Improved business performance	Improved supplier/customer relationship	Current benefit to be continued
Correlation coefficient Pearson's 2-tailed p-value (* # .05; ** # .01)	.2481 (.050)*	.1788 (.164)	.3888 (.002)**	.1869 (.146)

The result shows that as the percentage of competitors online increases, there is significant evidence showing that a small firm would feel it is more competitive than its non-online competitors and has improved supplier/customer relationships. This is possibly due to the use of Internet which helps it to reach out to customers better than its non-online competitors. However, there is no evidence that an increased percentage of competitors online leads to better performance or instils confidence in future benefit.

The second hypothesis (IC2) examined whether peer pressure to use the Internet for communication has an effect on experiencing benefit. One-way ANOVA was used to examine such effect and the result is shown in Table 3.

Table 3 shows that inclination to communicate over the Internet has no significant effect on Internet Commerce benefit, although those under such pressure have more positive experience overall. This indicates that despite email is becoming an important way to communicate, those who prefer to use email to communicate do not necessarily experience more benefit than those who do not or do not have any preference.

In addition to the percentage of competitors on the Internet, the issue of competitive advantage gained from Internet Commerce was investigated (IC3). This was done in addition to (IC2) because a high percentage of competitors online may not automatically translate into competitive disadvantage. The responses between the two groups show a significant difference in Internet Commerce benefit (see Table 4). Those who expressed non-adoption as a competitive disadvantage clearly had more positive responses than those whom did not say so, suggesting actual competitive advantage is an important influence of benefit. Together with the result in Table 2, we conclude that the actual experience of competitive disadvantage is a more important influence of benefit than how many competitors are online.

Table 3. One-way ANOVA analysis of mean scores for hypotheses IC2

	Comp. advantage over non-online competitions	Improved business performance	Improved supplier/customer relationship	Current benefit to be continued
Prefer to use other media (mean values)	3.2	3.0	2.9	4.0
Prefer to use Internet (mean values)	3.6	3.6	3.4	4.2
Use both Internet and other media (mean values)	3.4	3.0	3.3	4.1
F-ratio	.3771	.9315	.8822	.2116
(p-value: * # .05; ** # .01)	(.6874)	(.3994)	(.4190)	(.8099)

Quality information is key to shaping the strategic direction of a small firm (Clemens, 1992). One of the important functions of Internet Commerce is to access and exchange business information. Through testing IC4, we discover that those who found the Internet convenient to obtain information support also experienced more benefit (see Table 5). The difference between the two groups is significant across all four indicators of benefit, suggesting that the Internet as a tool to access and exchange information is a strong influence of benefit.

Table 4. T-test results for hypotheses IC3

	Comp. advantage over non-online competitions	Improved business performance	Improved supplier/customer relationship	Current benefit to be continued
Yes, experienced comp. adv (mean values)	3.8	3.5	3.7	4.5
No, not experienced comp. adv (mean values)	2.9	2.6	2.4	3.5
T-test (p-value: * # .05; ** # .01)	.013*	.009**	.000**	.002**

The results in this section indicate that from an industry sector perspective, experiencing competitive disadvantage and the usefulness for information support are key influences of Internet Commerce benefit. Neither being a preferred medium of communication nor percentage of competitors online has the same effect. Based on these findings, we can conclude that if a firm is in an industry which Internet Commerce will lead to the experience of competitive advantage and generate convenient information support, it will directly contribute to Internet Commerce benefit.

Table 5. T-test results for hypotheses IC4

	Comp. advantage over non-online competitions	Improved business performance	Improved supplier/customer relationship	Current benefit to be continued
Yes, good info support (mean values)	3.6	3.4	3.5	4.4
No, not good info support (mean values)	2.6	2.0	1.9	3.0
T-test (p-value: * # .05; ** # .01)	.015*	.000**	.000**	.007**

The effect of value system on Internet Commerce benefit

Within a value system, a small business carries out business activities with its suppliers and customers, a co-operative setting typically found within value systems. Therefore, if there is a high percentage of firms at both ends of the value system online or adopting Internet Commerce, a small business is likely to experience more benefit. The relationship between the critical mass at both ends of the value system and Internet Commerce benefit was investigated using a regression model.

The model has low p-values (<.005) and reasonable R-values across the four benefit indicators suggesting it has good predictability. Table 6 shows that there is a consistent effect from the downstream value-chain on the experience of Internet Commerce benefit. The percentage of customers who participate in Internet Commerce is the most critical factor of Internet Commerce benefit in a value system.

The lack of influence from the upstream value-chain maybe due to the sample nature where most small firms are in non-manufacturing industries. This finding is also consistent with what has been found in another study (Poon and Swatman, 1998) which discovers that over a twenty-month period, the Internet has helped to develop better customer relationships but not supplier relationships.

The result in Table 6 may not be generalisable because given a different sample (e.g. using small manufacturing firms instead) it might have generated a different result pattern. This is yet to be confirmed when a sector-based study is carried out in the future.

Table 6. Multiple regression model of the value system hypotheses (p-value: * # .05; ** # .01), § = unstandardised coefficients shown				
	Comp. advantage over non-online competitions	Improved business performance	Improved supplier/customer relationship	Current benefit to be continued
• Constant	2.28**	2.216**	1.842**	3.163**
• % of customer on Internet§	.0053	.00092	.0124*	.0071
• % of customer participate in IC§	.0017**	.015**	.0116*	.0092 (Sig.=.058)
• % of supplier on Internet§	.0042	.0397	.0044	.0054
• % of supplier participate in IC§	.0030	.0066	.0058	.0015
	R=.586, F=7.323, Sig.=.000	R=.540, F=5.648, Sig.=.001	R=.636, F=9.334, Sig.=.000	R=.488, F=4.383, Sig.=.004

Nonetheless, it is well understood that small businesses are often highly customer-focused.

CONCLUSION

Our results show that certain elements of a business environment have an influence over Internet Commerce benefit. By abstracting the business environment into a industry sector dimension and a value system dimension, the influences from each dimension were investigated separately. Along the industry sector dimension, the experience of competitive advantage and information support are key to Internet Commerce benefit. Whereas along the value system dimension, the percentage of customers willing to participate in Internet Commerce is the most significant factor of Internet Commerce benefit.

There are limitations to generalise from these results. Firstly, the sample is biased towards non-manufacturing small firms and this might have diminished the influence from the supplier side value-chain. Secondly, there might be other factors which have not been included in this study but are important to predict Internet Commerce benefit. These factors need to be further explored. The next stage of this study is to investigate additional issues such as adoption strategy and the effect of technology-business alignment.

REFERENCES

1. Abell, W. and Black, S. (1997) Business Use of the Internet in New Zealand: A Follow-Up Study. http://www.lincoln.ac.nz/ccb/staff/abell/webnet.htm.
2. Abell, W. and Lim, L. (1996) Business Use of the Internet in New Zealand: An Exploratory Study. http://www.scu.edu.au/ausweb96/business/abell/paper.htm.
3. Auger, P. and Gallaugher, J. M. (1997) Factors Affecting the Adoption of an Internet-based Sales Presence for Small Businesses. *The Information Society*, 13(1), 55-74.
4. Barker, N. (1994) *The Internet as a Reach Generator for Small Business*. Masters Thesis, Business School, University of Durham.
5. Barker, N., Fuller, T. and Jenkins, A. (1997) Small Firms Experiences with the Internet. In *Proceedings of the 20th ISBA National Conference*, Belfast, Northern Ireland.
6. Benjamin, R. and Wigand, R. (1995) Electronic Markets and Virtual Value Chains on the Information Superhighway. *Sloan Management Review*, Winter, 62-72.
7. Bennett, R. (1997) Export marketing and the Internet: experiences of Web site use and perceptions of export barriers among UK businesses. *International Marketing Review*, 14(5), 324-344.
8. Cash, Jr., J. I. (1987) Interorganizational Systems: An Information Society Opportunity or Threat? In *Towards Strategic Information Systems* (Somogyi, E. and Galliers, R., Eds), pp. 200-220, Abacus Press, Kent, UK.
9. Clemens, T. (1992) Small Business Perception of Time, Information and the Strategic Process: A Longitudinal View. In *Proceedings of the SEAANZ and Institute of Industrial Economics National Small Business Conference* (Renfrew, K.M., Hutchinson, P.J. Eds), pp. 215-224, Sydney, Australia.
10. Costello, G. (1995) Electronic Commerce Inter-organizational System Conceptual Models and Their Applicability to Strategic Alliances in *The Eighth International Conference in Electronic Data Interchange & Inter-Organizational Systems* (Clarke R. Gricar J. and Novak J, Eds), pp. 100-114, Bled, Slovenia.
11. DIST (1995) *Small Business in Australia - Fifth Annual Review*. DIST, Australia
12. Fink, K., Griese, J., Roithmayr, F. and Sieber, P. (1997) Business on the Internet - Some (R)Evolutionary Perspective. In *Proceedings of the 10th International Bled Electronic Commerce Conference*, (D. Vogel, et al., Eds), Vol. 2, pp. 536-555, Slovenia.
13. Forrest, J. E. (1990) Strategic Alliances and the Small Technology-based Firms. *Journal of Small Business Management*, 28(3), pp. 37-45.
14. Fuller, T. and Jenkins, A. (1995) Public Intervention in Entrepreneurial Innovation and Opportunism: Short Cuts or Detours to The Information Superhighway?. In *Babson Entrepreneurship Conference*, London Business School, pp.
15. Hamill, J. and Gregory, K. (1997) Internet marketing in the internationalisation of UK SMEs. *Journal of Marketing Management*, 13(1-3), 9-28.
16. ITI (1998) Business Case: Electronic Commerce for Oshkosh Truck Suppliers (ECOTS). A report submitted to Cleveland Advanced Manufacturing Program (CAMP) by the Centre of Electronic Commerce, Industry Technology Institute, http://www.iti.org, Ann Arbor, MI, USA.
17. Konsynski, B. R. and McFarlan, F. W. (1990) Information Partnerships - Shared Data, Shared Scale. *Harvard Business Review*,

(Sep - Oct), pp. 114-120,

18. Konsyski, B. R. (1992) Issues in Design of Interorganizational Systems in *Challenges and Strategies for Research in Systems Development* (Cotterman W.W. and Senn J.A., Eds.), Wiley and Sons, USA.

19. Lederer, A.L., Mirchandani, D.A. and Sims, K. (1996) Electronic Commerce: A Strategic Applications?. *Proceedings of the 1996 SIGCPR/SIGMIS Conference* (Igbaria, M. Ed), Denver, Colorado, USA, pp. 277-287.

20. Malone, T. W., Yates, J. and Benjamin, R. I. (1989) The Logic of Electronic Markets. *Harvard Business Review*, (May-Jun), pp. 166-170,

21. Poon, S. and Swatman, P.M.C. (1996) Small Business Internet Usage: A preliminary survey of Australian SMEs in the *Proceedings of the Fourth European Conference on Information Systems*, Lisbon, Portugal, pp. 1103-1112

22. Poon, S. and Swatman, P.M.C. (1997) Emerging Issues on Small Business Use of the Internet: 23 Australian Case Studies in the *Proceedings of the Fifth European Conference on Information Systems*, (Galliers, R. *et al.,Eds)*, Cork, Ireland, pp. 882-895.

23. Poon, S. and Swatman, P.M.C. (1998) Small Business Internet Commerce – A Longitudinal Study. *The 11th International Bled Electronic Commerce Conference*, Bled, Slovenia, pp. ??.

24. Poon, S. (1998) *Small business Internet Commerce – A study of the Australian experiences*. Unpublished PhD thesis, School of Information Management and Systems, Monash University, Australia.

25. Porter, M.E. and Millar, V.E. (1985) How information gives you competitive advantage. *Harvard Business Review*, (Mar - Apr), pp. 134-142.

26. Rayport, J. F. and Sviokla, J. J. (1995) Exploiting the Virtual Value Chain. *Harvard Business Review*, (Nov-Dec), pp. 75-85.

27. Sieber, P. (1996): Virtuality as a Strategic Approach for Small and Medium Sized IT Companies to Say Competitive in a Global Market, In *Proceedings of the Seventeenth International Conference on Information Systems*, (DeGross, J.I., Jarvenpaa, S., Srinivasan, A. Eds.) S. 468, Cleveland, USA.

28. Webster J. (1994) Networks of Collaboration or Conflict? Electronic Data Interchange and Power in the Supply Chain. *Journal of Strategic Information Systems*, 4(1), pp. 31-42.

29. Zwass, V. (1996) Electronic commerce: Structures and issues. *International Journal of Electronic Commerce*, 1(1), pp. 3-23.

Business-to-Business Electronic Commerce: Possibilities and Challenges for Companies Entering the Electronic Age: Case Wallac Ltd.

Jussi Puhakainen

Turku School of Economics and Business Administration, Dept. of Information Systems Science, TUCS, Turku Center for Computer Science Lemminkaisenkatu 14-18, FIN-20520 Turku, Finland
E-mail: jussi.puhakainen@tukkk.fi, Telephone: +358 2 338311, Fax: +358 2 3383451

Katja Karjaluoto

Turku School of Economics and Business Administration, Dept. of Information Systems Science
E-mail: katja.karjaluoto@tukkk.fi

ABSTRACT

Electronic commerce is booming in some parts of the world but not in all parts. The big fortunes keep waiting. The Internet is a global network enabling global business, but for many local companies it is a quantum leap to become suddenly global. This paper addresses the most essential questions a company will have to answer before making the decision to establish a World Wide Web presence. These questions will also indicate what type of presence to establish. Without proper considerations most efforts will be in vain. Finally we offer some thoughts for solutions.

1. INTRODUCTION

The competitive environment around most businesses and companies is changing with accelerating speed, i.e. competition is becoming world-wide, organisations are becoming decentralized, new products are developed faster, new producing technologies are emerging and new delivery channels are available. Organisations are in the midst of whole new challenges and are seeking for better competitive position and productivity.

The rapid technological developments and an outstanding ability to transform technological advances into products for the masses have fuelled the information technology (IT) industry into one success after the other. However, with increasing competition and the emergence of electronic markets, of which the World Wide Web (WWW, the Web) is the most spectacular, technological excellence is no longer enough. The Web has opened up a whole new business arena with profound consequences for business practice and research (Glazer, 1991, Benjamin and Wigand, 1995, Rayport and Sviokla, 1994, 1995, Hagel and Rayport, 1997, Angehrn, 1997, Hoffman and Novak, 1997, Brännback, 1997, Brännback and Puhakainen, 1998).

Most of the discussion about these new business possibilities has revolved however around business-to-consumer electronic commerce. Success stories like Amazon.com are well known but the business-to-business side of discussion has been largely neglected (Timmers 1998, Charlton et al. 1998).

It is estimated that although the number of consumers on the net by the year 2000 could be several 100 millions the business-to-business part will constitute the larger part of electronic commerce.

Some estimates:
- B-to-B electronic commerce is 327$ billion in the year 2002
- 630 000 US companies and 245 000 European companies involved in full-fledged integrated B-to-B electronic commerce by the year 2002
- B-to-B penetration rate will grow from 10 % today to 90 % in 2001 (Timmers 1998)

One of the main reasons behind this development is the growth in general awareness of this new medium. Personal use is continually rising and the demographics of the Internet-user are more and more representative of the general public. This can partly be traced back to the decreasing costs of Internet access, also the encouraging governmental policies on Internet-usage (Guay et al. 1998).

In this paper we try to identify common problems and questions what companies starting B-to-B electronic commerce face. This is a practical analysis based on our work consulting Finnish companies. In the future we hope to include more case-examples to support the validity of these questions.

2. BUSINESS-TO-BUSINESS ELECTRONIC COMMERCE

Before starting Business-to-Business electronic commerce a company must be able to answer the following three questions: why, to whom and what added value will this new medium give to target groups.

2.1 Why?

The usual reason behind using Internet as a B-to-B tool or just establishing internet-presence has been "because our competitors are doing this"(Sterne, 1995, 1996, Angehrn, 1997). A company can however very rarely reap long-term benefits by just copying competitors service, so a more comprehensive analysis must be made before entering the age of electronic commerce.

One good reason to start B-to-B electronic commerce is to try to make single transactions as easy and cost-effective as possible. When considering the amount of time the companies are using in handling small, routine purchases it is obvious that a new way of purchasing could lower the handling costs by making both internal and external processes more efficient.

A practical example of this could be a company selling office supplies. Traditional way of doing business involves a customer who selects products from a catalogue and then calls or faxes in his/hers order. This order is then processed taking into account customers purchasing history and the prices and billing information is added. Usually the seller contacts the customer at this stage and gets his/hers approval for the prices and delivery/billing information. Then the order is shipped, if all required products are available.

Better way of doing this could be a customer-specific www-page which is connected directly into the company's selling/ inventory maintenance system. With this the customer can straight away look at different product availability levels and customer specific prices. With the technology available this can be done fairly easy and the customer can order routine-like purchases without contacting the seller. The customer in this analysis can be customer or sales company/agent.

Another reason, through not necessary one in gaining long-term benefits, is the will to offer this kind of service before the competitors. Although the competitors will probably enter the digital market being the pioneer can still be quite successful. There's always a barrier to change to new service so that the company can enjoy the position of market leader for a while.

Internet can also broaden company's markets geographically. The very nature of Internet is global and some B-to-C success stories have shown that it is possible to reach global markets. This should in our opinion however not to be the goal when starting B-to-B electronic commerce. There are, of course, exceptions but venturing to global electronic business without mastering regional or national electronic commerce is a quantum leap.

2.2 To whom?

This is the critical question when planning Internet-presence. With B-to-C electronic commerce it is possible, although not recommendable, to adapt the shotgun-approach: just aim at the masses and see how many hits we get. With the number of consumers in the net it is possible to make profit with this approach, but with B-to-B electronic commerce this style will probably be at most marginally profitable.

First to be targeted is logically company's existing customer base. We know who we are targeting and have means to reach them. We know individual customer's purchasing history, pricing, delivery information and contact persons. Thus we can start with them. This approach gives multiple benefits:
- We can lower the transaction costs of simple, routine-like purchases
- We show to our customers that we are willing to offer them new forms of service.
- Starting with new medium usually involves need to continually improve system. This is best done with existing customers because the risk of customer defection is low when compared to situation where all of the aimed customers don't have any bonds to the company. Improving the system with existing customers also gives the message that you do care, your customers can see their suggestions put into service.

Second group to be targeted should be the companies that:
- We do not classify them as loyal or regular customers, but have done business with them. With this new medium we can try to turn them into our loyal customers, a valid hope especially when our competitors have not yet entered Internet or when the quality of our system surpasses theirs.
- We know them to be potential customers to us but we have not had any interactions with them.

Third group consists of companies that:
- We have no knowledge of them. We can target also these companies but usually that involves using marketing to tell these potential customers about our internet-presence. We might also get some customers the way that they find our internet-site by themselves.

This classification is not based on any geographical base. A customer belonging in any of these three groups can be a regional, national or foreign customer. However the odds in getting foreign (and sometimes also national) customers usually diminish when moving from first group to third.

2.3 What added value for target-groups?

Having a clear reason or reasons to establish internet-presence and knowing target-groups is not sufficient if a company cannot offer their customers any added-value with the E-com system. However, if the system is jointly developed with customers it will probably meet this criteria without further development.

Internet-based electronic commerce systems can create added value:
- just because the service is open 24 hours a day. A customer can choose the most convenient time to do business with you. This is especially important with multinational systems when your customers office-hours can differ greatly from yours.
- saving customers time by making the ordering process simple, this can also gain monetary savings to your customer.
- By always giving correct, up-to-date information about products, services and prices. Paper catalogues are always out-of-date, but with a well-designed internet-site a customer can expect up-to-date information and personal pricing.
- By personal suggestions and information based on purchase history. Mass customisation is easy with www-applications. Mass customisation means that a company can broadcast different messages to different target-groups, usually this is done in internet by showing different prices, products etc. to different customers.
- And with numerous other features. This is a punch with Internet-based E-Commerce. It is easy to broadcast personified information, all information is based on the same database, you just decide how you want to show it to different customer-groups or even individual customers.

We do not, however, want to give an impression that a company should deal with it's customers solely with electronic systems. The way we see it, a company should always keep in touch with it's customers also by conventional means. A dialogue with customer is essential (Blattberg and Deighton, 1991), because with the internet it is very easy for a customer to switch supplier without you ever knowing why.

3. PROBLEMS THE COMPANY FACES WITH INTERNET-BASED B-TO-B: SOME SUGGESTIONS FOR SOLUTIONS

3.1 Problems

It is a well known fact in brand management that there is normally a huge gap between company intentions and the perceptions of these intentions (Aaker, 1991, Zeithaml and Bittner, 1996). Not understanding customer expectations can originate from inadequate marketing research activities, lack of upward communication , and failing to realise that services are about building relationships and not about transactions. Relationships are as important to new customers as well as old ones. Relationships contribute to loyalty.

When looking at Internet-based B-to-B commerce system as a relationship strengthening or creating tool we must first understand that a tool is useless unless the user finds it useful. As mentioned earlier a company must be able to pinpoint the needs of targeted groups and be able to create added-value for these groups. This is the first problem with electronic commerce.

Companies do not necessarily have the know-how, resources or time to create a value-adding system. Outsourcing is the obvious answer but the quality and pricing of companies designing internet-solutions varies greatly. This is due to the infancy of that particular market.

Outsourcing is not the answer when a company does not know there has been a question. Low capabilities for strategic planning is the major obstacle in IT-usage (OECD 1995).

Even if the firm is successful in creating a value-adding system there is the problem of spreading the knowledge of the existence of the system, particularly abroad. Depending on the target groups this can be a major problem.

There is also a problem of logistics. Logistics are usually not a problem within a country or within an economic region (EC) but if a company has little experience with foreign trade all the difficulties in monetary transactions, transport, insurance, duties and so on may constitute a major problem.

3.2 Some Thoughts for Solutions

Problems mentioned in earlier chapters can be classified roughly into following categories:
- Problems in strategic decision making ie realising there are possibilities in internet
- problems in designing the service
- problems marketing the service
- problems with logistics

The level of general knowledge of internet is low (internet as a commercial tool/market is only a few years old) and in our view two first categories will solve themselves in time when the level of knowledge rises. There are however ways in speeding this process and we call for governmental and educational policies aimed at spreading the knowledge. There really is no need for every company to repeat the mistakes of others when entering electronic age.

Last two categories constitute a problem that needs more drastic measures. Marketing is a huge problem if a company does not advertise regularly in conventional media and even if it does this advertising does not necessarily reach the aimed target groups. This problem is most imminent with target group 3. This is usually a problem for SME's (http://www.server.fi/~myfirm is not an url that is easy to find by itself) and for any company but the biggest multinationals when trying to reach potential customers abroad. Logistics is a same kind of problem, if a company's business has not involved exports it is quite difficult/costly to learn all the needed procedures when for example just wanting to generate some extra sales from abroad.

We suggest as a solution to these problems the creation of regional, national and later multinational (European) centres for electronic commerce. These centres should:
- have strong co-operation with governmental agencies
- offer easy access for companies to electronic commerce. In practice a company should be able to enter the e-com by just concentrating on it's core competencies. The centre in question (regional, national or multinational) would take care of all the needed technical work. A somewhat similar solution can be found at www.britishexports.com, which has over 90.000 British export companies.
- These centres would be linked:
- regionals to national and nationals to multi-national.
- The marketing would be mainly run by these centres. It is easier and more efficient to spread the word (500 companies in Western Finland in one address or all the business in Finland in one address) for government.
- There would be several ready logistic "pipes" for delivering the products.

We realise that this is not necessarily an free market economy view but the advantages of such centres in our view could be great. We must also bear in mind that for example in Finland the average company size is small (94 % of companies have less than 10 employees, only 498 companies have more than 250 employees) and these companies could greatly benefit from centres. Even the bigger Finnish companies might use the know-how of centres when starting internet operations. (Small Business Database. 1998)

To put it all together, it would be enough for a company to just make the decision to enter the electronic age.

4. A BRIEF CASE-STUDY

4.1 EG&G Wallac

EG&G Wallac develops, manufactures and markets analytical systems for use in research and clinical diagnostics laboratories. With headquarters at Turku, Finland, the company employs some 700 people worldwide and consolidated turnover is around 110 MUSD. Together with the bioanalytical division of EG&G Berthold, EG&G Wallac forms EG&G Life Sciences, a strategic business unit of the United States-based EG&G, Inc.

In this field Wallac has been an early adapter of electronic commerce (website since year 1994, http://www.wallac.com) Since then the development has been moderate: internet approach has shifted from the online-catalogue to the information source for existing customers, but no attempts to employ internets interactive capabilities has been made. This is made intentionally because the new media itself has been evolving and there hasn't been any certainty about its future development. Now when it seems to be sure that internet is the media of future the company has started to regard it as potential tool of make business processes more effective and efficient.

We are currently working with Wallac rethinking the uses of internet. The work is still in the early stages, so the following findings are not complete.

In case of Wallac the three questions could be addressed in following way:

WHY:

Although the present ordering process is functioning well the customers needs for fast consumable deliveries (compare with JIT) could be addressed with internet based ordering system could. It would be in some cases a radical change to the order processing: At the moment the situation can be the following (worst case scenario): agent in middle-east sells a product to customer. During the selling process the agent makes numerous inquiries about availability and prices by fax or phone. The order is faxed to sales office in Greece, where it is processed and faxed to regional headquarters in Vienna. In Vienna the order is checked and modified (takes 2-4 days) and finally faxed to production facility. This is ordering process works but it is quite clear that Internet-based system like one described earlier could be an easy and more efficient alternative.

TO WHOM:

Wallac sells both through company owned sales offices and independent agents. These are both important target groups. They could use internet as a sales tool. Wallac might also consider direct sales in certain products, mainly in different filters, reagents ie. consumables the machines need to operate. The company knows who are using Wallac's products and also the potential users are easy to identify (hospitals and universities for example). These target groups need all customised information.

WHAT:

Added-value: because internet is "open" 24 hours it can help global operations in multiple ways (for example for an agent in far-east it is now hard to check inventory levels and production queue because of time-difference). A customer on the other hand might find valuable a personified web-page which tells about Wallac technology that the customer is using and makes ordering supplies and updates simple.

CONCLUSIONS

Before a company enters electronic commerce there are some very basic questions that need to be answered, which are essentially the same required at the start of any business. Why do we enter into this business? Who are our customers and what are their needs? What added value can electronic commerce provide for our targeted customer.

Additionally it is essential to realise that electronic commerce is a truly global business and this is problematic for many small and medium sized enterprises. It is a quantum leap to transfer from a local community company into a global company. We suggest that some regional, national and multinational co-ordination centres would be established, which would provide the necessary technical support and help in planning otherwise out of reach for small companies. This idea may seem somewhat orthodox and contrary to all principles of free market activities, that we suggest some return to hierarchical structure. However, it is obvious that small companies – as well as bigger ones for that matter – need considerable amounts of serious advice on what it really takes in terms of resources in reaching electronic commerce success.

REFERENCES

Aaker, David A. (1991), Managing Brand Equity, New York, Free Press

Angehrn, Albert A. (1997), "Designing Mature Internet Business Strategies: The ICDT Model", European Management Journal, August, pp. 361-369

Armstrong, Arthur. G and Hagel, John III (1996), "The real Value of On-Line Communities", Harvard Business Review, May-June, pp. 134-141

Benjamin, Robert and Wigand, Rolf (1995), "Electronic Markets and Virtual Value Chains on the Information Superhighway", Sloan Management Review, Winter, pp. 62-72

Blattberg, Robert C. and Deighton, John (1991), "Interactive Marketing: Exploiting the Age of Addressability", Sloan Management Review, Fall, pp. 5-14

Brännback, Malin (1997), "Is Internet Changing the Dominant Logic of Marketing?" European Management Journal, Vol. 15. No. 6., pp. 698-707

Brännback, Malin and Puhakainen, Jussi (1998) "Web marketing: Has the distinction between products and services become obsolete?", Journal of Market-Focused Management, Vol. 3, No.1 pp. 47-58

Glazer, Rashi (1991), "Marketing in an information-intensive environment: Strategic implications of knowledge as an asset" Journal of Marketing, October, pp. 1-19

Guay et al. (1998), "Internet Commerce Basics", International Journal of Electronic Markets, 05/98.

Hagel III, John and Rayport, Jeffrey. F.(1997) "The Coming Battle for Customer Information", Harvard Business Review, January-February, pp. 53-65

Hoffman, Donna. L. and Novak, Thomas. P.(1996), "Marketing in hypermedia computer-mediated environment: Conceptual foundations", Journal of Marketing, July, pp. 50-68

Hoffman, Donna. L. and Novak, Thomas. P. (1997), "A New Marketing paradigm for Electronic Commerce", The Information Society, Vol. 13, No. 1, pp. 43-54

"Information technology (IT) diffusion policies for small and medium-sized enterprises (SMEs)". (1995) OECD.

Jarvenpaa, Sirkka, L. and Ives, Blake (1994). The Global Network Organisation of the Future: Information Management Opportunities and Challenges. In Journal of Management Information Systems, Spring 1994.

Rayport, Jeffrey F. and Sviokla, John J. (1994), "Managing in the Marketspace", Harvard Business Review, November-December, pp. 141-150

Saffo, Paul (1997). Looking Ahead: Implications of the Present, In Harvard Business Review, September - October 1997

Schwartz, Evan (1997). Webonomics. Nine Essential Principles for Growing your Business on the World Wide Web. Broadway Books.

Small Business Database 1998. Small Business Institute, Turku and Statistics Finland.

Sterne, Jim (1995), World Wide Web Marketing, New York, John Wiley & Sons

Sterne, Jim (1996). Customer Service on the Internet. Wiley Computer Publishing.

Timmers, Paul (1998). Business Models for Electronic Markets. In EM-International Journal of Electronic Markets. vol. 8, no.2

Zeithaml, Valerie, A. and Bitner, Mary Jo (1996), Service Marketing, New York, McGraw-Hill Companies Inc.

Global Information Management: A Review of Expert Viewpoints

Freddie Quek

Connect-World, Elsevier Science London, London School of Economics, Unicorn House, 3 Plough Yard, London EC2A 3LP, UK
Freddie@connect-world.com, Freddie@biomednet.com, Tel: +44 (171) 422 1600, +44 (171) 323 5348

Gurpreet Dhillon

College of Business, University of Nevada Las Vegas, Las Vegas, Nevada, 89154-6009, USA
Dhillon@ccmail.nevada.edu, Tel: +1 (702) 895 3676; Fax: +1 (702) 895 4370

INTRODUCTION

Academic papers usually start with the identification of a problem, followed by a critical review of existing literature. Usually such a literature review helps researchers to not only ground their thoughts in reality, but also set the tone for empirical work. As opposed to this classic way of doing research, which is perhaps best suited for well established problem domains, we felt that issues relating to global information management are still emerging and there is perhaps no agreement as to what the consequence of globalization on world business would be. This was especially so when we consider the manner in which information and communication technologies (ICT) are impacting our lives. We believe that the visions and actions of opinion leaders, cultural innovators, technological role models and moral figures are important and critical in starting a global process of re-examination and implementation of these priorities. Therefore we approached a cross-section of established as well as upcoming visionaries to solicit their visions on the development of the future global world.

From our synthesis of the various expert viewpoints, we establish a number of emerging themes that should be focused on for the study of global information management. One of which is the convergence and interplay of technologies and the emergence of 'networked societies'. In recent years information systems and business management literature has suggested that the use of ICT by organizations as a result of the accessibility and affordability of computing power, indicates the advent of an era dominated by 'information networks' and a borderless economy. This networked world is epitomised by the Internet, a symbol of the growth and explosion of this era, which has revolutionized the way in which organizations and individuals communicate, work and add value to the businesses.

Another emergent theme is that of empowering the individual. Technologies offer dramatic new possibilities for personal growth. Millions of individuals can now define their own use of technology. They can demand and pay for it, for work, entertainment, or to facilitate relationships with others. It can also empower individuals in their work. Already, we are seeing on the Internet, areas where the individuals are able to compete in the same market with the big corporations.

GLOBALIZATION

In recent years information systems and business management literature has suggested that the use of information technologies by organizations has set the tone for a borderless economy. A number of factors are facilitating this phenomenon. For example, the World Bank estimates that by 2010 the cost of a transatlantic telephone call will fall to about 3 cents per minute. Such a free commodity orientation and the accessibility of computing power to a vast majority of people indicates the advent of an era dominated by 'information networks'. Advances in IT, its confluence with telecommunication technologies and the consequent emergence of networked societies have revolutionized the way in which individuals communicate, work and add value to the businesses. The growth and explosion of the Internet is a symbol of the growth and explosion of the 'information networks' and a borderless economy. It is estimated that currently there are over 55 million people worldwide who have connections to the Internet, growing to 550 million by the new millennium, representing 10% of the world's population. There was a time when 'to be global' was equated 'to being multinational' with physical presence in foreign markets. Today almost any service can be digitized and transmitted electronically.

As Ken Ohmae suggests, we are seeing the emergence of many interlinked economies. This is true at least of the developed countries. Even in emerging economies we are witnessing pockets of development that are directly linked to a globally linked economy. Such an interlinked economy is transforming the world in many fundamental ways - from the development and distribution of computer software to medical information provision, educational programmes and architectural services. Our future is inadvertently tied to the viability of national and regional economies — and to their ripple effect globally. The recent economic crisis in Asia, Russia and Brazil stands testimony to such dependencies.

EMERGENT GLOBAL INFORMATION MANAGEMENT ISSUES

The world has already witnessed the globalization of economic activities with the international information and communications network serving as a backbone. The old series of poorly integrated national economies is giving way to the creation of one interlinked global economy as they become deeply intertwined with each other. Statistics from the WTO and UN showed rapid growth in the volume of cross-border trade and investment in the last three decades. The expansion of economic activities that eventually render national borders meaningless, will be further accelerated by the construction of undersea cables, the provision of global mobile telecommunications services via satellite, the cost reduction of telecommunications services and the rollout of many practical and easily accessible services on the Internet.

Liberalization of Trade and Services

Along with technological progress came the global trends of deregulation, liberalization and privatization to stimulate growth and provide a platform for sustainable economic development in the future. The historic WTO Agreement on Basic Telecommunications Services, which came into effect on February 5th 1998, represents 72 countries and accounts for more than 93% of the total domestic and international revenue of US$ 600 billion generated in this sector annually. The Information Technology Agreement signed on March 26th 1997 by 39 countries accounted for 90% of the world trade in IT. In statistical terms, these two Agreements cover international business worth over a trillion US dollars, which are symbolic of the progress made in the liberalization process on a global scale.

As world markets become increasingly competitive, the need for efficient and reliable info-communications networks is more compelling than ever before. The World Bank, ITU, WTO and many governments believe that infrastructure development (telecommunications in particular) is fundamental to a country's economic well-being.

New Global Society

The new global society can make knowledge available at one's fingertips. Email is one good example of how we are all connected by the technology available. There will be more broad-based tools for interaction, work and entertainment. People in the professional and academic world have already exploited and benefited. Many online clubs and virtual communities have sprouted on the Internet, and technologies have enabled their integration across national boundaries.

In the past we used to gain knowledge through connecting with our cultural backgrounds. Now, with access to a global structure, those connections are not so obvious. A global information society (GIS) is based on the concept of global connectivity where it removes the penalty of geographic remoteness from centers of world commerce and culture. For rural communities which used to depend on traditional economic foundations like farming, ICTs and access to the GIS can totally transform a region's economic base.

The high-speed, fibre networks are the deep water ports and railway exchanges of the 21st century.

EMERGING THEMES

Issues relating to global information management are still emerging, and there are perhaps no agreements as to what the consequence of globalization on world business would be. We believe that the visions and actions of opinion leaders, cultural innovators, technological role models and moral figures are important and critical in starting a global process of re-examination and implementation of these priorities. Therefore we approached a cross-section of established as well as upcoming visionaries (see appendix for complete listing) and identified the emergent themes from their responses.

'Networked Society'

The new global economy, based on socio-economic restructuring and technological revolution, has led to the emergence of "networked societies", revealing the role technology plays as the most important social infrastructure working as a driving force for economic growth in the competitive business environment. Cheap information, based on advances in microelectronics and communication technology, has replaced cheap energy as the key factor in driving production of goods. According to Castells, this is the key to the social changes taking place now.

In his book, The Rise of the Network Society, Castells describes the network society as a new kind of social organization that offers a new paradigm as a means to make sense of the rapidly changing economic, social and technological environments. This networked form of organization and working is characterized by the transformation of work and the growth of the service sector; the integration of electronic communications (television, computer, multimedia); the new topology of network space and its relation to the local space we live in; and the change in time perception caused by the instantaneous yet asynchronous nature of network time.

The legendary John Doerr, a hugely successful venture capitalist in the famed Silicon Valley, refers to the 'Networked Economy' as a new paradigm for the functioning of business. According to Doerr, virtual businesses will aggregate markets across the globe, transact business and transport electronic goods and services throughout the network. Commenting on the nature of networked societies and changes in management, Drucker writes that management theories, assumptions, policies, and practices of the past may not apply in the future. The new information-based organization is founded on knowledge, the executive's principal resource. Specialized knowledge integrated into a task becomes productive knowledge.

Drucker also comments that the changes in trade and investment, the relationship between the world economy and the domestic economy, and trade policy are transforming the way business will be conducted. He says that a lesson learned from the last 40 years is that there is a direct relationship between increased participation in the world economy and increased domestic economic growth. Drucker provides insight into the Pacific Rim countries and the world economy, highlighting China and Japan. The new world economy has changing centers of power and new growth markets.

Numerous authors have drawn the attention to the creation of a knowledge-based economy whose two pillars are knowledge and information. The transformation of society has changed from that of a farming society to blue-collar workers and then knowledge workers. Formal education is essential for the knowledge worker. Similarly a networked world will transform enterprises, both public and private from the way companies and government agencies interface with their customers to the way individuals interact among themselves. For example in the US, the federal government is creating innovative ways to deliver government services to the public, such as filing income tax returns and Social Security claim forms, renew passports, get disability checks - basically, transact all their business with government agencies.

The basis for the networked society was founded on building the information superhighways, initiated at the 1994 ITU World Telecommunication Development Conference which mandated the modernising of the world's existing infrastructures and using them to induce economic growth and create jobs. The Internet Society is also working towards having at least one point of presence for the Internet within every country and territory of the world. Political and industry leaders at the G7 Conference in Belgium in 1995 provided more momentum by focusing on the development of an Affordable and high-speed communications GIS that can link virtually everyone together.

Empowerment

With knowledge comes empowerment. The era of Information Age is rapidly evolving into the Interactive Age. ICTs have made possible the collection, storage, transmission, and linkage of enormous amounts of information and they are now expanding to engage the individual consumer in a variety of activities. They are now integrated with every fabric of daily life, from home computers and mobile phones, to email and the Internet, they give many people access to the tools with which to experience aspects of life that they never had access to before. They offer dramatic new possibilities for personal growth, from developing personal senses of mastery, forming new kinds of relationships, to communicating with friends and family all over the world instantaneously.

The individual is no longer a passive consumer. For instance, interactivity makes possible real-time notice and choice options that acknowledges a direct relationship between individuals and the companies with which they do business. The power shifts are happening in many other areas such as transactions of goods, education, and organization management. Networks will gradually replace the old organizational and institutional setting which are based on vertical, over-rationalized, large scale bureaucracies. Mobility, interactivity, and pervasive connectivity are transforming our operational modes, making everything more productive, effective and adaptive. Individuals included in the network are therefore being empowered by this transformation.

Turkle of MIT reminds us that we need to think of ways to make the resources, available online, to have a positive impact on real life. Online communication, in many ways, is a return to print, to reading and writing. Already, many online communities are not only civil but actively encourage friendships and networking, and we certainly can have the best of both the virtual and real worlds. A powerful combination of liberalisation and innovation has provided an environment where developments are application and user-driven rather than dictated by technology. With strong competition at all levels of the information society, user choice will be infinite.

Seamless end-to-end interoperability of applications will be the common standard. Electronic commerce will make production processes more efficient and environment-friendly. It will help drive down prices of all goods and services, and thus lead us into the next phase of competition-driven, sustainable globalisation.

SYNTHESIS

At the macro level the global economy should certainly be a strong beneficiary based on the facility for increased international trade via electronic commerce, and the businesses which can meet the needs of society in general and users in particular, will see tremendous opportunity with all the developments discussed above. As is epitomised by the Internet, this networked world enables the customers to serve themselves at Web sites which provides 24 hour service, faster responses than traditional telemarketing and at a lower cost to service. However, there are also new challenges and problems. Rapid technological developments, introduction of multimedia applications, success of the Internet, and the conclusion of the WTO basic telecommunications negotiation are posing a new market environment, completely different from the previous ones.

Better or Different World?

The telephone and television have become the main drivers of changed awareness and information networks with global news, email and web pages are accelerating the pace of change even more. In this networked world, we can organise our society in a completely different way. The exciting implication of the Internet and the convergence of technologies may not make people realise that it is going to radically change the way we work, play and live.

Castells proposes that instead of considering market mechanisms in a mechanistic manner, we need to develop a sociological perspective in studying the newly emerging networked society. He examines data from global sources in each of the above categories, focusing mainly on Europe, North America, and the Far East, which he sees as the chief local/cultural influences on the networked society. With meticulously cited research from each area, he shows Europe pulling itself together to survive in the global economy, North America as the center of unfettered individualistic capitalism and the Far East as the example of carefully managed government sponsorship of economic development. He argues that the ultimate beneficiary of this cornucopia will be the entire humanity. Some even predict that the GII will usher in the 'Digital Utopia', providing the necessary momentum for economic development and narrowing the gap between the rich and the poor.

The pessimists on the other hand have their doubts. Angell of the London School of Economics questions whether the future is necessarily better, or that it becomes different. According to him, the stresses and strains of today's society are just lying dormant, waiting for a catalyst that will trigger a chain reaction of change. He quotes Alvin Toffler in suggesting that we are going to feel the explosive impact of the 'third wave' in our own lifetime which is going to tear apart families, shatter the economies and paralyse the political systems. The question that arises is whether these developments are a change for a better future, or are they inevitable changes which may or may not lead to a better future?

All countries of the world are faced with major challenges, such as the provision of health services, education, employment, sufficient income to meet material needs, a sense of personal security within the law, and a sense of security as a nation. Although individual countries may disagree about how to go about achieving those goals, there is agreement in a general sense about what the goals should be.

New Responsibilities?

To attain empowerment, the onus is on the individual to acquire knowledge — the knowledge of how to exploit the technologies for one's own use. The quest for access to developing knowledge and relationships according to Downton, is to enrich the way we work and the diversity in our lives. In this sense, the enabling technologies empower us to be liberated in these aspects, and give us the ability to do things in completely new ways.

Empowerment should however, not be discriminatory. The disabled must be considered. The effect of the technology is going to depend on what people do with it. We confront many questions and choices as we try to assimilate technology. But this scenario assumes that we will all be able to deal with the responsibilities that come with individual empowerment. Among the most difficult questions include: Can we expect information technologies to replicate democratic decision-making and replace today's model of representative democratic leadership with the immediacy of consumer choice?

In order to shift to a new world economic order, and to raise our achievement in the existing world social order, countries must have the political will and the preparation to join in. The bilateral arrangements between countries, the natural monopolies in the provision of public goods and services such as electricity, water, gas and telecommunications by governments are very quickly becoming obsolete in the modern world. The very essence of political governance and its relationship to commerce, and commerce itself is being seriously challenged. Yesterday's policy tools and regulatory structures can no longer work.

Global or Local?

Castells' analysis of the actual role of government in the global economy and in the development and application of technology will be a useful reminder to many in the Internet world who do not think it has one but is instead withering away into the marketplace. The new economy, based on socio-economic restructuring and technological revolution will be shaped, to some extent, according to political processes laid by the state. While most economic activity is not global, and most people do not work in the globalised segment of the economy, the fact remains that everybody's livelihood, everywhere, ultimately depends on global economic management, information and trade.

All societies ultimately depend on what people, individually and collectively, want and decide. Policies could be designed to allow for a softer social transaction to the Information Age, and to share the extraordinary harvest of the information technology revolution. It would take a major effort at educating, and retraining the entire labour force, starting with a computer literacy campaign for the adult population which has been undertaken by the young. It would take a concerted international policy to install the technological infrastructure of the Information Age throughout the planet. It must include a global, social and environmental agreement that would link the expansion of international trade and production to shared international standards, along the lines already elaborated by the International Labour Office.

Unprecedented Social and Cultural Impact

The changes in work patterns and economic development that Castells examines are daily newspaper fare as people and social institutions struggle to come to terms with the network society. Social patterns are changing quickly, and there is a growing sense of unease, an undercurrent of uncertainty. In some quarters, information technology is seen as a great cure for social ills, in others as a dispenser of toxins and a tool for crime. Castells' work can provide a coherent framework for a more realistic discussion of the true role of information technology and how it fits with the other factors driving social change.

For most people in the world, globalization, informatization and networking appear as threatening processes of disenfranchisement of their rights, and of confusion in their lives. Thus, people everywhere are resisting becoming passive subjects of global flows, by affirming their identity as an alternative value system. Religion, locality, ethnicity, nationality, gender or cultural preference are being used to build communal trenches of resistance.

CONCLUSIONS

This paper presents a summary of opinions expressed by a cross-section of leaders and visionaries. These leaders and visionaries have played an active role in creating and implementing their visions for the future. Our aim for future research is to develop a framework to map the articulation of visions to a clear plan of action which can be 'measured'. We are also interested at Morgan and Smircich's (1980) proposal to look at other research modes for established frameworks of observation that can offer a unique range of insights unobtainable by existing methods, such as one that constitute a specific hermeneutic mode located at the 'subjective' end of the spectrum. Such a review is important since most of the academic work done in global information management is way behind practice. We therefore plan to work with some of these visionaries to develop this framework.

METHODOLOGY, APPENDIX AND REFERENCES

Please contact the authors for details.

Client-server Computing: Lessons Learned and an Application in the Healthcare Industry

Ann Shou-an Char
Systems Analyst, Parkland Health & Hospital System, 6300 Harry Hines Blvd., Bank One Tower, Suite 500, Dallas, Texas 75235
Telephone: (214) 590-4772, Fax: (214) 590-4794, E-mail: achar@parknet.pmh.org

Mahesh S. Raisinghani, Ph. D.
Assistant Professor, University of Dallas, 1845 East Northgate Drive, Braniff #118, Irving, TX 75062-4736
Telephone: (972) 721-5173, Fax: (972) 721-4007, E-mail: mraising@gsm.udallas.edu

INTRODUCTION

Client-server computing is a phrase used to describe a model for computer networking. In this shared processing model, a server has an intelligent database engine functioning as a service on the network. This model offers an efficient way to provide data/information and services to many users as needed. A network connection is only made when a user needs to access the information or obtain the needed service. This lack of a continuous network connection provides network efficiency. Any change made in the server is transparent to clients.

A client is a requester for networked data/information and service. A client is usually a PC or workstation that can query database and/or other information from a server. Typical client functions are to display the user interface, perform basic input editing, format queries to be forwarded to the server processor, communicate with the server, and format server responses for presentation.

A server is a computer that stores information for manipulation by networked clients. Examples of servers are a mainframe, a high powered workstation, a mini computer, etc. A server is passive and it does not initiate conversations with clients although it can act as a client of other servers. A server waits for and accepts clients, presents a defined abstract interface to client, and maintains the location independence and transparency of client interface.

A client/ server system allows one or more clients to request data from one or more servers and put the data to a convenient place for clients. An underlying operating system and inter-process communication system is required to form a composite system for distributing computation, analysis, and presentation.

CHARACTERISTICS OF CLIENT-SERVER COMPUTING

The major characteristics of a client-server include the logical separation of the client processes from the server processes as well as the ability to change a client without affecting the server or other clients.

Client-server computing is distinct from ordinary distributed processing. There is a heavy reliance on bringing user-friendly applications to the user on his or her own system. The client-based station generally represents the type of graphical interface that is most comfortable to users. This gives the user a great deal of control over the timing and computer uses and gives department-level managers the ability to be responsive to their local needs.

The following two paragraphs were taken from material found at http://empire.lansing.cc.mi.us/course/wdavis/130/client_server.html:

When the applications are dispersed, there is an emphasis on centralizing corporate databases and many network management and utility functions. This enables management to maintain overall control of the total capital investment in computing and information system and enables management to provide interoperability so that systems are tied together.

At the same time, it relieves individual departments and divisions of much of the overhead of maintaining sophisticated computer-based facilities, but it enables them to choose just about any type of machine and interface they need to access data and information. There is a commitment, both by user organizations and vendors, to open and modular systems, which means that the user has greater choice in selecting products and in mixing equipment from a number of vendors. Networking is fundamental to the operation. Thus, network management and network security have a high priority when you organize and operate information systems.

TYPES OF CLIENT-SERVER

There are three types of client-server architectures and what makes the client-server system work is the software application process on the client.

A) Software Architectures

The three layers of software application are: the presentation layer, business logic layer, and data management layer.

The presentation layer takes the incoming data from external stimuli and edits it. The language paradigm for this layer is mostly object-oriented nowadays. This layer is almost always located on a client machine, but it is not a strict rule. Some PC's may be used as mainframe screens that it does not keep the origin of the presentation logic. The presentation layer also will present the response from the server to the outside world.

The business logic layer is the heart of the client-server system. The code that executes the business policy, rules, and regulations is in this layer and it can be located on the client, the server, or in between the client and server. The language paradigm for the business logic layer depends on the development tool chosen. It can be a mixed language layer, but the trend is towards object-oriented constructs.

The data management layer is charged with access and corporation of data. When this layer receives the data request, it will read and write the data and send the data to where it was requested. The language paradigm for this layer is normally a relational database. As the need of video, multi-media, sound, and hypertext objects, unstructured data is also collected here.

The overview of the software structure flow can be described as a circular system as indicated in Appendix 1. The presentation layer (a PC) receives an input (data request), it informs the business logic layer to analyze the request to match against the code and search in the data management layer. When the data request is matched in the data management layer, the data is then sent back to the presentation layer through the business logic layer.

B) Fat Client vs Thin Client

With a **fat client (thin server)** the client has ability to control the data. The execution is mostly performed on the client machine. The server is responsible for sending data to the client and back to server.

With a **thin client (fat server)** the client is restricted to the presentation layer and the majority of business logic is performed on the server.

The first generation of development tools Graphic User Interface (GUI) like Visual Basic and PowerBuilder encouraged two-tier hardware architecture. The user-friendly development tools enabled the user's presentation performance. The second GUI development tools generation separated presentation from business logic. The characteristics of the second GUI generations are reusable, portable, and maintainable. It promoted the reusability because they are very mechanical in nature. It is portable because it separates presentation & business logic. It is maintainable because business logic is separated and kept in one place so that the change is transparent to both client and server.

C) Hardware Architectures

The software structures do not function alone. The software structures and hardware structures are inter-dependent on each other. They need each other to make the client-server system function. There are three hardware tiers: two-tier, three-tier, and n-tier client-server architecture. The choice among these three should be based on the scope and complexity of a project, the time available for completion, and the expected enhancement or obsolescence of the system.

The two-tiered architecture contains of a client and a server where the logic areas are combined on the client as shown in Appendix 2. When the client requests data from the server in the two tiered architecture environment, the software layers concept starts running among the hardware architecture. The presentation and business logic layers take place on the client and the data management layer is as the server. The language paradigm used is typically SQL.

In most cases, a two-tier system can be developed in a small fraction of the time it would take to code a comparable but less-flexible legacy system. It also interacts well with prototyping and Rapid Application Development (RAD) techniques, which can be used to ensure that the requirements of the users are accurately and completely met. Two –tier architecture works well in environments that have fairly static business rules.

When there is a change in business rules, it would require a change to the client logic in each application. System security in the two-tier environment can be complicated because a user may require a separate password for each SQL server accessed. The proliferation of end-user query tools can also compromise data base server security. Client tools and the SQL middleware used in two-tier environments are also highly proprietary, and the PC tools market is extremely volatile. The volatility of the client-server tool market raises questions about the long-term viability of any proprietary tool to which an organization may commit therefore to complicating the implementation of two-tier systems.

The **three-tier hardware architecture** contains clients (presentation layer), local application server (functionality layer), and central server (data management layer). Unlike the two-tier hardware architecture, the software architecture applied to it is logically separated (please see appendix 3). The C language is used in the three-tier hardware architecture.

In the three-tier hardware architecture that the roles of client and central server are the same as in the two-tier hardware architecture, but the role of local application server is not a fixed role. It can be a client to the central server and a server to the clients depending on the direction of communication.

The **n-tier client-server architecture** is the compound model of the three-tier hardware architecture. It lets the PCs connect directly to the database server and bypass the local server as indicated in Appendix 4.

ADVANTAGES OF CLIENT- SERVER

Client-server is an open system. It uses powerful graphical workstations, servers, and mainframes to distribute data process across networks. The client-server model enables rightsizing, the selection and location of computing resources according to the individual's and work group's changing requirements. Over time, depending upon the needs of the business, the cost of a client-server system can be lower then other system architectures. Another is increased productivity from the individual to the enterprise. It results from better access to information for requesters and better distribution of resources throughout the enterprise. Additional benefits of client-server include: client-server (key components) and network work together; any of the key elements may be replaced without major impact on the other elements when the need to either grow or reduce or increase processing for that element dictates; using less expensive MIPs available on each platform insures cost effectiveness; new technology may be incorporated into the system; domain, entity, and referential integrity may be maintained on a single database server; data may be accessed from WANs and multiple client applications, performance may be optimized by hardware and process; and data security (only in the application lever) is centralized on the server.

DISADVANTAGES OF CLIENT-SERVER

There is no right or perfect solution for all businesses on management decision even though client-server computing provides innovative services for a number of businesses. Careful strategic planning is required up front because of the flexibility of the client-server systems and the complexity of networking. There are some other disadvantages.

The following bullets were taken from material at http://www.personal.kent.edu/~jnattey/spage7.html:
- The hardware, software, and communications technology is neither mature nor entirely stable, nor easy to assemble.
- Because client-server is not well understood it is frequently sold inappropriately or oversold to management and unsatisfied expectations result.
- Support costs can run three times the price of system hardware and software.
- Redesign and reprogramming are not trivial exercises.
- Backup and recovery in a client-server environment can be expensive.
- The more distributed the network, the greater its vulnerability.
- Client-server is an evolving technology and as such there is no standardization.

Client-server computing allows an organization to rapidly create applications that reflect changing business needs. However, underneath the surface are costs that can make client-sever systems more expensive to operate than centralized host-based systems. Thus, total life cycle costs must be considered.

SOME MYTHS OF CLIENT-SERVER DEVELOPMENT

There are a number of myths associated with client-server development. For example, David R. Ruble in his book Practical Analysis & Design for Client/Server & GUI Systems discussed some of them.
1. "Client-server technology will make users more productive."
Client-server technology can enable users to be more productive because it is usually used to provide information to those who need it. It does not guarantee a greater productivity if one uses client-server systems for business purposes.
2.1 "Client-server is less expensive."
Some people may just look at the hardware cost and forget about the invisible costs like manpower-related costs for reengineering the business and associated training, and loss of long-term employees because they cannot adopt the new system.
2.2 "We can use the new system to enable improvements in the business process."
This statement is persuasive only if the employees are satisfied and can be more productive. The business process improvement is supported by effective software, trained users and supporters, and improved procedures.
2.3 "Hardware costs will go down."
It is easier to request data by using new software so that more people request more information. This increases the need for processing power which increases costs for the additional hardware needed to respond to the increased demand.
3. "PC stands for personal computer."
Some employees abuse their freedom of access to the Internet or other personal uses. Sometimes these actions damage the PC (the company's property). That is why PC does not stand for personal computer. Therefore, some companies control employees' personal usage of the company's property includes computer.

4. "It's not easy to build windows using these new RAD tools."

This statement is true especially for GUI development tool vendors. If you know how to write short effective code, it is sure productive to build windows using these new RAD tools.

5. "The next version of the development tools will fix our current problems."

It depends on what you have and how the vendor is going to upgrade it.

6. "The manager does not need to know the methodology."

How can you supervise an accountant on the billing process if you do not know the billing process? If you are a manager, you need to know everything that will be required for a project.

7. "We do not have to do any of this analysis and design stuff because we are going to purchase packages rather than build systems."

Coding may not need to be performed, however the system to by purchased must be analyzed to ensure the requirements of the business are met.

8. "Standards will emerge as the project goes on."

The project may soon die if it starts with no standards. One can adapt standards established by another project and modify them for use on your project. Or, just create new standards for the project.

9. "We need one standard methodology and one standard CASE tool."

In the current client-server environment, hardware and software of different paradigms are used. There is not always one standard methodology to solve a problem. Many times, more than one methodology is needed in order to complete a project. Some CASE tools have enough techniques and management tools built in to support a full life cycle methodology. But methodology and CASE tools change over time.

RISKS OF CLIENT-SERVER DEVELOPMENT

1. There is a common risk that technical management may overlook the capacity requirements of the system. This may cause unexpected failure in the future.
2. The client-server environment may be complex. The operation, maintenance, and support, and administration of a large number of machines requires consistent application of standard methods of implementation to keep the job manageable.
3. Some assumptions that were appropriate for a small network may not scale up well to a large network.
4. Poor deployment planning is a bad sign for managing client-server systems. Many IT managers are accustomed to only managing the host computer. This end-to-end system may be a challenge to IT management.
5. Management may face employees' resistance to the installation of new system and in-coordination of installation activities.
6. Client-server system provides more flexibilities on software applications for the requester/user. But, the user may frequently use two or three applications out of ten. The more flexibility the client-server system provides; the greater the change for confusion by the user. Education on software applications may be required to train employees to effectively use the system.
7. Vendor competition can be a hidden and the biggest risk to business organizations utilizing client-server computing. Software Company A may buy out Software Company B & C to eliminate its competitors. Software Company A may stop supporting the X & Z applications sold by Software Company B & C later on for its own business purpose. The business organization buyers may have big problems when this situation happens.

FUTURE TRENDS IN CLIENT-SERVER COMPUTING

Information technology is a very volatile area that it is continuously and rapidly changing. Business strategies need to be changed as the information technology advances in order to make the business more competitive and keep up-to-date business information skills.

The trend in the client-server environment can be looked at in two different ways. Fat client is more favored in academical environment and research centers because of its ability to provide user control over various software applications. The professors, students, and researchers need as many tools as they obtain to perform their jobs.

On the other hand, thin client tends to be more favored by more disciplined business processes. Where they prefer minimizing the costs on the fixed procedures and structures. A large healthcare organization is a good example of a business that may favor the thin client. Many healthcare organizations have disciplined and fixed procedures and structured business environments. The implementation of thin client (fat server) may minimize their budget problems and provide better security and data controls regarding sensitive patient information.

Since information sharing and building solutions are important functions of client-server computing and many businesses are going globally, we should not be surprised to see client-server computing taking a step into the global business environment.

AN APPLICATION

Healthcare information technology was an area that was a slow and quiet growing area a decade ago. There has been dramatic growth and internal expansion within information systems in healthcare since the Health Care Financial Administration (HCFA) established so many new rules and regulations to monitor and manage Medicare, Medicaid, and the whole healthcare system. Healthcare organizations need a system that can handle their growth easily and efficiently while meeting the stringent control and reporting requirements imposed by the government. Client-server computing can be an efficient tool for healthcare organizations' information system's needs.

One of the authors is working for a large county health and hospital system where a client-server architecture is gradually replacing the mainframe architecture. We are currently using a mainframe system called Patient Management/Patient Account System (PMAS) for all patient accounts, admissions, discharges, and transfers. The mainframe system (MDX) has been used by The Community Oriented Primary Care (COPC) to handle complete outpatient appointment, schedule, and account information for outpatient visits. MDX has been in use for about seven years and it currently does not have the capacity required for COPC to keep up with its patient information. MDX does not have the capacity for all outpatient information so that COPC can only keep its patient information for two years (from the current working day back to two years ago). Epic was selected to replace MDX. Epic is a client-server model and therefore, has client-server characteristics.

Like most other healthcare organizations, we are not a risk taker on information technology. Over the intermediate term, we plan to utilize the PMAS system for all inpatient information and the Epic system for all outpatient use. Since the Epic system was recently installed and the client-server model has existed for several years, we should not have much of a "technological crisis" until a new and improved efficient system is on the market.

SUMMARY

Client-server computing offers businesses the potential for increase in flexibility and cost effectiveness in processing, managing, storing and sharing data/information. But before a decision is made to implement client-server computing, many factors must be carefully considered. The technology continues to undergo rapid change. For example, thin client-server computing is based on breakthrough technology.

Therefore, it is essential in selecting a solution to a business' computing requirements, that a system's approach to take. First, the requirements must be established, not only current requirements, but forecasted long term needs. Potential solutions, including client-server computing, need to be identified and evaluated with respect to performance, technology insertion, maintenance and support, training and total cost of ownership. This approach should reduce risks and provide management the visibility for decision making.

REFERENCES

1. Haight, T. "The Steady Increase of Client/Server.", Client/server Computing:The Strategic Edge For A changing Landscape – A Supplement To Information Week, (1993):80.
2. Hachtel, George. "A Best of Breed Approach to Client/Server", Data Management Review, vol 4. No. 1 (January 1994) pp: 17-19.
3. Huff, Richard A. "Client/Server Technology: Is It A Bill of Goods?", Information Strategy: The Executive's Journal, v12n1, (Fall 1995), pp:21-28.
4. Diamond, Sidney "Client/Server: Myths & realities", Journal of Systems Management, v46n4, (Jul/Aug 1995), pp: 44-48.
5. Parr, Harvey. "Can Client server live up to its promise?", Insurance System Bulletin, v11n4, (Oct 1995), pp: 6-8.
6. Rifkin, Glenn, "Information technology: The Client/server challenge", Harvard Business Review, v72n4, (Jul/Aug 1994), pp: 9-10.
7. Ramarapu, Narender K. "Client/server computing: Is it the right choice", Information Strategy: The Executive's Journal, v12n2 (Winter 1996), pp: 39-41.
8. Renaud, Paul E. (1993). Introduction to Client/Server Systems. New York: John Wiley & Sons, Inc.
9. Ruble, David A. Practical Analysis & Design for Client/Server and GUI Systems. New Jersey: Prentice Hall, Inc.
10. Vaskevitch, David. Client/Server Strategies. Boston Massachusetts: IDG Books Worldwide, Inc.
11. http://empire.lansing.cc.mi.us/course/wdavis/130/client_server.html
http://www.personal.kent.edu/~jnattey/spage7.html

Information Technology Opportunities and Challenges in Argentina

Mahesh S. Raisinghani, Ph.D. and Claudia Montoya
University of Dallas, Graduate School of Management, Irving, TX 75062
Phone: (972) 721-5173, Fax: (972) 721-4007, Email: mraising@gsm.udallas.edu

ABSTRACT

The intent of this descriptive and exploratory research is to provide a good foundation for research in global information technology (IT) with a focus on Argentina. Global IT Research is in its infancy. However, even in this short span, a theoretical base for global IT has evolved from reference disciplines in international management, history, sociology and psychology. This article first provides framework for diffusion of IT with experiences from other world regions, and then goes on to examine IT in the regional context of Argentina and its implications for IS; the cultural, social, political, psychometric factors and contingencies influencing IS in Argentina; and the issues that are unique in some way to Argentina.

INTRODUCTION

With the increasing integration and globalization of Latin American economies, there is both an opportunity and a challenge for IT management to quickly (re)build world-class operations even in the presence of limitations in public infrastructure, resources, skilled labor and technology. Since advanced and industrialized nations such as United States (US), Western European countries, Japan, and Australia among others are regarded as the major players in both the production and consumption of technology, there are lessons to be learned from successes as well as failures in the management of IT resources in top performing companies of the developed economy.

This article first provides framework for diffusion of IT with experiences from other world regions, and then goes on to examine IT in the regional context of Argentina and its implications for IS; the cultural, social, political, psychometric factors and contingencies influencing IS in Argentina; and the issues that are unique in some way to Argentina. A conceptual model of the global IT environment shown in Figure 1 illustrates the diffusion of IT based on the level of economic growth. The proposed comprehensive model for global IT environment shown in Figure 2 aids the understanding of the cultural, political and economic aspects involved in IT management situations that deserve to be studied and documented. Figure 3 evaluates the practices of IS organizations by classifying them into Hofstede's quadrants. Table 1 shows the examples of countries that can be grouped into Hofstede's quadrants.

Argentina's recent growth in technology has principally been spurred by heavy external investment in telecommunications. Since this telecommunications growth is relatively recent, most of the systems development has been fueled by non-Argentine companies. Subsequently, no dominant geographical location has evolved into a center for technical development similar to the Silicon Valley in the US. The next section evaluates the economic outlook in Argentina and its impact on IT.

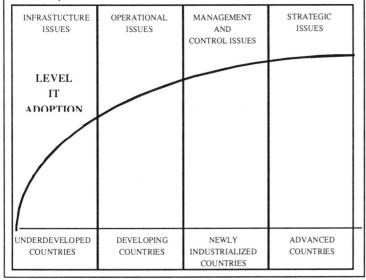

Figure 1. A Model of Global information Technology Environment Level of Economic Growth
Source: Palvia C. Prashant & Palvia C. Shailendra; (1996); "Global Information Technology and Systems Management." Ivy League Publishing, Limited, New Hampshire.

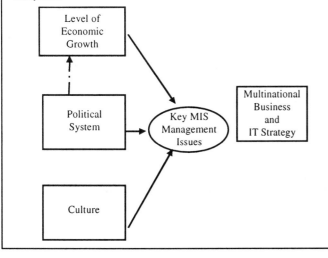

Figure 2: A Proposed Comprehensive Model For Global IT Environment
Source: Palvia C. Prashant & Palvia C. Shailendra; (1996); "Global Information Technology and Systems Management." Ivy League Publishing, Limited, New Hampshire.

ARGENTINA'S ECONOMIC OUTLOOK

For several decades, Argentina suffered economic decline and constant inflation. In 1989 changes were instituted by President Menem. He recognized the fact that without changes Argentina was certain for economic disaster.

One of the first steps taken to lead Argentina towards economic recovery was the enactment of the 1991 Convertibility Law. This established guidelines to lead to price stability and monetary policy. Through this law, the government privatized most of the state-controlled companies, relaxed foreign trade and investment, improved tax collection, and created private pension and worker's compensation systems.

Through the implementation of these acts, Argentina's economic growth was phenomenal. Along with this growth came a great challenge of how to continue the growth with more equitable distribution of income. Due to the reforms previously mentioned as well as to a stabilization of the Argentine currency, there has been new investments in the industrial sector, specifically in food products, petroleum products, automotive, mining, and metals. Argentina's exports doubled in a five-year period and imports experienced a two-fold increase during this time period.

During the 1995-1996 time frame, the peso suffered a severe devaluation. However, due to previously enacted programs and support by other countries, Argentina was able to weather the financial crisis with little impact. The government continues to make economic adjustments to meet the country's needs.

There are some challenges that Argentina still faces. Those are: the ability to create jobs for the citizens through aggressive measures in the labor arena, to continue the policy of reforms in the banking industry, and finally, the simplification of the tax laws and fighting tax evasion.

Banking
Banking reforms as mentioned above,

Figure 3: Practices of IS Organizations Classified into Hofstede Quadrants

Low
Uncertainty
Avoidance

MARKET
Scanning for opportunities (Cooper, 1994).
Participation by end-users (Mouakket et. al., 1994).
Use of groups or teams (Wetherbe et. al., 1994).
Connectivity (Nelson et. al., 1992).
Wide-spread access (Nelson et. al., 1992)
Distributed processing (Wetherbe et. al., 1994)
Innovation (Cougar, 1990)

FAMILY
Highly centralized IS organizations (Sicar and Rao, 1986).
Limited end-user involvement (Burn et. al., 1993).
Limited use of networking (Sicar and Rao, 1086, Goodman and Green, 1992).
Preference for centralized data storage (Sicar and Rao, 1986).
Lack of equality among team members (Odedra-Straub, 1993).

LOW ———————— POWER DISTANCE ———————— HIGH

MACHINE
Improve existing operations (Schwarzer, 1995).
Less preference for reengineering (Schwarzer, 1995).
Difficulty in balancing centralized and decentralized architectures (Schwarzer, 1995, Ein-Dor et. al., 1992).

PYRAMID
Automation of routine processes (Azuma and Mole, 1991).
Focus on accounting, manufacturing, and operations (Azuma and Mole, 1991).
Limited end-user involvement (Nelson et. al., 1992).
Little Emphasis on distributed environment (Nelson et. al., 1992).

Focus on
order

---

led to record investments. By the end of 1997, peso and dollar deposits had reached 70 billion dollars. Foreign-controlled banks now hold about 40 percent of Argentina's bank deposits. Rapid growth demonstrates that there is a high level of confidence in Argentina's reforms. Nevertheless, the problem of high financing and lending costs still remains as compared to other industrialized nations. Relaxed lending for small and medium size firms must be implemented to stimulate job creation.

Table 1: Examples of Countries which can be grouped into Hofstede's Quadrants
Source: Shore, Barry; (1996); "Global Information Technology and Systems Management." Ivy League Publishing, Limited, New Hampshire.

MARKET	MACHINE	PYRAMID	FAMILY
Denmark	Finland	France	Hong Kong
Sweden	Switzerland	Japan	Singapore
Ireland	Germany	Mexico	India
New Zealand	Israel	Greece	Philippines
USA	Argentina	Arab Countries	West Africa
Great Britain	Costa Rica	Korea	Malaysia

Foreign Trade

Foreign trade has been a key element in Argentina's economic surge of 1990's. Trade has been essential for Argentina to meet its external payments. Along with this came the cooperation between Brazil and Argentina in MERCORSUR, which is one of the largest markets in the developing world. Being a member of MERCOSUR will have a greater importance in the future. The recent financial crisis suffered in the Asian market stresses the fact that Argentina must be aligned with a trading partner in order to suffer as little effect as possible from external factors.

Through the alliance in MERCOSUR, Argentina has been able to gain access to the East Asian markets. However, trade with the United States continues to be in a deficit situation for Argentina. From 1993 to 1997, Argentina experienced a 13 billion trade deficit with the United States. In 1998, the total was 3.6 billion dollars. This was due to continued demand by Argentina for capital goods and the recovery of the local economy. This trend demonstrates the importance of Argentina to modernize and improve competition in Argentina's industrial sector.

Investment

The United States invested 12 billion dollars by mid-1997 in Argentina. These investments are concentrated in telecommunications, banking, electricity, petroleum, food processing, and auto manufacturing. According to a 1994 investment treaty between Argentina and the United States, U.S. investors can invest in any segment of the market except shipbuilding, fishing, nuclear power generation, and uranium production. The treaty has provisions for international arbitration in case of disputes.

Exchange Rate Policy

Argentina has no exchange controls. The Central Bank buys and sells dollars at the rate of one peso per dollar.

Foreign Competition

U.S. suppliers such as Microsoft and Novell dominate the local market for networking software. Japanese software is reputed to be user-unfriendly, and local business people are aware that European technological levels are lower than those of U.S. suppliers.

The excellent reputation earned locally by Microsoft and Novell still leaves a wide-open space for other U.S. suppliers to tap the expected surge in demand.

INFORMATION TECHNOLOGY IN ARGENTINA

The Argentine market of hardware, software and services related to IT reached 1,930 million dollars in 1997. This figure shows 20 percent increase in relation to 1996.

The Argentines bought 927 million dollars in equipment, 48 percent of the total market billing. Software reached 345 millions (17.9 percent) and services, 658 million (34.1 percent). In units, 370 thousand computers were sold during 1997. This takes the total estimated number of computers installed in Argentina to 2.1 million. Of this number, 730 thousand include multimedia technology (www.tradeport.org/ts/countries/argentina/, 1998).

Evidence of software market growth in Argentina is the local presence through subsidiaries of the principal world suppliers including: J.D. Edwards, SSA, IBM, Microsoft, Lotus, Novell, Computer Associates, Informix, Oracle, and Autodesk among others. The growth in PC software sales has been helped by the constant growth of microcomputer sales. Microcomputer sales may also be used to project the market for PC applications software.

A characteristic of the IT market in Argentina is its concentration in a few companies. In 1994, the $ 1.2 billion in supply sales was divided in the following manner: IBM, 43 percent; HP and Compaq, 6 percent each; NCR-AT&T, Unysis and Epson, 4 percent each. Three companies compose 50 percent of total industry sales and twelve companies represent 80 percent (including Xerox, TTI, Microsistemas, Sisteco, Bull and EDS, each one with annual sales of more than $20 million) (United States Department of Commerce, 1996).

The market of notebooks witnessed an increase of 36 percent in the first three quarters of 1997 (with respect to 1996). During this period, 18,044 units were sold. The leading brand names are Compaq, Texas Instruments, IBM, ACER and Toshiba. The market of servers also grew significantly in 1997. The first quarter reflected a 31 percent growth in relation to the same period in 1996. The surge in the sale of notebooks is due, not only to the expansion of mobile technology as a common working tool, but also to a considerable price reduction and the penetration of new and high capacity models into the market. Argentina follows clearly the worldwide trend toward internetworking and the convergence of all telecommunications services into one single screen (IDC Argentina, 1998; U.S. Department of Commerce, 1998).

The best prospect sectors for U.S. exporters to Argentina are in the computers and peripherals sector as represented in Table 2.

The density of personal computers in comparison to the other Latin American countries and US is shown in Table 3.

Software

PC software and software for mid-range and mainframes differ not only in its characteristics but also in its channels of distribution. The price of software for medium and large machines also includes the high cost for service. This makes it difficult to separate services from software, considering that the same software publishers sell the software, the integration and customization of the product.

Local Competition

Local production of networking software is negligible, accounting for less than 2 percent of the total market. This factor is brought about by high local labor costs. No local firm is in a position to make investments as large as those of Microsoft and Novell to develop new solutions. Local end users are also used to working with U.S.-developed software, and moderately comfortable with working in English. Applications in Spanish could, however, enjoy a slightly higher demand than similar solutions in English.

Table 2: Computers and Peripherals Sector in Argentina (US$ millions)

	1996	1997	1998
Total Market Size	630	760	888
Total Local Production	50	60	70
Total Exports	5	6	7
Total Imports	575	706	825
Total Imports from U.S.	504	495	487

Exchange Rate: One peso equals one dollar.
Source: www.tradeport.org/ts/countries/argentina/

Table 3: Personal Computers Per 1000 People in Latin America and US

Argentina	24.6
Brazil	13.0
Chile	0.0
Uruguay	22.0
United States	328.0
Venezuela	16.7

Source: ITU World Telecommunications Indicators Database, 1995

Table 4: Total of 17,211 nodes; 0.455 nodes per 1000 inhabitants of Argentina.

1,477 Web servers
5088 registered domains
429 FTP Servers

Source: Reporte de nodos Latinoamerica y el Caribe

Table 5: Internet Hosts in Argentina Per 10,000 People As of July, 1996

Argentina	2.72
Brazil	2.90
Chile	9.27
Uruguay	2.76

Source: ITU World Telecommunications Indicators Database, 1996

INTERNET STATISTICS

As of April 25, 1997, Argentina (.ar domain) had the following Internet statistics shown in Table 4:

It appears from the proliferation of the .ar domains and large growth of Argentine ISPs that Argentina is quickly becoming a "wired country." Another example of this is the emergence of the "cyber cafe" phenomenon in Argentina. The causes for this trend are the appearance of credit, economic stability, and the favorable exchange rate for the Argentine currency (one Peso equals one Dollar), combined with constant price reductions. The following table compares Argentina's number of Internet hosts to other representative countries:

Another important feature of the local IT sector behavior is the growing market share (in units and Dollars) of microcomputers, peripherals, and software. Within the hardware category, personal computers (PC's) have more than compensated for the shrinkage in sales of midrange computers and mainframes.

The next section discusses the IT opportunities and challenges in Argentina with its implications for management.

OPPORTUNITIES, CHALLENGES AND IMPLICATIONS FOR MANAGEMENT

The three broad categories of IT opportunities and challenges in Argentina are wireless communications, telecommunication equipment, and software development (http://gurukul.ucc.american.edu/initeb/dh7566a/argentin.htm, May 1997).

Wireless Communications

The two regional telephone companies, Telecom Argentina Telecom and Telefónica de Argentina, are aggressively moving to deploy new networks and improving the country's reputation for poor service. In wireless communications, the February 1994 award of regional cellular licenses to a consortium led by GTE and AT&T has established
a strong U.S. presence in this market long dominated by European service companies.

The mobile wireless penetration rate in Argentina is growing at rapid rate. Argentina will probably see higher rates of wireless growth than more developed countries, due to the large costs for wiring a country for telephones.

Telecommunication Equipment

Imports have traditionally supplied about one-third of the telecommunications equipment market; however, privatization and increased competition have increased the ratio of imports close to one half of the total market. Argentina is a good candidate for IT manufacturing due to the growing demand for information technology and telecommunications equipment. Most of the investment in this market is coming from international sources. Argentina will slowly grow their domestic IT manufacturing, assisted by the technology transfer from the developed countries.

Software Development

According to the Economist Intelligence Unit Limited (1996) and the Argentina National Telecommunications Commission (CNT), 62% of Argentina's GDP comes from the service sector, Argentina's strong growing economy continues to encourage purchases of imported goods and services. Given the high expansion in the computer base, significant software purchases will follow. Application software of universal applications should find a growing market which will comprise the newly privatized public utilities, banks, and insurance companies.

Argentina is not a good candidate for offshore software development due to the lack of substantial software development experience. Besides, Argentina's strong currency continues to encourage purchases of imported goods and services.

SUMMARY

Argentina's telecommunications privatization has led to rapid growth and innovation that benefits all industries. For example, Telefónica de Argentina has an advanced "smart card" with a chip inside it, which allows customers to use any phone at their reach as if it were using their own home phone. Since the network is digitized, Telefónica de Argentina can provide advanced services such as call blocking, automated dialing, and credit limits. The electronic linkages are nearly in place to allow businesses to take advantage of advanced supply chain management.

With heavy foreign investment in the areas of telecommunications and information technology in Argentina, the technical expertise will slowly be absorbed into Argentina's workforce. Within 3-5 years, Argentina will have the labor supply to support business to business EDI and strategic linkages. Investments in Argentina's small scale distribution centers can take advantage of Argentina's favorable labor costs and growing agricultural and manufacturing industries for international trade. As the distribution centers grow and business relationships are made, the country's communications infrastructure will have matured to a point where international inventory management and ordering systems will be advanced enough to offer a direct competitive advantage over other distribution centers.

REFERENCES

Gibson, Rick (1998), "Three Missing Pieces in Global Information Technology," Journal of Global Information Technology Management, Vol. 1 No. 2, April.

IDC Argentina, (1998), "Computers Market in Argentina," International Market Insight.

Palvia Prashant (1998), "Global Information Technology Research: Past, Present and Future," Journal of Global Information Technology Management, Vol. 1 No. 2, April.

Reinhard, Nicolau (1998), "IT in Latin North Americas," Journal of Global Information Management, Idea Group Publishing, http://www.idea-group.com/jgim986.htm

U.S. Department of Commerce (1998), National Trade Data Bank, September 2.

United States Department of Commerce (1996), "Argentina - Local And Wide Area Networks", International Trade Administration, Market Research Reports, Mar 2.

Achieving Interaction Quality in Marketing-oriented IT Projects: Focusing on the Cultural Effects

Hindupur V. Ramakrishna and Xiaohua Lin

Penn State Great Valley, School of Graduate Professional Studies, 30 E. Swedesford Road, Malvern, PA 19355

Fax: (610)725-5224, (610)648-3371 (hxr7@psu.edu) and (610)648-3223) (hxl165@psu.edu)

INTRODUCTION

As competition intensifies, businesses have an increasing need for timely information (Maltz and Kohli 1996). The growing emphasis on marketing intelligence is based on the belief that a firm's capability of using information will increasingly determine how it performs against competition in an age of information (Moorman 1995). Evidence abound that organizations known to be equipped with effective marketing information systems are inevitably leaders in their fields, including UPS, MCI, and L. L. Bean. Unfortunately, although the advancement of information technology has increasingly enabled the companies to meet their information need, many firms have difficulties to effectively manage their IT projects designed to offer marketing solutions (Cleaver 1998). As is known, the overall failure rate for IT projects including marketing-oriented ones is very high (Lyytinen and Hirschheim 1987). These failures result in billions of dollars of financial losses and cost companies many opportunities. To better take advantage of information technology in a firm's marketing endeavor, academicians and practitioners alike have to answer this question: Why are some IT projects more successful than others?

Remarkably, this crucial issue has not been addressed fully in empirical research to date. In particular, previous research has largely overlooked a key aspect of IT project implementation: the ongoing interaction between IT function and user groups. In the cases of marketing-oriented IT projects, for example, the inability to effectively manage ongoing interaction by marketing and IT managers has been found to be a major cause for failed or unsuccessful marketing-oriented IT projects within firms. In this paper, we present a conceptual model that focuses on the quality of ongoing interaction in implementing marketing-oriented IT projects. Drawn on previous research, the model includes two cooperation-centered constructs – trust and relationship commitment as important antecedents of interaction quality. The model further considers a set of "cultural" factors, i.e., orientation toward IT, organizational culture, and national culture that are posited as influencing interaction quality in IT project implementation process. In the current US IT environment where there are thousands of jobs unfilled, organizations do not have the luxury of hiring IT candidates for their fit with organizational culture but are bound to hire them for their knowledge, skills, and abilities. In addition, due to widespread outsourcing of IT activities and the typical composition of IT personnel pool, an increasing percentage of IT professionals working in US organizations would be non-US born. By investigating the potential impact of organizational and national culture as well as orientation toward IT function, this research attempts to make a significant and timely contributions to the US businesses that endeavor to sharpen marketing tools with advanced information technology. The conceptual model is portrayed in Figure 1.

INTERACTION QUALITY AND IT PROJECT SUCCESS

To successfully implement an IT project, many conditions have to be in place, such as management commitment and well formulated working plans (Swanson 1988). However, these antecedent conditions do not simply translate into desired project outcomes. A well-funded and planned project may fail because of the lack of productive interface between IT and marketing personnel during the implementation process. From a process perspective, the way marketing and IT interacts on a daily basis casts a positive or negative tone of the working relationship, channels more or less energies into joint actions, and ultimately determines the success or failure of an IT project. In the language of communications theory, when communications between IT and marketing functions are frequent, bidirectional, and integrative, marketing-oriented IT projects have better chance to succeed. Stated formally, we propose that:

P1. As interaction quality increases, the likelihood of IT project success increases.

TRUST AND RELATIONSHIP COMMITMENT

Given its significance, what determines the quality of interactions between IT and marketing groups? Management and marketing literature identifies two key antecedent variables within an organization – trust and relationship commitment that exert crucial influence on interaction and communication between functional areas within firms. Trust, as a feature of relationships, indicates a willingness to rely on a partner in whom one has confidence (Moorman, Zaltman, and Deshpande 1992). As with other types of IT projects, the success of marketing-oriented projects should be ultimately judged by how the marketing function's needs are served with the implemented information systems. Obviously, this requests an adequate dialogue between the two departments on a continuing basis during the implementation process. Compared to other functional areas, marketing demands more from its information systems the ability to be flexible and responsive to evolving marketing. It is not surprising, therefore, that constant changes may be requested by the marketing function during an IT implementation process, especially if it spans a long period of time. To effectively address the changing needs, marketing and IT people have to communicate, not only frequently, but in an integrative fashion. Yet, to achieve such interaction quality, marketing and IT people have to overcome the distrust that unfortunately prevails in many US corporations (Bresnahan 1998). Trust not only opens the door for information exchange, but reduces the fear for confronting disagreements. The above discussion suggests the following proposition:

P2. As trust increases, interaction quality increases.

Relationship commitment exists when a partner believes that "an ongoing relationship with another is so important as to warrant maximum efforts at maintaining it" (Morgan and Hunt 1994). Successful IT projects demand high quality interactions which go beyond routine-type interface. However, such interactions can be secured only if marketing and IT people are committed to the common goals, to the working relationship, and by essence to the other party. As is known, identifying with one's department rather than interdepartmental goals is a major obstacle to any corporate projects that require team efforts across functional areas (Fisher, Maltz, and Jaworski 1997). To overcome this, it is imperative for team members to identify with the collective goals and interests, that is, to become committed to the relationship within a specified time frame. When IT and marketing people attach themselves to the working relationship, they are more likely to share concerns, address problems, and resolve disagreements in an integrative manner. In other words, the following linkage can be expected:

P3. As relationship commitment increases, interaction quality increases.

Propositions 2 and 3 imply that the effects of trust and relationship commitment on IT success are indirect through quality interaction. In addition, previous research suggests at there is direct association between relationship effectiveness and trust/relationship commitment (Morgan and Hunt 1994). Accordingly, we model both indirect and direct effects of trust and relationship commitment on IT success.

P4. As trust increases, the likelihood of IT project success increases.

P5. As relationship commitment increases, the likelihood of IT project success increases.

CULTURAL PERSPECTIVES OF INTERACTION

Modeling trust and relationship commitment as key antecedents of interaction quality, the research emphasizes psychological aspect of relationship process. This orientation leads to one group of factors that uniquely influence or moderate the associations conceptualized in P2 and P3. These factors include: (1) orientation toward IT; (2) organizational culture; and (3) national culture. For the purpose of convenience, we use a broad term – "culture" to refer to the three factors. With these cultural variables, the research is able to address an often-raised research question: Does relationship effectiveness demand congruence in perceptions, beliefs, and attitude?

Orientation toward IT

Orientation toward IT (OIT) refers to the way IT function is perceived by IT or other functional areas. Dahlbom and Mathiassen (1997) described three views of IT functions: support; equal in value to any other function; or the driver for the entire business, as summarized below:

As far as interaction is concerned, our attention is on both parties' views of the IT function. Depending on which view is taken, the nature and pattern of interaction between marketing and IT can be rather different. Organizational literature shows that the nature of communications between organization members depends largely on the power relationships

Perception	IS as a Support function	IS as equal in value to any other function	IS as driver for the business
Slogan	I build things	I help people	I change things
Focus	Artifact	Culture	Power
Approach	Construction	Evolution	Intervention
Role	Engineer	Facilitator	Emancipator

(Jablin 1987). For example, if IT people self-claim as the driver for the entire business, they may not proactively seek inputs from marketing people, even in marketing-oriented projects. On the other hand, marketing people may focus on the "ownership" of the system to be implemented and treat IT people as "support" team. In both circumstances, two-way, integrative communications are unlikely. Specifically, we propose the following direct effects of OIT on interaction quality:

P6a. The more the IT function is perceived as equal, the higher the interaction quality will be in marketing-oriented IT projects will be.

P6b. The more the IT function is perceived as Support or Driver, the less integrated the ongoing interactions.

Organizational Culture

Organizational culture (OC) is defined as "the pattern of shared values and beliefs that help individuals understand organizational functioning and that provide norms for behavior in the organization" (Deshpande and Webster 1989, p.4). Organizational culture plays a bonding role for members to collectively pursue effectiveness within an organization (Cameron and Freeman 1991). As such, the nature, direction, and magnitude of interactions between IT and user groups will to certain degree depend on the prevalent culture of the entire organization. Two types of organizational culture, often considered as contradictory, are clan and hierarchy cultures. Clan cultures stress cohesiveness, participation, and teamwork, whereas hierarchy cultures emphasize order, rules and regulations, uniformity, efficiency, and control (Cameron and Freeman 1991). Since clans emphasize the development of shared organizational understanding and commitment, communications tend to flow freely and interactions occur across functional boundaries. By contrast, hierarchies tend to disintegrate an organization, so that effective interaction and communications exit only within each subunit (Moorman 1995). We thus propose that:

P7. Compared with hierarchy cultures, clan cultures are more likely to have quality interactions between IT and marketing groups in implementing marketing-oriented IT projects.

National Culture

National culture (NC) is "the collective programming of the mind which distinguishes the members of one human group from another" (Hofstede 1980, p.21). One of the striking facts in the US IT sector has been the employment of increasing number of international employees, a trend reconfirmed by the recent legislative initiative in the Congress. This phenomenon has created a peculiar situation with respect to the IT activities in the US firms: the marketing and IT functions tend to be performed disproportionally by Americans and internationals, respectively. When this happens, additional difficulties are witnessed in IT development projects designed for marketing solutions. As is known, diverse national cultures make interaction and communications problematic as they subscribe their members to different norms (Hofstede 1980). Take an example of a marketing manager born in the US. When he needs to talk with the IT department for issues involved in an IT project, there is an increasing chance that his/her counterpart is a member of a different national culture. As a product of the American culture, the marketing manager is likely to prefer openness in information exchange but confrontation in resolving disagreements. However, his/her partner, born in a different culture, may be used to more ambiguous communications and avoiding or accommodating styles in conflict resolution. If this is the case, the ongoing interaction between the representatives of marketing and IT functions can be frustrating or inadequate at least. The above discussion suggests that:

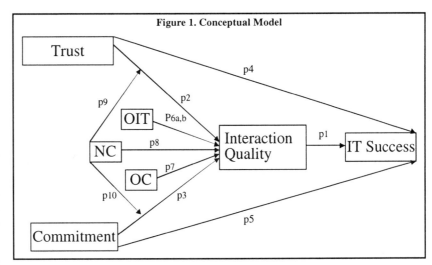

Figure 1. Conceptual Model

P8. As diversity of nationality increases between marketing and IT groups, interaction quality decreases.

National culture may not only have a direct impact on interaction quality, but also moderate the effects of trust and relationship commitment on it. While different cultures may conceptualize trust the same way, they may vary in the degree of reliance on trust in exchange relationships. In the context of conflict resolution, for example, the association between trust and open communications is likely to be moderated by parties' nationality (Lin and Miller 1997). The effect of relationship commitment on interaction quality may also vary in strength depending on a party's national culture. Cross-cultural psychologists reveal the so-called in-group effect that members of collective cultures, compared to members of individualistic cultures, are more likely to behave differently depending on whether the interaction partner is an in-group member or an out-group member. As a result, the effect of relationship commitment should have a stronger effect among members of collective cultures than among individualistic cultures (Lin and Miller 1997). Using nationality as a proxy for national culture and focusing on Americans (likely to be individualistic; marketing position) and their international counterparts (likely collectivist; IT position) in IT projects, we suggest:

P9. The effects of trust on interaction quality depends on whether marketing and IT personnel belong to the same nationality group.

P10. The effects of relationship commitment on interaction quality depends on whether marketing and IT personnel belong to the same nationality group.

CONCLUSION AND FUTURE RESEARCH DIRECTIONS

We attempt to make theoretical contributions in two areas. First, we explicitly examine quality of ongoing interaction and its important antecedents in marketing-oriented IT projects. Successful IT projects need strong resource commitment and well-formulated plan and designs; then a quality interaction process needs to be in place to turn these important inputs into desirable outcomes — effective marketing information systems. Corporate management's task thus is not limited to resource allocation, but includes making sure that there is a productive relationship between IT and marketing personnel. Attention should be paid to nourish a trusting relationship and set up procedures and systems that help IT and marketing people to identify with each other and with their working relationship. Second, we identify a set of "cultural" variables that exert important influence on interaction quality either directly or indirectly through their interaction with trust and relationship commitment. Importantly, these are the areas where management can work on. With well designed education programs to promote proper attitude toward IT, to nourish an integrative organizational climate, and to eliminate or at least reduce distance created by national cultural difference, the chance of successfully implementing marketing-oriented IT projects can be greatly enhanced.

A logical next step is to empirically test the model presented in this paper. The model may be tested using data collected from US companies that have recently carried out marketing-oriented IT projects. To reflect the dyadic views of ongoing interaction, IT and corresponding marketing personnel should be identified to participate. In addition to reliable, valid research instruments, securing a sufficiently large sample of paired respondents poses a major challenge to research projects such as this.

REFERENCES

Bresnahan, Jennifer (1998), "Improving the Odds," CIO Enterprise, November 15, 36-48.

Cameron, Kim S. and Sara J. Freeman (1991), "Cultural Congruence, Strength, and Type: Relationships to Effectiveness," in Research in Organizational Change and Development, Vol. T, R. W. Woodman and W. A. Passmore, eds. Greenwich, CT: JAI Press inc., 23-58.

Cleaver, Joanne (1998), "Ground Zero: Marketing, IT Battle over Web site Control," Marketing News, Vol. 32 (18), 1, 15.

Dahlbom, Bo and Lars Mathiassen (1997), "The Future of OUR Profession," Communications of the ACM, Vol. 40 (June), 80-89.

Deshpande, Rohit and Frederick E. Webster (1989), "Organizational Culture and Marketing: Defining the Research Agenda," Journal of Marketing, Vol. 53 (January), 3-15.

Fisher, Robert J, Maltz, Elliot and Bernard J. Jaworski (1997), "Enhancing Communication Between Marketing and Engineering: The Moderating Role of Relative Functional Identification," Journal of Marketing, Vol. 61 (July), 54-70.

Hofstede, Geert (1980), Culture's Consequences, London, Sage Publications.

Jablin, Frederic (1987), "Formal Organization Structure," in Handbook of Organizational Communication: An Interdisciplinary Perspective, F. Jablin et al., eds. Newbury Park, CA: Sage Publications, 389-419.

Lin, Xiaohua and Stephen Miller (1997), "Joint Venture Ongoing Negotiation: Strategies, Relational Contexts, and Effect of National Culture," working paper.

Lyytinen, K. and R. Hirschheim (1987), "Information Systems Failures: A Survey and Classification of the Empirical Literature," Oxford Surveys of Information Technology 4, 257-309.

Maltz, Elliot and Ajay K. Kohli (1996), "Market Intelligence Dissemination Across Functional Boundaries," Journal of marketing Research, Vol. 32 (February), 47-61.

Moorman, Christine (1995), "Organizational Market Information Processes: Cultural Antecedents and New Product Outcomes," Journal of Marketing Research, Vol. 32 (August), 318-335.

Moorman, Christine, Zaltman, Gerald and Rohit Deshpande (1992), "Relationships Between Providers and Users of Market research: The Dynamics of Trust Within and Between Organizations," Journal of Marketing Research, Vol. 29 (August), 314-328.

Morgan, Robert and Shelby D. Hunt (1994), "The Commitment-Trust Theory of Relationship Marketing," Journal of Marketing, Vol. 58 (July), 20-38.

Swanson, (1988), Information Systems Implementation, Homewood, Illinois: Irwin.

Kids & the 21st Century: Shaping the Future… Towards Information Society "Little Horus Web Site"

Heba Ramzy, MSc
Kids Information Highway and Electronic Publishing Dept., Director, RITSEC, 11A Hassan Sabry St., Zamalek, Cairo, Egypt
Tel. (202) 341 1761 – Fax (202) 341 2139, Hramzy@ritsec1.com.eg

Computers are going to change the way kids think and learn just like tractors changed farming. However, computers are the means by which student orchestrates the use of IT to share knowledge and communicate with each other. IT is the organization of knowledge and a vital aspect in today's world for our future leaders. As we are approaching the 21st century, it is very important that our decision-makers would pay much attention and time to our future leaders to prepare them for next millenium through the use of IT and communication. In today's world we find that the Internet has become the vital means of information provision in today's world, from a CEO to a clerk, from a school principle to a 1st grader. This information reservoir is stored on what is called the network of the networks "the Internet", is of high importance. In that respect, no one can ignore such a tool. The Internet is the fastest, easiest, and richest tool not only as information provider and knowledge disseminator but also as network connector around the world regardless of time, space, difference and similarity. This connection has helped in making the world closer, leading to the realization and the formation of the Global Village.

The Internet has a wealth of knowledge and information sources for both kids and adults. If we are looking in a couple of year's time, we have to think of the future makers, our Kids. One third of the world population are kid under the age of 15 and one half under the age of 20 while only 15 million of them are Internet users. These kids need more than a game, e-mail. They need to benefit from such a device in a much more elaborate way. They need more informative, educative but at the same time entertaining sources in both the real world and the Cyber space. In that respect, the world should be mobilized and work towards preparing our kids for the 21st century and putting this issue on top of all countries' agendas. In Egypt, an initiative was put together "Investing in Our Future" to prepare the kids for the next millenium. The initiative was developed to help kids talk today's language, communicate with their peer group in different parts of the world and allow them to compete and work in a global environment. It includes a number of activities among which are the establishment of the 21st Century kids clubs, the development of place in the Cyber Space, and help develop the software industry for kids in Arabic. Although we realized that we were doing pioneer work, we never realized how much ahead we were of many other countries, both in connections and activities locally and internationally.

This working document is to highlight the directions and the activities that are carried out in Egypt in the area of kids, technology and the next millenium. It will also allow us to share our success stories with experts and professionals helping us to making a difference in the world of our future leaders to assist in our future plans.

VISION
Investing in Our Future… Preparing the kids for the 21st Century

A CASE STUDY FROM EGYPT:
The initiative, "Investing in Egypt Future" to prepare the kids for the 21st Century was put together to help kids talk today's language, communicate with their peer group different part of the world and allow them to compete and work in a global environment. These activities have been designed in a way to help us meet our objective. They include establishing 21st Century Kids Clubs, a place

in the Cyber Space and initiation of the kids software industry in Egypt

Our Objectives are:

- Creating the environment and providing the tools for the kids and youth to learn about today's language and practice the use of IT and communication facilities
- Building bridges between today's kids principle of peace, tolerance, harmony, love
- Exposing today's kids to new ways of thinking to be able to compete tomorrow in a global environment
- Creating collaboration among kids and youth around the world to help create circles of knowledge among themselves
- Mobilizing the whole country to work towards preparing the kids for the next millenium
- Improving the quality of educational and cultural tools and material on the Internet for the kids and youth

The presentation is built upon a remarkable successful initiative that is taking place in Egypt, which started in 1996 with the development of the first Information Highway for kids Little Horus. In addition we found it important to introduce the concept of the 21st Century Cyber Café.

THE 21ST CENTURY CLUBS:

As we are approaching the 21st century, and as the importance of the use of IT and communication increased, the introduction of the concept of the 21st Century Cyber Café for kids in 1996 was of high importance. It is an IT empowered library that has software library, traditional library and cutting edge computers. The first pilot club, which was so successful, was inaugurated in June 1997. This has encouraged us to spread it across the Nile valley in all cities and village of Egypt. Today, we have 16 up and running in 10 different governorates. Our focus is to serve the half the population under the age of 20 not only the haves but also more importantly the have-nots.

In less than two months (summer 98), 16 centers has been implemented. It is a great collaboration where private sector, government, NGOs have partner together to realize this. It started very modest but the exponential is unbelievable. There are more than 4500 students who have attended the summer program and more than 92% of their parents want to attend the same program. We have more than 7 are expected to start functioning before the end of the 1998.

Capitalizing on the success implementation of the 21st Century Clubs during the year 1998, where 34 were established in 17 different governorates, a plan for establishing 150 more in Egypt and three countries of the region. The idea of these clubs has proven to be appealing not only at the kid's level who represents one third of the population but also on the youth and the family level. Having these Clubs spread all over the country will help Egypt to be an Information Society by the turn of the Century.

LITTLE HORUS WEB SITE HTTP://LITTLE-HORUS.COM

Little Horus, the first Egyptian web site for kids in the Cyber Space both in Arabic and English. It contains more than 300 pages of information and illustrations covering Egypt's 7000 years of civilization, telling the kids about the land of civilization with its Ancient, Greco-Roman, Coptic, Islamic as well as Modern civilization. It gives snapshots of Egypt today, including its economic, culture and social life. Kids can have fun while visiting selected favorite places in the tour section and also playing games in the entertainment section. Under the Motto of "Make One Friend A Day", kids can make friends, exchange ideas and enjoy being a member of "Little Horus" club. Kids get to learn how to deal with each other regardless of time, distance, differences & similarities and form a network where they will be able to share our motto One Friend A Day.

This site was developed specially for kids to get training, and learn while having fun. They will have the chance to learn about Egyptian culture, business areas.

H. E. Egypt's First Lady, Mrs. Suzanne Mubarak, forwarded little Horus web site to the world June 1997. Ever since, it has proven success. In Nov 1998, the number of hits has reached 3.5 million hit. It was recognized by a number of international organizations for its content. In addition, it is being used by 5th and 6th grade students in North America 22 different states as a reference for their studies. Because of its educational value, it was chosen to be published on a CD-ROM and distributed among 17,000 schools in Australia. The site is being updated weekly.

For the international exposure, we share our experience through the participation in a number of international events and competition. In that respect, Little Horus site was mentioned in the white paper that was forward by Bill Gates called, "Empowerment 2001, Government Technology for the 21st Century" in Jan. 1998. It was also selected to be published among 300 other sites in the book called Cyber Space for kids (in two volumes for different age groups) in 1998. It has also been translated to Iclandise to be taught for their kids.

THE IMPACT OF LITTLE HORUS

Periodically we review how the site is being perceived and received by kids, parents, educators, Internet users and other interested parties all over the world and its impact worldwide.

- Number of visitors per week is more than 1,500.
- Most requested pages (in order) according to the visitors are History, About Little Horus, Egypt today, Entertainment, Tour, Arabic Version, Write to Little Horus.
- Most active countries according to the number of visitors to the site (USA, Canada, UK, Egypt, Australia, Germany, Sweden, France, Spain, Finland, Brazil, Italy, Israel, Ireland, Japan, Netherlands, Denmark, Singapore, New Zealand, Norway, Belgium, Mexico, Peru, South Africa, Iceland, UAE, Amman, Kuwait). The majority of visitors come from the US, which represents about 87% of the total hits. This number is justified where there is about 10 million out of 15 million kids is the using the Internet in the US.
- Most active States according to the number of visitors to the site (Virginia, California, Ohio, New Jersey, Minnesota, Massachusetts, New York, Georgia, Washington, Ontario, Pennsylvania, Texas, Illinois, Oregon, North Carolina, Missouri, Florida, Maryland, Arizona, Michigan).

- The site has received a number of awards and was recognized by different international organizations.
- The average number of messages on a daily basis is between 30 messages. These messages contain different subjects among which are, making friends from Egypt, wants to know more about particular issue related to Ancient Egypt, contemporary & kids games, recipes, and many others.
- The site is being updated regularly on a weekly basis.

SOFTWARE FOR KIDS

One of the most important activities is to build the software industry for kids in Arabic. A number of activities have taken place for the creation of awareness of the establishment of the Arabic Software Industry for kids. In efforts to prepare the receipt of such efforts a contest for both professional and beginners was announced in 98. The impact of contest has created the interest among the software industry leaders to start investing in area. Also, a workshop was conducted to surface the importance to developing Arabic software. This workshop has help in putting such issue on top of the agenda of the country.

Within the framework of allowing the students to participate in international projects, we are currently introducing ThinkQuest program. It is an international program that will allow the Egyptian students to work and compete with their peer group from different countries in the world leading to a true glob village. Students will be working and developing their projects on the Internet in one of their preferred areas.

This project will help leverage the knowledge level of the whole society though it is mainly targeting kids & youth. During the two months of summer 98, we have witnessed how the number of students and youth attending the Clubs program. These kids were able to transfer the knowledge and attack the interest of their families where than 92% of their parents wanted to attend the same program. It is basically a bottom up approach, which will help the Egypt to be an Information Society by the next century.

Through Little Horus, the Egyptian kid was put on the Cyber map and was able to play an active role in this virtual world. The realization of the global village among kids from different part of the globe was achieved where channels of communication and circles of knowledge were created.

Through this project, we were able to create a place in the Cyber Space, avenues for the kids and youth to share and communicate with their peer group from different parts of the world and develop software in Arabic for the 21st Century Clubs. Thus, we were able to create a place in the virtual world and another in the physical world where each will serve the other. In addition students will be able to collaborate and compete in a global environment through the participation in Think Quest programs. Our motto is "the Sky is the Limit.... Mind, Soul & Body", where everything is taken care of and handled for our future leaders to make a difference in their tomorrows world.

An Object-Relational SE-Repository with Generated Services

N. Ritter, H.-P. Steiert, and W. Mahnke,
Department of Computer Science, Database and Information Systems Group
Universty of Kaiserslautern, P O Box 3049, 67653 Kaiserslautern, Germany
{ritter / mahnke / steiert}@informatik.uni-kl.de

R. L. Feldmann
Department of Computer Science, Software Engineering Group, University of Kaiserslautern, P O Box 3049, 67653 Kaiserslautern, Germany
feldmann@informatik.uni-kl.de

ABSTRACT

Several activities around the world aim at integrating object-oriented data models with relational ones in order to improve database management systems. As a first result of these activities, object-relational database management systems (ORDBMS) are already commercially available and, simultaneously, are subject to several research projects. This (position) paper reports on our activities in exploiting object-relational database technology for establishing repository manager functionality supporting software engineering (SE) processes. We argue that some of the key features of ORDBMS can directly be exploited to fulfill many of the needs of SE processes. Thus, ORDBMS, as we think, are much better suited to support SE applications than any others. Nevertheless, additional functionality, e. g., providing adequate version management, is required in order to gain a completely satisfying SE repository. In order to remain flexible, we have developed a generative approach for providing this additional functionality. It remains to be seen whether this approach, in turn, can effectively exploit ORDBMS features. This paper, therefore, wants to show that ORDBMS can substantially contribute to both establishing and running SE repositories.

Keywords: Software Engineering, Repositories, Object-Relational Database Systems, Extensibility, Reuse, Experience Database, Generic Methods.

1. INTRODUCTION

1.1 Project

The *Sonderforschungsbereich 501 'Development of Large Systems with Generic Methods' (SFB 501)*, which was founded by the *Deutsche Forschungsgemeinschaft (DFG)* contains (among others) the (sub-)project *Supporting Software Engineering Processes by Object-Relational Database Technology*. In this project we consider new object-relational database technology [13, 17] with respect to developing systems, allowing comprehensive data management in software engineering (SE) processes, and, in cooperation with the infrastructure (sub-)project that runs the *SE Laboratory of the SFB 501*, we want to provide a corresponding SE-repository. *Comprehensive data management* encompasses both, managing project data (project database) related to a current development process as well as managing experience data (experience database, [4]), i. e., information gained during (completed) processes and showing a high potential of being efficiently reused in subsequent processes.[1] Throughout this paper, we use the term *SE repository* as a kind of superordinate concept encompassing both, project data as well as experience data management. We will discuss to which extent object-relational DBMS can be directly exploited to fulfill requirements of SE repositories, and, additionally, how they can substantially contribute to generate repository manager functionality.

1.2 Object-Relational Database Systems

Currently, the approved (key) features of relational database systems (RDBMS), e. g., transactions, queries, views, and integrity maintenance, are integrated with the advantageous features of object-oriented database systems (OODBMS), e. g., support for complex objects and user-defined data types, leading to so-called *object-relational database systems* [13, 17]. ORDBMS are currently considered to be the most successful trend in DBMS development (see the evolving SQL3 standard [22]). Many of the *properties of current-generation-ORDBMS*[2] do effectively support the special needs of SE applications. From our viewpoint, the most important benefits are:

• *Enriched Modeling Concepts and Extensibility*

ORDBMS offer a rich type system which allows to define abstract data types, arrange types in inheritance hierarchies, map relationships as references and define complex data types with the help of type constructors. Furthermore, an infrastructure for handling large objects is provided. The set of predefined data types may be extended [14] by user-defined data types (UDT), which, in turn, may be used to construct even more complex UDTs. Additionally, extensibility allows to express behavioral aspects by means of so-called user-defined functions (UDF). As we will see below, these mechanisms are extremely beneficial w. r. t. the SE application area.

• *Access to External Data*

Several mechanisms are provided to extend database processing to data that is not directly stored in the database, but, e. g., held in the file system. These mechanisms allow development tools to store data in files, but, simultaneously, these data can be accessed and controlled via the database interface of the SE repository manager.

• *Infrastructure for Managing VITA Data Formats*

Most ORDBMS vendors offer predefined extensions for managing video, image, text, or audio data. Text (and image) facilities, for example, are helpful to manage documentations, technology descriptions, or annotations. Even video/audio management may be reasonably exploited in SE, e. g., to store videos of inspection meetings or oral documentations and training material.

• *Infrastructure for Access via WWW*

Also among the predefined extensions of most ORDBMS vendors are mechanisms to connect database applications to the WWW. These are extremely helpful to bridge heterogeneity and, thereby, provide appropriate interfaces in a distributed system environment.

Obviously, the mentioned features of ORDBMS can efficiently be exploited to fulfill requirements of SE applications. The following section will discuss this issue. Nevertheless, current ORDBMS are by far no panacea; there are many data management demands that cannot be directly fulfilled by exploitation of an ORDBMS, but must be met by providing additional system components. We think that this additional functionality can be provided by generic methods, which, in turn, may be based on object-relational database technology, as we will show in a separate section below.

2. DIRECT EXPLOITATION OF ORDBMS FEATURES

The enriched object-oriented modeling features of ORDBMS help model the complex object structures of SE applications. Project as well as experience data can be structured adequately by means of object-orientation, especially inheritance, type constructors, and references. For example, in our SE repository the primary experience data is (logically) structured into the areas *process modeling, qualitative experience, technologies, component repositories, measurement*, and *background knowledge* [8, 10]. Actually, the experience elements [7] (each associated with one of the mentioned areas) are large objects, which can be stored in the database by using the management features for CLOBs (character large objects) or BLOBs (binary large objects) offered by ORDBMS. Considering experience elements as large objects has the following reason.

During a running SE process, design tools are applied that store data in proprietary formats by using the file system. Since these data are needed by the originating tool or other tools in the proprietary format, it is not reasonable to transform and store them in the database. Nevertheless, due to consistency reasons, a more integrated data management is wanted. In this regard, ORDBMS offer the possibility of linking external file system data with database data. This concept offers referential integrity, access control, and coordinated backup and recovery for database related file system data. A file system filter intercepts file system requests to the linked data and, thereby, controls access (w. r. t. the database access rights). This means that design tools may further access file system data, but the data is closer integrated with the database data. In cases where the data written by tools is not in a binary format, it is, furthermore, possible to extend database search to external data. For example, search on (internal[3]) database data and search on (external) HTML files may be combined by making the database engine interoperate with external search engines via special extensions. Even modifications on external data are possible (via the database interface), although these should be applied extremely carefully, in order not to corrupt (external) data needed by tools in subsequent phases of the design process.

While we are extensively using the mechanisms mentioned in managing project data (data associated with a running development process), the management of experience data [8] is slightly different. Here, as already mentioned at the beginning of this section, we decided to store experience elements exclusively as internal data, in order to achieve absolute consistency. Those data, created by a design process and considered to have a high potential of reusability (after a corresponding analyzing process) are relocated into adequate database structures and further on considered as experience elements. For the primary experience data, as mentioned above, the CLOB/BLOB mechanisms offered by ORDBMS are exploited.

In order to support designers (or managers, respectively), who want to initiate a new design process, in finding experience elements suitable for reuse in the new process, each experience element is associated with a so-called *characterization vector* [8]. The characterization vector contains descriptions concerning all relevant aspects of corresponding reuse artifacts and spans meaningful relationships among experience elements, or between experience elements and associated data in the project database. This enables us to offer comfortable search functions at the experience base interface. We think it is crucial to offer a similarity-based search, since it is usually not possible to specify queries exactly. Here, again, ORDBMS render a substantial contribution. Similarity functions can be realized as UDFs and, thereby, be 'pushed under' the (SQL-)interface of the database system. Now, these functions can easily be used within database queries and a lot of work can be delegated to the database system. Furthermore, handling these functions is still flexible enough, because most DBMS vendors (intend to) offer Java [2] as a programming language.

Another advantage of ORDBMS, which is extensively used in our SE repository, is the usually predefined infrastructure for connecting the database (application) to the WWW. Thus, appropriate interfaces for a distributed, heterogeneous system environment may be offered.

The facilities discussed so far, are some out of a number of advantages –all of which we cannot discuss here due to space restrictions– of ORDBMS, which are extremely helpful in realizing an SE repository and which, consequently, are extensively exploited in our approach.

Nevertheless, object-relational database technology is no panacea. There are many deficiencies that must be overcome by providing additional system components. The basic question here is, to what extent extensibility is the appropriate mechanism for realizing repository manager functionality. We think that there are many requirements of SE applications that are too complex to be naturally 'pushed under' the database interface. As an example, let us consider *versioning* of experience elements. Since versioning follows a certain model, the corresponding versioning facilities cannot adequately be realized as database extensions without getting too large a 'cognitive distance' between the mental user model and the model implemented. Therefore, we decided to provide application servers which are (logically) located on top of the database system. Our special concern in this regard is to show that application server functionality can be effectively provided by generic methods, as the following section is going to discuss.

3. VERSIONING AS AN EXAMPLE FOR GENERATED SERVICES

As already discussed in [12], there are very many facets that versioning models may differ in. We think that many of the different concepts that lead to (lots of) different version models are very application-specific. Consequently, a generic version model

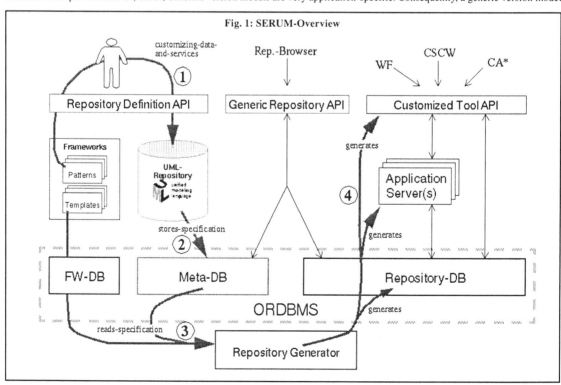

Fig. 1: SERUM-Overview

cannot support *all* applications properly, but rather serves some more, some less appropriately. Our goal is to be able to support all applications by providing basic versioning facilities which may be refined and which are the foundation for generating application-specific functionality. In Fig. 1 a graphical illustration of our generative approach called the SERUM[4] approach [15, 16] is given.

If new versioning facilities are supposed to be generated, it must first be chosen from a set of half-fabricated components. We call such a half-fabricated component a *framework*. The framework has to be customized by adapting, refining, completing, and specializing the chosen components (1). The customizing process takes advantage of object-oriented concepts, such as, for example, subclassing (specialization), overloading, late binding of interfaces, etc. Several of the *reuse* techniques identified in [9] are exploited in our approach. Each framework consists of two parts, a technology-independent part containing so-called *design patterns* and a technology-dependent part containing so-called *templates* (see below). The result of the customization process (including the application of design patterns) is a *UML[5] specification of the new repository manager*, which is stored in the SERUM meta-database (2). This UML-specification is used as input for the SERUM *repository generator* (3), which generates the *repository database schema*, the *customized tool API*, and (several) *application servers* (4). Here, the previously mentioned design templates are exploited. SERUM design templates provide mappings of the given UML model to the object model of different implementation technologies, like programming languages (C++, Java, ...), ORDBMS, strategies for architectural design (client-centric, server-centric, repository servers, caching and buffering strategies), and communication mechanisms (CORBA, OLE, RPC, ...). All the (generated) value-added data management services together establish the new repository manager. Because we are using an ORDBMS, the *repository database schema* not only consists of tables, but also includes UDTs and UDFs. Sample UDFs are the similarity functions supporting search on experience elements. Generated *tool API functions* must meet the requirements of the associated design tools and allow for adequate access to the generated services. Additional functionality, which cannot (or should not) be implemented neither at API level nor at database server level, must be implemented by specialized *application servers*. For example, functions mapping the object structures of the specified versioning model to the structures provided by the ORDBMS data model, or functions for synchronizing access to versioned objects, are located at this level.

Regretfully, due to space restriction, we cannot further detail the SERUM approach in this paper and have to refer to the corresponding literature [15]. Nevertheless, the previous brief description should have shown that the enhanced modeling features, and, especially, the extensibility features of ORDBMS are very beneficial in our approach. The repository generator reads all its (input) specifications from the ORDBMS and integrates most of the functions it generates as UDFS. For example, besides the already mentioned similarity functions, UDFs for version manipulations, for checkin/checkout, as well as for embedding version manipulations into object-oriented programming languages are provided this way.

4. RELATED WORK

Triton [11], one of the object management systems developed in the Arcadia project [19, 11, 18, 21], is based on the Exodus [5] database system toolkit. Heimbigner describes Triton as follows: '*It is a serverized repository providing persistent storage for typed objects, plus functions for manipulating those objects*' [11]. While we, on demand, link the stored data objects from the ORDBMS to the file system, so that different (commercial) SE tools can use them, Triton uses Remote Procedure Calls (RPC) for communication between client programs (SE tools) and the repository. Obviously, it is very difficult, often even impossible, to make commercially available tools collaborate with the repository this way, since their source code is not available. As a result, a variety of mediators [20] would have to be used in order to bridge the gap between a repository like Triton and the tools to be applied in our environment. As we think, our approach of storing experience elements as large objects within the database and making them available in the file system as soon as they are to be accessed by tools, is easier to realize, easier to administrate, and, therefore, more practicable. Finally, as described in [11], versioning, another important feature of our SE repository, is not supported by Triton.

In [3] a hybrid system for delivering marketing information in heterogeneous formats via the Internet is described. An object-oriented client/server document management system based on an RDBMS is used for storing the documents of the repository. Standard attributes, like creation date, author, or a version number are automatically assigned to the repository entries by the document management system. Additional attributes, which further characterize a document, have to be included as HTML metatags. Web servers are running search engines to index the repository with the help of these tags. Since we are not using HTML metatags in our repository, all describing attributes are summarized in the characterization vectors assigned to each experience element. Based on these characterization vectors, we offer tailored search mechanisms, including similarity-based search functions, for the different SE tasks, whereas the system described in [3] offers the standard web functionality for search and retrieval.

The given examples illustrate the shortcomings and advantages of existing repositories based on different DBMS and contrast them with our approach based on ORDBMS. A more detailed discussion and a comparison with AI systems (like Case-based reasoning systems [1]) is, due to space restrictions, beyond the scope of this paper.

5. CONCLUSION

In this position paper, we have discussed the potential of ORDBMS w. r. t. to the provisioning of SE repositories handling both project data and experience data. We have shown that ORDBMS can significantly contribute in this concern. The enriched modeling concepts and the extensibility features, especially, can directly be exploited for realizing repository manager functionality. For provisioning those facilities, e. g., versioning, which cannot exclusively be implemented by ORDBMS mechanisms, we propose the generative SERUM approach, which effectively puts into practice the basic idea of reusability and, thereby, provides an efficient way of provisioning repository manager functionality. Here, ORDBMS extensibility is again helpful, since (implementations) of generated functions can either adequately be managed by the ORDBMS or interoperate with the ORDBMS.

As future work, we intend
- to refine concepts for generating repository servers, i. e., functionality the DBMS may not be extended by,
- to take software versioning and configuration models as well as activity management models [6] developed in cooperating sub-projects of the SFB 501 as examples for generating repository manager functionality with the SERUM approach,

- to develop a flexible processing model for ORDBMS allowing to dynamically determine the processing location (client or server) of an UDF managed by the ORDBMS,
- to validate our overall approach in sample software engineering processes.

ACKNOWLEDGMENTS

The authors would like to thank Prof. Dr. T. Härder and Prof. Dr. H. D. Rombach for their support. Part of this work has been conducted in the context of the Sonderforschungsbereich 501 'Development of Large Systems with Generic Methods' (SFB 501) funded by the Deutsche Forschungsgemeinschaft (DFG). Last but not least, we would like to thank Sonnhild Namingha from the Fraunhofer Institute for Experimental Software Engineering (IESE) for reviewing the first version of this paper.

[1] Due to simplicity we will use the notion *experience elements* [7] for both kinds of data throughout this paper.
[2] Although we are using a certain commercially available ORDBMS to implement our approach, we do not want to detail specific features of different systems. Thus, we use the term ORDBMS as providing a union of features offered by the leading commercially available DBMS or provided in the SQL3 standard.
[3] From the viewpoint of the database engine.
[4] 'SERUM' stands for: SE Repositories based on UML
[5] Unified modelling language [23, 24].

REFERENCES

[1]   Aamodt, A., Plaza, E.: Case-based reasoning: foundational issues, methodological variations, and system approaches. AI Communications, 7(1):39-59, 1994.
[2]   Arnold, K., Gosling, J.: The Java Programming Language. Addison-Wesley, 1996.
[3]   Balasubramanian, V., Bashian, A.: Document Management and Web Technologies: Alice Marries the Mad Hatter. Communications of the ACM, 41(7):107-115, July, 1998.
[4]   Basili, V. R., Caldiera, H., Rombach, H. D.: Experience Factory. Marciniak, J. J. (ed), Encyclopedia of Software Engineering, Vol. 1, John Wiley & Sons, 1994, pp. 469-476.
[5]   Carey, M., Dewitt, D., Graefe, G., Haight, D., Richardson, J., Schuh, D., Shekita, E., Vandenberg, S.: The EXODUS Extensible DBMS Project: an Overview. In Zdonik, S., Maier, D., editors, Readings in Object-Oriented Databases, Morgan Kaufman, 1990.
[6]   Dellen, B., Maurer, F., Münch, J., Verlage, V.: Enriching Software Process Support by Knowledge-based Techniques. Int. Journal of Software Engineering and Knowledge Engineering, 7(2):185-215, 1997.
[7]   Feldmann, R. L., Münch, J., Vorwieger, S.: Towards Goal-Oriented Organizational Learning: Representing and Maintaining Knowledge in an Experience Base. Proc. 10th Int. Conf. on Software Engineering (SEKE '98) San Francisco, CA, June, 1998.
[8]   Feldmann, R. L., Mahnke, W., Ritter, N.: ORDBMS-Support for the SFB 501 Experience Base. Technical Report 12, Sonderforschungsbereich 501, Dept. of Computer Science, University of Kaiserslautern, 1998, in preparation.
[9]   Gamma, E., Helm, R., Johnson, R., Vlissides, J.: Design Patterns: Elements of Reusable Object-Oriented Software, Addison-Wesley Publishing Company, 1995.
[10]   Geppert, B., Rößler, F., Feldmann, R. L., Vorwiger, S.: Combining SDL Patterns with Continuous Quality Improvement: An Experience Base Tailored to SDL Patterns. Proc. 1st Workshop of the SDL Forum Society on SDL and MSC (SAM '98), Berlin, Germany, 1998.
[11]   Heimbigner, D.: Experiences with an object manager for a process-centered environment. Proc. 18th VLDB Conference, Vancouver, British Columbia, Canada, August 1992.
[12]   Katz, R.: Towards a Unified Framework for Version Modeling in Engineering Databases. ACM Computing Surveys, Vol. 22, No. 4, December, 1990, pp. 375-408.
[13]   Kim, W.: Object-Relational - The unification of object and relational database technology. UniSQL White Paper, 1996.
[14]   Loeser, H.: Exploiting Extensibility of ORDBMS for client/server-based Application Systems. Proc. 10. GI-Workshop Grundlagen von Datenbanken, Konstanz, June, 1998, pp. 77-81, in German.
[15]   Mahnke, W., Ritter, N., Steiert, H.-P.: Towards Generating Object-Relational Software Engineering Repositories. University of Kaiserslautern, Proc. Datenbanken in Büro, Technik und Wissenschaft (BTW '99), Freiburg, Germany, March, 1999.
[16]   Mahnke, W., Ritter, N., Steiert, H.-P.: A Basic Versioning Framework for SERUM. Technical Report, Sonderforschungsbereich 501, Dept. of Computer Science, University of Kaiserslautern, 1999, in preparation.
[17]   Stonebraker, M., Brown, P., Moore, D.: Object-Relational DBMSs. Second Edition, Morgan Kaufmann Series in Data Management Systems, September 1998.
[18]   Tarr, P., Clark, L. A.: PLEIADES: An object management system for software engineering environments. In Notkin, D. (ed), Proc. of the 1st ACM SIGSOFT Symposium on the Foundations of Software Engineering, ACM Press, December, 1993, pp. 56-70.
[19]   Taylor, R. N., Belz, F. C., Clarke, L. A., Osterweil, L. J., Selby, R. W., Wileden, J. C., Wolf, A., Young, M.: Foundations for the Arcadia Environment Architectur. Proc. ACM SIGSOFT/SIGPLAN Software Engineering Symposium on Practical Software Development Environments, ACM, November, 1988, pp.1-13.
[20]   Wiederhold, G.: Mediators in the Architecture of Future Information Systems. IEEE Computer, 25(3):38-49, March 1992.
[21]   Wileden, J. C., Wolf, A. L., Fisher, C. D., Tarr, P. L.: PGraphite: An Experiment in Persistent Typed Object Management. In Third Symposium on Software Development Environments (SDE3), 1988.
[22]   ISO Final Committee Draft - Database Language SQL'ftp://jerry.ece.umassd.edu/isowg3/dbl/ BASEdocs/public/', 1998.
[23]   OMG, UML Notation Guide, Version 1.1, OMG Document ad/97-08-05, September, 1997.
[24]   OMG, UML Semantics, Version 1.1, OMG Document ad/97-08-04, September, 1997.

Design and Implementation of ATM Network Algorithms with Link Failure

Ali Salehnia

Computer Science, South Dakota State University, Brookings, SD 57007

Phone: 605-688-5717, Fax: 605-688-5822, Salehnia@mg.sdstate.edu

ABSTRACT

In the last decade the need for transporting high volumes of data and for high-speed, time sensitive communication have grown immensely. Current LAN technology does not provide enough bandwidth for the enterprise-wide use of emerging applications such as multimedia and real-time video[1]. Shared LAN media such as Ethernet can quickly become saturated with traffic loads that prevent real-time applications from performing on a timely basis. Other existing protocols such as token-ring and fiddi don't scale well across the WAN. ATM technology will provide high bandwidth, low latency networks that can provide time sensitive delivery of voice, video, and data through private networks and across public networks.

In this paper, three techniques for providing single link restoration in ATM based networks, considered to be the core networks for the deployment of future broadband ISDN (Integrated Services Digital Networks) services, are designed and simulated.

ATM CONCEPTS

Among other things, an ATM network can be described as: a set of rules; a communications protocol; a replacement technology for local area networks; a replacement technology for campus networks; a high band- width service of public carries; and a transfer mode [10], ATM was first proposed by Bellcore, the research facility for AT&T in the U.S., and a few other telecommunications companies in Europe. It was originally described as "fast packet switching with short fixed length packets," [2]. The basic idea of ATM is to segment data in small cells and then transfer them by the use of cell-switching. Such cells have a uniform layout and a fixed size of 53 bytes, which greatly simplifies switching. Being more complex. packet-switching is not nearly fast enough to be of use for isochronous data (i.e. real-time video and sound). Cell-switching gives maximum utilization of the physical resources [3].

ATM CELL FORMAT

The first five bytes of the cell make up the header, and the next 48 bytes are the payload. Out of those 5 header bytes, 24 bits are for the VPI (virtual path indicator) and VCI (virtual channel indicator) labels, 8 are for control, and 8 am for header checksum. The 48 bytes of payload may contain a 4 byte ATM adaptation layer (AAL) with 44 bytes of real data; this all depends on a bit in the control field of the header. Fragmentation and re-assembly of cells into larger packets at the source and then the destination are affected by this optional adaptation layer [2]. The first 8 bits of VCI label is the virtual path identifier (VPI) which is a number between I and 255, and the last 16 bits is the virtual channel identifier (VCI) which means there can be 65535 active channels [3]. A virtual channel is equivalent to a virtual circuit-that is both terms describe a logical connection between the two ends of a communications connection. A virtual path is a logical grouping of virtual circuits that allows an ATM switch to perform operations on groups of virtual circuits. ATM switches use the VPI and VCI fields of the cell header to identify the next network segment that a cell needs to transit on its way to its final destination [5].

With the exception of the GFC field, the format of the NNI header is identical to the format of the UNI header. The GFC field is not present in the format of the NNI header. Instead, the VPI field occupies the first 12 bits, which allows ATM switches to assign larger VPI values.

CONNECTIONS AND SIGNALING

ATM is a cell-switching and multiplexing technology that combines the benefits of circuit switching (constant transmission delay and guaranteed capacity) with those of packet switching (flexibility and efficiency for intermittent traffic).

The main function of an ATM switch is to receive cells on a port and switch those cells to the proper output port based on the VPI and VCI values of the cell. This switching is dictated by a switching table that maps input ports to output ports based on the values of the VPI and VCI fields [5]. Before two end-points can communicate with each other, a logical or virtual path must be established between them. When the path is established, many applications can communicate independently through it, using virtual channels. Such connections are made between all ATM switches and user equipment [3].

CONNECTION CONTRACTS

It is necessary to be able to specify which requirements we want for a connection (such as traffic type, peak and average bandwidth requirements, delay and cell loss requirement, how much money to use, etc.). This is called the Quality Of Service. (QOS) and is given when a virtual path is established. All the virtual channels in a path have the same QOS, which simplify the switching of the cells through the network. It is also possible to establish more than one virtual path between end-points, if there is a need for different quality between the same end-points [3, 4].

At the connection setup time, user specifications dictate the requirements for sending and receiving data via the network. The system will try to stay within these requirements for the duration of the transmission. There may be several kinds of network interfaces in the future. the ATM Forum is responsible for defining interfaces required to operate and manage ATM networks[2].

ATM networks rely heavily on user-supplied information at connection setup time in order to provide the desired connection for transmission. They can secure a fixed bandwidth for an isochronous (repeating in time such as voice samples) connection carrying a continuous bit stream and a plesiochronous (variable frequency such as compressed video) connection for a variable bit stream as well as rely on statistical sharing with no specific bandwidth for bursty sources [2, 3, 9].

In ATM networks, the transmitter and receiver performances are also independent of one another. The transmitter side is constrained by flow control of the simultaneous connection streams with respect to hand- width and other user requirements. The receiver side is constrained by asynchronous reception of cells at a variable rate and whether or not the adaptation layer is used. If the AAL layer is used, the re-assembly of these cells into a higher layer protocol data unit (PDU) would also be done in the hardware of the receiver side[2]. The network will then try to ensure that the connection stays within those requirements and that the QOS parameters for that connection remain satisfied for the entire duration of the connection.

ATM REROUTING WITH LINK FAILURE

Computer networking has changed enormously over the past five years, especially due to the ever-expanding Internet. The productivity and profitability for both organizations and individuals have been enhanced significantly by these revolutionary tools. Hardly a day goes by without an individual using computer networks to conduct personal and professional business. This trend is accelerating day by day.

Fast, robust, network restoration is a key factor for improving overall network performance and reliability. In this paper, three techniques for providing single link restoration in ATM based networks, considered to be the core networks for the deployment of future broadband ISDN (Integrated Services Digital Networks) services, are designed and simulated .

The first technique is a hardware method. It is fast but needs extra capacity and ends up being very costly. The second technique is a software method. It is slow, using a spare capacity hunting algorithm to find an alternate route, but uses no extra hardware. The third technique is combination of the above two strategies and hence the performance of the algorithm lies in the middle of these strategies. The control structure used here is distributed instead of the usual centralized approach. Generally speaking, there is a trade-off among restoration speed, processing/memory burden, and restoration capacity.

These three algorithms achieve this trade-off in different ways and to varying degrees. These single link restoration techniques are generalized to restore multiple link failures and are simulated by using the results of single link failure restoration techniques.

There have been some studies carried out on ATM network recovery [11, 12, and13]. It has been noted that there are several intrinsic features that could potentially be exploited to provide improved restoration techniques beyond those established for synchronous transfer mode (STM)-based networks. Some of these features are: ATM cell level error detection, inherent rate adaptation, and nonhierarchical multiplexing. In this paper, we attempt to extend some of the previous work by: 1) testing some untested existing techniques and some modified techniques; 2) proposing new strategies; 3) addressing the trade-off issue.

REROUTING OUTLINES

Following the guidelines in [11], we studied and tested two approaches. In the first approach, when a failure occurs the affected traffic is retorted to the extent possible on facilities with spare capacity. A capacity search algorithm must be used to find spare capacity. A contention-resolution protocol is employed to assign routes to VP's in order to prevent dead-lock in the event that more than one VP is trying to establish a route on the same facility. The flooding algorithm described in [12] is an example of this approach. The main drawbacks of this method are: 1) Considerable time is required in discovering paths with spare capacity; 2). Restoration is limited to the extent of available spare capacity.

To overcome these problems, one can provide redundant capacity on the channels. The channels are allocated on the first come first serve basis and that may make this approach suboptimal. The restoration may not be complete or full in all scenarios of single link failure. We may overcome this problem by providing more than the minimum amount of channel capacity for all channels. The restoration may be slow due to the time for alternate routes to be computed. The second approach described in [1] solves the above problems by providing redundant capacity and pre-computing alternate paths for all VP's under all failure scenarios. The pre-computed alternate routes are stored in network nodes. Upon receiving failure information, every node carrying VP's affected by the failure activates the stored alternate paths for the affected. The time required to affect restoration consists of the time taken to propagate the failure information to all nodes and time taken to activate alternate paths at all nodes. Fast and guaranteed restoration is critical to the successful operation of high-speed networks.

There is a tradeoff between restoration speed, processing/memory burden and restoration capacity. There are several techniques, which achieve this tradeoff in different ways and to varying degrees. The control structure can be either centralized or distributed. In the centralized approach, alternate route computation and activation of alternate routes is done by a centrally located processor. In the second approach, route computation is done and activated by the nodes, which are affected by the link failure. In the centralized approach when the central processor receives the link failure message, it compares the link failure identifications in the received messages and correlates this with a span ID. Then the processor identifies the failed link and indexes the failed span number. Next it creates the list of VP's affected by the link failure. Then all the alternate paths for these affected VP's are fetched and it sends the setup messages and the alternate route table to all the nodes that must carry the affected VP's. One advantage of this method is that there is no burden on any of the nodes. The disadvantage is the large amount of time taken to activate the alternate paths.

In the distributed approach, each node computes its own alternate routing tables and stores them. When there is a link failure, the affected node sends the link failure information to all the nodes, by a flooding algorithm. Then each node will search through its routing tables and activates the appropriate VP's. The advantage is that the restoration is fast and the disadvantage is the requirement of processing power in each node. We prefer a hybrid approach consisting of a combination of the central and distributed approach by using the best of both architectures. In this hybrid approach, individual nodes send status reports, either synchronously or asynchronously. The central controller takes a global view of the state of the network and sends routing commands or information back to the nodes in the light of its global view. The central portion of the algorithm keeps track of information, reacting fairly slowly to the global situation. Local discretion is allowed to the individual nodes so that they can react rapidly and independently to any changes in the network like link failure. The global information is somewhat out of date, but takes the widest view. The local information is up to date, but is myopic. In the fully distributed approach when a span fails at a given node, VP's traversing a certain path may have to be alternately routed on to a different path. The node needs to compute alternate paths not only for those VP's that may pass through it before failure, but also for those VPIs that may pass through it after a span failure. And this should be done for every span failure. The result is that considerable processing is required at each node to compute alternative paths, specifically in a large network and where there are a large number of VP's. We implement the following algorithms based on ideas described in [11].

ALGORITHMS

1. Local rerouting: In this strategy, when a link fails all the VP's carried on that link are rerouted locally, around the failed link, without regard to their point of origination or the destination.
2. Source-based rerouting: In source-based rerouting each VP affected by a link failure is processed and rerouted individually. Each affected VP is traced back to its source node, which reroutes the VP on the pre-computed alternate path.
3. This scheme is a combination of local rerouting and source based rerouting. In this scheme VP's are rerouted locally but with two differences: a) VPIs are rerouted individually based on their destination. This allows the local node to determine the best alternate route for each VP from itself to the VP destination; and b) Backhauling is avoided.

IMPROVEMENT AND ANALYSIS

In all the algorithms presented in this paper, the fact that it is not always possible to go around the failed link, has not been considered. For instance, if the link failure involves the outer nodes or the end nodes of the computer network. We solve the problem by adding a number of extra redundant capacity. Finding more information on the neighbor nodes could decrease the number.

Based on our testing results, we find that local rerouting algorithm is very simple to implement as it treats all the VP's carried by a link as an aggregate unit. This simplicity is at the cost of higher restoration capacity.

Since redundant capacity has to be assigned on new each hop, this results in unnecessary assignment of redundant capacity. Since all the VP's are processed locally, this scheme requires the fewest number of nodes to be involved in the rerouting process and could potentially be the fastest in terms of restoration speed. Because VP processing and activation take considerable time, it may create a bottleneck. The memory requirement in this scheme is relatively small.

The source based rerouting is optimal from the point of view of restoration capacity, the memory burden placed on the network nodes is much larger than in the case of local rerouting as any given node could be affected by many more link failures. The restoration time may be longer than in the case of local rerouting as the failure information has to propagate back to the source nodes before restoration can be effected. If processing for VP activation is the bottleneck, this scheme may even achieve better restoration speed, as the VP activation is distributed among many more nodes than in the case of local rerouting.

The restoration speed, as well as memory requirement, of the local-destination scheme is intermediate between the local rerouting and source based' restoration schemes. Also this requires lower restoration capacity than the local rerouting scheme.

CONCLUSION

In this paper, we reviewed and tested several previous techniques of rerouting with faulty links in a ATM network. The objective is to provide quick restoration and at the same time not to place undue burden on the node processors. Here we should note that any specific node is not affected by all failures and even if a given node needs to reroute VP's on a link affected by a span failure, it needs to carry only a fraction of the affected VP's. Source based rerouting is more efficient than local rerouting in terms of redundant capacity, and the local rerouting is intermediate in terms of redundant capacity and time needed for restoration. Clearly, more work is needed to find more effective approaches to compromise the factors of speed and cost.

REFERENCE
[1]. Sheldon, Tom, LAN Times Encyclopedia of Networking. New York, NY: McGraw-Hill, 1994.
[2]. Asynchronous Transfer Mode & Its Many Advantages., http://www.ece.orst.edu/ - dajanis/e478p2.html
[3]. ATM (Asynchronous Transfer Mode),, http://www.ifi.uio.no/-karlo/atm.html.
[4]. ATM Service Categories: The Benefits to the User. http://www.atmforum.com/atmforum/service_categories.html.
[5]. Asynchronous Transfer Mode., http://www.combinet.cornlunivercd/data/doc/intmettito/55755.htm.
[6]. De Prycker, Martin, Asynchronous Transfer Mode, Bookcraft, Great Britain, 1993.
[7]. Tanenbaum, Andrew, Computer Networks, Prentice Hall, Upper Saddle River, New Jersey, 1996.
(8). The ATM Forum, ATM, User-Network Interface (UNI) Specification, Version 3. 1, Prentice Hall, Upper Saddle River, New Jersey, 1995.
[9]. Black, Ulyess ATM: Foundation for Broadband Networks, Englewood Cliffs, NJ: Prentice-Hall, 1993.
[10]. Gadecki, Cathy and Heckart, Christine, ATM for Dummies, Foster City, CA: IDG Books, 1997.
[11]. J. Anderson, B. Doshi' S. Dravida, P. Harshavardhana, "Fast Restoration of ATM Networks," IEEE Journal on Selected Areas in communications. Vol. 12, No. 1, Jan. 1994, pp.128-136.
[12]. T. Landegegem, P. Vankwikelberge, H. Vanderstreten, "A Self-Healing ATM Network Based on Multilink Principles," IEEE Journal on Selected Areas in Communications. Vol. 12, No. 1, Jan. 1994, pp.139-148.
[13]. R. Kawamura, K. Sato, 1. Tokizawa, "Self-Healing ATM Networks Based on Virtual Path Concept," IEEE Journal on Selected Areas in Communications. Vol. 12, No.1, Jan.1994, pp.120-127.
[14] . A. Alles, "ATM Networking," Cisco Systems, Inc. May 1995
[15]. R. Vetter, "Asynchronous Transfer Mode: An Emerging Network Standard for High Speed Communications," Chapter for Advances in Computers. Vol. 44, To be published.

A Methodology for Profiling Users of Large Interactive Systems Incorporating Neural Network Data Mining Techniques

Philip Sallis
Computer and Information Science, University of Otago, Box 56, Dunedin, New Zealand
Tel: +64 3 479-8143, Fax: +64 3 479-8311, psallis@infoscience.otago.ac.nz

Linda Hill, Greg Janée, Kevin Lovette, and Catherine Masi
Alexandria Digital Library Project, UCSB, Santa Barbara, California, USA
{lhill,gjanee,kal,masi}@alexandria.ucsb.edu

INTRODUCTION

This paper and its associated appendices with graphical and tabular output can be found at http://www.alexandria.ucsb.edu/eval/papers/IRMA/

The research in progress described here concerns the development of a methodology for computing profiles of users and patterns of use for large interactive information systems. In particular, it describes a methodology being developed in connection with the Alexandria Digital Library (ADL) based at the University of California, Santa Barbara (Frew, Freeston, Kemp, Simpson, & Smith, 1996).

Processes for capturing both user registrations and session logs have been designed and incorporated into ADL to support evaluation of user characteristics and use patterns. The registration form collects a small set of information that can be used to characterize classes of users. The session logs record actions taken by the user in creating queries and evaluating results, including the query statements submitted to the system. The design of the registration form and the system itself reflect lessons learned from previous ADL evaluation studies (Hill et al., 1997). The existence of the registration data for ADL users permits the categorization of users into meaningful groups (*stereotypes*) (Paliouras, Papatheodorou, Karkaletsis, Spyropouls, & Malaveta, 1998) which can be further augmented with associated characteristics from patterns of use.

The research described here is an exploration of an alternative method for mining the data of the registration files and the session logs for patterns of system use related to user characteristics. It applies connectionist methods, using artificial neural networks (specifically self-organizing maps), and fuzzy clustering as one part of an overall evaluation framework that also makes use of basic statistical techniques. All of the techniques applied are being evaluated for their worth in revealing user and use patterns to inform the continuing development of ADL.

First, descriptions of the ADL system, its user interface, the user registration process, and the format of the session logs are given to describe the environment in which this research is taking place. Second, the particular neural network data mining tool employed, *Viscovery* (Eupadics,1998) is described and a rationale is given for this approach to data mining. Next, some of the processes established to process and analyze the data are given in some detail as well as some preliminary results. In summary, we give our evaluation of the analysis process itself and the current status of the research.

THE ALEXANDRIA DIGITAL LIBRARY

The Alexandria Digital Library (ADL) is a georeferenced digital library (Alexandria Digital Library, 1998). It is one of the six Digital Library Initiatives funded by the NSF, DARPA, and NASA between 1994 and 1998. ADL is in the process of becoming an operational component of the UCSB library system and the California Digital Library. All kinds of information can be georeferenced with latitude and longitude coordinates. You might think primarily about maps, aerial photographs, and remote sensing images but text items, specimen collections, pieces of music, people, and gazetteer entries can also be georeferenced to places. In ADL, all collection objects are georeferenced with latitude and longitude coordinates that provide *footprint* representations of the areas they are about. The user interface presents the user with a Map Browser that can be used to draw a box around the area of the world that he or she is interested in. This *query area* and other selected query parameters, such as Type, Format, and Date, form a query. The items that match the query are returned in a list. The user can use the Map Browser, thumbnail images, and the metadata to evaluate the results. Selected items can be downloaded, if they are online. If they are offline, the contact information for getting them is given.

New ADL users fill out a registration form before beginning; on subsequent visits they fill in their user name and password. The user is asked for eight pieces of information (sex, age, affiliation, primary function role, primary subject interest area, highest educational degree, the number of times that previous versions of ADL were used, and how they discovered ADL in the first place) plus a self-report on proficiency in four areas (geospatial data, online searching, WWW, and computers). Answers for all questions are required but "decline to answer" and "other" options are offered for some questions. Names are disassociated from the registration details and all reference to individual registration data is done by number.

ADL operates in a distributed client-server environment. The client records the actions taken by users and sends the log back to the server. Only "click" actions are recorded, not complete cursor movements. Actions are time-stamped and identified by a session identifier that includes the user identification. Actions include that actual query sent to the system.

When users exit an ADL session, they are presented with an exit poll and given the opportunity to comment and grade the performance of the system during the session. They are asked to state the purpose for their use of ADL as specifically as they can. They are asked to give ADL a "grade" on the interface and the collections. They are given the opportunity to type in comments and questions and they are asked if they would like someone from ADL to contact them.

Conventional summative statistics are generated for registration statistics and session counts. The research description that follows is an exploration of other means of analyzing and mining the data for user and use patterns.

Artificial Neural Networks and *Viscovery*

Artificial Neural Networks (ANNs) are increasingly being used across a variety of application areas where imprecise data or complex attribute relationships exist and are difficult to quantify using traditional analytical methods (Kasabov, 1996). ANNs include tools such as self-organizing maps (SOMs), which generate multi-dimensional data space models and provide for the dynamic juxta-position of vectors from the problem space with others that are related by similarity measure. In the case of this research, the input vectors are those that characterize individual users and their use of the information system. Each attribute from the problem space that represents one of the independent characteristics, is contextually dependent on all others within the attribute class by virtue of being part of the summative whole that is 'averaged' to produce a normalized user profile against which all individual profiles are matched. The 'learning' or self-modifying aspect of the SOM is intrinsic to any ANN analytical environment. It is made obvious through the 'training' function of the SOM. It takes each set of attributes for individual users (defined as vectors of attributes) and retains every value for comparison with others in the whole data set. In this study all attributes are binary values that reflect the presence or absence of a personal characteristic, which facilitates this kind of analysis. Attribute sets are, therefore, binary vector arrays.

Viscovery is a commercially available ANN product. It utilizes the Kohonen self-organizing map concept. It accepts data input as contiguous adjacent pairs of values that become network nodes for relationship with others in the sample. In the case of this research, these nodes have a binary value of either '0' or '1'. The software requests parameter bounding values to determine the number of epochs (iterations) of the comparisons made in order to calculate a geometric mean (centroid) for the entire sample against which individual vectors (sets of attributes within an attribute class) can be measured for closeness of fit to the centroid. The software has a graphical interface with color intensity for attribute classes enabling visual comparisons to be made. Primarily, this distinguishes *Viscovery* as an ideal data-mining tool for this research task.

ANNs are especially powerful data mining tools when linguistic, fuzzy concepts (fuzzy labels such as 'young', 'medium', 'warm') are associated with their nodes. The methodology presented here makes use of the combination features of ANNs and fuzzy terms.

The Methodology

The methodology is based on the premise that each user has certain individual characteristics that may change over time but pertain for adjacent sessions. Therefore, for each and every session logged by the ADL server, a set of concomitant individual user characteristics can be 'bracketed' with that data to reflect a unique set of use attributes. For any individual user therefore, a profile can be generated and compared with a summative or 'mean' profile of all system use.

The methodology follows a sequence of data gathering steps from both the registration and session log files, then applies an *a priori* classification scheme (fuzzy labels) to both duration and frequency of use for each user, which are appended to the registration data. The software used and programs developed to carry out this processing are detailed below.

Each of the data items from the registration data file is coded so that a binary value is assigned for individuals. For instance, if the user is female a value of '1' is assigned and if not, a value of '0' is assigned. The same is true for male users and other attributes such as age range and skill levels.

The duration is recorded in the session log data in real time. Times are assigned a 'fuzzy' label for one of *low, medium* or *high* duration. These in turn are assigned a binary value for each with a '1' if the condition is true and '0' if false. For a *medium* duration therefore, the binary vector pattern would appear as "010"; whereas a *low* duration would be "100" and a *high* duration would be "001". In this way, each session event generates a composite binary vector. This is concatenated with the registration data binary vector. A set of binary vectors for sessions relating to each system user is then produced. Conclusions can be drawn from this data to indicate use patterns and individual user behavior. In this research, these become user profiles.

Individual user profiles are clustered for each independent variable. Each variable has a binary value indicating its presence or absence as a characteristic of individual user profiles. When put together a binary vector is built, which represents each user's profile. Using Kohonen self-organizing map technology from a neural network toolset, (in this case *Viscovery*), these binary vectors are input to a 'training' simulation that calculates a centroid (geometric mean) from which patterns of system use emerge. The centroid becomes the 'norm' with which each individual user profile is compared. These results are currently observable in the form of clusters of attributes around variables such as duration and frequency of system use, sex, age, professional group or proficiency rating.

THE PARSING PROGRAMS AND DATA MANAGEMENT SOFTWARE

A sample of the session log data in its original form is shown below as Figure 1. The data in this form had to be processed in order to extract what was needed for use and user profile analysis.

The PERL programming language was chosen for this parsing task because of its task-specific string search and text manipulation capabilities. Imbedded within this process was the assignment of fuzzy labels to individual session duration (short,medium,long) that could then be computed for each user over their total session events and for frequency of use (single,low,medium,high) in a similar manner. These labels are currently assigned arbitrarily according to an *a priori* classification criteria. It is envisaged that these will be statistically derived once there is sufficient and reliable data from which co-efficients can be computed.

The algorithm for determining session duration using PERL is as follows:

Figure 1 – Sample of original log data

```
00000874.0000.0005I897435248I00000874.0000.0005-897435248Istart_sessionI1.6.4
00000874.0000.0005I897435265I00000874.0000.0005-897435248Iclient_data_beginI
00000874.0000.0005I897435398I00000874.0000.0005-897435248Iclient_actionILib: SessionID: 00000874.0000.0005-
897435248
00000874.0000.0005I897435398I00000874.0000.0005-897435248Iclient_actionILib: Load Collections
00000874.0000.0005I897435399I00000874.0000.0005-897435248Iclient_actionIMap Mode: ZOOM IN
...
00000874.0000.0005I897435404I00000874.0000.0005-897435248Iclient_actionIMap: Button Pressed: east
00000874.0000.0005I897435405I00000874.0000.0005-897435248Iclient_actionIMap Mode: SELECT
00000874.0000.0005I897435407I00000874.0000.0005-897435248Iclient_actionIMap: Query Region(s) Modified
...
00000874.0000.0005I897499663I00000874.0000.0005-897499637Istart-searchI1   collections: adl_gazetteer   knf: (and (loca-
tion (or (overlaps (rectangle (coord -129.69488721804512 47.13827067669173)(coord -103.98060150375942
25.935263157894738)))))(or (type "Military")))
00000874.0000.0005I897499663I00000874.0000.0005-897499637Isqllselect con_num, west, south, east, north, '', '', type_is,
'', title, '' from oct_admin where ( ( Overlap(HG_Box(-129.694885,25.935263,-103.980598,47.138271),location) ) AND ( (
type_is = 'military' ) ) );
00000874.0000.0005I897499682I00000874.0000.0005-897499637Isqllselect con_num, west, south, east, north, '', '', type_is,
'', title, '' from oct_manmade where ( ( Overlap(HG_Box(-129.694885,25.935263,-103.980598,47.138271),location) ) AND ( (
type_is = 'military' ) ) );
...
00000874.0000.0005I897499758I00000874.0000.0005-897499637Istop-searchI1075693856
00000874.0000.0005I897499762I00000874.0000.0005-897499637Iclient_data_beginI
00000874.0000.0005I897499781I00000874.0000.0005-897499637Iclient_actionILib: SessionID: 00000874.0000.0005-
897499637
```

Sort file by session id, time/date stamp
Read and parse record to extract userID, time/date stamp, sessionID, action, action_data
Find the start and end of each session
  Note: This was complicated by the fact that a session end did not always accompany a session start. Thus the end of session could only be determined by a new session beginning. Previous session information was retained so that duration could be determined. Then processing of the new session data began.
Eliminate sessions with duration of 0.
Assign vectors and fuzzy labels as follows:
if ($duration >= 1 and $duration <= 359) {
    $vector = "10000000";
    $fuzzyD = "short";}
elsif ($duration >= 360 and $duration <= 659) {
    $vector = "01000000";
    $fuzzyD = "medium";}
elsif ($duration >= 660 and $duration <= 959) {
    $vector = "00100000";
    $fuzzyD = "long";}

The algorithm for determining session frequency using PERL is as follows:
Sort file by userID, sessionID
Read and parse record to extract $userID, $time_stamp, $sessionID, $action, $data_for_action
Count sessions per user
Assign vectors and fuzzy labels as follows:
    if   ($session_count == 1) {
                $vector = "1000";
                $fuzzyD = "single";}
elsif ($session_count >= 2 and $session_count <= 5) {
                $vector = "0100";
                $fuzzyD = "low";}
elsif ($session_count >= 6 and $session_count <= 10) {
                $vector = "0010";
                $fuzzyD = "medium";}
elsif ($session_count > 10) {
                $vector = "0001";
                $fuzzyD = "high";}

The session log file is stored in a database located on a server that is accessible via ODBC connection. Thus all processing can be done within *Microsoft Access* using their SQL. The *Microsoft Access* software facilitates development of integrated tables, queries, forms and reports and expedites 'import to' and 'export from' other *Microsoft Office* software products, such as *Excel* and *PowerPoint*. This is useful for data display and report generation.

The algorithm for determining session duration using MS Access queries is as follows:

Sort by sessionID, time stamp.

Weed out remaining garbage records by looking at length and contents of sessionID field.

For each unique sessionID, determine min and max time stamp.

Calculate duration.

Create duration vector and fuzzy label table per specifications.

Assign vector and fuzzy label to each record.

The algorithm for determining session frequency using MS Access queries follows:

Count sessions by user id excluding sessions with duration = 0.

Create frequency vector and fuzzy label table per specifications.

Assign vector and fuzzy label to each record.

Create session frequency report.

Export as html.

The session log data is then joined with the registration data using the following algorithm.

Extract current reg vectors and data definition from the registration attribute assignment table

Replace white space with blanks and to insert a delimiter after the user_id. Imported into Access as reg_vectors table.

Join registration vector table to duration and frequency table.

Created table with aggregated fields defined.

Aggregated vectors based on attributes.

SOM output and data mining results

In order to see the best illustrations of output (in color) from the SOM, the sample results can be viewed at http://www.alexandria.ucsb.edu/eval/papers/IRMA/som_output.html. An example cluster for the sample data set being used at present is reproduced below (Figure 2) in black and white as an illustration of the attribute (component) distribution. The lighter polygons (in these black and white versions) are those with the greatest correlation. In color it is the darker polygons that have the highest correlations. The geometric mean (centroid) for this particular clustering is denoted by the small dark circle (dot) in the lightest of the polygons. The other dots denote correlation points in the data that illustrate the convergence of multiple components within the entire set.

The output in Figure 2 is a visualization of the ADL registration data and shows how the components for all users (their individual registration data and system use data) are clustered according to their occurrence across the entire set of data. Conventional output from a statistically derived cluster analysis would depict the relative proximity of components (attributes) as bunches of data points. The clustering in Figure 2 uses polygons that appear in color as different shades to depict the correlative intensity of individual components. The data mining tool allows analysts to skip from cluster-to-cluster examining the relative component presence in the polygons.

The clustering in Figure 2 is for all components but the two that are depicted below in Figure 3 (AGE and SEX) are from the registration data only. The fuzzy labels for DURATION and FREQUENCY do not influence the output in these examples.

The following two outputs (Figure 3), provide an illustration of the patterns produced by the SOM for two of the convergent components. The two highly correlative components are 'AGE' and 'SEX'. This illustration depicts MALES and the age-group 30-34 as being most influential on the overall SOM clustering.

SUMMARY AND FUTURE DIRECTIONS

The objective of the research is to analyze system-user interaction as part of an evaluation framework based on individual profiles of use. Results of this approach will be correlated with what can be discovered about users from other sources, such as

Figure 2 – Output from the SOM clustering

Figure 3 – Output clusters for 'AGE (30-34)' on the left and 'SEX (Male)' on the right

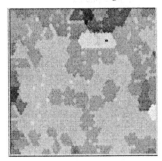

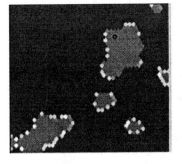

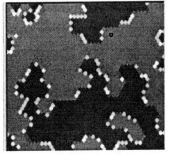

interviews, observations, and questionnaires. It is suggested that the methodology outlined in this paper could be used generally for any large system evaluation project.

There is no point in speculating about actual use patterns emerging from the data at this time because most of the current output is related to system testing and does not reflect 'real' use. Once the system is operational, use patterns can be derived and the results reported.

The data mining capabilities of software products such as *Viscovery* enable us to determine the relative proximity of user and use attributes as they inter-relate and form clusters to show how they combine to produce a typical user at any snapshot of time based on the incremental data at hand. The graphical output from Viscovery is particularly advantageous for interactive data mining visualization.

By comparing the output from standard statistical clustering with that of *Viscovery*, it can be seen that SOMs provide a rich alternative for conducting 'lets see' and 'what if' analyses of user and use patterns. The connectionist approach using artificial neural networks also enhances the ease of profiling system user behavior and can be capitalized upon by publication of the summative results by way of a webpage, which in turn facilitates an enriched user-feedback environment.

The continuing work in this project will concentrate on examining innovative ways to conduct data mining, especially using connectionist methods with ANNs. It will also experiment with self-modifying structures that can 'learn' about user behavior and thus predict future trends in system use. As the methodology is worked out, more actions will be extracted from the session logs for analysis. In particular, 'time on use' intervals will be derived for the stages of user interaction during a session (e.g. time using Map Browser, time setting up the query, time evaluating the results) and the system components used during a session will be analyzed. Concurrently, standard statistical techniques will be used to further extract use and user profile characteristics.

REFERENCES

Alexandria Digital Library. (1998). Homepage . http://www.alexandria.ucsb.edu.

Deboeck G. and Kohonen, T. (eds). *Visual Explorations in Finance with Self-Organizing Maps.* Springer, 1998.

Eudaptics Software. *Viscovery: SOMine Lite (V 2.1),* 1998.   http://www.office.eudaptics.co.at

Frew, J., Freeston, M., Kemp, R., Simpson, J., & Smith, T. (1996). The Alexandria Digital Library testbed. *D-Lib Magazine*(July/August 1996). http://www.dlib.org/dlib/july96/alexandria/07frew.html.

Hill, L. L., Dolin, R., Frew, J., Kemp, R. B., Larsgaard, M., Montello, D. R., Rae, M. A., & Simpson, J. (1997). User evaluation: Summary of the methodologies and results for the Alexandria Digital Library, University of California at Santa Barbara. *Proceedings of the ASIS Annual Meeting, 34,* 225-243. http://www.asis.org/annual-97/alexia.htm.

Kohonen, T. The self-organizing map. *Proceedings of the IEEE* 1990, 78(9): 1464-1480.

Kasabov, N.K., *Foundations of Neural Networks, Fuzzy Systems, and Knowledge Engineering.* MIT Press, 1996

Paliouras, G., Papatheodorou, C., Karkaletsis, V., Spyropouls, C., & Malaveta, V. (1998). Learning User Communities for Improving the Services of Information Providers. In C. Nikolaou & C. Stephanidis (Eds.), *Proceedings of the Second European Conference on Research and Advanced Technology for Digital Libraries (ECDL'98), Heraklion, Crete, Greece, Sept. 1998* (pp. 367-383). Berlin: Springer-Verlag.

Does IT Lead to Diversification?

Namchul Shin
College of Business, Rowan University, Glassboro, NJ 08028
Phone: 609-256-4500, Fax: 609-256-4439, Shin@rowan.edu

ABSTARCT

Firms diversify their operations to achieve economic benefits by utilizing business resources across multiple markets. Economic benefits are, however, often not realized due to costs of coordinating the resources in multiple markets. Because information technology (IT) is widely used for achieving efficient and better coordination of business resources and activities, IT may facilitate diversification by reducing costs of coordinating business resources across multiple markets. This paper examines the relationship between IT and diversification, both related and unrelated diversification. Based on microeconomic theory of diversification, transaction cost economics, and previous information systems research, this paper develops hypotheses and an explanatory model, and describes a methodology for an empirical analysis.

INTRODUCTION

Information technology (IT) has been widely used for supporting and integrating various business activities such as procurement of raw materials, production and service. Applications of IT such as electronic data interchange and communication networks have also facilitated better interorganizational coordination (Malone, Yates, Benjamin 1987; Gurbaxani and Whang 1991). With the use of IT, firms are radically changing the way of doing business to improve their performance.

Firms make strategic decisions such as diversification or vertical integration to enhance their organizational effectiveness and efficiency. Firms diversify their business lines into multiple markets for more efficient utilization of their resources. Firms also integrate vertically their business activities within their boundaries for better coordination. Because IT is widely used for achieving efficient and better coordination of business resources across multiple markets and of economic activities between different organizations, corporate managers may have to consider their diversification or vertical integration strategy aligned with the use of IT.

This paper examines the relationship between IT and diversification. Based on microeconomic theory of diversification, transaction cost economics, and previous information systems research, this paper develops a theoretical framework for the relationship. This paper develops hypotheses and an explanatory model, and also describes a methodology for an empirical analysis.

HYPOTHESES AND THEORETICAL BACKGROUND

The main hypothesis of this study is that IT facilitates related diversification, but not necessarily unrelated diversification. When firms pursue related diversification, sharing and coordinating business resources across multiple markets is essential for achieving economic benefits. IT reduces costs of coordinating business resources across multiple markets and thus facilitates related diversification. Unrelated lines of business do not necessarily exploit common business resources such as managerial expertise and technical knowledge for achieving economic benefits.

According to microeconomic theory, a firm is a collection of physical, human and intangible resources capable of undertaking a number of separate activities. Some resources may be relatively product-specific and thus they are utilized in producing a particular good or service through one business line, whereas other resources may have value in producing a number of goods or services in multiple business lines. If such resources are insufficiently utilized in the firms' current operations, then it may be worthwhile using them elsewhere. In that case, the firm will use the resources by diversifying its operation into multiple business lines (Clark 1985).

Firms pursue related diversification to achieve economic benefits by sharing human or physical resources across multiple markets. On the other hand, firms pursue unrelated diversification to achieve economic benefits by exploiting excess capacity in their capital because capital can be more efficiently allocated in an internal market than external markets. When firms pursue related diversification, there exist costs of coordinating the resources, including costs of information processing, across multiple markets (Williamson 1975). Unrelated business lines do not require as much coordination as related business lines do because unrelated diversification is pursued mainly for financial reasons. Thus, unrelated diversification does not need as much as coordination of business resources as related diversification.

IT can be used to coordinate business resources, e.g., physical resources, managerial expertise, technical knowledge, and market information across multiple markets (Malone, Yates, and Benjamin 1987; Gurbaxani and Whang 1991; Clemons and Reddi 1992). Through increased coordination, IT improves resource utilization, lowering costs of coordinating resources. In other words, IT enables scale and scope economies by achieving efficient utilization of common business resources across multiple markets or industries in which firms operate. Inherent scale or scope economies in these resources are often not realized due to costs of coordinating the resources in multiple markets. Thus, by reducing costs of coordinating business resources across related business lines and by providing better means of coordination, IT can facilitate related diversification.

METHODOLOGY AND MODEL

To empirically analyze the relationship between IT and diversification, we employ firm-level data for IT spending and entropy measures for both related and unrelated diversification. The methodology used for this analysis is ordinary least-square (OLS) regression analysis. This model measures the relationship between IT and diversification for a given sector in a given year, while controlling for several firm characteristics such as R&D expenses, advertising expenses, capital stock, and for industry- and year-specific effects. To correct the heteroskedasticity problem, all the independent variables are adjusted for firm size (the number of employees). The basic econometric model is as follows:

$$DIV_{it} = \beta_0 + \beta_1 IT_{it} + \beta_2 R\&D_{it} + \beta_3 AD_{it} + \beta_4 CAP_{it} + \beta_5 INDUSTRY_{it} + \beta_6 YEAR_{it} + \varepsilon$$

where

DIV_{it} = related diversification or unrelated diversification of the ith firm in year t

IT_{it} = IT spending per employee for the ith firm in year t

$R\&D_{it}$ = R&D expenses per employee for the ith firm in year t

AD_{it} = advertising expenses per employee for the ith firm in year t.

CAP_{it} = capital stock per employee for the ith firm in year t.

$INDUSTRY_{it}$ = a dummy for each sector or industry where the ith firm is operating in year t

$YEAR_{it}$ = a dummy for year for the ith firm.

ε = an error term with zero mean

CONTRIBUTION

Although the relationship between IT and organization of economic activities has been reviewed in the literature (Malone, Yates, and Benjamin 1987; Gurbaxani and Whang 1991; Clemons and Reddi 1992; Bakos and Brynjolfsson 1993), there has been very little empirical research on the relationship between the two. By empirically examining the relationship between IT and diversification, this research attempts to build the cumulative tradition for the above information systems research. This research is also valuable for practitioners. Because strategic decisions such as diversification are closely related to firm performance, this research provides corporate managers with implications that firm performance can be improved by the use of IT, aligned with strategic diversification.

REFERENCES

Bakos, J.Y., and Brynjolfsson, E., "Information Technology, Incentives and the Optimal Number of Suppliers," Journal of Management Information Systems, September 1993.

Clarke, R., Industrial Economics, Basil Blackwell Ltd., 1985.

Clemons, E.K., and Reddi, S.P., "The Impact of Information Technology on the Organization of Economic Activity: The 'Move to the

Middle' Hypothesis," Working Paper, The Wharton School, University of Pennsylvania, 1992.

Gurbaxani, V., and Whang, S., "The Impact of Information Systems on Organizations and Markets," Communications of the ACM, 34(1), 60-73, January 1991.

Malone, T.W., Yates, J., and Benjamin, R.I., "Electronic Markets and Electronic Hierarchies," Communications of the ACM, 484-497, June 1987.

Williamson, O.E., Markets and Hierarchies: Analysis and Antitrust Implications, New York: Free Press, 1975.

Assessing the Motivational Quality of Websites

Ruth V. Small

School of Information Studies, Syracuse University, 4-297 Center for Science & Technology, Syracuse, New York 13244-4100
drruth@mailbox.syr.edu, (315) 443-4511

Marilyn P. Arnone

President for Research & Evaluation, Creative Media Solutions, 716 East Washington Street, Syracuse, New York 13210
arnone1@ibm.net, (315)422-9605

INTRODUCTION

As millions of people "surf the net," how can businesses be assured that their websites will (1) attract surfers, (2) interest them long enough to thoroughly explore the site, (3) motivate them to purchase their product or service, and (4) encourage them to return to the site and recommend the site to others. As the number of commercial World Wide Web sites continues to grow at an explosive rate, the need for interface design guidelines and evaluation criteria also increases.

Although there are a number of resources that provide guidance on the structure and content of web interfaces, few focus on the motivational aspects of websites, i.e. those features that motivate customers to visit, explore, and return to a website. Since motivation may be the ultimate goal for a website, motivational quality of websites becomes an important issue to be addressed. In response to this need, the Website Motivational Analysis Checklist (WebMAC) was developed to help diagnose, analyze, and assess the motivational quality of websites.

There are a growing number of companies offering web evaluation services. Most of those services involve an expert assessing the quality of the website and offering ways to improve it, largely from a marketing perspective. WebMAC differs from other instruments because it (1) has a theoretical base, (2) is user-centered, (3) uses a research approach, and (4) allows feedback for improvement from multiple viewpoints (Nielsen, 1994). This article outlines some general criteria for evaluating websites and describes WebMAC, an instrument that focuses on the motivational quality of websites.

EVALUATIVE CRITERIA OF WEBSITES

Because of their dynamic, interactive nature, networked electronic information resources like websites require different criteria for evaluation than other types of media (e.g. print, video). There are two major factors for website evaluation: critical content and motivational quality.

Critical Content

Critical content criteria constitute the "bottom line" of website evaluation; i.e. the overall content must be both valid and appropriate for the intended audience. If either of these characteristics is absent, the user will likely not spend much time at the website. Therefore, content is the first consideration that must be considered in evaluating a website.

There are also a number of content features that characterize the relevance of a website; i.e. information and interface characteristics of the website. Schamber (1993), building on and synthesizing the work of Taylor (1986) and others in the information science literature, describes a number of content-related features that affect the relevance of documents within a system, several of which are likely to have a direct or indirect impact on the motivational quality of a website, our second major factor for website evaluation.

Some content-related features are:
- accuracy, currency, and credibility of information;
- ease of intellectual access to information within the website;
- an interface that provides both help and orientation;
- logical organization of information;
- clarity of directions on how to use the website;
- interesting and useful information;
- appropriate type, amount and difficulty level of information.

Motivational Quality

Motivation explains the "why" of behavior. In a web context, motivation explains why a user chooses, becomes engaged in, and revisits a website. Critical content, as described above, is one factor that will influence motivation in this context. Motivational quality also incorporates functionality features; i.e. those features that affect access and performance. In a Web environment, functionality describes the technical aspects that cause various functions within the website to work the way they should. Taylor (1986), in his Value-Added Model for information systems, describes several functionality-related issues that directly affect a user's motivation to visit and spend time at a website. They include:

- ease of physical access to the website;
- consistent, standardized format (e.g. navigation buttons maintain consistent shape and location);
- browsing capability (e.g. ability to explore information within a website);
- linkage (e.g. to other relevant websites);
- response speed (e.g. use of quickly loadable graphics);
- selectivity (e.g. user-control of where to go and what information to access);
- variety of access points to information (ability to access information in more than one way and from various points in the system).

Functionality has a direct impact on customer motivation because when one or more of these features malfunctions, the customer is likely to become frustrated and leave the site, possibly never to return. This explains why some current web evaluation instruments appear to emphasize functionality of a website (e.g. Caywood, 1997). Although our instrument considers both content and functionality issues, it frames those issues in terms of motivational quality.

Theoretical Framework

Expectancy-value (E-V) theory (aka expectancy-valence theory, expectancy theory) (Vroom, 1964) helps define individual motivation (Ferris, 1977). E-V theory attempts to explain why a person chooses to expend effort on certain tasks or activities rather than others and proposes that motivation occurs only when a person both values and is successful a given task or activity.

Until recently, the application of E-V theory has been largely confined to the workplace environment; i.e. focusing on ways to increase the level, amount, and quality of production, using output as a measure of motivation. More recently, researchers have applied this theory to a variety of electronic environments, focusing on ways to promote the motivation to use a particular information system, using engagement and satisfaction as a measure of motivation. For example, a study by Burton, Chen, Grover, and Stewart (1992-3) strongly supports E-V's appropriateness for assessing the motivation to use an expert system. Snead and Harrell (1995) and DeSanctis (1981) found the theory appropriate for evaluating the motivation to use a decision support system.

Expectancy-value theory may also be useful for understanding motivation in a web environment; i.e., why a person visits a website, explores that website, and returns to that website. In E-V theory terms, the site must have value and promote positive expectancies for successful use.

There are several factors that contribute to the value and expectancy aspects of a website, which we have synthesized into four attribute (see Fig. 1). Sites must provide value by being engaging as well as useful to the user. Websites that are organized for ease of access and use and are satisfying promote an expectancy for success. The degree to which these attributes are present in a website comprises its motivational quality. Fig. 1 below illustrates the relationship of the four attributes to the value and expectancy components.

Based on these four attributes, an instrument for assessing motivational quality in a web environment has been developed and tested. That instrument is described below.

Engaging	Useful	Organized	Satisfying
\	/	\	/
VALUE		EXPECTATION FOR SUCCESS	

Fig. 1. Attributes That Contribute to Value and Expectation for Success in a Web Environment.

The WebMAC Instrument

The WebMAC instrument (Small & Arnone, 1998) differs from other web evaluation instruments in the following ways:

- It was founded on sound motivation theories applied to the web environment.
- It is intended to identify areas for improvement of an existing website and/or to provide guidance for the development of a new website.
- It focuses on motivational quality but also includes functionality- and content-related items framed in terms of their effect on motivation.
- While most other instruments are expert-centered, it is user-centered, i.e. intended to provide feedback from actual potential users of the website.
- It is also useful as a checklist when designing a new website.

WebMAC consists of an evaluation instrument, administration directions, and scoring guidelines. Before beginning, the evaluator is encouraged to spend some time exploring the targeted website in order to have some familiarity with its content and structure before completing WebMAC's 40-item Likert-type scale. On the WebMAC Scoring Sheet, the evaluator records his/her agreement ratings for each item on a four-point scale from 0 (strongly disagree) to 3 (strongly agree). If the evaluator believes an item is not applicable to that site, he/she is instructed to designate NA for that item. Twenty items are related to each of the E-V components: Value and Expectation for Success. These two components are further broken down into four general attributes (10 items per attribute): Engaging (E), Useful (U), Organized (O) and Satisfying (S).

Engaging (E)

The (E) attribute emphasizes website features that stimulate curiosity and engage the customer's interest in the site. ES features include mechanisms that will immediately attract the customer's attention at the home page and engage the customer as he/she proceeds through the website. Some of WebMAC's E items include:

- The colors and/or background patterns used in this website are pleasing.
- There is an eye-catching title and/or visual on the home page of this website.
- This website provides interesting examples of the concepts presented.

- This website had unique features that made it more interesting.
- I found surprising things at this website.

Useful (U)

The (U) attribute emphasizes those website features that add value to the information presented, provide a meaningful context, and improve the relevance of the site to the customer. Some U items are:
- The information contained in this website is current and up-to-date.
- The purpose of this website was always clear to me.
- The information at this website is accurate.
- All visual information (e.g. videos, photographs) included in this website is relevant to the topic covered.
- The website's information was provided by credible sources.

Organized (O)

The (O) attribute emphasizes features that provide a logical overall structure and sequence. OE features include ease-of-use and build customers' confidence in their ability to successfully access needed information or browse through the site easily and quickly. Examples of WebMAC's (O) items include:
- This website is logically organized.
- At all times, I could control what information at this website I wished to see.
- No matter where I am in this website I can return to the home page or exit.
- There is an introduction or table of contents at the beginning of the website that describes the scope of the content contained within it.
- This website provides overviews and/or summaries with large amounts of text.

Satisfying (S)

Most potential customers explore the World Wide Web for one of two motives: (1) to find information needed for business or professional purposes or (2) to find information desired for personal use. The (S) attribute emphasizes those features that affect customers' overall feelings of accomplishment and satisfaction from visiting the website, regardless of their motivation. These features influence the customer's tendency to revisit the website and to recommend the site to others. Some (S) items are:
- I found the amount of information I needed at this website.
- All of this website's hyperlinks were active and fully functioning.
- This website provides links to other relevant websites.
- I found the amount of information I needed at this website.
- I would use this website again.

After rating all of WebMAC's items, the evaluator transfers each score into one of four columns (one for each of the WebMAC attributes). Each column is then totaled and total scores for each attribute recorded on the WebMAC Scoring Sheet, allowing the evaluator to compare numerical scores on each of the four attributes. A score of less than 20 indicates a need to improve the motivational quality of that attribute. The evaluator may wish to plot total scores for the four attributes on WebMAC's line graph for a quick visual assessment of specific strengths and weaknesses of the site.

The WebMAC Scoring Grid allows the evaluator to combine the (E) and (U) scores into one Value (V) score and the (O) and (S) scores into one Expectancy for Success (EX) score. These two scores and their midpoint are then plotted on a grid. The midpoint falls into one of four quadrants. Each quadrant corresponds to an overall assessment for the website. High scores on both (V) and (EX) earn an "Awesome Website" rating.

VALIDATING WEBMAC

WebMAC provides an opportunity for structured analysis of the motivational quality of World Wide Web sites. Testing and validation of the WebMAC instrument has been ongoing over the past year. WebMAC has been tested with both undergraduate and graduate students. A group of 23 graduate students was asked to independently evaluate an assigned website using the original 60-item WebMAC that included an open-ended question that solicited suggestions for improvement. Items were randomly ordered to prevent clustering and categorization. Analysis focused on the distribution of scores for each question, represented by histograms. Items with a wide spread of scores (standard deviation of 1.00+) were either revised or eliminated. The results were used to test reliability and to identify ways to improve the instrument.

A second test was performed to gather information concerning the understandability and redundancy of the instrument. Researchers individually observed eight graduate students as they evaluated one of two pre-selected websites that were considered moderately motivating. Students were asked to use the instrument to evaluate several websites and provide the authors with feedback on each item and on the usefulness of the instrument. This test identified redundant and ambiguous questions and provided feedback as to the organization and length of the instrument.

Pilot testing resulted in several changes to the original instrument. The yes-no scale was changed to a Likert-type scale to more precisely reflect the evaluator's rating. An item analysis revealed problematic items. Those items that were considered vague or poorly worded were modified; irrelevant or redundant items were eliminated. Final testing of the instrument was conducted with 21 graduate and five undergraduate students during the spring and summer of 1998, providing feedback for the final revisions of the instrument. Testing of the instrument for international use is currently in progress.

During the testing and validation of WebMAC, some interesting findings deserve mention. In general, subjects spent only 5-10 minutes exploring the website before using the instrument, even though they were told they could spend longer (up to 20 minutes) reviewing the site. In addition, as they began to complete WebMAC, they tended to stay on the home page to evaluate as many items as possible, only navigating other pages when they could not find a particular feature on the homepage. Subjects with more experience exploring and using the Web tended to spend more time overall than novices completing the evaluation. All of these findings suggest that website visitors make a determination as to its quality and usefulness very quickly. This may indicate the importance of focusing on the motivational quality of the home page.

Final testing for validity and reliability of the instrument is now underway with approximately 250 college students at a major northeastern university. Results will be included in our presentation at IRMA in Hershey, PA in May 1999.

CONCLUSIONS

Businesses that depend on their websites to generate business and market products or services must be concerned with the motivational quality of those websites. This article describes the theoretical foundation, organization, and testing of an easy-to-use, 40-item diagnostic instrument for evaluating websites. The Website Motivational Analysis Checklist (WebMAC) focuses on the motivational quality of websites; i.e., those features that cause the visitor to come to the site, explore the site, revisit the site, and recommend the site to others. Motivational features are defined in relation to expectation-value theory and four general attributes: Engaging & Stimulating, Useful & Credible; Organized & Easy-to-Use; and Satisfying & Effective.

Businesses expect their website to attract both first customers and return customers. A high motivational quality rating of that website becomes an essential goal for achieving that purpose. WebMAC provides quick and easy recognition of areas that are strong in motivational quality and areas in need of improvement. Beyond its usefulness as an evaluation tool, WebMAC provides a set of guidelines for web designers to create exciting and useful websites.

Versions of the WebMAC have been developed for use in non-business settings. Three instruments (WebMAC Junior, WebMAC Middle, and WebMAC Senior) are intended for use in educational settings by elementary, middle, and high school students. WebMAC Broadcast/Cable allows producers of television series to assess their related websites.

To date, WebMAC has been adopted in a number of different settings, including:
- evaluation of the website of a federally-funded project at Oklahoma State University
- evaluation of the website of a nationally televised children's television program
- translation of the instrument into Portuguese and cross-cultural validation in research projects at two universities in Brazil.
- evaluation of U.S. Department of Education websites as part of a federally-funded project at Syracuse University.

For more information on any or all of these instruments, visit our website at <www.MotivationMining.com>.

REFERENCES
Burton, F.G., Chen, Y., Grover, V. and Stewart, K.A. (1992-3, Winter). An application of expectancy theory for assessing user motivation to utilize an expert system. Journal of Management Information systems, 9 (3), 183-198.

Ferris, K.R. (1977, July). A test of the expectancy theory of motivation in an accounting environment. The Accounting Review, 52 (3), 605-615.

Nielsen, J. (1994). Heuristic evaluation. In J. Nielsen and R.L. Mack (Eds.). Usability Inspection Methods. New York: John Wiley & Sons.

Schamber, L. (1994). Relevance and information behavior. In M.E. Williams (Ed.). Annual Review of Information Science and Technology, Medford, NJ: Learned Information, Inc.

Small, R.V. (1997, Fall). Assessing the motivational quality of World Wide Websites. Syracuse, NY: ERIC Clearinghouse on Information & Technology, ED Document #407930/

Small, R.V. and Arnone, M.P. (1998) WebMAC: Website Motivational Analysis Checklist (3.1). SMALL packages: Fayetteville, NY.

Snead, K.C., Jr. and Harrell, A.M. (1995). An application of expectancy theory to explain a manager's intention to use a decision support system. Decision Sciences, 25 (4), 499-513.

Taylor, R.S. (1986). Value-added processes in information systems. Norwood, NJ: Ablex.

Vroom, V. H. (1964). Work and Motivation. New York: Wiley.

Embedded Multi-criteria Decision Support for Automated Resource Allocation of Deep Space Network Equipment

Jeffrey H. Smith, William Heinrichs, and Chet Borden

Jet Propulsion Laboratory, California Institute of Technology, 4800 Oak Grove Drive, MS 601-237, Pasadena, California 91109-8099 U.S.A.

Phone 818-354-1236; FAX: 818-393-9876; jeffrey.h.smith@jpl.nasa.gov.

ABSTRACT
Growth in demand for telecommunications by the Jet Propulsion Laboratory's Deep Space Network (DSN) has created increased interest in methods and techniques for reducing costs and improving efficiency. Responding to this increased demand, NASA

and the Jet Propulsion Laboratory have been moving toward standardization of telecommunications services and the process for allocating resources to those services.

This paper describes an automated, embedded multi-criteria decision making approach used to allocate telecommunications equipment. Mission users requiring telecommunication services generate service requests containing information about technical parameters of the spacecraft, distance from Earth to the spacecraft, and type of service needed. A technical analysis of each ground antenna is performed to determine whether the antenna can communicate with the spacecraft.

The objective function of the multi-criteria decision problem is to maximize the data rate of communications subject to constraints that characterize the spacecraft communications system and the ground-based antenna communications system. The solution to this decision problem is obtained using lexicographic methods implemented across multiple databases. The outputs of the embedded multi-criteria decision process are rank ordered lists of feasible equipment sets. Examples are presented and discussed.

INTRODUCTION

There has been considerable interest at NASA in reducing the cost of operating space missions [1, 2, 3]. To this end, the process of delivering telecommunications has transformed a paradigm of providing highly customized and varied capabilities to one of delivering standardized services. Numerous organizations involved in delivering these services have been examining a variety of technologies for accelerating the definition of missions, selecting needed services, identifying equipment resources, scheduling those resources for each mission, and eventually delivering the requested services to the project "customers."

This paper describes an application of multiple criteria decision techniques to the selection and identification of equipment resources to deliver standard telecommunications services. The approach combines multi-criteria decision concepts with advanced computer networking, database, and object-oriented technologies to produce feasible resource combinations based on customer selections. Figure 1 outlines the components of the telecommunications resource allocation problem.

THE RESOURCE ALLOCATION PROBLEM

The telecommunications resource allocation problem spans three stages involving multiple objective functions, multiple constraints, and multiple criteria.

Stage 1.   Feasible antenna identification based on service
Stage 2.   Equipment set synthesis
Stage 3.   Ranking of equipment sets by multiple criteria

At Stage 1, service selection maps telecommunications services to multiple decision criteria used to identify feasible antennas. The key parameters are stored in a Mission and Assets database for access by mission users and other service-related tools (Table 1).

Service selection criteria are used as inputs to a telecommunications link budget analysis model [4]. The service selection criteria are augmented by technical parameters that characterize the performance of the various antennas [5]. These technical parameters are also stored in the Mission and Assets database.

Stage 2 criteria identify supporting equipment required to complete the communications link. These criteria are affiliated with each of the equipment items stored in the database of resources. An Equipment Mapper connects each of the feasible antennas to a string of support equipment required to complete the telecommunications link. For example, if the signal is to be transmitted to a spacecraft, there are numerous transmitters available for allocation. If the signal is to be received from the spacecraft, there are numerous receivers that may be used. The Equipment Mapper identifies all combinations of equipment capable of providing the requested service subject to the constraints of equipment performance, availability, and customer specifications. The intersection of the service criteria, feasible antennas, and associated equipment sets yield feasible equipment sets capable of providing the requested service. However, the number of feasible equipment configurations will be large for many inner solar system distances. At Stage 2, these configurations would be in no specific order of preference or priority.

Stage 3 uses multiple criteria to rank order feasible equipment sets before allocation (scheduling) of resources. Costs and equipment availability for scheduling are two im-

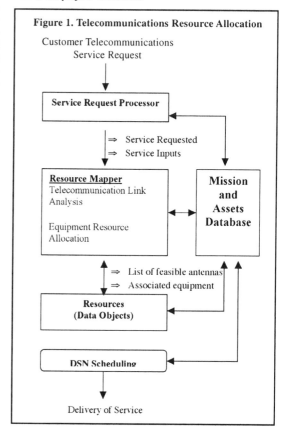

Figure 1. Telecommunications Resource Allocation

Customer Telecommunications
Service Request

↓

Service Request Processor

⇒ Service Requested
⇒ Service Inputs

Resource Mapper
Telecommunication Link Analysis

Equipment Resource Allocation

Mission and Assets Database

⇒ List of feasible antennas
⇒ Associated equipment

Resources (Data Objects)

DSN Scheduling

↓

Delivery of Service

Table 1 . Stage 1 Multiple Decision Criteria	
Criteria for Service Selection	Units
Radio frequency band	X, S, K_a
Spacecraft transmitter/receiver frequency	MHz
Distance between Earth and the spacecraft:	km
Elevation angle of the ground antenna	degrees
Weather condition assumption	Attenuation model
Command data rate (Maximize)	Bits per second
Spacecraft antenna gain	dB
Spacecraft system noise temperature	Degrees Kelvin
Spacecraft antenna-related losses, dB	dB

portant criteria for rank ordering the scheduling of equipment sets. Feasible equipment sets have an operating cost and equipment availability that depends on spacecraft view by the ground resource, downtime for maintenance, and equipment reliability.

The resource allocation problem outlined above uses multiple decision criteria to produce a simple mapping from customer service selections to final equipment set allocations. This is done using a network-based user interface, on-line databases, and automated analysis tools.

Figure 2 illustrates the Stage 2 resource allocation "variables" that define a potential telecommunications link. Each subsystem represents a placeholder for an equipment resource that is connected into a link. Given a selected service, the link is composed of resources drawn from an array of possible choices in each subsystem category.

The challenge of this resource allocation problem is to maximize the amount of data transferred per unit time by choosing a link from thousands of possible equipment configurations which number on the order of more than 10^5 combinations. However, numerous equipment-specific constraints on each service and resource reduce the actual number of combinations to between 10^3–10^4. Determining the exact number of configurations is confounded by the variability in constraints—each resource has a unique (and sometimes complicated) constraint set defined by the resource's purpose, performance, and availability characteristics. The objective was to embed a decision support system in the process of identifying equipment sets to provide automatic updates to resource allocation decisions.

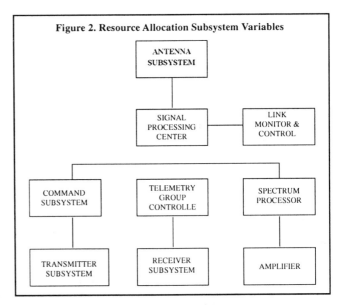

Figure 2. Resource Allocation Subsystem Variables

APPROACH

The Resource Mapper uses an object-oriented approach for the definition of equipment resources. Each resource object contains all the relevant information about the resource and the constraints on the use of that resource. The equipment object functionality is simple in structure with three levels of complexity: (1) class, (2) type, and (3) instance; so that each level inherits all the properties of the previous level.

A class hierarchy was used to represent the component objects for each resource in Figure 2 resulting in objects defined by a Resource Type Name shown in Table 2.

The 23 resources within the 9 classes were composed of specific "instances" of each type. For example, the 70m "Antenna" has 3 instances: DSS14 at the Goldstone, California Complex; DSS43 at the Canberra, Australia Complex; and DSS63 at the Madrid, Spain Complex. The different instances of equipment represent the physical resource entities identified by geographic location.

The manner in which resources can be connected is maintained in a table that contains the parent-child relationships between each equipment item and its connectivity to other equipment instances. These parent-child relationships constitute a series of lexicographic constraints that determine permissible connections between equipment resources. The embedded decision algorithm is maintained within the data table definitions for each of the decision criteria.

The availability of a resource also constrains its inclusion in a link. While the Resource Mapper scans available resources for assignment to a link, the resource's availability determines whether it can be included. An antenna may be planned for operation at some future date so the resource object instance for that antenna contains the date when the antenna would become available. Similarly, if the antenna were to be decommissioned at some future date, the resource object would not be included in service requests after that date. If an equipment resource is an X-band frequency element, it can only be included with other

Table 2 . Resource Object Classes and Derived Types	
Resource Class	Resource Type Name
Antenna	70 meter 34m Beam Wave Guide 34m High Efficiency 34m Standard 26m
Signal Processing Center	Standard SPC
Link Monitor and Control	Standard LMC
Command Subsystem	Standard CMD
Telemetry Group Controller	TGC-A, TGC-B
Spectrum Processor	DSP-R (Radio Science) DSP-V (Very Long Baseline Interferometry)
Transmitter	TXHS, S-band high power TXLS, S-band low power TXHX, X-band high power TXLX, X-band low power
Amplifier	S-FET, S-band SHMT, S-band S-TWM, S-band XHMT, X-band X-TWM, X-band
Receiver	BVR (Block 5 receiver) REC (Block 3 receiver)

X-band frequency equipment. Thus, constraints affiliated with each resource are contained within that resource's object definition (instance). In this manner, new resources can be added and decommissioned resources can be removed with minimal impact on the resource allocation process.

Results

After parent child relationships were defined for all equipment instances, a list of all valid equipment sets was created in a resource allocation table. The parent-child relationships stored in the data table form a simple tree structure that can be traversed to collect each equipment resource stored in the vertices. A complete equipment set was denoted with an end-to-end path spanning the tree. Once the tree had been traversed through all possible paths, a complete list of possible equipment configurations was available for resource allocation.

Table 3 displays a partial list of allocations for the services: Command Radiation (transmission "to" a spacecraft) and Telemetry Service (transmission "from" a spacecraft). Each row in the table is derived using the pre-defined parent-child relationships for each object. Each row constitutes a feasible option based on the antenna link analysis indicating the stated antenna is a feasible solution. The headings of the table correspond to the generic equipment resources shown in Figure 2 with the exception of "Signal Processing Center" which is common for both Command and Telemetry services. The first series of equipment sets are for antenna "DSS12" or the 34 meter standard antennas. The first row indicates that telemetry service can be provided with antenna DSS12, requires a link monitor and control subsystem; a telemetry group controller (unit "B" in this case); a Block V Receiver (Block V is the model version); and an S-band amplifier (S-FET unit "A"). The suffix of "10" on some equipment names indicates the location of the equipment (10 = Goldstone, California).

The next step was to merge the output of the Stage 2 multi-criteria decision problem that identified the feasible antennas with the resource allocation table of all equipment combinations. This stage of the resource allocation problem filtered all *infeasible* antennas from Table 3 resulting in equipment sets capable of providing the service to the requesting mission with its unique characteristics. At this point the inputs were available for the embedded decision algorithm to prioritize the feasible equipment sets.

While there are multiple criteria available for prioritizing equipment sets, the operating cost based on antenna fees was identified as a particularly important criterion for ranking equipment sets. The algorithm for computing DSN Antenna (Aperture) fees embodies incentives to maximize utilization efficiency [6]. It employs weighted hours to determine the cost of DSN support. The following equation was used to calculate an hourly Aperture Fee (A_F) for DSN support:

$$A_F = R_B[A_W(0.9 + F_c/10)]$$

where:

A_F = Weighted Aperture Fee per hour of use.

R_B = Contact dependent hourly rate, adjusted annually ($560/hr. for FY98).

A_W = Aperture weighting (=0.1 for 11-meter stations (stations have <u>very</u> limited capability); = 0.5 for 26-meter stations; = 1.0 for 34-meter stations; = 4.0 for 70-meter stations)

F_c = number of station contacts, (per calendar week).

The value of station contacts, F_c, is set equal to one for each service request. A Resource Mapper function that integrates performance across multiple service requests uses the frequency of requests to further refine the equipment sets for the "package" of services requested in a particular contact. When the equipment sets are identified by the Resource Mapper, a field in the database containing a pointer to the cost model automatically computes the cost of each set. Another field associated with each equipment set is automatically set to the relative ranking with respect to cost (lowest cost ranked 1, highest cost ranked N). In this manner, scheduling algorithms can assign equipment sets in priority order based on the embedded cost analysis.

DISCUSSION AND CONCLUSIONS

The use of embedded decision support for resource allocation and assigning valid equipment sets to user defined services was demonstrated in the study. An object-oriented approach to the definition and management of telecommunications resources was shown to be effective for integrating and simplifying the complex processes of antenna feasibility analysis, link equipment assignment, and allocation of equipment sets to service requests. The process was implemented successfully in prototype form using Open Database Connectivity (ODBC) to connect the analysis components written in the C++ language with data stored in the Mission and Assets database. The entire process was developed for use on network servers.

The resource allocation approach is one component of a new Service Request Processor for telecommunications services. The automated, multiple criteria decision methodology used to identify feasible antenna alternatives and map physical equipment resources to those antennas represented a first step in a simplified, service-based telecommunications process. A unique feature of this application was embedding object-oriented resource constraints within the resource definitions in a manner that automated the formation of equipment configurations using database architectures.

In addition, embedding multiple criteria objectives in the structure of the Resource Mapper provided a natural environment for embedding multiple criteria decision-making methods in the process. The advent of software technologies capable of facilitating the integration of dissimilar resources and functions were instrumental in developing the prototype for this study.

ACKNOWLEDGMENTS

The authors would like to thank Chet Borden and Joe Wackley at JPL for their support. The authors also acknowledge the help of Sil Zendejas and Rick Covington whose support enabled elements of this work to be performed. This work was carried out by the Jet Propulsion Laboratory, California Institute of Technology, under contract with the National Aeronautics and Space Administra-

Table 3. Resource Mapper Output Showing Equipment Sets Composed of Resource Instances (see Figure 2 for definitions of equipment instance names)

SpcName	LmcName	CmdName	TgcName	AntName	RecName	TxrName	AmpName
SPC-10	LMC-10	---	TGC-B-10	DSS-12	BVR-1	—	S-FET-A
SPC-10	LMC-10	---	TGC-A-10	DSS-12	BVR-1	---	S-FET-A
SPC-10	LMC-10	CMD-10	---	DSS-12	---	TXLS-A	---
SPC-10	LMC-10	—	TGC-B-10	DSS-12	BVR-1	---	X-TWM-A
SPC-10	LMC-10	---	TGC-B-10	DSS-12	BVR-1	—	S-TWM-A
SPC-10	LMC-10	---	TGC-B-10	DSS-12		TXLS-A	---
SPC-10	LMC-10		TGC-A-10	DSS-12	BVR-1		X-TVVM-A
SPC-10	LMC-10		TGC-A-10	DSS-12	BVR-1		S-TWM-A
SPC-10	LMC-10		TGC-A-10	DSS-12	.	TXLS-A	---
SPC-10	LMC-10	CMD-10	---	DSS-12	BVR-1	—	X-TWM-A
SPC-10	LMC-10	CMD-10	---	DSS-12	BVR-1	---	S-FET-A
SPC-10	LMC-10	CMD-10	—	DSS-12	BVR-1	---	S-TWM-A
SPC-10	LMC-10	—	TGC-B-10	DSS-14		TXLS-A	---
SPC-10	LMC-10	---	TGC-A-10	DSS-14		TXLS-A	
SPC-10	LMC-10	CMD-10	—	DSS-14		TXLS-A	
SPC-10	LMC-10		TGC-B-10	DSS-14	BVR-H		X-TWM-A

tion.

REFERENCES

1. National Aeronautics and Space Administration, Space Operations Management Plan, Document JSC 27527, Lyndon B. Johnson Space Center, Houston, Texas, February 28, 1997.
2. Smith, Jeffrey H., The Challenge of Doing More With Less: Finding the Right Portfolio of Technology Investments, JPL Document No. D-11776, Jet Propulsion Laboratory, Pasadena, California, May 1994.
3. Smith, Jeffrey H., "The New Millennium Technology Program: Streamlining the R&D Planning Process," *Proceedings of the 25th Annual Meeting of the Decision Sciences Institute*, Seattle, WA, 1996, pp. 518-520.
4. Smith, Jeffrey H., "Algorithm for Service Request Processor Antenna Selection Using Mission and Assets Database (MADB) Inputs," JPL IOM 311.8/97-14, Jet Propulsion Laboratory, Pasadena, California, July 28, 1997.
5. TDA, Deep space Network/Flight Project Interface Design Handbook, JPL Document 810-5, Rev. D, Volumes I, II, Jet Propulsion Laboratory, Pasadena, CA, March 29, 1997.
6. NASA, NASA's Mission Operations and Communications Services, (this description applies only to proposals in response to NASA's Announcement of Opportunity for Discovery Missions), NASA Document AO 98-OSS-04, National Aeronautics and Space Administration, Washington, D.C., February 1998.

Digital Video in a Twenty-First Century Classroom

Maj Todd L. Smith, Maj Doug Wolfe, and Bernard J. Jansen
Department of EE & CS, United States Military Academy, West Point, NY 10996
Voice: (914) 938-5562, FAX: (914) 938-5956, Todd-Smith@usma.edu
Voice: (914) 938-2200, Doug-Wolfe@usma.edu
Voice: (914) 938-3233, jansen@exmail.usma.edu

ABSTRACT

Digital Video is an exciting new medium with the potential to revolutionize the way organizations train their employees. However, there are questions that must be answered. What is the best use of video? How much video do you need? Is ATM required, or can you achieve multiple streams of thirty frames per second over a collision based protocol? Is the payoff worth the cost? In this paper, we explore the quality of video over a 100 Mbps Switched Ethernet Network using a RealVideo Server. We compare the performance and quality of the RealVideo Stream with MPEG-1 distributed from a File Server using various client and server combinations.

1. INTRODUCTION

The United States Army has approximately 475,000 soldiers that are deployed across the United States, Europe, Asia, and Central and South America. Regardless of their occupational specialty or rank, they require continual technical and professional training. This includes refresher training, new equipment training, and training associated with new positions, units, environments, or ranks. In fact, the main mission of a peacetime army is to train.

In the past, most training has been conducted at the soldier's duty station. Officers and noncommissioned officer plan for and schedule sustainment or refresher training, and experienced soldiers provide the instruction. However, it often occurs that the required expertise does not exist in a unit, and either instructors are sent as a temporary duty (TDY) to the post or soldiers are sent TDY to a central school. This centralized instruction is very effective, but it is also very expensive.

In 1995, the Army's Training and Doctrine Command [11] initiated a plan to reduce expenses incurred when soldiers travel for training. Through distance learning, TRADOC hopes to leverage technology to provide quality, centralized instruction to soldiers located all over the world. Their plan has two components central to this paper. The first is Classroom XXI, where soldiers at a training post will be able to access digital materials. The second is the Distance Learning [11] Program. Those soldiers not located at training centers will access multimedia-training materials from a digital library through a distributed database. These materials will consist of text, graphics, audio, and video files accessed through either a Hypertext front-end or as a stand-alone application.

TRADOC requested that the Department of Electrical Engineering and Computer Science at the United States Military Academy, West Point, New York review current technology and assist with the planning and design for Classroom XXI. This initiative will result in the creation and fielding of over 500 classrooms during the next few years. For an overview of the Classroom XXI and US Army Distance learning plan see Adams and Jansen.

One of the primary considerations in the design of the digital library is the role of digital video, and we have divided this issue into two areas:

(1) How much video do we need?
(2) How much video can we deliver?

We are currently exploring both of these issues. The goal of this paper is to: (1) Describe the configuration of the network and classroom, (2) Identify successes and problems, and (3) Discuss future plans.

2. RELATED WORK

In addition to cost reduction, schools, businesses, and governmental organizations are turning to Distance Learning [11] to bolster enrollments, share expertise, extend the geographical extent of training programs, and broaden their customer base [1], [3]. Within an educational environment, DL provides a means to keep faculty employed and low enrollment courses viable through video-conferencing and digital libraries [4], [7]. The mechanisms required to deliver an instructor's video taped lecture or printed material to students at various locations and times are fairly well documented and routine. The challenge is to distribute interactive, multimedia resources on a large scale, in a timely and cost-effective manner.

Research is continuing on the most effective utilization of networks for DL [7]. Current DL programs are using a mixture of 3.5" floppy disks and CD-ROMs to distribute multimedia files to students [5]. The 1.44 MB size restrictions of a floppy disk make it impractical for anything but text files or application files to be distributed. Likewise, CDs present two challenges to instructional developers. First is the 650-MB capacity limit of the compact disk. With a typical MPEG-1 file averaging 12-18 MB per minute of video, this storage limitation is quickly reached. Second, because of the "write-once, read-many" nature of compact disks, changes to any file on the disk, no matter how slight, require a new master and all of its accompanying charges, effectively erasing most of the savings realized through the use of CDs in the first place.

To provide learning materials quickly and efficiently to students, many schools have turned to digital libraries. Some institutions like the University of Minnesota, utilize a type of monolithic storage arrangement to provide learning material to a continuing education student population that is scattered over several hundred miles of the northern United States [2]. Others, like Virginia Tech use digital libraries as a reference store for local students [4]. While the exact methods of storage and retrieval may differ, both examples allow students access to repositories of multimedia information through some type of network connection. These server-based edifices allow any student with network access, either through a local area network or dial-up access, to access or browse learning material of any type. Because of the immediacy of server access by instructors and developers, the material is current. It does not have the lag time of disk mastering or disk distribution. As such, digital libraries become a natural extension of any distance learning plan.

However, multimedia applications stress the entire digital library, network, computer infrastructure, including data storage, servers, bandwidth, and processors. We were extremely interested in the effect of multimedia applications on our networking infrastructure during the planing and development of Classroom XXI [1]. Specifically, we attempted to locate research data and information concerning how much video was needed and how much could be delivered on a given network.

3. NETWORK AND CLASSROOM CONFIGURATION

As always, there were several competing requirements that limited the potential designs of the classroom network. Since portable computers are becoming ubiquitous in Army Units, TRADOC wanted us to determine their utility in a classroom environment. This restricted the use of ATM to the desktop. A facility at Fort Eustis, Virginia has implemented ATM (155 Mbps) to the desktop in a similar trial. Funding and personnel were also limiting factors. There exists insufficient funding to hire network administrators for the design and maintenance of the classroom, so instructors installed the network and are responsible for its maintenance. This is a constraint that will be imposed in an operational setting as TRADOC fields the classrooms.

However, we were able to use a T1 line provided through a grant from MCI for Internet access. This capability freed us of the limitations of the existing Campus Network. Based on these considerations, we choose a combination of switched 10BaseT and 100BaseT Ethernet using Category-5 twisted pair cabling. The Network Interface Card in the client machines determines the speed of the network connection.

Figure 1 shows the network infrastructure as it stands today (May 1998). Each client workstation in the classroom has a switched Ethernet 10/100Base-T connection. All of the machines are connected to a CISCO Catalyst 2924 Ethernet Switch. This switch is then connected to a CISCO Catalyst 2908 Ethernet Switch via Full-Duplex 100BaseT. The Catalyst 2908 is used to support the servers where the web, training database, and video content of the training courses are maintained. The Catalyst 2908 also provides an uplink to the department's T1. The T1 would be used for distance learning via the Internet.

The client machines consisted of Pentium 166 Notebooks with 80 MB of RAM. They have 10/100BaseT 3COM Fast Etherlink PCMCIA Network Interface Cards. The servers included two Dual Pentium 200 MHz machines each with 160 MB of RAM, a Dual Pentium 90 MHz with 48 RAM, and a Pentium 200 MHz with 32 MB of RAM. These servers provide web, database and video content to the students.

In our test, we utilized two types of video, MPEG-1 and RealNetworks RealVideo. Students accessed the MPEG-1 files through a file server located on a switched 100 Mbps segment. We also connected the server to a 10 Mbps segment for performance comparisons. We are currently installing a Video Server capable of MPEG-1 streams for further study. The RealVideo Server was installed on a 100 Mbps segment off of the Cisco 2908.

RealNetworks states that their architecture "is a framework of client and server API's for the development of streaming multimedia applications. It is the third generation client-server system created by RealNetworks, designed to allow independent software companies to build or adapt their software to be streamed from servers and played by clients which support" [9] the architecture. RealNetworks uses their proprietary protocol, The Real Time Streaming Protocol (RTSP). RTSP is a communications protocol for the "control and delivery of real time media" [9]. We chose the RealNetworks products because of their dominance in the video server market. We are currently exploring other technologies, as well.

The classroom operating system was Windows NT 4.0. NT provides diagnostics that allow the monitoring of processor and memory utilization. However, we had difficulty installing and maintaining different combinations of PCMCIA cards and installing some software programs. Several MPEG-1 players had difficulty under NT 4.0, but the Microsoft plug-in for Media Player worked on all platforms and on most files. A few files recorded with a digital video camera worked under Windows 95, but not under NT.

Finally, we used the NetXray/Dual Version 3.0.0 sniffer to look at the network utilization, collisions, and errors. We first tried to run the sniffer on a Pentium 166 notebook, but it could not handle the network load and locked up. We then switched to a Pentium 200 desktop, and were able to measure the impact on the network.

4. DISCUSSION

As stated, our target client was a notebook with a 166 MHz Pentium processor and 80 MB RAM. We also looked at other clients to determine the impact of the client on system performance. None of the clients had MPEG hardware, but the video cards, video memory, cache, and bus architecture varied greatly in the available machines. Table 1 illustrates the performance our notebooks compared to other systems. The P166 was able to play the MPEG-1 file full screen without degradation of quality. The audio was synchronized sufficiently that speech and lip movement seemed natural.

We first streamed/transferred the video file from the Pentium 200 MHz machine with 32 MB of RAM. When using the RealVideo, the server could stream to the maximum number of clients on the network with no performance degradation from either the network or the server. The network utilization varied from 4-7% with no collisions or network errors. At the advertised 45 Kbps, nineteen clients should have registered 855 Kbps or less than 1% of the 100 Mbps segment (8.55% of the 10 Mbps segment). But, when we attempted multiple transfers of the MPEG-1 file, the server degraded to the point that we had to disconnect it from the network. We were only able to achieve five simultaneous transfers. The network utilization was 7% at the time of system

Table 1 - Client Utilization		
Client Machine	RealVideo	MPEG-1 File
Pentium 100 MHz 80 MB (Desktop)	45%	99%
Pentium 133 MHz 32 MB (Notebook)	70%	100%
Pentium 166 MHz 80 MB (Notebook)	70%	100%
Pentium 233 MHz 128 MB (Desktop)	12%	13%
Pentium 300 MHz 128 MB (Desktop)	2%	11%

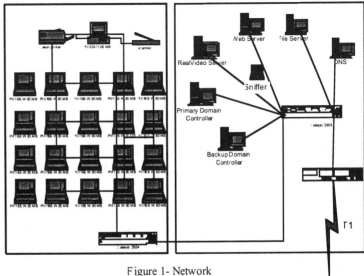

Figure 1- Network
Configuration

failure. Assuming a transfer rate of 1.5 Mbps for a MPEG-1 file, five files would require 7.5 Mbps or 7.5% of available bandwidth (75% of the 10 Mbps segment).

Second, we used the Dual Pentium 90 Server located on a 10 Mbps segment. The server showed an average of 5% CPU utilization when streaming 19 RealVideo Streams. The network utilization varied between 7 and 9% with no errors or collisions. This configuration only supported four MPEG-1 files prior to the degradation of video quality. The server was at 32% utilization and the network varied from 65% to 68% utilization on the fifth stream. The audio on all five were unintelligible when the fifth file began.

Finally, we used the Dual Pentium 200 MHz and 160 MB of RAM. As before, there was no degradation in the RealServer streamed video. The significant difference came with the MPEG video file transfer. We were able to achieve nineteen simultaneous MPEG transfers with no degradation of video quality. The maximum network utilization was 32% with no collisions or errors. The server CPU utilization was only 25% on one processor and 4% on the other.

Network utilization was not a factor when the server was connected with a 100Mbps Ethernet segment. The segment never exceeded 35% utilization and we did not see any collisions on the segment. It was not until we connected the server to a 10 Mbps Ethernet segment that we saw degradation in the video. We were only able to have four simultaneous transfers of the MPEG file without any loss in quality.

Table 2 - Network Utilization, 200 MHz Server, 100 Mbps Segment

	RealVideo	MPEG-1 File
Number of Streams before degradation	19	5
Network Utilization	4%	10%
Collisions	0	0
Errors	0	0

Table 3 - Network Utilization, Dual 90 MHz Server, 10 Mbps Segment

	RealVideo	MPEG-1 File
Number of Streams before degradation	19 (no degradation)	5
Network Utilization	9%	68%
Collisions	0	30
Errors	0	5

Table 4 - Network Utilization, Dual 200 MHz Server, 100 Mbps Segment

	RealVideo	MPEG-1 File
Number of Streams	19 (No degradation)	19 (No degradation)
Network Utilization	7%	32%
Collisions	0	0
Errors	0	0

5. FUTURE WORK

As stated, we are attempting to answer two questions: how much video do we need and how much video can we deliver. Our results show that fifteen frames-per-second video can be delivered to a classroom at a fairly low cost. Full screen, that is thirty frames per second video is possible at a higher but still reasonable cost. However, scaleable systems require video servers that are currently expensive and difficult to maintain.

We are currently installing a Video Server that is scaleable to 1000 MPEG-1 streams to validate streamed video over the campus network (CAN). We plan to validate simultaneous delivery of high bandwidth streams over the CAN and alternative low bandwidth streams over a Wide Area Network.

The second question is why. We are working with the Engineering Psychology Department at West Point to determine the best use of video in an educational environment. Currently, we have compared a live lecture with various digital video formats, i.e., speaker only, alternating speaker and slides, and slides only. We showed the RealVideo to an Information Systems course, and they unanimously agreed that even this quality was sufficient to be of benefit. However, as digital video becomes more available, expectations will rise. We are exploring the possibility of storing key lectures, guest speakers, and student presentations in digital form. We are confident that we have an infrastructure that can support video. We are not sure of the demand.

6. CONCLUSION

In this paper, we examined the feasibility of digital video in an educational environment using standard paradigms. We used a variety of client, server, and network configurations and compared the suitability of each.

7. REFERENCES

[1] Adams, William and Bernard J. Jansen, *Distributed Digital Library Architecture: The Key to Success for Distance Learning.* Proceedings of the 8th International Workshop on Research Issues in Data Engineering. 23-24 February 1998. 2-8.

[2] Dance, Muriel. *The Promise of Distance Learning.* http://weber.u.washington.edu/~jamesher/mdance.htm. Accessed November 1997.

[3] Duin, A. Hill, and E. A. Nater. *Designing and Managing Virtual learning Environments for Secondary, Post-Secondary, Graduate, and Continuing: An Education Land Grant Perspective.* Proceedings of the World Conference on Educational Multimedia and Hypermedia 1996. Pp. 202 - 207.

[4] Etter, D.M.; Orsak, G.C.; Johnson, D.H. *A Distance Learning Laboratory Design Experiment in Undergraduate Digital Signal Processing.* 1995 International Conference on Acoustics, Speech, and Signal Processing. Conference Proceedings. p. 2885-7 vol. 5.

[5] Fox, Edward. *Digital Libraries, WWW, and Educational Technology: Lessons Learned.* Proceedings of the World Conference on Educational Multimedia and Hypermedia 1996. P. 246 - 251.

[6] Harris, J.A.; Murden, C.; Webster, L.L. *The Potential of Interactive Multimedia on CD-ROM to Enhance Laboratory Work in*

Physical Science and Engineering. 1994 IEEE First International Conference on Multi-Media Engineering Education Proceedings. p. 296-301.

[7] Lollar, R.B. *Distance Learning for Non-Traditional Students to Study, Near Home, Toward a UNC Charlotte BSET Degree.* Proceedings IEEE Southeastcon '95 Visualize the Future. p. 366-7.

[8] Palounek, Andrea P. T., et.al. *Distributed Computing Network for Science and Math Education in Rural New Mexico.* Proceedings of the World Conference on Educational Multimedia and Hypermedia 1996. P 557-562

[9] RealNetworks Home Page, http://www.real.com/corporate/index.html, accessed 19 November 1997, last modified on 28 October 1997.

[10] Stanford. *An On-Line Distance Learning System Using Digital Video and Multimedia Networking Technologies.* http://minas.stanford.edu/project/project.html. Accessed November 1997.

[11] U.S. Army Training and Doctrine Command. *The Army Distance Learning Plan.* Available on-line from http://www-dcst.monroe.army.mil/adlp/adlp.htm. Accessed 1 December 1997.

Some Essential Concepts and Tools for Creating and Maintaining a Web Page Infrastructure for Classroom Use

Robin M. Snyder

Department of Information and Operations Management, UNC Charlotte, Charlotte, NC 28223-0001

(704) 547-2908, rmsnyder@email.uncc.edu

ABSTRACT

Creating an HTML file for a web page is actually one of the easiest aspects of creating a web page system. But there are a number of other systems aspects that are often overlooked that play a key role in creating and maintaining a web page infrastructure for classroom use. The aspects discussed are those that were faced and addressed by the author. Although the author often uses custom programming to address the issues, the same techniques could be used for standard off-the-shelf applications suites such as Microsoft Office. This paper should be of interest to anyone using the web in the classroom.

INTRODUCTION

The author started experimenting with HTML in the summer of 1995 and, by the summer of 1996, began using HTML in the classroom and has used HTML and the Internet in every class taught since then. This paper describes some of concepts and tools that have been developed in order to do this easily, efficiently, and effectively.

SIZE OF THE WEB SYSTEM

Creating an HTML file for a web page is actually one of the easiest aspects of creating a web page system. Given the proper web tools and web system infrastructure, a web system can grow very quickly very fast. To provide some idea of the scale of the system, here is a quick summary (provided by the web spider, to be discussed later).

File summary: 1998-10-16 at 11:46		
393	.spr	document files
897	.htm	HTML files
11	.exe	executable files
6	.xla	Excel Add-In's
437	.jpg	JPEG image files
265	.gif	GIF image files
99	.bmp	BMP image files
24	.???	other files
2132		total files in 173 directories
0		archive files
3486		inter-file references checked.

In this case, there are **2132** file in **173** directories in the entire system with **3486** inter-file references (just in the HTML files). Since the author has just started at a new institution, there are no archived files from previous classes (see details below).

The techniques that work for just a few files in a few directories may not work well for thousands of files in hundreds of directories. The rest of this paper provides an overview of the concepts and tools used to create and maintain this system.

DOCUMENT TO HTML FORMATTING

The author maintains identical HTML files in two forms. One form is for slide presentations in class via the local hard drive (for efficiency reasons), the teacher-side system. One form is for notes for students via the Internet, the student-side system. The author uses a very flexible and powerful word processor that provides a fully customizable printer interface, screen interface, editor macro interface, and formatter interface patterned after the UNIX EMACS word processor, but with a nicer screen interface. The word processor is the Borland Sprint 1.0 for DOS word processor from 1988. In 1995, the author created a new format file for HTML (under a thousand lines now, but originally started as a few hundred lines) that provided HTML support. For example, in the formatter, bold text is created by using the **B** macro. The text

This is @B(bold).

is formatted to the following.

This is **bold**.

Sprint actually provides a nice color-coded text screen interface whereby the text to be bold-faced starts with a **Control-B** and ends with a **Control-N** (both are inserted by editor macros). The Control-B in the text file is interpreted by the text formatter as invoking the **B** macro. The generic **B** macro is defined as follows.

@DEFINE(b, font bold, ifnotfound, overstruck)

To convert this to HTML, the macro is redefined for an HTML printer as follows.

@MACRO(b()="@NOTCT(<B>)@EVAL()@NOTCT(</B>)")

So, for the HTML printer,

This is @B(bold).

is formatted to the following.

This is <B>bold</B>.

The **NOTCT** command insures that no character translation is done on the enclosed text argument. In this case, the following character translation needs to be added to the HTML printer.

Such formatter macros are quite easy to write. Again, a 1988 DOS word processor was easily adapted to HTML in 1995. Sprint does run out of memory occasionally, but works well for books up to 400 pages where the table of contents, index, list of figures, etc., do not exceed 64KB of memory.

Other formatting features allow different formatting actions to be taken depending on whether the output is teacher-side HTML, student- side HTML, PostScript (i.e., a paper or article as opposed to an HTML summary), etc.

For example, whenever a link is made, the formatter also generates an HTML comment that contains source document location so that, if the link is deemed not valid, the word processor (via an editor macro) can automatically find the source of the bad link. This saves a lot of time.

Editor macros are very important in being able to do actions automatically in real time that either cannot be done with formatter macros or, because of real time requirements, need to be done on the screen.

It is important to note that WYSISYG (what you see is what you get) word processors, by their very nature, do not lend themselves to text formatting, since with formatting you cannot see what you are going to get until you do the formatting. Such systems, such as Microsoft Word, provide just editor macros and not formatter macros (although some simple formatting features can be provided in WYSIWYG mode). The problem with editor macros is that they introduce nontrivial copy- update problems. For example, in a WYSIWYG word processor, if one redefines what "bold" means (or "Chapter", or "Section", or "SubSection", etc.) one must find every occurrence of that format and change it. This is not too much of a problem with one file, or several files in one directory, but with thousands of files in hundreds of directories, it is just too difficult.

With the text formatting method, if any aspect of formatting is changed, such as the appearance of a "Section", just reformat all of the documents. This can be easily done with 4DOS batch files and a web spider.

A WEB SPIDER

A web spider was written to determine which HTML files need updated (based on file time and date stamps) and reformat those files. Note that all document files are formatted into both a teacher-side version and a student-side version. Both versions share the same image files. For example, the document

C:\F\I3239-8C\notes&02.spr

is formatted to the teacher-side file

C:\W\I3239-8C.HTM\notes&02.htm

and also to the student-side file

C:\W\I3239-8C.WEB\notes&02.htm

Any bad links (or other errors) are identified and located automatically in the source document within the editor. This allows any changes made to the web system to be updated before publishing the changes on the Internet, as is done at the end of each class period.

ARCHIVING WEB PAGES FOR CLASSES

During the semester, web files are organized in a manner that is convenient to the teacher. Thus, web files are spread out over 20 to 40 directories. At the end of the semester, however, a program written by the author is used to consolidate all web files for each class in one subdirectory. The archived class web files thus form an audit trail of what went on during the class. Duplicate file names are resolved internally, since the file names themselves are not important, as long as all links are appropriately changed. Not only does this give the teacher and student an audit trail of the class, but it frees the teacher to reorganize the current web system without concern (or work) from having to maintain link consistency for those files. One can get an idea of the growth of the web system from the number of files in the archived classes over time. Here, the QM course is the MBA quantitative methods for business course and the IS class is the MBA management information systems class.

In many cases, once course content is created, it is easy to add it to a course as needed. This is a great benefit, for example, if content is covered that the students should know, but do not remember very well. If the teacher has content from a prerequisite course, that can be linked into the current course so that, after a brief recap, the students not remembering very well can check out the detailed notes on-line outside of class.

Trimester	QM	IS
Fall 1996	105	54
Spring 1997	144	
Summer 1997	102	
Fall 1997	282	286
Spring 1998	600	
Summer 1998	872	

DATABASE GENERATION

There are parts of the web system that should be stored in the database and generated automatically, typically via a database web report feature or via custom programming from a database. The author uses this for the following reports.
• List of students in the class, with links to their web pages.
• Lists of students for project/presentation assignments, etc.

BACKUP SYSTEM

The web system must, of course, be backed up. The author uses a custom program to back up all files, at the source level, to a backup medium. The Iomega Zip disks work well, but, since the backup is done at the file system level, other media could be used as well. The author has developed a special hash-code to determine whether a directory on a slow backup media (such as a Zip disk) needs to be updated, which, in the case of about 10,000 files in 300 directories, speeds up the backup check of a Zip disk (that needs no updating) from about 40 seconds to about 2 seconds.

If the web system resides on a NetWare file server, as might be the case when a Windows NT server maps the teacher's URL to that NetWare file server, the same backup system can be used to "backup" the web directories to the NetWare file server, thus updating the web system. Used for two years by the author, this is a nice alternative to the standard FTP route.

FTP AUTOMATION

In most cases, FTP must be used to update a web server. With thousands of files and hundreds of directories, it is best if this is done automatically. The 4DOS batch file language is an extended and powerful superset of the DOS batch file language (which is tedious, not very powerful, and a pain to use). It is used to tie together many aspects of the web system. For example, the author uses 4DOS batch files to automate update via FTP. Briefly, the 4DOS batch file maintains a date and time of the last web update, and then searches through all of the web directories, and dynamically creates an FTP command script (as a text file) that is then given to the command line **ftp.exe** program to execute. This works very well and does not require the author to keep track of which files need updating. In fact, it works so well that the author uses it to maintain two identical web sites, http://www.uncc.edu/~rmsnyder is on a UNIX web server maintained by the University and http://www.sit.uncc.edu/rmsnyder is on a Windows NT web server maintained by the School of Information Technology. Since links to files on the UNIX web server are case sensitive, the web spider was modified to insure that all filenames matched in a case sensitive way.

PICTURES

The author takes pictures of students at the start of each class. A personal decision support system, developed by the author, allows the picture acquisition, processing, organizing, and updating to be done very easily. These pictures are used for a variety of purposes during and after the semester.

If the students have network accounts, the pictures so taken are provided to the students for use on their web pages, should they so desire.

It is also important, during and outside of class, to be able to grab screen images, process them, organize them, and add them to the web system. The author has written a simple screen grabber (in Delphi), a more sophisticated image organizer (also in Delphi), that work together (as separate programs) to make grabbing screen images and adding them to documents easy and very organized. This can be done in real time (i.e., during class) such that students are not overly distracted while images are added to the class notes in real time.

MICROSOFT OFFICE

Although the author often uses custom programming to address the issues, the same techniques could be used for standard off-the-shelf applications suites such as Microsoft Office. The primary reason that Microsoft Office, or some other application suite, was not used was the real-time penalty for using such software. The software is just too sluggish to provide a satisfactory response time for real-time classroom use. In addition, the copy-update problems of skipping the formatting stage, in order to achieve some form of WYSIWYG mode, creates practical problems that are just too difficult to program around.

SUMMARY

This paper has presented an overview of those concepts and tools that the author has found essential in creating and maintaining a large and dynamic web system for classroom use. As with most web systems, the author's web system is continually growing and (hopefully) improving.

A Personal Decision Support System for Acquiring, Processing, Organizing, and Using Student Pictures in a Classroom Setting

Robin M. Snyder

Department of Information and Operations Management, UNC Charlotte, Charlotte, NC 28223-0001

(704) 547-2908, rmsnyder@email.uncc.edu

ABSTRACT

It is important for teachers to learn and connect student names with student faces. This can be difficult when class sizes are large, and even more difficult after the semester has ended and new classes have started. This paper describes a personal decision support system, designed and implemented by the author, that is used to acquire, process, organize, update student pictures. Applications and uses of these pictures are also discussed. There are a number of interesting design, implementation, practical, and human aspects of this problem that should make this paper of interest to a wide audience.

INTRODUCTION

The author has found student pictures to be a significant advantage in learning and connecting student faces with student names, both during the semester and after classes have ended. Since the advent of computerized picture acquisition, the main problem has been creating a system that was easy and fast to use. This paper describes a system that fills this need.

DESIGN CONSIDERATIONS

Although many institutions do take student pictures, those pictures are usually not made available to teachers, for a variety of reasons. Thus, a personal decision support system for acquiring, processing, organizing, and updating these pictures becomes an important alternative. The goal is to make this as easy and fast as possible.

THE STUDENT DATABASE

A database is maintained of all students and classes that the author teaches. The important fields in the student part of this database are as follows.

- **FullName** is the full name of the student, as recorded by the institution.
- **StudentId** is the student ID, as prescribed by the institution.
- **UserId** is the user ID that the author assigns to the student (which may or may not correspond to the user ID assigned by the institution).
- **LastName** is the last name of the student.
- **FirstName** is the first name of the student.
- **NickName** is the name the student prefers to be called.
- **Email** is the preferred email address of the student.
- **HomePage** is the preferred home page of the student.

Of these fields, **FullName** and **StudentId** are usually provided by the institution in electronic form. The field **UserId** is determined the the author. The fields **LastName**, **FirstName**, **NickName**, **Email**, and **HomePage** are provided by the students via electronic submission (and not discussed further here).

For security reasons, the author has found it useful to use a **UserId** to identify the student rather than the **StudentId**. Thus, the **UserId** can be made public, but the **StudentId** is kept private (and only used in order to submit final grades for the class).

Typically, the **UserId** is formed by using the first initials of the first and middle name, followed by up to six characters of the last name. So, the student

Tamara Frances Snyder

would be assigned the **UserId**

tfsnyder

unless the **UserId** is already in use, in which case the last letter would become a digit to form a unique **UserId**.

The picture for student **tfsnyder** is saved both as a bitmap file **tfsnyder.bmp** and as the JPEG file **tfsnyder.jpg**. The pictures are not stored in the database, but are stored as bitmap (i.e., **.bmp**) file in the **USERS.BMP** directory (for bitmaps) and in the directory **USERS.JPG** (for JPEG images). These directories are not made public, but are for the teacher's use.

For example purposes, a class size of 40 students will be assumed.

PICTURE ACQUISITION

The author started taking student pictures in 1992. A slow, expensive, and somewhat tedious process then, the current crop of video acquisition devices has greatly improved the quality of the pictures, greatly reduced the cost of the hardware, and greatly reduced the time necessary to acquire the pictures. Currently, the author uses a Connectix QuickCam/VC camera that connects to the parallel port of the author's laptop computer, although the methods to be described should work with most any camera on the market today. Most similar cameras today are in the $100 range.

For classroom presentations, the author uses a laptop on a cart that is wheeled from/to the office to/from the classroom. Thus, the camera is always available, and, in fact, comes in handy in getting real- time images (e.g., textbook pictures, hardware pictures, etc.) for inclusion in the class notes published at the end of class on the Internet (the system for doing this is not discussed here). Thus, the laptop and camera setup are sunk costs, since they are always available in every class.

At the start of the first (or second) class meeting, the students are asked to line up to have their pictures taken. It is important, though, to announce something similar to the following.
- The pictures to be taken are for the teachers personal use in connecting student names and faces. No one else will have access to the pictures.
- Each student will be provided with the picture taken in electronic form, should they wish to use it for their web page.
- Having the picture taken is a class requirement.
- If you do not like the picture taken, you can chose to have it taken again (and again, and again, etc.).

To save time, the author usually goes over the procedure at the end of the first class, and then starts taking picture before the start of the second class, as student arrive (already knowing what is going on, if they remember it from the first class). This reduces the amount of class time used for picture taking, processing, and organizing.

To start the picture taking, a chair is positioned so that the background is plain (to make the compressed JPEG file smaller) and the camera is adjusted appropriately. The author has found it useful to use a small tripod to keep the camera from moving during picture taking. Otherwise, students will seem to have crooked heads.

One this is done, pictures can be taken at a rate of about one student every **5** to **10** seconds. After a while, one gets used to determining and pressing the "take picture" key at the exact moment when the student cracks a smile. It is easy to take **40** pictures in about **5** minutes.

Most picture acquisition software will store the pictures in a directory. This directory must be determined so that the decision support software, written by the author, can find those pictures.

PICTURE PROCESSING

In order to take pictures quickly, it is difficult to get the student face lined up properly. The first part of the DSS is a program that takes the bitmap picture created by the camera software and allows the teacher to adjust a rectangle (i.e., dotted lines on the screen) to properly frame the picture, saving the framed picture to another directory. This takes about **2** to **4** seconds per picture so that **40** pictures can be framed in about **2** minutes.

The rectangle size selected was a width of **160** and a height of **224**. The prime factorization of each is as follows, keeping in mind that the resizing of images works best (computationally and visually) if it is done in powers of **2**.
$$160 = 2 * 2 * 2 * 2 * 2 * 5$$
$$224 = 2 * 2 * 2 * 2 * 2 * 7$$

PICTURE ORGANIZING

The second part of the DSS is used to match the pictures with the names of the students. The program that does this, displays the unassigned student names for that class on the left, the unassigned pictures in the middle, and the assigned pictures and names on the right. For the currently unassigned picture, the teacher asks, who is this. The teacher then clicks on the unassigned name on the left, and then clicks on the "**Assign**" button. Other buttons include "**Recover**" to undo an assigned picture and "**Replace**" to replace an assigned picture with a new picture (as is done when a student has a new picture taken). The process of assigning names to pictures starts out slow, since there are **40** names to pick from, but speeds up as each unassigned name on the left is paired with a unassigned picture, and moved to the right part of the screen. This process takes about **3** to **6** seconds for each picture, or, for **40** students, about **3** minutes.

TIME SUMMARY

The time summary for **40** students is as follows.

Spending **10** minutes during the first (or second) class period is well worth the benefits of having the student pictures.

Of course, makeup pictures are always required, but these can be done before or after class or during breaks.

Acquisition:	5 minutes
Processing:	2 minutes
Organizing:	3 minutes
Total:	10 minutes

USES OF THE PICTURES

The author has used the pictures taken using the method just described for a number of purposes. Some of these include the following.
- An attendance program was written that displays the pictures of the students on the screen in a rectangular grid. The pictures can be dragged to another spot on the screen, to take advantage of the fact that most students tend to sit in the same place every class period. If a student moves, just move their picture. Student seem to take this attendance system much more seriously than the manual method. The program knows when each class meets, so it can automatically load the desired class. The background is color-coded for the three display modes: all (blue), absent (red), present (green). Clicking on the picture records the time that a student was arrived (i.e., absent to present) or departed early (i.e., present to absent). Hints appear that display the name of the student over which the cursor is positioned. If a picture is not available, a dynamic bitmap is created that displays the name of the student on a white background.
- Part of the program used to organize the pictures includes a capability to look up the picture of a student, even if only part of the

student name is specified. This is very useful in visually identifying a student when a student calls up on the phone, or sends mail, etc. Often, after classes have ended, a student who took classes years ago will call and request something (letter of recommendation, etc.). In such cases, it is very useful to be able to visualize the student.
- Each student is provided with their own picture in electronic format. This is easy on a network where each student has their own network userid. Otherwise, email must be used to send the picture to the student.
- The JPEG versions of the pictures are used in an automatically generated teacher-side web page that links each picture to the student's home page on the Internet. This makes it easy to go to each student's home page in class. Not only does the teacher learn the student's name, but the students start to learn the names of the other students. Displaying student web pages in class is a good way to "raise the bar" for what is expected in a web page. Most students become motivated to improve their own web pages to keep pace.

FUTURE DIRECTIONS

Some future directions include the following.
- The author uses Microsoft Outlook as an email system and has experimented with VBA to automate tasks in Outlook. One useful feature would be to see the picture of the student whenever email is opened from that student. This would be very useful since the author (automatically) collects and processes assignments via email, in addition to student inquiries via email.
- The attendance system (described above) will eventually be improved to conveniently interface (via double-click on the student picture) to either the grading system or the Outlook mail system (where textual student information is being maintained).
- The author has written a program to keep track of student scores in an easy and flexible manner. Adding pictures to the program would make the system more teacher-friendly.
- The author has, from time to time, considered recording students saying their own names as an way to learn the proper pronunciation of student names. The same methods discussed here would apply. Although tried a few times, this is still an area for future research.

SUMMARY

This paper has described a personal decision support system, designed and implemented by the author, that is used to acquire, process, organize, and update student pictures. These pictures are used to learn and connect student names and faces in a variety of useful ways, as discussed in this paper.

Is EDI the Best Alternative to Implement Electronic Commerce?

Khalid S. Soliman
Fogelman College of Business and Economics, University of Memphis, Memphis, TN 38111
Tel: (901) 678-3699, E-mail: ksoliman@memphis.edu

ABSTRACT

Organizations today are striving to gain competitive advantage. Electronic commerce has become a key element in establishing strong business-to-business relationships. Until recently, electronic data interchange (EDI) has help developing strong inter-organizational links. However, many companies have reported several problems in using EDI. The explosion of the Internet have made many companies think of utilizing it to implement business-to-business truncations. This study explores some of the advantages and the disadvantages in EDI environment. EDI on the Internet approach is introduced as an alternative to traditional EDI.

INTRODUCTION

Competitive advantage is the key for survival in today's market place. More and more companies are adopting inter-organizational systems in order to increase their competitive advantage (Riggins and Mukhopadhyay, 1994). Inter-organizational links establish strong alliance among companies along the supply chain. Cycle time reduction is one of the immediate benefits of inter-organizational linkage. Although many companies have come a long way in reducing internal costs by reengineering their internal processes, reengineering the inter-organizational supply chain may hold benefits of greater magnitude than those associated with internal reengineering efforts (Nichols et al., 1995).

Porter (1980) has presented three basic approaches for gaining competitive advantage: 1) be the low cost producer, 2) differentiate, 3) fill a market niche. Of these three strategies, becoming the low cost producer is the riskiest. "If price is the only reason customers are doing business with you, lower prices from a competitor will result in fewer customers for you and possibly a price war," (Wetherbe, 1998). Improving the supply chain will give all the trading partners on the supply chain the chance to reduce their costs externally while at the same time reducing inventory levels, implementing just-in-time inventory policy and improving customer service. One significant impact in Linking organizations is the faster cycle time and reduced personnel costs.(Riggins and Mukhopadhyay, 1994)

Responding to customer trends is considered to be a great customer service skill for the survival of any organization. Improving the supply chain will put the retailer in a position to be able to address customer trends as quickly and as efficiently as possible.

Electronic commerce is a viable option to many organizations to improve the supply chain in order to remain competitive. The idea is to be able to identify consumer trend quickly and then electronically communicate those movements through the supply chain (Abcede, 1997). Companies have used technology to reduce costs and improve customer service (Gurley, 1997). Technology advances have made software package applications more valuable than ever, with capabilities one has never imagined just ten years ago. Also, connectivity improvements via electronic data interchange (EDI) and the Internet now make it easier to focus on the entire supply chain, as does improved inter-operability between systems (Harrington, 1997).

The purpose of this paper is to acknowledge the importance of a strong supply chain among organizations and its impact on simply "staying in business" in a very competitive market place. This study highlights the features of EDI as a viable option for linking all trading partners. The advantages and disadvantages of EDI are discussed and another alternative is introduced, EDI on the net. Also, the study discusses the concerns about establishing EDI on the net and some of the available technologies to address those concerns. Finally, the article presents a collection of recommendations from the industry's experts to IT professionals to be better equipped in the information technology age.

EDI

EDI allows computer to computer communication of business information across company's borders. (Haugen and Behling, 1995) In other words, it establishes a line of communication of information in a standard format between organizations or parties that permits the receiver to perform a specific set of business functions such as purchasing and invoicing. It takes advantage of the existing communications technology and takes data from one computer-based information system and places it into another (Carr and Snyder, 1997).

The figure below depicts a purchasing example within EDI framework.

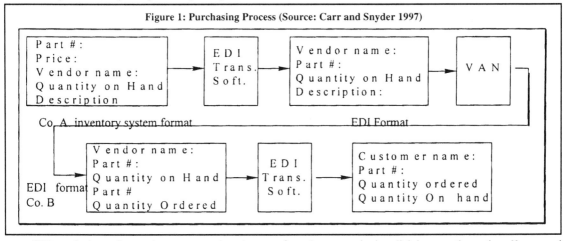

Figure 1: Purchasing Process (Source: Carr and Snyder 1997)

EDI standards require certain components in order to perform the communications link between the parties. Haugen and Behling (1995) have explained the various components of EDI:

1) Local applications that generate record data relevant to the business transaction.
2) EDI software needed in order to translate messages between systems. Software includes:
   - Application interface to interact with the system.
   - Document database to store messages.
   - A preparation module for translating and batching outgoing messages.
   - A Processing module to process and translate incoming messages.
3) A hardware platform that ranges from microcomputer to mainframe.
4) Access via value added network (VAN) to an EDI clearing house service. The VAN translates data from one format to another and facilitates message storage and retrieval.

Advantage of EDI

EDI by its basic definition allows companies to generate electronic purchase orders, invoices, bills of lading, and a variety of other documents and send them instantly to trading partners anywhere in the world. From a financial point of view, that means increased cash flow and lower trading costs (Adams, 1997). It increases the accessibility of information that will have an impact on the supply chain. Hence, it enhances the business relationships between trading partners as well as reducing transaction costs (Haugen and Behling, 1995).

According to Porter and Miller, "Careful management of linkage is often a powerful source of competitive advantage" (1985). Companies are striving for new ways to create a competitive advantage. Strong links across the supply chain can provide companies with the tools to implement the just-in-time inventory management. Outbound logistics can play an important role in improving competitive advantage and strengthening the supply chain through the use of Electronic Data Interchange (Shore, 1996).

Providing the best service to customers is what business is all about. Companies that create a competitive edge pay close attention to customer service and customer needs. Companies, in assessing customer's needs, should be able to define consumer trends quickly, act in a timely fashion, and provide customers with their needs. EDI can address these requirements. It equips companies with tools to establish efficient response to customers' needs (Haugen and Behling, 1995)

Disadvantages of EDI

While the advantages of EDI have been discussed, there have been several reported disadvantages in implementing EDI. The first issue regarding EDI is the cost that comes associated with VAN. Companies pay a pretty hefty VAN bill $5,000 to $6,000 per month just for the network (Bartholomew, 1997). It was estimated in a cost analysis of an EDI system at a large manufacturer that the cost to link that manufacturer to its 12 plants and 120 trade partners exceeded $23.5 million (Riggins and Mukhopadhyay, 1994). Given the prohibitive cost of the VANs, many of the small suppliers may not be able to afford the cost associated with infrastructure necessary to adopt the inter-organizational systems with EDI.

Another consideration is the standards in establishing EDI. In order to avoid any difficulties, establishing EDI between trading partners requires hardware at both ends to have a certain degree of compatibility. In other words, the communications infrastructure at both ends must be up to a certain standard in order to have seamless processing (Haugen and Behling, 1995). In short, The idea of working with several partners and creating communications through the use of EDI can be very costly for any organization.

Another disadvantage of using EDI through VANs is that the customer and suppliers are tied in a long-term relationship. Although this is beneficial for the health of doing business, it may have some drawbacks. Over time, other suppliers may come up with a similar, but higher quality product with lower prices or better service. The high costs associated with establishing the linkage may prevent companies from switching suppliers even when such a decision is the right one to take.

EDI ON THE NET

Given the disadvantages discussed above, companies are continuously searching for alternatives to improve links of the supply chain and at the same time reduce associated expenses. Because of the explosion of the Internet, companies start looking to the Internet as a new avenue for conducting business. In addition, the exponential increase in consumer purchases on the net has added a new dimension to the debate. However, most established companies will enter this arena only after someone else takes the lead and implements EDI on the Internet (EDI/Net) concept (Gurley, 1997). The ultimate winner in this case is the consumer.

Advantages of EDI on the Net

There are several advantages in adopting the EDI/Net approach. A major advantage of EDI/Net is that the standards are common for all partners as well as the interoperable systems (Dykeman, 1997). The Internet is a network of computers. It has no regulating body and it has no owner. This gives any business freedom to conduct business on the net practically cost free. EDI/Net utilizes all the aspects of the Internet. The Internet and the ease of adoption of its standards allow organizations to contact any other organization anywhere in the world (Dykeman, 1997). It has the potential to reduce geographical, cultural, and language barriers between partners worldwide. For smaller organizations that can't afford the cost of VAN-based EDI, using the Internet may open a whole new world of trading partners. For larger organizations that already understand the intricacies of VAN-based EDI, the openness of the Internet promises the expansion of a successful business practice. It also offers the opportunity to reduce costs by a substantial margin. On one hand, it provides any organization with the maneuverability it needs to switch trading partners with the least expense in the quest for higher quality, lower cost producers. On the other hand, it reduces the power of the trading partner at the beginning of the supply chain due to gained power at the end.

EDI/Net allows the organization to be more sensitive and responsive to consumer trends. According to Abcede (1997) it creates electronic efficiencies within the entire supply chain in order to achieve Efficient Consumer Response. The result here is lower inventories, faster turnovers, and quicker responds to consumers' demands.

Another advantage of EDI/Net is that it eliminates the high costs associated with the VANs. EDI on the net presents a great potential in savings for both suppliers and marketers (Abcede, 1997).

Most companies are looking for ways to cut costs. Once they begin to feel comfortable with the Internet, IS managers will take the opportunity to rid themselves of expensive VAN services.

Concerns about Security

Many companies already using EDI are reluctant to switch from a closed, secure trading environment to the open, risky one of the Internet. However, the emergence of hybrid EDI has encouraged some to develop similar systems with their own partners or to look at other ways of combining EDI and the Internet. This can include transmission of EDI messages to a value-added network supplier for translation into text or form-based information and onward remittance to the trading partner over the Internet.

There is an abundance of new technology and tools on the market today designed to make cyber commerce safe. McCartney (1997) has suggested some of the options available with regard to security: Firewalls, Digital-ID, and Certification.

Firewalls: Can be either a hardware or software device that is deployed to block unauthorized communications across network gateways and that filters information between the Internet and the intranet. In order to provide sufficient security for the connectivity, organizations have to follow certain rules in applying firewalls. Lister (1998) has proposed critical keys for successful implementation of Internet connectivity with trading partners: 1) authenticating users' identity, encrypting data as it travels over the Internet, and administering security that spans multiple organizations, 2) having a dedicated product that always provides better security than the "built-in" security features of the company's off-the-shelf servers and applications, 3) considering more secure methods of authentication such as digital certificates, smart cards, or hardware tokens, 4) controlling access to information after the organization has authenticated the user's identity, including providing outside partners selective access to corporate information based on their relationship to the organization, 5) forcing trading partners to adopt and use the security solutions the company chooses; in some cases, suppliers may be required to use smart cards for authentication or purchase encrypting routers or firewalls to create secure communication between the organizations, 6) examining applications to determine potential security holes, and evaluating how the security can be hardened, and 7) copying corporate data onto servers that are outside the corporate's firewall, an area often called the demilitarized zone. Then external users are limited to these exiled systems, presenting little risk to the systems that sit behind the firewall.

Digital IDs: Digital-ID helps businesses know who published the software they're downloading, provide audit trails, and, in some instances, can be used to secure an entire transaction in exchange for giving the ID vendor a percentage of the purchase price.

Certification: Certification is given to a web site when it meets the specified criteria.

Other Concerns

There are some other concerns that many companies have with regard to utilizing the Internet as a mean of communication:

Bandwidth

Bandwidth problems are very similar to the problems companies had with the speed of computers in the early days of personal computers. The request for larger bandwidth will stay around for a while. The improvement of technology and the pressure from business to push forward innovation will have a great impact on the future of bandwidth.

Network Reliability

This is another concern of many companies specifically those who are doing business abroad. Many countries around the world are still building their infrastructures. This will have an impact on the implementation of EDI/Net with trading partners from those countries.

Cultural and Political Issues

Companies who are doing business globally understand the dimensions of this problem. Cultural and political issues are always a concern for those companies. Although trading on the Internet may make cultural matters more sensitive, some efforts from the trading partners in the U.S. might be fruitful.

Assessing the Risks

In order to adequately adopt the appropriate technology for your company, you have to assess the risks associated with the implementation of this technology. McCartney (1997) lists the factors that affect the implementation of internet communications: 1) the kind of business you're in, 2) the size of financial transactions involved, 3) your position in the supply chain, and 4) Whether you're doing business outside the U.S.

Whether or not you're willing to open part of your intranet to business partners depends on the amount of trust you put in your partner and the amount of security you are willing to implement.

FINAL THOUGHTS

The idea here is not to promote EDI whether it is on the net or not. The main idea is to present the technology available to improve the supply chain to information technology (IT) specialists. There are many lessons learned that I would like to share with IT people:

Information is our middle name

It is crucial for IT professionals to be continuously searching for information. New technologies are emerging every day. With the role that information technology plays in positioning organizations in the market place, IT people have to understand the evolving technologies, evaluate them, and determine those that can fit with the organization's strategy. Educating top executives about the new technology is part of the IT professionals' job. In short, to educate executive, IT professional have to be educated and well informed themselves.

Don't be left in the cyber dust

The Internet is exploding. Many businesses are taking advantage of the information age and the array of benefits offered by the Internet. Online shopping is one of the booming activities on the Internet. On one hand, consumer shopping on the Internet was around $500 million in 1996 and is estimated to be around $ 7 billion by the year 2000. On the other hand, in the business-to-business arena, the amount of business that trading partners have done on the Internet was less than $1 billion in 1996 and it is estimated to reach $66 billion by the year 2000 (Stevens, 1997). All these companies have found the right technologies to provide security and to implement electronic commerce.

It is of great importance to IT professionals to understand all the aspects of EC in order to recommend the appropriate choice to their top management. Furthermore, it does not mean that if security concerns are legitimate today, that these concerns will hold true tomorrow.

In summary, many IT professionals get caught up with the day-to-day activities of supporting end-users or maintaining existing technology. IT people have greater responsibility: to guide their organizations through the information age in order to position themselves in a competitive manner.

REFERENCES

Abcede, A., "EDI, Internet connect as data goes electronic," National Petroleum News, Vol. 89, No. 11, pp. 110-114.
Adams, E. J., "Second Coming for electronic data interchange" World Trade, Vol. 10, No. 11, November 1997, pp.36-38.
Anonymous, "How to get from 80 to 100 percent in EDI," Datamation, Feb. 1993.
Bartholomew, D., "Clinging to EDI," Industry Week, June 23, 1997, pp. 44-47.

Carr, H. H., Snyder, C. A. The Management of Telecommunications, the McGraw-Hill Companies, 1997.

Haugen, S. and Behling, R., "Electronic Data Interchange as an Enabling Technology for International Business," Journal of Computer Information Systems, Fall 1995, pp. 13-16.

Gurley, J. W., "Seller Beware: The Buyers Rule E-Commerce," Fortune, November 10, 1997.

Harrington, L. H., "New tools to automate your supply chain," Transportation & Distribution, Vol. 38, No. 12, December 1997, pp. 39-42.

Lister, T., "Ten Commandments for converting your Intranet into a secure extranet," UNIX Review's Performance Computing, Vol. 16, No. 8, July 1998, pp. 37-39.

McCartney, L., "A Safety Net," Industry Week, April 21, 1997, pp. 74-78.

Nichols, E. L., Frolick, M. N., and Wetherebe, J. C., "Cycle time reduction: An inter-organizational supply chain perspective," Cycle Time Research, Vol. 1, No. 1, 1995, pp. 63-81.

Porter, M. E. Competitive Strategy, The Free Press, New York, NY 1980.

Porter, M. E., and Millar, V. E., "How Information Gives You Competitive Advantage," Harvard Business Review, July-August 1985, pp. 149-160.

Riggins, F. J. and Mukhopadhyay, T., "Interdependent Benefits from Inter-Organizational Systems: Opportunity for Business Partner Re-Engineering," Journal of Management Information Systems, Vol. 11, No. 2, Fall 1994, pp. 37-57.

Shore, B., "Using information technology to achieve a competitive advantage: A study of current and future trends," Journal of Computer Information Systems, Summer 1996, pp.54-59.

Stevens, T., "Set sales on the net," Industry Week, April 21, 1997, pp. 56-68.

Wetherbe, J. C., "Time and Technology: Competing for Customers in the Future," Cycle Time Research, Vol. 4, No. 1, 1998, pp. 1-13.

Integrating Insurance Transaction Streams into Electronic Markets

Brian Subirana and Patricia Carvajal

MIS department, IESE International Graduate School of Management -University of Navarra, Barcelona, Spain

Tel: 34-3-2534200, Fax: 34-3-2534343, subirana@iese.edu, carvajal@iese.edu

INTRODUCTION: CONFIDENCE, BRAND AND INSURANCES

It can be noticed that there is a lack of confidence in on-line products and services (Choi, et al. 1997). Security poses serious challenges to the growth and wide adoption of electronic commerce (Bhimani, 1996; Froomkin, 1996). In order to respond to aspects related to security, technological tools have been developed such as cryptography, firewalls and digital certificates. Even if there are solutions in some of these areas, they have not gained users interest or trust so far (Pernul, et al. 1997).

The lack of confidence stems, in part, from time asymmetry and information asymmetry. In effect, even if Internet does reduce the time for some transactions to be completed, most real world transactions require some form of movement of goods or services, thereby introducing time asymmetries in the process of exchange of assets between transacting parties. Time asymmetry brings the notion of risk (perceived or real) to each of the agents involved in the transaction who must invest resources before receiving a return (Salam et al., 1998). In many situations, information asymmetry has significant implications on the operations of Markets (Caillaud, 1990; Greenwald, 1990). Information asymmetry also affects the on-line market; in electronic markets the physical product is not examined, only a representation of it. This situation imposes certain limitations on knowledge of the product and, therefore, uncertainty regarding its quality or that of the vendor. (Choi et al. 1998; Grace 1998).

Confidence is pervasive in all the client relationship process. The notion of confidence implies the deposit of resources (money, time, personal information) into the hands of another party for use for his/her own benefit, or of the buyer, or both. Without the appropriate level of confidence, the exchange of information between individuals and organizations will be limited (OECD, 1997, 10). There are three essential aspects related to confidence: to be led to a selection in which the end is foreseen as a happy or a painful event, to realize that the event depends on the behavior of the other party and finally to perceive the intensity of the negative event superior to that of the positive one.

The management of confidence has been historically affected by brand-name recognition. In the nonvirtual world, the mere presence of brand name is sufficient to create confidence in relatively unimportant decisions, as for example the purchasing of little amounts of products or repetitive purchases, and in generic products of easy specification. In effect, brand name recognition performs different functions: a) An identification function; the brand identifies the product according to its main characteristics. It also leads to a specific configuration of attributes. Therefore, the brand itself constitutes valuable information of the characteristics related to a specific product offer. b) A reference function: the brand helps the buyer to identify himself, brand contributes in structuring and organizing the market offer. c) A guarantee function: the brand is a public commitment of quality and performance. It is a given promise. It assures the permanence of quality that is expected of it. d) A personalization function: the selection of certain brands allows individuals to place themselves in relation to their desired social status. In making a selection a person shows his desire to be different from his peers or, on the contrary, to integrate himself. e) A playful function: it corresponds to the pleasure that is experienced when purchasing. The presence of multiple brands makes certain buyers experience a feeling of true animation and results in a source of stimulus. f) A practical function: instead of having to repeat a complete decision process on each occasion, the brand facilitates the memorization of previous selection processes and the conclusions of consumption experiences. The brand is in this sense, a summary of information related to past purchasing experiences. Taking into consideration that the brand name is memorable and easy to recognize, it gives the buyer the possibility of following repetitive processes and, as a result, generates confidence in the client.

When such confidence does not exist, users try to compensate its lack with endorsements, licenses and insurance. In the nonvirtual world these practices are used in important transactions (with high monetary value) or to complement the brand. However, in the virtual world we can see how these endorsements and insurance are used even in small transactions without greater importance nor volume. Confidence management in the virtual world is bringing about a fast and sustainable growth of the insurance role, a development that, in turn, goes against global brands. In this article we will analyze new models of confidence management.

TRANSACTION STREAMS

The simplest representation of an interchange process online involves at least three roles: buyer(customer), seller (Supplier) and shipper (distribution service). A market transaction corresponds to a finite number of interaction processes between market participants in various roles. The goal is to initiate, arrange and complete a contractual agreement for exchanging of goods and services in the most efficient manner. The involved interaction processes are grouped into classes and form the phases of a market transaction (Schmid and Lindemann 1994).

Before a transaction is completed five processes need to be enacted: player selection, contract condition setting, contract signature, contract storage and transaction action. We will refer to them as the transaction processes (Subirana 1998). These transaction processes can be represented graphically as it shows figure 1:

Underneath each process many related actors take part and create more relations and transactions as well. We have passed the traditional model to a series of transactions streams, in which more than one organization controls the first four transaction processes.

In this flow of transactions, which operates so differently from the real world, users are required to compensate the lack of

Figure1:Transaction processes

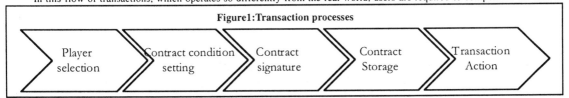

| Player selection | Contract condition setting | Contract signature | Contract Storage | Transaction Action |

confidence with endorsements, licenses and insurance. For that reason, the lack of effective ways of managing the need for endorsement, security and insurance is a well recognized barrier to the full acceptance of transactions on the Internet (Tapscott 1996) (Schwarz 1997). One area in which transactions are becoming more streamed is in the insurance and endorsement of the signature and contract storage (Hodges 1997)(Markey 1997).

INSURANCE TRANSACTION STREAMS

First we will study the application of the 5 transaction processes to insurance function. Then we will analyze under the view of transaction streams, the electronic representation of endorsements, licenses and insurance policies, in order to elicit how the implications of the insurance industry in the electronic commerce allow the creation of an atmosphere of confidence between insurer and the insured, getting a closer and richer client/insurer relationship.

Player selection involves the selection of the economic agents that will be involved in the transaction. An insurance contract represents an agreement between the service provider and the party insured. It can also represent an agreement among three parties, the surety, the obligee and the principal. This contract is called a policy and specifies the obligations of the involved parties. The policy covers damages inflicted by the insured upon a third party if the damages were caused by an accident or occurrence. The insurer does not relieve the insured from responsibility for committing malicious acts.

The contract condition setting refers to the process by which the involved parties negotiate the details of the action to be performed. This activity observes the situation of negotiations, the interactive exchange of messages between players involved (Runge, 1998). When a policy is requested, insurance providers calculate the risk to be assumed by the insurance policy and fix the premium at an adequate level to reflect this risk. Insurance providers will need to assess a service provider about procedures and past behavior to determine risk and to set a premium. Policies require an assessment of the assumed risk and settling claims requires judgment, neither of which are easily automated. In other words, policy purchasing transactions are, in general, too complex for current electronic market models.

Contract signature refers to the binding step in the process in which the transaction players agree on a course of action that clarifies how the transaction activities will be performed. This can be a short and standard agreement or a long, detailed and customized contract. Policies are agreements certified by the signatures of the parties. The electronic representation of a policy will include the following information:

1. The names of the parties: The name of the insurance provider, the name of the service provider and a description of the obligee(if *needed*)
2. The subject of the insurance and the insured risks.
3. The period during which the policy will be in force
4. The limits of liability (an individual limit, an aggregate limit of liability or possibly no limit in the cases of endorsement or license)

Licensing and endorsements are mechanisms that may be used to gain confidence in the service provider and playing the role, described by Ba et al. (1998), of a trusted third party for electronic commerce transactions. A license is a credential that indicates that a service provider is legally authorized to provide a service. It indicates that the service provider has been found to meet certain minimal qualifications required by law, and that is subjected to regulations and sanctions if it violates the law. An endorsement provides assurance that a service provider meets more rigorous requirements determined by the endorser, and usually provides information about the quality of a service provider. The confidence in an endorsed service provider depends in part on one's confidence in its endorsers. Endorsements do not provide compensation for damages incurred while interacting with service providers. They provide a mechanism for clients to better evaluate and reduce the risk involved in dealing with service providers. Licenses proving the legal authority to offer a particular service and require of the service provider to follow certain policies of protection of its clients. The concept of an insurance policy, licensing and endorsements are related, differing only in the limits and source of compensation in the event of a loss. Insurance policies provide a contractual responsibility to the insurance providers. The development of "institutional trust" will lead to a decrease in the consumer-perceived level of risk of transactions over the Internet (Salam et al., 1998; Sarkar et al., 1998).

Before a transaction contract is signed, an assurance credential is granted to a server after knowing the requirements imposed by the server, who issues the credentials. Assurance credentials can be defined as proxies. Furthermore, proxies can be set in such a way that all the transactions realized by a given organization are endorsed and certified by an independent and trusted firm.

The verification of the insurance credential shows an example of how transactions streams are implemented. When an assurance credential is received from a service provider, the client validates the credential in two steps. First, the proxy is verified cryptographically. It may require further interactions with others servers. Second, the information presented in the proxy is extracted and compared against the user's and application's policy for server selection. Furthermore, the service provider must authenticate itself to the client using the authentication protocol used by the system (Lai, et al. 1997).

INSURANCE INDUSTRY CONFIGURATION

Nevertheless, the presence of assurance credentials should not by itself improve confidence in a service provider. This confidence must depend in part on the confidence in the endorser or insurance provider. An extensive network of relations can be activated to create confidence. Figure 4 shows an example of the network of company roles that are emerging.

In this example, client C requests service from service provider S2. To provide this service, S2 subcontracts to service provider S1. C's confidence in the composite service depends on the assurance provided for both S1 and S2. To improve customer confidence, S1 and S2 obtain a liability insurance policy from insurance provider I1. As long as C has confidence in I1 it is assured that C will be compensated in the event of damages caused by S1 or S2. In this example C does not have confidence directly in the insurance provider, but will accept the endorsement of E3, an organization that rates insurance companies. Client C will also find that service providers S1 and S2 are licensed by licensing agency L2, indicating that L2 has found each server competent in offering its services. The licensing authority L2 has not been endorsed directly, but is recognized as the appropriate licensing agency by C (Lai, et al. 1997).

In this way a new model of confidence' management is config-

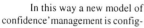

Figure 4: Network of Trust Relationships

ured. This necessity of confidence is generating a fast and sustainable growth of insurance, with the effect of rendering less important the value of the global markets

CONCLUSIONS

This need for confidence is generating a rapid and sustainable growth of insurance, potentially diminishing in importance the value of global brands. While the booming of companies constituted as confidence drivers, as for example Bizrate.com and @guard is appreciated, licenses, endorsements and insurance as mechanisms to increase confidence in the system are also needed.

In a stable system built on these contributors to the confidence management model, it is clear how the insurance industry allows the formation of a trustful ambiance between insurer and insured, with the effect of creating a huge net of transaction streams, and ultimately facilitating a closer client/insurer relationship. Through this process a new model of confidence management is being formed, and thus, the appearance of a new role is anticipated: the role of the Insurance Agent.

Figure 3 illustrates the infrastructure underlying transaction streams. As can be seen, many players are involved in simple, routine transactions. Nine layers have been identified: customer layer, customer management layer, service provider layer, payments layer, attention management layer, navigation selection layer, insurance layer, predictive modeling layer and information layer. To see how these layers afe being called into action, Figure 4 provides an example of the cascading effect of transaction streams. In the example we have plotted the players involved when our example user clicks an insurance robot to purchase a product. The robot itself, calls a set of licensing agencies and endorsement agencies. These in turn search for insurance brokers that, through third-party predictive modeling and endorsement agencies, assess what is the risk premium that should be offered. The robot then collects all the answers and provides the aggregated response to the user. Observe that insurance brokers nurture their systems with information provided from the information layer companies in combination with predictive modeling results. This enables an optimization of their hit-ration while minimizing risk. The transaction stream diagram also illustrates transaction streams related with advertising. In an attempt to capture attention, advertising networks maximize their advertising effectiveness by leveraging audience profiles with predictive modeling techniques. Observe that the information layer is similar for the advertising and insurance streams while the modeling techniques are of different nature: the former is geared towards managing attention while the latter results in insurance quotes. In both cases, click-yield management techniques are required to optimize the available "click inventory".

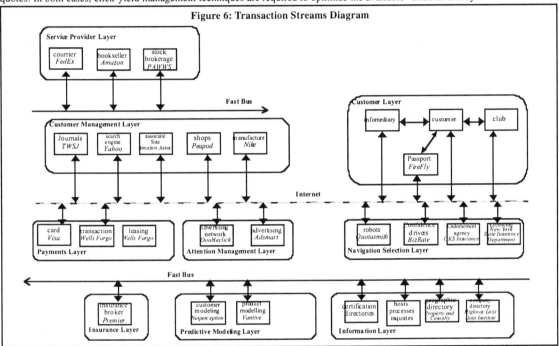

Figure 6: Transaction Streams Diagram

The future will belong to those companies that can successfully add value in the wave of transaction streams. A secure transaction ownership may only be possible when ownership occurs at the transaction activity level. Transactions on the Internet will evolve into an ever increasingly complex environment where management will struggle to capture future profit arenas. The Internet provides tools to facilitate the streaming process. The Internet enables different transaction participants to establish protocols to perform each of the five basic transaction components in a myriad of different ways. The insurance landscape can provide means of managing confidence both from user-centered and provider-centered views. Insurance providers should seek opportunities in linking their products and services with transaction stream layers. Ultimately, insurance providers may perform many of the current brand roles.

REFERENCES

Ba, Sullin, Whinston, A.B:, Zhang H. (1998) *"The Design of a Trusted Third Party for Electronic Commerce Transaction"* Association for Information Systems (AIS) Americas Conference.

Bhimani, Anish (1996) *«Securing the Commercial Internet»* Communications of the ACM, Vol.39, Nª 6.

Booz-Allen & Hamilton Financial &Health Services Group (1997) Internet Insurance: *A Study of Current Use and Future Trends»* New York. (February) http://www.bah.com/press/insurance.html

Caillaud, B. (1990) *Regulation, competition and Asymmetric Information.* Journal of Economic Theory. 52 (1).

Choi, S.Y., Stahl D.O. and Whinston A.B. (1997) *The Economics of Electronic Commerce.* Macmillan Technical Publishing.

Choi, S., Stahl, D.O., Whinston, AB (1998) *Intermediation, contracts and Micropayments in Electronic Commerce. Electronic Markets-* International Journal of Electronic Markets, 8(1), 20-22.

Datamonitor, Inc, 1996, *«Insurance on the Internet, 1996-2000.»* New York.

Froomkin, A.Michael.(1996) *«The Essential Role of Trusted Third Parties in Electronic Commerce».*75 Oregon Law Journal 49

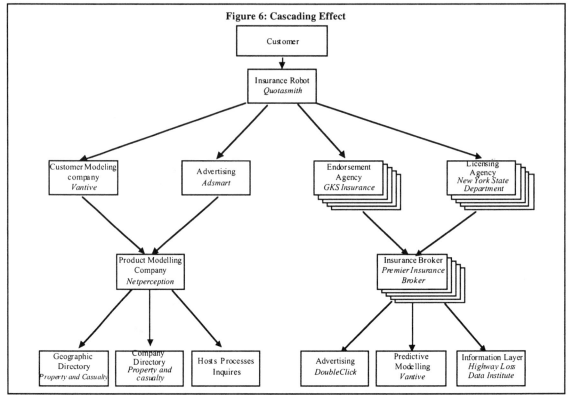

Figure 6: Cascading Effect

Gazala, M. E., Weisman, D.E., Doyle, B., Trevino, V. (1998) «*Revitalizing Agents and Brokers*» Cambridge, MA: Forrester Research, Inc (January).

Garven, M.F. (1998) *Electronic Commerce in the Insurance Industry: Business Perspectives*. Working Paper 98-3. Georgia State University.

Grace, M.F. (1998) «*Regulatory and Economic Issues Involving Electronic Commerce in the Insurance Industry*» Center for Risk Management and Insurance Research, Working Paper Series Number 98-2 (March).

Greenwald, B.C. (1990) *Asymmetric Information and the new theory of the firm: financial constraints and risk behavior*» American Economic Reviiew. May.80(2)

Guttman, R., Moukas, A., Maes, P(1998) *Agents as Mediators in Electronic Transactions.*Electronic Markets-International Journal of Electronic Markets, 8(1).22-26

Hodges, M. *Building a Bond of Trust*. MIT"s Tecnology Review, August/September, 1997.

Lai, C., Medvinsky, G and Clifford, B. *Endorsement, Licensing and Insurance for Distributed Services*. Cambridge MA: MIT Press, p. 417

Markey, E.J. *A privacy safety net*. MIT"s Tecnology Review, August/September, 1997.

Organization for Economic Co-operation and Development (OECD) (1997). "*Dismantling the Barriers to Global Electronic Commerce*" http://www.oecd.org/dsti/sti/it/ec/prod/dismantl.htm, November 1997.

Pernul, G., Rohm, A.(1997) *Integrating Security and Fairness into Electronic Markets*. Fourth Research Symposium on Electronic Markets: Negotiation and Settlement in Electronic Markets.Euridis. Erasmos University

Runge, A. (1998) The Need for Supporting Electronic Commerce Transactions with Electronic Contracting Systems. Electronic Markets-International Journal of Electronic Markets, 8(1), 16-19.

Salam, A.F, Rao, H.R., Pegels, C.C.(1998) «*An investigation of Consumer-percerved Risk on Electronic Commerce Transactions: The role of Institutional Trust an Economic Incentive in a Social Exchange Framework*»Association for Information Systems (AIS) Americas Conference.

Sarkar, M.B., Butler, B. Steinfield (1998) *Intermediaries and Cybermediaries: A Continuing Role for Mediating Players in the Electronic Marketplace*. Journal of Computer-Mediated Communication Vol1, Nª. 3

Schmid, B.F and Lindemann, M.A. *Elements of a Reference Model for Electronic Markets*. International Jounal of Electronic Markets, Vol. 4 Nro.1, 1994.

Schwarz, E.I. *Webnomics*, Broadway, New York, 1997.

Selz, D. Schubert, P(1997) *Web Assesment-Applied to the Agreement and Settlement Fase*.Fourth Research Symposium on Electronic Markets: Negotiation and Settlement in Electronic Markets.Euridis. Erasmos University

Subirana, B. *Transactions Streams and Value Added: Sustainable Business Models on the Internet*. New Managerial Mindsets: Organizational and Strategy Implementation. Edited by M.A.Hitt, J.E.Ricart and R.D.Nixon, 1998.

Tapscott, D. *The Digital Economy*. London:McGraw-Hill, 1996.

Exploring the Intellectual and Social Dimensions of Strategy-IT Alignment: A Cognitive Mapping Investigation

Felix B Tan

MSIS Department, The University of Auckland, Private Bag 92019, Auckland, New Zealand

Tel: +64 9 3737999, Fax: + 64 9 3737566, f.tan@auckland.ac.nz

ABSTRACT

The purpose of this paper is to report on a research-in-progress and in particular to introduce a cognitive mapping method. The proposed study examines the intellectual and social dimensions of strategy-IT alignment. Research in the field is predominantly behavioural in focus. There is virtually no studies investigating alignment from a cognitive perspective. The proposed project is therefore a response to calls for more cognitive emphasis in strategic management research. It proposes to use a cognitive mapping technique, known as the repertory grid, to explore the social dimension of alignment and its relationship to the intellectual dimension. This article begins by placing the proposed study in context of published research on alignment and highlights the proposed research objectives. The concept of cognitive mapping is then introduced and the repertory grid process discussed. The conclusion outlines the research deliverables and the potential contribution of the study to both management and research.

INTRODUCTION

One of the top two concerns of business and information systems (IS) executives in the 1990s, is the need to improve the alignment between the organisation's business strategy and its deployment of information technology (Galliers, 1993; Galliers et al., 1994; Broadbent, 1989; Moynihan, 1988; Davies et al., 1995; Watson & Brancheau, 1991). This issue, termed as strategy-IT alignment, is an important concern to the practitioner community - an issue management has been grappling with since the mid 1980s (Watson, Kelly, Galliers & Brancheau, 1997). Empirical investigations on this subject thus far have tended to focus on the business strategy - IT relationship and its impact on firm performance (Chan & Huff, 1993; Chan, Huff, Copeland & Barclay, 1997; Tan, 1995a & 1997; Burn, 1996). These studies agree that alignment is important to IS effectiveness and firm performance. In another study, Reich & Benbasat (1996) suggest that there are two dimensions to alignment - social and intellectual. The latter represents the state of alignment in the organisation, while the former describes the mutual (ie. shared) understanding between business and IS executives of business and IT objectives and plans. A good number of alignment studies focus on the intellectual dimension (Floyd & Woolridge, 1990; Zviran, 1990; Broadbent & Weill, 1993; Burn, 1993 & 1995; Chan & Huff, 1993; Tan, 1995 & 1997; Chan et al, 1997). The few which studied the social dimension (Nelson and Cooprider, 1996; Enns, Murray, & Huff, 1997) agree that shared understanding between business and IS groups is linked to higher levels of IS effectiveness.

A closer examination of research into both the intellectual and social dimensions of alignment indicates that these studies are behavioural in focus. They explore the alignment issue by examining the way organisations conduct themselves. In contrast, few studies have attempted to investigate the issue from a cognitive perspective. Managerial cognition is an area of growing interest and importance in strategic management (Huff, 1990; Walsh, 1995). Researchers in this field argue that shared managerial cognition (beliefs and values held in common - ie. shared understanding) is integral to organisational development. By bringing a cognitive perspective to bear on strategic management, numerous studies have focussed on the concerns of individual managers and the commonalities among groups of managers. These studies highlight how cognitive mapping methods can be used to illustrate and evaluate management thought. (Stubbart, 1989; Ginsberg, 1989; Huff, 1990; Langfield-Smith, 1992). One such method is the Repertory Grid, developed by and grounded in Kelly's (1955) Personal Construct Theory.

Despite the increased popularity of cognitive theories of strategic management and the importance of strategy-IT alignment, there appears to be a lack of studies examining the link between managerial cognition (ie. shared understanding) and strategy-IT alignment. This research project is a therefore a response to calls for more cognitive emphasis in strategic management research (Stubbart, 1989; Huff 1990).

PROPOSED RESEARCH OBJECTIVES

Empirical studies cited earlier have examined separately the intellectual and social dimensions of alignment. The proposed research will attempt to study both aspects together, with the following aims:

- To examine the relationship between shared understanding (ie. managerial cognition) and strategy-IT alignment, that is the link between both the social and intellectual dimensions of alignment;
- To explore the nature of the shared understanding* between business and IS executives regarding strategy-IT alignment (*cognition held in common and distributed cognition).

PROPOSED METHODOLOGY

The proposed study plans to investigate shared understanding and strategy-IT alignment constructs by:

- exploring the cognitive construction system of individual IS and business executives toward strategy-IT alignment;
- analysing the extent to which these construction systems are shared amongst these executives (shared understanding); and

• examining the relationship between the shared understanding and strategy-IT alignment.

Most extant theory of psychology has little to say about the method of research. The research design is not derived from theory, but from standard scientific procedures. According to Bannister (1981), "a developed psychological theory should have clear and extended implications for research method. It should not only generate topics for research, …… it should propose appropriate methods of inquiry, the form and logic of experiments." (p. 191). This investigation draws heavily on Kelly's (1955) Personal Construct Theory. Kelly not only propose a theory about how individuals construe or make sense of his or her own environment, but also integrate an appropriate research design into his theory. Personal construct theory has generated a number of tools of psychological inquiry, the most notable of which is the repertory grid method. The grid method is now an accepted research tool in psychology (Bannister, 1981) and in the management field is the preferred methodology for mapping the cognitive constructs of individuals (Dutton et al., 1989; Reger, 1990a & 1990b; Brown, 1992; Reger & Huff, 1993; Daniels et al., 1995; Hunter 1997). Kelly's (1955) procedure is a part of a broader set of techniques in the study of managerial cognition. These approaches have been generally termed as cognitive mapping techniques (Huff, 1990).

The research proposes to employ a cognitive mapping methodology known as the repertory grid technique to collect data through a series of interviews. The repertory grid is the methodological extension of Kelly's (1955) Personal Construct Theory. The technique provides a means of accessing both the commonalities (cognition held in common) and differences (distributed cognition) between these executives - ie. their shared understanding. Interviews will be done with the assistance of RepGrid 2, repertory grid software package, installed on a laptop computer. Separate interviews will be conducted with individual business and IS executives in each organisation. The data collected during the interviews will also be analysed using RepGrid 2, which employs cluster and principal components analyses to create individual cognitive maps. Normative (group) cognitive maps will be constructed using individual differences multi-dimensional scaling. The alignment construct will be measured using Chan & Huff's (1997) STROBE-STROIS instruments.

The Concept of Cognitive Mapping

The term "cognitive map" was first used to mean an internal representation of concepts and relationships among concepts that an individual uses to interpret events and form expectancies in a particular problem domain. At the theoretical level, a cognitive map is a mental model, which allows complex problems to be framed and simplified so that they can be understood. This understanding then enables decisions to be made about a solution or set of potential solutions to the problem. At the empirical level, a cognitive mapping technique is a way of uncovering the essential elements of the representations held inside someone's head and portraying these externally so that they can be viewed by observers (Swan and Newell, 1994).

A number of cognitive mapping techniques can be used to investigate cognition in organisational settings. The maps these techniques produce tend to vary along a continuum from those that look at simple concepts to those that examine deeper underlying meanings (Huff, 1990). The following broad categories of cognitive maps have been identified in the literature:

1. Maps that assess attention, association and importance of concepts;
2. Maps that show dimensions of categories and cognitive taxonomies;
3. Maps that show influence, causality and system dynamics;
4. Maps that show structure of argument and conclusion; and
5. Maps that specify schemas, frames and perceptual codes.

Cognitive maps can be produced several ways. For instance, at the surface level of analysis are techniques such as content analysis which identifies key concepts by looking at frequency of word usage in verbal and written communications (results in category 1 maps). At the deeper level, techniques such as the repertory grid can be used to cluster concepts together into underlying dimensions or to categorise them into hierarchical order (produces category 2 maps). At a deeper level still are causal mapping (category 3 maps) techniques which can be used to identify the key element of a persons beliefs for a particular problem domain and to describe the cause and effect relationships among these elements.

Cognitive mapping is a generic term which subsumes a variety of research methods. The common theme binding these together is that all cognitive mapping methods seek to represent cognitive structures used by research participants, either individually or collectively, to shape their experiences into patterns that guide their actions. Causal maps (category 3 maps) have attracted particular attention from strategy researchers because they form a basis for predicting the likelihood of future occurrences from past events and this are believed to be closely tied to strategy formulation and decision making (Huff, 1990; Swan & Newell, 1994). However, dimensional analyses (category 2 maps) have also been applied extensively to define competitive space (Reger & Huff, 1993), the strategic environment (Dutton et al., 1989), managerial competencies (Cammock et al., 1995), and strategic diversity (Ginsberg, 1989). These studies focus on individual cognitive maps. An exception is the work of Simpson & Wilson (under review), who develop a gross cognitive map of the strategic team for each of the organisations studied.

Mapping Individuality and Commonality

The study proposes to construct (category 2) maps showing cognitive dimensions or constructs of business and IS executives toward strategy-IT alignment. A cognitive mapping method known as the repertory grid will be used. Two elicitation techniques are used - the full context and minimum context elicitation. The repertory grid process and its elicitation techniques will provide both detailed constructs at the level of individual business and IS executives, as well as data which can yield similarities amongst these executives. The repertory grid (a) provides a means of accessing both the commonalities and differences between constructs which are being applied to strategy-IT alignment within the companies being studied; (b) do not impose the researcher's frame of reference on the participating executives, ie. it is free from observer bias; (c) provides data that can be analysed through statistical methods and leads to results that can be replicated and validated (Ginsberg, 1989; Simpson & Wilson, under review). The repertory grid approach and it grid products are firmly grounded in George Kelly's (1955) Personal Construct Theory.

The Repertory Grid – Some Basics

The repertory grid, pioneered by George Kelly (1955) is a group of procedures for uncovering the constructs which individuals use to structure and understand their environments. It is both a structured interview *process* in which respondents classify and evaluate elements on a numerical scale according to their own personal constructs, and a grid of elements by constructs that is the *product* of these procedures (Ginsberg, 1989). In the management field, repertory grid has been the preferred methodology for mapping the cognitive constructs of individuals (Dutton et al., 1989; Reger, 1990a & 1990b; Brown, 1992; Reger & Huff, 1993; Daniels et al., 1995; Hunter 1997).

Elements are the subject within the domain of the investigation. For instance, Hunter (1997) explored the similarities and differences between systems analyst in order to ascertain the qualities which can lead to an 'excellent' systems analyst. The elements Hunter used are the systems analysts in each of the organisations he studied. The constructs are the attributes the participants employ to differentiate between the systems analyst.

So, the basis of the interview is a repertory of elements representing the domain of interest. The elements are used to elicit constructs that the individual applies to sensemaking. Once a construct is defined, all other elements in the repertory are rated or ranked along this dimension. By repeating this process a number of times, a grid of *m* elements and *n* constructs is developed for each participating executive. The grid can then be analysed to yield measures of the structure and content of each executive's cognitive construction system. An example of the grid produced by a single participant in Hunter's (1997) study is portrayed in figure 1.

On the left of the example are the constructs employed by a single participant (in this instance, it is the CEO) to differentiate between the systems analyst in his organisation. Each analyst is then rated along each elicited construct. The rating employed in the above example is a 1 to 9 scale.

Two elicitation techniques will be employed in this study. Firstly, is the "minimum context form" or "triadic sorting" method. Selecting three factors at a time from the repertory, each executive will be asked to identify some way in which two factors are

Figure 1: Example of a Repertory Grid (adapted from Hunter, 1997)

Participant: Mr. CEO

CONSTRUCTS	ELEMENTS					
	A	B	C	D	E	F
1. Delegator - Does work himself	7	2	5	4	2	6
2. Informs everyone - Keeps to himself	8	2	3	3	8	6
3. Good user rapport - No user rapport	5	2	4	2	4	2
4. Regular feedback - Inappropriate feedback	6	1	5	3	5	3
5. Knows details - Confused	2	1	4	3	5	1
6. Estimates based on staff-Estimates based on himself	8	3	4	6	4	6
7. User involvement - lack of user involvement	6	2	5	5	3	3

Note: Elements A to F represent the individual systems analyst

similar and different from the third. This process may be repeated until the researcher is satisfied that all relevant constructs have been identified.

The second eliciting technique is the "full context form" to elicit the similarity judgements to be used in statistical analysis. This method will involve each executive sorting the full set of factors from the repertory into any number of discrete piles based in whatever similarity criteria the individual chooses to apply. Once the sorting is completed, the executive will be asked to provide a 2-3 word descriptive title for each pile of factors. These titles along with the identifiers of the cards in each pile will be recorded for analysis.

Repertory Grid Process

Figure 2 summarises the research process undertaken. A company specific repertory of elements will be used as the stimulus for the generation of personal constructs. The repertory for each company lists the factors important to successful strategy-IT alignment within that company. This repertory will be developed *a priori*, based on published research into the enablers and inhibitors of alignment. Constructs are then elicited through interviews using both full and minimum context

The interviews will be structured in three parts:

a) *introduction to the repertory*. Executives will be presented with a randomly ordered list of the repertory factors. Each factor will be rated according to its importance to successful strategy-IT alignment.

b) *minimum context elicitation*. The triadic elicitation of constructs will be illustrated first using a neutral example to familiarise the executives with this stage of the interview. Three cards with the words 'Barina', 'Corona', 'Lancer' (models of passenger cars) will be used as the example. This is followed by the actual triadic sort of the factors in the repertory. This is done using RepGrid 2, an interactive software, designed to aid the researcher in eliciting and in

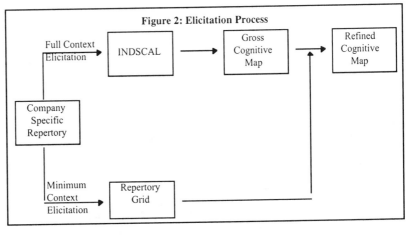

Figure 2: Elicitation Process

analysing repertory grid data.

c) full context elicitation. The participating executive will be asked to sort all of the elements in the repertory into piles based on their judgement of similarity or dissimilarity. A short descriptive title will be given to each pile.

Grid Analysis

The product of the minimum context form of elicitation is the repertory grid. The grid consists of m number of elements and n number of constructs. This means that there are $[n+m.2(poles)+n.m]$ pieces of information to consider in looking at a grid. For example, a grid with 5 elements and 7 constructs will present 35 entries in the grid, 5 elements and 7 pairs of constructs. This gives a total of 52 pieces of information to be analysed. There are several approaches to reorganising the raw grid data published in the repertory grid literature (Bell, 1990; Beal, 1985, Ginsberg, 1986). These approaches allow the researcher to examine the relationship amongst element and amongst constructs as well as between elements and constructs. These approaches are not discussed in this paper.

The product of the full context form of elicitation is a gross cognitive map. Using INDSCAL to analyse this data will produce a set of gross dimensions which are shared across the entire company. The results from the minimum context elicitation (ie. the repertory grids) are then used to refine this cognitive map and identify constructs which are less universally held.

PROPOSED RESEARCH DELIVERABLES

For each participating organisation:
- An assessment of the state of strategy-IT alignment.
- A cognitive map of the decision making group (ie. business and IS executives) - a visual representation of the quality of their shared understanding.
- Cognitive maps of individual business and IS executives - these individual maps will allow executives to make comparisons and appreciate the viewpoints and perceptions of others.
- A set of management processes critical to effectively align IT and your organisation's strategy.
- An assessment technique to assist organisations in examining the nature of the cognitive processes applied to the alignment issue and to assess the state of alignment over time.

POTENTIAL RESEARCH AND MANAGEMENT CONTRIBUTIONS

The application of cognitive theory and mapping techniques to the study of strategy-IT alignment is a significant step forward in the understanding of the phenomenon. The study deliverables will provide insights into the nature and extent of the shared understanding between business and IS executives in each participating organisation. This will allow management to become more aware of the cognitive commonalities and differences amongst their executives and can provide the platform upon which the overall group can collectively diagnose disagreements. The investigation will also contribute to a better understanding of the relationship between the social and intellectual dimensions of alignment. Implications for research and management practice are discussed below.

Research Contributions
- This project proposes to examine strategy-IT alignment (intellectual) and shared understanding (social) from a cognitive perspective. The study draws heavily on Kelly's (1955) Personal Construct Theory and its cognitive mapping methodology known as the repertory grid. The application of this technique is in itself a significant methodological advancement in the field.
- Using cognitive maps as surrogate measures of the shared understanding construct can provide insights into the nature and extent of shared understanding between business and IS executives.
- Little is known about the relationship between shared understanding and strategy-IT alignment. The study hopes to find support for the notion that a high quality of shared understanding between business and IS executives is more likely to be associated with a higher level of alignment between the firm's IT and its business strategy.

Management Contributions

This investigation can contribute to the practice of information systems by providing suggestions for organisational action at two levels - group and individual.

i) Group Intervention

The resulting cognitive maps can provide insights into the quality of shared understanding between business and IS executives within an organisation. The maps can display the understandings held in common by the group as a whole. Furthermore, the maps can also reveal the differences in perception between individuals and between business and IS executive groups. These maps can provide the platform upon which the overall group can collectively diagnose disagreements.

ii) Individual Intervention
- When a balance between unity and diversity of collective thinking is not achievable, individual executives must become aware of the nature of the individual cognitive maps operating in their organisations. This study can reveal the nature and extent of commonality and individuality within and between business and IS executive groups. Each executive and executive group can gain greater awareness of what the issue looks like to other executives and executive group. This can provide a basis for increasing shared understanding through collective diagnosis and management of disagreements.
- Cognitive mapping techniques, particularly, the repertory grid can be used to improve the shared understanding within and between business and IS executive groups in two ways :

a) diagnostic - maps can help individual executives focus attention, trigger memory, highlight priorities, supply missing information and reveal gaps in information, leading to more creative problem-solving;

b)intervention - maps can assist individual executives in the subjective analysis of their own understanding, leading the individual to modify this understanding.

REFERENCES

Available upon request.

A Paradigm Shift: From IT to ICT

Andrew Targowski
Professor of Computer Information Systems, Western Michigan University, Department of Business Information Systems,
Kalamazoo, MI 49008
targowski@wmich.edu

Omar Khalil
Professor of Information Systems, University of Massachussetts Dartmouth
okhalil@umassd.edu

ABSTRACT

Information and communications technology (ICT) contribution in the workplace has evolved over the last forty years. Focus has shifted from procedure automation, to communications and on line access to information and networks, and currently to cognitive computing. With such a paradigm shift, IS professionals are expected to use ICT tools to design systems that augment and support the knowledge work of humans. To meet the challenge, IS academicians and practitioners must collaborate in order to advance the theory and practice of effective and efficient management of information and knowledge. Effective communications is a key to such a collaboration; and the consolidation of the IS discipline's terminology facilitates such communications.

INTRODUCTION

Helping organizations and individuals to use technology more effectively to achieve their goals is the *raison d'être* of the information systems (IS) discipline (Westfall, 1998). A strong relationship between IS academicians and practitioners is essential to the IS role. However, the apparent disconnection between the two communities has led to a similar disconnection between the way of educating graduates in information technology (IT) tools and systems and the industrial/business practices. Such a disconnection is evidenced by:

1. The different IT tools found in the two environments (academia vs. industry),
2. The level of systems thought in academia and those developed in the industry,
3. The lack of ongoing, effective communications between academia and the business/industrial environments, and
4. The different titles of information professionals that are used in academia and in business/industry.

The last issue is the focus of this paper. Academic and professional terminology should be similar. The existence of too many synonyms and homonyms in the field will broaden the gap between education and business/industry, with all negative consequences for both sides.

The scholar and professional terminology determines the way of thinking and acting. Different terms reflecting the same object, process, or issue lead to miscommunication between the communities of academicians and practitioners. In result, education and practice may be ineffective. For example, the academia in 1980s forced the term DSS (Decision Support Systems), which was not accepted by the practitioners. Just about 10 years later, the software industry came out with the term Data Warehousing, and to a certain degree includes DSS functionality. This example seems to suggest that academicians have lost time educating IS graduates in DSS.

Information processing as a profession is relatively old, since it began in the 19 century, when punched card equipment was introduced to public and commercial practice. However, the modern stage of that profession is about 50 years old, since it is marked by the emergence of computers. The modern stages of the business-oriented profession that one can recognized are:

- 1950s-1960s Electronic Data Processing (EDP) personnel
- 1960s-1970s Data Processing (DP) personnel
- 1970s-1990s Information Technology (IT) or Information Management (IM) specialists
- 1990s-2000s?

Additionally, different names have been used to describe IS academic departments and curricula. The following names are popular:

- Data Processing
- Management Information Systems (MIS)
- Computer Information Systems (CIS)
- Computer-Based Information Systems (CBIS)
- Information Resource Management (IRM)
- Information Systems
- Decision Science

- Systems Science, or
- Combination of above terms.

This disagreement on a curriculum name among academicians is very symptomatic. In addition to the previously mentioned disagreements, these symptoms of serious incongruity between academic and practitioners communities should be a signal to begin a serious discussion of the essential aims of the IS profession. One approach to begin such a discussion is a paradigmatic one.

A paradigm is a model or a way of thinking that defines a set of rules that guide actions and behaviors (Baker, 1992). A paradigm changes when the context and, consequently, the rules for success change. It is essential to recognize the shifts in the information technology (IT) paradigm so that academicians and practitioners can make appropriate decisions, and operate in the context of future changes rather than the past ones.

The purpose of this paper is to elaborate on the paradigm shift in IT teaching and practice and its consequential changes. In doing so, a historical perspective of the root differences between the European and American approaches to IT education is presented first, followed by a characterization of the ongoing paradigm shift in IT education and practice, and the paper ends with conclusions.

THE EUROPEAN APPROACH

In Europe, the computer industry began in two countries; Great Britain and France, followed by Sweden, Italy, Central and Eastern Europe, and later in Germany. Europe generated such terms as a *robot, computer, cybernetics*, and *informatics, ICT (Information-Communication Technology)*. Czech writer Karel Czapek, who wrote a play "Rozumny Universalny Robot", coined the term robot in 1921. In the Czech and Polish languages, a *robot* means a job. A *robot* in English means *a jober*.

The British, who at the beginning, in the 1940's and 1950's coined the term *computer* by applying this name to an accountant, coined the term computer. In late 1960s a *computer* was used to name a digital machine, in Great Britain and in the US. In addition, the term *cybernetics* was applied first by an English physician, then by Ross Ashby and Stanford Beer and French Jean Ducroux in the 1950s. However, an American, Norbert Wiener, gave this discipline, then unnamed a comprehensive definition in 1948.

In the 1960s, when it was just obvious that punch card equipment was being replaced for ever by computers, the French introduced the term *l'informatique. l'informatique* was assembled from two words; *information* + *automation*. This name was just one name for everything which was associated with computers and information. It was a term similar to construction, manufacturing, transportation, and so forth. In this sense it was a fortunate term, one for the whole scholar discipline and industrial practice.

In Poland, in 1971 the term *informatics* was introduced by one of the authors (Targowski, 1971) and was immediately accepted by the industry, government and scholars. To describe sub-disciplines, the following names were used (Targowski, 1980):

- Theoretical Informatics
- General Informatics (broad strategies, policies, and structures)
- Computing Informatics
- Technical Informatics
- Commercial Informatics
- Public Informatics
- Infostrada (1972 project)
- National Information System (1972 project) (National Information Infrastructure)

In the 1990s, the Americans begin to talk about the *Information Superhighway* (Infostrada) as a metaphor for the convergence of information technology, telecommunications technology, and broadcasting. The Europeans, always careful about the right name, begun to talk about the *Information-Communication Technology (ICT)*.

THE AMERICAN APPROACH

The U.S. is not a disputable world leader of information technology developments. Even punch card equipment was developed in this country in the 19th century. Ever since, American companies, such as NCR, IBM, CDC, Honeywell, Boroughs, Univac, Digital Equipment Corporation, Unisys, Hewlett-Packard, Compaq, Sun, Microsoft, and others are shaping the developmental directions of the information processing and its profession.

However, despite such a decisive role played by the American computer industry, this country straggles with the application of right names for the discipline. Historically speaking, the first term for the industrial applications, coined by John Diebold in 1964, was *information technology*. The academicians did not accept this term and the Association of Computer Machinery (ACM) in 1968 introduced its own term of *computer science*. Ever since, academia and industry disagree on the terminology.

Computer science has roots in the 1940's and the first computer science department was created in the 1950's at the University of Ohio. Its long time chairman, Peter Denning, was a *spiritus movers* of a new definition of computer science, which is now just called computing (Denning, et al 1989).

Computer science was a misleading term, since the discipline was, and still, lacking its scientific rules. In fact, this new academic discipline was about system programming, including such software components as an operating system, computer languages and utilities. The term *science* indicated rather that this discipline is to be part of the Colleges of Arts and Sciences. It was not, however, a comprehensive discipline, since it excluded the tasks of hardware design and computer applications in organizations. Computer engineering was "assigned" to Engineering Colleges, and organization applications have been left to Business and Public Administration Schools. In such a manner, the communication gap among these three sub-disciplines has been created and broaden in the academia.

After 10 years of applying computer science, the ACM came out with an updated curriculum, shifting from computer science to computing. A new name suggests that the discipline includes everything associated with system software development and scientific computing.

In organizational practice, the *information technology* term is still popular. However, the *information management* (IM) is increasingly favored. In light of the convergence of information and communications technologies, the IT term does not reflect what is taking place in the organizational and personal practice. The IT term is misleading and is not properly directing the academic and business-industrial programs.

A NEW PARADIGM OF COMPUTER-DRIVEN PROFESSION

Apparently, Corporate America is going through a paradigm shift that is driven by the demands of the new, competitive business environment and profound changes in the nature of computers (Tapscot and Caston, 1993, p. xi). It is a new era of IT in which business applications of IT, the nature of IT itself, and the leadership for use of IT are all going through profound change (Tapscot and Caston, 1993, p. 13). The new IT users are more sophisticated and more demanding. They are no longer content to depend on IS departments to achieve the benefits of IT, and more capable in using IT applications (Schwrz and Brock, 1998).

The Americans who once overlooked the opportunity to adapt the European term L'informatique should not miss the opportunity to substitute the *Information-Communication Technology (ICT)* for *Information Technology (IT)*.

By the end of the millennium, the information processing is decisively evolving towards the computer-networking environment, whose new paradigm can be defined as:

The integration and connectivity of different media, technology platforms and application systems within the entire organization, which can be local, spread-out or virtual.

The information processing discipline, also, should apply the same paradigm towards its undertakings. A new paradigm of this discipline is:

The integration of sub-disciplines and connection of their all members.

By the end of the 1990's in the U.S. a new term *informing science* is pursued by Ali Cohen (Cohen, 1998). It is a noble effort, however, it seems too innovative to be accepted widely by both academicians and practitioners. It is the authors' view that a strategy of gradual improvements of such terms should be adopted.

TECHNOLOGY VERSUS APPLICATION SYSTEMS

The presented dilemma in a subtitle reminds us of a question "What comes first a chicken or an egg?" Does a given technology define our discipline or an organizational function such as information management (so called back office)? looking at the structure of Gross National Product (GNP), we may observe that the term IM, rather than IT, is applied to describe a volume of money spent on the application of IT in the American economy. As well, if we look at the business function, we may observe such terms as marketing, finance, accounting, management, production, which are technology neutral. The industrial practitioners did not replace the term production by the term *computer integrated manufacturing (CIM)*.

Hence, we should agree that both terms should be applied:
• Information-Communication Technology (ICT) to describe complexity of solutions.
• Information Management (IM) to describe a new organization function, which manages the applications of ICT.

A SCOPE OF ICT

A scope of ICT under the form of an Enterprise Information Infrastructure (EII) is provided as follows:

I. Info-Communication Services
   1. Computing Environment
     a) Silicon Components and Processors
     b) Storage, Monitors, and Others
     c) Computers Platforms
       (1) Personal Computers
       (2) Mid-range Computers
       (3) Main Frame Computers
       (4) Network Computers
       (5) Digital Assistants
       (6) Others
     d) System Software
       (1) Operating Systems
       (2) Programming Languages
       (3) Software Servers
       (4) Browsers
       (5) Search Engines
       (6) Security Systems
       (7) Utilities
       (8) Others
     e) Information Engineering
       (1) Developmental Environments
       (2) Database Management Systems
       (3) Data Warehousing
       (4) Data Mining Tools
       (5) Others

   2. Networking Environment
     a) Transmission Media
     b) Modems, Switches and Access Tools
     c) Internetworking Modules
     d) Standards and Protocols
     e) Network Operating Systems
     f) Network Management Systems
     g) PBX
     h) LAN
     i) MAN
     j) WAN
     k) GAN
     e) VAN
     f) Internet
       (1) Intranet
       (2) Extranet
       (3) Intranet
   3. Information Superhighway (multimedia)
   4. Others

II. End-user Computing
   1. Word processing (Word, WordPerfect)
   2. Spreadsheet (Excel, Lotus)
   3. Desktop database (Access, SQL)
   4. Presentation (Power Point)
   5. Computer graphics (Canvas, McDraw)
   6. Publishing (Page Maker)

7. E-mail (Pegasus, Eudora)
8. Internet browsing (Netscape, MS Internet Explorer)
9. Personal information systems (calendaring, activity management, address and contact management)
10. Online information services (America On Line)
11. Desktop conferencing
12. Decision Support Systems (DSS)
13. Executive Information Systems (EIS)
14. Others

III. Enterprise Information Systems
1. Organization IS
   a) Product IS
   b) Operation IS
   c) Inter-organizational IS
   d) International IS
2. Cross-Functional IS
   a) Transaction Processing System
   b) Databases
   c) Data Warehouse System and Data Mining
   d) Management Information Systems
      (1) Management Control Systems
      (2) Executive Information System

(3) Decision Support Systems
(4) Expert Systems
   e) Work Flow Systems
   f) Document Management System
3. Computer Integrated Manufacturing
4. Others

IV. Info-Communication Systems
1. Voice Mail
2. E-mail
3. E-meeting
4. Computer Conferencing
5. Discussion Forum
6. Groupware
7. Teleconferencing
8. Telecommuting
9. Fax
10. EDI
11. E-commerce
12. Online Information Services
13. Others

Out of the four EII categories (I, II, III,IV) only one subcategory (I,1.) reflects IT and two categories (I but .1, IV) reflect ICT. Even the categories II and III identify applications that used to be IT-driven, and nowadays are rather ICT-driven.

A SCOPE OF INFORMATION MANAGEMENT (IM) DISCIPLINE

The IM discipline involves the systematic study and practice of ICT (computers, telecommunications, television) and applications (systems, services, infrastructure) at the organizational and individual levels. The fundamental question underlying IM is: What can be informated (automation with added value)?

One mission of an information management discipline is to effectively manage a solution and/or perception to the appropriate degree anytime, anywhere in the synchronism of events. Information management becomes a new organizational (business) function, which optimizes some other functions such as management, marketing, product development, production/service, finance, accounting, legal, inter-organizational relations, and international relations.

The following nine areas that cover the information management discipline are selected (Targowski 1998):
1. Ecology of Information
2. Information Science
3. Programming Languages
4. Computing Environment
5. Networking Environment
6. Information Engineering
7. Application Software Engineering
8. Information Infrastructure Engineering
9. Information Resource Management

A curriculum model for each area can be divided into the scope of theory, architecture (modeling), and design. This concept of a new IM discipline does not contain such areas as artificial intelligence, since this area is heavily covered in computing. A domain of application expert systems is covered in information engineering, among other information systems.

WHAT IS NEXT? KNOWLEDGE MANAGEMENT (KM)

Earlier era was characterized by relatively slow and predictable change that could be deciphered by most of information systems applications. Systems based on programmable recipes of success were able to deliver their promises of efficiency based on optimization for given business contexts (Malhotra, 1998). However, the new and growing world of knowledge-based industries puts emphasis on precognition and adaptation, in contrast to the traditional emphasis on optimization based on prediction (Malhotra, 1998). This new business environment is characterized by radical and discontinuous change and demands anticipatory responses from knowledge workers, who need to carry out the mandate of faster cycle of knowledge creation and action based on this new knowledge.

Knowledge is the information resident in people's minds that is used for decision-making in unknown contexts. Knowledge and information are distinct. While information generated by computer systems is not a very rich carrier of human interpretation for potential action, knowledge resides in the user's subjective context of action based on that information. There is a need for variety and complexity of interpretation of information outputs generated by ICT systems. This mandates the shift from the traditional emphasis on transaction processing, integrated logistics, and workflow to systems that support competencies for communication building, people networks, and on-the-job learning.

KM is a concept under which information is turned into actionable knowledge and made available effortlessly in a usable form to the people who can apply it (Angus et al., 1998). It encompasses management strategies, methods, and technology for leveraging intellectual capital and know-how to achieve gains in human performance and competitiveness (Sullivan, 1998).

While KM goes beyond information management, KM is a relatively new field and the business world is still feeling its way forward. KM focuses on the management of information, knowledge and experience available to an organization—its creation, capture, storage, availability and utilization in order that organizational activities build on what is known and extend it further (e.g., Angus et al., 1998). However, KM is still difficult to understand because the business processes it aims to computerize do not exist in the real world for most organizations. Additionally, with the exception of the specialized organizations whose entire business is KM, there is no obvious, proven model to follow (Angus et al., 1998).

Nevertheless, KM is not simply a technological issue (Haapaniemi, 1998; (Sullivan, 1998). ICT provides only the tools and systems— e.g., groupware, internet, intranets, data warehousing and other foreseeable tools—that support knowledge creation, discovery, and distribution. A purely technological approach also runs the risk of overloading employees with information, rather than arming them with knowledge (Haapaniemi, 1998). More attention is given to the organizational, cultural, and behavioral factors, which are usually the biggest part of the problem.

Recent IS literature (e.g., Davenport and Prusak, 1997) emphasizes the shift from the knowledge economy to the knowledge ecology, where the focus is on the ecosystem and its interrelated components. It's a shift in focus from the individual to the community of practice. Knowledge ecology looks at knowledge practice more than production. It requires ICT to provide both reach and reciprocity, since knowledge creation depends on relationship as well as on access to information (Cohen, 1998). It requires, in tun, a shift from IM to KM. Such a shift to KM suggests adding new dimensions—e.g., ecology of knowledge, auditing of knowledge assets, publishing and editing--to the above mentioned nine areas of IM.

CONCLUSION

As it is well documented in the literature (e.g., Toffler, 1990), the most successful in the information age will be the individual, group, community, society, or nation that has access to information and the ability to process. Corporate America witnesses a paradigm shift that is driven by the demands of the new, competitive business environment and profound changes in the nature of computers (Tapscot and Caston, 1993, p. xi). It is a new era of ICT in which business applications of ICT, the nature of ICT itself, and the leadership for use of ICT are all going through profound change (Tapscot and Caston, 1993, p. 13).

Networking of humans through technology and the formation of networked intelligence must be the target of ICT applications. The new ICT users are more sophisticated and more demanding. They are no longer content to depend on IS departments to achieve the benefits of IT, and more capable in using IT applications (Schwrz and Brock, 1998). Even though network and computing technology provide automation and connectivity, it's the information that translates into business transactions, products, service and applications.

This new challenge is shifting the focus of IS education and practice towards effective and efficient information and knowledge management (IM and KM). 'Connectivity/operability' among and within IS academicians and practitioners is a must in order to advance the IS profession. In order to maximize the outcomes of such connectivity/operability:
- The information management professionals must pursue a strategy of consolidating the discipline's terminology applied in its theory, architectures (models), and design, otherwise, the incoherent discipline cannot produce coherent research and specialists.
- IS researchers need to enter into formal dialogues with practitioners (e.g., Saunders, 1998), to identify their unsolved problems and the research issues that are considered important to the application of ICT tools in support of information and knowledge management in organizations.
- IS faculty— with feedback from practitioners and in light of the evolving ICT tools— need to continually review and revise IS curricula in order to best prepare IS students, and the organizations that hire them to cope with this challenge of rapidly changing ICT and its expected roles in organizations.

REFERENCES
ACM (1968), "The Computer Science Curriculum," ACM Communications, vol. 11.
Ackoff, R. L (1967). "Management Misinformation Systems," *Management Science*, No. 14, pp. 147-156.
Angus, J., Patel, J., Harty, J. (1998). "Knowledge management: Great concept…but what is it?," *Informationweek*, March 16, pp. 58-70.
Baker, J., (1992). *Paradigm: The business of discovering the future* (N.Y.: Harper Business, 1992).
Cohen, D. (1998). "Toward a knowledge context: Report on the first annual U.C. Berkeley forum on knowledge and the firm," *California Management Review*, Vol. 40, No. 3, Spring, pp. 22-39.
Davenport, T. H., and Prusak, L. (1997). Information Ecology: Mastering the
Information and Knowledge Environment (N.Y., N.Y.: Oxford University Press).
Denning, P.J., D.E. Comer, D. Gries, M.C. Mulder, A. Tucker, A. J. Turner, and P.T. Young (1989) "Computing as a Discipline," *Communications of ACM*, vol. 32, no. 1, January. pp. 9-23.
Cohen, E. (1998), www.informing.edu
Diebold, J. (1964), Beyond Automation, New York: Praeger Publishers.
Haapaniemi, P. (1998). "We've got too much information—and not enough knowledge," *Chief Executive*, pp. 26-27.
Malhotra, Y. (1998). ""mailto:Tooks@work: Deciphering the knowledge management hype," *The Journal for Quality and Participation*, July/August, pp. 58-60.
Nowell, A., Perils, A., and H. Simon (1967). "What is Computer Science?" Science 1957: 1373-1374. (reprinted in *Abacus* 4 Summer 1987).
Saunders, C. (1998). "Editorial Preface: The Role of Business in IS Research," Information Resources Management Journal, Winter, pp. 4-6.

Schwarz, G., and Brock, D. (1998). "Waving hello or waving good-bye? Organizational change in the information age," *International Journal of Organizational Analysis*, Vol. 6, No. 1, January, pp. 65-90.

Sullivan, C. (1998). "AIIM '98 report: Industry experts evaluate the show in Anheim," Inform, July, 1998, pp. 12-17

Tapscot, D., and Caston, A. (1993). *Paradigm Shift: The new promise of information technology* (N.Y.: McGraw-Hill Taylor).

Targowski, A. (1971), Informatics a Key to Prosperity (in Polish), Warsaw: PIW.

Targowski, A. (1980), Informatics, Models of Systems and Developments (in Polish), Warsaw: PWE.

Targowski, A. (1998), " A Definition Of Information Management Discipline," The Journal of Education for MIS, The Fall.

Toffler, A., Powershift (N.Y.: Bantam Books, 1990).

Westfall, W., "An IS Research Relevancy Manifesto," 1998, www.cyberg8t.com/westfalr/relevant.html

National and Global Information Infrastructures: Explanations and Implications

Andrew S. Targowski and Alan I Rea, Jr.

Department of Business Information Systems, Haworth College of Business, Western Michigan University, Kalamazoo, MI 49008

andrew.targowski@wmich.edu, Phone: 616-387-5406, FAX: 616-387-5710

alan.rea@wmich.edu, Phone: 616-387-4247, FAX: 616-387-5710

ABSTRACT

Targowski (1996) explores the formation of the "New Information Civilization" (NIC) that will carry us into and beyond the 21st century as a civilization. Within this NIC, various components , such as infactories, infomalls, and infohighways (1-6) work together to create and sustain not only a "National Information Infrastructure" (NII) but also ultimately form a "Global Information Instructure" (GII). It is the purpose of this paper to explain and elaborate on these concepts and then explore how and if they are being implemented in society today as we prepare for the 21st century.

INTRODUCTION

Alvin Toffler (1980) discusses the three waves of civilization: Agricultural, Industrial, and Information. If we look at histories of most developed nations, his assertions hold true. Agriculture enables civilizations to forgo their nomadic ways, Industry allows civilizations to produce material goods, and Information brings us closer even still to the connectivity needed for the 21st century democratic structures. However, not all cultural pundits see this move into an Information Age as warranted or wanted. Neil Postman (1992) discusses the concept of the "Technopoly" which "eliminates alternatives to itself" (48) by making the only choice one of technology instead of social codes or other moral choices.

There is "truth" in both these views, and we explore both the pros and cons of the Information Age and discuss the structure and implementation of a National and a Global Information Infrastructure. We hold that technology is neither inherently good of bad. Rather, it is in specific implementation and use of technology that these designations arise.

NATIONAL INFORMATION INFRASTRUCTURE

Most developed countries are always looking for mean to enhance their infrastructures. In the United States, the federal, state, and local governments work together to create the most viable means of physical transportation structures: interstates, toll roads, etc. Vice President Al Gore (1995) has called for a Global Information Infrastructure (GII), more commonly referred to as the "Information Highway." We must admit this "construction" is driven by market supply and demand with any type of planning initiatives taking the back seat to capitalism. However, there are ways to loosely organize these information structures.

Targowski (1996) puts forth a model (Figure 1) of the NII. He discusses the components in great detail, but for now a short list of each component is warranted so that we might discuss how to implement and coordinate this structure in our models:

1. Infohighways: telematic network services treated as information utility
2. Electronic Knowledge: takes the form of the National Digital Library
3. Electronic Health: a seamless matrix of telematic networks and interorganizational computer applications of health care services
4. Electronic Money: eventually will replace paper money
5. Electronic Commerce: seamless matrix of telematic networks of business
6. Electronic State: can take the form of "Big Brother" or Electroni Republic
7. Enterprise Information Infrastructures of virtual educational institutions
8. Local Information Infrastructures
9. National Cyberspace
10. Electronic Global Users
11. National Information Policy

As the NII develops, there is a need for more contact with other NIIs. Just as the U.S. policies of isolationism in the past have proved ineffective, so to are policies that work against expanding infrastructures beyond those of a national level. One of the means by which a NII expands and remains viable is through global expansion (Figure 2).

GLOBAL INFORMATION INFRASTRUCTURE

With this global expansion, comes the need to interact with other NII and information centers. No longer do the physical or political boundaries separate the exchange of information as in the past. However, until the actual physical development (communication lines, equipment, etc.) are in place, the means to expand and become a Global Information Infrastructure are hindered (Figure 3).

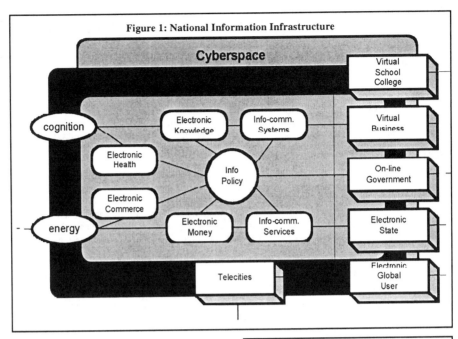

Figure 1: National Information Infrastructure

CONCLUSION

In our research, then, we look at how expansion can occur and what conditions and criteria need to be present and met to form Global Information Infrastructures. However we also discuss implications of slowed and decreased growth versus expanded growth of the GII and what this means to our Global Economy.

Figure 2: The Growth-oriented Relationship Between the Global Economy and the Global Information Intrastructure

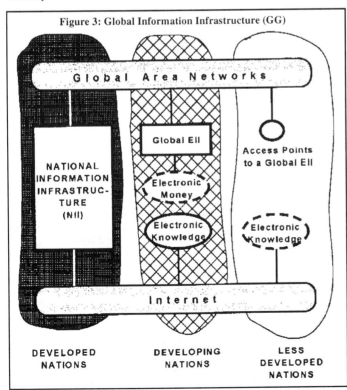

Figure 3: Global Information Infrastructure (GG)

REFERENCES

Postman, Neil. (1992). Technopoly: The Surrender of Culture to Technology. New York: Vintage Books.
Targowski, Andrew. (1996). Global Information Infrastructure: The Birth, Vision, and Architecture. Harrisburg, PA: Idea Group Publishing.
Toffler, Alvin. (.1980). The Third Wave. New York: Morrow.

A Component Model for an Inter-organizational Agent-based Coordination

Klement J. Fellner, Claus Rautenstrauch, and Klaus Turowski
Otto-von-Guericke-University, Institute for Technical and Business Information Systems, P.O. Box 4120, D-39016 Magdeburg,
Germany
phone: +49 (391) 67-18385, fax: +49 (391) 67-11216, Email: {fellner|rauten|turowski}@iti.cs.uni-magdeburg.de

ABSTRACT

Organizations are faced with growing competitive pressure and the movement to buyer markets. To fulfill the customer requirements of customer individual products at low costs, high quality, and short shipment deadlines, manufacturer have to cooperate closer with suppliers and dealers as well as deploy an efficient and economical inter-organizational logistic. Therefore, a fast exchange of relevant information is necessary across all participating organizations. To achieve this, a component model for an internet based multi-agent-system is presented as a means to improve inter-organizational communication to automate the coordination of the production process. The component model is used to implement the different parts of the multi-agent system, thus supporting re-use and easy adaptation to changing process requirements at lower costs.

COMPETITIVE ADVANTAGES THROUGH AN OUTOMATED INTER-ORGANIZATIONAL COORDINATION

Business processes have been stretched across organization borders already before to gain competitive advantage through the combination of individual core competencies, or solely because of individual organizations lack specific knowledge. Nowadays, organizations worldwide are faced with growing competitive pressure through open markets and the movement from seller markets to buyer markets, and they seek to replace their "legacy" information systems with better, network-based architectures. The constant spreading use of (inter-)network technology involves new possibilities and adds a new quality to inter-organizational cooperation. Companies may now cooperate not only locally, but globally with any company offering needed know-how (knowledge as well as products) at best quality and lowest costs to gain competitive advantage. This is especially necessary when marketing strategies, like mass customization (cp. e. g. Pine II 1993), are succeeding. A network of manufacturers, suppliers, and retailers has to be established to put mass customization (a way for businesses to offer individual products at prices comparable to mass production and comparable short shipment times) into action (cp. Kotha 1996, pp. 447-449).

Better integration of suppliers as well as the coordination of inter-organizational production processes are critical success factors for mass customization (Moad 1995, p. 35). Availability of technologies, that enable communication across organizations and between (heterogeneous) information systems, like protocols (e. g. TCP, HTTP), or platform-independent programming languages (e. g. Java), only solve the technical problems of executing inter-organizational business processes. Especially the individual, usually heterogeneous, application systems are now supposed to work together improving process execution and allowing participating organizations to gain competitive advantages.

A COMPONENT MODEL FOR AGENT-BASED COORDINATION

Integration of supply chains, coordination of production processes, and security issues in internet banking represent a selection of well-discussed, but still open problems fields of information system development. Leaving out security issues, these problems can be partly addressed using software agents. Agent architectures are widely discussed since the late 1950's as a means to automate tasks within the computer's world (for an overview cp. Bradshaw 1997). Tasks, like exchanging information for communication purpose or coordination processes are well-suited to be executed using software agents. Software agents themselves consist of several different elements, e. g. (Corsten; Gössinger 1998, p. 176) identified three main parts constituting the minimal set-up for agents used in the area of production planning and scheduling (PPS): the communication processor, the local knowledge base, and the problem solver. Furthermore, an ontology which is suitable for the application area is needed. An ontology is a common agent communication language that allows the agents to understand each other semantically.

Implemented in a certain way, agents serve as a basis for automating major parts of the inter-company business processes, as they are well-suited to coordinate the production of individualized products in the early phases of negotiation between manufacturer and suppliers. Taking these parts, a core component model of an agent-based coordination system can be derived (cp. figure 1). Possible software components are: listener/manager agent, conversion agent, negotiation agent, communication processor, problem solver, and the knowledge base.

According to figure 1, we distinguish between three classes of agents: agents that fulfill a conversion task, agents that fulfill a negotiation task, and agents that supervise the execution of a conversion or negotiation process. Conversion agents translate the data into languages that may be understood by the application systems (mostly PPS systems) of the respective participant of a production network. Negotiation agents are used to coordinate the production itself. Listener/manager agents supervise the execution of any other agent.

There must be two conversion agents in a given system implementation, if a connection to an application system (e. g. PPS) is desired. One for each direction of the transformation. Both, of course, may use the same knowledge base for the matching of terms.

Because a company usually implements more than one kind of negotiations (e. g. auction-based, contract-based or combined forms) there may also be more than one negotiation agent. Depending on business rules for a concrete object of negotiation the

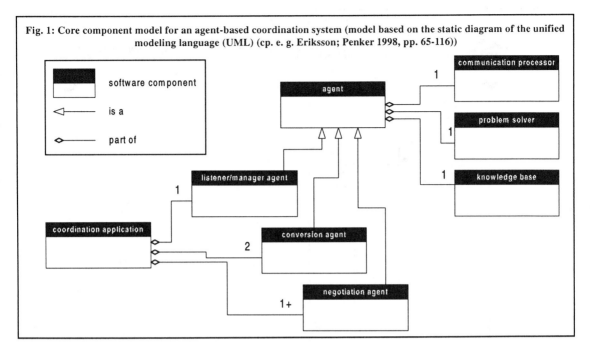

Fig. 1: Core component model for an agent-based coordination system (model based on the static diagram of the unified modeling language (UML) (cp. e. g. Eriksson; Penker 1998, pp. 65-116))

listener/manager agent chooses the suitable negotiation agent for every new negotiation process.

The communication processor in this model is responsible for the local as well as the remote communication between agents. This agent is identical in every agent of a given system implementation. However, the implementation of the problem solver and the knowledge base is different in each class of agents. The problem solver of a negotiation agent consists of rules how a negotiation has to be carried out, whereas the conversion agent need to know how to transform application specific data into an application independent exchange format. The contents of the knowledge base may also vary between different agent implementations. A conversion agent, e. g. may use the knowledge base for a thesaurus of terms and their definitions. Hence, the knowledge base of negotiation agents consists of information regarding suppliers, shipment terms and conditions.

Apparently, there are several parts of the model, which may be re-used extensively. To enable re-use, an implementation as independent software components is suggested. According to (Orfali et al. 1996, p. 34) a software component can be sold independently from other components, does not form a complete application, has an open and well-specified interface, is system-independent, and extendable. Following this definition, agents may also be build using other agents, or parts of other agents.

INTER-AGENT COMMUNICATION

To establish and improve communication between manufacturer and supplier in a mass customization scenario the implementation of electronic data exchange (Electronic Data Interchange (EDI)) is necessary. The implementation of EDI additionally lead to organizational information-based surplus values (cp. Kuhlen 1996, esp. p. 90), e. g. an improved organizational as well as operational structure or time and cost savings. The most important standard for inter-organizational data exchange was established by the United Nations - the UN/EDIFACT (Electornic Data Interchange for Administration, Commerce and Transport) (UN 1995). However, the standard did not get the expected recognition and implementation extent because of fundamental drawbacks (cp. Zbornik 1996, pp. 92-93, Goldfarb; Prescod 1998, pp. 106-110):

• Absence of semantic rules (e. g. for quantity or packaging units),
• the implicit assumption that every organization implements the same business processes and scenarios,
• economic (e. g. high implementation costs) as well as
• organizational shortcomings (e. g. slow adoption to changing business processes, complicate adjustment of established business process and rules).

On the one hand there are several ongoing efforts to establish uniform business scenarios and semantic rules (cp. TMWG 1998, Harvey et al. 1998, pp. 25-26, Steel 1997). The XML/EDI-Initiative on the other hand concentrates on the economical and organizational drawbacks of the standard using the Extensible Markup Language (XML) (cp. Bray et al. 1997) to lower the implementation costs and increase its flexibility. XML, like HTML (HyperText Markup Language), is based on the SGML (Standardized Generalized Markup Language) standard, but in contrast to HTML provides the possibility to define new tokens (tags) as well as user-defined document structures through Document Type Definitions (DTD). DTD describe the syntax of a certain data token. XML/EDI, as a way to utilize XML for inter-organizational communication, is based on well-known EDI-Standards, like UN/EDIFACT, templates representing organization-specific business rules, and DTDs.

Further on, we utilize XML/EDI, resp. the persistent use of XML for inter-organizational data exchange using a multi-agent system to improve inter-organizational communication. As a first approach we use the UN/EDIFACT segment names as standardized field descriptors for the multi-agent system.

Fig. 2: Message exchange for procurement

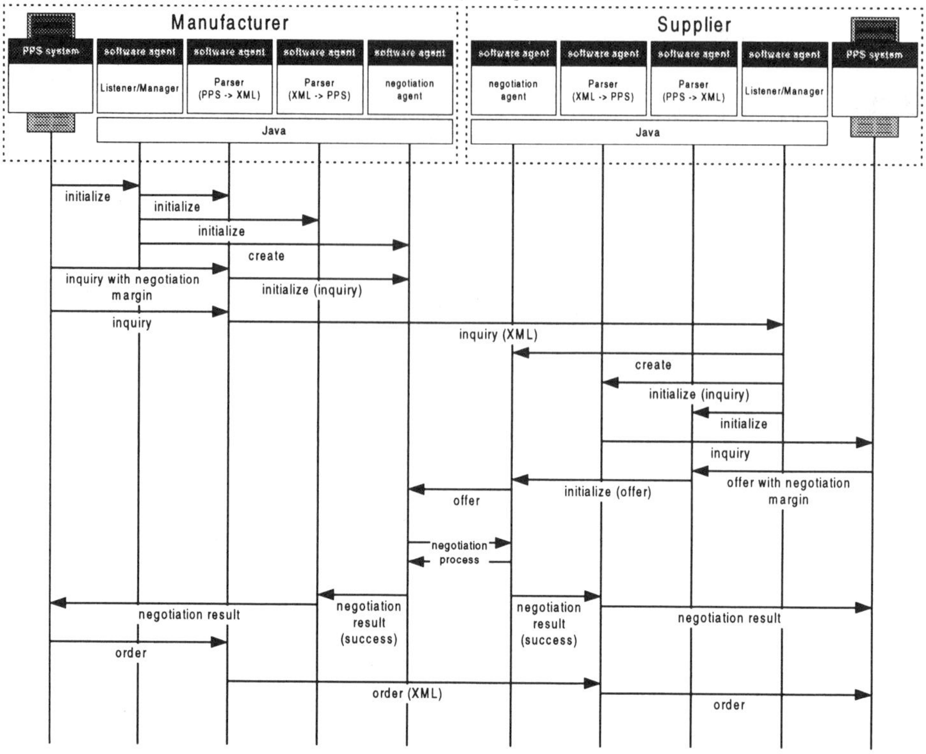

The following explanation of our approach is based on the message exchange diagram in figure 2. To keep it manageable, we restrict our example to one supplier. For an in deep explanation of its connection to mass customization and the multi-agent system itself see (Turowski 1999).

Figure 2 shows the software agents used by the manufacturer resp. the supplier, the application (PPS system), and the message exchange between these components. Manufacturer as well as suppliers use a PPS system which provides at least a proprietary interface for exporting and importing data in a non-standard format. After the product configuration the parts for procurement are determined and bought from suitable suppliers. The manufacturers PPS system therfore generates the necessary inquiries. Ideally, these reports are forwarded automatically to all suitable suppliers using EDI. Utilizing our approach, the output of the PPS system (the inquiry) is transferred to a software agent (the conversion agent "Parser (PPS -> XML)"), which transforms the output to XML. Afterwards, the XML output is transferred to the supplier using the standard internet protocols (as TCP/IP). The conversion agent ("Parser (XML -> PPS)") at the supplier-side transforms the inquiry into the format required by the suppliers PPS system. The conversion agent matches the content of the XML document with the arguments needed by the PPS system using the standardized XML-tags which categorize every transferred information.

Next, the inquiry is processed by the PPS system resulting in an (automatically) generated offer, which is transferred to the manufacturer using the same mechanism as described above.

Besides the described simple communication process between manufacturer and supplier, more complex coordination processes including additional sub-processes may occur. The above, simple process, assumes, that conditions, like date of shipment, quantity, deadlines or prices are fix for all participating parties. In real world processes these conditions are most likely subject of a negotiation process. To include and automate this process we use the negotiation agent. Objects of the negotiation process are parts that have to be produced in order to assemble a customer individual product. Negotiation agents do not need to know much about these objects. They only get an identification and certain constraints, e. g. due dates or quantities. This information is created by the conversion agents based on the data given by the PPS system of the supplier or manufacturer. As a result the negotiation agent returns the conditions on which one (or more) suppliers agreed to deliver.

Strictly speaking, the manufacturer generates an additional inquiry with negotiation ranges for several conditions, like price, date of shipment, etc. After the inquiry for negotiation is parsed by the conversion agent, the output is used to initiate the negotiation agent. On the supplier-side an offer is generated matching the inquiry. When receiving an offer, the manufacturer-side negotiation agent extracts all relevant (negotiable) information and generates a counteroffer, accepts the offer, or aborts the negotiation process. The routing and the necessary conversion for this process is done by the conversion agents. After termination of the negotiation process, the negotiation result is transformed by the corresponding conversion agent ("Parser(XML -> PPS") and transferred to the PPS system, which generates an order based on the negotiated offer.

In case that all conditions are negotiated and corresponding orders are triggered, the same multi-agent system can be used to coordinate the production process, e. g. adjustment of production plans in case of failure. The system which failed to meet the agreed

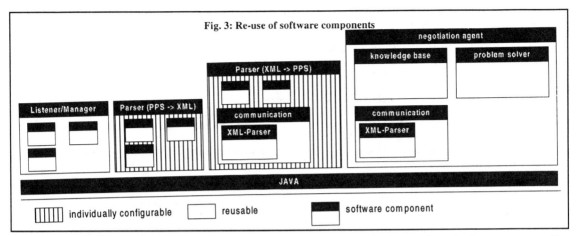

Fig. 3: Re-use of software components

conditions creates a suitable software agent to negotiate any changes. The opposite side, of course, has to implement a corresponding software agent for negotiation.

The negotiation agents in the presented scenario all use the same software components for inter-organizational communication. This allows the re-use of appropriately implemented agents for similar tasks in different processes.

IMPLEMENTATION ASPECTS

So far, the implementation of agents took place in special-purpose programming languages and environments, therefore resulting in proprietary systems (Bradshaw 1997, pp. 377-378) (for an overview of programming software agents cp. (Shoham 1997)). In case of production processes that involve multiple suppliers, as mass customization, where systems of the manufacturer have to communicate with different suppliers, maybe unknown at system implementation time, an open implementation of agents is absolutely necessary.

Consistently, we propose a component-orientated implementation of agents that communicate with each other using protocols of the internet. When software parts are implemented as components, applicable in different application areas, like the communication component, maybe re-used extensively, thus cutting down implementation costs.

A possible scenario of re-use is presented in figure 3. The software agent "Listener/Manager" serves as the coordinating unit, responsible for the initialization resp. creation of other agents as required by the application scenario. Hence different negotiation processes or conversion tasks can run parallel to each other. Whereas the "Listener/Manager" and the negotiation agent may be re-used in different system environments without any change, the conversion agent has to be adapted for every new application system (e. g. PPS system). As mentioned, the application system has to provide an interface, where the input and output format is known. The complexity of the conversion agent depends solely on the application system interface. A simple conversion agent e. g. parses a text-file generated by the application system and adds the corresponding XML-tags to the detected data fields. A more complex agent can access the information directly using e. g. remote function calls (RFC) in the application system. Additionally, the conversion agents which transforms the data fields from XML to an application specific format has to be adapted. Since several XML-parser are available for free (e. g. XML2Java from IBM or XMLParser from Sun), the remaining effort to adapt this parser is low.

Besides conversion agents, there also exist negotiation agents responsible for the execution of negotiation processes. The communication component, which is responsible for the communication between negotiation agents, includes an additional XML-Parser to interpret the received documents for the problem solver. This output of the XML-parser depends on the used problem solver. Hence, it is reusable together with the problem solver. The problem solver implements negotiation mechanisms (e. g. auction based negotiation). The extent of its re-use depends on the number of application scenarios where the same negotiation mechanism may be applied. After configuring the agents with organization specific information and the adaptation to the information infrastructure (e. g. PPS system, etc.) the agents are usable for both, the manufacturer and the supplier.

As prototype language, Java (Sun Microsystems 1998c) has been chosen. All agents are implemented as Java applications, therefore requiring the existence of a Java Runtime Environment (JRE). Above all advantages (e. g. object-orientation or platform-independence), Java comprises a component model, the JavaBeans (Sun Microsystems 1998a), providing the features for a straight-forward implementation of the presented approach. JavaBeans are by definition implementations of self-contained components (c. p. Englander 1997), i. e. a single component can be distributed and used alone as well as in combination with others. Also, the needed functionality to implement inter-agent-communication is part of the standard Java API (java.net) (cp. Sun Microsystems 1998b).

Allowing an easy way to compose applications visually, Sun's Java Studio, is used to implement the prototype components. In fact, JavaBeans may be implemented in every other bean container, whereas a bean container is defined as visual design environment, which uses a set of standard interfaces provided by the components through introspection.

OUTLOOK AND CONCLUSIONS

The deployment of an efficient and economical information logistic is a key success factor for organizations implementing strategies like mass customization. In this paper we introduced a component model for a multi-agent based architecture to support the implementation of such concepts. Where available, we use public standards (like HTML, XML, etc.) or open industry standards (like Java) to implement our approach. Furthermore, we concentrate on the re-use of essential software components. We achieve a high degree of platform independence through the use of Java as implementation language, therefore allowing organizations to adapt the components fast and at lower implementation costs. In addition to the support of inter-organizational communication processes the introduced approach enables also the support of nearly all kind of procurement processes as well as inter-organizational coordination of production processes using the same information infrastructure. Another advantage is the possibility to implement the mentioned concepts and techniques step by step. E. g. starting with communication agents to support only the transfer of information, followed by a multi-agent system including the negotiation in the second step, and third, a multi-agent system to coordinate an inter-organizational production process.

At the time we are working on the multi-agent prototype based on the component model presented in this paper to support our approach. The prototype is entirely written in Java using development environments from Sun (JavaWorkshop and JavaStudio). Additionally, we make use of free XML-parsers and the integrated business application system R/3 from SAP to implement the communication with existing application systems.

Furthermore, the advances in the definition of communication standards have to be taken into account, as the UN/EDIFACT standard serves only as a starting point for the definition of our XML tags.

REFERENCES

Bradshaw, J. M. (1997): An Introduction to Software Agents. In: Software Agents. Ed. J. M. Bradshaw. Seattle, p. 3-46.

Bray, T.; Paoli, J.; Sperberg-McQueen, C. M. (Eds.) (1997): Extensible Markup Language (XML). http://www.w3.org/TR/PR-xml.html. 12.06.98.

Corsten, H.; Gîssinger, R. (1998): Produktionsplanung und -steuerung auf Grundlage von Multiagentensystemen. In: Dezentrale Produktionsplanungs- und -steuerungs-Systeme: Eine EinfÅhrung in zehn Lektionen. Eds.: H. Corsten; R. Gîssinger. Stuttgart, p. 174-207.

Englander, R. (1997): Developing Java Beans. 1. ed., Cambridge.

Eriksson, H.-E.; Penker, M. (1998): UML Toolkit. New York.

Goldfarb, C. F.; Prescod, P. (1998): The XML Handbook. Upper Saddle River.

Harvey, B. et al. (1998): Position Statement on Global Repositories for XML. ftp://www.eccnet.com/pub/xmledi/repos710.zip. 01.12.1998.

Kotha, S. (1996): From Mass Production to Mass Customization: The Case of the National Industrial Bicycle Company of Japan. European Management Journal 14(5), p. 442-450.

Kuhlen, R. (1996): Informationsmarkt: Chancen und Risiken der Kommerzialisierung von Wissen. 2. ed., Konstanz.

Moad, J. (1995): Let Customers have it their Way. Datamation 41(6), p. 34-39.

Orfali, R.; Harkey, D.; Edwards, J. (1996): The Essential Distributed Objects Survival Guide. New York.

Pine II, J. B. (1993): Mass Customization: The New Frontier in Business Competition. Boston.

Shoham, Y. (1997): An Overview of Agent-Oriented Programming. In: Software Agents. Ed. J. M. Bradshaw. Seattle, p. 272-290.

Steel, K. (1997): The Beacon User's Guide: Open Standards for Business Systems. http://www.cs.mu.oz.au/research/icaris/beaug1.doc. 01.12.1998.

Sun Microsystems (Ed.) (1998a): JavaBeans 1.0.1 Specification. http://www.javasoft.com/beans/docs/beans.101.pdf. 20.08.1998.

Sun Microsystems (Ed.) (1998b): JavaBeans: API Specification. ftp://ftp.javasoft.com/docs/beans/beans.101.pdf. 21. Jan. 1998.

Sun Microsystems (Ed.) (1998c): JDK 1.1.6 Documentation - Java Development Kit. http://www.javasoft.com/products/jdk/1.1/docs/index.html. 21.08.1998.

TMWG (Ed.) (1998): Reference Quide: "The Next Generation of UN/EDIFACT": An Open- EDI Approach Using UML Models & OOT (Revision 12). http://www.harbinger.com/resource/klaus/tmwg/TM010R1.PDF. 01.12.1998.

Turowski, K. (1999): A Virtual Electronic Call Center Solution for Mass Customization. In: R. H. Sprague (Ed.) Proceedings of the 32nd Annual Hawaii International Conference On System Sciences, Maui, Hawaii, (CD-ROM).

UN (Ed.) (1995): United Nations Directories for Electronic Data Interchange for Administration, Commerce and Transport. http://www.unece.org/trade/untdid/Welcome.html. 01.12.1998.

Zbornik, S. (1996): Elektronische MÑrkte, elektronische Hierarchien und elektronische Netzwerke: Koordination des wirtschaftlichen Leistungsaustausches durch Mehrwertdienste auf der Basis von EDI und offenen Kommunikationssystemen, diskutiert am Beispiel der Elektronikindustrie. Konstanz.

Trust in Electronic Commerce

Craig Van Slyke
Ohio University, College of Business, 236 Copeland Hall, Athens, OH 45701
(740) 593-0819, vanslyke@ohiou.edu

Rosann Webb Collins
University of South Florida, College of Business Administration, 4202 East Fowler Avenue, CIS 1040, Tampa, FL 36612-7800
(813) 974-5524, rcollins@coba.usf.edu

Christie Lynn Comunale
The State University of New York at Stony Brook, Harriman School for Management and Policy, Stony Brook, NY 11794
(516) 632-7428, ccomunal@coba.usf.edu

ABSTRACT

Conducting business via electronic commerce (e-commerce) is becoming increasingly popular. Organizations view e-commerce as a potential vehicle for increasing their reach, improving customer service and reducing costs. However, if e-commerce is to reach its potential, customers must have an appropriate level of trust in the organizations with which interact via e-commerce. This paper discusses some issues related to the role of trust in e-commerce and presents a theoretical model that may help guide further investigations into trust and e-commerce.

INTRODUCTION

Organizations of all sizes are turning to electronic commerce (e-commerce) as a means of improving efficiency and effectiveness. Commerce conducted over the Internet is increasing at a phenomenal rate. It has been estimated that U.S.-based e-commerce transactions will exceed $300 billion by 2002 (Wilder, 1998). If transaction-oriented e-commerce is to be successful, the parties involved must properly assess the level of trust they should have in each other. Many potential consumers are reluctant to provide personal information such as credit card numbers to e-commerce outlets. Clearly, one partner's lack of trust in the other may lead to a reluctance to engage in the transaction.

In this paper, we propose a theoretically-based model of trust in e-commerce. The model draws from previous research on trust, information technology and e-commerce in an attempt to draw a comprehensive picture of the components and consequences of trust as they relate to e-commerce.

THE IMPORTANCE OF TRUST IN ELECTRONIC COMMERCE

Every business relationship involves trust (Hart & Saunders, 1997). Business conducted electronically is no different. In fact, the introduction of technology into a relationship may challenge existing trust between parties (Hart & Saunders, 1997). Electronic commerce is one example of a technology-mediated relationship where the introduction of technology may impact trust. If e-commerce practitioners do not adequately understand how trust is built in these technology mediated relationships they may find that their efforts are less successful.

The model presented here can help e-commerce practitioners better understand their potential customers and how those customers perceive the antecedents of trust. This understanding may enable practitioners to take appropriate actions to increase trust. Researchers should also benefit, since the components and relationships represented in the model can guide research on e-commerce and the role trust plays in its effectiveness.

ELECTRONIC COMMERCE TRUST MODEL

In this section we describe the proposed model, which is shown in Figure 1. Each component of the model is described. In addition, propositions are offered concerning the relationships among the components as noted in the model. In addition, the theoretical basis for the model is discussed.

Trust

Trust has been defined in a number of ways. In the context of an economic exchange (as in e-commerce) it may be appropriate to consider trust to be the expectation that the other party will behave in accordance with commitments, negotiate honestly, and not take advantage, even when the opportunity arises (Hosmer, 1995). This definition is used in this research.

While most definitions of trust deal with exchanges and relationships between individuals, these concepts can be extended to interorganizational exchanges, since relationships between organizations are managed by individuals (Aulakh, et al., 1996).

Outcomes of Trust

In order to understand the role of trust between customers and organizations in e-commerce, it is important to consider the possible outcomes of trust. There are two outcomes of trust included in the model, use and monitoring, which are discussed below.

<u>Use</u>: There are two components of use that are impacted by the customers' assessment of the organization's trustworthiness: frequency of use and type of use. If a potential customer deems the organization untrustworthy, it seems likely that the frequency of that customers interaction will be impacted. The more trust the customer is willing to place in the e-commerce organization, the more frequent will be the use.

The type of e-commerce interaction may also be impacted by trust. Even if customers lack trust in the organization, they may still be willing to engage in interactions with low risk, such as gathering product information. However, when trust is high customers may be willing to take part in higher risk interactions, such as providing personal information, and participating in economic exchange.

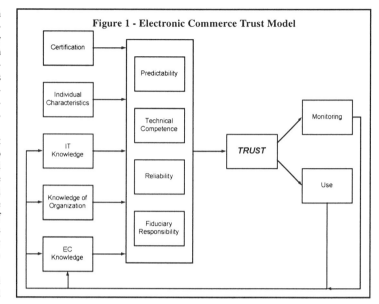

Figure 1 - Electronic Commerce Trust Model

In order to better understand how trust impacts e-commerce it is proposed that two types of use be considered, those perceived by customers as being high risk, and those perceived as being low risk. It should be noted that it is the perception of the e-commerce user, rather than an objective assessment of risk that is important. In addition, while it is expected that increasing trust will positively impact both high and low risk use, the magnitude of the impact may differ.

A number propositions can be offered that concern the relationship between trust and use. These propositions are stated below.

P1: Trust in an organization has a positive relationship with the use of electronic commerce to interact with that organization.

P1a: Trust in an organization has a positive relationship with the frequency use of electronic commerce to interact with that organization.

P1b: Trust in an organization has a positive relationship with the use of electronic commerce to interact with that organization when the interactions are perceived as being high risk.

P1c: Trust in an organization has a positive relationship with the use of electronic commerce to interact with that organization when the interactions are perceived as being low risk.

Monitoring: In any relationship, a lack of trust in another may lead to more monitoring of the other and the relationship. Similarly, lack of trust in an e-commerce organization may lead customers to monitor the relationship more frequently. Simply put, the higher the trust , the lower the monitoring. For example, a customer who has provided credit card information to an low risk e-commerce organization may spend considerable time checking for unauthorized charges. If the level of trust is higher, the customer is less likely to engage in such behavior. This monitoring behavior impacts the efficiency of the e-commerce relationship. Any gain from interacting through e-commerce may be offset by the time and effort spent monitoring.

Following the thinking above, the following proposition may be put forth.

P2: Trust in an e-commerce organization is negatively related to monitoring of that organization.

Having discussed the outcomes of trust in the context of e-commerce, attention is now turned to perceptions that impact trust. These are discussed in the following section.

Perceptual Components

A number of perceptions are important when one makes an assessment of the trustworthiness of another. Several of these apply in the context of e-commerce. It is important to note that the following are perceptual. In other words, what matters is the individual's perceptions, not the objective evaluations of some expert.

Predictability: Consistency is the foundation of predictability (Rempel, et al., 1985). One party in an e-commerce transaction may reasonably expect a trading partner to behave consistently. Predictability is not synonymous with consistency, however. Predictability pertains to the trusting party's ability to "know" what the actions of the trustee will be. It is possible that actions will change, which impacts consistency. However, if the trusting party understands the reason for and anticipates the change, predictability will not suffer.

In interpersonal relationships, predictability is positively related to trust. In other words, the more predictable an individual views another to be, the higher the trust in that party. It may be expected that this holds in e-commerce relationships. If so, then P3 can be reasonably offered.

P3: Perceptions of predictability are positively related to trust.

Technical Competence: Competence is an important dimension of trust (Barber, 1983). Its importance has been demonstrated in a number of organizational contexts (Hart & Saunders, 1997). As perceptions of competence increase, so does the willingness to trust. Even if a trusted party is willing to act appropriately, if they lack the technical competence to do so, trust may suffer.

The perception of technical competence may be particularly applicable in e-commerce relationships, due to e-commerce's technical nature. In e-commerce, if the trusting party is not confident of the other party's competence in carrying out a transaction successfully and securely they will be less willing to trust and less willing to engage in that transaction. This leads to the following proposition.

P4: Perceptions of technical competence are positively related to trust.

Reliability: The consistency between what an actor says and does is known as reliability (Hart & Saunders, 1997). This is conceptually similar to dependability, which is the correspondence between how an actor behaves and how the actor *should* behave (Johnson-George, & Swap, 1982). If a trusting party feels that a trusted party is not acting in accordance with statements and agreements, trust suffers.

Reliability has been included in IT-related models of trust (Hart & Saunders, 1997). As a result, it is expected that the influence of perceptions of reliability on trust will hold in e-commerce. If this is the case, Proposition 4 can be offered.

P5: Perceptions of reliability are positively related to trust.

Fiduciary Responsibility: Fiduciary responsibility is an important component of trust (Barber, 1983). Fiduciary responsibility can be thought of as the obligation of the organization to act on behalf of the customer when the customer has insufficient knowledge or experience to judge the organization's actions. For example, an attorney is required to act on a clients behalf, even though the client may not possess the expertise to evaluate the attorney's actions. When perceptions of fiduciary responsibility increase, so does trust.

In some e-commerce applications perceptions of fiduciary responsibility may impact trust. For example, a customer of a Web-based travel agency must trust the agent to faithfully act on their behalf (to, for example, identify lowest cost fares), even though the agent knows that the customer's knowledge is insufficient to accurately judge the agent's actions.

P6: Perceptions of fiduciary responsibility are positively related to trust.

Antecedents to Perceptions

Perceptions of the components of e-commerce trust may be impacted by a number of factors. While each of these is thought to affect the perceptions that impact trust, the direction of the impact is not clear, with the exception of third-party certification. As a result, no propositions are offered, with the exception of third-party certification.

Individual characteristics: A number of individual characteristics may impact the individual's trust in e-commerce. Among these is the individual's propensity to trust (Mayer, et al., 1995). Some people are simply more prone to trust another. Other possible characteristics include attitude toward technology and attitude toward e-commerce. Depending on the characteristic studied, a number of propositions can be put forth.

Information technology knowledge: Individuals' knowledge of information technology (IT) may impact their assessments of the components of trust. This is particularly true of perceptions of technical competence.

Knowledge of the organization: An individual's knowledge of the trusted organization plays a role in perceptions of the components of trust. This is particularly interesting in the context of e-commerce. In many traditional forms of interaction, the trusting and trusted parties may have mutual contacts. This is more likely in a highly dense social network than in less dense networks. Even when two parties do not know one another, they may have mutual third-party ties which enable the trusting party to gain knowledge of the trusted party. This may be less likely in an e-commerce context due to the wider geographic dispersion between the parties. Of course, knowledge of the trusted organization can be gained through direct interaction. In order to ascertain the nature of the relationship between knowledge of the organization and the perceptions associated with trust it is necessary to conduct additional research.

Electronic commerce knowledge: This antecedent is similar to IT knowledge. However, it is possible that a trusting party's knowledge of e-commerce is different from his or her knowledge of IT. Prior knowledge of e-commerce may impact assessments of predictability, technical competence and reliability.

Third-party certification: Certification of third-parties may become an important component in e-commerce trust. In e-commerce, there may be less opportunity to gather information about a potential trading partner from others in a social system. This opens the door for initiatives such as the American Association of Certified Public Accounts' and Canadian Institute of Chartered Accountants (AICPA/CICA) joint effort, CPA Web Trust (Williams, 1997). CPA Web Trust is a seal of assurance which when granted to an e-commerce Web site provides potential customers with assurance that the site meets AICPA/CICA criteria for business practices, transaction integrity controls and information protection.

As the name implies, the CPA Web Trust program is directly targeted at increasing the level of trust customers have in e-commerce. According to a recent study, forty-six percent of those surveyed indicated that the seal would increase the likelihood of purchasing on-line (AICPA, 1998). This leads to the following proposition.

P7: The presence of third-party certification is positively related to perceptions of predictability, technical competence, reliability, and fiduciary responsibility.

CONCLUSIONS

Electronic commerce is an increasingly important application of technology. Researchers and practitioners must understand the role of trust in e-commerce relationships. The research model presented here represents a first step at gaining this understanding.

REFERENCES

AICPA, "Key Findings," http://www.aicpa.org/webtrust/kfind.htm, March 1998.

Aulakh, P., Kotabe, M, and Sahay, A. "Trust and Performance in Cross-Border Marketing partnerships: A Behavioral Approach," *Journal of International Business Studies*, (27:5), 1996, pp. 1005-1032.

Barber, B. *The Logic and Limits of Trust*, Rutgers University Press, New Brunswick, NJ, 1983

Hart, P. and Saunders, C. "Power and Trust: Critical Factors in the Adoption and Use of Electronic Data Interchange," *Organizational Science*, (8:1), January/February 1997, pp. 23-42.

Hosmer, L. "Trust: the Connecting Link Between Organizational Theory and Philosophical Ethics," *Academy of Management Review*, (20:2), April, 1995, pp. 379-403.

Johnson-George, C. and Swap, W. "Measurement of Specific Interpersonal Trust: Construction and Validation of a Scale to Assess Trust in a Specific Other," *Journal of Personality and Social Psychology*, (43:6), December 1982, pp. 1307-1317.

Mayer, R., Davis, J. and Schoorman, F. "An Integration Model of Organizational Trust," *Academy of Management Review*, (20:3) , July 1995, pp. 709-734.

Rempel, J., Holmes, J. & Zanna, M. "Trust in Close Relationships," *Journal of Personality and Social Psychology*, (49:1), July 1985, pp. 95-112.

Wilder, C. "Clinton's Call: No New Internet Taxes," *Information Week*, March 2,1998

Williams, K. "AICPA Launches Electronic Commerce Seal," M*anagement Accounting*, (79:4), October 1997, p. 16.

An Empirical Study on Internet Topic Searching (Using Standalone Internet Search Engines) by Computer Study Students.

Melius Weideman

Cape Technikon, Cape Town, P.O. Box 3109, Tygerpark 7536, South Africa

melius@commerce.ctech.ac.za, 27 21 9134801, tel: 27 21 9135515

BACKGROUND

The aim of this paper is to disseminate the results of research done into the searching process followed by computer study students when looking for subject information on the internet.

The author has adjusted lecturing methods and implemented new ideas over time in an attempt to make the learning process of his computer study students more successful. During an early informal experiment it was proven that students are prepared to put in extra work if it involves their own evaluation directly.

As internet access became the norm in computer labs, it was noticed that students' attention was easily absorbed by aimless surfing and chatting, rather than completing given tasks during practical sessions. A second experiment during the 1998 academic year proved that students would use the internet for academic purposes, if a reward was offered. The author attempted to combine these two sets of results to use the time otherwise spent on aimless surfing to the students' own advantage.

ISSUES

The hypothesis for the main research tour was whether or not students had the ability to (without prior guidance) successfully search for information on the internet, which, if found, would supplement their study material. A formal pilot study done by the author during 1998 provided enough feedback to refine a questionnaire to be used to measure students' ability to find relevant academic information on the internet. Some issues which this pilot study has identified are:

• the fact that students suffer from the halo effect
• bandwidth problems in labs cause serious bottlenecks
• many students are unable to describe a search clearly in natural language.
• some students do not read simple instructions

The questionnaire was adjusted accordingly, and used during a country-wide research tour (October/November 1998). The purpose of the experiments done on the tour was to measure the % success achieved when students have to search for academic information on the internet (without any prior training of any kind).

FINDINGS

A total of 293 students from four race groups (both genders) at 12 different institutes following 13 different courses were involved in the research tour. They were asked to identify any one resource (handbook, notes, etc) used in any one of the subjects they were enrolled for. Furthermore they had to describe a problem area in terms of missing information they experienced with this resource. Finally they had to search for this information in a controlled environment, within 30 minutes. The results follow.

Student ages varied between 17 and 42 years, with an average of 21.56 years. The spread between genders were 32.3% female, 67.7% male. A question was posed: "How many hours of formal instruction have you received on the use of the internet?" More than 75% answered "Less than one hour".

A total of 46% of the students use the internet at least once per day. Furthermore, 82% have used a search engine to find information before. The subject: "Computer and Information Technology" appears to be creating most problems for students --74% of the respondents who are enrolled for it have identified it to pose a problem. Figures for other subjects include 55.2% (Technical Programming), 48.3% (Computer Science), 36.3% (Information Systems), 31% (Informatics), 27.3% (Business Information Systems, 26.3% (Psychology), 25% (Chemistry), 24.2% (System Software) and 23.1% (Education).

A total of 46.4% of the participants indicated that their handbooks had the most gaps in the information they provide, while traditional lectures came second with 30.3%. Videos and libraries posed the smallest problem.

When asked to choose any search engine to use in the final step of the experiment, four out of every ten students chose Yahoo -- a far greater figure than any other search engine.

The number of hits listed before students started visiting websites varied between 1 and 53,469,078. The number of sites visited within the allotted 30 minutes varied between 1 and 42. Almost 25% of the students spent the full 30 minutes on the search, including successful and unsuccessful candidates. The average time spent before finding the information or giving up before it was found was 20.7 minutes.

If the unknown figure is omitted, only 38% of the students found the information they identified initially, within the allotted time.

CONCLUSION

This last result has proven that without a researched, tested and proven model to guide them, students cannot be expected to make use of the internet as an alternative information source to traditional resources. A minor conclusion reached is that bandwidth and the general level of computing facilities in laboratories will both have to increase to make the successful implementation of serious internet searching possible.

At the time of reading this paper (May 1999), the author will have completed the model referred to above. Testing this model on a worldwide audience of students will be in an advanced stage at this time. Final figures to indicate its success or failure could possibly be divulged at a future IRMA conference!

Libraries, Users, Librarians, Information and the Internet: how do they interact to change a world?

Andrew Wenn

HPS University of Melbourne & Department of Information Systems, Victoria University of Technology
email:AndrewWenn@vut.edu.au, phone: 61 3 9688 4342, fax: 61 3 9688 5024

INTRODUCTION

The State Library of Victoria (SLV), located in Melbourne, Australia, is the main repository and access point for information about Victoria and Victorians for Victorians and peoples from the rest of the world. This research was prompted by a statement I came across in the library's mission statement:

A significant program in 1994-95 will be the establishment of an electronic gateway to provide Victorians with direct access to databases worldwide via home personal computers or via their local public or educational institution library. Victorian information will also be made available to Victorians and others.

(State Library of Victoria, 1994)

and by another description of the way information was stored and disseminated to the population of Victoria in the later part of the nineteenth century:

[t]he Annual Report of 1870 stated with some satisfaction that books, in numbers varying from 100 to 200 or 300, were being lent to public libraries, mechanics' institutes or athenaeums; they were packed in cases of oak, bound with brass and lined with green baize; the boxes or cases were closed with sliding doors and were covered with a waterproof tarpaulin to protect them when on their journeys.

...

By 1870 the cases were circulating amongst eighteen towns and suburbs, covering a population of 130,000 people.

(anon, 1956)

To me these statements conjured up a whole world of changes and I began mentally asking questions like "What is happening to libraries?", "How is the internet changing what libraries are doing?", "How are library users really using the internet; are they using it as a means of accessing information or for other purposes?"

This then really set the scene for a qualitative study of libraries and the ways they were using the internet.

METHODOLOGY

From the outset, it was fairly clear that there were at least two different groups involved with the internet in libraries – the users and those responsible for taking the bookings and other administrative and policy making aspects.

After some preliminary discussions with staff at the library it became clear that I was going to be studying a fluid and changing situation. Policies were being determined as I spoke to staff and new equipment was being installed or moved on a regular basis. It seemed to me that the best way to study theses changes was to sit and observe what was happening, look at the way the organisation worked, the practices that were employed, the consequences of implementing decisions and new policies. In short this was to be a mainly qualitative study with some quantitative data collected to obtain demographic information and provide some useful triangulation. (Creswell, 1998; Hammersley, 1992; Trauth, 1997)

Initially the SLV was to be the site of the data collection but, in order to provide a richer data set the study has been expanded to include two libraries in the metropolitan area and a fourth from rural Victoria. The bulk of the data has come from the three city libraries. The methods used include participant observation, semi structured interviews and informal discussions with library users.

Twenty librarians have participated in semi-structured interviews and I have observed the internet booking and other procedures at all three libraries. Survey data was collected using a mixture of closed and open ended questions. Eighty surveys have been distributed and all except one have been returned. I have been collecting documents and audio-visual data also.

PRELIMINARY FINDINGS

Although the research has been conducted at three sites, at the time of writing only the results from the SLV have been examined in enough detail to report here. Some preliminary analysis has been done to reveal themes that need further analysis and more follow-up fieldwork. It is already possible to see themes based around the concepts of:

- access
  - who authorises it,
  - who has access,
  - what does access really mean?
- frustration
- fear
- power
- anxiety
- excitement
- what is meant by information?
- negotiated discourses of practice
  - how did the booking procedures arise?
  - how did the conditions of use arise?
  - where did the SLV's policy of no assistance for email users come from?
- the reconfiguration of physical space and a thing I am calling information space
  - the physical space of the library being reconfigured by the users, the technology and the library staff.
  - the space where information is stored and accessed is being altered
- the library as the *post restante* of the new millennium
- the material semiotics of information
  - things that point to information (URLs, email addresses, discussion list names, usenet names)
  - where information is stored

Throughout the interviews with the Reference Librarians, I have seen the internet referred to as a tool, "*I see it as a tool*", "*Its another reference tool*". The internet is another reference tool it is not something to be taken as totally new, or separate from everything else. So they just integrate it into their current practices when they are using it for information retrieval. It is subsumed as another tool in their arsenal alongside the CDRom's, Online subscription databases, print-based items and so on. There are differences here though depending on the type of reference work that that particular librarian is responsible for. Genealogy resources on the web are particularly valued and as such the librarians in that area tend to use it more and refer people to internet based resources. The type of information Reference Librarians see the WWW as most useful for is the obscure or the very up to date. There are concerns with the veracity of information obtained from the web and a number of staff I talked to were at pains to point out that the "moving sands" nature of many web-based resources was a source of frustration. But it comes separate from that if they have got to do things like book people in to use the internet. It becomes a source of frustration. It (the internet) is manifesting itself in a number of different ways and I will illustrate these in my presentation.

There are interesting tales to tell about the library patrons too. In the main they are backpackers (about 80% of the users at the SLV) in their mid-twenties who use the internet to stay in contact with friends and family in their home country. Table 1 shows a breakdown by country of origin for a small sample of users. Interestingly enough, there is only one Victorian amongst the Australian users the remainder are from interstate. As such they form an itinerant set of users, a fluid group, who nevertheless have manage to shape parts of the system to serve them better.

Backpackers use the internet to keep in contact with parents, relatives and others in their home country, specifically they will use email for this. They also use it to keep in contact with others they meet whilst travelling. Ask any of the backpacking community why they use email and they will almost certainly reply "It's fast, its cheap, convenient and easy to use." They also like the idea that delivery is instant rather than there being a five to ten day delay before the addressee receives their mail. For instance, Ellen is using terminal 4 and in a conversation with her later on, she is very enthusiastic about email. "*I like using email its great - you get a buzz out of it. It's fun. It is a good way of keeping in contact with people you meet whilst travelling. I collect email addresses.*" During my observations I saw many people with diaries or scraps of paper which had email addresses written on them. It seems that the email address is, at least for one group of people usurping the role of the postal or street address.

Table 1 Breakdown of country of origin for internet users at the SLV

Country of origin	Count	% of total
Australia	4*	9
Belgium	1	2
Canada	1	2
Czech Republic	1	2
Denmark	1	2
France	1	2
Germany	2	4
Hong Kong	1	2
Israel	1	2
Italy	2	4
Japan	6	13
Malaysia	1	2
Netherlands	9	20
New Zealand	1	2
Philippines	1	2
Thailand	1	2
United Kingdom	6	13
USA	5	11
Wales	1**	2
Total	**46**	

* NSW 1, Qld 1, Tas 1, Vic 1
** Most insistent that I put Wales not U.K. or England

One of the SLV staff members I talked to identified the backpackers and their use of email and the fact that they come in droves at opening time to book as the reason why many people are no longer making reference enquiries *"When people see a huge line at a desk they're, um, scared away because they think well my enquiry is going to take up more time and they're really busy. Whereas we would really rather be dealing with proper research enquiries."* Similar sentiments were expressed to my by a number of other staff members too and is one of the reasons why the booking procedures were altered during the time I spent at the site.

FURTHER INVESTIGATION

There are obviously many other aspects of the internet and public libraries that could be discussed in a much longer paper. In the presentation accompanying this, I will touch and hopefully discuss in more detail some of these. The research is at a preliminary stage and more analysis, including analysis of data from the other two libraries, is needed to help identify some of the more abstract issues and to aid the development of further ideas and theories. It is anticipated that further field work will be undertaken during 1999.

CONTRIBUTION TO KNOWLEDGE

This research can be seen as providing an insight into how public access internet facilities in libraries are being used and how they are developing. Early research results point to the fact that there is a strong sense of co-constitution of the system between the users, management, staff and the myriad of non-human actors involved. Understanding the type of interactions that take place and the how they arise should provide organisations with the knowledge to furnish a better, more useful and accessible service.

REFERENCES

anon (1956). The Public Library of Victoria 1856 - 1956. Melbourne.

Creswell, J.W. (1998). Qualitative Inquiry and Research Design: Choosing among five traditions. Thousand Oaks, CA, Sage Publications.

Hammersley, M. (1992). What's wrong with ethnography. London, Routledge.

SLV (1994). L21 State Library of Victoria Strategic Plan. Melbourne, SLV.

Trauth, E.M. (May-Jun, 1997) Achieving the Research Goal with Qualitative Methods: Lessons Learned along the Way. From: Information Systems and Qualitative Research. Proceedings of the IFIP TC8 WG 8.2 International Conference. Eds: Lee, A.S., Liebenau, J. & DeGross, J.I. London, Chapman & Hall, pages 225 - 245.

Design and Management of Wireless Communications Networks

Shin-yi Wu and Frank Yeong-Sung Lin

Graduate Institute of Information Management, National Taiwan University, Taipei, Taiwan R.O.C.

TEL: 886-2-28366659, E-mail: shin_yi_wu@hotmail.com

ABSTRACT

In this paper, we consider the optimal wireless communications network design problem with respect to carrier-to-interference ratio constraints, user demand constraints, and cell capacity constraints. Major components of costs when constructing a wireless communications network are identified and a mathematical programming model is derived to determine the system configuration with minimum construction cost. To the best of our knowledge, this is the first time this overall design problem is mathematically formulated. To solve the proposed mathematical programming model, a number of heuristic solution procedures based on Lagrangean relaxation methods are developed and are tested with large-scale numerical examples for their efficiency and effectiveness. From the computational experiments, our Lagrangean relation based algorithms for the overall design problem has significant improvement compared with other one-parse algorithms. Based on the test results, it is suggested that the proposed algorithms may practically be used for the overall wireless network design problem.

1. INTRODUCTION

To provide efficient and effective uses and management of the scarce resources in the wireless communications networks, we deeply investigated the whole wireless communications network design problem and found that this design problem is actually the combination of four tightly coupled and self-difficult subproblems: MTSO allocation, base station allocation, power control, and channel assignment. Previous researchers have carried out intensive researches on one or some of these four subproblems, while the whole design problem with the consideration of the four subproblems all together remained unsolved. However, since these four subproblems exist strong coupling effects, solving these four subproblems separately/sequentially may not be the best policy. We are convinced that solving the four subproblems jointly at the same time will not only theoretically but also practically achieve better performance, measured by construction costs, than the cases where these four subproblems are considered separately/sequentially. A mathematical programming model is derived to determine the system configuration with minimum construction cost in this paper.

2. PROBLEM FORMULATION

By using management science methods, we can transform the joint design problem for wireless communications networks as the following mathematical formulation.

2.1. Notation

Given Parameters:

A: an upper bound on the number of channels that can be assigned to a base station (e.g. equal to 120 in GSM systems)

D_{ri}: distance between mobile station r and the base station at location i

$E(S_i)$: number of channels required to serve user demand S_i (in Erlangs) such that the call blocking probability shall be no greater than 5%

F: the set of available channels

G_i: an arbitrarily large number

H_k: present value of the installation, operation and maintenance cost for an MTSO at location k

J': an upper bound on J_k

K: user demand of each mobile station (in Erlangs)

L: the set of possible locations for a base station

N_{ik}: present value of the connection, operation and maintenance cost of the link between an MTSO at location k and a base station at location i

O: the set of possible locations for an MTSO

$Q(J_k)$: equipment cost of an MTSO with capacity J_k

R': an upper bound on R_i

S': an upper bound on S_i

T: threshold of acceptable C/I ratio

U_i: present value of the installation, operation and maintenance cost for a base station at location i

V: present value of the license cost for using a channel

$W(\alpha)$: present value of the transponder cost for a base station with number of channels a

t: the set of mobile stations

Decision Variables:

B_i: the decision variable which is 1 if a base station is installed at location i and 0 otherwise

C_j: the decision variable that is 1 if channel j is used and 0 otherwise

$I_{ii'}$: Interference factor between the base stations at locations i and i' and it is a function of the fourth power of R_i.

J_k: capacity of the MTSO at location k

M_k: the decision variable which is 1 if an MTSO is installed at location k and 0 otherwise

P_{ijk}: product of X_{ji} and Z_{ik}

R_i: transmission radius of the base station at location i

S_i: total user demand (in Erlangs) of the base station at location i

X_{ji}: the decision variable which is 1 if channel j is assigned to the base station at location i and 0 otherwise

Y_{ri}: the decision variable which is 1 if mobile station r is assigned to the base station at location i and 0 otherwise

Z_{ik}: the decision variable which is 1 if an MTSO at location k is connected with a base station at location i and 0 otherwise

2.2. Mathematical Formulation

Primal Problem IP:

$$\min \sum_{k\in O} H_k M_k + \sum_{k\in O} Q(J_k) + \sum_{k\in O}\sum_{i\in L} N_{ik} Z_{ik} + \sum_{i\in L} U_i B_i + \sum_{i\in L} W(\sum_{j\in F} X_{ji}) + \sum_{j\in F} VC_j \qquad (IP)$$

s.t.

(1) $M_k = 0$ or 1	" $k\in O$
(2) $B_i = 0$ or 1	" $i\in L$
(3) $C_j = 0$ or 1	" $j\in F$
(4) $Z_{ik} = 0$ or 1	" $i\in L, k\in O$
(5) $X_{ji} = 0$ or 1	" $i\in L, j\in F$
(6) $Y_{ri} = 0$ or 1	" $r\in t, i\in L$
(7) $P_{ijk} = 0$ or 1	" $i\in L, j\in F, k\in O$
(8) $0\le J_k \le J'$	" $k\in O$
(9) $0\le R_i \le R'B_i$	" $i\in L$
(10) $0\le S_i \le S'B_i$	" $i\in L$
(11) $Z_{ik} \le M_k$	" $i\in L, k\in O$
(12) $X_{ji} \le B_i$	" $i\in L, j\in F$
(13) $E(S_i) \le \sum_{j\in F} X_{ji}$	" $i\in L$
(14) $\sum_{j\in F} X_{ji} \le A$	" $i\in L$
(15) $D_{ri} Y_{ri} \le R'$	" $r\in t, i\in L$
(16) $\sum_{i\in L} Y_{ri} = 1$	" $r\in t$
(17) $-P_{ijk} \le 0$	" $i\in L, j\in F, k\in O$
(18) $P_{ijk} - Z_{ik} \le 0$	" $i\in L, j\in F, k\in O$
(19) $P_{ijk} - X_{ji} \le 0$	" $i\in L, j\in F, k\in O$
(20) $X_{ji} - P_{ijk} + Z_{ik} - 1 \le 0$	" $i\in L, j\in F, k\in O$
(21) $\sum_{k\in O} Z_{ik} \le B_i$	" $i\in L$

(22) $\sum_{i \in L} \sum_{j \in F} P_{ijk} \leq J_k$ " $k \in O$
(23) $\sum_{i' \in L, i' \neq I} I_{ii} X_{ji} \leq G_i + (1/T - G_i) X_{ji}$ " $i \in L, j \in F$
(24) $X_{ji} \leq C_j$ " $i \in L, j \in F$
(25) $\sum_{r \in t} K Y_{ri} \leq S_i$ " $i \in L$
(26) $Y_{ri} \leq B_i$ " $r \in t, i \in L$
(27) $D_{ri} Y_{ri} \leq R_i$ " $r \in t, i \in L.$

    The objective function is to minimize the sum of the following items: (i) the present value of the installation, operation and maintenance cost for all MTSOs required, (ii) the equipment cost of all MTSOs required, (iii) the cost of the connections between all MTSOs and their slave base stations, (iv) the present value of the installation, operation and maintenance cost for all base stations required, (v) the present value of the equipment cost for all base stations required, and (vi) the present value of the license cost for all channels required. These six items are the major costs involved in configuring a cellular network.

3. SOLUTION APPROACH

3.1. Lagrangean Relaxation

    By using the Lagrangean relaxation method, we can transform the primal problem (IP) mentioned above into the following Lagrangean relaxation problem (LR) where Constraints (19) ~ (27) are relaxed:

Problem LR:

$\psi(a, b, c, d, e, f, g, h, l) =$
min $\{ \sum_{k \in O} H_k M_k + \sum_{k \in O} Q(J_k) + \sum_{k \in O} \sum_{i \in L} N_{ik} Z_{ik} + \sum_{i \in L} U_i B_i + \sum_{i \in L} W(\sum_{j \in F} X_{ji}) + \sum_{j \in F} V C_j + \sum_{i \in L} \sum_{j \in F} \sum_{k \in O} a_{ijk}(P_{ijk} - X_{ji}) + \sum_{i \in L} \sum_{j \in F} \sum_{k \in O} b_{ijk}(X_{ji} - P_{ijk} + Z_{ik} - 1) + \sum_{i \in L} c_i(\sum_{k \in O} Z_{ik} - B_i) + \sum_{k \in O} d_k(\sum_{i \in L} \sum_{j \in F} P_{ijk} - J_k) + \sum_{i \in L} \sum_{j \in F} e_{ij}[\sum_{i' \in L, i' \neq I} I_{ii} X_{ji} - G_i - (1/T - G_i) X_{ji}] + \sum_{i \in L} \sum_{j \in F} f_{ij}(X_{ji} - C_j) + \sum_{i \in L} g_i(\sum_{r \in t} K Y_{ri} - S_i) + \sum_{r \in t} \sum_{i \in L} h_{ri}(Y_{ri} - B_i) + \sum_{r \in t} \sum_{i \in L} l_{ri}(D_{ri} Y_{ri} - R_i) \}$ (LR)
s.t.

(1) $M_k = 0$ or 1   " $k \in O$
(2) $B_i = 0$ or 1   " $i \in L$
(3) $C_j = 0$ or 1   " $j \in F$
(4) $Z_{ik} = 0$ or 1   " $i \in L, k \in O$
(5) $X_{ji} = 0$ or 1   " $i \in L, j \in F$
(6) $Y_{ri} = 0$ or 1   " $r \in t, i \in L$
(7) $P_{ijk} = 0$ or 1   " $i \in L, j \in F, k \in O$
(8) $0 \leq J_k \leq J'$ " $k \in O$
(9) $0 \leq R_i \leq R' B_i$ " $i \in L$
(10) $0 \leq S_i \leq S' B_i$ " $i \in L$
(11) $Z_{ik} \leq M_k$ " $i \in L, k \in O$
(12) $X_{ji} \leq B_i$ " $i \in L, j \in F$
(13) $E(S_i) \leq \sum_{j \in F} X_{ji}$ " $i \in L$
(14) $\sum_{j \in F} X_{ji} \leq A$ " $i \in L$
(15) $D_{ri} Y_{ri} \leq R'$ " $r \in t, i \in L$
(16) $\sum_{i \in L} Y_{ri} = 1$ " $r \in t$
(17) $- P_{ijk} \leq 0$ " $i \in L, j \in F, k \in O$
(18) $P_{ijk} - Z_{ik} \leq 0$ " $i \in L, j \in F, k \in O.$

    We can further decompose the Lagrangean relaxation problem into 5 independent, easily solvable sub-problems.

3.2. The Dual Problem and the Subgradient Method

    According to the weak Lagrangean duality theorem, $\dot{E}$ is a lower bound on the optimal objective function value of the Primal Problem (IP). We then construct the following dual problem to calculate the tightest lower bound and solve the dual problem by using the subgradient method.

    max $\psi(a, b, c, d, e, f, g, h, l)$ (D)
    s.t. $a, b, c, d, e, f, g, h, l >= 0.$

    After the implementation of the subgradient optimization procedure, we got a lower bound on the optimal objective function value of the primal problem. However, as we have predicted, the tightest lower bound we get was very loose and no primal feasible solution was found in the process. In order to get the primal feasible solutions, we try to utilize the optimal dual solutions to develop some heuristic algorithms for the primal problem.

4. GETTING PRIMAL FEASIBLE SOLUTIONS

    Due to the complexity of the primal problem, a divide-and-conquer method is proposed to get the primal feasible solutions. As we have mentioned before, the whole joint problem is the combination of 4 subproblems. They are (i) MTSO allocation, (ii) base station allocation, (iii) power control, and (iv) channel assignment. If we can solve the base station allocation and power control subproblems first, we can divide the whole joint problem into three parts. The first is the base station allocation and power control subproblem. The second is the MTSO allocation subproblem. And the third is the channel assignment subproblem. For each of these subproblems, two kinds of algorithms are proposed: iterative and one-parse procedures.

4.1. Base Station Allocation and Power Control Subproblem

In this part, we have to decide the following decision variables:

B_i: the decision variable which is 1 if a base station is installed at location i and 0 otherwise

$I_{ii'}$: Interference factor between the base stations at locations i and i' and it is a function of the fourth power of R_i.

R_i: transmission radius of the base station at location i

S_i: total user demand (in Erlangs) of the base station at location i

Y_{ri}: the decision variable which is 1 if mobile station r is assigned to the base station at location i and 0 otherwise

In the process of the Lagrangean dual search procedure, we have coefficient $(g_iK + l_{ri}D_{ri} + h_{ri})$ for each Y_{ri} and coefficient $(U_i - c_i - \Sigma_{r\in i}h_{ri})$ for each B_i. Coefficient $(g_iK + l_{ri}D_{ri} + h_{ri})$ is a function of D_{ri} (distance between mobile station r and base station i), and if we sum $(g_iK + l_{ri}D_{ri} + h_{ri})$ of each Y_{ri} in the largest service area of base station i (and under the capacity constraint of base station i), the sum can be viewed as the indicator of customer density to some degree (it also can be viewed as the cost of assigning mobile station r to base station i). On the other hand, coefficient $(U_i - c_i - \Sigma_{r\in i}h_{ri})$ is a function of U_i (the construction cost of the base station located at i). We are more willing to construct a base station with lower U_i and with higher customer density. So we can utilize these coefficient vectors to determine B_i, $I_{ii'}$, R_i, S_i, and Y_{ri} by the following iterative algorithms:

Algorithm BA&PC1:

Step 1. For each base station i, sum $(g_iK + l_{ri}D_{ri} + h_{ri})$ of each Y_{ri} in the largest service area and under the capacity constraint. Then add $(U_i - c_i - \Sigma_{r\in i}h_{ri})$ to the sum.

Step 2. Sort the base stations based on the number of potential users and the sums calculated in Step 1. That is the base station with more potential users is considered first, but if two base stations have the same numbers of potential users, then the one with the smaller sum calculated in Step 1 is considered first.

Step 3. According to the rank decided in Step 2, set the B_i one by one to 1 until all mobile stations are served. That is when we set a base station i, we try our best to utilize all its capacity until no other mobile stations can be served by it. Set all corresponding Y_{ri} to 1, others to 0, and calculate all S_i.

Step 4. Set all R_i to be large enough to cover the farest mobile station assigned to base station i, and calculate all $I_{ii'}$.

Algorithm BA&PC2:

Every time when we need to construct a new base station, we go through Algorithm "BA&PC1". That is, we choose a base station to construct by repeatedly applying Algorithm "BA&PC1" rather than sort the candidate base stations once.

Algorithm BA&PC3:

Step 1. For each base station i, sum the smallest K $(g_iK + l_{ri}D_{ri} + h_{ri})$, where K is the maximum number of mobile stations that can be served by a base station. Then add $(U_i - c_i - \Sigma_{r\in i}h_{ri})$ to the sum.

Step 2. Sort the base stations based on the sums calculated in Step 1. That is the base station with the smaller sum calculated in Step 1 is considered first.

Step 3. According to the rank decided in Step 2, set the B_i one by one to 1 until all mobile stations are served. That is, when we set a base station i, we try our best to utilize all its capacity until no other mobile stations can be served by it. Set all corresponding Y_{ri} to 1, others to 0, and calculate all S_i.

Step 4. Set all R_i to be large enough to cover the farest mobile station assigned to base station i, and calculate all $I_{ii'}$.

Besides utilizing the coefficient vectors in the process of the Lagrangean dual search procedure to determine B_i, $I_{ii'}$, R_i, S_i, and Y_{ri}, we could also simply utilize D_{ri} and U_i in similar ways to develop some one-parse algorithms.

4.2. MTSO Allocation Subproblem

In this part, we have to decide the following decision variables:

J_k: capacity of the MTSO at location k

M_k: the decision variable that is 1 if an MTSO is installed at location k and 0 otherwise

Z_{ik}: the decision variable which is 1 if an MTSO at location k is connected with a base station at location i and 0 otherwise

We can construct another mathematical model for the MTSO allocation problem:

Primal Problem MAIP:

$$\min \Sigma_{k\in O}H_kM_k + \Sigma_{k\in O}Q(J_k) + \Sigma_{k\in O}\Sigma_{i\in NL}N_{ik}Z_{ik} \qquad \text{(MAIP)}$$

s.t.

(1) $M_k = 0$ or 1	" $k \in O$	
(2) $Z_{ik} = 0$ or 1	" $i \in NL, k \in O$	
(3) $0 \le J_k \le J'$	" $k \in O$	
(4) $\Sigma_{k\in O}Z_{ik} = 1$	" $i \in NL$	
(5) $Z_{ik} \le M_k$	" $i \in NL, k \in O$	
(6) $\Sigma_{i\in NL}E(S_i)Z_{ik} \le J_k$	" $k \in O$	

where NL is the set of all base station locations decided in Section 4.1.

Again, we solve it with the Lagrangean relaxation method and subgradient method, and then we proposed 6 heuristics for this subproblem to get the primal feasible solutions.

4.3. Channel Assignment Subproblem

In this part, we have to decide the following decision variables:

C_j: the decision variable that is 1 if channel j is used and 0 otherwise

X_{ji}: the decision variable which is 1 if channel j is assigned to the base station at location i and 0 otherwise

We also can construct another mathematical model for the channel assignment problem:

Primal Problem CAIP:

min $\sum_{j\in F}VC_j$ (CAIP)

s.t.

(1) $C_j = 0$ or 1 " $j\in F$
(2) $X_{ji} = 0$ or 1 " $i\in NL, j\in F$
(3) $E(S_i) \leq \sum_{j\in F}X_{ji}$ " $i\in NL$
(4) $\sum_{i'\in NL,\ i'\neq i}I_{ii'}X_{ji'} \leq G_i + (1/T - G_i)X_{ji}$ " $i\in NL, j\in F$
(5) $X_{ji} \leq C_j$ " $i\in NL, j\in F$

where NL is the set of all base station locations decided in Section 4.1.

Again, we solve it with the Lagrangean relaxation method and subgradient method, and then we proposed 3 heuristics for this subproblem to get the primal feasible solutions.

5. COMPUTATIONAL EXPERIMENTS

A number of test examples are used to test the algorithms proposed above. The major assumptions and parameters used in this study are as follows:

1. Demand is uniformly distributed in the region.
2. The mobility of the mobile stations is ignored. This assumption is valid in areas with relatively low levels of mobile station mobility e.g. a residential neighbor-hood.
3. Calls arrive according to a Poisson process.
4. Mobile station density = 0.0001 MSs/m^2.
5. Mean call blocking probability = 5%.
6. Mean user demand of each mobile station = 0.1 Erlangs.
7. Available number of channels = 1000.
8. Service area = 100 km^2 or 400 km^2.
9. Maximum number of channels which can be assigned to a base station = 120.
10. Cost of a MTSO = 30 million NT dollars.
11. Threshold of acceptable C/I ratio = 18 dB.
12. Cost of a base station = 5 million NT dollars.
13. Cost of the license of a channel = 200 thousand NT dollar.
14. Cost of a transponder (each can serve 8 channels) = 400 thousand NT dollars.
15. Unit connection cost between base stations and MTSOs = $NT 300/m.
16. Possible power radius of a base station = 500m or 1000m or 1500m or 2000m or 2500m.
17. MTSO equipment cost structure:

Table 5-1 Cost Structure of MTSO Equipment	
Channels	Cost ($NT)
500	5 million
1000	9 million
1500	12 million
2000	14 million
2500	15 million

From the computational experiments, our Lagrangean relaxation based algorithms for the three modules and the overall design problem have significant improvement than other one-parse algorithms. For example, our algorithm for the channel assignment module achieves up to 10.14 % improvement compared to the algorithms proposed by other researchers and our recommended iterative algorithms (based on the Lagrangean relaxation method) for the MTSO allocation achieve up to 14.30% improvement compared to other one-parse algorithms. As for the overall design problem, our Lagrangean relaxation based algorithms also result in very good performance. They achieve up to 37.20% improvement compared to other one-parse algorithms. Based on the test results, it is suggested that our algorithms may be practically used for the overall wireless network design problem.

6. SUMMARY AND CONCLUSIONS

This paper investigates the overall wireless communications network design problem under the assumption that the mobility of the mobile stations is ignored and with respect to carrier-to-interference ratio constraints, user demand constraints, and cell capacity constraints. For the problem, a mathematical programming model is derived and some heuristic solution procedures are exploited based on Lagrangean relaxation. These heuristics are tested extensively with practical-size problems to show how efficient and effective they are. To the best of our knowledge, this is the first time this overall design problem is mathematically formulated and we are the first who try to solve the overall design problem at the same time. The solid result is not only the first attempt in academics but also could be applied directly to the industries. This paper may be extended to consider the effects of mobile station mobility together.

REFERENCES

[1] C. S. Ya. "Power Control and Channel Assignment of Wireless Communications Networks.", National Taiwan Technology University Master Degree Thesis, 1997.
[2] L. Y. Wei, "The Research of the Channel Assignment in Mobile Communications Systems with Unregular Cells.", National Taiwan Technology University Master Degree Thesis, 1997.
[3] A. M. Geoffrion. Lagrangean Relaxation and Its Uses in Integer Programming." Math. Programming Study, 2: 82-114, 1974.
[4] B. T. Polyak. A General Method for Solving Extremal Problems. Soviet Mathematics Doklady, 8: 593-597, 1967.
[5] B. Gavish and S. Sridhar. Economic Aspects of Configuring Cellular Networks. Wireless Networks, 1(1): 115-128, February 1995.
[6] K. Feher. Wireless Digital Communications: Modulation & Spread Spectrum Applications. Prentice Hall PTR, 1995.
[7] E. B. Carne. Telecommunications Primer: Signals, Building Blocks and Networks. Prentice Hall PTR, 1995.
[8] F. Y. -S. Lin. "Aquasi-static Channel Assignment Algorithm for Wireless Communications Networks." ICOIN '98, Japan, January

1998.

[9] I. G. Tollis. Optimal Partitioning of Cellular Networks. IEEE International Conference on Communications, 3: 1377-1381, 1996.

[10] J. L. Goffin. On the Conver gence Rates of Subgradient Optimization Methods. Math. Programming, 13: 329-347, 1977.

[11] K. Pahlavan and A. H. Levesque. Wireless Information Networks. John Wiley & Sons, 1995.

[12] M. L. Fisher. The Lagrangean Relaxation Method for Solving Integer Programming Problems. Management Science, 27(1): 1-18, January 1981.

[13] M. S. Bazaraa, H. D. Sherali and C. M. Shetty. Nonlinear Programming: Theory and Algorithms, 2nd Ed., John Wiley & Sons, 1993.

[14] S. Papavassiliou and L. Tassiulas. Joint Optimal Channel Base Station and Power Assignment for Wireless Access. IEEE/ACM Transactions on Networking, 4(6): 857-872, December 1996.

Managerial Issues of Electronic Commerce

Vincent C. Yen

Department of Management Science and Information Systems, Wright State University, Dayton, Ohio 45435

ABSTRACT

Electronic commerce has been recognized as an integral part of business. Because of its richness in ways the technology could provide, it is difficult for information systems developers and managers to effectively plan and manage such projects. The paper highlights practical elements that should be considered by a Web-based electronic commerce project team.

INTRODUCTION

In the last five years, electronic commerce (E-commerce) on the Internet has been growing at an exponential rate. The phrase EC is broadly defined as any portion of business activities conducted on the Internet. Currently, there are two categories of EC in operation: business-to-business and business-to-consumer. ECs conducted in the business-to-business class uses tools such as Electronic Data Interchange (EDI) and extranets. Recently, growing availability of Internet development software has enabled companies to develop their own EC Web sites. Since most of business activities can practically be transformed to the Web-based, launching a new EC project requires planning and management. It is particularly so for a full range of commercial activities on the Internet. Yen (1997) suggested a list of E-commerce activities for planning considerations. These activities are given in the following model.

AN INTEGRATED MODEL OF E-COMMERCE

The elements of the integrated e-commerce model is briefly given below.
1. Requirements – help establishing requirements and specify products and services
2. Search - select source of suppliers
3. Marketing
   • Product presentation– Presentation and demonstration (multimedia)
   • Product information – Written descriptions and warranty policies.
   • Product pricing - Products/services pricing policies
   • Product promotion - Products/services promotion and sales
4. Order processing
5. Payment and settlement
   • Payment mechanism selection
   • Refund/return policies
6. Logistics - specification and coordination of delivery of goods and services to customers
   • Delivery methods [sea, air, ground, electronic]
   • Routing
   • Scheduling and tracking
7. Customer service
   • Inquiries – via e-mail
   • Maintenance
   • Satisfaction survey
   • Purchase records
   • Return and settlement
8. Information Access in Supply Chain
9. Linking with Backroom Systems
10. Recognizing Barriers in E-Commerce

E-COMMERCE PROJECT MANAGEMENT

It is useful to understand the breadth of e-commerce project components. But, at the beginning of a project, the scope should be kept to a manageable size. The selection of the components must be closely aligned with business goals, policies, and resource availability. The development team for an e-commerce project must consider additional areas on top of the model components. We briefly point out tasks and/or questions must be investigated under marketing, customer communications, the business, customer information, technology platforms, staffing, and, legal and regulatory barriers.

MARKETING

The goal is to draw in and interact with customers, act on their wishes, and react to their concerns. That is to design for attracting traffic, personalize content, allowing for self-service and conduct e-commerce transactions.
(1) Who are your target audience, business or consumers?
(2) What are your promising products/services.

CUSTOMER COMMUNICATIONS

An important part of EC is the interactive activities between customers and the Internet. Business would like to remember customers or potential customers they are dealing with. In addition, businesses would also like to know customers shopping behavior, personal interests, etc. Some of the issues relate to the collection of customer information are:
(1) How would you convince consumers to register at your site and provide accurate data?
    One of the tasks might be posting a privacy policy.
(2) What information will you collect and report about each customer?
(3) Should customer approval be needed in uses of customer data?
    For example, should you notify and seek customer approval for the selling of the mailing-list information.
(4) How can consumers review and correct that information?
(5) How do you position your site in search engines?
(6) How do you collect registration information?
(7) How is feedback solicited and organized into useful form?
(8) Which site you would like to maintain links?
    Business-to business communications issues:
(1) How will the product catalog be provided and maintained?
(2) Should suppliers' order entry system be launched?
(3) What emerging standards: OBI (open buying on the Internet), EDI (Electronic data interchange) must be maintained?

THE BUSINESS

Understanding business strategies, policies, functions and procedures are relevant to the development staff. Some of the questions must be asked are:
(1) What is the business mission, goals and objectives?
(2) What is the business' competitive model?
(3) Is the message aligned with corporate goals?
(4) Is the EC project cost-effective?

TECHNOLOGY PLATFORMS

Questions need to be evaluated are:
(1) What should be the components of the Integrated Model of E-Commerce?
(2) What would be the interactive tasks performed or processed on the Web-based e-commerce?
(3) What would be the kinds of technologies most appropriate for the required tasks?
(4) Should the components be made in-house or purchased from vendors? Managers much keep abreast of Internet technologies, and maximize the use of such technologies in the most cost-effective manner.
(5) What development tools/languages should the in-house developers use? The criteria of choice may depend on staff skills, and the ease and speed of the tools/languages. Some examples of the tools/languages are: Java, XML, InterDev, and NetObjects Fusion.

STAFFING

The crux of any project is people. Staff drawn from various departments across the company must support the Web-based e-commerce. For Web marketing, some marketing staff should participate or contribute their expertise in determining, designing, and on-going maintenance of the Web. The same can be said for Web production, systems administration, networking, database management, account management and customer service. The permanent nature of the Web-based e-commerce justifies the need to have a managing committee and/or an organizational unit in charge of all activities.

Since the development tools used in the Web-based e-commerce are still evolving, and some areas have no standards or different standards, staff developers must keep abreast with the technology. To this regard, companies should offer training opportunities to its staff. Major issues in staffing are:
(1) Should a task force or a permanent unit be established to develop and operate the EC?
(2) What should be the staff composition for the unit or task force?
(3) What is the relationship of this unit with the rest of the company?
(4) How to manage staff training and retention?

LEGAL AND REGULATORY BARRIERS

Management shall anticipate the legal and regulatory issues that might be relevant to the e-commerce. Again, Yen (1997), points out the areas for critical thinking are: marketing and advertisement contracting, payment systems, and dispute settlement. Other areas are interoperability, Internet security, standards, and format conversion and data interchange; cultural issues in global electronic trade; tariffs and taxation; uniform commercial code for e-commerce; intellectual property protection; and privacy.

CONCLUSION

In this paper, we reviewed the components of the Integrated Model of E-Commerce. Since management activities are on planning, resource management, scheduling, and controlling, we discuss their counter parts in managing Web-based e-commerce projects. In particular, we raised many important issues for consideration in the process of EC development. We do not claim the issues are complete and comprehensive, however, they do cover a broad range. We will be continuing doing this research in such a practical area. In conclusion, understanding the E-Commerce model and knowing the managerial issues involved are critical to the success of e-commerce project development.

REFERENCE

Austin, Thomas W. (1997). Betting on Digital Money. EC.COM, May, 8-10.

Charles, Carol A. Editor (1996). Globalizing Electronic Commerce. The Center of Strategic and International Studies, p. xviii.

Gould, Janet (1997). JEPI and Internet Payment Protocols. EC.COM, 3(4), May, 24-26.

Griffith, Griff (1996). Barriers to Electronic Commerce. Globalizing Electronic Commerce. Charles, Carol A. Editor, The Center of Strategic and International Studies, Washington, D. C., 29-38.

Kambil, Ajit (1997). Doing Business in the Wired World. Computer, 30(5), 56-61.

Kalakota, R. and Whinston, A.B., Editors. (1997). Readings in Electronic Commerce. Addison Wesley Longman, Inc.

Rapp, James B. (1997). Electronic Commerce: A Washington Perspective. Readings in Electronic Commerce. Kalakota, R. and Whinston, A.B., Editors. (1997), Addison Wesley Longman, Inc.

Tenenbaum, Jay M., Chowdhry Tripatinder S., and Hughes, Kevin (1997). Eco System: An Internet Commerce Architecture. Computer, 30(5), 48-55.

Tom, David, (1993). Effective Supply Chain Management. Sloan Management Review, Summer, 35-46.

Verity, John W., Hof, Robert D., Gaig, Edward C., and Carey John (1994). The Internet: How It Will Change the Way You Do Business, Business Week, November, 80-88.

Walsh, Brian (1998). Building a Business Plan for an E-Commerce Project. Network Computing, Vol. 9, No. 17, September, 69-75, CMP Media Inc.

Yarbrough, Lincoln (1997). EDI Over the Internet: DEIINT. EC.COM, 3(7), September, 22-26.

Yen, Vincent (1978). In Integrated Planning Model for Electronic Commerce.

A Case for Case Studies via Video-Conferencing

Ira Yermish, Ph.D.

Department of Management and Information Systems, Haub School of Business, St. Joseph's University, 5600 City Avenue, Philadelphia, PA 19131

610.660.1636 - 610.917.0165 (fax), IYermish@sju.edu

ABSTRACT

Demands are being placed on educational institutions to provide course content in new and complex forms to address the needs of an ever more mobile student body. This paper explores the issues of delivering a normally highly interactive graduate level course using these new technologies within the demands of organizational missions and constraints. The paper will argue that some course covering topics of organizational technology assimilation, is the ideal place to begin this process. It will describe the problems and issues that were faced in one typical course. We will also suggest that this is an ideal area to focus future research in organizational adoption of new technologies that address missions and strategies.

INTRODUCTION

The "passing of remoteness" is how one commentator described the phenomenon of the rise of the Internet and other distance-shrinking technologies. Ever since the advent of television, educators have wrestled with the viability of using this technology to reach wider audiences. Educational television facilitated the distribution of high-quality program content in a one-directional fashion. Yet for many educators, this approach lacked the interactive give-and-take so important to the educational process. Video-conferencing has been used heavily in industry to reduce the costs of travel within far-flung organizations. This technology made it possible to meet "face-to-face," even if the faces were a little blurry and movements were jumpy at best. The visual cues so often considered important in determining if messages were being properly communicated were now available.

Educational institutions have always lagged behind industry in adopting these technologies for financial reasons. The investment in the infrastructure to support these technologies was usually beyond the means of the organization. Yet these same constraints are tipping the balance toward the requirements to adopt these technologies. Resource constraints, particularly in the area of a scarce, high-quality faculty, competition among educational institutions for market share, and the declining technology costs and improvements in transmission quality are combining to drive experiments in this area.

In graduate business education, there has always been an emphasis on the interactive approach to education. Universities pride themselves on, and like to print glossy brochures about the interactive classrooms where the faculty and students conduct highly charged dialogues on topics of immediacy. One popular form of this dialogue is the case study approach. Similar to the kinds of activities one might find in a law school moot-court experience, potential managers must, with often limited and yet at the same time overwhelming data, process situations, explore options and develop recommendations. The instructor may provide a gentle push based upon the direction the class takes but shouldn't, assuming good case study pedagogy, be dominating a one-sided presentation. Unlike a lecture in nuclear physics, there is no way to predict the exact direction of the class interests - a very dynamic approach is required. How can the video-conferencing technologies address the needs of this very complex form of the educational experience? This paper will review one professor's experiences and organizational issues surrounding this issue and raise some future research questions that should be addressed to improve the quality and efficiency of this specific form of education.

INSTITUTIONAL BACKGROUND

St. Joseph's University is a medium-sized institution serving primarily the Delaware Valley markets. With 2,800 full-time undergraduates and nearly 5,000 part-time undergraduate and graduate students it has, especially since the 1960s served the "non-traditional" student market. Part-time MBA, Executive MBA, and industry specific masters' programs (e.g., Food Marketing, Pharmaceutical Marketing and Public Safety) were developed to reach specific educational market niches important within the general geographic area. As one narrows the focus of particular programs the need to serve larger geographic areas is inevitable. From the point of view of the program directors, any means of expanding this reach and hence filling up classrooms (read: generating more income) is desirable. This region has a large concentration of pharmaceutical companies and this market has been an especially valuable one for St. Joseph's. But, given the vagaries of highway arteries, students can be excused for their reluctance to brave rush-hour traffic to attend courses at our main campus. The approach frequently taken at institutions like St. Joseph's is the creation of "satellite campuses" in corporate training centers or in the facilities of other educational institutions closer to the students but without similar programs. Though only thirty miles from the main St. Joseph's campus, the campus of Ursinus College in Collegeville, Pennsylvania, has provided an excellent alternative for students to attend the evening MBA program. This campus is located near a concentration of pharmaceutical companies from which we draw a significant student population.

The approach to these "distance-education" sites has been simple: have the faculty face the Expressway rush-hour traffic, or fly to the remote city, instead of the students. A "customer-first" business strategy if ever there was one. From the administrator's point of view this worked beautifully and would continue to work well if it weren't for a countervailing pressure. In the effort to add more sections at the remote sites for student flexibility, the academic department chairs found it necessary to hire adjunct faculty to cover the increased number of sections. This actually exacerbated the problem, making these distance education sections even more profitable. Unfortunately, the pressures of perceived quality, largely brought on by the requirements of accreditation (AACSB, in this case) made the situation untenable. Full-time regular faculty coverage demands made scheduling problems a nightmare.

The president of St. Joseph's University, Nicholas S. Rashford, S.J., has always been interested in the use of technology in delivering education. He, and his academic cabinet, has been a strong supporter of technology. To this end, he created an *ad hoc* committee, the Distance Education Task Force, to explore how technology could be used to address these frequently conflicting organizational goals:
• Expanding Geographic Reach
• Expanding Programmatic Content
• Improving Educational Quality
• Reducing Educational Costs

One of the outcomes of this Task Force was a joint program with Ursinus College to establish a direct link between two technology-equipped classrooms. These facilities would be used to provide simultaneous classes on the two campuses, particularly to serve a number of graduate education programs (e.g., MBA and Health Administration). The two institutions agreed to invest in the technology to implement these classrooms to address these needs. Each site included a PictureTel facility for two-way video and audio including their LiveShare computer projection facility. This facility makes it possible to share computer applications running on PCs at either end of the T-1 dedicated line connection (with ISDN backup). On a large projector students could see PowerPoint presentations, videotapes, slides, or share comments on a whiteboard while the instructor or other students were being shown on one of the two monitors at the front of the class.

From a programmatic point of view, the most significant issue was the scarcity of faculty resources. For many narrowly focused courses, it was impossible to adequately cover the needs of the two campuses. This seemed like an ideal opportunity. As a member of the task force, I volunteered to offer my upper division, MBA course "Case Studies in Information Resource Management" as one of the first courses using the new facility.

COURSE DESCRIPTION

This course has been an integral part of our management information systems specialization in the traditional MBA (evening) program at St. Joseph's for many years. Using traditional textbooks (e.g., Applegate, et al 1996), updated Harvard case studies as well as some additional sources of special cases (e.g., Leibowitz and Khosrowpour 1997 or Wysocki and Young 1990), students explore through written and oral presentation, the current issues in strategic information technology management. During the fifteen-week semester students prepare individual case analyses and make formal group case presentations. Table 1 shows an outline of the assignments and course flow. A major goal of the course is to improve analytical and critical thinking skills. Creativity and cross-functional thinking is stressed throughout. There is very little lecture, just enough to emphasize critical conceptual issues.

The course is divided into three major phases.
* Individual Case Analysis
* Group Informal Presentation
* Group Formal Presentation

During the first phase, all students prepare the same set of cases for general class discussion. Short two or three page analyses are submitted at the time of the class to guarantee student preparation. The major goal of this phase is to address the conceptual issues and to give students feedback on the quality of their analytical processes. It is here that we can correct many of the defects in logical analysis. For example, students will frequently make one-sided recommendations without adequately exploring the possible negative arguments.

In the second phase, the class is arranged in teams of three to four students. Each team is responsible for the presentation and discussion of a case. All students are required to read all cases. To foster creativity and to give students an opportunity to get more comfortable with the process of presentation, this phase is ungraded. This does not mean, however, that there is no feedback. On the contrary there is much greater feedback from both the instructor and the students. Each presentation is evaluated by the class on the basis of content and presentation quality. There are often lively debates in this phase concerning the styles used. The only grading that is done during this phase addresses student participation.

In the final phase, each team makes a formal presentation of one of the cases (or case series). This presentation is formally graded by the instructor for content, flow, graphic presentation and ability to reply intelligently to questions.

I'm not sure I knew what I was getting myself into when I volunteered for this course. Despite participating in a short seminar for faculty describing the techniques of video-conferencing courses, I was not prepared for the new environment. As a free wheeling instructor, rarely locked into one place in a classroom, the demands of the technology often were frustrating and negatively affected the quality of the instruction. Add to this a problem of over-subscription (thirty-five students at the two sites instead of the normal twenty-five student limit) and we have the ingredients for disaster. Fortunately, we were able to get by some of the technical glitches which are almost guaranteed for a new facility. There were times when I would lose the train of thought as I was trying to make sure that each student was properly being shown on the screen for the remote site. Within about six weeks, we could handle to controls and still maintain control of the class content. But the lessons were learned. More about the administrative issues later.

From the students' standpoint there were a number of interesting opportunities in this first attempt in the Fall of 1997. For most of the students, despite working for large companies with corporate communications operations including video-conferencing, this was their first opportunity to engage in discussions that crossed the electronic video frontier. It didn't take too long to get both sides of the connection to participate in normal class discussions. The interesting events began during the informal presentation phase. Working with document cameras, presentation programs, automatic following video cameras and the like was a good experience for the students in learning one of the key concepts of the course: technology assimilation. They quickly learned that

Table 1 - Course Outline		
Date	Instructor Location	Assignment
Sep 1	SJU	Introduction, Minicases
Sep 8	URS	Text Chapters 1-5 (read text material only) Case 5-1 Mrs. Fields Cookies
Sep 15	URS	Text Chapters 6-9 Case 2-1 KPMG Peat Marwick: The Shadow Partner HBR 9-397-108 KPMG **Written case assignment number 1** on KPMG series
Sep 22	SJU	Text Chapters 10-13 Distance Education Workshop, Chat Rooms, Minicase
Sep 29		**Yom Kippur - No Class**
Oct 6	URS	Case 9-1 Toyworld Discussion, Developing Presentation Strategies that use the technology to its fullest
Oct 13	SJU	Electronic Commerce and the Virtual Organization Case 1-1 Veriphone, HBR 9-398-030 Veriphone Case 4-4 Open Market, HBR 9-198-006 Ford Motor Company **Written case assignment number 2**
Oct 20		**Spring Break - No Class** Paper evaluations will be e-mailed
Oct 27	SJU	**Informal presentations (with immediate evaluations)** **Written case assignment number 3 due with presentation** Group 1 Presentation: HBR 9-396-283 China's Golden Projects Group 2 Presentation: Case 4-5 Proctor and Gamble
Nov 3	SJU	Group 3 Presentation: Case 10-1 Xerox: Outsourcing ... Group 4 Presentation: Case 11-3 Chemical Bank: Tech Support
Nov 10	URS	Group 5 Presentation: HBR 9-198-007 Network Computing at Sun Microsystems
Nov 17	SJU	Review Evaluations - Group Meetings for Formal Presentations
Nov 24	SJU	**Formal presentations (e-mailed evaluations)** **Written case assignment number 4 due with presentation** Group 3 Presentation: National Mutual Series Group 4 Presentation: Air Products Series
Dec 1	SJU	Group 5 Presentation: Singapore Series Group 1 Presentation: Frito-Lay Series
Dec 8	URS	Group 2 Presentation: Burlington-Northern Series
Dec 15		Chat Room with Final Comments, Etc.

it was not easy to walk up to the podium, press the buttons and make a quality presentation. The interaction of technology and content became obvious to them.

A number of technical issues that are not present in local presentations surfaced. For example, the high quality graphics with complex color schemes that could be incorporated into a local presentation often took noticeable and annoying minutes to be transmitted between the stations. "Cute" presentation tricks like dissolves and fades didn't work smoothly. For this ungraded opportunity to gain facility, they were very grateful. During the second, a graded phase, they demonstrated significant improvements, demonstrating that most had learned the lessons of the first phase. These were translated into quality distance presentations that used the media to convey the message without being an intrusion.

In short, the students were able to learn how one information technology could be best incorporated within an organizational context. They learned how to modify their approaches to deliver messages and to engage in creative dialog across distances. Ideas easily flowed across the electronic barrier.

ADMINISTRATIVE ISSUES

This facility addressed one critical issue quite easily: faculty coverage. Given the number of students in this upper division course across the two campuses it resolved a need for adjunct faculty. This has been an important issue as St. Joseph's as it strives for AACSB accreditation. The requirement for greater coverage by regular full-time faculty has also been marketed by the University as providing a higher quality educational opportunity. Increasing opportunities and flexibility for students has always been a desire of the program directors while at the same time creating scheduling nightmares for the academic department chairpersons.

Another important institutional benefit from both the St. Joseph's and Ursinus perspectives has been the publicity associated with the electronically based alliance. As institutions compete more intensely for shrinking populations, this advantage could be significant.

From the academic standpoint, the faculty is gaining experience in using new technologies to deliver course content in new ways. In addition to the video-conferencing mode, we are beginning to use web-based technologies to share comments and conduct discussions. In this second semester of this course (Fall 1998) I have added a small component of this to the course structure. MBA students, often working full time and traveling in their work, appreciate the ability to write cases, transmit messages and get feedback from any location in the nation. Where some institutions are going toward completely remote distance education, St. Joseph's maintains the critical importance of a "home base" around direct student/teacher interaction within the structure. The terms of the alliance required that the instructor be at both locations during the term (see Table 1). From a business standpoint, students are addressing case issues in remote modes so similar to the kinds of problems described in some of their cases (e.g., Veriphone in Applegate, et al 1996).

Not all, however, is "sweetness and light" with this concept. From a student standpoint, there must be some diminution of perceived quality when the instructor is a small figure on a TV screen instead of a live being in a face-to-face environment. This must be balanced by the students with the increased flexibility in their educational opportunities afforded by this structure. From the faculty point of view there is a course organization is much more complex. There are issues of materials distribution (via FedEx, fax, e-mail, courier) and personal travel. There is the difficulty in getting to know students at remote locations. When dealing with a course like "Case Studies" these issues can be quite complex.

From the organizational perspective, these advances do not come cheap. In addition to the technology infrastructure required for the operation of these courses, there is additional overhead (e.g., technicians, hardware and software maintenance and equipment upgrades). The bar has been raised in education and institutions must invest to maintain growth and reputation.

Finally, there is the faculty compensation issue, an issue that St. Joseph's is struggling with at this time. Given the increased workload associated with distance learning course structures, how should faculty be compensated? A highly interactive course like "Case Studies" brings these issues to light rather clearly.

SUMMARY

"Case Studies in Information Resource Management" provides an excellent laboratory for studying how new technologies can be implemented in education. At a "meta" level, we can examine how the institution explores and adopts this technology for its educational "value-chain." How do we integrate video-conferencing, web-technologies and traditional printed materials in a seamless, effective way? When is it appropriate and how do the organizational missions and strategies affect the technology implementation strategies? This author sees this as an important new line of research in technology management within a critical industry.

BIBLIOGRAPHY

Applegate, Lynda M., F. Warren McFarlan, James L. McKenney, **Corporate Information Systems Management**: Text and Cases, Fourth Edition, Irwin, Chicago, IL, 1996,

Liebowitz, Jay and Mehdi Khosrowpour (editors), **Cases on Information Technology Management in Modern Organizations**, Idea Group Publishing, Hershey, PA, 1997.

Wysocki, Robert and James Young, **Information Systems: Management Practices in Action**, John Wiley & Sons, New York, 1990.

On a Unifying Notation of Uml Diagrams Based on Natural Language Paradigm

Alexandra Galatescu
Research Institute for Informatics, 8-10 Averescu Avenue, 71316 Bucharest 1, ROMANIA
Fax: 40 1 224 05 39, E-mail: agal@ std.ici.ro

ABSTRACT

Unified Modeling Language (UML) is recommended by Object Management Group as an object-oriented method for complex system analysis and design. It is intended to cover almost all aspects of OO modelling combined with process modelling and to facilitate distributed OO arhitectures. But, its overwhelming representation combined with the perspective of new symbolic extensions for future requirements of the object and process modelling entail the need for a uniformly represented and more flexible meta-model. The first part of the paper proposes a new notation for objects and processes analysis and design, called activity-centred graphs and based on natural language morphologic and semantic units and functions. It relies on the idea that natural language is an universal meta-model, able to describe any kind of information and activity. The second part of the paper compares this representation with UML basic notation and exemplifies the mapping of UML diagrams into activity-centred graphs.

1. INTRODUCTION AND MOTIVATION

UML (Unified Modeling Language) is recommended by OMG (Object Management Group) as a method for specifying, visualizing and documenting OO systems under development, during their requirements analysis, analysis and design steps (see [UML97a-g], [Booch96], [Harmon97] etc). It is intended to satisfy an old requirement of the systems' developers: a unique model from analysis to implementation, gradually detailed. The OO approach of such a model has become much more necessary since C++ and, lately, Java (i.e. OO programming languages) are going to have the greatest impact on the implementation of the today's information systems. UML is not intended to specify a methodology but, mainly, to provide and standardize a set of notational conventions, describing dedicated diagrams (use case, class, sequence, collaboration, state, activity, implementation diagrams). At least four reasons recommend UML:

- it unifies three already spread OO notational conventions: Booch notation, OMT (Object Management Technique) or Rumbaugh notation and Jacobson's OO Software Engineering (OOSE) notation. The benefit is that already exist modelling tools for these notations which, put together, would encourage the automatic representation of UML diagrams (a list of tools is given in [Harmon97]).
- it takes into account all three perspectives in information system development, previously separated in OMT [Rumbaugh91]: 1) *data perspective*, aiming at modelling the essential information to be represented in a system, 2) *functional perspective*, aiming at modelling the functions and the data flow between functions and 3) *control perspective*, aiming at modelling the dynamic, time-dependent behaviour of the system. The benefit is that both data-centric and problem-centric modelling approaches can use UML. Last approach is an important objective of business engineering and workflow modelling, detailed in [Taylor95], [Lawrence97], [Sheth96, 97], [Eder96] etc.
- UML diagrams provide conceptual means for information system developing, from analysis to their implementation. These diagrams anticipate the spreading of the three-tiered distributed OO architectures (client tier, Internet server tier and legacy application tier, exemplified in Figure 11(a)), as well as the use of object request brokers (based on CORBA standard architecture proposed by OMG and detailed in [OMG95], [Miller96], [Harmon97] etc).
- UML diagrams have a natural mapping to OO programming (even, automatic mapping by some existing OO modelling tools). The benefit is the increasing efficiency of the OO programming.

Nevertheless, from the viewpoint of the developers of the information systems, that are users of modelling tools as well, UML has shortcomings that cannot be overlooked for a long time:

- in its both manual and automatic use, UML has the psychological defect of being overloaded with symbols and notations, that the user (analyst or designer) should memorize;
- the main cause of UML overwhelming representation is that it is intended to cover almost all aspects of OO modelling combined with process modelling. However, any new requirement in object or process modelling will entail a new symbol/ notation in UML, or at least a new icon/ marker for a new stereotype, property or constraint (the build-in extensibility mechanisms of UML). For example, regarding the multidatabase objects, special types of attributes and relationships should be explicitly revealed in order to represent the global class vertical or horizontal fragmentation, the replication, the global-to-local mapping, the distributed topology etc. Also, new types of business or infrastructure objects are usually necessary, like objects with disjunctive meanings, groups of heterogeneously typed objects, expression-like objects etc. Or, we need explicit relationships among operations (e.g. operation subtyping), new inter-operation constraints, new constraints on the object interoperability etc.

In order to unify the notations in conceptual and process modelling, avoiding, as much as possible, the symbolic representation and foreseeing future extensions, the paper proposes a stylized linguistic notation, that observes the main units and functions in NL (Natural Language) morphology and semantics. Other functions may further refine its linguistic features. It relies on the idea that NL is an universal meta-model, able to represent any kind of information and activity. In this paper, UML plays the role of model (it answers the question "what to model?") and the proposed notation plays the role of meta-model (it answers the question " how to model?").

The paper is made up as follows: Section 2 presents the basis of the proposed notation; Section 3 compares it with NL and

UML main units and functions and exemplifies its abilities for representing the UML diagrams.

2. MOTIVATION AND PRESENTATION OF THE ACTIVITY-CENTRED GRAPHS

After the activity-centred graphs motivation in Section 2.2, their presentation will focus on the most important modelling requirements for the three determinatives of the real world: activities, objects/ concepts and processes.

2.1 Case Grammar and Thematic Roles

[Filmore68] has introduced the notion of 'case', that has evolved to what is called today 'case grammar'. Case grammar emphasizes the importance of the semantic/ thematic *roles* (cases) that the *nouns* play *relative to verbs* and the *adjectives* play *relative to nouns* in the sentence. Such roles are: AGENT, INSTRUMENT, PATIENT, EXPERIENCER, LOCATION, GOAL, SOURCE, DESTINATION etc. In order to be standardized, the abbreviated form of these roles and their classification appear in [ANSI95].

2.2 From Conceptual Graphs to Activity-centred Graphs in Conceptual Modelling

The appropriateness of the *semantic networks* (graph structures with labelled nodes and labelled links) in NLP (Natural Language Processing) has been revealed so far in the specialized literature (e.g. [Allen87]). In their common use, the word senses are represented as *nodes* and the relationships between the words senses, usually expressed by cases (thematic roles), are represented as *links*.

Conceptual graph (CG) *formalism* ([Sowa84,88,91a,91b], [ANSI95], [Catach85], [Fargue86], [Chein92] etc) is the most important example of this common use of the semantic network paradigm to NLP. CGs can be used for the semantic interpretation of the NL-based DB interfaces [Levreau91]. Also, CGs are a visual form of logic, with a natural mapping to first-order logic. CG abilities and previous use in modelling are synthesized in [Lukose96]. CG-based modelling languages previously developed (e.g. [Moller95], [Lukose96]), though based on 'extended' CGs, preserve two of their *basic rules*: 1) to represent only binary relationships among words and 2) to represent by nodes (called 'concepts') any category of words (object, property, action, event, state, point in time etc), excepting the prepositions, conjunctions, some adverbs, which are replaced by cases (called 'conceptual relations').

The consequence of the first rule is that the representation diagrams become overloaded for middle or large systems and only complicated and indirect structures could solve complex aspects in the real world. The consequence of the second rule is the uniform representation (see example in Figure 1(a)) of the nouns and verbs, hence, of the objects and activities, their counterparts in conceptual modelling. This might be acceptable for a data-centric modelling approach, where the interpretation and control of the system dynamics (object behaviour and functional activities) are less important as a modelling goal.

Star graphs [Chein92] change the CG first rule, allowing conceptual relations (cases) among *more ordered concepts* (see Figure 1(b)).

Activity-centred graphs (ACGs) ([Galatescu95, 97]) change the CG second rule mentioned above. They are star graphs with *two distinct categories of nodes* (concepts and activities) and *two main categories of links*: 1) thematic roles (<<role>>, see Sect. 2.3), standing for 'concept—operation' links or for 'active concept—attributive concept' links, and 2) inter-operation connectives (Sect. 2.5.5), as control statements.

As CGs, activity-centred graphs also allow the coreference link between two *coreferent concepts* (that refer to the same individual), see the dashed lines in Figure 1(a), 9(b), 12.

Figure 2 presents the graphic, linguistic and logical notation of an ACG.

ACGs main objectives are: 1) the representation of the main elements of the real world: *activities* and *objects/ concepts* that define *processes*, together with the *constraints* upon them and the *links/ dependencies* among them, 2) a unique notation for all phases of the system development cycle, from analysis to its implementation, 3) the approach to NL morphological rules, 4) the logical consistency of the representation, 5) the equidistance relative to various models for object and process analysis, design and implementation.

2.3 ACTIVITY Abstraction, Description, Specialization and Subtyping

2.3.1 Activity Abstraction and Description. Intended for abstracting and describing a real world activity integrated in a process/ system, an activity-centred graph unifies:

- *activity (operation) name* (type) in the process/ system definition;
- a *domain dependent description* of the activity, composed of: 1) the domain dependent *dynamic signature* of the corresponding operation, unifying the input, output and input-output concepts involved in the operation execution, as *actual parameters*; 2) local concepts participating in the operation execution, composing its *static signature*. Being directly involved in the activity execution, the concepts in this description are called *active concepts*.
- a *domain independent description* of the activity, composed of: 1) the domain independent dynamic signature of the operation, unifying the *unique roles* of the input, output and input-output concepts *relative to the operation* they are involved in. These roles stand for *formal parameters* in the operation description. 2) roles of the local concepts relative to the operation they describe.

Figure 3 represents the two-level description of a generic activity. Concept roles relative to operations may be abstracted by acronyms (see also [ANSI95]) like: AGNT (agent of the activity, i.e person or object that produces the activity), PTNT (patient, i.e object the activity operates upon), RSLT (result of the activity), INST (instrument to achieve the activity), RCPT (recipient, i.e person or object receiving the result of the activity), LOC (location of the activity), CHRC (characteristic of the activity), SRC (source of an activity or its initial state), DEST (destination of an activity or its final state), PART (part of another concept meaning a whole), TIME (point in time when the activity begins), DUR (duration of the activity), EVNT (event that stimulates the activity execution), DSCR (activity description), STAT (state of the activity), CAUS (activity cause), GOAL (activity goal), QTY (activity measure/ quantity/ degree/ approximation), COND (activity pre-condition), EXPT (activity exception) and so on. These roles force the designer think of the meaning of the concepts he is going to model and help build his model by *ACG sentences*, interpreted as in Figure 2(b).Each of the above roles has one or more prepositions, conjunctions or adverbs as *linguistic synonyms* such as: 'by' for AGNT, 'of', 'upon' for PTNT, 'into' for RSLT, 'with', 'through' for INST, 'at' for TIME, 'when' for EVNT, 'as', 'of' for CHRC, 'at','in', 'on', 'over', 'to', 'into' for LOC, 'from', 'out of' for SRC, 'to' for DEST, 'of', 'out of' for PART, 'like' for DSCR, 'for', 'to' for RCPT, 'for' for DUR, 'in', 'as' for STAT, 'because of' for CAUS , 'in order to', 'to' for GOAL, 'about', 'as' for QTY, 'if' for COND, 'unless' for EXPT.

With the above description of an operation, its processing may be achieved either by utilizing its domain dependent component or only by utilizing its domain independent one. The first case is the common use of the operation, which facilitates the implementation of the *operation polymorphism* (the same operation behaves differently when it is applied to objects from different classes), a feature of OO programming. The benefit in the second case is that, the domain independent description of the operation facilitates the *reusability of the operation processing* (the same procedure for the operation implementation can be executed for different types of concepts (or different classes, in OO modelling), only depending on the concept/ object roles). See for example the operation (ENTER) in Sect. 3.3.3. The standard meaning of these roles further helps for the operation reusability.

2.3.2 Activity (Operation) Specialization. Whereas the pure OO conceptual models only allow method-like operations, ACGs allow the definition and description of different types of operations.

Concept definition operations are dedicated to structuring the definition (intension) of different types of concepts (e.g. complex/ multiple/ group/ list concept types as well as their subtypes, see Sect. 2.4). In order to structure the class intension, pure OO models basically indicate the *tuple_of* and *part_of* operators.

Functional operations are dynamic operations that accomplish the system's functions (tasks) during its execution period. Processing the functional operations may be determined/ constrained by events (event concepts or event operations) or pre-conditions.

The simulation of the functional operations in OO conceptual models is not natural and increases the design complexity. In UML, they are naturally represented only in use case and in the activity diagrams.

As special kinds of functional operations, four groups might be separated:
* *event operations* that, besides the specific tasks they may accomplish, they also stimulate the execution of other operations. In OO approach, sending a message is the event that stimulates the corresponding operation (method).
* *knowledge acquisition operations* intended for accomplishing the static (declarative) functions of the system, operational in its modelling/ acquisition period;
* *dependence operations* as a special type of association operations. They reflect the way how one or more (*source*) *concepts* dynamically depend/ impact on one or more (*destination*) *concepts* (on their intension/ extension/ aggregation structure/ state etc).
* *interrogation operations* on the process repository, as knowledge retrieval units, used independently or as components of more complex interrogations.

2.3.3 Subtyping A Functional Activity. Using ACGs, the developers may define *activity subtypes by concept restriction* (denoted by $<_r$). It means the restriction to certain individuals/ conditions of one or more concept types involved in the structures describing a functional operation, such as: 1) *operation signature* (as in Fig. 9(a)) or 2) *operation identifier* (Sect. 2.4.4) or 3) *operation qualification structure* (Sect. 2.4.5). Activity subtyping partly solves the *activity polysemy* (different, usually non-disjunctive, meanings of the same activity-like word).

2.4 CONCEPT Abstraction, Quantification, Structuring and Qualification

2.4.1 Concept Typing. This is the first abstraction rule upon the concept representation, meaning that a concept has a domain dependent unique type, e.g. PERSON, CAR for individual persons and cars. A concept in a process will be identified by the unique pair [Concept_Type: individual], which addresses an object/ document/ image/ property/ event/ state/ identifier/ structure/ expression / (comparison/ logical etc) operator etc. Comparing with OO models, the concept type corresponds to the class name and 'individual' corresponds to a particular object.

2.4.2 Concept Subtyping. This is a lower-level abstraction rule upon concepts. It separates the concepts that have the same type into more categories, generally non-disjunctive. It solves the *concept polysemy* (different and non-disjunctive meanings of the same concept type [Sowa88]).

A concept subtype derives from a concept type, by applying to it one the following operations:
* *attribute restriction* (denoted $<_r$) of one or more:
* *identifying attributes* of the initial concept. A special example is the restriction of [Activity_Type] in the activity identifier [ActivityID] (an infrastructure complex concept type like in Fig. 4). It allows the directly use of the subtypes [atomic_activity] or [subprocess] that refine and restrict the activity identification and significance. Other examples are in Figure 7(b).
* *qualifying attributes* of the initial concept type. A special example is the subtype [suspended_activity] obtained by restricting the qualifying attribute [Activity_State] associated to the activity identifier in the qualifying graph in Sect. 2.4.5.

Concept subtyping by attribute restriction is a special kind of activity subtyping by restriction, applied either to the concept definition operation (Sect. 2.4.4) or to the concept (implicit or explicit) qualification operations (Sect. 2.4.5). On the other hand, when necessary, subtyping a functional activity is achieved by the restriction of the activity attributes unified in the activity identifier, which is a concept type as well.

* *type specialization* (denoted by $<_s$). Examples are: 1) [PRE_Condition], [POST_Condition] that specialize and may further be used instead of the general multiple type [MC_Constraint] (Figure 4(b)) or 2) [Time_Based_Condition], [Resource_Based_Condition] and [Cost_Based_Condition] that specialize the general list concept type [LC_Expression] (Figure 4(d)).
* *type renaming* (denoted $=_n$), e.g [Agent] could replace the type [Actor_Role] in Figure 3.

Concept subtyping is a special kind of definition operation. Other definitions appear in Sect. 2.4.4.

Unlike class subtyping in OO models, that may determine the creation of new physical classes, the concept/ activity subtyping here is just a virtual operation. Subtypes implicitly inherit the identification, description and qualification attributes of their supertypes, possibly restricted to certain values/ conditions. If a subtype needs new attributes (as in OO models), they will compose a new identification/ qualification structure for the subtype, appended to the structures already inherited from its supertypes.

Main benefits from concept/ activity subtyping are: 1) it accelerates the representation understanding, by refining the meaning of the concepts/ activities, 2) it accelerates the operation processing, by restricting the range of individuals involved in the operation execution. The extensions of the subtypes by restriction/ specialization are subsets of the extensions of their supertypes. 3) it facilitates inter-ontological requests by means of subtypes as inter-ontology relationships, similarly to the *synonyms* and *hyponyms* in [Mena98].

2.4.3 Concept Quantification. In an activity-centred graph, concept quantification has two forms:

* *logical quantification*, by means of 1) the universal quantifier " for 'any', 'all', 'every' and 2) two existential quantifiers: ∃ for 'must exist' (compulsory existence) and ∃? for 'may exist' (optional existence). Logical quantification facilitates 1) the logical interpretation of the operation description as a *rule* with the concepts preceded by " in its *premise* and with the concepts preceded by ∃, ∃? in its *conclusion* (see Sect. 2.6); and 2) the explicit specification of the compulsory or optional presence (instantiation) of the concepts in the operation execution.

* *associative quantification*, by means of the *concept plural*. Each concept may be either singular (an instance) or plural (composed of more instances). A plural concept may be either collective (whose elements represent together the respective plural concept) or distributive (whose elements may separately represent the concept and participate in operation). Collective plural is denoted by C{ } and the distributive one by D{ }. If necessary, the *plural cardinality*, is mentioned by C@n{ } or D@n{ }.

The distinction between the collective and distributive plural 1) gets the representation closer to NL and 2) refines the possibilities of the concept association during the operation execution.

2.4.4 Concept Structuring. It must help us create at least: 1) the definition/ identification structure of a concept type and 2) the dynamic composition structure of an aggregate concept.

Definition/ identification structure of a concept type is an activity-centred graph that describes the *definition operation* of the respective concept type. As examples, four definition operations might be useful in the infrastructure or business component of a process/ system:

* *complex type definition* is the operation that defines a *complex concept type* by means of (generally, immutable across sessions and internally used) attributes, usually identification attributes of the complex concept. In Figure 4(a), [ActivityID] is defined as an infrastructure complex type. Similarly, one can define identifiers for processes, users etc or business complex types as in Fig. 7, 9, 11.

Complex concept types correspond to both flat and complex (composite) objects in OO modelling.

* *alternative meaning selection* enumerates more disjunctive predefined meanings (represented by other concept types/ subtypes) of a *multiple concept type*. Usually, this is an infrastructure concept that allows the designer/ automatic process to select the appropriate meaning of the concept during the modelling/ execution session. In Figure 4(b), the multiple concept type [MC_Constraint] enumerates the three (suppose disjunctive) possibilities of constraining an activity: by time-based, resource-based or cost-based conditions. Multiple concept types solve the *concept homonymy* [Sowa88]. See also [MC_CustInfo] in Figure 7(b).

* *group composition* gathers more predefined (usually heterogeneous) concept types that have a common higher-level meaning (which may be called *group concept type*). Figure 4(c) defines a group concept that gathers the three kinds of conditions constraining an activity: pre, post and transition condition.

* *list concatenation* is the operation that concatenates predefined concept types. It creates a *list concept type*. For example, an expression is a list of concepts and operators (including NULL as list terminator), obtained by a recursive concatenation operation as in Figure 4(d).

Similarly, any new type of concept and the corresponding new definition operation might be further introduced, using the same representation rules as any ACG. The concept types with structured definition have, as individuals, instances of the corresponding ACGs instead of values.

The concepts involved in definition operations might have structured definitions as well (see Fig. 11).

Composition structure (tree) of the aggregate concept, as in OO models, may be considered the result of the dynamic synergy of three operators: aggregation (tuple_of), reference (part_of) and inheritance (consequence of an is_a operator). General examples of aggregate concepts are: organization structure of a company, assembling structure of a car, hierarchical structure of a process, hierarchical structure of a multidatabase schema, class intension etc. A predefined aggregate concept is [Salesorder] in Figure 7(b). Representing the three operators by ACGs has the following advantages: 1) it allows the uniform representation of the three operators, 2) it introduces an additional semantics on the composition tree, with impact on its domain independent processing, by the roles of the concepts it involves, relative to the composition operators.

2.4.5 Concept Qualification. It means the association of external properties (*attributive concepts*, possibly changeable across sessions) to active concepts (direct participants in operations). A straight way for concept qualifying is by *attributive roles* (e.g. CHRC (characteristic), POSS (possessor), DSCR (description) etc): [attributive_concept] ──ROLE──► [active_concept]

When we need to control the concept qualification (e.g in an acquisition process), this role-like relationship (as in CGs) may be simulated by an operator-like relationship (as in ACGs):

[active_concept] <<PTNT>> (SETTING) <<ROLE> > [attributive_concept]

In Figure 12, one may notice the difference between the qualifying role CHRC of the attributive concept [DILIGENT] (standing for adjective in the respective ACG sentence) relative to the active concept [BOY] and the role <<CHRC>> of the concept [DISTANCE:'near'], standing for adverb relative to (GO).

Activity qualification may be similarly solved using the infrastructure concept [ActivityID]. For example, the state of the activity, a permanently checked property, can be associated by:

[Activity_State:{inactive/ active/ suspended/ completed}] ──STAT──► [ActivityID]

Unlike other representations (including OO models), the attributive concepts (primitive or structured) are represented here as any concept and can become active concepts in other circumstances.

Qualification structure of an active concept joins all the attributive graphs that qualify it.

2.5 PROCESS Definition, Structuring, Integration, Navigation and Control

In order to master its complexity, the ACG-based process can be organized as a controlled diagram of *declarative and procedural modules*, simplified by *declarative and procedural encapsulation* and integrated by the *conceptual and procedural connectivity*, during both the process modelling and execution.

2.5.1 Declarative Modules. As declarative modules, one can use stand-alone, joint or coreferenced ACGs, externally represented during the process modelling and internally accessed during its execution. They are either the identification/ composition/ qualification structures of the concepts or the (possibly combined) descriptions of the functional/ acquisition/ dependence/ interrogation activities.

2.5.2 Procedural Modules. They define *subprocess-like activities* as controlled hierarchical subdiagrams of (atomic or subprocess-like) activities, components of the process diagram. A subprocess-like activity is the root (entry point) of the corresponding procedural module (see O-o, O2_1, O2_9 in Figure 5).

2.5.3 Declarative and Procedural Encapsulation. It is needed in process modelling and execution, in order to simplify and gradually reveal the complexity of the process. It is possible due to the contraction and expansion of the declarative and procedural modules (see the sample diagram in Figure 5).

Declarative contraction means the external compression of a declarative module to the name of the concept, structure or activity that module defines or describes.

Procedural contraction means the external compression of a procedural module to the name of the subprocess-like activity that module represents.

Declarative/ procedural expansion is the inverse operation versus the declarative/ procedural contraction. It reveals details on a concept, structure or atomic/ subprocess-like activity.

Nested declarative/ procedural encapsulation is needed when repeated embedded declarative/ procedural contractions and expansions are required during the process modelling or execution.

2.5.4 Conceptual and Procedural Connectivity. This is an important aspect of the process integration that reflects the *conceptual and procedural constraints* imposed on the process structure and execution.

Conceptual connectivity means the relationships (or conceptual dependences) among two or more activities belonging to the same process or to different processes. Conceptual connectivity is closely related to the software engineering principles of module coupling and cohesion. There are three types of inter-concept relationships that can be defined among two or more ACGs: 1) by join on a common concept/ subgraph, 2) by concept coreference and 3) by concept transfer among operations (activities).

Join on a common concept/ subgraph determines the simplification of the process external diagram and space saving in the process repository, by representing the common concept just once. One can join:
- *a non-definition operation and the definition structures of the involved concept types.* For instance, the generic (OPERATION) in Figure 3 with the identifying structures of the concept types [ActivityID] and [GC_On_Activity_Constraint].
- *two or more non-definition operations.* For example, (OPERATION) in Figure 3, as main operation, with a possible operation describing [Invoked_Application], as a collateral operation;
- *a non-definition operation and the qualifying structures of the involved concepts* like in Fig. 12; etc.

Concept coreference associates two (different or identical) concept types that address the same individual concept within two different graphs, separately processed. An example is the coreference between the operations activated by the same agent (see the dashed lines in Figure 1(a), 9(b), 12). It solves what may be called the *concept anaphora*.

Figure 12 shows how ACG sentences are correlated by join and coreference. The graphs (I), (II) and (II), (III) are coreferent because the concept [BOY:John] is coreferent with the concept [PERSON:John]. The graphs (I) and (II) are joint on the concept [HOME]. The graphs (II) and (III) are joint on the concept [SCHOOL]. Without the contextual correlation between them, the graphs (I), (II), (III) may be considered independent of each other. The operation (HAVE) may be represented and stored as *collateral operation* for the operation (GO).

Concept transfer (data/ knowledge flow) among atomic operations (described by ACGs) is a function that associates the input concepts of an operation with some output concepts issued from previously executed operations. A transfer function can be processed either domain dependently, or domain independently, by correlating the domain dependent or independent descriptions of the involved operations.

Procedural connectivity in a process means the logical/ semantic constraints among atomic/ subprocess-like activities, belonging to the same process or to different processes. They mainly consist of 1) *navigation and control rules* throughout the process structure (e.g. parallel or sequential routing, AND-Split, OR-Split, AND-Join, OR-Join met in UML), 2) *decision conditions* on the sequence of activities within a process (e.g. transition conditions in UML) and 3) *transfer functions* among subprocesses, in addition to the concept transfer among atomic activities (see above). Next subsection will sketch these three aspects of the procedural connectivity in ACG representation.

2.5.5 Control Statements in the Process Structure. An ACG-based process may be represented as a diagram of functional operations (ACG sentences), standing for *executable statements*, whose execution is controlled by *control statements* (that correlate ACG sentences, see Figure 5, 6, 9(b), 10(b)). The control statements that constrain the navigation throughout the process structure are represented as inter-operation connectives (acronyms) and may have the following meanings: 1) *operation semantic grouping* (GROUP); 2) *operation refinement*, inferred from connectives that specify the *semantic specialization* (SPEC), *compulsory or optional execution* (MUST or MAY), *alternative* (but not necessarily disjunctive) *execution* of the child operations (CASE); 3) *execution timing*, by THEN, BFOR, AFTR between two operations; 4) *(exclusive) disjunctive execution* (OR, XOR); 5) *execution conjunction* (AND); 6) *execution negation* (NOT); 7) *imperative execution* of the operation that follows DO or RSLT; 8) *conditional alternative execution*, by IF-THEN-ELSE, depending on a procedural decision condition (see below); 9) *conditional repetition*, by

WHILE-DO, depending on a procedural decision condition; 10) *unconditional,* compulsory or optional, *repetition,* by MUST RE-PEAT or MAY REPEAT; 11) *purpose subjunctive execution* of an operation, by GOAL (preceded by an operation whose execution is motivated by the execution of the operation that follows GOAL); 12) *operation description,* by DSCR, that introduces the description of an operation as one or more correlated operations; 13) *execution stimulation,* by EVNT, that introduces an *event operation* stimulating another operation; 14) *execution starting point in time,* by TIME, that introduces the starting point in time of the operation as a *time condition* (a predicate condition of operations, whose true value is automatically associated to a certain point in time). This list may be enlarged. Each control statement has a natural counterpart in logic (e.g. in predicate calculus, see Sect. 2.6), that ensures the correctness of its processing and helps us control the logical consistency of the process.

A general and flexible implementation of such a core of control statements first impacts on the process modelling, that becomes closer to a visual programming and an appropriate frame for implementing visual expertise (or debugging) functions. Secondly, it impacts on the activity scheduling and control that, lately, requires a flexible and domain independent approach, broader than the techniques currently used. The standard meaning of each control statement, as well as its implicit logic, allow its processing independently of the actual operations it connects (similarly to the programming language processing). Third, these NL-oriented connectives of the ACG sentences improve the process understanding during its modelling period and facilitate the process linguistic interpretation, in a more formalized way than the additional texts usually used as explanations.

2.5.6 Decision Conditions. The decision strategy, composed of transition (continuation) conditions, generally unifies two kinds of conditions, that both naturally complete the ACG representation:

- *conceptual conditions,* as predicate expressions composed of concepts and logical/ comparison operators. During the process execution, they are verified at certain decision points along the process structure and are correlated with the control statements at the respective points. The true value of a conceptual condition depends on the current values of the involved concepts, matching certain predefined values or subconditions. See CASE connective in Figure 9(b), 10(b).
- *procedural conditions,* as predicate expressions composed of activity identifiers and logical operators. They are intrinsic components of the conditional control statements (e.g. IF-THEN-ELSE, WHILE-DO) and their true value depends on the truth values of the component activities at the current moment during the process execution. For example, an activity may be true if it has already been executed and false otherwise. These conditions are necessary because, although the activity identifiers are concepts (see Figure 4 (a)), generally they cannot be used in conceptual conditions, because of the different interpretation of their true values.

2.5.7 Transfer Functions (data /knowledge flow) Among Subprocesses (procedural modules). Concept transfer between a parent (caller) process/ subprocess and the child (called) subprocess is reflected in the signature of the subprocess-like operation, the root of the procedural module that refines it. This signature, say SUBPROCESS ($I_1, I_2, \supset, I_m, O_1, O_2, \supset O_n$), is composed of non-disjunctive sets of input and output concepts and has a domain independent counterpart (composed of the invariant roles of the parameters relative to SUBPROCESS operation). There is a one-to-one correspondence between any input concept in this signature and an output concept of a previously executed activity (within a parent or ancestor subprocess), where the concept was defined. The input concepts for SUBPROCESS are further passed to its child operations. The output concepts from SUBPROCESS may be defined (instantiated) in and acquired from its child operations. They are passed to a subsequent activity inside of the parent (sub)process.

For both forward and backward transfer, among atomic or subprocess-like activities, if the correspondence is among the domain independent descriptions of the activities, the transfer becomes domain independent as well. This approach together with the preoccupation for *decreasing the number of concepts in the dynamic signature of the operations* help us loosen the strength of the (declarative or procedural) module coupling. This is an important objective of the module coupling, as a software engineering principle: minimizing the number and strength of the inter-connections between modules.

2.6. Logical Consistency of the ACG-based Processes

Logical consistency of an ACG-based process basically derives: 1) from the logic of the ACG notation, sketched in this section, 2) from the validity (already proved in the specialized literature) of the structured design and software engineering principles like modularity, encapsulation, connectivity, 3) from the rigurous control of the user and system actions relative to that process. The theoretical support of this control also relies on the logic of the ACG declarative and procedural/ transactional notation.

This section deals with the logical inference (for simplification here, in first order logic) inside both the declarative and procedural modules representing ACGs and their connections. It tries to suggest 1) the generality of the ACG notation, 2) the support for a general processing of ACGs, meaning the processing of combinations of logical rules corresponding to the modelled ACGs.

2.6.1 Activity-centred Graph as an n-order Predicate. Each operation OPERATION(Concept_Type$_1$, $\supset$, Concept_Type$_p$) (and, implicitly, the graph that describes it) is an n-order predicate if there exists at least one structured concept CONCEPT$_i$, "i Œ1:p, which is an (n-1)-order predicate, because its l-definition (see below) contains (n-2)-order predicates and so on.

2.6.2 Logical Inference Inside Activity-centred Graphs. Universal quantifiers in ACG notation help us impose the following *rules on the logical inference inside an ACG*: 1) the premise is a conjunction of the concepts preceded by a universal quantifier; 2) the conclusion is a conjunction of the concepts preceded by a (compulsory or optional) existential quantifier; 3) the same conclusion should be valid for each component of a plural concept in the premise of the inference; 4) an operation uniquely associates a concept (or a component of a plural concept) in the premise with each concept in the conclusion.

These rules suggest a partition of an ACG like:

(I) "[concept$_1$]   ∃[concept$_2$: C{}]
        <<role$_1$>   <<role$_2$ >>
        (OPERATION) <<role$_3$> ∃[concept$_3$]

into its premise (II) and into the two components of its conclusion ((III) and (IV)):

(II) [" [concept$_1$:x]]   **(III)** [[x] <<role$_2$> (OPERATION) <<role$_2$> ∃[concept$_2$:C{}]]
(IV) [[x] <<role$_1$ > (OPERATION) <<role$_3$ > ∃[concept$_3$]]

After a further transformation of the plural, the inference inside the graph (I) becomes:

(V) ("x) ((concept$_1$(x) ∧ role$_1$(x)) ⊃ (∃S) (∃z) (set(S) ∧ ("y∈S) (concept$_2$(y) ∧ role$_2$(y) ∧ concept$_3$(z) ∧ role$_3$(z) ∧ OPERATION (x,y,z))))

The above rules can be applied to complex declarative modules (joint or coreferent graphs) as well.

In formula (V), the roles and the plural notations have been transformed into monadic predicates. Variables 'x', 'y' and 'z' have a *double semantics*: 1) that of the domain dependent concept types they refer to and 2) that of the OPERATION-dependent roles. This second meaning of the concepts helps represent the graph by a non-positional and domain independent predicate: OPERATION (role$_1$, ⊃, role$_3$).

2.6.3 Logic of the Attributive Graphs and Qualification Structures. An attributive graph like: [attributive_concept] ROLE [active_concept] that qualifies an active concept is represented by a binary predicate ROLE (attributive_concept, active_concept). It is a positional, domain dependent and, possibly, an n-order predicate. The logic inside an attributive graph may be represented in predicate calculus by:

("a) (attributive_concept (a)) ⊃ (∃c)(active_concept(c)) ROLE (a,c). Hence, each attributive concept must be associated with at least one active concept. Qualification structure of a concept 'c' unifies its attributes 'a$_1$',..., 'a$_n$' by the conjunction of its attributive graphs: Q(c)=Role$_1$(a$_1$, c)∧...∧Role$_n$(a$_n$, c).

2.6.4 Logical Consistency of the Procedural Modules. It is mainly ensured by the logic of the inter-operation connectives. Each connective may be associated with a *constraining inference rule*, whose *premise* is the last activated operation (denoted by PO) and, implicitly, all the previously activated operations for a given concept and whose *conclusion* is the conjunction (or disjunction) of the operations proposed for the process continuation and denoted by O, O$_{i1}$,⊃, O$_{in}$.

In order to represent the mapping rules of the inter-operation connectives into predicate calculus, the following notations will be used: 1) *x, y* individuals of output concept types of PO operation, transferred to its child operations, 2) ⊃ the compulsory activation of the implied operation, 3) ∧ the conjunction of the operations or rules, 4) ∨ the disjunction (exclusive or not) of operations or rules, 5) ==> the transformation into predicate calculus of an inter-operation connective, 6) NULL, a null (ineffective) operation.

The transfer (or sharing) of at least an output concept of the operation in the premise to the operations in the conclusion of the inference rule is implicitly supposed. It justifies the logical correlation between operations, aiming at operating on, at least, a common concept.

Sequential Execution of the Operations

PO *THEN / BFOR* O ==> ("x) ((PO (x) ⊃ O (x)) ∧ ¬ (O (x) ⊃ PO (x)))

PO *AFTR* O ==> ("x) (∧(PO(x) ⊃ O(x)) ∧ (O (x) ⊃ PO (x)))

PO *MUST* Oi$_1$, ⊃, Oi$_n$ ==> ("x) ((PO (x) ⊃ Oi$_1$ (x)) ∧ ⊃∧ (PO (x) ⊃ Oi$_n$ (x)))

PO *MAY* Oi$_1$, ⊃, Oi$_n$ ==> ("x) ((PO (x) ⊃ (Oi$_1$ (x) ∨ NULL)) ∧ ⊃∧ (PO (x) ⊃ (Oi$_n$ (x) ∨ NULL))) **Or**

PO (*MAY* ∧ *conceptual_condition*) Oi$_1$, ⊃, Oi$_n$ ==> ("x) (((PO(x) ∧ *conceptual_condition*) ⊃ (Oi$_1$(x) ∨ NULL)) ∧⊃∧ ((PO(x) ∧ *conceptual_condition*) ⊃ (Oi$_n$(x)∧NULL)))

PO *SPEC* Oi$_1$, ⊃, Oi$_n$ ==> (∧PO) ∧ (∃x) (Oi$_1$(x) XOR ⊃XOR Oi$_n$(x)), PO usually is a virtual operation

PO *DO / RSLT* O ==> ("x)(PO (x) ⊃ O (x))

Alternative Execution

IF *procedural condition THEN* O$_1$ / *ELSE* O$_2$ ==> (∃x) ((*procedural condition*(x) ⊃ O$_1$ (x)) ∧ (∧ *procedural condition*(x) ⊃ O$_2$ (x)))

PO *CASE* Oi$_1$, ⊃, Oi$_n$ ==> ("x) (PO(x) ⊃ Oi$_1$ (x) ∨ Oi$_2$(x)∧⊃∨ Oi$_n$ (x)) **Or**

PO (*CASE* ∧*conceptual_condition_value*) Oi$_1$ ⊃,Oi$_n$ ==>("x) ((PO(x) ∧ *conceptual_condition _value$_1$*) ⊃ Oi$_1$(x)∨ (PO(x)∧*conceptual_condition _value$_2$*) ⊃ Oi$_2$(x)∧∨(PO(x)∧*conceptual_condition _value$_n$*) ⊃Oi$_n$ (x))

Iterative Execution

WHILE procedural condition DO O ==>(∃x)((procedural condition(x)⊃O(x))∧(∧procedural condition(x) ⊃ NULL))

PO *MUST REPEAT* ==> ("x) (∃y) (PO (x) ⊃ PO (y)). To avoid the infinite loops, NULL will be instead of 'y' when the repetition ends. This is a declarative end. PO stops after its expansion/ start.

PO *MAY REPEAT* ==> ("x) (∃y) (PO (x) ⊃ (PO (y) ∨ NULL)). This is a procedural end of the repetition that stops before PO expansion/ start.

Logical Execution

PO *AND* O ==> ("x) ((PO (x) ⊃ O (x)) ∧ (O (x) ⊃ PO (x))) (sequential AND)

PO *OR* O ==> ("x) ((PO (x) ⊃ (O (x) ∨ NULL)) ∧ (O (x) ⊃ (PO (x)∨ NULL)))

PO *XOR* O ==> ("x) ((PO (x) ⊃ ∧ O (x)) ∧ (O (x) ⊃ ∧ PO (x)))

NOT O ==> ("x) (∧ O (x)), x an input concept of O .

Grouped Execution PO *GROUP* Oi$_1$, ⊃, Oi$_n$, (with compulsory Oi$_1$, ⊃,Oi$_k$ and optional Oi$_{k+1}$, ⊃, Oi$_n$) ==> ("x) (PO(x) ⊃ (Oi$_1$ (x) ∧⊃∧ Oi$_k$ (x)∧ (Oi$_{k+1}$(x) ∨ NULL) ∧⊃∧ (Oi$_n$ (x) ∨ NULL)))

Operation Description PO *DSCR* DO ==> ("x) (PO (x) ⊃(∃d) DSCR(d)), where DSCR(d) = (Id) l-definition(DO)[d] 'd' is an instance of PO description defined by the operation DO.

Operation Motivation PO *GOAL* O ==> ("x) ((PO (x) ⊃ O (x)) ∧ (∧O (x) ⊃ ∧PO (x)))

Operation Stimulation EO *EVNT* O ==> ("x) ((∃e) EVNT (e) ⊃ O(x)), where EVNT(e) = (Ie) l-definition(EO)[e] 'e' is a particular event and 'l-definition (EO)' is the l-expansion of the event operation EO.

Operation Starting time_condition *TIME* O ==> ("x) ((∃t) (time_condition (t) ⊃ O(x)))

't' is a certain point in time when the time_condition becomes true.

A *conceptual condition* on one of the above control statements changes the logic of the statement. It either facilitates the automatic selection among alternative operations, like in the second form of CASE or just refines the decision for continuation like in the second form for MAY.

Operation modality is another constraint that, in the present form of the ACG notation, is reduced to the operation obligation (by 'must' and 'may' verbs preceding the operation type). It may be extended to verbs expressing possibility, intention, wish, belief, etc., relative to the operation execution.

2.6.5 Logical Support of the Declarative and Procedural Encapsulation. Declarative and procedural encapsulation relies on the l-definition of the declarative modules (stand-alone, joint or coreferent ACGs) and of the procedural ones, as presented in this section.

l-*definition of A Stand-alone Operation.* Each operation has a corresponding l-expression that defines it. For the operation represented in a linear notation: (OPERATION) -

$$<<role_1>> \quad " [CONCEPT_1]$$
$$<<role_2>> \quad \exists [CONCEPT_2] \supset\supset$$
$$<<role_p>> \quad \exists?[CONCEPT_p]$$

the respective l-expression in predicate calculus will have $x_{i1}, \supset, x_{ik}$ (the input/ output/ input-output parameters, with $\{x_{i1}, \supset, x_{ik}\}\tilde{A}\{x_1, \supset, x_p\}$) as bound variables:

OPERATION = $l(x_{i1}, \supset, x_{ik})$ $(x_{j1}, \supset, x_{j(p-k)})$ $("x_1)(CONCEPT_1(x_1) \wedge role_1(x_1)) \supset (\exists x_2) \supset (\exists x_p)$
$(CONCEPT_2(x_2) \wedge role_2(x_2) \wedge \supset \wedge (CONCEPT_p(x_p) \vee NULL) \wedge (role_p(x_p \vee NULL))$ OPERATION $(x_1, \supset, x_p)$

NULL helps represent the concept optional existence ($\exists$? in the ACG graphic or linear notation).

l-*definition of A Structured Concept.* Each structured concept 'x' has a corresponding l-expression for its definition graph. In predicate calculus, the respective l-expression will have x as a bound variable:

STRUCTURED_CONCEPT= (lx) $(x_1, \supset, x_n)$ $("x)(STRUCTURED\_CONCEPT(x) \wedge RCPT(x)) \supset$
$(\exists x_1) \supset (\exists x_n)(CONCEPT_1(x_1) \wedge role_1(x_1) \wedge \supset \wedge (CONCEPT_n(x_n) \vee NULL) \wedge (role_n(x_n \vee NULL))$
DEFINITION_OPERATION $(x, x_1, \supset, x_n)$

l-*definition of A Procedural Module.* Suppose that a procedural module is a controlled hierarchical diagram composed of OPERATION$_1$, $\supset$, OPERATION$_n$, with OPERATION$_1$ the root of the module. And $O_{ij=}$(OPERATION$_i$, IOC, OPERATION$_j$) are the tuples representing direct connections (by means of interoperation connectives) between two component operations of the module. Each tuple O_{ij} will be a rule in predicate calculus, according to the corresponding IOC transformation in Sect. 2.6.4.

l-definition of the procedural module, with OPERATION$_1$ as root, will be the conjunction of O_{ij} tuples (and implicitly of the rules they represent): OPERATION$_1$ = $l(x_{11}, \supset, x_{1k})$ $(\wedge O_{ij})_{i,j}$, with $(x_{11}, \supset, x_{1k})$, the parameters of OPERATION$_1$, as bound variables.

3. A UNIFYING NOTATION OF UML DIAGRAMS USING ACTIVITY-CENTRED GRAPHS
3.1 UML Diagrams in the System Development Cycle

[Harmon97] summarizes the five phases of the system development cycle (requirement analysis, analysis, design, code and test) and the UML diagrams distributed to the first three phases. These phases compose an iterative (cyclical or spiral) approach of the system development, allowing the developers to gradually increase the complexity of the system project and, finally, of the system prototype. This cyclical approach becomes much more efficient when a unique model is used along all the five phases and new details are added from a phase to the next one and from a cycle to the next one. Such a unique model is intended to be UML. UML diagrams can be used alone or together with other non-official, but accepted, diagrams, mainly for the requirement analysis phase, such as: LOVEM (Line of Vision Enterprise Methodology) diagrams for BPR (Business Process Re-engineering) workflow analysis, Jacobson's OOSE (Object Oriented Software Engineering) Ideal Object Model or CRC (Classes, Responsabilities and Collaborators) Cards.

Officially, the distribution of the UML diagrams along the first three phases is as follows:
- for the requirements analysis phase, UML provides the notation for use case diagrams;
- for the analysis and design phases, UML provides four groups of diagrams:
- static structure diagrams: class diagram and object diagram;
- interaction diagrams: sequence diagram and collaboration diagram;
- state diagrams: state diagram and activity diagram;
- implementation diagrams: package diagram, component diagram and deployment diagram.

Generally, for each group of UML diagrams, new symbols and notations have been introduced ([UMLa-g]). Section 3.3 will exemplify how all these groups of UML diagrams can be represented by ACGs, whose main notations are summarized in Section 2.

3.2 Conceptual Comparison of the UML and ACG Notations
The intended comparison is synthesized in Table 1 that advocates for the following general conclusions:
- all notations (CG, ACG, UML) have a counterpart to NL main morphological units, structures and functions, but ACG and CG mapping into NL constructions is natural, direct and general. Most UML symbols are indirectly associated with NL morphological constructions.
- a wide range of UML symbols and notations can be represented by a small and unitary set of symbols in ACGs. The implicit meaning of the UML symbols and notations have been transferred to the explicit meaning of the names of the ACG nodes (concepts, operations) and links (roles, connectives). The same symbol is used for whatever concept/ operation/ connective. Only the concept/ operation/ connective name and intrinsic meaning are changed. The benefit is that the symbols associated to the same kind of nodes/ links will be implemented by similar types of internal structures. Only the procedures (for operation execution, concept definition or inter-operation control) will differ, depending on the nodes/ links meanings.
- CG formalism has a more reduced set of conceptual elements. It has only one type of nodes and one type of links. But, the same application has a more complicated solution using CGs instead of ACGs. The main reasons are that ACG representation 1) unifies more binary CGs in the operation description, 2) adds structuring rules, close to the software engineering principles: modularity,

encapsulation and connectivity, already familiar to the system developers and users, 3) introduces (relative to CGs) or extends (relative to UML) the explicit procedural semantics of the operation and process control, in earlier phases (analysis and design) of the system development cycle.

• ACG and CG notations are equidistant relative to any particular model (relational, OO, workflow, functional etc) in comparison with UML which is mainly dedicated to OO reasoning and modelling. Consequently, a one to one correspondence between the ACG/ CG external structures and their internal counterparts becomes natural, whatever is the implementation model.

Table 1 Comparative study on the conceptual characteristics in Real World, Natural Language, Activity-centred Graphs, Conceptual Graphs and Unified Modeling Language

Real World	NL	ACGs	CGs	UML
Complete assertion, attitude, question etc	Sentence	An ACG	One or more CGs	- Diagram - Subdiagram
Complex idea, situation, application	Phrase/ Paragraph etc	- Decl. module - Procedural module	Context	Use Case/Package/ Diagram
Object, abstract notion, place, event, quality (simple/complex)	Noun (simple/ compound)	Active Concept (primitive/ with structured def.)	Concept (primitive/ complex)	Object (flat/ composite)
Action, state, attitude (simple/ complex)	Verb (simple/ compound)	Operation (activity) (atomic/ subprocess)	Concept (primitive/ complex)	- Message (method) - Complex transition
Object feature, quality (simple/ complex)	Adjective (single/multiple)	- Attributive concept - Qualif. structure	Concept (primitive/ complex)	Object attribute (value/complex struct.)
Action characteristic	Adverb	- Active Concept - Descrip. operation	Concept	- Operation property - Attribute of assoc.
Anaphora (backward reference)	- Pronoun - Anaphoric art.	- Concept coref. - Procedural cond.	Concept coreference	- Reflexive assoc. - Object lifeline
Role of Object in Action	Preposition/ Conj. / Adverb	Concept-operation role	Thematic role	- Role in association - Role in interaction
Inter-object Relationship	Conjunction (copulative/ disjunctive etc)	- Depend. operation - Implicit AND in operation descrip.	Thematic role	Association/Dependency /Aggregate composition / Message
Inter-operation Relationship	- Conjunction - Conjunctive adverbs	Inter-operation connective	Thematic role	-Simple/complex transition - Control icons both in activity diagrams
Object Plural	- Cardinal of individual noun -Collective noun	Concept plural (distrib./ collective)	Concept plural distrib. / collective /default/ cumulative	- Object multiplicity in association - Multiobject
Object Quantification and Modality	-Noun quantifier - 'there is' construction	Concept quantifiers "(any, all)/ ∃(must exist)/ ∃?(may exist)	Concept quantifiers (universal (") / existential (∃))	Object multiplicity in association
Action Modality	Modal verb	Modal verbs must/ may before operation name	Conceptual relation PSBL -possibility OBLG-obligation etc	Decision symbols in activity diagram
Object Type–Instance Dichotomy	Noun, Proper noun	[Concept Type: individual]	[Concept Type: referent]	object:Class
Specialized meanings of Objects/ Actions	Word Polysemy	- Activity subtyping - Concept subtyping	Concept subtyping	- Class specialization - Interface
Encrypting the knowledge on Objects/ Actions	-Human Knowl. - Metonymy - Anaphora	-Decl. encapsulation - Procedural encapsulation	Contraction/ expansion of the concept λ-definition	Packing - class definition - diagram
Disjunctive meanings/ possibilities of Objects/ Actions	Word Homonymy	- Multiple concept - CASE connective - Activity specialization	Separate concept types	- Separate classes - Decision among activities - OR split in transition - Stereotypes
Question	Interrogative sentence	Interrogative operation with (?) before concept	Proposition with (?) instead of referent	' Query' property of the operation
Embedded Objects/ Ideas / Actions etc	Embedded sentences	Nested declarative/ procedural modules	Nested contexts	- Composite objects - Nested states

3.3 Mapping UML Diagrams to Activity-centred Graphs

A straight way to make understandable the UML-ACG mapping is by comparative examples of the two representations. The brief SalesWeb application defined in [Harmon97] will be resumed here and transformed into ACG representation. For space saving, the ACG linear notation will be used.

3.3.1 Mapping UML Use Case Diagram to Activity-centred Graph Notation. A UML use case diagram is intended to describe the main processes (use cases) in a system and the interaction between processes and external systems or individuals, called actors. Graphical diagram is completed with use case descriptions (scenarios). Each scenario is a set of *sentences* that describe a step of the interaction between the use case and an actor. Later, in the design phase, each sentence will be transformed into more types of diagrams.

Using ACGs, the UML diagram in Figure 6(a) becomes the procedural module in Figure 6(b) (that groups the three subprocess-like operations) together with the initial descriptions (ACGs) of the three operations. The UML scenario that describes each use case will be replaced by one or more procedural modules that refine the initial process together with the declarative modules that describe the new operations. Describing scenarios by ACGs instead of texts forces the analysts to better and sooner organize their ideas on the intended system.

3.3.2 Mapping UML Static Structure Diagrams to Activity-centred Graph Notation. *Class diagram* shows the classes to be included in the system and the relationships among them. *Object diagram* usually instantiates parts of the class diagram, in order to show context-specific properties of and relationships among certain objects of the previously represented classes. UML class diagram contains more kinds of symbols for representing: the class intension (attributes and methods), their association (physical/conceptual connection between two or more classes), dependency relationship (that indicates whether one of the elements in the association changes when the other one changes), the class inheritance, interfaces, part-whole relationships, constraints etc.

Figure 7 exemplifies the mapping of some UML symbols to ACG notation. One may notice that all types of relationships in UML have become operations described by ACGs (definition, dependence, subtyping or functional operations). Object multiplicity has become concept plural combined with concept quantification. 'Custinfo' specialization has been solved by three infrastructure concepts (a multiple concept and two subtypes). The operations (Accounting_ACCESS) and (Inventory_ACCESS) might be subtypes of a generic operation (Application_ACCESS), because they have the same domain independent description. But, they are redundant here because the two operations directly appear as invoked methods (checkCredit) and (checkItem) in Figure 9.

3.3.3 Mapping UML Interaction Diagrams to Activity-centred Graph Notation. *Sequence diagram* (or event trace diagram) shows the relationships between specific objects, namely, how messages (events) are sent between objects and how long the objects remain active. Objects participate in the interaction by their lifelines (vertical lines showing their active existence) and the messages they exchange are arranged in time sequence. *Collaboration diagram* shows the ordered flow of the messages between objects. The links between objects are here numbered and labeled with the names of the operations called by the corresponding messages between objects. Figure 8 represents the sequence and collaboration diagrams for the sales example in [Harmon97]. One may notice that, in the sequence diagram, the messages that activate the objects are texts that should be later described, by the description of the methods they activate.

In the corresponding ACG notation in Figure 9, the correlation between objects is directly expressed by the name of the methods (operations), that have here their initial description (ACG), comprising at least the correlated concepts/ objects. The diagram in Figure 9(b) looks rather overloaded because of the concepts and concept-operation roles, additionally represented in the ACG procedural modules. They might be missing in the process diagram, without losing information, because they necessarily appear in the signatures of the respective operations in Figure 9(a).

Other conclusions which one may draw from Figure 9 are:
- UML sequence and collaboration diagrams are simultaneously represented by ACGs, because the operation control (Fig. 9(b)) intersects the objects connection in the operations description (Fig. 9(a)).
- the diagram can be divided into modules: 1) procedural modules (e.g. the module corresponding to the subprocess operation (Item_ENTER) in Figure 9(b)) and 2) declarative modules (ACGs), as those represented in the linear notation in Figure 9(a).
- ACG notation refines the operation control in comparison with the UML interaction diagrams, where the messages appear only in their sequential (chronological) order. As one will notice later, the diagram in Figure 9(b) functions instead of a UML activity diagram as well.
- the roles of the objects/ concepts in the operation execution, revealed in the ACG diagrams, help the developer identify the class which that operation would better belong to (in OO implementation).
- using the domain independent signatures in the operations processing, all three ENTER-like operations in Fig. 9(a) can be processed by a unique procedure for the generic operation ENTER (AGNT, PTNT, PART). PART might be the role of a multiple concept, whose disjunctive meanings, corresponding to the components of the aggregate concept [SalesOrder] (Fig. 7(b)), are consecutively selected by the sales person. This is an example of *operation reusability* for different concept types (Sect. 2.3.1).

3.3.4 Mapping UML State Diagrams to Activity-centred Graph Notation. *State diagram* shows how a specific object changes its states. This diagram is important for tracking the object evolution (see more aspects in [Edelw97]). *Activity diagram* is, in UML, a special type of state diagram. It describes the activities, data flows and the decisions between activities. In UML, the activity diagram is attached to a class, to the implementation of an operation (method) or to a use case. The state diagrams are mainly used when asynchrounous events occur, whereas the activity diagrams represent the procedural flow and control of the events (which mainly mean the completion of internally-generated actions). Figure 10(a) represents a UML state diagram. A corresponding activity diagram will use the same notations, but instead of direct correlations between the three activities (states), a decision symbol (the traditional diamond shape) will be used to indicate the alternative activities.

The corresponding ACG diagram (Fig 10(b)) just adds new nodes (operations, concepts) and links (connectives) to the previously represented ACG diagrams.

3.3.5 Mapping UML Implementation Diagrams to Activity-centred Graph Notation. *Package diagrams* show how classes could be divided into modules. They are logical diagrams that do not necessarily imply a physical division of the classes. *Component diagrams* are used to show the intended physical modules. Each package has a component counterpart. *Deployment diagrams* allow the representation of the physical (distributed) platforms, as well as the needed network connections. Each of these diagrams introduces the symbols shown in Figure 11(a).

In ACG notation (Figure 11(b)), a UML package becomes the implementation instrument of a procedural module that describes the procedural flow of a subprocess-like operation (the root of that module). For instance, [SalesWeb_program] is the main instrument of the subprocess (Report_Sales) in Figure 6(b). The logical location (parent process) or the physical location (site) of this subprocess can be both mentioned in the definition of this instrument or in the signature (ACG) of the subprocess-like operation. The sites, on the other hand, can be described and linked inside ACGs, as any concept type.

4. CONCLUSIONS

Apparently, the model notation is less important while modelling tools offer an automatic help to the developers of complex systems. However, real life has proved that the popularity of a model depends on its simplicity, in both notation and semantics, and on its approaching to human reasoning (e.g. ER model and its variants). On the other hand, the system complexity has so much increased lately that very simple models are not satisfactory any more. Today, models/ representations from more computer science domains (e.g. DB, AI, BPR, workflows) tend to combine. OO models and now UML are examples in this respect.

All these models abstract parts of real life, that people usually describe in NL, as the lowest-level abstraction of their life. ACGs are a new attempt to close the conceptual modelling to NL, considered an universal meta-model. They might be an appropriate starting point toward this objective. ACG notation is liable to improvements, additions or changes. An intended change regards the symbolic notations of the nodes and links in order to obtain a user-friendly interface of these graphs. ACG linguistic features may also be improved. Concept and activity subtyping using ACGs also deserves a thoroughgoing study for the future creation, correlation and comparison of different (distributed) domain ontologies.

The comparison with UML notation was, firstly, intended to reveal the diversity of aspects that might be represented by ACGs. Secondly, it was intended to emphasize the main general advantage of ACGs versus UML: its natural extensibility, issued from the different approach of the conceptual abstraction. As in NL, in the ACG approach, the meaning of the symbols used in other models (including UML) has been transferred to the meaning of the words (nodes and links). Along the paper, other particular advantages have been revealed.

So far, the activity-centred graphs have been experienced for automating a general multidatabase modelling process and for the analysis and design of a hospital information system.

5.   REFERENCES

[Allen87] Allen J.: Natural Language Understanding. Benjamin/Cummings Publishing Comp., Inc., USA, 1987.

[ANSI95] IRDS Conceptual Schema. Part 1: Conceptual Schema for IRDS. Part 2: Modeling Language Analysis. ANSI Report X3H4/93-196, appeared in 1995

[Booch96] Booch g., Rumbaugh J, Jacobson I.: The Unified Modelling Language for Object-Oriented Development. Rational Software, USA, 1996

[Catach85] Catach L.,Fargues J.: Deduction et operation pour le modele des graphes conceptuels.IBM Paris Scientific Center, 1985

[Chein92] Chein M.,Mugnier M:Conceptual Graphs: fundamental notions. Rev. d'intellig. artif.,vol. 6-no 4/1992

[Edelw97] Edelweiss N., Oliveira J.:Roles Representing the Evolution of Objects. JAIIO'97 Conf., Brasil, 1997

[Eder96] Eder J., Groiss H., Liebhart W.: Workflow Management and Databases. Proc. 2eme Forum International d'Informatique Appliquee, Tunis, 1996

[Fargue86] Fargues J., Landau Marie-Claude, Dugourd A., Catach L: Conceptual graphs for Semantics and Knowledge processing. IBM Journal of Research and Development, vol. 30, nr.1, Jan.1986

[Filmore68] Filmore C.J.: The case for case. In Bach. E, Harms R. (Eds): Universals in Linguistic Theory, New York, Holt, Rinehart and Winston, 1968

[Galatescu95] Galatescu A: An Activity-based Ontology Using Conceptual Graphs. Intl. Symp. KRUSE (Knowledge Retrieval, Use and Storage for Efficiency), Santa Cruz , USA, 1995

[Galatescu97] Galatescu A: Toward a Unifying Representation of Concepts, Processes and Knowledge Flows using Activity-centred Graphs. 7th Workshop on Knowledge Engineering: Methods & Languages (KEML97) (ftp://swi.psy.uwa.nl/pub/keml/keml.html), Milton Keynes, UK, 1997

[Harmon97] Harmon P., Watson M.: Understanding UML: The Developer's Guide. With a Web-base Application in Java. Morgan Kaufmann Publishers, Inc., USA, 1997

[Lawrence97] Laurence P. (Ed): Workflowf Handbook. John Wiley&Sons, 1997

[Levreau91] Levreau G., Meunier J., Bouzeghoub M., Metais E.: Definition d'une Interface Language Naturel pour la Conception de Bases de Donnees. Rap. tech. MASI91.45, Inst. Pascal, Paris, 1991

[Lukose96] Lukose D.: MODEL-ECS: Executable Conceptual Modelling Language. Proc. of Knowledge Acquisition Workshop (KAW96) (http://ksi.cpsc.ucalgary.ca/KAW/KAW.html), Banff, Canada, 1996

[Mena98] Mena E.,Kashyap V.,Illarramendi A.,Sheth A.: Domain Specific Ontologies for Semantic Information Brokering on the Global Information Infrastructure. Conf. on Formal Ontologies in Inform. Systems, Torino, 1998

[Miller96] Miller J., Sheth A., Kochut K., Wang X.: CORBA-Based Run-Time Architectures for Workflow Management Systems. Journal of Database Management, Special Issue on Multidatabases, 7(1), 1996

[Moller95] Moller J., Willems M.: CG-DESIRE: Formal Specification Using Conceptual Graphs. Proc. 9th Knowledge Acquisition Workshop (KAW'95), Banff, Canada, 1995

[OMG95] Object Management Group: Common Facilities Architecture 4.0, 1995

[Rumbaugh91] Rumbaugh J., Blaha M. et al..: Object-Oriented Modeling and Design. Prentice-Hall, 1991

[Sheth96] Sheth A., Georgakopoulos D., Joosten S., Rusinkiewicz M., Scacchi W, Wileden J., Wolf A.: Report from the NFS Workshop on Workflow and Process Automation in Information Systems. UGA-CS-TR-96-003, (http://lsdis.cs.uga.edu) Univ. of Georgia, USA, 1996

[Sheth97] Sheth A., Kochut K.: Workflow Applications to Research Agenda: Scalable and Dynamic Work Coordination and Collaboration Systems. Proc. of NATO Advanced Study Inst. on Workflow Management Systems and Interoperability, Turkey, 1997

[Sowa84] Sowa J.: Conceptual Structures: Information Processing in Mind and Machine. Addisson Wesley, Reading, Mass., USA, 1984

[Sowa88] Sowa J.F.: Lexical Structures and Conceptual Structures, in Semantics in the Lexicon. Edited by J.Pustejovsky, Kluwer Academic Publishers,1988

[Sowa91a] Sowa J.F.(Ed): Principles of Semantic Networks. Explorations in the Knowledge Representation, Morgan Kaufmann Publ., USA, 1991

[Sowa91b] Sowa J.F.: Toward the expressive power of the natural language. Principles of Semantic Networks. Explorations in the Knowledge Representation, Morgan Kaufmann Publ., 1991

[Taylor95] Taylor D. : Business Engineering with Object Technology, John Wiley, 1995

[UML97c] UML Semantics, v1.1. OMG (http://www.omg.org). 1997

[UML97d] UML Notation Guide, v1.1. OMG (http://www.omg.org). 1997

[UML97e] UML Extension for Objectory Process for Software Engineering. OMG (http://www.omg.org). 1997

[UML97f] UML Extension for Business Modeling. OMG (http://www.omg.org). 1997

[UML97g] Object Constraint Language Specification OMG (http://www.omg.org). 1997

A Framework for Representing and Reasoning with Information Systems

Choong-ho Yi

Dept. of Information Technology, University of Karlstad, S-651 88 Karlstad, Sweden

Tel: +46-54 700 11 61, Fax: +46-54 700 14 46, E-mail: choong-ho.yi@kau.se

ABSTRACT

This paper presents a formal approach to ISE, where an IS is viewed from two perspectives, namely representation of IS and reasoning with it, but still within one framework, using a first order many-sorted temporal logic. A formal semantics has been provided for some fundamental aspects of an IS in an integrated manner, i.e. temporal (time, action duration), static (state) and dynamic aspects (the effects of action, state change).

1 INTRODUCTION

Most of traditional approaches within Information Systems Engineering (ISE) have been based on using a collection of several graphical symbols, e.g. boxes, circles and arrows, as their main language. Such languages are usually given semantics in an informal manner. Consequently, it's difficult to represent clearly the basic concepts necessary for an IS, e.g. state, action, change, which, in turn, makes it more difficult to maintain and utilize systematically the information expressed in such a way. To cope with the difficulties a number of formal approaches have been proposed during the past decade. While each of them has certain advantages for the domain it has been designed for, some fundamental aspects of an IS are still missing in one or more approaches. For example, 1) *time* is not considered in, e.g. Z [Spivey 92], VDM [Andrews 88] or Statechart [Harel 87] and it is not clear how time can be integrated into them. 2) While in reality actions have *duration*, and different actions may have different length of duration, they are often considered without time, e.g. in OASIS [Lopez et al. 92] and ERAE [Dubois et al. 88]. In other words all actions are understood to be instantaneous, and we cannot express that some business activities (e.g. a supply from USA to Sweden by ship) may take longer time (say, a month) than others (e.g. an order by telephone). 3) In some object-oriented approaches, e.g. TROLL [Jungclaus et al. 96], a *state* is defined w.r.t. an object, i.e. state of an object. However, it may cause difficulties when reasoning about several objects at the same time unless all the states of the objects involved are synchronised. 4) Most of them focus on representation issues, e.g. the expressive power of a proposed language; whether the language supports any method for structuring, e.g. classification, complex concepts. But, connection to *reasoning* level, i.e. how to manipulate the represented information to obtain more and useful information of sorts, e.g. simulating the behaviour of the system in different situations; proving that the system satisfies some desired properties, has not been studied enough yet.

This paper outlines a formal approach to ISE, suggesting solutions to the drawbacks of previous approaches pointed out above. An IS is viewed from two perspectives, namely representation of IS and reasoning with it, but still within one framework, using a first order many-sorted temporal logic. A formal semantics has been provided for temporal (time, action duration), static (state) and dynamic aspects (the effects of action, state change) of an IS in an integrated manner, based on Features and Fluents [Sandewall 94].

2 A MANY-SORTED TEMPORAL LOGIC FOR INFORMATION SYSTEMS ENGINEERING

The key features of the language will be illustrated by defining it for an example of IS which contains typical business objects and processes: Customer orders a product from a supplier; supplier supplies a customer with an item of the product type which has been ordered; supplier invoices a customer for an item; customer pays a supplier for an item. For a complete definition of the logic, please refer to [Yi 99].

2.1 Syntax

As in any many sorted logic the syntax begins with defining symbols for different types: A set P= {Agent, Product, Item, Nat} of symbols for the object types agents (customers and suppliers), products, items and natural numbers (to describe, e.g. price of a product), respectively, and the symbols Time for time points, Property for properties of objects, and Action for actions.

Then a set F of constant, function and predicate symbols that are typed over the above types are introduced:

constant symbols of types $\mu \in \Pi \cup \{Time\}$

function symbols Prop: $\pi_1 x...x\pi_n \rightarrow$ Property

function symbols Act: $\pi_1 \%...x\pi_n \rightarrow$ Action

predicate symbol holds: Property x Time

predicate symbol occurs: Action x Time x Time

The binary function symbols + and – over numbers (i.e. Time and Nat$\in \Pi$), and the binary predicate symbols < over numbers and = for equality will be used. The triple Σ = <Π, Time, Φ> is a *signature*. In addition typed variable symbols I for Item, P Product, Ag Agent, N Nat and T Time (may be indexed, e.g. Ag1, Ag2 etc), propositional connective symbols $\{\neg, \wedge, \vee, \rightarrow, \leftrightarrow\}$, quantifier symbols {®, ∃}, and parenthesis symbols {(,)} will be used in the language.

Function symbols Prop of type Property (simply property symbols in the sequel) are intended to describe relations between objects of different types. For example, given in F the function symbol

price_of: Nat x Item $\rightarrow$ Property

the function price_of(N, P) represents the assertion that "The price of the product P is N". Properties are used as objects in the predicate holds, which has been defined over properties and time in order to deal with time-related assertions. The predicate

holds(price_of(N, P), T)

states that "The price of the product P is N at time point T". Other properties that will be used for our example are as follows: item_of(I,P) "I is an item of product P"; owner_of(Ag,I) "Ag is the owner of I"; ordered(Ag1,Ag2,N,P) "Ag1 has ordered P from Ag2 with order number N"; supplied(Ag1,Ag2,N,P) "Ag1 has supplied P to Ag2 with order number N"; invoiced(Ag1,Ag2,N1,N2) "Ag1 has invoiced Ag2 with amount N2 for order N1"; paid(Ag1,Ag2,N1,N2) "Ag1 has paid N2 to Ag2 for order N1". This presupposes, of course, the corresponding property symbols, e.g. item_of: Item% Product ‡ Property be defined in F.

Function symbols Act of type Action (simply action symbols in the sequel) denote actions involving, as their arguments, objects of different types p_i. For example, given in F the action symbol

order: Agent x Agent x Nat x Product $\rightarrow$ Action

the function order(Ag1, Ag2, N, P) stands for an action "Agent Ag1 orders product P from agent Ag2 with N as a unique reference number assigned to the order ". The agents pair is used to represent communications between multiple agents, and to trace capabilities and responsibilities of the agents concerning the action. The predicate

occurs(order(Ag1, Ag2, N, P), T1, T2)

asserts that the action order(Ag1, Ag2, N, P) occurs over the time period T1, start time point, and T2, end time point. Therefore *action duration* can be represented. Other actions needed for our example include, e.g. supply(Ag1, Ag2, N, P, I) meaning that "Concerning the order with reference number N, Ag1 supplies Ag2 with an item I of product type P". Again, the action symbol be defined in F.

The *vocabulary* Λ of the language consists of a signature Σ = <Π, Time, Φ> and a set D of domains, where D is a set of object domains $D\pi_i$ and time domain D_{Time}, i.e. Λ = <Σ, D>. For our example we assume a small set D as follows: $D_{Product}$ = {p1, p2}, D_{Item} = {i1, ..., i4}, D_{Agent} = {ag1, ag2, ag3} and D_{Nat} = D_{Time} = {0, 1, 2, ...}, i.e. the set of natural numbers is used for both Nat and Time.

2.2 Semantics

Let Λ = <Σ, D> be a vocabulary. Then a *state* S is a mapping from terms of type Property all of whose arguments are object names, e.g. item_of(i1, p2), to {t, f}. However, for syntactical convenience, a state will be expressed as "an interpretation of properties", i.e. as a mapping from property symbols to a set of the ordered tuples of objects which, together with the property symbols, constitute property terms that have been mapped to t. For example, the mappings item_of(i1, p1) x f, item_of(i1, p2) x t, ..., item_of(i4, p2) x t will be compressed simply as item_of x {(i1, p2), ..., (i4, p2)}. Therefore we are using *system states*, not object states. The state S below describes a state of our system where i1 and i4 are items of the product p2, and i2 and i3 are of p1; the agent ag1 owns i4, ag2 i3, and ag3 i1 and i2; the price (of every item) of the item p is $28; no order, supply, invoice or payment have been made.

S = {item_of x {(i1, p2), (i2, p1), (i3, p1), (i4, p2)}, owner_of x {(ag1, i4), (ag2, i3), (ag3, i1), (ag3, i2)},

price_of x {(28, p1), ..}, ordered x Ø, supplied x Ø, invoiced x Ø, paid x Ø }

A *state log* SL is a mapping from D_{Time} to states. Given a time point T, SL(T) then represents the state of the system at the moment of time. An *action log* AL is a mapping from D_{Time} to a set of tuples <A, T1, T2> where A is a term of type Action, all of whose arguments are object names, and T1 and T2 are time point names for start and end time. Thus given a time point T, AL(T) then represents the set of actions with their duration that have been completed successfully at that time T. The pair <SL, AL> is a *history*. Then an *interpretation* I is a tuple

<D, K, SL, AL>

where K is a mapping from constant symbols to their domains. The predicates holds and occurs are evaluated as follows.

If Prop(O1, ..., On) is a Property term and T is a Time term, then I(holds(Prop(O1, ..., On), T)) = true iff SL(I(T))(Prop(I(O1), ..., I(On)) = t.

If Act(O1, ..., On) is an Action term and T1, T2 and T3 are Time terms, then I(occurs(Act(O1, ..., On), T1, T2)) = true iff I(T1)<I(T2) and AL(I(T2)) u (Act(I(O1), ..., I(On)), I(T1), I(T2)).

For example, in an interpretation I= <D, K, SL, AL> where, for time point 5, SL(5) is the state S described above, and AL(5)= {<order(ag1, ag2, 1001, p2), 4, 5>}, the atomic formulae holds(owner_of(ag1, i4), 5) and occurs(order(ag1, ag2, 1001, p2), 4, 5) are assigned the truth value true. However, the formula holds(owner_of(ag3, i4), 5) is false in I. Note, object names, e.g. p2, and time point names, e.g. 5, are mapped to themselves in any interpretation: I(p2)=p2 and I(5)=5. The predicates = and < are interpreted as usual.

3 REPRESENTATION OF INFORMATION SYSTEMS

In order to represent an IS in our logic, we define a vocabulary $\Lambda = <\Sigma, D>$ for the system first, where Σ is a signature $<\Pi$, Time, $\Phi>$ and D is a set of object domains $D\pi i$ and time domain DTime. Then the system is described successively by those components that characterise the system. As such components we identify invariants I, a set A of pre- and postconditions of actions, a set R of business rules and a pair G for business goals. The pair

$<\Lambda, <I, A, R, G>>$

then represents the system. This component-oriented structure is motivated to provide in one framework the overall view of the system, but also to maintain the representation in a modular way.

3.1. Invariants

The component I is a collection of logic formulae expressing constraints on the states of the system, i.e. constraints on relationships between object types that must hold in all states. For example, the formulae

"T"I∃!P holds(item_of(I,P), T)

"T"N holds(∃!Ag1∃!Ag2∃!P ordered(Ag1,Ag2,N,P) ∨ ¬∃Ag1∃Ag2∃P ordered(Ag1,Ag2,N,P), T)

describe that at any moment of time, for all items, exactly one product exists; that at any moment T, for every order number N, at most one order, i.e. a tuple (Ag1, Ag2, P), may exist, respectively. Here we are using syntactical sugars. ∃! is used as a quantifier denoting "exactly one". Thus the first formula above is an abbreviation of "T"I (∃P1 holds(item_of(I, P1), T) ∧ "P2 (item_of(I,P2) → P1=P2). Also, let φ, φ1 and φ2 be property terms, and • denote any of the connectives ∧, ∨, → and ↔, then holds(φ1, T) • holds(φ2, T) ≡ holds(φ1•φ2, T); ∧holds(φ, T) ∫ holds(∧φ, T); "Vholds(φ, T) ∫ holds("Vφ, T); ∃Vholds(φ, T) ∫ holds(∃V φ, T).

Actually, the formulae in I are obtained by translating E-R style diagrams, and the two formulae above are partial translation of the diagram below.

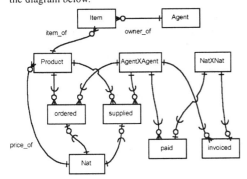

Notice in the graph, while Product, Item, Agent and Nat are object types (and are associated with object domains), ordered, supplied, invoiced and paid are compositions of the object types and are expressed as properties, like item_of, owner_of and price_of, in logic. In addition, other classification methods like partition, specialisation and generalisation etc. can be formalised similarly, though they are not presented in this paper. The one-to-many constraints, e.g. that from Product to Item ("for a given product, none, one or many items exist"), will hold in any state. That's why they have not been translated in the formulae above.

3.2 Actions

The pre- and postconditions of actions are defined in the component A. Let A be an action, then the functions precond(A) and postcond(A) return the preconditions and postconditions, i.e. effects, of the action. These conditions are expressed as a mapping from a subset of Property terms to {t, f}. For example, given

precond(supply(Ag1, Ag2, N, P, I)) =
{ordered(Ag2, Ag1, N, P) x t, item_of(I, P) x t, supplied(Ag1, Ag2, N, P) x f, owner_of(Ag1, I) x t }
postcond(supply(Ag1, Ag2, N, P, I)) =
{owner_of(Ag1, I) x f, owner_of(Ag2, I) x t, , supplied(Ag1, Ag2, N, P) x t }

the preconditions of the action supply(Ag1, Ag2, N, P, I) are: P has been ordered between Ag1 and Ag2 with order number N; I is of type P; P has not been supplied yet, (i.e. no item of the product type has been delivered); I is available to Ag1 (for delivery). The postconditions can be understood in the same way.

3.3 Business Rules

Business rules in *R* are intended to prescribe what and how to do in different business situations. The rules are expressed as logic formulae using properties, actions, time and predicates over these entities. For example, the rule

max_delivery_time(T) ≡
"Ag1"Ag2"N"P"T1"T2 (occurs(order(Ag1, Ag2, N, P), T1, T2) →
∃!I∃!T3∃!T4 (holds(item_of(I, P), T3) ∧
occurs(supply(Ag2, Ag1, N, P, I), T3, T4) ∧ T2≤T3 ∧ T4-T2≤T))

states that whenever a customer Ag1 orders a product P over [T1, T2], after order is completed (T2≤T3), an item I of the product type is to be delivered exactly once within T days (T4-T2≤T), assuming that all time points are expressing dates. Business rules represented as such, i.e. capturing dynamic, static as well as temporal aspects, provide rich expressiveness and flexibility, and are suited for implementing goals.

3.4 Goals

A characteristic of goals is that they are usually highly abstract, e.g. customer_satisfied ("the customers should be satisfied").

In order to make such a goal operational, we decompose it into subgoals at a lower level using AND/OR graphs, e.g. AND(prompt_delivery, purchase_on_credit) which means "the customers should get prompt delivery" and "the customers should be allowed to make a purchase on credit". Decomposition process continues until the subgoals can be implemented in terms of business rules described in Subsection 3.3. For example, the subgoal prompt_delivery can be implemented by the rule max_delivery_time(7); purchase_on_credit may be either decomposed further into subsubgoals or implemented by a rule, etc. Formally, G is a pair of goal decompositions and goal implementations.

4 REASONING WITH INFORMATION SYSTEMS

One major benefit of formal representation is that it serves as a base for *formal reasoning*. As a connection from representation to reasoning, this paper outlines reasoning with goals where goals are used as guiding principles for (business) activities. State log and action log (see, Subsection 2.2) play a main role here. As time elapses, the logs are extended for successive time points according to what happens in the system: If an action is evoked in a state which satisfies its precondition, then the action will be performed successfully, which results in i) changing the state of the system with the action's postconditions (see, state update function below), and ii) adding the action to the action log; if the precondition does not hold in the start state, the action can not be completed and the system state is not changed. Precise definitions follow:

Let S be a state and let postcond(A) be given for an arbitrary action A, then the *state update function*

S ÷ postcond(A)

returns a new state which results from updating S by postcond(A) such that every mapping $\rho\xi\tau$ in S, where ρ is a property term and $\tau\in\{t,f\}$, is changed to $\rho\xi\upsilon$ if $\rho\xi\upsilon\in$ postcond(A) and $\upsilon\in\{t,f\}-\{t\}$, but remains unchanged otherwise.

As an example, if S= {q(a)xt, q(b)x t, q(c)xf, ...}, or S= {qx{a, b}, ...} using syntactical simplification, where the property symbol q is defined over an object domain {a, b, c}, and postcond(A)= {q(a)xt, q(b)xf}, then (S ÷ postcond(A))= {q(a)xt, q(b)xf, q(c)xf, ...}, or simply {qx{a}, ...}.

Let S be an initial state. As time passes, the now time n of the system advances from the initial time 0 with one unit successively and, accordingly, the state log SL and action log AL are defined for every n such that

1) if n= 0, then SL(n)= S and AL(n)= ∅;

2) if an action A is evoked over time period [T, n] with 0£T<n and precond(A)⊆SL(T), then
SL(n)= (SL(n-1) ÷ postcond(A)) and AL(n)∈ <A, T, n>;

3) SL(n)= SL(n-1) and AL(n)= ∅ otherwise.

Reasoning is then performed in model theory of logic, i.e. using interpretations I = <D, K, SL, AL>, each of which assigns true or false to logic formulae (see, Subsection 2.2). The main idea behind the formal reasoning is, that a business goal is satisfied in a business process if at least one interpretation exists which assigns true to both (the formulae expressing) the process and (the business rule implementing) the goal. The reasoning is described in detail in [Yi 99], but roughly in three steps below:

1) A business process is constructed as a set of predicates occurs(A,T1,T2) and formulae describing constraints on the action occurrences in the language. The process may exist already in the enterprise, or be proposed as a possible process in the future.

2) Check whether at least one interpretation exists which assigns true to the business process. Such an interpretation is then a model of the process. If yes, it means that the process may take place successfully. Continue to 3). But if no, the process can not be performed in any way. Go to 1).

3) Select one or more goals of interest. Check whether the formulae implementing the goals are also true in the model of the process from 2). If yes, the goals are achieved in the process, which is a desirable situation. If no, however, the goals are violated by the process. Then we may find an alternative process by modifying it or constructing a new one. Go to 1).

5 CONCLUSIONS

We have shown how an IS can be not only represented but also reasoned about within a single framework. An IS has been represented as a structure consisting of vocabulary, invariants, actions, business rules business goals. A formal semantics has been provided in an integrated manner for some fundamental concepts within ISE, i.e. time, duration, state, the effects of action and state change. Then as an example of reasoning we have shown reasoning with business processes (actions) and goals based on the semantics. It is our hope that our work complements previous formal approaches suggested within ISE.

REFERENCES

[Andrews 88] D. Andrews. Specification Aspects of VDM. *Information and Software Technology*, Vol. 30, No. 3, pp. 164-176, 1988.

[Dubois et al. 88] E. Dubois, J. Hagelstein and A. Rifaut. Formal requirements Engineering with ERAE. *Philips Journal of Research*, Vol. 43, pp. 393-414, 1988.

[Harel 87] D. Harel. STATECHARTS: A Visual Formalism for Complex Systems. *Science of Computer Programming* 8:231-274, 1987.

[Jungclaus et al. 96] R. Jungclaus, G. Saake, T. Hartmann and C. Sernadas. TROLL- A Language for Object-Oriented Specification of Information Systems. *ACM Transactions on Information Systems*, Vol. 14, No. 2, pp. 175-221, 1996.

[Lopez et al. 92] O.P. Lopez, F. Hayes and S. Bear. OASIS: An Object-oriented Specification Language. Proc. of the CAiSE'92, Ed. Loucopoulos, pp. 348-363, Springer, LNCS 593, 1992.

[Sandewall 94] Erik Sandewall. *Features and Fluents, A Systematic Approach to the Representation of Knowledge about Dynamical Systems*, Oxford University Press, 1994

[Spivey 92] J.M. Spivey, *The Z notation*, Prentice Hall, 1992

[Yi 95] Choong-ho Yi. Towards the Assessment of Logics for Concurrent Action. AAAI Spring Symposium: Extending Theories of Action, Stanford University, March 1995.

[Yi 99] Choong-ho Yi. PhD thesis manuscript in preparation.

A Neural Network Model of Treasury Bill Rates

Milam Aiken and Bart Garner
School of Business Administration, University of Mississippi, University, MS 38677
601-232-5777, aiken@bus.olemiss.edu, bart@bus.olemiss.edu

Luvai Motiwalla
College of Management, University of Massachusetts, Lowell, One University Avenue
Lowell, MA 01854 , luvai_motiwalla@uml.edu, (978) 934-2754

ABSTRACT

Neural networks have been used to forecast many economic and financial time series with varying degrees of success. The research described here shows how a neural network using leading economic indicators as inputs was used to forecast annual-average 91-day Treasury Bill rates one year into the future. Results show that the model's accuracy was superior to naïve, expert, and T-Bill futures estimates. The paper also describes the steps necessary to design neural network models.

INTRODUCTION

The simplest method to forecast a time series such as Treasury Bill (T-Bill) rates is the "naïve" forecast. Using this technique, a future time period is assumed to have the same value as the current time period, i.e. there is no change. Perhaps the most commonly-used technique to forecast T-Bill rates, however, is based upon the Delphi method, a consensus opinion of expert forecasts. A third technique proposed recently is based upon using T-Bill futures, a method which was demonstrated to be superior to a survey of 50 financial experts for annual forecasts made one year in advance (Babin, 1997). In addition to being more accurate, the futures forecasts are more readily available because data on T-Bill futures are published daily in many financial periodicals. A fourth technique relies upon neural network modelling, and in one study, was demonstrated to be superior to the experts' and the futures' estimates (Aiken, 1995). This paper extends this prior research by further analyzing the components of the model and making additional analyses of its accuracy.

NEURAL NETWORKS

Since the mid-1980s, the use of artificial neural networks (ANNs) or artificial neural systems (ANSs) to approximate nonlinear, dynamic systems has increased. Usually called simply neural networks (NNs), these systems can be found in many disciplines including, but not limited to engineering, computer science, medicine, psychology, and business. In business, the predictive and pattern recognition capabilities of NNs have gotten the most attention. Some applications include, forecasting of stock prices (Margarita, 1991), mortgage risk assessment, credit-authorization screening, and bankruptcy prediction (Odom & Sharada, 1990).

A neural network is a computer-based simulation of what occurs in the mind (Wasserman, 1989). When humans learn, neurons in the brain adjust their connections, thus making associations in concepts. A computer-based neural network models these connections mathematically. Through repeated trial-and-error, a neural network is trained with a set of historical data until its accuracy reaches an acceptable level.

A neural network is typically developed in a three stage process (Aiken, 1996). First, decisions must be made about what the input variables will be, how many layers and nodes in each layer the network will have, the transfer function, and other training (or learning) parameters. Next, the network is trained using a subset of the data until the average error between the forecast and the actual values is reduced to a minimum (typically as close to zero as possible). Finally, the trained neural network is used to forecast with the remainder of the data to test whether or not the decisions made in the first stage were appropriate. For example, if the forecasts are poor, new variables may need to be added, the numbers of layers and nodes in the network may need to be changed, or a different transfer function may need to be used.

The development of a neural network may take several iterations until a sufficiently accurate network model is generated.

DEVELOPING THE NEURAL NETWORK

As described above, the neural network to forecast T-Bill rates was developed in a three-stage process:

1. Choosing the inputs: Using the Business Cycle Indicators (BCI) software from Media Logic, Inc., approximately 250 quarterly and monthly macroeconomic and financial data series over a period of about 50 years are available for viewing through graphs. Through subjective visual inspection, several related time series chosen through theory and intuition were compared to the T-Bill rates. *Figure 1* shows a sample screen from the software with the target variable's graph at the top and two possible input variables at the bottom. In this figure, recessionary periods are automatically marked with darker lines, and the series are automatically scaled for the best fit on the screen.

Many of the series seemed to have no correlation at all, were coincident, or lagging. For example, most of the financial data series (bonds, interest rates, etc.) were highly correlated but were coincident (changing along with the T-Bill yield) and had no predictive ability. However, the leading economic indicator series — Department of Commerce Leading Economic Indicator Composite Index (LEI), Center for International Business Cycle Research Short Leading Composite Index (Short), and CIBCR Long Leading Composite Index (Long) — and the Money Supply (M1) often turned before T-Bill yields, giving a high degree of predictive value. The annual average data are shown in *Appendix I*.

Figure 2 shows that the LEI had a fairly strong positive correlation (.60) with T-Bill rates for three prior years. The other correlations were mixed for the three prior years: M1 (.25), Short (.60), and Long (.50). These correlations indicate that for developing the model, four observations (the current year plus the three prior years) for each input and target variable may influence the next year's target (T-Bill rate).

2. Training the network: Using the four inputs and the target, a neural network was developed using NeuroForecaster 3.1, a product of NewWave Intelligent Business Systems, Inc. All of NeuroForecaster's default training parameters (e.g., learn rate, momentum, output processing, normalization, etc.) were used with the exception that "serial presentation" was chosen instead of "random presentation." In addition, the network used the genetic algorithm which is often more accurate (but slower) than the other backpropagation techniques also offered as choices.

Figure 3 shows that using rescaled-range analysis (a tool provided with NeuroForecaster), approximately 35 observations (where the tail narrows significantly) are necessary for training the network. That is, 35 observations should be the minimum in-sample set size (NeuroForecaster, 1994). Initially, the network was trained on annual average indicator data and three-month T-Bill rates from January 1949 to January 1974 (the averages reported covered the 12 months preceding each date) and a forecast was made for the following year (the annual average for 1974). Next, the network was trained on annual data from January 1949 to January 1975

and a forecast was made for 1975's average three-month T-Bill rate. Similar iterations covered the period up to January 1994. In the later iterations, the older data was omitted. For example, the last training set consisted of annual data from January 1969 to January 1989. In each case, the network was trained until the learning error was reduced to approximately 10%.

Appendix 4 shows the accumulated error indices for the inputs and target provided by NeuroForecaster after training. As indicated, the most significant variable was the Short-leading index with a value of 100 (100 = most significant). The correlation analyses discussed earlier also indicated this to be an important variable.

3. Testing the network: *Figure 4* shows a NeuroForecaster sample screen with a forecast (circled) for 1989 (the record date is January 1990). Data to the left of the vertical bar in the figure was used for developing the network (the "in-sample" data) and data to the right of the vertical bar was used for testing the accuracy (the "out-of-sample" data). As shown in the "Peek Window", the forecast for 1989 (the data point just to the right of the vertical bar) was very accurate (an actual average of 8.12% versus a network estimate of 8.06%). The network trained with data up to 1989 was also accurate up to 1994, although additional accuracy is usually obtained by training with the most recent data.

CONCLUSIONS

Table 1 shows that the neural network estimates were far superior to the competing techniques with a mean absolute error of 0.19 and a mean absolute percentage error of 3.3% for this ten-year period. Further testing over a 20-year period from 1974 to 1994 showed that the mean absolute percentage error in annual average 91-day T-Bill rate neural net forecasts made a year in advance was only 0.20; very close to the 0.19 of the ten-year period.

This research has demonstrated how a neural network developed using NeuroForecaster 3.1 and economic and financial data from Business Cycle Indicators may make accurate one-year forecasts of annual average Treasury Bill rates. Future research includes investigating other types of Treasury Bills, forecasting horizons, and input variables.

APPENDIX I

Model Data

Date	T-Bill	LEI	M1	Short	Long
490101	1.040833	71.40833	518.8333	53.83333	51.65833
500101	1.100833	69.53333	519.0166	48.80833	52.51666
510101	1.2175	75.25000	527.0000	57.79999	56.64166
520101	1.5525	74.67499	509.8999	58.72500	53.60833
530101	1.7675	73.90833	524.0333	58.89166	54.82499
540101	1.94	73.43333	532.2333	60.77499	55.70833
550101	0.95	73.28333	538.4499	61.31666	59.60833
560101	1.745833	78.05833	557.1083	70.36666	64.61666
570101	2.659166	77.67500	555.2999	69.95000	62.10833
580101	3.2625	75.23333	540.5500	68.29166	60.89166
590101	1.838333	75.16666	532.7083	69.45833	63.42499
600101	3.413333	78.89166	547.4833	78.04999	67.13333
610101	2.946666	77.48333	539.8333	75.84166	67.92500
620101	2.375833	79.31666	544.25	79.70833	73.57500
630101	2.779166	80.75833	550.7166	83.19999	79.50833
640101	3.1575	82.74166	560.8499	87.15833	87.93333
650101	3.5525	84.92499	574.6916	93.10000	93.55833
660101	3.949166	87.00000	589.9916	97.61666	99.48333
670101	4.881666	87.28333	599.2333	100.4583	97.30000
680101	4.330833	86.65833	605.9333	100.0083	99.99166
690101	5.344166	88.59999	620.9916	107.1249	102.8916
700101	6.685833	88.96666	624.2583	111.625	100.9916
710101	6.439166	85.16666	612.5750	107.0416	97.42499
720101	4.3375	88.00833	626.2583	113.2000	113.1749
730101	4.0675	92.23333	649.6749	122.6333	125.7916
740101	7.025833	93.20833	656.6583	130.6666	127.7749
750101	7.871666	87.94166	621.3333	123.125	112.3416
760101	5.821666	84.93333	594.3333	117.0166	118.5250
770101	4.996666	90.80000	593.3916	132.2833	131.5499
780101	5.265	92.30833	600.0500	137.8999	142.1333
790101	7.2225	93.29166	603.5749	145.1750	143.0499
800101	10.04166	92.10833	584.0583	146.8416	137.1333
810101	11.61416	88.57499	546.2333	141.8249	126.2583
820101	14.07666	88.77499	531.5833	147.5333	128.0833
830101	10.72333	87.11666	533.6750	145.2749	137.0416
840101	8.62	93.58333	574.4916	163.6999	165.5333
850101	9.573333	95.25833	589.2833	171.0250	174.2333
860101	7.489166	95.26666	619.8500	174.8749	187.7666
870101	5.9725	97.66666	690.8583	184.3499	200.6416
880101	5.825833	100.0000	743.7166	195.1083	212.4916
890101	6.671666	100.0666	745.1416	197.4583	220.3166
900101	8.115833	99.65833	718.0166	202.7249	227.0333
910101	7.51	98.42500	706.0166	201.3333	230.4166
920101	5.409166	97.12500	717.5666	202.1833	232.3416
930101	3.46	98.09999	782.9166	213.9083	243.7750
940101	3.019166	98.72499	848.8499	224.1166	259.1000

REFERENCES

1. Aiken, M. (1995). "Forecasting T-Bill Rates with a Neural Network," *Technical Analysis of Stocks and Commodities*, Vol. 13, No. 5, May, pp. 85-89.
2. Aiken, M. (1996). "A Neural Network to Predict Civilian Unemployment Rates," *Journal of International Information Management*, Vol. 5, No. 1, Spring, 35-45.
3. Babin, Charles. (1995). "An Efficient Crystal Ball," *Forbes*, January 30, p. 141.
4. Beltratti, A., Margarita, S., and Terna, P. (1996). *Neural Networks for Economic and Financial Modeling*. International Thomson Computer Press, pp. 171.
5. Konstenius, Jeremy. (1994). "Trading the S&P Using a Neural Network," *Technical Analysis of Stocks and Commodities*, Vol. 12, No. 10, October, pp. 40-45.
6. Margarita, S. (1991). *Neural Networks, Genetic Algorithms and Stock Trading, in Artificial Neural Networks*. (eds T. Kohonen, K. Makisara, O. Simula, J. Kangas), North-Holland, Amsterdam.
7. Mendelsohn, Lou. (1993). "Training Neural Networks," *Technical Analysis of Stocks and Commodities*, Vol. 11, No. 11, November, pp. 40-48.
8. *NeuroForecaster User's Guide*, NewWave Intelligent Business Systems, Singapore, 1994.
9. Odom, M. and Sharda, R. (1990). "A Neural Network Model for Bankruptcy Prediction," *Proceedings of International Joint Conference on Neural Networks*, Vol. 2, IEEE, San Diego CA, pp. 163-168.
10. Wasserman, P. (1989). *Neural Computing: Theory and Practice*. Van Nostrand Reinhold: New York.
11. Yuret, D. and De La Maza, M. (1994). "A Genetic Algorithm System for Predicting the OEX," *Technical Analysis of Stocks and Commodities*, Vol. 12, No. 6, June, pp. 58-64.

FIGURES

Figures available upon request to authors.

Towards Effective IT Risk Management Structures Across the Organisation

Piotr Krawczyk

Department of Computer Science and Information Systems, University of Jyvaskyla, P.O. Box 35 SF-40351 Jyvaskyla, Finland
tel:+358-(14)-60 24 77, fax:+358-(14)-60 25 44, e-mail: piotr@jytko.jyu.fi

ABSTRACT

Though, both academics and practitioners, recognize the importance of IT as a source of business risk, relatively little attention has been paid to this problem. This study will result in the refinement and validation of a framework for IT-Risk Management (ITRM). In the IT literature, risks are discussed in terms of four types of IT- related activity, representing four levels of IT concerns:

- the development of an organisation's IT strategy (the strategy level);
- the selection of a portfolio of IS projects (the planning level);
- the management of a system development (management level);
- the management of the IT infrastructure (the operations level).

We have defined a preliminary model of risk areas which will serve as a starting point for this study (see Figure 1).

Senior IT executives need to be aware of all these risks and their interrelationships, though they cannot be heavily involved with all of them. Responsibility for the various risks is probably best handled if the risks can be partitioned by management level and functional level. We need guidance for how such a partitioning could be developed and managed.

In this paper we evaluate the importance of identified risk factors and CIOs ability to manage them. We offer simple mechanism for risk classification (see Table 2). Also, we present cognitive map of IT management competence based on relation between the level of risk importance per factor and CIO's ability to manage it (see Figure 2).

INTRODUCTION

Strategy Level

The business impact of a poor fit between business strategy and technology strategy can be assessed in terms of opportunity costs (options lost) to the organisation due to its inability to act (see, e.g., Clemons, 1995 and 1998). (Henderson and Venkatraman 1993) have proposed that IT infrastructure investments can be analysed using the theory of real options. Another type of strategy level risk deals with the increased vulnerability of the organisation due to a high level of technological dependency. (Perrow 1984) provides an insightful analyses of the ways that system complexity and tight couplings can result in unanticipated modes of operation and consequent performance failures.

However, little attention has typically been paid to risks at this level in either the practitioner or research literature.

Planning and Portfolio Level

At this level the major organisational risk deals with the difficulty of reconfiguring the hardware and software infrastructure in order to implement the organisation's technology strategy (Henderson and Venkatraman, 1992). Failure at this level may result in insufficient infrastructure capacity to meet growing demands for IT services, inability to deliver specific services, lack of integration among IS applications, poor data quality, high training costs.

There has been considerable attention paid to pieces of this level in IT management literature (e.g. Ward and Griffiths 1996; Ciborra and Jelassi 1994), including: mechanisms of analysing and managing risks of the overall systems portfolio and technology platform development (e.g., Elam et al. 1988, Chapter 5); developing and appropriate balance of risk in the portfolio of IS development projects (e.g. Mc Farlan, 1981); and, adjusting the architecture of choices to comply with these strategic planning contingencies (Earl,1989).

Management Level

The major risks at this level deal with the failure to design a system with the needed capabilities or to implement the selected system in a timely and cost effective manner. This level has been the focus of a large body of research, including work on software risk management and the substantial literature on systems implementation (Boehm 1988). Textbooks (e.g., Charette, 1989) and tutorials (e.g., Boehm, 1989) have been devoted to clarifying major risks in software development and to establishing mechanism for effectively dealing with them. A good summary and analysis of the major studies in this area has recently been completed by (Lyytinen et al., 1994).

Overall, this level of IT risks has been much more thoroughly investigated and is better understood than two higher levels.

Operational Level

At the forth level of the IT risk framework, the concern shifts to the day-to-day operation of the organisation's capability. Broadly, the risk at this level is that a failure in IT operations will result in the organisation not having the necessary support it needs to continue its operations.

(Ginzberg et al. 1990; Neumann 1995) describe two broad classes of failure which subsume many of the potential risks in this area (their classes, though, are broader, and include some risks we have defined as project level risks).

The risks at this level are typical concerns of EDP auditors, and there has been substantial work especially in the practitioner community, on defining procedures for addressing them (see, e.g., Clark and Wilson, 1987)

Interaction between levels- Holistic Approach

An important characteristic of the IT risk framework is the interactions between risk levels across the company structure (see ITRM model Figure 1). For example, a choice of a technology architecture at the Planning Level affects directly the formulation of the systems development projects and project level risks at the Project Level. These interactions, however, run in both directions and may affect multiple levels at the same time. Though not depicted in Figure 1, each level in the hierarchy should provide feedback to each higher level. Consequently, a failure at the operations level may impact an organisation's thinking at the Portfolio or Strategy levels. These interactions have not been well documented, and are not completely understood. Yet, it is a key aspect of the CIO's responsibility to manage these interactions and to understand the associated risk impacts (see, e.g. Osterle, Brenner and Hilbers, 1993). Therefore, the main goal of this study will be to develop a better understanding of these interactions and to formulate guidelines for managing them.

METHODS

Measurement

We developed ITRM research model operationalized by 30 latent variables (see Figure 1 and Table 3).
Likert scale was applied upon each risk factor in form of two major questions (see Table 1).

Sample

In our pilot study we conducted 15 structured interviews with CIO's and senior IT managers in the years 1997/98. From the database of 2080 Finnish CIOs and IT managers (over 90 percent of the population), addresses were chosen randomly, and an interview based questionnaire was sent to 500 of them (over 20 percent).

Design

In order to triangulate our research with independent views 23 software engineers were interviewed from companies subcontracting to the aforementioned organisations.

Content Validity

Based on (Heikkinen 1996) thesis, a list of risk factors was elaborated by referring to over 20 publications on IT management uncertainty (see Table 3). In order to check if the instrument measures cover all vital properties under investigation (Burt, 1976, p.4), 28 CIOs and senior IT managers were asked to list top three risks at each level of organisational structure (with 50 percent respond rate achieved). The emerging profile of risks is organised by the percentage of respondents claiming the importance of a given risk factor (see Table 5).

Construct Validity

Independent Samples Test was applied to check stability of measures across two different methodologies: interview vs. questionnaire data gathering, (tables 8 and 9) (Campbell and Fiske, 1959; Cronbach, 1971).

Reliability

All measures but first, related to importance of identified risk factors at strategic level (.52 Cronbach alpha), evidenced strong reliability and validity (see example of measures for IT management performance at strategy level Table 7). Internal consistency reliability estimates using Cronbach's alpha ranged from.72 for evaluation of IT risk management performance at strategy level to.84 for evaluation of IT risk management performance at planning and portfolio level. However, it was an overall Cronbach alpha.91 for the 30 items across the four levels that showed strong reliability of the applied measures (Cronbach, 1951). The high Cronobach alpha gives empirical support for advisability of the holistic 4-level approach.

Procedure
Validated instrument will be sent to 2080 Finnish CIOs and Senior IT managers (over 90 percent of the population).

Sampling bias
We obtained 5 percent respond rate comparing to 10 percent achieved by E&Y Global Annual Information Security Survey based on the same CIO/IT Managers database. The higher respond rate of E&Y survey could be explained by maturity of the instrument with regard to its content and structure, the portfolio of E&Y clients included in the sample, and professional editing of questionnaire form. We investigated carefully reasons for not responding. Direct e-mails were sent to 128 managers which failed to fill the IT Risk Management enquiry form (see Table 5).

RESULTS

Shared Understanding
CIOs vs. Software Engineers
Survey results showed much agreement between CIOs and SE- Software Engineers on many areas of IT risk management (see Figure 2 and Table 6). Both parties share understanding, and acknowledge independently, big risks related to rigidity of ISS, strategic information and technology management (Ward J, Grffiths p. 1998 pp 359-441; Corder 1989.); portfolio of IS and data-communication architecture; communication, authority, performer and structure at project level; as well as information security and established practices and procedures at operational level.

Differences
CIOs vs. Software Engineers
Some differences in IT risks assessment among the two groups may be explained by heterogeneity of the actors involved (different status in the organisation, technical vs. business background, different levels and areas of job responsibility and distinctive to every individual "world of thoughts"). Characteristic pattern can be found in ITRM performance assessment. Software Engineers as an independent control group claimed that areas like strategy formulation (see e.g. Ward and Griffiths 1998 pp 490-539), strategic technology management, portfolio of hardware and data communication architecture (see e.g. Ross and Beath 1996), organisation of work (with underlying issues of communication within a team, use of authority and skills of project members) as well as general rules and procedures for personnel, are seriously under-managed. From the risk perspective, formulation and implementation of IS strategy is of paramount importance to CIOs, whereas SEs were concern with complexity of structure-task-technology relations at management level (see Cash, McFarlan and McKenney 1992) and personnel related risks at operational level. Software engineers in contrast to senior IT managers seems to underestimate importance of IS strategy formulation. This may lead to serious breaches in ISS implementation process due to lack of commitment, shared understanding and mutual support for IT and Business strategy alignment. In fact 50 percent of senior IT managers reported lack of IT strategy as the major thread. 45 percent of CIOs reported lack of alignment between IT and business strategy as high risk , yet common problem.

The differences in risk and related management performance should be analysed and appropriate course of action should be assign.

Top Risks Across 4-Levels
By a Pool of Fourteen CIOs and Senior IT Managers

Strategy
Lack of IT strategy was evaluated as a principal risk and claimed by 50 percent of senior IT managers (see Table 5). This in consequence was followed by risk of business and IT strategies being not aligned (43 percent). Non-commitment from company executives represents thread recognised by 14 percents of respondents (see e.g. Kemerer and Sosa 1991 p17,20 and Clemons 1995 p 11-31).

Planning and Portfolio
Senior IT managers identify lack of IT architecture as a major pitfall in risk management at planning level (28 percent). Inadequate cost benefit analysis, errors in prioritisation, lack of resources to implement strategy were reported as common obstacles at the planning phase (see e.g. Ward 1998 p 96-155). Also 14 percent of managers identify lack of IT-business strategy alignment as a risk factor affecting directly planning level.

Management Level
Management (project) level is mainly concerned with risks of changing timetables (vendors related), wrong people selected to perform a tasks, selection of development tools and general risk of new technology (21percent) (Leavitt 1965; Bessant 1991; Griffiths and Newman 1996; Mitev 1996). 14 percent of IT managers report lack of clear division of duties, no support from executive level (low priority for IT development), and inadequate quality control as serious candidates for risk analysis.
Operations
At this level 35 percent of IT managers view exposure to technology and data security as major threats experienced and caused by personnel and 14 percent of them refer to lack of cost management.

Multilevel Risk Factors

It can be seen (Table 5), that lack of alignment between IT and business strategy has direct impact on both strategy and planning levels. Problem of not reliable vendors (Kemerer, Sosa 1991 pp 217) arise at both planning and management level. Cost management problem spans all three levels from the bottom up. Two risk factors apply to all four levels. These are: resource allocation and general threat of dynamic changes in ever more complex couplings of new technologies (see e.g. Kemerer, Sosa 1991 pp. 111). There is lack of feedback from operational level resulting in lack of executive insight into operational level. At the same time both CIOs and IT managers would like to see more support from the top executives (Fiegener, Coakley 1995 pp 56-61).

Table 1: 2.5 Management of The Information System Portfolio

a) Is there a systematic method in use for examining the coverage of the systems portfolio in the organisation? y/n
b) What method ?_____
   i.e. BSP (Business Systems planning) by IBM
   Other: _____
c) Is there a systematic method for the evaluation of current system portfolio in terms of business
   value added and technical quality improvement ? y/n
d) What method are used in evaluating/examining the systems portfolio?i.e. (Systems audit grid)
   Other:_____
e) What risks, might be triggered by lack of systematic IS portfolio management ?
   _____

In your opinion, how important is the risk factor (Lack of systematic IS portfolio management) to your organisation?

1	2	3	4	5
meaningless	minor	mediocre	important	very important

How well do you think, in your organisation, the factor (Lack of systematic IS portfolio management), and risks it causes, are managed?

1	2	3	4	5
poorly	tolerably	mediocre	well	very well

Table 2: Mechanism for Risk Identification (i.e. Management Level - IS development project)

Risk Sheet (example)	Check List (sample)
Error! Bookmark not defined. **General:** Identifier: 1 Name: Ambiguous quality level Description: The requested quality level is so ambiguous that it is impossible to understand what is to be reached. Owner: IT Manager Classification: Technology Nature: Specification Domain: Software	Management Level **Risk Definitions:** The requested quality level is so ambiguous that it is impossible to understand what is to be reached. Customer asks for changes which are not documented, treated and planned, do not lead to contract negotiation. Management is not kept informed. Data are numerous and complex, leading to performance problems in storage, treatment and exchanges.
Causes: Identifier: Name: 1 Undecided customer. 2 Quality plan missing. 3 Uncomplete quality plan.	**Cause Definitions:** Undecided customer . Quality plan missing. Uncomplete quality plan. Users' requests badly managed. Users remarks not known.
Impact: Description: Product quality is not adapted to user's needs (sub or over-quality).	**Impact Descriptions:** Product quality is not adapted to user 's needs (sub or over-quality). Every user 's remark is considered as a request for change (project drifts in cost and time scale) or no request is taken into account (client is unsatisfied).
Strategy: Risk management strategy: **Actions:** Identifier: Name: 1 Write a quality plan 2 Re-formulate quality requirements. 3 Give users a test version.	Product performance during execution does not address requirements (problems due to inputs/outputs). Ef ficiency of resources is insufficient.

Towards Effective IT Risk Management

We argue that there is a need in IT domain for risk classification mechanism which would enable sharing fragmented expertise of various stakeholders within a broader context of organisational learning. Risk approach, when applied to management of ambiguity in sense-making communities and management of uncertainty in organisation as decision-making system, could facilitate the process of IT and business strategy alignment.

Risk Classification

We present simple mechanism for enhancing communication between different actors through risk classification. (see Table 2).

SUMMARY AND CONCLUSIONS

We developed ITRM research model operationalized by 30 latent variables (Figure 1, and Tables 1 and 3).

In addition 28 CIOs and senior IT managers were asked to list top three risks at each level of organisational structure. The emerging profile of risks is organised by the percentage of respondents claiming the importance of a given risk factor (see Table 5).

Survey results showed much agreement between CIOs and SE- Software Engineers on many areas of IT risk management (see Figure 2 and Table 6). Both parties share understanding, and acknowledge independently, big risks related to rigidity of ISS, strategic information and technology management; portfolio of IS and data-communication architecture; communication, authority, performer

Table 3: Risk Factors Itemised Across Four Levels of IT Management	
Identified Risk Factors	Source by Author (for full description see list of references)
STRATEGY LEVEL	
Lack or Imperfection of IS Strategy	Earl 1989, p 67
IS Rigidity	Clemons 1995, p 65-66
Difficult Implementation of IS Strategy	Henderson & Venkatraman 1992, p 7
Faulty Organising in Information Management	Lacity & Hirschheim 1992, p 5
Inadequate Control /Supervision	Earl 1989, p 119, 159, 166; Ginzberg & Moulton 1990, p8
Inadequate Technology Management	Lyytinen 1994, p 11
PLANNING & PORTFOLIO LEVEL	
Lack or Imperfection of Information Architecture	Leppanen 1996
Lack or Imperfection of IS Architecture	Halttunen 1990a; Ginzberg & Lyytinen 1995
Lack or Imperfection of Hardware Architecture	Ginzberg Moulton 1990, p 5, 6
Lack or Imperfection of Data Comm. Architecture	Turban, McLean &Wetherbe 1996
Lack or Not Systematic Portfolio Management	Earl 1989, p73, 74; Mc Farlan, 1981
MANAGEMENT LEVEL	
Task Difficulty	Beath 1983, p138; Lyytinen 1994
Communication	Mantei 1981
Authority	Fiegener & Coakley 1995 p 58
Organisation of Work	Margetts & Willcocks 1994 p 8-17
Actors Involved	Boehm & Ross 1989, p 902; Lyytinen 1994, p10
Technology	Lyytinen 1994, p11
Task-Performer	Lyytinen 1994, p11
Task-Technology	Lyytinen 1994, p11
Task-Structure	Mantei 1981
Performer-Technology	Lyytinen 1994, p11
Performer-Structure	Lyytinen 1994, p11
Technology-Structure	Lyytinen 1994, p11
OPERATIONAL LEVEL	
Personnel	Ginzberg & Moulton 1990, p 5,7; Ginzberg & Lyytinen 1995, p4 Finne 1995, p 105
Outsiders	Boehm 1989, p72,73; Finne 1995, p 102, 114
Hardware	Finne 1995, p 111
Software	Boehm 1989, p 66; Finne 1995, p 112
Information	Clark and Wilson, 1987
Premises	Clark and Wilson, 1987; Neumann 1995, p 174-176
Practices/ Procedures	Ginzberg & Moulton 1990, p 8,9; Clark and Wilson, 1987

and structure at project level; as well as information security and established practices and procedures at operational level. Software Engineers as an independent control group claimed that areas like strategy formulation, strategic technology management, portfolio of hardware and data communication architecture, organisation of work as well as general rules and procedures for personnel, are seriously under-managed. In contrast to senior IT managers, software engineers underestimate importance of IS strategy formulation. This may lead to serious breaches in ISS implementation process due to lack of commitment, shared understanding and mutual support for IT and Business strategy alignment. In fact 50 percent of senior IT managers reported lack of IT strategy as the major thread. 45 percent of CIOs reported lack of alignment between IT and business strategy as high risk , yet common problem.

We offered simple mechanism for building and sharing organisational knowledge on IT related risks and ways to manage them (see management level example Table 2). Also, we present cognitive map of IT management competence based on relation between the level of importance per risk factor and CIO's ability to manage it (see Figure 2).

Validated instrument will be sent to 2080 Finnish CIOs and Senior IT managers.

Table 4: Reasons for Not Responding to the Questionnaire

One or More Declared Reasons for Not Responding to the Questionnaire	N
Total Number of Enquiries for Respond Failure	128
Total Number of Explained Cases (including 15 returned mails by post office)	65
Returned mail due to unknown recipient (incl. 5 people not working anymore)	15
Never received the questionnaire	4
No experience/expertise in the area	7
Forgot to fill it	4
Too busy	27
The questionnaire was too long	14
The information asked is confidential	14
Did not like the content of the questionnaire	2
Did not like the structure of the questionnaire	2
Simply did not want to answer	4
Other :	
died	1
claiming personal harassment	1
** will consider filling-up the questionnaire if resent	14
forwarded questionnaire or referred to another person	5

REFERENCES

Burt R.S. "Interpretational Confounding of Unobserved Variables in Structural Eqution Model" Sociological Methods & Research. Aug 1976 Vol.5, pp. 3-52

Beath C.M. " Strategies for Managing MIS Projects: A Transaction Cost Approach. Computers and Information Systems Graduate School of Management, University of California, Los Angeles.

Bessant J. " Managing Advanced Manufacturing Technology: The Challenge of the Fifth Wave, NCC-Blackwell, Manchester, 1991.

Boehm, B.W. "A Spiral Model of Software Development and Enhancement", Computer IEEE, 1988.

Boehm B.W., "Software Risk Management" IEEE Computer Society Press 1989.

Boehm B.W., Ross R. "Theory of Software Project Management: Principles and Examples" IEEE Transaction on Software Engineering 15 (7), 902-916, 1989.

Cash, J., McFarlan, W. And McKenney, J. 1992 "Corporate Information Systems Management , Irwin, Boston.

Charette R.N., " Software Engineering Risk Analysis and Management", McGraw-Hill, 1989.

Campbel l , D.T. Fiske D.W. "Convergent and Discriminant Validation by the Multitrait-Multimethod Matrix", Psychological Bulletin (56), March 1959, pp. 81-105

Choo1997 "

Clark D.D., Wilson D.W. " A Comparison of Commercial and Military Computer
Security Policies", Proceedings of the 1987 IEEE Symposium on Security.

Clemons E. "Using Scenario Analysis to Manage the Strategic Risk of Reengineering", Sloan Management Review, 1995 pp.61-71.

Clemons E.K., Thatcher M. E., Materna R. " Strategic Implications of Infrastructure as a Consumable Resource (Taking the "Real" Out of Corporate Real Estate), 1998.

Clemons E.K., Thatcher M.E., and Row M.C. "Identifying Sources of Reengineering Failures: A Study of the Behavioral Factors Contributing to
Reengineering Risks". Journal of Management Information Systems/ Fall 1995.

Corder, C. "Taming your Company Computer" McGraw-Hill 1989.

Cronbach L.J. "Coefficient Alpha and the Internal Consistency of of Tests" Psychometrica (16), September 1951

Cronbach L.J. ""Test Validation " in Educational Measurement, 2nd Edition, R.L. Thorndike(ed.), American council on Educatopm, Washington D.C.., 1971, pp.443-507.

Earl M. "Management Strategies for Information Tecnology", Prentice Hall, 1989.

Elam J., Ginzberg P., Zmud R. " Transforming the IS Organization, Washington , ICIT Press, 1988.

Fiegener M., Coakley J. " CIO "Impression Management- Problems and Practices", Journal of Systems Management, Nov/Dec 1995.

Finne T. "A Knowledge-Based DSS for Information Security Analysis. Licentiate Thesis. Abo Akademi , Ekonomisk-Statsvetenskapliga Fakulteten. 1995

Ginzberg M., Moulton R. "Information Services Risk Management", Proceedings of the 5th Jerusalem Conference on Information Technology, 1990.

Ginzberg M., Lyytinen K. "Information Technology Risk at the Top: The Definition and Management of Risk By Senior Executives. A Proposal to the SIM International Advanced Practices Council. September 12 1995.

Griffiths C. And Newman , M. "Theme Issue: Management and Risk in Information Technology Projects", Journal of Information Technology, 11, (4). 1996.

Heikkinen K. "Tietohallinnon Riskitekijat ja Niiden Arviointi" Master Degree Thesis, Department of Information Systems, Unversity of Jyvaskyla 1996.

Henderson J. C. and Venkatraman N. 1992, Strategic Alignment: A Model for Organisational Transformation through Information Technology in Kochan and Keen P.G.W 1991, Shaping the Future : Business Design Through Information Technology, Harvard Business School Press, Boston MA.

Henderson J C. Sussman S.W. " Creating and Exploiting Knowledge for Fast-Cycle Organizational Response: The Center for Army Lessons Learned

Hunter A. " Uncertainty in Information Systems" McGraw Hill 1996 pp 95 and 102

Kendall R.A.H " Risk Management for Executives (A practical Approach to Controlling Business Risks " Pitman Publishing 1998.

Kemerer C.F. Sosa G.L. "System Development Risks in trategic Information Systems". MIT " Information and Software Technology, vol..33 no 3 April 1991

Table 5: Top IT Risks Across Four Levels of Organisational Structure (by 14 CIOs and Senior IT Managers)

	Emerging Risk Profile Across 4 Levels of Organisational Structure	%
Strategy Level	Lack of strategy	50
	IT and business strategies not aligned	43
	Non-commitment from executives	21
	Lack of knowledge about available technology	14
	Strategy is too strict in rapid change of environment	less than 10
	Lack of resources to implement strategy	less than 10
	Difficulties in implementing IT strategy	less than 10
	Strategy not being followed	less than 10
	Strategy not detailed enough to allow planning at the operational level	less than 10
	Unreliable Vendors	less than 10
Planning & Portfolio Level	Lack of IT architecture	28
	Inadequate cost/benefit analysis	14
	IT and business strategies not aligned	14
	Errors in prioritisation	14
	Lack of resources to implement strategy	14
	Lack of feedback from operational level	less than 10
	Pressure of changing technologies on existing applications	less than 10
	Too big, redundant resources	less than 10
	Unreliable vendors	less than 10
	Hardware architecture is wrongly defined	less than 10
	Lack of hardware architecture	less than 10
	Missing elements of IS architecture	less than 10
	Software architecture is not suitable for tasks	less than 10
	Personal agendas	less than 10
	Incorrect or inadequate documentation	less than 10
Management Level	Risk of new technology	21
	Changing timetables (vendors related)	21
	Wrong people selected to perform tasks	21
	Selection of development tools	21
	Responsibilities not clearly defined	14
	No support from executive level (low priority for IT development)	14
	Inadequate quality control	14
	Lack of internal and external resources	14
	Strong dependence on existing technology solutions	less than 10
	Task not defined clearly enough	less than 10
	User interface	less than 10
	Insufficient end-user involvement	less than 10
	Poor project organisation	less than 10
Operational Level	Exposure to technology and personnel related risks	35
	Weakness of data security	35
	Lack of cost management	14
	Management has not enough insight into this level	less than 10
	Wrong choice of technology	less than 10
	Risk of Internet	less than 10
	Rapid infrastructure development	less than 10
	Lack of resources	less than 10
	Lack of technical aids	less than 10
	Program errors	less than 10
	Inefficient use of resources	less than 10

Lacity M., Hirschheim R. "The Information Systems Outsourcing Bandwagon: Look Before You Leap". Working paper. 1992

Leppanen M. "Contextual framework for the analysis and design of information systems development methodologies", Manuscript, University of Jyväskylä, 1996.

Lyytinen K. Mathiassen L. Ropponen "An Organizational Analysis of Software Risk Management Approaches", University of Jyvaskyla, working paper, 1994.

Mantei M. The Effect of Programming Team Structures on Programming Tasks". Communication of the ACM, March , vol. 24, 3.

Margetts H., Willcocks L. "Informatization in public sector organizations: Distinctive or common risks?" Information and the Public Sector , Vol. 3, No. 1 p 8-17, 1992.

McFarlan W.F. " Portfolio Approach to Information Systems" Harvard Business Review, 1974.

McFarlan W.F. " Portfolio Approach to Information Systems" Harvard Business Review, vol.59(4), pp 42-150, 1981.

Mitev N."Social, Organizational and and Political Aspects of IS Failures: The Computerized Reservation Systems At French Railway"., in Coehlo, J.Jelassi, T Krcmar, H., O'Callaghan R., Saaksjarvi Proceedings of ECIS 1996.

Neumann P. "Computer Related Risks" ACM Press, Addison Wesley 1995

Osterle H. ,Brenner W., Hilbers K. "Total Information Systems Management" p 5 Wiley 1993

Perrow C. Normal Accidents: Living with High Risk Technologies, New York: Basic Books, 1984.

Ross J. W., Beath C.M. Goodhue D.L. " Develop Long-Term Competitiveness Through IT Assets, Sloan Management Review 1996.

Turban E., McLean E.and Wetherbe J. " Information Technology for Management", chapter 9, by New York: John Wiley & Sons, 1996.

Ward J. Griffiths P. "Strategic Planning for Information Systems". Wiley 1998

Table 7: Cronbach Alpha and Correlation Matrix (Strategy Level Example)
Strategy Level   Risk Management
RELIABILITY ANALYSIS - SCALE (ALPHA)

			Alpha if Item Deleted
1.	ST11RM	IS Strategy Formulation Mngmt	.6398
2.	ST12RM	IS Strategy Rigidity Mngmt	.7141
3.	ST13RM	Management of IS Strategy Implementatio	.6727
4.	ST21RM	Information Management	.6622
5.	ST22RM	Control and Supervision Mngmt	.6883
6.	ST23RM	Management of Technology	.7357

Correlation Matrix

	ST11RM	ST12RM	ST13RM	ST21RM	ST22RM	ST23RM
ST11RM	1.0000					
ST12RM	.5815	1.0000				
ST13RM	.3691	.3608	1.0000			
ST21RM	.4648	.1829	.3628	1.0000		
ST22RM	.4022	.1464	.2690	.4563	1.0000	
ST23RM	.1631	.0290	.3125	.3164	.2560	1.0000

N of Cases =   58.0
Reliability Coefficients   6 items
Alpha = .7245   Standardized item alpha = .7308

Information and Communications Technology Assessment Process

Martha Gorman, Director
Institute for International InfoStructure
637 South Broadway, Suite B231, Boulder, CO 80303
303 494 4488; 303 494 4787 fax; marthagorman@worldnet.att.net
http://home.att.net/~marthagorman/infostructure.html; www.cesii.com

The nature and structure of computer applications change as technology evolves. The mainframe-centric era, characterized by monolithic, enterprise-wide, transaction processing applications, which were accessed by "dumb terminals," gave way to the PC-centric era. The PC-centric era witnessed the emergence of desktop productivity software (word processors, spreadsheets, and personal databases). The hallmark of this era was the growth of decentralized, departmental computing. While this allowed for increased productivity and autonomy within departments, from the enterprise perspective, it also resulted in the proliferation of isolated, independently managed systems. These systems were often based upon fundamentally different methods of information collection and processing, which were irreconcilable at the enterprise level. Decision making at the enterprise level was often impaired as a result.

As the bandwidth of data communications networks grew and latencies decreased, the PC-centric era began to give way to the network-centric era. Today the Internet, essentially a "network of networks," allows for the inter-linking of computer networks on a global basis. As a result, isolated applications dedicated to specific tasks such as accounting, inventory management or manufacturing are being replaced by highly integrated, network-based, web-enabled applications. Some have even predicted the death of the PC as network computers or appliances (today's "dumb terminals") begin to emerge. These devices link end-users to centralized, large-scale application servers that can be more easily and effectively managed and maintained (see "The Future of Computing" in The Economist, 9/12-18, 1998).

What does this mean for developing countries? Access to global networks could promote a much broader participation by developing countries in global markets for goods and services. It could also facilitate information exchange and collaboration among developing countries, or between developing countries and Europe, North America, Japan and Australia. As such, the information revolution, made possible by the network-centric computing era, has the potential to enhance socioeconomic development processes and help eliminate many of the current North-South technological and economic inequities.

There are, however, a number of constraints which make it difficult for organizations in developing nations to share in, or benefit from, the communications revolution. For instance, these organization frequently lack easy, low-cost access to global data communications networks, especially those located outside of major cities. They also often lack sufficient capacity to build, operate, manage and maintain the information and communications technologies involved. And trade regulations, legal systems and government policies in developing countries are not always conducive to the widespread growth of affordable telecommunications and the free exchange of information.

Recognizing both the opportunities and the threats posed by the information and communications revolution in developing areas, local governments, multilateral development banks, private industries, and non-governmental organizations are seeing the wisdom of budgeting adequately for information and communications technologies in development projects throughout the emerging nations of the world. This priority shift and these burgeoning initiatives have raised a number of important issues which must be systematically addressed:

* How can one best determine if the Information and Communications Technology (ICT) of the Organization hosting a development project is able to support the Project and the Host Organization's goals? This will entail determining what the Project goals are and how they relate to the operation and management of the Project from the point of view of the organization, primarily in terms of data collection, data-flow and information systems integration. The goal is simply to help the selection, installation and deployment of an ICT system that has the capacity and capability to support the project's goals effectively and efficiently.
* Does the Host Organization have the tools and skills needed to effectively manage the project? If not, what training program or recruitment program needs to be implemented in order for the project to be effectively managed?
* What is required to ensure that the ICT infrastructure is flexible enough to adapt to changing business conditions?
* Will the proposed ICT infrastructure yield the necessary information required to manage and control the project throughout its lifetime?
* Under what conditions will the ICT infrastructure need to be enhanced? What will future enhancements cost, and how will they be paid for?
* Are there training and recruitment programs which should be instituted to meet the needs of future enhancements of the Program's ICT?
* Will the proposed ICT tie into and help a sectoral strategic information infrastructure to emerge?
* How will the sectoral strategic information infrastructure tie into and help a national information infrastructure to emerge? What potential benefits will these systems generate in the future, and how can they best be utilized to improve the economic well being of the people in the country in which the Project is located?
* What legal, institutional and regulatory reforms are needed or would help to facilitate the development and growth of a sectoral strategic information system?

Recognizing that an business objectives-based ICT Assessment Process is needed to answer these questions, the Institute for International InfoStructure commissioned a team of IS experts to devise such a process that would be applicable in developing areas. The resulting Information and Communications Technology Assessment Process (ICTAP) is based upon the Control Objectives for Information and Related Technology (COBIT). COBIT, an authoritative source on IT control objectives and IT audit, was first released by the Information Systems Audit and Control Foundation (ISACF) in 1996, and updated in 1998. It is the result of a major global research initiative that was undertaken to develop generally applicable and accepted standards for good practice of information technology control.

Funding for a Pilot Project to help further define, refine and enhance the ICTAP is currently under consideration by the Information for Development (infoDev) group of the World Bank. This Pilot Project, if funded, will take place in Cartagena, Colombia. Aguas de Cartagena, a water and wastewater utility, has agreed to host this Pilot and cooperate in the Assessment Process. The target project involves the expansion of Aguas de Cartagena's physical plant and facilities, and is also under consideration for World Bank development funding. It is hoped that the Pilot Project will begin in March, 1999. The Assessment Process itself would then be complete by July, 1999, and the analysis of the experience and Process improvement implementation would be finalized by September, 1999.

Three important outcomes of this Pilot Project are:
1. Demonstrate the feasibility, costs and benefits of formally implementing an ICT Assessment for Projects under consideration by lending institutions.
2. Help establish the standards and criteria required of an ICT assessment to ensure that the Assessment provides valid and reliable recommendations.
3. Demonstrate the benefits of making a standard practice of conducting formal ICT assessments for international development projects within the multilateral lending institutions.

The ICT Assessment process that is to be tested by the Pilot Project is comprised of four Phases:
Phase I evaluates the information and communications infrastructure of the Borrower:
a) hardware/software evaluation
b) data reliability determination
c) missing data set identification, and

d) business system interface scope and efficiency evaluation

Phase II produces an information and communications infrastructure reinforcement and data tie-in analysis of the Borrower:

a) system entity relationship attribute diagrams

b) system data flow diagrams, data source recommendations

c) system process flow and timing diagrams

d) hardware/software requirements and corresponding cost model, and recommended data interface plan.

Phase III provides a plan to reinforce any inadequate ICT infrastructure within the Borrower, the cost of the hardware, software and services required to achieve best practices, and also provides the automated tracking required to compare project/cost data against the defined project goals.

Phase IV monitors and audits the new ICT system, creating mechanisms for upgrading and improving the system over the long term.

It will be possible to implement all four Phases of this Process at three different levels of depth and detail, according to need:

1. Management level, Strategic ICT Requirements

2. Administrative level ICT Requirements

3. Operational level ICT Requirements

The ICT Assessment Process which will be developed via the proposed Pilot Project is, at one level, really an attempt to help further formalize the way in which we determine whether or not funded projects are achieving the development objectives of the corresponding lending institution.

At another level, the implementation of the standards and criteria developed by the proposed Pilot Project will reduce the need to create and fund isolated ICT development projects. Rather, it will make it possible to build and strengthen the infostructure of developing nations at the same time that the physical and social infrastructure is being funded and developed. Moreover, this ICT infrastructure will be based on real applications and business objectives and tied to existing projects, from whence the funding will be derived.

Finally, by using existing projects to develop essential infostructure in developing areas, the pace of the growth in the region's information infrastructure could take place quickly enough and across a broad enough range of sectors and organizations to allow ICT to level the global playing field, rather than create even greater disparities.

Dr. Oscar Arias, speaking at the Executive Conference on Integrated Information Systems-Cesii '98 in Miami last September, spoke eloquently of the "moral obligations" imposed by IT. He said that IT is not just an opportunity for developed nations, but that these same nations have a moral obligation to use Information Technology wisely and to make it available to unify the globe and create an inclusive global marketplace.

The Institute for International InfoStructure, a non profit organization, was founded to accelerate the systematic enhancement of the Information and Communications Technology infrastructure of the developing world. The widespread, institutionalized implementation of the Information and Communications Technology Assessment Process is an enormous step in the direction of realizing both Dr. Arias' enlightened vision and the Institute's valuable mission.

Choice of Internet Technology: Java or ActiveX

Liang Yu
Krannert School of Management, Purdue University
West Lafayette, IN 47906
Email: liang_yu@mgmt.purdue.edu

The debate over the key Internet technology rages on: Java versus ActiveX. Recent theme articles on leading Information Systems magazines (Computer World, Information Week, Byte, etc.) show that the choice between Java and ActiveX is a great concern of the Internet community. It is also of great interest to academic researchers. Especially, we are interested in the end users' behavior in adopting technology/standard and the network externalities involved here. This paper provides an empirical study on the choice of ActiveX and Java technology, using a multinominal logit model. The main purposes of this paper are: 1) to find out the factors that affects the users' choice; 2) to explore empirically issues of network externalities. The data used is from the GVU Internet Survey (April 1997). The results indicate that the choice of the technology greatly depends on the relative experience of users as well as the relative technology they are using. We try to explain our findings using theory of indirect network externalities. The limitations of this paper and further research directions are discussed at the end of the paper.

I. INTRODUCTION

When you want to implement some dynamic executable contents on your web page, which technology will you choose: Java Applets or ActiveX controls? The debate over this key Internet technology rages on nowadays. To understand the debate, it is important to understand the features of ActiveX controls and Java Applets as well as their technological and economic implications.

The rationale underlying both Java Applets and ActiveX controls is that they are active components that can be downloaded via internet (especially web) to a host computer and are executable on the host machine in real-time. By enabling distributed computing, they greatly enlarged the value of the Internet. They are both based on the client-server architecture and object oriented technology, they both support "download once run many times", however, they have different approaches. In the case of Java applets, the Java virtual machine (JVM) in each host computer interprets the byte code and controls access to the system resources. The JVM removes the applets from the details of the host OS and thus applets can run on any platform that supports JVM. Currently most platforms do. ActiveX controls, in contrast, are written as DLLs, so they must be loaded into some kind of container, and they have to register themselves with Windows registry and execute as native Windows applications.

Downloading executable content from unknown web sites may be very risky. Who knows what this little application will do once it is on your system, therefore, security is one the primary concerns of Internet users. ActiveX use an mechanism called code signing technology to verify the origin of a control so that if a control destroys your system, at least you'll know who do it, but the author of the ActiveX control need to buy certificate authorities (CA) from independent CA provider. While Java applets will use Java sandbox mechanism which provides highly restrictive security. For example, an applet can't perform unauthorized system functions (e.g. allocating memory); it is simpler, cheaper and safer in some way but is limited in certain functions.

The basic trade-off is portability versus performance and the security issues. What we need to keep in mind is that both "Java" and "ActiveX" are labels applied to a broad range of technologies. They are like standard, although they are partially compatible, they perform better if working with software in the same technology/standard. Basically, ActiveX stay in line with the typical Microsoft technology such as OLE, while almost all the competitors of Microsoft rally under the flag of Java, among them, there is the producer of the most popular web browser-Netscape. Especially as technology works on the web server side, ActiveX and Java Applets works better with the web browser of similar technology: Microsoft Internet Explorer and Netscape Navigator respectively. As we shall see, this brings up interesting indirect/complementary network externalities.

II. PREVIOUS WORK

Choice between Java and ActiveX is a choice of standard. Standard choice issues have long been of interest to economists. Grindley (1995) summarized six well known cases of technology/standard choice: Beta vs. VHS, DOS/Windows vs. Macintosh, compact discs, high definition television, QWERTY keyboard, and open mainframe/mini computer system. The cases show that network externalities play an important role among the standard choice.

There is a growing body of largely theoretical literature on the economics of network externalities and standards. Katz &Shapiro (1985) has classified the network externalities into direct network externalities (e.g. telephone network) and indirect network externalities (e.g. hardware and software) which result from the complementary property of goods.

Although there are some empirical work with respect to the standards and network externalities, Gandal (1994) notes that "the modeling exercises have run well ahead of the solidly established fact base". Almost all of empirical work used the hedonic price model approach. Gandal(1994) provides the evidence that the personal computer spreadsheet market exhibits network externalities. In particular, consumers are willing to pay a premium for spreadsheets that are compatible with the LOTUS platform, the dominant spreadsheet format. Addressing the same issue, Brynjolfsson and Kemerer(1996) used the data of installed base of spreadsheet and found out the price increases as the product's installed base increases.

However, hedonic models have their defects. For example, in computer software market, the list price is often not the actual market price, software sometimes goes with hardware. The market price is hard to find. In particular, when complementary network externalities occur in the market, competing firms will offer strategic price (for example, Microsoft will give out Microsoft Internet Explorer free and gain profits from complementary goods), thus disguised the price indicator (Yu (1997)). This paper tries to take on a different approach -discrete choice model approach.

III. MODEL

Choosing between Java and ActiveX, Users basically have four alternatives (all of them are technologically possible):

0: not use either of them   1: use Java but not ActiveX.
2: use ActiveX but not Java   3: use both Java and ActiveX

It is reasonable to assume that the utility of user i for choice j depends on his decision on both technologies, the characteristics of these technologies and the characteristics of the user himself and a random error term. For discrete choices, we can use multinominal logit model. The model can be described as P (user i choose j) = $(1+\exp(-b0-BX))^{(-1)}$ where X is a vector of all explanatory variables, B is a vector of coefficient.

Our candidate explanatory variables include:

General individual data: professional training background (Communication, Computer Science, Fine Arts, ...), Education Level (High School, College, Master, Doctoral), Age, Gender, Household Income, Geographical Location(USA, America other than USA, Europe, Asia, other).

Individual data concerning Internet and computing: Years on Internet (including email, ftp, etc.), Years of programming, Primary Computing Platform(Windows, Unix, Macintosh, others), Web Browser (Microsoft Internet Explorer, Netscape Navigator, others), Topics of Authoring Documents(News, Ads, Research, Sports, Entertainment, ...)

Individual data concerning Java and ActiveX: Experience with ActiveX (Yes/No), Experience with Java (Yes/No), Perceived Security level of Java, Perceived value(contribution) of Java

IV. DATA ANALYSIS

Data Source: The data used in paper is from the Graphic, Visualization & Usability Center in Georgia Institute of Technology (GVU) 7th WWW user Survey (http://www.gvu.gatech.edu/user_survey/survey-1997-04/). Our data is taken from the HTML Authoring Survey (3467 respondents), Web and Internet Usage survey (16,012 respondents) and general demographics survey (16,028 respondents). After linking data from different surveys and deleting data that miss key values (missed the Java and ActiveX choice in our case), we get a sample of size 2685.

The meanings of those variables that finally enter the model are as follows:

1. JA is the dependent variable. It has four values, it takes on 0 if the respondent does not plan to use either of them, 1if plan use Java but not ActiveX; 2 if plan to use ActiveX but not Java; 3 if plan to use both Java and ActiveX

2. BG_COMP is the dummy variable that takes on value 1 if the respondents have received professional training in computer science, 0 otherwise.
3. Ujava takes on value 1 if the respondent has used Java before, 0 otherwise.
4. UActx takes on value 1 if the respondent has used Java before, 0 otherwise.
5. JSECU is the variable measuring the perceived security level of Java. It takes on value 1 if the respondent think Java is very insecure, 2 if somewhat insecure, 3 if somewhat secure, 4 if very secure, 0 if don't know.
6. VJAVA is the variable that measure the perceived value adding of Java, 0 stands for don't know, 1 for fluffy, 2 for Aesthetic (make things prettier), 3 for functional , 4 for revolutionary .
7. TP_ADS is a dummy variable. = 1 if the documents that the respondents are mainly for advertisement or marketing, 0 otherwise.
8. BR_IE is a dummy variable. = 1 if the respondent uses Microsoft Internet Explorer as web browser, 0 otherwise
9. BR_NE is a dummy variable, = 1 if the respondent uses Netscape Navigator as web browser, zero otherwise
10. Pform_W is a dummy variable. = 1 if the respondent's primary computing platform is DOS, Windows, Win95 or Windows NT, 0 otherwise.

Since our data varied across individuals rather than choices, or in other words, our variables are all alternative - specific variables, we use a multinominal logit model to estimate the model, the result is shown in Table 1 (coefficients for LHS=0 are set to 0).

With respect to alternative 1 (plan to use Java rather than ActiveX), all the variables are significant at .05 level. We won't be surprised to see that BG_Comp has a positive sign since Java is kind of sophisticated technology, those who have professional training in computer science are more likely to be able to use it. If a user has used Java before, he tends to use it again (increase the probability of choosing 1 by .34 , please refer to the marginal effects in Table 2). At the same time, the more secure or the more value-added he feels about Java, the more likely he will choose Java rather than ActiveX.

We are especially interested in the signs of BR_IE, BR_NE and Pform_W since they reflect the effect of indirect network externalities. As we expected, choices of Java is positive related to their choice in using Netscape Navigator as web browser while negatively related to their choice of Microsoft Internet Explorer. If the primary computing platform is windows-based (that is Windows 3.1, Windows 95 or Windows NT), the probability of choosing Java but not ActiveX will decrease. Similar significant results can be seen in other alternatives (LHS=2, LHS=3). These can be viewed as evidence of complementary network externalities.

One thing notable in (LHS=2, users choose ActiveX but not Java) is that JSECU, VJAVA are insignificant. This indicates that they are committed to Microsoft technologies regardless their opinion of Java. One reason for this is that they want to capture the installed base of Microsoft platforms.

Table 1. Estimated coefficient (values in brackets are p-values)

	Y=1	Y=2	Y=3
Constant	0.2100560	0.6407790E-01	-0.2522012E-01
	(0.00000)	(0.00000)	(0.17089)
BG_COMP	0.8010206E-01	-0.7352330E-02	-0.1530411E-02
	(0.00001)	(0.32003)	(0.90551)
UJAVA	0.2377857	-0.4658158E-01	0.2200096E-01
	(0.00000)	(0.00000)	(0.12547)
UACTX	-0.3061071	0.1321291	0.3204333
	(0.00000)	(0.00000)	(0.00000)
JSECU	0.2092481E-01	-0.7800648E-03	0.8883568E-03
	(0.00233)	(0.77851)	(0.85425)
VJAVA	0.7224224E-01	-0.8469770E-02	0.2720606E-01
	(0.00000)	(0.00905)	(0.00000)
TP_ADS	0.3739433E-01	0.4130912E-02	0.8209989E-02
	(0.05178)	(0.59442)	(0.54394)
BR_IE	-0.6769201E-01	0.2750764E-01	0.4507330E-01
	(0.00000)	(0.00000)	(0.00000)
BR_NE	0.6759320E-01	-0.2750033E-01	-0.4506434E-01
	(0.00000)	(0.00000)	(0.00000)
PFORM_W	-0.8288578E-01	0.1527837E-01	0.1215271
	(0.00000)	(0.03680)	(0.00000)

The partial derivatives (marginal effects) are listed in Table 2. We can see the strongest effects among dummy variables come from the experience in using Java or ActiveX.

Table 2. Partial derivatives (Marginal Effects)

	Y=0	Y=2	Y=3	Y=4
Constant	0.4377285	-0.1077301	-0.3450707E-01	-0.2954913
BG_COMP	-0.8683955E-01	0.9292004E-01	-0.4894702E-02	-0.1185782E-02
UJAVA	-0.3376293	0.3424751	-0.2262591E-01	0.1778006E-01
UACTX	-0.6993363E-01	-0.1875049	0.4385968E-01	0.2135789
JSECU	-0.2515626E-01	0.2547309E-01	-0.1820512E-03	-0.1347817E-03
VJAVA	-0.9422665E-01	0.7507557E-01	-0.4506003E-02	0.2365708E-01
TP_ADS	-0.6670098E-01	0.5354706E-01	0.1952590E-02	0.1120133E-01
BR_IE	0.2478185E-01	-0.7098168E-01	0.8362194E-02	0.3783764E-01
BR_NE	-0.2464470E-01	0.7088063E-01	-0.8365026E-02	-0.3787091E-01
PFORM_W	-0.6068870E-01	-0.1011974	0.1316519E-01	0.1487209

Table 3 gives the actual versus predicted results, we can see that they are reasonably close.

Table 3. Actual versus Predicted results

Actual	Predicted				
	0	**1**	**2**	**3**	**Total**
0	450	343	13	24	830
1	242	1044	3	77	1336
2	17	15	23	44	99
3	47	140	10	193	390
Total	756	1542	49	338	2685

V. DISCUSSION

This paper represents a step in using discrete choice model in the study of the key Internet technology choice: Java versus ActiveX. We also examine indirect/complementary network externalities. The results of the empirical analysis are consistent to the theory and our expectation. The managerial implication of our findings will be: for the users, if may bring greater user satisfaction if we can make the choice of web authoring tools together with choice of the platforms and web browser. For vendors, it may be profitable to strategically price under marginal cost, or to bundle the complementary products together. For example, Pricing ActiveX browser aggressively can attract a big user base for ActiveX authoring tools. Bundling the web browser and the web authoring tools with the operating systems may also be a way to attract users.

This study has certain limitations. Due to the limitations of data, some variables are unavailable, some variables are obscure in meaning. We are also subject to the sampling problems of GVU surveys. This paper uses a static model, but the software technology is characterized by continuous development. In a static model, the economic meaning of each alternatives (2*2 choice of Java and ActiveX) is not very clear, however if in a dynamic model, the transmission from one status to another may make more sense and bring more insight.

REFERENCES:

Brynjolfsson, Erik and Chris Kemerer "Network Externalities in Microcomputer Software: An Econometric Analysis of the Spreadsheet Market", Management Science, 42(12), 1627-1647, December 1996.

Gandal, Neil "Hedonic price indexes for spreadsheets and an empirical test for network externalities", Rand Journal of Economics, 25(1), 160-170, spring 1994.

Gandal, Neil "Competing compatibility standards and network externalities in the PC software market", Review of Economics and Statistics, 599-608, 1995.

Grindley, P. "Standards strategy and policy: Cases and stories", Oxford University Press, 1995.

Katz, M.L and Shapiro, C. [1985] "Network Externalities, Competition and Compatibility", American Economics Review, 75:424-440.

Yu, Liang "Complementary Network Externalities", Purdue University Krannert School of Management, working paper, 1997.

Use of Recurrent Neural Networks for Strategic Data Mining of Sales Information

Jayavel Shanmugasundaram, University of Wisconsin
M. V. Nagendra Prasad, Andersen Consulting
Sanjeev Vadhavkar & Amar Gupta, Massachusetts Institute of Technology

An increasing number of organizations are involved in the development of strategic information systems for effective linkages with their suppliers, customers, and other channel partners involved in transportation, distribution, warehousing and maintenance activities. An efficient inter-organizational inventory management system based on data mining techniques is a significant step in this direction. This paper discusses the use of neural network based data mining and knowledge discovery techniques to optimize inventory levels in a large medical distribution company. The paper defines the inventory patterns, describes the process of constructing and choosing an appropriate neural network, and highlights problems related to mining of very large quantities of data. The paper identifies the strategic data mining techniques used to address the problem of estimating the future sales of medical products using past sales data. We have used recurrent neural networks to predict future sales because of their power to generalize trends and their ability to store relevant information about past sales. The paper introduces the problem domain and outlines how data mining helps to formulate the strategic vision of information technology (IT) in the company. In the technical part of the paper, we first describe the implementation of a distributed recurrent neural network using the real time recurrent learning algorithm. We then describe the validation of this implementation by providing results of tests with well-known examples from the literature. The description and analysis of the predictions made on real world data from a large medical distribution company are then presented.

1 INTRODUCTION

With the advent of data warehousing, companies have started storing large amounts of historical data. One way of exploiting this information is by using such data to predict the future. In this paper, we address the specific problem of predicting future sales using information about past sales. An accurate prediction of future sales could lead to significant savings in inventory costs etc. In this project, we used recurrent neural networks to predict future sales using past sales obtained from a medical company, Medicorp [1,2]. The results of this experiment suggest that recurrent neural networks are a good way to predict trends in sales. However, it appears that this technique is not appropriate for predicting accurate sales figures for this application. This limitation could mostly be attributed to (a) the insufficiency of data, which makes it difficult to detect long-term dependencies and (b) the uncertainty and pronounced effects of exogenous variables in the real world data, rather than to a deficiency in the technique itself. We provide a justification for the above statement by studying the predictive performance of recurrent neural networks on noisy mathematical functions, where the noise is intended to model the effects of exogenous factors. We show that recurrent neural networks are very effective at learning functions with a small amount of noise and that the performance degrades substantially as the noise level increases. The major phases of the projects involved the following. First, a general recurrent neural network was implemented. This implementation, which could easily be adapted to run in distributed environments, was done using C++. The real-time recurrent learning algorithm, with appropriate modifications made to make the implementation distributed, was used. This implementation was then tested on some standard problems from the literature. Recurrent neural networks were then used to predict some real world data provided by Medicorp. The nature of the predicted results were then investigated and possible explanations for these results were put forth based on the ability of recurrent neural networks to learn noisy mathematical functions.

The main contributions of the paper are
* Data mining techniques for strategic information systems.
* Distributed design of a recurrent neural network architecture for strategic data mining
* Building of a general recurrent neural network simulator which can be instantiated with different network topologies and node activation functions.
* Investigation, analysis and explanation of the predictions and results based on real world data from a large medical distribution company.
* Suggestions for alternative data mining architectures which could prove useful.

The rest of the project report is organized as follows. Section 2 describes the problem to be solved in some detail and section 3 explains why the recurrent neural network architecture was chosen over other architectures for this problem. The implementation of the recurrent neural network is described in section 4. Section 5 presents and analyzes the prediction results on Medicorp data. Section 6 provides the conclusions and the lessons learned from this endeavor.

2 THE PROBLEM DOMAIN

With hundreds of chain stores and with revenues of several billion dollars per annum, Medicorp is a large retail distribution company that dispenses pharmaceutical drugs to customers in a number of states in the United States. Just as any other retailer in its position, Medicorp is forced to carry a large standing inventory of products ready to deliver on customer demand. The problem is how much quantity of each drug should be kept in the inventory at each store and warehouse. Medicorp incurs significant financial costs if it carries excess quantities of drugs relative to the customer demand. Unsatisfied customers frequently turn to competing stores, and Medicorp loses potential profits in such cases. Because of negative experiences, unsatisfied customers may switch company loyalties, relying on other pharmaceutical chains to serve them. On the other hand, Medicorp incurs a financial cost if it carries excessive inventory levels, especially because pharmaceutical drugs have limited shelf-lives Historically, Medicorp has maintained an inventory of approximately a billion dollars on a continuing basis and has used traditional regression models to determine inventory levels for each item. The corporate policy of Medicorp is governed by two competing principles: minimize total inventory and achieve highest level of customer satisfaction. The former principle is not quantified in numerical terms. On the latter issue, Medicorp strives to achieve a 95% fulfillment level. That is, if a random customer walks into a random store, the probability for the availability of the particular item is 95%. The figure of 95% is based on the type of goods that Medicorp carries, and the service levels offered by competitors of Medicorp for the same items. Medicorp has about 1000 stores, and maintains information on what is sold, at what price, and to whom. The last piece of data has not been utilized in any inventory-modeling endeavor at Medicorp. After reviewing various options, Medicorp adopted a "three-weeks of supply" approach [1]. This approach involves the regression study of historical data to compute a seasonally - adjusted estimate of the forecasted demand for the next three week period. This estimated demand is the inventory level that Medicorp keeps, or strives to keep, on a continuing basis. Each store within the Medicorp chain orders replenishments on a weekly basis and receives the ordered items 2-3 days later. Overall, this model yields the 95% target for customer satisfaction. Medicorp would like to explore the use of strategic data mining techniques to achieving the strategic corporate goals for customer satisfaction and cutting down on the current inventory.

The best way to manage an inventory is to be able to develop better techniques for predicting customer demands and stock inventories accordingly. In this way, the size of the drug inventory can be optimized to keep up with demand. To find the best solution to the inventory problem, we looked at the transactional data warehouse at Medicorp. The Medicorp data warehouse is hundreds of gigabytes in size containing all sales information from 1986 to the present. From this vast data warehouse, we extracted a portion of the recent fields (Jan. 1995 - Sept 1996) which we felt would provide adequate raw data for a preliminary statistical analysis:

Date field - Indicates the date of the drug transaction
Customer number - Uniquely identifies a customer (useful in tracking repeat customers)
NDC number - Uniquely identifies a drug (equivalent to a drug name)
Quantity number - Identifies the amount of the drug purchased
Days of Supply - Identifies how long that particular drug purchased will last
Sex fields - Identifies the sex of the customer
Cost Unit Price - Establishes the per unit cost to Medicorp of the particular drug
Sold Unit Price - Identifies per unit cost to the customer of the particular drug

The preliminary statistical analysis was utilized to help search for seasonal trends, correlation between field variables and significance of variables, etc. Our preliminary statistical data provided evidence for the following conclusions:

* Women are more careful about consuming medication than men.
* Sales of most drugs showed no or little correlation to seasonal changes.
* Drug sales are heaviest on Thursdays and Fridays.
* Drug sales (in terms of quantity of drug sold) show differing degrees of variability:
  Maintenance type drugs (for chronic ailments) show low degrees of sales variability.
  Acute type drugs (for temporary ailments) show high degrees of sales variability.

3 REASONS FOR CHOOSING RECURRENT NEURAL NETWORKS

In this section, we explain the rationale behind choosing recurrent neural networks as the prediction technique for the problem at hand. After a survey of the time series prediction literature, we found that neural networks performed at least as well as other techniques in a majority of cases. For example, the results of the Santa Fe competition on time series prediction [11] suggest that the performance of neural networks is better than that of other techniques for predicting the future trends in stock prices. A paper authored by Mozer [9], which explains the details of the neural network architectures used in that competition, served as a starting point for the exploration of different neural network architectures. The problem of predicting future sales, as with other time series prediction problems, requires the network to maintain some sort of state1 so that it can detect and use trends in the data to make future predictions. Of the neural network architectures with state, we decided to choose from either recurrent neural networks or time≠delay neural networks because they seemed to be the most well studied, with a large body of work describing how to set parameters etc.

The results in [9] indicate that the predictive performance of recurrent neural networks and time delay networks do not differ greatly. We chose the recurrent neural network architecture because the length of the delay in time≠delay networks has to be set in advance [7] and because recurrent neural networks are more general than time delay networks. The reason for the latter is that recurrent neural networks could learn to delay the inputs to any arbitrary length in time2.

4 IMPLEMENTATION OF RECURRENT NEURAL NETWORKS

In this section, we first describe the reasons for choosing a particular learning algorithm for recurrent neural networks. We then explain the details of this algorithm and the modifications made to make the algorithm distributed. A distributed design for recurrent neural networks is also presented. Finally, we describe experiments used to validate the implementation of the distributed design.

4.1 Selecting the Learning Algorithm

The three main algorithms that exist for training recurrent neural networks and their advantages and disadvantages are listed below:

1. Back Propagation through Time: This is an extension of the regular back-propagation algorithm used in feed≠forward neural networks. However, at each time instance, the back propagation algorithm takes time proportional to the number of time ticks after the start time. Also, the storage needs increase with time. Thus, this approach is impractical when the length of the sequence is unbounded and is computationally expensive when input sequences are long.
2. Time≠Dependent Recurrent Back≠Propagation: This algorithm is for training a continuous≠time recurrent network. This algorithm has very modest space and time requirements. However, this algorithm does not allow for real-time learning.
3. Real≠Time Recurrent Learning: This algorithm can be used to train general recurrent neural networks and has space and time requirements which are independent of time (though still more than the requirement for Time≠Dependent Recurrent Back≠Propagation algorithm). An advantage of this algorithm is that it can be run on-line without waiting for the sequence to be complete.

Since we wanted to have a general implementation which could be used for many time series prediction tasks, we chose to use the Real≠Time Recurrent Learning [14, 13] (RTRL) algorithm. Though this implementation is more expensive in terms of space and time when compared to the time≠dependent recurrent Back-Propagation algorithm, the on-line nature of the RTRL algorithm allows for continuous learning and prediction over arbitrarily long sequences (such as what might be expected in our domain of interest).

4.2 Design of the Neural Network

The design of the neural network was made to facilitate implementation in a distributed environment. Nodes and Edges in the neural network were modeled as objects and interactions between these components occurred only through well-defined interfaces. These interactions could be directly translated into messages in a distributed environment. Modifications were also made to the RTRL learning algorithm so that maximum parallelism could be exploited in a distributed implementation. These modifications ensure that nodes in a network have to communicate only with nodes connected to them (the output nodes, however, have to communicate with all the nodes in the network).

The implementation of this distributed design was done using C++ because the object≠oriented concepts in the language matched the design well. The implementation was made general enough so that arbitrary topologies of networks could be instantiated and activation functions could be specified independently for every node. The learning rate can also be varied and a momentum term can be specified to filter out high frequency disturbances on the error surface that the network traverses during the learning phase.

4.3 Validation of the Implementation

We tested the implementation of the recurrent neural network by making it learn (a) Exclusive Or with Delay [14] and (b) to be a Shift Register [10]. We present the learning results on the Delayed Exclusive Or problem in this report.

4.3.1 The Delayed Exclusive Or Problem . This problem involves giving the network a continuous stream of two inputs. The Exclusive Or of the inputs at time t is the required output at time t + 2. Thus, the recurrent neural network should not only learn that the output is the Exclusive Or of the inputs but should also learn that the output is to be delayed by two time units. No information other than the input and the expected output is given to the network. Table 1 shows an example trace of inputs and outputs presented to the network.

Time	Input 1	Input 2	Output	Comments
1	1	0	0.5	Output undefined, so arbitrarily set to 0.5
2	1	1	0.5	Output undefined, so arbitrarily set to 0.5
3	0	0	1	Exclusive Or of inputs at time 1
4	1	1	0	Exclusive Or of inputs at time 2
...	...	...	...	...
N	0	1	0	Exclusive Or of inputs at time N-2
N+1	1	0	0	Exclusive Or of inputs at time N-1
N+2	0	0	1	Exclusive Or of inputs at time N

Table 1: Traces of Input and Output in Delayed Xor

4.3.2 Experimental Results. A recurrent neural network with 3 nodes was presented with the time delayed Exclusive Or patterns. A learning rate of 0.1 was used and training was done over 100000 test inputs. The momentum term was set to 0.5. The output of the network at some time t was said to be correct if it differed from the actual output by no more than 0.25 (thus, the squared error for a "correct" output should be less that 0.0625). As figure 1 shows, the network learned the relationship between the inputs and the output. We also tried training a five node recurrent neural network with a 3-time delay Exclusive Or pattern and this function too was effectively learnt. The results that we obtained are consistent with those presented in [14]. A recurrent neural network with three nodes was also trained to be a shift register with two time delays between input and output. From the positive outcome of these experiments, and by carefully studying the execution traces of the program, we concluded that the implementation of recurrent neural networks was "correct" and could be used for real≠world problems.

5 SALES PREDICTIONS

In this section, we present the prediction results on real≠world data obtained using recurrent neural networks. We first discuss how the recurrent neural network was trained and how over≠fitting was avoided. We then discuss the value of parameters chosen for the predictions and reasons for the choice. Finally, we present an analysis of the prediction results and investigate the appropriateness of recurrent neural networks for this prediction task.

5.1 Architecture and input/output format

Since the requirement was to predict the sales one-day in advance, we chose to treat each day as one unit of time. Thus, we had 365 data points, which corresponded to each day in 1995, as the training data set. At each time instance t, the sales for the day t were given to the network and the sales for day t + 1 were obtained as the output of the network. No other input was given because Medicorp provided no information about other variables. We used an implicit representation of time [6], i.e., time was not an explicit parameter, which was input to the recurrent neural network but was implicitly represented as the training period of the network.

The input sales were scaled between -1 and +1 using the formula: scaled_sales = 2 * (actual_sales / max_sales) - 1 (1) where scaled_sales is the scaled value of actual_sales, given that the maximum sales of the product in a day is max_sales. The output sales predicted by the neural network, which lies between 0 and 1 for logistic units, were scaled to give the predicted sales using the formula: predicted_sales = (predicted-value - x) * max_sales / (1 - 2 * x) (2) where predicted-value is the value predicted by the network corresponding to the sales for the next day (the day after the current time step with respect to the network). The value of x served to scale the output to between x and 1 - x because logistic units have difficulty predicting extreme values (near 0 and 1).

The information about the actual value of the next day sales is provided to the network for updating its weights. The transformation performed to these sales before being given as the required output to the network is the inverse transformation of the one presented above. Required prediction sales is determined the formula required prediction = x + [actual_future_sales * (1 - 2 * x) / max_sales] (3) where actual_future_sales is the actual value of sales on the day of after the current day.

The 365 data points available for the year 1995 were used as the training data set. Since repeated training (many epochs) was sometimes required when we used small learning rates, the outputs of each unit was set to 0.5 (a neutral value between the extremes 0 and 1) at the beginning of each epoch.

5.2 Avoiding Over≠fitting

One of the problems faced in training neural networks is over≠fitting to the data used for training. After the network learns the general trends present, it tries to fit its predictions to the actual data that is presented for training. This leads to prediction results that are skewed to the idiosyncrasies of the training data set. To avoid this, we used the half-year data available for 1996 as the test data set to avoid over-fitting. The sum of the squared errors of the predicted sales for the first half of 1996 was measured after each training epoch. When this error started rising, it meant that the neural network was starting to over≠fit with respect to the training data [12]. This technique proved to be very effective for most of the predictions. This was because the minimum sum of the squared errors on the test data set far exceeded the sum of the squared errors on the test data set when the network "converged". Figure 2 shows a typical over≠fitting curve.

5.3 Determining Appropriate Parameters for the Architecture

There are four parameters, which have to be determined before using a recurrent neural network to predict values. They are
(a) The number of nodes in the recurrent neural network.
(b) The learning rate of the neural network
(c) The momentum rate used to remove high frequency variations in the error surface
(d) The variable x defined in section 5.1.

The momentum term was not experimented with as part of this project and was set to 0 in all the simulations. The details as to how the other parameters were determined are given below:

5.3.1 Learning Rate . The learning rate was chosen to be low enough so that the curve got by plotting the mean square error on the test data set (and the training data set) versus the number of training epochs was a smooth curve. What this meant was that the mean square error on the training data set monotonically decreased over time and the mean square error on the test data set decreased monotonically till the point of over≠fitting, after which it increased monotonically. We experimented with various learning rates for the problem at hand and finally arrived at the learning rate of 0.001 for fast moving drugs and 0.01 for slow moving drugs. These learning rates give rise to smooth mean square error curves like the one given in figure 2. A higher learning rate of 0.01 for fast moving drugs gives rise to noisy error curves like the one shown in figure 3. Even a higher learning rate of 0.1 does not lead to any learning at all.

5.3.2 Number of Nodes . Initially, we hypothesized that the larger the number of nodes in the neural network, the better the prediction is likely to be. However, on running experiments, we found that this was not the case and that there were networks with a certain number of nodes that were better suited for the task than other networks. We feel that the reason for this is over-generalization when there are too few nodes and under≠generalization when there are too many nodes. That is, when there are too few nodes, the network is unable do enough processing and has enough information to detect trends and predict good output. However, when there are too many nodes, the network acts like a lookup table and stores specific variations in output. Thus, the network is unable to generalize and pick up trends. In the case of fast moving drugs, surprisingly, the recurrent neural network with just 4 nodes performs better than most architectures with more number of nodes. This is probably because trends are more short-term in fast moving drugs and/or because a lot of generalization is required. Figure 4 shows how the error varies with the number of nodes in the network for a particular fast moving drug. This pattern was roughly followed for the other fast moving drugs too (only in one out of the 4 cases did the error for the four node network exceed the error of a network with a different number of nodes). We also notice that the error starts to decrease as the number of nodes is increased past 10. This decrease is however very gradual and the error of the 4 node network continues to be better than networks having any reasonable number of nodes. In our experiments, we used networks with 4, 10 and 20 nodes for predicting fast moving drugs. For slow moving drugs, the variation in error is roughly similar to the variation in figure 4 with the exception that the error for networks with 10 nodes is almost the same as the error for networks with 4 nodes. We used networks with 4, 10 and 20 nodes for predicting the sales of slow moving drugs too.

5.3.3 Output Scaling . Since each node in the recurrent neural network has a logistic activation function, it is very difficult for the network to output extreme values (i.e., near 0 and 1). In order to overcome this difficulty, we studied the effect of scaling output in the range x to 1-x linearly so that the effective output range was between 0 and 1. Figure 6 gives the minimum sum of the squared error on the test set of a fast moving drug for different values of x. This figure is similar for slow moving drugs. We see that the error increases with the value of x. The reason for this is twofold:

(a) As the value of x increases, even slight differences in the output are magnified when the scale is adjusted to the [0, 1] range.

(b) The networks do not make high amplitude predictions for this application (reasons will be given in later sections).

Since the error when x = 0 is about the same as the error when x = 0.1 and because slow moving drugs require the network to predict 0 sales, we chose to use the latter setting for our experiments.

5.4 Prediction Results

In this section, we present some graphs, which show the prediction results of the recurrent neural network. For the sake of brevity, sales prediction results are shown for only two of Medicorp's products. These two were selected as representative samples from the ten products whose sales were predicted. Figure 6 shows the actual sales of drug 1 (a fast moving drug) on each day of the year 1995 and figure 7 shows the actual sales of drug 1 for the first half of 1996. Figure 8 shows the predicted results of a recurrent neural network having 4 nodes (this prediction had the minimum square error on the test set). Figures 9 and 10 show the predictions of architectures with 10 and 20 nodes. The predictions of these two architectures do not minimize the squared error on the test set but these figure are included so that the predictions of recurrent neural networks with varying number of nodes could be compared. Note that the scales of the graphs are different because each graph was scaled to show the maximum amount of detail. Thus, for example, figures 7 and 8 look different although they show the same trends.

5.5 Analysis of Prediction Results

On interacting with Medicorp management, we found out that they were interested primarily in two prediction results:

(a) The trend of the sale for the next day, i.e., whether sales were going to increase, decrease or remain the same and

(b) The actual amount of sales for the next day. An accurate determination of would automatically provide the information requested in (a).

However, the Medicorp management suggested that trend analysis would be very useful even if accurate prediction for the next day were not possible. This is because any indicator of trends is likely to lead to savings. In this section, we determine how the predictions of the recurrent neural networks measure against these two metrics.

5.5.1 Trend Analysis . In general, the predicted results seem to follow the trends well for fast moving drugs. The predictions in figure 8 follow the actual trends 70% of the time. If the prediction was always up or always down (fast moving drugs rarely have the same sales for two consecutive days), the expected percentage of correct trend predictions is 50%. Thus, we can see that the neural

Fast Moving Drug Number	% of Right Trend Predictions
1	60.55%
2	62.77%
3	70.00%
4	65.00%

Slow Moving Drug Number	% of No Changes	% of Right Trend Predictions
1	52.77%	55.56%
2	51.11%	61.11%
3	50.00%	52.33%
4	46.11%	52.78%

Table 2: Trend Predictions for Fast Moving Drugs   *Table 3: Trend Predictions for Slow Moving Drugs*

network uses regularities in the data to predict future trends. In general, the prediction of trends was good for all the fast moving drugs we investigated. Table 2 shows the percentage of correct trend predictions for four fast moving drugs.

The trend prediction in the case of slow moving drugs is also good. For instance, the predictions in drug 4 match the actual trends 52.78% of the time. This is better than always predicting that the sales would remain the same (the most frequent category), which gives only 46.11% accuracy. Thus, we see that the neural networks learn some sort of patterns in the sales of slow moving drugs too. The percentage of correct trend predictions for four slow moving drugs is given in table 3.

5.5.2 Error in Sale Prediction. Unfortunately, recurrent neural networks do not predict the actual sales figures too well. This can be seen by comparing figures 7 and 8, representing sales and predictions of fast moving drugs. Although the predicted results follow the trends rather well, the amplitude of the predictions is much less than that of the actual results. The results are worse in the case of slow moving drugs. Even the constant prediction does not fall to 0 because of uncertainty about the next peak.

We use the root mean square error (scaled between 0 and 1 using the formula used to scale the actual output sales) of the predicted sales with respect to the test set as the measure of the deviation between the predicted output and the actual output. Tables 4 and 5 tabulate these values for four fast moving and four slow moving drugs respectively.

Fast Moving Drug Number	Root Mean Square Error
1	0.17
2	0.23
3	0.20
4	0.22

Table 4: Prediction Error for Fast Moving Drugs

Slow Moving Drug Number	Root Mean Square Error
1	0.20
2	0.23
3	0.25
4	0.19

Table 5: Prediction Error for Slow Moving Drugs

This root mean square error for fast moving drugs is very high (approximately 20% of the total variation). This coupled with the fact that the output varies within a range of only 0.6 about 90% of the time suggests that the amplitudes predicted are not likely to be too useful. In the case of slow moving drugs, although the output is usually 0, the network cannot predict this because of uncertainty about the height of the next peak.

We feel that the prediction of the amount of future sales is not very accurate mainly due to the uncertainty introduced due to the effects of exogenous variables. This hypothesis is consistent with that presented in [9]. Recurrent neural networks can effectively learn some fundamental mathematical functions and this learning rapidly deteriorates in the presence of noise (which is intended to model the effects of exogenous variables).

The prediction results suggested in the previous sections suggest that, although recurrent neural networks perform well in detecting trends, they do not always predict the correct magnitude of sales. The effect of exogenous variables on Medicorp's sales could be a major cause for this difference in prediction and actual results. Predictions will become weaker as the amount of noise (which could be construed as the effects of exogenous variables) becomes more pronounced.

6 CONCLUSIONS AND FUTURE WORK

The rapid growth of business databases has overwhelmed the traditional, interactive approaches to data analysis and created a need for a new generation of tools for intelligent and automated discovery in data. Knowledge discovery in databases presents many interesting challenges within the context of providing computer tools for exploring large data archives. Inventory control is a nascent application for neural network based strategic data mining and knowledge discovery techniques.

The paper presents preliminary data from research effort currently underway in the Sloan School of Management in strategic data mining [1, 2]. Earlier efforts from this research group concentrated on the use of multi layer perceptron (MLP) and time delay neural networks (TDNN) for inventory control. Prototype based on these networks was successful in reducing the total level of inventory by 50% in Medicorp, while maintaining the same level of probability that a particular customer's demand will be satisfied.

In this paper, we designed and implemented a recurrent neural network and used it to predict sales. The predicted results were a good indicator of the trends but did not have strong (high amplitude) predictions. We have put forth one possible explanation for this phenomenon in terms of exogenous variables. More specifically, noise weakens the predictions of recurrent neural networks, which otherwise are able to accurately predict data. One possible reason for the weak prediction of Medicorp's sales could be the pronounced effects of exogenous variables on sales. Since the effects of these variables would appear as noise to the neural network (in the absence of any information about the variables), the predictions are conservative and not too high in amplitude. However, the trends in sales are predicted accurately, in spite of the influence of these exogenous variables.

During the course of this project, we also investigated alternatives to the recurrent neural network architecture. Barto et. al. [3] use Associative Reward Penalty (ARP) units instead of standard logistic units in a neural network. A modified architecture could use these units in place of logistic units in a neural network and use eligibility traces so that the units remember the past and use it to predict the future. Since the ARP units are stochastic, they have fewer tendencies to get stuck in local minima. Though using the architecture will not avoid the problems due to exogenous variables, this architecture may be better suited for prediction tasks. Including exogenous variables in the predictions and exploring this new architecture are plans for future work.

Acknowledgments. We thank Aparna Agrawal for her help in building training data for the neural network. We also thank Gerardo J. Lemus Rodriguez, Auroop Ganguly and Neil Bhandar for their helpful ideas and discussions. Proactive support from the top management of Medicorp throughout the endeavor is greatly appreciated.

Figures available upon request from authors.

REFERENCES

[1] Bansal, K. Vadhavkar, S. and Gupta, A., "Neural Networks based Forecasting Techniques for Inventory Control Applications" in International Journal of Agile Manufacturing, Vol. 2. No. 1, 1998.

[2] Bansal, K. Vadhavkar, S. and Gupta, A., "Neural Networks Based Data Mining Applications For Medical Inventory Problems" in Data Mining and Knowledge Discovery, Vol2. Issue 1, 1998, pp. 07-102.

[3] Barto, A.G., "Adaptive Neural Networks for Learning Control: Some Computational Experiments," Proceedings from the IEEE Workshop on Intelligent Control, 1985.

[4] Barto, A.G., Jordan, M.L., "Gradient Following Without Back≠Propagation in Layered Networks," Proceedings of the IEEE First Annual International Conference on Neural Networks, June 1987.

[5] Barto, A.G., Sutton, R.S., Anderson, C.W., "Neuron like Adaptive Elements That Can Solve Difficult Learning Control Problems," IEEE Transactions on Systems, Man and Cybernetics, Vol. SMC≠13, No. 5, Oct. 1983.

[6] Elman, J.L., "Finding Structure in Time," Cognitive Science, vol. 14, pp. 179≠211, 1990.

[7] Hertz, J.A., Krogh, A.S., Palmer, R.G., "Introduction to the Theory of Neural Computation," Santa Fe Institute Studies in the Sciences of Complexity, Lecture Notes vol. I, Addison≠Wesley, 1991.

[8] McClelland, J.L., Rumelhart, D.E., "Explorations in Parallel and Distributed Processing," MIT Press, Cambridge, 1988.

[9] Mozer, M.C., "Neural Net Architectures for Temporal Sequence Processing," Predicting the future and understanding the past (Eds. A. Weigend and N. Gershenfeld), Addison≠Wesley, 1993.

[10] Rumelhart, D.E., McClelland, J.L., "Parallel Distributed Processing: Explorations in the Microstructure of Cognition," MIT Press, Cambridge, 1986.

[11] Weigend, A.S., Gershenfeld, N.A., "Time Series Prediction: Forecasting the Future and Understanding the Past," A Proceedings Volume in the Santa Fe Institute Studies in the Sciences of Complexity, Addison-Wesley, 1994.

[12] Weigend, A.S., Huberman, B.A., Rumelhart, D.E., "Predicting the Future: A Connectionist Approach," International Journal of Neural Systems, vol. 1, pp. 193≠209, 1990.

[13] Williams, R.J., Peng, J., "An Efficient Gradient≠Based Algorithm for On Line Training of Recurrent Network Trajectories," Neural Computation, vol. 2, pp. 490≠501, 1990.

[14] Williams, R.J., Zipser, D., "Experimental Analysis of the Real-time Recurrent Learning Algorithm," Connection Science, vol. 1, no. 1, pp. 87≠111, 1989.

Endnotes

1 This is not necessary if the sales data for x days is given as input to the network, where x is large enough to subsume the period of any pattern in the data. However, in real world situations, one is unlikely to know the periods of such trends and hence, this workaround is not always feasible.

2 The length to which the recurrent neural network can delay the input signal increases with the number of units in the network.

Approximate k-Nearest Neighbor Search Algorithm for Content-Based Multimedia Information Retrieval

Kwang-Taek Song and Jae-Woo Chang
Dept of Computer Engineering
Chonbuk National University
Chonju, Chonbuk 560-756, Korea
Tel: +82 652-270-2414 {ktsong, jwchang}@dblab.chonbuk.ac.kr

Hakgene Shin
Dept. of Office Automation
Chonju Kijeon Women's College
Chonju, Chonbuk 560-701, Korea
Tel: +82 652-280-5265: shin@kns.kijeon-c.ac.kr

ABSTRACT

The k-nearest neighbor search based on similarity is one of very important issues for content-based multimedia information retrieval(MIR). The conventional exact k-nearest neighbor(k-NN) search algorithm is not efficient for the MIR applications because multimedia data should be represented as high dimensional feature vectors. Thus, the approximate k-nearest neighbor search algorithms have been addressed because the performance increase may outweigh the drawback of receiving approximate results. In this paper, we propose a new approximate k-nearest neighbor search algorithm for high dimensional data to achieve fast retrieval. In addition, the comparison of the conventional algorithm with our approximate k-nearest neighbor search algorithm is performed in terms of retrieval performance. Results show that our algorithm is more efficient than the conventional ones.

1. INTRODUCTION

Since internet, computer hardware, and network have been rapidly developed, users should handle various multimedia data. To fulfill the requirements of handling multimedia data, the similarity search in multimedia database has become an important issue. The similarity search is briefly defined as searching for the set of similar objects to a given query object. Mostly, similarity is not measured based on the objects directly, but rather based on the abstractions of objects, called features. In many cases, features are described as points in some high-dimensional vector space. The similarity of two objects is assumed to be proportional to the similarity of their feature vectors, which is measured as the distance between feature vectors. Thus, the similarity search is implemented as a nearest neighbor search within the feature space. In the content-based multimedia retrieval system, it is important for the system to efficiently support k-nearest neighbor search query. Since the conventional GIS applications handle relatively small number of objects, the exact k-nearest neighbor search has not considered the efficiency much. However, in case of query against large multimedia database, the searching for exact k-nearest neighbor objects requires significantly high disk I/Os. To overcome this overhead, approximate k-nearest neighbor search algorithm were proposed [Ary94]. Although these algorithms generally work well for low-dimensional spaces, their performance is known to degrade as the number of dimension increases, which is called ëdimensional curseí phenomenon In this paper, we propose a new approximate k-nearest neighbor search algorithm suitable for content-based multimedia database in dynamic database environments. Our algorithm reduces disk I/Os with reasonable false drops. We show that the performance increase of our algorithm outweighs disadvantages of receiving approximate results. We also show that our algorithm outperforms other approximate search algorithms and it is useful for the environments with very frequent user queries.

The organization of this paper is as follows. In Section 2, we will review some conventional k-nearest neighbor search algorithms. In Section 3, we propose a new approximate k-nearest neighbor search algorithm for high dimensional multimedia data. In Section 4, we compare our new approximate k-nearest search algorithms with the conventional ones in terms of precision and the number of page I/Os. In Section 5, we draw our conclusion.

2. RELATED WORKS

In this section, we review previous nearest neighbor(NN) search algorithm, exact k-NN search algorithm, and approximate k-NN search algorithm for data-partitioning index tree. [Rou95] proposes an approach using the R-tree for nearest neighbor search. The algorithm reduces the number of visiting nodes by computing the minimum distance (MINDIST) and the minmax distance (MINMAXDIST) between a given query point and minimum bounding rectangle (MBR) representing sub-branches or objects. Given a query point P and an object O enclosed in its MBR, MINDIST is based on the minimum distance of the object O from P and MINMAXDIST is based on the minimum of the maximum possible distances from P to a face(or vertex) of the MBR containing O. MINDIST and MINMAXDIST offer a lower and an upper bound on the actual distance of O from P respectively. These bounds are used by the nearest neighbor search algorithm to efficiently prune the paths of the search space in an R-tree.

In order to guarantee significantly better query time than brute-force search with a modest amount of space, the alternative approach of finding approximate nearest neighbors is worth considering[Ary94]. Consider a set S of data points in R^d and a query point $q \in R^d$. Given $\varepsilon > 0$, we say that a point $p \in S$ is a $(1+\varepsilon)$-nearest neighbor of q if DISTANCE (p,q)/DISTANCE$(p^*,q) \leq (1+\varepsilon)$ where p^* is the true nearest neighbor to q. In other words, p is within relative error ε of the true nearest neighbor. More generally, for $1 \leq k \leq n$, a k-th $(1+\varepsilon)$-nearest neighbor of q is a data point whose relative error from the true k-th nearest neighbor of q is ε. For $1 \leq k \leq n$, we define a sequence of k $(1+\varepsilon)$-nearest neighbors of query point q to be a sequence of k distinct data points, such that the i-th point in the sequence is an i-th $(1+\varepsilon)$-nearest neighbor of q. [Loh97] defines MAXDIST which is used for increasing the performance of the k-NN search. The distances between the query point P and every objects included in MBR R are smaller than MAXDIST(P, R). Based on the approximate rate ε, [Loh97] applies the approximate k-NN algorithm to R*-tree.

3. NEW APPROXIMATE K-NEAREST NEIGHBOR SEARCH

In this section, we propose a new approximate k-nearest neighbor (k-NN) search algorithm for fast retrieval in high-dimensional feature space.

3.1 Motivation

The feature vector generated from multimedia object is high dimensional. But, when the conventional k-NN search algorithms are applied to high dimensional data, the performance is dramatically degraded. Therefore, it is necessary to provide an approximate k-NN search algorithm which is quickly responding to user query. While keeping the approximate error rate smaller than acceptable level in query results, the algorithm should have reduced search space by a pruning strategy, in order to perform fast retrieval operations. The conventional approximate k-NN algorithm shows faster response than the exact k-NN algorithm in low dimensional data. However, the conventional k-NN search algorithm does not improve its retrieval performance if it is applied to high dimensional data(as shown in Figure 1). As the dimension increases, MINDIST decreases and MINMAXDIST increases respectively, and so the distance between MINDIST and MINMAXDIST used for pruning strategy is sharply increasing. As shown in Figure 1 (b), when the pruning strategy is applied to the high-dimensional data, the search space is not reduced because it cannot find any MBR which has MINDIST greater than the k-th smaller MINMAXDIST.

To perform fast approximate k-NN search query for high dimensional data, it is necessary to provide more efficient pruning strategy. The pruning strategy for the fast approximate k-NN search should support the followings.

1. It should be able to efficiently reduce the search space
2. While increasing the number of pruning, it should be able to keep the false drop low.

3.2 New Pruning Strategy of Approximate k-Nearest Neighbor Search

To overcome the problems mentioned in section 3.1, we introduce new distance concept (i.e., metric) for an efficient prun-

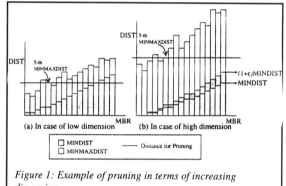

Figure 1: Example of pruning in terms of increasing dimension

ing in high dimensional data space.

Definition 1. The distance of a point P from a rectangle R in the same feature-vector space, denoted $\text{MINMAXDIST}_\beta(P,R)$, is the following. ($0 \leq \beta < 1$)

$$\text{MINMAXDIST}_\beta(P,R) = \text{MINDIST}(P,R_k) + (1-\beta)\text{MINMAXDIST}(P,R) - \text{MINDIST}(P,R_k))$$

For an efficient pruning in the first step, we use MINMAXDIST_β which is the reduced MINMAXDIST by β-value. Since the difference between MINMAXDIST AND MINDIST increases in high dimensional data, we use the β-value, which is an arbitrary rate from 0 to 1, so as to reduce MINMAXDIST. If we don't reduce the difference using the β-value, the pruning rarely happens in the initial stage of the pruning strategy. $\text{MINDIST}(P, R_k)$ means the MINDIST of k-th MBR in the list of MBRs ordered by MINDIST. $\text{MINMAXDIST}_\beta(P, R)$ is smaller than $\text{MINMAXDIST}(P, R)$ and is larger than $\text{MINDIST}(P, R_k)$. Therefore, in case of pruning by $\text{MINMAXDIST}_\beta(P, R)$, we can avoid pruning too much because the pruning leaves at least k number of sub-nodes

Definition 2. Given a point P and a rectangle R of the same dimensionality, we define $\text{MAXDIST}_\beta(P,R)$ as follows. ($0 \leq \beta < 1$).

$$\text{MAXDIST}_\beta(P,R) = \text{MINDIST}(P,R_k) + (1-\beta)\text{MAXDIST}(P,R) - \text{MINDIST}(P,R_k))$$

The MAXDIST_β reduced by β-value provides an efficient pruning in the second step. $\text{MAXDIST}_\beta(P, R)$ is a metric which overcomes the shortcomings of the pruning step using MAXDIST(P, R) proposed by [Loh97]. We use the β-value in order to reduce MAXDIST(P, R). Thus, in case of pruning by $\text{MAXDIST}_\beta(P, R)$, we can avoid pruning too much because the pruning leaves at least k number of sub-nodes.

Definition 3. Given a point P and a rectangle R of the same dimensionality, we define $\text{DISTANCE}_\beta(P, o_k)$ as follows. ($0 \leq \beta < 1$).

$$\text{DISTANCE}_\beta(P,R) = \text{MINDIST}(P,R_k) + (1-\beta)\text{DISTANCE}(P,R) - \text{MINDIST}(P,R_k))$$

The $\text{DISTANCE}(P, o_k)$ is a metric between P and the k-nearest neighbor object which has been found. The $\text{DISTANCE}_\beta(P, o_k)$ is a metric reduced by β-value. Using the DISTANCE_β, we can reduce the search space. To avoid too much pruning leading to many false drops, we limit the reduced metric to $\text{MINDIST}(P, R_k)$. Based on the definition 1, 2, and 3, we propose new pruning strategies (PS) for approximate k-NN algorithm to prune MBRs during the search as follows:

PS 1. An MBR R with MINDIST(P, R) which is greater than the $\text{MINMAXDIST}_\beta(P, R')$ of MBR R' with k-the nearer MINMAXDIST from query point P is discarded .

PS 2. An MBR R with MINDIST(P, R) which is greater than the $\text{DISTANCE}_\beta(P, o_k)$ of o_k with k-th nearer DISTANCE from query point P is discarded.

PS 3. When MBR R_1, R_2, ..., R_i include more than k number of object (i < k), an MBR R with MINDIST(P, R) which is greater than the $\text{MAXDIST}_\beta(P, Ri)$ of R_i with the farthest MAXDIST from query point P is discarded .

Figure 2 shows an example of the pruning using the MINMAXDIST_β of PS1 in case of k=5. D1 is the 5-th nearer MINMAXDIST to the query point and D2 is the 5-th nearer MINDIST. By the definition1, P is the distance for the actual pruning which is a reduced D1 using β-value. The pruning strategy using P resolves the problem such that D1 can not prune any nodes when it is applied to exact k-NN search. Also, the pruning strategy avoids pruning too much because it leaves at least k number of sub-branches.

3.3 Our Approximate k-Nearest Neighbor Search Algorithm

We refine the approximate k-NN search algorithm using the pruning strategies such as PS1, PS2, and PS3. The k-NN algorithm manages the nodes to visit by using BranchList as Queue structure. Thus, the search space can be efficiently reduced to perform the optimal approximate k-NN search. While visiting the node with the shortest distance from the query point to the child node in the directory node, the rest of the nodes in the directory are stored into BranchList. If the distance from the query point to the node to visit is farther than the distance to the k-th object ok in the list R containing the search results, the visiting of the node is canceled. If a terminal node has an object which is nearer to the query point than ok in the list R, the object is added to the list R. And the nodes with farther MINDIST than the $\text{DISTANCE}_\beta(P, o_k)$. are discarded from BranchList. The algorithm continues until there is no active node in BranchList. The following is the pseudo-code description of our approximate k-NN search algorithm.

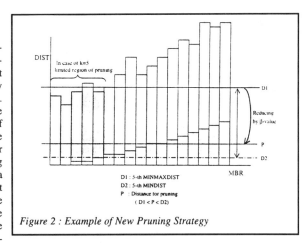

D1 : 5-th MINMAXDIST
D2 : 5-th MINDIST
P : Distance for pruning
(D1 < P < D2)

Figure 2 : Example of New Pruning Strategy

[Approximate k-NN Search Algorithm]

Input:

        Q : query point, $\{q_i \mid q_i \in Q,\ 0 \leq i < n,\ n \text{ is an integer}\}$

        K : number of object to retrieve

Ouput:

        R : result list for k-NN, $\{o_i \mid o_i \in R,\ 0 \leq i < k\}$

Variable:

BranchList : candidate node list , $\{node[i] \mid node[i] \in \text{BranchList},\ 0 \leq i < \text{BranchSize}\}$ node[i] {

```
mindist;      /* MINDIST */
minmaxdist;         /* MINMAXDIST */
maxdist;      /* MAXDIST */
```

```
                    pointer;    /* pointer to child node */
                    }
BranchSize : current number of candidate nodes in BranchList
BetaMinmaxdist : MINMAXDIST_β(P, R)
BetaMaxdist : MAXDIST_β(P, R)
BetaDist : DISTANCE_β(P, o_k)
NearestDist : Distance from query point Q to k-th object in R or k-th MINMAXDIST
Node : current node
NodeSize : number of MBRs or objects in current node,
Node Process: Expand root node and add its all mbr in BranchList;
Sort all nodes in BranchList by using its mindist;
Perform search & pruning using BetaMinmaxdist and BetaMaxdist in BranchList; while( BranchSize > 0 ) {
          Make Node as child node of node[0] from BranchList;
          if( Node.type == LEAF ) { /* in case of leaf node */
                    checkflag = FALSE;
                    for( i=0; i<Node; i++ ) {
                              dist = ObjectDIST(Q, Node.objecti);
                              if( dist < NearestDist ) {
                                        Insert Node.objecti to R;
                                        Calculate NearestDist from R;
                                        checkflag = TRUE;
                              }
                    }
                    if( checkflag == TRUE )
                    Perform search & pruning using BetaDist in BranchList;
}
      else {          /* in case of internal node */
          Add all Node′s mbr in BranchList;
          Sort all nodes in BranchList by using its mindist;
          Perform search & pruning using BetaMinmaxdist and BetaMaxdist in BranchList;
}
          }
End:
```

4. EXPERIMENTAL EVALUATION

4.1 Implementation and Experiment Environments

We experiment the performance of the approximate k-NN search algorithm using X-tree[Ber96] on Solaris 2.6/SUN Enterprise 150. The table 4.1 shows the experiment factors. In the experiment, we use randomly generated feature vector for each dimension.

We consider two aspects to evaluate the performance of our approximate k-NN search algorithm. First, we evaluate the quality of query results using precision. Secondly, we evaluate the response time by measuring RDPA(rate of decreasing number of page access). The precision can be obtained by the following equation. precision=NNA/NNEx100(%).

Table 4.1: experiment factors

	20 DIM	40 DIM	60 DIM	80 DIM
Number of Objects		200,000		
Page Size		4,096 bytes		
Number of nearest neighbor, k	10, 50, 100			
β-value	$0 \leq \beta < 1$			

NNA : number of true Nearest Neighbor retrieved by Approximate k-NN search
NNE : number of true Nearest Neighbor retrieved by Exact k-NN search (=k)
RDPA is computed by comparing the number of page I/Os required for our approximate k-NN search with the number for the exact k-NN search. The following equation shows how to compute RDPA. RDPA=(EPN-APN)/EPN x 100
EPN : Page Number for exact k-nearest neighbor search
APN : Page Number for approximate k-nearest neighbor search
To find β−value for optimal retrieval performance, we define CPV(Combine Performance Value) using the precision and RDPA.

Definition 4. CPV(Combine Performance Value) is defined as follows:CPV=w_1 x precision+w_2 x RDPA where
RDPA : rate of decreasing number of access page
w_1, w_2 are weights for precision and RDPA respectively.

4.2 Performance Comparison on Precision and RDPA.

The first experiment measures the precision rate and the number of page I/Os using the proposed k-NN search algorithm. In the pruning strategy of our algorithm, the β-value plays an important role in reducing search space for k-NN search. Therefore, as the β-value increases, the number of pruned node increases so as to reduce the number of page I/Os. By reducing the number of page I/Os, the retrieval performance improves while the precision rate decreases.

Figure 3 shows the precision and the RDPA values of each dimension. When the dimension is 20 and β-value is 0.91, our algorithm has 96.5% for RDPA and holds 80% for precision. In other words, when the exact k-NN needs 100% of the number of page

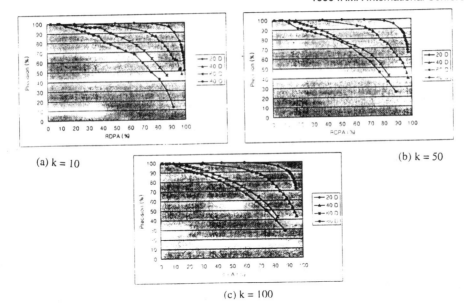

(a) k = 10

(b) k = 50

(c) k = 100

Figure 3. Precision and RDPA for each dimension

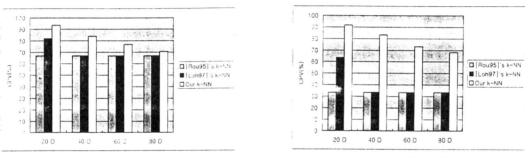

Figure 4. In case of δ_2, k=100

Figure 5. In case of δ_3, k=100

access I/O, our approximate k-NN search needs just 4% of number of page access I/O and our algorithm holds 80% precision value. When the dimension is 40, 60, and 80 and precision values is 80%, the RDPA has 83.4%, 60%, and 41.4%, respectively. When the β-value is fixed, the precision value increase but the RDPA decrease as the k-value increase.

4.3 Performance Comparision on the CPV

We use the CPV(Combine Performance Value) to show superiority of our algorithm, compared with the conventional exact k-NN algorithm and the approximate k-NN algorithm. The CPV has 3 types, i.e., δ_1, δ_2, and δ_3, based on the definition 4. δ_1 means that the priority of the precision is the same as that of the RDPA, i.e., the value of w_1/w_2 is 1. δ_2 means that the priority of the precision is more important than that of RDPA, such as that the value of w1/w2 is 2. δ_3 means that priority of RDPA is more important than that of precision, such that the value of w_1/w_2 is 1/2. For example, because the result of the exact k-NN has 100% for precision and 0% for RDPA over all dimensions, we get the 50%, 66.7%, and 33.3% for CPV value in the case of δ_1, δ_2, and δ_3, respectively. The Figure 4 shows the CPV value of δ_2 and δ_3 when the k value equals 10.

Figure 4 and 5 shows the CPV value of the approximate k-NN search algorithm of [Loh97], the exact k-NN search algorithm, and our algorithm in the case of δ_2, and δ_3 . For this, we use 0.25 to 0.97 for β value when the dimension is 20 and 40, and use 0.8 to 0.98 for ?-value when the dimension is 60 and 80. From the result, in the case of δ_2, our approximate k-NN search algorithm has 93.4%, 83.7%, 76.7% and 70.5% for CPV when the dimension is 20, 40, 60, and 80, respectively. When the dimension value is 80, our approximate k-NN search algorithm has nearly the same CPV values as exact k-NN and approximate k-NN. This is because the increasing of dimension makes precision more decreasing than that of RDPA. But in all dimensions except 80, our approximate k-NN search algorithm has a good performance than the other k-NN search algorithms. In the case of ?3, our approximate k-NN search algorithm has highly performance than that of the exact k-NN search algorithm and the approximate k-NN search algorithm of [Loh97]. Though the CPV decrease as the dimension grows, our approximate algorithm has 68.1% for CPV, i.e., more 35% than those of the approximate k-NN search algorithm of [Loh97] and the exact k-NN. Our approximate k-NN search algorithm is superior to the other k-NN search algorithms over all dimensions in terms of retrieval performance.

5. CONCLUSION

The content-based multimedia retrieval requires similarity search for feature vectors extracted from multimedia objects. Recently, the k-NN search have been an important issue. However, as the dimension increases, the performance of conventional exact k-NN search algorithm and approximate k-NN algorithm is decreased. The conventional exact k-NN and approximate k-NN search algorithm need to access most of the directory and data pages for more than dimension 40.

In this paper, we defined new metrics, $MINMAXDIST_\beta$, $MAXDIST_\beta$, and $DISTANCE_\beta$ for efficient pruning strategy on high-dimensional data space. Also, we propose the new efficient approximate k-NN search algorithm for high-dimensional data and evaluate the performance of our algorithm. From the result of experiment, our approximate k-NN search algorithm improved 40~80% of the RDPA when our algorithm holds 80% precision. At moderate and high dimensionality (d≥20), our approximate k-NN search algorithm can outperform the conventional k-NN search algorithm. Although our algorithm allows some false-drops, it is faster than the conventional algorithm for high-dimensional data space. However, we should find the optimal β-value for each by experiment. Future research will focus on the extension of our algorithm to a robust approximate k-NN search algorithm that can overcome the problem of false-drops.

REFERENCES

[Bec90] Beckmann N., Kriegel H.-P, Schneider R. and Seeger B., 'The R*-tree: An Efficient and Robust Access Method for Points and Rectangles', Proc. ACM SIGMOD Int. Conf. on Management of Data, Atlantic City, NJ, 1990, pp. 322-331.

[Ary94] Arya, S. et al., 'An Optimal Algorithm for Approximate Nearest Neighbor Searching", In Proc. ACM-SIAM Symposium on Discrete Algorithms, pp. 573-582, 1994.

[Rou95]] Roussopoulos N., Kelley S. and Vincent F.: 'Nearest Neighbor Queries', Proc. ACM SIGMOD Int. Conf. on Management of Data, 1995, pp. 71-79.

[Ber96] Berchtold S., Keim D. and Kriegel H.-P., 'The X-tree: An Index Structure for High-Dimensional Data', 22nd Conf. on Very Large Databases, 1996, Bombay, India.

[Loh97] Woong-Kee Loh and Kyu-Young Whang, ëA Fast k-Nearest Neighbor Search Algorithm for Multimedia Content-Based Retrievalí, Proceedings of the 25th Korea Information Science Society(KISS) Conference, Vol. 24, No. 2, p167~170, 1997.

The Control of Crucial Knowledge

G. Blaauw and Dr. Jacques S.K.Th. Boersma
Department of Information and Knowledge Management, Faculty of Management and Organization, University of Groningen, The Netherlands
+31-50-3633372, Fax: +31-50-3633850, E-mail: G.Blaauw@bdk.rug.nl
+31-50-3633864, Fax: +31-50-3633850, E-mail: S.K.Th.Boersma@bdk.rug.nl

0 INTRODUCTION

This proposal explains the organization of the research project entitled "The Control of Crucial Knowledge". Section 1 describes the theoretical framework underlying the research and the reasons for undertaking it. This provides the basis for the formulation of the primary research question and the secondary research questions derived from it (section 2). These sections explain "What" will be researched. The rest of the proposal explains "How" this will be done. Section 3 describes the development of the conceptual model for the core elements of the study, while section 4 is devoted to the type of research and the methodology used.

1 BACKGROUND OF THE RESEARCH

There is a growing insight that the vitality of organizations is determined, to a large extent, by knowledge (Quinn 1992; Nonaka and Takeuchi 1995).

Technological developments and modern economic and management insights have led to a situation in which the management of knowledge is high on the agenda of corporate managers. To put this development into perspective, I will first provide an overview of the historical background, before presenting the case for knowledge management in the light of macro-economic and meso-economic developments in relation to management concepts.

1.1 Historical background

Boersma (1995) states that the dynamics and complexity facing organizations is continuously increasing. Following Hammer and Champy (1993), he mentions four factors that are responsible for this development: increasing customer demands, fiercer competition, shorter product life cycles, and permanent, constantly accelerating technological change.

These economic and management developments have made the management of knowledge a highly crucial issue for companies. Many authors (among them Bell 1976; Drucker 1993; Senge 1994) state that the industrial society as formed by the industrial revolutions is currently in a state of transition. According to Bell, Drucker and others we are now entering a new era, which is characterized by products and processes with a high knowledge intensity that have hardly outgrown the initial stage yet. In this post-industrial information or knowledge era, organizations are considering knowledge at the meta level. Corporate managers have thus become responsible for the control of knowledge and the results of such control. Knowledge is being applied to determine what knowledge is necessary and to analyse how goals may be reached with the help of this knowledge. Seen from this perspective, the traditional production factors - labour, capital and natural resources - have been supplemented by a new and decisive production factor: knowledge.

Because of this shift of emphasis, economic theories no longer regard knowledge as a feature of other factors, but as an entity in its own right (Boisot 1997; Jacobs 1996; Ministry of Economic Affairs 1994). Traditionally, economic theories viewed knowledge as an exogenous factor, i.e. a factor that is fixed and cannot be influenced (Penrose 1959: 76-80). Within this traditional paradigm, there is no reason for developing any form of Knowledge Management. In modern growth theory, this viewpoint has changed , knowledge is regarded as an endogenous factor, which means that the value of knowledge may change when influenced by certain factors. In addition, knowledge is seen as reproducible. Knowledge obtained may lead to higher growth without resorting to additional labour (Ministry of Economic Affairs 1994). Knowledge can be regarded as a reproducible production factor (Penrose 1959; Boisot 1997).

In the light of these developments, Knowledge Management is a highly necessary activity.

1.2 The role of knowledge in management
Following on the developments mentioned above, a new perspective on knowledge in organizations is being created. In analogy with the concept of organizational metaphors formulated by Morgan (1993), Spender (1989) regards organizations as "bodies of knowledge". He pays particular attention to organizational specialization. From the perspective of knowledge management, organizational specialization is a method for organizing increasingly large amounts of knowledge. As products and production are increasingly being based on knowledge, the functions and structures within organizations are changing (Jacobs 1995).

Quinn (1992) states that knowledge management is a key factor in certain strategic decisions made by service businesses. Considerations regarding the use of vital corporate knowledge - the Core Competence (Prahalad and Hamel 1990) - and the knowledge available in other organizations play an important role in numerous strategic decisions about whether to outsource activities and whether to engage in relationships with other companies for the purpose of such outsourcing, purchasing and sales, and other strategic cooperations. On the basis of modern growth theory, Nooteboom (1998) - who integrates notions from games theory, transaction costs theory (Williamson 1985) and network theory (Johanisson, 1986) into his cognitive theory of the firm - points to knowledge management considerations as important motives for entering into cooperative relationships with other companies.

Nooteboom refers to the dilemma of focus versus scope:
- On the one hand, a company should concentrate on its own Core Competence (Prahalad and Hamel 1990): focus;
- On the other hand, it should take its environment (in the broad sense) into account to ensure that it does not overlook any threats and opportunities (Competitive Advantage, Porter 1985; Williamson 1985): scope.

If one assumes that the knowledge available within an organization will directly or indirectly lead to some form of activity, the appreciation for such activities may serve as a measure for the value placed on the underlying knowledge. The Core Competence concept is based on the notion that an organization has one or more core activities that generate the highest added value for this organization. Such activities are considered to constitute the core of the organization. The organization's other activities only support or supplement these core activities.

Another factor plays a role in determining the relative value of knowledge within companies: the scope. This concerns the value of knowledge for the organization within a larger context, which is usually called the environment. The company's competitors are obviously a major environmental factor. At this point, the Industrial Organizations theory developed by Porter (1985) should be considered. This theory is based on the idea that organizations may have a Competitive Advantage at industry level. Naturally, this has repercussions within the company itself. Apart from the size of an organization or its access to markets, knowledge may also be a factor in achieving a Competitive Advantage.

As stated above, knowledge is in in our post-industrial society considered to be an important resource (Boersma 1995). Resources are the tangible and intangible assets that are tied semi-permanently to the firm (Caves 1980). These resources are being used in the processes conducted by an organisation

The primary processes are the processes wich lead directly to the products or services offered to the costumer. The primary processes consist of all activities, communications and task-synchronization mechanisms that are directed to sustain and support the primary flows in an organization up to the client or end user. (Foster et al. 1995).

Resources are not only necessary to conduct these processes, they also determine its effectiveness and its outcome. Organizations achieve their level of performance via the products and services that result from their primary processes. This means that there is an important influence of the knowledge in an organisation to the conduct and the outcome of the primary processes. The alignment of processes requires coordination and communication. To achieve this, knowledge and information is a necessity. The right information and knowledge should be at the right place at the right time (MacGee et al. 1996). Information can be used for knowledge work and for communication. It is required for knowledge work to enable the employee to perform a knowledge intensive activity. Information that is used for communication enables employees to adjust and coordinate their activities. A second form of communication involves the tranfer of knowledge itself.

According to the resource-based theory resources offer Competitive Advantages because a firm is a unique combination of resources. This uniqueness enables the organisation to offer more value (differentiation or lower costs) than the competitors.

Resources lead to longer-lasting competitive advantages if they cannot be easily copied. This is especially the case for of resources that have been developed over longer periods of time.

If resources can be copied, they will gradually change into competitive necessities (Mata et al. 1995; Parker et al. 1989).

In certain cases, the Competitive Advantage is solely based on the company's geographical location or a regional monopoly. Such organizations may continue to exist despite the use of generally available knowledge. If the Competitive Advantage is based on knowledge, then this is unique knowledge that gives the company an advantage not shared by its competitors.

Thus, there is a relationship between Core Competence and Competitive Advantage, in the sense that the relative value of the knowledge within the organization may be deduced from it. The relevance of an insight into the organizational knowledge base when considering strategic decisions is thus evident.

The concept of Core Capabilities is related to the concept of Core Competence. The Core Competence is determined by testing and classifying the skills present within the organization. Only those activities that are most highly developed within the organization and on which most of the products and services are based are regarded as the Core Competence. The concept of Core Capability, however, also uses the positive ways in which the organization distinguishes itself from its competitors as a relative yardstick.

According to Leonard-Barton (1996), the basis for managing knowledge is understanding and capitalizing on the Core Capabilities and - for technology-based organizations - Core Technological Capabilities. The Core Capabilities of industrial organizations primarily consist of production technologies and the mutual interdependence of these technologies and their coordination by experts or systems.

Core Capabilities therefore are connected to the Competitive Advantage of an organization. Such capabilities have been built up over a relatively long period of time and cannot be imitated easily. Supplemental Capabilities are capabilities that add value to the core activities but can be imitated easily. Enabling Capabilities are necessary for the company, but in themselves not suitable for creating a Competitive Advantage. Core Capabilities differ from both Enabling Capabilities and Supplemental Capabilities, since neither of these gives the company an advantage over its competitors; instead, they only create suitable conditions for utilizing the Core Capabilities. According to Leonard-Barton, a Core Capability has the following elements:

1. The knowledge and skills of the employees;
2. Knowledge existing as a physical system. This includes production systems and computer hardware and software;
3. The management system, which stimulates and regulates the transfer, application, and creation of knowledge;
4. The value system on which the use of knowledge is based.

1.3 The concept of 'Crucial Knowledge'

To take the decision to invest in knowledge, it is very important for a organization to know what knowledge is relevant to the organization and what knowledge adds value. It is also important for the organization to be able to keep this knowledge and the resulting benefits and advantages to itself, at least temporarily and/or partially. If this is not the case, the organization will not be able to gain a Competitive Advantage and the investment in knowledge will not be worthwhile. Protection often takes the form of patents, confidentiality clauses, and competition clauses. However, in the course of time it will not be possible to stop the dissemination of knowledge: patents will expire and imitation will occur, for example through product imitation or reverse engineering. Thus, knowledge gained by one organization will eventually become available to other organizations. In other words, in due course knowledge developed by individual companies will acquire the characteristics of a collective commodity. This means that an organization should be capable of acquiring fast and accurate insights into this Crucial Knowledge, which means that it should determine:

- What knowledge should be acquired;
- What knowledge should be disseminated;
- What knowledge is confidential and should therefore be protected;
- What knowledge should be given commodity status by means of patents and licences;
- What knowledge should be protected against loss (Boersma 1995).

Thus, for an organization the concepts of Core Competence, Core Capabilities, and Competitive Advantage are related to unique and valuable knowledge. This also means that this Crucial Knowledge has often been developed within the organization or specifically for the organization.

Crucial Knowledge includes at least the - ever changing - knowledge that is necessary to operate within the industry at an acceptable level. In many cases, Crucial Knowledge is incorporated within experts in the form of (partially) tacit knowledge (Polanyi 1958) that manifests itself as problem-solving behaviour. The crucial aspect of knowledge is therefore primarily viewed as the availability of such problem-solving behaviours in the light of the continuity of the organization.

When identifying and observing knowledge, it is important to realize that each of the four types of knowledge (human knowledge, documented knowledge, mechanized knowledge, and computer-based knowledge) is also a specific source of knowledge (Boersma 1995). Managing experiments for the transition from tacit to explicit knowledge and vice versa seems to be a core responsibility of management (Nonaka and Takeuchi 1995). Apart from making tacit knowledge explicit, the incorporation or application of knowledge should also involve the transition from tacit to explicit knowledge; in this area, too, the company should experiment to make the knowledge suitable for application. One of the elements of this research project is the design of a practical method for the identification of relevant sources of knowledge, for querying these sources, for experimenting when knowledge should be made explicit, and for structuring the information acquired in this manner. After Crucial Knowledge has been identified and described in a structured way, the organization should formulate a Crucial Knowledge policy.

The analysis of fields of knowledge that are relevant to the company may reveal that knowledge should be built up in a particular field. This means that the knowledge in question should first be acquired and then be incorporated into people, machines and business processes. There are various alternatives to building up knowledge, such as purchase, training, imitation, and experimenting.

Crucial Knowledge is the knowledge within an organization which can provide Competitive Advantage and is the basis for the Core Competence, it is also related to the primary processes of an organization.

Crucial knowledge can be identified by considering the Core Competence, Competiitve Advantage and the primiary processes of an organisation. It can be made more explicit by identifying and describing the carriers of this knowledge. It can be operationalised by a desciption and classification method.

2 GOAL AND RESEARCH QUESTIONS

This empirical research starts with a research question that is based on the concepts of knowledge and organizations described in section 1.

The fact that knowledge has become increasingly important to organizations appears from practical data, social and economic issues, and developments in management theory and Organization Studies. The theory has provided several concepts and hypotheses that seemed suitable for the research project, especially Core Competence (Prahalad and Hamel 1990) and Core Rigidities (Leonard-Barton 1996). Porter's notions of Competitive Advantage in industries are also relevant.

Competitive forces determine the relative value of a company's private knowledge. Operationalization of Michael Polanyi's tacit-explicit knowledge dichotomy and its development within a dynamic model by Nonaka and Takeuchi (1995) are also useful. Finally, this research has aspects in common with strategic management, benchmarking, Organization Studies, and Knowledge Management. These concepts provide the basis for the research. The combination of these concepts and the description of the organization and the activities based on this background provide a structure for the identification of Crucial Knowledge. Thus, these theoretical concepts enable the construction of a measurement technique, which is the main goal of the research:

Goal: The development of a method for identification and control of Crucial Knowledge within organizations.

With this goal in mind, the central research question has been formulated as follows:

Research question: How can Crucial Knowledge be identified and controlled within organizations?

The goal and the research question constitute the heart of this study. When the research question has been answered, the goal of the research will be achieved.

To answer the research question, four secondary research questions have been derived from it.

Secondary research questions: I What is Crucial Knowledge?

                                                II How can Crucial Knowledge be identified?

                                                III How can Crucial Knowledge be controlled?

Answers to these secondary questions are essential for answering the central research question.

The main issues of this study have now been explained. The research focuses on the development of an instrument to be used for the identification and control of Crucial Knowledge. The conceptual model developed as part of the research ties the various elements together and is based on indicators of Crucial Knowledge within organizations.

3 MODELS USED IN THE STUDY

This section describes the methodological aspects of the research. The study focuses on the design of a method for identifying, classifying, and controlling Crucial Knowledge within organizations.

To model Crucial Knowledge, theories will be used that develop the concepts of Core Competence, Competitive Advantage, and Core Capabilities. To develop the conceptual model of the knowledge carrier, notions will be used from theories that deal with the role of knowledge in organizations and the relationship between the strategy of the organization and the primary processes. These notions will be combined to formulate the conceptual model. Finally, I will briefly describe how the model will be tested by studying several cases by means of action research.

3.1 Modelling Crucial Knowledge

The description of Core Competence at the end of the previous section provides the starting-point for the conceptual model. This model contains a reflection on the way in which knowledge manifests itself within organizations and ways to describe it adequately. It is the basis for the inventory and consultancy method described later. Figure 1 indicates how an adequate description of knowledge may be given.

Figure 1 is a diagram of the conceptual model and the way in which the concepts of which it consists are related. The conceptual model introduces various concepts that will be used to describe the knowledge within organizations.

These concepts - required knowledge, specific knowledge, Crucial Knowledge, and scarce knowledge - will now be described in more detail.

Required knowledge

Required knowledge must be available because the mere existence of the company has organizational consequences. Each company requires a certain amount of knowledge to monitor its processes and to communicate. This is independent of the industry in which it operates. The knowledge is inherent to the existence of the company and is usually not part of the Core Competences. We can define required knowledge as basic knowledge that is necessary for the mere existence of every organization.

Examples of required knowledge are the administrative apparatus (secretaries doing the typing and answering the telephone) and simple bookkeeping procedures (keeping records of debtors and creditors).

Specific knowledge

Specific knowledge is knowledge that is specific to the industry in which the company operates. It is related to the type of product made or the type of process occurring within the company. It is knowledge that must be present to analyse and solve particular problems. For a textile company, for example a weaving mill, specific knowledge is knowledge about weaving and textiles. Each company within the weaving industry must have this specific knowledge. In principle, the primary process that may be identified in one such company should be partially or completely applicable to other weaving mills. The fields of knowledge that may thus be defined are therefore specific to the industry and the knowledge concerned therefore arises from the nature of the company.

Crucial Knowledge

Through Crucial Knowledge, a company can distinguish itself from other companies in the same industry. Crucial Knowledge is essential to a company, determines its identity, and distinguishes it from its competitors. Crucial Knowledge can appear in several ways:
- The cruciality is determined by a very specific expertise on a particular field of interest and activity in the organization.
- The cruciality arises from an unique combination of knowledge from several fields of interest and activity in the organization
- The cruciality lies in the ability to generate creative and innovative solutions in product-, service-, or process development.

In some cases, the company has taken the initiative to develop and implement this knowledge, which makes it unique and crucial. Market developments may require the company to seek out new Crucial Knowledge and to relinquish or modify existing Crucial Knowledge. Crucial Knowledge is essential to the survival of the company.

Crucial Knowledge forms the basis of the Core Competence and Competitive Advantage of an organization.

Scarce knowledge
Scarce knowledge may be required, specific, or crucial knowledge, for example because the knowledge concerned only resides within a few employees, machines, documents, or computer system. The more crucial the knowledge in question is, the more problematic scarcity may become (see Figure 1). If required knowledge is scarce, any loss of such knowledge does not threaten an organization. After all, many businesses possess required knowledge since they need it to exist, and it can therefore easily be replaced. This is less threatening than a situation in which Crucial Knowledge is scarce. If Crucial Knowledge is scarce, the organization is vulnerable. Because this knowledge has usually been developed within the company, loss of a carrier will often mean that the knowledge will have to be developed anew.

The fields of knowledge identified by the measurement instrument therefore concern specific knowledge and Crucial Knowledge. What needs to be determined is the extent to which these fields of knowledge are crucial and thus highly important for the identity of the organization concerned. It is also important to describe what specific or Crucial Knowledge is scarce.

3.2 Modelling the knowledge carrier
The conceptual model shown below indicates how knowledge possessed by knowledge carriers in the organization may be identified and described adequately.

The model has been formulated within the context of an organization. For this purpose, an organization is regarded as a set of coherent goal-directed activities. The sequence and interaction of these goal-directed activities constitute the processes within the organization.

The model concentrates on the activities for which knowledge is applied.

It is assumed that these activities are carried out by knowledge carriers. Van der Zwaan & Boersma (1993) state that knowledge may exist in the form of human knowledge (the knowledge carrier is a person), documented knowledge (the knowledge has been documented), mechanized knowledge (the knowledge is stored in a machine), and automated knowledge (the knowledge is incorporated into a computer).

The activities of a carrier constitute its tasks. The sequence and interaction of the various tasks are therefore part of the processes. Knowledge is regarded as the capability that enables goal-directed activities. It is assumed that this knowledge itself cannot be observed. However, since the activities can be observed, they may serve as indicators for the knowledge available. A second indicator for the presence of knowledge is not the activity, but the entity engaged in it. This entity is referred to as the 'carrier'. A carrier is not only a storage medium for knowledge but also the entity that actively applies it. If the knowledge has been explicitly stored, but the storage medium itself is not capable of using it, this is indicated in the model by the storage bin with the added label 'passive'. The degree of coherence of the organization's activities is not only demonstrated by the functions of the activities within the process, but also by the communication between the various carriers. Part of this communication is intended for the coordination of activities, another part for the transfer of knowledge that is required for the performance of a task. The latter form of communication is also shown in the diagram above.

In the following sections more detailed descriptions will be given of each of the entities and the relationships shown in the model:
The entities and their definitions;
The relationships between these entities;
The ways in which they will be operationalized.

3.2.1 Entities
The following definition of Knowledge is used in this study:
Knowledge is a meaningfully ordered stock of information (interpreted data), and understanding, plus ability to transform it into actions (skill), which yields performance (Nooteboom 1996).

The knowledge **Carrier** is a human carrier (sometimes also a automated system) (Boersma 1995).

A **Task** is defined as follows (Roe and Zijlstra 1991):
1. The instruction to do work in such a way that a given initial state is transformed into a given final state (instruction);(or)
2. The goal to be realized by means of a particular activity as set by the person engaged in the activity (objective);(or)
3. The activity itself as carried out in response to a command or objective (activity).

Process is defined as follows:
"All activities, communications and task-synchronization mechanisms that are directed to sustain and support the primary flows in an organization up to the client or end user." (Foster et al. 1995)

The definition of **Communication** is:
The transfer of task-related or activity-related knowledge from one carrier to another.
Storage is defined as follows:
The explicit codification of task-related or activity-related knowledge within a storage medium.

3.2.2 Relationships
The relationships between the various components of the model are defined as follows:

1a knowledge -> carrier
1b carrier -> knowledge
2a knowledge -> task
2b task -> knowledge

These relationships are assumed to exist, but they cannot be operationalized. However, they can be inferred from other data.

3a carrier -> task	The carrier has one or more tasks.
3b task -> carrier	The task is performed by a carrier.
4a task -> process	The task is part of a process.
4b process -> task	The process consists of tasks.
5a carrier -> storage	The carrier is able to explicitly store his or her knowledge in a storage medium.
5b storage -> carrier	The carrier can obtain knowledge from a storage medium.
6a carrier -> communication	The carrier can transfer knowledge through communication.
6b communication -> carrier	The carrier can acquire knowledge through communication.

3.2.3 Variables
The entities and relationships listed above need to be worked out in the form of operational variables. Not all entities and relationships can be operationalized, however.

Component 1: Entities
Since knowledge is not tangible, its presence will have to be ascertained indirectly.
However, the carriers can be identified, and the same applies to the tasks.
The 'communication' variable has been restricted in the sense that it is assumed to concern the knowledge that may be used by carriers to perform their tasks; in other words, communication for the sake of the transfer of knowledge.
The **Carriers** will be identified by means of:
- Lists of employees;
- Lists of functions.

The **Tasks** will be identified by means of:
- The transformations to be realized (task analysis/task description);
- Their functions within the process (job descriptions).

The **Process** will be outlined in the form of
- A work flow diagram or a primary process diagram.

Communication may be measured by:
- Identifying the communication channels between carriers;
- Determining the frequency of these communications;
- The number of other carriers involved in the communication;
- Social networks;
- The tasks and functions of the other carriers within the process (identification of 'experts').

The **Storage** of knowledge may be observed in:
- Handbooks;
- Reports;
- Technical drawings;
- Descriptions of procedures;
- Formal regulations.

Component 2: Relationships
As has been stated before, not all relationships can be operationalized explicitly. Relationships 1 and 2 are not explicit. They are assumed to operate implicitly. These relationships can be described by means of an analysis (deduction or induction) of other data that can be obtained through measurement.

1a knowledge -> carrier
1b carrier -> knowledge
2a knowledge -> task
2b task -> knowledge

The relationships listed below can be measured in the ways described. The measurement technique is not presented in great detail here, but will usually involve several variables for each relationship that will be aggregated to describe the relationship.

3a carrier -> task	The carrier has one or more tasks. By relating the carriers to tasks, they may be specified. The tasks of each carrier can be described.
3b task -> carrier	The task is performed by a carrier. The carriers involved in each task can be listed.
4a task -> process	The task is part of a process. The relationships between the tasks and the process can be described, for example by listing other tasks involved, such as preceding and subsequent tasks or simultaneously performed tasks.
4b process -> task	The process consists of tasks. The process is broken down into its component tasks.
5a carrier -> storage	The carrier is able to explicitly store his or her knowledge in a storage medium. The amount of knowledge stored by the carrier can be used as an indicator for the extent to which the carrier has made his or her knowledge explicit.
5b storage -> carrier	The carrier can obtain knowledge from a storage medium. This relationship can be measured by observing to what extent the carrier accesses the knowledge stored.
6a carrier -> communication	The carrier can transfer knowledge through communication. This relationship can be measured by observing to what extent the carrier communicates with other carriers for the purpose of knowledge transfer.
6b communication -> carrier	The carrier can acquire knowledge through communication. This relationship can be measured by observing to what extent the carrier communicates with other carriers to acquire knowledge.

3.3 Synthesis

The relevance of knowledge is thus expressed by the model of Crucial Knowledge. To locate Crucial Knowledge within organizations, models of carriers will be constructed and subsequently used.

The carrier is therefore also important for the description of Crucial Knowledge. As has been stated before, this carrier may, for example, be a machine (mechanized knowledge) that is supplied by an engineering factory.

A third characteristic that will be used is the extent to which Crucial Knowledge can be made explicit (Polanyi 1958; Nonaka 1995). In other words: can it be described or stored in some way or easily verbalized? If the knowledge is explicit, it will be easier to transfer. If the knowledge is available but has not been described, it is referred to as implicit or tacit knowledge. It is more difficult to transfer this kind of knowledge. Although it can be applied, it is difficult to put it into words. Employees with many years of experience are a good example. In the course of time, they will have acquired enormous expertise, but they will often be unable to explain why a particular solution is the best, because they are not consciously aware of the mode of reasoning they have developed as a result of their long experience. This phenomenon is very important for the description of Crucial Knowledge, because it may make it more difficult to transfer knowledge or to make it explicit.

Finally, the study will make use of the distinction made by Boersma &Stegwee and others between declarative knowledge, i.e. knowing 'what' (factual knowledge); procedural knowledge, i.e. knowing 'how' (declarative knowledge); and background knowledge, i.e. knowing 'why'. (Cf. Section 3.2). It will be investigated to what extent there is a relationship between this classification and Crucial Knowledge. The classification also provides an insight into the formal structure of the knowledge available.

To sum up, this study therefore describes knowledge in terms of:

1. Its relevance;
2. The carrier;
3. The extent to which it may be made explicit;
4. The way in which it is structured.

The fields of knowledge to be distinguished by the measurement instrument are classified on the basis of these criteria. This classification and the conceptual model (which in turn has been specified by the theoretical framework) provide a basis for developing the measurement instrument. The methodology to be used in the study is explained in the following section.

4 METHODOLOGY

This research proposal focuses on the phenomenon of Crucial Knowledge. Crucial Knowledge is not an isolated phenomenon. It is closely linked to other variables within and outside the organization, which is why it is necessary to investigate it within the context of the organization and to take relevant environmental factors into account. These considerations will have to be reckoned with when developing the research design.

It should be considered which research method applies to the present study. Yin (1989) provides a framework for linking various types of research, the research question, and the extent to which the situation should be manipulated (Table 1).

Table 1. Relevant situations for various research strategies (adapted from Yin 1989: 17)			
Strategic type of research	Research questions	Requires control over behavioural events?	Focuses on contemporary events?
Experiment	how, why	yes	yes
Survey	who, what, where, how many, how much, how often	no	yes
Case study	how, why	no	yes
Action research	how, why	yes	yes

It is clear from the conceptual model that we are dealing with a large number of variables. This means that the phenomenon of Crucial Knowledge can only be investigated in a real-life situation. Research into a phenomenon with the above-mentioned characteristics may be conducted by means of case research. This methodology concentrates primarily on 'how' and 'why' and much less on 'how many' or 'how often'. The present study searches for similarities between organizations concerning Crucial Knowledge. This allows imposing a structure on a large number of variables and relationships. Thus, it will be possible to describe the essential and typical characteristics of the phenomenon of Crucial Knowledge.

However, for the part of the study that deals with the control of Crucial Knowledge the condition that the researcher is not allowed to interfere is too restrictive. Although Yin concludes that case research is relevant to 'how' or 'why' questions, practical tests - and thus interference - are in order when it comes to the study of design issues. Such issues concern contemporary events that can hardly be controlled by the researcher, if at all (Yin 1989: 20). Case research relates the explanation of human behaviour to the context. Action research aims at a better understanding of behaviour and takes interactions with the researcher into account (Checkland 1992). It is therefore implementation-oriented.

4.1 Case research

Biemans and Van der Meer-Kooistra (1995) sketch how case research should be conducted in a business context to ensure that it will yield reliable scientific knowledge.

Yin regards a case study as a form of empirical research a) which investigates an as yet unclear contemporary phenomenon and its context; b) in which the boundary between the phenomenon and its context is not clear either; and c) which uses several sources to obtain evidence. The instrument to be designed will provide an answer to the question 'how' Crucial Knowledge may be identified. Furthermore, case research explicitly investigates the context. It is difficult to separate the situation that is being investigated from its context (Hutjes and Van Buuren 1992: 23; Swanborn 1984: 337).

Depending on the goal of the research, Biemans and Van der Meer-Kooistra distinguish the following type of case research:

Explorative case research (to answer the 'what' question);
Explanatory case research (to answer the 'why' question);
Descriptive case research (to answer the 'how' question).

Explorative case research is primarily used to develop hypotheses. If the goal is testing a theory or theoretical concept for purposes of generalization and expansion of theories, explanatory case research is the preferred type. If the research is conducted to investigate how a phenomenon manifests itself in a concrete situation, descriptive case research is in order. The latter method is also applied as part of explorative or explanatory case research, since a description of the investigated phenomenon and its context is required before it can be explored or explained. The current study into Crucial Knowledge employs the descriptive method, since it investigates in what ways Crucial Knowledge exists within organizations. Since this is the first study into Crucial Knowledge as used in practical circumstances, it may also be called explorative.

Van der Zwaan (1990: 70-75) distinguishes four types of case research.

The simple case study, in which one object of research is observed during a single period.

The multiple case study, in which several similar cases are compared.

The longitudinal case study, in which the situation is observed for several periods.

The stratified case study, in which a comparison is made with other objects at a lower aggregation level within the investigated situation.

In our case, longitudinal research would only be possible after the conceptual model and its operationalization have been completed. Since this project will only run for four years, the time remaining for the actual empirical research is too short to allow longitudinal research.

4.2 Action research

Although case research is suitable for testing the research instrument to be developed and determining whether it is a useful tool for deciding balancing issues, it is less well suited for testing the consultancy model, since the researcher is not allowed to interfere in case research (Checkland 1992). This part of the project will therefore consist of action research. Action research enables the researcher to influence the organizations being investigated, which means that this type of research is the best methodology for this part of the study (the testing of the consultancy model).

Action research is a more far-reaching methodology than case research because the researcher has the explicit intention to influence the situation. In case research, the role of the researcher is limited to observing or gathering information.

4.3 Validity and reliability

As with all forms of research, case research and action research have their advantages and disadvantages.

This section will discuss validity, reliability, the presence of the researcher, and generalizability, and indicate the ways in which the disadvantages will be kept to a minimum. If the study is to be worthwhile, it will have to be both reliable and valid. To meet these requirements, the principle of triangulation (Patton 1990) will be applied. This means that the following steps will be taken:

Data triangulation: the use of various data sources: documents, informants, etc.

Theory triangulation: the use of various theoretical perspectives

Researcher triangulation: the use of several researchers. The presence of the researcher may cause or change aspects of the situation ('control effect') and give a false impression of the situation through selective perception ('biased viewpoint effect', Hutjes and Van Buuren 1992: 56).

Methodology triangulation: the use of various methodologies (experiments, questionnaires, and case studies)

By applying the principle of triangulation, the object of research, Crucial Knowledge, and the inventory method can be investigated without interference by the factors listed above.

Case research gives greater insights into the object of research and improves the *validity*, while decreasing replication and *reliability*. The disadvantage of the lack of replication will partly be counteracted by including several cases (i.e. organizations) in this study. Another important way to reduce the influence of these disadvantages is the member check: making the results known to the people involved to check if they square with their ideas. In this study, the results will be discussed with the companies involved. The *generalizability* (external validity) of case research is somewhat limited. However, the generalizability of experiments and surveys is also limited. In principle, the conclusions cannot be extended beyond the context in which the research took place.

In itself, this criticism is true, although this only applies to statistical generalizability. Theoretical and analytical generalizability is possible, in the same way as with experiments and surveys. The generalizability of a case study improves when cases are carefully selected and when more than one case is involved (Hutjes and Van Buuren 192: 60). Yin (1989: 32) states that analytical generalizability can be claimed when two or more cases support the same theory. If 'critical cases' are selected, for example, and they do not support the core of the conceptual model, it may be expected that this support will be lacking in other cases too (Hutjes and Van Buuren 1992: 63).

4.4 Practical research activities

The preferred methodology of multiple case research requires that the number of cases to be investigated and the criteria for selecting the objects of research and their contexts be specified. Essentially, this issue revolves around the quality of the conceptual model. The less robust the model, the greater the effort required to ensure analytical generalizability.

The organizations that are willing to cooperate in this research have allowed the researchers to work within their organizations for several weeks. Prior to this period, documents such as strategy plans, annual reports, handbooks, production statistics, market figures, and internal memos will be studied. The primary process will be studied with the help of the available documentation and observations by the researchers. Interviews with ten to fifteen employees that may be assumed to be involved with Crucial Knowledge have also been planned, as are interviews with the board of directors. The questions they will be asked concern the areas of expertise or the positions within the company of the interviewees. All operationalized questions will be posed to all interviewees. The decision to interview several employees is a deliberate one, because it will give the researchers the opportunity to talk to all the employees that are directly involved with crucial areas of expertise. Moreover, this will enable the researchers to determine whether there is consistency within the organization about Crucial Knowledge.

REFERENCESAND FIGURES

Available from the authors upon request.

ABSTRACTS

National Strategy for Information Technology Case of Iran ICT1400

Amir Albadvi, Ph.D.
Tarbiat Modarres University, School of Engineering, Industrial Engineering Dept.
P.O.Box: 14155-4838 Tehran, Iran, +9821 8011001 ext. 3343 Fax: +9821 2070381, albadvi@net1ef.modares.ac.ir

INTRODUCTION

In the current situation in which the principal means of generating economic value has shifted from manufacturing to intellectual activity and the value of human resources is becoming increasingly diverse, the sophistication and enhanced productivity of intellectual activities are essential to achieve further economic development and higher standards of living. Although the sophistication of intellectual activities and enhanced productivity are possible with the rapid development of information and communications technologies (ICT), information technology is not being fully exploited in Iran.

The purpose of this research-in-progress is to clearly define Iran's vision for the year 2021 (year 1400 in the local calendar) toward an advanced information infrastructure society. The objective is to propose a national strategy with specific policy programs for each field in which information technology should be promoted.

THE STRATEGY DEVELOPMENT PROCESS

Different explanatory theories as the nature of the strategy development process have been postulated. Much literature emphasizes a deliberate process of *strategic planning approach*, an intentional process involving a logical, sequential, analytic and deliberate set of procedures. The research is structured around a three-dimensional configuration of strategy development process. Three dimensions of strategy development were derived from the literature and generally fit to the context of information and communications technologies (see figure1). These dimensions are *key technologies* (a set of technology clusters which have high impact on the development of ICT); *economic sectors* (major economic and social sectors of Iran with potential use of information technology opportunities); and *applications* (information technology applications which serve as different strategic choices).

RESEARCH APPROACH AND FINDINGS

According to the Delphi method, a panel is used with expert members in communication remotely through three rounds of questionnaires transmitted via email. Through the process of expert opinion survey, consensus has been approached among participants in the following clusters contributing to the leading edge of information technology:

1. Components and hardware technologies (e.g. high performance computers)
2. Software technologies and toolkits (e.g. fault tolerant system, real time systems)
3. Networking technologies (e.g. TCP/IP, internet, extranet, wireless networking)
4. Communication technologies (e.g. frame relay, packet switching, VSAT)
5. Knowledge engineering (e.g. soft computing, fuzzy systems, neural networks)
6. Human-Computer interfaces (e.g. multimedia, virtual reality, web technology)

By using AHP (Analytic Hierarchy Process) method, pairwise comparisons of clusters under multiple criteria were designed. The output is a ranked list of the key technologies with the highest invest-

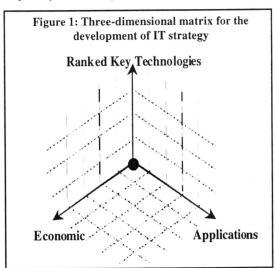

Figure 1: Three-dimensional matrix for the development of IT strategy

Ranked Key Technologies

Economic

Applications

ment potential in Iran.

The research also tapped the practical and visionary expertise of more than 100 experts in different economic and social sectors to see how information technology can pervasively applied to improve their sector's performance. According to NGT (Nominal Group Technique) method, a collection of individuals were brought together for generating ideas and priority setting of development plans in each sector. The output is a ranked list of development plans with the most potential use of information technology opportunities.

Third dimension of the research is identification of strategy enablers, application flagships of information technology, which were employed in different countries to enhance the definition of information age. By using the benchmarking method, the best-practice application flagships in different countries were studied. The output is a comprehensive list of application flagships like digital economy, teleworking, smart school, telemedicine, electronic government that can form strategic choices for Iran.

EXPECTED RESULT

A cross-sectional analysis of the three-dimensional matrix should result in a set of strategic choices of application flagships for Iran. Application flagships which have the most effective impact on the success of the development plans of different economic sectors as users of those applications, and which were also ranked as the best investment choices on key technologies for Iran[1].

ENDNOTE

1 This research is sponsored by Iran Telecommunication Research Center and IMPSC (Iran Management & Productivity Study Center)

The Need for MIS Training for Elementary School Teachers

Marsha Bialaszewski
Warren Elementary School

Dennis Bialaszewski
Indiana State University, Department of Systems and Decision Sciences, School of Business, Terre Haute, Indiana 47809, 812-237-2113, sdjessie@mama.indstate.edu, dennis@polishrose.com

One area where educators seem to be lagging behind industry is in the need to provide and direct teachers to the appropriate training they should receive to be able to better teach in the information age. Whereas industry pays to send employees to obtain appropriate training so they may continue to be competitive while serving customers, too often elementary school teachers must pay for the entirety of their continuing education with little counseling as to the most appropriate courses to take. Typically a teacher may sign up for a course which might not even employ current technologies and thus perhaps fortify bad teaching habits that may have developed. Also, teacher certification too often relies on what the traditional course has been rather than to make use of perhaps a series of seminars that would update a needed skill set.

Too often teaching pedagogy gives way to immediate issues such as what other certification should I get rather than to look at new technologies. Even at the elementary school level students are fairly computer literate but not necessarily information resource literate. When studying history are proper web sites being developed to enhance teaching and are teachers accessing these web sites. Too often determining proper web sites is more of a happenstance procedure rather than employing a systematic approach.

What about the attitude of relying on web sites rather than texts to keep current. If zoo animals are being discussed are teachers accessing available video for students to view and discuss? Have they considered a real time view of some famous zoo in order to view in real time what those animals are doing? Have they considered viewing animals in zoos located around the world and wondering why there are differences? Might they have to actually spell the animals name in order to view the animal? There is a very strong movement for active learning but how are elementary teachers being led to information system tools and technology to benefit the students as active learners?

What is the relationship between a university's MIS area and their elementary education area and what is currently being considered appropriate information systems literacy for the new and also the veteran elementary school educator? Too often the elementary school teacher is still given a narrow course on a latest particular version of some software without a continued immersion of internet development and no real vision of the importance of managing information systems technology. Knowing about the importance of managing information systems technology is not just the job for the CEO of that particular school nor is it only for some information systems specialist. However, managing this technology in a way which will benefit students must be a complete commitment if there is to be success through the school. It must be prioritized as a need and resources obtained to make it a reality - it is not just in the prioritizing of some computer acquisition and giving some training to a selected few on some specialized software!

What is the attitude of the school principal to obtaining the necessary resources to keep abreast of the information age and how committed is the school superintendent on these issues. Moreover, are they able to convey to the school board their needs in this area and obtain appropriate support from them. Are the teachers understanding the limitless possibilities or are they mired in a thought process of a lack of funding and too much effort on their own part to obtain appropriate training. And do the few who understand give up because they are spending too much out of their own pocket to do the job while others who are not committed but retained spend ledd and work less.

Many of these problems can be smoothed out if their is quality communication between the teachers, principals, and relevant others with Information Educators at the local universities. But, unfortunately, in some areas there is no quality communication between those in a School of Education and those Information System educators at the university itself. Unfortunately, at times politics and course loads and isolation between area faculties impede necessary action. Who is leading the movement at various universities to provide quality information system education for elementary school educators?

At a local midwest university their is a strong corporate advisory board where industry leaders provide input for the Management Information Systems major. There has been discussion about someone from the area of education being asked to serve on the advisory board. There have been questions as to the level of person asked to join and whether it should be at the local or state level. At the same time there are some who evaluate school accreditation who say is a good school is a five star school now why meddle in pushing technology into the curriculum. This is a short sighted view with no vision of the potentiality.

Aside from curriculum issues there could easily be structured a web page yearbook for the students. The schools own history and advancements could be more easily documented but is there a desire and commitment to do this. The paper that is unnecessarily used and many local schools in enormous. Yet with existing security and file attachment procedures most of this waste in truly the result of a lack of vision. But, who should shoulder the blame for this lack of vision or is there the word blame inappropriate. What we believe is that proper training and demonstrations to top level administrators may be a first step.

Not long ago a midwest university's MIS area and volunteer students offered seminars to three area junior high schools. While some teachers attended and a few selected students were invited not one of the three invited principles chose to attend. Did they already feel completely knowledgeable in the area or was this absence a demonstration to their teachers that they have not yet committed to a high priority in this area. While a money commitment is very important sometimes that can be blamed on school boards and local citizenry. However, one of the most difficult commitment that one can make and one that is a completely outward examplification of one priorities is the commitment of one's time to an issue.

In the MIS area students have worked on electronic teams with students from other universities as they write a joint paper. For example, students from Indiana State University worked with students from Pretoria University of South Africa while at the same time working on another project with students from the University of the Pacific. Many became "friends" with their electronic teammates. What about electronic teams of sixth graders from a rural school in the midwest teaming on some very short project with students from an inner city school in the west? The gain would be in the process. Students with very different backgrounds could learn they could easily work together while learning some simple facts perhaps about weather or geography. If this short project had to result in a very simple written report even some writing skills could be enhanced. Obviously the importance of working as a team would be unveiled. The technology exists today for such experiences. Has their been a conscious effort to ignore such endeavors or is it simply because of the lack of training and continuing education paths taken by some. Is it also because information system educators have narrowly focussed on developing a product for traditional business and have ignored those not involved with "higher education."

We end this discussion for a plea for a close dialog between those in elementary education and the information system educators. Only until the vision is realized by leaders in both areas will we be able to provide the highest quality of education for our students and also provide a methodology for the most appropriate continuing education so that the process may thrive.

Attitudes Toward Information Technology: A Regional Look

Karen D. Loch, Ph.D.
Decision Sciences, J. Mack Robinson College of Business, Georgia State University, Atlanta GA 30303-3083
404/651-4095; 404/315-8412, kloch@gsu.edu

We often fail to acknowledge differences between countries, particularly if we are not from that part of the world. This may be due to physical proximity, such as the United States and Canada, economic trading blocks, such as ASEAN or EU, or similar religious leanings or political forms, such as the Middle East and Eastern Europe. This failure results in, among other things, less than optimal transfer and adoption of information technologies. This study surveys participants from five countries in the Middle East: Egypt, Jordan, the Sudan, Saudi Arabia, and Lebanon, on their attitudes toward, perceptions of, and experiences with information technology.

The Sample was drawn from knowledge workers. Within countries, samples were drawn from both public and private institutions. Total sample size is 270. Data explore cultural differences, attitudes towards technology such as ease of use, perceived usefulness, and the likelihood of successful transfer of technology in a particular context. The preliminary findings support the need to understand the micro-levels beliefs and behaviors as a key component in successful transfer of information technology into organizational and business environment. While there are similarities across country, there are also significant differences that are of import to organizations conducting business in the region. Practical and research implications are addressed.

A Prototype to Transform Legacy Systems Into Object-oriented Systems

Virginia Mauco and Hernán Cobo
Instituto de Sistemas de Tandil, Depto. Computación y Sistemas - Fac. Cs. Exactas
Universidad Nacional del Centro de la Pcia. de Bs. As.
Campus Universitario - (7000) Tandil - Pcia. Bs. As. - Argentina, Fax: 54 - 2293- 431963
vmauco@exa.unicen.edu.ar, hcobo@rec.unicen.edu.ar

INTRODUCTION

Software evolution is an inevitable process for software systems. Actually, there are many systems developed 20 or more years ago which are still used. These systems are called legacy and may be defined as large software systems people don't know how to cope with, but that are vital to organisations. Hence, the decision on how to manage them is crucial because they may represent years of accumulated experience and knowledge. Besides, the software may be the only place where organisations business rules exist.

Although these systems were developed with the best technologies available in that moment, repeated and continuous changes may have altered their structure transforming them in large and unstructured systems. Remedial actions are then required to manage such systems.

In this work, a project whose aim is to develop a tool to simplify the maintenance of systems written in an imperative language is described. This tool, only considering the procedural source code of the systems, transforms them to improve their original structure. Besides preserving the original functionality, the new code generated should be structured, legible, modular, reusable, and more easily maintainable. Some of these features may involve changing the source language, making necessary to rewrite the system with different syntax or in a different paradigm.

STRUCTURES DEFINED TO REPRESENT PROGRAMS

As part of this project two structures have been defined to represent all the information extracted from imperative programs. One of them, called Intermediate Language (IL), was specially designed to allow the tool to be used with programs written in different imperative languages. An advantage of this structure is that the algorithms designed to enhance code quality are independent from the original source code. It also allows rewriting the improved programs in a language different from the original one. The languages considered were Pascal, Cobol, C and Fortran. The IL maintains two different views of the control structure of a program. It gives a global view, by means of block statements, and it also maintains all the primitive statements with control flow level of detail to allow regenerating automatically the original code. In consequence, it represents a tree structure that shows a hierarchical view of the program, in which the leaves compose a directed graph that reproduces the original control structure.

The other structure is the Extended Program Dependence Graph (EPDG), which is an extension defined over the Program Dependence Graph. It was designed to store and manipulate in an easy way the information represented in the IL. It is a directed graph whose nodes are connected by different types of edges. The nodes correspond to program statements (assignments and control predicates), and the edges represent data or control dependencies among these statements. The set of these dependencies induces a partial ordering on the statements in a program that must be followed to preserve the functionality of the original program.

OUTLINE OF THE TOOL

This tool is structured into three main steps. The first one, called Syntactic Restructuring Step, turns an arbitrary imperative program into a structured one by means of transformations defined over the EPDG, according to the rules imposed by structured programming. It doesn't modify the portions of the program already structured. The second one, referred to as Modularization Step, decomposes a monolithic structured program into a functionally equivalent collection of smaller modules, combining program slicing techniques and a set of criteria like cohesion, coupling, fan-in, fan-out, factoring, etc. A variant of output-restricted slice was defined to capture all relevant computations involving a given variable. Following this definition, a slice is constructed for each different use of each variable in the program. Starting from the lattice of the slices computed ordered by set inclusion, candidate modules are automatically detected and extracted. Each potential module is then analysed considering some criteria before its implementation. Since object-oriented programming increases maintainability and reusability of systems, the last step, called Object-oriented Conversion Step, aims at turning a structured and modular imperative system into an object oriented one. Potential classes are identified (including the instance variables and methods), using two complementary methods based on an analysis of global variables and data types. Although this step is still under analysis, a first prototype that transforms imperative systems into object-oriented ones written in Smalltalk, has been developed.

The two first steps of the tool are completely implemented in a prototype that can receive as entry an imperative program written in Pascal, Cobol, C or Fortran and produces as output a structured and modular program written in any of these languages.

CONCLUSIONS

This tool works, but its complete development is a challenging task and several steps need to be improved.

User intervention is sometimes necessary to resolve conflicts and supply domain knowledge so that the resulting objects are more meaningful. The user is also required to assign a meaning name to the isolated functions.

Although the use of the prototype in a set of case studies has preserved the functionality, a formal demonstration is still under analysis.

The Evolution of Information Resources Management

Karen S. Nantz, Ph.D. and Jeannette Francis, Ph.D.
Eastern Illinois University

Information Resources Management (IRM) is a discipline within management information systems (MIS) that considers information as an organizational resource that requires managing in the same way as more traditional organizational resources.

The concept of IRM, first introduced in 1979, has experienced an unforeseen evolution. IRM was initially used in the government sector as a way to deal with the discontent caused by excessive paperwork and reporting requirements. The Paperwork Reduction Act of 1980 was a response to governmental IRM. A similar impetus in the private sector, led by the records management area, led to more effective and efficient clerical functions. The IRM concept has since been embraced and expanded by various disciplines like Library Science, Office Management, Database Management, and Information Systems Science.

Today there are many associations and journals dedicated to the advancement of IRM, but there has yet to be a unified review of what exactly Information Resources Management entails. What is its place in the spectrum of management fields and its functional importance to corporate end users and IS professionals? The only aspect of IRM that most researchers agree upon is that information resources are valuable corporate assets and should be managed accordingly. Divergent views have been expressed in an attempt to define what constitutector as a way to deal with the discontent caused by excessive paperwork and reporting requirements. The Paperwork Reduction Act of 1980 was a response to governmental IRM. A similar impetus in the private sector, led by the records management area, led to more effective and efficient clerical functions. The IRM concept has since been embraced and expanded by various disciplines like Library Science, Office Management, Database Management, and Information Systems Science.

Today there are many associatit the perception that IRM emerged from the fields of database management, library science, and records management?
• What body of knowledge constitutes the field of IRM?
• Are the contributors to IRM building upon each other's ideas by testing and refining early perceptions about IRM?
• Is there a sufficient body of competing theories about IRM to signal the emergence of an IRM paradigm?
• What shifts have taken place in the IRM identity? What are the present trends, and what themes and/or topics are expected in the future?

METHODOLOGY

A comprehensive database and literature search was conducted to identify journals having titles or topics associated with IRM. Journals were classified as database management, records management, information resources management specific, library science, government, and information science.

A systematic and direct analysis of all the mainstream IRM articles (over 200) published between 1979 and 1998 were assessed. Articles were classified and coded according to: subject or topic, type (conceptual, model, theoretical, or applied), and the orientation (research or practical). This classification is consistent with the Alavi and Carlson MIS study (1972) and also closely parallels content analysis research methodology used by Culnan and Swanson (1986). In addition, the researchers applied the multidimensional model, proposed by O'Brien and Morgan (1991) to all non-governmental articles.

Based on the analysis, the researchers present an IRM matrix showing the evolution of IRM since its inception twenty years ago.

BIBLIOGRAPHY

Alavi, Maryam and Patricia Carlson, 1992, "A Review of MIS Research and Disciplinary Development," Journal of Management Information Systems 8(4), 45-62.

Cheon, Myun J., C. Lee Choong, and Varun Grover, 1991, "Research in MIS—Points of Work and Reference: A replication of the Culnan and Swanson Study," Data Base 23(2), 21-29.

Culnan, Mary J., 1986, "The Intellectual Development of Management Information Systems, 1972-1982: A Co-Citation Analysis," Management Science 32(2), 156-172.

Culnan, Mary J., 1987, "Mapping the Intellectual Structure of MIS, 1980-1985: A Co-Citation Analysis," MIS Quarterly, September, 1987, 341-353.

Nolan, Richard L. and James C. Wetherbe, 1980, "Towards a Comprehensive Framework for MIS Research," MIS Quarterly 4(2), 1-19.

O'Brien, James A. and James N. Morgan, 1991, "A Multidimensional Model of Information Resource Management," Information Resources Management Journal 4(2), 1-11.

A Project Manager's Perspectives on Added Value to Projects by Implementing SEI Guidelines

Dr. Ramamurti Sridar, PMP

IBM Global Services/Adjunct Faculty at University of Phoenix at San Jose, San Jose, CA 95193

Tel: 408-256-6591; Email: rsridar@aol.com or rsridar@us.ibm.com

Increasingly, organizations (both public and private) are embracing the project management discipline to achieve their bottom line. In this regard, Project Managers are viewed as strategic resource contributing to the ultimate success of the organizations. This scenario has placed the project managers in the hot spot, constantly impressing up on the management as to the added value provide to the projects during their life cycle. Project Managers look for a generally accepted/proven guidelines that they can adopt during various phases of project life cycle - initiation, planning, execution, Closure, and Control.

Software Engineering Institute (SEI) has established a series of guidelines that project managers can follow to achieve certain maturity level. The author of this paper is going to address the 'added value' from the point of view of attaining the level 2 maturity level. The level 2 maturity level dictates the project's process to be under the effective control of project management system based on performance of previous successful projects. The key here is to gather the repeatable successful tasks in previous projects and incorporate into subsequent projects to enhance the success rate.

The author's aate success of the organizations. This scenario has placed the project managers in the hot spot, constantly impressing up on the management as to the added value provide to the projects during their life cycle. Project Managers look for a generally accepted/proven guidelines that they can adopt during various phases of project life cycle - initiation, planning, execution, Closure, and Control.

Software Engineering Institute (SEI) has established a series of guidelines that project managers can followg & oversight

Software subcontract management

Software Quality assurance

Software configuration management

The author would like to discuss the added value to project's stakeholders by following the guidelines for each of the above KPAs.

ADDED VALUE ON REQUIREMENTS MANAGEMENT

A good and solid Requirement Management calls for a sound Requirements document that captures the customer's request for the functionalities to be incorporated into the application system. This requires a back and forth dialogue between the customer and the analyst/ developer which enables a common understanding with the customer on the requirements. The added value provided to various stakeholders as a result of sound Requirement definition is summed up as follows:

a. The final acceptance rate of deliverables is enhanced for the project sponsor and the customer.

b. The cycle time for development and final delivery is reduced considerably (possibly 20 percent) by the elimination of rework on the part of developer.

c. A sound software development plan with higher certainty rate of achieving the target by the Project Manager.

d. Easy to implement change control with a sound baseline requirement in terms of customer acceptance of change.

e. Streamline the resource allocation process in terms of hardware, software, and resource skill for project sponsor, customer, functional manager, and project manager.

ADDED VALUE ON SOFTWARE PROJECT PLANNING, TRACKING AND OVERSIGHT MANAGEMENT

A detailed statement of work (SOW) is the basis for a sound software project planning which includes the goals and constraints. This establishes a common understanding among the project stakeholders in terms of project deliverables, project duration, project risks, and project resources. The subsequent activity that follows the SOW is the software development plan which encompasses detailed project tasks associated with a planned time horizon and planned sizing of work effort. A documented procedure for estimating the tasks is stipulated by SEI to achieve a standard estimating process.

Software Project Tracking and Oversight management is critical to the successful execution of the project. A clearly spelled out policy on frequency of tracking and reporting should be part of the project plan. The tracking entails the measurement of project task achievement against the original plan. The project tracking report is shared among stakeholders. Project tracking and serves aand Oversight Management

A detailed statement of work (SOW) is the basis for a sound software project planning which includes the goals and constraints. This establishes a common understanding among the project stakeholders in terms of project deliverables, project duration, project risks, and project resources. The subsequent activity that follows the SOW is the software development plan which encompasses detailed project tasks associated with a planned time horizon and planned sizing of work effort.that they could plan for managerial reserves.

c. The customer can make a pro-active planning on needed end user documentation and training procedures.

d. The project team members attain the skill of a disciplined estimating approach which could be successfully used in future projects.

e. The project manager firms up the commitment of resources with project sponsor and functional managers.

f. Functional managers could foresee a definite resource redeployment schedule for the resources after the conclusion of the project.

g. The project manager can foresee any possible delay in the execution of the project and alert the project sponsor/customer as a result of tracking.

h. The project task variances as a result of tracking brings to focus on future tuning of estimates more realistic which is a real benefit to project team members and project manager.

i. Instill a sense of ownership and commitment on the part of project team members when they are tracked for their performance on project tasks.

j. Enable project manager to implement changes to commitments as a result of tracking schedule variance resulting from possible added requirement.

ADDED VALUE ON SOFTWARE SUBCONTRACTOR MANAGEMENT

The task of identifying skilled resources with respect to a project always goes beyond looking at project manager's own resource pool. The project manager is faced with two key choices: a. grow the needed skill for the project within the project manager's own resource pool by way of on the job training or education. b. Bring in external contractors with the required skill. In the former case, the project manager has to absorb the learning curve effect in the project schedule. In the latter case, the project manager has to absorb the additional responsibility of subcontractor management.

The task of software subcontractor management entails evaluation of subcontractor bid/skill level, tracking the performance of subcontractor, and ensure that the subcontractors follow the established project implementation guidelines.

The added value provided to various stakeholders as a result of software subcontractor management is summed up as follows:

a. The project sponsor/customer can achieve savings in project direct labor cost resulting from low cost country subcontract resources.

b. The project manager/functional manager can grow the skills of their resource pool by letting them work side by side with the subcontractors.

ADDED VALUE ON SOFTWARE QUALITY ASSURANCE

Quality Assurance is a key component of project management. The outcome of quality assurance bears a direct relationship to the outcome of the project (success or failure).

Quality Assurance (QA) starts from the very beginning of the initiation of the project and flows through the entire project life cycle. As part of the QA activities, SEI recommends the following:

a. Technical Risk Assessment (TRA) during the project planning phase.

b. Prepare Solution Assurance Review Checklist (SARC) during the project planning phase

c. Project Management Review report during development and and delivery of project.

The added value provided to various stakeholders as a result of software quality assurance management is summed up as follows:

a. The technical risk assessment brings to focus the high impact risk exposure items - new technology used in project timeliness of delivery of business critical function etc.- to the project sponsor/customer which enables them to make an effective contingency plans.

b. The project manager can make his project plan more realistic by incorporating risk mitigation tasks along with the rest of the project tasks for tracking.

c. The Solution Assurance Review Checklist provides an early warning to the project manager in case of any deficiency in project initiation/planning/execution/delivery like incomplete DOU (Document of Understanding), lack of funding for the project, lack of skill identification, lack of sound estimation of tasks for scheduling etc.

d. Force the project team members to focus on solution delivery matching the customer requirements as a result of project management review done both during solution development and before solution delivery to the customer.

e. The customer is assured of quality solution delivery that meets his/her requirements.

ADDED VALUE ON SOFTWARE CONFIGURATION MANAGEMENT

Software Configuration Management entails the adoption of a mechanism by which the software work products (like source code, executable module, user documents, requirements, test scripts, test data etc.). are maintained in a software repository. The purpose is to control changes to the baseline and to ensure integrity and traceability of changes to software work products during the life cycle of both development and production system.

The added value provided to various stakeholders as a result of software configuration management is summed up as follows:

a. Reliable recovery of the last workable software work product in the event of any failure of the production version of the software work product which enables the customer feel more secure.

b. Project development team members have controlled access to software work products thereby preventing accidental overlay of code to the same module.

c. The software repository control report serves as an effective auditing trace which the project manager can use for the project audit.

REFERENCES

1. Paulk, Weber, Garcia, Chrissis, Bush. "Key Practices of the Capability Maturity Model" V1.1, CMU/SEI-93-TR-25, 1993

2. Paulk, Weber, Curtis, Chrissis. "The Capability Maturity Model/: Guidelines for Improving the Software Process". Addison-Wesley, 1995.

3. Judd, Maureen. "Introduction to the Software Engineering Institute Capability Maturity Model (SEI CMM)". IBM Global Application Delivery Presentation, January 1999.

Activity Based Costing for Libraries and Non-profit Agencies

Virginia Anne Taylor
William Paterson University, 8 Linda Drive, Jackson, NJ 08527
taylorv@nebula.wilpaterson.edu, 732-367-3907 (phone), 732-730-1362 (fax)

Caroline M. Coughlin
Rutgers University, New Brunswick, NJ 08903, coughli@scils.rutgers.edu, 732-249-9716

The case research approach is used to develop a cost behavior analysis tool and an application of activity based costing (ABC) techniques in a typical not-for-profit based library or information agency. The relationships between library services and standard costs are uncovered and discussed. Our paper explains how a standard cost measurement system evolves using people, things, processes and results as building blocks.

Library Directors are often asked to develop alternative budgets that reduce their base funding by five or ten percent. Because the traditional lump-sum and line item budgets issued by institutional management merely describe the cost of providing a library, the library is often viewed by the parent organization as a cost center rather than a production center. As such it is a prime areas for belt- tightening and easy target for cost cutting. One key goal of this groundwork is to present the library as center that generates valued products.

First, in order to facilitate a better understanding of the overhead concept presented later in the ABC procedure, we begin with an explanation of the difference between fixed and variable cost behavior. Examples of many cost behavior patterns are graphically illustrated to highlight the behavioral differences among library costs. Second, cost allocation approaches are developed. Drawing on the familiar budget formula, a line -item budget listing the costs to operate the library unit, we develop two main program budgets, the Organization and Distribution Program and the Interpretation Program. The emphasis here is on linking expenditures with broad goals.

Next, the main services or products for each program are defined to create a program budget formula. Services that fulfill the needs of our various constituents are defined as outputs or products. Finally, a transaction cost approach is designed to assign activity costs on a product by product basis, develop an ABC format, and estimate standard costs for the various information products delivered within a program area. Fixed costs are viewed as capacity producing costs. Transaction is broadly defined as a unit of activity that has a conclusion and a well defined result, i.e. question answered. Upon identifying the cost driver for each activity, costs are allocated according to the proportion of each cost driver consumed by the product / information service.

The study indicates the application of ABC procedures improves the gathering, processing, and disseminating of cost and budget information within the library unit. Results suggest using cost behavior analysis as a management tool enhances the evaluation of alternate solutions. It improves library directors' operational level decisions about library expenditures such as outsourcing or ownership. In addition, the procedures yielded evidence for a program defense.

Since ABC techniques uncover the direct impact of proposed budget cuts on service delivery, they are useful tools to influence the allocation of organizational resources at the strategic management level. This example provided evidence indicating compliance with a five percent overall budget reduction request would require a significant reduction in a particular reference service product, answering complex research questions. Long-term commitments in the overhead and personnel cost pools necessitate applying the total dollar amount of any reference program funding reduction to the materials budget. This would severely affect the ability to answer complex reference questions upon which reference staff spend 95% of their time. As the parent organization strives to accommodate the changing external environments with existing organizational capacity, they may decide the endangered product is vital to their mission and restore funding. Since in this situation the resultant ABC techniques show that every dollar of restored funds has a triple positive effect on reference services, the data generated could also have a positive affect on outside funding.

PANELS

Information Technology Diffusion in the Public Sector

Moderator: A. K. Aggarwal, University of Baltimore
Members: Rajesh Mirani, University of Baltimore; Mike Carleton, Health and Human Services;
Sonali Aggarwal, R.V. Engg College

Information is the key to survival for organizations of tomorrow. How effectively organizations manage and use technology will determine their very existence in the twenty-first century. Computer usage is diffusing upward in the organizational hierarchy, creating significant growth in new applications aimed at middle- and top-level managers. Though much has been written about technology in the private sector and even third world countries, there is still lack of information about technology diffusion in the public sector.

Management theory suggests that the decisions and decision processes of public and private sectors differ considerably. A potential implication of this is that differences in decision processes translate into differences in the IT usage. However, this has never been empirically tested, although the use of computer modeling in Federal agencies has been the focus of at least one study. Most of the available research literature on IT usage focuses on specific modeling tools or is prescriptive in nature.

This panel will explore some of the following issues: Are there differences in IT usage in the public and the private sector? How is IT diffusing in the public sectors? Are IT needs different in the public and private sector? What are the implications of these differences? Who dictates IT issues in public sector? Is the government ready for Y2K?

Distance Education - Tools & Pedagogy

Panel Moderator - Dennis Bialaszewski, Indiana State University
Panelists: Alan Rea, Western Michigam University; Laura Hall, University of Texas, El Paso; Nancy Thomson,
Northwest Missouri State University; Ira Yermish, St. Joseph's University

This panel will discuss issues which are leading edge in Distance Education delivery. Panelists have experience with video conferencing, and many internet based tools in the classroom. Panelists also have experience with the delivery of graduate courses over the web. The panelists backgrounds are divergent as are their course offerings. This panel should provide insight to those contemplating heavier reliance on internet based pedagogy as well as added perspective for those already integrating many of the tools and techniques.

We will outline the different levels of implementation of web based courses and internet delivery and discuss how instructors can best synthesize contenet and a new medium. This discussion takes into account the learning curves (for both instructor and student), the situation (technology avaialbe, institutional support and merit) and many other factors one must consider as we embark upon a new era of education in the 21st century.

Ultimately this discussion does see us moving in the right direction but how we get there is a matter of debate. First time offerings of courses which are mediated by new learning tools require redefining of many assumptions from those of the regualr classroom delivery. Decisions need to be addressed as to how to handle these new assumptions created by mediated learning.

These issues are broad based and involve the registrar, financial aid, faculty allocation and management, technology provisioning and articulation/transfr agreements with other academic institutions. They center around programatic issues such as establishing policies, technology, student and faculty expectations, technology training and support, ownership and copyright, etcetera.

Specifically issues such as the following should be thoroughly discussed and determined in order to insure success of delivery:

• Costs of marketing Courses

- Recording of Transfer Credit
- Faculty Ownership, load, and evaluation
- Logistics of Testing, Materials development and collection
- Technology training and support
- Differences between competencies with these tools by students
- Differences between tools/methodologies available at different sites
- Consideration of the development of new interdisciplinary courses

    Although many question remain unanswered we must develop an appropriate paradigm at our respective institutions in order to insure success. We have many possibilities to increase diversity in many many ways. We can now have globally offered courses. This panel should serve as a stimulant for our appropriate involvement.

Distance Education - Classroom Issues

Moderator: Dennis Bialaszewski, Indiana State University
Panelists: Joe Williams, Colorado State University; Jimmy Issac, India; Raymond Papp, Central Connecticut State University; Tom Pencek, Meredith College

    Often times the entire focus in discussions of distance education is only on the learner who is distant. And yet sometimes delivery is in an environments where there is also a local learner ... what impact do these deliveries have upon local learners. Oor panelists will look at issues such as this. Moreover, there are issues of impacts of different cultures and different environments for distance education delivery. There are also issues related to language barriers and the like if distance education is intended for those in different countries. How are these isses be explored today. This panel will focus on what sometimes is viewed as more peripheral issues but they are no less important issues in formulating quality distance education delivery.

    Moreover, as part of the Connecticut State University's initiative to offer courses via th internet, onlineCSU was piloted during the Fall 1998 semester with an initial offering of some two dozen courses. CSU has partnered with REAL EDUCATION, a leader in online education using the internet. A panelist has extensive experience in this project and will share website and hypertext links with participants so they may view the course in a real time setting.

Global Diversity in IRM Education

Moderator: Eli B. Cohen (chair), Informing Science Institute and Leon Kozminski Academy of Entrepreneurship and Management
Members: Jakov Crnkovic, College of Saint Rose; Robert RC Childs, National Defense University; Jacky Swan, Warwick Business School, University of Warwick; Philip Sallis, Dept of Information Science, University of Otago, University of Otago; Shirley Fedorovich, Embry-Riddle Aeronautical University; Karen D. Loch, Decision Sciences, Georgia State University; Peter Goldschmidt, Faculty of Commerce and Economics, The University of Western Australia; Dimitar Grozdanov Christozov, Faculty Office, American University in Bulgaria; Duöan Lesjak, University of Maribor, School of Economics and Business; Jessie Wong, National Institute of Education, Singapore; Syed Mahbubur Rahman, North Dakota State University; Gail Thornburg, Online Computer Library Center Inc.

EXECUTIVE SUMMARY

    Information Resource Management is viewed differently in different countries. The panelists have taught in diverse countries and so bring together their views of the field and of the challenges in teaching students.

    The very content of the field is conceptualized differently around the globe. The American approach considers empiricism the premier source of knowledge of this field. In contrast, the European approaches to understanding IRM are more inclusive and cross-disciplinary. In Australasia, education in this field tends to be housed within a Faculty of Infomatics with emphasis placed on the technical aspects.

    Some of the topics of this roundtable session include the following:
- How should the IRMA/DAMA model curriculum be revised to be more inclusive?

- Do students' needs differ from culture to culture?
- Do curricular needs vary from country to country? Can one model curriculum fit all?
- What impact has distance education had on teaching and on the research/teaching demands on IRM professors?
- What Web resources are available to improve IRM education? The Global Informing Sciences Education web site at < http://gise.org > is one such resource.

One of the purposes of this panel is to draw together individuals (from the panel and the audience) who are interested in this area with an eye toward working on revising the IRMA/DAMA model curriculum.

Primer for Disaster Recovery Planning: A Tutorial for Information Resource Managers/Faculty

Dr. Charlotte J. Hiatt

Craig School of Business, California State University, Fresno, 5245 North Backer Avenue, Fresno, California 93740-8001, (209) 278-2823, Fax: (209) 278-4911, charlotte_hiatt@csufresno.edu

INTRODUCTION

Corporate information is the life's blood of an organization. Companies have become more sophisticated in their use of information systems and thus, more dependent on these systems for survival. Despite the care taken to protect critical assets, the possibility of losing information in a disaster, such as fire, flood, earthquake or power outage, always exists. Usually, buildings and equipment are adequately insured; the information they contain is often not afforded equal protection. An unexpected disaster can strike an organization at any time. If not adequately prepared, the company may not recover the information that enables it to function normally; in fact, it may not recover at all.

Considering the potential catastrophic impact of a major information loss, careful and thorough preparation must be conducted in anticipation of such an event. This preparation can be accomplished through disaster recovery planning (DRP).

OBJECTIVES OF THE TUTORIAL

Unfortunately, all the MIS texts currently being used to teach the standard MIS course (graduate and undergraduate levels) only include a limited discussion of these issues (usually less than one page). Most of the emphasis tends to be on security and control measures. Today, more than ever before, information is a vital business resource. The loss of vital records could be devastating and may even lead to the ultimate closure of a business. Typically, industry does not become concerned about planning for a disaster until one happens to them or to someone else. It is important, therefore, that MIS graduates, faculty, and business managers have access to a synthesis of the current (but broadly-dispersed) documentation on disaster recovery planning. This tutorial will:

- Review the common terms used in the DRP field.
- Present strategies for obtaining management support for DRP development.
- Layout a framework for plan development.
- Discuss the major elements included in a disaster recovery document.
- Provide an overview of commercial DR software, facilities, and services.
- Suggest some criteria for selecting the appropriate software, facilities, and services.
- Discuss how the information in outline on the next page might be used to supplement an MIS course.

DRP TUTORIAL OUTLINE

I. Introduction
II. Definition of a Disaster
III. Identify Disaster as a Possibility
IV. Need for a Disaster Recovery Plan
V. Secure Top Management Support and Resources

A. Building Reliable Support
B. Securing and Preparing Resources
VI. Organize Plan Development Team
VII. Conduct Risk and Business Impact Analyses
A. Identify and Prioritize Assets and Functions
B. Identify Threats to Assets and Functions
C. Prioritize DRP Efforts
VIII.   Identify Data Storage and Recovery Sites
A. Data Backup
B. Off-site Storage
C. Identify the Information Asset
D. Select an Off-site Storage Vendor
IX. Formulate Strategies for System Backup/Recovery
A. Recovery Site Alternatives
B. Alternate Site Selection Criteria
C. Common Concerns
D. Asses Business Recovery Needs
E. Avoid Common Misconceptions
F. Select a Hot-site Facility
G. Contract with a Vendor

X. Evaluate Alternatives for DRP Development
A. Consultants
B. In-house Development
C. PC-based Software
XI. Define Assumptions and Limitations of the Plan
XII. Write the Plan
A. Organization of Plan
B. Body of Plan
XIII. Develop Primary Procedures for Emergency Response
XIV. Write Emergency Management Plan
XV. Designate Disaster Recovery Teams
A. Types of DR Team
B. Team Member Characteristics
C. Team Tasks
XVI. Develop a Notification Directory
XVII. Other Resources for DR Information
A. Research the Literature or the Web
B. Professional Organizations and Certification

Knowledge Management: An Army Perspective

Panel Moderator: Miriam F. Browning, Director, Information Management, Office of the Secretary of the Army, Director of Information Systems for Command, Control, Communications and Computers
Panel Members: LTC(P) Stephen E. Broughall, Director, Strategic and Advanced Computing Center; DR (COL) Roger J. Channing, Industrial College of the Armed Forces; LTC John F. Kendall, HQ, Department of the Army, Personnel Command; COL Mike Heimstra, Center for Army Lessons Learned

Knowledge management is an integrated, systematic approach to identifying, managing and sharing all of an enterprise's information assets, including databases, documents, policies, and procedures, as well as previously unarticulated expertise and experience resident in individual workers. Fundamentally, knowledge management is about making the collective information and experience of an enterprise available to the individual knowledge worker, who is responsible for using it wisely and for replenishing the stock. As the Army transitions from a platform centric land battle doctrine to the advent of the knowledge based platform doctrine suggests that the battle will be won using sophisticated information technologies and knowledge management based tools.

The 21st century warrior's reliance on new advanced weapons systems has forever changed the nature of modern warfare. In the next century, the ability to effectively leverage these sophisticated weapons systems as part of our defense strategy must become an integral part of our national security policy. The need for implementing new strategies is vital to protect communications, intelligence, military deployments and scores of other information.

Army Knowledge Online is the operational entity responsible for achieving this mission and will be the focus of the panel discussion. The panel will consist of an introduction of Army knowledge management and four presentations:

Introduction: Overall Army Introduction of the Army and Army Knowledge Management
I. Army Knowledge Online Overview
II. Mentor and Virtual Reality Training for Senior Decision Makers and Leaders
III. Officer Professional Management System XXI
IV. Army After Next

Conclusion: The Army Knowledge Online initiative is a key element in the transformation of the institutional Army into a true knowledge and capabilities-based organization. When the First Digital Division is fielded in 2000, it will leverage information and technology to create a more lethal and situationally aware force. To keep pace with this warfighting force, the Institutional Army must be ready to support the Army's digital operations in the 21st century.

To meet this challenge, General Dennis Reimer, the Chief of Staff, U.S. Army established the Army Knowledge Online initiative. The Army has established the following vision and mission for its application of knowledge management within the Institutional Army:

Vision – Transform the Institutional Army into an information – age, networked organization that leverages its intellectual capital to better organize, train, equip and maintain a strategic land combat Army Force.

Mission – To embed knowledge management into the Army culture and processes to achieve a sustaining momentum that will carry it into the 21st century. This will be accomplished through changes in organizational structure, culture, processes and technology.

The Role of Information Technology in the Delivery of Student Financial Assistance in the New Millennium

Panelists: Jerry Russomano, Director of Program Systems Service, Office of Student Financial Assistance Programs, U.S. Dept of Education, (202) 708-7701, Fax: (202) 708-4828, Jerry_Russomano@ed.gov; Jim Cornell, Systems Area Manager, Office of Inspector General, U.S. Dept of Education, (202) 205-9538, Fax: (202) 205-8238, Jim_Cornell@ed.gov

In the past two years, the U.S. Department of Education (ED) has developed Plans to transform its expensive, stovepiped Office of Student Financial Assistance Programs (OSFAP) information systems into an efficient, integrated and comprehensive student financial aid delivery system. The current vision is a paperless, seamless and customer centered process that supports all aspects of SFA management. This panel will discuss the Department's planned Information Technology (IT) solutions to achieve this vision and its collaborative approach to developing them.

BACKGROUND

The U.S. Department of Education (ED) Office of Student Financial Assistance Programs (OSFAP) recently became the Government's first Performance Based Organization (PBO). OSFAP oversees the delivery of approximately $40 billion per year in student financial aid and manages a $120 billion loan portfolio, qualifying it as one of the largest lending institutions in the U.S. In administering the Department's need-based financial assistance, OSFAP partners with guaranty agencies, lenders and nearly 8,000 educational institutions to make federal grants, loans and work-study funding available to nearly 8 million eligible undergraduate and graduate students annually.

IT DRIVEN CHANGE

To accomplish its vision for the 21st century, OSFAP has embarked on several initiatives. They include conducting a comprehensive Year 2000 readiness program, using GSA's virtual data center contract to gain system integration and efficiency, incorporating EDI and web-based applications to improve the speed and efficiency of the SFA delivery system, and implementing the Project EASI vision to create other efficiencies and enhance OSFAP's customer service.

OIG'S ROLE AS A PARTNER FOR PROGRESS

In an effort to provide more timely input to ED on IT matters, the Office of Inspector General (OIG) is transforming its role. While some traditional audit work continues to be conducted, the role of the IT Systems group is evolving into one focused on quick response audit products and providing ongoing advice and assistance. This has served to build customer trust and support OSFAP's transition into the 21st century.

CONCLUSION

Through the opportunities granted by the PBO, its new leadership team, and the supporting role of the OIG, OSFAP is anticipating the successful implementation of its vision for the 21st century. Audience input will be sought on lessons learned from the private sector that could benefit OSFAP in its modernization effort.

A New Pennsylvania: Using IT to Help Reengineering within State Government

Panel Chair: Charlie Gerhards, Commonwealth of Pennsylvania

The panel presents the conceptual framework of Business process reengineering through information technology in the commonwealth of Pennsylvania. IT strategic planning initiatives undertaken by the commonwealth are discussed; and the ways are defined on how IT can enable fundamental change that will eliminate waster, cut bureaucracy, reduce costs and improve the level of government services to the citizens of the Commonwealth. The emphasis is on how information technology is used to enable and transform the way the commonwealth conducts its business. Special topics include: The IT Strategic Planning Initiative: An Enterprise-wide Perspective of the Commonwealth; Delivery of Business Results through IT: Strategies and Success Stories: Managing the Organizations IT Resources in the Year 2000.

Teaching with Technology, Teaching about Technology

Session Organizer and Chair: Nancy C. Weida, Bucknell University, Dept. of Management, Lewisburg, PA 17837, phone: 570-577-1399; fax: 570-577-1338; e-mail: nweida@bucknell.edu
Panelists: Douglas E. Allen, Bucknell University, Dept. of Management; David Jensen, Bucknell University, Dept. of Management; John Miller, Bucknell University, Dept. of Management; Christopher J. Zappe, Bucknell University, Dept. of Management

MOTIVATION AND FORMAT

As technology pervades every aspect of business education, it is natural (and essential) to step back and assess the effects of technology use on learning. This year's conference theme of "Managing Information Technology Resources in Organizations in the Next Millennium" provides an excellent opportunity to analyze and discuss correlation between technology and learning.

The purpose of this panel is to bring together a diverse group of business educators, from fields such as strategy, the decision sciences, marketing, organizational behavior, and accounting, to discuss these important pedagogical issues.

In particular, the discussion will center on how the new technologies and pedagogies affect such issues as:
• The classroom environment
• The student-teacher relationship in the virtual age
• Actual learning
• Reaching students with different learning styles
• Student expectations
• Professor expectations
• Teaching *about* technology, and teaching *with* technology

The structure of the session is as follows. Following brief remarks from panelists, the floor will be opened up for discussion.

Two Recent Decisions To Buy, Not Build, Clinical Information Systems Make or Buy Decisions With Respect To Healthcare Applications

Panel Chair: Laurie Williams, RN, BSN, MHA, Superior Consultant Company, Inc.,
Panelists: Sue Paone, Corporate Regional Vice President, RN, BSN, MHA, Client Services Manager, University of Pittsburgh Medical Center; Betsy Thornquist, Project Leader, Physician Communications Network (PCN), Health System, Yale-New Haven, Health System

ABSTRACT

Professionals from two leading-edge healthcare delivery systems will critique their processes to buy an enterprise-wide Clinical Information System (CIS) rather than build. Both the UPMC and Yale-New Haven Health Systems built CIS products before. Both will compare the products considered and recap the strategic differences between their CIS finalists.

BACKGROUND

Superior Consultant Company, Inc. will preface this expert panel discussion with an overview of the enterprise-wide CIS selection process. As moderator, Superior will introduce the various methodologies and panelists, then facilitate an interactive discussion. To balance perspectives, the panelists represent two different Integrated Delivery Networks (IDNs) and different results. The panelists from vast urban university-affiliated IDNs with multi-state and international clientele will detail their respective experiences. All will engage in an interactive discussion emphasizing specifics to "separate the facts from fiction" about CIS products.

Unlike at other international conferences, this panel is committed to being specific about what they saw at the various demonstrations, site visits and corporate visits; and what their CIS functionality, technology, cost, implementation, support, client satisfaction and corporate stability comparisons yielded. Throughout this discussion between the moderator, panelists and 1999 Information Resources Management Association (IRMA) audience, we will offer useful and detailed information to bolster the audience's efforts to embark on their own CIS selections. Because the panelists selected different CIS solutions, each can comment on their contract negotiation and implementation successes to date — WITHOUT endorsing the named products, but focusing on the general attributes, benefits and drawbacks of a given CIS.

APPROACH

1. Each IDN formed a task force of interested physicians, nurses, clinicians, information systems and management engineering professionals and administrators to meet periodically throughout the six to twelve month CIS selection timetables.
2. Each objectively compared the functionality of the industry's top CIS products via customized Request For Proposals (RFPs) and extensive on-site demonstrations to educate the entire medical, nursing, and clinical staffs.
3. Each scrutinized client satisfaction with the CIS vendors' support services, implementation efforts, products and productivity gains (or lack thereof) via exhaustive telephone reference checks, peer networking at user groups, conferences, word of mouth, consultant knowledge databases and research, and Internet searches of vendor Web pages and List Serves.
4. Each analyzed if the vendors' Research & Development (R&D) vision and other claims matched their various strategic business needs (e.g., by comparing delivery dates documented in the RFP vs. detailed co-development discussions).
5. Each evaluated the CIS technologies against operating requirements and legacy system interface requirements.
6. Each recapped the major risks and benefits (e.g., with respect to functionality, technology, cost, implementation, support, client satisfaction, and corporate stability) to select a partner-of-choice and facilitate contract negotiations.

RESULTS / RECOMMENDATIONS

1. While each panelist had a different timetable, task force structure, decision-making authority, budget and vendor mix, all reached consensus to select the CIS that best addressed their enterprise-wide IDN strategic and tactical needs (by prefacing the selection with a thorough Information Systems Strategic Planning process). Each prefaced their CIS selection with an cost:benefit analysis of past efforts to build applications.
2. All conducted key user interviews to prioritize functional requirements before issuing the RFP. Rather than distributing "yes-no" checklists, each customized the RFP to ask for "essay" responses that identified if the CIS had the requisite functionality and how it would help achieve key business objectives.
3. Each weighed RFP responses differently but all established scoring mechanisms in advance to ensure an equitable and comprehensive review of the CIS products and vendor partners. To implement caveat emptor [let the buyer beware], the audience must "Trust But Verify" and empower your CIS Selection Committee and Task Forces to conduct rigorous due diligence — after instructing the vendors that all their statements must be scrupulously accurate or they risk elimination.
4. All insisted the CIS finalists follow scripted demonstration formats to nformation Systems Strategic Planning process). Each prefaced their CIS selection with an cost:benefit analysis of past efforts to build applications.
2. All conducted key user interviews to prioritize functional requirements before issuing the RFP. Rather than distributing "yes-no" checklists, each customized the RFP to ask for "essay" responses that identified if the CIS had the requisite functionality and how it would help achieve key business objectives.
3. Each weighed RFP responses differently presenter went through each step.
5. Rather than visiting only the handful of showcase sites where the vendors maintain strategic alliances and provide ample support, all aimed to visit comparable facilities in terms of size, complexity, legacy system interfaces, academic vs. lay users, live application portfolios, etc. Some also traveled alone to uncensored site visits where they randomly asked CIS users for their opinions, not just those of the hosts on the scripted agenda.
6. All used best efforts to obtain comprehensive cost comparisons for the start-up and true long-term operating expenses; make certain that the hardware configuration was more than adequate; and negotiate enterprise software licenses rather than traditional fees based on fixed volume statistics.

TRACK OBJECTIVES AND BENEFITS TO IRMA'99 ATTENDEES

Track attendees will be able to:
1. Provide an objective framework for CIS evaluations.
2. Ensure an equitable and comprehensive review of the available "best selling" CIS products and vendor partners.
3. Examine helpful CIS comparison tools and valuable marketplace research.
4. Discuss methods used to successfully involve the medical and nursing staffs in replacing a legacy CIS — and embracing the full use of new technologies.
5. Evaluate lessons learned (e.g., buy vs. build, guard against subjective grading of the best-looking Graphical User Interface (GUI) vs. most robust functionality, minimize "shopping" vs. taking the first step toward implementation, involve the critical users and decision-makers from the outset).
6. Perform a rigorous analysis of all selection criteria that will enable audience to better negotiate a fair risk-sharing contract — with payments tied to timely performance, measurable milestones (e.g., live interfaces, product delivery dates) and productivity gains. Translating promises into strict contractual penalty clauses is vital.

DOCTORAL SYMPOSIUM ABSTRACTS

Exploring the Transition to Enterprise-wide Software Solutions

Marie-Claude Boudreau
Georgia State University, 35 Broad St., 9th floor, Atlanta, GA 30303
gs04mcb@panther.gsu.edu, (404) 651-3880, Fax: (404) 651-3842

INTRODUCTION

At the heart of the highly competitive emerging marketplace, enterprise-wide software solutions, more commonly called "enterprise resource planning" (ERP) packages, provide a promising means for companies to achieve business breakthroughs. ERP packages are integrated sets of business applications that allow companies to manage almost all aspects of operations including manufacturing, human resources, finance, and logistics. It is predicted that the global ERP market will grow at a compound annual rate of 37 percent over the next five years; indeed, the worldwide ERP market of $11 billion in 1997 is expected to reach $52 billion by 2001 (AMR Report 1997).

High risks frequently accompany the high payoffs potentially attainable through the transition to an ERP package. In fact, about half of ERP projects fail to achieve hoped-for benefits (Appleton, 1997). The consequences of such failures are considerable, given that an organization can spend millions of dollars and require many years of effort in such a project. Because the successful implementation of an ERP system is contingent upon an accurate assessment of the associated organizational changes (Appleton, 1997), there is a need to investigate the nature of such organizational changes in the specific context of an ERP transition.

THEORETICAL BACKGROUND

A process approach (Mohr 1982) to study ERP transition is proposed. Studies using a process approach to research are better suited to explain how organizational change emerges, develops, grows or terminates over time (Van de Ven and Huber 1990). While studying how ERP transition unfolds, we want to specifically focus our attention on two dimensions frequently stressed when deciphering patterns of change: the *form* and the *content*. The form deals mainly with the amount and frequency (pace) of change, and the content describes the specific theoretical constructs associated with change.

Form of Organizational Change

The two main views on the form that may be taken by an organizational change are known as *evolutionary* and *revolutionary*. The evolutionary view generally portrays change as consisting of minor improvements or simple adjustments (Quinn 1980). The revolutionary view rather describes organizational change as being fundamental and discontinuous (Miller and Friesen 1984). Whereas authors generally polarize their attention on either kind of changes (Dewar and Dutton 1986), alternative views have also been proposed. The punctuated equilibrium, for instance, is a particularly well-known view on change that claims to integrate the evolutionary and revolutionary perspectives (Tushman and Romanelli 1985; Gersick 1991). Other variations of the evolutionary / revolutionary dichotomy have been proposed by Henderson and Clark (1990), Bartunek and Moch (1987), Nadler and Tushman (1989), Brown and Eisenhardt (1997), and Choi (1995).

Content of Organizational Change

Robey and Boudreau (in press) recommended the use of theories employing a logic of opposition to study the organizational consequences of information technology. A logic of opposition includes a dialectical process (Van de Ven and Poole, 1995) according to which forces promoting and impeding change must be considered. Specific theories embedding a logic of opposition have been shown as especially appropriate: organizational politics, organizational culture, institutional theory, and organizational learning. Because none of those theories are deterministic in their nature, they are helpful in better understanding the frequent contradictory consequences of information technology.

Issues

The literature on form and content of organizational change is suggestive of multiple perspectives according to which change may be apprehended. Accordingly, the form of an ERP transition may be interpreted as being an evolution, a revolution, or some alternative form of change. The form of change may be also be understood dissimilarly at different organizational levels, as demonstrated in Taylor's (1998) study of organizational change. As to the content of the organizational change associated with an ERP transition, one should expect to see different forces to be at play to promote and impede the changes associated with an ERP transition. Such forces may belong to a specific theory or may rather combine elements from many theories. As a consequence, ERP research should proceed by not excluding potential forms and contents of organizational change. To stay open to this multiplicity of perspectives, an interpretive stand will be taken while studying the process of ERP transitions. An interpretive position, indeed, is explicitly appropriate when one wants to capture complex, dynamic, social phenomena that are both context and time dependent (Orlikowski and Baroudi 1991).

EXPECTED OUTCOME

We are only beginning to understand the nature of change, especially with respect to organization (Goodstein and Burke 1991). Those organizations that will embrace enterprise-wide software solutions will go through an important technological change. The organizational change associated with such technological endeavor, however, is hard to assess given the dearth of empirical literature on ERP transitions. It is our contention that the elaboration of a specific theory explaining the ERP transition process will both benefit from and contribute to the enrichment of the existent literature. For practitioners, this research will permit the development of general managerial guidelines to help organizations planning to acquire an ERP package to be successful in their implementation process. For researchers, the main contribution will be in the enrichment of the different views on organizational change and organizational theories.

The Role of Adaptive Learning Systems in the Successful Implementation of Information Technology (IT) for Small Business Entrepreneurs

Dessa David

Zicklin School of Business - Baruch College; Graduate Center, City University of New York, New York, New York 10010, Dessa_David@baruch.cuny.edu

ABSTRACT

The enticement of information technology (IT) to a businessperson is magnetic. IL promises to dramatically reshape the way business functions are conducted. The potential benefits that IT promises to a business are alluring. Today, there exist a competing climate among businesses to adopt IT. To the small business entrepreneur, the pull to adopt IT is no different from that of the multinational corporations. The *competitive and strategic advantages, status, increase productivity,', automation of tedious tasks, reduction of errors, the internet and its advantages, business leveraging, a new technologically savvy consumer, decreasing hardware* prices are just a few of the motivators of information technology adoption. Despite its promise, IT implementation poses many challenges. IT implementation can be costly and risky. Generally, a small business entrepreneur cannot afford such risks. An incorrect decision or lack of the decision can he the difference between success and failure of his business. **The small business entrepreneur remains virtually unassisted in their decision-making and control for implementing IT technology.**

Small businesses are fundamental to the United States economy. The [Small Business Administration, Office of Advocacy, The Facts About Small Business, 1997; Small Business Answer card 1998] shows that small businesses account for the majority of businesses in the United States today. They are responsible for 99% of the 23.3

nonfarm businesses and 51% of the gross domestic product. To this end, it is imperative that researchers continue to explore ways in which small businesses can utilize IT for strategic and competitive advances.

Tremendous attention has been focused on IT and its value to businesses. Studies have been done to evaluate factors that influence IT success [Delone, 1988; Seddon, 1997]. [Delone, 1988] determined that the knowledge of the CEO was the most important determinant in successful IT implementation. [Raymond, 1988; Cragg, 1993] stated that computer knowledge are essential factors to promote information technology implementation. For a small businessperson, the decision to adopt IT must bring benefits to his business. [Seddon, 1997] concluded that in order for the CEO to decide to implement technology he must perceive potential net benefits of IT to his/her organization. With limited resources in a small business, the knowledge to evaluate **the potential benefits of IT is not always available.**

In computer science, expert systems, decision support systems and executive information systems play significant roles in supporting the decision making process [Agarwal, 1994; Marakas, 1998; Sharma, 1998, Sullivan, 1989]. However, the scopes, of all of the mentioned paradigms, remain limited and lack the flexibility to adapt to the various cognitive styles and environments that the decision-maker must consider to make effective decisions. To fully assist the small business entrepreneur with his/her complex decision process regarding IT implementation, tools that are adaptable to these changes must be developed.

This project proposes that an **Adaptive Learning System (ALS)** is the answer. This system utilizes Artificial Intelligence and combines the strengths of existing decision support technologies with intelligent systems to make a hybrid of an Intelligent adaptive agent [El-Najdawi, 1993; Fazlollahi, 1997; Holsapple, 1993; Piramuthu, 1993]. The ALS will assist the entrepreneur in making effective decisions about IT implementation. The system will be adaptable, nurturing and encouraging to the entrepreneur's needs. It will provide support for decisions over time. The dynamic adaptation characteristic of the ALS enables it to disperse expert advice at an appropriate level to the user. Basically, this system will become his *'consultant in a can'*.

The *'consultant in a can'* is expected to improve the quality of IT decisions, significantly reduce the risks that small business entrepreneurs face as they embark on IT implementation, and reduce the level of dissatisfaction felt when IT fails to meet their needs. Incorporating the businessperson ideas in the model places the entrepreneur in a unique position making IT decisions and retaining control of the process. He can now feel a level of support and increased confidence about his decisions. The entrepreneur is no longer a passive participant but an active one.

A review of the literature exposes the lack of research attention on small business IT issues. The bulk of research is generalized for large corporations. Small businesses need research tailored for them [Ein-Dor et al 1978; Pollard, 1998]. Tools and practices to assist the small business entrepreneur exploit the benefits of technology can be developed from grounded research. This project contributes to the advances of small business effective utilization of IT. Future research projects include: developing a prototype for the ALS; other uses for intelligent systems within the small business environment.

References available upon request from author

Individual, Group and Organisation Goals that Contribute to the Continuous Acceptance and Success of Executive Information Systems: An Empirical Investigation

George E.M. Ditsa

Department of Business Systems, University of Wollongong, Australia

+61 2 4221 4034, Fax: +61 2 4221 4474, george_ditsa@uow.edu.au

INTRODUCTION AND BACKGROUND

"'Failures' of technology have been quite common throughout history - every major innovation starts out with a lot of hype and hope. Within a few years the euphoria is replaced with disappointment and cynicism. If the technology proves itself however, the cynicism eventually yields to reality and success. The automobile, the radio, television and personal computers have all experienced such an acceptance cycle. Now EIS are having their turn of the bat" (Burkan, 1991, p. vii).

Executives of organisations are charged with the responsibility of making strategic decisions that will ultimately affect the survival of the organisations. The formulation of these strategic decision-making activities requires a myriad of information from both the internal and external environments of the organisation. And to obtain the necessary information, executives monitor both environments of their organisations continually in an attempt to assess the threats and opportunities that may impact on the organisation's survival. In recent times, the complexity of the business environments has increased due to market globalisation coupled with the growth in the number of products and services produced in multiplying markets (Matthews 1992). To complicate matters, competition and pressures from financial markets have intensified, while more and more government legislations, policies and regulations are ever affecting industries (Matthews, 1992; Frolick et al. 1997). These factors must seriously than ever be taken into account by any visionary executives in making any strategic plans for their organisations. Due to today's rapidly-changing business environments and fierce competition in the market, there is also the dire need and growing challenge for executives to make strategic decisions promptly in order to remain competitive and stay ahead in business.

To assist executives in obtaining some of the necessary information needed in their decision-making process from computer-based information systems, Executive Information Systems (EIS) were designed. These systems were thought of as being specifically tailored to meet executives' information needs for decision-making. EIS are nowadays the most innovative in high information technology as an aid of managerial work (Bergeron and Raymond, 1992; Watson et al., 1992; Harvey and Meiklejohn, 1990; Johansen, 1988; Holsapple and Whinston, 1987). However, as indicated in the opening quote, there has been some disappointment and cynicism replacing the euphoria that greeted the birth of EIS. Whereas there are some reports of success stories in using EIS, there are as well a good number of reports of EIS failures (Waston and Frolick, 1993). These failures revealed the "risky and fragile" nature of the development and implementation of these systems (Houdeshel and Watson, 1987; Rockart and DeLong, 1988; Watson et al. 1997).

As a result of the reported EIS failures, some organisations that are yet to implement EIS are reluctant to do so (Byun and Sub, 1994; Waston and Frolick, 1993). Study also revealed that relatively few EIS are fully operational. In Australia, for example, there are relatively few EIS which are fully operational, though there has been an increase in the past five years and many are now under development and implementation (Pervan and Phua, 1997).

Understandably, EIS are still a relatively new phenomenon and problems still exist in their development and implementation. Little research has so far been carried into EIS. In Australia, for example, very little research into EIS has been conducted (Pervan and Phua, 1997). More research is therefore needed into EIS if it is to prove itself

so that the "cynicism eventually yields to reality and success". It is the primary aim of this research therefore to contribute to the achievement of this goal.

THE ISSUES AND THE RESEARCH QUESTIONS

There are several factors that contribute to EIS failures: some technical, others are managerial and organisational (Watson et al. 1997). Above all, some of these failures will result from the failure of the intended users, the executives, to use the systems because they do not satisfy their needs. Some users may initially support and accept the systems but reject them later on because their requirements are no longer being met.

Following from the literature review, there are various studies to identify factors that contribute to the success and failure of EIS. However, there has not been a reported study that investigates whether individual goals, group goals and organisational goals contribute the success or failure of EIS.

An EIS is a class of information systems designed to facilitate the decision-making processes of executives. The success of an EIS depends upon many factors. One is that an EIS should support the strategic management process (SMP). The SMP is comprised of four phases: environmental analysis, strategy formulation, strategy implementation, and strategic control. If an EIS is to support the accomplishment of organisational objectives, then it should support all the four phases of SMP. However, in formulating strategic plans, various motives come into play: some organisational, some group and some individual (personal). The organisational behaviour literature suggest that the success or failure of any organisation should be analysed at three distinct levels of behaviour - individual, group and organisation (Campbell, 1979; Lewin and Minton, 1986; Koppes et al., 1991; Ivancevich and Matteson, 1993). Behaviour is viewed as operating at individual, group and organisational levels. This approach suggests that when studying organisational behaviour, one should identify clearly the level being analysed - individual, group or organisation. The effectiveness of the individual contributes to the effectiveness of the group, and the effectiveness of the group contributes to that of the organisation. However, there always exist conflicts of interest among these three distinct categories in any organisation. For example, while the individual may have the motive of using an information system as a tool to enhance his/her job appraisal and promotion, a group may be using it to enhance its position and reputation in the organisation, while at the organisation level the use of this system may be for competitive advantage in the industry. The conflicts of interest will appear to be higher at the executive position. Thus the central research questions to be addressed therefore in this study are:
1. Do individual executive goals contribute to the continuous acceptance and success of EIS?
2. Do group goals contribute to the continuous acceptance and success of EIS?
3. Do organisational goals contribute to the continuous acceptance and success of EIS?

RESEARCH OBJECTIVES

This research has three primary aims. The first aim is to identify the primary uses of Executive Information Systems (EIS) and the primary goals for each of these main uses in Australia. The second aim is to investigate whether individual goals, group goals and organisation goals contribute to the continuous acceptance and success of EIS. And the third aim is to develop a holistic approach to the development and implementation of EIS to incorporate the identified user goals.

THEORETICAL CONSIDERATIONS AND FRAMEWORK

The Theory of Reasoned Action (TRA), the Technology Acceptance Model (TAM) and Activity Theory (AT), in addition to the Information Richness Theory, the Social Presence Theory and the Social Influence Theory are considered and form the theoretical framework for this research.

Fishbein and Ajzen's (1975) (Ajzen and Fishbein 1980) TRA is a widely studied model from social psychology which is concerned with the determinants of consciously intended behaviour. According to TRA.
1. A person's performance of a specified behaviour is determined by his/her behavioural intention to perform the behaviour and the behavioural intention is jointly determined by a person's attitude and subjective norms.
2. A person's attitude is determined by his/her beliefs about the consequences of the action multiplied by the evaluation of the consequences.
3. Subjective norms are determined by the multiplicative function of a person's normative beliefs, that is, the perceived expectations of specific referent individuals or groups, and the person's motivation to comply.

The technology acceptance model (TAM) which is an adaptation of TRA, introduced by Davis (1986), is especially meant to explain computer usage behaviour. TAM uses TRA as a theoretical basis for specifying the casual linkages between two key beliefs: perceived usefulness and perceived ease of use, and users' attitudes, intentions and actual computer adoption behaviour. TAM posits that the two particular beliefs, perceived usefulness and perceived ease of use, are of primary relevance for computer acceptance behaviours. TAM is considerably less general than TRA and designed to apply only to computer usage behaviour.

Activity Theory (AT), propounded by the Russian psychologist Vygotsky and developed by Leontiev and others in the first half of the century, has the basic unit of analysis of all human endeavour as an activity which is undertaken by a human actor and motivated towards an object. Such activity is composed of goal-oriented actions and is only meaningful in its social context. Of particular relevance to EIS is the AT concept of activity as mediated by tools.

CONTRIBUTION OF RESEARCH

It is envisioned that after the successful completion of this research, the following contributions will be made to the field of information technology, especially in the areas of EIS.
1. An understanding of the motives of executives for using EIS.
2. Identification of some user goals that contribute to the continuous acceptance and success of EIS.
3. An understanding of the use of EIS by executives to EIS developers and how user goals can be factored into the development and implementation of EIS to enhance EIS success.
4. An understanding and direction for research into EIS in particular and IS in general.
5. An understanding of the use of EIS to practitioners leading to a better IS management.

Modeling of Electronic Markets Based on the Concepts of Hybrid Multi-Agent Systems and Generic Electronic Markets Services

Markus A. Lindemann
mcm Insitute for Media and Communications Management, University of St. Gallen, Mueller-Friedberg-Str. 8, 9000 St. Gallen, Switzerland
++41 / 71 – 224 2792, fax: ++41 / 71 – 224 2771, Markus.Lindemann@unisg.ch

INTRODUCTION

The concept of electronic markets (EM) with its roots in capital markets has been a research topic for more than two decades. Based on the tremendous growth of the Internet EM received wide attention in business and major research progress has been made during the past few years (e.g., convergence of markets, platforms, and technologies; better knowledge about the concept of EM; increasing economic relevance of electronic commerce (EC) applications; expansion of applications of multi-agent systems within organizations; proof of concept of reference models for IT applications). The economic importance of EM and EC applications are stressed by different institutions. However, the proponents of EC often do not know how markets work and behave. The establishment of an EC system does not automatically create an electronic market in an economical sense. This research attempts to take note of this issue by modeling EM based on the concept of multi-agent systems and the notion of generic EM services.

HYBRID MULTI-AGENT SYSTEMS

From an organizational, design-oriented perspective EM can be viewed as (hybrid) multi-agent systems. Similar approaches are described in literature. Three of the five basic organizational modeling concepts for EM according to Schmid are agents, roles, and protocols. Compared to the proponents of distributed artificial intelligence *hybrid agents* are modeled within the proposed model i.e. agents can be of an artificial or human nature. An agent participates in an electronic market transaction, so an agent is an active entity in an electronic market. In this course, primary and secondary agents can be distinguished. A primary agent is directly involved in a market transaction (e.g., buyer and seller), whereby a secondary agent provides special services and supports the market transaction (e.g., information broker or electronic notary). *Roles* are abstracts of concrete agents and describe behavior patterns of market participants. A *protocol* is a set of rules and organizes the interactions between roles.

Therefore, roles and protocols should represent testable modeling knowledge. The following issues have to be observed:
- Design and characteristics of (artificial and human) agents;
- Architecture of multi-agent systems and possible forms of agent interaction.

Even if there is no agreed upon definition of the term "agent", according to the theory of agency, agents can be characterized by the three primitive modalities "belief", "desire", and "intention" (BDI agents). This approach is widely used and often extended. A conjunction of this research is that the concept of BDI agents can be used to model hybrid agents. Further, the proposed architecture of EM will be based on the contract net approach in which a dedicated co-ordination agent is responsible for matching the bids and "clearing" the market. By means of communications channels and a common language agents communicate to negotiate and sign contracts for offered and demanded products and services. Among others, for example, a common "contracting protocol" with negotiation rules is needed.

GENERIC ELECTRONIC MARKETS SERVICES

From a technological viewpoint generic EM services will be discussed. Mainly, these services are based on EC packages already provided on the market to support the interactions between market participants in the single phases of a market transaction technologically. From a more theoretical perspective, they must be generic i.e. they must be of a universal character to support different kinds of actors in various situations. For this, these applications should be independent of a concrete context. Additionally, these applications must be integrated in a way that a permanent and fluid support of a market transaction can be guaranteed ("plug-and-play" solutions).

OVERVIEW OF THE INITIAL MODEL

The figure below summarizes the explained approach above of how to model EM. EM, which are based on these modeling concepts, promise to be able to cope with the unstable situation of the permanently changing economical environment by providing a maximum of flexibility.

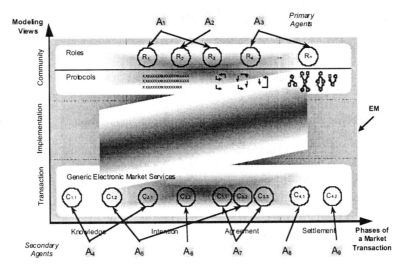

FURTHER WORK AND OUTLOOK

The areas of EM are an ongoing research field and economical awareness is still growing which leads to innovative solutions to design and build EM. An ongoing discussion within financial theory is related to the optimized design of stock markets. The discussion is based on the knowledge that different organizational shapes, rules, processes, and structures of different systems can have provable effects on the efficiency of the market process and therefore on the whole market result. Market microstructure theory deals with the behavior of market participants and tries to conclude about course and results of market processes. In this context, markets can be divided into three categories: brokered markets, dealer markets, and auctions. According to these categories, three comprehensive cases will be selected to validate the proposed model. In addition, the model will be reflected against the background of – and probably supplemented with – various issues of market theory, for example, efficiency criteria of markets such as liquidity and immediacy, or special roles in stock markets such as market makers or specialists.

Impact of Information Technology (IT) in the Performance of Brazilian Banks

Antonio Carlos Gastaud Maçada

Federal University of Rio Grande do Sul, Management School, Brazil, Information and Decision-Making Support Systems Research Group, Av. João Pessoa, 52 Sala 11 90040-000 Porto Alegre - RS Brazil 55-51-316-3474 Fax: 55-51-316-3991, acgmacada@adm.ufrgs.br

INTRODUCTION

Industry and service organizations have invested time, money, even their own future in Information Technology (IT) (Wang, Gopal and Zionts, 1995). According to a number of authors, competition and rivalry between these organizations are the main factors justifying these high investments in IT (Parson, 1983; McFarland, 1984; Clemons, 1986; Mahmood and Soon, 1991; Nolan and Crosson, 1996). However, Venkatraman (1994) stresses the necessity of caution, as the effects produced by introducing IT give a new shape to business strategy and, in many cases, can redefine the firm's own purpose. It is not totally evident yet if IT investments improve competitive positions of organizations in the various sectors of American economy (Strassmann, 1997). It is, then, extremely important to understand how IT resources are applied and managed and what possible effects on organization strategic variables it will cause.

Banking are among the organizations with the highest investments in IT, planning their strategies based on its use and application (Nolan e Crosson, 1996). "Retrospectively, the bank sector is the most evident place to seek information technology manifestations in the 21st century" (Peters, 1993, p.137). Indeed, IT investments made by the bank industry, in countries such as the United States and Brazil, have amounted to a total of 18 billion dollars in 1996 (Institutional Investitor, 1996) and 1.5 billion reais (Febraban, 1997), respectively. It has become a survival factor for several banks, and, as a result of this, it is necessary that their executives understand and manage their resources as a tool to reach competitiveness.

BACKGROUND AND DESCRIPTION OF PROJECT

Although there is a significant amount of research made in this area, a great number of authors fail to explain conclusively the strategic and economic impact that IT investments have on productivity and organizational performance (Mahmood, 1997). For the authors, only one study has found a positive and clear relation between IT investments and performance (Hitt e Brynsolfsson, 1996). For Barua, Kriebel and Mukhopadhyay (1995), the results of studies of IT impacts are not conclusive either, because their analysis is supported on works published between 1980 and 1990, which, according to the authors, have the only effect to point out that impacts were positive or negative, and their assumptions are based on issues such as productivity and economic return. The research results of IT impacts are faulty and inconclusive due to errors in their measuring process Brynjolfsson (1993) and Wilson (1993). The study concludes that more studies in this area are necessary, taking into account the organizations and their executives' needs. (Mahmood, 1997). The development of appropriate tools for this investigation, however, is essential.

The objective of this thesis project is to identify the impacts on the performance of Brazilian banks regarding IT implantation and use. The great motivation to develop this work is the possibility to combine methods aiming at providing researchers and managers with tools to measure and later evaluate the impacts brought about by the introduction of IT in the organizations. This objective intends to answer the following questions:

1a. How to measure the impacts of IT?

In a preliminary literature review, it was identified that traditional methods of financial economic nature have not been producing satisfactory responses. This led the researcher to identify the impacts through the perception of people who use IT in organizations and, later, to select strategic variables to supply the mathematical model (DEA) which will measure the investment conversion effectiveness, thus leading to a new research issue.

2a. What is the perception of the Brazilian banks that use the IT as a strategic tool regarding the possible impacts of the strategic variables in banks?

3a. Which are the strategic organizational variables supported by IT that most produce impacts on Brazilian banks?

RESEARCH METHODS

Survey and Data Envelopment Analisys.

SURVEY

Research on Information Systems (IS) have suggested that a variety of factors affecting organizations in their strategic approach and pursuit of competitive advantages (Mata, Fuerst and Barney, 1995). Mahmood and Soon (1991) and Palvia (1997) criticized the validity of these models, because: a) none of them was developed as explanatory models; b) none of them was empirically tested; and c) none of them led to conclusions considering strategic decision making.

Factors selected to achieve this research objectives are based on the research developed and validated by Mahmood and Soon (1991) and Palvia (1997). The models proposed by the authors aims at measuring IT effects over the strategic variables at domestic (national) and global (international) levels. Palvia's model is an extension of Mahmood and Soon's model, which is composed by ten strategic variables and has been applied only in American firms (domestic context). The model expanded by Palvia (1997) to measure IT strategic impacts at a global level is composed by twenty variables: ten domestic variables adapted to the international context and other ten variables derived from literature, still embryonic, that relate IS with the globalization process.

The choice of domestic and global variables to compose the model reflects the current competitive economic scenario in which Brazilian banks are involved, which are the unit of analysis of this work. The respondents are the executives of Brazilian banks. In order to avoid bias in answers, for every questionnaire delivered to the technology area, two were given to executives that use IT to keep and implement strategies in banks.

DATA ENVELOPMENT ANALYSIS (DEA)

The DEA method is a technique used to measure the relative efficiency of a number of similar units, named Decision Making Units (DMU). They may be firms, agencies, hospitals, people, etc. according to the objectives of the study. For instance, in this paper the relative efficiency of bank organizations is studied. The model applied is the model CCR (Charnes, Cooper and Rhodes, 1978, 1979), that assumes constant returns of scale.

The DEA model offers various advantages as an empirical tool in studies on the IT impacts on organizational performance (Wang, Gopal and Zionts, 1995). It is a mathematical model to measure efficiency or performance of units (in this case, banks) that need information or factors which allow the generation of answers, providing, then, the evaluation of the Brazilian banks.

DEA will be a tool that the student will use to measure the performance of Brazilian banks, and survey will supply the information that make this evaluation process possible, based on the organizational strategic variables related with the investments made on IT. The integration of the survey with DEA will be a challenge to the researcher.

RESULTS - PILOT TEST

The process of validation of constructs and the measurement tool followed the steps described by Benbasat and Moore (1992) and Straub (1989) with the aim of achieving a reliable and robust tool. The reliability of each variable was examined. The coefficient are in the range between 0.60 and 0.98. The coefficient 0.92 for the instrument as a whole ensures its reliability. In order to include only relevant items in each variable, a new correlation analysis total-item corrected was carried out. This procedure eliminated twenty-nine items of the instrument. The remaining items present corrected total-item correlation coefficients, varying from 0.42 to 0.97, what suggests that these items are significantly correlated with the content of their constructs. The convergent and discriminating of the model was achieved through the multi-trace/multi method matrix method (MTMM). 30 executives of 2 Brazilian banks participated in the pilot test. After the pilot test, changes in the questionnaire were made and it was sent to 135 banks.

CONCLUSIONS AND CURRENT STATUS

The process of validating the instrument and adaptation of the constructs for application in Brazilian banks was very long and hard.

During this period, I noticed the interest of the banking industry executives in obtaining a tool capable of evaluating the impacts of IT based on their perception. It was identified that more research in the area is necessary.

Currently, together with the accountants of Brazilian banks, we are studying how to adapt the variables selected in the final model resulting from the survey in order to supply DEA, and how to collect this data in the banks' reports. The pilot test has been concluded. The research is now in the data collection stage in 135 banks.

The variables identified as impact variables, once it is verified at the conclusion of the study, will provide other students with its use when formulating other instruments to measure impacts in other organizations.

Hard and Soft Data- A Look at Data Quality in Management Decision Making

M. Pamela Neely
State University of New York at Albany, Center for Technology in Government, 1535 Western Ave., Albany, NY 12203, (518) 442-3924, fax (518) 442-3886, pneely@ctg.albany.edu

BACKGROUND INFORMATION

Corporations, government agencies, and not for profit groups are inundated with enormous amounts of data they must process as they make decisions. Management decision making has been enhanced in recent years by the development of decision support systems, executive information systems, expert systems and data warehouses. Decisions based on the additional information that these systems provide can be more beneficial to the decision making process, but it is imperative that the issue of data quality be addressed. If the incoming data is of poor quality, then the decisions based on this information will also be of poor quality.

Skilled managers use all of the data available to them, hard and soft, to arrive at decisions. They consider the quality and the source of the data when evaluating alternatives. While the decision support systems, executive information systems and data warehouses facilitate the decision making process, the final decision rests with the manager and his/her experiences in similar situations.

FINDINGS AND DISCUSSION

Hard data, such as data generated by a transaction processing system, can be analyzed and cleaned with software tools that are available on the market today. In this paper I have defined the types of tools that are available, and the specific data quality issues that these tools are designed to address. These tools, though they differ in specific features, all use an underlying assumption, that the data can be compared to an external source. The validation of the incoming data against an independent source is a key component of the data quality tools on the market today. The validation may be against a set of business rules or a Postal Zip Code reference, but it is a vital part of the system.

A look at soft data reveals that it is used in a different way than hard data. While hard data can be used alone, soft data is used in conjunction with hard data. While management recognizes that soft data may not be verifiable, the data is necessary in the context of the overall process and managers will attempt to confirm the data. In many instances, the percentage of soft data used in the decision is greater than the percentage of hard data. Thus, they need to trust that the data has some meaning.

Managers routinely compare the data, both hard and soft, to external sources and to their own experience. Whether the decision involves the educational plan for a severely handicapped child or a complete revision of the menu in an alcohol rehabilitation unit, the decisions are arrived at with a combination of resources that include hard and soft data, and the conscious consideration of the quality of that data.

CONCLUSION

Poor data quality in a tool that supports management decision making, such as an executive information system or data warehouse, will yield poor quality decisions. However, 100% clean data is cost prohibitive and unrealistic. The dimensions of data quality should be evaluated in the context of the decision to be made to determine where the greatest benefit for the cost will be derived.

Managers implicitly and consciously consider the quality of the data. When dealing with hard data, they expect it be accurate. It is assumed that tools will have been used so that the data they are given will be accurate, relevant, complete, and consistent.

Managers spend more time verifying the soft data. When managers use soft data in the decision making process, they will make the effort to check the cleanliness themselves. They will frequently consult additional resources, and will always rely on experience in similar situations. They realize that the data has not been processed through software tools and will need to be taken with less assurance of accuracy and consistency. Further research in how soft data can be cleaned is suggested.

Formalising the Information Resource Management Role in Business Processes

Karen Nelson

Credit Union Services Corporation (Australia) Limited (CUSCAL)

+617 3214 1700, Fax +617 3214 1711, knelson@cuscal.com.au

BACKGROUND INFORMATION

Credit Union Services Corporation (CUSCAL) an unlisted company, owned and funded by its member credit unions, is the major of two special service providers to credit unions in Australia. The Corporation exists to provide benefits of aggregation through economies of scale, in the production and supply of products and services which credit unions acting alone would not be able to provide to their members. The products offered include retail and institutional banking, treasury, information technology and systems, insurance, market research, marketing other business services, publications and bulletins.

In December 1997 the credit union movement had assets totalling $A17.7 billion, from 253 credit unions, which in turn had memberships totalling $A3.5 million, meaning that one in five adult Australians has relationship with a credit union. On asset size, credit unions appear after the four major banks (National Australia, Westpac, Commonwealth and ANZ) and the amalgamated St George - Advantage Bank.

CUSCAL is predisposed towards managing information as a resource like other business resources such as people and finance. Since 1996, the Corporation has performed a number of projects that could be generally categorised as information management. These projects have ranged from the development of a Quality Management System and the creation of an Information Technology Strategy to analysis of specific information flows and use. CUSCAL wishes to consolidate these components and coordinate all information activities in a formalised approach to information management.

This case study provides a base line and framework for coordination of information resources management within CUSCAL. It is proposed to build on this baseline in subsequent action research work to articulate a model for information resources management within business processes.

DISCUSSION OF THE ISSUES

There are few practical demonstrations of how information resources management (IRM) can be achieved within organisational contexts. This lack of explicit examples has meant that those responsible for the information management function have often resorted to the management, acquisition and maintenance of information technology resources. That is, attention has been focused on the carrier of information or data, while the content and the context (in the form of organisational business plans) are often seen in a subordinate role. This focus means that senior managers still don't get the information they need despite some massive investments in new technologies and systems. Many organisations face a conundrum where there is an over supply of much information, but good, high quality, relevant, and timely information is scarce. Scarcity has been an impetus for instigating strategic management of other resources, and in this context information also requires management to ensure the information resource is effectively utilised.

A focus on technology management instead of on policies or strategies which specifically refer to information and its management, combined with the absence of suitable responsibility for information strategy implementation, and little overall coordination of information activities within normal business processes may lead to situations where organisations don't know what information they have or need to meet business objectives. This confusion may be exacerbated if a positive information culture is compromised due to information sharing decreasing as an organisation becomes more information intensive.

Service organisations, such as CUSCAL, are under pressure to improve customer service because customers are demanding to be treated as individuals rather than members of a large group. This means that knowledge and information about the customer - supplier relationship and needs to be implicit in all interactions. One challenge for IM is to transfer this information into accessible and useable corporate information.

A descriptive case study with embedded surveys has been used to describe how information resources management is achieved within a specific financial services environment. The research questions addressed were: (1) how is the scope of CUSCAL's information domain determined, (2) what is the current organisational context for information resources management, (3) how does the management of technology fit in terms of information resources management, (4) what is the organisational culture of the organisation and the dominant political model.

FINDINGS

The scope of CUSCAL's information domain is determined by integration with the annual business planning process. The information required to meet objectives and indicate goal achievement is identified and documented during planning activities, and then made available for information strategy development within each business unit.

CUSCAL has recently adopted an enterprise level information management (IM) policy which has the objectives of ensuring *"the right information is acquired externally and generated internally to achieve what the corporation needs to do; that information is exploited fully to meet current and future needs; and that there is a framework for the coordination of all information activities"*. IM activities such as resource, functional or business unit strategies are guided by the key concepts, critical success factors and basic principles for IM articulated in this policy. There is a new division (Information Resources) which is responsible for administration of this policy and acts as an internal consulting group to the rest of the organisation in terms of information management initiatives.

The management of information technology and systems is the responsibility of a separate division under the direction of the Chief Information Officer (CIO). This area includes administration of the local and wide area networks, the National Credit Union Network, telecommunications, desktop hardware and software, and internal technology (operates data centre and develops applications for data processing and transfer between credit unions and other business entities). Senior management from this division work closely with the Information Resources group on all information management projects.

Case study findings indicate that the current information culture resembles (in the worst case) a anarchic or feudalistic model of information politics. In an anarchic model, there is an absence of any overall information management policy (adopted by CUSCAL in April 1998) which leaves individuals to obtain and manage their own information. CUSCAL's dominant culture exhibits symptoms of a feudalistic state where the management of information is performed by individual business units or factions, who define and manage their own information needs and report (or share) only limited information to the rest of the enterprise. Some business units have well developed end user capability which has lead to development of information systems meeting specific business unit requirements without much attention to the information itself as an enterprise wide resource rather than being "owned" by individuals or business areas. An example of this activity occurs in the finance area which has a MIS group who have implemented an enterprise resource planning tool with little involvement from either Information Resources or Information Technology personnel or planned consultation with their internal customer base.

CONCLUSION

CUSCAL has adopted an integrative approach to information resources management which in this organisation has meant the separating (for the time being anyway) the responsibility for information resources management (the content and context) from the means of storing and disseminating system based information. Although initially this separation was contentious the two divisions have built a solid working relationship which has resulted in a number of successful information projects. The linking of organisational information requirements to the business planning process is a new initiative and greater participation from the business units in this exercise should be apparent during the next round of planning commencing in February 1999. The current information culture is gradually moving from rampant to mild feudalism through improved understanding and demonstration of the benefits of coordinated information resource management and active support for business unit goal achievement. Positive changes in attitudes to information sharing are also apparent within some areas where cost efficiencies are to be gained by not maintaining information that is already present in the enterprise. Further action research work is now required to build these findings into practical model for information resource management that can be applied and tested in a wider environment.

Continuous Evaluation of Information System Benefits

Ming-chuan Wu

Lally School of Management and Technology, Rensselaer Polytechnic Institute, Troy, NY 12180
wum3@rpi.edu, 518-276-5695

RESEARCH PROBLEMS

The issue of IS evaluation becomes more important and problematic as organizations are investing more in information technology while finding no effective ways to justify the investments. While issues of IS/IT investment evaluation may be various in scope, our research only discuss within the level of a certain IS development project. We believe that the newly heightened strategic use of IS requires a new evaluation framework that addresses specifically intangible benefits and overall accountability by integrating the evaluation process across the life cycle of the system. Therefore, we propose a multi-stage evaluation framework incorporating previous methods into an adaptive process to guide the evaluation practice. The framework will feature constructs that evaluate benefits at the design stage, connect evaluation methods across different stages, and provide feedback to these methods as the process progresses. As such, the research will contribute to the evaluation of intangible benefits as well as the continuous evaluation of strategic IS projects for overall accountability.

LITERATURE

The notion of multi-stage IS evaluation is not new. Enterprise information systems are typically developed and implemented within a corporate social context that often involves a long time frame (in months or years), different interest groups, and interrelated activities and processes. Due to the dynamic and uncertain nature, a system's attributes such as users' requirements, organization's needs, and system consequences tend to change over its life cycle. Hence IS evaluations are often conducted at different stages of the life cycle, focusing on different evaluation domain.

Benefits, in particularly, are mostly evaluated either at the beginning or at the end of a projects. Traditional approaches work fine when IS benefits are mostly tangible, but may be inadequate for more current IS applications where intangible benefits dominate.

The above conceptual diagram in Figure 1 illustrates the problem from the perspective of uncertainty. Accuracy of IS benefit evaluation can be conceptualized to depend on two factors: the level of benefit tangibility for a certain IS project and the uncertainty level of IS development, which generally decreases along system time line. The inside curve represents the estimate error range for systems with mostly tangible benefits, which do not change much among different stages. Therefore, an evaluation made at the initial planning stage is sufficient to justify a go-no-go decision for this class of projects. On the other hand, for IS applications with more intangible benefits, justifying their economical value is difficult even after the systems are implemented. Predicting their benefits at the initial stage is problematic, as they are subject to high level of benefit uncertainty.

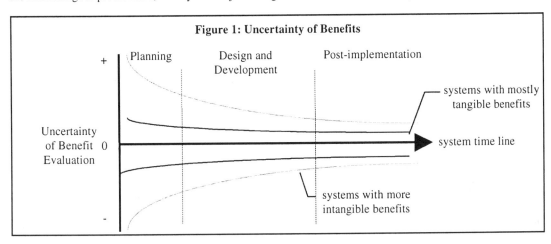

Figure 1: Uncertainty of Benefits

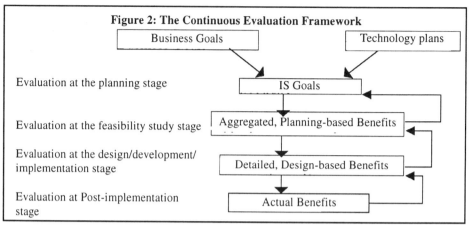

Figure 2: The Continuous Evaluation Framework

Evaluation of intangible benefits in the planning stage is more difficult than in later stages. Many researchers have devoted their efforts to this problem. A major result is the finding that different types of IT/IS have different kinds of value for an organization and thus necessitate different techniques in the analysis of the differing values. Therefore, some researchers turn their focus on how to categorize IS projects and existing evaluation methods. Both matrices and ladder-like hierarchies have been used to classify IS project and methods. However, the results vary greatly in logic, to a point that their relevance is discussed. Several studies have reflected a frustrating fact that most organizations still use finance-based methods to evaluate IS benefits while expressing doubts on the result of their evaluation.

We argue that the inherent uncertain nature of intangible IS benefits makes accurate evaluation in the early stage impractical. However, as illustrated in Figure 1, we believe that the evaluation process can be extended systematically along system life cycle to incorporate the information that will become available as the process moves on, to better assess intangible benefits. This view is corroborated by recent research calling for treating evaluation process as an organizational process for deeper organizational learning.

SOLUTION APPROACH

Based on the multi-stage evaluation concept, we propose a continuous and adaptive framework for evaluating IS benefits, as illustrated in Figure 2. This framework aims to enable an integration of the "islands of evaluation" for (strategic) investment on IS/IT. The objective is to provide a new basic result to assist the evaluation processes assuring the projected benefits for organizations. A benefits evaluation matrix is designed to support the framework.

Specifically, the proposed framework will accomplish the following three goals:
• Adaptability of evaluation methods

The evaluation methods available in the literature will be adopted to determine the benefit concepts and indicators at each stage. The goals and the measurement could either be generic or be particular for each project. The benefit concepts and indicators will be developed at an appropriate abstraction level for each stage. In addition, this research will also determine appropriate benefit concepts and indicators to reflect the detailed projections at design/development stage. All methods used will be adjusted to provide suitable granularity as required in the evaluation matrices.

• Creation of evaluation linkage between stages

Linkages are created between stages. The goals identified at the first stage (e.g. gaining market share) will be used to formulate benefit concepts by incorporating other information such as user requirements (e.g. providing internet service) at feasibility stage. Benefit concepts can then be more accurately projected at the design stage while the functions and capacity of the system are determined. This research will provide a mechanism based upon the benefits matrix to help the continuous evaluation process more forward at each stage, with feedback to the preceding stage.

• Collaboration with system development process.

The benefit evaluation process is logically coupled with that of system development. To capture this nature, and to facilitate the processing requirements of the benefits matrix, this research will devise a coupling methodology to allow these two processes to share efforts and results. System development efforts provide natural results (such as user requirement, process analysis, and design) that can be used to evaluate benefits. Specific classes of information that both processes can share will be determined.

Author's Index

Journal of
End User Computing

Editor-in-chief Mo Adam Mahmood
University of Texas, El Paso

The *Journal of End User Computing* (JEUC) focuses on providing coverage of research findings and expert advice on the development, utilization and management of end user computing in organizations. The original articles in each issue deal with the trends, usage, failure, successes, solutions, policies, and applications of information technology resources in organizations. Along with the highly regarded peer reviewed manuscripts in each issue, is the *Industry and Practice* section featuring practical-oriented submissions, such as case studies, expert interviews and editorial/opinion pieces that are selected based on their usefulness to our readers.

ISSN 1043-6464 • Published quarterly • Annual subscription rate: • US$85 Individuals; US$175 Institutions

Journal of
Database Management

Editor-in-charge Shirley Becker
Florida Institute of Technology

The *Journal of Database Management* (JDM) is an international journal aimed at designers, developers, educators, researchers, consultants, and administrators of database management systems. The major emphasis of topics in JDM is on database issues ranging from strategic planning to issues concerning the greater utilization and management of database technology. Along with the highly regarded peer reviewed manuscripts in each issue is the Industry and Practice section, featuring practical-oriented submissions, such as case studies, expert interviews and editorial/opinion pieces that are selected based on their usefulness to our readers.

ISSN 1063-8016 • Published quarterly • Annual subscription rate: • US$85 Individuals; US$175 Institutions

Idea Group Publishing
1331 E. Chocolate Avenue
Hershey PA 17033-1117 USA
Tel: 717/533-8845 • Fax: 717/533-8661
http://www.idea-group.com